For Susan –

Enjoy!

TEXAS EXTRA

A Newspaper History of the Lone Star State 1835-1935

CASTLE BOOKS

Credits & Permissions

The publisher thanks the following companies and publishers for their kind permission to reprint the following pages and articles:

The Anvil Herald *(Hondo):* August 31, 1894 *(Hondo Herald) Small size emergency format due to flooding,* Welcome rain, disastrous flooding *(page 166)*; August 19, 1898 *(Castroville Anvil),* Advertisements *(page 173)*, and Article on Buffalo soldiers *(page 174).* ***Austin American Statesman:*** May 25, 1934 *(Austin Statesman),* Bonnie and Clyde burial *(page 216).* ***Beeville Publishing Company:*** November 8, 1907 *(Beeville Bee)*, "A Texas Ranger Fight" and Advertisements *(pages 188 and 189)*; January 31, 1908 *(Beeville Bee),* "Early Days of Slavery in Texas" *(page 190)*; and February 28, 1908 *(Beeville Bee),* Cynthia Ann Parker & the Comanches *(page 191).* ***The Coca-Cola Company:*** January 4, 1919 (*The Dallas Democrat Annual Edition),* Coca-Cola Advertisement, with an invitation to visit the local soft drink bottling plant *(page 202).* ***The Cuero Record:*** August 19, 1895 *(Cuero Daily Record),* "How Bill Doolan, a Notorious Bandit, Won a Schoolma'am's Love" *(page 167)*; August 21, 1895 *(Cuero Daily Record)*, "He Bit the Dust Quick / J. Wesley Hardin Shot Dead in El Paso *(page 168)*; and June 3, 1898 *(The Constitution, Cuero),* Texas reads about the Spanish American War *(page 175).* ***The Dallas Morning News*** *(Reprinted with the permission of the Dallas Morning News):* May 24, 1894, Candidate Reagan, Bill Dalton and the Longview Robbery *(page 162);* May 25, 1894, "He was hanged," Bill Dalton pictured *(page 163)*; August 27, 1896, "Afro-American Fair" *(page 171)*; January 17, 1901, The Beaumont Gusher *(page 179)*; January 18, 1901, "Cap on the Well / Big Deals are Made" *(page 180)*; January 19, 1916, Houdini visits Dallas *(page 195)*; April 15, 1917 *(News Magazine Supplement)*, Bathing beauties at Galveston beach *(page 200)*; April 2, 1934, Clyde Barrow kills two policemen *(pages 210 and 211)*; and May 24, 1934, Posse kills Clyde Barrow and Bonnie Parker *(pages 214 and 215).* ***The Galveston Daily News:*** May 25, 1894, The Dalton Gang and the Longview robbery, "The Bandits Corralled" *(page 164)*; September 11, 1900**,** Single sheet edition published right after the hurricane, List of Deaths *(page176)*; September 12, 1900**,** "Story of the Hurricane Which Swept Galveston" *(page 177)*; and August 14, 1901, **"**A Train Held Up" near Denison *(page 185).* ***The Houston Chronicle:*** August 21, 1895 (*Houston Daily Post),* "Wesley Hardin Killed" *(page 169)*; May 12, 1901 *(Houston Daily Post),* Full-page map of Beaumont oil fields, Stock offering for Beaumont Spindle Top Oil Company *(Pages 183 and 184)****;*** October 20, 1929 *(Houston Post Dispatch),* What the well-dressed and well-heeled women of Houston wore at the close of the roaring twenties *(page 203)*, Photo, article, and ad for *Miller bros. famous 101 Ranch and Wild West Show (page 204)*; October 26, 1929 *(Houston Post Dispatch, gravure section)***,** Woolworth's lunch counter priced menu *(page 205, Copyright 1929 Houston Post. Reprinted with Permission. All rights reserved)*; October 27, 1929 (*Houston Post Dispatch*), South Texas Agricultural and Industrial Exposition, "Texas Gulf Coast Boost Oil production" *(pages 206 and 207, Copyright 1929 Houston Post. Reprinted with Permission. All rights reserved)*; October 27, 1929 *(Houston Post Dispatch, gravure section)***,** "Texas children" *(page 208).* ***Muskogee Daily Phoenix Times Democrat:*** April 2, 1934 *(Muskogee Times Democrat)*, Bonnie and Clyde on the run *(page 209).* ***The Palestine Herald Press:*** May 23, 1934 *(Palestine Daily Herald),* **"**Barrow and Bonnie Parker Riddled with Bullets" *(page 213).* ***Paris News:*** April 7, 1898 (*The Texas Herald),* "A Great Ten Days Sale!" *(page 172).* ***Rockdale Reporter:*** September 13, 1900 *(Rockdale Messenger),* Advertisements *(page 178).* ***The Rocky Mountain News*** *(Reprinted with the permission of the Denver Rocky Mountain News)****:*** July 11, 1904 *(Rocky Mountain News, Denver),* Harvey Logan, "the world's most notorious bandit and train robber" and leader of the "Hole-in-the-wall" gang, is cornered and kills himself *(pages 186 and 187).* ***Scripps Howard Newspapers:*** April 5, 1934 (*The El Paso Herald Post)***,** "Desperado and Cigar Smoking Pal" *(page 212).*

Special thanks to ***Stephen A. Goldman Historical Newspapers*** for: ***Texas Chronicle (Nacogdoches)*** *three pages, October 28, 1837:* Life in early Texas *(pages 12, 13, and 14)*; ***Tri-Weekly Telegraph (Houston)****, July 29, 1863:* Death of General Sam Houston *(page 84)*; ***The Illustrated Police News****, October 19, 1878:* Contemporary wood cut portrait of Bill "the Butcher" Longley *(page 117)*; ***Dallas Morning News,*** *May 25, 1894:* "He Was Hanged," Bill Dalton Pictured. *(page 164).*

This edition published by Castle Books,
a division of Book Sales, Inc.
114 Northfield Avenue
Edison, N.J. 08837

Compiled by Eric C. Caren
from the collection of Caren Archives, Inc.

ISBN 0-7858-1082-X
Printed in the United States of America

Texas Extra

Table of Contents

1850's

1860's

1860's

1870's

1870's

1880's

1880's

1890's

The Connecticut Courant.

VOL. LXXI.....NO. 3693. HARTFORD, MONDAY, NOVEMBER 2, 1835. PRICE TWO DOLLARS.

CONNECTICUT COURANT.
PUBLISHED BY
GOODWIN & CO.
FIFTEEN RODS NORTH-WEST OF THE STATE-HOUSE, HARTFORD.

Price Two Dollars per annum, payable in advance—a liberal discount made to companies.

Advertisements not exceeding a square inserted three times for One Dollar—every after continuation Twenty Cents.

No accounts will be opened for Advertisements sent from a distance.

WEEKLY ALMANAC.

NOVEMBER.	☉ R.	☉ S.	D. DEC.	R. ☽ S.
2 Monday,	6 54	5 6	4 48	3 25
3 Tuesday,	6 55	5 5	4 50	4 27
4 Wednesday,	6 56			
5 Thursday,	6 57			
6 Friday,	6 58			
7 Saturday,	6 59			
8 Sunday,	7 0			

Full Moon, 5th,
Last Quarter, 13t
New Moon, 20th,
First Quarter, 26t

From the Religious Offering.

OMNIPRESENCE OF THE DEITY.

Who bids the billow heave its breast,
Then soothes its troubled throb to rest?
Who bids the coral greenly bloom
Around the sea boy's ocean tomb?
Oh Lord! The sky, the earth, the sea,
And all things else are full of Thee!

At whose command, when eve doth fall
With mantle dim, o'ershadowing all,
Do trooping stars come twinkling through,
And decking bright heaven's arch of blue?
Father! The sky, the sea, the earth,
Proclaim the author of their birth.

Thine are the mountains, Thine the caves,
Thou ridest on the winds and waves;
Thine is the bright, o'er-arching bow,
The thunder's voice, the lightning's glow;

Englishman would have, if he were to find such a custom in Lynn or Haverhill! Selkirk of itself has now but little to attract the traveller, though in history it makes an important figure. From Selkirk the usual detour is made up the Yarrow, and to Ettrick Forest—a district only twelve or fourteen miles in extent, and inhabited chiefly by shepherds, but which, it has been truly said, has been the subject of more verse than Temple itself. I had a letter for "Altive Cottage," the home of Hogg, the Ettrick Shepherd, but remembering that Scott has written—

"The scenes are desart now, and bare,
Where flourished once a forest fair"—

and feeling that the cold winds and "snaws" of Selkirk hills had frozen all the poetry in my veins, I had no heart for wandering—

"Up pathless Ettricke, and on Yarrow,
Where erst the outlaw drew his arrow."

associated them with himself as to make his name coeval with their existence. Though Melrose Abbey, therefore, every year, may crumble more and more away, yet the peaks of Eilden Hills will stand as long as earth can stand, and stand, too, as monuments to his memory.

Melrose Abbey was built by David I., in 1136. It is built in the most ornate style of gothic architecture, and is, therefore, decorated with an infinite variety of sculpture, most of which is excellently fine. The church, which alone remains, measures 287 feet in length, and 157 at the greatest breadth. It is said to be the most finished building in Great Britain of the kind—and the French taste is visible in some of its decorations. The crowding of other buildings around it takes away from the impression it would otherwise make; and this is perhaps the reason why (or it may be that the fresh feeling is already gone) I did not admire it so much as I did the solitary ruins of Fountain Abbey, near Studley Park. It stands examina-

From the New York Commercial Advertiser, Oct. 27.

WAR IN TEXAS.

The New Orleans papers, received this morning, contain advices from Metamoras, supported by a variety of official accounts, leaving little doubt that the quarrel between the Mexican government and the revolutionists of Texas, has at length assumed the aspect of actual hostilities. It is stated that by the order of Santa Anna general Cos had concentrated his forces on San Antonia, to fix there his head quarters for the invasion of Texas, with information that Santa Anna would shortly follow and overrun the province in two months. Exasperated at this movement, which the Texians are pleased to term a breach of faith, on the part of the Mexicans, the colonists are arming themselves at all quarters; and on the 23d ult. 700 of them had marched in a body from Brazoria for the capture of San Antonio, with a firm determination to make the present viceroy of Texas, Don Remon Masquia, governor of the state. A correspondent of the New Orleans Bee states that Santa Anna had written a letter to Matamoras, boasting that in less than two months he would overrun and conquer the whole of Texas; but vauntingly adds,—'although we consider this a mere gasconade, yet we wish he should have the temerity to pay the Texians a visit; and we should soon rid the republic of this would be Napoleon.'

Advices from Galveston to the 6th of October, state that the combatants of that place had armed themselves, to aid the people of Brazoria, in the event of an actual invasion by General Cos. Meantime the departments or jurisdictions of Texas have elected deputies to the general consultation to be held in Washington—on the 15th instant, and that their objects may be of a more decisive and determined kind than they had been led to suspect. With Zavala and Austin at their head, says a New Orleans editor, the Mexicans and Americans in Texas need apprehend little danger in their struggle for freedom and independence.

We have long believed that the troubles in Texas would ultimately end in an attempt at revolution. Indeed any man may have seen with half an eye, in the conduct of Col. Austin, an ultimate design of collision with Mexico, and it now only remains to be seen which will prove the strongest. The New Orleans papers are warmly espousing the cause of the Texians—or rather the American residents of Texas. The Bee of the 12th instant asks:—

"Shall the citizens of the United States, in their individual capacity, remain listless spectators of eventful efforts like those almost certain to occur in Texas before a few months shall have elapsed?"

The Commercial Bulletin of the same date, contains the following article:—

"The Texonians are now embarked in a glorious struggle for liberty; and call upon the sympathies of the American people, in the two-fold character of the founders of the equality of human rights, and their brethren. We will not permit ourselves to doubt the favorable issue of a conflict waged on one side by an odious despotism, and on the other by a brave people offering up their blood upon the altar of their rights.

The following notice has been handed us for publication, which we take pleasure in spreading before our readers:—

'Notice.—A meeting of the friends of Texas is respectfully called this evening, at 7 o'clock precisely—at the private committee room, Banks' Arcade; to deliberate on matters of importance to that country—all who are favorable to the cause in which the people of Texas are now engaged, are invited to attend.'"

In reference to this notice, the Louisiana Advertiser holds the following language:—

This call, we have no doubt, will be responded to by numbers—the interest felt in the welfare of our brethren of Texas is enthusiastic and sincere, and will prove itself on this occasion. To New Orleans the eyes of the colonists are directed, and in the moment of need they look for our support—they implore our succor—shall we be backward in the evidences of our friendship at such a crisis? Impossible! Their address to the citizens of New Orleans is anxiously looked for, and we shall give it, when received, all the publicity requisite. Yet fondly do we cling to the hope, that an amicable arrangement will prevent the threatened hostilities, and that the belligerents may become mutually reconciled. The next arrivals from Texas will be intensely looked for.

Now, with due deference to the citizens of New Orleans, we would inquire, whether the proceedings they are adopting, with an evident design of waging war against a nation with which the United States are at peace, are not only unauthorized, but absolutely illegal, and at war alike with the law of nations, and the spirit of the treaty existing between the two governments? As the Texians are Americans, who have gone thither to seek their fortunes, it is but natural that they should receive our sympathies—but at the same time, we have a treaty of peace and amity with Mexico, and our citizens have no more right to wage war against that republic, in behalf of Texas, now, than colonel Burr and general Jackson had to conspire against the government of Spain, in behalf of Mexico, thirty years ago.

Since the preceding matter was in type, we find that we shall not be able this evening to publish all the documents we had selected for that purpose. The following articles, which are of the most immmediate interest, must therefore suffice for to-day:

San Felipe, Sep. 19, 1835.—Dear sir: War is upon us—there is now no remedy. The answer of Cos is positive that the individuals demanded must be given up, and that the people must unconditionally submit to whatever the government chooses to do for them. He lays down the principle that the general government have the right to force us to submit to any reform or amendments, or alterations that congress may make in the constitution, &c. This is impossible—we had better leave the country at once, for we shall be under the Sos' doctrine, without any rights or guarantees of any kind. I therefore think that war is inevitable; we must prepare. What do you think of raising a volunteer corps to protect the consultation, and having it ready without delay? I think it probable Cos will attack the people on Guadalove in a short time—they expect aid, and ought to have it. I shall send to Nacogdoches immediately. S. F. AUSTIN.

W. D. C. Hall, Esq.

War.—Information was received last night by express that gen. Cos landed at Copeno with 400 men; arms and ammunition.

An expedition is now raising in the lower country to take the field at once. They are called upon to rendezvous at Leagua's old place on the Colorado on the 28th of this month.

Every man in Texas is called upon to take up arms in defence of his country and his rights. Those who can join the expedition on the 28th are requested to do so; or they can join it at James Kerrs on the La Vaca which will be the principal rendezvous.

A corps of reserve will be formed to march for and sustain the advance. Those who cannot gain the advance are requested to unite with the reserve and report themselves to the committee of safety in this place.

It is expected that each man will supply himself with provisions, arms and ammunition to march with.

Arrangements will be made with permanent supplies as soon as possible.

S. F. AUSTIN, Chair. of Com.

September 22, 1835.

The following is from the New Orleans Bee Extra, of October 13th. The intelligence is from the Red River Herald Extra:—

HIGHLY INPORTANT FROM TEXAS.

WAR IN TEXAS—GEN. COS LANDED NEAR THE MOUTH OF THE BRASOS WITH 400 MEN.

Isaac Parker has just arrived from Texas, bringing the intelligence that General Cos has landed near the mouth of the Brasos with 400 men, with the intention of joining the 700 Federal troops stationed at San Antonia de Bexar, and marching upon the people of Texas. He has issued his proclamation "declaring that he will collect the revenue, disarm the citizens, establish a military government, and confiscate the property of the rebellious." Messrs. Johnson and Baker bore the express from San Fellipe to Nacogdoches. Stephen S. Austin has written to several citizens of Nacogdoches, that a resort to arms is inevitable.

They have hoisted a flag with "The Constitution of 1834," inscribed on it, and two hundred freemen gathered around it, determined to stand or fall with it.

We subjoin the following letter from General Houston to the gentlemen who brought the intelligence.

San Augustine, Texas, Oct. 5th, 1835.

Dear Sir—At your request I hand you a memorandum, that you may be informed of our situation. War in defence of our rights, our oaths, and our constitutions is inevitable in Texas!!

If volunteers from the United States will join their brethren in this section, they will receive liberal bounties of land. We have millions of acres of our best lands unchosen and unappropriated.

Let each man come with a good rifle and one hundred rounds of ammunition,—and to come soon.

Our war-cry is "Liberty or Death!" Our principles are to support the constitution, and *down with the usurper!*

Your friend,
SAMUEL HOUSTON.

To Isaac Parker, Esq.—Present.

We have no time to make any comments. The people of the United States will respond to the call of their brethren in Texas!—*Red River Herald, Extra.*

Those gentlemen friendly to the rights of free and republic governments, are requested to meet at the Red River Exchange, this evening, at half past 7 o'clock, to take into consideration the situation of their fellow countrymen in Texas.

Natchitoches, Oct. 7, 1835.

more uncomfortable or dreary ride. Indeed a large extent of country here and further back is but a wilderness stripped of almost all its trees—with some large ruined fortress in every mountain pass glooming in the way like some wild ghost haunting a favorite spot. Never was there a better scene for wild and fearful story. The Germans would make this the very land of diabelrie.

The "Sutors o' Selkirk," are even now numerous in its principal streets, if not as numerous as when they made so many shoes for the Highland army in 1745. To be made a sutor of Selkirk even now, I believe, is but another phrase for being made a burgess—and every candidate for burgal honors is compelled to lick, or pass through his mouth a small bunch of bristles, such as are used by shoemakers, which too has been previously licked or smoothed by all the members of the town council, who may be present. This is called *licking the birse*, and signifies allegiance or respect to the craft who here have sway. How many horrors an

—and followed the stream of the now babling Tweed, for it had none of that furious tide at this season, which Scott sometimes describes, and sought yet one other object of interest, which the Lay of the Last Minstrel has made known to every American reader of the poem—I mean Melrose Abbey. After a walk of three or four miles, we found ourselves in a vale sheltered on every side by hills—a place which the monks had evidently selected for pleasantness and seclusion—and soon the towers of the abbey were in sight; and when we entered it, if not by the "pale moonlight," that Scott has enjoined in the hour of visitation, so as to avoid "the gay beams of lightsome day," which "gild but to flout the ruins gray,"—it was in the long twilight of this season—

"When the broken arches are dark in night,
And each shafted oriel glimmers white;
When the cold light's uncertain shower
Streams on the ruined central tower;
When buttress and buttress alternately
Seemed framed of ebon and ivory;
When silver edges the imagery,
And the scrolls that teach thee to live and die.

I have taken this quotation from the Lay of the Last Minstrel, because it is not poetry in its fictitious sense, but the very best description of a matter of fact—for

"The corbells* were carved grotesque and grim;
And the pillars, with clustered shafts to trim,
With base and capital furnish'd around,
Seem'd bundles of lances which garlands had bound."

and

"Thou would'st have thought some fairy's hand
'Twixt poplars straight the osier wand
In many a freakish knot had twined;
Then framed a spell, when the work was done,
And chang'd the willow wreaths to stone."

As our guide, who happened to be an intelligent man, quoted these and other passages, the accuracy of the description I saw, was remarkable,—and Scott has with a most happy facility seized upon existing objects to make out a poem, which is so connected with fact that it seems like history itself. I have not a doubt that two thirds of the uneducated people about here, believe that the wizard, Michael Scott, whose familiar spirit according to tradition cleft the Eilden hills in three, was buried here with the fatal book that William, of Deloraine, possessed himself of at dead of night, so vividly has the poet impressed upon the mind, his imaginations as facts. And the traveller on visiting any of these scenes, for miles and miles around is struck, as in visiting the seat of Wordsworth, with the idea that, Scott by his genius has given them all a charm which they had not before—and has thus erected for himself monuments as imperishable as the hills of which he has written, or so consecrated them, and

times, and this certain wonder of all future times. It is enough for me to stand in the ranks, and only to be counted as one of its defenders.

The Constitution of the United States, I am confident, will protect the name and the memory, both of its founders and of its friends, even of its humblest friends. It will impart to both something of its own ever memorable and enduring distinction; I had almost said something of its own everlasting remembrance. Centuries hence, when the vicissitudes of human affairs shall have broken it, if ever they shall break it, into fragments, these very fragments, every shattered column, every displaced foundation stone, shall yet be sure to bring them all into recollection, and attract to them the respect and gratitude of mankind.

Gentlemen, it is to pay respect to this Constitution, it is to manifest your attachment to it, your sense of its value, and your devotion to its true principles, that you have sought this occasion. It is not to pay an ostentatious personal compliment. If it were, it would be unworthy, both of you and of me. It is not to manifest attachment to individuals, independent of all considerations of principles; if it were, I should feel it my duty to tell you, friends as you are, that you were doing that, which at this very moment, constitutes one of the most threatening dangers to the Constitution itself. Your gift would have no value, in my eyes, this occasion would be regarded by me as an idle pageant, if I did not know that they are both but modes, chosen by you, to signify your attachment to the true principles of the Constitution, your fixed purpose, so far as in you lies, to maintain those principles, and your resolution to support public men, and stand by them, so long, and no longer, than they shall support and stand by the Constitution of the Country. "The Constitution of the Country!"

Gentlemen, often as I am called to contemplate this subject, its importance always rises, and magnifies itself, more and more, before me. I cannot view its preservation as a concern of narrow extent, or temporary duration. On the contrary, I see in it a vast interest, which is to run down with the generations of men, and to spread over a great portion of the earth with a direct, and over the rest with an indirect, but a most powerful influence. When I speak of it here, in this thick crowd of fellow-citizens and friends, I yet behold thronging about me, a much larger and more imposing crowd. I see a united rush of the present and the future. I see all the patriotic of our own land, and our own time, I see also the many millions of their posterity, and I see, too, the lovers of human liberty from every part of the earth, from beneath the oppression of thrones, and hierarchies, and dynasties, from amidst the darkness of ignorance, degradation and despotism, into which any ray of political light has penetrated; I see all those countless multitudes gather about us, and I hear their united and earnest voices, conjuring us, in whose charge the treasure now is, to hold on, and hold

The Connecticut Courant.

VOL. LXXII.....NO. 3704. | HARTFORD, MONDAY, JANUARY 18, 1836. | PRICE TWO DOLLARS.

CONNECTICUT COURANT.
PUBLISHED BY
GOODWIN & CO.
FIFTEEN RODS NORTH-WEST OF THE STATE-HOUSE, HARTFORD.

Price Two Dollars per annum, payable in advance—a liberal discount made to companies.

Advertisements not exceeding a square inserted three times for One Dollar—every after continuation Twenty Cents.

No accounts will be opened for Advertisements sent from a distance.

WEEKLY ALMANAC.

JANUARY.	☉ R.	☉ S.	D. INC.	R. ☽ S.
18 Monday,	7 28	4 53	0 22	Sets.
19 Tuesday,	7 28	4 55	0 23	6 3
20 Wednesday,	7 27	4 56	0 24	7 10
21 Thursday,	7 26	4 57	0 26	8 14
22 Friday,	7 26	4 58	0 28	9 18
23 Saturday,	7 25	4 0	0 30	10 23
24 Sunday,	7 24	4 1	0 32	11 26

Full Moon, 3d, 8h. evening.
Last Quarter, 11th, 11h. morning.
New Moon, 18th, 3h. morning.
First Quarter, 25th, 10h. morning.

AGRICULTURAL.

The following lines were sung at the recent annual exhibition of the Essex (Mass.) Agricultural Society.

THE FARMER'S SONG.

The Farmer's life we love, although
Fatigued by toil we be;
Contented to *hard work* we go,
None happier than we.
We love the lands we cultivate,
The cattle that we rear;
Sloth, Vice and Slavery we hate,
But count free labor cheer.

CHORUS.

We cast our seed on well tilled ground,
We dress our crops with care;
And when the harvest time comes round,
We earth's abundance share.

We envy not the rich and great;
The humblest farmer's lot
Is better than a vast estate,
By fraud or rapine got.
By healthful toil we win our bread
Beneath the glorious skies,
Enjoy the beauties round us spread,
And high God's bounties prize.

From early dawn to closing day,
To plow, plant, weed or mow,
The Farmer, whistling, hies away—
His wife is busy too.
To wash, to churn, to cook or sweep,
By turns her hand she plies,
Stops but to rock her babe to sleep,
Or hush her children's cries.

'Tis busy life but often here
Th' affections of the heart
In holiest purity appear,
And highest bliss impart.
We thankful take what God bestows,
And learn to feel and know,
That the best cure for human woes
Is industry below.

We strive to culture heart and head,
Our lives from vice to free,
And trust, like well filled grain, when dead,
Life giving bread to be.
To more successful enterprise,
Than we ourselves have known,
Or seeds, whence future crops shall rise
Superior to our own.

On the Feeding and Management of Milch Cows.

It is of great consequence in the management of a dairy that the cows should be treated with gentleness, so that they may not be afraid of being milked, or dislike the milker. A cow will not yield her milk willingly to a person she fears, hates, or apprehends ill treatment from. Young cows, in particular, may have their characters for gentleness and good milkers formed by the manner in which they are treated. This truth, of much importance to all concerned in a dairy or its products, is well established and illustrated by a communication from Mr. Russel Woodward, published in Memoirs of the New York Board of Agriculture, in substance as follows:—

Having formerly kept a large number of cows, I observed many amongst them dried up their milk so early in the fall, that they were not profitable, while others with the same keeping, gave milk in plenty until late in the season. I likewise have often heard my neighbors observe, that some of their cows, though very good in the forepart of the season, dried up their milk so early that they were unprofitable, and they would have to put them off; I accordingly found it expedient to find out the cause, if possible: and when I brought to mind the ways that some of my young cows had been kept and milked, I attributed the cause to the milking of them the first season they gave milk; and by many experiments since, I have found that young cows, the first year they gave milk may be made, with careful milking and good keeping, to give milk almost any length of time required, say from the first of May to the first of February following, and will give milk late always after, with careful milking. But if they are left to dry up their milk early in the fall, they will be sure to dry up their milk each succeeding year, if they have a calf near the same season of the year; and nothing but extraordinary keeping will prevent it, and that but a short time. I have had them dry up their milk in August, and could not by any means make them give milk much past that time in any succeeding year. I had two heifers, which had calves in April, and after getting them gentle, I set a boy to milk them for the season, (which is often done the first season on account of their having small teats:) he was careless, and dried them both up in August. Although I was satisfied I should lose the greater part of the profit of them afterwards, yet I took it upon me the following year to milk them myself and give them good feed, but to no purpose. I could not make them give milk much past the time they dried the year before. I have two cows now that were milked the first year they had calves, until near the time of their calving again, and have continued to give milk as late as ever since, if we will milk them.—*Genesee Farmer.*

BROOKS' LETTERS.

From the Correspondent of the Portland Advertiser.

NO. XXIX.
THINGS IN LONDON.

London, July 15, 1835.

"One man is nothing—at most but an atom, a mere atom, an anatomized atom!" Horror of horrors—how many times has this London been emptied in the many past centuries! What do they do with the dead? Can the earth hold them? How many feet deep of the dead, think you, there are under the earth, hereabout. If the resurrection will be as we think, what a spectacle will be exhibited here! The two millions of people over whom I am looking now, thirty years hence, will be half gone;—sixty years hence, quite gone. A new race will be in these streets. Our day will be *antiquity*. People will wonder how we looked and acted. The peoples' children's children will be trampling over us. Two millions more of dead will be added to the millions of millions under the earth. Other men will be in St. Stephen's then. The St. James will have another King and Queen if King and Queen then there be,—and the worms will be eating this one, if then he be not already eaten. Perchance his monument will stand up somewhere, as rusty as Charles the Second's. But old Thames will be what he now is. He will not change. Whip up quickly your heavy horses, ye draymen on Ludgate Hill. Others are hurrying to take your places. Drive on, livery boys. Who will drive when you are dead? What will a thousand years know of you?, What folly to pile up these huge masses of stone! Old Time sends abroad millions of messengers, eating and gnawing the very stone,—and by and by he comes himself, with his terrible sledge, and strikes down what they have loosened. And you, Westminster Abbey, must also fall. He is at work upon you. By and by, rubbish will fill your Poet's Corner. Aye, this old Tower, they are propping up and propping up. Its turrets look as if they shake. *There*, is the monument erected in memory of the great fire. Who knows, but another great fire will level even this dome in the dust. Sir Christopher Wren built this—and Sir Christopher Wren sleeps in a dark cell under my feet.

I have just been looking at Nelson's sarcophagus, under the very centre of this dome. Nelson died to lay in that gloomy place, to dispel whose darkness, torches must be lighted, ere his tomb can be seen. Oh, what is glory! A shilling is asked to see him, and the great painters, and some others—the same sum that is demanded for seeing the beasts in the Tower. What care all the mighty mass of human beings moving around this church, who lie buried here! The huge clock is striking. How many have died within the scan of the eye hence, since it first began to strike! Why cannot we arrest the march of Time, and keep young, and ever have such fresh feelings as I have now? The mischief is, I get used to every thing. What is new to-day, will be old to-morrow. Already London seems natural—not so strange, so awful, as when I came here almost frantic with astonishment. I cannot catch new thoughts, but I instantly lose them. What I see in the morning as wonderful, becomes old before night arrives. If I write down every thing as it first seems to me, I rave. If I wait till I am cool, the phantom is gone, and I am spiritless. The sound of the organ below, startles me again. I heard its loud notes swelling through the dome, and rolling through niche and gallery. The preachers in cathedrals ought to be giants, with giant's voices. If man had the power of the organ, a vocal power like that, then he could speak fitly of heaven in such vast aisles. He looks puny now, not like God's messenger. The service of religion is below, and the service of mammon about;—religion in the church,—money scrambling without. See the gold getters in the great Bank at my feet. In that Royal Exchange nearly full of rich merchants, the wealthiest on the globe, empires are bargained for. And then the forests of masts on the Thames, and in the huge docks far away. Myriads and myriads of streets and lanes!—who can count them,—all full of people—and who can feed them? Whence do the people of this empire obtain enough to eat? This puzzles me. If all this city drank from the little Thames, would they not drink it dry? How do they, I ask again, get enough to eat—so many eaters and so few producers!—What a slaughter too, there must be each day to feed them! What hecatombs of cattle slain!

Such were some of my thoughts confusedly crowded together, as I stood upon the top-most gallery around the dome of St. Paul's Church, and from this great height in the heart of the city, surveyed the masses of men and things all about me. In trusting you with these thoughts, such as must rush into every man's mind on looking at such a city, from such a place, I give you a better description than twice as many words in any other form can do. I can tell you to be sure, that I overlooked the dwellings of two millions of people, including the suburbs of London, and I might amplify upon the thickness of the smoke, and the dusty light it imparts to every thing. For miles you look upon dwellings. A rumbling confused sound swelling upwards, as of armies marching, falls upon your ears. You feel, and the feeling is a true one, as if you are looking with a glass upon the heart of all the world, whence blood is rushing every where,—for no other city any where exerts such an influence on all the world as London does. The whole world in fact, centres here. Here mankind, if I may use the expression, seem to have come to a focus. Whatever you want, or can imagine you want, money here will bring. Whatsoever you wish to see, you can see. Even this very scene of London, with a mock St. Paul's is kept for show at the Coloseum the other end of the city, and it is perfect too, with the smoke and all. And there, as if to mock nature, is kept a tropical climate with tropical plants; a cave too actually made, with a real waterfall, stalactites and all,—and then, as if this was not enough to astonish you, you are taken to Switzerland, shown Swiss cliffs, real cliffs, too, more waterfalls, really made and true to nature, and then from a Swiss cottage, you see Swiss mountains, (a painting this) and boats in actual motion over it! Here near Regent's Park, in thickly settled London is all this, all MADE—a steam engine (out of sight) pumping up the water, and turning water-wheels, and then cascades with their rainbows too! I call it the heart of the world then, for specimens of all the world are here. You can see any thing or have any thing you want to have—of fun or frolic—of literature or science,—of pleasure or of labor, of whatever there is, that the highest or lowest tastes of man can desire.

After a half-satisfying look from the dome of St. Paul's, I was fool enough to clamber up into the dark ball, the hot, pent up air, and the puffing of five or six fools like myself, made the air insufferable. I got down the narrow and dark steps again as soon as possible; and why I vexed myself to climb up in that dark place was more than I can tell. This height is 356 feet from the pavement of the church. The length of the church is 500 feet. The ground plot on which it stands, is two acres, 16 perches and 70 feet. Then I took a stroll through the whispering gallery, into the old library where there is nothing remarkable but the floor put together without a nail—by the geometrical staircase, which is a curiosity; and among the clock works, of the extent of which you will have an idea when I tell you that the dial is 57 feet in circumference, the length of the minute hand 8 feet, and that the bell which strikes the hours, weighs 11,474 pounds, and has been distinctly heard 20 miles! I had been into the crypt of which I have spoken before, and there saw where Wren, Nelson, Collingwood, Reynolds, Lawrence, Barry, West, and others are buried, and have told you too, that we were conducted about by the light of a lantern in this subterranean abode. The rest of my leisure time I spent among the monuments, which British pride and British generosity have clustered thickly together in the aisles of this great church. Pakenham and Gibbs who fell at New Orleans, stand on one monument here. Gen. Ross has a monument here. So has the Marquis of Cornwallis. Sir Isaac Brock who fell at Queenstown, (Canada) is represented as a corpse reclining in the arms of a British soldier, while an Indian mourns over his fate. The design of Gen. Ross's monument is *Valour* laying an American flag upon his tomb, over which *Britannia* is recumbent in tears, while *Fame* is descending with the laurel to crown his bust. The sculptor Flaxman, worked the monumental honors to Lord Nelson. His statue leans on an anchor. On his right, beneath, Britannia directs the attention of two young seamen to Nelson, their great example. The British Lion on the other side, guards the monument. The figures on the pedestal represent the North Sea, the German Ocean, the Nile and the Mediterranean. On the cornice are the words, Nile, Trafalgar, Copenhagen—but as to the last the less that is said about it the better, so I think. Sir William Jones, Dr. Johnson, Sir Joshua Reynolds, Admiral Rodney, Sir John Moore, Lord Collinwood, and the philanthropist Howard, each have monuments here,—with perhaps, some forty or fifty others. The best inscription of all, is that of the builder of the church, *si monumentum requiris, circumspice* on a plain marble slab over the iron gates leading to the Choir.

Thus do Englishmen pay their tribute to mind, manifest itself howsoever it may. The Poet as well as the Soldier, the Architect as well as the Judge, the Painter as well as the Sailor has his monument here. What an inspiring place for an Englishman! What a stimulus to ambition! But this much less so than Westminster Abbey, after visiting which, the traveller will understand why Nelson associated victory with its vaults and aisles, in the hour of battle.

English taste may love 'the venerable look' of St. Paul's as much as they please, but till I learn to love a coal pit, I shall have no love for such a mass of "lamp black" as this is on the outer side. The greatest piece of impudence of which John Bull is guilty, and I could not say a harder thing, for he is such an essence of impudence at times, is in bepraising the "solemn air" of his sooty buildings. He lives in a climate that rusts and begrims every thing exposed to it, and, therefore, his country's "venerable look"—and denounces the bright cheerful aspect of American dwellings. The London coal soot is over a half inch thick, I should judge from the view, on the walls of St. Paul's,—and we are really told, that this is "mellowed," "softened," "grand," "antique," "sublime." Why, we could make all America "sublime" in a week or so by our pitch, tar and lamp-black. Think now of the impudence of John Bull landing in New-York, for the first day in his life able to wear a clean shirt all the day, snuffing our dry air in contempt, and turning up his nose at our neatly painted dwellings. Think of his praising the "venerable aspect" of his smoked and sooty St. Paul's! Think of his thus extolling the vice of his climate, and ridiculing the purity of ours! Did you ever hear such ingenious impudence! I say nothing of the structure itself. I have had no opportunities as yet to compare and thus to criticise, for I have not seen St. Peter's nor have I been on the Continent where I am expecting to see wonders. Imagine a huge church to be in the centre of the Broadway of New York, or your own principal business streets, and you will have an idea of the situation of this, and a faint one of the bustle all around. Thick as are the people in Wall-street, they are three times thicker here. If they walked as rapidly as they do there, no man would soon know his own head and legs from his neighbor's.

B.

From the New York Observer.

LETTER OF REV. DR. EDWARDS.

To Rev. Wm. A. Hallock, Sec. of the American Tract Society.

Dear Sir,—In answer to yours of the 11th instant, I would observe, that from the slight attention which I have paid to the subject, I have always supposed that our Saviour used "the fruit of the vine" as one of the elements in the appointment of the ordinance of the supper; and that it is still a proper element to be used in the observance of that holy ordinance. This, so far as I know, is the common opinion of ministers and churches. And numbers are so desirous of exactly imitating their Savior and using only "the fruit of the vine" on such occasions, that they are in the habit of preparing it themselves, at each communion, as regularly as they do the bread, which is the other element that they think, as I do, it is proper to use, because this appears also to have been used by our Savior at the institution of the ordinance. All churches, however, are not so scrupulous about exactly imitating the Savior and using merely "the fruit of the vine." They think it enough to use what is considered and called wine, and that it is not necessary that they should know that it is merely "the fruit of the vine." And I have observed, in some cases, somewhat of a tendency in the more scrupulous to "despise" those who in this thing are less so; and in those that are less scrupulous, to "condemn" those that are more so. But I think it not unlikely, that Paul were he to address them, might say, "Let not him that is more scrupulous despise him that is less so, and let not him that is less scrupulous condemn him that is more so, for God hath received him." And "if you bite and devour one another, take heed that ye be not consumed one of another."

The American Temperance Society, however, and its officers have confined their efforts to the use of intoxicating liquor, as a beverage, or an article of diet, or luxury. By intoxicating liquor, they mean that which causes, or perpetuates drunkenness. In pursuance of this object they adopted, at their last annual meeting, the following preamble and resolution, viz:

"As it has been proved, by the experience of thousands in this and other countries, of all ages and conditions, and in all kinds of lawful business, that abstinence from intoxicating drink is not only safe but salutary; and as this is the only course in which it can be rationally expected that intemperate persons can ever be permanently reformed; and as the example and kind moral influence of the temperate is the grand means of leading the intemperate to adopt and pursue a course so essential to their present and future good, therefore, *Resolved*, that the more extensively and universally this course is adopted by all friends of temperance, the more rapid, in our view will be the progress, and the more complete the triumphs of the temperance reformation; and the greater will be the prospect that drunkenness and its evils will cease."

Here, you observe, they cautiously abstain from saying any thing about the use of intoxicating liquor in the arts, leaving that to artisans; and they say nothing about the use of it as a medicine, leaving that to intelligent physicians, who do not use intoxicating liquor as a beverage; and nothing about the use of it at the holy communion, leaving that to ministers and churches to do as they think will be most pleasing to the Lord, and most useful to men. The reasons which induce them to wish to have all men abstain from the use of intoxicating liquor as a beverage, are, they think that they will, by so doing, be more healthy, set a more useful example, and be better fitted for every good work. Nor are they aware that these views, as they understand them, conflict at all with the propriety of the use of "the fruit of the vine," or of the "bread," at the ordinance of the supper; while the evidence of the utility of abstinence from the use of intoxicating liquor as a beverage, is, in their view, conclusive.

Testimony in great variety and abundance is coming in upon them, and from many among the most respectable men in the country, like the following, which I copy from the Rev. Dr. Pierce, of Brookline, a man who, so far as I know, has never given any just ground for the charge of fanaticism, ultraism, or extravagance—bitter words, and often used when sound arguments and kind persuasion, would be more proper.

"For more than a quarter of a century," he says, "I have conscientiously abstained from distilled liquor. In the meantime, I have occasionally taken a little wine, when in company, and a tumbler of cider, at dinner. At length however, thinking it unnecessary, and having before me the example of a beloved father, who abjured the use of intoxicating beverage after he was 80 years old, and lived, with both bodily and mental faculties almost wholly unimpaired, till past the age of 91; and continually hearing that the habitual drinkers of ardent spirits exclaim, 'Give us your wine, and we will drink no more rum,' I resolved to abstain from the use of every thing which can intoxicate. This practice I have continued for more than two years; and the experiment has more than answered my most sanguine expectations. My health has been fine and uninterrupted. I have not had even a common cold. As to corporeal exertions, though in my 63d year, I walk ten miles in an afternoon, at the rate of four miles an hour, without fatigue; and what is better, without *thirst*. Since I have abjured cider, I often dine without drinking even water. As to mental efforts, I never feel so well prepared for close application, as immediately after I have walked ten miles without drink. Uniform health of body is almost necessarily attended with cheerfulness of mind. The saddest interruption that I find to the latter is, that, in the use of drinks, I cannot induce more to be as I am."

Should the example of Dr. Pierce, and that of 200,000 others in our land, of all ages, conditions, and employments, be followed by all sober men, and especially in our cities, while they would greatly promote their own benefit, they would set an example which would render others much more useful, and which would need only to be universally and perseveringly followed, to cure all the drunkenness in the world, and prevent that awful foe of God and man from any longer assisting the devil in driving men down to perdition. I am greatly obliged to you for your kind letter, and shall always gratefully receive from you, and and all others, any hints which may tend, by "light and love," to promote the good cause, temperance, which is so intimately connected with that of righteousness and preparation for the judgment to come. Any use of this letter, which will promote the public good, you are at liberty to make.

With great respect and esteem, I am truly yours, &c.

J. Edwards,
Cor. Sec. Am. Temp. Soc.

From the "South West by a Yankee."

THE CEMETERY AT NEW ORLEANS.

"This cemetery is quite out of the city; there being no dwelling or enclosure of any kind beyond it. On approaching it, the front on the street presents the appearance of a lofty brick wall of very great length, with a spacious gateway in the centre. This gateway is about ten feet deep; and one passing through it, would imagine the wall of the same solid thickness. This however is only apparent. The wall which surrounds, or is to surround the four sides of the burial-ground, (for it is yet incompleted,) is about twelve feet in height, and ten in thickness. The external appearance on the street is similar to that of any other high wall, while to a beholder within, the cemetery exhibits three stories of oven-like tombs, constructed in the wall, and extending on every side of the grave-yard. Each of these tombs is designed to admit only a single coffin, which is enclosed in the vault with masonry, and designated by a small marble slab fastened in the face of the wall at the head of the coffin, stating the name, age, and sex of the deceased. By casual estimate I judged there were about eighteen hundred apertures in this vast pile of tombs. This method, resorted to here from necessity, on account of the nature of the soil, might serve as a hint to city land-economists.

When I entered the gateway, I was struck with surprise and admiration. Though destitute of trees, the cemetery is certainly more deserving, from its peculiarly novel and unique appearance of the attention of strangers, than (with the exception of that at New Haven, and Mount Auburn) any other in the United States. From the entrance to the opposite side through the centre of the grave-yard, a broad avenue or street extends nearly an eighth of a mile in length; and on either side of this are innumerable insolated tombs of all sizes, shapes and descriptions, above the ground. The idea of a Lilliputian city was at first suggested to my mind on looking down this extensive avenue. The tombs in their various and fantastic styles of architecture—if I may apply the term to these tiny edifices,—resembled cathedrals with towers, Moorish dwellings, temples, chapels, palaces, *mosques*—substituting the cross for the crescent—and structures of almost every kind. The idea was ludicrous enough; but as I passed down the avenue, I could not but indulge the fancy that I was striding down the Broadway of the capital of the Lilliputians. I mention this, not irreverently, but to give you the best idea I can of the cemetery, from my own impressions. Many of the tombs, were constructed like, and several were, indeed, miniature Grecian temples; while others resembled French, or Spanish edifices, like those found in 'old Castile.' Many of them, otherwise plain, were surmounted by a tower supporting a cross. All were perfectly white, arranged with the most perfect regularity, and distant a little more than a foot from each other. At the distance of every ten rods, the main avenue was intersected by others of less width, crossing it at right angles, down which tombs were ranged in the same novel and regular manner. The whole cemetery was divided into squares, formed by these narrow streets intersecting the principal avenue. It was in reality a City of the Dead. But it was a city composed of miniature palaces, and still more diminutive villas.

The procession, after passing two-thirds of the way up the spacious walk turned down one of the narrow alleys, where a new tomb, built on a line with the others, gaped wide to receive its destined inmate. The procession stopped. The coffin was let down from the shoulders of the bearers, and rolled on wooden cylinders into the tomb. The mourners silently gathered around; every head was bared; and amid the deep silence that succeeded, the calm, clear melancholy voice of the priest suddenly swelled upon the still evening air, in the plaintive chant of the last service of the dead. Requiescat in pace! was slowly chanted by the priest—repeated in subdued voices by the mourners, and echoing among the tombs, died away in the remotest recesses of the cemetery.

THE WAR IN FLORIDA.

The following particulars of the state of things in Florida are published in the Charleston Courier, in the shape of extracts of private letters from Florida:

"St. Augustine, Dec. 26.—Although the enemy is 100 miles off, we experience all the vexations and troubles attending a besieged city; nothing is to be seen but the most inefficient militia, running from one quarter to another, a wild goose chase, without plans or well concerted measures, in order to give room to our detachment of troops. They are sent out in numbers of 20, 30, and 50, at the reasonable distance of 50 miles from each other, to procure intelligence and make reconnoissances where no enemy is known to be. Out of 240 men composing our militia, and 60 veterans, or alarm men, near 90 have left town upon these foolish excursions, and the remainder are constantly harrassed, by patrolling, mounting guard at head-quarters, and parading with military buttons in their hats (for uniforms or regular accoutrements are unknown) through the streets of this mighty city. All these movements are only productive of alarm, bustle, and noise, without advantage to any body. We are daily tormented by the most extraordinary reports, but nothing is positively known, except that within an extent of more than one hundred miles, six or eight individuals, personally obnoxious, have been killed by the Indians, and about the same number of houses burnt, which had been previously abandoned by the proprietors. The result of this is general confusion, notwithstanding there is no immediate danger, and a total stagnation of any sort of business, except for military contractors, who are in a hurry to bleed Uncle Sam."

"St. Augustine, Dec. 26.—Flattering myself with the belief that you always feel an interest in whatever concerns *us*, and in Florida generally, it was my intention to write, and give as far as I could a *correct* statement of our situation with respect to the Indians, now the one great and engrossing subject, but I have felt so gloomy for the last few days, that I deferred writing, in hopes of better spirits, till this moment that Southwick's signal gun warns me that I have only half an hour. It is so difficult even here to obtain truth, that I should not be surprised if many and gross misrepresentations find their way abroad. If however, we are represented in a hopeless and exposed condition, (in Augustine as well as throughout the country,) it is no more than the truth. The Indians have now openly commenced hostilities; General Clinch had issued orders to Colonel Warren, who had a party of 250 mounted men, to scour the country within a certain district, and to send on the baggage wagons to Mecanopi under a guard; the Indians, supposed about 80, lay in ambush, suffered the guard to pass on, and then attacked and captured three wagons; had taken out the ammunition and burnt two when Dr. M'Ilmore came up with 30 men, attacked them, retook the remaining wagon, and drove them into a hammock—I should say they retreated thither. The Dr. had two horses shot under him, and then, sword in hand, and on foot, called to his men to follow, but only twelve had courage to do so; he was therefore obliged to make good his own retreat with the wagon, and four men wounded. The Americans lost 15 horses in this skirmish.

"It is unknown what number of Indians may have fallen: all the plantations of Alachua are deserted except the General's and M'Intoshes'; at these two places the troops that were taken from this are stationed. At Newnansville there are 240 women and children endeavoring themselves to throw up entrenchments; they have only youths and old men to guard them. Mr. Watson was at that place when he wrote the above account. He further informs, that a plantation within two and a half miles of his, on the Suwanee, was burnt, and an attack expected to be made on his place on Monday last, and no tidings have since been received. Two days after the above intelligence, an express arrived from Major Putman, (stationed with about 30 men at Derley's Tomoka, saying that Henry Woodruff had been murdered at Volusia. Mr. Forester, and the others which were at Spring Garden, immediately made off for Tomoka, and were afterwards joined by Joseph Woodruff. You will easily imagine the injury that all this must be to Florida, even if the savages are ultimately conquered and sent off. What is to become of so many houseless wretches, who have fled from their homes, and left all to be destroyed by the ruthless enemy? Nor can there be any crops expected the ensuing year. Our express came in last night to say that Gen. Call had had an encounter, (with how many I know not,) but he had killed six and taken two captives. My greatest reliance is on the experience, judgment, and valor of this officer in this most dreadful of all warfare, but there is no knowing where the great body of Indians are. We are quiet as yet down South; no one attempts a journey now through any part of the country, but feel as if they might never return.—George is building a block house of cabbage logs, (which will not burn;) into this he means to convey what he can of his goods and chattels, and, if necessary, defend it. If I could only get them conveyed to him, I would try and get arms and ammunition from Charleston: if these could be sent them, I should have but little fear, for I know we could depend on our negroes, and there are, or were, 30 live oak cutters, but they were without arms, and James told me that Grice was apprehensive that they would return in the same vessel. The measures taken by Gen. H. seemed now more satisfactory; there are pickets placed over the bridge, outside the gates, and at the fort—but he has left in the whole town only about sixty men for this duty. A detachment has been sent to guard the Government stores."

"St. Augustine, Dec. 26—We are at war with the Seminoles. Much individual mischief will be done—many small settlements, and all, large or small, which are or shall be deserted, have been and will be burnt. Young Henry Woodruff, of Spring Garden, when out cattle hunting with a negro boy, was shot from his horse and killed; his brother Joseph, who had taken a different course, escaped. Forester and all the whites, immediately on getting intelligence from the negro boy who had escaped, deserted the plantation. Unless the slaves are very faithful it will be burnt. Lancaster has been shot in the neck, though not dangerously—Call is well—Clinch with 570 mounted volunteers. Bulow, Clinch, M'Intosh, Anderson, and some others, have their places guarded.

Destruction of the Kingston (U. C.) Hospital by fire with loss of life.—On Monday night the 21st of December, about 10 o'clock, the roof of the school-house attached to the hospital was discovered to be on fire, which spreading with amazing rapidity soon caught the roof of the hospital and quickly reduced the entire building to ashes. It is with deep regret that we have to add, that a man named John Carter, a paralytick, perished in the flames. It seems that at the time the fire was discovered, he was asleep in bed, but was immediately awakened and informed of his danger. He, however, did not appear inclined to pay much attention to the warning, and when last seen he was lying in bed. The rapidity of the flames was such, that even those who were earliest on the alert, had barely time to escape. The furniture, beds and bedding, provisions, &c. were destroyed.

IMPORTANT FROM MEXICO.

DEFEAT OF THE TEXIAN ARMY AT TAMPICO, AND THE EXECUTION OF TWENTY-EIGHT OF THE ARMY, MANY OF THEM NATIVES AND CITIZENS OF THE UNITED STATES.

New-Orleans, December 25.

The intelligence communicated to-day to our readers is rather of a serious and melancholy nature for the season; and is certainly of importance sufficient to cause sober reflection in the minds of our citizens who are not only solicitous for the success of our brethren in Texas, but are equally anxious to preserve faithfully the treaty ties of alliance between Mexico and the United States, and maintaining the integrity of our commerce and political relations.

The despatch of the Mexican Minister of Foreign Affairs to Washington is an able and guarded document, and well worthy the attention of the executive government. The President in his Message has stated that he had in part acted on the first suggestions recommended by the Mexican, when he asserts that he gave orders on the subject to the U. S. District Attornies; and we believe he might with the utmost safety act on the second in liberating Thompson and his crew as the prisoner has had a trial, and his jury could not agree on a verdict. Even this circumstance should inspirit to mercy if not to justice: for according to the law of nations, Thompson should not have been tried in any of our courts, for what he did as a Mexican citizen, in the Mexican seas, and under commission of the Mexican government. Thompson may doubtless have exceeded his authority, but the despatch points out the legitimate means of redress.

On the subject of the death by order of a court martial of 28 of our citizens at Tampico on the 14th inst., the minds of our citizens will be divided in opinion—some probably looking on it as but authorized butchery, deserving vengeance, while others more cautious and experienced, may think it lamentable, but also justifiable by necessity and the laws of nations. The invaders of a friendly country cannot be viewed as prisoners of war by right or courtesy, whether they have voluntarily or involuntarily taken arms against that country—the fact of having been found in arms against the peace and authority of a nation is a sufficient charge for condemnation, and justification for any mode of death conformable to military laws.—Those who went out in any of the expeditions from this place must have known the consequences: they went out in their individual capacity, as citizens, and the United States government is not responsible for their conduct: they have suffered in that capacity, and our government is not bound to take cognizance of their fate. Those who go to Texas should be prepared for victory or death, and certainly those who foolishly made an attempt on Tampico, dared the vengeance of the Mexican authority and laws. Their fate may be lamented by their immediate friends and the friends of humanity; but it is justified by necessity and policy, by right and law—precisely as the fate of any criminal becoming amenable to the penalties of justice for violated law.—[*Bee.*

The following is a copy of a letter from one of the unfortunate young men who joined in the expedition of General Mehia against Tampico:

Tampico, December 13, 1835. }
Nine o'clock, P. M. }

Dear Friends—I will in few words as possible give you intelligence of my fate which is an untimely one. To-morrow morning, before sunrise, I, together with twenty-seven of my companions, are to be shot, according to orders given by a court martial of Mexican soldiers, or officers, for an attack on this city on the night of the 15th November last. I, for my part, am perfectly reconciled to my fate. No use in giving particulars of the battle—I am pretty sure you must have heard them before. I, at the time of the engagement, got a wound in the head with a ball, and another thro' the right hand. I have been in the hospital until this afternoon, from the morning of the battle. No money can save us: even five thousand dollars was offered for any one individual.—There was likewise offered one hundred thousand dollars as a ransom; but the reason of the refusal was, that they want to deter others from the cause of Liberty. This is a regular *massacre*. We should have been treated as prisoners of war. I hope the American nation will revenge our lives. I have but a few hours to live, so God bless you all.

Farewell—Adieu.

JAMES FARRELL.

I cannot write well—excuse me.

To Messrs. Dubois & Garretson, New-Orleans.

We are politely furnished with the following letter from Tampico.

Tampico, December 14, 1835.

Dear Sir.—This morning twenty-eight unfortunate victims of treachery and villany, part of Meja's expedition were shot. I hand you enclosed a list of them, with a petition presented to the Military Commandant, by several foreigners and Mexicans, drawn up and signed by the prisoners; but alas, it was not in his power to meet their solicitations.

The papers enclosed, were sent to me by the curate who attended them in their last moments—they requested that they might be printed in New Orleans.

The letter from Jonas H. Steward, and the petition to the Commandant, were given to me at the prison grate, on Sunday morning—I had them translated into Spanish, and presented them myself to the Commandant, and am satisfied that had he the power, he would have complied with their last request.

You have here a full view, as well as the Government and people of the United States have, of the hideous crime committed in the port of New Orleans, against the laws of God and of honor, under the pretence of populating Texas. A number of distressed and unfortunate beings are entrapped and put on board the schooner Mary Jane, Captain Hall, under the express stipulation and understanding that they are bound for Matagorda and Galveston, in Texas, as the clearance of said vessel at the custom house in New Orleans, on the 6th ult. indicates. It was further understood that they were to have lands on their arrival there, and a free passage, and mark the result: such as has been the fate of these unfortunate men, was near to have been inflicted on every American in this place. Such enterprises may, in New Orleans, be termed mercantile speculations—they are worthy of such men as enter into them—and I do not envy them their feelings.

Extract from a letter of an American gentleman at Tampico, to a respectable house in this city, dated,

Tampico, 14th Dec. 1835.

I, in company with every respectable foreign merchant in this place, and I may add with every one throughout the country, most heartily deprecate the late attack made upon this port by Mehia and Peza supported as they were by troops raised abroad. You must be aware that the war in Texas, peopled as it is, principally by North Americans, naturally predisposes the minds of the uneducated portion of the Mexicans against our citizens resident here, and even against foreigners in general. This feeling is increased by the strongly inflammatory nature of nearly all the proclamations issued at the present moment by the commanding officers to their troops: and there is no double source of apprehension on account of the late attack upon Tamanlipas, for it is known that the expedition was fitted out from your port, that the men were greater than any one or two of the chief movers of the plan could advance.

Even those in this country who may have instigated this plan of operation have deceived themselves; for most of those upon whom they counted refused to act in concert with foreigners against their own country.

Why is it that the government of the United States does not take decisive measures to prevent the notorious embarkation of men, arms and money from her ports, and in a vessel which sails confessedly for the purpose of attacking a country at present at peace with her? And more, why after permitting this, and thus compromising her citizens resident here, does it not send out for their protection a sufficient number of citizens? I am aware that New Orleans is the only place in the U. States where the operations above mentioned can be carried on effectively; and I am still more surprised at it, as the capitalists of that place will be the heaviest losers should American property in this country be placed in jeopardy. All sensible merchants in Mexico wish for peace under whatever form of government the nation may think fit to adopt; and it is really vexing to think that our security and that of our property should be compromised at home.

We, the undersigned prisoners of war, condemned to be shot on Monday next, the 14th inst, at 7, A. M., by a military court martial, conformable to the established custom of the country, and composed of officers of the Mexican army, the sentence being read and interpreted to us on Saturday, at 4 P. M., by Captain Alexander Faulac of said army, as our last dying words, do declare ourselves innocent of the charge of either participating or colleagueing with any person or party having for its object the revolutionizing or disturbing in any way the tranquility of the government of Mexico, and that the testimony given before the honorable court of inquiry will corroborate this declaration, the facts and circumstances being briefly as follow:

That about 130 men, composed of Americans, French and Germans, two thirds of which being of the first named class, (including three who are natives of foreign nations but naturalized.) embarked on the 6th November last on board the American schooner Mary Jane, captain Hall, said to have been chartered or employed by a committee, of which Mr. William Christiy, of New Orleans, was the agent, to convey emigrants to the Texas, then understood to be at variance with the Mexican government. This opportnnity afforded many in pecuniary circumstances a passage free, which was readily embraced and accepted of. The terms agreed upon were, that it was optional whether the party took up arms in defence of the Texas, or not; that they were at full liberty to act as they pleased when landed on the Texian shore. That taking advantage of this favorable opportunity they accordingly embarked—the vessel proceeded on the voyage, and nothing transpired to indicate a belief but that all was right as it should be, until the 6th day we were out from the Balize, although it had been previously understood that a general, with his officers or staff, was on board the vessel, whose design was to act in concert with the Texians, and induce us to join him. Of this however we received no certain assent, but the truth is—Tampico was our destination and an attack upon the city, the design, which was now evident, and not before—the land being in sight and the vessel standing in it was announced that it was Tampico; that the steamboat then also in sight would have us in tow, and Tampico would be in our possession.—Elated with this harangue proceeding from the authority (through the instrumentality of Capt. Hawkins, one of the Aides,) of General Mehia, some were induced to join his standard, but of these the number could not have exceeded fifty, thirty-five of whom were French and Creoles, of New-Orleans, who doubtless had a previous understanding, they being exclusively privileged, having the quarter deck to themselves, and seemingly armed and equipped prematurely. The boat had us in tow soon, and all that could be crammed below were driven there until she struck the bar, and the steam boat soon afterwards. In this awful predicament, night closing on us, the sea breaking over us, efforts were used to reach the shore, which at imminent danger was effected safely, and were all landed during the latter part of the night and early part of the morning of the following day.

A formidable fort surrendered without an attack, and we built fires to dry our clothing. The party were now tendered arms and ammunition, and never having been soldiers before, some probably took them from curiosity, others from necessity and others from compulsion; and it is asserted and believed that no one person was or had been acquainted with two others of the number of us, before we could have an understanding we were commingled and bundled together more like a board or drove of swine than a company of soldiers competent to act as such, particularly against regular trained soldiery. At about 5 P. M. on Sunday we were formed and made ready for the attack, having added to our number about from 35 to 50 citizens, soldiers of adherents, and which were all judged to be Mexicans, a number being fellow prisoners with us, but without trial to this moment. Having no other resource we were necessarily compelled from obvious reasons reluctantly to join in the party, with a full determination not to act in concert with it, but submit ourselves as prisoners of war, having no design or intention to fight, and without one single exception every individual of the undersigned, from motives of conscience and oppression, added to the shameful abduction or deception practised on us, and chose to throw ourselves on the clemency and mercy of the authorities. And this being the substance of our testimony before the court, yet notwithstanding, mark the result which has terminated, not in an ignominous, but christian-like death. Trusting in God, and bearing in mind his promise, and with our trust in his mercies, we die both as Christians and men.

We have now but nine hours allotted us, and conclude hastily by requesting all who may hear of our fate to entertain no erroneous impression.

List of persons under sentence of death, by order of a military tribunal held at Tampico, to be shot on Monday, December 14, 1835.

Arthur H. Clement, native of Pennsylvania, aged 40, parents unknown.
Thomas Whitaker, of do., aged 30, father in Penn.
W. C. Barclay, of New-York, aged 20, parents in New-York.
Jacob Morrison, of do., aged 21, parents in Ky.
Edward Mount, of do., aged 23, mother in N. Y.
Charles Gross, of Penn. aged 23, mother in Penn.
Isaac F. Leeds, of New-Jersey, aged 30, parents not known.
Mordecai Gest, of Maryland, aged 53, father in Maryland; his own late residence in Ohio.
David Long, of Ohio, aged 25, mother in Ohio.
W. H. Mackay, of Virginia, aged 20, mother in Va.
Jonas K. Stewart, of Vermont, aged 33, mother in Vermont.
Daniel Holt, of Canada, aged 18, parents in Canada.
James Cramp, of England, aged 22, parents in Oswego, N. Y.
Lewis Jacobs, of do., aged 21, mother in L. Canada.
Thomas H. Rogers, of Ireland, aged 28, parents in Ireland.
Daniel Donnelly, of do., aged 20, parents in St. Johns, N. B.
James Farrel, of do., aged 23, father in Green County, New-York.
Jas. Martin Ives, of England, aged 35, no parents, two brothers in New-Orleans.
Augustus Laussear, of France, aged 22, } Parents in
—— Demoussent, do do. 25, } France.
Frederick Deboy, of Duntzic, aged 24, parents in Dantzic.
Fred. Wm. Mauer, of Germany, aged 22, parents in Saxony.
Henry Wagner, of Germany, aged 24, no parents, late from Philadelphia.
John Ivish, of Germany, aged 24, no parents.
Andreas Helen, of Germany, aged 50, no parents.
George Islein, do. aged 27, father in Germany.
Wm. H. Morris, of New-Providence, aged 28, no parents.
L. M. Bellepont, of Hanover, aged 25, no parents.
Three prisoners died in the Hospital, viz.:
—— Fleming, aged about 25, a native of Pittsburgh, Pa.
Harris Blood, aged 40, a native of England.
Jas. McCormick, aged 30, a native of Kentucky.

An enlightened and liberal Legislator.—We have seen this morning, an *envelope* addressed to Arthur Tappan and *gang*, franked by *J. Speight*, a member of Congress from N. Carolina, containing a piece of rope with this sensible, liberal and manly *envoi*.

"I herewith return you your protest, enclosing as a testimony of my high regard for your necks, a piece of rope. You will no doubt duly appreciate my motives.

J. Speight."

Washington, 2d Jan., 1835.

The paper thus returned, was the printed Protest of the American Anti-Slavery Society, against the denunciations of the President of the U. S. in his Message—a copy of which had been sent to each member of Congress—a document signed by *Arthur Tappan, William Jay* and others.—*New York American.*

Green old Age.—Mr. Eliphalet Hatch, of Southampton, is 91 years of age, and his wife a few months older. They have lived together almost 70 years. (I cannot give the exact period.) He is a blacksmith, and has labored at that trade 75 years. He labored some at that and other business the last summer. This winter he gets into his sleigh and drives 4 or 5 miles without difficulty. He stands erect, and walks *upright-ly*, and always has, in the best sense of those words. He read through the Bible three times during the year 1835. He gave up the use of ardent spirits some years since, without experiencing any inconvenience from total abstinence.—*Hampshire Gazette.*

The 26th of February has been named for a Convention of the people of New Jersey, opposed to Van Buren as a successor to the Presidency, to meet at Trenton, and select some suitable individual upon whom they are willing to bestow the highest office in the gift of a nation of freemen.

TELEGRAPH,

AND TEXAS REGISTER.

VOL. I. San Felipe de Austin, Saturday, March 12, 1836. NO. 19.

PUBLISHED EVERY SATURDAY, BY

JOSEPH BAKER & BORDENS.

TERMS: 5 dollars per annum, to be paid in advance. Advertisements (to be paid for when handed in,) occupying eight lines or less, one dollar for the first, and fifty cents for each subsequent insertion. Longer advertisements in the same proportion.

THE DECLARATION

OF INDEPENDENCE

Made by the Delegates of the People of Texas, in General Convention, at Washington, on March 2, 1836.

WHEN a government has ceased to protect the lives, liberty, and property of the people, from whom its legitimate powers are derived, and for the advancement of whose happiness it was instituted; and so far from being a guarantee for their inestimable and inalienable rights, becomes an instrument in the hands of evil rulers for their oppression. When the Federal Republican Constitution of their country, which they have sworn to support, no longer has a substantial existence, and the whole nature of their government has been forcibly changed, without their consent, from a restricted Federative Republic, composed of Sovereign States, to a consolidated Central Military despotism, in which every interest is disregarded but that of the army and the priesthood, both the eternal enemies of civil liberty, the ever ready minions of power, and the usual instruments of tyrants. When, long after the spirit of the constitution has departed, moderation is at length so far lost by those in power, that even the semblance of freedom is removed, and the forms themselves of the constitution discontinued, and so far from their petitions and remonstrances being regarded, the agents who bear them are thrown into dungeons, and mercenary armies sent forth to force a new government upon them at the point of the bayonet.

When, in consequence of such acts of malfeasance and abduction on the part of the government, anarchy prevails and civil society is dissolved into its original elements, in such a crisis, the first law of nature, the right of self preservation, the inherent and inalienable right of the people to appeal to first principles, and take their political affairs into their own hands in extreme cases, enjoins it as a right towards themselves and a sacred obligation to their posterity to abolish such government, and create another in its stead, calculated to rescue them from impending dangers, and to secure their welfare and happiness.

Nations, as well as individuals, are amenable for their acts to the public opinion of mankind. A statement of a part of our grievances is therefore submitted to an impartial world, in justification of the hazardous but unavoidable step now taken, of severing our political connection with the Mexican people, and assuming an independent attitude among the nations of the earth.

The Mexican Government, by its colonization laws, invited and induced the Anglo American population of Texas to colonize its wilderness under the pledged faith of a written constitution, that they should continue to enjoy that constitutional liberty and republican government to which they had been habituated in the land of their birth, the United States of America.

In this expectation they have been cruelly disappointed, inasmuch as the Mexican nation has acquiesced in the late changes made in the government by General Antonio Lopez Santa Ana, who having overturned the constitution of his country, now offers, as the cruel alternative, either to abandon our homes acquired by so many privations, or submit to the most intolerable of all tyranny, the combined despotism of the sword and the priesthood.

It hath sacrificed our welfare to the state of Coahuila, by which our interests have been continually depressed through a jealous and partial course of legislation, carried on at a far distant seat of government, by a hostile majority in an unknown tongue, and this too, notwithstanding we have petitioned in the humblest terms for the establishment of a separate state government, and have, in accordance with the provisions of the national constitution, presented to the general congress a republican constitution, which was, without a just cause, contemptuously rejected.

It incarcerated in a dungeon, for a long time, one of our citizens, for no other cause but a zealous endeavour to procure the acceptance of our constitution and the establishment of a state government.

It has failed and refused to secure, on a firm basis, the right of trial by jury, that palladium of civil liberty and only safe guarantee for the life, liberty, and property of the citizen.

It has failed to establish any public system of education, although possessed of almost boundless resources, (the public domain;) and although it is an axiom in political science, that unless a people are educated and enlightened, it is idle to expect the continuance of civil liberty, or the capacity for self government.

It has suffered the military commandants, stationed among us, to exercise arbitrary acts of oppression and tyranny, thus trampling upon the most sacred rights of the citizen, and rendering the military superior to the civil power.

It has dissolved, by force of arms, the state congress of Coahuila and Texas and obliged our representatives to fly for their lives from the seat of government, thus depriving us of the fundamental political right of representation.

It has demanded the surrender of a number of our citizens, and ordered military detachments to seize and carry them into the interior for trial, in contempt of the civil authorities, and in defiance of the laws and the constitution.

It has made piratical attacks upon our commerce by commissioning foreign desperadoes, and authorizing them to seize our vessels and convey the property of our citizens to far distant parts for confiscation.

It denies us the right of worshipping the Almighty according to the dictates of our own conscience, by the support of a National Religion, calculated to promote the temporal interest of its human functionaries, rather than the glory of the true and living God.

It has demanded us to deliver up our arms, which are essential to our defence—the rightful property of freemen—and formidable only to tyrannical governments.

It has invaded our country both by sea and by land, with the intent to lay waste our territory, and drive us from our homes; and has now a large mercenary army advancing, to carry on against us a war of extermination.

It has, through its emmissaries, incited the merciless savage, with the tomahawk and scalping knife, to massacre the inhabitants of our defenceless frontiers.

It has been, during the whole time of our connection with it, the contemptible sport and victim of successive military revolutions, and hath continually exhibited every characteristic of a weak, corrupt, and tyrannical government.

These, and other grievances, were patiently borne by the people of Texas, until they reached that point at which forbearance ceases to be a virtue. We then took up arms in defence of the National Constitution. We appealed to our Mexican brethren for assistance: our appeal has been made in vain; though months have elapsed, no sympathetic response has yet been heard from the interior. We are therefore forced to the melancholy conclusion, that the Mexican people have acquiesced in the destruction of their liberty, and the substitution therefor of a military government; that they are unfit to be free, and incapable of self government.

The necessity of self preservation, therefore, now decrees our eternal political separation.

We, therefore, the deligates, with plenary powers, of the people of Texas, in solemn convention assembled, appealing to a candid world for the necessities of our condition, do hereby resolve and DECLARE, *that our political connection with the Mexican nation has for ever ended, and that the people of Texas, do now constitute a* FREE, SOVEREIGN, *and* IN-

TELEGRAPH,

AND TEXAS REGISTER.

VOL. I. **San Felipe de Austin, Thursday, March 17, 1836.** NO. 20.

PUBLISHED WEEKLY, BY
JOSEPH BAKER & BORDENS.

TERMS: 5 dollars per annum, to be paid in advance. Advertisements (to be paid for when handed in,) occupying eight lines or less, one dollar for the first, and fifty cents for each subsequent insertion. Longer advertisements in the same proportion.

COMMUNICATION.

NO. III.

"Is life so dear, or peace so sweet, as to be purchased at the price of chains and slavery?"—PATRICK HENRY.

It is not necessary in order to show the identity in principle, of the Texas and the American revolution, to trace the parallel further, by enumerating the particular acts of tyranny or usurpation in the two governments of Great Britain and Mexico; for in the single claim of power to govern, the one her colonies, the other the STATES of the confederacy, in all cases whatsoever, the rights of the colonies and of the Mexican states are at once annihilated, and a declaration of indendence, that is, the erection of a new government for their future security, made, in both cases, the right and duty of the people. Yet it may gratify a useful curiosity to see how similar are the advances of despotism.

The American colonies enumerated among the wrongs, which they suffered from their government of Great Britain, the sending among them of *large bodies of armed mercenaries to harrass their people, and eat out their substance.* Precisely the same was attempted by the Mexican government. *To overawe their popular assemblies too.* So has the Mexican government overawed and dispersed popular assemblies, and has gone still further in attempting to take from the people their arms, one of the most important means in the present unsettled state of the country, both of their subsistence and defence. Indeed, had they but the power what would the Mexicans not do?

In 1775, the Congress of the British colonies of America proposed a declaration to be published to the army in orders, and to the people from the pulpit, in which, after particularizing the aggressions of Great Britain, they ask, "But why should we enumerate our injuries in detail? By one statute it is declared that parliament can of right make laws to bind us in all cases whatsover. What is to defend us against so enormous, so unlimited a power? Not a single man of those who assume it, was chosen by us, or is subject to our control or influence. We saw the misery to which such despotism would reduce us. We are now reduced to the alternative, of choosing an unconditional submission to the will of irritated ministers, or resistance by force. The latter is our choice. We have counted the cost of this contest and find nothing so dreadful as voluntary slavery. Honor, justice, and humanity forbid us tamely to surrender our freedom. We cannot endure the infamy and guilt of resigning succeeding generations to that wretchedness which inevitably awaits them, if we basely entail hereditary bondage upon them." And so may we well ask, why enumerate our injuries in detail, when the Mexicans assert the despotic power of making for us such a constitution of government as they shall see proper? What protection have we for our rights under a government claiming such an enormous, so unlimited a power. Not a single Mexican who claims this power was chosen by us or is subject to our control or influence. I trust, Texians, that like Americans you will deem nothing so dreadful as *voluntary slavery*—that justice, honor, and humanity will forbid you tamely to surrender your freedom, and that you cannot endure the infamy and guilt of resigning succeeding generations to that wretchedness which inevitably awaits them if you basely entail hereditary bondage upon them. "Is life so dear, or peace so sweet," asked the noble hearted Henry, "as to be purchased at the price of chains and slavery? Forbid it Almighty God.—I know not what course others may take, but as for me, give me liberty or give me death!!"

Such I am persuaded will be the language of every heart in Texas, when it is known, felt and understood, that Mexicans or any set of men have the impudence and effrontery to assert the right to bind them in all cases whatsoever—of compelling their submission to any constitution which they may think proper to impose upon us: for Texians cannot forget their origin, that they are Americans; and their birthright, that it is liberty. Then nothing will be wanting. Every citizen will be a soldier. "Every want will be made up by the spirit of the cause, and the soul within stand in the place of discipline, organization, resources;" and Texas, walking forth from the vile mire of dependence, will waive high the sword of proud defiance. A.

EXTRACT

OF A LETTER RECEIVED IN AUGUSTA.

Columbus, Ga. Jan. 27.

Dear Sir,—Our relations with some of the lower tribes of the Creek Indians, viz. the Euchees, Chehaws, Ohiwitchees, &c. have assumed a very serious aspect. It seems that in one of their plundering excursions on this side of the river a few days ago, one of the Indians belonging to the Chehaws was killed by the whites, in defence of their stock. This of course exasperated them, and as their morals embrace no law but retaliation, they gathered from 40 to 60 men and came over on this side to get two white men to appease the ashes of the dead. What success they had we know not; but as they were returning to recross the river into the nation, they were intercepted on the bank by Mr. John Watson, son of Gen. Watson, with 21 men, who gave them a fight of ten minutes, under great disadvantages. The Indians being under the bluff, and protected by it while the whites were out in the open field.

The party under Mr. Watson, with seven or eight exceptions fought bravely. Mr. Watson, with the courage worthy an American, rushed in front of his phalanx and urged them on with animated speeches. But such an unequal contest could not be maintained long. And after the few who braved the danger with Mr. Watson, left the field notwithstanding his repeated cries te rally, he left himself with two men dead, having received five bullet holes through different parts of his clothes. The men killed were of the names of Johnson and McBride.

After news of the skirmish reached here last night, a steamboat with 40 armed men went down to the scene of action, and recovered the bodies of the two men. No Indians were seen; but Johnson, (the only one that the savages are thought to have found,) was decapitated and otherwise horribly mutilated, and about his body the earth was turned up and made bare in a singular manner by these wretches, in their triumphant revels around him.

It is thought that one Indian was killed, as the tree behind which he stood (being the only Indian that was seen after the engagement began) was well marked, and behind it about a quart of bood on the ground. Yesterday there was a great panic, from rumors that the Indians to the number of 500, with an avowed determination to burn Columbus, had crossed the river below, and were advancing up. Consequently we were all under arms last night, and on guard until this morning, Every man has his gun on his shoulder, and seems resolved to die in defence of this town, and its fair inhabtants.

"To me a border war seems inevitable! And I for one (if it be not immodest to say so) am resolved to stay and meet it, whatever may be its horrors, as I have closed my imagination to every thing but revenge. We are in almost a defenceless situation! There are not 20 good muskets in the place, the 500 sent by Gov. Forsyth, to the contrary notwithstanding. Something should be done for us speedily. Either arms and ammunition or sufficient force to carry the the war into the enemy's camp, and route them out to extermination."

Industrious wisdom often prevents what lazy folly thinks inevitable.

cept a few articles of clothing. These sudden removals are attended with great hardships for women and children, in passing through a thinly settled country, often sleeping in the open prarie. The friends of humanity in the U. S., while providing for the security of the citizens of Florida, will surely think of the helpless women and children in Texas.

Since our remarks respecting the operations of the enemy were put in type, we have received the information contained in Thos. Gay's address to the people; and calculating upon Santa Ana's rapid progress to the east, and because San Felipe is thought to be one point of his destination, on account of the public archives and other reasons, it is thought prudent by the citizens to prepare the women and children for a removal across the Brazos river, over which we do not believe Santa Ana and the whole force of the Mexican nation will ever be able to pass, even should he succeed in crossing the Colorado. YET, we understand that some persons, living some distance east of the Brazos, and who were on their way to the post of duty, on hearing of the taking of the Alamo, returned, much frightened, with the intention of removing their families towards the Sabine. We beseech the people who are living east of the Brazos not to be alarmed from the apprehension of being molested by Mexican soldiery. No situation east of the Colorado river is, perhaps, more liable to be visited by our enemies than the one we occupy, in the open prarie, being the first house on the road from the Colorado. Our press is still in operation. We received the militia law yesterday, and hope to have it in circulation to-morrow; and, moreover, we expect to bring forth another number of the Telegraph next week.

We would persuade the inhabitants not to be alarmed because our troops are retreating from the Guadaloupe to the Colorado; for although General Houston might kill three times his number, he would not, we believe, lose the lives of his men with so little boot. Remember the retreat of Washington; and, like him, we believe General Houston is, by so doing, seeking an advantage of the enemy, as well as saving the precious lives of his men, and in the mean time making safe the retreat of the families.

In the present alarming situation of our country, we trust that the convention will not take up business which might properly be postponed as a fit subject for future legislation.

We are gratified that the Declaration, made by the Convention, is so generally approved by the people. Several persons, who were once opposed to the measure, say they will support it, and manifest the best evidence of their assertion by marching to the seat of war, to seal it, if necessary, with their blood.

TO THE PEOPLE OF TEXAS.

Fellow Citizens,—I have just received information by Col. William T. Austin of the fall of the Alamo, and massacre of our countrymen in that garrison. Goliad is attacked ere this and possibly has shared the fate of the Alamo. The enemy had advanced as far as Gonzoles on the evening of the 14th, with a detachment of about 2000 cavalry. Gen. Houston is on the retreat to Burnham's on the Colorado, with about 500 infantry! Gen. Santa Ana is at the head of the army, which is at this time from 6 to 7000 strong, so says Mrs. Dickinson who was in the Alamo when it was stormed. John Seguin gives the same information. Gen. Santa Ana is already advancing into the interior of our country. Our force in the field at this time does not exceed 1000.

The united action and exertion of all are now necessary to the salvation of Texas and the cause in which we are engaged. It is confidently expected that all will turn out and join the main body at Burnham's, or such other point as they may occupy. All—all, must be satisfied of the necessity as well as importance of making a desperate defence in support of their lives, fortunes, and sacred liberty. It is confidently hoped that none, in this hour of trial and danger, will prove recreant, but, like men and freemen, maintain all at the point of the bayonet.

Committee room, San Felipe de Austin, March 16, 1836. THOMAS GAY.
Attest, *Committee.*
F. W. JOHNSON,
EDWARD BAILEY,

San Felipe de Austin, March 12, 1836.

To Capt. JEREMIAH BROWN,
Comm. of the Gov't Sch'r Invincible.

Sir,—We the undersigned, in behalf of the passengers on board your vessel, during the voyage from New-Orleans to the mouth of the Brazos river, would beg leave most respectfully, to return you and the officers under your command, our heartfelt thanks for the gentlemanly treatment and kind attention extended to us during the passage. We have had an opportunity of testing your nautical skill, and know full well, that no man can feel a deeper interest in the cause of Texas, and that no one will go further to sustain her *true interests* than you will.

Persevere unto the end, and may success crown your efforts. Your cause is a *holy one.*—Let *Liberty* and *Independence* be your *motto*—prove yourself invincible and although you may, like *Brutus*, be sacrificed, remember it is for your country's good.

Wishing you, and those connected with you, health and happiness,

We subscribe ourselves
Your sincere friends,
B. HAMMETT NORTON, *Boston.*
WM. GREGORY, *North Carolina.*
WYATT HANKS, *Texas.*

THE FLORIDA INDIANS.

The report of the secretary of War in 1821, estimated the Indians in Florida at about five thousand souls, and gives a list of thirty five of their villages. The pure Seminoles, according to the statement of the agent, J. H. Bell, as reported by Dr. Moorse, were then only about twelve hundred in number, while the Creeks, which were divided into seven bands, were estimated at more than three thousand, and were said to have raised during the last war more than twelve hundred warriors. "Besides these," says the report, "are some remnants of ancient tribes, as the Houtehis, Chaas, Canaacs, &c. To this census, which would carry the Indian population (of Florida) to more than five thousand individuals, of both sexes, must be added five or six hundred maroon negroes, or mulattoes, who live wild in the woods, or in a state of half slavery among the Indians. These negroes appear to me to possess more intelligence than those who are in a state of complete slavery, and they have a great influence over the weak minds of the Indians." These extracts are observations of Mr. Peniere, in his letter to general Jackson, (July 1827,) and published in the appendix to the report, p. 311.

That the Creeks in Georgia and Alabama should make a common cause with the Florida Indians, a majority of whom are from their own tribe, is by no means a matter of surprise; and it is not improbable that the present war was a concerted measure between them. Nor will it be strange if their strength in the field should be greater than any of the estimates which have been made of their forces. Between their settlements on the sea coast and Cuba, the communication is easy, and as it has been the favored resort of pirates and smugglers, and the desperadoes of all nations, it is more than probable that they receive efficient aid from that source, especially in ammunition and military stores. And besides the refugee slaves aim for these settlements with a view of escaping to the neighboring islands, or joining in the conflict, and some of them, it is known, exhibit the full ferocity of their savage associates.

The Washington Globe contains an article in relation to the difficulty in Florida, from which we extract the following:—

Some three years since, a treaty was concluded by Col. Gadsden with these Indians, for a cession of their lands in Florida, and for their removal to the country procured for them west of the Mississippi. The execution of the treaty was contingent upon their approval of the country procured, which was to be examined by a delegation to be sent out for that purpose. This delegation was accordingly sent, approved of the country, and entered into a convention for the execution of the original treaty. Both of these instruments were duly ratified by the president and the senate. When arrangements however began to be made for the execution of the treaty, and the removal of the Indians, it was found that a portion of them were opposed to going. As they had ceded all their country in Florida, it was impossible to permit them to remain there, as they would unquestionably become a lawless banditti, committing depredations upon the inhabitants; and from the nature of the country, interspersed with marshes and swamps, it was feared that they might resort to these festnesses, and joined by runaway negroes, do much mischief in the country. But though it was impossible to permit them to remain, still it was desirable to remove them with as little injury as possible, and without the application of actual force. A considerable portion of them was at all times prepared to go, and the object was to get the refractory ones to join in the emigration. After many councils, and much discussion between them and the agents of the government, it was finally agreed that if their removal was postponed till this winter, they would all peaceably go. This position being fully agreed upon in open council, the arrangements then making were postponed, and it was determined to have every thing ready for their removal at the time prescribed.

Before however this perioda rrived, the disconted party began to commit murders, both upon our citizens and upon the chiefs friendly to a removal; and by degrees, they extended their aggressions till the frontiers were laid waste, and open hostilities commenced.

From the New Orleans Bee.

Louisiana has done her duty nobly and generously towards the national government; and proved that the spirit of her citizens is inferior in point of honor and liberality to the chivaly of no country in the world.

Soon as she had heard even the rumors of a massacre in Florida by the Indians, public meetings were held, subscriptions raised, and an amount collected of some thousands to levy and forward volunteers.

Immediately afterwards General Gaines having called on the governor in the name of U. States for eight regiments, they were raised in a few days by volunteers alone, without resorting to a draft on the militia. In every part of the state volunteers promptly presented themselves; and an army of 10,000 men could have been raised in a few weeks: so that the difficulty was to know whom to reject. 'First come, first chosen' was the only safe resort. The legislature instantly appropriated $80,000 to defray the expenses necessary to forward the troops raised; and the legion of New Orleans—the pink and pride of the militia of Louisiana, and vastly superior to the militia of any state in the union in all respects, except that of unmilitariness—paid for a splendid ensign given to the volunteers, to inspirit them with the feelings of conquest and of glory. Nearly 800 men under the command of the gay and gallant and charitable Colonel Smith were forwarded under these auspices.

Still our fellow citizens were not themselves contented with simply fulfilling the requisition of General Gaines. They poured in volunteers from all parts, west and east; and the legislature made another effort to gratify as well as satisfy this spirit of chivalry. In addition to the $80,000 previously appropriated, they authorised the governor to accept the services of those volunteers, and also a draft on the state treasury for $15,000; but this the governor, guided by the strict principles of duty and the constitution, thought proper to refuse. Yet the members of the legislature, while acceding to the force of the veto, laudably passed a resolution to defray all the contingent expenses of this auxiliary corps, amounting probably to $10,000.

Nor was the corporation of New Orleans deficient in generosity in this occasion. The city council made an appropriation of $5000 to forward 200 men to Florida, under the command of Dr. NcFarlane, late physician of the marine hospital in this city; and these have been forwarded to Mobile, at the rendezveus for the volunteers from the State of Alabama, under Col. Lindsay of the United States Army.

LATE FROM FLORIDA.

"Tampa Bay, on board the David Brown, February 14, 1836.

The conveyance I had written to you by yesterday has taken another route, and perhaps will not reach its destination, Mobile, in some time. We have been unavoidably detained here in wooding, discharging cargo, troops, &c. The army marched out in quest of the enemy, at half past 10 o'clock with all the pomp of war. Their red allies brought up the rear, seventy in number, and set up their wild war-whoop. Late in the afternoon of yesterday, there was a heavy firing heard, to the south of us, and it is supposed there was a general engagement. All the families, resident here, have taken refuge on board the shipping, during the absence of the army. We are getting under weigh for Havana, viâ Key West.

More troops required.—Last evening despatches were received from Gen. Scott, from which we learn that having received information that his present force would be inadequate for the emergency, he had made another call on his excellency the governor, for a full regiment of 750 militia, to consist of as many mounted men as could be furnished. It was required that they should rendezvous at Purysburg.

The apprehended Creek war is over. A few days since, Gen. McDougald who commanded the militia in service, was invited to meet the principal Creeks in a conference at Fort Mitchell. The result was a formal agreement by the chiefs to keep the peace—restrain their young men—cause parties on the frontiers to disperse—arrest and give up all offenders to the civil authority, and deliver all stolen proper at Fort Mitchell. It is believed that they will act in good faith, and that there is no farther danger of any disturbances of a serious nature.

PUBLISHED DAILY BY
JAMES GORDON BENNETT,
Office in the Clinton Buildings, at the corner of Nassau and Beekman streets.

THE HERALD.

VOLUME II. NEW-YORK, TUESDAY, APRIL 12, 1836. NUMBER 29.

☞ THE OFFICE OF THE HERALD IS REMOVED FROM THE CELLAR AT No. 148 NASSAU STREET, TO THE SPACIOUS OFFICE IN THE CLINTON BUILDINGS, CORNER OF NASSAU AND BEEKMAN STREETS.

TO OUR READERS AND SUBSCRIBERS.—We have to apologize to our patrons for the irregularity of the Herald yesterday—and probably to-day. The steam engine attached to the press from which the Herald is thrown off, broke a part of its machinery on Saturday, and we could not possibly get out earlier. The constant call for the Herald, yesterday, was beyond every thing that ever was seen in New York. Single papers sold at a *shilling* each, in Wall street. At our office, in the Clinton Buildings, corner of Beekman and Nassaw street, *we never charge more than a cent.* We could have sold thirty thousand copies yesterday, if we could have got them worked.

We trust no more ...

☞ The account ...
republished for the ...
fourth page. This p...
whole affair.

THE RE...

The excitement y...
city, was extraordina...
a horrible affair!"—"...
was received from T...
onists, but the privat...
absorbed all public a...

Her private histor...
ter equally so. She...
of Maine, and her rea...
this city she has ge...
Ellen Jewitt—in Bos...
orphan—her father ...
died while she was i...
lived a highly respec...
by name. Some of ...
pitying the bereave...
ted her to live at the...
cas was young, bea...
uous. Her good qua...
good feelings of the...
chere-amie of his da...
mate.

At an early age, ar...
was sent to a Femal...
it is called, over the ...
intellectual powers ...
markable brilliancy-...
appearance, and loo...
ers—she was belov...
obliging, good-tempe...

After having co...
time, Dorcas, during ...
the vacation at a dis...
town on Kennebeck ...
ta. Dorcas was the ...
the most lovely, inte...
appeared in that p...
ments, particularly ...
with brilliant wit a...
Yet even at this yo...
dications of a wild...
principles—or a kn...
morals. Her passi...
education only gav...
tions.

In this town, in th...
quainted with a yo...
Sp——y, a fine y...
to be a Cashier in o...
a short acquaintanc...
stitutes the honor ...
acter.

She returned afte...
situation soon beca...
quarrel ensued. S...
a moment of passi...
morality.

After having reco...
path of virtue, she r...
of Maria B. Benso...
among the young m...
town, she gave out ...
and that she had several connections of that name, at a short distance.

Her life at Portland was rather experimental. She was quite young, and retained some traces of modesty. Falling into a difficulty there, she took an opportunity one morning, and came to Boston. Here she assumed the name of Helen Mar, from a popular character in one of the young lady's novels. She lived in Boston about a year and a half, and left that city in company with a distinguished man for New York.

In this city she took the name of Ellen Jewett, and has lived at several houses round town. During the last winter she resided with a Kentuckian in a disguise for several weeks at one of our fashionable hotels. Her way of life in New York has corresponded with the terrible state of society in this city. At such fashionable houses, young men, married and single and all, meet together in the evening, spend their time and their money—exhaust their treasures and their sensibilities—and break down every moral tie that hitherto has kept the elements of social intercourse together.

The house No. 41 Thomas street, is occupied by Rosina Townsend, but this is not her real name. She is recently from Cincinnati, and is one of the most dashing in her infamous line of life.

Ellen Jewett was well known to every predestrian in Broadway. Last summer she was famous for parading Wall street in an elegant green dress, and generally with a letter in her hand. She used to look at the brokers with great boldness of demeanor—had a peculiar walk—something in the style of an Englishwoman. From those who have known her, we have been informed that she was a fascinating woman in conversation, full of intellect and refinement, but at the same time possessed of a very devil, and a species of mortal antipathy to the male race. Her great passion was to seduce young men, and particularly those who most resisted her charms. She seems to have declared war against the sex. "Oh!" she would say, "how I despise you all—you are a heartless, unprincipled set—you have ruined me—I'll ruin you—I delight in your ruin."

Her great intellectual passion was for reading the poems of Byron, and particularly Don Juan, which, however, has no doubt, produced more wretchedness in the world, than all the other moral writers of the age can check. With a happier destiny—and a steady moral principle, this young woman had talents calculated for the highest sphere in life. We know no private circumstance that has caused such a sensation in our city as the recent transaction. It is the whole topic of conversation wherever one goes. It is horrid. It creates melancholy. It produces horror. Will it work a reform? Will it make the licentious pause?

FURTHER PARTICULARS.—From the testimony of the witnesess examined before the Coroner's jury, it appears that Robinson came to the house about nine o'clock, with the cloak on. It was fully identified from the following circumstaness. There were two beautiful tassels attached to the cloak, which Ellen had frequent-...

... however, were so strong against him, that he was committed. His examination takes place this day, at two o'clock. Ogden Hoffman, Esq., is his counsel.

OTHER ACCOUNTS.—The accounts which crowd into us from all quarters, of the birth and parentage of the "remarkable creature," would confuse any ordinary mortal. We are cool and clear. Like Homer her birth place is claimed by natives of several countries.—The English protest she is a native of Birmingham, and came to this country young, like the daughter of Miss Foote by Mrs. M'Dermot. She was adopted then by Judge Western of Maine. Her original English name is Maria E. Benson. She came to New York eight years ago and first resided at Madame Post's Hotel in Howard street—then at the Laurence House in Chapel street—then at Madame Berry's Boarding Establishment, Duane street. She was born on the 13th March, 1813, and was 23 years of age and a few days when her awful murder took place.

During her residence here, she carried on an extensive country correspondence with every part of the Union. We learn from the Post Office that during last summer she usually received from three to eight letters a day. Her postage bill exceeded that of several brokers in Wall street. Her private correspondence is of a most remarkable character—resembling that of the famous Abellard and Eloisa. We are promised a choice selection from this correspondence, which are characterized by great talent, power, pathos and brilliancy.

Yesterday she was buried decently and privately, between 10 and 11 o'clock, at St. John's burying ground. A great crowd was collected all day in Thomas street. An immense excitement prevails. It is said by the friends of Robinson, that he can prove an *alibi* and that he is innocent. *Nous verrons.* He will be examined privately to-day in the Police office at 2 o'clock. He will be taken to the Police office in a carriage from the Bridewell. The Justices have agreed to exclude all reporters—and all the public. It is to be made a Holy Inquisition affair. The murder of a woman of bad character, would, in some quarters, be set down as nothing. We, man—unprincipled, heartless man—the lord of creation, and so forth—first ruin—and then cast frail woman from us, "like a loathesome weed away."—There is some mysterious juggle going on. Look to it—look to it.

MYSTERIOUS CIRCUMSTANCE.—On Monday morning, tracks of blood were seen in Anthony, near Church st., and traced up to Broadway, and thence to a physician's door. Some persons of that neighborhood, made a complaint yesterday morning, that a serious occurrence had taken place, in which one of the parties concerned, had his head dreadfully mangled with an axe.

A person was arrested yesterday afternoon, on suspicion of having been the perpetrator of the foul outrage, and as we learn, was, on his own admission, committed. No traces have as yet been discovered of the injured person, and thus the matter rests.

A GOOD ONE.—We w...
since, at the conduct of a ...
ing along Pearl street, bu...
They stopped in front of ...
Cedar street, where a ce...
pumping the water out f...
'Hillo Tom, just look ...
'Why! what's that.'
'D——n my eyes, To...
a leak, and they're pum...

☞ Dr. Sleigh is eng... Divine Revelation, in Philadelphia.

THE HERALD.

NEW YORK, TUESDAY, APRIL 12, 1836.

TEXAS—SAD NEWS.—The following is extracted from a New Orleans paper of the 28th ult. Will it not rouse the nation?

HIGHLY IMPORTANT FROM TEXAS.—We learn by the passengers of the schr. Cumanche, 8 days from Texas, that the War has assumed a serious character—on the 25th Feb. the Texian Garrison in Bexar of 150 men, commanded by Lt. Col. B. Travis was attacked by the advance division of Gen. San. Anna's army consisting of 2000 men who were repulsed with the loss of many killed between 500 to 800 men, without the loss of one man of the Texians—about the same time Col. Johnson with a party of 70 men while reconnoitering the westward of San Patricio was surrounded in the night by a large body of Mexican troops—in the morning the demand of a surrender was made by the Mexican Commander unconditionally, which was refused; but an offer of surrender was made as prisoners of war, which was acceded to by the Mexicans. But no sooner had the Texians marched out of their quarters and stacked their arms, than a general fire was opened upon them by the whole Mexican force—the Texians attempted to escape but only three of them succeeded; one of whom was Col. Johnson.

Between the 25th February and 2d March the Mexicans were employed in forming entrenchments around the Alamo and Bombarding the place; on the 2d March Col. Travis wrote that 200 shells had been thrown into the Alamo without injuring a man. On the 1st March the Garrison of Alamo received a reinforcement of 32 Texians from Gonzales having forced their way thro' the enemies lines, making the number in the Alamo consisting of 182 men.

On the 6th March about midnight the Alamo was surrounded by the whole force of the Mexican army commanded by San. Anna in person—the battle was desperate until day light when only 7 men belonging to the Texian Garrison were found alive who cried for quarters, but were told that there was no mercy for them—they then continued fighting until the whole were butchered. One woman, Mrs. Dickinson, and a negro of Col. Travis were the only persons whose lives were spared. We regret to say that Col. David Crocket and companion, Mr. Berton and Col. Bonhan, of S. C., were among the number slain. Gen. Cowie was murdered in his bed sick and helpless. Gen. Cos on entering the Fort ordered the servant of Col. Travis to point out the body of his master; he did so, when Cos drew his sword and mangled the face and limbs with the malignant feeling of a Camanche savage. The bodies of the slain were thrown into a mass in the centre of the Alamo and burned. The loss of the Mexicans in storming the place was not less than 1000 killed and mortally wounded, and as many wounded, making with their loss in the first assault between 2 and 3000 men.

The flag used by the Mexicans was a blood-red one, in place of the constitutional one. Immediately after the capture, Gen. San. Anna sent Mrs. Dickinson and the servant to General Houston's camp, accompanied by a Mexican with a flag, who was bearer of a note from San. Anna, offering the Texians peace and general amnesty, if they would lay down their arms and submit to his government. Gen. Houston's reply was, "True sir, you have succeeded in killing some of our brave men, but the Texians are not yet conquered." The effect of the fall of Bexar throughout Texas was electrical. Every man who could use the rifle and was in a condition to take field, marched forthwith to the seat of war. It is believed that not less than 4000 riflemen were on their way to the army when the Cumnche sailed, determined to wreak their revenge on the Mexicans.

Gen. Houston had burnt Gonzales, and fallen back on the Collorado with about 1000 men. Col. Fanning was in the Fort at Goliad, a very strong position, well supplied with munitions and provisions, with 4 or 500 men.

The general determination of the people of Texas is to abandon all their ocuupations and pursuits of peace, and continue in arms until every Mexican east of the Rio del Norte shall be extirminated.

☞ JOURNEYMEN MASONS.—At a large and respectable meeting of the Journeymen Masons of the City of New York, held at the 14th Ward Hotel, on Wednesday evening 6th inst. to take into consideration the existing rates of wages, and an advance on the same, Amos Roberts was called to the Chair, and Joseph Nutt and Oscar Bradford were appointed Secretaries. The call of the meeting having been read—

The following persons were appointed a Committtee to draft Resolutions expressive of the sense of the meeting—viz: Wm. Hopkins, Joseph Nutt, Samuel C. Reeves, Thomas Asten, James D. Kelly; who retired and presented to the meeting the following preamble and resolution.

Whereas, The present wages are insufficient to compete with the great increase of price of provision, rents, &c. and believing that the laborer is worthy of his hire, therefore

Resolved, That we, the Journeymen Masons of the City of New York, will require as an equivalent for labor $2 25 per day, on and after the 11th day of April.

AMOS ROBERTS, Chairman.
JOSEPH NUTT, OSCAR BRADFORD, } Secretaries. ap 11-3t

MARRIED.

On Friday evening last, by the Rev. Henry Chase, Daniel Baker, merchant, to Miss Mary Angelina, daughter of Mr. Thomas Eastburn, all of this city.

On the 7th instant, by the Rev. Thomas Brientnall, Mr. Albert S. Beach, to Miss Matilda, daughter of Daniel Updike, Esq., all of this city.

DIED.

On the 9th instant, Mr. John Kelly, of the firm of L. W. Kelly & Co., aged 31 years.

On the 9th instant, Mrs. Mary Hudson, wife of Mr. Wm. Hudson, in the 43d year of her age.

On the 10th inst. Miss Jane E. Mott, in the 20th year of her age.

On the 9th instant, Mr. Richard S. Schaeck, aged 73 years.

New-York American.

TUESDAY, APRIL 12, 1836. FOR THE COUNTRY. VOLUME VXIII. NUMBER 1519.

PUBLISHED FOR THE PROPRIETOR,
At No 13 Nassau st., corner of Pine st., New-York.
EVERY TUESDAY AND FRIDAY.

TERMS.—$4 per annum, *inadvance*, if paid at the office, or sent free of expense: $4.50, if paid *in advance* to the agents, or $5 at the end of the year.—*Five dollars* will be charged in all cases where a paper is discontinued without *arrearages being paid*.

☞ The NEW-YORK AMERICAN is also published DAILY at the same office, at $10 per annum. Also, *three times a week*, to country subscribers only, at $5 per annum, payable always in advance.

⁂ ADVERTISEMENTS in either of the above papes will be inserted at the *established* city prices.

NEW YORK AMERICAN.

THURSDAY EVENING, APRIL 7, 1836.

FROM HAVRE, we have, by the *Formosa*, dates to the 21st February, which give nothing new from Paris, whence by the way of London we have dates of 22d. The subjoined extract from a Havre letter of 21st, with accounts of sales on the 18th, may be deemed interesting.

"*Havre, 21st Feb.*

"The American question has been lost sight of during the ministerial crisis, but was brought into view two days ago by an article in the Journal des Debats, which blames the Message of the 15th of January, as taking away the good impression made by that of the 7th December. The opposition journals still consider the affair as if settled by the mediation of England; and so do most people.

"The war in Spain goes on without any decided advantage on either side. England, you will notice, continues to increase her naval force in the Mediterranean."

[COMMUNICATED.]

COLLEGE OF PHYSICIANS AND SURGEONS.—The Annual Commencement of this College was held on Tuesday, the 5th inst., at the College Hall. The following young gentlemen having complied with the ordinances of the Regents of the University and the laws of the State respecting graduation; and having on the day previous publicly defended their respective inaugural dissertations, were duly invested with the honors and privileges of the degree of Doctor of Medicine. The President, Dr. J. Aug. Smith, presided on the occasion, and delivered an address to the graduates. The Rev. Mr. Schroeder commenced and closed the exercises with prayer.

John Dayton—Epilepsy.
John Bates—Gastritis.
William Moore—Hœmoptysis.
Henry R. Lott—Medical logic.
Simon D. Hosley—Abortion.
J. R. Riggs—Scarlet fever.
A. W. Rogers—Phisiology of the circulation of the blood.
Edward Earle—Puerperal fever.
Abram Creveling—Uterine hœmorrhage.
James Bolton, A. M.—Marsh miasm.
John Doane—Actea racemosa.
John M. Carnochan—Surgical relations of the arch of the aorta.
Peter A. Stoutenburgh—Hydrocephalus.
D. L. Eigenbrodt, A. M.—Conjunctivitis.
John Wilson—Revulsives.
Joseph Stevermann—Trephining.
John E. Stillwell, A. B.—Trachitis.
Isaac H. Traver—Infantile remittent fever.
David M. Sayer—Acute hepatitis.
D. M. Schoonmaker—Dysentery.
Alex'r. M. Bruen, A. M.—Insanity.
William A. Matthews—Opium.
James Syme—Amputation.
James W. Andariese—Puerperal Fever.
William Miner—Scarlatina.
Alex. C. Castle—Tetanus.

WASHINGTON, Tuesday night.

The great trouble of the present day is the fast increase of the public treasure, and in truth it is accumulating so fast that it is coming in beyond our wishes. Alarm is felt at the amount lodged *ex necessate rei* in certain deposit banks, and in consequence of which, the wildest of all wild projects yet broached has been submitted by Mr. Benton, to-day, which, under the ostensible purpose of supplying the mint with bullion to be coined, is in reality a cover to make the mint a place of deposite for the public money hereafter; in other words, by and bye, we shall have a mint built here, and thus have the public money under our own (the party's) special and goodly keeping. This is carrying out the gold humbug with a vengeance. The bill was referred to the Committee on Finance. It proposed to transfer the public moneys *to* the mint, but not one word was said by Mr. B. as to how they were to come back.

The bill to repeal and reduce the duties on certain articles enumerated in Mr. Woodbury's statement, that might be so repealed or reduced without injury to the manufacturing interest, was taken up and some amendments agreed to. There being a proposition to reduce the duties on certain wines, it was laid on the table until the project is more fully considered, when the bill will doubtless be acted on

The bill to amend the act relative to the Custom House bonds given by sufferers by the late fire, was *passed*.

Mr. Leigh resumed and concluded a masterly refutation of the expunging process, and an exposé, irresistibly clear to the minds of all who were not willfully blind, of the consequences to which the doctrine will lead those who sanction it. Two instances will suffice: he alluded to their executive record of all appointments confirmed by them, and to their acting in a judicial capacity, imploring them in the name of God and of common sense to pause before they violate the Constitution. He fairly put the case, if a Senator wished to expunge any record of a preceding Senate, as to an appointment, was not such an expunction a virtual exercise of removal from office. In a judicial case he inquired, if a person was convicted by them and sentenced, would not expunging such conviction have the effect of expunging the sentence passed, and was the party, in such case, restored to his former standing? Again, in case of acquittal, and the sentence expunged, the party again put on his trial, could he plead or not the former acquittal, or submit to be tried twice for a crime, contrary to all former practice in courts of justice. My own candid impression is, that his remarks were so clear, cogent and conclusive, received as they were by marked attention and some applause from the galleries, that they *bar* all further necessity for discussion, in opposition to the resolution or arguments that may be henceforth urged. When he concluded, *no* Senator rose to gainsay him, and poor Benton had the pleasing duty to move to lay the resolution on the table—there, I hope, to sleep the sleep of death.

Executive business was taken up.

The House business was unimportant, nothing being done except the passage of the bill for the relief of the sufferers by the late fire.

[*From the Baltimore American.*]

TWENTY-FOURTH CONGRESS.

IN SENATE—Tuesday.

Mr. Benton, according to notice, introduced a bill for the better supply of bullion, and explained that he had been in correspondence with the Director of the Mint, to ascertain what quantity would be sufficient for the present, and he had provided by his bill that this sum should be transferred by the Deposite Banks to the Mint out of the public money in their possession. The bill was referred to the committee on finance.

A bill to admit, free of duty, certain articles of foreign produce and to lessen the duties on others, was taken up, and Mr. Knight moved to add pearl powder, linen tape, oil in jars, watches without cases, diamonds and precious stones, sextants, quadrants, telescopes, &c. An amendment was also added in the second section of the bill, changing the specified rate of duty ad valorem from 20 to 26 per cent. These amendments were agreed to, but in consequence of the absence of Mr. Webster, it was laid on the table.

A bill amendatory of the act for the relief of the sufferers by the late fire in New York, which was brought from the House, was taken up.

Mr. Davis suggested the propriety of immediate action on it, and it was read twice, and being in committee of the whole,

Mr. Wright explained the necessity for immediate action. He stated that by the construction put upon the bill, by the Collector of New York, all bonds given up to the date of the passage of the late bill were admitted to its benefits, and it thereupon became necessary to pass the present bill which limits the operation of the previous law to those bonds which had been given prior to December 15.

The explanation induced the Senate to dispense with the customary rules, and the bill was passed.

The Senate proceeded to consider the expunging resolution of Mr. Benton.

Mr. Leigh resumed his remarks, and with equal ability pursued his subject.

After Mr. Leigh had concluded, on motion of Mr. Benton, the resolution was ordered to be laid on the table and printed.

The bill to authorise contracts with Railroad Companies, and the resolution to retrocede the District of Columbia, were laid on the table for the present.

Mr. Calhoun then moved to take up the bill to prevent the circulation of incendiary publications, but before any action took place on the bill,

On motion of Mr. White, the Senate proceeded to the consideration of executive business, and thus occupied the residue of the day.

HOUSE OF REPRESENTATIVES.

By unanimous consent, Mr. Adams presented certain resolutions of the Legislature of Massachusetts, relative to the North Eastern Boundary—ordered to be printed.

Mr. Cambreleng, from the committee on ways and means, reported a bill supplementary to the act to establish the mint and regulate the coin of the United States—referred to the committee of the whole.

New York Relief Bill.

Mr. Smith, from the Committee of Ways and Means, reported a bill amendatory of the act for the relief of the sufferers by fire in New York. Its object is to limit the original bill to bonds prior to the fire. It was passed.

Mr. Wise renewed his motion to suspend the rules in order to submit his resolutions for the appointment of a select committee on the Deposite Banks. The motion was rejected—yeas 89, nays 91.

Naval Service Bill.

The House resumed the consideration of the above bill. The question being on the motion to strike out the appropriation for the Portsmouth Navy Yard,

Mr. Robertson, of Va., spoke at great length on the subject of the principles and measures of the present administration. At half past three he gave way to a motion that the committee rise, and Mr. Evans moved an adjournment—the yeas and nays are now taking on this motion.

[*Reported for the Courier and Enquirer.*]

PROCEEDINGS OF THE COMMON COUNCIL.

Wednesday evening, April 6, 1836.

BOARD OF ALDERMEN.

The Board met pursuant to adjournment.

The minutes were read and approved.

Petitions presented and referred.

Of J. D. Beers, S. Whiting and others, for lighting State street with gas; of John C. Morrison and Son, for the purchase of a gore of land; of Charles Hawkins, Joseph Delafield, R. F. Carman and others, for opening 10th avenue; remonstrance of 360 persons, against the appropriation by the Boston and Providence line of steamboats, of the exclusive use of pier at the foot of Murray street; of George C. Reed, Gabriel Mead, Saul Alley, and others, against the widening of Pine street, on the south side, between William and Nassau; of Isaac Vancleve and others, for a drain across the 3d avenue at 32d street; of a large number of persons of this city and Long Island, against the manner in which the ferry between Grand street and Williamsburg is conducted, and also for an enquiry into the alleged abuses and insufficiency of the boats; of George Law and others, for a well and pump in 15th street, near 10th avenue.

The Board of Assistants came into the Aldermens' Chamber, and the two Boards organized in Common Council, and proceeded to business in

Joint Meeting.

The minutes were read and approved.

The report of the Chief Engineer of the Fire Department, submitting the resignations and appointments, was received and adopted and filed.

The following appointments were made, viz: Asa Hall, Inspector of the Election in the 9th ward, vice Jacob Westervelt, resigned; Thomas S. McCarty, Inspector of Election in the 6th ward, vice William H. Hicks, resigned. The Joint Meeting then adjourned, and the Board come to order.

Two ordinances for the correction of nuisances, from the Board of Assistants, were concurred in.

Reports—Of the Street Committee, in favor of straightening the northerly line of Pearl street, between William street and Hanover square; was adopted.

Of the Committee on Wharves, in favor of extending the middle pier at the foot of Governeur slip; adopted.

Of the Committee of Conference, in favor of granting to the New Haven Steamboat Company the exclusive use of the pier at the foot of Pike slip, for one year; adopted.

Resolution by Ald. Labagh—That the Committee of Public Offices and Repairs inquire into the expediency of fitting up the room of the Circuit Judge, for the use of the Clerk of the Common Council and the Committees of the Boards; adopted.

By the same—For the extension of the sewer in Rector street, to the west side of West street, by means of a wooden trunk; adopted.

The Board receded from their former report against reducing the tax of Joseph L. Josephs, and concurred with the Board of Assistants in favor of reducing said tax.

Adjourned to Monday next.

BOARD OF ASSISTANTS, April 6.

The Board met pursuant to adjournment.

Reports.—Of Com. of Fire and Water, in favor of building an engine house for Eagle Engine Co. Committee of Wharves and Piers, in favor of leasing for one year west side of pier at the foot of Pike street. Same, in favor of leasing to Munson Hoit east side of pier 33 East River, for steamboat berth. Street Committee, in favor of widening Wall street on southerly side, from Exchange Place to property of American Insurance Co.

Mr. Curtis called up the papers from the other Board, relative to lighting Fifth Ward with gas, which, after discussion, was laid on the table.

The papers from the Board of Aldermen relative to straightening the northerly line of Pearl street were taken up, discussed, and laid on the table.

The Board then adjourned.

MELANCHOLY LOSS OF LIVES.—The packet ship Formosa, from Havre, arrived yesterday, on the 4th ult. in a gale, shipped a heavy sea, which washed overboard five of her men; also the cow and cow house, bulwarks, &c.

MARRIED,

Yesterday morning, by the Rev. Dr. McAuley, Leonard Perkins, of Norwich, to Helen R., daughter of Albert Wyckoff.

DIED.

On the 6th inst., Catharine, only daughter of William N. and Lydia H. Birch, aged 5 years and 3 months.

At Petersburg, Va., on the 27th ult., Mr. Charles P. Rogers, formerly of this city, aged 71 years.

PASSENGERS—

In the ship Franconia, from Liverpool:—Mr. and Mrs. Morris; Doct. and Mrs. Powell; Mrs. Crabtree; Doct Hatchell; Messrs. Broadbent, Wood and Hurst; and 160 in the steerage.

In the ship Formosa, from Havre; Joseph Landa, of Mexico.

In the ship Mexican, from Vera Cruz:—Mr O Bicieni, lady and two children, Mr Mercaido, lady and five children; C Paris, lady and two children; Capt J B Hotchinson; C Paris, A N Pellgrena, A Drugman, L F Braims, J Blanco, J Leguin, A Priends, C Bomiousa, and F Manleer.

NEW YORK AMERICAN.

FRIDAY EVENING, APRIL 8, 1836.

A brief absence has thrown us in arrears as to some matters, which, as recorders of the times, it is our business to note—and first, of the *Florida war*.

In the paper of last Saturday we commented upon an article from the Times, which struck us as extraordinary, concerning the movements of General Gaines. We find that in the next number the Times published a disclaimer, which, having inserted the original article, we also insert—not without a certain commiseration for a newspaper which inserts "with great pleasure" one day, what the next it does "not approve, and *believes the government does not approve*"!

[*From the Times of Monday.*]

The communication in relation to Gen. Gaines in our paper of Saturday, was inadvertently inserted without the knowledge of the editors. We do not approve, and believe government do not approve, the conduct of Gen. Gaines, which doubtless prompted as it was by the most patriotic motives, was still in violation of military discipline, and a high example of insubordination.

In connection with this subject, is the letter from Capt. Hitchcock, which will be found in our col-

the navigation is obstructed some five or six miles below, and at several points between this and Kingston. The rise of water has been inconsiderable.

In addition to the above, we learn that the river is open to *Crum Elbow*, a few miles above *Poughkeepsie*—then again from *Hudson* to the *light house* north of it—and from *Baltimore* to *Troy*. Another day or two must open the whole river.

The Senate of Massachusetts have rejected, by a very decisive vote, a bill from the House of Representatives abolishing, in some cases, the punishment of death.

NEW STORES.—Persons who are building new stores or warehouses, will do well to examine one now erecting on lot 117 Liberty, near Greenwich street. From present appearances, it bids fair to surpass any we have seen, both in the solidity of its construction, and security against fire and thieves. The superintendant (not a builder by the way) informs us that the floors are to be made like those in the warehouses of the London docks, that is, of slate two inches thick, which is found to be admirably adapted to the purpose, and concerning which we shall say more one of these days.

incautious speaker to overleap the bounds of philosopical investigation and political foresight, and array himself, by a species of paradoxical argument, against the very doctrine which he has volunteered to defend! But if Mr. Mann after this is not willing to avow his error, and plead inadvertence for his transgression, of what a grave political heresy does he acknowledge himself to be guilty!

Can he deem himself able to propogate such doctrines, and that too in despite of the community who have no doubt chosen him for his loyal adhesion to plebeian equality, and admiration of universal suffrage? And in fact has he not departed from the great principle which characterizes the right of franchise of his own State, which places the vicious and the virtuous, the ignorant and the educated, mental imbecility and intellectual power, the worthless vagabond and the independent freeman, the fugitive from foreign climes and the native born citizen, and, in fact, the basest satellite and the noblest man, upon the same level? Truly the exemplar of his public life seems to have faded from his view, and his holy horror of seeing the exercise of "*ministerial* duties" by irresponsible persons, has urged him to give utterance to the most astounding declaration, and the vilest proposition, that ever vibrated within the walls of the Capitol! He has deliberately asserted that the officers of the army have no identity with, and are not accountable to, the people, and necessarily when we connect it with the train of his argument, he has by implication asked that they be divested of their political privileges, or denied some of the common rights of citi-

[*From the Louisiana Advertiser, March 28.*]

THE FALL OF BEXAR—THE ENTIRE OF THE TROOPS IN GARRISON PUT TO DEATH—COLS. CROCKETT AND BOWIE KILLED!

We are indebted to a gentleman, passenger on board the steamer Levant, from Nachitoches, for the annexed letter, giving the particulars of the fall of Bexar—it is a copy of one addressed to the editor of the Red River Herald:

"Sir,—Bexar has fallen! Its garrison was only 187 strong, commanded by Lieut. Col. W. Travis. After standing repeated attacks for two weeks, and an almost constant cannonade and bombarding during that time, the last attack was made on the morning of the 6th inst. by upwards of 2000 men, under the command of Santa Anna in person; they carried the place about sunrise, with the loss of 520 men killed, and about the same number wounded. After about an hour's fighting the whole garrison was put to death, (save the sick and wounded and seven men who asked for quarter.) All fought desperately until entirely cut down; the rest were coolly murdered. The brave and gallant Travis, to prevent his falling into the hands of the enemy, shot himself. Not an individual escaped, and the news is only known to us by a citizen of Bexar, who came to our army at Gonzales—but from the cessation of Travis's signal guns, there is no doubt of its truth. The declaration of independence you have, no doubt, received, and you will, in a few days, receive the constitution proposed by the republic.

Cols. James Bowie and David Crockett are among the slain—the first was murdered in his bed, to which he had been confined by illness—the latter fell, fighting like a tiger. The Mexican army is estimated at 8000 men; it may be more or less."

A. BRISCOE.

FURTHER PARTICULARS.—We learn by the passengers of the schr. Camanche, 8 days from the Brazos River, that the war in Texas has at length assumed a serious character. Many of those who left this city, determined to lay down their lives in the cause of Texas, have bravely yielded them up at Bexar. Three young men from our office, we learn, are among the slain; the names of Wm. Blazeby and Robert Moore have been mentioned to us; that of the other we could not ascertain.

On the 25th February, the Texian garrison in Bexar, of 150 men only, commanded by Lieut. Col. W. B. Travis, was attacked by the advanced division of Santa Anna's army of about 2000 men, when the enemy were repulsed with the loss of many killed and wounded, variously estimated from 450 to 600, without the loss of a man of the garrison.

The great slaughter was ascribed to the fact, that every man of the garrison had about eight guns loaded by his side. About the same time, Colonel Johnson, while reconnoitering to the westward of San Patricio, with a party of 70 men, was surrounded in the night by a large body of Mexican troops. In the morning the commander sent in a summons to surrender at discretion, which was refused, and an offer to surrender as prisoners of war made. This was acceded to by the Mexican officer, but no sooner had the Texians marched out of their encampment, and stacked their arms, than a general fire was opened upon them by the whole Mexican force, when the prisoners endeavored to escape—three only of whom effected it, among them was Col. Johnson and one man who had been wounded.

Between the 25th of Feb. and 2d March the Mexicans were employed in forming entrenchments around the Alamo and bombarding the place. On the 2d of March Col. Travis wrote that 200 shells had been thrown into the Alamo, without injuring a man.

On the 1st of March, 32 men from Gonzales made their entry through the enemy's lines, and reached the Alamo—making the whole number in the garrison 182.

On the 6th March, about midnight, the Alamo was assaulted by the entire force of the Mexican army, commanded by Santa Anna in person. The Mexicans fought desperately until day light, when seven only of the garrison were found alive. We regret to say, that Col. David Crockett and his companion, Mr. Benton, also the gallant Col. Benham of South Carolina, were of the number who cried for quarter, but were told there was no mercy for them. They then continued fighting until the whole were butchered. One woman, (Mrs. Dickinson,) and a wounded negro servant of Col. Travis's, were the persons in the Alamo whose lives were spared. Gen. Bowie was murdered in his bed, sick and helpless. Gen. Cos, on entering the fort, ordered Col. Travis's servant to point out to him the body of his master; he did so, when Cos drew his sword and mangled his face and limbs with the malignant feeling of a savage.

The bodies of the slain were thrown into a heap in the centre of the Alamo and burned. On Gen. Bowia's body being brought out, Gen. Cos said that he was too brave a man to be burned like a dog; then added, *pew no es cosa eschade*—never mind, throw him in. The loss of the Mexicans in storming the place was estimated at not less than 1000 killed and mortally wounded, and as many more disabled—making with their loss in the first assault, between 2000 and 3000 killed and wounded. It is worthy of remark that the flag of Santa Anna's army at Bexar was a *blood red one*, in place of the old constitutional tri-colored flag.

Immediately after the capture of the place, Gen. Santa Anna sent Mrs. Dickinson and Col. Travis' servant to Gen. Houston's camp, accompanied by a Mexican with a flag, who was bearer of a note from Santa Anna, offering the Texians peace and a general amnesty, if they would lay down their arms and submit to his government. Gen. Houston's reply was, "True sir, you have succeeded in killing some of our brave men, but the Texians are not yet whipped."

The effect of the fall of Bexar throughout Texas was electric. Every man who could use a rifle, and was in a condition to take the field, marched forthwith to the scene of war. It was believed that not less of 4000 riflemen were on their way to the army when the Camanche sailed, to wreak their vengeance on the Mexicans, and determined to grant no quarter.

Gen. Houston had burnt Gonzales, and fallen back on the Colorado with about 1000 men.

Col. Fannin was in the fort at Goliad, a very strong position, well supplied with munitions and provisions, and from 400 to 500 men.

The general determination of the people of Texas seemed to be to abandon all the occupations and pursuits of peace, and continue in arms until every Mexican east of the Rio del Norte should be exterminated.

nesday night, and made a vast apartment.

Of her speed, sufficient is said, in noting the fact that her first trip was performed in considerably less than 14 hours; which, for a distance estimated at 200 miles, is fast enough.

Returning, the steamboat *President*, not second before certainly to any boat on the Sound, started from Providence six or seven minutes ahead of the *Massachusetts*, and a contest for superiority ensued—a generous emulation truly, for there was no undue excitement, no impropriety, nor any *unsafe* exertion made on board the Massachusetts, certainly; nor, we may say, we are sure, with every presumption of truth, on board the *President*. The *Massachusetts* bore away the palm, overtaking the President first abreast of Newport—and subsequently (the President having first, by some minutes, got away from the dock,) in the Sound, and arrived here several miles in advance of her competitor, in something less than fourteen hours from Providence. Of her commander, Capt. *Comstock*, it is hardly necessary to say more, than that to no hands could be more worthily confided so fine a vessel and so responsible a command; he may be likened to the engines of his boat, working silently, but very effectively.

The *Rhode Island*, another boat of the same class, and belonging to the same Company, was launched in safety yesterday, and will take place in the line in June. A third, to be called the *Narragansett*, of equal force and dimensions, is building, and when completed, the three will present to passengers a combination of power, speed, comfort and safety, not equalled, probably, on any waters.

These boats connect with the railroad line, so that on their arrival a train for Boston proceeds immediately, bringing, in fact, the cities of New York and Boston within easy and unfatiguing travel of from 15 to 18 hours.

[*From the Albany Argus of Wednesday.*]

THE ICE AND THE NAVIGATION.—The river is now entirely free from ice opposite this city; but

by the adoption of such a rule; and to them more emphatically belongs the remedy for such a wrong. And what more or less than this has Mr. Mann done, or expressed himself ready to do, in the speech before us? Aye, in this very speech in which he labors so hard to defend the people against the approaches of power, and the assumption of *ministerial* duties, he boldly asks, "*Are these officers* [of the Army] *accountable to the People, or identified with them in feeling to the extent necessary to a harmonious action?*" This is, indeed, a question which sets at once, common sense and common sympathies, at defiance. And does Mr. Mann, in truth, doubt the identity of the feeling of the officers of the Army with that of their fellow-citizens, and the accountability which duty, honor and affection are ever willing to render? Let us in our turn, ask the honorable gentleman if he has no faith in the lineaments which bind and characterize nations, in the bonds of consanguinity—in the sympathies of kindred habits, and customs, and instruction—in the ties of domestic life and public duties—in the incorrupt and incorruptible heart, which cherishes the love of virtue; or, in those sentiments and affection, which every man naturally bears for the land of his nativity? When all these—these which, by a beneficent Providence, are calculated to awaken the noblest feelings of our nature, are contrasted with the selfish rules which Mr. Mann would fain have us submit to, how insignificant and contemptible appears that radical spirit which would measure all objects by party interests, and reduce all sentiments to the level of dollars and cents!

In reading Mr. Mann's speech, we were surprised that one, who evidently prides himself as a champion of Republicanism, should have so far committed himself as to avow a principle which aims directly at the 'People's' rights, and, to use his own terms, "is not in accordance with the spirit of our civil institutions." But it is clear that Mr. Mann did not mean what he said, or suppose that it might have such an extended application, or go beyond the officers of the army, whom he wished by this kind of excision, to be separated from the body politic of the nation. It is another instance which shows how far oratorical fervor may lead the

bill was ordered to a third reading. The Senate, after some other ordinary business, went into secret session.

In the *House of Representatives* a bill for the better organizing, arming, &c., the militia, was reported. Mr. Sutherland reported a joint resolution repealing the restriction now existing by law, upon the appointment of additional Custom House officers—which, after being made to assume the shape of a bill, and upon statements from Mr. Lawrence and Mr. Cambreleng, that both in Boston and New York business was delayed for want of more officers, was ordered to a third reading. Mr. Wise made another ineffectual attempt to introduce modified resolutions for a committee of inquiry into the custody of the public deposites, &c. The resolution is in these words:

Whereas, since the custody of the public money has been under the entire control of the Treasury Department, the Secretary of the Treasury, by himself or his agents, has selected certain local State banks as places of deposite, without regulation by law; and whereas there is great doubt about the agency by which the said deposite banks are selected and regulated; and whereas said agency is alleged to be improper and corrupt, effected by some person or persons not officers of the Government, or appointed or responsible as such, or known in any manner to the laws, and who are secretly paid large stipends or amounts of compensation for procuring the custody and the use of the public deposites; and whereas the said banks, for which the public deposites are thus procured, are in possession of the public money without charge of interest or other charge whatsoever for the use of the same, and the said person or persons, their agent or agents, are alleged to be political partisans, wielding the public deposites for electioneering purposes, dangerous to the purity of the Government and to the liberties of the People: therefore,

Resolved, That a select committee be appointed, with power to send for persons and papers, to inquire into the mode or agency of selecting the banks of deposite for the public money; the contracts with the Treasury Department by which they are regulated; the manner in which, and the persons by whom, such contracts are made; into all correspondence whatsoever touching contracts for the public deposites; into all connexion or relation, official or unofficial, which exists or has existed between any person or persons and the Treasury Department, or between them and the deposite banks, or any other individuals or banks, touching the custody and the control and deposite of the public money, and into the amount and mode of compensation of all persons whomsover in any manner whatever connected with the Treasury Department or the deposite banks, having any agency whatever in negotiating between said Department and said banks, or any banks or individuals, touching the public deposites; and that said committee have leave to report by bill or otherwise.

The House refused to suspend the rules in order to receive this resolution, whereupon *Mr. Wise* said, that being satisfied "that the House was opposed to any inquiry for the purpose of resolving what was a reasonable doubt in relation to the connexion between the Government and the deposit banks," he would not renew his motion.

The Naval service bill was then taken up, and the House was still sitting on it—probably with the determination to pass it before rising.

LEGISLATURE, *Monday.*—In the *Senate*, a report was made and concurred in, *against* a bank at Oxford, Chenango co. The bill to improve the navigation of the *Albany basin*, was, after discussion, passed unanimously. The *Black River Canal* bill was passed, 17 to 10. Also, the bill repealing that appointing Commissioners to lay out a road from Poughkeepsie to Pine Plains.

In the *Assembly*, the following bills were passed:

To amend the act regulating the weighing of merchandise in the city of New York; ayes 74, noes 12.

To amend the revised statutes relative to the laying out of public and private roads.

The bill to incorporate the New Utrecht dock and steam navigation company, was read a third time and lost; ayes 79, noes 13. [Messrs. Clinch, Herttell, W. S. Paddock, Patterson, Richmond, Seaman, J. Sibley, Simpson, C. O. Shepard, Speaker, Tomlinson, Tubbs.]

The bill for reorganizing the Chancery Circuits, and the appointment of additional *Vice*-Chancellors, was killed by striking out the enacting clause, and the resolutions for such an amendment to the constitution as to authorize the appointment of *five Chancellors*, &c., were discussed for a time and laid aside. The bill introduced by Mr. Cutting for repealing the restraining law, and that for incorporating the Oneida Bank, came up as the regular orders of the day.

Mr. Cutting said that when this bill was first introduced by him, he conceived that all that would be necessary to ask would be to restore to individuals their original, inherent right of receiving money in deposit and of discounting notes. The bill extended no further, and contemplated the granting of no special privileges or favors. Since the introduction of the bill, a new state of things had arisen in this country, which, in the judgment of many, required that additional cautions and guards should be provided in the bill. He referred to the creation of the Bank of the United States, by the Legislature of Pennsylvania, with a capital of 35,000,000. It was apprehended that under color of this bill, either surreptitiously, through private agents, or publicly, that that bank might enter this State and wield its immense capital to the prejudice of individuals and the community. Without meaning to say how far he participated in these apprehensions, or to debate the question whether this would be likely to be the result of the passage of the bill, or whether that bank might not, by other means, enter this State in spite of our legislation—he was unwilling to yield to the suggestions of gentlemen, and to propose amendments, with a view to obviate objections of that kind. He would take the liberty to read the amendments before entering into the discussion at large, that the committee might have the whole ground before them, and see the nature and extent of his bill, that they might be able to determine, understandingly, whether there was any thing alarming in its features, or any thing which could operate otherwise than beneficial to the entire State. Before offering the amendment it might be well to state that the original bill left the right to issue bills or notes, to be put in circulation as money, precisely where it was left under the existing law, that is, individuals would be prohibited from issuing bills of their own. The object of his amendments was to extend these guards still further.

[The amendments were read. They propose in the first place, some verbal alterations in the original bill, one of them amending the title so as to read "To authorize the establishment of offices of discount and deposite, and to repeal," &c. as before, and another authorizing associations or individuals to issue notes of the Safety Fund banks of this State. The additional sections provide that no corporation shall keep any such office in this State, as that authorized by the bill—either directly or through its agents. They also prohibit such individuals or associations from dealing in, or receiving in deposite or payment, or issuing any bills of foreign banks. Another section imposes a penalty of $1000, for every contravention of either of these two last provisions, upon any person who shall, directly or indirectly, assent to or aid in such violation of the act.]

In order to the printing of these amendments, the Committee rose and reported. The Oneida bank bill was then considered, the first two sections passed, and on an amendment to the third offered by Mr. Cutting, prohibiting the issue of bills under the denomination of $20, the Committee rose.

Tuesday.—The bill for improving the navigation of the Albany basin, was recommitted, discussed anew, amended, and again passed—after which the Senate was employed in Executive business.

The Assembly was chiefly occupied with the bill repealing the restraining act, and the Oneida Bank bill, without result.

ASSEMBLY OF THE STATE OF NEW YORK.

FRIDAY, 25th March.

Distribution of the Avails of the Public Lands.

Mr. Bradish rose and said, that he held in his hand a preamble and resolutions, on a subject of deep interest to the people of this State, and the whole country. In calling the attention of the House at this time, to a subject so important and interesting to the whole people, he trusted he might be permitted thus early, to invoke in its consideration the candor and deliberation, due as well to the nature of the subject, as it would be in harmony with our responsibilities as representatives of the people. He therefore confidently indulged the hope that in the final disposal of this important matter, no other considerations than such as commended themselves to the House, as members of the House, and as citizens of this State, would have any influence. As the resolutions were concurrent, he supposed they would lie on the table one day of course.

The preamble and resolutions were then read by the Clerk, as follows:

Whereas, the United States, in entering into "articles of Confederation and perpetual Union," encountered serious impediments, arising from the claims of several of the States to the extensive unoccupied territory within their respective chartered limits; as well as from the views entertained by other States in relation to such claims:

And whereas the Congress of the United States, anxious to remove those impediments, did on the 6th day of September, 1780, resolve among other things, "that it be earnestly reccommended to those States who have claims to the western country, to pass such laws, and give their delegates in Congress such powers, as may effectually remove the only obstacle to a final ratification of the articles of confederation:"

And whereas Congress, on the 10th day of October, 1780, and before any State had in pursuance of its earnest request, made any cession of its territorial claims to the United States, did also resolve, "that the unappropriated lands that might be ceded or relinquished to the United States, by any particular State, pursuant to the recommendation of Congress of the 6th of September, 1780, should be disposed of for the common benefit of the United States, &c." and "that the said lands should be granted or settled at such times and under such regulations as should hereafter be agreed on by the United States in Congress assembled or any nine of them:"

And whereas several of the States, New York being the first, animated by a spirit of conciliation, and a patriotic desire to remove the impediments which existed to a cordial union and co-operation of all the States in the accomplishment of the great objects of the revolution, did, in pursuance of the earnest solicitation of Congress, make large cessions of territory to the United States, upon the conditions, and for the uses, declared by Congress in its resolution of the 10th of October, 1780; and which, by the express terms of the cession, were to be considered "as a common fund for the use and benefit of such of the United States as had become, or should become, members of the confederation or federal alliance of the said States, and were to be faithfully disposed of for that purpose, and for no other use or purpose whatever;" and which cessions proceeded not more from a spirit of conciliation than a sense of justice, and were induced by the consideration, that as by the united exertions and the common blood and treasure of the whole people of the United States, those immense tracts of fertile and valuable lands had been wrested from the British crown, so ought they to be considered as the common domain, and to enure to the common benefit of all.

And whereas the territory acquired by treaties with France and Spain, embracing Louisiana and the Floridas, were paid for out of the common treasure of the United States, which had been drawn from the people either by direct or indirect taxation, and is, therefore, and of right ought to be, the common property of the whole people of the United States, to be held and disposed of for their benefit:

And whereas it appears, from the returns of the Treasury department that there is now in the treasury upwards of thirty millions of dollars, of which twenty millions five hundred and seventy-one thousand, one hundred and twenty five dollars and seventy-five cents are the proceeds of the sales of the public lands; and that judging of the future by the past, there will be in the treasury, on the first day of January next, upwards of fifty millions of dollars; and that the average receipts from the sales of the public lands for the next ten years will probably exceed ten millions of dollars annually:

And whereas, the national debt has happily been extinguished, and it may be confidently estimated that, after all proper expenditures for the ordinary purposes of the government, and for putting the nation in an attitude of complete defence, both by land and by sea, there will still remain a large surplus, exceeding the amount of the proceeds of the sales of the public lands now in the treasury:

And whereas, such large accumulations of revenue are not only unfavorable to a wise economy in the public expenditures, and a pure administration of the government; but are corrupting in their tendency, and even dangerous to liberty itself; that instead of such dangerous accumulations, a sounder policy would suggest, and justice to the people seem to require, that a portion, at least, of their own money, now lying hoarded in banks, and neither necessary for the uses, nor profitable to the finances of the government, should be given back to the people, and be employed for their benefit:

And whereas, the right of the people to demand a distribution of the proceeds of the sales of the public domain, and thus become relieved and exonerated from burdensome and unnecesary taxation, is unquestionably not in contravention of the constitution, inasmuch as the cessions made by the several States were intended and expressly declared to be for the common benefit of the whole people of the U. S. and inasmuch also, as by the third section of the fourth article of the constitution of the United States, it is ordained, "that Congress shall have power to dispose of and make all needful rules and regulations respecting the territory and other property belonging to the United States":

And whereas, it appears by a report made to the Senate of the United States during the present session of Congrss that, should a distribution of the proceeds of the sales of the public land now in the treasury be made upon just and equitable principles, the State of New-York, in such distribution, would be entitled to receive the sum of three millions three hundred and nine thousand, five hundred and three dollars; and should such distribution hereafter continue to be made annually, this State would probably receive annually, upwards of one million and a half of dollars:

And whereas, the representatives of the people of this State would be unfaithful to their constituents, if they should be regardless of their right to demand and receive their just proportion of the *Fund* now held in trust for the United States by Congress—*a fund* which, if now justly distributed, would not only greatly relieve from the heavy burden of taxation, but would diffuse among the people manifold blessings, in useful and important works of internal improvement, and in multiplying and extending the advantages of education to every child of the republic: Therefore,

Resolved (if the Senate concur,) That our Senators and Representatives in Congress be, and they are hereby, earnestly requested to use every proper effort to procure the passage of a law which shall provide for a just and equitable distribution of the proceeds of the sales of the public lands, which are now or shall hereafter come into the national treasury, among the several States, according to their respective rights therein.

Resolved (if the Senate concur,) That his excellency the Governor be requested to transmit to each of our Senators and Representatives in Congress a copy of the foregoing preamble and resolution.

The ordinary motion to print, was made by *Mr. Carroll*, and decided as follows, ayes 28, noes 73:

Ayes—Messrs. A. Barker, Bradish, Brooks, Campbell, Carroll, Chambers, Comstock, Herttell, Jones, Keep, Lee, Marvin, Ogden, W. S. Paddock, Pardee, Patterson, Richmond, Robertson, Romeyn, D. L. Seymour, M. H. Sibley, Stimson, Switzer, Tomlinson, Tyrrel, J. J. Viele, S. L. Viele, N. West—28.

Noes—Messrs. Allen, Alsop, Arnold, Ayres, G. P. Barker, Barney, A. G. Benedict, D. Benedict, Benton, Berry, Bellinger, Blair, Borland, J. Chamberlain, Clinch, Connor, Cutting, Day, Dennison, Dimmick, Dorman, Duane, Dutcher, Ely, Fisher, Fitch, Floyd, Foster, Gay, Garritson, Graves, Gray, Griffin, Griffing, Guinnip, Hale, Hawks, Holland, Hough, D. Johnson, J. Johnson, Kiersted, King, Kirby, Knapp, Knight, Knowlton, Mead, Morgan, Munro, Parker, Pettibone, M. C. Robinson, O. Robinson, Seaman, Searles, J. Sibley, Simpson, Sharp, Shaver, Sly, C. E. Shepard, R. L. Smith, Speaker, Spencer, Stetson, Sutton, Topping, Tubbs, Van Etten, Walworth, J. West, Wilbur, Yates—73.

So the House refused to print the preamble and resolutions.

APPOINTMENTS BY THE PRESIDENT, by and with the advice and consent of the Senate:

Upton S. Heath, to be Judge of the United States in and for the District of Maryland, in the place of Elias Glenn, resigned.

John Murphy, to be Consul for the port of Cork, in Ireland, in the place of Reuben Harvey.

Edmund L. Rainals, to be Consul for the port of Elsineur, in the Kingdom of Denmark, in the place of Thomas H. Barker, resigned.

Edwin Bartlett, to be Consul for the port of Lima, in Peru, in the place of Asa Worthington, resigned.

MARRIED—

On Thursday morning, by the Rev. Dr. McVickar, HENRY S. HOYT, to FRANCES, daughter of WILLIAM A. DUER, Esq.

Yesterday morning, by the Rev. Erskine Mason, Mr W. O. Bokee to Miss Mary Archer.

DIED—

In Philadelphia, on Tuesday, the 5th instant, aged 69, Eleanor, wife of Rembrandt Peale, Artist, of this city.

At West Point, N. Y. of scarlet fever, Julia and Joseph Kinsley, children of Lieut. Z. J. D. Kinsley; the former aged 3 years and 6 months on Tuesday, the 29th March, the latter aged 7 years and 4 months on Friday, the 1st of April.

The Connecticut Courant.

VOL. LXXII.....NO. 3719. HARTFORD, MONDAY, MAY 2, 1836. PRICE TWO DOLLARS.

CONNECTICUT COURANT,
PUBLISHED BY
GOODWIN & CO.
FIFTEEN RODS NORTH-WEST OF THE STATE-HOUSE, HARTFORD.

Price Two Dollars per annum, payable in advance —a liberal discount made to companies.

Advertisements not exceeding a square inserted three times for One Dollar—every after continuation Twenty Cents.

No accounts will be opened for Advertisements sent from a distance.

WEEKLY ALMANAC.

MAY.	☉ R.	☉ S.	D. INC.	R. ☽ S.
2 Monday,	5 3	6 57	4 24	9 4
3 Tuesday,	5 2	6 58	4 36	11 21
4 Wednesday,	5 1	6 59	4 38	11 30
5 Thursday,	5 0	7 0	4 40	Morn.
6 Friday,	4 59	7 1	4 42	0 28
7 Saturday,	4 58	7 2	4 44	1 13
8 Sunday,	4 57	7 3	4 46	1 53

Full Moon, 1st, 3h. 11m. morning.
Last Quarter, 7th, 6h. 2m. evening.
New Moon, 15th, 9h. 20m. morning.
First Quarter, 23d, 1h. 8m. evening.
Full Moon, 30th, 11h. 12m. morning.

From the New-Orleans Bee, April 11.

FROM TEXAS.

The most distressing intelligence was received yesterday from this delightful (but at present unfortunate) country, by the arrival of the General De Kalb from Brazoria, whence she sailed on the 3d instant.

On the 23d ult. Col. Fanning had sent out a scouting party of about 50 men; they were massacred. On the 24th, he sent out a skirmishing party of 150; they were also cut off. He then resolved to destroy the fort of Goliad; burn the town; and cut his way thro' the enemy encamped in his neighborhood, as his provisions failed, and his garrison had diminished to 300. But in attempting this, he was surrounded by the Mexicans, and compelled to capitulate and lay down his arms—after which with characteristic treachery he and all were shot.

The detachment of volunteers from Georgia under Major Ward, has been also cut off, with the exception of three persons, one of whom had arrived in Brazoria before the De Kalb sailed.

On the 26th ult. General Houston found it necessary or convenient to retreat 20 miles rearward from the Colorado river, as one wing of the Mexican army had arrived on the opposite bank.

The Mexicans were advancing in two columns—one upon General Houston, the other towards the mouth of the Brazos.

The army under Houston was posted near the Brazos river on the 29th ult; and contained about 2000 men; that column of the Mexicans opposed to him had then crossed the Colorado, and numbered about 3000. The Texicans think and Houston has determined that the enemy shall never recross the Colorado; and we think and trust that they shall not pass the Brazos.

The Texicans have actually become desperate from the massacres, and situation of their affairs. They have burned San Felippe de Austin; and destroyed all the country in their retreat. They have sent hither their women and children, with whom the De Kalb and other vessels are crowded. They have resolved in case of necessity to burn Brazoria and Bell's landing on the approach of the Mexicans; and are transporting most of their effects to Galveston, for which place the sch'rs, Columbus and Flash, were ready to sail. The Pennsylvania and Shenandoah were bound for this port; the Santiano was at the mouth of the river; and the Julius Cesar within.

Extract of a letter dated Peach Point, March 28th.

Mr. Sharp has arrived from Houston's camp—he left there on the 24th in the evening—states that there were 800 Mexicans encamped in the prairie; and Sharp thinks there has been an engagement. Houston had resolved to attack them, and so sanguine was he of success, that he was about to take measures when Sharp left, to prevent their escaping by sending a body of 300 beyond the enemy. Prisoners taken by our men state that the enemies force did not exceed 5000 men after leaving Bexar. Houston had with him about 2000, and his force was daily augmenting—nothing certain had been heard from Fanning, the reports are that he is retreating, the garrison at San Patricio of 95 men had had an engagement with 1200 of the enemy, killed 150, and wounded as many more, and retreated without loss. Yours, &c. J. F. PERRY.

Extracts from the Texas Republican, March 23.

Twenty-seven men, under the command of Lieut. M. W. Smith, arrived here to-day, on their way to head-quarters; and will leave to-morrow morning.

To the Committee of Brazoria.

Caney, March 22d, 1836.

I have just arrived from Cox's Point, left about 30 armed men and some twenty-five unarmed, in charge of the public stores in that place, but fear from the general panic, that that place would be deserted, after bringing off as much as the lighters could bring, but if Colonel Wharton had arrived with the force, said to be with him, the point could have been protected against ten times the number. I repaired east, in order to rally all the disposable force of the retreating families, but found every man shifting for himself and helpless family, all of which were crossing Colorado, and on their way east; and this morning Captain Sharp brings the news from the advance of Fanning's army (who made their escape,) that Fanning was surrounded and fighting in the prairie, 6 miles east of Goliad, for life, when the advance guard made their retreat, which was under the command of Colonel Horton, and I fear Fanning and his brave companions are slaughtered. The news is that all Americans in Guadaloupe were butchered by the citizen Spaniards. Such is our situation, and all will be on their way to-morrow further east, and unless you can rally and send on men forthwith, to the cover of the retreat, all must be lost; —and I would recommend the procuring and detention of any vessel that may be in reach, to take off helpless families. And every man who can possibly do so, to rally and turn the enemy back faster than they came— I have the honor to subscribe myself, yours, respectfully, BENJ. I. WHITE.

Fellow citizens in Texas generally:—News of the most disastrous nature arrived here from the southern divisions of our army by the lieutenant and twenty men who formed the advance of Fanning's army; while trying to make their retreat from fort Defiance, they were attacked by twenty-seven hundred Mexicans in the big prairie. They are now advancing towards the Colorado. Help we want—and that speedily.— Time don't admit of my saying any thing more.

FRANCIS WELLS.

LATEST FROM THE SOUTH.

By the steam packet Columbia, which left Charleston on Saturday P. M. we have received papers to the hour of leaving, and later from all parts of the South. The news from Texas is confused and contradictory. It is however pretty evident that the Mexicans are advancing and the Texians retreating. The distress among the Colonists is very great; all active pursuits are at an end; families broken up, and a scene of terror and alarm appears to be the consequence. We extract all that appears of any consequence.

From Florida there appears to be nothing of a striking character. There has been no fighting with the Indians, nor do hostilities appear to be any nearer a close. The professions of the Indians that they were disposed for peace is not confirmed. Gen. Scott was marching down the Peninsula.—*N. York Daily Adv.*

LATEST FROM TEXAS.

The Louisiana Advertiser of the 13th inst. contains the following:

Texas.—The gentleman from whom we have the following statement (Capt. Horton,) left Goliad on the 19th ult. informs us that Col. Fannin, having taken up his line of march on that day, at the head of 306 men, was attacked by the Mexican army consisting of from 1500 to 2000, about nine miles from Goliad, our informant commanded the advanced guard, consisting of only 25 men, which was cut off from the main army; they remained in view of the battle for about three fourths of an hour, and in hearing of it for about two hours. During the time they were in view the Mexican cavalry made two unsuccessful charges on Fannin's army; the Mexicans, he thinks, must have lost at least half their number in these charges. The attack was made about 5 o'clock in the evening, and continued about two hours and a half. He is unable to state particularly how the battle terminated; he encamped within six miles of the battle field that night and heard the firing of cannon next morning. Having remained ten days within about ninety miles of the place where the battle was fought, he was unable during the time to get any correct account of its result. Capt. H. had two skirmishes with the Mexicans, about 250 in number the day previous to the attack on Col. Fannin. They could observe three of the Mexican horses going off unmounted—Capt. H's force in these skirmishes, consisted of about one to fiver

He also informs us that Col. Ward was despatched on the 9th ult. with a mission, (only 99 men) about 30 miles from Goliad, to the relief of Capt. King, who had been taken prisoner by the Mexicans with 23 of his men, six being killed. An engagement took place on the 11th, Col. W. was attacked within 23 miles of the mission by 1200 of the Mexicans; he retreated into the mission without the loss of a man; 62 of the Mexicans fell. He fought them from half past 4 P. M. till 9 of the same evening. Ward then retreated toward Copano. The latest accounts from him stated that he was making his way into the settlements, between the San Antonio and Guadaloupe rivers, towards Copano. On the same night, in the town of Waloope, three of our citizens were murdered by the Mexican citizens. Dr. Harrison, son of Gen. W. H. Harrison, of Ohio, was among the number of these unfortunate victims.

The Caroda has seventy passengers, nearly all women and children. The Brutus was ready to sail for New Orleans, full of passengers, women and children.

The New Orleans Courier of the same date says:—

Distresses of the Colonists.—The Schr. Coralla arrived this morning from Matagorda, (Texas) loaded with the unfortunate wives and children of the colonists—grief and despair is depicted on all their countenances—many who were in easy, if not affluent circumstances, are now reduced to abject poverty. A scene so distressing we feel assured has never before been witnessed in the United States—even the miseries of the unfortunate inhabitants of St. Domingo, with all their sufferings, can bear no parallel to this. Many of them being unable to escape with money, whereby they could supply their wants until such time as employment could be procured; but the people of Texas are pastoral, their riches were their flocks and lands, which they have been compelled to abandon, and are now flung on our shores destitute of every thing, and broken in spirit. It should be recollected they are Americans—their blood is ours; and it behoves us to alleviate their afflictions and sufferings. Many of them have lost their fathers, husbands, sons, and brothers—let therefore some of our worthy fellow citizens call a meeting for their relief—the call will not, cannot be made in vain—every man will throw in his mite, and even our ladies, who are proverbial for their benevolence, will not let such an occasion pass unnoticed. Any thing more from us, we deem unnecessary—the feelings of pity and charity in our inhabitants are such, that it is sufficient for them to know, that any of their fellow creatures are in need of a helping hand for them to extend it.

Slavery in Texas.—We copy from the American the annexed decree of Santa Anna, relative to slavery in Texas:

"His Excellency, the President of the Republic, Commander in Chief of the Army of Operations in the Territory of Texas, under the date of 16th inst. from San Antonio de Bexar, has issued the following decree:

"Whereas a great number of colonists, in contravention of the laws and institutions of the Mexican Republic which expressly forbid slavery and the slave trade in all its possessions and territories—availing themselves of the state of bondage, ignorance and almost destitution in which slaves are generally to be found in the states of the United States—found the means of importing, by sea and by land, and keeping in slavery, a great number of colored people, thus entailing that disgraceful system upon our country;— Resolved,

1. The laws and institutions of the Mexican Republic on slavery and the slave trade, shall, from this day, remain in full force in the whole Territory of Texas.

2. In compliance with said laws, the persons of all colored people, of both sexes, are from this moment declared free, and this whatever may be the nature of the contracts which bind them to their masters; should said contracts be, in a direct or indirect manner, contrary to the existing prohibitory laws of the Republic on slavery and slave trade, in which case they shall be considered as null and of no value.

3. Colored people, who may present themselves to the military governors or commanders, claiming the protection of the Mexican laws, shall be protected, allowing them their freedom, as well as the faculty of settling in whatever section of the Republic they choose, providing them with the necessary passport.

4. Those who shall, hereafter, contravene the Mexican laws on slavery and slave trade, shall incur the penalties prescribed in the latter.

San Felipe, 20th March 1836.

Signed, Prefecto de Cos."

The Connecticut Courant.

VOL. LXXII.....NO. 3720. HARTFORD, MONDAY, MAY 9, 1836. PRICE TWO DOLLARS.

CONNECTICUT COURANT,
PUBLISHED BY
GOODWIN & CO.
FIFTEEN RODS NORTH-WEST OF THE STATE-HOUSE, HARTFORD.

Price Two Dollars per annum, payable in advance—a liberal discount made to companies.

Advertisements not exceeding a square inserted three times for One Dollar—every after continuation Twenty Cents.

No accounts will be opened for Advertisements sent from a distance.

WEEKLY ALMANAC.

MAY.	☉ R.	☉ S.	D. INC.	R. ☽ S.
9 Monday,	4 56	7 4	4 48	2 20
10 Tuesday,	4 55	7 5	4 50	2 46
11 Wednesday,	4 54	7 6	4 52	3 10
12 Thursday,	4 53	7 7	4 54	3 34
13 Friday,	4 52	7 8	4 56	3 56
14 Saturday,	4 51	7 9	4 58	4 18
15 Sunday,	4 50	7 10	5 0	Sets.

Full Moon, 1st, 3h. 11m. morning.
Last Quarter, 7th, 6h. 2m. evening.
New Moon, 15th, 9h. 20m. morning.
First Quarter, 23d, 1h. 8m. evening.
Full Moon, 30th, 11h. 12m. morning.

NOTICE.
THE Trustees of the *Bishop's Fund*, are hereby notified that their stated Annual Meeting will be held at the County House, in New-Haven, on the 10th day of May, instant, at 7 o'clock, P. M. As there are several vacancies in the Board to be filled, and business of importance to be transacted, a punctual attendance of the members is requested.
ASHBEL BALDWIN, Secretary.
New-Haven, May 2. 2w19

NOTICE.
THE Co-partnership heretofore existing under the firm of LYMAN & GAY, is by mutual consent, dissolved. Amos W. Gay is duly authorised to close the business of the concern.
THEO. LYMAN,
AMOS W. GAY.
Hartford, April 23, 1836.

CO-PARTNERSHIP NOTICE.
THE subscribers have formed a Copartnership, under the firm of *T. R. & L. CASE*, for the purpose of transacting the Dry Goods Business.
THOMAS R. CASE,
LUKE CASE.
Hartford, April 21, 1836.

NOTICE.
THE Co-partnership heretofore existing under the firm of Cooley & Curtiss, is this day, by mutual consent, dissolved.
NOAH COOLEY,
A. L. CURTISS.
West-Granville, April 11, 1836.

The subscribers will continue business at the old stand, under the firm of *A. L. CURTISS & CO.*
NOAH COOLEY,
A. L. CURTISS.
West-Granville, April 11, 1836. 6w17

NOTICE.
THE subscribers have entered into Co-partnership, under the firm of *BURT & TOWNSEND*, and offer for sale an extensive assortment of *Boots* and *Shoes*, by the Case. Likewise, 200 dozen *Wax Calf Skins*; a good assortment of *Leather Findings*, &c. &c.
JAMES BURT,
DANIEL TOWNSEND.
Hartford, April 30, 1836. 19

NOTICE.
THE subscribers have formed a Co-partnership, under the firm of J. & A. CLARK, for the purpose of transacting the Retail Goods Business, in all its branches. By recent purchases in New-York, such additions have been made to the former stock of Jonathan Clark, as to make it an object for those in want of Merchandise to favor them with a call.
All kinds of Produce taken in exchange for Goods, and the highest price given. Also, Palm Leaf Hats. Straw Braid wanted.
JONATHAN CLARK,
ALBERT CLARK.
N. B. All those indebted to Jonathan Clark, are requested to call and settle their accounts.
Somers, May 2, 1836. 19

SCHOOL FOR BOYS.
THE Summer Term of the subscriber's School will commence on Wednesday, the 11th day of May. Scholars hereafter will recite in a room *seperate* from the school room. None but competent teachers will be employed; whose aim will be to have the studies *well understood*, and make the school worthy the patronage of the Public. The Teachers have a room connected with the school room, and thus the scholars while in it will be constantly under their supervision.
The Latin, Greek, and French languages are taught: and particular attention is bestowed upon the education of those, who are designed for a *business* life. Scholars are received at any time during the term; and are charged only from the time they enter; but it is preferred that they should enter at the beginning of the term, as there will then be adopted a regular plan of study for *twenty-two* weeks; and much is gained by going through the *whole course*.
Tuition, $6 a quarter of eleven weeks. A class of lads under ten years of age, who will attend only to the *elementary* branches, will be received at $4 a quarter. Scholars from abroad can board with the teachers, and be under their constant care, for $150 a year. Books and Stationery furnished at the customary prices.
NOAH B. CLARK.
April 25. 18

HARTFORD GRAMMAR SCHOOL.
A Term of this School will commence on Monday, the 9th day of May, instant, under the care of Messrs. Sophocles and Seymour, as heretofore.
Tuition, $6 per Term, of fourteen weeks, to be paid in advance, to Andrew Kingsbury, Esq.
Applications for admission, may be made to the Teachers.
ALFRED SMITH, } Committe of
T. C. PERKINS, } Trustees.
Hartford, May 2, 1836. 2w19

SELECT SCHOOL.
MISS J. R. BULKLEY'S Select School for Instruction in the various branches of Study and Needle Work, is now open for the reception of pupils. Lessons will be given in Music and French.
Hartford, May 2. 19

PRIVATE INSTRUCTION.
THE Summer Term of Misses Watson's School, will commence Wednesday, May 18th.
Hartford, April 18. 5w17

LITCHFIELD FEMALE SEMINARY
MISS M. A. SWIFT, PRINCIPAL.
THE Summer Term of this Institution, will commence on Wednesday, May 11th. French, Music, and Drawing, taught by Mademoiselle Genibrede.
Tuition, per Term of twenty-two weeks, as follows:

All English branches,	$10 75
French,	14 00
Drawing,	10 00
Music,	20 00

An extra charge is made for Latin and Greek.
Board may be obtained in respectable families for $2 per week.
Litchfield, April 25. 4w18

EAST-WINDSOR ACADEMY.
THE Summer Term in this Institution will commence on the 11th May, under the instruction of the Rev. Phillips Payson, and continue eighteen weeks.
The price for tuition, to be paid in advance, will be at the rate of from $4 to $5 for eleven weeks, according to the studies pursued. Mr. Payson will accommodate a small number of Lads in his own family, and pay particular and constant attention to their morals and deportment. His charge for tuition, room, board, washing, fuel, and lights, will be $150 per annum, payable half yearly in advance, with a reasonable compensation for the use of Beds and Bedding, if they are not provided by the students themselves.
References.—The Professors in the Theological Institute, East-Windsor: Rev. *Joel Hawes*, D. D.; Rev. *C. C. Vanarsdalen*; Rev. *T. H. Gallaudet*; *David Watkinson*, Esq.; *Eliphalet Terry*, Esq.; *J. L. Comstock*, M. D.
April 4. 7w15

CLASSICAL AND ENGLISH SCHOOL FOR YOUNG GENTLEMEN,
Pratt-street, nearly opposite the "Hartford Female Seminary."
THE Spring Term in this School, will commence on Thursday, February 25th.
Instruction is given in the studies preparatory for College, and in the branches usually taught in High Schools and Academies. It is the aim of the Teachers to give those whom they instruct a *thorough* acquaintance with the studies they pursue, rather than to urge them rapidly over an extended surface.
The year is divided into Quarters of eleven weeks each.
Terms Per Quarter.

Ancient Languages,	$7 00
English Branches,	6 00
For Instruction in French, by a native teacher, there will be an additional charge of	6 00

No deduction made for leaving the School, or for absence, during term time, except in case of sickness.
I. H. TUTTLE,
J. HENRY ELLIOT.
Reference may be made to the Right Rev. Bishop *Brownell*, The President and Faculty of Washington College, Rev. Dr. *Davis*, Rev. Mr. *Gallaudet*, Rev. Mr. *Hooker*, and Rev. Mr. *Burgess*.
February 8. tf 7

WANTED,
A HAT FINISHER.
CALLANDER, WATSON & CO.
Winsted, May 2. 2w19

WANTED,
A MAN to take charge of the Engine in a Paper Mill. Good recommendations will be required. Also, two Females to count, fold and assort paper. Letters may be addressed to me at New-Haven.
JAMES DONAGHE.
April 25. 18

TEXAS.

The annexed letter from the Columbus, (Geo.) Herald of April 19th, contains a more exact and connected view of the late events in Texas, than we have elsewhere seen. It was written by a Mr. Lambkin, late of Texas, to Gen. Bethune, of Columbus.

On board Schooner DeKalb, }
Mississippi River, April 7. }

Dear Sir—You are no doubt somewhat surprised at the heading of this page; but a few words will explain all. I am on board of one of a number of vessels that are laden with the unfortunate, who are flying from the terrors of war. You have perhaps heard of the storming of St. Antonio, and massacre of the Texian garrison. All, without an exception, perished, save a woman and two negroes. Davy Crockett was among the number. He had fully sustained his great character for intrepidity, during an unsuccessful attempt of the enemy to storm the Alamo, just one week before the massacre. A short time previous to this, a party of 60 or 70 under Col. Johnson, were cut off, save four. John Love was among the number who escaped. Reuben Brown fell there, and young Mitchell, of Harris County, fell in the Alamo. The taking of the Alamo was followed by the retreat of the main army from Gonzales, and by the extermination of Fannin's regiment, 500 strong.

Major Ward, and the Georgia battalion, (Capt. Wardsworth's company included,) had been detached by Col. Fannin, then at Bahia, to protect some families who were flying from the enemy; when they were attacked, and after fighting and retreating nearly two days, were at length overpowered by numbers, and all put to the sword, but five who escaped, and only two of them Georgians; one Richard Rutledge, formerly of Columbus, and the other David I. Holt.

In the meantime, Fannin had received orders to abandon the fortress of La Bahia, which he immediately executed, and returned towards the main army with the balance of his troops, 360 men, and seven pieces of artillery, when they were attacked in an open prarie by a large Mexican force, mostly cavalry. A small advance guard having been separated from the main body saw the fight, but could not tell the result. The termination to this unhappy affair, was explained by three men who escaped about the time of the catastrophe. Fannin sustained a great many charges in quick succession, sustaining some damage, and doing much execution; and kept retreating during the fight, which lasted during the greater part of a day, until he gained some post oak woods, when the Mexicans ceased their charges, but closely invested the place on all sides. Here Fannin received propositions from the enemy, and capitulated upon the promise of the Mexicans that they should be treated as prisoners of war. Their arms were immediately secured, and the next morning they were all shot, save the three who escaped. Mrs. Fannin had just arrived in Texas, but not in time to see her husband.

Many other barbarities have been committed. The army of Texas, after making a stand for a short time on the Colorado, has retreated to the east side of the Brassos. San Phillippe is burnt (by the citizens) and there is a probability that Brazoria and Washington have shared the same fate. I do not expect that there are half a dozen families west of the Brassos. The enemy is known to be marching into the country in two divisions of 200 men each; one through the interior upon the San Phillippe, and the other along the coast towards Velasco. They were constantly expected at the latter place when I left it, and the advance of the other division had already reached San Phillippe. The Indians had begun to be troublesome, and many negroes have run away—in some instances whole plantations of them had gone off in a body, but had done no further mischief. Very many families and negroes were going eastward, some for the United States by land and by water—others are making a stand in the east, covered by the army.

THE HERALD.

VOLUME II. NEW-YORK, TUESDAY, MAY 24, 1836. NUMBER 63.

PUBLISHED DAILY BY
JAMES GORDON BENNETT,
Office in the Clinton Buildings, at the corner of Nassau and Beekman streets.

TERMS OF ADVERTISING.

FOR TWELVE LINES, OR LESS.

1 day,	$0 50	4 days,	$1 25	7 days,	$1 87	10 days,	$2 25
2 - - -	0 75	5 - - -	1 50	8 - - -	2 00	11 - - -	2 37
3 - - -	1 00	6 - - -	1 75	9 - - -	2 12	12 - - -	2 50

FOR EIGHT LINES, OR LESS.

2 weeks,	$2 50	3 months,	$8 00
1 month,	3 00	6 months,	15 00

☞ All Advertisements to be paid for before their insertion.

TERMS OF SUBSCRIPTION.

City Subscribers, by leaving their names at the office, can be served daily by the Newsmen, to whom payment is to be made weekly.

Country Subscribers, in any part of the United States, or in Canada, can receive the Herald daily by mail, (postage paid by the subscriber,) on remitting $5 for one year in advance.

☞ No orders by mail are attended to unless the subscription is paid always in advance.

☞ Subscribers who want their papers left regularly at their houses, will please hand in their names at the office, in Clinton Hall, corner of Beekman and Nassau streets

☞Regular carriers supplied with the Herald at an early hour—newsboys and transient sellers not before 10 o'clock.

CORPORATION.—By a dexterous movement of the democrats in the Board of Assistants last night, Mr. Curtis was unanimously elected President of that body, Mr. Bruen and his antagonist being thrown to the dogs—the mad dogs. Mr. Talman rather disliked the dose, but he had to swallow it—it was of his own cooking. This piece of "olive branch," did not take with the Alderman. They went to voting, as usual, and came no nearer when we went to press, than they have yet been 8 to 8. Nothing settled.

IMPORTANT FROM TEXAS.

Texas is free and independent—Santa Anna is a prisoner of war—General Houston has obtained a victory even beyond the previous statements—and the cause of liberty is forever triumphant.

Such is the intelligence received yesterday morning by mail from New Orleans. The details, as far as known, will be found annexed. They are taken from the journals of that city, up to the 9th inst.

The misgivings in the public mind relative to this overwhelming victory are now swept away at a dash. Those who have attempted to throw suspicion over the brave deeds of the Texians, may think themselves well off if their insignificance preserves them from signal public indignation.

Every remark—every suggestion—every idea which we have heretofore thrown out on the victory will now be more than realized. The independence of Texas will not alone be secured—the liberty of Mexico—the regeneration of that land will be dated from the victory on the Brassos. The genuine spirit of political and intellectual liberty, as first promulgated by the republicans of England in the sixteenth century, will be infused by these American descendants into the Mexican institutions of the nineteenth. The highway to the capitol of Montezuma is now open to American enterprise and American adventure. Symptoms of revolution have already appeared—but general movements will follow.

Mexico will be regenerated—Texas is free. What further results may follow this magnificent victory, the imagination comes short of of picturing at this moment. General Houston, if he chooses, may soon plant his standard on the walls of Mexico. *At the commencement of this struggle we predicted the result*—at the very moment too, when the Courier and Enquirer was giving vent to the ferocious insults to Texian honor and bravery, prepared by the spy *Almonte* who is among the captured by the brave Texians.

The effect of this victory upon the public cannot be calculated. It will awaken a new passion and a new energy in the United States. It will open a new vista to the lovers of liberty, beyond the boundaries of this great empire. The republics of the South have been struggling for years with military tyrants. Mexico will first be regenerated by American arms and American principles. Colombia, Guatemala, Peru—all will follow. Meantime it remains for Congress to act wisely and energetically at the present crisis of affairs.—The independence of Texas may be acknowledged for it has nobly won it—but they had better wait and see the results of victory on the action of Mexico herself.

With these remarks we give the following extracts from the New Orleans papers:—

New-Orleans, May 9, 1836.

Texas.—Col. A. Houston of the Texian army has arrived in the steamboat Caspian, and confirms the news of the glorious victory of General Houston, and has favored us with the following list of the Mexican officers killed, wounded and missing.

Killed—General Castrillon, Colonel Batnes, Colonel Mora, Colonel Trevino, Colonel Don Jose Maria Romero, Lieutenant Colonel Manuel Aquirre, Lieutenant Col. Castillo.

General Cos, and many others supposed to be killed but not yet found.

Prisoners—General Antonio Lopez de Santa Anna, Col. Almonti, aid de camp, Cols. Cespedes of the Guerreror battalion, Bringas, aid to Santa Anna, Portilla de la Pedreguire aid to Santa Anna, Nuner, Valienti, Lieut. Cols. Felipe Romero, (wounded) Valenti, Don Pedro del Gardo, Fernando Urriza, wounded, aid to Santa Anna, Arcos, Encise, Mugla Don Ramon Curo, private secretary to Santa Anna, also five Captains and twelve Lieutenants.

Gen. Santa Anna made the following proposition—that his army should lay down their arms, Texas' Independence acknowledged, the expense of the war to be paid by Mexico, Santa Anna to remain as a hostage. General Houston had issued orders that a further advance of the Mexican army should be the signal for the slaughter of Santa Anna, and all the prisoners. The report of the terms of peace were not official but supported by a great number of letters from officers of the army. —*Com. Bulletin.*

Particulars of the capture of Santa Anna.—During the night of the 20th ult, after the skirmish between the Mexican and Texian forces, Gen. Houston made a movment with 600 men and all his artillery, and at day break met the Mexican force eleven or twelve hundred strong, also in movement, and gained a position within rifle distance of the enemy, before they were aware of his presence. Two discharges of small arms, and cannon loaded with musket balls, settled the affair—the Mexican soldiers then threw down their arms, most of them without firing, and begged for quarter, six or seven hundred killed. The officers broke and endeavored to escape—the mounted riflemen, however, soon overtook all but one, who distanced the rest—him they ran fifteen miles, when his horse bogged down in the prairie, near the Brassos timber—he then made for the timber on foot. His pursuers in the eagerness of the chase dashed into the same bog hole, left their horses and continued the pursuit on foot, following the trail of the fugitive, which was very plain, owing to the recent rains, until they reached the timber, where it was lost. The pursuers then spread themselves, and searched the woods for a long time in vain, when it occurred to an old hunter, that the chase might, like a hard pressed bear, have 'taken a tree." The tree tops were then examined, when lo! the game was discovered snugly ensconced in *the forks of a large live oak.*

The captors did not know who their prisoner was, until they reached the camp, when the Mexican soldiers exclaimed, "*El General! El Gefe! Santa Anna.* —*N. O. American.*

The officers and crew of the Invincible, were again brought up yesterday morning for examination, which took place in the United States District Court Room, before Judge Rawle. The Messrs. P. K. Lawrence, U. S. District Attorney, and Winthrop, Esq., appeared on the part of the prosecution. For the accused, the Messrs. Seth Barton, Randall Hunt, and O. P. Jackson, Esqrs. But four witnesses were examined on the prosecution, when an adjournment was made to this morning at 9 o'clock. We have never seen a finer collection of robust, and honest faced tars, than the prisoners, and in a good cause, we should ever hope, that they might prove invincible. Not wishing to give mutilated parts of the testimony taken, we shall defer publishing an account of the evidence &c., until we shall be enabled to present en masse.

By a gentleman, passenger on board the steamer Black Hawk, and who was in the battle of the 21st ult. we are informed that an individual was taken by the Texians, whom they generally believed to be the President Santa Anna. This individual, whoever he may be, made large offers for his ransom, and was captured while making his retreat to a bridge which crossed Symm's Bayou, which having been previously cut away, prevented his passing, and threw him into the power of the Texians. He was dressed in citizens clothing. Our informant adds, that Gen. Houston had at the time of the engagement 750 men, which were increasing very fast. The forces of the Mexicans amounted to 1200. Houston made it appear that he was retreating, and by this feint induced the Mexicans to advance towards Harrisburgh, while he was by this step more and more surrounding them. "Thus the work goes bravely on"—and as we prophecied from the first, so we find our prophecies rapidly realizing and all things, so far as Texas is concerned "working together for good.—*Com. Bul. May* 7.

NEW ORLEANS, May 6, 1836.

From private communications and other sources, the reported battle between the Texian forces and a large division of the Mexican army, published some days since, is now well confirmed. It is a sufficient matter for congratulation, that a battle has been fought and won, that freedom has triumphed in the contest, and the work of butchery at least checked if not entirely finished.

We are at this moment however informed, by a gentleman, passenger in the Jane, that the true Santa Anna is in Texas. All we add is, that the mystery will soon be solved.

FROM MATAMORAS.—Captain Williams reports that the Jane was detained at Matamoras 26 days by order of General Ditel Fernandez, and thus the neutrality of the American flag insulted. The sails of the vessel unbent and taken on shore; the captain imprisoned and otherwise maltreated. For what cause he could not learn, he having complied with every requisition of the Mexican Government, and possessing, (previous to his detention) every paper required by said goverment, even to his order for the pilot to take him to sea.

The fourteen persons who were sentenced to be shot on the 20th April, were reprieved until the 30th, and it was hoped that they would be finally pardoned; the most strenuous exertions being made in their behalf by all the foreigners of the place.

Captain W. states that a revolution had broken out in the city of Mexico, and it was further stated by a passenger on board the Jane, that the commander at Matamoras was only waiting for a favorable opportunity to renounce his allegiance to Santa Anna's Government.—*Com. Bulletin.*

BRIG JANE.—The captain of the Jane, reports the following:—the Jane was detained at Matamoras 26 days by order of General Fernandez—the neutrality of the American flag insulted—the sails of the vessel unbent and taken on shore—the captain imprisoned and otherwise most grossly maltreated, for what cause he could not learn, he having complied with every requisition of the Mexican government, and possessing previous to his detention, every paper required by that government, and his order for the pilot to take him to sea.

Captain Williams also states that a revolution had taken place in Mexico.

FURTHER FROM MONTREAL.—Further important intelligence has been received from Montreal. It appears that the *Ami du Peuple*, the organ of the French party in Montreal, has come out against the code of honor put forth by Campbell Sweeny and the Montreal Garrison. They cut up poor Campbell most savagely—almost as bad as if he were a Seminole. No matter. We have some consolation to pour into his wounded mind. If he makes his appearance in any part of New York, during the present season, Saratoga, Ballston, Lake George, or elsewhere, we are assured there is a set of prime fellows who have made up their minds to ride Campbell on a rail as a mode of expressing their thanks to him for the interest he has manifested in the affair of honor, between Tompkins and Neill. Seriously, however, we begin to suspect that the Montreal Garrison has been playing a joke on Campbell Sweeny, who is no British officer, but merely a white-livered hanger on upon their society.

RELIEF FOR BROADWAY.—This important street can no longer be used with safety by foot passengers, nor by private vehicles. By the worst kind of monopoly it has become the property of the owners of omnibusses. It is high time that the people should be restored to their rights, and this can be done by a very just and simple remedy.

1—Let the Corporation, if we have such a municipal body, pass an ordinance, fixing a tariff on licenses to use Omnibusses, in the different streets of the city, and let the tariff on Broadway be very heavy, say one thousand dollars.

2—Open a convenient thoroughfare to ease Broadway, and let the tariff there be moderate. This can be done by widening *Church street*, and opening it at both ends to run parallel to the whole extent of Broadway. Also open Center and Elm streets.

3—Let the whole angle of the Park, opposite to the Astor Hotel and the Park Theatre, be cut off, and converted into a paved square for omnibusses, to be called Park Square, and prohibit all omnibusses, hereafter, from going down to the Bowling green and Wall street.

The easy access to every part of Broadway from Church street, will be secured by allowing, under the license to travel Church street, a passage up the cross streets to Broadway, say at all points. This simple remedy will meet the convenience of all parties. The omnibusses instead of encumbering Broadway, while waiting for passengers, will take their stations at the corner in the cross streets, or in Park Square, and there likewise deliver their passengers as the end of their course. And should any spirited owners choose to encounter the tax on Broadway, the elegance of his carriage and its select character would make in an accommodation also to the ladies, whose convenience ought to be considered, and the increased fare would speedily remunerate him. Broadway would become then what it should be, a pleasant, agreeable, gay, fashionable street, and Park Square, with the Post office in the Brick church, *as it will be*, would be the centre of the city. Wall street, the Banks, brokers and Insurance offices, would then manage business quietly.

PAR VALUE.—A boy yesterday called at our office with a big Courier and Enquirer, of same day's date in his hand, "Will you give me a Herald for this Courier?" said he. As we had not read the trumpery of the big sheet, we replied, "O! yes, there's a Herald." The young fellow left the office, chuckling on the great bargain he had made—got a Herald for a Courier. This is pill No. 1, for this week.

RIOTS.—On Sunday last, two riots disturbed the peace of the city and the sacredness of the day—one in Rose street and the other in Cherry. The Saturday riot we gave yesterday.

The season of riots and rows is now approaching. In western New York, at Batavia, a very superior riot has been celebrated, and renewed several days in succession. Another riot, of a more inferior description, was held at Cincinnati, Ohio. In this city, we have had since the opening of the spring, probably, six or seven riots—besides hotel rows, and a few personal attacks. First—there was the riot of the Stevedores—secondly—the Journeymen Tailors—thirdly—the fashonable *fracas*, at Washington Hall—fourthly—the personal assault on the liberty of the press, in Wall street, by Webb—fifthly—the row among the Irishmen in the burnt district, last Saturday—sixthly and seventhly—the two riots of last Sunday.

More riots are expected soon. The weather is warm and no rain is apprehended for a month. Steam must escape. The following are the particulars of the latest riot:—

Christopher Merkle, constable of the 7th Ward, appeared at the Police office yesterday morning, and made affidavit to the following facts.

As he was passing down Cherry street, on Sunday afternoon, he saw a large mob collected before the houses Nos. 358, 360, and 362 Cherry street. As he approached the same, he observed Mr. Reeves, Street Inspector of the 7th Ward, on the ground, and several persons pummelling him pretty severely. Many of the mob were engaged in the intellectual employment of throwing stones and brick-bats at every passer by, and some of them were good marksmen too.

Mr. Mukle attempted to get the relief of Mr. Reeves, but the stones, and brickbats, and mud, flew so fast, and were thrown in such a marksmanlike manner, that he was glad to retreat, which he did, pursued by Regan, who was armed with a brickbat in each hand which he discharged successively at the *caput* of Mr. Merkle—but without doing any material damage to his upper works.

Once Mr. Merkle was out of sight, the mob commenced throwing stones, brickbats, and every missile that could be had at the windows of the above mentioned houses. Not a pane of glass or a sash of either are now visible so true was the aim of the assailants.

The row commenced in a most noted rum hole, kept by David Barry, at 358 Cherry street, and he was an active member of the corps. Thomas Brown, who keeps at No. 362, was also very busy upon the occasion, trying his skill as a marksman, by sending a stone or brickbat at the head of every passer by.

Several were arrested and safely lodged in prison, and unless discharged at the next sessions, may have the honor of working on Blackwell's Island in the same gang with Day and Beach. The names of those arrested, are James McConvin, Michael Lynch, Patrick Quinlon, John Campbell, and Thomas McCormick. Those who were known, but not arrested are Peter Hays, and ——— Regan.

The statements of Mr. Merkle was corroborated by four witnesses, who saw the whole transaction.

HORSEMANSHIP.—The mornings are so delicious that the young ladies who possess courage and sprightliness to get up at sun rise, are beginning to treat themselves to a canter long before the dust is kicked up by the cartmen or the Aldermen wake up from their deep slumbers.

Yesterday at half past five, a most beautiful creature—with a fine expressive face—bright eyes—auburn hair—arrayed in a splendid riding drapery and mounted gallantly on a roan steed passed our office attended by two cavaliers who sat most unguardedly and slouchingly on the outside of a pair of black horses. The fair lady—delicious creature—managed her steed with exquisite skill. The animal moved as if a part of herself—as her beautiful hair floated in the breeze sufficient to enrapture a saint. She passed the corner of Chatham and Beekman streets in an elegant canter—entered Broadway—and dashed out to Bloomingdale like Cleopatra Queen of Egypt—or the famous Zenobia of Palmyra. How beautiful!—how healthy!—how fresh!—how rosy she looked when she returned.

A handsome woman, on a handsome horse—and handsomely managed can lay the world in deep adoration at her feet.

MARRIED.

On Sunday evening, May 22d, by the Rev. Archibald McClay, Mr. Peter Kempt, to Miss Margaret Cado, all of this city. *

DIED.

On Sunday afernoon, after a short illness, Margaret, widow of the late Bernard Thompson.

On Saturday afternoon, Mrs. Hannah Van Cleef, in the 74th year of her age.

TEXAS CHRONICLE.

VOL. 1. Nacogdoches, Saturday, October 28, 1837. NO. 23.

THE TEXAS CHRONICLE

IS published weekly by J. W. BURTON, & W. W. BELL, at five dollars per annum payable in six months. No subscription will be received for less than six months. No papers will be forwarded to the United States, unless paid for in advance, or assumed by some responsible citizes residing in Texas.

TERMS OF ADVERTISING.

Advertisments will be inserted for one dollar per square for the first insertion, and fifty cents for each successive one. Eight lines is a square. If an advertisment makes less than a square, it will be charged as a full one, and if it exceeds a square it will be charged as two. Advertising accounts will bear ten per cent interest from due until paid. All articles of a personal character, whenever admitted, or Political Circulars, Public Addresses, for the individual benefit of the person or companies, it will be charged as advertisments. Announcing Candidates for office, will be ten dollars each. Professional Advertisments for eight lines or less, not alterable, for three months, twelve dollars; for six months, twenty dollars; for twelve months, thirty dollars.

No Advertisment inserted for less than two dollars.

LETTERS in all cases must be Post paid.

All Job work must be paid for on delivery.

ADVENTURE IN THE ROCKY MOUNTAINS.

(Original.)

In the fall of 1832, three companies of trappers assembled on the Missouri, a short distance below the mighty falls, so graphically described in the Narrative of Messrs Lewis & Clark. One of these companies, consisting of eighty men and twenty Indian warriors, was a branch of the Rocky Mountain Fur Company, led by Mr. Thomas Fitzpatrick. The other two companies were branches of the American Fur Company, enumerating, together, one hundred and twenty men, and were led by Mr. A. Dripps and Wm. H. Vanderburgh. A year previous to this time a small party had ventured here, in the heart of the Blackfoot country, and had made an extraordinary hunt, which led us to believe that this extensive portion of the mountainous region was yet untrapped, and would yield us a rich return of furs, for the dangers we should necessarily be exposed to in the prosecution of our employment.—Our trappers were ordered out in all directions in quest of beaver; but, to our mortification, returned with the report, that the country had been trapped by a party of Blackfoot Indians in the spring, and that the few remaining beaver were too cunning or too mild, to be taken.—A council of the leaders was immediately held, and, with their usual promptness of decision, it was determined that we should proceed southward up the Missouri, to the Three Forks, where the grand company should be subdivided, and each leader proceed with his party where his discretion might lead him to improve the short season for trapping yet left, and regain the expense incurred by a lengthy and fruitless journey. The country, at this time, to the northward, presented an interminable plain, bounded by the horizen and watered by Dearborn River and the Missouri. To the eastward and westward, lofty mountains arose above the clouds, extending parallel with the course of the river, and were twenty miles asunder; but the intermediate space was extremely broken, presenting countless mounds, and bluffs of every possible form and description. Whoever that has seen the admirable paintings of scenery and buffalo hunts, together with Indian portraits, recently exposed for public inspection in various parts of the United States, by that master hand, Mr. George Catlin, the American Artist—may form a pretty correct idea idea of the stupendous, the wild, the fantastic, the majestic and the picturesque freaks of nature, presented in many places on the borders of the Missouri. Here might be seen a high square bluff, with projections that had survived the war of the elements and the wear of time, that resembled a fort. There a cluster of them presented the *fac similic* of a village; one of them, unusually large, surmounted by a pointed pyramid of rocks that had thus far set decomposition at defiance, might be mistaken for the village church; and other lofty columns of the same character resembled monuments. Here and there were sprinkled over the earth magnificent domes of such perfect regularity that the beholder would hesitate to class them with the productions of nature, so closely did they resemble the works of art.

But the most singular feature of these most singular and nondescript productions was found in perpendicular projections that, at a distance, without the aid of imagination, were often mistaken for human beings. They were formed by the gradual decomposition of mounds composed of soft rock, of which the upper strata was much more durable than the others, and in many instances were worn to balls; the next strata being of more perishable materials, had undergone greater ravages, and presented the neck, whilst the remaining strata beneath formed the body. These figures, on near approach, might be compared to gate posts, covered with red clay, and surmounted by large round stones of a yellow cast; but at a long distance their rough aspect faded to an indistinctness frequently mistaken for perfection, that gave the appearance already noticed; and they several times were the cause of heedless chases to some of our companions, who mistook them for the living owners of the soil. These figures are numerous, and where several are seen on the summit of the same bluff are sometimes mistaken for a war party of Indians. In addition to these were bald or prairie hills, others of rock, either partially covered with soil or absolutely naked; and others of greater magnitude covered with pine and cedars. The country to the southward, on our course, was covered with mounds of the latter description, increasing in magnitude as we proceeded, until they finally became a connected spur of the grand chain jutting in close to the river. This spur was crossed by six or seven parallel trails, or paths, made by the Black foot villages, in passing and repassing to their hunting grounds, which guided us through the pines to the valley on the opposite side. On the summit of the mountain we found a quantity of broken bows and arrows, and remnants of tattered garments, that were supposed by some to be the tell-tale relics of a field of battle; but I believed, with others, that they were the clothing and arms of some unfortunate war party, who had returned disconsolate for the loss of their chief, and had destroyed their garments and arms, to excite greater sympathy in the village. We halted for the night in a beautiful little valley, occupied, when we approached it, by herds of deer and antelopes, but who fled when we entered it. On the following day, Wm. H. Vanderburgh, intending to hunt on the sources of the Jefferson, accompanied by the author of this sketch, and fifty men, separated from the main company, and directed his course for the head waters of Chark's Fork of the Columbia. After three days toilsome marching, we reached the *Deer House Prairie*, and halted on the margin of the principal stream—the Arrow Stone River, which flows one hundred miles northwestward, and unites with Bitter Root River, forming Clarke's Fork of the Columbia. The Deer House Prairie receives its name from the deer house, a natural but hollow mound of rock, covered with a slight coat of earth, about twelve feet high, and fifty feet in circumference; having a triangular apperture at the top, in which water is seen constantly boiling, but a few inches below the summit.—This mound rises out of a level prairie, about half a mile from the river; its waters hold sulphur ond salt in solution; and, in a clear cold morning, a fog rises from it resembling smoke, which gives it the appearance of an Indian lodge. It is also a great resort for deer, which may be seen at all times in its vicinity, *hence the name*. The surrounding valley is about sixty miles long and twenty broad, extremely fertile, but timberless, save narrow belts along the borders of the intersecting streams. Buffalo sometimes, though seldom, visit this valley, but are never seen west of it: moose deer are sometimes found here, though grizzly bears, deer, sheep and antelopes are the principal game.

Leaving this valley by its eastern extremity, we entered a deep winding defile, which brought us to the summit of the mountain, in full view of the plains of the Missouri, as well as those we had just left. Here, at the same glance, we could view the silvery waters of the Columbia and Missouri meandering through their respective vallies, and trace their sources to trickling rills that emanated from large banks of snow near us. Previous to this time we had passed two days without food; the hunters represented game numerous, but so wild that they were unapproachable, and daily returned to camp empty handed, which induced us to push forward without loss of time, to the Jefferson, where we were confident of finding buffalo.

We descended the mountain, and reached the margin of the river, on the following day, where, agreeable to our anticipations, we found a large herd of bison, and killed several in good condition. After this time we continued slowly up the Jefferson, until it became subdivided into three forks, called, by Messrs. Lewis & Clarke, the Philosophy, Wisdom River, and the Philanthropy, neither of which, at their junction, is more than thirty paces in width. We continued eastward up the Philanthropy to its source, and crossed a high mountain, decending to the Madison Fork of the Missouri. Here we were detained eight days by a snow storm, that continued that length of time without intermission. In the mean time, that branch of the Rocky Mountain Fur Company that had separated from us below the Three Forks of the Missouri, re-appeared and halted beside us. They separated from Dripps at the Three Forks, and had proceeded up the Gallatin several days, but finding the objects of their search rare, crossed on to the Madison, with the intention of trapping its sources. As this design clasped with our own, Vanderburgh determined to retrace his route, and finish his hunt on the sources of the Jefferson. Our hunters having collected their traps, rejoined us, and we returned westward through a defile to a small tributary to the Philanthropy, whilst our friends of the other company continued up the Madison. On the 14th of October we departed early, and ascended a succession of prairie hills, from the principal summit of which, we were in full view of the plains of the Philanthropy. The valley of the Philanthropy, from its junction with the Philosophy, twelve miles eastward, was a beautiful prairie, two miles in width, terminated by abrupt and lofty mountains to the north and south, a blue mountain fading in the distance terminated the view to the westward, where the Wisdom River took its rise, and a narrow defile formed by perpendicular walls of cut rock, marked the place where it burst forth from the mountains to the eastward. The river borders were garnished with scattering willow shrubbery, and an occasional cluster of aspen trees, might be seen at lengthy intervals, as the eye glanced down its serpentine course, nearly to the Jefferson, but no other timber appeared save the dark forbidding foliage of the pines, that encircled the bases of the frowning barriers that overlooked us, standing out in bold relief, against a meridian sky.

The eastern extremity of the plain, for miles in extent, was literally covered with buffalo, quietly grazing, and herds of antelopes were bounding over the prairie in all directions, or frisking about like lambs in conscious innocence and security. Previous to our departure from the Madison, we had suffered from the cold and raw state of the weather during the continuation of the snow storm; but now the plains were dry and dusty, and warmed by the genial influence of a cloudless sun. Such was the scenery and state of the atmosphere when we issued into the plains, directed our course angularly down the Philanthropy, intending to halt on its margin, six or eight miles below where it leaves the mountains. In the course of our march, one of the party pointed out several objects that were moving slowly along the borders of the river, but were rendered indistinct by the dark field of shrubbery behind them, which he asserted to be Indians, but we generally believed that they were buffalo.

In a short time one of our hunters returned and reported that they were Indians, he having been near enough to see them distinctly. Still our leader was incredulous, and ordered me to proceed in that direction until I should be perfectly convinced as to the truth of the report. I galloped over the undulating plain about half the distance to the river, and discovered the carcase of a buffalo just butchered, with the flesh cut up for transportation on a piece of the skin beside it, and a fire still laying upon it. From the situation of things I was convinced that the butchers were Indians, and that they had fled for safety or succour. So selecting the best of the meat, I fastened it to my saddle, and returned to the company. Our leader heard my report in silence, and continued his course, much to the displeasure of some, who believed that we should be attacked, and that our best course was to march to the nearest willows as soon as possible. During our progress a rumour was current that a party would go in quest of the Indians, to ascertain their strength and good or evil intentions. Presuming that it emanated from one partizan previous to unsaddling, I asked him if he intended to send out a party to seek further information on the subject. "No," said he, "it is unnecessary—if there are many of the Indians, we shall see them shortly, and if there are but few of them, they are already beyond our reach. Returning, I proceeded to unsaddle my horse, but ere I had accomplished it, Mr. Vanderburgh remarked that he had reconsidered the matter, and thought it necessary for some of us to go and ascertain whether the trappers might safely pursue their occupation or not. In the mean time, having saddled his own horse, he set out alone. Several of us immediately departed in pursuit—overtook him, and when we were all assembled, our number amounted to only seven. We proceeded up the river, at a round pace, three miles, and found a fire yet burning, with pieces of flesh, on pointed sticks, roasting around it. We charged through the thickets in the neighborhood of the fire, half expecting to find the Indians concealed in them, but returned disappointed. After carefully observing the traces and other signs, we at length came to the conclusion, that the Indians were about our own number, and had gone up the river. At the distance of three or four miles, just after the river bursts clear from the mountains, was a dense grove of aspen trees, one or two hundred yards in extent, which was the only place on the river where a war party could conceal themselves. To this point we directed our course, intending to proceed no further, for we were convinced that they would not pass this place, unless they had sought refuge in the mountains. As we rapidly approached this grove, all eyes were bent upon it with a penetrating and stedfast gaze; each waving leaf, and rustling twig, were watched with intense interest; expectation was at its height. Our horses slackened their speed, and we advanced slowly, and in a body. At length we crossed a deep gully, where a portion of the current flowed during the freshets in the spring; but we saw it not: our eyes were bent on penetrating the inmost recesses of the dark grove, where indistinct forms were gliding past each other; but they were trees: aught else we saw not. At this moment we were suddenly enveloped in a flash of vivid lightning, reverberating thunders rolled around us; the cloud quickly passed away, and more than a hundred flashing guns, glistening in the sun shine, met our gaze; whilst as many painted warriors, like the fabled genii of the East, rose from the earth on every side of us.

(*To be continued.*)

The Comet.—Is it not a grand and vast conception that this wan and misty orb has been travelling swifter than the swiftest cannon ball, through the dim realms of space, since our Saviour slept in the manger at Bethlehem, and the Star in the East lit its fires for the Wise Men's eyes? It is not like Divinity, that power of astronomic prophecy which pierced the curtains of the future, and foretold the events of this blazing world? Looks it not like sharing its attributes with Omnipotence, and 'circumventing God?'—And when this generation shall be slumbering in the dust, that predicted orb will again stream its 'horrid hair' across our sky.—When the lover who is now looked at with his mistress shall become a patriarch among his children; when the child now lisping its early inquiries of the wandering star, shall tell the tale in after years, to some grandbabe, throned on her knee—then the comet will come again! What changes, what revolutions, what convulsions of states and empires, will chance ere then! My soul expands into a sense of sublimity, as I reflect on the vast world of events between. How many ties will be severed, how many hearts be broken, how many tears shed! Yet these vicissitudes will advance and vanish, in that far element above and around us this luminous globe shall wander with its train; flashing and glowing through the fields of immensity. Though itself, imagination in her boldest flight, she sinks with wearied wing, unable to grasp the stupendous, boundless theme! Truly said the ancient minstrel:—'When I survey the heavens, the work of thy fingers; the moon and the stars which thou hast ordained, then I say, what is man, that thou art mindful of him, and the son of man that thou visitest him?'---Knickerbocker.

From South America. We are indebted to Mr. Coffee, of the Exchange, for Buenos Ayres papers to the 25th July, by the brig Maria Coffin arrived at this port. In their express news from Chili, they give an account of an insurrection, on the 3rd July, in one of the regiments at Quiilota, headed by Colonel Vidaurre. The minister of war Portales, and the general in-chief, Enoalada, with other dignitaries, were invited to a review by the Colonel, in order that they might assassinate them and thus neutralize the war with Peru. Portales and others attended accordingly, and were taken prisoners and put in irons. The mutineers then marched to Valpariso, but that city being apprised of their movement. was ready to receive them and repulsed them with great loss, 140 of 1459 being killed or wounded, while it sustained a very trifling loss. The insurgents previous to the battle forced the minister of war to leave a carriage in which he was confined, and shot him on the spot. He met his fate with great firmness. Vidaurre and his officers fled, but were captured, and it was expected would meet instant death. The British consul general, in acknowledging the circular of the government in relation to the event, says,—"an estamable and able minister, has perished a martyr in the cause of patriotism and true liberty, and a victim of the most foul and horrid treachery."

Extract of a letter dated

"Buenos Ayres, July 26.

"Markets dull for American produce generally; produce of the country scarce and high. The Indians had stolen a great many cattle from the plantations on the Southern frontier, and destroyed the Estancias. All business was at a stand in Buenos Ayres; the Governor had issued 4,300,000 more paper money in the month of June and July, and it was expected he would issue 5,000,000 dollars more before the year expires. Dollars 8 1-2 for one. National Gazette.

From the Savannah Georgian, Sept. 11.

FROM ST. AUGUSTINE.

We are indebted to Captain Curry, of the steam boat Cincinnati, for the St. Augustine Herald, of the 6th inst., from which we extract the following:

Our Indian Affairs.—Four negroes belonging to Major B. D. Heriot, who were captured by the Indians in 1736, made their escape and delivered themselves up at Fort Peyton (Moultrie,) on the morning of the 4th inst. They were delighted to rejoin the whites, and complain of hard fare among the Indians; they have been living on nothing but *coonty, Alligators and fish*, since they have been with the Indians. They represent the Indians entirely destitute of corn.

They state that there are a number of negroes now at at Major Heriot's Plantation engaged in prep ring coonty, under the superintendance of some Indians.

They communicate important information relative to the plan and situation of the enemy. The Indians, they say, have no idea of emigrating. Powell and Arpinki, are their master spirits.

The buildings at Volusia and Fort Mellon have been burnt by the Indians. This fact proves how far their promises are to be relied upon. They made a promise to Colonel Harney previous to the evacuation of Fort Mellon, that the buildings should be preserved.

We learn from Fort King that the Indians have left that vicinity.

Gen. Jesup is at Tampa Bay.

The post at Musquito is to be re-established by order of General Jesup. Troops have been sent down for that purpose.

Colonel Harney has been ordered to Washington for the purpose of getting men to fill up the companies of the 2d Regt. of Dragoons.

Brigadier General Hernandez left town yesterday for Musquito.

Captain Hanson's company, and Lieutenant Whitehurst's detachment of mounted volunteers, marched for Musquito on the 5th instant.

We find a novel balloon ascension described in the Nottingham (England) Journal. A young gentleman named Sneath, says that paper, residing at Mansfield, has made a large fire balloon, of fire proof canvas. On Wednesday evening he was anxious to try its buoyancy, and inflating it, he took it at 9 o'clock to the Bleak Hill, where he thought he had secured it to the earth. He got into the car to see what it would carry, when the sudden bounds given by the machine disengaged the cords, and he rose in the air. He remained in the balloon, floating about, until eleven o'clock, when the machine began to descend, and the grappling caught in a hedge near Spondon. Here, however, another difficulty presented itself; if he got out of the car the balloon would rise, so he determined to keep hid seat until the next morning, when to his great joy, he received the assistance of some countrymen about half past four, when he packed up his ponderous machine, and conveyed it to the nearest town, Derby, where it remains.

The following, copied from a Mississippi paper, is one of the neatest things of the kind extant:

IMPROMPTU.

Is there a heart that never sighed?
Is there a tongue that never lied?
Is there an eye that never blinked?
Is there a man that never drinked?
If so then heart and tongue and eye
Must tell a most confounded lie.

A Mr. Stubbell was killed instantly while blowing rocks at Beverly, Mass on Wednesday last. The drilling rod went through his head. Another person named Stephens was slightly wounded.

Poetry.

From the Southern Literary Messenger.

LIFE.

A brief history, in three parts, with a sequel, dedicated to a gentleman on his wedding day.

Part I.—Love.

A glance—a thought—a blow—
It stings him to the core;
A question—will it lay him low?
Or will time heal it o'er?

He kindles at the name—
He sits and thinks apart;
Time blows it to a flame,
Burning within his heart.

He loves her though it burns,
And nurses it with care;
He feels the blissful pains by turns—
With hope and with despair.

Part II.—Courtship.

Sonnets and serenades—
Sighs, glances, tears, and vows—
Gifts, tokens, souvenirs, parades,
An courtesies and bows

A purpose and a prayer—
The stars are in the sky—
He wonders e'en hope should dare
To let him aim so high.

Still hope allures and flatters,
And doubt just makes him bold;
And so, with passion all in tatters,
The trembling tale is told.

Apologies and blushes,
Soft looks, averted eyes;
Each heart into the other rushes—
Each yield sand wins a prize!

Part III.—Marriage.

A gathering of fond friends—
Brief, solemn words and prayer—
A trembling at the finger's ends,
As hand in hand they swear.

Sweet cake, sweet wine, sweet kisses—
And so the deed is done;
Now for life's woes and blisses—
The wedded two are one.

And down the shining stream
They launch their buoyant skiff,
Bless'd if they may but trust hope's dream,
Bu ah! truth echoes—*if!*

The Sequel.—IF.

If health be firm—if friends be true—
If self be well controlled;
If tastes be pure—if wants be few;
And not too often told.

If reason always rule the heart,
If passion own its sway—
If love in age to life impart
The zest it does to-day.

If Providence, with parent care,
Mete out the varying lot,
While meek contentment bows to share
The palace or the cot.

And oh! if faith, sublime and clear,
The spirit upward guide—
They're bless'd indeed, and bless'd for ever;
The bridegroom and the bride!

PUBLIC NOTICE.

HAVING been appointed Assessor for the County of Nacogdoches, I hereby notify the citizens thereof that the books are now opened at Colonel Thorn's store, in Nacogdoches, for receiving returns of their taxable property, where I shall attend until Saturday, the 28th of the present month, for the returns of this precinct, or any that may happen in town from other precincts. On Monday and Tuesday, the 30th an 31st, instant, I will attend at the house of John Walling, to receive the returns of that precinct. On Monday and Tuesday, the 6th and 7th of November, at the house of Captain Costley, for that precinct. On Monday and Tuesday, the 13th and 14th of November, at the house of Martin Lacy, for that precinct. On Monday and Tuesday, the 20th and 21st of November, at the Saline, for that precinct; and on Monday and Tuesday, the 27th and 28th of November, at the house of Wm. Elliot, for that precinct. That you may be prepared to make your returns, the law requires that you should, firstly, enter the number of acres of land; secondly, number of negroes; thirdly, number of cattle; fourthly, number of horses and mules; and fifthly, every other species of property, collectively as miscellaneous, each of which items you will value separately, and return them on oath.

Those who fail to make returns, or make false ones, will be subject to double tax, besides fine and imprisonment. It is to be hoped every citizen will promptly comply with the requisites of the law, however oppressive he may deem them, until constitutionally amended.

HADEN EDWARDS.

Nacogdoches, October 21, 1837. no 22-2t

JAMES G. HYDE,

ATTORNEY AT LAW,

HAS settled permanently at San Augustine; will practice in the different Courts of San Augustine, and the adjoining counties; also in the Supreme Court.

San Augustine, June 8, 1837. no 3-tf

NOTICE.

THE subscribers have this day entered into co-partnership, in the Carpenter and Cabinet Making business, in the first house on North street, opposite Mr. Emmanuel's dwelling, where they will attend to any business in their line, at the shortest notice. They having served a regular apprenticeship to their business, they hope they will be able to give general satisfaction to all who may entrust work in their care.

ABNER ALVIS,
WILLIAM STURROCK.

Nacogdoches, October 21, 1837. no 22-tf

FOR SALE.

ONE likely Negro Girl, about 18 years of age. She is a good Washer, and likewise a first rate Cook.—Terms of sale—Cash.

Those wishing to purchase will apply at the Printing Office.

Nacogdoches. October 21, 1837. no 22-tf

NOTICE.

THERE will be a Sermon delivered at the Masonic Hall every Sabbath, and also on Tuesday evening of every week. There will also be a Sunday School, under the charge of the Rev. J. Booth, which will commence at 8 o'clock on the Sabbath morning.

Nacogdoches, October 21, 1837. no 22-tf

NOTICE.

THE subscriber, living in Nacogdoches, will undertake the purchase and sale of Lands, collection of Notes and Accounts, on commission; draw deeds of conveyances of trust, and bills of sales, &c. at the shortest notice.—He is well acquainted with the eastern section of Texas. References—At Nacogdoches, Col. Frost Thorn, John S. Roberts, Charles H. Sims, and Col. Haden Edwards; at San Augustine, J. D. Thomas, Wyatt Hanks; at Velasco, Thomas F. McKinney; at Natchitoches, La., James Taylor, Esq.

W. R. D. SPRIGHT.

Nacogdoches, October 21, 1837. no 22-tf

TO RENT.

THE subscriber offers the following property to rent, upon reasonable terms, if early application is made, viz:

A Plantation, distance one quarter of a mile from the Town of Nacogdoches, with good house and spring, and other improvements.

A Plantation, seven miles from the Town of Nacogdoches, with good houses, improvements, &c.

A Plantation, two miles from the Town of Nacogdoches, with good houses and improvements.

A Plantation, five miles from the Town of Nacogdoches, with good houses, improvements, &c.

Also—two houses in the Town of Nacogdoches.

ALBERT EMANUEL.

Nacogdoches, October 21, 1837. no 22-tf

NACOGDOCHES HOTEL.

THE subscriber respectfully informs his friends, and the public generally, that he has taken the above named house in Nacogdoches, situated in North Street, nearly opposite the Printing Office. This House having been lately fitted up in a neat and comfortable manner, is well calculated to render his guests comfortable. His table will always be furnished with as good provisions as the country affords; and by giving his personal attention to his patrons, and by using every exertion, on his part, to accommodate those who may favor him with a call—he hopes to merit a share of public patronage.

In addition to the above named establishment is attached a Bar, where the choicest liquors can be found in Texas. And likewise there is a stable attached to the establishment, where he keeps a constant supply of corn and fodder, and a good hostler to keep and manage the concern.

T. T. McIVER.

Nacogdoches, October 7, 1837. no 20-tf

LAW NOTICE.

THE undersigned having associated themselves in business in the practice of Law, will attend to any professional business which may be entrusted to their charge, either in the District or Supreme Courts of the Republic.

All Land business will meet with strict attention.

THOMAS J. RUSK,
SAMUEL DEXTER.

Nacogdoches, Sept. 23, 1837. no 18-tf

CAUTION.

ALL persons are hereby cautioned against purchasing either of the two NOTES, given by me to Thomas J. Rusk, dated the 25th of March, 1837. One of the notes is for four thousand, the other for one thousand dollars. The notes were given without consideration—and I shall not pay either of them unless compelled to do so by law.

GEORGE A. NIXON.

Nacogdoches, September 30, 1837, no 19-tf

CAUTION.

ALL persons are hereby forwarned not to cut any timber on Squares No's 36 and 37, lately purchased of the Corporation. Said squares are situated north-west of Mr. Jones' property on the Hill.

ADOLPHUS STERNE.

Nacogdoches, October 14, 1837. no 21-3t

SHERIFF'S SALE.

WILL be sold in front of the Stone House, in the town of Nacogdoches, on Saturday, the 28th day of October next, the following described property, to wit:—

One tract of land, containing fifty acres, lying and being in the county of Nacogdoches—bounded south by the road leading from the town of Nacogdoches to San Augustine, south-west by the Bayou Lanan, and north by lands belonging to John Dorsett, east by lands belonging to Frost Thorn—levied on as the property of Jose de las Piedras, to satisfy sundry executions; one in favor of George Pollitt, against the said Jose de las Piedras; one in favor of Peter E. Bean, against the same; one in favor of J. S. Roberts, against the same, issued from a Justice's Court; one in favor of Adolphus Sterne, against Juan J. Gallard, Francisco Medina and Jose de las Piedras.

Terms, cash—purchaser to pay for titles.

DAVID RUSK, Sheriff.

Nacogdoches, September 30, 1837. no 19-5t

NOTICE.

THIS is to forewarn all persons from purchasing Town Lots in the Town of Cincinnati, (so called,) situated on the south bluff of the Trinity river, about twenty five miles below Robbins' Ferry—and also forewarning all persons who have bought lots in the said place, and given their notes for the same, to Mr. ——— De Witt, will withhold them from payment, for he has no legal claim upon the land whatsoever. I James Richards has a prior right to the said tract of land, as I did, in the month of October, 1834, procure an order of survey, of the said tract of land, from G. A. Nixon, which entitles me to a prior right.

JAMES RICHARDS.

Nacodoches, September 9, 1837. no 16—3m

DR. G. S. HYDE.

TENDERS his professional services to the citizens of Nacogdoches and its vicinity. He hopes that by strict attention to business, he will be able to merit a share of public patronage. He can always be found at the Emigrant's Hotel, unless professionally absent.

Nacogdoches, July 11, 1837. tf

LAW NOTICE.

THE UNDERSIGNED have entered into co-partnership, under the name and style of KAUFMAN & GOULD, for the practice of the Law. Any professional business, entrusted to their charge in Nacogdoches, San Augustine, and the adjoining counties, will meet with prompt attention. They may be found at the office of D. Lacy, Esq., Clerk of the County Court.

D. S. KAUFMAN,
C. M. GOULD.

Nacogdoches, June 20, 1837.

A CARD.

THE UNDERSIGNED, having been elected one of the Justices of the Peace, in and for the County of Nacogdoches, and having taken the oath of office, respectfully informs the citizens of this District, that his Office is on North Street, one door north of his dwelling house, opposite the Office of the Texas Chronicle, where he may generally be found, during business hours.

Nacogdoches, June 12, 1837.
no 3-tf WILLIAM HART.

ADMINISTRATOR'S NOTIC.

ALL persons indebted to the estate of Franklin J. Starr, deceased, are requested to make immediate payment; and those having demands against said estate, to present them as prescribed by law.

JAMES H. STARR, Administrator.

Nacogdoches, September 16, 1837.

DOCTOR A. HART.

[of New Orleans.]

INTENDS locating himself permanently in this place, and tenders his Professional services to the inhabitants of Nacogdoches and its vicinity. He can be consulted at all hours, and on any subjects concerning his profession, by calling at the residence of Mr. A. Emanuel.

Nacogdoches, August 26, 1837.
no 14-tf

NOTICE.

MY friends and patrons are hereby notified that, during my absence at the seat of government, Captain Wm. Y. Lacy and Mr. Warren A. Ferris, together or separately, will attend to all business in the surveying line, which has been entrusted to my care, and I am happy in being able to assure my patrons that these gentlemen have my utmost confidence, both as to integrity and scientific skill.

J. W. BURTON.

N. B. Captain Lacy is my authorized agent in business matters unconnected with the printing office. J. W. B.

Nacogdoches, September 16, 1837.

LAND FOR SALE.

THE subscriber offers for sale a tract of land, lying in the county of Nacogdoches, bounded as follows: on the south by the river Angelina, on the east by the brook of the Cariso, on the north by lands granted to Nicholas Morah, and on the west by De La Corda's lands. Said tract of land is twelve or thirteen miles in length on the west side of the Cariso, and one and a half miles in breadth. All persons are forbid in any wise to trespass on the above described lands, and they will be sold in suitable tracts for farms, or to suit the purchaser, and on accommodating terms. Any information in regard to said tract of land can be had by calling at the office of the subscriber in San Augustine, who is the authorized agent of Richard R Royal, proprietor of the land.

A. HUSTON, Agent
for R. R. ROYAL.

Nacogdoches, September 2, 1837. no 15-3m

NOTICE.

ALL persons importing goods of any description into the San Augustine district are required to enter them at the Custom House, at San Augustine, and to pay the duties on the same. And if any goods are unloaded, or pass the Custom House before the duties are paid or secured, the same will positively be seized as smuggled, and sold as such in thirty days—and the person importing them will be prosecuted without defalcation to the extent of the law.

JNO G. LOVE,
Collector of San Augustine District.

San Augustine, Sept. 18th, 1837. no 18-tf

NOTICE.

MESSRS KAUFMAN & GOULD are my duly authorised Agents, to transact all my business during my absence.

EDWARD DAVIS.

Nacogdoches, September 23, 1837. no 18-tf

NOTICE.

THE Subscribers take pleasure in informing the citizens of Nacogdoches and vicinity, that they have opened an establishment in this place for the purpose of manufacturing all kinds of Saddlery and Harness.

N. B.—Repairing done neatly and with despatch. A Journeyman Saddler will find employment by making immediate application to the subscribers.

JOSEPH BAIRD & CO.

Nacogdoches, September 23, 1837. no 18-tf

TOWN OF THORN-VILLE

THE Town of Thornville is situated in a fertile healthy and densly populated district, about nine miles east of Nacogdoches. The principal road leading to the Sabine passes directly through it. The adjacent country is well watered, crowned with extensive forests of the finest timber, and the soil and productions more rich and luxuriant than in any other portion of the country. It it is equi distant between the Sabine and Angelina rivers, in the centre of Nacogdoches county, and must ultimately become the county seat. The sight of the town is beautiful, being laid out on a height of sufficient elevation to carry off all the rains without leaving any pools for stagnation in the vicinity of the place. The proprietors are well aware that many of the new towns daily springing into existance in various parts of the country must sink into comparative insignificance. But on the other hand, there are many possessing the advantages of a healthy and salubribrious climate, unsurpassed for fertility of soil and wholesome spring water, where timber is inexaustable that must flourish, as the population of the country increases. So soon as our present difficulties with Mexico shall be adjusted and peace re-established, rail roads now in contemplation will be constructed and an impetus given to the inhabitants in pursuit of wealth and happiness, that will not fail to promote the advancement of the town of Thornville.—For terms apply to the proprietor on the premises.

HENRY BAILEY.

Thornville, October, 1837.

THE TOWN OF TRAVIS.

THIS TOWN is situated 12 miles South East of Nacogdoches, on the West bank of the Angelina, and is one of the finest BLUFFS on that River, 40 miles from the place where it empties into Snow river, which is susceptible of Steam Navigation. Keel Boats can ascend the whole year to this town, and Steam Boats 6 or 8 months in the year, it is in a decidedly healthy situation, being 8 feet above high water mark, and well supplied with good water, the road from this place to Nacogdoches is high and good, being free from stumps, Lagoons, &c.

PRICE OF SHARES.

Each Share, containing 4 Lots, 50 Dollars, 25 Dollars to be paid down, and 25 Dolls on delivery of Title, which will be given when the drawing of the lots is made.

For particulars, apply to

GEO. POLLITT,
A. STERNE,
C. CHEVALLIER,
J. M. DORR,
PATRICIO DE TORES.
} Share-Holders.

Nacogdoches, June 20, 1837. no 4 tf

THE NEW TOWN OF HUNTSVILLE.

THIS place is handsomely situated between the San Jacinto and Trinity, about fifteen or twenty miles from the latter on a beautiful elevated plain, the town is laid out so as to include in part a small sandy prairie, and has within its limits, on the north-east corner of the public square, three flush running and never failing springs of the best kind of cool and fresh free-stone water, and a bayou running full bold all the year, crosses the south-west corner of the town; heading one or two hundred yards above where it cuts the boundary lines.

This site certainly possesses such advantages of health as cannot be exceeded by any location for a town in the Republic of Texas. From its central position in the midst of a dense and richly populated, country. From its contiguity to navigation, it combines more commercial advantages than any other place within the limits of the country. It is sufficiently far from the river to avoid the poisonous miasma, that arises from the swamps and stagnant waters of the Trinity, and yet sufficiently near for all commereial purposes. Already a school has been established within the town; an impetus has been given to its commercial energies by the establishment of a mercantile house—an inn, with excellent accommodations—a black smith's shop, and establishment of saw and grist mills in the vicinity.

A more tempting opportunity for profitable investments has seldom been offered to the capitalists of Texas. For terms, which will be liberal, apply to the proprietor on the premises.

PLEASANT GRAY.

Huntsville, 11th September, 1837. no 17.

SURVEYING.

THE Subscriber respectfully informs the citizens of Nacogdoches, and its vicinity, that he will, with punctuality and accuracy, perform any jobs in this line that may be entrusted to his care. He will furnish neat plats and duplicates of his surveys and, if required, for any other surveys heretofore made. Charges reasonable.

W. A. FERRIS.

N. B. He may always be found either at Sims' Tavern or at the Printing Office.

Nacogdoches, September 9, 1837.

JAMES TAYLOR,

ATTORNEY AT LAW.

WILL attend regularly, the District Courts of Nacogdoches, San Augustine, Milam and Jasper.

Nadogdoches, August 26, 1837. no 14-tf

FOR SALE.

FIVE hundred or a thousand acres of first quality of LAND, within five miles of Nacogdoches; the title of which will be fully guaranteed. For further particulars, apply to ADOLPHUS STERNE.

Nacogdoches, September 23, 1837. no 18-tf

LAND AGENCY.

THE subscribers have entered into co-partnership as Land Agents and, in future, will transact any business of that kind under the firm of Sterne & Hyde.

JAMES G. HYDE,
ADOLPHUS STERNE.

Nacogdoches, September 23, 1837. no 18-tf

NOTICE.

A COMPLETE List of all the Land Laws, and their Amendments, passed in the Congress of Texas since the Declaration of Independence, for sale at this Office.

Nacogdoches, October 7, 1837.

From the Washington Sun.

"Or ravished with the whistling of a name,
See Cromwell damned to everlasting fame."

In all ages of the world a desire for posthumous fame has been an incentive to action. For this the student unremittingly toils. Casting the mind's eye through the vista of coming years, he beholds in prospective the laurels with which posterity is to encircle his brow; and, animated by cheering anticipations of the future, he trims the expiring taper, and dives again into his studies with renewed exertion. For this the soldier faces the martial array of his country's enemy, and amidst the din of battle, and the dangers that surround him, is cheered on with the reflection, that if he falls he will not die "unhonored or unsung." The statesman, too, in his efforts to preserve the civil liberties of his country, though, through the prevalence of injustice and corruption, his motives are ill-judged and his acts misconstrued, is still impelled to persevere in his course by the assurance that, in the revolution of time, justice will be awarded to him; and, for devotion to his country and her laws, which he manifested while living, he will receive due praise when he shall have long ceased to be.

This is well. But some have existed whose sole ambition was to be remembered, regardless whether that remembrance was accompanied with a curse or a blessing by those who should live after them. The poor wretch who burnt the temple at Ephesus, when asked why he did it, replied, in effect, that he despaired of doing any good, so as to ensure his being remembered by posterity; and, being determined to effect this, he had resolved on doing all the evil in his power. And to this day there are men who are actuated by the same feeling. This man burnt the temple dedicated to the Goddess of the Ephesians. The leaders of the party now in power, despairing of rendering themselves loved while living, or of being honorably remembered after death, determined their names shall be handed to posterity, though curses accompany them, have well nigh destroyed the temple of our liberties, by their reckless assaults upon its great outguards, the constitution, and the laws framed for its preservation. Their names will go down to posterity together with the sufferings of the people, whom they have so grossly deceived: and future generations, as they peruse the history of the present times, will name them as men who sacrificed every thing to the gratification of their own selfish ambition. How will they not wonder at the supineness of a people suffering under the oppressive measures of a tyrannical cabal, having the constitutional power of eradicating the evil, and yet refusing so long to exercise it.

A man with knowledge, but without energy, is a house furnished but not inhabited; a man with energy but no knowledge, a house dwelt in but unfurnished.

A LAWYER'S CRITICISM OF SHAKSPEARE.

I own that I never perused my favorite, the Merchant of Venice, without a mixture of melancholy to think that it has so many faults, and in particular that the distress turns chiefly upon embarrassments with which no lawyer can seriously sympathize. There are several striking flaws in this drama. In the first place, Antonio's difficulties arise entirely from his gross oversight in not effecting an insurance upon his various ragosies. He should have opened a set of policies at once upon the Rialto, where marine insurance was perfectly well understood, and where the brokers would have got him fifty names in a forenoon to any extent upon ship, freight, or cargo, lost or not lost. This prudential step would have given a totally different turn to the whole affair. When he wanted to help Bassanio with three thousand ducats for three months, he could easily have raised the money at four per cent on the security of an assignment of the policy. Shylock says of him, "Antonio is a good man; yet his means are in supposition, he hath an argosy bound to Tripolis, another to the Indies; I understand moreover upon the Rialto, he hath a third at Mexico, a fourth for England, and other adventures he hath squandered abroad. But ships are but boards, sailors but men; there be land rats and water rats, water thieves and land thieves; I mean pirates; and then there is the peril of waters, winds and rocks." Now these are the risks which the contract of insurance is intended to cover, as clearly explained in Marshall and our other writers, and as expressed in the following clause inserted in all policies: "Touching the adventures and perils which the said assurers are contented to bear, and to take upon them in this voyage, they are of the seas, men-of-war, fire, enemies, pirates, rovers, thieves, jettisons, &c. barratry of the masters or mariners, and all other perils, losses, and misfortunes that have or shall come to the hurt, detriment, or damage of the said goods or merchandise, and ship or vessels." With this precaution Antonio's means would have been no longer in supposition, but in certainty, and as good as hard cash, under deduction merely, of the premium of insurance.—Finally intelligence was received of Antonio's argosies being wrecked, it is plain that he might in the circumstances, have at once abandoned the underwriters and claimed for a total loss. It is painful to see so many amiable characters involved in grief and difficulties, which this simple and natural expedient would have obviated. My feelings at this reflection are something akin to those of a very susceptible medical friend, who declares that he can never set out Romeo and Juliet, from the thought that a judicious use of the stomach pump, in the last scene, would remove all the distresses, and make two lovers happy.—*Blackwood's Magazine.*

A public dinner was given to General Mirabeau B. Lamar, Vice President of Texas, by the citizens of Mobile, on the 6th instant. Below will be found the address of General Lamar, elicited by the following toast:—

8. Our Guest, General Lamar—distinguished for chivalry of character, intrepidity of conduct, and brilliancy of talents. In the gallant soldier and accomplished statesman of our sister Republic, we recognize one of the favored sons of our country. Success to him, and prosperity to the land of his love and allegiance.

[Here the following "Song of Welcome" to General Lamar, written by A. F. Keene, was sung by that gentleman to the tune of "Scots wha' hae," in his most melodious style, assisted in the chorus by the whole company.]

I.

We welcome to this board to-night,
A hero of renown in fight,
Who fought and won the glorious right
Of calling Texas free !!

Then welcome, Son of Freedom; here,
'Tis an hour to freemen dear,
We greet thee with a hearty cheer,
Who fought for Liberty!

II.

San Jacinto's plains can tell
A dreadful story, and the knell
Of scores of Mexicans, who fell
'Pon that victorious day.

Brave Houston's war cry sounded far,
'Twas echoed by the bold Lamar,
Who fought and conquered 'neath the Star
Of Texas, on that day.

III.

Then welcome to our board to-night,
The Chief of many a glorious fight,
Who drew his sword for Texas' right,
The brave, the good Lamar.

Now fill your glasses to the brim,
And standing up, we'll drink to him,
Who risked his fortune, life and limb,
For Texas! Brave Lamar.

After the rounds and rounds of deafening applause which followed the announcement of the third regular toast, and the singing of Mr Keene's "Song of Welcome," which was admirably executed.

General Lamar rose and delivered one of the most eloquent high-wrought and eminently poetical speeches we ever listened to on such an occasion. He occupied about an hour and a half in the delivery—but it did not seem that half of that space of time rolled away while he was speaking. We cannot attempt to do him justice.—The poetry of his description—the beauty of his imagery, and the chasteness and force of his language surpass all our ability to give any thing like an idea of either the one or the other.

He thought that after such a demonstration of friendly regard as had just followed the sentiment complimentary to himself, he might well cherish a love for Mobile. It came from many who knew him not, as well as from others who had known him long and intimately, and for whom he ever had a heart and a hand. In all his travels he had never found a truer, warmer hearted or more generous people, than the people of Mobile. But he could not think, no, not for a moment, that the compliment in the sentiment just drunk was intended for him—it was, and rightfully too, intended for the country and cause with which he was connected. If he had done any thing to make him in the least conspicuous in that country and its cause, it was nothing more than his duty—nothing more than what, he felt well assured, every gentleman there present would do. He knew that every one present had, as well as himself a heart to beat and a hand to strike for freedom against tyranny.

He went into a glowing description of the land of his affection and adoption, where, he said, the country was all beautiful and lovely beyond comparison—its daughters all fair—and its sons all brave.

He went into a history of the settlement of Texas, in consequence of the many strong inducements held out to the enterprizing people of the United States by the Mexican Powers—gave a vivid description of the subsequent repeated injuries inflicted upon the settlers of Texas, which in the end caused them to resist their oppressors, and to strike back the blow of freemen. He gave a graphic account of the war from its incipiency to its overwhelming conclusion, at the ever memorable battle of San Jacinto. He did able justice to his brave compatriots all—but modestly forgot himself, except to tell what he thought at the battle of San Jacinto. While all about him were uttering the war cry of "the Alamo! the Alamo!" in one continual loud roar, like the waters of a cataract, *he* thought only of the cruel butchery of his dear friends, Fanning and Ward, and rushed on to revenge their death. And a terrible revenge it was too.

He carried the company all with him to Texas; there pointed out to us all her manifold beauties; her salubrious air; her pure water; her beautiful vallies; her majestic hills; her fair women and her brave men; and then exclaimed, "this, gentlemen, is my home; the land of my adoption; the land of my love!"

He said the glorious sun, in its haste to go down to its bed of repose, did not allow him time to give his views upon one important subject; a subject which he intended should have been the principal theme of his remarks; but as it was getting late, he would take some other occasion to make his views known in full upon the subject. He meant the annexation of Texas to the United States.—He said the whole people of Texas were for the annexation. There was, however, one dissenting voice—and that was the humble voice which was then speaking.—Rather than have his own free, noble generous, beloved Texas joined to this Union with the turbulent and incendiary fanatics, the infuriated abolitionists, with Mr. Adams at their head, he would pray that she might, by some sudden earthquake, be cast out upon the ocean a lone island. And rather than be joined himself in a union with such fanatical enemies of the freedom, liberty and rights of the South, would prefer to be chained like Prometheus, to a rock, to be devoured by vultures; or like Mazeppa, bound to a wild horse, to be dashed down precipices until life should be extinct. Get rid of these fanatics, gentlemen, and Texas is yours with all my heart.

General Lamar's speech was listened to throughout with the most delighted attention and his well turned periods, breathing glowing sentiments of pure, unadulterated patriotism, were honored with the frequent burst of enthusiastic applause they so richly deserved.

THE TEXAS QUESTION.

HOUSE OF REPRESENTATIVES.
Assembled at Washington, U. S.
Wednesday, Sept. 13, 1837.

Mr. Adams, in reply to Mr. Howard, said that his object in moving the call upon the President relative to negotiations between the United States and Mexico, was not for the purpose of discussion, but that the information called for might be printed for the information of the House; and concluded by saying, that if, when the second resolution (calling for the correspondence, if any, between this government and the Republic of Texas in relation to the annexation of that Republic to the United States) come up for consideration, he would reply to such remarks as might be submitted in opposition to it.

The first resolution was adopted.

On the second, above referred to, Mr. Wise said that he was informed, from a source entitled to credit, that the correspondence between our Government and the Representatives of the Republic of Texas was not in a condition to be made public.

Mr. Adams said that the resolution was presented on the known instructions of the Congress of Texas to the Executive of that Republic, to open a negotiation for the annexation of that Republic to the United States. He believed that there was no constitutional right in Congress to annex. He went into an explanation of his views of the subject, and said that when the annexation of Louisiana was under consideration, he had raised the question in the Senate, and argued that no power but the people of Texas and the people of the United States alone could authorize the union; and declared that he believed that a large proportion of the people of the Union would prefer a dissolution of the Union to the annexation. He therefore demanded, in the name of the people of the Union, to know what is the correspondence on the subject, now carried on between this government and the Representatives of the Republic of Texas.

Mr. THOMPSON, of South Carolina, said that he was so far informed as to be able to say that the correspondence was not now in such a state as to justify its publication He reminded Mr. Adams that, as Secretary of State, he had argued that the United States had a just claim to the greater part of the Territory of Texas; and asked how the United States could be authorized to cede a Territory belonging to the United States, if, as Mr. Adams contends, they have no right now to obtain the same Territory by negociation?

Mr. Pickens said that he rose for the purpose of calling the attention of the House, and the Union, to the fact announced by the honorable member, (Mr. Adams,) that a large number of the people of the United States would prefer disunion to annexation. He expressed his gratification at hearing of constitutional limitation of power from that quarter; declared his desire to see the correspondence, and expressed his wish that the Executive was prepared to take his position on the new question thus made. He would not enter upon the discussion of the subject now, but wished Congress, and the people who controlled Congress, to be fully informed.

Mr. Petriken moved to lay the resolution on the table, which was decided in the negative; ayes, 74; noes, 144.

Mr. Howard said, after the remarks which had fallen from members, he was in favor of the adoption of the resolution; that he believed there was nothing in the correspondence which the Executive was ashamed or afraid to publish; and that, although he would not have originated the call, he would not, the call being made, oppose it.

Mr Grennell, of Massachusetts, insisted upon the adoption of the resolution without any limitation. He was not willing to leave any discretion with the Executive. He would pass the resolution making it imperative on the Executive to communicate all the correspondence.

Mr. Bynum was in favor of the resolution as amended, leaving it with the Executive to judge of the propriety of making the communication, because the discretion is properly placed in the Executive.

Mr. Wise was prepared to enter into a discussion of the constitutional power of Congress to annex. He quoted the clause in the constitution authorizing Congress to admit new States, but said as the question on the merits was out of order, he would not enter upon it. He rose to say that when he was up before, he had supposed that the correspondence was not in a condition to be published. Having been further informed, he withdrew his opposition to the resolution.

Mr. Bell was opposed to the resolution, on the ground that this subject, if brought before the House, would necessarily produce an excitement prejudicial to the due consideration of the other important question upon which the House are called to act; and implored the House to deliberate before they proceed, and with that view moved the order of the day. The motion was lost without a count.

Mr. Holsey, of Georgia, argued that, under the treaty making power, Texas could be annexed, and expressed his surprise at the ground assumed by Mr. Adams.

PHILOSOPHICAL PROBLEM.—Why has not Nature produced any square forms? Nature has produced circular, curvilinear, and poly-angular forms in endless variety; but not one square form. The public prints throughout the United States and Europe, are requested to publish the above question, a correct answer to which, will embrace the discovery of a universal law of nature, which has been lost to philosophy for several thousand years.—*N. Y. Star.*

Nothing new from Mexico or Texas. In New Orleans the fever is said to have disappeared, and business is reviving. The latest city papers mention the arrival of nine play actors, from New York—and five hundred and twenty-five dozen chickens, from St. Louis.—*Red River Gazette.*

General M. B. Lamar, Vice President of Texas, is at Mobile. He is mentioned as the most eligible candidate, and probably successor of General Sam Houston, in the Presidency of Texas. General Houston, it is said, will retire after the expiration of his present term.—*Red River Gazette.*

"The steamer John Linton has fine music. Those who are going to Red River are advised to travel on board of her."—*Picayune.*

We should like to hear some of it in Natchitoches; but alas, the river is as low as is the specie in the vaults of our banks; so low, that the Envoy, when on her way hither last Wednesday, found it necessary, on arriving at the head of the Bondieu, to suspend further progress, as it is a matter of grave speculation here whether the probability of a steamer arriving before Christmas day, is greater than that of getting a note discounted. We are glad to hear, however, that there is a considerable rise above, and that we may expect it here in a very few days.—*Red River Gazette.*

IMPORTANT CAPTURE.

PHILLIP AND UCHEE BILLY TAKEN.—DEATH OF LIEUT. MCNEIL.—We have the gratification of announcing to our readers the capture of the noted Indian Chiefs, Phillip and Uchee Billy, together with several warriors, squaws, and children, by the forces under General Hernandez, on Saturday and Sunday last.

On Thursday, the 7th instant, about 1700 men, comprising parts of company F., 2d Dragoons, under Lieut. McNeil, E. and H., 2d Dragoons, under Lieut. May, part of Captain Hanson's company, under Lieutenants Pellicer and Ferreira, and Lieutenant White's command of volunteer Florida horse, and company D., Artillery, commanded by Lieutenant Frazier, took up their line of march from Fort Peyton on an expedition to the south; the whole battalion under command of Lieutenant Peyton, 2d Artillery; General Hernandez in person superintending the expedition, with Lieutenant Graham, 2d Dragoons, Adj-de-Camp, Assistant Surgeon Motte accompanied the detachment.

On reaching Bulowville, the battalion took position for the night; the baggage train under Lieutenant Frazier, occupied St. Josephs. Whilst preparing to move the following morning, five negroes (four of them belonging to Major Heriot) came in and delivered themselves up.—They stated that they had left the Indians, and were anxious for the protection of the whites; that the Indians had no intention of emigrating, and that at that time there were parties of them employed south of the Tomoka, and east of the St. Johns, preparing *coonti*. Among the negroes was John, a slave of Phillip, who fled from his master on account of his attachment to his wife, one of the slaves of Major Heriot.

On Friday morning the battalion proceeded from Bulow's, and crossed the Tomoka near its head, with Phillip's John as a guide, leaving orders for the baggage to halt at Tomoka ferry. On Friday evening they saw the fires of an Indian camp at Dunlawton, about half a mile from the site of the burnt houses. They proceeded cautiously, and about midnight the volunteers under Lieutenant Whitehurst took a position in ambuscade on two sides of the camp. Just at daylight the regular dragoons, under Lieutenant Peyton, advanced to the attack. Lieutenant May's company charged; and Phillip, with another Indian, and a number of women and children, were immediately captured; only one, the younger son of Phillip escaping.

This capture was made without loss or bloodshed on either side. The Indian with Phillip, known as Tomoka John, offered to conduct the party to the Uchee camp about ten miles off. They took him at his word, and after a most fatiguing and circuitous march, came upon their fires early in the evening, halted about a mile from them until after midnight, when they carefully and completely surrounded them. From the barking of their dogs, however, and the fact that the fires were extinguished, the Indians must have suspected, or rather were fearful, that all was not right. At the dawn of day on Sunday, a charge was made by the whole force in two divisions, commanded by Lieutenants Peyton and McNeil. The Indians were on the alert, and gave one discharge of their rifles, by which Lieutenant McNeil was mortally wounded. Some little firing took place, by which two Inditns were killed, and two or three wounded.

The whole party, consisting of Uchee Billy, his brother Jack, three warriors and a number of women and children were taken: one only made his escape during the night, but without time or opportunity to give the alarm.

General Hernandez and his staff were present, and among the foremost on both occasions.

The whole number captured amounted to thirty-five, who were brought into town yesterday, accompanied by the whole battalion.

The gallant Lieutenant McNeil lingered till 10 o'clock on Monday night, when he expired. He was a promising young officer, and his loss is universally regretted.—His body was brought in and buried with military honors, at 7 o'clock yesterday afternoon.

As to the effect which this capture will have, speculation is varied. The non-combatant portion of our citizens think the captors ought to have sent in a flag and asked a surrender; others think that the party should have waited until the enemy had made their coonti, and come in to parley or deliver themselves up. Either of these speculations we throw aside, and look upon the event as a matter of fact, embodying more beneficial advantage to our territory than any preceding it, and giving promise in the capture of King Phillip and Uchee Billy, of a more speedy peace than all the military appointments which the last two years has made us familiar with.

General Hernandez and all under him are entitled to the warmest thanks of the country generally for having, with a very trifling force, penetrated the long-deserted, and in many places almost inaccessible, portion of our frontier, and thus brought into certain security the master spirits of Phillip, Uchee Billy and other desperate warriors.

The above details of the success of the battalion under Lieutenant Peyton have been hastily gathered, but from a source which admits of no doubt. The prisoners are among us, and secured in the Fort, with every attention and comfort consistent with the most liberal views of humanity—security of their persons being the principal aim.

ANOTHER STEAM BOILER EXPLOSION.

Louisville, (Ky.) Sept. 6.

EXPLOSION.—A dreadful accident occurred in the steam saw mill of Mr. Thomas Boyle, on Market street, above Jackson, on Monday evening. The wrist, or something connected with the wrist of the engine, was out of order—the engine was stopped, the water being low at the time in the double flue boiler. In about one minute after the stoppage, both flues collapsed, with a frightful explosion, and the boiler, weighing 9,000 pounds, was blown 100 feet from its bed, carrying away two of the main posts on which the frame of the saw mill rested, and the steam prostrating at the same instant a blacksmith's shop, situated in front of the saw mill. Of the persons engaged in the mill and shop, only one escaped unhurt. Eleven were injured in all—two died yesterday, and two others were said to be in a hopeless condition. The individuals killed were Jacob Boyle, son of the proprietor of the mill, aged about twenty-two, and Richard Rogers, who has left a helpless family. A fireman and a blacksmith, whose names we have not learned, are the persons said to be too much injured to recover. Those not mortally injured are, Thomas Boyle, Mr. Woodruff, Messrs. Spears, (father and son,) Mr Harris and Mr. Kendall.—Mr. Harris is a carpenter, and was in the blacksmith's shop; Mr. Kendall is a wagon maker, resides a few miles from this city, on the Salt River road, and happened to be passing in front of the establishment when the explosion took place.

This is, we believe, the most serious accident that has ever occured in this country by the explosion of a boiler of a land engine.—*Public Advertiser.*

The yellow fever in this city is believed to be on the increase. The interments for the last few days have averaged about sixty a day.—*New Orleans Bulletin.*

NATIONAL INTELLIGENCER.

PUBLISHED BY "DELIBERATE WITH CAUTION, BUT ACT WITH DECISION; AND YIELD WITH GRACIOUSNESS, OR OPPOSE WITH FIRMNESS." S. WHITING.

VOL. I. HOUSTON, TUESDAY, DECEMBER 11, 1838. NO. 41.

OFFICIAL.

By the President of the Republic of Texas.

A PROCLAMATION.

WHEREAS a convention between the Government of the Republic of Texas and the Government of the United States of America, to terminate the reclamations of the latter Government, for the capture, seizure and detention of the brigs Pocket, and Durango, and for injuries suffered by American citizens on board the Pocket, was concluded and signed at Houston, on the eleventh day of April, in the year of our Lord one thousand eight hundred and thirty-eight, which convention is word for word as follows:

Convention between the Government of the Republic of Texas and the Government of the United States of America, to terminate the reclamations of the latter Government, for the capture, seizure, and detention of the brigs Pocket, and Durango, and for injuries suffered by American citizens on board the Pocket.

R. A. Irion, Secretary of State of the Republic of Texas, acting on behalf of the said Republic, and Alcée La Branche, Chargé d'Affaires of the United States of America, near the Republic of Texas acting on behalf of the said United States of America, have agreed to the following articles:

ART. 1. The Government of the Republic of Texas, with a view to satisfy the aforesaid reclamations for the capture, seizure, and confiscation of the two vessels aforementioned, as well as for indemnity to American citizens who have suffered injuries from the said Government of Texas, or its officers, obliges itself to pay the sum of eleven thousand seven hundred and fifty dollars, ($11,750,) to the Government of the United States of America to be distributed amongst the claimants by the said Government of the United States of America

ART. 2. The sum of eleven thousand seven hundred and fifty dollars ($11,750,) agreed on in the first article shall be paid in gold or silver, with interest at six per cent. one year after the exchange of the ratifications of this convention. The said payment shall be made at the Seat of Government of the Republic of Texas, into the hands of such person or persons as shall be duly authorised by the Government of the United States of America to receive the same.

ART. 3. The present convention shall be ratified, and the ratifications thereof shall be exchanged in the City of Washington, in the space of three months from this date or sooner, if possible.

In faith whereof, the parties above named have respectively subscribed these articles, and thereto affixed their seals.

Done at the city of Houston, on the eleventh day of the month of April, one thousand eight hundred and thirty-eight.

(L. S.) R. A. IRION,
(L. S.) ALCEE LA BRANCHE.

And whereas the said Convention has been duly ratified on both parts, and the respective ratifications of the same were exchanged at Washington, on the sixth day of July, one thousand eight hundred and thirty-eight, by Fairfax Catlett, Chargé d'Affaires of the Republic of Texas accredited to the Government of the United States, and John Forsyth, Secretary of State of the United States, on the part of their respective Governments.

Now, therefore, be it known that I, SAM HOUSTON, President of the Republic of Texas, have caused the said Convention to be made public, to the end that the same and every clause and article thereof may be observed and fulfilled with good faith by the Republic of Texas and the citizens thereof.

(L. S.) In witness whereof, I have hereunto set my hand and caused the seal of the Republic of Texas to be affixed.

Done at the City of Houston this sixth day of November, in the year of our Lord one thousand eight hundred and thirty-eight, and of the Independence of the Republic of Texas the third.

By the President, SAM HOUSTON.
R. A. IRION,
Secretary of State. (Nov. 9—33-tf.

By the President of the Republic of Texas.

A PROCLAMATION.

WAEREAS, a Convention between the Republic of Texas and the Uninited States of America, for marking the boundary between them, was concluded and signed at Washington, on the twenty-fifth day of April, in the year of our Lord one thousand eight hundred and thirty-eight, which Convention is, word for word, as follows:

Convention between the Republic of Texas and the United States of America, for marking the Boundary between them.

Whereas, The Treaty of Limits, made and concluded on the twelfth day of January, in the year of our Lord, one thousand eight hundred and twenty-eight, between the United States of America on the one part, and the United Mexican States on the other, is binding upon the Republic of Texas, the same having been entered into at a time when Texas formed a part of the said United Mexican States; and

Whereas, It is deemed proper and expedient, in order to prevent future disputes and collisions between Texas and the United States, in regard to the boundary between the two countries, as designated by the said treaty, that a portion of the same should be run and marked without unnecessary delay—

The President of the Republic of Texas has appointed Memucan Hunt its Plenipotentiary, and the President of the United States has appointed John Forsyth their Plenipotentiary:

And the said Plenipotentiaries, having exchanged their full powers, have agreed upon and concluded the following Articles:

ART. 1. Each of the contracting parties shall appoint a Commissioner and Surveyor, who shall meet before the termination of twelve months from the exchange of the ratifications of this Convention, at New-Orleans, and proceed to run and mark that portion of the said boundary which extends from the mouth of the Sabine, where that river enters the Gulf of Mexico, to the Red River. They shall make out plans and keep journals of their proceedings, and the result agreed upon by them shall be considered as part of this Convention, and shall have the same force as if it were inserted therein. The two Governments will amicably agree respecting the necessary articles to be furnished to those persons, and also as to their respective escorts, should such be deemed necessary.

ART. 2. And it is agreed, that until this line shall be marked out, as is provided for in the foregoing article, each of the contracting parties shall continue to exercise jurisdiction in all territory over which its jurisdiction has hitherto been exercised; and that the remaining portion of the said boundary line shall be run and marked at such time hereafter, as may suit the convenience of both the contracting parties; until which time, such of the said parties shall exercise, without the interference of the other, within the territory of which the boundary shall not have been so marked and run, jurisdiction to the same extent to which it has been heretofore usually exercised.

ART. 3. The present Convention shall be ratified, and the ratifications shall be exchanged at Washington, within the term of six months from the date hereof, or sooner if possible.

In witness whereof, we the respective Plenipotentiaries, have signed the same, and have hereunto affixed our respective seals.

Done at Washington, this twenty-fifth day of April, in the year of our Lord, one thousand eight hundred and thirty eight, in the third year of the Independence of the Republic of Texas, and in the sixty-second year of that of the United States of America.

[L. S.] MEMUCAN HUNT.
[L. S.] JOHN FORSYTH.

And whereas, The said Convention has been duly ratified on both parts, and the respective ratifications were exchanged at Washington on the twelfth day of October, one thousand eight hundred and thirty-eight, by Anson Jones, Minister Plenipotentiary of the Republic of Texas, and Aaron Vail, Acting Secretary of State of the United States, on the part of their respective Governments,

Now therefore, be it known, That I, Sam Houston, President of the Republic of Texas, have caused the said Convention to be made public, to the end that the same, and every clause and article thereof, may be observed and fulfilled with good faith by the Republic of Texas, and the citizens thereof.

In witness whereof, I have hereunto set my hand, and caused the seal of the Republic of Texas to be affixed.

(L. S.) Done at the City of Houston, this sixth day of November, in the year of our Lord one thousand eight hundred and thirty-eight, and of the Independence of the Republic of Texas, the third.

By the President. SAM HOUSTON.
R. A. IRION, *Secretary of State.*

SAM HOUSTON,
President of the Republic of Texas;
[TO ALL WHOM IT MAY CONCERN.]

SATISFACTORY evidence having been exhibited to me that YOUNG J. PORTER, has been appointed Consul of the United States of America for the port of *Brazoria*, I do hereby recognise him as such, and declare him free to exercise and enjoy such functions, powers and privileges, as will be allowed to the Consuls of the most favored nations in the Republic of Texas.

(L. S.) In testimony whereof I have caused these letters to be made patent, and the Great Seal of the Republic to be hereunto affixed.

Given under my hand at the City of Houston, this 6th day of November, A. D., 1838, and of the Independence of the Republic of Texas the third. By the President,

SAM HOUSTON.
R. A. IRION,
Secretary of State. [Nov. 9—33-tf.

SAM HOUSTON,
President of the Republic of Texas;
[TO ALL WHOM IT MAY CONCERN.]

SATISFACTORY evidence having been exhibited to me that JOHN A. MONGES has been appointed Consul of the United States of America for the port of *Matagorda*: I do hereby recognise him as such and declare him free to exercise and enjoy such functions, powers, and privileges as will be allowed to the Consuls of the most favored nations in the Republic of Texas.

[L. S.] In testimony whereof, I have caused these letters to be made patent, and the Great Seal of the Republic to be hereunto affixed.

Given under my hand at the City of Houston this 6th day of November, A. D., 1838, and of the Independence of the Republic of Texas the third. By the President,

SAM HOUSTON.
R. A. IRION,
Secretary of State. [Nov. 9,—33-tf.

SAM HOUSTON,
President of the Republic of Texas;
[TO ALL WHOM IT MAY CONCERN.]

SATISFACTORY evidence having been exhibited to me that ELISHA A. RHODES has been appointed Consul of the United States of America for the port of *Galveston*: I do hereby recognise him as such, and declare him free to exercise and enjoy such functions, powers, and priviliges as will be allowed to the Consuls of the most favored nations in the Republic of Texas.

[L. S.] In testimony whereof, I have caused these letters to be made patent, and the Great Seal of the Republic to be hereunto affixed.

Given under my hand at the City of Houston, this 6th day of November, A. D., 1838, and of the Independence of the Republic of Texas the third. By the President,

SAM HOUSTON.
R. A. IRION,
Secretary of State. [Nov. 9—33-tf.

MISCELLANY.

BEAUTY OF SCIO.—'In the morning I rose early and walked out upon the terrace. Nature had put on a different garb. The wind had fallen, and the sun was shining warmly upon a scene of softness and luxuriance surpassing all that I had ever heard or dreamed of the beauty of the Islands of Greece. Away with all I said about Syria; skip the page. The terrace overlooked the garden filled with orange, lemon, almond, and fig trees; with plants, roses, and flowers of every description; luxuriant wilderness. But the view was not confined to the garden. Looking back to the harbor of Scio was a bold range of rugged mountains bounding the view on that side, on the right was the sea then calm as a lake; on both the other side, were ranges of mountains, irregular and picturesque in their appearance, verdant and blooming to their very summits; and within these limits for an extent of perhaps five miles, were continued gardens like that at my feet, filled with the choicest fruit trees, with roses and the greatest variety of rare plants and flowers that ever unfolded their beauty before the eyes of man; above all, the orange trees, the peculiar favorite of the Island, then almost in full bloom, covered with blossoms, from my elevated position on the terrace made the whole valley appear an immense bed of flowers. All, too, felt the freshness and influence of the rain; and a gentle breeze brought to me from this wilderness of sweets the most delicious perfume that ever greeted the senses. Dont think me extravagant when I say that, in your wildest dreams, you could never fancy so rich and beautiful a scene. Even among the ruins, that almost made the heart break, I could hardly tear my eyes from it. It is emphatically a Paradise lost, for the hand of the Turk is upon it; and a hand that withers all that it touches. In vain does the Sultan invite the survivors, and the children made orphans by his bloody massacre, to return; in vain do the fruits and the flowers, the sun and the soil, invite them to return; their wounds are still bleeding, they cannot forget that the wild beast's paw might again be upon them, and their own blood might one day moisten the flowers which grow over the graves of their fathers.'—*Stephens' Incident of Travel.*

A soldier being sent on a late Dutch expedition, said to the officer directing the drafts:

"Sir, I cannot go because I stut-ter."

"Stutter!" says the officer, "you don't go to talk but to fight."

"Aye, but they'l p-p-put me on g-g-guard, and a man may go ha-ha-half a mile, before I can say, wh-wh-who goes there?"

"Oh, that's no objection, for there will be another sentry placed with you, and he can challenge if you can fire."

"Well, b-b-but I may be t-t-taken, and run through the b-b-body before I can cry q-q-quarters."

OH, RUM!—A man killed himself a few days ago, by drinking a bottle of rum at a draught. "Sarved" the dead man right—and made Pope a liar when he said:

"Shallow draughts intoxicate the brain.
But drinking deeply, sobers it—*again.*"

The grand council of the Cherokees about which so much apprehension was excited in the West, has at length taken place. Mr. Stokes, U. S. agent writes the department of War, that it was from the first pacific, and that he himself wrote the invitations to the other tribes, among whom we note the Seminoles, Senecas, Delawares, Shawnees, Quapaws, and Sacs. They assembled at Takertanker, Sept. 21, and officially declared, that the report of their intentions to make war upon the United States was without the least foundation. That those tribes only who were friendly to the United States were invited, and that the object was to renew the amicable union that existed between our forefathers.

MEXICO, Sept. 22d, 1838.

The following resolution was approved by the Chamber of Deputies and transmitted to the Senate for discussion:

"That it is the will of the nation that the government should, during the difference with France, possess every facility necessary for maintaining the defence of the nation for preserving the integrity of its territory, the constitution, order and tranquility, without, however, possessing the power of expelling any Mexican from the republic, or prosecuting any for his opinions, or disposing of the property of corporations or individuals, save by general imposts prudently levied."

By a decree of September 15th, the government has imposed a direct and heavy tax on all professions, trades and avocations of every kind. This is done with a view to provide for the excessive expenditures required for the national defence. This impost, which is levied indiscriminately upon every public and private company, incorporation, public officers, and in short, upon every citizen whose annual stipend amounts to $50 per annum, varies from half per cent. to 12½ per cent. The two extremes of these contributions are half per cent. The latter proportion is levied upon those whose revenues exceed $12,000 per annum. Even the church, the object of such unqualified reverence to the Mexicans, is not spared.

The extracts from Mexico represent the country as entirely tranquil. The papers are filled with bulletins from different quarters, addressed to the minister of war, and informing him of the undisturbed condition of the people. By the last accounts it [illegible] that the news of the revolution of Tampico had not arrived [illegible] Mexico. It is not improbable that the intelligence of [illegible] discontent that will undoubtedly follow the decree of the Congress, which levies such onerous tribute upon all classes, will impair public tranquility materially. We should not, therefore, be at all surprised at learning that serious demonstrations of dissatisfaction prevail.

FREE TRADE TO THE LAWYERS.—A man from the country applied lately to a respectable solicitor in this town for legal advice. After detailing the circumstances of the case he was asked if he had stated the facts exactly as they occurred. "Yes, sir," rejoined the applicant, "I thought it best to tell you the plain truth; you can put the lies to it yourself."

A girl advertises in a New York paper, that she wants a husband, and that she would prefer a sub-treasurer. The object of that girl is variety; she means to have at least a dozen husbands before she dies. She intends to select a sub-treasurer each time, knowing that he will probably run away in a month and leave her free to choose a successor to fill his place.

MENAGERIE ELOQUENCE.—The honely genuine specimen in the huniwersal globe of the East Ingy rhinosycross, wot was cotched on the top of the north pole, by Capt. Ross, and of the vonderful hoorang-hootang as vollopped three hottentots in Wan Demon's land, and was only captured arter it had drank three gallons of rum toddy.

From the National Gazette.

Many of our readers have heard of, and some of them doubtless remember Rivington's Royal Gazette; published in New York, while that city was in the possession of the British army. Rivington was a royalist, and his paper, under the influence of Tories, was proverbially "a record of lies," quite as circumstantial as those of the Globe, and teemed with as much abuse of the whigs as some of the administration papers do at this day of the same men. Witness the following language from one of that class.

"The United States pay tribute to England's money jobbers and aristocrats, through the management of Jay, Hamilton, and the federal leaders of 1783, who had no other motive for joining the Revolution of '76, but because they wished to remove the fountain of state corruption in America from the palace in Westminister to the White House in Washington."

Robert Morris and Alexander Hamilton were abused by Rivington because they were true patriots, and in this respect the Royal Gazette does them more justice than the Government organ at Washington, which pronounces them to have been "unprincipled Englishmen."

The following *ju de'sprit*, from a cabinet of Revolutionary relics, which, in some respects, would be applicable elsewhere, may amuse our readers, and recall to their recollection men and events of former times:

RIVINGTON'S LAST WILL AND TESTAMENT.

Imprimis, to the King my dear master, I give a full set
(In volumes bound up) of the Royal Gazette,
In which he will find the vast record contained
Of provinces conquered and victories gained.

I know there are some that would fain be thought wise,
Who say my Gazette is a record of lies;
In answer to this I shall only reply,
"All the choice I had was to starve or to lie."

To Sir Henry Clinton, his use and behoof,
I leave my French brandy of very high proof:
It will give him fresh *spirits* for battle and slaughter,
And make him feel bolder by land and by water.

Yet I caution the knight for fear he do wrong,
'Tis "avant la viando apres le poisson."
It will strengthen his stomach, prevent it from turning,
And digest the affront of his effigy burning.

To Baron Knyphausen, his heirs and assigns,
I bequeath my old Hock and my burgundy wines;
To a true Hessian drunkard no liquors are sweeter,
I know the old man is no foe to the creature.

Provided, however, and nevertheless,
What other estate I enjoy and possess
At the time of my death (if it be not then sold)
Shall remain to the tories "to have and to hold."

As I thus have bequeathed them both carcass and fleece,
The least they can do is to wait my decease;
But to give them what substance I have ere I die,
And be eat up with vermin while living, not I.

In witness whereof, though no ailment I feel,
Hereunto I set both my hand and my seal;
As the law says, in presence of witnesses twain,
Squire John Coghill Knap and Brother Hugh Gaine.

Below is an article from the pen of Mr. J. S. Jones, of North Carolina. As the New York Star very justly remarks "the 'Old North' of the Southern has latent fires that burn with deep intensitsy and glowing colours. When awakened, as in Mr. Jones, we see what coruscations they can scatter around, of poeses of romance and of exact historical detail, pleasingly combined, and investing regions hitherto deemed barren of every interest, with associations that can never die, while love of country and admiration of her early patriarchs, comes to us in these sordid times, like some warning apparition, to recall us to those proud days of chivalry which were indeed the golden age of our history."

Extract from the Picturesque History of North Carolina, by James S. Jones, of Shacco.

ROANOKE ISLAND.

Such is the aspect of this shore,
'Tis Greece, but living Greece no more;
So coldly sweet, so deadly fair,
We start, for soul is wanting there.—*Giour.*

I have never wandered over the Island of Roanoke, without a feeling of melancholy, as intense as that of Byron, whilst contemplating the fallen greatness of Greece, the days of her glory are over, and gone with those beyond the flood; but still she is to me an island of the heart—for her shores are the graves of the warlike and the wise. The native Indian built his machicomack on her hills; and there too, stood the city of Raleigh, the birth-place of the Anglo-American—and thus was Roanoke known, long before the beach at Jamestown was settled, or the rock of Plymouth consecrated. She is the classic land of all English America, and will live in the future story of our Republic, as the mother earth of American liberty. The illustrious names of Raleigh, of Cavendish, of Grenville, and of Drake—the heroes of the reign of Elizabeth,—are a part and portion of her history. Hariot, the Mathematician and Philosopher of the age, for the space of a whole year, studied its natural resources and Indian history, and nearly two hundred and fifty years since, gave the world a book unequalled for the accuracy and interest of its details. It would seem, indeed, as if the chivalry and learning of that age had contributed this splendid representation, to give a dazzling brilliancy to the early history of that State, on whose shores the flag of England was first unfurled, and in whose valleys, and over whose hills, the mountain Goddess of Liberty first shouted the cry of American Independence. Bear witness, Mecklenburg, on the 20th of May, 1775.

But it is not historic associations alone, which makes sacred the shores and vine clad forests of Roanoke. Nature seems to have exerted herself to adorn it as the Eden of the new world. The richest garniture of flowers and the sweetest minstrelsy of birds, are there. In traversing the northern section of the Island, in the spring time of year, flowers and sweet scented herbs in the wildest luxuriance are strewn along your winding way, welcoming you with their fragrance to their cherished isle. The wild rose bush, which, at times, springs up into nurseries of one hundred yards in extent, 'blooms blushing' to the song of the thousand birds that are basking in her bowers.—The mocking bird, too, whatever ornithologist may say of its 'chimney habits,' makes this his favorite haunt; and I have, myself, seen him, pillowed on the highest cluster of roses, and swinging with his weight the slender tree, as he warbled out his most exquisite song. It may be, however that Roanoke is the very spot, where, in imitation of the Eastern queen of song, the mocking bird fell in love with the rose.

There are stately Pine forests extending along the centre of the Island—but the most beautiful of its trees are what are commonly called dogwood, the laurel, and a delicate species of the white oak. I have seen a forrest composed of these trees, the branches and limbs of which were literally entertwisted and knitted together by the embrace of the Roanoke vine, which, here, in its native garden, grows with extraordinary exhuberance.

Within the deep shades of these reclining vintages, the spirit of solitude at times reigns in undisturbed majesty. At mid day when the heat of the summer's sun is too glowing for exertion—there is not the chirp of a bird to break the solemnity of the spot. The long and slender vine snake, which at other hours is seen industriously threading his way through the mazes of the vintage, has now suspended himself on a twig, and hangs as idle and as still as a black silk cord. If you hear the tread of footsteps, it is not of man, but the stealthy retreat of an unsuspecting fawn, which hath slept too long, and which now like a woodland nymph, hies away on the approach of man. But in the morning and in the evening, this scene of quiet and of repose is all entirely changed. It is then that the granary of the Island, and the birds have all assembled and are warbling in bacchanal confusion, their morning or evening hymn. The scenery of Roanoke is neither grand nor sublime. There are no Alpine summits to mingle with the clouds, but a series of gentle undulations, and a few abrupt hills, in the valleys of which the richly dressed scenery I have described may be found. If it should ever be the lot of the reader to stray under the vintage shade of Roanoke—made impervious to the rays of the sun by the rich foilage and clustering grapes above him—he will not venture to discredit the highly wrought sketches of Hariot, nor mock the humble enthusiasm of the volume now before him. I remember once to have stood on the loftiest eminence of the Island, and to have watched the progress of a sunset. It was on a summer's eve, which had been made peculiarly clear by a violent thunder storm the preceding night—and not a film of a cloud or vapor was to be seen about the horizon, or in the blue vault of heaven. There was not a breath of air to stir the slender leaf of the few lofty pines that straggled around me, and even the mocking bird seemed to have hushed his capricious song, to enjoy the intense feeling of the moment. To the westward of the Island, the waters of the Albemarle crept sluggishly along—and in the winding current of the Swash, several vessels stood, with outspread but motionless wings. Away down to the South, Pamlico spread itself out like an ocean of gold, gleaming along the banks of the Chickamacomico and Hatteras, and contrasted with this, were the dark waters which separate Roanoke from the sea beach, and which were now shaded from the tints of the sunset by the whole extent of the Island.

"A sea of glory streamed along" the narrow ridge—dividing the inland waters from the ocean, and beyond this the boundless Atlantic heaved her chafed besom of saphire and of gold, against the base of yon stormy Cape. I enjoyed and lived in that sunset and twilight hour. I thought of the glorious destiny of the land on which I trod—as glorious as the waters and the earth then around me. I thought of the genius and the death of Raleigh—of the devotedness of Greenville—of the gallantry of Cavendish and Drake—of the learning of Hariot—of the nobleness of Manteo the Lord of Roanoke—of the adventurous expedition of Sir Ralph Lane up the river Moratock—of the savage array of the blood-thirsty Wingina—of the melancholy fate of the last of the Raleigh colonies—of Virginia Dare the first Anglo-American—of the agony of her mother—and I then thought of those exquisite lines of Byron,

Shrine of the mighty can it be,
That is all remains of thee?

On the ruins of the ancient city of Raleigh "the indolent wrecker now sits and smokes the pipe of oblivion—a very wreck"—ignorant of the glorious associations of the land of his birth. He can tell you nothing of the deeds of those whose early effort in the settlement of the Roanoke gave an impulse to English colonization in America, and thus laid the foundations of our great American Republic. He will speak vaguely of the name of Sir Walter Raleigh, and will regale you with legends and stories of pirates and wrecks, which it is the business of the novelist, and the historian, to record. Such of them as I could link with the Raleigh Colonies, I have engrafted upon more authentic material, and perhaps the traditionary history of no country is equal in interest to that of Roanoke Island. The legend of Sir Walter Raleigh's ship, of the great battle of Hatteras, and of the nativity of Virginia Dare, which I have perhaps, too painfully detailed, are the best assurances that the names of those who first planted the flag of old mother England on our shores, cannot die.

The Island of Roanoke is at present tenanted by a class of people as rude and as boisterous as their native seas. They are a race of adventurous pilots and hardy mariners, and in their light craft, seeks the remotest Islands of the West Indies, and occasionally, with their freights of naval stores, penetrates into the Mediterranean, to the ports of Gibraltar and Malaga.

A race of rugged Mariners are these,
Unpolished men, and boistrous as their seas,
The native Islanders, alone their care,
And hateful he who breaths a foreign air,
These did the Ruler of the deep ordain,
To build proud navies, and command the main;
On canvass wings to cut their watery way,
No bird so fleet, no thought so swift as they.—*Obyssey.*

Am I then too enthusiastic in the history of Roanoke Island? It is the birth-place of Virginia Dare—it was the the home of the faithful and noble Lord of Roanoke, and every hill, and every vale, is marked in its history of scenes of joy or woe. The battle fields of the warlike Wingina are there, and there the imagination may stretch itself backwards over the course of time, and dwell upon the Indian legends of wars, that had passed when the assembled host of barbarians fought upon the sea beach, that they might be cheered on by the music of the waves. I have dreamed away many a sunny day in the solitude of its wood, and while revelling in my fancy upon the present magnificence of our Republic, I have not forgotten that I stood within the paradise of the new world, in which Providence had decreed the nativity of the first-born of a great and mighty people.

CONGRESSIONAL.

SENATE CHAMBER, Dec. 3, 1838.

Senate met. Prayer as usual.

Journals read and approved.

The president pro. tem. presented a letter from the the Hon. Wm. H. Wharton, requesting leave of absence on account of the continued sickness of his brother.—Leave granted.

The orders of the day were taken up.

Joint resolution for the relief of Wm. H. Sanderson; read first time.

An act amending an ordinance, granting land to volunteers; read first time.

A bill uniting the war and navy department; read first time.

An act to incorporate the Bastrop Steam Mill Company; read first time.

Joint resolution for the relief of Samuel D. Marshall, referred to committee on Public Lands.

Joint resolution ordering one company of the regular troops now in this city, to march to Gonzales, was received from the House, by a substitute passing to its third reading.

Ayes and noes were called by Mr. Dunn.

Ayes—Messrs. Dunn and Wilson—2.

Noes—Messrs. President pro. tem., Barnett, Burleson, Burton, Greer, Jones, Kendrick, Rains, Seguin, Stroud—10.

So the substitute was rejected.

A bill granting a divorce to Sophia Aughenbaugh, was read second time, and referred to a special committee—Benton, Seguin and Burleson.

An act for the relief of John G. Love, Collector of the Port of San Augustine, was referred to Messrs. Benton, Reins and Everett.

An act to legalize certain marriages—read second time, and referred to Judiciary Committee.

Report of the committee on the act incorporating Neches Steam Mill Company.

Adopted with an amendment.

Mr. Everett was opposed to the amendment made by the Committee in regard to prohibiting Banking Privileges. It was not the wish of the incorporation to have Banking Privileges, and the amendment was only placed by the Committee to guard against that privilege.—He was entirely disconnected, and had no interest in the incorporation. He therefore could speak freely on the subject. He was requested by the Representative from Jasper to object to the amendment; he therefore hoped that as the amendment did not reach the object contemplated, to wit: The prohibition of issuing shin plasters, that the committee would allow the amendment to be lost. The charter was only a copy of the Matagorda Steam Mill Incorporation; there was no such guard attached to that bill, as now is attempted to be placed to the bill, under consideration. If Congress would pass a general bill prohibiting the issue of shin plasters, he would support it, but he disliked to see an invidious distinction drawn upon the same subject, only in different sections of the country.

Mr. Greer and Mr. Jones supported the amendment.

A resolution was received from the House of Representatives, ordering the meeting of both houses to fill vacancies in the Land Office Department; laid on the table until called up.

Joint resolution for the relief of P. T. Carneal, referred to committee on accounts and claims.

A joint resolution to repeal the section of the bill establishing the jurisdiction of the District Courts; referred to Judiciary Committee.

Joint resolution for the relief of Jno. Garrett.

Joint resolution for the relief of Wm. Walker.

Joint resolution for the relief of R. R. Royall; were all referred to Committee on Claims and Accounts.

Report from the Committee on the joint resolution for issuing bounty lands,

Was rejected and the original joint resolution requiring the Secretary of War to issue bounty lands for officers and soldiers, was read a second time.

Question—shall the bill be engrossed—ayes and noes were called.

Ayes—Mr. Wilson—1.

Noes—President pro. tem. Barnett, Burleson, Benton, Dunn, Ellis, Greer, Jones, Kendrick, Reins, Seguin, Stroud—so the bill was lost.

A message was received from the House, requesting the appointment of Joint Committee to enquire into the matters touching the Five Million loan.

An act to incorporate Protection Fire Company, No. 1, was referred to a Special Committee.

A Joint Reslution ordering the Joint Committee on Finance to procure information from the Secretary of the Treasury, in regard to the Five Million loan, was rejected.

A message from the President, was received by his private secretary, Z. L. Hoyle.

Joint Resolution requiring the Secretary of the Navy to grant bounty lands to seamen, referred to the Committee on Public Lands.

An act appropriating $5,000 to defray the contingent expenses of both Houses of Congress; passed.

Joint Resolution of Congress requiring the Secretary of War to grant discharges; passed.

An act to incorporate the towns of Beaumont and Jasper: passed.

A Bill making it penal to sell arms, munitions of war, &c., to the Indians; referred to the Committee on Indian Affairs.

A Bill prohibiting the destruction of timber, was laid on the table till called up.

Report on the claims of S. A. Saddler; adopted.

Report on the rate of interest; adopted.

Joint Resolution granting lands to each county, for certain purposes; referred to a Special Committee.

The Senate went into secret session—doors opened—adjourned till 3 o'clock, p. m.

THREE O'CLOCK, P. M.

Senate met.

Mr. Benton moved to call up the resolution ordering the election of officers in the Land Office Department; and offered a substitute, delaying an election; adopted.

The Senate adjourned until 10 o'clock, to-morrow.

DECEMBER 5th, 1838.

Senate met.

Prayer as usual.

Journals read and approved.

A message was received from his Excellency, the President.

Mr. Rains, from the Committee on the Judiciary, reported the act to repeal the 26th section of the bill establishing the jurisdiction of the District Courts; read a first time.

Mr. Burton made a report from the committee on the bill making it penal to sell arms, &c., to the Indians; read a first time; the bill laid on the table until called up.

Mr. Burton made a report from the Committee to whom was referred the Bill granting lands to certain counties, by presenting a substitute; read a first time.

Mr. Burton from the committee to whom was referred the bill granting a divorce to Sophia Aughenbaugh: reported; which, after much debate,—sundry motions and resolutions, was finally re-referred to a Special Committee consisting of Messrs. Burleson, Stroud, Barnett, and Kendrick.

A message was received from the House announcing the reconsideration of the resolution ordering the election of Chief Justices, and appointing the 11th December, for that purpose, which was taken up and concurred in by the Senate.

The resolution ordering the election of County Surveyors, was also announced to take place after the above election.

A Bill making appropriations for the Post Office Department; read a second time.

A resolution requiring the Secretary of the Treasury to pay out certain drafts—rule snspended—passed.

A bill for the relief H. Sanderson was read a second time, and referred to the Committee on Claims and Accounts.

The Senate adjourned until 3 o'clock, p. m.,

THREE O'CLOCK, P. M.

The Senate met.

A bill to establish the mail route to the city of San Augustine, from Houston; read a first time.

Joint resolution for the relief of H. C. White & Co.; read a fiist time.

A bill to incorporate the town of Milam; read a first time.

Mr. Burleson, by leave, introduced a petition from the citizens of Fayette county; referred to the Judiciary Committee.

An act to incorporate the Neches Steam Mill Company; passed.

An act prescribing the manner of locating Bounty Land; referred to the Committee on Public Lands.

An act fixing the rate of interest; passed.

A bill uniting the War and Navy Departments; read a second time, and referred to the committee on Military and Naval Affairs.

An act to incorporate the Bastrop Steam Mill Company; read a first time.

A message was received from the House, covering a resolution originating in the House of Representatives. for the appointment of a Committee to wait on the Treasurer and request him to keep his office open for the present week; which was unanimously rejected.

The Senate adjourned until 10 o'clock to-morrow morning.

HOUSE OF REPRESENTATIVES.

MONDAY MORNING, Dec. 3rd, 1838.

The House met.

Prayer by the Rev. Jno. McCullough, the chaplain.

Journal read and approved.

A message was received from the Senate, informing the House that the Senate had passed a resolution that the two Houses adjourn, on Thursday next, until Monday, the 10th inst. The resolution was amended by the House so as to adjourn on Wednesday, instead of Thursday; and the resolution so amended was concurred in by the Senate.

Mr. Kerr presented a petition in favor of Thomas Simmons, with accompanying documents; which were read and referred to the Committee on the Judiciary.

On motion of Mr. Cullen the Speaker appointed Messrs. Swift and Johnson, of Shelby, a Committee to wait on the Senate and inform them that the House was ready to receive their body for the purpose of telling out the votes for President and Vice President of the Republic.

The Committee discharged that duty and reported that the Senate had concurred and would meet the House immediately.

The Senate in conformity with the request of the House came into the Representative Hall, for the purpose of telling out the votes for President and Vice President.

The Speaker of the House invited the Honorable President pro. tem, of the Senate, to a seat at the Speakers table.

Messrs. Cullen and Menifee were appointed tellers.

The vote having been counted, the tellers reported that the Honorable MIRABEAU B. LAMAR had received, for the office of President, six thousand nine hundred and ninety-five votes; and the Honorable ROBERT WILSON, received for the same office, two hundred and fifty-two votes. Also, that for Vice President, the Honorable DAVID G. BURNETT received three thousand nine hundred and fifty-two votes; the Honorable ALBERT C. HORTON, one thousand nine hundred and seventy-one; and Dr. JOSEPH W. ROWE, twelve hundred and fifteen votes.

Whereupon, the Speaker of the House of Represntatives declared the Honorable MIRABEAU B. LAMAR and the Honorabls DAVID G. BURNETT duly elected President and Vice President of the Republic of Texas, for the next three years from the time of their induction into office.

The business for which the two houses met having been performed; the Senate retired, and,

On motion the house adjourned until to-morrow morning, 10 o'clock.

COMMUNICATED.

MR. EDITOR—When I was a lad, a neighbor of my father's built a very fine Saw-Mill—as near as I can recollect, it cost him some twelve or fifteen thousand dollars—it was completed in fine order—all he wanted was a crank to set it to work, this he expected to get from one of his friends hard by; and had made his flutter-wheel to suit this crank. All being finished, he mounted his horse, rode over to buy this crank of his friend; what was his surprise when he demanded the price? He asked him five times its cost—He swore he would be d——d before he would give it. The prospect of getting another was two hundred miles—he sent —two months was delayed—none to be had. The nearest then was New York, and it would require two months more—he took wit in his anger and got my father to buy it at six times its value, and went to work, and in a few days the profits of his mill paid for it. Now the situation of Texas.—Her domain is worth hundreds of millions; for the want of a few hundred thousand dollars, she will "squabble" whether she shall give 8 or 12 per cent. In one year from now by giving a small premium on money. At this time, her immense domain, by being protected; would be worth double, yea, treble,—but she will not be cheated or imposed upon, she will be d——d if she will. In another year she will take the crank and go to work, and it is paid for in a few days, by the increase in value of her currency, and the value of her domain.

VOX POPULI.

INAUGURAL ADDRESS.

Gentlemen of the Senate and House of Representatives, Friends and Fellow-Citizens:

INVITED by the suffrages of my fellow-citizens to the Chief Magistracy of the Republic, I embrace the opportunity which this solemn occasion presents, of tendering my deep and enduring gratitude for their distinguished favor. When I reflect upon the great unanimity of the popular voice by which I am called to this station, I cannot repress the painful apprehension that I may not be able to fulfil the high expectations which such general confidence implies; and if I did not feel assured that the co-ordinate branches of government, as well as the better judgement of those whom I may be able to call into my councils, would abundantly supply my deficiencies, I should be constrained to avoid a situation into which I bring abilities so inadequate to the discharge of its high and important duties. But indulging the pleasing hope that a warm hearted and liberal people, will continue to judge of my motives and my actions with the same generous indulgence heretofore extended to me as their public servant—forgiving what is wrong and sustaining what is right—I assume the duties of the Executive, with the solemn assurance to this august assembly, that every effort in my power shall be made to strengthen and retain the confidence reposed in my disposition to advance the happiness of the people, and to widen and confirm the foundations of our national institutions.

I place a high trust, my fellow-citizens, in the protection of the Great Ruler of nations who has never yet deserted a people whose virtues may have entitled them to the blessings of freedom. Driven into the assertion of our rights and the defence of our lives by the tyranny and oppression of those with whom it was our misfortune to be associated in government, Providential interference in our behalf, from the beginning of the revolution up to the present period—guiding us in the paths of victory, and sustaining us in the hour of difficulty when our own wisdom had failed us, has been so manifest and signal, that I cannot but indulge the cheering belief that the Great Dispenser of all blessings will still continue to prosper us in our future career; will be with us in all our trials and struggles, and in the end enable us to rear such a political superstructure for the preservation of freedom as tyranny cannot shake and time shall continually strengthen. Let then the warm oblations of the heart be freely offered to that Divine Being who hath thus far conducted us to glory and prosperity through so many trying scenes; and whilst we would supplicate a continuence of His protecting goodness, let it be our constant study to demean ourselves individually and nationally in such manner as not to forfeit all claim to the munificience solicited by the selfishness of our motives, or the folly of our measures. Nor should we in the fulness of prosperity forget those gallant spirits, whose military skill and manly energies, under the guidance of Providence, achieved our Independence, and laid the corner stone of a young Republic which we fondly hope may yet excel those nations which have arrived at maturity, in the purity of her institutions and the stability of her freedom. Whether the sons of the Revolution have sealed their devotion to liberty by the blood of martydom, or whether they still survive to participate in the fruits of their valor, it is equally our duty, in justice to our own feelings and as a bright example to those who are to come after us, to cherish the memory of the dead, and to reward the virtues of the living; and by so doing refute the slander of our foes, and enforce the solemn truth, that the generous and brave who draw in defense of Texas may rely with safety on the honor of her government.

In the new sphere in which I shall soon be called to act, I trust, I bring with me no feelings unbecoming the first officer of a free government. Nobler considerations than the gratification of selfish purposes and proscriptive passions must engage the Executive attention. We have peace to procure; the public credit to establish, and the resources of our country to develop. These, and similar are great concerns which should engross the attention of every department of government and call forth the highest energies of enlightened patriotism. But they are not to be attained, fellow-citizens, without union among the people, and without reciprocal confidence between the public despositories of power. If distrust and jealousy be allowed to take root in the different departments of government, and factions discensions spring up in the bosom of our present peaceful and united population, all the efforts of the patriot to advance the public weal will prove unavailing and abortive; and the nation, instead of moving onward to that proud elevation that awaits her, must necessarily recede into a debased condition, and possibly sink into irretrievable ruin. As one who is ever ready to make a sacrifice of all personal considerations to the nation's welfare, I entreat this enlightened assembly to receive the renewed assurances of my fixed determination, in the discharge of official duties to be guided solely by the good of our common country; and so far as my humble abilities will permit, fulfil the expectations of a generous and confiding people.

The character of my administration may be anticipated in the domestic nature of our government and peaceful habits of the people. Looking upon agriculture, commerce and the useful arts as the true basis of all national strength and glory, it will be my leading policy to awaken into vigorous activity, the wealth, talent and enterprise of the country; and at the same time to lay the foundation of those higher institutions for moral and mental culture, without which no government on democratic principles can prosper, nor the people long preserve their liberties. In the management of our foreign intercourse, I would recommend, that we deal justly with all nations, aggressively to none—preserve friendly and amicable relations with such as may be disposed to reciprocate the policy and avoiding all protracted and perplexing negociations, court free and unrestricted commerce wherever it may be the interest of our people to carry the national flag. Prefering peace, but not averse to war, I shall be ever ready to adjust all differences with our enemies by friendly discussion and arrangement, at the same time be equally prompt to adopt either offensive or defensive operations as their disposition and our own safety may render necessary. Unconscious of any selfish influences which are likely to draw me from the path of duty, I hope in the administration of our domestic affairs, to recommend by my example the spirit of justice and moderation in the exercise of official functions. I shall bestow preferment upon the virtuous and intelligent of all parties, who have the good of the country and not their own aggrandizement in view:—observe an equal and impartial balance between the rights, claims and interests of every class of our fellow-citizens, dealing justly with all, intentionally wrong with none:—sustain the freedom of the press, the purity of elections, the right of opinion; and the freedom and sanctity of religion:—maintain the integrity and independence of the Judiciary as the great dispensary of justice, and the correction of civil, criminal and constitutional abuses:—economize the public resources:—protect the frontiers:—recommend equality of taxation, burthening none of the brances of industry for the benefit of others:—discourage multiplicity of legislation:—patronize talents, integrity, and sobriety; and support with becoming liberality all laudable and patriotic institutions founded in reason and tested by experience. Above all things, my fellow-citizens, I shall feel it to be my imperious duty to execute the laws with impartiality:—to guard the public against fraud:—to hold every individual in official station to strict accountability:—and under all circumstances and at every hazard to maintain order and subordination *within*, and to repel all aggressions from *without*. If feelings like these shall animate my conduct, as I hope they will, and guide me through the toils, perplexities and responsibilities of my station, beneficial consequences cannot fail to flow to the public, and I shall find in a quiet the parentage of our revolution to the vagrant days of conscience and the smiles of a prosperous people, abundant remuneration for any sufferings, either of body or mind, which I may be doomed to encounter in the faithful performance of duty.

As this is not the occasion for the Executive to offer his recommendatory councils for the action of Congress, I must of course pass by, for the present, the development of those measures by which I hope to carry out the cardinal principles of my administration. Neither, until the Executive shall be installed into office, can he be supposed to possess the information necessary to be presented for the consideration of that body. At a peeiod, however, as early as practicable, I shall be pleased in complyance with the requirements of the constitution to unfold at length my views of general policy and to suggest such a course for legislative conduct as may seem to me the most essential to an energetic and successful direction of public affairs. And this I shall do the more cheerfully from the disposition which I see every where manifested, both by the people and the co-ordinate departments of government, not only to sustain the Executive in whatever is just and judicious, but also under all circumstances to adhere with fidelity to the constitution of the coun[illegible], and to walk in the light of those great principles [illegible]tional integrity and honor which constitute the pri[illegible] and glory of our young Republic.

There i[illegible] one question, of the highest [illegible]tional conc[illegible] which I feel it a privilege [illegible] a duty to address myself to the great body of the people themselves. I mean the annexation of our country to the American Union. Notwithstanding the almost undivided voice of my fellow-citizens at one time, in favor of the measure; and notwithstanding the decision of the National Congress at its last session inhibiting the Chief Magistrate from withdrawing the proposition at the Cabinet of Washington, yet still I have never been able myself to perceive the policy of the desired connection, or discover in it any advantage either civil, political or commercial which could possibly result to Texas. But on the contrary, a long train of consequences of the most appaling character and magnitude have never failed to present themselves whenever I have entertained the subject, and forced upon my mind the unwelcome conviction that the step once taken would produce a lasting regret, and ultimately prove as disasterous to our liberty and hopes as the triumphant sword of the enemy. And I say this from no irreverence to the character and institutions of my native country, whose welfare I have ever desired and do still desire above my individual happiness, but a deep and abiding gratitude to the people of Texas, as well as a fervent devotion to those sacred principles of government, whose defence invited me to this country, compelss me to say, that however strong may be my attachment to the parent land, the land of my adoption must claim my highest allegiance and affection; her glory and happiness must be my paramount consideration; and I cannot allow myself to speak in any other than the language of freedom and frankness on all matters involving her safety, dignity and honor.

When I reflect upon the invaluable rights which Texas will have to yield up with the surrender of her Independence—the right of making either war or peace; the right of controling the Indian tribes within her borders; the right of appropriating her public domain to purposes of education and internal improvement; of levying her own taxes, regulating her own commerce and forming her own alliances and treaties—when I view her divested of the most essential attributes of free government; reduced to the level of an unfit fraction of a giant power; or peradventure divided into Territorial districts, with Governors and judges and excise men appointed from abroad to administer laws which she had no adequate voice in enacting, and to gather imposts for the benefit of those who levy them—when I look upon her, as she soon will be, the Cornucopia of the world, pouring her abundant treasures into the lap of other people than her own; a tributary vassel to remote and uncongenial communities; communities as widely separated from her in feelings as in distance, who are known to be opposed to her peculiar and essential interests, and who are daily sending forth their denunciations against her from the fire-side, the pulpit and the council chamber:—and when I bear in mind that all this sacrifice of rights and dignity and character is to be made, for what?—for the privilege of going into a Union in which she carries wealth without proportional influence—for the glory of identifying her fortunes with a government in which a large portion of the inhabitants are alarmed for the safety of the very institution upon which her own hopes of happiness are based; a government embracing conflicting interests and irreconcilable prejudices, with lasting causes of domestic quarrel, where Texas can hope for nothing but a participation in the strifes that distract the public councils, and after passing through many throes and convulsions, be the means, perhaps, of producing or accelerating an awful catastrophe, which none could be more ready to avert, or sincerely deplore, than herself:—when I reflect upon these inevitable and fatal consequences of the proposed connection, and then turn from the darkand dreary picture to the contemplation of the high destiny that awaits our country; the great prosperity which lies within her attainment, if she will but appreciate her natural advantages, and not part with the right of developing and controlling her incalculable resources:—when I view her vast extent of territory, stretching from the Sabine to the Pacific, and away to the South West as far as the obstinacy of the enemy may render it necessary for the sword to mark the boundary; embracing the most delightful climate and the richest soil in the world, and behold it all in a state of high cultivation and improvement—her mountains of mineral yielding their vast treasures to the touch of industry; her luxuriant pastures alive with flocks and herds, and her wide fields whitening with a staple commodity, in the production of which she can have no rival; with the whole world for her market; and then consider the noble purposes to which this immense and exhaustless wealth may be applied, in adorning and beautifying the country, providing for its safety and defence, endowing institutions for the spread of virtue, knowledge and the arts, and carrying to the door of every citizen of the Republic, peace, plenty and protection—and when in addition to these glorious and grand results, I look still farther to the important improvements which she will be able to devise in government, and to the entire revolution which her example in free trade will effect on the commerce of other nations, emancipating it from the thraldom of tariff exactions, and placing it upon the high grounds of equitable reciprocacity, all of which will as certainly flow from the maintenance of her present independent position, as the sun courses the heavens—when I reflect upon these vast and momentuous consequences, so fatal to liberty on the one hand, and so fraught with happiness and glory on the other, I cannot regard the annexation of Texas to the American Union in any other light than as the grave of all her hopes of happiness and greatness; and if, contrary to the present aspect of her affairs, the amalgimation shall ever hereafter take place, I shall feel that the blood of our martyred heroes had been shed in vain—that we had riven the chains of Mexican despotism only to fetter our country with more indissoluble bonds, and that a young Republic, just rising into high distinction among the nations of the earth, had been swallowed up and lost, like a proud bark in devouring vortex.

That the people of Texas should have been in favor of annexation at the time their votes were given on the question, is not a matter of surprize, when we consider the then existing condition of the country. She was left, after the battle of San Jacinto, feeble and exhausted; without means and without credit; her settlements broken up; her villages desolated by ruthless invasion; and amid all, still threatened, in her defenseless situation, with a return of the foe and renewal of the sad calamities of war. Under such a state of things, no wonder that the people, harrassed and almost ruined—bleeding with present wounds, and apprehending a further accumulation of ills, should be willing to purchase momentary security by a surrender of their national Independence. Perhaps there was wisdom in the choice; but I am free to confess that even at that time, amidst the darkest period of our country's history, I never despaired of the Republic, but with unshaken confidence in the strength of our cause, and a full knowledge of what the energies of a free and determined people were capable of achieving; I raised my feeble voice against the sacrifice which we were about to make, without any reference to the difficulties of the moment, and with an eye exclusively directed to the future glory of the nation, and permanent prosperity and happiness of all.

But these imposing considerations, which, at one time, rendered the proposed political connexion seemingly desirable, have lost their validity and force. Indeed, they exist no longer. Our desolated plains have become green meadows and luxuriant fields. Where the iron car of war rolled with destroying energy, the ploughshare of the husbandman is driven in peace and safety; and instead of a sparse and suffering population, weighed down with poverty and blighted hopes, we behold a powerful and prosperous people, daily increasing in wealth and numbers, happy in their present possessions, and looking forward to still higher and more glorio[illegible] Invasion too, has lost its terrors. Conscious of our own strength, we know very well that the enemy had greater reason to apprehend danger from us, than we from him. A change has come over the aspect of our affairs. We have risen from our prostration with redoubled energies. And shall we now, in the midst of glorious hopes and increasing vigor, persevere in a suicidal policy, originally founded in necessity rather than choice? Would it not be far better for us, since the reasons which influenced our former verdict can have no farther application, to re-consider that verdict, and on good and valid shewing reverse the judgment?

Never were a people so favorably situated as we are for the establishment of a wise and happy government. We have already laid the ground work successfully and well, and it is only necessary now that we pay proper attention to the strength and symetry of the superstructure. As in the natural sciences, discoveries are daily being made, so in the art of good government, the great teacher, time, is continually suggesting new and important changes; which, as a wise people, we should be ever ready, advisedly, to adopt, undeterred by the dread of innovation; and with conscious rectitude for our guide, move boldly onward in the rapid march of improvement, and keep pace with the progress of successful experiment. The American Constitution is certainly the highest effort of political wisdom, and approaches more nearly to perfection than any other social compact for the government to man; yet a fair trial of fifty years has detected in that sacred chart many serious and alarming errors, which, if we will but wisely avoid, at the same time adopting its favorable features and availing ourselves of all the lights of modern experience, we shall soon be able to devise and perfect a system of our own which shall surpass its model as far as that has excelled all others. To achieve this desirable end, we must turn to the great volume of history that lies open before us, and profit by the lessons it teaches. We may gather from its faithful records not only a knowledge of what has been tested by other nations and found to be practically beneficial or pernicious; but we may be taught the more solemn and important truth, that the instability of governments has not resulted from any thing inherent in the nature of human institutions to flourish and decay like the vegetable kingdom, but from the fact, that all, with the exception of the American Constitution, have been [illegible] capacity, instead of being fashioned by reflection, and based upon the solid grounds of private integrity and public morals. The principles of virtue and justice are unchangeable and indestructable, and the government which shall be reared upon the one and administered upon the other, cannot fail to be an eternal bulwark to the rights of man.

The founding of government upon a *written* compact between the people and their rulers, is certainly a wise invention. By circumscribing the boundaries of power, it deprives ambition of the means of misrule. The chief excellence, however, consists in the confidence and safety which every individual must feel in the enjoyment of his rights, under a tenure of his own selection. He holds them, not by the uncertain dictum of an arbitrary potentate or privileged order of men, but by virtue of a high instrument, the standard of all rule and law, adopted by the special servants of the people—and clearly defined, approved and ratified by a whole community. But what would it avail a people, fellow-citizens, though they embody in their Constitution the wisest provisions and the most salutary doctrines, if they should be wanting in the necessary firmness and patriotism to respect and obey them. It is obvious that the advantages of such a system must rest upon a faithful compliance of all parties with the terms of the compact. If the people at large, and the different departments of government shall adhere with fidelity to its letter and its spirit, the nation will be able to preserve its freedom, happiness and independence. But if on the contrary, either the people or the public functionaries, unmindful of their obligations to its authority, shall suffer themselves to be hurried by the violence of baneful passions, or be seduced by the selfish suggestions of a temporary or narrow-minded policy, into a violation of its solemn injunctions, the inevitable consequence will be the loss of public credit, the destruction of private confidence and the subversion of all order, morality and safety. How important is it then to shield and protect the sacred charter of our liberties, alike from all encroachments, whether made by the people themselves or by those entrusted with official stations. There is a proneness in the nature of man to overleap the barriers that stand in the way of his selfish desires. As individuals, we are restrained from the violation of the laws, by the fear of punishment, but as communities we have nothing to withhold us from an infringement of the Constitution, except that high moarlity and honest pride which make the virtuous and enlightened bosom feel that its country's honor is its own. Hence I esteem it the first duty of a patriot, and highest evidence of his patriotism, to cherish and respect the Constitution of his country. Nor can I conceive of a more dangerous enemy to liberty than the popular chief who shall discard its authority under the hollow pretext that he is acting for the good of the people. No reasons of state policy nor exigencies can justify its volation. Under any and all circumstances its infraction is more dangerous than treason; and its dethronement is the death of liberty. Let me then invoke the people of Texas to stand by their constitution. Let us offer no violence to its precepts and restrictions. Let us bow to the supremacy of its authority. Let it be our cloud by day and our pillar of fire by night.

Having every confidence in the disposition and ability of the country to sustain itself from all invasions of it enemies, and fully satisfied that the Executive will meet with the hearty co-operation of an enlightened and patriotic people, in whatever may be necessary for the preservation of national integrity and honor, it only remains for me to pledge myself, under the solemn requirements of the Constitution, to a faithful fulfilment of my official duties.

MIRABEU B. LAMAR.

No. III.

Mr. Editor.—The Hon. John Quincy Adams has never drawn from the abundance of his malignant and hostile feelings against the honor and welfare of Texas, a more venemous and deadly shaft, than when he traced Gen. Sam Houston, when outlying on the skirts of Arkansas he fraternized with the squatter on the public domain and the [illegible]arthy Indian, without the industrious enterprize of the one, or the wild and savage virtues of the other. He sought not an h[illegible] home for his family, and his DULL LEAD COLOURED EYE, shone not with the bold and stern defiance of the Indian warrior.

It were painful to dwell long on the history of Gen. Sam Houston's connection with the Cherokees. After leaving Tennessee, he went to the west—was adopted as a son by *Old Gdly*, and in full council completely Indianized. Having attained this enviable distinction, and satiated his passion for show and parade, with all the paint, beads, feathers, flaps, nudity, and mocisons of a Cherokee brave, his vanity and ambition in an evil hour, induced him to aspire to be a *chief;* and to strengthen his claim, he married the widow Guitry, a homely old squaw with five children, but connected with many of the leading families and supposed to be wealthy for a squaw. But all would not do. Sam Houston had shown great aptitude for lazy lounging *civilized* Indian habits, but when they went out hunting, he was always borrowing bear skins and buffalo skins, and leather whangs from the young warriors, and the widow Guitry's little paposes, were always crying for something to eat, and he had no *scalps* to hang up in his wigwam, and was strongly suspected of having a forked tongue, and to be a s[illegible]ging bird, and so he would not do for a *chief*—and s[illegible]—and so—he went to Washington city.

It was at [illegible] period when Gen. Houston had never been in Texas, that the conversations with Dr. Mayo were held on which he predicates his letter of Dec. 1830, to President Jackson. The slightest perusal of that letter will show that there is no earthly connection between its developements and the revolution which took place in Texas near six years afterwards. From the moment the United States government determined to remove the Creeks, Cherokees, and other strong tribes beyond the Mississippi, speculation has been busy in conjecturing what would be the ultimate result. Some have predicted long and terrible wars on the whole frontiers of Arkansas and Missouri, and that the war hoop and scalping knife would sweep the whole right bank of the Mississippi. Others have thought that when the game became scarce, and subsistence hard to obtain, and the United States annuities were expended, the strong tribes would unite and force their way across the mountains to the shores of the Pacific, and there seek a home; and others have supposed that they would turn their united strength on Texas, and possess themselves of its delightful plains. It was under this latter speculation that Gen. Sam Houston made his communications to Dr. Mayo. His was a Cherokee plume, himself a Cherokee. "He descended on the immense field for enterprize *in the Indian settlement* beyond the Mississippi, and through that as a stepping stone to Texas." He said that he was organizing an expedition *against Texas*, which would and must take place in twelve months from that time, and recommended Dr. Mayo not to go with him to Texas, but to go and practice medicine amongst the Indians. Not one word is said about any confederacy or co-operation with the colonists in Texas, and in fact, he had no connection whatsoever with them. Doctor Mayo speaks of his "inflated schemes" and "romantic projections," and it is evident that President Jackson viewed them as the "baseless fabric of a vision." No expedition took place in the *twelve months*, and it is apparent that the whole matter would have slept in oblivion but for the accident that threw the letter into the hands of John Q. Adams.

The revolution did not break out in Texas till the fall of 1835, near six years after the conversations of Gen. Houston in Feb. 1830; and when it did occur it had no earthly connection with the Cherokees in Arkansas. In the year 1832, several revolutionary movements took place in Texas, predicated, however, on the mutations in Mexico, and having no tendency to a reverence; the garrison at Nacogdoches commanded by Piedras were defeated; the troops at Anahuac commanded by Col. Bradburn, were captured, and the fort at Velasco was stormed; and where was Sam Houston all this time with his Cherokees and *stepping stone into Texas?* Not one word of him; all his schemes had evaporated in smoke.

In the year 1833, near four years after the notable developements to Dr. Mayo, the mad hero of all the terrible machinations that have driven J. Q. Adams mad, came to Texas, and for the next two years was buffetted between the confines of civilized and savage life, with the vices of both and the virtues of neither; the only distinction he earned was the sobiquet of "Big Drunk" among the Indians. About that time the rage of "eleven league" speculations had seized on some of the *adventurous* spirits of the country, and Sam Houston was regularly taken into partnership with Mr. Sublett and others, which gave him some consequence, and which together with his Cherokee associations has formed the basis of all his after-greatness. And if there are any two things in which he has preserved his integrity, they are in his truth to his Cherokee brethren and his co-speculators in "eleven league grants." On them are founded his Indian policy, and his opposition to any system for settling the land titles of the country.

In the next, Gen. Houston's actual connection with the revolution will be shown, and the peculiar circumstances by which his name has been identified with a cause which he has never advanced but constantly injured.

One word to the editor of the Telegraph before this article is closed. If any misrepresentations occurred in relation to your article, it was from the loose and reckless manner in which your remarks were connected. You used terms that were improper, and you asserted *positively* what course the president would pursue without authority; in this you were wrong.

Your remarks were calculated to drive men who know the situation of the country, and would avoid any thing that would injure it, into a situation in which they must act at all hazards; but you disclaim that you wrote by authority, places matters as they were before.

The author of "Sidney" is not going into a crowd of challengers, nor into a street fight with the recreant ex-president of Texas.

It were hard to tell what course a man professing to belong to the school of honor and chivalry should pursue; if he challenges he is a "duellist and blackguard;" if he inflicts "personal chastisement," he puts himself on a level with "negro drivers and horse jockeys." What alternative is offered? I suppose he must sit down like a woman and cry, and exercise some of that extraordinary maguanimity of which the Telegrap speaks.

The author of "Sidney" knows his own course and will pursue it in his own time. He will not sue an insolvent debtor.

The former speaker of the House of Representatives, a man responsible for costs and *"rectus in curia"* both in Texas and the United States, has sued out regular process in the court of honor and chivalry against Gen. Sam Houston, and the defendant has taken the oath of insolvency.

SIDNEY.

UNITED STATES AND TEXAS.—The long tirades, long sermons and tedious dissentions on the annexa- of Texas to the United States can now be dispensed with. The continual hue and cry raised and kept up by various classes, has been happily terminated by the wise decision of the Texian government. The Hon. Mr. Jones, the young republic's minister at Washington, informed the United States Government, on the ratifications of the boundary convention, that the proposition of being admitted to this Union had been formally and absolutely withdrawn, and he wished to have it so understood throughout the States. This was reported in the southern journals of last winter, as having occurred; but some persons undoubtedly interested, continued to moot it from one end of this country to the other, until it had become finally the belief of a large number. The question is now settled, and so let it remain forever.—*New York Whig.*

NATIONAL INTELLIGENCER.

EDITED BY JAMES S. JONES.

Houston, Tuesday, Dec. 11, 1838.

The National Banner having been purchased by the present proprietor, he has determined to change its name and to date the establishment of the NATIONAL INTELLIGENCER from the commencement of the present administration, to which it will extend a full and cordial support upon the principles set forth in the President's Inaugural Address. His great talents, exalted worth and devoted love of country, render any other qualification of our course entirely unnecessary. We do not anticipate a departure of the President from the cardinal principles of Gov'nt which he so eloquently elucidated at his installation, and cannot therefore permit ourselves to indulge the slightest apprehension of opposition from any quarter to the establishment of our Government upon the liberal and magnificent basis marked out by the Executive. He has laid the corner stone upon a firm foundation, and we have no doubt (to borrow the idea of Ovid) that the great work he has undertaken to accomplish will be found to surpass the materials provided for its structure.

The support of the Executive and other departments of the Government in carrying out their liberal and patriotic views was one of the chief inducements to the establishment of this paper, and we are determined to conduct it in a zealous, but firm and dignified manner. We shall not intentionally profane the liberty of the press. No personal abuse, no hasty accusations upon slight and insufficient grounds, no uncharitable ascription of base or selfish motives shall ever soil the columns of this paper whilst it remains under our control. We are ever ready to condemn the licentiousness and support the freedom of the press. This liberty is indeed the great safe-guard of all others, and the most formidable enemies to free Government have been prostrated in a struggle with its power. Although a tremendous engine for the diffusion of useful knowledge, and the developement of the great interests of society, it has not unfrequently forsaken the dignity of its proper pursuits, in order to alarm the idol fears and awaken the most depraved feelings of mankind. Yet this is no argument in favor of the Tyrants decree to abolish or muzzle its freedom. Whilst therefore we claim to exercise the right of general and open discussion, we hope ever to avoid the habit of denunciation in which political Journals so freely indulge.

We shall inculcate the faithful observance of the constitutional powers appertaining to the several departments of Government—guard the reserved rights of the people with untiring vigilance, and endeavor to impress upon all, by frequent admonitions, the necessity for the preservation of the national faith without breach or suspicion of unfair dealing. We shall advocate a rigid economy and an impartial distribution of the funds in our Treasury—a strict accountability of all officers of Government, and an unrelaxed discipline in our military and naval departments. We shall oppose all monopolies—all untried experiments in currency or political economy—and all attempts to unite the purse and the sword of the nation. We shall endeavor to promote the establishment of a National Bank, a gradual reduction of the Tariff, and the claims of none but honest and capable men for office. With these views we submit our claims for patronage to the public.

We call the attention of the public to an article in the columns of this paper, over the signature of "Sidney." He writes in language bold, nervous, and animated with the spirit of truth. He, like many other bold spirits in the country who have felt the weight of Executive tyranny, regards Government as instituted solely for the good of the people, and not for the benefit of those who have *contrived to make a job of it.*

It has been remarked by a few, that these articles were written as a premeditated artifice to catch the favor and the affections of the people. We feel a pride in saying to those *gentlemen* that the author of "Sydney" has no occasion to resort to such petty artifices, either to gain or to hold the affections of the people. He holds them by a much higher and a firmer title; the simplicity of his manners, the benevolence of his disposition, the integrity of his life, his real devotion to the best interests of our country; that uncommon sagacity which enables him to discern those interests in every situation, and the unshaken constancy with which he pursues them in spite of every difficulty and danger with which he might be threatened.

From the earliest point of time at which he embarked in the service of the country, it is very certain he has never suffered any gale of fortune however high or prosperous, to separate him from the people; nor did the people on their part ever desert him. He was the man to whom they looked in every crisis of difficulty, and the favorite on whom they were ever ready to lavish all the honors in their gift.

His Excellency, MIRABEAU B. LAMAR, was inaugurated on yesterday, and took the oath of office, before a large and brilliant assemblage, who attended to witness the ceremony and to hear the address of the President elect, of the Republic. None were disappointed in his speech. Its elevated tone, orthodox principles, statesmanlike views and happy combination of energy and simplicity, entitle it to the first rank among similar productions which have attracted the admiration of mankind. The President, who enters upon the duties of his office with so many happy prognostics of political favoriteism, cannot fail to revive the slumbering energies of this Republic and to conduct her to a bright and happy destiny.

With a becoming expression of diffidence in his own abilities, the President has offered us the highest assurance of his power and inclination to serve the people of Texas. He is emphatically the man for the crisis—when his measures are matured in his own mind, he is prompt to execute them, as far as the powers entrusted to him under the Constitution may authorize him to proceed. His views are decidedly democratic tempered with a national pride, which must ever restrain the Executive from appealing to the passions of the people, when he fails to convince their reason or animate their patriotism.

The elder Cato once exclaimed before the Roman Senate "that it was not merely by force of arms that our fore-fathers raised this Republic from a low condition to its present greatness; No! but by things of a very different nature--industry and discipline at home, decorum and justice abroad, a disinterested spirit in council, unblinded by passion and uncorrupted by pleasure." Texas then cannot expect to be great by force of arms or the power of conquest but by an unwavering attachment to those principles of free and enligtened government set forth by President Lamar and rigidly adhered to like the fore-fathers of the Roman Cato. There is a dignity of thought—a devotion to liberty—a love of country—and a setiment of true greatness which characterizes his Inaugural Address, that cannot fail to excite the admiration of other civilzed nations and to lead them to the early cultivation of international civilities.

His opinions are delivered with a candour and independence which every man must admire and approve. He has pourtrayed the characteristic features of free government in a strain of eloquence, which would do credit to the most finished orations.—He has declared his determination to invite frienly intercourse with other nations and to enter into embarrassing negociations with none. Commercial freedom is advocated as one of the main pillars of our national edifice, whilst he clearly evinces his determiuation to maintain the preservation of internal order and a due observance of the laws and requisitions of government. He is pledged to sustain the independence of the judiciary—to support the freedom of elections—to mainiain the national faith—to respect the integrity of the Constitution—to economize the public resources—to protect the freedom of the press—to foster the arts and sciences---to encourage virtue, knowledge and religion; and to defend at all hazards the honor, the independence and the rights of the Republic. These are some of the leading principles to which he is pledged to adhere during the term of his service.

The address itself will be found in another column and we recommend its perusal to the people of this country and her friends abroad, as containing the best pledge we can offer for the successful maintenance of our independendence and the establishment of a high national character.

It is a pleasing and gratifying spectacle to witness the good order and decorum which prevail in both branches of our Congress. In this respect, as in many others, we can be permitted to boast that the sons of the American Union have not degenerated since their amalgamation with this Republic. The offspring is worthy of the distinguished mother which gave her birth. The present Congress can boast of a great deal of talent—an order of talent too, which the present situation of this Republic so imperiousiy demands. The members are intelligent and energetic men, and many of them distinguished for their forensic attainments.

In the Senate the presiding officer, the Hon. Stephen H. Everette, is remarkable for his accuteness of intellect, decision of purpose and great urbanity of manner. He has acted as President of the Senate for several sessions of Congress and has given universal satisfaction.

His efforts on the floor, are remarkable for their practical tendency. He makes no effort at unnecessary display, but comes direct to the point under discussion, which he never fails to handle with ability. He speaks with great ease and candor, and every man will readily perceive that he has uttered precisely what he thought.

In the House of Representatives, the Speaker, the Hon. J. M. Hansford, although a new member, and not familiar with the rules of the body, has given the most decided satisfaction. He has made most rapid improvement in the knowledge of the forms of parliamentary proceeding which bespeaks his talents and his industry. We regard Mr. Hansford as one of the most useful men in our country. His integrity, his intelligence, his firmness and his dignity of character, will always command any station which he may be desirous to fill.

There are many others of whom we would gladly speak, but whilst we are permitted to pay a just tribute to the virtues and talents of the presiding officers of Congress, we cannot undertake the invidious task of discriminating between the members.

The "Hymn of the Alamo," published in the poet's corner, from the pen of a Texan citizen, is truly poetical, and deserves to be ranked in a higher scale than the ordinary newspaper effusions of that character. The consecration of the memory of those gallant spirits, who fell in that sanguinary conflict, is worthy to be commemorated by the highest poetical genius. The day is not far distant, when the deeds of chivalry performed by our countrymen will pass into story and rank among the noted events of the world. In our plodding, money-making times, those daring feats are not properly appreciated. It was even so with the chivalric performances of the heroes of the middle ages.

We have been requested by a gentleman in the War Department to state that large numbers of counterfeit Land Scrip are almost daily presented to that Department for approval, signed Geo. W. Poe, Pay-Master General; and some bearing the signature of Barnard E. Bee, Secretary of War.

"Infelix" shall have a conspicuous insertion in our next paper.

☞ The reports from the 4th December, will be published in our next.

Extract from a Letter dated
NEW ORLEANS, Nov. 15, 1838.

I commenced writing to you about the cause, the country, and the population. Little, indeed nothing, need now be said about the first. That is settled. Her independence has been achieved; and she can never be again subjugated. An Anglo Saxon race hath done it. That is enough. Their march has always been onward and upward, and it will go on in the new world until not the Indian, the Gaul, the Frank, the Moore, the Castillian, or their descendants, will exercise dominion on this or the Southern continent. That indomitable spirit of *conquest*, calling it by its mildest term, is the only thing that is likely to retard the unprecedented growth and prosperity of Texas. She may too soon attempt to extend her boundary beyond the Rio del Norte, and thereby forfeit the sympathies of her sister republic and other civilized nations.

Of the country, I cannot command language adequate for description. Old Joe Craig, the Baptist preacher, we may suppose he was inspired, made an effort to describe Heaven, and in the attempt, after calling forth all the powers of his comprehensive mind and exhausting his fertile imagination with a wonderful flow of language concluded by saying: "In fine, my dear brethren, it is a Kentucky of a place."

I have seen, I may say, almost every acre of the State of Kentucky, which was in the mind's eye of the reverened divine, and I do believe that Texas has greatly the ascendency. Kentucky, when conquered from the savage, required long and unremitting toil to conquer it from the wilderness. Texas is, by nature, at onece prepared for the plough of the husbandman. About one third of Kentucky is fertile, and capable of successful settlement and cultivation. Nine-tenths of all explored Texas is of that character. And the soil and climate of Texas can produce advantageously every thing which Kentucky can, and many things requisite for the wants of man which Kentucky cannot. Sugar, cotton, rice, indigo, with all the tropical fruits, may be profitably cultivated and abundantly produced.

The stream, with their tributaries, running from the mountains in the Gulf of Mexico, and at appropriate distances for each other, are fringed on either side with fine timber and high, rolling, rich prairies in the rear. —The prairie regions are generally supplied with small tracts of timbered land, sufficient for the wants of the husbandman.

That laborious, expensive and protracted work of clearing a plantation, is necessary in but few places.—Time has not yet been allowed to explore its mineral properties---coal has been detected in many parts of the country---copper, lead, iron, and silver, are said to abound, and the latter but too abundantly, in the mountain regions.

Of salt, nature seems to have been as bountiful as though it was designed that all the cattle raisers of Kentucky and the north branch of the Potomac, with all the porkers of Ohio, were at once to be transplanted. There is, between the Nueces and the Rio Grande, a salt quary upon the shores of a small lake, which is perfetly inexhastible. Although it has been sold for twelve and half cents the mule load by the government, yet, according to the universal account, there is no apparent diminution of the salt. It is situated some thirty or forty leagues from Matamoras, and about the same distance from the Bay of Corpus Christi.

Of the population much might and should be said. I had formed the opinion that the great mass were refugees from the justice of other countries, and that it would be somewhat unsafe for a gentleman's person or pocket book to be in the country; and having both upon which I placed a high value, I invoked the guardianship of a fifteen inch Bowie knife, of whose companionship I became heartily tired and quite ashamed, for I was charged with being an adventurer from Arkansas.

It may be truly said, that vice pays homage to virtue. Those who have been suspected, and those who have been guilty of criems elsewhere, are vieing with each other in doing good. The temptation is greatest to be honest. All who are so, are wonderfully successful. I know of no country in which the temperate, industrious, honest man is more highly appreciated.

The character of imigration is essentially improving every day. Small landholders from the States, with their slaves, their stock and implements of husbandry—industrious mechanics, with their tools—enterprising merchants, with their goods—lawyers, physicians, and even ministers of the gospel and schoolmasters, are to be found wending their way to Texas, and settling throughout the Republic.

Although this communication has become already extended to a drowsy length, I cannot close it without a few suggestions of the social sytem, and political condition of this new republic. The courts of justice are organized througout the land, and the business is conducted with as much order and propriety as elsewhere. Justice is administered without any unnecessary delay. In many of the courts I atttended, the officers appeared to understand the duties and promptly to perform them. Debts are collectable with more than ordinary facility.—Injuries to the person, property and reputation of individuals are speedily repaired. And offences against the Republic, are punished with a certainty that would do credit to many of the States of the American Union.

The disposition heretofore manifested, to become one of the United States, has given way to a more enlarged policy, and their application for admission has been formally withdrawn. She has territory enough, with all the natural capabilities, to become a powerful Republic. She has wisdom in her councils. She has skill and daring in her camps, and a population understanding their rights; able, and determined to maintain them. A very favorabled moment now presents itself, to cause the independence of Texas to be acknowledged by Mexico. The domestic troubles of the latter, and the impending invasion of the French, would seem to invite a proposition from Texas to treat; but it may be that the Texian hot-blood and proud spirit would regard such a proceedure on their part as matter of humiliation, when the dispassionate statesman might consider it to be even noble and generous. Mexico is, in the estimation of others, in an humble not to say a degraded condition; and Texas does not, and never can entertain any fears of subjugaton from such a power. How much better then to propose peace with her, and stop that effusion of blood which must continue to flow along the borders, (however imbecile Mexico may be,) until their troubles are settled.

The descendant of the proud Spaniard, proud in the ratio of his insignificance, will never permit Mexico to sue peace with Texas, and a nominal war must exist, unless Texas will make advances. If she would do so, repudiate the idea of conquest and propose a purchase, I doubt not she would be at once successful; a success which would give her peace, credit, population, money, and insure a rapidity of growth in power, unparralled in the history of man.

She must even have some Indian troubles on her northwestern border, which will be increased or diminished by her Mexican relations. If she would treat with Mexico, the land system which she has adopted, and which cannot now be departed from, at least within the present undisputed limits, will greatly contribute to save expense to the government in keeping the Indians in check. The valuable unlocated lands along the Indian frontier which can now be had at a very trifling expense, will cause the associations of individuals sufficiently numerous to afford protection against Indian incursions, and save the necessity of a line of garrisons to be supported at the expense of the government.

The Congress which is now in session, and so far as I had means of judging, I am impressed that it is composed of such material as to promise much wisdom in its deliberations, and consequently much good to the country. The President and Vice President elect are to be inaugurated on the 8th of December. They are both very popular, and doubtless deservedly so. From their efforts, united with Congress, we may hope that ere long the Texian may repose under his own vine and fig tree, with none to make him afraid.

As this is the money age, I have concluded to reduce the amount of postage, by remitting you this through the medium of a newspaper. Very respectfully,

R. H. CHINN.

Gen. L- Combe, Lexington, Ky.

HYMN OF THE ALAMO.

AIR, "MARSEILLES HYMN,"

"Rise, man the wall, our clarion's blast
Now sounds its final revellie;
This dawing morn must be the last
Our fated band shall ever see:—
To life but not to hope, farewell—
Yon trumpet's clang, and cannon's peal,
And storming shout, and clash of steel,
Is ours, but not our country's knell:
Welcome the Spartan's death—
'Tis no despairing strife—
We fall, we die, but our expiring breath
Is freedom's breath of life."

"Here, on this new Thermopylæ,
Our monument shall tower on high,
And 'Alamo' hereafter be
In bloodier fields the battle cry."
Thus Travis from the rampart cried,
And when his warriors saw the foe,
Like angry billows move below,
Each dauntless heart at once replied,
"Welcome the Spartan's death—
'Tis no despairing strife—
We fall, we die, but our expiring breath
Is freedom's breath of life."

They come—like autumn's leaves they fall;
Yet, hordes on hordes, they onward rush;
With gory tramp they scale the wall
Till numbers the defenders crush.
The last was fell'd the fight to gain—
Well may the ruffians quake to tell,
How Travis and his hundred fell,
Amid a thousand foemen slain.
They died the Spartan's death
But not in hopeless strife,
Like brothers died, and their expiring breath
Was freedom's breath of life.

☞ JAMES M. MCGEE will be supported by a majority of the voters of this county, for Sheriff, at the next ensuing election.

INFORMATION WANTED—Of one Marinus Fitch, who left Cincinnati, Ohio, two years ago; or on the 24th of Sept. 1836, bound for Texas. Since that period his friends have not heard from him. He was about 23 or 24 years of age, 5 feet 8 or 9 inches high, black hair and black eyes. His dress good and plain—his habits perfectly moral; and he was acquainted with the dry goods business—could teach school, work on a farm, &c.

N. B.—He was naturally studious and fond of books.

Any information of such a person if communicated to his mother, Eunace Fitch, Pittsford, Monroe county, New York State, or to his brother, Willis O. Fitch, Rochester, New York State, would be most gratefully received and appreciated.

☞ Editors willing to confer a favor on a mourning family will please copy. Dec. 11-tf.

A CARD.

THE citizens of Houston are informed that Maj. S. WHITING, proprietor of the "National Intelligencer," is authorised to act as agent in this place and its vicinity, to receive subscriptions to the "NEW ORLEANS WEEKLY PICAYUNE." Those persons who wish to subscribe to this journal, are requested to call as above, and leave their names. One of the editors of the "Picayune" is now in the city, and is to be found, for a few days, at the office of the "Intelligencer." Dec. 4—40-tf.

CARD—At a meeting of the passengers, convened on board of the steamer COLUMBIA, Capt. Wade, from N. Orleans to Galveston Bay, Dec. 5th, 1838, Benjamin Taliaferro, Esq., of Ala. was called to the Chair, and Henry Baldwin, Esq., of New York, was appointed Secretary.

On motion of Gideon Hall, jr, Esq., of Connecticut, it was—

Resolved, That a Committee of five be appointed to draft and present resolutions expressive of the sense of the meeting; whereupon, G. Hall, jr. Esq., of Connecticut; Maj. Jas. S. Holeman, of Texas; J. W Quarles, Esq. of Virginia; B. Latham, Esq. of New York, and Dr. McAnelly, of Tennessee, were appointed on said Committee.

The Committee, after a short recess, returned, and by their Chairman, G. Hall, jr. Esq., reported the following resolutions which, on motion of H. Baldwin, Esq., were unanimously adopted:

Resolved, That the passengers, on the steamer Columbia, on its passage from N. Orleans to Galveston, on the 5th of Dec. inst., tender to John Wade, Esq., their warmest acknowledgments for the general attention and courtesy which he has shown; for the peace and order which he has maintained; for the neatness, convenience and accommodation of his boat; and for the rich and wholesome provisions of his table.

Resolved, furthermore, That the thanks of this meeting be also tendered to the other officers and crew of said boat, for the fidelity with which they have discharged their respective duties.

On motion of H. Baldwin, Esq. it was then

Resolved, That a copy of the foregoing minutes and resolutions be signed by the Chairman and Secretary, and also by the passengers, and that the same be presented to Capt. Wade, and published in the Texas and New Orleans papers.

The following is a list of passengers on board of the steam-packet Columbia, 50 hours from New Orleans—Mrs. M. A. Crosby, Mrs. Nancy Bonde, Mrs. Barrett & Son, Mrs. Barcharde, Mrs. Blackwell and 3 children, Mrs. Worcester, Mrs. Kelsey, Mrs. E. Conger, Mrs. Dr Forrest and 3 children, Mrs. T. Taylor and child, Mr. T. M. Miller, lady and son, D. Sherman and lady, E. Andrews and lady, Dr. Hartridge, S. Green, S. W. Kernon and servant, J. R. Jones, G. Hall, jr M. Booth, T. Nunn, T. M. Bagby, E. H. Crocket, J. B. Bigelow, G. P. Roberts, S. Folande, Mr. Kimball, F. Penny, R. C. Tood, A. Edwards, B. Latham, P. Phillips, D. Somers, W. Quarles, G. R. Frazer, Wm. O'Connell, A. Conry, H. Whitmore, Capt. Buckner, H. Baldwin, Jas. Goodall, T. R. Quinby, J. L. Doran, J. Dickinson, Maj. Holeman, T. M. Marston, G. W. Brodrick, G. M. Eddy, W. C. V. Dashill, S. M. Elliott, W. D. Turner, Maj. Lagrand, A. Byrne, J. Potter, F. Hunt, P. H. Bonham, John G. Moore, B. Taliaferro, D. S. Thompson, J. W. Blair, J. Scott, O. H. Hughes, E. M. Haynes, R. Mills, A. L. Clements, Dr M'Anelly, L. Young, H. W. Lewis, Wm. Wade, Capt. Ferguson,—34 passengers on deck.

REPUBLIC OF TEXAS,
COUNTY OF MATAGORDA. }

I, THOMAS HARVEY, Deputy Clerk of the Probate Court, in and for the County of Matagorda, do hereby certify that GEORGE COPELAND, has petitioned the Court for Letters of Administration, on the vacant succession of Edmond Huffty; that the same has duly advertised and no opposition filed in this Office.

Given under my hand and seal of Office in the town of Matagorda, the 27th day of June, A. D. 1838. THOS. HARVEY, Deputy Clerk of Probate.

Dec. 4—40-tf.

NOTICE.

PURSUANT to the second section of the "Act to provide for settlement of deceased soldiers estates," passed 18th May, 1838, requiring administrators to give sixty days notice, the undersigned is the lawful administrator of the estate of Washington Roward, deceased.

Dec. 4—44-8t. JOHN TEAL, Adm'r.

NOTICE.

MR. A. THOMPSON, Consignee of fifty Ploughs, received per Schr. Wolcott from New York, is requested to call or send for them at our office at Galveston, and pay freight and take them away. VANWINKLE BROTHERS.

Dec. 4—40-3t. Consignees of Schr. Wolcott.

Republic of Texas,
County of Nacogdoches, } *Court of Probates.*

WHEREAS, William Brunbey has filed his petition in the Probate Court of said County, praying for letters of administration on the estate of Horatio Daniels, a deceased soldier of the Army of Texas.

Notice is hereby given to all persons interested, to come forward at the November Term of said Court, and shew cause, if any they have, why the prayer of the petition should not be granted.

DANIEL LACEY,
Clerk of Probate Court.

September 28, 1838. 26--t

PROFESSIONAL.

Law Notice.

A. S. Thruston will attend the District Courts of Liberty, Brazoria and Richmond, and the Courts of this city. Office in Houston.
August 3 18-tf.

LAW NOTICE.

S. B. FIELDS, Attorney at Law, Lagrange, Fayette county, Texas. Refer to the Hon. Wm. M. Shepherd, Major G. W. Bonnell, and Gen. D. Y. Portis, Houston.
September 21. 1838. 25-tf.

LAW NOTICE.

JOHN R. REID, Attorney and Counsellor at Law, Office over the Auction Store of Hedenberg & Vedder, Houston Texas.
September 28, 1838. 26-tf

☞Telegraph will please copy and publish 12 weeks.

Thomas J. Rusk & James Reily,
ATTORNIES AND COUNSELLORS AT LAW,
HOUSTON CITY—Texas;

☞ Office with J. A. Newland, Notary Public. ☜
Gen. Rusk will be in this city so soon as the difficulties in the East will permit him. Nov. 6,—32-tf.

Law Notice.

J. H. HERNDON, will practice in the Courts of the Second Judicial District, comprising the counties of Brazoria, Fort Bend, Harrisburg, Austin, Colorado, and Matagorda, and the Supreme Court of the Republic.
Office in Richmond. [Aug. 17—19-tf.

J. H. HERNDON,

COUNSELLOR AND ATTORNEY AT LAW—Richmond, (Texas,) References:—Gen. M. Hunt, Dr. L. Jones, Col. James Love, Wm Jefferson Jones, Houston. [Nov. 30—39-tf.

LAW NOTICE.

PORTIUS & TARPLEY—Attorneys and Councellors at Law. Office over Hedenberg & Veeder's Auction Store, in the City of Houston, at which place one or both may always be found unless professionally absent.
August 24, 1838. 22—tf

Wm. H. Jack, P. C. Jack & Robert J. Towns,

HAVE associated in the Practice of the Law, under the style of JACK & TOWNS. Their offices are kept at Houston and Brazoria.

Reference,
Doswell & Adams, Houston.
McKinney & Williams, Galveston.
Mills & Burnett, } Brazoria.
Edmond Andrews, }
Wm. M. Beal, } New-Orleans.
James Reed & Co. }
Hon. Abner L. Lipscomb, Mobile.
Judge Wm. Vannerson, } Natchez.
Judge George Coalter, } aug.24-21-tf

Notary Public's Office.

THE subscriber having been appointed Notary Public for the county of Harrisburg, is ready at all business hours to execute any notorial acts, for those who may need services. Deeds, powers of Attornies, contracts and instruments of all kinds, done with accuracy and despatch. W. FAIRFAX GRAY.
Attorney at Law.

☞Office on Travis street, near the Capitol.
June 29—13-tf.

DOCT. TUCKER,

Respectfully tenders his Professional Services to the Public. He can generally be found at Captain Brunough's Store.
Houston, May 8, 1838. 3—tf

DR. CARAWAY,
Surgeon Dentist;

HAVING located in Houston, offers his professional services to the public. He performs every operation pertaining to Dental Surgery upon scientific principles. He cleans, files, plugs, levels, separates, extracts, and inserts, natural or porcelian teeth so as to appear natural.

☞Office with Dr. Dunn, in Sanderson's building on Main street adjoining the City Hotel.
Nov. 2, 31-tf.

Drugs, Medicines & Stationary.
COOK & EWING

RESPECTFULLY inform their friends and the public that they have now on hand, and will keep constantly, a general assortment of *Drugs* and *Medicines.*

All orders from the country will be punctually attended to, and Physician's prescriptions put up with accuracy and dispatch.

We have received per Columbia, a splendid assortment of Stationary, including English Letter, and Note Paper, Visiting Cards, &c.
April 25, 1838. 1:tf

BOOK-BINDERY,
HOUSTON.

THE SUBSCRIBER is prepared to receive and execute orders for Binding Books, of every description with taste, neatness and despatch.
LEDGERS, JOURNALS, DAY-BOOKS,
RECORD, BILL, RECEIPT,
And all kinds of *BLANK BOOKS*, made, bound and ruled, to any pattern that may be desired.
S. WHITING,
Government Printer, Intelligencer office.

INTELLIGENCER OFFICE.

LITHOGRAPHING
In all its Branches,
Maps of Cities and Towns, Letters, Circulars, Cards, Labels, Legal Notices, Bank Notes, Blank Checks, Bill-Forms,
And every description of
Work on Stone
Done in the most neat and expeditious manner.

BOOK AND JOB PRINTING.
Splendid extensive assortment of
TYPE,

For the printing of

Pamphlets.	Blank Deeds of Sale,
Catalogues,	Powers of Attorney,
Receipts,	Blank Bonds,
Notes,	Summonses,
Oaths of Allegiance,	Subpœnas,
Auction Bills,	Mortgages,
Circulars,	Transfers,
Show Bills,	Certificates,
Steamboat Bills,	Warrants,

&c. &c. &c.

All kinds of Blanks on hand and for sale as above.

Every description of Job Work that may be required, will meet with despatch, and on the most accommodating terms. Acts of the last Session of Congress are published at this Office. All orders for Book or Job Work of any kind, will be thankfully received and prompfly executed on application to
S. WHITING.
Houston, Nov. 2, 1838. Publisher, &c.

AWRENCE & HILL,

NO. 37 Camp street, New Orleans, are constantly supplied wit a full and complete assortmenf of every artical of PRINTING MATERIALS, Presses, Type, Ink, and Furniture of every discription, on the most accommodating terms.
Nov. 20 39-tf.

PROBATE SALE.

BY virtue of a decree from the Honorable Probate Court, for the county of Brazoria, I shall offer for sale on Saturday the 8th December, at the premises, near Francis Bingham's, all the personal property belonging to the estate of Achilles M'Farlan, deceased.

Terms—Cash for all sums under twenty dollars, and twelve months' credit, with good security, for all sums above that amount.
WM. P. SCOTT,
Probate Judge,
Brazoria, November 15, 1838. 33-tds

PROBATE NOTICE.
Republic of Texas—County of Harrisburg.

NOTICE is hereby given, in accordance with a law "toprovide for the settlement of deceased soldier's estates;" that I have heretofore applied for, and obtainedfrom the Probate Court of the aforesaid county, Letters of Administration on the estate of Robert Toler, a deceased soldier.
JNO. TURNER.
Houston, Oct. 4, 1838. 27—tf

PROBATE SALE.

BY virtue of a decree of the Honorable Probate Court for the county of Brazoria, I shall offer for sale at the door of the Court House on Monday the 10th December next, the following property, belonging to the estate of G. B. M'Kinstry, deceased, viz: The half Lot No. 1, in Block No. 13; and Lot 5, in Block No. 23. Terms—One half on 1st January next, and the remainder in six months, with bond and security.
WM. P. SCOTT, Probate Judge.
Brazoria, November 15, 1838. 38-tds

PROBATE SALE.

BY virtue of a decree of the Honorable Probate Court of Brazoria, I shall offer for sale at the door of the Court House, in Brazoria, on Monday the 10th day of December next, the following property, belonging to the estate of Abraham Durst, deceased. to wit: Two hundred acres of Land lying on the Mound League, twelve miles above Columbia, on a credit until 1st January next.

Bond and security will be required, and a mortgage on the premises, until final payment WM. P. SCOTT,
Probate Judge.
Brazoria, November 15, 1838. 38-td

CITY HOTEL.

THE subscribers under the firm of Henry Levenhagen & Co., beg leave to inform the public, that they have purchased of Messrs. Floyd & Collins the above establishment. The house has undergone a perfect repair---the proprietors will spareno pains nor expenses to make the same as comfortable as can be expected, and are ready now to receive travellers and boarders.

The stable will likewise be much improved---the best of attendance to horses, and the best of provender will be provided for. FERDINAND GEFLACH,
HENRY LEVENHAGEN.
Houston, September 14, 1838. 24—tf

Austin House.

THE proprietors of this Hotel having made such alterations and improvements as are necessary to the comfort of their Guests, are now prepared to receive them. Visitors will at all times find the comforts of life and as many of the luxuries as can reasonably be expected in a country so new. To the invalid more particularly, the town of Quintana offers all that can be desired, *health*; its situation upon the Gulf rendering it one of the most delightful and healthy resorts during the Summer months to be found in Texas.
SETTLE & WILLIAMS.
Quintana June 29, 13-tf.

TEXAS BOARDING HOUSE,
68 ROYAL STREET,
New Orleans.
Oct. 26, 30-tf.

Last Call.

ALL persons indebted to the subscribers, that don't intend paying us Cash, must call and settle their accounts by note, as travelling expenses are too high for us to wait on them with their accounts.
MARTIN CLOW & CO.
Columbia, June 1st, 1838—11-tf.

AUCTION HALL—GENERAL AGENCY,
Forwarding and Commission House,
No. 9 Main Street—Houston,
Under the immediate direction and sole control of
G. EVERETTE,

Who, from his many years practical experience as an Auctioneer, and in other mercantile capacity, flatters himself fully qualified to discharge all business entrusted him, to the entire satisfaction of all concerned.

References—His Excellency Sam Houston, Hon. S. H. Everitt, Hon. Robert Wilson, Messrs. Blackwell & Allen, Galveston; S. Newall, Esq., Galveston; Messrs. Ranlett & Co. and W. S. Johnson, Esq., New Orleans.
Aug. 17 19-tf

LAND AGENCY, BEXAR.

THE undersigned will attend to the buying, selling and locating of Lands in the County of Bexar, for all those who may wish to entrust him with their business. He has resided many years in the country, is well acquainted with every section of it; is a resident citizen of San Antonio De Bexar, and acquainted with all the original inhabitants and their language.

Terms reasonable.
July 6—tf HORATIO A. ALSBURY

City of Victoria.

ON the 15th day of August next, will be exposed for Public Sale, about
300 Building Lots, in this City.

Terms:—One quarter Cash, at the time of sale, the balance in equal payments of 6 and 12 months, secured by bond and mortgage on the property; the purchaser to pay the expense of conveyance, and to forfeit any instalments paid, should the terms not be complied with.

For general information, it may be necessary to observe, that *Victoria* possesses a Four League City Tract, unappropriated, 25 miles from the Espiritu and Matagorda Bays, and beautifully situated on the Guadaloupe River, which meanders through, dividing it in nearly equal parts. There is a large quantity of Timber on the river, which is navigable 25 miles above the town site; the water is good; the situation high and healthy. A Steam Saw and Grist Mill will shortly be in operation, and there is every facility and the best material for establishing a Brick Yard.

The County of Victoria is equally distant from the Sabine and Rio Grande, consequently is the most central part of the Republic. It enjoys a soil and climate equal to any other portion of Texas; is supplied abundantly with the best of water, and contains a large variety of the finest description of Timber.

Maps of the City are in preparation, and will shortly be laid before the public.
J. A. MOODY, Mayor.
City of Victoria, May 26, 1338—July 20-tf.

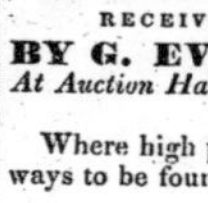
Horses, Mules,
Live Stock, Carriages
Waggons & Carts,
Farming Utensils, &c.
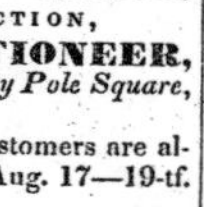

RECEIVED AND SOLD AT AUCTION,
BY G. EVERETTE, AUCTIONEER,
At Auction Hall No 9 Main street, Liberty Pole Square,
HOUSTON;

Where high prices and ready cash customers are always to be found waiting. [Aug. 17—19-tf.

WANTED,

AS an Apprentice to the Printing business, a boy 14 or 15 years of age, who can read and write and come well re-commended for moral and industrious habits. Apply at this office.
September 7, 1838. 23.

NOTICE.

THE Office of A. C. Allen, and the Office of the Houston Town Company, are now kept across the Bayou, at the Office of the Texas Steam Mill Company.
Nov. 6, 1838. 32-tf

NOTICE.

ALL persons having unsettled business with the firm of A. C. & J. K. Allen, and J. K. Allen, deceased, will please call on A. C. Allen surviving partner and settle the same, at his office in the office of the Texas Steam Mill Company.
November 6, 1838. 32-tf

Notice.

THE undersigned having been appointed Administrator, by the Hon. the Probate Court of Victoria County, on the Estate of Joshua Davis, deceased, intestate,—all persons having claims against the Estate are requested to present the same, duly authenticated, within the time prescribed by law, or they will not be attended to; and all persons indebted to the said Estate are notified by this publication, to pay their respective amounts immediately. JOHN DUNN
Aug. 10. 19-6m. Executor.

Notice.

ALL persons indebted to the Estate of John H. Cummins, deceased, are hereby notified to make immediate payment; and those having claims against said estate, will present them legally authenticated, within the time prescribed by law.
ELIZABETH BETHEA,
JOHN BETHEA,
F. W. JOHNSON,
Administrators.
Montgomery, May 26, 1838. 9-tf

NOTICE.

THE Carpenters Business of Daniels & Muncus will be continued under the same name as heretofore, R. R. Muncus acting as agent for Capt. Daniels during his absence, and the patronage of the public respectfully solicited.
DANIELS & MUNCUS.
Nov. 20, 36-3t.

NOTICE.

ALL those indebted to the subscriber by note or on account, will call at his office over his former store room now occupied by Dr. Everette, and settle the same, as no longer indulgence can be given; those having claims against the undersigned will present them for payment. J. G. Hutchinson is authorised to receipt for me, who can always be found at the above place.
WM. M. COOKE.
Nov. 23, 27-tf

Notice.

PERSONS wishing to obtain Lumber from the Steam Mill Company, are requested to present their orders for the same in writing, at the office of the Company. Orders will be uniformly filled up according to their dates. Several thousand feet of Roof-Boards on hand and for sale. Enquire at the Office of the Company.
Houston, June 7, 1838. 10—tf.

NOTICE.

Republic of Texas, }
Washington County }

HAVING been appointed by the Honorable Judge of the Probate Court of the aforesaid county, administrator on the estate of George Washington Daniell, late an officer in the regiment of Col. Fannin In compliance with an act of Congress in such cases made and provided, I hereby notify all persons indebted to said succession, to make immediate payment, and those having claims against said estate, are requested to present them duly authenticated, within the term prescribed by law, or they will be barred. H. BUTLER, Administrator.
November 21, 1838. 2m

ADMINISTRATOR'S NOTICE.

PURSUANT to the Second Section of an Act entitled an "Act for the setlement of the estates of deceased soldiers;" I, the second time, notify all persons concerned, that I have been appointed Administrator of the estates of E. D. Harrison, and J. S. K. Harrison, deceased soldiers of the Texian Army.
ACHILLES L. HARRISON, *Administrator.*
Sept. 20, 1838. 27—4t

NOTICE.

THIS is to certify that I have this day appointed Capt. W. Pierpont my lawful Agent and Attorney in the Republic of Toxas. All persons indebted to me are required to make payment to him, and any person having any business with me, can transact the same with my said agent. CLARK WOOSTER.
Houston, June 6—11-tf.

Republic of Texas, } In District Court,
County of Victoria. } September Term, 1838.

IN the case of John F. McGuffin, against Fernando De Leon, in an attachment upon the lands and tenements of the defendant, it is ordered by the Court that publication of the pendency of this suit be made in one of the public Gazettes published in this Republic, for six weeks, to be made at least two months prior to the next term of this Court, to be held on the third Monday in March next, that unless the defendant appear and answer on or before that time, the petition of plaintiff will be taken as confessed, and the lands attached will be sold to satisfy the same.

By order of the Court.
A true copy from the minutes.
J. A. MOODEY,
Deputy District Clerk, C. V.
Oct. 19, 29-tf.

Repulic of Texas, } In District Court,
County of Victoria, } SeptemberTerm, 1838.

IN the case of John S. Menifee and George Sutherland against Fernando De Leon, in an attachment upon the lands and tenements of the defendant, it is ordered by the Court that publication of the pendency of this suit be made in one of the public Gazettes published in this Republic, for six weeks, to be made at least two months prior to the next term of this Court, to be held on the third Monday in March next, that unless the defendant appear and answer on or before that time, the petition of plaintiff will be taken as confessed, and the lands attached will be sold to satisfy the same.

By order of the Court.
A true copy from the minutes.
J. A. MOODEY,
Deputy District Clerk, C. V.
Oct. 19, 29-tf.

Republic of Texas, } In District Court,
County of Victoria, } September Term, 1838.

IN the case of Thomas Menifee against Fernando De Leon, in an attachment upon the lands and tenements of the defendant, it is ordered by the Court that publication of the pendency of this suit be made in one of the public Gazettes published in this Republic, for six weeks, to be made at least two months prior to the next term of this Court, to be held on the third Monday in March next, that unless the defendant appear and answer on or before that time, the petition of plaintiff will be taken as confessed, and the lands attached will be sold to satisfy the same.

By order of the Court.
A true copy from the minutes.
J. A. MOODEY,
Deputy District Clerk, C. V.
Oct. 29, 29 tf.

Republic of Texas, }
County of Nacogdoches, } *Court of Probates.*

WHEREAS, William Brunbey has filed his petition in the Probate Court of said County, praying for letters of administration on the estate of Horatio Daniels, a deceased soldier of the Army of Texas.

Notice is hereby given to all persons interested, to come forward at the November Term of said Court, and shew cause, if any they have, why the prayer of the petition should not be granted.
DANIEL LACEY,
Clerk of Probate Court.
September 28, 1838. 26--t

$5,000 REWARD.

ON the night of the 7th February last, my Gin and Mill, to-gether with 100 bales of Cotton, were burnt. The door of the Gin House was broken open, and the foot-tracks of strangers were discovered in the vicinity of the building—furnishing indubitable evidence that it was the work of an incendiary. My relations with my fellow men, generally, are of such a nature that this act can be ascribed to one or two individuals alone; but I am not able to fix upon any one with certainty. I will therefore give the above reward of $5,000 for such information as will lead to the discovery of the wretch who perpetrated this infamous deed. I am satisfied that the individual who caused the burning employed others to do it, and I will hold harmless the informer, though he may have been a participator in the act.
WARREN D. C. HALL.
China Grove, June 27, 1838—jy 27-tf

$100 REWARD.

RANAWAY from my wagon at Mr. Hodges', 19 miles from Houston, about the 25th instant, a negro man named DOSSON, aged about 25 years black, complexion, about 5½ feet high, stout built, took with him a double barrel shot gun, and a bundle of clothes. Any person taking up said negro, and lodging him in jail for safe keeping, so as I may get him, or deliver him to me in the town of Matagorda, will receive the above reward. JAMES W. LANN.
Matagorda Sept. 22, 1838. 27--tf

$20 *Reward!*

STOLEN, from the Prairie near the city of Houston, a dark sorrel Horse, 6 years old, a small white spot in his forehead, one white hind foot, a small brand on his left shoulder, and new shoes on his fore feet. Twenty Dollars in Promissory Notes of the Government, or specie if required, will be given for the horse, and One Bit in shin plasters badly torn, for the thief, if delivered to Mr. Jackson at the Livery Stable, in Houston, or to the subscriber at La Grange.
MUSGROVE EVANS.
May 11, 1838. 5---tf

REWARD!

ONE hundred dollars reward will be given by me for the apprehension and delivery of my negro boy BOB, who is supposed to have been stolen from Washington by a white man, on the night of Monday, the first of October.

Said boy is a mulatto, about five feet four inches high, aged 32 years; he has a downcast look when spoken to, and is considerably bow legged.

I will give the above reward for the delivery of said slave, to me at Washington; and three hundred dollars for the detection of the thief, so that he may be dealt with according to law.
JEREMIAH CLOWD.
Oct. 12, 28-tf.

Treasury Department, }
City of Houston, 27th Oct. 1838. }

TEXAS PROMISSORY NOTES COUNTERFEITED.

THE public are hereby cautioned against the receipt of the Promissory Notes of Texas of the old issue in the printed form. The aptitude of swindlers in their avocation has become so great as to render it difficult for even the most skillful to determine between the genuine and counterfeit, of the old notes in that form. All collectors of public revenue are hereby notified and forbid to receive under any circumstances, notes of that description. And all persons holding such are requested to present them to this Department as they may fall due, where alone they can be properly scrutinized and redeemed by the engraved notes, and the interest paid.

However inconvenient this may be o the public, or however much they may suffer from this fraud, or however arbitrary this course may seem, I feel warranted as a public officer to pursue any course which would be best calculated to protect the Government from the ruinous frauds which would otherwise be practised.—And, inasmuch as this evil has grown out of measures which were originated and forced on the Department by the representatives of the people, it is confid ntly hoped that they, the people, will submit to and divide the evil among themselves, without reflection on this Department for assuming an attitude of self defence.
HENRY SMITH,
31 Secretary of the Treasury.

REMOVAL.

GEORGE STEVENS most respectfully informs his friends, customers, and the public generally, that he nas removed from where he formerly kept to the next door above that lately occupied by John Carlos, Esq., the second door above Mr. League's Houston House, where he will always keep as usual a general assortment of GOODS, and respectfully invites the public to call.

He will also attend to the general Storage, Forwarding and Commission business, which will be strictly attended to.
May 8, 1838.—3:tf

10,000 ACRES Bounty Land for sale at a low price, by
S. WHITING.

A CARD.

WE return our thanks to the citizens of Texas for the very liberal manner with which they have hitherto dealt with us, and solicit a continuation of their custom. They will always find at our establishment the best quality of every article in our line of business, and at fair prices. As we sell no garment except of our own make we warrant them in every respect; and should any article sold by us prove defective, it may be returned, and the price paid for it will be refunded, if required. Our stock comprises Dress Coats, Frocks, Pantaloons, Vests, Over-Coats, Cloaks, Drawers, Under-Shirts of Silk, Lambs Wool, Flannel and Cotton; also, fine Linen, Cotton, and Gingham Shirts, Socks, Stocks, Hdkfs. Gloves, Suspenders, Russian Robes, Russian Riding Belts, Silk & Beaver Hats, Umbrellas, Life-Preservers, Leather Travelling Trunks, Carpet Travelling Bags, and in short, every fashionable and useful article usually kept in clothing stores, to which we invite the attention of gentlemen wanting any article in our line. Orders promptly attended to:—Texas money taken at a fair rate.
ST. JOHN FABRE & Co.,
Corner of Camp and Canal Street, N. Orleans.
10-6m.

WEATHER BOARDING, &c.

2,000 feet Weather Boarding and Sheating, for sale Enquire at this office.
Nov. 2

Steamer "Correo."

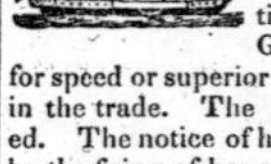

THE steamboat "Correo," H. Ferguson, master, will ply three times a week between this city and Galveston. She is not sur passed for speed or superior accommodations by any other boat in the trade. The strictest punctuality will be observed. The notice of her departure from either place will be the firing of her gun, and within one half hour from that time she starts.

☞ For freight or passage, apply on board or to
DOSWELL, ADAMS & CO, *Houston*,
Aug. 17.

LIQUORS, &c.

CHAMPAGNE and Claret Wines, Cider, Ale, and Raspberry Brandy in boxes; Raisins, Figs, Filberts, Pepper Sauce, Cayenne and Black Pepper, Starch, Lamp-black, Linseed and Lamp Oil, Wine biscuit, Water Crackers, &c., for sale by
Dec. 4—44-tf. WM. PIERPONT.

NAILS, Glass, Log Trace and Halter Chains, and Collins' Axes—just received and for sale by
Dec. 4—44-tf. WM. PIERPONT.

Moffat's Life Pills and Phœnix Bitters.

GENERAL REMARKS.—These medicines have long been known and appreciated, for their extraordinary and immediate powers of restoring perfect health to persons suffering under nearly every kind of disease to which the human frame is liable.

In many hundreds of certificated instances, they have even rescued sufferers from the very verge of an untimely grave, after all the deceptive nostrums of the day had utterly failed; and to many thousands they have permanently secured that uniform enjoyment of health, without which life itself is but a partial blessing. So great, indeed, has their efficacy invariably and infallibly proved, that it has appeared scarcely less than miraculous to those who were unacquainted with the beautifully philosophical principles upon which they are compounded, and upon which they consequently act. It was to their manifest and sensible action in purifying the springs and channels of life, and enduring them with renewed tone and vigor, that they were indebted for their name, which was bestowed upon them at the spontaneous request of several individuals whose lives they had obviously saved.

The proprietor rejoices in the opportunity afforded by the universal diffusion of the daily press, for placing his Vegetable Life Pills within the knowledge and reach of every individual in the community. Unlike the host of pernicious quackeries, which boast of vegetable ingredients, the Life Pills are purely and *solely vegetable*, and contain neither Mercury, Antimony, Arsenic, nor any other mineral, in any form whatever. They are entirely composed of extracts from rare and powerful plants, the virtues of which, though long known to several Indian tribes, and recently to some eminent pharmaceutical chemists, are altogether unknown to the ignorant pretenders to medical science; and were never before administered in so happily efficacious a combination.

Their first operation is to loosen from the coats of the stomach and bowels, the various impurities and crudities constantly settling around them; and to remove the hardened fæces which collect in the convolutions of the small intestines. Other medicines only partially cleanse these, and leave such collected masses behind, as to produce habitual costiveness, with all its train of evils; or sudden diarrhœa, with its imminent dangers. This fact is well known to all regular anatomists, who examine the human bowels after death: and hence the prejudice of these well informed men against the quack medicines of the day. The second effect of the Vegetable Life Pills is to cleanse the kidneys and the bladder, and by this means, the liver and the lungs, the healthful action of which entirely depends upon the regularity of the urinary organs. The blood, which takes its red colors from the agency of the liver and the lungs before it passes into the heart, being thus purified by them, and nourished by food coming from a clean stomach, courses freely through the veins, renews every part of the system, and triumphantly mounts the banner of health in the blooming cheek.

The following are among the distressing variety of human diseases, to which the Vegetable Life Pills are well known to be infallable:—

Dyspepsia, by thoroughly cleansing the first and second stomachs, and creating a flow of pure healthy bile, instead of the stale and acrid kind;—Flatulency, Palpitation of the Heart, Loss of Appetite, Heart-burn and Headache, Restlessness, Ill-temper, Anxiety, Languor, and Melancholy, which are the general symptoms of Dyspepsia, will vanish, as a natural consequence of its cure. Costiveness, by cleansing the whole length of the intestines with a solvent process, and without violence; all violent purges leave the bowels costive within two days. Diarrhœa and Cholera, by removing the sharp acrid fluids by which these complaints are occasioned, and by promoting the lubricative secretion of the mucous membrans. Fevers of all kinds, by restoring the blood to a regular circulation, through the process of perspiration in some cases, and the through solution of all intestinal obstructions in others. The LIFE PILLS have been known to cure Rheumatism permanently in three weeks, and Gout in half that time, by removing local inflamation from the muscles and ligaments of the joints. Dropsies of all kinds, by freeing and strengthening the kidneys and bladder; they operate most delightfully on these important organs and hence have ever been found a certain remedy for the worst cases of Gravel. Also, Worms, by dislodging from the turnings of the bowels the slimy matter to which these creatures adhere; Asthma and Consumption, by relieving the air vessels of the lungs from the mucus, which even slight colds will occasion, whichif not removed, becomes hardened, and produces those dreadful diseases. Scurvy, Ulcers, and Inveterate Sores, by the perfect purity which these Life Pills give to the blood, and all the humors; Scorbutic Eruptions, and Bad Complexions, by their alterative effect upon the fluids that feed the skin, the morbid state of which occasions all Eruptive complaints, Sallow, Cloudy, and other disagreeable Complexions. The use of these Pills for a very short time, will effect an entire cure of Salt rheum Erysipelas, and a striking improvement in the Clearness of the skin. Common Colds and Influenza, will always be cured by one dose, or by two, even in the worst cases. Piles,—as a remedy for this most distressing and obstinate malady, the Vegetable Life Pills deserve a distinct and emphatic recommendation. It is well known to hundreds in this city, that the Proprietor of these invaluable Pills, was himself afflicted with this complaint upwards of thirty-five years, and that he tried in vain every remedy prescribed within the whole compass of the Materia Medica. He, however, at length, tried the medicine which he now offers to the public, and was cured in a very short time, after his recovery had been pronounced not only improbable, but absolutely impossible, by any human means.

DIRECTIONS FOR USE.

The proprietor of the "Vegetable Life Pills" does not follow the base and mercenary practice of the quacks of the day, in advising persons to take his pills in large quantities. No good medicine can possibly be so required. These pills are to be taken at bed time every night, for a week or fortnight, according to the obstinacy of the disease. The usual dose is from 2 to 5, according to the constitution of the person Very delicate persons shall begin with two, and increase as the nature of the case may require: those more robust, or of very costive habit, may begin with 3, and increase to 4, or even 5 pills, and they will effect a sufficiently happy change to guide the patient in their further use. These pills sometimes occasion sickness and vomiting, though very seldom, unless the stomach is very foul; this, however, may be considered a favorable symptom, as the patient will find himself at once relieved, and by perseverence will soon recover. They usually operate within 10 or 12 hours, and never give pain unless the bowels are very much encumbered. They may be taken by the most delicate females under any circumstances. It is, however, recommended, that those in later periods of pregnancy should take but one at a time, and thus continue to keep the bowels open: and even two may be taken where the patient is very costive. One in a solution of two table spoons full of water, may be given to infants in the following doses—a tea spoon full every two hours till it operates; for a child from one to five years of age, half a pill—and from five to ten, one pill.

The Phœnix Bitters, are so called, because they possess the power of restoring the expiring embers of health, to a glowing vigor throughout the constitution, as the Phœnix is said to be restored to life from the ashes of its own dissolution. The Phœnix Bitters are entirely vegetable, composed of roots found only in certain parts of the western country, which, will infallibly cure Fevers and Agues of all kinds; will never fail to eradicate entirely all the effects of Mercury, infinitely sooner than the most powerful preparations of Sarsaparilla, and will immediately cure the determination of blood to the head; never fail in the sickness incident to young females: and will be found a certain remedy in all cases of nervous debility and weakness of the most impaired constitutions. As a remedy for Chronic and Inflammatory Rheumatism, the efficacy of the Phœnix Bitters will be demonstrated by the use of a single bottle. The usual dose of those is half a wine gloss full, in water or wine, and this quantity may be taken two or three times a day, about half an hour before meals, or a less quantity may be taken at all times. To those who are afflicted with idigestion after meals, these Bitters will prove invaluable, as they very greatly increase the action of the principal viscera, help them to perform their functions, and enable the stomach to discharge into the bowels whatsoever is offensive. Thus indigestion is easily and speedily removed, appetite restored, and the mouths of the absorbent vessels being cleansed, untrition is facilitated, and strength of body and energy of mind are the happy results. For farther particulars of Moffat's Life Pills, and Phœnix Bitters, apply to COOKE & EWING,
Druggists, Main street—Houston.

☞ Numerous certificates of the wonderful efficacy of both, may be there inspected.

In some obstinate and complicated cases of chronic and inflammatory Rheumatism, Liver Complaints, Fever and Ague, Dyspepsia, Palsy, Piles, injuries from the use of mercury, quinine, and other diseases of long standing, it may be found necessary to take both the Life Pills and the Phœnix Bitters, in the doses before recommended.

N. B.—These Pills and the Bitters will get all mercury out of the system infinitely faster than the best preparations of Sarsaparilla, and are a certain remedy for the rushing of blood to the head, or all violent headaches, tic douleureux, &c. All persons who are predisposed to apoplexy, palsy, &c., should never be without the Life Pill or the Bitters, for one dose in time will save life. They equalize the circulation of the blood, draw all pressure from the head, restore perspiration, and throw off every impurity by the pores of the skin. [Sept. 14. 24--tf.

SAMUEL SMITH & CO,

HAVING taken the stand recently occupied by C. C. Dibble & Co., on Main street, nearly opposite the City Hotel, offer for sale the following Goods on reasonable terms. They will be constantly receiving supplies of Goods of every description, and request their friends and fellow citizens to call and examiue for themselves:

25 Superfine broad-cloth dress Coats,
25 Elegant fancy Silk Vests, of superior quality,
4 Dozen fine Linen Shirts,
3 do Ruffled do, do,
6 do fine Linen Collars,
2[illegible] Pair Silk Bombazine Pants,
6 Dozen fancy silk Stocks,
3 do white and colored Bosoms,
4 do fine Drilling, Nankeen and Linen Pantaloons,
2 do Crimson Silk Handkerchiefs,
1 do Plaid do,
2 do half Hoes, (silk.)
2 do Roundabouts and Coatees,
1 do fine Sattin Stocks,
10 do Linen Cambric Hdkfs., colored borders,
20 do do do embroidered,
Saddles, Bridles and Martingales,

With an assortment of Groceries, Shoes, Boots, Hats and Hardware. They are prepared and have made arrangements to receive Goods on consignment, and persons consigning goods to them may rely on prompt settlement, and all orders will be thankfully received.
Dec. 4—40-tf.

Columbian Register.

EQUAL AND EXACT JUSTICE TO ALL MEN, OF WHATEVER STATE OR PERSUASION RELIGIOUS OR POLITICAL.—*Jefferson.*

Vol. XXVIII. | New-Haven, Conn. Saturday, February 15. 1840. | No. 1421.

Glorious chance for Girls.—It is well known that the Government of Texas, to encourage emigration from the United States, have offered a handsome bounty in land to any female who shall marry a citizen of Texas. A lady of Mobile, wishing to have a little more light on the subject, and to find out if possible what sort of an animal she would be required to wed, in order to obtain the land, addressed the editor of the Galvestonian for information. To all her questions he gives straightforward answers. He says that on the reception of the letter, he called a meeting of bachelors, and there was not one of them but agreed, in case an importation should be sent out to take and provide for at least one: and one chap went so far as to offer to take *six*, if they could do no better. As to the comeatability and quality of the land, he says that it will not come to them, but they can go and find it as good as ever lay out of doors, and well adaqted for raising soldiers, cabbages, lawyers, potatoes, pumpkins, cotton, sugar, dandies, ladies, babies, pigs, and chickens. Girls, Texas is the place. Pack up your dudds, take your knitting work, and be off in the first boat.

THE ILLUSTRATED LONDON NEWS

No. 6.] FOR THE WEEK ENDING SATURDAY, JUNE 18, 1842. [SIXPENCE.

[redacted]

PUBLIC DISTRESS.

It is a sad but too sure consequence of public calamity, of whatever kind, that the greatest pressure of its misery should, in almost every instance of human endurance, fall most heavily upon the poor. A larger amount of injustice—more farspread wrong—heavier sacrifices, and more unequal burthens, may be borne by the rich under any of the evil circumstanees of imperfect human legislation; but still, in any condition where society is well ordered—in any state short of anarchy or revolution—the maximum of personal and general suffering inflicted by the sins of the nation, the visitations of Providence, or the misfortunes of the time, is invariably endured be the classes to whom poverty is more familiar than plenty, and whose philosophy should be of that severe school which preaches "contentment under want." This evil is inherent in the nature of society, and the only barriers that communities and legislatures have been able to set up in amelioration of the condition of the lower and poorer classes, have consisted in a provision of means of employment to ensure comfort—in a cheapening of the ordinary *pabulum* of the labouring population—a system of emigration when the land is overpeopled—a redress of crying grievances engendered by any grown corruptions—a voice in the legislature for those to whom honest industry has brought the reward of toil—public schools, charities, and hospitals—and lastly, poor laws to guard against destitution, and punishments to check crime. There may be sects in society that will not admit of beggars—but there can be no great community without more poor than rich:—the wealthiest people are the fewest—the middle classes, ranging through all the channels of commerce, from retired enjoyment down to struggling, plodding work,—exceed the wealthier ranks in numbers (and perhaps in influence too under monarchical forms of Government); but the poor—the useful serving people of the land, the labourers, the artificers, the toilers for their daily bread—these make up the millions, to which the two other divisions of society only bear the proportions of thousands and hundreds, and by these the oppressions of public crime or affliction are always most practically felt. It is true that the pain recoils—that by the very sympathies of our nature, the suffering of the multitude is re-diffused through the whole social system, and becomes part of the common woe; but this affords only another reason why, when all the ordinary precautions of society have failed, when law is inefficient to stem the torrent of destitution, and when Famine, in spite of human foresight, stands and shivers under the lap of Luxury, and beneath the eye of Wealth, the energies of a nation ought to be invoked and active, and all men be taught to feel the claims, the importance, and the consequences of public distress.

We are led into these remarks by a reflective view of the aspect of the events of the times, as they follow each other with startling rapidity and effect. We do not write in a radical spirit, far from it. We are the advocates of religion, order, and the laws; but our politics are irrespective of all party—the politics of humanity—they are founded upon the high and broad basis of Christian brotherhood; and we are proud in the avowal, that it is our glory to championize the poor. Yet we would warn them also, and, while advocating their interests with the legislature, we would gag and stifle, as a foul and fell mischief, the dangerous doctrine which would seek for a redress of grievances less by the calm and manly appeal of justice, than with the simple clamour of agitating discontent.

The truth, however, is now, forced upon us, that, first, to raise the personal condition, and secondly, to purify the morals of the poor, have become considerations of immediate and paramount necessity; and we cannot refrain from the belief, that the means of gaining these desired ends are ramified through nearly every artery of our domestic policy, and embrace some of the most salient strongholds of our constitutional law.

The last winter was a dreadful one for the poor: the spring, while giving new fertilization to the soil, and fresh buds and flowers to the beauty of external nature, has held forth little promise of gladness to the thousands whom Christmas had well nigh starved; and now, in the heart and ripeness of warm and cheerful summer, the rags of misery are still fluttering to its breeze, and the voice of poverty is mocking the plenty of its reign. The workhouses are full—this is dreadful; but the prisons are full also, and this is worse. The cry for corn has swollen by hunger into the howling of the wolf, and the "clap-trap" of "cheap bread" has been almost made sacred by the bitter arguments of want. In the sister Kingdom dreadful riots have ensued, and at Ennis, in Clare, the tragedy which began with poverty has ended in blood. In our own manufacturing districts the people are pining with famine, and, as it were, under the shadow of death; and although the rich have got up festivities for their benefit, and wealth has opened its purse in their behalf—although benevolence has joined hands with charity, and the pulpit and the throne have spoken with appealing voices to win them succour; still there is a frightful and appalling wretchedness wherever the people swarm, and those who are not visited with the tyranny of the workhouse, or the retribution of the gaol, are either crushed by their misfortunes or only supported by their crimes. Their sufferings and their demoralization are horrible alike.

The poor-laws—the dreadful and distressing poor-laws—here present the ugly grievance which humanity is loudest in its cry to remove.

Again, the factory and mining systems have increased the amount of general pauper wretchedness, with individual horrors and corruptions that have startled the Legislature into action, and will not bear the public gaze.

The bad influences that have been exerted at elections—the frightful mass of bribery and perjury that has been recorded against the people—their desperate carelessness of the obligation of the franchise, and recklessness of honour in its exercise—all these are proofs of an abandonment of principle, which is too often the concomitant of poverty, led into temptation by the possession of a privilege to do wrong, without an impulse to prefer the right:—and *in* all these we find the worst mischiefs of deplorable suffering and growling discontent.

There is in fact, in the condition of the poorer classes, a mixture of sin and sorrow, which we heartily desire to see analyzed and cast away; we blame them less than we pity them—we sympathize more than we condemn; we give great preponderance to their grievances over their crimes, and therefore we invoke the energies of all thinking men and good patriots—we implore a full social consideration of the destitution which has been this year (and still is) climaxed in our land of liberty among the lower classes of our fellow-creatures, and we ardently pray for the exercise of such Divine mercy and human wisdom as shall temper the privations of poverty and make the lowly man sensible of his brotherhood with the rich.

This, we are persuaded, is only to be achieved by searching exposures and diligent political sagacity exercised upon every point of our domestic legislation, and *so* exercised as to make it one o the brightest and purest fountains of the happiness of the empire.

TEXAN MOUNTED MILITIA.

TEXAN MOUNTED MILITIA.

The latest accounts from Texas bring intelligence of threats of an invasion of the independence of that state, and of a probable call of her citizens to arms. The Texans are a young, but a gallant people; they have achieved their freedom with spirit, and now that the country is acknowledged by Great Britain in its separate condition, and that they are beginning to take rank for it as a nation, they will have fresh inducements to uphold their character for courage, firmness, and energy, in any political or warlike struggles in which they may engage. A strong interest has arisen in this country in all that concerns Texas of late years. The land was marked out to English enterprise as one full of temptations to emigration. The climate is salubrious and healthful beyond compare—the soil deliciously fertile—the natural scenery beautiful—the people enterprising, ambitious, and bold. At last the admirable work of Mr. Kennedy, and his vigorous letters in the *Morning Chronicle*, spread a more intimate knowledge of the Texas among the British public, and tended, in no small degree, to confirm the destinies of the country in a national point of view. The long-postponed recognition was given by the English Government—Mr. Kennedy himself was allowed to proceed, but in a sort of semi-official capacity; he returned the accredited *charge d'affaires* of the Texas to this country, and is now, we believe, the natural protector of her subjects upon the British shores. Doubtless we shall yet have a thousand illustrations of their land and manners from his own eloquent pen; and, in the meanwhile, in the spirited bit of grouping before the reader, we exhibit the character which chance has afforded us of the Mounted Militia of the New State, just as they are equipped for engagements such as those in which they may shortly have to contend.

VINDICATOR—EXTRA.

BY THE PRESIDENT OF THE REPUBLIC OF TEXAS.

A PROCLAMATION.

WHEREAS an official communication has been received, at the Department of State, from Her Britannic Majesty's Charge d'Affaires near this Government, founded upon a dispatch he had received from Her Majesty's Charge d'Affaires in Mexico, announcing to this Government the fact that the President of Mexico would forthwith order a cessation of hostilities, on his part, and the establishment of an armistice between Mexico and Texas, and requested that the President of Texas would send similar orders to the different officers, commanding the Texian forces:

And whereas, the President of Texas has felt justified, from the dispositions evinced by this act of the President of Mexico, and the nature of those dispositions, in adopting the proposed measure, and ordering the cessation of hostilities, on the part of Texas.

Therefore, be it known, that I, SAM. HOUSTON, President of the Republic of Texas, and Commander-in-chief of the Army and Navy of the same, do hereby declare and proclaim that an ARMISTICE is established between Texas and Mexico, to continue during the pendency of negotiations between the two countries for peace, and until due notice of an intention to resume hostilities (should such an intention hereafter be entertained by either party,) shall have been formally announced through H. B. M. Charges d'Affaires at the respective Governments, and the revocation of this proclamation; and all officers, commanding the forces of Texas, or acting by authority of this Government, are hereby ordered and commanded to observe the same.

In testimony whereof, I have hereunto set my hand and caused the Great Seal of the Republic to be affixed.

L.S.

Done at Washington, the fifteenth day of June, A. D. 1843, and of the Independence of the Republic the eighth.

SAM. HOUSTON.

By the President:

ANSON JONES, Secretary of State.

Vol. XXXII.

Daily National Intelligencer.

WASHINGTON: FRIDAY, MAY 17, 1844.

No. 9749.

PUBLISHED BY GALES & SEATON.

TERMS:

Daily Paper—$10 a year—$1 a month for any shorter period.
Country Paper—$6 a year—$4 for six months.
PAYABLE IN ADVANCE.

EXECUTIVE DOCUMENTS,

From which the injunction of secrecy was removed by the Senate, May 15, 1844.

A TREATY OF ANNEXATION, CONCLUDED BETWEEN THE UNITED STATES OF AMERICA AND THE REPUBLIC OF TEXAS, AT WASHINGTON, THE 12TH DAY OF APRIL, 1844

The people of Texas having, at the time of adopting their Constitution, expressed, by an almost unanimous vote, their desire to be incorporated into the Union of the United States, and being still desirous of the same with equal unanimity, in order to provide more effectually for their security and prosperity; and the United States, actuated solely by the desire to add to their own security and prosperity, and to meet the wishes of the Government and people of Texas, have determined to accomplish, by treaty, objects so important to their mutual and permanent welfare.

For that purpose, the President of the United States has given full powers to John C. Calhoun, Secretary of State of the said United States, and the President of the Republic of Texas has appointed, with like powers, Isaac Van Zandt and J. Pinckney Henderson, citizens of the said Republic; and the said plenipotentiaries, after exchanging their full powers, have agreed on and concluded the following articles:

Article 1. The Republic of Texas, acting in conformity with the wishes of the people and every department of its Government, cedes to the United States all its territories, to be held by them in full property and sovereignty, and to be annexed to the said United States as one of their Territories, subject to the same constitutional provisions with their other Territories. This cession includes all public lots and squares, vacant lands, mines, minerals, salt lakes and springs, public edifices, fortifications, barracks, ports and harbors, navy and navy yards, docks, magazines, arms, armaments, and accoutrements, archives and public documents, public funds, debts, taxes, and dues unpaid at the time of the exchange of the ratifications of this treaty.

Art. 2. The citizens of Texas shall be incorporated into the Union of the United States, maintained and protected in the free enjoyment of their liberty and property, and admitted, as soon as may be consistent with the principles of the Federal Constitution, to the enjoyment of all the rights, privileges, and immunities of citizens of the United States.

Art. 3. All titles and claims to real estate which are valid under the laws of Texas, shall be held to be so by the United States; and measures shall be adopted for the speedy adjudication of all unsettled claims to land, and patents shall be granted to those found to be valid.

Art. 4. The public lands hereby ceded shall be subject to the laws regulating the public lands in the other Territories of the United States, as far as they may be applicable: subject, however, to such alterations and changes as Congress may from time to time think proper to make. It is understood between the parties, that, if in consequence of the mode in which lands have been surveyed in Texas, or from previous grants or locations, the sixteenth section cannot be applied to the purpose of education, Congress shall make equal provision by grant of land elsewhere. And it is also further understood, that hereafter the books, paper, and documents of the General Land Office of Texas shall be deposited and kept at such place in Texas as the Congress of the United States shall direct.

Art. 5. The United States assume and agree to pay the public debts and liabilities of Texas, however created, for which the faith or credit of her Government may be bound at the time of the exchange of the ratifications of this treaty; which debts and liabilities are estimated not to exceed in the whole ten millions of dollars, to be ascertained and paid in the manner hereinafter stated.

The payment of the sum of three hundred and fifty thousand dollars shall be made at the Treasury of the United States, within ninety days after the exchange of the ratifications of this treaty, as follows: Two hundred and fifty thousand dollars to Frederick Dawson, of Baltimore, or his executors, on the delivery of that amount of ten per cent. bonds of Texas; one hundred thousand dollars, if so much be required, in the redemption of the exchequer bills which may be in circulation at the time of the exchange of the ratifications of this treaty. For the payment of the remainder of the debts and liabilities of Texas, which, together with the amount already specified, shall not exceed ten millions of dollars, the public lands herein ceded, and the nett revenue from the same, are hereby pledged.

Art. 6. In order to ascertain the full amount of the debts and liabilities herein assumed, and the legality and validity thereof, four commissioners shall be appointed by the President of the United States, by and with the advice and consent of the Senate, who shall meet at Washington, Texas, within the period of six months after the exchange of the ratifications of this treaty, and may continue in session not exceeding twelve months, unless the Congress of the United States should prolong the time. They shall take an oath for the faithful discharge of their duties, and that they are not directly or indirectly interested in said claims at the time, and will not be during their continuance in office; and the said oath shall be recorded with their proceedings. In case of the death, sickness, or resignation of any of the commissioners, his or their place or places may be supplied by the appointment as aforesaid, or by the President of the United States during the recess of the Senate. They, or a majority of them, shall be authorized, under such regulations as the Congress of the United States may prescribe, to hear, examine, and decide on all questions touching the legality and validity of said claims, and shall, when a claim is allowed, issue a certificate to the claimant stating the amount, distinguishing principal from interest. The certificates so issued shall be numbered, and entry made of the number, the name of the person to whom issued, and the amount, in a book to be kept for that purpose. They shall transmit the records of their proceedings and the book in which the certificates are entered, with the vouchers and documents produced before them, relative to the claims allowed or rejected, to the Treasury Department of the United States, to be deposited therein; and the Secretary of the Treasury shall, as soon as practicable after the receipt of the same, ascertain the aggregate amount of the debts and liabilities allowed; and if the same, when added to the amount to be paid to Frederick Dawson and the sum which may be paid in the redemption of the exchequer bills, shall not exceed the estimated sum of ten millions of dollars, he shall, on the presentation of a certificate of the commissioners, issue, at the option of the holder, a new certificate for the amount, distinguishing principal from interest, and payable to him or order, out of the nett proceeds of the public lands hereby ceded, or stock of the United States, for the amount allowed, including principal and interest, and bearing an interest of three per cent. per annum from the date thereof; which stock, in addition to being made payable out of the nett proceeds of the public lands hereby ceded, shall also be receivable in payment for the same. In case the amount of the debts and liabilities allowed, with the sum aforesaid to be paid to Frederick Dawson, and which may be paid in the redemption of the exchequer bills, shall exceed the said sum of ten millions of dollars, the said Secretary, before issuing a new certificate, or stock, as the case may be, shall make in each case such proportionable and ratable reduction on its amount as to reduce the aggregate to the said sum of ten millions of dollars, and he shall have power to make all needful rules and regulations necessary to carry into effect the powers hereby vested in him.

Art. 7. Until further provision shall be made, the laws of Texas, as now existing, shall remain in force, and all executive and judicial officers of Texas, except the President, Vice President, and heads of departments, shall retain their offices, with all power and authority appertaining thereto, and the courts of justice shall remain in all respects as now established and organized.

Art. 8. Immediately after the exchange of the ratifications of this treaty, the President of the United States, by and with the advice and consent of the Senate, shall appoint a commissioner, who shall proceed to Texas and receive the transfer of the territory thereof, and all the archives and public property, and other things herein conveyed, in the name of the United States. He shall exercise all executive authority in said territory necessary to the proper execution of the laws, until otherwise provided.

Art. 9. The present treaty shall be ratified by the contracting parties, and the ratifications exchanged at the city of Washington, in six months from the date hereof, or sooner if possible.

In witness whereof, we, the undersigned, plenipotentiaries of the United States of America and of the Republic of Texas, have signed, by virtue of our powers, the present treaty of annexation, and have hereunto affixed our seals respectively.

Done at Washington, the twelfth day of April, eighteen hundred and forty-four.

J. C. CALHOUN. [SEAL.]
ISAAC VAN ZANDT. [SEAL.]
J. PINCKNEY HENDERSON. [SEAL.]

MESSAGE.

To the Senate of the United States:

I transmit herewith, for your approval and ratification, a treaty, which I have caused to be negotiated between the United States and Texas, whereby the latter, on the conditions therein set forth, has transferred and conveyed all its right of separate and independent sovereignty and jurisdiction to the United States. In taking so important a step, I have been influenced by what appeared to me to be the most controlling considerations of public policy and the general good; and in having accomplished it, should it meet with your approval, the Government will have succeeded in reclaiming a territory which formerly constituted a portion, as it is confidently believed, of its domain, under the treaty of cession of 1803 by France to the United States.

The country thus proposed to be annexed has been settled principally by persons from the United States, who emigrated on the invitation of both Spain and Mexico, and who carried with them into the wilderness which they have partially reclaimed the laws, customs, and political and domestic institutions of their native land. They are deeply indoctrinated in all the principles of civil liberty, and will bring along with them, in the act of re-association, devotion to our Union, and a firm and inflexible resolution to assist in maintaining the public liberty unimpaired—a consideration which, as it appears to me, is to be regarded as of no small moment. The country itself, thus obtained, is of incalculable value in an agricultural and commercial point of view. To a soil of inexhaustible fertility it unites a genial and healthy climate, and is destined, at a day not distant, to make large contributions to the commerce of the world. Its territory is separated from the United States, in part, by an imaginary line, and by the river Sabine for a distance of 310 miles; and its productions are the same with those of many of the contiguous States of the Union. Such is the country, such are its inhabitants, and such its capacities to add to the general wealth of the Union. As to the latter, it may be safely asserted that in the magnitude of its productions it will equal in a short time, under the protecting care of this Government, if it does not surpass, the combined production of many of the States of the Confederacy. A new and powerful impulse will thus be given to the navigating interest of the country, which will be chiefly engrossed by our fellow-citizens of the Eastern and Middle States, who have already attained a remarkable degree of prosperity by the partial monopoly they have enjoyed of the carrying trade of the Union, particularly the coastwise trade, which this new acquisition is destined in time, and that not distant, to swell to a magnitude which cannot easily be computed; while the addition made to the boundaries of the home market, thus secured to their mining, manufacturing, and mechanical skill and industry, will be of a character the most commanding and important. Such are some of the many advantages which will accrue to the Eastern and Middle States by the ratification of the treaty—advantages the extent of which it is impossible to estimate with accuracy or properly to appreciate. Texas being adapted to the culture of cotton, sugar, and rice, and devoting most of her energies to the raising of these productions, will open an extensive market to the Western States, in the important articles of beef, pork, horses, mules, &c., as well as in breadstuffs. At the same time the Southern and Southwestern States will find, in the fact of annexation, protection and security to their peace and tranquillity, as well against all domestic as foreign efforts to disturb them; thus consecrating anew the Union of the States, and holding out the promise of its perpetual duration. Thus, at the same time that the tide of public prosperity is greatly swollen, an appeal, of what appears to the Executive to be of an imposing, if not of a resistless character, is made to the interests of every portion of the country. Agriculture, which would have a new and extensive market opened for its produce; commerce, whose ships would be freighted with the rich productions of an extensive and fertile region; and the mechanical arts, in all their various ramifications, would seem to unite in one universal demand for the ratification of the treaty. But, important as these considerations may appear, they are to be regarded as but secondary to others. Texas, for reasons deemed sufficient by herself, threw off her dependence on Mexico as far back as 1836, and consummated her independence by the battle of San Jacinto, in the same year; since which period Mexico has attempted no serious invasion of her territory; but the contest has assumed features of a mere border war, characterized by acts revolting to humanity. In the year 1836 Texas adopted her Constitution, under which she has existed as a sovereign Power ever since, having been recognised as such by many of the principal Powers of the world; and contemporaneously with its adoption, by a solemn vote of her people, embracing all her population but ninety-three persons, declared her anxious desire to be admitted into association with the United States as a portion of their territory. This vote, thus solemnly taken, has never been reversed; and now, by the action of her constituted authorities, sustained as it is by popular sentiment, she reaffirms her desire for annexation. This course has been adopted by her without the employment of any sinister measures on the part of this Government. No intrigue has been set on foot to accomplish it. Texas herself wills it, and the Executive of the United States, concurring with her, has seen no sufficient reason to avoid the consummation of an act esteemed to be so desirable by both.

It cannot be denied, that Texas is greatly depressed in her energies by her long-protracted war with Mexico. Under these circumstances, it is but natural that she should seek for safety and repose under the protection of some stronger Power; and it is equally so that her people should turn to the United States, the land of their birth, in the first instance, in pursuit of such protection. She has often before made known her wishes; but her advances have, to this time, been repelled. The Executive of the United States sees no longer any cause for pursuing such a course. The hazard of now defeating her wishes may be of the most fatal tendency. It might lead, and most probably would, to such an entire alienation of sentiment and feeling, as would inevitably induce her to look elsewhere for aid, and force her either to enter into dangerous alliances with other nations, who, looking with more wisdom to their own interests, would, it is fairly to be presumed, readily adopt such expedients; or she would hold out the proffer of discriminating duties in trade and commerce, in order to secure the necessary assistance. Whatever step she might adopt, looking to this object, would prove disastrous, in the highest degree, to the interests of the whole Union. To say nothing of the impolicy of our permitting the carrying trade and home market of such a country to pass out of our hands into those of a commercial rival, the Government, in the first place, would be certain to suffer most disastrously in its revenue by the introduction of a system of smuggling, upon an extensive scale, which an army of custom-house officers could not prevent, and which would operate to act injuriously the interests of all the industrial classes of this country. Hence would arise constant collisions between the inhabitants of the two countries, which would evermore endanger their peace. A large increase of the military force of the United States would inevitably follow, thus devolving upon the people new and extraordinary burdens, in order not only to protect them from the danger of daily collision with Texas herself, but to guard their border inhabitants against hostile inroads, so easily excited on the part of the numerous and warlike tribes of Indians dwelling in their neighborhood. Texas would undoubtedly be unable, for many years to come, if at any time, to resist, unaided and alone, the military power of the United States; but it is not extravagant to suppose that nations reaping a rich harvest from her trade, secured to them by advantageous treaties, would be induced to take part with her in any conflict with us from the strongest considerations of public policy. Such a state of things might subject to devastation the territory of contiguous States, and would cost the country, in a single campaign, more treasure, thrice told over, than is stipulated to be paid and reimbursed by the treaty now proposed for ratification. I will not permit myself to dwell on this view of the subject. Consequences of a fatal character to the peace of the Union, and even to the preservation of the Union itself, might be dwelt upon. They will not, however, fail to occur to the mind of the Senate and of the country. Nor do I indulge in any vague conjectures of the future. The documents now transmitted along with the treaty lead to the conclusion, as inevitable, that if the boon now tendered be rejected, Texas will seek for the friendship of others. In contemplating such a contingency, it cannot be overlooked that the United States are already almost surrounded by the possessions of European Powers. The Canadas, New Brunswick, and Nova Scotia, the islands in the American seas, with Texas trammelled by treaties of alliance, or of a commercial character, differing in policy from that of the United States, would complete the circle. Texas voluntarily steps forth, upon terms of perfect honor and good faith to all nations, to ask to be annexed to the Union. As an independent sovereignty, her right to do this is unquestionable. In doing so, she gives no cause of umbrage to any other Power; her people desire it, and there is no slavish transfer of her sovereignty and independence. She has for eight years maintained her independence against all efforts to subdue her. She has been recognised as independent by many of the most prominent of the family of nations, and that recognition, so far as they are concerned, places her in a position, without giving any just cause of umbrage to them, to surrender her sovereignty at her own will and pleasure. The United States, actuated evermore by a spirit of justice, has desired, by the stipulations of the treaty, to render justice to all. They have made provision for the payment of the public debt of Texas. We look to her ample and fertile domain as the certain means of accomplishing this; but this is a matter between the United States and Texas, and with which other Governments have nothing to do. Our right to receive the rich grant tendered by Texas is perfect; and this Government should not, having due respect either to its own honor or its own interests, permit its course of policy to be interrupted by the interference of other Powers, even if such interference was threatened. The question is one purely American. In the acquisition, while we abstain most carefully from all that could interrupt the public peace, we claim the right to exercise a due regard to our own. This Government cannot, consistently with its honor, permit any such interference. With equal if not greater propriety might the United States demand of other Governments to surrender their numerous and valuable acquisitions, made in past time, at numberless places on the surface of the globe, whereby they have added to their power and enlarged their resources.

To Mexico the Executive is disposed to pursue a course conciliatory in its character, and at the same time to render her the most ample justice, by conventions and stipulations not inconsistent with the rights and dignity of the Government. It is actuated by no spirit of unjust aggrandizement, but looks only to its own security. It has made known to Mexico, at several periods, its extreme anxiety to witness the termination of hostilities between that country and Texas. Its wishes, however, have been entirely disregarded. It has ever been ready to urge an adjustment of the dispute upon terms mutually advantageous to both. It will be ready at all times to hear and discuss any claims Mexico may think she has on the justice of the United States, and to adjust any that may be deemed to be so on the most liberal terms. There is no desire on the part of the Executive to wound her pride, or affect injuriously her interest; but, at the same time, it cannot compromit by any delay in its action the essential interests of the United States. Mexico has no right to ask or expect this of us; we deal rightfully with Texas as an independent Power. The war which has been waged for eight years has resulted only in the conviction, with all others than herself, that Texas cannot be reconquered. I cannot but repeat the opinion, expressed in my message at the opening of Congress, that it is time it had ceased. The Executive, while it could not look upon its longer continuance without the greatest uneasiness, has nevertheless, for all past time, preserved a course of strict neutrality. It could not be ignorant of the fact of the exhaustion which a war of so long a duration had produced. Least of all was it ignorant of the anxiety of other Powers to induce Mexico to enter into terms of reconciliation with Texas, which, affecting the domestic institutions of Texas, would operate most injuriously upon the United States, and might most seriously threaten the existence of this happy Union. Nor could it be unacquainted with the fact, that, although foreign Governments may disavow all design to disturb the relations which exist under the Constitution between these States, yet that one, the most powerful amongst them, had not failed to declare its marked and decided hostility to the chief feature in those relations, and its purpose, on all suitable occasions, to urge upon Mexico the adoption of such a course in negotiating with Texas as to produce the obliteration of that feature from her domestic policy, as one of the conditions of her recognition by Mexico as an independent State. The Executive was also aware of the fact that formidable associations of persons, the subjects of foreign Powers, existed, who were directing their utmost efforts to the accomplishment of this object. To these conclusions it was inevitably brought by the documents now submitted to the Senate. I repeat, the Executive saw Texas in a state of almost hopeless exhaustion, and the question was narrowed down to the simple proposition whether the United States should accept the boon of annexation upon fair and even liberal terms, or, by refusing to do so, force Texas to seek refuge in the arms of some other Power, either through a treaty of alliance, offensive and defensive, or the adoption of some other expedient, which might virtually make her tributary to such Power, and dependant upon it for all future time. The Executive has full reason to believe that such would have been the result, without its interposition, and that such will be the result, in the event either of unnecessary delay in the ratification, or of the rejection of the proposed treaty.

In full view, then, of the highest public duty, and as a measure of security against evils incalculably great, the Executive has entered into the negotiation the fruits of which are now submitted to the Senate. Independent of the urgent reasons which existed for the step it has taken, it might safely invoke the fact, which it confidently believes, that there exists no civilized Government on earth, having a voluntary tender made it of a domain so rich and fertile, so replete with all that can add to national greatness and wealth, and so necessary to its peace and safety, that would reject the offer. Nor are other Powers, Mexico inclusive, likely, in any degree, to be injuriously affected by the ratification of the treaty. The prosperity of Texas will be equally interesting to all, in the increase of the general commerce of the world: that prosperity will be secured by annexation.

But one view of the subject remains to be presented. It grows out of the proposed enlargement of our territory. From this, I am free to confess, I see no danger. The federative system is susceptible of the greatest extension compatible with the ability of the representation of the most distant State or Territory to reach the seat of Government in time to participate in the functions of legislation, and to make known the wants of the constituent body. Our Confederated Republic consisted originally of thirteen members. It now consists of twice that number, while applications are before Congress to permit other additions. This addition of new States has served to strengthen rather than to weaken the Union. New interests have sprung up, which require the united power of all, through the action of the common Government, to protect and defend upon the high seas and in foreign parts. Each State commits, with perfect security, to that common Government those great interests growing out of our relations with other nations of the world, and which equally involve the good of all the States. Its domestic concerns are left to its own exclusive management. But if there were any force in the objection, it would seem to require an immediate abandonment of territorial possessions which lie in the distance and stretch to a far-off sea; and yet no one would be found, it is believed, ready to recommend such an abandonment. Texas lies at our very doors, and in our immediate vicinity.

Under every view which I have been able to take of the subject, I think that the interests of our common constituents, the people of all the States, and a love of the Union, left the Executive no other alternative than to negotiate the treaty. The high and solemn duty of ratifying or of rejecting it is wisely devolved on the Senate by the Constitution of the United States.

JOHN TYLER.

Washington, April 22, 1844.

Mr. Van Zandt to Mr. Webster.—[Extracts.]

Legation of Texas,
Washington, December 14, 1842.

Sir: The undersigned, Chargé d'Affaires of the Republic of Texas, (under the instructions of his Government,) begs leave to submit for your consideration a subject of general concern to civilized nations, but of peculiar interest to Texas, viz. *the character of war at present waged against Texas* by Mexico. From the nature of the facts involved, it is believed that this step will be deemed not only admissible, but entirely proper.

The civilized and Christian world are interested in the unimpaired preservation of those rules of international intercourse, both in peace and war, which have received the impress of wisdom and humanity, and been strengthened through a long course of time by the practice and approval of the most enlightened of modern States. To these rules, in their application to the pending difficulties between Texas and Mexico, your attention is respectfully invited.

Whenever a people, separate and sovereign, are admitted into the great community of nations, they incur responsibilities and contract obligations which are reciprocal in their character, and mutually binding upon all the members of that community, the extent and force of which depend upon that code of ethics which prescribes the reciprocal duties and obligations of each sovereign member. Hence arises the right to supervise the mode and manner of warfare pursued by one nation towards another, and the corresponding duty of inhibiting the perpetration of acts at variance with the laws of humanity and the settled usages of civilized nations.

In view of the character of hostilities at present waged by Mexico and Texas, and of those principles which it is believed have been so frequently and flagrantly violated by Mexico, the hope is confidently indulged by my Government that the direct interference of nations, mutually friendly, will be exerted to arrest a species of warfare unbecoming the age in which we live, and disgraceful to any people professing to be civilized.

The course of conduct uniformly observed by the Government and people of Texas towards Mexico, stands in palpable contrast with the manifold enormities and wanton aggressions of the latter, and will, it is confidently believed, furnish abundant ground for the exercise of the right of interference now invoked. * * *

What is most to be deplored in a war of this character is, that the unoffending and defenceless become victims of the most relentless cruelty. War, in its most generous and noble aspect, is accompanied by great calamities. Nations are seldom benefited by it, and it must be productive of great individual suffering. But when individuals and nations are exasperated by repeated wrongs, even cruelty may be rendered tolerable, when it is used as retaliation for injuries long endured. The massacres and cruelties which have been inflicted upon Texas since the commencement of the revolution have been responded to by a generous forbearance. But that forbearance cannot be expected much longer to exist.

The object of Mexico in her course cannot be misunderstood. By incursions of the character complained of, she may depress our husbandmen and farmers; the cry of invasion that is kept up, and the excitement incident to a state of war, may prevent emigration and embarrass our revenue, by deterring men of enterprise and capital from making importations of goods into our country: these for a time may avail her something, but the aggregate of human suffering will be a poor recompense for the advantages thus gained. The origin, genius, and character of the people of Texas are guaranties for her ultimate success. Nations that contribute to her advancement will command her gratitude.

Never since eighteen hundred and thirty-six has Mexico attempted any thing of the character of a general invasion of Texas, or conducted the war upon any plan calculated to test the superiority of the two nations upon the field of battle, and bring the war to a close by the arbitrament of arms. Her hostile demonstrations, thus far, have consisted exclusively in the clandestine approach of small bands of rancheros from the valley of the Rio Grande, accompanied by Indians, (both of whom are actuated from purposes of plunder and theft,) but sometimes associated with fragments of the Mexican army, composed, for the most part, of convict soldiery, fitted for nothing either honorable in enterprise or magnanimous in conduct.

The people of Texas being for the most part agriculturists, and engaged in the tillage of the soil, the consequences of this predatory warfare have been to them extremely vexatious and harassing, without in any degree hastening the adjustment of the difficulties existing between the parties. Entirely different is the general character of the Mexican population: they are literally a *nation of herdsmen;* subsisting in a great measure from the proceeds of their flocks and herds, they can move about from place to place, and make their homes wherever inclination or convenience may prompt, without detriment.

Hitherto the conduct and disposition of the Government and people of Texas have been diametrically opposed to those manifested by Mexico. While Mexico has been depredating upon the property of our exposed and defenceless frontier, murdering the inhabitants in cold blood, or forcing them away into a loathsome and too often fatal captivity, inciting the numerous tribes of hostile Indians who reside along our northern frontier to plunder our exposed settlements, stimulating them to the most cruel and barbarous massacres and inhuman butcheries even of our defenceless women and children, and to commit every excess of savage warfare, Texas, animated by the hope of avoiding a further resort to arms and the attendant calamities, for injuries received returned forbearance; her President has sought to abstain from the effusion of blood, and with that aim has uniformly restrained the impetuosity and calmed the excitement of his countrymen, so often aroused by a course of conduct which violates every right, both private and national, and a cruelty and depravity which would disgrace the darkest ages of feudal barbarism. The popular impulse might have been turned upon the enemy upon their own soil; the result might have proved that a free people, burning with vengeance long restrained, could levy a heavy retribution.

Such being the character of hostile operations against Texas on the part of our enemy, which being plainly violative of every principle of civilized, Christian, or honorable warfare, and at the same time so little calculated to achieve the professed object of the war, the reconquest of Texas, the President confidently hopes the Government of the United States will feel not only justified but even called upon to interpose its high authority to arrest this course of proceeding, and to require of Mexico either the recognition of the independence of Texas, or to make war upon her according to the rules established and universally recognised by civilized nations. It is believed that this subject addresses itself to the Government of the United States with peculiar force, having been the first to welcome us into the family of nations. Many of her citizens were thereby induced to emigrate to Texas, some of whom have gone only for purposes of trade, others to become citizens and share the common fate of our young Republic, but both of whom are alike exposed to the outrages alluded to. Again: the United States being the leading and oldest independent Power on this continent, and long famed for the correctness of her principles, her highly enlightened and magnanimous policy both in peace and war, entitle her to the exercise of the interposition invoked, without subjecting her to the imputation of arrogance.

If Mexico believes herself able to resubjugate Texas, her right to make the effort will not be denied; on the contrary, if she chooses to invade our territory with that purpose, the President, in the name of the people of all Texas, will bid her welcome. It is not against a war with Mexico that Texas would protest. This she deprecates not. She is willing at any time to stake her existence as a nation upon the issue of a war conducted upon Christian principles. It is alone against the unholy, inhuman, and fruitless character it has assumed, and still maintains, which violates every rule of honorable warfare, every precept of religion, and sets at defiance even the common sentiments of humanity, against which she protests and invokes the interposition of those powerful nations which have recognised her independence.

The Government of Texas has already given an earnest of her disposition to consult the wishes of other nations, when those wishes do not conflict with the general interest and convenience of the country. Fully appreciating the friendly sentiments of the United States and other Powers who had acknowledged the independence of Texas, and relying much upon their ability and influence in securing an early and permanent adjustment of our difficulties with Mexico, the President, in compliance with the desire of the United States and other Governments, expressed through their representatives to the Texian Government, revoked the late proclamation of blockade against Mexico, and at a time when our navy was preparing to enforce it with greater rigor, and thus removed every cause of embarrassment to those nations in their intercourse with our enemy.

Having thus yielded the opportunity of retaliating upon our enemy for the many injuries we had received at their hands, less reluctance is felt in making this representation, and invoking the interposition of the United States to put an end to a mode of warfare at once disgraceful to the age, so evil in its consequences to civil society, so revolting to every precept of the Christian religion, and shocking to every sentiment of humanity.

The undersigned avails himself of the occasion to offer to Mr. Webster renewed assurances of his distinguished consideration.

ISAAC VAN ZANDT.

Hon. Daniel Webster,
Secretary of State of the United States.

Mr. Upshur to Mr. Murphy.

No. 6.] Department of State,
Washington, August 8, 1843.

Sir: A private letter from a citizen of Maryland, then in London, contains the following passage:

"I learn from a source entitled to the fullest confidence that there is now here a Mr. Andrews, deputed by the abolitionists of Texas to negotiate with the British Government. That he has seen Lord Aberdeen, and submitted his *projet* for the abolition of slavery in Texas, which is, that there shall be organized a company in England, who shall advance a sum sufficient to pay for the slaves now in Texas, and receive in payment Texas lands; that the sum thus advanced shall be paid over as an indemnity for the abolition of slavery; and I am authorized by the Texian Minister to say to you, that Lord Aberdeen has agreed that the British Government will guaranty the payment of the interest on this loan, upon condition that the Texian Government will abolish slavery."

The writer professes to feel entire confidence in the accuracy of this information. He is a man of great intelligence, and well versed in public affairs. Hence I have every reason to confide in the correctness of his conclusions. There is, however, some difficulty in understanding the terms of the proposition as he has given them. If the money to be advanced is to be repaid in Texas lands, it can scarcely be regarded as a loan, and of course there is no necessity for any guaranty on the part of the English Government. I think it probable that alternative propositions have been made: the one for an advance to be repaid in lands, and the other for a loan to be guarantied by the English Government. But, whatever the precise terms of the proposition may be, there seems to be no doubt as to the object in view, and none that the English Government has offered its co-operation.

A movement of this sort cannot be contemplated by us in silence. Such an attempt upon any neighboring country would necessarily be viewed by this Government with very deep concern; but when it is made upon a nation whose territories join the slaveholding States of our Union, it awakens a still more solemn interest. It cannot be permitted to succeed without the most strenuous efforts on our part to arrest a calamity so serious to every part of our country.

If such an attempt were confined to the "abolitionists of Texas," it would scarcely merit grave consideration. Their numbers, it is believed, are very small; and the state of public opinion in that country is by no means favorable to the success of their enterprise. But if it be a fact that it has engaged the attention of Lord Aberdeen, and that he has pledged the co-operation of the English Government to a certain extent, it possesses an importance which demands our

NEW-YORK WEEKLY TRIBUNE.

BY GREELEY and McELRATH. | OFFICE TRIBUNE BUILDINGS. | VOL. V. NO. 36. WHOLE NO. 244.

$2 A YEAR, IN ADVANCE. | NEW-YORK, SATURDAY, MAY 16, 1846. | 10 COPIES FOR $15

MAY.....For The Tribune.

BY W. H. C. HOSMER.

"Day's harbinger
Comes dancing from the East, and leads with her
The flowery May."—*Milton.*

I.

Airs from the clear South-West have borne
A fairy hither on their wings,
And pining Grief forgets to mourn,
Transported by the psalm she sings.
Pale Want, in ragged, thin attire,
Who found no faggot for his fire
When howled the wintry storm,
Quitting his desolate retreats,
Looks forth, and with a blessing greets
The sunlight free and warm.

II.

The deep, orchestral wood gives ear,
Thrilled to its heart by joyous song.
And in the laughing fields I hear
Old voices that were silent long;
In a rich suit of gold and black
The Oriole hath wandered back
To weave her hammock light;
And the brown Thrush, a mimic wild,
For many weary moons exiled,
From bough to bough takes flight.

III.

A sea of verdure overspreads
The rushy banks of pond and cove,
And wild flowers lift their jeweled heads,
Frail, air-swung censors of the grove.
Tall blue-bells, in my woodland walks,
Nod gracefully their leafy stalks
In welcoming to me;
With luscious wine, by Night distilled,
Their cups to overflowing filled,
Allure the gauze-winged bee.

IV.

The rose-lipped shell on Ocean's beach
Hath less of beauty in its hue
Than fragrant blossoms of the Peach
That twinkle diamonded with dew;
The Cherry lifts its snowy crest—
In white the Plum and Pear are drest,
Diffusing odor round;
Detached, in orchards, by the breeze
The painted drapery of the trees
Falls, carpeting the ground.

V.

Our sires thronged forth from cot and hall
When, sooty and grotesque of look,
Round May-poles, garlanded and tall,
His bells the morris dancer shook.
By loyal hands a Queen was crowned,
And manly pastimes Labor found
While cloth-yard shafts were drawn.
With laughing sky and festal earth
Comported well that scene of mirth
Upon the daisied lawn.

The merry-making games of old
Unlocked the portals of the heart,
And rarely man his honor sold
For booty in the crowded mart;
When Woe appealed to Wealth for food
He owned the tie of brotherhood,
Giving without disdain;
A generous valor warmed the soul
Where love of Country held control.
Not low desire for gain.

VII.

Capricious April sighed away
His perfumed breath with closing eyes,
And, leaving crown and realm to May,
Within a grave of beauty lies.
Shelley, if living, would declare
A tenement of rest so fair,
Undarkened by a cloud,
In love with death would wanderer make,
And, in his heart enamored, wake
A yearning for the shroud.

VIII.

Bright drops on floral cup and bell
When breaks the first fair morn of May,
No longer, blest by fairy spell,
Can charm the freckled mole away;
But, ah! this season of delight
Hath magic yet to make more bright
The tomb-stone of the Past;
And Memory 'a-*May*ing' goes,
Reviving many a withered rose
In gardens dim and vast.

IX.

Called by the flowery Queen of Spring,
Dispensing bliss without alloy,
The sportive insect tribes take wing,
And Nature's holiday enjoy:
Oh! not in gaudy trappings clad,
Alone the proud and mighty glad
At her bright Court are made;
Alike upon the great and small
Her royal favors freely fall—
Her sunshine and her shade.

X.

Thou art the May of other hours—
Undimmed thy locks of golden sheen—
And still, with dandelion flowers,
Is starred thy plaid of living green;
But Time, alas! in me hath wrought
Drear changes, both in form and thought,
Since Boyhood's blissful time
When, lulled by bird and running stream,
I couched me on thy flowers to dream
Of Heaven's unshadowed clime.

Avon, May 9th, 1846.

☞ The Governor of Connecticut sent his Message to the two Houses on Friday. It is particularly savage against the Registry Law, which is pronounced unconstitutional and an infringement of the rights of voters. His Excellency recommends the passage of a stringent law to prevent the employers from controlling the votes of their laborers by threats of dismission, &c. He also recommends the passage of a law limiting the number of selectmen in each town to six, (or such other convenient number as the Legislature may prescribe) and providing that in their choice each elector shall deposit a ballot containing four names only, and that the six having the greatest number of votes shall be declared elected. This he thinks would secure to the minority in every town the voices of at least two members of this important board, to be heard whenever oppression, injustice or partiality should be practiced.

The License Law is assailed with great unfairness, coupled with specious professions of regard for the cause of Temperance!

The School Fund of the State is $2,070,055, the interest of which, during the year—$119,385—has been appropriated to the benefit of 85,275 children, between the ages of four and sixteen. The Governor recommends the abolition of the office of Assistant School Fund Commissioner.

The State Prison has yielded over its expenses the sum of $7,000, which the Governor thinks ought to be appropriated for the benefit of the Deaf and Dumb, or to some other beneficial purpose.

Various Judiciary changes are also proposed, with a view to economy.

There is a balance in the Treasury of $14,704 73. The Governor thinks, notwithstanding, that it will be necessary to borrow money to pay the debentures of Members of the Legislature, and he takes occasion to expatiate with the usual Loco-Foco pathos on the inequalities of taxation, the burdens of poor men, &c.

The Banks are said to be in a sound condition, but the Governor thinks they should be closely watched.

On the subject of the Tariff and Sub-Treasury the Governor talks after the fashion of his party. The Annexation of Texas is dwelt upon with the usual emotion. In relation to Oregon his tone is somewhat blustering, but he goes for compromise on the parallel of 49°.

The Libel Case.—We understand that the case against Mr. F. Thomas, of Maryland, for a libel, has been this day continued till the fall session of the Court of this city. Much debate had taken place at the bar upon the motion of Mr. Thomas's counsel to take Mrs. Linn's testimony by deposition—which failed. The case is continued to give the opportunity of having her testimony taken before the court in person. [Wash. Union.

Topographical Sketch of Matamoros and vicinity, showing the position of the Army of Occupation.

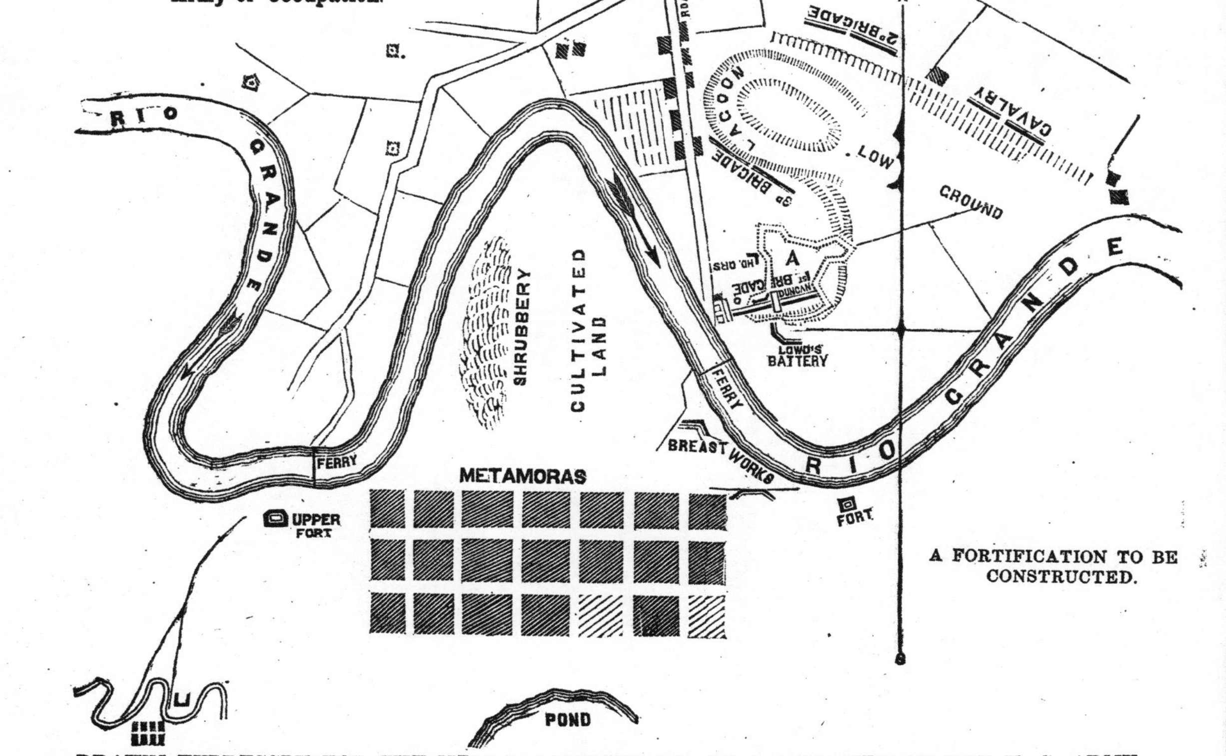

DRAWN EXPRESSLY FOR THE NEW-YORK TRIBUNE, BY AN OFFICER OF THE U. S. ARMY.

WAR WITH MEXICO!

ARRIVAL OF STEAMSHIP GALVESTON AT NEW-ORLEANS.

Requisitions on the Governors of Louisiana, Mississippi, and Alabama for 8,000 Troops.

AMPUDIA SUPERSEDED BY Gen. Arista!

POSITIONS OF THE MEXICAN AND U. S. FORCES!

COL. CROSS MURDERED AND LT. DEAS CAPTURED!!

Lieut. Cairn and 13 men killed, Capt. Thornton missing, and Capt. Hardee and 46 men Prisoners!!

CONGRESS APPROPRIATES $10,000,000 AND PROPOSES TO RAISE 50,000 VOLUNTEERS!

$100,000 APPROPRIATED BY THE LA. LEGISLATURE.

The War Bill Passed BY THE HOUSE.

THE WAR MESSAGE.

INTERVIEW BETWEEN GENS. WORTH AND VEGA.

FATE OF THORNTON UNCERTAIN!

No Mexicans between Pt. Isabel & Gen. Taylor.

Steamer New-York with the Recruits ashore!

RE-INFORCEMENT OF POINT ISABEL!
By Crews of U. S. Vessels Flirt and Lawrence!!

Gen. GAINES again in the Field.

GREAT EXCITEMENT IN NEW-ORLEANS.

DEPARTURE OF TROOPS.

&c. &c. &c.

The steamship Galveston arrived at New-Orleans on the morning of the 2d inst. confirming the intelligence received the previous day, that *Lieut. Porter and four men had been killed by the Mexicans.* On the 1st inst. the Galveston boarded the steam schooner Augusta, from the Brazos St. Iago, and brought to New-Orleans, Col. Doane, bearer of important dispatches from Gen. Taylor, and a requisition on the Governors of Louisiana, Mississippi and Alabama for 8,000 troops.

Ampudia has been superseded by Gen. Arista, who had addressed a polite note to Gen. Taylor, informing him that he, Arista, had assumed the command of the Mexican forces.

On the morning of the 10th ult. when Gen. Taylor found himself exposed to the enemy's fire, with his right and left unprotected in consequence of the peculiar bends of the river, he ordered one division of his army to take position in the bend above and the bend below the town, while with the main army he maintained his first position, where he still remains. Gen. Taylor has used all diligence to strengthen his position by throwing up breastworks, by entrenchments, fortifications, &c. and the Mexican General, Ampudia, has been equally industrious in fortifying the town defensively, keeping his soldiers employed, night and day.

Gen. Taylor's heavy ordnance of eighteen-pounders are said to be situated within point-blank shot of Gen. Ampudia's house in the middle of the City, at a distance of 300 yards. Thus the two armies have been situated for upward of two weeks up to our present dates, neither having committed any positive act of hostility upon the other. On the 10th inst. Col. Cross, Commissary-General of the Army, rode out by himself about 10 o'clock in the morning, to the house of a German, about two miles from the army, where (as was afterward ascertained) he was taken prisoner by a party of Mexican Rancheros. As soon as he was missing, Gen. Taylor sent a detachment of men, who scoured the country in search of him, but to no purpose.

Two or three days after Capt. May, of the 2d Dragoons, took a runaway negro in the neighborhood of the same place where Col. Cross was captured; and from this negro the above information of the taking of Col. Cross was obtained. Immediately after Gen. Taylor sent a messenger to the Mexican General, requesting information whether Col. Cross was a prisoner with him or not. The next day Gen. Ampudia sent several officers to the American camp, with the answer that they knew nothing of Col. Cross, but they had made Lieut. Deas a prisoner.

This officer, it appears, had previously crossed the river (but without orders) in search of Col. Cross, (who was his particular friend,) and had fallen into the hands of the Mexicans. Much uncertainty and many surmises prevailed in regard to the fate of Col. Cross. But the more probable opinion appears to be that his capture was unauthorized by, and unknown to Ampudia; and it is to be feared that he has been murdered by the party by whom he was taken, and his horse, money and clothing divided among them.

On the 14th, Gen. Ampudia sent a formal notice to Gen. Taylor, ordering him to leave his present position within 24 hours, and to evacuate the whole territory West of the Nueces, or that his refusal would be considered a declaration of war. Gen. T. immediately returned for answer, that his orders were to maintain his position on the East bank of the river, and that he should do so, especially as the roads were muddy, and it was unpleasant retreating at this season. Shortly after the reception of this answer, the Mexican army partially withdrew from the town, and a portion of the troops disappeared from the West bank of the river.

General Taylor was prosecuting the fortifications at Point Isabel with steady perseverance, and expected to have them completed so as to be able to open fire on Matamoros on the morning of the 28th.

From the Galveston News, Extra, April 30th we learn that on Thursday morning, 23d ult., a Mexican came to Gen. Taylor's camp and reported 2000 Mexicans crossing the river some twenty miles above. The same afternoon Captains Hardee and Thornton were sent with two companies of cavalry, 63 men in all, to reconnoitre. On Friday morning they fell into an ambush of the enemy, when Lieut. Cairn and 13 men were killed, Capt. Thornton missing, and Capt. Hardee and 46 made men prisoners. On Saturday afternoon the Mexicans sent in a wounded man, who made the above report. These Mexicans, it is stated, were commanded by Canales and Carabajal. After the fight, the Mexicans on this side of the river were largely reinforced, and have surrounded Gen. Taylor's camp, cutting off all communication with Point Isabel, at which place is the train and all of the stores belonging to the Army—Gen. Taylor not having on hand over ten days' provisions. There are at Point Isabel 90 artillery-men, 20 dragoons, about 250 teamsters, and about 150 citizens and laborers; and the entrenchment not half finished.

A company of 50 Mexican cavalry were seen on the night of the 26th within five miles of Point Isabel. They were supposed to be a corps of observation.

The steamer Monmouth landed Mr. Catlett on the night of the 28th ult. at Port Tobacco with dispatches from Gen. Taylor, calling on Gov. Henderson for 40 companies of riflemen, 60 men each, 20 of the companies to be mounted men to rendezvous at Corpus Christi, when they will be mustered into service and supplied with provisions; the foot companies will rendezvous at Galveston.

General Memucan Hunt was to leave Galveston on the evening of the 28th by way of Velasco and Victoria, to rendezvous at Corpus Christi, preparatory to marching for the relief of Gen. Taylor.

The same Extra contains a call 'To Arms,' signed by the Commander of the Galveston Volunteer Battalion, and stating that a rendezvous would be immediately opened for volunteers to increase the ranks of each of the volunteer corps of the city, and also to organize an additional company of Infantry or Riflemen.

If 150 or 200 men, with the proper officers, could be raised by the next morning, they would be supplied with arms and accoutrements, and take passage on board the steamer Monmouth, for Point Isabel.

The Governor of Louisiana has issued his requisition for 2,500 volunteers, and they were all ready in the streets, on the morning of the 2d, actively preparing for departing. They expected to leave the next day. The Louisiana Legislature has appropriated $100,000 for the service. The city of New-Orleans was in a great state of excitement—drums and flags, parading through the streets calling for volunteers.

On the 22d, Gen. Taylor received from Gen. Ampudia, by means of a flag of truce, a communication in very offensive terms, complaining of his having blockaded the Rio Grande; to which he replied that Gen. Ampudia had himself been the cause of the blockade, in having expressly declared that unless Gen. Taylor commenced his retreat behind the Nueces within twenty-four hours after his displaying his flag upon the left bank of the Rio Grande, he would consider *war* as being declared, and would act accordingly. Gen. Taylor farthermore stated that he would receive no farther communications from the Mexican commander, unless couched in language more respectful toward the Government and people of the United States.

From the last information that could be obtained, the force of the Mexicans is set down at seven thousand certain, and reports go as high as twelve thousand.

All communication is now cut off between the camp and Point Isabel, except running the gauntlet.

General Taylor is said to be as cool as a cucumber, and has so strengthened his position, that nothing can move him but starvation. The Mexican army was daily receiving large reinforcements from the interior.

From the N. O. Picayune, May 1.

The brig Apalachicola, Capt. Smith, arrived at this port yesterday from Brazos Bay, whence she sailed on the 24th ult. and reports that on the 22d she left Point Isabel, where Major Thomas, the acting Quarter-Master, informed Capt. Smith that the body of Col. Cross had been found about 4 miles from Gen. Taylor's Camp on the Rio Grande.—From the wounds upon the body it seems evident that he was killed by a lance.

It was farther reported that a person in Matamoros had acknowledged that he was the murderer, and had the watch and clothing of Col. Cross in his possession.

Gen. Taylor, it is reported, had made a formal demand for the murderer.

All open communications were permitted to pass by the Commandant at Point Isabel between that post and Matamoros.

The Mexican schooner Juniata, from this port for Matamoros, was taken into Brazos Bay on the 22d ult. by the pilots—no doubt by permission of the blockading force.

Still Later.—The schr. Cornelia, Capt. Stark, arrived last evening from Brazos Santiago, whence she sailed on the evening of the 24th inst. She reports that about three hours before she sailed an express arrived from General Taylor, stating that the Commander of the Mexican forces had made a formal declaration to Gen. Taylor that if he did not move his army from the position he then occupied within thirty-six hours, the Mexican batteries would be opened upon them.

The same express also stated that at that time a body of 2000 Mexicans had crossed the Rio Grande near Boretta—a small town about eight miles below Matameros, on the West bank of the river—and taken up a position between Point Isabel and General Taylor's camp. The design of this movement is evidently to cut off the American troops from their supplies.

A private letter was also received last evening from an officer in Gen. Taylor's camp, confirming in part the above report of the Mexicans having crossed the river, but stating the number at 1000 only. There had previously been so many rumors to the same effect in the camp, that little reliance was placed upon this one, which was first communicated by a Mexican, who was prudently detained, by order of Gen. Taylor.

The accounts by the Cornelia confirms the melancholy news given above as to the fate of Col. Cross. He was found entirely stripped and wounded, as before stated.

We have a letter from an officer in the camp, dated the 21st ult. the postscript to which states, what we had no doubt of, that the Americans "had not retired one foot from the bank of the river, nor does the General mean to do any thing that *can look like it*." "Our flag waves *over* the Rio Grande, and we have a fixed battery of 18-pounders that can 'spot' anything in Matamoros.

While upon the subject of the army, we may state that the steamer Col. Harney, which left here on Wednesday for Brazos Santiago, took with her a battery of ten long 12 pounders, and a quantity of munitions of war, and that she was to take in more at Galveston for the same destination.

The steamer Gen. Worth, twelve hours later from Brazos Santiago, and bringing, it is said, one day's later intelligence from Gen. Taylor's camp, was in the river last night, eight or ten miles below the city waiting for a tow. It is said a bearer of dispatches from Gen. Taylor was on board.

Col. Hunt immediately dispatched a boat to bring her up. Mr. Marks, attached to the Americrn Consulate at Matamoros, is on board the Gen. Worth.—There was a rumor brought by one of the schooners last night, that our Consul at Matamoros, apprehending imprisonment from the Mexicans, had left his post and repaired to Gen. Taylor's camp.

From the New-Orleans Correspondent of The New-York Tribune we have the latest intelligence up to May 3d.

A letter of the very latest date had been received from Gen. Taylor's Camp stating that Lieut. Cairn and ten men were shot; that Mason and Hardee were prisoners, and that the fate of Thornton was considered uncertain. It was the general belief in the camp, that Capt. Thornton, finding himself surrounded, had charged the Mexicans with a view of cutting his way through them.

The Governor of Louisiana had called on the Militia for four regiments of Volunteers. The Washington Regiment, Col. P. F. Smith, had already volunteered, and it was presumed that the whole number required, would offer their services, so as to leave on the morrow at the farthest.

Immediately on the receipt of the news contained in the *Tropic* Extra, the lower House of the Legislature, as soon as organized, appropriated by acclamation $100,000 for the equipment of Volunteers, and then adjourned. The Governor immediately made communication to Maj. Gen. Gaines relative to Volunteers.

A letter received from an officer of the U. S. Army in Texas, to an officer in New-Orleans, makes some explanation relative to Gen. Taylor's position. The affray of the twenty dragoons took place 23 miles *up the river*, which runs W. by N. from Matamoros; there whole of the Mexican force, 2,000 infantry and 12,000 cavalry across the river, *does not lie between Gen. Taylor and his supplies*, and it was believed that communication could be kept open with Point Isabel and his army.

The American Army, was as well fortified as circumstances and the extended lines would permit, and it was thought that in five days all would be ready for an attack on Matamoros.

A Marquée had been erected in Lafayette-square in New-Orleans, surmounted by the State and U. S. flags, and volunteers were flocking in. It was thought that 20,000 men could be raised, if necessary. It was thought that the Louisiana troops would be placed under the command of Gen. P. Smith of New-Orleans, who distinguished himself in the Florida War.

The Governor's Proclamation had been delayed, as he was waiting for a written communication from Gen. Gaines.

The steamer New-York, which left New-Orleans on April 30th, for Brazos Santiago, got ashore near the S. W. Pass, and it is feared, will have to discharge before she can be got off. She has 180 recruits on board, one piece of artillery, and some munitions of war.

It was presumed that the crews of the brig Lawrence and schooner Flirt, would be called upon to lend their aid to the command at Point Isabel.

Gen. Taylor had persisted in following to the letter his instructions from the Department, and from motives, apparently of pride, refused to make a call for volunteers until he had been reduced to a humiliating position.

Great excitement exists in New-Orleans, caused by the news by the Galveston. The roar of artillery was summoning the citizen soldiers to their duty. Capt. Farno's Native American Company was to leave by the steamer Alabama on the afternoon of the 2d. Col. Oakley and the 47th Regiment of Louisiana Militia were to leave in a few days.

Minutes of an interview between Brig. Gen. W. J. Worth, U. S. A., and Gen. Romulo Vega, of the Mexican Army—held on the right bank of the Rio Grande, 28th March, 1846.

On exhibiting a white flag on the *left* bank of the Rio Grande, a boat with two officers—represented as cavalry officers—with an interpreter—the same who appeared at the crossing of the Colorado—and a fourth person, crossed from the right bank of the river.

It was stated through an interpreter—Mr. Mitchell—that a general officer of the U. S. Army had been sent by his commander general, *with dispatches*, to the commanding general at Matamoros, and to the civil authorities; and that an interview was requested.

After some conversation explanatory of the above, the Mexican party recrossed the river, to report to the Commanding General at Matamoros and return with his reply. An open note for the American Consul at Matamoros, with an endorsement on the back in pencil, was delivered to the Mexican officer. He replied that he should hand it to the Commanding General. "Certainly, of course," was Gen. Worth's remark in reply.

On the return of the same party, Gen. Mejia sent word, that if the commanding general of the American forces wished a *conference* with the commanding general of the Mexican forces, it would readily be acceded to; but as a junior to the commanding general, on the part of the American troops, had requested a *conference*, Gen. Mejia could not entertain such a proposition; but that an officer of corresponding rank and position, in the Mexican forces, would be ready to receive any communication sent by Gen. Taylor.

It was perceived that the relation of the parties was misapprehended, they supposing that a conference was requested; this was corrected immediately, and it was reiterated that Gen. Worth was merely *bearer of dispatches*, with authority to relate verbally certain matters of intest to the commanding general at Matamoros.

The proposition of Gen. Mejia was then acceded to, with the remark that this was a mere question of form, which should not be permitted to interfere with any arrangements necessary to the continuance of the friendly relations now existing between the two Governments.

The Mexican party recrossed to the right bank, and after a short absence returned, stating that Gen. Romulo Vega would receive Gen. Worth on the right bank of the river—their own selection—for the reception of any communication which Gen. Worth might have to make from the commanding general.

Gen. Worth crossed the river, accompanied by Lieutenant Smith, *Aid-de-Camp;* Lieuts. Magruder, Deas and Blake, attached to his staff; together with Lieut. Knowlton as interpreter. On arriving at the right bank of the river, Gen. Worth was received by Gen. Vega with becoming courtesy and respect, and introduced to the "authorities of Matamoras," represented in the person of the Licenciado Casares. On the Mexican part were present, Gen. Vega, the Licenciado Casares, two officers—represented as cavalry officers—an interpreter, with a person named Juan N. Garza, *Official de Defensores.*

After the usual courtesies on meeting, it was stated by Gen. Worth that he was the *bearer of dispatches* from the Commanding General of the American forces to Gen. Mejia and to the civil authorities of Matamoros. A written and unsealed document was produced, and Gen. Vega desiring to know its contents, it was carefully read, and translated into French by Lieut. Knowlton, and afterward translated into Spanish by the Mexican interpreter. Gen. Vega then stated that he had been directed to receive such communications as Gen. Worth might present from his Commanding General, going on to say that the march of the U. S. troops into a part of the Mexican territory, Tamaulipas, was considered as an act of war.

Gen. Worth.—"I am well aware that some of the Mexican people consider it an aggressive act, but [interrupted by the Mexican interpreter, and after a light discussion of the international question on the part of Gen. Vega], Gen. Worth repeated the above remark, adding that it was not so considered by his Government; that the army had been ordered *there* by his Government, and *there* it would remain; whether rightfully or otherwise, *that* was a question to be settled between the two Governments. Gen. Vega, still disposed to argue the merits of the case, was told by Gen. Worth that "he came to state facts, not to argue them."

Gen. Worth then stated that he had been sent with dispatches from his Commanding General to Gen. Meija; that Gen. Mejia had refused to receive it from him personally, adding, with emphasis and some degree of warmth, "I now state that I withdraw this dispatch, having read it merely as an act of courtesy to Gen. Vega; that in addition to the written dispatch to Gen. Meija, I am authorized to express verbally the sentiments with which the commanding General proposed to carry out the instructions of his Government, in which he hoped to preserve the peaceable relations between the two Governments, leaving all questions between the two countries to be settled between the two Governments; and if hereafter Gen. Mejia wished to communicate with Gen. Taylor, he must propose the means—assuring Gen. Vega that, should Gen. Mejia present himself or send his communications by a subaltern officer, in either case he would be received with proper courtesy and respect. The question of right of territory was again opened by Gen. Vega, who asked how the United States Government would view the matter should the Mexican troops march into or occupy a portion of the territory of the United States.

Gen. Worth replied that General Vega might probably be familiar with the old proverb, "Sufficient for the day is the evil thereof," and that it "would be time enough to consider such matters when the act was perpetrated."

This proverb did not appear to have been translated by the Mexican interpreter, but was received by Gen. Vega with a smile and slight shrug.

Gen. Worth.—"Is the American Consul in arrest or in prison?"

Gen. Vega.—"No."

Gen. Worth.—"Is he now in the exercise of his proper functions?"

Gen. Vega, after apparently consulting with the Licenciado Casares for a moment, replied that he was.

Gen. Worth.—"Then as an American officer, in the name of my Government and my commanding General, I *demand* an interview with the Consul of my country."

No reply.

Gen. Worth.—"Has Mexico declared war against the United States?"

Gen. Vega.—"No."

Gen. Worth.—"Are the two countries still at peace?"

Gen. Vega.—"Yes."

Gen. Worth.—"Then I again demand an interview with the Consul of my Government, in Matamoras—in presence, of course, of these gentlemen, or any other that the commanding General in Matamoros may be pleased to designate."

Gen. Vega reiterated that he was in the proper exercise of his functions; that he was not in arrest, nor were any Americans in Matamoros in arrest; that he would submit the *demand* to Gen. Mejia, adding that he thought there would be great difficulty. This *demand* was repeatedly made, in the most emphatic manner, and a reply requested, Gen. Vega stating that the Consul continued in the exercise of his functions, and that the demand would be submitted to Gen. Mejia.

Here the interview was suspended, while the Licenciado left the party, to submit, as we understood, the demand for an interview with the Consul to Gen. Mejia. While engaged in friendly intercourse, Gen. Worth stated to Gen. Vega, in an informal manner, as an evidence of the good faith, intentions and dispositions of his commanding general, that he was well aware of the importance of Brazos Santiago to the commerce and business community of Matamoros; that he would respect their laws and customs, and freely grant entrance and exit to all Mexican and other vessels trading with Matamoros on the same terms as before its occupation by the United States, leaving all questions arising therefrom to be settled hereafter by the two Governments. At the expiration of about a quarter of an hour the Licenciado returned, and reported that Gen. Mejia would not accede to the request for an interview on the part of Gen. Worth, saying nothing, however, relative to the question of the Consul.

Gen. Vega was then again informed that the dispatches intended to be delivered to General Mejia by General Worth in person would be returned by him [Gen. W.] to his commanding general, considering any other disposition of them as disrespectful to him, repeating that they had been read to General Vega in courtesy to him, and that General Mejia must take his own means of communicating with Gen. Taylor; that whether Gen. Mejia sent a superior or subaltern officer to Gen. Taylor, at all times accessible, he would be received with becoming courtesy and hospitality, presenting, at the same time, a written and sealed document for the civil authoritis of Matamoros, which was received by Gen. Vega and immediately transferred to the Licenciado Casares.

Gen. Vega.—"Is it the intention of General Taylor to remain on the left bank of the Rio Grande?"

Gen. Worth.—"Most assuredly, and there to remain until directed otherwise by his Government."

Gen. Vega remarked that "we" felt indignation at seeing the American flag placed on the Rio Grande, a portion of the Mexican territory. Gen. Worth replied, "that was a matter of taste; notwithstanding that, *there* it would remain." The

SEE FOURTH PAGE.

CAMP OF THE ARMY OF OCCUPATION IN TEXAS

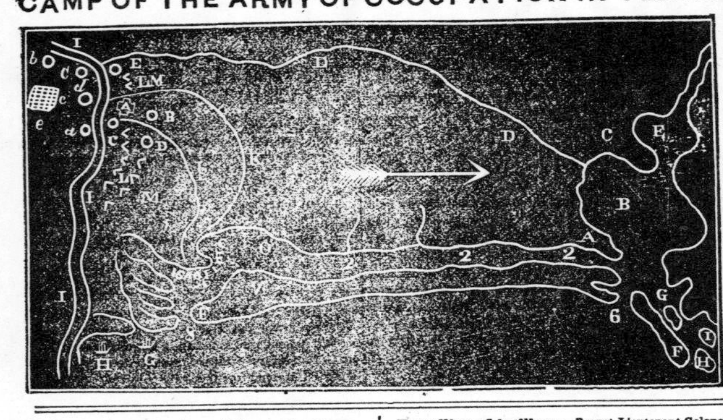

War News Continued from 1st Page.

army had been ordered to occupy its present position by its Government; it come in a peaceful rather than belligerent attitude, with a determination to respect the rights and customs of those on the right bank of the Rio Grande, while it offers protection to all on the left bank within their own territory.

No reply having been received from Gen. Vega relative to the demand for an interview with the American Consul, the question was again introduced by Gen. Worth, and the demand for the last time reiterated.

Gen. Vega promptly refused to accede to the demand, replying, without waiting for the interpretation, "No, no."

Gen. Worth.—"I have now to state that the refusal of my demand to see the American Consul is regarded as a belligerent act; and in conclusion I have to add, that the commanding General of the American forces on the left bank of the river will regard the passage of an *armed* party of Mexicans, in *hostile array*, across the Rio Grande, as an act of war, and pursue it accordingly.

The interview here terminated, and Gen. Worth and staff returned to the left bank of the river.

The above contains the substance of the interview between Generals Worth and Vega, and, as far as possible, the exact words and expressions used on the occasion. Lieutenants Knowlton and Magruder, of the 1st Artillery, of the Topographical Engineers, and Lieut. Smith, of the 8th Infantry, were present at the interview.

The War in Texas—Excitement in New-Orleans—Gen. Taylor's Movements.

Correspondence of The Tribune.

NEW-ORLEANS, May 4th, 1846.

Messrs. Greeley & McElrath:—The excitement here increases hourly—our whole city is in confusion—squads of fine-looking men are every where parading the streets, headed by the fife and drum.—We now have war, a thing that has been much talked of, without, we fear, calculating the costs. Public opinion here is that Gen. Taylor's orders were not such as should have been given, and that from his inability to act decisively, the Mexican War may be prolonged, or involve other powers in the matter. Gen. H. Davis, Secretary of the Senate, will resign his office on taking command of a company of volunteers—Capt. Fulton, late of the Army, has offered his services to the Governor. From Capt. F.'s well known reputation as an officer in the Florida war it is hoped he will get a commission.

I send you a Map of the seat of War. It is correct, and was made from the direction of an officer direct from Gen. Taylor's army. I also send a list of officers, with particulars, &c.

From a statement known here, taken from a private letter of Gen. Taylor, good reason is had to believe that a general action has taken place between the American and Mexican forces. It was stated that at a given time Gen. T. would leave five hundred men in the main entrenchment opposite Matamoros *and march the remainder of his army to Point Isabel.* Nothing can exceed the expectation of the citizens to hear of the result of the battle, or rather of the expected one. * * *

List of U. S. Officers of the Army of Occupation.

Gen. Taylor's camp extends about four miles along the river bank—two miles above, and two miles below Matamoros. The entrenchment to erect it required twenty-three hundred men for thirty days. It is made of sand, and covered over with twigs woven together like basket work, surrounded by a very wide and deep ditch. The walls of the magazine, in the interior of the fortification, are formed of pork barrels filled with sand, seven tier thick, four tier high, covered over with timber, on which sand is piled ten or twelve feet. Twelve heavy pieces of ordnance are so placed as to command the town of Matamoros. Five hundred men could defend the fortification against any force the Mexicans could bring against it at present.

Description of the Map given above.—American side.—(*a*) The Fort, with the batteries commanding Matamoros; sufficiently large to contain the whole army under command of Gen. Taylor; occupied by Maj. Ringgold, 3d Artillery. (*b*) Gen. Taylor's head quarters, at which are Col. Twiggs, of the 2d Reg't Dragoons, second in command; Lieut. Col. J. Garland, commanding 4th Infantry; Lieut. Col. J. S. McIntosh, commanding 5th Infantry, and Brevet Lieut. Col. Thos. Childs, commanding Battalion of Artillery. (*c*) Breastworks. (*d*) Encampment. (*e*) Encampment. (*f*) Brasos. (*g*) U. S. schooner Flirt. (*h*) U. S. brig Lawrence. (*i*) Rio Grande. (*j*) Short road from Point Isabel to Matamoros, twenty-seven miles. (*k*) Long road do., thirty-five miles. (*l*) Tents. (*m*) Horses of Gen. Taylor's army. (*n*) Padre Island. (*o*) Layguna del Marthe. Figures 8, 6, 6, 2, 2, 2, depth of water.

Mexican side—(*a*) (*b*) (*c*) and (*d*) batteries. (*e*) Matamoros.

Corpus Christi Bay.—(*a*) Flour Bluffs. (*b*) Corpus Christi Bay. (*c*) Kenny's Rancho. (*d*) Old Road to Matamoros. (*e*) Nueces. (*f*) Mustang Island. (*g*) McGowan's Bluff. (*h*) St. Joseph's.

The point of action where Capt. Thornton, Lieut. Cairn, and fourteen men were killed and forty men taken prisoners, is above Matamoros, and not on the map.

Maj. Munroe, of 4th Artillery, commands Point Isabel. Quarter Master General Maj. Thomas, and Ass't Quarter Master Maj. S. McRee, with 300 men, are at Point Isabel. By the death of Col. Cross, Maj. Thomas is the senior Quarter Master of the Army of Occupation. It is supposed that Col. Hunt, of our New-Orleans, will be ordered to take Col. Cross's place.

UNITED STATES ARMY IN TEXAS.

General Staff.—Brigadier Gen Z Taylor, commanding; Capt W W S Bliss, Ass't Adjutant General; 1st Lieut JH Eaton, 3d infantry, aid-de-camp; Lieut Col M M Payne, 4th artillery, Inspector General "Army of Occupation;" Col T Cross, Ass't Q M Gen, (killed;) Major C Thomas, Quarter Master, (Point Isabel); Major S McRee, do do do; Assistant Quarter Masters, Capt G H Crossman, Capt E S Sibley, Capt E A Ogden, Capt W S Ketchum; Commissary of Subsistence, Capt G G Waggaman; Surgeon P H Craig, Medical Director; Surgeon N S Jarvis; Assistant do, B M Byrne, (St Joseph's,) Assistant do, J R Conrad; Paymasters, St Clair Denny, Lloyd J Beall, Roger S Dix.

Engineers.—Capt J K Mansfield, Capt John Sanders, 1st Lieut J M Scarritt.

Topographical Engineers.—Captain T J Crain, 1st Lieut J E Blake, 2d Lieut George Meade.

Ordnance Department.—Capt G D Ramsey, 2d Lieut C P Kingsbury.

Light Artillery.—Major John Erving, 2d artillery; Ass't Surgeon J B Wells, General Staff; 2d Lieut S Fahnestock, 4th artillery, Act'g Adj't.

Brevet Majors—John Munroe. 4th Artillery; S Ringgold, 3d Artillery.

First Lieutenants—James Duncan, 2d Artillery; Braxton Bragg, 3d do; J. F Roland, 2d do; R. Ridgely, 3d do; W. H. Snover, 3d do; E. Bradford 4th do; J. C. Pemberton, 4th do; J H Thomas, 3d do.

Second Lieutenants.—Wm. Hays. 2nd Artillery; J. F. Reynolds, 3d do; J J Peck, 2d do; S L. Fremont, 3d do; M. Lovell, 4th do; J. P. Johnston, 4th do; S. G. French, 3d do.

Second Regiment of Dragoons—Colonel D. E. Twiggs, commanding; Assistant Surgeon, L C. McPhail, general staff; First Lieut. H. H. Sibley, Adjutant.

Captains.—Croghan Ker; C. A. May; S. B. Thornton (killed;) W. J. Hardee, (prisoner.)

First Lieutenants.—W H Saunders; F Hamilton; A Lowry; O F Winship, A C S and A Q M.

Second Lieutenants.—R P Campbell; George Stephens; R H Anderson; W Steele; Lewis Neill; G T Mason. (killed;)——Kane; D B Sackett.

First Brigade.—Brigadier General W J Worth, commanding, (resigned;) First Lieutenant Larkin Smith, 8th infantry, A D C; Surgeon H S Hawkins General Staff; Surgeon J J B Wright, do do; Assistant Surgeon D C De Leon, do do.

Battallion of Artillery.—Brevet Lieutenant Colonel Thomas Childs, commanding; Second Lieut R S Garnett 4th artillery, acting Adjutant.

Brevet Majors.—J Dimick, 1st artillery; W W Morris, 4th artillery.

Captains.—Giles Porter, 1st artillery; S Mackenzie 2d do; Martin Burk, 3d do; A Lowd, 2d do; C F Smith 2d do; J B Scott, 4th do; R C Snead, 4th do.

First Lieutenants.—M Knowlton, 1st artillery; E Deas, 4th do, (prisoner;) R A Luther, 2d do; G Taylor, Brevet Captain 3b artillery; A Ebsey, 2d do; W H Churchill, 3d do; J B Magruder, 1st do; J S Hatheway, do; C B Daniels, 2d do; W H Fowler, 1st do; W Gilman, 3d do; J P McCown, 4th do.

Second Lieutenants—L Chase, 2d Artillery; A B Lansing, do; A A Gibson, do; W S Smith, 1st do; S K Dawson, 1st do; J F Irons, 1st do; H M Whiting, 4th do; S Williams, 1st do; H F Clarke, 2d do; S Gill, 4th do; J F Farry, 4th do; G W Ayres, 3d do; C Benjamin, 4th do; C L Kilburn, 3d do; A Doubleday, 3d do; J J Reynolds, 4th do; T J Curd, 1st do; L B Weld, 1st do.

Eighth Regiment of Infantry—Brevet Lieutenant Colonel W G Belknap, commanding; 2d Lieutenant John D Clark, acting Adjutant.

Captains—W R Montgomery, W O Kello, R B Screven, H McCavett, J V Bomford.

First Lieutenants—J V D Reeve, G Lincoln, J Selden, C R Gates, A L Sheppard, A T Lee.

Second Lieutenants—R P Maclay, J Beardsley, C. D Jordan, T L Chadbourne, E B Halloway, C D Merchant, T J Montgomery, J G Burbank, C F Morris, J J Booker, J Longstreet, H M Judah, George Wainwright, J S S Snelling.

Second Brigade—Lieutenant Colonel J S McIntosh, 5th Infantry, commanding; 1st Lieutenant C L Stevenson, 5th Infantry; Brigade-Major-Surgeon R C Wood, General Staff; Assistant Surgeons, J W Russell and H C Crittenden, do do.

Fifth Regiment of Infantry—Major T Staniford, commanding; 1st Lieut G Deas, Adjutant.

Captains—Martin Scott, M E Merrell, A Drane, E K Smith, A S Hool, C C Sibley, J L Thompson, W Chapman.

First Lieutenants—B B Marcy, A C S and A Q M; J H Whipple; N B Russell; D Ruggles, A C S, 5th Infantry; W Root; J A Whitall.

Second Lieutenants—S H Fowler; S Norvell; H Whiting; M Rosencrants; T G Pitcher; R L Brooke; J C Robinson; P Lugenbeel; J P Smith; W L Crittenden.

Seventh Regiment of Cavalry—Major J Brown commanding; Second Lieutenant F N Page, Adjutant.

Captains—E L Hawkins; D S Miles; J G Rains, Brevet Major; T H Holmes; D P Whiting; F Lee; W Seavell, Brevet Major; S W Moore; R H Ross; R C Gatlin.

First Lieutenants—F Britton; N Hopson; J R Scott; A Montgomery, A C S; C Hanson; C H Humber.

Second Lieutenants—L Gantt; E Van Dorn; J H Potter; A Cruzot; J M Henry; S B Hayman; F Gardner W K Van Bokkelen; E B Strong; H B Clitz; W H Wood

Third Brigade—Col W Whistler. Fourth Infantry, commanding; Second Lieutenant G O Haller, Fourth Infantry, Brigade Major; Assistant Surgeons, J B Porter, M Mills, J Simmons, A W Kenedy, General Staff.

Third Regiment Infantry—Lieut Col E A Hitchcock, commanding. Brevet 1st Lieutenant D S Irwin, Adjutant.

Captains—L N Morris, J Van Horne, G P Field, H Bainbridge. J L Coburn.

First Lieutenants—P N Barbour, Brevet Capt L S Craig, W H Gordon, W H Henry, Brigade A C S; J M Smith, D T Chandler, A A Q M; O L Sheppard.

Second Lieutenants—W B Johns, D C Buell, W T H Brooks, A J Williamson, J C McFeran, J J C Bibb, Thomas Jordon, J B Richardson, A W Bowman, R Hazlitt, G C McClelland, J P Hatch, B E Bee.

Fourth Regiment of Infantry—Lieut. Col. J. Garland, commanding. First Lieut. C. Hoskins, Adjutant. Brevet Major, G. W. Allen, acting Major.

Captains—John Page, P. Morrison, G. Morris, W. M Graham Brevet Major, G. A. McColl, R. C. Buchanan, C. H Larnard.

First Lieutenants—B. Alvord, R. E. Cochrane, A A M; R. H. Graham, E. G, Elliot, A C S, St. Josephs.

Second Lieutenants—T. H. Porter, *killed*, H. D Walen, C. C. Augur, J. S. Woods, Sid. Smith, J. Beaman, U. S. Grant, J. A. Richey, P. A. Farelly.

Lieutenants D. F. McPhail, 5th infantry, commanding.—Lieutenant N. B. Rossell, 5th infantry. Lieutenant S. Hamilton, 13th infantry, left here Saturday, May the 2d, with one hundred and eighty-nine men in the steamer New-York, for the Army on the Rio Grande

☞ We are rejoiced to learn, by this evening's mail, that Captain Seth B. Thornton, and Lieutenant Mason, with two dragoons, had arrived safe in Gen. Taylor's camp.

Capt. Thornton, discovering the ambuscade too late to retreat, had plunged gallantly through the enemy's ranks, and cut his way with his own sword, with a boldness and intrepidity that is almost incredible. It seems he is not to be killed by accidents of flood or field. He is the same gentleman who so narrowly escaped when the Pulaski was blown up. He had the yellow fever several times in Florida, and has passed through many other hair-breadth 'scapes.

When Gen. Worth left the camp, Captain Thornton asked him for his sword. The General buckled it upon him; and when he heard yesterkay of Captain T.'s gallantry, he exclaimed "That was *my* sword. I knew it would never be disgraced in his hands. He is as noble and gallant a fellow as ever held sword in hand." [Union.

MILITARY MOVEMENTS.—We learn from the St. Louis Republican of the 30th ultimo that the following companies and officers of the 6th Regiment United States Infantry, stationed at Jefferson Barracks, were under marching orders for Texas, and were to leave as soon as possible:

Lieut. Col. Wilson, Commanding. Company K—Bt. Maj. Abercrombie. Company E—Capt. A. S. Miller, 2d Lieut. Plummer, Bt. 2d Lieut. Dilworth. Company G—Capt. E. Backus, 1st Lieut. G. W. F. Wood, 2d Lieut. S. D. Carpenter. Company C—Capt. J. H. Lamotte, 1st Lieut. G. Barry, 2d Lieut. J, Terrett.

DEPARTURE OF VOLUNTEERS.—A Company of Volunteers, numbering fully one hundred, left here last evening, on the steamboat Fashion, for New Orleans, whence they will proceed with all possible dispatch to the American Army on the Rio Grande.

Before leaving, the Company elected Gen. Robert Desha Captain, and Capt. Thomas Adrian Lieutenant—Gen. Desha immediately took charge of the Company and departed with it last evening. He is a gentleman of great energy, of undoubted bravery and has "seen service." A better man could not have been selected to take command of the Mobile Volunteers.

For an hour before their departure last evening, the wharves in the vicinity were lined with spectators, and as the boat shoved off, the air resounded with the shouts and cheers, "three times three," of the assembled thousands, in honor of the gallant and patriotic Volunteers, who so nobly and promptly responded to their country's call. May the God of battles protect them!

[Mobile Adv. 5th.

THE BLOCKADE OF THE RIO GRANDE.—We learned last evening that formal protests had been made before the British Consul by the English houses which had shipped cargoes on board the schooners Equity and Floridian, for Matamoros, which were turned back by the United States brig Lawrence, off the mouth of the Rio Grande.

[Picayune, 1st.

WAR! WAR.—The Phila. U. S. Gazette says: "We understand Messrs. Savery & Co. iron founders of this city, have received an order from Government, to supply at once one hundred tons of cannon balls."

☞ The Mayor of Philadelphia has called a public meeting of the citizens of that city and county, which was to be held in Independence-square yesterday, to express their opinion upon the state of public affairs, and to adopt such measures as are required by the present emergency of the country.

TEXAS.—A correspondent writing from New-Orleans, April 29, says: The Texas Congressional election was yet undecided. The Houston Star thinks there is little doubt that Judge Pillsbury is elected. The Galveston News thinks the chances are in favor of Col. Williams.

The election for Free Schools took place at Galveston on the 23d. The vote was all in their favor.

It is neck-and-neck now with our Country and Mexico, which is most ridiculous in this war on the Rio Grande. Lieut. Porter's death will be deeply lamented He was married but a short time since. Lieut. P. was a brave and gallant officer, and worthily bore the name of his hero father. We fear that his death will be unrevenged. It is very amusing indeed to see the Government concentrating its energies to meet a few ill-disciplined troops of Mexico, and yet clamoring for war with England! The mail is about closing. In haste. * *

☞ THE LEGISLATURE of Rhode Island adjourned on Friday to meet again on the fourth Monday in June.

The War News—Things in Washington.

From the Philadelphia North American Extra.

WASHINGTON, May 10, 1846—5 o'clock, P. M.

From the news which has arrived, it is clear Gen. Taylor has been deceived by the specious pretences of Ampudia; and from what I have gathered within a few days, I am convinced this deception extended itself to other important officers. Gen. Worth, two nights ago, stated to Gen. Roger Jones that the Mexican Commander had sent over a message to Gen. Taylor, warning him against marauding bands of Mexicans, that would commit murder or any other crime for the sake of the most miserable booty.—There is hardly any doubt now, but, it was a scheme to restrain the vigilance and activity of our scouting parties, and to cover the secret operations of the Mexicans.

Since the arrival of Mr. Slidell three days ago, there have been various consultations between him and the President and the Cabinet, as to the proper measures that should be pursued; and it was determined yesterday morning, before this last intelligence had reached here, to send in a MESSAGE TO-MORROW, RECOMMENDING A BLOCKADE OF ALL THE MEXICAN PORTS.

After the news by the evening mail was authenticated, the *Cabinet was again convened and adjourned until this morning*, resolving to put in requisition such disposable force as is at the command of the Executive. I do not pretend to speak in other than general terms of the determination taken to-day, but it is sufficiently known to be depended upon, a Message will be communicated to-morrow, giving a Declaration of War, and submitting a recommendation for an immediate augmentation of the defences by suitable appropriations and by calling upon the contiguous States for volunteers and drafted troops, if necessary. To what lengths the President will feel it incumbent to go, I am not prepared to say, for his policy thus far has given us no indication of what he will do. At such a time I would not cavil, but Mr. Polk has invoked upon his head a responsibility which he can never satisfy.

A letter has been received here from Captain Ramsay, of the Ordnance Department, who is in command at Point Isabel, wherein he states the force consists of *eighty men!* Some one or two hundred camp followers are about, on whom no reliance can be placed. To show the exigency to which the post is reduced, he mentions that he and two private soldiers are allotted to work a howitzer. The others are disposed among the guns.

The Military Committee of the House met this morning, for the purpose of putting its affairs in train to meet the demands for information, and to suggest estimates and ready resources to-morrow.

A letter was received here recently by a respectable gentleman from a merchant in Vera Cruz, dated April 2, in which he remarked that the movements of the Mexican army toward Texas would depend upon advices then expected from England, and which reached there very shortly afterward, whereupon the signal for these operations was given, and the result is now before the world. *It is argued from this strong fact, that Great Britain* is an actor behind the scenes in this attempt of Mexico. I do not pretend to endorse the inference, though it carries much plausibility upon its face.

Why the Message, which will be transmitted to-morrow, has been delayed until this, the eleventh hour, *after* the blow has been struck—perhaps the fatal one—is more than all practical sagacity can unravel. When I stated to the public some weeks ago, that the administration had taken its purpose, and the President would lay the subject before Congress in a "few days," I had the most *immediate authority* for the declaration, and was as much surprised as any one else, when I learned to my astonishment, he would delay all action for the arrival of Mr. Slidell, who had previously communicated every tittle of official information in his possession. INDEPENDENT.

Correspondence of The N. Y. Tribune.

WASHINGTON, May 10, 1846—Midnight.

Gen. WORTH who had resigned and came home was sent back to the camp this morning and probably took out some farther orders to Gen. TAYLOR.—His resignation, I believe, never reached the Department here. It is said that had it arrived, it would have been accepted. It is said that Dispatches have been in the city several days, from Gen. Taylor, foreshadowing what has come to pass; and yet the President delayed to communicate with Congress.

The bar-rooms and other public places to-night were echoing with the voices of brandy and water Patriotism—some of the more sober scarcely suppressed their maledictions on the President for his treatment of Gen. Taylor, while others seemed to blame the conduct of the General himself.

Many think that the vote to make large appropriations should be accompanied by an impeachment of the President. Some members of Congress say that they will vote fifty millions to carry on the War, if Polk, Dallas, and the Cabinet, and others who got us into the scrape can only be made to go and fight in the front rank.

You will see by the proceedings in Congress, yesterday, that several members of the Committee which was to impeach Mr. WEBSTER, have asked to be excused, because the House would not allow a clerk, or on account of sickness. These are but foolish excuses by which to sneak out of the hopeless and despicable task in which they are engaged.

There is a report that Gen. HOUSTON of Texas is going home to take part in the war. In this way he would probably do us more good than in any other capacity. But will he go?

As to the men required for service in Mexico, common soldiers, however well disciplined, are not well suited to the kind of warfare in which the Annexationists have involved us. The *chaparels*, which you see mentioned in the late news, are clumps of trees in which Rancheros, or drovers, and bush-fighters, find shelter. They are generally composed of short prickly shrubs or stunted trees, covered with sharp thorns, in which to take shelter it is necessary to be clothed as the Rancheros are, in leather or buckskins. These chaparels, you will see, are numerous around the seat of war, and none but those accustomed to fight and hunt among them can succeed. RICHELIEU.

Correspondence of The New-York Tribune.

BALTIMORE, May 11, 8 o'clock, P. M.

U. S. TROOPS FOR THE RIO GRANDE.—An express arrived on Monday from Washington to Col. Bankhead, to dispatch four companies of the 2d Artillery, under his command, immediately to the Seat of War. They will be taken as follows—one company from Fort Trumbull, New-London; one from Fort Hamilton; one from Governor's Island; and one from Fort Mifflin, Delaware River. We also learn that eight other Companies of Artillery on the Atlantic coast are ordered off to the Rio Grande, making twelve Companies in all.

LATER.

Correspondence of The Tribune.

The bill which passed the House is in substance as follows:

Whereas, by an act of the Republic of Mexico a state of war exists between that Government and the United States:

Sec. 1. The President is hereby authorized to accept the service of Volunteers not exceeding **50,000**, for twelve months or to the end of the war.

Sec. 2. **$10,000,000** are hereby appropriated to carry the above into effect.

Sec. 3. Volunteers are to furnish their own clothing and horses, but when mustered into active service are to be armed and equipped by the Government.

Sec. 4. They are to be subject to the articles of war, and, except as to clothing and pay, to be placed on the same footing as the army, and in lieu of clothing they are to receive an equivalent in money.

Sec. 5. The Volunteers to be officered according to the respective laws of the States to which the companies belong.

Sec. 6. The President, if he thinks it necessary, is empowered to make nominations to the Senate of Generals of Brigade and Divisions, and of the General Staff, as now authorized. The Generals will appoint their own Aids, and the President will apportion the officers among their respective States tendering Volunteers.

Sec. 7. The Volunteers received will be entitled to all the benefits conferred on persons wounded in the service of the United States.

Sec. 8. The President is authorized to complete all the armed vessels now authorized by law; to purchase or charter merchant vessels and steamboats to be converted into public armed vessels, in such moneys as are necessary to protect the sea board and harbors, or general defence.

Secs. 9 & 10. Provides the rate of pay and the continuance of the act for two years. Privates of foot companies will receive $10 per month; the mounted men $20 per month, including the use and risk of horses.

But two hours were allotted to the discussion in the House. Rhett, Holmes and others argued pro and con as to the case of War. Adams took ground against the Bill.

An amendment declaring war was voted down by an immense majority, as not necessary, the act of Mexico having made a state of war.

In the SENATE this discussion on the Message from the President was all closed. It was warm, and strong comments were made against the course of the Executive on removing so small a force as Taylor's to a position so hazardous.

Mr. CRITTENDEN was particularly eloquent and impressive, and spoke in the highest terms of Gen. Taylor.

The SENATE adopted the bill increasing the companies in service to a hundred men each. The bill for raising a regiment of mounted riflemen was taken up and postponed.

From the Washington Union Extra, May 11.

THE PRESIDENT'S MESSAGE.

To the Senate and House of Representatives:

The existing state of the relations between the United States and Mexico, renders it proper that I should bring the subject to the consideration of Congress. In my Message at the commencement of your present session, the state of these relations, the causes which led to the suspension of diplomatic intercourse between the two countries in March, 1845, and the long-continued and unredressed wrongs and injuries committed by the Mexican Government on citizens of the United States in their persons and property, were briefly set forth.

As the facts and opinions which were then laid before you were carefully considered, I cannot better express my present convictions of the condition of affairs up to that time, than by referring you to that communication.

The strong desire to establish peace with Mexico, on liberal and honorable terms, and the readiness of this Government to regulate and adjust our boundary, and other causes of difference with that power, on such fair and equitable principles as would lead to permanent relations of the most friendly nature, induced me in September last to seek the reöpening of diplomatic relations between the two countries. Every measure adopted on our part had for its object the fartherance of these desired results.

In communicating to Congress a succinct statement of the injuries which we had suffered from Mexico, and which have been accumulating during a period of more than twenty years, every expression that could tend to inflame the people of Mexico, or defeat or delay a pacific result, was carefully avoided. An envoy of the United States repaired to Mexico with full powers to adjust every existing difference. But though present on the Mexican soil, by agreement between the two Governments, invested with full powers, and bearing evidence of the most friendly dispositions, his mission has been unavailing. The Mexican Government not only refused to receive him, or listen to his propositions, but, after a long-continued series of menaces, have at last invaded our territory and shed the blood of our fellow-citizens on our own soil.

It now becomes my duty to state more in detail the origin, progress, and failure of that mission. In pursuance of the instructions given in September last, an inquiry was made, on the thirteenth of October, in 1845, in the most friendly terms, through our Consul in Mexico, of the Minister of Foreign Affairs, whether the Mexican Government "would receive an envoy from the United States entrusted with full powers to adjust all the questions in dispute between the two Governments;" with the assurance that "should the answer be in the affirmative, such an envoy would be immediately dispatched to Mexico."

The Mexican Minister, on the fifteenth of October, gave an affirmative answer to this inquiry, requesting, at the same time, that our naval force at Vera Cruz might be withdrawn, lest its continued presence might assume the appearance of menace and coercion pending the negotiations. This force was immediately withdrawn. On the 10th of November, 1845, Mr. John Slidell, of Louisiana, was commissioned by me as Envoy Extraordinary and Minister Plenipotentiary of the United States to Mexico, and was entrusted with full powers to adjust both the questions of the Texas boundary and of indemnification to our citizens.

The redress of the wrongs of our citizens naturally and inseparably blended itself with the question of boundary. The settlement of the one question in any correct view of the subject involves that of the other. I could not, for a moment, entertain the idea that the claims of our much injured and long suffering citizens, many of which had existed for more than twenty years, should be postponed, or separated from the settlement of the boundary question.

Mr. Slidell arrived at Vera Cruz on the 30th of November, and was courteously received by the authorities of that city. But the Government of Gen. Herrera was then tottering to its fall. The revolutionary party had seized upon the Texas question to effect or hasten its overthrow. Its determination to restore friendly relations with the United States, and to receive our Minister, to negotiate for the settlement of this question, was violently assailed, and was made the great theme of denunciation against it.

The Government of General Herrera, there is good reason to believe, was sincerely desirous to receive our Minister; but it yielded to the storm raised by its enemies, and on the 21st of December refused to accredit Mr. Slidell upon the most frivolous pretexts. These are so fully and ably exposed in the note of Mr. Slidell of the 24th of December last, to the Mexican Minister of foreign relations, herewith transmitted, that I deem it unnecessary to enter into farther detail on this portion of the subject.

Five days after the date of Mr. Slidell's note, Gen. Herrera yielded the government to Gen. Paredes without a struggle, and on the 30th of December resigned the Presidency. This revolution was accomplished solely by the army, the people having taken little part in the contest; and thus the supreme power in Mexico passed into the hands of a military leader.

Determined to leave no effort untried to effect an amicable adjustment with Mexico, I directed Mr. Slidell to present his credentials to the Government of Gen. Paredes, and ask to be officially received by him. There would have been less ground for taking this step had Gen. Paredes come into power by a regular constitutional succession.

In that event his administration would have been considered but a mere Constitutional continuance of the Government of Gen. Herrera, and the refusal of the latter to receive our Minister would have been deemed conclusive, unless an intimation had been given by Gen. Paredes of his desire to reverse the decision of his predecessor.

But the Government of General Paredes owes its existence to a military revolution, by which the subsisting constitutional authorities had been subverted. The form of government was entirely changed, as well as all the high functionaries by whom it was administered.

Under these circumstances, Mr. Slidell, in obedience to my direction, addressed a note to the Mexican Minister of Foreign Relations, under date of 1st of March last, asking to be received by that Government in the diplomatic character to which he had been appointed. This Minister, in his reply, under date of the 12th of March, reiterated the arguments of his predecessor, and in terms that may be considered as giving just grounds of offence to the Government and people of the United States, denied the application of Mr. Slidell. Nothing, therefore, remained for our envoy but to demand his passports, and return to his own country.

Thus the Government of Mexico, though solemnly pledged by official acts in October last to receive and accredit an American Envoy, violated their plighted faith and refused the offer of a peaceful adjustment of our difficulties. Not only was the offer rejected, but the indignity of its rejection was enhanced by the manifest breach of faith in refusing to admit the Envoy, who came because they had bound themselves to receive him. Nor can it be said that the offer was fruitless from the want of opportunity of discussing it: our Envoy was present on their own soil.

Nor can it be ascribed to a want of sufficient powers: our Envoy had full powers to adjust every question of difference. Nor was there room for complaint that our propositions for settlement were unreasonable: permission was not even given our Envoy to make any proposition whatever. Nor can it be objected that we, on our part, would not listen to any reasonable terms of their suggestion: the Mexican Government refused all negotiation, and have made no proposition of any kind.

In my Message at the commencement of the present session, I informed you that upon the earnest appeal both of the Congress and Convention of Texas, I had ordered an efficient military force to take a position "between the Nueces and the Del Norte." This had become necessary to meet a threatened invasion of Texas by the Mexican forces, for which extensive military preparations had been made.—The invasion was threatened solely because Texas had determined, in accordance with a solemn resolution of the Congress of the United States, to annex herself to our Union; and, under these circumstances, it was plainly our duty to extend our protection over her citizens and soil.

This force was concentrated at Corpus Christi, and remained there until after I had received such information from Mexico as rendered it probable, if not certain, that the Mexican Government would refuse to receive our Envoy.

Meantime, Texas, by the final action of our Congress, had become an integral part of our Union. The Congress of Texas, by its act of December 19th, 1836, had declared the Rio del Norte to be the boundary of that Republic. Its jurisdiction had been extended and exercised beyond the Nueces.

The country between that river and the Del Norte had been represented in the Congress and in the Convention of Texas, had thus taken part in the act of Annexation itself, and is now included within one of our Congressional Districts. Our own Congress had, moreover, with great unanimity, by the act approved December 31st, 1845, recognized the country beyond the Nueces as a part of our territory by including it within our own revenue system; and a revenue officer, to reside within that District, has been appointed by and with the advice and consent of the Senate.

It became, therefore, of urgent necessity to provide for the defence of that portion of our country. Accordingly on the thirteenth of January last instructions were issued to the General in command of these troops to occupy the left bank of the Del Norte. This river—which is the South-Western boundary of the State of Texas—is an exposed frontier. From this quarter invasion was threatened; upon it and in its immediate vicinity, in the judgment of high military experience, are the proper stations for the protecting forces of the Government.

In addition to this important consideration, several others occurred to induce this movement.—Among these are the facilities afforded by the ports at Brazos Santiago and the mouth of the Del Norte for the reception of supplies by sea, the stronger and more healthful military positions, the convenience for obtaining a ready and more abundant supply of provisions, water, fuel, and forage, and the advantages which are afforded by the Del Norte in forwarding supplies to such posts as may be established in the interior and upon the Indian frontier.

The movement of the troops to the Del Norte was made by the commanding General, under positive instructions to abstain from all aggressive acts toward Mexico, or Mexican citizens, and to regard the relations between the Republic and the United States as peaceful, unless she should declare war, or commit acts of hostility indicative of a state of war. He was specially directed to protect private property and respect personal rights.

The army moved from Corpus Christi on the 11th of March, and on the 28th of that month arrived on the left bank of the Del Norte, opposite to Matamoros, where it encamped on a commanding position, which has since been strengthened by the erection of field works. A dépôt has also been established at Point Isabel, near the Brazos Santiago, thirty miles in rear of the encampment. The selection of his position was necessarily confided to the judgment of the General in command.

The Mexican forces at Matamoros assumed a belligerent attitude, and on the 12th of April, General Ampudia, then in command, notified General Taylor to break up his camp within twenty-four hours, and to retire beyond the Nueces river, and in the event of his failure to comply with these demands, announced that arms, and arms alone, must decide the question. But no open act of hostility was committed until the twenty-fourth of April.—On that day, General Arista, who had succeeded to the command of the Mexican forces, communicated to General Taylor that "he considered hostilities commenced and should prosecute them." A party of dragoons of sixty-three men and officers were on the same day dispatched from the American camp up the Rio del Norte, on its left bank, to ascertain whether the Mexican troops had crossed, or were preparing to cross the river, "became engaged with a large body of these troops, and after a short affair, in which some sixteen were killed and wounded, appear to have been surrounded and compelled to surrender."

The grievous wrongs perpetrated by Mexico upon our citizens throughout a long period of years, remain unredressed; and solemn treaties, pledging her public faith for this redress, have been disregarded. A Government either unable or unwilling to enforce the execution of such treaties, fails to perform one of its plainest duties.

Our commerce with Mexico has been almost annihilated. It was formerly highly beneficial to both nations; but our merchants have been deterred from prosecuting it by the system of outrage and extortion which the Mexican authorities have pursued against them, whilst their appeals through their own Government for indemnity have been made in vain. Our forbearance has gone to such an extreme as to be mistaken in its character. Had we acted with vigor in repelling the insults and redressing the injuries inflicted by Mexico at the commencement, we should doubtless have escaped all the difficulties in which we are now involved.

Instead of this, however, we have been exerting our best efforts to propitiate her good will. Upon the pretext that Texas, a nation as independent as herself, thought proper to unite its destinies with our own, she has affected to believe that we have severed her rightful territory, and, in official proclamations and manifestos, has repeatedly threatened to make war upon us for the purpose of reconquering Texas. In the mean time, we have tried every effort at reconciliation. The cup of forbearance had been exhausted, even before the recent information from the frontier of the Del Norte. But now, after reiterated menaces, Mexico has passed the boundary of the United States, has invaded our territory, and shed American blood upon the American soil. She has proclaimed that hostilities have commenced, and that the two nations are now at war.

As war exists, and, notwithstanding all our efforts to avoid it, exists by the act of Mexico herself, we are called upon, by every consideration of duty and patriotism, to vindicate, with decision, the honor, the rights, and the interests of our country.

Anticipating the possibility of a crisis like that which has arrived, instructions were given in August last, "as a precautionary measure," against invasion, or threatened invasion, authorizing General Taylor, if the emergency required, to accept volunteers, not from Texas only, but from the States of Louisiana, Alabama, Mississippi, Tennessee, and Kentucky; and corresponding letters were addressed to the respective Governors of those States.

These instructions were repeated; and in January last, soon after the incorporation of "Texas into our union of States," General Taylor was farther "authorized by the President to make a requisition upon the Executive of that State for such of its militia force as may be needed to repel invasion or to secure the country against apprehended invasion." On the 2d day of March, he was again reminded, "in the event of the approach of any considerable Mexican force, promptly and efficiently to use the authority with which he was clothed to call to him such auxiliary force as he might need."

War actually existing, and our territory having been invaded, General Taylor, pursuant to authority vested in him by my direction, has called on the Governor of Texas for four regiments of State troops—two to be mounted, and two to serve on foot; and on the Governor of Louisiana for four regiments of infantry, to be sent to him as soon as practicable.

In farther vindication of our rights and defence of our territory, I invoke the prompt action of Congress to recognize the existence of the war, and to place at the disposition of the Executive the means of prosecuting the war with vigor, and thus hastening the restoration of peace. To this end I recommend that authority should be given to call into the public service a large body of volunteers, to serve for not less than six or twelve months, unless sooner discharged.

A volunteer force is, beyond question, more efficient than any other description of citizen soldiers; and it is not to be doubted that a number far beyond that required would readily rush to the field upon the call of their country. I farther recommend that a liberal provision be made for sustaining our entire military force, and furnishing it with supplies and munitions of war.

The most energetic and prompt measures, and the immediate appearance in arms of a large and overpowering force, are recommended to Congress as the most certain and efficient means of bringing the existing collision with Mexico to a speedy and successful termination.

In making these recommendations, I deem it proper to declare that it is my anxious desire not only to terminate hostilities speedily, but to bring all matters in dispute between this Government and Mexico to an early and amicable adjustment; and, in this view, I shall be prepared to renew negotiations, whenever Mexico shall be ready to receive propositions, or to make propositions of her own.

I transmit herewith a copy of the Correspondence between our Envoy to Mexico and the Mexican Minister for Foreign Affairs; and so much of the Correspondence between that Envoy and the Secretary of State, and between the Secretary of War and the General in command on the Del Norte, as are necessary to a full understanding of the subject

JAMES K. POLK.

WASHINGTON, May 11th, 1846.

From Washington.

From our Regular Correspondent.

WASHINGTON, May 7, 1846—5 P. M.

The Committee of Investigation into the manner by which C. J. INGERSOLL obtained access to the Private Papers in the State Department met this morning.

Mr. BUCHANAN, Secretary of State, appeared before them, and gave all the information on the subject which he possessed. I believe he did not pretend to know much, but answered with cheerfulness every question put to him.

The Committee will meet again on Saturday and pursue their investigations, and have other witnesses before them.

In SENATE several reports were read, after which the bill for the settlement of the claims of New-Hampshire against the United States coming up

Mr. ATHERTON hoped that the vote would now be taken.

Mr. DAYTON hoped that the vote would not now be taken in a Senate so thin as it is at present.

After some conversation the vote was taken on the passage of the bill and the President said the Noes seemed to have it.

The Ayes and Noes were then ordered and resulted Yeas 18; Nays 10. This was one vote short of a quorum. The President declared the vote and added that no quorum voted. It was a strictly party vote. The 18 voting for it being Locos and the 10 voting against it Whigs.

Mr. SPEIGHT hoped that if there was any rule by which a call of the Senate might be made to compel the attendance of Senators it might be enforced.

Mr. BREESE read a rule of the Senate which seemed to authorize a call.

Some remarks were made by several Senators, particularly by Mr. MOREHEAD, who stated that the Senate never resorted to this expedient to compel attendance. He referred to a speech made on this subject in the Senate two or three years since by Mr. BENTON.

The bill was finally passed over informally. Several Senators came in during the conversation, which made more than a quorum present. Some ten members, in addition to those who answered to their names, were in the Hall in a few minutes after the call of the roll—making in all some 38 members.

The Senate then passed to the consideration of other matters of a more private character, without again calling the Yeas and Nays on this bill.

On motion of Mr. MANGUM, the Senate agreed to adjourn over till Monday next, for the sake of putting the Senate chamber in summer order.

Some private bills were then taken up—among which was one for the relief of J. J. BULOW, for the destruction of his property by Indians in Florida, which created a long discussion between the Florida Senators, J. M. CLAYTON, CRITTENDEN, &c.—It was finally laid on the table, and the Senate adjourned till Monday at 12½ o'clock.

In the HOUSE, after some ineffectual attempts to proceed with business, Mr. GIDDINGS moved to reconsider the vote ordering the President's message of yesterday to be printed, and was proceeding to make some remarks amid much confusion, when, before the objects of his remarks could be fully comprehended, he was ruled out of order, and the whole matter laid on the table.

Mr. ADAMS of Miss. offered the following Resolution:

Resolved, (the Senate concurring,) That the President of the Senate and the Speaker of the House of Representatives adjourn their respective Houses *sine die* on Monday the 13th day of July next, at 2 o'clock P. M.

This coming up out of order, it required two-thirds of the members present to carry a suspension of the rules.

The Yeas and Nays were ordered, and resulted Yeas 101, Nays 62. This looks as if the Resolution would be carried the first opportunity that may be had of voting upon it. The country would feel much relieved by their absence from this city.

The House then went into Committee of the Whole and took up the Post-Office Appropriation bill, upon which a discussion of some two or three hours took place, after which, it was reported to the House with some slight amendments, and passed.

The House then adjourned.

The proceedings in both wings of the Capitol to-day were of very little interest. RICHELIEU.

Reported for The Tribune................By Telegraph.

FRIDAY, May 8, 6½ P. M.

The SENATE was not in session to-day.

In the HOUSE OF REPRESENTATIVES, Mr. TIBBATTS, from the Select Committee on the subject, reported a bill for the benefit of the blind, authorizing three townships of Public Lands, to be sold by the Secretary of the Treasury, and the proceeds to be appropriated to purchase books for the use of the blind. After some discussion as to whether the bill should be now considered or referred to Committee of the Whole, it was finally referred to said Committee.

The bill to retrocede Alexandria back to Virginia was next taken up in Committee of the Whole, Mr. DOUGLASS in the Chair. Mr. HUNTER of Virginia made a very able and eloquent speech in favor of the bill. Mr. CULVER of N. Y. moved to strike out the word *white* in the bill so as to secure equal rights to colored men. This motion was lost.

Mr. PAYNE of Alabama, made a vehement speech against the Bill, in which he charged Eastern Virginia with a design to add the votes of Alexandria to their strength in State elections. Mr. PAYNE said the object of Eastern Virginia in thus seeking to increase its vote was to defeat Western Virginia in its efforts to extend the right of suffrage. This accusation of Mr. P. brought all the Virginia members, except Mr. PENDLETON, to their feet to reply to the charge.

Mr. BAYLY got the floor and came down on Mr. PAYNE like a thousand, nay, like ten thousand brick. He charged Mr. P. with impertinent interference in the domestic affairs of Virginia, of which he, Mr. P. knew nothing. Mr. BAYLY is still speaking and bearing down upon Mr. PAYNE most severely, Payne looking iron spikes and taking notes There will be a scene.

From our Regular Correspondent.

WASHINGTON, May 8th, 1846—5 P. M.

Mr. WEBSTER is expected back in this city in two or three days. He will probably be in New-York to-morrow or Monday.

Mr. SLIDELL and family arrived at Coleman's from the South, by the way of the Ohio river, last night. We may, therefore, soon expect to hear something from the Executive about Mexico.

The weather is still hazy, cold and rainy.

The SENATE was not in session to-day. Workmen are employed in the chamber in putting it in Summer repair. The chairs, desks, curtains, &c. are strewed about the rotunda. They have adjourned over till Monday, but it is understood that there will be no business transacted till Tuesday. Five or six Members will meet on the floor and adjourn *pro forma* as they cannot adjourn for a longer time than three days without the consent of the House of Representatives.

In the HOUSE, this morning, Mr. TIBBATTS of Ky. reported a bill from the Select Committee appointed for that purpose for the benefit of the blind.

Mr. ATKINSON of Va. moved to lay it on the table, which motion was lost.

It was finally read twice and referred to the Committee of the Whole on the State of the Union, by a vote of 103 to 54.

The following is the bill as reported, which may be interesting to the numerous friends of the blind:

A BILL FOR THE BENEFIT OF THE BLIND.

Be it enacted, That there be set apart for the benefit of persons in the United States afflicted with blindness, a quantity of land equal to three townships, which may be selected and located by a competent and fit person appointed by the Secretary of the Treasury, out of any of the Public Lands of the United States, in sections corresponding with any of the legal divisions in which the public lands are authorised to be surveyed, so as not to interfere with private land claims or the rights of preëmption: which lands, when so located, shall be disposed of under the direction of the Secretary of the Treasury, to procure the printing of a Library of Books for the use of the Blind, which books shall be distributed among the States and Territories of the United States by the Secretary of the Treasury, as near as may be practicable, in the ratio of the number of blind persons in each State and Territory respectively, at the time of such distribution: *Provided*, That the said lands shall not be sold for less than $1 25 per acre.

The House then went into Committee of the Whole, Mr. DOUGLASS in the Chair, and took up the bill to re-cede to Virginia the County of Alexandria in the District of Columbia.

A spirited discussion ensued, in which a rather severe controversy occurred between Mr. BAYLY of Va. and Mr. PAINE of Ala.

Mr. McDOWELL of Va. made a very eloquent speech in favor of his bill, which wast listened to with more interest than any other speeches I have heard delivered, except Mr. Adams's.

Some slight amendments were adopted, when the Committee rose and reported to the House.

The bill with the amendments finally passed the House by a vote of 95 to 66. The House then adj.

The Daily Delta.

VOLUME I.] NEW ORLEANS, SATURDAY MORNING, MAY 30, 1846. [NUMBER 199.

THE DELTA.

THE undersigned have made arrangements for the permanent publication in this city of a daily newspaper, to be styled THE DELTA, the first number of which will be issued from their Office, No. 112 Poydras street, on the 12th October.

Instead of following the hackneyed course generally resorted to on occasions like the present, of setting forth in florid phrase and pointed period what THE DELTA will be, they will confine themselves in this instance to stating, that in politics it will be *strictly neutral:* in all the other attributes—commercial, literary and miscellaneous—of a valuable and interesting journal, it will be the object and aim of the undersigned to make it worthy of a liberal public patronage.

The subscription to the daily paper will be TEN DOLLARS per annum, payable semi-annually in advance. They will also issue, once a week, a large sheet in quarto form, the subscription to which will be THREE DOLLARS per annum, in advance.

DAVIS, CORCORAN & CO.

New Orleans, October, 1845.

Business Cards.

JOSEPH O. PIERSON, *Steamboat and General Agent*, 75 Poydras street, New Orleans. m14

REMOVAL.—FELIX CONNOLLY has removed his Auction Store to No. 66 Camp street. o12

P. DOWNEY, PUBLIC WAREHOUSE KEEPER *No. 86 DELORD St.*, New Orleans. n29 1y

JAMES DUNLAP, *Attorney at Law, No. 3 ST. CHARLES ST., Room No.* 11. jy18 6m

DAVID L. McCAY, *Notary Public*, 71 Canal street, (up stairs.) o12-tf

THOMAS CONNOLLY, *Wholesale and Retail Clothing and Dry Goods Store*, 32 New Levee. n6-1y

JOSEPH H. MOORE, *Commission Merchant*, 107 Poydras street. o13—1y

P. ROTCHFORD, *Commission Merchant*, 39 New Levee. o12tf

J. J. BROWNE, *Cotton Broker*, 33 Camp street, New Orleans. o12

D. ISRANG, *Military and Fashionable Tailor*, 81 *Magazine street.* o12

H. BONNABEL, *Wholesale and Retail Druggist*, corner of Tchoupitoulas and Natchez streets, New Orleans. o12 1y

WILLIAM GRAY, *Steamboat, Plantation and Family Groceries*, 58 *COMMON STREET, New Orleans*, next door to Hewlett's Exchange. m6 tf

MATTHEW MARTIN, *Wholesale Grocer and Commission Merchant*, No. 54 *NEW LEVEE STREET*, New Orleans. m5 1y

CHARLES BEDFORD. *Commission Merchant and Shipping Agent*, 48 Customhouse street, New Orleans. fy3

JOHN CRAGG—Successor of Dents Corcoran—*Notary Public*, 60 Banks' Arcade, (up stairs) Magazine street. d4 tf

REMOVAL.—*CHARLES A. LABUZAN, AUCTIONEER*—duly commissioned—has removed his office to No. 27 Camp street. n7

ABRAM A. GREEN. JOHN M'DOUGALL.
GREEN & McDOUGALL, *Commission Merchants*, No. 75 Poydras street. o12

J. E. HYDE. J. H. OGLESBY.
HYDE & OGLESBY *Commission and Forwarding Merchants*, 12 Poydras street, N. Orleans. o12

J. B. THOMPSON. J. O. NIXON.
THOMPSON & NIXON, *Fashionable Ready-Made Clothing and Outfitting Establishment*, 44 Canal reet, near Chartres street o12

SAMUEL LOCKE, *Importer and Dealer in Hardware*—also Manufacturer of Tin and Copper Ware—Nos. 7 and 8 Front Levee, between Customhouse and Bienville streets. o13

COLEMAN & DUDLEY, *Manufacturers of Corn Meal, Flour, &c.*, corner of Tchoupitoulas and St. Andrew street, Lafayette. M. R. DUDLEY, 51 Tchoupitoulas street, New Orleans. o19 6m

H. SCHOONMAKER. ANDRE BROUSSEAU.
A. BROUSSEAU & CO., (Successors to H. SCHOONMAKER,) *Importers and Dealers in Carpets, Floorcloth, Matting, &c.; Jeans, Linseys and Cottonades, by the case.* 23 *CHARTRES ST.* fy22

BOYLE & MACCORRY, *Wholesale and Retail Dealers in DRY GOODS AND CLOTHING, No. 26 POYDRAS ST., corner of Tchoupitoulas, NEW ORLEANS.* ☞ Constantly on hand a general assortment of PLANTATION GOODS, &c. jy8 1y

J. RANDOLPH BURNS, *Attorney and Counsellor at Law, and Commissioner of Deeds, &c., for the State of South Carolina.* Office, 45 Customhouse street, New Orleans, La. The German and French Languages are spoken in the office. Office Hours from 9, A. M., to 6, P. M. m11 1y

GUION & CO.,

T. F. GUION, W. S. GUINNESS, JOHN BUSH.

CORNER OF ST. CHARLES AND CANAL STS., NEW ORLEANS, *Importers and Wholesale and Retail Dealers in Fine Fancy Articles, Cutlery, Perfumery, Combs, Brushes, Toilet Articles, Umbrellas, Walking Canes, Gloves, and Gentlemen's Furnishing Goods.* Warehouse, 19 Maiden Lane, New York. m4

THOMAS N. GRAVES, *Blank Book Manufacturer and Stationer*, No. 54 *GRAVIER STREET, opposite Canal Bank building. New Orleans*—who, in addition to the usual articles of STATIONERY, keeps constantly on hand the most extensive stock of BLANK BOOKS, of all descriptions, manufactured under his own immediate superintendence. oct28 1y

A CARD.

J. M. JONES, *No. 8, Strand, Galveston, Texas*, DEALER IN BOOKS, STATIONERY, JEWELLERY and FANCY GOODS. Persons visiting Texas will please call and examine our general assortment of everything in the above way. Also, agent for the sale of cheap publications, Magazines, &c.

N. B.—Maps, Charts and Histories of Texas always on hand and for sale. d31-tf

W. F. HYDE & G. W. MOSS, *Auction and Commission Merchants*, W. F. HYDE, *Auctioneer, Nos. 37 and 39 COMMON STREET, corner of Magazine, New Orleans.*—Special and strict attention will be paid to the sale of Real Estate, and Property of every description, at all times and in every part of the city.

References.—Messrs. Maunsel White & Co.; A Ledoux & Co.; G. & C. Urquhart; A. & L. Addison; Wm. Frost & Co.; J. W. Stanton & Co.; Norcross & Fosdick; Dudley & Nelson; Alexander Grant, Esq., and T. R. Hyde, Esq. n25

COPARTNERSHIP NOTICE.

THE undersigned have formed a copartnership under the firm of BEARD, CALHOUN & CO., and will continue the business of *Auctioneers*, for the sale of Real Estate, Bank and other Stocks, Slaves, and Merchandize; and will also act as Appraisers and General Brokers, for the sale and purchase of all descriptions of property. ☞ Office No. 8, Banks' Arcade.

J. A. BEARD,
JNO. CALHOUN,
Oct. 1st.—o29 J. R. BEARD.

M. C. QUIRK, *Cabinet Maker and Undertaker*, corner Camp and Poydras streets, near Lafayette Square. Orders for funerals, at all hours, promptly attended to. o14-1y

JEWELRY.

W. S. MORGAN, WORKING JEWELLER and WATCHMAKER, *No. 27 CAMP street.*—Mr. Morgan announces his removal from Natchez to this city. He offers for sale, on terms the most reasonable, every variety of articles of Jewelry and Watches, and is prepared to repair every thing in his line with despatch. n2 6m

WATCHES, JEWELRY, PERFUMERY, AND FANCY GOODS.

E. A. TYLER, *No. 39 CAMP STREET*, has for sale a good assortment of Gold and Silver WATCHES, Gold Guard, Fob and Vest CHAINS, Keys, Pencils, Pens, &c.; Broaches of every kind; Finger Rings; Gold and Silver Thimbles; Spectacles of all kinds; Silver Table, Tea, Mustard Salt and Sugar Spoons; Ladles, Tongs, &c.; Fine Razors, Scissors and Pocket Knives; Cologne, Lavender, Fancy Soaps, and a great variety of Perfumery and Fancy Goods, any of which will be sold at extremely low prices.

☞ Watches, Clocks and Music Boxes carefully repaired and warranted. Jewelry Manufactured and Repaired. Hair neatly braided for Bracelets, Necklaces, &c. o12

BOAT-SAILS AND AWNINGS.

H. CASSIDY, Plain and Fancy BOAT-SAIL AND AWNING MAKER, *No 22 NEW BASIN, between Circus and St. John Streets, New Orleans.*—Every description of Wood and Iron-frame Awnings for stores, galleries, offices, steamboats, &c., made to order at the shortest notice, and waranted proof against rot or mildew. Every description of *Military Tents, Markees, Tarpolins, &c.*, made in a superior manner. ☞ Fall and Purchase-ropes of every description spliced and furnished at the shortest notice. o25-1y

JOHN McCARTY, PLUMBER,

No. 134 CAMP STREET.

HAS just received a new assortment of French Water Closets; also, Force and Lift Pumps, Beer Pumps, &c., Bathing Tubs and Shower Baths. Laying and repairing Lead Pipes; Sheet Lead work of every description; Ship work, &c., promptly put up and repaired. All orders punctually attended to. Charges moderate. o18 1y

NICHOLAS DOBBINS,

Copper, Tin and Sheet-Iron Worker,

No. 8 TRIANGLE BUILDINGS, (near Louisiana Bakery.)

SHIP BLACKSMITHING—in all its Branches—attended to with despatch. ☞ N. B. All kinds of Cooking Utensils made to order, and repaired.—Ships' Pumps, Cabooses, &c., furnished to order and repaired. o24 6m

BLACKSMITH AND WHEELWRIGHT.

The subscriber is prepared to furnish DRAYS and CARTS, finished in a superior manner, with iron axles. Ship Blacksmith Work and Job Work in general, done with care and despatch. Workshop on Tchoupitoulas street, between Hunter and Roffignac streets.

y11 ALEXANDER WATERSTON.

STORAGE.

10,000 BARRELS or the bulk thereof will be STORED IN FIREPROOF WAREHOUSES, on moderate terms, by

d 19 6m P. DOWNEY, 86 Delord st.

Colleges and Schools.

FOR YOUNG LADIES.

MR. E. J. GOMEZ respectfully informs the parents of young Ladies, that he will begin a *Course of Lessons* in the SPANISH LANGUAGE, about the 12th of January, in the house of a respectable family living in the 2d Municipality. The number of pupils will be limited, and those who would avail themselves of this opportunity will oblige him by addressing a note to the office of this paper, No. 112 Poydras street.

Mr. Gomez's method for teaching his native language s a new and easy one, which will enable any person o learn it in ONLY FOUR MONTHS.

☞ For further particulars, references, &c., apply at Mr. G's Rooms, *No. 42 CUSTOMHOUSE st.* jy2

HIGH SCHOOL FOR YOUNG LADIES,

Carondelet street, near St. Joseph st.,

AS BOARDERS OR DAY PUPILS—*under the superintendence of the MISS ALLISONS.*

In this institution the most competent Instructors are employed in every department essential to a highly finished education. Particular care is bestowed on the formation of the manners of the Young Ladies, and the most unwearied attention is devoted to their mental improvement. The mode of discipline pursued by the Miss Allisons is one of uniform gentleness, as calculated to produce the happiest effects upon all dispositions, and to create a truly feminine and ladylike deportment and character.

The study of the French Language forms a part of the daily employment of all the pupils, under the superintendence of a Professor from Paris, and is included in the terms of tuition: all other Languages with the accomplishments of Music, Singing, Drawing and Dancing, are the seperate charges of the teachers and masters engaged in the institution.

The Miss Allisons refer to—

W. Freret, Esq.,	Rev. Dr. Wheaton,
S J. Peters Esq.,	Judge Rawle,
H C. Cammack, Esq.,	W. P. Converse, Esq.,
Theodore Shute, Esq.,	A. Lanfear, Esq.,
H. Palfrey, Esq.,	L. C. Duncan, Esq.,
H. Lockett, Esq.	o12

SPANISH LANGUAGE. Evening Class.

REMOVED TO No. 90 CONTI St.

DON E. GOMEZ, Professor of Spanish Literature, has the honor to inform the public that he will open an EVENING CLASS, for the purpose of teaching his native language to those who would acquire the Castilian idiom, now become so useful throughout the U. States.

Mr. G. possesses an intimate and perfect knowledge of the language, and follows a method of instruction so natural and easy, that he does not fear to assure any person that he may SPEAK SPANISH IN FOUR MONTHS.

☞ Terms are moderate. Private lessons attended if required. For further particulars apply at the office of this paper. n5 6m

Restaurats.

TREMONT HOUSE AND RESTAURAT,

ST. CHARLES ST., adjoining the Theatre.

THE subscriber respectfully informs his friends and the public, that he has had his establishment thoroughly repaired, and is now fully prepared to accommodate those who may favor him with their custom, with BOARDING AND LODGING—*by the Day or Week*—on as favorable terms as any similar establishment in the city. The Table shall be supplied with the best the Markets afford. *Meals at all hours*—to suit all occupations. The BAR is supplied with choice Liquors.

☞ THE RESTAURAT will be open until a late hour in the evening. OYSTERS served up in every style. [o23 3m] P. IRWIN.

FRANKLIN HOUSE.

LAKE END OF THE SHELL ROAD.

THE subscriber having leased from the Canal and Banking Co., the FRANKLIN HOUSE, at the Lake End of the New Shell Road, respectfully informs the patrons of the old firm of Hunter & Lathrop, and the public generally, that he is prepared fully to meet the expectations of his guests. The excellence of his table shall not be surpassed; his servants shall be courteous and obliging. His larder is supplied with the best the markets afford, including Game, Fish, Crabs, Oysters, Turtle, Terrapin, &c.

o12 JAS. W. LATHROP.

MILES' AMERICAN OYSTER SALOON,

ST. CHARLES street, next door to O'Meara's American, and opposite the St. Charles Hotel.

THOMAS MILES informs his old customers and all who would become new ones, that he has completed his arrangements for the winter business. He will keep constantly on hand, oysters fresh from the best beds of the Gulf and the Lakes, which he will serve up in every variety of style as called for.

As heretofore, he will use all dilligence in procuring the best Beefsteaks and Mutton Chops to be found in the market. They will be served up at the shortest notice, as will be Game and every other delicacy of the season.

His charges will continue to be moderate, and his waiters as usual, polite and attentive.

☞ Private parties can be accommodated with boxes for their exclusive use. o12-tf

GLASS AND CROCKERY WARE.

MICHL. O'CONNOR, dealer in GLASS AND CROCKERY WARE, *NEW BRICK ROW. NORTH SIDE OF POYDRAS MARKET. between the Amphitheatre and Philippa street,* sells Tumblers, Wine, Cordial, Champagne, and Jelly Glasses, Lamps, Decanters, &c.

The patronage of Hotel and Coffee-House Keepers is respectfully solicited. n13—nov2 1y

PHILADELPHIA SADDLERY WAREHOUSE,

No. 6 MAGAZINE STREET, near Canal st.,

SIGN OF THE GOLDEN HORSE HEAD.

MAGEE, KNEASS & CO., from their long experience as Manufacturers and Importers of SADDLERY, *expressly adapted to this Market*, are enabled to offer a Stock of Goods to select from, unsurpassed for assortment and manufacture in the country, and can with certainty insure satisfaction to all, as they are determined not to be undersold. Their stock comprises all kinds of Saddlery, Harness, TRUNKS, Leather, and Coach Trimmings; also, Saddlery, Hardware, Coach and Harness Furniture, Ploughs, &c. nov23 1y

CARRIAGES.

The subscriber is now receiving a few superior built GIGS AND BUGGIES, suitable for Doctors' use or business purposes. On hand, COACHES, BAROUCHES, ROCKAWAYS and BUGGY WAGONS, all of which bearing comparison can be sold as low as at any other establishment in the Southern country. Persons wishing to purchase will please give me a call, as I am determined to dispose of my present stock at a sacrifice. A. E. CRANE, 66 St. Charles street,

ap21 6m Opposite the New Exchange.

NEW ORLEANS CARRIAGE WAREHOUSE,

AT Nos. 118 and 120 GRAVIER STREET, (Rear of the St. Charles Hotel.)

The undersigned has just received in store from his Manufactory, and will receive by every packet from New York, CARRIAGES AND HARNESS of every description, with the latest improvements, and designed expressly for this market.

Though the undersigned does not, like some other establishments in the trade, propose to sell his stock at a sacrifice, for quality and prices he confidently invites comparison with any in New Orleans. Purchasers are invited to give me a call. E. W. HALE.

Also, for sale, COACH TRIMMINGS, VARNISH, &c., &c. ap25 d&W

ECLIPSE STABLES,

On Philippa and Circus Streets,

Between Gravier street and the Poydras Market.

Are now under the Management of Mr. B. FORDNAY, and are prepared to receive HORSES for sale. Livery Horses also kept with care in the best manner, at $15 per month. Carriages, Cabs, Horses, Buggies, and Saddle-Horses for Hire, on the MOST REASONABLE TERMS. Expresses sent to any part of the Coast with despatch, by a careful and efficient person. Horses Bought and Sold on Commission.

A CARRIAGE REPAIRING SHOP is attached to the premises, where all kinds of Wood-work, Smith-work, Horse-shoeing, Painting, and Trimming are executed in the best possible manner.

fy14-1y WILLIAM J. WHITING.

FAMILY GROCERIES.

250 SACKS Rio Coffee;
20 do Old Java do.;
5 do Mocha do.;
75 boxes Tomato Catsup;
10 do Walnut do.;
5 do Mushroom do.;
25 barrels No. 1 Mackerel
30 do No. 2 do.;
20 do No. 3 do.;
100 packages assorted do., Nos. 1, 2 and 3,
20 hogsheads Sugar;
50 barrels Molasses;
20 half barrels Syrup;
75 boxes Sperm Candles;
10 tierces Rice;
200 boxes Soap;
20 boxes Castile Soap;

A general assortment of fine Liquors; Segars; Pickles; crushed and pound Sugar; Tobacco; and every thing in the Grocery line for sale by

fy28 4m JOHN C. SHANNON, No. 53 New Levee

Fashionable Clothing.

CLOTHING!—CLOTHING!!

At No. 34 NEW LEVEE.

THE best selected and cheapest stock in New Orleans. Also, a large assortment of DRY GOODS, of the latest and newest styles, and a complete assortment of HATS, BOOTS and SHOES, for sale low at the store of JAMES CORLIS, 34 New Levee,

d14 n1 6m—n8 A few doors above Poydras st.

☞ Planters and strangers visiting the city would find it to their interest to call and examine my extensive stock of Domestics before purchasing elsewhere. J. C.

S. M. RON,

Corner CARONDELET AND COMMON STREETS,

RESPECTFULLY informs his friends and the public that he is now prepared to make New Garments out of Old, by thoroughly renovating and cleaning them; also to DYE Gentlemen's and Ladies' Garments ANY COLOR, at the shortest notice.

TAILORING—Civil and Military.—The strictest attention will be paid to this branch of the business; and those favoring me with their custom, can be assured that their work will be done to their satisfaction, in a thorough workmanlike manner. n12-6m

REMOVAL.

THE subscribers have removed their *Wholesale Clothing Establishment* from No. 1 Magazine street to the GRANITE STORE, NO. 35 MAGAZINE, corner of Gravier street, opposite the Arcade.

They are now receiving from their manufactory in New York a large stock of the finest and most fashionable CLOTHING, such as

Super Cloth Cloaks;
" " Overcoats, Frock and Dress Coats;
Cloth Paletots, of all styles;
Black and fancy Cassimere Pants;
Cashmere, Satin, Silk and Velvet Vests;
Linen and Linen Bosom Shirts, of latest styles;
Silk, Cotton and Flannel Under Shirts and Drawers,
Satin Scarfs, Cravats and Stocks; Hosiery, &c. &c.

All of which will be sold at low prices, wholesale and retail. o12 TAYLOR & HADDEN

Hats, Boots & Shoes.

St. Charles' Shoe and Hat Store.

U. LAROUSSINI would respectfully inform his friends and the public that he has removed his store from 175 Poydras street, (one door from the corner of Baronne,) to the *Corner of ST. CHARLES AND POYDRAS.* He has now on hand, and is prepared to sell at the lowest prices, a large assortment of FASHIONABLE HATS, and Gentlemen's BOOTS, SHOES and BROGANS. Also, every description of Ladies', Misses', Children's and Servants' SHOES, just received from the best manufactories of Philadelphia, New York and Paris. dec6 6m

REMOVAL.

THOMAS HILLMAN would respectfully inform his friends and the public in general, that he has removed his SHOE STORE from No. 40 to 98 *CAMP ST.* He has now on hand and is prepared to sell at the lowest prices, a large assortment of Gentlemen's Boots, Shoes and Brogans; all descriptions of ladies work, servants and childrens. He is going largely into the local manufacturing of gentlemen's wear of all kinds, and has now a large supply of French Calf Skins, also Philadelphia and New York, of the best quality. Patent Leather and Findings, all of the choicest descriptions.

n13tf THOMAS HILLMAN, 98 Camp st

ALL TASTES SUITED.

Just landed, per last packet ships from New York and Havre, a splendid assortment of all the different qualities and newest styles of fashionable HATS.

ALSO—The ne plus ultra moleskin Hat, extra quality, celebrated for its beauty and durability, a few cases only, the splendor of which is unsurpassed.

Youths' and men's CAPS of the latest fashion. All for sale cheap for cash at

CALDER'S Fashionable Hat Store,
n2 tf No. 4 Camp street.

HATS AND CAPS.

JOHN ROBERTSON & CO., 31 *Canal street*, New Orleans, have just received per ships Clyde and Clifton, from New York, a large and complete assortment of HATS and CAPS, consisting of gentlemen's Extra Fine Moleskin, Superfine Short and Long Napped Beavers, Russia Cassimere, Brush and Silk Hats, latest New York and Paris Styles; Square and Round Crown Sporting Hats. Also, Medium and Broad Brims of every description; Gentlemen's Dress, Cloth, Velvet, Otter, South Sea Seal, Muskrat, Warspite and Glazed Caps; Youth's and Children's Fancy Cloth and Velvet Caps; Ladies' Riding Hats and Caps with Plumes, newest styles. All of which are offered on the most reasonable terms, and no pains spared to give entire satisfaction to purchasers. o29

Maguire's Daguerreotype Rooms,

NO. 6 CAMP STREET.

J. MAGUIRE has been awarded the FIRST PREMIUM at the late State Fair, for the finest specimens of DAGUERREOTYPE in Louisiana.

LIFE-LIKE PORTRAITS guaranteed, or no charge made.

Apparatus (guaranteed the genuine Voigtlander Camera) with Instructions; Plates, Cases, &c., &c., for sale on the most reasonable terms. m12 tf

SHIP AND STEAMBOAT LUMBER YARD.

No 4 TRIANGLE BUILDINGS, on the Levee, in front of St. Mary's Market.—The undersigned keep constantly on hand Wheel Arms, Bucket Plank, Brace Stuff, Live-oak and White-oak Plank and Timber, Knees, Decking, Donage, White and Yellow Pine, Cypress, Walnut, Cherry, Mahogany, Hickory, Ash, Cedar, Gum, Poplar, &c. &c.

All Orders filled with promptness by

n1 tf FILKINS & BRADY.

FIFTY DOLLARS REWARD.

Absconded, on the evening before last, the Mulattress VIOLETTE. She is about 38 years of age; 5 feet 2 or 3 inches high; of rather bright color; regular features, and wanting a good many of her front teeth. She is slow of speech and very intelligent. The above reward will be paid to any person who will deliver her as indicated, and give evidence to convict the person or persons who are suspected of concealing her, or $20 for the slave alone. Apply at No. 11 Old Levee street. m2

$20 REWARD.

LOST, OR STOLEN, on Wednesday, the 11th inst., somewhere between the Hotel at the Lake-end of the New Shell Road and the St. Charles Exchange, a Green POCKET-BOOK, containing $45 or $47 in cash, and three notes—a description is left at this office, where the finder is requested to leave the same, and receive Twenty Dollars reward. m15 tf

FOR SALE.

A FIRST RATE COOK (Mulatress) talks English and French. She is about 38 years of age, and has been 16 years in the family.

An excellent HOUSE SERVANT, and a pretty good Washer and Ironer. This Negress is about 19 to 20 years of age, and is affectionate to children.

A mulatto BOY about 13 years of age. He is very intelligent and would be valuable to a Physician, or as a house or body servant. Creole of this city.

They speak both languages, and are offered for sale for no other reason than the owner's breaknig up house keeping. Apply at this Office. fy17

ALEX. HILL'S HOUSE FURNISHING STORE,

56 CAMP STREET, New Orleans.

Where families can find all articles of HOUSE-KEEPING, comprising a general assortment and select stock of—

KITCHEN FURNITURE—Cooking Utensils, Tin and Iron Ware, Fire Sets, brass and steel; Shovels and Tongs and Kitchen Fire Irons.

Enamelled and Patent Metal Tinned Hollow Ware; Fire Dogs.

German Silver, Block Tin and Britannia Tea and Coffee Urns.

TABLE CUTLERY—German Silver, Britannia and Iron Tea and Table Spoons.

WOOD WARE—Brass and Iron Bound Cedar Pails, Churns and Tubs.

Rattan Bound Cedar Ware, a new article.

WILLOW WARE—Baskets, Cradles, Nurse Chairs and Wagons.

BRUSHES—Fancy and Plain, Dusting, Sweeping and Hearth Brushes.

MATS—Jute, Manilla, Alicant, Palm and Husk Mats.

Waiters and Trays.

Brass, Britannia and new metal Candle Sticks and Lamps. Steamboat and Hall Lanterns.

COOKING STOVES and FURNACES.

D. and J. Wright's patent Premium Cook Stoves, for wood or coal, with fixtures complete, the most approved pattern in use.

☞ Hotels and Steamboats furnished at reduced prices. o26—6md&W

ORLEANS SPICE MILLS

BOLEN & VERNON having taken the Store on the *corner of LAFAYETTE and MAGAZINE sts.*, will continue to supply Grocers, Hotels, Restaurats, Steamboats and the public, with a superior article of ROAST AND GROUND COFFEE; SPICES, of all kinds; HOMINY and FRESH CORN MEAL. Country Merchants supplied on reasonable terms.

jy30 BOLEN & VERNON.

50 SLAVES—Just received from Virginia and for sale by

dec13 6m S. N. HITE, 100 Union st.

OIL VITRIOL—For Soda Manufacturers, received by H. BONNABEL,

m7 corner Natchez and Tchoupitoulas sts.

Fancy and Dry Goods.

Linens, Linen Sheetings, Nettings and Checks of Direct Importation.

JUST received, per ships Nestor and Waldron from Liverpool, twenty-five packages of—

Super Undressed Family 4-4 Linens, Fine Lawns, &c.;
6-4, 10-4 and 12-4 Linen Sheetings—Grass Bleached;
8-4 and 10-4 Damask Table Linens—various qualities;
8-4, 10 4, 16-4 and 24-4 Damask Table Cloths; Napkins;
Huckaback Linen Towels, Diapers and Crash;
Superfine Linen Checks and Stripes; Heavy do. do. for coarse use;
Planters' Linens and Osnaburgs;
Linen Nettings, finest Bleached and Brown;
The genuine Patent Double 12-4 Bobbinet, for Musquito Bars, such as were never before imported here, and *only to be had at NOLAN'S.*

The above Linen Goods are fully warranted, being expressly manufactured to the order of and for the trade of the subscriber.

The Fancy Dress and Staple Stock of Dry Goods will be sold at *very reduced prices* for the balance of the season. JAMES P. NOLAN,

corner of Chartres and Canal streets.

N. B.—Plantation and Family Dry Goods put up at the lowest wholesale prices at retail, to suit country purchasers. ap30 1m

FRENCH MILLINERY, &c.

MRS. BANISTER, *Importer of French Millinery and English Straw Bonnets, No. 66 ROYAL STREET, corner of Bienville,* has just received her Spring Stock of SUMMER BONNETS, PARASOLS, BAREGE SCARFS, &c. She is also receiving, by every arrival, a select assortment of Ribbons, Flowers Caps, Plumes, Veils, Corsets, Gloves, Ladies' and Infants' Embroidered Robes, Collars, Handkerchiefs and Fancy Goods. m12tf

A CARD.

DOCTOR BANKS takes this opportunity of informing the citizens and inhabitants of New Orleans that he has taken an Office at the corner of Girod and Carondelet streets, where he may be consulted every day before 12 o'clock. He was formerly a Surgeon in the Honorable East India Company's service, and possesses testimonials from the leading Medical Men of London.—Amongst others, the following from Sir Astley Cooper, whose pupil he was for some years at the Borough Hospitals.

"It is with the greatest pleasure that I certify to my opinion of the high professional attainments of Mr ABRAHAM BANKS, whom I consider worthy in every way of the highest professional confidence.

ASTLEY COOPER.

Guy's Hospital, April 2d, 1834.—m29 3m

Marine and Fire Insurance.

TENNESSEE MARINE AND FIRE INSURANCE COMPANY—Capital $300,000.

DIRECTORS.

John M. Hill,	Jacob McGavock,
Geo. W. Martin,	Wm. Eakin,
F. B. Fogg,	Jno. M. Bass,
W. W. Woodfolk,	Jos. B. Knowles,
Alex. Allison,	G. M. Fogg.
Sam Seay,	

JNO. M. HILL, President.

JAMES J. GILL, Secretary.

This long established Company, with the most ample means for the protection of its policies, continues to take RIVER, SEA and FIRE RISKS on the most liberal terms, at its Agency in New Orleans, at the office of

m21-6m ALLISON, ALLEN & CO., 67 Magazine st.

EXPRESS MAIL ROUTE.

EXPRESS MAIL ROUTE FROM NEW ORLEANS TO BALTIMORE, *via Mobile, Montgomery, Augusta and Charleston.*

Through in 6 1-2 Days!

New Orleans to Mobile—Fare $5, by the Daily Line of Steamboats.

Mobile to Montgomery—Fare $8, by the Steamboat Lines on the Alabama River. $10 to $15 by the Daily Mail Stage Line.

Montgomery to Charleston—Fare $26 50. Time 49 hours.

WINTER SCHEDULE:

On and after November 1st, 1845. 24 hours in advance of the Savannah Line.

Leave Montgomery,	8	o'clock,	A. M.
" Chehaw,	12½	"	P. M.
" Atlanta,	5	"	P. M.
" Augusta,	6	"	A. M.
Arrive at Chehaw,	12	"	M.
" " Atlanta	4½	"	P. M.
" " Augusta	4½	"	A. M.
" " Charleston	2	"	P. M.

DISTANCES:

From Montgomery to Chehaw, by Railroad	40 miles
" Chehaw to Atlanta, by Post Coaches	136 "
" Atlanta to Augusta, by Railroad	173 "
" Augusta to Charleston, by Railroad	136 "

Three Daily Stage Lines between Chehaw and Atlanta.

The Express Mail, the Georgia Railroad, and the South Carolina Railroad Lines, running in connection, passing through West Point, LaGrange and Newnan, over one of the best roads in the Southern country.

This Route has recently been improved by a change in the stage road, by New Coaches on the Stage Lines, by New Cars on the Carolina and Georgia Railroads—those on the latter fitted up with STATE ROOMS AND BERTHS.

Charleston to Baltimore—Fare $21, by the Washington City, or Chesapeake Bay Route.

☞ For *Through Tickets* between Montgomery and Charleston, apply to

J. C. RIDDLE, Montgomery, Ala.

☞ The undersigned will be prepared to furnish information relative to the entire route, at the Verandah Hotel, New Orleans. WM. REYNOLDS,

jy 8m Travelling Agent.

FEED AND CORN MEAL

At the Arcade Mill, 18 St. Joseph st.

GROUND FEED for Cows and Horses always on hand, or ground to order, at the Arcade Mill, 18 St. Joseph street, and for sale on the most reasonable terms.

Also, FRESH GROUND CORN MEAL of superior quality constantly supplied to customers. All orders for Corn Meal, Grits, or Hominy promptly attended to.

m5 1m ALONZO HITCHCOCK.

ANGLO AMERICAN.

CHARLES HESTER having been appointed the New Orleans Agent for this valuable publication, would be happy to receive subscriptions to the same. He will also attend to any other business connected with said paper. Communications left either at his residence, on *APOLLO STREET*, near the corner of Polymneum, or upon his slate, at the Office of the New Orleans Price-Current, *CORNER OF CAMP AND GRAVIER STREETS*, will meet prompt attention.

N. B. C. H. is also a COLLECTOR OF ACCOUNTS, and pays particular attention to the collection of rents. a10 1m

Slates, Flag and Gutter Stones, &c.

SLATES, FLAG AND GUTTER STONES, FIRE BRICKS, &c.—

2,000 Squares SLATES, assorted;
800 Yards YORKSHIRE FLAG STONES;
500 do. do. GUTTER STONES;
100,000 FIRE BRICKS;
50 Casks ENGLISH CEMENT.

Apply to JOHN W. WALSH, Slater,

fy11 3taws4m 120 Rampart st.

SUNDRIES.

IN store and for sale by the subscribers:—

2 pipes fine old Montillado Sherry Wine;
20 demijohns, 5 galls. each. do. do.;
60 casks XXX London Brown Stout Porter;
25 do. XX Dublin do. do.;
40 do. superior fine English Ale;
60 bbls. Butter, Water and Boston Dyspepsia Biscuit, also Soda Crackers, neatly packed in boxes;
50 dozen Pickles, assorted, in large & small size jars;
75 do. foreign and domestic Preserves, assorted;
40 do. Jellies do., in large and small size jars;
25 do. Sauces and Ketchups, assorted;
700 lbs. superior fine Spanish Chocolate;
1000 lbs. Zante Currants, in large and small packages;
70 boxes sweet shelled Almonds;
30 do. bitter do.;
35 do. Maraschino and Curacoa;
20 do. Spices, put up qr. lb. papers;
75 do. Genoa Citrons;
60 do. French Capers;
40 do. of the celebrated Aromatic Bitters;
25 do. Wine and Stoughton Bitters;
18 do. French Fruits in their own juice, assorted;
2500 do. wholes, halves and qrs. Sardines in oil;

ALSO—Candy neatly packed in boxes, to suit country merchants, and at reduced prices; Syrups of all kinds manufactured and packed in boxes of 1 dozen each; Liquors of all kinds in bottles, expressly for families, such as fine old London Dock Brandy and Port Wine, (very old,) Madeira and Sherry do., old Jamaica Rum and Monongahela Whiskey; also Lime Juice by the bottle, dozen or gallon; Honey do. do. do.; Raspberry and Strawberry Vinegar in pint bottles; Canton Ginger by the jar or case; Prunes do., and a great many other articles too numerous to mention may be found at

R. F. NICHOLS & CO., Wholesale Confectioners,

m24 3t 76 and 78 Camp st.

CHERRY BRANDY, &c.

A FRESH supply of this delightful beverage, so much admired for its *cooling and healing qualities*—just received.

Likewise, a superior article of GOSHEN BUTTER; CHEESE; FAMILY MESS BEEF; SCHOOLEY'S HAMS; 50 bbls. OLD WHISKEY; &c., &c., for sale by

WM. GRAY, 58 Common st.,

m21 3t next door to Hewlett's Exchange.

Hotels & Boarding-Houses.

PRIVATE BOARDING at MRS. MILLIKEN'S, 120 *POYDRAS Street., corner of St. Charles st.* Entrance on Poydras st. m8 3m

BOARDING.

MRS. J. H. WILSON, 27 *BIENVILLE STREET*, is now ready to receive gentlemen, for permanent or transient Boarding, on the most reasonable terms. o28 tf

COMMERCIAL HOTEL—CARD.

In order to suit the convenience of Boarders, more particularly Day Boarders, there will be two Dinners set each day from and after the 1st May—one at 1 o'clock and the second at 3 o'clock. Rates for Board only, during the summer season, per week, $4.

a30 HENDRICK & BELL.

FAMILY BOARDING-HOUSE.

MRS. E. OVIATT, *No. 9 CANAL STREET*, having leased the adjoining building, is now able to accommodate from twenty to thirty families. Families visiting the South, will find it one of the most desirable and healthy locations in the city. A continuation of the liberal patronage that she has received, is most respectfully solicited. o23—6m

BOARDING.

MRS. PROCTOR informs her friends and the public that her house has been thoroughly refitted and arranged for the coming season. She is now ready to receive boarders, and trusts that her central location and moderate prices will insure her the same liberal patronage as formerly. Families or single gentlemen can be accommodated with rooms and board on as favorable terms as at any house in the city. Entrance, fourth door from Canal street, on Royal. o30 1y

Cheap Board to Suit the Times

At the NORTH AMERICAN HOTEL, *corner of Bienville and Levee streets*, New Orleans—By Mrs. ANN E. BRUCE.—This Hotel is convenient to the Texas steamship landing. It has been thoroughly cleaned, and newly furnished, for the reception of FAMILIES AND SINGLE GENTLEMEN. Day-boarders, and gentlemen wishing only to have Dinner, can be accommodated. The most liberal arrangements will be made, with families and gentlemen, for the season; and nothing will be wanting on the part of the Proprietress, to make the guests comfortable. jy14

WAVERLY HOUSE---MOBILE.

This Establishment has been thoroughly repaired, painted and furnished throughout, and is now in complete order, and open for the reception of boarders. The accommodations of this house are equal to any in the city, and the proprietor will spare no pains or expense to make his guests comfortable.

dec13 JO CLEMENT.

PLANTERS' HOTEL.

This well-known establishment, after undergoing a thorough renovation and being newly furnished, is now open and ready for the accommodation of Travellers and Boarders, and the proprietor pledges himself that no exertion shall be wanting on his part to render this Hotel one of the most desirable in the city. The table and bar will at all times be supplied with the best the city can produce, and that in abundance.

Board and Lodging, per day,	$1 50
Board only, per month,	20 00

J. W. YOUNG.

Late of Henrie House, Cincinnati, Ohio.

☞ Prices moderate, to suit the times. n25 tf

COMMERCIAL HOTEL.

THE undersigned would inform the citizens of New Orleans, and the public in general, that they have taken the above establishment, situated at the corner of *GIROD and NEW LEVEE STS.*, which, after a thorough renovation, is now open and ready for the reception of boarders, both citizens and transient—also, Day Boarders. The spacious bar-room attached has also been thoroughly cleaned, furnished with the best wines and liquors, and will be kept so as to make it equal to any bar in the city. The interior of the whole establishment will be under the management of THOS. W. THOMPSON, who is so well known in this city and St. Louis, Mo., as an experienced manager of such an establishment. It is the intention of the Proprietors to make the Commercial Hotel equal to any similar establishment in the city. Its location is one of the most desirable in the city, being situated opposite the principal steamboat landing in the Second Municipality.

a8 R. C. HENDRICKS & BELL, Proprietors.

☞ Picayune please copy.

AMERICAN HOTEL AND RESTAURAT.

EXCHANGE street, between WATER and COMMERCE stoeets, MOBILE.—The above well known and popular establishment having undergone a thorough repair, is now open for the reception of visitors or permanent boarders. To planters and business men generally, the above establishment is the most convenient in the city, being in immediate proximity to the wharves and principal thoroughfares, and can accommodate from 50 to 60 with sleeping apartments, and from 150 to 200 with board.

The Eating Department is on the RESTAURAT PLAN—where they can get their meals at ANY HOUR of the day, and not be compelled to be there at a certain hour or go without. The proprietor flatters himself that he has hitherto had the good fortune to give satisfaction. He is provided with the best cooks that can be procured in the city, and attentive and civil waiters; all the substantials, delicacies and varieties that the market affords are provided with a liberal hand, and his charges the most moderate of any house in the city.

☞ The utmost order and cleanliness is observed throughout the establishment.

The proprietor hopes that with these recommendations and a strict attention to business to merit a share of their patronage. [d13 tf] JAMES J. DYER, Proprietor

For Rent.

TO LET.

STORE No. 35 Common street. Apply on the premises. m8 12t

TO RENT.

A HOUSE on Conti street, containing four rooms in the house, besides kitchen and bedroom. Rent $10 per month. Inquire of A. BOWERS,

m5 1m 180 Tchoupitoulas st.

TO RENT.—*Possession given immediately.*—A comfortable and well finished two story brick dwelling house on Gravier street, next to the corner of Philippa street, having four rooms, with servants' rooms, kitchen, a good cistern and yard. Apply on the premises, or to M. GERNON,

m3 1m At Judge Jackson's Court, 60 Royal st.

OFFICE AND STORE TO RENT.

A well finished and very desirable COUNTING ROOM on the second floor, with a finished sleeping room above.

ALSO—A STORE ROOM on the first floor, for rent, by [o14 tf] JOS. H. MOORE, 107 Poydras st.

TO RENT—A two story Frame Dwelling and two story Kitchen; the dwelling has large galleries in front and rear; situated on Nayades street near the corner of Felicity street, near the Horse Station; a very comfortable residence. Rent for the balance of the season only $20 per month. Immediate possession given. Apply to

jan14 FELIX CONNOLLY, 66 Camp st.

TO RENT.

A comfortable DWELLING-HOUSE, containing 10 rooms, good yard and hydrant, will be rented on moderate terms, furnished or unfurnished. This house has at present a number of permanent boarders who would wish to remain during the summer.

—ALSO—

Would be rented with the house, a WOMAN SERVANT, who is a good cook, washer and ironer, and every way trust-worthy.

For further particulars inquire on the premises, 166 Poydras street, or to

ap17 tf A. MARMION, 96 Camp st.

NEW CANAL.

The Passenger Barges on the New Canal will commence running their regular trips on SUNDAY, the 26th inst., leaving the Depot at the New Basin for the Lake at the following hours:

ON SUNDAYS.

From City to the Lake—At 6 and 8 o'clock, A. M.; at 2, 4, 5 and 6 o'clock, P. M.

From Lake to the City—At 8 and 10 o'clock, A. M.; at 4, half-past 6, half-past 7 and 9 o'clock, P. M.

ON WEEK DAYS.

From City to the Lake—At 6 o'clock, A. M.; at 4 and 5 o'clock, P. M.

From Lake to the City—At 8 o'clock, A. M.; at half-past 6 and half-past 7 o'clock, P. M.

Passage each way 20 cents; Children and servants half price; Children under 8 years old gratis.

☞ Office—New Canal Depot.

a24 1meod JAS. STOCKTON, Sup'dt.

CARPETING AT REDUCED PRICES.

THE subscribers wishing to cut down their present large assortment of BRUSSELS THREE-PLY AND INGRAIN CARPETINGS, offer them now at very REDUCED prices. They invite the attention of persons furnishing Steamboats and Hotels, who will find it their interest to purchase at the present low rates.

fy22 A. BROUSSEAU & CO., 23 Chartres st.

OIL STORE.

SAMUEL W. CUTTER, *No. 104 POYDRAS ST.*, keeps constantly on hand SPERM, WHALE, LARD, LINSEED and TANNER'S OIL. Families supplied by the gallon with the best winter strained LAMP OIL, on the most moderate terms. jy6—d4 1y

THE DAILY DELTA

IS PUBLISHED

BY DAVIS, CORCORAN & CO.,

AT NO. 112 POYDRAS STREET.

TERMS:

Subscriptions received for twelve months for $10—half yearly and quarterly at the same rates. All subscriptions in advance. Single copies, 5 cents.

Advertisements, not exceeding twelve lines, inserted for $1 the first, and 50 cents for every subsequent insertion. Those of greater length charged in proportion.

Advertisements, not specified as to time, will be published one month, and charged accordingly; but no advertisement or subscription will be stopped, until all arrearages are paid, unless at the option of the proprietors.

Advertisements published at intervals, viz: weekly, semi weekly, tri-weekly, or monthly, are charged $1 per square for every insertion.

A liberal discount will be made to those who advertise by the year.

THE DELTA.

Capt. Samuel H. Walker.

This officer is one of those rare spirits which a state of war will bring out from our citizen soldiers. His late unequalled conflict with the Mexicans, in which he lost nearly every man under his command, and his daring heroism in cutting his way to Gen. Taylor's camp, have excited in the public mind a strong desire to know more of him. He is the same gentleman so frequently and honorably spoken of in Gen. Green's journal of the Mier expedition. In 1842 he went to Texas, and during the invasion of that Republic by Gen. Woll, he was marked for his bold and daring conduct. After the Mexican General had retreated from San Antonio, and when he lay upon the Rio Hondo, Walker and Captain McCullough crawled through his camp one night and spied out his position, and the next day with the gallant Hays, led the attack upon his rear guard. He then joined the celebrated expedition against Mier, and on the morning of that sanguinary battle, he, with three others—being the advance scout of the Texans—was taken prisoner and carried with his hands tied behind him to the head quarters of Gen. Ampudia. The Mexican General questioned him as to the Texan forces, and when Walker informed him that the Texans had only three hundred men, Ampudia pompously replied: 'Does that audacious hand full of men presume to follow me into this strong place and attack me?' 'Yes,' says Walker, 'make yourself content upon that subject, General, they will follow you into hell and attack you there.' He was, with his comrades, then marched a prisoner to the city of Mexico.

At Salado, with the lamented Capt. Cameron and Dr. Brenham, he led the attack upon the guards, overpowered them, and marched for Texas, when, after eating up all their horses and mules, and living for days upon their own urine, surrendered to the Mexican Generals Mercier and Ortago. He was again marched to Salado, where, with his comrades, he was made to draw in the celebrated black bean lottery, and every tenth man was shot. Those that remained of the Texans were marched to the Castle of Peroté and the city of Mexico. Here, while working on the streets in that city, he was struck by a Mexican corporal for not working faster, when with his spade he knocked down the corporal, which caused the guards to beat him nearly to death. His life was a long time despaired of, and upon his recovery, he with two companions scaled the walls of his prison after nightfall, and made his way to Texas, over a distance of more than a thousand miles. Before, however, they got out of the country, they were twice more imprisoned, and each time effected their escape. When he reached Texas again, he joined Capt. Hays, who, with fifteen others, armed with Colt's repeating pistols, fought 96 Camanches, and defeated them, leaving 36 killed upon the ground. Here Walker was run through the body with a Camanche spear, and his life again despaired of. We now hear of him, with 70 Texans, attacking 1500 Mexicans, and all perishing in battle but himself and six others; and then, to crown his wonderful life of daring, he cut his way, single-handed, into Gen. Taylor's camp from Point Isabel.

To such men Texas is indebted for her emancipation from Mexico. Few as they are, they have won her liberty, and have miraculously maintained it for ten years against all the boasted power of Mexico. We trust that the President of the United States, in making his appointments, will not overlook them and fill his army with the carpet knights who never smelt gunpowder, and whose only merit may be a *political* endorsement and a reverential devotion to the courtesies of the White House.—*N. Y. Globe.*

THE ARMY.—A correspondent of the New York Mirror remarks—"The following is the enrollment of troops ordered by the Executive in the several States, and mustering eighty-six regiments and a half. If the companies are full, the force will be equal to, and beyond, the 50,000 men ordered by Congress."

ENROLLMENT.

New Hampshire,	2	Illinois,	3
Massachusetts,	3	Indiana,	4
Maine,	3	Kentucky,	4
Vermont,	2	Ohio,	6
Connecticut,	2	Michigan,	2
Rhode Island,	1	Wisconsin,	1
New York,	8	Iowa,	1
New Jersey,	2	Florida,	1
Pennsylvania,	6	Louisiana,	4
Maryland,	2	Texas,	2
Delaware,	1	Tennessee,	4
Virginia,	5	Dis. of Columbia, 1 battal'n.	
North Carolina,	3	86 regiments,	
South Carolina,	2	500 men each,	
Georgia,	3		
Alabama,	3	43,000	
Mississippi,	2	250 half regiment,	
Arkansas,	2		
Missouri,	2	43,250	

THE MAN OF LEISURE.—"You'll please not to forget to ask the place for me, sir," said a pale blue-eyed boy, as he brushed the coat of the rich man of leisure at his lodgings.

"Certainly not," said Mr. Inklin, "I will be going that way in a day or two."

"Did you ask at the place for me yesterday?" said the boy on the following day, with quivering lip, as he performed the same office.

"No," was the answer, "I was busy, but I will to-day."

"Heaven help my poor mother," murmured the boy, and gazed listlessly on the cent Mr. Inklin laid in his hand.

The boy went home. He ran to the hungry children with a loaf of bread he had earned by brushing the gentlemen's coats at the hotel. They shouted with joy, and his mother held out her hand for a portion, while a smile flitted across her face.

"Mother, dear," said the boy, "Mr. Inklin thinks he can get me the place, and I shall have three meals a day; only think, mother, three meals, and it won't take me three minutes to run home and share it with you."

The morning came; and the pale boy's voice trembled with eagerness as he asked Mr. Inklin if he had obtained the place.

"Not yet," said the man of leisure, "but there is time enough."

The cent that morning was wet with tears.

Another morning arrived.

"It is very thoughtless in the boy to be here so late," said Mr. Inklin. "Not a soul to brush my coat!"

The child came at length, his face swollen with weeping.

"I am sorry to disappoint you," said the man of leisure, "but the place in Mr. C.'s store was taken up yesterday."

The boy stopped brushing, and burst afresh into tears. "I don't care now," said he, sobbing, "we may as well starve—mother is dead!"

The man of leisure was shocked, and he gave the pale boy a dollar.

Mr. Inklin was taken ill. He said often that he thought religion might be a good thing, and meant to look into it. An anxious friend brought a clergyman with him. He spoke tenderly, but seriously, to the sufferer, of eternal truth.

"Call to-morrow," said the man of leisure, "and we will talk about these matters."

That night the man of leisure died!—*Morris' National Press.*

☞ It is said that there is a place in Duchess county, N. Y., where the children are so fat that that they have to be rolled in sand to keep them from slipping out of bed.

NEW-YORK WEEKLY TRIBUNE.

BY GREELEY & McELRATH. OFFICE TRIBUNE BUILDINGS. VOL. V. NO. 38. WHOLE NO. 246.

$2 A YEAR, IN ADVANCE. NEW-YORK, SATURDAY, MAY 30, 1846. 10 COPIES FOR $15

FREEDOM'S MARTYRS.

BY GEORGE S. BURLEIGH.

HEROES there are whose memories never die;
Their glorious deeds to after times are told,
In thrilling songs, by gray-haired bards of old,
Whose harp strings vibrate to Eternity;
And harmless sweeps the flood of ages by
Their names, in deep-wrought characters enrolled
High on the rock of Glory's mountain hold,
And o'er the track where storm and tempest fly.
Their deeds of fame, from History's glowing pages,
Stand forth, the watchwords of another clime,
Thrilling the stern souls of succeeding ages
With fire electric down the chain of time;
And from their record, years that roll along
In their destroying strength, but sweep the stain of wrong.

Round Glory's temple-walls preëminent,
The martyred spirits, crowned with honor, stand,
Who brought their offerings with a willing hand
To thy pure altar, Freedom! Fame hath lent
The brightest stars that gild her firmament
To deck the garlands of that glorious band,
Amid the splendors of the spirit land,
Where their bright hours in living joys are spent.
What though on earth their path seemed dark and [lowly,
With fervent zeal, and hearts for ever strong,
And souls which burned with aspirations holy,
Earnest for truth, they battled with the wrong,
Triumphed o'er fate and earth's malignant frown,
And won, in warfare stern, the martyr's thornless crown.

Through scorn, derision, hatred, blood, and fire,
The fearful baptism of the true and tried,
They pressed, unshaken and unterrified,
To Death and Victory. Every fond desire
Of Earth was laid on Pleasure's funeral pyre:
Wealth, with its damning blight; unhallowed pride;
Quiet and fame, and all of earth beside—
A holy incense to the Spirit-Trier.
Triumphant, through heroic self-denial,
A conquered world beneath their feet was trod;
Freer and purer, over every trial,
Th' aspiring soul was drawn unto its God;
And while around them howled the tyrant's wrath,
Heaven's gorgeous light was shed resplendent on their path.

Freedom, bright zoned and glorious Goddess, hath
Her *living* Martyrs, who may never shrink
From the stern conflict, even though they drink
The cup of fierce affliction. Strong in faith,
That looks beyond the opening gates of death,
They gaze, untrembling, from the fearful brink,
On the dark wave where meaner millions sink,
And shriek their terror in their dying breath.
Sternly they circle round her holy altar,
When gloomiest rolls Oppression's gathering storm,
With purpose fearless, hearts that never falter,
And souls that glow with holiest passions warm,
Breasting the tempest in its wild uproar, [leys pour.
When Scorn and red armed Wrath their mingling vol-
Their souls in calm, unbroken sunshine swell,
Though clouds around them gather, fast and black,
And fling dark shadows o'er their stormy track.
Harmonious songs their guardian angels swell,
On viewless harps, o'er Hate's discordant yell;
And Heaven's own portals roll, obsequious, back,
To pour its glory on them, and the rack
Of the fierce storm their spirits cannot quell.
They stand, like mountains, when the deep-toned roar-
Of warring elements is round their breasts, [ing
While on their summits Heaven's rich light is pouring,
And silent Peace in radiant beauty rests;
There the first beams of new-born morning play,
And lingers, with soft light, the sun's last dying ray.

PRAY FOR ALL.

BY VICTOR HUGO.

"Daughter, to Prayer!"

PRAY thou for all who living tread
Upon this earth of graves;
For all whose weary pathways lead
Among the winds and waves;
For him who madly takes delight
In pomp of silken mantle bright,
Or swiftness of a horse;
For those who laboring, suffer still;
Coming or going—doing ill—
Or on their Heavenward course:

Pray thou for him who nightly sins
Until the day dawns bright—
Who at eve's hour of prayer begins
His dance and banquet light:
Whose impious orgies wildly ring,
Whilst pious hearts are offering
Their prayers at twilight dim;
And who, those vespers all forgot,
Pursues his sin, and thinketh not
God also heareth *him.*

Child! pray for all the poor beside;
The prisoner in his cell,
And those who in the city wide
With crime and misery dwell;
For the wise sage who thinks and dreams;
For him who impiously blasphemes
Religion's holy law.
Pray thou—for prayer is infinite—
Thy faith may give the scorner light,
Thy prayer forgiveness draw.

DISPATCHES FOR THE TRIBUNE

BY MAGNETIC TELEGRAPH

THE WAR WITH MEXICO.

TWO BATTLES!

The American Army Victorious!!

DEATH OF MAJOR RINGGOLD!

VEGA, THE MEXICAN GENERAL, TAKEN PRISONER.

American Consul and Residents at Matamoros Imprisoned!

Gen. Arista's Correspondence in the hands of Gen. Taylor.

EXCHANGE OF PRISONERS.

Paredes at the head of 15,000 Men on his way to Matamoros!

THE BLOCKADE VIGOROUSLY ENFORCED!

Boat Expedition against the Mexican Town, Barita, ordered.

8,000 TROOPS ARRIVED AT MATAMOROS!

MAJOR BROWN KILLED!

3000 Fresh Mexican Troops crossed the Rio Grande.

PHILADELPHIA, May 25, 1846.

There have been two engagements between Gen. Taylor and the Mexican troops: the first occurring on the 7th inst. when Gen. Taylor was returning from Point Isabel to his Camp opposite Matamoros, in which the Mexicans, numbering from 5,000 to 7,000, were repulsed.

The action lasted one hour and a half, in which time 600 Mexicans were killed or wounded, and the Americans took 300 prisoners and 8 pieces of artillery.

The total loss of the Mexicans in both actions was at least 1200.

The Mexican Army were so confident of Victory, that every preparation had been made to celebrate it, but all their preparations fell into the hands of the Americans.

In their flight many of the Mexicans took to the river and were drowned in their attempts to swim it.

Farther information has been received that the American Consul and all the American residents at Matamoros have been arrested and sent to Saltillo, a small town about 130 miles from Matamoros.

MAP OF THE SEAT OF WAR,

EMBRACING THE COUNTRY FROM NEW-ORLEANS TO THE CITY OF MEXICO.

Engraved Expressly for The New-York Tribune.

THE AMERICAN CAMP extends FOUR MILES on the United States side of the Rio Grande. Two Miles each way above and below the point facing Matamoros.

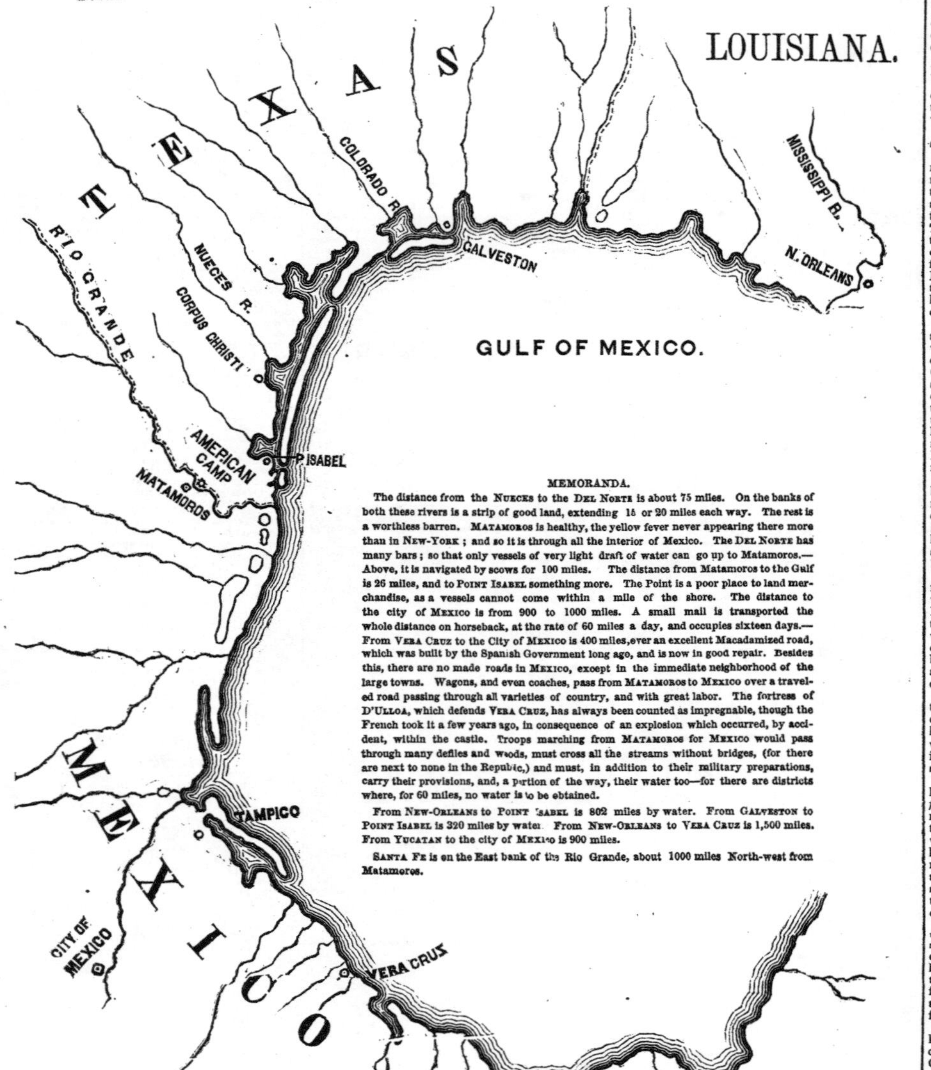

MEMORANDA.

The distance from the NUECES to the DEL NORTE is about 75 miles. On the banks of both these rivers is a strip of good land, extending 15 or 20 miles each way. The rest is a worthless barren. MATAMOROS is healthy, the yellow fever never appearing there more than in NEW-YORK; and so it is through all the interior of Mexico. The DEL NORTE has many bars; so that only vessels of very light draft of water can go up to Matamoros.—Above, it is navigated by scows for 100 miles. The distance from Matamoros to the Gulf is 26 miles, and to POINT ISABEL something more. The Point is a poor place to land merchandise, as a vessels cannot come within a mile of the shore. The distance to the city of MEXICO is from 900 to 1000 miles. A small mail is transported the whole distance on horseback, at the rate of 60 miles a day, and occupies sixteen days.—From VERA CRUZ to the City of MEXICO is 400 miles, over an excellent Macadamized road, which was built by the Spanish Government long ago, and is now in good repair. Besides this, there are no made roads in MEXICO, except in the immediate neighborhood of the large towns. Wagons, and even coaches, pass from MATAMOROS to MEXICO over a traveled road passing through all varieties of country, and with great labor. The fortress of D'ULLOA, which defends VERA CRUZ, has always been counted as impregnable, though the French took it a few years ago, in consequence of an explosion which occurred, by accident, within the castle. Troops marching from MATAMOROS for MEXICO would pass through many defiles and woods, must cross all the streams without bridges, (for there are next to none in the Republic,) and must, in addition to their military preparations, carry their provisions, and, a portion of the way, their water too—for there are districts where, for 60 miles, no water is to be obtained.

From NEW-ORLEANS to POINT ISABEL is 802 miles by water. From GALVESTON to POINT ISABEL is 320 miles by water. From NEW-ORLEANS to VERA CRUZ is 1,500 miles. From YUCATAN to the city of MEXICO is 900 miles.

SANTA FE is on the East bank of the Rio Grande, about 1000 miles North-west from Matamoros.

The Galveston Civilian of the 15th says that on the 13th Gen. Taylor received an express from his Camp stating that EIGHT THOUSAND FRESH TROOPS had arrived at Matamoros and that over **3000** had crossed the Rio Grande.

Gen. Paredes is at the head of FIFTEEN THOUSAND TROOPS, on his way to Matamoros.

It may possibly be that the fresh troops arrived at Matamoros are the advanced division of Gen. Paredes' army. No doubt the enemy was fully advised that Gen. Taylor had left for Point Isabel, and their plan is to try and capture him on his return, whilst a strong force crossing above is to come down upon his army.

Gen. Taylor appeared highly pleased with the intelligence, for since the war has opened, and no mistake, the excitement and activity attending operations open a new era to his victorious achievements and all have marked how much better he looks than when confined to the 'masterly inactivity' of the Corpus Christi campaign.

The Mexicans had continued their firing into the Fort opposite Matamoros nearly ever since Gen. Taylor left the works.

The brave and gallant Maj. BROWN died from a wound received in his thigh, by the explosion of one of the enemy's shells. His wounds were not considered dangerous, but he was placed in one of the bomb-proof burrows. Mortification ensued from the want of fresh air.

His death is deeply deplored by the Army. His intrepid conduct in foiling every attempt of the enemy to reduce the fort prepared them in a measure to anticipate the result of those conflicts with our brave Army.

The strength of the fort and the skill with which it is defended, are incomprehensible to the Mexicans, and indeed it might be, for they have thrown upward of 1,400 shot and shells into the works and every morning they present the same appearance.

The constant practice the enemy have had in firing at it has taught them the proper bearing to give to their guns, and almost every shot falls within the works.

The fort is never idle, and the ramparts and dwellings of Matamoros exhibit ruins of a hundred centuries, when gaping forth their lamentations of "Lo and behold what desolation is here!"

The sloop of war St. Mary's arrived from Pensacola on the 18th; steamer Mississippi on the 12th from Vera Cruz. The Bainbridge is off the Rio Grande, enforcing the blockade. The schr. Flirt sailed for New-Orleans on the 7th.

It is stated that an expedition is to be sent by boats of the squadron to take the town of Barita, 16 miles from the mouth of the Rio Grande, where there is a military force.

Gen. Vega was captured by the Texan forces at the slaughter of San Jacinto. He was also at the fall of the Alamo, and is a brave and accomplished officer.

A concentrated attack on Matamoros is contemplated by the land forces, and Commodore Conner's boats. It is more probable that Barita is aimed at, where are stores and ammunition.

The Union publishes full details, which it thinks correct in the main, but doubts the arrival of Com. Connor and part of his squadron off Brazos.

P. S.—A letter in the New-Orleans Bulletin praises highly Capt. Blake's reconnoisance of the Mexican line. The enemy attempted a detour around the chapparal on our right to attack the train, and was met by the 58th Infantry, who met the Lancers in square, and then drove them by a volley during the cannonade.

The grass was set on fire, which so obscured the enemy that a cessation of firing for near three quarters of an hour ensued. This was the smoke seen on board the Flirt, I presume.

A pretty feat was accomplished by Lieut. Rolland, of Duncan's battery. He advanced with part of the train through the burning pass, the flames rolling 10 feet high, seized the prolongation of the enemy's right and enfiladed the enemy's flank completely. Gen. Taylor's general directions were to find the enemy with the bayonet.

Capt. May of the Dragoons, captured Vega as he was in the act of firing a piece himself. As soon as the Mexican batteries were uncovered, Taylor said to May—"Your time has come—here are the enemy's batteries, sir: take them, *nolens volens.*"—May charged gallantly—lost one-third of his squadron, but succeeded.

The battle is to be called Palo Alto, from a small stream. The other at Resaca de la Palma.

FARTHER PARTICULARS.

The Southern Mail of yesterday afternoon brought the Mobile Advertiser Extra, dated May 18th, 10 o'clock, A. M. in which we find the following particulars of the engagements reported by Telegraph.

Per steamer Col. Harney at N. Orleans..[Corr. N.O. Tropic.

BRAZOS SANTIAGO, May 13.

At the receipt of the news of the first battle I wrote you a short account; the result of the second is now on hand, and it is most decisive. It now appears that the Mexicans had only five thousand men in the field at the great battle, and four thousand stowed away in the chapporal near the battle ground. It was their intention to have made but a slight attack the first day, but being so closely pressed they were obliged to fight in order to make good their retreat to where the four thousand were in the chapparel. In the first fight a general officer had his head shot off; it is not yet ascertained who he was, as his body was not recognized by his dress as he lay upon the field.

Gen. Taylor advanced the morning of the first battle into the chapporal, then sent 860 picked men under the charge of Capt. McCall, to reconnoiter, he advanced unmolested until 3 P. M. (the army following at a distance,) when Capt. McCall sent word to Gen. Taylor that he had received a charge of grape from the enemy, and lost two men.

The army was then deployed, and Capt. May, 2d Dragoons, ordered to charge the battery that had thrown the grape, and to take it if he lost every man: he obeyed orders, took the battery of four guns and lost but one man. The battery was commanded by Gen. de la Vega, who was taken prisoner.

Our little army then rent the air with their huzzas, and rushed shouting upon the enemy, committing the most dreadful havoc among them, taking eight pieces of artillery, 155,000 rounds of cartridge, and 500 packed mules. Gen. Arista's camp bedstead contained all his private and public baggage papers, which latter will be of great value, as we now have the key to the whole campaign, which will enable Gen. T. to form his plans so as to entirely defeat their designs.

We took all and every thing they had, four hundred prisoners, and the army baggage. The enemy had between 8 and 9,000 troops in the two battles, but we, with 1,800 troops, completely routed them.

We exchanged prisoners, got Capt. Thornton, Hardy and his little band. Our officers while prisoners were well treated, having lived with Ampudia ever since they were taken. Gen. Taylor would not exchange for Lieut. Deas as a prisoner of war, as it would be sanctioning his crossing the river, which he did not, having reprobated his crossing in the severest manner.

In this second and glorious battle we lost about the same number of men as in the first, but had more officers wounded. Capt. Walker with his heroic band of Rangers, was the last that fired at the Mexicans. The army left him and his comrades on the bank of the rivers shooting them as they attempted to cross.

To-morrow General Taylor leaves here to make an attack on Matamoros, in connection with Com. Connor, who has sent a boat expedition up the river.

I forgot to mention that Gen. Taylor arrived here yesterday with all our wounded, between 50 and 60, with Gen. Romulus de la Vega, one Mexican Capt. and two Lieutenants, who go with this letter in the Col. Harney.

The Augusta from New-Orleans arrived last evening. The mules from Matamoros, some 500, were sent in to-day, as well as the Mexican wounded.

I should not forget to mention that all the shell, ball and grape shot of the Mexicans are made of brass or copper. This letter I must close, with details of glory enough for one day.

Correspondence of the Tropic.

Announcement of the coming of Volunteers—Unexpected arrival of Com. Connor at Brazos Santiago—Gen. Taylor starts for Matamoros—Com. Connor reinforces Point Isabel—Excitement—News from the battle-field—Retreat—Capture of Artillery—Mexican officer shot by his own men—Capt. Page wounded—Louisiana Volunteers—Uncle Sam's Sailors on shore.

BRAZOS SANTIAGO, May 10.

Since my last (not received) we have had two arrivals, the New-York and brig Millaudon.—The last brought the news that six steamboats with four thousand volunteers were about starting when she left. This news made us most cheerful, as we could not have then expected the result that has since taken place with our troops.

Dispatches had been sent to Vera Cruz by Gen. T., contents to us subs unknown, but rumor would have it that aforesaid Vera Cruz was to have been bombarded. Judge of our surprise then when at daylight on the morning of the 8th, after the whole squadron (Falmouth excepted) appeared off our harbor. The Commodore had not received the dispatches from her, but was informed at Vera Cruz, that the Mexicans had marched 6 or 7000 troops across by land to assist Gen. Arista in *whipping* Gen. Taylor.

Commodore C. therefore, thought very wisely that his presence here would do some good in the way of reinforcements. Gladly was he welcomed, as Gen. Taylor had marched out the evening previous o meet and conquer the enemy, taking with him wenty-two hundred men, teamsters included, with wo hundred and fifty teams loaded with ammunition, provisions, &c. which the Mexicans were no doubt apprised of, as the teams had been loaded ever since Monday last, awaiting the orders for a march at a moment's warning.

Gen. T. left Point Isabel with little over four hundred men to defend it. Major Monroe, commanding here, sent a requisition to Com. Connor for as many men as he could spare, as we heard firing about 2 P. M. of the 8th, which continued with but little intermission until dark. Com. C. sent ashore 250 men, and on the 9th 4 or 500 more, which makes this place strong enough to withstand an attack against 20,000 men.

Believe me when I say there was the greatest excitement here all the afternoon of the 8th, as we could plainly hear the cannonading from the field of battle.

On the evening of the 8th, Mr. Murray and Mr. Bacon volunteered to go and find out the result.

On the morning of the 9th, a black boy came into camp, gave a history of the fight, which was about time, but as he had run away and left his team, he was not believed.

At 3 P. M. of 9th, Messrs. M. and C. returned, and stated as follows:

They got to Gen. Taylor's present camp, sixteen miles from here, at 3 A. M., there learned that the army marched until about 13 miles from here, when they saw the Mexicans drawn up in battle array across his road, he immediately gave his orders for the teams to halt until the 2d Brigade had passed.—The Mexicans were on the prairie near the edge of the chapp ral, when Taylor got within about three-quarters of a mile, they opened upon him with their flying artillery, Gen. Taylor arrived with Captain Duncan and Major Ringgold's companies, and at it they went until about sunset, when the Mexicans had retreated to the edge of the chapporal, and ceased firing.

After which Gen. Taylor fired ten or fifteen guns at them, and set to work throwing up two breast-works. At daylight the Mexicans were in the edge of the chapporal. A council of war was held by Gen. Taylor, and it was agreed that one brigade should advance up to the chapparal, in hopes to draw the Mexicans into a renewal of the fight; but the more the troops advanced upon them, 'the more they war n't there'—the Mexicans having retreated, leaving three pieces of artillery, any quantity of ammunition, and from FOUR to SIX HUNDRED DEAD upon the field; and God only knows how many wounded they took away.

One Mexican who was stationed at one of their batteries, says every body but himself at the batteries was killed—says the guns beat any thing they ever dreamed of, they were so quick. One of the Mexican officers in trying to rally his men, found he could not and commenced to cut them with his sword, when his troops shot him dead. We had 11 killed, and about 10 mortally wounded.

Capt. Page of the 3d, had all the lower part of his face shot off with a cannon ball—it is thought he will recover, though horribly mutilated. Major Ringgold had the fleshy part of both his legs shot through, and horse killed—none of his bones broken, which is wonderful. Our informant says the field of battle is strewed with the dead, and they could hear the groans of the Mexican wounded all night at Gen. T.'s camp. The Mexicans were commanded by Gen. Mejia.

There is no doubt that they have retreated across the river. When the volunteers arrive you may depend you will hear of them "reveling in the halls of the Montezumas," or peace and good will will be whipped into those bombastic Mexicans. It is a matter of surprise that so few were lost on our side.

The monotony of this place has been relieved the last two days by the drilling of '*Uncle Sam's web-feet,*' or '*barnacle-backs,*' that came from the Squadron. You would be surprised to see with what dexterity and precision they go through their evolutions with the muskets, and no one could resist a laugh to hear some of their sayings. One old salt said this morning, "Damn and blast my eyes! here is a ship ashore, and poor Jack on his beam ends." This speech was addressed to himself when looking on the tent that had been pitched, and was of sufficient dimensions to hold about fifty-two.

One-third of the whole number of the men from the squadron are Marines, the balance Tars. I should picture to myself a soldier riding *horseback* on a *cow* as soon as that I should see four or five hundred sailors going into war with muskets on their shoulders, but you could not restrain them from going against the Mexicans with only a knife and fork, if you will only show them only a chance, for they are all "eager for the fray." Yours, &c.

In the decisive battle Gen. Taylor lost about sixty killed and wounded, among whom there were three officers, viz: Lieut. Inges, of the Dragoons; Lieut. Cochran, of the 4th Infantry, and Lieut. Chadbu rn of the 8th Infantry. Among the wounded are Col. MacIntosh, of the 5th Infantry; Lieut. Col. Payne, 4th Artillery and Capt. Hooe, 5th Infantry—most of them slightly, and none supposed mortally.

Major Ringgold, well known as the Commander of the Flying Artillery, also died on the 11th, from wounds received in the action of the 8th.

Capt. Page, who was wounded in the same engagement, we are happy to state, is rapidly recovering. Lieut. Luther, also slightly wounded, is convalescent.

From the N. O. Tropic—Third Edition, 1 P. M.

Still Later from the Army.

THE GALVESTON ARRIVED!—The Galveston is just in, having left Brazos Santiago on the evening of the 13th. We hasten to lay the news by her before our readers.

From the Galveston Civilian of the 15th.

On the morning of the 13th, Gen. Taylor and his staff, with the guard that had brought down the train, &c. started for his camp. He was met by an express a few miles from Point Isabel, informing him that 8,000 fresh troops had arrived in Matamoros, 2,000 of which had crossed over, and 1100 more had crossed the Rio Grande at Barita, near the Bocachica, not more than 3 miles from Point Isabel.

Gen. Taylor returned to Point Isabel at once, and made preparations to leave the next day with such forces as were arriving. The steamship Galveston landed 450 Infantry, (Regulars and Volunteers;) the Augusta landed about 250; Capt. Price arrived via Padre Island from Corpus Christi, with his company of 70 mounted Rangers. They all reached the Point on the 13th.

The Telegraph and James L. Day will doubtless land their troops, amounting to upward of 800 at Point Isabel on the 14th. Great credit is due to Capt. Jeremiah Smith, of the steamship Cincinnati, and Capt. R. McBaker of the Monmouth, for the skill, energy and promptness, shown in management of their boats in transporting troops and supplies across the Bay at the Brassos Santiago.

Important from the Seat of War Direct.

Correspondence of The Tribune.

Camp at POINT ISABEL, May 9, 1846.

"The *fight* goes bravely on."—An express just in from General Taylor, tells us the gratifying story that he has succeeded in cutting his way through the Mexicans with a loss much less than could have been expected. The Mexicans may be regarded as routed.

This Camp (Santa Isabel) is composed almost entirely of Sailors, having about 800 of these brave fellows and 200 Marines from the squadron of Commodore Conner. There are about 200 Infantry here also.

We hourly expect reinforcements from New-Orleans, and shall doubtless make the best of our way to Matamoros as soon as our force is increased to 2,000.

General Taylor had only 2100 men with him when he left here on the evening of the 7th with about 200 baggage wagons loaded with provisions, for which he had left his Camp. Matamoros is *completely destroyed!* and our troops opposite that City, held their own bravely when last heard from, although much less than half the number of their opposers. Not over 350 at most.

I am sorry to inform you that Captains Ringgold and Page are wounded, doubtless mortally.

Col. Worth's loss is said to be irreparable. I am called for parade. Yours, MILES.

9 o'clock P. M.—We know nothing about the mails, and I write at random. I am told that my letter of the 8th has not yet gone—a disappointment of the worst kind, as it contained intelligence valuable only as far as it might be early.

I have just seen Lieutenant Steel, who left the battle-field at 5 o'clock this afternoon. He says the loss of the Mexicans, in killed, cannot be less than four hundred, one hundred and fifty of which were left unburied. General Taylor's loss was not over seventy killed and wounded, forty-three of whom are at this moment passing my tent on their way to the hospital tents. Almost every one has lost a limb. Lieutenant Blake was accidentally shot by his own pistol this morning. Major Ringgold is in, and is quite comfortable. His wound is through both thighs. Capt. Page's mouth and jaw are entirely shot away.

The force of the Mexicans making the attack on Taylor's detachment, is said positively to exceed six thousand, most of which is very good cavalry—the latter certainly, they say, over three thousand. A great many of Taylor's troops were with the wagons, and it is astonishing that he is not defeated.

Arista was with his troops yesterday, but Mejia is now in command. It is said, by three prisoners who came in last evening, that Arista was disgusted with the conduct of his troops, and refused to have any thing more to do with them. The firing recommenced an hour ago, after a suspension of nine or ten hours. Whether it is at Matamoros, or at Gen. Taylor's position, we cannot tell. The battle was fought eighteen miles from here.

As my guard mounts on the ramparts at 4 o'clock, I must try for a sleep. Yours, MILES.

10th.—The Mexicans rallied last night and made another vigorous assault on the wearied heroes of Taylor's party. The result has been a splendid victory on the part of our army, and the capture of Vega!! Our fellows deserve ten times the glory of heroes, as I suppose superior bravery to that exhibited by them was never imagined.

I have been through the hospitals to-day and can not express my feelings upon the glorious subject. Every man that I met, except three poor Mexicans, gloried in his fate. Poor Ringgold employs all his native fire in branding his description of the battle on the minds—the hearts—of his listeners. Doctor Foley, his physician, tells me that he has no hope of saving him. Page is worse than dead. Blake died yesterday afternoon. Major Brown, who was left by Taylor in command of the fort opposite Matamoros, has been killed. The express cannot tell the exact number of killed on either side in last night's engagement—but thinks our total loss less than seventy. The Mexicans fought very well, and their loss is tremendous. Arista is also said to have been captured, but the news is so good that I will not take the word of the express officer for the fact. But I am ordered to get ready to move upon Matamoros. Dispatches will leave at once for New-Orleans.

Yours, MILES.

The following letter from a brave and highly accomplished officer will be found to contain many importance particulars in detail which have not before reached us. The statements published in The Tribune from our correspondents may always be implicitly relied upon. It will be seen that the main facts of the letter have reached us from other quarters and have been already published.

Correspondence of The Tribune.

POINT ISABEL, Texas, May 6th, 1846.

MESSRS. GREELEY & McELRATH—*Gentlemen:* As to the affair of Capt. Thornton's, you are by this time well informed, and I need only say that himself, Capt. Hardee, Lt. Kane and 46 men are prisoners of war in Matamoros. The Captain succeeded in getting through the fence, and was not captured until he had arrived within five miles of our camp. Lt. Mason and several of the men were killed.—The Mexican force was about 2000, and Captain T. had between 50 and 60 men.

Lt. PORTER and a small party of Infantry were attacked by a party of *Rancheros* about the 10th or 12th of April. Himself and one of his men are supposed to have been killed.

After Capt. Thornton's affair, the General placed all hands at work on the Fort for the purpose of rendering it defensible, intending to finish it, to leave a suitable garrison, and then to move with all his available troops after his train of stores and provisions. For several days, every thing in Matamoros seemed to indicate a grand movement of their troops in some direction, and as far as we could judge, they were contemplating an attack on Point Isabel, which is our grand depot, and the base of all our operations. On the 1st, Matamoros appeared to be entirely deserted, and Gen. Taylor threw the 7th Infantry, *Lt. Bragg's Light Artillery* and *Capt. Lowd's Battery* of four 18-pounders into the work, and started with his army at 4 o'clock P. M. for Pt. Isabel. We marched rapidly but cautiously; for we expected to be attacked, and laid down on our arms in the prairies about 2 o'clock at night, having marched twenty miles without meeting any foe. We moved again at 5 o'clock, and reached Isabel about 12 M., on the 2d. The enemy had crossed the Rio Grande about ten miles from this place, and encamped a few miles from our camp in the prairies. Finding that we were in force, and that we had headed them off, they turned their course up the River, and moved toward our front. At 4 o'clock A. M., on the 3d, we were aroused by rapid and heavy discharges of artillery in the direction of Matamoros.

The firing was very brisk for near three hours, and then became less frequent. The bombardment was continued throughout the 3d, 4th and 5th, and still continues, night and day. Sunday evening, Capt. May started with a squadron of cavalry and a small command of Capt. Walker's for the purpose of observation, and of getting some communication with the Fort. He found bodies of troops in the prairies, and charged one Mexican squadron, but they fled for the chapporal. The gallant Captain smelt the rat, and gave up the chase. Capt. May returned in the morning, having left Capt. Walker behind. Capt. W. succeeded in getting through the chapporal, (nine miles,) although full of Mexicans, and communicated with Major Brown. He remained until night, and returned with great difficulty on the morn of the 5th. When Capt. Walker left, the Mexicans had fired 1500 shot at the work, and thrown a few shells into it, and only one man had been killed. They had three or four times as many guns as we.

Now for our artillery practice, which is highly creditable. At the third fire their 18-pounder was dismounted and the pieces thrown into the air, by American shot. After this the next most troublesome customer was similarly disposed of, and the same course pursued until every gun was dismounted. When the brave Capt. W. left the Mexicans had only two mortars, which they fired occasionally. This speaks well for our target firing, especially when it is a fact that we had but 150 rounds to each gun. Had the troops been furnished with a Paixhan gun and a few mortars Matamoros would have met a hard fate. The 18-pounders are under the command of Capt. Lord, who formerly was at Fort Hamilton; the battery of 6-pounders is under command of Lieut. Bragg, and will prove destructive in case of an assault. The enemy will doubtless assault the work, and are sure to be repulsed, for braver men never lived. The gallant Brown has nailed his colors to the mast and will never surrender. The Mexicans fired accurately, but their powder was weak and their shot had not sufficient momentum. Their shells would not explode, and hence so few of our men were killed or hurt. I hope my next may come from the city of Matamoros. Yours, &c.

Particulars of the Battle—Bravery of the American Officers and Soldiers—Their Humane Treatment to their Captured and Wounded Enemies—Arrival of Gen. Vega at New-Orleans, &c.

From the N. O. Com. Bulletin Extra, May 17.

The U. S. steamer *Col. Harney,* arrived at half-past two o'clock this morning, bringing as prisoners of war the Mexican General VEGA, and Lieutenants PRADA and VELEZ. Lt. Col. MARTINES, Aid-de-Camp to Gen. VEGA, accompanied his Chief voluntarily.

POINT ISABEL, May 12, 1846.

By the last departure I wrote you briefly of the operations of the Army up to the time of the bombardment of the Fort opposite Matamoros, and the movement of Gen. Taylor with the main body to this place, for the purpose of strengthening its defences. Having effected this, he marched, without waiting for reinforcements, on the evening of the 7th, and on the 8th, at 2 o'clock, found the enemy in position in front of a chapporal, which lies opposite to the timber of a stream called *Palo Alto.* The train was closed up, the troops filled their canteens, and Gen. TAYLOR promptly formed his line of battle as follows: On the right was *Ringgold's* Battery, 5th and 3d Infantry; then two eighteen-pounders; then the Artillery Battalion. The left was composed of the 4th and 8th Infantry and *Duncan's Battery.* A daring reconnoisance by Capt. *J. E. Blake,* showed the enemy's line to be of nearly twice the strength of ours, with heavy reserves in the chapporal.

The Mexicans opened the action with their artillery, the range of which was hardly great enough to reach our line which was moving slowly forward and some got into the hottest of their shot and their fire was returned from all our Batteries, and I venture to say that no field of battle ever displayed such skill or rapidity of fire and evolution. The first and only important movement of their artillery, was a detour around the church of chapporal on our right and attack the train—Capt. WALKER of the *Texan Rangers* promptly report-

SEE FOURTH PAGE.

THE WAR WITH MEXICO.

Continued from First Page.

ed this, and the 5th Infantry was detached to meet it, which it did handsomely, receiving the lancers in square and driving them by a well delivered volley. The cavalry then pushed on again for the train and found the 3d Infantry advancing in column of divisions upon them.—They then retired and as they repassed the 5th they received a fire from Lieut. *Ridgley's* two pieces, which had arrived at the nick of time. Two field pieces which were following the enemy's cavalry, were also driven back with them.

Meanwhile the enemy's left was riddled by the eighteen pounders which slowly advanced up the road—*Duncan's Battery* on the left neglecting the enemy's guns threw their fire into the Mexicans' Infantry and swept whole ranks. The 8th Infantry on the left suffered severely from the enemy's fire. The grass was set on fire at the end of an hour's cannonading and obscured the enemy's position completely, and an interval of three quarters of an hour occurred. During this period, our right now resting on the eighteen-pounders, advanced along the wood, to the point originally occupied by the Mexicans' left, and when the smoke had cleared away sufficiently to show the enemy, the fire was resumed with increased rapidity and execution. Duncan divided his battery on the left, giving a section to Lieut. *Roland* to operate in front, with the other he advanced beyond the burning pass, which was three feet high and the flames rolled 10 feet in the strong breeze and seized the prolongation of the enemy's right, enfilading that flank completely.

Night found the two armies in this position. On the 9th the General packed the heavy train, collected the enemy's wounded in hospital, buried their dead, arranged our own wounded, among which we have to regret the sudden death of Maj *Ringgold* and probably Capt. *Page*, and moved on in pursuit of the enemy on the Matamoros road. They had taken post in the chapporal the second time, occupying the bed of a stream called Resaca de la Palma with their artillery on the road at the crossing. I have no time for details of this affair. The General brought up his troops by battalions and posted them, with brief orders to find the enemy with the bayonet, and placed the artillery where they could act on the road. The Dragoons were held in reserve, and as soon as the advance of our line had uncovered the Mexican batteries, Gen. Taylor told Capt. May that his time had come—'Here is the enemy's battery, sir; take it *nolens volens*.' May dashed upon it with his squadron, and lost one third of it, but he cleared the battery and captured its Commander. Gen. Vega was in the act of raising a port-fire to fire a piece himself, when May took his sword, and brought the General off.

The enemy re-manned the guns and lost them the second time to the 5th Infantry. Captain *Barbour* of the 3d Infantry with his single company and a few men from the 5th who joined him in the chapporal, threw his back against a clump of bushes and gallantly repelled a charge of Cavalry. Capt. *Duncan* with his battery did terrible execution—he is a most promising officer. Lieut. *Ridgley* was also among the foremost.—In truth, it was a series of brilliant skirmishes and heavy shocks, in which 1500 fighting men met with 6000 hand to hand, overwhelmed them with the precision of their volleys and the steady coolness of the bayonet drove from the field with the loss of their artillery, baggage, pack mules, fixed ammunition, and near 2,000 stand of muskets.

The fort meanwhile had been summoned, with true Mexican duplicity, and told that Taylor was flying. The Matamoros newspapers and official bulletin called him a cowardly *tailor*. In answer to the summons the officers plunged their swords into the parapet and replied, 'To the hilt!'

Up to the evening of the 9th, 1500 shells and 3000 shot had been thrown, and the only loss was that of the brave commander, Maj. Brown, and one sergeant and one private killed and 10 wounded. The General returns to the army to-night, and will cross the river to-morrow or next day. The fort will be increased in guns, and especially provided with mortars, which will bring the town to terms. The navy will coöperate at the mouth of the river. The steamboats begin to carry supplies by that route.

Gen. Taylor has just given Gen. Vega a letter to Gen. Gaines and a letter of credit on his factor. The officers here and in the main body vied with their commander in delicate attentions to a brave and accomplished enemy, who won their admiration on the field, and was taken like a soldier in full harness and fighting gallantly to the last. Our loss about 30 killed and 140 wounded. Mexican loss at Palo Alto is set down by themselves at 450. At Resaca de la Palma 2,000 missing.

Since the battle our dragoons have been exchanged, grade for grade. The Mexican wounded were sent over to Matamoros. By the next arrival you will hear of the fall of the town and probably an offer from them to receive Mr. Slidell in any capacity. It ought to be mentioned that some of our regiments are full. Two of them only have about 300 men. Many instances have occurred of men handing their canteens to the wounded Mexicans and turning from them to fire upon others. There was not a single occurrence of cruelty toward the enemy. The morale of the army at its highest; it can now accomplish any thing, and they would die for a commander who does not ask them to go where he is not willing to lead, and one whose [illegible] they fully confide in.

The steamers Galveston and Augusta arrived at Brazos St. Iago on the 12th, and were discharging when the Col. Harney left. The steam schooner James Cage left Brazos St. Iago in company with the Col. Harney, with dispatches for Galveston; consequently, the next arrival to be looked for will be the steamship Galveston.

The officers killed and wounded on the American side are as follows:

Major Brown, killed; Major Ringgold, wounded, (since dead); Capt. Page, wounded; Lieut. Luther, do.

May 12th—Lieut. Inge, 2d Dragoons, killed; Lieut. Cochrane, 4th Infantry, do; Lieut. Shadburne, 8th Infantry do. Lieut. Col. McIntosh, wounded; Lieut. Col. Payne, do; Capt. Montgomery, do; Capt. Hooe, do; Lieut. Gates, do; Lieut. Seldon, do; Lieut. McClure, do; Lieut. Burbank, do; Lieut. Jordan, do; Lieut. Fowler, do. Number of non-commissioned officers and privates not known.

Correspondence of The Tribune.

THE BATTLES ON THE RIO GRANDE.

Extract of a letter from an intelligent Soldier of Capt. Duncan's Company, dated

"Camp near MATAMOROS, 16th May, 1846.

"We have just returned—fought two dreadful battles with the Mexicans on the 8th and 9th in returning to this place from Point Isabel.

The Mexican force was over 7000; we had not half the number, yet succeeded in driving and dispersing their army in all directions. We lost about 50 killed and several hundred wounded. Their loss is not far short of 500, and we captured 10 pieces of artillery, several hundred muskets, lances in abundance, 300 pack mules, about 150 prisoners, and among them their second officer in command, Gen. La Vega. The Mexicans made, during our absence, every effort to take the Fort. Major Brown, the commanding officer, was killed and one Sergeant. We lost several officers in the battles on the 8th and 9th—Col. McIntosh, Major Ringgold and many subalterns killed and wounded. In our company we lost but 5 horses, shot dead, Serg't. Wallender and three men badly wounded by cannon balls. The first battle was fought on the open prairie. Commenced at 12 o'clock and continued while we could see. Each army lay on the battle-ground during the night. The screams of the wounded and dying was heart-rending during that night. The next morning the Mexicans left the ground as soon as light, leaving us to bury their dead and take care of their wounded. They then took their position about four miles farther toward this place (about three miles from here) in the thick woods, and thought to drive us back to Point Isabel. We overtook them at 2 o'clock, P. M. and the second battle commenced and continued about two hours.

I will give you all particulars when I get a tent pitched and some place to write."

The Bombardment of Fort Taylor.

The following is an extract from a letter of one of the Officers of the Army at the Camp on the Rio Grande:

"Gen. Taylor left here with his troops on the 1st inst. for Point Isabel, leaving the 7th Regiment of Infantry, about 400 men, together with Capt. Lowd's and Briggs's Companies of the Artillery to defend the Fort until his return. On the 3d (Sunday morning) at day-break the Mexicans attacked the Fort with their batteries and four mortars at different points. They fired from 5 o'clock A. M. until 11 A. M. During this time Capt. Lowd's battery of four 18-pounders fired 356 balls, destroying one of their batteries and injuring another; they then stopped firing, to repair, for a short time; they kept up their attacks on all their batteries generally at day light, again at 2 P. M., and at sunset. Their attacks lasted 7 days from 8 cannon and 4 mortars. They did us but little harm, and killed but two persons: Major Brown, commanding officer, and one soldier. Gen. Taylor returned on the 9th. On his way back he had two fights with the Mexican Army, on this side the river: the first on the 8th, the next on the 9th. At the last of which, he completely routed them. They amounted to about 6,000. The last fight took place about 3 miles from this Fort. He took Gen. La Vega prisoner, and many other officers and troops, and all their field artillery—8 guns, and an immense pile of baggage, 4 or 500 muskets, and musket and cannon cartridges. The field was covered with their dead and wounded, and not until just now have they all been buried."

[This makes more sure that only 2 persons (above named) were killed in the Fort, and that the report of 263 being killed was a mistake.]

Almonte's Secretary Imprisoned—Mexican Plan of Warfare—Bombastic Dispatch.

From the New-Orleans Commercial Times, May 16th.

The Sardinian brig *Providencia*, arrived here yesterday from Vera Cruz, which city she left on the 4th inst. Lieutenants NOLAND and MIDDLETON, U. S. N. came passengers by her. The United States squadron, consisting of the *Raritan*, *Falmouth*, *St. Marys* and *John Adams*, was off the port. The *Providencia* brought full files of papers from Vera Cruz, up to the date of sailing; and from the city of Mexico to the 28th ult. By the kindness of a gentleman of this city, we have been favored with a perusal of them, and we cull, for the information of our readers, the following paragraphs:

SANTA ANA AND HIS SECRETARY.—*El Tiempo*, of the 27th ult. states that Senor DON F. LERDO, the Secretary of Gen. ALMONTE, had been arrested at Vera Cruz and confined in the castle of San Juan d'Ulloa, in consequence of papers having been found in his possession, which reveal the true cause of his return from the Havana—compromising him to that degree, that he is to be forthwith tried, criminally. He was, on the 14th of April, forwarded to the city of Mexico, strictly guarded. He came from the Havana, doubtless, on a mission from SANTA ANA and ALMONTE.

MEXICAN PLAN OF WARFARE.—*El Expectador* of the 25th ultimo, furnishes its readers with the system of warfare which is to be adopted by the Mexicans in opposing the American army. It is to be emphatically a little, procrastinating, harassing, war, (*guerra en pequeno.*) The Government is adjured to abandon all idea of giving a pitched battle, campaign fight, but to confine the troops to a *guerilla* war. The Mexican army is to be split into fragments of 500 or 600 infantry and 200 cavalry, with which they are to intercept convoys to the American forces, cut off their communications, hang upon their flanks, pick off stragglers, and keep them, by unexpected attacks, in a continual state of alarm. They are to watch opportunities of making a sudden descent on their hospitals and magazines, lay waste the country through which they are to pass, and in this manner wear them out without giving them an opportunity of striking a single effective blow.

Important Official Dispatches.

Our Washington Correspondent has sent us the following:

HEAD QUARTERS ARMY OF OCCUPATION,
Camp at Palo Alto, Texas, May 9, 1846.

SIR: I have the honor to report that I was met near this place yesterday, on my march from Point Isabel, by the Mexican forces, and after an action of about five hours dislodged them from their position, and encamped upon the field. Our artillery, consisting of two 18-pounders and two light batteries, was the arm chiefly engaged, and to the excellent manner in which it was maneuvered and served is our success mainly due.

The strength of the enemy is believed to have been about six thousand men, with seven pieces of artillery, and eight hundred cavalry. His loss is probably at least one hundred killed. Our strength did not exceed all told twenty-three hundred, while our loss was comparatively trifling—four men killed, three officers and thirty-seven men wounded, several of the latter mortally. I regret to say that Major Ringgold, 3d artillery, and Captain Paige, 4th infantry, are severely wounded. Lieut. Luther, 2d artillery, slightly so.

The enemy has fallen back, and it is believed has repassed the river. I have advanced parties now thrown forward in his direction, and shall move the main body immediately.

In the haste of this first report, I can only say that the officers and men behaved in the most admirable manner throughout the action. I shall have the pleasure of making a more detailed report when those of the different commanders shall be received.

I am, sir, very respectfully,
Your obedient servant,
Z. TAYLOR,
Brevet Brigadier General U. S. A. Commanding.

The ADJUTANT GENERAL, U. S. Army,
Washington, D. C.

HEAD QUARTERS ARMY OF OCCUPATION,
Camp at Resaca de la Palma, 3 miles from Matamoros, 10 o'clock, P.M.—May 9, 1846.

SIR: I have the honor to report that I marched with the main body of the army at 2 o'clock to-day, having previously thrown forward a body of light infantry into the forest, which covers the Matamoros road. When near the spot where I am now encamped, my advance discovered that a ravine crossing the road had been occupied by the enemy with artillery. I immediately ordered a battery of field artillery to sweep the position, flanking and sustaining it by the 3d, 4th, and 5th regiments, deployed as skirmishers to the right and left.—A heavy fire of artillery and of musketry was kept up for some time, until finally the enemy's batteries were carried in succession by a squadron of dragoons and the regiments of infantry that were on the ground. He was soon driven from his position, and pursued by a squadron of dragoons, battalion of artillery, 3d infantry, and a light battery, to the river. Our victory has been complete. Eight pieces of artillery, with a great quantity of ammunition, three standards, and some one hundred prisoners have been taken; among the latter, Gen. La Vega, and several other officers. One General is understood to have been killed. The enemy has recrossed the river, and I am sure will not again molest us on this bank.

The loss of the enemy in killed has been most severe. Our own has been very heavy, and I deeply regret to report that Lieut. Inge, 2d dragoons, Lieut. Cochrane, 4th infantry, and Lieut. Chadbourne, 8th infantry, were killed on the field. Lieut. Col. Payne, 4th artillery, Lieut. Col. McIntosh, Lieut. Dobbins, 3d infantry, Capt. Hooe, and Lieut. Fowler, 5th infantry, and Capt. Montgomery, Lieuts. Gates, Selden, McClay, Burbank and [illegible] were wounded. The extent of our loss in killed and wounded is not yet ascertained, and is reserved for a more detailed report.

The affair of to-day may be regarded as a proper supplement to the cannonade of yesterday; and the two taken together, exhibit the coolness and gallantry of our officers and men in the most favorable light. All have done their duty, and done it nobly. It will be my pride, in a more circumstantial report of both actions, to dwell upon particular instances of individual distinction.

It affords me peculiar pleasure to report that the field work opposite Matamoros has sustained itself handsomely during a cannonade and bombardment of 160 hours. But the pleasure is alloyed with profound regret at the loss of its heroic and indomitable commander, Major Brown, who died to-day from the effect of a shell. His loss would be a severe one to the service at any time, but to the army under my orders, it is indeed irreparable. One officer and one non-commissioned officer killed and ten men wounded, comprise all the casualties incident to this severe bombardment.

I inadvertently omitted to mention the capture of a large number of pack mules left in the Mexican camp.

I am, sir, very respectfully, your ob't. serv't.
Z. TAYLOR,
Bt. Brig'r. General U. S. A., Com'g.

The ADJUTANT GENERAL of the Army, Washington, D. C.

HEADQUARTERS ARMY OF OCCUPATION,
Resaca de la Palma, May 11, 1846.
[ORDERS No. 59]

1. The commanding general congratulates the army under his command upon the signal success which has crowned its recent operations against the enemy. The coolness and steadiness of the troops during the action of the 8th, and the brilliant impetuosity with which the enemy's position and artillery were carried on the 9th, have displayed the best qualities of the American soldier. To every officer and soldier of his command, the General publicly returns his thanks for the noble manner in which they have sustained the honor of the service and of the country. While the main body of the army has been thus actively employed, the garrison left opposite Matamoros has rendered no less distinguished service by sustaining a severe cannonade and bombardment for many successive days. The army and the country, while justly rejoicing in this triumph of our arms, will deplore the loss of many brave officers and men who fell gallantly in the hour of combat.

2. It being necessary for the Commanding General to visit Point Isabel on public business, Colonel Twiggs will assume command of the corps of the army near Matamoros, including the garrison of the field work. He will occupy the former lines of the army, making such dispositions for defence and for the comfort of his command as he may deem advisable. He will hold himself strictly on the defensive until the return of the Commanding General.

By order of Brig. Gen. TAYLOR:
W. W. J. BLISS, Act. Adj. General.

HEADQUARTERS ARMY OF OCCUPATION,
POINT ISABEL, (Texas,) May 12, 1846.

Sir: I am making a hasty visit to this place, for the purpose of having an interview with Commodore Conner, whose squadron is now at anchor off the harbor, and arranging with him a combined movement up the river. I avail myself of the brief time at my command to report that the main body of the army is now occupying its former position opposite Matamoros. The Mexican forces are almost disorganized, and I shall lose no time in investing Matamoros, and opening the navigation of the river.

I regret to report that Major Ringgold died the morning of the 11th inst. of the severe wounds received in the action of Palo Alto. With the exception of Capt. Paige, whose wound is dangerous, the other wounded officers are doing well. In my report of the second engagement, I accidently ommitted the name of Lieut. Dobbins, 3d Infantry, among the officers slightly wounded, and desire that the omission may be supplied in the dispatch itself. I am under the painful necessity of reporting that Lieut. Blake, topographical engineers, after rendering distinguished service in my staff during the affair of the 8th inst. accidentally shot himself with a pistol on the following day, and expired before night.

It has been quite impossible as yet to furnish detailed reports of our engagements with the enemy, or even accurate returns of the killed and wounded. Our loss is not far from 3 officers and 40 men killed, and 13 officers and 100 men wounded; while that of the enemy has in all probability exceeded 300 killed; more than 200 have been buried by us on the two fields of battle.

I have exchanged a sufficient number of prisoners to recover the command of Captain Thornton. The wounded prisoners have been sent to Matamoros—the wounded officers on their parole. General la Vega and a few other officers have been sent to New-Orleans, having declined a parole, and will be reported to Maj. Gen. Gaines. I am not conversant with the usages of war in such cases, and beg that such provision may be made for these prisoners as may be authorized by law. Our own prisoners have been treated with great kindness by the Mexican officers.

I am, sir, very respectfully, your obedient servant,
Z. TAYLOR,
Bt. Brig. Gen. U. S. A. com'dg.

The ADJUTANT GENERAL of the Army, Washington, D. C.

Com. CONNER *to the Secretary of the Navy, dated*
U. S. Ship Cumberland,
Off VERA CRUZ, May 18.

"The decided tone of the Manifesto of the Mexican Republic, in connection with other indications, seem to leave no doubt that orders have been given to Gen. Arista to attack the American Army on the Del Norte, should a favorable occasion offer, under the belief that an attack is contemplated. I have considered it advisable and have determined to sail to-morrow morning for the Brazos Santiago, with the Cumberland, Raritan, Potomac, John Adams and Somers. The Falmouth I will leave to protect our interests and to watch the course of events. The appearance of the squadron at that place, with a knowledge of the considerable reinforcements it can afford to our army will, I think, cause the Mexican Generals to pause, if not altogether to abandon their designs of attacking Gen. Taylor. All accounts concur in stating the Mexican army to amount to nearly 8,000 men. I feel assured the Government has not the means of maintaining this force for any length of time in the field,—indeed there is not even now a dollar in the Treasury; hence, delay will either cause the army to disband, or another revolution to take place, either of which events it is believed cannot be otherwise than favorable to the wishes of our Government in bringing about an amicable settlement of our difficulties with Mexico. The latter would undoubtedly contribute to that end, as it would place in power men wholly opposed to the policy at present pursued. Considerable activity has prevailed at this place since my arrival in .... and strengthening the defences of the Castle and the Town of Vera Cruz. As far as I am able to ascertain there are now nearly if not quite 200 guns mounted in the Castle of St. Juan de Ulloa, and as many as 50 in the two Forts, and walls of the City, commanding the anchorage. Their guns are all new and of heavy calibre, most of them being 32 and 42 pounders, with a number of eight and ten inch Paixhan guns. There are said to be nearly 2,000 in the fortress and about the same number in the town.

"Your ob't. serv't. D. CONNER.

"To Hon. G. BANCROFT, Sec'y. Navy."

U. S. Ship Cumberland,
Off the Bar of BRAZOS SANTIAGO.

"SIR: As stated in my communication to you of the 3d, the squadron left the Roads of Sacrificios on the morning of the 4th, and has just anchored off the Bar of Santiago, where I have just been apprised that hostilities have actually taken place, some days since. As the opportunity by which I send this communication cannot be delayed, I have only time to add, that after communicating with Gen. Taylor, and ascertaining the situation of affairs at Matamoros, I shall remain here no longer than the presence of the squadron may be required. After which, it will be necessary for this ship, the Potomac and John Adams, to repair to Pensacola to replenish their provisions and water; in meantime, orders will be given to carry into execution your instructions in relation to the Blockade of the Mexican coast, and to meet and repel in the most decisive manner the hostilities of the Mexican nation. Some more small vessels are required, also one or two small steamers of a draft of water not exceeding 8 feet. These vessels will be necessary to enforce a strict Blockade of the coast. Yours, D. CONNER.

"To Hon. GEO. BANCROFT, Sec'y. Navy."

Affairs in Mexico—The War—Difference with France, &c. &c.

From our Mexican Correspondent.

VERA CRUZ, May 4th, 1846.

Messrs. Greeley & McElrath:—I wrote last on the 23d ult. since which date matters have daily worn a graver aspect. It seems that War is inevitable, or rather that Peace is impracticable, between this nation and the United States. It is a contest not only wicked but foolish, and it has been brought about by political dishonesty originally, and by political blundering recently.

The American Commodore proposed to President Herrera that a *Commissioner* should be received from his Government to that of Mexico, and upon information of the acceptance of that proposition the American President sent a *Minister Plenipotentiary and Envoy Extraordinary*, as Paredes says, as a resident Minister near this Government.

This foolish blunder gave Paredes a pretext for rejecting the whole matter, and sending Mr. Slidell home again "with a flea in his ear."

Santa Ana does not see proper to time his advent with the views of his partisans, and we are left in happy uncertainty with regard to his intentions. It is pretty clear, however, that his landing at this port would not be a safe operation while old Nicholas Bravo is Commander-in-Chief of the Eastern Division.

Paredes drives things along pretty much as he pleases, and a good deal after the military fashion.—If a law is needed he issues a "decree" which becomes at once the law of the land. His ingratitude to the press is worthy of remark. To its license he was principally indebted for his present station, and he now turns upon it as an enemy, enforcing the most violent provisions of common and statutory law.

A recent decree punishes all publishers and printers who may be concerned in issuing any sentiments in advocacy of the principles of any invader of the Republic, or which may favor any efforts to change the established order of things or which may calumniate the supreme powers of the nation, &c. &c. the provisions of which went into immediate effect, in the seizure of Garcia Sorres, the popular head of the "Monitor" periodical. He was sent off in charge of a party of soldiers, without any show of a trial, "toward the Northern frontier."

I have seen nothing from Mazatlan later than the 8th ult., at which date the Savannah, the Constitution, the Levant and the Warren ships of war and the store ship Erie were at anchor in that harbor, the sloop Portsmouth and schooner Shark having sailed on the 1st. While writing, however, I observe a notice of seven of our men-of-war lying at anchor in that harbor. One of them may have been the Congress, but the paper does not say so.

I have not seen in any of the United States periodicals the slightest reference to Felix Clavé's well written observations on the "Mexican question."—A translation of them has appeared in the columns of "El Republicano," and I have read it with great interest—so great as to induce me to retranslate a part of its conclusion for your excellent journal. Some of the hints to be found there might well be pondered over by the people who are now sending our troops into a doubtful territory, to take it for ourselves. Right or wrong, it is an ill-judged and badly conducted measure, inasmuch, at least, as it involves the chance of particularly ill-timed defeat. There are far greater faults in war or politics than to despise one's enemy, and yet our Government sends fewer than four thousand soldiers to *seize upon* a territory guarded by nearly, or quite, double that number of regular troops, and treble that number of people fighting to protect their homes and their hearths. But like highwaymen, and robbers generally, we have counted more upon the weakness and terror of our opponents, than upon our own strength, and we may, as highwaymen have sometimes done, discover our error at the very moment when a remedy is impossible.

Clavé says that France has suffered many injuries from Mexico, for which the former must have redress. That "the annals of our (French) relations with Mexico reduce themselves to a series of outrages, which we have suffered either without notice or imperfect redress, for twenty years past," &c. &c. And after recounting some of the circumstances, proceeds in this fashion:

"However deplorable, in some points of view, our differences with Mexico may appear in their immediate consequences; however disagreeable to France may be the necessity of fighting at such a distance enemies with whom we can only exchange the expenses of our enterprises and the blood of our soldiers; we shall find, upon a close examination, that the Mexican question presents another aspect, far less fearful in its character. An occasion is indeed offered to France to reëstablish her tottering influence throughout the New World! Will she improve it?

"Surely not by attempting—as in 1838—to take San Juan de Ulloa, nor to dismantle Vera Cruz! The Mexicans safely entrenched beyond the reach of our fire, will laugh at our fleets, and quietly wait till the Yellow Fever and the 'Nothere' compel us to accept the most evasive terms, in concluding an unsatisfactory treaty.

"Neither will we turn our steps, with designs of conquest, toward California or Sonora, or establish ourselves in the Gulf of the Pacific in order to watch the American Continent more closely. No one now has such a thought. It is not the interest of France to found Colonies on the other side of the Atlantic. What is of more value to us than lands is a direct influence over all the Republics of the South, and the explicit protectorate of all the old Spanish Colonies.

"Let us suppose that, taught by experience, we go with well calculated and established resources, with strong fleets; and troops for land operations, to dictate a peace to Mexico.

"This proceeding would involve a great expense, without producing a corresponding result, for this reason: Supposing even that the stipulations for peace were such as the honor of our country, and the interests of our commerce, should dictate, who would guaranty their fulfilment? What Government would be responsible for the observance of these conditions? Is it not well known that Governments in Mexico succeed each other more rapidly than years, and that that of to-day pays no regard to the acts of its yesterday's predecessor? If, when our troops have retired, the Government with which we treated should be overturned by one of their popular movements, would not the national vanity attribute the defeats and humiliation of Mexico either to the incapacity or the treachery of that Government? And would we not, sooner or later, again be compelled to declare against the nation? To dispute this by hypothesis would be to declare one's ignorance of the Mexican people, and of past events. Any compact with Mexico must be illusery, as long as her laws and institutions are so variable. In order to treat with any security with Mexico, it would be necessary to establish there a real, effective, substantial power, one which could guaranty the observance of stipulations. In fact, to create there what has been created in Europe in the case of Greece; that is to say, a Government, a Nation. The Mexicans, humbled by a long period of Slavery, are, like the Greeks, enemies of foreigners, and divided in opinions, in families, and in interests—less energetic and active than that people, and more behind hand—so to speak; they are yet more docile, and consequently the enterprise of establishing such a power would be the more easy of accomplishment.

"Two methods present themselves to us as means of establishing in Mexico the wholesome influence of a stable and respectable power. One of these methods as shadowed forth by an English journal. "The Times," consists of constituting Mexico into a Kingdom, and to place the crown upon the brow of a foreign prince. The Times recommends for this purpose an individual of a Spanish family, as less repugnant to the country in many respects," and of course "more easily to be controlled by English influence," &c. &c.

"The second method appears to us more feasible.—From the parties which dispute their claims to public favor, one should be selected, which would offer for the future, the strongest political guaranties; and which would devote itself to the duty of supporting, fortifying and directing them. Three opinions divide the public sentiment in Mexico, and which the leaders use both to reach the Presidency and to maintain themselves in it. These give their names to the parties, which are: Absolutists or Centralists, the Moderatists, and the Federalists or Liberals."

The writer proceeds to analyze these parties too much in detail to permit me to transfer them to my sheet. He arrives, at length, at the choice of the Federalist party as the one best qualified to redeem the country, and to fix forever French influence as the controlling principles of South American policy. He thinks, however, that "for the Federalist party to succeed in establishing order in Mexico, it is necessary that it be directed by a force entirely foreign to the passions of the country, that it be ensured against its own excesses, and protected against itself—otherwise it must fail at once, from impotence induced by the defects in the national character!!"

Poor Mexico, her best friends will not praise her—her own children blacken her character!

I have not time to give you any details of the floating news. The American Squadron will move to-day, doubtless for Matamoros, as we learn that Arista has positive orders to cross the Bravo, twenty leagues above the city, and attack Gen. Taylor.

Very respectfully, &c. C.

Seven Regiments of Volunteers.

The President has at length made a requisition upon the Empire State for her share of the Volunteer Force ordered by Congress. A dispatch was received at Albany on Friday from the War Department, requesting the Governor of this State to cause to be enrolled and held in readiness for muster into the service of the United States, seven Regiments of Volunteer Infantry. Notice is to be hereafter given when the service of the volunteers will be required, at which time an officer of the United States Army will be sent to muster them into service, at such place as may be designated.

The seven Regiments will constitute a force of about 5,500—officers, non-commissioned officers and privates.

THE LOUISIANA VOLUNTEERS.—We learn from the N. O. Commercial Bulletin that the four regiments called for by Gen. Taylor were fully organized, enrolled into the service of the United States, armed, clothed and completely equipped, in the short space of ten days—a remarkably short period when every circumstance is considered; and in addition to these four regiments there have been organized in New-Orleans, and arrived from the interior of the State, additional companies sufficient for another Regiment; but unless a farther requisition is made the men will not have an opportunity to repair to the seat of war. The following is the official report of the volunteers so far furnished by Louisiana:

Washington Regiment, commanded by J. D. Walton, total strength	675
Jackson Regiment, commanded by S. F. Marks	866
Montezuma Reg. commanded by J. H. Dakin	733
Louisiana Volunteers, commanded by Horatio Davis	734
Brig. General Persifor F. Smith and Staff, 4	3,008
Louisiana Legion, 10 companies of Infantry and a Battalion of Artillery, (to be enrolled to-day,) commanded by Brigadier General D. Augustin, about	1000
Fifth Regiment, composed of companies and squads, who were too late, say	750
Total number of volunteers, so far organized	4,753

The first three regiments, with the exception of one company, have embarked.

VOLUNTEERS.—The following companies have arrived since our last publication: From the parish of Iberville, 64 volunteers, Capt. Geo. K. Shiel, first Lieut. F. Gayne. From Natchitoches, 80 volunteers, Capt. John Waddell, first Lieutenant J. Doslin. From West Baton Rouge, 75, Capt. Robertson. From Madison Parish, 82, Capt. McKiernan. From Alabama, 100, Capt. Pratt.

The steamer Florida, and the brig Orleans, sailed last night, with the remainder of the companies, under the command of Col. Dakin. [N. O. Com. Bulletin.

THE ROAD TO MEXICO.—A friend has furnished us from his route-book with the distance from San Antonio, Texas, to the city of Mexico, including all the intermediate halting places. Just at this moment it possesses [illegible] questions put to us as to the distances from point to point in Texas and Mexico. They are given from the journal of an actual traveler, and the recruits who have not yet left here may improve the opportunity of the passage to Brazos Santiago to study the road which they may have to traverse.

DISTANCE FROM SAN ANTONIO TO THE FOLLOWING PLACES:

	Miles.		Miles.
Rio Grande, at the Presidio,	150	Hacienda San Juan de Vanegas	25
San Juan de Nava	22	Village of Cedral	10
San Fernando	15	Town of Matagula	20
San Juan de Mata	15	Hac. Represadara	25
Rosita	23	" Laguna Seca	20
River Sabinas	35	Village of Benado	30
Hacienda of Alamas	20	Hacienda Bocas	33
" Encines	20	" Peñasco	20
" Hermanes	15	City San Luis Potosi	10
" Ajuntas	23		
Town of Monclava	17	Total	800
		Hacienda Pila	15
Total	355	Town of Jeral	30
Castano	10	Hacienda Cubo	20
Ranche of Bajan	30	Town of Dolores	35
Tank of San Felipe	33	" S. Miguel Grande	30
Hacienda Aleno	20	Hacienda Santa Rosa	34
" Messia	22	City of Queretero	13
Village Capellanillo	25		
Saltillo	10	Total	977
		Hacienda Colorado	15
Total	505	Town San Juan del Rio	28
Hacienda Agua Nueva	15	Hac. Arroya Saco	30
" Incarnacion	35	Village of Tula	30
" San Salvador	30	City of Mexico	50
" Salado	22		
		Total	1130
Ranche las Ancinas	607	[N. O. Pic. May 17.	

QUARTER-MASTER'S CERTIFICATES AT A DISCOUNT.—The *Baltimore American* publishes the following extract of a letter from New-Orleans.—Like many other movements in connection with our Mexican difficulties, it discloses gross mismanagement on the part of the Government at Washington:

"It will hardly be credited that with the large force in Texas, requiring constant and heavy supplies, and with the emergency now existing, the Quarter-Master's Department is entirely destitute of funds, and it has to buy supplies, charter steamboats, and make all its arrangements *on credit*, of course paying an exorbitant addition in the price of everything; and the Quarter-Master's certificates for money due, are hawking about in the streets and at every shaving shop in the city at heavy discounts, disgraceful to the credit of the Government, who boast of having some 10 or 15 millions of surplus funds in the Treasury! These certificates, though payable on demand so soon as funds are received, are selling at 8 or 10 per cent. discount, and if they accumulate much longer, will be at a still heavier rate."

PRESBYTERIAN GENERAL ASSEMBLIES.—The two Presbyterian General Assemblies organized in Philadelphia on Thursday. The N. S. elected Dr. S. H. Cox Moderator, and Rev. Mr. HATFIELD, Clerk. The session was principally occupied by a discussion on the organization of a new Synod.

The O. S. Assembly elected Dr. HODGE, of Princeton, Moderator, and Rev. Mr. RODGERS, temporary Clerk, in absence of Rev. Mr. Engles, detained by sickness.

☞ The only Banks of the State which have suspended during the past year are the *Lewis County Bank*, a Safety Fund Institution; the *White Plains* Bank under the General Banking Law, and the *Farmers' and Drovers'* Bank of Buffalo. The bills of the White Plains Bank, amounting in the whole to $28,000, are secured by bonds and mortgages and New-York State stocks in the hands of the Comptroller. Those of the Farmers' and Drovers' Bank, amounting in the whole only to $10,000, are secured wholly by New-York State Stocks, and will of course in a very short period be redeemed in full.—There are no other Banks in the State which are in any way doubtful. Some miserable, unprincipled fellows attempted on Saturday last to excite the fears of small up-town dealers against several of the heaviest and safest institutions of the country, by circulating a written list of what the paper termed *broken Banks*. What their object could have been we can not imagine. The act was base and pitiful.

FIRST ARRIVAL OF COPPER—A RICH CARGO.—We have at length something from the Copper Region of Lake Superior, besides rumors of the richness and value of its minerals. The steamboat Franklin, Capt. Edmunds, arrived yesterday morning, having on board SEVENTY-FIVE TONS of copper, from the Cliff mines, belonging to a Pittsburgh and Boston Company. The cargo, we understand is valued at *three hundred thousand dollars*. In the masses we saw, there was a large sprinkling of silver, which gives them their great value. We saw a finger ring, which we are informed was hammered from the native metal, being about half and half silver and copper. [Buffalo Pilot.

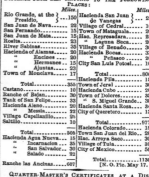

Designs of the Administration.

It is asserted in various quarters with the utmost confidence that the Administration has deliberately determined to invade Mexico, and that this undertaking—so full of peril and responsibility—has been confided to Gen. SCOTT, who will commence his march for the Mexican Capital as soon as a sufficient force can be concentrated. The *Express* gives, on the authority of "gentlemen from Washington who ought to know and probably do know," the following plan of the campaign:

Mexico, it is said, is to be invaded at four points,—with the eye upon the Capital, where is intended the ultimate concentration.

To preserve our forces from the *vomito*, our columns are to march on the high regions of Central Mexico, which are said to be as healthy as New-York or Pennsylvania.

The Commander-in-Chief is to be in Major General Winfield Scott, who, report says, is to lead one column, Gen. Wool another, and Gen. Taylor another. The fourth leader we have not heard named.

The great Western division of the army from Missouri, Illinois, Iowa, Wisconsin, &c. will proceed direct into the gold region of Santa Fé and New-Mexico, sending a detachment into California by the short route discovered by Captain Fremont. This will be a column of hunters, trappers, wagoners, settlers, armed wandering tribes, that fight with the rifle in one hand, and work with the plow in the other. The "Mormons," probably, will be in this column.

A column from the Southwest will rendezvous, it is said, at Fort Towson, on the Red River, Louisiana, whence there is an ancient military road, in good order, across the high table lands of Upper Texas to the city of Chihuahua, in Northern Mexico, there uniting with the roads from Santa Fé, California and the Pacific, which all join the great military road at Chihuahua, leading to the city of Mexico. Both these routes are most delightful for a Summer campaign.

The main garrison will probably be established at the Presidio del Norte, on the right bank of the Rio Grande, on the road from Fort Towson to Chihuahua, which seems to be the most central place for keeping up uninterrupted communication with all poits. Chihuahua is exactly in the centre of Mexico, due West of Bexar, Texas; and due East of Guayamas, a port on the West Coast, in Lower California.

Meanwhile the Mexican forces are to be diverted as much as possible from assailing our columns by a continued bombardment of the castle of San Juan d'Ulloa, and the occupation or blockade of every port of importance on the Gulf of Mexico, or on the Pacific.

Proclamations in Spanish are to be broadcast, promising protection and liberty to the Mexicans from their military rulers; security to their Churches and their Priests, and denouncing all who contemplate "a revel in the halls of Montezuma," or the sacking of the Churches, and the robbing of the gold mines.

Pecuniary Effects of the War.

Behold the beginnings of evil as described in the following extract of a letter from New-Orleans to the Courier and Enquirer:

Alarm and distrust pervade the commercial community—exchanges have rapidly fallen—Sterling 6 per cent. sight checks on New-York 2½@2¾ per cent. discount—60 day bills 3½@4 per cent, and can only be negotiated at those rates with difficulty, and in limited amounts. Produce falling still more rapidly—Flour was offered yesterday at 2⅞ and could probably have been bought at $2½. Corn which 5 days since was at 45c is to-day down to 32c. Cotton has declined 1c per lb. All kinds of merchandise are unsalable, except at ruinous rates. Real Estate property dead. Money has probably never been scarcer not even in the general crash of 1837.

Failures have already begun, and so many more anticipated, that confidence is dreadfully shaken. It is also throwing all the freights into foreign bottoms, who not only obtain the preference, but higher rates than American vessels. British ships are asking 1d on Cotton—this high rate has not yet been submitted to, but I have little doubt will be shortly obtained. Two American ships were taken up yesterday at ¾d.

The state of affairs will react severely on the West, and as a small specimen of the effect of war upon the value of their produce—It will also react in New-York when the Government call upon the deposit banks to place heavy funds at this place, which they will have to do in specie, as it would be impossible to negotiate bills here or buy them at the North on this place, in sufficient amounts except at a loss greatly exceeding the cost of sending specie, which must either be sent over the mountains and down the river, or by a ship of war as the present premium in packet ships is 3 per cent, and would be three times that, on the first knowledge that a privateer was afloat against our commerce.

Mexico.

The attention of our people having been withdrawn from Oregon to Mexico, we shall embrace the opportunity of occasionally publishing in The Tribune statistics of the latter place, which it is hoped may prove of more than mere temporary interest.

According to the best authorities we have been able to consult, the population of Mexico in 1842 was 7,200,000, of whom 4,000,000 were estimated as Indians; 1,000,000 whites; 6000 blacks; and 2,000,000 of various castes, such as Tambos, Mulattoes, &c. &c.

In the City of Mexico there are several Collegiate Institutions of respectable grade and standing, and within the last few years Schools have rapidly multiplied throughout the entire Republic. About Fifty Newspapers are published in the Cities and various Provinces.

The population of the Republic is made up, in round numbers, as follows:

Mexico	1,400,000	Sinaloa	150,000
Jalisco	675,000	Chiapas	140,000
Puebla	660,000	Sonora	120 000
Yucatan	580,000	Queretozo	120,000
Guanajuato	510,000	Nuevo Leon	100,000
Oajaca	500,000	Tamaulipas	100,000
Michoacan	500,000	Coahuila	75 000
San Luis Potosi	320,000	Aguas Calientis	70,000
Zacatecas	275,000	Tabasco	60,000
Vera Cruz	250,000	Nuevo Mexico	60,000
Durango	160,000	California	35,000
Chihuahua	150,000		

THE EXPORTS from the Republic of Mexico amount to about $20,000,000 annually. Not less than $12,000,000 of silver are coined in the various Mints, of which there are some six or eight in the Republic.

CHAPPORAL.—The Charleston News says that the word "Chapporal" has been frequently mentioned in reference to the Mexican War, as furnishing shelter for a party in ambush; the word is used as synonymous with Mattorales. CHAPPORAL, signifying a compact mass of bushes matted together; whilst MATTORALES means a good many not compact. These clusters occur in great numbers, some being merely a collection of bushes covering small spaces, and separated by intervening openings. Others extend over many acres, and for miles; they are composed principally of thorny bushes and the prickly pear. These plants of course grow wild, but are collected and planted so as to form hedges and fences around the cultivated grounds, which will keep out all animals, even hogs. It is said that the Chapporals afford excellent shelter and concealment for an army in ambush, as the men may conceal themselves in parties of 5, 10 or 20, behind the clumps of bushes, where they may remain unseen and unnoticed. The whole country between the Nueces and the Rio Grande is interspersed with these Chapporals and salt lakes, with but a small, a very small, sprinkling of fresh water or grass.

SQUADRON IN THE PACIFIC.—We have received advices from our squadron in the Pacific, principally lying at Mazatlan, under command of Commodore Sloat, to the 8th of April, at which time, we are glad to learn, the officers and crews of all the vessels there were in good health, and the squadron in most efficient condition for any service it may be required to execute.

No blockade has as yet been enforced, though the Governor of the province and his officers, together with most of the inhabitants, were in the greatest state of excitement and alarm, by reason of a report having been circulated that the American commodore intended blockading the port. The Governor had marched all his troops some miles out of town; all the papers of the Custom House and town were removed into the interior, and many of the poor people with their families had fled into the country to seek a place of safety from the apprehended attack of the barbarous Americans; and all without the least cause or even demonstration of any kind from our squadron. The letter says:

"We have still lying here most of the squadron, viz. Savannah 54, Constitution 54, Warren 24, Levant 22, Portsmouth 22, Erie 4, and the Congress 54; Captain Stockton and the Cyane, daily expected. The Shark, 12, has gone to the Sandwich Islands to repair, after which she will return to the coast again." [Com. Adv.

YUCATAN.—The Union publishes the following extract of a private letter recently from Yucatan:

"The people of Yucatan, it appears now, are in earnest in throwing off the yoke of the Central Government, and are determined to invoke the aid of the United States to effect this. The bearer of the demand from Gen. Paredes, (I am advised,) upon the Yucatan Government for its quota of troops to operate against us, was indignantly ordered to leave Merida immediately, for that the only troops that Yucatan would furnish, would be to operate against Mexican tyranny."

Benton's Speech on the Oregon Occupation Bill.

Correspondence of The Tribune.

WASHINGTON, May 22, 1846—5. P. M.

The Galleries of the Senate were crowded to-day in anticipation of a rich treat in Mr. BENTON'S Speech on the Oregon Occupation Bill.

His Speech was about two hours long, and this is only preliminary to the body of the speech which will be given on Monday, to which time the Senate adjourned. He only wants to be a little more excited to make it a great speech.

Mr. BENTON said that he had looked for a settlement of this question of boundary by Negotiations, not by Legislation. As Negotiations lagged, events advanced. He would correct several errors on this subject.

The first is that 54° 40′ is the boundary between the U. S. and Russia. So far from it, the fact is that that line was suggested, and that too by the United States as the Northern boundary of Great Britian.

Mr. BENTON here gave the history of the convention with Russia of 1824, showing that there is really no such boundary line as 54° 40′.

He then referred to Greenhow's Map, which was copied correctly, for it seems that while he confines himself to copying he does right well, but when he goes to expounding the treaties of territory the Lord deliver us from it—but he gives no such line as 54° 40′ in his map.

Here is another map with the line of 54° 40′ laid down running over every thing, seperating neighboring ports, streams from their springs, and true only to the imaginary line from the sea to the mountain.

And this map we issued in an extra number of 10,000, deceiving hundreds of thousands by this nonsense. The whole country has been excited to war on a line. If they should rally to march to that line they would find that when they got there that they could not find it!

"*Dulce et decorum est pro patria mori.*" It is sweet and becoming to die for our country, but it is necessary to know where to die. Yet this whole continent has been agitated by the cry of an imaginary line, having really no existence. Oh! mountain that brought forth a mouse—henceforth thy name shall be 54° 40′!

Mr. Monroe and his Cabinet, in 1823—the men who acquired this Territory and who were all ripe in knowledge—offered to make 55° the northern boundary for Great Britain. We make it *our* northern boundary. They offered to give Great Britain 6 degrees on the Pacific; we try to squeeze her out altogether, and for this the 54° 40′ men are willing to involve us in war. The proposition of Mr. Monroe and the wise patriots surrounding him was that this North Western Territory should be divided into three parts—the northern to Russia, the middle to England and the southern part to us. We now bring the Northern or Russian possessions jam down on our boundary.

Upon this part of the subject he hoped he had shown the falseness of the supposition of such a boundary line as 54° 40′, and he hoped that henceforth we should hear no more of this exploded humbug. Another error he would expose was the unity and indivisibility of our title to the whole of Oregon, and its flippant corollary, "all or none." Our claims arose from different causes. Our title to some parts arose from settlement consequent on discovery. North of the Columbia, our title was founded on that of Spain. How ridiculous then it is to talk of these different titles being the same, and that therefore we should have all or none.

Another pernicious error was denying the existence of the line of 49° by the treaty of Utrecht, for it has been the misfortune of the 54° 40′ men to find lines where there are none, but actually not to find them where they are. Yet upon this title and line alone the United States forced out the British from Louisiana. In support of this he read several authorities. He also sent to the Clerk's table a letter from Timothy Pickering, now of Utica, N. Y. to Hon. DANIEL WEBSTER on the question of boundary. Mr. B. said that he had examined the documents referred to by Mr. Pickering and found them to be correct. He made some beautiful allusion to Mr. Pickering's history, recounting the circumstances under which he saw him in the Halls of Congress.

The clamor of all the organs, great and small, had been raised to drown these truths.

He then read an extract from the Royal Geographer, THOMAS JEFFRIES, who states that the boundary line was seen by Commissioners under the Treaty of Utrecht, and that it had been settled on the parallel of 49°.

We have heard much of the map with a red line, but he would venture to prophesy that whenever that map was restored to the public Library another red line would be seen marking the 49th parallel as the boundary.

Mr. BENTON concluded this part of his speech by saying that on another day he would proceed to speak of Oregon itself, having succeeded in clearing off the false position in which it had been placed by the 54° 40′ men. Their efforts he characterized as the struggle of mud-puddle-lane against all history.

His speech is terrifically severe on the 54° 40′s, who wince under his blows like whipped hounds.—He will continue on Monday. RICHELIEU.

WASHINGTON, May 23d, 1846—5 P. M.

Gen. SCOTT will leave this City, probably, in eight or ten days for the South, and precede the army, which you will see has been called out pretty extensively by the President and Secretary of War, whose circular to the Governors of the different States appears in last night's Union. The Administration is going about this work so deliberately that it would seem as if the entire subjugation of Mexico was what they want.

It is said that the President has appointed Father McIlroy of Frederick, and the Vice President of the Georgetown Catholic College, to repair immediately to the Army on the Rio Grande, as Chaplains, to prevent desertion. This is like every thing Polk does. It is the act of a demagogue. Does Mr. Polk think that even eloquent Catholic divines could make those of their own faith believe that an unrighteous war is a just one?

Let this country engage in a just war, and no Priest is necessary to hold the Catholics, whether native or foreign, to their allegiance, even if the Pope himself should be an enemy. Mr. Polk is too much acquainted with Loco-Foco demagogues to understand the feelings of the Catholics and naturalized citizens of this country. I may have more remarks on this point hereafter.

There is a rumor, which I presume has no foundation in truth, that Bishop Hughes, of New-York, has been requested to go to Mexico as a kind of Pacificator. Does Mr. Polk think that he could blind the eyes of such a man as Bishop Hughes by his Low-co-Foco trickery?

I understand that the President has pardoned Babe, the pirate, and that he will be set at liberty on Monday next.

WASHINGTON, May 25, 1846—5 P. M.

Mr. BENTON continued his speech to-day on the Oregon question. He spoke about two hours. He will take another day at least to finish it. No sketch can give you an idea of the way he is using up the 54° 40′ men. If you could make room for it you should publish it at length when it is concluded. He will continue it on Wednesday next.

His speech to-day was highly argumentative, being full of quotations from books, histories and public documents, showing that Monroe and other distinguished patriots recognised 55° or 54° 40′ as the Northern boundary of the English possessions.—These authorities he said he would not forsake for that of those whose knowledge of the Oregon question extended only as far back as the Baltimore Convention, when this great National question became a party watchword.

These great men he had cited were not for "all or none." They were for some, and for that some that belonged to us. His speeches on former occasions had been misquoted. He was always for 49°. It is the line of right—the line of propriety—the line of mutual advantage—it was the line of our fathers. The records show that they stood upon it, and show also that formerly he stood upon it. He would make an offer to great Britain on that line, and he would make that offer an *ultimatum*. It would yet be an *ultimatum*, and he would make it so now.

He showed that England and the United States were both committed for that line. Even Sir Robert Peel's disapproval of the hasty refusal of that line by Mr. Pakenham showed that the English Government would not deny that that line was the proper boundary.

I trust Mr. BENTON will not support Mr. Polk should he send our army North of 49°, and thereby get us into a war. Yet he has supported him in taking possession of territory which was said by this same Mr. BENTON to be as clearly the property of Mexico as he has shown that New Caledonia is the property of Great Britain.

The Committees on the Webster and Ingersoll affair still pursue their investigations. As I mentioned in a late letter, there was a difficulty in the Committee of which Mr. Pettit was Chairman. Mr. Vinton was next on the list, and an attempt was made to pass him over, contrary to the practice in such cases. It was finally abandoned, and Mr. Vinton is Chairman of the one Committee and Mr. Schenck of Ohio, Chairman of the other.

The Senate had an executive session this afternoon which continued some time. I understand that they rejected the nomination of Mr. HORN as Collector of the Port of Philadelphia, by a vote of 29 to 22. RICHELIEU.

PORTRAIT OF GEN. SANTA ANNA AND AIDS.

THE above is a very fair representation of General Santa Anna, who, after singular reverses and banishment, has been restored to Mexico, and is at this day in command of her armies. He has been a soldier of fortune. Born and educated among revolutions, he appears incapable of appreciating the blessings of peace and of a mild, liberal and tolerant Government. He is certainly a cool and brave man, though we very much doubt whether he can be called a skilful General. If he is so, he will have an opportunity now to show it. He is a cunning, intriguing, plausible politician, and his position is one of great danger and delicacy.

The Texan Infantry Resisting the Mexican Cavalry.

AT the assault on the strongly defended City of Monterey, almost the first who gained the summit of the Hills were the Texan Rangers, shouting to the top of their voices and crying Alamo and Goliad, the scenes of Texan slaughter by the Mexicans. They rushed into the thickest parts of the City, driving the cavalry before them and struck them down with the butt end of their muskets. It was a terrific assault. With axes they broke through the walls of houses, ascended the terraces, and fired down upon the Mexicans. In that siege the Texans performed prodigies of valor.

BROTHER JONATHAN

GREAT PICTORIAL BATTLE SHEET.

AN ILLUSTRATED HISTORY OF THE VICTORIES AND CONQUESTS OF THE AMERICAN ARMY IN MEXICO.

BY WILSON & CO. 15 SPRUCE St. NEW-YORK. Entered according to Act of Congress, in the year 1847, by Wilson & Company, in the Clerk's Office of the District Court for the Southern District of New-York. PRICE 12½ CENTS—10 COPIES FOR ONE DOLLAR.

MAJOR GENERAL ZACHARY TAYLOR, U. S. A.

DRAWN AND ENGRAVED FOR THE BROTHER JONATHAN BATTLE SHEET.

IN the following pages will be found a record of the life and deeds of the distinguished General, a faithful portrait of whom is given in the above engraving. General Taylor is represented on horseback, in full military dress, as he may be supposed to appear in battle. His glass is raised as if about to observe some distant movement of his own troops, or reconnoitre those of the enemy. On his right is a battery of flying artillery, whose rapid and deadly discharges have rendered to this arm of the service the foremost distinction, and the highest utility in an open field. It was this artillery that fought and won the battle of Palo-Alto, and it was the right arm that saved the little band at Buena Vista, and scattered destruction in the ranks of the grand army of Santa Anna. At the front of one of the batteries is seen the gallant Ringgold, under whose experienced skill the flying artillery of the American army has received those improvements in its tactics, giving to it a celerity of movement, a rapidity of fire, a fatal precision of aim, which, as evinced in the late battles in Mexico, have no parallel on the most skilfully fought fields of the world. This accomplished artillerist has just sighted one of his deadly pieces, when, turning the flank of his horse to the enemy's fire, he is shot through his legs, and the horse and rider fall to the plain, pierced with mortal wounds. Major Ringgold is represented in the engraving at the moment of receiving the fatal shot, while Col. Payne, in the distance, starts with horror at the sight, and involuntarily stretches out his hand in aid. On the right is seen the mild, brave and accomplished Major Bliss, the chief of General Taylor's staff, his secretary, and friend. The appearance of General Taylor on horseback is dignified, graceful and noble. He is said to have short legs in proportion to the length of his body, but this does not detract from his making a commanding figure on horseback. He has a noble head, and wears a benignant countenance, while his white hair gives him a venerable appearance. In person he is inclined to corpulency. Though he is represented in the engraving in full military costume, yet he generally pays little regard to the etiquette of military dress. He prefers to appear in a roundabout, with linen pantaloons, and a broad-brimmed hat. His appearance is described as resembling more that of a Pennsylvania farmer than of a general officer.

The North American.

By W. C. TOBEY. "Press Onward." PRICE ONE SHILLING.

VOL. 1. MEXICO, WEDNESDAY, SEPTEMBER 29, 1847. NO. 1.

THE BATTLES OF MEXICO:

The public expect an account of the battles that have been fought in the valley of Mexico. We should be glad to furnish all the details of the six glorious encounters which it was the fortune of our troops to realize, and are sorry that it is not in our power to do so,—our opputunities of soliciting information do not allow it. We shall, therefore, give our own account of the different battles, as we saw them, trusting that our friends in the army will correct any errors we may commit. The Mexican people have been grossly deceived by the accounts given of these battles by their officers. Every man having a command seeks to cover his discomfiture with some excuse, and we regret to say, a majority seem to have forgotten the prominent principle to be observed in such matters—Truth. With this preface we shall first give an account of

THE BATTLE OF CONTRERAS.

During the whole of the 18th of August, the batteries at the hacienda of San Antonio had been firing at intervals upon Gen. Worth's command, which lay upon the San Augustine road within a short distance of the spot where early in the day the gallant Thornton was killed.—The engineers were occupied in making reconoisances and most of the firing was upon small parties under their command. On the morning of the 19th Gen. Pillow's division was put in motion on the road leading to San Angel by the field of Contreras. At the hill about two miles from the latter the command was obliged to halt and cut a road for the light batteries to pass, which was effected in about an hour and a half, and the troops again moved forward, filling up and crossing a deep ditch which had been made by the enemy, but abandoned. As the head of the column reached the rocky ground, General Twiggs arrived with his division and passed on by the path to the left, Gen. Pillow's command marching in a straight line for the village of Tizipan in which a large number of Mexican Infantry were seen supported by the cavalry under Gen. Santa Anna. About 2 o'clock our troops had arrived within reach of the long guns in the works at Contreras, and a heavy fire was opened upon them from several pieces. The works on Conteras were admirably planned for the defence of the narrow and only pass our troops could take, twenty-seven pieces of artillery being placed so as to bear directly upon the difficult path and steep decent to, and the ascent from the river. Besides these there were thick breastworks of stone and sods, so constructed as to protect the Mexican infantry who commenced a heavy fire upon our skirmishers.

Added to these temporal advantages, nature had interposed almost insurmountable obstacles in the deep ravine traversed by the swollen and rapid stream, and a mile of broken country covered with rough stones and rocks of volcanic origin, presenting at every step a surface dangerous alike to light troops and horsemen. No better stand could have been taken by General Valencia for the defence of the city of the Aztecs. On entering this pass the two brigades, composing the second division became separated; Gen. Smith, with the 1st artillery, 3d Infantry and mounted Riflemen, taking ground in the small trees to the left, where he soon became engaged with the enemy's light troops, and Col. Riley with the 2d and 7th Infantry and 4th artillery, passing on towards the church on the plain to the north of Contreras. Gen. Pillow's division, under command of Brigadier Generals Pierce and Cadwallader, took ground on Col. Riley's right to cut off the retreat of the enemy, should Col R. succeed in driving him from his stronghold, and also to dislodge the large force of infantry which skirted the woods below the church, and which was effected in gallant order.

But the assault of Contreras was not a matter to be effected in a moment. Independent of its strong defences and superior force Gen. Santa Anna, with a long line of cavalry and infantry, threatened the advancing party on the hill to the right, defending the road to San Angel and ready to close in upon our troops the moment they should be thrown between him and Valencia.—The experienced eye of the veteran Riley detected the plan of the enemy at a glance, and he was not a loss for resources. His command was put in position in a lane near the village and halted while a reconnoisance was made by Lieut. Tower of the engineer corps.

Several skirmishing parties having been thrown out by the enemy, two companies of the 2d Infantry were sent to drive them in and finally the entire regiment, headed by Captain T. Morris was detached for that duty, under the immediate command of Col. Riley. The action now became highly interesting to the numerous spectators on both sides. The little force under Col. Riley had nearly gained a position upon the plain west of the village when the batteries on Contreras were opened with renewed vigor and a large force of cavalry was sent to dislodge the regiment. Col. Riley formed a square, received the charge and repulsed it. The enemy, however, soon rallied, returned within pistol shot and commenced a fire of escopetry. Col. Riley immediately broke his square, formed in line of battle and charged and drove the cavalry, scattering it in all directions. A stand of colors, several horses, &c. were captured in this brilliant charge the flag by Capt. Casey in person. A colonel of lancers was among the killed in this encounter. He, with a few others dashed recklessly upon the bayonets of the infantry, urging on their comrades, but the steady aim and destructive fire of those veteran troops was too deadly to be long withstood. The lancers again collected and retired to the hill behind the batteries.

During the whole afternoon the hill facing the scene of operations on the east was covered with interested spectators. Though within point-blank range of the heavy pieces in the enemy's works, Generals Scott and Pillow, Col. Harney and many staff officers and citizens were anxiously watching the progress of the battle. From the first commencement our men have been closely engaged with the light troops of the enemy and the roll of musketry was continual. Capt. Magruder had placed his light battery in position and opened a destructive fire upon the mass of soldiers in the Mexican works and the rocket and howitzer battery was also in effective use. Several of Lt. Callender's rockets fell within the entrenchments and we could readily see the slaughter they made, without glasses. About 5 P. M. the long guns in Contreras were brought to bear upon these batteries and handled them very roughly. Three howitzers were dismounted and Lt. Johnson mortally and Lt. Callender severely wounded. Several of the men serving the pieces were killed or wounded at the guns.

The news of the disasters to our light batteries had reached the hill where we watched the fight just as the cavalry advanced upon Col. Riley's square. Many anxious eyes watched the progress of the lancers as, with their gay apparel and bright arms, they swept down the slope upon the little band of infantry that awaited them, and when they were within pistol shot one could have heard a loud breath yards distant. But when the combattants met; when the white smoke rose along the line of musketeers and the horsemen were sent flying in disorder from the field, the air was rent with shouts and every man felt that victory would be ours. There were no long faces on our side after that. If any had doubted the result before none doubted it then. The ice was broken with the magnificent line of Valencia's lancers. At this moment Gen. Shields arrived with the Palmetto and Empire men and passed on under a heavy fire of shell and round shot to the support of the second division, amid the cheers of the officers and citizens assembled on the hill and the cavalry who were chafing for a hand in the conflict. Till night-fall the firing from the works on Contreras was kept up with unceasing fury. Thousands of cannon and musket balls, and grape and cannister shot by bushels flew growling and singing and whistling over the heads of our gallant soldiers, but they faltered not and but few fell. Towards evening the enemy moved two pieces of cannon from Contreras to the hill occupied by Gen. Santa Anna and his cavalry, and opened upon Gen. Pillow's command, but they wasted shot and shell, firing far above the troops.

Night at last came and with it a cold, drenching rain that lasted without intermission until daylight. About dark Gen. Smith joined Col. Riley and at 10, P. M., formed the plan of attack for the morning. Our troops lay on their arms in the rain until 3 A. M. next morning, when Col. Riley's brigade moved silently up the ravine between the two bodies of the enemy and having got into position waited for the dawn. The march in this difficult ravine was one of great toil and danger, yet it was effected without discovery or accident. The men lay down in their wet clothes, the rain still falling heavily, but every soldier preserved his firelock and not one missed when the contest came.

Daylight found our little storming force in the deep ravine directly in the rear of Contreras. Gen. Valencia's forces were up and preparing to resume the cannonade and a party of lancers held the hill occupied by Gen. Santa Anna on the previous day. Gen. Cadwallader, with the Voltiguers and the 11th Infantry, had taken up a position on Col. Riley's left, to protect him from an attack from the cavalry and succor him should Valencia prove too strong for his little party. At a little after 7 o'clock, the rain having ceased, the sun shone out brightly and discovered to those on the east hill the exact position of both partie. At this time the charging brigade was formd for the assault in two columns at hlf distance, emerging from the ravine with threecheers that were more terrible to those in the works than the deep roll of musketry that foloved. The Mexican General exerted himsef to avert the calamity which threatened him. Sveral light pieces were turned round and discharged at the advancing columns, but the gunnrs were frightened and shot in the air. Several rgiments of infantry were formed and opened aire on our line, which was returned when the bie-jackets arrived near enough to see their advrsaries wink. After firing four rounds Col. Fley deployed two small parties to skirmish on h right and heading the colums called out "*now bys, forward and give them hell!*" The men srang forward at a run and the work was soon fished. But as they neared the works the fire c musketry and light artillery was teriffic. Gpt. Hanson, of the 7th Infantry, fell mortally wounded at the head of his Company, and simtaneously the Color Sergeants of the 2nd Infatry and 4th Artillery were shot down. Capt. Vessels of the 2nd caught up the colors of his giment and was pressing forward with them when he was shot in the leg and was for the moment disabled. Lt. Benjamin seized the flag of te 4th and gallantly planted it on the breastworks beside those of the 2nd and 7th.

The Mexicans were completely routed and sd precipitately towards the city. When the treat commenced the Voltiguers and 11th Intry poured into their disordered ranks a deadfire and at the foot of the hill the Riflemen, d Infantry and 1st Artillery and the Volunteer giments under Gen. Shields gave them such a arm reception that throwing down their arms ey dispersed in all directions or yielded themlves prisoners of war. While Col. Riley's igade was advancing on the works a body of valry attempted to gain his rear. These were llantly met and repulsed by Captains Guther's and Irvin's companies of the 11th.

One of the most flattering features of this cont was the re-taking of O'Brien's pieces by the giment (4th Artillery) to which they belonged. apt. Simon Drum, whose gallant deeds at Mo10 del Rey, Chepultepec and at the Gareta are e admiration of, and whose death is lamented 7 the whole army, laid hands on the first piece, apt. Casey of the 2nd securing the other.

We will not prolong this narrative by a rehearsal of incidents that will at another time have mention. Our account is made up from memory, without notes or a glance at the reports of the officers commanding. If we have, as is doubtless the case, failed to give in this hasty sketch, credit to any who took part in that brilliant victory, we shall be glad to make the amende in some future number. Descriptions of the other battles will follow as rapidly as the circumstanses will allow.

The spirit with which our army came to the lists of battle in the plains of Mexico, may be best illustrated by a knowledge of that which pervaded even those who followed it in the peaceable character of citizens. To that end we publish the following preamble to the muster roll of the "McKinstry Volunteers," together with the orders of the Commander in Chief organizing and disbanding them.

Preamble.

"We, the undersigned, citizens of the army, feeling the importance of the present crisis, and anxious to contribute our mite to the honor of the American Army, and to share the glories of the second "conquest of Mexico" hereby enroll ourselves as Volunteers under the command of Capt. J. McKinstry, and agree to be subject thereto until the issue of the approaching struggle."

Upon which was issued the following "special order:"

Head Qrs. of the U. S. Army
Inspr. General's Department,
Chalco, Mexico, Aug. 15th, 1847.

Captain Justus McKinstry, of the United States Army, is hereby excused from duty in the Quarter Master's Department to which he belongs, and, at his own request, is recognised as the commander of a body of Volunteers, citizens of the United States, to be known as the McKinstry Volunteers who, under the influences of a noble patriotism, have enrolled themselves for service in the United States Army, pending the approaching contest of arms before and at the capitol of the Mexican Republic. He will be obeyed and respected accordingly,

By command of Maj. Genl.
WINFIELD SCOTT.
E. A. Hitchcock,
Lt. Col. and Inspr. Gen'l.

After the battles of Cherobusco, and Contreras, and pending the Armistice, Genl. Scott issued the following

Special Order,

Head Qrs. of the Army
Inspr. Gen'l. Department,
Tacubaya, Aug. 31, 1847.

The "McKinstry Volunteers," voluntarily organized to serve before the capital of Mexico, having handsomely consummated the design of their union, is hereby dissolved, and their gallant commander, Capt. McKinstry, will report to the chief of his Department with this Army for duty.

The General in Chief tenders his thanks to the "McKinstry Volunteers," for their valuable services on the memorable days of the 19th and 20th inst., in the battles before Mexico.

By command of Maj. Genl.
WINFIELD SCOTT.
E. A. Hitchcock,
Lt. Col. and Inspr. Genl.

Did'nt know he was Wounded.—At the battle of Churubusco a German soldier belonging to Lt. Lyon's company, 2nd Infantry, was wounded early in the afternoon, but nearly forgot to discover it. After the fight was over he assisted in bringing in the wounded until night, ate his supper and was rolling himself in his wet blanket when he felt a slight pain in his hip. On examination it was found that a grape shot had entered his hip and lodged in the groin on the bone, making a very ugly wound This fact reminds us of the old story of the two soldiers who agreed if either fell the other should take him to the surgeon. In the fight one lost a leg and his comrade, according to promise, took him on his back and started for the surgeon, but on the way a cannon ball took off the wounded man's head. His faithful friend, however, travelled on unconscious of the severe mishap, when some one observing him called out, "where are you going with that dead man."—'To the surgeon," said the soldier. "Why what can the surgeon do for him," said the other, "his head is shot off." The soldier laid down his load and on seeing that he was rightly informed, exclaimed. "Well, by Jabers, he tould me it was his leg was aff."

Revived.—Most of the city newspapers have been revived. Santa Anna feared the press and tied it; Gen. Scott has set it free again.

The North American.

WEDNESDAY, SEPT. 29, 1847.

GENERALLY.—Our arrangements in regard to translations and other important matters are yet in a very unfinished state, and we have to ask the indulgence of our friends for a few days, when we hope to have all things satisfactorily arranged.

THE NORTH AMERICAN is in the Capital of Mexico—our flag floats over its national palace. To achieve this consummation much has been sacrificed by our invincible little army, many of the bravest of the brave have fallen. The world will do ample justice to the living and the dead who have participated in the severe struggles and brilliant victories which it has been the fortune of the American troops to encounter.—We shall not enlarge upon a subject so pregnant with glorious recollections. The object of this article is purely introductory.

With something of that ambition which prompts men to love to see their names in print, yet with a stronger desire to employ the least unprofitably the time which circumstances render it necessary for us to sojourn in this city, we have determined to publish a newspaper; trusting to the kindness of friends and a liberal patronage for the wherewithal to freight our little bark and keep it afloat. And we have to ask a large share of indulgence for this, the first number. All who are in any way conversant with newspaper publishing will readily appreciate the many embarrassments to be contended against in a commencement. The ice once broken, we expect to get over the little of blank paper we have to spoil more pleasantly, both for reader and editor.

Our paper will be governed by the same general rules as those of the United States. Communications touching incidents of the war or political or general subjects, will be published upon the responsibility of the authors—the editor always reserving the usual censorship. We know many officers in our army possess eminent qualifications to aid us in carrying out the objects of our enterprize, and invite them to favor us with contributions. This invitation is also extended to such of our Mexican friends as desire an independent channel through which to address their countrymen upon the important topics which at present command a large share of interest in the two republics.

ASSASSINATIONS.—A citizen told us the other day, that some of the lowest orders of the population are flattering themselves with the idea that they can decimate our army by assassinations—To say nothing of the villainy of such a mode of warfare, we can assure all who entertain such an idea that it is preposterous in the extreme.—During the first three or four days after our army entered the town, some half dozen assassinations occurred, but of late we have heard of none.—Our men are generally on the look out for such favors and are as handy with a bowie-knife as most people, and extremely cunning in the use of the revolver. We should suppose that all citizens who desire peace and good order would frown down any attempt, come from what quarter it may, to incite the mob to such an infamous proceeding. Any serious demonstration of that nature will be prejudicial to others than the mere actors. While it could result in little or no injury to the American Army the citizens generally would be the sufferers. We apprehend however, that all sober men, whether soldiers or followers of the army, have little to fear. Those who invite personal injury by their excesses, deserve little sympathy.

ONE OF THE BENEFITS arising from the occupation of the city by the American army, may be witnessed at the Custom House, where hundreds of indigent females are employed at higher wages than they have ever before recieved for like labor, in making clothing for the troops.—Many of these, we are told, are relatives of officers and soldiers in the Mexican army, the absence or death of whom has left them destitute. It is a source of gratification that, while our officers could not avert the calamities which have befallen these people, they are doing everything in their power to alleviate their afflictions.

WE ARE REQUESTED by Lt. BARBOUR, of the Kentucky Cavalry, to state that from earnest inquiries he has learned that the report that the Prisoners sent from this city to Tampico are starving and dying of starvation is undoubtedly exaggerated. That our men have suffered a great deal is undoubtedly true, yet it is hardly probable that the report given in the "Star" of yesterday is in every particular correct.

TO BEGIN WITH.

It has become an almost universal custom for editors to mark out in the beginning the course of policy they intend to pursue in regard to all prominent questions affecting the political and social interests of the people, and it may be expected by some that we should honor the practice with a formal "declaration of principles." "Situated as we are, and unaccustomed to" Mexican politics, such an effort would perhaps prove a task of more than ordinary magnitude: to start out with a specified line of policy that time and a better knowledge of the character of the people to whom our journal is addressed, might render impolitic, would be productive of results unpleasant alike to reader and writer. We shall, therefore, throw out such suggestions as, under the circumstances, arise in our mind, desiring all to understand that we claim no infallibility in morals or politics, and ask for our opinions no greater considerations than they intrinsically merit.

The present condition of affairs affords much matter of speculation for the political economist—much room for the labors of the philanthropist. The immutable laws of Destiny must be obeyed; progress, improvement and the enlightenment of the masses are the instruments with which she is working out momentous results for the benefit of the human race. Men may advance or retard these results according to their influence upon society, but no earthly power can stay the tide of Progress that is rapidly overspreading the world—blessing all within reach of its invigorating influences. A mighty moral revolution is pervading the nations; mind is overcoming the thraldom of matter; truth is silently dispelling the shadows of error, and mankind are awakening to a proper appreciation of their birthright. The signs of the times teach us that a new era is dawning: shall we not heed them and profit by their foreshadowings?

A new era is dawning upon Mexico. The despotic power that has blighted her glory and driven peace from her borders, has fallen. May no phœnix rise from the ashes of military tyranny to revive the scenes of tumult and blood that for years have estranged her children, made foes of brothers, and dimmed the lustre that once encircled her name! The flag of a sister republic is upon her capitol; the hand of a brother republican holds the balance of justice in her national palace. These meteor stars, reviving the lustre of the sun of Anahuac, shall give light to the blind masses who are ever groping after, yet have never found the jewel Freedom. Those red-and-white stripes and the blue that binds them, will teach the reckles and unreflecting advocates of strife the virtue and happiness that lies in union, fraternal confidence and social purity. That brother's hand would uplraise the oppressed as it has stricken down the oppressor. Casuists may cavail at our professions of friendship; military men may still cr war and vengeance; national pride may continue to nurse sentiments of mortification and distrust; but the "sober second thought" that has obtained among the peace-loving and the just of the republic will ere long vindicate the truth.

The genius of North America is opposed to military oppression and unrestrained power.—Our motto is "eternal hostility to every form of tyranny over the mind of man." The glorious principles of civil and religious liberty are born with us and held as sacred as our love for the God we worship. With us parties rise and fall, as with you, and our government is one year administered by men who are politically opposed to their predecessors; but the just principles upon which our constitution is founded never change. They are planted in the hearts of the people and nothing can eradicate them.—That great lever of human greatness and human liberty and happiness—Education—is a more invulnerable guardian of our institutions than all the armies and navies of the world. An enlightened people, blessed with the sublime attributes of self-government, need no armament, no legions of soldiers to protect their rights, for then the government is the heart of the whole mass, regulating the system which sustains it.

Are the people of Mexico prepared to believe that a nation so constituted desires their degradation? are they willing to suppose that a people blessed with perfect freedom of conscience and action would attempt their enslavement?—Such an anomaly would command the title of "the eighth wonder of the world"—a possible impossibility. We know that cunning aspirants for power will say that the objects of this war are conquest and the dismemberment of Mexico; we know too, that every act of generosity and magnanimity on the part of our General-in-chief is perverted and misrepresented. But we know also that truth, though "crushed to earth will rise again," and that however the minions of tyranny may deceive the people, justice will at length be done us by the good.

This war was not of our seeking. At its commencement and during its progress the American government, following the dictates of the nation, presented the olivebranch again and again, only to be insulted by those who governed Mexico by the power of the sword. We shall not rehearse the incidents that have occurred since our army entered the teritory of Mexico. The results of the battles that have been fought and the moral which arises from those results are or should be known to and felt by every intelligent citizen of the republic. Suffice that General Scott sat down before the gates of the capital and again invoked peace; that the agent of our government offered terms of honorable settlement of the existing difficulties and recieved in return unstable promises and broken faith. We are not prepared to establish who were the parties to that dishonorable mockery which spoke of peace while it prepared for butchery. Those who controlled the government must stand sponsors for it before the world. Gen. Scott had then but one alternative and he did not hesitate to embrace and accomplish it. All Europe would have condemned him had he acted otherwise You would have laughed at his generosity and your military rulers would have insulted him with pot-valiant challenges and blustering bravado.

Citizens of Mexico—the merchant, the artisan and the tiller of the soil—to you we address these remarks, and we do it on all kindness.—We would not remind you of the reverses of your armies save to exhibit the impotence of military power when wielded for unworthy purposes. The strong arm that oppressed the peaceful citizen, despoiled the industrious poor and laid contributions upon your temples of religious worship, was powerless when called upon to defend your city. All the advantages of long discipline and constant practice in internal warfare availed nothing when opposed to men who, taught to love peace and respect the rights of mankind, in war fight for principle and know no such word as defeat. A country governed by a military despotism can never prosper. A people who continually war with each other, though every man be educated in the science of arms, cannot sustain themselves against a foreign enemy. The same ambitious aspirations, the same distrusts and heart burnings which destroy internal peace and confidence render them powerless when they would be united in a common cause. The history of the past tells you this; will you not learn a lesson from it? The time has arrived when you may without fear vindicate yourselves. Disband your armies and bid those whose trade is war go till the fields or labor in the workshop for a livelihood. Elect for your Governors, men of peaceful habits and unambitious natures. Establish schools upon the ruins of your barracks and educate your children that they may govern themselves, if they would govern others. Rely upon general intelligence and fraternal union and confidence in each other for the protection of your household. Other people live securely under such government, and why cannot you? You possess all the elements of national greatness enjoyed by your northern brothers. You dwell in the most lovely country the sun ever shone upon; why not be worthy of it? Adopt a form of government equal to your capacities and be republicans in fact as you are in name. Leave fighting and the military arts to monarchies and be the free, happy people God intended you should be.—The same mild form of government that we enjoy in the United States will in a few years be your inheritance. If you will not seek it, it will be brought to you. Progress is the order of the age and "press onward" should be your motto. The little fire of freedom that was kindled by the Pilgrims on Plymouth rock is destined to extend its glorious influences until not a son of man upon the American continent shall breathe the chill air of the despot's dungeon or wear the galling chains of tyranny. This may be the prophecy of a dreamer—but think of it.

THE CHURCHES and buildings near the grand plaza are terribly riddled with musket balls, fired during the many revolutions that have taken place in this city. A soldier on being told the other day that it was done in the fight between Gomes Farias and the church party, said he thought it must have been a hole-y war.

OLD ZACK IN MEXICO.—In the street running from the center of the plaza to the alameda, we notice a handsome sign with the words, "AMERICAN TAYLOR." This is the first intimation we have had that General Taylor was "revelling in the Halls of the Montezumas."

THE PRISONERS.—Capts. Heady C. M. Clay and G. W. Smith, (A. Q. M.) and Lieuts. W. F. Barbour, T. J Churchill and Geo. W. Davidson and several of their men, arrived in this city a few days since from Toluca in fine health and glorious spirits. Among the men are Sergt. White, of Capt. Heady's comyany, privates John Seabough, Geo. W. Crawford, and A. T. Waterberg, of Lt. Barbour's company and Paul Williams, of the Arkansas Cavalry.

THE CIRCUS.—Mr. Bensley opened at the Teatro Principal on Sunday afternoon and has given nightly performances since that time. His company is a very good one, composing several excellent performers. In addition to the regular troupe, Madame Armand has been engaged and nightly exhibits her skill in equestrianship. We are pleased to see that Mr. Bensley is well patronized.

OUR OFFICE.

Is at No. 2, CALLE DE LOS PLATEROS, about one square from the grand plaza, where subscriptions and advertisements may be left and specimens of job work examined.

JOB WORK, such as, Quarter Master's blanks, cards, hand bills, circulars, bills of exchange, and every kind of fancy and plain printing, will be executed at the *North American Office*, No. 2, Calle de los Plateros, in a style superior to any establishment in the city.

THE GENIUS OF LIBERTY.

Vol. 1. VERA CRUZ, FRIDAY, NOVEMBER 12, 1847. No. 42.

THE GENIUS OF LIBERTY.

PUBLISHED DAILY, [EXCEPT SUNDAYS.]

R. C. Matthewson & M. J. Quinn,

EDITORS AND PROPRIETORS.

OFFICE—Corner of Principal and Vicario street.
ENTRANCE 659 VICARIO STREET.

TERMS.—Subscriptions received for one month for $2 00—payable in advance. Single copies 12½ cents.

ADVERTISEMENTS not exceeding ten lines, inserted in English or Spanish, $1 for the first and 50 cents for every subsequent insertion. Those of greater length charged in proportion. When advertised in both languages a deduction of 25 per cent will be made.

Persons advertising by the month, will be entitled to ten lines, each day, in either language, for $10, or in both languages for $15. A deduction of 25 per cent. will be made on advertisements for subscribers. No advertisement will be discontinued till all arrearages are paid.

General Order, No. 11.

ALL vessels except Army Steamers and Transports, arriving at ports in Mexico held by the United States forces, are to be visted by a boat from the guard ship of the day, or any single vessel of the Squadron, that may be in port, for the purpose of tendering the usual compliment of services to foreign vessels of war and of detecting any irregularities in foreign mail steamers or merchant vessels whether foreign or American.

It is desirable when it be practicable, that the boarding officer should be a Lieutenant.

M. C. PERRY, Com'dg Home Squadron,
U. S. Flag Ship "GERMANTOWN."
Anton Lizardo, August 18, 1847.

Regulation of Pilots by the Board.

1st. All pilots are required to cruise in a suitable vessel and keep at sea.

2d. The rate of pilotage is two dollars and fifty cents per foot on all vessels over sixty tons—under sixty and over thirty, ten dollars—under thirty tons, six dollars in and out.

3d. Vessels spoken inside the reef are not bound to take a pilot or to pay half pilotage.

5th. Vessels spoken outside the reef and refusing a pilot will be subject to half pilotage.

The pilot is considered *pro. tem.* responsible both to the Court and this Board for all violations of the port regulations.

Rates for vessels of war as heretofore under the Mexican regulations.

(Signed)
FRANKLIN BUCHANAN, U. S. Navy.
E. G. ELLIOT, U. S. Quarter Master.
F. M. DIMOND, Collector.
Vera Cruz, September 1st, 1847.

To Boat Owners.

THE owners of the different boats traficing in the harbor, are requested to present themselves at the office of the harbor master, in order that they may take out their trading licenses and have their boats numbered.

Be it also known, that the owners of the said boats will be held responsible for all the frauds, felonies, and other illegal acts which may be committed by the respective crews.

N. B.—All persons who do not take out their license before or on the 15th instant, shall be fined Five Dollars.

oct 9 FELIX PETERS, Harbor Master.

Notice.

ALL passenger boats will be hereafter licensed and the number of each will be printed on the bow, and the passage to and from the shipping fixed as follows: For each and every passage, 50 cents; to go and return without detaining the boat, 75 cents, and in northers, the price fixed by the parties. Any boat caught smuggling will be confiscated, and the owners fined and imprisoned, and any boatmen detected in exacting more than the prices above fixed, will be fined for every offence, Five Dollars.

FRANKLIN BUCHANAN, Commander.
F. M. DIMOND, Collector.
E. G. ELLIOT, CaCapt. A. Q. M.
Vera Cruz, Oct. 9th, 1847.

VERA CRUZ:

Friday Morning, November 12, 1847.

Gen. Wade, of Ohio, has offered to the War Department, to raise a brigade, arm, equip and transport it to the seat of war at his own expense; the cost thereof to be met hereafter by the Government.

The Court of Common Pleas in Boston has decided, in the case of Wm. White *vs.* Asaph E. Buss, that money lent at a card-table, while the parties were playing, is not recoverable at law.

TURPENTINE.—The North Carolia Newbernian furnishes some statistics in relation to the manufacture of turpentine in North Carolina. The number of barrels of turpentine annually made in the State is estimated at 800,000, not more than 200,000 of which are shipped in its crude state, the largest portion being distilled in the State. The estimated value to the maker is over $1,700,000 annually. About 4000 or 5000 laborers are engaged in making it. There are now ln operation 150 stills, valued at $225,000. This number of stills to have steady work, would require 600,000 barrels annually more than is now made; which is an indication that the distilling houses are overdone.

ENGLAND.—The editors of the New York *Journal of Commerce* have been favored with the following extract of a letter written by a merchant of New York, who has long been a resident in one of the most populous manufacturing districts in England. The letter is addressed to his partner in New York:

"You will learn from the papers the frightful state of the mercantile world on this side of the water. Confidence is almost annihilated, and the distress for money is unparalleled. Loans are now being made in London, Liverpool, and all the important manufacturing and shipping marts, of money payable on demand, and on undoubted security, at ten per cent. per annum interest. Say what they may, the harvest is only an average for corn, (meaning the cereals,) whilst the peas, beans and turnips are fearfully short—and the potato crop is doomed—to add to the alarm, we are advised that the cholera has, in its westward march, already reached Poland, and it is feared we shall be visited with that scourge this winter. The track it follows is almost identical with that of 1831–2."

Notice.

A GLEE CLUB, or FREE AND EASY, will be formed at the house of Capt. George Stephens, at the sign of the Gun, opposite the Ten Pin Alley of Capt. Peters. The first meeting for organization will be held on Saturday evening, the 13th of November. Gentlemen who have attended the preliminary meetings will please be punctual at the hour above specified.

Gentlemen wishing to enrol their names as members of the aforesaid Club, will have the kindness to present their names to Capt. Stephens, on or before the hour of 11 o'clock, Saturday morning.

By order of the President:
H. LATHROP WILLIS, Sec'y Glee Club.
Vera Cruz, Nov. 12, 1847.–2t

POETRY.

The Ultimatum.

BY LYDIA JANE PIERSON.

A song on the proposition to surrender to Mexican barbarity and tyranny the land between the Nueces and the Rio Grande—the battle-fields of Palo Alto and Resaca de la Palma.

It may not be! Forbid it, God!
  Forbid it, all that patriots prize:
That land has tasted freemen's blood;
  Their dust within its bosom lies.

'Twere madness to resign the soil
  On which our conquering feet have trod;
Battling our way with glorious toil;—
  It may not be—forbid it, God!

Can we relinquish lands where now
  The striped and starry banner wave?
No, never! We engrave our vow
  On every fallen brother's grave.

They could not sleep, (the slaughtered brave
  Who in their beds of glory rest,)
And feel the footstep of the slave
  Pollute the soil above their breast.

Resign the field where Ringgold fell!
  The spot where gallant Stephens lies!
Where Cochran felt his bosom swell
  Triumphant in death's agonies?

Where brave and virtusus hearts poured out
  The life so dear to hope and love,
Invoking with their dying shout
  Our country—and our God above?

No! By our country and our God,
  We will not yield that dear-bought soil!
We still have hearts with generous blood,
  And soul's to dare the conqueror's toil.

On! To the rescue! Hearts of steel—
  On! To the rescue! Souls of fire—
Let kindred blood inflame our zeal
  To conquer—triumph or expire.

Huzza! Press on where Taylor stands
  Invincible in conquering might;
We must prevail where he commands,
  And God sustains our sacred right.

Ask Taylor to retrace his way,
  And leave his conquest to the foe!
And this broad land, from sea to sea,
  Shall echo his emphatic No!!

No, never! This is holy ground,
  Bought and baptized with patriot blood;
See! with her fetters half unbound,
  She lifts her hands to Freedom's God!

By Freedom's God, she shall be free!
  Huzza brave hearts, press boldly on:
Strike home, nor pause till victory
  Shall put her olive garland on—

'Till o'er that land to utmost parts
  Our Eagle's sheltering wings are spread;
And Taylor throned on freemen's hearts
  Enjoys his laurels in the shade.

CLERICAL JOKE.—A few years since when the Rev. Dr. Hawks was about leaving New York for the South, he was waited upon by the vestrymen of a small church in Westchester county, and urgently solicited to take charge of the same. The Reverend Doctor graciously received the committee but respectfully declined their proposal, urging as a chief objection that the salary, though liberal for the parish which they represented, would be inadequate for his expenses, having a considerable family of small children to educate and provide for. One of the committee replied, "the Lord will take care of them; he has promised to hear the young ravens when they cry, and to provide for them." "Very true," said the Reverend gentleman, "but he has not promised to provide for the young Hawks."

A celebrated steamboat builder at New York has just concluded a contract to build a steamboat *four hundred feet iong!*

THE FREE AMERICAN.

VOL. 1. VERA CRUZ, SATURDY, DICEMBER 4, 1847. NO. 12.

The Free American.

PUBLISHED DAILY, [SUNDAYS EXCEPTED.] BY
F. A. DEVILLIERS & J. A. EPPERSON.

OFFICE—Corner Compañia & St. Maria streets.
ENTRANCE NO. 269 COMPANIA STREET.

TERMS.—Subscriptions recieved for one month for $2 00—payable in advance. Single copies, 12½ cts. Twelve copies 1 00.

ADVERTISEMENTS not exceeding 10 lines, inserted in English or Spanish $1 for the first and 50 cents for each subsequent insertion. Those of greater length charged in proportion. When advertised in both languages a deduction of 25 per cent will be made.

Persons advertising by the month, will be entitled to ten lines each day, in either language, for $10, or in both languages for $15. A deduction of 25 per cent. will be made on advertisements for subscribers. No advertisement will be discontinued till all arrearages are paid.

REGULATIONS OF PILOTS BY THE BOARD.

1st. All pilots are required to cruise in a suitable vessel and keep at sea.

2d. The rate of pilotage is two dollars and fifty cents per foot on all vessels over sixty tons—under sixty and over thirty, ten dollars— under thirty ton, six dollars in and out.

3d. Vessels spoken to inside the reef ar not bound to take a pilot or pay half pilotage.

4th. Vessels spoken outside the reef and refusing a pilot will be subject to half pilotage.

5th. The vessel that takes Pilots into port, is obliged to employ the same Pilot to take them out; if to the contrary, to receive half pilotage extra.

The pilot is considered *pro. tem.* responsible both to the Court and this board for all violation of the port regulations.

Rates for vessels of war as heretofore under the Mexican regulations.

(Signed)
FRANKLIN BUCHANAN, U. S. Navy.
E. G. ELLIOTT, U. S. Army,
F. M. DIMOND, Collector,
Vera Cruz, Nov, 22nd, 1847

HEAD QUARTERS.

Department of Vera Cruz, (*Mexico,*)
NOVEMBER 19, 1847.

ORDER NO. 115.

NO PERSON shall be permitted to land in the Department of Vera Cruz, from any public or private vessel, belonging to, or employed by, the United States, as a transport, or for other purpose, unless said person belongs to, is attached to, or has business with, the army or navy; and in the latter case, it must be clearly established to the satisfaction of the commanding officer of Vera Cruz, previous to their debarking. Persons who reside or who have legitimate business in Mexico, are of course not included amongst these who are prohibited from landing.

By order of Col. H. WILSON.
B. A. ARTHUR,
Adjt. 1st Inft. U. S. A., and
A. A. A. G., Depart. of Vera Cruz.

Head Quarters, Department of Vera Cruz,
NOVEMBER, 3, 1847.

ORDER No. 110.

COMPLAINTS having been made that the practice exists in this city of discharging fire arms in houses, yards, &c., to the great annoyance of the Guards and others, it is strictly forbidden that fire-arms be discharged within the walls of the city; and any person detected in the infringement of this order, will be arrested and dealt with accordingly

The Police and Guards of this city are required to aid in carrying out this order.

By order of COL. H. WILSON,
B. H. ARTHUR, Adjt. 1st U. S. In'ft. and
Nov.5, '47. A. A A. G, Dep of Vera Cruz.

HEAD QUARTERS.

Department of Vera Cruz,
November 24th, 1847.

ORDER NO. —.

FROM and after this date, all Mexicans coming to this market, are notified that, at the Gate of Mexico, at 10 o'clock, each morning, there will be a detachment of Dragoons to escort them safely through tde Sand Hills on the Orizaba road. Persons thus interested, are particularly advised to be punctual to the hour. H. WILSON,
nov 24-6t Col. U. S. A., and Gov. Vera Cruz.

TO OWNERS OF BOATS & LAUNCHES

IN accordance with the following agreement, I, the undersigded, notify all owners of Boats and Launches to pay into my hands their monthly tax. FELIX PETERS, Harbor Master.

We, the undersigned, agree to allow Felix Peters, the Harbor Master, the monthly tax on the Boats and Lauches as named and numbered in this document, and the said Peters is held accountble to us for his faithful performance of his duty, both towards the boatmen and the public.

FRANKLIN BUCHANAN, Commander.
F M DIMOND, Collector.
E G ELLIOTT, A. Quartermaste.
Vera Cruz, Nov. 25, 1847. nov 25-tf

NOTICE.

THE Partnership heretofore existing in Vera Cruz, Mexico, between F. L. Walsingham and Teiesfora Lartigue, is dissolved by mutual consent. The debts outstanding will be collected by F. L. Walsingham, and all lawful claims will be paid by the same.

The Auction and Commission business will be conducted as usual by the subscriber, at his Auction Store, 584 St. Juan de Dios street, Vera Cruz. F. L. WALSINGHAM,
U. S. Auctioneer and Insurance Agent.
Vera Cruz, October 28, 1847.

Poetry.

☞ The authoress of this, calls it "A Life Scene," and so it is, and very tenderly painted; though we recognise tint and drawing as we read. But it is a touching picture in a changed light, and so we give it place—*N. Y. Paper.*

Spring came—and she was fair;
White violets bloom her hair
As she tripped, in youthful pride,
By the river's sedgy side.
And no sweeter sound was heard
Than a voice, which, like a bird,
In ringing rapture rose
To brak the morn's repose.

Then Summer came—and bright
As starry gleams of light
Her springing form was seen
To cross the village green.
Blush roses, bathed in dew,
Their fragrance round her threw,
But faint her smile had grown
And low her voice's tone.

Next autumn came—aud mild
Her soft eyes on us smiled:
But tears had worn away
Their former brilliant play.
No more she twined her hair
With rose and violet fair;
Her footsteps sought no more
The river's sedgy shore.

Last Winter came—and low
She slept beneath the snow,
Secure from every grief;
For death had brought relief!

That Love's hot breath consumes;
Thus fall the blighted flowers
Beneath Love's scorching showers.

PORT OF VERACRUZ.

LIST OF VESSELS IN PORT.

STEAMERS.	MASTERS.	CONSIGNEES.
Severn, (Eng.)	Vincent,	Maning, Macintosh, &c.
Ann Chase,	....	"
Severn,	Vincent,	Manning & co
Mary Burt,	....	"
SHIPS.	MASTERS.	CONSIGNEES.
Rhode Island,	Fletcher.	Quartemaster.
BARKS.	MASTERS.	CONSIGNEES.
Epervier,	Robbins,	Bastina, Busing & Co
Washington,	Bartlett,	Quartermaster.
Gen Worth,	Cheney,	"
Etrarian,	Branseen,	"
Monaco,	Lewis,	"
Pensacola,	Hallett,	"
Peterson,	Peterson,	"
Village Girl, (Eng)	Wooff,	G de Drusnia & Co.
BRIGS	MASTERS	CONSIGNEES
Rosa, (Sardinian)	Gueirolo,	Viya & Brother
Elizabeth Louise,	Tachtman,	Batre & Uhthoff
SCHRS.	MASTERS.	CONSIGNEES.
Peruvian,	........,	J. Saulnier.
Mississippi,	Clarke,	"
Eleanor Stephens,	Hall,	Quartermaster.
Renaissance,	Derbes,	Master.
May,	Allen.	Juan Saulnier.
John Rowlett,	Hanlon,	Master.
John Drew,	Searles,	"
William Tell,	Dyer.	"
Martha Louisa,	Simpton,	Quartermaster.
SLOOPS.	MASTERS.	CONSIGNEES.
Wm R Crach,	Peterson,	Master.

POCKET BOOK FOUND.—A small Pocket Book was fonnd, containing a bank note and some change.

The person who has lost it, will find it at the Quartermaster's office. Dec 4-3t

VERA CRUZ:

SATURDAY MORNING, DECEMBER 4,

Relations of the Sexes.—The editor of the *Nntional Era*, in reply to a correspondient, says: "As to our own creed, we think it highly orthodox. We believe that woman was taken at first from the side of man, but that ever since man has been born of woman; that they are both very indispensable to each other, and that "if man, the hermit, sighed till woman smiled," she would have done the same thing, had not her full gaze, on first awaking to Life, rested upon him; that if, in a certain sense, man is the head of the woman, woman is the heart of man in a good many senses; that there is no conflict of rights, or, so far as we have ascertained, no natural hostility, between the sexes; that the crowning glory Earth is the well-ordered Family, where husband and wife rule each other by Love and Reason, without rude appeals to prerogative on one side, or necessity of sufferring submission on the other, both equally love and respected by their children, both equally loving and reverencing the great Father of All.

THE RED SEA AND THE MEDITERRANEAN.—The London correspondent of the Nation Intelligencer writes that influential parties in England, France and Austria have united for the construction of a canal across the isthmus of Suez with the entire concurrence of the Viceroy of Egypt. Surveys have been made, and the work has been fonnd practicable; the chief difficulty, which is at the Mediterranean termination, can be mastered; a ship canal, wide and deep enough to float a first rate man of war, is to be constructed from Suez to Pelusium, on the Mediterranean. English, French and Austrian engineers are on the ground, Mr. Stephenson, the celebrated English engineer, is to construct the port at Suez, M. Nigrelli, and an Austrian engineer of celebrity, undertakes the port at Pelusium, whilst the execution of the ntermediate canal has been intrusted to a French engineer of great eminence.

SLAVE TRADE.—Lieut. Com'g Bell, of the U. S. Brig Boxer, has addressed a letter to the Navy Department, from Porto Praya, in which he states that he had overhauled an American brig (the J. W. Huntington) on the night of the 31st August, owned in New York, from Rio Janeiro, with the usual assorted slave cargo on board, and lumber enough for a slave deck. He was informed also, that the Malaga had precisely such a cargo except the lumber. The American brig Senator, boarded in March last, was out from Rio with such a cargo, and similarly chartered. The master of the J. W. Huntington reports she [the Senator] now lies scuttled in Rio. Having safely landed 500 slaves at Cape Frio, she proceded into Rio under Brazilian colors, where her owners were suffered to strip her of all her furniture, and then the Government seized as a no-document vessel—the American crew having left her at Loargo, where the slaves were taken ion board.

Lieut. Bell has been informed, that about 30 American vessels arrive on the south coast of Africa from Brazil, some of which are known to take a return cargo of slaves. They are freighted by Brazilians for Africa, where their American crews leave them. "In these transactions," says Lieut. Commanding Bell, "you perceive the mode in which the American flag covers and promotes a trade which no other flag can, and the base uses to which it is applied by foreigners who have not the manliness to vindicate the freedom of their own."

A Wild Cat.—We understand a large quadruped, ycleped a wild cat, was slain on Wednesday night last, on the premises of Mr. J W. Vanwickle, whose plantation is situated about a mile above us.—*Point Coupee Echo.*

Daily American Star.

VOL. I. MEXICO, TUESDAY, JANUARY 18, 1848. NO. 92.

THE DAILY STAR
Will be published every day (Mondays excepted) by
PEOPLES & BARNARD.

THE LATEST FROM WASHINGTON.

The following interesting summary of Congressional news, etc., we copy from files of the the Picayune, received on Sunday:

Congressional Proceedings of Wednesday, Dec. 15.—The Petersburg Intelligencer furnishes a brief report of the proceedings of Congress on Wednesday, the 15th inst. The resolutions of Mr Calhoun will command attention:

Senate.—Mr. Calhoun offered the following resolutions:

Resolved, That to conquer and hold Mexico, either as a province or incorporating it into the Union, is inconsistent with the avowed objects of the war, contrary to the settled policy of the Government, in conflict with its character and genius, and, in the end, must be subversive of all our free and popular institutions.

Resolved, That no line of policy for the further prosecution of the war should be adopted which may tend to consequences so disastrous.

The resolutions were ordered to be printed.

House of Representatives.—A long debate occurred on Mr. Vinton's resolution for the appointment of a new committee to be designated as the Committee on Internal Commerce.

A message was received from the President giving his reasons ... Harbor bill.

Mr. Wentworth ... Committee on Con...

Mr. Vinton mo... committee—upon ...

Mr. Isaac Holm... tion to the Mexica...

Monday, Dec. ... introduction of sun... bills. Mr. Calhoun ... gard to Mexico:

Resolved, That to con... a province or to incorp... sistent with the avowe... prosecuted, a departure... ernment, in conflict wit... end subversive of our f...

Resolved, That no lin... of the war should be ad... ces so disastrous.

Mr. Calhoun ca... submitted by him ... to make them a sp... On this matter he ... gether by the wish... sired was that the... If agreeable to the... second Tuesday in... be made the specia... motion was agreed...

Mr. Allen intim... be to refer the s... Foreign Relations, ... ensued, in which ... Dickinson, Niles, ... pated.

Mr. Dickinson ... day for the consid... after some debate...

A message was... Representatives, a... Dromgoole, of Vir...

Mr. Mason addr... choly occasion, an... customary resolu... adjourned.

In the *House* M... annexed:

Resolved, That the m... and Territories, as a l... revenue, be now called... States before resort be...

Mr. Richardson... tions:

Resolved, That the ... and necessary on our p... sole purpose of vindica... of securing an honorab...

Resolved, That the ... peace leaves this gov... vigorous prosecution of... with the law of nations... calamities and burdens... and honorable peace, ... money or territory for... of the war.

Resolved, That the a... depend upon the obstir... the war.

Mr. Richardson...

Mr. Botts move... table.

A motion was h... now adjourn, and... yeas and nays—ye...

Mr. Schenck m... which motion the...

A motion was h... adjourn, and deci... negative—yeas 96... refused to adjourn...

The yeas and na... ing a call of the H... and nays 84. So t... be a call.

And then the H...

Tuesday. *Dec.* ... of petitions and m... appropriately refe...

In the *House of Representatives*, the Speaker announced that the presentation of petitions and memorials would be the first business in order. He then commenced calling the States for that purpose, commencing with the new States.

Many petitions and memorials having been presented, Mr. Giddings submitted one for the abolition of slavery in the District of Columbia, and moved its reference to the Judiciary Committee.

Mr. Jones, of Tennessee, moved to lay said petition on the table.

Mr. Jacob Thompson requested the reading of the document, and it was read for the information of the House.

On the motion to lay it on the table, the yeas and nays were called for and taken. They stood 97 in the affirmative and 97 in the negative.—The Speaker said that he had been accustomed to give a fair hearing to petitions couched in respectful terms, and he should therefore vote in the negative. So he declared the motion to lay the petition on the table lost.

Mr. Giddings said he would press the reference of the matter to the Judiciary Committee, and so it lies over.

On motion of Mr. Vinton, the House agreed to go into Committee of the Whole to-morrow, and take up an appropriation bill to meet a deficiency in the appropriation for the last fiscal year. ...The Speaker now announced the unfinished...

nays. The question of non-reception being put, as a matter of course, Mr. Berrien moved to lay that question on the table, and the yeas and nays being required by Mr. Hale, in reference to the first of these petitions, it was decided in the affirmative—yeas 33, nays 9. The yeas and nays are as follows.

Yeas.—Allen, Ashley, Atchison, Atherton, Badger, Bell, Berrien, Brandbury, Breese, Bright, Butler, Calhoun, Cass, Davis of Mississippi, Dickinson, Dix, Downs, Fairfield, Felch, Foote, Hunter, Johnson of Maryland, Johnson of Louisiana, Mangum, Mason, Niles, Rusk, Sevier, Spruance, Sturgeon, Turney, Westcott, Yules—33.

Nays.—Baldwin, Clarke, Corwin, Greene, Hale, Miller Phelps, Underwood, Upham—9.

The second petition, after some few remarks from Mr. Hale, in defence of the course which he had deemed it his duty to take, took the same course.

A bill was reported by Mr. Cass, from the Military Committee, to raise for a limited time an additional military force, and Mr. Cass gave notice that he would take the earliest opportunity to call this bill up for consideration.

In the *House*, Mr. Robert Smith presented a petition from sundry citizens of Illinois, praying indemnity for losses in the Black Hawk war.

Mr. Lincoln presented resolutions calling on the President for information touching the causes which led to the war and the right of the United States to the territory between the Nueces and the Rio Grande...

REMARKS OF MR. DIX, OF NEW YORK.

In the Senate, Dec. 20, 1847, upon a Retiring List, and Relief of Widows and Orphans of Officers.

I rise to present two petitions, to which I desire to invoke the attention of the Senate. It was not until yesterday that I was apprised of their contents, or I should have brought them here at an earlier day. They were left on my table in the city a week or ten days ago, when I was absent, sealed and addressed to an honorable Senator from Missouri, (Mr. Benton), not now in his place, who served for many years as Chairman of the Committee on Military Affairs, with distinguished honor to himself and advantage to the country; and I greatly regret that he is not here to take charge of them. I am not in the habit, sir, as you know, of accompanying the presentation of papers with introductory remarks. In ordinary cases it is doubtless more proper to await the action of appropriate committees on the subjects to which they refer. But I trust the nature of these may be deemed by the Senate to justify a departure from the usual practice.

They are petitions signed by the officers of the army at Puebla, on the 1st day of August last before it commenced its march towards the city of Mexico. The first is styled "a petition for a retiring list." It contains two hundred and thirty-three signatures, and prays for certain ... provisions in respect to aged and dis... ...cers, which, without casting any new ... the public treasury, would, in the ... the petitioners, add greatly to the ... of the army, and at the same time do ... those who perform the drudgery and ... the perils of military service in the ... ill only say further in reference to this ... hat the plan suggested corresponds, to ... nt, though not fully, with one proposed ... commander of the army, (Gen. Ma... ...d I believe recently recommended by ... adjutant general with a view to the ... ...ts.

...cond "a petition for widows and or... is signed by two hundred and twenty-... and I believe the names, as far as ... are identical with those borne on the ... also dated at Puebla, on the 1st day ... last, almost at the moment the army ... march for the valley of Mexico: and, ... nsidered in connection with the sur... circumstances, and the brilliant events ... followed, with a rapidity of succession ... xceeded by those which signalized the ... rance of Bonaparte into Italy, it ... itself, with great force, to the feelings, ... the justice, of Congress and the coun...

...ot detain the Senate by entering into ... d review of these events with a view ... the appeal contained in the petition on ... ition. I hope, however, I may be in... saying, in justice to those who bore a ... m, that the first conquest of Mexico ... it appears to me, be compared with ... either as to the obstacles overcome, ... the relative strength of the invaders. ... phs of Cortez were achieved by poli... superiority in discipline and in the im... ...f warfare. The use of firearms, until ... own to the inhabitants of Mexico, was ... itself to make his force, small as it ... itible. In the eyes of that simple and ... us people he seemed armed with ... n power. Other circumstances com... ...cilitate his success. The native tribes, ... he country was possessed, were dis... ...unities, not always acknowledged the ... and often divided among themselves ... ble hostility and resentments. Cortez, ... summate prudence and art, turned ... ntions to his own account; he lured ... s to them into his own service, and ... presented himself at the gates of the ... xico, he was at the head of four thou... e most warlike of the natives, as auxil... e band of Spaniards, with which he ... d his march from Vera Cruz. Thus, ... ccesses were as much the triumph of ... arms. Gen. Scott, and the gallant ... d, had no such advantages. The ... ulation of the country from Vera Cruz ... was united as one man against him, ... ted by the fiercest animosity. He was ... y military forces armed like his own, ... ter disciplined, occupying positions ... themselves, strong by nature, and forti... ding to the strictest rules of art. These ... were overcome by his skill as a tacti... d by a corps of officers unsurpassed for ... wl dge of the art of attack and defence, ... he indomitable courage of his follow... h half his force left on the battle-field ... hospital, and with less than six thou... after a series of desperate contests, he ... ession of the city of Mexico, containing ... wo hundred thousand inhabitants, and ... by the remnant of an army of more ... thousand soldiers. I confess I know ... modern warfare which exceeds in ... the movements of the American army ... half to the city of Mexico. I shall not ... speak of them in the language of

---

Samuel Lewis, W. T. Wilson

FLAG OF FREEDOM.

VOL. I.] PUEBLA, (MEXICO,) SATURDAY, NOVEMBER 20, 1847. [NO. X.

PUBLISHED EVERY WEDNESDAY AND SATURDAY,
On the Main Street, near San Jose Church,
BY KRITSER AND COMPANY.
PRICE HALF DIME.

POETRY.

"PUEBLA DE LOS ANGELES."

The city of Puebla has the additional cognomen of "Los Angeles," or the angels—so called from the following legend. During the building of the magnificent Cathedral in the *plaza*, (one of the most beautiful ecclesiastical edifices on our continent,) it is said, that when nearly completed, the angels one night descended from heaven, and put the finishing stroke to the stately pile. The following morning the beautiful church appeared to the astonished "*Poblanos*" finished! and a large, sonorous bell, which previously had baffled human endeavors to place it in the steeple, by independent agency already suspended.

'Tis night! the valley's sweetly sleeping,
The moon she beams o'er dale and hill;
The twinkling stars their watch are keeping,
And nature's voice is hushed and still,
Save when the balmy scented air
Breathes perfumed o'er the landscape fair.

Behold where yonder stately towers
Unfinish'd, in their pride arise:
Where, 'midst Puebla's slumbering bowers,
They rear their turrets to the skies!
Whose starry glories seem to smile
Upon the sacred, stately pile.

Truthfully the solemn structure seems,
In uncompleted majesty,
To watch the slumbering city's dreams,
And from the constellated sky,
To bid celestial glory bless
Its fanes, with heaven's lovliness!

Deeper the shades of night are falling,
And darkness reigns—above—around;
Silence, how breathless—how appalling!
Surrounds the couch of sleep profound—
When lo! a beam refulgent bright,
Illumes the church with heavenly light.

Whence shines that light? what distant notes
Of seraph music, soft and clear,
In the night's solemn silence float,
Embracing every slumberer's ear!
Why gleams the fair Cathedral's spire,
With strange, seraphic, mystic fire!

Hush! this is holy ground—the bright bands
Of dazzling cherubims complete
The work which brave, devoted hands
Of man commenc'd—the dwelling mete
For God and angels—whence should rise
Devotion's incense to the skies.

Ah, holy hour, how brightly beaming,
The stately, fair Cathedral stood;
It's aisles with heaven's effulgence gleaming!
No wonder dreams serene and good
Hover'd around each slumbering head,
And blest the city's sleepers' beds.

Morn in the eastern sky is breaking,
The sun comes up in majesty;
To life the dewy vale is waking,
What wonder fills each wondering eye,
Completed the Cathedral stands,
Completed by no *human* hands.

Forth from its noble towers resound
A bell's deep toll which calls to prayer;
Amaz'd, the people kneel around,
When they discover suspended there,
A bell, which angel hands alone
Could raise to the recipient stone!

Sons of the Aztec's faded race,
Well may ye view with pious awe
The holy, consecrated place,
Whence seraph erected towers soar!
And well with pious reverence kneel,
When tolls the angelic bell its peal!

Fort Loretto, Nov. 15th, 1847. QUIZ.

VARIETY.

A Mexican Lariated.—We were told last evening that a few days ago a number of horses belonging to the Quartermaster's department were "stamped" and they ran off. Three or four Mexicans in the public employ were sent after them. After huddling them together and while engaged in throwing ropes over their necks, a strange Mexican was observed officiating his services in the same line. Quick as thought a lariat was cast over his head and the noose drawn. The suddenness and force of the action threw him to the ground and dislocated his neck. Several horses, we learn, have been ridden off in this way at various times. Some six or seven horses, on this occasion, escaped without the United States brand being burnt upon them.—*Matamoras Flag.*

A Curious Verdict.—A strange verdict has been rendered in Ireland under the following circumstances:—An inquest was held recently in Galway in the work house upon the body of a mendicant, and the jury rendered the opinion thus: We think the deceased came to his death by exhaustion and misery caused by the want of the necessaries of life; and as Lord John Russel, head of her Majesty's Government and Sir Randolph Routh, by not taking the necessary measures to prevent famine and to save Ireland from the deplorable situation in which she now finds herself, have contributed to distress the Irish nation, we think that the said Lord John Russel and the said Sir Randolph *are guilty of wilful murder* upon the person of the deceased. The coroner refused the verdict thus rendered; but the jury would not consent to change it.

Rogers and Rakes were amusing themselves lately in a *pungent* contest of pun-making. 'Now,' said Rakes to Rogers, 'can you tell me, Sam, why the Roman Catholic clergy are richer than the Protestant Clergy?' Rogers studied till the time was up. 'Why, then, Sammy,' cried Rakes, 'are they not a-*mass*-ing every day of their lives.' Rogers was so delighted, that he threw a somerset, and dashed his heel through a chimney-glass.

'Well, Nimrod, how long were the children of Israel in the wilderness? 'Till they found their way out.' Who was cast into the lion's den? 'Van Amburg.' 'Who was compelled to seek refuge in the land of Nod?' 'Gov. Dorr.' 'Why?' 'Because he got up the *King's* ebenezer and *Providence* wouldn't protect him.

'Ha! is that a dagger I see before me?' said a young actor, who was practising histrionics in his attic. 'No, sir,' said his landlord's red-haired daughter, "it's only mamma's bill for seven week's board and washing!"

A drunken youth got out of his calculation, and was dozing in the street, when the bells roused him by their ringing for fire. 'Nine, ten, eleven, twelve, thirteen, fourteen,' cried he. 'Well, if this isn't later than ever I knew it!'

To be moderate in prosperity, is to know how to walk on the ice.

Annual Pictorial Herald.

Number 5. NEW YORK, JANUARY 1, 1848. Price Sixpence.

THE

Major General Zachary Taylor.

The First Encampment of the American Army, under Major General (Then Brevet Brigadier General) Taylor, at Corpus Christi, July 31, 1845.

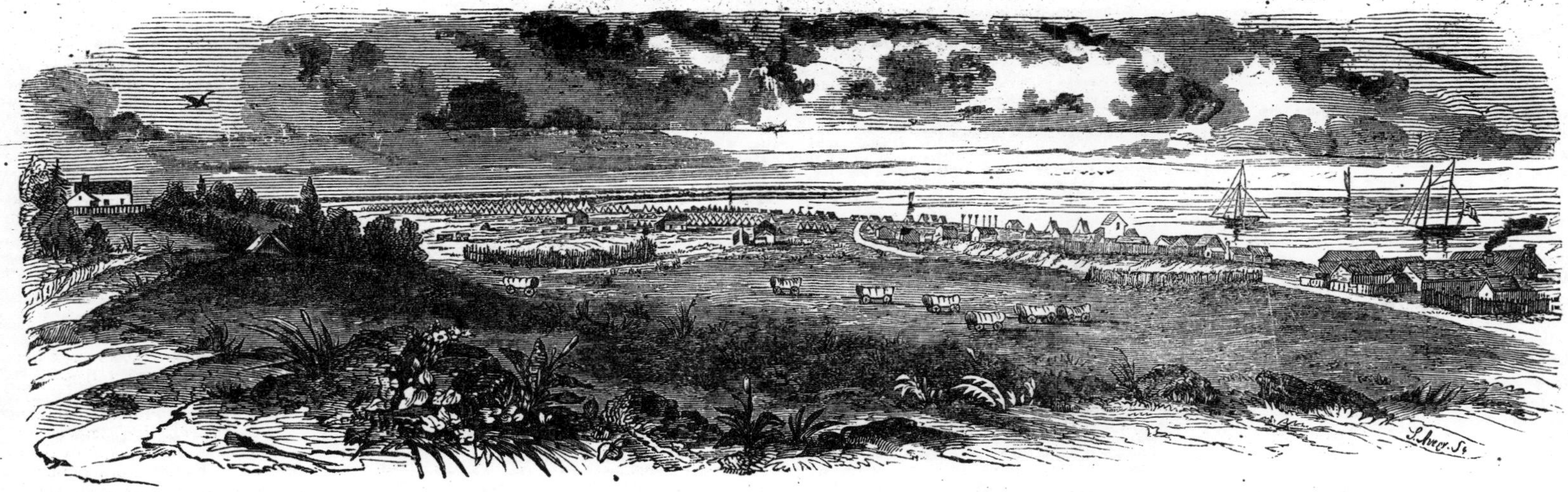

OF THE

Major General Winfield Scott.

The Texian Advocate.

PUBLISHED WEEKLY BY JOHN D. LOGAN AND THOMAS STERNE, AT $3 IN ADVANCE, $4 IN SIX MONTHS, OR $5 AT THE END OF THE YEAR.

VOL. 3. VICTORIA, TEXAS, THURSDAY, JUNE 1, 1848. No. 5.

THE
TEXIAN ADVOCATE
WILL BE PUBLISHED EVERY THURSDAY BY
LOGAN & STERNE.

TERMS.

The Texian Advocate will be devoted to Agriculture, Morals, Education, Health, Science, Art, the diffusion of practical and useful information, and to the General Interests of the People of Western Texas. It will be sent to subscribers in any part of the United States at the very low price of Three Dollars in advance; Four Dollars in six months; or, Five Dollars at the end of the year.

Each number will generally contain one or more interesting tales, several pieces of Poetry, Hints on Domestic Economy, Practical Receipts for the Farmer, Mechanic, and House Keeper, Miscellaneous Articles selected with great care, Religious Thoughts and observations, together with a fund of Wit, Humor, Anecdote, &c.

—AND ALSO—

The Latest News from all parts of the United States and Foreign Countries; the state of the Markets, and all other matters of interest to the general reader.

ADVERTISING.

One square (10 lines or less) 1st insertion,	$1,00
Each subsequent insertion,	50

Longer advertisements in the same proportion.

CONTRACTS BY THE YEAR,
PAYABLE QUARTERLY.

One square, six months, renewable,	$12,00
Two squares, six months,	18,00
Three squares, six months,	23,00
Four squares, six months,	28,00

Longer advertisements in the same proportion.

One square, one year, renewable,	$20,00
Two squares, one year,	30,00
Three squares, one year,	36,00
Four squares, one year,	40,00

Longer advertisements in the same proportion.

Business Cards per annum,	$10,00

Announcements of Candidates will be inserted as other Advertisements, and charged for accordingly.

Political circulars will be charged as advertisements.

All letters must be post paid.

Single copies of the paper, 10 cents

Legal Advertisements.

We could not find a more fitting occasion than the present to say a few words to persons having *legal advertisements* to make in the columns of the Texian Advocate. In future no advertisement the publication of which is required by law will appear in our columns, unless paid for in advance. We have been driven to the adoption of this rule by the extreme difficulty we meet with in collecting this description of debts.

In order, therefore, that all may act understandingly, we here submit such instructions as may enable the Clerks of the District Courts and others to calculate the cost of a given advertisement for any period of time: Ten lines of ordinary manuscript will be counted a square, and will cost one dollar for the first week, and fifty cents for each subsequent week it is required to be published. Any number o lines over ten and not exceeding fifteen, will count a square and a half; over fifteen and not exceeding twenty, two squares, and so on: thus, an advertisement of forty-seven lines will count five squares, and will cost, for one week, five dollars; for two weeks, seven dollars and a half; for eight weeks, twenty-two dollars and a half. In counting the lines, there is no deduction to be made for those only partially filled, as captions, signatures, &c.

Proposals for a Loan.

TREASURY DEPARTMENT,
April 17, 1848.

SEALED proposals will be received, under the act of 31st March last, until 3, P. M., on Saturday, the 17th June, 1848, for sixteen millions of dollars of United States stock, reimbursable twenty years from and after the 1st day of July, 1848, bearing six per cent. interest per annum, payable semi-annually, on the first days of January and July of each year. No bid will be received below par; nor will any bid be considered unless one per cent. thereof is deposited in some depository of the United States at or before the date fixed for opening the proposals. The bids, in all cases, must be unconditional, and without any reference to the bids of others, and should state distinctly the premium offered. The proposals should be sealed and endorsed "*Proposals for loan of* 1848," and addressed to the Secretary of the Treasury, Washington City, D. C. The sums which may be accepted will be required to be paid to the depository of the United States nearest the places of residence of the persons respectively whose offers may be successful; but the amount of the accepted bids from bidders not residing in the United States, must be deposited with the assistant treasurers at New-York, Boston, Philadelphia, or New-Orleans.

To give an opportunity to all persons to participate in the investment of funds in this stock, bids will be received for the lowest denomination of certificates authorized by law—being for fifty dollars—as well as for the highest sum.

All certificates under one thousand dollars will be transferable on the books of the treasury, or by delivery with coupons attached, at the option of the bidder. To avoid expense, confusion, and multiplication of accounts, all certificates with coupons attached will be for the sum of one thousand dollars.

The successful bidders will be required to deposite the amount awarded in five equal instalments in each of the months of July, August, September, October, and November of the present year, except for sums not exceeding twenty thousand dollars, where the bidder may be desirous of making immediate payment, in which case the whole amount may be at once deposited. The stock will bear interest in all cases from the date of deposite.

The bids will be opened at the Treasury Department at 3 P. M., on Saturday, the 17th of June, 1848, in the presence of all persons who may desire to attend; but, under a provision introduced into the act of 31st March last, no bidder will be permitted to withdraw his bid. On all bids not accepted, the amount deposited in advance will be immediately returned. The whole premium on the amount awarded must be deposited as part of the first payment required in July next.

R. J. WALKER,
Secretary of the Treasury.

Each of the daily papers of Boston, New-York, Philadelphia, Baltimore, Charleston, and Orleans, and in all the other States the papers selected to print the laws of the United States, are authorized to publish this advertisement.—*Union.* 4-f17J.

POETRY.

My Mother.

MOTHER: O, how my bosom thrills,
Oft as I hear thy honor'd name!
It wakens nobler feelings than
Are waked by hopes of wealth or fame;
It brings before my dreaming gaze
The cherished scenes of other days.

The sweetest cord that ever sounds
Among the strings of memory,
Is that which oft, at fancy's beck,
Can bring me back to youth and thee:
I hear the songs which lull'd me then—
Such sounds I ne'er shall hear again.

Since thou hast gone, misfortunes oft
Their shadows dark have o'er me cast;
The future now seems bright no more,
And joy is found but in the past;
And of that *past* thou seem'st a part,
Which ne'er shall vanish from my heart.

When seeking joy in pleasure's halls,
Amid the mazes of the dance,
I've felt thy care was o'er me still,
And seem'd to meet thy chilling glance,
And heard thee whisp'ring, "Son, beware,
O, seek no more for pleasure there!"

And mid that throng I've trac'd the past,
Till mem'ry dwelt on other years,
And brought to mind her mild reproof,
Which once could melt me into tears;
And oft I've left those scenes, and thought
Upon what once that mother taught.

Though years have pass'd, a mother's care
I often feel is circling round;
And when I stand beside her grave,
I feel as if on holy ground;
While scenes in which she bore a part
Came thronging round my stricken heart.

And oft upon that hallowed spot
I've knelt to tame this heart so wild,
And sought in prayer that purity
My mother taught me when a child;
And oft methought my spirit there
Has heard the accents of my pray'r.

O, when this changeful, earthly scene,
Is fading from my failing sight,
May my glad spirit plume its wings,
To try a loftier, nobler flight,
To heaven's blest real! O, may I flee,
Mother, from earth to God and thee.

To my Daughter Lily.

Six changeful years are gone, Lily,
Since you were born to be
A darling to your mother good,
A happiness to me.
A little, shivering, feeble thing
You were to touch and view,
But we could see a promise in
Your little eyes of blue.

You fastened on our hearts, Lily,
As day by day wore by,
And beauty grew upon your cheeks,
And deepened in your eye;
A year made dimples in your cheek,
And plumped your little feet;
And you had learned some merry ways,
Which we thought very sweet.

And when the first sweet word, Lily,
Your wee mouth learned to say,
Your mother kissed it fifty times,
And marked the famous day.
I know not, even now, my dear,
If it were quite a word,
But your proud mother surely knew,
For she the sound had heard.

When you were four years old, Lily,
You were my little friend,
And we had walks and nightly plays,
And talks without an end.
You little ones are sometimes wise,
For you are undefiled;
A grave grown man will start to hear
The strange words of a child.

When care pressed on our house, Lily—
Pressed with an iron hand—
I hated mankind for the wrong
Which festered in the land;
But when I read your young, frank face,
Its meaning sweet and good,
My charities grew clear again—
I felt my brotherhood.

And sometimes it would be, Lily,
My faith in God grew cold—
For saw I virtue go in rags,
And vice in cloth of gold;
But in your innocence, my child,
And in your mother's love,
I learnt those lessons of the heart
Which fasten it above.

At last our cares are gone, Lily,
And peace is back again,
As you have seen the sun sink clear,
After the gloomy rain;
In the good land where we were born
We may be happy still;
A life of love will bless our home—
The house upon the hill.

Thanks to your gentle face, Lily!
Its innocence was strong
To keep me constant to the right
When tempted by the wrong.
The little ones were dear to him
Who died upon the Rood—
I asked his gentle care for you,
And for your mother good.

There has been an organization of the whig party at Galveston in this state.

HISTORICAL.

Joan of Arc, or the Maid of Orleans.

From the moment the supreme command of the French army was entrusted to this remarkable woman, she displayed the most consummate skill in military plans and movements. She seemed indeed to possess intuitively a knowledge of what ought to be done in every emergency. And whenever she differed from her Generals, or rather they differed from her. and their counsels prevailed, which was the case in one or two instances at the commencement of her public career, the issue proved conclusively that she was right and they wrong. That a young, uneducated peasant girl should surpass in military skill and strategy the veteran officers of the French army, was to them humiliating in the extreme. It was, however, borne without resentment or apparent jealousy, so long as her services were absolutely necessary. After the coronation of Charles at Rheims, when the fortunes of the French might be said to be partially retrieved, the French Generals seemed to brook their subjection to her authority with reluctance. To dismiss her from the army they could not; for both the army and the king would have opposed it. Consequently but one way appeared feasible by which to rid themselves of a superior who entirely eclipsed their talents and genius—and that way was to permit her to fall into the hands of the enemy! This was done at Compeigne.

The joy of the English at her capture was excessive. They had regarded her as an impersonation of the devil, come forth to thwart all their plans, and defeat their measures; and like the Philistines in the case of Samson, they determined to glut their vengeance with the blood of their victim. The Duke of Bedford was determined upon her death. As a prisoner of war this could not be accomplished, unless clandestinely and by assassination. To gratify his malignity, he formed the plan of having her tried before an *ecclesiastical* tribunal, upon the charge of heresy and witchcraft, care being taken that her judges should be of the right stamp to effect his diabolical purpose. She was carried to Rouen and there imprisoned. Not satisfied with confining her in its great tower, her captors placed her in chains; and Turner, in his history, says, "A cage of iron was sworn to have been made fore her, in which she was fastened by the neck, feet, and hands, from the time of her arrival at Rouen to the first day of her trial. Three Englishmen passed the night in her chamber, and two more watched on the outside. It is with pain we remark that they behaved to her with great brutality; but the imputation of witchcraft had made her an outcast from human nature."

The account of her trial and sufferings is given in the language of her historians.—We quote from Sharon Turner's History of England:

"The Bishop of Beauvais, and the deputy of the Grand Inquisition consulted on the form of the process; and what was called her trial was arranged according to the forms of the Inquisition in the following January, and actually began in the next month.—These men seem to have been her presiding judges. Depositions were taken as to the circumstances of her life and actions. Her person was examined by the Duchess of Bedford, and some matrons, and she was fifteen times brought before her judges, and very minutely interrogated, between the 21st of February and the 17th of March. But the event depended neither on her answers nor on the evidence. Her answers clearly showed that she had been guilty of no crime, but patriotism and enthusiasm, mingled with impressions, which her personal manner and countenance must have satisfied her examiners were mental hallucinations, not impious impostures. The unprejudiced and the humane would have admired and pitied her; but policy and bigotry condemned her, and to a cruel death. The English bravery was seduced from its habitual generosity, by the mistaken hope that her disgraceful execution would destroy the talisman which had reversed their successes, and it stooped to avail itself of the credulity, trick, injustice, and cruel prejudice, which doomed a prisoner of war to be burnt for sorcery and witchcraft.

"The sequel is painful to read and narrate. She became ill, and the Earl of Warwick sent physicians to her, with this injunction: 'The King would not have her by any means die a natural death. He has bought her dear, and is desirous that she should die by justice, and be burnt. Visit her, therefore, and cure her.' They found her in a fever, and told him they must bleed her. 'Beware of that,' the Earl replied, 'she is cunning, and may kill herself.' She recovered. Her sentence was read to her. She refused to lay aside her male attire, except to take the sacrament. She was at one time threatened with torture; but she calmly braved it. 'If pain should draw from me false confessions, it will be your violence that will force them from me.' It was not inflicted. The Duchess of Bedford kindly brought her female clothes, to lessen the irritation against her; she declined them; and when the tailor put his hand on her neck to take off her dress, she struck him with indignation at the affront. New efforts were made to induce her to appear in the garments of her sex, to confess the crimes imputed to her, and to abjure them. She exclaimed, 'All that I have done, and all that I do, I have done well, and am doing well to act so.'—They promised her liberty; she was shaken for a moment, but at last said, 'You will have a great deal of trouble to seduce me.' On further urgency, she agreed to sign the abjuration they brought, if the clergy and the Church advised it. 'Sign now,' said Erard, a doctor of theology, 'or you will finish your life to-day in the flames.' She told him she would rather sign than be burnt. The English secretary put a paper into her hands. She said she could neither read nor write. They gave her a pen, and made her repeat the abjuration after them. She did so, and smiled, and drew a circle at the bottom of the paper. The secretary took her hand, and made her mark a cross. She consented afterward to put on female attire; but she soon repented of her acquiescence, and resumed her male dress."

The final scene is so beautifully and touchingly, as well as truthfully painted by Turner, that the reader will thank us for quoting it entire, in preference to any attempt of our own to portray it. The execution took place on the 30th or 31st of May, 1431, in the market-place of Rouen. Says Turner:

"It was announced to her in the morning that she was to be burnt that day. She cried out most piteously on hearing it, wrung her hands, and tore her hair. 'Am I to be treated so horribly and so cruelly? Must my body, which has always been wholly pure, be consumed to-day to ashes? I would rather be beheaded seven times than be burnt! O, I appeal to God, the great Judge, for all the wrongs and injuries they have done to me!' But recovering herself, she resumed her usual piety and resignation, and made her confession. She received the sacrament very devoutly, shedding tears profusely, and with inexpressible humility. When the prelate of Beauvais, one of her severest enemies, entered, she said to him, 'Bishop! I die through you, and I appeal against you before God.' Seeing Peter Morice, an ecclesiastic who had befriended her, she exclaimed, 'Ah! monk Peter, where shall I be to-day?' 'Have you not good hope in the Lord?' he answered. 'Yes,' was her reply, 'if God help me, I shall be in paradise.'

"She was dressed in female habiliments, and at nine in the morning was taken on a car with her confessor, and guarded by eight hundred men, armed with axes, swords, and lances, was carried to the market-place of Rouen. Her tears, and lamentations, and prayers, all the way, melted the spectators. Arriving at the fatal spot, she cried out, 'Rouen! Rouen! must I die here?' She was placed on the scaffold, with the wood that was to consume her. A vast multitude filled the place. The Cardinal Bishop of Winchester was one of the prelates that attended. A doctor in theology made a sermon to her and the people. She heard him patiently. When he had done, she fell on her knees, and uttered such fervent prayers to God and her saints, and asked for those of the spectators so earnestly, that the English themselves, and the Cardinal wept profusely, and pitied her; but none stepped forward to release her. A vindictive and defamatory address was read to her that could only embitter her last moments. She asked in return but for a cross. An Englishman present immediately made one from the end of a stick, and gave it to her. She took, kissed, and put it in her bosom, and petitioned to have one from the church, that she might look on it till she expired. It was brought, and she eagerly and long embraced it; but her persecutors became impatient, and exclaimed, 'Do you mean, priest, to make us dine here?' The clergy had before given her up to the secular power, and the fire was now ordered to be applied. 'Execute your office,' was the last command; but two seargents approached to draw her from the scaffold. She saluted them, and came down. Men at arms then seized her, and dragged her back with great fury to the stake. She made piteous outcries, invoked her Savior, and moaned, 'Rouen! Rouen! will you be my last abode?' Several persons, unable to support the sight, quitted the place. The degrading mitre of the Inquisition was placed on her head, having the conspicuous words, 'Heretic, relapsed, apostate, idolater.' She was tied to the stake. The faggots were set on fire. She cried with a loud voice, as she felt the flames, 'O, Jesus!' Seeing her friendly friar in danger from the heat, she bade him retire, but to hold up the cross to her till she was dead. She refused to deny the revelations she believed she had received. She declared her conviction that she had done nothing but by the Divine order, and that her voices were not illusions. The scaffold being plastered, the flames advanced slowly, though the executioner, in pity, wished to hasten their operation, that he might shorten her sufferings. As the fire and smoke distressed her, she called out for holy water. She implored fervently the Divine assistance, calling on her saints, at times shrieking, at times groaning and praying. At last her head was seen to fall on one side; and the name of her Savior, pronounced with the loud voice of agony, was the last words she was heard to utter."

Thus perished, in the twenty-first year of her age, one of the most remarkable characters that ever appeared upon the stage of human action; and her death has stamped eternal infamy upon both French and English, but more especially the latter.

Many attempts have been made to account for the singular apparitions which continually accompanied her. Some, as we have seen, imputed them to the direct agency of the devil: others supposed them an emanation from above. In latter days, some have attempted to account for them upon some acknowledged philosophical principles; while others, among whom, as we have seen, is Tytler, suppose the whole an imposture suited to the age, and the object to be achieved. The probability, however, is, that the key to the whole is to be found in an enthusiastic temperament, and a mind possessing a highly excitable imagination, slightly diseased. This might cause her, as in a multitude of other cases which have been subject to rigid investigation, to mistake her own imaginings for realities; while her enthusiastic patriotism and devotion would probably cause these imaginings to invest themselves with a patriotic and religious character.

A statement setting forth some of the advantages of a Rail Road from Matagorda Bay to the Pacific Ocean.

[From the Pamphlet of Dr. Levi Jones.]

The climate is thus adapted to the constitutions of emigrants from all other countries. None of the diseases usually incident to warm climates prevail to any extent here, and the hardy settler from Vermont or Maine, or from Scotland or Switzerland, enjoys as vigorous and robust health, as if he had been born and nurtured on the soil.

Besides this important section of Texas, at least five of the North-eastern States of Mexico, will find this place their natural outlet to market. It is well known, that there are no roads in that country, and that the immense chains of mountains, preclude their construction, were that wretched government even disposed to undertake them.—The mule paths to the coasts of the two oceans, will be immediately abandoned, when American enterprize opens the road to the interior, through the western part of Texas. The productions of this portion of Mexico, are similar to those of western Texas, and the population is the most industrious and efficient in that country. The population of these Mexican States is very considerable. Several large cities exist there, Chihuahua has a population of about 30,000, and the province or State of this name, is rich in mines, and produces a large quantity of wool. Intelligent Mexican merchants set the consumption of foreign goods, in this State, down at upwards of two millions of dollars a year. Durango has a population of 25,000, and the State produces four millions of dollars annually from the mines.—Its consumption of foreign goods is greater than that of Chihuahua. The capital of Coahuila has a population of about 30,000. We make a few extracts from the publication to which we before referred to, in relation to the Santa Fe trade:

"The extent of this trade, (the Santa Fe,) has never been accurately known—or, if known, has never been published to the world. Those who knew most about it have been engaged in the trade, and had therefore, strong motives for keeping their information to themselves. Gen. Almonte, in his elaborate report to the Supreme Government in 1834, estimated the amount of bullion, annually passing to the United States through this channel, at two millions of dollars.

"That the Santa Fe trade has contributed largely to build up, enrich and give importance to St. Louis, is most certain; and that the flourishing town of Independence on the Missouri is indebted for its origin and subsequent prosperity to the same cause, is no less true. For more than twenty-five years this trade has been perseveringly carried on, often with immense and never without large returns. Narratives of the stirring border incidents of the present season (1846) have given a degree of publicity to the details of its importance and extent, which they had never before obtained.

"It is now well ascertained that more than one million of dollars, in gold and silver, has been invested in merchandise for the 'prairie voyages' during the past year. These goods have been sent over the mountains, down the Ohio, and up the Mississippi to St. Louis. From that place to Santa Fe, the distance is 1200 miles, over bad roads and through predatory tribes of Indians. As a protection from the latter, squadrons of United States troops have, on several occasions, by order of the Government, accompanied the large caravans.

"Independence has of late years become the point of departure for a majority of the Santa Fe traders. Some, however, have gone and continued to go by way of Van Buren, up the Arkansas river, and from thence eight hundred miles by land, over the prairies. A trade must be profitable that will justify, year after year, such distant and costly over-land transportation, and any new line that will relieve it from the enormous transit charges referred to, must—other things being equal—command the bueiness.

"David Waldo, a highly intelligent and respectable merchant, for twenty years engaged in this overland trade estimates its amount during the past season at nine hundred and thirty-seven thousand five hundred dollars worth of merchandise—as follows:

Value of goods, first cost,	$937,500
400 large ox and mule wagons,	75,000
1700 mules,	70,000
1000 yoke of oxen,	35,000
550 men for the trip,	75,200
Freight, insurance, &c., to St. Louis,	93,000
Provisions, and outfit of all kinds,	61,000
	$409,780

No better authority can be given than that from which the above estimate is derived. It shows the cost of transportation on less than one million dollars worth of goods to be nearly four hundred and ten thousand dollars to Santa Fe. Further shipments of goods were made after the date of Mr. Waldo's estimate, and with a fair allowance for the additional vehicles, &c., required to transport them, the aggregate for the past season may be set down at five hundred wagons, besides pack mules, and nearly one thousand men. This would seem to indicate, what no doubt is the fact, that considerably more than one million of dollars have been invested in this bold traffic, during the past year, and that the expenses have been proportionately heavy. Indeed, such are the unavoidable expenses by this circuitous route, that the merchants whose sales have averaged only one hundred per cent. on the first cost, have deemed it a good years business, whether their net profits have reached forty per cent."

In addition to this, a considerable trade has sprung up between some of these Mexican States and San Antonio, which, under all disadvantages, shows the natural current of this business, to be through Western Texas. In short, nothing can be more certain, than that the Mexican States of New Leon, Coahuila, Durango and Chihuahua, from the difficulty and danger, not to say absolute impracticability of navigation of the Rio Grande, will find La Salle their true market. The most remote of them is not more than 700 miles from this point, and large portions less than half that distance. From these States, two-thirds of all the gold and silver extracted from the mines of Mexico are procured, and this fact will, of course, quicken the enterprize and energy of those who are contending for the trade of these rich provinces. The restoration of peace will turn the attention of capitalists to the opening of a road, to reach it by the shortest and best route. The position and advantages of La Salle, cannot fail to attract their immediate notice. The result of this, we shall now briefly advert to.

It will be understood at once, that we allude to the construction of a railway, westward, to reach, when completed, San Diego or some other suitable port on the Pacific. This is no longer a matter of doubt. It is a moral certainty, and we trust we shall show, that when it is undertaken, La Salle must be its Atlantic *terminus*. The best guarantee for the achievement of this great work, is the conviction of all the far-sighted portions of the commercial world, that it is practicable, and that it is necessary, to keep pace with the improvements that characterise the present age. Railroads and steam power have revolutionised the intercourse of mankind. They have almost annihilated space and brought into contact the most remote inhabited regions.

The material question is not now whether it can be, or shall be completed, but *what is the best route for it to run?* Shall it be the Northern route, advocated by Mr. Whitney, or shall it be the one near the isthmus of Tehauntepec, or the central route, from the Gulf of Mexico, through the Passo del Norte, of the Rio Grande? These three routes alone, present themselves as practicable for this mighty undertaking. Which shall be preferred?

It is not intended to argue the matter fully, or to exhibit all the facts urged in behalf of each. It will be enough to state here, that the great length of the northern route; the barren country through which it must pass, the difficulty to be surmounted in crossing the several mountains, and the rigor of the winters lasting for many months during which time the ground is covered with deep snows, prove at once the impolicy of adopting this route. The southern or Tehauntepec route cannot be relieved from objections equally formidable. It is in a foreign country—it is in a region of exceeding insalubrity—the route itself is a bad one—the harbors at each end, are not suited to the immense business, which must necessarily be done on such a line of communication; and the dangers, difficulties and distance of the navigation, to a point so far south as that would be, are insuperable objections. For these reasons, and others, that might be stated, neither of these routes can meet with ultimate favor.

The central route only remains, and on this must the choice fall. Recent explorations in California, New Mexico, on the coast of the Pacific, and on the way thither, show this to be the true route. Scientific men generally agree now upon this subject. A treaty with Mexico, which gives the United States the Gila river for its southern boundary in the west, and the Rio Grande in the east, will secure all that is necessary to induce this selection.

Intelligent travellers and scientific officers of the army agree, that from the Passo del Norte to the Pacific, along or near the Gila river, to the Port of San Diego, or to some other point in that vicinity, a route for a railroad can be found, which offers no serious difficulties to its construction. The mountains are cut down almost to their base—the passage across them is smooth and accessible—the country healthy—the climate mild—wood, stone, and all the materials for constructing a railroad, abundant and readily procured. San Diego is represented to be a port of great safety and extent, and admirably adapted to the purposes of a depot on the Pacific, for the immense business, which this highway of nations would command.

The Passo del Norte is a point on this route, which the road must inevitably touch, and the only question for us to consider now is, from this point, what is the most expedient and feasible route to the Atlantic coast? Would it be down the Rio Grande river, or to Galveston, or the Red River, or to La Salle? All these routes have been suggested.

The Rio Grande from its length, and its importance as our southern boundary, would present great advantages, if it were navigable for steamers of any considerable draft. The experience, however, of Gen. Taylor, and of private individuals, who have made vigorous efforts, and lost large sums of money in attempting to run steamboats in it, above Comargo and Mier, has put that matter to rest forever. All these efforts have signally failed. The hope of running steamboats above Comargo, must be utterly abandoned. And if it were even navigable, the bar at the mouth of the river would always oppose serious obstacles to its navigation, for any useful purpose on a large scale.

A road to Galveston or Red River, would necessarily have to cross all the intervening streams, from the Rio Grande to either point, and of course the belts of highlands, or table lands, that stretch between them. It would be much longer than a road to La Salle, and if completed, would possess not a single, assignable advantage, over the other. Increased length, increased cost, and no advantage, will certainly afford but slender ground of preference for either of these routes.

It is stated without fear of contradiction, that the route from Passo del Norte to the head waters of the San Saba, and thence to La Salle, is not only practicable, but is one of extraordinary facility and cheapness. It would cross no large streams; the country is high, smooth, and healthy, and timber and other necessary materials, within convenient reach.

The entire distance from La Salle to the Pacific, would but little exceed one thousand miles, and a portion of this distance, from the Gulf of Mexico, nearly to the Passo del Norte, is through a country of unsurpassed fertility and beauty, rapidly filling up, with a thriving population. Lateral roads would be speedily made in various directions, not only to penetrate the rich valleys of Texas, but to reach the Rio Grande in several places, and thus divert the trade and business of all northern Mexico into this channel. However mountanious large portions of north western Mexico, and that part of Texas extending towards Santa Fe may be, there are yet extensive valleys of surpassing productiveness, which will ultimately attract and sustain a numerous and flourishing people. Mines of the precious metals will no doubt be discovered, and these will give life and energy to Anglo-Saxon enterprise in these solitary wilds; build towns, open roads, cultivate fields, reclaim the wildness, and smooth the rugged asperities of nature.

It is a curious fact, well worth recording, that about forty years ago, the late John Jacob Astor, of New York, then extensively engaged in the fur trade on the Pacific, made application to the Spanish Government for permission to construct a road and line of military posts, across the continent, from a point on the Pacific near San Diego, by way of Passo del Norte and San Antonio, to Matagorda Bay in Texas. For some cause not known, this application was refused.—Thus did this sagacious man, at that early day, suggest what scientific discoveries have recently confirmed, that the true route for a communication between the Atlantic and Pacific Oceans, is the very one which we advocate.

We state this important fact on the authority of Mr. Astor himself, who imparted it to Lieut. Slacum, late of the U. S. Navy.

In 1837, Lieut. S. was specially appointed by Mr. Van Buren to make reconnoisances in that quarter, and consulting with Mr. Astor previously to setting out on the tour, was assured by him that the route indicated was the most eligible one for free communication of trade between the two oceans; the climate, distance, and character of the face of the country through which the road would pass, being all in its favor. Soon after his return, Lieut. S. assured a gentleman of high respectability in Texas, that this impression was strengthened and confirmed in his mind by the results of his observations.

It can be scarcely necessary to refer to the magnitude and importance of the trade, which would take place on this road, were it constructed, between the eastern and western countries of the world. Suffice it to remark, that few cruisers would hereafter double Cape Horn; the vast current of trade that has taken that course, would be at once diverted to this route. Its value and extent cannot be adequately described, nor can we refuse its increase. With danger averted—time abridged—capital invested, thus reduced, its augmentation would be almost unlimited. And let us not forget that this vast trade and commerce, which have, from the earliest ages of civilization, been the great desideratum of nations, and have built up and sustained the most populous and powerful cities and monarchies described in history, will be brought directly under the supervision of our own government, and rendered immediately conducive to its prosperity and glory. Who can predict the consequences which may follow, from holding in our hands and controlling the grand *fulcrum*, on which the lever, that moves the commercial affairs of the world, must inevitably rest?

In relation to the state of affairs in Ireland, the last London Times gives the following:

Great and influential bodies continue to pour in addresses to the Lord Lieutenant, expressive of their determination to support the Government; but the train of discontent seems now to be laid so extensively, and with such mischievous effect, that we doubt whether the whole weight of the Government, with even the support of the O'Connells, will be able to prevent some great explosion. Another significant feature attends this unhappy state of things. The run on the savings banks in Cork and in the South of Ireland, goes on with accelerated speed. The depositors desiring their funds are paid in Bank of Ireland notes, which are speedily converted into gold. Mr. Mitchell's language, in the United Irishman, increases in violence daily. The Nation also vies with the younger journal, in disseminating treasonable doctrines. A late number contains a letter from a parish priest, setting forth the doctrine of Catholic resistance. It inculcates the duty of arming quietly, and goes on to say to the people: "Make your peace with God; put your houses in order, and prepare to die." It then teaches them to bide their time; and then, when it comes, every man must vow, "before God and his country, to lesen, if he can, by one man at least, the enemies of his native land, and then to die." Such language as this, coupled as it is with minute instructions from the United Irishmen how to drill, carry, and use the pike and the rifle, can only be productive of some mighty catastrophe. The feeling as to the efficacy of repeal in staying the mischief, appears in some quarters to gain ground, but there is not the smallest appearance of such an idea being entertained by the Government. Amongst the converts to repeal, however, is said to be no less a persouage than the Earl of Shrewsbury, who, no doubt, trembles for his estates.

"White man berry onsartin, nigga [illegible] shure."—*Modern Philosophy.*

The Advocate.

OFFICE IN WHEELER'S NEW BUILDING.

VICTORIA, TEXAS:
THURSDAY MORNING, JUNE 1.

Agents for the Advocate.

PORT LAVACA, James T. Lytle.
TEXANA, N. McNutt.
GOLIAD, John F. McKinney.
SAN ANTONIO, James L. Trueheart.
SEGUIN, Tho's H. Duggan.
GONZALES, Benj. B. Peck.
LAGRANGE, A. L. Vail.
COLUMBUS, A. C. Hunt.
RICHMOND, M. M. Battle.
HALLETSVILLE, C. Ballard.
ROCKY MILLS, B. H. Stribling.
CUERO, C. Cardwell.
CUNNINGHAM'S P. O., James Robinson.
INDIAN POINT, S. A. White.
CORPUS CHRISTI, H. W. Berry.
SAN FELIPE, James Hillyard.
REFUGIO, Dan'l O'Driscole.

WILL THE FRENCH REPUBLIC STAND?—This is a very fruitful theme just now, and opinions are quite variant. That it will have to pass through fiery trials is beyond all doubt. Louis Philippe's government left the French nation in the most dreadful financial and commercial derangement; the Banks have since suspended, and the clamors of disappointed creditors have been general. Besides these things, the commercial classes have been greatly injured by the change of government, and the stringency of the times. Still, we are permitted to hope that it has passed the worst. M. de Lamartine has certainly proved himself equal to any emergency, and stands confessedly at the head of the Provisional Government. A salutary measure of the new government was the abrogation of all synacures, and the reduction of all salaries.—For our part our fears have almost passed away. We think we can begin to see the working out of that magnificent problem which the world has so often attempted to solve. If we should be pointed to the defunct ancient republics, we would reply that the *Representative System*, to them unknown, has cured many of their defects.—Their changes were never the result of a desire to conform to even an ideal standard of right; their wars were servile or civil, the result of rival factions in arms, of selfish jealousies, and of the grossest corruption; their greatest victories were ever over the liberties of their country. These republics had no printing presses and no Bible; neither a power of expressing widely correct sentiments, nor a correct moral guide by which to shape them. Their knowledge of the practical arts of life was confined to a very few branches, and while they had beautiful temples, they did not know the comforts of a well constructed dwelling.—The acquisition of territory was but another name for plunder, and commercial pursuits had scarcely the form of a regular business. The extension of territory was solely for the purpose of gaining wealth without industry, and of making men eminent by their trophies.

All this is changed in modern times, and changed lately in most respects by the new era of American representation. That human nature *per se* is the same radically in all ages we admit, but its developments differ under the influence of favorable circumstances.

Our own system is one of these controlling circumstances, the consequence of intelligence, self-denial, and much endurance. The colonial yoke borne by our forefathers was probably the lightest ever borne by men, so far as it affected their personal comfort, but it was thrown off under the influence of a strong conviction that it was to be superseded by an equitable and rational enlargement of individual rights, and of rights that might be permanently protected and established by a rational form of government.

We hear that our friends of Goliad are exerting themselves to navigate the San Antonio river. They have built a keel boat and taken her out into the Bay, and some of them have gone to San Antonio City to make an effort to get the merchants of that place to give them their freight. The plan as we understand it, is to bring the freight up the Guadalupe in steamboats to the mouth of the San Antonio, and from thence to Goliad in Keel boats. It is an enterprize worthy of all praise, and we wish it success.

Western Texas continues very healthy, with warm and dry weather. Crops of every kind very fine—though a good rain would be of material service to late plantings of corn. If the worms do not injure the cotton, the people of the "States" may look out for some of the *tallest* yields that ever they went any place. Two hundred and fifty bales to the acre wont be a *patching!!*

CAN'T COME IT.—A correspondence between Paredes and one Rubio, of France, has been gotten hold of and forwarded to the State Department at Washington, in which Louis Philippe's French Government had pledged itself to place the Duke de Montpensier upon the throne of Mexico. We rather guess he can't come it.

The Hon. WM. K. SEBASTIAN has been appointed U. S. Senator from Arkansas, to fill the vacancy occasioned by the death of Senator Ashley.

A Retrospect.

In looking back upon the events of the past few months,—their rapid succession and momentous character,—the mind is filled with profound astonishment. Revolution upon revolution—reform upon reform—man asserting the dignity of his nature, and planting himself upon the immutable basis of rational liberty—these are some of the startling scenes that we have just been called upon to record, and that have passed before the world's view with an almost panoramic swiftness. We are not superstitious; but it really seems difficult to discard the impression that a more than human agency is at work in rescuing millions of human beings from the most inexorable bondage. How else can we account for the simultaneous rising of the mighty masses in France, Italy, Austria, Prussia, Poland, Hungary, Naples, Ireland, the minor German provinces, and even in Great Britain itself, the 'mistress of the world,' as she is sometimes called. In nearly all these cases the rotten fabrics of feudalism and monarchy have fallen to the ground, and upon their ruins are growing up wholesome and durable institutions, based upon the imperishable bulwarks of human rights, and firmly grounded in the affections of mankind.

Every editor can bear witness that such a succession of important events cannot be found in ancient or modern history.—None but the largest daily prints could find room for more than a mere synopsis of the events as they occurred on the continent of Europe; and even the great London Times itself acknowledged that what would ordinarily have occupied one of its pages, must now be crowded into six lines. Our Mexican war and Presidential election, subjects certainly of no ordinary interest, have been lost sight of in the more exciting news from abroad.

Ladies' Fair.

We understand that the Ladies of Port Lavaca are making great preparations for the purpose of giving a Fair on the evening of our National Anniversary. The proceeds of the entertainment are to be appropriated to charitable purposes. The fair ladies of Texas, as elsewhere, are always foremost in every good work, and we would suggest to our bachelor friends generally, that they will meet with few such opportunities to supply themselves with all the little fancy articles of the toilet and the wardrobe, or indulging in the almost forgotten luxuries of ice cream, &c. &c., with which the table will be supplied. Beauty and ice will be attractions almost irresistible.

THE EFFECTS OF THE REVOLUTIONS AND WAR.—Almost every branch of commerce as well as the great industrial interests of our country feels the pressure produced by the revolutions abroad and by our protracted war at home. But perhaps no class suffers so severely as the cotton planter of the south. A combination of circumstances has brought down the great staple of the south to an insufferable extent, and it may require considerable time in which to recover from its extreme state of depression.

As soon, however, as quiet and permanency are restored abroad, and peace established at home, we anticipate the most marked revival in business. The ubiquity of our commerce, the trophies of our arts, and the power of our arms, too, will be seen, felt and acknowledged by all the nations of the earth.

A general restoration of peace and permanent commercial relations among the different nations of the world would be of vast benefit to trade of every kind. They would advance the arts and sciences, promote the cause of education, morality, and religion, and thereby greatly add to the happiness of mankind; whilst at the same time by the excellent working of our institutions, we should be most effectually carrying out the great *mission* given us to perform.

The sum of $242,000 in money and provisions has been subscribed in the United Stater, for the relief of Ireland.

THE MODEL ARTISTS AGAIN.—A Mrs. Johnson, of New York, has complained to the police that her three daughters, Isabella, Louisa, and Elizabeth, all under the age of eighteen, were nightly exhibiting themselves as Model Artists, in tights, at Palmos, to the disgrace of themselves, and in contempt of her authority. A warrant was issued for their arrest.

Gen. Scott arrived at Elizabethtown, N. J., in safety, where he was warmly received by his neighbors.

On the 15th May two small boats belonging to the U. S. Steamers Vixen and Iris, were swamped on the bar of Tuspan, by which Commander W. S. Harris, of the Iris, and Commander Henry Pinkney, of the Vixen, together with a Frenchman of Tuspan, and two seamen were drowned. The accident occurred in trying to cross the bar at the mouth of the river.

The N. Y. correspondent of the Boston Chronotype says that some parties in that City went into a flour speculation on the strength of the foresight and predictions of A. J. Davis, the Clairvoyant. The predictions turned out fallacious, and the credulous parties lost $30,000. Served them right.

The office of the Philadelphia Spirit of the Times was destroyed by fire on the 19th May.

Late and Important.

We have a slip from the Galveston Civilian of the 23d May, containing intelligence from New Orleans to the 21st. The European news is more pacific; and, as a consequence there is a slight improvement in cotton. Yucatan still continues to be the scene of terrible events, and calls loudly for the intervention of our government.

BRITISH INTERVENTION IN YUCATAN.—The British Minister residing in Mexico, has accepted, on the part of his country, the offer made by Yucatan, some time since, and has sent a frigate to take possession of the country.

A Campeachy paper publishes the following: "The British Minister in Mexico has accepted the offer simultaneously made by Yucatan to the United States, England, and Spain, of the dominion and sovereignty of Yucatan, on condition that she should be saved from ruin and destruction by the Indians."

This movement, on the part of the English Minister will most probably accelerate the movement of our Congress in relation to Yucatan affairs.

The Black Vomit has made its appearance at the City of Vera Cruz. Mr. M. F. Beebee, late Sutler at that place died of its effects.

A *Conducta* had arrived at Vera Cruz from the City of Mexico with one million of dollars in specie. The money was consigned to a Commercial house in Vera Cruz.

THE TREATY.

ORGANIZATION OF THE MEXICAN CONGRESS.

From the American Star of the 11th May, printed at the city of Mexico, we make the following extracts:

As we stated would undoubtedly be the case, the Senate was organized at half-past seven on Sunday evening. The committee presented their report of nominations for President and Secretaries which was approved, the oath was administered, and a formal announcement was made that the Chamber of the Senators was constitutionally and legitimately installed. The two branches of the National Congress then immediately commenced their sessions, and it is said that the treaty will be the first, if indeed not the only business to come before them.

The Senators and Deputies met at the Academia, and President Pana y Pena made his appearance, accompanied by all the members of the cabinet. He then delivered an address, occupying three quarters of an hour—a copy of which has not been received, it being still in press when the Diligence left. The President of the Chamber of Deputies replied in general terms to the President's discourse. After a few complimentary remarks, Florrign proceeds as follows:

'Your excellency has maintained the standard around which the people may assemble, either to be vanquished in war or be re-organized by peace. Your excellency, in fine, having been entrusted with the tremendous responsibility of granting a truce to their severe sufferings, arresting the ponderous sword of the conquerer, has received the tribute of acknowledgment which, under such circumstances, the victims of an unjust war are accustomed to offer to their Government—the homage of a respectful silence. But from this day, also, begins the judgment of the nation in regard to your excellency, exercised through its representatives. These profoundly penetrated with the convictions that the resolution to which they arrive, is about to decide irrevocably the present and future welfare of the people and of the Mexican name, will not for a moment lose sight of the duties prescribed in such a situation, by the high confidence reposed in them by their constituents.—They will sacrifice, if necessary, their convictions and feelings, to become the organs of the popular will, and the sentence which they shall pronounce will be dictated by conscience and a stern regard for the laws of honor and of duty."

The Monitor here publishes the proceedings of the late preliminary meetings of the chamber of Senators, but they possess nothing of interest for our readers. We observe that at the first meeting one Senator only was wanting to complete a quorum. It was determined to call upon Rosa, Minister of Relations, to fill the vacancy. He, however, refused to attend as a Senator, because he was in doubt whether he could discharge the duties of that office, while he held his place in the Cabinet.

We understand that the members have all received their pay, and as a quorum in both houses is at last in attendance, we shall look for speedy action upon the treaty. The indications are encouraging that its ratification will be carried by both branches, and become the law of the land. Unless the disorganizers persist in their violent opposition, we see not why the treaty, as modified may not receive the warm approval of Congress. It is certain that, if violent measures are attempted by any of the radical Puros, their originators and abetters will receive severe punishment from the hands of the Supreme Government. Hereafter the Congressional proceedings will be watched with intense interest, and we hope that those entrusted with the performance of high and responsible legislative duties, at a period like the present, will not fail to meet the reasonable expectations of the people.

FOREIGN.

The steamer Cambria arrived at New York on the night of the 13th inst. from Liverpool, whence she sailed on the 29th April. Her advices are consequently seven days later.

The French elections went off quietly. The moderate party is said to be in the ascendency.

The Pope of Rome had given a cordial reception to the U. S. Charge. Political affairs in the Papal States remained unchanged.

The troops of the Confederation have captured the Schleswig, after several severe engagements. The Danish artillery and fortifications were carried at the point of the bayonet. The conflicts were bloody—the Danes having lost twenty thousand men in killed and wounded. The Prussians lost three thousand.

The war is still progressing in Lombardy. King Charles Albert gallantly maintains his position in Messina—his quarters are at Volta.

The Sicilian Commons dreading Ferdinand, as one of the Bourbon dynasty, which has always been unsuccessful, have determined to govern themselves.

Spanish affairs are very much disturbed. A revolution is in prospect. Lord Palmerston had addresded a letter to the Spanish Government, which was returned in an insulting manner. Madrid was in a state of great excitement; business of all kinds was at a stand in that capital.

Portugal is on the verge of a Revolution. The Queen is reported to be about to abdicate in favor of her son.

England still retains her peaceful aspect, but it is the omenous stillness which precedes the storm, and the expected announcement of an outbreak in Ireland is not destroyed but prolonged.

The Russians have obtained a victory over the Danes and much blood has been shed in a cause which is not wholly that of liberty, and the philanthropist will have to deplore the loss of human life without feeling that aught has been done for the freedom of the masses.

There appears to have been no decided action between the Sardinians under Charles Albert and the Austrians. The former have, however, maintained their position.

Revolutionary Excitement in Canada.

Late papers from the far North intimate the probability of another revolutionary attempt in portions of Canada. The Buffalo Express of the 29th ult., says that, from the tone of the conservative press in Canada East, it infers that the recent momentous proceedings in Europe have created a profound sensation throughout that Province, and especially among the inhabitants of French extraction. The Montreal and Quebec journals, of the class above mentioned, are considerably alarmed at the indications, and are striving to suppress the excitement, by referring to the events of 1837 and 1838, and denouncing the present agitation as equally feverish and equally dangerous to rational liberty. A manifesto has been issued in favor of an immediate agitation, for a repeal of the Union of the two Provinces. This the French Canadians say is necessary to save themselves from political subserviency and national suicide. The movement, of course, is denounced by the conservatives. There was a meeting of young French Canadians in Montreal on Friday, the 21st ult., at which an address was adopted to the young men of Paris, in the name of the young men of Montreal, congratulating them upon the late events in that capital, which have created such intense interest in every part of the world. This step is strongly censured by the conservative papers.

A new French paper has just been established in Montreal by a number of young men, under the auspices of the famous Papineau. In a late number, the editor, referring to the late proceedings which led to the arrest of the agitators in Dublin, copies a resolution adopted by their followers afterwards, and follows it up by the following remarks:

"This resolution, adopted in the midst of a thousand bravos, was preceded and followed by inflamatory speeches—in one of which we remark the following curious phrase, which cannot fail to interest our readers: "Our enemies have struck the first blow; but the echo of it will be heard in Paris, in Vienna, in Berlin, in Washington, and in Montreal, which is on the poi t of becoming the capital of a new independent State.'"

A gentleman who has recently visited the settlements on the Guadalupe above Gonzales, and on the St. Marks, has informed us that those settlements are improving with astonishing rapidity. The whole line of frontier from the St. Marks to the Cibolo, is thickly studded with new farms, and the clearings indicate that numerous thriving villages will soon be found on all the principal streams. The village at the head of the St. Marks now contains more than forty houses, and large and flourishing farms are scattered in all directions around the place. The settlements around New Braunfels are also rapidly increasing. The season has been remarkably favorable, and it is believed that the crop of corn will be the most abundant that has ever been raised in that section. Very little cotton has yet been planted as the settlers in anticipation of a great emigration during the ensuing fall have turned their attention chiefly to the raising of grain.—*Houston Telegraph.*

ANOTHER CONTRIBUTION TO SCIENCE.—Messrs. Andrews & Boyle are publishing, in the Anglo-Saxon, a series of articles on "Phonetics, or The General Principles of the Pronunciation of all Languages," from the pen of Herr Zsbdiel Hauritz, a distinguished German philologist, now on a visit to this country. Herr Hauritz has devoted many years to the investigation of this subject, having resided in various countries with a view to making the most extensive observation upon all the phenomena of human speech, and acquiring a partical kowledge of the languages of Europe and Asia.

This treatise, though bearing the indubitable marks of profound learning, such as we have seldom had the pleasure of seeing exhibited in this country, is nevertheless written in a style of extreme simplicity and adaptation to the common comprehension, worthy of admiration. Judging from those portions of the treatise which we have been able to peruse, we should say that this series of articles, alone, would be of far more value to any reader interested in the study of his own language, or engaged in acquiring a foreign one, than the yearly subscribtion price of the Anglo-Saxon.—*New York Tribune.*

In connexion with the above we take occasion to say that the Anglo-Saxon is an interesting and well conducted paper, the greater portion of which is printed in Phonotype, or the method of Spelling by sound. The subscription price is $2 00 per year.

The Picayune of the 27th contains despatches from the City of Mexico to the night of the 18th May. They were transmitted from the city to New Orleans in seven days and seven hours, the shortest time on record—another feat of newspaper enterprize.

For the Texian Advocate.

MESSRS. EDITORS:—In these most extraordinary days of improvement in the arts and sciences—say phrenology, mesmerism, telegraphic communication, rail-road from ocean to ocean, Mosely-Bakerism, the Mexican war, the second exile of the Napoleon of the South, the electro-magnetic power applied to the propelling of boats, and I might mention, but with more patriotic reverence, the French revolution and general overturn of the ancient dynasties of Europe, and the establishment of a republican form of government, and in religion we have had our German reform, partly in obedience to the dictate of the Pope. But all these things, Messrs. Editors, sink into insignificance in comparison to a recent discovery in the chemical properties possessed by the waters of the Guadalupe river.

I have been a practicing physician in the town of Gonzales for eight years, accustomed the whole time to drinking and bathing in the waters of this river, but never discovered nor even suspected that plunging in the stream was a cure for all the maladies of this life. But recently a *man* who operates on many persons at an appointed time, informed his astounded audience, that such an operation in the river was an infallible cure for all hereditary or contracted diseases; but that the shower-bath would produce no other effect than to give the individual so sprinkled a disposition to wrangle and quarrel with his neighbors and brothers, and superinduce a jealous, backbiting, envious temper, and frame of mind.

But hear, if you please, how this man in vain tries to wash out this most unfortunate temper and strange frame of mind by his favorite mode of plunging; but in place of washing out, it seems as if indellible ink to set the dye deeper, being dyed in the wool! I have heard much said about how pleasant it was for brethren to dwell together in love and unity, but so far as water plunging in this river is concerned, it appears to me to have the contrary effect; it makes those who should be brothers in unity and love strive to see how unpleasant brethren can live together, encouraging discord and a disposition to deny his brother a morsel of bread to sustain life, or a drop of wine to cheer his desponding heart.

Now, I have no preference as to the mode of curing the man; but if the remedy for one disease generates many others of a more malignant and unmanageable kind, I think it might be well to pause and consider if it were not better to try the shower bath a short time longer, amongst other reasons because it can be used with great safety in the most protracted cases, such as affect the more vital organs of the system; more especially is it applicable to the healing and preservation of a diseased intellect, which of all organs we should be most diligent to protect.

I am a warm admirer of all benefactors of mankind, whether in church or state, in the pulpit or at the bar, in popular assemblies, or the humane physician alleviating the pains of the body to which my fellow beings are incident, and especially when they are journeying to that undiscovered country from whose bourn no traveler returns. But above all I love the pious minister of the gospel, who in the midst of his congregation or at the bed-side of his dying fellow mortal, while smoothing his path to a land of spirits, of joy and eternal life, that will encourage his patient in the salvation of his soul in the eleventh hour, even in the absence of much water, by if it were necessary sprinkling him with a few drops of clean water, which per chance might be suited to the extreme emergency of his case. But being as I am a non-professor, as truth compels me to say, I cannot admire or encourage any man or set of men who seek to rise upon the downfall of others, or who love no water but that composed of the tears of society into which they baptise their patients. By the way, Messrs. Editors, our river runs by your town. I suppose you too drink of the waters of the Guadalupe. I wish to advise you not to drink or bathe any more in this stream, for———; but I do not like to tell you why; however I must whisper it in your ears for your good, that you may not when I see you refuse me a crumb of bread or a drop of wine, (for you ought to know how pleasant it is for brethren to dwell together in love.)

There was a little talking man that guesses, sometimes between words, that plunged—yes, head and any, or as some would have it *splunged* a poor African dying the wool in the water of the Guadalupe, and the river has not boiled over since, and the water will not be fit for use till it does run over. Our citizens do not much like it, for they want to live in love and unity. But gentlemen, I had like to have forgotten to tell you that this little guessing man had notified the citizens that he was prepared rub off some of the *green* of the disbelievers in plunging if they would come out and hear him explain, but true it is that he did not even get the black off the poor African patient. Whether he will be a wrangler or not I cannot tell.

But Messrs. Editors, to be more serious, I had thought that the voluminous commentaries written by so many of the ablest divines on earth, on the different modes of baptism would have superseded the necessity of any little guessing men troubling themselves about that which the great Dr. Clark of England, who could speak twenty-seven different languages, ventured an opinion with fear and trembling. Messrs. Editors, if we have any more rubbing off of the green here I will let you know.

UNION.

POSTSCRIPT.

THE TREATY RATIFIED.

We have just seen and conversed with Mr. C. Cardwell, of Dewitt county, who left Port Lavaca on yesterday evening. He reports that he saw the N. O. Picayune of the 29th May, brought over by the Steamship Yacht, and that it announced unequivocally the ratification of the Treaty of Peace. We have ourselves perused the Picayune of the 27th, and judging from the tenor of the Mexican news in it, there is no doubt of its truth.

We have delayed the publication of our paper several hours in hope to get some of the particulars of the news, but the mail from Lavaca brought us nothing.

The Picayune of the 29th contains the organization and first proceedings of the Democratic National Convention. Considerable sparring was going on between the friends of Cass and those of Woodbury.—Gen. Quitman was spoken of for the Vice Presidency.

The impression was general that Cass' prospects for the nomination were better than any others, and there is a great probability that he is to be the democratic nominee.

MEXICAN ITEMS.

Pena y Pena has been elected President *ad interim.*

It is said that after a full representation shall be had, that Herrera will be elected President for the period prescribed by the Constitution.

A revolution was attempted in Morelia, but was put down by the civil authority.

MURDER AT LA GRANGE.—Some time last week *John A. Paxton* killed *John Cronkrite.* The circumstances, as they have come to us are something like these: Cronkrite kept a Hotel last winter in Lagrange, and Paxton, who is a merchant, and was one of his boarders, became, as it is said, excessively fond of Cronkrite's wife, in consequence of which Cronkrite parted from her a short time ago and went off. His recent appearance at Lagrange was to obtain reverge, making threats against Paxton's life. It was under these circumstances Paxton sought a private opportunity and shot him.

Paxton gave himself up, was taken into custody, and discharged by the examining Court.

The climate of Texas is as varied as the productive qualities of its soil. On the Gulf and near large rivers, especially those towards the East, which are occasionally overflowed, it resembles that of the neighboring States of Louisiana, Mississippi and Alabama, with an ample abatement of injurious influence. The reason of its greater salubrity is this; The Texan forests are as free from the rank undergrowth of the heavily wooded districts of those States, as the level region of Texas generally is from those putrid swamps which under the almost vertical sun of the South, exhale the elements of disease and death. In Texas, from river to river, the country consists of a series of open acclivities; while in Louisiana and Mississippi the land similarly situated, being covered with compact and level forests rerains the annual inundations, and the stagnant moisture with the dense vegetation it nourishes, acted upon by the solar heat, generates noxious miasma, the ever fruitful cause of malignant fever. Intermittent fevers—such as are common in all new countries, when the process of clearing and cultivation first expose to the sun's heat the vegetable deposit of ages—are not unknown on the low alluvial soil of Texas; but with the progress of population and improvement these fevers diminish in violence, and ultimately disappear.—*Kennedy's History of Texas.*

An Evangelical Alliance at Constantinople.—We should like to have been present at the meeting described by a writer in the *Day Spring*, of Constantinople, Jan. 4, 1848. He says:—"Yesterday was the great Monthly Concert—the first Monday of the year—and a glorious day it was at Constantinople. Think of a great union prayer meeting, consisting of Armenians, Jews, Americans, English, Scotch, Germans, Catholics and Greeks; and all sitting down together at the table of the Lord—Congregationalists, Presbyterians, Episcopalians, Lutherans, Baptists, Methodists, Baptized Jews and Protestant Armenians. Prayers were offered in three languages; Turkish, English and Armenian. Remarks and exhortations were made in four languages, German, English, Armenian and Turkish. And hymns were sung to the same tune, at the same moment, in three different languages, Armenian, German and English. The first tune was Old Hundred, the same that will be sung in the Millennium; and the second was Martyn. There was no confusion, no discord. No one was out of time or out of tune. The harmony was perfect; while each with the spirit and the understanding, and with the greatest power and might, was singing in his own tongue wherein he was born, or with which he is now familiar, '*the high praises of our God.*' The effect was overpowering. It was 'the voice of a great multitude,' redeemed out of many nations, kindreds and tongues, and it rose on high like '*the sound of many waters.*' Our chapel was crowded with communicants, and our hearts were filled with emotions too big for utterance."—*S. C. Advocate.*

From the Austin Democrat.

SUPREME COURT DECISIONS.

DECEMBER TERM.

Opinion of the Court delivered by A. S. LIPSCOMB, Associate Justice.

Mason, appellant,
vs.
The heirs of Russell ap'lee.

Appeal from the District Court of Shelby County.

The appellees brought their suit against the appellant to recover land, and obtained a verdict and judgment, from which an appeal was taken to this court.

There was a motion for a new trial, on several grounds stated; the motion does not appear to have been acted on by the court below; the appellant contends, and we think justly, that as the motion was not granted, that it was overruled by operation of law. It is not however important to the interest of the parties, as the most material points will arise on the face of the record. We shall cousider however the motion for a new trial as overruled, and if it was a case that required it, would reverse the judgment, if in our opinion the court below erred in so doing. We see nothing of error in the overruling the motion for a new trial from the evidence that was permitted to go to the jury. The correctness of the opinion of the court in rejecting evidence, will be noticed hereafter. One of the grounds only for a new trial will be considered. The affidavits of several of the jurors going to show their own misconduct, were presented to the court as grounds in support of the motion. The permitting such evidence cannot be too strongly reprobated, as leading to improper tampering with the jurors to procure such affidavits after verdict; and further, a juror so shamelessly disregarding the obligation of his oath, as to be guilty of such irregularities, after a cause had been submitted to him, justly deserved punishment, and ought to have received it. Such affidavits, when offered, should only have been received and made a part of the records of the court, as the grounds of the punishment of the affiants.

We shall now proceed to examine other questions of law presented by the record.

The first in order will be the striking out a part of the answer of the defendant in the court below. The suit was brought on a grant for a league of land issued by George Antonio Nixon, commissioner for Zavalla's Colony.

The defendant, in the first part of his answer, puts in a general denial of the allegations in the petition. He then further answers, by making several distinct averments, which it is not necessary to notice, excepting one of them, charging that the survey of the grant was made without the limits of Zavalla's Colony, all of the answer was stricken out, except the general denial. It is difficult to conceive on what principles the averment recited was stricken out, because although the general denial would put the plaintiff to proof of good title, yet it is surely no objection that the defendant should in his answer, by an averment advise the plaintiff that the validity of the deed would be impeached on the trial, and it is only by referring to the decision of the Court on the trial, that the reason for striking out the averment, was found to be that the defendant could not be permitted in this action, to impeach the validity of the grant, under which the plaintiffs claimed title. If the title could be impeached, we believe it could have been done under the general denial, as well as under a special averment, therefore it was not of much importance to the defendant, that his averment was stricken out, yet we believe that it ought not to have been stricken out unless it be true, that the defence set up by the defendant in the averment, was not good in law. To which inquiry we will proceed, being the point on which the case mainly depends. On the trial, the defendants offered in evidence, the Colony contract of the Empresario Zavalla, with the Government of Coahuila and Texas. And for the purpose of showing that the land in question was not within the limits of the Colony, he then offered the evidence of Adolphus Sterne and George W. Smyth, taken by Commissioners, which testimony was rejected by the court, as incompetent and inadmissible. The counsel for the plaintiff below, (the appellee in this court) has attempted to assimilate the grant to a record judgment, and denies that it can be collaterally enquired whether it was correct or not; that its correctness cannot be drawn into the controversy. Now we conceive that there may be a material difference between a deed and a judgment of record, yet admitting its effect to be the seme, the conclusion would not follow, that it could not be inquired into in any case. The distinction is this, if it is a court of competent jurisdiction and has adjudicated on a matter within its jurisdiction, the judgment so rendered cannot be enquired into in a collateral way, it is *rese adjudicata.* But if there is a defect of jurisdiction, the judgment is a nullity, and may be shown in any suit, where it may be offered as evidence of a right. And this distinction has been rendered easily to be understood by classifying them as void and voidable judgment. No one is concluded by the first, every one is to some extent concluded by the latter.—This doctrine was fully examined in the case of Southerland vs. De Leon, at the last term of the Court. It is fully laid down in Rose vs. Himley, by the late Chief Justice Marshall, he says: 'A sentence professing on its face to be the sentence of a judicial tribunal of evidence by a self-constituted body, or by a body not empowered by its government to take cognizance of the subject it had decided, could have no legal effect. The power of the court then is of necessity examinable to a certain extent, by that tribunal which is compelled to decide whether its sentences has changed the right of property. The power under which it acts must be looked into, and its authority to decide questions which it professes to decide, must be considered upon principle. It would seem that the operation of every judgment must depend on the power of the Court to render that judgment, or in other words, on its jurisdiction over the subject matter, which it has determined. Hickley et al, vs. Stewart et al, 3 Howard, U. S. C., 760; Elliott et al, vs. Piersol, 1 Peters, 340.' The appellee's counsel further contends that parole testimony could not be received, to impeach the grant of the Commissioner Nixon, and refers to a case in 4 Bibb, 329, to show that the grant cannot be resisted by parole evidence; that if it was illegally issued, that it must be vacated by

The California Star.

EXTRA.

FRIDAY MORNING, (8 o'clock,) FEB. 4, 1848.

From the Army !---Great News ! !

Arrival of the "Troubador" from Mazatlan---Disposition of the American Forces--Gen. Taylor--Santa Ana --The Mexican "Congress," &c. &c.

Battle of Contreras ! !

Death of Sam. Walker, Texan Rangers---United States News,---Foreign Items, &c. &c. &c.

We deploy from our paper columns on this occasion, at the solicitation of numerous City readers. By the arrival, on the 20th ult., at Monterey, from the S. Islands, we have Honolulu papers, to Jan. 1st. From the Polynesian of this date we copy the summary of interesting intelligence, below given, entire.

Just as we were preparing our paper for the press yesterday, the cry of "sail ho!" caused us to delay "making up" a little to ascertain whether any answers to our questions propounded in another column were on the way. By noon, it was ascertained that one of the vessels arrived was the Troubadour from Mazatlan, bringing important news from Mexico, Europe and the United States. By delaying our paper, we are enabled to present our readers a brief summary.

The particulars of the Mexican war we obtain from files of "The Daily American" and "American Star," newspapers published in the city of Mexico jointly in the English and Spanish language by Yankee editors. We have copies to Nov. 5th. By them it seems Mexico was entered by the American army early in September, after several hard fought battles, of which we are not able to obtain any official reports. We gather however that the Americans lost 361 killed, including 23 officers and 1830 wounded in all these engagements. A spirited account of that of Contreras will be found below.

The Mexican Congress had adjourned to Quepetero, and were sqabbling about the election of a new President.

The Mexicans besides heavy losses in killed and wounded, lost 9000 men prisoners and their army was wholly disorganized. Santa Ana was wandering about the country sustaining a guerilla warfare. A strong party opposed to him had grown up, and many Mexicans were in favor of the entire occupation of their country by the American forces to put an end to the tyranny of their military chieftains. Still there was no prospect of peace. Commissioner Trist had been recalled by the U. S. government, and the Mexicans notified that the Americans would make no further proffers of peace. If Mexico desired it, she must send an agent to Washington to treat.—The victories in the valley of Mexico had greatly excited the American people, and they were now in favor of the entire occupation of the country. Orders had been sent to occupy all the capitals of the Mexican States. Gen. Worth with 4000 men left Mexico, Nov. 4th, for Quepetero. A revolution had occurred in Oajaca. Sixty deserters from the American army, taken fighting in the Mexican ranks, had been hung. Assassinations of American soldiers were daily occurring in Mexico, and severe measure of retaliation were resorted to. The horrible tragedies which attended the occupation of Spain by France appear to be renewed in Mexico among the lower classes. The rights of property, religion, &c., have been scrupulously respected by the Americans, and many valuable improvements are being made under their auspices. In Mexico, the papers advertise American theatres, circuses, hotels, shows, stage coaches, &c., as if it were a Yankee town.

Gen. Taylor had gone home. Gen. Quitman succeeds to his command. Taylor is still the most popular candidate for the Presidency. The public debt of the U. S. July 1, was $30,000,000.

In England great distress prevailed among the grain speculators. Mr. Robinson, Governor of the Bank of England, had failed—the failures in London among the flour and grain merchants amounted to $15,000,000. The crops in Europe and the U. S. were very abundant and prices low. This was to the 1st of October. News to the 19th from Boston had reached Mexico, confirming the account of the failure of Prime, Ward & King, of New York, and the general depression in the money market.

Mazatlan was taken 11th Nov. Col. Telles with 800 men left on the 10th. 1,000 men were on their march thither from Guadalajara. Some skirmishing outside had taken place.—The Mexicans lost 2 killed and many wounded. The Americans 1 killed and 18 wounded.—The American garrison at Mazatlan consisted of 400 men with Artillery, the fleet commanding the town. At La Paz and San Jose, Lower California, where small commands only had been left, the inhabitants incited by a Mexican General who had crossed over, had risen and besieged both places, putting the Americans in much jeopardy. This was the last of Nov.—The Mexicans were finally repulsed, losing many killed and wounded. The Americans lost 1 killed and 3 wounded. It was reported that the Mexicans in besieging La Paz had seized the Hawaiian Schooner Louise to assist in their operations. Com. Shubrick had despatched the Cyane and Portsmouth to the relief of those ports.

The Chilean brig Argo, hence, was seized by the Americans for an infraction of her neutrality, ransomed by her supercargo for $4,000 The American brig Cayuga, at Mazatlan, was also under seizure for having touched at San Blas, an enemy's port. Capt. Mott and family were expecting to leave in December in that vessel for this port.

THE BATTLE OF CONTRERAS.

During the whole of the 18th of August, the batteries at the hacienda of San Antonio had been firing at intervals upon Gen. Worth's command, which lay upon the San Augustine road within short distance of the spot, where, early in the day the gallant Thornton was killed. The engineers were occupied in reconnoisances, and most of the firing was upon small parties under their command. On the morning of the 19th, Gen. Pillow's division was put in motion on the road leading to San Angel by the field of Contreras. At the hill about two miles from the latter, the command was obliged to halt and cut a road for the light batteries to pass, which was effected in about an hour and a half; and the troops again moved forward, filling up and crossing a deep ditch which had been made by the enemy, but abandoned. As the head of the column reached the rocky ground, Gen. Twiggs arrived with his division, and passed on by the path to the left; Gen. Pillow's command marched in a straight line for the village of Tizipan, in which a body of infantry was seen, supported by the cavalry under Santa Ana. About two o'clock our troops had arrived within reach of the long guns in the works at Contreras, and a heavy fire was opened upon them from several pieces. The works on Contreras were admirably planned for the defence of the narrow, and only pass our troops could take; twenty-seven pieces of artilery having been placed so as to bear directly upon the difficult path and steep descent to, and the ascent from the river. Besides these, there were thick breastworks of stone and sods, so constructed as to protect the Mexican infantry, which commenced a heavy fire upon our skirmishers.

Added to these temporal advantages, nature had interposed almost insurmountable obstacles in the deep ravine traversed by the swollen and rapid stream, and a mile of broken country covered with rough stones and rocks of volcanic origin; presenting at every step a surface dangerous alike to light troops and horsemen. No better stand could have been taken by Gen. Valencia for the defence of the city of the Aztecs. On entering this pass the two brigades composing the second division became separated; Gen. Smith, with the 1st Artillery, 3d Infantry, and mounted Riflemen, taking ground in the small trees to the left, where he soon became engaged with the enemy's light troops, and Col. Riley with the 2d and 7th Infantry and 4th Artillery, passing on towards the church on the plain to the north of Contreras. Gen. Pillow's division, under command of Brigadier Generals Pierce and Cadwallader, took ground on Col. Riley's right to cut off the retreat of the enemy, should Col. R. succeed in driving him from his stronghold, and also to dislodge the large force of Infantry which skirted the woods below the church, and which was effected in gallant order.

But the assault of Contreras was not a matter to be effected in a moment. Independent of its strong defences and superior force, Gen. Santa Anna, with a long line of cavalry and infantry, threatened the advancing party on the hill to the right, defending the road to San Angel, and ready to close in upon our troops the moment they should be thrown between him and Valencia, His command was put in position in a lane near the village and halted while a reconnoisance was made by Lieut. Tower of the engineer corps.

Several skirmishing parties having been thrown out by the enemy, two companies of the 2d infantry were sent to drive them in and finally the entire regiment, headed by Capt. T. Morris, was detached for that duty, under the immediate command of Col. Riley. The action now became highly interesting to the numerous spectators on both sides. The little force under Col. Riley had nearly gained a position upon the plain west of the village, when the batteries on Contreras were opened with renewed vigor, and a large force of cavalry was sent to dislodge the regiment. Col. Riley formed a square, received the charge, and repulsed it. The enemy, however, soon rallied, returned within pistol shot and commenced a fire of escopetry. Col. Riley immediately broke his square, formed in line of battle and charged and drove the cavalry, scattering it in all directions. A stand of colors, several horses, &c. were captured in this brilliant charge, the flag by Capt. Casey in person. A colonel of lancers was among the killed in this encounter. He, with a few others dashed recklessly upon the bayonets of the infantry, urging on their comrades, but the steady aim and destructive fire of those veteran troops was too deadly to be long withstood. The lancers again collected and retired to the hill behind the batteries.

During the whole afternoon the hill facing the scene of operations on the east was covered with interested spectators. Though within point blank range of the heavy pieces in the enemy's works, Generals Scott and Pillow, Col. Harney and many staff officers and citizens were anxiously watching the progress of the battle. From the first commencement our men had been closely engaged with the light troops of the enemy and the roll of musketry was continual. Capt. Magruder had placed his light battery in position and opened a destructive fire upon the mass of soldiers in the Mexican works and the rocket and howitzer battery was also in effective use. Several of Lt. Callender's rockets fell within the entrenchments and we could readily see the slaughter they made, without glasses. About 5 P. M., the long guns in Contreras were brought to bear upon these batteries and handled them very roughly. Three howitzers were dismounted and Lt. Johnson mortally and Lt. Callender severely wounded. Several of the men serving the pieces were killed or wounded at the guns.

The news of the disasters to our light batteries had reached the hill where we watched the fight just as the cavalry advanced upon Col. Riley's square. Many anxious eyes watched the progress of the lancers as, with their gay apparel and bright arms, they swept down the slope upon the little band of infantry that awaited them, and when they were in pistol shot one could have heard a loud breath yards distant. But when the combatants met; when the white smoke rose along the line of musketeers and the horsemen were sent flying in disorder from the field, the air was rent with shouts and every man felt that victory would be ours. There were no faces on our side after that. If any had doubted the result before none doubted it then. The ice was broken with the magnificent line of Valencia's lancers. At this moment Gen. Shields arrived with the Palmetto and Empire men and passed on under a heavy fire of shell and round shot to the support of the second division, amid the cheers of the officers and citizens assembled on the hill and the cavalry who were chaffing for a hand in the conflict. Till night-fall, the firing from the works on Contreras was kept up with unceasing fury. Thousands of cannon and musket balls, and grape and cannister shot by bushels, flew, growling, and singing, and whistling over the heads of our gallant soldiers, but they faltered not, and but few fell. Towards evening, the enemy moved two pieces of cannon from Contreras to the hill occupied by Gen. Santa Ana and his cavalry, and opened upon Gen. Pillow's command, but they wasted shot and shell, firing far above our troops.

Night at last came and with it a cold, drenching rain, which lasted without intermission, until daylight. About dark Gen. Smith joined Col Riley and at 10 P. M., formed the plan of attack for the morning. Our troops lay on their arms in the rain until three A. M. next morning, when Col. Riley's brigade moved silently up the ravine between the two bodies of the enemy, and having got into position waited for the dawn. The march in this difficult ravine was one of great toil and danger, yet it was effected without discovery or accident. The men lay down in their wet clothes, the rain still falling heavily, but every soldier preserved his firelock, and not one missed when the contest came.

Daylight found our little storming force in the deep ravine directly in the rear of Contreras. Gen Valencia's forces were up and preparing to resume the cannonade, and a party of lancers held the hill occupied by Gen. Santa Ana on the previous day. Gen. Cadwallader with the Voltigeurs and the 11th infantry, had taken up a position on Col. Riley's left, to protect him from an attack from the cavalry, and succor him should Valencia prove too strong for his little party. At a little after 7 o'clock, the rain having ceased, the sun shone out brightly and discovered to those on the east hill the exact position of both parties. At this time, the charging brigade was formed for the assault in two columns at half distance, emerging from the ravine with three cheers that were more terrible to those in the works than the deep roll of musketry that followed. The Mexican General exerted himself to avert the calamity which threatened him. Several light pieces were turned round and discharged at the advancing columns, but the gunners were so frightened that they shot in the air. Several regiments of infantry were formed and opened a fire on our line, which was returned when the blue-jackets arrived near enough to see their adversaries wink. After firing four rounds, Col. Riley deployed two small parties to skirmish on his right, and heading the columns, called out, "Now boys, forward and give them hell!" The men sprang forward at a run and the work was soon finished. But as they neared the works, the fire of musketry and light artillery was terrific. Capt. Hanson, of the 7th infantry, fell mortally wounded at the head of his company, and simultaneously, the Color Sergeants of of the 7th infantry, and 4th artillery were shot down. Capt. Wessels, of the 2d, caught up the colors of his regiment and was pressing forward with them when he was shot in the leg, and was for the moment disabled. Lieut. Benjamin seized the flag of the 4th, and gallantly planted it on the breastworks beside those of the 2d and 7th.

The Mexicans were completely routed and fled precipitately towards the city. When the retreat commenced, the Voltigeurs and 11th infantry poured into their disordered ranks a deadly fire, and at the foot of the hill, the riflemen, 3d infantry, and 1st artillery, and volunteer regiments under Gen. Shields, gave them such a warm reception, that, throwing down their arms, they dispersed in all directions, or yielded themselves prisoners of war. While Col. Riley's brigade was advancing on the works, a body of cavalry attempted to gain his rear. These were gallantly met and repulsed by Capts. Getheren's and Irving's companies of the 11th.

One of the most flattering features of this contest, was the re-taking of O'Brien's pieces by the regiment (4th artillery) to which they belonged. Capt. Simon Drum, whose gallant deeds at Molino del Rey, Chapultepec, and at the Gareta, are the admiration of, and whose death is lamented by the army, laid hands on the first piece, Capt. Casey of the 2d securing the other.

Gen. Patterson, Marshall, and Cushing combining a force of over 6000 men, have arrived at Vera Cruz, and will march immediately for this capital.

Capt. Sam. Walker was killed at Huamantia on the 11th, whilst charging upon the enemy's cannon. Both his legs were shot off by round shot, and he died just as his men had carried the place and taken the cannon of Santa Ana.

Gen. Hoppins, we hear, is dead. Col. Taylor, brother to the General, is in Washington.

From the same source we also learn that a great revulsion has taken place in the commercial community in the United States, arising from the great depreciation in the price of bread stuffs. Messrs. Prime, Ward & Co., of New York, among the heaviest bankers in the Union, had stopped payment from this cause.

Gen. Kearney has returned from California to the United States. He made the trip to Jefferson city in sixty-six days. On reaching that city, he placed Lt. Col. Fremont, (who accompanied him,) under close arrest. The private letter conveying this intelligence, does not state the cause of Col. Fremont's arrest.

A part of Col. Hay's Texan Rangers have arrived at Vera Cruz.

Capt. Tilghman's company of Baltimore artillery, have arrived at Vera Cruz.

Major Hughes, of and with the Baltimore battalion, is stationed at, and occupies the National Bridge.

The Whigs will have a majority in the next Congress beyond a doubt.

Troops are being raised all over the United States, with the greatest facility, for the Mexican war. More volunteers have offered their services than can be received.

At no season, for a number of years, has the yellow fever raged to such an extent in New Orleans as at present. Scarcely an unacclimated person has escaped it.

From an article in the Washington Union we infer that 35 or 40,000 men will be sent to Gen. Scott, so that, if a peace is not speedily made, he will have enough to send to any place that the army may wish to occupy. Contributions will also be levied upon the different towns.

We extract the following from the New Orleans Delta of Sept. 27:

Gen. Kearney arrived at Washington on the night of the 18th inst. from Missouri. He is said to be in good health, and is desirous of joining the army in Mexico as soon as he can be released from his engagements at Washington. Col. Fremont is expected at Washington in a few days.

Here we are compelled from very lack of room, to abruptly close this highly interesting abstract of the general news. In the STAR of to-morrow morning we publish complete.

The Texian Advocate.

PUBLISHED WEEKLY BY JOHN D. LOGAN AND THOMAS STERNE, AT $3 IN ADVANCE, $4 IN SIX MONTHS, OR $5 AT THE END OF THE YEAR.

VOL. 2. VICTORIA, TEXAS, THURSDAY, APRIL 27, 1848. No. 52.

THE
TEXIAN ADVOCATE
WILL BE PUBLISHED EVERY THURSDAY BY
LOGAN & STERNE.

TERMS.

The Texian Advocate will be devoted to Agriculture, Morals, Education, Health, Science, Art, the diffusion of practical and useful information, and to the General Interests of the People of Western Texas. It will be sent to subscribers in any part of the United States at the very low price of Three Dollars in advance; Four Dollars in six months; or, Five Dollars at the end of the year.

Each number will generally contain one or more interesting tales, several pieces of Poetry, Hints on Domestic Economy, Practical Receipts for the Farmer, Mechanic, and House Keeper, Miscellaneous Articles selected with great care, Religious Thoughts and observations, together with a fund of Wit, Humor, Anecdote, &c.

—AND ALSO—

The Latest News from all parts of the United States and Foreign Countries; the state of the Markets, and all other matters of interest to the general reader.

ADVERTISING.

One square (10 lines or less) 1st insertion,	$1,00
Each subsequent insertion, - - -	50

Longer advertisements in the same proportion.

CONTRACTS BY THE YEAR,
PAYABLE QUARTERLY.

One square, six months, renewable,	$12,00
Two squares, six months, - - -	18,00
Three squares, six months, - - -	23,00
Four squares, six months, - - -	28,00

Longer advertisements in the same proportion.

One square, one year, renewable, -	$20,00
Two squares, one year, - - - -	30,00
Three squares, one year, - - -	36,00
Four squares, one year, - - - -	40,00

Longer advertisements in the same proportion.

Business Cards per annum, - -	$10,00

Announcements of Candidates will be inserted as other Advertisements, and charged for accordingly.

Political circulars will be charged as advertisements.

All advertisements to be paid for in advance or the payment assumed by some responsible person.

BY AUTHORITY.

Acts and Resolutions passed at the first Session of the thirtieth Congress.

[PUBLIC—No. 20.]

AN ACT further to supply deficiencies in the appropriations for the service of the fiscal year ending the thirtieth of June, eighteen hundred and forty-eight.

Be it enacted by the Senate and House of Representatives of the United States of America in Congress assembled, That the following sums be, and the same are hereby, appropriated to supply deficiencies in the appropriations for the service of the fiscal year ending the thirtieth of June, eighteen hundred and forty-eight, namely:

For pay of one additional clerk in the office of the Fifth Auditor, rendered necessary by the increase of light-house business, at eight hundred dollars per annum, from the first of June, eighteen hundred and forty-seven, to the thirtieth of June, eighteen hundred and forty-eight, eight hundred and sixty-five dollars and ninety-four cents.

For extra clerk-hire for the settlement of the increase of business in the office of the Secretary of the Navy, occasioned by the Mexican war, six thousand dollars.

For salary of the judge of the southern district of Florida, per act of twenty-third February, eighteen hundred and forty-seven, from third March, eighteen hundred and forty-seven, to thirtieth June, eighteen hundred and forty-eight, at two thousand dollars per annum, two thousand six hundred and sixty-one dollars and twelve cents.

For salaries of district attorney and marshal of the southern district of Florida, per same act, from third March, eighteen hundred and forty-seven, to thirtieth June, eighteen hundred and forty-eight, at two hundred dollars each per annum, five hundred and thirty-two dollars and twenty-two cents.

For salaries of the two keepers of the public archives in Florida, per act of third March, eighteen hundred and twenty-five, one thousand dollars: *Provided,* That so much of said act of third of March, eighteen hundred and twenty-five, as authorizes the appointment of two keepers of the public archives, shall be, and the same is hereby, repealed from and after the thirtieth June, eighteen hundred and forty-eight; and, in the mean time, it shall be the duty of the Secretary of the Treasury to cause the said archives to be removed to some public office in the State of Florida, to be designated by the President of the United States, there to be safely kept.

For expenses of thirty-five light houses, including oil and other annual supplies, delivering the same, and repairing the lighting apparatus for four hundred and twenty lamps; salaries of thirty-five keepers, at the fixed average of four hundred dollars per annum, and also all other expenses for six months, twenty-two thousand seven hundred and forty dollars.

For one new floating light, including the keeper's salary at six hundred and fifty dollars, and all other expenses for nine months, two thousand three hundred and sixteen dollars.

For additional expenses of sundry new buoys for six months, one thousand six hundred and ninety dollars.

For additional expenses of a temporary floating light at Sand Key, Florida, in lieu of the light-house destroyed there, one thousand five hundred dollars.

For superintendent's commission on twenty-eight thousand two hundred and forty-six dollars, at two and a half per cent, seven hundred and six dollars and fifteen cents.

For contingent expenses under the act for the collection, safe-keeping, transfer, and disbursement of the public revenue of sixth August, eighteen hundred and forty-six, five thousand dollars.

For contingent expenses in the office of the Treasurer of the United States, five hundred dollars.

For per diem compensation for clerk employed in the Adjutant General's office, one thousand dollars.

For per diem compensation of clerk employed in the Ordnance office, one thousand and ninety-eight dollars.

For per diem compensation for eight clerks employed, and such additional number of clerks as the exigencies of the public service may require to be employed temporarily, by the Commissioner of Pensions, with the approbation and consent of the Secretary of War, during the present fiscal year, on bounty land business in the Pension office, at a rate not exceeding three dollars and thirty-three cents per day, fifteen thousand six hundred and ninety dollars and ninety-six cents.

For contingent expenses of the Pension office, one thousand dollars.

For clerks in the office of the Secretary of War, being an unexpended balance of the appropriation remaining on the thirtieth June, one thousand eight hundred and forty-seven, for that purpose, two hundred and ninety-one dollars and eighty-five cents.

For outfits of charges des affaires to Naples, the Papal States, and the Republics of Bolivia, Guatemala, and Ecuador, twenty-two thousand five hundred dollars.

For one quarter's salary for each of the charges des affaires to the Papal States, Bolivia, Guatemala, and Ecuador, four thousand five hundred dollars.

For salary of the consul at Beyroot, from the fourth of August, eighteen hundred and forty-six, to the thirtieth of June, eighteen hundred and forty-eight, nine hundred and fifty-three dollars and eighty cents.

For compensation for such additional number of clerks as the exigencies of the public service may require, to be employed temporarily by the Secretary of the Treasury in the office of the Second and Third Auditor, and in the office of the Second Comptroller, at a rate not exceeding one thousand dollars per annum, and for contingencies, seventeen thousand dollars.

For compensation to eight additional clerks to be employed in the General Land office, at the rate of one thousand dollars per annum each, the sum of two thousand dollars.

For the relief and protection of American seamen in foreign countries, twenty thousand dollars.

ARMY.

For regular supplies, incidental expenses, and transportation in the Quartermaster's department of the army, five million dollars.

For clothing of the army, camp and garrison equipage, including one hundred and sixty thousand dollars for clothing to volunteers in lieu of commutation therefor, one million one hundred and twenty thousand dollars.

For subsistence in kind, (in addition to the sum of one million dollars appropriated at the present session,) two million nine hundred and thirty-seven thousand nine hundred and thirty-nine dollars and seventy-four cents.

For pay of volunteers called into service during the present fiscal year, three million six hundred and eleven thousand dollars.

For medical and hospital department, sixty-four thousand five hundred dollars.

For purchase of ordnance, ordnance stores, and supplies, three hundred thousand dollars.

For expenses of arbitrating the title to the Pea Patch island, five thousand dollars.

MARINE CORPS.

For provisions, sixteen thousand one hundred and four dollars.

For clothing, thirty-six thousand three hundred dollars.

For fuel, three thousand seven hundred and seventy-seven dollars.

For military stores, three thousand five hundred dollars.

For transportation and expenses of recruiting, five thousand dollars.

For contingencies, six thousand dollars.

For paying James Crutchett for lighting the Capitol and grounds, three thousand dollars and ten cents.

For contingent expenses of the Senate, twenty thousand dollars.

For contingent expenses of the House of Representatives, fifty thousand dollars.

For payment for printing of one thousand copies of list of patents, by Commissioner of Patents, two thousand dollars, to be paid out of the patent fund.

SEC. 2. *And be it further enacted,* That the sum of eight hundred thousand dollars be, and the same is hereby, appropriated for clothing in kind to volunteers for the fiscal year ending the thirtieth of June, eighteen hundred and forty-nine, agreeably to the act entitled "An act to provide clothing for volunteers in the service of the United States," approved the twenty-sixth of January, eighteen hundred and forty-eight; and that so much of said sum of eight hundred thousand dollars as the President shall direct, is hereby authorized to be applied to the purchase of said clothing during the current fiscal year.

ROBT. C. WINTHROP,
Speaker of the House of Representatives.
G. M. DALLAS,
Vice President of the United States, and
President of the Senate.

APPROVED March 27, 1848.
JAMES K. POLK.

For the Advocate.

MESSRS. EDITORS:—Being aware that you always feel a deep interest in every thing which concerns the fame of Western Texas, you will allow me to call your attention to a remarkable surgical operation which has lately been performed in this place.

On Friday the 24th of March, Isaac Piles received a wound in the shoulder by a charge of small duck shot, which fractured the upper end of the arm bone, and lacerated the flesh so severely, that on the next day the outer and forepart of the shoulder was mortified, and it was found necessary to remove the arm at the shoulder joint.—This has always been considered one of the most difficult and dangerous operations in surgery, and in a majority of cases proves fatal, the patient expiring under the knife.

In consequence of the head of the bone being much fractured, it was found impracticable to arrest the flow of blood during the operation by pressure in the axilla, and some of the shot being lodged in the region of the clavicle, the swelling and inflamation was so great, that it was impossible to make pressure on the artery upon the first rib. This increased the difficulty of the operation.

The incision was commenced four or five inches down the arm on the back side, brought over the top and front, removing the deltoid, and a portion of the subclavium and pectoral muscles, and continued down the foreside to the place of beginning, leaving an inch or two containing the subclavium artery undivided.

The head of the bone was now dissected out and removed from its socket, several small arteries tied, and yet the pulse was beating regularly in the wrist. Dr. Dallam then seized the part which remained undivided, compressing it to stop the flow of blood, while Dr. Johnson made the final incision, and ligatured the artery.

This operation lasted about *five* minutes and the loss of blood but moderate.

In nine days after the amputation, the patient was so far recovered as to be able to walk about the street.

This operation was first performed, I am told, within the last century, and from its magnitude is now comparatively rare. It probably never has been performed in Texas before.

Another operation was performed by Dr. Johnson a few days after, which, although not of such magnitude as the first, yet is of considerable importance in our State at the present time. Mr. Morris Simonds, son of Capt. Simonds of Jackson county, was shot on the Rio Grande, and lost his leg in consequence of the wound. The ball however lodged in the hip, and he has suffered extremely with it for the last twelve months. He was brought to Dr. Johnson to have the ball cut out. By an operation lasting *less than a minute* the ball was removed, and Mr. Simonds starts home to-day much relieved, with a prospect of speedy recovery.

I have taken the responsibility of reporting these cases without asking the permission of the operator. Dr. Johnson already ranks high in the profession as a practical surgeon, and these operations will add to the reputation he already deservedly enjoys. It must be gratifying to the whole community to know that we have living in our midst a scientific physician who is able by his skill to heal the wounds and alleviate the sufferings of those who are afflicted amongst us. Yours, J. T. L.

Port Lavaca, April 14, 1848.

For the Advocate.

MESSRS. LOGAN & STERNE:

Gentlemen—Inasmuch as we are dignified with the title of city, it becomes us to exercise some of the high functions appurtenant thereto. The empty subriquet of city, town, or borough, is as sounding brass or a tinkling symbol, unless we realize some of the beneficial results thereof—or otherwise let us assume a village attitude.

In the instance to which I shall call attention, it is not for formes sake that I desire it; but from a higher and more worthy motive—its practical usefulness, and most salutary results. I refer to the organization by our city council of a Board of Health, consisting, say of four members selected from the different sections of our city, whose special province it shall be to abate any local cause that may exist, calculated to generate disease, and to cause individuals to remove all nuisances upon their premises, or otherwise be subject to such fine as the council may affix.

But it may be thought by some wiseacre that the city council can do this. I admit it—but its a fact as fixed as any other, that that which is every body's business, is exactly nobody's. Besides, sirs, are we to expect the members of our city council, the dignitaries of our city, to explore the frog ponds of our vicinity to ascertain their miasmatic exhalations? an act of supererogation on their part that a person must be soft indeed, to believe in. "Listen not with credulity to such whisperings of fancy," for they assuredly will not do it. But a Board of Health would, it being their business—a body to whom the citizens might repair with a confidence of attention, as they would to a coroner to organize an inquest, or to a Sheriff for the arrest of a culprit.

To drain stagnant waters, or such other improvement as might involve an expenditure of money, let them present the object and probable cost to the consideration of the city council, and ask an appropriation.—We have public spirited citizens enough to to do this, and who would cheerfully officiate.

Did such a Board exist, think you that the stagnant pond of water opposite the residence of Mr. Phillips, and which intercepts the travel of Gonzales street, the main inlet to our city from Spring creek, would be permitted to remain as it is, a repulsive emblem of inattention? No sirs—for in the phrase of Lloyd's, it may be denominated a nuisance as A No. 1—insufferable were it not for the aquatic music with which it enlivens the neighborhood. Yes, gentlemen, we have a full toned orchestra there, whose accommodating disposition is such, they need no encore to musical entertainment.

Perhaps it were better to administer to our body corporate only in broken doses. I will therefore refrain from a farther prescription, except this suggestion, which I feel impelled to by a species of coacathes scribendi. If our city treasurer has not at present any surplus funds upon hand, he doubtless will have upon the sale of our timbered lands, rendering his purse so plethoric that I recommend an application of the lancet. Yes, sirs, a gentle bleeding will be of service, inducing the convalescent condition which will enable him to walk around our public squares, investigative of the proprieties of an enclosure—warding off all damage to those beautiful shade trees, with which our city council will doubtless decorate them, and upon whose lofty boughs birds of the gayest plumage shall sit, warbling their praise.

Where on earth a more inviting spot for trees than Victoria? They not only subserve the purpose of shade, but evince taste on the part of any community. All writers affirm that flowers around and about a house denote a lady of refinement within. In like manner the embellishments of a city, gives the impress of its citizens features. Let us make this a sort of oasis in the desert, for the travelling emigrant, where he may repose in luxury and sigh to become one of its inhabitants.

I am done, sirs, with this remark to those who may say that this is mere moonshine, that there is more in this world, Petrucio, than is dreampt of in thy philosophy.

Victoria, April, 1848. H.

From the Lady's Book for March.

Aunt Magwire's Account of Parson Scrantum's Donation Party.

BY THE AUTHOR OF "THE WIDOW BEDOTT PAPERS."

Concluded from last week.

Just then the door was thrown open, and we was invited out to supper. So we went squeezin' and crowdin' into the settin'-room. Some o' the folks pushed and jammed as if they was afeard that they shouldn't git the best chance. Glory Ann Billins sot at one end o' the table a poorin' coffee, and Jo Gipson's wife at 'tother end a poorin' tea; and I tell, 'twas as much as ever they could dew to poor it fast enough. Jeff, he flew around and helped the ladies. For my part, I didn't feel like eatin' much—I was jammed up agin the wall and couldn't stir hand nor foot. So I told Jeff te fetch me a cup o' tea and a nut-cake, and he did; and I took 'em, and managed to eat the nut-cake, but somebody hit my elbow and made me spill the heft o' my tea; so I stood and held my empty cup, and looked on to see the performance. I say for't, if 'twant worth seein', I'm mistaken. Why, if I was a starvin' to death, I shouldn't be willin' to act as some o' them folks did. They pushed, and elbowed, and pulled, and hauled, and grabbled like crazy critters. 'Twas amusin' to see 'em put down the vittals—I'd a gin a sixpence, Nancy, to a had you there;' twould a ben fun for you to look on and see the dewins. You'd a thought that the biggest part o' the company hadn't had nothing to eat since the last donation party, and didn't expect to have nothin' more till the next one. The wimmin, as a gineral thing, took tea, and eat the cake and pies, and so forth.—And the men, they let into the coffee, and biscuit, and cheese, and cold meat, and such like. I actilly see Deacon Skinner drink six cups o' coffee, and eat in proportion.—And Dr. Lippincott, my grief! 'twas perfectly astonishin' to me that one mortal body could hold as much as that man put in—no wonder he's so fat—they say he gits the heft of his livin' away from home—contrives to git to one patient's house jest as dinner's ready, and to another's jest at tea-time, and so eats with em. And I wish you'd a seen the Widder Grimes. Grammany! how the critter did stuff! I took particular notice of her, and I see she had an awful great work-bag on her arm, and every little while she'd contrive to tuck a piece into't, when she thought nobody want a lookin'. As soon as I got a chance I hunched Jeff, and says I—"For pity's sake, Jeff, dew obsarve the Widder Grimes.' So Jeff, he watched her a spell. 'By George!' says he, 'if that aint rich!' I tell ye, 'twas fun for Jeff. Bymeby—after she'd got her bag party well filled, says Jeff to me, says he—'Now, mother, may I stir her up a little?' 'I don't care,' says I. So he reached forrard and hollered across the table tew her, loud enough for everybody to hear—'Miss Grimes, may I come to your party?' 'My party?' says she; 'what do you mean?' 'Why,' says Jeff, says he, 'I reckoned from the size o' your bag, and the quantity o' provisions you was a layin' in, that you was calculatin' to make a party, and I thought I'd like to come.' Everybody looked at Miss Grimes; and, I tell ye, she looked as if she'd like to crawl into some knot-hole—and I don't know but what she did—for she made her disappearance amazin' soon after. And, then, them siminary gals—gracious! how they did eat! I 'spose they was half starved at Miss Pinchim's. Afore long the table was purty well cleared, and Miss Scrantum had to go to the buttry and bring on all 'twas left. I guess everything in the house that could be eat, without stoppin' to cook it, was made way with that night.—When the siminary gals had eat all they wanted, they amused themselves a throwin' hunks o' cheese and buttered biscuit at the young men. After most o' the other eatables had been disposed of, Dave Runyon, great gump! went into the buttry and brought out the box o' raisins that was to go towards Cappen Smalley's pew rent, and handed 'em round. Everybody grabbed, especially the siminary gals and children, till ther want one left in the box. When supper was about finished, Jane Elizy Fustick, (she's always a tryin' to dew somethin' cunnin',) she went into the store-room and got a chain o' sassages, that old Miss Crocker brought, and come along slily and throw'd it round Liph Peabody's shoulders. Liph, he was a standin' by the tea board, a drinkin' a cup o' coffee. When he felt the sassages come floppin' round his neck, he was skart, and whisked round suddenly and hit the tea board, and knocked it off onto the floor, and smash went everything on it!—What made it more aggravatin' was, ther was a dozen Chany cups and sarcers on it that Miss Scrantum had fetcht out after the folks come out to supper. They was some that she sot a great deal by; her mother gin 'em tew her, and her mother was dead.—She didn't bring 'em on at first, for fear they'd git broke. She sot on all her common crockery, and borrered a good deal at Cappen Smalley's store, calculatin' if any on't was broke to pay for't. But when she see so many folks come crowdin' out, she was afeard ther wouldn't be cups enough, so she fetcht out her mother's Chany cups and sot 'em on the tea board. But Glory Ann got along without usin' 'em, and there they sot, and when the tea board fell, they fell tew, and every one on 'em was broke or cracked. Gracious! how Miss Scrantum looked when she see her precious Chany all to pieces. She didn't say a word, but her lips quivered, and she trembled all over.—But she seemed to overcome it in a minnit, and went and brought a basket and begun to pick up the pieces, and I and Jeff took hold and helped her. A good many o' the company had gone back into the parlor; but there was enough left to track the sassage round, and, my goodness! what work they made with 'em! While we was a pickin' up the crockery, all of a sudden ther was a terrible holerbaloo in the parlor—Jeff and me rushed in to see what was the matter, and gracious gransfather! what do you 'spose it was? Why one o' them pesky siminary gals had throw'd a hunk o' cheese and hit Miss Scrantum's parlor lamp that was settin' on the table, and knocked it over and broke it all to flinders. But that want the wost on't—where it tumbled over it fell right onto that plum-colored satin bunnit, and the ile run all over it in a minnit. Afore anybody could ketch the bunnit, one side on't, ribbin and all, was completely ruined. Such a sight as 'twas, you never sot your tew lookin' eyes on! All the ile that didn't go onto the bunnit was soaked up in the paper that Jeff took, that was a lyin' right aside on't, and the biggest part o' that was spiled tew. My grief! how I *did* feel when I see that beautiful bunnit in such a condition! And poor Miss Scrantum turned as pale as death, and Susan cried like everything. I axed Sam Lippincott (the doctor's red-headed boy) who 'twas that throw'd the cheese—he pinted out the gal, and I goes up to her and, says I—'You good-for-nothing little huzzy, haint you no better manners than to be a throwin' cheese at other folkses lamps in that way?' She was a real sassy little thing, and didn't care a straw for what she'd done. She looked up and grinned as impredent as could be, and says she—'Excuse me, marm—I hadn't the most remote idea o' hittin' the lamp.—I meant to aim at Sam Lippincott's head, and mistook the lamp for it. I'm sure you cant blame me for makin such a *natral* mistake.' Did you ever! I was a good mind to hit her a cuff aside o' the head, but I didn't. I told Miss Pinchem on't, though, the next day—and she punished the huzzy by keepin' her on bread and water a week. Jeff said 'twas a very *equinomical* kind o' punishment. Well, the party broke up purty soon after this scrape, and Jeff and me went hum. Jeff went off to bed. Yer uncle was out; dear me! how I *did* dream meetin' him! Afore long he come in. 'Well,' says he, 'how did the party go off?' 'O, well enough,' says I; 'but I'm tired and sleepy, and we won't talk about it to-night.' The fact is, I felt tew mean to tell him the truth—but in the mornin', when Jeff come down, he let it all out. My grief! how yer uncle did crow over me. 'Didn't I tell ye so?' says he; 'don't ye wish you hadn't a went?'—'Yes,' says I, 'if it's any satisfaction tew ye to know it—I *dew* wish so.' 'I know'd ye would,' says he. I verily believe he was glad the bunnit got spiled. I don't 'spose he'll let me hear the last o' that donation party as long as he lives—he *is* such a critter to hang onto anything.

The next mornin', as soon as I got my chores done up, I went over to Miss Scrantum's to see how they come on, and help 'em regilate a little. Murder-alive! such a sight as that house was, from one end to 'tother, I never sot my tew lookin' eyes on! The carpets was all greased up with butter, and cheese and sassages. And then the lamp ile had done more mischief than we know'd on the night afore. It had run off the table, and made a cruel great spot on the best carpet; and I found Miss Scrantum a tryin' to wash it out. I sot tew and helped her—but 'twant no use—'twouldn't come out. Susan, she was a settin' on a little stool a scourin' teaspoons, and cryin' as if her heart would break. 'What's the matter, dear?' says I—but the poor child couldn't answer me. So her mother said she was cryin' about the bunnit bein' spiled. 'No wonder,' says I, 'it's enough to make anybody cry. I 'spose you can't dew nothing with the bunnit, can you?' 'O yes,' says Miss Scrantum, says she; 'I've ben lookin' at it this mornin', and I think I can get enough out of it to make a bag of. It'll make a very nice bag—and I shall keep it as long as I live, for your sake, Miss Magwire.' I looked at the woman with surprise. Ther she sot on the floor, a rubbin' away at that grease spot, and a talkin' as calmly about that six dollar bunnit as if it hadn't a cost more'n six cents. I was kind o' vexed at her for not makin' more fuss about it. I actilly begun to think she hadn't no feelin', and didn't care for nothin. 'And then', says I, 'to think o' their breakin' your beautiful Chany—'twas shameful—a present from yer mother, tew; and you sot *so* much by it; and I've heerd you say it was the last thing yer mother ever gin ye.' I was a runnin' on in that way when I thought I heerd Miss Scrantum sob—I looked up and she was a cryin' dretfully. She couldn't hold in no longer when I spoke o' the Chany. I was sorry I said a word about it; but it convinced me that Miss Scrantum had feelins, deep feelins; but she'd larn't to control 'em, poor woman! Well, I staid a little spell and helpd 'em clean up, and then I went hum. Susan went to the door with me. When we got outside I axed her whether ther was many provisions brought in the night afore. She told me to come to the store-room and look. So I went into't and took a view, and there was tew or three pumpkins, a couple o' spare-ribs (*spare* enough, I tell ye), three or four cabbages, a chicken, what was left o' Deacon Peabody's cheese, and a cod-fish. 'Is that all?' says I. 'Yes,' says Susan, 'and half o' the cheese, and one o' the spare ribs and the chicken, are to go for pew rent—I heerd pa tell ma so; but you musn't let 'em know I told you about it—for they'd think it wrong for me to speak about it; you won't tell 'em, will you, Miss Magwire?' 'No, my darlin,' says I, 'I wont let it out.' So I went hum—and as I went along considerin' the matter, I come to a *unanimous* conclusion in my own mind, that *donation parties was a humbug.*

Well, the next Sunday Parson Scrantum requested the male members of his congregation to meet him the next evenin' at the meetin'-house. Yer uncle went to the meetin'. I was in a wonderful fidgit to know what was the object on't—and quite impatient for husband to come hum. When he come, I observed he was oncommonly tickled about something. "What *is* the matter? dew tell, for pity's sake,' says I. 'Why, the Minister's axed a dismission,' says I. 'You don't?' says I. 'Jest so,' says he; and then haw-haw'd out a laffin. 'What ails ye, man alive?' says I; 'I don't see what ther is to laff at in that; for my part, I look upon't as a great misfortin to Scrabble Hill, to lose such a minister as Parson Scrantum. I'm astonished to see you laff.' 'Well, you won't be,' says he, 'when I tell you about the meetin'.' So he went on and gin me the hull description. He said that when Mr. Scrantum told 'em he wanted a dismission, they was wonderful surprised—Deacon Skinner he riz and axed the reason. So Mr. Scrantum stated that he found it onpossible to support his family on his salary. Deacon Skinner said *that* was curus—he thought four hundred dollars was *purty well up.* Deacon Peabody said he thought so tew, especially with a *donation party* besides. Deacon Fustick, he put in, and said 'twas rather a queer time for a minister to complain of his congregation, jest after they'd gin him a *bee*—and he axed Dr. Lippincott what was *his* opinion. (Now Dr. Lippincott never had an opinion in all his life, on any subject—if he had, he never expressed it for fear of injurin' his practice; 'taint even known what his politics is—he always contrives to be away on election days.) So he hemmed and hawed, and said that really he hadn't *made up his mind*—he hoped Mr. Scrantum 'preciated his donation party—he hoped the congregation 'preciated Mr. Scrantum; he wished—he wished—in short, he wished things wasn't sitiwated jest as they was sitiwated; and that was all they got out of *him.* Old Parker observed that minister's families, somehow, took more to support 'em than anybody else. Mr. Scrantum said that his family lived as equinomical as they could be, but he had a good many children, and 'twas purty difficult to dew as he'd ought tew by 'em on four hundred dollars a year; axed 'em whether they thought ary one o' them could dew it. Cappen Smalley, rich old curmudgin, stuck up his head and said, he guessed *he* could dew it—especially with the help of a donation party every year; but he hoped Mr. Scrantum's request would be granted unanimously; for his part, he'd long ben of opinion they'd ought to have a *cheaper* minister, and one that hadn't such a snarl o' young ones. I don't 'spose Parson Scrantum would a said anything severe if it hadn't a ben for Cappen Smalley's speech. He seemed quite stirred up by it. He riz up considerable flustrated, and says he—'I thank God, that whatever else I lack, He has ben pleased to give me plenty o' the *poor* man's blessins—yea, a quiver full of them. And it's for their sakes, not my own, that I come here to-night. If I was alone in the world, I could and would dew on a'most nothing—though the Scripter says the laborer is worthy of his hire. Brethren, since I come among you, I've done my best to be a faithful pastor—if I've fail'd, I hope to be forgiven. At first I had an idee that I should be able to rub along on my small salary; and I don't know, but what I might a done it, if it hadn't a ben for *one thing,*' Here he paused. 'What was *that?*' says Deacon Peabody. Mr Scrantum continued—'I've ben here tew years, and you've had the kinkness to give me tew donation parties. I've stood it so far, but I can't stand it no longer; brethren, I feel convinced that *one more donation party* would completely *break me down.* I will now retire and leave the meetin' to decide as they see fit.' Yer uncle said that for about five minutes after he went out universal silence prevailed.—The first to speak was Deacon Skinner.—'Strange!' says he. 'Curus!' says Deacon Peabody. '*Ree*-markable!' says Deacon Fustick. 'Onaccountable!' says Cappen Smalley. 'Singular circumstance!' says Dr. Lippincott. Then yer uncle got up, and, says he—'Gentlemen, I don't see as anything's to be gained by settin' here and wonderin' all night. For my part, I think all Parson Scrantum's said is true—and I move it be put to vote.' So 'twas put to vote and granted.

A few days afterwards the minister's folks packed up and started off to Miss Scrantum's father's. to stay till they could git another place. Yer uncle gin 'em ten dollars when they went. He'd a ben glad to give fifty if he'd a ben able. They was very thankful for't, and the parson gin us his partin' blessin' and I'd ruther have *that* than all Cappen Smalley's money. We all felt bad enough when we said good-by. Miss Scrantum cried hard—she didn't try to conceal her feelins then. Susan cried tew, and so did I—and we had a gineral time kissin' all round; as true as I live, Jeff, he kissed Susan tew—but don't you teaze him about it; I was glad to see him dew it, though Susan did blush awfully. They made us promise to come and see 'em if ever they got another sittiwation. We've heard lately that the parson had got a call to Bangtown. I don't know nothing about the village, but I hope to gracious it's a place where *donation parties* is a thing unknown.

The New York Sunday Mercury has a genius in his 'Nimrod,' whose brightness the editor developes in the following lesson in catechism:

"Well, Nimrod, how long were the children of Israel in the wilderness?"

"Till they found their way out."

"Who was cast into the lion's den?"

"Van Amburg."

"Who was compelled to seek refuge in the land of Nod?"

"Governor Dorr."

"Why?"

"Because he got up the *King's* ebenezer, and *Providence* wouldn't protect him."

"That will do Nimrod for this week."

MARYLAND.—The Legislature of Maryland, at its late session, passed 386 laws, besides resolutions and various matters.

From the N. O. Delta.

Texas:

Its soil, climate, agricultural advantages, stock raising capacity, &c.

GALVESTON, April 8, 1848.

Dear Delta—Being in the habit of reading your very interesting columns, and finding therein the history of the present age, carefully and correctly gathered together from the whole "four quarters," tastefully arranged, and judiciously recommended to the attention of those who are, at one and the same time, your patrons and your pupils, I sometimes "think to myself," "Mr. Delta, you are neglectful of Texas." Texas has already made some figure in the world, young as she is. She is now about to become, after a conclusion of peace, the most interesting of the new States. Combining, within her limits, all the varieties of soil and climate of all the Union, she presents the only example of a State totally independent, or with capacity to become so, of all the other States.

Some portions of the soil and climate of Texas, embracing an extended area, are adapted to the cultivation of all cereal grains. Water power, and all the facilities for manufactories are abundant. Texas is admitted, by all who know any thing upon the subject, to be the best stock country in the world. Besides all this, cotton, sugar, tobacco, and all the other productions of the South, flourish with vigor, unknown in the other States. Here we find the resources of all the States united in one.

But Texas has been laboring under disadvantages which no one of the other new States has encountered. *They* grew up under the fostering and parental care of the Union, while Texas passed the first twelve years of her existence under the malignant eye of an unnatural stepmother, and the last twelve in open and continuous warfare. But, now that peace is about to be *conquered,* things will take their natural course.

As fine sugar lands as ever broiled in the sun, can be purchased in Texas, at prices ranging from two to ten dollars. So of cotton lands. This being the case, planters will not shut their eyes upon it, but will speedily commence the work of planting in Texas. It is not necessary to discuss the question of the superiority of Texas lands; the disparity in prices between them and lands of a similar quality in the old States, determines all questions in their favor.

Next to the planting interest, no other will be so important in Texas as that of raising stock and growing wool. Those who have paid some attention to this subject, all say, that an estimate, based upon reasonable probabilities, would appear so extravagant, as to forfeit the reputation of the most discreet grazier. For instance—sheep may be sheared twice a year, will have lambs twice a year, and, as a general rule, produce twins. It will, however, be perceived at once, that an estimate based upon these grounds would find credit with none. It is to be hoped, that a very few years of peace will bring the knowledge of the advantages of Texas home to all those who are now laboring, in all parts of the Union, to keep soul and body together.

Inland navigation and transportation are just beginning to receive attention. During the last winter, a steamer has been placed upon the Guadalupe, another upon the Brazes, two others upon the Trinity, and yet another upon the Neches. Roads are being constructed through the low country, bordering upon the coast; and after the completion of these, travel upon horseback and in carriages, through all the parts of Texas, will be delightful.

But there is one particular element which will enter into the future prosperity of Texas, and which deserves peculiar notice.—Texas lands are cheap, and are owned in all parts of the nation. Hence there are numerous persons, scattered abroad, whose interests are partially identified with the prosperity of this State. Texas is about to throw her wide domain into the market, and it cannot be supposed that United States lands will find ready sale at one dollar and a quarter per acre, whilst finer, or as fine lands, in a finer climate, can be purchased in Texas for one-third of that amount. At the last session of the Legislature, which has just closed, two bills passed the House, one of which provided for ascertaining the amount of the State debt, and the other for permitting the holders thereof to enter lands in payment, at twenty-five cents per acre. The former bill passed the Senate, and, therefore, became a law; the other did not, but failed for reasons creditable to the Senate. By it, priority would have been given to audited claims, since they could have been exchanged for lands immediately; whereas all other claims were required to be audited, before they could be in a proper shape to entitle the holder to lands. The holders of these claims will speedily be repaid for the confidence with which they have relied upon their final liquidation. Lands at twenty-five cents per acre, for the original amount and interest thereon for nearly or quite ten years, will foot up a handsome speculation upon present prices.

But I am wandering from the proper object of my letter; it is to the consequences of this policy I desire to direct your attention. By it the taxable property of the State will be greatly increased; by it the prices of lands will be confined to a proper standard; and by it the number of those whose interests are identified with our prosperity will be enlarged.

There are many other points connected with this subject, and which I desire to bring to your notice, but they must be reserved for a future communication. Two very important considerations, are: First—The effect of this war upon the South, and particularly upon Texas, by way of dispelling prejudices against the healthiness and institutions of the South and Southern character. Secondly—Texas, considered as the terminus of the institution of slavery, and the only new State where slave labor would be profitable, Of these I will treat hereafter. Yours, &c., A TEXAN.

Flight of the Mexicans at the Battle of Churubusco.

The accompanying plate represents a terrific scene at the close of the battle of Churubusco on the afternoon of the 20th of August. The Mexicans are completely routed, and fleeing, are pursued by Colonel Harney and his dragoons to the very gates of the capital. In this pursuit our horsemen fell upon their rear, and trampled beneath their horses' hoofs, and cut down by the sword vast numbers of the fugitives. Friend and foe mingled in one mass, with arms clashing, roll along together in this disastrous retreat. The Mexican cavalry, thanks to their early flight and their fleet horses, are safe, and are already pouring into the city; out the infantry, who stood their ground and were the last to leave the field, are overtaken, by the American dragoons, who fell upon them with a furious onslaught. One of the Mexican officers, more humane and brave than his associates, had fallen back to the rear to protect and aid his men in their precipitate flight. In his anxiety to save his men he is overwhelmed by a party of the pursuing horsemen. He is perceived by an American Lieutenant of dragoons, who, selecting him as his prize, dashes on to him with full speed, and with uplifted sword calls on him to surrender. The Mexican answers with a back stroke of his sabre, which the American parries, and follows up by a well directed blow that fells his plumed foe to the ground.

In the back ground, and near at hand, is seen the city of Mexico—the capital of the Mexican republic, once the famed city of the Aztecs, which three hundred and twenty-six years before, had beheld the last of its Montezumas expire, and Hernando Cortez, the conquering Spaniard, enter in triumph within its walls. Now on the afternoon of the 20th of August, 1847, the last rays of the setting sun linger and play on the summit of the cathedral-spire that is reared on the site of the Halls of the Montezumas, another conquering race is at the gates of this famed and ill-fated city—it is the Anglo-Saxon of the North. The haughty Spaniard has subdued and ruled the native Aztec for many generations! now the Spaniard in his turn must yield up the fruits of his conquest to the white-faced Saxons who assume for themselves the dominion of the North American continent.

The battle of Churubusco was a continuation of the engagement, during which, on the morning of the 20th of August, the fortifications of Contreras were taken by the artillery and bayonets of seven thousand American troops, driving Gen. Valencia and fifteen or twenty thousand men from a strongly fortified position. The greater portion of the troops fled to their main works at Churubusco, a distance of almost three miles, and within but four of the Capital. Santa Anna had already arrived, and with the reinforcements from Contreras was in command of twenty-five thousand men, and one hundred guns. The army of General Scott, in three divisions, under the command of Generals Twiggs, Worth, and Pillow, numbering in all about seven thousand men and with but twenty-seven guns, came up and commenced an attack early in the afternoon. The action was commenced by Gen. Twiggs, and Generals Pillow and Worth soon joined in the fight which continued with destructive fury for upwards of two hours, when the Americans charged on the foe and at the point of the bayonet drove him from his strong-hold. This was the most sanguinary contest of the war. The New York and South Carolina regiments of General Shields's brigade lost half their numbers in killed and wounded. Colonel Butler, of South Carolina, fell in the early part of the engagement, and Colonel Burnett of New York was severely wounded. The loss of the Americans on this day in killed and wounded was one thousand and seventeen; that of the enemy has been estimated at more than double that number. In the two actions there were nearly four thousand prisoners taken, among whom were several generals and three ex-presidents of the Mexican republic. We captured also fifty pieces of artillery, and a large quantity of small arms, ammunition, and camp equipage. Among the prisoners were taken seventy deserters, in the Mexican uniform, styled the Legion of St. Patrick, and led by O'Riley, the chief of the deserters. Fifty of these renegades were subsequently hanged, and the remainder flogged, branded, and sentenced to work in chains during the remainder of the war, and then be drummed out of the army.

FLIGHT OF THE MEXICANS A

In this battle t two light batterie daring manner in superior numbers one battery of si tack a fort defe guns, among whic and three eight

HE BATTLE OF CHURUBUSCO.

ricans employed
a instance of the
r forces attacked
e mentioned that
was ordered to at-
h twenty three
ighteen-pounders
witzers; each of

the latter being the same calibre as sixty-eight pound Paixhan guns. The battery to reach the fort advanced without any covering to within range of the Mexican grape, and amid a destructive fire held its position during the fight, until the storming parties turned the enemy's flank, and put him to flight. The battery in this bold charge had three pieces dismounted and three officers killed and mortally wounded. Gen. Shields, who, in addition to his own brigade had command of the brigade of Gen. Pierce, highly distinguished himself on this occasion. He was ordered to gain the rear of the enemy, but finding this impossible, he was the first to charge on the works of the enemy. He advanced, in the face of a most destructive fire of artillery which swept down nearly half his men, and at the point of the bayonet stormed the works, took several pieces of artillery and many prisoners, among whom was Riley's band of deserters. In the pursuit Gen. Shields was the first to lead, and continued till passed by Col. Harney and his dragoons. Some of the infantry of Gen. Shields, however, continued in the pursuit and advanced with the dragoons to the gates of the city, until night coming on they were recalled. In the engraving may be seen the officers of the New-York regiment. One of them has seized by the jacket, one of Santa Anna's veterans who has paused to fire on the American dragoon officer that has just passed him. Before, however, he can pull the trigger he falls, pierced upwards through the bowels to the heart, by the sword of the New-Yorker.

Col. Harney paused not until he had reached the very walls of the city; and some of his fearless riders actually entered within the gates. Had he not been recalled, it seems as if he would have rode to the main Plazza and demanded the surrender of the city. It is the opinion of some that had the whole army of Scott joined in the pursuit, the city might have been taken possession of that very night, and Santa Anna driven from the capital. The pursuing party was recalled for the night, and active operations from that time were suspended. On the 22nd an armistice was agreed on, which being terminated on the 7th of September, General Scott again advanced, fought the bloody battles of Molino del Rey, Chapultepec, and on the 14th entered the city of Mexico.

The Texan Rangers.

The Texan Rangers appear to have a terrible reputation among the Mexicans. The following extract from a Buena Vista letter, which we find in the National Intelligencer, shows that they have good cause to be afraid of even the approach of a Ranger:

In their capacity of rangers, the Texans, of course, have an almost boundless field of movement. If sent out from a city or a camp they are never expected to return before or until after night, or the next day. If attached to a train, they are only expected to show themselves occasionally, to signify that they are on the alert. Now, it has frequently happened that a stray ranger has been cut off while on one or the other kind of duty, by perhaps depending too much on his own prowess and strength in a gang of Mexicans with whom he may have fallen in, or he may have been caught asleep, or in some other way have given them the advantage of him, and his life is lost. He is missed; search is made for him by his comrades; his body is perhaps found, perhaps not. The nearest Mexicans to the vicinity of his disappearance are required to account for him; they will not, or cannot. The bowie-knife is called upon, and deliberately every male Mexican in that rancho is speedily done for, guilty or not guilty. But these are not enough to make an offset for the life of a Texan. Another rancho receives the fearful visit, and again blood flows. The number killed on some occasions in this way has been fearfully great, as has been gathered from what fell from the Texans, but no one but themselves knew about it, as a report of any such doings to the nearest commanding officer would only be followed by a tenfold retaliation on the nearest "customers." This is all horrid, it is true, but it has had the salutary tendency of causing the well-disposed and honest Mexicans to ferret out and inform on those who practise murder and robbery. Going about at some distance from camp is consequently much more safe. A lansiero's (lancer's) fear of a ranger is most remarkable,—remarkable even to ludicrousness, as we learn from the Mexicans in the vicinity of the American camp and from our officers.

STATE GAZETTE.

VOL. 1. AUSTIN, TEXAS, SATURDAY, OCTOBER 20, 1849. NO. 9.

THE TEXAS STATE GAZETTE.
Is published on Saturdays
BY WILLIAM H. CUSHNEY.

TERMS.

SUBSCRIPTION.—Four Dollars per Volume of fifty-two numbers. Single numbers, Ten Cents. In all cases, payment in advance will be required of Subscribers living out of the County of Travis; or the amount assumed by a responsible resident of the City of Austin, or the Agent. In this particular, there will be no respect of persons or deviation from our terms on any account whatever.

ADVERTISING.—Advertisements will be inserted at One Dollar per square of seven lines, or less, for the first insertion, and fifty cents for each continuance. One-half these charges will be made to those who advertise by the year, with the privilege of changing quarterly.

Business Cards, of not more than one square, will be inserted for ten dollars per annum.

Announcements of Candidates for Office, and all political, personal and business Communications promotive of individual interests, will be charged as Advertisements.

All Advertisements, the publication of which is required by law, must be paid for in advance.

The twenty-second section of the law regulating fees of office, provides that in all cases where a citation, or other process, is required to be served by publication in a newspaper, the officer whose duty it may be to make such service, shall be furnished with the printer's fee for such publication, before he shall be required to have such service made.

The first section of the act of February 5, 1841, regulating the sale of runaway slaves, provides also, that where any slave is committed to jail as a runaway, a notice of the apprehension and commitment, with a full description of such slave, shall be published weekly in one of the papers at the Seat of Government, for the space of one month, and printed copies thereof furnished to the Clerk of the County Court of the county where the commitment shall have been made.

To facilitate the computation of our charges for advertising, one hundred words or less may be considered as constituting a square; over one hundred and under two hundred words, two squares, and so on.

Advertisements not marked with the time for which they are to be published, will be continued until forbid, and charged accordingly.

Subscribers, Advertisers and Agents may remit money at our risk and expense. All communications must be addressed to the Publisher, *post paid*.

LIST OF AGENTS FOR THE GAZETTE.

☞ Agents will be allowed twenty per cent. on all moneys received and paid over by them for subscriptions and advertising.

C. Erhard, San Marcos.
James Nicholson, Bastrop.
W. B. Coffee, Lockhart.
W. Basel, New Braunfels.
T. H. Duggan, Seguin.
S. A. J. Haynie, Webber's Prairie.
Edw'd. Malloch, Gonzales.
M. Johnson, Port Lavaca.
John Henry Brown, Indianola.
Alexander Somervell, Saluria.
W. L. Hunter, Goliad.
B. F. Neal, Corpus Christi.
James L. Trueheart, San Antonio.
W. J. Jones, Columbus.
J. F. Crosby, Brenham.
J. B. Robertson, Independence.
H. R. Cartmell, Washington.
M. K. Snell, Houston.
H. W. Raglin, Anderson.
J. R. Henry, Springfield.
George W. Glascock, Georgetown.
C. M. Hubby, Cameron.
Thos. P. Collins, Crockett.
John H. Reagan, Buffalo.
S. G. Newton, Dallas.
John Welch, Melton's P. O.
S. A. Venters, Alton.
G. W. Barnett, McKinney.
James N. Smith, Cuero.
P. U. Pridham, Victoria.
J. W. B. McFarlane, Refugio.
Peter Mahony, San Patricio.
R. Howard, Brownville.
A. G. Stakes, Rio Grande City.
H. P. Bee, Laredo.
John Hoffman, Castroville.
Geo. F. Holcamp, Fredericksburg.
W. H. Crutcher, La Grange.
M. M. Battle, Richmond.
A. Underwood, Columbia.
R. D. Johnson, Galveston.
Hugh B. Boston, Montgomery.
Isaac McGary, Huntsville.
John H. Potts, Leona.
W. F. Henderson, Corsicana.
John Lund, Franklin.
S. W. Kellogg, Wheelock.
Harvey Mitchell, Boonville.
W. W. Hill & W. A. King, Caldwell.
W. H. Huggins, Liberty.
John P. Kale, Livingston.
A. E. McClure, Palestine.
A. P. Sullivan, Kaufman.
James Bradley, Greenville.
J. Jordan, Jordan's Saline.
E. Hopkins, Tarrant.
W. D. Fitch, Sherman.
H. G. Hendricks, Bonham.
W. H. Millwee, Paris.
G. F. Lawton, Clarksville.
S. H. McFarland, Boston.
Jefferson Cooke, Mt. Pleasant.
S. F. Mosely, Jefferson.
John H. McNairy, Gilmer.
W. P. Hill, Marshall.
Thos. J. Hays, Tyler.
Jas. R. Armstrong, Henderson.
J. H. Anderson, Carthage.
L. H. Ashcroft, Shelbyville.
W. P. Brittain, Rusk.
Thomas Barrett, Nacogdoches.
O. M. Wheeler, San Augustine.
Austin & Clapp, Sabinetown.
A. C. Caldwell, Marion.
M. Priest, Woodville.
Z. Wms. Eddy, Jasper.
Tho's J. Booker, Burkeville.
J. P. Pulsifer, Beaumont.
C. T. Hilliard, Hilliard's P. O.
Rev. John Haynie, Rutersville.
Geo. Burkhart, Matagorda.
G. Eagan, Wharton.
Eli Mercer, Egypt.
Edw'd Purcell, Brazoria.
N. H. Munger, San Felipe.

THE LAW ON NEWSPAPERS.

1.—Subscribers who do not give express notice to the contrary, are considered as wishing to continue their Subscription.

2—If Subscribers order the discontinuance of their papers, the Publisher may continue to send them until all that is due be paid.

3—If Subscribers neglect or refuse to take their papers from the office to which they are directed, they are held responsible until they have settled their bill and order their papers discontinued.

4—If Subscribers remove to other places, without informing the Publisher, and the paper is sent to the former direction, they are held responsible.

5—The courts have decided that refusing to take a paper or periodical from the office, or removing and leaving it uncalled for, is *prima facie* evidence of fraud.

Also, that where a Subscriber to a periodical failed to notify the Publisher to discontinue the paper, at the end of the time for which he subscribed, or pay up the arrearages, he was bound for another year.

And also, that where a Post Master failed to notify the Publishers of Newspapers that their papers were not taken from the post office, he rendered himself liable for the amount of subscription.

CALENDAR FOR 1849.

	S	M	T	W	T	F	S
SEPT'R,	-	-	-	-	-	-	1
	2	3	4	5	6	7	8
	9	10	11	12	13	14	15
	16	17	18	19	20	21	22
	23	24	25	26	27	28	29
	30						
OCTOB'R,	-	1	2	3	4	5	6
	7	8	9	10	11	12	13
	14	15	16	17	18	19	20
	21	22	23	24	25	26	27
	28	29	30	31			

	S	M	T	W	T	F	S
NOV.,	-	-	-	-	1	2	3
	4	5	6	7	8	9	10
	11	12	13	14	15	16	17
	18	19	20	21	22	23	24
	25	26	27	28	29	30	
DECEMBER,	-	-	-	-	-	-	1
	2	3	4	5	6	7	8
	9	10	11	12	13	14	15
	16	17	18	19	20	21	22
	23	24	25	26	27	28	29
	30	31					

ARRIVALS AND DEPARTURES
Of the Mails at Austin.
S. G. HAYNIE, City Postmaster.

GALVESTON MAIL, *via* Webber's Prairie, Bastrop, Cunningham's, La Grange, Rutersville, Shultz's, Montville, Independence, Washington, Perriman's, and Hamlin's to Houston, by four horse coaches; thence to Galveston by steamer: Arrives on Sundays and Thursdays at 6 p. m., and departs on Sundays and Wednesdays at 6 a. m.

WESTERN MAIL, *via* San Marcos and New Braunfels to San Antonio, in four horse coaches, and thence to Castroville on horseback: Arrives on Tuesdays and Saturdays at 6 p. m., and departs on Mondays and Fridays at 6 a. m.

SOUTHWESTERN MAIL, *via* Lockhart, Gonzales, Cüero, Victoria, Port La Vaca, Indianola, Saluria, Goliad, Refugio, Lamar, San Patricio, Corpus Christi, Brownsville and Rio Grande City to Laredo, on horseback: Arrives on Tuesdays at 4 p. m., and departs on Wednesdays at 6 a. m.

NORTHERN MAIL, *via* Georgetown, Waco Village, Weyman's, Richland, Mitchell's, Dallas, McKinney, Greenville, Alton, Sherman, Bonham and Paris to Clarksville, on horseback: Arrives on Thursdays at 4 p. m., and departs on Fridays at 6 a. m.

COLONIZATION CONTRACTS.

CONTRACT with Charles Fenton Mercer and his associates: January 29, 1844.

This contract, made the 29th day of January, eighteen hundred and forty-four, between Sam Houston, President of the Republic of Texas, acting in behalf of the Republic, of the first part, and Charles Fenton Mercer, late of the State of Virginia, but now of the city of Tallahassee, in the Territory of Florida, in the United States of America, and such associates as he shall choose, of the second part, witnesseth that, Whereas, by an Act passed by the Congress of Texas, entitled "An Act, granting lands to emigrants," approved, February the 4th, 1841, the President of the Republic of Texas was authorized to make a contract with sundry persons, named in the said Act, for the introduction and settlement of emigrants, upon the vacant lands of the Republic of Texas, upon certain terms and conditions, therein expressed: the provisions of which Act, were extended and made general, and perpetuated by a subsequent Act, amendatory thereof; approved the 5th of February, 1842: and Whereas, by a Joint Resolution of the Congress of Texas, "to modify the provisions of an Act, entitled an Act, granting lands to emigrants, approved, the 16th of January, 1843," the President of the Republic of Texas was authorized to make such further contract or contracts with the grantees, named in the aforesaid Act, or with their assigns, or legal representativves, as shall be deemed by him, for the benefit of the Republic, and as shall not be inconsistent with the provisions of the said Act: and Whereas, the said Charles Fenton Mercer is the legal representative of part of the said grantees; one of whom died in London, prior to the passage of the Act of the 4th of February, 1841, before mentioned; and five others of whom assigned to the said Charles F. Mercer, among others, their interests in the said Act, and all contracts made pursuant thereto, by an assignment and transfer of their interests, dated in London, the 22d day of September, 1841; and the said Charles Fenton Mercer is desirous to make a new contract, in behalf of himself and others, his associates, to be united in one Company or association, for the purpose of colonizing part of the ungranted or unappropriated lands of the Republic of Texas. Now this contract witnesseth, that the parties thereto have mutually covenanted and agreed, and do hereby covenant and agree to the terms and conditions of this contract, and bind themselves to each other, for the faithful fulfillment of the same, as follows, viz: The party of the second part, for himself and his associates, his and their heirs, executors, administrators and assigns, covenant and agree, with the party of the first part, acting in behalf, and for the Republic of Texas, to introduce and settle, within the limits hereafter described, by the party of the first part, or within such other limits as may be hereafter prescribed by the President of the Republic of Texas, for the purpose aforesaid, and in accordance with the provisions of the Acts aforesaid, and the said Joint Resolution, and within the term of five years from the date hereof, as many emigrant families as he and his associates can settle within the said limits, to be hereinafter described as aforesaid, at the rate of one family for every section of one mile square, of vacant or unappropriated land within said limits: and, for this purpose, the party of the second part, and his associates, or their legal representatives, shall cause the unappropriated lands within the prescribed limits, to be surveyed as needed, for the purpose of settlement, into sections of six hundred and forty acres, or half sections of three hundred and twenty acres each, at their option, and shall cause to be built, from time to time, as needed, such number of log cabins, or small houses constructed of other materials, as circumstances shall require, for the comfortable accommodation of each family introduced and settled as aforesaid. The number of families to be settled in each of the five years, succeeding the date hereof, shall not be less than one hundred, in each and every year of the said term; and for the better and more definite description of what is meant by the term family, the following meaning shall be understood to be expressed thereby, viz: That each family shall consist of at least a man and his wife, or of a widower and two or more children, if males, under the age of seventeen years; if females, unmarried; or of a widow and two or more children, unless one be a son above seventeen years of age; in which case, one child shall suffice; or of two single men over the age of seventeen years.

And the party of the second part, and his associates, further covenant and agree with the Republic of Texas, the party of the first part, that as soon as they shall receive a title from the Government of the Republic, to any tract or tracts of 640 acres, or of 320 acres of land, for the introduction and settlement of the families aforesaid, they will convey to each and every family aforesaid, such number of acres of land, as shall be agreed between them, the said party of the second part, and his associates, and the said families respectively; but not less than 160 acres, nor more than 640 acres, to any one family; and that they will include in each deed of conveyance to a family, a clause of *defeasance*, requiring such family to enclose, with a good fence, and cultivate at least fifteen acres of the land, so conveyed; and to reside upon the same for three years, or forfeit their title to the Republic; or the party of the second part shall name the number of acres stipulated to be given to each family, as aforesaid, and request that the deed of conveyance be made therefor, to the several families respectively, or their legal representatives, directly from the Government of the Republic; and in that case, the deed for the remaining portion of a section, or of two half sections, as the party of the second part may desire; shall be made by the government to the said party, or their legal representatives.

And the party of the first part, in behalf of the Republic of Texas, hereby covenants and agree, with the party of the second part, their heirs, executors, administrators and assigns, or legal representatives, that they shall be authorized to introduce and settle emigrants within the limits hereinafter described, until they shall have settled therein, as many families as will entitle them to each and every alternate section of 640 acres; or to each and every alternate half section of 320 acres included, (as well as to all other sections,) therein, according to the terms and conditions herein provided. But the said party of the second part, shall not be required, in any case, to settle or receive, or purchase any lot or tract of land, section or half section, or fractional part of a section, which is not of fair quality, for agricultural purposes; or which is so far situated in the interior of a prairie, as to render it inconvenient for settlement: *provided*, however, that all the lands which have been legally located within the limits hereinafter prescribed, according to the provisions of subsisting and valid laws, shall not be settled, received, occupied or purchased, by the party of the second part, under, or by virtue of this contract: but no location within the said limits, made subsequent to the date of this contract, shall constitute any *bar* to the purchase or settlement of any part of the lands, hereby set apart and appropriated for colonization, by the second party to this contract, or their legal representatives.

And the said party of the first part, further covenants and agrees, in behalf of the Republic, to give, grant and convey, to the said party of the second part, and associates, or their legal representatives, one section of 640 acres of land, for each family; or two half sections of 320 acres, for each and every family, which they shall introduce and settle upon the lands hereinafter described and set apart for colonization: *provided*, that each alternate section or half section of 640 or 320 acres, shall be reserved to the Republic, to be purchased or not, by the party of the second part, on the terms hereinafter stipulated. And a full, absolute and perfect title shall be made, in the usual mode and form, to the party of the second part, or their legal representatives, for each and every section, half section, or other fractional part of a section, to which they may become entitled, under the provisions of this contract: and the same shall be conveyed to them as soon as, and whenever they shall exhibit, to the Commissioner of the General Land Office of this Republic, or other proper officer thereof, in manner and form hereinafter prescribed, the evidence of having surveyed the portion of land for which such conveyance is desired, and that there are comfortable small houses or cabins, erected thereon, and families residing therein, who have been settled thereon by the said party of the second part, or their legal representatives: the said party paying, or causing to be paid, the expenses of such conveyances, as provided by the act of the 4th February, 1841, as aforesaid. Or, if the said party of the second part shall so request, the government shall convey the title of such number of acres, as the party of the second part shall have stipulated to convey, to the several families respectively, to said families or their legal representatives, directly; and the title to the residue of each 640 acres, or of any fractional part thereof, shall be in such case or cases, made directly to the party of the second part, and their legal representatives.

And the said party of the first part, further covenants and agrees, on behalf of the Republic of Texas, that the said party of the second part shall be allowed, and receive from the Government, as a further compensation for their services, and recompense for their labor and expense in introducing and settling the families herein provided for, *a premium of ten sections of 640 acres, or twenty sections of 320 acres of land, for each and every hundred families introduced and settled as aforesaid; but no premium for any fractional number of one hundred families shall be allowed.* And, whenever due evidence shall be adduced, that the party of the second part, or their legal representatives, have settled one hundred families aforesaid, the said party or their legal representatives, shall select said premium sections within said limits, from among those reserved to the Republic: *provided*, That such selections shall be, where practicable, of continuous alternate sections, or fractional parts of sections, equivalent in extent to ten sections of 640 acres each; and a full and perfect title to said premium sections, so elected or chosen, shall be made to the party of the second part, or to their legal representatives from the Government of Texas.

And the said party of the first part, on the behalf of the Republic of Texas, further covenants and agrees, with the party of the second part, and their legal representatives, to give and grant to each settlement of one hundred families, made in pursuance of this contract, one section of 640 acres; to be located as near the centre of the settlement as practicable; and on the payment by such settlement, or by the said party of the second part, on their behalf of the sum of twelve dollars, in gold or silver specie, into the Treasury of the Republic, to grant one other section of six hundred and forty acres, to each settlement of one hundred families, in addition to the former; both to be conveyed directly to such settlement, to aid them in erecting the necessary buildings for religious public worship, and elementary or primary schools.

And the said party of the first part, in behalf of the Republic of Texas, further covenants and agrees, with the party of the second part, and their legal representatives, that, on paying into the Public Treasury, and obtaining the Treasurer's or other proper officer's receipt for twelve dollars, paid into the same; and also of the delivery for cancelment to the same, or other proper officer, of any bonds, promissory notes, or other audited liabilities of the Republic, to the amount of six hundred and forty dollars; the party of the second part, or their legal representatives, shall be entitled to demand, and shall receive from the government, a full and absolute title to six hundred and forty acres, of the alternate sections, reserved as aforesaid: *provided*, that previous to any such grant or conveyance, the said party of the second part, or their legal representatives, shall furnish due evidence that, for every section or fractional parts of a section, or sections, amounting to six hundred and forty acres of the reserved alternate sections, not comprehended in the twelve sections of every hundred, granted as premium sections, or for purposes of religious worship and schools, an emigrant family has been introduced and settled in the manner aforesaid; and for every part of a section stipulated to be granted to such family, a conveyance, if desired, shall be made directly to such family, or to their legal representatives, on the terms and conditions prescribed, as aforesaid, relative to the conveyances to be made to the families introduced and settled in the other sections, not reserved as aforesaid; and the conveyance for the residue of each alternate section, or of the balance remaining of the six hundred and forty acres of fractional sections, shall

Correspondence.

STOCKTON, CALIFORNIA, August 25, 1849.

W. H. Cushney, *Dear Sir:*—Since I last wrote you, I have visited the gold regions, and washed out some of the raw material—the pure gold itself. Large quantities of this precious metal are to be obtained by the process of digging and washing. If pounds could be generally procured by a single day's labor, as in some instances, it would be extremely gratifying; but this is seldom the case. Take it all in all, I would prefer some other business at even one half the profits. The labor, to render it lucrative, is worse than that applied in the digging of canals or the grading of railroads.

The prices of everything in the mining districts are high. Flour sells for 75 cents per pound, pilot bread 50 cents, raisins $1 00, sugar and coffee 50 cents, corn and barley, for horse feed, $37\frac{1}{2}$ cents, or $19 00 per bushel, a good size loaf of bread 75 cts., a bottle of whiskey $4 00, and a single meal $2 00. Lumber is selling for $500 per thousand feet. Freighting on pack mules to the mines, seventy miles, $20 00 per hundred pounds—on wagons $25 00. The trip is made to the diggings in three days by the usual mode of conveyance. A stage (uncovered wagon) has been running from here to the Sonorian camp, seventy miles, through in fourteen hours—charges $32 00.

I am domiciliated, at present, with our old friend J. F. Stephens, who has a store here, and has made $25,000 within the last five months. He will return to Texas rich.

Although there is much gambling going on here, the town is very quiet and orderly. Two men were hung lately for stealing.

Capt. Haynie's company* from Austin, arrived lately at the mines, and all well—George Evans in particular.

Alfred Luckett has had his trading house, at the Sonorian camp, burnt lately, and all his effects destroyed. Col. A. A. M. Jackson, Maj. Roman and Maj. Barry all have trading houses at the mines.

Mr. Stephens wishes to be remembered to you; and Dr. Wm. M. Shepherd, who is here, sends his regards to Mr. Shaw and all his old friends and associates now at Austin.

Yours truly,
CHAS. MARINER.

* Capt. Haynie, with his company, left Austin on the 18th April last, by way of Fredericksburg and El Paso. He has accomplished the distance from here to the mines, in about ninety days, including a delay of some time at El Paso.—*Editor.*

Chihuahua--Maj. Chevallie and the Indians.

We take the following information from a letter written by a citizen of Brazoria county, dated at the city of Chihuahua, July 6th, and published in the Civilian. We were reluctant to credit the report that Major C. had contracted with the authorities of Chihuahua, to furnish Indian scalps at a stipulated price for each. There is, however, no longer any room to doubt that such was the case. The correspondent says:

The Legislature of this State has authorized the employment of companies of rangers, or Indian hunters, upon these terms:—The members to arm themselves—to have no regular pay, but to receive $200 for the head of each Indian warrior, $100 for the head of each woman or child, and somewhat higher rewards for each prisoner, and to have all the plunder.

When Major Chevallie arrived here with the first company of emigrants to California, he entered the service upon these terms, and made two expeditions with a small company against the Indians. Many of the men were without the means of going on.—The fulfilment of the terms on the part of the government was guarantied by individuals of wealth and standing, and some of the more public spirited of the citizens, principally Americans, aided in fitting out the expedition. The result was the killing and capturing of I don't know now many men, women, and children, for whom the money was punctually paid—I never enquired the number. I was told by one of the company, that he saw a child no higher than his knee killed in cold blood and scalped. They also captured a number of horses and mules.—The members of the company made some $300 apiece by the operation. Not one of their number was wounded. In one of their expeditions, they went more than one hundred miles to an encampment where there were between 150 and 300 Indians, and at daylight charged into it.

Chevallie has withdrawn from this business. He started on to California—not far from town shot himself accidentally—was brought back, and is still here, not entirely recovered from the effects of the wound.

Another company is out under John Glanton from San Antonio. It numbers perhaps 30 men. They expect to go some 200 miles to find the Indians. They are splendidly mounted and armed. Many of the young men in our company had made up their minds to go on this heat, and would have done so but for my remonstrances.

Heretofore the Apaches have been friendly with the emigrants. They have shown this disposition in more than one instance where they have encountered small parties. Now it is war to the knife. They avow it, and swear they will have vengeance.—Now we shall have to move with caution and in force, and may expect all stragglers to be cut off.

From Santa Fe.

Advices from Santa Fe as late as the 9th ult., have been received at St. Louis.

Fort Bent was a short time ago surrounded by Indians and burnt. William Bent and several other Americans are supposed to have been murdered. The Indians are represented to be very hostile to the whites, and have been very troublesome to travellers.

At Santa Fe preliminary meetings had taken place for the purpose of holding a Convention, in order to form a State Government.

The Indians lately stole 200 Government horses at Los Vegos, and burned two Americans.

The Science of Mining.

The mines of California have baffled all science, and rendered the application of philosophy entirely nugatory. Bone and sinew philosophy, with a sprinkling of good luck, can alone render success certain. We have met with many geologists and practical scientific men in the mines, and have invariably seen them beaten by unskilled men, soldiers and sailors and the like. The simple secret is that gold has been thrown about promiscuously by volcanic power, and distributed along the margin of streams and in river beds by mountain torrents, and it is the hard-working and lucky man who may restore it.—*Placer Times.*

The mother and sisters of John Mitchel, the Irish patriot, lately arrived in Philadelphia. They will probably reside with their son and brother, W. H. Mitchel, who has an office in one of the Departments at Washington.

☞ Col. Martin K. Snell has been removed, and Isaac E. Wade appointed Postmaster at Houston.

A Description of California.

A California correspondent of the N. Y. Tribune draws the following picture of El Dorado:

Why have Col. Fremont, Farnham and others so studiously misrepresented this parched, barren, mountainous country? The entire Northern portion of Upper California is inferior to New England in every respect, while the Southern half of the same territory is baked and burned by a scathing, scorching sun for nine months in the year, without rain or dews and deluged during the other three.

The timber is sparse and almost valueless. It is so dry, that a tree of one-and-a-half or two feet diameter will become thoroughly seasoned in forty-eight hours after cutting.

Ought intelligent, fore-handed farmers to be induced to leave comfortable homes and bring their families to a land, however rich in mineral wealth, where Indians positively cannot live?

The harvest of gold will be gathered in two years, and the gleanings will be poor indeed. After that, woe unto him whose cupidity or stupidity brings him hither.

Latest from California.

The steamship Falcon arrived at New Orleans on the 4th inst., having made the run from Chagres in five days and eighteen hours—the quickest passage on record. She brought $70,000 in gold dust.

The dates by the Falcon are from San Francisco to Sept. 1st.

The number of miners multiplied during the month of August. There are no accounts of large pieces being found. The streams are low. New washings have been discovered and old ones abandoned.

A party is operating with sub-marine armour in the middle fork of the Sacramento. They think when they get their apparatus fairly at work, they will average $10,000 per day. Two steamers are plying on the Sacramento. There had been considerable sickness at the mines, at last accounts. At San Francisco the general health was good.

A severe diarrhœa, believed by some to be the cholera in a mild form, and by others to be the precursor of that disease, had caused a good deal of suffering.

A new tri-weekly paper called the Pacific News has been established at San Francisco. Improvements are going on with remarkable rapidity. New wharves are being built to facilitate the landing of goods.

There are six churches in full activity in San Francisco.

Quicksilver is known to be very abundant in the territory and some of the richest mines are to be wrought forthwith.

A theatre is about to be built at San Francisco, and a Merchants' Exchange was being opened at last advices.

Texas Cotton Crop.

Our information from every section of the State, enables us to state positively, that the yield of cotton will fall one half short of the reasonable expectations of the planters. The causes have been mentioned from time to time, and we need not repeat. The picking goes on rapidly, and the planter will find time this year to enjoy the holidays.—*Houston Advertiser.*

Texas Sugar Crop.

Preparations are rapidly making to commence sugar grinding. The crop is remarkably heavy and forward, and by taking the cane by the forelock before Jack Frost makes his appearance, the yield will be great and the sugar of a fine quality.—*Hous. Adv.*

Yucatan.

Late accounts from Yucatan *via* Havana, represent that the Governor and people were much agitated by a report that England was about to intervene with arms for the pacification of the peninsula, by virtue of a contract with the President of the Republic, on condition that the port of Bacalar and its jurisdiction be ceded to England. A communication, it is said, had been received by the Governor of Yucatan, from the Mexican Minister of Foreign relations, embracing the project of pacification initiated by the British Government, one feature of which is said to be, that a portion of the peninsula be ceded to the Indians, where they may live entirely independent of the Spanish race, governing themselves under British protection. This looks like another ambitious project on the part of Great Britain, and so it appears to be considered in Yucatan, as it is stated that the government of the peninsula will reject the intervention on the proposed basis. The progress of events in the peninsula, and the action of the British agents should be closely watched by the cabinet at Washington. The little speck in that quarter may soon become a portentous cloud, threatening severe injury to the interests of the United States. Has Secretary Clayton any time, now he has so many difficulties with foreign powers on his hands, to pay some attention to British intrigues for obtaining a predominating influence in the immense extent of country bordering on the Gulf, and stretching from Mexico to the Isthmus of Panama? We shall see.—*N. O. Courier.*

California Mail Routes.

The Special Mail Agent for California and Oregon, advertises in the Alta California for proposals to carry the mails from the 1st of October, 1849, to the 30th of October, 1850, between the following places:

1. From San Francisco, weekly, *via* Benicia and Sutterville, to Sacramento City and back.
2. From San Francisco, weekly, to Stockton and back.
3. From Sacramento City, weekly, to Vernon and back.
4. From Sacramento City, weekly, to Culloma and back.
5. From San Francisco, weekly, *via* Pueblo San José, to Monterey and back.
6. From Monterey, weekly, *via* Santa Barbara, to Pueblo Los Angeles, and back.
7. From Pueblo Los Angeles, weekly, to San Diego and back.
8. From Benicia, weekly, *via* Napa, to Sonoma and back.

☞ The New York Express, a whig paper, alluding to M. Poussin's recall, says:

"We fear there are Cabinet social difficulties deeper than any of those things which have led to, or stimulated this quarrel.—We hear of scenes somewhat similar to those which occurred in the early part of General Jackson's administration."

A Republic converted into a Monarchy, and a President turned Emperor!

A matter of very serious import, ridiculous though it may appear, in these times of tottering thrones and fallen kingdoms, has come to pass in the Negro Republic of Hayti. Late accounts from that Island represent the astonishing fact that the Republic of Hayti has become an Empire! and the President Soulouque declared an Emperor, by legislative enactment! *King* Soulouque was invested with the Imperial Crown on Sunday, the 26th ult., at the Catholic Church, in presence of the people, and with all the "pomp and circumstance" of royalty. The event was gotten up by the legislative council of the Island, not "by and with the advice and consent" of the people, who, it seems, were taken by surprise, and amazed at the movement, but with the aid and "fraternization" of the troops. What the issue will be, of such singular proceeding, it is impossible to divine. A Republic changed into a Monarchy is something very notable in this age of enlightenment and progressive democracy.

☞ Semi-official letters from Belyrane state that Dembinski was far from intending to imitate the conduct of Georgey, as he had determined to fight to the last, but that the flight of Kossuth had compelled him to relinquish the idea. The last interview between Kossuth and Georgey was very bitter. All Kossuth's eloquence and presence of mind is said to have forsook him, and next day he was in full flight for the Turkish territory, and Georgey for the Russian camp.

The Question.

The only question, therefore, which the people should really and truly discuss is: Does Austin possess sufficient facilities for the people, or does some other place possess them in such greater degree as to warrant the expense incidental to such removal, and the loss that must inevitably accrue to the State in the value of the public buildings and lands now owned by the State at Austin, and which of course will, by the removal, be rendered entirely valueless?—*Houston Gazette.*

☞ Over twelve hundred sheep have just been driven in from Illinois. They are full-blood Merino. The wool clipped from this flock last season brought $37\frac{1}{2}$ cents per lb. in market. They belong to Mr. Clinton Harris, and will be pastured in Grimes county. By furnishing fine fleece breeders, this flock will prove a great desideratum to Texian wool-growers.—*Houston Advertiser.*

A Big Lump.

Maunsel, White & Co., of New Orleans, received a lump of gold from California, by the Falcon, weighing fifty ounces—all in one solid mass, picked out at one dig. The value of this lump is $800.

The health of Houston remains good. Business has opened with unusual activity. Our merchants are receiving a heavy stock of merchandise. Cotton is coming in freely. Many wagons are in from the interior, which go out heavily laden with goods. Our steamboats are plying regularly in the Bayou, with heavy freights. We notice considerable improvement going on in various parts of the city.—*Houston Presbyterian.*

Meteorological Observations---Austin City.

OCTOBER, 1849.		THERMOMETER.				WIND.	REMARKS.
		SUNRISE.	NOON.	SUNSET.	MEDIUM.		
T.	11,	56	78	78	$70\frac{2}{3}$	South.	Clear,
F.	12,	61	83	$81\frac{1}{2}$	75	SW, S, E, NE.	Clear, [showers
S.	13,	64	$74\frac{1}{2}$	74	$70\frac{2}{3}$	NE, E, SSE.	Cloudy and occasional
Sun.	14,	72	79	$65\frac{1}{2}$	72	SSW, W, NW	" and much rain.
M.	15,	56	$63\frac{1}{2}$	59	$59\frac{1}{3}$	North.	Clear,
T.	16,	46	67	64	59	"	Clear,
W.	17,	45	70	68	61	"	Clear,

Official.

Qualifications and Resignations reported to the State Department, since the 13th October, 1849.

ANDERSON COUNTY.

A. E. McClure, elected District Clerk, July 13, 1846; qualified July 25, 1846.
William Jones, Notary Public; qualified Oct. 3, 1846.
James M. Perry, do. do. March 30, 1849.
Darius H. Edens, Surveyor, elected Feb. 10, 1849; qualified Feb. 20, 1849.
William R. Anglin, Justice of the Peace, prect. No. , elected Feb. 10, 1849; qualified Feb. 23, 1849.

CHEROKEE COUNTY.

John Conner, District Clerk, elected July 13, 1846; qualified August 1, 1846.
Nathaniel Killough, Notary Public, qualified November 6, 1846.
Stockton P. Donley, do. do. ———.
Jesse Gibson, Assessor, elected August 6, 1849; qualified Aug. 20, 1849.
W. W. Wilburn, J. P., prect. No. 3, elected Aug. 6, 1849; qualified Aug. 20, '49.
W. L. Coleman, J. P., prect. No. 3, elected Aug. 6, 1849; qualified Aug. 20, '49.

FORT BEND COUNTY.

Thompson H. McMahan, District Clerk, elected July 13, 1846; resigned March —, 1848.
George W. McMahan, Notary Public, removed from County, March —, 1848.
Philemon T. Herbert, do. do. do. April —, 1849.
John S. Peck, Surveyor, elected, Nov. 7, 1848, resigned, April —, 1849.

HOUSTON COUNTY.

Riley B. Wallace, District Clerk, elected Sept. 7, 1846; qualified Sept. 18, 1846.

JACKSON COUNTY.

Nicholas McNutt, District Clerk, elected July 13, 1846; qualified July 30, 1846.

LEON COUNTY.

William Keguin, District Clerk, elected July 13, 1846; qualified July —, 1846.
David M. Brown, Notary Public, qualified Oct. 12, 1846.
Henry Tiebout, do. do. Feb. 1, 1848.
Thomas W. Blake, do do. Nov. 21, 1848.
John Patrick, do. do. Nov. 27, 1848.
George W. Ellis, do. do. May 10, 1849.
David M. Brown, do. resigned ———.

RUSK COUNTY.

John P. Grigsby, District Clerk, elected July 13, 1846; qualified July 23, 1846.
J. B. Oliver, Notary Public; qualified July 24, 1848.
John McClarty, do. do. May 16, 1849.
Julien S. Devereux, County Commissioner, elected Aug. 7, 1848; qualified——.
S. Slade Barnett, do. do. do. ——.
William M. Ross, do. do. do. ——.
Mark Stroud, do. do. do. ——.

WALKER COUNTY.

Jesse W. Wilson, District Clerk, elected ; qualified Nov. 13, 1837.
John S. Besser, Notary Public, qualified, Sept. 8, 1846.
Josiah Merritt, do. do. Aug. 3, 1846.
Isaac Tousey, do. do do. 13, 1846.
George W. Rogers, do. do. January 11, 1847.
Joseph W. Hackett, do. do. March 3, 1847.
W. H. Davis, Justice of the Peace, prect. No. , elected ; qualified Oct. 19, '49.

WASHINGTON COUNTY.

William Love, Notary Public; qualified Sept. 28, 1846.
Moses Park, do. do. do. 27, do.
Stephen R. Roberts, do. do. July 27, 1846.
Lozenski Gilbert, do. do. Sept. 2, 1846.
Robert B. Wells, do. do. July 31, 1847.
David M. Estis, Coroner, elected ; qualified, August 27, 1849.
Lozenski Gilbert, Notary Public; died June 6, 1847.
Robert B. Wells, do. resigned Feb. 19, 1849.
Moses Park, do. do. Oct. 18, 1849.

The Texian Advocate.

PUBLISHED WEEKLY BY JOHN D. LOGAN AND THOMAS STERNE, AT $3 IN ADVANCE, $4 IN SIX MONTHS, OR $5 AT THE END OF THE YEAR.

Vol. 5. VICTORIA, TEXAS, FRIDAY, JUNE 21, 1850. No. 8.

Statement of the Officers of the Expedition under Gen. Lopez.

To all who may be concerned, be it known, that the undersigned, officers of the Liberating Army of Cuba, being desirous of rendering General Don N. Lopez, commander-in-chief of said army, the amplest justice, do, freely and voluntarily, make the following statements of events and facts, viz:

At the time we embarked on the Isle of Women, where we went to join Colonel O'Hara, and remained there some time for the purpose of filling our water casks, Gen. Lopez, on learning that some men were displeased with the object of the expedition, issued a general order, stating that all those that were unwilling to follow him, could return to the United States in the barque Georgiana, where they would find provisions and all necessaries for the voyage. In accordance with that order, some thirty men were embarked on the Georgiana, and the rest, to the number of six hundred and nine, rank and file, including the General, went into the steamer Creole, and left for Cardenas. We arrived in Cuba and landed at the town of Cardenas, of which we took possession, capturing the Governor, and the garrison joined us, with the exception of the officers, as soon as they were informed of our motives, stating that they did not know Gen. Lopez during the fight.

We entered the town about half past four o'clock, A. M., having had some delay in landing on account of the boat being aground near the wharf, which delay caused our landing to be discovered by the people of the town and reported to the Governor, who immediately ordered the garrison under arms, and prepared to defend themselves and the town. Gen. Lopez, knowing that there were some enemies around the town, and and having to send the steamer water and coal necessary for her to return to some port in the United States, was compelled to remain in the town all day to protect the boat and crew, and some wounded men, who were to be sent back on the steamer, several men and officers having been wounded in taking the town in the morning.

The difficulty in getting the coal and water on board of the boat, gave the enemy ample time to destroy the railroad, so that it was impossible to leave by means of it, and, as we understand by the General himself, he being aware that the steamer could not be ready to leave before 8 or 9 o'clock P. M., he thought convenient to change his plan of operations, and evacuate the place, embarking the men on board the steamer, and effecting a landing in some other part of the Island of Cuba.

As the troops were withdrawing from the town, they were attacked by a small body of Lancers, and a promiscuous assemblage of armed persons on foot, according to the observation of our officers, or by twenty-two lancers and forty-five infantry, according to the report of a prisoner taken that evening, and of those who turned on our side in the morning—all of which force were repulsed with great loss, allowing our column to embark in good order, on board the steamer. This being done, at 9 o'clock P. M. we got out to sea, and after getting some short distance out in the bay, the boat got aground, and as there was ample time to receive intelligence in Mantanzas, of our landing in Cardenas, and considering that any delay would bring the most disastrous consequences, by the arrival of some armed vessel from Mantanzas while we were aground, therefore, it was of the last importance to lighten the steamer at any sacrifice, rather than endanger the lives of all in a defenceless and desperate situation.

Consequently, an order was given to lighten the boat, and some provisions and a large quantity of ammunition was thrown overboard, leaving only some 30,000 rounds, beside those each private had. At daybreak the boat was afloat, and after getting out of the bay, the steamer stood in a northeastern direction, until she was entirely out of sight, when she changed her course to the west. At about 8 o'clock in the morning General Lopez learned from one of the field officers that many of the men were dissatisfied and wanted to be returned to the United States, using their rights as American citizens. To which General Lopez replied that he intended to communicate to the field officers the change in his plan of operations. Soon after, the field officers assembled in the General's quarters, and after hearing that the object was to effect another landing at Mantua, (west of Havanna,) where he had many friends that would assist him, and where there was no garrison at all, and by the manœuvre divert the attention of the government of the Island, which was already called to the east of Havana. A majority approved the plans of General Lopez, and the dissenting gave it to be understood that they were willing to follow the General, provided they could be assured of a similar willingness of all on board. The question then arose as to whether there was any such willingness. The result of an investigation as to the sense of our whole force on the subject was, that about three-fourths of our whole number refused to land again on the Island of Cuba, without reinforcements of men and artillery, and being short of ammunition, they insisted upon being conveyed to Key West. The reserved rights of men required that should be the course pursued. Gen. Lopez opposed it strongly, on the ground that he had left New Orleans for Cuba, and that he would remain there at the risk of his life; for if we were to go to Key West, or any other point of the United States, the vessel would be confiscated, and other consequences, which would ruin the whole affair. Some time afterwards, one of the officers asked Gen. Lopez whether he had given any orders to the captain of the boat as to the course she should pursue. To which General Lopez replied, "yes, to Mantua." The officers stated that the men were very uneasy and dissatisfied, and determined to go to Key West. General Lopez still objected to it, further saying, that he could not go from Key West to Cuba, on account of the reasons already given, and also of the danger of meeting some Spanish man-of-war; but if the men had decided they ought to give such orders to the Captain, he would not.

Consequently, the order was given to the Captain of the boat, and some men posted by the compass to prevent any deviation from Key West. Just as we were near Key West, we saw a Spanish steamer of war, (the Pizarro,) pursuing us so closely, that we could hardly have escaped, had she not got aground, and remained so for half an hour. However, we had only time to get into the bay, close to the town, for she came in nearly the same moment. After landing here, the boat was seized by the Government, and the men went ashore with their baggage, &c. In the delicate position in which General Lopez was placed, he has done all in his power to facilitate means of transportation for these men, having also placed in the hands of the field officers eighty-six doubloons, which money was taken from the treasury at Cardenas, and counted before many witnesses, and for which he gave a receipt to the Collector of said place. This money went to attend mainly to the wants and necessities of the wounded.

We conclude this by simply adding that our respects for Gen. Lopez is unbounded, and that it was with the most poignant sense of regret that we found ourselves unable to carry out the General's views, especially since they were coupled with entreaty, and imploring us to land himself and personal friends, together with the Spanish troops that joined us there in Cardenas, even should we leave him there without any of our force.—*Mobile Register*, 1st.

Singular Occurrence.—We learn from a very reliable source, that not many weeks —it may have been years—since a married man residing in Charleston went home rather unexpectedly one night, and on entering his accustomed room found all in darkness, but from the quiet breathings of the "partner of his cares and joys," knew that she was there, and began to disrobe himself preparatory to retiring. He had not proceeded far in this operation, when the wife awoke, and called out, as if alarmed—

"Who's there?"

"It's only me, my dear."

"What, you, husband? I did not expect —oh—I'm so glad you have come—I'm in such dreadful pain—do run to the apothecary for a little laudanum—or paragoric—or peppermint—do, dear, quick—oh!—oh!"

And the woman appeared in such agony, that the husband became really alarmed, and quickly donning some of his attire again, started, without his coat, post haste for the medicine.

Reaching the apothecary shop, he procured the curatives, and proceeded to pay for them, when, in feeling in his pockets he hauled out what he at first supposed was a silver half dollar—but on examination, it proved, to his amazement, to be a *twenty dollar gold piece*. Wondering how such a piece of money came into his pocket, he delved again, and lo! another double eagle appeared!—again was the operation repeated—and again—with similar results—so that he found himself the mysterious possessor of the snug sum of two hundred dollars in gold when he thought he was not worth as many cents. We may as well here state, in order to avoid any apparent incongruity, that as double eagles have but lately appeared from the mint, this curious affair must have been of recent occurrence.

Pleased—gratified—yet nevertheless a little alarmed, but much more astonished at this sudden windfall, our hero returned hurriedly to his domicil to dose his better half, and to acquaint her with his remarkable good fortune. Scarcely had he entered the room, however, before he found that his lovely wife had entirely recovered, and, at the same moment, the astounding fact was made known to him that *he had on another man's pantaloons*.

Almost paralyzed with this discovery, he yet managed to examine further, and discovered that *his* inexpressibles were missing—together with his coat,—but in place of the latter, an elegant blue broadcloth garment was left, which from the amount of gilt buttons, and the peculiar devices upon them, rendered it pretty certain that its rightful owner belonged to Uncle Sam's naval service.

What transpired afterwards we do not know—but the "net-work of complicated circumstances" seemed to point with irresistible force to an act of conjugal infidelity, which the moral sense of this community is sometimes shocked in being compelled to read of.—*Boston Herald.*

A Rational Dutchman.—An honest and pious Dutchman, in training up his son in the way he should go, frequently exercised him in Bible lessons. On one of these occasions, he asked him:

"Who vas dat vat vould not shleep mit Botipher's vife?"

"Shoseph."

"Dat's a coot boy? Val, vat vas te reason vy he vould not shleep mit her?"

"Don't know—shpose he had anudder voman whom he vas engaged to sleep mit."

Seeing the Elephant.—The St. Louis Intelligencer says that no less than eighty returning California emigrants came passengers on the St. Paul from St. Joseph.—The majority of them made a start across the Plains, met with the elephant, counted the two rings on his tail, were satisfied, and backed out.

"If you ever marry," said a Roman Consul to his son, "let it be to a woman who has judgment enough to superintend the getting of a meal of victuals—taste enough to dress herself—pride enough to wash her face before breakfast, and sense enough to hold her tongue when she has nothing to say."

"Sealed proposals," as the chap said when he kissed his sweetheart.

Making Diamonds.—Chemistry has long since discovered that the purest diamonds were nothing but carbon, and they have been reduced into this latter by the action of heat. The question has frequently been asked, if *diamonds* can be changed into *carbon*, why *carbon* cannot be changed into *diamonds?* This question, it appears by the following article, from the Paris Correspondence of the London *Times*, has at last been satisfactorily answered, and henceforth we suppose diamonds will be as abundant as charcoal, and when we see one of the large black wagons with an hundred or more bushels of this latter article traveling through our streets, we may imagine it is on the way to some diamond manufactory. So soon as the art becomes perfected, we shall no doubt have pure qualities of carbon shaped out into the form of water and wine glasses, decanters, salt-holders, plates and dishes, and having undergone the needful process, thus obtain entire dinner services of pure diamonds. With the aid of gas lights they would certainly make a most brilliant display.

The writer for the *Times* says:

"The scientific world has been in a state of commotion during the whole week, in consequence of the publication of the discovery of the long sought for secret of the fusion and crystallization of carbon. The Sorbonne had been crowded for the last few days to behold the result of this discovery in the shape of a tolerably sized diamond of great lustre, which M. Desprezt, the happy discoverer, submits to the examination of every chemist or savant who chooses to visit him. He declares that so long ago as last autumn he had succeeded in producing the diamond, but in such minute particles as to be visible only through the microscope, and, fearful of raising irony and suspicion, he had kept the secret, until, by dint of repeated experiments and great labor, he had completed the one he now offers to public view. Four solar lens of immense power, aided by the tremendous galvanic pile of the Sorbonne, have been the means of producing the result now before us. M. Desprezt holds himself ready to display the experiment whenever it may be required. The diamond produced is of the quality known in the East as the black diamond, one single specimen of which was sold by Prince Rostoff to the late duke of York, for the enormous sum of twelve thousand pounds.

A Touching Story.—The following beautiful and touching story was related by Dr. Schnebly, of Maryland, at a meeting held in New York, to hear the experience of twenty reformed drunkards:

"A drunkard, who had run through with his property, returned home one night to his unfurnished house. He entered his empty hall—anguish was gnawing at his heart-strings, and language is inadequate to express his agony as he entered his wife's apartment, and there beheld the victims of his appetite, his lovely wife and darling child. Morose and sullen, he seated himself without a word; he could not speak; he could not look upon them. The mother said to the angel by her side, "Come, my child, it is time to go to bed," and the little babe, as was her wont, knelt by her mother's lap, and gazing wistfully into the face of her suffering parent like a piece of chiseled statuary, slowly repeated her nightly orison; and when she had finished, (she was but four years of age,) said to her mother, 'Dear ma, may I not offer up one more prayer?' 'Yes, yes, my sweet pet, pray!' And she lifted up her tiny hands, closed her eyes, and prayed: 'O God, spare my dear papa!'

That prayer was wafted up with electric rapidity to the throne of God. It was heard —it was heard. The responsive "Amen!" burst from the father's lips, and his heart of stone became a heart of flesh. Wife and child were both clasped to his bosom, and in penitence he said, "My child, you have saved your father from the grave of a drunkard. I'll sign the pledge."

Horrible Suicide.—A correspondent of the Boston Transcript, writing from Nashua, N. H., under date of the 14th ultimo, says:

I have just returned from a horrible sight indeed—the drunkard suicide and his murdered child. Scarcely recovered from the shock of a suicide in the case of a hard drinker by the name of Foster, at the close of last week, we were quite unprepared for the still more tragic scene of this morning. There lies the father, (a Mr. Allen,) ghastly in death, just cut down from the fatal cord; and there, mute in helpless innocency, lies the corpse of his little daughter, two years old to-day, the youngest of eleven children, just strangled by the murderous hand of the father, by means of a cord that had cut through the skin, and nearly separated the head from the body. All this was done while the wife and mother had gone, at 5 o'clock in the morning, to an upper chamber to dress the diseased limb of a sick and suffering daughter.

One day last week the discouraged and distressed wife said to the husband; "We cannot live so. If you will not do anything for the support of yourself and family, and if you will continue to take the children's earning to buy rum, I must make complaint to the Selectmen," (putting on her bonnet to go.) "If you will wait till next Tuesday," replied the drunken husband, "I will either go to work or take myself out of the way." Tuesday came, and its deeds are done. And now when the worthless carcass of the drunken suicide shall have been buried, he will be "out of the way." But who shall pluck the sting out of that mother's heart? There she sits, with her dead baby in her arms, anxiously waiting the magic work of the daguerreotype. "Oh, give me at least this," she said, "all that will soon remain of my child."

Lord Byron once said "with all his follies, he was never guilty of stopping his paper because its editors happened to displease him.

Crops in Arkansas.—From every section of the State (says the Little Rock Gazette, of the 24th ultimo,) the accounts are very unfortunate. A letter dated Plum Bayou, Jefferson county, says:

The prospect for crops is any thing but flattering in these parts. I do not know of a farm where they have not had to plant their cotton a second time, and it is doubtful whether we will get stands this time or not. It still continues wet and cold. Corn stands are also bad. It is not possible for a full crop of cotton to be made now, as a full month of the cotton season is already lost.

Another letter, of the same date, from Arkadelphia, Clark county, says:

It has been raining here for a month, almost every day, and sometimes it pours.—Stands of cotton, as a general thing, in South Arkansas, are very bad, and of corn, worse. The birds take it up as fast as it comes up. Some of our planters have planted three or four times, and have no stands yet.

BY AUTHORITY.

Public Acts

Passed during the first session of the Thirty-first Congress.

[Public—No. 4.]

AN ACT, Providing for the taking of the Seventh and subsequent Censuses of the United States, and to fix the number of the members of the House of Representatives, and provide for their future apportionment among the several States.

1.—OF THE DUTIES, LIABILITIES, AND COMPENSATION OF MARSHALS.

Be it enacted by the Senate and House of Representatives of the United States of America, in Congress assembled, That the marshals of the several districts of the United States, including the District of Columbia and the Territories, are hereby required respectively to cause all the inhabitants to be enumorated, and to collect all the other statistical information within their respective districts, in the manner provided for in this act, and specified in the instructions which shall be given by the Secretary of the Interior, and in the tables annexed, and to return the same to the said Secretary on or before the first day of November next ensuing, omitting from the enumeration of the inhabitants Indians not taxed; also, at the discretion of said Secretary, any part or all the statistics of the Territories except those of population: *Provided, however,* And if the time assigned for making the returns shall prove inadequate for the Territories, the said Secretary may extend the same; *Provided, further,* If there be any district or Territory of the United States in which there is no marshal of the United States, the President shall appoint some suitable person to discharge the duties assigned by this act to marshals.

Sec. 2. *And be it further enacted,* That each of said marshals shall, before entering upon his duties, take and subscribe the following oath or affirmation, before any circuit or district judge of the United States, or before any judge of any State court, to wit:

I, marshal of the district of , do solemnly swear (or affirm,) that I will to the best of my ability enumerate, or cause to be enumerated, all the inhabitants of said district, and will collect, or cause to be collected, the other statistical information within the same, and will faithfully perform all the duties enjoined on me by the act providing for the taking of the seventh census. And when duly authenticated by the said judge, he shall deposite a copy thereof, so authenticated, with the said Secretary of the Interior, and no marshal shall discharge any of the duties herein required, until he has taken and subscribed this oath, and forwarded a copy as aforesaid.

Sec. 3 *And be it further enacted,* That each marshal shall separate his district into subdivisions containing not exceeding twenty thousand persons in each, unless the limitation to that number causes inconvenient boundaries, in which case the number may be larger; and shall also estimate, from the best sources of information which he is able to obtain, the number of square miles in each subdivision, and transmit the same to the Department of the Interior: *Provided, however,* That in bounding such subdivisions, the limits thereof shall be known as civil divisions, such as county, parish, township, town, ward or district lines, or highways, or natural boundaries, such as rivers, lakes, &c.

Sec. 4. *And be it further enacted,* That each marshal shall appoint an assistant for each subdivision, who is a resident therein, to whom he shall give a commission under his hand, authorizing him to perform the duties herein assigned to assistants, which commission shall set forth the boundaries of the subdivision, of which appointment so made, and the boundaries so specified, the marshal shall keep a true and faithful record

Sec. 5. *And be it further enacted,* That each marshal shall seasonably supply each assistant with the instructions issued by the Department of the Interior, the blanks provided for the enumeration of the population, and the collection of other statistics, and give to him from time to time all such information and directions as may be necessary to enable him to discharge his duty. He shall carefully examine whether the returns of each assistant marshal be made in conformity with the terms of this act, and where discrepancies are detected, require the same to be corrected. He shall dispose of the two sets of the returns required from the assistant marshals as hereinafter provided for, as follows: one set he shall transmit forthwith to the Secretary of the Interior; and the other copy thereof he shall transmit to the office of the Secretary of State or Territory to which his district belongs. He shall classify and determine the rate of compensation to be paid to each assistant marshal according to the provisions of this act, subject to the final approval of the Secretary of the Interior. He shall from time to time make himself acquainted with the progress made by each assistant marshal in the discharge of his duties, and in case of inability or neglect arising from sickness, or otherwise, appoint a substitute.

Sec. 6. *And be it further enacted,* That if any marshal shall, by any arrangement or understanding whatever, secure to himself any fee, reward, or compensation for the appointment of an assistant, or shall in any way secure to himself any part of the compensation provided by this act for the services of assistants, or if he shall knowingly neglect or refuse to perform the duties herein assigned to him, he shall, in any such case, be deemed guilty of a misdemeanor, and if convicted in any such case, shall for such offence forfeit and pay not less than one thousand dollars.

Sec. 7. *And be it further enacted,* That any marshal of the United States may, for any purpose not inconsistent with the duties of the assistants herein provided for, appoint a deputy or deputies, to act in his behalf, but for all official acts of such deputy or deputies, the marshal shall be responsible: *Provided, however,* An appointment to collect the social statistics shall not be deemed an interference with the duties of the assistants.

Sec. 8. *And be it further enacted,* That whenever the population returned in any district shall exceed one million, the marshal thereof shall be entitled to receive as a compensation for all his services in executing this act, after the rate of one dollar for each thousand persons; but if the number returned shall be less than a million in any district, the marshal thereof shall be allowed for his services at the rate of one dollar and twenty-five cents for each thousand persons: *Provided, however,* that no marshal shall receive less than two hundred and fifty dollars; and when the compensation does not in the whole exceed the sum of five hundred dollars, a reasonable allowance for clerk hire shall be made, the amount whereof shall be determined by the Secretary of the Interior: *And provided, further,* That the marshal of any district may at his discretion perform the duties of an assistant in any subdivision in which he may reside, and when he shall personally perform the duties assigned by this act to assistants, he shall receive therefor the compensation allowed to assistants for like services.

II.—OF ASSISTANTS, THEIR DUTIES, LIABILITIES, AND COMPENSATION.

Sec. 9. *And be it further enacted,* That no assistant shall be deemed qualified to enter upon his duties, until he shall have received from the marshal, under his hand, such a commission as is provided for in this act, and shall take and subscribe the following oath or affirmation, which shall be thereon endorsed, to wit:

I, , an assistant to the marshal of the district of , do solemnly swear (or affirm) that I will make a true and exact enumeration of all the inhabitants within the district assigned to me, and will also faithfully collect the other statistics therein, in the manner provided for in the act for taking the seventh census, and in conformity with all lawful instructions which I may receive, and will make due and correct returns thereof as required in said act. (Signed.) Which said oath, or affirmation, may be administered by any judge of a court of record, or any justice of the peace empowered to administer oaths, and a copy thereof duly authenticated shall be forwarded to the marshal by such assistant, before he proceeds to the business of the appointment.

Sec. 10. *And be it further enacted,* That each assistant, when duly qualified in manner aforesaid, shall perform the service required of him by a personal visit to each dwelling house, and to each family, in the sub-division assigned to him, and shall ascertain, by inquiries made of some member of each family, if any one can be found capable of giving the information, but if not, then of the agent of such family, the name of each member thereof, the age and place of birth of each, and all the other particulars specified in this act, the tables thereto subjoined, and the instructions of the Secretary of the Interior; and shall also visit personally the farms, mills, shops, mines, and other places respecting which information is required as above specified, in his district, and shall obtain all such information from the best and most reliable sources; and when in either case the information is obtained and entered on the tables, as obtained, till the same is complete, then such memoranda shall be immediately read to the person or persons furnishing the facts, to correct errors and supply omissions if any shall exist.

Sec. 11. *And be it further enacted,* That each assistant shall, within one month after the time specified for the completion of the enumeration, furnish the original census returns to the clerk of the county court of their respective counties, and two copies, duly compared and corrected, to the marshal of the district. He shall affix his signature to each page of the schedules before he returns them to his marshal, and on the last page thereof shall state the whole number of pages in each return, and certify that they were well and truly made according to the tenor of his oath of office.

Sec. 12. *And be it further enacted,* That each assistant shall be allowed as compensation for his services after the rate of two cents for each person enumerated, and ten cents a mile for necessary travel, to be ascertained by multiplying the square root of the number of dwelling-houses in the division by the square root of the number of square miles in each division, and the product shall be taken as the number of miles traveled, for all purposes, in taking this census.

Sec. 13. *And be it further enacted,* That in addition to the compensation allowed for the enumeration of the inhabitants, there shall be paid for each farm fully returned, ten cents; for each establishment of productive industry, fully taken and returned, fifteen cents; for the social statistics, two per cent. upon the amount allowed for the enumeration of population, and for each name of a deceased person returned, two cents: *Provided, however,* That in making returns, of farms and establishments of productive industry, the instructions given by the Secretary of the Interior must be strictly observed, and no allowance shall be made for any return not authorized by such instructions, or for any returns not limited to the year next preceding the first of June next.

Sec. 14. *And be it further enacted,* That any assistant who, having accepted the appointment, shall, without justifiable cause, neglect, or refuse to perform the duties enjoined on him by this act, shall be guilty of a misdemeanor, and upon conviction be liable to a forfeiture of five hundred dollars; or if he shall wilfully make a false oath, it shall be deemed perjury; or if he shall wilfully make a false certificate, it shall be deemed a misdemeanor, and if convicted or found guilty of either of the last named offences, he shall forfeit and pay not exceeding five thousand dollars, and be imprisoned not less than two years And each marshal shall be alike punishable for the two last named offences when committed by him.

Sec. 15. *And be it further enacted,* That each and every free person more than twenty years of age, belonging to any family residing in any subdivision, and in case of the absence of the heads and other members of any such family, then any agent of such family shall be, and each of them hereby is required, if thereto requested by the marshal or his assistant, to render a true account to the best of his or her knowledge, of every person belonging to such family, in the various particulars required in and by this act, and the tables thereto subjoined, on pain of forfeiting thirty dollars, to be sued for and recovered in an action of debt by the assistant, *to the use of the United States.*

Sec. 16. *And be it further enacted,* That all fines and penalties herein provided for may be enforced in the courts of the United States within the States or Territories where such offence shall have been committed, or forfeiture incurred.

Sec. 17. *And be it further enacted,* That the marshals and their assistants are hereby authorized to transmit through the post office any papers or documents relating to the census, by writing thereon "Official business, census," and subscribing the same with the addition to his name of marshal, or assistant, as the case may be; but this privilege shall extend to nothing but documents and papers relating to the census, which shall pass free; and the sum of twelve thousand dollars is hereby appropriated out of any money in the Treasury not otherwise appropriated, for the purpose of covering the expense of transmitting the blanks and other matter through the mail, to be paid to the Post Office Department.

Sec. 18. *And be it further enacted,* That if any of the Territories or places where the population is scarce, the officers of the army or any persons thereto belonging, can be usefully employed in taking the census, the Secretary of War is hereby directed to afford such aid, if it can be given without prejudice to the public service.

Sec. 19. *And be it further enacted,* That the Secretary of the Interior is hereby required to carry into effect the provisions of this act, and to provide blanks and distribute the same among the marshals, so that the enumeration may commence on the first day of June next, and be taken with reference to that day in each and every district and subdivision of districts; to draw up and distribute at the same time printed instructions, defining and explaining the duties of such as collect the statistics, and the limits by which such duties are circumscribed, in a clear and intelligible manner; to see also that all due diligence is employed by the marshals and assistants to make return of their respective doings, completed at the times herein prescribed; and futher, as the returns are so made, to cause the same to be classified and arranged in the best and most convenient manner for use, and to lay the same before Congress at the next session thereof. And to enable him the better to discharge these duties, he is hereby authorized and required to appoint a suitable and competent person as superintending clerk who shall under his direction have the general management of matters appertaining thereto, with the privilege of franking and receiving free of charge all official documents and letters connected therewith; and the said Secretary shall also appoint such clerks and other officers as may be necessary, from time to time, for the efficient management of said service. And the compensation to be allowed and paid to the officers connected with the census office shall be as follows: For the superintending clerk two thousand five hundred dollars per annum in full for his services; and for other assistants and clerks the compensation usually paid for similar services, to be fixed and allowed by the Secretary of the Interior: *Provided,* That no salary to a subordinate clerk under this section shall exceed the sum of one thousand dollars per annum. The blanks and preparatory printing for taking the census shall be prepared and executed under the direction of the census board; the other printing hereafter to be executed as Congress shall direct.

Sec. 20. *And be it further enacted,* That, for the purpose of carrying into effect this act, and defraying the preliminary expenses, there is hereby appropriated out of any money in the treasury not otherwise appropriated, one hundred and fifty thousand dollars, out of which the said Secretary of the Interior may allow to the person employed as secretary of the census board a compensation after the rate of three thousand dollars per annum, during the period he has been in their employ.

Sec. 21. *And be it further enacted,* That whenever a marshal shall certify that an assistant has completed to his satisfaction, and made return of the subdivision confided to him, and shall also certify the amount of compensation to which, under the provisions of this act, such assistant is entitled, designating how much for each kind of service, the Secretary of the Interior shall thereupon cause one half of the sum so due to be paid to such assistant, and when the returns have been carefully examined for classification, if found executed in a manner satisfactory, then he shall also cause the other half to be paid. And he shall make payments in the manner and upon like conditions to the several marshals for their services.

Sec. 22. *And be it further enacted,* that the tables hereto annexed, and made part of this act, are numbered from one to six, inclusive.

Sec. 23. *And be it further enacted,* That if no other law be passed providing for the taking of the eighth, or any subsequent census of the United States, on or before the first day of January of any year, when, by the Constitution of the United States, any future enumeration of the inhabitants thereof is required to be taken, such census shall, in all things, be taken and completed according to the provisions of this act.—

Sec. 24. *And be it further enacted,* That from and after the third day of March, one thousand eight hundred and fifty-three, the House of Representatives shall be composed of two hundred and thirty-three members, to be apportioned among the several States in the manner directed in the next section of this act.

Sec. 25 *And be it further enacted,* That so soon as the next and each subsequent enumeration of the inhabitants of the several States directed by the Constitution of the United States to be taken, shall be completed and returned to the office of the Department of the Interior, it shall be the duty of the Secretary of the Interior to ascertain the aggregate representative population of the United States, by adding to the whole number of free persons in all the States, including those bound to service for a term of years, and excluding Indians not taxed, three-fifths of all other persons; which aggregate population he shall divide by the number two hundred and thirty-three, and the product of such division, rejecting any fraction of an unit, if any such happen to remain, shall be the ratio or rule of apportionment of representatives among the several States under such enumeration; and the said Secretary of the Department of the Interior shall then proceed, in the same manner, to ascertain the representative population of each State, and to divide the whole number of the representative population of each State, by the ratio already determined by him, as above directed; and the product of this last division shall be the number of representatives apportioned to such State under the then last enumeration: *Provided,* That the loss in the number of members caused by the fractions remaining in the several States, on the division of the population thereof, shall be compensated for by assigning to so many States having the largest fractions one additional member each for its fraction, as may be necessary to make the whole number of representatives two hundred and thirty-three: *And provided, also,* That if after the apportionment of the representatives under the next or any subsequent census, a new State or States shall be admitted into the Union, the representative or representatives assigned to such new State or States, shall be in addition to the number of representatives herein above limited; which excess of representatives over two hundred and thirty-three shall only continue until the next succeeding apportionment of representatives under the next succeeding census.

Sec. 26. *And be it further enacted,* That when the Department of the Interior shall have apportioned the representatives in the manner above directed among the several States under the next, or any subsequent enumeration of the inhabitants of the United States, he shall, as soon as practicable, made [make] out and transmit under the seal of his office, to the House of Representatives, a certificate of the number of members apportioned to each State under the then last enumeration; and shall likewise make out and transmit without delay to the Executive of each State a certificate, under his seal of office, of the number of members apportioned to such State under such last enumeration.

Sec. 27. *And be it further enacted,* That the Secretary of the Interior, in his instructions to the marshals, shall direct that the statistics in regard to all other descriptions of hemp, not embraced in the denomination of dew and water-rotted, shall be taken and estimated in the returns.

SCHEDULES TO CENSUS BILL.

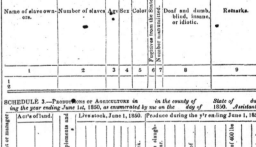

SCHEDULE 1.—Free Inhabitants *in* *in the county of* *State of* *enumerated by me, on the* *day of* 1850. *Assistant.*

Dwelling houses numbered in the order of visitation.	Families numbered in the order of visitation.	Name of every person whose usual place of abode on the first day of June, 1850, was in this family.	Description. Age	Sex	Color. White, black, or mulatto.	Profession, occupation, or trade of each male person over 15 years of age.	Value of real estate owned.	Place of birth naming the State, Territory or country.	Married within the year.	Attended school within the year.	Persons over 20 years of age who cannot read and write.	Whether deaf and dumb, blind, insane, idiotic, pauper, or convict.
1	2	3	4	5	6	7	8	9	10	11	12	13
1												1
2												2

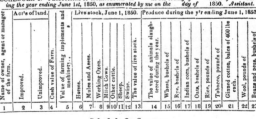

SCHEDULE 2.—Slave inhabitants *in* *in the county of* *State of* *enumerated by me, on the* *day of* 1850. *Assistant.*

Name of slave owners.	Number of slaves	Description. Age	Sex	Color	Fugitives from the State.	Number manumitted.	Deaf and dumb, blind, insane, or idiotic.	Remarks.
1	2	3	4	5	6	7	8	9
1								2
2								2

SCHEDULE 3.—Productions of Agriculture *in* *in the county of* *State of* *during the year ending June 1st, 1850, as enumerated by me on the* *day of* 1850. *Assistant.*

Name of owner, agent or manager of the farm.	Acr's of land. Improved.	Unimproved.	Cash value of Farm.	Value of farming implements and machinery.	Live stock, June 1, 1850. Horses.	Mules and Asses.	Working Oxen.	Milch Cows.	Other cattle.	Sheep.	Swine.	The value of live stock.	Produce during the y'r ending June 1, 1850. The value of animals slaughtered during the year.	Wheat, bushels of	Rye, bushels of	Indian corn, bushels of	Oats, bushels of	Rice, pounds of	Tobacco, pounds of	Ginned cotton, bales of 400 lbs each.	Wool, pounds of	Beans and peas, bushels of
1	2	3	4	5	6	7	8	9	10	11	12	13	14	15	16	17	18	19	20	21	22	23

Schedule 3.—Continued.

Produce during the year ending June 1, 1850.—*Continued.*

Buckwheat, bushels of	Barley, bushels of	Potatoes. Irish, bushels of	Sweet, bushels of	Value of orchard products in dollars	Wine, gallons of	Value of produce of market garden.	Butter, pounds of	Cheese, pounds of	Hay, tons of	Clover seed, bushels of	Other grass seeds, bushels of	Hops, pounds of	Hemp. Dew rotted, tons of	Water rotted, tons of	Flax, pounds of	Flaxseed, bushels of	Silk Cocoons, pounds of	Maple Sugar, pounds of	Cane Sugar, hhds. of 1,000 pounds	Molasses, gallons of	Honey and Beeswax, pounds of	Value of home-made manufactures
24	25	26	27	28	29	30	31	32	33	34	35	36	37	38	39	40	41	42	43	44	45	46

[*Concluded on second page.*]

[*Concluded from 1st p-ge.*]

CENSUS BILL.

SCHEDULE 4.—Products of Industry *in in the county of State of during the year ending June 1, 1350, at enumerated by me. Assistant.*

Name of corporation, company, or individual producing articles to the annual value of five hundred dollars.	Name of business, manufacture, or produce.	Capital invested in real and personal estate in the business.	Raw material used, including fuel. Quantities.	Raw material used, including fuel. Kinds.	Raw material used, including fuel. Values.	Kind of motive power, machinery, structure or resource.	Average No. of hands employed. Male.	Average No. of hands employed. Females.	Wages. Average monthly cost of male labor.	Wages. Average monthly cost of female labor.	Annual Product. Quantities.	Annual Product. Kinds.	Annual Product. Values.
1	2	3	4	5	6	7	8	9	10	11	12	13	14

SCHEDULE 5.—Social Statistics *of , in the county of , and State of compiled by me. Assistant.*

Name of town, county or city.	Aggregate valuation of real and personal estate	Aggregate amount of taxes assessed.	Public Schools
	Real estate, $ Personal estate, Total, $	State $ County, Parish, Town, Total, $	No. of Colleges. Do. Acade ies. Do. Free Schools. Do. other Schools. Do. Schoolhouses. Amount of money raised by tax for schools last year—$
	How valued.	Road tax—$	Raised in other ways for Schools last year—$
	True valuation—$	How paid.	Received from public funds for schools last year—$

SCHEDULE 5—Continued.

	Public Libraries. No.	Volumes	Name.	Class.	Periodicals, including newspapers. How often published.	Number of circulation.	Seasons.
Social. Colleges Academies. Public schools. Sunday schools							Has this season produced average crops! What crops are short? To what extent? What is the average per year!

SCHEDULE 5—Continued.

Public Paupers.	Criminals.	Cost of Labor.	Religious Worship.
Whole number of paupers supported during the past year.	Number convicted of crime during the year ending 1st June, 1550.	Average wages to farm hand per month, hired by the year and boarded—$	No. of churches.
Number supported on the 1st day of June.	In prison on the 1st June 1850.	Average wages of a day laborer, without board —$ With board—$	
Native {White. Black.	Native {White. Black.	Average payment to a carpenter per day without board—$	No. of persons each will accommodate.
Foreign.	Foreign.	Average wages to a female domestic per week with board—$	Value of churches—$
Cost of supporting paupers during last year.		Average price of board to a laboring man per week—$	

SCHEDULE 6—Persons who died *during the year ending 1st June, 1850, in the of in the county of , and State of enumerated by me, Assistant.*

Name of every person who died during the year ending 1st June, 1850, whose usual place of abode at the time of his death was in this family.	Description. Age.	Description. Sex.	Description. Color—White, black, or mulatto.	Free or slave.	Married or widowed.	Place of birth, naming the State, Territory, or country.	The month in which the person died.	Profession, occupation or trade.	Disease, or cause of death.
1	2	3	4	5	6	7	8	9	10

Approved, May 23, 1850.

We confess that we feel some misgivings as to the prospect of the passage of the Compromise Bill by Congress. The defeat of the measure must be eminently productive of mischief, while its adoption, in our estimation, would have a most happy influence in allaying the jealousies which have distracted certain sections of the Union, and diverted so much of the action of Congress from the legitimate business devolving upon that body. While we have been gratified beyond measure to witness, during the last few months, the most palpable evidences of reaction at the North against the abolition and Free Soil hobbies, and in favor of the South and the Compromises of the Constitution, we have been surprised and grieved to see manifested among some of the politicians of the South a steady desire to resist all the reasonable and probable means suggested for the purpose of allaying the public discontent, and restoring harmony and fraternity of feeling to the different sections of our hitherto happy and prosperous Union. We cannot look upon any man, who is instrumental in defeating the plan of Compromise now before the Senate, as the real friend to the South, no matter what his motives may be. Mr. Benton on the one hand and Mr. Clemens and his coadjutors on the other, whether influenced by a partiality for Free Soilism or Nullification, are equally mischievous and injurious to the country, so long as they unite with Hale and the Abolitionists of the North in defeating the only hope of conciliation and harmony which now holds out to the nation.

No Southern State can better afford delay in the settlement of the questions which now agitate the country than Texas. She has no fear of the loss or prejudice of her territorial claims from the lapse of time.—She is under no necessity and feels no solicitude for the sale of her public lands. She is the farthest removed of any state in the Union from Abolition excitement and influences, and would be the farthest from the scene of hostilities in the dreadful event of a war between the different sections of the Union. She embraces within herself all the elements of self-preservation; has once maintained a separate existence as a nation and is perfectly able to do so again.—Nevertheless, Texas feels no desire to sever her connection with the Great North American Union, and as little to form one with a Southern Confederacy, in which she would be bound to bear arms, and send her sons to die, for the abstractions, whims and ultraisms of the Souhern Hotspurs, who see no remedy but blood-letting, for the fever into which they are thrown by their differences with the North. Happily for us, the feeble efforts which have been made to get up an excitement in Texas against the entire North and against the Union, have failed. Our citizens are undisturbed by the agitations on the subject; and prepared either for a reasonable adjustment, by the present Congress, of the matters in controversy, or for reasonable delay—"a masterly inactivity"—by which these questions will ultimately solve themselves. But we are not prepared for disunion or a Southern Confederacy. We will abide by the Union, as it is, as long as we can do so without being greatly oppressed. When that can be no longer preserved, Texas will consult her own interests, by reverting to the state in which she stood before annexation, and avoiding "entangling alliances" with all other powers.

Our Southern friends may deem as many "great principles" at stake as they choose in the present issues—the only real interest at stake is the safety of slave property. The compromise bill proposes to use all practical means to secure this. How the return of fugitive slaves to their owners can be better effected by a dissolution of the Union, we cannot imagine. Slaves hitherto escaping into the free states of the Union have been considered in danger of being lost—those escaping into Canada, Mexico, or other countries *out* of the Union have been looked upon as actually lost—to their owners. What Canada and Mexico are now, the free states would become, on the dissolution of this Union—complete asylums for runaway negroes.—*Galveston Civilian.*

A series of most extraordinary outrages has recently been committed upon a young lady in Buffalo. A few weeks ago, she was knocked down, gagged, robbed, and left in the street, with her hands and feet tied. On Thursday week, she was suddenly seized at night, in the hall of her boarding-house, tied, and carried to a pond, where a large stone was placed upon her person; and, one night since, she was again seized in the back yard of the house, bound, and thrown into the canal, where she was discovered, nearly dead, by some men who had sought the place to water their horses. Two or three of the gang of rowdies supposed to be implicated in this extraordinary affair have been arrested. The particulars are given in the Buffalo Commercial Advertiser.

The Advocate.

Office in the brick building near the Court House.

VICTORIA, TEXAS:

FRIDAY MORNING, JUNE 21.

ANNOUNCEMENTS.

☞ We are authorized to announce John McGrew, Esq. as a candidate for the office of Sheriff of Victoria county, at the ensuing election in August next.

☞ We are authorized by the friends of Mr. George W. Wright, to announce him as a candidate for the office of Sheriff of Victoria county at the ensuing election in August. If elected, he will discharge the duties of the office faithfully, and to the best of his ability.

☞ We are authorized to announce Wm. S. Glass, Esq. as a candidate for re-election to the office of District Attorney of the Tenth District.

☞ We are authorized to announce N. T. Gaines, Esq. as a candidate for the office of Clerk of the District Court of Victoria county, at the ensuing August election.

☞ We are authorized to announce G. Wm. Garnett as a candidate for the office of Clerk of the County Court of Victoria county at the ensuing August election.

State Comptroller.

☞ We are authorized to announce JAMES B. SHAW, Esq., as a candidate for re-election to the office of Comptroller of the State of Texas, at the ensuing August election.

☞ We are authorized to announce E. STERLING ROBERTSON, Esq., as a candidate for the Office of Comptroller of the State of Texas, at the ensuing August election.

State Treasurer.

☞ We are authorized to announce JAMES H. RAYMOND, Esq., as a candidate for re-election to the office of Treasurer of the State of Texas, at the ensuing August election.

Attorney General.

☞ We are authorized to announce A. J. HAMILTON, Esq., as a candidate for the office of Attorney General of the State of Texas, at the ensuing August election.

We are authorized to announce Judge Geo. W. Paschal, of Galveston, as a candidate for the office of Attorney General for the State of Texas at the ensuing August election.

☞ We are authorized to announce Samuel B. Mixon, as a candidate for re-election to the office of Constable of the Victoria Precinct at the ensuing August election.

☞ We are authorized to announce S. R. Van Norman, as a candidate for the office of Constable of the Victoria Precinct at the ensuing August election.

William P. Miller solicits the votes of the electors in the Victoria precinct at the ensuing election, for the office of Constable. If elected, he will serve them faithfully.

We are authorized to announce Edward Linn, Esq., as a candidate for re-election at the ensuing August election, to the office of District Surveyor, composed of the county of Victoria, and also of parts of the counties of Calhoun, Jackson, Lavaca, and DeWitt, formerly Victoria county.

Chief Justice.

We are authorized to announce Wm. Ragland, Esq., as a candidate for the office of Chief Justice of Victoria county, at the ensuing election in August next.

We are authorized to announce Judge John C. Cleland as a candidate for the office of Chief Justice of Calhoun County.

PUBLIC MEETING.

The Citizens of Victoria County will meet on Tuesday next at 5 o'clock, P. M., at the Court-House, to take into consideration the Report of Major R. S. Neighbors relative to his mission to Santa Fe.

MANY CITIZENS.

June 21st, 1850.

☞ We are requested to state, that a Quarterly Examination and Exhibition of the Sunday School of this place will be held (Providence permitting) on next Sabbath morning, commencing precisely at 10 o'clock. A discourse, relevant to the occasion, may be expected from the Rev. Joel T. Case. A general attendance of all who feel interested in the moral and religious education of the young, is respectfully solicited.

The National Intelligencer, of June 1st, contains a long letter from Ex-President Tyler to the Hon. H. S. Foote, in favor of the compromise plan. The Hon. A. Stevenson, of Va., and ex-Speaker of the House of Representatives has also, in a letter to Senator Foote, taken decided ground in favor of the compromise.

The compromise still lingers in the Senate. Its fate is still uncertain. No new developments as to its strength have been made since our paper of last week.

The Washington Union.—In the Union, of the 31st ult., there is a card from Mr. Burke, announcing that his connexion with that paper ceased on that day.

South Carolina U. S. Senator.—The Governor of South Carolina has appointed Robert W. Barnwell, U. S. Senator, in place of Mr. Elmore, deceased Mr. Barnwell was formerly member of Congress, and president of the college of South Carolina. He was at Nashville as a delegate to the Southern Convention at the time of his appointment.

The Compromise.—*Andrew Stevenson.*—The Washington Union, of the 31st ult., says:

Just as our paper was going to press, there was placed in our hands for publication an admirable letter from that veteran statesman, Andrew Stevenson, of Virginia, addressed to Gen. Foote, in warm support of the leading features of the adjustment now pending in the Senate of the United States. Mr. Stevenson having been a warm and efficient advocate of the Nashville Convention, and a fearless defender of southern rights at all times, his support of the compromise may be viewed as quite a decisive indication from Virginia on this subject.

The Cuban Investigation in N. York.—The N. Y. Evening Post of the 3d says:

We understand that the Grand Jury, in the United States Circuit Court, this morning, reported that no evidence had been produced before them which justified any proceedings against persons in this city, suspected of conniving at or abetting the late invasion of Cuba by General Lopez.

The Prisoners in Cuba.—A Washington letter, of the 3d, in the N. Y. Tribune, says:

The Secretary of State, this morning, has transmitted by telegraph to Mobile, and thence to be dispatched by the most speedy conveyance to Cuba, an official letter to the Spanish authorities of that Island, informing them that the authorities of Spain have no right to anticipate a criminal or illegal intent on the part of any American citizens found upon any island in the neighborhood of Yucatan, and that the seizure of any such persons under such circumstances will not be recognized or permitted by this government.

Treasury Notes Outstanding.—According to the statement of the Register of the Treasury, the amount of Treasury notes outstanding on the 1st, was reduced to $445,489 31.

The Iowa Electi n Case.—The N. Y. Tribune has a dispatch from Washington, which says:

The committee on Elections, in the House, has decided that Daniel F. Miller, (whig) the contestant in the Iowa disputed election case, is the rightful member from that State, instead of William Thompson, (dem.) who has held the seat since the organization of the House. The vote in the committee stood 5 to 4. The report is delayed by the absence of Mr. McGaughey, who has gone home to Indiana, but is expected to be soon here again.

By Magn tic Telegraph.

Arrival of the Canada.

Baltimore, June 11.—P. M.

The steamer *Canada*, with dates from Liverpool up to the 1st of June, arrived at Halifax to-day. She reports a further advance of *one-eighth* in Cotton, Fair Orleans being quoted at 7⅜d. The sales for the week were 65,000, of which speculators took 20,000, and exporters 4000. Flour was firmer, but no change in price. The same may be said of Wheat. Corn was dull at prices from 6 pence to 1 shilling lower. In Provisions, Beef is held at full prices. In Pork there is no improvement, and prices are in favor of buyers. Irish Bacon Shoulders are in good demand.—Hams neglected. In Lard, the large arrivals have checked operations. Sales have been made at 31s to 39s. Prices have receded during the week.

Favorable accounts have been received from the manufacturing districts.

Liverpool Markets.—*Baltimore*, June 11, 5 P. M.—Brown & Shipman's circular, dated the 28th ult., says: "Yesterday, under the influence of the advices received by the Canada, the demand for cotton improved. The sales of to-day have amounted to twelve thousand bales, at a shade advance, but not amounting to one-eighth.

There was a general apprehension of another short American crop, which was causing considerable excitement in the market.

Nashville Convention.—The committee of this body has unanimously reported in favor of extending the Missouri compromise line of 36 deg. 30 min. to the Pacific.

Congress.—In the Senate, on Monday, Mr. Benton made his expected motion for an indefinite postponement of the compromise bills, and made a long speech on that side.

General Cass had the floor for Tuesday, (yesterday.) The vote will be taken on Thursday.

The general belief is that it will pass by 3 majority.

[We suppose that this means that the compromise bill, not Mr. Benton's motion will pass.]

The Cotton Crop in Mississippi.—The Mississippian of the 7th says:

Since publishing our last statement of the crops of Mississippi, we have received letters from about fifteen additional counties. We are sorry to say that we have never in our life known a more gloomy prospect. We shall not make 250,000 bales in the State—the number ought to be 700,000 bales, at least.

Dreadful Tragedy at Memphis.—We learn from the N. O. True Delta of the 12th inst., that a dreadful street fight occurred at Memphis, Tenn., on the 8th inst., growing out of the prosecution of the parties connected with the Farmers Bank affair, in which Colonel Coe, Dr. Fowlkes and Mr. Gaines were killed, and Mr. Twigg mortally wounded.

The new census bill apportions the number of Representatives, in the lower House of Congress, at two hundred. The present number is two hundred and thirty. The ratio of representation under the new bill, will be about one hundred and twenty thousand. The present ratio is about seventy thousand six hundred and eighty.

On Monday the 3d inst., the Governor opened the election returns for the seat of Government. The vote stood thus: Washington, 1145; Palestin , 1884; Huntsville, 1216; Tahuacana, 3142; and Austin 7679—being a majority of 270 votes over all other places voted for, and is therefore elected the seat of Government until the year 1870, unless the State is sooner divided.

A meeting of the Royal Arch Masons of this State, will be held at the city of Houston on the 24th inst., for the purpose of forming a State Grand Chapter.

Gen. Lopez has surrendered himself to the United States Marshal for the District of Louisiana, and was at the latest dates undergoing his trial. The opinion prevails that he will be acquitted of any violation of the laws of the United States.

VICTORIA,

Its Prospects—Duties of its Citizens.

The last lingering doubt in regard to the *navigability* of the Guadaloupe is at length removed. He that now expresses doubt is either *ignorant* or *insincere*. With neither class will we stop to reason. The Kate Ward has made about 30 trips and some of them in very quick time. So quick, indeed, as to place it beyond question that a trip to the Pass and back to Victoria can be made regularly in 48 hours. She made the passage up in 17½ hours, and the downward passage can be made in a shorter time. All obstructions are now removed. Navigation may now be *regular, safe*, and *expeditious.*

These qualities being admitted to belong to our river navigation, we will premise another fact which will doubtless be admitted to be true by all conversant with the subject, which is, that enough freight passess through our town from and to the Bay, to keep a steamboat constantly employed; or at least to furnish sufficient employment to make the capital invested yield a fair profit.

There is another general fact which we merely name but which we cannot stop to enforce, for it indicates an intellect beneath the reach of argument, to question its truth. This general fact is, that water transportation is *cheaper* than that by land. There are no circumstances connected with the Guadaloupe navigation between Victoria and the Pass which makes it an exception to the general rule. The navigation being *safe, regular, and expeditious*, the price of transportation less, and enough of freight to justify the running of a boat, it would seem almost *incredible* to a stranger, that wagons are used instead of boats as means of transportation. There are a few reasons which combine to bring about this result, to which we shall for a moment advert.

The first is, that wagons have been hitherto the only means of transportation, and experience has proved, that it always requires time, and is sometimes attended with much difficulty, to change established usages for the introduction of *new*, though much superior plans. If our citizens desire to see *at an early day*, all the trade from the bay come to our town by the river, they must make some exertion to divert it from the old channel.

The second reason is, that the persons having control of the trade through the Bay are desirous that it should not be diverted from its old channel. We do not censure them for this. Perhaps it is even commendable in them. The diversion of all the trade now passing through our town from its present route to its new channel via the river, would be a heavy stroke, if not a death blow upon the towns of Port Lavaca and Indianola, and would build up our city upon their downfall. To expect the citizens of those places to make efforts to change the present mode of transportation, is to expect them to commit an act of folly, tantamount to their own commercial suicide. To expect them even not to make strong efforts to retain it as it is, is to suppose them both deaf and blind to the promptings of their own interests. But their interests do not stop at making efforts at retaining the wagon transportation. If, from the nature of things, a change must take place sooner or later, the interests of both these places will lead them to make a landing point at any other place than Victoria. That point will suit them best which has fewest advantages to concentrate the whole trade, and is least adapted to the building up of a rival town or city. We have no hesitation in saying, it is their true interest to have as many landings as possible on the river, and to keep up as much as possible, a fair division of the trade among them all. If this is their true interest, and it does seem to us to be so, beyond all reasonable question, will they not use efforts to carry out every thing which may be to their advantage. The merchants of those places are *intelligent, enterprising*, and *possess capital*. They will not see Victoria built up at the expense of the trade and commerce of their own towns, without an effort in their behalf, and such an effort as will require the counter united and concerted efforts of all the citizens of Victoria to overcome it. Already has a warehouse been erected at Kemper's Bluff, and a gentleman has gone to the region of the Ohio with the avowed purpose of bringing a suitable boat with him, which he destines to ply between that point and the towns on the Bay. It is believed that the San Antonio trade can be diverted from Victoria, to that as its landing point.

In this state of things what are the citizens of Victoria, and planters in the interior interested in the building up of Victoria, to do, in order to the development of our own advantages as the point of depot for all the trade of the interior? We answer, their duty is plain. It consists

1st. In the purchase of a suitable boat to be owned and controled by them. This boat should make regular trips, and always meet the steamer at the Pass, and transport freight and passengers to Victoria, *cheaper*, and in *quicker time*, than can be done on the present route. This is all of easy accomplishment. Our citizens have the capital. They have the enterprise, and nature has given the advantages. Nothing is lacking but some one to move first, and actively, in the matter. Let this be done and no landings between this and the Bay will be hereafter talked of. Kemper's Bluff will always indeed be a landing for a small section of the lower San Antonio; but the trade of Bexar and the trade of San Antonio River from Goliad up, will make the depot of land transportation at this place.

Now is the time for our citizens to move in the matter. The rivalry of the towns on the Bay, the division of the trade among them, and the uncertainty as to what point will ultimately swallow up the rest, is peculiarly favorable to the concentration of the trade at Victoria. Another consideration should not be over-looked, the Bexar trade now crosses our river at this place, and can, by reasonable efforts, be stopped at this point—but if a boat should be put in the river, with arrangements to meet that trade at Kemper's Bluff, it will require very considerable efforts to get it back—far greater that to retain it.

Besides, the public expectation of the interior has long fixed the period of the clearing out of the obstructions of the river, as the period when Victoria would be their depot. "Hope deferred maketh the heart sick." Every delay introduces an element of scepticism in the public mind as to our advantages, and consequently increases the obstacles to any diversion of the trade from its present channel.

2nd. This boat should be owned by our prominent citizens generally, in order to enlist every interest among us in its support. For a union of effort is absolutely necessary for success. Every other mode of transportation must be broken down by it, and every other landing blotted from the map. This must be done by cheap rates, quick time, and punctuality.

3d. Our merchants should become commission and forwarding merchants for all the trade to and from the country.

4th. A commodious ware-house should immediately be built at this place. We are informed that there is a new wharf just completed by Mr. Decrow at the Pass. A ware-house here is absolutely necessary. Will not our citizens wake up to a sense of their true interests? Will they fold their hands in apathy and supineness at the most critical moment in the history of their town. Now is the golden moment. The fruit of our toil for years is now within our power, if we will only reach forth the hand and clutch it. This opportunity passed away unembraced, and difficulties will increase upon us on every hand. Other landings will spring up, other channels of trade will be opened up, other boats having other interests will be put in the River, and merchants in the interior, and planters, will form other mercantile associations.—All of which must be broken up before we can be restored even to our present position.

ORGANIZATION OF SANTA FE.

It will be perceived by the report of Maj. Neighbors which we publish to-day, that he has been unsuccessful in the objects of his mission—that the public authorities and people of Santa Fe utterly refuse to come under our jurisdiction, or to acknowledge our sovereignty. Although this conduct on the part of the government and people of Santa Fe is not entirely unexpected, it is nevertheless a subject of the most profound regret to every Texian, because it necessarily devolves upon the State high duties, which cannot be otherwise than painful in their performance. Obedience to the laws is, in a Republic, the first duty of the citizen. It is the basis of all social law and order. Disobedience is in such a government, peculiarly the fruitful mother of discord and anarchy, and as such must be checked in the bud. Yet to enforce this obedience, and to punish this disobedience, by the musket and the bayonet, although sometimes demanded by the public welfare, can never be resorted to by freemen, except on the demand of honor, or as the reluctant choice of alternative evils. The fact, as in the case before us, that the mass of the disobedient citizens are Mexicans, and alienated from us in manners, in language, and religion, and connected to us by no ties growing out of a common origin, or by associations springing from a common history, may palliate, but cannot remove the regret ever attending the discharge of this highest, because most painful, duty of the citizen. But painful as a resort to arms against his fellow citizens must ever be to the American citizen, yet it sometimes becomes a high duty of State, and as such *must be performed*. Circumstances has brought about such a position of affairs. A crisis now exists in the history of Texas, which imperatively demands of her citizens the exercise of this high duty, this last resort.

We have reflected upon the present position of affairs with an anxious and sincere desire to find out a mode of adjustment of the matter which would avoid a resort to arms. But we have been able to think of none, which could be adopted without a sacrifice of honor, and the true interests of the State.

What is the state of facts? Texas claims Santa Fe as an integral portion of her Territory. Nine tenths of her citizens regard her claim as valid beyond the shawdow of a doubt. Her legislature, with great unanimity, at the session of 1849–50, passed an act organizing the county of Santa Fe, and appointed a commissioner to carry the provisions of the law into effect. The commissioner in obedience to the requirements of the law proceeded to the designated point and attempted an organization, but the public officials, and the people set at defiance his authority, refused utterly to recognize the sovereignty of the state, denied all allegiance to it, and coolly set to work to form a State Government for themselves.

In this state of facts, what is Texas to do? We again say we can see no alternative compatible with honor, other than to send a military force, well armed and equipped, with full authority to enforce obedience to the law. There is another alternative, but one which we presume no Texian would entertain for a moment, that of surrendering the country at discretion, without an effort to retain it—an alternative which, if adopted, would mar the lustre of every victory of the revolution, and dim the bright fame won by her heroes in that proud and eventful struggle.

It may be asked what influence the pending compromise and propositions for purchase of that territory, should exercise over the course of Texas in reference to Santa Fe in the present emergency. We reply, the conduct of Texas, so far as *preparation* for action is concerned, should in our opinion, not be influenced by any action on the part of the United States Congress.—Texas should take immediately the initiative of such steps as honor demands for the subjugation of her rebellious subjects. The time for the starting of the expedition may be delayed or hastened by the action of Congress. But this is a matter to be determined by events as they arise. For the present we see no good reason why Texas should not take immediate preparatory steps for sending a military expedition at a suitable time. Indeed we think we perceive many reasons in favor of a prompt initiative. This state of preparation should not be abandoned until the actual *assent* of Texas is given to whatever propositions Congress may make.

We advocate prompt preparations in view of the *possibility* of a necessity arising out of the conduct of New Mexico, in the attempt to form a State government, for immediate ultimate action on the part of Texas; yet we would in the present position of affairs at Washington, advice no hasty setting out of an expedition. A turn of affairs there for or against our interests, may hasten or retard operations against Santa Fe. We perhaps would best express our idea by the words, *prepare and wait the turn of events.* A month may decide us.

OUR SANTA FE TERRITORY.

Executive Department,
Austin, Texas, June 4th, 1850.

To the Editor of the State Gazette:

Sir:—I have received from Maj. Robert S. Neighbors, (special Commissioner, appointed by and with the advice and consent of the Senate, to extend the laws of the State over the unorganized counties of its North-western portion,) important information connected with his mission, and as it is deemed by me highly proper that the people of Texas should possess it as early as possible for consideration, I respectfully request that you publish the same in your next paper. The information referred to is herewith transmitted.

Very respectfully, your obdt. serv't,

P. H. BELL.

Major Neighbors' Report.

City of Austin, June 4th, 1850.

Sir:—I have the honor to inform you that I arrived in this city on yesterday, having left Santa Fe on the 24th April and El Paso on the 11th of May.

I herewith enclose for your especial consideration, a copy of a proclamation issued on the 23d of April by Col. John Munroe, U. S. A., commanding 9th military department. By it you will perceive that the people of New Mexico are about to go into a separate State organization. This movement I am induced to believe, has been brought about by the encouragement given them by the President of the United States through his instructions to Col. McCall, U. S. A., as they were published, and very generally circulated through that territory.

Having since my arrival, been informed that you did not receive my letter of the 12th of April, which I forwarded with other documents and letters to you by the military mail, via El Paso, I deem it proper to call your attention to my movements after the organization of the county of El Paso. Having received a copy of Col. Munroe's circular letter to the commanding officers of the 9th military department, ordering "a strict non-interference" with me in the discharge of my duties, and several letters from private individuals in Santa Fe advising me to come on to Santa Fe, I lost no time, and arrived at that place on the 8th of April, under the impression that I should be able to effect an organization. I was well and courteously received by the inhabitants. As soon as possible after my arrival, I commenced an investigation of public sentiment, and endeavored to ascertain the practicability of organizing.

I deemed it my first duty to call upon Col. Munroe, the military Governor. I found by his conversation that he would give me no encouragement, nor adopt any measures or policy that would forward the views or wishes of Texas. On the contrary, he expressed himself as decidedly favorable to the then existing state of affairs, "and believed it best that the present government with the Mexican laws now in force, should be maintained until Congress shall establish some other." During the conversation I asked him the plain question, "are you willing to acknowledge the jurisdiction of Texas, provided I hold the elections and qualify the proper civil officers?" His answer was, "I am not prepared to say so. I have no right to abolish the present government. The judges and other officers are commissioned by the United States government, and I have no power to remove them, unless instructed to do so by my government." I called his attention to the probability of the Executive of the State (in the event of my failure to organize,) extending our jurisdiction by proclamation and enforcing the laws by a military force.

His reply was, "that would be the proper

The Texian Advocate.

PUBLISHED WEEKLY BY JOHN D. LOGAN AND THOMAS STERNE, AT $3 IN ADVANCE, $4 IN SIX MONTHS, OR $5 AT THE END OF THE YEAR.

VOL. 5. VICTORIA, TEXAS, FRIDAY, AUGUST 30, 1850. No. 18.

For the Advocate.

THE WILD PEOPLE OF TEXAS.

MR. EDITOR:—You have, no doubt, heard of the circumstance of wild people having been seen upon the lower Colorado, on the return of the settlers after having been driven from their homes during the revolution of 1835–6. Much has been said, and I think something written upon this subject. I have been told by persons who lived in that section at the time, that a man was frequently seen, and other human tracks in the river bottom, of various sizes, but that this man could never be approached near enough to assertain whether he could speak any language or not.

On the return however of the settlers, and the country becoming more densely populated, he was less frequently seen, and finally all traces of him, or his companions, was lost sight of on the Colorado.

By this time, those settlers who had taken flight from the Navidad and Lavaca rivers in the general "runaway," began to feel safe in returning to their homes again; and on doing so, many of them found that the Mexicans, on their retreat, had driven off all their stock, both cattle and hogs, and they were compelled to resort to the wild game of the forest for a sustenance. On penetrating the deep morasses and timbered bottoms, skirting the lower parts of those rivers, they were much surprised to find human foot prints mixed up with those of the wild bear, panther, leopard, cat, and other animals of the woods.

This circumstance created much curiosity among the few settlers of this portion of the country. It was not long, however, until they heard the account of the man and tracks that had been seen, and disappeared from the Colorado, and no doubt was then entertained but it was the same persons, who, on the country along the Colorado valley becoming somewhat settled up, had broke across the big prairie and made their way to the timbered lands of the Navidad and Lavaca.

The people of these rivers became quite interested upon this subject, many plans were laid, and drives with hounds taken, and chases on fleet horses to catch some or all of these people—but all in vain. A gentleman even came from the Brazos with his blood hounds, which he said would follow a human track to the verge of "old mother earth," but they were completely foiled and out-witted, and the gentleman had to give up the "corn" and return home unsuccessful.

This subject became vastly interesting, and was one which lay near and pressed heavily upon the hearts of the settlers. It began to be plainly developed that there was a community of them, and the idea of a race of human beings—more wild than the savage races that roam over the great prairie plains of the Rio del Norte—being raised up in the midst of civilization, was one harrowing to every *mother*, and *women in general*, to say nothing of the sympathy felt by the rougher sex. But what could be done? Many searches were made into the deep recesses, where the sun never shone, and from the overhanging cane, the matted vines, and the rich heavy foilage of the trees, mid-day was converted into dark twilight. In these dark haunts the hunter's dogs would gather around him, whine, turn their hair the wrong way, and show every disposition to get out. The same feeling would seize the hunter himself, and he would instinctively break, for the prairie hills. On one occasion, a large camp was found on the bank of the river, supported by a large live-oak tree across the horizontal branches of which poles were placed, and on them a quantity of black moss, and other things piled, which formed quite a good roof, and under this roof they had raw hides stretched above high-water-mark, upon which they slept. At this camp was any amount of bones of all kinds of animals and fowls, and quantities of corn cobs.—The raw hides were secured by platted raw-hide ropes, and a very ingenious *snare* for catching hogs was found near this camp, formed of the same kind of rope. The settlers had been convinced for some time before this camp was found that these people depredated upon their stock, poultry, and corn fields, and some times articles of female and children's clothing would be missing from the clothes-line when hung out to dry and left out over night. It was now supposed that this family at least could be caught by watching the camp, but not so. So soon as they found the settlers had discovered it, they never visited it again.

At this juncture all attempts to force this community into civilized life was abandoned by the settlers, and a new line of policy adopted, which was one of non-interference; at the same time, if opportunities offered, acts of kindness, mercy and love, was to be exhibited towards them. This change towards them had a happy effect, for the community soon finding that they were neither hunted nor pursued, commenced sallying forth from their hiding places, and in a short time even the females could be seen gliding about the farms, and farm houses of the settlers, at twilight-hour, looking more like faries or spirits from another world than human beings.

The spirits of the settlers began to be greatly revived, and sanguin hopes were entertained of redeeming, at no very distant day, this community from a life of nature, and wildness, and bringing them under a more *benign* influence.

The world may be considered as one large mansion, where man is permitted to enjoy the works of nature, and to admire the hand that called it into life. Blessed with talents, and endowed with sense, he feels himself the lord of earth's domain; but, whilst he contemplates the superiority of his station, he is apt to forget from *whom* it is *derived*. Amidst the many advantages which the mind enjoys from tracing nature through her varying course, that of finding it raised with admiration to the power which formed it, is one of the most beneficial that can be produced; for it is impossible to observe its nice dependencies, without beholding an *Almighty hand*.

In taking a view of animated nature, and beholding the connexion which exists in every part, we cannot but observe the exact resemblance which subsists between the *human* and the *animal race*. If Providence has bestowed upon *us* the gift of *intellect*, they are endowed with *sagacity*, or *strength*; and so great is the similitude in the formation of our bodies, that we might be termed animals erected on the hinder legs.

This resemblance between man and beast, though it may degrade the *body*, should elevate the *mind*, and point out the folly of *personal arrogance*, when we reflect that our form bears affinity to a brute's.—Man's superiority consists in *virtue*, and of that possession he may well be vain.—There he enjoys that pre-eminent distinction which raises him above every other tribe—leaving man to the possession of that superiority which the benevolent Author of his being has designed.

How very important then that man, being endowed with reasoning faculties, and especially those who once enjoyed the blessings of civilization, should not be suffered to run wild, and roam through the forests with the wild beasts and animals of the woods, in a savage life.

It was now perceptible that this wild community looked upon the settlers with less suspicion, and showed evident signs of wishing to form alliances of friendship.—This was cheering to the settlers, who exerted themselves in every possible way they could, to bring about a state of things so devoutly desired; and to encourage them, such articles as it was thought they understood the use of, or desired, were placed in their reach, and to the inexpressible joy of the ladies of the neighborhood, they were usually taken, particularly such as would be desirable for female or children's use.

About this time a beautiful sand-beach was discovered on the bank of the river, to which they evidently resorted. Here many experiments were tried, if possible to ascertain the language they spoke, if any, and what knowledge they still retained of civilized life; for it was quite evident that they had once enjoyed the happy influence of civilization, if not christianity. Letters were written in various languages, folded up and directed to them, by splitting the ends of small sticks, placing the letters in the split end, and sticking the other end in the sand. In this way their attention was invariably called to them, and the letters were *always taken, opened*, and folded up again *inversly* and replaced in the sticks. But no answers were ever received, or hopes entertained that they could read them, or if by possibility they could read and write, they possessed no facilities for doing so.—Notwithstanding all the discouragements and difficulties, which seemed to present themselves in this *noble* and *philanthropical undertaking*, the settlers never gave over, but appeared to entertain "hope against hope," and each "remove of a lengthening chain," seemed to redouble their energies, and they went forth in this "labor of love," exhibiting at every step a zeal and perseverance, worthy of all commendation and imitation.

As it always has been, and ever will be, so it was in this case. The unceasing cries, the holy ejaculations of a whole people, borne upon the "wings of the wind," to that ear ever open to the prayers of the righteous, must and will prevail. Light, as a sun-beam, as an emination from the great central throne of the combined system of worlds, broke upon the settlers, and rejoicings, such as are heard when "*the dead's alive and the lost is found*," filled the settlement. A male person of medium stature and something under middle age, was discovered to linger around the habitations of the settlers, not only at night, but during the day, showing evident signs of wishing to hold more close communion with the inhabitants. It was soon discovered that he left off returning any more to the community in the swamp—nor in fact was it entirely certain that he ever belonged to that community, although supposition placed him there. Every overturn on his part, was met in a becoming gentle manner by the settlers, and in a short time he would in the day venture up quite near to the settlers, look very earnestly at them, and then make off without attempting to speak a word. He presented an uncommon *wild* and *romantic* appearance, with his long hair and tremendous heavy long *red goatees* and beard! He appeared to be in deep mental concern, and many were the surmises to arrive at the cause of his distress. The gentlemen of the neighborhood supposed that some dreadful rencounter or quarrel had taken place between him and his male companions; but the ladies, as usual, were of a decided and very different opinion.—They were *determined* to make a *love affair of it*, and so they *fixed* it, in spite of all their *fathers, brothers*, and *lovers* could say, "he had been *discarded*, so he had," or in other words "*kicked*," and hence "the poor man's distress." And there was no use in arguing the question any further, for the ladies had decided the matter, and the gentlemen, (as we poor *he* mortals generally have to do,) gave it up, whether really convinced or not. So, be the real cause what it might, there was no finding it out. However, he soon threw off all restraint—came into the houses of the settlers, partook of food, and in a short time was found "clothed and in his proper mind;" though his *look* was *wild* and *glaring*, and for a considerable length of time he kept a profound silence. Gradually, however, he began to imitate talking, though his gibberish could not be understood for a great while.

This circumstance greatly encouraged the settlers, who used every means in their power to render the new comer comfortable and happy, and to induce him to return to habits of civilized life. The progress which he made, more than met their fond anticipations, for in an uncommon short time, considering the case, he evinced a disposition to engage in the common daily transactions of life, and by exercising and practising in letters, his knowledge of education soon returned, and he was enabled to enter into business transactions with quite a degree of facility. Finding that *land* was held by *tenure*, he soon became quite desirous of its acquisition; and so infatuated had he become with the notion of unbounded freedom, while roaming wild through the world's wide domain, that he regarded not the lines or land marks of any one, but set his compass both deep and wide, as though he would "take in all the shore." There is one savage habit, however, which he clings to with great tenacity, and that is of wearing his long *red* goatees, which he utterly refuses to part with under any circumstances. All attempts to draw from him any account of his origin, or his wild habits of life, were unavailing, it being a subject upon which he will have nothing to say. And all his movements—his *wild* and romantic appearance—*truly* and *emphatically* points him out to be what he is usually *denominated*—"THE WILD MAN OF THE WOODS."

Well, I suppose by this time you are ready to enquire, and what became of the balance of this wild community? Be patient gentle reader, and you shall hear the whole story. You are not to suppose that, while such untiring attentions were being paid to the "*wild man of the woods*," the balance of the community were neglected. On the contrary, in another part of the neighborhood every effort was used to get them in, and rapid and successful strides were made to that end. It was not long before they could be seen passing through the neighborhood in day-time, and by gentle approaches and kind treatment they would venture up to the settlers during day light. Three females, three grown males, and several children, constituted the remaining community. The eldest of the females is quite *dark complected*, and it is rather difficult to determine to what *race* of people she belongs; the other two females are much younger and lighter *complected*, and supposed to be the daughters of the eldest.—The children are still lighter, and some of them would be taken for dark-skined white people. They number at this time some ten or twelve, and are from one to twelve or thirteen years of age. The males all appear to be entirely *white*, the youngest quite *fair-skined*; two of them appear to be about the age of the eldest female, and the youngest I would suppose rather under that of the two youngest females. How the children are divided among them I cannot tell.

The balance of this community did not pursue the same course which the *wild man of the woods* did. Instead of taking up at the dwellings of the settlers, they came out and pitched their camp at an out-of-the-way place, on the high lands adjoining the Navidad swamp, near a large lagoon or pond of water, and on the west side of that river. At this place they have lived for several years, and appear to be advancing slowly, or rather we might say returning, to civilization. They have a small farm, which is cultivated rather poorly, and all kinds of stock and poultry, and appear to enjoy themselves very well. They are fond of being visited by strangers, and seem fully to understand that they are objects of curiosity. The *patriarch* of this community (for one of them appears to bear that relation to the balance, and they must have been governed under the *patriarchical* form,) is a man who seems to possess a good mind, and is uncommonly fond of hunting, and well acquainted with all the streams, swamps, and hiding places in all that section of country. Here can be seen fair (that is *tolerably* fair) woman in all her native loveliness and beauty, forms presenting the most perfect symmetry, being well developed in the most particular minutiæ, (without the additional paraphernalia, such as bustles, silks, jewelry, and other articles usually worn by ladies,) sparkling black eyes, jet black hair, such as would vie with the raven, complexion, a most lovely nut-brown—a very *brunette*. They refuse to say any thing of their wild life.

There is, at this time, a gentleman engaged in teaching the children of this community, and a most laudable and praiseworthy labor it is, to learn those young and untutored minds to *shoot*, and to direct them in a proper and virtuous channel. Some of the children are quite sprightly and promising, and all are advancing very well in learning the common branches of an English education, and strong hopes are entertained that the whole community will soon embrace christianity. The writer not long since visited these "children of nature," and the unassumed kindness and hospitality, which they seemed perfectly willing to extend to him, has made quite an impression upon his mind, and especially will the courtesy, kind treatment, and bland manners of their praiseworthy teacher, a native son of "Old Erin," be long remembered.

And those lovely females, so kind and so clever.
When they laughed they seemed to laugh all
over,
Like any fair lake, that the breeze is upon,
Dances to the wind—and dimples to the sun.

Now, reader, if you enjoy the reading of this story as well as the writer did its relation to him, he will be amply repaid for the imperfect manner in which he has thrown it together. After travelling hard all day, he called at the hospitable dwelling of Mr. ——, and his horse and himself being well cared for, and being seated in an easy chair, a gentleman, (not the landlord,) inquired, "Stranger are you fond of *history*?" and being answered in the affirmative, he related something like the foregoing story.

A TRAVELLER IN THE WEST.

PRESIDENT'S MESSAGE.

WASHINGTON, August 6, 1850.

To the Senate and House of Representatives:

I herewith transmit to the two Houses of Congress a letter from his Excellency the Governor of Texas, dated on the 14th day of June last, addressed to the late President of the United States, which, not having been answered by him, came to my hands on his death; and I also transmit a copy of the answer which I have felt it my duty to cause to be made to that communication.

Congress will perceive that the Governor of Texas officially states that, by authority of the Legislature of that State, he dispatched a Special Commissioner, with full power and instructions to extend the civil jurisdiction of the State over the unorganized counties of El Paso, Worth, Presidio and Santa Fe, situated on its northwestern limits.

He proceeds to say that the Commissioner had reported to him, in an official form, that the military officers employed in the service of the United States, stationed at Santa Fe, interposed adversely, with the inhabitants, to the fulfillment of his object, in favor of the establishment of a seperate State Government east of the Rio Grande, and within the rightful limits of the State of Texas. The four counties which Texas thus proposes to establish and organize, as being within her jurisdiction, extend over the whole of the territory east of the Rio Grande, which has heretofore been regarded as an essential and integral part of the department of New Mexico, and actually governed and possessed by her people, until conquered and severed from the Republic of Mexico by the American arms.

The Legislature of Texas has been called together by her Governor, for the purpose, as is understood, of maintaining her claim to the territory east of the Rio Grande, and of establishing over it her own jurisdiction and her own laws by force.

These proceedings of Texas may well arrest the attention of all branches of the government of the United States; and I rejoice that they occur while the Congress is yet in session. It is, I fear, far from being impossible that, in consequence of these proceedings of Texas, a crisis may be brought on which shall summon the two Houses of Congress, and still more emphatically the Executive Government, to an immediate readiness for the performance of their respective duties.

By the Constitution of the United States, the President is constituted Commander-in-chief of the Army and Navy; and of the Militia of the several States, when called into the actual service of the United States. The constitution declares also that he shall take care that the laws be faithfully executed, and that he shall, from time to time, give to the Congress information of the state of the Union.

Congress has power, by the constitution, to provide for calling forth the militia to execute the laws of the Union; and suitable and appropriate acts of Congress have been passed, as well for providing for calling forth the militia, as for placing other suitable and efficient means in the hands of the President to enable him to discharge the constitutional functions of his office.

The second section of the act of the 28th February, 1795 declares that whenever the laws of the United States shall be opposed, or their execution obstructed, in any State, by combinations too powerful to be suppressed by the ordinary course of judicial proceedings, or the power vested in the marshals, the President may call forth the militia, so far as may be necessary to suppress such combinations, and to cause the laws to be duly executed.

By the act of March 3d, 1807, it is provided in all cases of obstructions to the laws, either of the United States, or any individual State or Territory, where it is lawful for the President to call forth the militia for the purpose of causing the laws to be duly executed, it shall be lawful for him to employ, for the same purposes, such part of the land or naval force of the United States as shall be judged necessary.

These several enactments are now in full force; so that if the laws of the United States are opposed or obstructed, in any State or Territory, by combinations too powerful to be suppressed by the judicial or civil authorities, it becomes a case in which it is the duty of the President either to call out the militia or to employ the military and naval force of the United States; or to do both, if in his judgement the exigency of the occasions shall so require, for the purpose of suppressing such combinations. The constitutional duty of the President is plain and peremptory, and the authority vested in him by law for its performance clear and ample.

Texas is a State, authorized to maintain her own laws, so far as they are not repugnant to the constitution, laws and treaties of the United States; to suppress insurrections against her authority, and to punish those who may commit treason against the State, according to the forms provided by her own constitution, and her own laws.—But all this power is local, and confined entirely within the limits of Texas herself.—She can possibly confer no authority which can be lawfully exercised beyond her own boundaries. All this is plain, and hardly needs argument or elucidation. If Texan militia, therefore march into any one of the other States or into any Territory of the United States, there to execute or enforce any law of Texas, they become at that moment trespassers; they are no longer under the protection of any lawful authority, and are to be regarded merely as intruders; and if, within such State or Territory, they obstruct any law of the United States, either by power of arms or mere power of numbers, constituting such a combination as is too powerful to be suppressed by the civil authority, the President of the United States has no option left to him, but is bound to obey the solemn injunction of the constitution, and exercise the high powers vested in him by that instrument and by the acts of Congress.

Of if any civil posse, armed or unarmed, enter into any Territory of the United States, with intent to seize individuals to be carried elsewhere for trial, for alleged offences, and this posse too powerful to be resisted, by the local civil authorities, such seizure or attempt to seize is to be prevented or resisted by the authority of the United States.

The grave and important question now arises, whether there be in the Territory of New Mexico any existing law of the United States, opposition to which, or the obstruction of which, would constitute a case calling for the interposition of the authority vested in the President.

The constitution of the United States declares, that "this constitution, and the laws of the United States which shall be made in pursuance thereof, and all treaties made, or which shall be made, under the authority of the United States, shall be the supreme law of the land." If, therefore, New Mexico be a Territory of the United States, and if any treaty stipulation be in force therein, such treaty stipulations is the supreme law of the land, and is to be maintained and upheld accordingly.

In the letter to the Governor of Texas my reasons are given for believing that New Mexico is now a Territory of the United States, with the same extent and the same boundaries which belonged to it while in the actual possession of the Republic of Mexico, and before the late war. In the early part of that war, both California and New Mexico were conquered by the arms of the United States, and were in the military possession of the United States at the date of the treaty of peace. By that treaty the title by conquest was confirmed, and these territories, provinces or departments separated from Mexico forever; and by the same treaty certain important rights and securities were solemnly guarantied to the inhabitants residing therein.

By the fifth article of the treaty, it is declared that—

"The boundary line between the two republics shall commence in the Gulf of Mexico three leagues from land, opposite the mouth of the Rio Grande, otherwise called the Bravo del Norte, or opposite the mouth of its deepest branch, if it should have more than one branch, emptying directly into the sea; from thence up the middle of that river, following the deepest channel, where it has more than one, to the point where it strikes the southern boundary of New Mexico; thence westwardly, along the whole southern boundary of New Mexico, (which runs north of the town called Paso) to its western termination; thence northward, along the western line of New Mexico until it intersects the first branch of the river Gila; (or if it should not intersect any branch of that river, then to the point on the said line nearest to such branch, and thence in a direct line to the same;) thence down the middle of the said branch and of the said river until it empties into the Rio Colorado; thence across the Rio Colorado, following the division line between Upper and Lower California, to the Pacific ocean."

The eighth article of the treaty is in the following terms:

"Mexicans now established in territories previously belonging to Mexico, and which remain for the future within the limits of the United States, as defined by the present treaty, shall be free to continue where they now reside, or to remove at any time to the Mexican republic, retaining the property which they possess in the said Territories, or disposing thereof, and removing the proceeds wherever they please, without their being subjected on this account to any contribution tax, or charge whatever.

"Those who shall prefer to remain in the said Territories may either retain the title and rights of Mexican citizens, or acquire those of citizens of the United States. But they shall be under the obligation to make their election within one year from the date of the exchange of ratifications of this treaty; and those who shall remain in the said Territories after the expiration of that year, without having declared their intention to retain the character of Mexicans, shall be considered to have elected to become citizens of the United States."

"In the said Territories property of every kind now belonging to Mexicans not established there shall be inviolably respected. The present owners, the heirs of these and all Mexicans who may hereafter acquire said property by contract, shall enjoy with respect to its guaranties equally ample as if the same belonged to citizens of the United States."

The ninth article of the treaty is in these words:

"The Mexicans who, in the Territories aforesaid, shall not preserve the character of citizens of the Mexican Republic, conformably with what is stipulated in the preceeding article, shall be incorporated into the union of the United States, and be admitted at the proper time "to be judged by the Congress of the United States) to the enjoyment of all the rights of citizens of the United States, according to the principles of the Constitution; and, in the mean time, shall be maintained and protected in the free enjoyment of their liberty and property, and secured in the free exercise of their religion without restriction."

It is plain, therefore, on the face of these treaty stipulations, that all Mexicans established in Territories north of the line of demarkation already mentioned, come within the protection of the 9th article; and that the treaty, being a part of the supreme law of the land, does extend over all such Mexicans, and assures to them perfect security in the free enjoyment of their liberty and property, as well as in the free exercise of their religion; and this supreme law of the land, being thus in actual force over this territory, is to be maintained and enforced until it shall be displaced or superseded by other legal provisions; and if it be obstructed or restricted by combinations too powerful to be suppressed by the civil authority, the case is one which comes within the provisions of the law, and which obliges the President to enforce those provisions. Neither the constitution nor the law, my duty or my oath of office, leaves me any alternative or any choice in my mode of action.

The Executive Government of the United States has no power or authority to determine what was the true line of boundary between Mexico and the United States before the treaty of Guadalupe Hidalgo; nor has it any such power now, since the question has become a question between the State of Texas and the United States. So far as this boundary is doubtful, that doubt can only be removed by some act of Congress, to which the assent of the State of Texas may be necessary, or by some appropriate mode of legal adjudication; but, in the mean time, if disturbances or collisions arise, or should be threatened, it is absolutely incumbent on the Executive Government, however painful the duty, to take care that the laws are faithfully maintained. And he can regard only the actual state of things as it existed at the date of the treaty, and is bound to protect all inhabitants who were then established and who now remain north and east of the line of demarkation, in the full enjoyment of their liberty and property, according to the provisions of the 9th article of the treaty; in other words, that all must be now regarded as New Mexico which was possessed and occupied as New Mexico, by citizens of Mexico at the date of the treaty, until a definite line of boundary shall be established by competent authority. This assertion of duty to protect the people of New Mexico from threatened violence, or from seizure to be carried into Texas for trial for alleged offences against Texan laws, does not at all include any claim of power on the part of the Executive to establish any civil or military government within that Territory. *That power* belongs exclusively to the Legislative department, and Congress is the sole judge of the time and manner of creating or authorizing any such Government. The duty of the Executive extends only to the execution of laws and the maintenance of treaties already in force, and the protection of all the people of the United States in the enjoyment of the rights which those treaties and laws guaranty. It is exceedingly desirable that no occasion should arise for the exercise of the powers thus vested in the President by the Constitution and the laws. With whatever mildness those powers might be executed, or however clear the case of necessity, yet consequences might nevertheless follow of which no human sagacity can foresee either the evils or the end.

Having thus laid before Congress the communication of his Excellency the Governor of Texas, and the answer thereto, and having made such observations as I have thought the occasion called for, respecting constitutional obligations which may arise in the further progress of things, and may devolve on me to be performed, I hope I shall not be regarded as stepping aside from the line of duty, notwithstanding that I am aware that the subject is now before both Houses, if I express my deep and earnest conviction of the propriety of an immediate decision, or arrangement, or settlement of the question of boundary between Texas and the Territory of New Mexico. All considerations of justice, general expediency, and domestic tranquility call for this. It seems to be, in its character and by position, the first, or one of the first of the questions growing out of the acquisition of California and New Mexico, and now calling for decision.

No Government can be established for New Mexico, either State or Territorial, until it shall be first ascertained what New Mexico is, and what are her limits and boundaries. These cannot be fixed or known till the line of division between her and Texas shall be ascertained and established; and numerous and weighty reasons conspire, in my judgment, to show that this divisional line should be established by Congress, with the assent of the Government of Texas. In the first place, this seems by far the most prompt mode of proceeding by which the end can be accomplished. If judicial proceedings were resorted to, such proceedings would necessarily be slow, and years would pass by, in all probability, before the controversy could be settled. So great a delay in this case is to be avoided, if possible. It would be every way inconvenient, and might be the occasion of disturbance and collisions.

For the same reason, I would, with the utmost deference to the wisdom of Congress, express a doubt of the expediency of the appointment of commissioners, and of an examination, estimate, and an award of an indemnity to be made by them. This would be but a species of arbitration, which might last as long as a suit at law.

So far as I am able to comprehend the case, the general facts are now all known, and Congress is as capable of deciding on it justly and properly now as it probably would be after the report of commissioners.

If the claim of title on the part of Texas appear to Congress to be well founded, in whole or in part, it is in the competency of Congress to offer her an indemnity for the surrender of that claim. In a case like this, surrounded as it is by many cogent considerations, all calling for amicable adjustment and immediate settlement, the Government of the United States would be justified, in my opinion, in allowing an indemnity to Texas, not unreasonable and extravagant, but fair, liberal, and awarded in a just spirit of accommodation.

I think no event would be hailed with more gratification by the people of the United States than the amicable arrangement of questions of difficulty which have now for a long time agitated the country, and occupied, to the exclusion of other subjects, the time and attention of Congress.

Having thus freely communicated the results of my own reflections on the most advisable mode of adjusting the boundary question, I shall nevertheless cheerfully acquiesce in any other mode which the wisdom of Congress may devise.

And, in conclusion, I repeat my conviction that every consideration of the public interests manifests the necessity of a provision by Congress for a settlement of this boundary question before the present session be brought to a close. The settlement of other questions connected with the same subject, within the same period, is greatly to be desired; but the adjustment of this appears to me to be in the highest degree important. In the train of such an adjustment, we may well hope that there will follow a return of harmony and good will, an increased attachment to the Union, and the general satisfaction of the country.

MILLARD FILLMORE.

EXECUTIVE DEPARTMENT,
Austin, (Texas,) June 14, 1850.

SIR: By authority of the Legislature of Texas, the Executive of the State, in February last, dispatched a special commissioner with full power and instructions to extend the civil jurisdiction of this State over the unorganized counties of El Paso, Worth, Presido, and Santa Fe, situated upon its north-western limits.

That commissioner has reported to me, in an official form, that the military officers employed in the service of the United States, stationed at Santa Fe, interposed adversely with the inhabitants to the fulfilment of his object, by employing their influence in favor of the establishment of a seperate State Government east of the Rio Grande, and within the rightful limits of the State of Texas. I transmit to you herewith the proclamation of Colonel John Munroe, acting under the orders of the Government of the United States, under the designation of Civil and Military Governor of the Territory of New Mexico.

I have very respectfully to request that your Excellency will cause me to be informed, at your earliest possible convenience, whether or not this officer has acted in this matter under the orders of his Government, and whether his proclamation meets with the approbation of the President of the United States?

With assurances of distinguished consideration, I have the honor to be your Excellency's most obedient servant,

P. H. BELL.

To his Excellency Z. TAYLOR,
President of the United States.

DEPARTMENT OF STATE,
Washington, August 5, 1850.

SIR: A letter addressed by you to the late President of the United States, and dated on the 14th of June last, has, since his lamented decease, been transferred to the hands of his successor, by whom I am directed to transmit to you the following answer:

In that letter you say that, by the authority of the Legislature of Texas, the

[*Concluded on second page.*]

[CONCLUDED FROM 1ST PAGE.]

Executive of that State, in February last, dispatched a special commissioner, with full power and instructions to extend the civil jurisdiction of that State over the unorganized counties of El Paso, Worth, Presido, and Santa Fe, situated upon its north-western limits; and that the commissioner has reported to you, in an official form, that the military officers employed in the service of the United States, stationed at Santa Fe, interposed adversely with the inhabitants to the fulfilment of his object, by employing their influence in favor of the establishment of a separate State Government east of the Rio Grande, and within the rightful limits of the State of Texas. You also transmit a copy of the proclamation of Colonel John Munroe, acting under the orders of the Government of the United States, under the designation of Civil and Military Governor of the Territory of New Mexico, and respectfully request the President to cause you to be informed whether or not this officer has acted in this matter under the orders of his Government, and whether his proclamation meets with the approval of the President of the United States?

In the events which have occurred, I hardly know whether your Excellency would naturally expect an answer to this letter from him. His predecessor in office, to whom it was addressed, and under whose authority and direction the proclamation of Col. Munroe was issued, is no more; and, at this time, the proclamation, whatever may be regarded as its true character, has ceased to have influence or effect. The meeting of the people of New Mexico, by their representatives, which it invited, is understood to have taken place, although the Government has as yet received no official information of it.

Partaking, however, in the fullest degree in that high respect which the Executive Government of the United States always entertains towards the Governors and the Governments of the States, the President thinks it his duty, nevertheless, to manifest that feeling of respect, by acknowledging and answering your letter. And this duty, let me assure your Excellency, has been so long delayed only by uncontrollable circumstances, and is now performed at the earliest practicable moment, after the appointment of these heads of Department, and their acceptance of office, with whom it is usual, on important occasions, for the President of the United States to advise.

In answer, therefore, to your first interrogatory, viz: whether Colonel Munroe, in issuing the proclamation referred to, acted under the orders of this Government, I have the honor to state that Col. Munroe's proclamation appears to have been issued in pursuance, or in consequence, of an order, or letter of instruction, given by the late Secretary of War, under the authority of the late President, to Lieut. Col. McCall. Of this order, which bears date on the 19th of November. 1849, your Excellency was undoubtedly informed at the date of your letter. A full and accurate copy, however, is attached to this communication. Col. McCall is therein instructed that if the people of New Mexico, for whom Congress has provided no Government, should manifest a wish to take any steps to establish a Government for themselves, and apply for admission into the Union, it would be his duty, and the duty of others with whom he was associated, not to thwart, but to advance their wishes. This order does not appear to authorize any exertion of military authority, or of any official or even personal interference, to control, or affect in any way, the primary action of the people in the formation of a Government, nor to permit any such interference by subordinate officers. Col. McCall and his associates were not called upon to take a lead in any measures, or even to recommend any thing as fit to be adopted by the people. Their whole duty was confined to what they might be able to perform, subordinate to the wishes of the people. In this matter it was evidently contemplated that they were to act as the agents of the inhabitants, and not as officers of this Government. It must be recollected that the only Government then existing in the Territory was a quasi military Government, and as Congress had made no provision for the establishment of any form of civil Government, and as the President doubtless believed that under these circumstances the people had a right to frame a Government for themselves, and submit it to Congress for its approval, the order was a direction that the then existing military Government should not stand in the way of the accomplishment of the wishes of the people, nor thwart those wishes, if the people entertained them, for the establishment of a free, popular, republican civil Government, for their own protection and benefit. This is evidently the whole purpose and object of the order. The military officer in command, and his associates, were American citizens, acquainted with the forms of civil and popular proceedings, and it was expected that they would aid the inhabitants of the territory, by their advice and assistance, in their proceedings for establishing a Government of their own.—There is no room to suppose that Colonel Munroe, an officer as much distinguished for prudence and discretion as for gallant conduct in arms, meant to act, and did act, otherwise than in entire subordination and subserviency to the will of the people among whom he was placed. He was not authorized to do, nor do I understand him as intending to do, any thing whatever in his military character, nor to represent, in any way, the wishes of the Executive Government of the United States.

To judge intelligently and fairly of these transactions, we must recall to our recollection the circumstances of the case, as they then existed. Previous to the war with Mexico, which commenced in May, 1846, and received the sanction of Congress on the 13th of that month, the Territory of New Mexico formed a Department or State of the Mexican Republic, and was governed by her laws. General Kearny, acting under orders from this Government, invaded this Department with an armed force; the Governor fled at his approach, and the troops under his command dispersed; and General Kearny entered Santa Fe, the capital, on the 18th of August, 1846, and took possession of the Territory in the name of the United States. On the 22d of that month he issued a proclamation to the inhabitants, stating the fact that he had taken possession of Santa Fe, at the head of his troops, and announcing his "intention to hold the Department with its original boundaries, (on both sides of the Del Norte,) and under the name of New Mexico." By that proclamation he promised to protect the inhabitants of New Mexico in their persons and property, against their Indian allies, and *all others*, and assured them that the United States intended to provide for them a free Government, where the people would be called upon to exercise the rights of freemen in electing their own representatives to the Territorial Legislature. On the same day he established a Territorial Constitution by an organic law, which provided for executive, legislative and judicial departments of the Government, defined the right of suffrage, and provided for trial by jury, and at the same time established a code of laws. This Constitution declared that "the country heretofore known as New Mexico, shall be known hereafter and designated as the Territory of New Mexico, in the United States of America," and the members of the lower House of the Legislature were apportioned among the counties established by the decree of the Department of New Mexico, of June 17, 1844, which counties, it is understood, included all the Territory over which Texas has lately attempted to organize counties and establish her own jurisdiction. On the 22d of December, 1846, a copy of this Constitution and Code was transmitted by President Polk to the House of Representatives, in pursuance of a call on him by that body. In the message transmitting the Constitution, he says that "portions of it purport to establish and organize a *permanent* Territorial Government over the Territory, and to impart to its inhabitants political rights which, under the Constitution of the United States, can be enjoyed permanently only by citizens of the United States. These have not been approved and recognized by me. Such organized regulations as have been established in any of the conquered Territories, for the security of our conquest, for the preservation of order, for the protection of the rights of the inhabitants, and for depriving the enemy of the advantages of these Territories, while the military possession by them of the forces of the United States continues, *will be recognized and approved*." Near four years have now elapsed since this *quasi* military Government was established by military authority, and received, with the exceptions mentioned, the approval of President Polk. In the meantime a treaty of peace has been concluded with Mexico, by which a boundary line was established that left this Territory within the United States, thereby confirming to the United States, by treaty, what we had before acquired by conquest. The treaty, in perfect accordance with the proclamation of General Kearny, declared that the Mexicans remaining in this Territory should be incorporated into the Union of the United States, and be admitted at the proper time (to be judged by the Congress of the United States) to the enjoyment of all the rights of citizens of the United States, according to the principles of the Constitution;" and in the meantime "should be maintained and protected in the free enjoyment of their liberty and property, and secured in the free exercise of their religion without restriction." Thus it will be perceived that the authority of the United States over New Mexico was the result of conquest; and the possession held of it, in the first place, was of course a military possession. The treaty added the title by cession to the already existing title by successful achievements in arms. With the peace, there arose a natural expectation that, as early as possible, there would come a civil Government to supersede the military. But, until some such form of Government should come into existence, it was matter of absolute necessity that the military Government should continue, as otherwise the country must fall into absolute anarchy. And this has been the course, generally, in the practice of civilized nations, when colonies or territories have been acquired by war, and their acquisition confirmed by treaty.

The military Government, therefore, existing in New Mexico at the date of the order, existed there of inevitable necessity.—It existed as much against the will of the Executive Government of the United States as against the will of the people. The late President had adopted the opinion that it was justifiable in the people of the Territory, under the circumstances, to form a Constitution of Government, without any previous authority conferred by Congress; and thereupon to apply for admission into the Union. It was under this state of things, and under the influence of these opinions, that the order of the 19th of November last was given, and executed in the manner we have seen. The order indicates no boundary and defines no territory, except by the name of New Mexico; and so far as that indicated any thing, it referred to a known Territory, which had been organized under military authority, approved by the Executive, and left without remonstrance or alteration by Congress, for more than three years. It appears to the President that such an order could not have been intended to invade the rights of Texas.

Secondly, you ask whether the proclamation of Colonel Munroe meets with the approval of the President of the United States?

To determine this question, it is necessary to look at the *object* of the proclamation and the *effect* of the proceedings had under it.

If the object was to assume the authority to settle the disputed boundary with Texas, then the President has no hesitation in saying that such object does not meet his approbation, because he does not believe that the Executive branch of this Government, or the inhabitants of New Mexico, or both combined, have any constitutional authority to settle that question. That belongs either to the Judicial Department of the Federal Government or to the concurrent action by agreement of the Legislative Departments of the Governments of the United States and Texas. But it has been sufficiently shown that Col. Munroe could have had no such object, and that his intention was merely to act in aid of the people in forming a State Constitution to be submitted to Congress. Assuming, then, that such a Constitution has been formed, what is its *effect* upon the disputed boundary? If it compromits the rights of either party to that question, then it does not meet the President's approbation; for he deems it his duty to leave the settlement of that question to the tribunal to which it constitutionally belongs. It is sufficient for him that this boundary is in dispute; that the territory east of the Rio del Norte seems to be claimed in good faith both by Texas and New Mexico, or rather by the United States. Whatever might be his judgment in regard to their respective rights, he has no power to decide upon them, or even to negotiate in regard to them; and therefore it would be improper for him to express any opinion. The subject matter of dispute is between the United States and Texas, and not between the inhabitants of New Mexico and Texas. If those people should voluntarily consent to come under the jurisdiction of Texas, such consent would not bind the United States or take away their title to the territory. So, on the other hand, if they should voluntarily claim the title for the United States, it would not deprive Texas of her rights. Whatever those rights may be, they can only be affected by her own acts or a judicial decision. The State Constitution formed by New Mexico can have no legal validity until it is recognised and adopted by the law-making power of the United States. Until that is done, it has no sanction, and can have no effect, upon the rights of Texas or of the United States to the Territory in dispute. And it is not to be presumed that Congress will ever give its sanction to that Constitution without first providing for the settlement of this boundary. Indeed, no Government, either Territorial or State, can be formed for New Mexico, without providing for settling this boundary. Hence he regards the formation of this State Constitution as a mere nullity. It may be regarded, indeed, as a petition to Congress to be admitted as a State, but until Congress shall grant the prayer of such petition, by legal enactments, it affects the rights of neither party. But as it is the right of all to petition Congress for any law which it may constitutionally pass, this people were in the exercise of a common right when they formed their Constitution with a view of applying to Congress for admission as a State, and as he thinks the act can prejudice no one, he feels bound to approve of the conduct of Col. Munroe, in issuing his proclamation.

I am directed also to state that, in the President's opinion, it would not be just to suppose that the late President desired to manifest any unfriendly attitude or aspect towards Texas, or the claims of Texas.—The boundary between Texas and New Mexico was known to be disputed; and it was equally well known that the Executive Government of the United States had no power to settle that dispute. It is believed that the Executive power has not wished—it certainly does not now wish—to interfere with that question in any manner whatever, as a question of title.

In one of his last communications to Congress, that of the 17th of June last, the late President repeated the declaration that he had no power to decide the question of boundary, and no desire to interfere with it, and that the authority to settle that question resides elsewhere. The object of the Executive Government has been, as I believe, and as I am authorized to say it certainly now is, to secure the peace of the country; to maintain, as far as practicable, the state of things as it existed at the date of the treaty; and to uphold and preserve the rights of the respective parties, as they were under the solemn guaranty of the treaty, until the highly interesting question of boundary should be finally settled by competent authority. This treaty, which is now the supreme law of the land, declares, as before stated, that the inhabitants shall be maintained and protected in the free enjoyment of their liberty and property, and secured in the free exercise of their religion. It will, of course, be the President's duty to see that this law is sustained, and the protection which it guaranties made effectual; and this is the plain and open path of Executive duty, in which he proposes to tread.

Other transactions of a very grave character are alluded to and recited in your Excellency's letter. To those transactions I am now directed not more particularly to advert, because the only questions propounded by you respect the authority under which Colonel Munroe acted, and the approval and disapproval of his proclamation. Your Excellency's communication and this answer will be immediately laid before Congress, and the President will take that occasion to bring to its notice the transactions alluded to above.

It is known to your Excellency that the questions growing out of the acquisition of California and New Mexico, and among them the highly important one of the boundary of Texas, have steadily engaged the attention of both Houses of Congress for many months, and still engage it, with intense interest. It is understood that the Legislature of Texas will be shortly in session, and will have the boundary question also before it. It is a delicate crisis in our public affairs, not free, certainly, from possible dangers, but let us confidently trust that justice, moderation, and patriotism, and the love of the Union, may inspire such counsels, both in the Government of the United States and that of Texas, as shall carry the country through these dangers, and bring it safely out of them all, and with renewed assurances of the continuance of mutual respect and harmony in the great family of States.

I have the honor to be, with entire regard, your Excellency's most obedient servant,

DAN'L. WEBSTER.

To his Excellency P. H. BELL,

Governor of Texas,

The following impressive counsel by Jas. Madison should, at the present time, sink deep into the heart of every American:

As this advice, if ever it see the light, will not do so until I am no more, it may be considered as issuing from the tomb, where truth alone can be respected, and the happiness of man alone consulted. It will be entitled, therefore, to whatever weight can be derived from good intentions, and from the experience of one who has served his country in various stations a period of forty years; who has espoused in his youth, and adhered through his life, to the cause of its liberty; and who has borne a part in most of the great transactions which will constitute epochs in its destiny. The advice nearest to my heart, and deepest is, that the Union of the States be cherished and perpetuated. Let the open enemy to it be regarded as a Pandora with her box opened, and the disguised one as the serpent creeping with his deadly wiles into Paradise.

The Advocate.

Office in the brick building near the Court House

VICTORIA, TEXAS:

FRIDAY MORNING, AUGUST 30.

The President's Message.

We publish to-day the message of President Fillmore, the letter of Mr. Webster to Gov. Bell, and the bill as it passed the Senate, proposing to purchase a portion of our territory. We would recommend all of them to the careful perusal and thoughtful consideration of our readers. To the full understanding of the difficulties which now surround us, it is important to clearly apprehend the position of the Executive of the Union, as well as the feelings and views of Congress.

From the hasty consideration which we have as yet been able to give the message and letter, we understand the position of the Executive Department to be as follows: First, that the United States has a *claim* to New Mexico; and that under the treaty of Guadalupe Hidalgo, the General Government is bound to protect the inhabitants against aggression from every quarter, and that the Executive will feel it his bounden duty to do so, until the rival claim of Texas is adjudicated.

Second. That there are but two constitutional modes of settlement of the conflicting claims—the one by referring the matter to the Supreme Court; the other by agreement between the Congress of the United States on the one part, and the State of Texas on the other. He prefers the latter, as likely to give most satisfaction, and warmly and eloquently urges it upon Congress to make, without delay, a proposition to Texas to purchase her claim to a portion or all of the disputed territory.

Third. Denies any right in the Executive to decide the dispute, and therefore desires not to be understood as expressing any opinion on the comparative merits of the respective claims.

Fourth. The Executive is opposed to the organization of either a Territorial or a State Government for New Mexico, until after the dispute relative to the Texas boundary is fully adjusted.

We understand these to be the principle positions assumed by the Executive. Of course we do not approve the first position. We believe, and nine-tenths of the people of Texas believe, that the territory east of the Rio Grande, from its source to its mouth, belongs to Texas by clear and indisputable title, and that it was the duty of the General Government to have surrendered the possession of it to Texas, so soon after the conclusion of the war as it might be demanded. But the Executive of the United States, and, we fear, Congress, have taken a different view of the subject. It will be perceived by reference to our summary of Congressional proceedings, that whilst the bill proposing to purchase a portion of Texas territory for $10,000,000 (which subsequently passed that body) was pending in the Senate, Mr. Mason, of Virginia, moved to amend the bill by striking out the whole, and substituting therefor a claim embracing a full recognition of the title of Texas to all the country east of the Rio Grande.—This amendment was voted down by an overwhelming majority—37 to 14—not one-half, even, of the Southern Senators voting for it. If this vote is to be regarded as a test of the feeling of the Senate as to the validity of the Texas title, then, indeed, are we in a woful minority; and if it is to be regarded as an index to the feelings of the people of the whole United States, well may it cease to be a matter of surprise that the President shall feel it his duty to keep the possession of New Mexico even by force, until the matter of boundary is finally adjudicated and settled.

These are pregnant facts, which the people and Legislature of Texas would do well at this juncture to consider. It is not alone the Executive, but the Congress and Executive united, which is against us; yet, whilst they refuse to recognise the title of Texas, for the sake of peace, and to avoid collision between the different members of the confederacy, they propose to purchase the disputed territory. What should Texas do? We say emphatically, *accept the proposition*—take the *ten millions*—part with the territory. If the Congress should even recognise our title to be good, we would not be willing to retain the territory if we could sell it for any fair price. What do we want with 20 or 30,000 Mexican voters way up in an extreme corner of the State, to hold the balance of power and control our elections and legislation? The only real value to Texas, of New Mexico, is to *sell*. Then, as we are offered a fair price for it, let us accept the offer made us, and be rid of an unhappy controversy with the United States,—be rid forever of a comparatively (to Texas) worthless and difficult to govern territory, and be rid forever of a mongrel population, the mass of whom are *peons*, and fitted for no social position above that system of pseudo-slavery in which they were born—certainly not fitted, by intelligence or morality, to have extended to them the right of suffrage, that boon so inestimable to freemen, and which our Constitution has so lavishly and unwisely extended to them.

The U. S. Boundary Survey Commission arrived at Indianola on Thursday last, on the steamer Galveston, and may be expected here sometime next week.

The cotton in this section of country is very promising, and the bolls are maturing and opening fast. The planters are busily engaged in picking. As yet we have had no sign of the worm, and if they do not appear within the next few weeks, the crop will be safe from their depredations. Indeed more than half a crop is now open and ready for picking—notwithstanding the spring was so unfavorable, and the plant is full three weeks later than usuall, the prospect now is encouraging, that our planters will make better crops than they did during either of the previous five years.

Capt. Reid's hands are now picking from 170 to 180 lbs. each per day.

We learn that in Gonzales county, the cotton crop looks very well, and promises an abundant yield.

The Legislature.

By the last Austin mail, we have the proceedings of the Legislature up to the 15th inst. Apart from the election of officers and the appointment of several important committees, but little business of interest has been transacted. The Senate have passed a resolution, declaring that no business other than that recommended to the Legislature by the Governor, shall be entertained during the present extra session.

Senator Robertson introduced the following bill, which was read a first and second time, and referred to the Select Joint Committee of both Houses:

A Bill to be entitled an act to raise a certain number of Volunteers, to suppress Insurrection in the county of Santa Fe.

SECTION 1. *Be it enacted by the Legislature of the State of Texas*, That the Governor be, and he is hereby authorized, to call five thousand volunteers, to be organized into five regiments of one thousand men in the aggregate each; the companies to consist of one hundred men each in the aggregate, and to be officered according to the regulations of the United States army.

SEC. 2. That each volunteer be required to furnish his own horse, arms and equipments, and shall receive the same pay that is allowed to troops of the United States of a like character; and in addition to said pay, each volunteer receiving an honorable discharge for services contemplated by this act, shall receive as a bounty, a quantity of land proportionate to the time he serves, that is to say, for three months service three hundred and twenty acres, for six months, six hundred and forty acres, and for twelve months, twelve hundred and eighty acres. The presentation of an honorable discharge to the Adjutant General, shall be a sufficient voucher for that officer to issue the bounty land warrants contemplated by this act.

SEC. 3. That two regiments of said volunteers be mustered into service immediately, and that the other three be required to hold themselves in readiness to march at a moments warning.

SEC. 4. That should the exigencies require the other three regiments in the field at any time, the Governor is authorized to call them into the service and march them to the scene of rebellion; but said reserve of three regiments is not to be called into the service for any other purpose than to enforce our lawful jurisdiction over the soil of the State, as defined by the law of 1836.

SEC. 5. That for the payment of said troops for the services contemplated by this act, the proceeds arising from the sale of any portion of the public lands that this State may hereafter sell, is hereby specifically appropriated.

SEC. 6. That the Governor is hereby authorized to take command of said troops in person.

SEC. 7. That all moneys in the Treasury not otherwise appropriated, are hereby appropriated for the purpose of carrying into effect the provisions of this act; and that this act be in force and take effect, from and after its passage.

Telegraphed to the New Orleans Picayune.

Arrival of the steamer Pacific.

BALTIMORE, August 12.—The American steamer Pacific arrived at New York on the evening of the 11th.

English Markets.

Since the sailing of the Cambria, cotton had advanced ⅛ to ¼d. The sales of cotton for the four days prior to the departure of the Pacific, amounted to 47,000 bales.—Baring's circular quotes an advance of ⅛d.

Congressional.

The *Senate* was to take up the California Bill on Monday (12th). It is believed that the *House* will pass the Texas bill, though the northern and southern ultras continue to combat it.

Battle between the Danes and the Holsteiners.

On the 25th ult. a great battle took place between the Danes and Holsteiners, in which the former were victorious. The Danes were 40,000 strong and the Holsteiners 30,000. The killed, wounded and missing amounted to 7000. The Danes lost the greater number. The Holsteiners were compelled to retreat; but the Danes proposed a truce of three days, which was declined by the former.

The Hanovarians have determined to side with the Holsteiners.

Germany.

Austria refuses to abide by the decision of the Frankfort Parliament.

Congressional.

BALTIMORE, *Tuesday*, August 13.—On Monday, (12th), the amendment of Mr. Davis, of Mississippi, proposing a division of California, was rejected by a vote of 30 to 20. The bill admitting California, was then ordered to be engrossed for a third reading by 23 to 19. The Senate then adjourned.

Cotton.

Cotton at New York has an upward tendency.

A Southern Caucus.

BALTIMORE, *Tuesday*, August 13th.—A caucus of Southern members of Congress has been held. Thirty members were present. They resolved to oppose the Texas and California bills by all the constitutional means in their power, unless the territorial question is previously settled. Their resolutions are published.

Congressional.

The California bill has passed the Senate by a vote of 34 to 18.

Editorial Correspondence.

WASHINGTON, Aug. 8, 1850.

DEAR STERNE:—The times are exciting here as I doubt not they are with you in Texas. Since the defeat of the Omnibus or Compromise bill, Mr. Fillmore, the new President has sent in a special message to both Houses of Congress confined to the Santa Fe and Texas questions. The message is quite lengthy, and is on the whole regarded here as an able, mild, and conciliatory document, quite different in its tone from President Taylor's last message on the same subject. I enclose you the message, and hope you will lose no time in laying them before the readers of the Advocate.

The movements in Texas are not without their influences here, and there is no doubt but they formed one of the strongest reasons that induced the new President to urge so earnestly, as he does in his message, the speedy settlement of the Texas Boundary question by Congress. It is not to be doubted that he feels that he is placed in a delicate position; for he must see that if he attempts to use the military power of the United States to prevent Texas extending her jurisdiction over Santa Fe, he will that moment kindle an excitement throughout the country that will shake this Union from one extremity to the other. The opinion prevails here that had it not been for the action of Gen. Taylor the present Administration would not insist upon holding possession of Santa Fe at all, but would withdraw in favor of Texas. Certain political reasons, however, conspire against this course now—among which I doubt not is a sentiment of respect and deference for the memory of the late President.

Mr. Pearce, of Maryland, who has the immortal honor of defeating the Omnibus, has introduced in the Senate a bill to settle the Texas Boundary and indemnify Texas for the surrender of the Santa Fe country. Towards the measure I feel entirely friendly, and there is no doubt it will be supported by both our Senators. Rusk told me, indeed, that he should support it, though he expected that course would defeat his re-election. I hope not. I should exceedingly regret that for such a praiseworthy act as that Texas should withhold her support and countenance from one who has rendered the State such signal service, and who enjoys such an enviable position in the Senate. I think Kaufman is disposed to support Pearce's bill, whilst Howard is opposed to it. It is but proper to state that by Pearce's bill Texas is to give up all the country North of a line beginning at the 100th degree West of Greenwich and running due West on the parallel of 36 to the 103 degree West of Greenwich, thence due South to the 320 parallel, thence due West to the Rio Grande. For this country the United States is to pay Texas ten millions of dollars. The lines give more satisfaction than did those in the Omnibus bill, and I make no doubt the bill will pass the Senate, and perhaps the House, and that too pretty soon.

The arrival here yesterday of Ex-Gov. Henderson, Ex-Gov. Wood, Judge Watsons, and other citizens of Texas has created quite a stir here. These gentlemen report the excitement in Texas as at the very highest pitch, and give it as their very decided opinion that no such bill as Pearce's or the Omnibus would meet the approbation of Texas—in other words that she will not sell Santa Fe at all. Can this be true? I cannot think so. All my information is to the reverse. No doubt the people of Texas felt greatly incensed, as I myself did, at the course of the late Administration, and at the conduct of the military authorities at Santa Fe. But events have rapidly and materially changed, and my advice to the people of Texas is not to be too exacting. Let us not exhibit any factious spirit now by refusing to accept any liberal overture for the settlement of the vexatious question.

Should Congress, however, fail to take measures for the settlement of the question at its present session, it will be incumbent upon Texas to use every means to get possession of Santa Fe. I have no fears but she will be successful. The first gun that fires against her in any attempt she may make to extend her rightful jurisdiction will kindle a flame in the breast of every man South of the Potomac, and thousands will rush to the relief of the "lone star" State.

Still, I hope the matter may be settled in a pacific manner, and that the people of Texas will not reject any fair proposition having for its object so desirable a consummation.

California is not yet admitted, though there is very little doubt but she will be soon. Mr. Douglass' bill is pending in the Senate, by which body it will be passed so soon as a vote can be had upon it—say in a week or so. The appropriation bills are all behind, and those in the public service here have the delectable prospect before them of being *shaved* at five per cent per month.

I can assure you the pressure in favor of settling all the vexing questions of the day, is becoming very great, yet the Representatives of the people seem to take little heed. They really appear emphatuated. Indeed, it is not to be disguised that love for peace, security, and the Union, is not half so deeply grounded as has been supposed, and there are numbers of men in Congress from both sections of the Union, that would rejoice if the great crisis were to take place to-morrow.

Mr. Clay, upon the defeat of his Omnibus scheme, went to Newport, Rhode Island, to recruit his strength, worn down as he had been by so many months of unceasing toil in his noble effort to reconcile the conflicting interests of his country. How nobly he deserves of that country may the fidelity of history not fail to record.

The summer has been a hot one here—the thermometer since the middle of June rising daily to 90 in the shade, and frequently up to 95. Health moderate—no cholera. Yours, LONE STAR.

Arrivals in the Bay.

LA SALLE, August 21, 1850.

DEAR STERNE: The fine steamship Galveston, Captain Henry Place, arrived along side our new wharf, drawing nine and a half feet water, on yesterday, from New York via New Orleans. She brought over Col. McClelland, and 115 civilians, and Col. Long and 100 soldiers, all belonging to the commission to run the boundary line between the United States and Mexico, together with a great amount of baggage, provisions, wagons, &c., &c., attached to the same. These officers and men proceed by land from Indianola to Victoria, there to fit out under the arrangements of Mr. Quartermaster Myers. They are a fine looking set of men.

The Galveston has been thoroughly overhauled, and under the command of Captain Place, one of our best seamen, now resumes her station in the line between this and New Orleans.

The schooner Jane Elizabeth is also discharging one thousand barrels of stone coal on the wharf at La Salle, for the Government.

On yesterday, the wharf at La Salle was graced by the presence of the following vessels, all fastened to it at the same time, viz: steamers Galveston, Envoy and Mary Somers; schooners Jane Elizabeth, from New Orleans; Wave, Dayton, and Tom Paine, from Matagorda; and the Colonel Brown, from Texana, besides seven small sails, making a total of *fifteen* large and small crafts at one wharf. It was, indeed, a charming sight.

Mrs. Eberly will open a Hotel here in a short time; and Mr. Mason will have his warehouse and residence up in a few days.

Yours, &c., M.

THE TEXAS BOUNDARY BILL.—The following is the bill which has passed the Senate relative to the settlement of the Boundary question of Texas:

A bill proposing to the State of Texas the establishment of her northern and western boundaries, the relinquishment by said State of all territory claimed by her exterior to said boundaries, and of all her claim upon the United States.

Be it enacted, &c., That the following propositions shall be and the same hereby, are, offered to the State of Texas, which, when agreed to by the said State, in an act passed by the General Assembly, shall be binding and obligatory upon the United States, and upon the said State of Texas: *Provided*, That said agreement, by the said General Assembly, shall be given on or before the 1st day of December, 1850.

First. That the State of Texas will agree that her boundary on the north shall commence at the point at which the meridian of 100° west from Greenwich is intersected by the parallel of 36° 30′ north latitude, and shall run from said point due west to the meridian of 103° west from Greenwich; thence her boundary shall run due south to the 32° of north latitude; thence on the said parallel of 32° of north latitude to the Rio Bravo del Norte; and thence with the channel of said river to the Gulf of Mexico.

Second. The State of Texas cedes to the United States all her territory exterior to her limits and boundaries, which she agrees to establish by the first article of the agreement,

Third. The State of Texas relinquishes all claim upon the United States for liability of the debts of Texas, and for compensation or indemnity for the surrender to the United States of her ships, forts, arsenals, customhouses, customhouse revenues, arms and munitions of war, and public buildings, with their sites, which became the property of the United States at the time of the annexation.

Fourth. The United States, in consideration of said reduction of boundaries, cession of territory and relinquishment of claims, will pay to the State of Texas the sum of ten millions of dollars, in a stock bearing five per cent. interest, and redeemable at the end of fourteen years, the interest payable half-yearly at the Treasury of the United States.

Fifth. Immediately after the President of the United States shall have been furnished with an authentic copy of the act of the General Assembly of Texas, accepting these propositions, he shall cause the stock to be issued in favor of the State of Texas, as provided for in the fifth article of this agreement.

Provided also, That [illegible] of said stock shall not be issued until the creditors of the said State, holding bonds of Texas for which duties on imports were specially pledged, shall first file at the Treasury of the United States releases of claims against the United States for or on account of said bonds.

THE AUSTRIAN PLOT FOR THE ASSASSINATION OF KOSSUTH.—A man named Bard has left Constantinople for London, in a sailing vessel. He is the bearer of documents which tend, by strong circumstantial evidence, to show the participation of the Austrian authorities in the plot for the assassination of Kossuth. The Austrians had seized and imprisoned him, but failed to obtain his papers, and he has at length managed to escape from their clutches with these important documents in his possession.

BOSTON MUSEUM.

BY CHARLES A. V. PUTNAM & CO. | A LITERARY CHRONICLE OF THE TIMES. | PRICE, $2 50 A YEAR, BY CARRIER; $2 BY MAIL; IN ADVANCE.

VOLUME 4. | BOSTON, MASSACHUSETTS, SATURDAY, JUNE 14, 1851. | NUMBER 1.

THE BOSTON WEEKLY MUSEUM

IS PUBLISHED EVERY SATURDAY, AT No. 12, SCHOOL STREET, BY

CHARLES A. V. PUTNAM & Co.

TERMS.—To City Subscribers, who receive their papers by a Carrier, the terms will be $2.50 a year, or $1.25 for six months, invariably in advance.

☞ Persons who receive their papers by mail, will be furnished for $2.00 a year, or $1.00 for six months, in advance.

⁂ Letters and communications should be addressed to "CHARLES A. V. PUTNAM & Co., PUBLISHERS OF THE BOSTON WEEKLY MUSEUM, Boston, Mass.," (*Postpaid*).

☞ For sale, Wholesale and Retail, by HOTCHKISS & Co., REDDING & Co., W. R. DAVIS, FETRIDGE & Co., and BEERY & Co.

DEXTER & BROTHER, No. 43, Ann street, New-York.

WM. TAYLOR & Co., Nos. 4 and 5, North street; L. B. BROWNE, No. 1, Jarvis Building, Baltimore.

A. WINCH, No. 116, Chestnut street, Philadelphia.

Biographical Sketch.

[WRITTEN FOR THE BOSTON WEEKLY MUSEUM.]

GEN. SAMUEL HOUSTON.

THIS gentleman having been informally nominated as a candidate for the next Presidency, and his nomination having met with unexpected favor in many parts of the country, his history has become a subject of very general interest among the people of the United States.

Within a few days, accident has placed in our hands a volume of over two hundred octavo pages, entitled—"*Sam Houston and his Republic*," which we have perused with a high degree of pleasure. It is from the pen of Mr. C. Edwards Lester, of New-York, an author of considerable notoriety, who has written several entertaining works on popular subjects, and whose style is bold, vigorous, elegant, and occasionally far superior to that of most American authors.

The work before us was originally published in 1846, by Burgess, Stringer & Co., and, of course, could have had no reference to the next Presidential election, or to the Presidency at any time. It is handsomely printed, and, at the present moment, when "Sam Houston and his Republic" of Texas are so much talked about, cannot fail to receive considerable attention.

We know not whether General Houston will be a candidate for the Presidency at the next election; but, as he is a MAN OF THE PEOPLE, and has always run well and successfully, on his own hook, "at home"—both in Tennessee and Texas—outstripping all competition, we should not be surprised to find him a candidate.

There is much in the character of General Houston that is romantic. His life abounds, from his youth upward, with "wild and wonderful" incidents—some of them of a very startling character. Indeed, the volume before us, although a faithful history of Sam and his Republic, teems with the beauties of *romance* from beginning to end; and no unprejudiced reader can peruse its pages without feeling a deep sympathy for the man, and for his sufferings and persecutions, from his youth until Texas became one of the United States; a warm admiration for his fearless bravery as a soldier, in many hard-fought battles, and great respect for his talents as a statesman.

As the first President of Texas, he had difficulties to encounter of a serious and most vexatious character. These are sketched with minuteness and fidelity by Mr. Lester, who appears to have written to enlighten the public mind, and not with a view to flatter General Houston, or to magnify his exploits, in council or in the field, in both of which, as is well known, he has distinguished himself in an eminent degree.

We have been so much delighted with, and have received so much instruction from, Mr. Lester's book—although published four years ago—that we have made a number of notes in relation to it, which we can confidently commend to the notice of our readers as matter well deserving of their perusal. In many instances we have quoted the language of our author; but in merely giving a bird's-eye view of a volume of over two hundred pages, we cannot be expected to have done this extensively.

GENERAL SAMUEL HOUSTON was born March 2nd, 1793, in Rockbridge County, Virginia. His ancestors, on both his father's and mother's side, were Scotch. His father was a man in moderate circumstances, and had a passion for military life; he served in the revolutionary war, as inspector of brigade, and held that office in Virginia till 1807, when he died. He was a man of powerful frame, fine bearing, and indomitable courage, which qualities his son inherited, and they were the only legacy, the only "real and personal property," he had to leave him. His mother was an extraordinary woman—rather tall, and possessing a full, matronly form, a fine countenance, and superior intellectual powers; her beneficence was universal.

Such were the parents of our hero, who never entered a school-house until he was eight years of age, and then, according to our author, to very little purpose. His father died when he was thirteen years of age, at which time he could read, write and cypher tolerably well. This event changed at once the fortunes of the family.

Mrs. Houston was left with the heavy burden of a numerous family—six sons and three daughters. She immediately sold out the homestead, crossed the Alleghany Mountains, and settled on the banks of the Tennessee river. That was forty-five years ago, at which time the State was sparsely populated. She pushed her way to her forest home through unpeopled regions of country. "Fired still with the same heroic spirit which first led them to try the woods in Virginia, our daring little party stopped not till they reached the limits of the emigration of those days. They halted eight miles from the Tennessee river, which was then the boundary between white men and the Cherokee Indians."

Young Houston was now set to work, with the rest of the family, in clearing the soil and providing the means of subsistence. As soon as he could be spared from hard labor, he went to an academy in West-Tennessee, for a while, and made considerable progress in his studies. It is stated that he derived much benefit from Pope's translation of the Iliad, which he read so constantly that he could repeat it from one end to the other. He had two or three other books, and became an enthusiastic admirer of translations from the Latin and Greek. So decided did this propensity become that, on being refused, when he asked the master's permission to indulge it, he turned on his heel, and declared solemnly that he would never recite another lesson of any other kind while he lived! He kept his word, in part.

Leaving the academy, young Houston went into the store of a retailer, but not feeling at home behind the counter, he suddenly disappeared. Search was made for him, but he was nowhere to be found for several weeks. At last intelligence reached the family that he had crossed the Tennessee river, and gone to live among the Indians, where he appeared to be as happy as a West-Indian planter.

When Sam was found, he was questioned by his elder brothers, who had often crossed his wishes, as to his motives for doing as he had done. He coolly replied, that he preferred measuring deer-tracks to tape—that he liked the wild liberty of the red man better than the tyranny of his own brothers, and, if he could not study Latin in an academy, he could, at least, read a translation from the Greek, in the woods, and read it in peace. So they could go home as soon as they liked. His family, after this, gave themselves no uneasiness about his absence, supposing that the evil would soon cure itself; but they were mistaken—he did not return until his clothes were worn out, and he wanted a new suit. He was then kindly received by his mother and brothers; but the first act of tyranny the latter showed, drove him to the woods again, where he passed a long time with his Indian mates, chasing the deer through the forest with a fleetness little short of their own, engaging in all those happy sports of Indian boys so peculiar to savage life, and wandering along the banks of the streams by the side of some Indian maiden. In all, he was three or four years or more among the Cherokees, running wild, sleeping on the ground, chasing game, making love to Indian women, and reading Homer's Iliad. He certainly must have been in clover at that time—in a position which thousands of young men, even in New-England, would envy him—if they could start right off!

His early residence among the Indians afterwards proved of great advantage to him. There it was he found a father and a friend, and became initiated into the mysteries of the red man's character; and there a taste was formed for a wild forest life, which made him, many years after, (while he was Governor of Tennessee) abandon once more the habitations of civilized men, with their coldness, their treachery, their hypocrisy, and their vices, and pass years among the children of the Great Spirit, till he finally led the way to the achievement of the independence of Texas. No white man has ever lived on this continent who has had so complete a knowledge of the Indian character—none who could sway so powerful a control over the savage mind.

During the six years that Houston was President of Texas, not an Indian violated a treaty with that republic; but, under the administrations of Lamar and others, not a tribe was known to regard one. His life among the Indians lasted till his eighteenth year. Leaving them, he returned among the pale-faces, and tried his hand at teaching school, in which vocation he succeeded beyond his expectation.

His price of tuition for scholars was *eight* dollars per annum—one-third to be paid in corn, delivered at the mill, at thirty-three and one-third cents per bushel—one-third in cash, and one-third in variegated domestic cotton cloth, an article in which the school-master was dressed; he also wore a snug cue. When he had made money enough to pay his debts, he shut up his school, and went back to his old instructor to study; but finding in the problems of Euclid a stumbling block, he abandoned the academy once more.

This was in 1813; but fortunately an event now took place which was to decide his destiny—the second war with Great Britain. A scouting party of the United States army having appeared in the vicinity of his residence, with music and the stars and stripes, young Houston enlisted, at once, against the advice of his friends, who were opposed to his joining the army as a common soldier. He then made his first speech, to this effect:—

"And what have *you*, craven souls, to say about the *ranks*? Go to —— with your stuff. I would much sooner honor the ranks than disgrace an appointment. You do n't *know* me now, but you shall soon *hear* from me."

They cut his acquaintance; but his mother gave her consent, and, while standing at the door of her cottage, she handed her boy a musket, and thus addressed him:—

"Here, my son, take this musket, and never disgrace it; for, remember, I had rather all my sons should fill an honorable grave, than that one of them should turn his back to save his life. Go, and remember, too, that while the door of my cottage is open to brave men, it is eternally shut against cowards!"

He marched off with the recruiting party, joined the ranks of the army, and was soon promoted to a sergeant, became the best drill officer in the regiment, and in a short time was promoted to an ensign. He thus commenced his military life on the full tide of prosperity. His first engagement with an enemy was under General Jackson, at the great battle of the Horse-Shoe, with the Creek Indians, March 27th, 1813. A brief account of this bloody battle will not be unacceptable to the reader. We condense it from the book before us:—

Battle of the Horse-Shoe.

The Cherokees, friendly Indians, were under General Coffee. General Jackson had a force of over two thousand men, while the Creek warriors, the chivalry of that warlike nation, numbered one thousand, who had taken their last stand, resolved to risk all upon a single struggle. Ensign Houston was in the thickest of this sanguinary battle. He distinguished himself by scaling the breast-works of the Creeks, calling out to his brave companions to follow him, as he leaped down among the Indians, cutting his way as he went. Soon after he reached the ground, a barbed arrow struck deep into his thigh, which was pulled out by his lieutenant with great difficulty, on the third trial, tearing the flesh as it came. A stream of blood followed, and Houston re-crossed the breast-works to have his wound dressed; and while in the hands of the surgeon, General Jackson came up to him and ordered him not to return. But he disobeyed this order, and in a few minutes was with his men again fighting the Indians.

The action had now become general, and more than two thousand men were struggling hand to hand. Arrows and spears and balls were flying—swords and tomahawks were gleaming in the sun, and the whole peninsula rang with the yell of the savage and the groans of the dying. The Indians had been made to believe by their prophets that the Great Spirit was with them, and would crown their efforts with victory, and the complete and final destruction of their foes. This awakened in them a feeling of superstition, and they fought with unusual desperation and malignity. The account says:—

"Not a warrior offered to surrender, even while the sword was at his breast. Hundreds were already weltering in their gore—multitudes of others had been shot or drowned, in attempting to swim the river—the ground was covered with the dead and dying, and the battle was supposed to be over; but, to the last moment, the old prophets stood firm, and gazed up toward the sky; around them warriors clustered, feeling to the very last moment that victory would come. Hope expired only with the expiring groan of the last prophet, and the warrior who gasped at his side."

Houston, after his first wound, distinguished himself for daring bravery in this battle, in an attack upon a large party of the Indians who had secreted themselves. He led the charge, and received two rifle balls in his shoulder; his arm fell shattered to his side. He stood in his blood as long as he could, then withdrew and sank down exhausted to the earth. "The sun went down over the ruin of the Creek nation. Where, but a few hours before, a thousand brave savages had scowled on death and their assailants, there was nothing to be seen but volumes of dense smoke, rising heavily over the corpses of painted warriors, and the burning ruins of their fortifications."

After all the perils of this hard-fought battle, in which he displayed a heroism that excited the admiration of the entire army, and received wounds which to this day are unhealed, Houston was taken from the field of the dead and wounded, and committed to the hands of the surgeon; but it was supposed he could not long survive. One ball was extracted—the other was not. He was finally left to die; but after a night of severe suffering, he found himself, in the morning, much easier. He was removed, on a litter drawn by horses, to Fort Williams, some sixty miles distant, where he remained, suspended between life and death, for some time. Nearly two months after the battle, he was removed to his mother's house, worn down to a skeleton from his extreme suffering. Subsequently, having recovered a little strength, he was carried to Knoxville, for surgical aid; and when he had become strong enough to ride a horse, he set out, by short journeys, for Washington, and reached that city soon after the burning of the capitol. Thence he proceeded to Virginia, his native State, where he remained among his old friends till spring. Our author says:—

"The military prowess and heroism displayed by Houston at the bloody battle of the Horse-Shoe, secured for him the lasting regard of General Jackson, whose sympathies followed him through all his fortunes. More than thirty years after, when the venerable old chief was trembling on the verge of life, looking out with undimmed cheerfulness from the dark inn of mortality upon the summer-path of light that opened before him, he sent for Houston to hurry to his bed-side to see him die."

But, we believe, although Mr. Lester does not mention the fact, that General H. did not reach the Hermitage until after the venerable old man had drawn his last breath.

Rapid rise of the General—His unfortunate Marriage, and its singular effect upon him—His sudden abandonment of his wife, and his residence among the Indians.

HOUSTON had an unlimited furlough. From Virginia he went to Tennessee. Having reached Knoxville, he heard of the glorious battle of New-Orleans. After peace was proclaimed, he was retained in the service as a lieutenant, and stationed at that city. In 1817, he was appointed a sub-agent to make a treaty with the Cherokees. Subsequently, he resigned his place in the army, and went to Nashville to read law. He was now in his twenty-fifth year. He entered the office of Hon. James Trimble, and so rapid was his progress as a student that, in six months, he was admitted to practice at the bar.

Soon after this, he was appointed Adjutant-General of the State, with the rank of Colonel. In October, of the same year, he was elected District Attorney of the Davidson district, and was obliged to come in collision with all the talent of one of the ablest bars in the Union. But he was found quite equal to the task. In 1821, he was elected Major-General of the Militia. In 1823, he was elected to Congress, without opposition. In 1827, he was chosen Governor of the State, by a majority of twelve thousand votes. His personal popularity was unlimited, and his accession to office found him without an opponent in the legislature! In 1829, he married a young lady of respectable family and of gentle character, whom he suddenly and mysteriously left, after living with her a few months only, and went among the Indians again, abandoning forever, as it was then said, all the charms of matrimony and of civilized life. The affair, at the time, as we well remember—for it was one of the most romantic, startling, unaccountable freaks that was ever recorded in the annals of matrimony—created a very general amazement among the American people, and everywhere was freely commented upon in the newspapers, some of which, without knowing *anything* of the causes which induced him to make so strange and unnatural a movement, denounced him in unmeasured terms. As might have been expected, there was a general sympathy for the lady; and yet, even to this day, the *cause* is unknown. The secret will die only with the General. The following account of this interesting affair we copy from Mr. Lester's work:—

"Owing to circumstances, about which far more has been conjectured than known by the world, the union seems to have been as unhappy as it was short. In less than three months a separation took place, which filled society with the deepest excitement. Various reports flew through the State, all of them unfounded, and some of them begotten by the sheerest malignity, which divided the people of the State into two hostile parties, and inflamed popular feeling to the last point of excitement. As usual on such occasions, those who were most busy in the affair were the very ones who knew least about the merits of the case, and had the least right to interfere. But unfortunately for the peace of society, there is everywhere a class of impertinent busybodies, who make it their special business to superintend and pry into the domestic affairs of their neighbors; and whose curiosity must be satisfied at any expense to private character. And as such persons always like to believe the worst, the secrets of no family are exempt from their malignant intrusions. These are the disturbers of the peace of society, whom the law seldom punishes, although they perpetrate more crimes than highwaymen and assassins—burglars of the domestic tranquility of families—robbers of others' good name—assassins of the characters of the innocent.

"Thinking, most probably, that they were doing her a kindness, the friends of the lady loaded the name of Houston with odium. He was charged with every crime man ever committed. The very ignorance of the community about the affair, by increasing the mystery which hung over it, only made it seem the more terrible. In the meantime, Houston did not offer a single denial of a single calumny—would neither vindicate himself before the public, nor allow his friends to do it for him. He sat quietly, and let the storm of popular fury rage on. From that day, even among his confidential friends, he maintained unbroken silence; and whenever he speaks of the lady, he speaks of her with great kindness."

This is all very well, and commendable to the General, who would never recognize the right of the public to interfere in this matter—and he treated them as though it had never happened. He considered it a painful, but a private affair. He had been elected to every office which he held in the State by acclamation, and he determined instantly to resign his office as Governor, and forego all his brilliant prospects of distinction, and exile himself from the habitations of civilized man. He went to his adopted father, the "King of the Cherokees," in Arkansas, knowing that he would be greeted there with the old chief's blessing. Nor was he mistaken: his reception was everything that he could have desired. His separation from his friends at the steamboat is spoken of as a touching scene. He was but about thirty years of age, in the vigor of early manhood, and had filled the highest stations, and been crowned with the highest honors his State could give. His friends knew the history of his early life, and they felt proud of his character.

With one more short extract, we shall close this portion of our article. The subject of broken matrimonial engagements is always a delicate one, and it most generally leads to broken reputations, and not unfrequently to broken heads. That law which separates "those whom God hath joined," ought to be trampled under foot, and then thrown in the faces of the judges who would administer it. Our author says:—

"But notwithstanding Houston's unbroken silence about his difficulty with his wife, and the sacrifice of all his hopes, he was denounced by the journals of the day, and hunted down with untiring malignity by those who had the meanness to pursue a generous man in misfortune. After his determination to leave the country was known, they threatened him with personal violence; but in this he bearded and defied them. His friends did not desert him while the sun of his fortune was passing this deep eclipse. They gathered around him, and the streets of Nashville would have flowed with blood, if Houston's enemies had touched a hair of his head. But such cowardly ruffians never execute their vows, when they have brave men to deal with."

Houston's New Residence.

Houston, after resigning his office, took leave of his friends, and quietly left the city of Nashville, for the Falls of the Arkansas, a distance of several hundred miles.* The dwelling of the Cherokee chief was only two miles from the Falls, and it was night when the steamboat which conveyed the General arrived there. But the old Chief had got wind of his coming, and in a short time he came down to meet his son, taking with him all his family. They embraced with great affection, and the venerable Oolooteka thus addressed him. We transcribe his speech as a beautiful and touching specimen of Indian eloquence, of paternal regard and affection for one whom he had adopted many years previously, while yet a boy.—

"My son," said he, "eleven winters have passed since we met. My heart has often wandered where you were; and I heard you were a great chief among your people. Since we have parted, I have heard that a dark cloud had fallen on the white path you were walking, and that when it fell in your way you turned your thoughts to my wigwam. I am glad of it; it was done by the Great Spirit. We are in trouble, and he has sent you to give us council, and take trouble away from us. I know you will be our friend, for our hearts are near to you, and you will tell our sorrows to the great father, General Jackson. My wigwam is yours—my home is yours—my people are yours—rest with us!"

Gen. Houston now passed three years among the Cherokees. Well has it been remarked, that the red men on this continent have had few better friends than he. His works, and his associations, have shown it.

And now we will inform the reader what kind of a home Houston had with his adopted father. "Oolooteka's wigwam, (says Mr. Lester), was large and comfortable, and he lived in patriarchal *simplicity* and abundance. He had ten or twelve servants, a large plantation, and not less than five hundred head of cattle. He never slaughtered less than one beef a week throughout the year for his table: his wigwam was always open to visitors, and his bountiful board surrounded by welcome guests." This is a pretty tall description of Indian life.

Leaving the Cherokees, Houston went to Washington, for the purpose of exposing the gross and inhuman impositions practised by some of the government agents among different Indian tribes. He induced Gen. Jackson to turn half a dozen of the most corrupt and dishonest of them out, in consequence of which he subsequently met with much abuse in Congress, and in the newspapers—those faithful "chroniclers of the times." He severely chastised one member of Congress,* a deserter from the Jackson ranks, who was about to shoot him, (his pistol missed fire!) by knocking him down on Pennsylvania avenue, for which offence he was brought to the bar of, and censured by, the House of Representatives. After a variety of difficulties and persecutions, at the seat of the general government and elsewhere, he returned to his exile among the Cherokees. We have not room for a more particular account of this portion of his life, which appears to have been surrounded by a "sea of troubles." We think there is not another public man in this country who has suffered so much persecution at the hands of his political rivals as this brave, eccentric, and talented individual.

General Houston in Texas.

Houston had no more ambition to gratify. Posts of honor and emolument, proffered by Gen. Jackson, he rejected, for he would never suffer the foes of the old warrior and statesman to heap opprobrium upon his name for showing favor to a proscribed man. He had made up his mind to spend the rest of his life in the tranquility of the prairie solitudes. But, in 1832, when symptoms of revolutionizing Texas began to appear, he was invited to join the Texans, and head any movement that might be determined on. Filled with the military enthusiasm and chivalry of his earlier days, he accepted the invitation. About two thirds of the book before us—and the most interesting portion of it—treat of important events in Texas, with the whole of which the General was closely identified. A more complete, full, and interesting history of that country, from 1832 to 1844, a period of twelve years or more, cannot probably be found. We certainly have never heard of one, and regret that our limits will not permit us to give an extended account of it.

The opposition and difficulties which Houston had to encounter, from the start, to the time that the independence of Texas was acknowledged, and she was, finally, enrolled among the stars and stripes, under the administration of Mr. Tyler, were enough to discourage, to appal, any other heart but that of Sam Houston.

The civil and military movements are all noticed with accuracy, and the details, most of them, are highly exciting. The barbarous *massacre* of Col. Travis and the whole body of his brave companions, in the Alamo; that of Col. Fanning's regiment, of several hundred men, at Goliad; Houston's brilliant victory, and the capture of Santa Anna, at San Jacinto; these, and many other startling events, are all recorded with minuteness and fidelity, and in a style at once graphic and beautiful. The description of the great and bloody battle of San Jacinto, and there have been but few like it in the annals of ancient or modern warfare, is especially exciting. It was this battle that decided the fate of Texas, and achieved her independence. We should like to republish the whole of it, if we had room.

There were only seven hundred Texans on the field, and Santa Anna's army numbered over eighteen hundred. The former fought with great desperation; their war cry was—"*Remember the Alamo!*" They knew that they were fighting for their lives, and that there was no escape for them except in victory. Houston spurred his horse, at the head of the centre column of his little army, right into the face of the foe. Several balls struck his horse in the breast, and one ball shattered the General's ankle. It was close fighting on both sides. The Mexicans fought with unusual bravery. It was a desperate struggle, hand to hand; but the fierce vengeance of the Texans could not be resisted; they were fighting for their homes, their families, and their dead kindred. Their enemies fell thick and fast; and the Texans stamped on them as fast as they fell, and trampled the prostrate and dying down with the dead—and clambering over the groaning, bleeding mass, plunged their bowie-knives into the bosoms of those in the rear!

* The Cherokees had removed from their old "hunting grounds," to their new home in Arkansas.

* Mr. Stansbury, of Ohio, if we mistake not.

When they saw that the dreadful onset of their foe could not be resisted, the Mexicans either attempted to fly, and were stabbed in the back, or fell on their knees to plead for mercy, crying—"*Me no Alamo!—Me no Alamo!*" They received their deserts, precisely *such* mercy as they had shown to the Texans, at Goliad and in the Alamo!

Of a division of five hundred infantry, upon which General Houston, even after he was wounded, made a gallant charge, only *thirty-two* lived to surrender as prisoners of war. The slaughter among the Mexicans was terrible, and their flight became general; they were hotly pursued, however, until there was scarcely a show of them left alive. Houston's horse fell dead at the close of the battle, with seven balls in his body, when his rider was thrown to the earth, and his companions discovered, for the first time, that he was wounded. He was taken to his tent, to have his wounds dressed.

Thus ended the bloody day of San Jacinto—a battle, as we have before said, that has scarcely a parallel in the annals of war. The spoils amounted to nine hundred muskets, three hundred sabres, two hundred pistols, three hundred mules, one hundred horses, twelve thousand dollars in silver, a large quantity of provisions, clothing, tents, &c. This was a considerable haul for the Texans, in their then weak and feeble state. As a republic, they were in their infancy, with a sparsely settled population, and without an army, the implements of warfare, ammunition, money, or credit. Such was Texas at that day.

The Mexicans left *dead* on the field six hundred and thirty men, including many officers; multitudes, also, perished in the morass and bayous. Of the survivors, two hundred and eighty were wounded—making in all over nine hundred killed and wounded, and there were eight hundred prisoners. Only *seven* men were known to have *escaped* from the field. And yet, incredible as it may seem, the Texans lost only *seven* men, killed, and less than *thirty* were wounded!

The morning after the battle, Santa Anna was found, disguised in a miserable rustic dress, and brought before General Houston, who was lying on the ground enjoying a comfortable sleep. Santa Anna came up behind him, and took his hand, which waked him. He then formally surrendered himself, as a prisoner of war. With his subsequent liberation, against the wishes of a large majority of the Texans, who were anxious to have him shot, our readers are probably acquainted.

There are some amusing anecdotes related in the account before us. One old man, by the name of Curtis, carried *two* guns. When asked why he did so, he answered—"D——n the Mexicans! They killed my son and son-in-law, in the Alamo, and I intend to kill two of them for it, or be killed myself." He killed his two men, and afterwards wanted to cut out a razor-strop from the back of Santa Anna!

Houston, while in Texas, as was his custom for a long time, was dressed in buckskin breeches and a Mexican blanket. In regard to this freak of his, in dressing in the style of an Indian, General Jackson is reported to have said—"He thanked God there was one man at least in Texas, whom the Almighty had had the making of, and not the tailor."

The Conclusion.

But we have made so long a story of this that we have room only for one more short extract—from page one hundred and ninety, near the conclusion of the book:—

"We know all of Houston's history. We know, too, that just as he was stepping upon the theatre of a high and brilliant fame, a cloud came over the sky, and wrapped his heart and his home in sadness and in gloom. There is a sorrow which even the hero cannot bear. The storms of life may beat against the frail dwelling of a man as wildly as they will, and the proud and the generous heart may still withstand the blast; but when the poisoned shaft of disappointment strikes the bosom where *all* we love and live for is treasured, the fruit of the world turns to ashes, and the chain of life is broken. Then it is that too often reason and bliss take their flight together. When this dark cloud fell over the path of Houston, he buried his sorrows in the flowing bowl. His indulgence began with the wreck of his hopes, and, like many other noble and generous spirits, he gave himself up to the fatal enchantress. But the days of his indulgence have long since passed away. When the sunlight of domestic happiness again shone through his dwelling, and he was sustained once more by that great conservative principle of a man's life, *a happy home*, illumined by the smile of an affectionate and devoted wife, his good angel came back again, and for years no man has been more exemplary in all the virtues of the citizen, the father, and the husband. From that moment,* he espoused the great cause of virtue and temperance, with all the earnestness of his nature. Whenever an opportunity has been presented, he has eloquently spoken, in public and private, in favor of that beneficent movement, which has restored many thousands of generous but misguided men to the long abandoned embraces of weeping families, and to the noble duties of citizenship."†

That General Houston is one of the leading men of the day is a fact that will not be disputed; and it is not at all probable that his substance or his shadow will become less within the next two years. That is our opinion. We see that the latest honor conferred upon him was by the legislature of the State of Pennsylvania, who invited him to honor them with his presence on the 22nd of last February, the anniversary of the birth of Washington. He afterwards attended a great temperance celebration at the Tabernacle, in New-York, for the purpose of delivering an address before a crowd of teetotalers.

A New-York journal says of the General as a temperance lecturer:—

"General Houston is a most efficient speaker. Too many of our temperance speakers, like too many of our pulpit speakers, have everything cut and dry for the occasion, and consequently exhibit a great want of vitality, so to speak, in their efforts. They have the body of an argument certainly, but they want the soul. Not so with General Houston; he speaks to the heart, he speaks to intemperate men as Mark Antony spoke over the dead body of Cæsar to the Romans. 'He tells them that which they themselves do know;' presents his own practical experience of men and things, and bids them 'speak for him,' like 'Cæsar's wounds.'

"To see one whose early life had its own waywardness, who has commanding talents, who led successfully the armies of the 'Lone Star' through a thousand life-perils to victory, and to the establishment of her independence; who presided over her destinies as President, and who, when she joined our constellation, was her first Senator in the Congress of the United States, to see such a one coming up to the work in the great temperance movement, speaks well for him and for us, and well for the success of our cause. And it gives us great gratification to have repeated evidences of the fact, that the General is not only in the field, but in active and conquering service."

* His second marriage.

† The hero of San Jacinto was one of the United States Senators who supported the resolution inviting Father Mathew to a seat within the bar of the Senate chamber, as a token of respect for his philanthropic works. In alluding to temperance, the stalwart soldier remarked, with fire flashing from his dark eyes—"I, sir, am a disciple. I needed the discipline of reformation, and I embraced it. I am proud upon this floor to proclaim it, sir; and would that I could enforce the example upon every American heart that influences or is influenced by filial affection, conjugal love, or parental tenderness. Yes, sir, there is love, purity and fidelity inscribed upon the banner that he bears. It has nothing to do with abolition or with nullification, sir. Away with your paltry objection to men who come bearing the binnacle above the turbid waters which unfortunately roll at the foot of this mighty republic!"

☞ "I was once," said Judge Douglass, "on the stump in Illinois, surrounded by a party of canalers, one of whom regarded me somewhat significantly, measuring with his eye my diminutive and then attenuated person. Presently he addressed me.—'Mr. Douglass, are you a descendant of the great Black Douglass?' 'Yes, I am.' My health had been bad for some time, and I was reduced to about one hundred and ten pounds. The Irishman scanned again my puny limbs. 'Fath and be jabers,' said he, 'and a divil of a *descent* it is.'"

[Written for the Boston Weekly Museum.]

STANZAS.

To E—— C——.

I tread the halls where laughing Mirth,
 Or bright-eyed Beauty reigns supreme.
Ah, such to me are little worth!—
 As waking from a brilliant dream
We find each fair creation flown,
 These fade as thought of thee comes through;
And my lone heart perforce must own—
 "Si je te perds, je suis perdu!"

I linger oft in Nature's courts
 When summer-blooms are sweet and fair,—
And with his mate the wood-dove sports,
 Or moans in notes of sorrow there:
All sights of joy, all sounds of ruth,
 Give thy dear semblance to my view;—
Enstamping deeplier the truth—
 "Si je te perds, je suis perdu."

And when the night's calm influence
 Is o'er each wayward passion flung,—
When quelled is ev'ry meaner sense,
 And slackened chords to praise are strung,—
The chastened thoughts that swell my breast,
 Direct the way I should pursue;
Still showing on my heart impressed,—
 "Si je te perds, je suis perdu!"

B.

[Written for the Boston Weekly Museum.]

A TALE FOR THE SCHOOLGIRLS.

Composition.—*Subject*—HOPE.

BY ADALIZA PERRY, AUTHOR OF "MARY MAHONY," ETC.

CHAPTER I.

"In this world of sorrow, this vale of tears, this"—— It was the beginning of Mary's composition. For a whole hour she sat there at her mother's desk, pen in hand, the sheet laid out fair and smooth before her, traced upon thus, in chirography unexceptionable, and there affairs stood still, a dead stand. Poor Mary! The "'world of sorrow' was capital. Everybody talks about *that*, though why people make such a point of it, I'm sure *I* do n't know," thought the poor girl within herself, looking down approvingly upon the phrase, "and then—'vale of tears'—nothing can be better; hum, this—what else *shall* I call it?"

Never was there a girl like our Mary Hughes. So bright she was, so obliging, so womanly, so—everything, that Mary Hughes or any other mortal Mary could be that was worth being—pardon the digression, good Mr. Editor, but *I* believe Mary is a charmed name, and I never marvel at any amount of perfections marshaled under its banner, not I, and I veto your doing it, so put on your credulity-glasses. I will not tell how Mary looked, because I have not the time, and you can find her description drawn in full in any "last novel" you have a mind to open, besides, for my Mary has set for the portrait of every heroine that has been described these ten years, that I am sure of.

Now, to return to the subject in hand. "This—this"—— Mary looked up at the clock and it ticked on and on that Wednesday afternoon, as barren in suggestions, as meaningless, and disagreeable, as though it had been studying some part on purpose to annoy her; the grave old family pictures that hung around were full enough of speech, but then, they sent Mary's thoughts sky-larking away over quaint cap-borders, and storing up models of ancient cues and shirt-frills. She could read anything off them but just the things needed. Out of the window was just the back of one towering block of stores—mightily suggestive for the theme in hand, that, surely.

Well, the subject had been given and something *must* be done. It was awful enough to face Mr. Tracy, the great head teacher, and a man terrible in his correctness, with only a minor blunder, and a missing composition—why! At any rate, Mary was not a girl to be balked in an undertaking, let the fates meddle as they would. Sitting there, waiting for "the Muse," or whatever name the poor drudging genius of school composition might have, was all foolery, *she* would not do it. True, she had been nervous and from that disheartened, but now, all at once, Mary grew desperate, and the pen went flying along the sheet like very sport.

"This—this composition exercise;" there, nothing could be better; it followed "Vale of Tears," like a book, and if anybody understood the connection, she did, she guessed, just then. It gave the whole a sort of comic turn, too, those melancholy first passages, that was worth everything—then followed a dashing flourish about "drooping spirits," despondency, and the like, and at last, in a graceful sweep, Hope herself was introduced, likened to spring, and sunrise, and rainbows, and—the cry of "Land" to Columbus, and *finis*. Bravo! not less than six lines Mr. Tracy had stipulated, here were eight, full measure. Mary wiped her pen, folded the sheet, peeped into the mirror (she was a beauty, and I am afraid she knew it, too) clapped her hands, and skipped away in a perfect ecstacy.

CHAPTER II.

Bright faces, quick footsteps, and loud laughter, and chat were there about the Academy buildings early on the morrow.

"Ah, Mary Hughes! Good-morning, Mary," cried a sallow-faced sentimental-looking girl, seizing our Mary's hand the moment she entered the yard.

Mary said "Good-morning," with great cordiality, for that terrible non-composition spectre she had carried about like a nightmare on her mind, the whole week past was laid at last, and her spirit was so light she felt cordial towards everybody.

"Oh, Mary, and have you your composition?"

"Yes, all finished, Ann, every word, and signed and folded."

"Ah, how I envy you, Mary;" and here Ann grew very grave and rigid, and Mary was certain she was going into some kind of a scene. Ann Rawson was nervous, and used to put on heroine airs sometimes, and look broken-hearted, and sometimes it had been rumored "she was going to faint," though she had never actually done that. All this was very fine and interesting to the school-girls, and it was conceded on all hands that Ann was to be petted and humored, and that every possible sacrifice should be made by every one for her peace of mind. At this moment appearances foreboded almost everything.

Mary felt sure in her own mind, if her composition was not *very* extraordinary, she might well envy *her*; but it *might* be that. So she exclaimed very cheerily in her own heartsome way—

"Envy me, Ann? Why, I'm sure, yours is a thousand times better."

Ann shook her head, and after a long, long silence, and a deal of murmuring incoherence, at length, gasp by gasp, it came out, that really Ann had got no composition at all.

"Bravo!" here broke out one Fanny Scribe, a noisy, dark-complexioned girl, who, it seemed, was enjoying the scene mightily. "Give her yours, Mary."

"Shame, shame, Fanny Scribe!" was the cry of almost every voice in the yard; for Fanny was a kind of outlaw among good society. She would be uncourteous, she would say what she liked on all occasions, and as for her having the least faith in Ann Rawson's nervousness, she had not, and declared she never would have.

"Shame, shame, shame, Fanny Scribe!" cried the indignant girls again, for the first had scarce ceased, when poor Ann had sunk powerless to the ground.

"Shame, indeed!" retorted Fanny, not in the least put down. "Pretty dear! I understand her faintness; just give her up your composition, Mary; see how it will revive her."

"My composition? No, indeed! I would, though, Miss Fanny, with my whole heart, I would, after all, if it was right, and would do her good. There, *that* I would."

And Mary stood proudly erect, her cheeks flushed, and her eyes sparkling with the thought of her generous sacrifice, looking down on the malicious Fanny with just the degree of contempt her insinuations deserved.

"Would you, Mary?—oh, oh, would you?" here, to the surprise of everybody, broke forth the drooping Ann, suddenly reviving, and seizing Mary's hands with unlooked for energy.

"Indeed, I would, Ann," said Mary, mildly, "only it would n't be right, you know, to pass off mine for yours."

"Right? Alas, Mary! not right to save me—*me*, with my poor shattered nerves, from Mr. Tracy's displeasure? Oh, Mary!" and away reeled Ann, overcome again by excess of emotion, and all the girls, just Fanny excepted, circled around, and pitied the sensitive girl so touchingly, and argued so eloquently on the sacrifice, Mary was half-distracted herself, bless her. Fanny Scribe would say her say though, and Fanny had such a way of maintaining her own independent opinions, she was shamefully unwomanly.

"There, let her alone," she was heard calling out shrill and piercing, a voice above all the hubbub. "Lazy jade! Why did n't she write for herself? Ask her. Oh, oh, she 's insensible! *I* know; she 's too lazy. Lazy? no, she 's *stupid*, she is, there, I know she is, to write her own! and so she comes wheedling the work out of a good, generous girl in that way. Well, she shows some discernment, anyhow, in fastening where she is sure to get the best. Mary may take it as a compliment."

Away whirled Fanny in high wrath, marching into the schoolroom and placing herself at her desk as though her spite were more than she could trust herself to move about with.

She knew no more about it, only that Ann Rawson read a composition, a most beautiful composition, and she read it with great effect, too; something must have brought her to life; cause unknown. And Mary had none; and Mary was made to stand in the middle of the floor in consequence, and listen, oh, to such a terrible reprimand, while all the time her sweet, kindly face was telling as plainly as *she* could wish, how undeserved it was.

Well, well; might not she get up and betray the whole? Once she made up her mind to do it, but then, no; after all she would n't. She admired Mary's nobleness, and it would seem like throwing a damp over the whole glory of it. The girls understood it, of course, and held their peace.

"Very well," thought Fanny, glancing from Mary into Ann's simpering, yet just now exulting face; "very well; and now, Miss Ann, if you do n't behave just right, look out for revelations!"

Mr. Tracy did not notice it—Fanny was not aware of it herself, but I am sorry to say she accompanied this mental threat with an ominous shake of the fist, "in school" it was, too.

I know not what Mary's thoughts were. She looked rather gratified, when the composition read so gloriously, though whether it was the success of the theme, or a friendly rejoicing over the recovery of Ann's spirits, there was no guessing. Ann, too, was promoted for the same, and Mary degraded; but Mary bore that heroically. It was only when she tied her bonnet-strings, and turned her face homewards, that any change could be detected in our Mary, and then something was discernible like self-condemnation. Perhaps as the action began to be reviewed with associations of home and fireside teachings, it did not have quite the look of honesty, for Mary's perceptions of right and wrong were exceedingly acute, her conscience did not really justify the thing. There was no telling, only she was not herself.

CHAPTER III.

Somehow, nobody could tell why, Mr. Tracy never had the least charity for Ann's spasms. He was very hard-hearted, all the girls agreed; sure as she was seized with one in her class, away he would march her to her seat, and the way he would storm at, and scold her, used to be terrific. His regimen had great efficacy, however, for when everything else failed, that would restore her instantaneously, only the remedy was quite as dreadful as the disease.

The following morning he was in a great ferment at the disappearance of a little book, called "Key to ——'s Arithmetic." The examples in the arithmetic used in school, had none of them their solutions given, as Mr. Tracy preferred his pupils should learn to rely upon their own reasoning faculties, and the only key (published accompanying the work) allowed in school, he kept in his own possession, to produce and illustrate from as occasion required. This had been kept on a particular shelf, particularly deposited, inside of his desk, usually guarded by lock and key, and when not, certainly, one would suppose, quite as safe under his strong word of prohibition, outlawing any culprit guilty of touching aught within said desk. Because of this, the morrow was a dismal day. Then Mary entered school with a very grave face. She scarcely returned Ann's greeting at all, answered the other girls coldly, and when Fanny Scribe approached her with some boisterous witticism about "Hope," she merely drew down her long eye-lashes, pursed up her lips, and deigned no reply. All at once, Mary was found out to be proud and disdainful. She took her degraded place in the class with a look that some of them interpreted something like this—"Well, even here, I can look down on all the rest of you."

Fanny did not read it so, though; there was no reading it at all. She would have given the world to have ferreted into it; but no, there sat Miss Mary, that good, generous, sunshiny Mary Hughes, metamorphosed into an icicle. What could that yesterday's transaction have had to do with it? A great deal, it seemed. Could it be that Mary's eyes were opened, and she had found out Ann's trick, and felt the humiliation of having been gulled? "I hope so, that I do," muttered Fanny to herself, and she looked into Mary's calm, brown eyes, and tortured herself with the mystery. How unlike they were; Fanny with the thought of being gulled, overreached, &c., and Mary, our Mary, only troubled with the thought of doing wrong.

Time wore on, and really it was evident that that "Hope" affair *had* wrought a miracle; for it was wonderful what a change had come over Ann. From the dullest, most backward scholar in her class, she was fast assuming rank, and moving upward. "To one word of judicious praise," as Mr. Tracy remarked very solemnly to a visitor, "wisely administered," might be attributed that great salutary change. She was still subject, in the recreation times, to attacks of the old malady; but what was remarkable, she could no longer fasten upon Mary. No, Mary held herself aloof, and seemed to be quietly scrutinizing her conduct, as though seeking to penetrate her motives for some unknown purpose of her own.

Ann's seat was next hers, and in all past times she had very comfortably copied her sums, and saved her poor nerves a deal, by availing herself of Mary's honest labor in all departments. But now Mary's books were arranged on her own particular desk, and all her doings were kept as secret as though she had belonged to the "Council of Ten."

"What has come over you of late?" shouted Fanny Scribe, one recess, after this state of things had continued for nearly a week.

She put her arm through Mary's very affectionately, for she had determined in her own mind to forget all seeming oddness, and be Mary's friend. She really loved Mary.

Mary did not return or repulse the caress, she only looked very calm and unfathomable, and said, quietly—"Nothing."

"Nothing? Pshaw! You do n't deceive *me*, Mary! I know, I guess; it's that Ann Rawson; she read your composition last week. Nuisance!—jade! Think I did n't guess, Mary? She write that?—*she!* and about Hope, too! I sup-

THE TEXAS STATE GAZETTE.

H. P. BREWSTER, Editor:---J. W. HAMPTON, Associate Editor.

City of Austin, October 4, 1851.

Mr. F. T. ALEXANDER has been appointed a travelling agent for the Gazette, and will in a few days start on a trip through the counties of Bastrop, Fayette, Colorado, Matagorda, Jackson, DeWitt, Lavaca, Calhoun, and ohers adjacent. We hope our subscribers and other friends will be prepared to settle up arrearages, and send us many new subscribers.

☞ E. W. WILEY, No. 57 Camp street, New Orleans, is a duly authorized agent for the *Texas State Gazette* in that city, to receive subscriptions and advertisements, and receipt for the same.

☞ J. W. NOWLIN, of Waco Village, is a fully authorized agent for the *Texas State Gazette* in that locality.

☞ With emotions of deep regret, we announce the death of the Hon. John H. Rollins, United States Indian Agent for Texas. He died at San Antonio, on Thursday, the 25th ult. Since his residence in Texas, Judge Rollins, by his urbane and courteous deportment, had won the kind regards of many warm friends, who deeply deplore his death.

Late and Important from the Rio Grande.

We learn from a member of Capt. Ford's company who arrived yesterday, that a large insurgent force, numbering about five hundred men, composed of Americans and Mexicans, attacked and took the town of Camargo and got possession of the custom-house, and with it a large amount of property. There was a severe fight on the occasion between them and the Government troops stationed there, in which a man named Smalley, who formerly lived on Brushy, had his arm shot off. Our informant learned these facts from a Mexican just arrived from Laredo, who further stated that there was a strong feeling in favor of the movement throughout the country between the Rio Grande and the Leona made, and that the insurgent force was daily increasing. It was understood that the troops at Matamoras and other points on the river had been sent for, to assist in quelling the outbreak, and that a large force was moving on Camargo from the interior, and it was supposed that an attack would be made on the insurgents about the 22d of last month.

Ford's company were mustered out of the service of the United States on the 24th, and about fifty men of his command left with the Captain to take a hand in the game. Men were being raised and organized to join the revolutionists throughout the valley of the Rio Grande, and there seems to be no reason to doubt that there will soon be a force of Americans there in arms, sufficient at least to be troublesome.

Canales and Cabajal are said to be the leaders, they are both shrewd and capable men, but in our opinion, utterly void of principle or patriotism; and let the present affair result as it may, they will reap the benefit.

Speech of General Sam Houston.

We are indebted to the kindness of a friend at Huntsville for a slip from the *Presbyterian* office containing a synopsis of Gen. Houston's speech at that place on the 22d ultimo. The crowded state of our columns at the time we received the slip enables us to give only the synopsis of the speech, without note or comment—omitting even the remarks of the *Presbyterian* accompanying the synopsis.

☞ We are gratified to see that Messrs. Gray & Duffau have received at their drug store a large assortment of school and other books, which they offer on accommodating terms. An establishment of this sort was greatly needed in our city, and we hope such encouragement and patronage will be bestowed upon Messrs. G. & D. as will not only amply repay them for their enterprize, but stimulate and justify them in enlarging and improving their stock to a degree commensurate with the wants and what should be the literary character of our city.

☞ On the fourth and fifth pages of to-day's paper, will be found some very interesting articles. That from the New Orleans *Delta*, headed "The South again Deluded," contains much truth and warning, though there are some remarks in it we do not approve. The article from Solon Robinson we trust will arrest the attention of the northern people: for we sincerely believe he does not misrepresent the state of public opinion at the South in regard to the repeal of the fugitive slave law. And it is equally true, that the preservation of the Union rests with the people of the North. By doing their plain, simple duty, all danger of disunion will be forever dissipated.

☞ Gen. Henry Whitney, who recently visited Texas on a tour of inspection, died at St. Louis on the 16th ult.

☞ According to the recent census, the entire population of Bexar county, is 7,023. Qualified voters, 2,337; slaves, 389; free persons of color, 57.

☞ The following are the officers of Metropolitan Division for the current quarter:

Geo. H. Gray,	W. P.,	Truman B. Beck,	T.,
Musgrove Evans,	W. A.,	Rob't M. Elgin,	C.,
D. J. Miller,	R. S.,	P. H. Adams,	A. C.,
J. T. Price,	A. R. S.,	George Kerr,	I. S.,
A. N. Hopkins,	F. S.,	Wm. Davenport,	O. S.,
Jo. W. Hampton,			P. W. P.

The New Governor.—The number of strangers present at the inauguration of Lazarus W. Powell, as Governor of Kentucky, on the 2d ult., is estimated at fifty thousand. The inaugural address is said to be an excellent one.

Texas and Her Creditors.

When the Government of the United States was driven by the fanaticism of the free soil politicians into a position, where it was necessary for it to join issue with the State of Texas on the question of her boundary, and submit to a determination, a proposition was made by the Federal Legislature to adjust the question upon certain terms and conditions, clearly and distinctly set forth in an enactment of that body known generally as Pearce's bill.

Ten millions of dollars were offered Texas as an indemnity for a portion of her territory; of this sum, five millions were required to be withheld until Texas should file with the Secretary of the Treasury of the United States releases from all her creditors, who were holders of that species of her debt for which the revenues arising from imports were specially pledged. This proposition was submitted to the people of Texas for their acceptance or rejection, under circumstances, however, which scarcely allowed them an alternative; for upon her act in reference thereto, seemed at the time to depend the very existence of the Union. It was an act of deliberate patriotism by a people, smothering the indignant resentment naturally excited by the course of the General Government towards their State; at one moment threatening her like a slave with the rod, at another insulting her with a bribe. The proposition was accepted by the State *modo et forma*, with great unanimity, and the Union was thus relieved from a crisis which threatened to shake it to the foundation, if not scatter it on the earth.

In carrying into effect the terms of the adjustment made by the General Government and Texas, it became necessary at the very outset to determine the question, to what class of our debt the proviso above stated, applied to—in other words, what particular species of our debt was secured by a special pledge of the revenues arising from imports. It is well known that when the proposition was received in Texas, and its merits were under discussion during the pendency of the question of its acceptance before the people of the State, that it was insisted in argument, and not denied even by those who opposed its acceptance, that only the interest on the debt created by the act of June, 1837, was so secured, and that this portion of our debt only, responded to the description in the proposition. As a legal proposition, this, as far as we have seen, has not been disturbed by any argument. In fact, to adopt any other conclusion, it seems that we must invite construction where none is required, and amplify by some arbitrary and Procrustean process, the meaning and force of language. In reference to the terms employed in the proposition to Texas, we must either assume that they were used in reference to the distinction made in the laws of Texas to the different issues of her debt, or as expressive of a fact which, independent of them, attached to the class intended to be covered by the proviso. The first is certainly the most natural and just assumption, for only by a reference to these laws could the fact be known, that a species of debt responsive to this description existed; and from the same source, and at the same time, they were compelled to see that there were other descriptions of debt recognized by Texas in this respect essentially different. If this be the true light in which to view the matter, it is too plain for controversy. Argument could not strengthen our proposition. To state it, is to decide it.

If, on the other hand, it be insisted that Congress in the terms employed, intended to express a class of debt to which some quality was common, and had no reference in their words to the laws of the State, we do not see that this can militate against our views. Taking the proviso in this light, and subject it to the test of legal criticism, it becomes without meaning or force; for it is settled law, that nothing can be the subject of a pledge which is incapable of manual tradition and possession. The revenues of a State, then, a thing not in existence, resting only in speculation, could not be made the subject of such a contract—they could not be pledged. It is, however, profitless at this time to pursue this argument; for let the truth be on which side it may, for us or against us, the President of the United States has assumed to decide, that all the debt created previously to 14th of January, 1840, is protected by the proviso, and that no portion of the five millions reserved can be issued to Texas, until the releases of the holders are filed; and it only remains for the State of Texas to adopt such measures as her Legislature may deem wise to protect herself from injustice and imposition.

That such would be the decision of the General Government through its present authorities, we never entertained a doubt. The secret outside influence which secured the passage of Pearce's bill, and which, no doubt, interpolated the celebrated proviso, did not expend all its influence in that measure; it had a reserved capital for the occasion which has arisen, and no one who was acquainted with the accessible character of the present whig administration, as demonstrated in the Galphin and Gardner transactions, could have any ground to doubt that potent reasons for such a decision would, at the proper time, be thrown into the scales. Apart from that, Texas has ever been with the whig party a favorite abomination; and since its installation into power, she has received at its hands the treatment of a step-child, and to have expected from Mr. Fillmore and his cabinet a decent measure of justice, was to sin against light and knowledge.

The administration seems to have adopted the idea of Congress, that there was an indigenous dishonesty in Texas, against which it is his duty to guard our unwary creditors, who wrung from our necessities promises, like the wretch might wring from a drowning man before he would throw him a plank to save his life.

Through the recent elections in the State, there has been a significant and authoritative expression of public opinion on this subject. Coming fresh from the people, with this actual issue before them, their representatives can neither doubt the sovereign sufficiency of the injunction, nor question the authority from which it comes. The people of the State have declared that Texas ought not to pay her debt, except at a rate ascertained to be the fair value of what she received, and this principle it will be the duty of the Legislature to carry out.

Although since the acceptance of the proposition by Texas, there has been many circumstances calculated to irritate her sensibilities, and arouse a spirit of resentment, still we hope the Legislature will approach the question of our public debt, with feelings and purposes as little as possible influenced by them. No sooner had the acceptance of Texas been made known, than certain creditors of the State began to ply the General Government for payment of their demands, without deigning to notice Texas in the matter. To this, the authorities at Washington could not accede, it was too grossly preposterous even for their latitudinous liberality in favor of stale demands, by which cabinet members are wont, in these degenerate days, to replenish their own purses and reward their favorites. Failing in this, the State of Texas became the theme of an army of letter writers; some hoping to drive her from her position by abuse, others to seduce her from it by flattery. Then comes all sorts of propositions—some for receiving half in money and half in lands—and some, complicated with stupendous and visionary schemes of public improvements, out of the stock or profits of which, our whole debt was to be paid, and the country from the Rio Grande to the Sabine, and from the mountains to the seaboard, to be gridironed with railroads.

These sprats, though skillfully thrown, caught no gudgeons, and the people of Texas have said they will adhere to the principle announced in 1848, and persisted in to the present moment. All this gratuitous and indecent interference we can pass by, and take up the question at the next session of our Legislature, with a dispassionate and deliberate purpose of doing what we conceive complete justice in the premises, both to creditors and to ourselves.

Under this state of the question, it will be impossible for the Legislature at its next session to make arrangements for the payment of any portion of the first class debt, without an abandonment of the principle, in favor of which there has been such solemn and repeated expressions of public opinion, by accepting some of the many propositions which will, no doubt, be made by the holders of this debt.—We have no apprehension of such a course on the part of the Legislature, and consequently can entertain no other expectation than that the whole of it will be suspended until the proviso shall be repealed, or so modified, that those who may be willing to accept payment at the scaled rate, can receive their debt out of that fund. All attempts to wheedle or worry us into a submission to their exactions, we hope will be met with a stern rebuke teaching them the truth, that Texas having fairly ascertained what is just, will mete it to her creditors, and no more—their potent auxilliary, Mr. Fillmore, to the contrary notwithstanding.

The following is the letter of Mr. CORWIN, announcing to Gen. HAMILTON the decision of the President:

TREASURY DEPARTMENT,
September 15, 1851.

SIR: The President has decided in the matter of the Texas Public Debt:—First, that only five millions of stock can be delivered to Texas until releases, as provided in the act of Congress of the 9th of September, 1850, are filed in the Treasury Department for all that portion of said debt which issued prior to the 14th of January, 1840; as in his judgment the act of the Republic of Texas of the 14th of January, 1840, specially pledged the duties on imports for all the public debt of Texas created prior to the passage of that act.

Second. That all the issues of Texas bonds, certificates of stock, or notes made receivable for "all public dues," are claims for which the duties on imports are pledged within the meaning of the act of Congress of the 9th of September, 1850; and releases of all such must be filed in the Treasury Department, as provided in the last named act, before he can be justified in delivering the remaining five millions of stock to the authorities of Texas.

The President has instructed me to communicate this decision to you, in compliance with your request made in behalf of the creditors of Texas.

Very truly, your obedient servant,

THOMAS CORWIN,
Secretary of the Treasury.

Gen. JAMES HAMILTON,
Chairman Committee of Creditors of Texas.

☞ We have beeen applied to, to publish the reply of Gen. Bates to an article over the signature of "Travis," addressed to him in relation to the federal court, and his connection therewith. We have declined to do so, because we have, during the progress of the controversy, of which this forms a portion, studiously avoided compromitting ourselves with either party. Not having published the article of "Travis," or any other of the strictures upon the federal court, or its officers, we feel entirely justified in declining to adopt a different course towards the latter. Had we done so, however, we should have felt it a duty to have published their defence.

☞ We often see articles copied from the *Gazette*, into the columns of our cotemporaries, without the due credit being given. An occasonal omission of this sort we can look over and attribute to inadvertence; but when a wholesale business comes under our notice, we must be permitted to enter an humble protest, and claim the courtesy due from one member of the craft to another. The editor of the *Western Star*, at Paris, in his paper of the 6th ult., copies verbatim, or as nearly so as his own errors will permit, nearly a whole column from our paper, leaded and inserted as editorial, without credit; and in his next number, he again inserts immediately under his editorial head, and leaded, no less than *six* articles from the *Gazette*, also without credit. Now, it is a pleasure to us to be able to furnish paragraphs or articles that our cotemporaries may deem worthy of spreading before their readers; but in doing so, it is very ungenerous to withhold from us the credit due. And we respectfully request of the *Star*, that when next he finds it necessary to appropriate our editorials as his own, he will not disfigure them with such horrible blunders. He should at least send forth our productions in as decent a garb as they possessed when he laid violent hands upon them.

☞ His numerous friends throughout the United States, will hear with deep regret the news of the death of the Hon. Levi Woodbury. He died at his residence in Portsmouth, New Hampshire, on the 4th ult. Mr. Woodbury, as a statesman, was among the ablest, purest and most consistent of his day. He was honored by the people of his native State with the most important and honorable offices in their gift; was a member of the cabinet of two Presidents, and at his death, was Associate Justice of the United States Supreme Court.—He was a democrat of the old school, understood and practised the principles he professed, and at his death, was the choice of a large portion of his party for the Presidency—a station, though the most exalted on earth, he was most eminently capable of filling with honor to himself and usefulness to his country.

☞ A treaty of international copy-right has lately been concluded between France and Austria.

The Episcopal Church.

We have just received the printed Journals of the Second Annual Convention of the Protestant Episcopal Church for the Diocese of Texas, held at Galveston in May last. From it, we gather the following facts: The Convention is composed of 14 Parishes, supplied by 8 ministers—Rt. Rev. G. W. Freeman, D. D., Provisional Bishop. The report of the Committee on the State of the Church says:

"That from statistics laid before them, they find a steady increase in the church in this Diocese. Although the number of our parochial clergy has been increased during the past year, by an addition of but one, yet we think we see everywhere marks of progress and growing interest in the church. Two of our brethren, who were with us a year since, have felt themselves called upon to labor in other fields, and have consequently left the Diocese. Two from other Dioceses have come to cast in their lot among us, so that by removals, in point of numbers, we are neither losers or gainers. One has been ordained within our own borders, giving us an increase of one laborer in the gospel harvest during the year. There are at this time no candidates for orders. There have been *four* new Parishes organized during the past year. Reports have been received from only five of these, which renders the statistical matter furnished to this Convention very meagre. These five Parishes report *forty-five* baptisms; *eighteen* marriages; *thirty-three* funerals; *sixteen* confirmed in two Parishes—the Bishop, as yet, having made no visitation of the others. Present number of communicants 178—giving an increase, as reported by three of the Parishes, of 18. Amount contributed for church purposes in four Parishes, is $3,874."

The Convention resolved to establish a Diocesan School, to be under the charge of the Rev. Charles Gillet, which school, we understand, has been located at the flourishing village of Anderson, Grimes county. The Trustees of the school are Dr. Anson Jones, P. G. Merritt and John S. Rhea.

☞ We most cordially approve the positions assumed by the *Redland Herald*, as summed up in the following article by the *Galveston News*:

"The *Redland Herald* is opposed to this State taking a single dollar's worth of stock in any work whatever of internal improvement, whether for clearing out rivers or constructing railroads. The editor very justly instances the waste, extravagance, bad management, speculations, frauds, and the thousand swindling operations to which States are always subjected when such public works are undertaken under the direction of the Legislature. He instances Georgia, which State undertook a railroad eight years ago, 130 miles in length, and which has but recently been completed at the enormous cost of $25,000 per mile, having involved the State in debt without being of any utility, and yielding only one or two per cent. on the capital; while the roads of the same State, built by private enterprise, have cost only ten or fifteen thousand dollars per mile and yield a handsome income on capital stock. He also refers to the thirty or forty millions expended by the "Keystone State" in improvements which have involved the State in an onerous system of taxes, ruined her credit abroad, and yield at the outside but one or two per cent. He also cites Illinois, Indiana and some other States which have involved themselves in bankruptcy and the disgrace of repudiation by engaging largely in similar public improvements."

A New Dance.

The votaries of dancing will doubtless be highly gratified to learn that a new dance of a very striking character has just been introduced into the fashionable world at the watering places North. It is called the *Somersetski*, and is thus described by the editor of the Petersburg *Intelligencer*, who saw it performed recently at Old Point:

"The Somersetski is the name of a new dance which bids fair to knock the Waltz, the Mazourka, the Polka, the Rodowa, and the Scottish, into a cocked hat. This last named dance is by far the most rediculous affair that was ever participated in by sane people. We never see it without thinking of a gander balancing himself on one leg, and nodding affectionately and amorously on his favorite goose. But from all accounts, the Somersetski is the dance of the age. It is danced by four persons—two gentlemen and two ladies. The ladies are dressed in a frock reaching up to the knee, and the continuances are of stockinet, fitting as close as possible to the skin. One lady wears a white and a black stocking, and the other wears a green and a red. The gentlemen are dressed in shorts, their stockings of pink and purple colors. The dance begins by the gentlemen turning somersets over the ladies, after which the ladies turn somersets over the gentlemen, and then the whole party turn somersets over each other, rapidly, promiscuously and miscellaneously. During this last movement, the performers, with their variegated costumes, present all the changes of the kaleidoscope. Those who have seen this dance, admire it greatly. It will doubtless soon be in vogue at all the watering places."

Communicated.

Mr. Editor: I have heard it suggested that the name of the Hon. H. R. Runnels would be presented to the next House of Representatives for the office of Speaker of that body. For the two preceding terms, Mr. Runnels has been an able and efficient representative. He is a gentleman of sterling integrity and great firmness of character, familiar with the mode of legislative procedure, and would, I am inclined to think, fill the Speaker's chair in a manner eminently satisfactory. Permit me to express my conviction, that the House could not do better than to select him as its presiding officer.

An Observer.

Revolution in Italy.

There appears to be a general impression among the observant minds of Europe, that Italy is again on the eve of a violent and sanguinary revolution. Almost every foreign newspaper that we read—every one which dares to intimate its opinions—is full of forebodings as to some great trouble at hand. Even the conservative papers of London and Paris do not suppress their fears, and the silent military preparations of Austria, show that the Government are not unaware of what is in the wind. American travelers, recently returned from Europe, with whom the editor of the *New York Post* has conversed, bring with them the same conviction.—*N. O. Picayune.*

From the Presbyterian of the 27th inst.

GEN. SAM HOUSTON'S SPEECH AT HUNTSVILLE.

In the outset, Gen. Houston paid a high and deserved compliment to his noble colleague, Gen. Rusk. He alluded to their past services together in the early struggles of the country, and spoke eloquently of their joint efforts in support of the adjustment measures of the last Congress. He adverted to his Oregon vote. He had been abused for it—had been denounced as a traitor, and held up to the reprobation of mankind, when that vote was given in strict accordance with the Missouri Compromise; when the passage of the Oregon bill was but a re-enactment or acknowledgement of the line of 36 30. Oregon territory all lay above that line. The South did not contend for the right to carry slaves there. That matter was settled by the act of 1820. All Oregon was then declared to be freesoil. Besides, the people of that territory when they asked for a government, petitioned Congress to prohibit the introduction of slavery there. He had planted himself upon the Missouri line of 36 30, he had adhered to that compromise, regarding it as invested with the sanctity of the constitution itself, until it had been abandoned and denounced by the South.

He voted also for the admission of California. For this he had been denounced. California was admitted as other States have been admitted. The people adopted a republican form of government: they had prohibited slavery themselves. There was nothing in this repugnant to the constitution of the United States. It was the very principle that the Democratic party had always contended for,—the principle that he had always contended for, and that he would always contend for—that the people have the right to make their own domestic and municipal regulations and laws. It was necessary for California to have a State Government; the emergency—the extraordinary state of things—demanded it absolutely; the salvation of the people depended upon it; the peace of the Union itself—perhaps its very existence depended upon it. California was a remote territory. It was rapidly populating—the character of the population was anomalous. A great majority of the people were good people, but there was a large intermixture of bad men among them—reckless and abandoned and lawless characters, whom it was necessary to intimidate and restrain by the strong arm of the law. The people needed protection against such men, and protection could only be afforded by a well regulated State Government. If that had been denied them, they would not have been treated as American citizens. They would have felt it, and would it not have weakened their attachment to this Government? Nay, who will say that such act of injustice on our part—a disregard of their interests and their rights—might not have resulted in a renunciation of their allegiance to this Government! What then would have been the result? Could we have forced them into subjection? Could we have conquered them? Even admitting that this were possible, it was not the way to preserve the Union—it would have endangered its existence. We regard the people of California as our equals, entitled to all the benefits and privileges and blessings that we enjoy.

But, what was stranger than all, he had been abused for voting for the ten million proposition to Texas. It was his fate to be abused—he had been abused for everything that he had ever done for the country. But he did not look for it in this instance. He was called a coward at the battle of San Jacinto: if he was a coward, he was a most unfortunate one, for it had been his fate, in every battle that he had ever fought, to be severeley wounded. He was called a coward for the retreat from the Colorado—which proved the salvation of Texas. He had been charged with treason in endeavoring to sell Texas to England and France, when these very slanders, which he suffered to go abroad uncontradicted, about his intrigues with these powers, was one of the means that hastened on the consummation of the great measure of annexation. He had been abused for vetoing the land bill, which was finally passed over his head, and which has entailed incalculable evils upon the country. He was abused for vetoing the war bill, in 1842, when it was proposed to invade Mexico. Some then thought that Texas could conquer Mexico without men or means: he thought it would require both. When Uncle Sam undertook it, it required fifty thousand men, and sixty millions of dollars. He had been abused and denounced for these and for many other things that he had done for Texas, but really he did not expect to meet abuse for his agency in the settlement of the Texas boundary question—a measure so fraught with benefits to Texas and blessings to the Union. This part of Gen. Houston's speech was very interesting. He reviewed the history of the boundary question. It was a clear elucidation of the whole subject, and was the more interesting as it disclosed much of his own private history in this connection that had not before been published.

General Houston disposed of the Southern Ultras and Northern fanatics very summarily. He placed them in the same category—classed them together—they were governed by different sentiments, but they aimed at the same object—a dissolution of the Union. Fortunately for the country, there were but few of them in either end of the Union. The people at the North and South were satisfied with the adjustment of the slavery question. The country had nothing to apprehend from the few restless spirits, who were still endeavoring to keep up the agitation. They were powerless, for the sympathies of the people were not with them.

Of the disunionists in Texas, or those who opposed the acceptance of the ten million proposition, Gen. Houston made equally as hasty work. He met their arguments triumphantly, and expressed his surprise that there was any oppositoin to a proposition so immensely advantageous to Texas. He alluded to the proposition that we once made to England, to give her five millions of dollars to secure a recognition of our independence by Mexico. There appeared to be no opposition to that measure At another time, Texas made overtures to the United States for annexation. She was willing to surrender all her public domain on condition that the government would annex her, and assume the payment of her debt. There was no opposition heard to that proposition. But we had now made an infinitely better bargain—we were in an infinitely better position than we would have been, had either of the other propositions been successful. We had been annexed—we had ten millions of dollars, and we still had a vast public domain of one hundred millions of acres! What more could we desire? had not everything conspired to render us eminently prosperous and happy as a people? And all this has been acquired without a single sacrifice of principle or honor on our part, and without jeopardizing, in the least, the interests of our sister States of the South. On the contrary, Texas, while regardful of her own interests, gave peace to the country. It was upon the acceptance of the proposition made to her, that the whole system of compromise turned. She had it in her power, by rejecting that offer, to open afresh the fearful agitation of the slavery question between the North and South. She acted as became her, conscious of her duty to herself and the Union. It was urged, that Texas in accepting the ten millions proposition would devote a portion of her territory to freesoil. This, so far from being the case, had the effect to take off the slavery restriction that already applied to a large portion of her territory. By the joint resolutions of annexation, the Missouri line of 36 30 was extended through Texas. No State could have been admitted above that line as a Slave State. That restriction is now removed and New Mexico can come in as a Slave State, if the people desire to do so; nor is there anything now to prevent the slaveholder from carrying his slaves into any part of the ceded territory.

We regret that we cannot give a more satisfactory report of Gen. Houston's speech here on Monday. We have noticed it but imperfectly, merely hoping to give something like a faint outline of its general features.—It is impossible for us to do more.

☞ The following letters from the Cuban prisoners in Havana, written just before sailing for Spain, need no comment, so far as they speak of the conduct of the *American* Consul:

Havana City Prison, Sept. 7, 1851.

We, the undersigned officers and men, now incarcerated in the City Prison of Havana, on account of our participation in the late expedition against the Island of Cuba, under the command of General Lopez, being about to embark for Spain, cannot refrain from expressing our heart-felt gratitude to Mr. Joseph T. Crawford, Consul-General of Her Brittanic Majesty, and to Mr. W. Sydney Smith, British Consulate at this place. To Mr. J. S. Thrasher, and to the American and British citizens of Havana generally, we also owe a debt of deep and lasting gratitude. To them we owe all, for by their kindness and generosity we have been able to overcome many of the difficulties and sufferings we should have otherwise undergone. To them we owe a debt of gratitude we would willingly express by words, but language fails us; hoping, however, that should we be spared to return to our homes, we may have the opportunity of repaying in part the debt we owe. Should such not be the case, we sincerely pray that God, the ruler of the universe and lover of good acts, may repay them, by bestowing upon them in this world all the blessings a Divine Providence can bestow, and, after death, by a reward more lasting still—life eternal.

Capt. Robert H. Ellis, Lieut. E. H. McDonald, Lieut. David Winborn, Maj. Louis Slessinger, Capt. F. H. Grider, Lieut. J. D. Baker, and one hundred and thirty-three others.

Havana City Prison, Sept. 7, 1851.

We, the undersigned, prisoners incarcerated in the city prison of Havana, on account of our connection with the late Cuban expedition, under the command of General Lopez, cannot withhold an expression of our feelings towards the American Consul—Mr. Allen Owen, of Georgia—now at this place. Since our arrival at this place, he has *honored* us once with his presence, but since that time, although repeatedly solicited, has always steadily refused to revisit us, either in his private or official capacity. Placed as we are, we feel an act of this kind far more deeply than if otherwise circumstanced. How to account for it we know not, but can only ascribe it to that worst of all feelings—inhumanity—or that more degrading still—cowardice. We write this so that our fellow-countrymen at home may know what kind of a man is placed at the head of their affairs at this place. [Signed,]

Robert M. Grider, Capt. Com. Company B, Edmund H. McDonald, 1st Lieutenant Company A, Charles A. Downer, Peter Lacoste, Michael Geiger, and others.

From Corpus Christi.

The *Nueces Valley* does not pretend to know whether the seat of Col. H. L. Kinney for the Senate will be contested or not, as reported. The editor says, however, that his opponent, "Davy," would have been elected by a large majority, *if he had received votes enough.*

The same paper, of the 7th instant, regrets that so many delays have prevented the men on Mustang Island from going to Cuba. The editor presumes the chief cause for this delay is the want of funds in New Orleans to pay their transportation. A number of the *Filibusteros* have abandoned the enterprise, being impatient of this delay, and the balance are very restless in their "pent-up Utica."

The same paper gives the information that *Legs* Lewis has proposed to the *Hombres* on the other side of the Rio Grande, who want another revolution, to lead them to certain victory, and put them in possession of the Sierra Madre Republic, for the sum of $175,000, paid in advance—as all printers' bills should be. The patriot *hombres*, however, it is said, prefer Col. Kinney shall be their leader in carving out the new Republic, rather than have it done by *Legs* by contract.

Methodists.—A statistic article on Methodism in New England appears in *Zion's Herald*, which reports in the six Conferences 66,206 members and 559 preachers. Vermont has the largest number of members in proportion to the population, it being 1 to 21. The Methodist population of New England, including families, is estimated at nearly 400,000 or about equal to the population of Connecticut.

☞ The District Court for the county of Walker, commenced its session in this town on Monday last, the Hon. Judge Meggison presiding. The amount of business on the docket, is said to be very large.—*Huntsville Item 27th September.*

☞ John Ross has been re-elected Principal Chief of the Cherokee Nation. He has held the office of Chief since 1828.

Dr. Dickson of Grimes county, and Dr. Evans of Polk county, both representatives to the Legislature, spent several days in our town in the fore part of the week.—*Huntsville Pres.*

☞ At the recent session of the District Court of Houston county, John Risley was sentenced to 18 months in the Penitentiary for larceny. He arrived at his new lodgings on Wednesday night.—*Huntsville Item, 20th ult.*

F. GLEASON, {CORNER OF BROMFIELD AND TREMONT STREETS. BOSTON, SATURDAY, JUNE 26, 1852. $2 00 PER VOLUME. 10 Cts. SINGLE COPY.} NO. 26.—VOL. II.

CATCHING WILD HORSES ON A PRAIRIE.

It is a rapturous vision to gaze upon the prairies—those "gardens of the desert;" but how few ever enjoy the luxury! Few countries are adorned with these beautiful scenes, and none more bountifully than America. In no portions of America do they exhibit more beautiful or more varied aspects than in Mexico and Texas. The prairies of Texas especially are as wonderful in their vast extent as they are peculiar in beauty and singular in fertility. The adventurous colonist, attracted by the paradisiacal scene, who is, perhaps, the first

"—— of that advancing multitude,
Which soon shall fill these deserts,"

finds himself not in this great solitude alone. It is thickly peopled with myriads of gaudy insects that flutter over the flowers, with sliding reptiles, beautiful birds, graceful deer, bounding buffaloes, and numerous troops of fine and noble wild horses. The settler selects his spot; builds himself a dwelling in a shady island, and by conforming to certain requisitions of the government, becomes at once the rightful proprietor of nearly as much territory as his eye can at once survey; and when he finds time to enclose it with substantial landmarks, he feels secure against intrusion. He plants his sugar and his cotton, and whatever else he may choose to cultivate, and the benignant climate and prolific soil shortly yield him the most abundant crop, and he reaps more than a hundred fold. The soil is easily subdued, and with little care, whole herds of cattle grow up to enliven the wide domain, where they roam throughout the year without barns and without the northern haystacks or granaries. If he wishes a horse or a drove of horses to ride, to travel, to hunt, to work, he has only to ride into the prairie, and the animals cost him only the trouble of catching them. The horses of Texas are small, run wild in numerous droves over the prairies, and are easily taken and rendered serviceable. They were probably originally introduced by the Spaniards, and are called *mustangs*. To illustrate the manner of taking these animals, is the object of the engraving presented by our artist below. The pursuer provides himself with a strong noosed cord, made of twisted strips of green hide, which, thus prepared, is called a *lasso*, the Spanish word for a band or bond. He mounts a fleet horse, and fastens one end of his lasso to the animal, coils it in his left hand, leaving the extended noose to flourish in the air over his head. Selecting his game, he gives it chase; and as soon as he approaches the animal he intends to seize, he takes the first opportunity to whirl the lasso over his head, and immediately checks his own charger. The noose instantly contracts around the neck of the fugitive mustang, and the creature is thrown violently down, sometimes unable to move, and generally, for the moment, deprived of breath. This violent method of arrest frequently injures the poor animal, and sometimes even kills him. If he escapes, however, with his life, he becomes of great service to his master, always remembering with great respect the rude instrument of his capture, and ever afterwards yielding immediately whenever he feels the lasso upon his neck. Being thus secured, the lassoed horse is blindfolded; terrible lever jaw-breaking bits are put into his mouth, and he is mounted by a rider armed with most barbarous spurs. If the animal runs, he is spurred on to the top of his speed, until he tumbles down with exhaustion. Then he is turned about and spurred back again; and if he is found able to run back to the point whence he started, he is credited with having bottom enough to make a good horse; otherwise he is turned off as of little or no value. In various parts of South America, Mexico and California, this mode of catching wild horses is constantly practised at the present day, and, indeed, forms the regular business of a large class of wild and careless Spaniards, Indians and half-breeds, who eschew civilized society, and prefer to live a life of savage freedom and as their own masters. Probably some of the finest shaped and fleetest horses in the world are thus taken every year, and put to the most common manual service among our frontier settlers, and Southern and Western hunters; horses which cost nothing but the catching, and which, at the North, would bring from $300 to $400 each. As a sketch, our artist, while he has followed nature truthfully, has also given us below a very capital and effective picture, which our readers cannot but be pleased with, as an embodiment of stirring and hazardous adventure.

MODE OF CATCHING WILD HORSES ON THE PRAIRIES, TEXAS.

ILLUSTRATED NEWS.

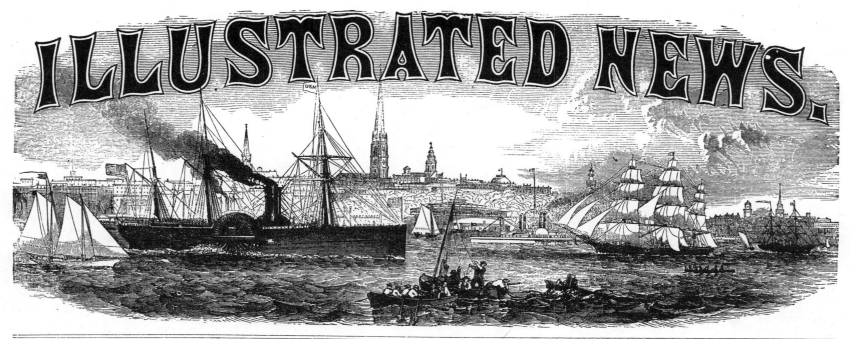

No. 18. Vol. I. NEW YORK, SATURDAY, APRIL 30, 1853. Price Six Cents.

SANTA ANNA.—THE MEXICAN REPUBLIC.

A few weeks since we presented our readers with a sketch of the British mail steamer Avon, entering the port of Vera Cruz, Mexico, having on board General Santa Anna, the newly elected President of the Mexican Republic, whose public career we then briefly reviewed. Later advices mention his enthusiastic reception at Vera Cruz, the authorities of which city waited upon him on board the vessel, and conducted him on shore with great ceremony. Santa Anna afterwards left for Mexico, from which city an escort of one thousand men started forth to meet and welcome him.

The following manifesto was published by him on the day following his arrival at Vera Cruz:

Mexicans: On placing my foot on the shores of my country, I salute them with the liveliest emotion. My heart has palpitated with tenderness from the time when my eyes commenced to discover around our coasts the lofty mountains which indicate the proximity of a land in which everything is dear to my heart, in which everything brings to me the dearest reminiscences.

You have called me, believing me useful to save you from the state of anarchy and superstition into which you had fallen, and I have not delayed in responding to your summons. You already have me on your soil, resolved to employ all my energies in an object of such essential importance. But if I have been quick to come at your call, it is from reckoning upon your efficacious operation. Of no use will be my firm resolution to consecrate myself entirely to the salvation of the country if every one of you do not assist me, co-operating with all his ability to the attainment of these ends.

Far from me is the thought of avenging ancient grievances. Those who have been my enemies may dismiss all fear. Everything is forgotten; and in touching the shores of my country, I present to all the hand of friendship. Neither do I come to make any party prevail. I come only to raise the sacred standard of union, summoning to follow it all Mexicans, whatever may be their opinions. Every man whose heart swells and is moved at the voice of his country, he is my friend, he is my companion.

Mexicans, too long have we permitted ourselves to be deceived by chimerical ideas. We have lost too much time in intestine dissensions. A sad reality has come to drag us from such a deplorable deception. To what have we arrived at the end of thirty years of independence? Cast an eye over the map of your country, and you will find that a great portion of your territory has been lost. Examine the state of your finances, and you will meet nothing but disorder, abuse, ruin. What is your credit abroad. What is the opinion which you enjoy in foreign nations? Where is that army in whose lines I have had the honor to serve, that army which gained your independence, in which I glory of having had no small part—that army which I led through the deserts, conquering difficulties which appeared insuperable, to the frontier of the republic—at whose head I repelled an inimical invasion, and with which I fought, with little fortune, but not without honor—when your capital was occupied by the enemy.

ANTONIO LOPEZ DE SANTA ANNA.

Mexicans, let us become ourselves again. Let us improve the hard lessons of experience. Let us repair the errors we have committed. Here you have me to contribute my share to this honorable reparation. Toil with me in good faith in this glorious work, and we still have country, national honor, and a name which we will not be ashamed to own.

Soldiers! comrades in arms! Behold anew at your head your old general, him who has conducted you sometime with glory; him who has not abandoned you in the moment of misfortune; him who bears on his body an honorable mutilation, and who, with you, has exposed his breast to the balls of the enemy in the days of your misfortunes. Listen to a voice which is not unknown to you. Follow your general and friend, let us restore to our noble profession the lustre of which it has been deprived; and although the relations of friendship which exist with all nations, and which I shall cultivate with all care, may not at present make your gallantry necessary, let us be ready, should national honor require it, to prove in the face of all the world what the Mexican soldiers have always sheltered in their breasts.

Mexicans, of all classes. Let the day of my return to the country be the day of general reconciliation, and let the joy which it causes me to find among you, exhibit itself in all assembled around the national standard, and let us hear all shout with the same union and enthusiasm as in 1821, *Viva la patrie, viva la independencia!* (Long live the country, long live independence.) These are the wishes with which I present myself at your call, these the vows of your compatriot and friend.

Antonio Lopez de Santa Anna.

One thing seems certain; Santa Anna returns to supreme power, nominally the President of Mexico—in reality he intends to be its Dictator. He is aware that extreme measures, and those only, will rule the country. He has watched the course of Louis Napoleon. He intends to *Napoleonise* the Mexicans. A new, vigorous and determined policy may be expected in Mexico. It is not unlikely that his favorite idea—the confiscation of the church property—may be the first *coup d'etat* attempted by Santa Anna. Its results would place some money at his command—which is the key of all power; and if he would then open the doors of his country to the enterprise, industry, and energy of the North—copy their railroad systems—encourage the establishment of manufactories — invest confiscated wealth in building up profitable business for foreigners, he may yet benefit his country. Left to itself and the resources of its citizens, the Mexican Republic ends in dissolution. Sooner or later it seems likely to become part of our own territory.

THE GARDINER TRIAL.

As the case now stands, the evidence in favor of Dr. Gardiner is materially strengthening. Important witnesses, occupying high positions in society, have testified to his integrity and good standing. Having reviewed the evidence when against his reputation and interests, we take pleasure in alluding to it now that it has become favorable.

M. M. BALLOU, {CORNER OF TREMONT AND BROMFIELD STS. BOSTON, SATURDAY, NOVEMBER 17, 1855. $3,00 PER ANNUM. 6 CENTS SINGLE.} VOL. IX., No. 20.—WHOLE No. 228.

STATE OF TEXAS.

The fine picture on this page was drawn expressly for us by Billings, and exhibits the usual grace and felicity of his pencil. The device of the State arms is a "lone star." On one side of the picture is seen an Indian on horseback shooting a buffalo, and on the other a train of settlers, both characteristic of the State. The original inhabitants of this region were among the fiercest and most warlike tribes encountered by the Spanish adventurers. Prior to 1690, there was a small French colony here, but they were driven out by the Spaniards. In 1810, the North American provinces of Mexico revolted against the Spanish crown. The settlers of Texas, a large majority of whom were from the United States, weary of the constant revolutions of Mexico, asserted their independence, and finally achieved it by the battle of San Jacinto in 1836, in which a handful of Texan riflemen defeated a vastly superior force, commanded by General Santa Anna, the "Napoleon of the southwest." In 1845, Texas was annexed to the United States, and admitted into the Union. The State is of irregular form, and embraces an area of about 237,320 square miles. The existing constitution of the State is wise and liberal. A constitutional provision provides for the support of public schools, and Texas has many respectable educational institutions. The revenues of the State are estimated at $110,000, and the average annual expenditures at $100,000. The surface varies greatly, being very mountainous in the west, and sloping down towards the seacoast. A large part of the area is exceedingly fertile and productive. The prairie region is, perhaps, the richest. The State is well wooded throughout, its sylva embracing oak, hickory, elm, walnut, sycamore, cedar, pine, etc. Fruits, including some of the choicest fruits of the tropics, and every variety of vegetable, are easily raised. The great staple is cotton. Grain crops thrive well. Rice and tobacco are cultivated, as well as the sugar cane. Indigo, vanilla and various medicinal shrubs are among the natural productions. The noblest river of the State is the Rio Grande, 1800 miles long. The Roman Catholic religion prevails among the descendants of the earlier settlers, but the Catholics are largely outnumbered by other denominations of Christians. The population at the last census was 212,592. The climate is said to be remarkably healthy. The wet and dry seasons constitute the winter and summer; the former lasts from December to March, and the latter comprehending spring, summer and autumn.

The Advertiser.

BASTROP, TEXAS.

WM. J. CAIN, Editor.

Saturday, May 29, 1858.

Special Notice.

Legal advertisements MUST *be accompanied with the* CASH *from this time henceforth. We find it almost worth the amount for publishing such notices to collect it after the work is done. The same rule will hereafter apply to job-work and will not be departed from.*

Rates of Advertising:

One square, (10 lines or less,) one insertion....	$1 00
Each subsequent insertion..................	50
Business Cards, one square, one year........	10 00
For six months...........................	6 00
For three months.........................	4 00
One column, changed quarterly, one year....	90 00
Half " " " " "	50 00
Quarter column...........................	35 00

☞ The Hons. Sam Houston, J. H. Reagan, J. P. Henderson, and Guy M. Bryan, have again placed us under obligations for interesting public documents.

☞ Rev. Henry Renick will hold a two days meeting in the Union Church, commencing 1st Saturday, 5th of June.

☞ Since our notice of the examinations was put in type, we have received notice from Col. ALLEN, stating that the Cadets would deliver addresses on Thursday night, 10th June; also, addresses will be delivered by L. W. Moore, Esq., and by the Superintendent.

☞ The light fingered gentleman who purloined Webster's large Unabridged Dictionary from the Nicholson House, with the name of R. H. Hall in it, is requested to return it forthwith, immediately if not sooner.

NEW GOODS.—Our young friend, ED. NICHOLS, has just received a beautiful assortment of new goods; see his advertisement in another place. He is a tip-top clever fellow, and advertises liberally.

NEW STORE AND GROCERIES.—Read the advertisement of friend ROSENTHAL in another column. He has opened a Dry Goods and Provision Store, on the Corner, near the Post Office, and has just received Groceries direct from the coast. He is clever and accommodating and sells goods and groceries very low for cash. Give him a call.

☞ We call attention to Mr. Baker's advertisement for the sale of cabbage and turnip seed. He pronounces these seed to be superior to any ever had in this market, and says he has not been without cabbage a single week during the last two years. He gives double the quantity usually bought in papers at the stores, for the same price. Call at Mr. Nichol's store, and get some before it is too late.

OUR BOOK TABLE.—We have received GODEY'S LADY'S BOOK, for June, edited by Mrs. SARAH J. HALE, and L. A. GODEY, published at Phila'd. Pa., at $3 per annum.

THE LADY'S HOME MAGAZINE, edited by T. S. ARTHUR and VIRGINIA F. TOWNSEND, for June, is also, before us—published at Philad., at $2 per annum.

PORTER'S SPIRIT OF THE TIMES.—This inimitable and amusing journal is on our table.—Published every Saturday at No 346 and 348 Broadway, New York, at $3 00 per annum.—WM. T. PORTER & GEORGE WILKES, editors.

The above are the best and most worthy and interesting periodicals published, and the numbers before us, are not a whit behind former ones. Their enviable position is universally known, and requires no commendation or endorsement from our pen.

MELANCHOLLY.—We have been shown a letter written to Mr. C. K. Hall, of this place, by Mr. Kirk, dated Lampasas Springs, which announces the melancholly tidings of the death of Mr. WM. EARBEE, a worthy young man who has lived for several years past in Bastrop, but recently joined the company of Texas Rangers, under the command of Col. Jno. S. Ford. The letter does not mention any of the circumstances connected with his death; but it is presumed, it occurred from the accidental shot of his own pistol. He was killed about four weeks since. He attended the last term of the District Court, held in Bastrop, and met with this unfortunate fate about a week after leaving here, while on his return to the camp of Col. Ford, at, or near Lampasas Springs. The writer of the letter stated that he would send his horse and gun and such other articles which he had in his possession at the time of his death, back to Bastrop, at his earliest convenience.

P. S.—Since the above was put in type, we have been shown a letter from Mr. J. T. Hart, dated Camp Runnels, May 21st, to Col. R. H. Hall, of this place, which states that our young friend came to his death by the accidental discharge of his rifle, which he had carlessly left tied to his saddle, on his horse, while he had dismounted to refresh himself with a nap. The horse in grazing about came near some bushes, and brought the gun in contact with a limb, which caused it to fire, the contents lodging in Mr. E's head, scattering his brains for several yards around the spot where he lay, killing him instantly. Mr. Hart says he will bring his effects to Bastrop, and deposit them with some of the friends of the deceased for safe keeping, until his relations can get them.

Democratic County Convention.

We observe, from the uumerous placards posted round town, that the Democratic party of Bastrop county, have resolved to hold a meeting on Saturday next, 5th of June, for the purpose of nominating candidates for county offices, and to take into consideration the action of the meeting held on the 15th inst., at the Court House, which appointed delegates to attend the Lockhart convention, to be held on the 12th of next month, and who were instructed to vote for Mr. White of Seguin, as the choice of the Democracy of this county, for the candidacy for District Attorney, of the 2nd Judicial District.

There now appears to be two dissenting parties in the Democratic ranks of this county.—While one advocates the convention system of nominating candidates for offices, which come under the jurisdiction of the Executive or Judicial departments of our Government, the other are directly antagonistic to such measures of placing incumbents into office. The latter assume the position, that offices which come under these heads, should not be entrameled into the meshes, of politics, or influenced by them—that when an officer is elected through party intrigues, such means of election, naturally, has a corrupt tendency, in spite of all the good qualities which may combine the nature of the officer elected,—therefore, they urge the importance of candidates taking the field upon their own merits, and let the old Jeffersonian test be applied to every aspirant, "is he faithful, is he honest, is he capable."

It is a "fixed fact," that the fortunate individual who receives the nomination for any office in the State of Texas, from the Gubernatorial Chair down to Beat Constable or town Marshall, needs no further endorsement to insure his election, and the truth of this saying will be verified by the next August election. In future, we intend to take an independent stand, and vote for the man we may like best, and whose qualifications entitle him to the position to which he may aspire, we care not whether he may be convention or anti-convention democrat,—nevertheless, for small petty offices, we think every patriotic man, who feels that he is worthy of a position and merits an office, by the requisite qualifications necessary to fill such offices, and whose general deportment entitles his claims to due respect and consideration, should announce himself a candidate independent of any party or clique, assemble in caucus to dictate to the masses, who they shall or shall not vote for. We are an independent *man* and an independent *democrat*—notwithstanding our nature has been strongly tinctured with Know Nothing proclivities—and we shall try to publish an independent paper.

Examinations.

The examinations of the students of the Female College, and of the Military Institute, in Bastrop, will commence on Thursday next, 3d, and conclude on Thursday following, 10th June. On Wednesday night following, after the examination exercises are concluded, the cadets will deliver addresses, and on Thursday night following, the ladies will close the exercises with an exhibition. The patrons and friends of these institutions are respectfully invited to attend during the examinations and exhibitions. They will no doubt, prove very interesting and entertaining to the public. The principals of these worthy Institutions have spared no pains or labor in discharging their respective duties toward the scholars during the past session. Our educational institutions have already made a reputation which may be envied by adjacent towns and cities, and we would be pleased to see these branches of education continue to prosper in our midst, with double the ratio which they have within the last twelve or eighteen months; and under the present auspices, and under the supervision of the present principals, we may hope to see a continued prosperity in them, and an increasing interest manifested by our citizens to sustain these indispensibles to the welfare and advancement of our city of Bastrop. There is no branch of life which has a tendency to cause a town or city to flourish with renewed activity more than that of education; and it is to the interest of every individual, we care not whatsoever pursuit of life in which he may be engaged, to succor the educational institutions of his town; while it builds up the school or college, it also advances the interest of his business in the same ratio. Let our citizens, one and all, attend the examinations, see the prosperity of our colleges, and, in future, unite and build up colleges, which shall ever claim to be inferior to none in the Southern States in any respect. We have the material, we have the funds, we have one of the healthiest locations in the State, we can have the *will* and the *assistance*; and all that is required, is *united action*, to accomplish this great purpose.

TO TEMPERANCE SOCIETIES.—We are sorry to learn, from the notice we publish below, that our enterprizing friends of the TEMPERANCE BANNER, which was published at Galveston, have been compelled to suspend the publication of the BANNER, indefinitly, for want of means adequate to support their noble purpose. We should think there were, certainly, enough friends of Temperance in Texas, to support one sheet, advocating its hallowed principles. We would like to see the friends of Temperance throughout the State arouse from their lethagy, and rally to the support of a first class Temperance Journal—a home journal—devoted to the best interest of the family circle. Come friends, put a shoulder to the wheel and help our enterprising friend, HANSON, in his noble work:

Notice.

Owing to circumstances uncontrolable, the "TEMPERANCE BANNER" will be suspended for a short period, or at least until arrangements can be made, which will warrant its support.—We hope our temperance friends will come forward to our assistance, as we have now published the work nearly six months, and during that time have not received enough money to pay for the paper the work has been printed on. This may seem strange, but it is nevertheless true. We are desirous to continue the work, and hope our temperance friends throughout the State will readily come forward to our assistance.

We hope our bretheren of the press will oblige us by copying this notice with such comments as they deem proper.

HANSON & WHEAT.

☞ A woman's heart is like a fiddle—it requires a beau (bow) to play upon it.

Texas Volunteers.

The Act to increase the Army has passed Congress, as many of our readers are already aware; and as we have had many interrogatories put to us in reference to the Bill authorizing the organization of the two regiments for that purpose, we publish the following for general information:

"HOUSE.—The house took up the Senate's amendment to the Volunteer Bill.

"Mr. Quitman said he preferred the original number of regiments, four, but as the troops ought to move immediately, he would consent to the reduction of two.

"The house concurred in all the Senate's amendments, which leaves it to the discretion of the President to accept the services of one mounted regiment of volunteers for the defence of the Texas frontiers, and two regiments, for the protection of supply and emigrant trains, and the suppression of indian hostilities. This was agreed to, by eleven majority." And so the bill has finally passed.

"*Be it enacted, &c.*, That the President of the United States be authorized to receive into the service of the United States one regiment of Texas mounted volunteers, *to be raised and organized by the State of Texas*, for the defence and protection of the Texas frontier thereof, to continue in service from the time that the whole regiment shall be mustered into service, *for the term of eighteen months, unless sooner discharged by the President.*—Said regiment shall be composed of one Colonel, one Lieutenant Colonel, one Mayor, and Adjudant with the rank of first Lieutenant, one Quarter-master and Commissary with similar rank, one Surgeon and two Assistant Surgeons; one Seargeant Major, one Quartermaster and Commissary Sergeant, *and ten companies, each of which shall be composed of* one Captain, one first Lieutenant, one second Lieutenant, four Sergerants, four Corporals, two Buglers, one Farrier, *and seventy-four privates*. Each of said officers below the rank of Major,—non-commissioned officers, Musicians, Farrier and privates—*shall furnish and keep himself supplied with a good serviceable horse and horse equipments, for the use and risk of which, in addition to the pay and allowances herein provided, he shall receive forty cents a day while in service with his horse;* and if any non commissioned officer, musician, farrier, or private, shall, from carelessness or neglect, injure or render his horse unfit for service, *and shall fail to supply a serviceable horse within the period of ten days from the loss*, such soldier shall, from such time be entitled only to the pay of a private of infantry.

SEC. 2.—That the officers, non commissioned officers, musicians, farriers, and privates of said regiment shall, when mustered into the service of the United States, be subject to the rules and articles of war. Shall be armed at the expense of the United States, as the President shall direct; and shall be allowed the same pay, rations and allowances in kind, including clothing, and be subject to the same rules and regulations as are provided for the regiments of cavalry now in the service; but no field officer shall receive forage for a greater number of horses than he may, from time to time, actually have in service. No pay or allowance shall be due until said regiment shall be received into the service; but each officer and man, shall then be entitled to one day's pay and allowance for every twenty miles he may have been required to travel from his residence to the place of muster."—This is the kind of troops asked for by the people of Texas. Much efficiency has been promised to the public service, if such troops should be organized; and we have little doubt that all these promises will be realized, if the regular officers, under whose command this regiment is to be placed, will lead them to the charge, in active service. The ten companies are to be raised by the State of Texas; Organize therefore, and tender your services to the Governor. These companies will be received by him in the order in which they are tendered; first come, first served, is the rule.

INDIAN FIGHT.—We are under obligations to the State Gazette for a copy of their extra, of the 27th inst., containing a full account of an engagement with the Comanche Indians, by Capts. Ford and Nelson, on the north side of the Canadian river, on the 12th instant. The report occupies a space of near three columns, giving full particulars of the proceedings of the engagement. We have not sufficient room to publish the whole report; but will give the most important items. There were 76 Indians killed, 18 taken prisoners, and many wounded, and over 300 horses captured. The Rangers numbered 213, including friendly Indians. Two of the Ranging force were killed.

☞ The following despatch from Birdville, we find in the Dallas Herald Extra, dated May 18th:

BIRDVILLE, May 17, 1858.

JUDGE LATIMER:—We have the most horrid news here. All is excitement and confusion. Several expresses have arrived from Parker county, stating that the Reserve Indians, and others combined numbering, many thousands, were killing all before them. They were at Loving's Store, at the West edge of Parker county, yesterday morning. All believe the news, for there appears to be no room to doubt it. It is believed here that the main force of the Indians will come down through Denton, from the North-west, as they have stolen, within a few days past, all the horses on the head waters of Denton, Hickory and Elm creeks.

We have started some 150 men from this county to Parker, and some North.

If one-fourth of the news be true, it is awful indeed, and none appear to doubt it.

Dallas should send all the help in her power forthwith, up through this county, and thence in a North-west direction. In great haste,

Your ob't serv't,

A. G. WALKER.

☞ The Richmond Reporter says we have just been shown a letter from Waco, which speaks favorably of the position of Judge Bell. A spirit of investigation seems to be abroad in the land, and is every day gaining ground. The inquiry appears to be, wherever a self-constituted clique have morally, politically, or constitutionally, the right to control the votes of free citizens. If so, we are living under an oligarchy of the most despotic kind.

CHARMS.—A fortune of twenty thousand pounds. COUNTER CHARMS.—Pretty shop-girls.

Mass Meeting.

From the Lagrange True Issue of last Saturday, we clip the following resolutions, which are recommended to the consideration of the people of Fayette county, to be acted on at the meeting to be held on the 14th June.—We publish them that our readers may see the sentiment and feeling of the Democracy of our adjoining county of Fayette:

There will be a MASS MEETING of the Democracy of Fayette County, on the Second Monday in June, (the 14th,) to which all true State Right's men, without distinction of party, are invited to attend and participate.

It is proposed to submit to the consideration of the meeting the resolutions below.

FRED TATE, JAS. L. GAY,
F. GAITHER, A. R. GATES,
CHAS. S. LONGCOPE.

Whereas, the late action of the Congress of the United States, on the admission of Kansas under the Lecompton Constitution, shows a fanatical determination on the part of a large portion of the Northern States, too recklessly override and violate the most sacred guarantees of the Federal Constitution, the tendency, and ultimate end, of which, is to reduce the Southern States to a condition worse than dependency, in which they will cease to be recognized and treated as equals in the Union; we the people of Fayette county, deem it the proper time when the Southern States should lay aside all party differences heretofore, and unite, as a band of brothers, embarked in a common cause, wherein our interest is a unit, to secure there equality in the Union or their independence out of it.

Therefore—Be it resolved that we solicit and invite our fellow citizens of the State, also the people of the entire South, to assemble in primary county and State Conventions, for the purpose of consulting upon the proper action which it behooves the South now to adopt; and that we will cordially co-operate with them, to secure our equality, even if it serves the Federal compact.

Resolved 2d—That we consider harmony and unity among the Southern people, as the only vital elements to secure our liberty and equality, either within or without the Union; and to effect so necessary and indispensable an object, all party differences, all party prejudices, and all party animosities, should now be sacrificed on the altar of Southern patriotism.

Resolved 3d—That we suggest and recommend to his Excellency the Governor, H. R. Runnels, the necessity and propriety of calling on the people of the State to take into consideration the present crisis, and adopt such measures as will effectually meet the emergency of the times.

Resolved 4th—That our thanks and gratitude are warmly tendered to James Buchanan and those patriots of the North, who have so nobly and firmly co-operated with the people of the South in defending the letter and spirit of the Federal Constitution; and that whatever our fate may be, be it for weal or woe, we shall always appreciate the self sacrifices they have made for us and our country; and shall ever consider them as brothers of the same revolutionary ancestry, who acquired our independence, and made us all equals in the Federal Union.

Resolved 5th—That for the purpose of harmony, and effecting a coalition of all parties in the South, we will make no State or County nomination hereafter; but shall consider every man who believes in the doctrine of State rights, Southern rights, and a strict construction of the Federal Constitution with other necessary qualifications, to be worthy of our suffrages.

COL. KINNEY.—The Star publishes a letter, dated Panama, April 16, in which it is stated that Col. Kinney has been for some time treating with the Mormons, with a view of settling them on the Mosquito coast; that by the last California mail he received intelligence that his proposition had been favorably received by the Mormons, and that this information had enabled him to raise $30,000 in cash, and $80,000 more in merchandize and supplies, with which, accompanied by twenty followers, he has sailed to Greytown. He expects to obtain, through Gen. Lamar, permission to colonize the country under the Nicaraguan flag, obligating the Colonists to help to defend Nicaragua against the filibusters.—Failing to obtain this privilege, he will hoist the Nicaraguan flag, and as this is under British protection, he expects no opposition from any quarter.

CAMELS.—We learn from the San Antonio Herald that the parties with whom the Government has contracted for a supply of camels are to deliver 160 at New Orleans on the 1st of October, and have started two vessels from New York to procure them at Tangier.

ATTEMPTED MURDER AND QUICK RETRIBUTION.—On Wednesday evening Mr. Thomas O'Neal made a brutal assault upon his wife, with a butcher knife, cutting her in three or four different parts of her person, injuring her so severely that her life is despaired of. This morning, Mr. O'Neal was found hanging by the neck, outside of the calaboose.—*Lavaca Herald.*

RIO GRANDE CROSSING.—We learn from the S. A. Texan that a new crossing of the Rio Grande has been discovered within the last few days, that bids fair to make a new era in our inter-communication with Mexico. This crossing is about sixty miles above San Fernando, near a point called San Vicente, and seems to be the place marked out by nature as the *great point* of crossing in our trade with Mexico. It is by far the nearest route to Chihuahua, from most of the posts and towns in Western Texas; and the Texan has no doubt but it will be the point where the great Pacific railroad will cross on its way to Chihuahua and the Pacific.—*News.*

HOUSTON.—The Telegraph furnishes us with the following items:

The subscription books to the telegraph line between that city and Galveston, are now opened, and some progress has been made.

The work of laying the track of the Central Road, now lacks but two miles of completion to Hempstead. There is yet, however, considerable work to be done on that section.—The grading of the Texas and New Orleans Road is being carried forward with energy.—The annual report of the H. T. and B. Road, will show a very prosperous condition of the affairs of that company. The prospect of the early completion of the line to Columbia is very bright.

THE LATEST NEWS.

WASHINGTON, May 18.—In the Senate today the bill providing for the admission of Oregon into the Union is under discussion.

In the House, Joaeph Wright, of New Jersey, a Democrat, has been elected Door-Keeper, in place of Hackly, removed.

THE SEARCHING OF AMERICAN VESSELS.

The U. S. vessels-of-war Saratoga and Dolphin have been ordered to join the home squadron; and communications have been addressed to various collectors of customs requesting them to forward to Washington official reports of searches of American vessels by British vessels, which may have come to their knowledge.

The President, it is stated, will await the receipt of definite intelligence and of explanation from England, before taking any decisive action in the premises.

Washington News.

The Committee of Ways and Means have resolved on reporting a bill to authorize the raising of a loan of $15,000,000 to meet the wants of Government.

Brig Wingold which arrived at Boston on the 17th, was fired into after leaving Sierra Morena and the ball passed near the Captain's head.

H. W. Herbert, Esq., an extremely versatile writer, better known by the *nom de plume* of "Frank Forrester," committed suicide in New York on the 16th inst.

Orders have been issued to the home squadron to prevent further outrages on American vessels by British cruisers.

An indignation meeting was held at New York on the 18th., by the ship masters on the subject of outrages committed on American vessels by British Cruisers in the Carribean Sea, searching them. It is said Gen. Cass had addressed Lord Napier in strong terms on this snbject.

The steamship North America which left Liverpool on the 5th inst, brings news of a slight advance in cotton of about ⅛.

A telegram from St. Louis gives interesting news from Camp Scott, April 10th, to the effect that the Mormons had laid down their arms and that Governor Cummings had entered Salt Lake City without an escort, at the invitation of Brigham Young. Many of the mormons had gone to the Southern part of the Territory, followed by their wives and children. A party of bandits, 250 in number, armed and mounted, were reported to be in the vicinity of Fort Scott, defying the United States troops. They were commanded by the notorious Montgomery. One hundred and fifty families had been robbed and driven into Missouri. Gen. Harney reached Leavenworth on the 12th.

It is stated that the Government has given orders to the Home Squadron to prevent further outrages on American shipping by British cruisers.

The Secretary of the Treasury invites proposals for $4,000,000 for coin.

Utah Affairs.

WASHINGTON, May 18.—The government intends to keep a large force in Salt Lake Valley, and make Salt Lake City a depot for stores and equipments, even if the late intelligence be true, which is confirmed by further dispatches.

It is also reported that the general feeling of the Mormons is in favor of peace.

Oregon Passed the Senate.

WASHINGTON, May 18.—In the Senate to-day the bill for the admission of Oregon into the Union was passed by a majority of 18.

The bill providing for the running of the boundary line of the State of Texas, without the making of scientific investigation was passed.

ST. LOUIS, May 19.—We have intelligence here to-day that Gen. Persifer F. Smith died at Fort Leavenworth on Sunday night last at half past 12 o'clock.

The command of the Utah expedition now devolves on Gen. Harney.

ST. LOUIS, May 20.—We have intelligence here to-day, announcing the arrival of Col. Kane at Fort Leavenworth from Salt Lake, on Sunday last, with the news that Brigham Young had resigned the Governorship of the Territory.

British Outrage on Cuba! Troops Landed.

NEW YORK, May 20.—By the steamship Black Warrior, Capt. J. T. Smith, which arrived here to-day from New Orleans via Havana, we have intelligence from the latter announcing that great indignation had been aroused there, as well as in official circles as among the population generally, in consequence of the landing of a force of British marines at one of the outports of the island under the pretence of searching for Bozal negroes, or recently introduced slaves.

The Captain of the Port had been ordered to Havanna by the Captain General for trial for not having resented the insult.

THREE CHEERS FOR MEXICO.—We have just recieved the intelligence from the "Brownsville Flag," that the liberal party, under Col. Zuazua, and officer of Oidauri, has taken Zacetecas, and holds as prisoners Gen. Manero, several other officers, and a large number of troops, with 12 cannon and 200 stand of arms. This dispatch is dated Zacetecas, April 27th.—*S. A. Texan.*

COL. KINNEY IN CENTRAL AMERICA.—A Washington despatch, of 29th ult., says:

The Panama correspondent of the States says that Col. Kinney is negotiating, and with every prospect of success, for colonizing the Mosquito coast with English Mormons, under either the Nicaraguan or Mosquito flag.

Other advices state that Col. Kinney has been assisted by English capitalists in raising a considerable amount of money and large quantities of provisions, and sailed for Greytown.

OREGON.—We notice that the Constitution under which Oregon is now applying for admission, prohibits free negroes from residing in that State. Several of the free-soil members contended that such a clause was repugnant to the Constitution of the United States, as by it, those who might be citizens of the Free States, could not go there, and they were therefore disposed to vote against the admission of Oregon on that ground. But Seward, seeing the folly of making an objection to the admission of a Free State, particularly at this time when they were trying to get the control of this government into their own hands, overruled this objection, and Oregon will doubtless be a State of this Union before the close of this session.—*News.*

☞ Col. Fremont carried out with him a release given by the United States government of all the mineral wealth in the Mariposa claim; and as the decision of the California court rested wholly on this United States claim, that decision does not in any way affect Col. Fremont's title to the mines:

☞ A severe hail storm occurred in Chesterfield co., Va. Many of the hail stones were large as hen's eggs and in some places laid two feet deep.

Texas Items.

HOUSTON AND ORLEANS RAILROAD.—The Houston Republic says twenty-seven men, carpenters and others, have arrived there from New Orleans, to work on the Houston, Opelousas and New Orleans R. R.

THE NEW COURT HOUSE.—The Belton Independent says: We understand that the contract for our new Court House has been awarded to Messrs. Keller & Bramlett of Waco, for $13,625

☞ The "Weekly Independent" says that J. Henry Brown, has purchased property in the immediate vicinity of Belton, and that he is now reckoned as a denizen citizen of that town.

☞ Notwithstanding the brightened aspect of the times, and the cheering prospects on every hand, some of the people of Western Texas are now grumbling—we learn from the San Antonio Herald—because they will have to build new corn cribs, in order to house their coming crops.

☞ The Houston Telegraph learns that Mr. Groesbeck has bought for the Central Road, 80 new freight cars, one 22 tons locomotive and a machine shop complete. Bills of lading for the cars have been received in Houston.

GEN. HENNINGSEN.—This distinguished gentleman stopped several days in our city last week, on his return from Mexico, where, it seems, his proffered services were not accepted. He took passage on the steamer Texas which sailed for New Orleans on Saturday. So says the Indianola Courier.

DISTRICT COURT—Is in full blast. Judge Terrell is unquestionably, one of the most business men we have ever seen on the bench; and if our opionion would weigh well, it should be thrown into the scale thus: he's clear-headed.—*Journal.*

☞ We learn from the Houston Republic that a turtle four feet six inches long, and twenty inches across the shell, was caught in Bray's Bayou, by Mr. Perkins' negroes. He weighed 118 pounds. A *post mortem* examination is to take to-day.

☞ The San Antonio Texan says we have heard of no new cases of small pox since our last, and we understand the hospital is now closed. We were sorry to hear through a gentleman from Atascosa, that two cases had occurred in that county, and we have learned that some persons from there came to San Antonio to be vaccinated,

METHODIST CHURCH.—Nightly, during the week, crowded meetings have been held at this church, the clergymen officiating being the Rev's. J. C. Wilson, B. F. Perry, A. Davidson, R. H. Belvin and Thos. A. Smith.—The meetings are said to have been remarkably interesting, and with our neighbor of the Herald, we trust that they will result in much good to the community.—*S. A. Texan.*

ROASTING EARS.—The Austin Sentinel says we are indebted to our friend, Major John Hampton, for a fine lot of roasting ears. They were grown in a field within the limits of the corporation, and are the earliest we have seen during the season.

☞ The True Issue says the District Court—Judge Bell presiding, convened at this place on the 17th inst. The business of the Court this week has progressed rather slowly, and but few important cases have been finally disposed of. The docket will occupy the time of the Court for perhaps three weeks.

☞ The vote was taken on Monday in Houston to repeal the ordinance for closing liquor shops on Sunday, and was defeated by a majority of 91, who voted in favor of continuing the old ordinance. The whole vote cast was 357, and shows conclusively that Houston is in favor of good moral city government.

☞ The True Issue says Judge Bell is giving universal satisfaction, on the District Bench, and will secure we suppose, a majority of the democrats of this county, for the office of Associate Justice of the Supreme Bench. The more the public see of him, the better are they satisfied of his peculiar fitness for the position he seeks.

NEW ORLEANS MAIL.—The Galveston News says we learn from Capt. Place that the new mail contract will embrace one mail boat per week from New Orleans via Sabine Pass, two mail boats via Berwick's Bay, to extend the trip to Powderhorn, and two on the outside route, which will also go to Powderhorn, thus giving us five mails per week with four to Powderhorn and one to Sabine Pass. The boats also are to leave so as to arrive on separate days.

HENDERSON, OF TEXAS—It is said that this gentleman, the Senator elect from Texas, is far gone in consumption, and will not probably enter upon the duties of his post. If such should unfortunately be the case, there is a probability that Col. Louis T. Wigfall, formerly of South Carolina, will succeed him.—*Edgefield Advertiser.*

☞ The True Issue says the Fayette county Agricultural Society met on last Monday, at which time an address was delivered by A. R. Gates, Esq. We regret that circumstances were such that it was out of our power to be present. Mr. Gates is a finished scholar and planter, and takes deep interest in everything affecting the subject of agriculture.

PROSPECT FOR CROPS.—During the past week we have conversed with reliable gentlemen who have visited the different counties east, west, north and south of us, and they all declare that without a single exception, the present prospect for crops in Western Texas has never before been equalled. The rain has been abundant and the damage by grasshoppers, which no doubt was greatly exaggerated, is now scarcely seen or felt.—*S. A. Texan.*

☞ The Board of County Commissioners awarded 10 cents per day to indigent pupils from the school fund appropriated to this County. After this amount has been paid out to the Teachers who have complied with the requisition of the Law, and make their applications for the fund, if there is a balance on hand, it is to be divided *pro rata* among the other pupils.—*Belton Independent.*

☞ Hugh Cooper, the murderer of Benj. J. Fortson, was again convicted at Corsicana Court and sentenced to be hung.—*Dallas Herald.*

MECHANICS' INSTITUTE.—$10,000 has been appropriated by the Legislature of the State of Tennessee, for the purpose of erecting a Mechanics' Institute.

HYMENEAL.

☞ We received a letter by yesterday's mail from our young friend, M. W. YOUNG, ESQ., noting his arrival at Galveston, and which also, conveys the gratifying intelligence of his happy union with the beautiful and accomplished Miss MARTHA JANE ANDREWS, of Monroe county, Mississippi, which took place on the 12th May, instant.

A pleasant and happy voyage to you and your fair bride, friend BILLY, over the sea of life; may peace and plenty follow in your wake, and may your dearest anticipations be crowned with unalloyed love, pleasure and prosperity.

MARRIED—On Wednesday, 26th instant, at the residence of the bride's father, Rob't. Moore, by the Rev. J. A. Kimball, Mr. J. D. ROBERTSON, of Williamson county, to Miss HARRIETT A. MOORE, of Bastrop county.

The Bastrop Advertiser.

Independent Journal----Devoted to Politics, Agriculture, Education, Temperance, Internal Improvement, and General Information.

VOL. VI. BASTROP, TEXAS, SATURDAY, JULY 24, 1858. NO. 21.

THE

"BASTROP ADVERTISER."

Issued every Saturday by

WILLIAM J. CAIN.

Editor and Proprietor.

TERMS:

TWO DOLLARS AND A HALF A YEAR, *in advance* THREE DOLLARS, if payment be deferred longer than Three Months.

ADVERTISEMENTS will be inserted at the rate of ONE DOLLAR A SQUARE, *for the first insertion*, and FIFTY CENTS for every subsequent insertion. *Ten Lines* (or less,) constitute a square.

All articles of a personal character will be charged double the above rates—*cash in advance when admitted.*

The number of insertions required must be stated or marked on the advertisement, or they will be inserted until ordered out, and charged accordingly.

A liberal deduction will be made from the above rates to those who advertise by the year.

No subscription will be discontinued until all arrearages are settled.

POETRY.

The Welcome.

BY JAMES A. BEVERIEGE.

One year ago—one little year—
And we were all at home;
A thousand miles divide us now,
But still I know thou'lt come.

Come! when the autumns saddest wails,
Come through the winter's wind,
Come to me as ye always came
And a welcome you shall find.

Come to me if the summer sun
Should bronze thine own fair face
I'll clasp thee still to this fond heart,
And in thy soul find grace.

'Tis said that absence conquers love;
'Tis but a poet's dream,
A love like ours should not be thought
An evanescent gleam.

Nor time, nor chance can ever change
Two hearts that love so well,
For the saddest hour we ever felt
Were when we spoke farewell.

MISCELLANEOUS.

Death of Senator Henderson.

Speeches of Hon. Guy M Bryan, of Texas, and Gen. Quitman, of Miss.

Mr. Bryan, of Texas, rose and addressed the House as follows:

MR. SPEAKER—The announcement just made from the Senate reminds us that another has been stricken from the rolls of great men. Texas again sorrows. She has lost her Rusk and her Henderson! She comes among you, representatives of the States united, a stricken State. Her mighty men have fallen. She weeps for the loss of the gifted and the able, the eloquent and the chivalrous. Henderson was a soldier by nature, a statesman by experience, knowledge and wisdom; a good man from heart and reason. He stood in the front rank of southern patriots and Texan heroes.—True to his friends, false to no man or cause, he was elevated to the seat that death has just vacated by the *unanimous* voice of the representatives of his State—a place once filled by Rusk, and which, had health and life been accorded to him, would have been honored by a Henderson.

You cannot know him as *we* in Texas knew him. Had he been spared to us in his usefulness and vigor of health and mind, you would have admired, esteemed and loved him. His character was frank and liberal, of indomitable will and purity of purpose, with great originality of thought and action. He scorned everything like trick and artifice; with a free spirit and an untrammeled mind, he would have been the Rusk and Clay of the Senate. This may strike some as language too strong. It is what I mean, and because believing it to be true, I speak it. Engaged by his bed-side in his last moments; and since in his behalf, I have had no time to prepare such remarks as are appropriate to the occasion. Consequently I can give but little information as to his early life. Born in Lincoln county, North Carolina, on the 31st of March, 1809, he grew up in that State, in body and mind, as straight as the pines of the old North State. He fitted himself for the law, and was practicing with success his profession, when the wail of Goliad, and the stern cry of the Alamo, reached his ears.

His noble soul was moved to decisive action. He left the scenes and friends of his childhood for the rough life of a Texan soldier. He came to Texas as a volunteer in 1836, and entered the army as a Brigadier General. When the army was disbanded he was appointed Attorney General in the cabinet of the President of Texas. He was afterwards appointed Secretary of State. In 1838, he was sent as Minister to France, where he remained three years. He here met with his wife, Miss Cox, of Philadelphia. On his return to Texas he was offered a situation in the cabinet, which he declined.—He commenced the practice of the law with General Rusk as partner in Eastern Texas. In 1843, he was associated with the resident Minister at Washington, Mr. Van Zandt, to negotiate a treaty of annexation with the United States government. He was a member of the convention that framed the State constitution of Texas, and was inaugurated the first Governor of the State after annexation.

In the war with Mexico as Major General he commanded the Texan troops called into the service of the States. His gallantry at Monterey placed upon his brow the laurel of the soldier, while his ability as a statesman had previously obtained for him the civic wreath.

Upon the expiration of his gubernatorial term he returned to his home at San Augustine, and resumed the practice of his profession with eminent success until he was called by the voice of his State to fill the place of the illustrious Rusk. This position he did not seek, it was thrust upon him. Would that he had never accepted it for, had he not, he would now be within the influence of the balmy clime of Cuba. He was in Havana when the political strife upon the Kansas question within these halls was at its height. Believing that his duty to the South and country required his presence here, he came; he came to fall a martyr to his fidelity, to the State of his love and the institutions of his section.

Although for a long time he refused to accept office, yet, in retirement, he never forgot the duties of the citizen. He was an active State-rights Democrat, of the Calhoun school, and, as such, contributed as much, if not more than any other man in his State to bringing Texas to the present high position she now occupies among her sisters of the South. He regarded the continud agitation of the slavery question as full of peril to the Union, and as humiliating to the sovereign States of the South, and destructive of their rights in the Union.—He regarded the opposition to slavery as having entered into the head and heart of the great masses of the people at the North, and that they were honest in entertaining this opposition. He believed that nothing could save the South in the Union, but union and decisive action on the part of the South. For he thought, until the South convinced the North that they were united in wisdom, feeling and action, upon that great question, which rises superior to every other, so long would they of the North regard the protests of the South as idle tales made for the political effect only. Hence he was opposed to any concession in the late contest upon the Kansas question. We cordially conferred and acted together up to the vote upon the conference bill.

A short time before the vote was taken in the House, he sent for me to come to him in the Senate Chamber. We then finally determined our course. We were both opposed to the measure. He said he could not vote for it; but, rising superior to and far beyond the feelings of the politician, looking at the future with the forecast of a statesman, he said, I cannot vote for the bill, but I cannot be instrumental in dividing the South; I would rather know that I am right than aid error for the sake of appearing right. Consequently, I will not vote at all. These statements I make as an act of justice to the lamented Senator, so that it may go back to his people that he was ever mindful of the interests and honor of Texas. He died on yesterday of disease of the lungs, at five and a half P. M., with his accomplished and bereaved wife, his physician, my colleague, and myself at his bedside.

He retained his consciousness to the last.—His last intelligible words were, "It is my last prayer." He has too soon followed (to join) his friend and partner, the noble Rusk. Texas mourns the loss of her noble sons. A great people weep over their bier.

"There is a tear for all who die,
A mourner o'er the humblest grave,
But nations swell the funeral cry,
And triumph weeps above the brave."

Mr. Speaker, I offer the following resolutions:

Resolved, That the House of Representatives of the United States has received with the deepest sensibility the intelligence of the death of J. P. Henderson, a Senator from the State of Texas.

Resolved, That the officers and members of the House of Representatives will wear the usual badge of mourning for thirty days as a testimony of the respect this House entertains for the memory of the deceased.

Resolved, That the officers and members of the House of Representatives in a body will attend the funeral of J. P. Henderson, on to-morrow at 3 o'clock, P. M. in the chamber of the Senate.

Resolved, That the proceedings of this House in relation to the death of J. P. Henderson, be communicated to the family of the deceased by the clerk.

Resolved, That, as a further mark of respect for the memory of the deceased, this House do now adjourn.

MR. QUITMAN—It was but an hour before the meeting of the House that I received a notification that the members from Texas desired that I should take part in adding a tribute to the memory of their deceased Senator. Without any preparation, therefore, I come before the House to give my full approval to all that has been so eloquently said by my friend from Texas (Mr. Bryan) in regard to the talents, character and virtues of the lamented senator from Texas. It was, sir, not long since that I was called upon similarly in this House, to make some remarks upon the melancholly announcement of the death of the late Thomas J. Rusk, senator from Texas. Since that time our sister State, yet grieving for the loss of her distinguished and deceased senator, proceeded to select from among her most patriotic and well-tried men, a representative of her sovereignty to fill the place vacated by the death of the lamented Rusk. Following the direction of general public sentiment, the legislature unanimously selected for this prominent and responsible station J. Pinkney Henderson, whose lamented death has just been announced by the member from Texas, (Mr. Bryan.)

The garlands cast upon the tomb of the late illustrious Rusk are scarcely withered ere we are again called upon to sympathize with our sister State in the loss of an equally worthy and distinguished successor, who had scarcely taken his seat before he was summoned to another and better world. Thus, in the short space of a year, we have twice been called upon to mourn with Texas in her irreparable bereavements. There is, Mr. Speaker, a remarkable paralell between the history and character of these two men, who have succeeded one another so rapidly in the Senate. They were friends, and at one time partners in the practice of their profession. Both, for similar reasons, emigrated to Texas in 1836; both took prominent part in the war of their independence, and in the construction and afterwards the administration of the government, which was founded upon the success of that war. Both were ardent friends of annexation and, at last, both were appointed representatives of their State in the Senate of the United States, and died in the performance of their duties. Both enjoyed the entire confidence of the people of their State, and both departed to their long homes without a stain or imputation upon their private character.

General Rusk had, from his long services in the federal councils, acquired more reputation beyond the limits of Texas, but it is believed by all who knew General Henderson, that had he been favored with an opportunity of displaying his talents and statesmanship, the high traits of character which he possessed, he would soon have been placed amongst the first statesmen of the country.

I knew him personally well, both as a soldier and statesman. We were associated in the attack upon Monterey, in the war with Mexico. We assimulated in political creeds, and after the Mexican war we frequently corresponded upon political subjects. Gen. Henderson's public and private character was unblemished and without a stain, and he had traits of character which at once attracted the attention of all who had the good fortune to form his acquaintance. He was frank, high-toned, and honorable, without guile or dissimulation. Abhorring deception in political matters, as well as in private transactions, he gave his opinions on all subjects with candor and truth, never practising or countenancing dissimulation on any subject. It was these bold and prominent traits that acquired for him in his own State that high reputation and confidence which few ever acquire among their fellow men. It was these noble qualities that drew forth my admiration and respect. I rose, however, Mr. Speaker, merely to add a few words to what has been said by my friends from Texas, and to second the resolutions which have been presented by him.

The question was taken, the resolutions were unanimously adopted, and the House adjourned.

The Lower Class.

Who are they? asks a cotemporary. The toiling millions—the laboring men and women—the farmers—the mechanic—the artizan—the inventor—the producer. Far from it. These are nature's nobility—God's favorites—the salt of earth! No matter whether they are high or low in station, rich or poor in pelf, conspicuous or humble in position, they are the "upper circles" in the order of nature, whatever the factious distinctions of society, fashionable or unfashionable decree. It is not low, it is the highest duty, privilege and pleasure, for the great man and the whole-souled woman to earn what they possess—to work their own way through life—to be the architect to their own fortunes. Some may rank the classes we have alluded to as only relatively low; and in fact, the middling classes. We insist they are absolutely the *very highest*. If there is a class of human beings on earth who may be properly denominated low, it is those who spend without producing, who dissipate on the earnings of their fathers or relatives without learning or doing anything in aid of themselves.

We are all mariners on this sea of life,
And they who climb above us up the shroud,
Have only in their overtopping place,
Gained a more dangerous station and foothold,
More sincere.

[*Bowling Green* (*Ky.*) *Standard.*

IRRESOLUTION.—Irresolution is a habit which imperceptibly creeps upon its victim with a fatal facility. It is not vicious, but it leads to vice, and many a fine heart has paid the penalty of it at the scaffold. Trifling as it appears in the wavering steps of the young, as they grow older its form changes to that of a hideous monster, which leads them to destruction with their eyes open. The idler, the spendthrift, the epicurean and the drunkard, are among its victims. Perhaps in the latter, its effects appear in the most hideous form.—He knows that the goblet which he is about to drain is poison, yet he swallows it. He knows, for the example of thousands has painted it in glaring colors, that it will deaden all his faculties, take the strength from his limbs and the happiness from his heart, oppress him with foul disease, and hurry his progress to a dishonored grave, yet he drains it under a species of dreadful spell, like that by which small creatures are said to approach and leap into the jaws of the loathsome serpent, whose fiendish eyes have fascinated them. How beautiful and manly is that power which the resolute man passes unmoved through these dangers.

THE MORMON PROPHET'S HAREM.—Bigham Young it is said, has the best conducted harem in the place. His wives have al their seperate duties assigned them. One is a teacher of all the children, others do the house-work, others work weaving in his facory, while the original Mrs. Brigham superintends.

WHY A MAN MAY MARRY A DECEASED WIFE'S SISTER.—One argument in the British Parliament in favor of letting men marry their deceased wives' sisters was, that by doing so a man had only one mother-in-law instead of two.

☞ Moving for a new trial—courting a second wife.

POETRY.

Would that We might meet Again.

Ah! would that we might meet again,
Nor part till life's decline;
For know that thou a golden chain,
Doth bind this heart to thine;
A chain whose tendril will entwine
While on this earth I rove—
Which naught but love can ne'er dissolve,
The magic chain of love.

Ah! would that we might meet again,
For lone and dreary are
The hours, when thou art far away;
Yet love's my guiding star;
And still amidst the darkest hours,
'Twill sweetly point to thee;
For thou this heart's best treasure art,
And thou shalt ever be.

Yes! would that we might meet again;
Thy smile I fain would see:
But dost thou, when, 'mid other scenes,
Still cast one thought on me?
Doth thy fond mem'ry e'er recall
The hour when first we met?
The hour with joy and gladness fraught,
This heart can ne'er forget?

Ah! would that we might meet again;
I would the hour might come
That "where thou goest I may go,"
And there shall be my home.
Yet still as days glide swiftly by,
Though joy or sadness reign,
This hope I'll fondly cherish still—
That we may meet again.

MISCELLANEOUS.

Spurgeon on the American Revival.

The celebrated Spurgeon, whose stirring eloquence has produced such intense excitement in England, recently delivered a sermon in London on the great revival in America. We subjoin a passage:—

"You never saw such people. The outsiders called these fanatics. It is blessed fanaticism. Others say, they are nothing but enthusiasts. It is a heavenly enthusiasm. Every thing that is done is done with such spirit!—If they sing, it is like the crashing thunder; if they pray, it is like the swift sharp flash of lightning, lighting up the darkness of the cold-hearted, and making them for the moment feel that there is something in prayer. When the minister preaches, he preaches, like a Boanerges, and when the church is gathered together, it is with a hearty good-will. When they give, they give with enlarged liberality; when they visit the sick they do it with gentleness, meekness and love. Everything is done with a single eye to God's glory; not of men, but by the power of God. Oh, that we might see such a revival as this!

"But, blessed be God, it does not end here. The revival of the church then touches the rest of society. Men who do not come forward and profess religion, are more punctual in attending the means of grace. Men that used to swear, give it up; they find it is not suitable for the times. Men that profaned the Sabbath and despised God, find that it will not do; they give it all up. Times get changed; morality prevails; the lower ranks are affected. They buy a sermon where they used to buy some penny tract of nonsense. The higher orders are also touched; they too are brought to hear the word. Her ladyship in her carriage, who never would have thought of going to so mean a place as a conventicle, does not care where she goes so long as she is blessed. She wants to hear the truth; and a drayman pulls his horses up by the side of her ladyship's pair of grays, and they both go in and bend together before the throne of sovereign grace. All classes are affected.

"Even the Senate feels it; the statesman himself, is surprised at it, and wonders what all these things mean. Even the monarch on the throne feels she has become the monarch of a people better than she knew before, and that God is doing something in her realms past all her thought—that a great King is swaying a better sceptre, and exerting a better influence than even her excellent example. Nor does it even end there. Heaven is filled. One by one the converts die, and heaven gets fuller; the harps of heaven are louder, the songs of angels are inspired with new melody, for they rejoice to see the sons of men prostrate before the throne. The universe is made glad; it is God's own summer; it is the universal Spring. The time of the singing of birds is come; the voice of the turtle is heard in our land. Oh, that God might send us such a revival of religion at this!"

How to Take Life.

Take life like a man—take it by the forelock, by the shoulders, by the spine, by every limb and part. Take it just as though it was—as it is—an earnest, vital essential affair. Take it just as though you personally was born to the task of performing a merry part in it; as though the world had waited for your coming. Take it as though it was a grand opportunity to do and to achieve; to carry forward great and good schemes; to help and cheer a suffering, weary, it may be, heart-sickened brother.

The fact is, life is unvalued by a great majority of mankind. It is not made half as much of as should be the case. Where is the man or woman who accomplishes one tithe of what might be done? Who cannot look back upon opportunities lost, plans unachieved, thoughts crushed, aspirations unfilled, and all because of the lack of the necessary and possible effort? If we knew better how to take and make the most of life, it would be far greater than it is. Now and then a man stands aside from the crowd, labors earnestly, steadfastly, confidently, and straightway becomes famous for wisdom, intellect, skill, greatness of some sort. The world admires, wonders, idolizes; and yet it only illustrates what each may do if he takes hold of life with a purpose—by the head and shoulders. If a man but say he will, and follows it up by the right kind of effort, there is nothing in reason he may not expect to accomplish. There is no magic, no miracle, no secret to him who is brave in heart and determined in spirit.

JENNY LIND.—Mrs. Goldschmidt (Jenny Lind,) recently gave birth to twins—one of each sex. Here we have another edition, in two volumes, of "Goldsmith's Animated Nature."

A Gang of Thieves.

The Waco Democrat reports the statement that a gang of horse thieves and robbers have been discovered in the upper portion of Navarro county, extending through various other counties of the State. That paper says—

About the 10th inst., (June) whilst a gentleman by the name of Graves and his wife, living on the line between Nevarro and McLennan counties, were absent from home, their house was entered in the day time by two villians of the darkest dye for the purpose of *robbing* and if necessary to accomplish their purpose—*murder*. Four children of Mr. Graves'—a little girl aged about 11 years and the others still younger, were there *alone*.—Immediately on entering, these villians presented a pistol to their heads and with horrid curses and imprecations, told the children if they moved or spoke, they would blow their brains out. They then proceeded to search for money—breaking open trunks, closets, chests, &c. It was their belief, as they afterwards confessed, that Mr. Graves had a large quantity of money, for which he had sold a stock of cattle a few days before. It was true that he had sold the cattle, but fortunately for himself, sold on *time*. They also confessed that they entered the same house on the two succeeding nights, whilst Mr. Graves and family were absent, to *avoid* them—believing that Mr. Graves was absent during the day carrying the money with him, and expecting to find him at home at night—intending to murder him, if necessary, to get the money.

Mr. Graves now saw too plainly the perilous situation of himself and family, and immediately aroused the neighborhood to his assistance—and likewise warned them of the insincerity of themselves and families from the same desperadoes. Active and energetic preparations were instantly put on foot to ferret out the villians and secure their arrest. From the descriptions given of them by the eldest of Mr. Graves' children, suspicion rested upon two bad characters named Bill Mitchell and Jim Warren, living on Pin Oak creek. The citizens proceeded to their house and surrounded it before the guilty party was aware, that he was in the grasp of Justice—Jim Warren was found alone in the house.

On seeing the situation he was in—that escape was impossible, and resistance madness—he surrendered and *voluntarily* confessed that he was one of the two who entered Graves' house, and Bill Mitchell the other.

He furthermore stated that there was a regular organized band of horse thieves, &c.,—extending through the counties of Navarro, Limestone, Falls, Milam, Bosque, Bexar and Burlerson—with signs grips and passwords. He disclosed the names of all he could recollect. He then told where Mitchell might be found; search was made and he was soon caught. He was examined separately and apart from Warren and made the same confession that Warren did, giving the names however, of ten more than Warren did. The names of the gang as disclosed, was as follows:

Jim Warren and Hardin Warren, of Pin Oak, Nevarro co., Esquire Pogue, Weatherford, Parker co., formerly of Limestone county; Dr. Carmel, Lawrence Carmel, Alex Barnes, Laughlen Barnes, Charley McGuyer, Bill Cunningham, of Rush creek, Navarro co., Hiram Sharne, Steel's creek, Limestone county; Bill Mitchell and Tom Mitchell, Milam co., Geo. Miller, Geo. Fry, Marion Hughes, Geo. Kellin, Bill Jones, Tom Middleton, Gal Brown, Willis Wills, Bill Wills, Dan Wills, of Milam county; Tom Hughes, Bill Hughes, Geo. Hughes, of Yeawah, Burlerson co; Henderson, Peters, Jim Burks, formerly of Limestone; Bill Jones, Mart Jones, of San Antonio; Bill Ward, Bill Moss, Barton Moss, Tom Gordon, John Gordon, Robertson county; Jesse Parsons—dead; Jim Arnett, Zina Aggleston, Jim Spindle, Tom Black, Boatwright, Tom Jeffers—John Wardick, Bryant Wardick, Tom Rogers, Tom Rusk, Shuts, Hence Kellin, John Miller, Tom Smith, Tom Jackson, Tom Miller, and Jim Owen—residence not given.

Two in Heaven.

"You have two children," said I.

"I have four," was the reply—two on earth, two in Heaven.

There spoke the mother! Still hers, only gone before! Still remembered, loved and cherished, by the hearth and at the board; their places not yet filled, even though their successors draw life from the same breast where their dying heads were pillowed.

"Two in heaven!"

Safely housed from storm and tempest.—No sicknes there, nor drooping head, nor fading eye nor weary feet. By green pastures, tended by the Good Shepherd, linger the little lambs of the heavenly fold.

"Two in Heaven!"

Earth less attractive. Eternity nearer. Invisible cords drawing the material soul upwards. "Still small voices" ever whisper, "Come!" to the world-weary spirit.

"Two in Heaven!"

"Mother of angels!" Walk softly! Holy eyes watch thy footsteps! Cherub forms bend to listen. Keep thy spirit free from earth taint; so shalt thou go to them, though they may not return to thee.

☞ A man very much intoxicated was sent to jail. Why did you not bail him out? inquired a bystander of a friend. Bail him out! exclaimed the other; why you couldn't pump him out!

Reflections.

"Appearances deceive,
And this one maxim is a standing rule:—
All men are not what they seem."

We are not much given to criticism. We were once disposed to contemplate with charity the frailties and infirmities of our fellow creatures, and to look with an eye of credulity upon the world of mankind. We supposed that all persons, with whom it became our duty or pleasure to associate in our intercourse with society, to be our friends; nor did we ever think of suspecting the fidelity of any one's professions, until positive demonstrations convinced us of their insincerity.—As we grow older, however, and are compelled to plunge into the troubled current of business transactions, we are reluctantly constrained to look upon a world in a light different from what they were wont to do. To analyse the motives of men—to study the anatomy of human character—and to discriminate the vices that pollute, and the virtues that adorn society—indeed requires an acute perception. Sometimes they are so delicately and nicely blended in the composition of man, that they almost neutralize each other, and present a subject whose moral features it is almost impossible to comprehend. Again, the depravity and turpitude of the heart stands out in bold relief, and the destructive thunderbolt slumbers in the cloud, gilded with the brightest rays of sunshine, presenting a practical illustration of the remark, that "a man may smile and be a villian still." Hypocrisy, ingratitude, and a multitude of other infirmities, seem to find a nest in their bosoms. They apparently delight to prey upon character, be it ever so pure, and to bring it down to a level with their own.

Had we the power, our pen would indite reformation upon a heart so desperately wicked; and our voice would invoke, in strains of earnest importunity, the soft and delicate hand of virtue to cleanse the receptacle of vice of its impurities, and to melt, with true penitence, the soul corroded with sin and deformed with iniquity.

We are indulging in no personal allusions; but it has been our misfortune, if a misfortune it be, to meet with just such characters in the course of our short pilgrimage through life.—*Southern Intelligencer.*

Honest Labor.

Labor, honest labor, is mighty and beautiful. Activity in the ruling element of life, and its highest relish. Luxuries and conquests are the result of labor; we can imagine nothing without it. The noblest man of earth is he who puts his hands cheerfully and proudly to honest labor. Labor is a business and ordinance of God. Suspend labor and where is the glory and pomp of earth—the fruits, fields, and palaces, and fashionings of matter, for which men strive and war? Let the labor-scorner look around him, look to himself and learn what are the trophies of toil. From the crown of his head to the sole of his foot, he is a debter and slave of toil.—Where gets he the garniture and equipage? Let labor answer. Labor—which makes music in the mine, and the furrow, and at the forge. Oh! scorn labor, do you—man who never yet earned a morsel of bread! Labor pities you, proud fool, and laughs you to scorn. You shall pass to dust forgotten; but labor will drive on forever, glorious in conquests and monuments.

A BEAUTIFUL EXTRACT.—There lies in the depth of every heart that dream of our youth, and the chastened wish of manhood, which neither cares nor honors can ever extinguish—the hope of one day resting from the pursuits which absorb us; of interposing between old age and the tomb, some tranquil interval of reflection, when with feelings not subdued, but softened with passions, not exhausted but mellowed, we may look calmly on the past without regret, and on the past without apprehension.

But in the tumult of the world, this vision forever recedes as we approach it, the passions which have agitated our life disturb our latest hours, and we go down to the tomb, like the sun in ocean with no gentle and gradual withdrawing of life back to the source which gave it, but sullen in its firey glow long after it has lost its power and splendor.

CAN'T PLEASE OLD MAIDS.—The editor of a country paper, having been taken to task by a female correspondent for noticing Dr. Hall's receipe to prevent ladies from taking cold, viz: "to keep the mouth shut"—hits back as follows:

"We never could make ourselves popular with old maids. Do what we would—squeeze 'em behind the door, which they dearly love—flatter 'em on the sofa—dance with 'em at parties—take 'em to sleigh rides, and treat 'em to ice cream, oysters, 'kisses'—in short, attend ever so gallantly all their wants save making them a direct offer—and the moment our back was turned they would turn too and show their teeth, (false ones of course. Well, hope deferred maketh the heart sick, and we never blamed 'em."

☞ "Hans, did you ever see any sassafras?" "Sassy *frau!* mine cot! yaw. I schleeps mit him every nichts!" "Vos you means, you schleeps mit him?" "Vy, Mose, dats mine wife, saucy frau!"

☞ An exchange notices the marriage of Miss Angelia Braham, a daughter of the great vocalist, and adds:

"We congratulate the bridegroom upon his privilege of reposing, even on earth, upon A. Braham's bosom.

FRANK LESLIE'S ILLUSTRATED NEWSPAPER

No. 163—VOL. VII.] NEW YORK, SATURDAY, JANUARY 15, 1859. [Price 6 Cents.

THINGS IN AND ABOUT SAN ANTONIO.

By Richard Everett.

On the morning of September 2d, 1858, the train of the Santa Rita Silver Mining Company, bound for Arizona, came in sight of the ancient city of San Antonio, Texas. It was a bright, pleasant morning, and the scene was quite Oriental. After twelve days of slow travel across the prairies from the sea coast, meeting with very sparse evidences of civilization, San Antonio appeared to us like the Mecca of some wearied caravan. The view of the city and surrounding country helped out the similarity. Over a mass of low white buildings, located on the verge of a boundless plain, swelled the dome of the old Mission Church, while clumps of oaks and mesquites served for the palms and date trees of Eastern lands. Two rivers wind through the city, flowing from living springs only a short distance beyond the suburbs. One, the San Antonio, boils in a vast volume from a rocky basin, which, environed by mossy stones and overhanging foliage, seems devised for the especial dwelling-place of nymphs and naiads. The other, the San Pedro, runs from a little pond, formed by the outgushing of five sparkling springs, which bear the same name. This miniature lake, embowered in a grove of stately elm and pecan trees, is one of the most beautiful natural sheets of pure water in the Union—so clear, that even the delicate roots of the water-lilies and the smallest pebbles may be distinctly seen. In this grove we packed our wagons, and beneath the shade of the thick foliage built our campfires. The tired mules, turned loose upon the neighboring prairie, manifested their delight by repeated rolls upon the thick carpet of

TEXAN HERDSMEN.—FROM A SKETCH BY OUR OWN CORRESPONDENT.

mesquite grass, which is, in this portion of Texas, the much-relished food of every description of live stock.

Tradition says that more than two hundred years ago there were Spanish settlements in the San Antonio valley. Be this true or merely romance, we have historical proof that in 1581 the Jesuit Fathers, those indomitable pioneers of civilization, explored and founded missions in what is now New Mexico. In the course of investigations made in the valleys around Santa Fe, the ruins of walls and houses, evidently of Spanish workmanship, have been discovered, of earlier date than those of a similar character in Texas, which proves that the first settlements were made at points far north of San Antonio. History tells us with what zeal the early apostles of the Catholic faith carried their explorations into the uttermost corners of the earth. They were the first to penetrate the mysterious empire of the Chinese, they wandered over the steppes of Tartary; they went out with infidel caravans to the sacred city of the Mahomedan; they sat down at the gates of Japan; and again explored, in their bark canoes, the great lakes of the North American continent. A Marco Polo traverses the East Indian realms, a Marquette and a Joliet track the Mississippi from Lake Pepin to the Gulf of Mexico. Two hundred years ago their missions were established on the coast of California, and before the American continent was discovered they had set up the index of their faith upon the icy shores of the Arctic Sea. Religious zeal was the greatest, perhaps the only characteristic of the old Jesuit explorers: they indulged in the vain idea, not yet eradicated from the minds of missionaries, that men can be Christianized before they are civilized—an idea chimerical and vain, as illustrated by the universal failure of all those laborious and hazardous enterprises into savage lands, which have been undertaken by missionaries of the Catholic Church. The only evidence we have of the toils and dangers attendant upon those missions are vague traditions and piles of mouldering ruins. Saxon civilization, the civilization of labor, which felled trees, built roads, laid out towns and established laws, came after; a civilization which progressed instead of degenerated, and elevated instead of debased, the people upon whom it dawned.

In the year 1715 a fort was established near the present site of San Antonio, and named Fort San Antonio de Valero. Time has eradicated all traces of this old fortification, and even tradition does not indicate its site. Ten years after a mission building was erected, said to be one of the three whose ruins are now in existence, and irrigating ditches or "acequias," constructed to carry water upon the cultivated fields. From the year 1730 we have authentic data taken from the old Spanish records preserved among the archives of the county in which San Antonio is located. In that year, says the old record, came twelve families of pure Spanish blood, from the Canary Islands, who laid out and founded the city of San Antonio. Among the settlers was a Garcia, a Flores, a Navarro and a Garaza, names afterwards prominent in the revolutionary history of Texas, while it was claimed as a Spanish colony. One year after their arrival the colonists, assisted by the Jesuit fathers and their crowds of Indian converts, erected the quaint church which now, defaced and battered by the storms of one hundred and twenty-seven years, stands in the main plaza of the city, a monument of the almost buried past. Its evening bells echo sweetly their chimes as in the days of long ago, and crowds of worshippers still kneel upon the old stone floor and bow before the venerable picture of the Crucifixion which hangs, all dim and discolored, above the altar.

Four other missions were erected upon the banks of the San Antonio river, and named respectively San Jose, La Espada, San Juan and Concepcion. They were large, strong, half-church, half-fortress edifices, in appearance something like the feudal castles of olden time, whose ruins are scattered all over Europe, surrounded by a high and massive stone wall, with only one entrance. The buildings, which consisted of chapels, dormitories, halls, cells and kitchens, were all built of limestone, the quarrying and transporting of which must alone have been an immense labor, as some of the edifices were of great extent. Each mission was surrounded by an extensive farm, whose acequias and irrigating ditches are yet visible. Among all the missions of this section that of San Jose must have been conspicuous from its size, its strength, and the rude splendor with which it was decorated. Still may be seen carvings of saints and sacred relics upon the walls and ceilings. Over the main entrance, which is garnished by many ornaments, there is yet a battered representation of the Virgin and her Infant, and the patron, San Jose, cut in the hard limestone. Profane heretics have used the eyes and nose of the venerable saint, and "the place where his heart ought to be" for targets where they have chronicled their skill as marksmen. The chapel front is ornamented with coarse fresco painting in red, yellow and blue, in its day doubtless to the ignorant beings who worshipped there a grand exhibition of art. From San Jose we visited the mission of Concepcion, which was once a lofty structure with two tall towers and a dome, surrounded by a thick arched wall. We found a lot of Mexican cattle-herders in full possession, and the main chapel room filled with filth and rubbish. The outbuildings and arches are overgrown with moss and weeds. In the soft twilight which was slowly stealing over the San Antonio valley the scene was solemn and sad, and we startled at our own footsteps upon the desolate pavement, half expecting to see the cowled figure of some ghostly monk start from the gloomy arches to rebuke our unhallowed intrusion.

Crossing the San Antonio river from the main plaza, we came to a quaint old edifice, whose seamed and battered front betokens an acquaintance with shot and shell. It was built after the Moorish style, and although of late a modern roof has been added, is the same old edifice memorable as the Thermopylæ of Texan independence—the Alamo! a name familiar to the American people as a "household word"—a name associated with a siege and a defence the like of which can scarcely be found in the history of any State. The place where fell Bowie, Travis, Crockett and a band of as brave spirits as ever upheld struggling freedom in any quarter of the globe. The history of the Texan Revolution is yet to be written. The struggles and sacrifices, the suffering and martyrdom of those who fell in the short but terrible strife which was the prelude to Texan Independence, deserve to be recorded as glorious examples of patriotism, as noble as that which immortalized a Leonidas, a Tell, or an Andreas Hofer.

The Alamo was never intended for a fortress, although the walls are very strong; yet it has been the scene of several severe conflicts. The last one, which gave it a widespread renown, was in 1835. In 1835, General Cos, commanding a strong Mexican force, was besieged in San Antonio by a small irregular body of Texans. Divided into bands under different leaders, the latter made poor progress. Dissensions broke out, and there was a prospect that the siege would be abandoned. At this crisis, Colonel Benjamin Millman one morning mounted his horse, and riding through the camp, called out, "Who will go into San Antonio with old Ben Millman?" It was just at the close of a council of war, where it had been decided by a close vote not to make an attack. At first there was no movement, but as the gallant old man repeated his challenge the border blood fired up, and a score of bold spirits swore they would "follow Old Ben hellwards if his route laid in that direction." Volunteers then turned out by hundreds, Old Ben told off the storming parties and selected the officers. At a signal they rushed, rifle and bowie knife in hand, to the assault. A long and ferocious conflict followed, for the Mexicans were two to one against the attacking force. At length, after both parties were exhausted, and heaps of dead and dying encumbered the approaches to the city, General Cos surrendered, and was permitted to march out of San Antonio, and with his remaining force retire from Texas with the honors of war. He did so, and it was supposed that such a humane and generous example would be reciprocated should the fortune of war place Texans in the hands of their enemy. The expectation was vain. About one year after, Santa Anna, with a strong force of infantry, cavalry and artillery, entered San Antonio. The small battalion of Texans under Colonel Travis, numbering only one hundred and eighty-seven men, retired to the Alamo. Loopholes were quickly made in the walls, and the best marksmen took position on the flat roof. Santa Anna immediately laid siege and commenced a furious bombardment with six and twelve pounders, at the same time hoisting a blood-red flag, and ordering his men to give no quarter. The Texan force, composed entirely of riflemen, conducted the defence with wonderful skill and bravery, never throwing away a shot, and picking off every Mexican who came within range. Many anecdotes are told of this deadly conflict. One rifleman, a borderer named Hallett, is said to have shot thirty-three men in two days, and each victim was pierced between the eyes. Another, creeping into the Mexican camp, killed and scalped two captains and regained the Alamo in safety, although fired at by a whole company of the enemy. John Bowers, a gallant son of Ohio, fell shouting, "Hurrah for Texas and Liberty!" Another brave spirit, shot through both legs so as to be disabled from standing, made his comrades prop him up at a loophole, where he fired the rifles as they were handed up, never missing his aim although suffering dreadful pain.

The Mexicans continued to pour in their shot; in order to wear out the defenders they kept up the bombardment night and day. There was suffering for food and water in the Alamo, and the ammunition was rapidly giving out; in this dire extremity, Colonel Travis wrote to the Constitutional Convention of Texas, then in session, for aid, and Colonel Fermin in attempting to relieve him was taken prisoner, and with over three hundred of his men massacred in cold blood. A more base and treacherous act never disgraced a nation, and a day of retribution came for the Mexican Government. When the news came to Travis, he wrote to a friend: "Take care of my little boy. If the country should be saved, I may make him a fortune, but if the country should be lost and I perish, he will have nothing but the proud recollection that he is the son of a man who died for his country!"

After considerable time spent in bombardment, Santa Anna ordered a general assault. Having received a strong reinforcement, his army amounted to over four thousand effective men, while the garrison of the Alamo was reduced to about one hundred and thirty. One Sunday morning, at two o'clock, the Mexican army, completely surrounding the Alamo, advanced to the assault. Santa Anna formed his cavalry in a circle outside his infantry, with orders to cut down any soldier who hung back or retreated without orders. Placed between two alternatives, his troops advanced to the assault with a species of desperation, under express orders to give no quarter. Travis and his men prepared for the final death struggle. It is said that many of the men shook hands with each other and said "Good-bye" before going to their respective posts.

The cannonade ceased, and the Mexican soldiers, goaded on by the officers, who took good care to keep in the rear, rushed to the attack. Four times were they beaten back, leaving the ground covered with dead and dying. At each charge fresh troops were sent, and Santa Anna himself was seen urging on his reluctant soldiers. At the fifth assault the remnant of the garrison ceased to defend the walls, and in little groups, knowing they were doomed to death, fell back into the courtyard, fighting hand to hand. In an angle of the wall, still pointed out, fell Colonel Crockett, bowie-knife in hand, but not until he had covered the ground around him with dead men. Directly opposite, Colonel Travis sank down with a cheer upon his lips. Every man of the brave band fought until his last breath escaped. None called for quarter, none shrank, none fled; all perished, a sacrifice to their country. A nobler nor a grander spectacle the world never beheld—as sublime and heroic as the martyrdom of saints. Colonel Bowie (inventor of the deadly knife that bears his name), confined to his bed by illness, was discovered and massacred. Major Evans, in attempting to fire the magazine so as to blow up friend and foe, received a death-wound. Nor did Mexican atrocity cease with the death of every Texan. The dead bodies were mutilated and then burned, and the heads of Bowie, Crockett and Travis displayed from the walls of the Alamo.

Farmer and his men, who had surrendered a few days previous, were promised free and unmolested passage to the United States. In all there were some three hundred and seventy-five men, mostly volunteers from the cities of New Orleans and Mobile. The evening before their execution they were full of hope, and sang "Sweet Home" and other songs dear to the heart. All were happy with bright anticipations, for the dark veil of the future had not been lifted. The next morning, under pretence that they were going to be told off into squads to march homewards, they were taken out and shot, and died shouting defiance to their cowardly captors. The day of vengeance came, when upon the field of San Jacinto the troops of Santa Anna heard the dreadful battle cry—"Remember Goliad!" "Remember the Alamo!" and pleaded in vain for mercy. The rifle and bowie-knife did their work, and the Alamo was avenged. The old edifice, new roofed, is now occupied by the Quartermaster's Department of the United States Army, as a storehouse.

San Antonio is like Quebec, a city of the olden time, jostled and crowded by modern enterprise. The latter-day American building with its four or five stories and half glass front, overtops the grim old Spanish wall and the dilapidated Mexican "hacal," which betoken a by-gone era. Here have the Germans settled in large num-

(Continued on page 102.)

DOMESTIC MISCELLANY.

Congressional Summary.

Senate.—JAN. 4.—The Senate met at noon in the old hall, from which the desks had been removed, but a supply of cane-bottomed chairs had been provided for their accommodations. The galleries and floor were crowded notwithstanding the heavy snow storm, it having been understood that the Vice President, Mr. Crittenden, and other eminent men would speak. A spark of gallantry lighted up the commencement, for Mr. Stuart moved that as many ladies were unprovided with seats in the gallery they should be accommodated on the floor of the house. This, however, was effectually quenched by Mr. Hamlin, who maintained that the admission of crinoline would impede legislation. The ladies consequently were not admitted. Upon Mr. Davis's submitting the report that the new chamber was ready Mr. Crittenden moved the adoption of the report in a most appropriate address. He was followed by the Vice President, who gave an historical sketch of the great men whose presence had hallowed the ancient hall. The Senate then proceeded in a body to the new hall.

Mr. Mallory, from the Naval Committee, reported a bill to build ten additional sloops of war, which was laid over. He said he would make an effort to obtain an early vote upon it.

Mr. Mallory also introduced a bill to raise the pay of the officers of the navy.

Quiet being restored, the Senate appropriately devoted the rest of the day to discussing Mr. Johnson's (Tenn.) motion instructing the Finance Committee to investigate into the expenditure of the public money, and to report the means to bring the expenses of the Government within rigid economy.

Messrs. Johnson, Seward, Bigler, Fessenden, Toombs, Shields, Davis, Collamer, Mason, Stuart, Clingman, Green, Reid and others took part in the debate. All agreed in the necessity of retrenchment, the only point debated being whether to refer it to the Finance or a Special Committee.

Without action the Senate went into executive session, and on the opening of the doors Mr. Hunter introduced the first appropriation bill of the session, namely, the Indian Pension and the Military Academy bill, when the Senate adjourned.

JAN. 5.—There was little business done this day. The chief subject of interest being the addresses on the death of General Quitman, whose memory received elegant tributes from the lips of many eminent members of the Senate.

JAN. 6.—After a short discussion on French Claims, the Pacific Railroad bill was brought up. Mr. Harlan urged the necessity of locating the route.

Mr. Ward spoke in favor of the parallel of 32, comparing its advantages of level and distance over the central and northern routes, maintaining that the southern route can be built with the smallest amount of money, and in the shortest time.

Mr. Iverson made a strong sectional speech, and moved that the bill be recommitted, with instructions to report a bill for the construction of two roads; a northern and a southern one. He admitted the constitutional power of Congress to grant the public lands, but was astonished that Southern Senators should vote for such a magnificent donation to the North. It is a fact that all the southern roads pay seven to eight per cent. dividend, while the northern ones pay nothing. So small an opinion had northern capitalists of southern investments, that he believed if the wealthy Senator from South Carolina, Mr. Hammond, offered a mortgage on his plantation and negroes, worth half a million of dollars, for a loan of ten thousand dollars in New York, he could not get it, notwithstanding the popularity of his Barnwell speech.

JAN. 7.—Mr. Seward presented a resolution, which was adopted, calling on the President for recent correspondence between the British Government and the American Minister at London, relative to the abuses of the American flag in the African slave trade, and especially touching the case of the yacht Wanderer. A resolution, offered by Mr. Harland, of Ohio, calling for information respecting the ships, officers and pay of the navy was passed. It was then agreed to take up the French Spoliation bill, but on account of the illness of Mr Davis, of Mississippi, who was entitled to the floor, its consideration was postponed, and the Pacific Railroad bill came up, the debate on which occupied the rest of the day. The Senate adjourned over until Monday, Saturday being the anniversary of the Battle of New Orleans.

House of Representatives.—JAN. 4.—On motion of Mr. Bernhisel, the Committee on Territories were instructed to inquire into the expediency of providing for the territorial capital of Utah.

Mr. John Cochrane, of New York, presented a petition from the Canal Board for an appropriation for the lakes and harbors in connection with the canals of the State of New York.

Various reports were presented from the standing committees, including the following:

By Mr. Washburn, of Illinois, the Senate bills, making appropriations for the improvement of the mouth of Milwaukie river and Chicago harbor.

By Mr. Faulkner, of Va., the Senate bill, providing for the payment of the claims of Maine, for expenses incurred by that State, in organizing a regiment for the Mexican war.

On motion of Mr. Phelps, of Missouri, the House went into Committee of the Whole on the state of the Union on the Indian appropriation bill. Without coming to a conclusion, the Committee rose, and the House adjourned.

JAN. 5.—There was little business of importance. General Quitman received many complimentary eulogisms. His death was very eloquently treated by Mr Thompson of New York.

JAN 6.—The special order was the codification of the Revenue laws, and for other purposes, which was considered in Committee of the Whole. John Cochrane made a speech in favor of the bill, after which its further consideration was postponed until next week. The Indian Appropriation bill was next considered in Committee, and gave rise to a spirited debate,, which continued until the adjournment, and during which Messrs. Gidding, of Ohio, and Bryan, of Texas, entered into a discussion of the relative good and evil resulting from the annexation of the latter State.

Mr. Colfax, of Indiana, has introduced a bill for the organization of a new Territory, to be called Colona. The Territory will embrace all the recently-discovered gold region of Pike's Peak, Cherry Creek, &c., and will extend from the one-hundred and-third parallel of longitude to the crest of the Rocky Mountains, and from the thirty-seventh to the forty-second parallel of latitude—making nearly a square. It will include part of the present Territories of Kansas, Nebraska, Utah and New Mexico—the greater part being taken from Kansas. Mr Colfax believes that by the coming summer there will be a population of at least twenty thousand persons in the proposed Territory.

JAN. 7.—A bill was introduced by Mr. Blair, of Missouri, to establish an assay office at St. Louis. Mr. Stephens, of Georgia, announced that he was ready to report the Oregon bill whenever the Committee on Territories should be called. A bill was reported from the Committee on Ways and Means, making appropriations for fortifications. A resolution was passed calling on the Secretary of the Interior to report under what law and by what authority the "Advisory Board of Agriculturists to the Patent Office" is assembled, and for other information relative to them. After the passage of eleven private bills in Committee of the Whole, the House adjourned.

Utah.—A rather singular state of things, judicially, exists in the Territory of Utah. Judge Sinclair seems to be very anxious to have plenty of business, and in his charge to the Grand Jury, opposed the interpretation given to the President's pardon by the Commissioners and Governor Cumming, and claimed that the judge sees only with judicial eyes, and knows nothing respecting any particular case, of which he is not informed judicially; consequently, the pardon not having been extended to the people through him, it amounts to nothing, and he goes in for having everybody before the court. The judge includes in his charge the consideration of the subject polygamy. The jury are to find out if it exists in the Territory, and to what extent, and the judge winds up: "It is probable that no grand jury in the United States ever held in its grasp questions so grave and comprehensive as those which ought to occupy your minds."

The prosecuting attorney, Mr. Wilson, addressed the jury in opposition to the course pointed out by the judge, and defended the position taken by the Executive, the Commissioners and the new Governor. He set forth the right of the Chief Executive of the nation to pursue the course he did; that the Commissioners were invested with authority to carry into effect the provisions of the proclamation, which they did, and returned home; that Governor Cumming, in his first proclamation from Great Salt Lake City, declared "the proffered pardon was accepted, with the prescribed terms of the proclamation, by the citizens of Utah; peace is restored to our Territory, &c."

The attorney concluded with: "Wherefore, gentlemen of the grand jury, it only remains for me to say, for the reasons given, that there are now no acts of sedition, treason or rebellion, against the government of the United States in this Territory, which the prosecuting attorney of the United States for the Territory of Utah, with the President's proclamation and pardon before him, and the Governor's solemn announcement of its acceptance, can charge before you against any of the inhabitants of this judicial district, or of the Territory of Utah."

The Ten Governors.—There was a little horse play at the last weekly meeting of these famous gentlemen. It is thus described by a daily:

"On motion, the Board balloted for President and Secretary. On the second ballot, Governor Anthony Dugro received eight votes, and was declared duly elected President of the Board for 1859. On the second ballot, Benjamin F. Pinckney was elected Secretary of the Board. A very animated contest then occurred, at the instigation of Governor Oliver, about a very small matter. The Ten Governors sit about a table that is perhaps ten feet long, and at one end of which is the President's chair, and as some of the members seem to think that the easiest way to slide into the Presidential chair was to sit close to it, they made a tremendous struggle to get as near as possible to the favorite end.

"Governor B. F. Pinckney suggested that Governor Oliver would probably never get to the Presidential chair, and therefore it was natural he should aspire to get close to it. Governor Oliver gave public notice that one year hence he would be President of the Board. Governor Maloney made some remark in support of a proposition to draw lots for the seats. President Dugro, who had taken his seat, wished Governor Maloney to address him respectfully. Governor Maloney gave notice that he would respect every other man's rights, and would defend his own to the most desperate extremity. Governor Oliver hoped the old members would not be eternally rooted out of their places. The lots were prepared, and seats designated by numbers. Governor Oliver said that he was lucky in lotteries, but he hoped there would be no huggy muggering, and 'let the tickets be shook up well and all fair.' After prolonged dawdling, the lots were drawn, and Governor Oliver got a little farther from the Presidential chair than he was before. Some political sparring ensued, and then a motion to allow keepers of the Penitentiary, during the inclement season, to land at the Penitentiary dock, instead of the ferry stairs, was discussed, and referred to the Committee on Ferry."

There is something very appropriate in Governor Oliver's confessing that he was lucky in lotteries. We recommend that Mayor Tiemann and Mr. Birney be put upon his track!

Nicaraguan Heroes.—There has lately been so much of the Bombastes Furioso about the filibusters, that burlesque is made commonplace by their deeds. They start in the Susan, determined to die rather than submit to the British cruisers. Hip hip hurrahs are discharged over toasts utterly destructive to the British Lion. They sail in defiance of the United States authorities, carrying off as either hostage or captive an officer of the Federal Government. They escape the British cruisers, and are on the point of landing when the Susan runs aground, and the invaders are shipwrecked and helpless men. To increase the sarcasm, a British vessel of war comes up and lands them tenderly at the very port they sailed from. Verily, the way of the filibusters is funny!

The Slave Case.—The case of the yacht Wanderer has been investigated at Savannah. Dr. Duke testified that he visited some negroes on Montmolin's plantation, sixteen miles up the river, and they could not speak a word of English. They understood Spanish, however, very well. The men implicated in this affair were committed for trial.

The Bennett Divorce Case.—This remarkable case has resulted in Judge Waldo granting Mrs Mary A. Bennett's application for a divorce from Dr. Bennett, the famous pillmaker. She is to have an alimony of $4,000 and to possess the custody of her three children. The judge was very severe on Dr. Bennett and some of his witnesses.

John Brougham, the Wit and Dramatist.—This famous wit was asked the other day to write an epitaph upon himself. Taking a copy of the *Constellation*—he likes to be surrounded by stars—he requested that brilliant sheet should be his shroud, and wrote as follows:

MY EPITAPH.

Here, reader, turn your weeping eyes,
My fate a useful moral says,
The hole in which my body lies,
Would not contain one-half my plays!

Missionary Matters.—A meeting of the ministry and brethren of the Methodist Episcopal Church of the city was held at St. Paul's Church, corner of Fourth avenue and Twenty-second street, on the occasion of the departure, as missionaries to British Columbia, of the Rev. Dr. Evans, superintendent of the mission to that place, Rev. Mr. White, Rev. Mr. Robinson, and the Rev. Mr. Browning, four gentlmen of the Canada Conference of the British Wesleyan connection. Mr Hall (*Commercial Advertiser*) occupied the chair, and the Rev. Bishop Janes made a very interesting address to the departing missionaries. We think a mission to the Common Council ought to be now projected. What is a Feejee Islander to such a splendid cannibal as McSpedon, the President of the Board of Aldermen, who celebrates his advent to that position by a rough and tumble fight with some hackdrivers?

Bunsby's Himself Again!—A paper which has reached its 11th number and 2d volume, says: "I regret that I have no more space to devote to a criticism of this performance, as I feel that Mr. Sullivan as an artist of intelligence demands a more extensive appreciation. I am, however, of the opinion that it is but of little consequence to the interests of the stage, the gratification of the play-goer, or the reputation of Shakespeare whether Hamlet is ever performed again or not." We should like to ask how the writer feels after such a

SKETCHES IN SAN ANTONIO—THE FANDANGO.—FROM A SKETCH BY OUR OWN CORRESPONDENT.

THINGS IN AND ABOUT SAN ANTONIO.

(*Continued from page* 96.)

bers, bringing good old-fashioned industry along with their lager bier. Their neat cottages and vegetable gardens are noticeable all about the suburbs. As a general thing, they are a better class of emigrants than those found in our large cities, and are doing for Texas a work of civilization very much needed. Among the native population there is a little or no energy. There is not a steam engine nor a flour mill in San Antonio. All the dry goods, groceries and manufactured articles needed for a city of eight thousand or ten thousand people, whose trade with the frontiers amounts to millions every year, are hauled from the sea coast, one hundred and fifty miles, upon wagons and rude carts. Flour, potatoes and onions are among the articles of import, the attention of the inhabitants being concentrated upon cotton and cattle. There is not a good bakery, a first nor even a second class hotel in the city. Ice, cut from the ponds of Massachusetts sells, whenever there is a load in town, at from fifty to seventy-five cents per pound. Nothing is cheap but the tough, stringy grass-fed beef, which may be bought in the hoof for from two to two and one-half cents per pound. One of our New Englanders who spent a day or two in the city, declared that the opportunities for making money were so many and varied for a man of small capital, that the very contemplation made him feel worth at least half a million.

Walking about the city and its environs, you may well fancy yourself in some strange land. The houses, many of them built of adobe, one story high, and thatched, swarm with their mixed denizens, white, black and copper-colored. The narrow streets, the stout old walls which seem determined not to crumble away, the aqueducts, along which run the waters of the San Pedro, the Spanish language, which is spoken by almost everybody, the dark, banditti-like figures that gaze at you from the low doorways—everything, in the Mexican quarter of the city especially, bespeaks a condition widely different from what you are accustomed to behold in any American town. To conduct trade successfully, it is necessary to employ clerks who understand Spanish, or the tongue spoken by Mexicans and called Spanish, as a large amount of trade is done by Mexicans.

The better class of people, Americans and foreigners, speak of "The States" and "News from the States" when referring to any other portion of the country than Texas, except to the West.

A large element of the population of San Antonio is Mexican. There are a few respectable, intelligent and wealthy families, but the majority are of the lower order, with all the vices and none of the virtues belonging to the better situated. The men, whenever they work, are employed as teamsters, herders and day laborers. It is the general belief, founded as I believe on fact, that a Mexican is good for nothing unless in service over cattle, horses and mules. The bend of their talent is towards live stock. As little Cape Codites divert themselves by playing whalemen, and in that amuse-

MAIN PLAZA, SAN ANTONIO, TEXAS.—FROM A SKETCH BY OUR OWN CORRESPONDENT.

ment harpoon kittens and chickens, so does the juvenile Mexican take at once to the lasso, and with precocious skill lariat dogs, goats and calves; and thus, growing up in constant practice, the lariat becomes in his hands a deadly snare. Its throw is swift and certain, and it is alike dreaded by man and beast. Every cattle farm and horse-range has its lasso men or "ropers," as they are called in Texas, whose duty it is to catch runaway and refractory mules, horses and cattle, and in this business they become wonder-expert. It is ludicrous to see the chopfallen air which at once comes over an old mule when the lasso has tightened around his throat. Experience has taught him that all attempts to escape are vain, and with a miserable look of resignation he submits to be led off.

The free-and-easy style of life which is characteristic of the lower order of Mexicans is sure to surprise a stranger. He sees children of both sexes, from two to six years of age, strolling about in the economical and closely-fitting costume bestowed upon them by nature. Women, short and dumpy, with forms guiltless of artificial fixtures, and in the single article of attire usually denominated a petticoat, brief at both ends, are observed in-doors and out, manifesting not the slightest regard for the curious glances of the passers-by. Parties of men, women and children bathe in the San Antonio river, just outside the corporate limits, without the annoyance of dresses. This comfortable fashion was formerly in vogue within the city, until the authorities concluded it might with propriety be dispensed with.

Mexican amusements, in the shape of cockfights and fandangoes, help to elevate and refine the people of San Antonio, such as choose to participate. Every Sunday, just after mass at the old Mission Church, there is a cock-fight, generally numerously attended. The pit is located in rear of the church, about one square distant. On last Sabbath, going past the church door about the time of service, I observed a couple of Mexicans kneeling near the door in a pious attitude, which would doubtless have appeared very sober and Christianlike, had not each one held a smart gamecock beneath his arm! Pious souls! They had evidently paused a moment on their way to the cockpit, in order to brush over their little shortcomings for the past week.

The fandangoes take place every evening, and are patronized by the lower orders of people, who, as the sapient circus proprietor in "Hard Times" would declare, "must be amushed." A large hall or square room, lighted by a few lamps hung from the walls, or lanterns suspended from the ceiling, a pair of negro fiddlers and twenty or thirty couples in the full enjoyment of a "bolero," or the Mexican polka, help make up the scene. In the corners of the room are refreshment tables, under the charge of old women, where coffee, frijoles, tortillas, boiled rice and other eatables may be obtained, whiskey being nominally not sold. From the brawls and

MISSION OF CONCEPCION, NEW MEXICO.—FROM A SKETCH BY OUR OWN CORRESPONDENT.

PRIMITIVE BATHING, NEAR SAN ANTONIO.—FROM A SKETCH BY OUR CORRESPONDENT.

free fights which often take place, it is surmised that the article may be had in some mysterious manner. At these fandangoes may be seen the muleteer, fresh from the coast or the Pass, with gay clothes and a dozen or so of silver dollars; the United States soldiers just from the barracks, abounding in oaths and tobacco; the herdsman, with his blanket and the long knife, which seems a portion of every Mexican; the disbanded ranger, rough, bearded and armed with his huge holster pistol and long bowie-knife, dancing, eating, drinking, swearing and carousing, like a party of Captain Kidd's men just in from a long voyage. Among the women may be seen all colors and ages from ten to forty; the Creole, the Poblano, the Mexican, and rarely the American or German—generally, in such cases, the dissipated widow or discarded mistress of some soldier or follower of the army.

San Antonio is rapidly improving. Near the Alamo a fine hotel of stone is being erected by an enterprising German. The new Catholic Church is a grand edifice for Texas. Near the city is a quarry of limestone, so soft that it can be cut with a common knife. Exposed to the air for any length of time, it hardens and becomes solid. Some fine warehouses have just been completed; one is rented by the United States for a storehouse and barrack building. The wealthy and refined portion of the inhabitants do not seem disposed to erect costly dwellings, probably for the reason that a building of any pretensions to style and finish is a remarkable costly affair. Everything but the stone must be imported; iron from Cincinnati; window frames from Boston, and pine lumber from Florida. Even shingles are brought from Michigan, and glass from Pittsburgh. A railway from some point on the coast is needed to develop and improve the country, and until one is constructed San Antonio will be a peculiar and isolated city.

COCK FIGHTING—THE MEXICAN NATIONAL SPORT.—FROM A SKETCH BY OUR OWN CORRESPONDENT.

The Intelligencer.

FOR THE CAMPAIGN.

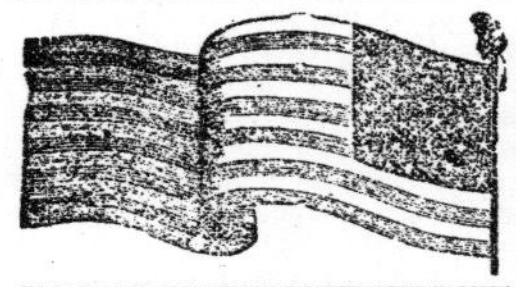

AUSTIN,
SATURDAY, JULY 2, 1859.

DEMOCRATIC TICKET.

FOR GOVERNOR,
GEN. SAM HOUSTON,
OF GALVESTON COUNTY.

FOR LIEUT.-GOVERNOR,
COL. ED. CLARK,
OF HARRISON COUNTY.

FOR LAND COMMISSIONER,
FRANCIS M. WHITE,
OF JACKSON COUNTY.

FOR CONGRESS, FIRST DISTRICT,
HON. JOHN H. REAGAN,
OF ANDERSON COUNTY.

FOR CONGRESS, SECOND DISTRICT,
GEN. A. J. HAMILTON,
OF TRAVIS COUNTY.

FOR SENATOR,
E. D. TOWNES,

FOR REPRESENTATIVE,
ROBERT J. TOWNES.

FOR FLOATER.
C. C. McGINNIS.

PLATFORM.

Resolved. 1. That all men who are opposed to the re-opening of the AFRICAN SLAVE TRADE, SECESSION, and other DISUNION issues; all who are friends to the National Democracy and the Administration of James Buchanan, and who are willing to allow the people to express their adherence to the UNION and the CONSTITUTION, at the polls, are requested to unite with us in the election of Gen. SAM HOUSTON for Governor, and A. J. HAMILTON for Congress, 2d District.

Resolved 2d. That we approve the bold defense, by Gen. Sam Houston and John H. Reagan, of the people of Texas, their conservatism, love of the Union and of the National Democracy, as the only party opposed to the Black Republicans, and think them entitled to the fullest confidence of the people of Texas.

BLANKS.—We have now on hand a very large stock of neatly printed Blanks, on a superior quality of paper. Among our stock may be found "Attachments, Bonds, Indictments, Deeds, Executions, Depositions to be used in the Federal Court, &c." Send in your orders. We can fill them all.

TO NEW SUBSCRIBERS TO OUR CAMPAIGN PAPER.—In consequence of the unparalleled augmentation of our subscription list, we are induced to offer our Campaign paper to new subscribers, at the reduced price of fifty cents. All who desire, may now avail themselves of the opportunity of obtaining one of the cheapest political journals in the State.

☞ Col. Henry [illegible] spoke on Monday last in reply to Franky [illegible], and all agree that notwithstanding the horns of the "little" bull, he pushed him entirely off the Cincinnati platform. Want of space prevents our giving a full review of the speech.

☞ Our *pro tem.* Judge F. M. GIBSON, has gone to Houston. We commend him to Cushing, as the gallant writer has a delicate labor question before him. And to all our friends we have to say, that braver champion never crossed swords with a foe. We commend him to the hospitalities of the Bayou City.

☞ The Waco Southerner charges, that secret ms. circulars went out from this city. We have heard talk of the mare's nest. But we can hear of nothing except the advertisements of the Runaway negroes of Dr. Philips.

Programme

FOR CELEBRATING THE ANNIVERSARY OF AMERICAN INDEPENDENCE ON THE FOURTH DAY OF JULY.

At 4 o'clock, A. M., there will be fired a salute of 33 guns.

The Quitman Rifle Company and Band will meet at the Armory at 8 1-2 o'clock, A. M.—The procession will form in front of the Armory in the following order: 1st. Band; 2nd. The company; 3d. Ladies; 4th. Citizens, etc.—The procession will then move up Pecan street to Congress Avenue, thence up Congress Avenue to Mulberry street, thence down Mulberry to the Methodist Church. On arriving at the Church the ceremonies will be conducted in the following order:

1st. Prayer by Rev. Wm. H. Seat.
2d. Reading of the Declaration of Independence, by a member of the Company.
3d. Oration by a member of the Company.

The public generally are invited to attend and participate in celebrating the day.

Committee. { R. M. ELGIN, B. P. HOLLINGSWORTH,

The members of the company will assemble at the Armory dressed in black frock coats, white pants, patent leather belts and forage caps. By order of the Captain.

A "Junius" Come to Life.

We extract the following well-timed communication from the correspondence of the Bonham Era, a paper which supports Judge Reagan and Runnels:

"You quote from the State Gazette, the stale fustian concerning K. N.ism. I wish you had found better authority. The editor of that sheet is not remarkably scrupulous in the matter of assertions, and every ounce of his bread comes through and depends upon his PROFESSION AS A POLITICIAN. To expect truth or candor from him is like asking a dissertation on honesty from a professional black-leg." * * * * "The condition of our State affairs stands in its own peculiar attitude, and need not be mixed up with K. N.ism, bleeding Kansas or any other defunct issue. From a plethora of over $5.000-000 our treasury has become empty,—the settlements on our frontier retrograding instead of advancing. Our educational fund is abridged by Executive neglect to submit a constitutional amendment. Our Executive communications to the President have been so rude that that functionary has refused to notice them. We know no better remedy for all these matters than to re-call the public servant in whose hands our poor treasury became rich—whose policy peopled our frontier as if by magic—in whose safe hands no domestic interest ever suffered from neglect, or perversion to purposes of speculation—and with whom President Buchanan has consulted more frequently, and with more implicit confidence than any other Senator. Let us make SAM HOUSTON OUR GOVERNOR, and we shall find remedies for all the evils which now retard the advancement of our State. JUNIUS."

The Governor's Circular.

As one of the evidences of wailings of despair, a circular has appeared bearing the signature of that intense embodiment of Southernism, H. R. Runnels. It bears evidences of the work of many pens. But the temper of the defeated candidate runs all through it.

We are told that the "two steam power presses" sent out 5,000 Platforms containing this precious document; that it went also in sheets and in pamphlets. That it has been in fact a real "rule and figure work, long number" job.—But whether paid for out of the public treasury *contingently*, our informant saith not. We trust it will be every where read. Without marring its beauties, we make a few extracts, and give some running comments, which naturally suggest themselves to every unprejudiced mind:

"As there seems to have been much misapprehension of the powers and duties of the Executive, at the same time that my course has been most *grossly and wilfully misrepresented*, I must ask indulgence for their brief explanation."

"Grossly and wilfully misrepresented," is too harsh language from the man of "prerogatives" to his erring subjects. Throw the mantle of charity around the Frontiers-men, Governor.

"There are bounds which the officer dare not transcend in obedience to his obligations to the Constitution."

Just so. And when your Excellency, in the hurry of appointing a host of "fire eaters" to the Vicksburg Convention; and in going to Houston to help Chilton out with the "platform," and to secure your nomination, forgot to publish the proclamation "three months in the public prints of the State," you should not have expended three thousand dollars in publishing it from seven to three weeks, in the vain hope that the illegal fee would silence the printers. If the Constitution stands in the way of defending the frontier, it should not be prostrated for an electioneering trick.

"So much, then, for the erroneous impressions made prevalent in certain localities, by designing persons, or those uninformed of the facts—that I have neglected the frontier, and that the Governor, by virtue of his office, has either control over the treasury, or power to call out armies."

By what authority then, did you get money out of the Treasury to send electioneering "Commissioners" to the frontier? or, if you prefer, men "to prevent a collision between the citizens and the troops?" or to act as a "barrier between the Citizens and the Reserve Indians, after it was discovered that they had done "all the mischief?"

"Yet the entire blame has been taken from the shoulders of the U. S. Government, which has been deaf to all remonstrance and petition, and thrown upon the State Government, *which of right has nothing to do with the question*."

Nothing to do with the frontier troubles—the loss of life and of half a million of property—the receding of the line and the abandonment of homes!—No, nothing! This explains the inaction and inefficiency of the Governor, until he felt the necessity of securing the vote.

"By act of the 5th Legislature, passed in 1853-4, jurisdiction was expressly ceded to the U. S. Government over them, before the Indians were permanently located there, and thus for the time being, the State parted with all authority over them, the act of cession placing them as much beyond the control of either the Executive or Judiciary of the State, as if they had been situated in the remotest State or Territory of the Union."

Nothing but a blind reliance on unscrupulous advisers could justify so reckless an assertion as this.—Texas had no power to confer jurisdiction upon the Courts of the United States, over the reserves. Congress never extended the Intercourse laws over the Indian reserves in Texas. But even if it had, the concurrent jurisdiction of our State over the country, would not have been removed. This notion, that because a small portion of Texas land has been temporarily dedicated to Indian purposes, therefore Texas had parted with jurisdiction, civil and criminal, and all rights of sovereignty over the area, is "squater sovereignty" with a vengeance!! That the [illegible] has no jurisdiction there, has been settled by the highest authorities, hence our able District Attorney, R. B. Hubbard, never had any indictments found there. Only the other day, the Supreme Court of the United States held, that in such and much stronger cases, the State Courts, did not lose jurisdiction.

This was the great question in Georgia, where the sovereignty and rights of the States were so gloriously sustained by President Jackson. We wish the lawyer who wrote this dodge would show his face. It is a miserable subterfuge at the expense of State sovereignty.

"Accusations too ridiculous and contemptible for any but madmen to believe, have been made by demagogues from the stump and published by an incendiary and licentious press to fan the flames of discord, by which alone they expect to gratify the feelings of private spite and succeed in accomplishing their political ends."

What liberal minded *gentleman*, to say nothing about the dignity due to the office of *Governor*, ever indulged in such a pitiful diatribe—such a contemptible ascribing of motives towards his masters, who, in an evil hour, elevated him to a position for which he has no capacity? If Runnels really claims to have done his duty, he should yet remember, that those whose servant he is, have a right to express their own opinions, as to the efficiency of his administration. Danton said, "In the palmiest days of Louis 16th, I called him 'My fool of a king,' and now for questioning the perfection of the directory, I am to lose my head." Here is an humble creature clothed with a little brief authority, insulting the public sentiment of a bleeding frontier, "with motives of private spite;" and he who has paid *one* press by the "rule and figure work system," to say nothing of "mistakes" of a "thousand dollars at a time," and who has encouraged its arrogance, has the presumption to talk about "an incendiary and licentious press," and "demagogues from the stump"!! Where was there ever a greater little demagogue than this little governor of Bowie county, *hardin r. runnels!* The man is paid $3,000 a year, and is given the use of a fine mansion, in which to hold his caucuses with his virtuous clique. He is clothed in raiment and fine linen at the expense of the State; he travels out of the State; he saith to this man go, and he goeth even to a treasonable Vicksburg Convention, or upon a frontier electioneering mission; he saith to another come, and he cometh, even from making speeches against Reagan, into the secret circular conclave; but it is hardly fair, that the governor should proclaim the "I am more holy than thou," from the top of the capitol. He should punish the clique who wrote it.

POSITION.

"My political position is fully defined in the resolutions of the Convention from which I received the nomination."

You don't say so. Do you mean the inside or outside resolutions?

"THE ENEMY."

"Though claiming the name of Democracy, of whom is the Opposition composed? Is it not the old foes of Democracy leagued with factionists and disorganizers of every other shade of opinion? Missouri compromisemen, Squatter Sovereigns, opponents of the Dred Scott decision, slave trademen, anti-conventionists, secession and disunionists, whose eyes the lights of patriotism have so recently opened to past error, all represented by candidates whose political antecedents have made them the appropriate captains in such a cause."

Governor, you have thus described your own crowd with graphic pen.—Thus viewed, you are relieved from the charge of want of truth, fairness and candor, which would otherwise sully the writers of the circular for the Executive of Texas.

CONDEMNS HIS OWN WORK.

"Sad, however as is the picture, it is even darkened by an attempt to array class against class, in urging the antagonism between white and slave labor, as taught by Seward and his co-laborers, thus insidiously calling to its aid whatever anti-slavery feeling may be supposed to exist."

And why was the Governor silent when his own organs commenced preaching that "labor is degrading;" that the "poor man's son was at work in the field, when he ought to be at play or at school;" that "the laboring white man is reduced to the level of the negro;" that we should import Africans, until a laborer can only earn "forty or fifty dollars a year;" and that where there was another "class of laborers," "free men should be elevated above it?"

Who but the organs, fed and fattened by the patronage of the government of Governor Runnels, ever preached this doctrine? Who sought to profit by it, even to the encouragement of a contraband trade? Who visited Lamar? Who subscribed to fit out piratical, contraband vessels?

When Gov. Runnels signed the above sentiment, he knew that he was slandering nine-tenths of the people of Texas. He knew that none but such Aristocrats as himself ever talked about "class against class." We have no classes however, in America, except the honest against the dishonest classes. Snobs, such as surround Runnels, are forever prating about "classes, laboring classes," "upper tendom," "best society," and such nonsense, as they read in European literature. And unfortunately there are weak Republicans who believe it. But who could make Houston and Hamilton thus think and reason? To which "class" do you belong, Governor? Do you set yourself above the "class" of Artizans and laborers in the field? For shame man! recant the libel!

And what "anti-slavery feelings" does the Governor suppose exists in the land? We deny that there is a single Texan opposed to negro slavery. It is easy to see, that the Governor alludes to the "classes" who have been charged with it, by his clique of Ex-Know Nothings. He was thinking of the practical works of his aids in preparing his circular, in expelling the Mexicans, lest they *might* injure the slaves; of the "Germans" whom *they* never defended; of the Northern Texans, against whom the News has again and again made the charge; of Reagan who is now charged by several of the Governor's organs with Abolition sentiments; of all, in fact, who oppose the re open the African slave trade abomination; and who maintain, that white gentlemen can and do work in Southern fields. These were the "classes" who were passing before the vision of the Bowie county planter, who always kept at a safe distance from this "dangerous Mexican population."

"Fellow-Citizens, permit me to say, that I shall discuss no outside issues."

Then why have you been going outside of the facts to insult your betters? Why have you been prating about "slave traders" and the "classes?" Is there one word in your fanfaronade deducible from the Democratic platform?

"And yet, with an insolence finding its parallel only in the most unblushing falsehood, such issues as are attempted to be forced on the candidates of the democracy, by this Babel of opposition, to distract and divide its counsels."

Governor, you are positively losing your temper. Such language is only befitting Billingsgate. It is as unpardonable, in an address from a dignified Governor, as would be profane swearing in his daily intercourse on the streets. If you have no respect for your "enemies," you should have some little for the Executive office you are to fill so short a time.

"The charge of disunion and secession has been made against the nominees of the Houston convention and particularly upon myself. The charge is false. I have never uttered a sentiment in my whole life inconsistent with loyalty to the Union and the Constitution."

Then Governor your whole life; your inaugural; your Kansas message; your "Sirocco blast;" your militia organization; your associates; your Southern Congress; your organs; your open advocacy of re-opening the slave trade, which is *per se* a disunion measure; the claims of your friends, that you are a "fire-eater;" your Vicksburg African slave trade Convention to which you were appointing Delegates, when you should have been issuing the proclamation for amending the Constitution; these have all belied you. But Wigfall, Judge Crosby, Lott, Britton, Maverick, Throckmorton and others will recollect, that amidst your secret caucuses at the Executive mansion, we told them that whenever you and your treasury fed dynasty saw, that your secession movements were laying you on your backs, you would become the loudest "Union shriekers in the land!" To save pap and power, we verily believe you would not only shriek for the Union, but for "free soil" itself.

If you would not the clique would. Better employ your Mississippi friend, Frank Gildart, next time. He has been tried at Inaugurals.

From the Galveston Union.

GALVESTON, June 15th, 1859.

Lt. Gov. F. R. Lubbock, Present—Dear Sir:

Have you any objections to answer categorically the following queries:

1st. Are you in favor of or against the re-opening the African slave-trade?

2d. Do you believe the law which declares the African slave trade Piracy, unconstitutional? [illegible] strictly to enforce the slave trade [Piracy] law?

3d. Do you believe, that causes now exist which make a dissolution of the Union desirable?

By straightforward answers you would oblige your friend. F. FLAKE, Editor Union.

No answer has ever been received, although Gov. Lubbock promised to answer in a few days, if possible next day. This shows, that *He* is trying to evade the issue now before the people.

We now respectfully call upon Gov. H. R. Runnels and Gen. T. N. Waul to answer the above questions, and we would further ask of Gen. Waul, whether, as a representative in Congress, he would propose or vote *for* a proposition to repeal the present laws on the subject of the slave trade. We would ask of Gov. Runnels, whether in case the Legislature should pass a bill declaring the laws of Congress on this subject to be unconstitutional and assuming that the State has entire control of the matter, he would approve or veto such a measure.

COPY OF MR. LUBBOCK'S LETTER.

"F. FLAKE, Editor Galveston Union."

Dear Sir: Your favor of the 15th June reached me some time ago.

Press of business has prevented my giving you an earlier reply.

In answer to your first and second interrogatories

"1st, Are you in favor of or against the re-opening of the African Slave trade?

"2nd, Do you believe the law which declares the African slave trade piracy" constitutional?"

I beg leave to say that in accepting the nomination of the Houston Convention I determined to confine myself to the platform of principles enunciated by said Convention.

I approve of the action of said Convention, in refusing to discuss, or make the re-opening of the slave trade an issue, and shall not discuss the constitutionality or policy of said measure.

In answer to your third interrogatory,

"Do you believe that cases now exist which make a dissolution of the Union desirable?"—I answer, No.

In answer to your fourth interrogatory.

"Do you believe that our courts ought strictly to enforce the slave trade piracy law?"

I answer that every law until repealed, or declared unconstitutional, should be enforced by the courts of the country.

F. R. LUBBOCK.

Austin 25 of June, 1859.

ANSWER OF GOV. H. R. RUNNELS.

MAJ. JOHN MARSHALL,
Chairman of State Committee,

Dear Sir—I cheerfully reply to your note of to-day, that I fully endorse the sentiments of the Hon. F. R. Lubbock, in his letter to F. Flake, Esq. I am now, as I have ever been, for the Union under the Constitution, and the strict maintainance of the Supremacy of the laws, and I do not consider that there is any cause for a dissolution of the Union at this time.

My acceptance of a nomination under the Platform of the State Democratic Convention forbids me, had I desired it, but I have never done so, to make any outside issues, or seek to add any new test of Democracy. That platform meets my most hearty approval, and I have already pledged myself to maintain it inviolate.

Respectfully,
H. R. RUNNELS.

AUSTIN June 27, 1859.

MORE BLUNDERS.—Why could not Lubbock have answered the letter *put into his hands* by Mr. Flake, without waiting until he got to Austin and consulted the *clique*? Why could not Runnels concur in Lubbock's evasive answer without first being civilly ordered to do so by the chairman of the *clique*? Who wrote or dictated the answers of Lubbock and Runnels? As they have denied that they are secessionists, and have not denied that they are in favor of the re-opening the African slave trade, is it not now clear, that *they are in favor of the re-opening of the African slave trade?* And to contend for re-opening the slave trade is *per se* to contend for secession.

Such being the case, can any Buchanan Democrat give them his support?

ALL RIGHT!!
The Battle goes on Well!
The East girding on the Armor for the Fight.

REAGAN'S NAME AT THE MAST OF THE TEXAS REPUBLICAN, AND DIFFERENCES HEALED!!!

[*Texas State (Platform) Gazette.*

THE TRUCE BROKEN!

The Republican hauls Reagan and White Down!

What will the Chairman of the Central Committee do? Will he notice the fact, or will he keep Loughery's stale story capitalized in his paper?

The Republican *cum multis aliis* says:

"WE HAUL REAGAN DOWN.—We understand, from reliable authority, that Judge Reagan in his recent speech at Crockett planted himself back again on his circular, and that his speech at that place, was, if anything, more offensive than the circular itself. It was with great reluctance he could be brought to acknowledge that he would support the State ticket, and not until he was driven to the position. This speech at Crockett was a violation of the agreement with his friends here, and this, coupled with the tone of the presses in his interest in this district, renders it impossible for us longer to continue his name at the masthead of our paper. The compromise made with Judge Reagan by a portion of his friends in this place, contemplated that the discussion of the African slave trade, should be ignored, and that there should be union in support of the State ticket. The tone of the presses in his interest, show clearly that this is not to be the case, and that while they are nominally supporting Runnels and Lubbock, they are really in favor of Houston, and are using the extent of their influence to promote his election. We are now satisfied that this compromise was extorted from Judge Reagan's fears We were willing to make any sacrifices, except those of principle, to keep the democracy united, and inasmuch as Judge Reagan had explained away the offensive portions of his circular, and had made such ardent professions as a Southern man, we disregarded our instincts, and agreed to support him. We can do so no longer, and can only regret that we ever agreed to hoist his name."

"Judge Reagan's canvass presents a singular anomaly. He occupies a position condemned by nearly every leading member of the party in this district. Yet they permitted him to take the field without opposition, when they knew that his circular and the speeches that must be made in defence of it, were calculated to destroy the harmony of the party and promote, if they did not secure, the election of Houston—that the defeat of the party necessarily leads to its demoralization, and would ostracise them from its councils. We and others made the issue at Henderson. Had we been properly sustained, Houston and Reagan would have been beaten five thousand votes in this district. Can they not yet do something to redeem this district and to save the State?"

"WHITE OVERBOARD."—"We publish this week the correspondence between George W. Paschal, editor of the Austin Intelligencer, and F. M. White, the Democratic nominee for Commissioner of the General Land Office. Mr. White's position in relation to the re-opening of the African slave trade was very well known by the delegates in the Houston Convention, and his claims were most warmly urged, as we understand, by gentlemen in that body holding what are termed ultra views on that subject. Why he should be giving countenance to the introduction of this impracticable and distracting issue in the present canvass, when the Democracy have expressly ignored it, we are at a loss to understand, unless he intends to aid in the election of Houston. The entire tone of his letter [illegible] a desire to see the Democratic ticket beaten. While we are entirely indifferent, therefore, as to whether Mr. White is in favor of, or opposed to, the re-opening of the African slave trade, we cannot recognize him as a good Democrat in giving countenance to the agitation of that question. We have recently learned that he said, while a member of the Legislature, that he would rather see slavery abolished than the Union destroyed. We cannot consistently vote for or support such a man, and we, therefore, take his name from our mast-head. Other Democrats can do as they please; as for ourselves, henceforth we shall execute such men without the benefit of clergy. Mr. White cannot blame any Democrat for voting against him; for he says that he does not consider the support of the nominees of the party a test of Democracy. Doubtless there are thousands who will take him at his word, and vote against him."

The conservative Democrats—the national Democracy—the friends of the Union—the supporters of Buchanan—the opposers of re-opening the African Slave Trade, Higher Lawism and a dissolution of the Union, have now but one way to preserve their own self respect; and that is to treat those candidates who are not for them as against them, and to vote accordingly. Take the advice of that sterling Democrat, GEORGE W. SMYTHE,—make the issue. Settle it.

Waul, Lubbock and Runnels are Know Nothings—The Kentucky Democracy being the Judges.

We copy the following from that old Democratic paper, the Frankfort Kentucky Yeoman, the leading Organ of Vice President Breckinridge and the Kentucky Democracy:

"THE RIGHT POSITION.—The Whigs and Americans of the fifth Magistrates' district in this county, at their precinct meeting last Saturday, to appoint delegates to the county convention, passed the following admirable resolution:

Resolved, That we hold the doctrine of non-intervention for the protection of property in negro slaves in the Territories, as taught by BERIAH MAGOFFIN, the Louisville Democrat, Lexington Statesman, Frankfort Yeoman, and other organs of the Democracy, as practical Abolitionism of the deepest dye—deserving the reprobation of all friends of Southern rights and institutions, as well as all true lovers of our glorious Union.—*Shelby News. (K. N.)*

In response to this, we hold that all "the Whigs and Americans of the fifth Magistrates' district," who endorse the above are long-eared asses. It is superfluous to add that the editor of the News is an ass. By consulting the official statistics, we find that Shelby is noted for its mules and asses, and we apprehend from reading the above resolution that the crop of asses for 1859 will largely exceed an average. If some of the "Whigs and Americans of the fifth Magistrates' district" should be sent to the next State Fair, we will bet a lead pencil, or something of equal value, that Shelby takes the premium on asses."

We do not set down the nominees of the Houston Convention, which changed the platform, as asses. But certainly they are with the Kentucky Know Nothings, and no consistent Democrat can support them.

ONE OF THE SIGNS OF THE TIMES.—As Gen. Houston and Col. Clark are supported by *three* Campaign papers, while Runnels and Lubbock are advocated by only *one*, (a very small one, and much of it in small capitals,) it is apparent that the real democracy outnumber the slave trade and secession minority in a ratio of three to one.

Unpardonable Dereliction of Duty by the Executive—He is the Enemy of Education, as well as all Printers except the Public Printer.

The people of Texas, including voters, women and school children, who know not the total inefficiency of Governor Runnels, and how completely he and his managers have been absorbed in their African slave trade project, and the secondary effort of securing the election of Runnels and Lubbock, will be astonished at the total disregard of the popular will in the great and sacred cause of education.

The mode of amending the Constitution of Texas, is as follows:

"SEC. 37, ART. 5.—The Legislature, whenever two-thirds of each House shall deem it necessary, may propose amendments to this Constitution, *which proposed amendments shall be duly published in the public prints of the State, at least three months before the next general election of Representatives*, for the consideration of the people."

"The Governor shall take care that the laws be faithfully executed."—*Sec. 10.*

There is a provision in regard to the cause of education, the inconvenience of which had been long felt. It reads as follows:

"EDUCATION.—Sec. 3.—All public lands which have heretofore, or which may hereafter be granted for public schools, to the various counties, or other political divisions in this State, shall not be alienated in fee, nor disposed of otherwise than by lease for a term not exceeding twenty years, in such manner as the Legislature may direct."

A domain worth millions of dollars has been appropriated to aid the cause of education. It is scattered through the various counties, and is subject to continual trespasses. Every one knows, that in Texas, wild, uncultivated lands cannot be "leased;" nor could they, should the Governor, and his organ, and keepers, carry out their contraband notions of importing Africans.

The Legislature, almost unanimously, at its last session, proposed the following amendment to the Constitution, so as to make the school lands available to the children "of the poor, who have to work in the field, while they ought to be at play or at school."

"JOINT RESOLUTION PROPOSING AN AMENDMENT TO THE STATE CONSTITUTION:—

"Be it resolved by the Legislature of the State of Texas, that the 3d section of the 10th article of the Constitution of the State, shall be so amended as to read as follows, viz:—

"SEC. 3.—All public lands which have heretofore, or which may hereafter be granted for public schools, to the various counties in this State, may be sold by the county courts of each county to which the lands belong, or by such tribunals as may succeed to their jurisdiction, by consent of a majority of the legal voters in said counties, and under such general rules as the Legislature may from time to time prescribe. *Provided* that the principal of the proceeds of the sale of such lands shall be retained and invested as a permanent school fund, for the counties owning the same, and the interest only shall be used for educational purposes.

"Approved February 16th, 1858."

This joint resolution should have been "duly published in the public prints of the State," on the first Monday in May, but unfortunately on that day, a matter of more vital interest to the Executive was on hand. The Houston convention was in session. Of what importance was this amendment of the Constitution, almost universally demanded by the people, compared to the nomination of Runnels, secession, and the re-opening of the African slave trade?

Runnels has no children, the Secretary of State has none, and we are not advised about the Lt.-Governor. At any rate the Governor, Lt. Governor, Secretary of State, Public Printer, the Digester, who took the responsibility of advising the removal of Dr. Perry, when there was no power, according to Judge Terrel, the Governor's notary and clerk in the Senate were all gone, and, we believe, all were at Houston, complotting for making Governors. Congressmen &c. There was no one here to attend to issuing the [illegible] it was not issued. The will of the people is thus defeated; the practical application of the trust fund is delayed four years longer; the lands are being despoiled, and the children of the poor are growing up in ignorance.

☞ The Gazette, having been unable to find the amiable Susan to take the accident upon herself, or even to get the "street opinions" of ex-Chief Justice Hemphill, or any other decent lawyer, that "THREE MONTHS" in the Constitution, may mean three weeks; and the Governor and his Secretary, and the Secretary of State and his Secretary, having failed to answer our interrogatories, as to *who* prepared, and *who* forgot to publish the proclamation in the public prints of the State, three months before the next general election of Representatives, "FOR THE CONSIDERATION OF THE PEOPLE," a judgment by default may now be taken, and it may be recorded, that the Governor has no "consideration for the people," nor "their Representatives."

We ought, perhaps, to qualify the statement about the Governor's enmity to the Printers.—In this instance he shows a remarkable affection for them, at the expense of the people.—Some of the papers published by practical printers, are asserting that the cost of the illegal and unauthorized publication, will actually be three thousand dollars! The *per diem*, journal and statute printing, (counting the "invisible lines,") have already cost five thousand dollars. And, as a man with the Governor's bold views, will still endeavor to maintain his error, of course even though a majority of the voters fail to record their names for the amendment, the Governor will hold that the consulting of the people is merely directory, and therefore, the amendment can be made by "his Excellency's prerogative," and the advice of the Legislature. With the same propriety with which he published *too late*, the Governor can and will recommend, that it shall be adopted, notwithstanding the "proposed amendment was NOT PUBLISHED THREE MONTHS before the election, "*for the consideration of the people*," and notwithstanding they did not consider, and did not vote, as required BY THE CONSTITUTION.

For cannot those who would swear by Gov. Runnels, should he assert, with Cushing, that a poor white man is a negro, quote all the convention papers, and say: "The amendment was proposed by the Legislature, and the joint resolution sanctioned by the Governor; it was printed in the book, with so many invisible lines, by the public printer; it was advertised *fifty* days in the organ of the Governor, and *ten* days in some of the lesser organs; it was talked about a great deal; the people did not vote to be sure, but that was their own business, since they had an opportunity; and are they not just as much bound, as are the people of Bexar bound by the action of the THIRTEEN who sent Dr. Graves to the Houston Convention? it is according to the usage of the organizers, and therefore it is Constitutional. "*Quod erat demonstrandum.*"

This is the logic with which the imbecile Gov. Runnels "appeals to the virtue and intelligence of the people."

Now, if the publications are legal, they are legal by relation; that is, the "Executive prerogative" makes ten days count three months, and therefore the printers may all charge for three months, with a better apology than the Public Printer charges for "rule and figure work, and invisible lines." But what will Major Johns say to the accounts? or will he refer them to the Chairman of the Committee on Printing, who have a right to "measure" pages, as well as to *measure* the distance from Brownsville to Austin?

Will the people submit to such a trampling under foot of the constitution and laws? such a profligate expenditure of the public money? such wanton insults to their understandings? Answer at the polls.

General Waul's Platform.

Resolved, That the laws of the Federal Government, making the African Slave trade piracy, and all other laws which tend to the absolute prohibition of the introduction of African Slave laborers into this country from abroad; is without constitutional authority, and ought, therefore, to be repealed.

Resolved, That it is a matter of *vital importance* to the Southern States that the uncultivated lands of the Western and Sothern districts of country, now lying idle, *should be cultivated by slave labor.*

That we now scarcely have slaves enough in the South to cultivate the lands already in use, and that the increase being only that of reproduction, is not sufficient to supply the demand, *and to compete with the immense influx of white labor from other countries.* That our experience teaches us that cotton can and will be raised successfully by white labor at ten cents per pound, and that, in the end, IF A COUNTER MOVEMENT IS NOT MADE BY SLAVE OWNERS, their slaves will become a mere unit in the great army of laborers in the South. We therefore recommend the subject to the earnest attention of the State Convention at Houston, *and instruct our delegates* to introduce and advocate measures for the accomplishment of the introduction into the Southern States from abroad of additional slave laborers."

We understood Gen. Waul to deny that the Gonzales resolutions were shown to him before the meeting; but he admitted that he served as a Delegate in the Houston Convention under them. Then as a Democrat, Gen. Waul must either have obeyed his instructions in good faith, or he must acknowledge, that Delegates to a Convention are not bound by the instructions of their constituents; and therefore the whole machinery is anti-Democratic and anti-Republican. These resolutions were Gen. Waul's "commission" in the Houston Convention. Did he obey them? or if he went there to disobey them, did he act in good faith? We fear he has Wigfall's notions about instructions. But now he says, that the Democratic platform is his "commission;" and therefore he will not answer upon his Gonzales "commission." But if the Delegate disobeyed one commission given him by a County Convention, will he better observe the "commission by the State Convention," which he calls an army commission, of all things, most despotic?

But when pressed with questions by Gen. Hamilton, he (W.) would not answer whether he agreed in sentiment with the Gonzales resolutions. In his zeal, however to denounce such Abolition sentiments, as the second resolution contains, and are constantly preached by the Telegraph, the News, and some other such Editors, he did admit that the said Gonzales resolution was wrong.

The Gen. is in a sad dilemma, and we don't see how he is to be relieved. Gen. Waul said, "he was responsible to the Democracy of Gonzales County alone." But that would be no answer to the people of Texas, should he, like his predecessor, "tie to" the little disunion squad, and destroy his influence by voting for re-opening the African slave trade, or even by urging his own extreme views against the non-intervention principle of the Cincinnati platform.

With Gen. W's loose notions about "commissions and instructions" he can not be trusted.

Lieut. F. R. Lubbock's Platform.

In his speech here on Monday last the explosive orator, Lubbock, admitted that he is part owner of the Houston Telegraph. Therefore he is responsible for the following sentiments from that paper:

"In the sweat of thy face shalt thou eat thy bread" was never intended as any thing else than a CURSE and but for the capabilities which the Almighty has given to human nature to rise from this ABJECT AND DEGRADED CONDITION, this condition to which they were degraded by the disobedience of the parents of the race, the curse would have had a bitterness which we can illy comprehend, and DEGREDATION A FULNESS WHICH WOULD HAVE LEFT NO ROOM FOR AUGHT BUT BRUTISHNESS IN OUR HUMANITY."

* * * * *

"Labor as an end is despicable, as a means a blessing. WE CONDEMN our worst *criminals* to hard labor as an end for years or for LIFE. In so doing we intend to condemn them to the WORST CONDITION OF HUMAN LIFE in which that life can be sustained, as a reward for their crimes, which have rendered them unworthy to share with their fellows a better condition."

* * * * *

"But again THAT MANUAL LABOR IS A DEGRADATION IN ITSELF CONSIDERED, let us look at those persons who devote themselves to it for life, and see what of intelligence, refinement, or indeed (to make a word) humanheartedness they possess. With occasional exceptions they are *below the average scale of humanity.* Their faculties—sometimes good—are allowed to remain undeveloped, their minds inactive, the better part of them in a word coated with rust."

"Hence we have said and maintained that in a land like ours, where there is a RACE OF MEN who are by nature deficient in these higher attributes of humanity, the tilling of the soil, the hewing of the wood, and the drawing of the water should be left to them, and still further, WHENEVER THIS CONDITION IS FAR SUPERIOR TO THAT IN WHICH THIS RACE IS FOUND IN NATURE, IT IS THE PART OF HIGH PHILANTHROPY TO REMOVE THEM, AND THUS ADVANCE THEM TO THE PLACE WHICH PROVIDENCE HAS EVIDENTLY MARKED OUT FOR THEM."

Lubbock could have controlled Cushing. These were part of the sentiments in favor of re-opening the African Slave trade. For them, Lubbock is responsible. In all the contest about re-opening the African Slave trade, he must have endorsed the sentiments of his own paper. He now refuses to disclaim, or to answer questions. Let the people say how far they approve of the above from his own organ.

THE UNANSWERED LETTER.—The last issue of the Platform contains a curious electioneering document—the Letter of Gov. Runnels to President Buchanan, that has not yet been honored with an answer. Any one that will wade through it, will be at no loss to conjecture why a man of President Buchanan's sense of propriety thought it proper that the correspondence should proceed no farther until another Governor is elected.

THE BANNER.

A. N. VAUGHAN, EDITOR.

BEAUMONT, TUESDAY, JAN. 22, 1861.

☞ As the last two weeks have been full of stirring incidents in the progress of that great and noble movement, which is now working out the deliverance and liberty of the people of the South, we will give our readers a summary of the most important, which have occurred during that time.

The Custom-House, the United States Arsenal, Fort Moultrie and Castle Pinkney have been taken by South Carolina. The United States sloop-of-war—Star of the West—has been fired into, and made to hunt some other harbor than that of Charleston.

The United States Arsenals and Barracks at Baton Rouge, and Forts Jackson and St. Philip at the Mouth of the by order of his Excellency, Thomas O. Moore, Governor of the State of Louisiana. The armament of the United States Cutter has also been taken possession of in the name of the State of Louisiana.

Fort Morgan, at Mobile has been taken possession of, in the name of Alabama. Fort Barancas, and Warrington Navy Yard at Pensacola, have been taken by Alabama and Florida. Forts Johnson and Caswell have been taken by North Carolina. Alabama, Mississippi and Florida have seceded from the Union.—The sudden abandonment of Fort Moultrie by the United States troops, and the occupation by them of Fort Sumpter, seems to have filled the people of South Carolina with military enthusiasm.

Gallant South Carolina is no longer alone in the great drama of secession. Other actors are now upon the stage.—Other States have seceded from the Union. Other ports have turned their guns upon the enemy.

The spirit of the South is thoroughly aroused to meet the great emergency her safety and honor require, and as State after State withdraws from the Union, the fixed attention which South Carolina drew upon herself, will be turned to the grand aggregation of free and independent Southern States, seeking, in a common assemblage those new means of preserving their liberties and institutions, which their separate organization renders necessary.

☞ Our readers will see from the telegraphic dispatches in this issue, that the political sky is becoming obscured with angry clouds, and that the long expected storm is near at hand. South Carolina, Alabama, Mississippi and Florida, are all out of the Union. Georgia, Louisiana and Arkansas will soon follow their example, nor will Texas be far in the rear of her sisters. The border slave States will undoubtedly follow in quick succession. The South has gone so far, that she will either be compelled to advance, or retreat in disgrace, and the latter, we are satisfied she will never do.

The State Gazette of the 3rd inst. says:
—On Monday last, Miss Sallie Moss, one of our loveliest young ladies unfurled from the summit of Pilot Knob, with her own fair hands, a Lone Star Banner. On the same day, Mrs. McGee, the accomplished lady of Capt. William McGee, hoisted the same proud emblem of our liberties, in front of her husband's beautiful residence.

The same paper of the same date says:
—We have just had the pleasure of a vis- missioner appointed by the Legislature of Alabama, to visit Texas. He has been received with great cordiality and enthusiasm by our citizens.

LONE STAR FLAG RAISED.

The Liberty Gazette of the 11th inst., says:

At a meeting of the citizens of this place on the public square, on Wednesday last the Lone Star Flag was suspended from a pole one hundred feet high and her folds unfurled to the breeze amid the greatest enthusiasm. The Meeting was ably addressed by Messrs. Cleveland, Trowell and Stewart, each vindicating the right of a State to secede from the Union at pleasure. Mr. Cleveland discussed at some length the excited condition of the country, and said that a dissolution of the Union was inevitable. He also stated that he, as a Delegate to represent the counties of Liberty and Polk in the Convention, which is to assemble on the 28th inst., in the city of Austin, would urge to the extent of his ability, the repeal of the articles annexing Texas to the United States. During the delivery of the speeches frequent bursts of applause greeted the speakers, and volleys of Musketry made the welkin ring in token of the intense approval of the step Texas is about to take in going out of the Union. The meeting then adjourned to the Court House, for the purpose of organizing a company of Minute Men, to hold themselves in readiness in case of any emergency.

LATEST BY TELEGRAPH.

SECESSION OF ALABAMA.

PASSAGE OF THE ORDINANCE.

Montgomery, Jan. 11.—The following ordinance, to dissolve the union between the State of Alabama and the other States of the Union, under a compact styled "The United States of America," passed the Convention at half past two o'clock to-day.

Whereas, The election of Abraham Lincoln and Hannibal Hamblin to the offices of President and Vice President of the United States of America by a sectional party, avowedly hostile to the domestic institutions and the peace and security of the people of the State of Alabama, following upon the heels of many and dangerous infractions on the Constitution of the United States by many of the States and the people of the Northern section, is a political wrong of so insulting and menacing a character as to justify the people of the State of Alabama in the adoption of prompt and decided measures for their future peace and security; therefore,

Be it declared and ordained by the peo- *Assembled*, That the State of Alabama now withdraws, and is hereby withdrawn, from the Union known as the United States of America, and henceforth ceases to be one of said United States, and is, has a right, and ought to be, a sovereign independent State.

Sec. 3, *And be it further declared and ordained by the people of the State of Alabama in Convention assembled*, That all powers over Territories in said State and over the people thereof, heretofore delegated to the Government of the United States of America, be, and they are hereby withdrawn from said Government, and hereby resumed and vested in the people of the State of Alabama; and as it is the desire and purpose of the people of the State of Alabama to meet the slaveholding States of the South who approve of such a purpose, in order to frame a provisional as well as a permanent Government upon the principles of the Government of the United States.

Be it also resolved by the people of Alabama in Convention assembled, That the people of the States of Delaware, Maryland, Virginia, North Carolina, South Carolina, Florida, Georgia, Mississippi, Louisiana, Texas, Arkansas, Tennessee, Kentucky, and Missouri, be and are hereby invited to meet the people of the State of Alabama, by their delegates in Convention, on the fourth day of February next, at the city of Montgomery, for the purpose of consulting each other as to the most effectual mode of securing concerted and harmonious action in whatever measures may be deemed most advisable for the common peace and security; and

Be it further resolved, That the President of this Convention be, and is hereby instructed to transmit a copy of the foregoing preamble of ordinance and resolutions to the Governors of the several States named in said resolutions.—Done, by the people of the State of Alabama, in Convention assembled, at Montgomery, this eleventh day of January, A. D. 1861.

The preamble of ordinance and resolutions were adopted, by ayes, 61; nays 39.

After the adoption of the ordinance the hall was opened to visitors. A splendid flag, presented by the ladies of Alabama, was conveyed to the President's stand and formally presented to the Convention, through Mr. Yancey, in a handsome and patriotic address.

Mr. Smith, delegate from Tuscaloosa, followed in a feeling reference to the stars and stripes, and invoked blessings on the new flag.

Mr. Alpheus Baker, of Eufaula, returned the thanks of the Convention to the ladies, in eloquent terms.

The ordinance will be ratified Monday, when it is believed many other delegates will sign it.

An immense mass meeting is now in front of the capitol. Distinguished Co-operation delegates are pledging their constituents as a unit to sustain the secession flag now waving over the capitol, amid the ringing of bells, the firing of cannon, and the most intense enthusiasm.

THE UNITED STATES ARSENAL AND BARRACKS AT BATON ROUGE SURRENDERED TO

Special Dispatch to the Delta.

Baton Rouge, Jan. 11.—The companies compesing the expedition to this city from New Orleans, for the purpose of taking possession of the United States Arsenal and Barracks, were ordered out at daylight this morning for company drill, and at noon they formed on the north side of Boulevard street. This street is in the lower part of the city, the Arsenal and Barracks being just beyond its uper limits. The order to take up this posisition was issued by the Governor to Colonel Walton, of the Washington Artillery in command of the New Orleans detachment. Immediately after forming on the North Boulevard the troops received orders to move towards the Arsenal and other United States buildings, for the purpose of taking possession of them. On a demand from Colonel Walton, the posts were surrendered without any resitance on the part of the United States forces. In fact resistance would have been totally useless, and could have had no other result than the useless effusion of blood. On the surrounding of the buildings, a strong detachment of New Orleans troops took possession of them, and posted a guard at each point of ingress and egress. The main body of the troops remained without the grounds of the Ordnance Department.

The Barracks and officers' quarters are informally surrendered, but are still occupied by Federal soldiers. These, however, will leave within thirty-six hours. They are to go ub the river to Fort Washington, under command of Lieut. Todd. The New Orleans detachment, under Col. Walton, will remain on duty until further orders to-morrow. On Sunday, they will start for home. At present, all are in good health.

MISSISSIPPI STATE CONVENTION.

All the delegates elected to the convention, which meets in this city to-day, have arrived.

Jackson, Jan. 7—9 A. M.—Governor Pettus, of this State, has ordered the military companies to prepare ball cartridges.

Jackson, Jan. 7.—The Convention organized at 12 o'clock to-day.

Hon. W. S. Barry, of Lowndes county, was elected President on the third ballot.

A prayer was offered by the Rev. Marshall Warren, invoking the assistance of Almighty God in the deliberations of the people's servants.

The President, in his remarks, strongly favored State secession.

A resolution was adopted that a committee of fifteen be appointed by the President of the Convention, with instructions to prepare and report as speedily the withdrawal of Mississippi from the Federal Union, with a view to the establishment of a new Confederacy, composed of the seceding States. The names of the gentlemen on this committee will be announced to-morrow.

A committee of three was also appointed to wait on the Governor for communications of importance to the Convention.

The Convention then adjourned till 10 o'clock to-morrow

CAUCUS OF DELEGATES.

A majority of the delegates assembled in caucus this morning and adopted a resolution requesting the President of the Convention to draft the ordinance of secession.

Jackson, Jan. 8.—The Convention met at 10 o'clock this morning, pursuant to adjournment.

The President announced the following standing committees, this day appointed: On Citizenship; on Federal Jurisdiction; on the State Constitution; on Military and Naval Affairs; on the formation of a Southern Confederacy.

The Governor's communications will be presented to-morrow.

A resolution was offered for the appointment of commissioners to Alabama and Florida, to inform those States that the Convention would adopt resolutions providing for the formation of a Confederacy. A long debate on the resolution ensued.

The Commissioners from South Carolina and Alabama, were invited to seats on the floor of the Convention.

A resolution was adopted to amend the Constitution of the States and authorizing the borrowing of money for the purpose of military defense. Much of the morning session was consumed in dicussing the power of the Convention to amend the Constitution of the State.

A resolution was passed inviting the Judges of the High and Circuit Courts to seats on the floor.

A dispatch from Georgia announcing her determination to secede immediately was read, and created much applause.

The Convention then adjourned till ten to-morrow.

The gallery was well filled with ladies who honored the Convention with their presence.

The military of the State are on parade mimic warfare and skirmishing.

The hotels are thronged with interested citizens from abroad.

The prevailing excitement is intense. The committee on the ordinance of secession are now in caucus.

Jackson, Jan. 9.—The Mississippi Convention went into secret session at half past ten o'clock this morning.

Jackson, Jan. 9.—The ordinance declaring the immediate secession of the State of Mississippi from the Federal Union, passed the Convention by a vote of 84 against 15.

The delegates from the States of South Carolina and Alabama, took seats on the floor of the Convention amid great applause.

An effort to postpone the action of Mississippi was made, but afterwards voted down.

The fifteen opposing voters will sign the ordinance to-morrow, making it unan The most brilliantly illuminatod to-night, guns are being discharged, and rockets fired.

The most intense excitement prevails.

FLORIDA STATE CONVENTION.

THE STATE PROBABLY OUT.

Tallahassee, Jan. 10.—It is reported here, on reliable authority, that Florida will pass the secession ordinance to-day.

NAVAL RESIGNATION.

Captain Randolph, of the United States Navy, resigned his position yesterday, and immediately tendered his services to the Governor of Alabama.

OFF FOR FLORIDA.

A number of Editors and Compositors, in companies, have left for Pensacola.

ALABAMA.

THE U. S. ARSENAL AT MOBILE TAKEN.

Mobile, Jan. 4, P. M.—The United Statesarsenal at this place was talen by Mobile troops this morning at an early hour.

Twenty thousand stand of arms, fifteen hundred barrels of powder, thre hundred thousand rounds of musket catridges, with other munitions of war, fel into the hands of the Mobile soldiers.

No defence was made on the partof the Federal troops.

It is rumored that Fort Morgan, at the entrance of the bay, was also catured last night.

SOUTHERN PROVISIONAL GOVERNMENT

A special dispatch to the commercial says that the Southerners in Washington are greatly excited from the tenor of the dispatches which pour in from all quarters South.

Southern members of Congress say the President must recognize the rights and facts of secession, order the evacuation of Government forts, and surrender other public property at the South.

The Vice-President abandons all hopes of peace, unless Mr. Crittenden's propositions are adopted.

In some quarters a provisional Southern Government is talked of.

Senator Hunter, of Virginia, mentioned as President, Hon. Jeff. Davis, of Mississippi, as Commander-in-Chief of the army, and Mr. Mason, of Virginia, as Secretary of Foreign Affairs.

THE WAR COMMENCED!

Charleston, Jan. 9.—A constant watch has been kept for the last two days in expectation of the arrival of the steamship Star of the West, with reinforcements, and provisions for Fort Sumter. At 6 o'clock this morning the Star of the West hove in sight. As soon as she was discerned the new battery on Morris Island, lying outside of Sullivan's Island, was put in preparation for active measures.—The drums beat to quarters, and the men were ordered to man the guns. In the meantime the steamer kept steadily approaching, and when she arrived within a distance of half a mile, she hoisted the American flag.

A warning gun was then fired across her bows, but elicited no attention whatever, the steamer keeping steadily on her course. As soon as it was perceived that she was determined to attempt an entrance into the harbor, the battery opened fire upon her. In a short time she was struck three times, when, finding it would be impossible to achieve her purpose, she put out to sea again in a northeasterly direction.

In the meantime, Fort Moultrie had also opened fire on the steamer, but the distance was so great that the vessel could not be reached. Fort Moultrie fired nine shots, which, for the reason stated, were ineffectual.

The Star of the West was accompanied by a steam tender, heavily laden, supposed to be with provisions for Fort Sumter. The Star of the West is known to have been much injured by the fire from the battery.

These events have produced the greatest excitement here, and the city is in a perfect blaze of enthusiasm.

Major Anderson has just sent a communication to the Governor, with a flag of truce; but the nature of the communication has not yet been made public.

Charleston, Jan. 9.—Major Anderson's communication to the Governor inquired whether the firing at the steamer was by his order. The Governor replied that it was, when Anderson notified him that Fort Sumter held command of the harbor and that no further communication by water would be allowed between the city and our forts. This will cut off all communication except by a circuitous land route.

The popular belief is that this must precipitate an attempt to storm Fort Sumter. All the reserved regiments are under arms, and a general fight can not be postponed many hours longer.

Charleston, Jan. 9.—As the State paid no heed to Major Anderson's threat, he sent another communication to the Governor to-night, saying he would defer the execution of his threat until his bearer of dispatches could return from Washington. Therefore all is quiet again, and the work of fortifying Morris Island is pushed forward with redoubled vigor.

The Jasper Clarion of the 12th inst. says:

Mr. Wicks, an old and respected citizen of Newton county, was killed about two weeks ago by Mr. Farris, of the same county. Farris has delivered himself to the authorities.

Street paving was first practiced in Carthage, when it was introduced to Rome. The Carthagenians were supplied with water from an aqueduct 50 miles in length, and so large that a man could stand erect in it. The cisterns for its reception and distribution were of corresponding mag- along the beach, travelers discover the remains of common sewers.

THE PACIFIC RAILROAD BILL.—The bill which passed the U. S. House of Representatives of the 20th inst., by a vote of 96 to 73, provided that the Northern road shall "start from two points--one on the Western borders of Iowa with two converging lines bearing westward and uniting within two hundred miles west of the Missouri river, and thence proceeding by a single trunk line by the nearest and best route and by the vicinity of Great Salt Lake to the city of San Francisco, or to the navigable waters of the Sacramento, in the State of California." The Southern road is likewise required to start "from two points—one at Fort-Smith, on the Western borders of Arkansas and the other on the Western border of Louisiana, with two converging lines bearing Westward, and uniting West of longitude 97°, and then proceeding by a single trunk line, and be the nearest and best route to the Pacific Ocean at or near San Francisco, crossing the Rocky Mountains South of the 34th parallel of North latitude." The corporation to which lands are granted to enable it to construct these railroads is to transpors therenpon the mails, troops and public stores of the United States, and to erect a telegraph along the roads in the most approved manner. It is also required to have five hundred miles of the road and of the telegraph line completed within six years after the passage of this act.

IMPORTANT FROM MEXICO.

THE CIVIL WAR ENDED.

VERA CRUZ, Mexico, Jan. 2.

The civil war is ended. On the 25th ult. the city of Mexico was the only place of importance that remained in the hands of the Church party, and on that day Christmas was there celebrated by the entrance of Ortego at the head of the Constitutional army whilst Miramon, at the head of 1000 men, decamped at an opposite gate. We have no authentic accounts of the whereabout of Miramon and Marquez since that date. One rumor places Miramon at the head of 2000 men at Peubla, which is not at all believed by the intelligent citizens here. Another is, that his forces have been disbanded, and the leaders are making tracks to the coast in disguise, no doubt, with the intention of getting out of the country, but the Government having adopted such precautionary measures, and are so vigilant there, seems to be but little chance of their escape.

There seems to be no strong feeling against Miramon, further than that if he is caught, a fair trial will be given him, and he will be put to death as a traitor, with the grace of clergy; but Marquez the butcher, who had four American doctors shot in cold blood, whilst they were engaged in the christian act of administerin to the sick and wounded of both armies, will be knocked in the head like a dog by the first party that catches him.

Several of the Bureau officers, with their clerks and archives of office, have already gone up to the city, the rest of the Govment, with President Juarez, will go this week. Our Charge d'Affairs, Mr. Elgee, will go up with the property of the Legation on the 5th inst.

The effect of these changes will be immediately felt on the commerce of the country. Already things are brisker here. Trade with the interior will open, and the long pent-up wants of the country must be satisfied.

There are now in port only two American vessels, one Spanish, three French, one Hamburger, one Sardinian, and one Danish. The American war vessels Sabine, St. Louis, Pocahontas, Cumberland, and the flagship Powhatan are at Sacrificios; also, the English steamers Valorous, Gladiator and Jasper; the French brig Mercure; and the Spanish steamer Blasco de Gurro. The Powhatan moved up from the Castle last week, but as the small-pox is on board the Cumberland, and she quarantined, the flag officer for the present remains in the Powhatan.

I am sorry to say that Uncle Sam's credit has gone down in this place. U. S. navy bills have been eagerly sought at par, and the paymasters of the squadron had no trouble in raising funds to support their ships. Since the last arrival of the Tennessee their bills have been refused at an offer of discount. They would not be taken at any price.

The Abolition fanatics of your country have brought ruin ane disgrace upon their country, and to us it seems strange that the Northern people, who are so much interested in remaining with the South, ever permitted their fanatacism to run so rampant. As neighbors and allies we would feel happy to see the Union continue, but if you do divide, our sympathies are with the South. You are our neighbors and friends, and our interests are more identified.

Apropos, in the event of the dissolution of the North, the first civil war in this country will lead to the union of the North-eastern States of Mexico to the Southern States of the North; and it will be a movement inaugurated by our people. It will promote our interest, peace and safety. We are tired of revolutions, and, with the example of the North before us, we can see plainly that our destiny and future hope are with you.

The Gladiator will leave to-day at 12 o'clock, and I send this by her.

From the White Man Extra.

Indian Fight---Thirteen Killed and Scalped and Three Prisoners taken by Capt. Ross.

We hasten to lay before our readers the gratifying news contained in the following letter. Capt. Ross has done his duty as a soldier, and enemy as he is, we cannot withhold from him the praise he is justly entitled to. He has taught the Indians that white men can kill and scalp and that they can be followed to their homes and punished.

That they were the perpetrators of the recent murders in Jack and Parker counties, there is no doubt. We sincerely hope Capt. Curenton and his gallant company may meet with like success, and we think they will, for they are not the men to turn back on the trail, where it is fresh. Success to the gallant rangers, and may they continue to kill the villainous rascals, who have desolated our frontier.

CAMP AT LOST VALLEY. DEC. 25 1890.

To the citizens of Jacksboro—

I have just arrived at my camp and found Judge Harmason, of Young county, in camp, having the news that Capt. Ross had a fight on last Wednssday with the wild Camanches, 16 in number, killing 13, and took the Chief's son who is about seven years old, and a white woman and her child prisouers, the white woman having been with them from a child.—There was found with the Indians Mrs. Sherman's Bible, with her name written upon it. Copies of the White Man, with Mr. Riley's name upon them, and other articles, indicating that they were the ones who committed the late depredations in this county. There was with Ross some 25 of the regular cavalry at the time.

The woman states that five days before the fight, 25 warriors left camp for the settlements, for the purpose of stealing, &c. From all the facts it appears that there are Indians in the country at this time quite numercus, and it behooves every man to be at his post on the frontier.

E. W. ROGERS.

A NORTHERN RELIGIOUS PAPER SPEAKING OUT.—The New York Churchman (Episcopalian) says:

Peace can never be restored to the country until the agitation of the slavery question is put down, entirely and absolutely. The continued excitement kept upon this question must, sooner or later, produce a dissolution of the Union, and is therefore plain treason, neither more nor less. The Union was formed under a Constitution which recognized the right of all the States to legislate upon their own internal affairs, and it cannot be supposed that the South would have entered into an alliance which might have ever defraueded them either of their political; religious or moral right to continue the practice of domestic servitude, so essential to their material prosperity, or which would exclude them from their fair share of the common territories. Any arrangement attempted by the North having for its object either one or the other of these results, is a destruction of the original compact entered into by the States, and affords strong ground for dissatisfaction on the part of the aggrieved section.

General Henningsen has written for publication a letter on the present crisis and the right of secession. The General is, of course, with the South in feeling. In reply to the inquiries of former companions-in-arms and others, he announces that he "will be one of many to carry a musket or saber in defence of the first seceding State against which coercion shall be attempted." General Henningsen also pledges the services of his stepson, John M. Berrien Connelly, of Jefferson county, Ga., now fifteen years old, and at present a member of a Northern Military Institute--in the same cause.

THE STATE OF TEXAS, }
COUNTY OF JEFFERSON. }

In obedience to a proclamation of His Excellency, Sam Houston, Governor of the State of Texas, I A. J. Ward, Chief Justice of Jefferson county, do hereby order and direct that a poll be opened and an election held at the several Precincts in said county on the 4th day of February, A. D. 1861, for the purpose of electing one Delegate to a Consultation of the Southern States from the District composed of Galveston, Jefferson, Chambers, Liberty, Polk, Trinity, Madison, Brazos, Walker, Grimes, Montgomery, Harris, Austin, Fort Bend, Wharton, Brazora, Matagorda, Jackson and Calhoun counties, and returns make to me within ten days thereafter; said election to held and conducted in due form according to law, by the following presiding officers: Precinct No. 1, G. W. O'Bryan, no. 2, John S. Johnson, no. 3, Neill McGaffy, no. 4. C. W. Saladee, no. 5, Levi Carr.

Given under my official seal and signature, at Beaumont this 8th day of Jan. A. D. 1861.

A. J. WARD, Chief Justice of Jeffersoncounty, Texas,

January, 15th, 1861.

Notice.

Is hereby given to all persons interested in the Estate of Stephen W. Turner, deceased, that at the Regular January Term, A. D. 1861, of the Honorable county court of Orange county in the State of Texas, holding sessions for Probate Business, R. A. Neyland will present for probate a certain nuncupative Will, made by the deceased in his last sickness.

All persons interested in said Estate, are hereby cited to be and appear at and before said court and contest the same if they please.

Witness S. F. Baker, Clerk of the County Court of Orange county, Texas.

{ L. S. } Given under my hand and official seal this the second day of January A. D. 1861.

S. F. BAKER, C. C. O. C.
by C. H. SAXON, Deputy.

The State Gazette.

BY JOHN MARSHALL & CO.

SUBSCRIPTION, (IN ADVANCE)..............$3 00.
SUBSCRIPTION, (NOT IN ADVANCE)..........$4 00.

Clubs and Democratic Associations furnished at liberal Cash rates.

State Gazette.

VOL. XII. SEAT OF GOVERNMENT, AUSTIN, TEXAS, SATURDAY, FEB. 2, 1861. NO. 26.

AN ORDINANCE to Dissolve the Union between the State of Texas and the other States United under the Compact styled "The Constitution of the United States of America."

SEC. 1. Whereas, the Federal Government has failed to accomplish the purposes of the compact of Union between these States, in giving protection either to the persons of our people upon an exposed frontier, or to the property of our citizens; and whereas the action of the Northern States of the Union is violative of the compact between the States and the guarantees of the Constitution; and whereas the recent developments in federal affairs make it evident that the power of the federal Government is sought to be made a weapon with which to strike down the interests and prosperity of the people of Texas and her sister slaveholding States, instead of permitting it to be, as was intended, our shield against outrage and aggression; therefore

We, the People of the State of Texas, by delegates in Convention assembled, do declare and ordain that the Ordinance adopted by our Convention of delegates, on the fourth day of July, A. D. 1845, and afterwards ratified by us, under which the Republic of Texas was admitted into the Union with other States, and became a party to the compact styled "The Constitution of the United States of America" be, and is hereby repealed and annulled; that all the powers which by the said compact were delegated by Texas to the Federal Government are revoked and resumed; that Texas is of right absolved from all restraints and obligations incurred by said compact, and is a separate and sovereign State, and that her citizens and people are absolved from all allegiance to the United States, or the Goverment thereof.

SEC. 2. This Ordinance shall be submitted to the people of Texas for their ratification or rejection by the qualified voters, on the 23rd day of February, 1861, and, unless rejected by a majority of the votes cast, shall take effect and be in force on and after the 2nd day of March, A. D., 1861. Provided that in the representative district of El Paso, said election may be held on the 18th day of February, 1861.

Done by the people of the State of Texas, in Convention assembled, at Austin, this first day of February, A. D., 1861.

T. J. CHAMBERS,
Chairman of Committee on Federal Relations.

Mr. Ochiltree, from the Committee on Federal Relations, made the following report:

To the President of the Convention:

The members of the Committee on Federal Relations concur fully with the majority in recommending the adoption of the ordinance reported by the said committee; but, we ask leave respectfully to dissent from the resolution accompanying the ordinance, which proposes to refer said ordinance back to the people for ratification or rejection. The minority are of the opinion that the best interests of the people of the State would be served by giving an immediate operation to the ordinance of secession.

[Signed] W. B. OCHILTREE,
A. W. O. HICKS,
WM. S. TODD,
P. T. HUBERT.

Mr. Scott moved a suspension of the rules, in order that the reports might be taken up for action.

On motion of Mr. Rainey, the Convention adjourned, to meet at half past 7 o'clock in secret session.

SOUTHERN FORTIFICATIONS.

It is to be presumed that immediate measures will be taken to partially garrison the numerous forts on our Southern coast; which form our internal system of defence in that quarter. Those forts are now wholly without garrisons, and thus in a totally defenceless condition, without, I believe, an exception. It is of the highest importance, in view of the threatening demonstration of the Gulf States, that these forts should be at once manned and put in a posture of defence. With those important works in the hands of the insurgents, a blockade of the Southern ports would be difficult, from the fact that they guard the approaches to nearly all the Southern harbors. The long shore line, destitute of shelter, would prove very embarrassing to a blockading squadron, unless those harbors could be reached. But with those forts in possession, the entire control of both ingress and egress from the Southern ports is established.

I append a list of these fortifications, taken from Col. Totten's report made to Congress several years ago, giving the cost of each, and the number of guns they severally mount:

Table of Navy Yards and Principal Forts South of Mason and Dixon's Line, showing the Position, Cost and Strength of each.

WHERE LOCATED.	COST.	NO. OF MEN, WAR GARRISON	NO. OF GUNS.
Fort McHenry, Baltimore, Md.	$146,000	350	74
Fort Carroll, Baltimore, Md	135,000	800	159
Fort Delaware, Del. River, Del.	539,000	750	151
Fort Madison, Annapolis, Md.	15,000	150	31
Fort Severn, Maryland	6,000	60	14
Fort Washington, Pot'c River	575,000	400	88
Fort Monroe, Old Pt. Com't, Va.	2,400,000	2,450	371
Fort Calhoun, H. R's, N'lk, Va.	1,664,000	1,120	224
Fort Macon, Beaufort, N. C.	460,000	300	61
Fort Johnson, C. Fr, Wil., N. C.	5,000	60	10
Fort Caswell, Oak Island, N. C.	571,000	400	87
Fort Sumter, Charleston, S. C.	677,000	650	146
Castle Pinckney, Chs'n, S. C.	43,000	100	25
Fort Moultrie, Charleston, S. C.	75,000	300	54
Fort Pulaski, Savannah, Ga.	923,000	300	150
Fort Jackson, Savannah, Ga.	80,000	70	14
Fort Marion, St. Augustine, Fla	51,007	100	25
Fort Taylor, Key West	----	1,000	185
Fort Jefferson, Tortugas	----	1,500	293
Fort Barancas, Pensacola	315,000	250	49
Redoubt, Pensacola	109,000		26
Fort Pickens, Pensacola	759,000	1,260	212
Fort McRae, Pensacola	384,000	650	151
Fort Morgan, Mobile	1,212,000	790	131
Fort St. Philip, M. Miss River	113,000	600	124
Fort Jackson, Mouth Miss. Riv.	317,000	600	150
Fort Pike, Rigolets, La.	472,000	300	49
Fort Macomb, Chief Menteur, La	447,000	300	49
Ft. Livingston, Barrataria, La.	342,000	300	52

In addition to these are incomplete works at Ship Island, Mississippi River; Georgetown, S. C.; Port Royal Roads, S. C.; Typree Islands, Savannah; Galveston, Brazos, Santiago and Matagorda Bays, Texas.

The guns which were lately stopped at Pittsburg were designed for those at Galveston and Ship Island.

Hampton Roads is the great naval depot station and rendezvous of the Southern coasts, and the only good roadstead on the Atlantic, South of the Delaware.

Pensacola is very strong, and the only good harbor for vessels of war, and the only naval depot on the Gulf.

The fortresses at Key West and Tortugas, on the Southern point of Florida, are among the most powerful in the world, and every vessel that crosses the Gulf passes within sight of both.

The protection of this great system of fortifications, it is now believed, will engage the immediate and earnest attention of the War Department.—*Washington Cor. N. Y. Tribune.*

DRAW YOUR BLADES.

Draw your blades; prepare for battle,
 Ere the ruthless hosts are here;
Wait not till the sabre's rattle
 Heralds war's red legions near.
Watchful ever, never dreaming,
 With your armor girded on,
Firmly wait, with falchions gleaming,
And with all your banners streaming,
 Till the foeman presseth on.

Let no dastard shade of pallor
 O'er your features, soldiers, spread.
Ye are favor'd sons of valor,
 Offspring of a noble dead.
Where the war steeds, wildly tramping,
 Snuff and paw the gory ground,
When the boldest foes are camping,
Where the hireling hordes are tramping,
 There let Southern steel be found.

Pause not till the last invader
 Reeling from our borders, flies;
Give no quarter—each crusader
 Who would fly or falter, dies.
Let not Mercy, interceding,
 Turn stern Justice from her path;
Look ye to your kindred bleeding,
Look where virtue, vainly pleading,
 Sinks beneath the foeman's wrath!

Up! that ye may live in story!
 Rise! and prove your Spartan birth!
Bards shall sing ye "Sons of Glory!"
 Patriots' tongues proclaim your worth;
Generations hence will name ye
 Noblest of this stormy age;
And, tho' jealous foes defame ye,
Loyal hearts will ever claim ye,
 Guardians of their heritage!

New England in the War of the Revolution. It is part of the Revolutionary record that during the whole war New England did not send one single company South of the Potomac. General Washington's correspondence shows how difficult he found it to obtain military aid in Massachusetts. Let the protest of Virginia to the Continental Congress be read. It says to New England:

"We were with you at Boston and at Quebec; we missed you at Savannah and at Guilford; we were alone at Trenton and Princeton; and now, when our Continental contingent is full; when Virginians are defending New Jersey against the British in New York; when we have 10,000 troops of our own in the field at home; when all our titheables are heavily taxed, and when the British forces are invading our borders, you refuse, after frequent appeals, to send any continental troops to our assistance. Exhausted in fighting the battles of the country on every field from Canada to Georgia, we warn you that unless assistance be speedily given, we shall withdraw our contingent, and fight by ourselves and for ourselves alone."

This is the same New England that in the war of 1812 refused to fight outside of New England, because the "war was unconstitutional."—*N. O. Delta.*

SAN PATRICIO, TEXAS, Jan. 5, 1861.

Major Marshall—

My Dear Sir—Noticing the patriotism of your editorials, and your strong advocacy of Southern rights, I take the liberty of giving you an item of politics and its incidents from the border counties. The counties of San Patricio, Goliad and Refugio vote together, and I am happy to say the people are as true as steel, though little of the element of slavery is among us, because in stock raising districts it is not profitable. There are four candidates in the field, (one Union). A. M. Hobby and Judge Lea, the disunion ticket, will no doubt be elected. Hobby made a powerful speech here to-day, and to him more than to any other man are we indebted for quashing the Union ticket and sentiment in the whole district. If elected, he will likely be the youngest man in your Convention, and if the people here are not very much mistaken, he will be the ablest. Give him a hearing in your Convention; he will do honor to the State and give strength to our cause. We hope that he and Lea will be the choice of the people.

Excuse the liberty I have taken.

Yours, &c., F. LOFTEN.

LEGISLATIVE PROCEEDINGS.

EIGHTH LEGISLATURE—EXTRA SESSION.

Austin, Thursday, Jan. 24, 1861.

SENATE.—Met pursuant to adjournment. Roll called. Quorum present.

Mr. Potter, chairman of committee on Judiciary, made the following report: The Judiciary committee have considered a bill to give additional time for holding the courts in the second judicial district, and to change the time of holding courts in certain counties in said district, and recommend its passage.

On motion of Mr. Throckmorton, the bill was taken up and read second time and ordered to be engrossed. Rule further suspended; bill read third time and passed.

Mr. Throckmorton introduced a bill to provide for the sale of land ceded to the United States for Indian purposes, by act of the legislature, approved Feb. 6, 1854. Read first and second times and referred to committee on Public Lands.

Mr. Miller offered a resolution to the effect that twenty copies of the Gazette be furnished each member. Lost.

Mr. Throckmorton introduced a bill to provide for the payment of the expenses incurred by special bearer of dispatches sent by the Governor to Washington city. Read first and second times and referred to committee on Finance.

Mr. Guinn offered the following resolution:

Resolved, That the Judiciary committee be instructed to inquire into the expediency of amending the penal code relative to tampering by white men with slaves, through free negroes or otherwise, and that they report by bill or otherwise. Adopted.

Mr. Potter introduced a bill providing what shall be sufficient *prima facie* evidence in certain cases of action brought by the State. Read first and second times and referred to committee on Judiciary.

A message was received from the House informing the Senate that the House had passed the bill making appropriation for the mileage and per diem pay of members and officers of the extra session of the 8th legislature.

On motion of Mr. Hyde, the bill was taken up and read first time. Rule suspended—read second time. Mr. Grimes moved to refer to the committee on Finance. Lost. The bill then passed to a third reading. Bill read third time and passed.

A message was received from the House informing the Senate that the House had concurred in the Senate's amendment to a bill making an appropriation for pay and mileage of members and officers of the extra session of the eighth legislature.

Mr. Parsons moved that delegates to the Convention be invited to seats within the bar of the Senate. Carried.

Mr. Hart moved to adjourn till 3 o'clock, P. M.

On motion of Mr. Stockdale, Senate adjourned until 10 o'clock, A. M.

Friday, Jan. 25, 1861.

SENATE.—Met, pursuant to adjournment. Roll called. Quorum present.

Mr. Potter, chairman of Committee of Judiciary, reported a bill providing what shall be sufficient *prima facie* evidence in cases of suit brought by the State of Texas, and recommended its passage.

Mr. Towns reported correctly enrolled a joint resolution, repealing a joint resolution in regard to the Governor's message on Kansas affairs.

Mr. Duggan introduced a bill to attach the county of Wilson to the Eighteenth Judicial District; and to amend the act entitled an act to provide for the time of holding the courts of the several counties in the Eighteenth Judicial District. Read first time.

On motion of Mr. Duggan, rule suspended, read second time, and ordered to be engrossed. Rule further suspended, bill read third time, and passed.

Mr. Blanch offered the following resolution:

Resolved, That the Committee on Finance be and are hereby instructed to inquire into the expediency of revising the tax law of the late session of this Legislature, and to report a bill, or otherwise. Adopted.

Mr. Stockdale introduced a bill to incorporate the Lavaca Wharf Company. Read first and second times, and referred to Committee on Internal Improvements.

Mr. Erath introduced a joint resolution to send delegates to a convention of border States. Read first and second times, and referred to Committee on State Affairs.

Mr. Towns, by leave, presented the memorial of R. T. P. Allen, asking an appropriation of lands for school purposes. Read first and second times, and referred to Committee on Militia.

Mr. Stockdale, chairman of Committee on Enrolled Bills, reported "a bill in relation to the procurement of money due by the United States to the State of Texas," correctly enrolled, properly signed, and presented this day to the Governor.

A message was received from the House, informing the Senate that the House had passed Senate's bill to define the time of holding courts in the Nineteetnh Judicial District.

A message was received from the House, informing the Senate that the House had passed a bill making an appropriation to pay the mileage and per diem of the Presidential electors, and a bill directing how the proceeds of the sale of the University Lands, now in the Treasury, shall be applied.

On motion of Mr. Parsons, a bill directing how the proceeds of the sale of the University Lands now in the Treasury shall be applied, was taken up. Read first and second times, and referred to Committee on Finance.

On motion of Mr. Parsons, a bill making an appropriation to pay the mileage and per diem of the Presidential electors, was taken up, read first time, rule suspended, read second time, and passed to a third reading. Rule further suspended, bill read third time, and passed.

A message was received from the Governor, transmitting the ordinance of secession of the State of Alabama, accompanied by a communication from the President of the Convention of that State.

On motion of Mr. Grimes, the communications were taken up and read, and on motion of Mr. Potter, the same were transmitted to the House of Representatives.

On motion of Mr. Parsons, the Secretary was directed to transmit a copy to the President of the Convention to meet in this city on the 28th inst., when that body shall be organized.

On motion the Senate adjourned until 10 o'clock A. M., to-morrow.

HOUSE.—Met. Roll called. Quorum present.

Mr. Branch, Chairman, reported, correctly enrolled and properly signed, a bill making an appropriation for the mileage and per diem pay of the members, and per diem pay of the officers of the extra session. Also, a joint resolution in reference to the Governor's message on Kansas affairs, and that the same had been presented to the Governor for his signature, and approved.

Mr. Stewart, Chairman of Committee on Finance, reported, recommending the passage of the bill making an appropriation to pay the mileage and per diem pay of the Presidential Electors.

Mr. Armstrong introduced a bill to amend article 1139 of O. & W.'s Digest. Read first and second times and referred to Judiciary Committee.

Mr. Ellett moved to take up bill to provide for the frontier protection. Lost.

On motion of Mr. Navarro, the Committee on Printing was instructed to contract for the translation and printing of 500 copies of the Governor's message in Spanish, and the same amount in the German language.

A message was received from the Senate, informing the House that the Senate had passed the bill to give additional time for holding the Courts in the 20th Judicial district, and to change the time of holding Courts in certain counties in said district.

Also laid before the House a message from the Governor.

On motion of Mr. Davis of Bastrop the message of the Governor, being a communication from the President of the Alabama State Convention, was taken up and read, and on motion of Mr Lewis of Montgomery it was referred to the Committee on Federal Relations, with instructions to lay a copy before the Convention, to meet in the city of Austin on the 28th of January.

A Message from the Governor in reference to land ceded to the United States by the State of Texas was taken from the Speaker's stand and read. On motion of Mr. Buckley, was referred to Judiciary Committee.

Mr. Stewart introduced a bill directing how the proceeds of the sale of the University lands should be disbursed. Read first time. On motion of Mr. Stewart, the rule was suspended and the bill read second time and ordered to be engrossed. On motion of Mr. Parker the rule was further suspended, bill read third time and passed.

Report from committee on Federal Relations, pending when the House adjourned on yesterday, was taken up and adopted by the following vote: Yeas 59, nays 17.

The resolutions reported by the committee, being before the House, Mr. Henderson proposed to amend by adding the words "in such form &c.," after the word taken, in second line third section.

Mr. Hancock offered a substitute for the resolutions and amendments.

Mr. Davis of Bastrop, moved to adjourn till 3 o'clock P. M. Lost by the following vote: Yeas 33, nays 36.

On motion the House adjourned till seven o'clock P. M.

Seven o'clock P. M.—House met. Roll called. Quorum present.

The substitute offered for the resolution, reported by the committee on Federal Relations, pending when the House adjourned was taken up.

Mr Haynes moved to adjourn till 10 o'clock to-morrow. Lost.

The question recurring on the adoption of the substitute, the House refused to adopt it by the following vote: Yeas 9, nays 53.

The question then being on the adoption of the amendment, the same was put and carried.

Mr. Mills offered the following amendment: "Provided that any member of said Convention, who may be a member of the Legislature of Texas, or an officer of the State receiving an annual salary from the Treasury of the State, shall not be entitled to receive the mileage and per diem herein mentioned." Adopted.

Mr. Davis of Bastrop, offered the following amendment, amend by adding the following caption—"A Joint Resolution to provide for the per diem and mileage of the members of the Convention, and to submit their action to the people," and by an additional section.

Mr. Foscue offered the following as a substitute for the amendment: Amend by adding this caption, "Joint Resolution concerning the Convention of the people the State of Texas."

Mr. Duncan moved to adjourn till 10 o'clock A. M. to-morrow. Lost.

On motion, the House adjourned until 9½ o'clock A. M., to-morrow.

Saturday, Jan. 26, 1861.

SENATE — Met. Roll called. Quorum present.

Mr. Sheppard, chairman of Committee on State Affairs, made the following report:

The committee to whom was referred the joint resolutions with regard to coercion, have respectfully considered the same, and instructed me to report the accompanying resolution as a substitute therfor:

Joint Resolution—That in view of the exigencies of the times, we deem it proper to declare, that when the sovereign States of this Confederacy entered into the compact of "union," they delegated to the Federal Government no power to compel by force of arms obedience by the States to the Federal authority, but, on the contrary, such power was especially denied. That employment, therefore, of force by the Federal Government to compel any State of this Union to perform its obligations under the Federal compact, or to compel a State against the will of the people to remain a member of this Confederacy, is in violation of the Constitutian, a dangerous usurpation of power, destructive of the rights of free government, and fatal to the existence of the Union itself, which, formed of equal and indpendent sovereignties, cannot be, as between conquering States and subjugated powers.

That should, as we have serious reason to apprehend may be in the present condition of the Union, the Federal Government attempt to coerce any of our sister States of the South, by force of arms, into subjection to Federal rule, we assure such State of the sympathies of our people, and that we shall make common cause with them in resisting by all means and to the last extremity such unconstitutional violence, and tyrannical usurpation of power.

On motion of Mr. Sheppard, the resolutions were taken up, substitute adopted, and ordered to be re-engrossed. On motion of Mr. Guinn, rule suspended. Mr. Grimes moved to strike out the words, "and fatal to the existence of the Union itself." Lost. The resolution was then passed by the following vote: Yeas, 58; nays, none.

Mr. Blanch offered the following resolution:

Resolved, That the committee on State Affairs be, and they are hereby instructed to inquire into the expediency of changing the existing law regulating the appointment of Physician of Lunatic Asylum, Superintendent of Deaf and Dumb Asylum and of the State Geologist. Adopted.

Mr. Erath offered the following resolution:

Resolved, That the committee on Finance, be requested to inquire into what amount of funds may be used from unexpended appropriations on deposit in the Treasury for public use. Adopted.

Mr. Quinan introduced the following resolution:

Resolved, That a committee of five be appointed from the Senate, and that the House be requested to appoint a committee of seven to act as a Joint Committee of both Houses to inquire and report whether any and what measures are necessary in the present State of our Federal relations, for the security of the School fund invested in United States bonds. Adopted.

On motion the Senate adjourned until 10 o'clock, A. M., on to-morrow.

HOUSE — Met. Roll called. Quorum present.

Mr. Davis of Bastrop, one of the committee on Enrolled Bills, reported correctly enrolled, a bill in relation to the procurement of money due by the United States to the State of Texas, and that the same had been presented to the Governor for his signature and approval.

Mr. Crooks chairman, reported correctly engrossed, the bill directing how the proceeds of the sale of the University Lands, now in Treasury shall be applied, and the bill making an appropriation to pay the mileage and per diem of the Presidential Electors.

ORDERS OF THE DAY.

Question pending when the House adjourned last night, viz: Mr. Foscue's amendment to Mr. Davis' of Bastrop, amendment to the resolutions concerning our relations with the Federal Government was taken up.

Mr. Foscue by leave, withdrew his amendment.

Mr Davis of Bastrop, offered the following as a substitute for his amendment, amend by adding the following caption: Joint Resolution concerning the Convention of the people of Texas.

Sec. 4. And it is further provided that said Convention should simultaneously with submitting the ordinance of secession to the people of Texas, also provide for the Election of Delegates to a Convention to assemble at Austin, for the purpose of forming a new Constitution, and making all necessary provisions for the then existing state of affairs. The number of Delegates to said new Convention should not exceed the number of Senators and Representatives, provided in the apportionment bill of 1860, and the election should be held under it, should the people of Texas, at the ballot box ratify the ordinance of secession, then the delegates elected at said election should assemble at Austin as soon as practicable after the rsult of said election is ascertained, to discharge said duty. The present Constitution and Laws of the State, remaining in the meantime, in full force and effect until a new one be submitted to them and ratified and adopted.

A message was received from the Senate informing the House that the Senate had appointed Messrs. Quinan, Throckmorton, Hall, Potter and Blanch, a committee of five to act with a committee of seven, to be appointed by the House, to inquire and report whether any and what means are necessary in the present condition of our Federal relations for the security of the School fund invested in United States bonds.

Mr. Buckley offered the following as a substitute for the resolutions and proposed amendments: Whereas, the people of Texas being much concerned for the preservation of the rights, liberties, and powers of the State and its inhabitants endangered by the political action of a majority of the States, and the people of the same have in the exercise of powers reserved to themselves, in the bill of rights, called a Convention composed of two members for each Representative in the Legislature from the various districts established by the apportionment law of 1860, to assemble on the 28th day of January 1861, at the city of Austin, which convention by the terms of the call made by numerous assemblages of citizens in various parts of the State, was, when elected and assembled, to have power to consider the condition of public affairs; to determine what shall be the future relations of this State to the Union, and such other matters as are necessarily and properly incident thereto, and in case it should be determined by said Convention, that it is necessary for the preservation of the rights and liberties aforesaid, that the sovereignty of Texas should resume the powers delegated to the Federal Government in the Constitution of the United States and by the articles of annexation, then the ordinance of said Convention resuming said delegated powers and repealing the ratification by the people of Texas, of articles of annexation should be submitted to a vote of the qualified electors of this State, for their ratification or rejection. Therefore be it,

Resolved, By the Legislature of the State of Texas, that the Government of the State of Texas hereby gives its assent to, and approves of the Convention aforesaid, and that this Resolution take effect and be in force from and after its passage.

Mr. Flewellen moved to postpone further consideration of the whole matter until Tuesday night.

Mr. Stewart moved to lay the amendment and the substitute on the table.

On motion of Mr. Dougherty, a division of the question was ordered. The question then being upon laying the amendment of Mr. Davis of Bastrop upon the table, the same was carried by the following vote; yeas 55, nays 17. The question then recurring upon tabling the substitute, the yeas and nays were ordered. The motion was lost by the following vote: yeas 39, nays 39.

Mr. Nelson moved the previous question, which was ordered. The question being, Shall the previous question be now put, the House refused to have it put, by the following vote: Mr. Nelson called for the yeas and nays; yeas 35, nays 43. The question then being on the adoption of the supstitute, was put, and the substitute adopted by the following vote: yeas 56, nays 24.

Mr. Walder offered the following amendment;

2d. The vote on any ordinance submitted by the Convention to to the qualified electors of this State, shall be taken at such time throughout the State as the Convention shall appoint; and the election shall be held by the officers now required by law to conduct elections for State officers, and shall be conducted according to the provisions of existing laws, as far as applicable, and the returns made at such time and to such person or persons, and to such place or places as the Convention may prescribe. All officers of elections are hereby required to conduct such election in pursuance of these resolutions, and the directions of the Convention, under such penalties as are now prescribed in like cases; and the said election is hereby placed under the protection of such laws, civil and criminal, as are, provided in cases of other State elections.

3d. Should said Convention, in addition to submission to the qualified electors of the State, any ordinance which they may pass, call a convention for the purpose of changing the present State Constitution, so as to vest the powers heretofore delegated to the United States in the State Government, then and in that case, election for delegates to such a convention shall be held at the same time, and conducted, and the returns thereof made in the manner provided in the second second section of these resolutions.

On motion of Mr. Henderson, the amendment was laid on the table by the following vote: yeas 53, nays 24.

On motion of Mr. Dickson, the main question was ordered, which being upon the engrossment of the bill, same was put, and the bill ordered to be engrossed.

On motion of Mr. Buckley, the rule was suspended by the following vote: Yeas, 58; nays, 15.

Mr. Nelson proposed to amend the caption as follows: "Joint Resolution, Concerning the Convention of the People of Texas, called in pursuance of the Bill of Rights." Adopted; and bill read third time, and passed. Yeas, 65; nays, 13.

On motion of Mr. Shannon, the bill to provide for the protection of the frontier was made the special order of the day for Monday next.

Mr. Walder moved to suspend rule and take up Senate's bill on the Speaker's stand, with the view of their reference to proper committees.

Mr. Branch, one of the Committee on Enrolled Bills, reported correctly enrolled and properly signed the bill to define the time of holding the courts in the Nineteenth Judicial District, and the same had been sent to the Governor for his approval and signature.

Mr. Davis, of Hays, moved to adjourn till 3½ o'clock P. M. Lost.

On motion, the House adjourned till 9½ o'clock A. M. on Monday.

Monday, Jan. 28, 1861.

SENATE — Met. Roll called. Quorum present.

Mr. Guinn chairman of committee on Finance, made the following report:

In obedience to a resolution of the Senate, requiring the Finance committee to examine what amount of funds may be used from unexpended appropriations or deposits in the Treasury, for the public use, they have obtained from the Treasurer a statatement of all the funds in the Treasury, from which they believe the following may be appropriated for the common purposes of supporting the State Government, to wit: Revenue of the State in specie $3,951,59. Sales of University Lands in specie $9,768,62. In 5 per cent, United States bonds $25,000. The two last amounts belong to the University fund. The University not being likely to go into operation soon, your committee are of opinion that the funds might be used by the State, and replaced from the State Revenue whenever the University shall be put into operation. Interest, Coupons not yet collected $3,550. Special deposits, settlements of estates, $17,313. This amount has been accumulating in the Treasury since the commencement of our State Government. Some portion thereof may be applied for, when it would be the duty of the Government to supply the means to pay the amount applied for, but the greatest part may never be applied for by the legal heirs or persons authorized to receive the same. Escheated property $2,183,01. Making in the whole the sum of $61,766,22, which your committee are of opinion may be used for purposes of the State Government.

Your committee have therefore offered the following substitutes for the two bills referred, and recommend their passage.

An act directing how certain funds now in the Treasury shall be applied, and a bill making an appropriation to pay for supplies furnished the Troops now on the frontier.

Mr. Erath introduced a bill to allow the holders of claims for money against the State, to take lands in lieu thereof, and to receive such claims for dues on lands; read first and second time, and referred to the Committee on Public Lands.

On motion of Mr. Parsons, Mr. Dulany, Senator elect from the fourteenth senatorial district, composed of the counties of Shelby and Panola, came forward and took the oath and his seat.

A message was received from the House, informing the Senate that the House had passed a joint resolution concerning the Convention of the people of Texas, called in pursuance of the Bill of Rights.

On motion, the joint resolution was taken up and read first time, rule suspended, read second time. Mr. Gentry offered a substitute therefor. Mr. Quinan moved to lay the substitute on the table. Mr. Throckmorton moved a call of the Senate, which was sustained. The Senate being full, the yeas and nays were taken on the motion to lay on the table, and stood as follows: yeas 20, nays 10; so the motion prevailed.

Mr. Townes then offered the following amendment: 1st. In the preamble, between the words "public affairs, and to determine," insert the words "with a view."

2. Strike out all after, and including the words, "then the ordinance of said convention resuming," and insert, "then the action of said convention be submitted to the people for ratification or rejection at the ballot box at the earliest practicable time after its adjournment."

3. In the first resolution, at the conclusion, add the words "for the purposes and to the extent aforesaid."

4. Add the following resolution: "The ordinance dissolving the relations of the State with the United States should, as soon as consistent with a full and fair vote, be submitted to the qualified electors of the State for ratification or rejection."

5. At the same time the vote is taken on said ordinance, the qualified electors should elect delegates to a general convention for the purpose of amending the State constitution, so far as to conform it to the relations of the State to the Union at the time the convention assembles.

6. If a new convention should not be ordered, and the convention elected 8th January, 1861, should adjourn to reassemble, there should be an election of delegates thereto on the same day, on which the ordinance is submitted to the people in each Representative District in which less than a majority of the qualified electors cast their votes on the said 8th January, to sit in the adjourned convention, with the delegates who did receive a majority of the votes of their Representative Districts.

Mr. Herbert moved to lay the amendments on the table.

Mr. Martin moved a call of the Senate. Sustained. Senate being full, the amendments were laid on the table. Yeas, 20; nays, 10. Rule suspended; bill read third time, and passed. Yeas, 25; nays, 5.

On motion, Senate adjourned until tomorrow 10 o'clock A. M.

HOUSE — Met. Roll called. Quorum present.

Mr. Darnell, chairman, reported as follows:

The committee on Federal Relations, to whom was referred the ordinance of secession passed by the Alabama State Convention, have had the same under consideration, and have instructed me to report the same back to the House with a request that the Speaker transmit the same to the President of the Convention of the State of Texas. They have also had under consideration a set of resolutions adopted by a portion of the citizens of Montgomery county, Texas, called main resolutions. The committee instructed me to report them back to the House and ask that they be laid on the table.

Mr. Crooks, chairman of the committee on Engrossed Bills, reported correctly engrossed a Joint Resolution concerning the Convention of the people of Texas, called in pursuance of the bill of rights.

Mr. Lewis of Montgomery, offered the following resolution:

Resolved, That in the opinion of this House, whatever ordinance or ordinances shall be passed by the Convention which is to meet here to-day, shall be submitted to the people for approval or disapproval.

THE BANNER.

A. N. VAUGHAN, EDITOR.

BEAUMONT, TUESDAY, MARCH 12, 1861

WHAT THE PEOPLE IN WASHINGTON THINK ABOUT OLD ABE'S INAUGURAL.

We learn from a special dispatch to the N. Orleans Delta, that the Southern men in the City of Washington, regard Lincoln's Inaugural as a declaration of war. John Bell advices Tennesse to prepare for war as the only means of preventing it. As soon as the coercion portion of the inaugural was read, dispatches were immediately sent to Gov. Pickens, advising him against attacking Fort Sumpter, and to await the action of the Confederate States.

WHAT THE PEOPLE IN WASHINGTON SAY ABOUT OLD ABE'S INAUGURAL.—Buchanan said: "I can't say what he means until I read his Inaugural." Mr. Douglas replied to Buck, and said that Abe did not mean coercion, from the fact that there was nothing said about retaking Forts or Federal property.

Senator Wigfall, says it is a most miserable paper.

It is said that Southerners generally look thereon as a precurser of war, while Thurlow Weed, (as might have been expected) is delighted with it.

WHAT THE PEOPLE OF MONTGOMERY THINK OF THE INAUGURAL.—Since the receipt of the Inaugural address of Old Abe, it is the universal conception of the people in Montgomery, that war between the Confederate States and the United States is inevitable. Mr. Benjamin, of Louisiana, thinks that there will be clashing of arms within thirty days.

As we have not seen the Inaugural, we will decline expressing an opinion as to its meaning, until we shall have read it, but we cannot forbear saying this much; that if he attempts to do what he says he will, *he* or some of his followers will get badly hurt. We allude to the following extract from the inaugural, where Abe says:

The power confided to me will be used to hold and occupy and possess the property and places belonging to the Government, and to collect duties on imports.—I must consider that in view of the Constitution and laws is unbroken, and to the extent of my ability I shall take care, as the Constitution itself expressly enjoins upon me, that the laws of the Union be faithfully executed in the States.

The above extract of the Inaugural, which we clipped from the Delta, is all that we have seen of that glorious document, which some call a conciliatory document. They call it cooncilatory, because Lincoln says there will be no invasion of the south except for the enforcement of the laws within the Confederate states, the collection of duties, retaking our Forts, &c. If that is Old Abe's peace document, we infer that a war document would be frightful indeed.

OLD ABE'S CABINET.

The Cabinet of Old Abe is composed as follows:

Secretary of State—W H. Seward of N.Y.
Secretary of the Treasury—Mr. Chase of O.
Secretary of War—Mr. Cameron of Penn.
Secretary of the Navy—Mr. Wells, of Con.
Postmaster General—Mr. Blair of Md.
Secretary of the Interior—Mr. Smith of Ind.
Attorney General—Mr. Bates, of Missouri.

It is said that the Senate confirmed the above appointments unanimously, with the exception of Blair as Postmaster General, and Bates as Attorney General, there being some four or five votes against each.

THE SUGAR CROP—POLITICS IN THE COUNTRY.

ST. JAMES, MARCH 4, 1861.

Editors Delta—At this time we are able to make an estimate of the next sugar crop. I am glad to say that the prospects for a large one are very flattering, and that the Confederacy will be able to export a large quantity to the United States. The seed cane was never better, and many have more than they want.—The ratoons are all good, even the second year's. Vegetation is very forward, and the cane already marks the rows in some lands; with favorable seasons henceforth, we may reach the crop of '53.

Our good parishioners who voted the Co-operation ticket so strongly, on account of the confidence which they placed in the Senatorial candidate of that party, have now opened their eyes to the truth that secession was not the bugbear it had been represented to them, and that the precipitate action of Louisiana, did not bring down on them a host of troubles, nor of Wide-Awakes. They acknowledge their delusion, and would now all vote against a reconstruction of the Union. This much I have written on politics to prove that the Co-operationists of this State, with few exceptions, are heart and soul with the South, notwithstanding the insinuations of the Yankee sheet whose articles have been deemed good capital against the South by all the leading Republican journals in the country.

Your's, COLONEL.

LETTER FROM GENERAL HENNINGSEN From the Montgomery Mail we extract the following:

The following report of the committees appointed respectively by the Governor and both branches of the Legislature of the State of Alabama to test the efficiency and safety of the so-called Law-Minnie muskets (or U. S. muskets altered into Minnies) confirms the opinion I expressed of them in a recent letter to the Montgomery Advertiser. The solution of this question might appear to be only a matter of State interest to Alabama, and of only limited interest to her, as these arms were but few in number, and as no others of the same character can, that I am aware of, anywhere be purchased.

I beg leave, however, to call attention to the matter, because in fact it is important to all Southern States. A large portion of their armament now consists and may for a long time consist, of various kinds of U. S. muskets. By recent returns the United States Congress it appears that since last spring over 100,000 United States percussion muskets and flint muskets altered to percussion have been sent to the United States arsenals in the Southern States. It became, therefore, a matter of public interest to determine by authenticated experiment that, by alteration, the range and accuracy of these arms could be many-fold increased up to the full efficiency of any heretofore manufactured by the United States Government, and that such alteration may be effected with perfect safety.

This, I submit has been fully established. I would remark in conclusion, however, that in the use of all long-ranging rifles, much depends on the shape and perfect manufacture of the shot, as regards accuracy and continued facility of loading. All the shot I have seen south, including those cast from the moulds furnished with the last United States Minnie rifles are deficient in one or other of these particulars. The shot furnished with the Law Minnie rifle, differ from the original form and are very badly cast.—The shot furnished with the United States last Minnie rifle are defective in shape. The former would often embarrass inexperienced hands to push down the barrel. The latter must often tear within the barrel, leaving in it a portion of the lead, which I hear those using them complain of. A slight alteration in the moulds will, however, obviate this difficulty. It is worth recording, that in the experiments above referred to, several hundred shots were fired from each Law Minnie musket without washing out, and without missing fire; the same result may be obtained with any Minnie rifle, even by the inexperienced, through the use of a properly made shot and by loading in a proper manner; otherwise, some difficulty and disappointment may be experienced.

I am, gentlemen, yours ob'd'ntly.

C. F. HENNINGSEN.

Evidently the time has not yet arrived for the entire unanimity of opinion in regard to some matters of public policy, even in the South. The Charleston Mercury does not concur in all that is done by the Montgomery Convention. It says:

We regret that any provisional government was formed at all, and in one or two important particulars confess to disappointment and surprise at the government and laws enacted. It seems that the United States protective tariff of '75 has been adopted, and that a positive condemnation of the institution of slavery, through the slave trade, has been inserted into the constitution itself. Neither of these did we expect. We did not suppose that any southern government, whether for a month or a year, would sanction the policy of protective tariffs.—The tariff of '75 is odious and oppressive in its discriminations. It was made to favor northern enterprise at the expense of the people at the South—a huge free list for them—the burden of taxation for us to bear, and we maintain is adverse to revenue, unjust in principle, and oppressive in practice. Whether this is brought about by a partial remission of duties or a partial imposition, it is still the same in effect. We enter our protest against the scheme and policy, both as regards ourselves and in the results so far as foreign nations are concerned and their friendship, at this time, valuable to us.—In each respect free trade is the policy of the Confederate States.

We deem it also unfortunate and *mal apropos* that the stigma of illegitimacy and illegality should be placed upon the institution of slavery by a fundamental law against the slave trade. In our opinion it is a matter of policy, and not of principle, to be decided now and hereafter, from the sound views of the necessities and safety of our people. We think it a proper subject of legislation.

THE IMMACULATE ABE.—In a late speech to a committee of Philadelphians, urging Mr. Cameron for a seat in the Cabinet, Mr. Lincoln said: "In the formation of my Cabinet, I shall aim as nearly as possible at perfection. I have already appointed Senator Seward, and Mr. Bates, of Missouri, and they are men whose characters, I think, the breath of calumny can not impeach. Any man whom I appoint to such a position, must be, as far as possible, like Cæsar's wife, pure and above suspicion, of unblemished reputation and undoubted integrity. I will not have any man associated with me whose character is impeached." This is what we had a right to expect. We always understood from Old Abe's neighbors and friends that he was a pink of purity and decency, and that when a Representative in Congress he never stooped to any job that brought on a vociferous remonstrance, signed by five hundred of his own party! By no manner of means! And therefore it is not at all wonderful that he should insist upon having a Cabinet made up of his own incorruptible materials, and worthy in all respect of sitting in Abraham's bosom. —*Richmond Dispatch.*

LATEST BY TELEGRAPH.

DOMESTIC INTELLIGENCE.

CONGRESSIONAL PROCEEDINGS

WASHINGTON, March 2.—In the House yesterday a bill providing for the admission of the Territory of New Mexico as a State in the Federal Union was tabled by 47 against 126.

The bill organizing the new territories of Neveda and Dacota was taken up, which after some discussion, passed.

In the Senate, Mr. Hunter refused to offer the Crittenden resolutions, saying, if they were adopted, the advantages of the Dred Scott decision would be lost.

Mr. Crittenden was willing to favor any propositions promising a pacific settlement of the difficulties.

Mr. Mason was against amending the Constitution, and denounced the Peace Convention plan as subversive to Southern rights.

Mr. Baker was willing to give ... a great deal to the border States, but nothing to secession.

Mr. Green said that th... ence propositions were t...

The House resolution ... special order of the 2d.

MISSOURI STATE C...

JEFFERSON CITY, ... Convention before adjou... to St. Louis, unanimo... resolution requesting its ... egates to swear to suppo... tion of the United St... State of Missouri.

A motion for secret se... mously defeated.

THE ELECTION IN ... OLINA

RALEIGH, March 2.— ... turns thus far received a... indefinite.

IMPORTANT FROM ...

WASHINGTON, March 2.—Telegraphic advices received to-day from Richmond say that an ordinance, providing for the withdrawol of the State of Virginia from the old Federal Union, has been drafted.

Ex-President John Tyler is doing all in his power to drive Virginia from the Union. It is believed he will succeed if Mr. Lincoln, in his inaugural address, entertains principles of a coercive nature.

SEWARD DECLINES A SEAT IN THE NEW CABINET.

WASHINGTON, March 2.—An unfounded rumor that the Hon. Wm. H. Seward had declined a Cabinet appointment, created great consternation among the Northern conservative and border State men. Some of the latter say they cannot sustain Mr. Lincoln's administration if Ex-Governor Chase of Ohio goes into the Cabinet.

LINCOLN'S CABINET.

WASHINTON, March 2,—The formation of Mr. Lincoln's Cabinet excites the most intense interest.

Mr. Lincoln was closeted till 2 o'clock this morning hearing suggestions on the subject, but nothing was concluded.

LINCOLN'S INAUGURAL.

WASINGTON, March 2.—The Inaugural was read last night to the members of the Cabinet, who have accepted it. It will occupy two columns in the National Intelligencer.

Mr. Lincoln's language is firm and decided. He will execute the laws, hold or recover the forts in the seceded States, and collect the duties.

He also advocates the holding of a National Convention.

Lincoln's safety on the inauguration day is regarded as secured beyond a doubt.

THE CORWIN RESOLUTIONS.

NEW YORK, March 2.—Special dispatches from Washington to the New York papers say the Senate will probably, by a two thirds, vote, concur in the adoption of Mr. Corwin's resolutien for non-interference with slavery in the States. The only chance for compromise now lies in the adoption of Mr. Corwin's resolutions.

PROCEEDINGS OF THE FEDERAL CONGRESS.

WASHINGTON, March 2.—The House has concurred in the Senate's Post-Office bill. The amendment annuls the present Butterfield mail route by El Paso, and gives them for three years and a half the central overland route daily to San Francisco, and tri-weekly-to Denver City and Salt Lake.

The amendment to the fugitive act which passed the House yesterday, provides that after the preliminaries where arrested, the fugitive is finally to have a jury trial in the State whence he escaped.

The House passed the Post-office bill as amended by the Senate.

In the House Mr. Dawes' resolution was adopted, censuring the Secretary of the Navy for accepting naval resignations.

Mr. Bingham unsuccessfully endeavored to get a bill providing for the collection of duties on shipboard, etc.

THE ELECTION IN NORTH CAROLINA.

RALEIGH, March 2.—There is a probability that North Carolina has gone against the holding of a State Convention.

FUGITIVE SLAVE CASE.

NEW YORK, March 2.—John Polhemus, a fugitive slave, was rescued from the United States Marshals. The officers had not a warrant.

STEAMER MONARCH SUNK.

LOUISVILLE, March 2.—The steamer Monarch, from Cincinnatti bound for New Orleans, sunk at the head of the falls in shoal water, by striking a rock. Her deck freight sustained no injury.

THE TARIFF BILL A LAW.

PHILADELPHIA, March 2.—A special dispatch to one of the daily papers says the President has signed the tariff bills, which consequently becomes a law.

SAILING OF OCEAN STEAMERS.

NEW YORK, March 2.—The steamer Kangaroo sailed from this port to Liverpool, the Saxonia for Hamburg, and the Fulton for Southampton and Havre. They took out on an agerage about $10-000 of treasure on freight.

DOMESTIC MARKETS.

NEW YORK, March 2.—Cotton closed dull and nominal; sales at 11½c per lb, for Middling Uplands. Flour closed dull at $5 05 to $5 15 for Superfine State. Corn—sales of 6750 bushels at 65½ to 78c. Pork quiet and steady; sales of 200 bbls at $17 25. Sugar closed steady, with sales of 940 hhds, at 4½ to 5c. for Cuba, and 5¾c. per lb. for New Orleans. Molasses—sales of 100 bbls, at 35 to 36 per gallon.

CINCINNATI, March 2.—Flour declining at $4 50 for Superfine. Corn steady, with sales at 33 to 34 c. per bushel. Oats are worth 27½ c. Whiskey is quoted at 15c. per gallon. Pork firm; sales of 700 bbls, at $17 for Mess. Coffee—sales at 13½ to 14c. per lb. The sales of

ADMISSION OF TEXAS INTO THE CONFEDERATION.

Montgomery, March 3.—The State of Texas was yesterday (March 2,) fully admitted into the Confederation of Southern States. Her delegates sworn in as members of the Congress, signed the articles of Confederation and are now fully entitled to vote, etc.. etc. Hons. Reagan and Oldham appeared and took their seats.

... Saturday, but at figures below the views of factors, and the sales were confined to 5000 bales at previous prices:

NEW ORLEANS CLASSIFICATIONS.

Inferior	—@—	Middling	10¾@11¼
Ordinary	7¼@7¾	Good Middling	12 @12¼
Good Ordin'y	8½@9	Middling Fair	nominal.
Low Midln'g	9¾@10¼	Fair	nominal.

STATEMENT OF COTTON.

Stock on hand 1st Sept. 1860....bales			74,138
Received since	1,661,176		
Received yesterday	8,289—		1,669,465
			1,743,602
Expoeted since	1,317,345		
Exported Saturday	25,150—		1,342,365
Stock on hand not cleared			401,237

TOBACCO.—We heard of 40 hhds. at private sales.

STATEMENT OF TOBACCO.

Stock on hand 1st September,....hhds.			20,570
Received since	14,037		
Received yesterday	37—		14,074
			34,644
Exported since	17,403		
Exported Saturday	306—		17,709
Stock on hand not cleared			17,935

SUGAR.—Sales of 1200 hhds, at previous rates. Fair to Fully Fair 4¾@5¼c. ℔ lb.

MOLASSES.—2000 bbls. sold at 26@28 c. for Prime to Choice and 300 half bbls, at 30c, ℔ gallon. Prices firm.

FLOUR.—The sales embraced 2532 bbls. of which 1000 Superfine, in lots, at $5 25, 232 Good Extra at $6 6½, 160 Extra at $7 25, 200 Fine at —. 500 Superfine at ---, 150 Low Extra at $6, 100 Extra at $7 50 and 200 bbls. Plant's at $9 ℔ bbl.

GRAIN, The sales of Corn embraced about 9700 sacks, including 1000 Yellow Mixed at 56@57, 4000 Mixed at 56, 1000 White Mixed at 60 and 1500 White at 62c. ℔ bushel. Of oats some 550 sacks were disposed of, comprising 250 at 40 c. 100 at 42 and 200 at 45c. ℔ bushel. In Bran we noticed sales of some 350 sacks, including 200 at 95c. and 150 at $1 ℔ 100 lb.

HAY, A lot of 90 bales Western was taken at $24 ton.

PROVISIONS, The transactions in Pork comprised 624 bbls. Mess on private terms. Retailing at $19 ℔ bbl. In Bacon Shoulders retail at 8@8½c., Ribbed Sides 10¾@11 and Clear at 11½@12c. ℔ lb. In Lard we did not hear of any sale of any moment.

WHISKY, 100 bbls. Rectified, in two lots, sold at 20c. ℔ gallon.

SPIRITS TURPENTINE, 30 (pine barrels) sold at 31c. ℔ gallon.

COFFEE, The sales amonted to 1246 bags Rio, viz: 50 at 11¾, 382 at 12⅜, 565 at 12½, 50 at 12⅞ and 150 at 13c. ℔ lb.

"PRINCE BOB."—Robert Lincoln, son of the President elect, who is known now as "Prince Bob," is destined to make his peculiar mark and be remembered by the people wherever he goes. Of the many good things told of this boy in Buffalo on Saturday, we heard the following: A few days since, when Mrs. Lincoln was on her way home from New York, attended by her son Robert, she found herself at Buffalo without a pass over the State Line Railroad. For that link in the chain of railway between New York and Springfield no provision has been made. After Mrs. Lincoln had taken her seat in the cars, at Buffalo, for the West, her son Bob entered the office of R. N. Brown, Esq., the gentlemanly Superintendent of the State Line Railway, and inquired if Mr. Brown was in? Mr. Brown responded, and inquired what was wanted? His interrogator addressed him in substantially the following language:

"My name is Bob Lincoln. I'm a son of old Abe—the old woman is in the cars raising h—l about her passes—I wish you would go and attend to her!"

Mr. Brown very promptly filled out the requisite papers to enable Mrs. Lincoln to ride over his road without payment of fare, and delivered them to her. It is probable that the old "woman" gave Bob no further trouble about the passes that trip.—*Rochester Democrat.*

"Too pure for earth!
He sparkled, was exhaled, and went to Glory."

Allen Neyland—son of Richard Neyland Esq., and Anna his wife—was born Feb. 15th, 1860, died Feb 24th, 1861—his funeral sermon was preached by Rev. J. P. Jones, a sermon, short, but impressive; and evidently calculated, to speak comfort, to the sorrowing hearts of the devoted parents.

Through the lone and dreary midnight,
Watched a mother by her child;
And the cold and tremling starlight.
Never fell on two more mild.

Softly now the cherub slumbers—
Slumbers on his little bed,
Angels warble sweetest numbers,
"Round the pallid infants head."

And the mother pale and weeping,
Breathed a low and fervent prayer:
"Trouble not the infant sleeping,
With the angels, round him there!"

And the angels whispered near her,
...e mother's ear,
...come to bear him,
...at wait him here."

...light was come,
...sement peeping,
...the spirit home;
...leeping.

...wly bed,
...round him.
...ngels tread,
...n hath found him.

...the silent years,
...above him,
...t mern appears,
...ence remove him.

LENA.

...d 1861.

...TON MATTERS.

[Correspondence of the Baltimore American.]

President Buchanan on coercion.—It is understood that President Buchanan will veto any measure that may be passed by Congress having for its object the coercion of the South, but it is evident from the course of his administration, since the reorganization of the Cabinet, that he does not view the protection of the forts and the energetic resistance of any attempt to seize them as coercion. He does not however, include in these measures the bill for the construction of seven steam sloops of war.

Lincoln's Speeches.—The Speeches of Lincoln have greatly lessened the public estimation of his character; and, as to statesmanship, his vacillation and contradictory harangues have had this effect of withdrawing from him all claims to this most essential qualification. His contest with Judge Douglas gave him a national character for shrewdness, tact and ability, but it is now regarded as evident that he has but little appreciation of the crisis in the affairs of the nation, and less capacity to meet the responsibilities that may devolve upon him. The possibility of his obtaining Cabinet officers from any eminence or standing, has been greatly lessened, if not altogether defeated, by these imprudent and irritating utterances, and there is no doubt that his friends in Congress are rather mortified and chagrined at the debut he has made on the national stage. The fact that Mr. Seward is to be leading mind of the administration is regarded as most fortunate for the future of the country.

A Republican Conflict.—The "irrepressible conflict" in the Repulican party has commenced in good earnest, a distinct line of demarkation having been established between the liberals and extremists. The attack on Judge Kellogg by the editor of the Chicago Tribune, which the Judge repelled with such emphatic emphasis as to leave his antagonist *hors du combat*, is an indication of the bitterness that prevails. The liberals are gaining ground, notwithstanding the speeches of Mr. Lincoln, as it is generally admitted that when he reaches Washington he will be under the control of Mr. Seward, Judge Kellogg, and those who agree with them in the present crisis,

Mr. Seward has invited the President elect to partake of the hospitalities of his house and home until the inauguration, as a means of separating him from the influence of the extremists. The latter, however, insist upon his taking quarters at Willard's, where they can have easy access to him. The question has not yet been decided, but the probability is that Mr. Seward will triumph, not only on account of the position he is to hold in the new administration, but from the fact, that the Presiden and his family, after the excitement and fatigue of their journey, will be glad to secure the privacy extended to them.

[Correspondence of the Baltimore Sun.]

Mr. Lincoln's premature disclosure of the policy upon which he is to conduct the government has hastened—what was, however inevitable—a rupture of the Republican party. It is now doubtful whether it can hold together till the 4th of March. Before that day Mr. Lincoln will find that no eminent man in the Republican party will come into his Cabinet upon the principle of coercion and no compromise which he has laid down.

The New Orleans Delta of the 6inst., says the public was rather astonished yesterday evening to learn from the telegraph reported of the Associated Press that Mr. Lincoln's inaugural was considered an eminently peaceful and conciliatory document. The reporter ought to have given the same information to the Arkansas Convention, which, it seems, has been determined in favor of secession by Mr. Lincoln's peaceful and conciliatory policy. If this absurd stuff is sent here to influence public opinion, previous experience ought to have sufficiently indicated utter futility of such expedients. To falsify is bad enough, but to falsify in a manner so thoroughly clumsy and ridiculous is unpardonable.

SIGNIFCATION OF CHRISTIAN NAMES. Benjamin, son of the right hand, i. e., of good fortune; Clement, mild tempered; Robert, famous in council; Sebastian, to be reverenced; William, golden helmet; James, a supplanter; David, well-beloved; Stephen, a garland; Alfred, all peace; Jesse, firm; John, gracious gift of Johovah; Judah, renowned; Charles, noble spirited; Albert, all bright; Daniel, a judge from God; Thomas, a twin; George, a husbandman; Joseph, addition; Simon, a hearkening; Andrew, courageous; Jacob, a supplanter; Solomon, peaceable; Lot, a veil.

Here we have given the signification of the Christian names of the Senators of the United States. It would seem that Benjamin Fitzpatrick was born to good luck; Clement C. Clay, Jr., of Alabama, is mild-tempered; Robert W. Johnson, of Arkansas, is famous in council; William M. Gwin, of California, is a golden helmet; James W. Grimes, of Iowa, is a supplanter; James Dixon has already manifested a disposition to supplant Republicanism; Stephen a Douglas may yet win the crown; but the idea of associating Alfred Iverson, of Georgia, with all peace is quite as much amiss as to say Jesse D. Bright is firm. Most of the people are beginning to think that John J. Crittenden is a gift of Jehovah. Judah P. Bejamin, of Louisiana will be renowned as a disunionist in the future history of America. The noble spirit of Charles Sumner, of Massachusetts, is not illustrated in his uncharitable speeches on American public affairs. Henry is recorded as uncertain. Albert G. Brown of Mississippi, is all bright, but he keeps much of his light under a bushel. Simon Cameron is hearkening, as they say in Nantucket, "the worst kind," for sounds from Springfield, Illinois, just now. So much for senators.

Rufus, red-headed; Josiah, whom Jehovah heals; Felix, happy; Ezra, is a helper; Susan is a lilly; Ida, happiness; Mary, means rebellion; Matilda; heroine; Deborah, will sing, for she is said to be a bee; Diantha, is a pink; Anne and Hannah are gracious; Jemima is a dove; Laura is a bay-tree; Margaret is a pearl; Miss Penelope is a weaver; Polly and Molly like Miriam; Phyllis is a green bough; Roda, is a rose; Miss Ursula is a she-bear; Abigail is her father's joy; but Almira, like Henry, is uncertain; Elizabeth is good; Hephzibah, my delight is in her; Roxana was the name of the wife of Alexander the Great; and Zenobia was the wife of Jupiter.

POPULAR NAMES OF STATES AND CITIES.

Virginia, the Old Dominion.
Massachusetts, the Bay State.
Maine, the Border State.
Rhode Island, Little Rhody.
New York, the Empire State.
New Hampshire, the Granite State.
Vermont, the Green Mountain State.
Connecticut, the Land of Steady Habits.
Pennsylvania, the Keystone State.
North Carolina, the Old North State.
Ohio, the Buckeye State.
South Carolina, the Palmetto State.
Michigan, Wolverine State.
Kentucky, the Corn Cracker.
Delaware, the Blue Hen's Chicken.
Missouri, the Puke State.
Indiana, the Hoosier State.
Iowa, the Hawkeye State.
Wisconsin, the Badger State.
Florida, the Peninsular State.
Texas, the Lone Star State.

CITIES.
New York City, Gotham.
Boston, the Modern Athens.
Philadelphia, the Quaker City.
Baltimore, the Monumental City.
Cincinnati, the Queen City.
New Orleans, the Crescent City.
Washington, the city of Magnificent distances.
Chicago, the Garden City.
Detroit, the City of the straits.
Cleveland the Forest City.
Pittsburg, the Smoky City.
New Haven, the City of Elms.
Indianapolis, the Railroad City.
St. Louis, the Mound City.
Keokuk, the Gate City.
Louisville, the Fall City.
Nashville, the City of Rocks.
Hannibal, the Bluff City.
Alexadria, the Delta City.

SPIES IN THE SOUTH.—The New York Herald, of the 1st inst., says:

Mr. Kennedy, the superintendent of the New York Police Department, has swarmed the city of Charleston and other Southern cities with detectives, whose duty it is to note vessels arriving from New York, which may have on board arms and other munitions of war, and finding out who are the shippers. This despotic and contemptible system of espionage, (continues the Herald) may word in the North with comparative safety to the persons of Mr. Kennedy's agents, but if their identity should be discovered in the Southern cities just now, as in all likelihood it will be, they will be treated in a very summary fashion.

QUEEN VICTORIA ON THE AMERICAN CRISIS.—In her speech on the opening of Parliament, Queen Victoria thus refers to our differences:

Serious differences have arisen among the States of the North American Union. It is impossible for me to look without great concern upon any event that can affect the happiness and welfare of a people nearly allied to my subjects by descent, and closely connected with them by the most intimate relations. My heartfelt wish is that these differences may be susceptible of satisfactory adjustment. The interest which I take in the well-being of the people of the United States cannot but increase by the kind and cordial reception given by them to the Prince of Wales during his recent visit to the continent of America.

SURRENDER OF EX-GENERAL TWIGGS, LATE OF THE UNITED STATES ARMY, TO THE TEXAN TROOPS IN THE GRAN PLAZA, SAN ANTONIO, TEXAS, FEBRUARY 16, 1861.—[See Page 182.]

FORT BROWN, TEXAS.—FROM A SKETCH BY A GOVERNMENT DRAUGHTSMAN.—[SEE PAGE 182.]

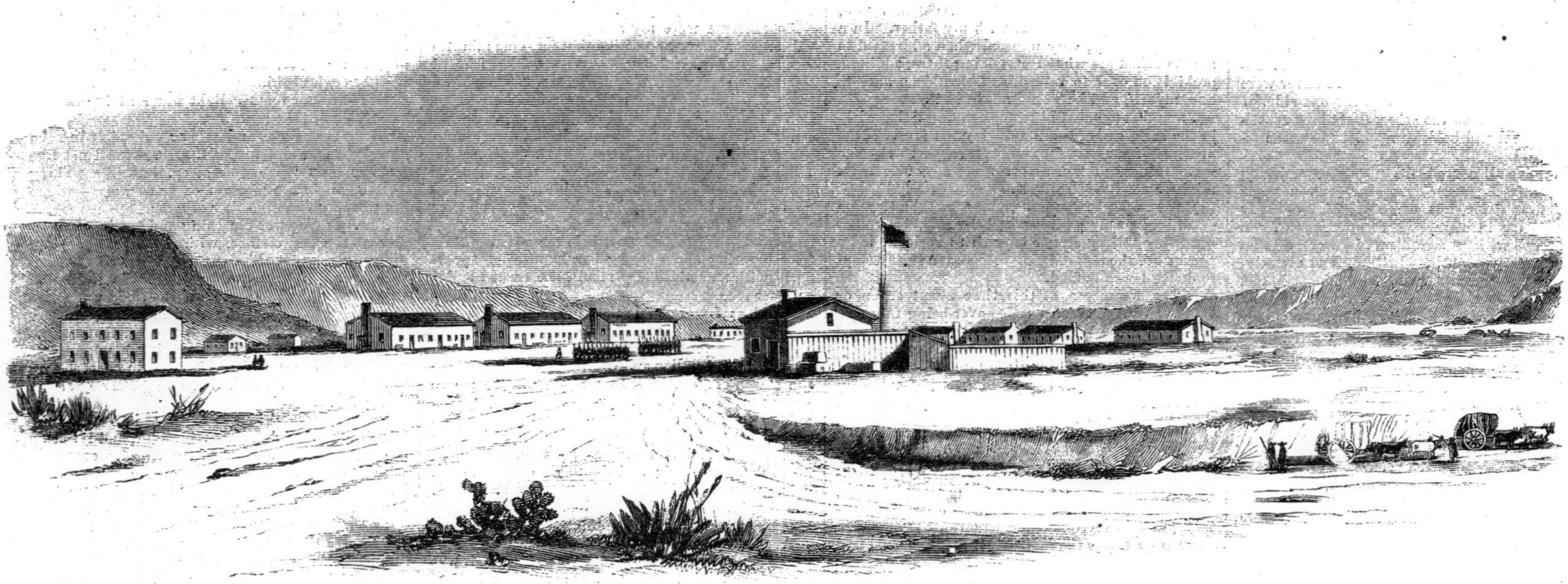

FORT LANCASTER, TEXAS.—FROM A SKETCH BY A GOVERNMENT DRAUGHTSMAN.—[SEE PAGE 182.]

THE ALAMO, SAN ANTONIO, TEXAS, LATE HEAD-QUARTERS OF EX-GENERAL [illegible]GGS.—FROM A SKETCH BY A GOVERNMENT DRAUGHTSMAN.—[SEE PAGE 182.]

BIVOUAC OF CONFEDERATE TROOPS ON THE LAS MORAS, TEXAS, WITH STOLEN U. S. WAGONS, ETC.—Sketched by a Member of the Corps.—[See Page 381.]

THE ILLUSTRATED LONDON NEWS

No. 1108.—VOL. XXXIX.] SATURDAY, SEPTEMBER 14, 1861. [WITH A SUPPLEMENT, FIVEPENCE

MEETING OF THE BRITISH ASSOCIATION AT MANCHESTER.

SCIENCE, like Wisdom, is justified of her children. Time was when the annual sessions of the British Association were held to be a capital theme for ridicule, and when journalists who cater for the instruction and amusement of men of business thought it became them to raise an uproarious laugh at what they described as talking, peripatetic, and wool-gathering philosophy. It is not the first time by a good many that the shadows which herald the approach of a majestic success, misinterpreted by men who believe that "there is nothing like leather," have excited wondrous ebullitions of noisy merriment, of which subsequent events have made the said men sheepishly ashamed. The British Association has not merely outlived the jeers of its early assailants—it has seen them converted into acclamations of praise.

ILLUSTRATIONS OF THE WAR IN AMERICA

TEXAN RANGERS (FEDERALISTS) RECONNOITRING.

SCARCELY anything more picturesque can be conceived than a troop of these rangers (as depicted on our first page) galloping wildly through the woody ravines of Virginia, between Alexandria and Fairfax, their carbines held ready for action at a moment's notice. To see them rattling along, draped in their loose ponchos, their stern, bearded faces shadowed by the overlapping brims of their sombreros, one might almost fancy them a troop of Cromwellian cavalry in grim pursuit of Cavaliers.

THE WAR IN AMERICA: TEXAN RANGERS (FEDERALISTS) RECONNOITRING BETWEEN ALEXANDRIA AND FAIRFAX, VIRGINIA.—FROM A SKETCH BY OUR SPECIAL ARTIST.

SEE SUPPLEMENT, PAGE 282.

THE TRI-WEEKLY TELEGRAPH.

VOL. XXVIII—NO. 12 HOUSTON, MONDAY, APRIL 14, 1862 WHOLE NO. 3507

BY SPECIAL & S. W. EXPRESS.

3 DAYS LATER.

A GLORIOUS VICTORY.

5000 Prisoners Taken!

ONE HUNDRED CANNON TAKEN.

Twenty Thousand Arms Taken.

GEN. A. S. JOHNSON KILLED.

ETC., ETC., ETC.

We have by the New Orleans train this (Saturday) morning, three days later papers, containing the following intelligence. The dispatches have full accounts of a great victory, but leave the second days contest still undecided. Let us hope for the best.

RICHMOND, April, 6.—Reports of a heavy skirmish near Yorktown yesterday, is confirmed by an official dispatch. The general opinion is fighting will be renewed to-day. Nothing later received this morning. there was a collision on the Central Road last night. Three killed and thirty wounded. Particulars not yet received.

MEMPHIS, April 6.—Last Friday night one of the enemy's gunboats succeeded in passing Island No. 10, is now at Madrid.

Fighting commenced this morning at 5 o'clock, near Monterey, on the Tennessee river. It was a general engagement. Gen. Hardee engaged the enemy at first, the other divisions taking part during the day, until the enemy were defeated. A large number of prisoners were taken, together with eight batteies. Gen. Grant commanded the Federals. The fight was terrific.

So far, we know of the capture of Gen. Prentiss and 6000 Federals by our forces. There is no doubt we have gained a glorious victory.

MEMPHIS, April 7.—Gov. Harris telegraphed yesterday evening to the Memphis Avalanche, from Corinth in regard to the great battle which commenced yesterday morning, about fifteen miles from Corinth, near the Tennessee river.

He reports our victory to be of a most decisive character. The relative loss was not known, but was great on both sides

Gen. A. S. Johnson fell at half-past 2 o'clock, P. M.

The fight between the land forces was supposed to have closed, but heavy firing had commenced between our forces and the enemy's gunboats on the Tennessee river.

It is impossible to know the precise number of prisoners captured from the enemy. But it was immense. Five thousand had already been brought to the rear, and the work of capturing the routed Federals, scattered and flying in all directions, was going on.

Gen. Prentiss, who was long in command at Cairo, was among the prisoners. Several other Federal Generals are reported to be also in our hands.

We have captured all the enemy's tents and camp stores, a large amount of ammunition and small arms.

Out of twenty or twenty-five batteries of artillery possessed by the enemy, it is believed that he has saved but an insignificant portion.

It is not known whether Buell effected a junction with Grant; but nothing reported from the battle field indicates that such was the case. It is believed that only Grant's column of fifty or sixty thousand, were engaged, and that our Generals will turn their attention to Buell at once.

MEMPHIS, April 7.

The following dispatches were received here this morning;

CORINTH, April 6, 2 o'clock.

A great battle commenced this morning at daylight. Our forces have driven the enemy back two miles, and our victorious columns are still advancing. The First Louisiana (Regulars) has taken a battery. Several other batteries have been captured Gen. Gladden, of New Orleans, had an arm shot off. It was reported that the left wing of our army had reached the Tennessee river, below the enemy's right. The loss is very heavy and the battle is still furiously going on. It is stated that Gen. Buell had crossed the river. Col. Kit Williams is reported among the killed.

We have the enemy's camp, all his amunition, stores, etc. The battle was very severe, and the loss heavy on both sides. Fighting is still going on near the river, the enemy having retired to their rifle pits. Gen. Polk is advancing and fighting.

Gens. Prentiss, Grant, Sherman, McClernand, Wallace and Smith commanded the Federal forces Gen. Smith was sick. It has been a glorious day for us. Report says that among the slain on our side were Col. Bote of Nashville, and Col. Brown of Mississippi. Gen. Hindman's horse was killed by a shell. The fall injured the General's leg.

A dispatch sent by a General high in authority, announces as his opinion that the entire Federal force gunboats and transports, are in the power of the Confederates. R

CORINTH, April 6, 3½ P. M.

The battle is still raging fiercely. Gen. Bushrod Johnston was wounded in the side. We have already captured four batteries. The enemy is still falling back.

BATTLE FIELD, April 6, 6½ P. M.

The battle of Shiloh has been fought and resulted in a glorious victory of the Confederate arms. The enemy have been driven to the river, and are now trying to cross in transports under cover of a heavy fire from their gunboats.

Gen. A. S. Johnston was killed while leading a charge.

Gen. Prentiss has been captured. He says that the enemy had 84,000 men in the field, and that only his division and Gen. Sherman's were engaged. They had 18 bateries engaged, which were almost all captured by us.

MEMPHIS, April 7—The latest from the field confirms our previous reports. At 6:30 P. M. the enemy were in full retreat down the river banks, the Confederates pressing them gallantly, led by Gen. Polk.

Gen. Johnston was killed instantly by a Minnie ball in his body, and a fragment of a shell shattering his leg.

The slaughter on both sides was tremendous.

Great havoc was made among the Federal officers.

Gen. Beauregard is now in command of the whole army. He pronounces the victory equal to that of Manassas.

It is reported that the Federals have abandoned their transports.

RICHMOND, March 7.—The following official dispatch was received here this morning:

To Gen. S. Cooper, A. A. G.:

The battle commenced on the 6th of April. We attacked the enemy in a strong position in front of Pittsburg, and after a severe battle of ten hours duration, thanks be to the Almighty, we gained a complete victory, driving the enemy from every position. The loss on both sides is heavy, including the Commander-in-Chief, Gen. A. S. Johnston, who fell gallantly leading his troops into the thickest of the fight.

G. T. BEAUREGARD,
General Commanding.

MEMPHIS, April 7.—The great battle of Shiloh commenced at daylight yesterday morning. The Yankees were driven back two miles. Our victorious columns are still advancing.

The 1st Louisiana Regiment took a Federal battery and several others have been captured.

Gen. Gladden, of the 1st Louisiana, had an arm shot off.

Col. Williams, of Memphis, was killed.

BATTLE FIELD, April 6, 6:30 P. M.—The battle of Shiloh has been fought, and resulted in a great victory to the Confederate arms.

Gen. A. S. Johnston was killed at 2 o'clock, when leading a charge. He was struck by a ball and a piece of shell.

Gen. Prentiss has been captured.

He says they had 35,000 men in the field. They had eighteen batteries engaged, the most of which was captured.

Gen. Buell had a portion of his force at Duck River.

We have captured the enemy's camp, all their ammunition, stores, &c.

The battle was very severe. The loss heavy on both sides. Fighting is going on yet.

Gens. Prentiss, Grant, Sherman, McClernard, Wallace, and Smith, commanded the Federals. Gen. Smith was sick. 2000 prisoners have been taken and sent to our rear.

It is reported that our forces are fighting Buel today.

Gen. Clark and Col. Brown of Mississippi, and Col. Rich of Missouri, are wounded.

The enemy have been driven to the river and are attempting to cross on transports. Many prisoners being brought in.

The latest reports from Gov. Harris, at Corinth, say: "We have had a hard fought battle. Our victory complete. Relative loss not known, but very heavy on both sides. Unfortunately Gen. Johnston fell at half past 2 o'clock, P. M.

"We have taken a large number of prisoners, among them, Gen. Prentiss, certain. Several other Generals reported. Land fight closed, but heavy firing from gunboats.

"We have captured all the enemy's tents, stores, a large amount of artillery. A large number of muskets and 2000 prisoners already sent to the rear."

FIVE MILES FROM MONTEREY, April 5, (Saturday) Our army is advanced to within five miles of the enemy's lines. Their camp is three miles from the Tennessee river, at Pittsburg.

Skirmishing has taken place all the morning, within a mile and a quarter to a mile and a half of our post. We are on a high ridge, between Owl Creek on the left and Licking Creek on the right extending three miles along the river.

CORINTH, April 6.—The great battle, for some days anticipated, commenced at sunrise this (Sunday) morning, by our attacking the enemy all along the line.

By 1 o'clock P. M. we had driven the enemy back two miles, with great slaughter, and gained the river (Tennessee) below.

We have a large number of pieces of artillery, and killed great numbers of men.

We have captured a large number of prisoners, who say their forces engaged number one hundred and twenty-five thousand men, and a large amount of artillery.

Sunday, April 6—4 P. M.

The battle commenced at 6 o'clock, this morning, our forces attacking. We have driven the enemy from his position to over five or six miles towards Pittsburg, taking camp after camp, and battery after battery, with an immense quantity of army stores. The enemy's tents were all left standing. The bayonet was used in taking every battery.

The Arkansas, Alabama, Tennessee, Louisiana and Mississippi troops all fought with heroic courage.

The slaughter was immense on both sides.

Gen. Gladden (1st Louisiana) lost an arm.

Gen. Hindman was wounded by a shell's bursting, which killed his horse.

CORINTH, Sunday, April 6.—The battle is still raging, and the advantage is all with our side. The enemy has been driven back three miles, through his encampments, rifle pits, and works, to within three miles of the Tennessee river.

A large quantity of cannon, ammunition, stores, tents and prisoners have been taken. Their slaughter has been terrible. They will doubtless be driven into the Tennessee river.

Prisoners taken from the enemy report that Buell's command was united with Grant's, from the beginning of the engagement. The whole of their army was engaged.

Beauregard commands the right, and is wherever the fighting is hottest and hardest. He says he has the enemy, and will make a sure thing of it.

We shall probably capture the entire army of the enemy, with their gunboats and transports. H. P.

April 6—I write at Gen. Beauregard's headquarters. He says the enemy are in full flight. He is organizing vigorously for the pursuit.

The enemy is flying down the Tennessee river, and most of them will be captured.

We already have thousands of prisoners, and nearly all the enemy's artillery.

It is a glorious and complete victory. The enemy was completely surprised, routed, cut to pieces, dispersed, and driven into the Tennessee river.

Beauregard says it is a better affair than that of Manassas. He calls it the battle of Shiloh, from a place on the river, and considers it a decisive victory.

I write this on the enemy's paper, with all their tents standing before me, and occupied by our men.

Gen. A. Sidney Johnston, I deeply regret to say, is among the slain.

Special to the True Delta.

MEMPHIS, April 7—Gen. Pillow arrived here today. He reports no fighting on the Tennessee line, except between the enemy's gunboats and our batteries erected on shore to intercept the boats in their descent.

He reports on the authority of Gen. Beauregard that the victory is complete.

From four to five thousand of the enemy have been taken, and prisoners are still being brought in.

From twenty thousand to twenty-five thousand stand of arms, one hundred pieces of cannon, all the enemy's stores and camp equipage have been captured.

It is generally supposed that the enemy's loss will amount to fifteen thousand and our loss to about four thousand.

Our forces and the wounded occupy the enemy's camp.

Lieut. Col. Patton, of Arkansas; Crews and Williams, of Memphis, and Col. Brown, of Mississippi, are reported killed, and many other officers wounded, but not fatally.

All quit at Island No. 10.

BATTLE FIELD, Sunday Night, April 6.—The day is ours. We have won a great and glorious victory, driving the enemy to his boats, and across the river.

The gunboats of the enemy played on our army a terrific fire, in the hope of driving us back, but were silenced by our batteries.

Our army bivouacked in the enemy's camp, and on the battle ground.

CORINTH, April 7.—Our victory, so far, is complete. The enemy was routed on both wings by Johnston and Bragg.

The enemy crossed the river this morning, but were repulsed.

Our loss is supposed to be about fifteen hundred killed and wounded, and that of the enemy three times that number.

Skirmishing still continues, and another conflict is anticipated to day.

Gen. Johnston's remains are to be sent to New Orleans, this evening, under an escort. His staff accompanies them, including Col. Preston and Maj Hayden, [on their way to Texas, we presume.—*Eds. Tel.*]

Our army is in high spirits, and confident of final success. It was the hardest fought battle ever fought on this continent.

The loss of arms and equipments by the enemy is immense. They lost all the guns in the several batteries engaged.

BATTLE FIELD, April 7, 10 A. M.—The night closed upon us yesterday before we could secure the full fruits of our victory, allowing a portion of the enemy to gain their river works and gunboats, from which they threw shells all night. The Confederates slept in the enemy's encampment. During the night, the enemy's transports went down the river to Crump's Landing, and brought up a new division of 7000 men.

This morning they appeared with reinforcements, and vigorously attacked our whole line. The firing was returned with spirit, and for an hour the cannonading and musketry were terrific. But the enemy have been repulsed all along the line, and are now falling back towards the river.

2 P. M.—The enemy appear to have been reinforced about noon, perhaps by Buell, and have vigorously renewed the attack, fighting along the whole line with varied fortune.

It is impossible to predict what the result of the battle will be, as both armies are fighting desperately, though it is believed that the Confederates will triumph.

Beauregard has commanded since Johnston's death, yesterday afternoon, assisted by Bragg, Polk, Hardee, and others. Bragg leads the attacking forces. H P.

LATER.

BY TELEGRAPH TO NEW IBERIA.

NEW ORLEANS, Tuesday, April 8th, 6 P. M.

Fight still going on. Result uncertain.

RICHMOND, April 5.—Nothing important in Congress to-day.

The contested election in the Third District of Arkansas occupied the House two days. The subject was re-committed to-day for further testimony. It is thereby postponed to the next session.

BAY ST. LOUIS, April 5.—About 2000 of the enemy landed yesterday at Pass Christian, and attacked our camp there.

Several shots were exchanged, but nobody hurt on our side.

Our troops retired in good order.

The enemy burned our tents and everything in the camp.

Several houses have been struck by the shells of the enemy's gunboats.

A launch, with one hundred men, came in the Bay of St. Louis and captured a schooner and cut the telegraph cable.

RICHMOND, April 4.—A letter to the Richmond Examiner says Col. Ashby was engaged fighting the enemy all day Wednesday, in Shenandoah county, first in the street of Woodstock, then in Edinburg.

We lost seven men. The enemy are reported to be advancing.

NORFOLK, April 4.—The steamship Jura arrived at Portland, with 20 days later intelligence from Europe.

Lincoln's emancipation message has been received in England.

The London Times denounces it as having destroyed all prospect of putting an end to the war.

Russell is praising the constancy of the Southern troops, and says the Northern troops are weary of the war, and clamorous for furloughs.

The Tangier prisoners have been transferred to the ship Harvest Home, bound for Boston.

France is sending more troops to Mexico.

Cotton has advanced from ⅛ to ¼. Stock 400,000.

Austria is strengthening the military posts on the Venitian frontier.

Northern dates to Tuesday have been received here.

The captured steamer Magnolia had arrived at New York on Monday, with cotton.

The Herald says the Virginia will be conquered without much bloodshed.

The New York stocks are languishing. Cotton slightly declined; some sales reported at 25 cents for Middling.

Gen Curtis, in Arkansas, has issued a special order of emancipation of three slaves, on account of their being employed in the rebel service.

The American, of Wednesday, says next month will be the end of active fighting—afterwards, there will be nothing to do but to restore order.

It is reported that the Federals captured Union City, Tenn., killing several Confederates, taking a large number of prisoners, 250 horses and a large quantity of stores.

LATER FROM NEW MEXICO.

MOVEMENTS OF SIBLEY'S ARMY.

Various Rumors, Etc.

We have the Mesilla (Arizona) Times of the 27th of March, from which we take the following intelligence:

The night after the battle of Valverde, Maj. Donnelson, of the Federal regular army, left Fort Craig with two companies of dragoons, for the purpose of destroying the stores in advance of our army.

The Governor of the Territory was in Fort Craig during the battle, and left that night for the purpose of rallying the militia of the Territory.

Two days after the battle, Lieut. Col. McNeill pushed on to the town of Soccorro, and took 250 militia prisoners, Col. Pino, of the N. M. volunteers, and several regimental staff officers, besides capturing a considerable quantity of flour, and 214 stand of arms. Capt. Barientos, of the volunteers, was taken prisoner two days after the fight.

On the 28th, Maj. Pyron, with a command of 500 men, with two pieces of artillery, started up the country to take Albuquerque.

The hospital of the Confederate Army of New Mexico, has been established at Soccora, thirty miles above Fort Craig.

Maj. Bagby has been promoted Lieut. Col., 3d Reg. Vice Col. Sutton, deceased. Capt. P. Jordan, Co. A, 3d Reg., has been promoted Major, Vice Maj. Bagby, promoted. Cpat. Shropshire, Co. A, 2d Regiment, promoted Major, Vice Maj. Lockridge, deceased.

The 1st regiment has been dismounted, and will hereafter serve as Infantry.

The enemy have extended their line from Fort Craig to the vicinity of Soccoro.

It has been reported here by Mexicans from above, that Albuquerque was taken by Major Pyron, with a loss of ten men, capturing four companies of regular.

The Mexicans report many desertions among the New Mexicans in the Federal army, and that they are perfectly disheartened by their defeat. They also report that at Fort Craig the first detail of volunteers sent out to bury the dead at Val Verde, deserted. The second detachment did the same; and the third time they sent out a detail of regulors with the volunteers, to watch them, who deserted *en masse*.

It has been likewise reported, by Mexicans, that Ft. Craig has been burned; and, also, that they were filling all the quarters with wood for that purpose. A thousand reports are in circulation, but few reliable, as communication is dangerous and irregular, and will continue to be so as long as the Federal garrison remain in possession of Fort Craig.

Our brave little army are in upper New Mexico, and will give a good account of themselves. We must be content for some time, without regular bulletins of their successes. But "bide a wee," and the capture of New Mexico will surely and certainly become a matter of record.

The Times says:

The Apaches of the Copper Mine tribe have sent in two delegations to Pino Alto lately begging a peace. They had agreed to send couriers to the Chirrichua and other tribes, and a general council was to be held in fifteen days for the purpose of making a general peace. On the morning of the 19th inst., the Apaches stole 15 head of stock near the ranch of Tortugas. This was done by the Mezcaleros, who have also committed many depredations lately in this and the El Passo Valley. The Navajoes are reported to be in numbers 20 or 30 miles back of Pino Alto, having been driven from their usual haunts by the New Mexicans.

The following additional particulars of the battle of Val Verde we also take from the Times:

The day was fiercely contested throughout, and until the latter part of the day, the enemy had gained some advantages. Firing had ceased upon both sides for over an hour, when the Federal General, deeming our forces routed, crossed the river in force and with his battery, to complete his victory, when the gallant charge was made which crowned our arms with success. In the terrible retreat of the enemy across the Rio Grande, many sank dead and wounded beneath its turbid and bloody waters, to raise no more forever! The current was strong, and the channel narrow, consequently to be wounded was but to meet death.

The loss of the enemy has not been accurately ascertained; but the killed and wounded must have been over five hundred. It was impossible to ascertain how many of the Federals perished in the river.

Col. Kit Carson's Regiment of New Mexican volunteers were covering the retreat, when a shell was thrown into their ranks, killing and wounding some twenty, when they became panic stricken and fled to the mountains.

The regulars fought with great bravery; and before the action both officers and men were sanguine of success.

The retreat across the river exhibited a perfect Leesburg rout; but the regulars of the enemy, formed upon the opposite bank, under a galling fire, and retreated to the Fort in the perfect order of a dress parade. The victory, though achieved gloriously over double our numbers, was dearly won; we have to mourn the loss of 46 heroes, and have 115 wounded

Lieut. Col. Sutton, of the 3rd Regiment, was mortally wounded in the charge, and died soon after the battle.

Major Lockridge was killed in the charge when the battery was taken, falling at the head of his column, and at the foot of a gun, but lived long enough to see victory crown our arms. His last words were, "NEVER MIND ME; GO ON BOYS!" In skill and bravery he was surpassed by none. In his death the Confederacy has sustained a heavy loss: and his name will fill a bright page in our country's history. Capt. Van Hovel, of the 2d Regiment, was also killed. He was a German, an old soldier, and a survivor of many campaigns.

Capt. Lang, commanding B company of Lanciers, of the 2d regiment, was dangerously wounded, and at last accounts was not expected to survive.

Lieut. Hubert, of Capt. Shropshire's company, (Co. A) 2d regiment, was killed. Maj. Raggle was slightly wounded. Lieut. Bass, of the 2d regiment was severely wounded, having both arms broken, one of which has been amputated. Lieut. Cartwright, Co. A, 1st regiment, was slightly wounded. Lieut. McCormick, of Capt. Crossan's company, 1st regiment, was mortally wounded, and has died since the engagement.

Capt. Lang's Company of Lanciers, of the 2d regiment, were severely cut up. Report says they had 8 killed, and 15 wounded. Capt. Tee's Company of Artillery covered themselves with glory, and did most effectual service. They had eight killed and wounded, and several horses killed. Major Pyron and command distinguished themselves throughout the action. But the same bravery pertained to the whole army.

The 2d Regiment (Col. Green's) sustained the heaviest loss, there being some twenty killed. In Captain Walker's company, Col. Baylor's regiment, one killed (Ed. Champion), John Cleghorn badly wounded, and two others slightly. In Capt. Coopwood's Spy Company, there were two killed.

In Maj. Pyron's Co., same regiment, Ryman was killed, Brown severely wounded, and two others slightly.

In Co. E, same regiment, (Capt. Stafford's Co.) Jas. Maloney and S. H. Nichols, slightly wounded.

The Federal force engaged was 5,000 men, 1,300 of whom were regulars, 200 Pike's Peak volunteers, and the remainder New Mexican volunteers and militia, under command of Brig. Gen. Canby. A reserve was left in Fort Craig of some 1,200 or 1,500 men under command of Brig. Gen. Hovey. The Confederate force engaged, including reserves and details, was not quite 2,300 men.

The two companies of volunteers from Pike's Peak, fought with unparalled desperation. One company was literally cut to pieces. It went into the action ninety-three strong and came out with only thirteen men.

About two hundred and fifty stand of small arms were taken. Numbers of the New Mexican volunteers were coming into camp and delivering up their arms. Courtesies were exchanged between the lines under flags of truce. We took six pieces of artillery—three six pounders, two twelve pounders, and one mountain howitzer—all unspiked and in good condition. A number of artillery horses were also taken, but we had two hundred horses killed in the action

The Federals have besides their force in Craig, which is a strong natural position, well fortified and almost impregnable, a considerable body of militia and volunteers elsewhere in the Territory, and five companies of regulars—one at Fort Union, two at Albuquerque, one at Fort Garland, and one at Santa Fe. This battle, however, is generally considered in this valley to have decisively ended military operations in New Mexico. The remaining force can make no considerable stand against our arms, and the garrison of Fort Craig will soon be compelled to capitulate for want of supplies.

LATEST FROM THE RIO GRANDE.

We have the Flag of the 3d, from which we extract the following intelligence:

Mr. Isidro Vela, Chief Justice of Zapata county, has written a letter to Gov. Vidaurri, in which he authorizes the Mexican authorities to cross the Rio Grande into Texas, after the fugitive Rojos. Considering that *vela* in Spanish means candle, we think Don Isidro is about the brightest one we have in Texas. If the Mexican authorities act on the Zapata county invitation, of which we have not the slightest apprehension, as Gov. Vidaurri is not only an intelligent man but a professed friend of ours, the chances are that they will have to take the Texas officer back with them.

From the adjoining States of Tamaulipas and Nuevo Leon, we learn that large and well appointed forces are still being sent into Tamaulipas for the pacification of the State, and for the purpose of meeting the European invasion should the negotiation at Orizaba not result in peace.

Several thousand troops from Durango and Chihuahua are now en route for Monterey to be used by Vidaurri in repelling the foreign invasion. Most of these forces are to be stationed in Matamoras and Tampico, so soon as the State of Tamaulipas is pacified. Gen. Comonfort will soon have a force of 6,000 or 8,000 troops under his command in Tamaulipas.

By private advices we learn that Gov. Serna has evacuated Victoria, the capital of Tamaulipas, and is now moving towards Tula. He attempted to fortify Victoria, to hold it; but Comonfort's forces were too strong, and he had to retreat. There is a report in circulation that Serna and Aramberri, of Coahuila, are working together, to produce a revolution in Nuevo, which will cause Vidaurri to recall his army from Tamaulipas to pacify his own State.

A disturbance occurred among the soldiers at Tampico, on the 6th of March, which was promptly suppressed by Gen. Tapia, and the ringleaders were caught and sent to serve in the army in distant parts of the Republic. Gen. Tapia recommends that the discontented leaders in the State, who may be caught creating disturbances, be sent away on the same principle, to remove them from their sphere of mischievous influence.

Col. Luckett returned to Brownsville on Tuesday from Hidalgo, whither he went last week to investigate the complaints made by the Mexican authorities that Caravajal was organizing a party in Texas to invade the State of Tamaulipas. He visited the camp of Caravajal near Hidalgo, and found about two hundred destitute refugees, unarmed, and feeding on beef and wild roots. They had no apparent organization, and looked more like runaways than revolutionists. Col. Luckett next visited Reynosa, where he was very politely received by the authorities, who very frankly stated their complaints, and pointed to Caravajal's camp.

Col. Luckett plainly stated the case that those men were unarmed, almost unclad, and without provisions—that they had been disarmed by his order, and that their guns were now in the custody of our militia authorities; and further that a guard was kept along the river to see that no harm was done. The authorities of Reynosa professed to be well satisfied, as they themselves could suggest nothing further that could be done to ensure peace. We believe we are justified in saying that the apprehensions which has existed of a collision between our authorities and those of Matamoros are entirely groundless, and that nothing at present disturbs the relations of peace between the two people. Our hands are full, and so are these of Mexico, with the wars which we have on hand.

The intimation by Gov. Lubcock, that he intended to draft troops if he could not obtain 15 regiments, is having the effect to weed out some of the dissatisfied spirits who have continued in Texas up to the present time, declaring themselves to be neutrals. Several of these hermaphrodites have passed into Mexico, and now bed with the nondescript representative of the universal Yankee nation in Matamoros. We congratulate the State on the happy riddance, and caution the Mexicans that a hypocrite in one country is a knave in all.

ITEMS OF INTEREST.

The New York Herald says: In the event of the passage of the bill agreed upon by the Territorial Committee in both branches of Congress to reduce the rebel districts, as far as they are conquered, to the condition of Territories, and put them through a rudimental course of Government, there will be a host of aspirants for the Gubernatorial chairs of the different Territories. The most prominent candidates now talked of are: For Governor of the Territory of South Carolina, Charles Sumner; Mississippi, John P. Hale; Texas, Henry Wilson; Louisiana, Wm. P. Fessenden; Georgia, John Sherman; Florida, Henry L. Dawes; Alabama, Martin F. Conway; Arkansas, Jim Lane; North Carolina, Roscoe Conkling; Tennessee, Benj. F. Wade; Virginia, Owen Lovejoy; Ship Island, John B. Alley, and Tortugas, John Hickman.

First catch your fish!

General Bragg is an officer not to be misunderstood. Here is a general order issued by his command from Bethel:

BETHEL, Tenn., March 16th, 1862.

With a degree of mortification and humiliation he has never before felt, the Major General commanding has to denounce acts of pillage, plunder and destruction of the private property of our own citizens by a portion of the troops of this command, which brings disgrace upon our cause. Men capable of such acts may swell our numbers, but will never add strength to our armies. They would do us less harm by serving in the ranks of the enemy, and if not prepared to abandon the vicious habits they have unfortunately contracted, had better lay down their arms and retire. Gallant men, not thus demoralized, stand ready to use them, and will do so with that firm reliance on an over-ruling Providence which a consciousness of right can alone give. The first step towards achieving success is to deserve it.

Commanders of all grades will be held responsible for the suppression of this great crime. Full compensation will, in all instances, be made from the pay of the offenders, and where this fails in its effect, summary punishment will be inflicted. The General will not hesitate to order the death penalty where it may be necessary, and will approve its execution by subordinates where milder measures fail.

By command of Major-General BRAGG.

The following is from the correspondence of the Cincinnati Gazette:

Clarksville is, next to Nashville, the most important point in the Western half of Northern Tennessee. A pleasant little city of five or six thousand inhabitants, with steamboating up to Nashville and down to Paducah, and railroad connections to Louisville and Memphis, with a larger shipping trade than Nashville, beautifully located on the rolling bluff of the Cumberland, with flourishing business houses, elegant private residences, full academies and female seminaries, tasteful churches, and the seat of not a little wealth and social refinement—so the rebellion found Clarksville.

It leaves her with trade destroyed, many of her business houses bankrupt, her costly bridges burnt, preventing railroad connection with either Louisville or Memphis, some of her best families exiles within the fast receding boundaries of the Southern Confederacy, a regiment and a half of her sons prisoners of war in the North, a victorious General's headquarters established in the residence of one of her absent traitors, sentries at every corner, an armed guard patrolling the streets, encampments of loyal soldiers around her treason-built forts, the cause of which they had given themselves, and forced to associate with and depend for the very necessaries of life upon the North they have been so industriously reviling.

Such are the rights secession has brought to Clarksville; and still the people pray the end may not be yet.

[It is rather singular that all this prosperity should depart with "Secessia!"]

We have all been curious to know the condition and feeling of the people in the rebel States. Here is a piece just cut of rebeldom, and still palpitating with its old life-blood. The people may eventually return to their allegiance, and become good Union men again; but just now they take particular pride in informing us that there are but six men in the whole city. They submit quietly to a force they know it would be madness to resist; but they are frank enough to make no secret of the fact, that all their hopes and sympathies are with rebellion, and that for us their best wish is that we may get soundly beaten on every field where we meet the Southern armies.

Strange as it may seem to those who, flushed with our recent successes, predict that a month will end the war, these people seem to believe in the ultimate success of their cause. Fort Henry they talk of as an affair hardly worth mentioning; and they insist that Fort Donelson wasn't so big a thing, after all. The gunboats were beaten, they say; the land forces were driven off on Thursday and Friday, and on Saturday forenoon they nearly made a Bull Run stampede of it for us; and, in short, but for the cowardice of Buckner, and the "excessive caution" (with due emphasis on "caution") of Floyd, Fort Donelson, they maintain, might still be theirs.

They cherish a very wholesome respect for our Mississippi fleet, (which a captured letter very mildly calls "the infernal hell-born contraptions known as Yankee gunboats,") but they insist that while "the Federals are dangerous on the river, we can whip 'em anywhere easy, on land."

Bells are now called for in all parts of the Confederacy for cannon. The Vicksburg Whig gives the composition of both bells and brass cannon:

For large bells there are three parts of copper and one of tin. A smooth or rifled six-pound bronze gun weighs 884 pounds, and is made of nine parts of copper and one of tin, or of 796 pounds of copper and 88 pounds of tin. Two hundred and twenty pounds of bell metal, by adding copper, which is cheap and abundant, will make a six-pound cannon; and in proportion for larger quantities.

Captain Morgan was returning alone toward Murfreesboro, and encountering a picket of six men, captured them and their arms. This is said to have been accomplished in this manner. He discovered a picket in a house, and, having on a Federal uniform, or, perhaps, overcoat, assumed a bold front and the confident air of a Federal officer, rode up to the picket and rebuking the officer in command for not attending properly to his duty, ordered him to give up his arms, which he did. He then directed him, under penalty of death, to call out the men one by one and surrender their arms, which was done, and all surrendered.

A story is told of a daring, reckless Secessionist, named Shields, who, when Kossuth Bull Nelson was in the State House square, at Nashville, attending the hoisting of the polluted stars and stripes, rode up to him and asked if he intended to afford protection to the women and children? Nelson replied that he should not answer that question. "If you do not," said Shields, drawing a pistol, "I shall blow your brains out on the spot!" "Certainly," replied Nelson, quaking with fear, "I intend to afford protection to the women, of course."

Some twenty ladies of Statesville, N. C., proceeded in a body to the railroad depot of the town, a few days ago, and with hatchets and hammer destroyed five or six barrels of whiskey and poured the liquid poison upon the ground; a fitting libation (says the Iredell Express) to the devil and his imps from the hands of patriotic women, whose mission, pending the war, is to "go about doing good."

We take the following from the Mobile Tribune:

THE GOVERNOR ON THE WHISKEY DISTILLERIES.—The Governor of Alabama has ordered that every distillery throughout the State for the distillation of ardent spirits shall be discontinued by the first day of April next.

Colonels of Regiments, Lieut. Colonels and Majors of Battalions, and commanding officers of camps, subject to the orders of the Governor, having good reason to believe that there has been any violation of this order, or upon the information of any proper person to that effect, is directed immediately to order out all, or such portion of his command as he may deem necessary, and without delay take possession of the still, all the apparatus and liquor, and transport the same to the court house of the county, where it shall be subject to his order for munitions of war and hospital supplies.

The order also declares that no ardent spirits shall be sold after the first day of April next within ten miles of any military camp in the State, established by the Confederate or State Executives, except upon the written prescription of a licensed physician, and any officer having good reason to believe that there has been any violation of this clause, or upon the information on oath of any reliable person to that effect, will immediately take possession of all the liquors, pack the same, and transport it to the nearest court house, where it shall be subject to the order of the Governor and commander-in-chief.

GEN. HUMPHREY MARSHALL.—Frequent inquires are made of the position now occupied by this vigilant and fortunate commander. We have sought the papers in vain to satisfy curosity. The last we heard of him was when he retired from a victorious field, in which with our ill clad, ill fed, ill armed handful of of men, he beat back a largely superior force, with heavy loss to the enemy. It is thought he went into quarters near Pound Gap, or between that point and Abirgdon, Va.

A gentleman assured us last evening that he had in June last received a long letter from Gen. Marshall in answer to one of his own (inviting the General, not ten [illegible] the service, to a brigadiership in south-western Missouri, but which he declined,) which was quite prophetic. Gen. Marshall sketched out the policy and course the Federals have since pursued, availing themselves of the Tennesse and Cumberland rivers. His topographical knowledge and quick military perception for the principal strategic points. It is regretted that they were not deemed advisable to be strengthened. A different tale might now be told. His counsel was not duly considered. We hope to see him reinforced, furnished with ample supplies, and early again in the field.—*Avalanche*.

HOW IT IS.—Can any one tell how it is men who absolutely cannot pay small debts can always find plenty of money to buy liquor and treat when happening among their friends? Can any one tell how young men who dodge their washerwomen and are always behind with their landlords, can play at billiards day and night, and are always ready for a game of "bluff" or "seven up." Can any one tell how men live and support their families who have no income and do not work, and why others, who are industriously and constantly employed, half starve? Can any one tell how it is that a man who is too poor to pay for a newspaper is able to pay fifteen cents a drink for liquor five or six times a day, and fifteen or twenty cents a day for cigars? Can any one tell how these things are done?—*Lynchburg Republican*.

From the Knoxville Register

A private dispatch received in this city gives a rumor current at Chattanooga, that Capt. John H. Morgan, who is acquiring distinction as "the Marion of the Revolution," has, within a few days past, turned up near Bowling Green, as the hero of another brilliant exploit. He is said to have burned a railroad bridge and several cars, captured 40 prisoners, including ten officers, besides one Yankee telegraph operator, the United States mail, and $50,000 in gold. If this is correct, Capt. Morgan's name will soon be such a terror to the Yankees, that the bare mention of it will be sufficient to scare a regiment out of a fortnight's sleep. We want a hundred Morgan's, with guerrilla squadrons in the field. The enemy must be harrassed in front and rear and on every side, wherever his infamous foot pollutes the soil of a Southern State. With a few such squadrons as Morgan's hovering as avenging spirits on his track, the vaunting foe will be confounded, "the current of his enterprises of great pith and moment will turn awry and lose the name of action." Who will contest the palm of this species of warfare with Capt. Morgan? Cannot East Tennessee produce a champion?

The Berlin Punch or Kladderadatsch, brings out his last number with a Christmas tree, richly illuminated and hung with presents for the surrounding potentates of Europe, in children's frocks. Master France is enjoying his little drum, with a "deficit" of eight hundred and twenty-nine millions, Master Yankee, two hundred and twenty-four millions of deficit, Master Austria one hundred and forty-six millions, Master Victor one hundred and fifty-nine millions scudi, and so on; while Master Prussia, with his two big boxes of cavalry and infantry, no deficit, is weeping bitterly, and wiping his eyes with his knuckles, crying, "I want to have a deficit, too!"

From the Columbus Sun.

Judging from all that we have seen and heard, there is little or no doubt that President Davis has, or will soon make, another requisition upon Gov. Brown for another quota of troops from Georgia, and that his Excellency will issue his proclamation to that effect.

It is certain that the Confederacy has not a sufficient number of men yet in the field to repel the myriads of Northern vandals pressing us upon all sides; and we hope the authorities will take such steps as will, if necessary, bring every able-bodied man into the field at an early day. The enemy has had the advantage in point of overwhelming numbers, and though we may not expect to equal them man for man, we can bring such a number into the field as will more than counter-vail their numerical superiority.

The Culpepper, Va., correspondent of the Columbus Enquirer, relates the following anecdote of General Toombs:

Quite an amusing scene occurred yesterday, near Warrenton. Gen. Toombs ordered the "fatigue" to "tote" rails and fill up a bad place in the road, when one soldier said that he could not tote a rail—whereupon the General dismounted and told the fellow if he would hold his horse he would do it. The man held the horse, and the General shouldered the rail and carried it to and threw it across the hole, which he had ordered filled. The soldier was a large, strapping fellow, and the rebuke the General gave him caused peal after peal of laughter, while the man looked as if he would have liked to have been in the hole, covered from sight by the rails he "could not tote."

On the 18th ult., the Governor and Executive Council of South Carolina adopted the following resolution:

Resolved, That the editors and owners of newspapers in this State be informed, that if any of their employees shall fall under the conscription, the Adjutant and Inspector General will be instructed to withhold from Confederate service such of said conscripts as the editor or owner of such newspapers shall declare by affidavit to be absolutely necessary to carry on their respective establishments, and that the work cannot be done by workmen within their command otherwise exempt.

Tri-Weekly Telegraph.

HOUSTON, TEXAS.

E. H. CUSHING, Editor and Proprietor.

MONDAY.....APRIL 14, 1862

THE GLORIOUS VICTORY.

We send forth to-day glorious tidings to the people. The great tide has turned. Our arms are again triumphant. We have routed the victorious hosts of Buell in a pitched battle of two days duration, closing each day triumphantly. Ten thousand of the enemy are taken prisoners. Largely over a hundred of their cannon have been captured, and many thousand of their soldiers slain. Our army has ere this been re-enforced by Van Dorn, and we may expect to hear of the victory being followed up and Tennessee relieved of the invader's columns. Glory to God for the victory.

NOTICE.—We have hitherto declined to receive shinplasters or tickets in payment of any dues to this office. We continue to refuse them under any and all circumstances. When sent from the country they are returned to the sender. Now that the stuff is wearing out, being counterfeited, and generally growing more and more worthless every day, many people wish they had pursued our plan of having nothing to do with them. As for counterfeits, it is almost impossible to detect them. The best way is to have nothing whatever

THE MONEY MATTER.

The complaints of both soldiers and people, of the failure of the Government to meet its obligations to them, have induced us to make some inquiry relative to the matter. The first thing to learn, is how the money gets here.

There are separate departments for which appropriations are made, and through which they are expended. For instance, guns are bought by Ordinance officers, with funds of the Ordinance Department. Provisions are bought by the Commissary, with funds of the Commissary Department. Troops are paid and transported by the Quartermaster's Department, &c. When the Quartermaster of any post wants money, he makes his estimates and sends them to the Division Quartermaster. He supervises and puts together all the estimates for his Military District into one estimate for the Quartermaster General at Richmond. In his office, they are again examined, and if approved, a request is made on the Treasury Department to forward the money. The money is then sent to New Orleans, and a draft for it is sent here. This draft is then endorsed and placed in the hands of a messenger to go and draw the money. This is what in common parlance is called the "circumlocution of red tape."

We are in receipt of information through our private correspondence in Richmond that the total amount of estimates that have been requested by the Quartermaster General's office in Richmond on the Treasury for the Texas military districts, including $850,000 for Sibley's brigade, from 1st Oct. to 22d of March has been $7,009,202,32.

We learn from official quarters here that for one considerable requisition for the Quartermaster of this district, which our correspondent refers to us, no draft has ever been received here. We also learn that estimates amounting to near two millions of dollars made in January, do not all appear to have been requested by the Quartermaster General from the Trea-

known. We are, however,
...as known to be on the way
is now no doubt that with
money will be received
to discharge most of
the Department here.
...ready received would have
...it for the fact that the exi-
...ve required that Quarter-
...iverted from the purpose
It has been necessary to
...odies of troops on unex-
...arge amounts on engineer-
...d not have been fore een.
..., the Quartermaster Gen-
...s revised estimates without
...xas to Richmond, and back
...when it is traveled through
...t is almost a wonder that
...assed. Besides this, money
...haps the wants of Texas
...ed. Somehow or other it
...d, as we have said before
...all is anywhere here. We
...ple to be patient. It will
...

GEN. A. SIDNEY JOHNSTON.

Another of the hero sons of Texas has been sarificed upon the altar of patriotism. Another has been added to the glorious list of Texians who have gained victory and death for the cause of Liberty. Lubbock and McLeod upon beds of sickness—Terry, McCulloch and Sidney Johnston upon the field of battle, though we shall see them no more on earth, will yet forever shine the brightest rays of the lustre which the Lone Star sheds upon the world. All honor to their memory!

SIDNEY JOHNSTON, though a native of Kentucky, has for six and twenty years claimed Texas as his home. The declaration of Southern Independence found him in Federal service on the Pacific coast. He had choice of three courses which he might pursue. First, he was offered the Command-in-chief of the Federal army. To this he was entitled, being second only to Gen. Scott in the old army. This he declined. He then had the privilege to remain in his command on the Pacific coast, far removed from the strife. This also he rejected. The third course was to resign and make the best of his way home. This he did on the very day he heard of the secession of Texas from the old Union.

But to get from California to Texas was no easy matter; and vessels were sent expressly to intercept his passage by sea. Of this he was apprised, and to escape the toils set for his capture, he undertook, with a party of friends, the overland route of 2,000 miles over a country infested with savages. The trip was both hazardous and difficult. It was, however, accomplished, and on the 26th of August, Gen. Johnston reached this city—his old home. Here he spent a day or two recruiting strength, and visiting his old friends. He seemed especially anxious that the causes of his long detention should be known to the people. He left here on the 28th for Richmond, where he was welcomed with open arms by the President, and at once commissioned a General in the regular army and assigned to duty in the Western Department. He at once took command there, and proceeded forthwith to prepare his defences to the advancing columns of the Federal forces. Of his repeated calls for troops, and how and why he failed to stay the tide of invasion on the Tennessee border, our readers are already informed. He fell back to the southern borders of that State. The disasters of Forts Henry and Donelson; the evacuation of Bowling Green and Nashville, aroused our people and brought them rapidly to the rescue. In the short space of forty days Johnston's army was increased from about 20,000 to upwards of 80,000; and seconded by Beauregard, he moved forward to give battle to the foe.

His noble and patriotic address to his troops, we published last week. The account of the battle is in to-day's paper. How he took 6000 prisoners, 2000 arms, 100 cannons, all in one day, and thus gloriously retrieved the fame which in some minds he had lost by the evacuation of Nashville, appears in those columns. But the fatal bullet struck him in the moment of victory, and the plaudits of a grateful people were wafted over the dead body of the hero who had given his life to save them. Let us hope that at least his departing spirit was conscious of the victory he had gained.

Gen. Johnston was a great man. Gen. Scott and President Davis, both regarded him as the first military man of America, and they were right. His retreat through Tennessee was one of the most masterly movements on the page of history. His subsequent reorganization in North Alabama and Mississippi. His rapid concentration of forces on the course of the enemy's advance; his meeting him, and defeating him in a pitched battle of great magnitude, all give evidence of his military genius. In his death the Confederacy has lost a tower of strength. Other Generals, and those of great ability we have, but as we believe, none like our Johnston. Let us mourn his loss and avenge his death!

The telegraph reports his remains en route for New Orleans. We presume they will be brought to Texas. Let our people be prepared to receive them and pay them the honors due a brave and noble soldier.

...emory of the Brave
...Sidney Johnston.

...Johnston fell at the head
...ng a charge against the
...s victory of Shiloh.
...f the army, and Secreta-
...ie, he was for 25 years a
...
...nud working at the plow
...the adjoining county of
...etary of War, now Presi-
...
...ing well the greatness,
...ion of his soul, gave him
...our Generals in the field.
...ts conspired to cloud his
...dy regained his place in
...untry, and all its hopes
...d his noble army on the
Those hopes have been
...ry is saved, but Johnston
...eath of the patriot, in the
...his country's independ-
...ed—for his country. *He*
...of young children, who,
...eir all.
...n the charity of the world;
..., among whom he was so
...ong whom he desired his
...heir abundance secure a
...as the best tribute to the
...ommander, whose heart's
...lorth has ascended a pro-
...favor of heaven on our

...be! Let the people come
...following form of subscrip-
...circulate it can procure

...pay the amounts annexed
...ted with W. J. Hutchins,
...to be invested to secure a
...ly of Gen. Johnston."
... and T. W. House have
...mmittee to secure sub-
...is hoped that the people
...the call, and that commit-
...ted in every county in the
...s for the purpose.
...office for that purpose will
...d to the Treasurer.

...other evening at Academy
...Dwyer's Company of Mili-
...e agreeably surprised to
...had become in the various
...r in so short a time. Capt.
..., and besides is over the
...empts men from military
...much interest in the thor-
...of the State troops, that he
...ith his usual spirit, made
...es, and will soon have a
...red to march with regular
...e State. His devotion to
...much commended. We
...e but one other comp ny.
...e must say that we never
...ter than that has under
...ructions. We believe all
...ll. The Colonel of the 1st
...any drills twice a week,
...week besides. Let this
...v months, and the Harris
...rank at the head of the

...receiving orders for Har-
...s copy to be had, so far as
...The only military work
...city is Gilham's Manual
...ly a few copies of them,
...of H. Sampson.

...s us that 37 of his com-
...ty. We gave the county
...t.

...ly assured that squads or
...gone on to take a hand in
...nce refused, unless they
...y have sought admission
...ol. Wharton has refused
...ow in excellent health.

...ng house and two small
...HENRY F. PERKINS.

BY SPECIAL EXPRESS!

ONE DAY LATER.

Second Days Fighting on the Tennessee River

OUR LOSS HEAVY.

More of the Great Victory.

Enemy Driven Across the River.

Ten Thousand Prisoners and Eighteen Batteries Captured.

ETC., ETC., ETC.

Our special expressman, Capt. Turley, arrived yesterday (Sunday) evening, at 6 o'clock, with one day later news, embracing the glorious intelligence of a complete victory over the enemy near Corinth, and the capturing of ten thousand prisoners and 18 batteries of artillery on the 7th. This was the second battle. Our news is taken from the Delta of the 9th, and is mostly special dispatches to that paper:

MEMPHIS, April 8, 1862.

A dispatch received here last night from the battle field on 7th, at 2 P. M., states that the enemy was reinforced by a division of seven thousand strong from below, and engaged us again in the morning at sunrise.

A desperate battle followed. All the morning our center and left were hotly engaged.

The enemy was driven back, but renewed the attack with great vigor with fresh troops, consisting probably of Buell's column.

The battle was raging and the fire was terrible.

Our loss was heavy. Gens. Bowen and Clark were wounded, and Gen. Cheatham injured. Col. Blythe, of Mississippi, killed, and Sanford's battery captured except one gun.

Our troops, up to last accounts, were behaving nobly.

A shell exploded inside of Gen. Hindman's horse. The General was seriously injured.

MEMPHIS, April 8, 1862.—A dispatch just received states that the Confederate victory is complete.

Yesterday was a more glorious day than Sunday.

We killed, captured and wounded from 10,000 to 20,000 of the Federals.

We drove the enemy across the river.

It is believed that his gunboats can not get down the river, on account of the low stage of water.

Two thousand prisoners arrived here to-day and two thousand will arrive to-morrow. There was a great loss of Confederate officers.

Capt. Bankhead says that the fight yesterday, opposite Pittsburg, was terrible. We drove the enemy across the river. Their gunboats saved them from utter destruction. We captured 18 batteries and 10,000 prisoners.

We are indebted to the courtesy of Dr. Austin for the following dispatch from his son. Capt. J. E. Austin, Captain of the Cannon Guard, Company D, 11th Louisiana Volunteers.

CORINTH, April 7.—We had a terrible and bloody fight yesterday and to day. Col. Marks, and nearly all the officers were wounded. The Eleventh cut up terribly. I am unhurt.

J. E. AUSTIN.

To Dr. W. G. Austin.

MEMPHIS, April 8.—A dispatch to the Avalanche, dated Corinth, April 8, says there was a terrible fight all day yesterday near the river.

The enemy's loss in killed, wounded and prisoners is fully 10,000.

Their rout was complete.

We captured eighteen batteries, with horses and camp equipage, and drove the enemy across the river. Their gunboats saved them.

We have been politely furnished with the following dispatch by Mr. J. R. Conway:

CORINTH, April 8, 1862.

We met the enemy yesterday and whipped them well. We slept on their field last night. I am safe and well.

C. A. CONWAY,
Serg't Twiggs Rifles, Crescent Reg't.

The following dispatch was received at the telegraph office here from the operator at Corinth.

To all offices.—The recent battle was fought in the interior, about 20 miles from Corinth. It is therefore, impossible to get answers to many of the messages sent here.

JNO. VAN HORNE.

The following dispatch has been received from Gen. Beauregard, and kindly furnished to us for the benefit of the public:

CORINTH, April 8, 1862.

We had another severe battle yesterday, and have returned to this place, which I can hold easily. The army is in good spirits.

The Louisiana troops behaved well. I am still untouched.

G. T. BEAUREGARD.

CORINTH, April 7, 1862.

We have had two days very severe fighting, and are now returning to our original position at Corinth.

[The above dispatch was sent from some point on the line of march from the battle field to Corinth, which is the nearest telegraph station.]

From the evening Delta of the 8th.

The latest intelligence from the scene of operations on the Tennessee river informs us that our army has returned to Corinth. The brilliant victory gained on Sunday last was the consummation of a strategy having for its object the defeat and demoralization of the Tennessee river expedition, and this object could be accomplished only while that expedition remained uncombined with Gen. Buell's column. A junction of the two Federal armies would have rendered the movement impracticable, and would have thrown the Confederate army on the defensive, in face of a powerful and exultant foe.

By assuming the initiative, by striking a powerful blow at Grant's army, we have crippled the enemy so greatly, that he is, doubtless, rendered incapable of taking any offensive measures. The opportune arrival of Buell, reinforcing Grant with a column of 30,000 fresh troops, saved that commander's army from total destruction, or dispersal. But the main object of the movement having been gained, our threatened communications being secured, having passed from the defensive to the offensive, we shall be enabled to strengthen our army, to concentrate our forces, to bring up Gen. Van Dorn's column, and, at a convenient season, to fall on the enemy with a preponderating force, and the prestige of victory.

From Delta, 9th

TE DEUM.—The victory of Sunday is, we understand, to be celebrated to-morrow in the various Catholic churches of the city by the chanting of the *Te Deum*. Archbishop Odin has issued instructions to that effect, and doubtless the occasion will be an imposing one.

From the Delta of the 9th.

FROM MISSOURI.—The Memphis Avalanche of yesterday, says it has heard, amid the exciting news nearer home, that a division of Price's army under Gen. McBride, had penetrated as far as Rolla (eighty miles from St. Louis) which place they burned, and completely routed the Federals stationed there. McBride's force was about 5000 strong. Also, that another detachment numbering 3000, was advancing on Springfield, with a view to capture the enemy's supplies collected there, which will doubtless be successful. Price is said to be advancing from Clarksville, and will again enter Missouri with increasing force.

Treasurer's statement of Concert conducted by Messrs. Chas. Otis and Theo Stadtler, on the evening of the 9th inst., for the relief of the families of Volunteers:

Total receipts from sale of tickets,		$596 95
" " " " books,		19 05
		$616 00
Paid for oil, candles and labor,	$32 00	
" " printing,	38 00	
" " music,	3 40	
" " tuning piano,	3 00	
" " moving piano,	4 00	$80 40
Nett,		$535 60

C. A. DARLING, Treasurer.

Received from C. A. Darling the above amount, $535 60, with bills and receipts for balance.

CHARLES S. LONGCOPE,
Treasurer Volunteer Relief Committee.

☞ See advertisement of Capt. Hargrove. The Texas Ranger has not yet appeared in Virginia. Gen. Hood wants a company in his brigade, and has sent Capt. Hargrove after them. We advise all who want service where they can gain glory to go. They must furnish their own horses and guns. Capt. H. will furnish the six-shooters. We hope he will have his company filled up at once.

☞ We have had the pleasure of meeting with our gallant young friend, Capt. I. C. Stafford, who has just returned from Arizona. He was in the battle of Valverde, at the head of his company. He is on his way to Richmond, with Col. Jno. R. Baylor, who will probably be here this evening.

LETTER FROM RICHMOND.

RICHMOND, VA., March 29th, 1862.

Dear Telegraph.—I have been told that in times of peace, my letters to you have afforded some satisfaction and information to your readers, and feel therefore, that I will not be considered a trespasser upon your columns now, in saying a word or two from the Capital of the Confederacy, when war is everywhere around us, and our horizon has recently become, to many, gloomy and beclouded.

The struggle for the next two or three months is to be an awful one, and upon the wisdom of our leaders, and the united efforts of our citizens, the question of an early termination of this war depends. How few there were either in the Federal or Confederate Governments, who looked far enough into the future, to measure the gigantic proportions of this terrible conflict, which was incident upon our separation. And how few there were, who could have imagined the perfidy, the grovelling submission, the bitterness which was so soon to characterize those with whom, thank God, we have dissolved all political and social connection forever.

Every day brings fresh evidence of the wisdom displayed by the Southern States in the step they have taken; for even the leading journals of the North are deploring the desperate condition of things in the Free States, where rights, privileges and liberty are yielded up by the citizens, and a tyranny and despotism mark the course of the Administration, "which Charles the 1st, and James 2d, in the utmost stretch of their power never durst attempt." The citizens have cried amen, to the unholy acts of the Government, and the Powers abroad are led to believe "that the Constitution of the Republic was not adequate to its own protection." The world has stood amazed at the quiet consent which the people of the North have given to the despotic sway of Mr. Lincoln and Secretary Seward, and the South should shout in exultation that she has no part or parcel with such a people, who bend the neck to the will of dictators, and look with complacency upon the frowning Bastiles which look down upon communities that once were proud of liberty. A constitution broken, disregarded and trampled under foot—honor, magnanimity, humanity, and every ennobling virtue thrown aside, like cast off garments, are the characteristics alike of the government and the governed, and the United States presents to the astonished world a people fallen in a few short months from an high estate to the very depths of degradation.

While we look with contempt and scorn upon the nation who so soon has forgotten the value of those liberties for which their fathers fought, and have proved themselves so unworthy of the boon obtained by suffering, peril and blood let us be wise, and consider how the recent evidences of their shame should affect us. If the simple *will* of Mr. Seward is *law*, if, as I have said, liberty and constitutional privileges are no more enjoyed, because Mr. Lincoln or Secretary Seward *wills* it to be so, and the people are *satisfied*, THIS WAR MAY BE WAGED AGAINST US FOR YEARS, and in its prosecution no regard will be paid to any recognized principles of civilized warfare, but cruelty and vindictiveness mark the steps of the invader wherever success shall attend his arms. The North is jubilant over its recent victories and hosannas are being sung to the fiends who have lit the incendiary torch, hurled their death dealing shells upon the defenseless and violated the chastity of Southern wives and Southern daughters.

The Federal Government will not, *cannot* stop this war and live. Upon it the present administration has planted itself, and with the facilities of creating money, with its commerce open and the acquiescence of the people in all it has hitherto done, we must expect that nothing will be left undone to subdue and subjugate us. It is the policy determined upon by the Dictator and the people uphold him in his efforts. Do not let us reckon without our host. Do not let us be too self-confident, or longer remain under the hallucination that this war will soon be over and our independence acknowledged. No matter what have been our opinions heretofore, no matter how much we may be unable to see how such an exhausting war is to be carried on by the North, no matter how we may expect England and France will be compelled to recognize us as a nation, because of the interruption to their commerce, and the necessity to them of a settlement of American affairs, let none of these considerations weigh a moment against what is every man's duty *now*. Merchandise, and occupations, and professions, and crops must all be mere *secondary* considerations, and war to the knife must be a household word, and resistance a part of every man's religion. Self-dependence must be the rock upon which Southern men and Southern soldiers plant their flag, and upon which they risk their all. The Northern hordes are upon us, the Yankee taskmasters but wait the cry of "the South has fallen," to make us worse than slaves... we have been asleep while they have rendered perfect their soldiers and inured them

to camp life, until now we...
ing taunts which come...
ginia, Kentucky, and Ten...
crated everywhere by the...
It may be that God has...
from us to learn us wisdom...
frowning Providence a...
Our reverses have roused...
old and young are flying to...
try determined to be free...
"From life without freedom...
For one day of freedom, oh...
Hark!—hark; 'tis the trum...
The death song of tyrants...
Our country is bleeding—h...
One arm that defends is w...

It is true we have outfo...
on every battle-field ma...
their slain.—True, that...
found wanting in courage...
a peace and speedily hum...
gant armies of the North...
one fails another must be...
Manassas has not proved...
points of view, for while...
from the field, and stood...
victorious, we were rende...
careless of the future by o...
The Administration of t...
the people, has been inac...
the proper time for fault-f...
man it must be evident tha...
besides many other places...
we were not in a conditio...
wanted the proper sort of...
diers with confidence. A...
"Politicians are not fit t...
appointments as have be...
continued, we might ha...
disaster, and defeat upon...
ties of the case, civilians n...
instances to office; but I t...
will no longer yield to imp...
ing placed many men in...
were not fitted. Our defe...
lected, and as the enemy...
realize the fact. If Roanc...
tended, what a check it...
Yankees: and if, after it h...
was getting ready to pene...
try, Newbern had been properly supplied with an army, and that army had been blessed with leaders, the troops that are now concentrating at Goldsboro' and Weldon might have been sent to strengthen Beauregard and Johnson.

There is much to lament on what has passed, but the battles which we have lost cannot destroy the South, and our duty now is, to lose no more, at least for want of men and proper precaution. We have been sadly deficient in our army, and as I have said before, if we would be free, every man must be willing to be a soldier, and forget all else but his country and its bleeding state. I am satisfied that my own State will send forth thousands of such men, as have already made the name of Texas terrible to the enemy, and that McCulloch and Terry, who fell at the head of their commands, and Lubbock and McLeod, and a thousand other brave Texans, who died at their posts, will yet be avenged, and that before many days have passed away.

Richmond is under martial law; and, notwithstanding the thousands of soldiers, whose tramp is heard continually in the streets, not a drunken man have I seen in the city. Oh! what a curse drunkenness has been among our officers and soldiers; and after seeing what I have seen of its effects, it is refreshing to find neither officers or soldiers permitted to stupify themselves when their country demands their health, their minds, their energies, their aid, in this, her time of need. Suspicious gentlemen are here handled without gloves, and it is neither healthy to speak or look treason in this latitude. We have all been too lenient to those who pollute our soil with their presence, and Texas, in many portions, needs purifying. There are men and women, too, in our communities, who should be banished at once from among us, for we have no place now for traitors, or those who are *not with us*. Our authorities should look to it.

There is no certainty as to when Congress will adjourn. My own impression is, they should sit continually, until something decisive takes place. The House of Representatives passed a resolution yesterday, to adjourn on the 31st. The Senate will not concur.

Yours, truly, HORACE CONE.

MERIDIAN, April 3.—Having noticed the number of volunteers for the war from the different counties, I send you the number of volunteers from this county as copied from the report of the Chief Justice of this county to the Adjutant General: Number of volunteers now in the service, 258; number of volunteers now ready for service, 100; total, 358. The largest number of votes ever polled in the county is 323. Now we challenge a better turn out from any county with the same voting population and being visited by the Indians as often. J. J. W.

ITEMS OF INTEREST.

The Federal report of the loss of men on the frigate Congress is, killed and missing, 120, out of a total of 484 men and officers on board.

The N. O. Delta atones for its strictures on Gen. Johnston's evacuation of Nashville, as follows, in an article about the battle of Shiloh:

It is profoundly sad, in contemplating this splendid triumph, to know that the able and gallant officer, the noble spirit and bright intelligence, who presided in organizing the battle, did not live to drink the music of the final shout of victory resounding from the field of glory. Like Wolf, he fell "leading his troops,"—according to the generous testimony of Gen. Beauregard—"into the thickest of the fight." Let us devoutly pray that, like Wolf, he died in the rapturous consciousness that the path of duty he trod so nobly was also the path of victory. The laurels that would have wreathed his brow must now wreathe his tomb. A nation's tears will bedew them, a nation's gratitude will keep them fresh; history will be proud to exhibit, poetry will fondly interweave them in lofty song, for all future time.

THE PENINSULA.—The grand army of the Federals seems to have been transported from the neighborhood of Washington to the Peninsula, which they have probably concluded is a shorter and easier road to Richmond than that via Manassas, which we have courteously placed at their disposal. But if the road by Manassas is bad, that by the Peninsula may not prove much better. Whether the movement is feint to cover an attack on some other point, remains to be seen. Gen. Magruder has not been asleep on his post at any rate, and at the present moment, he must be a napping. We have great confidence in this brilliant and energetic officer, and in the heroic veterans under his command.—*Richmond Dispatch.*

YORKTOWN.—Latest advices from this place represent the enemy as advancing in large force, and Gen. Magruder determined to give fight. Hampton refugees at Williamsburg and the ladies of the latter city were leaving for Richmond. A slight skirmish took place on Thursday between the advance forces of the enemy and our pickets, in which Lieut. Wray, of the Old Dominion Guard, was wounded in the hip. No other casualties reported on our side.—*Richmond Enquirer, 29th.*

THE ATTACK ON YORKTOWN.—The following is from a special despatch to the Memphis Appeal, dated Richmond, April 5th:

Under a heavy fire the enemy moved upon Yorktown this morning, from Ship Point at the mouth of York river. They attacked our entrenchments at Yorktown, the battle commencing at half past ten o'clock, and was still raging at three o'clock this afternoon. Our position is gallantly held. Gen. Magruder and staff were six miles below Yorktown at the commencement of the fight, but he has since reached his works safely, having passed within four hundred yards of the enemy, and received their fire. The cannonading was distinctly heard here.

THE DURATION OF THE WAR.—The following extract from the Richmond correspondence of the Charleston Courier gives the opinion of Gen. Lee and Secretary Benjamin on the duration of the war:

On emerging into open air again, I encountered our Commander-in-Chief. He looked the soldier and gentleman, as he undoubtedly is. Having related to him my adventures, I said: "General, are you hopeful?" "No, sir," he replied. "I am confident." "That is cheering," I observed, in the face of our disasters and defeats." "These," he said, have been the Bunker Hill victories of our enemy, and the providential mystery is how they have been so few. But the day of terrible retribution is nigh; he will be ruined; the North will be beggared and bankrupt, and the South will pass out of the ordeal respected by the nations of the earth, and with an imperishable name in history." And I am credibly informed that Mr. Benjamin said, a few days since, that the utmost duration of this war would be eight months; that in that time the North would be forced to succumb, no less to the prowess of our arms than to her own embarrassments and incapacity to prosecute a hopeless, expensive and irrepressible warfare.

NEW ADVERTISEMENTS.

PRIVATE BOARDING!

Inquire at No. 3, Perkins's Row, Main Street.
* tw3t.

NOTICE!

ALL persons who have contributed to the fund for raising 200 volunteers from Harris county, are requested to attend a meeting, to be held at the City Council room, on Monday, April 14th, at 3 o'clock, P. M., to receive the report of the treasurer.

CAVALRY
FOR VIRGINIA!!

I have a commission to raise a company of Cavalry for Hood's Texas Brigade, in Virginia. This is the only Cavalry company in the brigade.

Recruits will furnish their own horses and double-barrel shot guns. Forty cents a day will be paid for the horses. Six-shooters will be furnished to them. The men will be paid $50 bounty and $25 commutation on being mustered into the service. Men will report to me at Brenham till the 1st of May. Transportation to Virginia will be furnished.

April 12th, 1862-1t. R. W. HARGROVE.

HEADQUARTERS DEPT. OF TEXAS,
Houston, April 12, 1862.

GENERAL ORDER NO. 27.

I. Men already enlisted in the service of the Confederate States, who, without being regularly transferred or discharged by proper authority, leave their companies to join other companies, are deserters, by the 22d Article of War, and will be treated and punished as such.

II. Officers or persons enlisted in the service of the Confederate States inducing men to thus desert, will be punished to the extent of the military law bearing on such offences.

By order of
Brig. Gen. P. O. HEBERT.

GEO. R. WILSON, A. D. C. Apr 14—tf

ending June 30, 18[illegible], in the State of TEXAS, on the Routes and by the Schedules of Departures and Arrivals herein specified.

DECISIONS ANNOUNCED BY MAY 31, 1862.

[☞ BIDDERS should examine carefully the Laws and Instructions annexed, and especially the latter part of section 19.]

Route 6. (8506.)

From Galveston to Sabine City, 75 miles and back twice a week.
Leave Galveston Tuesday and Thursday at 11 a. m.
Arrive at Sabine City next days by 8 a. m.
Leave Sabine City Wednesday and Friday at 10 a. m.
Arrive at Galveston next days by 2 p. m.

Route 7. (8508.)

From Columbia, by Brazoria and Caney, to Matagorda, 50 miles and back, three times a week.
Leave Columbia Monday, Wednesday and Friday at 1 p. m. Arrive at Matagorda Tuesday, Thursday and Saturday by 3 p. m.
Leave Matagorda same days at 5 p. m. Arrive at Columbia next days by 7 p. m.

Route 8. (8511.)

From Galveston, by Wallaceville, to Liberty, 110 miles and back, three times a week, in steam boats.
Leave Galveston Tuesday, Thursday and Saturday at 3 p. m. Arrive at Liberty next days by 6 a. m.
Leave Liberty Monday, Wednesday and Friday at 3 p. m. Arrive at Galveston next days by 6 a. m.

Route 9. (8512.)

From Brenham, by Berlin, Vinegrove, Round Top and Rutersville, to La Grange, 36 miles and back, three times a week.
Leave Brenham Tuesday, Thursday and Saturday at 12 m. Arrive at La Grange by 8 p. m.
Leave La Grange Wednesday, Monday and Friday at 4 a. m. Arrive at Brenham by 12 m.

Route 10. (8512 A.)

From La Grange, by Reaganville, Cunningham, Alum Creek, Bastrop, Webberville and Hornsby, to Austin, 58 miles and back, six times a week.
Leave La Grange daily, except Sunday, at 4 a. m.
Arrive at Austin next days by 8 a. m.
Leave Austin daily, except Sunday, at 12 m. Arrive at La Grange next days by 4 p m.

Route 11. (8515.)

From Waller's Store, by San Felipe, Cat Spring, New Ulm, Industry and Fayetteville, to La Grange, 61 miles and back, twice a week.
Leave Waller's Store Tuesday and Saturday at 6 a. m.
Arrive at La Grange next days by 12 m.
Leave La Grange Wednesday and Sunday at 2 p. m
Arrive at Waller's Store next days by 6 p. m.

Route 12. (8516.)

From Cypress Top, by Rose Hill, Prairie Home, Montgomery and Goshen, to Huntsville, 59 miles and back, three times a week
Leave Cypress Top Tuesday, Thursday and Saturday at 10 a. m. Arrive at Huntsville next days by 9 a. m.
Leave Huntsville Tuesday, Thursday and Saturday at 6 p. m. Arrive at Cypress Top next days by 5 p. m.

THE TRI-WEEKLY TELEGRAPH.

VOL. XXVIII—NO. 44 HOUSTON, FRIDAY, JUNE 27, 1862 WHOLE NO. 3539

CITY ITEMS.

—— In view of the high prices now charged for the necessaries of life, we would suggest that "boots" makes a strike for higher wages, until the price of blacking is reduced, and that we dot no more i's nor cross our t's until the *raising* of blockade shall *lower* the price of ink. In the construction of buildings "Spalding's glue" should be used exclusively, so long as nails are selling at $50 per keg. "Radway's Ready Relief" should also be countenanced by the city authorities, if it will "relieve" us from prices now imposed on us. Matches—not those made in heaven—have also become very scarce and dear. To obviate this misfortune, all parents should encourage matches in all cases when practicable.

"Let tigers *match* with hinds,
And wolves with sheep."
Dryden.

Several cisterns in town are entirely empty and many others nearly so. Wood is selling in the streets at six dollars per cord, and starch is worth one dollar per pound. Consequently laundresses are charging $1 50 per dozen for washing.

—— We heard a Colonel of a Texas Regiment make a remark last evening that we cannot endorse. It was this, "I hope," said he, "that when this war is ended, we—the North and South—will resume our friendly relations." This "local" will never, under any circumstances, agree to that. What, again extend the hand of fellowship to the most barbarous foe the world ever saw!—Barbarism unparalleled, because civilized!—Again extend the hand to such creatures as Infamous Butler, and those who endorse his actions! Again extend the right hand of fellowship to those who have repeatedly desecrated the most sacred rights ever instituted by Almighty power! Again "be friends" with those who have so often forfeited during this war, all claims on their Maker and their fellow beings, to that respect ordinarily bestowed on an honorable foe! No. Sooner may this hand wither, and its possessor sink into oblivion, than be guilty of such infamy! Thenceforth, and forever, our motto is, no more communion, no more fellowship in any form, with that detestible nation, which has endeavored to enslave us, by means of the most unholy, tyranical and barbarous character. Let the wall of separation be built high and secure, and let a dart from heaven pierce him who would attempt to scale it. We have already "forgiven our enemies seventy times seven," or 4900 times. Let us do it no oftener than the scriptures require.

——When a person is quite fatigued, and the weather is unusually hot, and the mosquitoes uncommonly voracious, and the air is stagnant with unhallowed incense, it is truly refreshing to find that you are compelled to spend the night in a room—say in one of our hotels—where there are a dozen of other masculine victims, "bound on the same trtp." You turn in early and seek repose. Don't you wish you may obtain it! If you are endowed with the happy faculty of sleeping while that man in cot No. 1 is fighting fleas and mosquetoes with a boot-jack and umbrella, and those two "tight" specimens in cot No. 2, are discussing temperance, and that man in cot No. 4, is hourly shouting for water to cool his parched coppers, and Jake, in No. 4, is snoring by contract,, and two travelers in No. 5, have concluded to keep themselves awake by talking, so as to be "ready for the New Orleans cars," at four o'clock, and others are engaged at a *quiet* game of "draw-poker," &c., &c., you are indeed a fortunate being, and "will do to travel." We are not so constituted.

—— Wednesday, 25th inst.—hottest day of the season. At 12 M. 90 in the shade. Surplus flesh embarrassing. Paint and powder *running*—a great risk.

—— An abundance of vegetables can now be found in market—if you get there soon enough to find them. With a handful of shinplasters you can supply yourself with ripe cucumbers, green melons and antelopes, mellow squashes and tomatoes, &c., &c. This remark, however, is not applicable to all "sass" in market. We know of a stall where you can buy without being stalled.

—— The New York Herald is down on Infamous Butler for his order "No. 28." When that sheet gets down on a thing for its *immorality*, it is time that its author be suspended—by the neck!

—— We hear the word "skeedaddle" sometimes used. It is a Federal term, and is said to be more significant than "stampede." It signifies to "run from fear of Confederate bayonets, strewing the pathway with guns, haversacks, clothing," &c.

BLACK SHEEP.—Without wishing to speak or write at any time irreverently, we cannot refrain giving the reply of the school boy when told that with God all things are possible. Said he, "I would like to see him make Bill Stokes' mouth wider without setting his ears back!" He might have added, or I would like to see a black sheep washed white, or the dispositions of such traitors as Summers, Robb, Barker and the members of the "black list," published in our last, purified, without changing the present order of things. If it can be done, it is beyond our comprehension. Eternal infamy is their portion and everlasting disgrace their reward. This not properly a "city item," but it is the city opinion of this writer.

HEADQUARTERS,

DEPARTMENT OF TEXAS, HOUSTON,
June 16th, 1862.

General Order No. 55.

A MILITARY COMMISSION is hereby appointed to meet at Houston, on the nineteenth day of June, 1862, or as soon thereafter as practicable, to try and enquire into cases under Martial Law.

DETAIL FOR THE COURT:

1st. Captain G. Hunt, of Flournoy's Regiment.
2d. Captain H. Haldeman, Light Artillery.
3d. Charles Shearn, Esq.
Horace Cone, Esq., Judge, Advocate and Recorder.

By order of
Brig. Gen. P. O. HEBERT.
SAMUEL BOYER DAVIS, A. A. G. june23-3t

ESTRAYS.

ONE black horse mule about 15 hands high, 5 years old, branded on the left shoulder R. R., and some other brand not remembered.

Also one sorrel mare mule, about 15 hands high, 5 years old, and branded on left shoulder R. R. and J. N. Any information of said mules will be liberally rewarded by P. S. WILLIAMS.
ROUND ROCK, WILLIAMSON CO., TEXAS.
j 25-tw-3t

BY THE CENTRAL TRAIN.

We have an extra of the Shreveport News of the 20th, from which we take the following. We have had later telegraphic dates before:

GRENADA, June 13.—Northern dates to the 10th are received.

A special dispatch to the Chicago Tribune from Washington, states that Lord Lyons goes to England for 90 days. Steward, Secretary of legation, is charged with the duties of embassy during Lyons' absence.

Graver consequences are anticipated from Mercier's visit to Richmond.

Memphis papers of the 13th represent matters in that city as quiet, with few arrests.

Refugees are still arriving. The people are reported firm. Few business houses open.

A letter has been received from a perfectly reliable source which states that the editors of the Avalanche have promised the Federal authorities that they were gradually softening down the tone of the paper, and would come out in due season squarly for the Union. The Argus is to be suppressed.

RICHMOND, June 13.—Some cannonading was heard this afternoon in the direction of Mechanicsville. The expectation of another battle near the city has been revived to some extent to-day.

The passengers report that the enemy's gunboats have again made their appearance at Vicksburg on Monday the 16th inst. They were seven in number, and approached from below.

Picayune Butler is said to have established his headquarters at Baton Rouge.

The Federals are reported to be 15,000 strong at Baton Rouge.

Gen. Lovell is reported to have surrounded and captured 1,000 of the enemy in the vicinity of Baton Rouge.

CAPE RACE, June 7.—The North American, from Liverpool May 29th, via Londonderry 30th, was boarded off this point at noon to-day, *en route* to Quebec.

The defense commission appointed by the British government to inquire into iron-plated ships and fortifications, have unanimously concluded that the latter must continue to form an essential feature in the defense of the country.

The Daily News defends Gen. Butler's course at New Orleans.

The House of Commons inquired into the relations between England and the Federals and Confederates.

The Grand Duke Constantine is appointed viceroy of Poland.

The London News says there is nothing whatever in the proclamation of Gen. Butler to express the wrath or justify the indignant criticism of "rowdy sentimentalists." It contains provisions usual and necessary in such cases, and nothing more. The talk of coercing and tyranny is utterly absurd. In another article the Daily News reviews with satisfaction what has been done toward emancipation, and speculates upon what is to come. It looks upon the mean whine of the South as the greatest obstacle in the way of progress.

The Times replies to an article in the New York Journal of Commerce as to the hostility to England which prevails in both sections of the Union. It deeply regrets this hostility, and argues that no willful provocation has been given; but as to the course the Journal recommends England to pursue to remove this hostility, the Times points out its unreasonableness, and regrets that it cannot be complied with, and hopes that calmer and more reasonable pretensions may soon prevail.

Mr. Spencer had addressed another communication to the London Times, referring to the tactics of the Confedrates.

He says it is plainly useless to continue the war on the principle of "two men fighting three and a gunboat." Hence they resolve to call in their outlaying forces and concentrate upon Richmond, with the view also of falling back thence, unless tempted by circumstances to engage in general action. The business of tactics in an unequal war is to exhaust the strength of the enemy before grappling him in action. Gen. Halleck at Corinth appears unaccountable. He remains stationary on the ground fertile with fever and there may be truth in the statement that half his army is on the sick list.

More Skirmishing in Arkansas.

IN CAMP, NEAR SEARCY,
Arkansas, June 5th.

EDITOR TELEGRAPH: Since I wrote you last from Little Rock, we of the 17th Texas cavalry, Col. Jas. R. Taylor, have had stirring times. On the evening of the 27th ult., all those who were fit for duty, were ordered to cook five days rations, and be ready on the 28th to take up the line of march for Searcy Valley. In this valley the enemy have been estimated at from ten to twenty-five thousand strong, under command of Gen. Curtis, and so formidable was their strength that the possession of Little Rock, and other points Southward, seemed merely a question of time. Alf. Johnson's Spy Company—everybody in Texas knows Alf. Johnson—had been in the Valley for several days, and though it numbered less than one hundred men, it annoyed the enemy seriously, cutting off their foraging parties, killing their pickets, etc. It had ample time, and had gathered such information as would prove useful to Col. Taylor in the plan he had in view—attacking the enemy whenever and wherever he saw that he could do so without too much endangering his command.

Late in the evening of the 2d inst., information came to hand to the effect that some four or five hundred of the enemy were foraging north of Little Red River, some twenty miles distant from our encampment. Col. Taylor concluded to attack them with some three hundred of his command, and in a few hours our pickets were firing upon each other; ours on the south and theirs on the north side of the river. The Colonel did not deem it prudent to cross the river that night, but on the following morning moved his column over, and in a very short time the advance or picket guards, were engaged. The exact number of the enemy could not be ascertained and therefore concluded it was necessary to be cautious. By some means or other, I know not how the Yankees found out that the Texas Rangers were after them, and in less time than I am writing it they scattered and "skedaddled." We killed some four or five of them and took several prisoners, however, before they got out of our reach. The whole thing was managed on the part of Col. Taylor, in the most excellent manner; and had it not been for the base cowardice of the enemy—a thing not expected where the force was so unequal—the entire party would have been either killed or captured. They were, however, in such a *hurry*, that we captured at least fifteen hundred dollars worth of their transportation, &c.

Yesterday evening, a part of Cols. Taylor's, Parson's and Fitzhughs' Regiments got after the enemy again, and captured a half dozen or more prisoners, and wounded as many more of the "Feds." As is their custom, they fled. They have a great deal more fear of Texas Rangers than they have of the devil.

A more popular commander than Col. Taylor—with the people as well as his soldiers—is not in service in the Confederate States. Though he has been in command but a few weeks, and in but two engagements, yet his men all swear by him. I shall be greatly surprised if he does not do his country an immense amount of service, and win an enviable and glorious reputation.

The presence of our gallant little band here has scared Curtis. He is falling back upon Batesville now, and my own opinion is that he will have to "get further" if he escapes a just retribution.—There are no "Feds." south of Little Red River. I think it not unlikely that they will "take up" in St. Louis.

The outrages these fiends committed while in this valley are most horrible to relate. Not unfrequently, I am told, they would throttle helpless children and choke them until their parents would give up the last morsel of bread or meat in their possession. They insulted the women, laid waste the country, and stole hundreds of negroes.

All the forces now here are under the command of Major Gen. Hindman, and those of Texas under the immediate command of Brig. Gen. Rust.

Whenever anything turns up I will write you again. Until then, *adios*. C.

The Lines About Richmond—Flag of Truce Between the Lines.

From the Richmond Enquirer, 7th.

Throughout yesterday there was no movement that we can chronicle along our lines in front of Richmond.

By flag of truce between the lines yesterday we are placed in possession of information. General Johnston Pettigrew, of South Carolina, was not killed in the battle of the Seven Pines, before Richmond. Though severely wounded and a prisoner in the enemy's lines, he is now out of danger and doing well.

Col. Lightfoot and Lieutenant Col. Long, both of the 22d North Carolina regiment, were not killed as reported, and are both well. This gratifying information is furnished through Brigadier-General Sickles, of Sickles' brigade, and, though unauthenticated by any other testimony, we believe it is true.

At five o'clock yesterday afternoon some rapid firing of artillery was heard in the direction of Mechanicsville. The cause was not ascertained. The following are the particulars of the "artillery duel," indulged in by the opposing forces named on Thursday.

We have received more particulars of the artillery duel at Dr. Garnett's farm day before yesterday (6th.) Captain Squires's first company of the Washington artillery, together with the Maryland battery, Captain Andrews, and some pieces of Col. Lee's battalion, engaged the enemy's batteries across the Chicahominy at New Bridge. The cannonading continued two hours, and the enemy withdrew their batteries after losing one caisson (exploded) and several horses and men killed. In the evening a section of six pieces of Captain Squires's battery shelled a regiment of the enemy who were engaged in building a pontoon bridge across the river below Dr. Garnett's, scattering them and putting them to rout, leaving many men killed and wounded upon the unfinished bridge. The battery then took position near Dr. Garnett's house, and opened fire upon a house occupied by the Yankee pickets, about six hundred yards off. The shells failed to set it on fire. At this juncture Lieut. Edward Owen, of the Washington artillery; volunteered to head a party to burn the house. About a dozen of the 18th Mississippi regiment volunteered, and they started for the house at a double quick. Reaching the house, Lieut. Owen crept through a window and fired the staircase, and the place was soon wrapped in flames and reduced to ashes. The adventurous party then retired leisurely. All that now remains of the house are the chimneys. Contrary to expectation, our men did not receive a shot, although within fifty yards of the enemy's line.

Address to the Army of Richmond.

The President has issued the following address to the army:

I tender to you my grateful acknowledgments for the gallantry and good conduct you displayed in the battles of the 31st May and 1st inst., and with pride and pleasure recognize the steadiness and intrepidity with which you attacked the enemy in position, captured his advanced intrenchments, several batteries of artillery, and many standards, and everywhere drove him from the open field.

At a part of your operations it was my fortune to be present. On no other occasion have I witnessed more calmness and good order than you exhibited while advancing into the very jaws of death, and nothing could exceed the prowess with which you closed upon the enemy when a sheet of fire was blazing in your faces!

In the renewed struggle in which you are on the eve of engaging, I ask and desire but a continuance of the same conduct which now attracts the pride and admiration of the loved ones you have left at home.

You are fighting for all that is dearest to men; and, though opposed to a foe who disregards many of the usages of civilized war, your humanity to the wounded and prisoners was the fit and crowning glory to your valor.

Defenders of a just cause, may God have you in His holy keeping! JEFFERSON DAVIS.

The general will cause the above to be read to the troops under his command.

Executive Office, June 2, 1862.

MAJ. WM. W. WALLACE.

EDITOR TELEGRAPH: Though in the midst of a defensive struggle for our National existence, we should still not be unmindful of the importance of preserving on the Supreme Bench of the State the learning and ability by which it has so long been distinguished.

An election for Associate Justice, to fill the vacancy occasioned by the resignation of Judge Roberts, will take place on the first Monday in August next. Among all those from whom a selection might be made, there is, perhaps, not one better qualified to succeed Judge Roberts than Maj. W. W. Wallace of San Augustine. A native of the South, a profound lawyer, an accomplished scholar, an unostentatious gentleman, and just now in the full maturity of intellectual vigor, he seems to unite in himself, in an eminent degree, the essential requisites for the high office in question. It is understood by his friends that he will permit his name to be used as a candidate.

Maj. Wallace was formerly in politics a Democrat of the *Southern stamp*, and more recently has cordially co-operated in the political movement which has resulted in forming the Southern Confederacy. Seeking no political or other office, he has escaped all contact with the corresponding influences connected with the politician's trade, and for that reason would be all the better fitted for the bench. The Judicial ermine could not rest on the shoulders of one more worthy to wear it than Maj. Wallace. TYLER.

From the San Antonio Herald, 24th.

Latest from the West.

By Lieut. Robinson C. S. A. 2d regiment Sibley's Brigade, who arrived by last stage, we have the following information of affairs in the West:

The 1st, 2d and a portion of the 3d Regiment were under marching orders for San Antonio, the 1st was to leave Fort Bliss about the 3d inst. Col. Steele was ordered to remain with six companies of his Regiment, four companies of Phil Herbert's Battalion, and Capt. Teel's battery, for the purpose of holding Arizona. Col. Steele's command was at Dona Ana.

Gen. Canby had left with his main command for the States, leaving Col. Roberts in command at Fort Craig, his entire force probably exceed 2000. Kit Carson was at Fort Craig with his regiment. Canby was taking with him the prisoners taken at the battle of Glorietta.

Capt. Hunter had arrived at Mesilla and reports that in consequence of his belief that the Federals were advancing on Tucson he had retired his command to Arizona. The whole country was destitute of provisions, which was the real cause of Gen'l Sibley's evacuating New Mexico—and it is believed this is the cause also of Canby's leaving.

Maj. Pyron's command were at Fort Davis.—Capt. Walker's at Eagle Springs, and Col. Reily at Fort Lancaster with his [illegible].

HEADQUARTERS WAUL LEGION,
CAMP WAUL, June 24, 1862.

General Order, No. 19.

All officers and enlisted men of this command now absent on leaves of absence and furlough, are hereby notified to return to the camp by the 29th, in order to be present at the muster of the 30th of June, and to complete the preparations for taking up the line of march to Little Rock, Ark., without delay. By order of
T. N. WAUL, Col. Com'dg.
O. STEELE, Lieut. and Adj't. je 25-3t

Letters from Corinth.

CAMP OF WASHINGTON ARTILLERY,
CORINTH, Miss., May 11th, 1862.

Editor Telegraph—Dear Sir: After a safe return from attendance upon the General Assembly at Montgomery, in company with Dr. Bryan, I reached this military encampment on yesterday morning. I learned that the Rangers had left Rienza, 20 miles below, en route to Russelville, Ala. They were thrown in the command of Gen. Beall in connection with Morgan's and Scott's cavalry, and have crossed into Tennessee. Should events favor the movement, they expect to advance into Tennessee and on towards Kentucky. Col. Wharton has returned from New Orleans and left for the regiment. I found Maj. Harrison here entirely recovered from his severe sickness and only awaiting the great battle before following after the regiment. The Major is a gallant soldier and seeks every opportunity to join in the conflict upon the battle-field. Capt. Botts is also here, but has his furlough extended, not yet being sufficiently recovered to undertake the trip. I was delighted to grasp once more by the hand John Stewart, of company H, who was reported missing on the 8th of April, in the brilliant charge of Tuesday. He was crossing a bog, when they were falling back from the charge, and his horse sinking under him, before he was able to extricate himself and remount, some 20 Yankee cavalry were upon him, and there was no alternative but to surrender. He was allowed to ride to the river and there, with all our prisoners taken during the preceding days—some 400 in all—they were kept on the river's bank, without covering, exposed to the rain, cold and short rations until Friday, when they were shipped to St. Louis. The treatment was very harsh, and caused the prisoners to suffer exceedingly. Upon their arrival at St. Louis, before the prisoners were removed from the boat, Mr. Stewart was missing. Suffice it to say that after a good deal of exposure, fatigue and danger, he, with another prisoner, reached here safely a few days ago. He was the only one of our Rangers they were able to carry away with them. Thus our boys always escape the snare before entangled in its meshes.

We have an *army* here, all in readiness for the enemy. On Friday afternoon there was a brilliant skirmish on our right wing, where our troops, under Price and Van Dorn, chased two brigades, capturing their encampment; and, only by accident, failing to capture 8000 or 9000 prisoners. We are expecting the battle to open every moment. The enemy are cautiously advancing in heavy force, bringing their siege guns and preparing for a magnificent fight. It will be the turning point in this war. May the God of battles give our troops the strength to meet the enemy and put him to flight. Our trust is in God.

We have a large number of Texas troops here now. They will be ready for the conflict. The weather is clear and most propitious.

In haste, yours, R. F. BUNTING.

IN CAMP, THREE MILES SOUTH OF CORINTH,
May 13th, 1862.

Correspondence of the Telegraph.

Dear Telegraph:—Our regiment has been into the Corith fight and I am happy to report that we have none killed or wounded, or missing. The men were ordered to report to Gen. Van Dorn on the 9th inst., and he immediately led us out to attack the enemy's advance guard, who had taken Farmington, at some four miles to the east of Corinth. Our plans were somewhat frustrated by a sad mistake of his Arkansas regiments mistaking each other for enemies. They fired on each other, killing and wounding 6. Gen. Price's army made a forced march on the left wing of theirs, and attacked them. They resisted stubbornly for a while, but soon broke and run, leaving much property behind. Our loss I learn is some 16 killed and 28 wounded. That of the enemy killed, wounded, and prisoners, is from 500 to 800, besides a brass battery.

The battle raged awfully for a few hours, and the Federals suffered terribly. Our regiments were nearly exhausted by our long exposure, but they won from Van Dorn and Price, high praises for their good order in line. The following missing men at the battle of Shiloh are safe in St. Louis:

Lieut. Gallagher, B. Buddy, W. R. Anthony, Joe. Wright, James A. Rhea, H. Bartlett, and no doubt others are there. I obtained my information from a scrap of a St. Louis paper picked up on the battle field the other day. The health of the men is improving slowly, and all are ready for the next fight. Yours for the war,
SIOUX.

Ticklepitcher on Butler.

SIMZIS BYO, Joon 16, sicksty-2.

DEER TELEGRAPH.—Oin to a konfushun of the brace pan insydent upon, and okashuned bi, a too free imbybashun of schnapps, my last letter was dated egg sackly thurty dais ahed; but ef Kurnel Bill Skurry doant keer, and Rosencrantz has no pertikler objeckshuns, I feel prepaired two "strane a pint" and repoodyeight schnapps in futer.

Bengimmin, my fren "High Private," has "slitely" insinuaited that *you* ware "contemptible!" H P., are you not a leettle too severe? Pic, you shoud, by awl meens, except my fren's invitaish to visit Houston—becase whi, thar is a grate deel moar to be seen in that sitty than thar is in sum uther plaises whar thar is knot kwite as mutch to obzerve! Korse to akompany you, my deer Pic, 4½ staffs and ¾ doz. skillyton redgments, to proteck yer tender karkiss from "rebel gallitippers." Tha air good hands at "drilling," Pic, but knot very well "drilled," hents tha mite be kolled "raw rekroots." At any rait you doant know (konversant as you are with the subjeck of "ticks" and tac-ticks") that they possess the singular fakulty of redoosing wun to the consistency noan among butchers as "raw"—in which kais kunsidable "rekrootin" on your part wood be necessary. This reminds me, Pic that tha ar very mutch like your Yankee brethren, alwais "whine" be4 tha "drill" thar kusstomers. The onkommon skarsity of Yanky skippers in theas parts, is proof suffish uv ther remorseliss luv uv "drill." Ekwipt as tha air with a two-aiged soard, thar akootermens bein thar "war-rin' apparel, and thar "wings" alwais "on the moov," it is moarn likely they mai proov more terrible to your hoasts than has J. Morgan to Bewill's "bean-blowers."

Startling News.—The last nite's male by the U. G. R. R., brot the telegrams U C belo—

11 o'clock M.—Doant cum down on the Byo, fur the boys must skin ye and fling yer hide acrost a poal be4 yer dinner settled.

3 o'clock—The gals here, to a man, are ded agin ye, and yer kussid hide moutnt hoald sopegrese in kais uv an attack.

5 o'clock—Them gals on the Byo hev raised a ridgment of "lite infuntry," ekwipt and rashuned with brooms, raised in the last 5 owers, which is to wai anker on the 3 ultimow for New Orleens, the desine of the expedishun bein to "storm" the plais, "flank" the *soap factory*," maik shu-strings of "that standard sheat," and *sweap the dirt out of the St. Charles Hotel.*

In furtherants of the abuv aktiv moovments, I ev thot proper two issue this proklamaish:

HEDKWORTERS, DEPT. HARRISBURG,
Muskeeter Plais, Simzis Byo, Joon 17.

GINERAL ORDER No. 29.

Kno awl men by theas presents, That eye, Aitch Ticklepitcher, kommanding this Department—in vou of the *grate respeck* and *venerashun* in which B. Pic Butler is held by the "kontrybands" of Loozyanny, and havi g heerd of the *tender satisfakshun* which his "offishal koars" has okaishuned the "small fri" of the Kressent Sitty—do order and komand my subordynits to xecoot, that eech and every mail humun now lyin in sed Department, under 35 ears of aige and any hoo may be afterards bornd, who air alowed to anser two, or bar, the naim of Bengimmin, shall suffer deth. "Pervided, alwais," That sed proscripts be alowed 3 (three) dais in which to evacywait thea' presinks—it bein the cents of Department that as no mail humun has ever been naimed "Ben Arnolds since tue 1st Revolution, neether shood thar be alowed to bair, or hev sespended to thar naims, any sich ekklesyastickally damnibul wun of Ben. Butler, now hentsfourth and forever. Biorder of,
AITCH TICKLEPITCHER,
Brigydeer General Komdg.
M. BUGG, A. A. A. G.
Yours, in Confederate bonds, T.

FOR SALE—Several choice tracts of Land. Apply to COLMAN & LEVY.
Houston, June 11, 1862. je13 wlm.

WANNTED!

To know why true hearted Southern people will trade with merchants whose loyalty is questionable? And visit said merchants' wives, who give tea-parties when Fort Donelson falls, and dinner-parties when Nashville is surrendered?

WANTED,

To know why those miserable parched-peas of humanity, *old-black-republican-maids*, who bestow their starved grins on these wretched, union-loving-flop-eared, owlish-looking beaux, are still retained as teachers in professedly Southern families? Teaching the "young idea how to shoot!" Query.—In what direction will the aforesaid "young idea" shoot? Query second.—Would it not be better for aforesaid dames to teach aforesaid owlish beaux to "shoot," instead of lurking round of nights to see if any bad news comes?

WANTED,

A broom to clear this State of the stray "flees" that have hopped here from Yankee land.

Any person seeing above named "flees," may know them by this mark: They are like popcorn in a skillet. When secession gets too hot for them in one community or church, they hop into another; but they've settled pretty nearly now in one place, and it is awfully "flee"-bitten. Query.—Now that Lincolndom has gotten to be such a *hoggish-doggish* place? Wouldn't they be more in their *h—element*, if they would hop back again?

Any person furnishing the required broom will be liberally rewarded.

WANTED,

To know the exact estimate of character to be placed upon the *lady* ? ? ? ? who saw nothing in old Butler's infamously foul Order No. 28? Also the precise calibre of mind of said lady ? ? ? ? Query.—Is there any calibre to said lady's ? ? ? ? mind?

Any person imparting the information sought for will oblige an inquiring mind fully aroused by a strange combination of glaring inconsistencies.
PAULINE PRY.

Less than a thousand miles from Austin, June 18th.

Waco University—The Crisis.

CAMP SPEIGHT, Near Milican,
June 12, 1862.

Editor Telegraph: Allow me a small space in your widely circulated Telegraph to state that Waco University is not suspended, as reported. There are now between 90 and 100 students in daily attendance. 123 students have been matriculated during this session. The science of military tactics is taught daily in our University, and I have never seen a finer drilled company than the "University Guards." It is delightful to every patriot to see them on parade in full uniform, with martial music, performing so skillfully the varied evolutions. The rumor referred to may have originated from the fact that I have told all our students over 18 years old, that the crisis demanded us all to shoulder our muskets and win graves of glory or homes of freedom. I am here as a member of Col. Speight's regiment, and all our students over eighteen are now in the army; and you, I hope, will hear "a voice from Waco University" that will mean something more than "gas." All of our Professors, who are capable of performing military service, are now in the army, and we expect to fight on till the last Gothic invader is driven from our shores. In the mean time, Prof. R. B Burleson, who is the most experienced teacher in our faculty, aided by competent assistants, will carry on the Institution especially for such as are not old enough to go to battle.

In regard to the present crisis, I am rejoiced to know that the heroism of our people rises with our reverses. It could not be otherwise. Our all is at stake. We must be free or perish. If an inscrutable decree of Providence has ordained that we are not to succeed, let us at least fill our beautiful land with Alamos and Thermopylæs that shall loom up in the world's history and make the future generation a nation of heroes. Indeed it would be far cheaper to die than to live and work for Yankee tyrants. But I see no reason to despair—our reverses are not greater than any reasonable man might have expected from the superiority of the foe in numbers and the means of warfare. But, as the London Times has said, "The South is invincible from the vastness of her territory." VICTORY IS SURE. Our independence may cost us another seven yeasr war; if so, let it come. It may cost us rivers of blood and millions of treasure; if so, I repeat it, let it come. Liberty to a nation, like honor to a man, or virtue to a woman, is the gem of existence. Without it everything else, even life, is a curse, and not a blessing. Let us, therefore, arise as one man and swear by the Holy and Eternal One that the bones of 75,000 Texians shall whiten our prairies before Abolition despotism shall reign over this lovely land. Let us shake off the incubus, the nightmare, that seems to weigh upon all our military movements. Let us imitate the rapidity and wonderful dispatch of Alexander, Cæsar, Julian, Napoleon and all great military leaders. Napoleon or Julian would have conquered a province while our Generals are collecting their baggage wagons. There must be a change somewhere. Battles are oftener won by vigilance and rapid combinations of troops than by numbers or courage even. If the 30,000 brave Texians, now under arms and lingering in our borders, could only fall like a thunderbolt on the foe, we might decide the fate of our country, and make Texas free as long as the flowers bloom on our prairies or the waters of the Gulf beat on our shores.

RUFUS C. BURLESON.

Probable Movements on Charleston.

NEWARK, N. J., June 7.—The Advertiser publishes a letter dated "U. S. steamer Augusta, off Charleston, May 29," which says: "I have barely time to forward a letter by the prize just captured off this place, which is on its way northward. The news here is quite important. Our gunboats are within four miles of Charleston by way of Stono Inlet, and we expect soon to attack it."

PHILADELPHIA, June 7.—The United States gunboat Bienville arrived last night with three steamers in tow, which were captured off Charleston in attempting to run the blockade. Their names are the President, Lacroilla and Rebecca—all from Nassau.

The President's revokal of Gen. Hunter's proclamation was well received at Port Royal.

Gen. Hunter had organized a brigade of "contrabands," and was about to assign them to building intrenchments and fortifications.

A sharp engagement had occurred with the rebel batteries at Stono Inlet. The Union forces were virtually investing Charleston.

A rebel steamer was run ashore on William's Island while being chased by the blockading vessels, and is still aground.

The schooner Cora, prize to the Keystone State, is below.

HOUSTON, June 24, 1862.

Editor Telegraph—The officers and soldiers of Capt. Evans' company take pleasure in expressing, through your columns, their grateful thanks to the ladies of this city for the charity and kindness they have bestowed upon us during our sojourn here. The following ladies, Mrs. Heckle, Mrs. Casswell, Miss Lawyer, Mrs. Robertson, Mrs. Taylor, Mrs. Wood, Mrs. Cushman, Mrs. Furgerson, Mrs. Richardson, Mrs. Blount and Mrs. Anderson, have done much to alleviate the suffering of our sick, by furnishing them with such food and comforts as they could not otherwise obtain, and without which some of them would have probably died. We hope their kindness and generosity will not be lost upon us; and that upon the sanguine field of battle we will prove ourselves worthy of the attention and respect they have shown us. God bless the good ladies of Houston. H. C. RENFRO.

By request of the Company.

THE TRI-WEEKLY TELEGRAPH.

VOL. XXVIII—NO. 48 HOUSTON, MONDAY, JULY 7, 1862 WHOLE NO. 3543

BY THE CENTRAL TRAIN.

Vicksburg Still Holds Out.

BASTROP, TEXAS, DESTROYED.

ETC., ETC., ETC.

By the Central Train we have Shreveport papers of the 1st, and other Louisiana and Texas papers of corresponding dates. We have also a letter from Monroe, La., 28th from a correspondent just across the Mississippi. He says he counted 27 gunboats below the town. He says that Vicksburg will not be taken but by the most serious fighting. It is, he says, the Gibraltar of America.

Mr. John Clark, of the 2d, Regiment came by the cars. He crossed at Vicksburgh on the 24th. There were seven boats above and 32 gunboats, mortarboats and transports below. No great damage had been done to the place at that date. He crossed in front of Vicksburg.

Young Sam Houston has escaped from the enemy and is at his regiment.

We learn that Bastrop, Texas was destroyed by fire day before yesterday.

Richmond, June 20.—The Court of Inquiry convoked by order of the Navy Department, to investigate the destruction of the steamer Virginia, report that the destruction of that steamer, was in the opinion of the Court, unnecessary at the time and place it was effected, it being in evidence that the Virginia with very little more, if any lessening of draught could have been taken up to Hog Island, in James River, where the channel is narrow and there have prevented the larger vessels and transports of the enemy from ascending the river. The court is of the opinion that such a disposition ought to have been made of her.

The finding of the Court of Inquiry in the case o the destruction of the Mississippi is, that it was necessary to prevent her falling into the hands of the enemy.

Richmond, June 19th.—On Wednesday Kershaw's South Carolina Brigade was ordered forward by Gen. McLaws for the purpose of feeling the enemy on the nine mile road.

They advanced but a short distance in the woods when a brisk fire commenced along the line. The enemy was driven back. Our men pressed forward, took their camp, and brought off overcoats, arms, &c. Eight Confederates were wounded, including Col. Cuthbert, of the 2nd South Carolina regiment in the arm, and Capt. Walker of the 3d South Carolina, in the shoulder.

Northern papers of the 16th inst. have been received here. The London correspondent of the Philadelphia Inquirer says that the refusal of the English Government to give up the steamer Emily St. Pierre is couched in terms approaching, if not reaching insolence and insult.

The same correspondent says peremptory demand will be made, if it is not already done, for the release of the Bermuda.

Northern News.—The Richmond Dispatch, in its summary of late news from Baltimore, says:

The Government has taken possession of all the flour mills in the Valley of the Shenandoah, together with the grain and flour on hand. The Washington Star says that a camp of instruction for 50,000 troops is to be formed near Annapolis, Md., under the superintendence of Major John Wool.

In the U. S. Senate, Mr. Powell of Kentucky, introduced a resolution in relation to the formation of three negro regiments by Gen. Hunter.

Mr. Sumner introduced a resolution calling upon the President to revoke the appointment of Mr. Stanley as Military Governor of North Carolina.

Two hundred and forty-one prisoners captured by McClellan in the battle of Chicahominy, arrived at Fortress Monroe.

Gen. Johnston.—The Richmond correspondent of the Charleston Mercury, writing on the 8th inst. says: "Gen. Lee is getting the army in better trim, and Gen. Johnston is rapidly recovering. It is thought he will be out in the field within ten days."

The enemy are said to be extending their operations inland from Pensacola. A number of them came up the bay on a gunboat to Milton. at the head of Blackwater, and about twenty miles from Pensacola, on Saturday night last, suprising a portion of the 2d Alabama regiment.

Our Railroad.—The cars are now running to Quebeck on bayou Tensas within thirty miles of Vicksburg, and the company are still repairing the track further into the swamp.

We hear but little now from Beauregard's army at Oakalona. The Mobile News occasionally gets an inkling of news from that quarter. The sanitary condition of our army is much improved. It has better diet, good water, and a beautiful country. Meantime, the work of organization and discipline is going on, ready for new movements, which must depend largely upon those of the enemy. Gen. Pope, after following Beauregard down the road about twenty-five miles, retreated again with all haste, his men, scattered through the country in wild confusion, crying out for "water!" and damning "such a country," and Gen. Halleck for bringing them into it.

Bastrop, July 2, 1862.

We had a terrible conflagration here last night. The destruction of property was immense.

Three blocks were totally destroyed. The fire originated in the store of Louis Eilers. His clerk, a German lad, was burnt within the building. The gun manufactory is destroyed. Fire supposed to be accidental.

Enclosed please find list of sufferers.

Yours respectfully,

JNO. B. LUBBOCK.

List of Sufferers.—Nelson Burch, L C Cunningham, N B Tanner, Campbell Taylor, E D Barnett, Mrs Slocumb, McNeil, Mrs Redding, Fehere, Granger, T W House, R H Grimes, A Knittel, W Miler, Phil Claiborne, L Eilers, Price & Persons, M O Dimon, Brocop, Lewis, C K Hall, Mrs Beck, G Freidburger, Chas Ployer, Odd Fellows. L Eilers. N Burch, Cunningham & Co., M O Dimon, G Freidburger, and Dr. Chas Ployer are the principal sufferers. Their loss, sum total, is $75,000.

BY TELEGRAPH FROM GALVESTON.

MORE VESSELS ARRIVED.

Galveston, July 4.—Last night a skiff belonging to one of the wood schooners in the bay was stolen. This morning a skiff was seen near the Shntee by the look-out at Hendly's with one man in it. One of the Santee's boats took the skiff alongside, and the man went on board the Santee.

The prevailing opinion seems to be that the man is the notorious character Nicaragua Smith, and that he has made good his escape to the Federals.

The fleet off the bar was increased this P. M. by the arrival of a bark and a schooner. The whole number of vessels off the bar at present is 7, of following class: One first class frigate, two large barks, one large war steamer, three schooners—supposed to be transports.

Later.

July 4th, 6 o'clock P. M.—Another Steamer coming in from the west.

Galveston, July 5, 3 P. M.—One of the Steamers has left with the Santee in tow, going East. No other change.

VARIOUS ITEMS.

We take the following from the Franklin (La.) Banner, 28th:

The army worm is committing serious ravages on many plantations in this parish, destroying the cane and young corn in some places extensively.

Beef sells in the Franklin market at 20 cents per pound, and it is very difficult to get it, even at that price. This is about equal to paying 50 cents a pound for good pork. Necessity will soon compel our people to turn Grahamites.

Gen. Price was in Richmond on the 10th inst. The Richmond papers speak of him as the great leading spirit of the war. They say that "upon no single life and charactor do the people rely with higher hope and confidence to lead them to a successful issue through this dark and painful struggle. They honor and trust him as a soldier and a patriot."

A collision lately took place between a detachment of Col. Fournet's Battalion and about 60 Federals, on the Opelousas Railroad, between Bayou des Allemands and Raceland, resulting in wounding three Confederates and killing and wounding quite a number of Federals. Fournet's men were in ambush, and shot at the men as they approached in the cars. The train soon backed out, carrying with them the dead and wounded. Mr. Humble was among the Confederate wounded.

Our leading military men are stirring up the fighting men all over Attakapas, to be ready for the foe whenever they may have a chance at him. Gen. Pratt, Col. Fournet, the Swamp King, and Capt. D. Ker are in motion.

We notice a statement in the True Delta that the U. S. War Department has ordered 15-inch guns for some time, but a contract has now been made for a 20-inch gun, which, when rifled, will require an elongated shot weighing one ton, and, with a smooth bore, a round ball of 1,000 pounds.

The following infamous order we copy from the N. O. Delta:

Headquarters Detachment 21st Ind. Vols., Houma, La., May 16, 1862.

In compliance with an order from Major General Butler, I hereby order the following property of the parties herein named, destroyed by fire or otherwise, but in such manner as not to endanger or destroy adjacent property owned by parties herein not named; said property all situated in parish of Terrbonne to-wit:

Buildings, out buildings, and personal property of Howard Bond, near the town of Houma.
Buildings on premises of Col. Robinson.
Property of F. Gatewood, real and personal.
Property of Dr. Jennings.
Property of N. Wood (T. A. Wood) the Ceres newspaper establishment.
Parish Jail.
Property of B. Cooper.
Property of Gilbert Hatch.
House of E. N Dutrail.
Property of Crewel.

The parties above named, and whose property is to be destroyed, are known to be identified in a greater or less degree in the murder of two soldiers, and wounding of two others belonging the 21st Indiana Volunteers on the 10th day of May, near Houma. The Jail is destroyed because permitted to be employed as a place of confinement of the wounded

JOHN A. KEITH,
Lieut. Colonel 21st Indiana Volunteers Commanding Department.

The following is the published report of Lieut. Col. Keith, in the same number of the Delta, in regard to the execution of the above orders:

"In pursuance of said order, the following named property was burned or otherwise destroyed or seized upon, viz:

Property on premises of Howard Bond. Burned one dwelling house, furniture and contents; one other house, filled with sugar; from 50 to 100 negro houses, with out houses; one steam saw mill and one corn mill; three stables; two corn houses with contents; one cooper shop and blacksmith shop, with tools and other contents; one store house filled with molasses; two buggies and harness; stacks of hay and fodder. Taken from the above premises 35 mules, 20 sets of harness, 6 plantation wagons, 1 cart, 2 yoke of oxen, and 5 loads of forage.

"Property owned by Dr. Jennings burned. One dwelling house, other out houses, barn, stables, all their contents; buggy and a valuble library; other articles.

"Property owned by A. N. Dutrail, consisting of dwelling houses, stables and other outhouses, with all their contents, were torn down and utterly destroyed.

"Property of N. Wood (T. A.) consisting of the Ceres newspaper establishment, was completely destroyed, the type, and other material were thrown into the Bayou.

"The parish jail, a strong Brick building, by means of a Battering Ram, was demolished.

"The property of Crewel, consisting of a light one horse wagon, chest of carpenter's tools, was seized."

This, some Lieut. Col., in the same report, acknowledges that he carried off and delivered up to the quartermaster, 85 mules, 61 head of cattle, 8 horses, 43 sheep, 6 wagons, 2 carts, 1 spring wagon, 2 carriages, with other articles.

And all this was done because two Federal soldiers were shot, ane two others wounded, who went to Terrebonne, in company with other Federal soldiers, to seize a confederate vessel and arms in Southern territory.

Chappell Hill Female College.

Ed. Telegraph: The recent examination and concerts closing the present term of this institution well deserve a notice in your columns. Rev. John Carmer, the Principal, and Prof. Prohl, of the Music Department, with their respective assistants, have proved themselves worthy of a front rank in our very worthy corps of Texas teachers. We have never witnessed a more satisfactory examination. It was honest and thorough on the part of teachers, and a decided success with the students.

The concerts have added to the high reputation of Prof. Prohl in thts community. They were in beautiful harmony with the admirable examination. Prof. Prohl's large class of over seventy students shows significantly the public appreciation of his abilities.

The orderly, systematic character of everything in all the departments of this successful institution, is a very noticeable and most commendable feature of its merits.

In giving this merely sober statement to the public, we feel that we are doing but bare justice to a noble and meritorious school.

JAS. M. FOLLANSBEE,
THOS. WOOLDRIDGE,
Com. of Examination.

DONATIONS

Received at the C. S. General Hospital, Hempstead, for the month of June:

From the Ladies' Aid Society of Courtney, several valuable gifts of butter, eggs and chickens.

From Messrs. L. H. Wood & Co., Houston, 18 doz. spoons and 3 doz. knives and forks.

From the Hempstead Aid Society, through Mr. N. W. Bush, an assortment of crockery, tin ware, and domestics.

From Ladies of Huntsville, a quantity of clothing, sheets, towels, pillows, pillow cases, and twelve ½ bottles of blackberry wine.

From Mrs. Col. L. W. Groce and other ladies of Hempstead, many welcome donations of articles of diet and comfort for the sick soldiers.

WM. R. ROBINSON,
Surgeon General Hospital.

Pattersonville, La., June 28.

Dear Sir: Our company of Partizan Rangers had a fight with 200 Volunteers at Raceland Station last Sunday. We were in ambush, and they were coming up on the cars. We killed 47 and wounded 8 men. We had three wounded, none killed. We had double barrel shot guns loaded with buck shot, and fired at 20 yards. ——.

Continuation of Correspondence of the Civilian.

Letter from the Rangers.

Camp near Chattanooga, June 14, 1862.

In this camp life, it is difficult to keep up a connected thread of events as they transpire. In writing this morning, I find myself at fault, not knowing what I had last written. I will, however, endeavor to give you as well as I can, all that has occurred the last ten days, on our march from near Decatur to this mountain region.

I think on the day I last wrote, we received orders from our gallant Colonel, who had preceded us to this place. After a march of great danger in passing through and ahead of some 500 of the enemy, I have no stirring incidents to relate. We had a train of 26 wagons in charge, in all about 300 men. We had the invalids and the sick in charge. The efficient horses had been taken by the Colonel on his expedition across the Tennessee. We had, perhaps, 200 men under command of Major Harrison, who had joined us a few days before; so we took up our line of march for this place, 160 miles distant. Our pickets had been stationed on the south bank of the Tennessee, the enemy's on the north. Each morning as they were relieved, the new arrival would exchange a few rifle shots across the river, at a distance of six or eight hundred yards; then a white flag would be run up on one or both sides; an hour was allowed for bathing without being disturbed, and then each side had to look out and take care.

Our first day's march was ten miles. Nearing the river and passing through Courtland, which is the centre of a rich, cultivated and populous region of a highly cultivated and intellectual people, we encamped seven miles this side. Soon after, two supposed spies were brought in, captured in Decatur by an energetic citizen. One was an old Scotchman; the other had all the usual marks of a genuine "Down-Easter." They had papers from Gen. Mitchel, and, as their captor said, had done quite a business, on the other side, in theft and depredation on those who were obnoxious. They had been trailed by their captor for two days and nights, who ascertained they intended to cross at Decatur, preceeded them, made the capture immediately and hurriedly brought them on. They undoubtedly deserved death, but were turned over to Col. Scott, who was in our rear; their fate I know not. We passed within a mile of Decatur; took the right, thinking it more prudent to give the enemy as wide a berth as possible—who were going up the river opposite to us in large force, for an object which will be explained after awhile, but which was then unknown to us. On this day, we ascertained that the enemy at Whitesborough, just opposite Huntsville—which is ten miles from the river—had fitted up a steam ferry-boat, had barricaded her with cotton, mounted a cannon, and were going up the river. We had continued scouting on the river to watch her movements, as she still pursued her course up as we did. We did not feel quite secure as we slowly made our way up, the enemy close to us, and a boat to cross their troops. These Rangers, however, do not seem to fear man or devil, ready for fight at all times, no matter what the odds, and seemed as careless and indifferent to danger as if quietly reposing in their siesta at home. We crossed spurs of the Cumberland and the Sand Mountain, fell into Mills Valley, into the State of Georgia, and on the 7th day we received express from Col. Wharton for the efficient force to join him on the river here. This left us almost without protection. We then crossed the spurs of Stone Mountain, and encamped at its foot, intending in the morning to cross it and come down the Chattanooga Valley. This was Sunday. In the evening, our Chaplain, the Rev. Mr Bunting, in this wild region, in the open air, delivered us a fine sermon suitable to the occasion. Nearly all were present and attentive; a half dozen mountaineers were present also, who seemed to be well pleased. I could but think of the early Christian, who worshipped just at such places as they could find, and made the best they could of the circumstances surrounding them. Our Parson is well suited to his place; a fine scholar, a fine mind, an eloquent preacher. Above all he understands the world, and readily adapts himself to the ways of his *parishioners* without soiling his own garments. On the 16th day we reached this camp, having been joined the night before by the rest of the regiment. There was greeting, joy and gladness with all. All were interchanging in great glee the numerous incidents that had occurred during their separation. The general complaint of citizens against soldiers, is the free use they make of the property of citizens. With the part of the regiment I have been with for a month I have not heard a complaint of a single depredation. At every place we stopped they wished us to remain. We were undoubtedly in great danger, never more then twenty-five miles distant from the enemy, who had preceeded our arrival a day or two, and ineffectually shelled the town and retreated.

About a week before my arrival at the camp near Courtland, Col. Adams, in command of three skeleton regiments with about 800, of whom the Rangers were one, had crossed the Tennessee river above Tuscumbia for a foray into Tennessee. They had crossed their trains. Upon consultation the trains were recrossed just in time to save them; they were fired on as they crossed. Two days' rations were ordered and prepared. From some change I am not informed about, Colonel Adams attempted to recross and abandon the expedition, but he was interrupted by an overwhelming force. The only alternative left was to take their line of march through the enemy's lines avoiding them if possible, and make their way to the mountains sure. They could not do much fighting as they had but five rounds of ammunition, and that they reserved for an emergency. They were pursued to Winchester, Tenn., where they halted for several days When they left that place, or soon after, by some agreement Colonel Wharton separated the Rangers from the command, and successfully recrossed the river about 30 miles below this. The Adams commend were not so fortunate, they dallied, were attacked in an undefensible position and stampeded, with a loss of 150 horses, some killed and some prisoners.

Such was the indignation of his command, that on his arrival here he left it for headquarters, and it is said has resigned. Great sagacity and good fortune united saved the Rangers. It is now difficult to conjecture how, surrounded as they were by an overwhelming force, they successfully encountered all the perils that hourly attended them or three weeks, and made their way here without the loss of a single man. Great credit is due their Colonel, the officers and men. As I have said, the enemy followed them up, came opposite Chattanooga, shelled it for an hour, did little or no injury to the place, killed one man, wounded another, and retreated. Six new graves were found when they left. Opening one a 12-pound cannon was found buried; it had been dismounted by our shot and left three days since. There is a rumor this morning that they are crossing below. At midnight, last night, 150 of our men were ordered out to join others below, to see if this be true, and watch the various crossings of the river. We heard, too, yesterday that the enemy had crossed the Cumberland mountain and were in Powell's Valley; if this be so, (and it came from the Chief Quartermaster,) all our forces this side the Mountains, under the command of Kirby Smith, will be concentrated for a decisive battle, to protect Knoxville, the Railroads, and prevent an insurrection in East Tennessee by Brownlow's party. Where the Rangers are to go, is only conjecture. From the Gulf they have made their way to the top of the Alleghany range, and if I know them as well as I think I do, they are ready to go East, West, North or South, wherever the heaviest blows are falling, to do, or die, in a cause that gives but the alternative now of life or death, liberty or slavery. The late battle at Richmond, like that of Shiloh, is barren in its results. The life-blood of thousands of determined hearts has been poured out on the battle field, and in each case the ground for which they contended has been given up. How many thousands more are yet to bleed, is known only to the good God, before this unholy and unnatural strife is ended. The keenest intellect, and most piercing vision, cannot yet penetrate the Cimmerian darkness that lies beyond and around us. Even now, every household is in mourning, and the end is not yet. I can but have noticed, everywhere I have been, the unfaltering courage of our women; one and all they say, on to the battle field! Wives no longer weep openly for husbands slain; mothers for sons, or sisters for brothers. Their sorrows are confined to their own hearts, and if they weep at all, it is known only to God. The insults they have received everywhere in the South from those boasted *civilized* Yankees, have moved their hearts to desperation, until death itself is not looked on as a calamity. I hear to-day that our beautiful city is about to fall a prey to the spoiler; if so, no *lady* will remain there, that by any possibility can leave it.

The retreat of Beauregard seems to be approved by all, although it doubtless entails upon us the loss of Fort Pillow and Memphis. I was always at a loss to understand why Corinth should have been selected as headquarters: assailable on all sides, too near the enemy's base to gain the fruits of victory, after a battle gained, and besides when I left them a month since, the water was in a manner exhausted, and what was there very bad. Beauregard's present position is nearly equi distant from the Tennessee and Mississippi rivers, 60 miles or thereabouts from each. The enemy, to attack, must extend his line over a country difficult to advance, bad and scarce of water all the way. The deadly fevers that always prevail in this region, will doubly decimate his army in a month. If he should advance and be defeated, his whole army will be lost, or, at least, be entirely ruined. The regiment that arrived at New Orleans, 1003 strong, now number 700, a few more, perhaps; of this number there does not remain of those that left more than 500, the other 200 have been recruits. The other 500 have either died on the battle field, have been the victims of disease, or discharged on account of bad health. Those here are in fine health, not a dozen sick, none dangerous, as lively and cheerful as any in the land. They have had hard times from the beginning; their picket service constant and enduring. The last terrible winter in Kentucky did its work on many noble hearts that rest in a strange land. History may do them justice for their bravery on the battle field, but can never faithfully record what has been to them a thousand times worse than the casualties of any battle.

This is intended to give a mere outline of the movements and whereabouts of the Rangers, in whom so many in Texas are interested. I give you no stirring news. You can speculate as to the future as well as I—to speak of it at all can be but speculation. There is impenetrable darkness all around. I long to see the first gleam of light that will lead us on to honor, glory, and liberty.

GALVESTON.

Piedmont Springs, Grimes Co., Texas, Nine miles from Central Railroad, July 4th, 1862.

Readers of the Telegraph.—Feeling much in need of rest, recreation and sulphur water, that would be alkaline in its character, and contain 112 grains of solid matter to the gallon, and yield free sulphuretted hydrogen and carbonic acid gasses, the same to consist of alkaline sulphurets, sulphates and muriates, of lime and soda, together with smaller quantities of a salt of oxide of ion, I accepted the generous invitation of Leander Cannon, Esq., the proprietor of the "Piedmont Springs," and left Houston at 12½ P. M., the 2d inst., for a few days.

The cars made a quick trip to Navasota, but I held on to them and arrived there as soon as they did, or at 5 P. M. Jumping into an ambulance belonging to the proprietor aforesaid, I reached the Springs at 7 P. M. Time on the route, seven hours.

On arriving we were welcomed by a magnificent landlady and her beautiful daughter. Finding myself somewhat exhausted I took a drink of "sulphur," and retired to a comfortable room where I spent the night without seeing or hearing a single flea or mosquito! I deem this worthy of note, for I had supposed that no place in Texas was free from these plunderers.

Next morning, bright and early, I left my room in search of more "sulphur." Being alone, I walked a gallery about the length of Main Street, before I found a place of descent. Down I went one flight, and came to another gallery, which seemed longer than the first. When I reached the third, seeing others below me, I hailed a servant and enquired how much lumber there was in that house? He said there was ordinarily 600,000 feet, and that the walls of stone were somewhat extensive. I concluded I would "strike across" and see if I could not reach the ground by "shorter cuts." In this way I got things somewhat mixed. First I found myself in a ball-room 90 feet long, then in large and elegant parlors, then in enormous bed-chambers, all well ventilated, and finally brought up in a dining saloon 126 feet long. After resting a moment I rushed past the barber's shop, the "wine store," bath houses, ten-pin alley, store houses, and about a dozen other houses for guests, of various sizes, in pursuit of more "sulphur" from the fountain head.

After imbibing a few quarts from "Upper Spring," No. 1, I came to the conclusion that, in times past, I have visited many of the most famed and popular watering places in the North and South, and never had seen one that offered so many attractions to the invalid, or those in search of health and recreation, as "Piedmont Springs."

Here are accommodations for 600 persons, and nothing has been left undone that can add to the comfort of visitors. Situated in an elevated district, and surrounded by an atmosphere as pure as any in Texas, it is bound to remain free from malaria, and consequently healthy.

An abundance of cistern water can now be had for those who do not choose the spring water. The hunter and angler can find in this vicinity an abundance of game, and all can find whatever the lover of innocent amusement could desire.

The Hotel proper is four stories high, all *told*, and one of the most commodious and well ventilated buildings in the South. It is well furnished and managed. Nothing occurs to mar the pleasure or comfort of guests. The larders are crammed to overflowing, and the table is as well furnished and supplied as any in the State. If such accommodations do not attract visitors, and eventually render this one of the most popular resorts in the Southern Confederacy, this writer will doubt his ability to guess or foretell with any degree of certainty hereafter.

THE SPRINGS THEMSELVES.

There is no longer any doubt respecting the curative properties of these waters. Their merits are now acknowledged by all who have tested them.

But I seldom rely on the testimony of others, so I am experimenting with them myself.

One gallon drank before sunrise caused me to speak the truth all day, to recollect many things I had forgotten, and to guess right every time. Two gallons drank during one hour, set me to thinking—caused the scales to fall from my eyes, and gave me a lucid view of all the world.

Others were affected in a more remarkable manner. Old "stumps" held in these waters twenty minutes will shoot out to their original proportions. The ugliest looking men and women become perfect beauties in three days from their use, and they cause scolding women to become perfect paterns of meekness and docility in the same time, consequently they should be bottled up—the waters I mean—and kept in every family, for frequent use. The waters in spring No 1., are so strongly impregnated with sulphur or brimstone, that I have been afraid to explore it, not knowing where it might lead me! I am not anxious to come in contact with a pair of cast off hoofs.

But our limits are limited. Not so, however, with the waters of the Sulphur Springs; and I advise all ye who thirst to come here and try these waters Come on ye blind, halt and lame, and my word for it you will go away rejoicing at your cure. Come on, fair maidens and brave men, and you will leave none the less pretty or valorous.

H. P.

Correspondence Mobile News.

Letter from Chattanooga.

Chattanooga, June 17, 1862.

The Yankee General has no doubt found out by this that the blue clay mud holes, called Artesian wells. (!) some ten or fifteen feet deep, down which was lowered long, narrow, tin tubes, about the size of a common house water spout, in order to obtain the water, brackish with clay at that, were not so inviting as to render his stay at Corinth of any long duration. To push further South at this time of year in pursuit of our army, would be certain destruction, the retrograde movement of Gen. Beauregard being already equal to a defeat of Yankee arms. To fall back to the Tennessee river would be to demoralize and totally break up his army, so that he would seem to be between two fires.

It would seem, therefore, that there is but one outlet to his army that can save him, and that, too, is very problematical, though there can be no doubt but that the effort will be made. East Tennessee, under these circumstances, becomes of vast importance to the enemy to hold, as it commands the two great gates, the one leading to Virginia by Cumberland Gap, and the Cotton States through the mountain passes of Chattanooga. We already have reliable information that Buell's army is marching East, which is a sufficient indication to show that Halleck has no idea of retracing his steps over the fields of Shiloh to Savannah, on the Tennessee, with his whole army. At the same time, this movement clearly discloses the object of the enemy in gaining East Tennesssee, where he may hope to quarter his army in a more healthy climate for the summer. Under this view of the case, it looks as if there would be a struggle on both sides to reach this point by sending large reinforcements, and it simply becomes a calculation of time, which side has the advantage of reaching here first.

The distance is evidently in favor of Buell, but fortunately there is no rolling stock to move him over the Memphis and Charleston Road to Decatur, and his marches this hot weather must necessarily be slow, besides the great detention in crossing the Tennessee River, the Decatur bridge being destroyed. But for this their march to Huntsville and on to Stevenson and this place would be a rapid one, and a large force enter East Tennessee before we could reach it with our own troops. As it is, however, we have the advantage of the "land steamboats" over them, and can reach any point on our line before the enemy can move with his cumbersome forces.

Thus it looks to me that the summer campaign of Halleck's army, further South, is closed, and that he looks for new fields of operations in this direction. There was something more in Beauregard's retrograde movement than any of the Yankees dreamed of, and the results of that movement are now daily developing themselves.

The escape of Mr. Green Roberts, one of Col. John H. Morgan's men, from the Nashville Penitentiary, where he was held a prisoner, and who arrived here safe a few days ago, was very remarkable. He bribed the sentry to remove the iron grating from his window, which was in the second story, and then took the risk to jump to the ground, having to clear a wall beneath the window of some fifteen feet in height! It was a regular Sam Patch leap, of some forty feet. He made it, however, without breaking any bones, but he was so stunned by the fall, that he lay nearly an hour unable to move, but finally crawled off, and got away some two miles that night from town. He was afterwards twice captured, but was let go as an unoffending citizen, and finally made his way to this point.

Persons daily coming in from the interior report that 500 of our cavalry might have cut off the whole of Nagle's army, which so suddenly retreated from before Chattanooga. It is stated that a perfect rout prevailed; that the men were drunk, as well as officers, and straggled through the hills and mountains; that some thirty stopped at a gentleman's house, stacked their arms, and asked to be made prisoners.

ORA.

☞ A letter from Grayson county, of date 19th ult., says:

There has been no rain here for nearly three weeks, and some crops begin to show the effects of drouth. The yield of wheat in this county is only tolerable, though the breadth of land sown is so much greater than usual as to make more than an average crop. Corn will not be worth 25 cents per bushel here next fall if we have plenty of rain within the next two weeks.

The placing of Gen. Hindman in command in Arkansas is having a good effect. Rector and the family have "caved in," surrendered, and there is now no military authority in that State but the Confederate. Perfect unity of sentiment prevails, and troops are collecting at Little Rock in sufficient numbers to expel Curtis from the State. Gen. Pike's army of Indians have been furloughed for the harvest, and are to meet next Monday to reorganize under the Conscript Law.

From the New York Tribune, June 2d.

The Evacuation of Corinth.—A telegraphic dispatch from our correspondent at Cairo, gives us later news from Corinth. As it is approved by the military supervisor of the telegraph at that place, it may be received as, in a sense, official. From it we learn that the retreat of the Confederates from Corinth was conducted with perfect order; that they left nothing whatever behind them; That the forces have been, according to the statements of the inhabitants, moving for about a week, their provisions having gone some days before; and that their numbers were much less than has been generally supposed. This latter point, however may be matter of mere conjecture, or may be purposely misrepresented by the people. Why the evacuation took place, whither the enemy has gone, what is to be the next movement of Gen. Halleck—on these points we have no further light.

General Johnston's Wound.—A distinguished gentleman sojourning in our city for a time, has permitted us to make the following extract from a letter received by him on yesterday, from his accomplished daughter dated at Richmond, June 2d, where she was during the recent battles before that city, on Saturday and Sunday last:

"General Johnston was wounded by a Minnie ball in the shoulder. The ball passed down his back, and has not been found yet. At the same time a spent shell struck him in the breast. He fell from his horse, and broke two of his ribs; so, of course, he suffers very much. I spent all day yesterday with him. To-day he is much better, although the ball has not yet been extracted."—*Mississippian.*

Charleston to be Taken by the Yankees in Two Weeks.—The Charleston Courier says reports were rife in that city on Thursday, that a gentleman lately from Wasington stated that he had an interview with Secretary Stanton before leaving, and that the latter told him the Federal forces would certainly have Charleston in two weeks. This is (says the Courier,) from good authority.

If our Generals allow the enemy to land in force without opposition, and dig and entrench their way up to witin shelling distance of the city, it depends entirely on the industry of their "hedgers and ditchers" how long a time it will take to accomplish their object. But if they are pormptly met by our forces, and fought as our gallant 47th fought them on Monday last, the probability is that a large portion of the enemy will be permanently located on the island, and that the balance of them will go to Charleston under military escort.

The Chicago Post says the Lowell (Mass.) people, when the news of the Banks retreat came along, were so excited that they rang the (church) alarm bells! The fright could scarcely have been greater if "Stonewall Jackson" had turned up on Boston Common.

One hundred and eight Delaware slaves have disappeared since the rebellion.

In accordance with calls made by General Halleck, Governor Gamble, of Missouri, has issued a proclamation calling for recruits to fill up regiments of Missouri volunteers now in the service of the United States.

Last Notice to Tax Payers!!

ALL PERSONS in arrears for taxes due for the year 1861, are hereby notified to call at my office and settle up. Neglecting this Last Notice, will subject your property to advertisement and sale.

G. S. HARDCASTLE,
Assessor and Collector, Harris County.
Court-house, Houston, June 27th, 1862.
jne 30-tw2w.

THE TRI-WEEKLY TELEGRAPH.

VOL. XXVIII—NO. 52 HOUSTON, WEDNESDAY, JULY 16, 1862 WHOLE NO. 3547

CITV ITEMS.

——This town was much startled on Saturday last by the arrival of this "local." We came from "Piedmont," where we have been rusticating, masticating and sulphurating to such an extent that we feel like a bright, shining roll of clarified brimstone. The beauty congregated at the Springs from Plantersville, Anderson and Hempstead, nearly swamped our admiration, but we have providentially been spared to return to our duties, where we hope to be able to chronicle such facts as may enlighten and purify our readers "that their days may be long, &c.

We left the Springs with regret, for a more delightful place cannot be found in Texas.

——Capt. B. H. Andrews, who is now in camp on the Bay, near the mouth of Clear Creek, will give a ball at his camp this evening. Those who desire to attend should take the cars for Clear Creek Station, where they will find carriages in attendance.

To THE M. D. OF THE TELEGRAPH.—Is the "oxide of iron" and the "oil of spike" one and the same thing? EMETIC.

A physician as *rusty* as "Emetic" seems to be, should put a little more *oil* in his lamp, and *spike* the vent through which his senses are fast oozing.

—— The editor of the Item discourseth thus:

We ran down to Houston, on Friday last, to avoid work for awhile and see how the land lay; and were not much disappointed in our expectations. * * * "High Private" was at Piedmont Springs; thus we had no chance to crack jokes. He is one of those we were glad our presence ran off; for he is fast robbing us of our fame—his gills never being used in vain, while we, though ever on the strain, only bring forth with labor and pain. By the way, speaking of the Piedmont, we saw Dr. Cannon, ex-editor, and now owner of these Springs. He is a good humored fellow, and will make the sulphur of Beelzebub more profitable than the pinions of the eagle.

* * * * * *

We commend its (Houston's) sanitary condition for the balance of the summer to the especial care of "High Private," and hope he will issue his proclamation declaring all medicine, except whiskey, attempted to be brought in, contraband, and have it shipped up country! All the chance for the whiskey part of medicine is rotgut Yankee rum and brandy—and we all know what that is. The sight of a bottle makes you sick, and to drink it makes you steal!

We don't know what "rotgut is, but can guess. The "proclamation" shall appear in due time.

——Thirty or forty individuals will leave Houston, this week, for Piedmont Springs. There is room for at least six hundred. Turn out, all ye invalids and lovers of pleasure and recreation, and visit the springs for a month or two; and, our word for it, you will never regret it. You will there find more luxuries than this city can boast of at present.

——The number of strangers in the city has diminished somewhat of late; yet, even now the hotels are doing what may be called a flourishing business.

——During our late trip we saw many short ladies and received many short answers, when we ventured on the subject of domestic relations, but the shortest thing we saw was a breakfast at Navasota. Eight passengers who came in the stage from Huntsville, had just seated themselves at the table, when along came the cars. Just as they and taken seven mouthfuls and a half, toot! toot! said the engineer. The hungry ones made a rush and so did the landlord. They had time only to reach the train and threw overboard one four-bit shinplaster, before distance was lending edchantment to the view! How uncertain are human transactions!

—— In spite of all bristling and squealing, the four legged swine of this city have been compelled to succumb. No more do they enliven the streets with their presence. Retired porkers, adieu. Enjoy within your prescribed limits, with a grunt of satisfaction, all the pleasure you can, and never again aspire to that "area of freedom" to which you are no longer lawfully entitled. Here endeth the swine question.

—— Matches are now selling at two bits per box, or nearly one-half cent each. This is caused by the absence of so many of our young beaux. We venture to predict that when they "return from the wars," matches will be as plenty as Garibaldi hats. Keep up your courage. young ladies. There is a good time coming.

—— The city naver was much more healthy than at present. The same may be said of Galveston, all rumors to the contrary nothwithstanding.

—— Down with the dust. Where is the man with a watering cart? Who is there living on Main street that would not contribute a reasonable mite to lay this confounded dust? We venture to say none can be found who would not lend a hand. All are waiting to be called upon.

—— Others may remain incredulous respecting the news yesterday, but this "local" hesitates not to say that he believes the "Grand Army" is used up. McClellan may not have capitulated, but he is so completely routed and disorganized, that he will not come to time again for months, if ever.

—— We have received a handsome present in the shape of two new coats! For further information we refer to our worthy Mayor. If any one desires our "measure" for other articles of wardrobe, we will try and spare the time to accommodate them. Our modesty compels us to withhold further mention of this delicate subject. Ahem!

—— Young *gentlemen*(?) who promenade the streets on Sundays with "de colored fair sex," should see themselves for a few moments as others see them. More anon.

A NUT FOR OLD ABE TO CRACK.—On Saturday night last, the negroes of this city gave a ball for the benefit of sick soldiers. The tickets issued read as follows: "GRAND FANCY DRESS BALL, AT TURNER'S HALL. Sam Bowman has permission from Messrs. Geo. W. Frazier, T. W. House and Frank Mathews, to give a ball at Turner's Hall, for the benefit of the soldiers in the Hospital.—Admission, one dollar. Sam Bowman, Proprietor."

They were disappointed at a late hour in not obtaining the Hall, and were obliged, by permission of the Provost Marshal, to go to the Court House; consequently their receipts were comparitively small. Although much disappointed, they have paid over to the Mayor $51, to be applied as above stated. It is said that the ball was conducted with the utmost propriety. Put that in your pipe, Old Abe, and you blockaders who "read the Telegraph."

By-the-bye, how do you feel out there on your prowling mission, during this weather? If you had wool on your backs instead of bristles, you could not feel more sheepish when you read such accounts as the one given above.

HEADQUARTERS,

MILITARY SUB-DISTRICT OF HOUSTON, Houston, July 5, 1862.

Special Order No. 52,

ALL officers and men of Col. Flournoy's Regiment Texas Volunteer Infantry, now absent from the Regiment, *detached or otherwise*, will rejoin the Regiment at Hempstead immediately.

All persons absent on sick furlough, who are not able to move, will forward certificates of the fact from some respectable physician to the Adjutant of the Regiment at Hempstead.

By order of COL. GEO. FLOURNOY, Comd'g Military Sub-Dist.

R. L. UPSHAW, A. A. A. Gen'l. jly7-tw2w

BY THE CENTRAL TRAIN.

McClellan Bagged with all his Army.

We learn by passengers on the Central train that Gen. Van Dorn has published a general order to his troops with the official information that McClellan and his whole army has been taken prisoners.

Gen. Price has been ordered to the command. west of the Mississippi.

The Federals are marching on Monroe, La Carter's Brigade has been ordered to intercept them.

Vicksburg still holds out.

From the Shreveport News.

MONROE, LA., July 5.

Dear Sir: The Federals are advancing in this direction from Vicksburg with considerable rapidity, so much so that we fear they will be here in a few days, unless we can arrest them.

The object in this, to get 500 cavalry here from your place, as soon as possible.

Gen. Roane is looked for here hourly. McClellan's whole army has surrendered to Gen. Lee.

Have the cavalry forwarded as soon as possible, a little delay, and all is lost to us and you. Should they get here, they will proceed to your place without delay.

Yours,
C. H. MORRISON,

To Hon. R. WHITE, Shreveport, La.

The 500 men called for left here this morning for Monroe.

In addition to the above we will state that a passenger on the Beaumont train this morning, reported that the intelligence of the capitulation of McClellan had reached Woodville, Miss. as he left. Woodville is the last point on the telegraph line, which passengers by way of mouth of Red River would leave.

A Remarkable Scout.

Texians show their Training.

The following letter has been sent us by Mr. Franks. It contains an account of the most remarkable scouting skirmish we have seen yet. It beats Morgan, Scott and all the rest:

CAMP, NEAR RICHMOND, May 22d, 1862.

MR. F. G. FRANKS, Wharton, Texas.

Dear Brother:—As Judge Reagan has opened a mail route through to Texas, I have concluded to write again. I will now proceed to give you a history of my travels since I wrote you last, at which time we were encamped near Fredericksburg. Immediately after I mailed the letter, the long roll was sounded and we were marched out, formed in line. orders were read to the effect that each man should have cooked three days' rations, which should last him five days, and be ready to move at a moment's warning. In a short time after said preparations, we took up the line of march for Yorktown. After six day's and night's hard marching, we reached Yorktown—generally called the City of the Peninsula. We were camped there about two weeks, expecting the enemy to attack us. Our line of battle extended from town to Winn's Mills, distanced about eight miles, supported by about fifty strong batteries and one hundred and twenty thousand men—the flower of the army; and, I tell you, they gave our brigade as much as they needed. They have an idea that we had much rather fight than eat, and, judging the rest by myself, I will say that we do love to fight, but don't love to march twenty-five miles per day, fight all and eat none. While we were at Yorktown they kept scouts out from our brigade all the time, and our lines being not more than half a mile from the Federals, we had hard skirmishing with them every day. I was out in two scouts and was engaged both times. The first time I went there was only twenty of us. We passed through our pickets and got up within shooting distance of the enemy's pickets. We kept up constant firing at one another all day. We had one man killed and one wounded. We don't know how many we killed of them. At night we sent a courier back to headquarters, asking Gen. Hood for more men. He immediately sent eighty men, increasing our number to ninety-eight, with orders to act as we saw fit. By this time, we found out that the Yankees had holes dug all along their lines to stand picket in, we furthermore found that they came in those holes about an hour before day. So we, to get before them, got up and started at midnight, went there and placed a man in each pit—they being about fifteen steps apart.

We all took our positions, waiting very patiently for Mr. Yankey to show himself. but being so anxious to kill a Yankee, we were beginning to be impatient, we remained though in our holes. About half an hour before day we saw them kindling fires and cooking their breakfast. They soon got through and made a break for their holes; they marched in four ranks until they came in one hundred and fifty yards of us. By this time it was daylight. they being later than common; we then heard the captain give the command "Halt," "Left Dress," "Front." He then gave the command "As skirmishers take intervals," which they did most beautifully, then "Forward Guide Right," "March." Now every fellow made for his hole, not knowing that we were in a mile of them, but they advanced very slowly and seemed to be talking about how they should act. We sat perfectly still waiting for them to come on us. I heard one say "I guess them darned Texians will be in here again today." Another replied, "Yes, but it would be a darned good joke if them Texians as you call them should come in here and get into our holes." By this time the Yankee who was coming to the hole in which I was, had gotten in sixty yards of me, when one of our boys who was on the extreme left fired. At the sound of his gun, the Yankees broke for their holes, but to their great astonishment, their holes were occupied by those same "darned Texians. We let the rascals run right up on us before we fired, and nearly every man got his Yankee. We killed eighty and took thirty prisoners, and drove the rest of them clear inside of their inside pickets. We then returned to camp and was applauded very highly by our Colonel and General, Hood, Smith and Johnson. So ended our scout. Your brother,

R. H. FRANKS.

Letter from the 2d Texas Regiment.

CAMP NEAR PRICEVILLE, MISS. June 28th, 1862.

Editor Telegraph: Acting upon the supposition that anything concerning the "Bloody 2d" will be of interest to your readers, and feeling, moreover, impelled to make a "few feeble remarks" upon various subjects, I embrace the rare opportunity of somebody to send by, and the still rarer one of something to write on, paper being a scarce commodity in this "neck of woods."

Since our hegira from Corinth, as you probably know, we have had but little fighting to do, and the attention of the public mind has been gradually turned from the great army of the West to the still greater one in Virginia, and we have been allowed to rest quietly in camps; improving our health by the daily practice of the skirmish drill—a very pretty manoeuvre when executed upon the parade ground of camp Bee, with the accustomed congregation of fair spectators—but not considered so by the poor private, over a ploughed field, with the mercury standing at 90 degrees in the shade, with a momently increasing prospect of having to "rally on the reserve." some 400 yards in the rear, at a "double quick."

The romance of soldiering has pretty nearly worn off, and it has become reduced to facts and figures; I might with propriety say *bare facts*, for clothing, in common with other earthly things, will wear out—new supplies are "unavoidably detained." and *something* (a "military necessity," I reckon, as that is responsible for most all slight commissions or omissions,) keeps pay-day in the same place it has been for the last eight months, to-wit: still in the perspective, thereby preventing us from furnishing ourselves. When we first arrived at Corinth, we were told the Texians were readily recognized by being the *dirtiest* troops in the command; but experience proved to us that a new system had been adopted, as our retreat illustrated. In answer to the often repeated inquiry, "what regiment is that?" one of our boys merely raised the skirts of his coat, by way of a reply, and the dilapidated condition of his nether garments seemed to solve all doubts in the querist's mind, as he immediately rejoined, "Oh! yes, you are Texians." Well, we can console ourselves with the quotation that "a hole may be but the accident of a day; but a patch is the sign of premeditated poverty."

By-the-bye, friend Cushing. (not to fly off at too great a tangent,) our peace of mind has been rather disturbed by reports which have reached us from home, derogatory to a regiment which has been a favorite with Texians, and has won the good opinion of all, *worthy of notice*, it has been brought in contact with. One, which I particularly allude to is, that "the second day of the battle of Shiloh, our regiment ran before the fire of the enemy, and refused to rally when commanded—nay, even *entreated*, to do so, by our officers." No one who was with our regiment on that eventful day can, with truth, make the statement, that they dared not follow, where any dared to lead; and the only case when we were not close upon them, might have been in the retreat of that night to Corinth, and sufficient reason for that might be found in the fact, that the mud which impeded the footmen was more easily passed through on horseback. It must be borne in mind, that we had just undergone a march of nearly a month's duration from Texas, and were brought into action without a day's rest. Sunday morning, after double quicking since day-break, we came under fire at about 8 o'clock, and soon after were called upon by Gen. Johnston, with "Where is that Texas Regiment," and on our gallant Colonel answering, "Here they are," were ordered by the General to charge the enemy and drive them "out of that camp." After opening our fire and repulsing the enemy's charge three times, Col. Moore gave the command, "Charge bayonets," and with a yell, in we went; the Federals ran in great disorder, although we learned afterwards from prisoners, that they numbered 3000, whilst our regiment had less than 730. We made several other brilliant charges during that day and the following one, and were highly complimented by our Division Commander, General Withers. The fact that our field officers were promoted immediately after the battle, and that we received an order from Head Quarters to inscribe the word "Shiloh" on our battle-flag, show honors seldom granted to a "pack of cowards."

By the course of promotion, our regiment is now commanded by Col. W. P. Rogers, and a better or a braver man never led troops any where. He is universally beloved by his men, who have every confidence in his skill and bravery, so certain are they that victory awaits when he points the way.

Truly, yours,
CONFEDERATE.

A Tribute to the Memory of Miss Eva Harris.

Rarely has it fallen to the lot of a community to mourn the untimely death of so choice a spirit, and so perfect a character as hers, over whose mortal remains the grave has just closed. Death, with unsparing hand, has snatched from a wide circle of friends one whose life and daily walk have been a worthy commentary on her profession. A native of Texas, her early life was passed in the country, and in the dawn of womanhood she came to reside in this city. Possessing excellent mental abilities, and a taste both correct and refined, she was in a measure self-educated. She had seen enough of the world and its society to estimate it at its fair value, and though sociable in her feelings, and possessed of charming powers of conversation, she did not consider human life was bestowed merely for purposes of amusement or enjoyment. She thought it incumbent on her to do all the good in her power to accomplish; and she visited the sick and sought out the poor and friendless, and many an eye will now be moist with sad memories that used to glisten with joy at her approach.

Last winter, among the various claims pressing for attention and relief, she thought the case of the sick soldiers in the hospital, one of the most important. Many were sick numbers had died, and there was a lack of medicines and those comforts so essential to the sick. She, and a few others, undertook to procure means and see them properly applied. This involved not only time and labor, but no little exposure and hardship. Malignant colds were prevalent; she contracted one; and, with characteristic magnanimity, she neglected herself to attend to the wants of others, till she passed the line of relief, a rapid consumption set in, medical aid proved unavailing, and after a few months of prostration and suffering, she left us here, bereaved of her happy and cheering presence, but stimulated by her noble example in every good word and work.

Rest, sainted spirit! May the turf lie green and softly on your quiet grave, and may the sweet example you have left behind you animate and encourage others to "go and do likewise." *.

"Aye! thou art for the grave; thy glances shine
Too brightly to shine long. Again the spring
Shall deck her for men's eyes; but not for thine
Sealed in a sleep that knows no wakening.
The trees for thee have no medicinal leaf,
And the vexed ore no mineral of power,
And they who love thee wait, with anxious grief,
Till the slow plague shall bring the fatal hour.
Glide softly to thy rest, then; death should come
Gently to one of gentle mould, like thee;
As light winds wandering through groves of bloom
Detach the delicate blossom from the tree.
Close thy sweet eyes calmly, and without pain,
And we will trust in God to see thee yet again."

Houston, July 12, 1862.

THE BRIDGE BURNERS.—On yesterday evening seven of the bridge burners brought here for execution, were hung at a point not very far from the city. Arrangements were made for them all to be swung off at the same time. but two of the ropes breaking the men fell to the ground, instead of into eternity. But these two were quickly brought to their feet, new ropes adjusted to their necks, and an end at once put to their earthly career. We understand that seven others are to be hung at an early day, perhaps this afternoon.—*Commonwealth, 19th inst.*

Letter from Virginia.

RICHMOND, June 21st, 1862.

FRIEND CUSHING: Since the last battle time passes drearily away, nothing arising to increase the life or vigor of the scene in the entrenchments around our beleagured capital. This is strange, 'tis passing strange. Some eight weeks ago the commander-in-chief of the Yankee army represented himself to the authorities at Washington, and to the world, to be pursuing a routed, fugitive and demoralized army, which he intended to "push to the wall." He even doubted their ability to rally and make even a show of defence for Richmond. If they attempted to stand before the city, they would be captured or disposed of at a blow. It was altogether an impossibility for us to check the march of his invincible legions. Such was the substance of the bombastic dispatches which heralded the advance of the Yankee General on Richmond. For more than one month he has been in sight of the smoke of the city, and three weeks ago he was offered on opportunity of taking the city by battle if he could. But, instead of hailing the opportunity as a joyful epoch in his history, as we were led to expect from his many boasts and pledges, he skulked and dodged like an Indian, in the swamps and morasses of the Chickahominy; and therr he keeps himself.

It is now eleven months since the boaster, McClellan took command of this multitude of braves who, if accounts are to be credited, have been panting all the time for battle, with this invincible army Richmond was to fall and a quietus given to the rebellion in 90 day; yet he has made but one attack on the rear of our moving army, and in that he got terribly whipped. With the exception of this attack at Williamsburg he has shown no hostile intentions, except verbal ones, since his advent on the Peninsula. Every one North and South, await the sequel of his "masterly inactivity." In the city everything is quiet, order reigns supreme, and drunken soldiers are "like angels' visits," as the saying is rather misty. The hospitals have been cleared of three-quarters of the patients, the country citizens having taken them away by hundreds. All that were able to walk, received furloughs and have gone to their respective homes. One of our boys, A. Wolff, will probably start for Texas in a few days. Captured Yankees are being brought in every day and the prisoners present quite a lively scene. Gen. Sterling Price is still in the city. There is nothing new in the papers. Ben Wood's speech in Federal House of Representatives was the only thing of importance cut from the Northern papers. I send you a copy of it. He advocates the peace policy in strong terms but such as will not meet with favor in the Southern heart. There is at present more sickness than usual in our company, whooping-cough being the chief evil. None of the boys dangerously ill. Send a paper occasionally and oblige us all.

Yours, &c. P. P.

P. S.—Sick at present in Company A, W. A. George, F. M. Poland, H. C. Settle, O. F. Settle, W. A. Ceals, O. M. Douglass, J. H. Healy, C. P. Harn, Charles Sheldon, B. Wolf, L. Cramer, F. De Bulb, R. G. Howard, W. De Young, Dave de Grange, Wm. Denos, [illegible] Cohn, C. E. Stevens, Wm. H. Clark, G. Daily, F. Morse, Jasper Barron, Meyers, Limbs, John B. Hale, and B. P. [illegible]. Most of the above are under treatment in or near Richmond, and are being well cared for, so friends at home may reassure themselves in regard to their safety. P. P.

CITY COUNCIL PROCEEDINGS.

HOUSTON, July 10th, 1862.

Council met pursuant to adjournment, present, his Honor T. W. House, Mayor; Aldermen Thomas, Fleishman, Anders. Fisher and Taylor. The petition of sundry inhabitants of the City of Houston, representing that the surveys of the city by different city surveyors differed materially and praying the Council to establish a permanent survey was read and refered to a special Committee, viz: Aldermen Anders, Taylor and Fisher.

The following communication was received from the Fire Department:

To His Honor the Mayor and Aldermen of the City of Houston:

At a meeting of delegates from Protection Fire Company No. 1, Liberty Company No. 2 and Hook and Ladder Company, No. 1, convened at the Engine House of Protection Company No. 1, May 19th, 1862, the following Officers were elected for the Fire Department in accordance with an ordinance passed by your board, May 1st, 1862:

James H. Perkins, Chief of the Department; J. C. Baldwin, C. J. Granger, J. S. Cushman, Assistants; William Powars, Secretary. Which was read and ordered to be spread on the minits.

The Semi-Annual Reports and Reports for the month of June of the Assessor and Collector, and Secretary and Treasurer, were read and received and also the Reports of the City Marshal up to the first of May.

Report of the Finance Committee of the City of Houston, from Jan. 16, to July 1, 1862.

Am't Received from Assessor and Collector	$12,813 19	
Am't Rec'd from City Marshal	343 25	—$13,156 44
City Warrants Issued		6,259 00
Total		$19,406 44

Expenditures.

July 1, Expense acct. including appropriations for Military purposes	$5,070 14	
Street and Bridge acc't	3,815 38	
Dredge Boat	126 00	
Pauper acc't	365 40	
Police acc't	1,766 51	
Hospital and Physician	1,614 93	
Market account	169 34	
Licences Returned	119 82	
Camp Kyle	5 10	
Wharf acc't	4 50	
	13,057 21	
Old indebtedness taken up and cancilled	4,784 06	
Cash on Hand	1,526 76	
Warants on hand	38 50	—$19,406 44

WM. ANDERS, Chairman.

To the Mayor, Aldermen and Inhabitants of the City of Houston:

Your Committee on Finance beg leave to submit for your consideration the above Semi-Annual account of the financial condition of your city, showing the receipts and disbursements from the 16th of January to 1st of July, 1862. It will appear to your Honorable body that the Board in the expenditures has not over-stepped the revenues derived from collections. The actual expences fall a few dollars short of the income proper, but as there was a considerable number of old liabilities for which the city was paying interest. Your Committee authorized by resolutions of the Board have taken up nearly all the old liabilities and have issued Treasury Warrants to the amount of 6,250 dollars bearing interest. The old city bonds and drafts which used to float around in the community at and exorbitant discount, have entirely disappeared and your Committee has been able to meet its engagements with ready money. As far as the condition of the country would permit, important improvements have been made and they soon will be completed Owing to our political disturbances and falling off of our commerce, the revenues of the city have considerably decreased; some sources of revenues as wharfage tax, tax on goods and special licences have almost entirely ceased, that under those circumstances, the disparity between the receipts and expenses of the city is not greater or very gratifying to the city and in a great measure attributable to the energy, zeal and prompt actions of the Assessor and Collector, and Secretary and Treasurer, of the city to whom a great deal of credit is due for their valuable services.

Your Committee is informed by the Assessor and Collector, that he believes his collections for the half year from July to January next will equal his collections for the last six months, which will be more than sufficient to carry on the city Government and leave us some surplus for making improvements.

WM. ANDERS,
H. F. FISHER.

Report received and adopted.

The Street and Bridge Committee made the following report:

To His Honor the Mayor, and Board of Aldermen:

The petition of the Galveston and Houston Junction Railroad Company praying that Scrimpf street be opened as a public thoroughfare having been referred to your Committee, we, in the discharge of the duty imposed upon us have diligently investigated the subject, and from all the information we can obtain from other and personal examination of the survey and records we are led to the conclusion that the West line of the Sam Williams Survey upon which is located Schrimpf street, has been correctly traced by Mr. Convers and Mr. Powars. Believing this to be the case, your Committee, (though deploring the pecuniary loss to some who may have built on the street) must in duty bound recommend that the buildings be removed and the street opened to the public. All of which is respectfully submitted.

H. H. TAYLOR,
H. FLEISHMAN, } Committee.
W. E. THOMAS,

Which report was received and adopted.

On motion E. J. Sweney was appointed Deputy Marshal. The bill of W. R. Wilson was referred to the Finance Committee, and the bill of Behring & Bro. to the Street and Bridge Committee. The following bill were audited and ordered to be paid:

John Ross	$147 00	C. Koch	$ 7 00
A. M. Brooks	16 00	C. Fix	2 00
C. Koch	9 00	Kiay	4 00
R. Hilderbrandt.	24 00	W. R. Wilson	8 00
Stanley	18 00	T. W House	346 34
Dicoing	12 00	T. W. House	24 00
Staglish	12 00		

On motion the Council adjourned until Thursday 24th inst. GEO. EWING, Sec'ty.

GALVESTON, July 8th 1862.

EDITOR TELEGRAPH.—No doubt but a summary of news occasionally from this city would be acceptable to your many readers. Last Saturday the Santee took her departure in tow of a steamer, whilst a large steamer has taken her position as a blockading vessel. Nothing remains now of the formable fleet but the steamer and two schooners of diminutive size. Thus has Capt. Eagle taken his departure without carrying out his threat of bombardment at his "earliest convenience." This is hidden in obscurity, long may it remain so. The health of the troops on the Island is good and owing to the efficiency or our Provost Marshal, Mr. Massie, strict order reigns throughout the city, no drunkenness, fighting, or other necessary evils attending the selling of whiskey. All of the shops are effectually closed. There [illegible] had two [illegible] sudden deaths in the [illegible] being [illegible] one of Capt. [illegible] [illegible] The other, [illegible] company, [illegible] laid down on [illegible] motion to draw [illegible] in the room.

During the last few days we have had frequent and copious showers of rain which has filled the cisterns and laid the dust. The gardens are looking finely, many of which are covered with tomatoes and other vegetables, and no one to gather them, the proprietors being in the country. Watermellons in profusion, and can be bought at eight dollars per hundred. A few families are returning from the country, many of which are on the sick list from fevers contracted on or near the bayous, several have already died since their return.

The Telegraph and News are the only papers that we get and we have to look to them, with the exception of an occasional extra, for the news.

Sea bathing and a fine sea breeze during the day with cool nights, in a measure does away with laxity and debility of the system so plainly felt by a Galvestonian in and about your city, in fact anywhere in the interior at this season of the year. Many of our most intelligent citizens are of the opinion that the war is drawing to a close. The withdrawal of the would be capturer of "the forts and munitions of war in and about our city" has steadied our nerves, and we begin to think that Galveston is not a doomed city after all. So mote it be. H. C. B.

WHAT MEANS SUBJUGATION.

If any one has his doubts of the result of the subjugation of the South, let him read the following true copy of a letter, found upon the battlefield near Corinth, which was left behind by the author in his swift fight from the scene of conflict. Its contents serve to show the spirit by which the agrarian hordes of the North are actuated in countenancing and supporting this war upon us:

HAMBURG, TENNESSEE, April 27th, 1862.

My Dear Sue: I wrote to you a few days since. Fearing, however, that it has been miscarried or intercepted, I write again. We are at this place, and expect to move forward in a short time on Corinth, a distance of sixteen miles. We are expecting a hard contested battle, as we learn the rebels are in large force. Well, when that time comes up we will make the rebels feel the weight and power of our steel. I have seen many of the natives of this country. They present a woe-begone look. They look like they never had any advantages of an education. I noticed some of the women's dresses. You ought to be here to take one gaze at their huge appearance. Their hoops are made of grapevine and white oak splits. I feel sorry for the poor ignorant things. Well, we will teach them, in a few days, how to do without white oak and grapevine hoops. They are now the same as conquered, and one more blow and the country is ours. I have my eye on a fine situation, and how happy we will live when we get our Southern home. *When we get possession of the land we can make the men raise cotton and corn, and the women can act in the capacity of domestic servants.* The women are very ignorant—only a grade above the negro, and we can live like kings. My love to all the neighbors. Kiss all the children for me, and tell them pa will come back again. Adieu, my dearest Sue.

JAMES DONLEY.

MRS. SUE DONLEY, Mount Vernon, Illinois.
By the politeness of Mr. Allen.

From Havana—The Blockade.

NEW YORK, June 13.—The yellow fever is increasing at Havana.

The schooner Constitution arrived at Havana on the 27th ult. from Sabine Pass, with a rebel cargo conveyed to the British Consul, Crawford. Nassau dates to the 7th, note arrivals of rebel steamers Cecil on the 5th, and Kate on the 6th, from Charleston, with dates from rebeldom of the 2d inst.

The Bahama Herald says: "At last it appears that the Southern star is in the ascendant, and their noble courage is meeting some reward."

It then gives the rebel accounts of Jackson's raid in Virginia. The Steamer Nellie, attempting to run the blockade on the 27th, was run ashore after being shelled by Federal cruisers, and her cargo landed on Long Island, slightly damaged, but the vessel pretty badly used up. The steamer Tubal Cain, with a cargo for the rebels, arrived at Nassau from Liverpool, consigned to rebel agents, Addlery & Co. The inhabitants of Long Island were busily engaged in planting cotton seed.

THE TRI-WEEKLY TELEGRAPH.

VOL. XXVIII—NO. 55. HOUSTON, WEDNESDAY, JULY 23, 1862 WHOLE NO. 3550

CITY ITEMS.

PERSONAL.—Col. John A. Wilcox arrived in town last evening, as fresh and energetic as ever. He is "on to Richmond."

—— Judge Campbell lost a fine son on Sunday last. He was only ill a few hours, and died of congestion of the brain. Aged thirteen years. Sad loss.

—— We trust that when our Southern Confederacy becomes a fixed fact, which will be ere long, that we will have a National Academy, to regulate our language. Yankee ice, and Yankee Dictionaries, and Yankee everything else we must discard. Let us have our own language, unadulterated.

—— It is said that "Othello" was played in a masterly manner at *our* theater, the other night.

—— When we consider the state of the times, it is somewhat surprising that so many improvements should be going on, as at present in Houston. Building after builing is going up, and everything wears a healthy appearance. How do you get along with your subjugation, Lincoln—and how are the blockaders?

—— A substitute by the name of San Clair, belonging to Waul's Legion, was found dead last Sunday morning, at the corner of Main and Prairie streets.

—— Hard times for "locals." No town news afloat.

—— We hear complaints in certain directions, about airs that military officers are putting on. Such men should remember that this war will not last always, and those who look to "promotion", hereafter, should govern themselves accordingly.

—— The Victoria Advocate has a "Meteorology," or some such thing that regulates the weather. If it can regulate our weather—we would like to borrow it Monday was a little hotter than our grammar. For instance, Hot, Hotter, Hottest. Hottentot, Hottentotter. Hottentottest, Hot as——. Well, it was very warm. Then our "mean" temperature is about as mean to-day as temperature gets to be. During the past month we have had a fog, a velocity of winds, an average amount of clouds and the sun has set daily without interruption.

—— See notice of the death of Dr. MARSH, in another column. His death will be generally lamented, for he was universally respected in this community.

COL. JOHN MARSHALL.

The State Gazette pays the following glorious and worthy tribute to the memory of Col. Marshall. The people of Austin, it strikes us, are wanting in patriotic regard for the valliant dead, in making no public manifestation of their regret at his death:

John Marshall is dead. He fell on the field of battle and of victory, leading his gallant regiment against the entrenched batteries of the enemy. We can hardly realize the mournful fact that our friend is no more. We knew "when the hour that tries men's souls" should come, when our brave volunteers should be called upon to grapple with the invaders of our soil, that John Marshall would be in the thickest of the fray; and yet we hoped that his life would have been spared to have witnessed the final defeat and destruction of the enemies of the country. From early manhood to the hour of his death, he devoted his time, talents and fortune to the cause of the South, and during a political career of many years, never for a moment swerved from the true path of honor, and never sacrificed principles for men. We will not here attempt to give even an epitome of his life. He has gone to that bourne from which no one returns; but there is an imperishable wreath of glory about his brow; he died fighting for all he loved best on earth—for his countrymen, and their dearest rights; for his home, his wife and little ones, and for the soil that gave him birth. High-toned, chivalrous, generous to a fault, loving whatever was good and great, detesting whatever was mean, sordid and truckling, he of course had many warm and devoted friends, and many bitter, malicious and vindictive enemies. When those enemies, the most of whom are false to the South, shall have long since passed away, or be remembered alone with feelings of loathing and contempt, the memory of John Marshall shall live green in the hearts of his loyal countrymen, and his glorious death will stimulate to renewed acts of chivalrous daring the gallant and invincible soldiers of Texas.

BAYLOR UNIVERSITY, July 2d, 1862.

Soldiers of the Southland Braves.

Desiring to express our interest in the noble cause you have espoused, and wishing to evince our appreciation of your gallantry, we present you this flag, feeling assured that its folds will ever wave where

"Lofty deeds and daring high,
Blend with the notes of victory."

Hoping that you may return safely and speedily to your homes, crowned with the laurels of victory, we are your very sincere friends,

ELLA TRYON, MARY MASON,
CLARA MASON, NANNIE HOUSTON,
KATE CLARK, DORA PETTUS.

CAMP WAUL, July 3d, 1862.

To Misses Ella Tryon, Mary Mason, Clara Mason, Nannie Houston, Kate Clark, Dora Pettus.

FAIR DAUGHTERS:—In behalf of the "Southland Braves," we tender you our utmost thanks for the presentation of one of the most beautiful Confederate Ensigns that has ever been thrown to the breeze upon our tented fields. The interest ever manifested in our cause by the fair daughters of our own dear sunny land, will create the Archimedes lever with which your oppressed brothers will over-turn the sable shrine of Northern despotism, and roll back the tide of inhuman invasion, or with their bayonets, dig for themselves and their sisters, their own graves by the side of those of their mothers and fathers, now sleeping in Southland. But let us hope with you, that we may return in safety and victorious; and also hope, that we may be able to present you the same beautiful ensign, baptised in freedom's blood—consecrated to the God of Liberty, and forever embalmed in woman's patriotism.

We have the honor to be your kind friends and defenders.

W. R. SULLIVAN,
Captain "Southland Braves,"
Waul's Legion.

HEADQUARTERS,

TRANS-MISS. DISTRICT, South of Red River,
San Antonio, Texas, July 11t, 1862.

GENERAL ORDERS, No. 11.

I. With much concern the General Commanding this District has learned that officers of the Confederate army, have upon divers occasions seized and appropriated the private property of good and loyal citizens. That officers in the service should perpetrate such outrageously illegal acts would seem incredible, were it not for the irrefragable proofs furnished. Such conduct is in direct violation of all law, of the regulations and articles of war, and unbecoming an officer and a gentleman.

II. Any officer guilty of such conduct shall be promptly arrested by the nearest officer, whether he ranks him or not: charges preferred against him, tried by Court Martial and have inflicted upon him the severest punishment under the Articles of War and the Law Martial.

By order of Brig. Gen. P. O. HEBERT.
OFFICIAL. C. M. MASON, Capt. & A. A. A. G,
jy 16-tw3t.

BY THE CENTRAL TRAIN.

MORE GLORIOUS NEWS.

Baton Rouge Retaken.

Curtis Captured with 6000 Prisoners.

McCLELLAN'S DEFEAT ACKNOWLEDGED.

ETC., ETC., ETC.

We are in receipt of the Alexandria, (La.,) Democrat Extra of the 16th with the fellowing intelligence:

CHARLESTON, July 10.—The enemy landed in force yesterday on the main, near Port Royal Ferry, apparently for the purpose of making another attack on the Charleston and Savannah Railroad, but retreated on the approach of the Confederates.

GRENADA, July 10.—Passengers from Memphis last night say that intelligence was received there on Monday last, which states that Hindman had captured Curtis, with six thousand prisoners; and Fitch, being unable to reach Curtis with reinforcements, returned to Memphis with his command on Sunday.

GRENADA, July 7.—The St. Louis Republican of the 2d inst., which has been received here, still preserves a mystertous silence respecting McClellan's defeat, which it fears may mean disaster.

Farragut's entire fleet of gunboats and Porter's mortar fleet all passed down by the mouth of the river on Saturday morning. Their destiuation is supposed to be Mobile. For the present they have given Vicksburg a wide berth. The upper river fleet is still there.

RICHMOND, July 8.—The President has issued the following congratulatory address to our victorious army: SOLDIERS! I congratulate you on the series of brilliant victories which, under the favor of Divine Providence, you have lately won. And as the President of the Confederate States, I do heartily tender you the thanks of the country, whese just cause you have so speeially saved.

Ten days ago an invading army mustering superior to you in numbers and materials of war, closely beleaguered your capital, wantonly proclaiming its speedy conquest. You marched to attack the enemy in his entrenchments, and with well directed movements and death-daring valor, you charged upon him in his strong position, drove him from field to field, over a distance of more than thirty five miles, despite his reinforcements, and compelled him to seek shelter under cover of his gunboats, where he now lies cowering before the army he so lately derided and threatened with entire subjugation.

The fortitude with which you have borne the toil and privations, the gallantry with which you have entered into each successful battle, needs to have been witnessed to be fully appreciated. But a grateful people will not fail to record your deeds and bear you in loved rememberance. Well may it be said of you, that you have done enough for glory, but duty to a suffering country and to the cause of constitutional liberty claims from you yet further effort: let it be your pride to relax on nothing which can promote your future efficiency, your one great object being to drive the enemy from your soil, carrying your standards beyond the outer boundaries of the Confederacy, to wring from our unscrupulous foe the recognition of your birth-right and an independent community.

JEFFERSON DAVIS.

From the Alexandria Democrat, Extra, 16th.

GRENADA, July 9.—Northern dates of the 6th contain copious accounts of McClellan's defeat. They claim to have captured seven hundred Confederate prisoners. They acknowledge the loss of 20,000 men, thirty pieces of artillery, and a large amount of commissary stores and ordnance.

The following generals are confessed to be taken prisoners: Gens. Reynolds and McCall. Gen. Goslin was killed. The following were wounded: Gens. Meade, Burns, Sumner, Heintzleman and numerous field officers.

The strength of the Confederate army is stated at 200,000; loss at 30,000. The dispatch concludes by stating that the army is now encamped on high rolling ground on the banks of James river, 15 miles below Richmond. The transports are unloading supplies at the wharves.

The Commanding General is confident of successfully meeting any attack the enemy may make on their present position.

MOBILE, July 9.—The steamer Natchez, from New Orleans with a flag of truce, reports that the Confederates had captured Baton Rouge, with 1500 prisoners.

MOBILE, July 9.—The defeat is reluctantly confessed in the battle of Richmond by a few of the Northern correspondents.

The Cincinnati Commereial fears McClellan's defeat will precipitate foreign intervention, and advises prepartions to be put on foot to resist dictation from England and France.

On the fifth day of the battle Gen. McClellan's French Staff Officers left him on the first boat for home.

Another Federal gunboat is reported sunk by our batteries on White River.

MOBILE, July 8.—Gen. Shipley has been appointed military Governor of Louisiana and Picayune Butler displaced.

Gen. Van Dorn has captured Baton Rouge. All the Yankees were taken prisoners.

The partisans in the swamps opposite the city of New Orleans have driven in the pickets from Carrolton.

A Maine regiment mutinied because they did not want to go to Vicksburg, Two of them were shot.

Fifteen or twenty gunboats at Vicksburg have been badly damaged, some of which were sunk.

RICHMOND, July 8.—No intelligence has been received from the lines to-day.

The city is perfectly quiet, and the heat to-day has been oppressive.

Major-General McCall, of Pennsylvania, was captured in Friday's fight by a private in General Hill's division, of the name of Rawlings The General insisted upon receiving the prisoner from the hands of his captor, who had modestly retired and was doing his duty in the ranks when the distinguished prisoner was escorted to the presence of Gen. Hill by an officer.

Besides Gen. McCall Brig. Gen. Meade was captured here. Gen. McCall is at the Spotswood Hotel.

A correspondent of the Mississippian says that the enemy are now evidently attempting to flank us above on the Yazoo, and above Vicksbusg the battle will be fought. They cannot take our batteries, nor can they whip the forces we shall have at any point to meet them.

The greatest confidence prevails here now. We have a General in whom we all repose confidence; we have the best troops the army affords; activity is in all our movements; and "Liberty or Death" is the watchword.

Baton Rouge, with its garrison of 1500 Yankees, is said to have been captured by our troops last week. Our troops at Tupalo have advanced towards Tennessee. Bragg's army will soon be emulating the soldiers of Johnson and Lee in the East. It is rumored about the streets that there has been a fight in Arkansas, resulting in the capture of Curtis by Hindman.—*Shreveport News*.

HEADQUNRTERS,

TRANS MISSISSIPPI DIST., SOUTH OF RED RIVER,
San Antonio, Texas, July 9, 1862.

General Order, No. 8.

THE seizure by subordinate officer, of arms and munitions, the property of the State of Texas, is positively forbidden.

By order of Brig. Gen. P. O. HEBERT.
CHARLES M. MASON, Capt. & A. A. A. G.
jly16 3t

_ Some time since Pauline Pry asked through the Telegraph what was to be thought of a lady who could see no harm in Butler's Order No. 28. Mollie Hughes replies indirectly in the following expressive style. Her language is not as elegant as it might be, perhaps, but as she remarks in a note, "Evil be to him who evil thinks." It is expressive to say the least of it:

THE BUTLER.

BY MOLLIE HUGHS.

INSRIBED TO PAULINE PRY—Tune, "*The Man that Struck Billy Patterson.*"

There was a lady in Austin,
A lady very ancient, man,
And yet in spite of ruined teeth,
She fell in love with a Butlerman—
A nasty, ugly Butlerman,
A pole-cat smelling Butlerman,
A tearing, swearing, puking, knock-kneed,
Ranting, roaring Butlerman.

His face was no ways beautiful—
With poc-marked sores all marked across,
And the shoulders of the dirty dog,
Were big and red as a skinned hoss—
O, the lump of a Butlerman,
The whisky-devouring Butlerman,
The great he-rogue, with his Yankee brogue,
The ranting, rioting Butlerman.

Both of his eyes were bottle green,
And his nose was as red as a beat, my dear,
And the calves of his wicked looking legs
Would never meet by a foot, my dear—
O, the great big Butlerman,
The bandy-shanked Butlerman,
The stamping, ramping, swaggering, staggering,
Leathering, swash of a Butlerman.

The fellow had a monstrous paunch,
And he could'nt see his feet, my dear,
And shape and size the villian's neck
Was as big as a daddy's bull, my dear—
O, the horrible Butlerman,
The thundering, blundering Butlerman,
The stinking, slinking, blinking, drinking
Son-of-a-skunk of a Butlerman.

This name was a horrible name, indeed,
Being Picayune Rotgut* Butlerman;
And his breath that spewed a hog to death,
Was sweet perfume to Philisy-Ann—
The boozing, snoozing Butlerman;
The 'toxicated Butlerman.

This was the beast the lady loved,
Like all the girls of quality;
And she knew his order Twenty-eight
Was for the soldiers jolity—
O, the leathering Butlerman,
The barbarous, savage Butlerman.
That bothered the hearts of the Ancient Maids,
And fixed their love for the Butlerman.

* A kind of bad whisky.

Sylphide Swamp, July 4th, 1862.

Horace Greeley's Opinion of Weed,

As published in Punch, the organ of Lincoln's Administration, and the paper that describes successes, sorrows and scamperings of Yankee troops.

BY MOLLIE LEGRAND HUGHS.

Post me up in botanical phrases,
Expressive of raggydy Weedy things,
Growing by damp and dingy mazes,
Where the leech wriggles, and the frog sings.

Teach me words to express the infernal,
Root and branch and blossom and seed,
Flowers of the Albany Evening Journal—
Hemlock, night-shade, wormwood Weed.

'Tis well to say at Manassas battle,*
That we and the Tribune could have victory [won,
Or left a strait shirt-*tale* like Wilson,
To show that *We'd* made a Bully Run.

'Tis well to assert that Yankee courage
From mothers like mine Mrs. Greeley proceed,
Ugh! ugh! the ugly plant of the season.
Skunk Cabbage Henbane Hellebore, Weed.

'Tis well when the vessel keels to leaward,
To swear at the steersman for losing time,
Asserting that had he kept to *Sea-ward*,
Better luck would have favored him.

'Tis well to say that on all occasions
The Yankees show a commendable speed,
And so would you, before Texan rebels,
Lobelia Vermifuge Jim'son Weed!

Sylphide Swamp, July 10, 1862.

A Texas Skirmish.

Our letters from the Texas Brigade are sometimes so long coming that they lose much of their interest before reaching us. We extract, however from a letter from P. P., dated Richmond, June 13th:

Business has been so active lately that I have been unable to chronicle all the notable events that have transpired. Among the foremost of the interesting incidents that have occurred, was an affair that took place three days ago. A detail of five men from each company in the three Texas regiments, under the charge of two Lieutenants, were sent out at daylight to throw up rifle pits, and at the same time to observe the movements of the enemy in their immediate vicinity. While they were engaged at the work, a regiment of the enemy suddenly came upon them and opened a terrific fire. The little band fell back a short distance and prepared to give them battle in Indian style. The enemy, thinking they had fled, followed up their apparent success until within a very short range of our rifles, when the boys opened upon them and caused them to retire in confusion, leaving a number of their men on the ground. Another regiment took their place and attempted to drive our boys from behind their trees, but it was no use; the unerring Enfield brought a man every time, and at each volley at least 100 of the enemy were struck. Three volleys were fired, when the enemy retired, and evinced no disposition to renew the attack. They took nearly all their wounded from the field; 50 dead bodies were found, however, that had not been removed. Our loss was small—one of the 1st Regiment (D. D. Davis) was killed, and some 9 or 10 wounded. Among those wounded was F. C. Hume, of Capt. Powell's Co. D, 5th Texas, and A. Wolff, Co. A, same regiment. All of the wounded are faring well at present. A great deal of praise was awarded to the boys for the admirable display they made, and *mirabile dictu!* a notice of the event appeared in the Richmond papers, notwithstanding the fact that there was not a Virginian engaged in the fight.

Such notices are commendable, and show a desire to do justice to all engaged in the great struggle; though newspaper notices are not indispensably necessary to the cause, still they have a very salutary effect.

Our company has lost another member, Mr. F. S. Manuel, one of the recruits. He died a week ago at one of the city hospitals, having been sick but a very short time. He was with the company but a short while, but had made many friends, and had, on all occasions, exhibited the characteristics of a true soldier. His loss is regretted by all.

THE BATTLE ON JAMES ISLAND.

Brilliant Confederate Victory.

Correspondence of the Richmond Dispatch.

CHARLESTON, June 20th, 1862.

The late battle in the vicinity of this city was a far more brilliant and important affair than at first supposed. The enemy were so badly beaten that they have not fired a shot from their gunboats or batteries since, though previous to the fight they kept up a constant cannonade day and night. Considering the number of troops engaged on our side, and the length and fierceness of the combat, the battle is one of the most remarkable of the war. The rout of the invaders was complete. They abandoned their dead and fled in wild confusion to their gunboats. Two of their regiments—the 79th New York, (Highlanders,) and one from Michigan, fought well. One company of the former penetrated as far as our breastworks, and its captain was killed while mounting the ramparts. The enemy had five regiments in the fight. Our force engaged consisted of three companies of South Carolina artillery—the Charleston battalion, which numbered only 150 men; the Eutaw battalion, 400 strong, and Col. McEnery's Louisiana battalion. Other regiments came to the relief of these troops; but most of the fighting was already over. It will be seen, therefore, that the enemy outnumbered us two or three to one. Their greatest loss was occasioned in attempting to storm our entrenchments, behind which Colonel Lamar's artillery was stationed. Col. Lamar was the hero of the battle. He was severely wounded. Col. McEnery also deserves great praise. He led his Louisianians fearlessly into the fight, with the watchword, "Remember Butler."

Every day's exploration of the surrounding woods reveals additional dead of the enemy. It has been ascertained that a body of the Federals attempted to cross a swamp, where many of them stuck fast in the mud and were killed and wounded by our shells. Finally, the tide came up and drowned both dead and wounded. Two hundred and fifty of the enemy have already been buried by our troops, and fifty additional dead bodies were discovered yesterday. The total loss of the enemy in the battle cannot be far from—

Killed and left on the field	300
Taken prisoners	136
Wounded and dead carried off of the field, estimated at	700
Total loss of the enemy	1130

The Confederate loss in this glorious victory is

Killed	48
Wounded	106
Total Confederate loss	154

The enemy's attack was a surprise to our troops. Had a competent Confederate General been on the field and some plan of action arranged, the whole of the enemy's attacking force might have been cut off. As it was, the greater part of the battle was fought by the rank and file "on their own hook." We have four Confederate Generals in this quarter, but not one was in command. To the rank and file, then, be the glory given of having achieved one of the most brilliant successes of the war. If the Confederate Government is looking for material for more Brigadier Generals let promotion fall upon the lion-hearted Col. Lamar, who defended the entrenchments, and the gallant and chivalrous McEnery, who, like Blucher, came into the field just in the nick of time.

Since the battle, the enemy have been entrenching themselves silently at the lower end of James Island. As their plan of assault has proved impracticable, it is presumed they will be contented hereafter to advance by regular approaches—that is, if they are permitted to do so. Prisoners state that there are nine Federal regiments on the island and that Gen. Isaac I. Stevens, of Oregon, (the Chairman of the Brekinridge National Committee in the last Presidential campaign,) is in command. This man Stevens professed to be an ardent proslavery man before the war, and was here in Charleston, enjoying its hospitalities, only two years ago.

There is much dissatisfaction here with the military authorities of the department, and a strong wish expressed for a change in the commanding officer. The South Carolina troops are anxious to defend Charleston, and will do so successfully if they are permitted to. A report that we were to have the great services of Beauregard spread universal joy among the troops. If, however, we cannot have Beauregard, we would be glad to get Huger, Magruder, Hill of N. C., Whiting, Gregg, Joseph R. Anderson, or any other first class General. A change of some kind is necessary to restore confidence to the troops and people.

PALMETTO.

KEACHI, LA., July 6, 1862.

Editor Telegraph: Many of your readers might be interested to hear something from Carter's Brigade of Texas Cavalry.

We have been in this vicinity for some days, busy in making our tents, shoeing our horses, and preparing our arms the best we can for the campaign.

Since we have been here, Col. Wilkes has had several cruises up and down Red River, and they have in the main, been successful. Several parties have been trying to open up the trade from New Orleans, and some of the munitions sent up from that city out of the way of the Feds have, it appears, fallen into hands not very friendly to us! Against these have the expeditions been sent, and the result has been 5,000 lbs. powder, 10,000 lbs. lead, 15,000 pair cotton cards, 6,000 yards jeans, 2,000 yards Lowells, with quinine, caps, quicksilver, coffee, salt, &c., and the great bullet-moulding machine.

We will give you a little incident of the Colonel and one of his captains, Taylor, and the Governor of Louisiana. It appears that the Governor had purchased ten sacks of the salt illicitly introduced,—Capt. Taylor getting wind of it, went and took the salt. There was considerable opposition, but the stern Captain was not to be put off, so the salt had to come.

Yet another. In one of these excursions a French company was sent for to prevent the taking of some of the stores. The Texas Captain had only 20 men, but fell in with Lt. Col. Walker of Terry's Regiment, who had a few men with him. The gallant Colonel told Capt. T. he would send him a few hands in the fray if needed, but when Capt. T. saw the Creole company, he sent the Col. word he could whip them with his 20 Texians; but no fight took place, and Capt. T. carried off the stores.

The Committee of Public Safety have powerfully seconded Col. Wilkes' efforts to break up this Federal trade.

There is a great deal of sickness in the brigade—mostly measles—but not many deaths. We would have been at Little Rock but for the great numbers sick with measles, and it was thought best to let it take its course, and in the meantime to fully equip the command. The last two regiments are made up mostly of married men, who haxe left home only through a sense of duty, and wo be to the Yanks if ever they get a fair clatter at them.

The citizens of Louisiana treat us like true friends, and with a high-souled hospitality that has won all hearts; and the ladies, God bless them, by their kindness and solicitude for our well being, have made many a Texian's heart and arm stronger for the conflict.

You may hear from us again.

Yours truly, &c.,
J. E. F.

BY THE BEAUMONT TRAIN.

The only item of intelligence received by the N. O. train, in addition to what we received by the Central train yesterday is that a flag of truce steamer, having gone from Mobile to New Orleans with a load of flour, took back a cargo of merchandize purchased from the Federals, under a Federal permit to go through the blockade. On her arrival, the foreign Consuls in Mobile at once took measures to have the blockade of Mobile declared broken by the act of the Federals. It was expected that European war vessels would interfere at once.

The Texas Brigade.

ON THE LINES, June 9th.

To the Editors of the Dispatch.

A modern philosopher, whose teachings are to be valued more for their worldly wisdom, perhaps, than for their classic antiquity, whose proverbs are more practical than poetic, used to set before his son as a perpetual monitor, for his intercourse with his fellow man, this injunction—"Blow your own horn." At the risk of being numbered as one of this school, I claim a short space in your column.

In your account on the morning of the 15th, of the skirmish in which the Texians were engaged, there are some inaccuracies which I wish to correct, by simply telling the story as it is, myself being a witness on the spot, and a participator in the fight.

On yesterday morning, beneath the warm garb of the Sabbath sunshine, while yourself and other friends in the city were no doubt quietly performing your Sabbath ablutions, this skirmish took place, and inasmuch as military men here think it was creditable to us, I give you the facts:

A detail of one hundred and fifty men, from the 1st, 4th and 5th Texas regiments was made on that morning, *not to dig trenches*—that's not our style—but for the purpose of securing the woods in front of our line on the Nine-Mile road, seeing what Yankee force there was in the woods, and to drive them out if possible.

We found the enemy posted in the woods a few hundred yards from our front line of pickets. After reconnoitering, we discovered a strong force of the enemy—a whole brigade, it was supposed, in the left of the wood, and a large force, then unknown immediately in our front. The force on the left were silent, calculating that they had the dead thing on us, while those in front were bold and impudent, keeping up a constant fire at us from among the trees. We let them amuse themselves for a while in this manner, occasionally silencing one as he became too annoying, until our line was fully established and safegards placed against our friends on the left of the road.

The command was then given, "Forward, boys! Give them h—ll!" The Texas war-whoop rose on the air, and a thousand Yankees rose like dark spirits through the gloom of the forest. The voice of their officers could be heard amid the din of battle urging their men to stand, but it was in vain they essayed to stop our fast advancing line. They fired but one volley and took to their heels, our boys following. We pursued them out of the timber, under cover of their batteries, when they took refuge in their trenches, and fired back at us. Here we had a comrade killed; but regardless of the fierce fire poured upon them, four men bore him on their shoulders out of the field back to our camp.

In the meantime our friends on the left of the road attempted to succor their companions and to "suck us in." They started to come in our rear, but a small "family battery" we had in the right place opened on them and deterred them from their purpose. One well aimed shell fell in their midst, killing seven and wounding a number.

The enemy's loss in this engagement was forty five killed, including a Lieut-Colonel and two Lieutenants. We secured the sword of one Lieutenant, and a revolver from the other. On the pistol was engraven, "Presented to Lieut. M. C. Frost, by the citizens of——Ward, Philadelphia." The force against us, was one regiment, the 71st Pennsylvania, besides those gentry who threatened us on the left. We suppose the force that routed them did not exceed one hundred men, as a portion of our small party had to defend points in the woods to protect our flanks. Our men were under command of Lieutenant Barziza, of the 4th, Lieut. Jameson, of the 1st, and Lieut. Nash, of the 5th regiment, who acted discreetly and bravely, and led their men to the charge. Our loss was one killed, and four wounded, slightly.

Texas scouts run these same Yankees to their batteries a week ago, killing a number of them, and nothing was said of it. At West Point we killed 250, took a large number of prisoners, and stampeded three or four brigades, yet nothing but incidental allusions have ever been made to that fight by the Richmond press.

We are too much preoccupied to give details of our engagements, but we think that the same avenues by which you get the intelligence of every fight in which Virginians are engaged are open to the press, and ought to be brought into requisition. An opinion prevails with the army that you are disposed to magnify on the one side and to neglect the other.

Not partaking of this opinion, I send you this, with a simple prediction that when "the fight takes place the *Texas Brigade* will kill more Yankees, storm more batteries, and capture fewer prisoners than any brigade in the service.

A TEXAS SCOUT.

BLIND INSTITUTE, TEXAS.—We wish to call the attention of the public—especially of those who are more directly interested, to this important institution of our State. The existence of this fearful war, constitutes no good reason why the unfortunate should neglect their own dearest interests. The institution is located on a beautiful eminence handsomely enclosed and shaded with a good supply of forest-trees—and has every appearance of health. The buildings and outhouses are ample, for the accommodation of from twenty-five to thirty pupils, say fifteen of each sex. The rooms of the institution are furnished with everything that is necessary to make them comfortable. The institution has two exeellent cisterns furnishing a bountiful supply of pure, cold water. The water is thought to be the best about the city. The Asylum is furnished with a Globe, a Library of books, slates, and two fine pianos, all suited for the instruction of the blind.

The present Superintendent is a minister of the Gospel, of over thirty years standing in the Church, now occupies the relation of superannuated preacher of the M. E. Church, South. Not being able longer to pursue his favorite profession, is desirous still to be useful to his fellow-creatures, in some other sphere, as well as to secure a livelihood for his family. His long and unblemished standing gives every guarantee that the welfare of the pupils, mental, moral and physical, will be constantly aimed at. The Matron, Mrs. Smith, is noted for good taste and business qualities. No person committed to her care will suffer for want of attention. Miss S., the Music teacher and assistant in the School department, is highly accomplished and well qualified for the performance of her duties.

Not the least advantage occurring to the Blind in this institution, are the mechanical arts—such as broom-making, bottoming chairs, bead-work and knitting. We recommend all who intend to embrace the advantage afforded by this institution to address the Superintendent at Austin, immediately.—*Austin State Gazette.*

ADMINISTRATRIX NOTICE.

THE undersigned having qualified as Administratrix of the Estate of Alexander Keech, deceased, all persons having claims agains said Estate are hereby notified to present the same, duly authenticated within the time prescribed by law
jly9-w6w BETTIE S. KEECH, Admx.

THE SOUTHERN ILLUSTRATED NEWS.

J.W. TORSCH ENGRAVER

Vol. I.—No. 7. RICHMOND, SATURDAY, OCTOBER 25, 1862. Price 15 Cents.

GENERAL BENJAMIN McCULLOCH.

Gen. Benjamin McCulloch, whose picture we present in this number of our paper, was born in Rutherford county, Tennessee, about the year 1814. His father was aid-de-camp to General Coffee, and served under General Jackson in the Creek war. He fought under the latter officer at Talladega, Tallahassee and the Horse Shoe Bend, where he exhibited that reckless daring which often proves so efficient against savages and which has since rendered his son so famous. Young McCulloch was early placed at school, where he remained until his fourteenth year, at which time his father removed to the western part of the State, and settled in Dyer county. This neighborhood was then a wilderness, covered with swamps and dense forests, and infested by wild animals. Bears were so abundant as to form the principal meat of the settlers, and the hunting of them was an essential part of youthful education.

Young McCulloch soon signalized himself in this dangerous occupation, and became renowned throughout the settlement as a most successful hunter. A youth spent in this manner could not fail to engraft a love of enterprise and roving adventure in the bosom of the young and ardent Tennesseean. Accordingly, having reached the age of twenty-one, he set out for St. Louis, in order to join a trapper company destined for the Rocky Mountains. Much to his disappointment, he arrived in that city after the expedition had started. He then applied for admission into a company of Santa Fé traders, but here he was also unsuccessful, as their number was complete.

Disappointed in his ardent expectations, young McCulloch seems to have given up his intentions of roving, at least for awhile, as we hear little of him until the war between Mexico and Texas. This at once roused his daring spirit and he joined the standard of the Texans.

The following incident is replete with interest: "In September, McCulloch returned home, and soon after his arrival called on Col. David Crockett, who was making up an expedition to go to Texas, to take part in the revolution that had then broken out in Mexico; the whole Southwest at that time was alive with feelings of sympathy for the Texans, and numbers were daily flocking to their standard.—McCulloch agreed to accompany Col. Crockett to Texas. Nacogdoches had been appointed the place of rendezvous from which the expedition was to start, and the Christmas of 1835 was named the day for the meeting, when, as 'Old Davy' said, they were to make their Christmas dinner off the hump of a buffalo. Unfortunately, however, McCulloch did not arrive until early in January, and, finding that the party was gone, he proceeded on by himself to the river Brazos, where he was taken very ill, and did not recover until after the fall of the Alamo. McCulloch's disappointment was very great at not being able to join the gallant band of patriots at the time, but which afterwards proved very fortunate for him; for Colonel Travis, after having sustained a siege for thirteen days, with only one hundred and eight Texans against Santa Anna's army, fell with his brave little band, having previously killed *nine hundred* of the enemy.

"After his recovery, he descended the Brazos river in a boat to Grass Plant, where the Texan army had assembled, under General Houston."

He immediately entered the army as a private, and was attached to an artillery company, in which he remained until the battle of San Jacinto, where Santa Anna was made prisoner and his army of fifteen hundred killed or captured. He participated in that celebrated struggle, and was a sergeant in charge of the gun on the right. There were two guns, known as "the Twin Sisters," under the command of Captain Isaac N. Moreland, of Georgia. These guns subsequently fell into the hands of the Mexicans, but were eventually recaptured, and left at New Orleans, where they remained until a few years ago, when they were presented to the Texan government by the State of Louisiana.

McCulloch continued in service from time to time during the war. His operations were mainly upon the frontier in the battles with the Indians. He was very active in that respect and very often commanded parties who went out in pursuit of the savages, who looked upon him as their most formidable enemy.

At the termination of the Texan war, he settled in Gonzales county, where he remained for some time. But during the California excitement he went to that State, where, after a short residence, he was elected sheriff of Sacramento county. He, however, still retained an ardent attachment for the land of the "Lone Star," and, after an absence of a year or two, returned to Texas.

In the year 1846, he was elected as a member of the State Congress, as it was then called, which honorable position he held until the war broke out between the United States and Mexico. He then resigned his seat, and, like many of the Texans who had fought in the Texan revolution, he hurried forward to meet his old enemies. He raised a company of "Mounted Rangers," and joined General Taylor on the Rio Grande after the capture of Matamoras, not having been able to organize his command in sufficient time to participate in the first battles of the war. His company was used principally for scouting, and acted generally under his own direction, or the immediate command of General Taylor.

After the fall of Matamoras, McCulloch advanced to the town of Reynosa, where he remained for a while under command of Colonel Watson. Leaving this place with his company, he pressed further into the interior, and took possession of the town of China. Soon after, he entered Camargo, about the same time that General Taylor was marching to attack Monterey.

McCulloch's company formed part of the regiment of Texan Rangers, commanded by Colonel Jack Hays, which marched with General Worth to assist in storming the Bishop's Palace in Monterey. In all of the operations of General Worth's Division, McCulloch distinguished himself in a remarkable manner.

After the fall of the palace, the Texan Rangers were employed in breaking open the houses of Monterey and penetrating their walls inside toward the Central Plaza. They contributed most materially to the subsequent capitulation of the city.

Just before the battle of Buena Vista, Ben. McCulloch performed a most daring exploit. With one companion, he left camp in the night, and proceeded to make a reconnoisance within the lines of the enemy, then on the advance, with Santa Anna at their head. He entered the Mexican lines, where he spent several hours in close observation within hearing of the groups gathered around the watch-fires. He discovered their numbers, learned their plans, and obtained all the information necessary to General Taylor. He immediately returned and related to that officer the result of his reconnoisance, and upon that information General Taylor immediately acted by retreating to the strong point, "*Agues Nuevos*," where the battle of Buena Vista was fought.

In the battle of Buena Vista, McCulloch behaved with more than his accustomed bravery. "Maj. McCulloch," said Gen. Taylor, in his report, "rendered important services before the engagement, in the command of a spy company and during the affair was associated with the regular cavalry."

For gallant conduct during the siege of Monterey, McCulloch received an appointment in the quartermaster's department, with the rank of major, which position he either never accepted or never served in but a short time. In 1855, upon the organizing of four new regiments of horse in the United States Army, he was tendered, by President Pierce, the appointment of major in one of the new regiments of cavalry, which favor he declined, and returned to his home in Texas. He was afterwards appointed United States marshal for the District of Texas, which office he held up to the year 1859, when he resigned it.

The three latter years of his life, previous to the breaking out of the present war, were spent principally at Washington city. During that time, he was sent, under the administration of President Buchanan, and in company with Governor Powell, to

GENERAL BENJAMIN McCULLOCH—From a Photograph by Minnis.

Utah, to pacify the hostile tribes of Indians in that territory. While in Washington, Major McCulloch was upon terms of great intimacy with all Southern leaders, was an ardent advocate of secession from the beginning, and of the opinion that it would be followed by war. He was assiduous in his endeavors to stimulate the States to prompt action and to prepare themselves beforehand for any emergency.

The moment Lincoln's election to the Presidency of the United States was proclaimed, General McCulloch repaired to Texas, to take part in any movement that might be made in that State. He was selected unanimously by the Committee of Public Safety to raise the men necessary to compel the surrender of San Antonio, with its arsenal and the neighboring forts, four or five in number. Within four days, he had traveled one hundred and fifty miles, and stood before San Antonio with eight hundred armed men. It is almost useless to say he was successful. Shortly after, he was appointed a brigadier-general, and assigned to the command of the Indian territory.

General McCulloch rendered himself conspicuous in the Missouri campaign with Generals Price and Van Dorn. He was the ranking officer at the battle of Oak Hill, which is deemed one of the most bloody and fiercely-contested conflicts of the campaign in that quarter. In that struggle, his boldness, intrepidity and reckless daring were unparalleled.

At the battle of Elk Horn, this gallant hero poured out his heart's blood on the altar of his country. He was killed in the brush, on a slight elevation, by one of the sharpshooters of the enemy. He was not in uniform at the time, but his dress, together with his continued acts of daring, attracted attention, and he was picked out as a mark. He wore a dress of black velvet, patent leather high-top boots, and a light colored, broad brim hat. The soldier who killed him was a private in an Illinois regiment, who robbed the body of a gold watch.

The fall of General McCulloch was esteemed as a national calamity, and, in his official report of the battle, General Van Dorn declared that "no success could repair the loss of the gallant dead who had fallen on the well-fought field."

Ben. McCulloch was never married, but was socially inclined and rather fond of society. His mind was calm and vigorous; he was independent in his opinions and very firm; his manners and habits were very simple. He was noted for his strong friendship, and adversity had upon his noble nature but the effect of fire upon frankincense, causing the purest and finest essences to evaporate.

At the time of his death, the subject of our sketch was forty-eight years of age; his remains were taken to Texas and buried at Austin. His memory will ever remain green, and not a pulse among the thousands of brave hearts, who call the flag of the "Lone Star" their own, but will beat with emotion for the loss of him who defended it so nobly on every field, and not an eye of man, woman or child, but will drop a tear for the untimely end of the noble Ben. McCulloch.

DREAM LAND—A SKETCH.

Dreams, dreams! does it not seem like mockery, when the heart is sad and desolate, to dream of love, joy and happiness? yet it is a blessed respite from sorrow to fall asleep and fancy that life is joyous and beautiful, though we do sigh when we awake to find it but a dream.

We are all dreamers, even in our waking moments: for, do we not toil up the hill of life—pursuing some imaginary good that still eludes our eager grasp, and, bounding on, seeming to say in mocking tones, follow, follow! and we obey the call till death closes our eyes, and shuts out the phantom forever.

The infant in the cradle must have pleasant dreams; for, mark the pretty, rosy lips parting in a happy smile, and the little dimpled cheeks stamped with innocence and purity. Sweet babe, thou art doubtless dreaming of the angels. God bless thee.

The maiden, perhaps, dreams that her lover has returned from the field of battle, with his brow encircled with laurels, and the preparations go merrily forward for her marriage. She awakes with a happy smile, and hopes the dream may be soon fulfilled.

The mother dreams of her darling children that God has called from their earthly home, to dwell in heaven. They pass before her as angels, with their golden harps, and singing hallelujahs to God Almighty. She awakes contented, and looks forward with joy to the time when she shall join them.

The convict in his gloomy cell dreams of his childhood. Again he is by his father's side, listening to his kind words of counsel, and feels his mother's soft hand on his heated brow, as she draws back the brown curls and kisses him fondly. Then he hears the prayer rise up from that little cottage—his father's manly voice asking for protection and guidance, and praying that his only son may prove a blessing; and his mother's sweet, low voice saying, amen. He awakes, and hastily pacing his narrow cell, says, "Ah! if they had lived I should not now be a miserable felon. God forgive me."

The Christian dreams that with him time is ending; and before him is a glorious eternity. He sees the golden city of light, where sorrow and care cannot enter, and rejoices in possessing a passport through Jesus Christ. Surely, the Christian's dreams are bright and beautiful, and his waking moments are crowned with peace and joy.

A Beautiful Reflection.—Bulwer eloquently says: "I cannot believe that earth is man's abiding-place. It can't be that our life is cast up by the ocean of eternity to float a moment upon its waves and then sink into nothingness!—Else, why is it that the glorious aspirations, which leap like angels from the temples of our hearts, are forever wandering about, unsatisfied? Why is it that the rainbow and clouds come over us, with a beauty that is not of earth, and then vanish, leaving us to muse upon their faded loveliness! Why is it that the stars, who hold their festival around the midnight throne, are set far above the grasp of our limited faculties, forever mocking us with their unapproachable glory! And, finally, why is it that the bright forms of human beauty are presented to our view, and then taken from us, leaving the thousand streams of our affections to flow back in Alpine torrents upon our hearts? We are born for a higher destiny than that of earth; there is a realm where the rainbow never fades—where the stars will be spread out before us like islands that slumber on the ocean, and where the beings that here pass before us like shadows will stay in our presence forever!"

THE SOUTHERN ILLUSTRATED NEWS.

Richmond, Saturday, October 18, 1862.

The "Illustrated News" is published every Saturday afternoon, and can be had on application at our office, in the building occupied by Messrs. Samuel Ayres & Son, corner of Cary and Virginia streets. The Trade supplied at a liberal discount.

To Advertisers.—A limited number of advertisements will be inserted in the "Illustrated News," *at ten cents per line.*

Notice to Postmasters and Agents.—Any person sending us a list of ten subscribers, with the price of subscription, will be entitled to an extra copy of the "Illustrated News." Any one sending us a list of twenty, will receive three copies of the paper *gratis.* We call the especial attention of Postmasters to this fact.

OUR CONTRIBUTORS.

As an evidence that we are leaving no stone unturned to give the public a first-class literary paper, we take pleasure in announcing that we have secured the valuable services of the following named talented gentlemen and ladies, each of whom will contribute weekly to the columns of this paper:

W. GILMORE SIMMS,
JAMES BARRON HOPE,
HUGH R. PLEASANTS,
JOHN R. THOMPSON,
Dr. BAGBY—(Mozis Addums,)
Rev. J. C. McCABE, D.D.,
S. S. BRYANT,
MARGARET STILLING,
GRACE MILLWOOD,
Mrs. HERBERT—(Louise Manhiem,)
ZILLA BRYANT,
LAURA LEASON,
SUSAN ARCHER TALLEY,
MARY LOUISE ROGERS,

And many other writers, whose names are withheld from motives of delicacy.

THE TIMES.

The main body of the Army of the Potomac has been entirely quiet, since our last, in its old position near Winchester. The monotony of its life has, however, been greatly broken by two expeditions against the enemy—one under General Stuart and the other under Colonel Imboden. On the —— inst., Colonel Stuart left camp with a body of cavalry, estimated variously at from 600 to 3000, crossed into Maryland at Hancock, passed through the narrow slip of land which separates Virginia from Pennsylvania, and penetrated the latter a considerable distance. During the expedition, he passed through Mercersburg, Chambersburg, Emmettsburg, Liberty, New Market, Hyattstown and Burnesville. He thus made an entire circuit of the enemy, and returned by White's Ford. He cut the enemy's line of communication and destroyed many arms, captured a number of valuable horses and obtained quite a large number of recruits. On the 14th, General Stuart returned to camp without the loss of a man.

On Tuesday last, about one hundred and fifty prisoners, captured by Colonel Imboden in his late expedition, arrived in town. We have before us the official account of Colonel Imboden's proceedings. On the 2d inst., one of his scouting parties encountered a company of the enemy's cavalry at Hanging Rocks, in Hampshire county, and captured their captain (Battersley), five men and fourteen horses, army equipments, &c. The cavalry proved to be company B, 1st New York. On the morning of the 4th, in the midst of a dense fog, he surprised an entrenched camp of the enemy at the mouth of the Little Capacon. One of his companies actually got into the trenches before the enemy had the least intimation of danger. Captain Newhard, Lieutenant Chayner and fifty-five men, all belonging to company K, 54th regiment Pennsylvania volunteers, were taken, and eight killed or wounded in attempting to make their escape. Colonel Imboden burnt the railroad bridge over the Little Capacon, with all the company's buildings, &c. On the same morning, Colonel Imboden captured a company stationed at Paw Paw tunnel, by sending his cavalry across the river into Maryland to prevent escape, and surrounding the place by passing his infantry over a steep mountain. One captain, two lieutenants and ninety men (the whole company) were captured. They proved to be company B, 54th Pennsylvania. He took 175 Austrian rifles and accoutrements, and 8000 rounds of water-proof cartridges; destroying commissary stores, camp equipage, &c. for want of transportation. While thus engaged, about 200 Yankee cavalry from Romney fell upon his rear-guard at Capon bridge, dispersed the guard, which was weak, and 100 unarmed men whom he had left under Lieutenant Stone, burnt one of his wagons, attempted to carry off five others, but abandoned them, and burnt the carriages of two field pieces, carrying the guns in the wagons over the mountains. They captured also eight of his men and his medical chest. He subsequently recaptured all his wagons and ammunition. Like General Stuart, Colonel Imboden performed this important service without the loss of a man.

From Van Dorn's army, we learn that it is rapidly reorganizing, and have no doubt that it is already prepared for action. It held the railroad junction and was prepared to maintain it at any hazard. General Van Dorn has been superseded by General Pemberton.

Great uncertainty prevails with regard to General Bragg's position. The Yankee papers report a battle at Perrysville, and claim a victory, but in such subdued tones as to lead to the belief that they were defeated. A telegram from Chattanooga, on Wednesday, announced a great victory on the part of General Bragg, who, it is said, had killed, wounded and made prisoners 25,000 of the enemy. It soon became rumored that the President had received a telegram to the same effect from General Bragg himself. Much excitement was the consequence; but the rumor, as usual, turned out to be entirely false. The President had received no such telegram. The telegram to which we have alluded, and which was to the associated press, was copied, carried to the war office, and there read in the presence of several gentlemen, who did not enquire whether it had been addressed to the President or not. They spread the report and it flew like lightning. That there has been a great battle, we do not question. We shall leave this article open, to note the results, should they be received before we go to press.

Upon the whole, this has been a quiet week.

P. S.—The victory of Gen. Bragg seems to be confirmed. A telegram from Knoxville to the press of this city, dated 16th, quotes the Knoxville Register of that morning as saying that two couriers had arrived confirming it—that the battle commenced on Monday, 6th, Gen. Hardee commanding the right, Gen. Buckner the centre, and Gen. Marshall the left—that on the first day Hardee captured 1,500 prisoners—that on the second day (Tuesday) he captured 4,000 prisoners more—that Marshall and Morgan captured 3,200—and that the enemy was driven twelve miles with tremendous slaughter, our own loss being small. We captured also, forty pieces of cannon.—Confirmatory of this, the Register publishes an extract from a letter of Col. Palmer, who is at the Gap, and who says that two soldiers and a Tennessee captain wounded in the battle had arrived, who concurred in stating that Bragg had driven the enemy ten miles, capturing 9,000 prisoners. On Friday, it is added, Kirby Smith attacked them on the right, took 500, killed Gen. Jackson, and took Gen. Tom Crittenden. A despatch from Gen. Forrest, who participated in the battle of the 9th, dated Murfreesboro', 13th inst., to Knoxville, says he estimates the loss of the enemy in that battle at 20 to 25,000 men, and our own loss at 5,000. The Cincinnati Commercial, of the 11th, says Bragg has beaten Buell and driven him across the Kentucky river. Putting all these accounts together, we cannot but arrive at the conclusion that our troops have obtained a signal victory. The Louisville Journal, however, says Bragg is beaten. It acknowledges, nevertheless, the loss of four Generals—Jackson, Terry, Webster and Tonett killed, and two wounded—Gens. Curran Pope and Rosseau.

ODIUM THEOLOGICUM.

Not the least startling manifestation of animosity on the part of the Northern people towards the people of the Confederate States, has been the zeal shown by the Church in the prosecution of the war for the "crushing out of the rebellion." And when we say "the Church," we use the term in no restricted or sectarian sense, as meaning either this or that particular denomination of worshippers, but as embracing all who acknowledge the Christian faith in any manner, Trinitarians or Unitarians, Protestants or followers of Rome, from the disciples of Theodore Parker to the brethren of the Pennsylvania Conference bordering on the Pan-Handle, and from the applauding audience that attends the performances of Beecher to the devout flock that awaits the benediction of Archbishop Hughes. Not only are the religionists of the North unanimous in their support of the war, but they far outstrip the politicians in the rancor and hatred they exhibit. This is the more remarkable, as it seems wholly disconnected with any generally-shared sentiment against slavery. Long ago the Methodist and Baptist Churches of the old United States were rent in twain by the Abolition frenzy which had seized upon the Northern members of those establishments. The New School Presbyterian Church was not many years behind them in discovering that a fanaticism existed within the pale of its communion wholly incompatible with the brotherly feeling which should distinguish those who partook of the sacred elements at the same altar. The Old School branch of the same Church betrayed also, at every General Assembly, that the Northern brethren did not love the Southern brethren as was meet, because of the "deadly sin of slavery" resting on the latter. Still the institutions of the South had never been made cause of offence by Roman Catholic or Protestant Episcopal authority, and these two bodies of religionists appeared to exercise a conservative influence upon the country at large in restraining the growing dislike between the sections. *Mais la guerre a changé tout cela.* The war has wrought a change more extraordinary than was performed upon Moliere's worthy, when the heart was transferred from the left to the right side. The clash of resounding arms has so worked upon the Yankee soldiers of the Church militant, that they are become very ministers of wrath and agents of immortal vengeance. Never has the *anathema maranatha* been spoken with more of fearful vindictiveness than by the meek and lowly and gentle and sweet divines of Yankee-land in referring to their seceding brethren below the Potomac. One Yankee Presbyterian clergyman, in mentioning the Rev. Dr. Palmer, of New Orleans, said he hoped hereafter to meet the Dr. in heaven, but he ardently desired to see him hanged first on earth. Rev. Dr. Tyng gave his blessing to Billy Wilson's Zouaves. A regiment, recruited entirely from the Young Men's Christian Association of New York, has started for the seat of war, after praying that they might meet their "rebel" fellow-members on the field of battle. A Michigan flag was consecrated with refreshing solemnities at Detroit, upon which occasion utterance was given to many new varieties of malediction. And as if to show, in a special manner, that all denominations are united in this malignant crusade, two of the most eminent prelates of the North, long ago invested with lawn and mitre, forgetting all differences of creed, have visited Europe in company to bear false witness against their neighbor to the Courts of France and England. Three years ago it seemed in the highest degree improbable that any sublunary interest would prove strong enough to bring Bishop McIlvaine and Archbishop Hughes together, but the affinity has been established in a diabolical hatred of "the rebels."

Tantæne animis cælestibus iræ?

Very many of our readers must recollect the delightful season of religious exercises and social hospitality which was enjoyed in this city three years ago, when the General Convention of the Protestant Episcopal Communion of the United States of America held its sessions in St. Paul's Church. Everywhere the houses of our citizens

THE NEW YORK HERALD.

WHOLE NO. 9560. NEW YORK, SUNDAY, NOVEMBER 16, 1862. PRICE THREE CENTS.

NEWS FROM ALONG THE COAST.

Arrival of the Mail Transport Connecticut.

IMPORTANT FROM TEXAS.

The Whole Coast in the Possession of the Union Naval Forces.

A Negro Brigade in the Field at New Orleans.

Colonel Beard's Expedition from South Carolina

The Negroes in a Fight and Come Out Victorious.

Several Salt Works and a Tannery Destroyed,

&c., &c., &c.

The United States steamship Connecticut, Commander Haxtun, arrived at this port last evening from Galveston, New Orleans, Key West and Port Royal. She brings a mail from the squadron.

We are indebted to Commander Haxtun for late news and papers. The following is a list of her officers:—

Lieutenant Commanding—Milton Haxtun.
Executive Officer—J. W. Smith.
Acting Masters—J. W. Bentley, George E. Hill, Charles W. Lee, T. J. Linneken.
Assistant Surgeon—Samuel D. Flagg, Jr.
Acting Assistant Paymaster—Pilham W. Ames.
Engineers—First Assistant, Alex. McCausland; Second Assistant, Robert G. Pope; Third Assistants, David McArthur, James Campbell, Edwin F. Lewis, Lewis F. Swift.
Master's Mates—[illegible], John Daly, Jr., John Roberts, A. B. Langw[illegible], William H. Mead and Theo. E. [illegible].
Captain's Clerk and Special [illegible] for Government—Edmon Blankman.
Paymaster's Clerk—William [illegible].
Carpenter—J. P. Carter.
Gunner—George A. Parkhurst.
Paymaster's Steward—Charles [illegible] Curran.

The United States gunboat Connecticut sailed from the New York Navy Yard on the 12th day of October last, on a cruise through the Eastern and Western Gulf and the Providence channel.

At Apaco it was positively ascertained that no less than three vessels were being fitted out in the port of St. Georges, in the Island of Bermuda, to be employed in the rebel service against our commerce on the high seas; that whilst our own ships were denied coal every facility and aid was afforded the rebels in the construction and furnishing of these vessels.

Our cruisers on the coasts of Louisiana and Florida have of late been extensively engaged in demolishing the rebel salt works, and so effectually has the work of destruction been performed that salt in the cotton States is now worth $150 per sack, and very scarce even at that price.

Our naval forces, without the aid of the military, took Galveston, Texas, on the 8th day of October, and the place is now guarded alone by our gunboats. What is wanted now is for our government to send, without delay, a sufficient military force, not only to hold the place, but to protect the Union people who are there, and who have not the arms or the means to protect themselves against the atrocities of [illegible]. The gunboats now stationed there are doing all that they can to afford protection to the people. On the wharf at Galveston may be seen large numbers of people congregated together, immediately opposite to our fleet, where they remain day and night, so that if attacked by rebel soldiers they may be sheltered by the fire from our ships. But, notwithstanding that great watchfulness [illegible] strong force of rebel rangers and cavalry at nighttime come down to the city across the bridge, and seize upon good [illegible] men and force them into their ranks; and a refusal [illegible] them under such circumstances is instantly punished with death to the offender. Such a case occurred the night before the arrival at Galveston of the Connecticut. The rebel cavalry came down at night, made free with such property as they conveniently could carry with them, shot two Union men who refused to join them, and committed various other depredations, and then left for the interior. This might all be avoided had we but a single regiment stationed at Galveston, with a commander whose whole ambition would not be to grow rich too suddenly and keep his only brother's store filled at home.

At Aransas Bay we have several well armed vessels, which effectually keep out English as well as rebel traders.

At Matagorda Bay a sharp and most efficient blockade is kept up by Commander Renshaw's squadron. Within a few days our naval forces there captured very many vessels, both large and small.

On the afternoon of the 30th of October the United States steamer Connecticut, Commander Milton Haxtun, captured the English "whitewashed" brig Hermosa. She is deeply laden with a full cargo, consisting of drugs, dry goods, army blankets, hardware, powder, shoes, wines, quinine and a well assorted cargo generally. When captured she was close under the shore, say about two miles, and about fifteen miles to the eastward of Sabine. Her captain and second mate had already gone ashore to ascertain where best to land their cargo; but on their return to the brig they were convinced, if not satisfied, that Commander Haxtun had already determined to relieve them from the duty of discharging cargo at that point by putting a prize crew on board the brig and sending her to Key West for legal adjudication.

The United States steamer Connecticut has on board a cargo of cotton, also captured by her off the coast of Texas, in the schooner Rambler, having left the schooner at the Southwest Pass, protected by the guns of the United States ship Pampero, until she can be sent to a port for adjudication.

At New Orleans General Butler has put into the field four negro regiments. Should you visit that city and desire to make an excursion to Algiers, which is directly opposite to the city of New Orleans, the first object of curiosity that greets your ear is from the mouth of a negro soldier—the guard—"Who goes there?" "The countersign," &c.; and, unless the darkey happens to be "an intelligent contraband," the probability is that you will immediately thereafter require the services of a surgeon to extract the ball, or that of an undertaker to plant you in a becoming manner.

These four regiments are about being formed into one brigade, and doubtless the command of the brigade will be tendered to Mr. Sumner, of Massachusetts, or Cassius M. Clay, late of Russia, or to some other distinguished gentleman who happens to be afflicted with "nigger on the brain."

At Algiers, opposite New Orleans, there are quartered, at the expense of our federal government, over seven thousand contrabands. They are maintained and supported in large factory buildings on the levee, and not allowed to do any work. If your ship desires to coal, you cannot get one of these negroes for money or anything else. Should you apply to any of the officers in command to direct any of these contrabands to assist you in coaling, the answer is, "We have no authority to order them to work."

At Pensacola General Dow, the celebrated temperance preacher, is in command. During the week ending 1st of November he made quite a profitable business in and about Pensacola by seizing upon the property and furniture of women residing there. Among the articles which he captured—contraband of war, of course!—were seven elegant pianos, a large lot of female wearing apparel, and sundry silver forks and spoons.

At Port Royal the plantations there and in its vicinity are in command of Brigadier General Rev. Chaplain French, the famous abolitionist, who some months ago ostensibly went down to South and North Carolina to educate the untutored mind of the poor darkey. Since that, however, he has found that it won't pay, and he has turned his attention to quite another business, so that he can "turn an honest penny" at the same time. And really the change which he has made has put change into his pocket so fast that he has, by quick sales and large profits in the sales of calico and other domestics—which cost twelve and fourteen cents in New York, and are sold to these poor negroes at the figure of fifty cents and upwards—succeeded, as the Californian would say, in making his "pile."

THE CAPTURE OF CORPUS CHRISTI, TEXAS.

Additional Particulars of the Important Operations of the Gunboat Arthur, Captain Kittridge.

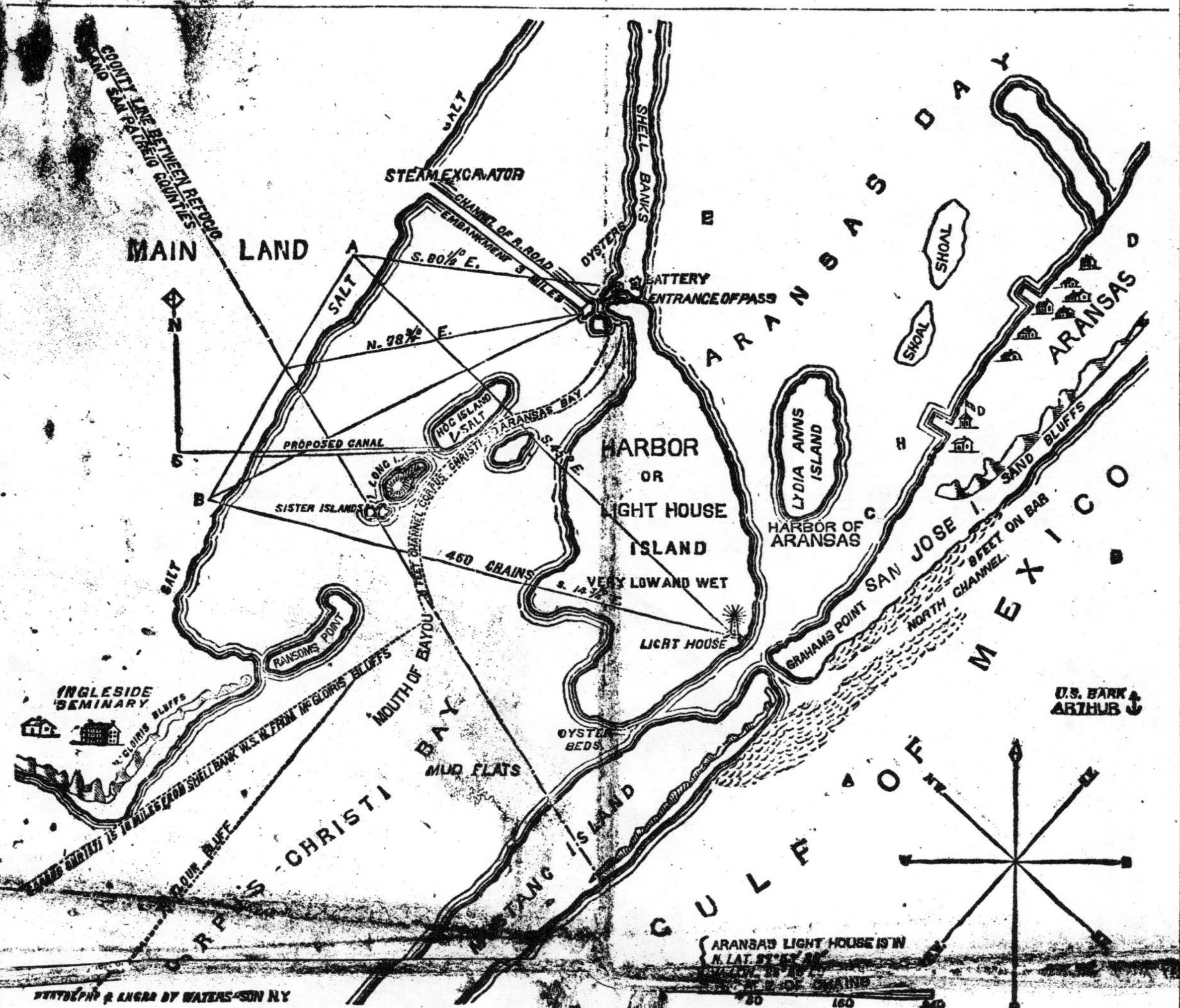

EXPLANATION OF CHART.

A—United States bark Arthur shelling rebel troops in February, 1862.

B—The Arthur shelling rebel cavalry out of Aranas in February, while the Arthur's boats (*C*) are advancing to attack them.

D—Rebel cavalry.

E—Yacht Coryphees bringing the sloop Belle Italia to, with shot from her Parrott gun—July 9.

F—Sloop Belle Italia.

G—Lighters filled with stone sunk in channel, to prevent the fleet getting into Corpus Christi bay.

H—Fleet at anchor at Aranas.

TEXAS.

The Capture of Corpus Christi.

OUR NAVAL CORRESPONDENCE.

UNITED STATES GUNBOAT ARTHUR, AT SEA, Oct. 12, 1862.

Additional Particulars of the Capture of Corpus Christi—Captain Kittredge Made a Prisoner—His Treatment by the Rebels—What He Saw in Texas—The Vessels Destroyed and Captured by the Arthur, &c.

On the 14th ult., while this vessel was absent at Galveston to land a lady passenger, taken in the prize schooner Water Witch, Captain Kittredge, commander of this vessel and of the naval forces at Aransas, Texas, was taken prisoner, with his gig's crew, while making a reconnoissance at Flour Bluffs, twelve miles from Corpus Christi. He had gone down to the latter place, by request of Admiral Farragut, to get Judge Davis' family for him (Judge Davis is a Union refugee, having escaped from Texas via Rio Grande in June last). As an express had to be sent to obtain General Bee's permission for his family to leave, some several days must elapse before an answer could be received from San Antonio, Captain K. used the time in exploring and sounding out the entrance Laguna Madre.

On the morning of the 14th, having observed two men ashore at Flour Bluffs, with arms, he gave orders to shell them, when they disappeared. A dwelling house near the spot was left untouched, as he did not wish to destroy private property.

Immediately after shelling them the Captain went ashore in his gig, with seven men, and ordered them to follow him (save the boat keeper); and with his usual daring, he led the men himself, and on going up to the house some fifteen or twenty armed men rushed out and surrounded him, and before he could draw his revolver he was seized. His crew following dare not fire, as their captain was in the midst of the rebels, and the disparity of their forces caused them to surrender.

There were two companies of infantry and two pieces of artillery behind a bluff near by, who now showed themselves.

The yacht and tenders opened fire upon the rebels; but they were satisfied with their prize, and left on the double quick for Corpus Christi.

The fleet came back to Aransas Bay. The next day a flag of truce went down to Corpus Christi, with two officers, who were allowed to see Captain Kittredge, who was to be sent to San Antonio for the action of General Bee, commanding this division of Texan troops.

On the 3d of October the yacht Corypheus came out from the inside, and on nearing us the Captain was discovered to be on board. The entire crew manned the rigging and gave three rousing cheers as he came over the gangway, in which the officers heartily joined.

Captain Kittredge was affected to tears at this expression of the estimation the crew showed for him, and by the cordial and warm hearted greeting of the officers. He was accompanied by his crew (who like himself had been paroled and released until regularly exchanged) and Major Hebbie and aid, of the rebel forces.

Capt. Kittredge speaks in high terms of the kind treatment he received at the hands of Gen. Hebert, Commander-in-Chief in Texas; Gen. Bee, commanding division Rio Grande; Major Hebbie, who accompanied Capt. Kittredge as escort; Major Gray, and all officers in his journey from Corpus Christi to San Antonio and back to Aransas. Crowds of people came out at the country villages to get a peep at the Yankee captain who had stirred them up so sharply in Corpus Christi and Aransas Bay. The men were as eagerly looked at as if they were beasts.

Great confidence was shown in Captain K.'s honor by sending him back to his own ship at Aransas, to go north from there. The bark is now at Pensacola for repairs. As the map you published of Aransas and vicinity was not properly made out, I send you a correct copy from regular survey. As Captain K. leaves by the Rhode Island, and as the bark has a new commander, I forward a *resume* of the vessels captured or destroyed by the vessels and tenders under Captain K.'s command:—

VESSELS CAPTURED AND DESTROYED BY UNITED STATES BARK ARTHUR WHILE UNDER COMMAND OF LIEUTENANT COMMANDING J. W. KITTREDGE.

Schooner J. G. McNeil.
Sloop Belleport.
Sloop Daniel Webster
Sloop Swan.
Sloop Mustang.
Schooner Reindee
Flat Lamar.
Sloop Belle Italia.
Schooner Monte Christo.
Schooner Breaker.
Schooner Elmer, sloop Hannah and steamer A B, armed rebel fleet, Corpus Christi.
Schooner Water Witch.

Our Galveston Correspondence.

UNITED STATES MORTAR SCHOONER HENRY JAMES, GALVESTON, Texas, Oct. 29, 1862.

Affairs off Galveston—Another Ram Preparing to Attack the Fleet—An Attack on Matagorda—Deserters from the Rebel Army, &c., &c.

As the Connecticut is off the bar, and leaves at twelve o'clock, I am compelled to use some haste in making my communication to your valuable paper. Everything is serene in this part of the country; we remain undisputed "lords of all we survey," although rumor says, as well as a deserter, that we are to be attacked by a ram now constructing and several sail vessels. We are prepared for anything like an emergency, and think that we can give them a very warm reception. The rebels have concentrated about eight thousand troops at Virginia Point, and fortified the place pretty strongly. The battery is placed so as to command the long bridge connecting the island and the mainland. The gunboat Owasco, Commander Guest, steamed up towards the bridge a few days since, and gave them a taste of her metal in the shape of an eleven-inch shell. Although using a charge of twenty pounds she could not reach the bridge. The water is too shallow to admit any vessel drawing more than six or eight feet. I think we shall try the mortar on them in a few days.

Commander Renshaw, with Lieutenant Commanding Law and Acting Master Pennington, left here on Wednesday last in the steamers Westfield and Clifton for Matagorda. We have not heard from them as yet, but are inclined to think that they took the battery at that place, and are now safely inside the harbor.

The rebels visit the town every night, impressing every man that is to be found. Only last night we heard the voice of a woman crying for help. We supposed that they were taking her husband off. In fact, the poor are worse off now than they were before, as they cannot protect themselves in any shape, and we can offer no protection while they remain in the city. No person is allowed in the city from the vessels, and I do not suppose anybody wishes to go there until we have a force stationed sufficient to hold it. I think it ought to be garrisoned, as there are a great many good Union men in the place, and it would be a good basis for operations in the interior.

Deserters come in every night. Their intelligence is nothing of importance, further than to say that one-half of the soldiers will desert as soon as we occupy this place by troops. They are all apparently disgusted with Jeff. Davis and his tools.

KEY WEST.

The Health of Key West.

TO THE EDITOR OF THE NEW YORK HERALD.

KEY WEST BARRACKS, Florida, Nov. 9, 1862.

As there seems to be a great misunderstanding in the North as regards the health of this place, I am most happy to say that this island is now perfectly healthy. We have had no case of fever for three weeks, and I think I can safely say we will be entirely free from it for this season.

We suffer very much here for want of mails. For instance, the last we had from New York was the 18th of October.

You will confer a great favor upon the army and navy, as well as the citizens here, by publishing this card and using your influence in prevailing upon the steamers leaving your city for the Gulf to touch here and leave the mails. Very respectfully, yours, &c.,

WILLIAM F. CORNICK,
Assistant Surgeon, United States Army.

PORT ROYAL, S. C.

Our Beaufort Correspondence.

BEAUFORT, S. C., Nov. 12, 1862.

Colonel Beard's Expedition in Search of Contrabands—The Rebels Driving Them Inland—The Expedition Destroys Several Salt Works and a Tannery—Capture of a Number of Negroes—A Fight between Rebel Sharpshooters and "Intelligent Contrabands"—Black Wins—Capture of Prisoners and Trophies, &c., &c.

The sudden and unexpected departure of a mail must be my apology for a very brief and somewhat disjointed letter.

The great theory is worked out—the doubt is solved—the same accomplished—the "intelligent contraband" will fight, and fight like a trump at that. An expedition has just returned from below, of which I can at this moment give but a meagre outline. The United States transport steamer Darlington, Captain Crandell, left here some two weeks since to gather up contrabands, and do such good to the Union and such harm to secesh as might conveniently come in her way. The expedition was commanded by Lieutenant Colonel Oliver T. Beard, of Brooklyn, an officer of the Forty-eighth New York Volunteers—an able, brave and efficient person. At St. Catherines they found that the rebel Colonel Braelsford had driven off the contrabands, and that he had killed some in so doing. They proceeded from there to St. Denis Island, where they spent a couple of days; from there a journey to St. Andrews Sound, where the party was enabled to render assistance to the United States transport steamer Neptune, from Hilton Head, S. C., with passengers (including 200 recruits) and freight for Fernandina. The men belonged to the Ninth Maine and Seventh New Hampshire. She took off her passengers and a portion of her freight. She next went into Fernandina, where she arrived safely, starting from Fernandina, after some delay, with sixty-two soldiers (colored) of the First South Carolina volunteers, under command of Captain Trowbridge. She pursued her way, breaking up salt works, destroying some seventy-five large salt kettles, also boilers, including a stray tannery, whose leather and fixings were suddenly confiscated. Contrabands to the tune of enough to stock a big plantation were also removed from further attendance upon secesh masters. Then came an attack on the boat from sharpshooters stationed in trees. The intelligent contraband, however, blocked this game, and picked off several from behind the Darlington's barricades in an artistic manner, proving that their turkey shooting experiences had not been entirely thrown away. Col. Beard stood outside like a man, and exposed himself most gallantly until the enemy had enough. The same is true of Capt. Trowbridge; and as for the darkeys, they covered themselves with glory, as witnesses the official report of the brave officer accompanying the expedition. When soldiers manage these sort of things, and are not interfered with, the material is sure to do its work. I have a funny yarn or two connected with these matters; but want of time forbids. Two of the colored soldiers were wounded; one in the head; the other, Achilles like, in the heel; but both stood up to their work and continued to load and fire until secesh was ready to quit, which he finally did suddenly. Among the spoils of war are all sorts of trophies, including four secesh prisoners, one from the State of Maine, and another from Massachusetts. An ill looking crowd they were. I saw them marched up under guard—a negro guard of the soldiers who captured them. One of these rascals was guarded by his former slave, and looked anything but amiable. The same fellow has a letter among his captured goods which he had just penned to his brother, wherein he enthusiastically requests him, "as a good deer shot, to make the fur fly from the Yankees every lick, as they are always, like a buck, jumping around." These worthies are now in jail here, and already take kindly to the oath of allegiance. They will probably be sent North for a change of climate.

Five new cases of yellow fever are reported "at the head;" but I think the scare, if any, is subsiding. We have had no mail for two weeks, which is a much more interesting matter than fever rumors to us.

Among the bad signs of ill feeling between the North and South, we may quote the following:—When secesh sent us a flag of truce the other day, the officer commanding our outer pickets asked the chivalry to take a "modest quencher"—as Dick Swiveller has it—which was declined upon the ground that they could not imbibe with the invaders of the sacred soil of musquito-breeding Carolina.

IMPORTANT FROM MISSISSIPPI.

Sharp Fight at Holly Springs—Six Rebels Killed and Seven Rebel Officers Captured—Death of General Villipigue, &c., &c.

CHICAGO, Nov. 15, 1862.

A special despatch from Lagrange, Tenn., dated the 14th instant, says that five regiments of rebel cavalry advanced last evening from Lumkin's Mills to within two miles of Holly Springs. Skirmishing commenced and continued for some time. The rebels lost six killed, and seven commissioned officers were captured.

The rebel General Villipigue died at Port Hudson a few days ago of pneumonia.

Sketch of the Rebel General Villepigue.

Brigadier General John B. Villepigue, whose death from pneumonia took place a few days since at Port Hudson, La., on the Mississippi river, a few miles above Baton Rouge, was formerly connected with the regular military service of the United States. He was a native of South Carolina and entered West Point Military Academy as a cadet in 1850. He graduated on the 30th of June, 1854, without particular honors. In the same class were General Howard, of Maine, the brave Lieutenant Greble, who was killed at Big Bethel, and other Union officers; the rebel General J. E. B. Stuart and several officers in that service. On the 1st of July, 1854, he was brevetted Second Lieutenant of the Second dragoons, and on the 27th of May, 1857, was promoted to a first lieutenancy, and was ordered to the Southwest. On the 31st of March, 1861, Lieutenant Villepigue sent in his resignation which was accepted. He at once offered his services to the rebel government, but for some little time he held but an inferior position. He was then made a brigadier general and ordered to the Mississippi. In May last he held the command of the rebel troops at Fort Pillow, and it was he who telegraphed to Gen. Beauregard that Gen. Halleck had sent two hundred exchanged prisoners, infected with smallpox, to his post; and when the statement was contradicted by Gen. Hallock he still persisted in his assertion. When Fort Pillow was evacuated Gen. Villepigue was ordered to Grenada, Miss., and was in command there during June and July of this year. He has since been in command in the extreme Southwest, and now has fallen a victim to the malaria of the district in which he was quartered.

Western Virginia.

ANOTHER BRILLIANT FEAT OF GENERAL KELLY.

MOOREFIELD, HARDY COUNTY, Nov. 10, 1862.

TO GOVERNOR PIERPONT:—I left New Creek on Saturday morning, the 8th instant, and after a continuous march of twenty-four hours, a distance of about sixty miles, reached Imboden's camp on the South Fork, eighteen miles south of this place, at half-past six o'clock yesterday morning.

We attacked him at once and routed him completely, killing and wounding many of the enemy; also capturing his camp, fifty prisoners, a quantity of arms, three hundred and fifty fat hogs, a large number of horses, cattle, wagons, &c. The infantry were routed and entirely dispersed, fleeing to the mountains. Their cavalry were, unfortunately for us, away on an expedition, or our success would have been complete. We burnt their camp and returned to this place this evening.

I had with me a detachment of the First New York cavalry, under the command of Col. McReynolds; the Ringgold cavalry, under the command of Captain Keys; the Washington cavalry, commanded by Captain Greenfield, Rourk's battery and three companies of the Twenty-third Illinois infantry, under the command of Major Moore.

The infantry companies were carried in wagons. The New York troops cannot be surpassed for patient endurance on the march or for gallant bearing when in action. Our attack was so unexpected and impetuous that our loss is trifling, three or four men slightly and one severely wounded; none killed.

B. F. KELLY, Brigadier General.

NEWS FROM EUROPE.

Arrival of the Etna Off Cape Race.

FOUR DAYS' LATER INTELLIGENCE.

Collision Between the Austrian and Italian Troops.

The New York Chamber of Commerce and the Alabama.

ADVANCE IN COTTON,

&c., &c., &c.

ST. JOHNS, N. F., Nov. 15, 1862.

The steamship Etna, from Liverpool on the 5th, via Queenstown on the 6th instant, passed Cape Race *en route* to New York at one o'clock this afternoon. She was boarded by the yacht of the press and a summary of her news obtained.

The dates per the Etna are four days later than those per the Europa at Halifax.

The political news per the Etna is not of any particular importance.

A slight collision had occurred between the Austrian and Italian troops on the frontiers of Austria and Italy, but quiet was soon restored.

The London *Times* again adverts to the action of the New York Chamber of Commerce, touching the rebel steamer Alabama, and denies that any blame can be attached to England.

The London *Daily News* takes altogether a different view of the case.

Mr. Bright has written a letter applauding President Lincoln's proclamation to liberate the slaves of the Southern States.

The steamship City of New York, from New York, arrived at Liverpool on the 4th instant.

The steamship Hibernian, from Quebec, arrived at Liverpool on the 5th inst.

Commercial Intelligence.

Cotton—Sales of the two days 15,000 bales, at an advance of two pence a three pence since Friday. The market closed buoyant.

Breadstuffs dull. Wheat declining.

Provisions very dull.

Consols, for money, 93½.

MAJOR GENERAL BANKS.

Meeting at the Astor House Relation to the Proposed Reception to General Banks.

In pursuance of invitation a large number of friends of General Banks met yesterday afternoon at the Astor House to confer together upon the best mode of extending a popular reception to Major General Banks.

Many of our most influential citizens responded to the invitation, and precisely at three o'clock the meeting was called to order by

Judge PEABODY—who being unanimously called to preside—addressed those present. He said we had among us a distinguished citizen and valiant soldier; a gentleman who all through the course of his life had held very eminent social and political positions, and whose fame depended much less on those positions, than as to the manner in which he had discharged the duties devolving upon him. The gentleman to whom he referred was now heart and soul engaged in matters of the utmost importance to the nation's welfare. He had no personal knowledge of the nature of the high trust imposed upon the gentleman, but he believed it to [illegible]. He alluded to Major General Banks. (Applause.) General Banks had commenced life without the advantages many present had enjoyed in their early start, and yet, by his own individual exertions, he was now in a position which the proudest man in the community might envy. Gen. Banks was now, or would be immediately, among them, and as report had it, as he had learned from the papers, he was engaged in a matter of great interest to the whole country, and upon which he would take an almost instant departure. In this view of the case it was thought that so eminent a citizen should receive at our hands—at the hands of the citizens of New York—that recognition which his past services entitled him to. General Banks would be but a few days among them, but there was yet ample time to them and to the citizens to extend to him their welcome as a proof of their appreciation of his past services and their assurance that he bears with him their best wishes for his future success. (Applause.) The compliment would be doubtless acceptable to him. So far as he understood the proposition, it was that the General should have a large and general reception from the citizens of New York—a reception, indeed, that would embrace both the General and Mrs. Banks. (Applause.) He thought the Astor House was eminently appropriate for such a purpose; and seeing that the papers had fixed Wednesday as the day, he saw no objection to that day. It was, however, for the committee to arrange the time and place, and for that purpose it was they had assembled together to confer.

Mr. STETSON here addressed the meeting. He said:—It is my duty, gentlemen, to make an explanation. When this matter was first spoken of both Mrs. Banks and the General said that such a compliment would be exceedingly gratifying to them; but the question had not been asked them if they could fix the time. Since the suggestion was made circumstances have transpired to make it almost impossible for the General to appropriate an evening. I am requested by the General to say to you, gentlemen, that however gratifying such an expression of kindness from the citizens of New York would be to him, he feared that he could not name a day upon which he could meet you.

Cephas Brainard, Esq., was then appointed Secretary of the meeting.

Colonel MONTGOMERY suggested the appointment of a committee to wait on General Banks when he arrived in the city, and fix the form and manner of the proposed reception.

General WETMORE, in the course of some laudatory remarks upon General Banks, said that such a compliment as that contemplated was eminently due to General Banks, the representative man of the republic, the representative man of one of the noblest States in the Union—Massachusetts. (Applause.) As a citizen of Massachusetts, Gen. Banks deserved honor as the commanding general of an important branch of the Union army; he deserved that honor now intended him. The whole community would turn out to do honor to a brave and successful general, and to the man who of the people had raised himself to his present high position. (Applause.)

Mr. ROBERT H. MCCURDY was in favor of a reception in which the whole people could take part, and opposed to a dinner where but a few could assemble. He wished the ladies of New York to have an opportunity of turning out in all the loyalty of their hearts, and which in so many ways they had hitherto given such undemonstrative evidences of. (Applause.)

Mr. FITCH proposed the appointment of a committee to wait upon General Banks, and to request the appointment of a day for the proposed reception. He felt convinced that fifteen thousand people at least would pay their respects to the General and his lady—besides the ladies.

Mr. EDWARD WARREN spoke warmly in favor of General Banks' claims to a public recognition.

After a few further desultory remarks a committee was appointed. It was intended to make the committee, on the suggestion of Colonel Montgomery, number thirty-four—one for each State of the Union. The Chairman, however, confined it to twenty-four, with power to the committee to add to its number. The Chairman, Judge Peabody, was elected chairman of the committee.

The following gentlemen were appointed a committee of arrangements:—

Colonel Montgomery, General Wetmore, Robt. H. McCurdy, Geo. W. Blunt, Chas. Gould, Jno. Paine, Moses Taylor, Captain W. A. Murfey, Henry E. Davies, Ethan Allen, Elliott G. Cowdon, Wm. G. Lambert, Edwd. Warren, J. A. Briggs, Geo. C. Ward, Geo. H. Ellery, Royal Phelps, Wm. M. Evarts, Geo. Opdyke, B. F. Manierre, Colonel J. F. Butterworth, Moses H. Grinnell, Chs. H. Marshall, Eyre Nye, Frank E. Howe, Hamlin Blake, Jno. H. Almy, C. W. Burton, A. J. H. Duganne, Jno. Chas. Noyes, R. E. Latham, Jno. Fitch.

A sub-committee of five was appointed to wait on General Banks for the purpose of fixing a day for the reception and the manner in which the compliment was to be made.

The meeting then separated.

The Steamship Nova Scotian.

FATHER POINT, Nov. 15, 1862.

The steamship Nova Scotian, from Liverpool on the 30th, via Londonderry on the 31st of October, passed this point at four o'clock this morning, *en route* to Quebec. She has forty-three cabin and one hundred and fifteen steerage passengers. Her news was telegraphed from Cape Race.

THE SOUTHERN ILLUSTRATED NEWS.

Vol. I. RICHMOND, SATURDAY, JANUARY 31, 1863. No. 21.

GENERAL ALBERT SIDNEY JOHNSTON.

[W. B. CAMPBELL, Engraver.]

GEN'L A. SIDNEY JOHNSTON.

(See cut on first page.)

Gen'l Albert Sidney Johnston, as brave and chivalrous a soldier as ever drew sword in defence of Southern rights, was born in Mason county, Ky., in 1803. He graduated at the West Point Academy in 1826, as Lieutenant in the 6th Infantry, and after serving in the Black Hawk war, left the army, and in 1836 emigrated to Texas, arriving there shortly after the battle of San Jacinto. He entered the Texan army as a private soldier, and was soon promoted to succeed General Felix Houston in the chief command—an event which led to a duel, in which Johnston was wounded. Having held the office of senior Brigadier General until 1838, he was appointed Secretary of War, and in 1839 organized an expedition against the Cherokees, who were totally routed in an engagement on the river Niches.

A Pontoon.

In 1840, he retired from the service, and settled upon a plantation in Brazoria county. He was an ardent advocate for the annexation of Texas to the United States.

He remained in the quietude of his home in Brazoria county until the breaking out of the Mexican war, when his naturally chivalric spirit caught the infection for the combat that swept over the South-west at that time, and, at the request of Gen. Taylor, he took the field against Mexico, as commander of the volunteer Texan Rifle regiment, in which capacity he served six months. Subsequently he was Acting Inspector General to General Butler, and for his services at Monterey received the thanks of his commander. We believe he was afterwards appointed to a prominent position on the staff of General Taylor, continuing with that distinguished old chieftain in all his operations in Northern Mexico.

Upon the election of General Taylor to the Presidency in 1848, he received the appointment of Paymaster in the United States army, and at the increase of the army, was made Colonel of Cavalry, and assigned command of the department of Texas. While in that position he signalized his military talents, and still further won the confidence of the country, by the vigorous and successful warfare which he initiated against the wild tribes of Indians, who were constantly engaging in marauding forays upon the early settlers.

We next find him in command of the celebrated Utah expedition, for which he was selected by James Buchanan, then President of the United States, owing to his unchallenged fitness for the enterprise.

He was next appointed to the responsible command of the Pacific, where he remained in service until the breaking out of hostilities between the North and the South. Immediately upon hearing that his adopted State, Texas, had passed the Ordinance of Secession, and cast her destinies with the new-born Republic, he resigned his position in the United States army, and began to make preparations with the view of at once removing South, to assist in repelling the threatened invasion of her soil by the Northern vandals.

On the inception of the war, General Scott, fully aware of the great military genius of Albert Sidney Johnston, made a vigorous but ineffectual effort to secure his services for the Lincoln Government, tendering him the chief command, to which his seniority and rank, according to army regulations, entitled him. But the noble Johnston spurned the offer—he would not sell his birthright, or draw his sword against his native State, as the old traitor Scott had done. Baffled in this piece of mean and malignant treachery, Scott took measures to have him arrested, so as to keep him out of the Confederate service. To attain this end, vessels containing police authorities were sent to intercept his passage around the sea, which circumstance accidentally coming to the knowledge of Gen. Johnston, induced him to take the overland route, by which he succeeded in arriving safe in New Orleans, whence he proceeded to Richmond. Immediately upon his arrival here, he was placed in command of the department of Kentucky and Tennessee.

When Gen. Johnston was appointed to this command, Kentucky had not yet ceased to claim that she was a neutral State, and it was therefore left to his option whether to occupy Bowling Green, a most important strategical position within the limits of that State, or not. Before he reached Nashville, however, that point had been decided—Kentucky had authorized the assemblage of troops threatening the borders of Tennessee—and General Buckner had already taken possession of Bowling Green. At Bowling Green, therefore, Gen. Johnston made his head-quarters. His high military reputation, and the exaggerated reports which soon became current, of his numbers, led the public to expect a glorious and crowning campaign in that quarter. Gen. Johnston was far from sharing in these hopes, or joining in these anticipations. He knew but too well the perilous position in which he was placed. On the other side of the river, in a position of immense strength, was Buell, with an army 50,000 strong. In his rear was the Cumberland river, liable to rise at any moment, and to admit the largest class steamers as high as Nashville. Still farther in his rear was the Tennessee, traversing the entire State of that name from South to North, a rise in which would give the enemy's gun-boats a free passage into Alabama. At the mouth of both these rivers—at Paducah and Smithfield—the enemy was collecting an enormous force, both naval and military. He could not but feel the deepest anxiety with regard to his situation; for he well knew the feebleness of his own force, and that while public opinion assigned him a splendid army of 130,000 men, he could not, in fact, muster the fifth part of that force. It has now, indeed, become well known, that he never had more than 25,000 men under his orders, during the whole time he was at Bowling Green. To this small force the enemy opposed a body of 100,000 infantry, 10,000 cavalry, and 3,000 cannoneers, of which force, Buell's army constituted a large proportion. That officer, in all probability, might have overwhelmed Johnston by a direct attack upon his camp, for he had an army of 50,000 men, of which at least 40,000 were effective, while Johnston had been compelled to send 12,000 men to Fort Donelson, the only fortification on the Cumberland which offered the slightest hope of retarding even for an hour, the advance of the enemy to Nashville, which it had now become certain was designed. Of the remainder, so many were sick that he could muster but 11,000 effectives. He had been representing the extreme precariousness and danger of his situation to the government for months, but no attention had been paid to his representations. Buell, probably, not knowing his weakness, determined to remove him from his position by operating in his rear. On the 15th of February, Gen. Johnston learned that Fort Donelson had fallen. No alternative was left but to retreat. It was accomplished without loss. A rear guard was left in Nashville, to secure as many stores and provisions as possible, and Gen Johnston fell back to Murfreesborough, where, uniting the remains of Crittenden's division and the fugitives from Fort Donelson, with the troops brought from Bowling Green, he found himself at the head of 17,000 men.

The line which General Johnston originally occupied having been irretrievably lost by these disastrous events, he determined to unite his forces with those of Gen. Beauregard, for the purpose of defending the Mississippi Valley, now greatly endangered by the advance of the enemy, and the siege of Island No. 10. Beauregard had concentrated his men at and around Corinth, where the Memphis and Charleston, and the Mobile and Ohio railroads meet. This junction was effected on the 1st of April, and on the 6th Island No. 10 surrendered. The united forces were farther increased by the arrival of three regiments from Louisiana, by two divisions of Gen. Polk's command, and a considerable body of troops from Mobile and Pensacola. The whole force was in the highest degree effective, was full of spirit, and burned for an opportunity to strike a blow. It was not long in presenting itself. Gen. Grant's army had advanced from Nashville, had crossed the Tennessee, and had taken up a position at Pitt's land, and the neighborhood. It was awaiting the arrival of General Buell, which was on the other side of the Tennessee. Gen. Johnston, who, by seniority, was in command of the whole force, determined to attack Grant before Buell could arrive, drive him to his transports, capture his artillery and stores, and retire to Corinth, the strategic point of the campaign. The troops took up the line of march from Corinth on Thursday, the 3d of April. It was the intention of the Generals to have made the attack on Saturday, the 5th. Had they done so, Buell would not have arrived in time, and Grant's army must have been destroyed. But the roads were in such a condition that they found it impossible to arrive within striking distance until Saturday evening, when the troops were worn out with fatigue. Some skirmishing took place that night, but the great battle was postponed until the next day.—General Johnston's whole force numbered 38,000; Grant's, between 55 and 60,000.

At daybreak next morning the action commenced by skirmishing along the whole line. The advance of the Confederates took the enemy completely by surprise, for they never imagined that they would have the audacity to oppose them. The ground was broken and undulating, and covered in a great measure by lofty trees, without any undergrowth.—After a tremendous cannonade, our troops advanced upon the enemy. They were received with great resolution, but nothing could effectually resist their impetuosity. For mile after mile they swept everything before them. At half-past two they had carried two of the three camps. Gen. Johnston ordered a charge to be made on the third and last.

Elated with the success of the day, he took his position before the brigades of Breckinridge and Bowen, and gave the order, "Fix bayonets." He then made a brief speech to the troops, and gave the command to "*charge!*"—The charge was made with a shout, the gallant chieftain leading in the van. The enemy was routed, and fled in great confusion. After this gallant charge, it was whispered that the "General was wounded," and some of his staff going in search of him, found him down in the ravine, a short distance from the field, reclining in the lap of Gov. Harris, who had gently lifted him from his horse.

The last words he ever uttered was some minutes after he was shot, when he said, "*Governor, I believe I am seriously wounded!*" Col. Preston, in an agony of grief, threw his arms around him, and called aloud and asked if he knew him.—Stimulants were administered, but he was totally unconscious, and quietly breathed his last at thirty minutes past 2 o'clock. His death was prudently concealed from the army for some time.

Thus fell one of the greatest Generals of the age. He fell where heroes love to fall—in the arms of victory upon the battle-field.

It is said that during the battle he was elated from the very beginning—asserting that victory was certain. His countenance, it is stated by his staff officers, gleamed with the enthusiasm of a great man, who was conscious that he was achieving a great success, that was to carry his name down to the latest syllable of recorded time.

His body was borne from the field by his staff officers.

When the remains of the distinguished chieftain reached New Orleans, then in possession of the Confederate forces, they were escorted to the City Hall by the military. The Governor of Louisiana, and staff, and Gen. Lovell and staff, and other prominent officers, besides the gentlemen who had escorted the body to the city, were also of the escort.

After the body had been deposited in the Mayor's parlor, the public were permitted to enter. Not a word was spoken. There was no simulated grief; there was the grief of a people who felt they had suffered a great loss, and whose sympathies were with the fallen. The offices of affection were not left unperformed on this occasion. Several ladies brought magnolias and other flowers, with which they encircled his coffin simply, but beautifully. Many looked with interest at the sword which lay sheathed by his side—so lately drawn in power and victory at the head of a mighty army, now dead, like the hand which would wield it no more on earth.

Many amusing and characteristic anecdotes were told of General Johnston during his campaign in Kentucky and Tennessee, by the correspondents of the daily journals.—Among them we find the following:

"One of his favorite officers, indeed, a messmate, accosted him pleasantly one morning, but the General scowled, muttered to himself, and never recognized the compliment. The unfortunate man felt not only slighted, but humiliated. He went to Major Rhett, related what had passed, and grievously protested that he knew not how he could have offended his superior officer. Dinner hour having come, our pining friend was not at the mess. "Where is ———?" inquired General Johnston. "He is mortified and afflicted by the slight which *you* put upon him this morning." "*Me* slight him!" exclaimed the General. "*I have not seen him to-day.*" An explanation ensued; the officer was sent for, Johnston apologized, and peace was again restored to the bosom of a loyal and sensitive soldier.

Soon after, however, while pacing in one of these moods by the door of his residence, an officer, with a saddle on his back, inquired of another, his superior in rank, if he knew where to direct him to a *shoemaker.* "There is one," was the waggish answer, pointing at the same time to Johnston, who was in citizen's clothes. Onward strode the interrogator until he reached the latter. He then threw down the saddle, and looking sternly at the General, with his hands in his pockets, gave the word of command, "That saddle must be ready in one hour, sir." He then turned to depart. "Hold!" said Johnston. "What did you observe?" "I said have that saddle ready in an hour," responded Captain Obstreperous. "Do you know who I am?" "Yes! you are a shoemaker, and I want you to hurry up, too!" "I am Gen. Johnston, sir," shouted the commander. In another moment, the saddle was picked up, and the Captain in retreat. "Halt!" shouted the General; "who told you I was a shoemaker?" "An officer, sir—I don't know his name." "Then leave the saddle and return in an hour *precisely.*" He heard and he obeyed. In one hour the saddle was mended and in his possession. "Now Captain," said the General, "endeavor to serve your country as I have endeavored to oblige you, and depart."

Written for the Illustrated News.

AN OLD MAN'S REVERIES.

About twenty-five years ago I was travelling in the stage-coach from Staunton to Charlottesville, a journey of thirty-six miles, which then required ten or twelve hours. Those were the famous days of stagemen, when the whole of Western Virginia was a horse-heaven, and the proprietors of mail coaches were among the magnates, almost as great in the social sphere as railroad directors and officials of the present day. The drivers were the best I have ever known, as indeed it was necessary they should be, for to pilot four-in-hand upon a zig-zag road, down the steep declivities of the Blue Ridge, especially in winter, when the ice rendered it difficult for horse or man to stand upright, was no child's play. Running for miles along the perilous edge of rocky precipices, the grandeur of the view could scarcely compensate for the unpleasant sense of insecurity which even a man of strong nerves might experience. My companions on the present occasion, however, seemed too much absorbed by the charms of the Switzerland of America, to observe the dangerous contiguity into which we were often brought

They have buried him, since then, beside the grave where he knelt in the moonlight the night before he went away. Only a foot of earth between the two who loved each other so dearly. Is there so much? Surely our dreams of the future are not all in vain. Surely somewhere, in the heaven which is "anchored off this world," where sickness and sorrow never come, and there are neither wars nor rumors of wars, somewhere in that still Land of Peace they are tasting the cup of joy which earth denied them.

John Morgan, and John Morgan's wife and children, will speak the name of Ash Thornycroft all their lives with such reverent tenderness as befits the memory of one who is enshrined in their hearts as saint and as deliverer. We know not yet for what good end he and those who fell with him laid down their lives—God grant that we may know hereafter—that the seed sown in tears we may reap with exceeding great joy.

MURFREESBORO, TENNESSEE.

WE publish on page 69 a view of MURFREESBORO, TENNESSEE, now occupied by General Rosecrans, from a sketch by our special artist, Mr. F. Beard. The *Times* correspondent says of the place:

Murfreesboro is a town which once contained some ten thousand inhabitants, is situated upon a level plain, has two colleges or seminaries—the Baptist Female Institute and the Soule Female College—and an academy for males, six churches, and one hotel.

In the centre of the town is a public square, containing a very handsome court-house. Around this square are the principal business-houses of the place. The streets are wide, and contain many handsome residences. At present the place is entirely deserted by its former residents. It was always strongly rebel in sentiment, and the few citizens who were imbued with Union sentiments have been refugees from home since the retreat of Buell's army. During my stay not a store was open save those taken for the use of Commissary and Quarter-masters' stores. No citizens were upon the streets, nor a woman or child visible—every thing in and about the town is military.

The other picture on the same page illustrates a curious spectacle which met the eyes of our army as they advanced to Murfreesboro. This was a forest of chimneys, which had been erected by the rebels to keep their huts warm, and had been left standing when they decamped. Mr. Beard counted these chimneys by hundreds. They gave a funereal aspect to the place.

THE LOSS OF GALVESTON.

WE publish on pages 72 and 73 two illustrations of the FIGHT AT GALVESTON, TEXAS, on 1st January, from sketches by our special artist in the Gulf. One of them represents the

GUN-BOATS ENGAGED.

The *Herald* correspondent thus described this scene:

When morning dawned signals were sent up from the flag-ship, which were responded to by all the gun-boats except the *Harriet Lane*, and now it was that the Commodore first discovered that she had fallen into the hands of the enemy.

The light also revealed the position of the enemy's fleet, and his preparations for an attack from the shore with artillery and riflemen.

It was now determined by the Commodore to retake the *Harriet Lane*, and he ordered the *Owasco* to round to and open fire. This gun-boat has an armament of one 11-inch and two 9-inch guns, and she opened with her heaviest.

No sooner had she sent one of her shells than the rebels crowded our prisoners—some of them wounded and dying—upon the deck of the *Harriet Lane*. They then raised a flag of truce, and paroled and sent the acting master of the *Harriet Lane*, and her only surviving officer, on board the flag-ship, with a message to Commodore Renshaw to the effect that if another shot was fired upon the *Harriet Lane*, every Union prisoner would be instantly thrown overboard. In consequence of this message Commodore Renshaw ordered the firing to cease, and made no further attempt to recapture the vessel.

The position of the enemy's fleet was at this time as follows: The two vessels which had accomplished the capture of the *Harriet Lane* were still lying near that vessel, swarming with sharp-shooters. Two more lay further off toward the bay, while the fifth held herself aloof at a considerable distance. This fifth vessel was reported to be the flag-ship, and, throughout the engagement, was said to have on board the precious carcass of General Magruder, whom the fortunes of war, since the outbreak of the rebellion, have carried from Yorktown to Galveston. But it is probable that General Magruder was on land.

During the morning the enemy opened fire upon our vessels from the shore and the city, of which they were now in full possession. Their sharp-shooters, breaking open the houses along the shore, took possession, and fired from the windows, while the batteries which had been placed in position also opened. They were responded to by our gun-boats, and this mutual exchange of courtesies continued for some time without much effect upon either side.

The rebels had placed two guns upon a point of land inside of and near the entrance to the harbor. The gun-boat *Clifton* was directed to silence these guns, and performed her work very handsomely. She fired first from her bow gun, then rounded and poured in a broadside; then turned and fired from her gun aft, then rounded again and delivered a broadside. This she did twice, when the enemy's guns were effectually silenced.

TERRIBLE EXPLOSION—DEATH OF COMMODORE RENSHAW.

The flagship *Westfield* was aground, and a little before ten o'clock in the forenoon the Commodore determined to burn her. The determination resulted in a terrible accident, which cost the Commodore his life. He covered the deck with turpentine, and made all necessary dispositions to insure her burning and had her set on fire. He then got into his boat, with Lieutenant Zimmermann, Chief Engineer William R. Green and two sailors, to proceed to another vessel. But the magazine had been left open, and scarcely had the Commodore and his comrades seated themselves in the boat when a terrible explosion occurred. The magazine, which was stored with ammunition, shells, etc., caught, and half the flagship and the Commodore's boat were scattered through the air in ten thousand fragments. Not one of the unfortunate men on board the vessel at the time or in the boat escaped instantaneous death. It is not known how many perished by this terrible explosion, but the number is estimated at ten to twenty officers and sailors. The explosion left the smoke-stacks standing and the vessel aft unharmed; but what remained was soon burned.

Meantime the rebels were making formidable preparations on shore to prevent the escape of the vessels. They were seen to drag artillery with heavy mule teams to the point commanding the bar, and were busily engaged in planting their batteries and training their guns to prevent the exit of our ships. The transport *Mary Boardman*, which is rigged precisely like a gun-boat, was lying near the flag-ship at the time of the explosion, and the fate of the Commodore was known only on board this vessel. It was supposed on board the other vessels that the Commodore had gone on board this ship. They therefore signaled her, asking "What shall we do?" Major Burt, a volunteer aid-de-camp on the staff of Governor Hamilton, told the captain of the vessel that they had no signals with which to reply, but that there was one signal which they could make which he thought would be heeded. He proposed to sail at once, and the captain, agreeing to this, immediately started. This was taken as a signal of retreat, and the *Boardman* was followed by all the other vessels in our possession. The passage over the bar was exceedingly dangerous, and the vessels were near grounding hopelessly several times; but they all escaped before the enemy had trained his guns sufficiently to do them any harm in crossing. The transports, which had gone to carry supplies to the island, immediately put to sea and returned to this city, the gun-boats remaining behind.

The other picture represents

THE FIGHT ON SHORE,

where the gallant Colonel Burrill with the Massachusetts Forty-second was overpowered by the enemy. A prisoner describing the affair to the *Times* correspondent spoke in the highest terms of the conduct of the Forty-second Massachusetts. He says they were completely shut in at one end of the wharf, where there was no probability of escape or manœuvring, and that they fought with the most desperate bravery, although outnumbered at least ten to one. Several times they fairly stemmed the rebel torrent that was rushing down upon them, and the enemy were at last compelled to take them by the bayonet. How many of our gallant fellows were killed he does not say, but he knows that the survivors were taken prisoners to Houston, and that the rebels had twenty-five killed in the struggle.

CHARLESTON, SOUTH CAROLINA.

THE illustrations on page 76 will give the reader some idea of the position of affairs at Charleston, South Carolina, and of fortifications and places of which more may be heard in the course of a day or two. How our illustrations were obtained is a mystery which we do not at present propose to gratify rebel curiosity by revealing. Suffice it to say that, while the rebels have been very active in strengthening their works, our gallant officers have not been idle, and the South Carolinians will probably find, when the tug of battle comes, that we know more of the nature and position of their defenses than they imagine.

ADVERTISEMENTS.

REBEL ATTACK UPON THE FORTY-THIRD MASSACHUSETTS VOLUNTEERS AT GALVESTON, TEXAS.—SKETCHED BY OUR SPECIAL ARTIST.—[SEE PAGE 79.]

Harriet Lane. Rebel Gun-boats. Owasco. Westfield being blown up. Mary Boardman.

ATTACK OF THE REBELS UPON OUR GUN-BOAT FLOTILLA AT GALVESTON, TEXAS, JANUARY 1, 1863.—SKETCHED BY OUR SPECIAL ARTIST.—[SEE PAGE 79.]

THE SOUTHERN ILLUSTRATED NEWS.

VOL. I. RICHMOND, SATURDAY, FEBRUARY 28, 1863. No. 25.

MAJOR-GENERAL JOHN B. HOOD.

We present in this number a portrait of the above named gallant chieftain, and transfer to our columns the subjoined biographical sketch, written by the Rev. Nicholas A. Davis, the Chaplain of the Fourth Texas Regiment:

"Major-General John B. Hood was born in Owensville, Bath county, Ky., June 29th, 1831, and was brought up at Mt. Sterling, Montgomery county. He entered upon his collegiate course at West Point in 1849, and graduated in 1853. He was then assigned to duty in the Fourth Infantry in California, where he served twenty-two months. And when the two new regiments, raised by Jefferson Davis, then Secretary of War, were called out, he was transferred July, 1855, to the one (2d cavalry) in which General Albert Sidney Johnston, who fell at Shiloh, was in command, and General R. E. Lee, the Lieutenant-Colonel. This regiment furnished many valuable officers to the South. General Earl Van Dorn, E. K. Smith, Fields, Evans and Hardee were from its ranks.

In the winter of 1855-6, General Hood entered upon the frontier service of Western Texas, where, in July following, he had a spirited engagement, and was wounded by the Indians on Devil's river.

A short time before the beginning of the present war, he was ordered to report for duty at West Point, as Instructor of Cavalry. But anticipating the present difficulties, he was allowed, at his own request, to return to duty in Texas—his object being, in view of all the prospects of impending dissolution, to be in that portion of the country which he most loved, and so greatly admired. He could see no hope of reconciliation or adjustment, but every indication of a fierce and bloody war; consequently, he had determined to cast his destiny with the South. On the 16th of April, 1861, he resigned his commission under the United States Government, and tendered his services to the Confederacy. His name was entered upon the roll with the rank of First Lieutenant, and ordered to report to General Lee, in Virginia, who ordered him to report to General Magruder, on the Peninsula. He was at once placed in command of all the cavalry of the Peninsula, with the rank of Captain of Regular Cavalry. Having several successful engagements with the enemy, he was soon promoted to the rank of Major. On September 30th, he was ordered to Richmond, and receiving the rank of Colonel of Infantry, was placed in command of the 4th Regiment Texas Volunteers, then in camp near the city. Very few of the men had ever seen him, and doubts were entertained whether a Colonel could be appointed, that would give satisfaction. For an attempt had been made to organize the regiment under Colonel Allen, of Texas; but in consequence of a protest of some of the Captains, the appointment was withdrawn. This produced a feeling with others, and it was thought that they would not be satisfied with any one that might be appointed. But in a few days the feeling was gone, and every one seemed to be perfectly satisfied. His commanding appearance, manly deportment, quick perception, courteous manners and decision of character, readily impressed the officers and men, that he was the man to govern them in the camp, and command them on the field. And his thorough acquaintance with every department of the service, satisfied every one with his competency for the position. For they found him able and ready to give all the necessary instruction, not only in drilling them for the field, but also in the forms and technicalities of the clothing, commissary, ordinance and transportation departments—for the want of which information, regiments entering the service frequently go hungry, and commissaries and quartermasters make many fruitless trips.

The General is about six feet two inches high, with full broad chest, light hair and beard, blue eyes, and is gifted by nature with a voice that can be heard in the storm of battle.

On the 8th and 9th of November, the 4th and 5th Texas Regiments left Richmond, and arrived at Dumfries on the 12th instant, where we were with the 1st to be organized into a Brigade, under Colonel Wigfall, who, to this end, had received the appointment of Brigadier-General. But, as he was the Senator elect from the State of Texas, after the meeting of Congress, he resigned. And on the 3d of March, 1862, Colonel Hood was appointed to take his place. Thus we see, within the short space of ten months and seventeen days, he was promoted from the rank of Lieutenant to that of a Brigadier-General. And having been personally associated with him during his term of service with the Texas troops, I take pleasure in saying that this rapid promotion, has not filled him with that official vanity and self-importance which so often kills the pleasure, and cuts the acquaintance of former friends. For while with him, there is no effort to make you feel the dignity of his official position; but you enjoy the pleasure of a social companion, familiar and kind friend. But as a companion, his friendship can not be cultivated to an extent that will allow a pretext to the neglect of duty, by either officers or men. He is a disciplinarian; and the discharge of duty is the way to his society and friendship. And, notwithstanding his rigid adherance to discipline, I am persuaded that he is as much admired and esteemed, by the men under his command, as any General in the army. And to this one thing I would, in a great measure, attribute his promotion in rank and our success in battle. Its importance is admitted by all. For it is this that makes the army of well-drilled soldiers so much more efficient than the raw militia. Our success depends upon it; and the sooner our people, our army and our Congress are willing to see it properly enforced, the sooner shall we see our enemy beaten, our liberty won and our country free."

MAJOR-GENERAL JOHN B: HOOD.

The following letter from the Commander-in-Chief of the army, shows what confidence he reposes in General Hood and the gallant soldiers composing his command:

GEN. LEWIS T. WIGFALL—

General: I have not yet heard from you with regard to the new Texas Regiments which you promised to endeavor to raise for the army. I need them much. I rely upon those we have in all tight places, and fear I have to call upon them too often. They have fought grandly and nobly, and we must have more of them. Please make every possible exertion to get them in, and send them on to me. You must help us in this matter. With a few more such Regiments as Hood now has, as an example of daring and bravery, I could feel much more confident of the campaign.

Very respectfully, yours,
R. E. LEE, General.

HEADQUARTERS ARMY OF VIRGINIA,
Near Martinsburg, Sept. 21, '62.

OLD age gives good advice when it is no longer able to give bad example.

PASSIONS often beget their opposites: avarice produces prodigality, and prodigality avarice; men are often constant through weakness, and bold through fear.

THERE is often more pride than goodness in our concern for the misfortunes of our enemies. We make them feel our superiority, by showing our compassion.

THE TRI-WEEKLY TELEGRAPH.

VOL. XXIX—NO. 56 HOUSTON, WEDNESDAY, JULY 29, 1863. WHOLE NO. 3711

BY PONY EXPRESS.

OUR SPECIAL DISPATCHES.

[Telegraphed from Beaumont.]

ALEXANDRIA, July 24th, 1863.

The following dispatches are found in the Cincinnati Commercial of the 8th inst.;

GENERAL MEADE'S DISPATCHES.

Headquarters, Army Potomac, near Gettysburg, July 3d, 1863, 8:30 P. M.

Major Gen. Halleck, General in Chief:

The enemy opened at 1 P. M. from about 150 guns, concentrating upon my left centre, continuing without intermission for about three hours, at the expiration of which time he assaulted my left centre twice, being upon both occasions handsomely repulsed with severe loss to him, leaving in our hands nearly 3000 prisoners, among the prisoners are Brigadier General Armistead and many Colonels and officers of lesser rank. The enemy left many dead upon the field and a large number of wounded in our hands.

The loss upon our side has been considerable. Maj. Gen. Hancock and Brig. Gen. Gibbon were wounded.

After the repelling of the assaults, indications leading to the belief that the enemy might be withdrawing, an armed reconnoissance was pushed forward from the left, and the enemy found to be in force. At the present hour all is quiet. My cavalry has been engaged all day on both flanks of t[he enemy, harassing and vigor]ously attacking h[im] ...

... has been ordered to make his Headquarters, until he can reorganize the 2nd Texas.

A similar order has been issued to Col. Waul respecting his Legion.

In accordance with instructions Col. Smith has and will furlough the members of Second Texas.—It is expected that all paroled prisoners from Vicksburg will be furloughed as soon as the order can be got from Richmond, to enable all to visit their home, due notice will be given when the members of the 2nd Texas will be required to assemble at Houston.

At present most of the prisoners paroled at Vicksburg will assemble at Enterprise, but their ultimate destinations is Demopolis where the parole camp is established. All of the Vicksburg prisoners are in good spirits, not at all demoralized and looking forward anxiously to the time when they can get another shake at the enemy.

The report that Pemberton sold Vicksburg is without foundation. Those who knew him best entertain no doubts of his loyalty, and the surrender was a matter of necessity to avoid starvation.

Major McKee informs me that Major Dick Howard is in New Orleans on parole.

Walker's army was within forty-five miles of this place yesterday. H. P.

FROM THE NORTH.

We continue our extracts from the St. Louis Republican of the 2d inst. The Republican says:

[From the National Intelligencer.

CONCENTRATION OF FORCES.

The New York evening Post earnestly urges upon ...

... 2 o'clock P. M., by a boat from the pirate bark Taconia—not Tacony—containing five men, under the command of the second officer.

After learning where the smack was from, the officer said: "You are a prize to the Southern Confederacy. I give you five minutes to get into your boats and go on board the bark."

After getting on board, as ordered, Captain Potter requested to be allowed to take his men and run the risk of getting on board some vessel or lose their lives. This was granted, and they left, the pirate captain giving them a basket of bread and some water.

They allowed the pirate, after he had set the smack on fire, &c., to get about five miles off, when they boarded the smack, hoping to put out the fire and remain on board until taken off, but they found the deck gone, and, the pirates being observed standing towards them again, they left. After rowing through the night, they reached the South Shoal lighthouse about six o'clock the following morning, having rowed a distance of twenty-eight miles. From here they were taken by the schooner Antietam, and soon after put on board the smack Eastern Star, which vessel brought them here. They report the pirate to be a bark of about three hundred and fifty tons, and think she has not over thirty men—regular cutthroats. Nothing was saved but the boats, quadrants and the clothes they stood in. The smack L. A. Macomber was a vessel of seventy tons, and owned in Noank. Captain Potter owned one half, and feels his loss severely.

They also report that she had destroyed twelve more vessels, and probably she will destroy more.—The smack Frances Ellen, of this port, was in sight, when the L. A. Macomber was burned, but it is hoped she has escaped.

Is it not time that our Government took this pirate in hand?

WASHINGTON, June 2?, 1863.

The following highly complimentary letter from the Secretary of the Navy to Captain John Rod[gers] ...

We take the following extracts from the New Orleans Era of July 7th:

From a Matamoras correspondent we clip the following:

Refugees arrive at Matamoras daily from Texas, and the number now amounts to over 5,000 which have arrived during the past fifteen months. Many of them are still in Matamoras, and in destitute circumstances. They are mostly poor men, depending upon their labor for means of existence.

Goods are continually being carried across the river into the State of Texas.

The following is the Era's account of an affair in Louisiana, of which we would thank some friend to give us a true statement. The Era lies so like his Satanic Majesty that we cannot believe a word it says.

On Saturday last a party of forty Texas cavalry came up to our outposts on the other side of the river under a flag of truce, escorting a number of our paroled prisoners. It seems that they came right up to our lines with the prisoners in a very unmilitary style, not halting as is usual at a respectful distance and sending the flag forward for a parley. The prisoners were duly received by the officers in command at the outpost, and after exchange of courtesies, the rebel escort took its departure. It rained that afternoon heavily. About dark a dash was made by a detachment of the enemy's cavalry upon the pickets with the intention of surprising and capturing them; but our boys were fully prepared for the emergency, and succeeded in cutting off and capturing the entire party. When brought in they were discovered to be the same escort that had brought our paroled men in under the flag of truce. They had concealed themselves in the neighborhood during ...

TEXAS ITEMS.

A correspondent of the Gazette charges upon the Telegraph an attempt to misrepresent Col. Herbert, in order to get him out of his seat in Congress. We beg the gentleman's pardon. We did no more than copy from the debates of Congress, as reported in the Richmond press, a speech of Mr. Herbert's, which we deemed anything but reflective of the sentiments of the people of this State, and to declare that Mr. Herbert would not be sustained in "erecting the standard of revolt," by his constituency. Mr. Herbert has disclaimed the speech, and we are glad of it. We trust if he is re-elected, he will see that the correction is made where the evil was done. Of course we take no part in the Congressional canvass in his district. We accord cheerfully to him the praise of noble heartedness, high toned honor, and an intellect by no means mediocre. His personal popularity is a proof of these qualifications.

The Huntsville Item expresses the general feeling when he says:

High Private is a truthful man,
Which none will deny;
He told us when Vicksburg fell,
And never told a lie!

We believe High Private as certain a reporter as there is in the Confederacy.

The LaGrange Patriot questions the propriety of impressing cotton, and wants to know the reason of the order. We can assure the editor that the reason was found in an imperious necessity for the purpose of putting the Trans-Mississippi District, and especially this State, in a posture of defence. The order emanated from Lieut. Gen. Smith, who is as free as any man can be from making any unjust or unnecessary assumption of power. And who, with the responsibilities now thrown upon his shoulders, deserves from the press ...

ANNOUNCEMENTS.

For Attorney General,
Col. N. SHELLY.
For the Legislature,
F. W. McGUIRE, of Washington county.
For Brig. Gen'l 17th Brigade, T. S. T.
J. W. BARNES.
For Congress, 1st District.
Col. JOHN W. BUNTON, of Hays county.
For State Senate, 2d District.
D. WILLIS.
For Representative, 48th District.
N. W. BUSH, for re-election.
For State Senate, 23d District.
CHANCY B. SHEPARD, of Washington county.
Col. N. HOLLAND, of Austin county.
For Congress 2nd. District,
C. C. HERBERT, for re-election.
Chancellor E. D. TOWNES, of Travis county.
For Senator 23rd District.
Judge GAB EFELDER.
For Floater from Washington and Fayette.
M. W. BAKER, of Washington county.
For Representative, Harris County.
JOHN T. BRADY.
M. A. DOOLEY.
HORACE CONE, for re-election.
A. S. RICHARDSON, for re-election.
GEORGE W. FRAZER.
For Congress, 5th District.
Col. JOHN R. BAYLOR.
For Representative, 37th District.
A. S. LIPSCOMB.
ISRAEL WORSHAM.
Dr. R. J. INGE
J. G. McDONALD.
For Representative, 47th District.
JOHN C. MITCHELL.
C. W. BUCKLEY.

DEATH OF GEN. HOUSTON

It is with deep and heartfelt sorrow that we announce the death of Gen. Sam Houston. It took place at his residence in Huntsville, on the 26th inst., at a quarter past 6 P. M. A letter from his physician, says:

"He died after an illness of five weeks. At one time during his sickness, hopes were entertained of his recovery, but his improvement was only apparent and it soon became evident that the hand of death was upon him. To his numerous friends it will doubtless be a matter of great satisfaction to learn that in his last hours he was sustained by the christian's hope and that he died the death of the righteous."

Thus has passed away one of the great men of the age. Say what we may of General Houston, we can but accord to him the merit of having filled his full share of the history of the last forty years. His life has been a remark[able] one.—Whether as Governor of Tenness[ee] ... but a little over thirty years [of a]ge, when he was [among] the Cherokees, or as a ... of age, or as chief of ... tion, or still later ... hero of the Texas revolu[tion] ... past years, ... the political arena of these last ... in the p[ublic] ... ublic consideration. He has not always bee[n] right, nor has he always been successful, but he has always left the impress of his mind upon the times in which he has acted.

What were the springs of action in his mind, who dare undertake to tell? What drove him when he was on the high road to fame, and the enjoyment of life, the Governor of a great State, the idol of a great people, to cast himself loose from them all and plunge into the wilderness of the West, and become the companion of savages? What led him afterwards, reinstated in the paths of civilization, the honored Senator of another great State, and the beloved idol of *its* people, to again cast himself loose from their convictions of right, and in defiance of their feelings yield his assent to the designs of their enemies? Who can tell? Whatever it was, the ease with which he regained the confidence of his fellow citizens, in both these instances, are among the most remarkable incidents in history.

After being lost for years in the wilderness, he re-visited Tennessee, and was received with the most flattering attentions by the whole people. He entered Texas, and was made little less than dictator. After being repudiated by the people of Texas twenty years later, denied his seat in the Senate, cast off by many who had always before voted for him, he took the field against a powerful and well organized party, and again the people flocked to his support and made him Governor.

Such power over men is unquestionably the most remarkable trait of his character. Therein lay the greatness of Sam Houston. It was not in his virtue, for in the course of his life he has passed through what would have been degradation to other men; and from the couch of the debauchee he has risen to the throne of power, his faculties unimpaired and his authority unquestioned. It was not in his generosity of heart, for a man who is as slow to forgive as was General Houston, is not a natural lover of his kind. But it was in the certain power of discovering the springs of human action, a knowledge of human nature, and an ability to use his knowledge, which few men possess.

To write a history of the life of Sam Houston is not our part. His history is t[oo] well known to make it necessary. To picture his character is also a task that may well be left to the public at large, to whom he was as well known as to us. We pity the heart that could now conceive evil of him. His noble qualities are before the people.

Let us shed tears to his memory, due to one who has filled so much of our affections. Let the whole people bury with him whatever of unkindness they had for him. Let his monument be in the hearts of those who people the land, to which his latter years were devoted. Let his fame be sacredly cherished by Texans, as a debt not less to his distinguished services than to their own honor, of which he was always so jealous and so proud.

... patch, from Sou[th] ... wherein he states, over his own signature, that he had gained a glorious victory over the enemy. The dispatch was dated July 5th. This evidence of Lee's success hourly accumulates. H. P.

ALEXANDRIA, July 26, 1863.

A St. Louis Republican of the 10th was received here this morning; it has but few dispatches; these state that Gen. Lee has fallen back to Hagerstown; that in the fight near Gettysburg General Lee gained ground during the two first days, and that on the third and last day of the fight there was a drawn battle; the enemy say our loss in killed and wounded was seventeen thousand, (17,000,) while their own did not exceed twelve thousand (12,000.) The death of Gen. Ewell is not confirmed.

A dispatch from Louisville, Ky., states that Morgan had crossed the Ohio at Corridon into Indiana, and was marching on to Indianapolis. At the time the dispatch was being sent, a large smoke was seen rising from New Albany, four miles below Louisville, and it was supposed the town was being burnt by a portion of the raiders.

Morgan's force was estimated at eight thousand.

Col. Ashbel Smith arrived here last evening from Vicksburg via Johnston's headquarters. From him I gather the following information:

Gen. Lee did not suffer a defeat, but he has fallen back to Virginia. Our loss had not been officially reported. His army is in good spirits, and not at all demoralized, as reported by the enemy.

The New York Herald of the 7th was filled with sensation articles expressly for the European market, as the steamer was to leave for Europe the next day.

The stores that Gen. Lee captured and stored away was immense.

Grants forces are concentrating at Jackson. It generally understood that Bragg and Johnston will unite their forces, now concentrating, all in one large army.

The Yankee raiders from Grants army have entirely overrun the line of the Jackson railroad, from Jackson to Brook Haven, burning the depots and other buildings all along the route, gathering up all the stock, and devastating generally with an unsparing hand.

Col. Smith is on his way to Houston, where he ...

SEC. 4. All slaves removed, by consent of their owners, to any seceded State after the passage by such State of an act or ordinance of secession, and hereafter brought into this State by their owners, shall thereupon be free.

SEC. 5. The General Assembly shall have no power to pass laws to emancipate slaves without the consent of their owners.

SEC. 6. After the passage of this ordinance no slave in this State shall be subject to State, county or municipal taxes.

PRIVATEERS TO BE HUNTED DOWN.

Hardly had the steamers returned: which were sent away a few days since, and reported their failure to discover the whereabouts of the pirates, than orders were received at New York to prepare once more all available vessels, and to charter every fast one to be had. The steamers Gertrude and Granite State, both captured prizes, are finishing rapidly at the Brooklyn Navy Yard, and will be sent to sea immediately. A tugboat was dispatched on Wednesday evening after the steam frigate San Jacinto, with orders to bring her back and dispatch her after the Tacony, but she was too far out to sea. Yesterday Rear Admiral Paulding succeeded in chartering the splendid ocean steamships Atlantic, Baltic, Star of the South and others.

The fleet arrived at the Navy Yard last evening, and will be outside the lights to day. The new steam corvette Shenandoah has received her sailing orders at Philadelphia, and will join the chase; the bark Ethan Allen has gone from the Boston Navy Yard, and the new steamer Hawquah, built at East Boston by Brown & Lovell, has been chartered for instant service. The steam frigate Susquehanna, which accompanied the Niagara on the cable expedition, has been hauled alongside the wharf, at the Brooklyn Navy Yard, to be fitted out; and, indeed, every vessel that possesses any sea-going qualifications will be in the hands of the constructors and fitters-out for the next few days. The following is a recapitulation of the squadron now about to participate in the chase:

1. Atlantic, chartered, New York. 2. Baltic, do. do. 3. Star of South, do. do. 4. Ethan Allen, bark, Boston. 5. Shenandoah, Navy-built corvette, Philadelphia. 6. Hawquah, steam corvette, Boston.

It was rumored last night that the Cambria, Blackstone and other craft have been chartered.

NOANK, Conn., June 24.—The crew of the smack, L. A. Macomber, Potter, of Noank, arrived here this afternoon. From one of the crew we learn that their ... was boarded June 20, at about half past ...

McCormick, 10; A F Sprott, 10 Russell Roark, 10; Stephen Watts, 10; Dr H W Johnson, 10; Charles Craighean, 10; Julius Day, 5; James L Goree, 5; M J Garner, 5; H McKinney, 5; J H Cleavland, 5; Saml E Goree, 5; Wm J Johnson, 10; Thrashley Mann, 5; A A Adew, 5; J H Lloyd, 5; J C Dear, 5; J L Miltrel, 5; Wm Sutton, 5; Geo Johnson, 5; Martin Hibbett, 3; J H Thompson, 2; N J Dobson, 2; Mrs Robt Robinson, 100; Mrs Henry Robinson, 75; Miss Jennie Robinson, (her daughter,) 25; Miss Mary Wood, 25; Mrs Larkin G Cleavland, 25; Mrs M F Kittrell, 20; Mrs M J Sprott, 5; Miss Mary Sprott, 5; Miss Rhoda Kelly, 5; Miss Mary Rives, 5; Miss Jane McAlpin, 5; Mrs Sarah W Goree, 100; Miss Susan E Goree, 5; Mrs S E Goree, 5, Mrs F A Bowdie, 5; Miss Julia Cleavland, 5; Miss M Cleavland, 5; Miss Lizzie Wheeler, 5; Miss Ella Wheeler, 5; Miss M Carter, 5; Miss Jane Carrer, 5; Miss Mattie Trezevant, 2 50; Mrs Torbut, 2 50; Mrs E Thompson, 5; Miss Mary Price 2; Miss Jane McGee, 2 50; Miss Lydia McGee, 1; Miss A H Thompson, 1; Mrs Dr Johnson, 5; Miss Maggie Lee, 10; Miss Lizzie Higgerson, 10; Miss Mag. McKinney, 5; Mrs Julius Day, 5; Miss Maggie Sutton, 5; Mrs H Johnson, 5; Mrs Cornelia E Palmer, 5; Mrs David Gindrat, 25; Miss Mollie Gindrat, 10; Mrs Mary Cunningham, 5; Mrs C C Johnson, 25; Mrs Sallie Moore, 8; A Harrel, 100:—Total, $1245 50.

We acknowledge receipt of the above sum.—ED. TELEGRAPH.

TREASURY DEPARTMENT, C. S. A., RICHMOND, May 11, 1863.

Notice is hereby given to all holders of two year Treasury Notes, issued under the Act of 16th May, 1861, that they must come in and present the said notes for funding at the Treasury or some one of its Depositaries, on or before the 31st day of July ensuing, or they will be debarred the privilege of funding. The said notes are entitled to be funded in eight per cent. Bonds payable in ten years.

(Signed,) C. G. MEMMINGER, Secretary of Treasury.

July 1-2aw1m

Speak no ill, but lenient be
To others' failings as your own;
If you're the the first a fault to see,
Be not the first to make it known;
For life is but a passing day—
No lip may tell how brief its span—
Then oh! what little time we stay,
Let us speak of all the best we can.

The European Times of the 9th instant says:

Small pox is raging at present with terrific violence in London and in various parts of the country, and, nowithstanding the great discovery of Jenner; this scourge of the human race, owing to the negligence of the public and apathy of the Government, is daily sweeping immense numbers to the grave, and disfiguring for life those whose lives the malady spares. In the metropolis, the hospitals are so crowded with cases that no more can be received, and it is now proposed to erect wooden sheds in the open air as was done when cholera was epidemic.

☞ We are indebted to a friend for the New Orleans Era of July 7th, with full Northern dispatches of the 27th. Lee's position is thus given:

It is now considered certain that Gen. Lee, with his whole command, is on the north side of the Potomac; that his left wing is in Pennsylvania; that Longstreet's corps is in the valley of Boonsboro,' between the town of Boonsboro' and the Pennsylvania State line, and that A. P. Hill's corps, accompanied by Gen. Lee himself, is not far from the battle-field of Antietam.

Immense rebel trains of wagons have returned across the Potomac from the valley of Boonsboro', loaded with all sorts of goods. They have made Charlestown, six miles from Harper's Ferry, the depot for those stolen goods, as wagons, after unloading at that place, return again to Maryland.

We have no room for further extracts to-day.

GOLDEN SPURS TO GEN. LEE.—We had the pleasure of examining, at the jewelry establishment of Mr. John Hill, 14th street, a short time since, a pair of very magnificent spurs, of solid burnished gold, which were imported through the blockade, from citizens of Maryland, as a present to Gen. Lee. They are each engraved on the inside, with the following inscription:

"STIMULUS DEDIT VIRTUS.

Presented to Gen. Robert Lee, by his friends and admirers of Prince George's County, Maryland."

The gift does honor to the patriotism and credit of the taste of the givers.—*Richmond Enquirer.*

... upon such subjects as shall suit their convenience and judgment.

Rev. Messrs. Hutcheson, Carnes, Castleton and Wagner; Judges Hill, Terril, Gray and Cole; Generals Magruder and Scurry; Messrs. P. H. S. Stanley, Horace Cone, Brown Botts, W. T. Ballinger, M. M. Potter, F. F. Chew, Alfred Richardson, George Goldthwaite and Capt. Marks.

Respectfully, LADIES OF HOUSTON.

CAMP NEAR CONCRETE, July 15th, 1863.

Editor Telegraph:—Allow me, through the columns of your paper, to return the thanks of the men of Wood's 32d Cavalry regiment to the citizens of Sweet Home, and those in the vicinity of our late camp on Rocky, for many favors furnished the men from their hands. Such treatment as we received from them is seldom extended towards the soldiery, especially in that section of country that we have been forced to march over in the past three months. If such a spirit of patriotism was manifested throughout the whole country towards the troops while on their marches, or in camps, there would not be so much discontent in the ranks; for if such a spirit is manifested toward the soldiers, such, they know, will be the treatment toward their families. Consequently, while they are ever solicitous of their families' welfare, they are content to remain at their post of duty.

And the young men's spirits have been aroused from the lethargic state into which they had fallen by inactiveness, by mingling with the Spartan daughters of that vicinity. I do not mean by this that we have been wholly inactive; but the barren country over which we have had to travel of late, without the hope of meeting the enemy, has made it of such a character to us. But, should we, upon the day of battle, be participants, we will teach the enemy that Texas mothers and daughters cannot be molested in their peaceful homes by the tramp of an invading foe. SOLDIER.

BRENHAM, July 24th, 1863.

Editor Telegraph:—Having just returned from Flournoy's Regiment, near Delhi, La., I have been much surprised to hear reports in circulation to the effect that Col. J. E. Shepard would not accept the office of Judge if elected—that his services were too important in the army, &c. Now, I take this method of informing the friends of Col. Shepard, that he has been lead to seek that high position for the reason that the state of his health and the affection of feeble eyes, renders his remaining longer in the field impracticable, whether elected or not.

G. T. MAROLD,
Capt. Co. E, 16th Reg't T. ... McCulloch's Brig., Walker's Div. July ...

... w shoe on his left
... ned with leopard
... le. Any one de-
... aid the above re-

D. ROBINSON.
jy27-tf.

INSTITUTE Will ... of pupils on the ... Charge for board ... 20 weeks. Currency rates. Address
P. P. ALLEN,
Bastrop, Tex.

—The Public Tan... under my direction is ... have capacity to ... every two months. In order to put this establishment, of such importance to the soldiers in the field, into successful operation, it is necessary to secure the services of at least 75 or 80 first class Tanners and Curriers, entirely familiar with their business. I therefore invite public attention to this important subject, and request all who are not in the army and exempt under the law, who are competent, sober and industrious, to offer their services to me with proper evidence of their capacity. And I call upon all soldiers in the ranks, who have experience in this line and who desire to do good service, to apply to me, and I will make application to the Major General commanding the District to detail them accordingly. In all cases, the most liberal wages will be paid to soldiers and citizens, and rations issued.

T. A. WASHINGTON,
Maj. & Q. M. C. S. A.
San Antonio, July 17, 1863.—jy24-1m

VALUABLE Real Estate for sale at Auction, Wednesday, July 29th inst. 50 acres Land, on the east side of Buffalo Bayou, with elegant dwellings, kitchen, negro houses, stables, cribs, orchard, and all desireable improvements.
Also desirable Blocks and Lots on Galveston Island, by
A. C. McKEEN & CO.
July 17-twtds.

FAYLE & BARNET,
COTTON FACTORS—and General Commission and Forwarding Merchants, Alleyton, Texas.
Personal attention given to the sales of Cotton, and the execution of orders entrusted to them.
Refer to T W. House, T M Bagby, and Smith and Shaw, Houston.
July 7tw1m

LADIES' RANGERS,
COL. JOHN R. BAYLOR, Commanding.
CAMP NEAR PIEDMONT SPRINGS, July 10, 1863.
VOLUNTEERS for the above corps can report to me at once, quarters and other accommodations being ready.
W. B. TEMPLE, Comd'g.
July 11-tw2w

T. W. Whitmarsh, Cotton Broker and Commission merchant, will purchase and sell for parties cotton, merchandize, produce, negroes, &c., &c., at J. H. Clark's store, Maine Street.
jy2-w&tw1m*

NOTICE.—I have about 1650 head of fine sheep which I will exchange for negroes. For particulars address the undersigned at Bastrop, or call at my rancho, 15 miles east of the town of Bastrop, near the old San Antonio road.
July 8. tw 3w
JOHN HEARN.

JOHN T. BRADY, is a candidate to represent the people of Harris county, in the next Legislature. July 3, d&w-tde.

THE NEW YORK HERALD.

WHOLE NO. 9923. NEW YORK, TUESDAY, NOVEMBER 17, 1863.—TRIPLE SHEET. PRICE THREE CENTS.

ADDITIONAL FROM EUROPE.

ARRIVAL OF THE MAILS OF THE ASIA

France and England Afraid of Recognition.

The Rebel Ram Question in England and France.

Building of Rebel War Vessels Stopped by Napoleon.

THE PRIVATEERS.

THE ALABAMA SEEN OFF CEYLON.

George N. Sanders on His Proposed Steam Fleet.

Secretary Chase's Financial Plans in England.

BEECHER'S FAREWELL TO THE BRITISH.

War Reports from Mexico and St. Domingo.

HOW RUSSIA RULES IN WARSAW.

Defeat of the English Fleet in Japan.

United States Consul Seward and a Chinese Footai on Burgevine's Secession.

THE FASHIONS, &c., &c., &c.

The European mails by the Asia reached this city from Boston at an early hour yesterday morning. Our files are dated in London and Paris on the 31st of October.

The letters of our special correspondents in London and Paris, with the compilation from the newspapers, given in the HERALD to-day, contain a very important *resume* of the events transpiring in the Old World when the Asia sailed.

The Paris correspondent of the London *Post*, writing on the 28th ultimo, says:—

The French government will not acknowledge the Southern States of America unless England does so first.

The *Journal de la Bourse*, of St. Petersburg, of October 22, attributes great significance to the presence of the Russian squadron in American waters. Closer relations with America would force England to a better understanding with Russia, whilst the Russian *rapprochement* to France would be synonymous with hostility to England.

The latest letters from Paris, in London, mention that, apart from financial matters, which are not quite satisfactory, the forthcoming speech at the opening of the Corps Legislatif by the Emperor excites intense interest. Poland, Mexico are America are expected to form important features in it. The approaching departure of Marshal Niel on a special mission to St. Petersburg is contradicted, but the Duc de Morny is spoken of as likely to proceed there. It was reported that, should the Emperor Napoleon previous to the 5th of November not receive from England and Austria their resolutions, the Emperor Napoleon will announce that he must withdraw from a joint action, and endeavor to obtain by other means, but pacific ones, a satisfactory solution for Poland as regards the present struggle. Such are the rumors in circulation in the French capital.

The French transport vessel Le Finistere left Cherbourg on the 25th of October for Vera Cruz, having on board five hundred Zouaves and six hundred add fifty other troops to fill up deaths and other casualties in the French army in Mexico.

Alderman Salomons, M. P. for Greenwich, England, addressing his constituents on the 28th ult., said;—

For his own part he was the advocate of the South in the present contest because they were fighting for independence; because they were the weaker side, and because he believed them to be honest and sincere. Was he, therefore, in favor of slavery? No; and that was an evil which he was happy to think would not survive the struggle.

THE REBEL RAMS.

Vigilant Exertions of the English Government to Prevent their Escape.

[From the Manchester Guardian, Oct. 29.]

There was a report in Liverpool yesterday that the rams had escaped; but the story was, of course, wholly unfounded.

[From the Liverpool Courier, Oct. 28.]

Inquiry shows that the government has been taking *most extraordinary precautions* to prevent any attempted departure of the rams. On Tuesday afternoon her Majesty's steamer Heron arrived in the Mersey, and took up a position in front of Messrs. Laird's dock, in which the least forward ram, El Monastir, is lying. The Heron did not anchor, but passed her cable through the side of the ferry buoy, so that it might be slipped at a moment's notice. In this position she now lies, with her fires banked and steam up. Marines were landed and sent on board El Monastir. Messrs. Laird's workmen were ordered off the vessel, which remains in the exclusive possession of the marines. No one is allowed on board and the workmen's tools have been sent ashore.

About the same time an additional force of marines was sent on board the other ram, El Toussoun, and all the workmen, with their tools and appliances, were ordered ashore. In her case also no person is permitted on board. The gunboat Goshawk continues to be moored ahead of the ram. It is understood that the iron-plated frigate Prince Consort is on her way to Liverpool, but it is difficult to ascertain whether this is correct or not. The authorities are very reserved. Her Majesty's steamer Majestic is already in the Mersey. These hostile preparations created much consternation, and it is believed that Messrs. Laird deem the seizure altogether illegal. The other vessel seized by government, the Alexandra, still lies in the Toxteth Dock, Liverpool, under embargo. Her case will come before the Court of Appeal early in the approaching term.

Will England Modify the Foreign Enlistment Act?

[From the London Post (government organ) Oct. 31.]

It is so manifestly *the interest of Great Britain to observe with strictness the obligations arising from neutrality* that it is extraordinary she should be more than suspected by the federal government of having disregarded in this respect the duties imposed upon her by international law. We do not now refer to the stereotyped abuse which, on all occasions and in the absence of any conceivable pretext, the Northern press and Northern statesmen think proper to launch against the government of this country. There is amongst a very large class of well educated and, as they believe themselves, unbiassed men in the federal States a strong conviction that the British government have, in every conceivable manner short of flagrantly outraging the law of nations, endeavored to aid the Southern confederacy in its efforts to achieve its independence. They close their eyes, unconsciously perhaps, to the fact that it is in English markets that the North has chiefly obtained the material of war which has been employed in the Southern campaigns, and looking only to the scanty supplies which have, at enormous risk, been obtained by the Confederate government protest against the facilities which have been afforded to those who are regarded as rebels against the established government. * * * * Should the Foreign Enlistment act prove a dead letter, the very important question will arise, whether, while the American civil war is still pending, it would be fitting to modify it, especially as the modification would operate solely against one of the belligerents. On the one hand the future interests of this country must be regarded, and on the other, the obvious infringement of the spirit, if not of the letter, of neutrality by legislating to meet the requirements of one of the contending parties. On the one side *policy and international law impress the necessity of preventing vessels intended to be used against a friendly State leaving our shores.* On the other, honor and dignity dissuade from introducing changes which can operate only against the weaker of the two belligerents, between whom we are desirous of standing perfectly neutral. The position is a difficult one for the British government, and it may be not less so for the Legislature. The modifications which have been introduced into naval warfare, and the construction of special engines of destruction, which were unknown to the framers of the Foreign Enlistment act, have made the course to be pursued by the government still more difficult and uncertain. The act is silent about the building of ships, and prohibits solely their being armed or equipped with the object of being used against a friendly State. But does the building of a vessel which can be employed as a ram for running down others constitute an infringement of the act? Some say yes, whilst other no less respectable authorities say no. Supposing the courts of law say no, ought the Legislature to interpose and supply the deficiency in the law? This question may, in fact be submitted to the Legislature. and if so its reply will demand the exercise of the greatest prudence and the greatest discrimination. To our mind the most fitting answer which could be given would be to the effect that this country had framed its laws with the view of enforcing neutral obligations, and that if those laws are proved to be defective it must await a time when suitable modification can be introduced without prejudice to the interests of a particular State.

The Crew from the Florida in Liverpool.

[From the London Times, Oct. 29.]

It may be mentioned that the rumors which have been current for some time, to the effect that a portion of the Florida's crew had arrived some weeks ago to take charge of the iron-clads, has no foundation in fact. The real fact is that these men became insubordinate at Brest because they were refused leave ashore, and were subsequently discharged by Captain Maffit. They made their way to Liverpool, and on their wages being paid they dispersed, and most of them immediately shipped in various merchant vessels.

George N. Sanders, His Son, and His Steam Line.

TO THE EDITOR OF THE LONDON TIMES.

SIR—"Historicus," in his reply to me yesterday, does himself great credit as an adroit special pleader, whatever judgment must be passed upon that candor which his chosen anonyme seems to claim.

He had set forth three documents, the first signed by me, the second unsigned, but on its face, manifestly imputed to the author of the first; the third, a so-called memorandum, said to be in the same handwriting with "the above letter." When I acknowledged the genuineness of the first, but repudiated the second letter, he now meets me by saying that no one had imputed to me that which I denounced as spurious. And yet "Historicus" himself, in his own first paragraph of commentary, connects them all together as referring to one transaction, which was the building of steamships under my contract; and, therefore, no one could read the whole without attributing to me the unsigned papers, even though "Historicus" now dodges my repudiation of them by saying that they are not attributed to me. Certainly not in so many words, the audacity of manufacture was not carried to the length of forging my signature. But I repeat, that no one can read them together without doing what "Historicus" himself distinctly did, ascribing them to me by direct and necessary implication, both as to authorship and as to handwriting. This is sharp practice, and proves the possession by "Historicus" of precisely that kind of legal talent upon which he will have to draw largely when he undertakes to make that, which he has not yet ventured upon, an answer to the exposure by "Vigilans" of the flat contradictions between his present arguments against Mr. Laird and the Confederate government and his recent statements of the law and of the clear rights of British merchants and shipbuilders. He comments with equal fairness on my expression of any papers having been "treacherously stolen," claiming (justly enough) that an enemy has a right to intercept despatches. My language evidently referred to an operation very different from ordinary open capture. The facts were simply these:—The Yankees sent to Richmond a scoundrel—unfortunately a relative of some of our best men in the confederacy—who so far wound himself into confidence as to be put in command of the yacht in which my son, Major Reid Sanders, undertook to get through the blockade. This villain carried the yacht straight into capture. My son sank his bag of despatches, believing it to contain everything; but it appears the spy had previously stolen from him some of my papers. This was the treacherous stealing to which I referred. It is easy to imagine how a rascal of his stamp, having his pay in view, might eke out by manufacture what was wanting to give a color of illegality to the transaction indicated by the stolen papers, so as to enable his employers to call on Earl Russell to arrest an operation really unimpeachable, by presenting pretended evidences going to distort and prevent it. I cannot acquit the Yankee State Department of some complicity in this, because they had the cruel meanness, not only to begin with casting upon my patriot and noble boy a charge of treachery, to give authenticity to the papers, but, although he was entitled by the then existing cartel to exchange in ten days, he was kept a close prisoner for over four months, while the cartel was in full operation, as he has been ever since, now nearly a year. This suppression of the evidence of the witness who alone could throw light on the whole matter, by a proceeding at once tyrannical and faithless, entitles me to challenge the genuineness of all and every of the stolen papers, though I have not hesitated frankly to acknowledge the one single letter which I do recognize as my own

Whether Mr. Mallory's letter to Mr. Mason, now again dwelt upon with renewed emphasis by "Historicus," as evidence that my steamers were to be war cruisers, has been honestly copied or not, or whether it has been a little twisted by the addition of a word or two, I neither know nor care. My steamers were to be mail and freighting vessels, designed to ply regularly to and fro, running all blockades of course, and of such strength of construction as to enable them to do so with probable impunity. Whether Mr Mallory, in alluding to them, may have called them "freighting and fighting vessels," is of little consequence. Of course, heavily plated vessels might be subsequently armed as any other vessels might be, and as some vessels after running the blockade have been; and the Confederate government could, with perfect legitimacy, promote their construction by giving me the contract in question. But has "Historicus," or has Lord Russell, yet gone so far in thick and thin identification with the policy (I will not say submission to the will) of the Yankee government as to deny me the right of ordering such vessels for *bona fide* freighting and blockade running purposes under a mail contract, because they may by possibility at some future period, in a Confederate port, be armed and converted, with a compensation to me for their diversion from the purposes of my contract? Does the Foreign Enlistment act forbid this? That question I leave to the merchants and shipbuilders, and to the common sense of England. It will be time enough to discuss it with "Historicus" after he shall have answered "Vigilans," who has already quoted against him passages from his own anterior letters, strongly asserting even much broader rights on the part of the mechanical industry and trade of neutral Powers.

I have already offered to submit my contract to Lord Palmerston himself. "Historicus" now asks me if I will tell Lord Palmerston where my vessels are building. He clearly means to insinuate that they may be Mr. Laird's "rams." This is neither handsome or fair, after my absolute declaration that Mr Laird's vessels have not, never have had, anything to do, directly nor indirectly, with my contract. But I hope "Historicus" will be satisfied with my response when I say that I am perfectly willing to give Lord Palmerston, with entire openness, the fullest information he may desire on the subject. Respectfully, GEORGE N. SANDERS

LONDON, Oct. 29, 1863.

Mr. Lindsay on Neutral Trade.

TO THE EDITOR OF THE LONDON TIMES.

SIR—Though "Historicus" is an able and learned writer, I am disposed to think that the cause he has now espoused is a weak one, or he would not attempt to misconstrue the language of those who differ from him

I did not "dispute the genuineness" of the intercepted correspondence. I knew nothing about that correspondence till I read it in the public press, and therefore I said in my letter to you that I could "not enlighten" him in regard to its authenticity. I expressed doubts as to its accuracy, and I supported those doubts by facts within my own knowledge.

If "Historicus" will take the trouble to refer to a very curt letter from the Foreign Office, which closes the published correspondence with Mr. Mason, he will find that I have not been "mistaken" in the reasons which induced the Confederate government to order the termination of that gentleman's mission to this country. That it was "timid" in case of inquiry about the Liverpool rams which are said to be for the Confederate government, or about the "six ships" which, so far as my knowledge extends, have no existence, is absurd.

I am not disposed, even if I felt myself competent, which I do not, to discuss with "Historicus" questions of international law. It may be quite wrong for vessels to leave the ports of this country and capture or destroy federal ships, but it is equally wrong to allow cannon to be sent to destroy Charleston, and if our government arrests the one they should stop the other, or our "impartial neutrality" becomes a farce.

In [illegible] impression of this morning Mr. Chase is reported to have said (I do not notice his unbecoming remarks concerning "old Mother England," or his threat about the "evidences of strength shown by the republic") that "England would consider it the best policy to pay for all the depredations of the Alabama and her consorts." Now, if the fitting out of that vessel was, as you state, "really an illegal adventure," and if the doctrines which "Historicus" has promulgated are sound, there may be more justice than would at first appear in the claims which the federal government have made upon us, and the tendency of the recent arguments of "Historicus" seems to me to be in favor of the opinions which Mr. Chase has just expressed.

As I may hereafter be called upon to give my vote for or against those claims, I am anxious to ascertain if they are really just, and to elucidate this point would "Historicus" favor me with an answer to the following questions?

1. Are the traders of this country, by our laws, interdicted from selling to belligerents in the ordinary course of their business such commodities in which they deal as, but for a state of war, they would have been entitled to dispose of? In other words, are they not to be allowed to pursue their lawful calling in their own country, because their customers happen to be at war?

2. As shipbuilding is quite as lawful a calling as the manufacture of guns or sabres, is it not as legal for Messrs. Laird to sell their ships in the Mersey to one belligerent as for the cutlers of Sheffield and the gunmakers of Birmingham to sell their sabres and their muskets to another belligerent?

3. If a cutler or cannon founder may by our law send sabres and muskets to New York, or mortars to bombard Charleston, or Greek fire to destroy its inhabitants, why may not a shipbuilder send a steam ram to New Orleans or Mobile?

4. Is not a rifle with percussion caps, balls and cartridges, or a bayonet fitted to its musket, or an Armstrong gun, with its munitions of powder, shells and fuzes, as fully equipped for injury to one belligerent as a ship with its cannon on board is to another? And is the stem of a steam ram built in a neutral port more clearly fitted for making a hole in a belligerent's ship than a rifle manufactured in a neutral town for drilling a hole through the head or body of a belligerent soldier or sailor?

5. If the Confederate government has violated our laws and invaded our sovereignty by contracting for ships in this country, how is it that the federal government has not done so also by contracting for, buying and transporting from our ports, even in our royal mail steamships, enormous quantities of contraband of war?

6. If the federals have a right to recover from us the loss they have sustained through "the depredations of the Alabama," will the Confederates not have an equal right to compensation for the destruction of their cities by the cannon which we sold to their enemies.

7. If it be the case that the federal government has ignored and instigated the Queen's subjects to violate the injunctions of her proclamation, is it in a condition, by the law of nations, to demand redress for the disregard of that proclamation by others? And are we to yield that to fear which has no support from either law or equity?

8. If it be the case that a violation of our sovereignty is an offence with which no government but our own has anything to do, and if, consequently, the steam rams have been arrested under our municipal laws, do not these same laws entitle this government to prohibit the transmission of arms and munitions of war as authoritatively as to place the broad arrow upon ships? And, if so, why does Lord Russell permit arms and munitions of war to go and order ships to stay?

9. The Confederates have said that if it were not for the Irish emigrants they would have finished the war long since Now, though the proof in neither instance may be very clear, still it is as clear that the federals get men from this country to fight their battles as it is that the Confederates get ships, can "Historicus" inform me why our government, when it stops the building of suspicious looking ships, does not stop also the emigration of suspicious looking men, of whom there are many thousand at present leaving Ireland for New York? And is the foreign nation that enlists these men entitled to claim at our hands the immunities of impartial non intervention?

When "Historicus" gives a satisfactory answer to these questions I shall be more able to comprehend and appreciate his arguments and his elaborate quotations, and, at the same time, understand more clearly than I now do what Mr. Chase means when he says that he would "like to take old Mother England by the hair and give her a good shaking."

In conclusion, allow me to add that, though I feel myself incompetent, and my knowledge far too limited, to deal with those great legal questions which affect the peace of nations, and which exercise so vast an influence over the interests and happiness of mankind, I nevertheless feel, in common, I believe, with many of my countrymen, that while we prohibit ships which are said to be for the South, and do not prohibit arms and men which are said to be for the North, our policy is not just. In a word, if we do not adopt the same measure of justice to both parties engaged in this most deplorable war, our professions of an "impartial neutrality" are mere empty words, and our policy is very different from that which has made England what she is. If we adhere to it—if we do not vigorously attempt to stop all, and, if we find it impracticable, cease to stop either ships or cannon, then I very much fear that our policy will be considered both inconsistent and unjust, and will go far to tarnish the fair fame of English statesmen. I am, sir, your obedient servant, W. S. LINDSAY.

SHEPPERTON, Oct. 28, 1863.

The Privateers.

PRIVATEER BUILDING STOPPED IN FRANCE.

[Paris (Oct. 30) correspondence of London Times.]

The French government has assured Mr. Dayton, the American Minister, that the vessels of war building for the South in France shall not be permitted to leave.

[From the London News, Oct. 30.]

The French government is said to have informed Mr. Dayton, the United States Minister in Paris, that the "autorisation" for the construction of certain vessels of war now proved to be building in France for the Confederates, and for certain cannon and munitions for their armament, has been withdrawn, and that the parties engaged in the business have been warned of the danger of prosecuting their work.

THE ALABAMA OFF CEYLON.

COLOMBO, Sept. 30, 1863.

It is reported that the Munlee, which arrived here yesterday, was sighted by the Confederate Alabama, and chased till British colors were exhibited The Alabama was in Simon Bay repairing on the 20th of September

THE AMERICAN QUESTION.

Secretary Chase as a Financier.

[From the London Times, Oct 31.]

Nothing is more agreeable than to listen to a highly successful man, who, in the evening of his life and the fulness of his fame, delights to narrate the causes which led to his greatness or the incidents which suggested his brilliant invention. The great mass of mankind, if incapable of doing great things themselves, take pleasure in knowing how great things are done, and the galling sense of inferiority is diminished when we see, as it were, the mechanism of mighty actions displayed before us like the machinery of a skeleton clock. That Columbus found out America when he was seeking for a short cut to India, and that Newton discovered the law of planetary revolutions while he was investigating the fall of an apple, are stories that will win the attention and excite the interest of all generations. Mr. Chase evidently thinks that he belongs to that class of great men whose reputation nothing can shake. He does not require that death should put the last seal on his renown, and stamp it for the benefit of all future time with the signet of immutability. He prefers to be the guardian of his own fame, and to supply as early as possible all that information which will be so greedily sought after when the great Chase has retired to that calm abode where there are neither loans nor greenbacks, and the art of the financier is neither known nor needed.

Mr. Chase does not stoop to defend his financial measures; they stand in no need of it; their triumphant success speaks for itself. He saw the want of his country; and he supplied it. The country needed a substantial, permanent and uniform medium of exchange, and Mr. Chase arose and gave it to them. He is at no trouble to prove that the present paper currency of the United States possesses these admirable qualities. That nobody can doubt, and we may be thought guilty of an impertinence if we offer any argument in support of so self evident a proposition. Uniform the American currency must be; for, if there were any diversity, the circulating medium which broke the law of uniformity must be either paper or gold. Paper it cannot be, for Mr. Chase has driven out of circulation the paper of the banks, and substituted the issues of the government in their place. Gold it cannot be, for gold Mr. Chase has succeeded in driving out of the country so effectually that there is no fear of its returning from exile to spoil the symmetry of a paper circulation. The greenbacks are clearly entitled to the praise of uniformity; nor can we deny to Mr. Chase's currency the attribute of permanency. *He has secured that by its depreciation.* There is not the slightest fear of his greenbacks sharing the proverbial fate of suddenly acquired wealth. *They will not take to themselves wings and fly to other lands. They are his, and his alone. We doubt if a single note has found its way across the Atlantic, unless as a curiosity.* Certainly Mr. Chase is entitled to claim for his currency the attribute of permanency A depreciated paper currency is an easy possession for a nation to acquire, and a difficult one to get rid of. Nobody wishes to deprive her of it; it is one of those blessings which excite no envy. Commerce does not touch it, war itself will not destroy it. Mr. Chase claims for his currency that it is not only permanent and uniform, but substantial. This may be proved by several arguments. In the first place, the bulk of it is very considerable. Printing presses have been at work for two or three years, day and night, in producing this currency, and it would be a curious calculation to estimate what kind of pile the whole issue of greenbacks would make should the government be ever in a position to buy them up and burn them. The substantiality of Mr. Chase's currency may further be proved by the immense weight which it supports Upon it rests the vast army and navy, the internal trade, the credit and the hopes of the United States. Surely that which supports all this mass must itself be substantial The utmost strength, however, of a machine is never known till it is broken, and we may possibly be called upon to witness this final proof of the substantiality of Mr. Chase's paper currency when we see the burden under which it is destined to give way.

* * * Let ordinary mortals toil and slave, let the Old World financiers rack their brains for fresh taxes, fresh loans, or further economies; Mr. Chase has found the philosopher's stone—he has got a uniform, permanent and substantial currency, which costs nothing and pays for everything, and he need trouble his head with none of these Old World embarrassments

We had certainly thought that there was nothing new in all this; we had thought that the art of issuing inconvertible paper, and declaring it a legal tender, had come into existence a little before the art of declaring national bankruptcies—nay, we had even gone so far as to speculate on some occult connection between the two. We now learn that we were mistaken, and Mr. Chase is good enough to give us a popular explanation of the steps which have led him to a discovery destined to relieve mankind from the primitive curse, and to make them rich without inflicting on them the slightest trouble or anxiety. The first thing that struck Mr. Chase was a declaration of our own, that no money would be advanced in this country to the Northern States by English capitalists. Reasoning deeply on this announcement, he came to the conclusion that as we would not lend he would not borrow from us; at any rate, till we came to ask him to do so—a qualification which we venture to think does not much diminish the absolute nature of the proposition. Having established this point of departure, this ingenious man began *by borrowing all the gold he could get in his own country and paying it away for war expenses.* In the course of this process his mind was struck by the remarkable fact *that the gold did not come back to him as fast as he paid it away*—an observation which, we apprehend, has been already made by every person who has entered upon a large expenditure of borrowed money and has not credit to borrow any more. This was exactly the state in which Mr. Chase found himself. Capitalists became exorbitant in their demands, and Mr. Chase came to the conclusion that instead of borrowing other people's notes he had better issue his own. As this was, however, only another form of borrowing, and as he had, as he tells us, previously exhausted his credit, people who were not willing to become creditors of the government, which was the case with many bankers, were unwilling to receive these notes in payment. Then the beautiful idea suggested itself to the mind of Mr. Chase of compelling them to take them in payment—that is, of making them legal tender. That, he triumphantly says, was the next step. You would have done exactly, he says, as he did. It is an affair of common sense and courage. No doubt any debtor whose credit is exhausted, whose bills nobody will take except at a ruinous discount, would, if he could, make them a legal tender. Mr. Chase could, and did, and therein lies his unapproachable superiority over the private debtor, who, when he cannot pay, has no resource but an ignominious declaration of insolvency.

But the greatest men are not consistent throughout. We are sorry to observe in Mr. Chase a lamentable confession of weakness. His next step was to borrow money on bond. This was quite right if he could get it; but, alas! in order to get it he promised to pay the interest in gold. Why in gold? Had he not at his absolute disposal—could he not create at will, that uniform, permanent and substantial currency to which labor must look for its reward, which represents the credit of the nation, and which, by the system of national banking, has received, as he informs us, the support of the capital of the country? He found, he tells us, that he could get gold, and so he used it; we clearly understand every other step of his career, but this recreant hankering for a metal which he had disgraced, superseded and driven out of the country is to us inexplicable. Was there nobody there to ask Mr. Chase what would be his next step? *Where does he intend to get more gold, or how does he propose to do without it?* Perhaps he had better perform his threat of making the capitalists of England press upon him the acceptance of their gold; perhaps he thinks that the payment of interest in specie for money which is gone and spent has lasted long enough, or perhaps he has discovered some secret for greatly increasing his paper circulation without diminishing its value. Nothing was ever at once found out and perfected, and we are bound to say that Mr. Chase appears to us to have been more successful in pointing out the steps by which he has ascended to his present eminence than in pointing out how he is to maintain it. Icarus is very near the sun, and we want to know how he is to prevent the wax in his wings from melting and burying him under a cloud of his own feathers.

How Secretary Chase Can "Shake" England.

[From the London Globe, Oct. 28.]

The obstacles put in the way of the fulfilment of Mr. Laird's ventures have had the effect of increasing the number of testimonies to the thoroughness of British neutrality in this American war. By the last mail we had a shriek from a Richmond journalist, who declared "the Palmerston administration" to be "the curse of Great Britain," because it has refused to join with France in the recognition of Mr. Mason and Mr. Davis. We, it appears, are answerable for the murder of thousands on thousands of Southern men, for the pillage of myraids of [illegible], and for the beggary, shame and outrage [illegible] about the Alabama, and his desire "to take old Mother England by the hair and give her a good shaking." Is that the Yankee [illegible] showing filial affection? But if Mr. Chase really wants to give England a thorough good shaking *there is one way of doing it, for which he is the fittest man in the world—let him get himself appointed Chancellor of the British Exchequer.*

The Elections in Ohio and Pennsylvania.

[From the London Herald (organ of the aristocrats), Oct. 27.]

The partisans of Mr. Lincoln, here and in America, are jubilant, of course, over the result of the State elections in Pennsylvania and Ohio. Those States are generally reckoned among the doubtful ones. The democratic party has always been strong there, but never so strong as to reduce its opponents to despair. * * * As neither the government organs in America nor the federal advocates here are likely to afford any explanation of the means by which this result has been achieved—as they are certain to treat it as a *bona fide* declaration in favor of the republican policy of proscription in the North and extermination in the South—as they will inevitably claim it as a condonation of the past tyranny of the administration, and a sanction for similar usurpations in future—it may be as well that we should point out briefly its real significance and the method by which it has been accomplished

In the first place the States in question are under martial law, the Habeas Corpus act having been suspended throughout the North with an especial view to these elections. This fact alone deprives the republican victory of all moral significance. *Who values a vote given, like those of Kentucky or Maryland, under the most violent form of compulsion? In England the scrupulous jealousy of the constitution removes the troops beyond the boundaries of a town where a poll is to be held, so that the civil power itself may not be strengthened by military support against the liberty of the electors;* in the Northern States military force is applied for the express purpose of forcing upon the constituencies candidates agreeable to the administration. We do not think much of the significance of a French election; but elections in France are patterns of popular freedom in comparison with those just held in Ohio and Pennsylvania. Again, every man who is seen to come up to the poll to vote for the democratic candidate—and, the ballot notwithstanding, it is almost always known in America how a man does vote—is a marked man, has proclaimed himself the enemy of a power which has rendered itself despotic, and is pretty sure, in one way or another, to pay its debt of vengeance. His republican neighbors may harass him at their pleasure; he will have no protection from a law which is interpreted either by federal courts martial or by Judges who are the mere creatures of the administration. If he be of military age he may feel pretty sure that the next conscription will, somehow or other, include his name. If he gets into any dispute with a drunken soldier or has his farm plundered by marauders from some German regiment, it will be sufficient for the culprit to say, "He voted for Woodward or for Vallandigham," and the complainant will be dismissed, not merely without redress, but with menaces and insults. In the cities there is a regular "reign of terror;" and a man of any note who takes an active part against the administration does so at the risk of imprisonment, banishment, or ruin, and with the certainty of malignant official and social persecution. Not satisfied with all this, the federal government has gone so far as to insist that the votes of soldiers in the field shall be counted; that is, that some twenty, thirty, or forty thousand votes shall be placed at its absolute disposal; for what soldier would dare to vote against the candidate of the government? An officer who did so would lose his commission; a sergeant would be reduced to the ranks; a private would have his life made a burden to him. It is not long since a federal general boasted of having reduced to the ranks a non-commissioned officer whose only offence was that, on being questioned by his superiors, he had avowed his disapproval of the policy of the administration. Finally, in Pennsylvania at least, the control of the ballot boxes was in the hands of the republican candidate, and scrutiny was of course impossible. Under these circumstances it is as impudent for the federal government to boast of its victory in Pennsylvania and Ohio as for the whigs to exult in the return of the Duke of Somerset's candidate for Totnes. In either case the election is a mere mockery. *Every man who voted for the opposition did so at the risk of ruin;* and a number of votes, sufficient to turn the scale, were held by men absolutely dependent on the mercy of the victorious party.

This is the country which is fighting for human rights and the extension of political liberty. This is the country which wages an internecine war on behalf of justice and freedom with a nation which has not, in the midst of invasion, found it necessary to suspend the writ of habeas corpus, or allowed military necessity to interrupt the course of civil law. In the South the press is free; in the North several papers have been suppressed, and even in the Empire City the Provost Marshal has warned the journals to publish no news unfavorable to the federal cause. In the South no State has for a moment been deprived of any portion of its rights; in the North, Kentucky and Maryland are subjected to a military despotism of the most hateful kind, their sovereign *status* being entirely ignored and their local governments overthrown at the point of the bayonet. In the South no man has been imprisoned, or banished without legal trial; in the North imprisonment and exile at the pleasure of the administration are habitually inflicted upon its leading opponents. And yet there are Englishmen besotted, ignorant, or dishonest enough to tell us that the defeat of the North would be a heavy disaster to the cause of human liberty; that the subjugation of the South and the extension of the iron tyranny under which Maryland and Kentucky are now suffering throughout the area of the Confederate States is an event for which all lovers of freedom ought to pray. Are these men in possession of their senses—*are they arrant hypocrites or merely frantic fanatics?* Are they really persuaded that martial law and the suspension of the habeas corpus at the pleasure of the Executive are the symptoms of a free government

THE TEXAS EXPEDITION.

Mouth of the Rio Grande and Vicinity, Brownsville and Point Isabel.

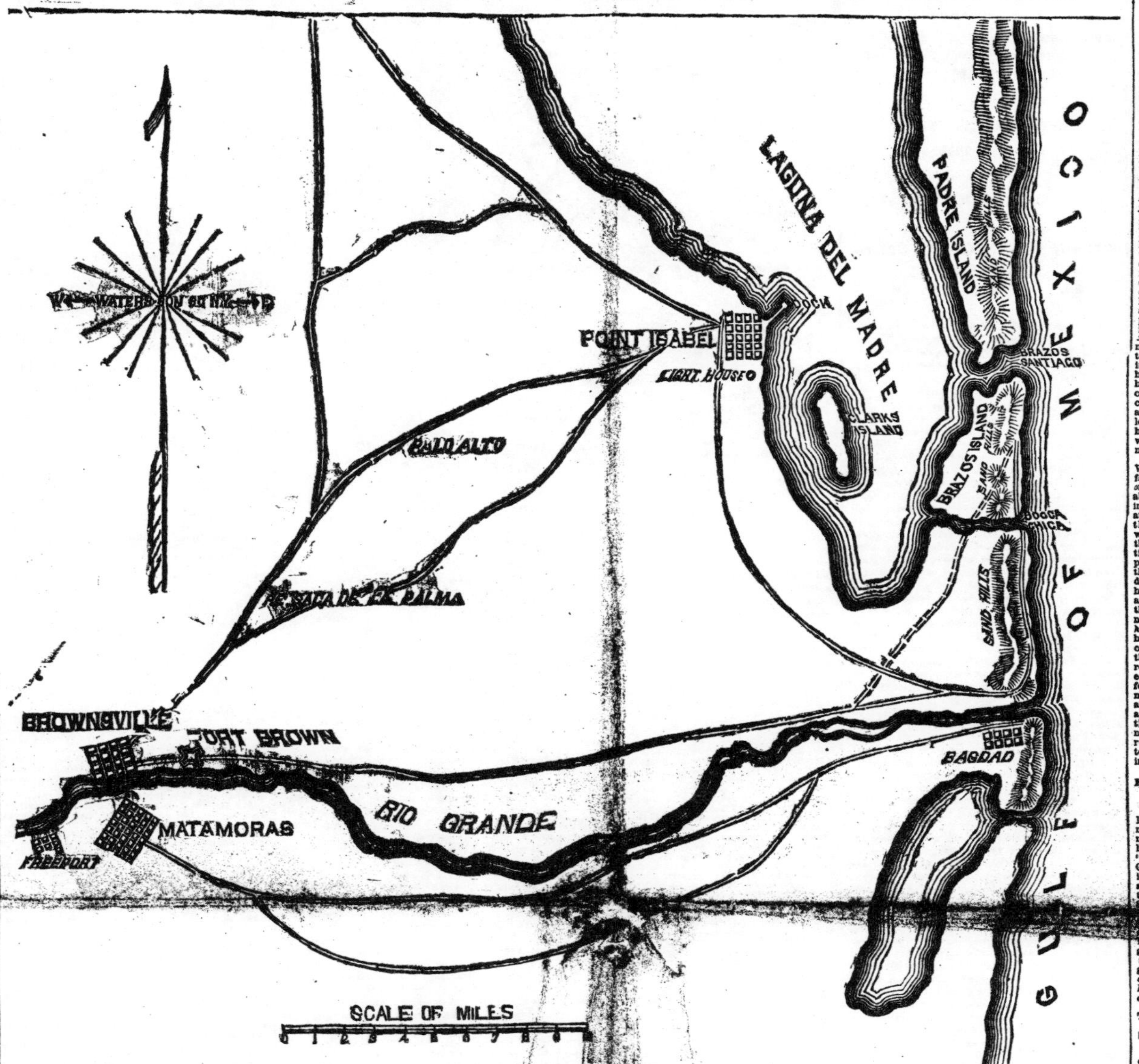

THE NEW YORK HERALD.

WHOLE NO. 9929. NEW YORK, MONDAY, NOVEMBER 23, 1863. PRICE THREE CENTS.

THE RIO GRANDE EXPEDITION.

Evacuation of Brownsville by the Rebels and Its Occupation by Our Troops.

How American, French and Mexican Interests Have Been Affected by the Movement.

Revolutionary Changes in the State of Tamaulipas.

THE FRENCH POLICY DEFEATED.

Necessity of Reinforcing General Banks' Army,

&c., &c., &c.

The steamship Star of the South, Captain Woodhull, arrived at this port yesterday from New Orleans, Pensacola and Key West. She reports that the steamship Mississippi sailed for Pensacola twenty-four hours previously, with her machinery disarranged.

Our Special Correspondence.

BROWNSVILLE, TEXAS, Nov. 9, 1863.

Here we are on the banks of the Rio Grande, with the old flag flying over the town, where it had not been seen before for the last two years and a half. We have got possession of this important place without a struggle, and we mean to hold it at whatever cost. Its importance will be more thoroughly appreciated after becoming acquainted with the history of the occupation and of its immediate consequences; and the military authorities at Washington should not delay a moment in so strengthening the army as to make it secure against all adversaries.

The rebels, who had been in possession of the place, under General Bee, becoming informed of the advance of our troops, under General Banks, prepared to evacuate it, and their preparations consisted chiefly in plundering the citizens, throwing the guns of Fort Brown into the Rio Grande, and then setting fire to the town. They burned the United States barracks and destroyed large quantities of property. This they were not permitted to do, however, without a serious resistance on the part of the inhabitants, who were organized for the purpose by a military officer from Mexico, General Cobos, who happened to be living at the time in Brownsville as an exile. The advance of General Banks' army entered it at ten o'clock on the morning of the 5th inst. This advance consisted of the Ninety-fourth Illinois Volunteers. General Banks and staff arrived at noon, and were followed, at about three o'clock, by a battery of the First Missouri Light artillery and the Thirteenth Maine Volunteers. The rest of the army is *en route* to this point, with the exception of those stationed at Brazos, at Point Isabel and at Brazos Island.

Our unexpected occupation of Brownsville has produced events which would not at first sight appear to have any connection with it, but which, nevertheless, flowed directly from it. The Mexican general whom I have already noticed as organizing the Brownsvilleites against the rebel incendiaries and plunderers, was a man of some note. His full name was—for he no longer lives—Jose Maria Cobos. He was a Peninsular, as they call them here—that is, a native of Spain—but came to Mexico when he was but thirteen or fourteen years of age. He had attained the age of forty-five and the rank of general of division in the Mexican army, in which he had served for the last twenty years. Although he had abstained from giving in his adherence to the French movement in Mexico, and was understood to be hostile to it, still he was on terms of close intimacy with General Miramon, who had gone over to the French, and both were known as reactionists, or adherents of the church party.

It was this connection, I believe, which led to the necessity of Cobos' retiring from the Mexican territory. You are aware that nearly opposite this place stands the town of Matamoros. This is the capital of the State of Tamaulipas. The whole State has been in a state of siege since early in 1862—still recognizing the Juarez government. Strangely enough, its coast was excepted from the declaration of blockade made by the French military authorities. This curious fact is susceptible of an easy explanation. It was an arrangement by which mutual advantages were secured to the French and to the rebels. The latter were enabled to get supplies from abroad through this gate, and to send cotton out in exchange for them; and as a *quid pro quo* for this advantage the rebels were to lend their aid in reducing Matamoros and the whole State of Tamaulipas to French jurisdiction. This nice little arrangement has been spoiled by the arrival of our troops just in the nick of time. But Cobos, finding himself at the head of from five to seven hundred men, made up from the ranks of the retreating rebels, from the residents of Brownsville whom he had organized to resist the plunderers, and from Mexicans attached to his cause, suddenly crossed the river, surprised the garrison of Matamoros, deposed the Military Governor of the State of Tamaulipas, and proclaimed himself Governor in his stead, under the following

PLAN.

In the heroic city of Matamoros, on the 7th day of the month of September, 1863, the undersigned having assembled to deliberate on the situation in which the republic is now placed—threatened on one side with the loss of its independence and with annihilation on the other, by the unbridled acts of a demagogism, represented by a band of men who, renouncing the principles which constitute order and the liberties of a free people, sustain its barbarous domination by means of terror and violence, in which is reflected the image of the dishonor of our country.

Considering that the Mexican nation cannot and must not abdicate its rights, thus investing a minority with the power of altering the fundamental form of our government;

Considering that it is an imperious necessity, in order to save our independence and to establish peace, which the people so much desire, that the unfortunate constitution of 1857 and the government which emanates from it should cease in every corner of the country—a government whose repeated and intolerable offences against all that our laws, institutions and customs hold to be most respectable call for prompt and efficacious reformation;

Considering that, in order to combine the means conducing to the end of suppressing the anarchy which afflicts the nation, and to give solidity to its future march of peace and progress, nothing can be done except all Mexicans of patriotism and firmness, whatever may be the political party to which they have been attached, shall band together around the glorious national banner, resolved to permit no power to be organized beneath its shadow which has not been sanctioned by the national will;

Considering that, if above the ruins to which at this day the edifice raised more than forty years ago, at the cost of the sacrifice of innumerable Mexicans, has been reduced, it be indispensable to construct a new edifice of our political regeneration, under the lawful protection and the good faith of the nations which profess true and disinterested friendship for us, it will never be admitted by the generality of Mexicans with the character and conditions now imposed on them; we therefore proclaim:—

Article 1. The constitution of 1857 and the government emanating from it shall cease to be exercised in the Mexican republic.

Art. 2. We proclaim the General of Division, Don Jose Maria Cobos, chief of the forces which shall be organized for sustaining this plan, and he shall issue such directions as will be necessary for its general adoption in the rest of the republic.

Art. 3. The different towns, on adopting it, shall remit their *pronunciamientos* to the chief above mentioned.

Art. 4. The General-in-Chief, already named, shall immediately convene a meeting of the people of Matamoros, that they may elect five persons of wisdom and discretion to draw up a plan without delay, having for its object the formation of a provisional government, which shall direct public affairs, and adopt such means as are necessary for the defence of our venerated independence.

Art. 5. In the meanwhile the funds coming into the public treasury shall be securely deposited under safe custody, and that only expenses necessary for war and government be liquidated, while the provision necessary to satisfy foreign agreements shall be duly set apart.

The deposed Military Governor, Don Manuel Ruiz, took refuge in this city. His deprivation of office was much regretted here, because he was recognized as an undoubted friend to the government of the United States. But Cobos did not long enjoy his triumph. A counter revolution against him took effect the very next day, headed by a colonel of cavalry named Cortinas. Cobos was defeated, captured, condemned and executed as a traitor, and

THE EXPEDITION TO THE RIO GRANDE.

Scene of General Banks' Movements in Texas---Occupation of Brownsville.

Ruiz recalled from Brownsville and reinstated in his post as Military Governor of Tamaulipas.

Cortinas published the following explanation and defence of his conduct on this occasion:—

TO THE PUBLIC.

The undersigned believes it to be his duty promptly to explain to the nation, as well as to the people of this heroic city and the armed garrison of the place which he has the honor to command, the reason for the execution of Don Jose Maria Cobos at eight o'clock on the morning of yesterday; and, as neither time nor the exigencies of the service to which I am dedicated for the maintenance of order and tranquillity among the people will permit me to enter into a diffuse relation of what has occurred, I limit myself to saying that, the garrison being convened to proclaim the removal of martial law from the State of Tamaulipas, and consequently re-establishing constitutional order, as the former condition of things was no longer tolerable in the State, for reasons which have been superabundantly represented to the government of the nation, Cobos evinced himself opposed to this idea, and sought to obtain the command of soldiers who, together with their chief, all belong to the country as Mexicans; and as liberals they are all ready to sacrifice their lives in sustaining and defending the constitution of 1857, no less than the government which emanates from it; when he made the first step of disagreement by issuing a proclamation in which he could not avoid manifesting the tendency of his ideas against the fundamental charter of the republic, and the government lawfully established by virtue thereof, crowning the work which he proposed to effect in Tamaulipas with the abortion of a plan which, reduced to writing and signed, should replace our constitution. What folly! At this juncture it was necessary to act as becomes the defenders of the code of the year 1857. Therefore Cobos was shot!

For the rest the garrison and people, with the corporation of this city, have expressed their views and decided to abolish martial law and to change the condition of the State in such a manner that it may enter into constitutional order, under which all its citizens and inhabitants will have those guarantees which the law secures to them, to which laws I have devoted the arms of the faithful soldiers who are under my command.

JUAN NEPOMUCENO CORTINAS.

MATAMOROS, Nov. 8, 1863.

But Ruiz enjoyed his restoration to office for no longer a period than poor Cobos enjoyed his usurpation. A third movement sent Ruiz rushing back to our protection in Brownsville, where he still remains. The state of siege was declared at an end, and the civil Governor of the State, Jesus de la Serna, a prominent Mexican citizen, was recalled to exercise his legitimate functions.

The document which announced this new change in the phantasmagoria of Matamoros movements is as follows:—

DECLARATION.

In the heroic city of Matamoros, on the seventh day of the month of September, the garrison of this station, under the command of Colonel Juan N. Cortinas, assembled in mass meeting, being convened by the people.

Considering that it is now a long time since the State has been suffering and lamenting the effects of the declaration of martial law in which it has been placed by the decree of the 4th of January, one thousand eight hundred and sixty-two, more especially as it has proved ineffectual to accomplish what was intended by its issue; for if the State has given its sons, as it has always done, to aid in the national defence, never failing the national government with its men or its resources, it nevertheless considers that it can do much more under the influence of its tutelary institutions: for these, derived from the general constitution of 1857, facilitate all those means which might be used to confront such an emergency, leaving to the citizen, at the same time, personally and in general, more liberty and desire to respond to his obligations when he reaps the fruit thereof; while this is threatened with extinction by the situation in which the State is now placed by the decree referred to, placing it under martial law, as well because this necessitates the suspension of some privileges as that others must disappear when authority is concentrated in the hands of functionaries who, in exercising it, draw upon themselves general animadversion, it may be, without thinking of it, whatever care and prudence they may have observed in the discharge of their official acts;

Considering that the State has never been truly found in circumstances under which it might with justice be placed under martial law, or rather in a state of war, according to the opinions of distinguished publicists, inasmuch as foreign invasion, which has threatened it at other times, and which it now suffers, has not and never has passed from one of its ports, like that of Tampico, a thing that is notorious;

Considering that this circumstance was, without doubt, the reason which induced the supreme government itself to issue another decree on the 12th of May last, removing martial law and authorizing the Governor, for the time being, to formulate such directions as were necessary for the re-establishment of constitutional order in the State—a decree which, without being expressly rescinded, has nevertheless been suspended;

Considering, lastly, that Tamaulipas is passing, in consequence of this restrictive state of affairs, without being able to contribute all that she can to the national cause, while its local progress is falling away, and that it is an exception in the federal balance, as perhaps there is no other State which is kept under martial law;

For similar public and notorious considerations, the armed garrison of this city and the people respectively spontaneously agree and conform together for the more punctual execution of the following articles:—

1. That the condition of martial law (*estado de sitio*) imposed upon this State by the decree of January 4, 1862, shall cease; and consequently the Governor elect, the citizen Jesus de la Serna, is called upon to resume the functions of his office, and that he take the necessary steps, in accordance with the constitution of the State, to organize and select the other constitutional authorities, whose term of service may have expired or whose places may be vacant through other causes.

2. The functions of the late Governor and Military Commander, Don Manuel Ruiz, who at present exercises both commands in this heroic city, therefore cease from this day.

3. Don Juan Fernandez shall also cease to exercise political authority, and until some person be appointed to succeed him the authority shall devolve upon the first alcalde, Don Raphael Quintero.

4. This resolution shall be transmitted to the supreme government, strongly representing to it that, this being a perfect and unanimous act of spontaneous agreement, it may give it its superior approbation.

Signed by the military commander, Juan Nepomuceno Cortinas, and all the officers of the garrison, some hundreds of non-commissioned officers, and the whole body of citizens.

General Cortinas, thus recalled to the civil Governorship of Tamaulipas, seems to have been associated in his public aims with Cobos. He is a Mexican by birth, of great influence, although of small pretensions to education or refinement, and is understood to be bitterly hostile to the French. So that, so far as we are concerned, we lose nothing by the change from Ruiz to Cortinas. He used to reside near Brownsville, and some two years since he got up a revolutionary movement against the Texan authorities of the county, which failed and necessitated his return to Mexico. He is represented as being in the interests of the United States, and it is supposed that he would, if necessary, encourage the enlistment of Mexicans in our military service.

His own continuance in office, however, is of the most precarious sort. Even before his arrival to resume his functions another rising was organized in Matamoros, and was to have come off last night. The American Consul there, fearing for the safety of his person and archives, notified General Banks of the danger, and measures were promptly taken by the General to give to the Consul the protection of our arms. The necessity, however, did not arise. *If it had arisen I should probably have been dating this letter from Matamoros, as the headquarters of the Texas-Mexican expedition. This might have involved us in hostilities with France; but it is impossible to perceive how, with that government persisting in its policy and our government persisting in its own, hostilities can be long delayed. It is, therefore, of the most urgent political necessity that our army here be reinforced to the extent of at least twelve or fifteen thousand men.* I presume that Gen. Banks takes the same view of the matter and has tried to impress it upon the authorities at Washington. *Our army must be strong enough not only to redeem Texas from the rebels, but to resist all further aggression by France upon the soil of Mexico.*

Tamaulipas, I repeat, has not yet come under the French yoke. I doubt that it ever will. The sentiments not only of its people, but of all Mexicans, are represented as being bitterly hostile to French influence. Even Spain and Spanish residents here regard it with much disfavor. At the same time the Juarez government is unpopular? What, then, is to be done? The medium course—between a French protectorate on the one hand, and a condition of chronic revolutionism on the other—commends itself to the popular heart, and that course is annexation to the American republic, or at least such an alliance with our government as may enable the Mexican people to expel the invader, reorganize their institutions on a firmer foundation, and make a new start in the career of self-government. Is the administration at Washington inclined to develop and foster this sentiment? If it is, no time should be lost in forwarding large reinforcements and supplies, thus enabling General Banks to kill two birds—rebel and French—with one stone.

There is no room for doubt that the French have been arranging a movement in Matamoros which would place that city and the whole State of Tamaulipas in their hands. The unexpected appearance of Banks at Brownsville, and the necessary evacuation of that town by the rebels, defeated the plan. Had it been successful the French would have attained their object without being exposed to any complications with our government, and the rebels would also have benefited by it. The movement of Banks has therefore proved not only opportune, but of the greatest importance in every aspect of the question.

Our New Orleans Correspondence.

NEW ORLEANS, Nov. 13, 1863.

The Thirteenth army corps, lately operating in the Teche country, embarked to-day at Brashear City for some unknown point in Texas, by way of Berwick's Bay.

The steamer Circassian arrived here to-day, and reports the disappearance of the yellow fever from the blockading fleet off Mobile.

Trade with St. Louis, on private account, is rapidly increasing.

A rumor is current to-day among secession sympathizers of a rebel defeat in Western Louisiana.

The War in Mexico.

ENGLISH NOTICE OF THE FRENCH BLOCKADE.

[From the London Gazette, Oct. 27.]

FOREIGN OFFICE, Oct. 27, 1863.

It is hereby notified that Earl Russell, her Majesty's Principal Secretary of State for Foreign Affairs, has received from her Majesty's Vice Consul at Vera Cruz a notification addressed to him by the Commander-in-Chief of the French naval forces in the Gulf of Mexico, and dated the 5th of September, 1863, of the blockade by the French naval forces, on and from the 6th of September, 1863, of the coast of the Gulf of Mexico, with the exception of Tampico, Vera Cruz, Alvarado, Coatzacoalcos, Tabasco and Carmen. The following is the official communication received by Earl Russell:—

We, the undersigned, Rear Admiral Commanding-in-Chief the naval forces of his Majesty the Emperor of the French in the Gulf of Mexico, in view of the state of war existing between France and the government of Juarez, acting by virtue of the powers which belong to us,

Declare, that from the 6th of September instant the ports and their outlets, the rivers, harbors, roadsteads, creeks, &c., of the coasts of Mexico which are not in the occupation of our troops, and which still acknowledge the power of Jaurez, from the lagoon, *ten leagues to the south of Matamoros*, up to and including Campeche, between twenty-five degrees and twenty-two minutes north, ninety-nine degrees and fifty-four minutes west, and nineteen degrees and fifty-two minutes north, and ninety-two degrees and fifty minutes west (meridian of Paris), shall be held in a state of effective blockade by the naval forces under our command, and that friendly or neutral vessels shall have a delay of twenty-five days to complete their cargoes and to quit the places blockaded.

The points excepted from the blockade are Tampico, Vera Cruz, Alvarado, Coatzacoalcos, Tabasco and Carmen.

Proceedings in conformity with international law and the treaties in force with neutral Powers will be taken against all vessels which shall attempt to violate the said blockade.

On board of the frigate Bellona, of his Majesty the Emperor of the French, anchored in the roadstead of Sacrificios, the 5th of September, 1863. A. BOSSE.

The Dramatic Fund Association.

TO THE EDITOR OF THE HERALD.

NOVEMBER 20, 1863.

Knowing the interest you take in all things relating to the welfare of the American Dramatic Fund Association and many kind offices received at your hands, I think it my duty to inform you of our latest good fortune.

Soon after the date of our late benefit in Brooklyn I made a statement to Barney Williams, Esq., of the proceeds, whereupon he gave us a donation of two hundred and fifty dollars, which made up, with our previous benefit and other donations, a trifle over one third of ten thousand dollars. This I stated to the gentleman who was the first to suggest the raising by donations, benefits, &c., the sum of ten thousand dollars, and that he would be one of three to do it, or one of two if the Fund would raise the other third. This gentleman was M. H. Sanford, Esq., of Boston, who has this day forwarded his check for the sum promised. The late J. H. Caldwell gave his check for the same sum, and the Fund has been enabled, by the kind liberality of Miss Cushman and others, to raise the other third, completing the full sum of ten thousand dollars. Making the interest of the Fund my excuse for thus troubling you, I beg leave to subscribe myself, yours, &c., CHAS. S. BERNARD,

Secretary American Dramatic Fund Association.

CHATTANOOGA.

Interesting from Gen. Grant's Department.

STRENGTH OF OUR POSITION,

&c., &c., &c.

Mr. T. C. Wilson's Despatch.

HOOKER'S ARMY, IN THE FIELD, Nov. 14, 1863.

REPORTED REBEL MOVEMENTS.

Reports reach us, through the medium of deserters from the enemy's forces, that the rebel generals are preparing for active service and an extensive move, with a view to severing or interrupting our communication with Louisville, Ky. How true this is remains for the future to show.

REBEL OFFICERS ON PICKET DUTY.

During the last ten days the number of deserters from the enemy is surprisingly large, and, what is still more strange, it increases every day. At last the enemy, having lost all faith in their privates, has stationed a commissioned officer at every picket post or point where it is at all easy for a man to desert. This foreshadows a state of feeling that cannot be over beneficial to the rebel cause or gratifying to the rebel leaders. The other night a sergeant, with the whole of the picket post, "reported" to our lines. What must have been the rebels' astonishment when they discovered this wholesale skedaddle.

PICKET LINE AMUSEMENTS.

It is a very curious thing to watch the actions of the pickets on both sides. The rebel pickets walk up and down across the narrow Lookout creek, whistling "Dixie," while ours immediately get up a counter whistle of "Yankee Doodle." Thus they whistle "down" the picket line.

"HE MUST BE A REAL YANKEE."

I want to tell you a truly interesting joke. I write "interesting" because it has a very large interest in showing how ignorant some of the Georgians are. The first night after we left Bridgeport General Steinwehr made his headquarters at a house located within the Georgia State line. One of his aids-de-camp had occasion during the evening to speak in German to the General's servant, in the presence of some of the female occupants of the building referred to above.

"I reckon, General," said one of the girls, "that man," pointing to the aid-de-camp, "must be a real Yankee. I can't understand him. Can you?"

"Not very well," replied the General. "He is lately from the Eastern States."

"And do they all talk that way?" again inquired the miss.

"Many of them do."

"Gracious!" said she, in evident surprise; "no wonder so many of them look wild."

"Why, did you think that any of them were as handsome as you are?"

"What is that you say?"

"I was remarking that you are really a very beautiful woman."

"Well, I'm as handsome as you are."

And here the conversation ended for the present.

CAPTAIN E. W. STOWE,

Assistant Adjutant General, United States Volunteers, leaves for Washington, D. C., to day, with letters and other papers of the highest character in recommendation. He seeks a position in the Invalid corps, in consequence of the wounds he received at Gettysburg having unfitted him for field service. Captain Stowe has proved a good officer, and a faithful one, and his absence will be regretted by the many with whom he has so often come in contact, both through business and social channels, and who have been highly prepossessed in his favor. Captain Stowe is the son of Mrs. Harriet Beecher Stowe.

THE TENNESSEE AND ALABAMA REBEL TROOPS WITHDRAWN FROM THE FRONT.

Last night the enemy withdrew all the Alabama and Tennessee regiments from our front as pickets. Their place is supplied by North Carolina troops, who say the others were sent away to prevent them from deserting. At about three o'clock this morning the enemy reinforced his picket line by one thousand five hundred men. Previous to this time the enemy had but very few men on the line of Lookout creek. Now the opposite bank is full of them and strongly guarded. The rebel generals have instructed their pickets not to talk with the Yankees, and if caught in the act they will be subjected to the severest penalties in punishment. These new pickets appear to be friendly. They have not fired as yet upon any of our men.

UNDER ARMS.

Our troops were under arms at daylight this morning, in consequence of the enemy manifesting a likelihood to disturb our present quiet. During the last week the rebel force stationed on Lookout Mountain has been busily engaged in the construction of strong earthworks. The other evening we forced them, for the time being, to discontinue their operations, in consequence of the accuracy with which our pieces dropped in the shells. Since then they have worked at night on these fortifications, which are located at a point adjacent to where the Chattanooga road crosses the lower slope or base of the mountain. Yesterday afternoon the rebels drew in their picket line. Perhaps it was done in order to make it more difficult for their disaffected soldiers to desert. At the time of the drawing in of the picket line a rebel brigade was observed manœuvering on one of the side roads of the mountain. Deserters who came in last evening report the rebels as preparing to shell us out of our camps, and to destroy our trains in the same way. It will do very well for them to attempt this, while it is a matter of extreme doubt whether they can be successful, or even succeed in doing us any material injury. Because we are not constantly banging away with our artillery it must not be taken for granted that we have no artillery that can reach or interfere with their position. What the end of this matter will be I cannot tell. Indeed there are none here now who can. An artillery engagement may open at any moment, and this is the most that can be said of it. This morning the weather is warm and rainy. A thick fog is also prevalent.

General Hooker has received a late rebel paper which fully admits that he out-generaled and drove the enemy with great loss on the occasion of the battle of Lookout valley.

Mr. E. D. Westfall's Despatch.

HEADQUARTERS, ARMY OF THE CUMBERLAND, CHATTANOOGA, TENN., Nov. 14, 1863.

THE BELEAGUERMENT.

One day's sojourn in Chattanooga would convince the most anxious and timid patriot at the North that there is nothing in the situation of "the besieged" at all calculated to awaken anxiety for their safety. The brilliant successes of Generals Joe. Hooker and Palmer, in opening the river route to Bridgeport, has insured full supplies and completely changed the aspect of affairs, which the rebels acknowledge. Provisions are even accumulating on our hands, and forage is once more plenty. Twenty-five paymasters, with seven millions of dollars, have reached here and commenced paying troops four months' pay, and sutlers are so muzzled by department orders that some benefit will result to the soldier and his family from this large payment. Clothing, camp and garrison equipage have come up in large quantities, and preparations for comfort during the ensuing winter among the soldiers seem to indicate a lengthy stay hereabouts. The army lives in peace and quiet in little huts improvised from bricks and barrel staves, secure from molestation by vicious rebels, by reason of the most complete system of defences on the American continent. This may read like a wild, ill-considered statement; but the impregnability of Chattanooga to direct assault is conceded by high rebel military authority, as well as claimed by the Union commanders. The town would hardly be recognized by an old resident, and there would no doubt be much weeping and gnashing of teeth if a few of the wealthy among that class were permitted to visit it now. There is not a superfluous tree on our manor south of the Tennessee river; hardly a superfluous building, certainly none which could afford shelter to an enemy from the effect of our guns. Mounds of earth, impassable moats and barriers are met in unexpected places, making it almost impossible for an enemy, without the key, to enter the town and "navigate" the streets, even though the hundreds of cannon and the thousands of rifles should maintain a most dignified silence at his approach. The distance—four miles—from town to Point Lookout, the only position from which the enemy ever attempted a bombardment in earnest, precludes the possibility of damage or loss of life by the enemy's fire from that quarter. If Bragg's men do not possess angelic temperaments—and I am inclined to believe they do not—they must be galled exceedingly at times to witness from Lookout the calm tranquillity of Union life in Chattanooga. As they sit shivering in the chill air, blanketless and forlorn, they command a view of comfortable log huts in the camps along the intrenchments; of suggestive smoke and steam arising from the chimneys of the town; of monster provision trains wending their way from Brown's and Kelley's landings; of fat and hearty soldiers encased in the great blue overcoat peculiar to Union men in this neighborhood; of sleek and frisky mules and negroes—a *tout ensemble* of healthy dont-care-a-damn-ativeness, observable only in confident armies securely situated. In the morning they are awakened by reveille in our camps; at night they listen to sterling patriotic airs, beautifully executed by the numerous Union bands, and dreamily covet a drop or two of the "Robinson county whiskey" used by loyal musicians to wet their whistles. Contrasting their daily life with ours, is there reason to be astonished at the disaffection known to exist among Bragg's troops? Is the mania of desertion unexplained?

A BIRDSEYE VIEW OF CHATTANOOGA AND VICINITY.

From the exalted position of Lookout Point the scene spread out to the visitor surpasses in grandeur and sublimity anything I have ever seen. I had an opportunity to visit the peak signal station several weeks ago, before the mountain slipped from our grasp, and the memory of the trip will ever be fresh with me. In a clear atmosphere the mountains of four States may be seen, though the Blue Ridge in North Carolina and the ridges of Alabama are more than fifty miles away. Of course the minutest points of our situation are spread out like a map before the rebel eyes on this peak; so a description of the view from my pencil will not be contraband.

THE GEOGRAPHY OF THE COUNTRY.

The ascent of the mountain from Chattanooga valley is by a winding, rocky road that gradually rises from the confluence of Chattanooga creek, two miles from the railroad depot in Chattanooga, and reaches the top of the mountain one mile in rear of Lookout Point. Here is or was a beautiful little summer resort, comprising three or four dwellings and a large hotel building, the whole known by the appellation of Summertown. The Point is about four miles from Chattanooga in an air line, nearly west, and its elevation two thousand feet above the river. The general course of the Tennessee river is from northeast to southwest; but, seen from Lookout Point, the shape of the river from above Chattanooga to Brown's Ferry—our nearest landing—is similar to the letter S, Chattanooga being in the southern bend and Moccasin Ridge in the northern. The abruptness of the lower bend is better represented by the Indian name, "Moccasin Bend," and the beholder is struck with the similarity of the neck of land embraced by this bend to a moccasin. Chattanooga town is on the instep, the confluence of Chattanooga creek is the toe, the confluence of Lookout creek the heel, and our pontoon bridge at Brown's Ferry is the ankle above the heel. Lookout Mountain is opposite the bottom of the foot, and Moccasin Ridge is the leg and foot. The distance from Moccasin Point to Lookout across the river is less than six hundred yards, to the Point about one thousand yards. The bend of the river from Chattanooga to Brown's Ferry is about six miles; across Moccasin Ridge the distance is only two miles. Missionary Ridge, upon which are Braggs' headquarters, and behind which lies the bulk of the rebel infantry, runs north and south, and is about two miles from Chattanooga. Chattanooga valley and creek are between Missionary Ridge and Lookout. This valley outside of our lines is densely wooded. Lookout valley and creek are west of Lookout Mountain, and between it and Raccoon Ridge, which is five or six miles from the Point. Walden's Ridge is on the north side of the river. The passage of the Tennessee between Walden and Raccoon is called "the suck." Kelley's Ferry, on the lower landing, is below "the suck," and one road to it passes through Lookout valley, under the rebel guns. So the attention of the gunners on Lookout is divided between Chattanooga, which they can barely reach, and the wagon road to Kelley's, which they cannot hit once in a dozen times. They have wasted a vast deal of ammunition, but have done no particular damage as yet. Occasionally our batteries on Moccasin Point reply to their fire, and sometimes reach the top of the mountain. A greater elevation is required than the pieces will stand, and the operation is somewhat risky in comparison with what we can effect. This, then, is the topography and geography of the country round about.

ITS REBEL OCCUPANTS.

There are now in front of us, according to the best information at headquarters, three full corps of rebels, viz:—Breckinridge's, Hardee's and Buckner's. Hardee has taken Polk's old corps and relieved Longstreet on Lookout Mountain. The latter has gone to East Tennessee, taking with him about half of Bragg's cavalry. The balance of the cavalry have gone to Lee's command in North Mississippi. Howell Cobb is in command of Georgia State troops, and a large number of paroled Vicksburgians are serving in the several corps. Isham G. Harris is "messing" with Bragg.

REBEL DESERTIONS.

Desertion has become an evil of such magnitude that rebel officers are represented to be in a "peck of trouble" about it. They come into our lines daily in squads of a dozen or twenty each, bringing their commissioned officers with them. The fever has spread so alarmingly that Bragg no longer knows whom to trust. For a time he consoled himself with the idea that disaffection existed only among a few Tennessee and Kentucky regiments, if at all. These he could easily keep within bounds, by keeping them off picket duty, thus giving them no chance to steal away. Recently, however, we have received invoices of South Carolinians, Mississippians, Alabamians and "Seminoles," stiff backed fire-eaters whom Braxton had a right to count on. I am not bold enough to say these men desert because they love secession less or the Union more, but from a desire to ameliorate as far as possible the lamentable condition of "number one," and take care of it in future. Last evening we had a batch of South Carolinians and Florida men, who had been in service only five days. They had been conscripted. They represent the draft officers as merciless. No man's age or infirmities will exempt him if he can stagger along under a musket. They are, moreover, required to equip themselves. Desertions are depopulating Chattanooga valley rapidly, yet they would be increased threefold if the rank and file of rebels were assured they would be treated like men when they reach our lines. All sorts of stories are circulated among them by their officers in reference to Yankee ridicule and abuse which will be heaped upon them if they desert—how they will be deprived of liberty and kept for exchange. Naturally they hesitate before taking the step.

ON THE CONTRARY.

Two Union deserters, Erastus C. Daly, Eighty-eighth Illinois Volunteers, and Valentine Benjamin, Company C, Forty-fourth Illinois Volunteers, were executed yesterday according to sentence of court martial. The execution was conducted in the usual manner of such affairs, and, as an example to the troops who witnessed it, its effect will be salutary. Benjamin fell from his coffin dead at the first fire, and tumbled into a nameless grave without a struggle. Daly was shot through the face, and died in pain.

CELEBRITIES.

General Grant, who has almost recovered his strength, occupies a delightful Chattanooga residence, and, with his briarwood pipe, walks to and fro and up and down the streets of the town, unattended, many times unobserved, but at all times observing. Quartermaster General Meigs has taken to a wall tent, from a regard for the fitness of things. His headquarters are in the field, and soldiers in the field inhabit tents. Generals Thomas and Gordon Granger are workers, and are preparing their grand machine for the next campaign, their consultations often extending far into the night.

Lieutenant Colonel Henry C. Hodges, Chief Quartermaster's Department, has been relieved by Major Langdon C. Easton. Colonel Hodges reports at Fort Leavenworth.

THE WEATHER AND THE RIVER.

We have at last fallen upon chilly times. Leaves have left the trees and disclose the rebel camps on Missionary Ridge and Lookout. There is a fair stage of water in the river and our pontoons are safe.

Complimentary Order to the Troops Composing Generals Turchin's and Hazen's Brigade.

GENERAL ORDERS—NO. 265.

HEADQUARTERS, DEPARTMENT OF THE CUMBERLAND, CHATTANOOGA, Tenn., Nov. 7, 1863.

The recent movements, resulting in the establishment of a new and short line of communication with Bridgeport and the possession of the Tennessee river, were of so brilliant a character as to deserve special notice.

The skill and cool gallantry of the officers and men composing the expedition under Brigadier General William F. Smith, Chief Engineer, consisting of the brigades of Brigadier Generals Turchin and Hazen; the boat parties under Colonel Stanley, Eighteenth Ohio Volunteers, and the pontoniers under Captain Fox, Michigan Engineers and Mechanics, in effecting a permanent lodgement on the south side of the river, at Brown's Ferry, deserve the highest praise.

The column under Major General Hooker, which took possession of the line from Bridgeport to the foot of Lookout Mountain, deserve great credit for their brilliant success in driving the enemy from every position which they attacked. The bayonet charge made by the troops of General Howard up a steep and difficult hill, over two hundred feet high, completely routing the enemy and driving him from his barricades on its top, and the repulse by General Geary's command of greatly superior numbers, who attempted to surprise him, will rank among the most distinguished feats of arms of this war.

By command of Major General GEO. H. THOMAS.

C. GODDARD, Assistant Adjutant General.

Rebel View of the Situation.

[From the Chattanooga Rebel, Nov. 10.]

As was stated in a recent letter, the enemy now holds Lookout valley, lying between the mountain of that name and Raccoon Mountain, and the entire line of the Nashville and Chattanooga Railroad, from Nashville to a point distant from Brown's Ferry not more than one mile. He also holds the Tennessee river from the ferry down to Bridgeport. Since getting possession of the valley he has fortified his position, and it is already almost, if not quite, as strong as that at Chattanooga. In his front, as he faces towards Lookout Mountain, is Lookout creek, which is too near his works for us to attempt to bridge it, and in his rear and on his flanks are the river and the Raccoon Mountain. This not all. If attacked in the valley, he can be reinforced from Chattanooga, by means of his pontoon bridges and across Mocassin bend, more rapidly and safely than we could reinforce our column of attack; for our reinforcements would have to pass around the north end of Lookout Mountain, where they would be exposed to the fire of the Mocasin batteries and the works in that vicinity of the ferry. So also if an attack were made upon Chattanooga the enemy would receive reinforcements from the valley and ferry more expeditiously than we could send troops from our left to the centre, or from the centre to the left; and this because the enemy would move upon a right line while we moved upon the arc of an circle.

From Brown's Ferry to the farthest point of the enemy's lines in front of Chattanooga the distance does not exceed two miles and a half, and from the ferry to the nearest point on the railroad it is not more than a mile. If not molested of course the enemy will extend the railroad up to the ferry, where there is a range of hills, behind which he can erect his depot buildings and protect his teams from the fire of our batteries on Lookout. When the railroad shall have been extended and the line from Bridgeport put in running order the distance he will have to haul his supplies will be reduced from sixty to forty miles down to a mile and a half and two miles.

This new move upon the military chess board, by which the enemy got possession of Lookout valley and the railway to Bridgeport, was a masterly stroke. The conception was a brilliant one. All the combinations admirable and faultless. All the combinations, from the building of the pontoon boats and floating them down the river at night, to the unexpected arrival of the forces at Bridgeport, were perfect. Indeed, the river and the railroad from Lookout Mountain to Bridgeport and the valley and Raccoon slipped from our hands so easily, or rather were taken from us so adroitly, that we hardly knew when it was done. The operation, however, has changed the whole aspect of affairs here. The question of subsisting the federal army in Chattanooga this winter is solved, and there is no longer any doubt about the ability of its commander to obtain all needful supplies, unless we dispossess him of the railroad.

VOL. III. • RICHMOND, SATURDAY, FEBRUARY 27, 1864. No. 8.

Rest.

"Jesus said unto Peter, 'follow me.' Then Peter, turning about, seeth the disciple whom Jesus loved following, which also leaned on His breast."—JOHN XXI, 19, 20.

Oft troubled and perplexed,
My heart within me vexed,
Fain would I flee away and be at Rest.

Even when all is bright,
My heart within me light,
The warning sounds: Lo! this is not Rest.

Griefs on my spirit weigh,
Joys lead my steps astray,
Where shall I cast them both and turn for Rest?

Full often have I heard
The Master's gracious words,
"Come unto Me, and I will give thee Rest."

Yet still I lingering stand
Without the Promised Land;
I look—I long—yet enter not its Rest.

Even when at His board
I meet my risen Lord,
Earth's cares intrude and mar the sacred Rest.

Fearful and far away,
A stranger guest I stray,
When on His bosom I might find my Rest.

For there, and there alone,
The human heart hath known
Brief, but bright foretaste of eternal Rest.

Forgotten there each fear,
Each doubtful point made clear,
On earth foreshadowing Heaven's perfect Rest.

O happy ones and blest
Who on the Saviour's breast
Find now and evermore the only Rest.

MAJ. GEN. JOHN A. WHARTON.

This gallant officer entered the army, at the commencement of the struggle, as a private, was afterwards elected captain of a company in the celebrated Texas Rangers, and subsequently colonel of that regiment. By true merit, towering genius and unrivalled courage, he has elevated himself with rapid strides from the volunteer ranks to the exalted position of major-general, and created for himself and the gratification of his followers a name that will be ever cherished by the survivors of the war and their posterity.

General Wharton was born on the 5th July, 1829, and has been a resident of Texas from his earliest infancy; his father, William H. Wharton, was Minister from the Republic of Texas to the United States, and one of the most prominent of the revolutionary heroes of that country. His mother was Sarah Ann Groce, a native of South Carolina, but moved to Texas in 1827, where she has since resided, beloved and esteemed by all who know her. General Wharton is her only child and the affection he bears to his mother is a noble trait in his character. He graduated at the South Carolina College, where he evinced an aptness for military life in the command, for three years, of a splendid company composed of the students. In 1854, he married Miss E. P. Johnson, daughter of Governor David Johnson of that State, a lady possessed of every accomplishment that adorns woman and contributes to domestic felicity. Before the war he was a planter and lawyer, never having been engaged in political life save as a Breckinridge elector, and as a member of the State Convention which passed the act of secession. His great ability as an orator and debater soon placed him at the head of the bar in his section. As a statesman, he is second to none in Texas, while the gracefulness of his figure and the force of his arguments carry conviction to all his hearers.

MAJOR-GENERAL JOHN A. WHARTON.

In a sketch so short as this it is impossible to give more than leading facts. Many gallant personal adventures and interesting details must be omitted. As a regular cavalry officer and as a picket to guard the front of our army he has no equal in his department; during a service of nearly three years his command has never been surprised by the enemy nor defeated in a fair fight.

For the service in which both Morgan and Forrest have rendered themselves so famous, he has no partiality, and has always opposed the sending his command on raids. He prefers his troops should be engaged in their legitimate service, so that in a *general engagement* he could use them as regular cavalry, believing that with his command, intact and in good condition, he could accomplish more than by numberless raids.

No officer in the service is more considerate of the rights of private citizens, always requiring commanders to be responsible for depredations committed by their troops. He has studiously avoided notoriety, preferring the approval of his senior officers to popular applause; and his worth will be attested by every general with whom he has been connected.—Strict in his official intercourse, and enforcing discipline, his troops are warmly attached and feel the utmost confidence in his capacity; well assured he will care for their wants, he possesses the happy faculty of endearing men to him, but requires from all his officers a faithful stewardship.

In four pitched battles, and over two hundred cavalry engagements, he has borne himself as a brave and gallant warrior, ever leading where the bullets flew thickest, as will be attested by his having been twice wounded and having had five horses killed under him; always self-possessed and of quick perception, he handles his troops with consummate skill, and disposes his forces to best advantage.

In November last, in view of his past services, the President promoted him to the rank of Major-General; and when the history of this war shall have been written, and a just tribute paid to the gallant chieftains who have battled so manfully for Southern Independence, the name of Wharton will be found enrolled among those who, by their gallantry, courage and skill, have been enshrined in the hearts of their countrymen.

ACCIDENTALS.

Accidentals produce a good effect when they occur in a piece of music; but in life they are apt to throw discord into many a pretty strain, and mar the harmony of society's quadrille, as, for instance, when one happens to pop unceremoniously into the apartment of a friend, and discovers the "head of the family," a temperance man forsooth, behind the closet door, with a mysterious looking jug to his lips, which, on beholding you, he relinquishes with a well feigned grimace, and shrug of disgust, uttering a ugh! which is followed by a grunt, and a lecture on debility, which etiquette compels you to swallow for the time being, but ever afterwards, when listening to the temperance addresses of said friends, his blossomed nose, and bitter jug whirl together in fantastic dances, frequently interrupted by a balance to your partner, as they glide through your imaginative brain.

Or when you discover one whom you believed a friend, in the act of playing you a false trick while you were trustingly reposing the utmost confidence in his sincerity.

To recount a choice bit of scandal to your confidant during an evening waltz, and upon suddenly turning, to discover the victim of your charitable remarks had been walking behind you.

To overhear Miss Primrose, who had kissed each of your faultless darlings, calling them little innocents, precious babes and sugar plums, tell your rival they were little pests, torments, and fit subjects for the house of correction, pointing out the spots on her cream-colored silk, which in the fullness of their hearts, and in return for her caresses and praises, they had plentifully bedabbled with a share of their molasses candy. Or start in the morning of life, fresh, vigorous, and full of hope, disheartened by the accidentals we encounter at noon, overwhelmed by them at sunset, and finally disgusted with them at the hour of retiring, or three score and ten!

PREFACE.

"The Old Flag" was published during an imprisonment of thirteen months in Tyler, Smith Co., Texas, upon a sheet of unruled letter paper, in imitation of *print*, a steel pen being employed in the absence of a Hoe Press with Conner & Son's Types, and Maynard & Noyes' Ink instead of Lightbody's. Of course, by this slow process, but one copy could be issued of each number, which was read aloud at the various cabins by some member of the "Mess;" and when all had read, or heard it read, the same was returned by the "Subscriber" to the "Office of Publication."

But one aim ever actuated the Proprietor in this undertaking, which was to contribute as far as possible towards enlivening the monotonous, and at times almost unbearably eventless life of Camp Ford—and to cultivate a mutual good feeling between all. Contributions were solicited upon matters of Local interest, Stories, Advertisements, etc., and many good Jokes were perpetrated upon each other, which were received purely in that light by the *victims*, and were the occasion of much enjoyment. It is therefore urged upon our patrons that they do not consider aught in these columns as embodying any ill personal feelings towards *anybody*, and desire to certify that the warmest affections and mutual kindnesses were unanimous with all the prisoners.

The Advertisements were most of them *bona fide*, genuine; especially those of a smaller paper published shortly before our departure from Texas, called the "Ford City Herald." As we have decided not to include the Herald in this volume, we will here insert some of its Advertisements, and other items of interest to the reader.

PARKER'S BAKERY,
No. 122 HESTER STREET,
BAMBOO PLACE,
Ford City, Tyler, Smith Co., Texas.
Always on hand, a fresh supply of DOUGHNUTS; Grape, Blackberry, and Custard
PIES.
By H. PARKER.

CITY BAKERY,
Corner *BROADWAY and FOX STREETS.*
FOR SALE, WHOLESALE AND RETAIL,
FLOUR, BACON, MEAL,
PIES,
CAKES, HARD-BREAD, BISCUITS, &c.
Terms—*Reasonable.*
BLANCHARD & CO.

P. CLARKE,
118 *HESTER STREET,*
BAKERY.

JOHN LEAN,
WHOLESALE
COMMISSION MERCHANT,
No. 5 Exchange Place, Speculation Street,
FORD CITY, TEXAS.

RARE BARGAINS!
READY SALES!!!
GIVE "WAX" A CALL!!!

Sign of the 3 Golden Balls!
MICHAEL SUGRUE,
COMMISSION AND EXCHANGE
BROKER,
No. 122 SPECULATION STREET,
FORD CITY, TEXAS.

WOODWARD & CO.,
MANUFACTURERS OF
CHESS-MEN, CHECKER-MEN, &C.,
CORNER SOAP AND FRONT STREETS.

WILLIAM JOHNSON,
Corner Battery Place & Broadway.
CHESS-MEN, CHECKER-MEN, &C.

PETER BALDWIN,
BAKER,
No. 240 SARSAPARILLA STREET.

SHEPPARD & CO.,
No. 442 Broadway,
BAKERS.

A. DODD,
No. 1 BROADWAY,
BAKERY.

REVIEW OF THE MARKETS—July 4, 1864

Wheat Flour	℘ 100 lbs.	$250 00
Meal, Corn	℘ bushel	15 00
Bacon	℘ lb.	5 00
Butter	℘ lb.	10 00
Eggs	℘ dozen	10 00
Molasses	℘ gallon	30 00
Sugar	℘ lb.	7 50
Soap	℘ lb.	7 50
Ripe Apples	℘ piece	1 25
Blackberries	℘ gallon	40 00
Grapes, green	℘ bushel	40 00
Milk	℘ gallon	20 00

REVIEW OF MARKETS—(*Continued.*)

Honey in the comb	℘ lb.	$ 7 50
" strained	℘ gallon	80 00
Whiskey	℘ "	200 00
" single drink		5 00
Segars	each	1 00
Tobacco, Chewing	℘ plug	30 00
" Conscript	℘ lb.	20 00
Cucumbers	℘ dozen	5 00
Cabbages	℘ head	2 50
Beans, String	℘ bushel	40 00
Straw Hats, camp make	℘ piece	25 00

The 22d day of February, 1864, was celebrated in camp, and proved a day never to be forgotten by any one of those who were witnesses of, or participated in, any of the exercises. These consisted of an *Oration* by Lt. Col. J. B. Leake, a Poem by Lt. Col. A. J. H. Duganne, *Voluntary Toasts*, and *Singing* by a *Glee Club*.

Hoping and trusting the style and correctness in which the following Lithograph copies of "The Old Flag" have been executed will meet the approbation of my late fellow-prisoners in Texas, and assuring them of having used every endeavor to produce them in the best possible shape, I remain,

Respectfully,

37 Park Row, New York.

J. P. ROBENS.

The Old Flag

Vol. 1. FORD CITY, MARCH 13th, 1864. No. 1.

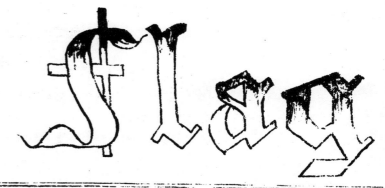

[WRITTEN EXPRESSLY FOR THE OLD FLAG]

HIGH-BIRD;

OR,

THE LEAGUE OF BLOOD!

A TALE OF THE MYSTERIES AND MISERIES OF FORD CITY, TEXAS.

BY MEIGH, D. K.

CHAPTER 1.

THE MIDNIGHT PROWLER.

Hark! dost hear the thunder roll?
Johnny, fill up the bowl!

IT was the still hour of midnight! The winds of a fierce norther whistled a mournful dirge at the doors of the shebangs of the inhabitants of Ford City, and the weary conscript more closely hugged—not the old flint-lock, but—the large log fire, blazing on his beat, while the Sergent of the Guard, wrapped his carpet-blanket still closer about his aged form, dreaming of

"The days of yore,
When he had more
Of Flour and meat,
Than he could eat,"

and d——d the "S. C"

At this lonely hour "a man might have been seen slowly wending his way" through the now quiet streets of this Yankee City. He was wrapped in a Confederate blanket, drawn closely about his face as a protection against the biting wind and sleet. Let us follow this man. Why does he dodge behind that large chimney! Ah! there comes that faithful guardian of the night—Watchman HAYLEY—it must be him this mysterious person avoids encountering.

"Past 12 o'clock and all is bully!" is the Watchman's cry, as he passes up Fifth Avenue, and is soon lost to view.

Now the mysterious night-prowler resumes his way, crosses a portion of Park Square and passing around to the rear of a low, one-story building, signals those within for admission.

One! two! three knocks, and a deep moan—a chicken crows within—the stranger answers by a noise much resembling the squeal of a pig!—the door is opened, and he disappears from our view.

CHAPTER II.

THE LOVIERS AND THE CRUEL PARIENT.

THE "God of Day" had sunk to rest behind a mountain of fire and pale Luna—if we remember correctly—on this occasion, arose in the East.

"Seated in a fine arm-chair which was "for streangth of back and durability of bottom a master-peice," in front of the Fifth Avenue House, was our lovely heroine, Miss Julia Wilhemena Dainah, engaged in the delicious pastime of smoking a pipe!

Many the aspirant for that hand had she turned away; among them one who had loved her almost to madness! This man—of powerful frame, and an imense beard, nearly reaching to the eyes—was well known as HIGH-BIRD: he had sworn a fearful oath, that on him she placed her pure heart's affections, his vengeance should fall, and the fair girl trembled for the life of her darling Phree Manchase.

We would describe our lovely heroine, but knowing our inability to do her beauty of mind or person justice can only refer the reader to that portion of "Milton's Paradise Lost" which describes her mother—Eve, and desire them to apply the same to JULIA.

Her gaze is fixed on a form coming up the Avenue. It is a tall, majestic, noble person—as straight as a rail—graceful in carriage, and as handsome in feature as "Honest Old Abe himself!

With a winning smile he flourishes a white handkerchief, bows his head with the grace of a mule, and with a meaning glance, passes by.

Directly she rises from her seat of ease, rushes into the house, and soon after appears, with her bonnet on, and slowly and gracefully meanders up the street in the direction the handsome youth has gone. She is passing thro Shin-bone Alley, when he again appears, rushes to her side, seizes her delicate fin, and clasps her to his gizard in an extacy of bliss!

"My precious Julia Wilhemena!"

"My darling Phree Manchase!"

"HARK! a step, me-thought I heard! cried Phree.

"I tremble lest pa mistrust us," responded the happy girl.

"O! that I had wealth—he would then own me worthy you. But the day will come when he will be proud to own the now humble mechanic as son-in-law! Know, darling, I have a plan laid for honors and riches! I feel, dearest, that I am a ——"

"SCOUNDREL!" cried the proud parient, suddenly showing himself in a towering passion. "Away! you d——d land-shark, and if I catch you cruising about these waters again, I'll hang you to a black jack as sure as my name is BRINEY AMOS!"

CHAPTER III.

THE LEAGUE OF BLOOD!

WE left the midnight prowler of the door of a suspicious looking house on Park Square; we will enter where he did at the close of our first Chapter, as there is that occurring within which greatly concerns our story.

Seated around a large, long table were a half dozen as villainous looking set of men as ever met for hellish purpose.

As the new-comer stepped into their midst, they all arose and cried.

"Welcome, worthy Chieftain! All hail!"

"No!" responded the grum voice, "nothing but a cold rain—no hail!"

As he gave utterance to this reply, he flung from him the Confederate blanket, and revealed the compacked form of HIGH-BIRD!

"Now," said he, "I have a job to be done, and will admit on the start, that I want none to engage with me in this work but those whose hearts are of iron, and whose hands grow stronger and more steady at flow of blood!"

"BLOOD! BLOOD!" cried one after another, in amazement, if not somewhat of horror.

"Ay! Blood! Red life-blood must flow!! Come, are ye old women that ye must needs repeat that five lettered word. I want volunteers—step forward those who would belong to HIGH-BIRD'S LEAGUE OF BLOOD!"

At once the whole moved forward as one man, and the Chief cried,

"Tis well—let it be so recorded!"

Then stepping to the table on which stood a large iron kettle filled with hot drink, each one filled his cup, raised it over his head, while the Chief rendered, and they repeated after him the following.

"To the LEAGUE of BLOOD! may the first blood shed under its new leader be a warning to all interlopers, hereafter, who may deem it safe to cross the path of HIGH-BIRD, to steer clear!"

All drank and caroused until the 'small hours' were come, and the last drop of that intoxicating Texian drink—Rye Coffee—was drunk.

CHAPTER IV.

THE LOWER 'MILLION!!

AT early candle-light that notorious Dance House of John, Son & Co, UNDAUNTED HALL, Corner of Battery Place and Shin-bone Alley, began to fill with the fancy-men of the city, who, insted of remaining at their homes, entertaining and instructing their families by readings from the "Tyler Reporter," or playing Chess, are to be found nightly in some of these bad places, dancing with lewd women—else at the Fifth Avenue House, playing at billiards, or on the pave making night hideous with their cries of debauchery.

The fiddler generally plays for his rum, getting disgustingly drunk, while a gay sport comes in on the banjo, winking at the g'hals, and drinking—when not fighting—with the b'hoys.

The light of the great log fire leant a strange and ghastly appearance to the revellers, as they sat and stood grouped about the room. At every fling or "jump-Jim-Crow" of the dancers were drawn out fierce Texan yells stamping of feet, encouragements by such exciting cries as "right smart!" "goin' old man!" "Bully for Mad Anthony!" re. "Go in on the GRAY mare!" and other immoral suggestions, or words to that effect —— when suddenly

A long, low, thrilling, shrilly shriek was heard!! All rushed to unbar the ponderous door, and emerging into the impenetrable darkness, beheld

"A sight to harrow up the soul—
Freeze the hot blood—
Make the wild eyes, like stars, start from their spheres,
The knotted and conjoined locks to part
And each particular hair to stand on end
Like quills upon the fretful porcupine!

CHAPTER V.

THE CONFLAGRATION.

IT was a fearful, yet a splendid spectacle. In the midst of the impenetrable murk and Cimmerian gloom which enveloped all the district of Ford City a fierce and baleful light was shining with such horrid glare as to cause each rocky pavement of the streets to gleam like molten lava, boiling in asphaltic pitts of red bituminous Tartarus.

A terrific conflagration was raging

The entire block adjoining the UNDAUNTED HALL was wrapped in a blue sheet of mingled smoke and flame: over this blue sheet the distracted inmates were vainly endeavoring to cast a wet blanket. The entire chimney of that palatial mansion occupied by the Duke of Wellington, and his soot, was a pray to the devouring element. and at all the lofty casements might have been seen the startled inmates, wildly wringing their hands and exposing charms which ought to have soothed to mercy even the demon of Arson himself. Vainly waving her white kerchief for aid, could be discerned the amiable Lady Tomasina O'Daign, then in an interesting situation—the result of her recent elopement—while at a dormer window, the Rt. Hon. Robin Redbreast, P.B., who writes for the "TYLER Reporter" was endeavoring to reconcile himself to the impending fate, by chanting in a voice like the dying swan or poor Low the Indian a meek and plaintive ditty on the overturn of the cruel war. It was indeed a heart-rending scene! The stout hands of our gallant firemen almost failed them at this crisis, but they were rallying at the stentorian shouts of Foreman Kerbre to repel the flames when, O! horror!—

A savage war whoop rang upon the midnight air!!

A legion of dusky forms danced defyingly around the flames, and the shuddering population of the city saw that they were surrounded by an invading war-party of Choctaws, Creeks and Cherokees.

CHAPTER VI.

THE RES Q!!!!!

TOMAHAWKS gleamed in the crimson light, and a chorus of yells and whoops affrighted every heart. A tall plumed Chieftain led the Cherokees,

MISCELLANEOUS.

A THRILLING LEAF FROM THE LOG OF AN OLD WHALER.' — Our crew were a young and villainous looking set of fellows; they were the off-scourings from nearly every nation, and quarrelsome words and desperate oaths in all languages, might be heard at almost any time. They were agreed in nothing but to try and shirk all duty and hate their officers.

These never appeared on deck, or gave an order but they were met with black looks muttered curses, and other evidences of insubordination that gave me great uneasiness. My officers were fine young men, but very high spirited, and I felt that some indiscretion might at any time precipitate a serious collision — possibly a mutiny and blood-shed.

To prepare against this, I caused all the arms to be removed to my state-room, kept my pistols carefully loaded and always near at hand. I was on the alert constantly and seldom left the deck.

Matters remained in this state nearly the whole passage, but when we had doubled the Cape and and entered the ~~trades of the latitudes~~, sun shine and the gentle breezes of the Latitudes seemed to influence even these savages, and better feelings prevailed.

Worne out by anxiety and watching I took this favorable opportunity to retire to my cabin, where sleep soon overcame me, and dreams transported me to different and happier scenes. My anxious voyage was ended — I was approaching my home — all ready I could see my wife and little ones I streatched out my arm — when a terrific scream and scuffling on deck brought me to my senses, and in horrified amazement to my feet. Apparently the event I had so long feared was upon us. The crew, knowing that I was asleep, had improved the opportunity to seize on the officers and take the ship! Those screams were no doubt from my murdered officers, and the same fate now awaited me! The dear faces of which I had dreamed, I should never see more, and only after years of heavy heart-sick waiting would they learn my sad fate.

Overwhelmed with dispair, but determined to sell my life dearly, I seized my pistols and rushed on deck! Gracious heavens!! what a sight met my eyes! Blood covered the decks — horror was in every eye. The cook, a fine looking Italion, stood over the fallen body, waving his long, gleaming knife, now crimsoned to the hilt! As he caught sight of me, he fell back, and I hastened to examine if life still remained, but alas! the blow was fatal — the pig was dead!

DEATH IN OUR BORROUGH. — In Ford City, on the night of March 4th, 1864, a youthful Pig — death caused by an over dose of Col. Nott's specific, "The Lion of the Day!" taken for the purpose of committing sow-i-side. [Too much care cannot be exercised in the use of Sumac, as its narcotic and stupefying effects have been experienced by many.] In reference to the deceased pig — we recommend that its remains be deposited in the tomb of that other tender martyr's the "pig Jim."

To our readers who are interested in Exchange, we are happy to be able to announce that Mr. King the Confederate Commissioner of exchange, has returned to Camp Ford, and has had an interview with our esteemed friend, MR. ROBBINS, the Federal Agent of exchange. MR. R—— assures us that he has strong hopes of soon effecting an arrangement by which we will be released from imprisonment and restored to our friends.

We have heard it suggested that as soon after the return of the prisoners of this place to N.O. a Ball be given, called "PRISONER'S UNION BALL."

Written for the OLD FLAG.

STANZAS. — To CLIANTHE.

Clianthe! while in lonesome thought,
I light my pipe, and smoke serenely,
I think of thee, with grace, so fraught,
With gentle brow and presence queenly.

A Federal bachelor, am I,
Who pines for one fond hearts communion
I pray thee list a captive's sigh,
And let me win you to the — UNION!

Methinks my hut a hall would be,
Were I in thy sweet heart a lodger,
And one bright smile of thine on me,
Would sweeten e'en my cold corn-dodger!

But true love ne'er runs smooth they say,
And fate with me has waged a quarrel;
One only sun-beam lights my way —
'Tis when thy foot trips thro' our corral.

Clianthe come! thou tender maid —
My jealous heart feels pangs eternal,
And Oh! don't stop at the stockade
To whisper to that other Colonel!

I'll bet two dollars and a half,
He seeks to win thy favor regal —
But at his rank, I scornful laugh,
He wears a Leaf and I an Eagle!

I've carved for thee a wond'rous bowl,
A goblet half, and half salt cellar;
And thee I'll pledge, my tender soul,
In sumach strong — my cloud dispeller.

Come, and I'll sit thee by my side,
And drink thy smiles like sunny weather,
A bran new chair I've made, so wide,
'Twill hold us both, dear maid, together!

CHAWLES

FOR THE OLD FLAG.

LINES ON THE DEPARTURE OF "ROSA."

Farewell, old friend! dear partner of my toil!
Go browse abroad and scour the Texan soil,
With lightsome hoof the turfy prairies tread,
And leave thy master in his lonely shed.

Ungrateful world! that still misfortune lends!
Remorseless fate! that parts congenial friends:
My mule departs — my Rosa flies my sight,
And leaves this tender heart to withering blight

How oft, enamored of thy growing charms,
I've borne thee corn-husks in my trembling arms,
How oft I've kissed thy cheeks and striven to trace,
As in a mirror, my own form and face!

Thy cause was mine, thy rights I deemed my own,
For day by day our sympathies had grown;
And when surrounding boors disdained thy form
To me thou camest, and found a kinsman warm

What though thy fairy-foot the garden spurned
And many an embryo plant in mirth upturned
What though thy youthful sports disturbed the ground
Till base born peasants on thy presence frowned

They knew thee not — they could not know nor feel.
The charms that thou to me would oft reveal.
Natures like thine all common contact spurn
Till love like mine, unites two souls in one!

Farewell, dear Rosa! far away thou goest —
Even in the hour I learned to prize thee mo-est!
The gates have closed behind thy waving rear —
I carve my pipes, and drop a briney tear!

AMOS.

ALL KINDS OF
JOB PRINTING
AT THIS OFFICE.

ADVERTISEMENTS.

PROSPECTUS!

THE first number of a semi-occasionally Newspaper entitled

THE CORN-DODGER ADVOCATE
AND
UNDAUNTED COMPANION.

will be issued
APRIL FIRST, — 1864.
bearing date, April 7th, '64, published one week in advance of date in order to reach distant subscribers on time. Devoted to the public good and filled with choice matter on Romance, Poetry, Local and Foreign News, Wit, and Humor, Advertisements and Correspondence.

The POETICAL Department will be under the special charge of FRANCIS MARIAN, JR. assisted by Molley Moore and a galaxy of Southern lyres.

HARRY, the celebrated companion of HUMBOLDT in his travels will attend to the Romance, and the first number will contain the opening chapters of a thrilling Novelette, entitled, the "PATAGONIAN GIANT;" or the DELAPIDATED MANSION ON THE RHINE. A Fearful Tale of Blood, Hair and Horror." Done in short-hand.

D.E.L. AMATER, TOM, SON, & co.
Publishers and Proprietors.
Shin-bone Alley, Head 5th Av.

WANTS.

A YOUNG WIDOWER, from South-America, desires Board in a private family where his society would be considered an equivolent for his meals and lodgings.
Address, H. HAYLEY, Soap Street.

A PROFESSED COOK; who understands baking CORN-Bread in plain style can find a permanent situation at the Undaunted Mess-room, Cor. Battery Place and Shin-bone Alley.

ABLE BODIED young men who can turn a WHEEL and answer all questions asked by others, concerning work going on, can find constant employment and Gymnastic exercise by applying at the Lathe-power Work Shop, rear of the Fifth Avenue Hotel. Graduates of the Paralelle Bars, etc. instructed in new muscular developments — gratis.

"THE OLD FLAG"

TERMS. —

PER ANNUM. $5.00
" PRICE .... .25

CONTRIBUTIONS,

Are respectfully solicited from all on Local News, Reviews, Poetry, Romance, Wit, and Humor, Advertisements, &c., &c.

W.H.M.
PUBLISHER & PROPRIETOR.

GALVESTON TRI-WEEKLY NEWS.

VOL. XXIII.] HOUSTON, MONDAY, JULY 18, 1864. No. 5.

TELEGRAPHIC.

SHREVEPORT, July 15th, 1864.

The following letter was received from an officer at Monroe, La., dated July 13th:

Lieut. D, from Harrison's command on the Mississippi river, reached this place this morning from the front. He read on yesterday, the 12th, a St. Louis paper of the 3d of July, in which it was stated that Grant had abandoned the siege of Petersburg, and had retired to City Point, and that Gen. Lee was advancing on him.

The campaign in Virginia was considered at an end. Gen. Breckinridge had whipped Hunter near Lynchburg, and driven him 150 miles. The news from Johnston is also favorable. Sherman had been repulsed in several attacks on our works, with serious loss. An expedition of from 8000 to 12,000 men had started a few days since from Vicksburg for Jackson, supposed to be a diversion in favor of Sherman. All the boats on the Mississippi river have been pressed for the movement of troops.

Canby has moved his headquarters to New Orleans and is supposed to be organizing a force for Mobile. A Chicago Times of the 4th has been seen in front, which is said to contain the same news as stated above with regard to Grant's abandoning the siege of Richmond. His whole army, by this paper, is reported North of James river.

The following summary is taken from the Memphis Bulletin, of the 6th:

Sherman telegraphed Stanton that Johnston has retreated across the Chattahoochie, within seven miles of Atlanta, and that he (Sherman) now occupied Marietta.

Sherman flanked Johnston at Kershow Mountain. Gen. Wilson had arrived at the army of the Potomac with the loss of some of his artillery and trains. Says he destroyed sixty miles of their railroads, which will take one month to repair. Siegel, at Harper's Ferry, says that Early, with Ewell's corps, occupied Martinsburg. No trains running on the Baltimore and Ohio Railroad. Hunter had arrived at Charleston, Kanawa Valley, while he says that he made a successful raid, some of his soldiers say that he lost several thousand prisoners, his artillery and wagon trains, and was badly defeated.

Grant was reported to have been attacked by Lee in his entrenchments at Bermuda Hundred, and to have repulsed the rebels.—*Telegraph.*

CAMDEN, July 16th, 1864.

News from the Memphis Bulletin of July 10th. The Chicago Tribune says there is to be a new call for troops, a half million will be called for. Drafting will be the order of the day. Hagerstown is in the hands of the Confederates. Gov. Curtin is calling loudly for help. Gold, in New York, 260@270.

A dispatch from Baltimore, dated July 7th, says the rebel force north of the Potomac is not a man less than thirty thousand.

The New York World says Wilson's loss has been greatly exaggerated.

Great distress, in consequence of the new rebel raid into Maryland, but the Northern public is induced to expect favorable military news. Grant had telegraphed the War Department, that a large portion of the rebel army had left his immediate front.

Gov. Curtin telegraphs that 28,000 rebels crossed the Potomac at Point of Rocks. Dispatches from Hagerstown of the 6th, report that a rebel force entered Hagerstown on that day and that the Federal force at that place after a spirited resistance was compelled to fall back on Green Castle.

The authorities of Pennsylvania call for 12,000 volunteers.

Advices from Green Castle report that the rebels are plundering the people about Middleton of their horses and property. CAMDEN.

TRINITY, LA., July 13—via Shreveport, 17th.

DEAR NEWS:—Dispatches just received from East of the river.

MARIETTA, July 2.—All quiet. The enemy made no advance since the fight of the 29th. Accounts from Petersburg, dated July 1st, the enemy threatening to bombard the place in case it is not evacuated.

RICHMOND, July 1.—Nothing new transpiring. Gold in New York 244. N.

SHREVEPORT, LA., July 11, 1864.

DEAR NEWS,—The Chicago Times of the 27 ult has been received and forwarded herewith. It is important, as showing the position of affairs in the North at this time.

I have news from Marmaduke's command dated 4th inst., stating that Gen. Shelby blockaded White River near Clarendon, captured one gunboat and whipped three others. The Federal force at Duvall's Bluff 4000 fortifying that place, and provisions and munitions moving from Little Rock to that point.

Col. Kelchen is operating to great damage of transports below New Madrid.

On the 5th inst our news from Marmaduke's command in which the items of the 4th are reiterated as to the fight of Gen. Shelby.

Gen. Cooper captured a transport loaded with supplies for the Federals at Port Gibson, at a point 25 miles above Fort Smith. The Federals anticipated a raid from Gen Cooper into Southwest Missouri. The Memphis Bulletin of the 29th ult., quotes gold in New York at 245, in Cincinnatti 270, in St. Louis 250, and the market closed in great excitement. Holders declining to sell at any price. The Bulletin is despondent and cannot imagine why gold should so rapidly and regularly rise in the market, in the face of signal and repeated victories in favor of the Federal armies.

I have enclosed the Extra of the Caddo Gazette of to-day containing some later news from the East, all through Federal sources. L.

☞ The Compositors of the "News" Office return their thanks to Mr. Mahan and Mr. Perkins, for a liberal present of mellons, and assure them that in these days of extortion their liberality is fully appreciated.

Caleb Cutwell's Talk to the Candidates.

I can't vote for you, sir, because you have not done your duty. You hold a responsible office. It matters not to me that you voted against secession, for it was a great question upon which many good men differed. But you did not come out boldly for the South after secession. You have been regarded by the enemies of our cause as with them, and you never told them that their claim was a lie; you never told the people that you were heart and soul with the South; you never spoke even when urged or invited to do so. It was your duty to come out boldly, actively, energetically, and to work untiringly for our cause—to cry aloud and spare not. You have had much leisure to work, and you have not done it. Your influence, thus exerted, would have been worth more to us than a regiment in the field. As it is, your position had done us more harm than several regiments of the enemy—silence in this war is influential. Those not actively and loudly for us, are in effect against us. Your election would be claimed as a triumph in favor of our enemies, and the Yankees would rejoice at it. You should shoulder your gun, sir, and go into the ranks and prove by your works that you are our friend. You are able to do this, have a good constitution, and could make a splendid soldier. Your competitor has done his duty fully. Go and imitate his example. You say you are with us in feeling—that your friends sincerely believe; but the mass of the true men do not, and it is your duty to convince them by stern actions of your sincerity. Your competitor is every way qualified for the office, and, though over the conscript age, went at an early day into the army and has battled manfully for us. He deserves the office by qualifications as complete as yours; and he deserves it, because he is also a soldier; and this you have never been. Let him now take the ease and comfort which office gives, and you the toil and hardships and dangers he has passed through. This will do you more honor than the office you seek by far. I do not think, sir, you ought to have run for this office, because you know how your silence and inactivity in our behalf had operated against us; and you also know, that you had no right to expect an election, if our soldiers were at home, and also that a large majority of the active war men would vote against you. Your only hope of reinstating yourself is by actions, actions, actions—in the army. Go there, and you may yet find honors you never can otherwise attain to.

I cannot vote for you, sir. You have held your present office long. You are a broad-shouldered, healthy, strong man, and ought to be in the army, and you know it. You have charged most exorbitant fees for your official acts, and let even the speculators give you the basis of fixing the value of Confederate States money, and you have charged specie rates and multiplied it by the speculators' table. You say that you take Confederate States money at par from soldiers and their families. That's a catch, sir, for popularity, because you know that they have none of your work to do. You have a large family, have you, that must be supported. So also have a hundred thousand and more of our soldiers, as poor as you, and many of them less able to do a soldier's duty. Others have charged as much as you. That does not justify you, sir. The Governor and all the State officers proper have been compelled to receive Confederate money at par, and you have claimed a right not accorded to them. Suppose the Governor, or any other salaried State officer, had multiplied his salary by 20, or 25, or 30, or 35, or 40, as you have done, and demanded the result. Why, sir, you would have joined in the hue and cry against him, and he would have been hooted out of his office by your help; and yet, you have done worse, because you have taken it from the people, and in the other case it would have come from the State. Those behind will take care of your family—the County will not let them suffer. But you can't bear for your family to live on charity. Poor fellow! Look around you and see thousands of families as respectable as yours, receiving assistance. It is not charity, sir—it is right—it is justice—it is law. Why, sir, how will you feel after this war is over, for your children to ask you, "Pa, were you in the army? Did you go to fight?" Look forward to this, sir, and be ashamed of yourself. Take up your gun, wallet and blankets, mount your horse, or go afoot, and hurry off to the wars, when you will find welcome, toil, hardships, battles, and victories. But, perhaps, you have got no competitor and think you will walk the track alone. Do not so flatter yourself, sir. The people know their duty and will do it, and before the election will find some man, over age or disabled, or, if need be, some soldier who has fought for us, to beat you as you deserve to be.

I can't vote for you sir. You ran for this office first when you found that you would have to go into the army, because you knew it would exempt you, and the same motive now spurs you on to run again, and on your sleepless bed you speculate every night upon the possibility of your defeat, and what you shall do, if defeated, and whether some other position you know to be accessible, or that you already have, will keep you out. Oh! I don't want to go to the army! This is your mental ejaculation every hour of the day, and until sleep seals your eyes.—And you have ever told the people that you are not able to do the duties of a soldier, or that you are exempt anyhow, either from disability or under some order of some officer, but go and tell them now, sir, that you are between 18 and 45 years of age; that all between those ages that can possibly do anything must do it, and that no officer can now, under the late law, give any order detailing men of your age, except in a government workshop. Not a man or woman who knows you, sir, that does not know you to be able to go into the army. How often have you been sick since your county people knew you. But you say you can't work, and therefore can't stand it in the army. Take that back, sir, and say you don't work and never did, and have been hunting office all your life to keep from it. Can't you drive beeves, drive a wagon, ride an artillery horse, pack and shoot a gun, and do ten hundred other things needed in the army?

And now, candidates, all of you, for high offices and low, from constable up, you who have never been in the army and have been kept from it by your offices, and you who have never had an office and now are seeking one to keep out of the army, and you who have dodged and managed, shifted and squirmed, ever since this war commenced, and done things to keep at home that you would have scorned to do and considered beneath you in peace times, and you who have had a nice time of it in offices made fat by multiplying specie rates by the speculators' figures and lived in the shade, and some of you even speculated yourselves; you, strong, healthy, active men, brawny armed, fat and sleek, who have lived high and enjoyed your good things—don't you feel ashamed of yourselves? How can you justify yourselves for not going into the army? Do you not know that the time is coming and near at hand when it will be a reproach upon you, if you fail to do it? Do you not know that you are even now the talk of every child, woman and man in your neighborhood? How can you look upon your wives and children, if you have them, and not feel it your duty to defend them?—How can you love your property and not feel it your duty to defend it? How satisfy your honor and not sustain it on the tented field? How expect the countenance of the fair women of our land, and not hasten to the ranks to help save them from dishonor? How see your country bleeding at every pore and not have a holy enthusiasm enkindled in your breasts to save it from ruin and slavery? Shame, shame upon you! Go and do your duty. Go, if need be, to blood and death for the land that you profess to love. Let the offices be given to the infirm, the over-aged, the maimed, or to soldiers who have worn themselves out in defending you and yours, or rather than to you, to soldiers who have met privations, toil and sufferings for even you.

CALEB CUTWELL.

EAGLE PASS, July 8th, 1864.

EDITOR NEWS:—I notice an article in the Houston Telegraph, of the 4th inst., "That a gentleman just from Eagle Pass states, that during the late scare from the raid, over 6000 bales of unexempted (so called) State Cotton was put across the river." He observes further, "That very grave suspicions were afloat concerning the raid," etc.

Now, Mr. Editor, this is either erroneous, or a designed falsehood, for some object or other. As, in the first place, no such quantity was at the time deposited here. I should say, that both Cotton Bureaus and individuals had not exceeding 2000 bales here; secondly, after the second night watching of all the male inhabitants, pretty much all business was neglected and suspeneed. And, I must say here, that I have never witnessed a more willing, unanimous and harmonious turn out for the common defence, than that which was manifested here during the days of trouble and excitement—old and young, regardless of rank, age, or position (with very few exceptions) met voluntarily at the place of rendezvous. Your Island citizens were represented by Gen. E. B. Nichols, J. A. Sauters, H. Rosenberg and others, in the watch for some six or seven consecutive nights—during which time I carefully observed every locality about the town and river, and I assure you that very little cotton passed over during the time. As regards the "very grave suspicions [that] were afloat concerning the raid," no one, I trust, acquainted with the facts as they transpired, will doubt the design of the renegades. I admit that various exaggerated reports existed and awakened apprehensions not justified by the sequel, but no one could at the time foresee what the strength and design of the enemy might be.

Since my last report, very little cotton has arrived, which has again caused an upward tendency, so that 21 to 23 cents may easily be realized in Piedras Negras.

Passengers by stage from Monterey arrived in Piedras Negras yesterday, report that the stage, as also private ambulances, *en route* for Monterey, have been stopped by an armed force of Governor Vidaurri, numbering some 300, and put into the rear under guard, with a design to make a raid upon Monterey, where they expect to meet with considerable sympathy. FRONTIER.

GALVESTON, July 16, 1864.

ED. NEWS—Yesterday Philip Connard, a private in Cook's regiment, who was arrested by one of the Provost Marshal's detectives a night or two since, was brought before the Commander of the Post for examination on the charge of making signals to the enemy at the time the Susana was leaving port, but no definite conclusions were arrived at, and the prisoner was remanded to the guard house to await further investigation. The registry list is now complete up to this date, showing the following result: Number of males registered, over 16 years of age, 1,481; females, over 16, 1,487; of the above number of males, there are employed in the marine service and in various other departments, including officers residing in town, 853, leaving a balance of 628 males over 16 years of age not in the service. There are 994 males and 1,063 female children, under 16 years of age on the registry. Total population of the city, 5,025, exclusive of the soldiery.

The members of Cook's Regimental Band gave an excellent musical entertainment at the Misses Cobb's Seminary, on last evening. Their performances were highly appreciated, though the patronage they received was not as liberal as their talents and former services really entitle them to. I learn they intend giving the Houstonians a musical treat in a few days.

The blockade this morning consists of flagship, side-wheel steamer, brigantine propeller, four gunboats, supply brig and prize schooner—total, 9.

Yours, ITEM.

☞ For Chief Justice of Fort Bend County, R. H. LEIGH.

List of Casualties.

In the 5th Texas regiment, in the battle of the Wilderness, Virginia, May 6th, 1864, Lieut. R. Bryan, commanding.

Field and Staff—Killed: None. Wounded: Lieut. Col. K. Bryan, severely in arm; Capt T T Clay, acting Lieut Colonel, severely, hand; Capt D C Farmer, acting Major, slightly, hip; Adjutant W P McGowen, slightly hip.

Company A—First Lieut B P Fuller, commanding—Killed: Private T P Bryan; wounded: Lieut B P Fuller slightly, hand, Sergeants G J Robinson, severely, face; J H Shepherd, slightly, legs; Private W H Clark (color bearer) severely, hand; J C Deloach, slightly, head; J E Landes, finger amputated. Total: Killed, one; wounded, six.

Co B—First Lieut Ed Collier, commanding—Killed: Private E Auerbach. Wounded: Privates E Besh severely, shoulder and head; W Cherney, slightly, arm; P Collins, severely, leg; R Graff, severely, arm. Total: Killed one; wounded four.

Co C—Captain J J McBride, commanding—Killed: None. Wounded: Captain J J McBride, both legs broken; Privates J T Allison, severely, arm; J E Ellis, slightly, side; John Garrison, slightly, hand; J E Lacy, severely, face; R Turner, leg amputated; H P Trawick, severely, head. Total: Killed, none; wounded, seven.

Co D—Capt W T Hill, commanding—Killed: Corporal W E Lewis; Privates W H Lewis; R H Griffin. Wounded: Capt W T Hill, severely, arm; Corporal W C Walke, severely, leg; Privates W W Alston, severely, leg; B Carrington, severely, arm and side; I E Gilbert, severely and missing; W H Myers, severely, both thighs; I Burton, severely, leg; W B Rome, leg amputated; W A Taylor, slightly, arm. Missing: Robert Stanton. Total: Killed one; wounded, nine; missing, one.

Co. E—2d Lieut B Eldridge, commanding. Killed—Private C E Farquehar. Wounded—Lieut B Eldridge, slightly, shoulder; Serg't W B George, slightly, hand; Privates John Daniels, severely, face; L Gee, severely, arm; W Leott, slightly leg; G W Williams, severely, both legs.—Total killed, 1; wounded, 7.

Co. F—Capt W D Williams, command'g. Killed—None. Wounded—Lieut R J McKennon, severely, leg; Privates O Copal, arm amputated; S Curvelo, arm and side; Jeff Chaisson, severely, hand; P Choate, severely, side; E Bouch, slightly, arm; Santos Rosas, slightly, leg; J M Dillon, slightly, leg; T Taylor, slightly, shoulder; E Tucker, severely, leg and foot; A N Vaughn, severely, leg. Total wounded, 11.

Co. G—Captain John Smith, commanding. Killed—Private W W Peeks. Wounded—Sergeants L Caldwell, severely, head; J G Sherrell, slightly, thigh; E D Williams, severely, head; Corporal T M Bigbee, slightly, leg; Privates S H Beller, severely, arm; G A Bennard, slightly, leg; J W Evans, severely, thigh; M D Garret, leg amputated; J C Gifford, severely, hand; A Huffman, severely, both legs; W W Hill, severely, shoulder; L W Miller, slightly, arm; E Pool, severely, hand; J A Sharp, severely, hand; J B Tomlinson, slightly, arm. Total killed, 1; wounded, 15.

Co H—1st Lieut W Robinson, commanding. Killed, none. Wounded—Lieut W Robinson, since dead; privates James Chesser, severely, arm; E K Gorree, leg; T L Hampton, slightly, leg; J Hemphill, severely, arm; D McCrackin, severely, both legs; J C Pinson, slightly, hand; James Robinet, slightly, leg; E Shaw, slightly, arm. Total: Killed, none; wounded, 10.

Co I—2d Lieut D R Ponce, commanding. Killed, private John Davis, George Baldwin. Wounded, Sergt C Clampit, severely in leg; privates W R Barlow, severely, abdomen; John Cooner, slightly, leg; John Dean, slightly, side; J W Dean, severely, face; R Flemming, severely, hand; J W Grant, severely, arm and thigh; W A Holmes, slightly leg; A B Hood, severely, hand, John Hoval, slightly, head; B J Baldwin, slightly, arm; E C Hawes, severely, face; O P Barton, severely, leg; J W Powell, severely, leg; W G Blue, slightly, arm. Total, killed, 2; wounded, 15.

Co K—2d Lieut Thomas Nash, company E commanding. Killed, Lieut Thomas Nash; private T McCrary; Thomas Henry, John McKee. Wounded, Sergt A B Green, slightly, side; Sergt D A Rowe, slightly, leg; private N Wily, severely, abdomen; W B Young, severely, thigh; H C Hirams, severely, hand, A Dunn, slightly, arm; E C Hubbard, slightly, leg; S D Waldrop slightly, leg. Total, killed, 4; wounded, 8.

Recapitulation—Killed, 13; wounded, 96; missing, 1. Aggregate, 110.

CASUALTIES OF FIFTH TEXAS REGT.

In the battles near Spotsylvania Court House, Virginia, May 9th, 10th and 11th, 1864, Captain D C Farmer commanding:

Co A, Sergt H G Settle, comd'g—Killed: Private Samuel Bailey. Missing: Private W B Ferrell.

Co B, Lieutenant Edward Collier, comd'g—Killed: None. Wounded: Private D Hurley, bayonet wound, face.

Co C, Lt E Anderson, comd'g—Killed: Private J J Pridgen. Wounded: Private J M Anderson, severely, leg.

Co D, Lt A C Woodal, comd'g—Killed: Private J T Shaw. Wounded: Private J T Alverson, severely, shoulder, since dead.

Co G, Capt John Smith, comd'g—Wounded: J B Small, severely, head.

Co H, Sergt L H Woodall, comd'g—Killed: Private W G Jones.

Recapitulation—Killed, 4; wounded, 4; missing, 1. Aggregate, 9.

W. P. McGOWEN, Adjutant.

Extract from a letter dated Camp Spring Bayou, June 29th, 1864:

"We have had a very fatiguing campaign for the past two months. Nothing of interest in camps at present. No movement on foot. Everything looks as if the wise heads intend sending us to Arkansas and Missouri again. We will have to move in some direction soon, for we cannot live here. We have been on half rations for the past three weeks, and some days not anything, although the troops are in fine spirits, and do not grumble at their living. Our regiment cannot remain so long—we will have to have a fight or something more to eat, one of the two.—*We do very well without rations as long as we have some excitement but when the excitement dies out then the men get hungry, and begin to make a noise.*

Lieut. Gen. Buckner passed through our camp yesterday, on his way to Department Headquarters, from the other side of the river. It is expected he will take command of the District of Arkansas and Missouri; but as Gen. Taylor has been relieved from duty here, he may be assigned to this District. He brings no news from the armies of Johnston or Lee."

[We hope our commanding officers are daily impressed with the truth of what the writer above says in the italicised lines. Texas troops must have action. *If the enemy won't come to them, they must be led against the enemy.*]

CAMP COLLINS, GALVESTON ISLAND, July 14, 1864.

ED. NEWS, *Dear Sir.*—Having noticed, in your paper a few days since, an account, given by your Galveston correspondent, of the burning of the blockade-runner, Carolina, by the enemy's gunboats on the 8th inst., after having been beached some 15 or 18 miles down the Island. I find the statement incorrect, and shall, in justice to the participators in the affair, endeavor to give a correct account of facts as they occurred: The boat was discovered by our men immediately after daylight. They were endeavoring at that time to beach her, being closely pursued by two of the blockaders. She succeeded in reaching the beach without being fired upon, and was instantly abandoned by her crew. The first gun was fired within five minutes after she was beached, and the firing was kept up upon her and flying crew for some fifty minutes, without serious damage to either. As soon as the discovery was made by us, we were ordered to fall in with arms, and were marched, by Lt Damon, then in command, to the scene of action with all possible dispatch, which was three miles distant. When we got within two miles of the vessel, we discovered the enemy proceeding in launches to board her. We were urged, by our Lieutenant, to quicken our pace and get within range of the boats before they reached the vessel, which we accomplished with great exertions. Our boys charged to the very surf, and fired, the launches turning immediately, reached the vessel as soon as possible, three in all, another having joined them. As soon as they discovered they could not board the Carolina, they opened fire on her with the intention of burning her, which they succeeded in doing in a very short time. In the meantime giving us the full benefit of the shell and shot, but as we took advantage of the protection the sand hills afforded, we experienced no inconvenience. One of the crew was killed while preparing to go on board to recover some property left behind by him, the shot striking the shoulder and penetrating the breast.

MEMBER CO. A., BROWN'S REGT.

Election of Judge of the First District.

H. Waller, Esq.—Each one of the candidates for Judge of the First District is deservedly popular, and entitled to the full consideration due to an intelligent gentleman and cultivated lawyer. But who (of the three) combines in his character, moral and professional, most of the other requisites indispensable in a faithful discharge of the duties of this important office? I would not be captious or hypercritical in canvassing the individual claims of these gentlemen, and surely it will not be so considered to allude to some facts and traits which peculiarly qualify one of them for the position, and seem to indicate him to the choice of the people. And first, I hold, that in the selection of a Judge he is preferable to all others, *ceteris paribus*, who has been educated and disciplined under the laws which he is called to administer. His perceptions, his sympathies, his attachments and his interests have all grown from and around them, and, in turn, afford him means and facilities in their construction and application which may not be acquired by years of study and practice. Do not understand me as contending for a system of judicial representation or sectional preference. All I mean to say is this: that in a State whose body of laws is derived from various and different systems, and founded upon local and obsolete usages and practices, it is of the utmost importance that these systems should be understood and these usages and practices known, and that I can conceive of nothing so conducive to this end as the knowledge and experience obtained by one trained and educated under the original and progressive application of these laws. I advance no new or startling idea. Let me ask gentlemen of the profession, how many and who best understand our process of garnishment, our process of special attachment, our trustee process, the proceedings under our community rights and the mode of proceeding in extending the execution upon lands? And let me ask, at the same time, how many and who are most competent in the decision of questions of title to land under our complication of claims? We have much "*judicial legislation*," and it is a practice universally condemned. Yet, in many cases, it is unavoidable and necessary, and in no State of the Confederacy more so than in Texas. All our titles to land depend, to a very great extent upon a series of judicial decisions, growing out of the several acts of the Congress of Mexico and the Legislature of Coahuila and Texas and the Legislature of the State of Texas—all providing for the disposition of the public domain, and each act founded in a policy peculiar to the condition and aim of its own Government. These legislative provisions are all voluminous, and the rights acquired under them often conflicting and seldom harmonious. In the midst of this conflict and want of harmony, the manifest perfection of right and title could only be sustained by judicial construction and determination. Hence, a system has grown up, at once complicated, artificial and argumentative. As a consequence of this, new questions are constantly being sprung upon the Court, and new decisions have to be made until the matter is settled by the Supreme Court. Open and vexed questions are presented, and Judges are left to adopt suddenly, or over-rule, mere *obiter dicta* which have been used and acted upon as settled authority. Now, in such important emergencies, is it not obvious that the lawyer who has been bred and educated under this peculiar system of laws—who has been thoroughly trained and disciplined, from his growth upward, in the usages and practices upon which these laws have been founded, is better able to state, or alter, or modify a general rule than another who until latter years has been a stranger to the State, a stranger to the usages and practices of the people, a stranger to all but the written law before him? Do not reason and duty call on us to select the man for Judge who not only knows the law in its letter but the law in the reason and spirit of its enactment—in the force and propriety of its application? Such a man is presented for the choice of the people in the person of Hiram Waller, Esq.

Again: it is desirable to select for Judge, if possible, a man who has made, and intends to make, the law *the one exclusive* business of his life. "The judicial office," says one who well knew, "ought to be filled by a man who is *wholly* a judge, *always* a judge, and *nothing* but a judge"—with intervals only for repose and recreation, his thoughts and labor should be turned to his official duties. He should be *omnis in hoc*. He has no time to devote to the cultivation of land, the sale of merchandise or the purchase of stocks. There is no greater mistake than prevails, of thinking that a Judge's duties begin and end with the spring and fall riding. The Court vacations are as much engrossed as are the sessions. Cases laid over for advisement, cases coming up on new-trial for error in judgment, reports, multiplying decisions and evolving new matter of doctrine and principles of law, requiring study and digestion, all force themselves upon the attention of the conscientious Judge, and leave him no time for outside employment. Indeed, the judicial office is incompatible with any other pursuit of life; and all the faculties of every man who takes it ought to be *exercised*, and exercised to this one great end. If Mr. Waller be called to the bench, we have an earnest in his past professional life of the exclusiveness of his future official one. For twenty years he has been sedulously and exclusively engaged in the duties of his profession—much of that time as an approved and efficient officer of the Government. All that he has, and all that he is, has been acquired in the one great business of his life. His only aim seems to have been to accomplish himself in his profession, with a view to future character and usefulness. For this he has frequently turned aside from opportunities of aggrandizement and preferment and followed, with steady aim, the narrow path of professional duty. With what success Mr. Waller has met in this single purpose of life, and how far it has qualified him to occupy official station, let the term of his service, his habits of application, the extent and success of his practice, the rank and position he has attained among his brethren of the profession attest. These bespeak what all accord to him—intellectual power, legal acumen and professional attainment of no ordinary character. But intellectual power and the *viginti annorum* in professional duty cannot of themselves qualify a man for the office of Judge. He must possess and illustrate in his life those high moral virtues which protect as well as adorn the ermine of office. With such virtues we presume no man in the State is more eminently endowed than Mr. Waller. Entertaining a strict sense of justice, his mind instinctively seizes upon the right, and adheres to it with the solemnity and tenacity of conviction. Courteous and amiable in his feelings, he investigates patiently, hears attentively, and decides promptly. Searching only for truth, his will is flexible to reason, but his purpose is as fixed as the pillars of the temple. "*Firmum ac tenacem propositi virum.*"

Such is Hiram Waller, and such his friends have presented him to the people of the First Judicial Circuit.

AMICUS CURIÆ.

—o—

Marlin, Falls Co., Texas, July 12, 1864.

Ed. News.—In your Tri-Weekly of the 8th inst., I see my name published as a deserter. In justice to myself, I beg leave to state, through your paper, how and why I am, and have been, absent from my command. About the 7th of March last, I obtained, from the proper authorities, a leave of absence for twenty days. At the expiration of that period not being able, from ill health, to return to my company, I applied to Surgeon D F. Baily, C. S. A., for a certificate of disability, which was given me for twenty days, and was duly forwarded through the mail to Capt. B A. Nally, of whose company I was a member. At the expiration of that time, being still unable for duty, I obtained another certificate from Wm Killbrew, M. D., which was also forwarded as above. In a few days after I forwarded the last certificate, though not well, I concluded to follow it in person. When I reached Galveston, I reported for duty to my Colonel, (Cook) who informed me my name had been dropped from the muster rolls, and I had ceased to be an officer in the regiment, and that he could not reinstate me, or replace my name upon the rolls. I remained in Galveston about two weeks or more, thinking that something would be done with my case, but nothing being done, I then made application to Lieut. Col. Manly, then commanding the regiment, for a court of inquiry, but it was not granted me. I still remained in Galveston for a week or ten days, hoping that some action would be had in the premises, but nothing yet being done, I returned to my home in Falls county, where I have been ever since, and always ready to respond to the calls of my country. No, Sir, I am no deserter, and I believe that an impartial people, when they know the facts connected with the affair, and from which alone the publication of my name as a dedserter has originated, will say that said publication was unjust, and certainly calculated to do me injury without cause. I went into the service voluntarily when in my 17th year, and have endeavored to do my duty as a soldier and as an officer. I have never regretted doing so, and am still ready to serve my country. I would state further that each of the certificates sent, as before stated, were authenticated with the seal of the County Court of my county, and each of them were duly recorded by Capt Nally.

Respectfully, JOHN WARD,
Formerly 1st Lt. Co. K. Cook's Regt. H. A.

The Galveston News.

BY W. RICHARDSON.

☞ Night before last some small boys who were swimming in the bayou got to quarreling among one another, and throwing missiles at one another. One of them, quite a small boy about fourteen years of age, finding himself assailed by a boy larger and stronger than himself, went home and having armed himself with a pistol, returned and meeting the larger boy presented his pistol and shot him in the abdomen, from which wound the poor fellow suffered extreme agony for near 24 hours when death finally relieved him. Cannot something be done to prevent our little children in the streets and during their amusements from carrying pistols and shooting each other? It is indeed a dreadful state of things.

☞ We notice in the list of killed and wounded between the 5th and 18th May, published in the Telegraph, the name of F. Gearing as severely wounded. It having been quite extensively reported that Mr Gearing had joined the Yankees at Brownsville, and was serving in their army, the above will assure his many friends that there is no foundation for the report.

Gonzales, July 12 1864.

Ed. News.—Col. Ford's recent capture of Yankees on the Rio Grande, sums up as follows: He went with a force up to within a few miles of Brownsville, and the Yankees supposing that to be all the force he had followed him out some 20 or 30 miles, and were surrounded by our men, whom Col. Ford had left behind. A sharp little fight ensued, which resulted in the capture of some forty, and killing and wounding of some 60 Yankees, also in capturing some 500 head of horses. This is the way we hear the news here, whether the particulars are as given or not, I cannot say, but certainly something has taken place.

More anon. OUT WEST.

Ed. News.—A private citizen seeking a controversy with an editor of a public newspaper, exhibits unpardonable weakness. I, therefore, disclaim every thing of this character, but as a member of the late Confederate States Grand Jury for the Eastern District of Texas, am unwilling that the *criminating* strictures, upon their generel presentation, which appeared in the "Telegraph" of the 13th inst., should go to the country without some member of that body attempting its vindication.

They charge that there can be no reasonable doubt of the existence of fraud and speculation in the Quartermaster, Commissary and Marine Departments, implicating the highest officials and the humblest agents, and that the business of speculating in government funds has been reduced to a perfect science, and that their books and accounts have been so kept as to render their detection almost a matter of impossibility.

The writer does not pretend to question the truthfulness of these grave charges, but accepts them as valid—as a part of the history of the country—attested in the most solemn manner by the most unimpeachable witnesses, that the officers of this military district, with but few exceptions, are dishonest, and are plundering the government. These astounding developments are (as they should be) well calculated to fill the country with alarm, and to excite untold fears in the public mind. In the general presentation, not a moity of the facts, as they existed in evidence, were presented to the public, and were it *now proper* to expose the mass and volume of testimony leading to implication and guilt that was so reluctantly presented before that body, it would be well calculated, also, to fill the minds, not only of the people, but of the implicated parties, with alarm, and their apologist would hide his head from very shame.

The members of that Grand Jury do not claim exemption or immunity from responsibility, and are answerable to God and to their country for the manner in which they discharged their duty upon that occasion, and I have no doubt will hold themselves personally responsible to any of the parties acknowledging themselves implicated in the charge. The few honorable exceptions have no interest in this controversy whatever, for there is not one syllable in the presentment pertaining to their case.

As regards our so-called premature adjournment, it was a matter of business pertaining to us alone, and we claim for ourselves to be the only proper judges of the appropriate time. We kept our own councils and sought no advice upon the subject, outside of the court and jury room, and it is well we did, for men must be very uncertain indeed, when we see one of the leading journalists of the country so far forget the dignity and responsibility of his position as to unblushingly become the *volunteer apologist* for crime and enormities of this magnitude and character.

His direct charge of malfesance on the part of the Grand Jury, will, ere long, receive the unqualified condemnation of all honest and honorable men in the District, and will be stamped as it well deserves, with *falsehood, infamy and detraction*. It has been suggested, (and very properly too,) that his unparalleled presumption in advising the Court to reempanel the Jury at once, and the *charge dictated* for deliverance upon their re assembling together, is only surpassed by his venality and overweening cupidity, and is in complete harmony and perfect union with his antecedents.

After a laborious session of six weeks, endeavoring to investigate crime and malfesance in office, for reasons best known to ourselves, the session was terminated under the conviction that violators of the law had cloaked their villainy so effectually, that to find bills of indictment against them *now, at this term of the court*, would be the extreme of folly.—The general presentment published was *intended* for the enlightenment of the people. It was intended for the information of the Lt. General commanding this military department, and also for the authorities at Richmond, whose aid has been or will be invoked in bringing official delinquents to justice and punishment. Its publication, instead of being "treasonable," and calculated to do harm as was intimated, will most assuredly result in incalculable good to the country—it will be as "bread cast upon the waters"—for it apprises the Lt. General and the Government at Richmond of the true and lamentable state of affairs in this military district, which will no doubt prompt an immediate, *vigorous*, *scrutinizing* investigation, as all the facts and evidences upon which that deliverence was predicated must have long since been forwarded to the proper heads of department of Government, and also to the President of the Confederacy. Its publication will result in further good, for it will constitute every true, loyal, patriotic citizen of the district, a sentinel on the watch tower of liberty—it will actuate and encourage him to report each sign of fraud. It will give to our brave soldiers in the field encouragement and confidence.

It will give them to understand, that whilst they are battling in the sacred cause of civil liberty—pouring out their life blood in the defence of human rights—the Government and the people are as a unit in their *resolve* to eradicate corruption from high places. And further: it will *aid* and *inspire* and *stimulate* succeeding Grand Juries in the *vigorous* prosecution of their labors and the full and impartial discharge of their duty.

That the Confederacy has been plundered and robbed to an enormous extent, there can be no reasonable doubt, and the authorities at Richmond will, most certainly, accept as *true* the averments set forth in the general presentment, upon the examination of the testimony. It will then find, not only something rotten in Denmark, but they will also discover that this rottenness has assumed the type and character of an *epidemic*; that it has been wonderfully contagious, approximating to pestilence, with which, *perhaps*, the writer in the Telegraph is *slightly* infected.

I seek no controversy with editors, and, if this communication is satisfactory to the public I am content to rest under it. ONE OF THE JURY.

Died—In Liberty, on the 12th inst., Sarah Sidney, aged 20 months, only daughter of Judge C. L. and Mrs Mary A Cleveland.

Died—At the residence of her son, Gen. J. B Robertson, near Independence, Washington county, on the morning of the 7th of July, Mrs C. Robertson, aged eighty-four years and six months.

Telegraph copy. july17tw1t.

Died—On Wednesday, 13th instant, Mrs. Helen Shaw, aged 56 years.

Died.—Was killed in a skirmish, on Red River, the afternoon of the 13th of May, W. H. Matthews, a native of Fayatte county, Tennessee, in the 38th year of his age.

Mr. Matthews was a true patriot and soldier, ever at his post of duty. Circumstances and the condition of his family prevented his joining the army at the beginning of the war, but when he saw his country needed his services, he volunteered and has since battled manfully in her defence. He was generous, noble and brave, always present in battles ready to perform any duty that might devolve upon him—lived and died a christian, beloved by all who knew him. He leaves a wife and five children to mourn his untimely death.

His company and friends deeply sympathize with the breaved family.

☞ We are authorized to announce R. N. PRYOR as a candidate for Assessor and Collector of Harris county.

☞ We are authorized to announce G. W. BRODRICK as a candidate for re-election to the office of County Treasurer, at the election in August next.

☞ Lt. STERLING FISHER is a candidate for County Clerk of Harris County.

☞ We are authorized to announce J. W. STELL, Esq, of Gonzales County, as a candidate for Attorney General of the State.

☞ If the people of Harris county will re-elect me to the office of Chief Justice, I will be happy to serve them. T. B. J. HADLEY.

☞ We have been authorized to announce the Hon. JAS. H. BELL as a candidate for the office of Chief Justice of the Supreme Court of the State.

☞ We are authorized to announce JUDGE R. A REEVES as candidate for the office of Associate Judge of the Supreme Court of the State.

☞ We are authorized to announce JUDGE C. W. BUCKLEY, as a candidate for the office of Associate Justice of the Supreme Court of the State.

☞ MAJ. W. L. ROBARDS is a candidate for Comptroller at the next August election. lawtd

☞ We are authorized to announce Mr. H. BRASHEAR, as a candidate for Chief Justice of Harris county.

☞ We are authorized to announce B. E. TARVER Esq., of DeWitt county, as a candidate for Attorney General of the State. my29

☞ Hon. GEO. W. SMITH is a candidate for re election to the office of Judge of the 1st Judicial District. my29*

☞ We are authorized to announce Col. O M. ROBERTS, as a candidate for Chief Justice of the Supreme Court of Texas. my27

☞ B P. LANHAM is a candidate for re-election of Sheriff, Harris county.

☞ We are authorised to announce Edward Bailey, Esq., as a candidate for the office of District Attorney, for the 1st Judicial District—election in August next.

☞ We are authorized to announce Col. JOHN SAYLES, of Washington county, as a candidate for Associate Judge of the Supreme Court.

☞ JOHN McMILLAN is a candidate for re election to the office of County Clerk.

☞ We are authorized to announce W. S. DELANEY as a candidate for re-election to the office of District Attorney for the 1st Judicial District.

☞ We are authorized to announce W. J. DARDEN, Esq, as a candidate for Judge of the 1st Judicial District.

☞ We are authorized to announce C. H. RANDOLPH as a candidate for re-election to the office of State Treasurer, at the ensuing August election.

☞ R. S ROBINSON is a candidate for Sheriff of Fort Bend county. jne24

☞ W. B. ROBINSON is a candidate for Treasurer of Fort Bend county. jne24

☞ D. FERGUSON, Esq., is a candidate for the office of County Treasurer for Fort Bend county.

Marshal's Sale.

Of Valuable Real Estate, in Houston, and also near Lynchburg, in Harris County, and in Trinity County.

UNDER and by virtue of an execution issued from the Confederate States District Court for the Eastern District of Texas at Galveston, in case No. 15, entitled, "The Confederate States vs. A. Blum & Bro., I will, on the first Tuesday of August 1864, being the 2d day of said month, sell for coin, Confederate notes or bonds, in front of the Court-house door of Harris county, in the city of Houston, within the hours prescribed by law, the following described real estate, to-wit: The south-east one half of Block No 99, in the city of Houston, the same consisting of lots one (1,) two (2,) three (3,) four (4,) and five (5,) and the one-half of lots eleven and twelve, being the one-half of said last named lots adjoining the lots first named, together with all and singular, the buildings and improvements thereon.

Also, Lots No. six (6,) and twelve (12,) and the half of three (3,) and the half of eight (8,) in Block 120, in the city of Houston, on the south of Buffalo Bayou, and also of that part of the same Block No. 120, as follows: one hundred and twenty-five feet front on Chene Verte street, and eighty five feet front on Capitol street, being a part of Lots Nos. three (3,) four (4,) and five (5,) containing an area of ten thousand six hundred and twenty-five feet.

The first described property, comprising what is known as the Blum residence, and recently occupied by himself and his brother, Leon Blum. The latter described property is situated in the same vicinity, all of which property will be sold with all improvements thereon.

Also—A Tract of three hundred and twenty acres of Land, in Trinity county, sold by R. A. Clippon to A. Felker, who sold the same to A. Blum.

Also—A Tract of three hundred and twenty acres of Land in Trinity county; sold by J. F. Moore, Sheriff of Trinity county, to James Poston, who sold the same to J. A. Felker, who sold the same to A. Blum.

Also—A Tract of three hundred and twenty acres of Land, situated on the east bank of the San Jacinto river in Harris county, adjoining the lands of David G Burnett and Charles P Kesches, and is the same tract of land which was sold by Othello Hare and Thomas J. Hare to A. Blum and his brother Leon Blum.

Also—Immediately after these sales are over, will be sold at the store of J. H. Morris, in the city of Houston, a large Fire Proof Safe, four desks, three large mirrors, and one small box of ink.

Also—Negro man Mortimer, 26 years old.

Also—Immediately after this sale is over will be sold at the house first mentioned above, a quantity of Household and Kitchen Furniture, Crockery and Glass Ware.

Also—One Piano Forte, one Copying Press, two Stoves, two Cooking Stoves, some Gas Fixtures, one Dray, one Cart, two Ladders,

WM. T AUSTIN, C. S. Marshal,
Eastern District, of Texas, at Galveston and Houston. jly10-tw-td

Flake's Bulletin.

F. FLAKE..............................S. RINKER

PUBLISHED BY F. FLAKE & CO.

GALVESTON:

Monday Morning Oct. 10th, 1864.

BY TELEGRAPH!

[SPECIAL TO FLAKE'S BULLETIN.]

—o—

From *Telegraph* Extra.]

CAMDEN, October 8th, 1846.

WASHINGTON, Sept. 26.—To Maj.-General DIX:—Dispatches from Sheridan to one o'clock Saturday night, dated 6 miles south of New Market, have been received. He had driven the enemy from Mount Jackson without being able to bring on a general engagement. Twenty pieces of artillery were captured at Fisher's Hill and eleven hundred prisoners. Breckinridge has gone to take command of the rebel Department of the Southwest.

Hood appears to be moving toward Alabama.

A strong force of rebel soldiers are reported operating against Gen. Sherman's communications, they captured Athens, Ala. Vigorous exertions are being made to overtake and destroy this force.

General Steele has been reinforced and assumed the offensive. E. M. STANTON, Sec'y of War.

NASHVILLE, Sept. 26th.—Forrest with his whole force advanced upon and destroyed Sulphur Springs trestle yesterday. Colonel Pace, commanding Elk river bridge, evacuated that post at daylight. Forrest took possession this morning. His force is estimated at seven thous nd strong, with three batteries.

Saturday, in the fight at Athens, five hundred men belonging the 6th and 8th Indiana Cavalry, were captured.

Forrest is reported to have butchered all negroes captured who were in Federal uniforms.

FORT MONROE, Sept. 25. — Secretary Seward arrived at 3 o'clock this morning and left immediately for City Point. Mr. Harrington, Assistant Secretary of the navy, arrived here this morning.

Late Richmond papers contain the following:

GRIFFIN, Sept. 21. — Farragut does not anticipate attacking Mobile at present.

General Sherman has issued orders forbidding all citizens to come this side of Nashville from beyond it.

BULL'S GAP, Sept. 22nd.—General Vaughn drove the enemy from Blue Springs this morning, capturing 120 prisoners.

The enemy are strongly fortified at Bull's Gap.

Early's defeat at Winchester is explained by facts generally understood in this city, but which it is not expedient at present to give greater publicity. It is sufficient to say, there is no use to reflect upon the commander or men: all that valor and skill could do was done in that fight.

TORONTO, Sept. 24.—Warrants have been issued here by the authorities for the arrest of several of the Lake Erie pirates, who have been seen in the city since the raid.

NEW YORK, Sept. 26th.—Gold opened with symptoms of great weakness, the price being eight cents below the lowest figures. On Saturday, at ten A. M., the price was 192, and in less than one half hour had touched 185, owing to the reported surrender of Mobile. It soon rallied, however, and sold for 189.

ST. LOUIS, Sept. 26.—General Price has entered Missouri, with a force estimated at 30,000 strong. He is supposed to march to the central portion with 3 columns and capture all important points. Kirby Smith is expected to join him with 12,000 men at Kansas. Guerillas are all concentrating aid to his numerous columns now in the southwestern part of the State, doubtless under Shelby, who has some 6—8,000 men.

Reports are in circulation to-night that a part of the force which occupied Fredericktown yesterday, captured Cape Giraadeau to-day, but it was doubtful. They may be demonstrating in that direction, but the p strong to be taken by cavalry.

ST. LOUIS, Sept. 25th.—Joe Shelby's cavalry to be 5—4,000 strong, they occupied Fred... miles frrm Pilot Knob, yesterday.

General Ewing, commanding the District of St. Louis, took a brigade of A. J. Smith's Corps down last night, and is otherwise fully prepared to meet the enemy.

Pilot Knob is well fortified and garrisoned, and Cape Girardeau can stand a siege, and the only damage the rebels can do is to temporarily cut off the railroad communication.

When Price crossed the Arkansas river some days ago, his forces moved towards Batesville, evidently with the design of joining Shelby in North or East Kansas, and with the combined commands to invade Missouri from the South East. The force occupying Fredericktown, doubtless the advance of the command, is estimated at six thousand strong.

ST. LOUIS Sept. 26th.—On recommendation of many leading citizens, Gen'l Rosencranz issued an order suspending all business, not absolutely indispensable, after twelve o'clock to-morrow for the purpose of organizing the citizens for the defense of the city. He appeals to the citizens of Missouri to take up arms and defend their homes.

DESOTO, Sept. 27.—The rebels in small force skirmished with our troops at Ironton this afternoon and without gaining any advantage. They appear to be concentrating a considerable force against Pilot Knob. General Ewing is in command at the latter place.

Price is reported to have passed through Farmingtown with a force a mile and a half in length.

NEW YORK, Sept. 27th. — The *Herald's* special from Sheridan's headquarters, dated ths 27th, says:

After his defeat at Winchester, Early withdrew his forces to Fishers Hill, leaving most of his wounded of the battle of the 19th and those which had accumulated from the various combats with Crook and Averill, in our hands. At Fisher's Hill he rested his right upon the Masaunthen Mountain and his left upon North Mountain, having his front about three miles in length, crossed by strong natural and artificial defenses. His right, which was about one mile in advance of his left, was considered almost impregnable. On the 21st a most important position in front of the enemy's centre was gained by General Wright's corps. They advanced their infantry to the heights in front of their centre, while Averill's division of cavalry attacked and drove the enemy at a gallop from his advanced position one mile back into his breastworks and held him there, while Crook's Corps, which had been concealed during the day, was transferred in the rear of Averill's division to the enemy's extreme left. At 5 P. M., Crook and Averill stormed the enemy's works, the cavalry leaping over barriers enclosed by the enemy, capturing two battle flags, 5 guns and over 100 prisoners, while Crook swept towards the enemy's centre. The sixth Corps furiously attacked, followed by the 19th, while Averill swept along the base of the North Mountain some seven miles, capturing one hundred and seventy-five cavalry horses, four caissons, fourteen negroes, eight ambulances and a number of fugitives from the enemy, having probably learned of the movement upon his right and rear, had commenced leaving this position some two hours before our attack. His departure was so hasty that he was compelled to leave sixteen guns and over a thousand prisoners in our hands. Yesterday morning the pursuit of the enemy was promptly continued by our cavalry and he was found in position on mount Jackson, 25 miles south of Fishers Hill, where he seemed disposed to offer stubborn resistance. Yesterday morning Early's rear was overtaken near Hawkins' bridge by General Averill, with his cavalry division, and driven to the top of Mount Jackson, where his entire force was found in position. Major Laddy, commanding the two battalions, was captured with several privates. Our cavalry pressed the enemy with great vigor and success till he brought an infantry division with artillery, and they held them in check until the sixth Corps arrived.

The *Herald's* New Orleans correspondent has the following:

The Trans-Mississippi rebels, numbering 25,000, are moving towards Missouri.

...TTANOOGA, Sept. 27th.—Forrest captured Athens, nd destroyed Elk river bridge and the garrison of ...ockade (colored) captured.

...eneral Averill was relieved from duty with his division this morning and granted leave of absence for twenty days. This order has caused a universal feeling of amazement in this army, and it is generally thought some question of rank between Averill and Gen. Torbert is involved, the former being the ranking officer, but the chief of cavalry of this military District.

The Nashville and Chattanooga railroad is not disturbed and ample provisions are taken to keep up uninterrupted communication between Chattanooga and Atlanta.

NASHVILLE Sept. 27th. — General Rousseau reached Pulaski yesterday about 3 P. M. Forrest's cavalry were within several miles of Pulaski and advancing. Heavy skirmishing commenced and continued until after dark by the advance of both forces.

Preparations are making at Florence to celebrate the six hundreth anniversary of the birth of Dante.

The great poet was born in 1865.

The N. Y. Herald, having failed to get a bid from McClellan's friends, has come out against the Chicago nominees.

OFFICIAL REPORT of Mr. MIKE CAHILL, the City Sexton, of Burials in all the City Cemeteries.

Sunday, October 9.

John Klenau,	19 y's,	Yellow Fever,	Dye's Battery.
John Gibson,	25 do	do	do	Wilke's Battery

THE STATE OF TEXAS—COUNTY OF GALVESTON

In County Court—October Term.

THE STATE OF TEXAS

To all persons interested in the Estate of the minor Antoinette Officiers.

You are hereby notified to be and appear at the October Term of the County Court of said County, to be holden at the Court House thereof, on the last Monday in October inst., then and there to show cause, if any you can, why the final account of E. H. Sieling, guardian of the estate of said minor, now of file in said Court, should not be audited and allowed, and to do such other things as may be ordered and decreed in the premises by the Court aforesaid.

{SEAL.} WITNESS, R. H. HOWARD, Chief Justice and Judge of the County Court of said County, with the seal thereo this 1st day, of October, A. D. 1864.

Teste: OSCAR FARISH, Clerk.

1m-b

Lost.

October 27th, the New York *News* and *World* of Aug. 31st. Whoever may have them will confer a favor on R. K. Hartley by leaving them at this office.

HEAD-QUARTERS DEPARTMENT TRANS-MISSISSIPPI, *Shreveport, La.*, September, 1864. [EXTRACT.]

GENERAL ORDERS, No 56.

* * * * * * * * * *

I. The following prices having been adopted by the Commissioners of the State of Texas, will remain in force until further orders:

SCHEDULE OF PRICES FOR TEXAS.

OFFICE OF BOARD OF COMMISSIONERS, *Marshall*, Sept. 1st, 1864.

Schedule of Prices adopted by Commissioners for the State of Texas, to take effect and be in force on the 1st day of September, 1864. Schedule for August 1st, ultimo, is hereby adopted and re-affirmed, and will remain in force till further notice, except in the following articles:

Transportation per mile, Stage	$	40
do do Railroad,		25
do do Steamboat,		05
Freight, per mile per 100 lbs in wagons,		06
Bacon, good, hog round, per 100 lbs,	50	00
Lard, good, per 100 lbs,	50	00
Sugar, white clarified, per 100 lbs,	125	00
do brown, prime, per 100 lbs,	75	00
do do common, per 100 lbs,	65	00

W. R. D. WARD, FRANK E. WILLIAMS, } Commissioners.

By command of GENERAL E. KIRBY SMITH.

sep22-4w S. S. ANDERSON, Ass't Adj't Gen.

Louisiana and Texas papers copy 4 weeks.

HEAD QUARTERS FIRST SUB-DISTRICT, *Galveston*, Sept. 24th. 1864.

GENERAL ORDERS, No. 49.

By direction of the Major-General Com'ding District of Texas, New Mexico and Arizona, the privilege heretofore granted vessels to run the blockade, is hereby cancelled. Steam and sail vessels drawing four feet water or less, will not be permitted to proceed to sea under any circumstances. And any vessel of this class attempting to run the blockade will be confiscated. The owners, crews, &c., of such vessels, heretofore exempted from conscription by virtue of said privilege, will be subject to enrollment in the army of the Confederate States, unless exempted for the purpose of trading to and from Galveston and the interior.

Vessels above this class (steam or sail) will not be permitted to leave the waters of Galveston and vicinity, without special permission from the Major-General Commanding District of Texas, &c.

Commanders of forts will fire upon any vessel (steam or sail) attempting to leave the waters of Galveston and vicinity without special permission from these Head Quarters of a date later than that of this order.

By command of Brig. General J. M. HAWES.

1wd-4tw sep26 WM. T[illegible]ER, A. A. Gen.

CUSTOM HOUSE, PORT OF GALVESTON, September 14th, 1864.

NOTICE.

The following goods were seized by officers of the customs, on the ground that they were imported into the Confederat States in violation of the Revenue Laws, viz:

THREE BOXES OF COGNAC on the 9th of July, 1864, at Galveston.

FIVE DEMIJOHNS OF RUM and ONE DEMIJOHN OF GIN on the 8th of August, 1864, on board a water-boat on the Bay of Galveston, Galveston County, Texas.

TWO DEMIJOHNS OF RUM, on the 16th of August 1864, at Galveston.

Any person or persons, claiming the above goods, are required to appear and make such claim within ninety days from the date of the first publication of this notice, *Provided*, that the same may file with the Collector a claim, stating his or their interest in the articles seized, and may execute a Bond to the Confederate States, in the penalty of Two Hundred and Fifty Dollars, with two securities, to be approved by the Collector or other officer authorized to approve the same, *conditioned*, that in case of condemnation of the articles so seized, the obligors will pay all the costs and expenses of the proceedings to obtain such condemnation.

3w JAMES SORLEY, Collector.

Henderson Times.

VOL. 5. HENDERSON, RUSK COUNTY, TEXAS, OCTOBER 22. 1864. NO. 38.

OBITUARY.

A tribute to the noble hearts who have shed their life's blood, in the defense of their country's rights, is due from far abler pens than mine, still, I offer and humble token to one whose life was sacrificed on the 27th August, 1864. I allude to William Hurst, of Co. "D" (14th) Texas Regiment. He fell while charging the enemy near Chattahoochie river.

Billy, (as he was familiarly called) was a good boy, noble soldier and a true patriot. Little would a casual observer think, when looking on his beardless cheek, his youthful brow, he was a fearless warrior. None can say he ever faltered when the command was, forward.

He was a moral, kind, noble boy. He bears a soldier's name untarnished. We have lost a friend, the South, a true soldier. His spirit has winged its flight to its Maker's presence. Sweet must be the welcome their, the brave receive, who die for liberty.

To his parents in the far off land of the "Lone Star State," who will mourn his loss, we offer the deepest sympathy of a soldier's heart.—Their son died in a noble cause. Sorrow loses half its sadness, when those we love, die as should a soldier. ONE WHO LOVED HIM

ITEMS.

Fremont's Withdrawal.

The following is Fremont's litter withdrawing from the canvass for the Presidency:

BOSTON Sept 21, 1864.—Gentlemen: I feel it my duty to make one step more in the direction indicated by my letter of the 25th of August, and withdraw my name from the list of candidates:

The Presidential question has in effect been entered upon in such a way that the union of the Republican party has become a paramount necessity. The policy of the Democratic party signifies either seperation or re establishment with slavery. The Chicago platform is seperation—Gen. McClellan's letter of acceptance is re-establishment with slavery.

The Republican candidate, on the contrary, is pledged to the re-establishment of the Union without slavery, and however hesitating his policy may be, the pressure of his party will, we may hope, force him to it.

Between these issues I think no man of the liberal party can remain in doubt. I am consistent with my antecedents in withdrawing, not to aid in the triumph of Mr. Lincoln, but to do my part towards preventing the election of the Democratic candidate.

In respect to Mr. Lincoln, I continue to hold exactly the same sentiments contained in my letter of acceptance. I consider that his administration has been politically, militarily and financially a failure, and that its necessary continuance is a cause of regret for the country.

There never was a greater unanimity in a country than was exhibited here at the fall of Sumter, and the South was powerless in the face of it; but Mr. Lincoln completely paralyzed this general feeling. He destroyed the strength of the position, and divided the North when he declared to the South that slavery should be respected. He built up for the South a strength which otherwise they could never have attained, and it has given them an advocate on the Chicago Platform.

The Cleveland Convention was to have been the open avoval of the condemnation which we had been freely expressing to each other, and which had ben fully known to the President; but in the uncertain condition of affairs, leading men were not found willing to make public a dissatisfaction and condemnation which should have rendered Mr. Lincoln's nomination impossible; and this continued silent and support established for him a character among the people which leaves no choice. United, the Republican party is reasonably secure of succes, divided the result of the Presidential election is at the least doubtful.

I am gentlemen,

Respectfully and truly yours,

J. C. FREMONT.

A St. Louis paper, on the day of the draft, heads its column with the following refrain:

The melancholy days are come,
The saddest of the year,
When drafted men feel verry cheap,
And substitutes are dear.

George H. Pendleton, in a speech made in New York last spring, said "that the prosecution of the war can lead only to union or seperation. If it leads to union, it will lead to an unmitagated despotism.

The Macon Confederate says:—It is said that Hardee's corps, in the late fight at Jonesboro, while it so reroically held at bay six corps of Yankees, killed and wounded fifteen thousand of the enemy. No wonder the soldiers are proud of being under, "Old Reliable."

THE FLAG OF PEACE—The Peace Flag has at last been flung to the breeze in New York city. For the length of an August day it waved from the Cooper Institute, gladdening many a heart with its mute prophecy. Too long had the ensanguined banner of Mars, or the baleful black of abolition waved triumphantly over our city; too long had the emblems of hate and force polluted the pure air of heaven and insulted the sorrows of our people; but at last—harbinger of the drawing of a better day—our eyes, offended by the gloom of the one and the glare of the other, rested on the Flag of Peace with its blessed blazonry and its inspired motto.

The flag, which was the gift of the ladies of New York, was costly and beautiful, worthy of the doners and the cause. It was of spotless white, and in the center a dove was represented bearing an olive branch, and beneath was the inscription, "Peace on earth. Good will toward all men."—Metropolitan Record.

The Confederacy publishes the following:

TRUE, BUT TREASONABLE.—A religious phamphle recently published in Philadelphia says:—"The Anglo-Saxon race kills races of men to get teritory to which it has no claim, makes treaties to plunder those who enter into them, breaks them to get lands, then blows the help less to atoms because they dare to remonstrate and seek self-preservation by force of arms; professes to be the messinger of peace, yet carries a sword even warm with blood, and often with the blood of its own immediate kindred.—Within the last three years it has slain a million and a half of men in a contest between brothers of one family."

Upon which the Mobile News makes the following comments:

"Treasonable it you please, but not true.—This cant about the brotherhood of Yankees and Southrons had a great deal to do about bringing on the war. Had the Yankees not supposed that we were the same craven stock as themselvs, they would have seen us d——d ere they had fought with us. The truth is, the population of the former United States was a mixture, of which the seperate elements were seperating, and, as in the process of crystilization, each particle seeks its lake, what was decent in the Yankee conglomerate had been for two generations or more gathering itself, by the instinct of race, around its kindred stock in the South, its place being meanwhile supplied by the importation of the scum of Europe, until it has been estimated that not one-tenth of the Northern population is decended from the old revolution population. The individual instances of Southern men who have relatives North must not be extended into a fancied relationship of the races, which, as to their bulk, are as distinct as were the Normans and Saxton on the day of the battle of Hastings."

The editor of the Wilmigton Journal, has figured, "on a goat" and "on a dog"—behold him now on a Jackass:

"Lend me your ears."—*Shakespear.*

Adam was a young man—he was a single man for Eve had not yet been created. The world was young, too, but Adam was younger—he was the last crowning work of creation. His rib had not yet been taken from his side, and he therefore felt not the aching void, that nameless want that so soon starts all his masculine decendents upon an eager hunt after *their* lost rib, and renders them discontented until they find it.

And Adam was in Eden, and the birds and the beasts came before him and he named them; and the lordly lion and the graceful stag and the noble horse passed in review; and there came also an animal with long ears, a gay and festive young fellow, and he marched up, slightly cavorting, and when he came opposite to Adam he halted and parted his ears and waited to be named, as the other beasts had been named; and Adam gave him his name also, saying unto him, "You are a Jackass!" and the animal with long ears thought it was a great thing to be a jackass and he said unto himself, "I'm a jackass" and he furthermore laughed and said "haw-a-chaw! haw? ughaw!" And his laugh was joyous, and he was proud. But since that time sin and sorrow have come into the world, and man having lost and found his rib, has been expelled from Eden, and is a conscript, and works hard for his rations, and all nature, animate and inanimate, seems to sympathise with him and suffer for that one great fall, and the song of the nightingale has caught a melancholy tone, and the notes of the jackass have a mournful cadence, the very ghost of that musical laugh with which the original donkey—the primeval *asinus*—made the groves of Eden resound, and the four rivers of paradise to leap and sparkle in their pebbly beds.

Alas for the fleeting hopes of earth! all that's bright must fade, and the brightest still the fleetest. It is no laughing matter to be a donkey now, or a man either, for that matter; and with the lengthening of [y]ears comes sorrow and lamentation. Let us pause.

This instructive fable has been translated by a learned friend from the original Arabic.

The New York correspondent of the London Telegraph refers to Henry Ward Beecher thus:

"I have the greatest difficulty in persuading myself that the course, vulgar, unbearded man who occupies the rostrum in American Dissecting churches, now spouting like an auctioneer, now like a strolling player, now lolling in an arm chair while the hymn is being sung—was a priest of any creed. This, of course, arises from predjudice and from having been brought up in the Church of England. To prejudiced persons the services of the church should be, to certain extent, a mystery, and elevated far beyond the petty environs upon the priest as a man set apart. When their priest is a funny priest, they are apt—in their prejudices—to look upon him not with admiration, but with horror. There is nothing mysterious about the religion of the masses here. The "Episcopal Methodist" have "hot turkey supper celebrations," and the "Chuch of the Holy Trinity" advertises a "clambake feast and strawberry ice cream festival."

The pulpits are draped with party flags, the preacher reeks from the last night's stump oratory, and the printer's devil is waiting with the proof of his last political sermon, to be inserted in the next week's "Independent." Everybody is familiar with the Scriptures; and Scriptural jokes of the most abominable and blasphemost kind are the choisest pearls in the garland of American humor. In fact, the money changers have got into the temple, and there are no means of driving them out; but then the Priests and the Levites have in their turn gone down town, and are great in Wall street and at Tammany.

TRIBUTE OF RESPECT.

Foremost among the mortal heroes of Co. "C." (14th) Texas cavalry, Ector's Brigade, whom it hath pleased an Alwise Providence, to take from us during this war, is color bearer, Henry White, who fell on the 31st day of August, 1862, in the battle of Richmond, Kentucky.

Privates, W. K, Hodges and G. L. Milford, both fell on the 31st day of Dec. 1862, in the battle of Murfresboro, Tennessee.

Private John Wagner, who fell on the 12th July 1863, in the battle of Jackson, Mississippi.

Private Wm. Gregg, who fell on the 19th Sept. 1863, in the battle of Chickamauga, Tenn.

Private John A. Harris, who fell on the 6th day of August 1864, in the defense of Atlanta, Georgia.

Private Daniel Oxsheer, who fell on the 27th of August 1864, in the battle of Chattahoochie river, Georgia.

They were enlisted by Capt. F. H. Garrison, on the 23d Dec. 1861, and since that time, they had been continually with their commands, passing through the perilous campaigns of Arkansas, Mississippi, Kentucky, Tennessee and Georgia, and each of them participating in each of the battles that the regiment was in, up to the date of their fall.

The writer of this humble tribute, knew them well, and was devotedly attached to them, as were also all of their comrades; they were intelligent, kind in disposition, pleasing in manners and appearances, generous to fault, and universally beloved by all who knew them.

We have lost in them seven dear friends; society seven of its brightest ornaments, and our country, seven of its most noble defenders.—

Their comrades deeply sympathize with their relatives, in their irreparable loss.

Oh! our friends are gone, never to return. Let us hope that our hearts may be so pure and bright, that we may meet them in another world.

ONE WHO LOVED THEM.

OBITUARY.

DIED, at her residence, near Henderson, on the 26th Sept. Mrs. E. P. GIBSON, aged forty-five years and nine months.

The deceased was born in Irwinton, Wilkinson Co., Georgia, and was the daughter of the late Mr. Samuel Beall, a man revered for his wisdom and piety. Her mother, a woman worthy of such a husband, still lives to mourn the loss of a daughter, whose proudest boast was, that she never spoke a disrespectful word to her parents. At the age of sixteen, the deceased married Mr. John Gibson. Two years after this marriage, both husband and wife, vowed to live a holy life, and many can witness how well they kept that vow. After a few years of happiness, the God who doeth all things well, called the husband home; the wife was left in a strange land, far from father, mother, brothers and sisters. Three little ones were thrown upon her for protection, and nobly did she buffet with the world for their sakes—early and late, did she instill into their young minds, a love for God and holy things, and, though, she did not live to see the full fruition of her labors, may we not hope that her spirit may yet be permitted to behold their consummation.

For fourteen years, she has been with us, walking in the straight way that leads to Heaven. She was the first at the house of God, and the last to leave the couch of suffering; to all she was kind and gentle, the aged blessed her, and the young honored and loved her. In sorrow and distress, all turned to her for aid and consolation. She who so sympathised with others, is now mourned, as one whose place cannotbe filled

After years of suffering, patiently borne, the weary spirit rests. She faded as the flowers, so gently, that we could not believe her dead, until the destroyer set his seal unmistakably on her calm brow. Like the flowers, she will bloom again in the spring-time, but it will be in the never-ending spring of Heaven.

When she found herself standing on the verge of Eternity, how joyously must her spirit have plumed its wing for its homeward flight; and how blissful the re-union of husband, babe and father with the just glorified soul, and the meeting with, the Savior, whom on earth she adored, in whose footsteps she so meekly trod. Ah! no mortal pen can describe the rapture of that meeting. She is happy, but the children around whom she had thrown the viewless arms of love, and drawn so closely to her sheltering bosom, are now doubly orphaned. In her, they found both father and mother. Alas for them, there still remains, probably, years of suffering and trial, before they, too, can be at peace. But there is a God above, who ruleth all things, and to Him, must they look, for consolation in their great sorrow.

Henderson Times.

J. M. DODSON, Editor and Proprietor.

HENDERSON, RUSK COUNTY TEXAS,

SATURDAY, OCT. 22nd, 1864

☞ We print fifteen or twenty extra copies of the 'Times' every week for gratuitous distribution in the army. We would be obliged to soldiers, from this county, absent on leave or furlough, to call at this office before returning to their command to get the latest issues to carry back with them.

☞ A specie basis store is now in full blast in this place.

☞ On yesterday morning and again this morning we had killing frosts.

☞ Our paper is small this week, but the news is not.

☞ According to "Sioux" the Telegraph correspondent, girls are plentiful in Western Texas, rating, *commercially speaking*, at five to one. Eastern Texas can beat that.

☞ Subscribers can use the margin of the "Times" this week for the purpose of writing negro passes and other small notes.

☞ We are anxious to purchase old merchantile books (Ledgers, Journals or Day-books,) we mean those that have been written up. We will pay a good price, in new issue.

☞ If any body has a half bushel, or even a peck of Irish potatoes that they would dispose of, and wish to get a good trade for subscription to the "Times," or for any thing else under our control, all they have to do is to speak out. We wish them for seed.

☞ A number of our subscribers have inquired of us, if Burke the "Great seed and book Man," at Houston, has any early cabbage seed, and if so, at what price. Will Mr. Burke please answer.

☞ We saw a fellow in town some time since trying to sell corn at $10 per bushel in new issue, who had his dinner in his pocket. Col. Davenport is charging $5 per meal in old issue; this fellow said he wound countenance no such extortion--he is the proper man to lecture on that subject.

SUPERIOR BLACKING.

Capt: A. G. Johnson, of this county, informs us that the best qualtity of blacking for shoes and boots, can be made from the berry of the white shoemake. It is prepared by boiling the the berries down to a strong tea, then straining and again boiling until it becomes of the consistency of fresh cream, when it is to be bottled up for use. Now is the time to gether the berries.

We will mail Extras to those who will deposit money with us, at one dollar each; or we will leave the Extras at the Post Office in this place, where parties desire it. News by telegraph is costly and those who desire it must foot the bill. If we are liberally patonized we we will keep up this arrangement. giving our patrons all the advantages of a Daily paper.

☞ We are authorized to say that Capttain John P. Grigsby, Assessor of Tax in Kind for Rusk Co.. will proceed to the discharge of his duties so soon as the necessary blanks are furnished, which will probably be in a few days.

☞ The following are the casualties in Co. "D." (14th) Texas Regiment, Ector's Brigade, in the recent fighting in the vicinity of Atlanta.

Lt. C. C. Doyle, right thigh broken by solid shot—left thigh severely bruised. Sergt. Z. W. Baily, severely wounded in cheek. T. J. Hunt, severely wounded in small of the back. Wm. Hurst, mortally wounded in lungs—died. W. S W. P. Wallace, mortally wounded in left thigh.

☞ The Quid Nunc in 'number six' Confederate Generals incidentally styles S. S. Printiss the great Southern traitor. If the warm hearted, chivalrous orator and statemen ever said or did any thing to call forth such an epithet as this we are not informed as to the time and place. True he was a Union man, but in the last political speech he ever made, which we believe was in 1850, a short time before his death, he declared that in the event of the withdrawal of the Southern States from the old Union he would be with the South. Some mistake about this; we regret that so unwarranted a [illegible] an elegant and deserved notice of the distinguished Govenor of Louisiana

☞ In last week's paper we expressed the opinion that in the event of McClellan's election some misguided citizens would favor reconstruction, expressing our unqualified condemnation of a movement of this kind Our opposition to reconstruction is not that we believe the McClellan party would fail to guarantee our rights to us under the Constitution—we think we would get all that we demanded for the time being.—But how long would they last? In four years there would be another election, with the chances in favor of all such guaranties being swept away, and a scene such as the last four years has presented, necessary to be re-enacted. No, whilst we are cut loose let us contend to the last. If the Northern States of the Mississippi valley will withdraw from the 'Old Concern,' we would gladly welcome them into our family, provided they would come in on our terms—the Eastern States we would receive upon no terms.

Our settled conviction is that the entire Mississippi valley ought to be under one Government, and we believe, if we are true to ourselves, in the course of time, it will be. Nature so intended it, and her laws, sooner or later, will work out their legitimate effects. Nature has created no affinity between the Mississippi valley and the Eastern States; but she has between the Southern Atlantic States and the Mississippi Valley. In the former case, the interests of the people is diverse, in the latter, they are similar. Texas and South Carolina, unite in the same Government, from natural affinity; Texas and Massachusetts, can only be united by force; such an union can not last. The old Union was to all intents and purposes, dissolved long before the secession of South Carolina. It never can be restored—unnatural force might bring the shattered fragments into a common mass, but it would only be a mixture, every part of which would go toitself so soon as the unnatural restraint was removed.

Man can accomplish wonders if he operates in conjunction with and under the established laws of Providence, but whenever he presumes to override those laws, a fearful fall is the result. The United States Government was a failure because the officials disregarded this great fact, in enacting unnatural and oppressive laws. It is now too late to make amends by retracing false steps—the legitimate effecte has been produced in the destruction of the Goverment. As well attempt to reconstruct a burnt city out of the ashes of the buildings as to reconstruct the United States Government as it was

Old Prices.—This is the theme just now among a large class of our people who have articles for sale or exchange. It is an easy matter to get corn, wheat or meat by giving sugar, coffee, or calico in exchange therefor at old rates. People appear to have forgotton that prices, before the war, were as variable as the wind, in consequence of the supply and demand being greater or or less at given times. We have known wheat, for instance, to sell at 50 cents per bushel one year and the very next at from three to five dollars; we have known cotton to sell at 4 cents per pound and we have known it to sell at 20 cents. There never was any such a thing as fixed prices and never will be while commerce continues. All this cry about exchange at old prices is the veriest humbug ever originated in the South—it is better suited to Yankeedom. Every body wants to sell wheat for sugar at old prices, but we have heard of no one offering thus to exchange, homespun domestic for wheat—eight yards to the bushel, for instance, this would have been the old rates of exchange—wheat at one dollar per bushel and domestic at 12½ cents per yard. The fact is that this cry in favor of exchange at old rates is only made when the party crying out will get a bargain by it. A great majority of our subscribers, living in Rusk county, are willing to exchange provisions to us for subscription at old prices but we have found only one who would thus pay for job work or advertising. The reason of this is that in the one case the subscriber gets a bargain, in the other we would get the bargain according to the rates we charge for such work

Oh consistency, thou art a jewel.

☞ In Mr. Seward's great campaign speech, delivered at Auburn, Sept. 3d, he announces that the emancipation measures of Lincoln, are only for war purposes, and will cease if a State should return to her allegiance to the United States' Government, so far as such state is concerned. Mr Seward says he gives this as his individual opinion, and not by authority of Lincoln—it is all the same Seward's opinion is the policy of the Lincoln dynasty, and *de facto* the Government of the United States, in a "nut shell." This announcement is the strongest evidence we have yet seen, that Lincoln recognizes the fact that he will not be able to "crush the rebellion," and that he entertains serious doubts as to his success in the Presidential campaign. It is a clear back donw, and in direct antagonism to all he has said or done for the past two years.

☞ "Hie, hie, hie, all you that want to get your money back come right along over here! Walk up gentlemen, trot up, run up, crawl up, tumble up roll up—no difference how you get here so you come." In olden times ere the incendaries had laid our flourishing village in ashes we were often enlivened by an harangue after the above style. Old men, young men, boys and all invariably responded by hastening toward the orator, not altogether for the purpose of purchashing the goods and capoodles which, by this time, the inevitable Dyke had displayed in front of the old "Mansion" "just a going, going, go-ing without a better bid." but from fear that they might loose the benefit of some of John's dissertations upon the "*cockadoodles and conflutements.*"

Those were halcyon days—we had almost ceased to think of them, and still fear it may be a long while before we are again permitted to enjoy such, but the running, tumbling and rolling up has been re-enacted, during the past ten days, not in that joyous mode of olden times, but with all the anxiety." This unwonted stir among the populace has been brought about by the issuance of some rather stringent orders, in refference to details and other classes of onecripts by Capt. Bagly Enrolling officer for this county. How long "the fun" is to continue we are not advised, but presume they will get through in a few days.

OUR LATEST.

The glorious news we publish this week is substantially confirmed by the latest telegrams. The enemy are driven from every point they gained around Richmond and Petersburg—our loss slight, that of the enemy heavy. Our forces captured 19 cannon and a large number of prisoners. Our greatest loss was in the death of Gen. Gregg of this State who fell at the head of his Brigade.

Sheridan is terribly used up by Early, and Burrbridge badly whipped in Western Virginia Hood is in Sherman's rear, on the North side of the Chattahooche, and it is reported a portion of his troops have re-occupied Atlanta.

On the 9th Price passed Jefferson City going in a North West direction.

The report of Beast Butler's death, we regret to say, is not confirmed—there is nothing said about it.

TELEGRAPHIC.

Camden, Oct. 18.—Major Blanks and other officers who have just arrived from the other side of the Mississippi river, bring important and reliable dispatches to Head Quarters here. They say that Gen. Early has completely routed Sheridan, and was still in pursuit of his shattered columns, when they left the other side of the river. He captured a great many prisoners, &c. Gen. Hood is now in Sherman's rear and in possession of Marietta, Ga., having defeated the force that Sherman sent back to protect, and keep open his communication. General Lee has defeated Grant, and driven him out of his works in front of Petersburg, capturing all his heavy artillery, and a large number of prisoners. Forrest and Wheeler, have complete control of the Railroad between Chattanooga and Nashville.

President Davis issued orders to all commanders in different portions of the Confederate States to fire a salute of one hundred guns in honor of our grand and brilliant victories.

A letter, dated Warren, Arks., Oct. 15th, was received at Head Quarters this morning. It says:

"The Memphis Bulletin of the 12th inst., is received. It reports the death of Beast Butler. He was killed in the late engagement near Richmond, and his command repulsed with great slaughter, and driven beyond their own works. The Bulletin also states that Sherman has evacuated Atlanta in consequence of Hood's forces being in his rear, and that he would have to fight his way out or surrender his whole army.

The Commanding General here has ordered sixty five guns to be fired in honor of our great and glorious victories.

Masonic Female Institute,
Henderson, Texas, Oct. 20th 1864.

At a meeting of the pupils of the Masonic Female Institute, the following resolutions were adopted:

Whereas, The schoolroom has been deprived of one of its most valued inmates, and the family circle of an affectionate and amiable daughter, by the death of CASSIE HAWKINS, who departed this life October 12th 1864, therefore,

Resolved, That we tender to the Mother and family, our warm and heartfelt sympathy, in their melancholy bereavement.

Resolved. That as a testimony of respect to the memory of the deceased, we wear the usual badge of mourning for thirty days.

Resolved. That we request that these proceedings be published in the Henderson Times and a copy of the same be presented to the Mother of the deceased.

[Shecial corrrespondent of the Rebel.]

Poisoned Texan—After the Battle.

Macon, Miss., Sept. 5, 1864.

At sunset on the 22d July, six miles southeast of Atlanta, the soldiers of Hardee's corps were bearing off the dead and wounded from the battlefield. In silence, as saddening as the melancholy duties of the wearied soldiers, the blood-stained bodies of fallen comrades were wrapped in their blankets and deposited in shallow graves. Anxious faces were grouped about each corps. None smiled, no word was spoken, not a tear fell from eyes that were humid, but never full. Hands blackened with powder, with touch as tender as a woman's, moved aside the tangled masses of hair, often clotted with blood, from the faces of the slain; with keen agonizing earnestness each attendant at the grave gazed upon the features of the fallen. A blanket thrown about the body, leaves strewn over it, and the cold clods enshrouded and coffined the mortal remaines of the true nobility of earth.

A wounded Texan was borne from the battlefield. A poisoned bullet had passed through his thigh. A Chaplain, Mr. C——, of Tennessee, when he looked at the wound and that neither the bone was broken nor the artery severed, rallied the stalwart soldier because of his apparent sadness. For a moment there was no answer, but looking the Chaplain steadily in the face he finally said, in steady tones, "I am dying."—His leg grew black, and soon the discoloration extended to his body. "I do not fear death," said the soldier. "Too often have I feared it." "Pray that God may pardon and bless me, and those I love."

I never heard a more eloquent and touching appeal to the Great Giver of all good, than this which fell from the lips of the man of God.—The body of the dying hero was racked with indescribable torture. A shudder would now and then convulse his muscular frame, but his thoughts were fixed steadily on the Invisible, the Unknown.

When the Chaplain arose, the Texan asked him to write to his wife. "Tell her that my boy may know it, how I died. Clasping his hands across his breast, he yielded up his life as calmly as if he, himself had willed it. Not a musle was distorted. He c l e n c h e d his teeth and closed his eyes and held his limbs motionless by the sheer force of his resistless will. In a moment of time, there was an eternity of agony, but the dying hero triumphed over death, as was his wont over mortal foes. He lay upon his blanket a model of perfect manly beauty.—There was, after dissolution, no trace of pain on his lip or brow. The long heavy lashes lay upon the sunburnt cheek; his long raven locks, damp with the dew of death, clustered profusely around his noble forehead; his firmly set lips, his muscular form, his attitude, that of a hero stricken down by a power which humanity is impotent to resist, were sublimely impressive.—There was no need of tears beside the body of a man like this. His proud and lofty spirit would contemn the spirit to his greatness. Soldiers, conscions of the majesty of departed worth, passed by respectfully with measured tread. "They said the bravest of the brave has fallen."

Shall we vainly imagine the anguish of the wife of such a man, or the utter desolateness of her home? Shall we speculate upon her and mar her moistened eyes and sad face, on which hope shall never smile again? The wakeful nights, when she shall place her cheek against the sweet fatherless child of her love, the efforts to live and impress upon the memory of her boy the virtues of the father—shall we reflect upon all this, and how that boy will hate the race with which coward's cunning and villain's device resorts to poison to give fatality to wounds?

That Texan widow is now an every day history. Its crushing weight is none the less keenly felt by the anguished sufferer. The son, inheriting the spirit of the father, will treasure up his wrongs. There will be two graves, one a shallow one, on a hill side in Northern Georgia, the other among the evergreens of Texas, whose occupants fell by the same murderous hand.

COMMITTED.

To the jail of Rusk county, Texas, on the 15th of October, 1864, two negromen, DANIEL and LEVI. Daniel is black, about thirty years old, about five feet high. Levi is about twety-eight eight years old, black complexion, about five feet three inches high. Both say they belong to Col. Jones, who lives on Black river, Louisiana, but that they were hired to Thos. Carrol, near Hthens, Henderson county, Texas, when they ran away. THOS A. JORDAN, Sh'ff R. C.

Oct. 18th, 1864. [v5:n38 tf.]

The Daily Telegraph

EXTRA.

HOUSTON. APRIL 21, 1865.

BY TELEGRAPH.

SHREVEAORT, April 21.—Gen. Lee with the army of Virginia has surrendered to Gen. Grant. Headquarters Armies of the United States, April 9, 4-30 P. M. To Hon. E. M. Stanton, Secretary of War. Gen. Lee surrendered the army of Northern Virginia this afternoon upon the terms proposed by myself. The accompanying additional correspondence will show the conditions more fully. U. S. GRANT, Lt. Gen'l.

April 9th, 1865.—General, I received your note of this morning on the picket line, whither I had come to meet you and ascertain definitely what terms were embraced in your propositions of yesterday with reference to the surrender of this army. I now request an interview in accordance with the offer contained in yours of yesterday for that purpose.

Very respectfully, your obd't serv't,
R. E. LEE.

CAMP U. S. A., April 9.—To Gen. R. E. Lee Commanding Confederate States Armies:—Your note of this date is but this moment 11:15 A. M., received in consequence of my having passed from the Richmond and Lynchburg railroad to the Danville and Lynchburg railroad. I am at this writing about four miles west of Walter's Church, and will push forward to the front for the purpose of meeting you.

Notice sent to me on this road where you wish the interview to take place will meet me. Very respectfully,
U. S. GRANT, Lt. Gen.

APPOMATOX C. H., April 8.—Gen. R. E. Lee, etc.:—In accordance with the substance of my letter to you of the 8th inst., I propose to receive the surrender of the army of Northern Virginia, on the following terms, to-wit: Rolls of all the officers and men to be made on duplicate, one copy to be given to any officer designated by me, the other to be retained by such officers as you may designate.

The officers to give their individual paroles not to take up arms against the Government of the United States, until properly exchanged, and each company or regiment commanders sign a like parole for the men of their commands. The arms, artillery and public property to be picked, selected and turned over to the officers appointed by me to receive them. This done each officer and man will be allowed to return to their homes, not to be disturbed by the U. S. authorities so long as they observe their parole and the laws in force where they may reside. Respectfully,
U. S. GRANT, Lieut. Gen.

Headq'rs, Army Northern Virginia,
April 9th, 1865.

To Lieut. Gen. Grant.

I have received your letter of this date, containing terms of surrender of the Army of Northern Virginia, as proposed by you, and as they are the same expressed by you in your letter of the 8th inst., they are accepted. I will proceed to designate the proper officers to carry the stipulations into effect. Very respectfully,

(Signed) R. E. LEE, Gen'l.

CLIFTON HOUSE, Va., April 9th.
Hon. E. M. Stanton, Sec'y of War

The following correspondence has taken place between Gen. Lee and myself. There has been no relaxation in pursuit during its pendence. U. S. GRANT, Lt Gen.

APRIL 7, 1865.—Gen. R. E. Lee—The result of the last week must convince you of the hopelessness of further resistance on the part of the Army of Northern Virginia in this struggle. I feel that it is so, and regard it as my duty to shift from myself the responsibility of any further effusion of blood, by asking of you the surrender of that portion of the Confederate States Army, known as the Army of Northern Virginia. Very respectfully,
U. S. GRANT,
Lieut. Gen.

April 7.—General: I have received your note of this date, though not of the opinion you express of the hopelessness of further resistance on the part of the army of Northern Va. I respect your desire to evade the useless effusion of blood, and therefore, before considering your proposition, I ask the terms you will offer of conditions of surrender.

(Signed,) R. E. LEE.

April 8, 1865.—Your note of last evening, in reply to mine of the same date, asking on what conditions I will accept the surrender of the army of Northern Virginia, is received, in reply I would say that peace being my first desire, there is but one condition that I insist on, that the men surrendered shall be disqualified from taking up arms against the government of the United States, until properly exchanged

I will meet you or designate officers to meet any officer you may name, for the same purpose, at any point agreeable to you, for the purpose of arranging definitely the terms on which the surrender of the army of Northern Virginia, will be received. Very respectfully,
U. S. GRANT,
Lieut. Gen.

HD. QRS. ARMIES OF THE C. S. '65.

General: I received at a late hour your note in answer to mine yesterday. I did not intend to propose the surrender of the army of Northern Virginia, but to ask the terms of your proposition. To be frank, I do not think the emergency has arrived to call for a surrender, but as a restoration of peace, should be the sole object of all I desire to know whether your proposals tend to that end.

I cannot therefore meet you with a view to surrender the army of Northern Virginia, but as far as your proposition may affect the Confederate States' army forces under my command and tend to the restoration of peace, I should be pleased to meet you at 10 A. M., to-morrow, at the old stage road to Richmond, between the picket stations of both armies.
R. E. LEE.

April 9, 1865.—Your note of yesterday is received I have no authority to treat on the subject of peace The meeting proposed for 10, a. m., to-day could lead to no good I am equally anxious for peace with yourself, and the whole North entertains the same feelings. Terms upon which peace can be had are well understood by the South.

By laying down their arms they will hasten that most desirable event, save thousands of human lives, and hundreds of millions of property, not yet destroyed. Sincerely hoping that all our difficulties may be settled without the loss of another life, I subscribe myself very respectfully,
U. S. GRANT, Lt. Gen'l.

Headq'rs, Trans-Mississippi Dep't,
Shreveport, La., April 21, '65.

Soldiers of the Trans-Mississippi Army, the crisis of our revolution is at hand, great disasters have overtaken us. The Army of Northern Virginia, and our commander-in-chief are prisoners of war. With you rests the hopes of our nation, upon your action depends the fate of our people.

I appeal to you in the name of the cause you have so heroically maintained, in the name of your firesides and families so dear to you, in the name of your bleeding country whose future is in your hands, show that you are worthy of your position in history, prove to the world that your hearts have not failed in the hour of disas and that to the last moment you will siu the holy cause which has been so iously battled for by your brethren Eastof the Mississippi.

You possess the means of long resisting invasion. You have hopes of succor from abroad. Protract the struggle, and you will surely receive the aid of nations, who already deeply sympathize with you. Stand by your colors, maintain your discipline, the great resources of this department, its vast extent, the numbers the discipline and the efficiency of the army, will secure to our country terms that a proud people can with honor accept, and may under the providence of God be the means of checking the triumph of our enemy, and of securing the final success of our cause.
E. KIRBY SMITH.

SHREVEPORT, April 21.—The New Orleans Times of the 15th, says that Mobile is now in possession of the Union forces, and that Forrest has met with disaster near Eastport. CONSCRIPT.

ELIZABETH STREET, BROWNSVILLE, TEXAS.—[FROM A PHOTOGRAPH.]

THE TEXAS OBSERVER.

JACK DAVIS & H. S. NEWLAND, INDEPENDENT. EDITORS AND PROPRIETORS.

VOLUME I. RUSK, CHEROKEE COUNTY, TEXAS, MARCH 24, 1866. NUMBER 18.

The Texas Observer,
IS PUBLISHED EVERY SATURDAY BY
A. JACKSON.

TERMS OF SUBSCRIPTION.
THE OBSERVER will be furnished to subscribers at $5 per annum, in currency, strictly in advance.

TERMS OF ADVERTISING.

One square, 10 lines or less, for the first insertion	$1 50
Each subsequent insertion	75
Professional or Business Cards, one square or less, one year	15 00
Six Months	10 00
Three Months	7 50
Announcing Candidates—For State or District Offices	15 00
County Offices	7 50
Beat Offices	5 00

A liberal deduction will be made to those who advertise by the year.
The above rates are fixed in National Currency.
☞ We wish it distinctly understood that the money will be required for every thing done in this office.

Business & Professional Cards

For the Observer.

Sketches of the Campaign of 1864.

WALKER'S DIVISION—RETREAT UP RED RIVER—BATTLE OF MANSFIELD.

BY COL. T. R. BONNER, 18th Texas Infantry.

SKETCH No. 1.

"A thousand glorious actions that might claim
Triumphant laurels, and immortal fame,
Confused in clouds of glorious actions lie,
And troops of heroes undistinguished die."
Addison's Campaign.

To make some record of their endurance, prowess and bravery, is due both to the surviving soldiers of the Trans-Mississippi Department, as well as to the memory of their gallant companions in arms, who so fearlessly met their fate in the camp and on the bloody field.

At the solicitation of some—perhaps too partial friends—I have consented to give a few desultory sketches of those movements and scenes which came under my more immediate observation, and "which I saw, and of which I was a part." It would be invidious in me to mention particular instances of individual fortitude and bravery, where every man was a hero; and in the campaigns and battles to which I may refer, I shall attempt to give only their brief outlines and those incidents more immediately connected with Walker's Division of the army, to which I had the honor to belong. Should more particular mention be made of the 18th Texas Infantry, it must be ascribed to the fact that I was connected with that noble body of troops, not for one campaign only, but during the whole period of the war. I shall be content if I can but impress more deeply upon the memory, the toils, hardships and glories of our gallant army, and incite others to record their recollections for the benefit of the future historian.

Though vanquished in the final result, we have the proud satisfaction to know that it was done by a brave and overwhelming foe; and they must and ever will do us the justice to say, that they "met a foeman worthy of their steel."

On the 13th day of March, 1864, the renowned Infantry Division of Maj. Gen. John G. Walker, composed exclusively of Texans, and which then numbered about 5,000 effective men and officers, abandoned its winter encampment near Marksville, La. [illegible] memorable retreat up the Red River valley, before the exulting and boastful legions of Gen. Banks. On the day after our departure, Fort DeRussey, situated on the bank of Red River, three miles from Marksville, was surrendered with its garrison of 400 Texans, after a brief and futile resistance to a combined land and naval force of the enemy. This garrison was composed of detached companies, one from each Regiment of Walker's Division, all under command of Lt. Col. Bird, of the 14th Texas Infantry.

Nothing was saved from the Fort, except two large 32 pounder Parrot guns, which were removed by order of Gen. Taylor, before the arrival of the Federals, and which accompanied our Division on its retreat. These huge guns, transformed into field pieces, and each drawn by a dozen yokes of oxens, presented such a novel appearance, that when first seen by our troops, they created no little merriment. Some witty soldier, incited by the comical idea of artillery being drawn by oxen, exclaimed at the top of his voice, "here goes your *Bull* battery;" and by that appellation these pieces were afterwards known during the entire campaign.

We were closely pressed by the enemy, who sometimes dashed upon the rear of our column, and having no cavalry force, our duties were necessarily much more arduous than they otherwise would have been. In addition to heavy guard and piquet duties, we were frequently compelled to march all night long. About the 20th of March we were joined by the Infantry Division of Gen. Mouton, and by the 2d Louisiana Cavalry, commanded by Col. Vincent. On the night of the 23d, we bivouacked in the piney woods, near Carrol Jones', about 35 miles north-west of Alexandria, which City had already surrendered to Gen. Banks.

Everything now betokened the greatest activity, and the prospect of stirring scenes was brightened every day. Gen. Taylor had taken the field in person, and had immediate command of the whole army. The Missouri and Arkansas Infantry, from Gen. Price's army, had been ordered to reinforce us, and the renowned Cavalry Division of Gen. Green was on the march from Texas and daily expected to arrive. The foe, encouraged by our continued retrogade movements, were becoming bolder and more daring. Our troops, accustomed to retreat, calmly obeyed their leaders, trusting that all would yet be well.—Walker's Division, unlike any other troops in the service, had so often advanced and so frequently retreated, that to do either had become to them alike a matter of indifference.

But while in the camp near Jones', an event occurred which spread a momentary gloom throughout the whole army. The splendid Cavalry Regiment of Col. Vincent, which had so recently joined us, had been posted, under direction of Gen. Taylor, as advanced piquets, on the Alexandria Road. While the Infantry were enjoying their quiet slumbers, the first for nearly two weeks, a large detachment of Federal Cavalry, guided by some traitor, made a circuitous march during the night and attacked Col. Vincent's command in the rear, capturing nearly 400 men, besides the guns and men of Capt. Edgar's Texas Battery. In consequence of this severe loss and the non-arrival of the troops from Texas and Arkansas, Gen. Taylor declined making a stand at this point, which had been previously contemplated. We immediately commenced the retreat, which was continued to four miles beyond Mansfield, on the road to Shreveport.

In the meantime, that magnificent body of Cavalry, known as "Green's Old Division," and three or four other Brigades of Texas Cavalry, all under command of that illustrious hero and chieftain, Gen. Tom Green, had arrived, and were daily engaging the enemy, chastising him whenever he ventured to make a dash upon our slowly retreating columns. The whole country, far and wide, was aroused to the highest pitch of excitement. The inhabitants all along the route of our retreat, were hurriedly quitting their homes, and fleeing before the approach of the invader. Consternation and alarm everywhere prevailed. Old men shouldered their guns and came to our assistance even from the interior of Texas. Notwithstanding every effort had been made by our leaders to collect as much available force as possible to meet the impending danger, yet the great distance of the troops in Arkansas, and the want of facilities for transportation, the advance of Gen. Steele, who had already crossed the Washita River, driving before him the army of Gen. Price, and intending to form a junction, about the middle of April, with Gen. Banks at Shreveport, prevented the concentration of more than 10,000 men at Mansfield. The army of Gen. Banks, in our immediate pursuit, was composed of the 19th Army Corps, with the 16th Army Corps in supporting distance. Besides these two Corps, Admiral Porter, with an immense flotilla of gun boats and transports had ascended Red River to within 40 miles of Shreveport. But with his apparently inadequate force, Gen. Taylor here resolved to give battle, and to this end every preparation was made on the night of the 7th of April.

The sun of the 8th, as it rose majestically in a cloudless sky, presented to the view of the astonished inhabitants of Mansfield [illegible] marching proudly back to meet that foe before whom they had so long retreated. As we passed through the streets of the beautiful town, they were thronged with fair ladies—misses and matrons—who threw their bright garlands at our feet and bade us, in God's name, drive back the Yankees and save their cherished homes. As their cheering songs of the Sunny South fell in accents of sweetest melody upon our ears, we felt that we were indeed "thrice armed," and though greatly outnumbered *would* drive back the foe. Alas! how many brave hearts which thrilled with patriotic emotion that morn, as we marched with flying banners through the town, were stilled in death before the last gleams of that day's sun rested upon the field of carnage! How many strong men, as they listened to the voices of those maidens and thought of their own loved ones at home, had ceased to think, or speak, or breathe, before that day had gone!

At 12 o'clock, our Division, in consequence of the near proximity of the enemy, after marching and counter-marching and manoevering, formed its line of battle in the edge of a large field about four miles from Mansfield, immediately on the right of the road leading to Ft. Jesup. The Division of Gen. Mouton, composed of one Brigade of Texans and one of Louisianians, occupied a similar position on the left of the road and half a mile distant from it. The intervening space between the two Divisions was filled up with several batteries of Artillery, some of which were in position on an eminence a few hundred yards in front of the main line. The Cavalry of Gen. Green, except that portion then skirmishing with the enemy, had been dismounted and occupied the right of our line. Here we remained inactive for about three hours, awaiting the expected attack of the foe, during which time the firing of our cavalry skirmishers became each minute clearer and more distinct.

This calm before the storm—the period which immediately precedes the conflict, when it is apparent that the deadly contest is near at hand—is more trying than even the battle itself. Unsustained by the reckless excitement and wild furor of the actual strife, the strongest mind must then shudder at the fearful thought that a few short moments more may usher the soul into eternity! Fondly, Oh! how fondly do we then recall the homes and loved ones far away, and the heart grows faint and sick with the thought that perhaps for the last time these associations rush upon the memory! In such a moment the hero is lost in the man!

Suddenly, at about the hour of half-past 2 o'clock, we were aroused from our momentary reverie by the rapid firing of the Artillery, followed in quick succession by the loud, long volleys of small arms, on the left of our line, which plainly announced that the work of death had indeed commenced. The Division of the brave but now lamented Gen. Mouton, numbering less than 3,000 men, had attacked a superior force of the enemy in strong position. For 20 minutes the echo of their guns swelled upon the breeze; and for minutes an awful feeling of intense anxiety and suspense filled our minds. The firing ceases—in a few moments a courier comes dashing at full speed over the hill—the dispatch is handed to General Walker—the moment is an anxious one, fraught with eagerness to learn, yet dread to hear the result. But soon the spirit-stirring word of "Victory" is conveyed to us from the General—Mouton had attacked the foe, and though he had himself fallen, and many of his daring soldiers had shared his fate, yet they had born the "Stars and Bars" again to victory. [illegible] of a 1,000 captured Federals and 6 pieces of Artillery, marching towards Mansfield, confirmed the glorious tidings.—Then did our long pent-up suspense give way to the wildest emotions of joy. As the welcome notes of triumph passed from regiment to regiment down to the right of the line, a shout of exultation, loud, and long, and deep, echoed and re-echoed far over the field, bearing congratulations of success to our victorious comrades, and foreboding a repetition of defeat to the astonished foe.

This was the turning point of the whole campaign, and to the indomitable courage and glorious success of this first charge of Mouton's Division, may we safely ascribe that series of brilliant achievements in the valley of the Red River, which shed such additional glory upon the Southern arms. Just at this critical period defeat would have been ruinous. But now, our Division, animated with the reckless exberance of feeling produced by unexpected success, were anxious to be led into action; and as the command "By the right of companies to the front" rang out loud and clear upon the evening air, every man moved quickly off with confident and determined step. Passing through the [illegible]

This momentary stand, however, gave time for the formation of a large Federal reinforcement, consisting of the 16th Army Corps. Entirely unconscious of the arrival of these fresh troops, who had formed at the upper edge of the field, their line extending far over the hills on either side of the road, we pressed on after those we had already defeated. By the time we had passed half way through the field, which enclosed a large peach and plum orchard, our flying foemen had taken shelter behind the line of their reinforcements. Then came the terrible shock. Volley after volley resounded from the hill, and shower after shower of [illegible] came whizzing down upon us. It was utterly impossible to advance, and to retreat beneath the range of their long guns seemed equally as desperate. Never shall I forget that moment, and what soldier was there who can ever cease to remember the "Plum Orchard" fight.—We lay down, arose again, and then involuntarily sought such shelter and protection as the ground afforded. Encouraged by their leaders, our brave men attempted again and again to charge, but human fortitude and human bravery were unequal to the task. Even Napoleon's "Old Guard" itself, in its palmiest days, must have quailed before that terrible fire. The very air seemed dark and hot with balls, and on every side was heard their dull, crushing sound as they struck that swaying mass, tearing through flesh, and bone and sinew. The position of our line could have been traced by our fallen dead. Within a few short moments many a gallant spirit went to its long home! Among these was the young and chivalrous Col. James R. Taylor, from Cherokee County, who commanded the 17th Consolidated Regiment Texas Cavalry, dismounted. His gallant bearing on the battle field had already won for him the admiration of the whole army. Here too, Lt. Col Cannon, of the 22nd, and Major M. A. Gaston and Capt. Jeff. Rogers, of the 18th Texas Infantry, were wounded. In fact every regiment of our Division suffered severe loss in both officers and men.

We were compelled to retire. As soon, however, as we reached the timber, the men were rallied, and though the sun had gone down behind the hills and night was fast closing upon that bloody scene, still it was resolved to make another effort to take the hill. Again the line was formed and the order given to charge. Right gallantly did we commence the task, but the enemy were fully prepared for our reception, and reserved their fire until we had advanced to within 100 yards of their position.—Then their rifles belched forth a bright-red sheet of flame along their whole line, lighting up the expiring day with an uneathly glare, while the the thunders of 10,000 guns resounded through the heavens and seemed to shake the earth to its very centre. For our wearied and almost exhausted troops to oppose such fearful odds with success, was utterly impossible, and the attempt to dislodge the enemy from his stronghold proved as unfortunate as it was ill-advised. Many a brave man, for there were no craven hearts in this last charge, whose life might have been saved to his country and his family, was slain in this vain attempt to drive the enemy. Here the impetuous Col. King, who was created a Brigadier General for his gallant conduct, was severely wounded. Had the battle closed when we first received our check in the orchard, no page in the history of the war would have recorded a more brilliant victory to Southern arms than that of the battle of Mansfield. As it was, much of the prestige of success gained in the day, was lost in the blood of the fearless heroes who fell in this deadly night-charge.

Having retired from the contest, un- [illegible]

From the Houston Papers.

State Convention.

AUSTIN, March 12, 1866.

The ordinance of secession is disposed of by the Convention. Mr. Slaughter's substitute was adopted, and ordered to be engrossed; it reads as follows;

Be it ordained by the people of Texas, in Convention assembled, That we acknowledge the supremacy of the Constitution of the United States and the laws passed in pursuance thereof, and that an ordinance adopted by a former Convention of the people of Texas, on February 1st, 1861, entitled an ordinance to dissolve the Union between the State of Texas and the other States, united under compact styled the Constitution of the United States of America, be and the same is hereby declared null and void, and the right heretofore claimed by the State of Texas to secede from the Union is hereby distinctly renounced.

Congress and the Freedmen's Bureau.

SPEECH OF HON. S. S. MARSHALL, OF ILLINOIS.

The Hon. Mr. Marshall, on the 3rd of February, made a capital speech in opposition to the proposed Bill extending and enlarging the powers of the "Freedmen's Bureau." Mr. Marshall said:

Every dollar that you take from the citizen without warrant of the Constitution is nothing more than robbery. Now what does this bill propose to do? It proposes to establish by Federal power, to be supported by Federal bayonets in all the States of this Union, and in every county thereof, if the Secretary of War sees proper so to do, a separate and independent jurisdiction and government, for the purpose of governing, feeding, clothing, educating and providing homes for the emancipated slaves, and of interfering with and controlling the local government and police of the people of those States; to establish an empire within an empire, providing one government for one race, and another for another.

It is a fundamental principle of American law that the regulation of the local police of all the domestic affairs of a State, belongs to the State itself, and not to the Federal Government. This is a principle which has never been denied until recently. The Federal Government has never attempted to act upon any other principle until this system of measures was inaugurated. Whence comes the power to carry out such measures as this? If no such power is conferred upon the Government by the Federal Constitution, then the attempt to thrust your hands into the pockets of the people to raise the money for this purpose, is, I repeat, nothing more than robbery, and it cannot properly be designated in any other way.

Now, the power to regulate their own domestic institutions and their own local policy is expressly reserved to the States. Sir, the Federal Government has never had any such power. So jealous, indeed were the colonies of this right to regulate and control their internal police, that during the throes of their terrible conflict for independence they refused to surrender to the revolutionary Congress any such power. They did so when the Declaration of Independence was made. They did so when the Articles of Confederation were adopted, and they did so when the Government was formed under which we are now sworn to [illegible] stitution which we are sworn to [illegible]. These facts are trite, but seem to have been forgotten, and men seem to act in these times as if the Government had the power to pass any law whatever without regard to the limitations of the Constitution.

The Convention of Maryland, on the 28th of June, 1776, before the Declaration of Independence was adopted, passed the following resolution:

"That the deputies of said colony, or any three or more of them be authorized and empowered to concur with the other United Colonies, or a majority of them, in declaring the United Colonies, free and independent States, in forming such further compact and confederation between them, in making foreign alliances, and in adopting such other measures as shall be adjudged necessary for securing the liberties of America, and that said colony will hold itself bound by the resolutions of the majority of the United Colonies in the premises:

Provided, *That the sole and exclusive right of regulating the internal government and police of that colony be reserved to the people thereof.*

As this resolution was laid before the Continental Congress some days before the Declaration was adopted, as a limitation upon the powers of the Delegates to bind the State of Maryland, and as an annunciation of the sense in which the people thereof accepted said Declaration.

Other colonies adopted similar resolutions. They were sent to the delegates and presented to the Continental Congress. It was understood at all times, and has been part of the public law of this country, that the Continental Congress acquired no right even during the throes of the revolutionary struggle to interfere with the internal police of the [illegible] of the States.

And, sir, when the Articles of Confederation were formed it was provided in Article two:

"That each State should retain its sovereignty, freedom and independence, and every power, jurisdiction and right which was not, by those articles of confederation, delegated to the United States in Congress assembled.

And when the Federal Constitution was adopted, establishing the Government under which we now live, although by a fair construction of that instrument, any court would have held that the Federal Government thereby acquired no powers except such as were delegated to it by the Constitution itself, yet for fear of a latitudinarian construction an amendment was adopted declaring that

"All the powers not delegated to the United States by the Constitution, nor prohibited by it to the States, are reserved to the States respectively or to the people."

No man who has any regard for the principles of the Constitution will controvert this exposition of the powers of the Federal Government. And as we are sworn here to have regard in all our acts to this great fundamental instrument I again call upon the advocates of the bill to tell me where they find in this Constitution any authority to take uncounted millions of the people's money to feed, clothe, educate, and buy lands and houses for the emancipated negroes of the South; and where the power to usurp the local jurisdiction of the States; and I will cheerfully give way to any one who will undertake to furnish the information.

I know that some have pretended that Congress acquires the powers asserted in this bill by virtue of the second clause of the amendment to the Constitution recently adopted. That amendment is as follows:

"Neither slavery nor involuntary servitude, except as a punishment for crime whereof the party shall be duly convicted, shall exist within the United States, or any place subject to their jurisdiction.

Sec 2. Congress shall have power to enforce this provision by appropriate legislation.

Congress has the power to enforce what? The abolition of slavery. This is not denied. Slavery is abolished throughout the entire land. But Congress has acquired not a particle of additional power other than this by virtue of this amendment. Whether it was right or wrong to abolish slavery in the manner in which it was done, none deny that is now abolished. No one man in the whole land is attempting, by virtue of local law or otherwise, to hold another man in bondage as a slave, in the sense in which this term is used in American law.

The power which one man claims to the service of another—the power to hold him in subjection to his will and sell him as property—that was slavery as understood at the time this section was engrafted into the Constitution.

Now, sir, under this same section, unquestionably if there is any attempt to reduce the men again to this kind of slavery, if any master refuses to allow his former slave to go at large, to have perfect right of locomotion, then it is within the power of the Federal Government, under this clause, to interpose, and to provide by law for a punishment for such an attempt. But, sir, does that empower this Government to correct or interfere with legislation in regard to different classes in the same State, or different peoples in this Government? Unquestionably not. In California legislation discriminates against a class of Asiatics that have settled among them. In the State of Illinois we do not grant to the African race all the privileges and im[illegible]. But, sir, is the black man in Illinois, in consequence of that, a slave? If unjust and unequal laws make all slaves who are injured thereby, then sir, we of the West are all now reduced to slavery.

Although we have the finest country on earth, our people are now borne down almost to the verge of poverty by a system of class legislation. The manufacturers and capitalists of the country, taking advantage of the power they have acquired in the national legislature, have imposed a most unjust and outrageous tariff and financial system upon us, by the combined effect of which the mass of the people in the West are now compelled to pay from two to four times as much for any article of merchandise they buy as they have ever been required to pay in any former time, and while this is so, their grain is rotting in their granaries for want of markets. And yet you have sent your tax gatherers to every man's homestead; they are in every county North and South; they are diving into the cellars, scrambling into the garrets, and prying everywhere, to find something on which to lay their inexorable grasp. Every article that the farmer buys is doubly taxed before it reaches him. A few years ago, during those administrations which the saintly patriots on this floor are so eloquent in denouncing, the poor man of the West could with one dollar by ten yards of the heaviest brown sheeting for his family. Now it takes five dollars to buy the same goods. And, sir, it is no exaggeration to say that of the larger part of this additional four dollars you are literally robbing him by the jugglery of class legislation enacted in part to add to the swollen hoards of the manufacturers of New England, and the bankers, speculators and bond holders of the country.—The farmer is taxed on every thing he eats, drinks or wears, on all that he owns, all that he buys, and all that he sells, on the bed on which he lies down to die, and on the coffin in which he is buried. And even then he does not escape you, for before the clods are settled upon his grave, your tax gatherer lays his grasp upon the heritage he leaves to his children.

All this he might endure if the burdens you impose fell equally upon all classes. But, sir, while the western farmer is thus literally hunted down, the wealthy bond holder, who counts his income by the thousand dollars, is by your legislation actually exempted from taxation, while the lordly manufacturer is protected—yes, that is the word—protected in the privilege of charging for his goods double what they could be bought for if free competition with the world were allowed by your laws. The increase in wealth of these favored classes is without a parallel. Their incomes are more than princely. They dazzle us with their lordly equippages as they dash by us. Their palatial residences whose glittering domes almost kiss the heavens, rise as if by magic, before our astonished gaze. And this political jugglery, this legislative system of robbery, has not only been permitted, but, sir, these laws have been enacted, without so much as a protest from the representatives of the West of the dominant party. These gentlemen have been so much occupied in glorifying and magnifying their own immaculate virtues and rampant patriotism that they have entirely forgotten the interests of their constituents. But, sir, the people of the West are beginning to understand this legislative hocus-pocus by which their money is conjured out of their pockets into the plethoretic coffers of the money lords of the land; and a storm is now gathering that will hurl from their seats many unrighteous patriots, who are so completely absorbed with the contemplation of their exalted virtues that they do not even now suspect the danger.

If, then, unjust legislation makes slaves of those who are wronged thereby, we of the West are this day being subjected and reduced to worse than Egyptian bondage. But this is not the sense in which the word was used in the Constitution. It referred to slavery only as it was known in the Southern States, the system by which one man held another as his property. That system of slavery is abolished, and the Federal Government has the right to see that men are not reduced to that system of slavery, but they have no power beyond that clause of the Constitution.

One of the poetical members of the Alabama legislature concluded a fervid speech as follows: "A man, sir, who would maliciously and in cold blood thus oppress the people, is not fit to live. He should be kicked to death by a jackass, and I'd like to do it."

A shrewd little fellow who had just begun to study Latin astonished his master by the following translation 'Vir, a man; gin, a trap, virgin, a man-trap.

We have beautiful weather to-day.

BRANDING CATTLE ON THE PRAIRIES OF TEXAS—MIRAGE IN THE BACKGROUND.—From a Sketch by James E. Taylor.—See Page 237.

DAILY EXPRESS.
OFFICE—MAIN STREET.

TERMS OF SUBSCRIPTION:

12 Months,	$16,00
6 "	8,00
3 "	4,00

ADVERTISING:
$1,50 per square of eight lines Nonpareal, first insertion; each subsequent insertion 75 cents.

Daily Express

WEEKLY EXPRESS.
ISSUED EVERY THURSDAY.

Terms of Subscription:

12 Months,	$3,00
6 "	1,50
3 "	1,00

Advertisements for Daily and Weekly 25 per cent. discount.

VOL. IV. SAN ANTONIO, TEXAS. FRIDAY. APRIL 22, 1870. NO 95.

TELEGRAPHIC

Domestic.

WASHINGTON, April 15.

A second delegation on the ratification of the Fifteenth Amendment visited the President. The President replied: "I could not say anything to those here assembled this evening, to convince them any further than I have done, of my earnest desire to see the Fifteenth Amendment a part of the Constitution. I will now only add, I hope those enfranchised by it will prove themselves worthy of the benefits conferred on them, and those who have the franchise without it, and that all be mutually benefitted by it. I feel confident that this will be the result, and if I had not thought so I would not have been so anxious for its ratification."

The President recognizes Mr. Bure Consul of France at Charleston; Xavier Weisenbach, Consul of the Swiss Confederation for Louisiana, Alabama, Tennessee, Arkansas, and Mississippi, to reside in New Orleans.

WASHINGTON, April 16.

Revenue receipts to-day $292,000; for the month, to date, $7,500,000.

The Banking and Currency Committee considered the bill increasing currency fifty million dollars. No result.

Foreign.

MADRID, April, 15.

The Spanish clergy persist in their refusal to swear allegiance to the constitution. Though the time within which they are required to take the oath is short, they have till now shown no disposition to yield.

Five men have been executed at Barcelona, for robberies and assassinations committed last month.

VIENNA, April 15.

The new ministry have issued a manifesto of their policy. They say they will endeavor to smooth difficulties end soften asperities, but without departing from constitutional ways or violating imperial rights.

The government will identify itself with the movements for national development on the basis of common right and liberty.

LONDON, April 15.

Newman Hall denies his intention to live in the United States.

Miscellaneous.

LEWISTON, Me., April 15.

The Grand Lodges of the temperance societies rosolved to take no direct action in politics at present.

NEW YORK, April 15.

Good Friday was more generally observed today, than ever before. The produce, exchange, stocks and gold boards and several mercantile and banking houses were closed. The courts adjourned yesterday till Monday.

All Episcopalean and Catholic churches were opened.

CHICAGO, April 15.

The Fenian Congress adjourned sine die, An executive committee of nine succeed it. The names of the members of the committee are to be kept secret for the present.

The expulsion of Richard McCloudy by General O'Neil was unanimously rescinded.

DENVER, Colorado, April 15.

Santa Fe telegrams report new mineral discoveries near Booming Station, New Mexico. The roads are lined with people going to the new mines.

SAN FRANCISCO, April, 15.

The agent of the Tennessee company of planters sent to China to procure laborers for the South, returned by the schooner American and says his mission was unsuccessful.

NEW ORLEANS, April 16.

Gold quoted at 113¼.

WASHINGTON, April 18.

New Mexico will be admitted. This makes thirty-eight States.

HOUSE—The usual number of bills were under regular call—none affecting the South.

In the Supreme Court other business pending, staves off the legal tender argument.

The Judiciary Committee recommend indefinity postponing the bill to prevent prize fighting.

Mr. Kellogg introduced a bill granting lands to the Vicksburg, Baton Reuge and New Orleans Railroad. Referred to the Committee on Public Lands.

Mr. Drake introduced the following as the Sixteenth Amendment:

The United States shall protect each State against domestic violence, whenever it shall be shown to the President such violence exists in such States. Congress shall have power to enforce the amendment.

Mr. Drake moved its reference to the Committee on Military Affairs, but it was finally referred to the Judiciary Committee.

Mr. Morrell introduced the following:

Resolved, The Judicary Committee shall be instructed to inquire whether corrupt means were employed to influence the vote of any Senator on the pending Georgia bill, with power to send for persons and papers. Passed.

INDIANAPOLIS, April 18.

Five inches of snow fell Saturday.

ST. LOUIS, April 18.

Defalcations of the city treasury amount to $167,000.

The rapid rise in the river here broke the main caisson surrounding the east pier of the bridge and the pier is now twenty-four feet under water. Work is progressing finely on the west pier.

PHILADELPHIA, April 18.

The Schuykill rose five feet last night and is still rising. A flood is impending.

COPENHAGEN, April 18.

Gen. R. Raasloeff, Minister of War, has tendered his resignation in consequense of the failure of the treaty for the sale of St. Thomas to the United States.

PARIS, April, 18.

A serious disorder has broken at O'Var, in Portugal. There has been some fighting, and several persons killed and wounded.

There has been a terrible water famine in Jerusalem. Dearth of this necessary has long been the great drawback of that city, and last year Miss Burdett Coutts, with extraordinary munificence, offered to spend £30,000 in providing it. The Turkish Government, from some ridiculous feeling of jealousy, it is supposed, declined the offer, and hinted its intention of taking measures to supply the want. However, nothing has been done, and latterly the distress has been terrible.

OFFICIAL.

LAWS OF THE UNITED STATES,

Passed at the Second Session of the Forty-First Congress.

ADDITIONAL CONVENTION.

To the Convention concluded on the 7th—24th November, 1868, between the general Post office of the United States of America and the General Post office of the United Kingdom of Great Britain and Ireland.

An additional Convention between the General Post office of the United States of America and the General Post office of the United Kingdom of Great Britain and Ireland naving established a reduced charge of six cents per ounce, or per thirty grammes, for the sea conveyance across Atlantic of letters sent in closed mails through the United Kingdom, the undersigned duly authorized by their respective governments, have agreed upon the following articles:

ARTICLE 1.

The postage to be collected in the United Kingdom upon paid letters posted in the Unlted Kingdom, addressed to the United States, as well as upon unpaid letters posted in the United States addressed to the United Kingdom, shall be three pence per half ounce or fraction of an ounce. Reciprocally, the postage to be collected in the United States upon paid letters posted in the United States addressed to the United Kingdom, as well as upon unpaid letters posted in the United Kingdom addressed to the United States, shall be six cents per fifteen grammes or fraction of fifteen grammes.

ARTICLE 2.

The British Post office shall account to the United States Post Office for ten cents an ounce on all paid international letters sent to the United States, and for ten cents an ounce on all unpaid international letters received from the United States; and the United States Postoffice shall account to the British Postoffice for ten cents an ounce on all paid international letters sent to the United Kingdom, and for ten cents an ounce for all unpaid international letters received from the United Kingdom.

ARTICLE 3.

Every internotional letter insufficiently paid, or wholly unpaid, received in the United Kingdom from the United States shall, in addition to the deficient postage, be subject to a fine of three pence, to be retained by the Postoffice; and every international letter insufficiently paid or wholly unpaid, received in the United States from the United Kingdom, shall in addition to the deficient postage, be subject to a fine of six cents, such fine to be retained by the United States Post Office.

ARTICLE 4.

The charge for the sea conveyance across the Atlantic of letters sent in closed mails through the United Kingdom, or through the United States, shall be computed at six cents per ounce or per thirty grammes.

ARTICLE 5.

The conditions of the convention agreed upon between the Post Department of the United States of America and the General Postoffice of the United Kingdom, signed at London the eigth day of November, and in Washington the twenty-fourth day of November, A. D., eighteen hundred and sixty-eight, so far as they are contrary to the preceding articles, are repealed.

ARTICLE 6.

The present convention, which shall be considered as additional to the convention of the 7th of November, 1867, shall come into operation on the first day of January, one thousand eight hundred and seventy.

Done in duplicate, and signed in Lon- the fourteenth day of December, eighteen hundred and sixty-nine, and Washington the third day of the same month.

[SEAL.] JNO A J CRESWELL,
Postmaster General.
HARTINGTON,
Postmaster General of the United Kingdom

I hereby approve the aforegoing convention, and in testimony thereof I have caused the seal of the United States to be affixed,

[U. S. SEAL] U. S. GRANT.

By the President:

HAMILTON FISH, Secretary of State.
Washington, December 3, 1869.

Notice.

All purchasers of land from the City of San Antonio, their agents or legal representatives, in cases where payments of principal or interest, or any part thereof, have been made in Confederate currency, or depreciated paper, and where interest is due and unpaid on such purchases, are required to come forward and make settlement. In accordance with city ordinance passed January 31st, 1870, and duly published, time is granted for settlement until the 1st day of May, 1870; after which time suits are authorized, and will be instituted against all delinquents.

In the absence of Davis & Murphy, Attorneys employed by the city, settlement may be made with

THO'S S. HARRISON,
Attorney at Law.
25-3-70d30d.)

The Daily Express.

A. SIEMERING & CO., Publishers.

STANLEY WELCH, Editor.

Official Journal of the United States.

Official Journal of Bexar County and City of San Antonio.

FRIDAY, APRIL 22, 1870.

Our Prospects.

By careful inquiry among the farmers who come to town, we learn that the fears expressed in regard to the evil affects of our late frosts are somewhat exaggerated. They speak of some little detriment to a few exposed localities, but taken generally speak hopefully and confidently of good crops.

Our seasonable and timely rains, together with the absence of winter severities, have caused all of our agriculturalists to strike out with renewed zeal and vigor, to reap from Dame Nature what she so generously bestows.

Old settlers and those who chanced to travel through the country many years ago, say that the country looks now as then a perfect garden of loveliness. In our raubbles ourselves, we have noticed unusual quantities of wild flowers that run riot over our vast prairies, and give it a bewildering fairy land semblance, to gladden not only the eye, but to touch the heart with those mystic influences that nature and nature's God evince in all their conceptions.

This brightness coupled with assurances of internal peace, fostered by an honest and incorruptible State Government, laboring for our weal, may well combine to put us in a good humor with ourselves and all others around us, and implant within us sentiments of gratitude to a merciful dispenser of all our blessings. In the great future to come when Texas shall have carried her standard to the heights now occupied by her more advanced sister States, may we look back to the prosperity of the year 1870 and from it date a period of uninterrupted good fortune.

All we need now is strong hands and willing hearts, and the problem that a few years ago agitated our people, as to whether Texas could be of utility to the general Government, will have solved itself by its showing of wonderful resources and its contributing of heavy revenues.

What can be Done.

The question of a railroad and the improvements it will bring with it, has been discussed by our populace thoroughly and freely, and yet we are as far off to-day from the reaching of our desires, as when we first began.

Now we do not desire the agitation of the railroad question to pass out of mind entirely, but we *do think* it unfair, that it should engross all of our attention, when there is so much else that can be done to improve our internal condition, while we are waiting for the railroad. On every side of us we see plain evidences of being behind the age, just one hundred years. Take for example what should be our first care and consideration, our public schools, true they have improved a little in the last few years, but are still far below the standard that our numerical strength and monied ability should have made them. We have not a school house, that is town property in the place, and the youth of the period are destined to grow up in almost utter ignorance, because we "lie supinely on our backs," and allow the matter to await railroads.

All through other countries we take the evidence of the prosperity of the people and of communities, from the standing of their public works; we in fact defy the producing of a single instance, wherein a community possessed of good public schools is not a flourishing place. Now what difficulties lay in our way, that from twelve to fifteen thousand people cannot have institutions of learning in keeping with the growth of the place? None that we can conceive of, save the old inert way our people have of "taking things easy."

This may have done in the past, but in a future wherein every disposition is shown to move onward with almost electrical rapidity, some other course is necessary, and we call upon our good people, our princely merchants, and our *well-wishers*, to take the matter in hand, at once, and evince a care for the education of those who are to live after us, and keep up the impetus of our growing city.

We want good schools with ample room, and with good teachers. The few paltry dollars invested, will return to your coffers with three fold interest, in the moral effect it will have upon dormant energies.

Again we want a town hall, one that shall combine utility with ornament; our Mayor, and our city counsellor, our Judges and other civil dignitares, are now crowded into filthy leaking hovels that can but detract from the dignity of the positions they hold in the eyes of any community.

If here again the paltry expenditure is the stumbling block, we can show a dozen plans how the thing can be made to pay. For instance build it so as to have a public hall wherein lectures, scientific, or otherwise may be given. Celebrations of societies, public gatherings, all will serve to provide a rental revenue that will pay interest on the money, and reduce the principal also. The Casino and Muench hall are now the only places that can be procured; the first mentioned suits very well, but belongs already to an institution who occupy it three-fourths of the time; the other is but an apology for a hall, it is small and in every way inconvenient. Come then worthy citizens, put on your thinking caps and let us be able to chronicle before long the fact of your making an effort in this, what seems to us, a move in the right direction.

By despatches received this morning we condense the order No. 74, of General Reynolds, in which he turns over to the civil authorities the State at large.

After citing the act of Congress, as approved March 30th 1870, he says:

"By virtue of the above act of Congress, the State of Texas resumes her practical relations to the National Government. All authority conferred upon the commander of the fifth military district, State of Texas, by the reconstruction l ws is hereby remitted to the civil authorities." Dated Austin, April 16th 1870.

Practically the passage of the act above alluded to gave us all that this order has given us, but we cannot forbear from returning to a subject so pleasing to us all, and enjoying as it were this long contemplated day of returning to the fair companionship of our sister States, with every right guaranteed to us that are originally heir looms of our grand old Constitution. While upon the subject we cannot forbear to remark that military rule is everything but pleasant, but in General J. J. Reynolds we have found the courteous gentleman and good statesman, so intimately blended in his composition as the military man, that we have suffered but scarcely any of the ills that the supersedure of civil by military authority generally gives. The gratitude of a warm hearted constituency will always be with him for his abilities shown, and his honorable course maintained.

And now for a good start. In a short time our legislature meets, and action will be taken upon all the matters of interest to the people east, west, north, and south in our State. We shall try to urge upon the public from time to time such measures as demand immediate attention. Our railroads, protection of our frontier, our public schools, and other internal improvements, that taken hold of in a proper spirit, will carry us up to a fair standard of excellence. All eyes are turned in direction of our able Governor, Edmund J. Davis; rest assured the country will have no fault to find with him, for if ever a man meant work, and work stamped with the impress of progressive ability, that man is he who so calmly stands at the helm of our ship of State, braced for any shock and able to ride our buoyant vessel over the turbulent waves of political malignity, and corruption, and anchor us safely in the harbor of peace and prosperity.

Exit Pere Hyacinthe.

The Pope has issued a decree secularizing Pere Hyacinthe, which, the cable mysteriously informs us, is "satisfactory to all parties." Pere Hyacinthe is, therefore, no longer a priest or a member of any religious ordes, but is simple, as before his ordination, M. Charles Loyson, a Catholic, without, however, resting under any ban or disgrace. Had he designed to enter the ministry of any Protestant Church, he would probably have preferred excommunication outright. The report confirms Pere Hyacinthe's declarations, while in this country, that he desired to remain a Catholic. Remaining a Catholic and no longer a priest, there would seem to be a necessity that a person of Mr. Loyson's great oratorical abilities should either enter upon political life, for which his talents and genius fit him in many respects, or return to the role of a teacher or professor, in which he spent the years preceding his debut as a pulpit orator.

If the story be true that Pere Hyacinthe's affections had been won from celibacy and the priesthood by a beautiful and accomplished lady of Boston, Mass., whom he has purposed to marry upon being released from the vows of the Church, we can easily account, not only for his visit to America, and, while in America, to Boston, but for the express satisfaction with which he and his friends receive the Pope's disposition of his case. If this be the direction in which the Hyacinthine zephyrs are blowing at present, they may be expected soon to waft again his fragrance to our shores. Verily, Solomon spoke from experience and with profound knowledge of his subject, when he declared that "There are three things which we cannot comprehend; yea, four that are past finding out: the way of an eagle in the air, the way of a serpent on a rock, the way of a ship in the sea, and the way of a man with a maid." We embrace this occasion to renew to the Pope the assurance of our distinguished consideration for the Church he represents, particularly in that feature of its discipline which ceases to look for works of vital piety in a man after he has fallen in love.

Old "Pap" Thomas.

HIS VIEWS OF SWEETHEARTS AND WAR.

Col. Watkins married the daughter of Gen. Rousseau about the close of the war—died in New Orleans, and his body was brought with that of his distinguished father-in-law, a few months ago, for interment in the beautiful cemetery at Cave Hill, Louisville. Just after the battle of Nashville, Col. Watkins, on Gen. Thomas' staff approached the General with a free and cordial manner, as if the request he was about to make could not be denied. "General, you know I have a sweetheart, Miss——Rousseau, whom I have not seen for——months. A leave of absence if you please, for——weeks." To the dismay of poor Watkins, Thomas shrugged his shoulders. Watkins, seeing that some intercession was necessary, reminded the General of his youth, the ardor of such years and such attachments, and referred to some probable history of the General in such matters. General Thomas quietly and soldierly replied: "Watkins, I've been there, and the truth is, that I, too, have a sweetheart, and have not seen her for weeks. And what is more, I have been married to my sweetheart, and want to see her as much as you do yours, and it is likely more. But I won't let her come to camp. A camp is no place fo a wife. She is out of her element, and it softens man. And I won't go to see my wife till my duty is ended and the war over. What I will not do myself I will not allow you to do. Besides, I have a 'raid' to make in Mississippi and Louisiana, and I decided this morning that you were the man to lead it. You will please report for duty at 6 A. M.

Southy says, in one of his letters, "I have told you of the Spaniard who always puts on his spectacles when he was about to eat cherries, that they might look the bigger and more tempting. In like manner, I make the most of my enjoyments, and though I do not cast my cares away, I pack them in as little compass as I can, and carry them as conveniently as I can for myself, and never let them annoy others."

It cost a New York dog $400 to bite a little girl.

DAILY DALLAS HERALD.

VOL. 1. DALLAS, TEXAS, SATURDAY MORNING, MARCH 22, 1873. NO. 35.

THE DAILY HERALD,

PUBLISHED EVERY MORNING BY

JNO. W. SWINDELLS & CO.

JNO.W.SWINDELLS. D.M'CALEB.

Terms of Subscription.

(PAYABLE IN ADVANCE.)

One year,	$10 00
Six months,	6 00
Three months,	4 00

Advertising.

One Square (ten lines of this size type) one insertion, $1. Each subsequent insertion, 50 cents.

Special Notices, next to reading matter, $1 50 per square each insertion. Local Notices in reading or editorial columns, 20 cents per line each insertion.

☞Special reduced rates made for longer periods

☞Advertisements payable in advance, unless with those doing a regular business under contract.

THE WEEKLY HERALD

IS PUBLISHED EVERY SATURDAY MORNING.

TERMS.—$2 50 per annum, or $1 50 for six months, in advance.

J. W. SWINDELLS & CO.

Official Directory.

DISTRICT OFFICERS.

HON. HARDIN HART, Dallas, Judge 14th Judicial District.
JNO. T. AULT, Esq., Dallas, District Attorney.

OFFICERS OF DALLAS COUNTY.

JOHN D. KERFOOT, Dallas, J. P. Precinct 1.
ROBERT S. GUY, Lancaster, " " 2.
MEREDITH MYERS, " " 3.
WILLIAM J. HALSELL, " " 4.
C. C. HUSTEAD, " " 5.
JOHN M. LAWS, Clerk of the District Court.
Z. E. COOMBES, } Deputy Clerks.
HENRY BOLL, }
JERE. M. BROWN, Sheriff.
M. V. COLE, Treasurer.
N. A. KEEN, County Surveyor.

CITY OFFICERS.

BEN. LONG, Mayor | JAS. H. FIELD, City Att'y
HENRY BOLL, Treasurer, | THOS. FLYNN, Marshal,
C. S. MITCHELL, Sec'y, | D. KING, Ass'or & Coll'or

ALDERMEN.—E. P. Bryan, C. Capy, G. M. Swink, Frank Austin, M. Thevenet, W. H. Gaston, Jno. W. Lane, A. M. Cochran.

SOCIETIES.

DALLAS CHAPTER, No. 47, Royal Arch Masons will meet at the Masonic Hall in the city of Dallas on the 1st Monday after the last Saturday in each month. WM. C. YOUNG, M. E. H. G.
HENRY BALL, Sect'y.

DALLAS COMMANDERY, No. 6, Knights Templar, will meet at the Asylum, in the town of Dallas, on the Thursday after the last Saturday in each month, at early candle-light.
E. G. BOWER, E. C.
J. E. BARKLEY, Recorder.

Companions. You are hereby summoned to attend a Stated convocation of Dallas Chapter, No. 47, on Monday evening, Dec. 30, 1872, at early candle lighting. By command of the M. E. H. P. THOS. WALKER, Secretary

TANNEHILL LODGE, No. 52, F. A. M., meets on the second and last Saturday of each month, at the Masonic Hall
HENRY BOLL, W. M.
RICHARD MORGAN, Sec'y.

RIDGELY ENCAMPMENT, No. 25, I. O. O. F., meets on the first and third Friday nights of each month, at the Odd Fellows' Hall.
F. A. SAYRE, C. P.
Attest: J. D. KERFOOT, Scribe.

DALLAS LODGE, No. 44, I. O. O. F., meets on every Wednesday night, at the Odd Fellows' Hall. E. W. HUNT, N. G.
F. H. DAVENPORT, Secretary.

THE DAILY HERALD.

D. McCALEB, Editor.

Our Agents.

Who are authorized to receive subscriptions and advertising for the Daily and Weekly HERALD:

J. C. Chew, 300 Broadway, New York; G. P Rowell & Co., 41, Park Row New York; Coe Weatherill & Co., Philadeldhia; Griffin & Hoffman, Baltimore; T. McIntyre, New Orleans; E. H Cushing, Houston; Hon. Jno. W. Lane, Austin.

DALLAS COUNTY.

INFORMATION FOR EMIGRANTS.

We have come to the conclusion that the best way to give information to emigrants is by answering such questions as are propounded by persons desiring to come to this country. In doing so we shall say something that we once thought was known to all the world "and the rest of mankind." People of this country who are not in the habit of receiving letters of inquiry can form no adequate idea of the ignorance that prevails in other States in reference to this country. Almost everybody knows that Texas is a good country, and especially Northwest Texas. It is tolerably well known that this is the only country in the world where both wheat and cotton grow to perfection; that we have a fertile soil, a healthy and salubrious climate are facts of general notoriety. But as to the products of this country, beyond wheat and cotton, the railroad facilities, the size of towns and cities, the churches, schoolhouses, public libraries, newspapers and state of society in general, they know absolutely nothing.

The questions that are asked about this county and city are not only surprising but mortifying. What do the citizens of this enterprising and flourishing city think of intelligent men in enlightened countries asking such questions as "How far are you from a railroad?" "How far from the Texas and Pacific railroad? Have you a newspaper published in your town?"

To many of our citizens it will seem incredible, but it is nevertheless true that scarcely a day passes that we do not receive a letter asking us if we have a newspaper published at Dallas, and if so, please send them a copy.

Have we a "newspaper" published in Dallas? Yes; we have three spicy weekly papers, and as live a daily as can be found anywhere, and hope soon to have a large book printing and binding establishment, and then we intend to print five hundred thousand copies of "What we know about Texas," and what everybody else ought to know. We will give some questions in the letters lying before us, and brief and truthful answers:

"Have you a good farming country?"

We have; wheat, corn, cotton, oats, rye, barely, millet and hungarian grass all grow finely in this county.

"Can you raise vegetables in your part of the country?"

We can raise every vegetable that grows in the temperate zone, and many that belong to the torid zone.

"Can you grow fruit in your country?"

For peaches this country is superior to any country we ever saw. Pears, plums, appricots and grapes grow very finely, and bananas and figs have been successfully grown in this country.

"Have you a good country for stock raising?"

Not in the sense in which stock raising is usually understood in Texas, that is to try to raise them on the range without any food; this is a prairie country, but it is being rapidly fenced up, so that the range will shortly be destroyed; but this is a very healthy country for cattle, and in the future it will pay to feed cattle in this coutry.

"What are lands worth?"

Lands in this county, first-class black-waxy soil from two to twenty feet deep, convenient to railroads, wood and water, are worth from four to eight dollars per acre.

"Is that a good country for mechanics?"

It is, especially for carpenters; a great deal of building is going on in this country, and more than four thousand people have settled in the city of Dallas within the last twelve months. There is a great demand for brick-masons in this city.

"What is the population of Dallas? Is it improving? Is it on the Trinity river—do boats ever run to Dallas?"

Dallas is on the east side of the Trinity river, and has a population of about 7,000—it has more than doubled itself within the last twelve months and is improving very rapidly—steamboats have run to Dallas but, on account of the snags in the river, navigation has for the present been abandoned.

"What are your Railroad facilities and prospects?"

The Houston & Texas Central Railroad runs through this city, and connects with the M. K. & T. at Red River, thus placing us in direct communication both with Galveston on the Gulf, and Saint Louis. The Texas & Pacific road is graded from here to Longview, the present terminus of that road. The track is being laid from here East, and we will soon be in direct communication with Jefferson, New Orleans, Memphis and Vicksburg. The Dallas & Wichita road has been commenced, running from here northwest. We will probably have the St. Louis, Springfield & Rio del Norte road, running thro' this county from Northeast to Southwest, and these with the Dallas & Palistine road, running from here to the Southeast, we will have railroads pointing to Dallas, not from the four, but from the *eight* points of the compass.

GALVESTON.—Mr. C. W. Hurley, an old merchant, (though a young man) has been elected Mayor of Galveston by a majority of 19 votes, over Mr. R. L. Fulton. The City Council stands politically, 7 Democrats to 5 Republicans. The cumulative system of voting was introduced in that election, thus giving the minority a representative.

Our thanks are due, and are hereby tendered to E. H. Cushing, Esq., Houston, for a piece of new music, entitled "O, let me breathe the air," a ballad; poetry from "Paradise and the Pere," in Tom Moore's Lallah Rookh; E. H. Cushing, publisher.

Also, to C. T. Sisson, Esq., Music Dealer, Austin, for the following pieces: "Ye Merry Birds," "Rudolf's Clange Waltz," "Tripping Schottische," "Amaryh's" "Bolero."

Judge H. G Hendricks, an old citizen of Northern Texas, and for several years past a resident of Fort Worth, died in that place last week.

TWO WOMEN ON THE BLOCK.

The Awful End of the Baby Farmers of Naples—The Necks of Two Murderesses Bared to the Axe—Rose Porro and Margarite Coraldi Expiating their Unparalleled Crimes.

The two bady farmers of Naples, whose appalling crimes have already been narrated in the volumes of the "North-East Georgian," recently paid the penalty for their deeds on the block in the Castle d'Nove, near Naples. The prisoners were brought before a judge and jury, and after a brief trial, during which the most revolting details of their terrible crime were elicited, both Rose and Porro and Margarite Coraldi were sentenced to death. The scene in the court room on their being pronounced guilty was effecting in the extreme, the women sobbing hysterically and kneeling in the dock to supplicate for mercy. A Naples letter thus describes the execution:

Early yesterday morning, when hardly a soul was astir in the narrow and boisterous thoroughfares of Naples, an omnious looking vehicle stood in front of the Perfect's chamber, near the Chiaja. On the uppermost floor of the prison is the chapel, where the condemned women were attending mass—their last mass—and the mourning strains of the "Miserere," chanted by the Sisters in the choir, could be heard gloomily wafting through the long coridors. The prisoners, still in black, knelt near the altar, and, at the appointed time, received their last communion.

TO THE EXECUTION.

Towards half-past six the prisoners flanked by an escort of ten gendarmes and preceded by three clergymen, move from the chapel to the van in front of the prison door. The van contained the prisoners, the chaplain and two assistants, two Sisters of Chariey, the prefect and his lieutenant and the usual guards on the outside. While the van was rolling over the pavement on its way to the Castle d'Nove, which is built right on the edge of the Bay of Naples, many harsh comments were made from groups of stragglers, while an occasional merciful one vouchsafed an ejaculation such as "The Lord have mercy upon them!" for well they all knew the mission of the rusty wheeled black van of the prison. During the tedious drive the prisoners prayed and sobbed alternately, and spoke little and only in whispers to the kind Sisters of Charity, who never ceased offering them religious consolation.

A guard of policemen occupied the gates of Castle d'Nove, and doffed their hats when the van drove up and the perfect made his appearance. The gates being thrown open, the prisoners were led thro' a long, stony passageway, darkened by high walls. Upon reaching the rooms of the jailor,

THE SISTERS,

assisted by other women, removed the cloaks and bonnets of the prisoners. The priests, sisters of charity and prisoners then knelt and prayed, the officers standing round with bowed and uncovered heads. At the close of the prayers for the dying, the executioner appeared, wearing a black mask and black single shirt. Assisted by the jailor, the executioner pinioned the arms of the criminals. The plain white collars around the doomed women's necks were removed, and all being ready, the living cortege moved through two passageways until the place of execution presented itself. It was a very unique sight.

At the extremity of a small, stone-surrounded and stone-bottomed yard is a flat rock shaped into a platform about eight feet square and two in height. On one end of this old stage, upon which only the last act is ever performed, there is a very narrow step, for only the executioner and his help, the jailer, use it. In the centre of the platform stood a block, the old block mentioned above, with a little bolt or hook in front for fastening the neck securely. The unfortunate women, when confronting this scene, prayed aloud and cried hysterically. The usual prayers were recited, and, when concluded, the jailor passed to the executioner a long instrument in an ancient looking scabbard of leather covered with steel and brass platings. The executioner, though evidently a young man, seemed familiar with the paraphernalia of his sorrowful craft. He adroitly unclased the heavy scabbard, drew forth a large,

GLISTENING AXE.

with a blade like a collossal razor, and took up his position on the rear of the platform. The criminal s eyes were bandaged with long strips of linen, which left enough to bind the head to the block.

Rose Porro was first conducted to the block, and when the jailer was about to place the linen over her eyes, she staggered back, and made a violent movement with her arms as if she would burst her pinions. But the chaplain's voice calmed her, and according to his admonition she repeated the Divine prayer, "Into Thy hands, O Lord, I commend my spirit," and fell upon her knees.

Margarite Coraldi was removed to the entrance of the yard, and prevented from witnessing her accomplice's death. The prison bell of Castle d'Novo was now tolling slowly, the clergy and nuns were praying fervently. and Rose Porro's white neck was made fast to the block; and exposed to the glittering axe of the executioner.

The chief warden of the castle, who may be called a sheriff, came near the platform in company with two medical men and the Sindaco. The chief warden motioned to all present to preserve strict silence, and then turning towards the executioner he raised his right hand—the signal for the fatal blow. The executioner, whose work had been staring weirdly at the sheriff awaiting that signal, lifted his weapon and stepped to the leff side of the prisoner. He raised the axe about one foot from the neck of Rose Porro by way of taking aim, and then swinging above her head, he brought the heavy blade down with all his might, and

THE HEAD DROPPED OVER THE BLOCK.

The trunk rose nearly a foot and a half, as if living, by the sudden spasmodic action of the severed nerves. a litter was immediately at hand, and the trunk and head of what was Rose Porro, the famous baby farmer, was removed, and Margarite Coraldi was led to the block. She prayed constantly, and did not evince any great fear until her head was forced on the fatal stann, when she uttered a brief, nervous scream. Her head was not completely severed at the first blow. The skin of the front of the neck remained uncut, and the body, springing back, exposed a ghastly gap which made every spectator shudder, and caused the platform to be smeared with blood. A pall was thrown over the body and its head, and both were removed in a litter to await, like Porro's corpse, burial in unconsecrated ground. The fulfilling of the executioner's contract was to wipe and whet the axe he used, and replace it in the scabbard fit for future emergencies.

THE SISTER OF EDGAR A. POE.—Miss Rosalie Poe writes the following note to the editor of the Newark (N. J.) Advertiser:

OAKLAND, Feb. 4, 1873.

KIND SIR:—I see a piece in your paper headed "Poe's Sister." There is a slight mistake in it. You say that Miss Poe is on James River. Mis Poe is living in Mathews county Va., and her post office is Hick's Wharf, Mathews county, Va. Any contribution to you will be thankfully received when forwarded to me, as I am in destitute circumstances, an invalid, and quite helpless at times, and need the comforts of a home. Yours respectfully,

ROSALIE POE.

Mrs. Martha Roberts, of Boon county, can boast of 192 children, grand children and great grand children—172 of whom are now living.

A TEXAS CATTLE RAID.

There are two sorts of cattle-thieves in the far Southwest—the wandering Indian tribes, and the white and half-breed marauders who come across the border from Mexico. They make their incursions in well-organized and well-mounted bands, generally under cover of darkness, and endeavor to get back across the border before the settlers can gather in sufficient number to make a successful pursuit. These predatory invasions are a source of great loss and vexation to the Texans who live within striking reach of the border, thousands of cattle being run off in this way every year. A very graphic representation of one of these raids is given in our illustration on page 100.

CATTLE RAID ON THE TEXAS BORDER.—[See Page 107.]

THE TEXAS CATTLE TRADE—GUARDING THE HERD.

THE TEXAS CATTLE TRADE.

The larger drawing on this page represents the interior of a cattle ranch on the northwestern frontier of Texas. A rude but comfortable log-cabin gives shelter to the herdsmen, who are, as a rule, generous, warm-hearted, brave, and fond of adventure. A stranger entering their camp might mistake them for lawless and dangerous characters, but they must not be judged by their rough appearance. Good comradeship, devotion, and disinterestedness are the rule among them, and hospitality is a sacred law. Nowhere is a traveler more cordially welcomed or more hospitably entertained than at a Texas cattle ranch. Indefatigable and excellent riders, they are perfectly familiar with the topography of the country over which they are continually roving, and as they are always well armed, and skillful in the use of the rifle and pistol, they are more dreaded by the Indians than all the United States soldiers ever sent into the State.

A herd of cattle is called a "bunch," and varies in number from five hundred up to ten or

THE TEXAS CATTLE TRADE—CALLING THE NIGHT GUARD.

SKETCHES IN THE FAR WEST—CURING HIDES AND BONES.

such places to protect the station against raids. Our second illustration shows a phase of the restless life led by many families in the far West. They are constantly on the go. From Arkansas to Texas, from Texas to Arkansas, and so back and forth, they wander up and down the face of the earth until the pilgrimage of life is ended. They are the genuine American nomads, as unsettled and restless as gypsies. The route usually taken by these "pilgrims" runs from Arkansas through the Indian Territory to Eastern and Northwestern Texas, and from three to four months are consumed in making the journey. The equipage consists of a rude covered wagon, crammed with odds and ends of household furniture and cooking utensils, dragged slowly along by a team of jaded horses; a milch cow is always in the rear of the wagon, and frequently a calf may be seen in the van. In this manner the pilgrims wind their way slowly over the tree-

SKETCHES IN THE FAR WEST—SUGAR-MAKING IN TEXAS.

BRANDING.

RODEO, OR

ON THE TRAIL.

CUT

HALTING-PLACE ON THE NINNESCAH RIVER.

THE TEXAS CATTLE TRADE.—Drawn

NG UP CATTLE.

T.

NZENY AND TAVERNIER.—[SEE PAGE 385.]

SHIPPING FOR THE EASTERN MARKETS.

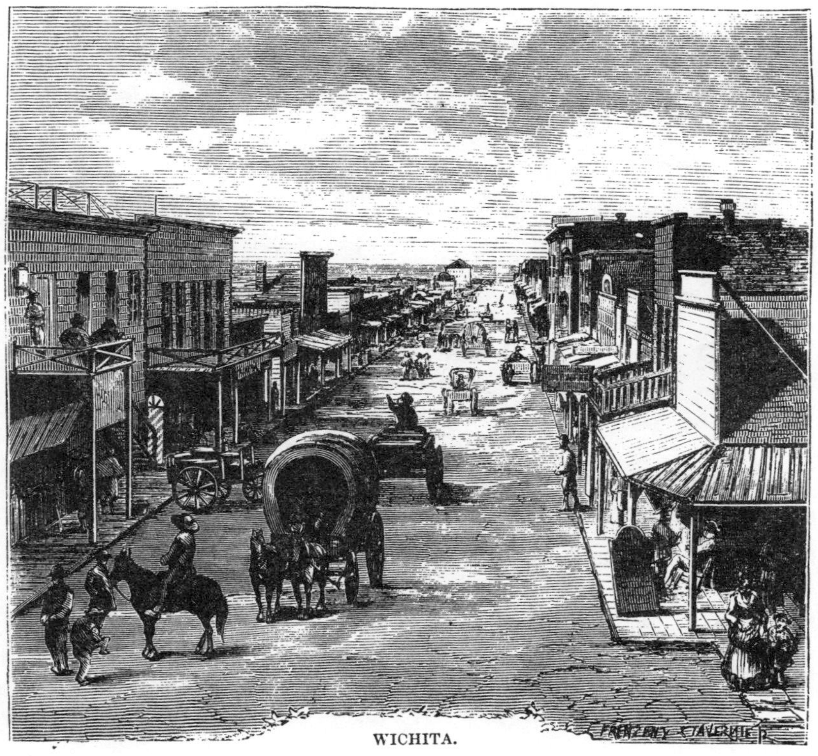

WICHITA.

HO, FOR TEXAS!

DRIVING CATTLE INTO A CORRAL.

Every body knows that a large proportion of the beef that finds its way to our tables comes from Texan cattle. These are driven in large numbers from the far Southwest up to Kansas, where they are transferred to the cars, and sent eastward by railroad. The droves vary from 500 to 8000, and are guarded by well-mounted and well-armed herdsmen, who are inured to fatigue and to fighting hostile Indians. The cattle feed during the long march on the luxurious grazing grounds of the Indian Territory. The entire journey from Texas to Kansas occupies from four to five months, as the herd must move very slowly, and what with stoppages to feed, water, and rest, only a few miles are made in a day. At various points along the route are great yards, called corrals, inclosed by tall, strong fences. These corrals are secure resting-places into which the cattle are driven temporarily. In our double-page illustration the herdsmen are seen in the act of driving a large number of cattle into one of these inclosures. One of the beasts, less manageable than the rest, has broken loose, and threatens to give the herdsmen plenty of hard work before they capture him.

DRIVING CATTLE INTO A CORR

THE FAR WEST.—[SEE PAGE 752.]

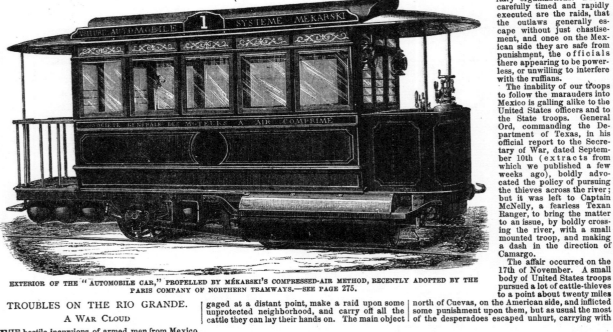

EXTERIOR OF THE "AUTOMOBILE CAR," PROPELLED BY MÉKARSKI'S COMPRESSED-AIR METHOD, RECENTLY ADOPTED BY THE PARIS COMPANY OF NORTHERN TRAMWAYS.—SEE PAGE 275.

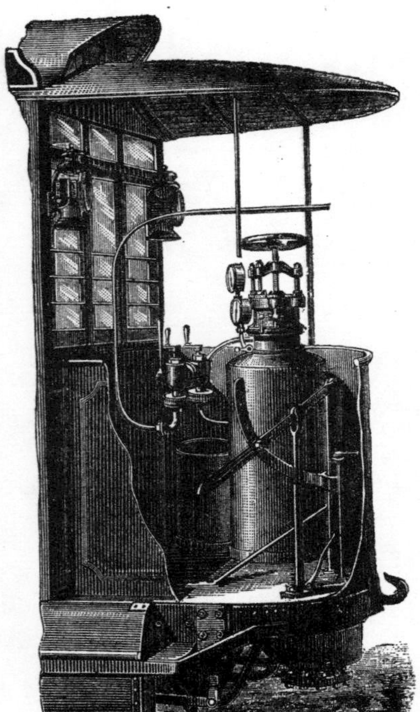

PRESSURE-REGULATING APPARATUS ON THE FRONT PLATFORM OF MÉKARSKI'S "AUTOMOBILE CAR" FOR TRAMWAYS.

TROUBLES ON THE RIO GRANDE.

A War Cloud

THE hostile incursions of armed men from Mexico into the territory of the United States have been a source of great annoyance for a long time to the settlers on the American side of the Rio Grande, and have lately become so frequent as to invite the serious attention of our Government. The matter was considered of sufficient importance to claim special mention in the President's message, and the preparations now being made to put our navy on a war-footing are looked upon by many as an indication that we may be again plunged into a war with Mexico.

Recent events have made the territory along the Rio Grande a point of general interest, and we have taken pains to obtain sketches of the operations now going on in that section. The United States Government have placed on the Rio Grande a small naval force, consisting of the light-draught steamer *Rio Bravo*, and two steam launches—the former carrying five guns, and each of the latter one Gatling gun. This flotilla is commanded by Lieutenant-Commander D. W. C. Kells, United States Navy, and its purpose is to render aid to the army in its endeavors to repress the depredations and outrages from which the American population along the river has so long suffered. The force of United States troops available for service on the extensive Rio Grande frontier is very limited, and quite inadequate to effectually guard the line, even at the points where the incursions are usually made, and the soldiers are kept hard at work in consequence of the disordered and lawless state of affairs. The military force consists of the Eighth Cavalry and Twenty-fourth Infantry, under the command of General J. H. Potter, United States Army.

The outrages that have caused so much trouble are committed by predatory bands of Mexicans, who cross the river, and, seizing an opportunity when the small body of United States troops is engaged at a distant point, make a raid upon some unprotected neighborhood, and carry off all the cattle they can lay their hands on. The main object of these incursions is robbery, but they frequently result in the murder of unarmed citizens, and in collisions with the United States troops and local military organizations. But so carefully timed and rapidly executed are the raids, that the outlaws generally escape without just chastisement, and once on the Mexican side they are safe from punishment, the officials there appearing to be powerless, or unwilling to interfere with the ruffians.

The inability of our troops to follow the marauders into Mexico is galling alike to the United States officers and to the State troops. General Ord, commanding the Department of Texas, in his official report to the Secretary of War, dated September 10th (extracts from which we published a few weeks ago), boldly advocated the policy of pursuing the thieves across the river; but it was left to Captain McNelly, a fearless Texan Ranger, to bring the matter to an issue, by boldly crossing the river, with a small mounted troop, and making a dash in the direction of Camargo.

The affair occurred on the 17th of November. A small body of United States troops pursued a lot of cattle-thieves to a point about twenty miles north of Cuevas, on the American side, and inflicted some punishment upon them, but as usual the most of the desperadoes escaped unhurt, carrying with them 250 head of cattle. Captain Randlett, in command of the United State forces, made a demand upon the Mexican Alcalde for the surrender of the thieves and the cattle, and received the usual equivocal answer that efforts would be made to capture the guilty parties, but none were turned over. In the meantime Major Alexander, with two companies of cavalry, had been dispatched on Nov. 18th, at noon, from Fort Brown as a reinforcement. He made the forced march of eighty-four miles and arrived at the crossing on the following day, but it was found that by this time some 400 or 500 Mexicans well armed, together with a portion of the regular Mexican troops, were defending the passage, making it folly for our small force to attempt to cross the river. The news of this outrage spread like wildfire through the country, and bodies of Texans rapidly armed and proceeded to the scene of action. Captain McNelly with a small body succeeded in making a crossing at another point, and meeting a party of armed Mexicans made a vigorous attack upon them, killing several Mexicans, but his enemies beginning to swarm about him, he wisely fell back to the river, where he intrenched himself. Protected by the guns on the American side, he was, however, unmolested, and he quietly crossed to the Texan shore.

The war feeling now runs high on both sides of the river, and unless the difficulty can be adjusted by diplomatic intervention, we may hear of startling news from that quarter which will revive the memories of the times when Fort Brown opened its batteries upon Matamoras, and old Zach Taylor marched his "boys in blue" over the Mexican border.

ON THE RIO GRANDE—MEXICAN CANNON AND "DOUBLED" GUARD THREATENING THE TOWN OF BROWNSVILLE, TEXAS, NOVEMBER 20TH, 1875.

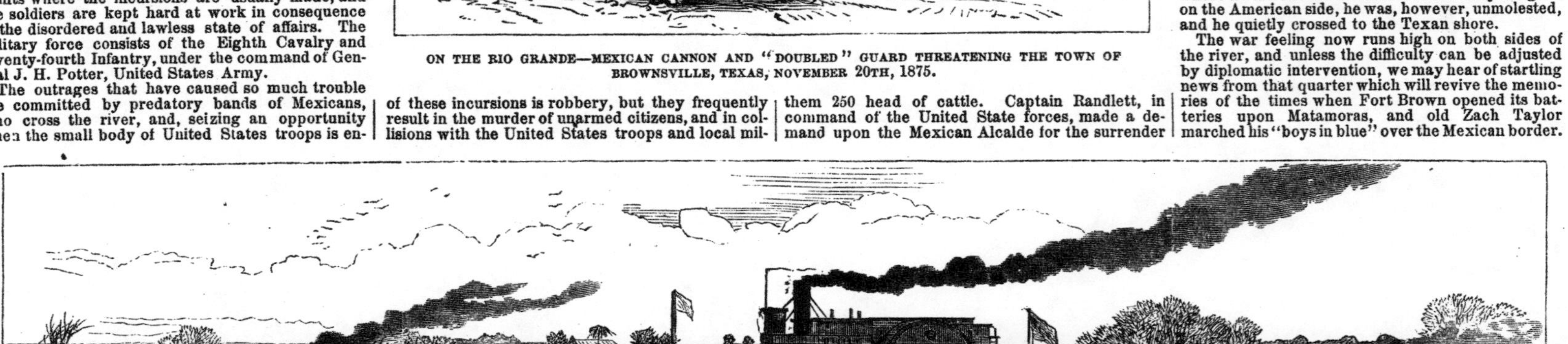

THE UNITED STATES FLOTILLA STEAMING UP THE RIO GRANDE.

UNITED STATES CAVALRY LEAVING FORT BROWN IN PURSUIT OF MEXICAN RAIDERS ACROSS THE RIO GRANDE.—FROM SKETCHES BY OUR SPECIAL ARTIST AT BROWNSVILLE, TEXAS.

Stockton Telegraph.

ARNOLD & REYNOLDS, *Valeat quantum valere potest.* Editors & Proprietors.

VOL. 1. FORT STOCKTON, TEXAS. March 26. 1876. No. 1.

SALUTATORY.

-:—:-

With this number, we commence the publication of a journal, and make our professional bow to the people of Fort Stockton, of Pecos County, of the state of Texas, the United States, and of the whole world. It will be our aim to furnish in each issue, the latest news derived from telegraphic reports, the mails, and other sources, on all subjects of interest to the army, citizens, and the public in general; to which end, we respectfully ask the assistance and support of the community, and we promise to use our best endeavors to give entire satisfaction; and in the words of our motto, ask the public to "let it pass for what it is worth".

Very respectfully,

Editors.

The U. S. Military Telegraph line is in working order, under the efficient management of Mr. E. M. Dunbar, and it is expected that the wire will reach San Antonio by the first of May—it is now working to Fredericksburg.

The outlook of the Post Garden is reported to be very favorable: it is to be hoped that "G. Hoppier, Esq." will not put in an appearance and spoil our calculations by taking all for toll.

LOCALS.

-:—:-

Does anybody know where Murray Hill City is?–See advertisement of lots for sale in that place.

J. Friedlander, of the firm of Friedlander & Co. Post Traders, left on the coach Saturday morning for Washington, D. C.

Attention is specially invited to the handsome preambulator invented and used by our enterprising Milk Merchant, Mr. Gaskey. Patent applied for.

Those who have not paid their taxes are respectfully requested to interview the accommodating County Treasurer, Morris Jacobs, Esq.–See advertisement on next page.

Major F. M. Coxe, Paymaster U. S. Army, arrived on the night of the 22. inst.–gave us our bi-monthly salary the next day, and left on a special coach the 24. inst. to make glad the hearts of our comrads stationed west of use.

The last detachment of the 8th Cavalry, companies "F." and "K." under command of Major Price, arrived at this post on the 21st inst. and left the next morning for Fort Clark. We will be glad to see the "Boys" again some day and hope they will be pleased with their new Station.

SCISSORINKTUMS.

-:—:-

—It is easier to take up a cross than to carry it.

—Every old maid can boast of two beaux, but they are elbows.

—The first water works in Texas are being established at Austin.

—San Francisco tradesmen seek to draw customers by offering to take silver at par.

—The Spanish army has 6 marshals, 77 generals, 136 lieutenant generals, and 335 major generals.

—A Cincinnati girl accidentally cut her tongue off, and all the young men are trying to shine up to her now.

—How cunning for the man who puts down carpets to leave the odd tacks business end up, like a church steeple for the sensitive soul.

—This being leap year men are not responsible if they do whatever women ask them to; and still this may lead to trouble in families.

—It is easy enough to write for newspapers. A man in Virginia offers to send "first class editorials" to all the papers in the country at the comparatively insignificant rate of $3 a column.

STOCKTON TELEGRAPH.

MARCH 26. 1876.

TERMS OF SUBSCRIPTION.

One copy, one year,	$1.00.
One copy, six months,	60c.
Single copy,	10c.

RATES OF ADVERTISING.

One column, one year,	$35.00.
Half " "	$20.00.
Quarter " "	$12.00.
Local Notices, per line,	10c

Collections for advertising will be made quarterly. Trancient advertisements in advance.

THE GREAT EVENT.

-:—:-

To the public—Our Press and material arrived on the 21. inst. just six months, to a day from the date of our order; and as it required considerable time to unpack and distribute our type, and get in working order, it was impossible to issue a larger paper this time, in the future we shall issue a four page paper on the 25th. of each month, and whenever there is important news by telegraph, that is of interest to our subscribers, we shall publish an extra and forward to them.

We have a fine stock of paper, cards, etc. and are prepared to do all kinds of Job Printing, promptly, and on reasonable terms, and we will guarantee satisfaction in all work entrusted to us.

This being the only paper published in northwestern Texas, it offers very superior advantages as an advertising medium, and we respectfully solicit the patronage of everybody who have anything to which they wish attention called.

Job Printing, of all descriptoins, done in the latest style at this office.

BY TELEGRAPH.

News, in brief, compiled from the associate press dispatches at Dennison, Texas, expressly for the U. S. Military Telegraph Lines.

:——:

Dennison, March 25th. Revolution in Mexico continues—The government General Labarra levies a forced loan of $30.000 on the people of Matamoras—Revolutionist General Diaz near Matamoris with one thousand men—Numerous uprisings in the interior states.

Mexican Border Committee vote unanimously to report joint resolution, directing the President to send at once to Rio Grande frontier, two full regiments of best Cavalry, each regiment to be twelve companies of one hundred men each, and to recruit sufficient number of men to bring these regiments up to standard; the second section directs the President to order troops across the border when necessary. The Committee unanimously adopt Schleickers report.

General Sherman gone to Washington to consult with Secretary Taft. It is thought there is a possibility of removal of Army Headquarters back to Washington.

It is stated that Treasurer New will resign upon selection of suitable successor.

The President, ex-Secretary Borie, Fred. Grant and others, said to be implicated in land transactions of doubtful character in connection with Denver and Rio Grande Railroad.

Ex-Minister Schenk in Washington. Stewart, of Emma Mine, swears that he (Schenk) had stock carried for him, and that his salary as director was $2.500 a year.

In Spencer investigation, connection of Spencer & Hines is established, which Carpenter tried to defeat.

Longfellow seriously canvassed as Schenk's successor.

Ex-Attorney General Williams, and Secretary Fish to be investigated in regard to Virginius affair.

Evans, Post Trader at Sill, before Investigating Committee confirms Marsh's statement, and says he paid General Rice one thousand dollars for introduction to Belknap. Rice wanted fifteen hundred. Ben. Butler, also before the Committee, says he knows nothing, but had his suspicions, and had been conducting an investigation of his own.

Judge Montgomery Moses of South Carolina found guilty of high crimes and misdemeanors, and formally dismissed.

Captain C. B. Penrose, C. S. ordered to San Antonio as Chief Commissary of the Department of Texas.

Bill passed repealing law forbidding appointment of ex-confederates to positions in the army.

British Parliament has passed a bill giving Queen Victoria title of Empress of the Indies.

COMANCHE STORE.

CONROY & FOURNELL.

Dealers in goods of all kinds.

WET & DRY.

SCHOOL BOOKS in VARIETY.

NO CROOKED WHISKEY ON HAND.

MURRAY HILL CITY.

A most desirable location, situated west of the garrison, just off the reservation.

-:—:-

Lots for sale by

J. FRIEDLANDER & Co.

MORRIS JACOBS.

County Treasurer.

Office at

J. Friedlander & Co's.

J. JACOBS.

WATCHMAKER & JEWELER.

First class work made a speciality.

Can be found at the store of J. Friedlander & Co.

M. F. CORBETT,

[POST TRADER]

Fort Stocton, Texas.

Keeps on hand a complete assortment of DRY GOODS, GROCERIES, and everything suitable for the *ARMY, CITIZENS,* AND Freighters Trains.

The Dallas Weekly Herald.

ESTABLISHED, 1849. DALLAS, TEXAS, SATURDAY, AUGUST 19, 1876. VOL. XXIII, NO. 49.

CAVE CANEM.

It has long been the opinion of the writer that if the canine race were extirpated everywhere, save in the pastoral districts, it would be a blessing to the human race. That opinion is much strengthened by an interesting article in the American *Exchange and Review*, detailing at length the evils resulting from man's companionship with this brute. There are many dangers which, in their aggregate results, are far greater than that of the horrible disease—hydrophobia. There are numerous parasitical worms, fungi and mites with which all dogs are infested, and which, either by direct communication with men, or through other animals, are continually causing most deplorable consequences, and as there is much less general information on this subject than respecting rabies, THE HERALD conceives the authorities worth quoting.

The dog is frequently attacked by the mange-mite, which in form resembles the cheese-mite. This parasite produces the mange in dogs and similar skin diseases in men. Another pestiferous mite, technically called the *acarus folliculorum*, often appears in dogs, occasionally an obstinate skin disease with pustules. A fœtid smell generally accompanies this disease, which is excessively disagreeable to delicate nostrils. The number of these mites to be found upon dogs are simply incalculable and they are frequently transmitted to men and children, occasioning a most obstinate skin disease. The scald mushroom is common to dogs and men, in the latter, generally attacking the scalp. This disease undoubtedly originated with the dog as of late years it has been discovered that this parasite fungus was the same on man as on dogs. There is scarcely a dog that does not have some of the various kinds of tape worms, either in its intestines, nostrils, brain, thorax, or uretha. The smaller tape worm *tænia coenurus*, with its stylet-like borers, often works its way into the brain of the dog, giving it a disease called the "staggers." The *tænia marginata*, a large worm, the *tænia serrata*, yet a different variety of tape worm, are to be found in nearly all dogs. There is a malady of the lungs and liver occasioned in man by fungi from dogs, called the *echinococcus* disease. In Iceland, where dogs live in the same apartments with families, every seventh man is said to have this disease. It is also frequent in Germany, especially in Thuringen and in Dresden, where thirty per cent. of the population are thus afflicted. There is another annulated worm formed frequently in the dog, which is wonderfully productive, sixty thousand eggs being counted in its oviparous sheath. By sneezing or blowing these embryos and disgusting parasites are dispersed from the nose of the dog, or flow in the nasal discharge, and as the dog is constantly rubbing his nose about, these eggs are often deposited on the food of animals, and possibly of man. In addition to these fatal objections to this miserable brute, we might name minor evils, such as fleas, pediculi, lice, etc., but we think the list collated from the *Review* already sufficiently formidable. The dog may be used to guard flocks of sheep, to hunt hogs or to guard the house, but he should never be used as a companion or be permitted to enter the dwelling. No dog should be permitted to appear in the streets without the name and residence of the owner upon its collar. But we very much question whether any dog licensed or unlicensed should be permitted upon our streets. If a quietus could be put to all dogs, the community would be better off, since the services and society of that brute does not compensate for the dangers attending his presence and for the heavy burden of his support.

THE enemies of the Texas and Pacific tried to get in an amendment, in effect, declaring that the Texas and Pacific had forfeited its right to its reservation, but the trick was discovered and defeated. They then abandoned the bill, showing very plainly that their only object in introducing it was to affect the vote on the Texas and Pacific extension bill. Praise is due to Senator Grace in this matter. It will be remembered that he fought the extension bill, but when it came to stabbing the company in an underhanded way, he was at once on his feet in its behalf. He charged on those now attempting to amend the bill pending, that they had gone back on their declarations of love for the school fund, and abandoned a bill over which they had made great parade while the extension bill was up. His speech was bold and to the point, and left no doubt that he had acted from a sense of duty in the matter of the Texas and Pacific extension, and now proposes to remain consistent. The bill passed without amendment.—*Martin's letter to the Register.*

We are glad to see the honorable Senator get right again. His head is now level and we believe he will keep it so. He has done North Texas some harm, but his heart was always right and we grant him the fullest absolution

WE are no admirer of a part of John Hancock's past career, but in view of the present crisis in the affairs of the Democratic party, we believe a sound and safe policy dictate that he should be returned. It is unwise to take any risks in such a time as the present, unless great gain is to overbalance the loss that might be sustained. We do not think the probable gain will compensate for the risk that is to be run—that of weakening the Democrats in the present canvass.—*Mexia Ledger.*

You were once very bitter toward Hancock, and it is high time for you to repent and fall into ranks with THE HERALD.

THERE was a bitter debate in the United States Senate on the 5th instant, in which the Hamburg riot largely figured. Senator Maxey, with wonderful patience and skill, repelled the vindictive attacks of Edmunds, Patterson and Boutwell. The spirit of intensified hate exhibited in that debate by Republican Senators towards the South, evidences anything else but a satisfactory condition of reconciliation in this Centennial year. They are summoning all their energies to raise up the bloody shirt and to trample down Southern States, that the battle in November may be won.

THE DALLAS HERALD crows over Bartow of the *Examiner* on the seventy-nine pounds melon question. It says: "Captain Jack Scott brought in a melon weighing ninety-two pounds." That's a whopper—the melon we mean—though it wouldn't require much to persuade us the other is a whopper too.—*Mexia Ledger.*

The Limestone county paper needn't grow jealous, for we will admit that its county grows extraordinary cabbage heads.

IN answer to ill-natured Republican birds who twit the New York Evening *Express*, for eating *crow*, it says that they must remember it does it for the Democratic cause.

PRACTICAL EDUCATION.

If THE HERALD prints a farmer's letter, taking a few liberties with it in order to make it a complete text, we believe our intelligent readers will not complain:

I am a farmer. My son is now eighteen years of age. He began to attend school at the age of six, and has attended two terms, or six months, in each year from that time until now. He is a boy of good health and of at least average mental abilities, and has never been considered less studious than his school-fellows and classmates. His teachers have been as competent as the average of those employed in country districts. His time in schools has been spent exclusively upon the seven rudimentary branches taught in the common district schools—spelling, reading, writing, arithmetic, geography, grammar, and the history of the United States. He is, nevertheless, a poor speller, reader, and writer, knows little of arithmetic and grammar except the rules, and has only a smattering of geography and history. I found out these things by asking him questions and setting him to do things for me. I take an agricultural paper, and one evening I asked John (my son's name) to take pen and paper and write for me a short article for the newspaper on the culture of corn, about which I thought I had some ideas worth communicating. I sat in my easy chair and dictated what I had to say, and John wrote it down. When the article was finished I told John to put my initials to it and send it to the office of the paper. Two weeks afterward, when the paper came, I looked for my article, but found instead the following editorial note:

"If our correspondent 'B. J. T.' knew one-tenth part as much about *orthography, punctuation, paragraphing*, and the use of *capital letters* as he does about '*corn culture*,' his article would have been gladly inserted. His ignorance of those matters, so important to editors and printers, seems as remarkable as his knowledge of the subject treated of. We advise him to write again, and get some intelligent school-boy to copy his article for him before sending it to us!"

My reflections on reading this gentle hint must be left to the imagination. Was not my John an "intelligent school-boy?" I would look further into the matter. I asked him to point out Salt Lake City on the map. He did so. By what name are the inhabitants of that city known? He could not tell. Is there anything peculiar in their religious notions and customs? Not that he knew of. How much sooner does the sun rise in Boston than in San Francisco? He did not know. Why should it rise *any* sooner? He could not say. Though only a farmer, I am fond of Shakspeare, and asked John to read me a scene from King Lear. It could not be called reading, and, in much pain, I soon desired him to stop. How many different sounds are there in the word *eight?* *Five, of course.* Did the colonies, prior to the Revolution, have the same form of government? Yes. What was it called? Colonial government. How many different kinds of national government have we had since the Revolution? Two, Democratic and Republican. "John," said I, "to-day I sold a load of hay weighing one thousand seven hundred and fifty pounds, and received pay for it at the rate of sixteen dollars and fifty cents per ton; how much money did I get?" He took his slate and went to work, while I read a fresh copy of THE HERALD. In an hour I had finished the paper, but John had not finished his sum. He said there were so many fractions in it, and he couldn't find a rule that would fit exactly. The next evening I told John that I had a little sum in practical farming for him to do: I rented forty acres of land to Mr. Jones, he to put it in corn and allow me one-third of the crop for the use of the land. Jones raised two thousand four hundred bushels, the total cost of which when cribbed was three hundred and fifty-five dollars. What did Jones' corn cost him per bushel in the crib? What was the cost of the whole crop per acre and per bushel? And if I sell my share at fifty cents per bushel, how much shall I get per acre as rent? John labored on it all the evening, but did not get correct answers to all the questions. I then gave him all of the items of cost and profit, and desired him to open an account with that forty-acre lot in due form, and prepare a correct balance-sheet of the same. He did not know what I meant.

Finding that my poor boy had very little to show for his twelve years of delving in the seven elementary common school branches; that he was a poor reader and a worse writer and speller; that he knew nothing of punctuation, and could not with the matter furnished him prepare a few pages of manuscript well enough to save them from the editor's waste-basket; that his stock of history and geography was meager in the extreme; while his knowledge of arithmetic, beyond the verbiage of the text-book, was unequal to simple ordinary business transactions connected with his father's farm—I thought that perhaps he had made up in general knowledge what he lacked in these respects, and continued my inquiries accordingly.

His reading books contained pieces from eminent orators, statesmen and patriots. Had his teachers told him anything of their biography, character, and services; of the occasions and circumstances under which their speeches and addresses were delivered? He said they had not. He had read descriptions of many lands and scenes, curious stories of beasts and birds, of insects and fishes; every day, all these years, he had walked over the earth with its many kinds and qualities of soils, its wintry wonders of frost and ice, its vernal freshness and beauty, the summer splendors of its trees and flowers, and the autumnal glories of its pictured woods and ripened fruits; he had heard the wild scream of the tempest, the Æolian murmurs of the zephyr, the deep bass of the thunder; had watched the sheen and sparkle of the stars at night, the brightening flash of coming day, and the gorgeous skies of sunset; he had lived and moved and had his being amid these omnipresent wonders of the material world—had his teachers sought to interpret them to him, to awaken his interest in them, and to bring him into loving relations with nature, with the objective, the visible, and tangible; had they in any way sought to redeem the dryness and litleness of words and books by showing their relations to the freshness and greatness of ideas and things; had they bidden him watch the curious growths and processes going on about him all the time, the perpetual marvels of plant-life and animated beings; and to move about with every sense awake and alert, eager to note the lessons and revelations coming up from every creature and thing that God has made? "Why no," said he, "they heard me recite what was in the books." "Of course," I pursued, "did they not do more than that? Did they not supplement and enrich the daily lessons of the books by information, facts, and illustrations drawn from their own reading, observation, and experience, so as to whet your appetite for general knowledge? Did they not tell you again and again that the few studies of the district school were chiefly valuable as necessary instruments for future acquisitions, that you might through them become intelligent, well-informed, useful, and happy?" They had not done any of these things, John said.

A day or two after this conversation I took a walk with my son through the gardens, stock yards, fields and prairies, resolved to bring this painful inquiry to a conclusion, and bitterly reproaching myself for having so long taken it for granted that all was well. Of the ground beneath our feet he only knew that it was a part of the earth's surface; of the gardens he knew that vegetables grew in one and flowers in the other; he knew the names of the various domestic animals, but he did not know which of a cow's jaws was destitute of front teeth, nor when she rose from the ground which end of her got up first; the grain in two adjoining fields was six inches high, one wheat, the other oats—he could not distinguish them; all he could tell of the meadows was that they contained grass; of forest trees he could tell the names of but few, while of their respective characteristics, and values for fuel, lumber, etc., he was ignorant. But the worst of all was that the boy's senses seemed inactive, his perceptions blunted, and his mind stupefied by the habit all these years of studying mere words instead of things also, and of regarding school-work as something separate and apart from the out-door world, having but a vague and unimportant relation to every-day life. Thenceforward I tried to arouse the child's dormant senses and faculties, and to show him what great things God had done for his education; to give him a fresh baptism into the spirit of nature and the world of realities from which, alas, his schooling had seemed to separate him.

This farmer's letter is no fancy sketch. It is a truthful portrayal of the results of the present educational system of Texas. It is for the intelligent public sentiment of Dallas and Dallas county to say whether this condition of affairs shall continue to exist. Whether their boys shall grow into an intellectual, highly cultivated race of men, or shall step down and out before the advancing culture and knowledge of the coming century.

PRACTICAL EDUCATION—ANOTHER FARMER'S EXPERIENCE.

I observed, Mr. Editor, in your last issue, the comments of a farmer upon his son's education, and his summing up of the results of his boys twelve years' schooling. If not consuming too much space and time I will offer you my experience in this regard:

I also have a boy about eighteen years of age who began to attend school when about seven years old. My boy possessed all the overflowing strength and ardor of a young, healthy and vigorous constitution. His brain was as active and as clear as that of ordinary boys, and his hours in the schoolroom were devoted to honest and faithful study, while with the bat and ball, and all the games of the play ground, no young athlete there surpassed him. His teachers have been grave, learned, diligent and conscientious men—men who felt the great responsibilities of their trust, and performed their duties with a devoted earnestness that has and ever will command my profoundest gratitude. My boy's time at school was spent exclusively upon the elementary branches, ordinarily taught in our schools, such as spelling, reading writing, geography, arithmetic, grammar and history. In these studies, so far as I have examined him, he evinces a proficiency that brings to my heart inexpressible pride and joy.

I take an agricultural journal, and some evenings since I request Robert (my son's name) to take pen and paper and write for me a short article for our county newspaper on the culture of cotton, about which I thought I had some ideas gained from a quarter of a centuries experience, that might be worth the publication. I dictated and Robert wrote, and when he had finished I directed him to place my initials thereto and send it to the office of our paper. In one week I received the paper and found my article printed in excellent style, but turning to the editorial page I found these words, "We publish with unusual pleasure the communication signed R. R. G., to be found in another column. If all of our correspondents would write as clear and open a hand, and would evince such perfect familiarity with punctuation, paragraphing and the use of capital letters, the labor of the printer would be materially lessened.

"The ideas advanced by our correspondent speak for themselves and are well worth perusal." A great feeling of satisfaction and pleasure came into my heart as I read this editor's kind comments on my boy's letter, and I felt thankful that it had been his fortune to be taught by able teachers. On the same evening in question, I was musing by my fireside after the labors of the day, and the thought occurred to me that I would try my boy in reading a brief act from Shakespeare, for though a farmer, I liked the book, and was ever charmed with the author's insight into human character. I handed him a scene from the Moor of Venice and bade him read.

I sat there entranced. The spirit with which that boy read, his clear and perfect utterance, every word falling rounded and beautiful like the coin from the mint; his correct intonation, the wonderful facility with which he seized upon the most subtle and airy meanings of the writer and gave them expression and life, was to me the very essence of good reading. The boy had evinced a thorough knowledge of reading, orthography, punctuation, emphasis, intonation, and he wrote so well that editors even stepped aside to compliment his hand; but how about arithmetic, the most essential of all? Was he proficient in this? I would try him. I would ask him questions outside of the usual routine; such questions as would require those general answers that demonstrate a perfect knowledge of details. So I called him to my side and said, "Robert, can you tell me how surveyors and astronomers obtain the value of distances between two inaccessible points?" A moment's thought, and the answer came: "They concieve those points to be connected by a system of lines, the value of which can be directly measured, and by these means we deduce the value of the unknown party. This problem of distances between inaccessible points generally resolves itself in the end into the solution of a triangle, some parts of which can be directly or indirectly measured, and so the value of the unknown parts calculated." "Well, Robert, is it upon this principle that the distance to certain stars is estimated."

"It is. We consider the problem the same as the solution of a triangle in which the base and adjacent angles are kuown, the star being apex of the triangle. By measuring the angle of elevation of the star from two given stations on the earth's surface and the distance of these stations from each other, we calculate the distance of the star."

"But suppose, Robert, the distance of the star is so great that the difference of the angular elevation, when viewed from the two extremities of any line that could be drawn on the earth's surface would be so slight that the other two sides of the triangle would not differ considerably from parallel lines?"

"In such a case, sir, the elevation of the star is taken at two different times of the year, six months apart, for this would give a base for the triangle equal to the diameter of the earth's orbit."

I was satisfied that my boy was fit to enter any college in the land. Although he might not be able to calculate the precession of the equinoxes, or to decipher the hieroglyphics upon the Rosetta Stone, he was nevertheless a fair practical mathematician, a good reader, and an excellent writer. His teachers had been scholarly and true men. They had given him practical, useful knowledge; the grain, instead of the chaff. They had imbued him with a lofty self-reliance, a will that hardened and grew stronger under difficulties, a purpose that never flinched in the face of disappointment or disaster. They had given him an expanded, cultured, thoughtful mind, that in the after years of life bid fair to light up with the splendor of its achievements the darkness that might surround him. He had been taught to interpret the "autumnal glories of pictured woods and ripened fruits, the wild scream of the tempest, the Æolian murmur of the zephyr, the deep bass of the thunder, the brightening flash of the coming day, the gorgeous skies of sunset," and with a heart swelling up with gratefulness and pride, I thanked Him, "who maketh the clouds His chariot, who rideth upon the wings of the wind," that He had vouchsafed to me such a boy, and that the country was blessed with such teachers.

TEXAS CROPS.

The monthly report of the agricultural department for July, makes an excellent showing for Texas. Taking the numeral one hundred as the representative of a full crop, the condition in July of corn was one hundred and twenty-one, wheat seventy-nine, rye eighty-eight, oats ninety-eight, barley one hundred and two, Irish potatoes one hundred and three, sweet potatoes one hundred and nine, beans one hundred and three, sugar cane one hundred and three, tobacco one hundred and three, cotton ninety-nine.

In corn and tobacco she is ahead of all the States. In barley three States excel her; in Irish potatoes four States are ahead; in sweet potatoes, one State; in sugar cane, two States. In Northern Texas the cotton crop, owing to the late opportune rains, will be largely in excess of the average, and the condition to-day is fifteen per cent. better than in July.

DALLAS has reason to be satisfied with her representatives in the Fifteenth Legislature.—[DALLAS HERALD.

It is sincerely to be hoped that Dallas will have no representatives in the Sixteenth Legislature, if Tom Scott has anything to do with it. Is Dallas satisfied with her representatives in the Fifteenth Legislature? But of course she is. Dallas is always satisfied with whatever is corrupt and treacherous. She is "satisfied" if her representatives return richer if not better men.—[Leon *Cabinet.*

This emasculated little sheet is malicious. We reprint its paragraph that a more extended exhibition of the *Cabinet's* editor's assinine qualities may be made.

WE give place to the following communication with pleasure, for THE HERALD is more than willing to pay tribute to the worth and capability of Senator Piner:

SENATE CHAMBER, AUSTIN, TEXAS, August 9, 1876.

Hon. James B. Simpson, Dallas, Texas:

DEAR SIR—I noticed in the DAILY HERALD of the 6th instant, a short communication signed "Uno," which, while it does justice in part, does not wholly do so. When the bill for the relief of the Dallas and Wichita Railroad Company came up in the Senate, there were others, as well as those mentioned in the communication, who rendered very material aid in the matter.

Among those not mentioned is the name of the Hon. F. E. Piner, of Denton, who was untiring in that, as well as everything else that has come before this Legislature for the benefit of Dallas and Northern Texas. Yours truly,

R. S. CUY.

THE WHISKY FRAUDS.

General Horace Porter's Yarn, as Taken Off the Grant Reel.

Origin of the Term Sylph again Mystified—The President Shocked by the Lewd Woman Recital—Further Examination Postponed Until December.

WASHINGTON, August 12.—General Horace Porter was before the subcommittee on whisky frauds to-day, in reference to Bluford Wilson's testimony. He said he did not allude to Sylph as a lewd woman in speaking of her to McDonald. If witness had thus spoken of Sylph, he would have been inventing a story which would have reflected on the President. The witness denied positively that he told Wilson the greatest favor he could do the President was to shield Babcock. Witness said he never heard General Babcock referred to as concerned in the speculations, except from newspapers.

Representative Cochrane asked the witness whether he did not know that certain papers shown to the President, implicating Babcock, was the reason why the President retained counsel to defend him. Witness replied he did not believe that any papers were placed before the President implicating Babcock. Witness stated the President intimated to him that nothing whatever had come to his knowledge which implicated Babcock, directly or indirectly, or in any manner, with the Black Friday speculations. In reply to a question as to what explanation General Babcock gave to the President and Attorney General Peirrepont about the Sylph despatch, witness said he did not attach much significance to it. He was not present with the President and Peirrepont when the explanation was made, he knew, however, that Babcock gave to them the origin of the term Sylph as was done during his trial at St. Louis. He did not know that the explanation made to the President and that in Court were different. Witness was positive in saying he did not tell Wilson that Sylph was a lewd woman and had given the President much trouble, etc. Wilson, however, did ask him what the explanation of Sylph was and he told Wilson what he had heard from others, although, as he had before said, he did not attach much significance to it. A question was asked whether the President, at any time, said anything to him about that matter and witness replied nothing was said by the President in his presence or hearing, and anything he may had heard as coming from the President, he declined to state. Subsequently, however, witness said he heard from the secretary that the President said the statement made by Major Wilson, before this committee, was incorrect that Wilson did not repeat this vulgar slander to him. Wilson commenced saying something about an improper woman, when the President stopped him instantly and said he did not permit the recital and discussion of the matter. The President never, either directly or indirectly, spoke to witness on the subject, nor did Wilson ever couple the term "lewd woman" with the "Sylph" dispatch. The witness explained his conversation with Babcock, the substance of which was that Babcock was a distinguished officer of the army, was a graduate of West Point, and therefore, every officer in the army felt an interest in the matter; that the President believed Babcock to be innocent, but that if guilty, he ought to be punished. Wilson did say to him, in the course of a conversation, that Babcock should be fairly dealt with and no injustice done to him, but further than that, he could not go. Witness did not assist Babcock in getting up his defense. He had not, since he had been summoned as a witness, been to see the President, but had purposely avoided calling on him at present; nor had he consulted with anybody, but had read some of the evidence and had a general idea of it.

General Porter was before the whisky committee again this afternoon, and examined at great length. He made various corrections in Bluford Wilson's testimony, and gave a history of his connection with the letter written by Wilson to General Henderson, at St. Louis, which has caused so much comment, and a copy of which, with the interpetration of the two initials, "W. H.," was sent anonymously to General Babcock. Wilson told witness this letter had no reference whatever to the President or Babcock, or to the visit of the President to St. Louis, but that it related entirely to whisky thieves in St. Louis. Wilson also gave what he understood as the origin of the term Sylph, which was the same as given at the trial of McDonald, and had no connection whatever with a lewd woman, as asserted. In other explanations the witness made a most emphatic denial that he ever gave an explanation of the term sylph, which could by any possibility be construed as casting any reflection upon the President. At the conclusion of his testimony the committee postponed further examination of whisky frauds until next session of Congress.

Crops, Cattle and Houses Destroyed by Fire.

MONTREAL, August 12.—A farmer wishing to clear a piece of land, between Hemmingford and Valley Field, started a fire, which spread so rapidly and so widely that crops, cattle, houses, etc., of the farmers in the neighborhood have been burned. The smoke from blazing farms interrupts navigation.

A pet dog of good size, belonging to a wealthy gentleman in New York, was buried in his master's lot in Greenwood Cemetery last week by an undertaker. A burial permit had to be obtained for him at headquarters, and the usual price for opening a grave was paid.

JAMES-YOUNGER GANG.

Confession of Hobbs Kerry, One of the Otterville Train Robbers.

He Participates in the Robbery, Receives Twelve Hundred Dollars of the Swag, is Arrested, and Blows—Movements of the Robbers.

ST. LOUIS, August 12.—Chief of Police McDonough, at a late hour tonight, gave out the confession of Hobbs Kerry, the Otterville train robber, which will be published to-morrow. It is quite a lengthy document, but the essential facts are that Kerry, Frank and Jesse James, Bud Younger and brother, Miller and William Chadwell, constituted the gang that robbed the train, and that Kerry got twelve hundred dollars of the swag. It appears that the train was not robbed in accordance with a previously concocted plan, but the party had been riding over a large extent of country for some time without finding anything for them to, and finally concluded to attack this train, acting apparently more from impulse than anything else. Kerry was not a regular member of the gang, but had been with them during their raid through the country, and was present at the robbery of the train and shared the spoils. It also appears that the police authorities here had information, early in June last, that the Youngers, James and other members of the band contemplated robbing a bank at Granby, in Southwest Missouri, and officers were sent there from here. This project was abandoned, however, and the officers returned. As soon as the robbery of the train occurred, Chief McDonough felt certain that it was done by this gang, and he immediately sent officers to Granby, Johnson and other places, and the arrest of Kerry and Bruce Younger was the result. McDonough had intercepted a letter written by Kerry to one of the band, and it was through this letter that he elicited the confession from him. All the parties mentioned above have been indicted by the Grand Jury of Cooper county, but whether vigorous measures had been taken to arrest them is not now known. There is no official notice of the capture. Chadwell and Pitts and officers here do not put much reliance in the reports to that effect. The confession gives a description of the robbery of the train, which is essentially the same as heretofore published, also the movements of the robbers for some time previous to the attack on the train, and their course to a point where the body was discovered, making quite a circumstantial account of all their proceedings.

THE INDIAN WAR.

A Sioux Squaw Reports a Terrible Battle in Which the Sioux Were Almost Annihilated.

The Report is Partially Confirmed by a Fort Laramie Dispatch from a Questionable Source—The Story Not Believed at Headquarters.

ST. PAUL, August 11.—A special dispatch from Bismarck, transmits the following from Terry's camp, at the mouth of Rosebud creek, dated August 5: Colonel Otis with six companies of the Twenty-second Infantry arrived on the second, and General Miles with six companies of the Fifth, reached camp the next day. The sight of these two fine battalions was most charming to our men, who are jubilant. Our fellows are in a temper which will render them dangerous antagonists. The entire command is being refitted and assembles on the South bank of the Yellowstone. The march will commence on the 7th. General Terry in an order dated July 26, expresses his thanks to

I have not yet been able to reinforce the garrison at Red Cloud. Spotted Toil or Standing Rock are strong enough to coral the warriors, or to arrest and disarm those coming in. I beg you to see the military committee of the House and urge on it the necessity of increasing cavalry regiments to one hundred men to each company. General Brook's total strength is one thousand seven hundred and seventy-four, Terry's one thousand eight hundred and seventy-three, and to give this force to them I have stripped every post from the line of the Monitobia to Texas. We want more mounted men. We have not exceeded law in enlisting Indian scouts, in fact we have not as many as the law allows us. The whole number in this division is only eleven thousand four hundred and eight. The Indians with General Crook are not enlisted or even paid. They are not worth paying; they are with him only to gratify their desire for a fight and their thirst for revenge on the Sioux.

(Signed) P. H. SHERIDAN, Lieutenant General.

Killing of Wild Bill—Indian Matters.

CHEYENNE, August 12.—A man arrived at Cheyenne this evening, who reports having crossed a fresh Indian trail between that point and Eagle's Nest. The prairie is on fire towards Chimney Rock, supposed to have been fired by them.

James B. Hickock, alias Wild Bill, known in Kansas and the Territories as a scout of some prominence in early days, was killed in a saloon at Dead Water on the 2d instant, by one Bill Sutherland, whose brother Wild Bill killed at Fort Hayes, Kansas, some years ago.

HELENA, Montana, August 13.—The Independent's, Boseman, Montana, special of August 12, says: A Sioux squaw who came into the Crow camp, reports a terrible battle, that General Crook has almost annihilated the Sioux, and had the remainder in such a position as to force their surrender. A scout from the Crow agency brings this news. It may be greatly exagerated, if not entirely false.

CHICAGO, August 14.—R. Williams, Assistant Adjutant-General, at Omaha, telegraphs to General Sheridan's headquarters here, that the following has just been received by him:

FT. LARAMIE, August 14, 1876.

The report of General Terry's fight with Sitting Bull, is confirmed through Indians coming into the Spotted Tail agency. They report a heavy engagement and defeat of the Indians, with great loss. Sitting Bull wounded.

TOWNSEND.

It is proper to say the accuracy of the information contained in this dispatch, coming as it does from questionable sources, is discredited.

ST. PAUL, Minnesota, August 14.—A Pioneer Press special from the Sioux expedition says: Preparations are at last complete, and we march at day break to-morrow, the route being up the Rosebud, and the objective points the Indians, wherever and whenever they may be found primarily. We expect to effect a junction with General Crook, but no deviation from our main object will be made for that purpose. Sickness is showing itself among the men, with a tendency to scurvy, and that which is to be done must be done soon. The weather is hot, the mercury indicating to-day, from 109 to 115 in the shade. General Terry's force, exclusive of the depot guard, consists of nine hundred and nineteen infantry, five hundred and seventy-four cavalry, forty artillery and seventy-four Crow and Ree Indians. The organization of the command is shown by following extract from general order No. 7: "Troops in the field to be organized for the coming movement as follows: The battalion of Fifth, Sixth and Seventh and Twenty-second infantry will constitute a brigade, under the command of Colonel Gibbon, of the Seventh infantry. The battalion of the Second and Seventh cavalry, battery of artillery and Indian scouts, will report directly to the department of the commander." One of the most formidable difficulties to be anticipated on this march is a want of water and grass. There has been no rain for many weeks and the Rosebud contains very little water at its mouth, and it is feared the grass which has survived the drought has been burned by the Indians.

LAWRENCE, Ks., August 14.—The Journal to-morrow publishes an account of the Custer battle, as reported by Agent Miles to Superintendent Nicholson. It is strictly the Indian version of the story, though it agrees in important particulars with that of the military. The Indians are said to have had forty men to Custer's one.

THE FIG BOX TRICK.

How It is Played on Immigrants.

Mr. M. C. Hangerford, of Clinton, Jones county, Georgia, and Mr. A. C. Williams, stopping at the Pacific hotel, who came in on the Texas and Pacific train last night at 10:30, from Georgia, called at THE HERALD office and made the following statement. That the man who sells newspapers and fruit on that train swindled a country boy emigrant, about eighteen years old, out of five dollars in this way. He sat down by him with a basket of dried figs in his lap. He then selected three boxes and pulling out twenty-five dollars, which he counted out, folded it up and put it in one of the boxes. Then he shut up all three boxes and shuffled them. Shuffling the twenty-five dollar box into his basket and dexterously replacing it with one out of the basket. "Now," said he "what will you give me for a chance."

The boy said he didn't want any chance. The man then said, "just give five dollars, being as it is you, and you can make twenty-five dollars easy enough." The greeny gave him the five dollars, and the boxes were opened, and, of course, there was no twenty-five dollars. Some of the passengers, who witnessed it, complained to the Conductor, Mr. C. L. Thorn, who said he would see about it, but who paid no attention to it until the train arrived, when he walked through the train, and reported the news and fruit man gone. The passengers had told him they intended to complain to Colonel Tom Scott, President of the road.

Mr. Hungerford's and Mr. Willams' address can be had at this office. If there are any confidence performances going on on this road, the officers should look into and remedy it, as it is calculated to injure the road. The gentlemen who made this statement and charge, declare their intention of writing back to the leading papers of Georgia a full account of their experience, and warning their emigrant friends not to come by the Texas and Pacific road. We are satisfied that the officers of the road will at once look into and punish all such practices as are complained of, and will see that they are not repeated, and that conductors are given special instructions relative to the protection of immigrants, and required to arrest confidence men or boys found on the train.

Grand Greenback Demonstration in Terrehaute.

TERREHAUTE, August 12.—The largest night rally, but one, ever held in Terrehaute was the independent greenback mass meeting held here tonight. Thirteen hundred torches were carried in the procession, and a large body of horsemen marched. Speeches were made by James Buchanan and N. W. Parker.

Railroad Strike Ended in a Compromise.

CINCINNATI, O., August 12.—The strike of the brakemen on the Ohio and Mississippi Railroad ended this afternoon, the strikers agreeing to go to work at reduced pay and the Company promising to restore the old rates as soon as the business of the Company will justify them in doing so.

Adams, the Coming Gubernatorial Candidate in Kansas.

MANHATTAN, Kas., August 12.—The delegates elected to-day to represent the Seventh district in the State Convention were Dr. J. Evans and Wm. F. Condroy. They were unanimously instructed to vote for N. Adams for Governor.

Miscellaneous Notes.

ST. ALBANS, Vt., August 12.—Leon Vandney and Arthur Roverts, of Montreal, fought a duel at Richford yesterday. Two shots were exchanged, in which Roverts was wounded. The participants were arrested.

NEW YORK, August 12.—The managers of the labor demonstration on Thursday have nominated James Gordon Bennett for Mayor.

THE GALLOWS.

Wesley Jones Hung for Committing an Horrid Outrage on a White Woman.

The Execution Witnessed by Eight Thousand People—Last Interview with the Condemned—Incidents, Etc.

His Victim.

Mrs. Benson was a very respectable white woman living in this county, who has been gradually sinking, and it is thought cannot long survive the injuries and brutal treatment received. Her mental sufferings are said to be great. Shame, mortification and the cruelty of the outrage are doing their work and the unhappy woman cannot long survive the horrors of her condition.

INCIDENTS.

The night before his execution, Wesley Jones had an interview with his wife and child, who had come from Upshur to see him. After parting with them he was very much overcome and walked his cell a good part of the night. The wife and child were again at the jail yesterday morning and had the usual affecting interview. He had been married four years and his wife said he had always been good to her. She was anxious to hear his speech, but had great horror to seeing him hung.

THE DAY.

At an early hour yesterday morning the streets began to be thronged with the country people, who came in from twenty miles around, in buggies, wagons, horseback and afoot, men, women and children. There must have been fully five thousand persons from outside the city. It is now many years since any one was hung in this city, and the peculiar atrocity of the crime committed had created a wide-spread feeling of curiosity, with a determination to see the law carried out. There was no rowdyism, noise or disorder. One would have imagined that there was a circus in own, and that the country people and town people were out for a holiday. Our reporters saw no drunkenness or lawlessness. The number of horsemen about the city was especially noticeable. The average Texan is not himself afoot, and glorious in being well mounted. There was about a brigade of cavalry turned loose here yesterday. The country people promenaded the streets, did some shopping, went sight-seeing, and regaled themselves with candies, peanuts and home made lunches. They had evidently come to make a day of it.

THE MILITARY

Consisting of the Lamar Rifles marched from their armory, under the command of Captain J. G. Eblen, to the jail, in front of which a large crowd of men, women and children, white and black and a good many of the men mounted had assembled. Arriving at the jail gate, the Lamar Rifles marched inside of the yard. The windows of the jail were crowded with prisoners who were clinging to the bars and staring out with breathless interest.

THE CONDEMNED BROUGHT OUT.

Sheriff Moon, assisted by two deputies and Marshal Morton, then brought out the condemned man, Wesley Jones privates James Bell, Wm. Evans and Benjamin Stewart, of company E. Seventh Infantry, for their bravery in taking dispatches to General Crook and returning. These men among others, volunteered to go through the hostile Indian country, when Indian scouts refused.

WASHINGTON, August 11.—The following is General Sheridan's letter to General Sherman, with his message asking for more cavalry or volunteers, and transmitted by the President to Congress, to-day:

CHICAGO, August 5, 1876.

To W. T. Sherman:

a burly negro with a coarse, sensual, brutal face dressed in black, with a white straw hat. A two horse wagon was in attendance and the prisoner was assisted up into the wagon and seated in a chair, Sheriff Moon, Marshal Morton, the Rev. J. R. Allen, of the Floyd street Methodist church, who had been specially requested to attend the condemned, and two colored ministers of the Gospel, Rev. George Allen, of the Free Mission Baptist church, and Rev. Mr. Marshall, of Waxahachie.

The fatal rope was then handed up into the wagon and deposited.

THE CONDEMNED.

The condemned man appeared serious but unconcerned, there was no nervousness at this time and no breaking down.

MORE MILITARY.

The Stonewall Greys here appeared marching down the street, under Captain E. G. Bower. They wore their caps and uniform pants but were in their shirt sleeves. They took up a position on one side of the wagon, the rifles on the other and

THE PROCESSION MOVES.

The procession moved on past the courthouse square to the gallows, which had been already erected on the Trinity river bottom, just above the bridge of the Texas & Pacific railway. About three thousand people followed the procession to the gallows, where the people began to assemble rapidly, until there must have been from six to eight thousand people present. The trees were swarming with spectators and every available standing point was packed with the expectant thousands, who preserved good order there was no demonstration. Any one who wanted to study the physique and characteristics of Texans, would have had a fine opportunity. The men were all strong, hearty sunburnt fellows, with brawny shoulders, horny hands and were the pictures of vigor and health. The crowd was evidently in a good humor. There were hundreds of negroes out in their best clothes, men, women and children mingling with the whites freely. None of them were in any way molested or interfered with and they conducted themselves with good order and decorum. They seemed fully impressed with the justice of the sentence and its execution.

ARRIVING AT THE GALLOWS.

When the procession arrived at the gallows they found an immense crowd of men, women and children had preceded them; even huxter wagons thronged the place, and the bluff, railroad bridge and trees were crowded with those eager to witness the execution. Many conducted themselves in a humorous manner and with an unbecoming air, while others plainly exhibited a realization of the solemn occasion.

The military were of valuable service in keeping back the crowd, for only a limited number could be accommodated within the hempen circle that surrounded the stand.

At twenty-five minutes of, three, Sheriff Moon escorted the prisoner upon the scaffold, and accompanying him were one or two deputies, Marshal Morton, Rev. J. R. Allen and two colored ministers. The prisoner's wife and child then came forward and mounted the stand to give their last farewell. They were together about five minutes, and the scene was pitiable in the extreme. His wife says he was a kind husband. After the parting she left the scene.

THE PRISONER'S REMARKS.

There was some disappointment from the few remarks of Wesley Jones; for many expected he would have much to say, much to confess, and say it boldly. But such was not the case, for, though ruffian that he has been, he was much subdued, and unmistakably labored under great mental anxiety, his protests to the contrary notwithstanding. He said little, but appeared to feel all that he said, as was quite natural.

"You have come to see me die. I, like all of you, have to die. I thank God I am going home to rest. I hope to meet you all in heaven. I know I have done wrong, as you all have. God will forgive me for what I have done, as quick as for what you all have done. I feel that Jesus is with me. I hope this will be a warning to you all. May God be with you all forever and forever. You can persecute the body, but not the soul. Do not scorn me because I have to be hung. I have said about all that I have to or can say. I want you all to pray for me."

One of the colored brethren then read a passage from the Holy Scriptures, followed by the hymn, "And must I be to judgment brought?"

Rev. J. R. Allen then offered up a fervent and appropriate petition to the Most High in behalf of the wretched man.

LAST MOMENTS.

There was then a shaking of hands and bidding the last good-bye, when all left the stand but the officers. Sheriff Moon then read the death warrant, after which he unshackled the prisoner and tied his arms behind him. He then had the prisoner step on the trap-door, tied his feet, placed the rope around his neck and the black cap over his head; and five minutes after the body dropped through the trap and hung by the neck. Not a kick was perceptible, only a slight shivering. At the expiration of fifteen minutes he was pronounced dead, dead. At this juncture a few shouts went up from among the crowd, which did not appear in accordance with the awful hour.

A COLORED MINISTERS LAST INTERVIEW WITH THE CONDEMNED MAN.

The Rev. A. R. Griggs (colored), pastor of the New Hope Baptist church here, wrote out and furnished THE HERALD the following account of his last interview with Wesley Jones, which we publish, that the colored people may known that the dead man had the consolation of religion.

Dallas, August 9th, 1876.

My sixth and last conversation with Wesley Jones was in the Dallas county jail. Mr. Jones was justly condemned on the 19th of January, 1876, for committing a rape on a white woman not far from this city, which he himself acknowledged and must on the 11th instant hang by the neck until dead, dead, dead.

The details of our conversation just two days before he dies is as follows:

I asked him how he felt, he replied. "Very well."

Are you prepared and willing to die?

"I am," said he, "all that I hate is that the time seems so long. I long to go there for my soul will be at rest."

You believe you will go to heaven when you die?

"I do."

Why do you think so?

"I have prayed and God has heard my prayers, moreover, I believe that I was converted when I was abo[illegible] eleven years old and would [illegible] joined the church in [illegible] county, Texas, but my [illegible] objected to it. I would [illegible] the Bethlehem Baptist [illegible] shur county, Texas, [illegible] met with an opportu[illegible]

"Do you know a[illegible] parents?"

"Very little. [illegible] when quite sm[illegible] either of the[illegible] father used t[illegible] boy."

"Why have yo[illegible] to me and send fo[illegible]

"I love to talk w[illegible] to want to do me all [illegible]

"When was the firs[illegible] saw me?"

"Last winter, [illegible] here sick."

"How old are you?"

"About 27 or 28 years old."

"Were you ever in much bad company?"

"Yes; when about fourteen years old I was driving cattle. The boys persuaded me to play cards and made me bet. From that I was led off."

After questioning him very closely and seriously about his conversion, as my custom was when there, I reached through the iron bars for a Bible one of the prisoners had. I read some in the nineteenth chapter of St. John, 25th, 26th and 27th verses. I referred to "the house not made with hands." (I Corinthians, 5.) Then to the Resurrection, "O, death, where is thy sting? O, grave, where is thy victory?" and how he would meet the Lord in the air, and even he would meet the Lord. I read to him of the things we would eat and drink when he got there and that God would give us light. (Revelations, 22 chapter.) I then bowed with him and offered prayer. While praying I thought of all the prisoners, and began to pray for them, thinking it probably my last visit in there. We rose with tears in our eyes. While there we sang the hymn commencing,

How happy are they,
Who their Savior obey.

We then shook hands to meet no more this side of the grave, knowing that in two days he must die. His last remarks to me were these:

"Mr. Griggs, you must come up and see these other prisoners when I am gone, and talk with them."

"I replied, that I would if they would accept, and to my surprise, white and colored said, "Come Mr. Griggs, we will be glad to see you at any time; and away I went with full heart and tears in my eyes.

ELDER A. R. GRIGGS

Pastor of the Colored Baptist church Dallas Texas.

THE LAW VINDICATED.

In conclusion THE HERALD congratulates the people of Dallas county upon their law abiding conduct from first to last relative to this outrageous criminal. The law has been carried out. Justice has been done. A jury composed of twelve good citizens tried the case, and convicted the man, who confessed the crime. The case was appealed, and the decision of the District court here confirmed and the prisoner sentensed and executed accordingly.

St. Louis Globe Democrat

Published Daily, Tri-Weekly, Semi-Weekly and Weekly, N. E. cor. Fourth and Pine sts., by the Globe Printing Company of St. Louis.

TERMS OF THE DAILY.

Single copies, per week, delivered by carrier....$ 25
By mail (payable in advance), postage paid by the proprietors, per year.................. 12 00
Five copies.............................. 55 00
THE SUNDAY GLOBE-DEMOCRAT—$2 50 per annum.
THE TRI-WEEKLY GLOBE-DEMOCRAT—(The Sunday Daily and the Semi-Weekly GLOBE-DEMOCRAT combined), by mail, $6 per year, (postage prepaid). Five copies, $25.
THE SEMI-WEEKLY GLOBE-DEMOCRAT is published every Tuesday and Friday morning—$3 50 per year. Five copies, $15 (postage prepaid).
THE WEEKLY GLOBE-DEMOCRAT is published every Thursday; ONE DOLLAR AND FIFTY CENTS per year (postage prepaid). No club rates.
NEWS-DEALERS can procure this paper regularly by sending their orders directly to us, or to the St. Louis Book and News Company, 307 North Fourth street, St. Louis, at 2¾ cents per copy, postage prepaid.
ALL SUBSCRIPTIONS are payable in advance, and may be sent, at our risk, IN REGISTERED letters.
ALL DRAFTS, checks and money-orders should be made payable to the Globe Printing Company of St Louis.
LETTERS, communications, telegraphic dispatches, whether on business or intended for publication, should be addressed to the Globe Printing Company, St. Louis.

TWELVE PAGES.

The War.

An important dispatch from Shumla asserts that the Turks, after a severe engagement at Papaskin, on Friday night, turned the Russian left wing, and that the Russians were repulsed along the whole line, suffering heavy losses. It is said Russian troops at Sistova, on Tuesday, rioted because of bad provisions, and threw 100,000 moldy loaves of broad into the Danube. A special dispatch gives thrilling details of the strange manner in which Aziz Pasha met his death in a recent engagement.

The weather indications for to-day are falling barometer, warmer, and clear or partly cloudy.

GOLD in New York yesterday opened and closed at 104.

HAS this country eaten $14,000,000 worth of Canadian fish? If it has not, we ought not to pay the indemnity. We call for a bill of particulars.

LOOK out for some great convulsion of nature. The Browns have won a game. We presume they couldn't help it. The other fellows must have blundered.

MR. FILLEY is forbidden to have anything to do with politics, but if you want an office under the "Reform" Administration of Mayor Overstolz, you must first get Mr. Filley's indorsement.

"Go and see Mr. Filley; if he says so, then I can give you a place." This is the response of several of the newly-appointed city officials to all applicants for positions. We mention it to show the extent to which Federal office-holders abstain from politics.

SENATOR MORTON'S condition is the subject of contradictory dispatches. Private advices represent the Senator as beyond hope of recovery, but the newspaper correspondents, pretending to be in receipt of authentic information, encourage the belief that the doctors will yet bring the Senator safely out of his ailment.

TOM EWING is not satisfied because America exports more than she imports. Three years ago he was remarking that the country imported more than she exported, and that "the balance of trade was agin' her." There is no emergency which can come upon an able-bodied politician like Mr. Ewing and find him unprepared.

THE great meat-shop question still agitates the municipal mind, and the House of Lords is puzzled to know how it can make the Commons recede from their amendments in favor of the butchers. If it could be satisfactorily shown that the meat-shopmen cast more votes and swing more influence than the butchers, the delegates would drop the butchers with the sudden surprise of an elephant dropping a plug of tobacco. This matter ought to be put in a proper shape, or there will be a deadlock between the lordly Capulets and the mighty Montagues.

THE Cuban League have circulated a lengthy and well-written petition asking Congress to recognize Cuban independence. It is unnecessary for us to print this document or any portion of it. There is nothing new to be said in favor of Cuban independence. It is an old story, and one which ought long since to have been properly heeded by the American Government. Every month increases the improbabilities of subjugation and adds to the reasons for believing that independence will be the ultimate result of the struggle. Belligerent rights ought to have been accorded to the Cubans long ago; they have succeeded, however, in spite of the denial of these rights, in making a most gallant fight, and now they are fairly entitled to full recognition.

MR. CURTIS, of the *Star* (the new "labor" organ), shares in the very common delusion that the American stock would die out if not re-enforced by fresh infusions from Europe; but Mr. Curtis does not explain how the American stock managed to show such vitality up to the year 1847, when the increase of population was out of all proportion to the infusion of foreign blood, nor has he mastered the physical statistics of the Boston public schools, which show that the children of American parents are taller, heavier and healthier than the children of foreign parents at the same age. The delusion about the decay of the American stock is a superstition almost as absurd as the belief in witchcraft, and any man who gives currency to it is either ignorant of the nature of statistics or careless of the value of his assertions.

THE National Board of Trade has given expression to the intelligent honesty of the American people in voting down the silver dollar, and it deserves thanks for having taken a manly stand on a question which offered so many temptations to dishonesty and demagoguery. The best argument we have heard in favor of the silver dollar came from the *Republican* when it pathetically remonstrated with Sherman, saying that if that noble coin had not been omitted from the coinage of 1873, it would have paid millions of dollars of debts public and private, "because it was the cheaper money." If they would only coin a silver dollar that would be worth say 75 cents, we should be still better off according to the *Republican's* logic; but there can be no question about the dishonesty of such logic.

THE duty of the Public School Board in the matter of awarding the city printing is clear. The advertisements calling for bids bound the Board morally, if not legally, to give the contract to the *Dispatch* as the lowest bidder. There was no question of circulation about it, because the proprietors of the *Republican* and the proprietors of the *Dispatch* both swore to the same city circulation, namely, 3,000 copies, and as the bid of the *Dispatch* was the lower, there should have been no question of the award. We hope that there is no crookedness in the committee, but the matter looks bad. There is an election coming off very soon, and it looks as if the committee was bidding for the post of brother-in-law to the *Republican*.

PATTI AGAIN.

The New York *Herald* prints a very funny story about Adelina Patti, declaring that the prima donna will sing no more; that in effect from and out of her late troubles at St. Petersburg she has experienced religion, and will retire into a convent, and thus imitate the example of Heloise, the famous pet of the yet more famous Abelard. The tale is possible, for it is difficult to calculate upon the eccentricities of a prima donna. It is improbable because these very eccentricities are generally more nearly allied to the delights of the world, the flesh, and the devil, than conventual seclusion and the tribulation where all the delights of the footlights
in the past must be tortured
remorse of the present, the medita
the enormity of trivial offenses mag
to unpardonable sins under the glo
veil and in the austerity of the c
Patti to choose such a part as that
almost equivalent to an abando
flirtation by Cleopatra, in the hey-d
beauty, when she boasted of the pas
which her Hercules, her Roman
leapt into her arms, contented the
It would be like Boadicea forge
fury when brought face to face wit
mans. It would be like Elizabeth
her dresses, or Mary her religion.
be a stranger fact than if Cor
forgotten her most precious
or if Prascovia Lopouloff, when s
stood before the face of the Czar A
had omitted to plead for the fate o
rents—the Exiles of Siberia. T
strange things in the history of fe
but for all that, if Patti abandons
and enters a convent, we shall be
the Ethiopian can change his ski
leopard his spots, with a faith far
plicit than that with which we ha
the dogma and the doctrines of any
has ever flourished, from the days of
otheism of Adam to the polytheis
last-discovered race of the South S
ers.

OUR ART CULTURE.

Mr. S. A. Coale, Jr., long know
city as an enthusiastic amateur of
collector of rare taste and judg
more recently brought into promine
strictures on the "Western pumpkin
in a letter to the New York *Worl*
has attracted a great deal of notice
its republication in the GLOBE-DE
has been compelled to vindicate h
best he can in a transparent intervi
Republican, and expresses a plai
about the condition of art cultu
Louis, which is not less severe than
although it is fortunately free from
garities which rendered the letter so
Mr. Coale is a gentleman who has
done more for the art culture of
than any other one man, and his o
any question connected with art is
a great deal of influence as soon a
freed it from the eccentricities w
art collectors an *irritabile genus*.
do to say that, because he acted fo
trying to prevent the loan of pictu
Fair, his censures are not well dese
fact Mr. Coale does not really desi
vent the exhibition of pictures in
he says that if the committee had
him he could (and of course he wo
secured by telegraph, in thirty-six h
loan of a hundred first-class picture
his chief reason for calling the Ex
pumpkin-show was that he was n
to by the committee. This is an ec
which entitles Mr. Coale to a full-p
bership in the *irritabile genus*, a
how strong is the contrast between
ment in choosing or approving a pi
his judgment in dealing with his fe
But suppose we leave Mr. Coale'
ality out of the discussion altogether, and confine ourselves strictly to an estimate of the standing of St. Louis as a center of art culture, what are we to say? The *Times* claims that St. Louis is very strong in "its appreciation of the old masters," when there are probably not fifty persons in the city who could tell an "old master" from a chromo. As there is not a single genuine "old master" in the city, there need be no false modesty about disclaiming acquaintance with them. But are we any better acquainted with the new masters? This is a very delicate question, but there is only one answer to it. If we were fond of art, if we knew anything of it or cared anything for it, this great city, with its swarm of population, its wealth, its vanity, its ostentation, would buy pictures even if it did not care to look at them, would affect an admiration for sculpture, architecture decoration, bronzes and bric-a-brac even if it were the merest dilettanteism. But we have not even gotten far enough to understand how far off we are from any art-spirit; we do not know enough to affect a taste which we do not possess. For all practical purposes it may be said that we simply ignore the existence of art.

The burden of proof rests on those who, in the face of the apathy and indifference of the population of St. Louis to all art interests, still affirm that we either know or care anything about it. There are less than five collections of amateurs, there is one dealer who has flourished (chiefly by the sale of window glass and putty), there is no art school, and last year an exhibition that should have drawn crowds did not pay the cost of the gas-light. This is a bad state of affairs, but there is only one way to mend it, and that is not by stirring up quarrels among those who have either time or means, either taste or good will, to devote to furthering the cause of art. Private amateurs can do a great deal, but public exhibitions can do a great deal more, and the best results can be achieved only when all pull together, as we trust all will do in the forthcoming exposition.

EUTHANASIA IN FLORIDA.

When they had drunk deeply of the wine of life, and age had begun to creep rapidly upon them, one of the chief aspirations of the Greeks of old was for euthanasia—a gentle and easy passage from this world to the next. Their literature teems with allusions to the idea, and no Greek thought that any of his people could truly be called fortunate unless a happy life was closed by a happy death. To make perfect such a journey to the shades of the invisible life, the last moments of the voyager must, above all things, be almost entirely free from physical pain. Such an exit was the crowning glory of a career blessed by the gods of Olympus. About two years ago the conception of this idea of euthanasia was seized upon and expanded by some of the leading scientific writers of England. They argued that, as certain diseases, after reaching a certain stage, were known to be incurable, and were attended with terrible pain, which frequently could scarely even be alleviated, and as the patient was then simply a burden almost intolerable to himself, his existence, from considerations of mercy, should be shortened by his physicians. The most ardent supporters of this new doctrine drew up a complete set of rules to govern the manner and practice of this species of euthanasia. They even drafted the legislation which would be necessary to enable the attendant physicians to kill instead of curing.

ST. LOUIS SOCIETY NOTES.

—Miss Hunt is visiting friends in Louisiana, Mo.

—Miss Addie Eads is visiting friends in Oconomowoc.

—Miss Alice Lyle is visiting friends at Bloomington, Ill.

—Miss Lizzie Porter is visiting some friends in Batavia, Ill.

—Miss Sophie Grindon has returned to her home in St. Louis.

—Mr. Houghton and family returned from St. Paul on Tuesday.

—Miss Garrison is visiting Miss Gertie Goodrich, of Milwaukee.

—Mr. Charles Chase has returned from a pleasant trip to Keokuk, Ia.

—Mr. T. J. Farrell left for New York during the early part of the week.

—Mr. J. C. W. Schmell is registered at the Cliff House, Devil's Lake, Wis.

—Mr. and Mrs. Quigley, of Quincy, Ill., are visiting friends in this city.

—Miss Allie Barney sailed from New York on the 22d inst. for Paris, France.

—Mr. J. C. Chapman has returned from a short visit to the Sweet Springs, Mo.

—Miss Vastine has arrived in London, England, and is charmed with the big city.

—Misses H. and L. Hinchman are visiting friends in Leavenworth and Salt Creek Valley.

—Messrs. D. K. Ferguson and B. Allen are registered at the United States Hotel, Saratoga.

—Miss Grace Metcalf left yesterday to spend a short time with some friends in Bridgeton, Mo.

—Mr. and Mrs. E. F. Chippell and family are stopping at the Finch House, Kilbourn City, Wis.

—Miss Julia Fife is spending a few weeks with her friend, Miss Gracie Greenlief, at Gray's Summit, Mo.

—Mr. Goodman King was during the early part of the week registered at Draper's Hall, Oconomowoc.

—Miss Amy Sparr is visiting Miss Lizzie Maxwell, in Keokuk, Ia. Both ladies were formerly of St. Louis.

A MAD LEADER.

The Bravest Man in the Ottoman Army.

Graphic and Thrilling Details of His Death.

A Severe Engagement at Papaskin on Friday.

The Russians Repulsed Along the Whole Line.

Political Points from France—Flashes from Afar.

Turkey.

Special Dispatch to the Globe-Democrat.

HOW AZIZ PASHA DIED.

NEW YORK, August 25.—A war correspondent, writing under date of Rasgrad, July 31, sends the following graphic and thrilling details of the death of a Turkish Pasha, one who was one of the bravest and most intrepid men in the Ottoman army, and who was killed at the recent engagement at Esirdje. The letter was written by an aide-de-camp present at the battle, and is as follows: I avail myself of the occasion to give you some details of the

LAST MOMENTS OF AZIZ PASHA.

Though one of the rarest Generals we possess, he has unfortunately, for the last few days, shown symptoms of insanity; to such a pitch had he arrived that his staff became alarmed. Usually so affable and tractable, he suddenly, only four days previous to the battle, soured in disposition

same work. It embraces a large number of the best scholars of this country, and has invited a society of European savants called the Congres de Americanistes to meet with it at Indianapolis, in 1879. Its officers at present are Hon. C. C. Jones, Augusta, Ga., President; Prof. S. F. Baird, Col. C. Whitlesey, Dr. Thomas E. Peckitt, and others, Vice Presidents; Rev. S. D. Peet, Ashtabula, O., Secretary; and Wm. S. Vaux, Esq., Philadelphia, Treasurer.

ELECTRIC FLASHES.

AT Iowa City, Albert Grenlich, fourteen years old, was drowned while bathing in the river yesterday afternoon.

THE hotel at Yellow Sulphur Springs, Va., burned yesterday. Loss $25,000; insured for $12,000. A colored boy was killed.

L. ROBERTS & Co., flour merchants, 17 South street, N. Y., yesterday made an assignment to Isaac Hoyt & Co. Liabilities estimated at $50,000.

AT Nyack, N. Y., Richard P. Eells, late Secretary of the Rockland Savings Bank, was arrested yesterday upon a charge of having embezzled funds of the bank.

AT Baltimore during an altercation Friday night between Chas. Pitts, aged twenty, and Chas. Wilson, aged nineteen, the former stabbed and killed the latter; both colored.

THE SICK STATESMAN.

Senator Morton's Struggle with the King of Terrors.

His Death Anticipated Almost Daily, Although His Physicians Have Not Given Up All Hope of His Recovery.

Special Dispatch to the Globe-Democrat.

RICHMOND, IND., August 25.—Your correspondent was not informed of the serious change in Senator Morton's condition as promised last night. He passed the latter portion of the night in pain, and was very restless. His condition at this hour,
10 a. m.—is much worse than at 10
t night, and is so acknowledged by Dr.
severe pains in the side returned
lock in the morning.

IN A CRITICAL CONDITION.

—Senator Morton's pains are extending
He is in a critical condition.

THE WORST MAY COME.

Senator Morton is very low now. We
edict the result, but think the worst

om Senator Morton's physicians and
ere are few people in Richmond, in-
medical fraternity, who consider his
r recovery as probable, and resident
of reputation say his restoration to his
h is almost impossible, and they an-
death daily. There is no question but
nator can not survive many such vio-
rms of pain as those of 3 o'clock and
this morning, when his family and
rrounded his bed, expecting death to
terrible sufferings. Dr. Thompson
called from Pennsylvania. Prominent
from abroad have arrived during
Among many telegrams of sympathy
eceived to-day was one from J. N.
ing: "President Hayes is deeply af-
he Senator's sufferings." His family
ians are awaiting with hopeful anxiety
of the next few hours.

RESTING WELL.

lock he is resting well.

AN HOUR LATER.

Morton has just been moved from his
easy chair, and seems to be resting
Dr. Bliss says he can not see how a
of the pain can occur.

DANGEROUS SYMPTOMS.

R. Holloway, Senator Morton's
-law, who has been constantly with the
ce his arrival here, has been increas-
ndeavors to furnish information, both
public, of the Senator's condition.
but natural that his views
hopeful, yet this morning his bulletins
eds of private answers to messages of
re utterly despondent. He had given
e. Dr. Bliss, in his official capacity,
to the Associated Press, at 11 o'clock,
Senator was out of danger. At
k Senator Morton's family
ily summoned to congregate around
elieved to be his deathbed before day-
heroic treatment the Senator was re-
he intense pains in the right side; but
eatly exhausted. Again at 9 o'clock
of pain returned, and for an hour his
momentarily anticipated. Again be
under the influence of medical
and dozed in nervous prostration
ut 4 o'clock, when his sleep
ed natural, quiet and healthful. At 5
again surprised even those who knew
former recuperative powers. He was
om his invalid chair, which is a favor-
during his illness, and was put to bed,
ESTED NEWSPAPERS TO BE READ,
d heartily into a discussion of various
nterest. At 8 o'clock he had what Dr.
ts was a voluntary movement of the
From that time until 11 o'clock there
tle change in his condition, yet his
watched with bated breath
of midnight, which has arrived, and
fatal pains in the right side have not re-
ne reason why his physician and family
n so anxious to have favorable
of his condition telegraphed to
rs is the fact that the Senator
every paragraph relating to his
and if the paper has had an unfavor-
clipped out, it must be produced to
is demand for news concerning
It is still claimed that the
malady is entirely the result of
. It is asserted that he has eaten al-
ng since the few mouthfuls of squirrel
lay which so nearly resulted fatally.
alled Dr. Bliss to his bed-
riends of the Senator, on last
emphasize his improved condition,
e departure of Dr. Thompson, his old
lis physician, for Pennsylvania. The
rs that Dr. Thompson was obliged to
s family, yet so alarming was the Sen-
dition this morning that telegrams were

RECALLING DR. THOMPSON,

robably arrive to-morrow. The Senator
ded by his entire family except one son, now en route from Alaska. Gov. Burbank has from the first been one of the strongest hopers for the Senator's recovery, and perhaps he of all other men should be hopeful, for he has stood beside the Senator's couch too often when all others expected death and seen the Senator rally in a few hours and occupy his seat in the Senate chamber. Your correspondent to-day interviewed four leading resident physicians outside the Senator's sick-room, for not half a dozen people outside the Senator's family have seen him for a week. These doctors have watched the progress of the disease, and know at least all favorable symptoms of his condition. One doctor says this pain in the side, which returns every alternate twenty-four hours, and each time earlier and more severe, with a tendency to creep up from the abdomen to the chest, is an ugly symptom. Bereft of medical terms, it is water in the cavity of the chest, and threatens fatal results. Another equally prominent physician asserts that the bleeding which has been resorted to will not save the Senator's life. The fact is, Senator Morton is

SUFFERING FROM A COMPLICATION

of his old enemy and present attack, which will in all probability result fatally in 48 hours. The third physician, and his name would be recognized throughout the West considers the Senator's condition alarmingly critical, and should he escape threatened paralysis of the heart he will be left a confirmed and helpless invalid who may await another attack for months. The last medical gentleman said, although he was conversant with the Senator's constitutional malady, yet from meager and unsatisfactory reports which his physicians and friends have seen and profess to divulge he could give no professional opinion, yet from all the facts as reported, he had very little hopes of the Senator's recovery, unless his physicians should succeed in averting these intense chest pains for the next twenty-four hours.

LATER.

1 A. M.—The dreaded midnight hour has passed. At 1 o'clock the Senator awoke from a natural sleep, which his attendants say was not the result of opiates. His mind is clear, no fever, pulse regular for first time since his attack. The Senator was delirious a portion of the time to-day, but to-night is perfectly rational. At 1:30 he called for a newspaper, but was persuaded to take a nap, and wait till morning, which he is now attempting to do, with a fair prospect of success.

LATEST.

RICHMOND, IND., Aug. 26—2 a. m.—The Senator's condition gradually improved since last report. Dr. Bliss is very anxious about what his condition would be at midnight, as pains of right side have heretofore occurred earlier each time. At 12 o'clock the Senator went to sleep, and has remained in that condition until this hour. Col. Holloway again very hopeful. The following message was received to-night from Washington, addressed to Col. W. R. Holloway:

I feel very much solicitude about Senator Morton. Please keep me advised as to his condition.
(Signed) R. B. HAYES.

THE CROOKS' CORNER.

Hardin, the Texas Outlaw, Captured in Florida.

The Latest Concerning the Rio Grande Outrages.

Three Prisoners Escape From Jail at Topeka, Kansas.

Frisco's Political Scandal—Curiosities of Crime.

Special Dispatch to the Globe-Democrat.

GALVESTON, TEX., August 25.—Special telegrams to the *News* to-night say that John Wesley Hardin, the most desperate man that has lived in Texas since 1868, was captured in Pensacola, Fla., two days since, where he has lived under an assumed name for several years. He was captured by two Texas State officers, who have equaled Pinkerton's detectives in this pursuit. They had to fight several of Hardin's friends, wounding one, killing one, and capturing Hardin and another. Hardin tried the habeas corpus scheme at Montgomery, Ala., without success. He has killed at least ten men, and been the leader of the Taylor party, whose feud with the Sutton family has cost DeWitt and surrounding counties three lives and a division of her citizens, until but few emigrants will go there, though the country is rich and fertile; but as it is in Western Texas, remote from the thickly settled sections, affects only their immediate neighborhood.

THE RIO GRANDE TROUBLES.

A *News* special from Brownsville to-night says State District Judge Russell arrived here Tuesday night from Corpus Christi. On Thursday he sent the following demand for the extradition of the parties engaged in the late Rio Grande City affair, as well as the parties delivered from jail, having previously sent demands from Rio Grande City to the authorities at Camargo, from which nothing has been heard. The Judge is earnest in his endeavors to bring about a rendition of these criminals:

United States of America, State of Texas, County of Cameron—To His Excellency Servado Canales, Governor of Tamaulipas, Mexico: SIR—I have the honor to call your attention to the fact that during the night of August 11, 1877, a band of marauders attacked the County Jail in Rio Grande City, Starr County, in this State, releasing therefrom Segundo Garsia, confined therein on a charge of murder, and Rudolpho Espronceda, confined on a charge of horse-stealing, and the said band shot and seriously wounded Noah Cox, Esq., the County Attorney of said County, as well as the Jailer. The said parties, so far as known, are, to wit: Rafael Garsia, Greagora Garsia, Seferno Juares, Rafael Trevino, Pedro Rodriguez, Brigado Olivarez, Pablo Parra and one Obispo, who, after committing the said assault upon the person of Mr. Cox and the Jailer, took refuge in the Republic of Mexico, crossing the Rio Grande, a few miles above Rio Grande City. Now, by virtue of the authority vested in me by the Governor of the State of Texas, under the treaty of December 11, 1861, between the United States and the Mexican Republic for the extradition of criminals, I ask and require that the said parties, to wit: Rafael Garsia, Gregoria Garsha, Seferno Juarez, Rafael Trevino, Pindro Rodriguez, Brigado, Olivarez, Pablo Parra and one Obispo, be delivered to me to answer the charge of burglary and assault with intent to murder, and that the said Segundo Garsia and Rudolfo Espronceda, so forcibly taken from jail, as aforesaid, and carried into Mexico, be delivered to me to answer the respective charges against them, to-wit: murder against Garcia, and horse-stealing against Espronceda.

I have the honor to be, very respectfully, your obedient servant,

(Signed) JOHN C. RUSSELL, Judge,
Twenty-fifth Judicial District of Texas.
Brownsville, Tex., August 23, 1877.

THE DEMAND

was given on Thursday by the Sheriff of this county to Gen. Canales in person in Matamoras, and up to a late hour of this Saturday no answer has been returned, and so far treated with silence if not contempt. It is not believed in Brownsville that Escobedo hired parties to break the jail, as stated in a previous issue of your paper. The conviction is strong that he had nothing to do with it, but that the friends and relations of Segundo Garsia, from Camargo, are alone responsible. It is asserted that Parra, Olivarez and Espranceda are in jail in Matamoras, but the authorities there have not informed our authorities. The most noted one (Garsia) has not been apprehended, nor do the people here believe he will be. Expect all sorts of quibbles and evasions until our Government takes a firmer and more threatening attitude. The stand taken by Gen. Ord is an expression of that entertained by all Texans.

was administered, not to bring about any temporary alleviation, but to hasten on an immediate and painless dissolution. It is true that, so far as we do know, it was thus given at the pressing request of the dying woman. But this will not remove it from a direct offense against the law. Under all the circumstances it would, perhaps, be too severe to call it murder. But so long as in law suicide is self-murder, a man who willingly hands a woman any deadly narcotic with the express purpose of enabling her to destroy herself, is technically guilty as an accessory before the fact. It is very dangerous to the community to allow husband or wife, in cases where death is apparently near, to constitute himself or herself the sole judge of its imminence, and to determine in how far it would be right and proper to abridge the pains of dissolution, as Mr. Keyes did in Florida two short weeks ago.

Unless Florida vindicates the majesty of the law by a prompt investigation, and a punishment, which need not be excessive, the example thus set may be imitated as a more expeditious mode of obtaining divorce whenever any slightly alarming fit of illness provides at once the opportunity and the probability of an escape from detection. If, indeed, such methods of quelling pain and providing euthanasia are to be sanctioned at all, it would be better to furnish some legal machinery like that talked of by the English enthusiasts, instead of opening wide a door for the possible commission of the worst of all crimes.

The First Bale.

Special Dispatch to the Globe-Democrat:

PRESCOTT, ARK., August 25.—The first bale of new cotton this season, raised by James Alexander, Nevada County, was sold here to-day to Clark Hamilton, and shipped by express to Gilkeson & Sloss, St. Louis. It classed good middling.

...s. W. Knapp, child and nurse; Mrs. John Whittaker, child and nurse; Misses Shepley and Kennett; Mrs. J. B. Swan; Capt. D. S. Carter; R. Sellew; J. G. Catlin.

—On Thursday evening last a very pleasant musical and reading entertainment was given, at the old St. Louis County Court House, by the young ladies and gentlemen of the Mount Olive Church. Social tete-a-tetes were indulged in by the young folks, after which a most attractive programme was carried out, followed immediately afterwards with refreshments of all kinds, and to which all did ample justice. Among the St. Louisans present were noticed the following: Mr. and Mrs. Smith, Mr. and Mrs. W. Clayton, Miss Nellie Hanley, Miss Annie Moore, the Misses Russell, Miss Ettie Saunders, Miss Morrison, Miss Lottie Moore, Miss Mollie Wash, Misses Sallie and Ella Heaps, Miss B. Walton, Miss Jennie Saunders, Miss Stella Smith, Miss Mattie Colburn, Miss Belle Morris, and Messrs. Wm. Morgan, Ben. Snow, O. Alexander, T. Smith, Wm. Howland, and many others.

Michigan Matters.

Special Dispatch to the Globe-Democrat.

DETROIT, MICH., August 25.—The Detroit Commandery Knights Templar will turn out strong for the grand tournament at Cleveland next week.

A special to the *Tribune* from Jackson says the body of Robert Allen, of Loni, was found in the Turbine water-wheel of the Ætna Mill, in that city, at 8 o'clock this forenoon. The mill stopped at 3 o'clock, but it was too dark at that time to ascertain the cause. The deceased was a farmer, and no cause for the accident has yet been ascertained.

A Busted Bank.

Special Dispatch to the Globe-Democrat.

LOGANSPORT, IND., August 25.—The People's Bank suspended business, and closed its doors to-day, owing to an insufficiency of funds to continue business. The failure is attributable to liberal interests on deposits. The depositors are mainly farmers and of the laboring classes. The deprivation of their savings is particularly hard. A statement of liabilities and assets will probably be made early next week.

Seriously Injured.

Special Dispatch to the Globe-Democrat.

UNION CITY, IND., August 25.—J. G. Harlan, of this place, was thrown from his buggy this afternoon and seriously, if not fatally injured.

and Plevna.

SULIEMAN PASHA TELEGRAPHS

confirming the report of Wednesday's desperate fighting, without decisive result. Fighting was resumed Thursday. The Russians are completely surrounded. We command their lines of retreat to Gabrova. To-morrow a decisive assault will be made. As the Russians have not profited by the darkness to retreat they risk being all captured.

THE GERMAN PROTEST.

BERLIN, August 25.—It is officially announced that all the Great Powers and Belgium, Holland, Sweden and Portugal have adhered to the German protest against Turkish cruelties.

France.

POLITICAL NEWS.

PARIS, August 25.—It is rumored that Father Hyacinthe intends standing as a candidate for one of the arrondisements of Paris, but his chances of success are considered to be small.

Ex-President Thiers, in receiving Republican deputations yesterday at St. Germain, said that a republic was the only government possible in France. He pointed out at the same time that it should be conservative, in order not to create alarm. Thiers said he did not doubt the triumph of the republican cause, and severely condemned its adversaries.

BRIDGES ACROSS THE DANUBE.

LONDON, August 25.—The Russians, it is said, have contracted with an engineering firm for construction of bridges across the Danube capable of withstanding ice.

RIOTOUS RUSSIANS.

It is said the Russian troops at Sistova, on Tuesday, rioted because of bad provisions, and threw 100,000 moldy loaves of bread into the Danube.

England.

GRANT IN LONDON.

LONDON, August 25.—Ex-President Grant and party arrived in London this morning.

The Past.

MANSFIELD, O., August 25.—The American Anthropological Association holds its first annual meeting in Cincinnati, Ohio, September 5, 1877. This is a society which has for its object the investigation of the prehistoric races of America. It was organized on the Centennial grounds, but has members scattered from Maine to California and from Minnesota to Texas—all engaged in the

THE CROOKS' CORNER.

Hardin, the Texas Outlaw, Captured in Florida.

The Latest Concerning the Rio Grande Outrages.

Three Prisoners Escape From Jail at Topeka, Kansas.

Frisco's Political Scandal—Curiosities of Crime.

Special Dispatch to the Globe-Democrat.

GALVESTON, TEX., August 25.—Special telegrams to the *News* to-night say that John Wesley Hardin, the most desperate man that has lived in Texas since 1868, was captured in Pensacola, Fla., two days since, where he has lived under an assumed name for several years. He was captured by two Texas State officers, who have equaled Pinkerton's detectives in this pursuit. They had to fight several of Hardin's friends, wounding one, killing one, and capturing Hardin and another. Hardin tried the habeas corpus scheme at Montgomery, Ala., without success. He has killed at least ten men, and been the leader of the Taylor party, whose feud with the Sutton family has cost DeWitt and surrounding counties three lives and a division of her citizens, until but few emigrants will go there, though the country is rich and fertile; but as it is in Western Texas, remote from the thickly settled sections, affects only their immediate neighborhood.

THE RIO GRANDE TROUBLES.

A *News* special from Brownsville to-night says State District Judge Russell arrived here Tuesday night from Corpus Christi. On Thursday he sent the following demand for the extradition of the parties engaged in the late Rio Grande City affair, as well as the parties delivered from jail, having previously sent demands from Rio Grande City to the authorities at Camargo, from which nothing has been heard. The Judge is earnest in his endeavors to bring about a rendition of these criminals:

United States of America, State of Texas, County of Cameron—To His Excellency Servado Canales, Governor of Tamaulipas, Mexico: SIR—I have the honor to call your attention to the fact that during the night of August 11, 1877, a band of marauders attacked the County Jail in Rio Grande City, Starr County, in this State, releasing therefrom Segundo Garsia, confined therein on a charge of murder, and Rudolpho Espronceda, confined on a charge of horse-stealing, and the said band shot and seriously wounded Noah Cox, Esq., the County Attorney of said County, as well as the Jailer. The said parties, so far as known, are, to wit: Rafael Garsia, Greagora Garsia, Seferno Juares, Rafael Trevino, Pedro Rodriguez, Brigado Olivarez, Pablo Parra and one Obispo, who, after committing the said assault upon the person of Mr. Cox and the Jailer, took refuge in the Republic of Mexico, crossing the Rio Grande, a few miles above Rio Grande City. Now, by virtue of the authority vested in me by the Governor of the State of Texas, under the treaty of December 11, 1861, between the United States and the Mexican Republic for the extradition of criminals, I ask and require that the said parties, to wit: Rafael Garsia, Gregoria Garsha, Seferno Juarez, Rafael Trevino, Pindro Rodriguez, Brigado, Olivarez, Pablo Parra and one Obispo, be delivered to me to answer the charge of burglary and assault with intent to murder, and that the said Segundo Garsia and Rudolfo Espronceda, so forcibly taken from jail, as aforesaid, and carried into Mexico, be delivered to me to answer the respective charges against them, to-wit: murder against Garcia, and horse-stealing against Espronceda.

I have the honor to be, very respectfully, your obedient servant,

(Signed) JOHN C. RUSSELL, Judge,
Twenty-fifth Judicial District of Texas.
Brownsville, Tex., August 23, 1877.

THE DEMAND

was given on Thursday by the Sheriff of this county to Gen. Canales in person in Matamoras, and up to a late hour of this Saturday no answer has been returned, and so far treated with silence if not contempt. It is not believed in Brownsville that Escobedo hired parties to break the jail, as stated in a previous issue of your paper. The conviction is strong that he had nothing to do with it, but that the friends and relations of Segundo Garsia, from Camargo, are alone responsible. It is asserted that Parra, Olivarez and Espranceda are in jail in Matamoras, but the authorities there have not informed our authorities. The most noted one (Garsia) has not been apprehended, nor do the people here believe he will be. Expect all sorts of quibbles and evasions until our Government takes a firmer and more threatening attitude. The stand taken by Gen. Ord is an expression of that entertained by all Texans.

Higby's Affidavit.

SAN FRANCISCO, August 25.—A Portland press dispatch says that W. B. Higby, who is under indictment for subornation of perjury, and in jail in default of bonds, has just made the following affidavit in regard to the Government investigation:

W. B. Higby, being duly sworn, would state that A. W. Waters, United States Marshal, and John D. Kelly, Collector of Customs Revenue, hired and induced W. H. Stiles to make the affidavit that he did, that I was present at the Cosmopolitan Hotel, in Portland, and heard and saw the above done; that John Kelly paid Stiles' way from Junction to Portland, and that he paid his way at the St. Charles Hotel while he was there, and that Kelly induced me, W. B. Higby, to procure the affidavit of E. A. Lake; that Morrison C. Athey wrote the affidavit of E. Lake; that he knows all about the transaction; that it was done in David Goodsell's office in the Holmes block; that I never induced, or tried to induce, any one to swear to what he did; that in payment to Lake for the above I gave an order on Waters, in accordance with John Kelly's orders. The object of the whole thing was to destroy any influence that the Governor might have for the United States Senate, and also to affect next June's election. I interviewed Morton at Ben Holliday's, in Porland, and informed him of the facts, and if he was put on the stand my testimony would be in accordance therewith. He said for me not to come before the Investigating Committee in Oregon, but to come to Washington, D. C.; that my mileage and fees would be paid, and that I would be kept out of the way under Morton's instructions.

Leg Bail.

TOPEKA, KAN., August 25.—While the workmen repairing the furnace in the County Jail were gone to dinner to-day, three prisoners escaped. The workmen had left a pinch bar where the prisoners, by using a broom and a string, could get hold of it. They did so, and with the bar knocked a hole in the partition between the furnace room and jail, got into the furnace room and walked out of the door which had been left open. Their names are Isaac Singleton, in for stealing a horse in Marion County; Wm. May, for stealing a gold watch in Jefferson County; a boy, J. T. Owensbee, of Shawnee County, for stealing a horse near Manhattan. Singleton once broke jail in Marion County, and was recaptured and sent here for safety.

Many Thousands Stolen.

BOSTON, August 25.—Bagnall & Loud, dealers in block and tackle, Fulton street, were robbed this afternoon of $29,000, $28,000 in notes, mortgages, etc., and the remainder in cash. Two men entered the store, when the salesmen all chanced to be busy and walked back to the counting-room and engaging a junior member in conversation asked to be shown something at the front store. During his absence it is supposed a confederate entered a side door near the counting-room and rifled the safe.

Robbed by Road Agents.

CAMP ROBINSON, NEB., August 24.—The Sidney coach, from Deadwood, was stopped last night above Buffalo Gap by five road agents, who fired into the coach before the word was given to halt. Ed. Cook, Division Superintendent of the Stage Line, was shot through the ear. The robbers secured $12 out of about $1,000 in possession of the passengers. One passenger, obeying the order to throw up his hands, drew up $500 with them. It being dark, the money was not noticed by the robbers.

Kicked by a Mule.

Special Dispatch to the Globe-Democrat.

CARROLLTON, ILL., August 25.—Last evening, as Jacob Schaefer, a well-known citizen living near here, was entering a stable behind a span of mules, one of them kicked him, inflicting very serious injuries about the face and head. He is confined to his bed.

EVERY variety of seaside evening mantelets are to be seen. The daintiest are of white cashmere, made in fichu patterns, with long ends and turned-over lapels, trimmed with colored silk embroideries or braidings, and edged with fringes of the combined shades. Other wraps are of darker hued cashmeres, in the same pattern, with long or short ends to be tied loosely below the bust, and all embroidered or braided in bright colored silks.

DENISON DAILY NEWS.

VOL. V. DENISON, TEXAS, THURSDAY MORNING, AUGUST 30, 1877. NO 17.

THE DENISON NEWS,

B. C. MURRAY, Proprietor.

TERMS:

Daily—Per mont ...	$1 00
" Per week, by carrier, ...	25
Weekly—Per annumn ...	2 50
" Six mon ns ...	1 50

ADVERTISING RATES:

One inch, first insertion ...	1 00
Each subsequent insertion ...	50
One-eighth columns, one month ...	6 00
Three months ...	15 00
One-fourth column, one month ...	10 00
Three months ...	25 00
Business cards 1½ inch, per month.	3 00

Local notices, 10 cents a line for the first insertion, each subsequent publication 7 cents per line

Double column advertisements, one-third extra.

Legal advertisements at legal rates.

Trantient advertisers will be expected to pay in advance.

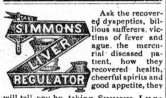

FRONTIER WAR.

A Party from Helena, Montana, Slaughtered.

Indians Having it all their own Way.

SALT LAKE, VIA HELENA, M. T., August 27.—The following has just been received:

FORT ELLIS, M. T., August 27.

Gen. John Gibbon, Helena:

On the 24th Indians struck the Helena and Radersburg party, killing seven men and taking two women and one man prisoners. The Indians released Mrs. Cowan, her sister and brother, who reached Schofield yesterday.

[Signed] BERHAM.

Capt. 7th Infantry, Salt Lake.

HELENA, M. T., August 27th.—A Herald special from the Mammoth Hot Springs of August 26th says: Our party were attacked to-day about noon. I am the only one so far as I know, that escaped. Probably they will come in to-night. I will give particulars from Bozeman.

[Signed] F. J. P. FISHER.

The party consistsd, among others, of of the following named persons, all residents of Helena: Joe Roberts, Andy Worker, Richard Kietrich and F. J. Paister.

GARDNER'S RIVER, August 26.—The Independent Extra from Hot Springs says: To Geo. Carpenter, U. S. Assay Office, Helena, Mont.: Emma, Ida and myself alive; Cowan and Olham killed; saw Cowan and Olham shot; balance missing. I think all are killed, but don't know; will send particulars when I reach Bozeman. The Helena party all gone except one missing; the Indians fired into their camp; Joseph, Looking Glass and Whitebeard were the chiefs.

SALT LAKE, Aug. 27.—A report from Bozeman says General Sturgis and six companies on the Yellowstone have gone to meet Joseph's band.

J. WESLEY HARDING.

Extraordinary Dilligence of a Detective.

Special to the Galveston News.

HOUSTON, August 27, 1877.

A gentleman down from Austin states that an old Chicago detective named Duncan worked up the arrest of John Wesley Hardin. He first sought out John Wesley's father in Gonzales county, bought a stock of goods, opened out in the old man's neighborhood and in less than a year became one of his most intimate friends and advisers. The old gentleman, in a gush of confidence, told his new friend that his son, whose whereabouts he minutely and confidently imparted, wanted to return to Texas. But the detective advised him against this and wrote a letter to John Wesley, which the old gentleman signed, telling him to stay a while where he was. The detective fixed up matters instanter, and, with Lieutenant Armstrong, reached John Wesley before his letter did. The rest is known.

Curious Freak of the Missouri.

The Missouri river is cutting a new channel opposite the city of St. Charles, and there is a strong probability that it will leave the present channel a mile or so to the north. This will render useless the magnificent bridge, which the people of that city have erected at so much expense. At that point the river makes a great bend, and the present indications are that it means to go straight through, making the base of a crescent. The accident, for it can scarcely be considered anything else, if it occurs, will be one of the greatest misfortunes that ever befell that section of the country.

THE EASTERN WAR.

Hills Around Shipka Covered with Dead Turks.

The Battle Still Continues, but no Further Details.

LONDON, August 28.—The Times Bucharest correspondent telegraphs: "It is said the hills around Shipka are covered with Turkish dead bodies, and that their loss has already been as great as the Russians at Plevna. The Russians still hold Shipka pass."

Telegrams from Adrianople announce that the Russians still hold Fort Nicholas, in Shipka pass. The Turks are attacking the highest Russian positions in the pass. Large numbers of the Turkish wounded are arriving at Adrianople.

A dispatch from Shumla announces that the Russians occupy Sophia, and a battle is expected.

No bulletin of Monday's date has as yet been received from Russian headquarters concerning fighting at Shipka pass, although they previously issued reports daily, and sometimes twice a day.

LIGHTNING.

Singular Experiences of a Missouri Gentleman.

[Sedalia Bazoo.]

In conversation with a gentleman from the southwestern part of the county, to-day, a representative of the Bazoo learned a remarkable incident, connected with Saturday's storm, which will go to form a part of the singular curiosities which make up the history of these elemental contests. It seems that Mr. Jas. Graham was out on the prairie

WITH HIS GUN

when the storm came up. At first he thought it would pass away, but when the rain begun to descend he started home, his gun across his shoulder. Before he had gone far a bolt descended, striking the end of the gun, running along the barrel, and tearing off the stock, and then leaping away, entered the ground a few feet in advance of

THE HORSE'S HEAD.

Both Mr. Graham and the horse were knocked senseless, but neither of them seriously injured. After a few minutes they recovered, and Mr. Graham continued his way homeward with his broken gun, glad to escape with its broken pieces as his only souvenir of his encounter with the lightning.

The New Orleans Democrat of a late date contains a stinging editorial criticism of Gen. Key's fawning policy, as developed in his speeches on his recent Northern tour. The Democrat says:

When he goes about the North with his cringing, unmanly professions of contrition for what not one gallant and true gentleman of the South ever thought of as a shame or cause of repentance, he is guilty of a misrepresentation which deserves, and shall not escape, prompt and indignant denunciation.

In 1834 Louis Napoleon, afterwards Napoleon III, Emperor of the French, was a bar-room loafer in New York, and a Mr. David Clark, a Hartford merchant, who met him at that time in a bar-room in New York, declares in the Hartford Courant that the loafer Prince then tried to swindle him out of a bottle of wine, and only desisted when he was threatened with being thrown out of the window. Truth is stranger than fiction.—*Ex.*

Rabbi Wise, editor of the Israelite, is said to have sent forth this challenge: "We defy any Christian clergyman or professor of Hebrew to write a Hebrew letter."—*Ex.*

That challenge was made three months ago and we have seen no response in the Israelite yet.

Notice is hereby given that the following certificates of indebtedness of the city of Denison are fraudulent and will consequently not be paid: 92, 44, 20, 6, 16, 10, 4, 11, 19, 15, 143, 13, 18, 21, 5.

Attest: R. M. GRUBBS,

J. S. BEST, Mayor.

City Clerk.

The Dallas Daily Herald.

By J. L. BARTOW—[VOL. VI. DALLAS, TEXAS, SATURDAY, FEBRUARY 23, 1878.——PRICE FIVE CENTS. NO. 11]—ESTABLISHED 1849

ROAD KNIGHTS.

The Central South-Bound Train Boarded by Six Masked Men at Allen Station.

The Express Car Run on the Siding---Safe Forced and Robbed of Contents.

The Messenger Shows Fight—In the Exchange of Shots Bores One of the Robbers, With Good Effect.

Daring Attack by a Rescuing Party on a Sheriff's Posse—A Running Fight in Which Wounds are Given and Wounds Received.

The Train Robbers and the Rescuing Party Thought to be One and the Same—Marshal Morton in Pursuit.

Last night the south-bound passenger train on the Central railroad was boarded at Allen station, six miles south of McKinney, by six men, who robbed the express car of twenty-five hundred dollars. The train had hardly drew up at the station when a man jumped up into the engineer's cab, covering the engineer and fireman with his revolver. Five other men attempted to enter the express car, when the messenger, J. S. A. Thomas, showed fight, firing three shots at the robbers, hitting one and it is thought killing him. The robbers fired five or six shots at the messenger, and rushing in, overpowered him, when they cut the bell rope and had the train in a swing. Uncupeling the express car from the train, they ordered him to pull over on the switch, which he did, when they went through the safe, getting some twenty-five hundred dollars. The robbers were all masked, save the one who covered the engineer. The passengers were completely demoralized, so sudden and unexpected had been the attack, and thinking that they would be visited, as a matter of course, a general scramble ensued in the secretion of money and valuables, yet they were not molested. One of the party proposed going through the passengers, but their leader commanded him to keep his place and come on, to the great relief of the passengers. After securing the money the robbers departed, going westward. There were enough male passengers aboard to have whipped the robbers out, but they were so badly demoralized that, with the exception of the express agent and Captain Will. Apperson, who attempted to arouse the passengers to action, there was no disposition of resistance shown.

About ten o'clock Marshal Morton received the following telegram, dated

CORSICANA, February 22.

Chief of Police, Dallas:

Train No. 4 was robbed at Allen tonight by a party of six men. Express car robbed. See conductor of train and get particulars. T. A. QUINLIN, Engineer and Superintendent.

Later in the night, about 12 o'clock, he received another telegram from Superintendent Quinlan, saying a car would be at his service by 1 o'clock to carry them up the road, to give chase to the robbers, and this morning at the appointed time they left.

It is thought that these are the same men who took the prisoner from Sheriff Reid, of Calcasien parish, Louisiana, while en route with him from Weatherford to Fort Worth.

A Louisiana Murderer Rescued from a Sheriff's Posse.

Last night the reporter learned from Mr. Reed, sheriff of Calcasieu, Louisiana, of one of the most daring attacks to rescue a prisoner that it has ever been his lot to record. A few weeks since the authorities of Parker county, having arrested a man named Doe Sharkey, who was wanted in Calcasieu parish, Louisiana, for the shooting ing and robbing of a man named Joseph Ray. Sheriff Reid, on being informed of the arrest, secured a requisition from the governor of the state of Louisiana. He arrived in Weatherford, Wednesday, and having secured his prisoner, Thursday, started on his return trip accompanied by Sheriff Lindsey, of Parker county, his deputy, Mr. Eddleman, a Mr. McFall, acting as guard, and a driver of a covered wagon in which they came, named McGeehe. Sheriff Reid and McFall rode in the wagon with the prisoner, while Sheriff Lindsey and his deputy rode in a buggy About one o'clock in the afternoon, when within some ten miles of Fort Worth, just as they were crossing a small stream, six men rode out of the bushes, coming between the wagon containing the prisoner and the buggy. One of the men rode in front of the wagon and leveling his pistol on the driver commanded him to halt, which on his refusing to do so—fired a fusilade into the wagon. The buggy in which was Sheriff Lindsey and Deputy Eddleman, was some forty yards behind, while the Weatherford stage was about one hundred yards ahead. Three of the party kept Sheriff Lindsey and Eddleman at bay while the others attacked the wagon containing the prisoner. Seeing that the prisoner was attempting to escape from the wagon, Sheriff Reid caught him around the neck, putting his head under his arm to hold him so as to prevent his escaping. The driver whipped the horses up, when a running fight ensued between the two parties. At the speed they were going, the parties in the covered wagon shot with difficulty. They passed the stage, going to the right, while the rescuing party went to the left, exchanging shots across the stage, to the great dismay of its passengers. While the wagon was going at this breakneck speed, Sheriff Reid took as good aim as he could, firing at one of the attacking party, whom he hit, when he reeled very much in his saddle, dropping behind, and taking no further part in the fight. It was while in the act of shooting that he released his hold upon the prisoner, who, with a powerful effort, succeeded in rolling from the wagon to the ground. The team was now going at lightning speed, while Sheriff Lindsay and Deputy Eddleman were conducting a running fight with three of the robbers in the rear. The prisoner, whose legs and hands were bound, was picked up by the attacking party, thrown on a horse, and carried of triumphantly. The officers not being on horseback were powerless to pursue the desperadoes, who rode away in a northern direction, going toward the Indian Nation. Deputy Eddleman received a flesh wound in one of his legs, and was shot through the overcoat, the ball striking and breaking a flask of whisky he had in his coat pocket. Sheriff Reid received a slight wound in the arm. He is on his way back to Louisiana, but thinks he will yet get his man and bring him to justice.

WASHINGTON.

The Irrepressible Chandler Comes Again with Visor Down and Lance in Rest and Tilts at the Presidential Fraud.

[Noon Associated Press Report.]

WASHINGTON, February 22.—The National Agricultural convention listened to Senator Windom upon the subject of water transportation being necessary for cheap transit and the national importance of improving the Missisfippi river. The convention resolved that the government might control the inter-state commerce; that congress be asked to take some action in regard to it.

[Night Associated Press Report.]

Ex-Governor Brown, vice-president of the Texas and Pacific railroad, concluded his argument to-day before the senate Pacific Railroad committee.

W. E. Chandler has written another letter, under the caption, "Was Governor Hayes a Bargainer?" The letter proceeds, "Unquestionably he was. Much of the coquetting with southern democrats during the winter was done by him. Messrs. Foster, Matthews and others kept him fully advised of what they were doing. Senator Sherman went to Columbus, reluctant to trade off Packard, and returned Secretary Sherman and joined in the trade. Mr. Hayes knew perfectly well that the price that he was to pay for the presidency was the betrayal of Packard and Chamberlain and the sacrifice of his own honor. But the fear of the loss of the presidency, with its $200,000 in money and its patronage, was too much for him and he deliberately paid the price. It would be cowardly to affect to think otherwise. If the subject is ever investigated by competent authority it will doubtless be found he confirmed in some way the assurances given by his friends before Mr. Levy proclaimed in the house that all was right, and Mr. Ellis told Mr. Hewitt that the count could proceed and changed his vote and opposed fillibustering. At all events, it is enough to convict him. His first act on arriving in Washington was to procure, or advise, an order from General Sherman withdrawing federal support from Packard and inviting the white leagues to crush him."

The silver bill cannot reach the president until Monday, when he may consider it ten days.

The agricultural congres adopted the following:

Resolved, That it is the sense of the national agricultural congres that the government ought to control interstate commerce, and that congress be asked to take some action in regard to it.

THE COURTS

Recorder's Court.

Mike Shival, drunk and down, fined $3 and costs.

William Wood, drunk and down, fined $3 and costs.

William Faber, drunk and down, fined $3 and costs.

Justice McLure.

State vs. Hattie Washburn, charged with shooting with intent to kill, was on trial yesterday. Argument of counsel to-day at two o'clock.

Justice Peak.

Meldon Bass, charged with the theft of a horse, put under $300 bond.

District Court.

State vs. Marion Dill, charged with murder, is being argued by counsel.

CENTRAL AMERICA.

Particulars of the Tidal Wave at Calloia—The American Steamer Sunbeam Boarded and Seized by Revolutionists at Greytown.

NEW YORK, February 22.—A correspondent of the Star and Herald, of Panama, writing January 17th, says of the tidal wave at Callola, that in the morning when the tide receded it was noticed that boats and coasting crafts along the shore were left high and dry and when the wave returned it passed with immense force over the walls of Muella Dorsena, pushing up over newly made ground, toward the station of the Oroga railroad for a distance of three hundred feet, carrying everything before it.

Launches, numerous little cane huts, built on the Esplanade and many enclosures around lumber yards, etc., were completely destroyed. The massive walls of Muella Dorsena, in front of the English railway station, were torn away, and in the station itself a train of freight cars were wrecked, such was the amount of water entering the station. The surf was tremendously high. The waters on the bar of Calloa during the day were so troubled as to render communication with the vessels almost impossible. So the damage done them could not be ascertained. For forty days previously several strong shocks of the earthquake were felt at Lima, but no serious damage was done. Iqueque, Callao and Arica experienced several earthquake shoks on the night of January 13, causing great excitement and some damage, while Payti was visited by a heavy rain storm, a phenomenon unprecedented there in the memory of man.

A correspondent writing the next day notes the drowning of five men, two being swept from the iron bridge connecting the shore with the docks. Although hundreds of persons witnessed the drowning, no assistance could be given. The sea was very violent, in which the ships rolled fearfully and the decks of the Peruvian man-of-war, Huascar, were repeatedly swept by the waves. The eight ton blocks of concrete, of which the coping of the Muelie Darsena was formed were knocked out and strewed about. Coal and goods and trucks on the railroad tracks were scattered in different directions, and a large amount of goods destroyed. Several vessels broke from their moorings, but were again secured. Almost all the wooden moles have been swept away. All forts fronting on the sea suffered.

From a letter from Borcas del Lord, the Star and Herald learns that on the 31st of January an armed band boarded the American steamer Sunbeam, Captain Kain, at Port Simon, and took forcibly possession. The captain was on shore at the time, and the officer in charge remonstrated and told them the United States government would regard their action as piracy. They replied that they did not care what the United States government said or did.

At 2:20 a. m., February 1st, another detachment arrived on board, and immediately gave orders to proceed to sea.

They were informed that the captain was not on board. An armed squad was sent to find him and did, he being in the company of the United States consul. The guard seized him and compelled him to go on board. When there he was forced to get under weigh on peril of being shot. The vessel proceeded with about forty of these people to Boscas del Toro, from whence leaders arrived. At Ceylon, on the way to Boscas del Toro, the British gunboat Contest was spoken, but the captain of the schooner was forbidden to make any signs for help on the fear of instant death. The authors of these acts of violence are defeated revolutionists of Greytown and elsewhere.

Grant's Defense of the Sumner Charges Mixed.

NEW YORK, February 22.—A published interview with General Grant, in Cairo, Egypt, reviews the controversies about Sumner and Motley. The general says of the discussion of the question: "If respect is due to the dead, truth and justice are due to the living, and I only speak in self defense and after many years of silent submission to the assaults from Mr. Sumner and his friends—only in the interest of truth and justice to Mr. Jay, as no one knows so well as Governor Fish and myself, makes a pretext of eulogizing the dead to attack Mr. Fish. If any one hated Mr. Sumner, it was Jay. At the time of the appointment of Motley as minister to England, Jay wanted to go to England and was sorely disappointed that a change would not be made in his favor, even after Motley had been fully assured of his appointment. Jay most probably forgave Sumner before the senator's death, but he blamed him for his failure to go to London.

Indications.

For the gulf states: rising barometer, winds mostly from the northeast and northwest, cooler and partly cloudy weather, and in the western gulf states occasional rains. Cautionary signals continue at Cape Henry, Cape May, Atlantic City, Barngate, Sandy Hook, New York, New Haven, New London, Boston and Portland, and are ordered for Indianola and Galveston.

HERE AND THERE.

Greenbackers in New Hampshire—Washington's Birthday Celebration in New Orleans—Mexican Veterans in Baltimore—Criminal Pocket.

NEW ORLEANS, February 22.—Business is generally suspended to-day. Salutes were fired this morning, noon and night, and the day celebrated by a military parade, a batalion of the Thirteenth infantry, a battalion of the sailors and marines, and volunteer military organizations participating. Weather clear and pleasant.

SAN FRANCISCO, February 22.—Chief of Police Beer, of Virginia City, Nevada, has been arrested, charged with having liberated a Chinaman in his custody on the charge of murder and putting a paid Chinese substitute in place of the prisoner.

BALTIMORE, February 22.—The annual meeting of the national association of Mexican veterans commenced to-day. Colonel James H. Ruddel, acting president of the Maryland association and a number of members, met at the assembly rooms and received delegates who had arrived in the city. After this ceremony, the Maryland association in a body, marched to Camden station, to receive and welcome a delegation of veterans from Washington.

NEW YORK, February 22.—DeRuca, the Italian consul general in this city, says the new pope had always been regarded as one of the most prominent members of the college of cardinals, and had distinguished himself in administration and diplomacy as a cardinal. His policy was understood to be moderate, and opposed to that of the party of Cardinal Antonelli.

The Times' Berlin dispatch says that Prince Bismarck's speech is disliked in the south of Germany, where the popular wish is to support Austria. Assurances counteracting the unfavorable effect of the speech, and calculated to persuade the public that Germany will not oppose Austria in any way, are circulated in more quarters than one.

HARRISBURG, PA., February 22.—The governor this morning granted thirty days' respite in the case of S. Fisher, sentenced to be hanged on the 26th instant. He also issued warrants for the execution of Patrick Hester, Peter McHugh and Patrick Tulley, to take place on the 25th of March, and for the execution of John Kehoe and Dennis Donnelly, to take place April 15th.

A resolution was offered in the house to-day asking congress to appropriate one million dollars to the centennial exhibition authorities as the government's share of the expenses of the exhibition.

RICHFORD, VT., February 22.—Walter N. Estes, a lawyer and special correspondent of the Boston Journal, died to-day, from the use of poisonous well water, making three deaths thus far. Several are not expected to recover.

PORTSMOUTH, N. H., February 22.—The greenbackers hold a state convention here, March 6th, and will nominate a ticket.

THE DILL CASE.

Examination of Witnesses and Argument of Counsel.

The interest in the Dill case is increasing as the trial progresses, as was evidenced yesterday morning by the crowd that thronged the district court room. The rehearsal of the details of the case within the past few days has made the murder of the negro, Reuben Johnson, green in the memory of the people, who are watching the case with increasing and unabated interest. The witness, Rice, having finished giving in his testimony, yesterday morning Colonel E. G. Bower, who was the prosecuting attorney at the time of the committing of the murder, was introduced upon the stand to rebut the evidence of Rice, who, during Bower's term of office, had made a sort of confession to him. In the details of the case, Rice's statement to him at the time, and his statement Thursday, were different, but in the main were the same. Mrs Dill, wife of the defendant, was next introduced by the defense, evidently to prove an alibi for the accused. Her statement conflicted no little with her statements upon a former trial, which had been reduced to writing and embodied in a statement of facts. The main point in her testimony was that the defendant had not left home the night the murder is alleged to have been committed. Mrs. Cameron, a married daughter of Mrs. Dill and a stepdaughter of the defendant, then took the stand, testifying that the defendant had not left home on the night of the murder.

Her testimony conflicted with that of her mother's in many respects. With this witness the examination of the witnesses ceased, when County Attorney Aldridge opened with an able speech. He was followed by Colonel Willard for the defense, who occupied the remainder of the evening in a most effective argument. The argument of the case will be resumed this morning by Colonel Hurt for the prosecution and Judge Thurmand for the defense.

At a wedding in Beaver Dam, Wis., recently one of the guests suddenly fell dead to the floor.

St. Louis Globe-Democrat.

VOL. 3—NO. 121. ST. LOUIS, FRIDAY MORNING, APRIL 12, 1878. PRICE FIVE CENTS.

NATIONAL NOTES.

Republican Prospects as Viewed by Secretary McCrary.

What May Be Accomplished in the Coming Campaign.

The Desire and Aim of the Administration.

Gould and Huntington Still Watching the Sinking-Fund Bill.

The House Fixes the Compensation of Pension Agents.

A Universal Opinion that the Bankrupt Law Will be Repealed.

THE ILLUSTRATED POLICE NEWS.

WILLIAM P. LONGLEY, CHIEF OF TEXAS "MAN-KILLERS." CHARGED WITH THIRTY-TWO MURDERS, HANGED AT GIDDINGS, LEE CO., OCT. 11, FOR THE MURDER OF WILSON ANDERSON.

BILL, THE BUTCHER.

An Interview with Longley, the Texas Man-Killer.

He Admits Having Murdered Thirty-two Persons.

Says He Hates to Hang, but Isn't Afraid to Die.

The Western Train Robbers Encounter a Plucky Crew,

But, Aided by Kerosene, Accomplish their Purpose.

The Blood-Curdling Confessions of an Eastern Assassin.

A Brute Murders His Industrious Wife and Commits Suicide.

The Misery Caused by Bugbee's Extensive Forgeries.

A Record of Rascality and Blood—The Criminal Calendar.

Special Correspondence of the Globe-Democrat.

GALVESTON, TEXAS, April 7.—This afternoon, at 3 o'clock, a correspondent of the GLOBE-DEMOCRAT had a short interview with William P. Longley, the notorious Texas desperado and murderer, who, according to his own account, has killed and murdered thirty-two men at different times within the last seven years.

The interview took place at the jail at Galveston, a strong and substantial brick building near the center of the city, and in one of the dungeons of the lower floor this noted character of the Southwest is now confined under sentence of death. Although incarcerated here, Longley was arrested, tried and condemned in Lee County, Middle Texas, for the deliberate murder of a man while plowing in a field, this being but one of the long list of victims which Longley, according to his own account, has planted.

HIS SENTENCE AFFIRMED.

Longley's death verdict having been affirmed by the Court of Appeals during the late session of that body at Galveston, nothing now remains to complete the stern demands of Justice but the sentencing of the murderer, which will have to be done by the District Court of Lee County. The dungeon occupied by the notorious Texas man-killer is as dark and dismal as any pictured in the pages of romance. A massive iron door from the rear opens into a corridor dimly lighted by rusty iron gratings. At the farther end is the cell of the desperado the strong iron door of which is secured by massive locks, and whose walls are also massive. At the sound of your footsteps, which fall on the brick pavement with an echo that almost startles you as well as the inmates of the neighboring cells, the indistinct outlines of a human figure, like an animal aroused in his lair, emerges from the gloom of the dungeon and approaches the bars

A DESCRIPTION OF LONG

It is Longley. He is rather inclined to be slim, but well proportioned and not gaunt and "with a lean and hungry look," as was Cassius. The first thing that strikes the beholder is the really handsome physiognomy of the Texas cut-throat. Scarcely yet in his twenty-fourth year, Longley has dark hair, worn rather long and slightly parted at the side; coal black whiskers and beard that shade a fine olive complexion; a nose rather after the Greek model; teeth white and beautiful as a woman's; eyes black as midnight, that seem literally alive with expression, which their possessor seems little inclined to curb or suppress. He looks anything but the cool man-slayer who has undoubtedly sent over thirty of his fellow-men to their long abodes.

Upon the occasion referred to, Longley wore much the same clothes as when first incarcerated—a dark cashmere coat, coarse hickory shirt, pants of some dark material, and a pistol belt, which the officers have allowed him to retain from the murdering outfit he used to wear.

A TALK WITH THE DESPERADO.

Since he was condemned the Jailor has had orders to allow no stranger to approach the prisoner. A GLOBE-DEMOCRAT correspondent, however, succeeded in being admitted to see him, and the following conversation ensued:

Correspondent. How are you, Longley? I have heard so much of you that I have come to see you.

Longley. That is all right. Glad to see you (smiling).

Cor. I must tell you beforehand that I have come to make up a newspaper article off you. May be you don't want any more said about you in the papers?

Longley. Oh, I don't care much what they say. They've said now about all they could. It don't matter.

Cor. I have myself written a good deal about you.

Longley. Yes, but I don't know that your paper has said anything against me.

Cor. Well, you have not, from your looks, become down-hearted, owing to the serious turn in your case.

Longley (smiling). Oh, I never allow myself to get so under any circumstances.

Cor. Have you anything to say

IN REGARD TO YOUR FATE?

Longley. This much: that I haven't had a fair trial; no trial at all, in fact. They were all my enemies.

Cor. If the worst comes to the worst I suppose you don't care much. I shouldn't think that a man like you, who has "planted" and killed thirty-two men, would be much afraid to die?

Longley. (Here the desperado looked down, and, eyeing the correspondent keenly, said:) No; I don't like to die, but if I have to die I'm not afraid to."

The interview was interrupted by the entrance of the Secretary of the Y. M. C. A., who gave Longley a number of tracts, sang a hymn, prayed, and, after reading a portion of the third chapter of Luke, made an exhortation to the prisoner. During the religious services the condemned desperado leaned his forehead on his left hand against the grating, apparently in deep meditation, at the same time regarding the exhorter with deep attention.

GOOD-BY TO THE DESPERADO.

After the Secretary had taken his departure, Longley asked the correspondent to approach the grating and have a further chat with him. A few words only passed, when the turnkey, presenting himself, intimated the interview must come to an end.

"Good-by, Longley," said the correspondent.

"Good-by, sir," replied the condemned man, offering his hand through the bars.

The correspondent took and shook it, saying, "We may meet again," at the same time regarding the desperado with a significant glance that might have been equivalent to filling out the sentence with "in the shadow of the gallows at Giddings, Lee County."

Lee Ward, of Harrison Township, was horribly burned by her clothing taking fire when she was standing near the stove in her mother's kitchen.

Burned to Death.

DETROIT, MICH., April 11.—Seven stores and five dwellings were destroyed by fire at Cadillac, this State, early this morning. Entire loss about $10,000; very little insurance. Mrs. Blount perished in the flames.

Killed while Hunting.

ERIE, PA., April 11.—Albert Smith, grocer, while hunting snipe on the lake beach, to-day, accidentally shot himself, the charge of shot going through his heart and the ramrod through his head. He leaves a wife and seven children.

Kicked by a Horse.

Special Dispatch to the Globe-Democrat.

GOSHEN, IND., April 11.—A son of Isaac W. Snyder, living in Goshen, was kicked in the face by a horse this evening and fatally injured.

Killed by a Tree.

Special Dispatch to the Globe-Democrat.

MORLEY, O., April 11.—While engaged in cutting a large tree, it fell unexpectedly and killed David Blank. He was a single man, thirty years old, and a resident of Muskegan.

Another Train Robbery in Texas.

Special Dispatch to the Globe-Democrat.

HOUSTON, TEX., April 11.—Robbers again attacked the Texas and Pacific train last night, about midnight, at Musquite Station, eleven miles east of Dallas. The gang numbered fifteen masked men. The engineer refused at first to stop, when they shot at him. He and the fireman were then arrested, and a battle ensued between the robbers and Conductor Alvord, who ran out and fired on them. All of them then turned and attacked, shooting at him, the bullets passing through the sleeping car. The conductor wounded one, it is thought fatally. He kept on shooting till a Winchester ball from one of the robbers struck him in the arm, breaking it. He then crawled under the car and kept on firing. Express messenger Curley and the armed guard, Gritz, opened fire on the robbers from the express car. One of the villains was wounded, and their leader called for a parley, telling the messenger he should not be hurt if he surrendered. He refused. The thieves talked a few moments, and

Continued on Third Page.

Daily Herald.

THE DAILY HERALD is published every morning, except on Monday, at $10 per annum in advance, postage prepaid; or 25 cents per week delivered in the city.
ADVERTISING RATES: One square (ten lines nonpareil) one time $1 50. each subsequent insertion, 75 cents Special rates for weekly monthly and yearly advertisers.

DALLAS, TEXAS.

THURSDAY MORNING : : : MAY 16

THE war cloud in Europe darkens once more.

THEY have commenced telegraphing about the health of the new pope already.

WASHINGTON city has a female communist. She delivers speeches "calm in tone" but wildcatish in language.

BROWN BOWEN will be hung at Gonzales to-morrow, the first legal hanging that has occurred in Texas for over a year.

ELIZA PINKSTON should be appointed to something, not necessarily for the benefit of the "something," but as an evidence of good faith.

MINISTER FOSTER gave an official dinner to President Diaz, April 30, and escaped without being lassoed by one of Diaz's noble patriots.

WHAT this country mostly needs at present is an eight-by-seven commission to decide against the delinquent yet wealthy taxpayer.

THE Marshall *Herald* is sad because circus companies do not come to Texas. The saw dust ring and "calico hosses" evidently have a charm for Uncle Bob.

THERE is nothing in the name of Smith is there? The county in this state named after that illustrious individual has no tax collector, any how.

MR. HEWITT's bill does not take with the army officers. They naturally object to being treated as the Pennsylvania coal corporations treat their miners.

THOSE Munchausen stories in two or three Hubbard organs about the "Hubbard ground swell" were certainly intended for humor, as the governor is an alleged farmer.

THERE is nothing in the report that Conkling, Hayes and Blaine have "made up." Conkling will cologne himself—a gallon of it is sprinkled on his shirt front every morning.

WITHIN the past two or three days people living in Chicago have had a foretaste of what is in store for them after the "coil is shuffled." They have been using furnaces up there to keep warm.

OH, well, there is no use in trying to pound anything like the truth into the Fort Worth *Democrat*, so what is the use in trying to straighten it out on the question of "that letter to a prominent republican in Grimes county?"

DOES the San Antonio *Herald* imagine for a moment that the candidates of the glorious state of Texas are orphans? Else why does it remark, "The people have enough to take care of themselves without supporting candidates."

MR. SHISKIN, the Russian minister at Washington, has asked to be recalled. He says the American newspapers make fun of him, and he can't stand it. He ought to hire Ben Butler as a substitute, and remain awhile to see how it works.

A WASHINGTON special to the Louisville *Courier Journal* says that since the speech of Governor Throckmorton against the reduction of the army and the need of protection on our Mexican frontier, the cabinet has determined to institute a more vigorous policy on the Mexican border.

GRANGER LANG's visit to Gainsville last week was immediately followed by a copious shower of rain, and now the farmers in that vicinity, who were suffering from drouth, say that Lang is surely the coming man for governor. There is nothing in politics like "fitness" for office.

BISHOP MCCOSKRY has addressed a letter to Bishop Smith, of Kentucky, withdrawing his resignation of March 11, and announcing his purpose to abandon his intended trip to Europe that he may hold himself in readiness to meet all definite charges against him, preferred by responsible parties.

THIS, from the St. Louis *Times*, is the undkindest cut of all at Blaine, of Maine: "The spectacle of James G. Blaine delivering an address at the opening of the Philadelphia exhibition was an eminently fit thing—a played out representative of a played-out party inaugurating a played-out show."

CONGRESSMEN MILLS is opposed to opening the Florida and Louisiana frauds. And Mr. Mills uses some good argument in behalf of his position, too. The question is, will it benefit the country? We think not, for every one is already satisfied that frauds were committed in these states without any investigation.

Now, this is a nice conundrum to be asked by as good a newspaper as the Chicago *Times*, as if every one couldn't answer it. The *Times* asks: "When Packard ascertains that in the Liverpool consulship there is an uncommonly good chance to knock down with no tell-tale bell-punch in the vicinage, will he hesitate to gather up his carpet-bag and go down to the sea in ships?

ESCAPE OF BASS.

The escape of Sam Bass and his men is certainly anything but gratifying to the law-abiding citizens in the counties in which he has had his rendezvous, and has operated as a highway robber. To say that any one officer or set of officers in pursuit of him are responsible for his escape would be unjust, when the nature of his escape is understood, yet there is a responsibility resting upon this escape which can not be overlooked. When the first robbery, at Allen, was committed it was *then* the duty of the local authorities to have been assisted by the state forces, in at least trying to capture the robbers, for they were evidently unable to cope with them singly. The sheriff of a county generally has from one to half a dozen deputies, who are expected to execute the laws, make arrests, etc., but to summon a promiscuous posse to undertake the capture of dangerous and well armed desperadoes is not always feasible. Bass committed robberies in one county, then another, and took refuge in the wilds of another. Then which of the sheriffs ought to have first attempted his arrest? Some would say, and naturally, too, the sheriff of the county in which he was hid. He, Bass, had six determined followers, all of whom were well mounted and equipped. They took refuge in the wilds of Denton county, where a promiscuous raid was made to no end. The sheriff of Denton county could at almost any time have either killed or captured the robbers
too late, if he had have ha
encouragement from the
well as a warrant for his
was not forthcoming until
other robberries had bee
It was then that the g
stimulated "to do somethi
lar indignation had bec
that it became an absolute
send state forces to the s
Jones placed the field in t
trusty lieutenant, who d
for the hard and endurin
made against the bandi
standing his failure to c
One thing, at least, was acc
Major Jones and his co-op
was driven out of the c
country in which the stat
been operating is almost a
Bass could have been with
yards of his pursuers at di
with impunity. The arres
fifteen men who are now l
Tyler, as accomplices show
robbers had aid and abetto
rounding country; and tal
facts into consideration, i
impossible to secure their
governor ought to have ac
in the beginning of the d
something might have l
plished. As the matter
remains for the detective
Bass' whereabouts, if th
ready know, and to secure
by strategy. This metho
tives claim, is the only
which Sam Bass and his
ever be taken.

Hon. J. W. Throckm[orton]

St. Louis Republican: I
on all hands that Gove
morton is one of the m
representatives that Tex
to congress. He rises fr
position of a mere politic
stand on the high plane o
manship and seeks to leg
a district, state, class or
advance the interest and
the whole people. With
gence, liberal views and
prehension of the needs
state and of the country
honestly, earnestly and
for the success of such me
pear best suited to insure
the whole nation. This
the state owes him m
faithful services. But sh
more, and should wipe
tempted stigma which fed
ty sought to fix upon him
deposed from the office of
which the people of Texa
him. The zeal, ability
views of government poli
in his congressional caree
qualities needed to make
ernor, and not only his hi
tions as a citizen, but a sen
towards a wronged man sh
him in the executive chair
socalled reconstruction re
While Governor Throc
earnestly advocated the c
the Texas and Pacific rail
done it more to secure a
way to the Pacific throug
west than on account of it
vantage to northern Texas; and he has shown just as much zeal since he entered congress in efforts for the establishment of an ocean line of steamers from New Orleans and Galveston to Rio and Vera Cruz. He is a democrat, but not a demagogue, and while favoring a wise economy in expenditures, believes the government was created to bless as well as rule the people, and gives his support to such measures of public policy as seem adapted to such a purpose. We are glad to learn that the approaching state convention of Texas is likely to nominate Mr. Throckmorton for the governorship.

A MEMBER of the national democratic executive committee writes that "They are heating the furnaces hot for Hayes in Washington, and our friends are determined to roast all who have been connected with the election frauds in the south. We cannot expect to oust the president, but we can demonstrate the connection of his fraudulency with the conspiracy so that no one can deny or doubt it."

Jay Gould and the Supreme Court.

Philadelphia Sunday Press: A sickening rumor fills the air, and threatens to still further depreciate the value of real estate. Some one has extorted from the administration the secret that Mr. Justice Swayne is to leave the supreme bench, and that Stanley Matthews will go on it. Let's see! Jay Gould contributed seventy-five thousand dollars to the Hayes campaign fund; Stanley Matthews is Jay Gould's attorney; the Pacific railroad bill will fight the new funding act in court; in course of time the case will reach the supreme court, with Stanley on the bench—oh, no! It cannot be!

Out in a Missouri town of nine hundred inhabitants, there are eight hundred members of a total abstinence club, and the habit of winking when ordering a lemonade has afflicted every man but one in the town with a chronic squint. That one is a drunken reprobate who won't reform.

ESCAPE OF BASS.

The escape of Sam Bass and his men is certainly anything but gratifying to the law-abiding citizens in the counties in which he has had his rendezvous, and has operated as a highway robber. To say that any one officer or set of officers in pursuit of him are responsible for his escape would be unjust, when the nature of his escape is understood, yet there is a responsibility resting upon this escape which can not be overlooked. When the first robbery, at Allen, was committed it was *then* the duty of the local authorities to have been assisted by the state forces, in at least trying to capture the robbers, for they were evidently unable to cope with them singly. The sheriff of a county generally has from one to half a dozen deputies, who are expected to execute the laws, make arrests, etc., but to summon a promiscuous posse to undertake the capture of dangerous and well armed desperadoes is not always feasible. Bass committed robberies in one county, then another, and took refuge in the wilds of another. Then which of the sheriffs ought to have first attempted his arrest? Some would say, and naturally, too, the sheriff of the county in which he was hid. He, Bass, had six determined followers, all of whom were well mounted and equipped. They took refuge in the wilds of Denton county, where a promiscuous raid was made to no end. The sheriff of Denton county could at almost any time have either killed or captured the robbers before it was too late, if he had have had the proper encouragement from the governor, as well as a warrant for his arrest, which was not forthcoming until after three other robberries had been committed. It was then that the governor was stimulated "to do something," for popular indignation had become so great that it became an absolute necessity to send state forces to the scene. Major Jones placed the field in the hands of a trusty lieutenant, who deserves credit for the hard and enduring campaign made against the bandits, notwithstanding his failure to capture them. One thing, at least, was accomplished by Major Jones and his co-operators, Bass was driven out of the country. The country in which the state troops have been operating is almost a jungle, and Bass could have been within a hundred yards of his pursuers at different times with impunity. The arrest of twelve or fifteen men who are now lying in jail at Tyler, as accomplices shows that the robbers had aid and abettors in the surrounding country; and taking all these facts into consideration, it was almost impossible to secure their arrest. The governor ought to have acted promptly in the beginning of the disorder; then something might have been accomplished. As the matter now stands it remains for the detectives to learn of Bass' whereabouts, if they do not already know, and to secure his capture by strategy. This method, the detectives claim, is the only one now, by which Sam Bass and his followers can ever be taken.

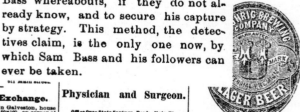

formed by him.
Sec. 4. No one shall sell or expose for sale any milk, vinegar, molasses, or anything else used for food or drink which is adulterated or which contains impurities injurious to health; and any one violating this section shall be deemed guilty of a misdemeanor, and upon conviction, be fined in any sum not exceeding fifty dollars.
Sec. 5. Any one having an analysis or test made by the City Chemist, shall pay for the same the sum of twenty-five dollars.
Sec. 6. It shall be the duty of the City Chemist to see that all articles shall be of the standard by ordinance to be established.
Sec. 7. The City Chemist shall perform such other duties as may hereafter be required of him in the ordinances establishing the standard of milk, &c., and providing for the inspection by him of any article.
Approved May 10, 1878.
J. B. HEREFORD, City Secretary.
W. L. CABELL, Mayor.
m11-d-10t

Denison Daily News.

Vol. VI. | Denison, Texas, Saturday Morning, May 25, 1878. | No. 80.

ANNOUNCEMENTS.

For Assessor and Collector.

We are authorized to announce the name of ARTHUR COFFIN for re-election to the office of Assessor and Collector of Denison, at the election on the 10th of June.

For City Treasurer.

We are authorized to announce O. E. O'MALEY as a candidate for re-election to the office of City Treasurer, at the ensuing election.

For City Marshal.

We are authorized to announce Mr, WM. HARDWICK, as a candidate for re-election to the office of City Marshal at the coming election.

County Judge.

We are authorized to announce J. P. Mills as a candidate for the office of Judge of Grayson county, at the November election. *

We are authorized to announce S. D. STEEDMAN as a candidate for Judge of Grayson county at the November election. *

For Representative.

We are authorized to announce G. C. DUGAN as a candidate for representative in the next Legislature at the ensuing November election. *

For County Assessor.

We are authorized to announce A. R. ANDREWS as a candidate for the office of Assessor of Taxes for Grayson county, at the ensuing election. *

Sheriff of Grayson County.

We are authorized to announce the name of W. C. EVERHEART as a candidate for re-election to the office of Sheriff of Grayson county, at the ensuing election, subject to the decision of the Democratic County Convention. *

We are authorised to announce E. G. Douglass, as a candidate for Sheriff of Grayson county, at the ensuing election, subject to action of the Democratic County Convention, if one is held. *

For County Clerk.

We are authorized to announce GEORGE A. DICKERMAN as a candidate for re-election to the office of Clerk of Grayson county, at the ensuing election, c

For District Clerk.

We are authorized to announce W. H. LANKFORD as a candidate for re-election to the office of Clerk of the District Court of the 27th Judicial District, at the ensuing election. c.

For County Treasurer.

We are authorized to announce J. P. LOVING as a candidate for the office of Treasurer of Grayson county, at the ensuing election. *

For County Collector.

We are authorized to announce THOMAS HOFFMAN, of this city, as a candidate for County Collector, at the November election, subject to the action of the Democratic Convention.

Arrival and Departure of Trains.

HOUSTON AND TEXAS CENTRAL.

	TRAINS.	ARRIVE.
No. 1.	St. Louis Express	12:01 A. M.
No. 3.	Chicago Express	11:00 A. M.
No. 5.	Way Freight	9:30 P. M.
No. 7.	Express Freight	4:00 A. M.
		DEPART.
No. 2.	St. Louis Express	4:20 A. M.
No. 4.	Chicago Express	4:00 P. M.
No. 6.	Way Freight	4:25 A. M.
No. 8.	Express Freight	4:05 P. M.

MISSOURI, KANSAS AND TEXAS.

		ARRIVE.
No. 1.	Chicago, Kansas & Texas Ex.	3:30 P. M.
No. 3.	St. Louis, Kansas & Texas Ex.	4:00 A. M.
No. 5.	Stock Train	1:00 P. M.
No. 7.	Through Freight	8:45 A. M.
		DEPART.
No. 2.	Texas, Kansas & Chicago Ex.	11:55 A. M.
No. 4.	Texas, Kansas & St. Louis Ex.	12:30 A. M.
No. 6.	Stock Train	5:00 P. M.
No. 8.	Through Freight	5:30 A. M.

DENISON & SOUTHEASTERN.

	DEPART.	ARRIVE.
Accommodation	8:00 A. M.	12:30 P.M.

Municipal Officers.

R. M. GRUBBS....Mayor
W. D. KIRK....President of Council
WILLIAM HARDWICK....Marshal
A. H. COFFIN....Assessor & Collector
O. E. O'MALEY....Treasurer
E. F. RADELEFF....City Clerk
G. G. RANDELL....City Attorney

COUNCILMAN—1ST WARD:
W. M. PECK, ED. N. ALLEN.

COUNCILMEN—2D WARD:
G. W. WILLIAMS, H. TONE.

COUNCILMEN—3D WARD:
H. ALEXANDER, W. D. KIRK.

COUNCILMEN—4TH WARD:
W. B. BOSS, JUSTIN RAYNAL.

OFFICIAL PAPER:
DAILY NEWS.

Regular meeting of Council, first Thursday in each month.

Proclamation.

WHEREAS: The city charter of the city of Denison, county of Grayson, State of Texas, provides that the regular charter election shall be held on the second Monday in June, of each year, and

WHEREAS: Said charter further provides that the Mayor shall give at least ten days notice before the holding of such an election. Now

Therefore, I, R. M. Grubbs, Mayor of said city, do issue this, my proclamation, ordering an election to be held by the qualified voters of said city, on the 10th day of June, A. D., 1878, for the purpose of electing one marshal, one treasurer, one assessor and collector and one councilman from each ward.

The voting places in the several wards shall be as follows:

1st ward, Hubschman's building, below Nolan Hall, on Austin Avenue.

2d ward, Randell & Peck's office, Main street.

3d ward, Mayor's office, on Skiddy street.

4th ward, building below Mr. Andiuss' grocery store, on Austin Avenue.

The following presiding officers are hereby appointed for their respective wards:

J. M. Sheeder, 1st ward.
L. A. Washington, 2d ward.
J. E. Mason, 3d ward.
J. A. Brenner, 4th ward.

The polls to be open from 8 a. m., to 6 p. m.

Given under my hand and the seal of said city, this 24th day of May, A. D., 1878.

[L. S.] R. M. GRUBBS, Mayor.
Attest.
E. F. RADELEFF, City Clerk.

Silver Dollar, Henry Clay, Infant Wonder, Babies, Champion, Non Plus Ulra, etc., only 5 cents a piece a Louis Lebrecht's.

DENVER DELUGED.

The Entire Western Portion of the City Flooded—Seven Bridges Swept Away, and a Large Lot of Public and Private Property Destroyed.

DENVER, COL., May 23.—A terrific storm of rain passed over a large area of Douglass and El Paso counties, this State, yesterday afternoon. It is believed to have been most violent along the span of the Rocky Mountains, which separates the headwaters of the Arkansas and Platte rivers. Cherry cleeck, which empties into the Platte and Denver rivers, which is ordinarily dry, was suddenly deluged at one o'clock this morning, and in thss than one hour the entire western portion of the city was flooded. Seven bridges were swept away and a large lot of other property destroyed.

Owing to the efficiency and industry of the fire department the entire population of the district devastated was aroused and in time to escape, and it is now believed that no lives have been lost in this city, other than that of an unknown man whose body was found in a freight car, where he had probably been asleep. The flood involved several streams on either side of the divide. The Denver and Rio Grande railroad lost a bridge near Colorado springs, interrupting the running of trains on this end of the road to-day. Three bridges were swept away on the Kansas Pacific railroad.

A freight train on the road, containing eighteen cars, broke through the bridge over the Kioma river, burying with it John A Baker, engineer, and Frank Selden and Pratt, firemen. Bodies not recovered. The debris and drift from Cherry creek lodged against the Colorado Central railroad bridge, across Platte river, and forced out a portion of the supports. This road also sustained considerable loss on its Cheyenne division, but probably its trains and those of the Denver division and Rio Grande railroad will move regularly to-morrow evening.

MURDERED BY INDIANS.

Thirteen Men Killed, and One Scalped Alive.

From the Nashville American.

CLAY COUNTY, TENN., May 12.—Some time last February I started with a party of men to the western edge of Texas on a buffalo hunt, about 160 miles from any settlement. On our trip homeward, toward the close of last month, about eighty-five Indians rushed upon us and killed thirteen men out of fifteen. Only myself and another made our escape. A certain Mr. Robert Black, from Giles county, Tennessee, lost his life in a very cruel manner. The Indians scalped him alive, and just when they began to mutillate his body we heard his last heart-rending cries. During this time we lay in a neighboring thicket.

Please publish this, as I believe Mr. Black has friends or relatives in your county. He married a widow—Mrs. Hewett—in Henderson county, as I understood. Mr. Black, in whose possession I saw during the hunt $500 and a receipt of $75 from John Hardeman, was scalped and killed April 20.

ALLEA PUCKET.

British Vice-Consul Interviewed.

PHILADELPHIA, May 22.—The British vice-consul at this place stated, in an interview with a reporter, that the English government was fully advised of all purchases made of vessels by the agents of the Russian government in this country. He said there was no authority to prevent the purchase of vessels in this country by either Russia or England under treaties, unless the purpose was to arm them in the country, and then interposition would be expected of the American government. There was no proof that the vessels already purchased were to be used for cruising purposes, and without that no interference could be offered.

305 Miles in Fifteen Hours.

NEW YORK, May 22.—Peralto, who started early this morning to ride 305 miles in fifteen hours, at Fleetwood park, finished his last mile in fourteen hours and thirty-one minutes, being twenty-nine minutes ahead of time. At the finish Peralto appeared as fresh as ever.

Philceter W. Gattes, a Chicago contracter, is bankrupt for nearly five hundred thousand dollars.

The Cattle Drive.

The following is a correct list of the herds that have followed the main trail from southern Texas, going north via. this eity:

J. P. Morris, 2,700 to Wyoming; John Blocker, 3,000, same place; Reed & Rachal, 4,000, Colorado; W. Moore, 2,560, Oyoming; John Hickey, 1,700, Kansas; Burris & Parker, 1,500, now on the market; Lee Comb, 3,200, Kansas; Henry Harvey, 500, Kansas; Goodin Bros., 950, to Wichita ranch; D. Rachal, 3,000, Kansas; W. Butler, 3,700, Kansas; W. Moore, 2,800, Wyoming; Clare & Little, 1,500, Kansas; W. Hock, 2,100, Colorado; J. Blocker, 3,700, Wyoming; Sol West, 3,100, Wyoming; Snyder Bros., 2,600, same; Joe Murray, 2,000, Kansas; J. F. Scott 1,200, Kansas; D. C. Choat, 2,000, Wyoming; C. W. Wood, 550, Kansas; W. S. Carrother, 2,000, Wyoming; Ed. Lott, 1,900, same; E. Pettus, 1,690, same; Bare & Bruce, 1,700, Kansas; Snyder Bros, 3,000, Wyoming; J. Scare 2,500, Texas ranch; John Dunn, 2,000, Kansas; Snyder Bros., 2,500, Wyoming; C. B. Lucas, 1,000, on this market; Snyder Bros., 2,200, Wyoming; Kingsbury, 1,000 Kansas; Armsby, 1,800, Colorado; Snyder Bros., 2,600, Wyoming; Henry Stephens, 9,000, 4,000, to Pan Handle, and 5,000 to Kansas.

They have been distributed through the following States as follows:

Wyoming Territory	38,550
Kansas	27,550
Colorado	7,900
Pan Handle, Texas	8,450
Total drive to date	82,450
Yet to report	20,000
Estimated drive for season	102,450

Of this nnmber Snyder Bros., have driven 25,000 alone to Wyoming.

To this date the branch trail to Fort Griffin, report 150,000 having passed. The total drive will fall 25,000 short of the estimate made at the commencement of the season, and will not exceed 275,000 head.—*Fort Worth Democrat.*

The Letter John Wrote.

The particular evidence which interests John Sherman in the Potter resolution is a photographic copy of his letter to Weber and Anderson, the supervising inspectors of East and West Feliciana, Louisiana. This letter authorized them to make out the protests against the results of those parishes on which the returning board threw out the democats' votes. These men at first hesitated, and the delay caused an open and flagrant violation of the law on the part of the returning board in receiv- the protests. Mrs. Jencks, a friend of Mrs. Weber, was in Washington in January with this letter, to make terms with Secretary Sherman. She disposed of the original to him, but first had it photographed; and this is the one that has fallen into the enemy's hand.—*Nashville American.*

A Sad Event.

Mention was made in these columns a day or two ago, of the departure of Mr. E. L. Dennis' family for Virginia. At Denison, their little boy Edward Walter died, which caused a return of the family to this city. The funeral will take place to-day from their residence on Main street. Only a month ago the infant daughter of Mr. and Mrs. Dennis was borne to Glenwood, and again the angel of death has visited them. They have many friends here who will mourn with them in their bereavement.

The Latest Tilton-Elizabeth Development.

The reason why the brethren of Plymouth church desire to delay action upon the subject of dropping Mrs. Tilton's name from the church rolls, is believed to be an astounding piece of information that they have lately received, and a delay of four or five months, it is hinted, will give the outside world proofs of Mrs, Tilton's condition when she wrote the confession. They believe that within the next three months Mrs. Tilton's resumption of marital relations with Theodore Tilton will be made manifest that the infant will be the pledge of restored love between the two—that is if it is certain that brother Beecher has not paid Elizabeth any pastorial visits lately.

The examination of R. W. Keeling, charged with the theft of a mare and colt, took place before Judge Kirk. It was established during the examination, that the defendant had taken up the animals under the estray law, and had not posted them according to law, because some party had claimed them, and asked him to keep the animals till his return. Keeling then placed them in charge of some one in this city, who loaned the animals to a party who forgot to return them. He was acquitted on the charge of theft, as well as on the charge of the violation of the estray law.

Finest line of perfumes in the city, in bulk or in bottles, at Guiteau & Waldron's. 25-tf

SPECIAL LOCALS.

At Mrs. Boldrick's,

All the latest styles and novelties in millinery and dress goods. Elegant in design and first-class in material these goods will recommend themselves to all who examine them. The ladies of Denison and vicinity are respectfully invited to call and see them. 5 10 2w

Rhine wines, of all kinds, at Louis Lebrecht's.

NEW MARKET.

A Profitable Word to Those Using Fresh Meats.

John Collett, son of J. A. Collett, the well known and popular butcher, has opened a No. 1 meat market on the northwest corner of Woodard street and Rusk avenue, called the Denison Meat Shop. There are no adjoining buildings, hence the pure air has free access, and the meats are kept cool and fresh. All kinds of the very best meats will be kept at greatly reduced prices.

A BRANCH MARKET.

Mr. Collett has a branch shop on Main street east of the school house, for the accommodation of residents in that vicinity. The same excellent meats will be kept, and the same liberal prices adhered to at this market as at Mr. Collett's other shop. 5-17 1w.

I have used several bottles of Simmons' Liver Regulator, and you may record the fact, that my feelings are so far changed that I can eat hearty, and am more like a well man than I have been for years past. I have suffered for four years and am grateful for relief.

J. RAFFERTY, Periodical Store,
1806 Market St., Phila.

To the Ladies of Denison.

Ladies, I take pleasure in informing you that I am just in receipt of a large and elegant assortment of millinery goods. For the past two months I have taken great care to observe the most approved styles, and can assure yon that I will keep nothing but first class goods, and I hope, as in the past, to have at least a share of your patronage.

Miss M. E. Carlat, a French lady of some years experience as a dress maker, and who comes highly recommended, has taken rooms with me, and respectfully invites the ladies to call and examine her work and prices. Remember the place of business, Singer office, opposite postoffice. H. H. VOSBURGH.
5-9 1mo.

You will save money by buying wall paper at Brown's. Choice new patterns just received.

Silver Dollars, Henry Clay, Infant Wonder, Babies, Champion, Non Plus Ultra, etc., only 5 cents a piece, at Louis Lebrecht's.

Brown's meat market, next door to Yeidel's saloon, is constantly supplied with the best meats of all discriptions. Bologna sausages, the best in the market, constantly kept on hand. 5-2 78 tf.

Five cases of wall paper, beautiful patterns, at Brown & Webb's—old Kansas City Store.

Boarders Wanted,

Mrs. N. S. George, at the Northeast corner of Gandy street and Austin Avenue, will accommodate a few boarders, with or without lodging. She sets the best table in Denison, and her rooms are cool, pleasant and well furnished. Refers to all the old citizens of the town. 1m. *

Brown is closing out the balance of his chromos and many other goods in that line, very cheap, at private sale, and persons needing any of the above goods can now find some rare bargains by calling at Brown's Bazaar. Great reduction in prices on fancy work, zephyr, splints, mottoes, card boards and canvass. Toilet soaps only twenty five cents per box.

Do you smoke? If so, call on Louis Lebrecht. He keeps a well assorted stock of cigars and sells the same reasonably.

Denison Daily News.

VOL. VI. | DENISON, TEXAS, SATURDAY MORNING, JUNE 8, 1878. | NO. 91.

FRED. CAMPBELL. CHAS. LEASE. ALEX. W. ACHESON.

NEW GOODS! NEW HOUSE! NEW PRICES!

—BUT THE—

SAME OLD RELIABLE MEN,

—AT—

Acheson's Drug Store!

225 WEST MAIN STREET,

DENISON, TEXES.

A COMPLETE ASSORTMENT

OILS, PAINTS, WHITE LEAD, DRUGS, MEDicines, Mediscinal Liquors, Dye-Stuffs, Glass-Ware, Etc., Etc.

All at Prices Astonishingly Low!

Machinist will find it to their advantage to buy Lubricating Oils here, both on account of Quality and Price.

NOW PUT UP YOUR

PRESERVES AND JELLIES

WHILE FRUITS ARE PLENTIFUL.

GAISMAN & CO.

Have all the Requisites.

Cooper's Gelatine!

All Grades of Sugar!

Pure Spices of all Kinds!

AND

Mason's Patent Fruit Jars,

THE BEST IN THE WORLD.

GAISMAN & CO.

Have also the best Assortment of

CHOICE FRESH GROCERIES

IN NORTHERN TEXAS.

And Manage to Keep Prices

BELOW ALL COMPETITION!

Miscellaneous.

CHICAGO,

BURLINGTON and QUINCY

RAILROAD.

Passengers from Texas and the Indian Territory, going east, take the

C. B. & Q. R. R.

AT HANNIBAL.

Through some of the finest Towns in Illinois:

Quincy, Galesburg, Mendota, Aurora, Etc., to Chicago.

BEST & CHEAPEST ROUTE

To all points

EAST OR NORTH-EAST.

Pawobroker and Jeweler.

R. N BROWN,

PAWNBROKER & JEWELER.

Watches and Jewelry Repaired.

No. 228 Main street,

AGENTS Something New, Rich and Racy. Secrets of life unveiled. The Great Sensation Book of the age! Agents coining money! Everyone that sees the book is sure to want it! Secure territory at once. 1000 agents wanted. Sure thing. Sample and instructions mailed on receipt of 50 cents. Address at once

AGENTS PUBLISHING CO., St. Louis, Mo.

$1200 SALARY. Permanent salesmen wanted to sell Staple Goods to dealers. No peddling. Expenses paid. Address S. A. GRANT & CO., 2, 4, 6 & 8 Home St., Cincinnati, O.

Educational.

WHAT YOU CAN GET FOR $5.00.

FOR $5.00 you can get, from us or any bookseller, Scribner's Monthly, the best of all the illustrated magazines, for one year and a half, beginning with the magnificent Midsummer number for August last, and containing all the chapters of "His Inheritauce," Miss Trafton's graphic story of Army Life; all of "Roxy," Edward Eggleston's New Novel, a story of Western life during the political campaign of 1840; and a large part of Boyeson's novel, "A Knight of Fortune," the story of a community of emigrants in the Northwest; besides shorter stories by Mrs. Burnett, Saxe Holm, Boyesen, etc.; and Illustrated Poems, Travel Sketches, Essays, Reviews, nearly a dozen of the splendidly illustrated series of "Out-of-Door" Papers, including many of the best of the series on "American Sports," and on "The Picturesque Aspects of American Farm Life," etc., etc.; including all the numbers of Scribner's Monthly from August, 1877, to January, 1879, inclusive, and also the splendid Christmas Holiday Number of St. Nicholas for December, 1877, containing one hundred pages—the finest number of a children's magazine ever issued in this or any other country; the whole containing more than 2,000 octavo pages of the best and latest illustrated literature. SCRIBNER & Co., 743 Broadway, N. Y.

See prospectus of St. Nicholas in another column.

Wholesale Grocers.

HANNA, OWENS & CO.,

Successors to Hanna & Waples,

WHOLESALE

GROCERS

Corner Main Street and Austin av.,

DENISON, - - - TEXAS.

2-9

$3 GOLD PLATED WATCHES. [illegible] Address A. COULTER & Co., Chicago.

Medical.

VEGETINE

For Dropsy.

CENTRAL FALLS, R. I., Oct. 19, 1877.

DR. STEVENS:—

It is a pleasure to give my testimony for your valuable medicine. I was sick for a long time with Dropsy, under the doctor's care. He said it was Water between the Heart and Liver. I received no benefit until I commenced taking the Vegetine; in fact, I was growing worse. I have tried many remedies; they did not help me. Vegetine is the medicine for Dropsy. I began to feel better after taking a few bottles. I have taken thirty bottles in all. I am perfectly well, never felt better. No one can feel more thankful than I do.

I am, dear sir, gratefully yours,

A. D. WHEELER.

VEGETINE.—When the blood becomes lifeless and stagnant, either from change of weather or of climate, want of exercise, irregular diet, or from any other cause, the Vegetine will renew the blood, carry off the putrid humors, cleanse the stomach, regulate the bowels, and impart a tone of vigor to the whole body.

VEGETINE

For Kidney Complaint and Nervous Debility.

ISLESBORO, ME., Dec. 28, 1877.

MR. STEVENS:—

Dear Sir,—I had a cough for eighteen years, when I commenced taking the Vegetine. I was very low; my system was debilitated by disease. I had the Kidney complaint, and was very nervous—cough bad, lungs sore. When I had taken one bottle I found it was helping me; it has helped my cough, and it strengthens me. I am now able to do my work. Never have found any thing like the Vegetine. I know it is every thing it is recommended to be

5 59-4w MRS. J. A. PENDLTON.

VEGETINE is nourishing and strengthening, purifies the blood, regulates the bowels, quiets the nervous system, acts directly upon the secretions, and arouses the whole system to action.

VEGETINE

FOR

Sick Headache.

EVANSVILLE, IND. January 1, 1878.

MR. H. R. STEVENS:—

Dear Sir,—I have used your Vegetine for Sick Headache, and been greatly benefitted thereby. I have every reason to believe it to be a good medicine.

Yours very respectfully,

MRS. JAMES CONNER.

411 Third St.

HEADACHE.—There are various causes for headache, as derangement of the circulating system, of the digestive organs, of the nervous system, &c. Vegetine can be said to be a sure remedy for the many kinds of headache, as it acts directly upon the various causes of this complaint, Nervousness, Indigestion, Costiveness, Rheumatism, Neuralgia, Biliousness, &c. Try Vegetine. You will never regret it.

VEGETINE

Doctor's Report.

DR. CHAS. M. DUDDENHAUSEN, Apothecary, Evansville, Ind.

The doctor writes: I have a large number of good customers who take Vegetine. They all speak well of it. I know it is a good medicine for the complaints for which it is recommended.

December 27, 1877.

Vegetine is a great panacea for our aged fathers and mothers; for it gives them strength, quiets their nerves, and gives them Nature's sweet sleep.

VEGETINE

Doctor's Report.

H. R. STEVENS, Esq.:—

Dear Sir,—We have been selling your valuable Vegetine for three years, and we find that it gives perfect satisfaction. We believe it to be the best blood purifier now sold. Very respectfully,

DR. J. E. BROWN & Co.,

Druggists, Uniontown, Ky.

VEGETINE

Prepared by

H. R. STEVENS, BOSTON, MASS.

Vegetine is Sold by all Druggists.

Meat Markets.

CENTRAL MEAT MARKET,

Next door to Mayor's office,

DENNEY & HYBARGER, Props.

Sausage Meat, Sausage, Head Cheese, Blood and Liver Worst, and

FRESH MEAT OF ALL KINDS,

And of the best quality, kept constantly on hand. 10-28 tf

Oculist.

DR. M. JOSEPHTHAL,

Formerly of Waco,

And Oculist of the State Blind Asylum at Austin, has permanently located at

SHERMAN TEXAS,

Where he is prepared to treat all the Diseases of the Eye.

wtf

BASS BACK.

He and His Staff Pay a Visit to His Old Home.

Retake Two Horses Captured From Them by Sheriff Eagen.

Citizens of Denton in Hot Pursuit.

From the Dallas Herald.

The startling information was received in this city last night, that Sam Bass and his gang had returned to Denton.

Early in the morning Sam Bass, Henry Underwood, Frank Jackson, Charles Carter and two others, one of whom is said to be named Barnes, rode into town and went direct to Work & Co.'s livery stable. The hostler, Charles McDonald, was just opening the livery stable. Underwood remained on the outside, while the others rode in and ordered McDonald to saddle two horses which had been previously captured from Bass by Sheriff Eagon, of Denton county, and placed in the stable by him.

When McDonald refused to saddle the horses, Jackson struck him over the head with a pistol. Carter and Jackson then saddled the two horses, Bass all the while keeping his pistol pointed at McDonald. One of the saddles taken was the property of Alex Cockrell.

John Work, the stage driver, was asleep over the stable at the time, and upon being awakened gave the alarm of "Bass! Bass!" But the robbers were two hundred yards away before the loss was discovered. McDonald joined in the alarm, and soon a dozen parties were in pursuit.

The robbers went in a northerly direction. After the alarm was given armed citizens left the town every few minutes for the chase after them until nearly fifty had gone, when the last account from there had been received. The robbers had got about two hours start of their pursuers and had probably arrived at their old stamping ground long before the pursuit commenced.

Caarter was in Denton Wednesday evening. He was not previously known to belong to the Bass gang. The authorities have a writ for him for catlte stealing, and tried to capture him when he was in Denton, but he eluded them and got away.

Wednesday a party of fifteen citizens chased Bass out of sight of Denton creek. the gang was followed all the way from Stephenson county, throngh Wise, by a party of rangers.

Major Penn.

Major Penn is now in Memphis, where the avalanche gives the following account of his work:

Major Penn, the lawyer evangelist, is meeting with his accustomed success in Memphis. Eighty conversions and sixty additions to the First Baptist Church had occurred up to the time the meetings were changed to the Central Baptist Church. Mr. Penn does not employ the ordinary altar exercises or anxious seat, as many term it, but invites all willing to know the truth, without regard to feeling, to test the truth of his work by presenting themselves for prayer, and claims that no one can continue to do so, and not become a Christian. He begs all to come and try what he terms his gospel plan.

The Dallas Bank Swindle.

Investigation into the bursted Dallas State Savings bank shows that concern to have been a first class thieving and swindling institution. In the first place it commenced business upon a lie, representing to the public that it had a paid up cash capital when it never had a dollar. The investigating committee have found a default of over $50,000 in bills receivable. Gruber, the president, manager, owner and manipulator of the rotten and rascally thing, is shown to have abstracted in two years $23,000 of the deposits, which he charged to his salary account and which should have only amounted to $12,000. Laighton, the cashier, has fled. He was a witness of too much value to the swindled depositors to remain around Dallas, and Gruber sent him off. The investigation is still going on with the bottom still to reach.—*Houston Telegram.*

The widow of Henry Timrod, the poet, of South Carolina, has been in Washington for some months, vainly trying to get employment in some of the departments.

FROM MEXICO.

Fight Between Mexicans and Indians—Escobedo.

Special to the San Antonio Express.

EAGLE PASS, June 4.—News from Mexico states that a party of Mexico and Kickapoo Indians, about forty in number, attacked a marauding Lipan camp, at a point near Santa Rosa, last Sunday morning, killing six warriers and capturing five others with ten women and children, who are now in the Santa Rosa jail.

Col. Martinez with about thirty revolutionists, was in Morales last Saturday recruiting for Gen. Escobedo's force, which numbers now, about two hundred men, and it is thought as soon as he raises a sufficient force of men he will make forced loans and terrorize the Mexicans into subjection. So far he has not molested anybody; only taken such stock as he requires. His exact position is not known, but we can expect to hear of him soon.

THE INDIAN RAID

One of the Colson Boys Dead, the Other Dangerously Wounded.

Special to the Galveston News.

ULVADE, June 5.—The two Colson boys, aged ten and twelve years, have been found, the youngest one dead with bullet holes through his head and breast; the other in a pool of water shot through the shoulder and arm, but still alive. When the Indians came on them the oldest fired one shot, when he was shot through the breast. The Indians, taking his pistol, shot him again through the arm, and left him for dead. The little fellow crawled into the water, where he was found next morning. The Indians, after a hard chase by the rangers, have got away, going east, having all their stolen horses, numbering over a hundred.

An Old Texan Heard From.

Col. N. B. Yard yesterday received a copy of the Anglo-American Times, published in London, and bearing date May 17. From it the following extract is made:

Capt. George Simpton, formerly of the Texas navy (when Texas was a republic), and for many years pilot and revenue officer of Galveston, is now living at Acton, near London.

Capt. Simpton was one of the early pilots who officiated at this port, and was the leader of a forlorn hope that carried supplies to the American troops when surrounded by Mexicans during the revolutionary times of the Republic. He was well known by all the old settlers, who hold in high esteem the recollection of his public servicees rendered to Texas and its people during the stormy days of the revolution.

England has approached nearer to free trade than any other nation. Tariff reforms were inaugurated in 1840 when the customs tariff comprised about 1,200 articles subject to duty. The imports, which were $310,000,000 in 1840, rose to $761,645 in 1850, to $1,052,654,365 in 1860, and in 1876 they had reached the enormous figure of $1,875,773,540. The exports, which were $550,643,580 in 1840 rose to $579,105,460 in 1850, to $822, 606,755 in 1860 and $1,283,833,010 in 1876—or an increase of imports and exports of 267 per cent in thirty-six years. These are results which stagger the protectionists. They cannot answer them.

"Free trade and sailors rights" is Col. Piner's motto.

Montague County Convention

Special to the Galveston News.

MONTAGUE, via HENRIETTA, June 4.—The county Democratic convention met to-day at Montague. Delegates to the State convention were instructed to vote for abrogation of the two-thirds rule; also to vote for Throckmorton for governor; Mabry, attorney general; Darden, comptroller; Dorn, treasurer; Harris, commissioner of the land office; Piner was recommended for congress. Refreshing rains have fallen and crops are good.

"A gentleman in the Pan Handle had our clerk to forward a marriage certificate to him. He now returns it endorsed, 'a square back down, and not my fault.'"—*Henrietta Journal.*

All kinds of bird seed at Guiteau & Waldron's. 25-tf

Safely and certainly that great external remedy, Glenn's Sulphur Soap, removes cutaneous eruptions by opening the pores whose obstruction was the cause of the difficulty. Test and you will endorse it.

Beautiful shades of black or brown are produced by Hill's Hair Dye.

Mothers, Mothers, Mothers.

Don't fail to procure Mrs. Winslow's Soothing Syrup for all diseases of teething in children. It relieves the child from pain, cures wind colic, regulates the bowels, and, by giving relief and health to the child, gives rest to the mother.

3-6-d&w-1yr.

A New Guide to Texas, Kansas, and the Beautiful Indian Territory.

FREE It tells you all about this wonderful country of the Great Southwest. It is full of beautiful pictures.

This Guide is sent FREE to everybody. It tells you about the entrance into Texas at its Gate, the beautiful city of Denison, and this Guide also contains pictures of scenes in the Beautiful Indian Territory, and also scenes in Texas and Kansas. It contains a scene at Hannibal Mo., showing steamers on the Mississippi river, and a railroad train starting for the Beautiful Indian Territory, and Denison, Texas. It tells you where to go to raise sheep and cattle.

This New Guide to Kansas and Texas tells you about the TEXAS wonderful Neosho Valley of Kansas, and a trip through it, commencing at Parsons, Kansas, and where to buy a splendid arm at very low figures. It also tells you how and where to get Excursion Tickets to Chanute, Humboldt, Emporia and Junction City, Kansas. It also tells you how to reach Fort Scott, Kansas.

This Guide tells you where to buy lands in Texas from 25 cents per acre up to $5 per acre. It tells you about the lands, the crops, the people, the churches, the schools, the rivers, etc., and is full of beautiful engravings of scenes in the wonderful Indian Territory and Texas.

KANSAS Send for a copy. We mail it to anybody free of charge

Address

JAMES D. BROWN,

Texas and Kansas Emigrant Agent, Sedalia, Mo.

You can get free guides at 101 Clark street, Chicago, Ill., or at 102 North 4th street, St. Louis, Mo.

Truss.

THE BEST TRUSS ON EARTH!

One person in every four is ruptured, and two-thirds thus afflicted desire to die, as they suffer from Dispepsia, Spinal disease, Paralysis, Mental derangement and Debility.

X "Howe's Spring Pad Belt Truss," X

For the treatment and cure of Rupture and Hernia, patented 1875, is the only scientific truss invented. Every physician endorses it at once, and patients buy it at sight.

Ruptured sufferers from old-fashioned metallic and hard rubber springs find comfort.

Send $3 for sample truss, circulars, and endorsements of thousands who have been cured, and of the leading physicians of the United States, including the great doctor and surgeon, Gregory, principal of the St. Louis Medical College. All say it is the best truss known. It has cured a 5-year rupture in five weeks, Send 10 cents for our weekly truss paper, etc. Rev. Howe, the patentee, is ruptured on both sides badly, and has been for 25 years, and he invented this great truss for himself only. We make them for

MEN, WOMEN and CHILDREN!

who daily bless Mr. H. for his invention.

THE HOWE FEMALE SUPPORTER is the best known for abdominal affections.

If you have a friend ruptured, do him a favor by sending us his name at once.

Address

X HOWE TRUSS CO., X

Box 1170. Council Bluffs, Iowa

5000 traveling agents wanted States, counties, and townships for sale

aug.16 tf.

Planesphere of the Heavens

AT EVERY MINUTE.

TO ASTRONOMY, WHAT A MAP IS TO GEOGRAPHY.

This is an invaluable substitute for the Globe, and is as much better as it s cheaper. A good ten inch globe will cost $20, and the Planesphere will solve the problems much quicker and in many cases with greater accuracy. There are two planespheres, making a complete set; one shows all the constellations handsomely painted, the other the stars on a dark ground like the sky. The two cost only $6.

Take one of these instruments in your hand any clear night, set it to the hour and minute marked by the clock, and you have a perfect map of the visible heavens before you, by means of which you can locate all the stars and constellations and learn their names. Then turn to the almanac, learn the situations of the planets in the constellations. Now with the aid of planesphere, you can easily find them in the sky. Ninety-nine problems in astronomy can be solved by this ingenious instrument. For the planespheres, or further information, address the inventor,

HENRY WHITEALL,

502, South 3d st., Camden, N. J.,

Who refers, by permission, to the editor of the Denison News.

Medical.

OLD,

TRIED,

AND

TRUE.

Texans are acquainted—or ought to be—with the wonderful merits of that great American Remedy.

MEXICAN Mustang Liniment,

FOR MAN AND BEAST.

This liniment very naturally originated in America, where Nature provides in her laboratory such surprising antidotes for the maladies of her children. Its fame has been spreading for 35 years, until now it encircles the habitable globe.

The Mexican Mustang Liniment is a matchless remedy for all external ailments of man and beast.

To stock owners and farmers it is invaluable.

A single bottle often saves a human life or restores the usefulness of an excellent horse, ox, cow, or sheep.

It cures foot-rot, hoof-ail, hollow horn, grub, screw-worm, shoulder-rot, mange, the bites and stings of poisonous reptiles and insects, and every such drawback to stock breeding and bush life.

It cures every external trouble of horses, such as lameness, scratches, swinny, sprains, founder, wind gall, ring bone, etc., etc.

The Mexican Mustang Liniment is the quickest cure in the world for accidents occurring in the family, in the absence of a physician, such as burns, scalds, sprains, cuts, etc., and for rheumatism, and stiffness engendered by exposure. Particularly valuable to Miners.

It is the cheapest remedy in the world, for it penetrates the muscle to the bone, and a single application is generally sufficient to cure.

Mexican Mustang Liniment is put up in three sizes of bottles, the larger ones being proportionately much the cheapest.

Real Estate Agents.

JESSE M. COOK,

NOTARY PUBLIC,

AND DEALER IN REAL ESTA T

Gun Block, up stairs,

DENISON, - - TEXAS.

10-2

LEONARD & COFFIN,

REAL ESTATE AGENTS,

Nelson House Building,

DENISON, - - TEXAS.

2-6 tf

WM. H. HUGHES,

REAL ESTATE AGENT,

Main street,

DENISON, - - TEXAS.

10-10 tf

H. TONE. J. T. MUNSON.

TONE & MUNSON,

Dealers in

REAL ESTATE,

—and—

COLLECTION AGENTS.

Abstracts of Titles furnished for the City of Denison and Grayson county.

CORRECTNESS GUARANTEED.

Office, 215 Mainstreet, up stairs.

DENISON, TEXAS.

Wholesale Liquors.

KENTUCKY WHISKY DEPOT.

EPPSTEIN BROS.,

Wholesale dealers in

KENTUCKY

WHISKY

Imported and Domestic

Wines, Brandies, Cigars, Tobacco.

The Oldest Wholesale Liquor House in Denison.

Next Door to the Star Store.

Lumber Dealer.

LONE STAR LUMBER YARD,

JOHN R. CARR, Prop'r.

Agent for the

STUDEBAKER WAGON,

DENISON, - - TEXAS.

oct 1 3m

Hotels and Restaurants.

WHITE HOUSE,

W. J. BUDD, Proprietor.

(Formerly Austin Avenue Hotel,)

Northeast corner of Morgan street and Austin avenue, and convenient to the

UNION DEPOT

—AND—

M., K. & T. STOCK YARDS.

Comfort in every respect guaranteed, and prices very reasonable.

3-12 tf.

J. M. LEA,

Proprietor

PLANTERS HOUSE,

Cor, Gandy st. and Houston av.,

DENISON, - - - TEXAS.

A New House, Newly Furnished, pleasantly located near the Railroad Depots and Business Centers. 1-13 tf

The most excellent attributes to the success of a first-class hotel are courteous treatment, a well appointed *cuisine*, and well furnished rooms. You can find all these at the Planter's House.

WASHINGTON HOTEL,

JOHN SUMMERS, Prop'r.

Corner Tremont and Mechanic streets

GALVESTON, TEXAS.

This house is centrally located convenient to business, and but two squares from Morgan Line Steamers, and one block from Union Depot.

Table unsurpassed by any house in the city

This house has a bell in every room, connected with the office.

9-19 tf

COSMOPOLITAN RESTAURANT.

CHARLES BURCKEL, Prop'r.

Open Day and Night,

MEALS SERVED A LA CARTE.

Reserved Rooms for Ladies and Parties.

GAME, FISH AND CELERY.

OYSTERS A SPECIALTY.

No. 107 Main street.

DENISON, - - TEXAS.

10-4 1m

Banks.

FIRST NATIONAL BANK,

DENISON, TEXAS.

Authorized Capital $500,000 00.

Does a legitimate Banking business.

Special attention given to collections in Missouri, Kansas and Texas.

SIGHT EXCHANGE BOUGHT ANO SOLD

On principal cities of the United States.

OFFICERS:

JOHN SCULLIN,	ED. PERRY,	W. H. SANFORD
President.	Vice-Prest.	Cashier.

DIRECTORS:

John Scullin,	D. W. C. Davis,
Edward Perry,	E. H. Lingo,
J. P. Rockwell,	A. H. Coffin,
Sam'l Star,	W. H. Sanford,

apr4tf

DROVERS' & PLANTERS

BANK

DENISON, - - TEXAS.

CAPITAL, - - - $200,000.

OFFICERS:

J. H. SLATER,	JOHN NEVINS,	W. J. HUGHES
Pres.	Vice Pres.	Cash.

DIRECTORS.

JAMES PORTER,	JOHN NEVINS,
J. H. SLATER,	SAMUEL HANNA,
W. J. HUGHES.	

Does a general banking business.

Gold, Silver, and Exchange bough and sold.

Interests allowed on Time Deposits Drafts drawn on all the principal cities of Europe. Oct. 6-tf.

Tobacconist.

J. E. MASON,

Manufacturer and Dealer in

CIGARS;

219 Main street.

DENISON - - TEXAS.

3-7 tf.

A. LENDORF,

Dealer in

HAVANA, KEY WEST,

—AND—

DOMESTIC CIGARS,

Tobacco and Smokers' Supplies,

Postoffice Building,

DENISON, - - TEXAS.

A. R. COLLINS & CO.,

GENERAL

LAND AGENTS,

AND BROKERS IN

City Real Estate,

DENISON, TEXAS.

SPECIAL ATTENTION TO THE LOCATION OF COLONIES.

Land Certificates

Bought, sold, or located on choice

Farming or Grazing Lands.

Abstracts furnished, taxes paid, home and foreign collections promptly made, collateral securieties negotiated, property exchanged, prompt attention given to subdivisions and surveys in city and county. Copies of state, city and county maps furnished, and correspondence promptly attended to. Business solicited and satisfaction guaranteed.

LOOK-OUT POINT.

Eighty acres choice black sandy land, two miles west of the city, on the wire road—25 acres improved, 35 acres enclosed with good fence, 5 acres stony, over which the road runs; 10 acres broken, covered with good timber: balance choice land, timber and prairie; small box house, good spring—price $10 per acre. Patent direct from the State, or will exchange for city property. More land can be bought adjoining.

Eighty acres university land, unimproved, all fenced with post and board fence; small box house, springs and everlasting water, six miles northwest from Denison; some timber, good tract—terms $5 50, part cash, part on time; will issue patent direct to the purchaser. Will exchange for desirable central city real estate.

Five hundred acres choice black sandy land, unimproved, three miles southeast of Denison, lays fine, 150 acres prairie, 30 or 40 acres broken, balance choice land, covered with fine timber, has several good springs—price $5 per acre; one-half cash, balance in one year, at 10 per cent. interest.

One hundred and sixty acres, six miles west of Denison; choice black sandy and waxy, all fenced and improved, good frame house and out buildings; about one mile from new station on the D. & P. railroad—price $10 per acre.

One hundred and sixty acres black sandy land, rare bargain, 10 miles southwest from Denison, three miles south of Pott's ranche, seven miles northwest from Sherman, all fenced, 115 acres under the plow; frame house, 4 rooms, granaries and stable, fine stock yard; never failing ponds of good water, stocked with perch and cat fish; fine groves of pecan timber, fine brick cistern, 224 assorted fruit trees bearing, grapes, blackberries, etc.; unimproved lands can be bought adjoining at $3 50 to $5 per acre; —price $15 per acre; good school near. The above is a choice location.

Seven University claims, unimproved, of 80 acres each, located five to eight miles northwest of Denison and one to three miles from the first station on the Denison and Pacific railroad—prices from $3 50 to $5 per acre; one-third cash, balance eight to ten years time, at 10 per cent. interest.

Sixteen improved University claims, of 160 acres each, from three to six miles west of Denison, choice lands; improvements only ordinary, good water, some timber—prices from $6 to $10 per acre, part time.

Five improved 80's, near the first station on the D. & P. road, all black sandy and waxy prairie, improvements only fair—price $6 to $15 per acre, time given on part.

Twelve hundred and eighty acres, 26 miles southwest of Sherman and seven miles south of Collinsville, all heavily timbered, two fine streams run through it; fine sandstone rock quarry—price $5 per acre.

Twelve hundred and eighty acres, four miles west of Collinsville, in the Cross Timbers, all choice timber, well watered on timber creek—price $1 50 per acre.

Four hundred and ninty-two acres, seven miles southwest of Sherman, unimproved, black sandy prairie—price $4 per acre.

374	acres	black	sandy	prairie.
100	"	"	"	"
320	"	"	"	"
320	"	"	"	"
200	"	"	"	"
400	"	"	"	"
640	"	"	"	"
640	"	"	"	"
374	"	"	"	"
1000	"	"	"	"
2000	"	"	"	"

The above tracts lay 10 to 15 miles west and south of Sherman, along the Government telegraph line on the route to Pilot Point—price $3 50 to $4 00 per acre.

Twenty-three hundred acres of prairie, on the line of the Trans-Continental railroad, eight miles west of Sherman, unimproved—price $5 per acre.

Six hundred and forty acres of prairie, five miles west of above tract, $5 per acre; choice land.

One hundred thousand acres choice black sandy prairie land in the "Pan Handle" of Texas; fine locations for stock farms—price from 40 cents to $1 50 per acre.

Three hundred thousand acres choice lands, improved and unimproved, in Cooke, Montague and Clay counties—prices from $1 to $3 50 per acre.

One hundred and fifty thousand acres choice and well selected lands, suitable for grazing and farming lands, in Jack, Wichita, Denton, Callahan and other northwestern counties.

New Advertisements.

THE MUTUAL LIFE INSURANCE CO., OF NEW YORK.

F. S. WINSTON, President.

Cash Assets, $85,000,000,

Or nearly $40,000,000 more than any other Life Company in the world. No premium notes.

Surplus over $10,500,000, or more than 4,000,000 above that of any other Life Company in the country.

Amount of insurance in force, $300,000,000, or $120,000,000 more than that of any other Life Company in the world.

Total income for 1877, $18,012,469.

Amount received for interest and rents in 1877, $4,882,307, $1,806,607 in excess of the death losses of the year, and $405,911 more than the death losses and expenses combined.

Paid to policy-holders since organization, in 1843, over $120,000,000.

Number of policies in force, over 90,000.

Ratio of expenses to income less than that of any other company.

Dividends larger than those of any other company.

The oldest Life Company in the country. A mutual company. No stockholders to control it, or to take any portion of its surplus. Issues all forms of regular life and endowment policies, but no tontines.

Pays dividends at end of first year, and annually thereafter upon every policy in force.

The undersigned, in announcing that he represents the Mutual Life Insurance Company of New York, asks the careful attention of the citizens of Denison and Northern Texas, to the strong points above presented.

This grand old company, which long since attained and now holds the foremost place among life insurance institutions of the world, offers to those needing insurance security terms unequaled by any similar institution. It has never disputed a claim shown to be just and right, and its surplus for yearly dividends is equitably apportioned each year among all its members, without geographical or other discriminations. Those who desire safe life insurance are invited to call upon me. By moderate payments now, they may make sure provision for themselves in advanced life, or for those dependent upon them after death, whenever that may happen.

THOS. HOFFMAN,

Office in McDougall Block, up stairs. 5-1 1mo.

Boots and Shoes.

A. UHLIG,

FASHIONABLE BOOT AND SHOE MAKER.

REPAIRING PROMPTLY AND NEATLY DONE.

Austin avenue, bet. Main and Skiddy streets. Denison, Texas.

Meat Market.

P. J. QUINN,

DENISON, - - - - TEXAS.

NEW ADVERTISEMENTS.

NEW RICH BLOOD!

PARSONS' PURGATIVE PILLS make New Rich Blood, and will completely change the blood in the entire system in three months. Any person who will take 1 pill each night from 1 to 12 weeks may be restored to sound health, if such a thing be possible. Sent by mail for 8 letter stamps. I. S. JOHNSON & Co., Bangor, Me. 1-4w

REVOLVER FREE Seven-shot Revolver with box cartridges. Address, J. Brown & Son, 136 & 138 Wood street, Pittsburg, Pa. 4 58-4w

PIANO Another battle on high prices. War **ORGAN** with **monopolies** renewed. See Beatty's latest Newspaper for full reply, **sent free.** Before buying **PIANO** or **ORGAN** read my latest circular Beatty's celebrated Pianos and Organs, beautiful Instruments! Challenge Comparison! Rivals are jealous of my success! Most successful house in America! Commenced a few years ago without a dollar, sales now nearly $2,000,000 annually, Lowest prices ever given, elegant Rosewood Pianos **$135.** 16 stop Church Organs, **$115,** **WAR** tremendous bargains now ready. Address **WAR** Daniel F. Beatty, Washington, N. J., 58 4w

THE GREAT MEN OF GOD

A new work of great interest to **EVERY BIBLE READER And STUDENT** in the land. Address for descriptive terms and circulars, NELSON A PHILIPS, Publishers, No. 805 Broadway, New York. 2-4w

PIANOS $675 Piano $175, PIANOS $1000 do $250, Elegant rose wood cases, magnificent 3 string upright **Piano** $210. *No risk.* See before buying. *This offer only where not introduced.* Trade pouring in. Agents wanted everywhere. Write for paper, free. THOMAS BROS., Catskill, N. Y. 1-4w

$50 For a Case of Catarrh That Sanford's Radical Cure for Catarrh will not instantly relieve and speedily cure. References: Henry Wells, Esq, Wells, Fargo & Co, Aurora, N Y; Wm Bowen, McHatton, Grant & Bowen, St Louis. Testimonials and treatise by mail. Price, with improved inhaler, $1. Sold everywhere. WEEKS & POTTER, Proprietors, Boston, Mass. **$50** 2-1-4 w.

ORGANS *Highest Honors at A Worlds Exhibitions.* LATEST CATALOGUES and CIRCULARS, with new styles, reduced prices and much information, sent free. MASON & HAMLIN ORGAN CO., Boston, New York or Chicago. 4w

LAME-BACK! BENSON'S CAPCINE Porous Plaster is the best remedy for lame or painful back, or weakness of the back, ever invented or known. It soothes, it strengthens, it cures, where other porous plasters, and all linaments fail.

Each **genuine** Benson's Capcine Plaster has the word Capcine cut through the plaster. Take no other. 1-4w

Painters.

HOUSE, SIGN,

—AND—

ORNAMENTAL PAINTING.

Having leased and refitted the paint shop on Rusk avenue, in rear of First National Bank, we are now prepared to execute

PAINTING,
GRAINING,
AND CALCIMIMING

In all the various branches, on short notice, and having secured the services of a practical artist, we guarantee perfect satisfaction in all cases or no charges.

Sign Writing, Graining, and Buggy Painting are specialties. Terms reasonable. **DRED PARKS & CO.**

N. B.—Mixed Paints furnished on short notice. 2-27 tf

Music Teacher.

M. L. WERNER,

PROFESSOR OF MUSIC

—AND—

TEACHER OF GERMAN.

Lessons given at the residences of pupils. For further information apply a the residence of M. A. Daugherty, or a the DAILY NEWS office.

To Music Teachers.

A new, natural and easy system, far superior to any ever before published. Pamphlet containing this system mailed free.

MILLER'S BIBLE AND PUBLISHING HOUSE 1102 and 1104 Sansom St., Phila.

Saloons.

OURAND'S SALOON

AND

RAILROAD OFFICE,

119 Main Street,

DENISON, - - TEXAS.

This old and popular resort is supplied with the

BEST LIQUORS IN THE MARKET

And all popular brands of Cigars.

READING ROOM ATTACHED.

10-1 tf

BANK EXCHANGE.

J. B. McDOUGALL, Prop'r.

EXCELS ALL OTHER SALOONS

In the city.

The choicest liquors and all the standard brands of imported and domestic cigars always on hand.

Call and try the best five cent cigar in the city.

227 Main street.

DENISON, - - - TEXAS.

9-5 dtf

J. A. BRENNER,

Dealer in

CHOICE LIQUORS AND CIGARS

Main street,

DENISON, - - TEXAS.

GRAND SOUTHERN SALOON,

J. RAYNAL & CO., Prop'rs.

Cor. Main st. and Austin av.

This is one of the oldest and most popular saloons in the city, and still preserves its popularity for keeping pure wines and liquors, and the best cigars.

FURNISHED ROOMS

Can also be had on reasonable terms.

8-18 tf

PALACE BEER HALL,

LOUIS LIBBIE, Prop'r.

CHOICE WHISKY, NO. 1 CIGARS,

ST. LOUIS ALE AND BEER

Constantly on draft.

South side of Main street,

DENISON, - - TEXAS.

The Palace Beer Hall has been recently fitted up in a neat and attractive style and furnished with

FINE BILLIARD TABLES.

The Wine Room, which has recently been fitted up, is nicely furnished.

Gents' Furnishing Goods.

E. H. HANNA,
Dealer in
HATS, CAPS, MEN'S FURNISHING GOODS,
NO. 112 MAIN STREET, - - - DENISON, TEXAS.

"I buy all my clothing of E. H. Hanna and this is the kind of a fit I get every time 1-5,

Furniture Dealer.

F. LEDRICK,

(Successor to John Nevins & Co.,)

DEALER IN

FURNITURE

GLASSWARE, QUEENSWARE,

Window Glass, Wall Paper, Carpet Paper, Baby Carriages, Bird Cages, Carpets, Matting, Mouldings, Picture Frames, Lamps and Lamp Fixtures, Window Curtains, Flower Pots, Etc., Etc.

A full supply of

HOUSE FURNISHING GOODS.

Also a full stock of

Metalic and Rosewood Coffins.

At the old stand, corner of Main street and Austin avenue. 3-1.

Business Notice.

After this date all notices of lodge meetings, (special meetings) tributes of respect, obituary notices over ten lines, and all publications of this character will be charged for at the rate of five cents per line, (which is half rate) for each insertion. Read this, and don't forget. We have to live and pay our printers, and there is no reason why we should work for nothing.

Denison, March 15, 1877.

Denison Daily News.

VOL. VI. DENISON, TEXAS, THURSDAY MORNING, JULY 25, 1878. No. 130.

CAPT. BASS.

To Whom Belongs the Glory of His Capture.

From the Sherman Register.

It is very evident that the treachery of the telegraph operator at Round Rock will result in robbing our worthy sheriff, William Everheart, of the credit that duly belongs to him for inaugurating the scheme that led to the capture of Sam Bass and one of his confederates. There is no doubt that William Everheart and a few of his most intimate friends, who were in the secret with him and were to assist in the capture of the outlaws only knew of the bank robbery that had been planned by Bass and his gang, to take place at Round Rock. The exact night that the bank was to be robbed was communicated to Sam Ball in this city, by spies working in the interest of our sheriff, while Everheart was quietly secreted at Round Rock waiting for matters to develop. Upon receipt of these tidings, word was dispatched to Everheart to be on his guard, and deputy sheriff Winters took the train to go to the assistance of Everheart. The miserable, treacherous, unprincipled operator at Round Rock, violated every principle of decency and the strictest instructions of his official capacity, by "giving our boys away" to a lot of shysters who have been roaming at ease over the prairies at the state's expense under the high-flown title of "State troops!" And through the contemptible treachery of this scab in human shape, these fellows get the credit and the reward for the capture, while our worthy sheriff, who has been following these bandits for weeks at his own expense, and laid the net into which the outlaws quietly walked, is left in the cold. For weeks he has been skirmishing Denton and other counties, losing his rest, neglecting his own affairs, and defraying every dollar of his own expense, and just at the moment when his labors are about to be rewarded, a miserable skunk steps in and thwarts his plans by putting into the hands of paid adventurers the very secrets upon which the very acme of his success depended. In the name of a grateful public, who recognize that the full credit of the capture belongs to Everheart, we demand the removal of the dirty, unscrupulous, treacherous dog that betrayed him, and further demand from our State authorities an ample and full recognition of his eminent services in the capture of the bandits.

ANOTHER VIEW.

Special to the Galveston News.

DALLAS, July 22.—The credit of the capture of Bass and a portion of his gang is given to Sheriffs Johnson and Everheart, who matured and urged the plan of arresting Murphy, releasing him on bail, and spreading the report that he had jumped his bond. The plan worked like a charm. Murphy hunted, apparently sought the camp of Bass for protection, and whenever opportunity offered, dropped information of the whereabouts and purchases of the gang to Johnson, Everheart and Capt Peak. The plan to rob the bank at Round Rock having been agreed upon, timely notice was dispatched by Murphy to Johnson at Austin. Details of subsequent events have appeared in the News. An officer from Austin says Everheart and Johnson would have been at the capture at Round Rock, but were advised by Major Jones to hold the fort at Austin. On the receipt of the dispatch from Murphy to Johnson giving Bass away, a consultation was held with Everheart and Major Jones; the latter urged that Murphy's information might be a ruse of Bass to get all the forces away from Austin in order to facilitate an attempt to release Pipes and Herndon. He left Everheart and Johnson to manage affairs at the capitol, and, accompanied by Capt. Hall, took the Round Rock affair in hand. The death of Bass creates sympathy for the newspaper men.

The statement that Everheart remained in Austin, when he knew from the spy that Bass was going to Round Rock, is decidedly too thin to go down with people in this section who know Everheart.

Sir Stafford Northcote has announced in the House of Commons the bethrothal of the Duke of Connaught, Queen Victoria's third son, with Princess Maria Louise, of Prussia, daughter of Prince Frederic Charles.

How it Happened.

The Denton Monitor gives the following version of the unfortunate shooting at McKinney:

We learn from W. R. Wetsel, Esq., just in from McKinney, that John Bingham, Esq., editor of the McKinney Enquirer, got into a difficulty with Mr. John Hunter, last Saturday evening, about sunset, and shot the latter twice through the thighs and mortally wounded a negro, accidentally, on the opposite side of the street. It occurred on the north side of the square. It seems that Mr. Bingham was under the influence of liquor at the time of the shooting. The difficulty grew out of a dispute about politics. "You are a friend of mine," said Bingham, "but you belong to a d—d clique." "You are a d—d liar," rejoined Hunter. When this was said, Bingham drew a four barrelled pistol, and as Hunter jumped behind a post, fired. The ball passed through his right thigh. He fired the second shot, and the bullet passed through his left thigh. The third ball missed, and the fourth mortally wounded a negro as above stated. Hunter was unarmed. Mr. Bingham was arrested and put in jail, but in a few minutes was taken out, arraigned before a Justice of the Peace; and placed under bond of two thousand dollars.

The above are the particulars as detailed to us by Mr. W. R. Wetsel.

All for Love.

SAN ANTONIO, July 20.—A Mexican living in the country south of here made love to a young lady, the daughter of his employer, and a marriage was decided on against the protest of the parents. On the day appointed for the event, the mother took the daughter, locked her up, and kept her confined two days. Upon being released she obtained arsenic, took the poison and soon died, no medical assistance being near.

Death Mystery.

SAN FRANCISCO, July 23.—The schooner Parallel reports that on the 17th instant, off coast about one hundred miles north of this port, she fell in with a Japanese junk, with not a living person aboard, but a number of corpses were found, some shackled together. They must have been dead a month at least. Some of the bodies were dressed in costly material. There was no food on board.

Another Bale.

ST. LOUIS, July 21.—The first bale of this season's cotton arrived here yesterday from Schulenberg, Fayette county, Texas, consigned to the St. Louis Cotton Exchange. It was graded strictly low middling, and sold at auction for 31 cents per pound. It will be taken to New Yord and sent thence to Liverpool.

Beaconsfield Gartered.

London, July 23.—The Times, on the subject of the bestowal of the garter upon Beaconsfield, says the highest social distinction which could be bestowed by a sovereign, is thus added to the applause which Lord Beaconsfield has won from the country at large.

The Treasury department is now furnishing depository banks with silver dollars free of express charges, This will no doubt result in placing a large amount of of silver coin in circulation. The order went into effect Thursday of last week, and applications to the amount of $310,-000 have already been received by the department.

Earl Beaconsfield is endeavoring to effect the reunion of the Roman Catholic and Greek churches, and the installation of the Pope as head ruler at Jerusalem. The Earl should not do that; he might defeat that pet prophecy of the christians, which looks forward to the restoration of the Jews.

When a man dies in Sherman from the effects of heat, the Courier calls it a stroke of apoplexy. There are no cases of apoplexy in Denison.

A carrier pigeon race of 500 miles, from Columbus, O., to New York City, has been arranged for July 25, for $100 in gold, offered by Joseph M. Wade, of Springfield, Massachusetts.

FROM AUSTIN.

How The Convention was Harmonized.

Special to the Dallas Herald.

AUSTIN, July 23.—The conference committee of eighteen, to select a candidate, nine from each side, which sat with closed doors has adjourned. Hubbard's and Devine's names were withdrawn, and agreed not to put forward any man heretofore ballotted for. No one name could be agreed upon, and each side are in caucus, each to name a candidate. The Hubbard men will probably name Stewart, of Harris, and the Devine men name Sayers, of Bastrop, or West, of Travis.

AUSTIN, July 23—4:25 p. m.—The two committees could not agree this morning, and another committee was selected. They reported the name of Oran M. Roberts, present Supreme Judge, at four o'clock, as the compromise candidate for Governor. No other man in the Devine caucus could be agreed on, and a number of delegates of the Hubbard caucus favored him from the first, but Reagan was the choice of the Hubbard caucus.

AUSTIN, July 23—5:50 p. m.—The convention met at five o'clock.

Herndon, of Smith, withdrew the name of R. B. Hubbard.

Bower, of Dallas, withdrew Thomas J. Devine.

Herndon nominated Oran M. Roberts, of Smith county. Said he (Roberts) would agree for his name to be placed in nomination only in the interest of peace and harmony, and would resign his high place of Chief Justice, if nominated. He paid a high tribute to his character and integrity, which was frequently applauded.

Crawford, of Marion, seconded the nomination of Judge Roberts.

Ex-Governor Stockdale, of De-Witt, seconded the nomination, and moved that he be declared by acclamation the choice of the democratic party for the next governor of Texas. Carried, and the chair announced that Mr. Roberts was declared the nominee.

Bower, of Dallas, placed in nomination for lieutenant-governor, Joseph D. Sayers, of Bastrop, and moved that his nomination be made by acclamation.

McLeary, of Bexar, seconded the nomination. Carried, and the chair announced Mr. Sayers as the nominee.

Herndon, of Smith, moved that a committee of three be named by the chair to notify Roberts and Sayers of their nominations. Herndon, Chenoworth and Bower were appointed as such committee. Balloting for attorney general has now begun.

AUSTIN, July 23.—10:30 p. m.—For attorney general, Ellis, of Lavaca county, nominated by George B. McCormick, of Marion, seconded by McLean, of Bexar; Martin, of Hunt, nominated by H. P. Mabry, of Marion, seconded by McLemore, of Galveston; Campbell, of Fannin, nominated by George T. Todd, of Marion, seconded by Young, of Bexar; Murray, of Collin, nominated by D. A. Nunn, of Houston, seconded by McCullough, of Leon; Martin, of Henderson, nominated Sam A. Wilson, of Cherokee, seconded by Rock, of Coryell. Nominations closed.

First ballot: McCormick, 652; Mabry, 323 2-3; Todd, 197; Nunn, 158 2-3; Wilson, 169 2-3.

Dallas county cast 39 votes for Mabry, and 6 for Nunn. Nunn and Todd withdrew.

10:32 p. m.—Before the conclusion of the second ballot, Wilson and Mabry withdrew their names. On motion of Mabry, the nomination of McCormick was made by acclamation. Adjourned to 8:30 o'clock tonight.

10:55 p. m.—The convention met at 8:30 o'clock. For comptroller S. H. Darden was nominated by Story, of Caldwell; John H. Cochrane, of Dallas, by Young, of Bexar; John Y. Rankin, by Coleman, of Harrison; John D. Stephens, by Jones, of McLennan.

First ballot—Darden, 618 1-2; Stephens, 335; Rankin, 243; Cochrane 146; scattering 141 1-2. Mr. Cochrane withdrawn.

MIDNIGHT.—Before the second ballot was concluded all the candidates but Darden were withdrawn, and Darden nominated by acclamation.

SAM BASS AND HIS BAND.

History of the Capture of the Train-Robber Chief, and the Story of His Career.

Bass' Last Moments—What He Said of Stage Robberies and Train Robberies.

Brigandage in the Black Hills and on the Union Pacific, Texas Central and Texas Pacific Roads.

[Special Cor. of the Galveston News.]

ROUND ROCK, July 22.—Sam Bass, who died at two minutes to 4 o'clock Sunday last, withheld till the last all knowledge that would tend to positively implicate his confreres. He would make no confession. He would not talk upon religion, and referred but briefly to his family. In reply to leading and cross questions as to his doings, and the records of those who are with him equally guilty, he made uniformly the same answer, viz.: "It is not my profession to tell what I know. It would hurt too many good men." He made this remark to one of his physicians and to Maj. Jones. To the latter he said: "It is agin my profession to blow on my pals. If a man knows anything he ought to die with it in him."

His utterances were plain and sensible, but illiterate. His general manner was one of absolute but unobtrusive defiance. He could neither read nor write. Among his men he ruled by exceeding great energy, courage, dash and generosity. The sentimentalist will call Bass a "noble" desperado. His last words were insignificant. To his colored nurse, James Chatman, who had tended him closely since he has been in town, he said only a few moments before dying: "The world is bobbing around." This was his last utterance. He was warned by his physician, twenty minutes before death, of his approaching dissolution, the expectation being that he might want to take advantage of the occasion for some statement of personal or public interest. He replied briefly to the warning: "Let me go." His death took place just two days after he was shot. No very severe struggles of suffering were observed till Sunday afternoon, when he showed intense agony. Even then he thought he would weather the trouble and recover—a delusion that never left him from the moment he was placed on his cot. His last moments were quiet and the end was characterized by a few short gasps, an interval of one minute with no breathing, and a short jerk of the head.

The object of attraction which has drawn many people from a distance on every train for two days being no more, the bright little town of Round Rock will once more assume her usual settled ways.

AUTHENTIC HISTORY OF THE PLAN OF CAPTURE.

Jim W. Murphy was incarcerated at Tyler at the time all the Bass party were indicted, as accessory, he being accused of harboring and giving information to the robbers. On the 19th of May, while in Tyler under bond awaiting his trial, he proposed to Maj. Jones to go and "get in" with the Sam Bass party and "give them away," upon condition that Maj. Jones would get the charge against him dismissed. The proposition was at once accepted, the agreement being that if Murphy would place Bass and his party in such position that they

COULD BE CAPTURED

The charge against him should be dismissed; or that if one or any of the robbers were captured through information received from Murphy, or if he would prove to Maj. Jones' satisfaction that he tried and had done all that was in his power to effect the capture and had failed through no fault of his, then Maj. Jones promised to appear in court in his behalf and give him credit on his trial for what he had done and do whatever he could legally to accomplish his acquittal. Murphy also appealed to Maj. Jones to intercede for his father, Henderson Murphy, who was indicted also, and begged that the charge against the old man be dismissed, saying that the old man had done nothing for which he should be tried. Maj. Jones promised to do all that he could for the old man. In pursuance of this agreement Murphy left Tyler secretly next morning, and it was promptly announced in the Galveston *News* that Jim Murphy

HAD "JUMPED HIS BOND."

Maj. Jones gave the information to a reporter of the *News* in the *News* office (Maj. J. arriving in Galveston just at that time), in the shape of a telegram from Tyler. The item was copied by state papers as a good one, the forfeiture of such a big bond as $15,000 was discussed, sympathy was expressed for Murphy's sureties, and the people got on none the worse for being no wiser. When court opened April 20, and the case of Murphy was called,

A FORFEITURE NISI

Was taken on his bond. The same day old man Murphy's case was called up and a nolle prosequi entered. This was done because it was announced that no testimony of sufficient strength existed against him, of which fact Maj. Jones was fully satisfied, and United States District-Attorney Evans showed no hesitation, from the lights before him, to recommend the action adopted in the case.

These developments will be remembered by those who have watched the progress of the train-robbery cases. To return to the

JONES-MURPHY AGREEMENT.

Capt. June Peak of the rangers, and Walter Johnson, deputy United States marshal, were admitted into the secret. Murphy was to report progress to them from time to time, as well as to Maj. Jones, and to call upon them or either of them for assistance in making arrests. Peak and Johnson were also to protect Murphy and prevent his being arrested and put in jail for forfeiting his bond.

Murphy went home to Denton county and at once made overtures to the Bass party, telling them that he had "jumped his bond" and wanted to join them, and would assist them in whatever they would undertake in their line of business, as he was on the scout and had to

LIE OUT IN THE BRUSH

Anyhow. He played the part of a fugitive, one evading notice, and showing anxiety for personal safety. Indeed, he would have been taken promptly by any officer of law who had not been let into the Jones-Murphy secret. But Bass and his men were suspicious of him and would not trust him fully or take him into their clan for some time. They finally formed an alliance, and on the 9th of June he went regularly in with them.

About this time Sheriff Everhart of Grayson county, to whom Johnson had communicated the secret, came to Murphy's house to assist in making the arrests. Murphy told him that he would have two of them back of his field that night, and that he could arrest them if he wanted to. But for some reason which Murphy does not know, the sheriff's party did not come. The plan was then made to arrest them at Bolivar, in Denton county, or on the road to Denton, where they were going to steal some horses, but this also failed. They then determined to leave that neighborhood, and went by Denton and stole a horse and saddle from Billy Mount's stable (Maj. J. has the horse in his keeping now for Mr. Mount), Murphy standing guard on the outside while Bass went in and got the horse. Thence they went down Elm, passed near Dallas and on to the Collins settlement, where they rested two days. Here the party received information that Murphy was with them for the

PURPOSE OF BETRAYING THEM,

And in a council of war they determined on his death. When the decision was made known to him he begged for his life, acknowledging that he had entered into the agreement, but that it was done to effect his escape from the clutches of the law, and with the intention of "giving Maj. Jones and the government away," and not them, and that if they would trust him he would take the lead in the first dangerous undertaking to prove his fidelity to them. He pleaded earnestly and long for his life. Jackson, fortunately for him, had been a friend of his youth, and now took his part. Murphy gives a concise account of

THE CRITICAL MOMENT.

He tells of how Jackson said he "would not believe Murphy would give them away; knew the boy well; would not lend his decision to a sacrifice, bloody and without a fair trial." In reference to this part of his experience, Murphy said to your correspondent: "I wouldn't go through it all again for $50,000 piled down on the floor before me—no, sir!—with all the anxiety and watching I had to suffer."

But said I: "Bass is no more and you are the man to thank for it, are you not?" Murphy struck his knees with his broad, brown hat, and said: "Well, it's all over now, and I am glad of it." He heaved a sigh of relief and was rising to go when I asked him if he did not feel kindly toward Jackson. He said he "hoped the good fates would be with the generous boy," and felt as though he owed him a debt of gratitude. For Underwood also Murphy expressed good feelings because of personal attachments. "They are good boys at heart, but on the wrong tack," said Murphy.

The protestations of fidelity by Murphy apparently satisfied Bass and party, but from that time on they kept so close a watch on him that he had no opportunity to communicate with any one who could assist him until the party reached Belton, when he wrote to Sheriff Everhart, and Georgetown, when he wrote to Maj. Jones.

Those persons who are at a loss to know why Maj. Jones was not better posted as to exact date of arrival and plans of Bass and party at Round Rock may here observe the cause. Oneone occasion Murphy had just dropped a letter in the post-office box when Bass came in and wanted to know what he was after. "After old newspapers to read in camp," promptly and discreetly lied Murphy.

Bass and party left Billy Collins' neighborhood about the 15th of June. Thence they went to Rockwall, reaching that place one week after they left Denton county; stayed one night and went to Terrell, remaining one night. Bass and Jackson examined the two banks here and concluded Hall & Co.'s was the best, but decided not to rob. Here it is proper to state that Murphy acted the part of the

CAUTIOUS MAN OF THE GANG.

He endeavored on every occasion when a robbery was proposed to defer it or defeat the design. His plan—the proper one—was to launch the party into the hands of the r angers without the perpetration of deeds of plunder and killing, or as little of this as possible. From Terrell they went to Kauffman, and finding no bank, Bass got an old man, keeper of a store in which he had a safe, to change a ten-dollar bill, but on seeing the situation thought the haul not worth making. They went next to Ennis, where Bass and Murphy ate dinner at a hotel and fed their horses at a stable. The Ennis bank was examined and found rather secure. They "passed" on it. Thence the party went to Waco and camped two miles from town on the east side of the river. Murphy and Jackson, detailed to look up the banks, saw a

PRIZE IN THE STATE SAVINGS BANK.

Jackson was enthusiastic, as he had seen quantities of paper money and gold on the counter. Murphy, as usual, was cautious, but had little to say till next day on the return of Jackson and Bass to camp from town. The latter had seen the prize, and concluded to capture it. Camp, which had been moved across the river from the place of first location, was now moved again to a situation that was more convenient for escape, the route of which was laid out. Murphy and Jackson went in to get provisions, and Murphy opened his persuasive batteries on Jackson, urging the danger of robbing a large bank in so much peopled a town. On their return to camp Murphy still cautioned against the daring move, arguing principally that the bank was too well banistered, and they would have too far to run in escaping. The enterprise was abandoned. Bass and Murphy went to town again, and took a drink at the Ranch saloon, where Bass had changed his last $20 gold piece,

ONE OF THE FAMOUS PIECES

Stamped 1874, and thus known as captured in the great $60,000 Union Pacific express robbery. They returned to camp, one mile south of Waco, and that night Barnes went back to the edge of town and stole a large dark bay mare with a little white in the face, white hind feet, and one rib broken causing a protuberance on the left side. The mare paces very fast.

Bass and party stayed around Waco three days altogether, and then went to Belton, where Murphy sold Barnes's old mare which he had been riding previously, to a little blacksmith, and gave a

BILL OF SALE

In his own name, viz.: J. W. Murphy. He explained this act by saying he wanted to leave some mark in his wake, showing where he was operating, and thinking, too, it might lead to detection of the party. One of the party gave Murphy a $5 bill to change, and while moving around to do this he managed to give them the dodge long enough to write to Sheriff Everheart on the 13th of June. Murphy also told his party that the bank of the town, being in the back of the store, was hard to get at, and not worth the risk of the descent upon it. Leaving Belton they moved to Georgetown, where Murphy found a chance to write to Maj. Jones, but came near being caught in the act of mailing and had to lie out of it to Bass. After a stay of one day at Georgetown the party moved to camp on the roadside two miles from

ROUND ROCK.

Camped next night nearer town, where the San Saba road crosses a creek, and afterward near old Round Rock, a mile from new Round Rock, south of the graveyard, near some negro houses. During these movements they were resting their horses and preparing to rob the Williamson County bank at Round Rock. Murphy pretended that his horse was nearly broken down in order to delay the robbery and give Maj. Jones time to arrive. In the meantime the party were in the bank several times. Bass and Murphy at different times got $5 bills changed. After the closest examination of the bank

THE FOLLOWING PLAN

Was fixed upon to rob it: They were all to go to the bank on foot, leaving their horses hitched in an alley near the bank. Barnes was to give the cashier a $5 bill to change—the last they had, by the way—and while he was doing this Bass was to level his pistol at the cashier and make him hold up his hands, when Barnes would jump over the counter, take the money and put it in a sack. In the meantime Jackson and Murphy were to stand in the door of the bank to keep anybody from coming in.

Bass, Barnes and Jackson came into Round Rock on July 19, the day the fight was precipitated, to make the final examination, leaving Murphy in charge of camp. Believing their horses were properly rested,

THEY FIXED ON SATURDAY,

July 20, for the descent on the bank. After getting the money they were to move out the San Saba road a short distance, then turn to the right, go up west of Georgetown and make their way to Denton, where they proposed to kill Deputy Sheriffs McGing and Wetzell of Denton county.

They swore death to Billy Scott, the witness, if they had to ride into Dallas for him. They say he wound himself into Collin's confidence, and through him got with the party under pretence of joining it; that the first time he was with them, Arkansas Johnson told them he was a spy, and insisted on killing him. Bass having confidence in Collins believed Scott all right, and would not consent.

OF THE MOVEMENTS

Of some of the Bass clan, not mentioned in the above narrative, it is known that in the fight on Salt creek Johnson was killed and Underwood and Henry Collins wounded. Collins ran off during the fight and has been seen by one of the party but only once. Since the fight neither Underwood, Carter nor Collins has been with Bass. Carter went home, but was sent out of the country by his father. Nothing has been known to Bass of Underwood since the fight in Wise county. William Collins, after "jumping his bond," promised to join Bass and go with him, but when they went to his house after him they could learn nothing of him. He owed Bass money, to which facts Bass attributes his disappearance.

MURPHY'S LAST LETTER—JONES' PLAN OF CAPTURE—THE FIGHT.

As to what Murphy had to say in his letter from Belton to Maj. Jones I posted myself in conversation with Murphy and Maj. Jones; also as to Maj. Jones' plan of capture. The following statement, in substance, I obtained from the major:

While Murphy was trying to get in with the Bass party he wrote to Maj. Jones several times, telling him what he was doing and the difficulties he labored under. He also communicated with Capt. Peak several times. After he got in with them he had no opportunity to write or communicate with him on account of being watched so closely by the robbers, one of whom always remained with him, and Maj. Jones knew nothing of their movements or whereabouts until he received a letter from Murphy written at Belton. This letter was mailed on the 18th, informing Maj. Jones that the party would be at Round Rock about that time; would camp in the immediate vicinity four or five days to rest their horses, which were very tired; would prospect around and then rob a bank or the train. Murphy begged that the letter should not be shown to any one; that if it was ever known the clan would kill him, and implored the major

"FOR GOD'S SAKE,"

To be on hand in time or he (Murphy) would have to join the robbery or Bass would kill him. He said he would see the major when he came to Round Rock or write to him and let him know as soon as their plans for the robbery were arranged. Maj. Jones at once started a courier with instructions to Lieut. Reynolds, who was at Lampasas with some men to meet him at Round Rock next morning, and at daylight next morning sent three men, whom he had in Austin, to Round Rock and went there himself on the first train. He took with him Maurice Moore, deputy sheriff of this county, whom he happened to meet on the street as he was going to the depot. Moore was formerly a sergeant in his command. Arriving at Round Rock he went to the post-office, expecting a letter from Murphy, but found none. He then warned the banker that the robbers were in the vicinity, and would probably attempt to rob him, and informed him of the steps he was taking to capture them. Called on Deputy Sheriff Grimes, who was once a member of his command, and took him and Mr. Albert Highsmith into his confidence. Theysent spies out to search the country round for the robbers' camp. At nightfall, having heard nothing of the robbers, and not knowing but that they had passed on to Austin, or concluded to strike the train at some other point, Maj. Jones notified Capt. Hall and the sheriff and United States marshal to look out for them in Austin, and telegraphed the railroad officers at Hearne and Austin

TO HAVE THE TRAINS GUARDED.

That night he had his men concealed at the depot here to protect the train, and also had the town thoroughly patroled. Next morning his spies were out by daylight, searching the country for the camp. His men were stationed at suitable points to watch for the robbers, and particularly to keep a lookout about the bank. About noon, having learned that Lieut. Reynolds had moved from Lampasas to San Saba, and fearing that he would not arrive in time, he telegraphed to Austin for Capt. Hall, who arrived at 2 o'clock P. M. After consultation they telegraphed to Austin for Lieut. Armstrong and some of Hall's men, as it was supposed the robbers numbered seven or eight men. About 4 o'clock P. M. the ranger who was keeping watch over the bank saw three men walk up the street and enter the store of Mr. Koppel. One of the men, he thought, had a pistol under his coat. He immediately informed Moore and Grimes, to whom he had been ordered by Maj. Jones to report, when Grimes, not suspecting who the parties were, but supposing they were cow-boys or countrymen, said he would go and see, and if one of them had a pistol he would arrest him for unlawfully bearing arms, and Moore went with him.

THE FIGHT.

They found the three men in the store purchasing tobacco. Grimes walked back to where they were, placed his hand on one of them and asked him if he did not have a pistol. The reply was, "yes," and instantly the three drew pistols and shot Grimes. As they fired Grimes said, "hold up, boys," but

DID NOT HAVE TIME TO DRAW HIS PISTOL.

They pushed or crowded him back towards the door, firing two more shots into him. As soon as they fired the first shots, Moore, who was near the door, drew his pistol and fired at them several times, one shot shattering the right hand of the man who turned out to be Sam Bass. They fired several shots at Moore, one of which passed through his left breast, which so disabled him that he could not pursue them further. In the meantime the three rangers had come from where they were stationed and fired on the robbers as they retreated across the street. Maj. Jones, who was coming from the telegraph office when the firing began, ran up to the Robinson corner, when, seeing the situation, he called on his men, drew his pistol, ran up the street, and when within fifty yards of the robbers, commenced firing upon them. One of the robbers turned as he reached the corner around which they were retreating and fired deliberately at Maj. Jones, the ball passing over his head and entering the wall of a building in his rear. At this time the

EXCITEMENT IN THE TOWN

Was fearful to witness. Men were running in every direction, some to get out of range of the whistling bullets and take shelter behind a friendly corner, tree or post; others to get such arms as they could lay their hands on and join in the fight; women and children were screaming and flying from the houses between and around which the robbers were retreating. All this presented a scene which beggars description. The robbers retreated across the street, half-way up the square and down the alley, at the lower end of which their horses were hitched, closely pursued and constantly fired at by rangers and citizens, but taking shelter and firing back at their pursuers at every convenient place. When half way down the alley, Bass received his second wound, the one which caused his death. Just as the robbers reached their horses, R. C. Ware, one of the rangers, took deliberate aim at one of them and shot him through the head, killing him instantly. As the other two mounted and ran off, Maj. Jones, Ware and Mr. J. F. Tubbs, a one-armed citizen who had taken Grimes' pistol and joined in the fight, fired several shots at them, but without effect. F. L. Jordan fired at the robbers from the back door of his store as they ran down the alley. Albert Highsmith shot at them from the back yard of his stable, and might have killed one of them had not a cartridge-shell hung in his Winchester.

WHO FIRED THE DEATH SHOTS.

As is always the case under such circumstances, there is some difference of opinion as to who fired the two fatal shots. Major Jones is quite sure that Ware killed Seaborn Barnes, as he was very near him and looking at both of them at the time. The coroner's jury decides that George Harrell, another ranger, fired the shot that proved fatal to Sam Bass.

LEE HALL TO THE FRONT.

Capt. Hall was at the hotel lying down when the fight commenced, but was quickly on the spot with Winchester and pistol in hand, mounted a horse which happened to be near and, accompanied by the three rangers, one of whom rode the dead robber's (Barnes') horse,

GAVE CHASE

To the flying robbers. Several citizens who had horses at hand went with him. As soon as Maj. Jones could get a horse he, accompanied by Maj. Dick Mangum and several other citizens, went in pursuit of the robbers also, but they did not go more than two or three miles before the old plug which the major had got from the livery stable played out and the party returned.

JIM MURPHY TURNS UP.

As they galloped through Old Round Rock Jim Murphy, who had come in from camp, stepped out from a crowd on the street corner and saluted Maj. Jones with a smile of gladness which his face had probably not worn for several months.

TRAIL LOST.

Capt. Hall pursued the robbers until the trail was lost in the brush and then returned to town, as it was too near night and his horses were too nearly broken down to follow further.

JIM'S STORY.

Jim Murphy soon came in and explained to Maj. Jones that it had been impossible for him to communicate with him since he left Georgetown without forfeiting his life, but that he had delayed the attack on the bank as long as possible, and would have communicated with him at all hazards before the time arrived for the robbery, which was fixed for the next day, Saturday, 20th, at 5 o'clock P. M.

NEVILL AND REYNOLDS ON HAND.

Abut two hours after the fight Lieut. Reynolds arrived with ten men, having ridden from San Saba, a distance of 100 miles, since 7 o'clock the evening before. He left his men a mile or two out of town and came in to report to Maj. Jones secretly before bringing his men in.

Later in the evening Lieut. Armstrong's party from Austin arrived. Next morning Sergt. Nevill of Lieut. Reynold's company, with eight men, accompanied by Deputy Sheriff Tucker of this county, took the trail of Bass and Jackson where it had been lost the evening before, but soon found that the two had separated.

THD CAPTURE.

After hunting round awhile they found Bass lying under a large tree in the edge of the prairie. As the sergeant approached him he held up his hand and said: "Don't shoot; I am unarmed and helpless. I am the man you are looking for;

I AM SAM BASS."

He had lain in the brush all night, but crawled out to the tree in the prairie about daylight, and had hailed a negro who passed him and tried to bribe him to haul him off and secrete him. The information of the capture was brought to Maj. Jones, who went out, accompanied by Dr. Cochran, and brought the prisoner in.

THE SPY HERO, J. W. MURPHY,

In the capture of Bass, is now of sufficient importance to warrant a notice. He led the gang into the snare and the death of two of them results. From the time of the secret agreement between him and Maj. Jones he has stuck as closely to the text as would appear possible in view of his ordinary degree of intellect. He exhibits a fair memory, as shown by the connected narrative he gives of the doings of the Bass party since he rejoined them as a spy. In essential particulars he has the same statements to make at all times and under all questions. But Murphy has shown a lack of fertility of resource in his capacity as spy; yet while he failed to keep Maj. Jones well posted by letter, he seems to have been as cautious as one could and should be in such a case. In fact, his caution and general reserve were apparently the best substitutes for daring designs and brilliant execution. Why the two plans laid between him and Sheriff Everheart to catch Bass and party failed, is not known, though Murphy feels his part was played well. Murphy was raised in Denton county, and has lived the last year near Crosstown, in Cook county, adjoining Denton. In personal appearance he is of quiet manner, slow gait, heavy cast of features, rather dull expression. Underneath all he carries a comfortable case and looks as though it would be hard to rouse his 200 pounds of flesh. He wears a red moustache and chin beard; has small blue eyes, and, while feeling elated at his achievement as the great Bass spy, always has a word of sympathy in reserve for Jackson and Underwood—the sympathy, it should be added, that is begotten by old friendship of better days.

THE WAY OF THE TRANSGRESSORS.

Of the seven men who were engaged in the train robbery at Mesquite, on the Texas and Pacific railroad, on the 10th of April last, some of whom were in all the train robberies which took place on the Texas Central and T. P. railroad previous to that time, five have been disposed of. Sam Pipes and Albert Herndon, arrested by Maj. Jones and Capt. Peak in Dallas county soon after the robbery occurred, have just been convicted in the federal court at Austin. Johnson, called "Arkansas," was killed by Sergt. Floyed of Capt. Peak's company, in the fight with the robbers of Salt creek, in Wise county, on the 12th of June. Sam Bass and Seaborn Barnes were killed by R. C. Ware and Henry Harrell, (as per verdicts of coroners' juries,) of Lieut. Reynolds' company, at Round Rock on the 19th day of July, 1878. Two of the band are still at large—Frank Jackson, who made his escape at Round Rock, and Henry Underwood, who left the band at the time of the Salt creek fight, and has not been with them since, and of whom nothing is certainly known since that time.

ALL HE WOULD SAY.

Every endeavor was made by Maj. Jones to secure Bass' confession. Your correspondent tried him in vain. Some one was nearly always near the prisoner with pencil and paper to take down what he had to say. In his moments of wakefulness he would talk guardedly to Dr. Cochran, his nurse Jim Chatman, Maj. Jones, some of the rangers, or myself. His utterances, though not of really great moment, are yet valuable and interesting; are disjointed and tempered with a reserve that was tantalizing. A book was kept to dot down his sayings in. From this book I copy verbatim: Joel Collins, Bill Heffridge, Tom Nixon, Jack Davis, Jim Berry and me were in the Union Pacific robbery. Tom Nixon is in Canada. Have not seen him since the robbery. Jack Davis was in New Orleans from the time of the Union Pacific robbery till he went to Denton to get me to go in with him and buy a ship. This was in last of April, 1878.

Grimes asked me if I had a pistol. Said I had, and then all three of us drew and shot him. If I killed Grimes it was the first man I ever killed. [Above statement made in presence of us. Dr. Cochran and J. B. Jones.]

Am 25 years old, and have brothers, John and Linton, at Mitchell, Indiana. Have four sisters. Have not seen Underwood since Salt creek fight. Saw two Collinses at old man Collins' since I left Denton.

Gardner, living in Atascosa county, is my friend. Was at his house last fall. Went to Kansas with him once.

Have been in the robbing business a long time. Had done much business of that kind before the U. P. robbery last fall. [This in presence of J. P. Jones, T. L. Hall, John Armstrong, McLee, Dr. Cochran and R. C. Ware.]

First time I saw Billy Scott was at Bob Murphy's; last time was at Green Hill's. Saw him at Billy Collins', but do not know the date. Never saw him but those three times. Don't pay any attention to dates, being always on the scout. Will not tell who was in the Eagle Ford robbery besides myself and Jackson, because it is against my profession. Think I will go to hell anyhow, and think a man should die with what he knows in him. [This in presence of J. B. Jones and Dr. Crawford.]

I do not know. [Qustion as to whereabouts of certain confreres—*Rep.*] They were with us about six months. Henry was with me in Salt creek fight four or five weeks ago. Arkansas Johnson was killed in that fight. Don't know whether Underwood was wounded or not at Salt creek fight. "Sebe" Barnes, Frank Jackson and Charles Carter were there. We were all set afoot in that fight but stole horses enough to remount ourselves in three hours, or as soon as dark came: after which we went back to Denton. Stayed there till we came to Round Rock.

Q. Where is Jackson now?

A. I don't know.

Q. How did you usually meet after being scattered?

A. Generally told by friends. [Declined to tell who these friends are.] Won't tell.

Q. How came you to commence this kind of life?

A. Started out sporting on horses.

Q. Why did you get worse than horse-racing?

A. Because they robbed me of my first $300.

Q. After they robbed you, what did you do next?

A. Went to robbing stages in Black Hills—robbed seven. Got very little money. Jack Davis, Nixon and myself were all that were in the Black Hills stage robberies.

[While he gives a cue sometimes, it will be seen he avoids the main facts, and refuses to tell what he knows is not known. It has been ascertained and published who were in the Black Hills and Union Pacific robberies. He tells where he has been as among friends, and gives names of those who were with him at times in fights and camp, but not a word as to who were with him in his train robberies.—REP.]

A Western Romance.

The wife of a merchant in San Francisco, finding, some six months ago, that the climate of the Pacific coast did not agree with her, as her lungs were rather delicate, decided to visit her relatives in Chicago, to see if the change would not benefit her. She went overland, her husband remaining in California because he was unable to leave his business. For two months after her arrival she wrote regularly and affectionately, declaring that her health was steadily improving, and that she hoped to rejoin him very soon. For the next three months her letters steadily decreased, both in frequency and fervor, becoming very rare and very cold toward the close of the period. He complained of the alteration in her feelings, which she denied in words, and proved by behavior. In two or three weeks more he set out for Chicago to ascertain the cause of her revolution, and reaching his destination went to the hotel where she was staying, went directly to her room, entered, found her talking pleasantly to a man, who appeared to be quite at home, but whom he had never seen before. The husband began upbraiding his wife, when the stranger demanded, "By what right do you thus address this lady?" "By the right of a husband," was the response. "That right is reserved for me, sir; I am her husband." "You? For how long, pray?" "For three months." "And I for six years." Both spoke the truth. The second marriage, as may be inferred, had been made after an irregular divorce, the woman having discovered that she liked the man present in Chicago much better than she liked the man absent in San Francisco. The two lieges talked revolvers, death and graveyards for a while; but after growing cool, resolved not to make fools of themselves. The woman frankly owned that she preferred No. 2, whereupon No. 1 expressed satisfaction, sensibly left her to her new-found felicity, bought a ticket for home, departed on the morning train, leaving a note for her saying that he would trouble her no further and do his utmost never to meet her again.

GRAIN SPECULATION.

Prodigious Proportions of the Milwaukee Wheat Corner.

[Special to the Chicago Times.]

MILWAUKEE, July 24.—This has been one of the most intensely exciting days ever experienced by the Milwaukee chamber of commerce. The rapid advance on July wheat, which the *Times* has all along foreshadowed in its dispatches, seemed to culminate at a jump to-day when $1 15 was reached and no wheat to be got even at that figure. Operators were fairly wild with excitement. Every effort seemed to be made toward "settlements," but it was observable that Mr. McGeogh, the king of the corner, was not at all anxious to square accounts; indeed, he no longer made overtures for settlement, as he did when July wheat stood at $1 02, $1 04 and $1 05. It would seem therefore that the end is not yet, and that the figure $1 25 suggested by the *Times* last week as the probable limit of the corner may yet be reached. Apropos of that price, a prominent receiver informed the *Times* reporter this evening that country customers in sending orders continually referred to the *Times* dispatches relative to the corner, and seemed to be largely governed in their actions by the information contained in those dispatches, having learned that such information was from bottom sources.

To-morrow will probably be an eventful day here, although it is claimed that most of the "shorts" have settled to day with McGeogh. The *Times* reporter is informed that the bulk of the money lost in the present corner will come from the "bear ring" of New York, St. Louis and Chicago, and that interior speculators in Minnesota and Wisconsin have mostly been on the "bull" or winning side. All of the crop reports received from the interior to-day claim that the wheat crop is damaged even more seriously than it was supposed could be possible. The corner is now supposed to have netted McGeogh over $500,000. There are now pretty strong indications that a powerful clique is at work with the intention of cornering August wheat. Some of the most successful corners ever manipulated have occurred in August, and the conditions are believed by many to be more favorable for a move of that kind than ever before. Rumor has it that Gov. William Young's sudden return from his trip to the mountains bears some relation to the move in August wheat.

The price at which the "shorts" have been able to settle to-day with McGeogh is claimed to have been $1 15 in most cases, although it is also claimed that in some cases the settlement was refused at that figure. The *Times* reporter was informed this evening, by what seems good authority, that one deal of twenty-five thousand bushels was settled at $1 20¾. The report, however, is denied by some who pretend to know.

There has been considerable feeling engendered on all sides by attempts and counter-attempts at influencing the inspecting. In an interview this afternoon with Inspector Holland, he informed the *Times* reporter that repeated efforts had been made to ring in poor wheat upon his inspectors; that he had had trouble with some of the "mixers;" that in one case where a lot of wheat had been rejected once as No. 2 at one of the elevators it was afterward put into cars and run on a side-track with a view to running into another elevator as wheat that had passed the inspection, and that in fact he had had great difficulty in keeping the inspection what it should be on account of the efforts to get in every bushel possible.

The feeling now is that McGeogh will force the corner to the greatest limit. The "shorts" can stand it, and the general expression tonight is that July wheat will reach $1 25. It is generally believed that not more than one or two firms here will suffer much, as the greater part of the short selling was by eastern men, mostly in New York and Philadelphia.

The most reliable information attainable places the amount McGeogh has settled at 125,000 bushels. It is believed that he yet holds fully a million and a half bushels. On that point, however, McGeogh himself refuses to make any statement.

A somewhat exciting scene occurred today, growing out of the differences in opinion concerning the wheat inspection. Mr. Charles Freeman had several car-loads that he thought ought to grade No. 2 inspected as No. 3. He met McGeogh and got into a dispute with him about the inspection, and finally, so some of the bystanders assert, Freeman told McGeogh that he had bought up the inspector. Then the lie passed and both parties saw their foolishness and resorted to apology instead of blows. Afterward a bet of $2,000 was made relative to the correctness of the inspection, and the bet was finally drawn and the subject dropped.

It is confidently expected that to-morrow will be the culminating day of the corner, and that every short who can settle will accept the opportunity. It is now conceded on all sides that it is an impossibility to get enough wheat in during the remaining days of July to break the corner, if McGeogh should conclude to be hard on his victims and force prices to an unreasonable figure. It is also conceded that a more successful corner in wheat was never manipulated.

Stampeding Cattle in Arizona.

An instance of what an Apache Indian will do in the way of cool daring, when the prize is worth the risk, once occurred on a ranch in Arizona.

The owner of the ranch was an American. To guard against the Apaches he had built a block-house, and, adjoining it, a court yard and corral, surrounded by an adobe wall eight feet high and two feet thick. In the corral the herd was nightly secured. He had a contract to feed and guard four hundred beef cattle, belonging to the United States fort, some thirty miles away. More than one attempt had been made by the Apaches to capture the herd, while feeding two or three miles from the block-house. But the vigilant herdsmen had driven the cattle at a gallop into the corral, before the Indians could "stampede" them.

One night there came a fearful storm. A solitary Apache, unarmed, and with nothing but a blanket to protect him from the cold rain, climbed over the corral's wall; crouching in the corner, he waited for day. Early in the morning, the storm having passed away, eight hundred herdsmen, mounted and armed, waited at the corral's gate for the herd to be turned out. The gate was opened. The stock poured out and filled the gateway. Suddenly up sprung the Apache; vaulting on the nearest horse, he clutched his mane with one hand, while with the other he waved his red blanket, and yelled like a demon. In an instant every "hoof" made a rush, and the stampede began. The horse, frightened, darted in the midst of the flying cattle. As in a frenzy they went through the gateway, the Apache clasped his arms around the horse's neck, and throwing his body on one side of the maddened animal, disappeared from view.

A thousand men ranged in solid column could not have stopped that rush of the crazed herd down the valley. The herdsmen fired a volley which wounded and killed some of the cattle. Two bands of Apaches darted out from opposite sides of the valley, closed up from behind the herd. Four hundred head of cattle were thus captured and run off by the daring and cunning of one Apache.

The Modern Treasurer.

[From the Philadelphia Times.]

The modern treasurer is a man to be respected and looked up to as a genius far surpassing the common every-day mortals surrounding him. His chief object in life is to stow away as large a proportion of the available funds as possible and live in fine style off the proceeds. This is what he is hired for, and he does his work well. There are common treasurers and uncommon treasurers. Their genius is estimated entirely by the market value of the paper upon which they have laid violent hands. Treasurer Tappan of Boston is an uncommon treasurer. He has enjoyed for years the confidence of everybody, and has had ample time to salt away considerably over half a million. He was found out the other day and rather liked it. It was a novel experience. Half a million is a good sum, and, of course, as he says, "there can be nothing said to affect his character or standing in the community." If he had only got away with a couple of thousand or so it would have been different, but when he causes the suspension of two or three big firms and drives all the banks of a whole city crazy his object in life has been attained. Next year he will run for congress.

AMONG the Long Branch politicians whose necks and wrists are just now even a shade more like raw beef than the ends of their nose is Emory Storrs of Chicago, counsel for Babcock in the whiskey trials. Mr. Storrs is more of a political keeper of the tally than a politician. Grant, as he has figured it out, is the only presidential candidate in Illinois; while Logan (the thunder of whose eloquence is directed at all times against the second era of secession and English grammar) is, as he has further calculated, the most popular senatorial contestant.

THE LAST OF LONGLEY—EXECUTION OF "BILL" LONGLEY, THE "MAN KILLER," AT GIDDINGS, TEXAS—See Page 6.

1—The desperado on the eve of the hanging. 2—A narrow escape—hanged as a horse thief, but cut down and resuscitated. 3—Fatal duel on horseback, on the prairie. 4 Assassination of Wilson Anderson, the crime which brought him to the gallows. 5—Acknowledging on the scaffold the justice of his doom.

THE TEXAN

Was established in 1870, and
Is a Democratic Journal,
Published in the Interest of
Robertson County.
GEORGE A. KUPFER, Editor and Publisher
Subscription
For one year....................................$ 2.00
For six months.................................. 1.00
For three months................................ 50

THE WIT OF THE PRESS.

A happy mother of male twins enthusiastically refers to her treasures as her "sweet boy and boy."

There is a fortune awaiting the man who invents a boomerang bootjack which you can throw at a cat and have it sail back to the window if it misses the mark.

If Mr. Edison will only invent a process for making confectionery out of sugar and five cent cigars out of Tobacco, he will be entitled to niche 1. section A, Temple of Fame.

"These Mongolians are improven," as the Gold Hill miner thoughtfully remarked, the other day, when the Chinaman quietly blew a hole through a white loafer who had just spit in his face.

She handed him a piece of smilax to admire, and after a fond gaze he gave it back saying. "Your smile lacks nothing in the line of beauty." She tried to look sad and wondered what it all meant.

The spirit of emulation in funerals is in strict obedience to public sentiment coming from the funeral of a friend, a Danbury young woman said to her mother: "Did you ever see such a cheap looking corpse?"

One of the great needs of this country is a vest pocket deep enough to take in the whole length of the extra cigar, so a man can look his fellow square in the eye and say, "No, I'm sorry, but this is the last, and I have already had it in my mouth.

The art of printing will never be complete till Proffessor Edison, or some one else, invents a means of conveying to readers' hears the shrill whistle that escapes a young husband's lips when he first learns that his wife has twins,

Some man with an eagerness for fame has invented a spring-seat saddle that wil rock a man to sleep on the hardest-going animal. What this country needs is some kind of a saddle that will hold a man down on the roof of a horse when he suddenly, and without warning, points at the sky with his tail.

When the modest young man is unexpectedly caught in a parlor full of woman one of whom has roguish eyes, and begins to try to think whether his hair is parted straight or not, the blushes start from his forehead and sweep over the top of his head and down his back, until he feels like a nutmeg grater with a tin ear.

A ROVING WOMAN.

She Takes to the Prairie and Lives Under a Bush.

(San Antonio Express.)

A few days since, our readers will remember, we made reference to the fact, that the wife of Hesse, a butcher, charged with beating a child almost to death a few days ago, had taken to the brush with her two children, and had been seen near the Leon creek, west of the city, by a Mexican. Yesterday, while riding about through the brush about four miles distant, and near the Castroville road, Mr. John Zoiler also came upon this woman. She appeared wild and careworn, and the two little ones with her looked hagged and hungry.

The camp of the trio was under the limbs of a bush, where there was evidence to lead to the belief that they had been at the place for several days. Mr. Zoller found the woman communacative, and she told him that her husband had induced her to take to the brush on account of the charges against him for beating his child. This Mr. Zoller told our reporter. One of the children remarked that they had nothing to eat for two days. After hearing their sad tales, Mr. Zoller turned his horse to the city, reported the facts to Judge Dwyer, and obtained a hack to bring this woman and her children to the city. This object accomplished, His Honor cared for them as best he could, giving the woman comfortable quarters in the second story of the county jail.

Mr. Bennett, jailor, informs our reporter that the woman and her children were all but starved. When food was placed before them they ate ravenously. The woman stated that she had been driven from home nearly two weeks ago by her husband, who made all kinds of threats. She was afraid to return home or even come to the city. She and her children had lived principally on a few potatoes they obtained in some way. When she sent home for food it was denied. Mr. Bennett says the children also corroborated her statements. They appeared to love their mother dearly The child that was recently beaten told the whole story, which is a horrible one, and fixed the outrage upon its father.

The peculiarity of the circumstances incident to the case of this woman and her children is almost without a parallel, and affords a big subject for the grand jurors now in session to work upon.

One of our city physicians was called to the country to see a patient, the early part of this week, some six or eight miles from town. The party sick was found to be an old lady, 75 or 80 years of age The case had been treated for several months by a local doctor as erysipelas. When first taken down in the early part of the summer the patient was violently effected with inflamatory sore eyes. Neglience upon the part of those attending her, permitted the screw fly to deposit its egg in the corner of the left eye, from which this most horrible and revolting case occurred. Upon an examination by our informant, the eye was found to be entirely eaten out by worms, and by a suffucating application to the wound, more than a quart mea-ure full of them were extracted. The physician thinks that in a little while longer the devouring vermin would have reached the patient's brain. Her recovery is hopeless—Paris *Banner*.

NEW ORLEANS Oct 30—Wether clear, windy and cooler. Deaths 13. New cases reported 34. Total deaths, 3,917. Total cases, 13,036.

A letter from Fort Concho, to the San Antonio *Express*, says the red devils are depredating in South Lano. Parties of them stole a number of horses near Junction city, and five men started after them on the 18th, inst. At the writing of the letter they had not returned or been heard from, and it is feared they have been murdered.

Spendthrift, two years old, by Australian, dam Aerolite, by Lexington, is the coming horse. He has started five times, winning every time. His first appearance was on the Association Course at this place. He is the property of Mr. Dan. Swigert, who has refused in the past week $10,000 for him, offered by parties at Nashville, Tenn. He is entered in stakes next year worth over $100,000. Mr. Swigert promptly refused the offer. Spendthrift was bred by A. J. Alexander. and purchased at his sale in 1877 for a thousand dollars.—Lexington (Ky) *Press*.

A short time ago there came to Lansingburg, a Salt Lake lady, to pay a visit to some friends and relaties. When she left home her husband had three wives, including herself, and she did not see any immediate prospect that the number would be increased, but she received a letter from her lord and master, only a few days ago, in which he informed her that he had found another lovely female, an imported woman, and had taken her into the flock.

Did this model woman "take on" when she read the letter? Not a bit of it! She simply smiled and then quietly remaked that she hoped the new wife would love him as much as she did.—Troy *Press*.

THE TWO PLATFORMS IN COMPARISON.

GREENBACK PLATFORM.

The representatives of the National Greenback Labor Party of the State of Texas in convention assembled. trusting in the integrity, patriotism and justice of the people of the State, do hereby announce the following as the political principles for the establishment and maintenance of which we pledge our earnest, united, unceasing efforts:

1. Want of harmony of sentiment on the financial question, in both the Republican and Democratic parties, renders it absolutely necessary that those who demand financial reform should abandon the old organizations and unite together in the National Greenback Labor party to save business men from bankruptcy, the working classes from starvation, and the whole country from revolution and the nation from repudiation.

2. We denounce as crimes against the people, the law making the greenback only a partial legal tender, the act creating the national bank system, the act changing currency bonds into coin bonds, the act exempting bonds from taxation, the act repealing the income tax, the act demonitizing silver, the act for issuing interest bearing bonds for the purchase of silver bullion to be converted into subsidiary coin, the act for the resumption of specie payments, the act for the indefinite increase of the national bank circulation and the enormous contraction of the volume of the circulating medium. We recognise the financial legislation of the government from the commencement of the civil war as the arbitrary dictation of a syndicate of bankers and ursurers, with the single and settled purpose of robbing the many to enrich the few.

3. We hold that the government of the United States has the power, and that it is its duty, to issue at once absolute greenback money in an amount equal to the United States treasury notes now in circulation, and the bonds of the United States sold, to money to be full legal tender for al debts, duties, taxes or purposes whatsoever, and redeem the treasury notes and bonds, principal and interest, immediately with such absolute greenback money. We further hold that no tariff should be imposed, except for the purpose of revenue; that all national banks should be promptly abolished; that no more bonds should be issued by the national government, and that all the money of the government should be taxable with other property.

4. We hold that the importation of servile labor from Asiatic countries should be prohibited under the severest penalties but that the immigration of the liberty loving from other lands should be encouraged.

5. We hold that the honest mechanic and laborer of the country should not be forced into competition with gangs of convicts sentenced to the penitentiary for crimes, and we demand that the contract system for this class of labor shall be abolished, and that all convicts shall be confined within the prison walls.

6. We recognize the mutual dependance of capital and labor, and depreciate all attempts to antagonize them. Combinations of capital to rob, and strikes of labor to resist robbery, are destructive of the true interests of both. We denounce alike the communism which demands an equal division of property and the infamous financial legislation which takes all from the many to enrich the few. We demand cheap capital and well paid labor.

7. We demand the abrogation of the odious and unjust occupation and smokehouse tax laws now in force in this State.

8. We are opposed to the general or State governments making further donations of the public lands to railroads or other corporations, and we insist that they shall be reserved for the benefit of actual settlers and the increase of the common school funds.

9. We demand the prompt abolition of all useless offices and a general and radical decrease of public salaries. and that county officers shall not be allowed to receive exceeding $1800 per year for their services, and whenever practicable, especially in judicial offices, the compensation should be fixed by specific salaries. and that in the future the government of Texas shall be conducted on the strictest business principles and on the most economical plans.

10. We pledge ourselves to re-establish in fact common free schools, and we denounce the Democratic party for its failure to carry out its promises in this regard

11. We declare in favor of an income tax based upon a constitutional limitation and graduating upwards, leaving untouched al. incomes under $1000.

12 We hold that all bonds now outstanding against the State of Texas should be funded in four per cent. bonds, the same to be taxed as other property.

13. We demand the passage of such laws as will prevent all combinations, discriminations and granting of rebate by ling transportation company, and compelany common carriers to furnish the same facilities and perform the same service for the same price to all men.

14. We demand a perfect and positive protection to our frontier, a protection that will guarantee safety both to the settler and to the vast interests of our herdsmen.

15. We demand that the rate of taxation for the year 1879 and subsequent years shall not exceed 37½ cents on the one hundred dollars as a State tax, and one half the amount as a county tax.

16. We demand that the exemption laws be so amended as to allow each family a comfortable homestead, not to exceed in value $2000.

17. That we remember with profound gratitude the struggles of the fathers of Texas in defence of the rights of themselves and their fellow citizens, and viewing the government which they consecrated with their blood as a rich and inestimable inheritance which has been handed down by them to us, we are pledged to aid in every way possible in securing its prosperity, and will oppose with all the earnestness of our natures every step looking to a destruction or to the impairing of its unity.

18. Finally, having thus set forth our distinctive principles and views, we invite the co-operation of all citizens of Texas, however differing from us on other questions, who substantially are with us in their affirmation and support.

DECLARATIONS OF PRINCIPLES ADOPTED AT THE CONFERENCE IN WASHINGTON.

WASHINGTON, Aug. 7.—The following is the declaration of principles adopted by the members of the Greenback party assembled in this city on Tuesday night:

We believe the two great political parties now constituted, to be so completely under the control of office-seekers, professional politicians, bankers, and money mongers, that it is unsafe longer to intrust to them this Government.

We believe that intelligent and pure men, regardless of former party associations, should fill all positions of trust and responsibility.

We are opposed to third terms for public offices, except those where skill and experience are indispensable to the proper performance of the required service.

We believe the powers of the general government are restricted to the express grants of the Constitution, and all powers not granted are reserved to the State and the people thereof.

We believe that the right of the States to tax property in the States is inviable, and that the United States bonds should bear the burden of government equally as with all other property, and any legislation that exempts said bonds from taxation is unjust and oppressive.

We favor a full legal-tender currency for the government and the people, the laborer and the office-holder, the pensioner and the soldier, the producer and the bondholder—a currency alike in value in every man's hand whereever the American flag floats as an emblem of sovereignity

We demand the immediate and unconditional repeal of the so-called Resumption act, the lawful liberation of the coin hoarded in the Treasury, and the removal of all restrictions to the coinage of silver.

While we favor the circulation of gold and silver as money, yet realizing that specie never has been and never can be sufficient to supply the commercial demands of the country, we therefor favor the issue of Treasury notes to such extent as will fully satisfy the requirements of trade, and that such notes be made a full legal tender.

We believe that the national bank system is oppressive to the people, and therefore demand the retirement of bank currency and the substitution of greenbacks therefor.

We declare that all bonds and obligations of the national Government ought to be paid in legal tender notes of the United States, except where it is otherwise provided by the original law under which they were issued; and all that can be called in and paid now should be paid at once, and the remainder as soon as it can be at once, and the remainder as soon as it can be lawfully done,

We oppose the further issue of interest bearing bonds, on any account, at any rate of interest, by the government,

While we oppose monopolies, subsidies, and special privileges, we favor a judicious expenditure of Treasury notes on internal improvements and in the construction of such rail highways as will furnish protection to our maritime and land frontiers, and open new markets for the products of American industry.

We believe that an economical expenditure of money in the construction of one or more lines of railway into Mexico, and the extension of a second and third line, that will create a competition to the Pacific coast, will be the means of making more accessible the market of that republic, as well as those of Australia, China, and Japan, whose trade will invigorate and sustain our manufacturing and industrial interests to a greater extent than any other system of internal improvements could possibly do.

We believe that the public lands are the common property of the whole people and should not be sold to speculators nor granted to railroads or other corporations, but should be donated to actual settlers in limited quantities.

We believe the interest of the industrial wealth-producing classes is the paramount interest of the whole people of the United States. Those, whose labor and enterprise produce wealth should be secure in its enjoyment. Our warmest sympathy is with the laboring classes who have been thrown out of employment by the ruinous financial policy and unjust legislation of the Republican party, and who must still continue to suffer under the system of false economy now established by the Democratic party, and we pledge the National party to a reversal of that policy, and the restoration of all the rights they are entitled to upon its ascendancy to power.

Upon this platform of principles the National party, feeling that the popular heart beat in unison with it, appeals to every lover of constitutional government whatever may have been his former party affiliations, to unite with us in our efforts to rescue the administration of the Federal Government from the hands of those who have and who still persist in centralizing power and oppressing the people.

TEXAS.—THE RECEPTION AND BALL AT THE OPENING OF THE NEW COTTON EXCHANGE, GALVESTON, FEBRUARY 21ST, ATTENDED BY MEMBERS OF THE AMERICAN INDUSTRIAL DEPUTATION, ON THEIR RETURN FROM MEXICO.

From a Sketch by H. A. Ogden.—See Page 39.

THE DEMOCRAT
AND RANCHERO.

VOL. 7. BROWNSVILLE, TEXAS, FEBRUARY 28, 1880. NO. 10.

A STRANGE STORY.

What a Young Lady Suffered By Blackmailing for Years—Her Brother, A Texas Ranger, Dying at the Hands of the Blackmailer.

Our citizens will probably remember a young man named Robinson, of McNelly's command, who was stationed here some years ago, and of his sudden departure from here by the steamer one day, which was a mystery to his intimate friends. His going was caused by the receipt of the following telegram from his sister: "I am in dire distress. Come home immediately," and the story of her wrongs and his death are clearly set forth in the following story. Robinson was also well known as a correspondent of the Austin *Statesman*, under the pseudonym of "Pidge," and his letters were well received by the press and people, for their dry, quaint humor, and picturesque descriptions of times, places and men, among whom it was his lot to fall in his peregrinations throughout the state.

LYNCHBURG, Jan. 17—One of the most remarkable scandals and tragedies recorded in the criminal annals of Virginia culminated in judicial proceedings this week in the county court of Campbell. This is the county in which Lynchburg is located, and the occurrence referred to took place for the most part at a farm house, situated about midway between the city and the court house, in the somewhat rugged region between Beaver and Opposum creeks. The parties to it belong to the most respectable class of Virginia yeomanry, not specially distinguished for wealth or culture, but industrious and well to do, and regarded with general respect as the bone and sinew of the land, whenever personal merit made claim to that recognition.

About six years ago a youth named Jesse E. Mitchell, while at work near the residence of a man named Robinson, in the neighborhood referred to, hurt himself badly with a saw, and was removed to the house to be properly cared for. Mitchell received at the hands of the family the utmost kindness and attention, so much so that in time he recovered from his injuries, though he ever afterwards suffered from a certain lameness. The family in which he found such timely and effectual refuge consisted of old Mr. Robinson and his wife, his son Thomas, and his daughter, Miss Lizzie May Robinson, the latter an amiable and attractive young lady. Between Mitchell and this young person, who had been specially kind to him during his illness, very intimate relations ensued, as was natural on the strength of their association and the sympathy which she manifested for his sufferings.

For some reason, however, an estrangement between the guest and his hosts soon followed, and Mitchell was forbidden the house by Mr. Robinson; Mitchell also got into a quarrel with young Robinson, the fruits of which were afterward fatal to one and nearly so to both of them; but at the time it appeared to blow entirely away. Robinson, moreover, about this time became involved in a scandal about a young woman of the county, and was arrested with a view to his criminal prosecution. While he was in the custody of the officers of the law he effected his escape by the aid, it is said, of his sister, and so made his way to Texas. Mitchell then began a system of espionage and persecution, of which Miss Robinson was the helpless victim, practicing on her fears in a thousand ways, and threatening her with disgrace and exposure of a kind most revolting to the sensibilities of a modest and innocent girl.

He is said to have threatened to deliver her to the authorities on account of her alleged connection with the escape of her brother from the constable, alleging that she had committed a felony in so doing, for which she could be subjected to the most severe punishment. It is said that he also accused her of a more flagrant offense, pretending that she was the mother of a babe born out of wedlock, and intimating his intention of exposing her shame to the public and fixing upon her a stigma of ineffaceable disgrace. While these things were going on the following postal card was addressed to Mitchell by the brother of the persecuted and unhappy girl:

"EL PASO, March, 1874.—Dare to harm a hair of any one who is of my blood, you cowardly dog, and I will have your life, if it be twenty years hence. I hear of all your tricks, and I'll settle all with you yet before I die. You can make war upon an unprotected woman now, but you are laying up treasures in heaven, or somewhere else, my lark, if you did but know it."

In July, 1876, Thomas Robinson moved, no doubt, by the reports that still reached him of Mitchell's proceedings, came to Virginia, and on reaching home found that Mitchell was on the premises. Mitchell attempted to retreat from the wrath of the brother, well knowing that wherever they met one or both must bite the dust. And so it proved. Young Robinson followed Mitchell and opened fire, striking him in the side, and receiving at the same time a ball from Mitchell's pistol in the abdomen. Mitchell fell, and was thought to be mortally wounded, but to make sure of killing him, Robinson thrust his pistol into his (Mitchell's) mouth and fired again, to give him the coup de grace.

The doctors, however, though unable to do anything for the relief of Robinson, did manage, after much ado, to rescue Mitchell from the jaws of death, which had gaped so wide to devour him. On his recovery began the extraordinary series of occurrences which furnish the basis of the proceedings that have been begun in the county court of Campbell, before John G. Haythe, the county judge. In August, 1876, the next month after the killing, and while he himself was but newly rescued from the grave, Mitchell is said to have extorted from the now unprotected Miss Robinson a bond for $1800. Procuring an interview with her, he is alleged to have stationed one W. E. Glass, a confederate, behind some bushes, with a view of making Glass a witness to what transpired between them. He again accused the girl of infamous conduct, and threatened her with exposure and legal penalties for her (pretended) crimes, and on her acquiescence under the accusation he bade Glass to bear witness that she had confessed her guilt. But this was only the beginning of the blackmail.

The next instance that the evidence developed was of a character even more shameless and heartless. When Thomas Robinson died he left $700 deposited with a firm of private bankers in Lynchburg. He gave this money to his sister. She secured a certificate of deposit; drew interest on the sum, and expended $200 of the principal, leaving $500 deposited to her credit. When the persecutions of Mitchell began she transferred this certificate to the charge of a person named Smith, that she might not be able to get it to satisfy the rapacity of her brother's slayer. Mitchell appears to have possessed such a powerful influence over the poor woman that she first gave him a written order for the money, and when the bank declined to recognize it, he compelled her to abstract the certificate from the papers of Mr. Smith, and thus was enabled to draw and appropriate the money, all that remained of the property of the man he had shot to death.

Pursuing his persecution, it is stated that Mitchell next obtained from the young woman a gold watch which had been given to her by her mother on her deathbed. It transpired in the examination that he used to frequent the heights and hills near the poor woman's home and keep a constant watch with a spyglass on all of her motions, knowing at all times where she was and what she was about, and what company she had, driving her almost crazy with the dread of him, which destroyed both her health and her spirits, and filled even her dreams, as she testified, with images of fear and horror. It seems hard to understand how such a series of wrongs could be perpetrated with impunity in a Christian land, but such is the woman's statement, borne out, too, by several respectable citizens of Campbell, who appeared before the grand jury. But the tragedy was hastening to its consummation. Old Mrs. Robinson is said to have died of a broken heart in consequence of these sorrows. Not long after her husband died also, and then Miss Robinson was left alone in the world to confront her relentless enemy.

When the old man died, his daughter, as sole heir, inherited the plantation on which the family resided. Not content with his spoils, Mitchell appears to have determined to possess himself of this property also. With this in view, he induced one J. C. Walton, a justice of the peace, to visit the young woman and take her deed on the plantation, in which Wm. E Glass, who had witnessed the former pretended confession of Miss Robinson, was made trustee and representative of Mitchell in the transfer. It was stated by Miss Robinson that Walton brought her a threatening letter from Mitchell, with the contents of which he professed himself acquainted, and that it was on the duress and intimidation exercised by this precious document that she acted in signing away her right to the property left her by her deceased father. After this instrument was executed, Mitchell appears to have ceased for awhile from the active pursuit of the unfortunate woman; but when, not long after, she made a sale of the plantation, the confederates then put forward their deed, which, until then, Walton had not recorded, and claimed the property as their own.

Miss Robinson, badgered at last beyond endurance, then employed counsel, and in the course of her disclosures the whole story came out. A general warrant for extortion was issued and the parties arrested. Intense excitement prevailed among the good people of the county, and especially those of the vicinage where these revelations transpired, and it is said that the threat of invoking Judge Linch's summary assistance was freely and favorably canvassed. Better counsel prevailed, however, and the case went to the Grand Jury of the County Court On Tuesday this body, after full examination of witnesses, found a true bill against J. E. Mitchell, Wm. E. Glass and J. C. Walton, for extorting, by threats, a deed of trust from Miss L. M. Robinson: a true bill vs. J. E. Mitchell and Wm. Glass for extorting a bond of $2300 from the same lady; a true bill vs. Jesse E. Mitchell for extorting, by threats, $500 from the same lady, and a true bill vs. J. E. Mitchell for extorting, by threats a gold watch from the same.

Mitchell was still in jail on the magistrate's original commitment; Walton and Glass were out on bail. All appeared and were arraigned, pleading, of course, "not guilty." Walton was bailed in the penalty of $250, and Glass committed to jail in default of $500 bail. Mitchell was remanded to jail, and, on motion of the prisoner's counsel, the case was continued till the next term of court.

Some of the most prominent lawyers of this section, among them Mr. Thos. Whitehead, formerly member of congress from this district, who assists the prosecution, are employed on both sides of this exciting and interesting case, which arouses great attention as something altogether novel in these parts.

A Medicine Should not be Gauged

By the suddenness and violence of its effects. Self evident as this proposition would seem, there are many foolish persons who are content only with a remedy which acts abruptly. The pill and other nostrum-vendors who trade upon the credulity of this class, find their "best holt," as poor Artemus Ward termed it, in the sale of violent purgatives. So long as they wrench the bowels of their dupes sufficiently, they are pretty sure of a certain measure of success. If instead of such pernicious rubbish, Hostetter's Stomach Bitters is used, the results are widely different. The bowels are relieved, but always gently, by this pleasant laxative, which does not weaken but invigorates them, and endows the co-operative organs of digestion and bilious secretion with activity and regularity, strengthens the constitution and physique, and while it is safe in its constituents, is sufficiently prompt in operation.

St. Louis girls have a way of teasing Chicago girls. They say, "My dear, I would not like to be in your shoes." Then the Chicago girl takes a hack, and after driving around the St. Louis girl's foot, says: "Of course you wouldn't like it. 'Twould hurt your corns to pinch them so."—Boston Post.

If your son has no brains, don't send him to college. You cannot make a palace out of a shanty by putting a French roof on it.

Did it ever occur to you why a lawyer who is conducting a disputed will case is like a trapeze performer in a circus? Didn't? Well, it's because he flies through the heir with the greatest of fees.

Gentleman to street Arab—Ain't you ashamed of yourself, using your fingers in blowing your nose?

Boy—Did yer expect me to blow me nose wid me legs?

Don't forget to call at the DEMOCRAT office for first-class job work.

El Democrata.

Tomo. 7. Brownsville, Texas, Febrero 28, de 1880. Núm. 10.

Administrator's Notice,

Notice is hereby given, that the undersigned has been appointed administrator, with full powers, of the estate of Justo Treviño, deceased, late of Cameron County, by the honorable County Court of the County of Cameron, at its present term thereof. All persons having claims against said estate are required to present the same properly authenticated, within the time prescribed by law, and all persons indebted to said estate, are required to make immediate settlement. The residence of the undersigned is at the Rancho de los Burros, Texas, and his Postoffice address is Santa Maria, Cameron County, Texas.

Any business with said estate. may be submitted to Messrs. Powers & Wells, of Brownsville, Texas, my attornies relating to said estate.

MARTIN HINOJOSA,
Administrator of Estate of Justo Treviño, deceased.
Brownsville, Texas, January 22, 1880.

Administrators Notice.

ESTATE OF PEDRO GALVAN, DECEASED.

Notice is hereby given to all persons interested, that the undersigned has been appointed administrator with full powers, of the estate of Pedro Galvan, deceased, late of Cameron County, by the Honorable County Court of Cameron County, on the 22nd day of January, A. D. 1880.

All persons having claims against said estate are required to present the same properly authenticated, within the time prescribed by law, and all persons indebted to said estate, are required to make immediate settlement.

The residence and post office address of the undersigned is at Brownsville, Cameron County, Texas.

ALEXANDER WERBISKIE.
Administrator of the estate of Pedro Galvan, deceased. Brownsville, Texas, February 4th, 1880.

El Democrata.

BROWNSVILLE TEXAS.

SECCION EDITORIAL

TERRENOS.

No es sin remedio la situacion de los dueños de tierras que han visto vender las suyas por falta del pago de las contribuciones, facilitan do la ley su recobro y librandoles de ese forzoso desasimiento. Un título cuando se ha registrado, constituye y una realidad ó una apariencia de tal y puede dar accion cuando se apoya en una posesion pacífica de cinco años, Los dueños de terrenos no deben exponerse á una venta fiscal para hacer pago de las contribuciones y evitar litigios costosos, ya sea pagando puntualmente cada año las que cause ó redimiendo los que les han sido vendidos. Con este objeto, reseñaremos algunas condicio nes con que acepta el rescate la actual legislacion del Estado, al tratar de esta materia.

Rescate de terrenos vendidos en pago de contribuciones. Todos los terrenos vendidos por ese motivo, pueden rescatarse pagando al que los haya comprado, dentro de dos años á partir del dia en que se verificó la venta, doble cantidad de la que el comprador pagó, junto con las contribuciones subsiguientes que hubiere satisfecho.

Si el comprador no residiese en el Condado en que está el terreno ó no se le pudiese encontrar, se hará la entrega del importe del rescate al colector de contribucion del propio Condado.

Los terrenos de que el Estado se hubiera hecho dueño por falta de comprador, previo al 24 de Julio de 1879, pueden rescatarse, pagando la contribucion que se está debiendo y, ademas, el interes de ocho por ciento por año á contar desde la fecha de la venta, y las costas originadas.

Al ser rescatados los terrenos que tiene el Estado, se pagará el dinero al colector de contribuciones del mismo Condado, pero es el Intendente de cuentas públicas quien dará el certificado de redencion, á peticion del dueño ó del colector.

El terreno del rescate está para espirar. El sistema de avaluo y cobro de contribuciones seguido conforme á la actual legislacion, se inauguró en 1876 aunque el cobro de las de aquel año, se sujetó á las leyes anteriores entonces en vigor. Las primeras ventas que bajo el sistema actual se hicieron en pago de contribuciones despues de 1° de Marzo de 1877, fueron solamente de los terrenos que se manifestaron y cuya contribucion correspondiente al año anterior de 1876, no habia aun sido pagada.

En 1877 y en los años siguientes, todos los terrenos que no fueron manifestados, se consideraron como de dueños desconocidos y las ventas que se hicieron despues de 1° de Marzo de 1878 para el pago de contribuciones correspondientes á 1877, recayeron sobre esos mismos terrenos cuya contribucion de 1877, estaba sin pagarse.

El plazo concedido por la ley para el rescate de los terrenos vendidos en 1878, espira para algunos Condados en Marzo próximo vendidos y para otros en los meses siguientes, segun la fecha de las ventas hechas en aquel año, de manera que el que pueda redimir con tiempo sus terrenos, selibrará de complicaciones á que darán lugar los titulos expedidos por no haber pagado la contribucion.

En cuanto á los terrenos que se apropió el Estado y de que hemos hecho mencion, si no son redimidos segun lo dispone la ley, se volverán á poner en venta y esta continuará siempre hasta que algun individuo los compre, quedando sujeto al rescate en el plazo de dos años de la fecha en que aquella se hubiere verificado.

Contribuciones atrasadas. No es menos interesante conocer este otro punto. Si el contribuyente que debe contribuciones, desde el año de 1873 se presenta á pagarlas, se verá relevado de pagar toda otra contribucion que deba anterior á aquel año, pero si da lugar á que se le obligue al pago ejerciendo la facultad coactiva, entonces, tendrá que pagar lo que esté debiendo desde el 1° de Enero de 1871, pero no lo que deba de esta fecha para atras. Sobre esto hay que hacer una aclaracion y es la siguiente. El pago de las contribuciones que se deban anteriores al año de 1877, no se admite hasta que un asesor forme los manifiestos ó inventarios con el respectivo avaluo, y no se puede saber cuando esto tendrá lugar, porque depende del estado ó listas que se estan ahora compilando en la oficina del Intendente de Cuentas públicas, y que han de facilitar á las Cortes de Comisionados de los Condados determinar que terrenos deben contribuciones por los años anteriores, y ordenar que se haga la liquidacion.

EXCELENTE SUGETO.

Parece que el nuevo juez del Condado trata de poner en movimiento todos los arbitrios que le dicte su vigilancia en favor de las escuelas públicas del mismo, y valerse de cuantos medios esten á su alcance y discurra oportunos para cumplir con sus deberes. Su aire apacible y modesto y su afabilidad le concilian la benevolencia de todos los que le tratan y en sus razonamientos, se descubre prudencia y buen juicio.

Larga y laboriosa debe haber sido la carrera de quien asi entra dan do cumplimiento con un conocimien to exacto de las cosas de su autoridad, y de esperarse es que á menudo entrará tambien en consejo su saber, sobre el remedio de algunos males y que verá abierto su camino para el cumplimiento de sus deseos. Hay gran diferencia entre un juez de Condado que todo lo embrolla y que está siempre dispuesto á hacer nacer dudas y buscar frívolas razones para hacer oposicion á los deberes anexos á su empleo, y un juez habil é inteligente que desde luego se da á conocer por su justificacion en el desempeño de sus obligaciones y por su exactitud en el oficio. Lo decimos con sinceridad pues no acos tumbramos á lisonjear ni á dejarnos seducir por las apariencias.

A PELEAR.

"Señor," nos dijeron muy de mañana á la puerta del cuarto en que dormiamos, "se ha presentado á la vista un bajel de bajo bordo que, segun informe del patron de una chalupa que pasó cerca de él, es pirata y que en su popa ha podido leer el nombre de EL DUENDE. Dice, ademas, que solo dos cabezas se han visto pero sospecha que su tripulacion es mucho mayor. Hay, señor, que estar alerta sobre algun salto repentino al arsenal de EL DEMOCRATA, guarnecerlo al momento de fortines y murallas, colocando alguna artilleria, y el número de tropa necesario para guarnecerlo."

No tengas miedo, no te acobardes, le contestamos, se dará providencia en todo, y entre tanto ponte de vigia en la gavia de nuestro bergantin velero que está amarrado en el arsenal, y expia los movimientos de ese corsario para echarle bala rasa si nos provoca á combate.

All right, nos dijo nuestro interlocutor que era un chico avieso de casta de bolillo como suele decir nuestro amigo B.........n.

WARRIOR.

El vapor de este nombre perteneciente á una linea Inglesa y que con destino á nuestro puerto salió de Liverpoold haciendo escala en Vera Cruz y Tampico fondeo en la bahia de Brazos ayer tarde.

Trae unos mil barriles de flete para este Comercio y probablemente saldrá para nueva Bleaus ésta tarde.

Entendemos que otro vapor de la misma empresa se halla ya en camino.

MOTIVO DE AFLICCION.

Un hijo del coronel J. S. Ford que reside actualmente en Austin, ha fallecido á consecuencia de una herida que recibio de un modo casual. Lo mismo que sus padres, ese jóven era querido en esta ciudad en la que ha nacido, pero el cielo lo ha determinado así. Tomamos parte en su desconsuelo.

FRANK LESLIE'S ILLUSTRATED NEWSPAPER

Entered according to Act of Congress, in the year 1881, by I. W. England, Assignee, in the Office of the Librarian of Congress at Washington.—Entered at the Post Office, New York, N.Y., as Second-class Matter.

No. 1322.—Vol. LI. NEW YORK, JANUARY 29, 1881. [Price 10 Cents. $4.00 Yearly. 13 Weeks, $1.00.

TEXAS.—CATTLE HERDERS INDULGING IN REVOLVER PRACTICE ON TELEGRAPH INSULATORS.
From a Sketch by Wm. F. Sparks.—See Page 363.

VOL. 2 BELTON, BELL CO., TEXAS, FEBRUARY 23, 1881. NO. 5

THE TEXAS FARMER.

Is Published Weekly.
AT
BELTON, TEXAS,
BY
W. P. HANCOCK & CO.

W. P. HANCOCK,..................J. F. FULLER
J. C. O'BRYAN.

—o—

TERMS:
$1.50 PER. YEAR.

The money invariably to accompany the names.

The Pirates' Arch.

We were off the Bahamas, in a small vessel, and having a considerable amount of specie on board, we were in fear of the pirates that we all knew infested the coast. Already we had a glimpse of a little, low, black craft that kept hugging the shore all day, without loosing sight of us; but having a six-pounder and a quantity of small arms on board, we set but little value upon the importance of the stranger.

I remember it as well as if it were but yesterday. We were running close reefed under a deserted island that jutted out into the sea in a singular archway of rock, through which we could see the billows toss their foaming crests in the distance as plainly as if we had been looking at them through some gigantic open window. The sight was at once sublime and wierd; for at the moment we discovered the fantastic cliff, a tempest of wind and rain, accompanied by thunder and lightening, was raging most frightfully.

We had not been long centemplating this wild and picturesque formation, when the first mate perceived a boat filled with armed men, shoot out from behind the perforated wall of rock, and bear directly down upon us. The captain, who was as brave as a lion, knew we were in for it, and instantly ordered the decks to be cleared for action. The pirate, for such it proved to be, was a bold fellow; for on he came, as if he fancied we should only make a mouthful for him. To be sure, his boat was a large one, and was filled with a fierce, formidable crew; but, then, so long as we could keep them from boarding us we knew we were all right.

I have often thought that the fate of the commander of the pirates was upon him, then and there, from the reckless way in which he exposed himself, not only in the conspicuousness of his dress, but the way he stood, towering above his crew in the fore-part of his craft. The captain, who was a native of one of the neighboring islands, was well acquainted with customers, and was now glad he had come across one of them at last; as of late, descents had been made upon several inhabitants of the group, resulting in plunder, abduction or murder.

The ball was opened handsomely, for the pirate had a swivel forward that he used to some purpose, but not with such dangerous effect as to do more than riddle our canvas and cripple our sailing for the time being. When, however, we found him within easy range of our small arms, we gave him a taste of the six-pounder, which we loaded with grape, and a well-directed volley of musketry, which astonished him. For the moment he was thrown into intense confusion; and preceiving this, we thought it advisable to repeat the dose before he had time to recever himself. This we did in a manner so striking and with such unprecedented effect, that to our utter surprise his boat went down in a twinkle before our very eyes, and what was more singular still, leaving him the only visible living thing, struggling with the angry billows, and throwing up his arm as if in an agony of despair. A chance shot had completed the work that we had begun so well; and now we were alone with our own wounded, none of our crew [illegible] killed, and I, the only passenger not having received a single scratch.

It was verging towards evening when we anchored off the archway of rock, and as the tempest had subsided, some of the crew had begun clearing up the decks, and putting things in ship-shape, while I induced the captain and two or three of the sailors to put off for the shore, and examine the rock more narrowly. Here we soon landed, and, to our surprise, at the mouth of a cave which opened upon the sea beneath the very arch of the rock already alluded to. Being armed and feeling that all the pirates had found a watery grave, this cavern was entered, unhesitatingly, and there to our utter astonishment, after a few paces, we perceived a young woman bound with cords, and seated leaning against the wall of rock. The moment the captain caught sight of her, he leaped forward with a cry that made the cavern resound throughout, and caught her in his arms.

We, who were looking on, were petrified, but the mystery was soon solved. The prisoner was his only sister, who had been dragged from her home in a neighboring island in the morning by "Pedro the Pirate." She had been walking alone among the rocks near her home, when she was suddenly seized and borne away in the craft we had just sent to the bottom with all the crew, among whom our grape had committed terrible havoc. Knowing that her family and friends were wealthy, the monsters had lain in wait for her, and borne her off in the hope of obtaining a heavy ransom, although the villain Pedro intimated that possibly she was reserved for another fate.

They had had information of our cargo and course, and had been on the qui vive. She had been lying bound in the boat for many hours, and just arrived at the rendezvous of the pirates, when the villains perceived us. They at once ran their bot ashore, and inhumanly thrust the por lady into the cave and then put o] to attack us, intending no doubt tc make short work of us and then retrn with their rich booty. Their degn, however, was frustrated as alredy seen; and now having unbound th fair creature we speedily explored he cave and turned the tables so farin our fayor that we had a more aluable cargo on board when we resued our voyage the same evening, than we had when we left the ship, ot to speak of the captain's lovely siter who had been rescued from imnnent peril by her brother, althoughunconsciously on his on his part, androm a lingering death by me, in onsequence of my having induced hii to visit the rock. The result of al this was that I took as my share of the booty the young lady found i the cave, who makes the best wife inhe world.

The New Year [illegible]

"Because, you know, fther, we didn't have any kind ofa good time last New Year's day," saiFred.

"Because you was toc sick," said John.

"And 'cause we couldn make one speck of noise," put in Luner.

Perley didn't say a wrd, but he looked as earnest as the rst, and was just as eager to hear hi father say yes.

They were begging or a New Year's party in the new house. It wasn't plastered yet, and 'ouldn't be ready to move into for som time, but the windows and doors wre in their places, and a stove had bee set up for the convenience of the masns, and to dry the plaster by-and-b when it should be ready.

"Yes, on one condition, said the father. "No one must nddle with the fire, or carry match into the house. Shavings are lyingabout, we can't be too careful."

The boys agreed to this.

"Can we make all the noiswe like?" asked Fred.

"Whistle, and drum, andoller all we want to," said Johnnie.

"'Cause we shan't 'sturbnybody," urged Luther.

"Yes, yes," said the father. "Whistle and sing, and shout, and dru, all you like. I've heard of raisingthe roof with noise, but I'll venture ine."

It wasn't to be a large pay. Only Cousin George and the tw Barrett boys. But only think of he noise seven boys can make, when ey have full license.

"You'll want plenty to eat noise is to be the chief amucement I guess I'd better fry doughnuts," id their mother.

"Yes, yes! doughnuts," saiFred.

"And can't we have hicky nuts, too?" asked John.

"Peanuts?" said Lutie.

"And 'lasses candy?" said Fley.

"Yes, yes, 'lasses candy!" sl they all.

"Yes," said their mother. "Only you must make that yourselves."

"Of course! That's just what we'd like to do," said the boys.

While they were carrying the invitations, Fred and Perley swept and cleared up the room where the party was to be.

Of course, the Barrett boys would come, and of course Cousin George wouldn't refuse. They came right along back with John and Luther, and the party began at once.

The first thing was to crack the nuts. They couldnt' find but three hammers, so the Barrett boys had to slide home and get two more. They only needed five, as Luther and Perley would be busy at the peanuts. When they were all cracked, the boys went to their mother for some old forks, with which to pick out the meats.

"When will you have your doughnuts?" she asked. "They are all ready now, a big plateful [illegible] up, nice and warm."

"I guess we'll have them now," said Fred.

So he carried out the plate of doughnuts, and a great pitcher full of milk to drink. John brought some tamblers. The carpenter's bench was the table, and the feast began.

While they were eating, they talked over their plans. The whole quart of molasses should be boiled, then half of it poured over the nuts, which must be arranged on the big platter. The rest they would work and pull till it was white, and then make it into sticks.

They were eager to begin, and did not linger at the table a minute longer than the doughnuts lasted. Then the kettle was put on, and soon the molasses began to simmer, and then to bubble and foam, till they had all they could do to tend it, so it need not boil over or burn.

Their mother brought out the big platter, well buttered, and their father came out to see to the fire and try the molasses, and as he didn't seem in a hurry to go, they invited him to stay, and he stayed and almost forgot he wasn't a boy.

The sun was almost down before they finished pulling the candy, and they had to hurry through, because candles couldn't be allowed in the new house. The father had marked the nut candy into squares before it was quite cool, so when they were ready to divide it, it broke apart easily. Each one had his share of both kinds, spread out on a clean bit of board.

"Have you had a good time?" said the father. "As good as you expected?"

"Yes, yes! better! A splendid time!"

"You haven't raised the root with your noise, as I see. Seems to me I haven't heard much noise, after all. I told you, you could make all you liked, you know."

"We've been so busy we forgot all about that part," said Fred, with a funny little smile.

"Then perhaps you would like to give three rousing cheers before you go?"

So they cried, "Hurrah! HURRAH!! HURRAH!!!" with a right good will, and repeated it again and again. But the roof didn't start a nail.—[Youth's Companion.

Ye Olden Days.

Thirty years ago Michigan people were a frank and truthful set. Strangers could come there and trade horses with their eyes shut, and breach of promise cases were known. Folks meant what they said, and when they gave their word, stuck to it.

Exactly thirty years ago a widower from New, York State appeared in Lansing on business. That same business carried him over to DeWitt, eight miles away.

While en route he stopped at a log farm-house to warm his cold fingers. Her [illegible] wife, both of whom were well along in years; and after some general talk, the woman queried:

"Am I right in thinking you are a widower?"

"Yes."

"Did you come out here to find a wife?"

"Partly."

"Did anybody tell you of our Susie?"

"Well, I've got as bouncing a girl of twenty-two as you ever set your eyes on. She's good looking healthy and good-tempered, and I think she'll like your looks."

"Where is she?"

"Over in the woods, here, chopping down a coon tree. Shall I blow the horn for her?"

"No. If you'll keep an eye on my horse, I'll find her."

"Well there's nothing stuck up or affected about Susie. She'll say yes or no as she looks you over. If you want her don't be afraid to say so."

The stranger heard the sound of her ax, and followed it. He found her just as the tree was ready to fall.

She was a stout, good-looking girl, swinging the ax like a man, and in two minutes he had decided to say:

Susie, I'm a widower from New York State; I'm thirty-nine years old, have one child, own a good farm and I want a wife. Will you go back home with me?"

She leaned on the ax and looked at him for half a minute and then replied:

"Can't say for certain. Just wait till I get these coons off my mind."

She sent the tree crashing to earth, and with his help killed five coons, which were stowed away in a hollow.

"Well, what do you say?" he asked as the last coon stopped kicking.

"I'm your'n!" and by the time you get back from DeWitt I'll have these pelts off and tacked up, and be ready for the preacher.

He returned to the house, told the old folks that he would bring a preacher back with him, and at dusk that even ing the twain were married.

Hardly an hour had been wasted in courting, and yet he took home one of the best girls in the State of Michigan.

THE WEEKLY NEWS.

A WEEKLY JOURNAL DEVOTED TO THE INTERESTS OF LIVE OAK AND SURROUNDING COUNTIES.

$2 Per Year. Lagarto, Texas, Saturday, August 6, 1881. Vol. I. No. 6.

LITTLE FROSTY.

Dark blue eyes with silken fingers,
Clinging curls of golden hair,
Where the sun-beams love to linger,
Near my darling baby fair.

Teeth as white as pearls of ocean,
Lips as red as ruby wine,
Dainty feet always in motion,
Little fingers clasped in mine.

What a blessing sent to cheer me,
All my griefs and joys to share,
With her precious arms around me,
Her baby-kisses on my hair.

N. St. G.

THE RAILROAD.
Here comes the Herald of a Noisy World.

Will the road be built? This is a question that is asked by many of our people. We are sure it will, and give the reasons for the faith that is in us. A road from San Diego to Houston is a *necessity*, linking the great chain of roads that is in construction by the Palmer-Sullivan Co. from the City of Mexico and the Pacific coast, to the cities of the United States. This surveyed route from San Diego to Houston is a direct line, and passing through the first tier of towns from the coast, and besides being the shortest, and most direct route from Laredo to Houston.

Its location so near the coast will necessarily absorb and control all travel and trafic that now seeks outlets by way of Corpus and Indianola. Without its connections the road would be a paying one all along the line; for in passing through the towns of Lagarto, Beeville, Goliad and Victoria, it would both accommodate and monopolize all the trades of these towns. The road has been located the greater part of the way, and it is thought work will commence early in the fall.

Now what effect will this rail road have upon the country? From the Colorado to the Rio Grande is a vast territory to be opened up, settled, and developed, and by the history of the past, it it is the mission of this coast-line road to accomplish that end. Before the first rail is lain, the property all along the line of this road will feel the influence of the coming change. Immigration will come, and homes will spring up, and progress and improvment will be the order of the day. Lands will appreciate in value, and horses, cattle, and other stock will find a ready market. The increase of population will provide a ready sale for the farmer's products, and the improved transportation will reduce the cost of what we have to buy. The railroad will enable the farmer and gardener to ship their early crops to the Eastern and Northern markets from two to four weeks in advance of other sections of this and other states. The stock raiser will receive for his beef here at the depot, a price corresponding to that of the cities North. The building of this road will give life and impetus to every interest of our country. It will give employment to our mechanics, clerks, and laborers. It will scatter money through the country, and place some within the reach of all. Finally, our mail facilities and every channel of intercourse, communication, trafic, travel and trade, will be made better by the railroad that is coming.

EXTRACTS
From an Unpublished Journal of a Trip to California in 1849.
(32 Years Ago.)
CHAPTER IV

July, 4.—A slight sensation was created yesterday by a raid from the Apaches. They carried off several mules. These Indians make frequent incursions upon the settlements near El Paso. The inhabitants are in constant apprehension of a raid. It is reported that the authorites offer $200.00 for Apache scalps. Parties are trying to organize a company of rangers for this service. I am told that Major Chavalle of Texas, with a squad of men has turned aside to hunt Indians. Some old friends called to see me to-day. They have traveled by way of Presidio del Norte, had to abandon their wagons in order to get through the mountains. They tell me my old friend Morris, turned back at San Antonio. It seems there are two routes from this point. We go the upper. Our company organization disbanded on reaching El Paso. Thompson and families have located at El Paso, on the Texas side of the river, and established a store. Mr. Coon, a Missouri trader, now owns the principal property at that place. He has a large store. The "great western," a female of notoriety in the late war with Mexico, is domiciled at this place.

July, 14.— After two weeks rest, and recuperation at our camp above El Paso, on the 12th inst. we resumed our march towards the far west. Traveling up the valley of the Rio Grande, we found the road good, and water and grass abundant. The river is skirted with cotton wood trees, some of them of very great size. The soil here is no doubt very rich, and all along this valley we notice evidence of former settlement and cultivation. The ditches used for irrigating, are yet plainly marked, but no houses or signs of recent habitation. In this region the principle rain fall is during the summer months, One half of the year is wet and the other dry.

July, 17.—Arrived at Donna Anna, a town situated on the Texas side of the river about sixty miles from El Paso, and near the United Staes boundry line. Two companies of United States troops are stationed here under command of Lieu. Sackett We are enabled to purchase supplies here, but the prices seem exhorberant, Bacon 50 cents per pound, and other articles in proportion. This is a very pretty little town, and contains some nice looking people. I met here three young ladies, sisters, aged from 12 to 18 The two youngest have auburn hair, and black eyes, all very fair and pretty. I took them to be Americans or foreign ladies, and addressed them in English. No comprehende senor was their reply. I then gave them a regular broadside of my Texas Spanish, and soon made a hasty retreat.

July, 29.— We are encamped thirty two miles adove Donna Anna on the west bank of the river. We crossed the river about twelve miles below this point. The river is about one hundred and fifty yards wide muddy, and swift. We were three days in crossing. This was the second time our boat was brought into requisition. the first time in crossing the pecos, as I have not heretofore described this convenient arrangement I will do so now. The boat belonged to Mr L. B. Harris, and was constructed with great care and fore-thought for the emergencies of the trip Imagine a wagon bed about fifteen inches deep, sloped up at each end like a scow boat, the bottom and sides all tongue and grooved together and well strapped with iron bands. The plank, good seasoned, inch cypress, well put together with white lead, and then painted. In the railing is inserted two sets of oar pins, the two end boards, which fit on top and hold the bows, make the seats, when propelling the boat. Here you have a good wagon bed, and a safe substantial, durable boat.

About sixty men are encamped at this place. We have again organized. Shackelford, Captain, and Harris, Sergeant. Twenty seven wagons, cows, oxen, mules and horses, without number. Several families are with us. Thorn's from San Antonio, among the rest. We are resting and recruiting the animals, repairing wagons, shoeing horses, hunting, fishing, etc. The range is excellent, and game plenty. We live well, and the time passes pleasantly. The weather is delightful, a fine breeze throughout the day, and the nights cool enough for a blanket. We make bread from wheat ground upon a steel mill. It is very wholesome and agreeable to the taste.

At this point our road leaves the Rio Grande, and reaches out towards that, to us yet undeserned country in the far west.

(TO BE CONTINUED.)

2000 immigrants looming into Texas every day. Trains all crowded, but the empire of Texas *can't* be crowed.

Napa county, California, produced 2,830,750 gallons of wine for the year 1880, valued at $500,000.

Texas is the home of the grape.

Thousands of tons of Mustang grapes on the Nueces river, (Live Oak county.) that are not made use of. If made into wine at 50c per gallon it would be worth $150,000. But the boom is coming.

San Antonio is the greatest horse market in the *world*. No other city handles more than half as many horses and mules. Sales in San Antonio from the first of January to July, horses, mares and mules, 31,000 head, not including private sales.

The Panhandle.

VOL. 1. MOBEETIE, WHEELER COUNTY, TEXAS, SATURDAY, FEBRUARY 25, 1882. NO. 27

Advertising Rates.

Yearly advertisements inserted at the rate of $1 an inch, per month, if two inches or more space is occupied; if less than two inches, $1.50 per month. Transient advertisements at higher rates.

Local notices and legal advertisements, fifteen cents per line first insertion, and ten cents per line each subsequent insertion. Must be accompanied by the cash, or they will receive no attention.

All bills payable monthly, unless otherwise agreed.

Subscription Rates.

THE PANHANDLE will be published every Saturday at the following rates:
One copy, one year..........$2 00
One copy, six months..........1 00
Payable in advance.

Subscriptions may be paid to A. S. Mercer, at the Henrietta Shield office, Henrietta, Texas.

Mr. F. G. Copeland is agent for THE PANHANDLE at Tascosa, and is authorized to receive payments for the same.

Mere Forms of Law.

One of the officials of Justice alley was the other day called upon by an old gray-headed farmer and his wife, together with a neighbor, and outside the door they hitched an old half-blind horse whose cash value was estimated at $25.

"You see," explained the old farmer, "nabur Jones wants to buy the old hoss out there, but he wants a bill o' sale signed by wife and I. We want you to draw up one for us."

The justice reached down one of the printed blanks, filled it out and then said:

"Now, you listen while I read this all over, and see if it is all right. All ready, now."

"Know all men by these presents, that—"

"Presents! Why, I'm not going to going to present him with the hoss!" interrupted the farmer.

"And we don't want any presents from him!" added the wife.

"That's all right—only a legal form," exclaimed his honor. "Listen."

"County Wayne—first part—consideration—sum of $25—grant—bargain and sell—party—second part—his executors, administrators—"

"I haven't got any executors or administrators!" interrupted neighbor Jones.

"No; all he's got is a wife and two girls!" added the owner of the horse.

"All form—all mere form," explained the justice, and went on:

"And assigns forever—covenant and agree—defend the same—heirs executors and administrators—"

"William, I shall never sign no such paper!" suddenly exclaimed the wife, as she rose up.

"Nor I either," stoutly replied the husband. "Why, I'd shake in my boots every time I met a constable."

"It is all mere form according to law," explained his honor. "All bills of sale read this way."

"Looks to me as if we were sort of tangled up," said neighbor Jones. "The old hoss is blind in one eye, and how can they warrant him?"

"And what has this hoss sale got to do with his heirs and covenants?" inquired the old man.

"I won't sign—I won't have anything to do with it!" exclaimed the wife, as she walked around. "We've always kept clear of the law, and we hain't going to get into no scrape and lose our farm now—not if we know it!"

The more the justice tried to explain the bigger the words looked, and the trio finally walked off. While they were unhitching the horse along came a house painter, and when he had heard their story he picked up a piece of paper in the alley, pulled out a stub of a pencil and wrote:

"We hereby sell this horse to John Jones for $25, cash down. We raised him from a colt, and his name is Andrew Jackson."

The paper was signed, passed over with the horse, and as the farmer received the money he said:

"That's all there is to it, law or no law, and it didn't take two minutes to do it. Why, I'd take Andrew Jackson back home and knock him in the head afore I'd put my name to that paper binding us to keep on covenanting and agreeing and assigning and administering a whole life time on an old hoss."

A Clown's Trick.

[London Daily News.]

Auriol, the celebrated French clown, whose death was recorded a few days ago in the columns of the Parisian press, was a man of remarkable courage, coolness and ready wit. During one of his professional tours in Russia he got into a terrible scrape, from which, however, his presence of mind enabled him to extricate himself triumphantly. He had been engaged, while at St. Petersburg, to perform at a private entertainment given by a wealthy nobleman resident on the Basil island. It was in the depth of winter, and the Neva was frozen hard. Auriol dressed himself in the clown's costume at his lodgings, wrapped himself up in furs, hired a sledge and started for his destination, instructing his driver to take the short cut across the river. Probably tempted by Auriol's costly pelisse, the driver, a tall, powerful fellow, pulled up suddenly when about half way across, jumped down from his perch, and letting fall his reins turned toward his fare with menacing gestures. A moment's hesitation would in all likelihood have cost Auriol his life, but he proved equal to the emergency. Throwing off his furs and revealing himself to his would-be assailant in the motley garb of his profession, he sprang out of the sledge and proceeded to execute some of his most amazing gambols on the ice. Paralyzed by so terrific an apparition, the driver made one ineffectual attempt to cross himself, staggered, and with an agonized cry of "The fiend himself!" fell flat and motionless upon his face. Without further loss of time Auriol slipped on his furs, picked up the reins, jumped into the sledge and drove off, safe and sound, to fill his engagement. Next morning the driver's corpse was found, stiff and stark, lying face downward on the frozen breast of the Neva.

About Polygamy.

Hon. George C. Bates, ex-U. S. Attorney of Utah, writing to the Denver Tribune, among other good things says, "that practicable polygamy in the mountains and valleys, outside of the cities and larger towns of Utah, almost invariably engenders incest among the children, which prevails all over the Territory, as will appear herein. In January 1875, it happened me to visit the southern parts of the Territory on business for the church, and, stopping to change horses and dine, I saw around one table five polygamic wives of one old bishop, and in and around the ranch some 36 large boys and girls of all ages from ten to sixteen and twenty years, and then and there learned that these young Mormons all slept in one large single room over head in the winter like so many pigs, and in the hot weather in summer they all huddled together in the straw in the stable, in promiscuous concubinage, and that several of the girls were bearing children to their brothers and cousins and uncles as so many cows and ewes would do, and that this was a matter of daily happening, and was not discouraged but winked at by the old bishop, who stood high in the church, as a natural consequence of their religious teachings, that every woman's future happiness was enhanced by the number of children she bore, no matter who be their fathers. But fearful as this crime may be, congress cannot legislate against the Mormon religion as such, and cannot and never will change or overthrow the rights of the people of Utah to a representative government, but can only take such steps and make such laws as shall exterminate, wipe out and end all polygamic crimes, and all bigamous connections; and this may easily be done and effectually punished by a brief amendment to the act of congress, July 2, 1862, making polygamy a felony and a crime."

Wonderful Lake.

In Colorado is a ten-acre field, which is nothing more nor less than a subterranean lake, covered with soil about eight inches deep. On the soil is cultivated a field of corn which produces thirty or forty bushels to the acre.

If any one will take the trouble to dig a hole to the depth of a spade handle he will find it to fill with water and by using hook and line, fish six inches long can be caught. The fish have neither scales nor eyes, and are perch like in shape. The ground is a black marl in nature, and, in all probability, was at one time an open body of water, on which vegetable matter had accumulated, which has been increased from time to time until now it has a crust sufficiently strong and rich to produce fine corn, though it has to be cultivated by hand as it is not strong enough to bear the weight of a horse. While harvesting the hands catch great strings of fish by making a hole through the earth. A person rising on their heel and coming down suddenly can see the growing corn shake all around him. Any one having the strength to drive a nail through the crust will find on releasing it that it will disappear altogether. — [Scientific American.

Mrs. Daguerreotype B. Watermellon called on Mrs. Americus Vespucius, a very fashionable Austin lady a few days ago. The following conversation took place:

"So your son is going to get married pretty soon, I hear."

"Yes, he will get married in a few months."

"He is so young. I should think you would make him wait until he arrived at the age of discretion."

"O, no," responded the mother, who has had five or six husbands, "if he waits until he arrives at the age of discretion, he will never get married at all."—[Siftings.

The Valley of Death.

The Valley of Death, a spot almost as terrible as the Prophet's valley of dry bones, lies just north of the old Mormon road to California, in Utah—a region thirty miles long by thirty broad and surrounded, except at two points, by inaccessible mountains. It is totally devoid of water and vegetation, and the shadow of a bird or wild beast never darkened its white, glaring sands. The Kansas Pacific railroad engineers discovered it and some papers which show the fate of the "lost Montgomery train" which came south from Salt Lake in 1850, guided by a Mormon. When near Death's Valley some came to the conclusion that the Mormon knew nothing about the country, so they appointed one of their number a leader and broke off from their party. The leader turned due west. So with the people and wagons and flocks he traveled three days and then decended into the broad valley whose treacherous mirage promised water. They reached the center, but only the white sand, bounded by scorching peaks, met their gaze. And around the valley they wandered, and one by one the men died and the panting flocks stretched themselves in death under the burning rays of the sun. The children crying for water died at their mother's breasts, and with swollen tongues and burning vitals the mothers followed. Wagon after wagon was abandoned, and strong men tottered and raved and died. After a week's wandering a dozen survivors found some water in a hollow of a mountain. It lasted but a short time, when all perished but two, who escaped out of the valley and followed the trail of their former companions. Eighty-seven families, with hundreds of animals, perished here, and now after thirty one years the wagons stand still complete, the iron works and tires are bright, and the shriveled skeletons lie side by side.

Railroad Accident.

WACO, Texas, Feb. 8.—A jury of inquest was empaneled, to-day, to investigate the cause and manner of the death of M. W. Stoll, wife and son, and Maj. Washburn, of the International Improvement Company, which occurred Tuesday night. Stoll and wife were killed outright, the son lived an hour. The jury viewed the remains of Maj. Washburn in his private car this morning. The body was badly disfigured.

The jury then went by special train, twenty-three miles to where the three bodies lay. Stoll was badly mutilated, beyond recognition and his wife and son almost as bad. The testimony was to the effect that Washburn wished to go to Waco, be with Stoll, wife and son, Mr. J. Painter and five negroes, employees of the latter took a hand car to run down to the switch two miles below where Maj. Washburn's car was, and learn the cause of the delay. On the way down the train suddenly appeared on the top of a hill, running toward them, and Painter ordered the negroes to turn the hand car back and run from the train. Painter then signalled the train to slack, and seeing he did not give the signal to stop, which the brakeman gave to the engineer, who put on the brakes, but the train was on the down grade and dashed into the hand car. Painter and the negroes jumped and landed unhurt. Washburn jumped, but did not land clear and was struck by the train. Stoll, wife and son remained on the hand car until thrown from it. Washburn's private car, draped in mourning, conveyed the remains to Fort Worth, and from there they will go to Ohio. The remains of the Stoll family go to New Jersey.

How to Judge a Horse.

The weak points of a horse can be better discovered while standing than while moving. If he is sound he will stand firmly and squarely on his limbs, without moving any of them, the feet planted firmly upon the ground, with plumb and natural ally poised. If one foot is thrown forward with the toe pointing to the ground and the heel raised, or if the foot is lifted from the ground and the weight taken from it, disease may be suspected, or at least tenderness, which is a precursor of disease. If the horse stands with his feet spread apart, or straddles with the hind legs, there is weakness of the loins, and the kidneys are disordered. Heavy pulling bends the knees. Bluish or milky-cast eyes indicate moon blindness, or something else. A bad tempered horse keeps his ears thrown back. A stumbling horse has blemished knees. A kicking horse is apt to have scarred legs. When the skin is rough and harsh, and does not move easily and smoothly to the touch, the horse is a heavy eater and his digestion is bad. Never buy a horse whose respiratory organs are at all impaired. Place your ear at the side of the heart and if a wheezing sound is heard, it is an indication of trouble—let him go.

"The six shooter must go," will be the sentiment expressed in a resolution that will be offered before the stockmen's convention at its March meeting by the Hon. E. M. Hewins. Mr. Hewins and James Hamilton could illustrate the wrong done by the indiscreet carrying of revolvers by cowboys in their experience with the Hunnewell case of Mills, Chustain and Carter. It cost each of these gentlemen six hundred dollars, simply because they were friends of the boys, and had not urged the boys to leave off their arms to any effect. The day of the six-shooter cowboy is passed, and that class should not be employed on the range. It is both dangerous to the party carrying arms, and the employers of the cowboys. This matter should receive the thought it merits, and every cowman on the neutral strip should place himself squarely on record against the carrying of six-shooters on the range. It will not take long to make it so unpopular that the cowboy will be glad to conform to the new order of things, and lay off his six-shooter. Peaceable citizens will gladly hail the day when this will be accomplished.—[Caldwell Post.

The New York Herald says: One of the most amusing incidents in journalism is found in the case of an editor in New Jersey. He is a delicate and humorous writer, with a "nose for news." He publishes a daily paper, which is brightly republican in politics; he prints a still brighter democratic weekly. In the daily he elegantly demolishes himself in the weekly paper; but in the weekly he gets even with himself by turning about and utterly annihilating himself as the editor of the daily journal. In some respects the daily has the most genius; but it must be confessed that the weekly has the most talent. The two-headed girl at Bunnell's has, we believe, recently applied for the editorship of the fashion columns on both papers.

The force of will is a potent element in determining longevity. This single point must be granted without argument, that of two men, every way alike and similarly circumstanced, the one who has the greater courage and grit will be the longer lived. One does not need to practice medicine to learn that men die that might just as well live if they resolved to live, and myraids who are invalids could become strong if they had the native or acquired will to vow they would do so. Those who have no other quality favorable to life, whose bodily organs are nearly all diseased, to whom each day is a day of pain, who are beset by life shortening influences, yet do live by will alone.—[Dr. George M. Beard.

He is a shrewd grocer, and when the lady who was going to have the sewing society came down for a jug of vinegar, he filled the jug with whisky. And folks quietly asked her where she bought her vinegar, and the next day the grocer sold six barrels of cheap vinegar to the customers who thronged his store. And though they were all pretty mad they couldn't very well kick, as he had given them what they called for, and then to say anything would be to get laughed at.

What a nuisance! exclaimed a gentleman at a concert, as a young fop in front of him kept talking in a loud voice to a young lady at his side. "Did you refer to me, sir?" demanded the fop. "O, no! I mean the musicians, who keep up such a noise with their instruments that I can't hear your conversation," was the stinging reply.

"Doctor," asked Brown, "why don't you put Frederson on a close diet? Don't you think it would be a benefit to him?" "Undoubtedly," replied the doctor; "but it would be no benefit to me. I might lose a patient; and when I lose a patient," he added, "I prefer to lose him in the regular way."

Latena: To a woman of delicate feeling the most persuasive declaration of love is the embarrassment of an intellectual man.

Stolen Respectably.

[El Paso Herald.]

Take it as a fact that the building boom continues, and there is no sickness in the city.

That a quarter million dollars worth of building will go up in the future immense in the next ninety days.

Take it as a fact that this city is believed to have no rights whatever that the Santa Fe railroad leech is bound to respect.

Take it as a fact that the young man who spends more money than he earns will bring up in the poor-house.

That the æsthetic craze has struck a few silly people in this city, and has made them the laughing stock of sensible folks.

Take it as a fact patent to all men of sense that a public hall is an insignificant desideratum compared with a public school.

[Caldwell (Kas.) Post, Feb. 16.]

Ben S. Miller and bride are in St. Louis, visiting, this week.

Two young Hereford calves sold in Barbour county last week for $100 cash. It pays to raise that class of cattle for this range.

Mr. William Larkin, captain of the Crooked and Pond creek winter pool, came to town Monday, very sick with malarial fever. His many friends among the cattle men wish him a speedy recovery.

Harry Spaun, one of Sedgwick county's cattle men, is in the city and called at this office yesterday. He reports that the cattle in and about Wichita have ceased dying from the disease that was prevalent earlier in the winter. He is roughing Missouri stock through this winter, and is having good success with them.

The Post, as one of the committee on invitation, spreads its wings all over Medicine Lodge and asks it, as a whole, to come over on March 1st and 2d and partake of the hospitalities of Caldwell and learn how to entertain stockmen, as the Lodge proposes to try her hand at it on March 17th. It takes experience in such matters.

We learn of destructive prairie fires having occurred on the ranges near the Medicine river in the I. T. A fire on Saturday of week before last burned off a scope of country nearly fifteen miles square from Driftwood to Medicine. A few big fires now would "knock the stuffin'" out of the range cattle, to a certainty.

[Caldwell, (Kas.) Commercial, Feb. 16.]

Two important decisions were rendered in Topeka last week, one by the supreme court and the other by Judge Morton of the district court of Shawnee county. The first decided unconstitutional so much of the prohibitory law as prescribes a punishment for drunkenness, on the ground that the provision was not expressed in the title of the bill. The court also says that persons legally in possession of liquor can drink, burn or give it away.

In the other case, Judge Morton held that the law which provides that when, in case of an appeal by the land owner from the award of the commissioners appointed to appraise land for railroad purposes, notwithstanding the appeal of the owner, the company to take possession of and occupy such land, upon giving a bond, is not complying with the provision of the constitution which requires compensation to be made in money, and is therefore unconstitutional and void.

It will strike the average citizen living on the border, who gives the subject a moment's thought as being rather queer that the U. S. army can be used to remove all persons from the Territory whom it regards as intruders, while it has no authority whatever to arrest horsethieves and murderers who make the territory a hiding place from justice. Call a man an "Oklahoma boomer" who crosses the line dividing the territory from the surrounding states, and the whole power of the army will be used to effect his arrest. Let it be known, however, that he is a thief or murderer, and the army folds its arms and says go to Fort Smith and get your warrant. How long is that condition of things going to last? If it existed in any part of the country on the Atlantic coast, it would not last longer than a bill remedying the evil could be rushed through congress. The west, however, has no rights congress or the cast is bound to respect.

THE TEXAS PANHANDLE

Entered at the Postoffice Mobeetie as second class mail matter.

A. S. MERCER, - - - MANAGER.
W. E. EDWARDS, - - - EDITOR.

SATURDAY, FEBRUARY 25, 1882.

Work was begun on the new state capitol building on the first of this month.

A telegram from Helena, Ark., says the levee there is broken and the city flooded.

The murderers of the Gibbons family, at Cattlettsburg, Ky., have been convicted and sentenced to be hanged.

The cattle men of Kansas will hold a general convention at Medicine Lodge, that state, on the 17th of the coming month.

The Chicago Drovers Journal reports the market for fine stock active, and the demand greater than the supply. Stockmen everywhere are grading up.

The territorial legislature of New Mexico has recently passed a bill dividing San Miguel county, the eastern portion to form a new county and be called Rio Colorado.

The grand jury in Kansas City have returned eighty indictments, and are still vigorously at work. And yet the Texas cowboys continue their pilgrimages there in droves.—[Galveston News.

Texas cow-boys of the better sort, those of to-day and the future, will continue to make pilgrimages to those places where there is evinced a leaning toward law and morality.

THE POLYGAMY BILL.

The Utah saints have received a set back in the bill passed by congress on the 16th inst. It provides that parties in any part of the United States on marrying more than one woman shall be deemed guilty of polygamy and punished by a fine of not more than $500 and by imprisonment for a term of not more than five years. That any person in any territory or other place over which the United States has jurisdiction, who shall hereafter live and cohabit with more than one woman shall be deemed guilty of misdemeanor, and on conviction be punished by fine of not more than $300 or be imprisoned for not more than six months, or both at the discretion of the court. In any prosecution of cases of this nature, it shall be a sufficient cause to challenge any person drawn or summoned as a juryman or talisman that he is or has been living in the practice of bigamy, polygamy or unlawful cohabitation with more than one woman; or that he believes it right for a man to have more than one living and undivorced wife at the same time. The president is authorized to grant amnesty to such offenders as have been guilty before the passage of this act, on such conditions as he shall think proper, but no such amnesty shall have effect unless the canditions are complied with. The issue of bigamous or polygamous marriages, known as Mormon marriages, that shall have been born prior to Jan. 1, 1883, shall be deemed legitimate. No polygamist, and no woman cohabiting with any persons as aforesaid, in any territory or other place over which the United States has jurisdiction shall be entitled to vote at any election, or be eligible for election or appointment to, or be entitled to hold any office or place of public trust, honor or emolument in under or for any such territory or under the United States. And all registration and elective offices of every description in the territory of Utah are hereby declared vacant. Such provisions are also made in the bill as to preclude the Mormon sect from having members in the legislative assembly of the territory, or any voice in that body.

From the reading of the bill it looks as though Mormonism must speedily be wiped out, and all that is needed to effect that consummation is a proper execution of the provisions of the bill and the enforcement of the laws. This beastly "religion" has befouled a fair territory, and through it the whole United States, altogether too long; and all moral people will rejoice that the passage by congress of this bill has made it possible to remove the plague spot, and take that disgrace from the history of this generation.

Kansas City Letter.

KANSAS CITY, MO., Feb. 19 1882.
Editor Panhandle:

A year ago at this time the severely cold winter was generally commented upon, while now the continued mild weather is the general topic of conversation. The question now being asked is: "What kind of March weather do you think we will have?" There are but two men in modern times who have ever had any reputation for being weather wise. I refer to Vennor and Tice; however they are not infallible prophets, therefore it is the height of folly to prognosticate as to what will and will not be. Rather let us content ourselves with the present and prepare for the worst. The worst of the season is about over and ranch men have not much to fear. I have written a great deal about the weather, but it is a subject of prime importance in every day life and cannot be disregarded.

I do not suppose your readers are interested in sensational matters in and around Kansas City, such as murder, robberies, etc., but rather in what affects their every-day business, such as gossip about cattle and live stock generally. If you wished me to write of the sensations, which occur here from day to day I would find it a much easier task than to make careful comments upon the condition of trade.

The markets for stocks, (not stock) grain and provisions have been topsey turvey for the past week or ten days, there having been such a general decline in values as to cause several failures in Chicago and St. Louis. The failures alluded to in Chicago and St. Louis were those of commission merchants who had taken option deals for their customers in the country, and the markets declining additional margins were demanded, which were advanced by the commission merchants, but not reimbursed to them. That is the story they tell, but the fact is, more likely, that the commission merchants had taken the deals for themselves, believing unwisely that values must still further advance. In other words, they were "bulls" and taking their chances, and they lost. It is useless for the writer to moralize on the ill-effects of speculation. Fortunes have been made and lost, as it were by a game of chance, but the most pernicious speculation is option dealing; it is to the one who starts in at it as whisky drinking is to the confirmed inebriate and card playing to the professional gambler. Once it gets its hold upon a man, no human agency can prevent him from keeping at it as long as a dollar can be had.

But enough of the weather and speculation, for the readers of THE PANHANDLE wish to know what has been going on in the stock trade at this point. Well, to commence with I can say that, to use a stereotyped phrase, "there has been no material change to the market" since I last wrote you. The cattle market appears to be unsettled, particularly for the better class of shipping steers. One day there will be an advance of 10 to 15c per 100 pounds for shipping steers; the next day there will be a decline amounting to the advance, then the receipts will fall off and the market will be steady; then receipts become larger and there is another decline. Of one thing you can rest assured—that cattle, as I wrote in my last letter, are not as high in price by 50c per 100 pounds as they were on the first day of last January. It is needless for me to reiterate here as to the cause of prices being lower, as your readers among stockmen ought to be pretty well posted by this time. But no cattle raiser can complain of the prices which are being paid at present. Just to think of it! Last week a lot of corn fed Texas steers, averaging 862 pounds, sold at $4.60. That price was not bad, but then it not as high as was expected, and there is where the trouble comes in.

The hog shipper has had a hard time of it for the past week, with values declining at the rate of 10 to 15c for three days in succession, and packers unwilling to purchase even at the decline in prices. There have been several buyers of hogs here for the New York and Boston markets, and they have taken at fair prices what the packers did not want.

L. A. Allen has not returned home yet from his trip south.

Ches. Shider was in the city during the week.

I caught a glimpse of Nick Eaton on the streets a day or two since.

Most of the Texas stockmen who make their headquarters here during the winter are absent in Texas now, where they have been attending the convention at Austin. S.

State Items.

A man was robbed in San Antonio recently of $4,500.

The public schools of Dallas have ceased to exist.

Burglars are still on the rampage at Fort Worth.

A new lodge of Odd Fellows is being organized at Beaumont.

Texas claims $2,000,000 from the government that she has expended in frontier protection.

Dirt was broken on the 1st, by sub-contractor C. Reecy, in excavating for the new capitol.

The citizens of El Paso burnt Guiteau in effigy. Their object was to teach the public a lesson.

George Brandon was arrested on Tuesday at Brackett, Texas, for the murder committed in May, 1877. He has been recently married.

Large anti-Mormon meetings were held on Monday at Portland, Maine, Chicago, Illinois, Kalamazoo, Michigan and St. Paul, Minnesota.

Carp have been extensively distributed throughout Texas by the United States Fish Commission, and in a few years we will see what Texas can do in the way of fish farming.

The attorney-general's report, made public February 1st, shows the following felonies in 1881: Murder, 354; theft, 2,130; arson, thirty-two; perjury, ninety five; rape, forty-six; robbery eighty; forgery, 121; burglary, 211; embezzlement, forty-two; other felonies, 1,095; total, 4,208; 889 convictions, against a total of 3,525, convictions in 1880. The attorney-general, in reply to certain railroad companies asking that suits against them for failing to meet their annual reports within the time prescribed by law, says: "I do not consider my duty as attorney-general extends to more than enforcing the law as I find it in the statute books."

[Gainesville Cor. Henrietta Shield.]

Gainesville merchants still keep up their courage and with few exceptions have had a fair winter trade.

Twenty five thousand pounds of merchandise left here this morning on wagons for Pala Dura canon, in the Panhandle of Texas. A new departure for Gainesville merchants, and one that may yet interfere somewhat with the Kansas merchants.

Henrietta has a good reputation, and everyone here recognizes the fact that she is the coming town of the west. The question of our getting the Fort Worth & Denver railroad being now settled, quite a number of men are thinking seriously of either moving out or establishing branch houses in Henrietta. There is a general spirit of inquiry about the west, and prospectors will soon be on the road in numbers.

[El Paso Herald, Feb. 15th.]

Yesterday evening about 7 o'clock Doc. Cummings, a brother-in-law of City Marshal Stoudenmire, and owner of the Globe restaurant, was shot and almost instantly killed by James Manning, a saloon keeper and owner of the Coliseum, and some other person. The feud is supposed to be the natural outgrowth of the tragic scenes enacted in this city last April, the resentment then engendered having lurked in the bosoms of parties affected by the untimely end of some of the persons who figured in that bloody affair. The burden of the testimony would seem to indicate that Cummings visited the saloon kept by Manning and after an altercation with him fired the first shot. Mr. Campbell, however, testifies that the slender man, meaning Manning, fired the first shot, and a Mr. Warren corroborates this testimony with the statement that he saw Manning fire the first shot. The true inwardness of the affair will, we hope, be disclosed by the application of Manning to Judge Falvey, of the district court, for release, and we believe the judge will see that the laws are executed and justice done without fear or favor from any quarter. Such things are a blot on the name of our city. The court adjourned at 6 o'clock p. m., and will meet to-morrow morning at 9 o'clock, when the question of bail will be decided.

Mrs. Scoville refuses to allow the enterprising Pennsylvanian to have Guiteau's body for exhibition. She says there is not money enough in the country to buy his dead body for the purpose of exhibition.

The trunks lines have advanced emigrant rates to figures that the western people fear will amount to prohibition in thousands of cases, and thus compel emigrants to remain in the east where there is neither room nor work for them.

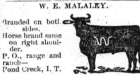

Changing Hands.

[Red Biver Chronicle,]

Never before in the history of New Mexico have there been so many transfers of ranges and stock animals, at good prices, as at present. There are two potent reasons for this: In the first place, the price of cattle last year reached such a maximum that stockmen think it a good time to sell their ranch and animals, at present good prices, and engage in something else where they can enjoy the benefits of civilization at a neighboring town or city, giving their wives an opportunity to see the world in company and allowing their children to go to school. The other reason is that monied men see a good opportunity to make money "hand over fist" by buying up small ranches and engaging in cattle raising on the wholesale.

Both sides are justified in their action. The frontiersman who commenced some years ago, roughing it to make both ends meet, after having increased his herd to such a number that he may now live comfortably on his income, entertains fears that the present high prices will not last and therefore jumps at the offer to sell at the good figures.

Owners of large herds and capitalists think differently, and we agree with them. The country is settling up rapidly all over the United States. Heretofore in the west and southwest it has been the custom of stockmen to stop at a nice watering place and let the animals graze on the public lands. As the settlements advance the public pastures are getting limited, and only the man with the patent of land in his pocket can feel comfortable; and stockmen are more and more getting into the habit of fencing their pastures to keep away trespassers and have less trouble in rounding up stock.

Taking into consideration the immense trade in live stock and beef now established with Great Britain, France and Cuba, the rapid increase of population in the west and consequent larger demand for butchering stock; the concentration of ranches into a few large ones, and there is but one decision to be arrived at—that all kinds of live stock are more apt to advance than decrease in value in the future. Our advice to our neighbors is to hold on to your lands and procure a patent for them as soon as possible. Do not decrease the number of your animals but keep on increasing the quality, and stock raising will be a more profitable business in the future than heretofore. By all means increase the size and quality, if not the number. Good, large animals will cost no more to herd than scrubs, they do not eat any more, and at the day of sale bring better prices.

Prices Have Doubled.

Mr. G. S. Plants, of Richland Springs, Texas, writing to a friend at Chicago under date of Jan. 17th, says in relation to the high prices of cattle in his country:

"Present prices of cattle are fully double what they were four years ago. This increase of price is capable of two solutions, based upon these facts: Either the prices have been stimulated by the demand for beef cattle, or capital is seeking investment at reduced profits. I have hardly given the subject close enough attention to venture my own judgment upon it. If the high prices are caused by the sympathy of stock cattle with the beef market, why, I conclude that present values are rather fictitious, for I do not think that present prices of beef cattle will prevail longer than till the present deficiency can be supplied by the northern corn-fed cattle crop, which will not prevail until a good crop season at the north, as it is only the scarcity of good beef in the north that has caused the boom in longhorns. On the other hand, if it is capital seeking investment at reduced profits, there is nothing fictitious about it. And furthermore, if such is the case there is no reason why cattle should not go still higher. They could stand considerable advance and still return a handsome profit; that is, compared to investments of large amounts at the north, if present prices are maintained with the probability of increase.

Trading among ranchmen is usually conducted on principles that would scarcely do in mercantile circles, yet among the rarest things one hears of is a crooked rancher. Occasionally a fellow turns up who is unable to meet his contracts, and cannot be held to them on account of the lax methods in vogue, as there is very much left to honor. Still, however, a man of dishonorable character cannot make much headway in the new country, and he is soon discovered. It would be better for all hands if contracts and the like were made in more business-like and systematic style, for no good man will object to having things done up in a manner that is legally binding, and if a man shows signs of weakening when strict business rules are introduced, it is better for the seller to learn his man then than wait till too late.—[Chicago Drovers Journal.

Russian proverb: People love truth, but invite the liar to dinner.

THE TERRELL STAR.

ONE DOLLAR PER ANNUM.

Entered at the post office at Terrell as Second Class matter.

CLEMENTS OPERA HOUSE

J. WHOMES, Manager.

Will seat one thousand persons. Elegant in all its appointments. New curtains, stage scenery and effects. Theatrical companies tendered every courtesy, and the hall placed at their command at ruling prices. For particulars address J. WHOMES, Manager.

LORDS OF CREATION.

"Blood will tell;" so be careful how you make confident of your relations.

Never do things by halves. That's the way the divorce court does business.

Scientific men have lately discovered that the crab does not crawl backward all the time.

When an obituary notice reads: "No further seek his failures to disclose," it means "Whisky killed him."

Just

Received at Underwood's the prettiest line of childrens' shoes in town.

Dr. Mosso, of Turin, has invented a machine for measuring thought, which he calls the "Plethysmograph."

The futile demands for ten-cent pieces show that the United States mint does not keep up with the dimes.

Some one says the man who is born to command is one made to order. It is not so in the case of a chief of police.

Go

To Underwood's if you want bargains in dry goods.

"What would you do, Mr. M., if your wife died?" asked Mrs. D. Mr. (who is very methodical)—"I would bury her."

"I aim to tell the truth." "Yes," interrupted an acquaintance, "and you are probably the worst shot in America."

The best thing about a rainbow is that it does not stay out after dark. It has not the absurd habits of the crank comet.

Money

Saved is money made, this you will do by buying your goods of Underwood.

Somebody says that "ballet girls are not so bad as they are painted." We hope not. They are painted frightfully.

The prophet who thinks everything will turn out according to his expectations should try turning out molasses from a cold jug.

As corpses are now frozen solid at the morgues in Paris, the gay Frenchman may be able to catch on to the American word "stiff."

Don't

Fail to price goods at Underwood's before buying, if you want to save money.

Catskin garments are the latest fashionable gewgaw. Everybody ought to be able to furnish his own, if his house has a French roof.

A Flatbush girl recently gave a quilting party, and all the girls contributed blocks captured by their respective bulldogs. They call it an "album quilt."

"Our young men are coming to the front," cries a political journal. It doesn't look that way at the theater. Just as many bald heads in the front rows as ever.

You

Will save money by buying your dry-goods, boots, shoes and hats at Underwood's.

He that is in trade is wise, all his goods to advertise; for that is the reason why half the people come and buy. Those who tread in wisdom's ways will sell most goods for holidays.

An observing person says: "Some men are like an umbrella with crook handle. They are always hanging around in out-of-the-way places, and are never to be found when they are wanted."

Nine-tenths of the unhappy marriages are the result of green human calves being allowed to run at large in the society pastures without any yokes on them. They marry and have children before they do mustaches; they are fathers of twins before they are proprietors of two pairs of pants, and the little girls they marry are old women before they are 20 years old. Occasionally one of these gosling marriages turns out all right, but it is a clear case of luck. If there was a law against young galoots sparking and marrying before they have all cut their teeth, we suppose the little cusses would evade it in some way, but there ought to be a sentiment against it. It is time enough for these bantams to think of finding a pallet when they have raised money enough to buy a bundle of laths to build a hen house. But they see a girl who looks cunning, and they are afraid there is not going to be girls enough to go around, and then they begin to get in their work real spry; and before they are aware of the sanctity of the marriage relation they are hitched for life, and before they own a cook-stove or a bedstead, they have to get up in the night and go after the doctor, so frightened that they run themselves out of breath and abuse the doctor because he doesn't run too, and when the doctor gets there there is not enough linen in the house to wrap a doll-baby.—Georgia Gazette.

Common Colds neglected, are the cause of one-half the deaths. Consumption lurks in ever cough, often using as masks, the rudy cheek, quickened pulse and sparkling eye, till it deeply plants its dreaded deadly seeds in the system. Every home should contain Ellert's Extract of Tar and Wild Cherry which prevents serious sickness if taken in time, and will surely cure colds, coughs, croup, catarrh, consumption and all Bronchial complaints. Don't wait for sickness to come, but this day take home a bottle of Ellert's Extract of Tar and Wild Cherry for it may save the life of a loved one, when delay would be death. Sold by Dansby.

A Mother's Responsibility.

"Mama," said a delicate little girl, "I have broken my china vase."

"Well, you are a naughty, careless, troublesome little thing, always in some mischief; go up stairs and wait till I send for you." And this was a mother's answer to a tearful little culprit who had struggled with and conquered the temptation to tell a falsehood to screen her fault. With a disappointed, disheartened look the sweet child obeyed; and that moment was crushed in her heart the sweet flower of truth, perhaps never again in after years to blossom into life. O, what were the loss of a thousand vases in comparison! 'Tis true "an angel might shrink from the responsibilities of a mother." It needs an angel's powers. The watch must not for an instant be relaxed; the scales of justice must always be nicely balanced; the hasty word that the overtaxed spirit sends to the lips must did there before it is uttered. The timid and sensitive child must have a word of encouragement in season; the forward and presuming, checked with gentle firmness; there must be no deception, no trickery, for the keen eye of childhood to detect, and above all, when the exhausted brain sinks with ceaseless vigils, perhaps, and the thousand petty interruptions and unlooked for annoyances of every hour almost set at defiance any attempt at system, still must that mother wear an unruffled brow, lest the smiling cherub on her knee catch the angry frown. Still must she rule her own spirit, lest the boy so engrossed with his toys repeat the next moment the impatient word his ear has caught. For all the duties faithfully performed a mother's reward is in secret and silence. Even he, on whose earthly breast she leans, is too often unmindful of the noiseless struggle till, too late alas! he learns to value the delicate hands that kept in unceasing flow the thousands of springs of his domestic happiness.

PHILLIP ALTBAYER'S

PRICE CURRENT.

Opera Block, TERRELL, TEX.

Largest and Cheapest CASH Grocery in the City.

☞ WEIGHT AND MEASURE GUARANTEED.

SUGAR.

Powdered,	8 lbs	for $1.00
Granulated,	9	" "
Standard A,	9	" "
Light brown,	10	" "
Brown,	11	" "

COFFEE.

Best (Little Green)	8 lbs.	for $1.00
Prime.	10	" "

CANNED GOODS—FULL LINE.

Pickles, 50 cents a gallon.
Chow Chow, 50 cents.
Mackerel. White Fish.
Maple Syrup, $1.25 a gallon.

SPICES, GROUND OR WHOLE.

Mace, per pound, $1.00.
Pepper, 25 cents; Alspice, 25; Marajam, 25; Thyme, Savory, 25; Laurel, 25; Celery, 25; Ginger, 20; Sage, 20; Cinamon, 35; Mustard, 35; Cloves, 50; Gelatin; 15; Poppy, 15 cents.

CROCKERY AND GLASSWARE.

Cups and Saucers, Dishes, Plates, Bakers, Spoon-holders, Sugar Bowls, Butter Bowls, Cream Pitchers, Ewers and Basin, Lamps, Lanterns, Looking-Glasses. Lamp chimneys, 5 cts. Raisins, 15 cents a pound; Currants, 8 cents; Fruit Butter and Mince Meat, 10 cents; Citron, 25 cents; Lemon Peel, 25 cents; Grand Duke Cigars, 5 cents; Parched Coffee, 15 cents per pound; Grits and Hominy, 4 cents.

TEA.

Oolong, 25 cents a pound; Young Hyson, 25 cts.; Imperial, 50 cents; Gunpowder, 50 cents.

BEANS AND PEAS.

Butter Beans, 14 lbs. for one dollar. Navy Beans, 16 pounds, English Peas, 16 pounds; Split Peas, 16 lbs.

RICE.

Best Louisiana, 12 pounds for $1.00.

In the charge to the Washington grand jury Judge Wylie took occasion to remark that newspaper libels were an offense creating more misery and working more injustice than any other form of crime. He rather suspected writers for periodicals had more than the usual proportion of liars among them. They were paid for lying and laughed at the idea of injustice in so doing. He believes, however, that there is some hope of improvement.

Edmund C. Steadman, Richard Grant White, John Burrough and other literary men living in New York, have organized an "Authors' Club" in that city. No intention exists to make it the champion of American copyright. Neither is it a literary club. It is merely designed to bring together, at intervals and in a simple and economical manner, men connected with literature in its various branches.

Remember This.

If you are sick Hop Bitters will surely aid Nature in making you well when all else fails.

If you are costive or dyspeptic, or are suffering from any other of the numerous diseases of the stomach or bowels, it is your own fault if you remain ill for Hop Bitters are a sovereign remedy in all such complaints.

If you are wasting away with any form of Kidney disease, stop tempting Death this moment, and turn for a cure to Hop Bitters.

If you are sick with that ferrible sickness Nervousness, you will find a "Balm in Gilead" in the use of Hop Bitters.

If you are a frequenter, or a resident of a miasmatic district, barricade your system against the scourge of all countries—malarial, epidemic, bilious, and intermitten fevers—by the use of Hop Bitters.

If you have rough, pimply, or sallow skin, bad breath, pains and aches, and feel miserable generally, Hop Bitters will give you fair skin, rich blood, and sweetest breath, health, and comfort.

In short they cure all Diseases of the stomach, Bowels, Blood, Liver, Nerves, Kidneys, Bright's Diseases. $500 will be paid for a case they will not cure or help.

That poor, bedridden, invalid wife, sister, mother or daughter, can be made the picture of health, by a few bottles of Hop Bitters, costing but a trifle. Will you let them suffer?

HOSTETTER'S

CELEBRATED

STOMACH

BITTERS

... remedies are rapidly giving ground before the advance of this conquering specific, and old fashioned ... in regard to depletion as a means of cure, have been quite exploded by the success of the great renovant which tones the system, tranquilizes the nerves, neutralizes malaria, depurates and enriches the blood, rouses the liver when dormant, and promotes a regular habit of body. For sale by all Druggists and Dealers generally.

THE BEST REMEDY

FOR

Diseases of the Throat and Lungs.

AYER'S

CHERRY

PECTORAL.

In diseases of the pulmonary organs a safe and reliable remedy is invaluable. AYER'S CHERRY PECTORAL is such a remedy, and no other so eminently merits the confidence of the public. It is a scientific combination of the medicinal principles and curative virtues of the finest drugs, chemically united, of such power as to insure the greatest possible efficiency and uniformity of results. It strikes at the foundation of all pulmonary diseases, affording prompt relief and rapid cures, and is adapted to patients of any age or either sex. Being very palatable, the youngest children take it readily. In ordinary **Coughs, Colds, Sore Throat, Bronchitis, Influenza, Clergyman's Sore Throat, Asthma, Croup, and Catarrh**, the effects of AYER'S CHERRY PECTORAL are magical, and multitudes are annually preserved from serious illness by its timely and faithful use. It should be kept at hand in every household for the protection it affords in sudden attacks. In **Whooping-cough and Consumption** there is no other remedy so efficacious, soothing, and helpful.

Low prices are inducements to try some of the many mixtures, or syrups, made of cheap and ineffective ingredients, now offered, which, as they contain no curative qualities, can afford only temporary relief, and are sure to deceive and disappoint the patient. Diseases of the throat and lungs demand active and effective treatment; and it is dangerous experimenting with unknown and cheap medicines, from the great liability that these diseases may, while so trifled with, become deeply seated or incurable. Use AYER'S CHERRY PECTORAL, and you may confidently expect the best results. It is a standard medical preparation, of known and acknowledged curative power, and is as cheap as its careful preparation and fine ingredients will allow. Eminent physicians, knowing its composition, prescribe it in their practice. The test of half a century has proven its absolute certainty to cure all pulmonary complaints not already beyond the reach of human aid.

Prepared by Dr. J. C. Ayer & Co.,

Practical and Analytical Chemists,

Lowell, Mass.

SOLD BY ALL DRUGGISTS EVERYWHERE.

KIDNEY-WORT

IS A SURE CURE

for all diseases of the Kidneys and

LIVER

It has specific action on this most important organ, enabling it to throw off torpidity and inaction, stimulating the healthy secretion of the Bile, and by keeping the bowels in free condition, effecting its regular discharge.

Malaria. If you are suffering from malaria, have the chills, are bilious, dyspeptic, or constipated, Kidney-Wort will surely relieve and quickly cure.

In the Spring to cleanse the System, every one should take a thorough course of it.

SOLD BY DRUGGISTS. Price $1.

KIDNEY-WORT

W. W WEST,

—DEALER IN—

SADDLES, HARNESS,

And everything pertaining to the Saddle and Harness line, and offers to sell as cheap as any house in northern Texas. Call and examine his stock for yourself, and you will not buy anywhere else. Moore ave., TERRELL.

☞ Agent for the New Home Sewing Machine—the best in the market.

Houston & Texas Central Ry

AND CONNECTIONS.

The only line running through the Central and best portions of the State of Texas.

Passenger Express Trains

—AND—

Daily Fast Freight Lines

Over the Entire Road.

PULLMAN'S PALACE SLEEPING Cars each way, daily without change, between **Galveston and San Antonio**, via Houston and Austin, and between Sedalia and St. Louis.

The Shortest Line Between Texas and Kansas City, Hannibal.

And all points North and West, and its position and connections render it especially desirable for reliable and comfortable travel between Texas and all points in the United States and Canada. Favorable routes, via Denison and Missouri Pacific Railway to Kansas City, Hannibal or St. Louis, or via the

Texas & N. O. All-Rail Through Line Via Houston and New Orleans. For the last named route, the DAY express trains of the Houston & Texas Central Railway make Direct Connections in Houston for New Orleans and all points in the Southeast, Northeast and East.

EUROPE!

Through tickets from or to any point in Great Britain or Continent of Europe, via the Houston & Texas Central Railway and all rail to New York, thence via

NORTH GERMAN LLOYD,
WHITE STAR, INMAN,
MISSISSIPPI & DOMINION,

Rotterdam and Italian Steamship Lines on sale at all important stations on line of this Railway, and at Galveston, Cuero, Victoria, San Antonio, Marion, Seguin, Weimar, LaGrange, Columbus, Flatonia, Shulenberg, New Braunfel, San Marcus, Round Rock, Rockdale.

Special inducements to people desiring to settle in the state.

A. FAULKER,
Texas Passenger Agent.

For information as to rates of passage & freight, routes etc., apply to or address,

E. D. TRUE, A. G. F. A.
G. B. GRAY, A. G. P. A.
J. WALDO, Traffic Manager,
Houston, Texas.

Marks and Brands.

FRANK HOUSTON.

Post Office, TERRELL, TEXAS.

F H on hip—underslope each ear. O on hip—crop in right, 2 underbits in left IRA on side, A D on hip—mark unknown.

Bow and Arrow on hip—underhalf crop in each ear. NU on hip F H on side—underslope in each ear. M on side—crop, split and overbit in right.

HOUSTON & HARDIN.

Road brand

MOORE & NICHOLS.

TOP—Crop off right, swallowfork and underbit in left.

SID WILLIAMS.

JOHN G. MOORE.

J. M—Swallowfork in right, swallowfork and underbit in left.

COG WHEEL—Underbit in right crop and two splits in left.

GRAY & HARDIN.

P. J. NORWOOD.

Hewitt Ranch, 8 miles south of Kaufman, L7 on side; underslope each ear.

MATTHEW CARTWRIGHT.

Post Office: TERRELL, TEXAS.

Ranches 5 miles east and 5 miles west of Kaufman. W. T. Gartwright, Manager, P. O. Kaufman, Texas. Owns all cattle in following brands and marks:

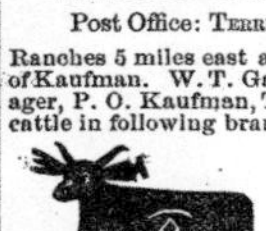

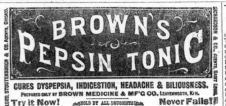

Same brand on horses on left shoulder. MAT on right side—various marks. Horses.

W. B. KERBY
Terrell, Texas.
XL on side or hip—mark crop left, underslope in right ear.
Horse brand, WK

The Cotton Market

Is now steady at settled prices If you desire to obtain the best in the State, ship your Cotton to

Wm. D. Cleveland,

the well known Cotton Factor and Wholesale Grocer, at Houston. Large receipts, extensive transactions, admirable system, prompt and correct returns; these features of his business enable him to guarantee satisfaction to all Shippers, and have made his business what it is. Send for his daily or weekly Cotton Reports.

Wagon Yard.

—WITH—

Grocery Feed & Store Attached

Comfort for men and teams at low rates. Remember the old stand formerly kept by J. J. Canada, now under control of

J. B. MADDING.

C. B. & J. J. CARTER

DEALERS IN

Rough & Dressed

LUMBER,

Doors, Sash, Blinds, Shingles

And a lot of FIRE BRICK, FIRE SAND and CEMENT.

Corner Broad and Francis Streets,

TERRELL, TEXAS.

SMITH & M'CLUNG

DEALERS IN

STOVES,

HARDWARE,

TIN WARE, &C.

Wallace corner, Moore Aye, TERRELL. Job work done promptly at low prices.

INGRAM & JACKSON,

DEALERS IN

MEAL, FLOUR,

And all kinds of

MILL-FEED STUFF.

We are thankful for the very liberal patronage that has heretofore been given us, and promise to do all in our power to merit a continuation of the same.

Central

MEAT MARKET

GRAY & HARDIN, PROPRIETORS.

The best meats the country affords will be kept, and our customers can rely on as low prices as possible. We are thankful for past liberal patronage and hope to merit a continuation of the same.

TEXAS AND PACIFIC

Railway Company.

An adjourned meeting of the stockholders and Board of Directors of the Texas & Pacific Railway Company, will be held at the office of the Company in the city of Marshall, Harrison County, Texas, on Tuesday, December 5th, 1882, at the hours of 12 and 1 o'clock, respectively.

C. E. SATTERLEE,
Secretary.

G. W. GRAY. J. D. GRAY.

G. W. Gray & Co.,

DRUGGISTS.

Moore Avenue,

TERRELL, - - - TEXAS.

Keep a large, fresh stock of Drugs and Druggists' Sundries. They also have the largest stock of Wall Paper in the city. Call and see them.

LEWIS DINELLY,

Watch-Maker

—AND—

SILVER-SMITH,

Houghton Block, Terrell, Texas.

Has the largest assortment of the finest Solid Gold Jewelry, Watches and Clocks in the city.

ADAM GRANT,

DEALER IN

FURNITURE,

Wood and Metalic Burial Cases and Caskets.

HARRIS BLOCK, TERRELL, TEXAS.

G. W. Sage, Manager & Funeral Director.

County Seat Merchants:

WATKINS & NORWOOD,

DEALERS IN

DRY GOODS,

Clothing, Hats, Boots and Shoes.

A large stock constantly on hand and fresh installments arriving daily. Highest ruling prices paid for cotton.

Bond & Carswell,

DEALERS IN

Fancy Dry Goods,

CLOTHING,

GENTS' FURNISHING GOODS,

Millinery Goods,

BOOTS, SHOES, HATS AND CAPS

Childress Block, TERRELL, TEX.

J. W. BRICE & CO.,

Grocers,

HARRIS BLOCK,

TERRELL, - - TEXAS.

A large, fresh stock on hand. The public is respectfully invited to call and get their supplies.

SELLING OUT.

Pat Layne is offering his farm for sale, which is three miles north of the city. Also the following property: One span of splendid mules, wagon and harness. A number one horse and single horse wagon. Horse gentle and suitable for family use. Five cows and calves, besides numerous other household goods and furniture at a bargain. Call on or address P. H. Layne.

RESIDENCE FOR SALE.

A comfortable residence on Rockwall Avenue for sale. Has attached good barn and out-houses; a fine well of water; four acres of land, two of which are in orchard bearing peaches, apples, pears and berries. Apply to

A. J. CHILDRESS.

GRAHAM & PHILLIPS,

—DEALERS IN—

FARM IMPLEMENTS,

Farm and Mill Machinery.

☞ STATE AGENTS FOR THE

Monumental Bronze Company,

—OF—

Bridgeport, Conn.

Office and Salesroom:

Corner Francis Street and Moore Avenue,

Terrell, - Texas.

Reliable Travelling Agents wanted.

LORD, STOUTENBURGH & CO. AGENTS, CHICAGO.

BROWN'S PEPSIN TONIC

CURES DYSPEPSIA, INDIGESTION, HEADACHE & BILIOUSNESS.

PREPARED ONLY BY BROWN MEDICINE & MF'G CO. LEAVENWORTH, KAN.

Try it Now! SOLD BY ALL DRUGGISTS **Never Fails!**

RICHARDSON & CO., AGENTS, SAINT LOUIS, MO.

C. L. JONES & SONS,

DEALERS IN

Dry Goods, Clothing

Hats, Boots and Shoes,

HARDWARE, QUEENSWARE, CUTLERY.

We carry a full stock of General Merchandise, in which is represented the latest and most desirable styles. Sole agents for Zeigler Bros. Hand made Boots and Shoes, the best in the market.

The condition as above indicated, exists in almost every family. With some the troubles are of recent standing, while many have become chronic and difficult to overcome. Old and young females are constant victims. Dr. Dromgoole's English Female Bitters makes positive and unmistakable cures of all lingering female weaknesses, excesses, irregularities and periodical obstructions; imparts strength and vigor to the feeble and emaciated; builds up and re-animates flagging, broken-down and worn-out constitutions; repairs damages inflicted by years of painful suffering; regulates, comforts and consoles the troubled maiden, and is a fast friend to mothers all along the troubled pathway of their married lives.

It cures ovarian diseases, uterine displacements and ulcerations, hysterics, leucorrhœa, chlorosis, weakness of the kidneys and back, revives the drooping, despondent and melancholy, calms the excitable and nervous. It is a never-failing iron tonic female regulator. $1.00. Sold every-where. Family Medical Adviser mailed *free* to any address. J. P. DROMGOOLE & Co., Proprietors, Louisville, Ky.

At the bedside, the physician's first question is, "How are your bowels?" proving that they must in all cases be properly attended to at once, by the use of some medicine that will cleanse the stomach, excite the liver, cause a free flow of bile and carry off these disease-making secretions. Pills, oils and other strong medicines, produce pain, griping, sick stomach, and often cause the loss of time.

Bailey's Saline Aperient is relieved of all these unpleasant effects; it acts mildly upon the bowels, causes a free flow of bile, relieves constipation, biliousness, sick headache, acid stomach, heartburn, colic, indigestion, etc.

It is a white powder, and is as cooling and pleasant as a glass of soda water. Large Bottles 50 cents.

G. & J. CARIKER'S

Grocery AND Supply House,

UNDER THE MANAGEMENT OF

J. B. WHITFIELD,

Childress Block, Terrell, Texas.

A full stock of groceries constantly in store and fresh goods arriving daily.

B. M. CHILDRESS & BRO'S,

BANKERS.

Francis Street and Moore Avenue, TERRELL, TEXAS.

Buy and sell Domestic and Foreign Exchange; make loans on approved collateral, and collect on all accessible points. As

MERCHANTS

WE ARE GENERAL DEALERS IN

FURNITURE, SADDLERY & SADDLERY HARDWARE,

Of which we carry large and complete stocks, and sell as low as the lowest for CASH.

FOR CASH ONLY.

The undersigned has opened a splendidly selected stock of

DRY GOODS,

Clothing, Boots, Shoes and Hats,

Queensware, Glassware, Cutlery,

Wood and Willow Ware,

In Houghton Block, Terrell, Texas, and respectfully solicits the trade of all who wish to buy goods cheap for cash.

A. J. UNDERWOOD.

Terrell Academy,

TERRELL, TEXAS.

School building in the grove a short distance west of the Methodist Church. The fall term of the seventh annual session, of this institution, will commence on MONDAY, SEPTEMBER 4th, 1882. And will continue four scholastic months. The principal takes this occasion to return his thanks to the friends who have shown an interest in the success of the school; and to assure all that no efforts will be spared to make the Academy equal to the best schools in the country. We educate the moral in connection with the intellectual mind, but studiously avoid sectarianism of every name and order. As regards our discipline, we govern rigidly—unswervingly; but none other than just powers will be exercised, since it is with the consent of the governed that we rule.

The Public Free School will commence with the opening of the session, and will continue until the public fund for this school is exhausted.

Pupils within the scholastic age (8 to 14 years) enrolled in this school, pursuing the studies embraced in the Free School Law will receive free tuition during free school term, those above or below that age will be charged the regular rate for tuition.

None but competent assistants employed. For terms and other particulars apply to

J. T. BURNETT, Principal.

SECOND YEAR.

Glendale Institute.

TERRELL, TEXAS.

H. Y. BLACK, PRINCIPAL.

This School for Young Men and Boys began its second session Sept. 4, 1882. Rates of tuition from $2 to $4 per month. In addition to the usual studies a thorough Commercial course will be given those who desire it.

Terrell

Female Institute,

TERRELL, TEXAS.

None but the best teachers employed. Course of instruction thorough and practical. For circulars and particulars call on or address,

JOHN VESEY, B. P., Principal.

BROWN'S

Lone Star Seeder.

DREW & BROWN, PATENTEES,

TERRELL, TEXAS.

This Seed Attachment runs on one wheel in the furrow behind, and between the molboard and landside of the plow, and the seed are sown broadcast in the bottom of the furrow. The feed is so arranged that it can be attached to all kinds of turning plows. It sows wheat, oats, barley, grass seed, and drops corn in the drill or in checks. The Seeder is made of the best of iron, and so arranged as not to be an impediment to the running of the plow. The advantages of the machine are: Every seed falls on damp ground and will come up, if it is good. It sows perfectly even and a uniform depth. The wind does not effect its work. It saves enough seed in forty acres to pay for itself. The birds get no wheat; it saves the trouble and the time of sowing by hand, and when you are done plowing you are done sowing and can harrow or roll the land at leisure. Price $10 to $15. Call and see sample machine, and leave orders with Drew & Brown for one.

Fall and Winter '82.

Go to the CASH HOUSE of

I. G. LAWRENCE & CO.,

—FOR—

DRY GOODS

CLOTHING,

HATS, BOOTS SHOES

NOTIONS, ETC.

Find them in the Phoenix Block, Moore Avenue, TERRELL, TEXAS.

No better place in North Texas to get anything you want, and at bottom prices.

W. H. COKER'S

Livery, Feed,

—AND—

Sale Stable,

Corner Broad and Francis Streets,

TERRELL, TEXAS.

Fine horses and carriages always on hand at reasonable rates.

C C. WILSON & CO.,

DEALERS IN

GRAIN AND FEED.

In warehouse west of the depot,

TERRELL, TEXAS.

They buy all kinds of grain, and pay the highest market price. Also weigh cotton and are agents for the Pacific Express company.

SAUL STERN,

WHO BECAME AN EXPERT FORGER TO SATISFY HIS MISTRESS' DEMANDS; NEW YORK CITY.

MRS. CARRIE FROST,

WHO SHOOK HER SANCTIMONIOUS HUBBY AND ELOPED WITH MAJOR POWELL; BROOKLYN, N. Y.

WILLIAM J. POWELL,

DEMOCRATIC POLITICIAN WHO ELOPED WITH THE WIFE OF HIS PIOUS FRIEND FROST.

Dodge City's Sensation.

The Luke Short affair in Dodge city, Kansas, has created much excitement in that section of the country. The main factor in the affair was Luke Short, a Texan, well known as one of the most fearless men in the Lone Star State. He fought a duel some years ago at Tombstone, Arizona, with one Storms, the fighter of the "Slopers," who had been imported to kill him. Storms himself, however, was killed in the duel, and Short became the "cock of the walk." His recent trouble in Dodge city grew out of a shooting scrape, in which no one was hurt. He gave bonds in $2,000 for his appearance and was released, but was rearrested on the following day and ordered by an armed mob to leave the city. Attorneys who came to defend him were prohibited by the authorities from stepping off the train.

Thus matters were looking very blue for our friend, when a number of his friends from different sections—chiefly sheriffs and marshals—came to Dodge city to dictate the terms of a treaty on the basis of Luke Short's return to his place of business in Dodge city without danger of future molestation. After some trouble the "peace commissioners," as they have been termed, accomplished the object of their mission, and quiet once more reigns where for several weeks war and rumors of war were the all absorbing topic.

All the members of the commission, whose portraits we publish in a group, are frontiersmen of tried capacity. The following is a brief but eloquent sketch of each of them, reported as sent to us by Harry E. Gryden, the able Dodge city reporter of the Associated Press, and an occasional correspondent of the POLICE GAZETTE:

"Bat Masterson, of whom so much has been written, arrived from the West prepared for any emergency and with a shotgun under his arm, on the next train after Short had returned. His record of having killed 26 men and being 27 years of age, is rather exaggerated. He has been sheriff of Ford county, in which Dodge city is situated, and has occupied positions as marshal of a number of rough border towns. All his killings were done in the discharge of his official duties, and he has never even been tried for an offence.

"Wyatt Earp, of California, is the celebrity who about two years ago went on the warpath at Tombstone, Arizona, against a mob of desperadoes who had assassinated his brother, Morgan Earp. In the terrible encounter which ensued he killed not less than eight of the assassins. Wyatt has been Marshal of Dodge city, Kan., and Tombstone, Ariz., and other frontier towns.

"M. F. McLean has an Arizona and Rio Grande record for wiping out Mexican ruffians, and came from Lower California to see that his friend Luke Short could 'stay in town' to attend to his business. He is cool and clear-headed. The great ability which he displayed in managing a fight has obtained for him the sobriquet of 'The General.'

"Charles Bassett was the first sheriff of Ford county, with his headquarters at Dodge city, being twice elected to that office, and succeeded by Bat Masterson. In those days men appeared always well armed, but he astonished the natives by taking post at the court house door, when the district court was in session, and disarming all persons desiring to enter. Of the small party that attended court he gathered no less than forty-two six-shooters and only killed one man (*sic*). He is now engaged in business in Kansas city, but came to Dodge to see if his friend Luke Short could take his regular meals without being molested.

"Neal Brown was formerly a marshal of Dodge city, and is a wonderful snap shot with both hands at once, with a cool and determined head in a fight. He came from his cattle ranch, forty miles south of here, to look out for Luke Short's interests.

"W. H. Harris is Short's business partner, and acted as manager of the commission.

"W. F. Petillon was secretary of the peace commission, and as such was instrumental in restoring law and order to Dodge city.

"Since their object in view was accomplished, all, with the exception of the two principals, Harris and Short, have left, and peace hovers like a white winged dove over the late turbulent city.

THE DODGE CITY "PEACE COMMISSION."

A GROUP OF PROMINENT FRONTIERSMEN WHO RESTORED QUIET IN A TROUBLED COMMUNITY.

No. 1 LUKE SHORT. No. 2—BAT MASTERSON. No. 3.—WYATT EARP. No. 4.—M. F. MCLEAN. No. 5.—CHARLES BASSETT. No. 6.—NEAL BROWN. No. 7.—W. H. HARRIS. No. 8.—W. F. PETILLON.

Saved from Death.

A thrilling spectacle was witnessed by a large number of persons on Monday, July 2, in the neighborhood of No. 121 West Eleventh street. Miss Susie Staver, who resides at the above locality with her mother and sister, while suffering under a spell of mental derangement, made her way to the roof of the house, and was about to throw herself over the parapet, when she was discovered by her mother and sister. The women had just time to grab the would-be suicide by the arms and hold on to her until their screams attracted the attention of neighbors, who succeeded in rescuing the girl from her perilous position.

SAVED FROM DEATH.

THE TERRIBLE STRUGGLE OF A MOTHER AND DAUGHTER WITH A MANIAC GIRL ON THE ROOF OF A FLAT HOUSE; NEW YORK CITY.

MURDER AND SUICIDE.

THE TRAGIC DEATH OF MISS FANNY SEAMAN AT THE HANDS OF HER BROTHER, AND SUICIDE OF THE MURDERER, AT THROGG'S NECK, N. Y.

THE DAILY FAIR NEWS

GRATIS. AUSTIN, TEXAS, THURSDAY, OCTOBER 18, 1883. VOL. VII.—NO. 34.

Capital State Fair.

THIRD DAY.

The Attendance Yesterday.

The Deer Chase and Races Yesterday.

The Outlook for To-Day.

And Generally All About the Fair.

Although the sun yesterday morning was rather backward in putting in a cheerful appearance, he amply recompensed us by shining out brightly and steadily when he did show up, and the day was one of the finest in all the calendar.

The roads leading to the Fair grounds were as smooth and solid as the best shell road. Over one thousand people put in an appearance on the grounds, and the exhibits, now fully placed in the most attractive manner, were reviewed with pleasurable interest by all. The stock pens were visited, and among the leading features were the Angora goats, owned by Mr. Moore, and a flock of fifty thoroughbred Merino sheep, owned by Mr. I. D. Kevan, of Taylor, Williamson county. In this flock twenty-five thoroughbred Merino rams, twenty thoroughbred ewes and four graded Merinos. This, we believe, is the largest exhibit of fine sheep owned by one person, ever exhibited at our Fair. The display of Messrs. Copes & Bass, successors to C. W. White, consisting of stoves, iron mantels, granite iron ware, etc., was highly creditable to the firm, and their exhibits being placed midway between the photographs and paintings, blended the useful and ornamental harmoniously.

Entering exhibition hall from the south, the first exhibit on the right, or eastern side of the house, is a very large case of fine needle and machine work in a hundred different varieties. Some of the embroidered imitations of peacock and other feathers on silk, linen, satin and worsted, interspersed with fine lace work, forms a large and handsome display. Right opposite is the elegant display of the Parlor shoe store of Messrs. Lewis & Peacock, which, being tastefully arranged in show cases, was much admired.

Right next to it is the display of Newman & Co., and here we paused to inspect the most elegant display ever made by a dry goods establishment at our Fair. It is arranged in a large case got up especially for the occasion with ends and sides paneled with large windows; the case is about eighteen feet in length by seven feet in breadth and about six

Concluded on fourth page.

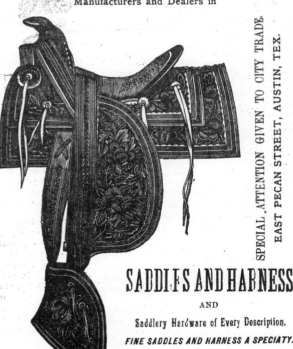

PROGRAMME

CAPITAL STATE FAIR

THIRD DAY—THURSDAY, OCT. 18.

IN THE ARENA:

12 M.—DIVISION B, HORSES—CLASSES 3, 4 and 6.

CLASS 3, CARRIAGE AND BUGGY HORSES.—Size, style, value and docility to be considered. Spans must be evenly matched in size, form and motion, and be owned and driven as a team. Color waived.
Best span of horses, $15; second best, certificate.
Best single horse, $10; second best, certificate.

CLASS 4, ROADSTERS.—This class includes horses too light for all work, and carriage horses not fully matched, but capable of speed and endurance to light loads on the road. Professional totters not eligible.
Best span of horses (set of harness), $15; second best, certificate.
Best single horse, $10; second best, certificate.

CLASS 6, SADDLE HORSES.—
Best saddle horse (fine cloak), $15; second best, certificate.
Best walking horse (boots), $10; second best, certificate.

STEER ROPING TAKES PLACE AT 12 M.

THE  RACES

FIRST RACE—SAN JACINTO DERBY—Three-year-old stake for colts and fillies, one mile heats. Entrance, $25; half forfeit. Association to add $150. First, $125; second $25.

SECOND RACE—TROTTING.—Mile heats to wagon, for horses owned in Travis county for a period not less than sixty days next preceding the date of race. No horse eligible unless used exclusively for road purposes. Owners to drive. Purse, $100. First, $75; second $25.

THIRD RACE—RUNNING.—One and a half mile dash, free for all. Purse, $150. First, $125; second, $25.

Entries for to-day's races are as follows: Running, mile and a half dash—Jim Brown's Glengower, Drok's Keystone Henderson, and Wataugа.

Trotting—Fred Turner, Burton; Bud Driskill, Kansas; Weed & French, Billy.

There are two ways of plugging a watermelon. One is to cut a piece out and the other is to put the melon into a high hat.

"Go in swimmin'!" exclaimed little Johnny Burlay. "Not much. The last time I went in father gave me a woodshed bath after I got home."

The Duke and the Dude.—The following story is told of an English nobleman, recently deceased: "The duke was once in church when a collection was announced for some charitable object. The plate began to go around, and the duke carefully put his hand into his pocket and took out a florin, which he laid on the pew before him, ready to be transferred to the plate. Beside him sad a little snob, who, noticing this action, imitated it by ostentatiously laying a sovereign alongside the ducal florin. This was too much for his grace, who dipped his hand into his pocket again and pulled out another florin. The little snob followed suit by laying another sovereign beside the first. His grace quietly added a third florin, which was capped by a third sovereign on the part of the little snob. Out came a fourth florin to swell the duke's donation, and then the little snob triumphantly laid three sovereigns at once upon the board. The duke, not to be beaten, produced three florins. Just at this moment the plate came around. The little snob took up his handful of sovereigns, ostentatiously rattled them into the plate and then turned defiantly toward his rival as if he would say, "I think that takes the shine out of you." Fancy his chagrin when the duke, with a grim smile, put one florin into the plate and quietly swept the remaining six back into his pocket."

The Man Who Leaves the Door Open.—While the Man Who Takes Your Umbrella has all seasons for his own, and the Man Who Has a Little Story to Tell fails not in seed-time nor in harvest, there is one particular fiend who becomes particularly numerous at about the time when there is a coolness in the morning breeze and no steam in the radiator. We refer to the Man Who Leaves the Door Open. He comes to the office on various ostensible errands, in fact on about every known pretext—excepting to settle a bill—but always his actual purpose is to go way leaving wide open the portal through which the autumnal zephyrs come cavorting with glacial coolness, and bearing in their chase embrace full many a token of the pervasive dust from which we spring and to which we shall return. It does no good to bawl at him to shut the door. Oh, no. He is meandering down the sunny street, watching the white-winged clouds playing tag in the deep-smiling heavens. But as we lay down the pen, and push back the chair, and walk to the door and close it softly and pensively, and then stoop to gather up the scattered papers that have whirled about our feet like fading forest leaves, the blessed Serosch whispers promises of a good time coming, and we are consoled with confidence that in that bright dawning era our autumn days will be free from carking care, for the Man Who Leaves the Door Open must go.

A Rich Man's Privileges.—One would think that with the advantages and opportunities offered to rich men in this country they would prefer it to any other country. But there is a great drawback on the value of this wealth, that the tenure is not secure. At present the rich man can buy legislatures, appoint judges, control politics, occupy the streets, grab the public lands, plant his telegraph pole on your sidewalk, run his trains in front of your third-story window, kill a passenger every day in his official capacity, and damn the public in the personal confidence of an interview. All this is very nice while it lasts, but it will not last. Even now it looks as if the money power was menaced, and as if the time was coming when the rich would have only their money to distinguish them from other people.—[New York World.

Young Man, Brace Up.—A lazy man is too contemptible to live, and has no rights his fellow-men are bound to respect. Young man, you may as well understand, first as last, that you have got to work for all you get in this world. You may not always get what you earn, as there are men in this world too mean and contemptible to give to others what really belongs to them, but if you would keep out of the poor house, and have a competency in your old age, you will have to work for it. To be sure there is a great difference in men. Some are endowed with greater intellectual powers than others, while some are greater physically. Some men are born low down in the scale of intellectualism, but mark you the physical of such a man. There is a way provided, however, for every man to better himself. You won't find it in the gin mill, neither is it to be found at the gambling table. Remember one thing, and that is, you have not the capacity to take into yourself all the strong drink made in this world, and you had better let the contract out before you attempt to work on it. Don't bet all you have on a bob-tail flush, or before you know that the other man will raise you out of the game or come in on a straight flush. Nine hundred and ninety-nine young men out of a thousand, who started with an idea of becoming suddenly rich by betting on a sure thing, get left, and are worse off than when they came into the game. The bay horse is more liable to get beat if you hold a pool check on him than he was before you put up your money. Such certainties are uncertainties, and never give up a certainty for an uncertainty. Don't fool with the tiger; you can't most always tell which way the beast will jump.

When a young man sits down in idleness, with an idea that the world owes him a living, it's high time his body was committed to the dust from whence it came. 'As for his soul, nothing will ever be known of it. It is so small that it would rattle around in the shell of a mustard seed, and when it leaves his lazy carcass, is forever lost on account of its infinite proportions.

A record of the young men who have been unfortunate enough to have a fortune left them, shows that eight in ten never amount to a single atom in the world, and seven out of the eight die bankrupts, financially, morally and otherwise.

When a father brings up his son in idleness, never teaching him the first principle of economy or the value of a dollar, he commits a terrible blunder. The father guilty of such a crime generally has to saw wood for a living in his old age. Nine out of ten of the boys with fathers who bring them up in idle luxury, ere they reach the meridian of life, are total wrecks. Wrecked on the rocks of total depravity which lie beneath the stream of life, and on whose sharp and ragged edges thousands of lives have been wrecked and ruined. Money bags may, like bladders, keep you above the waters of distress for a time, but puncture them, let their contents escape, and you sink.

Young man, you have undoubtedly meant to do well. No young man ever goes astray intentionally, but in some idle thoughtless moment he graduates from soda water and lemonade to something stronger, and before he is fairly aware of it, he has not only lost caste, but has a whole menagerie on his hands and is employing to a doctor to help dispose of his immense elephants and the snakes that laughingly cuddle in his boots. Yes, the world presents too many temptations for the minds of all to withstand, and the only safe way is for a young man to keep away from the temptations. If you see a man at a wheel of fortune win ten times running by betting on the red, you just keep your hands out of your pocket and see him lose all he made the next turn of the wheel and on the very color or number you knew would win.

Boys, the recklessness of youth is what has caused so many mothers' hair to turn as white as the driven snow. It's this that has caused so many fathers and mothers to give up by the way side and be laid in premature graves. The follies of our youth hang heavier upon the hearts of our fathers and mothers than the millstone that grinds the kernel into the finest flour. It is a pity that some of our young men of to-day didn't fall in between the millstones before they have caused the trouble they have.

Are Trichnae Killed By Salt?—The prohibition of the importation of American pork by the German government, on account of the alleged presence of the microscopic worm known as trichnæ, has awakened a large degree of interest among pork raisers and shippers in this country. That trichnæ are sometimes found in pork (and in some other food flesh) is not to be doubted. That proper cooking of meats for food destroys them is unquestionable. That all authenticated cases of injury to health arising from the presence of this microscopic worm, were traced to the eating of uncooked or half-raw meat is a fact. But that the salting of meat destroyed the parasite is still a matter of doubt, or, at least, it is a subject of dispute.

On this point, United States Consul John Wilson, stationed at Brussels, makes some statements, based on his own observations. He says:

"I have myself been present when officially appointed microscopists at some of the abattoirs of this country have been engaged in examining American pork for trichnæ, and have been invited by these gentlemen to see for myself, through their microscopes, the peculiar cell and spiral coil of the animal; but on carefully examining them, I have only observed, blended with the tissue and minute salt crystals, the entombed animal, evidently as destitute of life as the structure in which it was embedded.

"It is claimed by most trichinic observers that the process of generation and birth of this little animal invariably takes place in the stomach and intestinal canal, and that within a few days from its birth it has so matured as to penetrate the walls of the intestines and rapidly make its way through the various intervening structures to the remote muscular tissue of the animal it infects, there to be speedily encysted and endowed with a subsequent dormant existence of several years, during which time its presence occasions little or no inconvenience. Of this theory of the life and movements of this little worm, I can only say that it involves an almost unparalleled exception to the law generally regarded as determining animal life, and ought not to be accepted but upon the most positive proof. The law governing parasitic existence in living tissue usually involves the speedy death of the parisite after the pabulum upon which it feeds has passed from under the domain of force; hence, unless this tiny worm constitutes an exception to this law, its life be must short after the organic structure upon which it feeds has ceased to live."

Consul Wilson very pertinently adds that "if salt really kills trichnae, and of it I have scarcely a doubt, it is evidently an injustice on the part of foreign governments to lay an embargo on our pork product, which, of all others, in order to secure it against decomposition on a long journey to foreign markets, is better salted than that of any other country."

1. The Concert Hall, Spanish Fort. 2. The Louisiana Jockey Club. 3. Entrance to Chalmette. 4. Southern Yacht Club, West End. 5. Race Course.

LOUISIANIA.—SKETCHES IN AND ABOUT NEW ORLEANS.—BY A STAFF ARTIST.

PICTURESQUE POINTS AROUND THE CRESCENT CITY.

THE "Spanish Fort," on Lake Pontchartrain, is to New Orleans what Coney Island is to New York —a convenient and delightful resort for open-air festivity in summertime; and as there is a good deal more Summer in New Orleans than in the Northern metropolis, the lacustrine pleasure-ground, of which our artist has brought home a pictorial reminiscence, is the scene of an almost perpetual *fête-champêtre*. The Concert Hall is a veritable casino, like those of European cities, being a commodious structure fitted up with all manner of amusements and conveniences for the throngs of visitors. Excellent music is furnished here, and as the rich strains of "Night in Grenada," mingled with sounds of revelry and mirth, come floating to where the myriad lights of the rowboats twinkle on the dusky lake, the visitor feels that the sentiment is quite in keeping with the place. On Lake Pontchartrain, also, at the West End, is the club-house of the Southern Yacht Club, a quaint and hospitable-looking structure, approached by a broad plank walk leading over a causeway. On regatta days, when the wind blows free, and gayly-dressed crowds eagerly watch the course of the white-winged yachts over the broad blue expanse of water, the scene is one of beauty and animation. Another club-house, and one of the most charming places in New Orleans, is that of the Jockey Club, with its spacious and well-kept grounds. This club has some eight hundred members, of the *élite* of the city. The Jockey Club house was over a private residence, whose owner, suddenly widowed and made childless by an accident on the lake, and having no heart to return to a desolate home, disposed of it to its present occupants. It is a fine mansion, surrounded by trees and flowers, and approached by high steps. Within are parlors, library, dining-rooms, billiard-saloons and bowling-alleys. The house is a place of resort for members at all seasons, and to strangers of note its hospitalities are ungrudgingly extended—Saturday being especially "ladies' day." The mile racing-track of this club is said to be the finest in America, and the grand-stand can be entered from the club-house. Open-air concerts are frequently given of an evening during the season, and there is a platform for dancing.

Great is the change from these bright scenes to the peaceful shades of Chalmette. This beautiful cemetery, the resting-place of so many gallant soldiers, is a part of the historic battle-field where Andrew Jackson fought in 1815. Our sketch shows the shell-road entrance, where buried cannon guard the gate, and the fountain is descried as it leaps at the end of the vista.

THE TEXAS COW-BOY.

THE calling of the cow-boy of the prairies is one of peculiar hardship and peril. Often when a general "round-up" of cattle is in progress, he is in his saddle for sixteen hours daily for five months at a stretch. It is no uncommon thing for them to ride from fifty to one hundred miles a day; and to keep this up; each one is provided with from six to ten horses, while a wagon is provided for every ten or twelve men. Then, beside this hard work by day, when away from the ranch, the cow-boys always sleep on the ground, wound up in a blanket, and this covered with their tarpaulin or heavy duck cloth; and, moreover, those who are driving the beeves to the depot for shipment must by turns watch them through the night as well as drive them by day. And for all this they receive only from $30 to $45 per month and their board. One who has spent some time among these people writes of them as follows: "As you mingle with these cow-boys, you find in them a strange mixture of good-nature and recklessness. You are as safe with them alone on the plains as with any class of men, so long as you do not impose upon them. They will even deny themselves for your comfort, and imperil their lives for your safety. But impose upon them, or arouse their ire, and your life is of no more value in their esteem than that of a coyote. Morally, as a class, they are foul-mouthed, blasphemous, drunken, lecherous, utterly corrupt. Usually harmless on the plains when sober, they are dreaded in the towns, for then liquor has the ascendency over them. They are also as improvident as the veriest "Jack" of the sea. Employed as cow-boy only six months in the year—from May till November—their earnings are soon squandered in dissoluteness, and then they hunt, or get odd jobs, to support themselves until another cattle season begins. They are never cumbered with baggage. What little they may have besides the clothes they wear and their revolver or gun, is carried in a bag which they call their "war-bag." They are utterly reckless of their own lives. They never own any interest in the stock they tend. This dark picture of the cow-boys ought, however, to be lightened by the statement that there is occasionally a white sheep among the black. True and devoted Christians are found in such company—men who will kneel down regularly and offer their prayers in the midst of their bawdy and cursing associates. They are like Lot in Sodom. Our picture gives a good idea of the picturesqueness of the typical cow-boy, being supplied from a recent photograph.

TEXAS.—TYPES OF THE COW-BOYS OF THE PLAINS.

A WATCH WHICH GOES BY ELECTRICITY.

A JEWISH young man, nineteen years old, named Solomon Schisgal, has invented a watch which goes by electricity, and with scarcely any movement; it is, therefore, simple in construction and easy to handle; it is cheap, and, above all, keeps correct time. Herr Chwolson, Professor of Physics at the University of St. Petersburg, has written an article on the subject in the *Nowosti*, in which he says: "In its remarkable simplicity this invention can only be compared with the Jablochkoff system of electric lighting. The watches are without any springs, and consist solely of two wheels. Besides being true, they have the advantage of the second hand moving in single momentary leaps, as is usually the case only in very costly watches, and which is of the utmost utility for astronomical observations. These watches can also set in motion a certain number of watches of the same construction, so that they all keep exact time. The invention has convinced me that watches can be used for the purpose of telegraphy." After naming several other advantages, Professor Chwolson describes the invention as a wonder which will cause

OUTLAW BOGAN CASH.

He Commits a Dastardly Double Murder in Cheraw, S. C., and Escapes.

Taking Refuge in a Swamp—The Murderer's Father Surprised and Captured.

[Subject of Illustration.]

One of the most cowardly murders ever recorded in the South, occurred at Cheraw, S. C., on Saturday, Feb. 16, when W. B. Cash, son of Col. E. B. C. Cash, the noted duelist who killed Col. Shannon a few years ago, murdered Town Marshal Richards of that place, and a man named Coward.

The story of the murder by young Cash shows that it was a cowardly and brutal crime. Cash had been in Cheraw several days, and had had a fight with the Town Marshal, Mr. Richards. He said afterward that he had been drunk, and Richards had used him roughly. Cash promised the Intendant of the town that he would not molest Richards, and it is believed he then meant what he said, but when the Colonel came home and heard that his son had been ill-treated, he began to clean his gun, and announced that he was going to Cheraw to kill Richards. Bogan Cash, desirous of relieving his father of unnecessary trouble, took the job into his own hands, and reached Cheraw at 4 o'clock in the afternoon.

He took three horses with him, and hitched them here and there in the village. Richards was leaning against a tree in the main street. Cash walked past him twice, went to the telegraph office, and then came back, and, walking up to Richards, said:

"Hello! Are you watching me?"

Richards said no; that he was on duty, that was all. Mr. Coward was standing close by.

"Damn it, are you watching me, too?" Cash asked. His right hand was in his pocket. Coward did not reply. Cash walked away and suddenly stopped, wheeled about, and fired. His weapon was a self-cocking revolver. The shot struck Richards in the arm and killed Mr. Coward. A second shot gave Richards his death-wound, and a third missed both men. Then Cash pulled out a fresh revolver, mounted one of his horses, and set out for home. He shouted to the agent of the railroad as he flew past the station:

"I've got two of them, and am ready for as many more as may come."

When he reached home the Colonel was standing on the porch, gun in hand. He embraced his son and told him it was the best deed he had ever done.

The young murderer fled and concealed himself in a swamp. The Governor, learning that no efforts had been made to arrest Cash before he escaped, sent Chief State Constable Richbourg to Cheraw to learn why Sheriff Spofford had failed to take the assassin into custody. Capt. Richbourg reported that the sheriff was feigning illness, and that his deputies would not act. The warrant had been sworn out by J. T. Monair, Intendant of Cheraw, and the Intendant and a posse of ten resolute young men had tendered their services to the sheriff, who declined to accept them.

The Governor issued a proclamation offering a reward of $500 for the apprehension of the murderer, whom he described as "about 6 feet 3 inches in height, weight about 250 pounds, and about twenty-eight years old."

The last seen of young Cash was on Monday, March 3, when he was promenading the platform at Cash's Depot, armed with a Winchester rifle. There are ten thousand acres of swamp in the immediate vicinity of his home, and in the wilderness of the Peedee he could doubtless evade arrest much more easily than in another State, where requisition papers could reach him and officers be found to serve them.

About midnight on March 8, Chief State Constable Richbourg, with twelve picked men, armed with improved Sharps' rifles, left Columbia and arrived at Florence at 3:50 the next morning, where they were met by Sheriff Cole, of Darlington county, Sheriff Spofford, of Chesterfield county, still being "sick." The party took another special train from Florence, and reached a point a mile below Cash's house just before daylight. The house was at once quietly surrounded, and the posse waited for daylight. At about 6 o'clock the elder Cash arose and appeared at the front door. He espied the pickets about the house, and retired within. In about five minutes he reappeared armed with a Winchester rifle and two pistols, and tried to make his escape. He had not proceeded more than a hundred yards from his house before he was confronted by John H. Pearson, one of the sentinels, who presented his rifle and demanded Cash's surrender. Cash hesitated, and Pearson said:

"Drop your gun, or I'll shoot you in two seconds."

Cash dropped his gun quickly and admitted having been taken completely by surprise. When captured he was endeavoring to make his way to a log-house across the railroad track, where young Cash was said to be sleeping. The posse then closed in and searched the Cash mansion thoroughly, but could find nothing of Bogan Cash. A party then started for the log-house. When they were half way there Col. Cash, evidently becoming alarmed for his son's safety, made a proposition to go to the log house alone, if allowed to do so, and pledged his sacred honor that he would have his son surrender within two hours. His proposal was acceded to and the force recalled. Cash went and soon returned, saying that his son had left the house an hour before, and that he did not know where he had gone. He offered, however, if the posse would withdraw that his son would surrender before Wednesday. He frankly added that he only wanted "to come off with flying colors;" that neither he nor his son desired to be considered outlaws, but that he desired to effect a capitulation on his own terms.

The Colonel was taken to Columbia and placed in jail. Young Cash was seen on March 11 at a point about two miles from his father's house. He was mounted on a gray horse, and was armed with a rifle and two pistols. Three colored men met him. They gave him a supply of provisions and a package of newspapers and letters, after which he rode off rapidly in the direction of the Peedee Swamp.

Cash's Depot, where the home of Col. Cash and his son is, consists of a rickety depot, a few modest dwellings, a tumble-down store, and the great frame mansion surrounded by a double piazza and situated in a grove of majestic pines. It is a fine house, but its situation in the pine barren makes it a dreary place for a home. Here Col. E. B. C. Cash lives. His son, the outlaw, made the adjacent log-house his stopping-place directly after the shooting. This log-house and two stout barns are in a clearing framed with a worm-fence of pine rails. In one of these barns Cash was in the habit of taking refuge whenever any stranger approached the depot. He had a strong following, and his hiding place was picketed by scouts, who watched the neighborhood and brought him hourly bulletins of what was going on in the village. Col. Cash has said that neither he nor his son would fire upon any officer of the law who may come to arrest them. He said he did not want to see his son lynched, but would see to it that he gave himself up and stood his trial like a man. The new blood the Cashes are thirsting for is that of the posse that volunteered to capture Bogan after he committed the murder.

Col. Cash was arraigned before the Supreme Court at Columbia on March 13 on a writ of *habeas corpus*. A number of affidavits were submitted by the State, the tenor of which was to show that Col. Cash was an accessory, both before and after the fact, in the murder of Town Marshal Richards, of Cheraw. The prisoner was released on $2,500 bail.

After the Colonel had been released he was warmly congratulated by his friends, by whom he was escorted to the leading hotel for dinner, where the Colonel held an informal reception.

Bogan Cash, through one of his friends, got a citizen of Cheraw to telegraph to the Governor offering to surrender upon the condition that he should stay in Chesterfield jail until the next term of court, and be tried at that term. Gov. Thompson replied that he had no authority to make terms.

BEN THOMPSON'S DEATH.

The Noted Ex-Marshal of San Antonio, Texas, Dies at Last With His Boots On.

[With Illustration and Portrait.]

Ben Thompson and Ning Fisher were shot dead in the Vaudeville theatre Tuesday night, March 11. Joe Foster was shot in the leg, and will probably die of hemorrhage. Thompson and Fisher had been drinking together, and entered the theatre in company. They met Foster in the dress circle, and some words followed, when shortly after shots were exchanged. The dress circle was quickly cleared, the occupants jumping into the parquet below and through the side windows into the street. Before the theatre was fairly cleared of its occupants 1,500 persons on the outside were clamoring at the closed doors for admittance. Shortly after the shooting Thompson's brother appeared on the scene, but was promptly arrested.

The remains of the two victims were taken in charge by a host of friends, and the obsequies have been ordered on the grandest scale, regardless of expense. The theatre where the affray occurred was the scene last year of the killing by Thompson of Jack Harris, who was the proprietor of the place. Fisher and Thompson were probably the two most desperate and widely known men in Texas. They have each killed a large number of men.

Thompson possessed a wide reputation as a man-killer. He had frequently threatened to take San Antonia, and the San Antonia police were determined he should not. His desperate ferocity when roused, his fearless disregard of his own and other lives, and his fatal proficiency in the use of the revolvers were too well known to fail in acting as a warning to the employees of a house whose former owner had been killed some months ago. From the moment of his entrance to the theatre he was a doomed man.

Fisher was the younger man, but the greater desperado. He was originally from Goliad county, and his baptismal name was John King. His murders were innumerable. He was for years the captain of the celebrated Breeton gang, and in every town on the Rio Grande his name was a terror.

It is the irony of fate that men of such reputation for personal prowess as these two desperadoes should have been shot to death with not one life to render up in exchange for their own. Foster was accidentally shot by one of his own party.

GUISEPPE GUIDICE.

[With Portrait.]

The trial of Guiseppe Guidice, in the Kings County Court of Sessions, for murder in the first degree, in killing Maggiorini Daghiero, resulted, on March 4, in his conviction. The crime was committed on Nov. 30 1883, in front of No. 1 President street, Brooklyn. It was shown in evidence that the prisoner lurked in the vicinity to await his victim in the early hours of the morning, knowing when he would start for work. The jury deliberated for four hours, and then returned to the court-room, where many persons awaited the result. When the verdict, "Guilty, as indicted," was rendered, the prisoner appeared deeply moved, but soon recovered his composure. He was handcuffed and returned to Raymond Street Jail. He was brought into court on March 10, and sentenced to be hanged on Friday, May 2.

JAMES A. PARKER.

[With Portrait.]

Chief Detective Alf. W. Burnett, of West Virginia, arrested in Montgomery City, Mo., on Feb. 26, J. A. Parker, charged with committing a murder in Virginia on the 22d of December, 1877. The name of the man murdered was Gough. He was killed for his money, the amount obtained being $60. Parker left Virginia after the murder and was traced to St. Louis by Detective Burnett. There the trace was lost. It appears Parker has been in Missouri some years, being married in Lincoln county, Mo. He came to Montgomery City some months ago. He is about twenty-eight years of age, has a wife and one child. It is said Parker admitted having been in the town where the murder was committed at the time it was perpetrated, but claims he is not guilty of the charge.

PATSY DUFFY.

[With Portrait.]

Patsy Duffy, the premier rider of California, is the most successful jockey that has ever mounted a running horse on the Pacific Coast. His weight is, in condition, 105 pounds. He won the Garden City cup at Chicago, with Bell's Harry Gillmore, 1883, when he defeated John Davis and Lydia Stanhope and several others. He won the Pacific cup in 1880, 1881 and 1883. During his time he has ridden Winters, Pritchard, Baldwin, Haggin & Hearst, and all the prominent horses of the stables of the Pacific Coast. He is a genial, well-behaved and unassuming young man, with a very bright prospect before him. At the present time he is engaged by Haggin & Hearst as first rider. We wish him a grand success for the coming season.

TO CORRESPONDENTS.

M. W., Chicago.—No.

F. G., Ilion, N. Y.—Yes.

H. M. P., New York.—No.

X. Y., Foley, Mo.—A wins.

M. W., Rochester, N. Y.—No.

M. H., West Brookfield, Mass.—No.

S. J., East Mauch Chunk, Pa.—B wins.

Constant Reader, Rich Hill, Mo.—Yes.

D. J. W., Portland, Me.—Jack wins the game.

C. C. D., Minneapolis, Minn.—Thanks for items.

W. P., Trenton, N. J.—Lawrence is the middle name.

Harry Worth, Mineola, N. Y.—Second-class matter.

H. W. L., Chicago.—Yes, if you accomplished the feat.

G. W. H., Fall River, Mass.—Send on picture with record.

R. W., Wilkesbarre, Pa.—Yes, according to Hoyle's latest.

L. H. K., Bedford, Iowa.—It is not necessary to hold trump.

Geo. E. Pelton, Gray Eagle, Minn.—Price of book, 50 cents.

J. C., Buffalo.—In cutting for deal in euchre, jack is high card.

A. Young, Newark, N. J.—Costello, the jockey, was born in New York.

G. W. Benns, Fair Haven.—From Currier & Ives, Nassau street, N. Y.

Subscriber, Fort Bayard, N. M.—No, the number is out of print.

W. E. R., Easthampton, Mass.—Thanks for cut and matter received.

M. S., Bordentown, N. J.—Tom Sayers stood 5 ft 8½ in in height.

Mlle. J., St. Louis.—1. No. 2. We never published the picture.

T. H. S., Georgetown, Ky.—Harry Jennings, 395 Broome street, this city.

Geo. M. Walker, Davenport, Iowa.—Send $1.25 to this office for the book.

B. W., Scranton, Pa.—Send a forfeit, and we will publish your challenge.

Reader, Youngstown, Ohio.—Your wager on the City Counsel is a draw.

F. C., Saco, Maine.—Yankee Sullivan never killed a man in the prize ring.

Tody Mack, Providence.—See answer to G. M. Walker, Davenport, Iowa.

Wm. T. Merrick, Plainville.—See answer to H. W. S., Wheeling, W. Va.

W. L. P., Brownsville, Texas.—Henry Colin & Co., 79 Nassau street, N. Y.

J. Van S., Portsmouth, Va.—We will use the photo at the earliest opportunity.

City Ice Boat, Philadelphia, Pa.—On the evening of Thursday, March 1, 1883.

H. S., Rochester, N. Y.—A trade dollar was never recognized as a legal tender.

J. L., Albany, N. Y.—Your portrait is being engraved, and will appear shortly.

S. B., Pittsburg, Pa.—1. George W. Weisgerber was born Feb. 24, 1854. 2. No.

H. G., Philadelphia, Pa.—Constable, the English jockey, died on Feb. 17, 1881.

E. L. DeQuest, Franklin Co., Vermont.—Send $10, and we will mail you a pair.

Columbia Street, Utica, N. Y.—He will be twenty-six years of age next October.

H. M., Boston, Mass.—Richard K. Fox still owns "Police Gazette" (Emma B).

P. N. Hansen, Chelsea, Mass.—Address editor *Times-Democrat*, New Orleans, La.

Jerry Nevins, Nebraska.—J wins. There is no foundation for L.'s statement.

Constant Reader, Mahanoy City.—Yes, both paper and supplement, price 10 cents.

D. J. W., Hoboken, N. J.—Address Billy Edwards, care of Hoffman House, this city.

P. H. S., Rochester, N. Y.—The American News Co., 41 Chambers street, this city.

P. F. Nevaland, Brooklyn, N. Y.—We cannot give you the information you desire.

W. H. S., Canton, Ohio.—Acker, Merrill & Co., and B. W. Allen & Co., both of this city.

R. D. T., Brooklyn, N. Y.—If you desire your checker challenge published, send a forfeit.

M. G., Port Richmond, S. I.—George Slosson was born in De Kalb, N. Y., March 5, 1854.

J. M., Bridgeport, Conn.—1. No. 2. Write to James Keenan, 35 Kneeland street, Boston.

W. A. H., Auburn, N. Y.—1. Your scheme would not pay. 2. Send your photo and record.

M. S., Baltimore, Md.—1. We answer no correspondents by mail. 2. Send your portrait.

J. G. B., Pittsford, N. Y.—Charles Mitchell, the pugilist, was born in Birmingham, England.

J. R., Grand Island, Col.—Send $8, and we will forward you a standard pair of boxing-gloves.

H. A. G., New Haven, Conn.—Send $2, and we will mail you a book giving all the information.

J. S., Kensington, Philadelphia.—Do not know positively, but suppose about twenty-five years.

D. B., New York city.—We do not desire to enter you or any pedestrian in the April six-day race.

A. L., Auburn, Maine.—John C. Heenan's second, John McDonald, was born in Dublin, Ireland.

D. S., Duluth.—McLaughlin never defeated James Owens. It was Owens that defeated McLaughlin.

Capt. John Williams, New Orleans, La.—No challenge recognized unless accompanied by a forfeit.

J. A., Cleveland, Ohio.—It was Jerry Eaton. The affray occurred on June 11, 1868, at Philadelphia.

B. B., Albany, N. Y.—Write to the Boston *Globe*, Boston, Mass., and you will get the information you desire.

P. P. W. B., Wilkesbarre, Pa.—1. Yes. 2. Always glad to receive news. 3. We have no representative.

F. R. S., Pierceville, Pa.—1. The parties were never matched. 2. Will forward rules on receipt of 10 cents.

S. D. L., Milton, Pa.—1. Consult your town authorities. 2 and 3. Peck & Snyder, Nassau street, this city.

J. D., Providence, R. I.—They never fought as opponents in the ring, but they did engage in a bar-room row.

W. F., Allegheny, Pa.—1. *Banner of Light* and *Voice of Angels*, both published in Boston, Mass. 2. No.

Mrs. Elizabeth Day, Fall River, Mass.—Address Charles Day, manager Forepaugh's Circus, Philadelphia, Pa.

P. H. S., Rochester, N. Y.—Your questions were answered. If you let us know the book you want we will furnish it.

W. M., Detroit Mich.—We have already published Col. J. H. McLaughlin's photo and record in the Police Gazette.

D. C. N., Greenville, Texas.—1. Matter you sent was useless without names of parties. 2. Thanks for your kindness.

J. Colville, Co. C, Seventh infantry, Ft. Laramie, W. T.—"Waterford Jack," in Waterford, Ireland, 1855; died 1865.

M. W., Pottsville, Pa.—George Smith, of Pittsburg, did win a Sheffield handicap. On June 7, 1881, at Newall, England.

E. C. D., Bellevue, Ohio.—Send us a photo with names of the parties underneath. The one you forwarded has no names.

All Fours, Raleigh, N. C.—A good set of gloves will cost $8.00; book of instruction, 30 cents. Both can be had at this office.

F. N., State street, Chicago.—Write to James Keenan, 95 Portland street, Boston. The dog is owned by a party in Boston.

F. E. H., Navasoto, Texas.—Send 60 cents to this office for copy each of "American Athlete" and "Donnelly's Art of Boxing."

T. Q., New York.—Read the Police Gazette and *Fox's Week's Doings*, and you will find out what we thought of the decisions.

G. A. Dawson, Fayette Co., Pa.—Write to Robert Mace, Centreville, Newcastle Co., Del. He has a great breed of game fowls.

Subscriber, Baltimore, Md.—The park is closed at 9 P. M. in the spring and summer seasons, and at 6 P. M. in the winter season.

F. Fredericks, Catawissa, Pa.—1. Thirty-two takes first and second prizes; 31 third prize. 2. Broome won in 57 rounds; time, 1h 19m.

J. A. Smith, La Porte, Ind.—Will forward Police Gazette to any address in U. S. or Canada; price $4.00 per year, payable in advance.

M. S. W., Pottsville, Pa.—The Sullivan combination route is Los Angeles, through Arizona to Texas, and thence to New Orleans.

T. H. P., Detroit, Mich.—1. It is optional with referee to do so. 2. The rules as printed govern all contests, and will decide your question.

J. J. B., Lowell, Mass.—Paddy Ryan did win first fall, and threw Sullivan in the battle; they fought at Mississippi City, Feb. 7, 1882.

A. Blanchard, Fort Spokame, W. Ty.—Patrick McGowan was shot and killed by policeman John Delaney on the morning of Jan. 2, 1883.

Mattie, New York.—Jim Fisk was shot and killed, Saturday, Jan. 6, 1872; his assailant was sentenced to, and served, 4 years in Sing Sing Prison.

P. P. P., McAlister, Ind. Ty.—Alaska, New York to Queenstown, 6 days 18 hours 37 minutes; Queenstown to N. Y., 6 days 21 hours 40 minutes.

J. S., Peoria, Ill.—"The American Athlete," published by Richard K. Fox, is the standard book for athletes who engage in running and walking.

P. Dwyer, Brooklyn, N. Y.—John Morrissey was born at Templemore, Ireland, in 1831, and died at Saratoga, N. Y., May 1, 1878, aged forty-seven years.

A Reader, Middletown, New York.—1. Daniel O'Leary was born at Clonkelty, Ireland, June 29, 1846. 2. He stands 5 ft 7½ in in height and weighs 160 lbs.

C. J., Bogart, Sherman, N. Y.—1. The ace hand wins. 2. The ball does not count; he should have taken such precaution as would prevent the accident.

Chas. E. Boisor, Newark, N. J.—Sarony, Union Square; Marc Gambier, 16 West Fourteenth street, and John Wood, 208 Bowery, are among the best in their profession.

W. B. C., Boston, Mass.—1. Unknown. 2. Location, Winnipeg, Manitoba, Canada. 3. Clarence Whistler, born Jan. 12, 1856, near Delphi, Carroll county, Indiana.

J. O. G., Vinitia, I. T.—We cannot inform you the value of the coin. If you write to the Treasury Department, at Washington, you will probably gain the information.

Rich Hill Shoer, Bates Co., Mo.—1. Elliott was knocked out in 3 rounds when he met Sullivan. 2. Tug Wilson did not knock Sullivan down when they fought.

T. E. Julien, Butte, Montana.—Feather, under 115; light, 115 to 140; middle, 140 to 158; heavy, above 158, ("Police Gazette" revised Marquis of Queensberry boxing rules).

W. H. G., Baltimore.—Jem Ward, the ex-champion pugilist of England, visited New York, and gave an exhibition at the Old Bowery Theatre (now the Thalia), on June 29, 1868.

J. B. H., Cleveland, Ohio.—Sullivan and Coburn sparred together at the latter's benefit in Madison Square Garden, this city; also at exhibitions in Albany and Troy, this State.

J. M., Robertsdale, Ill.—Richard A. Pennell, on Jan. 31, 1874, put up a 201¾-pound dumb-bell, which was the best performance of the kind on record until Robinson beat it at San Francisco.

H. B. C., Gallatin, Tenn.—1. Joe Fowler, of Bristol, England, claims to be the feather-weight champion of the world. 2. Charley Norton, of Newark, N. J., holds the title of light-weight champion.

Sambo, New Britain, Conn.—1. Lew Ainsworth and Harry Hill wrestled for the collar-and-elbow championship of America, at Mozart Hall, New York city, on April 14, 1863. 2. Harry Hill won.

M. S., Oakland, Cal.—Bill Poole was born in Sussex county, N. J., in 1823. He died March 15, 1855, from the effects of a gun-shot wound, received in an affray at Stanwix Hall, Broadway, New York.

N. B.—We answer no correspondents by mail. All of our patrons desiring information will have their favors cheerfully replied to through the answer to correspondents column in the Police Gazette.

S. W., Indianapolis, Ind.—1. The New York Fire Department, for discipline, system and promptness in making ready, has no equal in the world. 2. Tom King weighed 182 lbs and Mace 176 lbs, the last time they fought.

W. G., Toledo, Ohio.—Tom Hyer and John Morrissey agreed to fight at the Abbey, N. Y., on Oct. 20, 1854. It was not Morrissey that proposed to fight with pistols, but Hyer produced revolvers and agreed to fight with them.

F. O. W., New York city.—A professional athlete is one who competes for money or makes a livelihood by athletic games. An amateur is an athlete who does not compete for money or engage in contests as a means of support.

J. M., Elmira, N. Y.—1. If you read the Police Gazette regularly, you must have read our criticism on the sketches of the Irish champions. 2. We said they were not correct, authentic or reliable, and proved it by dates and facts.

S. M., Dunkirk, N. Y.—1. Jem Mace beat Tom King and the latter defeated Jem Mace. 2. King won the last battle. 3. On Jan 28, 1862, Mace beat King in 43 rounds, lasting 68m. On Nov. 26, 1862, King beat Mace in 18 rounds, lasting 38m.

M. S., St. Louis, Mobille.—John Jackson, better known as Gentleman Jackson, was born in London, England, on Sept. 25, 1769. He beat Fewterell and Mendoza, and was beaten by George the Brewer. Jackson died at No. 4 Grosvenor street, London, Oct. 7, 1845.

J. H. S., Leadville, Col.—1. Jem Mace and Joe Goss fought three times. 2. It was their second match that ended in a draw, and it was fought at Longfield Court, near Mcopham, Eng., May 24, 1866. There was only one round fought in 1h and 5m, and then the referee declared the battle a draw.

Chas. Phillips, Ft. Pitt, N. W. Ty., Canada.—1. Sullivan and Mitchell fought with gloves at Madison Square Garden, this city, on May 14, 1883. 2. The fight was stopped by the police in the third round. 3. We have no record. 4. Edward Hanlan was born in Toronto, Canada, on July 12, 1855. 5. Capt. A. H. Bogardus, of Elkhart, Ill.

H. W. S., Wheeling, W. Va.—1. The American News Co., 41 Chambers street, this city, will furnish book. 2. By G. W. Hamilton, 14 ft 5½ in. 3. George Seward, in England, 9¼s, not authentic. 4. Jim Shaw's dog Jacko, London, England, killed 25 rats, 1:28, Aug. 20, 1861; 60 rats, 2:43, July 29, 1862; 100 rats, 5:28, May 1, 1862; 200 rats, 14:37, June 10, 1862; 1,000 rats in less than 100m, May 1, 1862.

J. S., London, Canada.—1. Mlle. Armaindo is a native of Canada. 2. She is 24 years of age, stands 5 ft 2½ in in height, and in condition weighs 135 lbs. Armaindo's first long-distance race was when she attempted to ride 600 miles in 72h at St. Louis, Mo., on March 19–20, 1882. She covered 617½ miles, which was then the best long-distance record in America. May 21–26, 1883, in Chicago, she rode against W. M. Woodside and W. J. Morgan, for the championship of America, and defeated both those famous professional riders, making her grand record of 843 1-11 miles.

Noah Young, Williamsburg, Col.—The fastest passage of the S. S. City of Paris was on her trip from Queenstown to New York in 1867. She left Queenstown at 4:11 P. M. on Nov. 21, and arrived at New York at 2:50 P. M. on the 29th, which, after adding 4h 28m for difference of time, makes the time of passage 8 days, 3 hours and 1 minute. The fastest passage of an Inman steamer was that of the City of Berlin, which left Queenstown Oct. 5, 1877, at 7 P. M., and arrived at New York Oct 13 at 4:50 A. M.; net time, 7 days, 14 hours and 12 minutes.

M. W., Baltimore, Md.—1. Col. J. H. McLaughlin defeated H. M. Dufur, at Detroit, Mich., Jan. 29, 1883, and on March 3, 1884. The conditions were collar-and-elbow, "Police Gazette" rules. 2. The following are the measurements of Dufur and McLaughlin: Height—McLaughlin, 6 ft; Dufur, 6 ft. Waist—McLaughlin, 40 in; Dufur, 34 in. Thigh—McLaughlin, 26 in; Dufur, 26 in. Calf—McLaughlin, 18 in; Dufur 16 in. Biceps—McLaughlin, 18 in; Dufur, 16 in. Forearm—McLaughlin, 16½ in; Dufur, 15 in. Chest—McLaughlin, 45; Dufur, 43. Weight—McLaughlin, 205 lbs; Dufur, 190 lbs.

G. W., Baltimore, Md.—1. Nat Langham fought several battles besides his battle with Tom Sayers. Langham beat Ellis at Hinkley, England, Feb. 3, 1843, in 8 rounds; beat Teddy Lowe in 43 rounds, 50m, at Long Reach, in 1844; beat D. Campbell in 27 rounds, 35m, near London, England, June 12, 1845; beat Gutteridge in 85 rounds, 93m, at Bourne, England, Sept. 23, 1846; beat Bill Sparkes, the Australian champion, in 67 rounds, 63m, at Working Common, England, May 4, 1847; beat Tom Sayers in 61 rounds, 2h 2m, at Lakenheath, Oct 18, 1853; fought a draw with Ben Caunt, at 196 lbs, for $200 aside, on the River Medway, Sept. 22, 1857. 60 rounds were fought in 1h 29m. 2. Langham was twenty-three years of age when he fought and defeated Tom Sayers. 3. He stood 5 ft 10 in and weighed 154 lbs. Sayers weighed 151 lbs, and was twenty-seven years old. 4. Langham never fought Aaron Jones.

BEN THOMPSON'S FINAL EXIT.

THE LAST ACT OF A FIERCE AND DESPERATE CAREER, AS PERFORMED IN A SAN ANTONIO, TEXAS, TEMPLE OF THE WILD AND UNTRAMMELED DRAMA.

SURRENDER OF GERONIMO!

HIS BAND ROUTED BY MEXICAN TROOPS.

Lieutenant Maus Takes Him Prisoner in Arizona and the Mexicans Threatening to Massacre the United States Forces.

TOMBSTONE, A. T., March 21.—News of the surrender of Geronimo to Lieut. Maus was brought here to-day by a soldier who has been under Lieut. Wheeler at Mud Springs. The circumstances of the surrender are as follows: Thursday afternoon, about ten miles south of San Bernardino, the Apache camp was attacked by Mexican forces. A hot skirmish followed, during which two Apaches were killed and the forces of Geronimo completed routed. Geronimo and his band fled in the direction of Lieut. Mau's camp for safety, and there made an unconditional surrender. The Mexican troops followed them across the line and demanded them as prisoners, and claiming that the fight occurred on Mexican soil and the victory was theirs. Lieut. Maus refused to give the prisoners up, which greatly incensed the Mexicans, who threatened to take them by force. Gen. Crook was hourly expected to arrive in camp, but at last accounts had not yet come. Two dispatches from Lieut. Maus have been received at Mud Springs, appealing for assistance. The situation is critical in the extreme, and the massacre of Lieut. Maus and his command may occur at any moment.

THE FIRE RECORD.

FLAMES IN FORT WORTH.

Special to The News.

FORT WORTH, March 21.—This afternoon about 5 o'clock a fire broke out in the parsonage of the colored Methodist Church on Elm, between First and Weatherford streets, and before the fire department could get to work the building was too far gone to save it from utter destruction. The building was of wood and burned like tinder. The church, which stood adjacent to the parsonage, caught and so rapidly did the flames spread that in a few minutes they were beyond control, and it was evident that the building was doomed. From the church the flames spread to a residence occupied by a negro family, and from that building to the residence of a Mr. Saunders. No efforts of the firemen, though they worked faithfully, could stop the fire, and in a short time the four buildings were reduced to a pile of blackened ruins. There was church service in the church when the fire broke out. As no one was in the parsonage, consequently everything in it was lost. Mr. Saunders and his family were out riding at the time, and all of his household effects were burned. He knew nothing of his loss until he returned after the fire was over and saw a pile of smoking ruins where his residence had formerly stood. He had a small insurance of his property. The entire loss will probably not exceed $6000.

ANOTHER FIRE.

Before the fire above mentioned was out another alarm was turned on from the southern portion of the city, caused by the burning of a small residence occupied by negroes, east of the Missouri Railroad track. The building was consumed in a short time with all its contents. The building was valued at $200, with no insurance.

RAIL SHOP BURNED.

BIG SPRINGS, March 21.—About 7:15 this evening fire was discovered in the oil house and paint shop of the Texas and Pacific Railway. This was a frame building 70x40 feet, distant from the roundhouse about fifty feet. The contents were about one hundred and twenty-five barrels of oil and a large quantity of waste. Before the alarm could be given the fire was beyond control but the town's people turned out en masse and worked with a view to saving the main shops. Ten locomotives were rolled out of the roundhouse. Then all efforts were directed toward saving the buildings. These efforts were successful, and at this writing their safety is assured. Nothing definite can be ascertained as to origin of the fire, but it was undoubtedly the work of an incendiary. The oil room was last visited by an employe at 5:30, but the door was forced by the firebug. A rumor was afloat that some of the guards stationed at the shops fired upon some person seen running from the oil house, but the rumor could not be traced to any reliable source. The loss, as near as can be learned, is about $5000 on contents of the building and $500 on the building.

STABLE AND RESIDENCE BURNED.

SHREVEPORT March 21.—D. Cooper & Sons' livery and sale stable, and residence in rear occupied by Mrs. D. Cooper, was entirely destroyed by fire to-night. The fire swept the whole corner from the new government building toward the street. Loss not known, but will not be great as nearly all the horses, vehicles, furniture, etc., belonging to those burned out were removed without much damage. The buildings were all frame and were old.

DWELLING BURNED.

SAN ANTONIO, March 21.—About 8 o'clock this evening a fire broke out in Beitell street and destroyed the dwellings of Mr. Green and W. W. Herron. The damage amounted to $3000, partially covered by insurance.

AT FALL RIVER.

FALL RIVER, Mass., March 20.—It is thought the walls of the City Hall are not materially damaged. The portion of the tower now standing will probably have to be taken down. The contents of the treasurer's and the city clerk's offices are believed to be uninjured. About three-fourths of the public library volumes were saved, many, however, in a damaged condition. During the progress of the fire Superintendent of Buildings Adams was severely injured by being struck on the head by a falling stone.

GROCERY BURNED.

SHREVEPORT, LA., March 20.—The frame building on Texas avenue, just below the Texas Wagon Yard, occupied by A. Luchmi as a grocery, was entirely destroyed by fire this morning. The building was insured for $1350 in the Mechanics' and Traders', of New Orleans. Luchmi had no insurance. Total loss about $2500.

SHOPS BURNED.

ABILENE, March 20.—Gilliand & Sharpe's blacksmith and wood shop, situated on North Walnut street, burned this morning at 3 o'clock. No insurance. Estimated loss of business and material, $3000.

How Chicago Papers "Get Their Work In."

CHICAGO, March 21.—To-day the Chicago Tribune announces that hereafter the retail price of its daily issue will be 3 cents a copy, a reduction of 2 cents. The Times and the Inter Ocean adhere to the old price. The Chicago Herald says of this: Among newspaper men this move of the Tribune is regarded as being in a great measure due to the marvelous success achieved by the Chicago Herald, a 2-cent paper, confessedly the brightest to be found in the city, strong and able in its editorial columns, and withal a model of typographical beauty. Although it is only in its fifth year, it is admitted to have eclipsed all its older contemporaries and stands first in point of circulation among the morning newspapers. Chicago has long been known as the home of the so called blanket sheets. Ten, twelve and sixteen pages are common issues of the Tribune, while all but the Herald, which is a folio, have followed closely in its footsteps. The reduction in price made by the Tribune naturally creates comment, and it is believed that the Times and Inter Ocean will be obliged to take the same course, and a repetition of the New York newspaper war is anticipated. Meanwhile the Herald will hold the field which it occupies and continue in its course of a steady and substantial circulation and prosperity.

CONDENSED STATE SPECIALS.

The mill company at Albany have failed to obtain water from the well dug on their property.

W. C. Zeiger, a prominent lawyer of Sulphur Ssrings, died last week of consumption.

Ladies of Albany realized $60 for their society from the dinner given on the day of the horse show.

The wife of City Marshal Whitlow, of Clarksville, died at the Commercial Hotel in that city Saturday.

Farmers in the vicinity of Mesquite are well up with corn planting, and are busily preparing land for cotton. They report splendid prospects for good crops.

In the District Court at Abilene the second hearing of the case of Wm. Cameron & Co. vs. Torry and wife, involving about $5000, resulted in a verdict dissolving the injunction.

Lewis Held, for many years connected with the hotel interests of Fort Worth, fell dead in the street yesterday afternoon. He had been on a protracted spree and his death is said to be attributed to alcoholism.

When the remains of Solomon Lawson, a young negro, were received from Somerville by his family in Brenham, on Saturday, a rope was found in the coffin. This suspicious circumstance led to an inquest. The jury has not yet reported.

Albert Johnson, a full blooded negro, 26 years of age, was arrested near Industry and turned over to the county authorities at Brenham. He is charged with committing an outrageous criminal assault on a young German woman. The crime was committed about two miles south of Brenham four months ago. The police have kept the matter very quiet. The young woman identified the negro. He claims to be a preacher.

Murder and War in Nebraska.

OAKLAND, Neb., March 21.—Henry A. Steadman, a farmer near here, quarreled with one of his men, Ed Johnson, yesterday and was killed. Johnson jumped on a horse and fled. An organized mounted posse started in pursuit. Johnson was overtaken twelve miles from the scene. He ran into a barn on the farm of Chas. Johnson and strongly barricaded himself, the chinks between the board affording excellent loop holes for the use of his weapons—a rifle and a revolver. The barn was surrounded and a fusilade begun. The murderer returned almost shot for shot. He was struck in the leg, but continued to fire and kept his pursuers at bay. Reinforcements were sent from Oakland by the Sheriff, with instructions to bring Johnson in, dead or alive. Chas. Johnson, the farmer, ventured too near the barn, and was shot down and will probably die. Constable Parker's horse was shot from under him and onother bullet ripped open his coat sleeve. The reinforcements arrived and were distributed with a view of preventing Johnson escaping in the darkness. In the barn with him were ten horses, some of which had been wounded or killed. Shortly after 8 p. m. Peter Johnson, a brother of Charles Johnson, was mortally wounded. A rush for the barn was made, but the murderer forced the assaulting party back with his well directed shots, some of which wounded the horses. At 1 a. m. this morning he was holding the barn and shooting at his pursuers. More reinforcements have left for the scene, which is now described as a veritable battle field.

Hello! Mr. Edison.

CINCINNATI, March 21.—Edison's claim to the invention of telegraphing from moving railroads is disputed by W. L. Silvey, of this city. Mr. Silvey says he invented the induction telegraph instrument, and has letters patent issued July 12, 1883. Mr. Silvey was then a resident of Castleton, Ind. The description of the apparatus which accompanied the letters patent is identical with the Edison machine, with one exception only. Mr. Edison uses a telephone receiver, and Mr. Silvey has what he calls a resonator. This is the only difference in the two machines. Mr. Silvey thinks his apparatus is superior to Edison's in that it produces sounds audible in a room.

Dissatisfied Street Car Employes.

PHILADELPHIA, March 21.—The Quaker City Protective Association, comprising the conductors, drivers and gripmen of the various lines in the city, held an all day meeting to-day, and passed a resolution instructing the conference committee appointed several days ago, to meet the board of street railway presidents on Tuesday and present their bill of grievances. The question of a strike will be governed very materially upon the disposition shown by the presidents. The bill of grievances was not made public, but it is understood to embrace twelve hours as a day's labor, with full pay.

Jaehne in the Jug.

NEW YORK, March 21.—Alderman Jaehne, who was arrested a few days ago on a charge of bribery, in connection with the Broadway Surface Railroad, and who was admitted to $15,000 bail, was surrendered by his bondsmen this evening and locked up. Mr. O'Donnell, his bondsman, said that he surrendered Jaehne because he had received positive information that he was about to leave the city, and not wishing to lose the money, he had surrendered him. Jaehne appeared very despondent and refused to make any statement, except that there was not the slightest truth in the rumor that he intended to leave the city.

A Friend of His Boyhood.

From the Pittsburg, (Pa.) Chronicle-Telegraph.

"My dear," said Mrs. Snaggs to her husband this morning, "I don't think I know your friend Mr. Pott, do I?"

"Pott?" asked Mr. Snaggs, in surprise.

"Yes, Mr. John Pott."

"John Pott? I don't know anybody of that name."

Oh, you surely must know him very well, for you talked about him in your sleep last night, and called him Jack as though you had known him all your life."

"Jack Pott! Ah, I must have been dreaming about a schoolmate of my boyhood days. I had almost forgotten him."

And Snaggs went down town cogitating on what a narrow escape he had.

Signs of Mental Derangement.

Philadelphia Call.

Mrs. Flunket—I am getting uneasy about my husband's intellect—or his memory, perhaps I should say.

Mrs. Dorsey—In what way?

"I asked him for $50 and he gave it to me without a word."

"Why, that was strange! But what led you to feel concerned about his memory?"

"Why, the fact that he didn't ask me what I had done with the 50 cents which he gave me last week."

SPECIAL BUDGET BY CABLE.

THE EASTERN WAR CLOUD AGAIN VISIBLE

Russia Assuming an Aggressive Attitude Over the Bulgarian Union—Another Tussle With Turkey the Czar's Desire.

LONDON, March 21.—The situation in the East is becoming serious. This time it is none of the Balkan States that are threatening trouble, for the belligerent order of Servia and Bulgaria and the aspirations of Greece have alike been throttled by the powers. The disturbing factor now is the captious and bullying attitude of Russia regarding the Turko-Bulgarian treaty. A few days ago she objected to the designation of a ruler of Eastern Roumelia as "Prince Alexander of Bulgaria," and insisted upon the "The Prince of Bulgaria." This being conceded, she now demands that the terms of the Prince's rulership, instead of being for life, shall be limited to five years. If this concession be also granted she will formulale a new condition to-morrow and thus prolong the crisis. The cause of this stubborn refusal by Russia to accept the Bulgarian union as an accomplished fact is a subject of much anxious speculation. It is well known that

THE CZAR HAS A CANDIDATE

for the throne of Bulgaria in the person of his brother-in-law, Prince Waldemar, of Denmark, and one theory is that the former is seeking to accomplish, by obstructive tactics, what he failed to do by more direct diplomacy for the deposition of Prince Alexander as a punishment for his coup d'etat of last September. But this theory is not broad enough to cover all the circumstances of the case, and the general belief is that a much deeper game is being played. Dispatches received to-day from St. Petersburg throw new light upon the situation, but do not wholly elucidate difficulty. The conscription is being enforced this year with unusual zeal and thoroughness. As fast as small squads of conscripts are obtained they are sent to small interior fortress or garrison towns, while corresponding numbers of veterans are drafted off to the great depots to be sent to join the force now being concentrated on the frontier of Roumelia. Thus the army, which is being formed in the south in apparent preparation

FOR A TUSSLE WITH TURKEY,

is getting some of the best material in the Russian service, which indicates the importance attached to its mission. The Czar, Czarina and Czarovitch are soon to start on a tour through the southwestern portion of their domain. The projected expedition is spoken of in the official paper as a pleasure trip, but it is believed to have a deeper significance. The route of the Imperial party includes Sebastopol, Kherson, Nikoli and Odessa. The official programme announces that a review of troops will be made at each of these places, and the general opinion is that the main object of the journey is to enable the Czar to personally inspect the vast army he is assembling, and to judge of its fitness for the important work before it. The visit to Sebastopol also doubtless means an inspection of the large dockyard and arsenal at that port where war-like preparations have lately been resumed with great vigor. Russian troops are also being massed at Batoum and other points in Trans-Caucasia, which fact seems to point to a Russian invasion of Turkey via Armenia, as an alternative or a support to an invasion by way of the Balkans. These extensive war preparations seem to mean that Russia is cast for and determined upon a final and decisive grapple with the Porte. This determination would be quite sufficient to explain Russia's search in the Bulgaria imbroglio for a pretext for invasions. An interesting side rumor bearing on this point is that Prince Alexander, though ostensibly an object of aversion to his imperial namesake, is really the latter's subsidized tool, and will not oppose the passage of any number of Russian troops across his dominion after being landed at Varna from Russian transports.

A CURIOUS STORY

is told as to the terms on which King George, of Greece, finally submitted to the mandate of the powers that there should be no Turco-Grecian war. The King has for months been willing enough to consent to peace and to discontinue his ruinous war preparations, but has been afraid of losing his throne through the desperate eagerness of the war party among his subjects. The honest broker of Berlin after a time saw where the shoe pinched and offered to guarantee the safety of the King's dynasty if he would disarm and renounce all idea of war. The young King timorously hesitated for a long time, but finally replied to Bismarck that he would obey his wishes if the powers would make some vigorous demonstration to show the Greek people that he only submitted under extreme pressure. This was agreed to, and in pursuance of this agreement, it is said, the allied fleet is now steaming from Suda Bay to blockade the port of Athens—not to coerce the King, but with his connivance, to coerce the subjects. This story, if true, explains many intricacies in recent occurrences in Greece and the willingness of the young King to save himself, no matter at whose expense, reveals a very kingly characteristic.

RIOT IN BELGIUM.

A Brussels dispatch says: Serious rioting occurred at Jemephe, Tilleur and Seraing, small places in the vicinity of Liege, Belgium, to-day, the leaders having apparently been encouraged by disaffected iron workers of Liege. Many shops were pillaged and houses of the municipal authorities looted. The rioters were plentifully supplied with revolvers, but these they used rather for the purpose of exciting terror than to inflict injury. The news of the disturbance created a slight panic here, but it was not serious and was quickly subdued.

SUMMONED BY GLADSTONE.

Mr. Gladstone has summoned Sir Robert Hamilton, permanent Secretary for Ireland, from Dublin to London to consult with him upon the subject of home rule. This is taken to indicate that the Premier contemplates modifications of his Irish policy.

Nothing Extraordinary.

Detroit Journal.

Mrs. Awjaw—Gough must have been a remarkable man. I have just read that he lectured 9000 times.

Mr. Awjaw—Nothing remarkable in that.

"No? Where is there a similar case?"

"Let me see. We have been married thirty years. Now, you have lectured about every night—let us say thirty times three hundred and fifty——"

(Seance breaks up in disorder.)

A SHOT AND SHELL TRAGEDY.

THE HORRIBLE DEATH OF FRED GOULD.

Blown Almost to Pieces by the Explosion of an Old War Missile Found in the Defenses of Galveston Island.

Special to The News.

GALVESTON, March 21.—For the defense of Galveston Island during the late unpleasantness the gallant Confederate, Gen. Magruder, established a fort in the western suburbs of the city in a locality now known as the intersection of Avenue N and Thirty-seventh street. Time and increasing population has, however, effaced all evidences of the fact, and, but for the recent discovery by a number of boys of a quantity of shrapnel shells in the numerous sloughs and lagoons in the vicinity, alrecollection would be but a matter of history. Among the boys were Edward and Henry Dippe, the oldest aged 15 years, and on finding that these sphericial case shot contained a number of leaden bullets which could be utilized for hunting, they took a number of them to their home on avenue N, near Thirty-fifth street. Among others

FRED GOULD,

living in the vicinity, was informed of the find. Fred was aged 18, a member of the Knights of Labor, Cotton Handlers' Assembly No. 4202. He was embloyed at the Factors and Taylor presses, and was one of the men who recently quit work in obedience to the mandate of the order. About noon to-day Fred called on the Dippe boys and, repairing to the yard in the rear of the house, they began the work of extracting the bullets from the shells. Fred removed the plugs while the Dippe boys, after soaking the shells in a bucket of water, shook out the bullets. Several of the shells had been thus treated, when Fred picked up one which he remarked would be difficult to open. The plug was covered with a lead cap, which he sought to remove with a hatchet and an old file. Mrs. Dippe was seated on the back gallery watching Fred as, with the shell between his knees, he worked away with hatchet and file. The Dippe boys were standing in front a few feet from him when suddenly the old file struck fire. The tin part ignited the fuse, which, after all these years and water soaking, had still kept dry beneath the leaden cap. There was a flash, an explosion, and Fred Gould

LAY DYING

on the ground, with a great rent in his side and his crotch and legs filled with bullets and his face blackened with powder. He lived about twenty minutes. Fragments of the shell tore through the house from rear to front, carrying away the sashes and making great holes in the weather boarding. The back gallery against which Fred was seated at the time, also bears the marks of shot and shell. Pieces of the shell were carried great distances, yet strange to say, though only a few feet away, Mrs. Dippe and her sons escaped uninjured. Gould was a native of Fon DuLac, Wisconsin. He is to be buried to-morrow at 3 p. m. by the cotton handlers.

CONGRESSIONAL FORECAST.

POINTERS ON THE WEEK'S WORK.

WASHINGTON, March 21.—Senator Edmunds intends cutting short the debate on his resolutions this week and the prospects are that a vote will be reached upon them by Wednesday. For several days complaints have been coming to him by Senators, who have various measures they wish considered, that the contest he is leading with the administration is consuming too much time, and he has expressed a determination to conclude it as soon as possible. Senator Colquitt has the floor to speak to-morrow. He will probably be followed by Senator Jackson and possibly two or three others. It is understood that Mr. Ingalls desires to speak on the subject. It has been rumored that a substitute will be offered by Mr. Edmunds before a vote is taken, as several Senators have expressed their dislike to the form of the second resolution, which says that no nomination shall be confirmed.

Mr. Logan intends occupying the hour for a day or two with his bill to increase the efficiency of the army of the United States by increasing the number of men, etc. As this is a broad subject, it may run along several days.

Mr, Platt intends calling up his bill for the admission of Washington Territory to the Union, as soon as the pending question is disposed of, and Mr. Frye, during the week, will seek a discussion of resolutions relating to the appointment of a commissioner charged with the settlement of fishing rights of the United States and Great Britain.

The bill to quiet title to the lands settled upon along the Des Moines River, vetoed by the President a week ago, will be called up by Mr. Wilson, who will ask for its passage over the veto if opportunity offers during the week.

IN THE HOUSE.

There is not much in view, aside from appropriation bills, in the House. Several private petition bills are to come up under previous question after call of roll to-morrow, among them a bill to pension the widow of Gen. Hancock, so that the Indian bill, which is unfinished business, cannot be disposed of before Wednesday. The postoffice appropriation bill will come next in order, and as it opens up a broad field for debate, may occupy much of the remainder of the week.

GENERAL WASHINGTON NOTES.

QUARANTINE RAISED.

WASHINGTON, March 21.—Official information having been received that the smallpox epidemic which has prevailed in the Dominion of Canada is now under control, the Treasury Department, with the approval of the President, has revoked the regulations issued Oct. 10, 1885, for the maintenance of quarantine inspections on the northern frontier of the United States.

A Bold Diamond Robbery.

From a New Orleans special dispatch.

Effie H. Hankins, of Chicago, a member of the demi-monde of that city, arrived here two days ago to enjoy the carnival. She had been very conspicuous on Canal street during these days through her massive and expensive diamonds. On one day she would wear splendid jewels of one pattern; the next day another lot, causing no little talk. She brought with her over $35,000 worth of diamonds, but to-day mourns the loss of half of them. Upon her arrival in the city she took apartments with May Banker, and she was robbed at 3 o'clock this morning by three men, who, with revolvers at her head, accomplished the deed. In a few moments they secured $17,000 of the jewelry. Hid away in the room were $18,000 more, which they overlooked.

"What lovely diamonds you have, Mrs. de Squint." "Really, it's very kind of you to say so, but those are only my market diamonds, you know."—Ex.

WINTER AND HEALTH RESORT EDITION

AUSTIN DAILY STATESMAN.

VOL· XVI. | PEGAN STREET, NEXT TO POSTOFFCE OFFICE OF PUBLICATION | AUSTIN TEXAS SATURDAY MORNING DECEMBER 25 1886. | ENTERED AT THE POSTOFFICE AS SECOND-CLASS MATTER. | NO. 123

AUSTIN.

SITUATED IN THE MIDST OF BEAUTIFUL EVERGREEN HILLS.

SURROUNDED BY SCENERY WHICH ENCHANTS THE BEHOLDER.

PUBLIC BUILDINGS AND RESIDENCES FINEST IN THIS COUNTRY.

Every Inducement Held Out to Sight-Seer and Health Seeker.

Finest Hotel Accommodations of Any City in the Southern States.

The Educational Advantages are the Best in the Southern States.

THE SITE OF THE CITY.

Austin is a city of 25,000 inhabitants. It was founded in 1839. It takes its name from Col. Stephen F. Austin, one of the early pioneers who brought out a colony to settle the country. Previously to the Texas war of independence and the defeat of Gen. Santa Anna and the Mexican power on the famous battle field of San Jacinto, April 21, 1836, Austin had no existence. It was the haunt of the deer and the buffalo; the hunting ground, the roaming place of the savage Indian. The capital of the Republic of Texas was formerly at Houston, but subsequently removed to Austin, which is now the permanent capital of a state with over 2,000,000 population, and a taxable wealth of $700,000,000.

Austin is beautifully situated in a high, broken, rolling country, with an unsurpassed water shed, and a natural drainage that cannot be excelled. The location is geologically in the great belt of cretaceous limestone which extends down to San Antonio. Geographically Austin is a little east of the 98th meridian; somewhat north of the 30th parallel, and, therefore, in the same latitude as New Orleans, La., and San Augustine, Fla. It is 150 miles from the gulf of Mexico in a straight line; 250 from the Rio Grande; 350 from the easternmost limits of the state; and about 600 from El Paso on the west.

The elevations of the city and surrounding country above the level of the gulf are as follows: At the postoffice, corner Sixth and Colorado streets, 500 feet; a little north of the new capitol, 550 feet; a the south gate of the university campus, 600 feet; just north of the lunatic asylum, 650 feet; some distance still further north of that asylum, 800 feet; six miles west of the city, 1000 feet. The channel of the Colorado, opposite and above the city, is

450 FEET ABOVE THE SEA-LEVEL.

Mount Bonnel, five miles west of Austin, rises almost perpendicularly from the banks of the Colorado, 450 feet above the channel bed, and consequently its summit is 900 feet above the gulf level.

The foundation underlying the soil on which the city stands is limestone, as is evident from the creek beds and the sides of the declivities which everywhere appear.

SCENERY.

Eastern travelers tell of the marvelous effect produced upon those who have traversed wild wastes of sand, and stand for the first time upon the mountains overlooking the valley of Damascus. A kindred effect is produced upon those who have crossed the boundless, monotonous prairie of the west, and catch the first view of the "Hill city of the south." From the lofty range, which bounds the elevated prairies on the south, the scene is truly imposing. Range upon range of hills, clothed with their perpetual green, descend by regular gradation to the plain below. The Colorado is seen fretting its impatient way round cliffs of jagged stone, until it bursts its shackles, and rushes into the broad alluvial valley to be lost again amid the luxuriant orchards and cotton fields to the east. A thin line of smoke on the south announces the arrival of a railway train bearing the fruits and products of Mexico and the tropics; a second marks the departure of one laden with the fleecy staple, and bound for the cotton markets of the east, while a third disappears among the blue hills on the north, where lie the immense quarries which are furnishing bone and sinew for the greatest state house of the union. Twelve miles away, through the clear southern atmosphere can be seen the city sharply out-lined against the green background of distant mountains. In the center rises the red granite pile on Capitol Hill, with its forest of derricks surrounded by the broad evergreen square laid out by the founders of the republic Around it cluster the towers and spires of white stone churches and government buildings; St. Mary's academy on its lofty eminence, overlooks the huge but graceful form of the Driskill hotel; to the right is the blind asylum and Tilitson institute; one mile west of the capitol, the lofty tower and bastions of the old Texas Military academy rise above the surrounding forest; far to the north, upon the highest elevation in the city, stands the University of Texas,

SURROUNDED BY THE PALATIAL HOMES

of the "cattle kings;" and still further north can be dimly discerned the outlines of the lunatic asylum, scarcely visible amid its extensive parks. These are the prominent features, but the eye lingers with pleasure upon the broad, regular streets, the forty hills crowned with stately residences and public buildings, and the varied topography of the scene. The pleasing effect is not lessened on descending from this elevated point. Taking a sail boat at the foot of Congress avenue, where the new iron bridge spans the Colorado, and, sailing up the river an afternoon of the long Indian summer, can be spent among scenery that resembles in no small degree the highlands of the Hudson. One mile above the bridge, bold, rocky bluffs close in upon the river, and follow its course to the northwest for more than one hundred miles. At some points naked limestone cliffs rise from two to five hundred feet above the stream, their summits clothed with cedars, and their base washed by the clear waters that foam and writhe in frantic efforts to escape. Such scenery is not complete without its romance. In a cave upon the side of one of these bluffs has dwelt for many years the "Hermit of the Colorado." His solitary abode can only be reached by water, and its wild surroundings would excite the interest of the most fastidious artist. Four miles above the city are Mormon Springs and Falls, deriving their names from a Mormon camp pitched there many years ago. A number of bold springs gush from the eastern slope and the river roars in a foaming torrent, over jagged rocks and against huge boulders for one hundred yards. One mile above this point is Mount Bonnell, which can also be reached by a shady, picturesque drive of four miles from the city. It has an elevation of 900 feet above sea level, and 450 feet above the river, into which a stone can be cast from its summit. From this point the scenery is wild in the extreme, and resembles that along the Kanawa. Below can be heard the roar of Mormon falls; far beneath wind the waters of the Colorado, along a channel rent in the solid limestone hills by some great convulsion of nature. To the northwest the hills and mountains are piled in indescribable confusion, resembling a battle ground of Titans. The sunset views from this point are gorgeous in the extreme, and present all the varied tints of the rainbow.

From fifty to seventy five miles beyond Mount Bonnel and easily accessible by the Austin & Northwestern railway, is scenery still more rugged and picturesque. At Marble falls the river disappears in immense fissures, worn through a bed of solid black marble, and reappears 90 feet below. Twenty miles beyond this, Fall creek rushes over a

SHEER PRECIPICE OF 100 FEET

into the Colorado, with a roar that can sometimes be heard for miles. Here are immense deposits of kaoline, lithographic stone, granite, marble, porphyry, fire clay, magnetic iron and copper ores.

A singular phenomenon in this region is that in many places the bed of a stream seems prefectly dry, presenting to the eye only a waste of sand; beneath this there is a constant flow of pure water, which can be obtained by excavations of from one to three feet.

Packsaddle and Long mountain, deriving their names from their peculiar shapes, are prominent features in the landscape, and have an elevation of 1,500 feet. Long mountain is three miles in length, one-half mile in width, and constitutes one of the finest cattle ranches in the west. Deer, turkeys and wildcats, besides smaller game, abound in this section, and the mountain streams are filled with bass and perch of every variety. The scenery upon the Perdinales river, twenty-five miles west of Austin, is also very attractive. The stream is perfectly clear, and grottoes, falls and rapids exist without number. In this section the evidences of volcanic agencies are clearly preceptible. At one point, known as "Dead Man's hole," an oval-shaped pit. 70x50 feet, exists in the bed of the stream; its depth has never been fathomed, and the evidences furnished by the surrounding formation tends to establish the belief that it is the crater of an extinct volcano. This region is the sportsman's paradise, and for fishing and hunting is not excelled in the west. In the immediate vicinity of Austin are many natural objects worthy of note. Crossing the iron free bridge across the Colorado, and turning to the west, a shady drive follows the course of the river for one mile, to the mouth of Barton creek, a bold stream, remarkable, even in this section, for its clear water, the beautiful moss which grows beneath, and the huge lilies and other water plants that line the channel. Turning abruptly to the south, the drive follows the bluffs along the course of this stream to the old dam and mill, one mile above. Crossing the dam on foot and entering a grove of lofty pecan trees, you stand upon the little eminence overlooking Barton's springs. In the centre of a small cave fifty feet in width, a volume of water boils up and rushes down the hillside in a stream of sufficient depth and power to float a large boat or turn the wheels of the most ponderous machinery. The water is as clear as crystal, and far below the surface can be seen masses of water cresses and luxuriant moss of every shade, from light silver to the darkest green. Turning to the west at Barton Springs a drive of ten miles through the highlands leads to Sulphur Springs; an

ISLAND OF NAKED LIMESTONE

rises above the center of the Colorado river; about the middle of this island is a stone basin 9 feet in length, 5 in breadth and 4 in depth, the spring fills this basin and seems to rise from the bed of the river, but in reality it first appears on the hill sides above and can be traced along deep fissures in the rock until it is lost under the limestone channel of the river, to appear again at this unexpected point. Its water has a strong mineral taste and possesses the finest medicinal properties, resembling that of Wooten Wells. Families are camped on the hills at all seasons of the year. Its beneficial effects are being constantly tested, and it is only a matter of time when it will be improved and have its hotel and other conveniences. Another natural curiosity is Carrington Springs, situated twelve miles northeast of Austin. A morning drive across the elevated, undulating prairie, brings you to an excavation of irregular shape on the brow of a grassy ridge; this is Carrington Springs, probably the most remarkable intermittent spring in America. For months its basin will be perfectly dry, then without warning, and without regard to rain or drouth, an immense body of water will issue from it and pour down the slope like a mill race for days or months, to cease as suddenly as it began. Its water is strongly impregnated with sulphur, has a decided mineral taste and smell, and changes the color of the grass over which it runs, to the purest white. The inhabitants, for a radius of many miles, watch anxiously for its flow, and during the periods of active operation a village of tents cover the slope and attest their faith in the efficacy of its waters.

THE CLIMATE OF AUSTIN AND VICINITY.

The climate of western Texas has long been celebrated among the people of our own vast empire, and of the adjoining states, as being peculiarly adapted to the amelioration and cure of chronic diseases of the organs of respiration, but it is only within the past ten years, or since the advent of railroads, that the advantages of this climate have been partially brought to the attention of the people of the north and east, who have hundreds of thousands of sons and daughters

DYING OF CONSUMPTION

and other diseases of the respiratory

THE NEW CAPITOL OF TEXAS.

tract. This part of Texas was traversed by Gen. Jackson and his armies during the war between the United States and Mexico, and to that campaign can be traced the first general notice its climatology received. But, for more than a generation after the termination of that conflict there was no means of reaching Austin and San Antonio, the distributing points for

THE GREAT HEALTH BELT

of the state, except by the old-fashioned stage coach, or the Mexican wagon train, and in consequence, the number of health seekers who cared to or dared avail themselves of the climatic advantages of this region was limited to a very small per centum, compared with the vast array who now seek here a restoration of their wasting vitality. Immediately upon the advent of railroads, however, western Texas, especially the neighborhood of San Antonio and vicinity, received considerable notice at the hands of the railroad management, and the advantages of the great southwest as a

WINTER RESORT FOR HEALTH-SEEKERS

was more generally advertised than ever before. As a result, the number of persons afflicted with chronic disease of the respiratory organs, who annually visit this part of Texas, has reached away up into the thousands, and the number grows larger each winter.

In proportion to its real merits, the climate of Western Texas has as yet received but feeble justice at the hands of the people of the United States. Thousands who have been blessed with a prolongation of life and resteration to health and strength, by a removal to this part of the state, stand ready and willing to testify in terms of laudation to the substantial virtues of the life giving atmosphere of this section, and living monuments to the health restoring atmosphere of Western Texas are to be found on the streets of every city, town, village and hamlet in the more than fifty counties comprising what is aptly styled the "Health Belt" of Texas.

AUSTIN IS THE GATEWAY

and chief distributing point of this great health section, and is, at the same time, the most beautiful and attractive of all the cities of Texas. Approaching from the north by way of the great Missouri Pacific, the road traverses a rich agricultural country until within a few miles of the capital city, where the scene changes, and the foot hills of the Colorado mountains, upon which Austin is located, are brought into view. The agricultural portions of Texas are not classed, in general, as possessing claims to healthfulness, and it is only when Austin is approached, that the visitor finds himself in the section whose climate claims special consideration as

A PULMONARY SANITARIUM.

When the journey to Austin is completed, however, a sanitarium is arrived at whose natural advantages equal, if, indeed, they do not altogether surpass, those of any of the more celebrated and more widely advertised pulmonary resorts of this or other portions of the United States.

We shall state briefly a few typical instances of its recuperative powers. One of our prominent citizens gives the following account of his case:

It was in the month of March, 1875, that I directed my footsteps to a southern climate for my health. My early years had been spent in Ohio and Kansas, the variableness of whose climate and the occasional severity of whose winters are now proverbial, but not more notably so than are those of all our northern and eastern states. Though naturally hearty and resistant, the severity of the northern winters told upon me, and ere the age of manhood had been arrived at, nasal and bronchial catarrh had well nigh sapped the foundation of my existence. Ozena in one of its worst forms, soon rendered life almost intolerable, and bronchitis so reduced my strength and weight that sympathizing friends predicted the early filling of a galloping consumptive's grave. A constant cough harrassed me, copious expectoration and sweatings reduced my strength, and slight bronchial hemorrhages occurred on several occasions. An uncle had died of consumption, and the outlook was not pleasing. A change of climate was decided upon, and early in the month and year named, the removal to Texas was made.

On the first day of March the train was boarded at a station near Kansas City, and the trip begun. The ground was covered with snow nearly a foot deep, all crusted with ice and sleet. The housetops were hidden by their snowy covering, while the eaves hung heavy with icicles. The trees were creaking and breaking in the wind with their heavy load of sleet and frozen rain, and all nature was

CLAD IN THE COLD GARB OF BLEAK WINTER.

The journey was a tedious one. But one line of railroad was completed to Austin at that time, and the trip was made in a round about way, necessitating three and a half days of travel, as against the forty hours run of to-day. A norther followed us down through the Indian Territory and north Texas, and it was not until we were well in the central part of the state that I was made to realize that a southern climate had been reached.

I shall never forget my arrival in Austin. But seventy-two hours before I had left the home of my childhood, in the lap of a cold, dreary winter. The winds were bleak and chilly, and no indications of the early approach of spring were apparent.

AT AUSTIN ALL WAS CHANGED.

The air was mild and balmy, and laden with the perfume of budding trees and flowers. The lark and mocker were whistling their sweetest notes, and so clear and pure was the atmosphere that the crowing of the chanticleer could be heard for distances almost beyond belief. The hills and plains and valleys were putting on the bright garb of spring, and all nature looked bright and inviting. The fields were already plowed and harrowed for the crops of summer, and in the valleys the corn was already sprouting from the mellow loam. The peach trees and plum trees were in blossom, and

BEAUTIFUL FLOWER AND VEGETABLE GARDENS

appeared on every hand. In my delicate health each breath of this God-given atmosphere seemed to impart a new lease of life, and ere my first day in this part of Texas was half over an affection for its winter climate was formed which has not to this day known any waning.

From Austin to San Antonio, a distance of eighty miles, the trip was made by stage on the 4th day of March, and so balmy was the atmosphere that nearly the whole of the journey was taken on top of the stage, and without a coat.

I spent the summer in San Antonio. An outdoor life was followed, hunting and fishing, and gaming, being our chief occupation for the period of several months. In the early fall, a camping trip of above six hundred miles was taken, and for a month we traveled and hunted over a number of the counties west and northwest of Austin and San Antonio, with the most gratifying result of

A COMPLETE RESTORATION TO HEALTH

and a gain of twenty pounds in weight in the period of thirty days. Our companion on that trip is still living, and this fact can be attested if necessary.

The experience of this citizen is not an unusual one. San Antonio has many notable instances of remarkable recoveries in the personnel of some of her citizens, and Austin citizenry is made up in fair part, of persons who have been attracted hither by the salubrity and curative abilities of her climate.

The two cities are equally favored in point of salubrity of atmosphere, which is rare, mild and balmy at the same time, but

AUSTIN IS THE MOST FAVORED

of the two in the matter of topography, geology and local surroundings.

San Antonio is located on black, heavy ground, in the valley of the San Antonio river, which pursues a very tortuous course from one end of the city to the other. It is traversed by numerous shallow irrigating ditches, which branch off in every direction, and which are extensively used for gardening purposes. From these and the winding river much moisture and fog is thrown off, while nothing of this kind obtains in Austin. San Antonio is much more compactly built than is Austin, and it lacks altogether, anything like the natural drainage the latter is blessed with, and in winter it is very muddy. The country around San Antonio in all directions, except to the south, is higher than the city proper, while to the south it is a vast mesquite flat. As remarked, the two cities are favored with the same pure, health-restoring atmosphere, and in this they are equal. But in point of topogra-

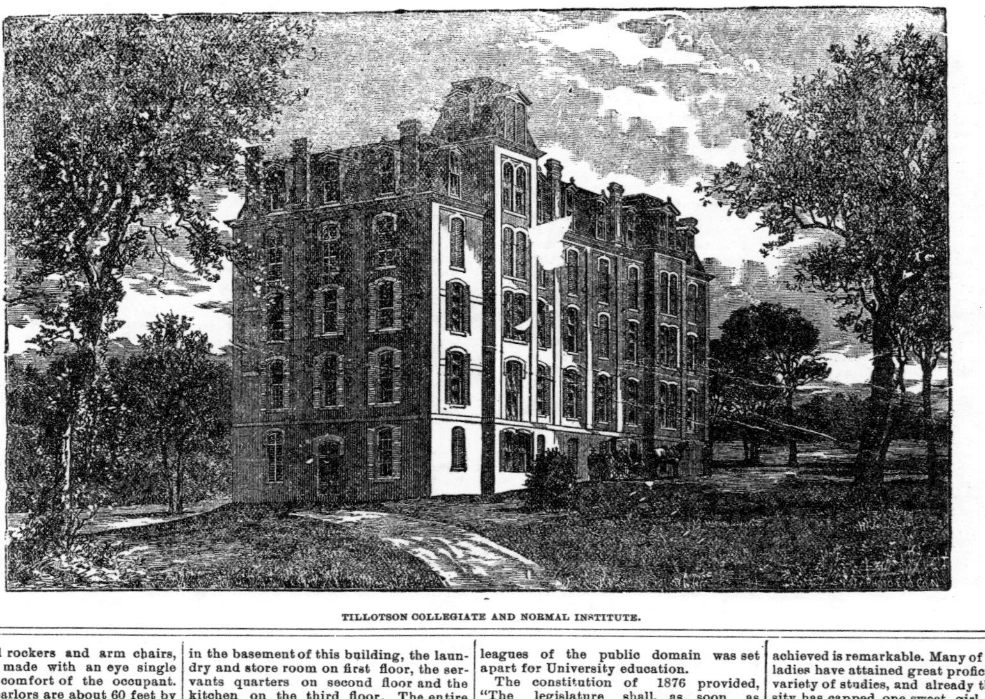

TILLOTSON COLLEGIATE AND NORMAL INSTITUTE.

whoie building is heated by steam and has grates in guest chambers.

THE SECOND FLOOR.

This floor it is that proves this building to be the finest in the south, and is the peer of any hotel in the country. Here we have reproduced the immense corridors of the first, sacrificing space for the comfort of the guests. In no hotel in the north or south can there be found such spacious corridors as are on this floor, which take the place of the narrow hallways found in all other hotels. The corridors on this floor are covered with heavy velvet carpets, 1,500 yards being required to cover them alone. The corridor running from east to west terminates on each end in an immense balcony. The one running north and south terminates on the south end on the handsome iron balcony overlooking the main entrance, the north end terminates at the entrance of the

GRAND DINING ROOM.

This room is sixty feet long and forty feet wide, and is lighted, in addition to four immense windows, by a blue glass skylight, 30x15 feet, thus giving soft light to the room, and at no time having an unpleasant glare. There are twenty-four dining tables in this room with a seating capacity of about 200. The chairs are of massive walnut, with maroon leather seats and back. Over the beautiful tile fireplace is a grand French plate, bevel edged mirror, 10x6 feet in size. The handsome mantels in this room, as well as the ladies and gentlemen's parlors, are elaborately carved in Romanesque style, and, like the furniture on the first floor, are in keeping with the exterior ornamentation of the building. The room will be lighted by ten 12-light chandeliers. In addition to this dining room there is just across a spacious hall the

LADIES ORDINARY,

the floor of which is covered with velvet carpet. There are three large windows in this room with lace curtains, ebony poles trimmed with brass and damask hangings. There are eight tables in this room with a seating capacity of seventy. The furniture is walnut, and similar to the main dining hall. Just back of this room is the children's dining room, covered with English Wilton carpet. The ladies' grand parlor is on this floor. The carpet in which is heavy moquette of Gobelin tapestry pattern, and the furniture is of walnut, upholstered with hair, and covered with plain, mottled, embossed and crushed plush. The curtains are lace with brass poles and trimmings, and velvet draperies, and an immense plate, bevel edged mirror is just above the tiled fire place. There are, at every door, turcoman portiers, with brass poles and trimmings. The gentlemen's parlor is a trifle larger than the ladies' parlor, and has a handsome moquette carpet, the potieres and draperies to windows being similar to the ladies' parlor. The furniture is walnut, upholstered in plush similar to that in the ladies' parlor, and has also large reed rockers and arm chairs, the latter being made with an eye single to the ease and comfort of the occupant. Both of these parlors are about 60 feet by 30 feet.

THE GUESTS' CHAMBERS

on the second floor are gorgeous in their appointments. The four main chambers on this floor have each a spacious bath room attached. Two of them have balconies overlooking respectively the southwestern and south-eastern portions of the city. The carpets are moquette. The furniture is massive mahogany, and each room contains a large plush couch and arm chair and reed rocker in addition to the regular chamber suits. The centre table is a beautiful solid mahogany affair. The mirrors in these and all other chambers are bevel-edged French plate. The curtains are flowered lace, with brass poles and trimmings, and silk draperies. The bureaus and washstands have each an immense slab of variegated marble. The fire place is tiled. The wood work in this and all the rooms is grained heart pine. Beside the four handsomely furnished rooms, with bath rooms attached, above

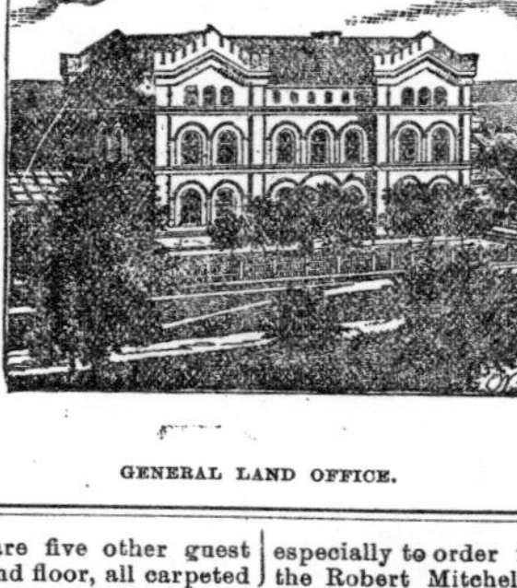

GENERAL LAND OFFICE.

referred to, there are five other guest chambers on the second floor, all carpeted with moquette, and one of which is furnished with mahogany, with trimmings to match, and the other four are solid walnut. The main staircase leading from this floor to the floor above, is carpeted with velvet, which is so thick and heavy that a footfall on it cannot be heard. The stairway is of carved heart pine, the rich grain presenting a splendid appearance. The ceiling of the second floor is sixteen feet high.

THE THIRD FLOOR,

in addition to the immense rotunda, has four spacious hallways, larger than are ordinarily found on the second floors of our finest hotels. The hallways are covered with body Brussels carpet. Corresponding with the four rooms on second floor fronting Sixth street,above described, are four guest chambers on the third floor, two of which have balconies, the view from which is picturesque in the extreme. These four rooms have each a large bath room attached. Two of them are furnished in walnut and two in mahogony, the bed and center table being handsomely carved. There are beautiful plush couches and arm chairs in each of these rooms. The curtains are lace, and the draperies are silk. The carpet is body brussels, each room having a different design.

Just across the hall from the rooms, and inside of the two hallways running from south to north, are four suits of rooms. Each suit is composed of two rooms, separated by handsome turcoman portieres with ebony pole and brass trimmings. One room of each suit is furnished in walnut and one in solid cherry, and carpeted with body Brussels. On each side of the building are two courts, thus giving the advantage of outside lighting for all of the rooms. There are, beside the rooms already mentioned on the third floor, twenty-five others, all carpeted with body Brussels, and are furnished in walnut, mahogony and solid cherry, with draperies, etc., to match.

THE FOURTH STORY

is carpeted with velvet tapestry. The ceiling is twelve feet high. On this floor will be found the continuation of the handsome chambers with bath attachment, thus completing a tier of six rooms on the southeast and southwest corners of the building, making twelve chambers with bath attachment, as handsome as possible to find in any hotel in this country.

These chambers are furnished in carved cherry and walnut, with draperies to match. All the chambers on this floor are furnished in solid cherry, with carpets and draperies to match. There is as much care displayed in furnishing these rooms on the fourth floor as the finest furnished chambers on the first floor.

The entire equitment of furniture—bar and office and news counters, was made especially to order for "The Driskill" by the Robert Mitchell Furniture company, of Cincinnati. The private and public bath rooms, water closets and stationary washstands, are all of the latest patterns, being constructed with especial reference to their sanitary requirements.

The building is as nearly fire-proof as is possible to build it, every partition wall being of brick from foundation to roof; every ceiling of corrugated iron; double floors, filled in with three inches of cement; so, in case of a fire starting in any room in the house, it would have to burn through a brick partition wall or through a corrugated iron ceiling with three inches of cement above it, before getting into the room above or beside it. In additien to this protection, the system of electric bells, above mentioned, through the house, enables the clerk in charge oft he office to instantly alarm the occupant of every room in the building at the same time.

THE CULINARY DEPARTMENT.

One of the principal features of the Driskill is the regard shown for the comfort of the guests, and in no way is this shown more than in the kitchen and laundry departments. These departments, as well as the servants quarters and boiler room, are in a separate three-story and basement building across a ten foot alley in the rear or north side of the house, and when it is remembered that the prevailing winds in this section are from the south and southeast, it will rebdily be perceived that the odor of cooking or from the laundry, will never pervade the house. The boiler is located in the basement of this building, the laundry and store room on first floor, the servants quarters on second floor and the kitchen on the third floor. The entire laundry and kitchen apparatus is of the most modern and approved kind and was furnished by the John Van Range company, of Cincinnati.

VENTILATION.

The most noticeable fact in connection with the hotel is the amount of floor space sacrificed to hallways and corridors to allow the free access of the breeze during the summer season, something very important in a southern latitude. When the skylights in the rotunda and all the windows in the hallways are opened, there will never be a time when a cooling breeze is not playing through the hotel. The immense public and private balconies, over a dozen in number, invite the guests to view the beautiful and picturesque scenery spread out before them. To the southward, just beyond the Colorado river, which is in plain view, are seen stretching ranges of high hills dotted here and there with beautiful residences within easy access of the city. To the west lifting the eye above the city stretching out all around, can be seen a beautiful low lying range of mountains, cleft in twain by the resistless action of the Colorado river. To the north can be seen the new Texas capitol, a mile farther off, the University building, and still another [illegible] beyond that the immense struc[illegible]ed as one of the State Lunatic asylum[illegible] Between these landmarks can be seen [illegible]alatial edifices and beautiful cosy little homes. To the east is seen near at hand the Roman Catholic Female Seminary, and beyond that the Tillotson Institute, and stretching out as far as the eye can reach, is a beautiful undulating plain.

This hotel has been leased from the owner, Col. J. L. Driskill, of Austin, by Mr. S. E. McIlheny, whose reputation as a landlord is too well established in Texas for Texans to require to be reminded of it. He is the veteran hotel keeper of the Lone Star state, and his experience is a valuable one to him as the landlord of such a grand hotel. He has surrounded himself with the best and most competent people to be found in service in this country, and his chef de cusine has a reputation in his line second to none.

Austin's pride in this building is double, first, because she possesses it; second, in that its architects, Messrs. J. N. Preston & Sons, reside here. These gentlemen have planned a building with which no one can find fault. It is peculiarly and especially adapted both to the guests who will stop at it and the climate prevailing in this latitude. The handsome wood carving, stone work, and in fact every class of work which could be done in Austin, has been done here, because our local mechanics bid a low and gave better satisfaction than any others.

The "Driskill" will be opened to receive guests Monday, December 20th, which day will commence a new era in the history of Austin.

THE UNIVERSITY OF TEXAS.

It was provided in the constitution of the Republic of Texas in 1836, that it shall be the duty of congress, as soon as circumstances will permit, to provide by law a general system of education. The act of congress in 1839, which authorized the commissioners to select a seat of government, provided that before the sale of lots in the site selected, "a sufficient number of the most eligible should be set apart for a capitol, arsenal, magazine, university, common schools, etc."

In accordance with this act the forty acre square on which the University of Texas now stands, was set apart for that purpose, and has ever since been known as "College Hill." At the same session fifty leagues of the public domain was set apart for University education.

The constitution of 1876 provided, "The legislature shall, as soon as practicable, establish, organize and provide for the maintenance, support, and direction of a University of the first-class, to be located by a vote of the people of this state, and styled "The University of Texas," for the promotion of literature, and the arts and sciences. This constitution also set apart one million acres of land for the University, in addition to the proceeds of sales of the land formerly set apart for the same purpose.

An act of the legislature establishing the university was passed in 1881, and provided, among other things, that it should be "open to male and female on equal terms, without charge for tuition."

The same year Austin was selected as its location by a vote of the people. In 1883 the legislature set apart one million acres more of land for the university. The corner stone was laid November 17, 1882, in the presence of probably the largest crowd ever assembled west of the Mississippi. The building was formally occupied September 15, 1883. Its government was vested in a board of regents, to consist of eight members, selected from different portions of the state, and appointed by the governor, with the advice and consent of the senate.

The act of 1881 provided for the erection of a building to cost not more than $150,000, to be constructed so as to admit of future additions.

In accordance with this act, the building already erected is merely the west wing of what will be the University building when completed.

The location is in the northern portion of Austin, on the highest elevation in the city,

600 FEET ABOVE SEA-LEVEL.

The building stands in the exact center of the forty acre lot, and when completed, will just cover the summit of the hill which slopes gradually in all directions. The building itself is four stories in height, and built of brick of the best quality.

A visitor to the university will find in the basement a thoroughly equipped chemical department, consisting of lecture room, store room, general laboratory, assay room, professors' labatory, etc. On the first floor he will find the physical department and the library. The former comprises a lecture room with seats arranged in the form of an amphitheatre, a museum containing a complete equipment of lecture apparatus and measuring instruments, costing $16,000, a general laboratory, etc. On the same floor is the library and reading room. The library already contains 5,000 well-selected volumes, and one wall of the reading room is covered with files of newspapers, which are sent regularly from all over the state. The visitor will find on the second floor a nicely-furnished room—there the young ladies assemble during the intervals between lectures, under the charge of the lady assistant. On the third floor he will find two carpeted rooms containing furniture which indicates that they are the halls of two literary societies—the Rusk and the Athenaeum. There is scarcely any finer sight to be seen within the university than these two halls on Saturday evening when a debate is going on. The young orator gets an audience which puts him on his metal, for not only do the young ladies, who are students, attend in force, but also quite a number of the ladies and gentlemen of the city.

As yet only the academic and law departments have been organized. The number of students at the time of writing is 225, of these 72 are law students. Of the academic students 47 are young ladies. To the University of Texas has fallen the task of solving the problem of co-education in university studies; the success already achieved is remarkable. Many of the young ladies have attained great proficiency in a variety of studies, and already the university has capped one sweet girl graduate. A candidate for admission to the university must be 16 years of age; the average age of the students is 20½ years.

The endowment of the University of Texas consists of 2,030,000 acres of land, and a permanent fund of $634,000. Its annual income at present is $47,000. The professors are paid fixed salaries, ranging from $4,000 to $3,000. A student pays no tuition fee, only $10 matriculation fee, if academic, and $20 if a law student. A student's principal expense is for room and board. The rate per month is now $13 to $20. A mess club has been successfully instituted which reduces the expense to $12 per month.

A course of public lectures is given each winter, one by each member of the faculty. These lectures have diffused a taste for literary and scientific culture. How well this university of the southwest has started in its career can best be seen by a perusal of the following account of the professors who have already been appointed.

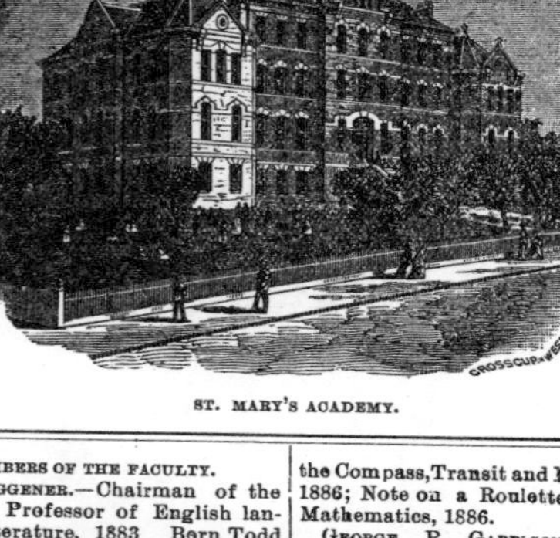

ST. MARY'S ACADEMY.

THE MEMBERS OF THE FACULTY.

LESLIE WAGGENER.—Chairman of the faculty, 1884. Professor of English language and literature, 1883 Born Todd county, Ky., 11 September, 1841. M. A., Harvard, 1861. LL.D., Georgetown college, Kentucky, 1876.

MILTON W. HUMPHREYS.—Professor of ancient languages, 1883. Born Greenbrier county, Va., 15 September, 1844. A. M., Washington and Lee, 1869. Ph. D., Leipzig, 1874. LL.D., Vanderbilt, 1883.

President of the American philological association, 1882.

Editor for United States of Revue des Revues.

Works and writings: Clouds of Aristophanes, in college series of Greek authors; Doctors Dissertation, on the function of the accent in Heroic verse; numerous papers in the American Journal of Philology.

HENRY TALLICHET.—Professor of modern languages, 1883. Born near Lyons, France, 1844. Student of Greiz gymnasium. Graduate Lausanne, 1861. Student at Leipzig 1861–3. D. Lit., Lausanne. Member of the Modern Language association of America.

Author of numerous critical papers in literary and other periodicals.

ROBERT L. DABNEY.—Professor of Philosophy, 1883. Born in Louisa county, Va., 1820; M. A. University of Virginia, 1842; D. D. Hampden Sidney, 1853; LL. D. Southwestern Presbyterian University, Tennessee, 1876. Fellow of the Victoria Institute, England, 1880. Works: "The Sensational Philosophy of the Nineteenth Century," New York, 1876; "System of Theology," three editions, 1872; "System of Rhetoric," Richmond, Va. Author of several works and papers in general literature.

GEORGE BRUCE HALSTED.—Professor of mathematics, 1884. Born in New York City November 25, 1853; M. A. Princeton college, 1878; Ph. D. Johns Hopkins University, 1879. Ex-fellow of Princeton college and of Johns Hopkins University; member of the Society for the Improvement of Geometrical Teaching, England. Works and writings: "Metrical Geometry," Ginn & Co., Boston, three editions; "Elements of Geometry," Wiley & Sons, New York, two editions, reprinted by Macmillan & Co., England. Author of fifteen papers in American Journal of Mathematics, Popular Science Monthly, Van Nostrand's Engineering Magazine, etc.

ORAN M. ROBERTS.—Professor of Law, 1883. Born in Lawrence district, S. C., July 9, 1815. M. A. University of Alabama, 1836; LL. D. University of Alabama, 1880. Elected to the supreme court of Texas, 1857, and several times chief justice. Governor of Texas, 1879–83. Work: "Description of Texas," St. Louis, 1881.

ROBERT S. GOULD.—Professor of Law 1883. Born in Iredell county, N. C., December 16, 1826. M. A. University of Alabama, 1844; associate justice of the supreme court of Texas, 1874–81; chief justice, 1882.

EDGAR EVERHART.—Professor of Chemistry, 1884. Born in Stokes county, N. C., April 8, 1854. M. A. Racine College, Wis., 1873; Ph. D. University of Freiberg, Germany, 1878. Member of the American Chemical society and of the German Chemical society. Writings on Doctor's dissertation: "Action of Nitric Acid on Naphtalene Tetrachloride," "Memoir on the action of Hydrates on Naphtalene, Addition Compounds," "Investigation of Mustards." Author of five papers in Journal of American Chemical Society.

ALEXANDER MACFARLANE.— Professor of physics, 1885. Born in Perthshire, Scotland, April 21, 1851. M. A. University, of Edinburgh, 1875; D. Sc., University, of Edinburgh, 1878; public examiner in matheematics, University of Edinburgh, 1881-4; fellow of the Royal society of Edinburgh, 1878; member of the British association for the advancement of science 1879; fellow of the American association for the advancement of science, 1885.

Works and Writings: Physical Arithmetic, Macmillan & Co., 1885; Algebra of Logic, Edinburgh, 1879; Analysis of Relationship, London, 1882; The Discharge of Electricity, four memoirs in transactions of Royal Society, Edinburgh; author of twenty-five scientific papers in Edinburgh, Proceedings, Nature, Philosphical Magazine, British Association Report, etc.

ALVIN V. LANE.—Associate Professor of mathematics, in charge of engineering, 1884, born at New Orleans, La., February 14, 1860, C. E. Vanderbilt, 1881, Ph. D. Vanderbilt, 1882.

Works and Writings: Adjustments of the Compass, Transit and Level, Ginn & Co. 1886; Note on a Roulette, Amer, Jour, of Mathematics, 1886.

GEORGE P. GARRISON.—Instructor in English Literature and History, 1884. Born, Carrollton, Ga., 19th Dec., 1853, L. A. Universtiy of Edinburgh, Scotland, 1881. First prize for poetry, University of Edinburgh, 1881.

CARLO VENEZIANI.—Instructor in Modern Languages, 1886. Born, Froenruola d'Ardo, (Italy,) 1857. Ph. D., Heidelberg, 1881.

JOHN D. NELSON.—Instruction in Ancient Languages, 1886. Born, Hanover county, Va., 26th October, 1860. Graduate of the University of Virginia, 1882.

SCHOOL SYSTEM.

Austin has, without any exaggeration, one of the finest, most successful public school systems in the south. The city has control of her own public schools. About 13 school houses are used, seven of which are owned by the city. Two of these latter are fine buildings—one, an imposing building of solid limestone rises out of dark foliage of stately oaks in the west of the city; its cost was $30,000. The other, recently constructed in Sixth ward, is of brick and a model of modern school architecture, costing $10,000.

Austin's public schools are flourishing, the total enrollment, 1885-6, being 2,291, average attendance 1,733, and number of teachers 47. The school system is ably managed and conducted; connected with it is a high school.

The public schools of Austin are financially on a solid basis. The receipts for 1885-6, were $42,036.35, comprising $16,135.60 from the state school fund, and $24,340.94 from the school tax levied by the municipal corporation. The disbursements including pay of teachers, rent and other items about cover the amount of receipts. The schools are separate for white and colored, with entire satisfaction to both races. The numbers of white and colored pupils, 1884-5, was 1,475 whites and 628 colored.

The estimated value of school lots unimproved is $7500; school lots and buildings thereon, $40,400; school furniture, $6320.

Besides the public schools, Austin has

MANY PRIVAE SCHOOLS

of high character. Among them a young ladies' school, St. Mary's academy, conducted by the Sisters of the Holy Cross. It occupies one of the most beautiful and commanding sites, and the highest eminence in the heart of the city, on East Bois d'Arc street—a site formerly selected for the residence of the president of the republic of Texas. The building is constructed of native stone,

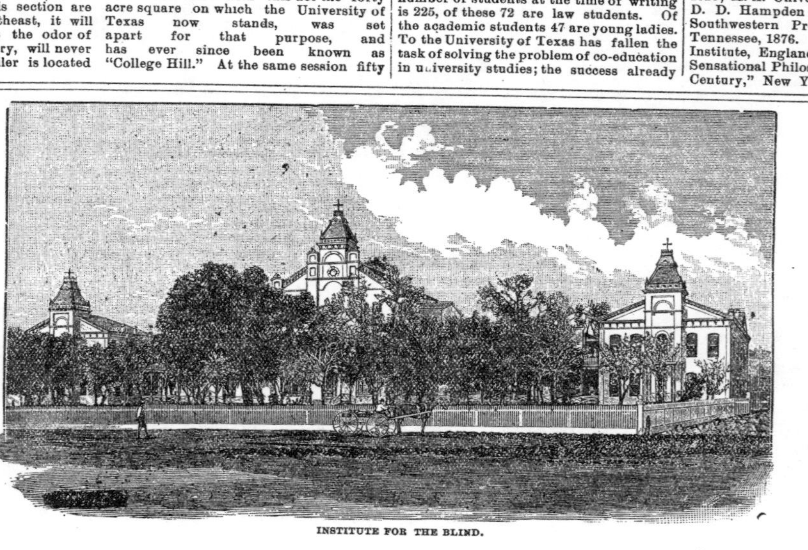

INSTITUTE FOR THE BLIND.

THE UNIVERSITY OF TEXAS.

THE COUNTY COURT HOUSE.

phy, natural drainage, dryness of soil and local altitude, Austin is far ahead. Coupling this with her better boarding facilities, her better churches and schools, her university and magnificent landscape surroundings, it is certain that Austin will become the sanitarium of northern pulmonary invalids as soon as her advantages are properly known.

By reference to the map it will be observed that Austin is in nearly the same latitude as southern Georgia and northern Florida, whose climates have been so highly lauded thtoughout the eastern and Atlantic states, while there is not a very great difference between her latitude and that of Southern California. At the same time,

HER CLIMATE POSSESSES A DRYNESS

unknown to that of Florida or of California, lying as it does midway between the Atlantic and Pacific, and far enough removed from the Gulf of Mexico not to be subjected to its fogs or moisture. In destructive affections of the lungs, the importance of this point of difference, cannot be over-estimated. Dryness of atmosphere is conducive to recovery, while moisture hastens decay; and neither Florida nor California, on account of their proximity to the great oceans can have the dryness of atmosphere peculiar to western Texas.

As illustrative of this feature of the climate of Austin and vicinity, we cannot do better than recite the experience of a correspondent of an Iowa paper, who told his story over the nom de plume, "Ferguson," in an open letter written years ago. For months before he came to Texas his health had been giving way, and early in the fall he had a hemorrhage from the lungs, dyspepsia had reduced him almost to a skeleton, and his physician informed him that unless he went south for the winter,

HIS DAYS WOULD SOON BE NUMBERED.

Acting upon this advice, "Ferguson" came to western Texas, so feeble that he had to be helped in and out of a carriage, and the outlook was in every way gloomy and discouraging. To use his own language: "As soon as I was able to carry my gun I went hunting. I kept in the open air as much as possible. I suppose that during my four months' sojourn in Texas there were not more than fifteen days that I did not spend a large portion of each day in the open air, sometimes on horseback, sometimes on foot. My health began to improve from the start. I was careful about my diet for awhile, but soon found I could eat anything I wished and digest it, and my appetite grew amazingly. There is something inexplicable about that Texas atmosphere.

IT MAKES YOU EAT LIKE A HORSE

and helps you to digest, all you eat. Invalids are the terror of boarding house-keepers in that country. If you ride or drive five or six miles in the open air, you feel like you had taken a strong stimulant. A bucket of stagnant water hung up in a tree for a few days becomes as sweet and pure as if it had just been dipped from a spring. Game will keep for a week or two, hung up, without salt.

Whatever there is anywhere to soothe the mind, give buoyancy to the spirits, to rebuild the wasted tissue of the body, it seems to me can be found in this surpassingly healthy country. There are more old people in Texas than I ever saw in any other state. It is said a native Texan was dilating on the healthfulness of his state. An astonished listener asked him if people ever died out there. The reply was: "Well, stranger, they don't exactly die; they just dries up!"

The same writer says: "I think it safe to say that if a person has no complication of diseases, besides

CONSUMPTION IN THE FIRST STAGES,

the chances for his recovery in southwest Texas are good, provided he lives much in the open air. If he does not make up his mind to stir around at a lively rate, he need not expect much benefit. For dyspepsia, an active outdoor life in Texas I believe to be a pretty sure cure."

The writer of the foregoing letter had tasted of the sweets of this climate and what he has said is worthy of careful consideration by all whose health is impaired. His statement is conservative and truthful, and his experience is but a reflex of that of hundreds of others who are to-day living monuments to the salubrity of the climate.

To the consumptive invalid whose case has not progressed beyond the earlier stages, the climate of

AUSTIN OFFERS GREAT INDUCEMENTS,

especially in the hemorrhagic and fibroid forms. Even in the more advanced stages the progress of the disease is arrested and life prolonged, in a much larger percentage of cases than would naturally be supposed possible. There are men walking the streets of Austin today who were brought here on their beds, almost as helpless as new born babes, and who are now in the full enjoyment of robust health. Among our business and professional men there are scores who have been prompted to remove to this city in search of health, who have been fully repaid for the confidence reposed in the climate. The circumstances of two cases at hand will serve as additional illustrations:

A gentleman formerly residing in St. Louis, Mo., had suffered severely from hemorrhages of the lungs, running him down in weight from 154 to 116 pounds. On advice of his physician, that to remain in St. Louis was certain death, and a change of climate to Southwest Texas might prolong his life for many years, he located in Austin in 1878, remained 20 months, improved rapidly; in fact, thought he had regained his health, when he returned to St. Louis, remaining 20 months, during which time his troubles gradually returned, and in 1881 he was obliged to return to Austin, bringing his family and locating permanently. Up to the present time he has continued in good health, without the aid of medicine, working continuously at his trade, and expresses himself as feeling better than he has felt for twenty years.

Another case is that of a physician, formerly a resident of Iowa, who had suffered from a severe cough all his life, and during three years previous to his locating in Austin had run down in flesh from 180 to 137 pounds. His family record was bad, a father and five sisters having died with consumption, and the doctor knew that grim death was hanging around in close quarters. So in 1882 he started in search of a desirable climate, and after trying several points, located at Austin, and from the start began gaining in flesh. He expresses himself as feeling better than he ever did in the northern climate, and that he is able to do a full day's work every day in the year, and believes he is good for a score of years yet.

Hundreds of people can be found in Austin from northern and eastern cities who have located to secure the benefits of the climate, and all of them are enthusiastic evidences of its advantages.

For the

HUMID FORM OF ASTHMA

there is no air superior. An illustrative case appears in the person of one of the most respected and well-to-do citizens of Austin, who, in early life, followed the sea. During his life as a sailor, he traveled in almost every climate in the world in quest of health, finally putting in at Galveston. At that port he learned of the claims of Austin, and at once visited this city with the result of complete immunity from his old enemy. His experience was so gratifying that he abandoned the sea, and has now resided in Austin for more than thirty years, without, at any time, suffering from his old complaint.

Within a month past a case came under observation in which the patient, the wife of a bishop in the Methodist church, who had been

A MARTYR TO HAY FEVER.

for more than thirty years, spent a part of August and all of September in this city and vicinity without having the first symptom of her old complaint, and herself and husband are so overjoyed at the fact that they have decided to remove from Georgia to Texas.

One of the most prominent of Austin's citizens, a public speaker of note, gives testimony as to the curative ability of this climate in throat affections. He was driven to the necessity of a change of climate, from his old home in Tennessee, by a constant and

ANNOYING IRRITATION OF THE THROAT,

which made public speaking unpleasant and difficult. He has been in Austin ten years, and his voice is as clear as a bell and as strong as a steam whistle. He never suffers from his former throat trouble, but is a perfect picture of robust manhood.

A druggist of considerable local celebrity had been a sufferer for years from irritative bronchitis, hemorrhages finally supervening, which seriously threatened his life. An outdoor life of several months, a portion of which time was spent across the Mexican border, has made him a sound man of robust physique. His general health and physical condition is better than it ever was before.

A capitalist, a former resident of Baltimore, had several hemorrhages from the lungs, and was sent to Florida in the winter of 1871, where he principally regained his health. But realizing that it was hazardous for him to return to Maryland to live, and dreading the summer climate of Florida, and seeing but small business inducements to locate in that state permanently, he removed to Texas in 1872, with the result of a satisfactory continuation of the improvement begun in Florida, and the enjoyment of perfect health to this day. This gentleman is one of the most enthusiastic admirers of the climate of Austin.

A prominent merchant cites his own case as follows: I had cholera in the city of New York in 1868, and so long as I remained in the north, never fully recovered from the dyspepsia and attendant bowel derangement which followed. To make the matter worse, my system became impregnated with malaria, and I came to Texas a walking skleleton. Following the advice of my physician, I pursued an outdoor vocation, and from the very commencement of my work improvement began. You see me now with an avoirdupois of nearly 180, and in the enjoyment of perfect health.

A merchant from Canada was seriously threatened with consumption and sought a residence in Austin four years ago, because of a predisposition to that dread disease, and the existence of initial symptoms which gave him great concern, such as a constant and harassing cough, pain throughout the chest, night sweats, debility, etc. Although closely confined in a store, he improved almost from the first and is in a fair condition of health.

A teacher of vocal music whose voice was so seriously impaired as to render it impossible for her to follow her vocation, came to this city six months ago and today the lady is enthusiastic in her praise of Austin's climate. Her voice is fully restored; her general health is greatly improved, and she numbers herself among those who have "come to stay."

In chronic malarial poisoning, the climate of west Texas is curative in almost every case. Austin is beyond the malarious district, and chills and fever are unknown, as are idiopathic affections. One of our most enterprising merchants reports the miraculous effects of a removal to this vicinity in the cases of his mother and sister, worthy of record in this connection. The family had resided for years in one of the most malarious districts in Ohio, and every member had been suffering with ague for months. The gentleman's mother had had

ONE HUNDRED AND FORTY CHILLS,

in alternate day order, and her health was completely shattered. She was but a living skeleton, a typical case of chronic malarial poisoning, with its attendant anaemia, dyspepsia, enlarged spleen, etc. A removal to Austin, Texas, completely cured her, and she had but one chill after reaching the state, even though exposed to inclement weather for a number of days immediately after her arrival.

It has been said that Austin is the gateway to the health belt whose claim as a pulmonary resort is under consideration.

TEXAS IS A GREAT STATE.

embracing an area of two hundred and seventy-four thousand square miles, an area greater than that of the New England confederation with New York and Pennsylvania combined, and it is but natural that so vast a territory should present a decided diversity of topography and climate. In the northern part of the state are to be found the wheat and oats and fruit growing lands; in eastern and southeast Texas are the lumber districts; in central and southern Texas cotton and corn receives the greatest share of attention, while in the tier of counties one hundred miles back from the Gulf, near the central longitude of the state, sugar is the chief product. To the western and southwestern parts of the state and to the Pan handle region, are the cattle interests mainly confined, and it is to these portions of Texas, more especially

SOUTH OF THE SNOW LINE,

that pulmonary invalids are invited. Austin and her neighboring city, San Antonio are the chief commercial marts of all this vast section, and also the distributing points for the traveling public, whether invalid or otherwise. Austin is first reached on the trip from the north. It is highly important that a rest should be taken here if any of the higher altitudes are to be visited. The growing town of Burnet, sixty miles distant on the line of the Austin & Northwestern railway, is alone accessible from this city. Its attitude is six hundred feet above that of Austin. Beyond Burnet, are the towns of Mason, Fredericksburg, Llano, San Saba and Menardville, with altitude ranging from fifteen hundred to twenty-two hundred feet above sea level, and from Burnet these points are to be reached by stage or private conveyance. The Austin & Northwestern railroad is the only line extending in a northwesterly direction into the health region of Texas, except via Del Rio on the Rio Grande, thence up that river toward El Paso, which gives an additional twenty-four hours of travel, with its attendant fatigue and expense. If a very high altitude is desired, the latter is the trip, the Sunset road at the crossing of the divide, near Fort Davis, attaining its maximum altitude of above six thousand feet. But, if a

PURE, DRY, BALMY ATMOSPHERE,

at moderate height above sea level is desired, and experience proves this to be exactly what is needed with a large majority of visiting health seekers, Austin and immediate vicinity is the place, and further travel is unnecessary.

The "northers" of Texas have a reputation which has had the effect of detering many from seeking health here, who would otherwise have come and been benefitted. It is true that this latitude is subject to variations of temperature which seem quite extreme and severe; but they are as nothing compared with the "blizzards" of Minnesota and Colorado, or the "cold waves" of the East Atlantic states; and instead of being a bugbear or a drawback to our climate, they are a decided blessing. In fact, but for their bracing and ozonizing effect, there are times, even in winter, when the atmosphere of this region is almost too balmy and comfortable for restorative purposes.

THE NORTHERS ARE A REAL GOD-SEND,

and as their coming is usually well known before hand, their ill effects, if indeed, there be any such, may easily be guarded against. It is seldom that it is cold longer than three days in succession in Austin, and even the most delicate invalid usually rejoices at the bracing effect of a Texas norther. The thermometer never registers zero in this city or vicinity, although at the highest atitudes mentioned, that point is often passed, and there is hardly a day throughout the winter when outdoor exercise is impossible.

A WHOLE VOLUME

might be written upon the climatology of Austin and vicinity, yet the half remain untold. As a winter climate for consumptives, bronchitic, and throat invalids, catarrhal and asthmatic patients, chronic dyspeptics, hay-fever sufferers, in fact, for health seekers in general, ours is hardly equalled, certainly not surpassed on the American continent and if the tide of health seeking travel was but directed hither, instead of so largely to the malarial state of Florida, and to the frozen regions of the Rockies, the per cent of recoveries in ailments of the classes described, would be greatly increased over the present figures.

TEMPERATURE AND RAINFALL.

With regard to the seasons and temperature, spring weather may be said to prevail all winter, with the exception of a very few days, now and then, during December and January, when a norther brings the mercury down to the freezing point, or a few degrees below. The grass, is green, the cedars and the live oaks also, and flowers bloom in the open air during every month in the year. Christmas dinner tables are usually

DECKED WITH VIOLETS AND TEA ROSES,

gathered from the lawns outside.

From April a slight but steady increase of heat goes on till the middle of July, from which time to the middle of September, the highest temperature of the year prevails. Mere figures, however, give a stranger an exaggerated idea of the heat of the summer. Ameliorating circumstances operate here to make 100° more endurable than 90° in the latitude of Ohio or New York. In the first place, the increase of the heat is so gradual that the system becomes prepared for it; and then the people adapt themselves to the requirements of the climate. The abundant fruit, vegetables and melons are freely used, and every one keeps, as much as possible, out of the sun; though it may be remarked in passing, that

NO CASE OF SUNSTROKE

has been known, except in a few exceptional instances of extreme dissipation. Again, the dryness of the atmosphere in summer prevents any feelings of languor and oppression, such as are experienced in a more humid situation. even in much higher latitudes; and finally, chief among the modifying causes, is the

THE DRISKILL HOTEL.

GENTLE BUT STEADY BREEZE

which blows from the Gulf of Mexico during the great part of the day, and all the night. Whatever its fluctuations during the day, and it has its caprices—it arises in the evening as unfailing as the twilight itself, so cool and soft, yet so persistent and steady, that those who have once enjoyed its refreshing breath are sure no other breeze was ever quite so delicious. The nights are thus rendered thoroughly comfortable even when the days are hottest, and this explains why people seem to suffer no ill effects from the long summers of this climate—the pleasant nights refresh the system sufficiently to counteract the ill effects, if there are any, of the warm days. One may sleep where the full force of this night breeze blows upon him without experiencing any ill effects; and it is remarked also as peculiar to this climate that exposure to inclement weather does not seem, as a usual thing, to be attended with the same danger to health as in other localities.

The leading farm products in the vicinity of Austin are cotton, corn, wheat oats and hay. All vegetables seen in Northern markets, and some not to be found there, are grown on the

NUMEROUS VEGTABLE FARMS

that surround the city. The finest that seem to thrive are the peach, fig, plum, apricot and grape. Pears and apples will also do well, when intelligently cultivated, although a few years ago it was held by old farmers that they could not be brought to perfection. A proper selection of soil and variety has, however, during the past few years, triumphantly proved this to be a mistake. Much enthusiasm has lately been brought to bear upon fruit culture in this locality, and new fruits and varieties are now being constantly produced. This gives reason to believe that some fruits now pronounced unsuitable to this climate will, in the near future, be abundantly grown here. Melons are plentiful and excellent; vegetables are in season from one to two months earlier than in St. Louis and New York, and as a second crop of many vegetables is produced in the early fall, the supply is continued far into the winter. Green peas, for example, are supplied till near December.

The following table shows the highest and lowest temperature reached, and also the amount of rainfall for the past eight years:

	Highest temp.	Lowest temp.	Rainfall.
1879-80	100	16	18.34
1878-9	96	23	21.34
1880-1	94	10	42.22
1881-2	98	12	25 14
1882-3	98	12	43.49
1883-4	101	24	43.27
1884-5	98	22	33.29
1885-6	103	6	32.60

Table showing monthly average temperature and amount of rainfall during the past two years, beginning November 1, 1884:

	1884-5. TEMP. Max.	1884-5. TEMP. Min.	1884-5. RAINFALL. Inches.	1885-6. TEMP. Max.	1885-6. TEMP. Min.	1885-6. RAINFALL. Inches.
Nov.	66.61	49.35	3.40	71.03	50.35	1.17
Dec.	57.30	41.84	1.68	64.00	43.89	2.69
Jan.	51.50	38.50	5.87	54.06	30.09	0.97
Feb.	51.27	49.57	0.78	67.56	42.00	2.18
Mar.	66.40	52.06	2.22	59.68	50.92	3.94
Apr.	77.40	64.12	4.71	77.68	59.68	5.04
May	85.50	67.40	8.40	90.83	69.09	—
Jn'e	92.63	74.87	0.63	91.93	74.13	0.92
July	93.00	74.25	1.68	98.83	76.12	3.24
Aug.	94.80	74.84	1.66	98.80	76.04	6.01
Sept.	87.40	72.70	8.97	93.00	72.76	12.23
Oct.	76.95	55.50	1 82	79.96	58.24	0.25

From the figures given above it will be seen that the country about Austin has a fair average rainfall sufficient to produce always reasonably good crops, and generally most abundant ones. Little rain falls between July and September, but during the other months of the year it is so distributed as to favor alike the farm, orchard and garden; a fact to which the blossoming lawns, vine-covered verandas and thrifty shade trees, seen everywhere throughout the city, bear testimony.

HOTELS AND PRIVATE RESIDENCES.

Hitherto the traveling public and visitors to Austin have had to depend chiefly upon two leading hotels, both located on Congress avenue. Outside of these a number of hotels of less note have competed for public patronage. It was long felt, however, that there was a want of better hotel accommodation. With this view there was begun in January, 1885, the construction of one of the finest hotels in the south, to be opened on 20th December. This magnificent building occupies an eligible site on Pecan street, or Sixth street, near corner of Congress avenue, in the business centre of the city. In architecture, the Romanesque style was followed, the arch being a distinguishing feature of the design. The "new hotel," to the beholder from a distance, looms up like a palace above the surrounding buildings—a vast, fire-proof pile of brick, iron and stone, and whose lofty columns and sculptural ornaments in front strike the spectator with imposing effect.

The Hotel Orr is located on West Seventh street, one block from Congress avenue, and has just been completed at a cost of $30,000. The building is of brick, three stories high, with broad southern verandas in front, and can accommodate 100 guests. It is furnished with telephone, gas, cistern and hydrant water and perfect system of electric bells.

The old Raymond House, on the corner of the Avenue and Fourth street, is being repaired and enlarged and will shortly be in first-class running order.

The Avenue hotel, three blocks above the Raymond house, can accomodate 150 guests and has been for some time under the excellent management of Mrs. Dill.

A large proportion of the private residences of Austin are of a size and style commensurate with its public buildings. No city in the country furnishes such a number of varied and beautiful building sites, and these have been turned to account by the combined skill of the architect and the thrifty wealth of the owner. There are sites within the city limits which, crowned with stately oaks, or beautiful cedars, and flanked by rocky or pebbly declivities, command a view of the Colorado river and its magnificent scenery for a distance of ten miles. Not a few of these sites have been improved and embellished by the hand of art, until, surmounted by attractive buildings, they become handsome and beautiful homes.

Most of the finer and more opulent residences are constructed of the durable white limestone, from quarries a few miles distant, or of brick and stone together. Many fine residences have of late years been erected by wealthy cattle and stockmen—some of the millionaires from distant parts of the state, who come to Austin as a desirable place of residence where they can have educational and other advantages for their families.

As proof of the progress of fine architecture in Austin, it may be mentioned that within the past year over half a million dollars have been expended in buildings of all descriptions, exclusive of the new capitol. Residences, many of them magnificent villas, have been constructed of brick or limestone, costing all the way from $500 to $50,000, and all in the most modern style. Generally, these beautiful abodes are as elegant and comfortable within as they are attractive and imposing without.

THE DRISKILL HOTEL.

In proportion as nature has endowed Austin over all other Texas cities, causing it to be selected as the capital of the state, so also can Austin justly boast of her superiority over any other city in the south in that this city now possesses a magnificent hotel building, whose appointments would be an ornament to New York, St. Louis, or San Francisco, being the peer of any hotels in those cities. Having chiefly in view the comfort and convenience of the most fastidious guest, the hotel has been constructed with good taste and sound judgment, costing, finished and furnished, $400,000. It has been named "The Driskill," in honor of its enterprising and public-spirited owner, and occupies an eligible site on East Sixth (East Pecan) street, near the corner of Congress avenue, in the business centre of the city. The dimensions of "The Driskill" are 150 feet south frontage on East Sixth (East Pecan), 170 feet east frontage on Brazos street, 260 feet west frontage, and 80 feet on East Seventh street (East Bois d' Arc) street—in all covering an area of a half square.

It is a fire-proof building, and is constructed of brick, the exterior being a pleasing combination of brick and dressed limestone, and is four stories in height. The design of the building is the Romanesque style of architecture, and is without doubt the purest example of that style to be found in this part of the country. Each of the principal facades is of presed brick dressed with white limestone. The plinth course, imposts, caps, keys, carbels, dragoons, tablets, etc., being also of limestone. The building presents an imposing and inviting appearance, as it looms up like a palace above all the surrounding buildings. On the south, east and west, are the three grand entrances, the main one being through a triumphal arch opening on East Sixth (East Pecan) street. On the first or ground floor, two spacious corridors, thirty-five or thirty-six feet in width respectively, intersect each other at the rotunda, which is open, airy and capacious.

THE FIRST FLOOR.

On this floor, just where the two immense corridors intersect, is the office, with all the handsomest and most approved appointments. One of these improvements is the system of bells connecting by means of an electric button with every room, thus enabling the clerk to learn whether any occupant of a room is in it without sending a bell-boy. In addition to this system of electric bells is, of course, the system of call bells from the room to the clerk's office. There is also in connection with the office an immense fire-proof vault. On this floor, in the rear of the office is located the spacious billiard and bar room. The bar side board and counter is one of the handsomest in the United States and was made especially for the "Driskill." The bar side board and counter, as well as the handsome office counter, news counter and cigar and telegraph counter, are all elaborately carved in the Romanesque style, and are in keeping with the exterior ornamentation of the building. The billiard room contains four of the latest and most modern billiard tables, and on the wall is the head of an immense Texas steer with its huge horns spanning about five feet.

The chairs and sofas for these corridors and other rooms on this floor, are made of solid walnut, with leather seats, and are very massive and heavy. The other rooms on this floor are the immense closets and wash rooms finished with marble slabs, the wood work being of heart pine, the barber shop with four bath rooms, and a beautiful reading room, large enough to accommodate 100 guests at one time. There is a large handsome passenger hydraulic elevator. The ceiling is twenty feet high and is of corrugated sheet iron, divided off in huge pannels by finely carved heart pine. On this floor there are three staircases, one at the ladies' entrance, a private one and the grand double staircase. The

four stories, massive and imposing, and commanding a magnificent view of the scenery of the river in the distance, the building having cost $60,000, and the site valued at $15,000. This school is for girls, the attendance being about 180. South of the Colorado and three miles from the centre of the city, and also beautifully situated, is St. Edward's college for boys and young men, conducted by the fathers of the Holy Cross.

In addition to these institutions there is a young ladies' select school of high rank, Hood Seminary, with sixty students, located on West Eighth street, occupying a desirable and central location. The appointments and building are all modern; value of the property, $15,000; within two or three blocks of the leading hotels. This school has a good library.

There is also a young ladies' school (Stuart Seminary), select and private, on East Ninth street, beautifully located, and patronized by the best families in the state. The students number fifty; value of property, including building, $15,000. This seminary has always occupied a high rank.

There is also located on the avenue a first-class business college, where a commercial education can be obtained. Also a German and English academy for boys, occupying a castellated building in the west of the city.

The Tillotson institute for colored youths of either sex, is a five story brick building, stone basement, situated on a commanding site one mile east of the city. The property includes twenty-three acres. It has about 150 students, from 14 years of age upward, 40 per cent. being boys, coming from different parts of the state. The property, including building, is owned by the American Missionary association, and is supported by the congregational churches of the United States and also receives help from the fund of $1,000,000 given by John F. Slater, of Norwich, Conn., to colored industrial schools. The institute has a library of 1,000 volumes. Value of property, including building, $40,000.

THE NEW CAPITOL.

For the past few years much has been written both in the local press and the press of the country in regard to the state house of Texas, the plans, specifications and perspective drawing for which were the creation of an able designing architect, combined with the intelligent co-operation of public servants of practical sagacity, and the construction of which requires on the part of the builders and supervisors special technical knowledge of a high order. It is somewhat difficult to present such a full description of this colossal structure as will be readily understood by the general reader; for, the truth is, it is well worth a trip to Austin, even from a distance, to visit and examine this granite House of State. In order, however, that the stranger may have some conception of its grandeur and magnitude, an outline is here submitted.

In coming up Congress avenue from the Union depot, the stranger will notice, directly at the head of this broad and stately street, some eight squares distant, situated on a beautiful hill, originally selected for the Capitol of the Republic of Texas, a monumental red granite building in course of construction, now with its third story nearly completed, towering over the business portion of the city, and running at right angles with Congress avenue, its third floor line being 115 feet above the Union depot, and the centre of its main front entrance facing south, being on a line with the centre of Congress avenue, which runs north and south. A short walk up Congress avenue, which is to Austin exactly what Pennsylvania avenue is to Washington city, brings the stranger upon Capitol Hill, where he can view the construction of the

LARGEST RED GRANITE BUILDING

in the world, examine the elaborate plans and beautiful drawings for this building, and witness the interesting operations of the various appliances and machinery used on this work, chief among which he will notice the sixteen tall and straight derricks with their projecting booms on various portions of the building, which are being continually raised higher and higher, as the work goes up, and which rise above the structure like the masts of a tremendous vessel, and by means of which pieces of dressed granite, weighing from ten to fifteen tons, limestone and other material are taken from the cars on the railroad track, that surrounds the building, and are placed where they belong in and upon the superstructure. There is no building anywhere that has as perfect and complete a building plant as is now in operation upon and in connection with the Texas state house. Three hundred men are at present at work upon the building, and there are about 2,000 men who are engaged in different sections of the United States and Europe, either in manufacturing or preparing material for various portions of the building. It is to be completed, under contract; not later than January 1, 1890, but from the rapid progress now being made it is evident that it will be finished early in 1889. The state of Texas gives a Chicago syndicate

THREE MILLION ACRES OF LAND,

located in a solid body in the extreme northwestern section of the state, comprising nearly all of nine counties, a territory larger than the state of Connecticut, for building this state house according to contract, plans and specifications agreed to by the state authorities and the syndicate, and it is estimated that the building, when completed, will have cost the syndicate about $4,000,000.

The exterior of the Texas state house is being constructed of native red granite from quarries in Burnet county, seventy-five miles west of Austin, where there are solid barren mountains of this durable material in inexhaustible quantities, pronounced by experts to be equal in every respect to the celebrated red granite of Scotland. The interior and dome walls of the building are, respectively, of rubble and dimension limestone from the quarries of this county.

The design of the new state house borders on the Doric, or, as it has been termed, a new Greek style of architecture. In form it approximates the Greek cross, with projecting center and flanks, having a rotunda and dome at the intersection of the main corridors. From east to west it is 562 feet long; from north to south 287 feet broad, and the height to the apex of the dome is 311 feet. The area of the building covers two and one-fourth acres.

The granite of the exterior of the first story is in large blocks, laying lengthwise, with the large window jambs standing upright, all being rough rock face work, showing the native richness of the material, while all the margins, including the window sills and their bases, are smoothly dressed, and the cornices are an imposing variety of smoothly dressed and rock face work. The exterior of the second, third and fourth stories have also considerable rock face work appropriately distributed, including the bases of the pilasters, the imposts, mullions and window jambs, but the stately feature of these upper stories is the numerous tall, clear cut and smoothly dressed granite pilasters that extend the full length of these stories, there being 176 of them around the building.

The basement is 11 feet 6 inches in height, the first story 22 feet, 1½ inches, the second story 20 feet, 10½ inches, third story 20 feet, and fourth story 19 feet in height.

The height to the first colonnade, or promenade, around the exterior of the dome above the roof is 126 feet; to the second colonnade above is 162 feet, and to the colonnade around the lantern of the dome is 217 feet, while the base of the bronze statue of of the Goddess of Liberty, that surmounts the lantern is 285 feet, the height of the statue being 12 feet, and to the

TOP OF THE LARGE GLASS STAR

emblematic of the Lone Star of Texas, which is secured above the statue, is 311 feet above the earth line of the building, which, including the elevation of Capitol hill above the city, places this star at a height of 376 feet, when viewed from the business portion of Congress avenue.

In the basement there are 63 rooms, to be nicely finished, and which will be used for storage of records and other purposes. The first floor is set apart for all the executive offices of the state government; the second floor for the legislative, and the third for the judicial departments; while in the fourth or central story there are a large number of handsomely finished rooms, not set aside for any special purpose.

The entire building will be lit by gas and electricity, and heated throughout by steam from a boiler house, already erected, a short distance to the east of the capitol grounds, and connected by a tunnel with the main building, through which the steam pipes pass. Passenger and freight elevators of the most approved style are provided for in the building, and every improved appliance and convenience used in any other complete modern public structure will be found in the new state house of Texas.

The distinctive feature of the main front entrance, facing south, is the triumphal arch that spans this entrance at a height of seventy-two feet, underneath which, in the vestibule of the first floor supporting a granite balcony, stand two magnificent columns, their bases and shafts of polished granite, with bands and caps of polished black and white marble. In striking contrast with this ornate entrance is the massive granite portico that dignifies the entrance on the opposite or north side of the building, facing university hill. The supports of the first story of this portico are large, rough blocks of granite laying lengthwise, while the columns of the second and third stories above are smoothly dressed. At the east and west ends of the building are open balconies with granite balustrades. In the four pediments of the building there will be large glass stars, with appropriate carving in the granite around them, which, together with the star on the dome of the building, are arranged to be illuminated by electricity.

All the broad and stately corridors throughout the building are laid in encaustic tiling of various appropriate colors and attractive designs. Each of the offices on the first floor has a large, fire-proof vault for records, and the state treasurer's office also has

A TREMENDOUS CHROME STEEL MONEY VAULT.

The two grand stairways are situated on both sides of the rotunda, near its east and west entrances to the long corridors that run the full length of the first floor; and these grand stairways ascend to the second floor near the entrances to the vestibules leading into the senate chamber in the east flank and the house of representatives in the west flank of the building, while the entire north projection on the second floor is occupied by the state library, and a large portion of the south projection is taken up by the governor's public reception room. These are the four grand state apartments on the second floor, and adjoining this last named room is the postoffice of the house and senate. West of the house of representatives, and also east of the senate chamber, in the two end pavillions of the building, are numerous rooms for the officers, clerks and committees of the legislature, and opening into the state library is a portrait gallery.

The house of representatives is ninety four by ninety-six feet, and the senate chamber ninety-four by seventy-nine feet. Both these legislative halls are open to the ceiling of the third floor, with galleries on the third floor line completely encircling their interior, the ceilings above being heavy, polished, cut stained plate glass, embossed and flashed, of superb design and color, and directly above these ceilings are the immense skylights on the roof of the building; while opening into the house and senate from the north and south are a double tier of windows. It will thus be seen that these two legislative halls receive an abundant supply of natural light, which will render them the most desirable assembly rooms that could possibly be constructed. The state library is sixty-eight by one hundred and twenty-four feet, and is also arranged like the house and senate for procuring an ample supply of natural light. Immediately above the state library, on the third floor, are the supreme and appellate court rooms, law library, attorneys' rooms, and clerks' offices, and in the front projection of the building, on the same floor, are the judges' consultation rooms. In the fourth or central story are twenty-three rooms not designated for any special use. There are in the entire building 256 apartments. Connected with the second third and fourth floors of the building is a balcony five feet in depth encircling the interior of the rotunda, sixty feet in diameter. The center of this rotunda, on the first floor, is of heavy plated glass, to give light into that portion of the basement directly underneath. There are also additional balconies in the interior of the rotunda, above the fourth floor of the building; and in the interior crown of the dome there is a canopy or diaphragm, circular in form, to be prepared for the reception thereon of allegorical or historical paintings. There is a flight of stairs leading from the fourth story to the exterior of the dome, and from this great altitude the variety of picturesque scenery in and around Austin will be interesting for the visitor to contemplate.

The dome of the Texas state house is the tallest of any capitol building in America, and the national capitol at Washington and the New York state capitol at Albany are the only two capitol buildings that can stand a comparison with the Texas state house, either in point of grandeur or magnitude.

OTHER PUBLIC BUILDINGS.

In the vicinity of the new capitol, at the head of Congress avenue, stands the temporary capitol building, constructed in 1882 for use till the completion of the capitol. The burning of the old state capitol in 1881 necessitated its building. It is a large, three-story, neat, though unpretentious building, occupied by the state government till the completion of the new building.

Opposite the temporary capitol is the court house of Travis county. Like most of the public buildings of Austin, it is constructed of white limestone. It is four stories, style ornate and dignified, and is one of the handsomest court house edifices in Texas. It was constructed in 1877 at a cost of $95,000, and in connection with the castellated jail and other buildings on the same premises cost altogether $150,000, the payment of which was completed by the county in the summer of 1886.

To the eastward of this building stands the General Land Office of the State of Texas. It stands in an area and enclosure of its own, on an elevation overlooking the court house. It is built almost exclusively of limestone, iron and solid concrete. It is a massive two story structure, one of the oldest in the city, and originally designed by a gentleman who was architect to one of the royal courts of Europe, and who probably copied the design from some of the old castles on the Rhine. This is not the least important state building about Austin, for it contains the titles, abstracts and records of every acre of land in Texas. Hence the building was made absolutely fireproof.

To the eastward of the land office, and on the heights that crown the farther banks of Waller creek, is the State Institute for the Blind. This is one of the largest institutions of the kind in the south. The central building is three stories, with wings of two stories, all having

A FRONTAGE OF 270 FEET,

and containing seventy rooms, halls and apartments. There is over 100 pupils, of either sex—from all parts of the state. It is an eleemosynary institution, supported by the state.

One of the most naturally beautiful places of interest in the vicinity of Austin is the Lunatic Asylum, situated on an elevated plateau, some two miles north of the city, and the dome of whose main building is visible from Capitol hill, looking up from the green foliage of the magnificent park surrounding the asylum. The buildings are of brick and stone, large, massive and roomy.

The total number of patients treated for the year ending October 31, 1886, was 773, of whom males 426, females 345. The total cost of running the institution during the same period, was $97,000, or about $168 per head.

The Lunatic Asylum buildings are two to four stories in height, and, from first to last, cost the state $300,000.

The institution for the Deaf and Dumb of Texas occupies commodious buildings, situated on the south bank of the river, amid beautiful groves of oak and other trees, and which looms up with fine effect as a prominent object in the picturesque scenery on the river at that point. It is reached from the splendid iron bridge, belonging to the county, elsewhere noticed.

The number of pupils, deaf mutes, cared for is 130. The situation is so salubrious that no death has occurred at this asylum during the year ending November 1, 1886, and only $100 was paid for medical services during that period. The Deaf and Dumb asylum commands a magnificent view of the city. It is said that Jefferson Davis, ex-president of the Confederate States, in the presence of several leading citizens of Austin, viewing Austin from the site of this asylum, remarked he had never in his travels seen such a beautiful natural location for a city as was there presented to him.

From the list of Austin's public buildings must not be omitted the United States postoffice, corner of Sixth and Colorado streets, erected by the government about five years ago, at a cost of $225,000. It is a handsome four-story stone structure.

CHURCHES.

No city in the state excels Austin in the beauty and elegance of its church architecture. Here there is the advantage not possessed by Galveston, Houston, San Antonio, Dallas, or Fort Worth, of beautiful and commanding sites, which greatly add to the stately magnificence of the buildings, which from eminences tower up above the city. Nearly all the leading churches of Austin are durably constructed of solid, massive limestone, taken from native quarries a few miles distant.

Among the churches is St. Mary's Roman Catholic church, of the Immaculate Conception, a fine and imposing structure of stone, situated on an elevated site on East Tenth or Mulberry street. The congregation comprises 200 families, and 500 members. Connected with this church, also, are several societies, notably the "Children of St. Mary," a sodality comprising 75 members, young girls of twelve to eighteen years old. Also, St. Joseph's sodality for boys, fifty members. Connected with this church, likewise, is a parochial school for boys. The Catholic church in Austin dates from 1853. The value of this church property is $60,000, including building.

The First Baptist church, corner Tenth and Colorado streets, is a commodious structure of brick and stone. Membership 300; Sunday school attendance, 250; value of the property, $16,000.

The First Presbyterian church, corner of Lavaca and Seventh streets, occupies a commodious building of limestone. Membership, 300; value of property, including building and ground, $15,000. Connected with this church is a chapel, situated on Robinson's hill, East Austin.

The Southern Presbyterian church also occupies a beautiful, somewhat imposing building of limestone, on an eminence on East Bois d' Arc, or Seventh street.

The inception of the Presbyterian denomination in Austin dates back to 1850, when this church was planted in the capital city by Rev. Wm. Baker, who was pastor till 1865. After the war the Southern church had but eleven members; in 1872 the membership had increased to seventy-one. In June, 1875, the present building was occupied. Now there are 274 communicants. Value of church building and property, about $20,000. Since 1869 this congregation has expended, for religious purposes, a

TOTAL OF $60,000.

The Tenth Street Methodist Episcopal church, south, occupies a fine building of brick and stone, corner of Tenth and Brazos streets, like the other churches on an eminence; membership, 550; Sunday school enrollment 400; value of building and ground, $32,000. The Methodist church started in Austin coeval with the beginning of the city.

St. David's Episcopal church comprises one of the finest congregations in the city. The corner stone of the church building, now occupying the corner of San Jacinto and East Seventh streets, was laid in 1855, and the church was rebuilt in 1885. It is a handsome, spacious building of native limestone. Value of property, including building, $20,000.

The Methodist church building is at the northwest corner of the Capitol grounds. It was built in 1880; value of property $20,000. There is also a Swedish church situated north of the capitol grounds.

The Congregation Beth Israel was organized in 1874, and comprises some thirty-five members, among them many wealthy and prominent citizens of Austin. The building occupied is a handsome two-story limestone structure, on an eminence over-looking the capitol grounds on the west, and Waller creek on the east. Value of property, $13,000. The congregation, though small, handsomely supports a regular minister.

Besides the churches above mentioned, there are the Christian church, West Hickory and Colorado streets, where a fair congregation worship; also, the Cumberland Presbyterian church, southeast corner West Seventh and Lavaca streets; also, German Methodist Episcopal church.

The African Methodist Episcopal church, corner Ash or Ninth and San Antonio streets, is a stone building, organized in 1874; membership, 360; value of building and property, $15,000. Other colored churches are Wesley Chapel, East Ninth street; Colored Baptist and Simpson Tabernacle; Wesley Chapel, (Methodist) valued at $14,000; membership, 450.

Connected with the churches are numerous ladies' aid societies, with a membership of fifty to one hundred each.

AUSTIN AS A BUSINESS CENTER.

Austin's business growth has steadily kept pace with its progress in other respects. It is the center of a healthy, increasing trade, drawn from one of the richest and most fertile regions of Central Texas—containing lands that, with a good season, make 30 to 40 bushels of corn, and one to one and a half bales of cotton to the acre. Besides, it is a good stock and grazing country—the soil being black land or red, or chocolate loam, noted for its fertility. The counties tributary to Austin's trade are Caldwell, Bastrop, Gillespie, Williamson, Llano, Burnet, Mason and Blanco. Being a railroad center, it is connected by rail with a large portion of this territory—and over the International & Great Northern, the Austin branch of the Houston & Texas Central, and the Austin & Northwestern Narrow Gauge. The latter road at present terminates at Burnet, 60 miles in the northwest, but is soon to be extended west to Mason, and penetrating a rich stock and grazing region.

The city is directly connected with the fine agricultural region south of the Colorado, by a magnificent free, iron bridge, owned by the county of Travis, and which cost the county $75,000.

The annual shipments from Austin, of leading products in round numbers, are as follows: Cotton, 30,000 bales; value, $1,500,000; wool, 700,000 pounds, value, $125,000; hides, 250,000 pounds, value, $40,000; lime, 75,000 barrels, value, $55,000; grain and hay, $15,000; live stock, $200,000.

The total value of shipments approximates $2,000,000. Nearly 50,000 bales of cotton are compressed here annually.

The total value of the manufacturing industries of Austin, including flouring mills, ice factories, brick and marble works, printing establishments, cotton compress, foundry and soap works, harness and saddle making, patent medicine manufactories, oil works, cigar making, copper, tin, zinc and iron works, manufacturers of furniture, brooms, etc., exceeds $500,000. In addition to these sources of revenue to the commerce of Austin, over $600,000 is being annually distributed by the contractors of the new state capitol for the construction of the same. Also the money turned loose by the state in payment of services of officials in the various departments, and in the purchase of supplies for the various asylums and public institutions, is estimated to approximate $500,000.

CITY WATER SUPPLY.

This has much to do with the health of a city. The citizens of Austin have, without question, the purest water supply of any city in the southwest. The works are situated on the Colorado, and the machinery is of the finest and most improved pattern of any in the south. About one and a half million gallons are daily driven out into the mains—the pipes reaching to the most remote parts of the city. The water is equivalent to spring water, being procured from the immense wells of an aggregate diameter of over one hundred feet, walled in with solid stone, twenty feet deep, and in which there is a depth of ten feet of water, so clear that a pin can be seen at the bottom. The water can be seen bubbling up from the pebbly bottom like a number of springs. The water is considered pure and healthful as spring water.

TAXABLE WEALTH.

The growing wealth of Austin is shown from the following city assessments for five years, taken from the official record and vouched for as correct:

Year 1882	$5,252,837
" 1883	5,887,748
" 1884	6,844,560
" 1885	7,208,442
" 1886	7,518,211

Austin, therefore, has a taxable wealth equal to the city of Houston; and while the debt of the latter is $2,000,000, Austin's debt is but $125,000, with a tax rate of 1 1-3 per cent.

MISCELLANEOUS.

Congress avenue, at the head of which stands the new capitol, and which reaches to the magnificent iron bridge across the Colorado, has beautiful paved sidewalks of native stone. A lady can, in wet weather, walk from the capitol to the river without getting her shoes wet.

Standing at the head of the Avenue, on an elevated point in the grounds belonging to the capitol, the view to the south is among the most attractive about the city. The Deaf and Dumb asylum, with its extensive grounds and new and splendid buildings, is situated on a prominence immediately to the right of the old stage road to San Antonio and the southwest, looking northward over the city. To the left and immediately opposite, lies Fairview Park, occupying a beautiful and commanding site, from which the eye can take in many attractive views on the north side of the river, to the east and west, with Austin and her magnificent capitol building occupying the central field. Immediately beyond Fairview, is an important and growing suburb, called "South Austin," while three miles and a half further to the south are the old confederate fortifications, bearing the name "Fort View."

During the late civil war General Magruder's forces threw up these breastworks and rifle pits upon the most commanding spot, immediately to the south of the city, for the purpose of protecting the capital of Texas from invasion by the federal troops from the government post at San Antonio. Fort View is a point of interest to northern visitors, and from the west of the fortifications the surrounding country can be viewed for many miles.

The country to the south of the river, for a distance of a mile or two, will eventually be a part of Austin, and its many beautiful sites will be occupied, as some of them already are, by stately residences of wealthy business men.

As the prevailing breezes of this country are from the south and southeast, that part of Austin will always be desirable as a location for homes. It would be a stroke of good business policy for some enterprising citizen, or wealthy health seeker from the north, to erect a sanitary hotel on one of the commanding locations south of the city, which enterprise necessity will eventually demand.

Connected with the water works is an electric dynamo, from which electric lights are supplied to any part of the city.

The average value of business lots on Congress avenue is $4,000 to $20,000.

Austin is out of the track of cyclones and violent storms, and outside the belt of coast country subject to yellow fever.

Austin has a street railway system reaching all principal points, with seven miles of rails laid. Capital stock $50,000.

The two leading cattle companies having their headquarters in Austin are the Day Land and Cattle company, capital $500,000, and the Dolores Land and Cattle company, capital $1,000,000.

The city is lit with gas as well as electricity. The gas works are among the finest in the state, the company being based on $100,000 capital.

On the river above the city are some falls, generating a water power capable of driving large factories or other machinery, and which only requires capital to utilize and turn to account.

Among the public buildings of the city is the city and county hospital, east Austin. It is constructed of limestone, commodious, with all modern improvements, and built with special reference to the purposes for which it is intended.

GEOLOGICAL.

SALIENT GEOLOGICAL FEATURES OF TRAVIS COUNTY, TEXAS.

From the United States Geological Survey.

Geographically Travis county is a portion of the coastal plain that borders the Atlantic ocean from New Jersey to Vera Cruz, the surface and underlying strata of which slope in a general direction normal to the nearest sea coast. The portion of this plain bordering the Gulf of Mexico attains its greatest width along a line drawn from the mouth of the Ohio to the mouth of the Mississippi. It contracts to the southwest, and finally narrows out in northern Mexico. The city of Austin, which is upon the western border of this plain, separates the county in two well-defined geological and topographical areas, locally known as the mountainous region, constituting the western half of the county, and the "black waxy" prairies the eastern. The bed of the International railroad approximately corresponds with this line of demarkation.

The surface of the county—once a much more level plain than now—has been sculptured into its present features by the erosion of the Colorado and its tributaries, and the atmospheric action. This river, in its general course from northwest to southeast, follows the direction of the surface slope, and the dip of the rocks of the region. The greatest altitude in the western portion of the county, is twelve hundred and fifty feet, and the lowest, at the intersection of the eastern boundary and the bed of the Colorado river, is four hundred—a total of nearly eight hundred feet in the width of the county.

The western or mountainous half of the county, presents a great thickness of rock exposure. The mountains are not primarily caused by serious local disturbances of the earth's crust, although slight displacement of the strata is evident, but are chiefly the result of the erosion of the Colorado, which has carved a deep canon through an immense thickness of strata there. The rapid weathering of the limestone through the atmospheric causes has aided in producing the broken features.

The eastern part of the county is a more level plain, underlying strata dipping at a much smaller angle than those of the mountain region. The rock substance is quite different in many respects, and readily decomposes on exposure to air and moisture, and consequently weathering into a more level region of country.

The rock strata of Travis county represents a deep sea sedimentation exclusively, no igneous or eruptive material being found anywhere in place. Certain volcanic rocks have been reported from Pilot Knob, ten miles south of Austin, but there is every reason to believe that it is a mistaken supposition. (See Buckley's first annual report.)

They all belong to the middle and later periods of geological time—mostly the Cretaceous—slight traces of the eocene tertiary being found in the extreme eastern portion of the county.

The Cretaceous strata in Travis county represent two well defined sub-divisions of that period, the one resting unconformably upon the other. These sub-divisions are well distinguished by their paleontological, lithological and stratigraphical differences. The uppermost of these correspond in aerial distribution to the black prairie region, and is locally known wherever it occurs in Texas as the "white rock." Dr. R. F. Shumard, state geologist, 1858–1859, applied the name of "Austin limestone" to it, but it is an unfortunate appellation, for it furnishes neither the valuable Austin limestone used for building purposes, or that used for burning into lime. The same formation underlies the black prairie lands of Mississippi, Alabama, West Tennessee, Arkansas, and northern and central Texas. In other states it is known as the "rotten limestone," from the readiness with which it decomposes on exposure to sun and moisture. This faculty, although rendering it unfit for building stone, makes it of incalculable value to the agriculturist, the rich black soil being largely a result of its decomposition. The lower member of the Cretaceous in Travis county constitutes the mountainous and hilly region to the west of the city, the contact between it and the above mentioned member, being easily traced along the lower portion of Shoal creek in the city of Austin. The formation is best seen along Barton's creek and the sides of Mount Bonnell. This member of the Cretaceous is found only in Texas, and is readily distinguished by its characteristic fossils, not one of which extends into the Austin limestone above it. The unlimited beds of stone from which the principal buildings in the city of Austin are constructed occur in it. The Austin marble, so-called, is a hard stratum of limestone occurring near the base of this member. Near the same horizon, beautiful springs are often found, such as those near the residence of Land Commissioner Walsh, two miles west of the city.

Concerning the minute geology of the extreme western and eastern portion of the county, the writer cannot speak with certainty, not having visited them in person, but it is not improbable, from the dip of the strata, that on the western [illegible] the old formations may be found while on the eastern the Cretaceous strata are succeeded by the eocene.

The formations in the immediate vicinity of Austin, as well as the adjoining counties, present to the geologist many points of scientific interest that cannot be mentioned here, but which makes the city a locality especially well adapted for the study of Texas geology, a fact that will always add much to its advantages as a state capital and a seat of learning. The geological features of the county, by the division into two regions, one a fertile plain adapted to the highest agriculture, and the other a broken mountainous region that will always furnish those recreations and benefits of nature so essential to the health and happiness of mankind, and that can be procured—only pure air and water and diversified scenery—will always make Austin one of the most desirable places of residence in Texas.

STATE FINANCES AND RESOURCES.

The following table shows the total assessed values of the state since 1870 to the year 1[illegible]

Total values 1871	$[illegible]
1872	[illegible]
1873	[illegible]
1874	[illegible]
1875	[illegible]
1876	[illegible]
1877	[illegible]
1878	[illegible]
1879	[illegible]
1880	[illegible]
1881	[illegible]
1882	[illegible]
1883	[illegible]
1884	[illegible]
1885	[illegible]
1886	[illegible]

In some years it will be noticed the increase for the year was over fifty million dollars.

In 1886 there was an increase in the value of lands of	$[illegible]
Increase in value of town lots	[illegible]
Increase in value of railroads	[illegible]
Increase in value of horses and mules	[illegible]
There was a decrease in the value of sheep of	[illegible]
Decrease in value of cattle	[illegible]

Owing to the drouth, cattle quarantine and other unusually depressing causes.

The assessed value of lands in 1884 was	$[illegible]
In 1885	[illegible]
In 1886	[illegible]

Showing a steady improvement in land values.

The State tax is 25 cents, and the school tax is 12½ cents on the $100 valuation.

The rate of county tax in the several counties in state ranges from 7½ cents (in San Patricio county) to $1.00 (in Cameron county), the average rate, taking all the counties, being 54 cents on the $100 valuation. The rate in this (Travis) county last year was just fifty cents

The occupation taxes last year amounted to	$[illegible]
Drummers' taxes last year amounted to	41,728
Railroad passenger tax	[illegible]
Tax on insurance companies	17,262

STATE FINANCES.

The following is a detailed summary of property in Texas and values thereof, as shown by the assessment rolls of the state for the year 18[illegible]:

Classes of property.	Numbers.	values
Land assessed in acres	114,763,682	$[illegible]
City or town lots		[illegible]
Railroads assessed in miles	6,133	[illegible]
Freight lines assessed in miles	7,474	[illegible]
Land certificates, acres	151,862	[illegible]
Steamboats, sailing vessels, etc	202	[illegible]
Carriages, wagons, etc	296,787	[illegible]
Manufacturing tools, implements, etc.		[illegible]
Materials and manufactured articles		[illegible]
Horses and mules	1,185,918	[illegible]
Cattle	6,955,248	[illegible]
Jacks and jennets	7,371	[illegible]
Sheep	4,543,765	[illegible]
Goats	592,486	[illegible]
Hogs	[illegible]	[illegible]
Goods, wares and merchandise		[illegible]
Money on hand		[illegible]
Miscellaneous		[illegible]
		$[illegible]
Add to above the approximate assessed value of lands in unorganized counties, owned by non-residents		[illegible]
Total value		$[illegible]
State ad valorem tax		$[illegible]
" school "		[illegible]
" revenue poll "		[illegible]
" school " "		[illegible]
Total tax		$[illegible]
Average value of land per acre		[illegible]
" " railroads per mile		[illegible]
" " telegraphs " "		[illegible]
" " steamboats, etc		[illegible]
" " carriages, "		[illegible]
" " horses and mules		[illegible]
" " cattle		[illegible]
" " jacks and jennets		[illegible]
" " sheep		1.16
" " goats		[illegible]
" " hogs		[illegible]

LAND MATTERS.

The cash receipts from sales and leases of lands by the state land board since the board was organized in 1883, were as follows:

For 6 months in 1883	$[illegible]
" 12 " " 1884	[illegible]
" 12 " " 1885	[illegible]
" 11 " " 1886	[illegible]
Total to November, 1886	$[illegible]

STATE LAND.

The report of Commissioner Walsh of [illegible] 1884 showed:

Total school land	32,71[illegible]
Total sales	8,[illegible]
Balance then to credit of fund	24,6[illegible]

Approximations by the legislature, [illegible] in round figures:

For construction of state capitol	3,00[illegible]
To the state university	2,22[illegible]
" " blind institute	[illegible]
" " deaf and dumb institute	[illegible]
" " lunatic asylum	[illegible]
Total	5,52[illegible]

Besides liberal grants to railroads, ma[illegible] and other internal improvement enterp[illegible] tional millions of acres.

Of the university lands about tw[illegible] acres, and of the free school lands ab[illegible] two million acres remain unsold. Larg[illegible] each, however, have been leased: some [illegible] eight cents, but mostly at six cents [illegible] grazing lands. About 3[illegible],000 acres, recent[illegible] for the university on the Rio Grande, [illegible] over $50 an acre, on account of water advantages.

The free school lands are worth on an average $2 per acre, without regard to the fact [illegible] valuable mineral developments on som[illegible] Some of them, as timber lands, are [illegible] $5 to $10 per acre, on account of the tin[illegible] alone.

The capitol lands, three million acres [illegible] Handle portion of the state, have passed [illegible] the control of the capitol building contracto[illegible]

Governor Robinson, of Massachusetts, in a recent speech to his fellow-townsmen in Chicopee, advised them to "give more attention to town meetings and [illegible] the governor and president take care [illegible] themselves."

Paul Balliet, of Ballietsville, who died on Tuesday last, was one of the best known citizens of Leigh county, having been county commissioner and county auditor. He was largely interested in the North White Hall mines and the [illegible] furnace.

TEXAS INVESTORS' GUIDE

TEXAS INVESTORS' GUIDE TO PROFITABLE INVESTMENTS AND HOW TO MAKE THEM.

By C. H. BREWSTER. DENISON, GRAYSON COUNTY, TEXAS, JANUARY 15, 1887. VOLUME I, NUMBER 2.

INTRODUCTORY.

The first issue of the TEXAS INVESTORS' GUIDE, distributed principally in Connecticut to the number of about 10,000. having performed the purposes for which it was intended, *i. e.*: To enlighten the investors of Connecticut regarding the stock interests of Texas; also, in a measure, to remove existing prejudices, and demonstrate by indisputable evidence the profits attending investments in land and cattle; has naturally brought out many inquiries, and awakened more or less interest; and at the same time been subjected to criticisms favorable and otherwise. I will in brief touch upon some of the criticisms and answer thereto:

The first to come to hand was from a party in New Haven, whose connections extend all over the world, and in the protection of its varied interests, felt called upon to pronounce me a fraud, &c., &c. He manages the "World's Collection Association," and from his monumental position deigns to notice me even in terms of disapproval, is of itself quite a compliment, and so I consider it. His main objection was to the table illustrating the number of stock that would be raised in five years. This particular table was supposed to be taken in connection with other statements presented, allowing the generally accepted percentage for loss under favorable conditions. Like any other business, unforeseen or unlooked for contingences are liable to arise which cannot be estimated. I expected from the data presented, that the reader should exercise his reasoning powers, and knowing what a cow in pursuance of natural laws governing multiplication, was capable of doing, he should be capable of arriving at his own conclusions. All farmers owning stock have the illustration at hand. But there are certain conditions of climate and attendant expense attached to the business, which makes it more profitable in certain sections of country as compared with others, as I have attempted to exemplify.

From other letters, the following criticisms:

"What is your object and purpose; you present nothing tangible." And from another: "What show does a man stand with a small capital, say from one to two thousand dollars;" and from others to give them the address of four or five reliable cattle companies, &c., &c.

I admit that it was somewhat blind as to the first objection. Its purpose was to draw out correspondence, and then formulate a plan of organization that would be the most acceptable, and as the result I submit a plan of organization which has been submitted to, and approved by, parties of high financial standing in Hartford. A financial agent selected who is universally respected and esteemed, in whom implicit confidence can be placed.

All I ask is that you give the plan submitted careful consideration, and make careful inquiry from the references submitted, and I am perfectly willing to abide by the result, well satisfied that they will be satisfactory.

I do not wish to speak in disparaging terms of the cattle business of the Northwest, just sufficient to draw comparisons, for I am well aware that there is a great deal of New England capital invested there. For among the letters which I have received, some are from parties who have invested in cattle companies operating in the Northwest, who are not satisfied with the returns, and consequently disgusted with the business. All I ask from such parties is that they will not condemn the cattle business of Southwest Texas, for the elements of success vary very materially as to the two sections of country, and hence no just comparison can be drawn.

I know what I am writing about when Texas is the subject. for I have cattle interests in the Southwest, and for the past ten years I have traveled most of the time on an average of four or five thousand miles a month, and coming in contact officially with from two to three hundred people daily, has given me an extended acquaintance, as well as a thorough knowledge of the State and its developments, and I have made the best use of the opportunities I have had, and now desire to benefit you as well as myself with the knowledge thus obtained.

Conditional application for stock conditions fully set forth in same, blanks for same, will be mailed upon application.

I request immediate attention and application, so that land can be purchased as soon as possible, for it is coming into more active demand every day; and by the purchase of cattle now we get the spring increase, and there being so many cattle on the outside, or free range, will enable me to buy at close figures.

C. H. B.

PLAN OF ORGANIZATION
—OF THE—
EQUITABLE
LAND, CATTLE AND INVESTMENT COMPANY.

In place of a board of directors, the management of the affairs of the company to be vested in the hands of a board of Trustees, three or more in number; one of whom will act as Managing Trustee; one as Attorney residing in Texas; one as Financial Agent residing at Hartford, Conn.

The first named to have the direct management of the affairs of the company, his duties to be: a personal supervision over the details pertaining to the operations of said company; keep a correct account of the receipts and expenditures; personally attend to the sales of beeves, the purchase of the land and cattle, assisted by the attorney; and to render an account of same to the Financial Agent at Hartford; together with said account, all bills of expense, &c. In the purchase of the land and cattle, duplicate deeds conveying title to said land. also bills of sale for the purchase of cattle and horses for the ranch, authenticated and duly recorded by the County Clerk of the county wherein same is located.

Managing Trustee to be assisted in management of the working of the ranch by a foreman or superintendent, who will permanently reside on the ranch, and to carry out or perform the instructions given by the Managing Trustee.

The second Trustee or Attorney, to assist the Managing Trustee in looking after the legal affairs of the company, supervise the transfer of titles, and see that same conform to the law; his compensation to be proportionate to services rendered.

The third Trustee to act as Financial Agent, with office at Hartford, Conn., he to be the custodian of the funds of the company; disburse money upon a requisition from the Managing Trustee; said requisitions to state for what purpose the money is required; said requisition to be kept on file in his office; also all bills of expense properly receipted in duplicate, one to be retained by the Managing Trustee; also duplicate bills of sale from the parties of whom horses or cattle are purchased, duly authenticated and recorded by county clerk of the county wherein the transactions are completed; these at all times to be open to the inspection of the stockholders. All revenues derived from the ranch to be remitted to him by the Managing Trustee, and by him deposited in the National Exchange Bank of Hartford, Conn., to the credit of the company. He is also authorized to disburse dividends to the stockholders, whenever the balance of cash to the credit of said company justifies it, and with the consent or concurrence of the Managing Trustee, taking proper receipt for same from each stockholder.

On or about the 1st. of January of each year, an exhibit of the company's business for the preceding year to be drawn off, and a copy of same mailed to each stockholder; together with said exhibit a copy of an inventory of cattle, horses, land and improvements, and value of same.

Said inventory to be made oath to by the Managing Trustee.

The capital stock af the company as designated in the Charter, is $100,000. If at any time it is deemed advisable to increase the capital stock of the company, due notice to be given to the stockholders, who will be given the preference in subscribing to a further issue of stock.

A meeting of the stockholders to be held at the office of the Financial Agent, at Hartford, some time during the month of January, after the inventory has been completed, and accounts of the preceding year audited by the Financial Agent.

At said meeting same to be submitted to the stockholders for their consideration and approval, and they as a majority to decide upon the policy to be pursued the succeeding year.

This meeting to be attended by, and presided over by the Managing Trustee, who must be prepared to answer all questions pertaining to the management of the company's interests.

C. H. BREWSTER.

LAND AND CATTLE PRIME FACTORS
IN THE
ACCUMULATION OF INDIVIDUAL WEALTH IN TEXAS.

Referring to the article reciting the accumulations of individual wealth, I will go back to the commencement of the career of a few of the more fortunate and successful. In the first place it will be necessary to give a brief description of the methods of doing business prevalent at that time, and also a brief comparison of the past to the present.

I will start off with a few of the millionaires residing at Galveston. Millionaires appear to be centralized at Galveston, and I have heard it stated, though I have not made the comparison myself, that it is, in point of wealth, the second or third wealthiest city in the United States in proportion to its population; reference to last census will inform you, &c.

This is owing to the fact that for many years it was the distributing mart for nearly all Texas. Distribution of supplies of all kinds, and in turn the distribution of the products of the soil, made Galveston the clearing house of the State, and all Texas paid tribute to its capital and commercial supremacy By advances of cash and extensions of credit through her merchants, to the interior merchants, and the entering into, for the time being, of a copartnership with the latter, which would be appropriately termed, "U, Catchem and We, Fleeceum & Co.," made of the farmer or producer a slave bonded to the Galveston merchants through their servants, "the interior merchants." There was an "*entente cordiale*" existing among the Galveston merchants, with one common end in view, a pull all together, to make all they could, the farmers being the principal sufferers, and oft-times the interior merchant was counted among the victims. The farmers were not deserving of much sympathy, for they possessed a perfect mania for obtaining all the credit possible. A great portion of the immigration to Texas is made up from the Southeastern Staies, i. e.—Mississippi, Alabama, Georgia, Virginia, &c.—and if, perchance, they should have anything left over, they would pack up and with their whole families journey back to their original States on a visit, returning in due course of time, with scarcely a cent in their pockets, to make another crop, depending upon the interior merchant to tide them over, advancing supplies, &c., he, in turn. taking a crop lien, chattel mortgage, &c., charging them a double price on all they purchased in addition to interest at 12 per cent. on matured notes, thereby, if interior merchants made all his collections, would be equivalent to 25 to 40 per cent. on capital invested. This applies to tenants. Now, if the merchant extending credit is a prudent and cautious business man he obtains an additional security by having the owner of the land guarantee the credits extended. Now, for a further illustration, we will take the history of an interior merchant, and style him "A."

"A" is engaged in farming and stockraising combined, and is ambitious to become a merchant; takes a trip to Galveston, interviews a few of the leading merchants, selects one or two that will do the best by him in the interchange of business relations.

To start in with he may have from $600 to $1,500 in cash, but has plenty of land. Galveston merchant agrees to stock him up. taking his cash, and deed of trust on his land, to secure his notes, and, if possible, obtain endorsements from a few of his friends owning land, &c. For mind that the Galveston merchant possesses all the experience as against "A's" ignorance, and the chances are that in due course of time the Galveston merchant will possess it all. As a retired Galveston merchant, in commenting upon the past, expressed it to me, "It was a rollicking style of doing business, with the advantages all on one side."

"A," in return, obligates himself to ship them all of his cotton. Now bear in mind that cotton was the staple crop, and they will advance him cash during the summer and fall to secure all the cotton they can. The Galveston merchant stocks him up with goods, for general merchandising, to the amount of $10,000 or $15,000. The first season results in a good cotton crop and collections fair. This oft-times proves to be the cause of his ultimate failure. Being ambitious, he concludes to spread himself, to outdo his competitor, and run the whole town, or at least the business portion of it, and, flushed with success, he ventures to indulge in a few luxuries to which he had hitherto been a stranger. And for the next season he increases his stock, takes more chances in his eagerness to increase his trade, by carrying farmers, takes more crop liens, and to such farmers as are already in his power, squeezes more juice out of them, and to new customers letting up a little on securities in order to secure them, and it is "come in, says the spider to the fly" and I will do better by you than any one else, or, as he says to himself, "till I can weave my web around you, then I will squeeze you, &c." In the meantime, "A" is under close surveillance by the Galveston merchant, through his adjuster or traveling financial agent, who is quietly preparing for a grand scoop of all "A's" earthly possessions.

"A" has shipped his cotton to his Galveston creditor, and has received his account sales, which includes the following items:

Freight, about	$4 00	per bale
Compressing	1 00	per bale
For selling—commission	2 00	per bale
Insurance	50	per bale
Storage and sampling	50	per bale
Drayage	15	per bale
Total	$8 15	

MERCHANDISE ACCOUNT.

To dry goods and groceries	$000 00
Interest on matured notes	12 per cent
To cash advanced to buy cotton	$000 00
Interest	12 per cent

The above is a very brief synopsis, amounts left out. Now, bear in mind, that "A" paid a certain price for his cotton, this is subject to any fluctuations in the market price, also to classification; mind, that "A" bought it a bale here and a few bales there, at a very rough classification, so that when it is tabled, and under a strong light, it is liable to considerable variation. It can readily be seen that "A" is at the mercy of the Galveston merchant, as to classification. Another very important item to "A" is the returns as to weight; that quite a difference exists against him, which is explained thusly by the Galveston merchant: Cow eaten in transit, sampling, &c., (and the cotton had not absorbed enough moisture in Galveston to even up.) The Galveston merchant, upon perusing the reports received from his financial agent, coucludes that "A" has gone to the length of his rope, proceeds to pull him in, makes a grand scoop and takes in all of the assets which includes a great deal of land and cattle. Occasionally the Galveston merchant gets left, but very seldom, for if he has the right kind of security he is safe; for instance, land; "A" can't run off with it very readily. Thus ends the career of "A," his star is set, and he retires to the shades of private life with experience alone to console him in the hour of his misfortune; his pride and ambition humbled, his daughters gathered in from the boarding school, and when the evening shades draw nigh, and the family circle is complete, they endeavor to shape their plans for the future; the daughters sit by silent and morose, weeping bitter tears of disappointment at their blighted career of social triumphs, presents a sad contrast to what might have been.

In the meantime the Galveston merchant goes careering onward, favoring breezes wafting him on to a million dollars.

How is it with the farmer? He still plods along, pursuing the same ceaseless routine, seldom in possession of any money, a victim to credit's extortionate demands. Talk about the condition of Russia's serfs, the victims of English landlordism, here we have its counterpart, and it does not excite but a passing comment. It is an incubus, a heavy weight holding down the agricultural masses of the Southern States. This is what produces lethargy, lack of ambition, loss of pride and self-respect. And on the other hand it presents an opportunity to enterprise and capital taking advantage of existing state of affairs to secure investments with prospect of returns that are far ahead of like investments East or West. Texas is undergoing radical changes; immigration pouring in from the Western and Eastern States, and capital is following as naturally as water follows its well defined channel. The extension of railroads opening up communication with other distributing trade centers, and the desire to obtain a share of the profitable trade of the State, and the influx of their drummers soliciting trade, have made decided inroads upon Galveston's territory, and offered indirectly to the farmer an opportunity of release from Galveston's tyrannical despotism. Galveston had the opportunity and took advantage of it, which was very natural, it was but history repeated: "making hay while the sun shines."

By referring to the brief biographical sketches of the Galveston millionaires, that outside of their legitimate business, they are Presidents, Vice-Presidents, or Directors in insurance companies, cotton compress companies, wharf company, banks, and banking companies. It can be seen at a glance, that there was nothing that slipped through their fingers, so that, eventually, they got it all; the farmer furnishing most of the blood which fed the Galveston leeches. You will also perceive that as other trade centers were made accessible, and competition diversified credits and reduced margins, the Galveston merchants incorporated Land, Mortgage and Loan companies, and are devoting their time and attention to these interests, looking after land interests accumulated through their peculiar business methods. One firm in Galveston accumulated in this way about 1,000,000 acres, and others in proportion.

While the New York and Eastern merchants, when it came to them in the way of assets from delinquent creditors, got rid of it as soon as possible, in many instances for a mere song, Galveston merchants held on to theirs, and the rapid appreciation of land values has contributed more than any other one thing toward making them millionaires. And it is the history of nearly all the wealthy men of Texas; the elements of their wealth made up by land, cattle and real estate interests.

Another very suggestive feature, showing the varied interests of the Galveston millionaires, and their land holdings, is their assessed valuation of property in Galveston, as compared to their estimated wealth.

Nothing in this article is intended to cast any reflections upon any one as affecting financial integrity or standing.

My object in commenting so freely upon Galveston merchants, is to better illustrate the business methods in vogue at the time referred to. When one becomes a millionaire he is a target, and one feels more or less privileged to shoot at it.

Galveston being represented by most of the millionaires in Texas, it became necessary to explain in a measure how this vast wealth was accumulated, in order to satisfy the curiosity of New England people, for whose benefit this paper is gotten up, and at the same time showing the possibilities of acquiring wealth in Texas, as compared with the New England States.

The farmers themselves are to be blamed for the prevailing methods of doing business, and have forged the fetters which hold them down; children follow in the well-beaten path marked out by their parents, and the ambition of their life is to be involved in debt.

C. H. B.

THE CATTLE BUSINESS IN THE NORTHWEST.

A party writing very interesting letters to the New York *Sun* over the signature of Frank Wilkeson, has been especially severe in his comments and description of the cattle business in the Northwest. I cannot say whether he is a disinterested writer on the subject, or whether he has invested, and lost his money, and thereby became soured on investments in that direction, but I will give you a portion of one of his letters; all the others are about on the same key, and you can judge for yourself:

"In the North Platte valley—I mean the land lying between the foothills of the Medicine Bow range and those of the Sierra Madre Mountains—the absence of all animal life is marked. There is not one head of stock there to-day where there were ten four years ago. Many extensive growers, who realize that the valley is ruined, have driven their cattle out of the region, Others have sold their brands at a loss. Where there were a hundred antelope four years ago there is not one now. Then great bands of game animals roamed carelessly and unconcerned at the approach of man. To-day a few vigilant wild animals hunt diligently for food on the bare, rocky hills, and ever keep watch for men. The prairie dogs—and they are lean prairie dogs, too—sit by their holes and bark feebly, as though discouraged and weary of life sustained on-sage brush roots, at the men they see, The valley is a desert. High, gray, rocky headlands, wide stretches of sage-brush covered plains, long reaches of gravel and deep ravines, waterless cross valleys, all bare of grass, and a most profound silence. There are a few houses along the small creeks, and in these dens of poverty live a few settlers who try to make a living out of the soil. There are a few ranches whose owners have seen better days, and who have become morose through brooding over their losses and the decay of their business. The grass on which the region's prosperity depended, is gone almost beyond redemption. One, two, three years' rest will not restore it, and annually the line marking the destruction of this once great grazing ground will rapidly recede further and further into the foothills until the green timber is reached, and then the valley as a grazing ground will be utterly destroyed. This result will be arrived at within three years.

As it is in this valley so it is in many others. I met and talked with cattle growers who graze their herds in the north, in the south, in the west, and on the plains, and, with few exceptions, all told the same story: That the native grasses on closely grazed grounds were almost extinct; that the grass had been trodden out of many valleys; that other extensive areas had been almost ruined by overstocking, and that disaster, serious and widespread menaces the whole cattle-growing industry west of the 101st meridian. Personal observation leads me to believe that about the wisest investment cattle men can make this fall would be for each of them to buy a dozen keen-edged skinning knives and prepare for the work which will surely have to be done before spring.

Cattle have fallen greatly in value during the past three years. And this fact, supplemented by the serious losses incurred by purchasers who unwisely bought book accounts of mythical cattle, or who trusted in the solemn assertions of ranch sellers and dealers in branding irons, has mentally depressed the cattle growers throughout the grazing region. Many of them have been struck down by bankruptcy during the past three years, and many others expect to become bankrupt this coming winter, and one and all are in serious financial peril. At last the Eastern and foreign investors realize that they have been badly swindled, and that the cattle-selling sharpers have defrauded them out of millions and millions of dollars. And now, when the range shows signs of exhaustion, they fear that they cannot sell their property for one-third its cost. In too many instances their fears are well groumded.

Throughout the grazing region there is an almost universal belief that the coming winter is to be an exceedingly hard one. This belief, founded on fear only, prevails in the offices of the merchants whose business it is to supply the ranches with provisions. The spectre of a hard winter sits in the back parlors of banks where the preliminary conversations relative to discounting cattle growers notes are held, and the spectre always works against the cattle growers' interests. Every man in the region is fearful of the future. All realize that the golden harvest days, when "tenderfeet" could be fleeced, and honest, trustful gentlemen be deceived with fraudulent book accounts and deceptive roundups has passed away forever. Joy has departed from the cattle grounds.

I have no doubt that the losses of cattle now grazing on the ranges of high altitude will be sufficiently large this winter to bankrupt many individual, as well as associated, cattle growers. And it matters not what the winter may prove to be. whether mild or hard, the condition of the grass on the range sharply indicates that a large portion of the cattle cannot rustle through it. They are doomed to die. There is but little good grass east of the mountains. FRANK WILKESON."

One thing I do know, that what first suggested cattle raising on the plains of the Northwest, was the immense herds of buffalo that grazed thereon, and always in apparent good condition, and acting on the supposition that cattle ought to do equally as well, it gave the business a start, and buffalo gave way to cattle, &c.

Thus started and found to be profiitable, it has grown to immense proportions; from individual investments it went on to immense corporations. And it has become a matter of fact that they have gone to extremes, and the cattle have eaten themselves out of grass, and tramped out the plains, so that no grass is coming up to sustain them.

The buffalo had a range all to themselves from the Gulf to the Northwest, free to roam at pleasure, and had nothing to intercept them in their race before the biting cold winds from the north.

How is it with the cattle? Those that have had the experience can best reply, and this coming winter will furnish additional evidence.

I will not attempt any farther comments or make any unjust criticisms.

It must appear evident to any reasoning mind that the cattle business carried on in an enclosed pasture, with favorable conditions of climate in your favor, and your cattle always under close inspection, cannot fail to be more profitable than in the Northwest.

It is often stated that the Northwest is the place to mature beef, and beeves from the plains of the Northwest are more salable and net more money than beeves from Texas. But give me a well selected ranch in southwest Texas, to breed stock, and a favorably located ranch in central or northern Texas in the feed belt, to mature and fatten beeves for market, and I am satisfied I could hold my own with the best of them. The property which I have discribed in central Texas I am very desirous of obtaining.

C. H. B.

WHAT WILL PRODUCE A CATTLE BOOM, ETC.

If the speculative view of trade is correct, any calamity or misfortune which may befall the cattle interests taken as a whole, will prove a blessing to the few at the expense of many consumers—for will it not prepare the way for a "boom" in the cattle market by destroying a certain percentage of cattle grazing upon open range, and thereby increasing the value upon the remainder, more particularly those that are confined within enclosed pastures under close inspection?

Prices will necessarily go up, and the cattle trade show a general improvement.

The price of meat will go up, too, and this proves a hardship to the poor. But the speculative view of trade takes no account of this part of the business; it considers only the interests of the few who sell, and leave the many who buy to look out for themselves.

C. H. B.

In conversation with a banker from Missouri, who was in the State recently prospecting, he stated that in N. E. Missouri prairie farming land, near large towns, ranged in value from $30 to $40 per acre; ten miles or more from town or railroad $10 to $25 per acre. Land of equal fertility as the Northern Central Texas lands would bring from $50 to $75 per acre.

MIDSUMMER **TRADE EDITION** 1887.	# El Paso Times.	CIRCULATION **25,000 COPIES!** 10 CTS. EACH.

EL PASO, TEXAS, AUGUST, 1887.

THE GATEWAY EL PASO TO MEXICO!

RECORD OF MAGIC GROWTH

From an Adobe Village in 1881 to a Modern City in '87!

The Crown Jewel of a New Commercial Empire.

Its Unrivaled Situation.

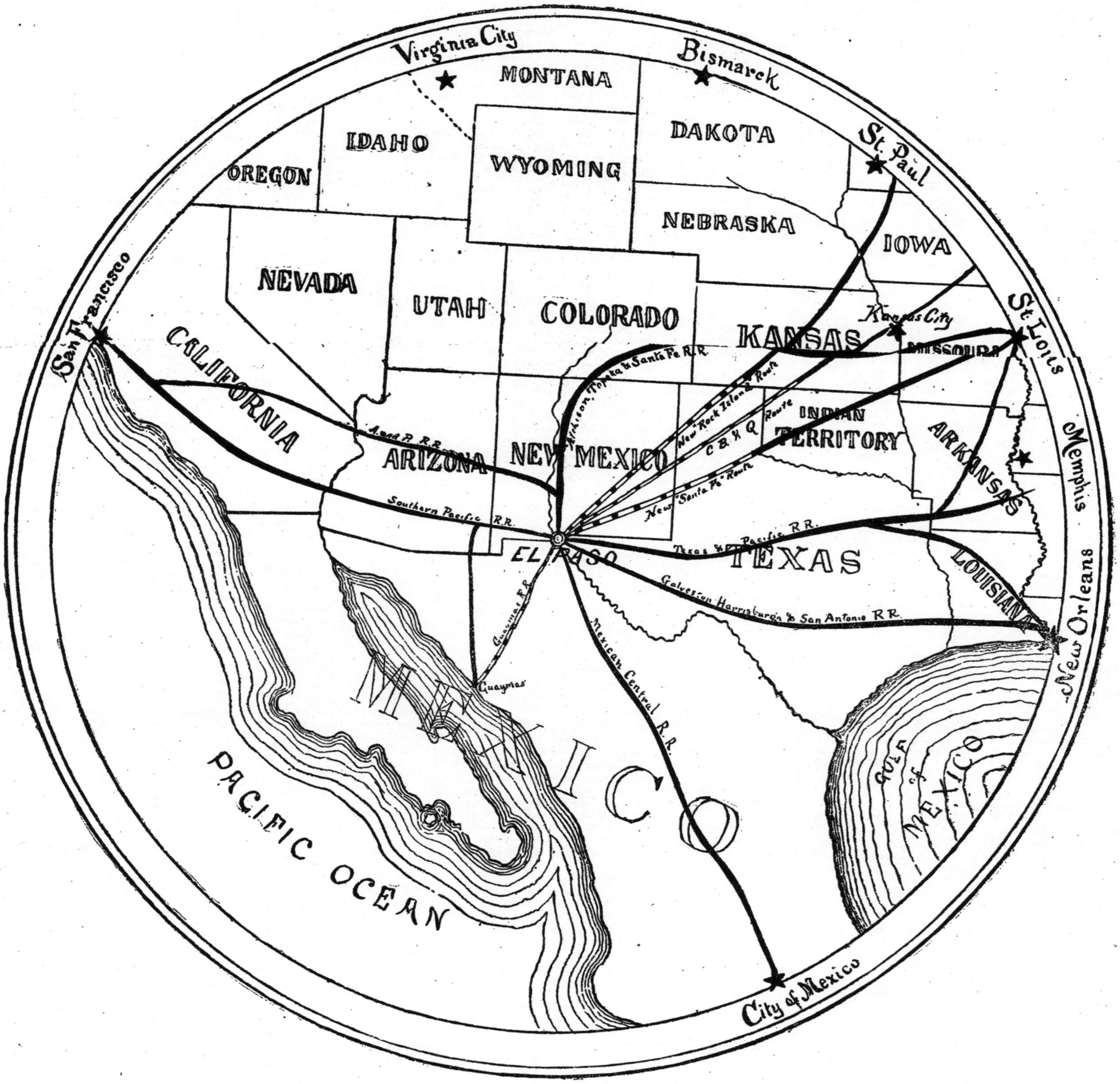

1200 Miles to the City of Mexico, 1200 Miles to San Francisco, 1200 Miles to St. Louis, 1200 Miles to New Orleans—The Hub of the Great Southwest—**A Great Railroad Centre**—The Terminus of Five Great Trunk Lines, the Atchison, Topeka & Santa Fe, the Texas & Pacific, Galveston, Harrisburg & San Antonio, Southern Pacific and Mexican Central Railroads—Three more Great Railroads approaching from the Northwest and Another Mexican Railroad in Prospect, Piercing an Unpenetrated Land of Silver and Gold—**Mineral Wealth**—El Paso the Distributing Point for the Gold and Silver Mines of Texas, Old Mexico, New Mexico and Arizona—An Unrivaled Smelting Point—One Smelter Completed and Another Large One Projected—**Natural Advantages**—Situated in the Valley of the Rio Grande, Fertile as the Nile, Growing the Productions of all Countries, the Fruits and Flowers of all Lands—The El Paso Grape, the Most Luscious on the Continet—Vine-Growing, Wine-Making---El Paso, 4000 feet Above Sea Level, with Dry Climate, Sunshiny Days and Delightful Nights is **One of the Great Sanitarians**---Constant Stream of Invalids from all the States---A Complete City---An Excellent Municipal Government---Churches---A Thorough Public School System---Large Hotels, Water Works, Gas Works---Good Sewerage System---Refrigerating Establishment---Slaughtering Cattle, Sheep and Hogs---Telephone---Electric Lights---Street Railway Systems, Connecting all Parts of El Paso with Paso del Norte, Mexico---$60,000 Opera House---United States Custom House---**Business Prosperity**---Prosperous Merchants---Solid Banks---International Trade---Real Estate---Advantages for Land Investments---Town Lots, Farm Lands, Fruit Lands and Vineyards, Cheap Compared with "Boom" Towns in the West---Farmers' and Fruit Growers' Opportunity---Read the Record---

Campbell Real Estate Company

Map of Campbell Real Estate Co.'s Property,

Showing Locations in El Paso, in Proximity to the Center of the City and Public Buildings. - - - - - - - - Street Railways. ———|———| Boundaries of the Original Mills' Map. Present Unsold Campbell Real Estate Company Lots and Blocks in Heavy Lines.

TOTAL SALES OF LOTS TO JULY 1st, 1887, $200,000.

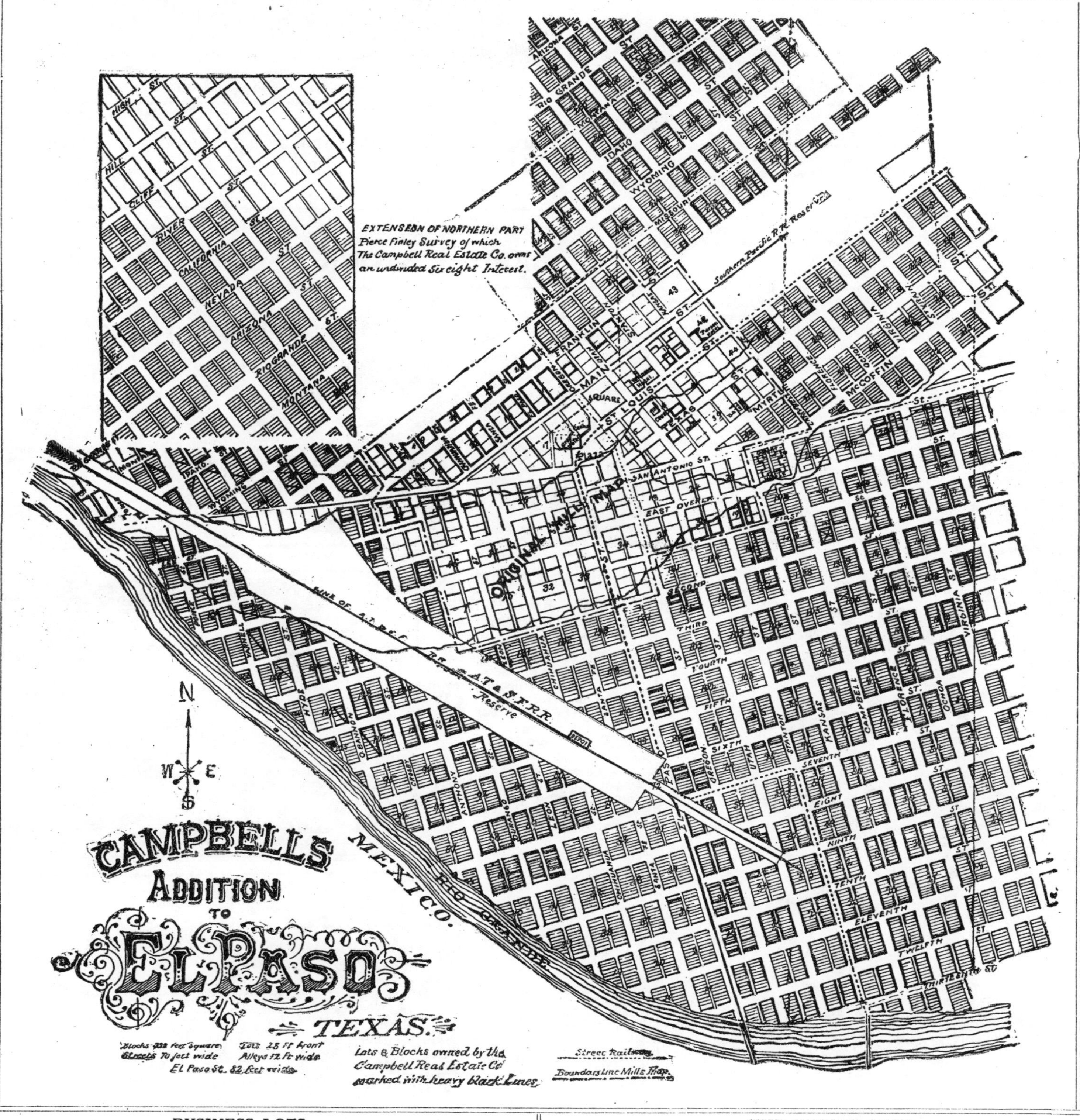

SALES DURING MAY AND JUNE, $80,000.

BUSINESS LOTS

On El Paso, Oregon, Utah, Stanton, Franklin, St. Louis, Texas, San Antonio, Overland, First and Second Streets.

RESIDENCE LOTS

On all Streets, in all parts of the City of El Paso, from the Mesa to the Rio Grande River bank. On the Mesa the sites are elevated and commanding, with fine views of the whole Rio Grande Valley, containing the noted acequias, trees, shrubbery, grasses and flowers.

PRICES

From $200 upwards, on such favorable terms as will satisfy purchasers.

THE UNSOLD LOTS

Are decidedly the most available and valuable within the present limits of the

RAPIDLY GROWING CITY

Of El Paso. They surround the magnificent court house, the elegant public school building, the Grand Central, Vendome and Pierson Hotels, the railway depots, the

NEW GOVERNMENT BUILDING

Soon to be erected on the Plaza, the Baptist, Catholic, Episcopalian, Methodist and Presbyterian Churches, the Banks and all other Public Places in El Paso.

E. S. Newman. G. T. Newman. S. W. Russell.

NEWMAN & RUSSELL,

AGENTS,

State National Bank Building, - - - - - - EL PASO, TEXAS.

B. H. DAVIS.

Among the distinguished citizens of the sonthwest, B. H. Davis, Esq., of El Paso, occupies a deservedly high position. His commanding presence, intellectual appearance, kind disposition, firmness, candor, energy, and love for his profession, combine to make him a central figure among the truly great men of Texas. Mr. Davis was born in Summerville, Tennessee, in 1834. His father, William Davis, was one of the most learned men of his generation, and for years one of the ablest jurists in Mississippi. He settled in Brazos county, Texas, in 1852. The son was educated at the best schools of his native Tennessee, and graduated with the very highest honors in Hanover College, Indiana. He was a student of law in the office of Judge Hughes, in Galveston, and was admitted to practice in the courts of the state in 1853. In 1852, in his eighteenth year, he came to Texas and after a brief residence in Galveston, removed to Brenham and engaged in the professional life, which has been his pride through an honorable career, with William Oldham, the leading attorney of that section of the state. When the war broke out in 1861, Mr. B. H. Davis joined Terry's Rangers, and after the extraordinary struggle, located in Bryan and associated with T. J. Beall, his present partner. It was the exceeding good fortune of these gentlemen to be engaged in almost every noted case in that district, and therefore were afforded opportunities to become known throughout Texas and the South.

The constitutional convention of 1876, one of the most remarkable of all the assemblages of the Lone Star, numbered Mr. B. H. Davis among its leading and most active advisers and workers. His general intelligence was wisely and efficiently exercised in behalf of the people of the whole commonwealtn. That was the only public position Mr. Davis friends and fellow citizens have been able to induce him to accept, notwithstanding he has been urged for judicial stations as well as the state senate and congress, but in all these efforts they have fallen still-born. He would not accept office.

In 1880, Mr. Davis came to this city, and until last year, the law firm continued as Davis & Beall. In January, 1886, Wyndham Kemp came here from Calvert, Texas, and soon after entered the same firm under the title of Davis, Beall & Kemp, with convenient and elegant offices over the State National Bank. They are safe counsellors, careful and conscientious advisers, well posted and able lawyers, and popular with the profession and the people.

Many admiring friends desire Mr. B. H. Davis to allow the use of his name for congress in the coming campaign of 1888, but without his consent up to this time. It is to be hoped he will carefully consider this matter and prepare for the race, inasmuch as several active friends in Parker county, the home of Mr. Lanham, are very anxious to make Mr. Davis the candidate of the democratic party, next year.

J. RUFUS CURRIE.

HON. JOSEPH MAGOFFIN.

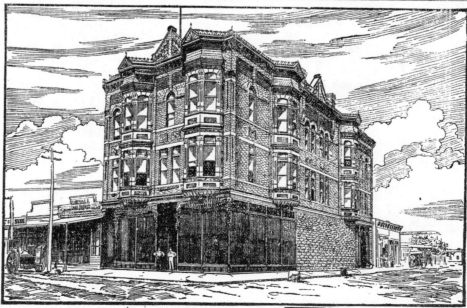

GENERAL SAM HOUSTON, GOVERNOR OF TEXAS AT THE OUTBREAK OF THE CIVIL WAR.

STEPHEN F. AUSTIN, FOUNDER OF THE FIRST AMERICAN COLONY IN TEXAS.

THE NEW CAPITOL OF TEXAS.

AUSTIN is situated on the left bank of the Colorado River, on the Austin branch of the Houston and Texas Railroad, at a point where this tortuous river runs like a thread of silver through a landscape variegated with patches of prairie, cedar-crowned hills, and low mountains in the blue distance to the west. The new Texas Capitol, of which Austin is the seat, is one of the finest red granite buildings in the world. The foundation was laid in 1884, and during the last year 300 men have been constantly employed on the last stages of the great work. The builders were a syndicate composed of the Messrs. FARWELL of Chicago and others; and it is estimated that from first to last it has expended in the construction of the building about $4,000,000, the compensation on the part of the State consisting of 3,000,000 acres of land—nine counties—situated in the "Panhandle" region.

The architecture of this magnificent new State-house is mainly of the Doric order. Its ground plan approximately resembles the Greek cross, with a rotunda and dome at the intersection of the corridors. Its front measures 562 feet from east to west, with a depth of 287 feet, and it covers $2\frac{1}{4}$ acres of ground. The altitude from the base-line of the building to the large glass star on top of the bronze statue of Liberty surmounting the dome lantern is 311 feet. The exterior is constructed of rough longitudinal blocks of granite, laid horizontally, but all the margins are beautifully dressed, and on the second and third stories there is considerable rock face work, through which are distributed a series of stately pilasters to the number of 176, covering the whole circuit of the building on these stories. All the broad corridors are laid in encaustic tiling of various patterns and attractive designs. The great rotunda is 65 feet in diameter, and encircled by a balcony five feet deep, connecting with the second, third, and fourth floors. The basement comprises 63 rooms, in which the records of the State and other things will be preserved. On the first floor are the Executive offices, while the second is set apart for the Legislative and the third for the Judicial departments of the State government. The Senate-Chamber, 94 by 70 feet, and the Hall of Representatives, 94 by 96 feet, are in keeping with the grandeur of the exterior. These great halls are both open through to the ceiling of the second floor above, and are completely encircled by galleries, the light being admitted through two tiers of windows and a ceiling of cut stained plate glass, above which are the immense skylights of the exterior roof.

The entire building will be lit by gas and electricity, and heated throughout by steam from a boiler-house situated a short distance to the east of the Capitol grounds, and connected by a tunnel with the main building. Passenger and freight elevators of the most approved style are provided for in the building.

The distinctive feature of the main front entrance, facing south, is the triumphal arch that spans this entrance at a height of seventy-two feet, underneath which, in the vestibule of the first floor, supporting a granite balcony, stand two superb columns, their bases and shafts of polished granite, with bands and caps of polished black and white marbles. In striking contrast with this ornate entrance is the massive granite portico that dignifies the entrance on the opposite or north side of the building, facing University Hill. The supports of the first story

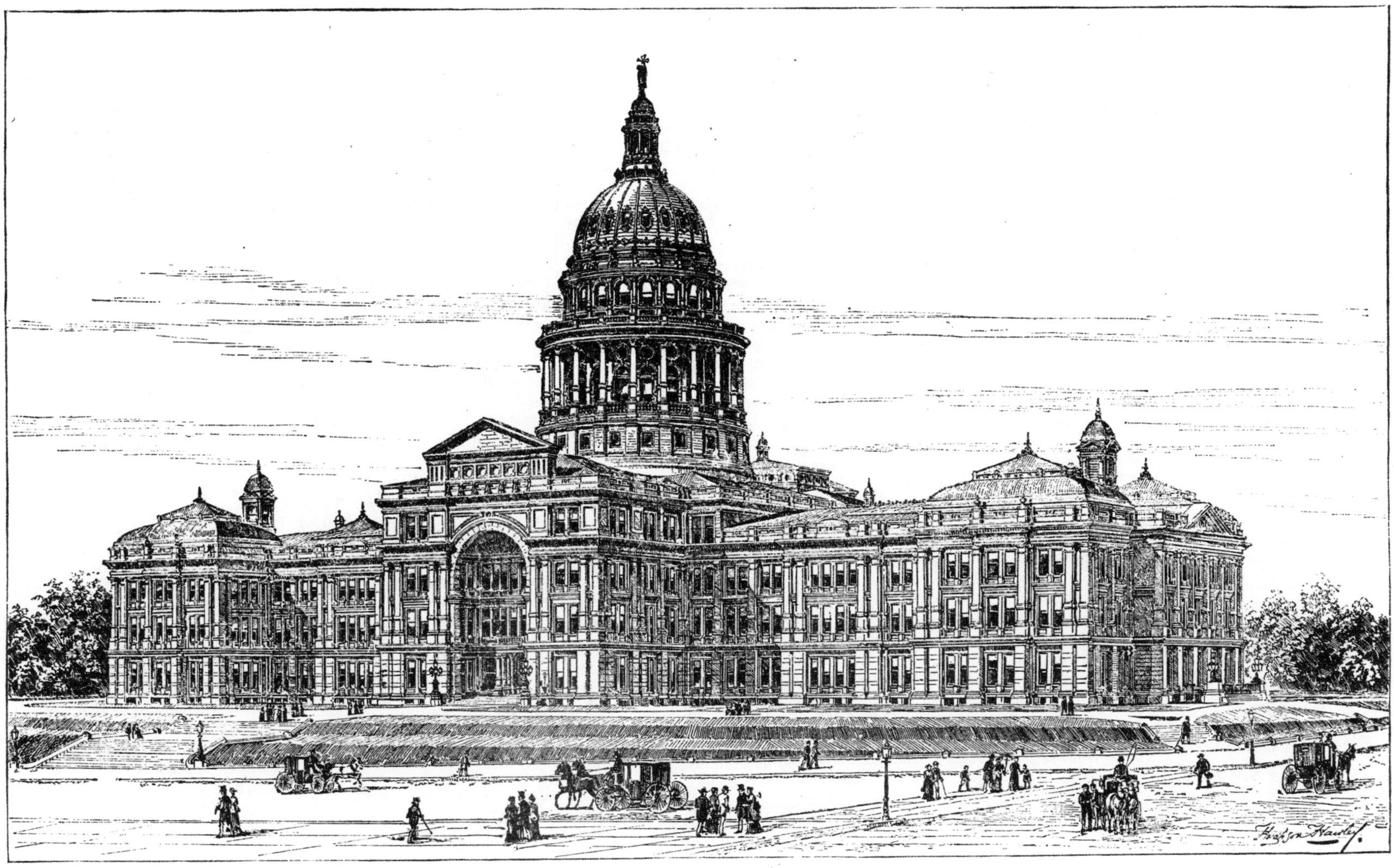

THE NEW STATE CAPITOL, AUSTIN, TEXAS.

The Texas Western.

AND

THE JONES COUNTY CALLIOPE.

THE TEXAS WESTERN and THE JONES COUNTY CALLIOPE Consolidated July 16th. 1889.

Then Gently Scan Thy Brother Man, Still Gentler Thy Sister Woman. Though Both May Gang A Little Wrang To Step Aside Is Human.

VOL. 7. ANSON, JONES COUNTY, TEXAS, THURSDAY AUGUST 22, 1889. NO. 22.

RAILROAD REGULATION.

Hon. S. W. T. Lanham Gives His Ideas on this All-Important Subject.

Commissions Have Been Tried and Indorsed in Other States and it Would Be Good Policy to Have One in Texas.

DALLAS, TEX., Aug. 9.—C. W. Harned, secretary Dallas manufacturers' association, has received the following letter bearing on the freight question:

WEATHERFORD, TEX., Aug. 7, '89.
C. W. Harned, Esq., Secretary Merchants' Exchange; Dallas, Tex.:

DEAR SIR—Your letter of the 15th ult., came during my absence from home. I do not hope to specially enlighten yourself, those for whom you institute inquiry, or the general public on the subjects indicated by your letter; nor do I feel able to give specific answers to some of your questions, for lack of the necessary information. The inter-state commerce acts, original and as amended, were passed during the period of my public service, and I gave them my support. To be candid I will say that aside from a conviction that some wholsome legislation in the regulation of railway corporations was necessary, I followed the lead of representative and more experienced legislators in all the matters of detail—those whose opportunities, experience and committee assignments and enabled them to specially investigate the subject in all its bearings. I believed then and believe now that such legislation could only be, in a great degree, tentative and experimental; that it was and is an extremely difficult question to solve. The line which separates the public character and responsibility of these corporations from the private rights belonging to the capital invested in them is not always easily traced. The blending of obligation to the public with individual privilege and personal right of the citizen incorporator, aside from considerations of evils to be corrected and the best policy to be pursued, surrounds the question with embarrassment and requires thorough and careful treatment. A recent discussion in the daily News by two of our ablest and most eminent men, each an ex-judge of the highest rank, and both sincere from their respective standpoints of observation on the railroad problem, cannot fail to attract the considerate attention of any one familiar with the personnel of the disputants.

The statement is credited to Mr. Choats that "railroads are made for the people, and not the people for the railroads." This is a captivating statement, and not without influence in any legislative body, state or federal. That it was necessary for congress to act upon the subject, when combination had absorbed competition, was generally conceded, and the public were prepared to receive with approval any proposition which contemplated a governmental regulation of the railroads in the popular interests. I did not believe when I voted for the original act that its provisions would at once relieve Texas—it being geographically at the end of a "long haul"—from all the ailments to which it was heir, in consequence of oppression, discrimination, etc., and I doubt, very capitally, if up to this good day, any very marked or material advantage has resulted to Texas specially, in consequence of its passage. Still it must not be condemned because its advantageous results are not instantaneous. It was an expression of the authority of the government and was designed for the good of the people. It is not yet perfect by any means. Time and tide will doubtless suggest and apply correctives and amendments. The commission feature of the act I do not think was fully approved by all who supported it. Indeed, I do not believe that our honored Judge Reagan, who so earnestly and honestly devoted so many years of his valuable service in opposition and intolerance of railway corporations and monopolies generally, wholly indorsed this provision. He regarded it, I think, as an experiment, if not with disfavor, in a very able and exhaustive speech made by him on March 28, 29 and 30, 1882, before the committee on commerce in answer to the opponents of his bill, he said among other things: "But I might defer to a commission as an experiment in addition to what is provided for in this bill, but not as a substitute for it. My fear as to a commission is that it would be more likely represent the interests of the railroad companies than those of the general public. The railroad companies can always combine their influence either directly, or if thought more prudent, indirectly, to influence the making of the appointment of such commissioners by whomsoever to be appointed. * * * This, I may add, seems to be peculiarly an era of congressional commissions. We had a commission to settle a controversy about a presidential election and the people were cheated. We had what is known as a silver commission, composed of good and able men, who went to Europe to learn whether an American congress should authorize the coinage of silver. We have provided for a commission on the rights of women and must await to see whether it can propose an improvement on the laws of God and the experience of the world. We have a commission on the traffic in alcohol liquors and must await to see to what extent it can promote temperance and to what extent we can safely violate the constitution of the United States. And we have before us a proposition for a commission to revise the tariff and must await to see how long it can delay that revision, and whether it can make our tariff legislation more monstrous and unendurable than it is at present. And this is still followed by the proposition to create another commission to make inquiries and reports in relation to railroad transportation. Whether the object of proposing this last commission is to defeat needed legislation on the railroad problem, or to do something of real utility, must be determined in the future. Whatever may be thought of the value and importance of these several commissions and proposed commissions, it seems to me the people might, with much advantage to themselves, constitute themselves into a commission to retire a sufficient number of mumbers of the two houses of congress and send others here who can and will legislate on subjects instead of putting them into commission to obtain information."

I am inclined to believe from the known character of the commissioners appointed, and such of their decisions as I have examined, tnat their investigations and recommendations may prove of value and importance as aids to future legislation and in adjusting grievance as far as the scope of their authority may contemplate. They are, in fact, mere auxiliaries to the real object of the act. Whether very useful or merely supplementary, I think they are there to stay as a permanent part of the legislation.

No action of congress on this subject can fully avail until it is met by sympathetic legislation on the part of the states. Its jurisdiction is limited and cannot reach all causes of complant wholly in a state. The states must meet it half way. I shall cheerfully vote for the amendment to the constitution as proposed by the Texas legislature. Twenty-five states and territories have adopted the system of a railroad commission. It seems that it has never been abandoned by any state that has adopted it, except Tennessee in recent years, and it is said that its abolition there was attributable to the opposition of railroads. While in my judgment the commission system has its defects and cannot fully meet all the requirements of the situation, still it seems to be sanctioned by the experience of the states which have tried it, and is to that extent commended to Texas. Where the tenure of legislators is so uncertain, where people are so immersed in their own business affairs and have not usually the opportunity to investigate the question of railroad transportation in advance should they be elected lawmakers—when the sessions of the legislature are limited as they are in Texas, it would seem expedient to afford them all possible lights for their guidance and to qualify them for a proper and well-advised treatment of and intelligent legislation upon one of the most important and delicate subjects which can engage their official consideration. As agents to assist the state in the detection and exposure of violations of such laws as it may pass, and in the accumulation of all pertinent and reliable data for the benefit of the state, which, in their official reports can be preserved and rendered accessible, in permanent form, to succeeding legislatures, being limited by legal authority and under specific directions as to the extent and operation of their functions, and wholly without power to make law themselves, it seems to me that it would be good policy to appoint a commission. If it has proved satisfactory in states territorially small, like Alabama and Georgia, how much the more is it likely to do so in a state like Texas, with its immense area and different conditions in its varied localities.

Permit me to say in conclusion, I think you and those whom you represent, in provoking a full and thorough discussion of this subject and inviting the thought and attention of the whole people thereto, are doing a good work. It must certainly be the wish of all patriotic men that safe conclusions shall be reached and fair and just legislation alike to railroads and people shall be enacted.

Respectfully, etc.,
S. W. T. LANHAM.

The Texas Western.
AND
THE JONES COUNTY CALLIOPE.
Official paper of Jones County.
Published Every Thursday,
AT
Anson, Jones County, Texas
BY
THE ANSON PRINTING CO.
HEC A. MCEACHIN, D. L. SMITH, M. R. ANDREWS, W. F. WRIGHT.
HEC A. McEACHIN, Managing Editor.
SUBSCRIPTION, $1. 50 Per Annum.
THURSDAY, AUG. 22, 1889.

Tired of Local Option.

Clifton Young of Abilene was here last week, and we understand that while here he expressed a willingness to open a first-class saloon in Anson, provided Local Option can be defeated. As soon as Mr. Young made this declaration, he found men in Anson who are actually pining to knock the stuffing out of the law; and forthwith, they began to talk it up. We understand a petition praying for an election is now being circulated.

Citizens of precinct 1, the same old enemy whom you stamped under your feet three years ago is again raising its head and threatening to strike. In a short time you will be called upon to repair to the polls and again give the jugwumps a lesson that will last them for three more years. Is there a business man in Anson who would enjoy having a saloon next door to him? Is there a father in Anson who desires that his sons shall have the benefit of a saloon? Is not the law we have, even with occasional violations, better than no restraint at all?

Local Option can be made effectual. If the county officers instead of winking at its violation, and perhaps, assisting in the same, will do his duty, if the physician can be made to realize that he is a man of honor, and punished for aiding in the violation of the law, if the court of the county would handle all violators without gloves, there would not be a drop of whiskey sold in Anson save upon cases of actual necessity. Citizens of Anson and precinct 1, we want no saloon in Anson. Be on your guard, keep your eyes skinned, and when the time comes for action, let us be up and at 'em. Let us show the jugwumps that true manhood and morality shall continue in the ascendancy in Anson, and if nothing but a saloon will do them, let them move to a saloon and not bring a saloon to us.

Charles Wilson and Hamp Willis, charged with the murder of James Sacre, of Sherman, in a pasture in the Chickasaw Nation, Dec. 18, 1888, have been acquitted. Milton Overton, the man who did the killing, died April 1, before he was brought to trial.

JOHN R. BROWN.

Formerly a Citizen of Jones County is Captured in Arkansas and Brought Back to Texas to Answer for His Crimes.

FRANKLIN, TEXAS, Aug. 19.—John R. Brown, alias John M. Brown, alias Col. C. Bryant, arrived yesterday morning for Arkansas in the custody of Deputy Sheriff John Moore. Requisition papers were issued by Gov. Ross upon two affidavits being made, one charging Brown with bigamy and the other with forgery. He was arraigned before Judge Dunn this morning, who fixed his bond at $1000 in each case, and failure to give the same he was remanded to jail. Brown was formerly editor and proprietor of the Central Texan. During his charge as editor he married a very estimable young lady at this place.

The party referred to in the above telegram came to Anson a few months ago from Franklin. For a short time he boarded with W. J. Power, just across the street from THE WESTERN office; and as he represented himself as an old newspaper man, he was well received at this office. He brought with him here his wife, and soon purchased a piece of land in the Metzger neighborhood. After buying the land he decided to build him a house and went to Abilene to purchase the necessary lumber. He lacked $100. of having the necessary funds, and asked Sheriff Tyson to endorse his note for that amount. Mr. Tyson told him that as he was a comparative stranger he could not comply with the request, but upon Brown agreeing to make him a bill of sale to his wagon and team, Tyson endorsed the note. As it was about train time and he was going East with an attached witness, Tyson, in the presence of the cashier of the First National Bank of Abilene, requested Brown to make the bill of sale and leave it with Frank M. Smith in Anson, which Brown promised to do. Brown procured the lumber, built his house, and becoming fearful that his former misdeeds had followed him here, he drove his wagon and team to Abilene, sold them for $270 and skipped for Arkansas, without having made the bill of sale as promised. He left Abilene the day Tyson returned, and they passed each other at Cisco. Brown's wife and her brother, Mr. Burrelsmith, who appears to be a perfect gentleman, are occupying the place Brown purchased, and Mr. Burrelsmith, so far as he has been able, has made good the acts here of his unworthy brother-in-law. Doubtless it will be a relief to Mr. Burrelsmith and his sister to know that Brown has been caught and will be punished as he so richly deserves. He is one of the most finished scoundrels and accomplished rascals that that ever set foot on Jones county soil.

A correspondent of the Gatesville Star from Phantom Hill, Texas, says that place raises pretty good sized watermelons. He claims that he was shown three that weighed 124 pounds each. Said correspondent may be a bigger man than we are, hence we won't call him a Joe Mulhaton.—Moody Monitor.

Phantom Hill is located in Jones county, Bro. Billings, and if the correspondent says those three melons weighed 124 pounds each, they weighed it. Forty and fifty pound melons sell daily on the streets of Anson at 5 cents each, but the largest we have heard from this season weighed 73 pounds.

James and Howe Pullen have been arrested at Kansas City on a charge of robbing the Wabash train on Aug. 3rd.

The wheat crop of Dakota has been cut off fully one half.

AN HISTORIC DOCUMENT.

Settlement of a Controversy Between James Collinsworth and Dr. Anson Jones.

The undersigned feeling the deepest interest in a matter of controversy which has arisen between Judge Collinsworth and Dr. Anson Jones, in mutual good feeling towards the parties, have presumed to investigate the circumstances in relation thereto, and have come to the following conclusions to which we hope the mutual friends of the parties will accede, viz:

That the cause of controversy having been an offensive remark of said Jones in relation to said Collinsworth in explanation of which the said Jones states that be always has and still does consider Judge Collinsworth too honorable and highminded in every respect to state falsehood or misrepresent facts. That the said Collinsworth be satisfied with the explanation and the matter end; and that the parties stand in relation to each other as they did previous to the matter of controversy in question.

THOMAS F. MCKINNEY.
WM. G. HILL

I agree to the above as the friend of Dr. Anson Jones.

R. R. BROWN.

I am perfectly satisfied with the above explanation as the friend of Judge Collinsworth.

WM. T. AUSTIN.

Brazoria, 9 March, 1837.

Talmage on Newspapers.

The Rev. Dr. Talmage, speaking of newspapers, says:

I have been betrayed by about every class of men in the world, but never by a newspaper man, and I believe there is a spirit of fairness abroad in the newspapers that is hardly to be found anywhere else.

Some times we take up a paper full of social scandals and divorce cases, and we talk about the filthy, scurrilous press; but I could preach a whole sermon on the everlasting blessing of a good newspaper. A good newspaper is the grandest temporal blessing that God has given the people of this century.

My idea is a good newspaper is a mirror of life itself. Some people complain because the evil of the world is reported as well as the good. The evil must be reported as well as the good, or how will we know what to guard against or what to reform? There is a chance for discrimination as to how much space shall be given to reports of such things as prize-fights, but the newspaper that merely presents the fair and the beautiful and the bright side of life is a misrepresentation. That family is best qualified for the duties of life who have told to them not only what good there is in the world, but what evil there is in the world, and is told to select the good and reject the evil.

The prospect for rain this morning is very flattering.

The Land Question.

By reference to a letter from Commissioner Hall to a party in Baird, published elsewhere in this issue, it will be seen that a man can not hold any part of another section of land than the one he makes his home upon, even though he may improve the same. Of course this ruling only applies to land sold under the act of 1883, which required settlement. But the commissioner goes further and says that men holding this class of lands can forfeit their claims to the state, allow the land to be re-classified and placed back on the market for sale, and that he will give the parties allowing the forfeiture preference to re-purchase this land over all others, under the provisions of section 22 of the act of 1887, which does not require actual settlement. There is something about the above that will fall like a pile driver on land jumpers.

Railroad Rumbling.

Brady is almost sure to get the San Antonio & Aransas Pass railroad. A committee from Taylor and Runnels counties have just recently returned home from San Antonio, where they made a proposition to President Lott of the San Antonio & Aransas Pass railroad to the effect that if the company would construct and operate the road through said counties with depots at the county seats, that said counties will grant right of way, depot grounds, and grade the road through the counties. After the conference, D. P. Gray, a member of the committee, and who is by no means a visionary man, is reported as having said there was hardly a doubt but that the proposition would be accepted. Brady is right on this route and the east and to the west of us renders it impracticable to miss Brady more than three miles. It will be remembered that Mason has agreed to pay $40,000 to the road when it is completed to that place. Brady has for a long time been a parasite but her manifest destiny for greatness is being seen by many.—Brady Sentinel.

A convention of cotton exchanges and boards of trade has been called to meet at New Orleans Sept. 11th, to consider the difference between cotton and jute bagging. The proposition is that from a certain date all cotton shall be sold by net weight, allowing 5 per cent of the gross weight for jute, and 3 1-2 per cent for cotton baggidg.

Mr. and Mrs. James M. Martin, of Minter, Lamar county, were in Abilene Tuesday. Mr. Martin has purchased land in the southwestern portion of Jones county, and will move out as soon as he can dispose of his property in the east. He is well pleased with the Abilene country as everybody is who sees it.—Abilene Reporter.

A Pleasant Contrast.

It is pleasant for brothers to dwell together in unity and perfect good humor, and this is as appicable to attorneys as to men in any other branches of the walks of life. Monday evening in the District court, a little scene occured which illustrates the truth of the above. One of the members of our bar, who tip the scales in the neighborhood of 300 pounds, closed his argument to the jury by telling them that he now yielded to the "Weeping Willow of the Anson bar," having reference to a brother attorney who is as prolific of gestures as a canine is of fleas, and who is rather noted for lightness of his avordupois. When the "Willow" took the floor, with a touching wave of his branches, he alluded to the compliment he had received, and retaliated by asserting that God gives some men brains and bones, while to others he gives an abundance of flesh. As for himself, he was perfectly satisfied with what he has received, and would not exchange with the honorable gentleman who preceded him. The court smole a broad smile, which was joined in with by jury and spectators and the case proceeded.

To the County Judges of Texas.

MERIDIAN, Tex., Aug. 18.—I suggest a convention of the county judges of Texas for the discussion of legislation needed in regard to matters of county government, which more than any other bears upon the citizen with direct and constant force. The schools, the roads, the judicial sytem in its local application, the burden of the jury duty, the relation of costs to penalties, the disposition of petty offenders and care of paupers, the county finances involving the expenditure for public improvement, the management of special and separate funds, and the whose subject of local taxation. These and other topics are always pressing and often full of perplexity, and the immediate interest of the people could hardly fail to be advanced by their discussion by a body of men who exercise in county affairs at once executive, legislative and judicial functions, and who as a body possess the freshest and most accurate information in regard to such affairs in every section of the state.

If a sufficient number of the county judges of the state will join me, we will try the experiment and make the call. Yours respectfully,

A. R. BARRY,
County Judge Bosque Co.

The Texas Western

AND

THE JONES COUNTY CALLIOPE.

The War is Still On.

From the Mobeetie Panhandle, we extract the following in reference to county politics in Roberts county. Our friend J. K. Little is county judge of that county, and we will wager a coon skin that he is a Digger, and can't be kicked or poohed out of his office. The Panhandle says:

"The trouble over the Roberts county election, which has been smouldering for months, emitting once in a while ominous sounds of coming trouble, came to a head on Monday last. The following extract from a private letter received here Tuesday gives an idea of the situation: 'We are having h—l; or at least things bid fair to have it. The Kickapoos have come over, all of them armed to the teeth with revolvers, and they have taken possession of the clerk's office. They took charge this morning early and have not left the room only long enough to eat, and then part of them guarded while the others ate. It is now late at night, and they still hold vigil. The Diggers are doing like-wise. We also have seven of the rangers here, Captain McMurray with them. There may be powder burnt before morn. I can't tell. I am going to crawl in a hole and pull the hole in after me.' The two factions in Roberts county are known as Kickapoos and Diggers. The former party had one of the latter (the county clerk) ousted from office on the plea of fraud at the election. An appeal was taken and is still pending, and we understand that the trouble on Monday grew out of the fact that the Digger clerk refused to accept the Kickapoo bond offered in that case. The district court decided that a man named Alcott had been elected, and the Kickapoos wanted to see him installed, but the Diggers don't want him, hence the trouble. Latest reports from the seat of war say that all is now quiet, the Kickapoos having changed the combination of the county safe, locked it and departed."

Denison is to have a cotton mill, as Boston capitalists are backing the scheme.

How to Proceed.

We extract the following from the Baird Star:

AUSTIN, Tex., Aug. 10, 1889.
J. J. Hendrix, Baird, Texas:

DEAR SIR:—Replying to your favor of the 7th inst. will state that your improvement of ½ section 125, University land, Callahan county, while living on adjoining tract, does not fulfil the requirement of actual settlement of lands purchased under act of 1883. Hence you can not receive the benefits of the "Validating act," passed by the 21st legislature, which is required in order to give you a patentable claim to your land. However, you can either forfeit your claim for non-payment of interest, or file your relinquishment to the State, and the land will be reclassified and placed back on the market for sale, when you can make your application to repurchase under the provisions of section 22, of the act of 1887, which does not require actual settlement in order to become a purchaser. Under such conditions as above stated, this department will be inclined to favor you above other applicants to purchase same, provided you are prompt in making your application to purchase after said land has been placed on the market for sale.

Respectfully,
R. M. HALL,
Commissioner.

One of our exchanges speaks of a millinery store kept by a very estimable lady, and says the editor was gratified to see her stocking up. The editor says he was never so astonished in his born days as he was when the paper came out to meet the lady and have her strike him across the head with an umbrella, and tell him he was a liar, and that she would tell his wife. He didn't know what she was mad at, and he had to read the item over a hundred times to see if there was anything spiteful in it.

Address John Hoeny, Abilene, for premium lists of the District fair.

JEFF DAVIS' SINCERITY.

In the course of an article on Jefferson Davis in the Chicago Inter-Ocean, over the signature of "Bystander," Judge Albion W. Tourgee writes: "Yet with all this, some things in fairness must be said of the aged chief of the Confederacy. He has been consistent and resolute in the maintenance of his views of government. Some years ago the bystander took the pains to collect and collate all the votes and speeches of Mr. Davis as a member of both houses of the national congress. It was a useless labor except from the fact that he desired to fill out and complete his own mental picture of one of the most notable men of his time—a man who has occupied an anomalous position in the world's history. As a result he does not hesitate to say that one making such a study and at the same time reviving in his own memory the sentiments of the time when the tempest broaded over our land, can not help a feeling of respect for the evident sincerity and ability of the man who was afterwards to stand on so strange a pinacle. From his belief in the constitutionality of secession, the righteousness of slavery, and the justice of the Confederacy he never wavered, from his earliest speech in the house of representatives to his latest letter, in which he confidently appeals to the future for a vindication of his views and conduct. What he then believed he still believes. One can not question his sincerity."

The Stephenville Headlight is undertaking to reform the world. It is a gigantic undertaking, but all things come to him who waits and serves the Lord—with the single exception of the Union Labor party, which the Headlight represents.

The Attorney-General's decision against combining against jute bagging, leaves every farmer the privilege of using any kind of bagging he chooses. It simply forbids a combination to down a combination.

The Texas Western.
AND
THE JONES COUNTY CALLIOPE.

☞Official paper of Jones county.

Communications on matters of interest, and Neighborhood news cordially invited.

Hill county is to have a new court house.

To the Throckmorton Times:—Fire that plate matter.

The range in Montana has been greatly injured by prairie fires.

G. H. Tyler has been nominated for lieutenant-governor of Virginia.

Chas. A. Hill's livery stable was burned at Greenville, Thursday. Loss $1500.

Haskell is getting there Eli. Mr. Eli has just opened a blacksmith shop up there.

A race-horse has been named for Amelie Rives-Chanler. Now she is truly great.

The Atchison, Topeka & Santa Fe railway system is said to be in a deplorable condition financially.

Mrs. J. H. Webb of McKinney is dead from burns occasioned by the explosion of a can of kerosene oil.

Joseph Maurer and his son, William, were poisoned Thursday, near San Antonio, from eating ham containing arsenic.

J. Forney, a rockmason engaged on a building at Breckenridge, fell from the building Friday, and a large rock falling on him crushed him to death.

Opinion of Marriage.

According to a bachelor editor, the following is why so many marriages prove a failure: He says "nine-tenths of the unhappy marriages are the result of green human calves being allowed to run at large without yokes on them. They marry and have children before they do mustache; they are the father of twins before they have two pairs of pants, and the little girls they marry are as old as their grandmothers in schemings. Occasionally one of these goslin marriages turn out all right, but it is a clear case of luck. If there was a law against young galoots sparking or marrying before they cut their teeth, we suppose the little cusses would evade it some way, but there ought to be a sentiment against it. It is time enough for these bantams to think of finding a pullet when they have raised money enough to buy a bundle of laths to build a hen house. But they see a girl who looks cunning, and they think there is not going to be girls enough to go around, and they begin to get in their work real spry; and before they are aware of the sanctity of the marriage relation they are hitched for life, and before they own a cookstove or a bedstead, they have to get up in the night and go after a doctor, so frightened that they run themselves out of breath and abuse the doctor because he does not run too, and when the doctor gets there there is not enough flannel in the house to wrap up a doll baby."

THE TEXAS WESTERN, of Anson, is booming its county with much style and we hope it may win.—Della Plain Review.

We hold a hand that always wins, Bro. McLain. Jones county is a full hand, and there is no necessity to call for more cards

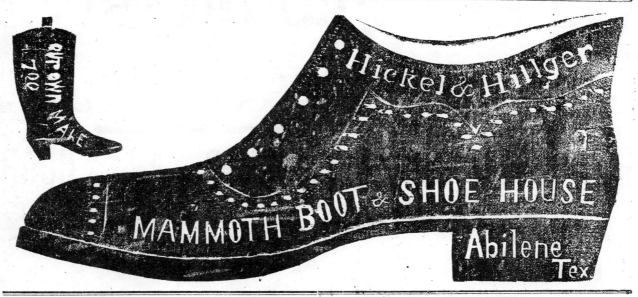

SULLIVAN SENT UP.

The Pride of the North is Given One Year in a Cold Southern Prison.

John L. Sullivan, the Boston brute who fought Kilrain in Mississippi, has received his just deserts in the shape of a sentence of one year's confinement in the county jail at Purvis, Miss. The following petition came from the grand jury:

"The undersigned members of the grand jury impanneled at the present term of the court and the petit jury who tried the case of the State vs. John L. Sullivan, convicted of prize fighting, respectfully show to the court that in view of fact that this is the first conviction for the offense named in this state, and for other reasons, they respectfully recommend and request that your honor will impose no higher penalty than a fine of $1000 and that no imprisonment be inflicted."

Ed Davis was the only petit juror who refused to sign. The grand jurors all signed as also did all merchants in the city, and a number of farmers round about, as well as the sheriff, clerk and other officers of the court, the justice of the peace before whom the case was first tried, and many others. Gen. Ford supplemented the petition by a few remarks.

Judge Calhoun also appealed for the clemency of the court. There was a pause, then there was a stir in the audience, and the champion turned up before the bar and speaking in a loud, clear and steady voice, said:

SULLIVAN SPEAKS.

"Your honor, I desire to make a few remarks. I can only ask for your clemency in this matter. No doubt I have done something wrong, but, as my counsel told you, I was ignorant of the laws. I am not as oratorical or as distinguished as the attorney on my right or my counsel, who have addressed you, and therefore I beg to remark that I am your humble servant, John L. Sullivan."

He then sat down and there was another pause, which was broken by Judge Terrell saying in his quiet way:

"Stand up, Sullivan."

The court did not say Mr. Sullivan this time. Sullivan stood up quickly. He threw out his chest and looked the court in the face, and had evidently determined upon perfect self control. Judge Terrell spoke slowly as follows:

THE SENTENCE.

"It seems to me this prize fight at Richburg, of which you stand convicted, was a gross affront to the laws of the state where the authorities personally forbade it. It seems to have been accomplished with systematic arrangements, and in the presence of invited thousands. It seems on the part of all connected in it to have been a studied disregard and contempt for law. They came from and through many states whose authority and civilization deterred them from any attempt at such public lawless conduct within their limits, and they chose the soil of Mississippi as the only fit ground for such combat, indicating their utter contempt of the sentiments of her people and the laws of her statute books. The sentence of the law is that for a punishment for the offense that you stand convicted of you shall suffer imprisonment for twelve months in the county jail."

Sullivan gloomily took his seat. He maintained his stolid look for a moment, but when attention was withdrawn from him his mouth put on the same appearance as when he met Kilrain in the ring, with little of sorrow tempering the ferocity. The feeling passed from him in another moment, and when he got under the railing to leave the courtroom he faced the sympathizing crowd with a broad smile.

The court then passed sentence on Mr. Fitzpatrick. Sixty days were granted to file a bill of exception and an appeal was taken to the supreme court. The district attorney announced that Kilrain would be here next week, and Fitzpatrick was subpœnaed as a witness and put under a $500 bond.

The re-union of Ross' and Ector's brigades was held at Sulphur Springs last week.

WEEKLY PROGRESSIVE NEWS

NEWS ESTABLISHED, 1885. PROGRESS ESTABLISHED, 1888. CONSOLIDATED JANU Y 1889. OFFICE OF PUBLICATON: TOBL BUILDING, MAIN STREET, BELTON, TEXAS

VOL IV. BELTON TEXAS TUESDAY, AUGUST 27, 1889 NO 27

Rev. R. M. Shelton's

Spirit Takes it's Homeward Flight.

A Sorrowing and Grief Stricken People.

Brief life, is here our portion,
Brief sorrow, short lived cares,
The life, that knows no ennding,
The tearless life is there.

At 4:20 o'clock Thursday evening, she spirit of Rev. R. M. Shelton, Pastor of the Methodist church of this city, took its flight from earth to heaven, amid a host of grief stricken relatives and sorowing friends. He died from continued fever, after an illness of about ten days.

"Death loves a shining mark." Bro. Shelton, was a young man about 29, years of age, just entering the prime of life, he was one of the best, most honored, esteemed and loved ministers, in this district conference. Was married on the first day of August, 1888, to Miss Mattie Mackey of Georgetown—who is left to mourn her irrepairable loss. He graduated at the Vanderbuilt University of Nashville Tenn. Has held the responsible position of Professor of English literature, in the Southwestern University at Georgetown Texas. Was ordained as an Elder at Weatherford Tex. in 1888, and has held several important appointments. Was appointed to Belton, M. E. church in December, 1888, which position he held at the time of his death.

His congregation and members of the church and infact the entire community, feel their loss most severly, but "God's will, not ours be done."

Had He asked us, well we know,
"We would cry, O, spare this blow!"
Yes, with streaming tears should pray,
"Lord we love him, let him say.
But the Lord doeth naught amiss,
And, since he hath ordered this,
We have naught to do, but still
Rest in silence on his will.

The funeral services took place, at the M. E. church, at 4, p. m., yesterday, and were conducted by the Rev. J. M. Barcus of Alvorado; Dr. Horace Bishop, Presiding Elder, of Georgetown District; Dr J. H. McClean, Vice Regent of the Southwestern University; and others. After which the remains were tenderly laid to rest in the north Belton cemetery, in a most beautiful casket, bearing the inscription "at rest," and in the earthly loss of Bro. Shelton.—The family, friends and church, have our sincerest sympaihies and condolence.

"For ever with the Lord;
Amen, so let it be."

AT THE CHURCH.

The church was suitably draped in mourning, and the services were conducted in a very solemn manner, and the many sad looking faces that attended the service told plainly of the immense sorrow that lay hidden in the hearts of every one present, appropriate hymns were solemly sung by the choir, and suitable passages of scripture read, and addresses delivered, in which the life of deceased was justly eulogized nd prayers for the afflicted family offered up. And altogether were very impressive, reminding those present of the uncertainty of life, and the sureity of death; after which the funeral services were finished at the cemetery, and the remains of a noble hearted christian gentleman, were placed in Mother earth, to sleep till Gabriel's trump shall awake.

He Hanged.

San Antonio, August, 23,—Jim McCoy, the one legged murderer of Sheriff McKinnly, of La Salle county, was hanged at 2 p. m., yesterday. He left a document with the sheriff which will probably throw light on the murder, when it is made public.

Commuted Sentence.

London, Aug., 23,—The death sentence of Mrs. Maybrick, has been commuted to penal servitude for life.

If you want to help advertise the get up and get of Belton, place "ads" in the PROGRESSIVE NEWS. Coppies of it go outside the state as follows—Chicago 2, New York 4 Atlanta Ga., 1, Cincinnati 1, S Louis 3, Pittsburg Pa., 3, Low Mass., 1, New Haven Conn., Warren Pa., 1, Sedalia Mo., 1, Kansas City 2, Philadelphia 1, Buffa. Ny., 1, Louisana Mo., 1, Louisville Ky., 1, Washington D. C, I, and in the state they go to Galveston, Dallas. Fort Worth, Waco, Austin, Houston, Brenham, Laredo, Temple, Nolanville, Troy, Holland, Salado, Caldwell, San Angelo, Linden, Moody, Corn Hill, etc., etc. While there is scarcely a state in the Union or a town in this state but what our weekly reaches.

Coal Oil Again.

Mineola, Tex., Aug, 23,—Mrs Ed Terry, tried the coal oil process of lighting a fire, and the result was she was burned to death, and her husband badly burned in attempting to put out the flames.

WICHITA HERALD.

Volume 8. WICHITA FALLS, WICHITA COUNTY, TEXAS, SATURDAY, OCT. 19, 1889. Number 5.

Its Soil! Its Water! It…

ITS PAS…

"Westward the star of …mpire takes …ay." It has

THE WONDERFUL WICHITA FALLS COUNTRY.

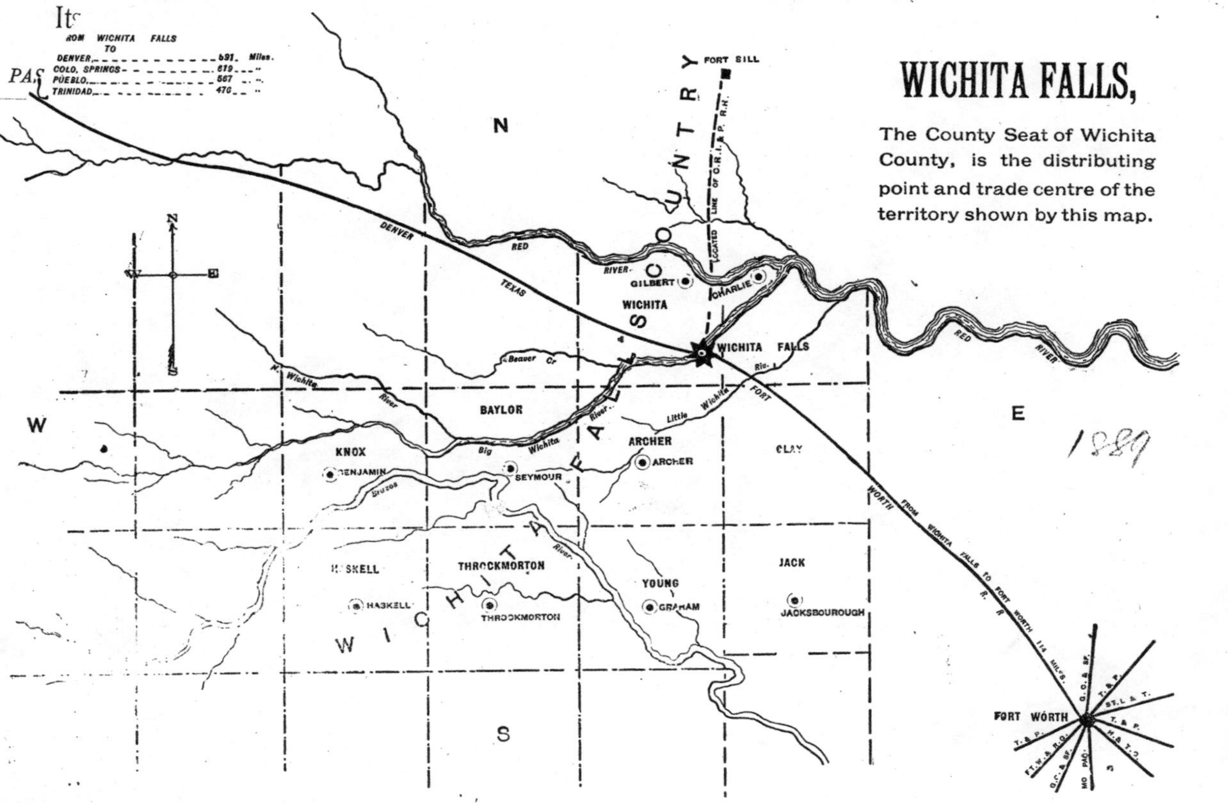

WICHITA FALLS!

The Plucky Little City that is Attracting Attention from Far and Near!

HER LOCATION! HER BUSINESS! HER PROSPECTS!

A little more than seven years ago the site where Wichita Falls now stands was part and parcel of a wide expanse of country bordering upon what the children of a former generation found laid down in their geographies as the great American Desert. The only sign of civilization for miles around was a rude log building occupied by a hardy pioneer who made it answer the double purpose of a dwelling and a grocery store, in which he sold tobacco and other supplies for the ranchman and the cowboy.

Herds of buffalo dwelt in the beautiful valleys or roamed over the sloping upland about him, and the Comanche Indian whose home was just across the Rio Roxo or Red river a few miles to the north, was a frequent and not always a welcome visitor. Countless numbers of cattle also, were to be seen in every direction grazing in the tall grass that waved to and fro in the breeze like the billows of the sea.

To-day the scene is wonderfully changed. The old log house still stands in the eastern part of the city, but instead of having for its environment only a boundless meadow of sedge grass, it is surrounded by handsome brick business buildings, a splendid brick and stone court house, churches, a school house and hundreds of substantial and attractive dwellings, the homes of a refined, intelligent, prosperous and happy people. They have converted the wilderness into a city and the cow pasture into a commercial mart.

Wichita Falls is the county seat of Wichita county. It is located 114 miles northwest of Fort Worth on the Panhandle route, the great trunk line railroad extending from Fort Worth to Denver, and is on the located line of the Rock Island now building from Caldwell, Kansas, to Cisco, which latter city is situated south of us on the Texas & Pacific and H. & T. C. railways. This road is already built and graded as far south as El Reno in the Oklahoma country, a point 103 miles south of Caldwell and only 130 miles from Wichita Falls. It is only a question of a few months when it will be completed to this point, when Wichita Falls will take rank with the most flourishing young cities of Texas.

Wichita Falls is the distributing point for a large scope of country lying immediately south and southwest of her, including the counties of Archer, Baylor, Knox and portions of Throckmorton and Young, and also portions of Clay and Wilbarger. She enjoys, unrivaled, the trade of this territory, being now a common freight point, which contributes largely to her growth and insures her solidity as a city. From these counties and from Wichita county as well she receives an immense amount of wheat, corn, oats and other farm products, cotton, live stock, wool, etc.

The city has six dry goods and clothing stores, eleven grocery stores, one exclusive clothing store, two jewelry stores, one shoe store, five grain stores, two hardware establishments, four implement houses, one saddle and harness and one furniture store, four drug stores, four hotels and several restaurants, five saloons, two newspapers, one national bank, four churches, a public school building, three blacksmith shops, three paint shops, a number of laundries, a bakery, an ice house, three livery stables, three wagon yards, a large patent roller flouring mill, a corn mill and cotton gin, numerous law, land and loan men and firms, two lumber yards and two brick kilns. This volume of business with but few exceptions, is transacted in one and two story bricks. There are but few frame business buildings. There are also to be built within the next few weeks two one story bricks 25x80 feet, one two story brick 25x75, and a two story brick 50x150 feet.

The contract is let for a $9000 jail, which is to be completed by the first day of January 1890. It will be located in the court house square, which with our $40,000 court house already built will add greatly to that portion of the city.

The city is admirably situated for drainage, sloping as it does from the eminence on which it is built, to the Big Wichita river which skirts the town plot. It has lately been incorporated and has a public spirited mayor and board of aldermen, and will soon enjoy the advantages of a first class city government.

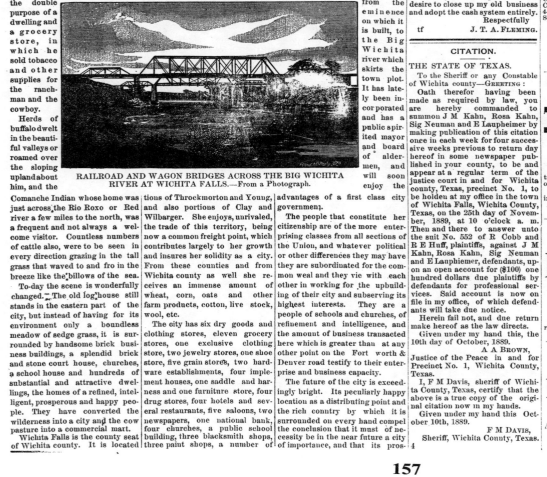

RAILROAD AND WAGON BRIDGES ACROSS THE BIG WICHITA RIVER AT WICHITA FALLS.—From a Photograph.

The people that constitute her citizenship are of the more enterprising classes from all sections of the Union, and whatever political or other differences they may have they are subordinated for the common weal and they vie with each other in working for the upbuilding of their city and subserving its highest interests. They are a people of schools and churches, of refinement and intelligence, and the amount of business transacted here which is greater than at any other point on the Fort worth & Denver road testify to their enterprise and business capacity.

The future of the city is exceedingly bright. Its peculiarly happy location as a distributing point and the rich country by which it is surrounded on every hand compel the conclusion that it must of necessity be in the near future a city of importance, and that its prosperity is as yet in its early infancy. It is to-day the best town in northwest Texas and its future cannot be pictured by the most vivid imagination.

To Whom it May Concern.

I will hereafter do a strictly cash business. By so doing I will be able to sell my customers goods at cheaper prices and with better satisfaction to them and myself. My patrons will please make a note of this. Those owing me accounts will please come forward and settle at as early a date as possible as I desire to close up my old business and adopt the cash system entirely.

Respectfully

tf J. T. A. FLEMING.

CITATION.

THE STATE OF TEXAS.

To the Sheriff or any Constable of Wichita county—GREETING:

Oath therefor having been made as required by law, you are hereby commanded to summon J M Kahn, Rosa Kahn, Sig Neuman and E Laupheimer by making publication of this citation once in each week for four successive weeks previous to return day hereof in some newspaper published in your county, to be and appear at a regular term of the justice court in and for Wichita county, Texas, precinct No. 1, to be holden at my office in the town of Wichita Falls, Wichita County, Texas, on the 25th day of November, 1889, at 10 o'clock a. m. Then and there to answer unto the suit No. 552 of R Cobb and R E Huff, plaintiffs, against J M Kahn, Rosa Kahn, Sig Neuman and E Lauphiemer, defendants, upon an open account for ($100) one hundred dollars due plaintiffs by defendants for professional services. Said account is now on file in my office, of which defendants will take due notice.

Herein fail not, and due return make hereof as the law directs.

Given under my hand this, the 10th day of October, 1889.

A A BROWN,
Justice of the Peace in and for Precinct No. 1, Wichita County, Texas.

I, F M Davis, sheriff of Wichita County, Texas, certify that the above is a true copy of the original citation now in my hands.

Given under my hand this October 10th, 1889.

F M DAVIS,
Sheriff, Wichita County, Texas.
4

"FIVE MINUTES TO GO BACK TO YOUR CELLS."

CONVICT MUTINY IN THE UNITED STATES JAIL AT FORT SMITH, ARK.—MARSHAL CRUMP, WITH A BEAD DRAWN ON THE MUTINEERS BY THE PRISON GUARDS, TIMES THE EXECUTION OF HIS ORDER TO "FIRE."

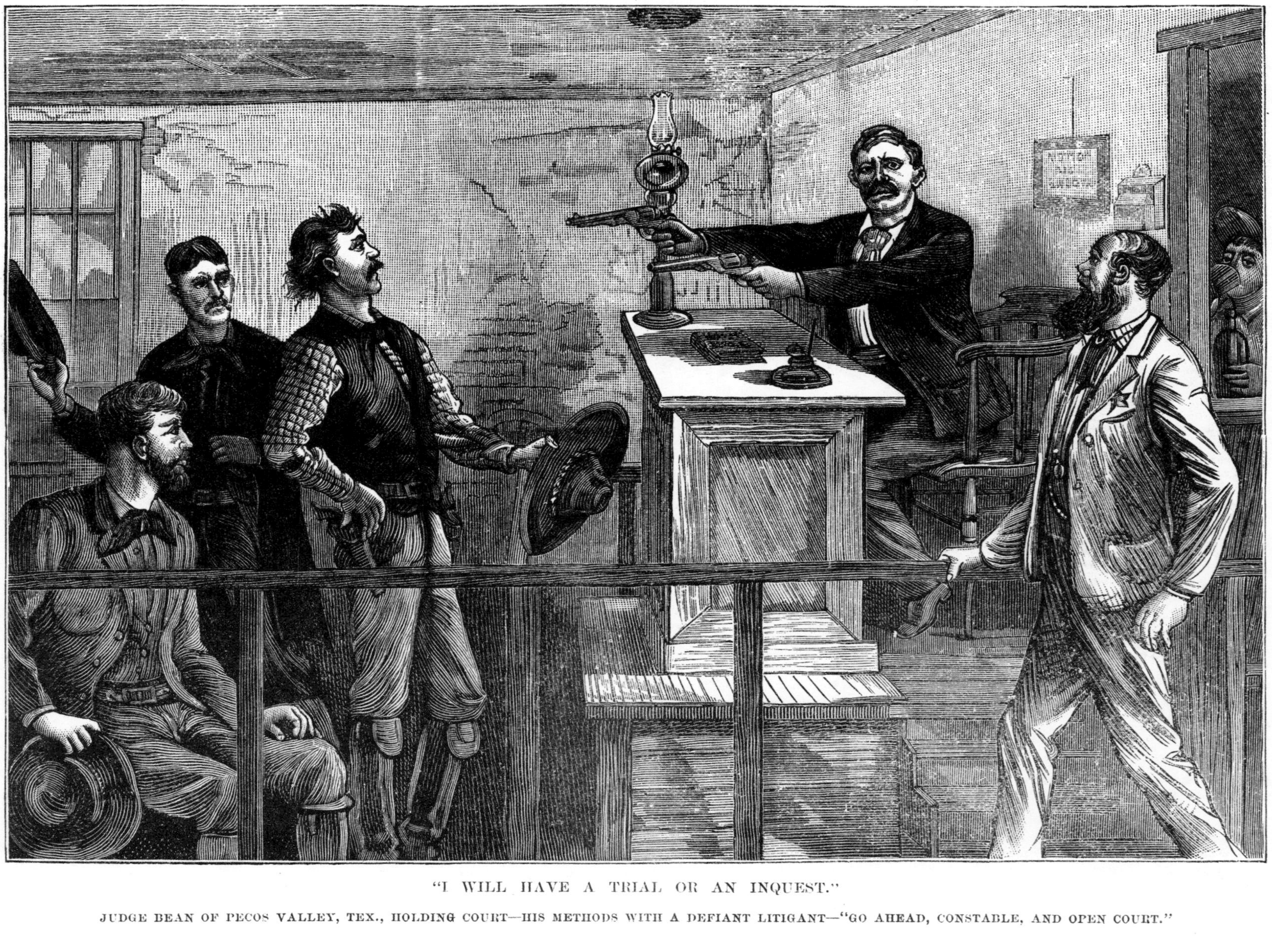

"I WILL HAVE A TRIAL OR AN INQUEST."

JUDGE BEAN OF PECOS VALLEY, TEX., HOLDING COURT—HIS METHODS WITH A DEFIANT LITIGANT—"GO AHEAD, CONSTABLE, AND OPEN COURT."

THE BOOMERANG.

FRIDAY, APRIL 8, 1892.

Union Pacific Mail and Express.

WEST BOUND.

No. 1, Limited,	Ar. 8:40 a. m.	Lv. 8:45 a. m.
No. 3, Fast Mail,	Ar. 10:25 a. m.	Lv. 10:30 a. m.
No. 7, Pacific Ex.,	Ar. 4:10 p. m.	Lv. 4:30 p. m.

EAST BOUND.

No. 2, Limited,	Ar. 2:20 a. m.	Lv. 2:25 a. m.
No. 4, Fast Mail,	Ar. 12:05 a. m.	Lv. 12:10 a. m.
No. 8, Atlantic Ex.,	Ar. 1:40 p. m.	Lv. 2:00 p. m.

It is the intention of the publishers of THE BOOMERANG that the paper should be delivered to every subscriber promptly and regularly. Subscribers will confer a great favor upon the management by reporting promptly every failure or defect in the service.

BOOMERANG CO.

STOCK TROUBLE NORTH

Johnson County Said to Have Been Invaded.

A VERY MYSTERIOUS TRAIN

It Conveys Pinkerton Men or Stockmen's Employes from Denver to Casper, Where They Left for the Northwest.

The Denver papers announce the startling information that a party of at least thirty-five Pinkerton detectives had been whisked through Cheyenne en route to the northern country to there begin the work of exterminating the rustlers. The work had been quietly enough performed so that only those who were into the secret were aware of what was transpiring.

At 2 o'clock on Tuesday afternoon a special train started from Denver. It had aboard somewhere between thirty-five and seventy-five men, probably about the first named number. This train reached Cheyenne before 5:30 o'clock in the evening and kept in the east end of the yards. Only certain individuals were allowed to go near it. It is now said that even the oilers were not permitted to oil the cars. A locomotive was attached to the train and soon after its arrival it steamed north.

The train as it left consisted, besides the locomotive, of a chair car with the blinds closely drawn, a baggage car, a caboose, three stock cars loaded with saddle horses and a Denver, Texas and Fort Worth flat car with several wagons aboard. In the chair car were the imported men, and it is said some fifteen or twenty stockmen. Each detective was armed with a Winchester rifle and two six-shooters. Everyone of the party seemed to have firearms of some sort. In the baggage car were the necessary number of saddles, blankets and paraphernalia. The trip to Casper, a distance of some 200 miles, was made long before daylight. A stop was made at the stockyards about a mile this side of Casper, and beyond that point the train did not proceed. In waiting there were found several men well acquainted with the country, some of whom reported the location of various men in whom the party was in search and gave such other information as seemed pertinent.

The details of the expedition had evidently been perfectly arranged. Each man knew his duty and did it quietly. The horses were debarked at the stock yards, the saddles removed from the baggage car and in a very short space of time most of the men were mounted, with their revolvers strapped to their well supplied cartridge belts and their Winchesters in scabbards at their saddle bows. The team horses and wagons were unloaded at the same time and the vehicles loaded with bedding and utensils. No one was masked and there seemed no desire to conceal identity. When everything was ready the signal to move was given, the guides took the lead and the cavalcade moved silently in a general northwesterly direction. By daylight not a trace or vestige of it could be seen in any direction.

Soon after the party had departed the train steamed back to Orrin and after remaining there a few hours started for Cheyenne, reaching there about 6 o'clock. The Leader says that none of the trainmen would say a word about it. When asked the object of sending an extra with such haste up north they replied laconically, "Coal," and refused to say a word further. It is now understood they were acting under instructions.

Telegraphic communication with Buffalo is by way of Douglas. From Cheyenne to the latter point is the railway telegraph line. From Douglas onward by way of Fort McKinney to Buffalo is a government line. Some time on Wednesday or that night the telegraph wires were cut or communication broken through other causes. No message can now either come or go in that direction, and the Johnson county region is therefore cut off except by mail.

It leaked out on Tuesday at Casper that some sort of an expedition had invaded that section but the report was quickly circulated that it was a party of surveyors whose purpose it was to secure and hold some of the important mountain passes which are a key to the situation in the building of a transcontinental road. This seems to have been generally accepted as a fact until yesterday when the true import of the invasion partially leaked out. At Douglas more definite news prevailed at an earlier stage. A strange and mysterious circumstance was then recalled. It was remembered that at least a week before the captain of the militia had received an official order to not obey any orders calling his company out except they came through the regular military channels.

Parties arriving from Douglas and Casper at Cheyenne last night claim that no excitement prevails in those sections and that they have no information beyond the fact that a surveying party has gone into the country. They are very guarded in what they say, which leads to the belief that they know or suspect a great deal more than they are willing to tell.

Rumor has it that the invading party intended to make a certain Powder river ranch in the first day out and radiate from that point. It is said that spotters have been at work in Johnson county for some time past definitely locating the men marked as rustlers. It is also stated, though where the rumor comes from no one can tell, that reports were made on Wednesday night by all the spotters and scouts at this Powder river ranch, and acting on this information the avengers took the trail.

In Northwestern Wyoming.

A dispatch from Billings, Montana, says that news has reached there of the finding of the bodies of two dead men and their horses on Alkali creek, a few miles north of Billings. The men are supposed to have belonged to a gang of horse thieves operating in southern Montana and northern Wyoming. The discovery of the bodies of the rustlers indicate that they met death while attempting to escape to the north with stolen stock.

This is believed to be the first successful work this spring in the extermination of the range rustlers of this section. The opinion seems to obtain that the coroner's inquest will throw no particular light on the mystery surrounding the death of these two operators in other men's range property.

J. B. Armour, alias McCoy, one of the range leaders of the rustlers' gang, is in jail at Billings on the charge of stealing a carload of horses near Buffalo, Wyoming, last August, driving them to Red Lodge, Montana, from whence he shipped to North Dakota. Armour's preliminary trial has been put off from time to time, awaiting the arrival of material witnesses for the prosecution from Wyoming. Armour may consider himself lucky that he escapes with a long term in the penitentiary.

THIS, THAT AND THE OTHER.

Fancy bananas at Paul May's.

Judge Brown is rooming at Mrs. M. B. Dawson's.

There will be a sociable at the Methodist church this evening.

Gentle winter is lingering in the lap of a very unaffectionate spring.

The Laramie Turners will hold a meeting at their hall Sunday afternoon.

When needing wall paper, painting or paper-hanging, call on Henry May.

No. 8 had a big train going east today. It was made up of thirteen cars.

Delicious fruit sherbets at Porter's.

Some ore brought in by a miner today has created some talk in mining circles.

Mrs. Howell's French class met at Mrs. Dr. Barnes' residence for the last recitation.

Cut flowers at Porter's Coffee House.

All the machinery has arrived here for the enlargement and re-arrangement of the laundry. The improvements are to be very extensive.

Mesdames Durlacher and Marsh are entertaining Miss Edith Gramm during her mother's absence. Mrs. Gramm will return next week with Mrs. Ivinson.

William Snyder has leased the D. Salsbury ranch and will move upon it with his family in a few weeks. His brother will occupy his residence on Sixth street.

A gentleman who just received a letter from Chugwater says that the Cable company has lost 100 cattle this winter and forty mares. Their colts have been dying almost as soon as foaled.

There will be a special service for women at St. Matthew's tomorrow afternoon at 4 o'clock. The service will consist of the litany and a reading on "The Joyful Mystery of the Presentation."

Confectionery, fruits, nuts. Pelton's.

Rock Springs Miner: The Sweetwater county delegation to the meeting of the state teachers' association speak very highly of the kind treatment received at the hands of the Laramie people.

Buy Kleeman's home made candies.

Miss Cora McDonald and Miss Hattie Knight of Evanston, Wyoming, will make their home this term at Mrs. Donkersley's on Fremont street. Miss Hattie has entered the senior preparatory class in the university.

Miss Lytle resumed her school duties Wednesday. During her absence and, on account of the necessity for a competent, experienced teacher to be in charge, Miss Wright kindly consented to conduct the various exercises.

Mrs. Cecilia F. Link has purchased from William Hunt lots 15 and 16, block 277, Sherrod's addition, with improvements. Consideration $1,000. The property is located at the southwest corner of Second and Kearney Streets.

Judge Brown today received a dispatch from Luther Fillmore saying that his son, Millard, was seriously ill and not expected to live. He is suffering from Bright's disease. He has been a prominent official on the Southern Pacific and is well known in this city.

During a late visit to the schools the following items were noted: The air of extreme quiet that prevails throughout the building; the orderly deportment during the sessions; the neat appearance of the pupils and their increased mental activities. All work seems to be conducted with military precision.

LUCKY SIX COMPANY.

They Will Meet to Decide About Diamond Drilling.

LA PLATA vs. CREEDE LEADS

If the Former Were at the Latter Camp They Would Create a Boom —Placer Mining in Lincoln Gulch.

As announced in THE BOOMERANG yesterday the drill recently purchased by the Diamond Drill Mining company has arrived and is at the depot. It was at first thought that it would at once be loaded and started for the La Plata in a day or two, but it has now been decided it will not leave the city until the first of the week. While the catalogue of the company shows that the drill itself weighs but about 850 pounds, the horse power and other attachments that come with the drill bring the weight up to over 2,200 pounds and this is about the amount that the company has had to pay freight on. The freight amounted to $48, a little more than was at first calculated. It is thought that the drill may be put in operation a week from tomorrow. It will take two days to make the trip to the Brooklyn mine.

The Lucky Six company will hold a meeting at once and decide in what manner they will have the drill put to work on their Brooklyn mine. The Diamond Drill Mining company will prospect with their drill for either a one-tenth interest in a claim or for a cash consideration.

La Plata Better Than Creede Leads.

John Travell says that he will probably remain in Laramie and not return to Creede. He says there are only about 300 miners employed there, 65 of whom are working in the Holy Moses. The formation is of such an easy character to work that 300 miners can do more than double that number at many other places. Creede, therefore, has not the pay roll and business is flattening out with marked emphasis. John says that if they had such leads at Creede as we have in the La Plata district they could be sold at big figures. Upper Creede will probably be a good, steady camp but lower Creede will probably become a dead letter. The snow up out of the gulch is from four to six feet deep.

Placer Mining in Lincoln Gulch.

P. Pfindler, who runs the postoffice and manages the store business for the Otris Mining company at Keystone, is in the city, having come here at the request of the postal inspector to appear against Charles Schabach, who has admitted his guilt in robbing the postoffice out there of $8.50. United States Attorney Fowler has failed to come over from Cheyenne to take up the case against Schabach and Mr. Pfindler says that if he does not turn up by Monday he will return to the Keystone.

He says they are working away on the Florence and are taking out good ore right along. He reports that there will be a great deal of placer mining on Lincoln gulch during the coming summer. Dick Ramey, Gus Hurley, Turner, Munson, Ekholm and others will devote their attention to placer mining. There is any amount of gold in the gulch and if they have any kind of luck they will have a profitable summer.

"THANK YOU,"

Is what Mrs. Paisley of Newburgh, New York, always says to Hood's Sarsaparilla. It cured her of a severe case of scrofula and eczema, and she has reason to be grateful.

If you are bilious, take Hood's Pills.

Choice Winesap apples at Cole's.

The Trabing Com'l Co. received and have to arrive within a few days the following 24 cars of goods:
Two of Defiance, Colo., flour.
Two of choice Colo. bran.
One of Minn. flour, Pillsbury's best.
One of oil cake.
Two of choice Nebraska oats.
Two of choice corn.
One of rye flour, buckwheat and corn meal.
One of salt.
One of oat meal.
One of California wine.
One of whisky.
One of straw and other paper.
One of syrup—barrels, kegs and cans.
One of chopped feed.
One of choice green apples.
Two of spring and farm wagons.
One of barbed fence wire.
One of lard, hams, bacon, pigs' feet.

REDUCED RATE TO DOUGLAS.
On account of democratic state convention at Douglas April 13, tickets at one and one-fifth fare for the round trip will be sold to Orin Junction from the 10th to 13th; good returning April 16th.
A13 G. C. RANDALL, Agent.

INNOCENT TENDERFOOT

His Experience in Coming Over Sherman Hill.

THE GREAT CATTLE KINGS.

The Tenderfoot Was Anxious to See One—Also Some Wild Cowboys Lasso Indians—He Was Heavily Armed.

It is often a matter of amusement to the people of this western country to learn of the ridiculous ideas that eastern people of have of this boundless western region, the home of the Indian and the land where the cowboy and the cattle king flourish.

The latest incident of this kind occurred recently while Clarence Covert was on his way home to this city after a visit with his parents at Hume, Missouri. On the Union Pacific train from Kansas City there was a young man with his wife and two children from Louisville, Kentucky. All the way to Denver the young man from the bluegrass state held no conversation with any one except his wife and children, but coming up from Denver he began to look about the country. He would occasionally look out suddenly with an anxious expression on his countenance as though expecting to see some one.

After leaving Cheyenne he could not stand it any longer, and Clarence being rather an unsuspecting looking individual the baker from Louisville approached him without fear of losing his scalp.

"Good morning."

"Good morning," replied Clarence.

"Where are the soldiers?" said the bluegrass tenderfoot.

"Guess they left them off this time," moodily replied the Laramie gentleman. The fellow gave a troubled glance at his family and Clarence said he commenced to "catch on" then that he had struck a tenderfoot and was sure there was a joke in sight.

"W-e-l-l, where are the Indians?" laconically replied the dough mixer from the bourbon region.

They were climbing up Sherman hill about this time and Clarence thought the altitude might be affecting the fellow so he was prepared for anything that the gullible eastern dime novel reader might drop from his plastic mind.

"Well, now, I would like to know how they capture these Indians anyway. Do they lasso them?"

Clarence nodded his head. After the fellow had taken another good look out of the window and scanning the horizon after the Cooper style he said:

"I'd like to see some wild cowboys lasso the Indians."

Clarence shifted his position and told the fellow that the Indians in these times rarely attacked the trains on the open plains but that it was a very common matter for them to ambush the trains in the tunnels and get a few scalps. Clarence had in mind the large snow sheds this side of Sherman about this time. The pastry monger's imagination of the west reached the climax when he said:

"I would like to see a Cattle King."

Clarence excused himself and went and told the brakeman of the joke and made him promise that when the train entered the snow shed that he would yell like a Comanche Indian. The brakeman followed instructions and as the train dashed out of the west end of the snow shed the paralyzed pastry compounder stood in the aisle by his wife and children with a new six-shooter in his hand determined to sell his life dearly. Clarence tried to induce him to stop off in Laramie to see a Cattle King but the fellow continued on west.

PERSONAL PARAGRAPHS.

George R. Eykyn and wife are in the city.

A. G. Lane was a visitor from Cheyenne today.

W. S. McDowell was in from the ranch today.

William Taylor of Rock Creek was in the city today.

General John Charles Thompson was in the city from Cheyenne today.

Arthur Parks of Fort Collins arrived in the city this evening on No. 7.

George Morgan has been out to the Sartoris ranch for the past two days.

Henry Gobleman left this evening for Rawlins and other points west for the brewery.

T. O. Minta, manager for the Beckwith Commercial company at Rock Springs, transacted business in Laramie today.

Mrs. Jens Hanson of Carbon, who has been visiting J. W. Johnson and family here for several days, returned home this morning.

Stormy weather has detained Mr. Myers in the city much longer than he intended. He returned this morning and will remain at the Keystone for some time.

Mrs. A. M. Decker and M. E. Stowers, relatives of Mr. and Mrs. W. B. Sutphin, are expected in the city tomorrow. They have been spending the winter in California and are on their way home to Scranton, Pennsylvania.

W. W. Breese returned last evening from a trip to Denver and Fort Collins. At the latter place he says there are 600 cars of potatoes that the people cannot get cars to ship them in. They are determined to build their new road. The potatoes have been sold several times but cannot be gotten into the market.

The Trabing Com'l Co. buy their goods right, get them from headquarters and in large quantities, hence will make prices lower than anyone.

MARION HARLAND.

The celebrated authoress, so highly esteemed by the women of America, says on pages 103 and 445 of her popular work, "Eve's Daughters; or, Common Sense for Maid, Wife and Mother:"

"For the aching back—should it be slow in recovering its normal strength—an Allcock's Porous Plaster is an excellent comforter, combining the sensation of the sustained pressure of a warm hand with certain tonic qualities developed in the wearing. It should be kept over the seat of the uneasiness for several days—in obstinate cases, for perhaps a fortnight."

"For pain in the back wear an Allcock's Porous Plaster constantly, renewing as it wears off. This is an invaluable support when the weight on the small of the back becomes heavy and the aching incessant."

Special prices made on grain, bran, flour, chopped feed and oil cake in ton lots, At TRABING'S.

Attend the sociable tonight at the Methodist church.

The Methodist General Conference at Omaha, May, 1892.

For the accommodation of those desiring to visit at points east of, in the vicinity of, or at Omaha, during May, the Union Pacific will sell tickets at one fare for the round trip. Tickets on sale April 28 to 30 inclusive, limited to June 1, 1892.

For tickets or additional information apply to G. C. Randall, agent Union Pacific system, Laramie. M1

BORN.

GREGG.—In Laramie, Wyoming, April 7, 1892, to the wife of C. R. Gregg, a daughter.

The Boomerang.

Tuesday, April 12, 1892.

Union Pacific Mail and Express.

WEST BOUND.

No. 1, Limited, Ar. 8:40 a. m. Lv. 8:45 a. m.
No. 3, Fast Mail, Ar. 10:25 a. m. Lv. 10:30 a. m.
No. 7, Pacific Ex., Ar. 4:10 p. m. Lv. 4:30 p. m.

EAST BOUND.

No. 2, Limited, Ar. 2:20 a. m. Lv. 2:25 a. m.
No. 4, Fast Mail, Ar. 12:06 a. m. Lv. 12:10 a. m.
No. 8, Atlantic Ex., Ar. 1:40 p. m. Lv. 2:00 p. m.

It is the intention of the publishers of The Boomerang that the paper should be delivered to every subscriber promptly and regularly. Subscribers will confer a great favor upon the management by reporting promptly every failure or defect in the service.

Boomerang Co.

NORTH STAR INVESTMENT CO.

Stockholders will meet in the hall Thursday April 14th, 8 o'clock p.m., to receive report from auditing committee and act on such questions that may be brought before the meeting. By order, 22eod3t E. Stendahl.

RUSTLER'S BEATEN

They Have Been Defeated by the Cattlemen's Army.

Nate Champion Was Shot and Somerville Burned.

STRAGGLING INTO DOUGLAS

Armed Ranchmen Have Been Retreating Into Douglas All Day Today—The Douglas Militia Company in Arms.

Excitement at Buffalo—It Is Said that a Riot Is Imminent at That Place—Straggling Ranchmen Are There Also.

Special to The Boomerang.

Cheyenne, April 12.—4 p. m.—The latest information received here from Douglas says that Sheriff Angus has just returned from north of that place and that he reports that Nate Champion was shot by the cattlemen.

The army surrounded Champion and Sommerville's ranch and opened fire on them, which was returned. When Champion and Sommerville had exhausted their ammunition Champion attempted to escape from his cabin. He ran about 200 yards from the building when he was killed by a volley of musketry.

Some reports say that it was not Sommerville who was in the cabin with Champion, but whoever it was refused to come out and surrender and the cabin was set fire and he burned with it.

Many ranchmen have been arriving in Douglas all day with arms and ammunition and the city is in a state of terror. The militia company have been assembled and are now resting on their arms. It is feared the cattlemen's army may attack the ranchmen who are in the city.

The ranchmen and rustlers have been scattered in all directions.

COMPANY A RECEIVES ORDERS.

They Will Meet at the Armory Tonight at 8 O'Clock.

At 4:40 o'clock this afternoon the commanding officer of Co. A of this city received orders to be ready to go to Johnson county.

The members of the company will meet at the armory this evening at 8 o'clock.

Champion and Somerville Lynched.

Special to The Boomerang.

Casper, Wyoming, April 12.—The report of the lynching of Nate Champion and Ray Somerville is fully confirmed this afternoon. They were both captured and hung. They are two of the best known men in the country. Champion was as fearless as a lion but he was overpowered by the cattlemen's army and with Somerwille was strung up.

It is understood that there will be several more parties lynched unless they leave the country.

The War About Ended.

Special to The Boomerang.

Douglas, Wyoming, April 12.—There is no doubt about the defeat of the ranchmen in the battle with the cattlemen's army. The war is thought to be practically over, although there may be some running fighting and smaller difficulties at other points.

Rustler's Defeated.

Special to The Boomerang.

Douglas, Wyoming, April 12.—The fight between the rustlers and the cattlemen's army has taken place and the latter has been victorious.

The small cattlemen are entirely routed and are fleeing in every direction. It is now known that the two men who were seen fleeing toward Fort Fetterman were rustlers who had been in the battle. One of them was wounded.

Owing to the fact that the cattlemen have control of the telegraph line it has been difficult to get any authentic information.

Some of the news that has been sent out is supposed to be from the cattlemen. The report yesterday that the rustlers had the cattlemen's army surrounded at the TA ranch is thought to be untrue.

Trouble at Buffalo.

Douglas, Wyoming, April 12.—It is reported here that there has been called out and a battle is liable to be fought at any time.

The defeated rustlers will have to forsake everything. All their accumulations are now to fall into the hands of some one else and the central part of the state will be run again by the cattlemen.

GENERAL COMMENT.

Great Interest Over the Situation Manifested in Laramie.

Until last evening there had been very little excitement in this city concerning the cattle troubles in Johnson county. People in the first place were hopeful that the situation would reach a peaceful settlement and without bloodshed.

When the news was published last evening in The Boomerang that there had been a battle and that a number had been wounded the feeling was at once different. It seemed to be the opinion that

Gov. Barber Was a Mere Stick

in the executive chair or else he was simply a stool pigeon. The expression was general that he should at once take an active hand in quelling any trouble in the state.

The opinion prevails that the armed force brought in from Colorado should be forced from the state and the executive should restore order. The governor is not obliged to leave these matters to the sheriffs of the different counties. The governor is empowered to move to restore

A Peaceful Condition of Things

so soon as he sees that the sheriffs are not preserving the peace. The Buffalo militia company has now been placed under orders and the Douglas company have been notified to be prepared for orders. It is said that two weeks ago the ranchmen and those denominated as rustlers met in Buffalo and laid out round-up districts to embrace Johnson county. This would indicate that they had considerable confidence in their own ability to cope with the stockmen upon equal terms.

These Round Ups

were not designated to begin until May and the intervening time these men usually spend close to their ranches making necessary repairs and getting everything in readiness for the spring and summer campaign. It was therefore generally believed that this time was selected with this object in view so that the men might be pounced upon individually or just as they were fonnd when they could offer but comparatively little resistance

Around the TA Ranch.

The battle between the stockmen's forces and the small cattlemen is supposed to have taken place near the TA ranch, owned by Dr. Harris of this city.

It is a beautiful section of country, but is not calculated for a long drawn out battle. The country is open and the parties would be obliged to face each other without protection. Dr. Harris' buildings are the best to be found upon any of the ranches in that country, and a force of men once fortified there could stand off a regiment.

Canton in Charge.

Casper, Wyoming, April 12.—While it is thought that Major Wolcott is one of the ringleaders of the cattlemen in the present war, it is very generally known that Frank Canton has probably had more to do with the management of the invading army than anyone else.

Everything taken together points to Canton as the great lieutenant of the cattlemen. His return to Wyoming was nicely timed. Soon after he came back it is now averred that the quiet report that a mob was to invade the country and clean out the rustlers.

Canton on his way from Chicago stopped in Denver and spent several days there, and it is thought he at that time made arrangements for the force they have in Johnson county.

Canton knows every foot of that country and has a large amount of property there. It is thought he did not dare return there alone since he is charged with the killing of Tisdale last December, and is now enjoying his liberty under $30,000 bonds.

About the time Tisdale was killed Champion and Somerville, who are reported killed narrowly escaped assassination.

Shrewdly Planned.

Cheyenne, April 12.—It is the opinion here that when the whole matter relating to the present cattle troubles is sifted to the bottom after the war is over that it will be found that the stock commission is at the bottom of the entire trouble.

The commission will undoubtedly attempt to justify itself in its present attitude against the smaller cattlemen of the central part of the state. The managers of the commission will attempt to show that they are justified by the law in sending an armed force into Johnson county.

By the law that reorganized the stock commission when Wyoming became a state, the commission is given authority to appoint a commissioner of round-ups and lay out the state in districts, the round-ups to be in charge of the round-up commissioner who has been appointed.

It is the opinion here that the commission will claim that the round-up commissioner had a right to employ sufficient men to take charge of the round-up and that they had a right to carry sufficient arms to proceed with the round-up.

The commission will undoubtedly be bold enough to attempt to set at naught the idea that they have brought an armed force into the state in violation of the constitution. An attempt will be made to surround every move with a "coloring" of the law.

The Attack Planned.

Douglas, Wyoming, April 12.—It has now leaked out that the present invasion of the state by an armed force under the direction of the big stockmen had been planned for some time previous to their appearance in this section.

Parties who were on the inside and got pointers as to what was coming some time ago offered to bet openly that there would be an armed force brought into the state to assist the cattlemen in running the country.

Fun for the Indians.

Special dispatch to the Boomerang.

Douglas, Wyoming, April 12.—A sensational rumor has reached here to the effect that some of the Wind River Indians are preparing to cross the Big Horn mountains and round up all the cattle they can find. While the attention of the cattlemen and the small stockmen is being taken they could live according to the Indian idea of living—with a full stomach.

PERSONAL PARAGRAPHS.

C. T. Gale is laid up with the rheumatism.

William Johnson of Rongis, this state, is in the city.

Johnny Dimmit arrived from Salt Lake this afternoon.

Ora Haley passed through the city last night on his way to Douglas.

Charlie Carter, well known in Johnson county as a range man, is in the city.

Bishop Talbot will remain in the city about ten days. Mrs. Talbot will return in May and Miss Annie will spend her vacation in Laramie.

Mrs. Howell and son left for Denver today. Since the illness of the latter he has been seriously affected with heart failure. At Denver they will meet a relative who will accompany the little boy to his grandmother in St. Louis.

Mrs. J. T. M. Kingstord went to Cheyenne yesterday to visit Mrs. Cox a former resident of this city. After Mrs. Kingsford had left on the 2 o'clock train she received a letter from Mrs. Cox saying that Mr. Cox's mother had just had a stroke of apoplexy and it was feared she could not live.

Rev. Mr. Goodale and wife, old friends of Mr. and Mrs. George, will spend a short time in the city. They are on their way home to Columbus, Nebraska, after having had a pleasant visit in California. While they were favorably impressed with the latter state they were not so enthusiastic as many. At Salt Lake, they attempted to gain an entrance to the newly erected temple. The rush of visitors at least 3,000, made the effort unsafe and they abandoned the idea. The statue of the angel, thirteen feet in height, which is placed on the central pinnacle of the temple, presents a beautiful appearance, especially at night. It is lighted from below by electricity and can be seen at a great distance.

UNIVERSITY BALL CLUB.

A and B Companies Will Each Have a Nine—A Strong Club.

The members of the university cadets have organized two ball clubs one from A company and one from B company. These two clubs will practice together during the season and when the university wants to pit a club against any outside organization they will pick the strongest nine they can to cross bats with other clubs. The members have not yet been assigned their positions, but this will be done in a few days. They will not go outside of the university for any players, and the games the club wins will be on their merits as a university club.

They will invite challenges from any of the Laramie clubs that may be organized. There are some excellent players among the cadets and with some of the new material in better shape they will be able to put up a strong game.

PROHIBITIONISTS.

A Meeting Last Night and Another Tonight—State Convention.

Rev. James P. Pinkham spoke at the court house last night on the subject of prohibition. Nearly every seat in the court room was taken and the reverend gentlemen held the close attention of all until after 10 o'clock. His remarks were full of wit and pathos and facts.

Mr. Pinkham will speak again this evening at the same place, at which time a temporary prohibition organization will be formed. Mr. Pinkham, after a trip further west, will stop at Laramie on his way back and the organization will then probably be perfected. It is the intention for the party to hold a state convention in the near future. It will be held either at Cheyenne or in this city, according probably to which place has the most delegates.

KILLED A TEXAS BOY.

James Jones a Bad Man Released From the "Pen."

REARRESTED FOR MURDER.

A Texas Sheriff Is En Route With Him to That State Where He Will Answer for Murder—Wyoming Crimes.

About 9 o'clock this morning James Jones, alias "Parker," "Sparks," "Harris" and other names, was liberated from the penitentiary, after having served a five-year term for robbing Paymaster Bash of the United States army of $7,600 at Antelope Springs, thirty miles north of Douglas. Jones escaped south at that time and was afterwards captured in Nebraska and was tried and sentenced to the state penitentiary.

His term expired this morning and as soon as he was released he was rearrested by Sheriff Yund, who was accompanied by Sheriff Moore of Wichita county, Texas. Sheriff Moore arrived in the city last evening. He had a requisition from Governor Barber for Jones, and procured the assistance of Sheriff Yund as he wanted a sheriff here to make the arrest.

Previous to coming to Wyoming Jones lived in Texas, where he committed a murder. Sheriff Moore said this morning that the murder for which Jones is wanted was committed in the summer of 1885. Two young men, Christiny and Ashby, were traveling through the country there and Jones fell in with them. They were going to the R2 ranch and Jones finally attempted to murder them both. He told them he knew a shorter route across the prairie than by the road and after getting them about four miles off the road he fell a short distance behind and shot Christiny. Ashby was mounted on a splendid horse and succeeded in getting away, although while stooping over on his horse he was shot in the back, the ball coming out of his shoulder. The young man killed was a mere boy, weighing only about 90 pounds.

When the warrant was read to him this morning he made no other reply than that he thought he might be wanted in Nebraska. It is said he stole horses there and in Colorado. It was feared that he would resist arrest even in the pen. He was brought over to the city and placed in the county jail until the train arrived at 1:30, when Sheriff Moore started for Texas with him.

Jones was located here by ex-Marshal Jeff Carr, who communicated with the Texas authorities. There was a reward of $500 for his capture and Sheriff Moore thinks Mr. Carr will have no trouble in getting the money as it was offered by the murdered boy's brother who is a prosperous business man in Texas. It is so long ago that it is not thought that Jones will be hanged.

THIS, THAT AND THE OTHER.

The Red Men met last night.

Fancy bananas at Paul May's.

Father Carmody will preach in the Catholic church Friday night.

Noah Wallace has been very sick since Saturday but is better today.

When needing wall paper, painting or paper-hanging, call on Henry May.

There will be a celebration of the holy communion at St. Matthew's tomorrow morning at 7:30.

Buy Kleeman's home made candies.

The W. H. Holliday company has the contract to refit the Beckwith Commercial company's store at Rock Springs.

Miss Wright was again called upon so assume the duties of teacher yesterday. Miss Yelton was unable to take charge on account of sickness.

Confectionery, fruits, nuts. Pelton's.

The will be evening prayer at St. Matthew's this evening at 7:30. The Rev. Mr. Goodale, of the diocese of Omaha, will make a missionary address.

Mr. Fisk, the tree man, is engaged in setting out 500 trees in the park for which work he has a contract with the city. He will receive $1 per tree for them when set out.

The lots which W. J. Hills will place on the market at $10 each with a chance for each purchaser to guess the number of grains of corn in a jar, are 24x132 feet in size.

The latest addition to the cycling fraternity in this city is in the person of W. B. Sutyhin's little 3-year-old son. He has a tricycle and in about thirty days will be open to challenges.

Delicious fruit sherbets at Porter's.

The trainload of machinery, which was mentioned in The Boomerang yesterday passed through the city this morning. It consisted of traction engines and threshing machines, and is en route to Portland.

Mr. and Mrs. Daniel McDonald, while out driving this afternoon were run away with and thrown from the wagon and injured. They had two children in the wagon with them, but they were not hurt. Dogs scared the team on north Second street.

Cut flowers at Porter's Coffee House.

P. J. Quealey, A. Johnson, and L. L. Laus of Rock Springs, J. W. Sammin and Joseph Reeves of Almy, the Sweetwater delegates to the democratic convention were in the city today. They left with the Laramie delegation this afternoon for the scene of the cattlemen's war.

Conductor Charlie Roberts and the brakemen who took the mysterious cattlemen's train up on the Cheyenne and Northern last week were in the city, but they will tell nothing of any importance about the expedition if they know anything. They say there were about 60 men and that they were well "heeled".

The best spring medicine is a dose or two of St. Patrick's Pills. They not only physic but cleanse the whole system and purify the blood. For sale by W. T. Winters, druggist.

If out of order, use Beecham's Pills.

BLACKBURN SOLD OUT.

R. Blackburn today sold his coal and street sprinkling business to A. H. Newton and A. Eastman, who come to the city from near Tie Siding. The transfer was made this morning and the new proprietors took possession of the business this afternoon. Mr. Blackburn will now give his attention to the ice business. Both gentlemen are somewhat acquainted in Laramie and they will start with good prospects of success. Mr. Blackburn sold no horses, but the sale included three wagons.

MARION HARLAND.

The celebrated authoress, so highly esteemed by the women of America, says on pages 103 and 445 of her popular work, "Eve's Daughters; or, Common Sense for Maid, Wife and Mother:"

"For the aching back—should it be slow in recovering its normal strength—an Allcock's Porious Plaster is an excellent comforter, combining the sensation of the sustained pressure of a warm hand with certain tonic qualities developed in the wearing. It should be kept over the seat of the uneasiness for several days—in obstinate cases, for perhaps a fortnight."

"For pain in the back wear an Allcock's Porous Plaster constantly, renewing as it wears off. This is an invaluable support when the weight on the small of the back becomes heavy and the aching incessant."

Hood's Sarsaparilla absolutey curesl where other preparations fail. It possesses medicinal merit peculiar to itself.

Constipation and all trouble with the digestive organs and the liver, are cured by Hood's Pills, Unequalled as a dinner pill.

THE BOOMERANG.

WEDNESDAY, APRIL 13, 1892.

Union Pacific Mail and Express.

WEST BOUND.

No. 1, Limited, Ar. 8:40 a. m. Lv. 8:45 a. m.
No. 3, Fast Mail, Ar. 10:25 a. m. Lv. 10:30 a.m.
No. 7, Pacific Ex., Ar. 4:10 p. m. Lv. 4:30 p. m.

EAST BOUND.

No. 2, Limited, Ar. 2:20 a. m. Lv. 2:25 a. m.
No. 4, Fast Mail, Ar. 12:05 a. m. Lv. 12:10 a. m.
No. 8, Atlantic Ex., Ar. 1:40 p. m. Lv. 2:00 p. m.

It is the intention of the publishers of THE BOOMERANG that the paper should be delivered to every subscriber promptly and regularly. Subscribers will confer a great favor upon the management by reporting promptly every failure or defect in the service.

BOOMERANG CO.

SURRENDERED!

The Cattlemen's Army Narrowly Escape Annihiliation.

Regular Fort McKinney Troops Alone Saved Them.

AT M'KINNEY UNDER GUARD

Judge M. C. Brown Is Being Urged to Go to Johnson County to Place the Invaders Under Bonds.

The Surrendered Force Consists of Forty-Five Men One of Whom Is Wounded—They Are Being Held for Orders.

Several Tragedies Are Expected to Follow, but the "War" Is Over "Squealing from the Cattlemen's Army Expected.

Forty-Five Men Surrendered.

CHEYENNE, Wyoming, April 13.—The following telegram was received by Governor Barber this afternoon from his aide, which confirms and explains the surrender of the cattlemen's army:

FORT MCKINNEY, April 13, 2 p. m.—Amos W. Barber's orders received 12:30 a. m. today by Col. Van Horn. He marched at 2 o'clock this morning with three troops of cavalry. I went with him to the scene of hostilities at 4:45. The beseiged party surrendered to Col. Van Horn forty-four men, one wounded, arms, ammunition. Parties brought to Fort McKinney to await instructions for disposal. Small bodies of armed men followed troops to Fort. Sheriff's party has disbanded.

C. N. PARMALEE.

An Earlier Dispatch.

DOUGLAS, April 13, 1 p. m.—The stockmen's army has now surrendered or agreed to surrender. It has not been learned that they have laid down their arms, but it is positively known that they have agreed to surrender to any proper constituted authorities, who will guarantee them protection.

A telegram has just been sent to Cheyenne asking that an attorney be sent to the scene of the hostilities for the purpose of placing each man of the cattlemen's army under bonds.

Those who cannot give bonds will be incarcerated in jail.

This is believed to practically settle the war and the company who entered the state so mysteriously and with such great intentions a few days ago are now in the clutches of the law and it is believed that every man will be successfully prosecuted.

Besides the killing of the three men before reported the only casualties were those that occurred last night when the ranchmen and settlers captured the supply wagons of the invading army. Two settlers were killed during the fight for possession of the wagon and several wounded. The stockmen had two men dangerously wounded and ten horses killed.

The cattlemen's army's were absolutely forced to surrender. Several of the men have escaped from the cattlemen's camp and report that they were hired in Texas for cowboys at $6 per day. Canton is said to be among the number who will have to surrender.

When the troops and the settlers first surrounded the invaders this morning and asked for their surrender they positively refused to do so. They had the TA ranch surrounded with entrenchments, and but for the capture of their ammunition and supplies, consisting of three wagon loads it is doubtful whether the situation would be as satisfactory as it is at present.

Judge Brown Going North.

CHEYENNE, April 13, 5 p. m.—Judge M. C. Brown arrived in the city a few minutes ago on No. 8 and it is understood that the people of Johnson county want him to go to the scene of the trouble to place the foreign invaders under bonds.

They have surrendered and the law must now take its course:

At this hour Judge Brown has not consented to undertake this perilous and particular piece of work. Considerable influence is being brought to bear upon him both in this city and from the north and it is probable that he will finally undertake the work.

GOVERNOR'S PROCLAMATION.

It Was Issued Last Night—Too Late to Do Any Good.

Governor Barber last night issued the following proclamation, and instructed his aid-de-camp to have a copy delivered to both parties to the hostilities:

"I, Amos W. Barber, acting governor of the state of Wyoming, do hereby command and direct each and all of the persons and parties now engaged in open hostilities near Buffalo, Wyo., to cease all hostilities. And I further direct that armed organizations do disperse and give their adherance to the laws of the state. I have asked the president of the United States for the troops at Fort McKinney to assist in suppressing the present hostilities and in restoring order and protecting life and property. AMOS W. BARBER, Commander-in-Chief.

The question has been raised whether Gov. Barber would ever have called out the regular army at Fort McKinney if it had not been that the cattlemen's army was on the point of being annihilated. Others want to know why he has delayed so long before taking the measures adopted at this time to quell the trouble.

There is a sentiment of pity for the governor mingled with censure with the belief that he has been imposed upon or that he has lent his silence to proceedings which he well understood. There is a question whether his proclamation to disperse includes the sheriff's posse. It reads so. Some have gone so far as to say that the proclamation shows that those opposed to the cattlemen have the best of the situation.

THIS MORNING'S DISPATCHES.

People Still Flocking into Buffalo—Cattlemen's Reinforcements.

BUFFALO, April 13.—Still the come. Rev. Mr. Rader and twelve men have arrived from Goose creek. The men have gone out to the camp and the preacher will go out in the morning. Over forty farmers have come down from Prairie Dog and as far north as Tongue river. The home party think two or three white caps have got through their lines. Last night was a very bad night. It is reported that reinforcements are coming from Billings for the cattlemen.

From Glenrock.

GLENROCK, Wyo., April 12.—A dispatch from Sheriff Angus says that three men were killed on Powder river. Forty white caps are surrounded by 300 settlers at the TA ranch nnd it is believed they will capture them all. The sheriff instructs the officers to guard all roads and arrest all suspicious parties.

INFORMATION OF THE DAY.

A Former Laramie Resident, Dr. Watkins Dies at Buffalo.

The first news received in Laramie this morning from the scene of the cattlemen's war in Johnson's county came through the medium of Judge M. C. Brown, who received the following dispatches:

CHEYENNE, April 13, 9:10 a. m.
M. C. Brown, Laramie:

Colonel commanding at Fort McKinney left wito the cavalry for the scene of hostilities at TA ranch at 3 o'clock this morning. Captain Parmalee of Buffalo, aide on the governor's staff, went with the troops as governor's representative. Nothing heard since then.

POTTER.

BUFFALO, April 13, 9:30 a. m.
M. C. Brown, Laramie:

Dr. Watkins died this morning. The Cheyenne band is not mobbed yet, but they are surrounded by 300 citizens and three companies of cavalry of the regular army from Fort McKinney.

J. T. WALL.

Former Laramie Resident.

The Dr. Watkins mentioned in the above dispatch was ten years ago a resident of Laramie. Judge Brown's message has been directed to the doctor and the reply accordingly mentioned the fact of his death. Dr. Watkins when a resident of Laramie was interested in the Cummins City mines. He purchased the mill now owned by Colonel Downey and which is now in operation at Gold Hill, having been taken there from Cummins City. It is supposed that Dr. Watkins was shot by the invaders as he was the chairman of the local cattlemen's organization which had asked the stock commission for representation on the regular round-up. It is therefore concluded that Mr. Watkins was shot by some of the white cap invaders and died as a result.

Regulars Called Out.

The latest news from Cheyenne this morning was that Governor Barber last night telegraphed to President Harrison asking for troops from Fort McKinney, only about twelve miles from the TA ranch, where the trouble has taken place, to assist in restoring order. It was stated to the president that the militia at Buffalo was needed there to protect the town and preserve order and that bloodshed could be prevented only by the use of the regulars. The governor also sent a dispatch to General Brooke, at Omaha telling him of the situation. The result was that the president this morning authorized General Brooke to call the cavalry at McKinney out and as shown by tha above dispatch they are now at the TA ranch.

The presence of the regular army there is for the purpose of preventing bloodshed. Without them there would be a battle and as the cattlemen's army is outnumbered it is safe to say that they would be entirely exterminated by the ranchmen who are swarming to the scene of the conflict.

Jack Flagg, who was reported killed last week, turns up alive and well, although he had a narrow escape. He was intending to spend the night at Champion's cabin with him and Nick Ray, who, it seems, was the one killed with Champion instead of Sommerville. Flagg and his step-son run into the regulators' camp accidentally and they opened fire on them. Flagg was on horseback and the boy was driving the wagon. The boy cut one of the horses loose and with Flagg escaped into the hills. Flagg says that he recognized Charlie Ford as one of the men who fired at him and he threatens to kill him.

The three settlers killed are: Nate Champion, Nick Ray and Roy Gilbertson. The latter was burned in his house.

The men who are assisting Sheriff Angus in preserving order and trying to arrest the invaders are said to be led by the best citizens.

The cattlemen's forces are still at Dr. Harris' TA ranch at last reports this morning.

COMPANY A'S MEETING.

Knapsacks and Ammunition Packed Last Night—Anxious to Volunteer.

Company A met at their armory last night in accordance with instructions. Besides the members of the company there were fifty or more present who came there for the purpose of enlisting if the company was called out. One member of company A said, "I believe we could raise 500 men in Laramie if they were wanted to go to Johnson county to arrest or drive out the invading army." That seemed to be about the feeling as near as an observer could tell.

The members of the company packed their knapsacks and cartridge boxes and are ready to leave for the north at short notice.

THIS, THAT AND THE OTHER.

Fancy bananas at Paul May's.

Regular meeting of the board of trade this evening.

The university center will meet this evening at the chapel.

Elder Charles Rowe will preach at the Methodist church this evening.

Mr. and Mrs. Gus Seigert have both been confined to the house by colds.

When needing wall paper, painting or paper-hanging, call on Henry May.

B. Sprague has purchased, the John McIntee property on Fremont street. Consideration $2,500.

Instead of the usual prayer meeting at the Methodist church tomorrow evening at 7:30, Elder Charles Rowe will preach. A cordial invitation is extended to all.

Buy Kleeman's home made candies.

Shirley, the little seven year old daughter of Mr. and Mrs. L. G. Graves has been dangerously sick for the past three days with bilious fever with brain and spinal complications.

Mrs. Dr. Kate Mitchell, the eminent English speaker en route for California, has been induced to stop over in Laramie next Monday evening and deliver a lecture at the Methodist Episcopal church.

James Roe is confined in the city jail, having stolen $40 worth of articles from Frank Mulhern's ranch. He was recently located near Sherman by Deputy W. J. Broadhurst, who arrested him yesterday.

Cut flowers at Porter's Coffee House.

Tomorrow being Maundy-Thursday, there will be two celebrations of the holy communion at St. Matthew's in order that all communicants may receive. The first will be at 7:30 a. m.; the other at 11 a. m.

There will be a special service and sermon for communicants and confirmation candidates at St. Matthew's this evening at 6:30. Bishop Talbot will preach on "The Holy Communion as a Means of Grace."

The Richard Mansfield opera company occupied two special cars on No. 1 this morning. They are en route from New York to San Francisco. Mr. Mansfield's special car, "Richard Mansfield," was attached to the train.

Twenty-six ladies enjoyed the kind hospitality of Mrs. Dr. Norris at the Presbyterian parsonage yesterday afternoon. The occasion was a "missionary tea" and it was a pleasant affair and reflected much credit upon the charming hostess.

The Laramie Cycling club will meet at THE BOOMERANG office tomorrow night for the purpose of electing officers for the year. All wheelmen of the city who are not members and wish to join the club are invited to be present. The meeting will be called to order at 7:30 o'clock.

Delicious fruit sherbets at Porter's.

Lawrence C. Phillips who is well known around Laramie as a member of the late ranching firm of Phillips Bros. & Barry was on Saturday last admitted to practice as an attorney-at-law in this state. Mr. Phillips is a solicitor of the supreme court in England where he practiced before coming to this country over six years ago.

FROM THE PEOPLE.

A Citizen Tells of Some Established Practices.

WHOSE BEEF THEY KILL.

It Is Asserted That Some of the Big Company Outfits Live on Other Than Their Own Brands—They Inaugurated Mavericking.

To the Editor of The Boomerang.

The principal topic for discussion at the present time is that of the condition of affairs in the northern part of this state. Newspapers are eagerly sought for the latest information from "the front." Speculation is rife as to the probable outcome.

Nearly everyone met on the street inquires, "Have you heard anything late?" Well might these inxuiries be made and anxieties felt, for there is an armed force within the state of our adoption, contrary to the statutes in such cases made and provided, and against the [illegible] The man [illegible] habitants thereof, and no effort, up to this time, has been made to stop it. The citizens stand aghast and powerless. The officials criminally silent and apparently unconcerned. The case as it now stands could be presented thus:

WESTERN HEMISPHERE, CONTINENT NORTH AMERICA. } ss.
Wyoming Stockgrowers' Ass'n.
vs.
State of Wyoming.

The cause of action in this case is the importation of Pinkertonians or others for the express purpose of "stopping the breed," as the hired mouthpiece of the concern says.

This cause of action is brought for the express purpose of testing the rights (whether by force, intimidation, murder or any effective method) of large steckgrowers to the further possession of the circumscribed ranges now left, the bone of contention being whether these ranges shall be surrendered up to honest settlers or whether their use will be coerced by reason of money power. A little retrospection may not be out of order.

When Wyoming was unsettled it naturally afforded grand opportunities for the raising of stock owing to that fact as well as that of being exceedingly well watered and the grasses being exceptionally nutritious. But as "the poor are always with us" it followed that smaller owners would seek homes for themselves and families so they too asked to share their humble part of the great government domain.

Here, then, is where warfare commences. Their rights are disputed for they are apt to covet a nice littie nook here or a grassy mead there. Naturally enough, they soon have neighbors who are willing to share privations and emoluments with their predecessor.

More trouble.

The time comes for an organization to be formed in order that stock may be better handled and that there may be a union of forces, thus expediting and facilitating the successful management of the only industry existing at this time. Round-ups are started and, like a new broom sweeps clean.

The Wyoming Stockgrower's association is created and it may be admitted with good intent, but like any other monopoly soon falls from grace and becomes tyrannical and overbearing. They control legislatures, pass stock laws that would be laughing stock of the whole world. Finally the time is ripe and power enough is mustered to get $10,000 appropriated for the support of a live stock commission or in other words the Wyoming Stockgrowers association branches out into two wings, one the legal, the other the real.

Now she's working!

As might be expect the new creation has almost unlimited discretion and power. Round-ups are now legal bodies, the foremen of which are called in legal parlance, commissioners. One legislator got so bold that he actually introduced a bill in the legislature prohibiting the rounding-up or driving of any stock whatsoever except during the "round-up period."

Before the legal creation mavericks were sold to the highest bidder, generally bringing about $7 but, alas, the value shrank until they were only worth one dollar a head after the commission was born. Ask Mercer about it. For a number of years past round- [illegible] year who in his mad endeavor to out do his predecessor would take almost a straight shoot through the country, gathering up what stock it was impossible to avoid. These are facts. So depleted did the service become that private owners had to actually hire men enough to round-up the whole range at an individual expense. So rotten did the association become that when a man was suspected of getting away with more mavericks than the average he was left to do his own rounding up, although remaining a prominent member of the association where all ills are righted and which was created by laws enacted by legislators "you and me" help create. These are not exaggerations but are stubborn and uncontrovertable facts.

A word as to "rustling." The writer hereof remembers well when the best mavericker (polite name for rustler) was held in high esteem, and his abilities as a "cow-man" were guaged by the fruits of his rietta. Cow boys particularly were retained at extravagant salaries if they had established reputations for mavericking.

Is it any wonder, then, if after serving an apprenticeship, those who had become proficient should start out for for themselves after being so tutored? None whatever. But here arises a cause for grief. I will undertake to prove in court, if need be, that one of the largest cattle companies in the northern part of the state gave standing orders to their employes that when a beef was to be killed it should not bear their own brand. And men arise in their might and say there is no God!

So far as rustling is concerned, I do not believe anyone, save those following that avocation, are in sympathy with the business, either directly or implied; but I do know that the majority of inhabitants of Wyoming are not going to tolerate the hiring of foreign forces and allow them to kill, burn and destroy their fellow citizens with impunity; and if any moving out is resorted to those who hire such awful work done will be the first to take a spin.

The small stockman neither asks nor will give qnarter. He is one of the people simply struggling for that which is his own, and of which no power on earth will or can deprive him.

I will have more to say at a future time about the motives that prompt them.

A CORRECT LIKENESS.

A Strong Piece of Evidence Against Jones, Who Was Arrested Here Yesterday for Murder.

Jones, the fellow discharged from the penitentiary yesterday and who was at once rearrested for a murder committed in Texas, is undoubtedly the man wanted there. THE BOOMERANG representative was yesterday shown a photograph of Jones taken in Texas about the time the crime was committed in 1885. It was a perfect likeness of the man arrested here yesterday with the exception that he has since cultivated a light moustache and chin whiskers. With his beard off it would be a perfect likeness of him today. He stated to THE BOOMERANG before leaving that they could do nothing with him in Texas.

BETTER THAN QUININE.

Quinine is not only an expensive medicine, it is a harmful one if taken too freely and too often. Of course the world insists in taking great quantities of it for fever and ague. Some persons think nothing else will cure fever and ague. We say positively, and testimonials back us up, that Brandreth's Pills have often cured bad cases of fever and ague when quinine has failed. Brandreth's Pills break up the worst attack.

Brandredth's Pills are purely vegetable, absolutely harmless, and safe to take at any time.

Sold in every drug and medicine store either plain or sugar coated.

Rubber Stamps of every description at this office.

The Dallas Morning News.

VOL. IX. DALLAS, TEXAS, THURSDAY, MAY 24, 1894. NO. 236.

CANDIDATE REAGAN

Issues Involved in His Nomination or Defeat Are

STATE AND FEDERAL.

The Former Number Thirteen Measures and the Latter Eleven Policies.

RESTORATION OF SILVER.

Tariff for Revenue Only, Tax Upon Incomes and the Repeal of the 10 Per Cent State Bank Tax.

FEDERAL COURT CONTROL

In the Matter of Receivership and Regulation of Interstate Commerce—Sustains the Recent Laws of Texas.

Austin, Tex., May 23.—Hon. John H. Reagan to-day issued the following address to the people, announcing his candidacy for governor:

Austin, Tex., May 23.—To the People of Texas: In answer to solicitations too numerous and respectable to be disregarded, I announce myself a candidate for nomination for the office of governor of Texas by the state democratic convention, which is to meet at Dallas in August.

In making this announcement it is proper that I should indicate some of the measures and policies, state and federal, which are necessary to the public welfare:

EXISTING LAWS.

I approve and will endeavor to have the following-named laws faithfully executed:

1. The railroad commission law of Texas as it now exists, subject to such changes only as may become necessary to its greater perfection.

2. The alien land law which prevents persons not citizens of the United States from holding title to land in this state for more than fifteen years.

3. The municipal bond law which prohibits the issuance of bonds by counties, towns and cities except for the purposes specified.

4. The corporation bond law, which prohibits the further operation of land corporations and requires those now owning lands in this state to sell them within fifteen years.

5. The railroad stock and bond law, which prohibits the issuance of fictitious stock and bonds and other indebtedness by railway companies.

6. The law which reserves all our public domain for the use of actual settlers in suitable quantities at low price on long time.

7. And generally all the laws for the protection of life, liberty and property.

PROPOSED MEASURES.

I will, if elected governor, unless otherwise directed by the state democratic convention, advocate such laws and policy as will insure:

1. The economical administration of the government in all its departments, preserving the efficiency of the public service.

2. The revision of the laws in relation to the fees and allowances to district attorneys, sheriffs and clerks, and a modification of the laws relating to the service of attachments on witnesses in distant counties.

3. A considerable reduction of the expenditures of the state could be made without injury to the public service by a reorganization of the judicial districts, a reduction of their number and an equalization of the duties of the judges.

4. Provisions for the transfer of fees over and above a reasonable compensation, to be fixed by law, to the several counties in which such officers respectively reside.

5. The reduction of the force and expense of the several departments and institutions to actual public necessity, consistent with the efficiency of the service.

6. Such laws as will render more perfect the policy of working the penal convicts on state account and prevent their competition with free labor.

7. Such legislation as will more perfectly protect laborers, material men and mechanics against loss and injustice.

8. Such legislation as may be necessary to complete the work of suppressing trusts, pools and combinations in restraint of trade, enabling the state by injunction or other legal process to restrain them.

9. Such measures as will insure the maintenance of the public free schools, as required by the constitution, for the full period of six months in each year.

10. Such measures as will promote the efficiency of the state university and its branches, the agricultural and mechanical college and the state normal institute.

11. The necessary appropriations to complete the improvements of the grounds around the state capitol, make proper repairs of the executive mansion and the necessary improvement of the other public property and buildings, as demanded by state pride and public necessity.

12. Such measures as will protect the live stock in this state from contagious diseases and against unjust discrimination by interstate quarantine regulations and such as will promote agriculture, horticulture and domestic material industries.

13. The passage of laws for the regulation of primary elections, to punish false swearing and fraudulent voting.

I will favor and support: 1. The action of the attorney general's department, began several years ago and still faithfully pursued, of recovering public lands unlawfully obtained by railroad companies for sidings and switches and by other methods and will jealously guard the rights of actual settlers in connection with them.

2. I favor the amendment of the constitution so as to give the state the power to endow, support and maintain a home for disabled and dependent confederate soldiers.

3. I also favor the amendment of the constitution so as to give the people the right to elect the railroad commissioners, so alternating the elections that but one shall be elected at a time, and thus retaining constantly two experienced commissioners.

4. I approve and adhere to the principles announced in the state democratic platform of 1892 and to the national democratic platform of principle.

FEDERAL ISSUES.

1. I am opposed to the reduction of the volume of money by taking silver from the class of standard redeeming money and the adoption of the single gold standard. Before this was done the gold and silver of the world measured all values and controlled the amount of bankable paper and exchanges. Now all values are measured by gold alone, and the reduction of all values of property and labor and of the volume of bankable paper and exchanges, the total derangement of the business of the country and an amount of bankruptcy never before known, with a vast increase of idle an unemployed men are the consequences. I therefore favor the restoration of silver, which is a part of the money of the constitution, to the place it occupied before it was demonetized in 1873—its coinage on the same terms as the coinage of gold at the ratio of sixteen of silver to one of gold.

2. I am opposed to the increase of the interest bearing public debt of the United States by the issue and sale of bonds.

3. I favor a tariff for revenue only, based as nearly as may be on the ad valorem value of imports, and limited to the needs of the federal government economically administered.

4. The regulation by authority of congress of interstate commerce so as to protect the people against unlawful exactions and unjust discriminations.

5. A tax upon incomes, so that the wealth of the country shall bear its due proportion of the expense of its protection by the government.

6. The repeal of the 10 per cent tax on the issue of state banks.

7. No further charters for national banks, and the winding up of the business of those now in existence when their charters expire.

8. Such legislation by congress as will limit and control the federal courts in the matters of receiverships and contempts, and give protection against their insidious encroachments on the reserved rights of the states. And as will require notice to the stockholders and others interested in such corporations as may be thrown into bankruptcy before receivers can be appointed, and as will require the assets of such bankrupt corporations to be collected and its debts paid as soon as that can be done. The circuit judges of the United States ought not to be clothed by their own acts with the duties of general superintendents of railroads for general business purposes.

9. A strict enforcement of the laws against the introduction of foreign paupers and criminals into the United States.

10. I would favor a change of the federal constitution so as to limit the tenure of office of federal judges to a prescribed number of years less than a life tenure.

11. I have for a good many years advocated the election of United States senators by the direct vote of the people, and still favor it.

To the foregoing declarations of principle I stand pledged, unless they shall be modified by the state or national democratic conventions.

ANSWERS TO OBJECTIONS.

It is objected by some that federal questions have no place in a state canvass; and that when a national convention has made its declarations on such questions the people of a state in their primary meetings and conventions are estopped from considering them. Why should this be so? In the monarchies of the old world the rulers, by whatever name they are called, are sovereign and the source of authority. In the United States, since the declaration of American independence and the adoption of the federal constitution, the people are sovereign and the source of authority. There is no power above them.

HON. JOHN H. REAGAN.

Another reason why such questions should be discussed is that the legislature which is to be elected this fall will have to elect a United States senator, to serve six years, and the people will elect thirteen representatives to serve two years. And they should be chosen with reference to their opinions on these and other federal questions. And to deny the people the right to consider these questions would be equivalent to an abandonment of the right and duty of self-government, and that they are subjects bound to obedience instead of sovereigns with authority to command.

Questions of coinage and currency, of tariff and other taxation, and of the regulation of interstate commerce affect directly and in an important degree the interests of every human being in the United States. Why should the people so affected be denied the right to express their opinions in their primary meetings and conventions on these questions? Why should they stand dumb before the president, or congress, or a national convention, and be denied the right, in their capacity as sovereigns, to declare their views and wishes on such uestions? To so hold is to deny the authority of the declaration of independence, and of the constitution of the United States, to overturn our theory of government and to deny the sovereignty of the people, and their capacity for self-government. And yet there are persons in this state who would do this merely to obtain a petty partisan advantage.

For expressing these views, now reiterated and emphasized, I have been charged with being opposed to the national democratic platform of principles. The people will judge as to the justice or injustice of this charge. If my whole political life is not a sufficient answer to such a charge I have nothing more to say.

It has been charged, and certain men and newspapers never weary of repeating the charge, that I was opposed to the adjustment proposed between the two wings of the democratic party at Dallas; and that I am opposed to the union and harmony of the democratic party. The only foundation there is or ever was for this charge is that I insisted, if real harmony was desired, and no political advantage was intended to be secured by either side, that meeting ought to refer all questions of principle and of political policy to the people in their primary meetings and conventions. That they, in their capacity as sovereigns, had the right to pass upon such questions, while no authority had been conferred on the committees there assembled for that purpose. Those who understand what had preceded that meeting will know why no advantage should have been sought by either side over the other. I was and am an advocate of the union and harmony of the democratic party. I was a member of the first state democratic convention which was ever held in Texas, in the Cass campaign of 1848. I have always regarded myself as a democrat of the Jefferson school and of the straightest sect. All my political honors have been conferred on me by that party. I have never failed to adhere to its principles, to fight its battles, and to sustain its organized action, whether in defeat and disaster or in the triumphs of victory. Every pulsation of my heart beats for the success of its principles and for its unity. And I ask the democracy of Texas to compare my political record with that of the men and newspapers who have been attempting to impeach my democracy.

Another charge which is made almost daily by certain newspapers and men is that I am opposed to and have denounced the present national democratic administration. The only pretext for this charge is that I have opposed and do now oppose the policy of the president and a minority of the democrats in congress for abandoning the policy of the democratic party on the questions of the coinage of silver and on financial questions, and their adoption of the policy of the republican party and their uniting with them to defeat the democratic majority in congress, and the great body of the democracy of the union, and to defeat and defy the known will of the American people on these questions. That is the full measure of my offending. In my published letter of May 3, I said:

"I, like the balance of the people, respect Mr. Cleveland where respect is due, but do not understand that he is the democratic party, or that his office exempts him from criticism where it is deserved. No doubt the next convention will indorse the Chicago national democratic platform, as the last one did; and it would be just to congress and to the president to indorse the repeal by the one and the approval by the other of the law authorizing the interference by the federal authorities with elections in the states. And if congress shall pass and the president shall approve a bill reducing tariff taxation and taxing incomes, and one repealing the 10 per cent tax on the issues of state banks it would be proper to indorse their action in these respects. But this does not make it necessary for the people to indorse the financial policy of the president."

I have never said one word in opposition to or in denunciation of Mr. Cleveland's administration as an administration. My criticisms have been exclusively of the position of the president and a minority of the democrats in congress on questions of coinage and the finances. And on these questions I am with about two-thirds of the democratic members of congress, with an overwhelming majority of the democratic voters, with the great mass of the American people, and for the money of the constitution; against the contraction of the volume of money, against the destruction of the value of labor and property, and against the bankrupting of all industrial interests, the impoverishment of the people, and the ruin of all debtors whether governments, corporations or people.

In asking the suffrage of the voters of Texas I thought it due to them and to me that I should make this explicit declaration of principles, policies and opinions.

It was not my intention to become a candidate for the office of governor, and I repeatedly so announced. But the call on me to be a candidate is so general from every part of the state that I have concluded that it is my duty to become a candidate. I do so with personal friendship and respect for each of the candidates for that office, so as to enable the people to select their choice among the candidates without strife or division in the party. And hope the canvass may be so conducted that when a nomination is made the defeated candidates may be willing to give a cheerful support to the one who is successful. I can and would support either of the candidates if nominated with a cheerful good will.

My official obligations will not permit me to make an extended canvass. I must in a large measure depend on the active support of those who wish me to be a candidate. I will speak on such of the questions herein named and others that may arise as I can at the following times and places:

Sherman, Saturday, June 2, 11 a. m.
Houston, Wednesday, June 6, 8 p. m.
San Antonio, Tuesday, June 12, 8 p. m.
Tyler, Monday, June 18, 2 p. m.

JOHN H. REAGAN.

FIRE RECORD.

BIG BLAZE AT NEW ORLEANS.

New Orleans, La., May 23.—[Special.]—Following the Pickwick club and the St. Charles hotel the West End hotel and all its belongings, together with various other buildings and appurtenances in the immediate vicinity, this morning went the way of all things combustible. Nobody appears to know how the fire started or pretends to account for it in any way, though the fact remains the same that nearly $100,000 has gone up in smoke in broad day light and at the very opening of the busiest season. The popular resort is in ruins.

The fire was first noted at 9 o'clock. Some say it was in the cupola, others declare the blaze burst forth in the northwest corner on the lake, overhead the rear of the kitchen and washroom, while others maintain equally positive that it made its initial appearance on the side of the building on the side toward tne canal. All, however, agree that it started in the third story and that there is no reason for it, not even an electric wire.

Simultaneous with the discovery an alarm was sent to the city, but before help in the shape of engines could be had the entire platform was ablaze involving the hotel, music stand, shooting gallery, theater and ice cream pavilion, conducted by Mannasier H. Vix, Gus Brill's saloon, the latter two places being on government property on the bank of the canal, extending from the bridge lakewards. In short, the entire area from the bridge along the revetment to the beginning of the garden, a distance of about 500 yards, thence out into the lake, almost a like distance, and to the canal. All the finest kind of platform work with everything on it was totally consumed. The roof of the Southern yacht club house at the end of the pier was damaged, the wind blowing off shore in that direction.

Across the road the refreshment buildings on the rear side of the revetment facing the hotel La Courts, Astredos, Mays and others were scorched more or less. Mays' small building was saved by the boy turning his soda water fountain on it. The Traction company's loss is partially covered by a blanket insurance policy for $75,000. The other losses are only partly covered.

The Eddy trio performing at the West End lost a part of their wardrobe, the musicians all their music and instruments. Manager Little of the Traction company will continue the band's engagement uninterrupted.

The hotel was a magnificent two-story structure, built in the gothic style of architecture, and was erected several years ago by the late Joseph A. Walker. Although it was constructed so that provision could be made for the accommodation of boarders if any parties desired to have such accommodation, there were very few guests of this kind there at any time. The place was occupied as a saloon and on the broad, shady verandas at the sides there were tables placed for parties who desired to enjoy the cool, invigorating breezes while partaking of their refreshments. There were several rooms for permanent boarders on the floor above and a number of apartments for private parties and picnics. The furnishings of the place were all modern and of the most handsome style. Larry Wilt was the lessee. It was owned by the New Orleans City and Lake Railroad and Traction company.

DWELLING AND CONTENTS.

Sweetwater, Nolan Co., Tex., May 23.—A dwelling belonging to Mr. Blosom, twenty miles south from here, caught fire and burned last Sunday afternoon while the family was absent. Parties from that portion of the county were here yesterday soliciting aid. Food, money and clothing were liberally subscribed and it is thought no serious drawback will befall Mr. Blosom, as his house will be rebuilt and clothing and food replaced.

HENRIETTA DWELLING.

Henrietta, Tex., May 23.—The dwelling owned by S. H. Powers and occupied by H. S. Cherry and G. D. Benson burned this morning. Loss on residence $2500; insurance in Lancashire $1500. G. D. Benson's insurance on household goods $250.

DWELLING AT ENNIS.

Ennis, Ellis Co., Tex., May 23.—A house belonging to Mrs. R. B. White and occupied by Mrs. S. Hale was destroyed by fire last night. Damage about $800; covered by insurance.

VACANT HOUSE.

McKinney, Tex., May 23.—A vacant house burned at a late hour last night in the eastern portion of the city. The house belonged to T. P. T. McLean.

MORPHINE POISON SYMPTOMS.

Corsicana, Navarro Co., Tex., May 23.—A man named Newell Muns, living three miles north of the city, died early this morning under peculiar circumstances. His symptoms point to morphine poisoning. He came here from Fort Worth last fall and had been in bad health and out of work for several years. He was a man of temperate habits. He was about 35 years old and leaves a wife and three small children.

MEN FOR TARGETS.

A Desperate Battle with Bank Robbers at Longview.

KILLED AND WOUNDED

One Robber and One Citizen Killed and Five of the Posse Wounded.

TWO HUNDRED SHOTS FIRED.

Two Men Worked Inside of the Bank While Two Others Stood the Citizens Off with Winchesters.

AMOUNT OF BOOTY SECURED.

Two Thousand Dollars Snatched from the Vault and the Fills Emptied—Officers of the Bank Escaped Uninjured.

Longview, Tex., May 23.—At 3 o'clock p. m. to-day two rough looking men walked into the First national bank. One had a slicker on, with a winchester concealed in its folds. He handed the following note to President Joe Clemmons:

"Home, May 23.—First national bank, Longview: This will introduce to you Charles Specklemeyer, who wants some money and is going to have it.

"B. and F."

It was written in pencil, in a fairly good hand, on the back of a printed poster.

The bank cashier thought it was an importunate subscription to some charity, and started to donate, when the robber pointed his winchester at him and told him to hold up. The other robber rushed into the side wire door and grabbed the cash.

Tom Clemmons and the other bank officials were ordered to hold up their hands.

The robbers hurriedly emptied the tills and went into the vaults, securing $2000 and three $10 No. 9 and nine $20 No. 27 unsigned Longview bank notes, which may lead to detection.

While this was going on two of the robbers were in the rear alley of the bank, shooting at every one who appeared, and were being fired on by City Marshal Muckleroy and Deputy Will Stevens.

The firing made the robbers in the bank very nervous, and they hurried the bank officers out and told them to run to the horses and mount.

This was done in order to keep the posse from shooting, but as bullets flew thick and fast, the bank men tore loose and ran around the corner, with several shots after them.

George Buckingham, who was shooting at the robbers, was shot and killed. While he was down the robbers shot at him several times.

City Marshal Muckleroy, who was shooting at another robber, received a winchester ball in the bowels. The ball glanced from some silver dolars which he had in his pocket, which may save his life. The ball pased through the cavity near the pelvic bone.

J. W. McQueen, a saloon keeper, thinking the shots were for the fire alarm, ran out in the alley and was shot in the body and it is thought is mortally wounded.

Charles S. Leonard was walking through the courthouse yard and was shot in the leg, necessitating amputation.

T. C. Summers was shot in the left hand.

Deputy Will Stevens was not hurt, though he stood in short range, and killed one of the robbers.

The bankers all escaped unhurt except T. E. Clemmons, who in the scuffle with the robber got his hand where the hammer of the robber's pistol came down and cut a hole in his hand.

The robbers who stood guard in the alley would yell at every one who came in sight and shoot at them instantly.

When the robbers rode away and saw one of their comrades dead they remarked: "Poor Bennett is dead," and the body of the dead robber was soon identified as George Bennett, a reckless fellow who had been here some months ago and married a daughter of a respectable farmer living near this place. He left here and went to the Indian territory. The dead robber was dressed like a cowboy, with high-heeled boots and spurs. He had on a belt full of cartridges and two double-action revolvers.

His horse, which was captured, had 300 rounds of ammunition strapped to the saddle.

Another of the robbers, the man who gave President Clemmons the note, was identified by several here. He married a respectable young lady in Panola county last fall, but later went to Mexico and has not been seen until to-day. He was well known here, having worked near here.

It is thought Bennett has a relative in the gang. If so, only one man remains to be identified.

The robbers rode rapidly out of town, displaying their firearms and the money they had got.

An armed posse was soon in pursuit, and when last heard of was fifteen minutes behind them.

The bank offered $500 for their arrest, dead or alive, and the citizens supplemented the amount by $200.

Deputy John Howard was shot at about fifteen times, but he was not hurt. He emptied his pistol several times and wounded one robber in the face.

No less than 200 shots were fired.

The robbers started out of town going by the home of George Bennett's wife and Brown & Flewellen's mill. They met a farmer four miles north of here and took his good hat and gave him an old one, and told him to tell the posse to come on; that they were going to keep on the big road.

CONDUCTOR'S STATEMENT.

The following statement of the robbery detailed in the foregoing account was given to The News last night by Mr. J. D. Jamison, a Pullman car conductor running between Longview and Fort Worth:

"I was asleep in my room two blocks from the bank when the robbery occurred," said Mr. Jamison. "The firing awakened me, and putting on a few clothes as hastily as I could I started for the place from which the sound of the shots came. I arrived just in time to see the robbers galloping out of town. The scene about the bank was one of the intensest excitement. The people were so excited that none could tell intelligently what had occurred, and one had to surmise for himself. In the center of a group of half-crazed people was a dead body, the body of one of the robbers, who had fallen a victim of one of the hundreds of bullets, which for a few seconds flew thick and fast. Another one of the quartette was wounded, but he escaped.

"The robbery occurred about 3 o'clock. The men, masked closely, rode up to the bank and demanded all the money in the vault. That which was lying on the counter, amounting to $1500, was taken immediately and thrust into a sack. But before they could secure more a clerk, regaining his senses, opened fire. This marked the beginning of a terrible fusillade. The robbers returned the fire, but before a second volley was fired crowds of men came running to the bank, and the few who had guns began using them vigorously. The sound of firing increased in intensity with each second and in a few moments it sounded like a mimic war. As the numbers increased the robbers began to retire, and, reaching their horses they mounted and galloped out of town, firing as they went.

"In the battle a citizen named Buckingham was shot, and he died a few moments later.

"As soon as possible the sheriff summoned a posse, and when I left he was in pursuit of the robbers."

H. C. TATUM'S STATEMENT.

Mr. H. C. Tatum of St. Louis, secretary of the Western Commercial Travelers' associaton, arrived in the city last night from Longview. He said of the robbery: "The robbers rode up to the bank about 3 o'clock in the afternoon and dismounted. Then one man held the four horses and then stood guard and the two others entered the bank and went behind the railing. They presented revolvers at the president and the cashier. The cashier attempted to resist and one of the robbers started to shoot him, but the cashier grabbed his pistol, the hammer striking on his hand. The robber tore away the pistol, lacerating the cashier's hand, and attempted to shoot again, but the cashier seized the pistol in the same manner with his left hand. The robber tore the pistol away again and both robbers then fled, making for their horses, the other robber in the meantime having grabbed about $1500 in silver.

"I understand that the wounded robber was caught and will be lynched. The robbers were evidently from the Indian territory, as the name of an Indian territory merchant was found branded on the sweatband of the wounded robber's hat."

Mr. Tatum is on business here for his association and is stopping at the Oriental.

HAD A RESERVE IN DALLAS.

Mr. Ed Tenison, cashier of the City national bank of Dallas, was met last night by a News reporter and asked if the First national bank of Longview had a reserve fund in Dallas. Mr. Tenison replied: "Yes; they always keep a large reserve with us. I knew personally the cashier of that bank, Mr. T. E. Clemmons, a very warm personal friend of mine. I last saw him about ten days ago when he was here attending the Baptist convention. I can say that his bank had every protection in the way of the safe and vaults."

PICKED MEN AFTER THEM.

Tyler, Tex., May 23.—Sheriff Smith of this county has sent some picked men in pursuit of the Longview bank robbers. They go north, with a view to intercepting them.

TO BURN HORSES.

An Oregon Company Has a Scheme to Better the Breed.

Portland, Ore., May 23.—A company has been organized here to use up the surplus supply of horses which now exist in the northwest and at the same time make it profitable for raising good American horses, thus furnishing another source of demand for the mongrel horse. It is proposed by this company to bring the horses to abbattoirs, a site for which has been chosen near this city, and there kill them. The flesh will be rendered of its oil and the residue with the bones and hoofs will be made into a fertilizer. The hides, that have always a market value, will be salted and the hair will be used in upholstery work. A portion of the meat will be compressed for use as chicken food. It is estimated that in Oregon, Wasnington, Montana, Nevada and Idaho there are at present 2,000,000 of half-breed, wild horses for which no market can be found.

M'ELROY & CO'S CIRCULAR.

New Orleans, La., May 23.—Liverpool surprised everybody by an advance of 2 to 3-64d, closing firm. Spot sales were 10,000 bales. The improvement was due to a rumor that Neill Bros. of London had issued a circular to the effect that the unfavorable feature in the market had been discounted and that an improvement should now be looked for. We understand that Mr. Henry Neill of this city contradicts this rumor flatly, but nevertheless it has had the effect of causing some shorts to cover, and the strength thus lent to the market was supplemented by a good spot demand. In this market spots were advanced 1-16c, with sales of 1550 bales. Futures closed 8 points higher than yesterday.

New York reports that quite a considerable quantity of cotton had been sold this morning for export, but that these sales would not appear in the official report until to-morrow. Galveston also reports a good spot demand. The situation presents nothing new, and unless there should be active buying by eastern spinners it would seem probable that the present improvement will be but a temporary spurt.

MOTION TO TABLE.

Teller Smokes the Democrats Out on the Tariff.

COMING OUT SOLID.

A Motion to Table the Tariff Bill Is Defeated by a Vote of 38 to 28.

GORMAN'S STRONG SPEECH.

He Defends the Tariff Bill and Recites the Difficulties Which His Party Had to Overcome.

TO ABOLISH THE CIVIL SERVICE.

Enloe Introduces a Bill to Bring This About. Investigating Carnegie's Armor Plates Taylor Confirmed.

Washington, May 23.—(Special.)—This has been a day of sensations in the senate. It was announced yesterday that Senator Gorman would probably make a speech to-day and some went so far as to state that he would make it at 12 o'clock, so there was more than the usual audience in the galleries to hear him. He got the floor before 12 o'clock and made his speech in a manner which impressed every one who heard it, and, moreover, elicited from even those who are opposed to him, or with whom he is unpopular, that it was a remarkably strong effort, and that it presented his side of the question as strongly as it could be presented. It is now evident that the days which he has been putting in ostensibly for his health over in Maryland have been mostly devoted to preparing this speech. True, he has been unwell, but not unwell enough to disturb his mental machinery, for his speech to-day is about as strong as any heard in the senate.

Of course he was given the greatest attention, because it was known he intended to say something, and, moreover that when he arose it was the signal that he considered the fight won for the democrats.

Gorman has the charcter, and very properly, too, of doing his fighting first and accomplishing his ends and then making his speeches. In fact, his speeches are not made to secure results, but to announce when results are secured. When the democratic caucus was held a prominent democratic senator and a member of the finance committee, said to The News correspondent: "D—n Gorman; he has been worming around in this bill, getting what he wants, and now he has bobbed up serenely in the caucus, urging everybody to stand to the measure and absolutely making it his bill," and that is about the general opinion of what he has done.

He announced in his speech that the democrats were a unit for the bill and that it must be passed.

This was a common place expression, but it was not such to the republicans, for Allison and others in replying to him admitted that this was the first declaration that could be called authoritative from the democratic side, which showed democratic unity. He stated that the bill in the house had not received the attention and discussion it deserved; that it would not raise enough revenue, and that members of the house knew this, and knew that the bill would have to be reconstructed in the senate. He said that when the bill came from the senate finance committee it was not satisfactory, and could not command the support of the democratic side, but when the amendments were agreed to then democratic harmony was secured and the sunlight of success shined on the measure.

This point was greedily seized upon by the republicans, who saw in it an opportunity to excuse themselves for the delay they had indulged in. They replied that, according to Gorman's statement, the bill had really only been before the senate since the 1st of May. He, in a very clear manner, explained the sugar schedule and other amendments brought in by the committee, and to all appearances made the action of the committee appear in a highly proper light.

He gave old man Hoar a very severe stab as he went along. Hoar in a speech several days ago in a heated way said that the democratic senators who were indorsing the amendments—said amendments giving protection here and there—were guilty of perjury. To this Gorman replied that a charge of perjury came in poor taste from a republican senator whose vote placed Rutherford B. Hayes in the presidential chair. Hoar turned very red at this remark, but he said nothing.

The speech of Mr. Gorman, as has been said, was a thoroughly prepared effort. He had studied every phase of the amendments, listened to all the complaints of delay and he had prepared himself to answer them. The answer may be said to have been adroit; may be said to have been sophisticated, but he answered them. His announcement of democratic unity was as pleasing to Teller, Dubois and that element of the republican party as it was unpleasant to Hoar, Aldrich, Chandler, Lodge and Hale, for Teller, taking the floor, said he was glad to hear the announcement; glad to know that there was a prospect of the disposition of the bill, and after making a few more remarks, said that he would test the real feeling of the senate on the question by moving to lay the bill on the table.

If some one had thrown a bomb from the galleries to the senate floor there could not have been more surprise, not to say consternation. Aldrich turned anxiously to Hoar and Hale, who sat near. It was evident that they did not want this done, and would like to check it. But how? If they objected in any way they placed themselves in the attitude of opposing the destruction of the bill, the motion to lay on the table being in this direction.

The democrats were as much astonished as the republicans. Senator Voorhees told [illegible]

The Dallas Morning News.

VOL. IX. DALLAS, TEXAS, FRIDAY, MAY 25, 1894. NO. 237.

INDIAN TERRITORY.

FOUL PLAY SUSPECTED.

Eufaula, I. T., May 24.—A man's hat with five holes shot through it was found yesterday by the side of a pool of blood on the banks of the Caledonian river, and foul play is suspected. The way the ground is torn up near the hat indicates that a murder has been committed and the victim thrown in the river.

HELD WITHOUT BAIL.

Ardmore, I. T., May 24.—William Allison was held without bail to-day by Commissioner Gibbins. He is charged with killing Pete Romero, a Mexican, near Red river, last fall. The parties were rivals for the affections of a young lady and engaged in a quarrel, in which Allison shot at Romero five times, one of the shots resulting fatally.

HERNANDEZ CASE.

The Mariage Held to Be Legal by the Supreme Court.

New Orleans, La., May 24.—[Special.]—The supreme court this morning handed down a decision in the famous Hernandez case, which affirmed the position taken by Judge King of the lower court and says that the marriage between Joseph Hernandez and Mrs. Augusta L. Church is legal. When Mr. Hernandez died he left several very handsome bequests to his second wife, formerly Mrs. Church. His children attacked the will on the ground that under the laws of Louisiana the marriage between Mrs. Church and the deceased was not legal. They also charged that she was his mistress. The allegations set forth in the petition was that the first Mrs. Hernandez had obtained a divorce from Mr. Hernandez in St. Bernard parish for committing adultery with Mrs. Church. Under the laws of Louisiana a divorced man cannot marry the woman with whom he committed adultery. The decision entitles Mrs. Hernandez No. 2 to the rich legacy left her by her husband. The amount involved is away up in the thousands of dollars. Mrs. Hernandez No. 1 is still alive and took an active part in the fight of the case.

STRING OF INDICTMENTS.

A Large Number of Parties Indicted Charged with Horse Theft.

Oklahoma City, Ok., May 24.—Startling news reached this city from Tecumseh, an Indian town fifty miles east of this place. Some thirty indictments have been returned against prominent residents and citizens of that community and elsewhere, charging them with horse stealing. Of this number seventeen have been arrested, thirteen are in jail, one out on bond and three have escaped and officers are in close pursuit. Thirteen have not yet been apprehended. seven of those arrested have already been arraigned and pleaded guilty.

Charles Patterson and a young man named Collins have turned state's evidence and a posse, accompanied by Patterson, has gone to the Seminole country to arrest the ringleaders.

The organization extends from Arizona to Arkansas and all along the route the members have caves and hiding places, from which they can pick off all pursuers and in which no lynx-eyed official can detect them.

Twenty-seven head of fine horses have been recovered.

A SERIES OF CRIMES.

Paris, Tex., May 24.—United States Marshal Williams has succeeded in unearthing what appears to be a most remarkable series of crimes. He now has in custody John Stevenson, Jim Stevenson and their mother, Mrs. Gay, a woman 60 years of age. The matter is being investigated.

HE WAS HANGED.

The Body of a Dead Bank Robber Decorates a Pole.

BURIED AS CARRION.

Two Funerals at Longview in Which There Was a Contrast.

REST OF THE GANG CORRALLED

Near Jefferson and Armed Men Are Pouring in to Hunt Them Down — The Latest Details.

Longview, Gregg Co., Tex., May 24.—The intense excitement caused by the robbery of the First national bank here yesterday afternoon continues. If there has been any abatement of the indignation and anger of the people for one of their best citizens and the thirst for revenge it has not been perceptible.

For once during a campaign east Texas quit talking politics to-day. Men forgot their differences and swore with locked hands that those fugitive robbers who killed Buckingham and wounded McQueen and Muckleroy and the rest were either to be killed in a fight or brought back here to be burned alive. And had the men been captured by officers of the law they would not have been prisoners longer than the time taken in preparing a bonfire to burn them.

All day long it has been talk, talk, talk. Every man had a new story that nobody else had heard and these men with their stories had little knots of patient, eager listeners in front of stores or on the street corners. Merchants and lawyers and bankers, even, forgot their business and were finding out about the robbery.

The scene of the tragedy was visited by hundreds and the fences and walls, which are numerously marked with bullet holes, were an unfailing object of curiosity. The ground where Bennett, the dead robber, was killed was as carefully marked as if it had been the burying-place of a president and the dark red spot where poor George Buckingham fell, a victim to his desire to see what was going on, was visited and the story of Buckingham's ending told again and again.

A stream of people have been to the bank to see Tom Clemmons, president, and Joe Clemmons, his brother, the paying teller. Their encounter with the robbers, their resistance, bitter and stubborn and finally their narrow escape at the hands of the marauders has been not the least exciting or dramatic chapter in one of the most exciting and dramatic occurrences of the last year or so.

Then the two men, Claude Lacy and Will Stevens, either of whom may have fired the shot which ended the dead robber's existence—nobody knows exactly which one did it—have been the heroes of a day and their praise is on every man's lips. It may sound a little odd to say that a killing is universally commended, but it is a cold fact.

There were two burials in the Longview cemetery to-day. One body was carried to the grave in a city cart, just as ordinary offal, followed by no mourners, uncased in even a pine box, literally unwept, unhonored and unsung. It was dumped into a hole in the ground in the potter's field and the earth hastily thrown over it. And thus, as the carcass of a cow, removed as a stench in the nostrils of the community, the remains of John C. Bennett, the robber, wait the final summons to appear at the place of readjustment, where all crooked things of the heart or body are made straight. One or two persons, including the brother-in-law of Bennett, went out and looked at the fresh grave and then proceeded to express their gratification at his removal and their entire satisfaction with the mode and manner of his taking off.

This afternoon there was another burial. Every store in town was closed. Every sound of busy life was still. Every face wore an expression of sadness and regret. From a little house near a church on Fredonia street issued crowds of people. A body in a handsome casket, with all the honors paid a hero, was followed to the grave by the longest funeral procession Longview has ever known. With uncovered heads the whole populace saw a body tenderly and reverently lowered into a grave to await the same resurrection that will come to the carcass of the other. Thus was the body of George Buckingham, citizen, honored, praised and consigned to its last abode.

Scarcely had the echoes of the prayers for the dead ceased to ring in their hearts before there came another paroxysm of excitement. A telegram was received from one of the pursuing party, John McCann, saying that the fugitives were corralled at Avinger, a little lumber camp on the East Line, sixteen miles west of Jefferson, and appealing for help. Volunteers were called for and fifty men responded in less time than it takes in the telling. Superintendent Trice of the Texas and Pacific had a special engine ordered to take the posse to Jefferson and soon twenty-five or more armed to the teeth were flying to the relief of the besiegers.

It was the first news from the pursuing party. There had been all sorts of rumors from time to time during the day that the fleeing and hunted men had taken this direction and that direction and had been seen in one place by one man and in another place by another man, but nothing definite had been or could be heard. Now all the town that is left is waiting for the capture.

If the robbers are taken alive there will be no expense to the state in the prosecution of them should they be brought back here. There is plenty of timber, plenty of matches and plenty of men willing to start a bonfire and anxious for a burnt offering to atone for the destruction wrought on yesterday.

GOING BACKWARD A LITTLE.

The story of the robbery has not yet been fully told. The outlines have been touched and results given, that is all. At 3 o'clock yesterday afternoon Longview was a very busy town. A criminal case which was a local cause celebre was at its climax in the courthouse and the courtroom was packed with men eagerly awaiting the finale. The Texas and Pacific train from the west, which marks an event in every day, had just arrived and all the tradespeople were at the depot attending to their business as usual.

Two men walked into the First national bank which is a little one-story building, famous principally because of Tom Campbell's connection with it.

One was a tall man over six feet high. He wore a rough, greasy, yellow slicker, such as are common among teamsters, and which was much the worse for wear and tear. He had a short, fuzzy beard all over his face about a week and a half old and appeared to be not over 25 years of age.

The other was a short, chunky man, about 5 feet 7½ inches high, with dark beard cut a la Boulanger, dark clothes. Both wore black slouch hats. The tall man walked up to the paying teller's window. The other one walked around to the left where Tom Clemmons, the president of the bank, was coming out of a wire door, the exit from his office. The tall man handed Joe Clemmons, the paying teller, a note. It was written in pencil on the back of a poster and read as follows:

"Home, May 23.—First national bank, Longview: This will introduce to you Charles Specklemeyer, who wants some money and is going to have it.

"B. and T."

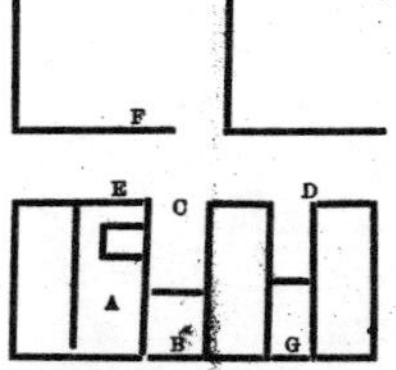

A—Bank building.
B—Store from which robber was killed.
C—Where robber fell.
D—Where Buckingham fell.
E—Where horses were tethered.
F—Cotton-yard.
G—Saloon out of which Buckingham and McQueen ran.

Joe Clemmons looked at the note and then looked up. A Winchester barrel was within an inch of his face and the tall man with a leer on his face was telling him to hold up his hands. He did so.

Just as Tom Clemmons opened the wire door the thick man sprang at him and shoved the muzzle of a six-shooter to his stomach. The man told Clemmons: "You —— —— ——, I am going to kill you or have money."

Just as he pulled the trigger Clemmons grappled with him and caught at the man's pistol. The fellow pulled the trigger and the hammer caught Clemmons' hand in the fleshy part between the thumb and forefinger. Three times the fellow tried to work the gun and three times the hammer caught in Clemmons' hand, making a hole in the flesh each time. Then Clemmons forced the man to his knees and was struggling with him. Clemmons usually keeps a pistol in a drawer of his desk. He worked the man around through the door to the desk and reached for the gun. It was gone. Clemmons' strength was nearly so. Finally the robber wore the banker out and at the point of a Colt's 45 told him:

"God — you, I have a good notion to kill you, but give me the money."

Clemmons replied: "You can have the money if you will not kill my brother or me."

During all of this time the tall man had been standing guard over Joe Clemmons at the paying teller's desk in front and all the time the tall man smiled.

When Tom Clemmons gave up the fight both robbers with both of the Clemmons in front of them walked to the money drawers and emptied their contents into a canvas bag which they picked up. One of them reached for Tom Clemmons' watch, which has a strong guard. He missed the watch, but caught Clemmons' vest, tearing it from shoulder to waist. The other got Joe Clemmons' ticker.

Before the men got to the safe firing commenced on the outside. One of the men said: "I guess we had better go now."

The men turned to the Clemmonses and said:

"God — you, get in front of us," and the Clemmonses did so.

The men then marched the Clemmonses out through the back door of the bank into the back yard and through a gate in the back yard to the alley where a regular fusilade was going on. There the Clemmonses broke and ran, and as Tom Clemmons said to me to-day:

"The only reason I am alive is that I outrun the bullets of everybody."

Neither of the Clemmonses were hurt beyond the injury to the hand above spoken of.

THE DEATH TRAP IN THE ALLEY.

While the struggle in the bank was going on Tom Clemmons yelled for help. John Wellborn, a cotton buyer heard the cries and started in the bank. He saw the situation and beat a retreat, spreading the alarm as he went. Mack Bartholomew heard it and he started in and somebody shot at him.

That shot was the alarm. Everybody heard it and everybody commenced running out to see what was the matter. People in stores east and west of the bank thought the sound came from the alley and they rushed out of back doors to get onto it. Those first in the alley saw a man standing down near the corner of Fredonia street with a Winchester in his hands and another almost in the rear of the bank with a similar gun and some horses hitched near by.

George Buckingham was almost the first man out. He ran within ten feet of the man with the gun. The fellow turned, saw Buckingham, coolly leveled his gun and fired. Buckingham fell mortally wounded. The man then poured three more shots into Buckingham's writhing body.

McQueen ran out of the same door as Buckingham, but before he got to the alley he got a ball in the hip and fell to the ground.

By this time the whole town was alarmed. The robbers were using Ballard needle guns and each report sounded almost as loud as a cannon. People left the courthouse and scampered across the cotton yard intervening to where the shooting was going on.

Among the first to reach the scene was Deputy Sheriff John Watson. He saw the men in the alley and reached for his pistol. It was only a little 38 and of little service. He emptied it at both men and was himself fired at a dozen times. The man standing at the mouth of the alley near Fredonia street and the other were wheeling right and left, shooting at every man who approached and yelling all of the time like a pack of Comanches.

Just as the Clemmons boys were marched out of the gate into the alley the man near the horses staggered and fell. The other at the end of the alley ran down to meet the two guarding the Clemmonses. One of them remarked:

"They have killed Bennett."

All three then mounted their horses and rode away.

When the citizens got to the fallen man he was dead, having been shot through the heart. He did not utter a word. A little farther up lay poor Buckingham and in the back yard of Buckingham's place McQueen had crawled to a safe place.

In all more than 250 shots were fired. Ex-confederate veterans said it sounded like the opening of a great battle. The wonder is that more citizens were not killed. They were running around looking for weapons and exposing themselves recklessly at every turn.

HOT PURSUIT.

As soon as horses and arms could be collected Sheriff Howard organized a posse and started in pursuit. The robbers had gone due north for several miles. About three miles from town the posse met an old negro woman who said one of the robbers was so badly injured that he had fallen off his horse in front of her house. The other two had ridden ahead to a skirt of woods and when the wounded man had remounted and caught up with them all three took off at a long gallop down the road.

At another place a little further along a negro man handed the sheriff two cartridges, a big one and a little one. He said three white men on horses had told him to give the big one to the sheriff and the little one to "that d—d little deputy," meaning John Watson, and to say there were plenty more where those came from.

Then they went through a cypress swamp about six miles off, heading a little to the north of east, and after that all trace of them was lost till the telegram came this afternoon announcing that they had been corralled at Avinger.

BENNETT IDENTIFIED.

When one of the surviving desperadoes seeing his comrade fall remarked: "They have killed Bennett," he gave the cue to the identification of the dead man. It was soon known that the fellow was J. C. Bennett, who came here last year and married a daughter of Mr. Green Renfro, a farmer living four miles from here. Shortly after the shooting was over Mr. Renfro himself came in and positively identified Bennett.

Then the dead body was raised against a barrel and the crowd commenced cutting off little strips of his clothing to preserve as mementoes. They cut away the greater portion of his coat, and of his boots the only thing that remained were the soles and heels. His hat suffered a similar fate. As the body, dressed in coarse, cheap hand-me-downs, with a gingham shirt, lay on the ground many persons spit upon it and kicked it.

Finally somebody hitched a rope to it and the carcass was dragged down the street to the depot followed by a tremendous throng. The rope was thrown over the arm of a telegraph pole and willing hands soon hoisted the lifeless mass of dirt and filth and flesh forty feet. There it dangled in mid air, reviled and jeered till the curiosity and spirit of revenge of the people were satisfied. Then it was cut down and lay in a street all night, unguarded. This morning it was picked up and buried.

In Bennett's saddle were found 300 rounds of ammunition. In one of his coat pockets was found a complete plat of the block in which the bank is located, showing all the exits and entrances as perfect and true with regard to every detail as the most experienced engineer could make it. This drawing is now in the hands of the sheriff.

Bennett's wife did not see the body and said she did not care to.

BEFORE THE ROBBERY.

For three or four days before the robbery the gang camped on a creek about four miles from here and spent the time hunting and fishing. Several of the farmers in the locality saw them and fished with them. They had a two-horse hack or carriage, a tent and cooking outfit and camping outfit. Two men rode in the hack and two men on horseback.

They arrived in town yesterday about 1 o'clock. Mr. July Garner, a farmer, had known Bennett when he was here last winter. He met Bennett on the street and shook hands with him. Bennett was accompanied by a man with a long beard. Mr. Garner asked when he was going to trade some more horses and Bennett said: "I will be back down this way directly and then you may see me." He did not seem to be in the least apprehensive, but was walking the streets as quietly as any other citizen.

To-day the hack containing the camping outfit was found in the woods. They had run it out of the road and deserted it in the brush.

MAY CAUSE FOUR DEATHS.

Before it is all over with the death list may foot up four. Buckingham and the robber are dead now and McQueen has a great hole clear through the abdomen from side to side and is not expected to live.

But another person whom no bullet touched is at the point of death and this evening the physicians have nearly given up all hope. That is Buckingham's wife. She has been very ill for a week or more and the news of her husband's taking off threw her into convulsions. Every thing that willing hands and loving hearts can do is being freely poured out for her recovery.

She is now almost beyond hope and it is one chance in a thousand if she lives. And the worst of it all is that five little children, helpless and alone, who are now fatherless, will be left motherless when she goes. The condition of Mrs. Buckingham has but accentuated public feeling and stimulated the desire for revenge in the minds of the people.

THE DEAD ROBBER.

THE BODY SWUNG UP.

AS OPEN AS DAY.

One feature of the robbery which may be considered remarkable is the openness of the whole thing. There was not the slightest pretense at concealment. When they were camping out on the banks of the creek, frolicking, the men would hail farmers passing and have chats with them. When they came to town yesterday morning they came like men and not like thieves.

There was not a single mask worn nor disguise of any kind attempted. Though more than one of the gang had been working around here and his face was familiar, they went around from place to place with the easy carelessness of farm hands who have some money in their pockets and have come to town to spend the day. They walked into one or two saloons and took several drinks and Bennett in the liberality of his heart set 'em up for the party.

T. J. CLEMMONS, president of the bank.

The only concealment was the weapons. The needle guns which did destruction in the afternoon were not visible in the morning. Nor did any of them wear a slicker. It is supposed that one man was left at the rendezvous to guard the weapons while the others came in to inspect the town and see how the land lay and make plans for the final assault.

THE BOOTY SECURED.

Various stories as to the amount of booty secured by the robbers have gone abroad in the newspapers and by word of mouth. Mr. Clemmons, president of the bank, says the amount secured was $2601 58 in silver and some small bills. The larger part of the money of the bank is kept in a vault, which is only opened on rare occasions, hence the smallness of the haul.

BENNETT'S HISTORY.

J. C. Bennett came to Longview last summer about the beginning of fall. He had a lot of horses which he traded with the farmers and paid considerable attention to the 18-year-old daughter of Mr. Green Renfro, a prosperous farmer of this county. He remained about two weeks and left, saying he was going to Las Vegas, N. M., from which place he claimed to have come, and where he said he had a ranch. He returned to Renfro's place in December, 1893, and in December married Renfro's daughter.

When he came the last time one of the Renfro boys saw in his trunk a roll of greenbacks amounting to more than $1000, which Bennett said was the proceeds of the sale of some horses and with which he intended to buy cattle. Bennett was accompanied by a man named Jim Jones, who, he said, was a friend of his working for him. He stayed at Renfro's during the winter and left about the last of January, stating that he had bought some cattle at Carthage and borrowed from Renfro the proceeds of a bale of cotton to pay the freight on the cattle to the ranch in New Mexico. Jones Bennett's friend, took one of the Renfro boys and went to Carthage to receive the cattle. When they got there Jones said that the best cattle had been sold, and he would not receive them.

The Renfro boy came back and Jones remained in that neighborhood for some three weeks, finally eloping with the daughter of a widowed school teacher. The mother protested, but Jones secured a license on his affidavit that the girl was over 18 years of age, when she lacked a few days of it. In a few days afterwards Jones drove to a store within a few miles of Renfro's house and left Bennett's saddle, saying he was afraid he was going to be prosecuted for perjury and had to 'light out.' Bennett and one of the Renfro boys overtook Jones and his wife some four miles from the store and Benett and Jones had a conference. Jones then drove off and Bennett and the Renfro boy returned home.

Coming back Bennett said that Jones had taken his money to buy the cattle, but, having failed, had left the money in a bank at Carthage, and that Jones had gone to the ranch in New Mexico. Nothing more was seen or heard of Jones. On the morning of Feb. 8, 1894, Bennett borrowed a horse from Renfro, saying he was going to meet some cattlemen who were camped near by and that was the last seen of him. The next day a note was received telling his wife that if he didn't show up by Saturday not to be alarmed. He didn't return and the first his wife or any of the family knew of his presence was when they saw his dead body on the street crossing after the battle.

Both Bennett and Jones were remarkably good shots, either with a pistol or with a rifle, and they frequently gave exhibitions of their skill with firearms. Bennett every morning when the papers came would ask, "Has there been another train robbery?"

Mr. Renfro, Bennett's father-in-law, told me to-day that Bennett's body was full of scars from bullet wounds. He said he had got them in a scrimmage with Mexicans in New Mexico in which five of them "stumped their toes while they were getting away." On another occasion Mr. Renfro says Bennett asked one of the Renfro boys: "John, could you shoot a Mexican down and rob him?" The boy said no and Bennett did not continue the conversation.

When Bennett left here last February Mr. Renfro wrote to Las Vegas to try and see if Bennett was known there. He wrote to people whose addresses Bennett had given him. The letters were all returned from the dead letter office. Mr. Renfro says Bennett pretended to be a United States deputy marshal and on one occasion exhibited a number of subpoenas for people living at Ardmore. Jones pretended to be a United States detective and wore a nickel-plated badge with the words "United States secret detective" under the lapel of his coat.

Bennett and Jones never traveled on a train. They came and went on horseback or in a wagon and nobody knew when or where they went. They never spoke of their travels beyond saying they went to Las Vegas always and came from there.

POSSE FROM DAINGERFIELD.

Daingerfield, Morris Co., Tex., May 24.—News reached here of the robbery of the bank at Longview yesterday, and that a posse of men from Longview had the robbers surrounded at Avinger, a few miles east of here. Sheriff J. W. High of this place and a posse of officers from Pittsburg went down this evening on the train to help out the posse and if possible capture the robbers.

REPORTED SURROUNDED.

Pittsburg, Camp Co., May 24.—The people are in a stir here over telegraphic reports that the Longview bank robbers are hotly pursued and are coming this way.

Sheriff Stafford received a telegram at 5 o'clock this evening from Cashier Clemmons at Longview, asking for a posse to go immediately to Avinger, a place thirty miles east of here, where a posse had the robbers surrounded.

REPORTED NEAR PITTSBURG.

Pittsburg, Camp Co., Tex., May 24.—A Mr. Latamore who lives east of here brought in the news at dusk this evening that the Longview bank robbers are being pursued by a posse five miles east of this place. Sheriff Stafford immediately summoned a dozen picked men and started in pursuit of the parties. Intense excitement prevails here and everyone is on guard. At this writing nothing can be heard of the posse who left here.

EXTRA PRECAUTIONS.

Plano, Collin Co., Tex., May 24.—The bank officials here after reading the tragic account of the bank robbery at Longview in this morning's News, have taken extra precautions against a daylight robbery. The Plano national bank is said to be as well fortified against burglary as any bank in the state.

REPORTED SURROUNDED.

Marshall, Tex., May 24.—Sheriff Perry received word that the Longview bank robbers were surrounded near Avinger and he and posse left here on a special train for the scene at 7:45.

ASHLAND DISTRICT.

BRECKINRIDGE WANTS PRIMARIES.

Frankfort, Ky., May 24.—The democratic committee meets here to-morrow to determine the manner and time of holding the election to nominate Congressman W. C. P. Breckinridge's successor. It is learned to-night that the Breckinridge people have decided to insist on a primary election to be held Sept. 12. It is understood that both his opponents, Owens and Settle, favor primaries. This will give Breckinridge six weeks to canvass the district after congress adjourns.

DENOUNCE HIM IN KANSAS.

Topeka, Kan., May 24.—At a meeting of the representative women of Kansas today an expression denunciatory of Col. Breckinridge in the shape of a preamble and resolution was adopted. The resolution states that the women of Kansas "join hands with our Kentucky sisters in demanding that no man henceforth be elected to congress who does not require in other men and exemplify in his own life the same standard of moral purity that is rightfully demanded of women."

The resolution as adopted was forwarded to the women of the Ashland, Ky., district.

BRECKINRIDGE TO SPEAK AGAIN.

Washington, May 24.—Representative Breckinridge of Kentucky will leave tomorrow for another round of speeches in his district. He speaks at La Grange Saturday and Owenton Monday. To-day he spent a good deal of time in court working on the bill of exceptions in the appeal from the decision in the Pollard suit.

FIRE RECORD.

BLAZE AT DE LEON.

De Leon, Comanche Co., Tex., May 24.—Six buildings burned here this morning at 2:15. Higginbotham company lost three houses, $1000, goods $300; no insurance. H. Taylor, stock of goods $1500; insurance $500 with the Providence. Buck Westbrook, carpenter tools, $150; no insurance. Thomas Blassingane, saloon and fixtures, light insurance on fixtures. P. G. Hilliard house, $500, goods $1000; $300 insurance on the house with the Teutonia. C. C. Morris, house $900; no insurance. Miller & Rucker, house $350; no insurance. Knights of Honor, lodge furniture $75; no insurance. A. Booth, goods burned $500; no insurance. F. L. Terrell, wall and roof to store building damaged $250; fully insured. The fire is supposed to have been the work of an incendiary.

FINE STABLES AFIRE.

Philadelphia, Pa., May 25, 2 a. m.—It is reported that the stables of Col. E. D. V. Morrell at Terrsdale are burning. The scene of the fire is eight miles from the city and details can not be procured tonight. If Col. Morrell's live stock is burned the loss will be heavy, as he has some fine horses and coaches, some of which were used in the recent coaching line to New York.

LONGVIEW ROBBERY.

It Has Resulted in Two Deaths and Will Be the Cause of Two More.

THE BANDITS CORRALLED.

Bennett's Body Strung Up to a Telegraph Pole—Burial of the Victims—Appeal for Help From the Posse.

Longview, Gregg Co., Tex., May 24.—The intense excitement caused by the robbery of the First national bank here yesterday afternoon continues. If there has been any abatement of the indignation and anger of the people for the loss of one of their best citizens, and the thirst for revenge, it is not perceptible. For once during a campaign, east Texas quit talking politics to-day. Men forgot their differences and swore with locked hands that those fugitive robbers who killed Buckingham and wounded McQueen and Muckleroy and the rest were either killed in a fight or would be brought back here to be burned alive. And had the men been captured by officers of the law they would not be prisoners longer than the time taken in preparing a bonfire to burn them.

All day long it has been talk, talk, talk. Every man had a new story that nobody else had heard, and these men with their stories had little knots of patient, eager listeners in front of stores or on the street corners. Merchants and lawyers and bankers even forgot their business and were finding out about the robbery. The scene of the tragedy was visited by hundreds and the fences and walls which are numerously marked with bullet holes were an unfailing object of curiosity. The ground where Bennett, the dead robber, was killed, was as carefully marked as if it had been the burying place of a president, and the dark red spot where poor George Buckingham fell, a victim to his desire to see what was going on, was visited, and the story of Buckingham's ending told again and again.

A stream of people have been to the bank to see Tom Clemmons, president, and Joe Clemmons, his brother, the paying teller. Their encounter with the robber, their resistance, bitter and stubborn, and finally their narrow escape at the hands of the marauders, has been not the least exciting or dramatic chapter in one of the most exciting and dramatic occurrences of the last year or so.

Then the two men, Claude Lacy and Will Stevens, either one of whom may have fired the shot which ended the dead robber's existence—nobody knows exactly which one did it—have been the heroes of a day, and their praises are on every man's lips. It may sound a little odd to say that a killing is universally commended, but it is a cold fact.

There were two burials in the Longview cemetery to-day. On body was carried to the grave in a city cart, just as ordinary offal, followed by no mourners, uncased in a pine box—literally unwept, unhonored and unsung. It was dumped into a hole in the ground in the potters' field, and the earth hastily thrown over it, and thus, like the carcass of a cow, removed as a stench in the nostrils of the community, the remains of John C. Bennett, the robber, awaits the final summons to appear at the place of readjustment where all crooked things of the body or heart are made straight. One or two persons, including the brother-in-law of Bennett, went out and looked at the fresh grave and then proceeded to express their gratification at his removal and their entire satisfaction with the mode and manner of his taking off.

This afternoon there was another burial. Every store in town was closed, every sound of busy life was still. Every face wore an expression of sadness and regret. From a little house near a church on Fredonia street issued crowds of people. A body in a handsome casket, with all the honor paid a hero, was followed to the grave by the largest funeral procession Longview has ever known. With uncovered heads the whole populace saw a body tenderly and reverentially lowered into a grave to await the same resurrection that will come to the carcass of the other. This was the body of George Buckingham, the citizen, mourned, honored and praised, consigned to its last abode.

Scarcely had the echoes of the prayers for the dead ceased to ring in their hearts before there came another paroxysm of excitement. A telegram was received from one of the pursuing party, John McCann, saying the fugitives were corralled at Avinger, a little lumber camp on the East Line, sixteen miles west of Jefferson, and appealing for help. Volunteers were called for, and fifty men responded in less time than is taken in the telling.

Superintendent Trice of the Texas and Pacific had a special engine ordered to take the posse to Jefferson, and soon twenty-five or more, armed to the teeth, were flying to the aid of the besiegers. It was the first news from the pursuing party.

There had been all sorts of rumors from time to time during the day. The fleeing and hunted men had taken this direction and that direction, and had been seen in one place by one man and in another place by another man, but nothing definite had been or could be heard. Now all the town that is left is waiting for the capture.

If the robbers are taken alive there will be no expense to the state in the prosecution of them should they be brought back here.

Going backward a little, the story of the robbery has not yet been fully told. The outlines have been touched and results given—that is all. At 3 p. m. yesterday Longview was a very busy town and a criminal case, which had become a local cause celebre, was at its climax in the court house, and the court room was packed with men eagerly awaiting the finale. The Texas and Pacific train from the west, which marks an event in every day, had just arrived, and all the tradespeople were at the depot attending to their business, as usual. Two men walked into the First national bank, which is a little, one story building, famous principally because of Tom Campbell's connection with it. One was a tall man, over 6 feet high. He wore a rough, greasy yellow slicker, such as is common among teamsters, and which was much the worse for wear and tear. He had a short, fuzzy beard all over his face, about a week and a half old, and appeared to be not over 25 years of age.

The other was a short, chunky man, about 5 feet 7½ inches high, with dark beard cut a la Boulanger, and dark clothes. Both wore black slouch hats.

The tall man walked up to the paying teller's window. The other one walked around to the left where Tom Clemmons, the president of the bank, was coming out of a wire door, the exit from his office. The tall man handed Joe Clemmons, the paying teller, a note. It was written in pencil on the back of a postal card:

"Home, May 23.—First National Bank, Longview: This will introduce to you Charles Specklemeyer, who wants some money and is going to have it. B. & T."

Joe Clemmons looked at the note and then looked up. A Winchester rifle was within an inch of his face, and the tall man, with a leer on his face, was telling him to hold up his hands. He did so.

Just as Tom Clemmons opened the wire door the thick man sprang at him and shoved the muzzle of a six-shooter to his stomach. The man told Clemmons: "Damn you, I am going to kill you or have money." Just as he pulled the trigger Clemmons grappled with him and caught at the man's pistol. The fellow pulled the trigger and the hammer caught Clemmons' hand in the fleshy part of the thumb and for three times the fellow tried to work the gun, and three times the hammer caught in Clemmons' hand, making a hole in the fleshy part. Then Clemmons forced the man to his knees and was struggling with him. Clemmons usually keeps a pistol in a drawer of his desk. He worked the man around the door to his desk and reached for his gun. It was gone. Clemmons' strength was nearly so. Finally, the robber, who wore the banker out, and at the point of the Colt's 45 told him: "G—d d—n you, I have a good mind to kill you, but give me the money." Clemmons replied: "You can have the money if you will not kill my brother or me."

During all of this time the tall man had been standing guard over Joe Clemmons at the paying teller's desk in front, and all the time the tall man smiled. When Clemmons gave up the fight both robbers, with both of the Clemmons in front of them, walked to the money drawer and emptied their contents into a canvass bag which they picked up. One of them reached for Tom Clemmons' watch, which has a strong guard, but caught Clemmons' vest, tearing it from shoulder to waist. The other got Joe Clemmons' ticker.

Before the men got to the safe the firing commenced on the outside. One of the men said: "I guess we had better go now."

The men turned to the Clemmons and said: "G—d d—n you, get in front of us."

The Clemmons did so. The men then marched the Clemmons out through the back door of the bank into the back yard, and through a gate in the back yard to the alley, where a regular fusillade was going on. There Clemmons broke and ran, and as Tom Clemmons said to me to-day, "The only reason I am alive is that I outran the bullets of everybody."

Neither of the Clemmons were hurt beyond the injury to their hands above spoken of.

While the struggle in the bank was going on Tom Clemmons yelled for help.

John Wellborn, a colored boy, heard the cries and started in the bank. He saw the situation and beat a retreat, spreading the alarm as he went.

Bartholomew heard it, and he started in, and somebody shot at him. That shot was the alarm. Everybody heard it and everybody commenced running out to see what was the matter. People in the stores east and west of the bank thought the sound came from the alley, and they rushed out back doors to get on to it.

Those first in the alley saw a man standing down near the corner of Fredonia street with a Winchester in his hand and another almost in the rear of the bank with a similar gun and some horses hitched near by. George Buckingham was almost the first man out.

He ran within ten feet of the man with the gun. The fellow turned on Buckingham, coolly leveled his gun and fired. Buckingham fell mortally wounded. The man then poured three more shots into Buckingham's writhing body.

McQueen ran out the same door as Buckingham, but before he got to the alley he got a ball in the hip and fell to the ground.

By this time the whole town was alarmed. The robbers were using Ballard needle guns, and each report sounded almost as loud as a cannon. People left the court house and scrambled across the yard intervening to where the shooting was going on. Among the first to reach the scene was Deputy Sheriff John Wilson. He saw the men in the alley and reached for his pistol. It was only a 38 and of little service. He emptied it at both men and was himself fired at a dozen times. The man standing at the mouth of the alley, near Fredonia street, and the other were wheeling right and left, shooting at everything that appeared, yelling all the time like a pack of Comanches. During the excitement some one fired at the man near the horses and he staggered and fell. The other three then mounted their horses and rode away.

When the citizens got to the fallen man he was dead, having been shot through the heart. He did not utter a word. A little further up lay poor Buckingham, and in the back yard of Buckingham's place McQueen had crawled to a safe place.

In all more than 250 shots were fired. An ex-confederate said it sounded like the opening of a great battle. The wonder is that more citizens were not killed. They were running around looking for weapons and exposing themselves recklessly at every turn.

As soon as a posse and arms could be collected Sheriff Howard organized a posse and started in pursuit. The robbers had gone due north for several miles. About three miles from town the posse met an old negro woman who said one of the robbers was so badly injured that he had fallen off his horse in front of her house. The other two had ridden ahead to a skirt of woods, and when the wounded man had remounted and caught up with them, all three took off at a long gallop down the road.

At another place a little further along, a negro man handed the sheriff two cartridges, a big one and a little one. He said three white men with horses had told him to give the big one to the sheriff and the little one to "that d—d little deputy," meaning John Wilson, and to say there were plenty more where these came from.

Then they went through a cypress swamp about six miles off, heading a little to the north of east, and after that all trace of them was lost until the telegram came this afternoon announcing that they had been corralled at Avinger.

When one of the surviving desperadoes, seeing his comrade fall, remarked, "They have killed Bennett" he gave the cue to the identity of the dead man. It was soon known that the fellow was J. C. Bennett, who came here last year and married a daughter of Mr. Green Renfro, a farmer living four miles from here. Shortly after the shooting was over Mr. Renfro himself came in and positively identified Bennett. Then the dead body was raised against a barrel and the crowd commenced cutting off little strips of his clothes to preserve as mementoes. They cut away the greater portion of his coat and his boots. The only things that remained were the soles and heels. His hat suffered a similar fate. As the body, dressed in coarse, cheap hand-me-down, with a gingham shirt, lay on the ground many persons spat upon it and kicked it. Finally somebody hitched a rope to it and the carcass was dragged down the street to the depot, followed by a tremendous throng. The rope was thrown over the arm of a telegraph pole, and willing hands soon hoisted the lifeless mass of dirt and filthy flesh forty feet. There it dangled in mid air, reviled and jeered until the curiosity and spite of the people were satisfied. Then it was cut down and lay in a street all night unguarded. This morning it was picked up and buried. In Bennett's saddle were found 300 rounds of ammunition. In one of his coat pockets was found a complete plat of the block in which the bank is located, showing all the exits and entrances as perfect and true with regard to every detail as the most experienced engineer could make it. The drawing is now in the hands of the sheriff. Bennett's wife did not see the body and said she did not care to.

For three or four days before the robbery the gang came here, and on a creek, about four miles from here, spent the time hunting and fishing. Several of the farmers in the locality saw them and fished with them. They had a two-horse hack or carriage, a tent, and cooking and caming outfit. Two men rode in the hack and two men on horseback. They arrived in town yesterday about 1 o'clock. Mr. July Garner, a farmer, had known Bennett when he was here last winter. He met Bennett on the street and shook hands with him. Bennett was accompanied by a man with a long beard. Mr. Garner asked when he was going to trade some more horses, and Bennett said: "I will be back down this way directly and then you may see me." He did not seem to be in the least apprehensive, but was walking the streets as quietly as any other citizen.

To-day the hack containing the outfit was found in the woods. They had run it out of the road and deserted it in the brush.

Before it is all over the death list may foot up four. Buckingham and the robber are dead now and McQueen has a great hole clear through the abdomen from side to side, and is not expected to live. But another person whom no bullet touched is at the point of death, and this evening the physicians have given up all hope. That is Buckingham's wife. She has been very ill for a week or more and the news of her husband's sudden taking off threw her into convulsions. Everything that willing hands and loving hearts can do is being freely poured out for her recovery. She is now almost beyond hope and it is one chance in a thousand if she lives. And the worst of it all is that the little children, helpless and alone, who are now fatherless, will be left motherless when she is gone. The condition of Mrs. Buckingham has but accentuated public feeling and stimulated the desire for revenge in the minds of the people.

One feature of the robbery which may be considered remarkable is the openness of the whole thing. There was not the slightest pretense at concealment. When they were camping out on the banks of the creek freely the linemen would hail farmers passing and have chats with them. When they came to town yesterday morning they acted like men and not like thieves. There was not a single mask worn nor disguise of any kind attempted. Though more than one of the gang had been working around here and his face was familiar, they went around from place to place with the easy carelessness of farm hands who have some money in their pockets and have come to town to spend the day. They walked into one or two saloons and took several drinks and Bennett, in the liberality of his heart, "set 'em up" for the party. The only concealment was the weapons. The needle guns which did the destructive work in the afternoon were not visible in the morning. Nor did any of them wear a slicker. It is supposed that one man was left at the rendezvous to guard their weapons while the others came in to inspect the town and see how the land lay and make plans for the final assault.

HAD THEM SURROUNDED.

Pittsburg, Camp Co., Tex., May 24.—The people are in a stir here over telegraphic reports that the Longview bank robbers are hotly pursued, and are coming this way. Sheriff Stafford received a telegram a 5 p. m. from Cashier Clemmons at Longview asking for a posse to go immediately to Avinger, a place thirty miles east of here, where a posse had the robbers surrounded.

GONE TO ASSIST.

Daingerfield, Morris Co., Tex., May 24.—News reached here of the robbery at Longview yesterday and that a posse from Longview had the robbers surrounded at Avinger, a few miles east of here. Sheriff J. W. High of this place and a posse of officers from Pittsburg went down this evening on a train to help the posse, and if possible capture the robbers.

POSSE IN PURSUIT.

Pittsburg, Tex., May 24.—A Mr. Latamore, who lives east of here, brought in the news at dark this evening that the Longview bank robbers are being pursued by a posse five miles east of this place. Sheriff Stafford immediately summoned a dozen picked men and started in pursuit of the parties. Intense excitement prevails here, and every one is on guard. At this writing nothing can be heard of the posse who left here.

FOUR STRANGERS AT PALESTINE.

Palestine, Tex., May 24.—Constable Henry Watts saw four strange hard looking men in town on horseback several days ago. Their movements aroused his suspicions and he watched them until they left the city. He is confident they are the same gang that robbed the bank at Longview yesterday.

NEW ORLEANS CHIEF.

Sequel to the Asa Gurney Imprisonment. Close Call for Gaster.

New Orleans, La., May 24.—[Special.]—Chief of Police Dexter S. Gaster had the closest kind of a call last night from being reduced to the ranks for his action in the Asa Gurney case. Gurney is an ex-employe of the American express company and was arrested by Gaster and Billy Pinkerton, charged with the theft of $50,000 from a money package. Gurney was acquitted and thereupon preferred charges against Gaster for the manner of arrest; that he, Gurney, was not properly recorded and incarcerated in the police station in the precinct in which he was arrested, but that he was spirited away first to one suburban station and then to another, not registered as a prisoner and kept for several days in secrecy, deprived of communication with his friends.

At the time it was thought that nothing would come of the trial before the police board, but to the surprise of a whole lot of people, the board treated it so seriously that it stood three to two in favor of a motion to reduce the chief to the ranks, virtually a dismissal.

The mayor was absent. Commissioner Beanham was in the chair and ruled that he had a vote as commissioner, which he cast, tieing the vote, and then as chairman cast the deciding vote. A subsequent motion to dismiss the charges against the chief was carried by Commissioner Beanham in the same way.

HERNANDEZ WILL CASE

Decided in Favor of Mrs. Church Hernandez, the Second Wife.

New Orleans, La., May 23.—[Special.]—The supreme court this morning handed down a decision in the famous Hernandez case, which affirmed the position taken by Judge King of the lower court, and says that the marriage between Joseph Hernandez and Mrs. Augustus Church is legal.

When Mr. Hernandez died he left several very handsome bequests to his second wife, formerly Mrs. Church. His children attacked the will on the grounds that under the laws of Louisiana the marriage between Mrs. Church and the deceased was not legal. They also charged that she was his mistress. The allegation set forth in the opposition was that Mrs. Hernandez No. 1 obtained a divorce from Mr. Hernandez in St. Bernard parish for committing adultery with Mrs. Church. Under the laws of Louisiana a divorced man can not marry the woman with whom he committed adultery.

The decision entitles Mrs. Hernandez No. 2 to the rich legacy left her by her husband. The amount involved is away up in the thousands of dollars.

Mrs. Hernandez No. 1 is still alive and took an active part in fighting the case.

CHARITIES AND CORRECTION.

Nashville, Tenn., May 24.—The twenty-first annual session of the national conference of charities and correction began today, President Lucius S. Storrs of Michigan presiding. Prayer was offered by Rev. R. K. Brown of Tennessee.

The president appointed as the committee on business and resolutions Dr. Hoyt of New York, Dr. Mills of Colorado, Dr. Johnson of Indiana, Dr. Hough of Ohio and Mr. Johnson of Massachusetts.

Mr. Byers of Ohio read the report of the committee on states, which announced that reports had been received from forty states. These reports contained much interesting information.

Hon. Levi L. Barbour of Michigan read the report of the committee of state boards of charity. The report said that much trouble had come from too great an influx of indiscriminate foreign immigration.

Mr. Neff of Ohio led in the discussion of this report. The subject of state charities as boards of control was discussed at length.

Invitations from Grand Rapids and New Orleans to hold the next annual convention in those cities were received.

The conference adjourned until 8 p. m.

After the adjournment of the general meeting of the charities and corrections convention this afternoon many special meetings were held. The committee on child-saving work, Mr. Homer Folks of New York chairman, met, and Mr. Folks spoke on the importance of the work.

A paper was read by Lyman Alder of Terre Haute on the construction, management and workings of an ideal institution for dependent children, indorsing the "cottage" plan. W. E. Faulkner of Atchison, Kan., and Mr. Kraus of Cincinnati also discussed the subject. Other speakers were S. A. Hassaway, Michael Heyman of New Orleans and J. W. Burkett of Boston.

"Instruction, Amusement and Discipline" was the next topic discussed, and remarks were made by Mr. Heyman, Mr. Savage, Mr. Alden, Rev. Thomas M. Yunot and others.

The section on charity organization met, John Glenn of Baltimore presiding. The session set for and discussed the educational work of the charity organization movement. A large number of delegates took part in the discussion.

The section devoted to consideration of reform in industrial schools also met, Hon. J. T. Mallahan of Nebraska presided. Hon. F. H. Nelbecker of Glenn Mills, Pa., read an extended paper on "The Basic Idea of Conducting and How Expressed." T. J. Charlton of Indiana read a paper entitled "Business Views of Institutional Relations."

Captain D. M. Burkett read a paper on "Qualifications Necessary to be a Successful Officer or Employe."

Miss Emma M. Gilbert of Chillicothe, O., read a paper, "Work Among Girls." Discussions followed the reading of the papers.

DALLAS DOTS.

VETO BY MAYOR BARRY.

Dallas, Tex., May 24.—Mayor Barry today filed with the city secretary his veto of the ordinance lodging power in the council to license saloons anywhere in the city. The existing ordinance which it is attempted to repeal prohibits saloons in residence districts.

George F. McMurchy, the well-known traveling man and single tax advocate, who went insane here about a week ago, was to-day sent to the lunatic asylum at Taylor.

The case of H. Blum of Galveston vs. William Bowen et al., is on trial in the United States court.

The remains of the man killed yesterday by an electric motor have been identified as M. Griffith, who has wealthy relatives in Memphis, Tenn.

SEVERAL ARE DEAD.

Striking Miners Attacked the Coal Pits at Stickle Hollow, Pa.

CONFLICTING TESTIMONY.

Other Labor Matters—Striking Miners Reinforced West of the Mississippi—Invaders Driven Back—Railway Telegraphers.

Uniontown, Pa., May 24.—The long threatened attack by striking miners on the pits of the Washington coal and coke company at Stickle Hollow in the Fourth pool district on the Monongahela river was made this morning, involving another of the grim tragedies that have characterized the irrepressible conflict. The fight was one of the fiercest in the history of the mining troubles in western Pennsylvania, and in the section where it occurred as well as throughout the whole coke region the situation it has developed is one of the most intense excitement and dread uncertainty.

To-night four strikers are lying dead, and double that number are badly wounded, some of them mortally. Thomas Keenan of Wood's Run is the only American killed in the encounter with the deputies. The other dead men are Slavs.

The wounded men who fell under the first volley from the deputies were taken off the field by retreating strikers, and even now the actual number of wounded is not really known, their friends having the strongest motives for concealing them.

It is perhaps too soon to attempt to apportion the responsibility for the killings. In the mass of confessed and contradictory statements there is testimony to show that the strikers, while threatening an attack, had committed no overt act of lawlessness beyond the possible offense of unlawful assembly; that the deputies fired on them absolutely without provocation that would warrant the use of deadly weapons, and that some of the killings were particularly cruel and unjustifiable.

Then there is equally abundant testimony to show that the deputies simply defended themselves and their charge from the rushing assault of an armed and bloodthirsty mob.

The strikers furnished all the dead men; not a deputy was fatally hurt and only three of them wounded.

The fight occurred at daybreak in the public roadway leading to the Stickle Hollow plant. Two thousand strikers, after camping near the works all night, came out there to intercept the men on their way to work and induce them to come out and help win the strike. A few of them carried Winchesters, while fully fifty others were armed with shot guns, muzzle-loading rifles and revolvers. Because of their threatening demonstrations, and the fact that they had given notice to the company that they would come to drive off the deputies if necessary, there were ball cartridges in the Winchesters carried by the guards, and the entire outfit at the works was in readiness to receive the raiders.

The deputies had specific orders, and it is admitted that the company had conveyed to them directions to shoot to kill.

Sixty-six of the strikers were placed under arrest and taken back to the company's ground, where they were closely guarded during the remainder of the day. The whole lot of them were later placed in box cars, which were closely nailed up, and kept there until this evening, when they were brought here to the jail in charge of twenty-five deputies. The men arrested are nearly all native born citizens, intelligent looking, and several of them are known to be men of influence and good reputation in the Fourth Pool district.

The situation at the mines to-night is alarming, and more serious trouble is expected within the next twenty-four hours. Reports from there late to-night are to the effect that 3000 strikers from the lower end of the Fourth Pool were marching on Stickle Hollow, thoroughly armed, for the purpose of storming the works, regardless of consequences. But these reports have not been verified.

None of the dead except Keenan have been identified. It is impossible to learn about the others that are dead. Fear muzzles the survivors and seals the lips of even the children of friends of the men in the fight. They will not even claim their dead, and nobody had come forward to speak for the remains of the poor fellows who are lying where they fell.

John Troy of Fayette City was badly wounded and will die. He is a prominent citizen of that place.

A MINE WRECKED.

Centralia, Ill., May 24.—About five hundred striking miners from Duquoin and the St. Johns mine arrived in this city today on an Illinois Central freight train and proceeded to the Big Four mine, operated by Pottinger & Davis, in the northern limits of the city. They demolished considerable of the machinery and filled the shaft with about fifteen feet of debris, dump carts and other loose material about the mine. Every glass and sash in the building was smashed. The total damage to the property is estimated at $2000.

The Big Four mine has for the past three days been running with about thirty men, and yesterday they refused to come out at the request of the local committee.

After the strikers had completed their work of destruction they left the city and two miles north separated in two gangs, one party going to Sandoval and the other to Odin. The mines are running at Odin, and it is expected that the destruction of property would follow their arrival there.

Sheriff Helms swore in 125 deputies, and after arming them chartered a train and started to Sandoval, where the west gang was overhauled, already headed for Odin. The train was quickly transferred to the Baltimore and Ohio tracks and the deputies reached Odin a few minutes in advance of the two branches of the mob. The strikers were surrounded and a few shots were fired, but no harm done. A portion of the mob surrendered and the remainder fled. About eighty men were arrested and brought here. This evening twenty more were brought in and all are now locked in the city hall.

Threats have been made that the prisoners will be released to-night and the city authorities have sworn in a large force of extra police to assist the deputies and guard the peace of the city.

RIOT AT SPRING VALLEY.

Spring Valley, Ill., May 24.—A Polish striker was arrested and locked up this afternoon for rioting. In the evening a mob of infuriated Poles and Lithuanians marched to the jail and liberated the prisoners. Later the police attempted to arrest the ring leaders of the mob in the Polish district, but they were set upon by another gang, armed with knives and missiles. Two of the officers were wounded. Mayor Jack has issued orders to the police not to make the arrest until the excitement had died down.

The Knights of Labor have posted a circular urging the strikers to keep within the bounds of the law and allow the fires to be extinguished.

RIOTERS AT LA SALLE.

LaSalle, Ill., May 24.—A mob of 1000 coal strikers, none of them English-speaking, raided the shaft of the LaSalle County carbon coal company here this evening and in a conflict with the sheriff and his deputies, five strikers, Sheriff Taylor, and Deputy Sheriffs Tom Holyhan and John Dwyer were painfully wounded. The mob closed in on the officers and a hand-to-hand fight ensued. Three men were arrested but one of them was released on the men threatening to tear down the jail and burn the city hall. The situation is alarming, and the governor has been telegraphed to with a request for state aid.

INVADERS MARCHED OUT.

Leavenworth, Kan., May 24.—Captain Steve Ryan of Napoleon, Mo., and 100 of his striking miners were marched through this city at 5.30 this afternoon in charge of Sheriff Rothenberger and hundreds of citizens and compelled to cross over the new steel bridge into Missouri, from whence they came. The rest of the mob gave up the invasion at Wallula, twelve miles south of this city, and are retracing their steps to Kansas City.

At 4.30 a message from Lansing announced their coming. As previously arranged, the court house bell began tolling, and within ten minutes fully 2000 prominent citizens and merchants among them and most of them armed, gathered around the court house, nearly all volunteers, and a company was at once organized and sent to reinforce sheriffs.

A few minutes after 5 o'clock the strikers, lead by the sheriff in a carriage, deputies on horseback and hundreds of citizens on foot and followed by supply wagons and many other business and laboring men with Garfield rifles, heavily armed, bringing up the rear, marched through the business portion of the city and on to the new bridge. They camped on the Missouri side to-night and will depart for their homes in the morning.

ILLINOIS TROOPS MOVING.

Springfield, Ill., May 25, 1 a. m.—Governor Altgeld has been in telegraphic communication all evening with the county and municipal officers at Centralia, LaSalle and other points where strikers were rioting during the day and shortly after midnight decided that troops must be called out.

Sheriff Taylor of LaSalle county wired at 11 o'clock that the situation was very serious, that his force of deputies were unable to cope with the rioters and that a mob surrounded the hotel in which he was lying wounded. Sheriff Helm of Centralia sent a report similar in character.

Orders are now being telegraphed for five companies of the Fourth infantry to report at Centralia, and four companies of the Seventh to report at LaSalle in the morning. Adjutant General Orendorff will go to LaSalle and Assistant Adjutant General Brill to Centralia.

THE RAILROAD TELEGRAPHERS.

Denver, Col., May 23.—The railroad telegraphers' convention to-day, by a vote of 70 to 62, decided to seat D. R. Brown of Buffalo, manager of the campaign of Thomas B. McMahon, for the position of grand chief. This is regarded as a victory for the anti-Ramsay forces.

Grand Chief Ramsay previously in the session presented his annual report. He congratulated the order on having obtained from railroads during the past year thirty-four wage schedules. The membership of the order had decreased, but a critical period in its history had been passed. There was now a revival of interest and the membership was likely to increase rapidly. The grand chief reviewed in detail the grievances adjusted during the year. He reported that he arrested the charter of Omaha division No. 2 because of the publication by it of a paper called the Wasp, which belittled the grand officers and injured the order. This matter, he said, was now before the convention and it would have to pass judgment. The grand chief opposed state divisions of the order as he favored state organization. He also favored federation. Changes in the by-laws agreed upon by the grand officers of various railway organizations were recommended for passage.

Mr. Ramsay told in full the story of his indictment and acquittal on the charge of having conspired to cut the wires of the Cedar Rapids railroad, with which the order was having trouble.

MORE MINERS STRUCK.

Little Rock, Ark., May 24.—All the miners in Coal Hill, the slope and at Denning struck to-day in sympathy with the United Mine Workers of the United States. The miners at Huntington are also out.

ROADS AGREED AT CHICAGO.

Chicago, Ill., May 24.—The Union Pacific will become one of the Western passenger association with emigrant clearing house on June 1 and the westbound emigrant rates between Chicago and the Pacific coast will be restored from their present rate of $16.10 to the old basis of $35 on June 3. Notice of the intended advance was to-day given the interstate commerce commission by Chairman Caldwell.

The Union Pacific comes in on the basis of 33⅓ per cent of through California business. The question of eastbound traffic will come up for discussion to-morrow, as will the matter of granting excursion rates during the summer.

The Missouri, Kansas and Texas requested the association some time ago to join it in making a 2-cent rate for parties of ten, but the association refused.

The presidents and general managers of the Western freight association to-day broke the time record on formulating and adopting an agreement. The committee of eleven appointed at yesterday's meeting presented a plan for the establishment of an executive committee composed of the executive officers of the leading lines. This committee is to have control of all the rates and no reductions will be made without notice being first given to the executive committee and then to the interstate commerce commission. Besides the executive committee, the Southwestern traffic association and the trans-Missouri committee of the Western freight association will have control of matters strictly in their own territory.

The meeting adopted the report without a dissenting vote or without making a material change in its wording.

All the roads in all the committees were represented, all were pledged to the restoration of the freight tariffs of May 1, not later than May 20, and the absolute maintenance of rates after that date. The agreement was the most quickly drawn and adopted affair of its kind in which the western lines have ever taken part.

AMERICAN NAVY HONORED.

London, May 24.—The banquet tendered to Admiral Erben, Captain Mahan and the officers of the United States cruiser Chicago by officers of the English navy and army and distinguished citizens of Great Britain was held to-night in St. James' hall.

The principal table was placed upon a platform underneath the organ loft, from which hung immense English and American flags.

A broad band inscribed "Blood is Thicker Than Water," was suspended from the gallery opposite the organ loft. Two British naval officers escorted each officer of the Chicago to his allotted seat. The American officers were in uniform; the other guests were in evening dress, but most of them wore orders and sashes.

Chaplain Sharman pronounced grace both before and after the banquet.

Lord George Hamilton offered a toast to the queen and President Cleveland. All then rose and drank to the toast amid tremendous enthusiasm.

Ambassador Bayard rose to reply and was received with prolonged cheering.

Admirable Hornby then toasted the United States navy.

Admiral Erben, responding to Admiral Hornby's toast, said that never before was such a compliment paid to the American navy.

Lord Robert Hamilton then proposed a toast to Captain Mahan and the officers of the Chicago. Captain Mahan responded felicitously.

Admiral Commerell briefly responded to Captain Mahan's toast, and the proceedings closed with the band playing the "Star Spangled Banner."

FIRE RECORD.

STORE AND CONTENTS.

Alice, Nueces Co., Tex., May 24.—Last night at 11.30 great clouds of smoke and leaping flames of fire were discovered to be issuing from H. B. Newberry's store and in less than fifty minutes the building and the entire stock of general merchandise, valued at $5000, were completely consumed. Insurance, $3000. A barber shop and an empty warehouse were also destroyed. Other adjacent buildings were saved by application of water and wet blankets.

COLONEL MORRILL'S STABLES.

Philadelphia, Pa., May 25, 2 a. m.—It is reported that the stables of Colonel E. D. V. Morrill at Torsdale are burning. The scene of the fire is eight miles from the city and details can not be procured to-night. If Colonel Morrill's live stock is burned the loss will be heavy, as he has some fine horses and coaches, some of which were used in the recent coaching line to New York.

PREMIER ROSEBERY.

He Makes a Point on Joseph Chamberlain--Will Reform the Lords.

IS GRATEFUL TO THE IRISH.

Ireland Tranquil and United With the Liberal Party—The People Cheer the Premier—Gladstone's Eye Treated.

Birmingham, May 23.—Lord Rosebery breakfasted with the Midland Counties liberal association at the Grand hotel. In the course of his speech the premier declared that the government was bound to bring forward the measures to which it was pledged. Joseph Chamberlain, Lord Rosebery said, was unable to support the measures which he once advocated lest the home rule bill should be passed with them. This was skating upon thin ice, and this great ardent reformer was obliged to sink every reform upon which he had set his heart because he was unable to agree upon the precise form which home rule should take.

In regard to the house of lords the premier said that a minister could not announce the details of the bill for its reformation until the government had received the country's mandate. He was a mender rather than an ender, because he did not know of any machinery by which the house of lords could be ended.

Touching upon the Irish question Lord Rosebery said there were points full of hope for its settlement. One was the closer union of the Irish party and the liberals. He felt grateful from the bottom of his heart for the way in which the Irish came to the assistance of the government during the recent critical division. The other was the tranquility of Ireland, an important factor in influencing the English in favor of home rule.

Lord Rosebery was loudly cheered while passing through the streets of this city on his way to the railroad station en route to London.

BRITISH BUDGET.

London, May 24.—The debate in the commons on the budget bill, which was expected in some quarters to prove the downfall of Lord Rosebery's ministry, was opened this afternoon by a gun fired by Sir John Lubbock, liberal-unionist, who moved that the budget committee be empowered to divide the budget into two parts and to embody the provision respecting the sinking fund in a different measure.

Sir William Harcourt said that the object of the motion was to revert to the system by which the house of lords would be able to overthrow the financial measures emanating from the house of commons. This system had already been condemned by Disraeli and Palmerston and by the committee of the house of commons. [Loud cheers.] Another reason for Sir John Lubbock's motion was to waste the time of the house by involving it in two bills and in two separate statements from the committee and in two third readings. At the present time also there were special reasons why the commons should preserve absolute control of the finances of the country.

Mr. Goshen and several minor conservatives supported the motion, after which a division was taken, with the result that it was rejected by a vote of 161 to 121.

The announcement of the government's victory was greeted with prolonged liberal cheers. Later two other conservative instructions to the budget committee were ruled out of order, and the house went into committee of the whole amid renewed liberal cheering.

MR. GLADSTONE'S EYE.

London, May 24.—Mr. Gladstone's right eye was successfully operated upon today. Drs. Nettleship and Habershon both attended the distinguished patient in Lord Rendale's house early in the day, and some time afterward they issued a bulletin stating that the eye had been operated upon for cataract and that the operation was quite successful. The operation took place at 9.30 a. m., Dr. John Bowerling Lawford assisting the two surgeons already mentioned.

Mr. Gladstone's health was well maintained after the operation and the doctors state that the result confirms the diagnosis of Dr. Grainger or Chester. The ex-premier is said to be in as good spirits as can possibly be expected.

SECRET CARTRIDGE FACTORY.

Belgrade, May 24.—The police have discovered a secret cartridge factory where ammunition for the Peabody rifle, with which the Servian militia is armed, has been turned out in large quantities. It is estimated that 3,000,000 cartridges have already been sent to the provinces.

M. Tajsic, the radical leader in the last skupstchina, has been arrested. The archpriest Gyuris has also been taken into custody.

FRANCE OPPOSES THE TREATIES.

Paris, May 24.—M. Delonele has announced his intention of introducing in the chamber of deputies the question of the British treaties with China, Italy and Belgium, alleging that they are a violation of French rights and existing treaties.

The Temps says that it is not so much the Anglo-Congo treaty as the fact that England wishes to establish a buffer state between the eventual possessions of France and Great Britain in Central Africa, following the example of the Siamese buffer state. There is also danger that Italy will ultimately absorb the upper Nile region.

M. PEYTRAL SUMMONED.

Paris, May 24.—M. Dupuy declined to form a cabinet and suggested that President Carnot should summon M. Peytral, ex-minister of finance, in the radical cabinet formed by M. Flouquet.

M. Peytral informed the president that he thought the task of forming a cabinet was beyond his power, but he would confer with his colleagues to-night and would give his answer to-morrow morning.

A HEALYITE PAPER.

Dublin, May 24.—The Irish Times learns that Mr. Labouchere is to advance the capital necessary to start a daily newspaper in Dublin devoted to the interests of the Healyite faction of the Irish party. The policy of the paper will be aggressive.

WANT A GOLD STANDARD.

Friedrichsrotha, Saxe-Coburg-Gotha, May 24.—At a meeting here to-day of the German banking association, at which thirty-five banks were represented, a resolution in favor of a gold standard was unanimously adopted.

BRECKINRIDGE'S CAMPAIGN.

Washington, May 24.—Representative Breckinridge of Kentucky will leave tomorrow for another round of speeches in his district. He speaks at LaGrange Saturday and Owenton Monday. To-day he spent a good deal of time in court working on the bill of exceptions in the appeal from the decision in the Pollard suit.

JOCKEY CLUB LOST MONEY.

Louisville, Ky., May 24.—For the first time in the history of the Louisville jockey club it has lost money on the spring meeting. The amount will be about $8000 and the club has decided to hold no more fall meetings unless the purses are guaranteed by the merchants and other beneficiaries of the meeting. Bad weather was principally responsible for the loss.

THE CHICAGO WORLD.

FOURTH YEAR.—NO. 15. CHICAGO, ILL., SATURDAY, JUNE 16, 1894. PRICE 5 CENTS.

A GAMBLING HELL.

Hot Springs, Ark., the Most Notorious Bunco Town On the Continent.

Here Highway Robbery Is Legalized and Plucked Victims Dare Not Squeal.

Three Hundred Blacklegs and Gamblers Thrive and Wax Fat in a Population of About 16,000.

Hot Springs, Ark., June 13.—This city is really and truly the gambler's paradise. Here everything in that line is "protected." In that regard this a high tariff city with free trade. There are thirteen gambling-houses in this city—ominous for the bettor. Of this number eight are of the "brace" variety, being so-called because the dealer pulls two cards instead of one when he sees that he is about to loose a large stake.

These games are "protected" by the payment of a sum monthly to the usual middleman who stands between them and some occult power or hidden force. There are about three hundred gamblers in this city, including the steerers and bunco men. The city has a population of about 8,000, with about an equal number of visitors. This shows a large percentage of the gambling element. The middleman receives a percentage of the profits of each gaming-house for and in consideration of his statesmanship in "fixing things dead to rights." He also receives 50 per cent of the stealings of the bunco men, and if the buncoist gets in jail he must fix things to get him out. The business is reduced to a system.

When a man is robbed of, say, $500, the buncoists hand the money to the middleman, not necessarily for restoration, but as guarantee of good faith. If the victim makes a "roar" he is given back a small portion. If nothing is heard from him in three or four days, the middleman takes his lion's share and the remaining half is divided among the buncoists. If a buncoist attempts to do business without first making a treaty with the middleman he is arrested after beating his first victim, and usually gets a long term in jail. If he attempts to hold back the middleman's half he likewise comes to grief, for the middleman must also be protected and has spotters on the streets. These buncoists have their signals, by which a confederate may know that a "sucker is on the string."

When a bunco thief starts toward Happy Hollow with a stranger or a Boston clergyman he signals to a confederate in waiting. When they have arrived at the cave in the glen, the favorite promenading spot, they find a game in full blast. The confederate, with his pasteboard layout, had cut across the hill. These fellows carry an assortment to please—faro layout, dice boxes, shells, three cards for monte and all the latest devices known to gambling and swindling. Another class haunt the hotels. These are mainly "steerers" for brace faro banks. They receive 5 per cent of the victim's losses.

There is still another class at the hotels, often boarders, who do not associate with the well-known gamblers, nor do they visit the gambling houses. These are the card sharpers. They cultivate acquaintances for the purpose of getting up a social game. They carry their own cards and shears to cut them with, so that they may prepare a deck for poker or for faro. They affect the airs of business men and repudiate the idea of even visiting a gaming-house, yet they are even more adroit thieves than the professional brace dealer. Private faro banks exist in some of the hotels, and visitors are nightly robbed of large sums. As a rule, they are the most interested in keeping the matter quiet. Very few men wish to proclaim that they have been fools or that they are impoverished.

Steering or roping is one of the chief industries of the town. It enters into almost everything. The physicians have cappers, to whom they pay from 25 to 50 per cent and tax the sick victim accordingly. The keeper of the bathhouse has steerers out on the streets, and he pays a per cent to the doctor or hotel-keeper who sends him a customer. The drug stores have cappers, and there are even cappers for the sale of bathing towels. The shops which sell antique curios (especially manufactured for tourists) also give commissions. As the visitor is here for only two or three weeks they endeavor to make his stay interesting and the nervous man will not soon forget it.

The gaming evil has given the city a bad reputation. Were the gaming-houses closed and the gamblers and their adjuncts, the bunco men, made to leave the city and remain away, there would be a greater number of health-seekers here every season.

MRS. PAT ROONEY DEAD.

The Famous Chimpanze of Cincinnati Follows Her Husband to the Monkey Heaven.

Mrs. Rooney, widow of Pat Rooney, was found dead in her cage at the Zoological gardens in Cincinnati the other morning. Consumption carried her off, as it did her husband three months ago. They were the finest chimpanzees ever in captivity and were all but human. They ate at a table, sitting on chairs and using dishes, knives, forks and spoons like human beings and had often been declared the missing link.

Since Pat's death Mrs. Rooney had been melancholy and would spend nearly all her time gazing earnestly at the stuffed form of her husband that stood near by. A month ago consumption developed and all efforts to save her life proved futile, Professor Garner, who studied the chimpanzee from a cage in the African forests, visited Mrs. Rooney last week and declared she could not live long. Mrs. Rooney's skin will be mounted and placed alongside the stuffed form of her late husband.

JUDGE BONNEY'S DEFEAT.

A reader of the World writes to the editor as follows: "I have noticed in the papers various theories as to the recent political revolution in the Fourth Illinois judical districe. There is, however, one cause for Judge Bonney's defeat which I have seen no mention—that is the intervention of that non-political organization, the A. P. A., which indorsed Mr. Carter and urged all its members to vote for him."

FELL ASLEEP ON THE RAILROAD TRACK.

William Christman, while walking home from Freeport, Ill., sat down on the railroad track and fell asleep. A freight train came along, struck him on the shoulder and hurled him several feet. He was picked up and taken to Freeport and afterward brought home.

SPIRITUALIST LEADER DIES.

Mrs. Minerva Merrick Orchardson, aged 84 and wealthy, died at Quincy, Ill. She has been the head of the spiritualistic colony here for years. A year ago she married Prof. Charles Orchardson of Chicago, who came here with the noted spook priestess, Vera Ava, now sojourning in Joliet.

JERRY SIMPSON CONVALESCENT.

Congressman Jerry Simpson, of Kansas, who was taken to Berkley Springs. Va., seriously ill is reported as mending rapidly. His wife writes he will soon be able to attend to his duties

THE THRILLING DEATH OF BILL DALTON NEAR ELK, I. T.

BILL DALTON DEAD.

The Notorious Western Bandit at Last Goes Down With His Boots On.

Surrounded by a Sheriff's Posse Near Elk, I. T., He Is Killed While Trying to Escape.

An Interesting Sketch of the World's Most Famous Bandit and Outlaw—One of Ten Brothers.

Ardmore, I. T., June 14.—There's no doubt of it this time, Bill Dalton is dead, and he died with his boots on, and a six shooter in his hands. The encounter was brief but it was telling while it lasted. It occurred near Elk a few miles from here.

Ever since the famous Longview, Texas, bank robbery which occurred May 23 last special posses and United States marshals have been on the chase for the notorious bandits, who of course were said to be no others than the Dalton gang. The details of that robbery are still fresh in mind.

On the morning of May 23, a man carrying a rifle concealed under his coat handed this note to President Clemmens of the Longview bank:

"This will introduce to you Charles Specklemeyer, who wants some money and is going to have it. B. and F."

It was written in pencil legibly on the back of a printed postal. The bank president thought it a subscription to some charity, and started to ask for particulars, when the stranger pointed his rifle at him and told him to hold up his hands. The other man rushed into the side wire door and grabbed the cash. Tom Clemmens, cashier, and other bank officials also were ordered to hold up their hands. The robbers hurriedly emptied the tills and then went into the vaults, securing $2,000.

While this was going on two confederates were in the rear alley shooting at every one who appeared. They were soon being fired upon by City Marshal Muckleroy and Deputy Marshal Will Stevens. The firing made the robbers in the bank nervous, and they hurried the bank officers out and told them to run. This was done to save their lives. Bullets flew thick and fast, and the bank men hastened around the corner with several shots flying after them. George Buckingham, who was shooting at the robbers in the alley, was shot and killed. While he was lying on the ground the robbers shot at him several times. City Marshal Muckleroy, who was shooting at another robber, received a ball in the abdomen. The robbers rode rapidly out of town shooting their rifles and displaying their money. That was the last seen of them.

Some days ago, however, word was brought to the marshals that a band of desperadoes had come in the country near Elk, and were making their headquarters with a man named Houston Wallace. When the Longview bank robbery occurred it was learned that the horses ridden by the men were stolen near Elk, also the last heard of their trail on their return from the raid they were going in the direction of this place.

Saturday morning Houston Wallace came to town, accompanied by two women. He had an unusual amount of money, and bought a wagon load of provisions, suitable for traveling with complete camp outfit. He visited the hardware store and laid in an enormous quantity of ammunition. Deputy Marshal T. Lindsey was suspicious that something was wrong, as Wallance is a man of very small means. After loading his wagon, Wallace had a large box put on from the express office. Deputy Lindsey resolved to search the outfit, and did so, finding three gallons of whisky. The large amount of ammunition and the various purchases further aroused his suspicion, and he resolved to go to Wallace's home, thinking the bank robbers were there.

The man and two women were held under arrest by Commissioner Gibbons on the whisky charge, while Deputy Lindsey secured as a posse Deputies Denton, Letherman, Booker, Reynolds, Hart, Freeman and E. W. Roberts, to raid Wallace's place. They left Ardmore Saturday night, riding by a circuitous route, and reaching Wallace's place about daylight the next morning. The house was quickly surrounded, but a woman had seen the deputies, and gave the alarm.

Dalton rushed to a rear window and leaped out, but was ordered to halt by Deputy Hart, who commanded him to stop three times. Dalton refused, and pulled his pistol, when Hart fired, striking Dalton in the left side. Dalton fell, and expired in a few moments.

Another of the band was seen at a window but escaped into a thicket near the house, where pursuit was useless.

The house was then entered and searched and over 150 letters besides numerous rolls of crisp bank bills were found.

There is not the least possibility of a doubt as to the identity of Dalton, as letters were found in his trunk, and the woman in the house with him proved to be his wife. Mrs.

Bill Dalton as He Looked Last Fall.

Dalton seems very much affected over the death of her husband, but says she always expected him to meet his death as he did. Dalton was married in California. He leaves his widow with two small girls, one of whom is a cripple.

The working up of the case and the execution reflects great credit on Deputy Lindsey, who had charge from beginning to end. The officers reached town with the body of Dalton about 6 o'clock in the evening. The streets leading to the undertaker's was thronged with an eager crowd trying to get a glimpse of the most noted outlaw in this country since the time of the James boys. The body was embalmed, to await officials from Longview, who had been wired to come. A sum of money was found in Dalton's trunk, along with a corn sack, such as is usually used by banks. The officers refuse to talk until the other two are captured. They are well-known as hard characters, and the marshals expect to effect their capture.

The body of the noted bandit was viewed at the undertaker's establishment where it was embalmed for shipment to San Fran-

RUDELY SNATCHED

From His Bride's Side While Congratulations Were Yet Exchanged.

Charles Lamb's Wedding to Miss Davis Is Followed by Prompt Arrest.

This Gallant Groom Fondled Others Besides Clara and Loved Minnie Neubert Not Wisely but Too Well.

Charles Lamb a handsome looking blonde conductor with fine chop siders and a delicately curled mustache that would be the delight of a tenor singer, is in deep trouble. He has just embarked on the matrimonial seas, and his frail bark is having tough weather. His troubles began literally, one might say, at the altar.

Lamb was married Wednesday to Miss Clara Davis. The wedding had just been solemnized and the two score invited guests and friends of the happy couple had scarcely concluded their congratulations, when an unfeeling policeman stepped in and said that he wanted the groom—and he wanted him right then. This took place at Burnside, a suburb of Chicago.

There's a little story in it, and of course another woman. Without another woman a story of this sort would necessarily be ridiculously flat. Miss Minni Neubert is the other woman, and, with the assistance of her mother, Mrs. Kate Neubert, caused the rumpus. They succeeded in separating the wedded pair before the groom's tip to the minister had had time to grow cold in the dominie's pocket.

The warrant sworn out by Mrs. Neubert, whose home is in Kensington, avenue, charges Mr. Lamb with assaulting her daughter. According to Minnie's tale of woe, Lamb had been keeping her company for a year or more, and matters had progressed in such fine style that their marriage seemed only a question of a little while; in short, that Lamb had offered to make Minnie "his'n" forever and had been promptly accepted.

While this appeared to be the case and there seemed to be no possible way of escape that glad day when their hearts should be glued together and beat as one there was no friction between Miss Neubert and her adored one. In fact, it is not of record that Mrs. Neubert placed large obstacles in the roadway of the couple.

But trouble brewed fast. Another charmer appeared. She is the young woman who until yesterday was Miss Clara Davis and later in the day secured the position coveted by Minnie. Their courtship must have been less boisterous, for no one knew that they were to be married until Sunday when Charles hunted his old flame and told her of his decision to make Miss Davis his bride. There was some exclamations of surprise; then a course of tears, a collapse upon the part of the jilted one and then followed threats of revenge. The couple finally parted in friendliness, at least so it seemed to Lamb, but here is where he knew not of woman's craftiness. Wednesday morning Minnie appeared at Charles' boarding house. She pleaded for her old love and sought by all sorts of artifices to kindle the dead embers. The appeal fell flat. It was then that dire revenge entered her little cabalistic head. She swore a warrant for assault on Lamb and it was served as related above.

Just what the nature of the assault was Miss Minnie didn't say, but she avers Mrs. Lamb will be interested in its recital.

CHASED THROUGH A CHURCH.

Father of a Girl, With a Big Revolver, Makes It Hot for Janitor Neile.

George L. Bellows, a Chicago printer, chased Willis Neile, an assistant janitor at the Moody church, on Chicago avenue, through several rooms of the church Wednesday with a revolver. Although Bellows told the assistant janitor several times that he intended to shoot him and during the chase was in range frequently he did not fire a shot. Neile ran into the apartments of Head Janitor R. R. Aitchison, on the third floor.

Mr. Aitchison then took a hand in the affair and called upon Bellows for an explanation. The party adjourned to another room, to which Mrs. Bellows and her daughter Nannie, 15 years old, who had accompanied Bellows to the church, were admitted. The parents of the girl accused Neile of planning to elope with her. He denied the charge and the girl also said it was untrue. Then Mr. and Mrs. Bellows wanted to know where Neile was last Thursday night, upon which occasion their daughter was away from home until a late hour. He satisfied them that he was at home sick, where he had been for a week. He also explained the buying of a new hymn book for the girl by saying he had accidentally broken the cover of her book and she insisted upon his buying her a new one. Then Mr. and Mrs. Bellows and Miss Bellows gathered up the revolver and returned to their home.

HE WANTED AN OFFICE.

And if You Will Carefully Read This You'll Learn What He Got.

Washington, June 15.—Mark Twain's story of the man who went to Washington as an applicant for a foreign mission and gradually abated his demands until he would have taken a janitorship if he could have got it is not nearly so pitiful as the case of A. C. Chewing, who was picked up senseless from hunger in the Smithsonian grounds a few nights ago.

Chewing came from Virginia six weeks before in the hope of obtaining a government situation. His money became exhauted, he was forced to leave his boarding house, and when he was picked up unconscious by a policeman he had eaten nothing for four days. It is to the credit of the people of Washington, who are not commonly credited with much sympathy for unfortunates like Chewing, that they have raised a comfortable sum of money and sent him back to his wife and children in Virginia, who, it turns out, were also starving.

The moral of the incident is plain. Any man who can make a bare living at anything else should shun the idea of getting a "political job" as he would pestilence. The best of these positions, even after they are secured, are neither permanent nor comfortable. The pursuit of them, in nine cases out of ten, results in disappointment and misery.

OUTLAWS ARE DEFEATED.

Officers in the Indian Territory Prevent a Wholesale Robbery by Timely Arrival.

Wagoner, I. T., June 15.—A battle took place the other day between a band of outlaws and deputy marshals at Claremoon, thirty miles northwest of here. Four armed men rode into town and hitched their horses in the rear of George Eaton's store. Two of the men were identified as horse thieves whom the authorities had long been hunting, and a posse of officers immediately placed them under arrest and started with them to the jail.

When about half way the two remaining bandits opened fire upon them with Winchester rifles, which was warmly returned by the marshals, driving the outlaws to their ponies and out of town. The firing was kept up by the officers as long as the bandits remained within range. One of the horses was riddled with bullets and his rider wounded, it is thought fatally, but he made his escape into the brush. Close investigation brought to light the fact that there was a big robbery on foot and has led to the arrest of eight or nine men of this place who it is thought were implicated with them.

BROOKLYN'S HAIR CLIPPER.

Six Inches Cut Off Mary Zimmerman's Braid in an Elevated Railroad Station.

The hair clipper has reappeared in Brooklyn, N. Y., and has clipped off part of a braid of pretty 14-year-old Mary Zimmerman. She went down town on an elevated train to attend a class at the Young Women's Christian association. Her glossy brown hair was shorn while she was on the platform of the Bridge street station. She thus describes how the clipper did his work.

"As I entered the gate at the station I felt a slight tug on my hair, which was closely braided and tied with a ribbon. I turned around in time to see a man who was close behind step back a pace and then move off quickly. It was not until I called at a friend's house that I discovered that my hair had been cut through about five or six inches from the end."

AFTER SUNKEN TREASURE.

A. Bauman, a capitalist of Johannesburg, South Africa, is floating an enterprise to recover $1,500,000 in sunken treasure. The gold is contained in two iron safes which went down with the ship Birkenhead off the African coast forty years ago.

MADE A BIG HAUL.

Newell B. Parsons, aged 24, and a society leader at Saginaw, Mich., has been convicted of stealing railroad bonds valued at $463,000, which he sent to Grand Rapids for safe keeping. The bonds were recovered.

BACK TO VATERLAND

Hundreds of Uncle Sam's Foreign Born Citizens Disgusted With This Country.

Hard Times and Labor Unions, They Claim, Have Forced Them Out of Good Jobs.

Scandinavians, Italians and Germans Are the Nationalities Most Affected—Low Rates an Inducement.

Our foreign born citizens are going back home. Since the 1st of March a tidal-wave of homesickness and discontent seems to have swept over the Scandinavian, Italian and German residents of Chicago. In some neighborhoods entire families are packing up their belongings and taking passage for the fatherland.

It is remarked that a large proportion of these emigrants belong to the higher class of artisans—carpenters, iron-workers and molders—and in perhaps half of the cases they have sold out all their possessions and are taking the money that remains after their tickets are procured to the old country, where it is their expressed intention to remain the rest of their days.

Among the Italians the lowest classes are remaining in America, principally for the reason that they cannot get enough money ahead to take them away.

Wednesday one of the waiting-room of Dearborn station was crowded with several hundreds of these emigrants and their baggage. They had all taken passage on a steamer leaving New York the last of the week, and a jollier crowd of travelers it would have been hard to find. They seemed wonderfully pleased at the prospect of getting out of the United States. Many of them had been in the country but a few years, and they had undergone a marvelous change from the shawl-headed stolid, practically penniless condition in which they arrived. All of them were neatly dressed, and by the number of bundles, valises and band boxes which they carried it was evident that they were far from being dependent on charity.

There were a great many different reasons assigned for leaving the country. First and foremost, all the men complained of hard times and of inability to obtain employment at living wages. One or two men said they could not get along with the labor unions, and cited several instances in which they had been forced out of jobs by the walking delegates. It had made them so disgusted that they concluded to go back to Norway.

"You see," said a brawny Swedish carpenter, "we can't make a living here and it is much cheaper for us to go home, especially when the rates of travel are so low. One dollar in Scandinayia will go as far as four here. Besides that, times are better all over Europe than they are in this country and we can probably secure employment at good wages."

The agents of the various steamship lines tell a convincing story of the emigration spirit. It was the general consensus of opinion among them that fully four times as many emigrants had left so far this spring as in any previous year. Among these the largest number are Scandinavians, but there are also many Italians, Germans, Poles and a few Scotchmen.

MAUD RUBLE'S MURDER.

Dr. Brown Is Formally Arraigned and Sam Payne, a Negro, Is Also Arrested.

Omaha, Neb., June 14.—Dr. William P. Brown who was arrested charged with the murder of pretty Maude Ruble has been arraigned. Little light has been thrown on the mysterious case. Yesterday, however, Samuel Payne, a negro who had occupied the house where the body was found up to within a few days of its discovery, and whose wife was found in possession of the girl's jewelry, was captured in Mystic, Iowa, and brought to Omaha. Payne fled from the city the night the girl's body was found. The day following Dr. Brown, with whom Miss Ruble had kept company, was arrested.

Payne says he met Brown on the street one night and the doctor handed him a bundle, remarking, "Here's a present for you." On opening it he found the Ruble rings. He will be subjected to a rigid cross-examination and the police are sure he will give the details of the murder. Their theory is that Brown murdered the girl in a fit of anger when she demanded that he fulfill his promise of marriage and then employed Payne to assist him in concealing the body. The defense claims that the body found is not that of Maude Ruble; that she is alive and well, and that she has absented herself in this manner to secure notoriety to enable her to go on the stage, for which she had a passion.

A POPULIST MURDERER.

Peyton G. Bowman, Leader of Kolb's Alabama Campaign, Shoots Down Eugene Jeffries.

Birmingham, Ala., June 14.—Eugene Jeffries, the mayor's son was murdered in cold blood yesterday by Peyton G. Bowman, the leader of Kolb's populist campaign in this state. Late in the afternoon while Bowman was drinking and talking in a loud voice in the saloon ex-Mayor Jeffries entered when, it is said, Bowman made an insulting remark to him. Jeffries replied by saying Bowman had had a confederate deserter for a law partner. The lie was passed, when Bowman struck Jeffries twice, knocking him down. Colonel Jeffries is an old and inoffensive man, small in size and feeble. Friends separated them, and Jeffries went his way.

When Eugene Jeffries, a mere stripling, heard of the insult to his father, it is said, he expressed his intention to have Bowman apologize About 8 o'clock young Jeffries entered the saloon Just as he put his head through the folding doors Bowman snatched out a pistol and fired at him. The ball entered the boy's neck, breaking it, and he died instantly.

Bowman surrendered, and was hurried off to jail. Immediately a great crowd of indignant citizens began gathering at the scene. Threats of lynching were freely indulged in, but it is not thought the threats will be put into execution. One story is that Bowman's brother held Jeffries while Bowman shot him. Bowman claims that Jeffries was armed, but this is denied. Excitement is intense, the general opinion being that it was a cold-blooded murder. The effect of the murder on Kolb's campaign will be most disastrous.

AMERICAN RAILWAY UNION CONVENTION.

Several hundred delegates are in attendance at the first quadrennial convention of the American railway Union now in session in Chicago. In his opening address President Eugene V. Debs paid his respects to the Pullman corporation in no uncertain tones. He then promised that the strike of the employes at Pullman would occupy the attention of the convention, and it is reported that these words mean no less than the tying up of Pullman cars on all railway lines. The union then proceeded to business, and passed a resolution denouncing the Tawney bill now before congress on the compulsory arbitration of labor troubles. The union will be in session several days.

IS THE STRIKE ENDED?

The miners' representatives and the operators assembled in Columbus, Ohio, and agreed upon a scale of wages for the miners in all sections of the United States. Some of the miners appear to be satisfied with it and some do not. Whether the arrangement wil actually end the strike cannot be foretold at this writing.

GOT $400,000 FOR KEEPING SOBER.

George Crocker, the youngest son of the California millionaire, has just been paid $400,000, the amount promised him in case he should keep sober for five years. Another $100,000 will be paid him if he keeps sober during the next five years. At that rate George will never land in the poor house.

BROKE HIS JAWBONE.

Perry Watkins, a colored pugilist of fame local to Jacksonville, Fla., is in the hands of the police for breaking the jawbone of Tom Reddick in a set-to. Watkins swears that the affair was a friendly scrap for points. Reddick will think differently till he can chew again.

A LAD MURDERED FROM AMBUSH.

Frank Richards, an 18-year-old lad of Mauckport, Ind., was shot from ambush and killed while returning home from church recently. The bullet hit young Richards behind the ear, killing him almost instantly. No cause is known for the attack, and no clue to the murderer.

TOO HOT FOR GROVER.

Washington, June 14.—Since the warm weather set in President Cleveland has been considerably indisposed and constantly under the doctor's care He is allowed no exercise and receives no callers. Mrs. Cleveland and the babies are at Buzzard's Bay, Mass.

THE SOLDIER BOYS WERE DRUNK.

The Canadian government has satisfactorily explained the incident of hauling down the stars and stripes at St. Thomas, Ont., on the queen's birthday, by stating that the militiamen were drunk and will be properly dealt with.

AVENGED HER HONOR

Alexander McKillop, Betrayer of Miss Keatley, Is Murdered by Her Father and Brother.

Had Scornfully Refused to Right the Wrong and They Took His Life.

Shocking Sequel to an Illicit Love Between a Gay Girl Cashier and a Street Car Conductor.

Alexander McKillop, a conductor for the Chicago City railway was murdered almost in front of his home on Wabash avenue shortly after midnight Tuesday. At first the shooting of the man was wrapped up in considerable mystery, and it was thought that footpads had done the deed. Subsequent developments however reveal quite a different story. The shooting occurred in front of the Haven school building on Wabash avenue near Fifteenth street.

When the detectives began investigating they did not have any trouble in finding a clew. They found that McKillop had boarded at 1536 Wabash avenue. He drew his month's wages Monday and in the evening left to go to Hyde Park. Shortly after he left two men called at the boarding house and asked to see McKillop. They were told that he was out. At 10 o'clock another man came and asked Mrs. Johnson, the colored woman, who occupies the basement at 1536, if McKillop had reutrned. He was answered, no. Shortly before 11 o'clock the first man came back. When asked what he wanted with McKillop, he answered: "That's all right. I'll wait till I see him."

McKillop came in about 11:20 and went out to the dining-room. He was eating when the door-bell rang. McKillop went to the door. Officer Rogers heard him make some laughing remark, and then he went away. That was the last time he was seen alive by any of the boarders. McKinley, who keeps the boarding house in Wabash aveneue, told the police that McKillop had compromised Miss Emily Keatley of 7840 Emerald avenue, and that her father and brother had insisted upon his marrying her. McKillop had said he would rather commit suicide than marry the girl. It was on this information that the real facts in the case were found out. The Keatleys were arrested and Orlando Keatley the son confessed.

According to his confession, McKillop had been acquainted with Miss Keatley for some time. The marriage of the two was opposed by the members of the family, but Mrs. Keatley finally consented to it. The wedding was set for several dates, but McKillop steadily failed to appear. It was set finally for last Saturday, but McKillop again remained away. The father and the son had in the meantime found out the relations existing between McKillop and Miss Keatley and they decided upon radical measures. They told McKillop that he must marry the girl. He refused. Then they planned his death.

They called again and again at the boarding house in Wabash avenue Monday night. They knew that McKillop was not working. When he saw them at the door he was evidently not frightened, for he joked with them and left a few moments later. They had gone but a few steps when the father and son turned on McKillop. The exclamation, "Then die, you cur," was heard. Five shots were fired, some by both men. Two of them took effect and death came almost instantly.

From persons who saw part of the tragedy it was ascertained that after McKillop had fallen and lay with his face to the ground one of the men struck a match, turned over the body and examined it to make sure that death had ensued. After the shooting the father held the small crowd that had come up at bay. Then both the men escaped.

The son, Orlando Keatley, is a lawyer, 28 years old. His father, Calvin F. Keatley, is an old resident in good circumstances.

GIVES BIRTH TO TRIPLETS.

Mrs. Jerry Brown, of Broadland, Ill., six miles north of Newman, gave birth Monday to three children, two girls and a boy. The girls weighed eight pounds each, while the boy tipped the beam at seven pounds. All are alive and going well.

DIED FOR LOVE.

Benjamin F. Cox, a prominent young Boston man loved Laura Wheelwright, and the day she was married to a young Englishman, who came over after her, Benjamin took a sip of cold paison and died.

THE HONDO HERALD.

VOL. 4. HONDO CITY, TEXAS. AUG. 31, 1894. NO. 28.

OUR APOLOGY.

THE HERALD is much reduced in size owing to the fact that our paper is held over in San Antonio on account of the wash-out. This issue is gotten out in small calibre merely as a diversion. It may help you to fight off ennui while you are waiting for the resumption of traffic.

RAIN AND RUIN.

Another glorious rain visited this section Wednesday night and Thursday morning. It is difficult to estimate the quantity of water that fell, but it is generally agreed that this is the heaviest rain in fourteen years.

Cotton is safe, winter range is assured and all tanks, waterholes and even hogwallows are full to overflowing. The Hondo river was full—in fact, was on a regular tear. There was a greater rise than is known since 1880, and the adjacent territory was threated with inundation, the water being 8 feet deep in some houses.

At D'Hanis the flood caused sad havoc. The Seco railroad bridge, the section house and four miles of track were washed away. Two children of Mr. Benedict Deckert were drowned, and it was only after a long search that the corpses were found. The poor man lost everything he had and steps are now being taken to alleviate his distress.

The scene at D'Hanis beggars description. The company has a large number of men at work repairing the damage, but the work has been delayed by rain, and it is impossible to tell when trains will run again.

The Leona bridge was washed away and half the town of Uvalde flooded. Six lives were lost. Reports from there are meager, as telegrams have to go by way of El Paso. Charley Metzger, who went to Uvalde the other day, telegraphed that he is safe, but lost both his horses.

No trains were run yesterday, except those carrying materials and men to the scene of disaster, and at this writing (Friday noon) traffic has not been resumed. Our postal facilities are completely stopped by reason of this tie-up.

The telephone line between here and Castroville is grounded and communication has not yet been established.

—The board of trustees have secured the services of Prof. S. M. Grubbs of Pearsall as principal of the Hondo City Academy for the ensuing year, with Miss Vannie Fourqueron of San Marcos for assistant. Both come well recommended as teachers and we trust that under their management the school will be kept up to its present high standard. The time for the opening of the public term has not yet been decided on, but the private term will September 17.

—Celeste Pingenot is the only man who can travel these days. He came in on the convict train after laying over at Lacoste a day or so.

A Shocking Tragedy.

A deed terrible in its nature and horrible in its results was enacted in San Antonio Tuesday morning. Dr. Andrew O'Malley committed the deed, and his little 3-year-old babe was the victim.

Between the hours of 1 and 2 o'clock Dr. O'Malley was awakened by a noise in the front part of his house, and as, according to his own statement, he had been disturbed several times by burglars he thought that the cause, and taking his pistol, cocked the weapon and proceeded in search of the intruder. The front room was examined and the doctor then went into the room occupied by his son ,Justin, and a nephew aged 10 years. Here he ascertained that the noise which aroused him was caused by the door bumping against the cot on which the boys were sleeping. Justin, the baby boy, was lying on the edge of the cot with one arm and a leg hanging over. The father endeavored to turn the child over, keeping the cocked pistol in his hand, and as he did so the pistol was discharged. The ball entered the child's right side going clear through its body ranging down and landing under the skin on the lefs side. The boy awoke and seeing his father cried:

"PAPA, IT HURTS AWFUL!"

The father glanced at his child for a moment before he realized what an awful deed he had done. Then, supposing that the wound was fatal and aendered insane by the fearful accident, he deliberately placed the pistol to the child's forehead and fired again, killing the little one instantly.

Several hours after he notified a neigboring physician who summoned the police, and Dr. O'Malley was lodged in the county jail on a charge of lunacy.

The unfortunate man has lived in San Antonio but a short time, but had made many friends, who admired him for his brilliancy and attainments. He is believed to be insane, caused by injuries received several years ago and the habitual use of cocaine.

Public Meeting.

The people of Hondo City and vicinity will please take notice that Prof. C. Vincent of Indianapolis, Ind., will deliver lectures on reform in Medina county at the following places, to-wit:

Devine, September 4, 1894.
Hondo City, September 5, 1894.
Castroville, September, 6, 1894.

Prof. Vincent is an able speaker and everybody who wishes to hear a good speech should come out to hear him.

M. SAATHOFF, Chairman.
A. B. BRUCKS, Secretary.

—Miss Rose Bailey is visiting friends in picturesque Castroville.

—Joe Carle and Earnest Leinweber took in the festivities at Castroville Saturday.

—The Divine Providence school will open next Monday.

—Miss Georgia Bailey returned from a visit to San Antonio Wednesday.

—The Misses McLemore of Lavernia are visiting Mrs. Herring.

—All kinds of job printing executed in the highest style of art at this office. Call and see samples and prices.

SHERIFF'S SALE.

STATE of TEXAS, }
County of Medina. }

By virtue of an Order of Sale, issued out of the Honorable District Court of Medina county, on the 31st day of July, A. D. 1894, by the clerk thereof, in the case of Louis Oge versus John B. Moeur and John K. Moeur, No. 1047, and to me, as Sheriff, directed and delivered, I have this 31st day of July, A. D. 1894, seized and taken into my possession, the land hereinafter described, and will proceed to sell the same for cash, within the hours prescribed by law for Sheriff's Sales, on the

irst Tuesday in September,

A. D. 1894, it being the 4th day of said month, before the court house door of said Medina County, in the town of Hondo City, the following described property, to wit:

Situated in Medina county, Texas, being lots One (1) to Twenty (20) inclusive, in Block Number 3, as per map of J. K. Moeur's Addition to Hondo City, recorded in Book A. No. 25, page 623, of Record of Deeds of Medina Co., Texas, in office of clerk of county court of Medina county, Texas; said block No. 3 being the Southwest quarter of a 20-acre tract conveyed by the G. H. & S. A. Railway Co. to J. B. Moeur, by deed recorded in Book A, No. 19, page 217, of Record of Deeds of Medina county, Texas, levied on as the property of John K. Mouer to satisfy a judgment amounting to $296.65, with interest at 10 per cent per annum from June 29, 1894, in favor of Louis Oge, and all costs of suit.

Given under my hand, this 31st day of July, A. D. 1894.

JOE NEY, Sheriff
Medina Co., Texas.

In France the population averages about 187 to the square mile. In this country the average is 21.

Sandwiches.

At this time of year flies and men are alike—both are liable to get in the soup.

Some school boys, like postage stamps, have to be licked before they will stick to their letters.

Fishermen may not tell a straight lie, but they are mighty apt to angle in that direction.

Don't think less of a man because he runs from his creditors. He is only footing his bills.

The ladies should remember that if they are given equal political privileges with men they will have to work the roads as long as they live, for no woman ever gets past 45.

There is danger that some member of congress may after a while commit suicide by an accidental discharge of his duty.

The reason why boarding house butter generally lasts so long is that boarders have too much respect for old age to stick a knife into it.

THE Populist representative convention convened at Pearsall yesterday. Who will be nominated can not even be conjectured as Populist conventions are as inscrutable as a jury in a justice of the peace's court.

The town of Hubbard in Ohio is running itself. Both the mayor and city marshal are in jail, the former for intoxication and the latter for not obeying orders.

—Candidates should have their cards printed at THE HERALD office.

A Sad Death.

Death, with its icy hand, has been among us, and Mina Graff, beloved wife of Mr. Emil Graff has departed from this vale of sorrows to a brighter realm above.

To one who knew her from early infancy and has seen her grow up into blushing maidenhood, to one who has seen her wedded to the man of her choice and face the stern realities of life with all the ardor of youth, this announcement causes ineffable sadness, but even to strangers this visita of the angel of death causes a sigh and a tear.

When a woman is taken away from her husband and babes who is there so callous as not to pay at least the "passing tribute of a sigh?"

Such is the case here, and what makes it so peculiarly pathetic is that her husband is lying critically ill with typhoid fever and is not yet aware of his great loss.

The deceased was born in Quihi and is a daughter of Mr. and Mrs. F. L. Boehle. She married about three years ago and at the time of her death was the mother of two children.

The last sad rites were performed upon the remains Tuesday afternoon, in the presence of a large concourse of relatives and friends.

THE HERALD extends its warmest sympathy to the bereaved family.

—Mr. and Mrs. Joe Ehlinger attended the celebration at Castroville Monday.

—For a general tie-up a wash-out beats Debs all to smash.

—Mr. Victor Euen of Black Creek was in the city Monday. He reports heavy rains and the finest of prospects for a big cotton crop. Victor is a staunch Democrat, but condemns the action of the San Antonio convention, and says the Democrats of his precinct are indignant at the methods employed in defeating Judge Paschal.

—We are pleased to say that we are not a bit envious at the success Mr. Chancey is attaining in the rainmaking line; we only feel pangs of remorse because we did not turn it over to him long before we did.

—The colored people have had a religious revival out on the creek, conducted by Rev. L. F. Fitzgerald of Yoakum. The oldest colored man in the county, Reuben Knowles, among others, got religion.

—Mr. B. M. Simmons and family returned Tuesday from an extended visit to friends and relatives in Brazos county. Although Mr. Simmons is short one daughter he seems to be in good spirits.

—Prof. H. L. Stewart left Tuesday for Sabinal to enter upon his duties as principal of the public school in that town. He is a teacher of ability and experience and we wish him success.

—We erroniously stated last week that Prof. Woolls had moved to Pearsall. The fact is he has not yet moved but will do so shortly.

—H. B. Taylor, candidate for assessor, spent several days in the ancient town of Castroville last week.

—Mr. M. D. Stewart and family removed this week to Sabinal, where they will in future reside.

—August Kempf and Celeste Pingenot went to Castroville Monday to attend the picnic.

—Sheriff Ney is on the sick list.

The Cuero Daily Record.

VOLUME 3. CUERO, TEXAS MONDAY EVENING, AUGUST 19, 1895. NUMBER 30

ROMANCE OF THE BORDER.

How Bill Doolan, a Notorious Bandit, Won a Schoolma'am's Love.

About two years ago Bill Dalton, Bill Doolan and their gang held up a train near Gainesville, Tex. While the members of the band were rifling the express car Doolan held the passengers in their seats by the persuasive use of a Winchester. On the car back of the smoker, says a correspondent of the Philadelphia Press, was a pretty girl who was going to the Chickasaw country to teach school, and her face seemed to attract the outlaw, for he inquired where she was going and her business.

A few months later a good-looking fellow began to be seen in the vicinity of Purcell, where the girl, Belle Bailey, taught school. The two became friends and then lovers. People warned the girl against Ballard, as the man called himself, but the young lady paid no attention to them. About a year ago Deputy Marshal Spears happened to ride into the place where Miss Bailey taught school, and found there this man Ballard. The recognition was mutual. Both went for their guns, but the stranger was the quicker of the two.

"Get down off your horse," he commanded, when he saw he had the drop on the officer. Spears obeyed.

"I won't kill you," said Ballard, "because I want to reform, if you'll let me, but I don't propose to be shot in the back. Unbuckle your belt and throw it away. Be careful how you do it, or you are a dead man."

The deputy obeyed and was left bound with his own handcuffs. During the melee the girl stood as though petrified. As she saw her lover about to turn away she said: "Who and what are you?"

"Bill Doolan," replied the man. "I want to reform, but they won't let me."

Common rumor has it that Miss Bailey did not give up her outlaw lover even after she knew who he was. She lost her school, and six months ago she disappeared. No one knows just where the pretty school-teacher drifted to, but it is a fact that for the past year Doolan has been very quiet, and for four months no one has seen him in the territory. Sensational telegraphic reports sent out in regard to fights with the "notorious Bill Doolan" have proved fakes in every instance.

A CENTURY OF WAR.

Soldiers Killed During the Battles of One Hundred Years.

When the revolution broke out France's effective army was only 120,000 men. For the wars waged during ten years, in Belgium, on the Sambre, the Meuse, the Rhine, the Alps, the Pyrenees, in the Vendee and in Egypt, there were called out 2,800,000. At the census made in the ninth year of the republic, says the London Lancet, there remained of these only 677,598. In the killed and in dead by disease the wars of the first republic cost France 2,122,402 men. From 1801 to Waterloo, 3,157,398 men scarcely sufficed to fill the blanks, which in an incessant war against combined Europe France incurred at Austerlitz, Jena, Auerstadt, Friedland, Saragossa, Eckmuhl, Essling, Wagram, Taragona, Smolensk, Moscow, Lutzen, Bautzen, Dresden, Leipzig and Waterloo.

Under the restoration of Louis Philippe and the second republic, in spite of the war in Spain (1823), the conquest of Algiers (1830) and the taking of Antwerp, France passed through a comparative calm. The army numbered about 213,748, and the mortality averaged 22 per 1,000. In 1853-5 commenced the epoch of the great wars—the Crimea, Italy (1859-60), China (1860-1), Mexico (1862-6) and the disasters of 1870. In the Crimea, out of 300,268 men, 95,615 succumbed; in Italy, out of 500,000, there died 18,673; in China, 950, and in Cochin China 48 per 1,000. The second empire cost France about 1,600,000 soldiers. According to Dr. Langneau's demographic tables the century from 1795 to 1895 witnessed the death in battle or by disease of 6,000,000 French soldiers.

CURIOUS TONGUES.

Those of the Woodpecker, the Parrot and the Humming Bird.

Some fresh information about the tongues of birds has recently been gathered by a German naturalist. Many people suppose that woodpeckers use their sharp-pointed tongues as darts with which to transfix their prey. It is true that the woodpecker, like the humming-bird, can dart out its tongue with astonishing rapidity, and that its mouth is furnished with an elaborate mechanism for this purpose; yet investigation shows that the object of this swift motion is only to catch the prey, not to pierce it. For the purpose of holding the captured victim, the woodpecker's tongue is furnished with a sticky secretion.

Considering its powers of imitating speech, it is not surprising to learn that the parrot's tongue resembles that of man more closely than any other bird's tongue does.

It is not because the parrot is more intelligent than many other birds, but because its tongue is better suited for articulation than theirs, that it is able to amuse us with its mimicry.

The humming-bird's tongue is in some respects the most remarkable of all. It is double nearly from end to end, so that the little bird is able to grasp its insect prey with its tongue, very much as if its mouth were furnished with a pair of fingers.

Shoes of the Olden Time.

During the reign of William Rufus, Henry I. and Stephen all sorts of extravagant shoes were worn. The toes were sometimes long and pointed and sometimes made a curl like a ram's horn. Occasionally they were twisted in different directions, as though the feet were deformed. In 1462 English ladies and gentlemen wore the points of their shoes a yard long and fastened to the garter with golden chains ornamented with bells. The custom was prohibited under pain of being cursed by the clergy, but, as it showed no signs of abating, a fine of twenty shillings was assessed for every public appearance in such shoes.

The Cuero Daily Record.

VOLUME 3. CUERO, TEXAS WEDNESDAY EVENING, AUGUST 21, 1895. NUMBER 32

COMPLETELY SURPRISED.

Miss Annie Clark of Victoria Complimented by a Surprise Party.

Yesterday the RECORD mentioned a surprise party to take place last night and it came off exactly as pre-arranged. The young people assembled at the home of Mrs. Nitsche and in a body went to Mrs. Wassermann's to surprise Miss Clark, Miss Georgia Wassermann,s guest. Those of the party were: Misses Katie and Bertha Knopp, Kossbiel, Ida and Pauline Kunitz, Letsch, Nitsche, Keller, Mangold, Ott, Gohmert, Lillie and Mamie Schnaubert, Heyer, Irene Galley of Yorktown and Josey Haller of Victoria. Messers. Able, E. and H. Verhelle, Lewis, Robt. and Geo. Heyer, Ragel, Mayne, Gus. and E. Wassermann, Zedler, Nitsche, Dromgoole, Kunitz, Keller, Gus. and R. Kleinecke. Miss Wassermann evidently had caught an inkling of what was going to happen as she was up and prepared to receive the party on its arrival, but Miss Clark was completely surprised, having retired for a night's sweet repose. She was 'roused however, hurriedly made her toilet and appeared to welcome the surprisers in a very short time, and as one of the boys expressed it, "looked simply lovely." (Can you guess the fellow?) Well, social conversation and merry making continued until the midnight hour approached when one and all said goodnight and expressed themselves as having been highly entertained.

Why buy trash when you can go to Barnes & Bunker's and get a solid silver belt pin for 25 cents; also side combs at 15 cents a pair.

IN THE VALLEY.

While out on the plains oft our eyes
Are careless in noting the view;
But down in the valley, the skies
Are dear as we look for their blue!

When flushed with our triumph we go,
We think not of God and his might;
But down in the shadows of woe,
The soul will turn Godward for light.

—Will T. Hale.

LETTERS UNCALLED FOR.

Letters remaining uncalled for in the post office at Cuero for the week ending August 20th, 1895:

Alexander, W. J.	Stowe, Mrs. L.
Arnold, Lila,	Smith, Mrs. G. W.
Banks, Miss Lucy	Sullivan, Lizzie
Brown, Miss Mary	Treal, Matta
Drake, Dock	Verner, Witte
Hill, Marion	Verner, Miss
Joneson, Josie	Welton, John
McDonald, Mrs. Jane	Williams, Mrs. F.A.
Pleasants, Tom	Wright, Chas. P.
Ryon, J. J.	Whatley, Mrs.
Slade, Littleton.	

MEXICAN LETTERS.

Albiar, Gregoria G.	Linsalda, Hinacio
Castanedo, Jesuesita	Romero, Juan
Garcia, Eligis	Tijarino, Agapito
Habes, Jose.	

RETURNED DEAD LETTERS.

Garcia, Ponciano	Rodriguez, Eulogio
Powells, Celia.	

D. W. NASH.

W. H. Sartain is at home again after a few weeks' run over the country, stopping at Yoakum a few days among other places.

All kinds of fresh bread and pies every day at the bakery of Paul Zucker, corner Main and Gonzales streets.

HE BIT THE DUST QUICK

JOHN WESLEY HARDIN SHOT DEAD IN EL PASO.

He Became Desperate and is Slain by City Marshal Sellman—A Noted Desperado Gone.

Albert Wood killed by a train at Denison.

The Lavaca grand jury found sixty indictments.

Silver men boldly defeated in the Ohio convention.

Quay probably wins the fight in Pennsylvania.

Cotton closed three to four points up yesterday in New York.

State Alliance and labor organizations in session at Lampasas.

Unknown Mexican torn to pieces by a train near Crockett, Tex.

The reform democrats won in the South Carolina elections.

E. H. Phillips committed suicide at Brownwood, using strychnine.

Chas. Rundle killed Joe Richardson with a baseball bat at Brenham.

Twelve bodies so far removed from the Denver hotel. Ten more are believed to be in the ruins.

The president has refused to pardon Edgar Bailey convicted of manslaughter in Eastern Texas.

Bud Johnson and his sister, both children, burned fatally at Benchly, Tex., by an explosion of coal oil.

A Union Pacific train held up in Nebraska and one also on the Chicago & West Michigan. No particulars were obtainable.

A. J. LaRose shot fatally by his pretty little wife at Galveston. She was driven to commit the deed because of his brutality.

The bond syndicate again prevented the gold reserve from falling below the $100,000,000 mark by depositing $2,000,000 in gold at the sub-treasury.

An unknown man took morphine in Dallas and then laid down in an ant bed. The insects partially devoured his person and he was alive when found but past recovery.

The Stockmens' Protective Association of Southern Texas is in session at Houston. It was decided to offer a reward of $50 for all persons caught setting fire to the range.

THE FORT BEND MURDER.

Wharton, Tex., Aug. 20.—No trace of the person or dead body of Sheriff Brown's murderer has yet been found. He is said to be still alive and, further, that he will be hanged to-night, but there are so many rumors that it is impossible to trace any of them. It is generally believed that he will be dead when found.

TONIGHT'S RECEPTION.

The season will be opened up tonight, by the society people in a complimentary reception and ball to Mr. and Mrs. G. A. Lackey at Turner hall. The entertainment gives promises of being, and all things point to, a most delightful occasion and everyone is looking forward to it with no little pleasure. Under the efficient management of the young gentlemen who have the affair in charge there's but little doubt that every anticipation will be wholly realized. No less than fifty couples, including married and single, will grace the occasion with their presence. The hall will be arranged in surperb condition and the entire string band will furnish music for the entertainment, so the event is bound to be a swell one. Tomorrow's RECORD will contain full account of the affair.

Better by far have no city hall than a hall that would not answer every purpose and be an ornament to the town as well as a monument portraying the enterprise and push of our "city dads." Come again.

A MATTER OF PRIDE.

Today a small lot of uncompressed cotton was shipped out of Cuero. Such action is incompatible with the growth and prosperity of the city and the RECORD trusts it will not be repeated. It matters not whether the local cotton men (who could have controlled the compressing of this lot) are stockholders in the Cuero compress or not the fact remains it is a home enterprise, and as such should move them to a better sense of their duty and we might say obligation. Their pride in home and ambition to see success crown such enterprises, which mean the future life and growth of the city, should impell them to demand the work done here. No citizen with Cuero's every interest really at heart will permit cash gain or increment of this character to leave the confines of home's sacred precincts. Cuero's institutions, both public and private, WILL always be uppermost in every true citizen's heart. The RECORD trusts it will never again have to chronicle a shipment of cotton out of the city to be compressed. It is an unpleasant duty, and the man or men who permit it, without first exhausting every legitimate means to circumvent it, are certainly unmindful of their patriotic duty to home.

REAL ESTATE TRANSFERS.

Caroline Olson to Mary Pauline Miller, south west ½ of block 28 for $10.00 and other considerations.

Ex. Stockdale and Geo. J. Schleicher executors to R. A. Pleasants and J. M. Hamilton, 17½ acres of the J. A. V. Y. Gonzales league, for $431.25.

J. W. Burns to R. A. Pleasants, undivided interest in 531 acres of the Elihu Moss league, for $75.00.

Emily Bulwer to Ida Pettitt, 95 acres of the Stevens R. Roberts' league, for $10.00 and other considerations.

Emily Bulwer to Lena Dedear, 80 acres of the Stevens R. Roberts' league, for $10.00 and other considerations.

May Smith to Chas. G. Smith, undivided interest Jno. York survey, for $2,500.00.

Wm. Mirbe to Leopold Moscheck, one lot in Yoakum, for $400.00.

S. A. & A. P. Town Site Co. to C. C. Niles, south ½ of block 68, Yoakum, for $1000.00.

Ex. Stockdale and G. J. Schlicher to W. H. Terry, lot 12, block 91, for $250.00.

W. H. Terry to A. V. Palmie, lot 12, block 91, for $475.00.

HIS FIRST "OFFENCE."

Twilight had set in and Justice Stokes, after a hard day's labor on the bench, had just taken his seat at the supper table Monday evening to do justice to a sumptuous repast, when lo! and behold! a summons came. His presence was desired at once—aye, demanded—at the county clerk's office, where two loving hearts pined for unity and awaited his coming to be made one. Noble man that he is, he responded promptly and though it would be his first offence, under such a charge, he acquitted himself with credit. (He don't always acquit.) A marriage ceremony is not always easily performed and a "marrier" who never before had the experience, to attempt to tie a Mexican knot, and that after dark with but an excuse of a lamp and neither end of the contracting string acquainted with his own language, does well to say "It is enough, I pronounce you man and wife;" but when he goes through the entire ceremony without a bobble, except in calling the names, he deserves credit and prompt pay, both of which he got and the couple left contented and happy and Stokes did it.

Character reading from the teeth is the latest. Those that are long and narrow denote vanity. Long projecting teeth indicate a grasping disposition; treachery is known by small, white separated teeth; inconstancy, by overlapping teeth, and the possessor of wide separate front teeth is sure to tell all he knows.

Trust a woman who sits with her thumbs elevated—she may be determined but she is truthful. The one who conceals her thumbs is quite apt to be deceitful. Observe the thumb also if you desire to judge intellectual strength, for the longer it is; proportionately, the greater the strength of the brain.

These warm days a plunge in the Natatorium will help things wonderfully—have you tried it?

FOR SALE.

Ten acres of land, fenced, with two houses on it, fronting on Aransas Pass railroad near cotton compress. Also two stores on Esplanade street, occupied by telegraph and post offices. Terms, part cash; balance on long time. Also four head thoroughbred Holstien cattle.

W. H. CRAIN.

MARRIAGE LICENSES.

Marriage licenses issued since Aug. 19: Chas. M. Taylor to Miss Annie Hepsebeth Dowlearn. James C. Merritt to Miss Pearl Lee Roader. Valentine Basquez to Clemencia Sauches.

Cuero's brag violinist, Chas. Flick, is back from a several weeks' visit and summer outing to Port Lavaca. Charley speaks in glowing terms of his sojourn on the bay and says he is now ready to resume his duties. He will organize his music class again this fall.

The scarcity of carpenters is a noticable fact in Cuero. Those that are here are kept as busy as bees constantly and the demand seems to be steadily increasing. This speaks volumes for a growing town. And still we grow.

A better meal for 25 cents cannot be had in the state than that served by Chas. Lenz, at his famous restaurant.

NO TRACE OF THE NEGRO.

Disappearance of Deputy Brown's Murderer Still a Mystery.

TOBACCO OF MONTGOMERY COUNTY

Will Be Made Into Cigars at Willis. Burglars Entered Many Houses at Lexington—Suicided.

Wharton, Texas, August 20.—(Special Correspondence.)—A veil of mystery seems to hang over the recent tragedy as to what has been the fate of the murderer of Deputy Sheriff Brown. That strip of the county in which the search for the escape has been going on is the most remote and inaccessible portion of this section. The larger part of the territory is covered with heavy timber, reinforced by thick and impenetrable undergrowth. As to local happenings a long time transpires before the matter became public property. Grave doubts are now entertained by a very large body of people as to the truth of the report that the negro escaped from the custody of the posse who had him last in charge. But people who seem to know show a very firm disinclination to discuss the whole affair and maintain that the "negro escaped." Today Constable Heartt tells The Post reporter that he is certain that the negro who committed the murder was not an escaped convict, but had been at work several days prior to the tragedy in and about town, and that he decamped suddenly from this locality about the time the murder took place. He has other matters bearing upon the subject, which he refused to let The Post representative publish.

This morning Mr. W. M. James, who has been near the scene of action and who was present with the posse when the negro was in their possession yesterday morning, tells the reporter substantially the following story:

"There were about twelve or fifteen men in the party who had the prisoner in charge; they had a rope or a chain around his neck, I think chain, for there was also a padlock on it. He was fully questioned by different men of the posse, and he was induced to confess to the killing, which he did voluntary, saying in brief that while the deputy was in advance horseback, he (the prisoner) having a pistol concealed in his bosom, took a favorable opportunity and shot the deputy in the back; the first shot disabled him; he fired twice with the pistol and taking the dead man's gun, fired once again into the body. He told where he hid the gun, etc."

James says that he lingered only about ten or fifteen minutes with the posse and firmly maintains that he does not know what became of the prisoner after he left.

Sheriff Rich returned from Spanish Camp last evening and brought the two negroes arrested at that point by M. S. Anderson, and supposed to be two of the escaped convicts.

This morning Adam Howard, a colored man, brought in a negro who confesses to being one of the escapes from the State farm in Matagorda county.

Sheriff Rich has gone down in the lower precinct to the scene of the recent tragedy.

At 5 p. m. Sheriff Rich returned from the lower precinct, where he went this morning, as indicated above, in search of some traces of the murderer. The sheriff says though he interrogated several parties no one can furnish him the least information as to what has become of the escape. All affirm that the prisoner escaped. There are, however several rumors afloat, the last one—which is given the most credence—is that the negro is alive and under a strong guard, hidden away and that tonight the crowd will meet and take a vote on the disposition to be made of him—whether he will hang or be brought to the county seat and placed safely in jail to await the action of the courts. W.F.L.

Montgomery County Tobacco.

Willis, Texas, August 19.—Contractor Leslie has resumed work on the brick tobacco warehouse for T. W. Smith, after a suspension of work of two weeks on account of being out of brick. The building will be ready for business in thirty days. It is rumored there is a project on foot by which this building will be converted into a large cigar factory. It is the object of those interested to form a joint stock company with sufficient capital to buy up all of last year's crop of tobacco here and employ about twenty cigarmakers, putting out 50,000 cigars per month. The demand for Willis cigars has increased to such an extent that it is impossible for Blohm Brothers to fill the orders. The fact that these men have never had a salesman on the road and have never sent out any advertising matter, and receive orders for cigars from all over this and several other States is sufficient guarantee that a large factory here would pay well if properly managed.

Mr. C. B. French of Kansas City, a leading tobacco man of that city, accompanied by Mr. C. F. Rhode, a cigar man of Galveston, spent two days here this week on business connected with hese tobacco firms. They had quite a leasant time mingling with tobacco rowers and talking tobacco.

Besides being a tobacco man Mr. French an old hog raiser and is now negotiang for a 300 acre tract of land near here, which he says he will start a "long ... hog ranch.

. Barth from Iowa, who owns 800 land south of here, will soon nice residence on his place and is on letting a contract for it to be brick.

A Most Horrible Death.

, Texas, August 20.—An unknown ridently about 45 years of age, ghing 170 pounds, was found lying river bank near the brick yard rning. A negro woman discovered d furnished assistance. He died The physicians say that he swalnorphine yesterday and had evipeen exposed to the sun of the dews of the night for twelve or hours. Worse than all, the unrtunate man had selected for his resting place the home of a colony of red ants, and when found they had swarmed in his ears, eyes and mouth. His nostrils vere crowded with the insects and the ests had partially devoured him. He ngered in great agony for three hours ter the negress found him, and death ist have been a Godsend. The police icers say that it was the most sickening ne they have been called on to witness many years.

Palestine Camp U. C. V.

Palestine, Texas, August 19.—Palestine camp No. 44, United Confederate Veterans, met tonight in Glenn's hall, with J. W. Ozment, commander, presiding and Adjutant John Young as secretary. The minutes of the previous meeting was read and approved. Little business was done except to hear reports of committees appointed at last meeting. This camp has reorganized and its officers and members are fully determined to keep up the same.

A Sailor Burned.

Orange, Texas, August 20.—This afternoon the captain of the schooner A. J. Perkins, loading at Wingate's mill, sent aboard an empty whisky barrel to be used on deck as a water cask. A sailor, Henry Elfstone, cut a square hole in the barrel and started to charr it on the inside; when he dropped the fire into it the gas exploded, the flames leaping out and completely enveloping the sailor's body, burning his breast, left arm and mouth severely before assistance could reach here. The injuries are not dangerous, but painful and precludes the possibility of his working for some time. Elfstone's home is in Galveston, where he has a family, and he had only shipped with the Perkins yesterday, having came from Galveston on the Annie Root.

PREACHERS. SUSPENDED.

Investigating Committee Deem a Trial Necessary.

Galveston, Texas, August 20.—The committee appointed by Bishop J. C. Keener to investigate the reports in circulation in reference to Rev. E. H. Harmon and Rev. W. Wimberly has been in session for two days and concluded its inquiries at 10:30 o'clock tonight. The committee was careful and thorough in its investigation. More than a score of witnesses were examined, and information was sought from all available sources. After considering the case fully the committee rendered the following decision:

"We, the committee appointed by Bishop J. C. Keener to investigate the rumors and reports seriously affecting the moral and religious characters of Rev. E. H. Harmon, presiding elder of the Brenham district, and Rev. W. Wimberly, preacher in charge of Brenham station, have made thorough inquiry into these matters, and from the evidence before us we deem a trial necessary. Therefore, in due time, bills of charges and specifications will be formulated and copies of the same will be furnished the accused in time to allow them ample opportunity for the preparation of their defense." Signed by G. C. Rankin, O. T. Hotchkiss, C. A. Lamar.

As a result of this decision the gentlemen accused are suspended from the ministry until their cases are finally disposed of by the Texas annual conference which meets in Brenham, Texas, on the 4th day of next December.

Seth Ward,
Chairman Committee.

Anti-Class Resolutions.

Halletsville, Texas, August 20.—The Negro Anti-Class Legislation club of Lavaca county at their meeting here Saturday passed the following resolutions, which were handed to your correspondent for publication in The Post:

1. That we, the members of the Colored Men's conference, will not support any party or any candidate who aspires for representative or any office where the powers invested in him for control of the same and will not give equal representation to the negroes as a race as that of any other race.

2. That if any party or candidate uses the slightest attempt of discrimination against the negroes politically as a race that we as members of the Anti-Class Legislation organization will not support such party or candidate.

3. That it shall be the object of this conference to use every effort to secure recognition for negroes of Lavaca county.

W. J. Stephens, Chairman.
W. W. Scott, Secretary.

Corpus Christi Cullings.

Corpus Christi, Texas, August 20.—Engineer Ripley of Galveston arrived at Aransas Pass yesterday and will proceed at once to make a survey of the old channel and the jetty work now under construction.

Another new quarry has been opened seven miles this side of Laredo, making four quarries in all now being operated.

Contractor Clarke says from now on twenty-five carloads of rock will arrive here daily.

A few nights ago a Mexican woman on the bluff had trunk robbed of $130 in money, diamonds valued at $300 and all her wearing apparel. The empty trunk was found next day in the Arrayo. No clue to the robbers.

Major James Moore of Hondo City left here yesterday morning for Hebbvonville, where he will receive 1000 head of cattle purchased for himself and John Merriman from Ed Corkill.

Cuero's New Compress.

Cuero, Texas, August 20.—An event of no small value to the commercial importance of Cuero transpired yesterday evening when the new compress began to press the fleecy. A crowd of citizens interested in the city's growth assembled, and at 4 o'clock the lever was pulled. The press worked as though many a bale had gone the same way before. The compress was built entirely by local capital and is complete in every detail. The visitors were regaled by the management with barbacued meats, drinkables, etc. This scores another success for Cuero's enterprising citizens.

Today is the ninth anniversary of the great storm of 1886, which devastated this section to such an alarming extent.

The many friends of The Post and Mr. C. S. E. Holland read with pleasure the announcement that he had assumed his former relations with the paper. He is a very popular newspaper man in this section.

Comanche Cullings.

Comanche, Texas, August 19.—Bishop Garrett of Dallas will preach at the Episcopal church next Sunday.

The Alliance at Cottonwood is to give a picnic the 22d instant.

Frank Chancellor of the Exponent, with his family, are to start for the Colorado river today, and will be gone a week.

Rev. W. W. Patrick of Cleburne preached at the Episcopal chapel yesterday.

Judge T. H. Conner convened district court this morning.

Captain F. M. Browne, who has been North purchasing goods, has returned.

Comanche's cotton crop, from prospects at present, will not be more than half as large as in 1894.

W. B. Riley, an enterprising groceryman, has his bottling works ready for use.

Burglars at Lexington.

Lexington, Texas, August 20.—This town was visited by burglars last night. B. F. Budd & Fowler's store was broken into, but only two pairs of pants have been missed.

F. Vanderworth's saloon was robbed of two gold watches, one silver watch, a pistol, shotgun and $9 in money.

Two men are held on suspicion, and officers are hard at work on the case.

Torn to Pieces.

Crockett, Texas, August 20.—Last night about nine miles south of this place, a Mexican whose name is unknown, was run over and killed by some northbound train. He was literally torn to pieces. Section Foreman Brooks made the discovery this morning and notified Justice Newton, who held an inquest and returned a verdict in accordance with the foregoing.

Shooting Scrape.

Velasco, Texas, August 20.—Last night Jim Parker and Mary Eagleton became involved in a quarrel, which resulted in the latter being shot in the shoulder with a 32-caliber revolver. Parker is in jail. Both negroes.

Suicided.

Brownwood, Texas, August 20.—E. H. Phillips, late of Ellis county, committed suicide one mile in the country this morning by taking strychnine, aged 26 years. Family troubles.

Post Readers Pleased.

Palestine, Texas, August 19.—The fast mail train arriving here from Galveston at 6 p. m. is hailed with delight by the numerous readers of The Post.

WESLEY HARDIN KILLED.

Another of the Few Bad Men Laid Low in a Saloon.

HE WAS SHOT BY A CONSTABLE

Whose Life He Had Threatened and Who Acted in Self-Defense—Hardin's Record of Crime.

El Paso, Texas, August 20.—Last night just before midnight another of the few remaining bad men of Texas went the way blazed out by victims of his own murderous revolver.

Constable John Sellman shot and instantly killed John Wesley Hardin in the Acme saloon. Hardin, it is said, had made threats to shoot Sellman on sight; the latter walked into the saloon and as quick as Hardin saw him he made a motion as if to draw his weapon; without a moment's loss of time Sellman drew and fired, the bullet being a center shot and ending the career of Hardin. He didn't get in a shot.

The remains of John Wesley Hardin were laid in the grave today.

For the last three weeks Hardin has been drinking considerable, writing a story of his life and making life a burden to the police, whom he threatened to run out of the country. Several days since on the complaint of Mrs. McRose, who he had kept begging for her life several hours at the point of a pistol, he was arrested by a batch of five officers, who he made read the warrant twice over before he would surrender.

The trouble which resulted in his death last night was brought on by his telling Constable Sellman in the Acme saloon he did not like his (Sellman's) son, who was one of the party of officers who had arrested him a few nights before. One word brought on another and it ended by his telling Sellman to get out in the middle of the street and he would come soon and come "a smoking."

Sellman waited for him several hours but he did not come out. Then Sellman went into the saloon with a friend and stepping up to the bar near Hardin they both watched one another through the mirror in front. After Sellman had taken his drink he says Hardin reached for his gun and he pulled his own and turned loose. The first shot crashed through Hardin's brain and killed him instantly. He received two more shots while falling to the floor. He had a gun in each hip pocket but did not get a chance to pull either. Thus ended the career of the man who has for several months been feared by the public in general.

Constable Sellman is an old officer and has a record as a killer of smugglers and thieves. Some years ago he fought a band of cattle thieves in Dona Ana county, New Mexico, and killed two and captured the rest, four in all. He killed Bass Outlaw in this city a year ago. Outlaw was a deputy United States marshal and had come to Texas in such a hurry that he had neglected to bring his right name along, and in an emergency picked up the one he died under in Western Texas. Outlaw was killed by Sellman in self-defense a few seconds after the former had killed Ranger M. C. Kittridge.

Wes Hardin, as he was familiarly known over Southwest Texas, was easily the most noted of the living Texas desperadoes. Hardin's early career was spent in De Witt county, and he was a terror in that section in the 70's, or until he was sent to the penitentiary. He was sentenced to fifteen years, but got a time allowance for good conduct, which enabled him to secure his discharge eighteen months earlier than would have been the case had he been compelled to serve out his full time.

After spending some time in Cuero and afterwards at Gonzales, where he nearly got into trouble in the excitement of the county election last year, he came to El Paso about three months ago. On his way out here he stopped in San Antonio and renewed many old acquaintances of former days. During his stay in San Antonio he was sober and quiet, but there was the same dare-devil look in his eyes and the same old restless spirit burning inside of him, which indicated to his old acquaintances that he would soon break out again. He was a prominent figure around the vicinity of Main Plaza and Soledad street for several days.

Soon after his arrival here he became the leading figure in a case where in it was attempted to induce a fugitive from American justice to come back to this side of the Rio Bravo, and which resulted in the killing of the fugitive on the bridge that connects El Paso with Juarez. Hardin, however, could not long restrain his old propensity to drink and gamble, and when in his cups was very quarrelsome and threatening.

One night shortly after his arrival he made a losing of $75 against a crap game in one of the gambling houses. Being exasperated at his loss he pulled his pistol and compelled the dealer to hand him the money back. He then walked out to the middle of the room, flourishing his pistol and declared if any — — didn't like his style, let him say so and "get out in the road."

On another occasion, in a poker game with four men, he lost a big pot and compelled the winner to give it back to him.

Nearly everybody got out of his way when he was in an ugly mood, and this led him to believe he was cock of the walk and bore a charmed life.

Hardin was the son of a Methodist preacher, and was born in Trinity county, being 45 years of age at the time of his death. He was sent to the penitentiary

In 1868 John Wesley Hardin entered upon his career of crime and bloodshed at the early age of 17. At that time originated the Taylor-Sutton feud; his nerve and daring soon placed him at the head of the Taylor faction, and between the years of 1868 and 1874 forty or more of the Sutton faction were extirminated, sixteen deaths being laid at Hardin's door. Two years after the conception of the feud Hardin became the leader of seventeen desperadoes, who terrorized and controlled the town of Comanche at intervals, for two years or more openly defying law and order. The gang did not confine their operations to the town of Comanche alone, but roamed over the counties of Comanche, Gonzales and DeWitt, stealing cattle, demanding supplies at the points of their pistols, and for excitement exterminating all stray members of the Sutton crowd who came across their paths.

In February of 1874 while Hardin and his crowd were carcusing in a saloon at Comanche Deputy Sheriff Webb of Brown county rode up and entered the saloon by the back door. Seeing himself outnumbered he attempted to pass through, but was accosted by Hardin, who demanded to know if he had a warrant for any of his (Hardin's) crowd and if he expected to execute it.

Upon Webb replying in the affirmative Hardin drew his gun and Webb gamely gave up his life in defense of his duty. This aroused public indigation to such a pitch that Hardin became an outlaw and a price was set on his head. Shortly before this time he killed Captain Jack Helm, a man of note in his day, who was in command of a Ranger company which wherever it went in Southern Texas left a trail of blood behind it.

Helm got into a dispute with a 14-year-old boy, of whose father he was the murderer. While Helm was in the act of stabbing the boy with a knife Hardin's pistol cracked and Helm turned up his toes. The Rangers took after him and run him near Yorktown, but Hardin killed three of his pursuers and escaped.

After the killing of Deputy Sheriff Webb Hardin's band dwindled to a mere handful and owing to vigilance of the Rangers the leader was forced to seek safety in flight. Going to Jacksonville, Fla., in 1875 he entered the butcher business under the assumed name of Swain. In six month's time his whereabouts became known to detectives, who had been on his trail. Becoming uneasy, the fugitive started for his old haunts in Texas and was captured and brought back to Comanche, tried for the killing of Webb, receiving a sentence of twenty-five years penal servitude. Seventeen years of this was served before being pardoned by the governor.

During his confinement he applied his leisure hours to the study of law and upon his release was admitted to the bar at Pecos. He came to this city last October in the capacity of attorney for J. P. Miller, who was to be tried on the charge of conspiracy against the life of Sheriff Bud Frazier of that place.

His next move was to send word to a local saloon man that he wanted to be his partner and he, thinking discretion the better part of valor, gave him a half interest next day. Going to a local wholesale liquor house he ordered all the wet goods he thought necessary and had it charged. The liquor house not only charged this, but told him the store was at his disposition whenever he wanted it. He published a card to the effect that while he was in the saloon he would see that belligerents had a fair deal and no dead sure thing would go if he knew of it. In consequence the saloon was given a wide berth and soon closed for want of patronage.

Hardin was well connected and has many relatives in all parts of the State. Three hundred and sixty pages of closely written manuscript was found in his trunk today, which purports to be a history of his life. The police refuse to allow any one to read it, and will hold it until the arrival of relatives, who will reach here tomorrow. Joe Hardin, a brother of John Wesley, was lynched in Comanche in 1874, principally because he was a brother of the latter.

from Lampasas county in 1876 for the killing of the sheriff of Comanche county, who was attempting to arrest him. He was released in 1894, and stood his last trial for murder in Cuero in the same year. The jury failed to agree at the trial, and as it was an old case in which it was difficult to secure testimony, the case was subsequently dismissed.

In his personal appearance John Wesley Hardin was as typical a Texas desperado of the earliest type as was ever portrayed in the dime novel. He was of medium weight, nearly six feet tall, straight as an arrow and light complexioned, with an eye as keen as a hawk. As an expert shot he was the peer of either King Fisher or Ben Thompson in their palmiest days.

He could shoot as quickly and aim as straight as either of them. It was almost sure death for anyone who was in front of his gun when Hardin drew a bead.

Seventeen scalps are said to have dangled from his belt and it is likely that the number of human lives that he has taken will exceed that number.

Louis Dreyfous, formerly a San Antonio gambler, was dealing monte once at Cuero in the early days of Hardin's career. Hardin walked up to the table where Dreyfous sat. He wore two pistols and a very boyish look. Dreyfous had heard of Hardin's exploits but did not know him by sight and did not recognize Hardin when the latter walked up to where the game was being dealt. Hardin asked for a "lay out," but Dreyfous remarked that he was too fresh and did not need so many sixshooters.

Hardin laughed his peculiar laugh and the men about the table began to fall back. Dreyfous asked what was the matter, when one of the players whispered in his left ear, "Why, you blasted idiot, that is Wes Hardin." Dreyfous ran out of the room as fast as his legs could carry him and has never been seen since in that vicinity.

Fortunately for him Hardin considered Dreyfous' ignorance as a good joke, called for a fresh dealer and the game proceeded until Hardin "busted" the game.

Hardin had a National reputation as a desperado and the news of his tragic taking off is being sent all over the world by the enterprising newspaper correspondents.

RELIGIOUS.

Meeting at Georgetown.

Georgetown, Texas, August 20.—The three meetings held at the old fair grounds Sunday by the First Baptist church were well attended and much interest manifested. The singing, conducted by Val C. Hart of Galveston is a feature He has organized a splendid choir and they succeed in making the woods ring with harmonious melody. The grounds are well shaded and watered with cool springs. About two dozen families occupy tents on the grounds and others are expected to join them this week.

Rev. Isaac Sellers, the pastor, who is a splendid outdoor speaker, is doing every thing in his power to make the meeting a grand success.

Fifteen Accessions.

Caldwell, Texas, August 20.—Rev. A. S. Blackwood has just returned from Cook's Point, where he has been engaged for the past ten days in conducting a camp meeting. He reports fifteen accessions to the Methodist church, twenty-five reclamations and more than forty who expressed their intention to lead a better life. He will begin next Friday a camp meeting on the Yegua in Lee county.

Religious News.

Comanche—The Baptists are holding a protracted meeting near Whattville under the auspices of Rev. T. S. Bomar.

Comanche—The third quarterly conference of the Comanche Methodist church met in this city today.

Palestine—A big Methodist camp meeting is going on at Brushy creek, sixteen vW*S2fafiaaokr fd..eGfl Pa,fi(z miles north of this city. Presiding Elder Fowler and Rev. Timmons of this city are assisting in the services.

Bartlett—Rev. Story is conducting a protracted meeting at the Methodist church which is daily growing in interest.

Josserand—The Presbyterians began a protracted meeting here Monday night to continue for several days, conducted by Rev. Will Junkin.

THE DEATH ROLL.

Mrs. Ella Dean.

Victoria, Texas, August 20.—Mrs. Ella Dean died yesterday at the home of her son, Mr. A. A. Dean, at the age of 66. The funeral occurred this morning from the Presbyterian church.

Lemmie Sykes.

Lexington, Texas, August 20.—Lemmie Sykes, who has been suffering for the past few weeks with blood poisoning on account of an operation performed on his foot, died this morning at 9 o'clock.

Major Holmes.

Austin, Texas, August 20.—From letters received here today it is learned that Major Holmes, formerly private secretary to Governor Ross, died at Mason on August 17.

Other Deaths.

Cuero.—Mr. C. L. Brown died on the 19th.

Taylor.—Mrs. W. W. Mumford died August 18, aged 53 years.

FARMERS AND LABORERS.

The Alliance and the Federation in Session at Lampasas.

A CONFERENCE WILL BE HELD

Between the Two Organizations—Officers Elected by the Federation. Speeches Attacking Democracy.

Lampasas, Texas, August 20.—The great meeting of the laboring masses is in progress. Several hundred people are encamped about Hanna Springs and more are expected tomorrow.

The State Alliance was in session today, with President Evan Jones of Dallas in the chair and Secretary Fanny Leak at her desk. In his annual address President Jones called attention to the harmony and prosperity of the order, stating that its members had more than doubled in the year.

Committees were appointed on revision of the constitution and for conferring with a committee from the Federation of Labor.

The Federation of Labor met tonight and elected permanent officers as follows: George M. Beach, Dallas, president; J. E. Scott, Dallas, vice president, and W. B. Ross, Copperas Cove, secretary. The body is still in session, with a probability of doing nothing tonight.

While the alliance and federation were in session, the large dancing hall of the Hanna Springs bath house was filled with listeners to various speakers. J. S. Bradley of Abilene spoke in the afternoon and Secretary McMeans of the alliance occupied the evening. Both men were heartily cheered, especially when they most bitterly assailed the democratic party or any of its leaders. McMeans declared that Roger Q. Mills is dead and Bradley said Reagan had passed his usefulness, and the crowd yelled.

George Clark is billed for a speech, but he will not be here. Harry Tracy speaks tomorrow.

The Farmers' alliance had its origin in Lampasas county, Texas. First organization was effected the latter part of the summer of 1877 on Donaldson creek upon the premises of John R. Allen, about nine miles northwest of Lampasas Springs. John R. Allen was its founder. He originated the idea and worked it up among his neighbors. The first alliance was christened Pleasant Valley Farmers' alliance No. 1. Pleasant Valley also became the name of the place of its meeting. In the fall of 1877 it adopted a constitution and by-laws containing a declaration of purpose. Captain L. S. Chevose was the chairman of the committee that framed the constitution, and the Farmers' alliance is mainly indebted to him for its organic law. John Spears was the first president. The original members were small farmers, combining stock raising with farming. Most of them were in comfortable circumstances. None of them were educated in books. In the course of six months Pleasant Valley numbered forty or fifty members. Other alliances sprung up in the country around, taking their names Farmers' alliance and their constitution from Pleasant Valley alliance.

February 25, 1878, the county alliance and May 4, 1878, the State alliance were organized at Pleasant Valley. They were confederations of the parent alliance and those which had sprung up under it. They adopted the declarations of purposes of the parent alliance and its constitution was modified to suit their enlarged organizations. July 13, 1878, the State alliance met at Pleasant Valley, represented by twenty-five subordinate alliances—fourteen in Lampasas county and eleven in adjacent counties. Some time after the first alliance was organized W. Y. Baggett of Coryell county, Texas, joined it. It was he who a few years afterward organized a Farmers' alliance in Parker county, Texas, from which the alliances of this State, I understand, have mainly ramified.

The declarations of principles as contained in the constitution of Pleasant Valley No. 1, and adopted by the county and State alliances, are as follows:

1. Profoundly impressed with the truth that we, as Farmers' alliance, should set forth some declaration of purpose, united by the strong and faithful tie—political and home interest—we mutually resolve to labor for the alliance and its purpose.

2. To indorse the motto: In essential things unity, liberty and in all things charity.

3. To endeavor to advance our cause by laboring to accomplish the following objects:

1. To develop a better and higher state, politically and financially.

2. To strengthen our attachments to our cause.

3. To a better mutual understanding to sustain our laws.

4. To constantly strive to secure entire harmony, good will and vital brotherly love among ourselves.

5. To suppress personal, local, sectional and National prejudices, all unhealthy rivalry and all selfish ambitions.

6. To perpetuate our alliance.

7. And a faithful observance of these principles will insure ur mental, moral and political advancement.

The above is substantially the same as the "declaration of purposes" of the Farmers' alliance at this time. Much of the very language is the same. There has been quite an improvement made in its grammar, some elimination and some evolution, but all of these fundamental ideas of the organization are in this crude original. However, an exception is to be noted in their first idea of purpose, enunciated in their present declaration enjoining the "education of the agricultural classes in the science of economic government in a strictly non-partisan spirit," which, as expressed, is a confused conception, evidently not originating with the farmers. The present declaration also adds some details of charity and fidelity, but their substance is in the original. Evidently, beyond doubt, the principles of the Farmers' alliance as set forth in its most recent and authentic declaration originated with the farmers of Lampasas county, Texas. They conceived the idea, gave it form and promulgated it. There have been some evolutions, it may be, but the germ in all of its distinctness and completeness from which the Farmers' alliance, both as State and National organizations, has grown and expanded, is to be found in the constitution of Pleasant Valley alliance, adopted in 1877 on Donaldson creek, in Lampasas county, by John R. Allen and his associates. Not only were their principles the same as those of the Farmers' alliance at this time, but it seems that their plan of operation, the number, style and duties of their officers (with an exception hereafter to be noted), the qualification for membership and the obligation of members have remained substantially the same. From the start it seems to have been a social and educational institution. The women and youths of 16 and upward were admitted. It was a secret society, having its secret officers and secret work, its degrees, signs, passwords and pledges.

The pledge was as follows:

"I hereby pledge myself to meet the brothers of the alliance as often as possible and assist my officers in keeping peace and harmony in the country; and I now pledge my sacred honor before Almighty God and the brothers of this alliance not to, in any manner whatever, knowingly wrong or defraud a brother of the alliance, nor will I permit it to be done in my presence if in my power to prevent; and I furthermore will report all estray stock to the secretary that may be or come in my range, and I now pledge myself to support the constitution of the alliance."

The pledge of the ladies was as follows:

"I pledge my sacred honor to use my influence to advance the cause of the Farmers' Alliance, and I now pledge myself before Almighty God and the brothers of this alliance not in any way whatever, by word, action or writing, directly or indirectly, divulge or make known any of the signs or secrets of this alliance, nor will I permit it to be done in my presence if in my power to prevent it."

The third degree pledge was:

"In addition to my former obligations I hereby pledge myself to speak the truth and nothing but the truth to any brother of this degree, and furthermore I will believe anything told me by a brother of this degree concerning the business of this degree, so help me God."

THE STATE CAPITAL.

Military Commissions Issued to Members of T. V. G.

Austin, Texas, August 20.—The following commissions were issued by the adjutant general today:

N. H. Ricker, colonel, Third regiment.

John Dowell, lieutenant colonel, commissary department.

Isidore Moses, major, commissary department.

W. B. Brush, major, commissary department.

George Estes, captain; W. L. Frame, first lieutenant; J. B. Gibson, second lieutenant; Pecos Valley Guards.

James Lawlor, captain; J. J. Hussey, first lieutenant; J. M. Browne, second lieutenant; Emmet Guards.

J. S. Oglesby, captain; C. C. Overaker, first lieutenant; C. E. Saigling, second lieutenant; Piano Rifles.

TAX VALUATIONS.

The following counties, whose tax rolls were received by the comptroller today, show increases and decreases as follows, as compared with last year:

	Valuation.	Increase.
Bandera	$1,121,066	$50,757
Uvalde	3,315,665	59,700
Orange	1,695,248	215,754
Kerr	1,867,603	9,902
Kaufman	7,066,738	208,359
Menard	1,320,495	79,080
Nueces	6,032,714	183,799
Haskell	2,470,773	50,822

	Valuation.	Decrease.
Moore	$569,371	$96,239
Mitchell	1,997,978	171,144
Blanco	1,369,523	47,391
McCulloch	1,445,908	43,896
Cherokee	2,965,097	105,754
Midland	1,235,282	11,638
Refugio	2,117,225	60,323
Henderson	2,479,896	32,543
Randall	797,954	81,599
Zapata	834,360	125,000
Hood	2,000,833	82,600
Hall	1,408,979	$79,572

NOTES.

The charter of the Colorado County Abstract company was filed in the department of state today. Place of business, Columbus. Capital stock, $10,000. Incorporators, Fred James, M. H. Townsend, A. M. Waugh, D. B. Gray, W. D. Hart.

Ground was broken in the capitol yard this morning for the State Firemen's monument.

Secretary of State Mayfield, who has been in bad health for some time, has gone to Wootan Wells.

Judge H. Clay Pleasants and wife of Cuero are in the city visiting their son, John J. Pleasants, secretary of the State democratic executive committee.

Judge J. H. Robertson has returned from Wootan Wells.

The railroad commission will dispense with the services of one of its expert engineers on September 1, the work of valuing railroad property in the State being about completed.

The university regents today leased seventy-two sections of university land in Tom Green county at 3 cents per acre.

SHORT TEXAS SPECIALS.

FLATONIA—Cotton is coming in pretty lively and is selling at 7 cents.

HUNTER—An unknown Mexican was killed here, supposedly by two men, who have not been arrested.

SHERMAN—William Gruildstoff, postmaster at Tom Bean, was held in a bond of $750 to answer the charge of embezzling government funds.

HILLSBORO—Two children of Samps Richardson, colored, were burned to death in a fire which consumed their home. The parents were at church.

TEMPLE.—The new $22,000 school building is nearing completion and will be ready for the opening the first week in September.

LULING—While driving cows at his father's ranch near Staples, Willie Marcy was thrown from his pony and so badly injured that his life is despaired of.

LOCKHART—Mr. A. J. Meiars, who was so seriously stabbed by Alexander at Dale, a few days since, as reported by The Post, is recovering and will get well. Alexander surrendered and is now under bond.

BENCHLEY—A young boy named Bud Johnson dropped a lighted match near a kerosene can, which exploded. The clothing of the boy and of his sister caught fire, Bud being burned to a crisp; the little girl is not expected to live.

COLD SPRINGS—At the meeting of the commissioners court, held here Monday, the resignation of H. D. Thompson as county treasurer was accepted and Mr. J. H. McClanahan appointed to fill the office. He was given twenty days in which to make bond and qualify. Mr. McClanahan is a young business man of this place, of sterling worth and high business integrity and is well qualified to fill the office.

Yardmen Hurt.

Orange, Texas, August 20.—This afternoon at 2:15 o'clock as the switch engine was backing down to the Miller shingle mill to bring out a load a rail suddenly gave way and the tender jumped the track and fell over on its side. W. H. Porter, yardmaster, and Tom Tatum, brakeman, were standing on the footboard and as the tender went over the footboard pinned them in the mud, catching Porter on the heel and Tatum on the right shoulder. A brakeman had to run forty yards for an axe and chop the footboard in two before they could be liberated. On being rescued from their perilous position and examined by physicians it was found that Tatum's right ankle had a broken bone, his shoulder badly bruised, back strained and left ankle considerably bruised. Porter's right foot was squeezed terribly, but it is thought no bones are broken.

Beaumont Budget.

Beaumont, Texas, August 20.—The Ladies' Aid society of the Baptist church request The Post to announce that the ice cream festival that was to have been given at the city park tomorrow night has been postponed until next week. Inclement weather makes the postponement necessary.

The steamer Lunnira is to clear from Sabine Pass tomorrow with a cargo of 360,000 feet of railway ties and timbers from the Reliance Lumber company of this city.

Political Notes.

Bryan, Texas, August 20.—Colonel Hindman of Illinois, a populist of the first water, addressed the citizens at the court house tonight on the economic questions of the day.

Chilton-Buman.

Comanche, Texas, August 19.—J. B. Chilton and Miss Clara Buman were married last Thursday, Rev. R. W. Benge officiating.

ISLAND CITY NEWS ITEMS.

Saloonman Shot and Fatally Wounded by His Wife.

SAYS SHE ACTED IN SELF-DEFENSE.

The Shooting Was the Result of a Quarrel—Colored Baptists in Session—Fresh Water—Notes.

Galveston, Texas, August 20.—Emma La Rose, the pretty 25-year-old wife of Al La Rose, a saloonkeeper, shot and probably faatly wounded her husband this morning at 8 o'clock at their residence on Fourteenth street and avenue N.

Two shots were fired and both reached their mark. One entered the neck and came out under the right eye and the other imbedded itself in the upper portion of the right leg. Both wounds are dangerous and death may result.

There were many rumors as to the cause of the shooting, but all agree that prior to the shooting La Rose and the woman had a row, in which she was considerably bruised. Her eye is black, and there are several bruises on her body

Immediately after the shots were fired Mrs. La Rose put away her revolver and started to the police station to surrender herself to the authorities. On her way to the station she was met by Mounted Officer Frank Sommers, who placed her under arrest and escorted her to police headquarters, where a charge of assault with intent to murder was preferred against her.

As soon as possible the wounded man was conveyed to the Sealy Hospital and every attention given him. On the way to the hospital La Rose seemed to suffer great pain and repeatedly asked Officer Plummer if his wounds were dangerous. "I feel as if I was going to die," he said; "I am suffering terribly."

At the hospital the man was tenderly lifted from the patrol wagon and carried into the building, where the surgeons commenced the work of probing for the bullets.

Immediately after the shooting great crowds surrounded the La Rose residence and it was with great difficulty that the officers kept the curious and excited crowd from entering the house.

Everything was confusion within. There were marks of blood in the room in the upper story of the residence where the shooting occurred and on the walls were the imprints of bloody hands, where La Rose staggered down the stairway in pursuit of his wife. On the porch where he fell was a pool of blood.

When the officers arrived at the residence La Rose's life was apparently fast ebbing away. Physicians were telephoned for and immediately after they arrived the flow of blood was stopped.

Half an hour after Mrs. La Rose arrived at police headquarters a Post reporter saw her. The detectives' office was the place of the interview and here is what she told The Post man:

"At an early hour this morning I arose as usual and got breakfast for Al. After breakfast was over I walked upstairs, and while there heard Al and his mother talking together. His mother said something about me, and I heard Al exclaim: "Is that so?" There was some further conversation between them concerning me, and then Al came upstairs. We had a talk and finally I remarked that if he would give me $100 I would leave him, and he could live with his mother. His mother did not like me and made it very unpleasant for me around the house. To my request for money he said I could go rustle for it. One word brought on another and pretty soon he went to the wardrobe to get a shirt. I told him not to disturb things, but I would get it for him.

"He then cursed me and struck me a severe blow in the eye. I was knocked almost senseless and saw him run in an adjoining room and try to open a trunk. Knowing that he always kept a gun in it, I ran to my sewing machine, got a revolver from under the cover and blazed away. I then ran down stairs and he followed me. At the foot of the stairs his mother caught him and he finally got away from her and kept advancing towards me. It was then that I fired the second shot, and he fell on the porch. If his mother had not held him I believe he would have killed me.

"After the shooting I put the pistol away and came down to the city to give myself up to the police. On my way to the station I met Officer Sommers, who placed me under arrest. These are all the facts concerning the shooting."

Mrs. La Rose told the story in a straightforward way, although she appeared a trifle nervous.

Mrs. LaRose has resided in Galveston for a number of years and has lived with LaRose about seven years. She is a brunette of pleasing appearance and quite a bright woman. At the time of her interview with The Post man her sister was with her.

LaRose has been in the grocery business here for several years, but lately engaged in the saloon business. He is well known in the city.

The Post man called at the hospital this afternoon to see LaRose, but he could not be disturbed. His condition is serious.

COLORED BAPTISTS.

The Colored Baptist Young People's union convened in the city today. About 400 delegates are in attendance at the convention, which will be in session six days. The meeting was called to order by President William Taylor of Seguin, and an interesting programme was carried out. The principal features of today's programme was the president's annual address, vocal selections by visiting delegates and what is known as a model church reception, conducted by Professor E. H. Blackshear of Austin.

Two hundred and twenty-five of the delegates present came from points along the line of the Southern Pacific.

The residents of Galveston are now consuming fresh water, obtained from the wells at Alta Loma. The water was turned on Sunday and the big jubilee to celebrate the event will be held on August 31.

INJURED IN A RUNAWAY.

Mrs. Clara McGraw, who resides on Market near Nineteenth street, went yesterday in a buggy down the island, where she owns a farm. In returning home the horse became frightened and Mrs. McGraw was thrown from the buggy and two ribs were broken. She was conveyed to her residence. Her condition is precarious.

LOUISE FOUND.

The schooner Louise, which capsized Sunday, was located today near the marine ways on Bolivar Point, to which place she had drifted and was towed to this port by the yacht White Wing. She will be repaired and put in commission again.

NOTES.

Stafford Wheeler of Arcadia was in the city today.

C. H. Milby of Houston spent the day in the city.

James McCormack of Houston is spending a few days in the city.

Professor Phil Underwood, who was shot yesterday by Everett Smith, is improving and the attending physician says the chances are favorable for his recovery.

Mrs. Ruby Holmes, after visiting her uncle, H. M. Knight, clerk of the court of civil appeals, for the past several weeks, has returned to her home in Shreveport.

FIRST BALES.

McKinney, August 20.—McKinney's first bale brought 7 cents and a premium of $15.75 today.

Whitesboro, August 20—The first bale of new cotton was ginned at W. H. Marshall's gin and was sold here today by J. T. Hough to H. H. Robertson. Fifteen dollars in premiums.

Brenham Budget.

Brenham, Texas, August 20.—The Post columns have already contained an account of the striking of Joe Richardson on the head with a baseball bat by Chas. Randle, during the progress of a scrub game of baseball in Watsonsville Sunday afternoon.

This morning Joe Richardson died from the effects of the wound.

Justice Ewing held an inquest and decided that he came to his death from the blow with the bat.

The examining trial before Justice Ewing this afternoon resulted in his bail being fixed at $1000, which he failed to give, and he now languishes in jail.

John Meyers' 4-year-old boy fell off a bench at the table at his home, near Gay Hill, yesterday, and broke his right leg.

Sheriff Teague and James Marable returned from Galveston this morning, where they went to get Mr. Marable's watch, which was burglarized from his house here a few nights since. The watch was identified and recovered, but the thief who pawned it has not been captured yet.

A Shooting Affray.

Forney, Texas, August 20.—Two young men got into an altercation this morning about 1:20 o'clock over a game of cards. It is said that one of them had won the other's money and gave $1 back, whereupon the loser asked him if he did not think that he ought to give it all back to him. The winner replied in the negative and said that he would not. The other, it is said, replied: "I'll have it or kill you," and began shooting. Four shots were fired, all missing his target. The second shot, however, struck John Davidson in the face, just below the eye, seeming to range down the neck toward the shoulder. Davidson was asleep when the firing began. The first shot awoke him, and he raised up just in time to get the second ball. Officers are in pursuit. No arrests.

Alleged Bogus Checks.

Mexia, Texas, August 20.—A young man who came to Mexia one year ago, and who had done but little work since his arrival, succeeded in working the business men here Saturday. Late Saturday evening he expressed a desire to run down to Galveston, and as the banks had closed he went to several business men and gave his check for amounts ranging from $5 to $20, totaling something over $100. He then left, and not until the various parties went to turn in their checks yesterday was it discovered that he had no money in the bank, and that they had been worked to perfection. Nothing has been heard of him.

INTERRUPTED THEIR LOVE-MAKING.

THE HORSE OF A LEADING OFFICIAL OF PRESIDIO COUNTY BREAKS THROUGH THE ROOF OF A HOUSE AT THE SAN CARLOS MINES, NEAR CHISPA, TEX.

KHALID MUST BOW.

UNLESS HE SURRENDERS IN SHORT ORDER THE PALACE WILL BE BOMBARDED.

WAR SHIPS HOVER ABOUT

Ready to Turn Loose at Any Moment. Terrell Writes a Note to the Turkish Government.

Zanzibar, Aug. 26.—Admiral Rawson this afternoon received cabled instructions from the British government and a message was also received here by the British consul from the foreign office.

As a result the admiral and the consul held another conference at the end of which an ultimatum was sent Said Khalid. He was ordered to haul down his flag and surrender with his forces no later than 9 o'clock to-morrow morning. If he fails to do so the palace will be promptly bombarded by the British warships. All British subjects have been requested to embark on board the warships here by 8 o'clock to-morrow morning.

Zanzibar, Aug. 26.—The night passed quietly. Said Khalid is still in possession of the palace square, the guns of which are trained on the British warships, Philomel, Bush and Sparrow, which have landed sailors to protect the British consulate where all the ladies are lodged.

The warships are moored opposite the palace square and their commanders are awaiting orders from the British government.

As already cabled the Khalid took possession of the palace immediately after the announcement of the death of Sultan Hamid and proclaimed himself sultan. He has barricaded himself in the palace with 700 armed Askaris following the example of his father, who took the same steps, but was overawed by the British forces which established the late sultan instead.

The British first-class crusier St. George, twelve guns, the flagship of the Cape of Good Hope and west coast Africa station with Rear Admiral Harry W. Rawson on board, has arived here and landed 250 additional men to protect property and maintain order.

Kilkenny Journal's Comments.

Dublin, Aug. 26.—The Kilkenny Journal, commenting upon the release of John Daly, the Irish political prisoner, from Portland prison, says:

"The red Indians' torture of captives is humane when compared with the torture inflicted upon Daly in England."

Continuing the periodical mentioned refers to the allusion in the queen's speech to the outrages in Armenia and adds:

"The queen can find nearer home more vent for her hypocritical tears than among the Kurds," and asks: "Where is the queen's clemency? Daly was released a few months before death would have released him, and three others have been driven mad by tortures in penal servitude."

Venezuelan Blue Book.

London, Aug. 26.—The new Venezuelan blue book, which will be issued here shortly, was forwarded to Washington on Saturday last.

In an editorial this morning commenting upon the issuance of the blue book the Times says: "We presume the government's object in issuing the blue book containing exclusively Dr. Schomburgk's reports and letters relative to the boundary mission stations from 1841 to 1844 was for the purpose of refuting the Venezuelan allegations relative to alteration and extension of the Schomburgk line twenty years after Schomburgk's death."

News from Nicaragua.

Managua, Nicaragua, via Galveston, Aug. 25.—United States Consul Paul Wieske and family have arrived. All are well.

Gen. Cabezas, of Mosquito reservation fame, is dead. He was buried at Masaya.

Several natives have petitioned the government to abolish the freedom of trade now existing. The petitioners favor the restoration of the full import duty.

Ex-President Adam Cardenas, who has just returned from New York, has reached San Juan del Norte.

A Battle Near Cuenca.

New York, Aug. 25.—A dispatch to the Herald from Guayaquil, Ecuador, says: Hard fighting is still going on between the government and rebel forces in the vicinity of Cuenca. From Naranjal heavy canonading could be heard on the morning of Aug. 22.

Advices from the Herald correspondent in Alemst state that Gen. Alfaro is now only two miles from Cuenca, which Vega is preparing to defend. The terror-stricken inhabitants are leaving by the hundreds.

Scheme for Cretan Reforms.

London, Aug. 26.—The Chronicle this morning says: "It is learned that Russia, France and Great Britain agreed a month ago that no Cretan reforms could be effective unless carried out under the continuous control of the foreign consuls. The present scheme, which advices from Constantinople indicate has been accepted by the sultan, grants virtual autonomy to Crete."

Deranged on Seeing His Mother.

Skibbereen, Aug. 25.—Alfred George Whitehead, Irish-American political prisoner who was released from Portland prison last week and who arrived here yesterday evening, became completely deranged after seeing his mother and disappeared soon after. He has not been seen since, although searchers are scouring the neighborhood all night long.

What the Globe Thinks.

London, Aug. 26.—The Globe referring to the political campaign in the United States expresses the opinion that the avoidance of spread eagleism by Major McKinley and Mr. Bryan may be accepted as a sign that Monroeism as advocated by Messrs. Cleveland and Olney no longer dazzles American minds.

Terrell Not Satisfied.

Constantinople, Aug. 26.—United States Minister Alexander W. Terrell has notified the Turkish government that the latter's answer to the demands of the United States for indemnity as a result of the burning of the American missions at Kharput and Marash is not satisfactory.

Rebel Stronghold Falls.

New York, Aug. 26.—A dispatch to the Herald from Panama, Colombia, says:

"A correspondent in Ecuador sends word that the rebel stronghold in the mountainous districts of Cuena has fallen, practically putting an end to the revolution in Ecuador against Alfaro, headed by one Vega and openly supported with money and arms by the clergy."

Bottle Washed Ashore.

London, Aug. 26.—A bottle which has just washed ashore at Arranmore contains the following inscription:

"December 27, Ocean Maid, New Brunswick to Liverppool, is foundering in latitude 47 and longitude 57:45.

"J. B. GILMORE."

Meeting of Oil Companies.

Glasgow, Scotland, Aug. 26.—A meeting of the Scotch oil companies has been called for to-day in order to consider the fact that American oils are selling in Scotland at below the Scotch agreement prices.

Bullion for America.

London, Aug. 26.—The Daily News in its financial column says:

"It is learned that the bulk of the £300,000 in bullion which left the Bank of England yesterday is destined for America."

Foreigners Must Register.

New York, Aug. 25.—Senor Arturo Baldasano y Topete, the consul general for Spain in this city, to-day received the new decree of the captain general of Cuba extending to Oct. 31 the time for all foreigners resident in Cuba to register and procure their certificates. When the decree is in full operation it will do away with a number of certificates now used by people claiming a dual nationality. Many of them, foreigners, it is alleged, are rebel agents, and when arrested claim British, French or American citizenship. The new decree, it is thought, will facilitate the maintenance of public order in the island.

City of Mexico Budget.

Mexico City, Aug. 25.—The daughter of ex-President Santa Ana, who has just died here, leaves a fortune of $3,000,000, all of which goes to her children. The will was opened to-day.

The new governor of the federal district ordered a search for a clandestine convent yesterday and the suspected building was searched by detectives who, however, found nothing to prove any violation of the reform laws. It is rumored that all hidden convents will be suppressed.

The Spanish colony in this city is now contributing $50,000 monthly for the Spanish cause in Cuba.

The bicycle is to be introduced in the army and a plan for giving thorough instruction in the use of the wheel has been prepared.

Much interest in Mexican investments is being shown by north of England and Scotch capitalists, who are picking up good properties.

Plantations Destroyed.

New York, Aug. 25.—A dispatch to the Herald from Havana says:

A correspondent in Santiago de Cuba communicates details of a widespread destruction of foreign property before the insurgents in the district. In the great Cauto coffee zone more than thirty plantations, including the magnificent estates of Aurora Delerita and Hampatia were destroyed and owners driven to Santiago for refuge. The proprietors of the majority of these plantations, it is said, are Frenchmen.

Great celebrations will take place in Havana on the arrival of the new reinforcements from Spain. The municipal authorities and the local patriotic Spanish societies are arranging an enthusiastic reception to Gen. Rey, who succeeds Brig. Gen. Bosch in command of the operations around Manzanillo.

Sultan of Zanzibar Dead.

Zanzibar, Aug. 25.—The sultan of Zanzibar, Hamed Bin Thwain Bin Said, is dead. He was about 40 years of age and was a nephew of the late sultan Ali Kahlifa and Burghash and succeeded to the sultanate on the death of Sultan Ali, March 5, 1893. He was one of a number of claimants and was selected as being the most fitting, by the British government which exercises a protectorate over the sultanate.

Washington, Aug. 25.—The state department has received a cable message that the sultan of Zanzibar died at 11 o'clock this morning. The cable message adds that "Said Alld holds the palace; sailors and marines landed, rioting to-night feared."

As to Gold Contracts.

London, Aug. 25.—The Daily News this morning in an article discussing the powers of the United States supreme court and a possibility of a decision in opposition to the validity of gold contracts, says:

"The point is complicated by one decision, and the future course of the United States supreme court in this particular is by no means so certain as that Wall street and Lombard street would like to believe it, but the conservatism shown by the supreme court and its special respect for property, as demonstrated by its verdict against the income tax, indicates that the chances are in favor of the validity of gold contracts being maintained under all circumstances."

Troubles in Brazil.

London, Aug. 26.—A dispatch to the Times from Rio Janerio says that the disorders caused originally by political conflicts between the Brazilians and the Italians continue throughout Brazil, the mobs seeking to attack the Italians who are apparently conducting themselves peacefully. It is claimed that the trouble is due to Brazilian demagogues and especially in the province of San Paulo.

Forbidden Immigration to Brazil.

Rome, Aug. 26.—The Italian government has forbidden all immigration to Brazil in consequence of the recent Brazilian-Italian riots there and the cruiser Umbria has been ordered there.

Movement of Troops.

Havana, Aug. 26.—It is reported here that the insurgents recently burned over thirty coffee and cocoa plantations in the province of Santiago de Cuba. Among the larger plantations burned were the splendid estates of Aurora, Sempatia and Dolorita. It is estimated that more than $1,000,000 worth of property was destroyed. These estates were owned by French citizens who were not sympathizers with the insurgents, but who have remained neutral from the commencement of the troubles in Cuba.

At a meeting of the board of trade to-night it was deliberately announced that the decree prohibiting the planting, cutting and harvesting of the sugar and coffee crops would be strictly enforced.

The recent report circulated that the Havana university would be closed and the building used as a military hospital is pronounced untrue by the Spanish authorities.

The Laurada Arrived.

Philadelphia, Pa., Aug. 26.—According to two cablegrams received in this city the steamer Laurada, which sailed from this port for Cuba, Aug. 6, landed one of the most formidable filibustering expeditions yet shipped to Cuba. The cargo was landed on the southern coast of Cuba, in Santa Clara province, the Cubans aboard the steamship landed with the cargo. The cargo consisted of 53,000 pounds of dynamite, eleven fixed guns, four cannons, seven gatlings, a quantity of ammunition and nearly 200 men.

FIRE RECORD.

Destruction of Ontonaga.

Milwaukee, Wis., Aug. 26.—A special to the Wisconsin from Houghton, Mich., gives particulars of the fire which destroyed Ontonaga. The fire originated in the swamp just south of the Diamond Match company's mill. A strong wind swept the flames before it and the planing mills, box factories and the immense dry-kilns of the match company were soon a mass of ashes. The flames descended on the business and residence quarter of the city and finally lodged in 65,000,000 feet of sawed lumber on the dock. The destruction of the village was complete, barely a dozen houses in the suburbs remaining standing. The onslaught of the flames was so sudden that barely one in twenty succeeded in saving anything of their effects. The heat from the burning mills and lumber was so intense that the people were compelled to seek shelter under the trees and driftwood along the lake shore. Many walked to Rockland, fifteen miles away. There are about 1800 men, women and children without food or shelter. Many are insufficiently clothed and they suffered severely last night. The Diamond Match company lost two fine saw mills having a daily capacity of about 450,000 feet and other mills and buildings worth in all nearly $2,000,000 and lumber worth nearly $1,000,000. Insurance to the extent of $75,000 was carried. The loss on the balance of the village will foot up about $2,000,000 with $300,000 insurance. The fire is still burning in the lumber piles and it is impossible to go among the ruins. Houghton & Hancock are raising provisions and clothing. Money is needed badly. A special from Green Bay, Wis., says a carload of provisions, clothing and tents was sent to Ontonaga this morning.

Dwelling.

Thornton, Limestone Co., Tex., Aug. 25. —E. Z. Kidd lost by fire a house and Mr. John McCaig lost all of his household goods and 2000 pounds or more of seed cotton. Caused by matches in the hands of children. No insurance.

Cotton Gin.

Groesbeeck, Limestone Co., Tex., Aug. 26. —J. T. and W. M. Prichard's cotton gin was destroyed by fire to-day. Loss $6000, insured for $2500.

Union Depot Project.

Galveston, Tex., Aug. 26.—The new union depot project assumed a new phase to-day in the announcement that the Missouri, Kansas and Texas had withdrawn from its proposition to jointly build the new structure with the Santa Fe, which it is said, will be the finest passenger depot in Texas. The Katy will use the depot for its passenger depot under the same conditions as all other roads, will be admitted as tenants.

RIOT IN CONSTANTINOPLE.

Mob Takes Possession of the Ottoman Bank—Numbers Killed.

Constantinople, Aug. 26.—At 1:30 this afteroon a score of men armed with revolvers and bombs invaded the Ottoman bank, killing a number of gendarmes. Closing the bank to prevent the inward movement of the mob, the employes escaped to safe quarters in the bank building occupied by the syndicate which has control of the tobacco in this country. The invaders climbed upon the roofs and from the windows fired upon the police. The police returned the fusilade in a vigorous fashion and several were killed and wounded. The riot then became general. Shops were sacked and bazaars invaded and the wildest excitement prevailed throughout cercertain quarters of Constantinople.

A later report says there is no doubt that the movement was revolutionary in plan and scope and that it had its origin at the secret meetings of the Hintchakiste Armenians. About forty of the rioters were still in possession of the Ottoman bank at a late hour this evening, despite all the efforts of the government forces to remove them from the building. Advices from the disorderly sections of the city late to-night were to the effect that the riot still continues; that mobs are constantly increasing in the Galata quarter. A bomb exploded in Constantinople near Galatia guard house. Many soldiers were wounded.

GLUT IN SHIPPING.

Grain Steamers for Either New Orleans or Galveston.

New Orleans, La., Aug. 26.—"Beginning with October and November we will charter all grain vessels with the option of loading either at New Orleans or Galveston," said George W. Kelley, agent for the big New York ship owners. W. W. Hutbert & Co., the second largest grain exporters out of this port, to The News correspondent to-day.

This is the first time the company has made this condition in their charters and it is right in line with the same action taken by Charles F. Orthwein & Co., and the beginning of the season, all of which means that large exporters are finding it advantageous to place ships at Galveston. Mr. Kelley said he wished they had a dozen big ships here now, that he could easily place them at reasonable rates in this port and at Galveston. The reports of the congested state of grain in that port created much interest here to-day and led to the discovery that much the same condition of affairs exists here, there now being over 1,000,000 bushels of grain waiting tonnage.

The recent railroad rate war in grain rates from Missouri river points has caused a vast movement of grain to the two gulf ports at a time of year when but few vessels were under charter and it has produced an unprecedented glut in shipping. It was estimated to-day that fully twenty-five grain steamers could be placed here at reasonable rates, but they are not here, the English owners holding them for exorbitant freight rates.

Speaking of the Galveston congestion, W. J. Orthwein of the large exporters firm, said that they had three steamers there which would greatly relieve matters. The steamship Europa, loaded yesterday, carried out 55,000 bushels of grain. Mr. Orthwein said: "To-day we are loading the Sir Walter Raleigh, which holds 80,000 bushels, and the Bendi is at quarantine with which we will carry out 44,000, all going to European ports."

COMMERCIAL MATTERS.

Hilton, Hughes & Co. Assign.

New York, Aug. 26.—The dry goods firm of Hilton, Hughes & Co. (once A. T. Stewart & Co.) have made an assignment to G. M. Wright.

Among the banks in Wall street the failure of Hilton, Hughes & Co. is regarded as due to the gradual decline in business. The firm's credit for the last five years has been badly impaired and it is understood they have been taking stock for several weeks past and recently was understood to have received $750,000, which has been used in reducing the liabilities of the firm.

Mr. Wright was not at his office when reporters called this morning, but in his absence a clerk answered questions. "The trouble was caused by the stringency in the money market," he said. "It was found, in justice to creditors, that this was the best way of liquidating the affairs of the firm. It is impossible to make any statement at present. One will be issued later. More than that I am not at liberty to say."

It is reported that Siegel, Cooper & Co. will take over the stock of Hilton, Hughes & Co. The assignment was made by Albert B. Hilton, who comprises the firm. No statement has yet been made as to the liabilities and assets. After the close of business in the house last night there was a conference between Mr. Hilton and the managers of his various departments. The books were gone over carefully and the exact status of the firm was presented. At an early hour this morning there came the decision that the house must close its doors. Accordingly when the employes hurried up to the building they found on each door this notice: "All employes are notified that their services are no longer required and that they will be paid in full to and including this day." The following statement, which had been prepared by Assignee George M. Wright, was given out later:

"Parties in interest became satisfied that the business was not making a profit. It was therefore determined to close it. It was at first supposed that this could be done by an ordinary 'closing out' sale without any general assignment. With this end in view Judge Hilton within the last month advanced $250,000 to the firm to pay on account of merchandise claims. He has during the last few years advanced very large sums. As claims were pressing, there seemed no other way to close the business with justice to other creditors and protect the property from sacrifice but by a general assignment without preferences.

"It is believed that all the merchandise and general debts can be paid in full out of a sale of the stock and the collection of outstanding accounts. The bank paper is secured and will, of course, be all paid.

"Negotiations are pending for the sale of the whole stock, which if carried through will result in a settlement of the debts in a very short time."

No Tangible Assets.

Chicago, Ill., Aug. 26.—The governing committee of the Stock Exchange in its report on the recent attempt to corner Diamond Match and New York Biscuit stock by W. H. and J. M. Moore say an examination of the books of the Moore Bros. discloses no tangible assets. The most important fact disclosed by the report is that $785,000 of Diamond Match funds was used as margins in the speculation without the authority of the directors of the company. The Moores allege, however, that it was by authority of the executive committee. A pool of wealthy men whose names are withheld is declared to have been behind the Moores in the deal, and they have been forced to assume a full share of responsibility.

Not only has the entire surplus of the match company been practically wiped out, but there is a loss of more than $1,000,000 on the stock carried for the "pool." There has been a drop of 70 points in Match since the exchange closed. On the stock it means a loss of $7,000,000. The revelation of the unauthorized use of company funds has raised the question of the criminal liability of the Moores.

Chattel Mortgage.

Houston, Tex., Aug. 26.—J. M. Heiser, doing business on Washington street, today filed a chattel mortgage, naming C. M. Becker as trustee for the amount of $4411.

AFRO-AMERICAN FAIR.

THE OPENING WAS GIVEN UNDER VERY AUSPICIOUS SURROUNDINGS.

CREDITABLE STREET PARADE

The Opening Address Points to the Progress of the Race and Contains Food for Reflection.

Houston, Tex., Aug. 25.—The Afro-American fair of the state of Texas was opened to-day according to programme by a street parade that was highly creditable. The weather was warm but otherwise very favorable and of course the streets were thronged with people anxious to see the parade. The formation was made on Milam street about the crossing of Leeland, Polk and Dallas avenues, and was under the direction of Grand Marshal Ed Jones and a corps of assistants wearing uniforms of the old continental variety, with the tripointed hats. Before 10 o'clock the crowd began to gather at the point of formation and there awaited the various features to compose it. The component parts poured in from all directions with a promptness that was highly commendable. There were two colored bands on hand and while the delay existed they relieved the fatigue with occasional selections. But the military was absent, something rather unusual. There was a hitch somewhere and people along the line of parade grew very impatient. They caused a delay of over an hour. It occurred in getting them from the camp into the city, but as the long line began to move shortly after 12 o'clock, the military was pardoned by the expectant crowds.

The Houston colored brass band headed the line and the remainder moved as follows:

Fife and drum corps, Brazos light guard of Bryan, Sheridan guards and Cocke rifles of Houston, Excelsior guards of San Antonio, the Capital City guard of Austin, the last the colors of the First battalion, T. V. G., colored, sponsors uniformed in a carriage, Dr. Bowen of Atlanta, Emmett Scott and two other speakers, temples Nos. 1 and 2 of uniform rank, Knights of Tabor of Houston, juvenile zouave company, forty bicyclists of Galveston, Dallas and San Antonio with decorated wheels, appearing very pretty, Alamo baseball club of San Antonio, Houston baseball club, both in uniform, President Ed Banks and other officers and prominent personages, including the wives of many of the leaders and the committee in charge of woman's work exhibit; first carriage (open) was drawn by two milk white horses in white harness, white reins, white wheels, body covered and profusely bedecked with green artificial rosettes and wreaths. It was followed by nine open carriages and buggies, each covered with white and trimmed profusely, each with a different colored flower, as orange, pink, red, yellow, blue, pale pink and various shades of some of these colors. The spokes of the wheels were encircled by wreaths of its color. The occupants were generally dressed in white. These were really very beautiful. The decorations were done by J. T. B. Johnson, colored, and was complimented on all sides. There were ten other carriages, the occupants of which were attired in pink, red, blue and white.

Behind the carriages came a large float bearing fifteen girls dressed in blue, with silvery caps. It was the Second Ward yacht club. Behind it was another wagon bearing girls (the broom brigade), dressed in white skirts and blue waists. This closed the parade, and it was highly creditable to the fair. The parade moved down Milam to Dallas avenue, across to Main street, along it to Franklin avenue, across to Travis, up to Texas avenue, along it to San Jacinto, thence toward the bayou and across to the Grand Central depot, where the train for the driving park was boarded, and all hands went out, where the programme was continued by speaking and the execution of the following programme:

Invocation, Rev. D. J. Hull of Houston.

Patriotic hymn, "The Star Spangled Banner," and military salute to national colors.

Dedicatory ode.

Chorus, "Great and Marvelous." (Farmer.)

Opening address, Emmett J. Scott, vice president of the Afro-American state fair association.

"The Woman's Department," Mrs. Emma A. Williams, president board of lady managers.

Chorus, "For Unto Us," from "The Messiah."

Welcome to the city, Mayor H. Baldwin Rice.

Chorus, "March Onward." (Giebel.)

Address, His Excellency Governor C. A. Culberson.

Chorus, "Gloria." (Mozart.)

Oration, Prof. J. W. E. Bowen, Ph. D., D. D., of Atlanta, Ga.

Chorus, "Hallelujah," from "The Messiah."

Master of ceremonies, Edward Banks, president.

The programme was rendered from a stand facing the grand stand and capable of seating 170 people. The musical selections and recitations were very creditably rendered and greeted with applause. The address by Mayor H. B. Rice was interrupted with frequent applause. He in substance said that it was the custom these days to deliver a few words of welcome and retire, but he wanted, as a member of the Anglo-Saxon race, to welcome the colored people to the city and to wish them success, and he wanted to see them win on their merits. The speaker paid a pretty compliment to Emmett Scott, the colored speaker who had just spoken. He then spoke of what the race had achieved in the past thirty years, and, looking at it, what might they not accomplish in one hundred years. (Great applause.) Their success, he held, was in education. It was the key to the situation. He recalled the fact that only a few days ago he had issued a diploma to the first colored male graduate of the schools here, but he hoped that he and his successor would in future hand them many more. (Applause.) He wanted to see them win on merit—in fact it was the only way they could win, and when merit calls for it the Anglo-Saxon will extend the hand of encouragement. He was raised in the south and knew the negro, and he would say there was no man from any nation would help the negro more than the southerner. He again welcomed them to Houston, and with it closed amid applause.

The address of Dr. Bowen of Atlanta was very long and much of it he had said before in an address at the Atlanta exposition. Some of his points were made in comparing individuals and races, and wound up by showing the superiority of the black race in more ways than of any other, and held out the idea that in future it ought to be so that the color of a man's skin would never be looked or asked when he came up for consideration. There were a few white people out who heard the address. He displayed a great deal of learning, and he was often, perhaps, too deep for his audience in his reference to craniology. His remarks were frequently applauded by the colored people. It was after 6 o'clock when he finished.

Following is the opening address delivered by E. J. Scott, vice president of the association:

OPENING ADDRESS.

Mr. President, Ladies and Gentlemen: As an indivisible and indispensable factor in American life Afro-Americans are recognized and are pursuing the even tenor of their way toward the attainment of the higher privileges of citizenship, with no thought of the bitterness of the past; with but one thought—the promise of the future.

This Afro-American state fair and exposition, to which you have been invited, is the conception of a number of gentlemen of this city, whose idea is to here, in these buildings and on these grounds, accentuate the claim of the black citizenship of Texas to the confidence and respect of all men, who believe with Pope that "Worth makes the man, and want of it the fellow." The result of their labors is here for your inspection and your criticism. It has not been hoped that you would be startled with its gorgeousness. The aim has been to exhibit here substantial representations of what the black men and the black women of Texas have done and are doing industrially and educationally.

Scarce three months have passed, and I speak the entire truth, since the first meeting was held and an association formed. At that meeting the chances for success and failure, in view of the short time intervening between the conception the idea and the time set for its realization, were thoroughly canvassed. The enormous amount of work involved was not underestimated, nor has it been shirked.

With an entire consciousness of foredoomed failure without the active support and cordial assistance of the press of the state and of their fellow citizens, white and black, they solicited and have received such co-operation as the merit of the project, to my mind, deserves. The directors are not unmindful of the fact that no labor of theirs would in itself have brought about the magnificent results which here attract the eye and delight the fancy, and they extend their thanks to these influences which have been so helpful and to those citizens who by counsel and in a more substantial manner have conserved to promote the object which this exposition seeks.

Texas, with her genial climate, her boundless possibilities and her expanding greatness, must needs have the activities of all her citizens quickened; every resource of our grand state must be developed and every contributing factor for such development must be utilized to the fullest extent, to the end that this empire in itself may take its rightful place in the world of commerce as one of the richest commonwealths of our country.

The people of Texas, nor of the south, nor of the union, can not afford to be indifferent toward any element of its population, be that element white or black. The conversion of the waste products of humanity into good citizens and useful men will repay a thousand fold for whatever of active sympathy and assistance is expended in the effort. It is a self evident fact, a philosophical axiom, that a chain is no stronger than its weakest link; that a community prospers only in such a degree as all elements of its population prosper. If I may be permitted then to suggest to the people of Texas, I will say, utilize the forces which are all about you for developing your great agricultural possibilities and for the material upbuilding of the El Dorado which a kind providence has laid at your feet. I should like to commend for especial favor the people whom this exposition is designed to represent. I can not forget their quiet forbearance in the face of certain repressions and distinctions which they do not deserve and which have not the sanction either of logic or of gratitude. I can not forget their usefulness as citizens in the past, and I shall not fail to remember that as a labor force they have not been a turbulent factor, nor have they forced upon you distracting labor strikes nor wars. You of the south know them and they know you. When treachery meant destruction to your firesides they were loyal, and when an all wise God decreed their emancipation they were not less loyal.

We have a new south, and the new south has a new negro. Bravely fighting up from the dependent condition of the slave to the self-reliant condition of the man, he finds himself opposed by adverse conditions, but with a deathless optimism that's always his. He fights on, conscious that the proper reward awaits him. He has surprised his enemies and maligners in the past. He has accumulated more than $250,000,000 worth of realty possessions. He has developed more than 25,000 school teachers and professors in colleges. He has built 30,000 churches of costly design and finished architecture and has doubled and trebled with his labor the possessions of the south.

Black men recognize the fact that certain elements of their own race bring to them nothing but dishonor and disgrace. They know that discriminatory and repressionary restrictions are the reaped reward for the conduct of the "commoner" elements of the race, who care nothing for the newer civilization; but they know at the same time that if a race is to be judged by the fittest and not by the untutored masses that the achievements of her Douglasses and her Washingtons and her Bowens and her Fortunes and her Cuneys entitle them to a conspicuous place in the world's history. I wish even now that the captious and unfair critic could view this scene. I could wish no more than that he might see the thoughtful and intelligent faces which greet me. I could only wish that an opportunity be provided to note the evidences of thrift and industry which the splendid and magnificent exhibit here betokens. I could wish that he might know, as I know, that a startling array of professors from Texas schools and colleges, that doctors from standard schools of medicine, that lawyers from Ann Arbor and Boston university and Howard, that clergymen of repute and scholarship, that editors and writers of Afro-American newspapers, that men of national renown, that pure women from Christian homes and firesides, from intellectual associations and pleasant and happy surroundings, that one who is considered eligible to the bishopric of a great church, receiving nearly enough votes to elect on the first ballot, contribute to make up this audience; and then I would turn to him and ask if these people, these Afro-American citizens, deserve any worse treatment than that which is accorded any other race. I might appeal for them from the standpoint of justice, morality and religion, but it is preferable to seek for the fullest liberty for every citizen of this section through the medium of this section's commerce. Weak, but aspiring, it seeks development, to the end that it may become great and rich and powerful. Vexed racial questions, then, may hereafter find their solution in this proposition: That that which aids one element must necessarily aid all; that that which oppresses or does not encourage retards and militates against the fullest realization of our commercial hopes.

Let us, too, remember the improvement of such opportunities as are ours is of infinitely more benefit than lamentations and fault findings; that a state which is generous in the distribution of her school fund for all her children, and philanthropic in the establishment of three state eleemosynary institutions, whose citizens accord us a fair opportunity to earn an honest living, and who have sought to emphasize their sympathy for and their willingness to care for the needy and the weak, is not undeserving of our gratitude.

This exposition will have accomplished desirable results if the interest of both races is incited and cognizance secured to the fact that the material interests of both races are inseparably and indissolubly one. And so we welcome you here, and pray the benedictions of heaven that an era of good fellowship, of recognition for deserving mankind, of thriftiness and a desire to deserve every privilege accorded and conceded, may follow this exposition now formally opened and which seeks these results.

AT THE GROUNDS.

The display of exhibits at the grounds will be very good. The articles were in nearly all cases demonstrative of what the negroes of this state are capable of doing and have done to their credit.

There were many specimens of what negroes have produced in the field, garden and orchard and many creations of the skilled hand and eye of the negro. They were all creditable and in many cases extraordinary. The display had been arranged in the building known as the cooling paddock, a large, square structure, pretty well lighted and ample to hold the exhibits apportioned to it, and they were nearly all on the grounds. It was south of the grand stand.

Among the most noticeable exhibits may be mentioned a patent car coupler, an invention by Jacob Calvin Smith, colored, of Luling. He had been a railroad man, and his invention resulted from years of experience. He had two little freight cars, each perhaps a foot long, a railroad track for their operation, and there on a little table demonstrated the practicability of his improvement. A coupling could be made from the top or side of the car without the brakeman standing between the cars when they came together. Provision was made for the difference in height of cars, bumpers and all other requirements. It was operated from the side by a lever and from the top by a rod and spiral spring. It was patented by the government, good for seventeen years, and is a sure preventive of injury to brakemen. He also had an appliance for airbrakes, invented by A. J. Conley, also of Luling, so that on cars of both kinds the safety brake can be placed.

A box containing tools made of steel was exhibited by Ed Jones of this city. The contents were a razor blade, a razor, a hammer, small ice hooks, callipers and the like.

A very pretty toy house, complete in every detail, made by a son of Storkie Watson, was creditable work. It was painted, had glass windows, and was quite pretty. A set of furniture, made by the same boy, stood beside the little house and was almost as good a piece of work.

A guitar, complete in all parts except strings, was there from San Antonio.

A cistern in miniature, made by A. N. Raiford, was well done.

Fine products of the field were specimens of rye, hay, corn, cotton in boll and on stalk, and seeds of several kinds.

An exhibit by Neil Simmons, living near Houston, of turkeys, ducks, chickens of several kinds, pigeons, including the fantail and one or two other kinds, were all superior specimens and highly creditable to Harris county.

A miniature full-rigged steamship "the Lillie," was exhibited by John Washington of Galveston. It appeared to be complete to the smallest detail. It was six feet four inches in length and twelve inches beam, painted and full rigged. There was another smaller one from Seguin, but no name was attached. Both were excellent specimens of handiwork.

A very small (toy) stationary engine was steamed up and in operation just outside the east door of the hall. It was the work of Bussie Wade, a colored boy about 17 years old, and a very skillfully constructed piece of machinery.

A chest filled with small tools showed an artist's touch.

Prairie View school had exhibits in the way of drawings by its pupils. They included geometrical and architectural figures, building plans and masonry structures in outline.

A collection of flowers and plants adorned the central portion of the space, and was very pretty. Many of them were semi-tropical specimens. Cured tobacco plants from the near country made a very good display.

There were a numebr of other exhibits in the hall, but it was difficult to give credit to whom it was due, from the fact that the managers decided not to allow the names to be attached to the exhibits, but to have them identified by a number. This was to enable the judges of the various competitions to consider the entries solely on their merits, not knowing to whom any belonged. It was a very creditable aim to reach perfect fairness.

In another part of the ground there were several stables of blooded horses, and some very fine ones. Bailey Sparks and Ned Brown had fine horses on the grounds, and some good races are promised.

In the grove south of the grand stand and near the artesian well are located the tents of the five companies of colored militia. General Mabry and several officers visited the camp during the afternoon, and the place is under strict military discipline. Major Wilson, colored, is the officer in command, and orders were issued this evening enforcing all the rules and regulations of an encampment. The companies will have their drills, guard mount and battalion formation and maneuvers. The men have the best provision for a soldier's life in camp that could be asked. They have a cool place and well watered grounds.

A number of exhibits arrived to-day and will be in place to-morrow.

There are a number of amusements on the ground.

It is estimated that there were 1500 visitors to the grounds to-day.

Trains leave on the hours, and returning leave the grounds on the half hours. They are composed of eight coaches.

Ancient Order of Pilgrims.

Houston, Tex., Aug. 25.—To-day the Ancient Order of Pilgrims, colored, of the state met here in fourteenth annual session in the market house, and there were 180 present.

Prof. J. H. Crawford of Houston, H. C. P. of the order, called the house to order and introduced Van H. McKinney of Houston, who welcomed the delegates.

Response was made by J. P. Harris of Austin. He gave a history of the race as well as of the society.

Rev. W. B. Crawford led the song, "It's the Promise of Gdo." Prayer by R. W. Osbourne of Hempstead, after which the H. C. P. appointed the following committees:

Resolutions: T. D. Ubtshall, N. C. Washington and Annie Taylor.

Credentials: J. A. Mathews, Alice Hount, G. Watrous, L. W. Osbourne and W. L. Blockshall.

Adjourned for dinner.

The H. C. P. called the house to order. Rev. C. H. Smith and J. S. Tibbett were appointed to fill places. The committee on rules and order of the day reported. Officers made their reports, and then came the reading of the constitution.

Among the delegates are Revs. W. H. Davis of Calvert, A. A. Gooden of Austin, C. H. Smith, W. B. Crawford, Prof. Perkins of Conroe and Hon. J. T. Harris of Austin.

There will be two sessions each day. The body will get down to business to-morrow, commencing, perhaps, on reports of committees and officers. There are thirty sanctuaries in the state, with a membership of about 1600.

Decoy Letter Victim.

Shepherd, San Jacinto Co., Tex., Aug. 26. —Several registered packages containing money have disappeared from the mail between Cold Springs and Houston during the present month aggregating some $115. Postoffice inspectors disguised as drummers threw this town into consternation by arresting a young man yesterday named Eddie Sharman, who was employed as postoffice clerk at Shepherd and out of whose pockets they extracted $96 in greenbacks, among which was $25 in marked bills which the detectives had that day sent in a decoy letter through the mail, which would pass through Sharman's hands on its way from Cold Springs to Houston.

Trouble Brewing in Karnes.

Houston, Tex., Aug. 26.—It is unofficially learned to-night that Gen. Mabry has received a message from the sheriff at Karnes City asking for a company or squad of rangers at the point to prevent serious trouble. Nothing was said about the nature of the trouble, but it appears that the rangers were only recently removed from there under the advice of the captain. It appears that it is the same old trouble renewed.

Injunction Petition Denied.

Cleveland, O., Aug. 26.—Judge Stone in the common pleas court to-day denied the petition of the striking Brown Hoisting company employes for an injunction to compel the company to reinstate the old men as agreed. The court decides that the strikers have an adequate remedy at law in an action for damages for breach or contract. The court also denies a mandate or order to compel the Brown company to take its men back on the ground that the contract is too indefinite.

Killed by a Tram Car.

New London, Conn., Aug. 26.—While Sunday school excursionists from this city were landing at Gale's ferry this morning, a heavy tram car was let loose down an incline by a party of boys. The car dashed into the excursionists. One woman was killed and several persons seriously injured. A dozen of more were thrown violently into the water. A panic resulted in which others were injured.

Campaign Contributions Forbidden.

Washington, Aug. 26.—The civil service commission has issued an order to federal officeholders warning all employes against seeking or making contributions for campaign purposes. The order is sweeping in its character and affects all branches of the government service. Violaters of the law will be prosecuted.

Fatal Sunstroke.

Galveston, Tex., Aug. 26.—George Andre, a Frenchman nearly 70 years old, was found last night on the beach nearly two miles below the city. The body was in a decomposed condition. Death was due to sun-stroke while under influence of alcohol.

Lost Three Fingers.

Wharton, Wharton Co., Tex., Aug. 26.—A white man named Stafford, who runs Hudgins' gin at Hungerford, got his arm caught in the saws yesterday and lost three of his fingers.

Minnesota Populists.

Minneapolis, Minn., Aug. 26.—The populist party of Minnesota met in state convention here to-day and finished its work late to-night. The nominees are: Governor, John Lind; lieutenant governor, J. H. Bohler; secretary of state, Julius J. Henry; state treasurer, Alex McKinnon; attorney general, John A. Keyes.

Festival Tragedy.

Sandy Point, Brazoria Co., Tex., Aug. 26. —At a colored festival on the Ramson place on Saturday night Wade Richardson and Tom King were shot. Richardson died instantly and King is not expected to recover. The party who fired the shots made his escape. King has been constable of this precinct for a number of years.

Oil and Natural Gas.

Beaumont, Jefferson Co., Tex., Aug. 26.—Instructions have been received here to stop boring in the wells at Gladys City. Something like $3000 has been spent there in the attempt to secure oil and natural gas, the wells being now 360 feet deep and still no indications of a successful result.

Cut His Own Throat.

Burton, Washington Co., Tex., Aug. 26.—Henry Dahlmeyer, a German farmer living four miles north of here, suicided last night by cutting his throat with a razor. Temporary mental derangement is given as the cause of the deed.

Report Not Believed.

South McAlester, I. T., Aug. 26.—The report sent the press that Green McCurtain, the governor-elect of the Choctaw nation, had been assassinated, is not believed to be true. No trouble of any kind has been reported from this section of the country.

Cut Her Throat.

Hearne, Robertson Co., Tex., Aug. 26.—While picking cotton on the Scott place, two miles south of Hearne, a negro disagreed with his wife and in a fight the woman had her throat cut from ear to ear, dying almost instantly.

Cotton Worms.

Bryan, Brazos Co., Tex., Aug. 26.—A. G. Davis, a farmer of this county, reports that cotton worms have made their appearance in the uplands and are looking after what little there may be of the top crop.

The Texas Herald.

Politically, a Scientific Free Government in the General Interest of the People.

VOL. III. PARIS, TEXAS, THURSDAY, APRIL 7, 1898. NO 1

A GREAT TEN DAYS SALE!

During which we will offer bargains from every department of the store. These will be bargains such as cannot be heard of at any other house in Paris.

Our Reasons For This Great Sale Are These:

Ten days from now our buyer will leave again for the eastern markets on his Second Spring Trip. Our First Spring Trip was made 30 days ago. Now to close out for Spot Cash—to convert into money—which we can use while in market next week to great advantage. We shall place our entire stock before the public at prices positively never heard of before at this time of the season. Remember we want the cash and are making prices that will tempt you to spend your money if you need the goods.

STAPLE DOMESTICS.

Percales worth 7 cents, sales price	4c per yard.
Percales worth 10 cents, sales price	6c " "
Percales worth 12 1-2 cents, sales price	7 1-2c " "
Bleach Domestic for	2 1-2c " "
Bleach Domestic yd-wide, no starch, worth 6c for	4c " "
Bleach Domestic yd-wide, extra good	5c " "
Unbleach Domestic 36-inch wide	3 1-2c " "
Unbleach Domestic 36-inch wide, heavy	4c " "
Peperal Sheetings, full width, worth 18 cents	12 1-2c " "
Bleached Peperal Sheetings worth 22 1-2 cents	15c " "
Good Drilling	4 1-2c " "
Heavy Pants Cottonade	10c " "
A nice Dress Ging	4c " "
Apron check Ging	3 1-2c " "
Bonnet Chambra worth 10 cents for	7 1-2c " "
Zephyr Ginghams worth 12 1-2 cents	7 1-2c " "

These are only a few of the good things in this department. You will be delighted when you see the quality which these prices represent

DRESS GOODS DEPARTMENT.

A linen Batiste worth 15 cents, sale price	6 1-2c
A beautiful figured Challie worth 17 cents	8c
Dimities, very fine cloth 40 inch wide, only	7 1-2c
Organdies, dainty colors 40 inch wide, only	7 1-2c
Black Brocaded Skirting goods worth 40c, sale price	25c
Brown Serge well worth 40 cents	25c

These goods are also in blue and gray.

WHITE GOODS.

It seems unreasonable to be slaughtering the price on these at this time of season, but every article in the house goes. No reserve.

DRESS LININGS.

The 5c Cambric going at only	4c
The best grade of Celicia going at only	8c

BLACK SATTEENS.

8½c quality will sell at	6c
10c quality will sell at	7½c
12½c quality will sell at	8½c
20c quality will sell at	12½c

Corsets.

A Ladies' Corset for the small sum of	20c
An extra good Ladies' Corset, well worth 75c, for	45c
The dollar quality you can buy at	65c

We think these prices will move them.

Hats--Men's and Women's.

A ladies nice sailor hat	25c
" " sailor well worth	75 for 40c
" " " " "	1.00 " 50c
Men's Hats	45c
A wide brim black worth	1.25 for 75c
" " " " "	2.00 " 1.25

Clothing.

Jean Pants best quality Doeskin worth $1.00, only	73c.
" " good quality " 75 "	50c.
Men's good ducking pants " 50 "	35c.
" " " " " 65 "	45c.
Boys' Knee Pants	15c.
Men's Suits for	3.50.
" " "	5.00.

We take orders for tailor made clothing from cheapest to the finest at the very lowest prices.

Men's Shirts and Furnishings.

A Man's Shirt worth 35 cents for	20c
" " " 40 " "	25c
" " " 50 " "	35c
" " " 75 " "	50c
Undershirts from 15 cents to	50c
Good heavy Jumpers	25c
Men's Drawers	20c
Good bleached Jean Drawers, double seat, worth 40c,	25c

Table Linens and Towels:

In this department we have put the knife in to the hilt and you can buy a towel for	6c a pair.
A nice bleach Marseils Towel	15c "
A very large linen Huck Towel	20c each.
Bleach Table Linen for	20c a yard
" " " "	40c "
" " " "	50c "

Skirts and Shirt Waists.

See our window display of shirt waists.

A waist worth 90c for	48c
" " $1.50 for	75c
A skirt worth $1.25 for	90c
" " $2.50 for	$1.50
" " $5.00 for	3.50

Shoe Department.

A Ladies' Slipper for the low price of	25c a pair.
" Dong. Button Shoe for	75c "
" " " " worth 1.50 price	1.00 "
" " " " " 1.75 now	1.25 "
A Man's good work Shoe, all solid, for	85c "
" nice medium quality worth 1.50 for	1.25 "
" " Dress Shoe worth 2.00 for	1.50 "
A full Dress Shoe for men, vesting tops, in chocolate and tans, worth 4.00 for	2.50 "

Notions--Small Things.

Men's Suspenders for	10c a pair.
" good heavy Hose	5c "
" Handkercheifs	2 1-2c each.
" 4-ply pure linen Collars	2 1-2c "
" " " " Cuffs	15c a pair.
A nice silk Necktie	10 cents.
Ladies' Belts	10 "
Ladies' Hose	5 "
Hair pins	4c a box.
Pins	1c a paper
Thimbles	2 1-2c each.

Laces and Embroideries.

Look through these and get the prices when you are in the store.

The above prices can give you only a slight idea of what good things will be offered in this GREAT TEN DAYS SALE. We cordially invite your personal inspection of the goods and we say positively that the lowest prices you will see for many days are being made on merchandise at this store during this SLAUGHTER SALE. Bring your cash and give us a trial.

CRITTENDEN & SPIVY,

The Low Price Leaders.

THE CASTROVILLE ANVIL

DEVOTE[illegible] [illegible]TEREST OF [illegible]

VOl XIII | Castroville, Medina Co Texas Friday August 19th 1898 | No 1

Official Organ of Medina County

FINANCE REPORT.

On this the 9th day of August A. D. 1898, the Commissioners Court of Medina county, Texas, compared and examined the quarterly reports of County Treasurer C. B. Leinweber, and found the same correct and approve the same as follows:

GENERAL FUND.

RECEIPTS:—April 1-98, Balance on hand..	$5,794.04	
Receipts since	400.38	
DISBURSEMENTS		$ 4,024.95
Balance on hand		2,169.47
	$6,194.42	$ 6,194.42
July 1-98. Balance on hand	2,169.47	
Aug. 9-98. Balance on hand	2,418.88	

ROAD AND BRIDGE FUND.

RECEIPTS:—April 1-98. Balance on hand..	$2,855.37	
Receipts since	1,836.76	
DISBURSEMENTS		$ 609.79
Balance on hand		4,082.34
	$4,692.13	$ 4,692.13
July 1-98. Balance on hand	4,082.34	
Aug. 9-98. Balance on hand	4,128.94	

COURT HOUSE FUND.

RECEIPTS:—April 1-98. Balance on hand.	$2,901.49	
Receipts since	193.14	
DISBURSEMENTS		$ 2,977.27
Balance on hand		117.36
	$3,094.63	$ 3,094.63
July 1-98. Balance on hand	117.36	
Aug. 9-98. Balance on hand	117.36	

PERMANENT COUNTY SCHOOL FUND.

Cash account:		
RECEIPTS:—May 10-98. Balance on hand.	$ 141.19	
Receipts since	2,000.000	
DISBURSEMENTS		$ 2,000.00
Balance on hand		141.19
	$ 2,141.19	$ 2,141.19
Aug. 9-98. Balance on hand	141.19	

AVAILABLE COUNTY SCHOOL FUND.

RECEIPTS:—Sept. 1-97. Balance on hand.	[illegible]	
Receipts since	[illegible]	
DISBURSEMENTS		$ 8,799.50
Balance on hand		404.25
	$ 9,203.75	$ 9,203.75
Aug 9-98. Balance on hand	404.25	

RECAPITULATION.

Aug. 9-98. Balance on hand	
General Fund	$2,418.88
Road and Bridge Fund	4,128.94
Court House Fund	117.36
Permanent School fund	141.19
Available School fund	404.25
Total	$ 7,210.62

Cash on hand belonging to Medina County, in the hands of County Treasurer C. B. Leinweber, as actually counted by us to-day.

ASSETS.

Due and invested for Medina County Permanent school fund.	
Note of Louis Heath	$ 1,000.00
Land note of Grenwelge	5,000.00
Note of John Ihnken	500.00
Due by Medina County	3,428.34
18 Medina County Court House Bonds.	18,000.00
Due by Joe Lamon on land	1,634.00
Total Permanent fund	$29,562.34

BONDED INDEBTEDNESS

26 Court House Bonds @ $1000	$26,000.00
8 Jail Bonds @ $1000	8,000.00
Due by Medina county to Perma. fund	3,428.34
Total	$ 37,428.34

Ordered that the treasurer have proper credit, that this report be entered in the minutes and published one time in the official organ, THE CASTROVILLE "ANVIL."

Witness our hands, officially this 9th day of August A. D. 1898.

Attest:
AUG. KEMPF
County Clerk

HERMAN E. HAASS
County Judge
Medina Co. Texas.

FRED. NEUMAN
F. KILHORN
JOHN B. NEY
C. A. DUNCAN
County Commissioners Pr. No. 1, 2, 3 and 4, Medina County Texas.

Sworn to and subscribed this the 9th day of August 1898.

{L. S}

AUG. KEMPF,
County Clerk,
Medina Co. Texas.

—THE ANVIL $1.50 a year

COMMISSIONERS COURT.

August term, Monday the 8th met at Hondo Texas, all members present, when the following proceedings were had:

The returns of special school tax election in Dist. 15 Devine was opened and canvassed being 76 votes cast for the tax and 16 votes against, the assessor was ordered to make out special rolls and assess said tax of 20cts. as levied.

A County line consolidated school district was granted petitioners of a part of Dist. No. 18, on the E. Verde creek.

The painters reporting the 2nd coat painting of the court house finished the court inspected the work and ordered the three coat proposition of $250 of Contractor Banks accepted.

The finance report as ordered published was prepared.

Assessor Taylor submitted the rolls, as printed in last issue and as per summary below which was adopted and warrant ordered issued to him for $595.13 as ½ of his fee, payable by the county.

ASSESSED VALUES.

The assessed value of all the taxable property in Medina county on Jan'y. 1-98 was $2,845,626. (an increase over last year of $60.476, as follows: 755,573 acres of land at $1,778,820; town lots $174,689; 6388 horses and mules at $79,875; 28,549 cattle at $237,750; 44 jacks and jennets at $1515; 5135 sheep at $4180; 1861 goats at $975; 728 hogs at $805; 1 dog at $25; 1295 vehicles at $28,710; goods wares and merchandise $63,150; machinery $27,970; money $45,265; miscellaneous $20,300; 41 miles rail road G. H. & S. A. Ry. Co. $328,725, rolling stock $47,481; (the I. & G. N. R. R. not taxed) 72 miles telegraph $3430; a grand total of $2,845,626; on which the state taxes are $12,111.49; or 38cts. on $100 valuation and the county taxes are $17,860.26 or 62cts. on the $100, a grand total of $29.971.76, or $1 on the 100 valuation.

A special school tax of 20cts is levied in School Dist. No. 9 Chicon on $31,860 worth of property, amounting to $63.72 taxes.

Petition of H. M. Burton and others for election for hogs running at large in part of Justice Pr. No. 5 was rejected, because the boundaries did not describe an established sub-division of this county.

The regular tabular semi-annual statement of the county was prepared, and ordered published next week.

A new Justice Precinct was established, coextensive with election precinct No. 12 Tehuacana to be known as justice precinct No 7, and J. C Newton appointed Justice of the peace and J. P. Nixon constable, and term of court on the last Saturday of each month, at Hardt school house.

The road matter for 3rd class road of Jos. Tschirhart from Haas settlement to Lacoste was dropped at request of petitioners.

Petitition for 2nd class road from Baders ranch to Medina river was granted and Joe Rift, John Rohrbach, Aug. Hutzler, Ed. Meyer and Chas. de Montel appointed a jury of view to lay out road etc.

Petition of H. B. Balzen for change from 2nd to 3rd class road of a past of upper Sturm hill road was granted.

Reviewers heretofore appointed to lay out 3rd class road from Yancey to Devine were ordered to lay out the now traveled gated road from W. E. Newtons house to where same intersects Pearsall road.

Petition of F. J. Craddock for 2nd class road from Lytle to intersect Lacoste road was granted and J. F. Briscoe, Gust. Koenig, J. V. Reicherzer, Aug Weber and Jac Kempt appointed a jury of view to lay out the road.

Petition of F. P. Seekatz and others to close certain lanes on upper Medina road was read the court having no jurisdiction same were not acted on.

Report of jury of view on Devine-Cemetary road was adopted and J. H. Smith, G. T. Briscoe and Rev. Metzinger each allowed $15 as damages.

Teachers Examinations

The following compose the board of examiners of Medina County. Prof, W. T. Calmes, Hondo, Prof. A. B. Brucks, New Fountain, and Prof. J. R, Davis Devine.

Examinations are held on the 3rd Friday and following Saturday of each month, except January, March May and July. All applicants should notify Co, Supt. H. E. Haass, at Hondo Tex. at least one week in advance.

—THE ANVIL $1.50 a year

A GUARDSMAN'S TROUBLE.

From the Detroit (Mich.) Journal.

The promptness with which the National Guard of the different states responded to President McKinley's call for troops at the beginning of the war with Spain made the whole country proud of its citizen soldiers. In Detroit there are few guardsmen more popular and efficient than Max R. Davies, first sergeant of Co. B. He has been a resident of Detroit for the past six years, and his home is at 416 Third Avenue. For four years he was connected with the well known wholesale drug house of Farrand, Williams & Clark, in the capacity of bookkeeper.

The First Sergeant.

"I have charged up many thousand orders for Dr. Williams' Pink Pills for Pale People," said Mr. Davies, "but never knew their worth until I used them for the cure of chronic dyspepsia. For two years I suffered and doctored for the aggravating trouble but could only be helped temporarily.

"I think dyspepsia is one of the most stubborn of ailments, and there is scarcely a clerk or office man but what is more or less a victim. Some days I could eat anything, while at other times I would be starving. Those distressed pains would force me to quit work.

"I tried hot-water treatment thoroughly, but it did not affect my case. I have tried many advertised remedies but they would help only for a time. A friend of mine recommended Dr. Williams' Pink Pills for Pale People, but I did not think much of them.

"I finally was induced to try the pills and commenced using them. After taking a few doses I found much relief. I do not remember how many boxes of the pills I used, but I used them until the old trouble stopped. I know they will cure dyspepsia of the worst form and I am pleased to recommend them."

Dr. Williams' Pink Pills are sold by all dealers, or will be sent postpaid on receipt of price, 50 cents a box or six boxes for $2.50, by addressing Dr. Williams' Medicine Company, Schenectady, N. Y.

You may advise your son to push, but he may prefer to pull.

Important to Mothers.

The manufacturers of Castoria have been compelled to spend hundreds of thousands of dollars to familiarize the public with the signature of Chas H. Fletcher. This has been necessitated by reason of pirates counterfeiting the Castoria trade mark. This counterfeiting is a crime not only against the proprietors of Castoria, but against the growing generation. All persons should be careful to see that Castoria bears the signature of Chas. H. Fletcher, if they would guard the health of their children. Parents and mothers, in particular, ought to carefully examine the Castoria advertisements which have been appearing in this paper, and to remember that the wrapper of every bottle of genuine Castoria bears the fac-simile signature of Chas. H. Fletcher, under whose supervision it has been manufactured continuously for over thirty years.

The watering place exodus is on; the exoduster is off.

In some instances curiosity becomes criminal.

Thermometers are higher now than in winter; they are then low.

Beauty is Blood Deep.

Clean blood means a clean skin. No beauty without it. Cascarets, Candy Cathartic cleans your blood and keeps it clean, by stirring up the lazy liver and driving all impurities from the body. Begin to-day to banish pimples, boils, blotches, blackheads, and that sickly bilious complexion by taking Cascarets,—beauty for ten cents. All druggists, satisfaction guaranteed, 10c, 25c, 50c.

A sack coat often hides an indifferent figure.

Is Health Worth Ten Cents?

Man suffers many mysterious ailments from unknown causes, and nine-tenths of them have their origin in the digestive canal somewhere. It does any person good to clean out this canal occasionally in a rationaly way, provided it is not done in a violent manner. The proper cleansing and disinfecting preparation is Cascarets Candy Cathartic, which are very gentle, but at the same time thoroughly effective. A 10c box will purify the whole system and in most cases remove the cause of ill health. When "feeling bad" take Cascarets. They will do you good, and can do you no harm.

We call ourselves harder names than we allow others to.

Thinking of the one you particularly dislike tends to create hate.

We tip the scales to find our weight; the waiter, to save wait.

Too much success sometimes produces serious failure.

The fad of the summer girl is said to be the monogram fan.

Coffee sherbet is a delicious summer dish if well made.

Some of the pretty new Japanese paper fans are unique.

Some people are blue because they have nothing to be blue about.

Some men fall in love because they think it is a matter of business.

The new baby oft puts the pet poodle's nose out of joint.

DAIRY AND POULTRY.

INTERESTING CHAPTERS FOR OUR RURAL READERS.

How Successful Farmers Operate This Department of the Farm—A Few Hints as to the Care of Live Stock and Poultry.

About the Poultry House.

E. T. Abbott, before Kansas state board of agriculture: I said a while ago that you needed a house for your poultry. I want to tell you about one or two things that you need about a poultry house. You not only need to keep a hen warm, but you need to give her a comfortable place for the night. She not only needs to be comfortable so far as inclemency of the weather is concerned, but she needs to be in the same condition that a man needs to be in order to rest. If you don't believe it, just go out some night in the barn and lie down on a crooked board or on a pole and undertake to sleep there all night. Well, people will go to the woods and get knotty, crooked poles, and lay them up, starting at the ground and running up at an angle of about forty-five degrees, until the last pole is generally about even with the top of the house. They simply rest on something; they are seldom ever nailed fast, and are large as my wrist at one end and small as my finger at the other end, all filled with knots, with crooked places in them so that as the fowls move from one place to another the poles are unsteady; and yet the people expect their fowls to get up on those poles and rest comfortably during the night. A monkey might wrap its tail around such a pole and hold on, but it is no place for a hen to sit down and rest; and if she did sit down, along would come another hen directly and sit down on a crooked place in the pole, making a leverage, and causing the pole to flop over and throw her off, knocking half a dozen other down with it. Not only that, but if you build a roosting place that way—that is the old orthodox roost, the kind they had when I was a boy, the kind that is proper if you follow tradition—not only are they liable to fall off these crooked, unsteady poles, but every fowl tries to get the top pole. Did you ever go into a hen-house where roosts are made that way and listen to see what a commotion there is? Every hen tries to get to the top pole, and every rooster tries to get there, too, and they crowd in, and work and work and push themselves in until one gets pushed off and falls down and creates a great commotion. Why, it takes an hour every night for the poultry to get settled down and become quiet. Now, instead of doing that way, make your roosts all down on a level.

Foreign Cheese Made in America.

The Michigan Farmer states, upon the authority of a prominent cheese dealer, that in this country "the business of manufacturing foreign cheeses has grown to an industry aggregating about $10,000,000 a year." New York, Ohio, Minnesota and Wisconsin dairies supply most of the home markets with Camembert, Roquefort, Gorgonzaba, Stilton, Cheshire and Swiss cheese, besides a Limburger that in six weeks cannot be distinguished from the genuine article of seven or eight months old. This last is made in Jefferson county, N. Y. The Roquefort is made on the shores of the great lakes, mostly in Minnesota and Wisconsin, and the Swiss can only be made in Wisconsin and Ohio, where the pasturage and water are just right. St. Lawrence county turns out tons of Stilton, Parmesan and other kinds, and Camembert and Brie are made in other parts of the state. The products are claimed to be equally good as the imported article, "and the deception is aiding in the development of an American industry."

General Purpose Cows.

There are two sides to every question, but when a final analysis is arrived at there is seen to be a right and a wrong, and however closely they may lie alongside of one another, they never really mix in the sense of amalgamating, says Jersey Bulletin. In most discussions of such topics as the general purpose cow, the difference of opinion is found to grow out of and rest on a confusion of certain terms. Strictly speaking, a cow that is moderately well fitted to several different uses is a special purpose animal—that special purpose being to meet the various wants of the general purpose farmer. In this case the scrub cow is a special purpose cow, her special purpose being to suit the scrub farmer. But this is not the sense in which special purpose is generally used and commonly understood. According to the generally accepted use of the term, a special purpose cow is either a dairy cow or a beef cow, and belongs as a rule to some one of the breeds that have been developed for the one purpose or the other. In this, its proper sense, the term is not applicable to the scrub cow or to that rarity—the general purpose cow. The physical conformation and physiological structure that enables the dairy cow to do her work well disqualifies her for doing equally well the work of the beef cow. So, for similar reasons, the beef cow is disqualified for doing first class dairy work. These facts are so simple, so plain and so familiar to any person who has any acquaintance even with the two types of cattle, that it requires considerable patience to listen to their discussion. The point involved in the general purpose cow discussion is not so much the kind of cow to be used, as the kind of farming to be followed. If the sale of dairy products or of dairy cattle is to be the object, then common sense points out the necessity of resorting to some one of the developed dairy breeds. So on the other hand if beef making be the object. If, however, no one thing is to be made a specialty, then the farmer is at liberty to suit his own fancy. Such farmers will, as a rule, be content with the scrub. The exceptional men will select some one of the beef breeds, or of the dairy breeds, as their circumstances or fancy may dictate, and breed in that direction, grading up and improving their scrubs along the chosen line.

Dairy Notes.

Patrons of all factories where milk is consumed should support the managers in making a fight for good milk. It frequently happens that the buyers do not dare reject the milk of certain patrons for the reason that to do so would make them powerful enemies. It is unfortunately the case that patrons frequently side with a patron when he is in the wrong. Especially is this so if the factory manager or butter or cheese maker be a new man. The patrons need to be stirred up on this matter.

* * *

Do not lose sight of the cow's feed, even if it is summer. It sometimes happens that a cow is well fed all through the winter, but when summer comes she is allowed to take care of herself. This is all right so long as the pasturage lasts, but little by little the herbage fails and the feed becomes dry. The change is so slow that the owner does not notice it till irreparable injury has been done, at least injury that cannot be repaired till the cows come in again. By all means look after the cows that are in milk and see that they have a full feed every day.

* * *

The adulteration of food seems to have no limit. We thought when they began to adulterate butter with oleomargarine that the business would be profitable enough to the promoters and they would be satisfied to sell that article at least pure. But now they have begun to adulterate the oleomargarine with starch, paraffine and so forth. Next we may expect they will adulterate the starch with something still cheaper. Verily greed is both blind and insatiable. If we allowed these manufacturers of bogus products to have their way we would soon be feeding on sawdust and sand. This all shows the need of pure food laws, both for the states and the nation.

Wheat and Corn as Pig Food.

Purdue University has been conducting some experiments to ascertain the value of wheat and corn as pig food. This experiment had for its purpose a comparison of the feeding value of corn and wheat singly or in combination, when fed to growing, fattening pigs. This involved a consideration of several points of importance, all of which had a direct bearing on the experiment. The pigs used were farrowed October 20, 1896, were high grade Chester Whites, and the product of two pigs that were full sisters. Each sow had nine pigs, and the two litters were very uniform and furnished unusually good material for experimentation. They were placed in the experiment soon after weaning. Sixteen of the pigs or eight from each litter, were divided into four lots of four pigs each, consisting of three barrows and one sow in each lot.

The foods fed were as follows, with skim milk: Corn, wheat (dry), corn and wheat (half and half), wheat (soaked). The grain was fed whole, in regular pig troughs resting on platforms in small pig lots, and in the case of lot IV, the wheat, after being weighed out, was soaked for twenty-four hours in cold water up to the last of March, after which it was soaked only twelve to fourteen hours, that the wheat might be fed unfermented. In addition to the grain ration, each lot was fed daily about 1 p. m. from 10 to 12 pounds of separator skim milk. The summary of the experiments are as follows:

1. Pigs fed exclusively shelled corn for grain, in cold weather, made a gain per day of 1.16 lb.
2. Pigs fed whole wheat dry, for grain, made a gain of 1.02 lbs. per day, while those fed soaked whole wheat gained 1.05 lbs.
3. Pigs fed corn and wheat whole, half and half, gained 1.12 lbs. per day.
4. To produce one pound of live pork with shelled whole corn cost 1.49 cents.
5. To produce one pound of live pork with dry whole wheat cost 4.57 cents, while it cost 4.69 cents if the same kind of wheat was soaked.
6. To produce one pound of gain with the pigs fed a mixture of half and half whole shelled corn and whole wheat, it cost 2.97 cents.
7. The influence of the food on the organs and fleshy parts of the body, did not seem to be materially different.
8. Where corn was fed exclusively the bone was softer than where either wheat alone or corn and wheat were fed together.

Why You Should Keep Hens.

1. Because you ought by this means to convert a great deal of the waste on the farm into money, in the shape of eggs and chickens for market.
2. Because with intelligent management they ought to be all-year revenue-producers, excepting, perhaps, about two months during moulting season.
3. Because poultry will yield you a quicker return for your capital invested than any of the other departments of agriculture.
4. Because the manure from the poultry house will make valuable compost for use either in vegetable garden or orchard. The birds themselves if allowed to run in the orchard will destroy many injurious insects.
5. Because while cereals and fruits can only be successfully grown in certain sections, poultry can be raised for table use or to lay eggs, in all parts of the country.
6. Because poultry-raising is an employment in which the farmer's wife and daughter can engage and leave him free to attend to other departments.
7. Because it will bring the best returns, in the shape of new laid eggs—during the winter season—when the farmer has most time on his hands.
8. Because to start poultry raising on the farm requires little or no management; poultry can be made with little cost a valuable adjunct to the farm.—Ex.

Successful Sale of Shorthorns.—Recently one of the most important sales of Shorthorns in the Midlands was conducted by Messrs. Alfred Mansell & Co., of Shrewsbury, at Sherlowe, some few miles from Shrewsbury, England. The Sherlowe herd was established some 60 years ago, and has had a great reputation for having been bred on practical lines. Mr. Alfred Mansell conducted the sale, and in his opening remarks alluded to the encouraging nature of Shorthorn sales during the present spring and the healthy foreign and home demand, the latter of which proved that breeders had confidence in the breed and its future. Thirty-three cows and heifers were sold at an average of 47 pounds and 12 shillings each. Twelve bulls were sold at an average price of 35 pounds and 14 shillings each.

BLACK MEN IN WAR.

NEGROES RECOGNIZED AS CAPABLE ON ALL SIDES.

Colored Citizens Accepted as Officers in the Volunteer Troops—Radical Prejudices Greatly Diminished by Recent Events—Change in Sentiment.

One thing seems to have been settled in the war with Spain. That is the right of the negro to be a soldier, to have command as well as be commanded. Officers of the African race have been sent out in command of regiments not wholly of their race. Others have gone to the front in command of companies, the remaining companies of the regiment being white. If Illinois is called upon for another regiment of volunteers that regiment, first of all, will be a regiment of negroes, officered by men of the same race with the rank and file. This, too, to the exclusion of proffered regiments well organized by white men, some members of congress, others former cadets at West Point, and all of experience in military affairs.

No better indication of the change of front of the public has been observed than the attitude toward the former enslaved race. No man versed or experienced in military matters can or does fail to accord to the negro his full mead of praise for his conduct under fire and in conditions which many people might well shrink from. The conduct of the "buffalo" soldiers in the Indian wars has been such as to inspire unbounded confidence in the negro as a fighter. This has all taken place since the dictum was published by General Benjamin Butler that the colored troops fought nobly. It has taken over thirty years to batter down race prejudice to a sufficient extent to gain even a reluctant admission that a colored man is capable of command. Cadets at West Point, if of black face, have been "sent to Coventry" as "plebs" and kept there until dismissed from the army. Few have been graduated. Not a man of black skin has come at Annapolis. Today there are several negro officers in command of regiments, battalions and companies in the service. With the outbreak of war a leading southern journal took the position that in the very nature of things the negro would come to the front not only as a soldier but an officer, but few in the south felt that the thing could be possible. The negro in most of the southern states has no part on police, constabulary or other peace footing. But the first manifestation of actual war was the confinement in Atlanta of some Spanish prisoners of war, guarded by colored troops. The whites stared, breathed hard and finally took a broader view of the situation.

In 1861 the people of Baltimore stoned the Sixth Massachusetts regiment of volunteers when the command passed through the city. The vast dieffrence was shown when a regiment bearing the same designation passed through the other day on the way to Camp Alger. One of the companies was composed entirely of [illegible]ks, from Capt. Williams to th[illegible] recruit on the roster. But [illegible] [illegible]id not stone the regiment; they [illegible]eered the black boys in their blue uniforms as heartily as they did the white. In 1861 the war was sectional, today it is the nation against a foreign enemy. This makes a difference even so far as the color of the faces of the troops may be concerned. This incident, significent as it is, pales in comparison with the march of the Ninth Ohio. When this regiment passed through the capital on its way to Camp Alger, its commanding officer was a negro. He was major Charles B. Young, a West Pointer, who holds the rank of first lietenant in the Seventh cavalry. Major Young's command included three companies of colored men and seven of whites. None of the captains of the seven objected to reporting to a black officer. He knew his business, was a trained officer and was named by the governor from a school detail. The governor of North Carolina has decided to form a regiment of colored troops, officered in whole by men of their own race. He has named as colonel, James H Young, a politician of Raleigh. By so doing Governor Russell has taken advanced ground beyond that taken by any executive of any southern state. He is a republican to be sure, but his action can be contrasted with that of Governor Bradley of Kentucky, who wishes to do the same; with Governor Atkinson of Georgia, who refused to accept colored men, and Governor Johnston of Alabama, who refused commissions to colored officers. Owing to the feeling engendered all over the land colored men have been reluctant to enlist for fear their own race would not be recognized in the official grades. The matter having been laid before Secretary Alger that officer stated bluntly that colored men would be accepted and when qualified their officers of their race would be recognized. This has settled the status so far as the official recognition of the negro is concerned. The people have learned to believe that if a black man is a good soldier he might be a good officer if properly trained. If in the present war he shows this to be true his standing will be materially aided.

Floors of Paper.

In Germany, it is said, paper floors are well liked because, having no joints, they are more easily kept clean, they are poor conductors of heat and of sound, and they cost less than hard wood floors. They are put down in the form of a paste, which is smoothed with rollers, and after it has hardened, painted of any desired color or pattern.

"Bicycle Uncles."

Frankfort and Paris pawnbrokers have found it necessary to enlarge their premises for the storage of bicycles. The Paris municipality has voted $2,600 to convert one of the halls at the Mone de Pieto into a bicycle storeroom.

Waltzing and Hugging Not Alike.

Ethel—I just left Miss Elderly. She says she can't see any difference between waltzing with a man and letting a man hug you. Bessie—She would if she had ever been hugged.

COFFEE AND INSURANCE.

The Connection Between the Two Shown in New York and London.

From New York Sun: There might not seem to be any direct connection between coffee and insurance, but that one exists is attested by many episodes in the history of early New York. In 1759 the Old Insurance Office, as it was called, was open from noon to 1 o'clock and from 6 to 8 o'clock in the evening every day at the Coffee house, under charge of Keteltas & Sharpe, and gave marine insurance to merchants, secured by subscriptions of underwriters. In 1778, as the destruction of vessels by American privateers increased the risk of navigation, a new insurance office was opened at another coffee house, and from that time on the insurance business of New York was carried on generally in coffee houses. There was a precedent for this in another coffee house indissolubly connected with insurance—Lloyd's, in London. Edward Lloyd was the enterprising proprietor of a coffee house in Tower street patronized by shippers and merchants. The first mention of it is to be found in the London Gazette of Feb. 21, 1687. During the reign of Charles II., and toward the close of the seventeenth century, merchants greatly affected coffee houses, though it was not until 1691 or 1692, when Lloyd removed to the corner of Abchurch lane and Lombard street, that his house became the headquarters of marine insurance with which the name of Lloyd's is now associated. Steele, in the Tatler, and Addison, in the Spectator, notice Lloyd's coffee house, the resort of merchants and shipowners, and the Spectator of April 23, 1711, gives an insight into the manners and customs of its frequenters. It might reasonably be inferred that coffee, which is a soporific and taken to quiet rather than excite the nerves, would reduce the speculative tendencies even of nautical men and thus offer little inducement to those desirous of procuring hazards on ships. But what seems to have been the case was this: Something stronger than coffee was indulged in at the coffee houses, and, moreover, they were the places of meeting of those who interchanged maritime experiences. Each patron of the coffee house reported what he had heard—and, perhaps, some things he hadn't. The result of these conferences was a more general understanding of the risks attending navigation, and the practice of insuring ships against loss led gradually to other diversified and larger items of insurance.

Mississippi's New Senators.

From the Washington Post: Senator Sullivan, who will take his seat this week as successor to the late Senator Walthall, by appointment from Gov. McLaurin of Mississippi, will be one of the youngest members of that body. He has been in Mississippi for over a week, his selection for senator having been assured, as the Post stated several days ago. Although this has been his first term in the house, Mr. Sullivan has taken an active and creditable part there for a new member. He has made two or three speeches at the day sessions of the house and has participated actively at the Friday night sessions. Although a southern man by birth and associations, Mr. Sullivan has shown himself especially free from sectional prejudice and has never opposed reasonable pensions to the veterans of the civil war. He was one of David B. Hill's followers in the south, and, while he is a free silver man, he is not radical in his views. Like Representative Bailey, his brother-in-law, his course in the past has been for a conservative policy that would not estrange the gold democrats. In personal appearance Senator Sullivan is a man of medium size. He is very erect and precise in his bearing and converses with a frank but positive tone. He has a keen eye, an aquiline nose, and features that are rather thin and convey an impression of severity. Notwithstanding this, Senator Sullivan is a very pleasant man socially, and during his service in the house has been popular. He was appointed by Speaker Reed as a member of the committee on claims and of the committee on Pacific railroads.

Wooden Shoes Worn in Europe.

It is estimated that there are no fewer than 70,000,000 Europeans who wear wooden shoes. Basswood is ordinarily employed for sabots, but willow is the best material.

PEOPLE WITH TITLES.

Baron Siegfried, the young Bavarian lieutenant who in 1893 carried off and married Princess Elizabeth, granddaughter of the regent of Bavaria, was naturally expelled the kingdom. His wife's maternal grandfather, the emperor of Austria, after a very severe interview with the young couple, gave the baron a commission and has now raised him to the rank of count.

Presents to the sultan from the Emperor William are becoming almost as numerous as his majesty's speeches and telegrams. It is said that the kaiser intends sending his Ottoman majesty a handsome and excellently trained war dog, at present attached to a regiment of the garrison in Berlin. Two officers who have trained it are commissioned to convey the imperial present to Constantinople.

Mme. la Duchesse d'Uzes, the well-known society woman of Paris, has the distinction of being the first "chauffeuse" in Paris, having passed her examination as manager of a motor car before the government engineers. She accomplished the test journey of forty kilometers with the greatest assurance and skill, and her example is sure to be largely followed. The next fair candidate is Mme la Princesse de Montiglione, who goes up for examination in a few days.

There was a distinguished visitor in the house of commons recently, namely, H. H. Aga Khan, the Bombay Mohammedan chief, who was introduced by Sir Mancherjee Bhownaggree. He is a young man of pleasant appearance and manners. He listened with interest to Sir William Harcourt and Mr. Balfour's speeches and showed an intelligent appreciation of the parliamentary system. But his interests are those of the sportsman rather than of the politician. His stud of Arabs in Bombay is perhaps the best that exists anywhere.

THE CONSTITUTION.

VOL. II. CUERO, TEXAS, FRIDAY, JUNE 3, 1898. NO. 6

The War!

BATTLE OF SANTIAGO.

Spaniards Tryed to Torpedo the Americam Battleship Texas in theDark, But They Did Not Succeed.

May 31.--The first engagement between Commodore Schley and the Spanish fleet commanded by Admiral Cervera took place last night.

Two torpedo boat destroyers, about midnight, slipped quietly out of the harbor, bent on mischief. They crept along in the shadow of old Castle Morro and the mountain for two miles to the westward before they were discovered by the lookout on the Texas, where the men were sleeping by the guns, so that the battleship could be quickly manned. An instant after the lookout gave the alarm the white stream of the Texas' searchlight flashed along the shadow and under the mountain revealing the desperate game of the imprisoned Spaniards.

The torpedo boat destroyers, when they found they had been discovered, dashed toward the Texas, which, with the cruiser Brooklyn close beside her, was lying inshore.

The Texas promptly opened fire with her port forward batteries and her crack six-pounders, and the hiss of the armor-piercing shells thrown in the direction of the advancing torpedo boat destroyers startled the whole feet.

The Broyklyn also came into action, firing several rounds at the Spanish craft, but the bulk of the shooting was done by the Texas. The entire fleet went to general quarters, and soon their searchlights were playing around the narrow entrance of the harbor, in the expectation that Admiral Cevera's whole fleet would emerge from its haven and fight it out. The torpedo boat destroyers made a plucky dash through the rain of shells from battleship and cruiser, but, failed in their attempt to surprise the watchful Schley, turned and ran back into harbor. No attempt was made to pursue them. It is thought that they were not struck. as they retreted quickly and made small targets in the uncertain moonlight.

FROM RABKE.

Editor, Constitution:

The excitement of war seems to be monopolizing the attention of the people at present to such an extent that they are failing to give due attention to the civil affairs of state and nation. This should not be. The actions of Congress will affect the material welfare of our country more than the success or failure of Sampson's fleet in its endeavor to blocade Cuba.

Let every citizen protest against the issue of interest bearing bonds and demand, and pledge themselves to accept the legal tender paper money of the government in payment for services and all other claims against the government.

The voters of Texas should not lose sight of the imperative need of reform in the management of state affairs

They should not forget that over $600,000,00 of school funds is now lying idle in the treasury or being used by favorite bankers and not bringing in a cent to the rapidly decreasing school fund of Texas.

They should not forget that our attorney General who compromised a number of cases against the rail roads of Texas because he had no time to prosecute them has found time to "stump" the state in the interest of his own candidacy while he was drawing a $4,000, salery for the "faithful" discharge of his official duties.

They should not forget that a R. R. commission appointed to equalize and fix a just and equatable freight rate in Texas have failed miserably to accomplish the purpose for which the commission was created. Shall we continue paying them to help the R. R.'s fleece us?.

Have the people forgotten the $2,500, of their money given by the C. C. C's to Ex Gov. Hogg, to find out what an atty. General of the state of Texas ought to know?.

He, (the atty. Gen.) should be able to correctly interpret the constitution of Texas, it seems to me. Are the people going to sanction by their vote a law, which in order to supply funds for an extravagant state house ring to squander, saps the life blood out of almost every business or occupation?

Are the people going to be satisfied with the miserable makeshift known as the "fee bill"? Certainly not.

An extra election which will cost the state over $40,000, caused by the criminal carelessness or utter incompetence of the last legislature, will serve to remind the voters of their duty to themselves and their country in Nov.

Let us discuss these things, and see if it would not be fair and right to give the people a direct vote on laws under which they must live.

Some fear the people would have too much power, they are not competent to use that much power. Jefferson said all power was inheront in the people, then how can a man have too much of what is his from the first?

A. M. Coats.

SHOT ACCIDENTALLY.

Wednesday evening about 7 o'clock Mrs. Rhoad Fisher, Jr. who had just returned home with her mother, from an evening walk and evidently gone up stairs to put away some clothing or get something out of a trunk and it is supposed the revolver was in the tray of the trunk and when she lifted the tray out the revolver fell out and discharged, shooting her through the heart. When a Constitution reporter arrived on the scene life was almost extinct. She died about ten minutes after the accident occured.

This is one of the sadest accidents that has occured in the history of Cuero and has cast a shadow of gloom over the entire city

The Constitution extends its most heart-felt sympathy to the heartbroken mother and husband.

WAR NOTES.

Key West, Fla., May 30.–The cook of the United States auxilary gunboat Hawk, a native of Manila, deserted his post three days ago and was arrested as hore today.

Atlanta, Ga., May 30 —One thousand and thirty-three recruits left Atlanta today for Tampa over the Southern & Central Railroad of Georgia. The men were not uniformed and lacked guns.

One thousand men will be started for San Francisco for service in the Philippines as soon as their equipmont reaches Fort McPherson.

Mobile, Ala., May 30.–(Special.)—Clothing, of which the men stood greatly in need, has been distributed to part of the First Texas. No one knows when the rest of the First and the entire second are to be provided for.

Galveston News.

TUESDAY, SEPTEMBER 11, 1900.

Ward Headquarters.

The headquarters of the ward chairmen were announced as follows:

First Ward—Thomas Doyle, 917 Market street.

Second Ward—Charles Wallis, 1426 Post-office street.

Third Ward—Jake Davis, Center and Mechanic streets.

Fourth Ward—A. C. Torbett, Y. M. C. A. building.

Fifth Ward—Mart Royston, Y. M. C. A. building.

Sixth Ward—George Stenzel, 34th and Winnie.

Seventh Ward—Forster Rose, 29th street and Avenue N.

Eighth Ward—Edmond Bourke and Sealy Hutchings, Garten Verein bowling alley, Avenue N.

Ninth Ward—Clarence Ousley, residence of R. Spillane, Tremont near Avenue N.

Tenth Ward—W. F. Coakley, 2018 Ave. O

Eleventh Ward—Jno. Goggan, St. Mary's University, Eighth and Market streets.

Twelfth Ward—Edger J. Berry, Cracker Factory, Avenue A, near Tremont street.

WIND'S VELOCITY.

Reached One Hundred Miles an Hour When the Instruments Broke.

Galveston, Sunday.

The United States Weather Bureau office lost all records of the storm after 6:30 p. m. At this moment the anæmometer or wind gauge blew away from the top of the five story building. The wind reached a velocity of 100 miles an hour, which was recorded by the wind gauge just before it was carried away. Whether it blew at a higher rate after that hour is not positively known, but the weather men seem to think there were gusts that reached a velocity a trifling over 100 miles an hour velocity. The weather bureau records only five minute blows. The anaemometer records every minute blow, but the reports as kept only show the records for every five minutes. The last five minutes recorded before the wind gauge was destroyed showed a velocity of 84 miles an hour. But two minutes of this five minutes recorded a velocity of 100 miles an hour. The wind blew a steady gale from the north and northeast and reached its highest velocity from the northeast. At 3 p. m. the wind was blowing at the rate of forty-four miles an hour and steadily increasing in force and fifteen minutes later the gauge showed 48 miles an h ur. From four o'clock until 6.30 it steadily increased in force until it registered this 100-mile an hour velocity. It did not decrease rapidly in violence after this high blow, and in fact kept up a steady gale until late into the night. The weather bureau records do not show the exact velocity, but there were gusts that challenged the highest rate registered early in the evening.

The wind blew from the north from about 1 p. m. until 2:30 p. m. when it began to shift around to the northeast and maintained this direction till 8 o'clock, when it shifted to southeast and then to south.

The rainfall record was also lost. The rain gauge recorded a fall of nearly two inches up to 5 p. m. and was wrecked by the terrific wind that swept the apparatus from the roof of the Levy building. The rain fall, however, for the twenty-four hours, ending Sunday morning, was not exceptional and would not have been but an ordinary rainstorm had it not been for the hurricane accompaniment.

APPEAL FOR AID.

To the Humanity of the World.—Thous to be cared for.

Galveston, Sunday.

The following telegram was written Sunday afternoon and effort was made to send it to Houston. The tug Brunswick was placed at the disposal of the public committee by General Manager Spangler of the Gulf & Inter-State Railway. But the fireman and engineer had been drowned, or, at least, were missing, and the captain did not feel it safe to venture out on the Bayou with its rafts of driftwood with a strange crew. Hundreds of telegrams had been filed at the telegraph offices and with the committee to be sent by this tug. An effort was than made to get the tug Cynthia, but it was found that she drew too much water to make the trip up the bayou. General Manager Bailey said he would be glad to see the tug go had it been possible for her to make the trip. The official telegram was as follows:

ASSOCIATED PRESS, MEMPHIS OR CHICAGO—GALVESTON, SEPT. 9.—Following message sent to president United States, governors states, mayors cities, all public officials. Unspeakable calamity been visited upon Galveston, utterly beyond local relief. Large proportion population shelterless, without food or raiment. Not one family has escaped serious injury. Local banks and financiers have advanced generous fund for immediate relief, but so great and universal is damage to unflaging industries many weeks or months must elapse before people can become self-sustaining, Galveston has always been quick to respond to disterss of others. We confidently appeal to humanity of the world in greatest calamity that has befallen any community in century. Tomorrow we must begin feeding and clothing thousands of destitute. As soon as possible in next few days this committee will communicate detailed information as to suffering and devastation; Meanwhile we urge promptest relief to prevent death by starvation and disease. Send funds and supplies to John Sealy, Chairman Finance Committee.

W. C. JONES, Mayor.
M. LASKER, President Island City Savings Bank.
J. D. SKINNER, for Galveston Cotton Exchange.
C. H. MCMASTER, for Chamber of Commerce.
R. G. LOWE, Manager Galveston News.
CLARENCE OUSLEY, Manager Galveston Tribune.

700 BURIED.

Taken Out by the barge Monday. All Effort to Identify Dead Stopped.

GALVESTON, Tuesday.

The good citizens of Galveston are straining every nerve to clear the gronnd and secure from beneath the debris the bodies of humans and animals, and to get rid of them. It is a task of great magnitude and is attended by untold difficulties. There is shortage of horses to haul the dead, and there is a shortage of willing hands to perform the grewsome work. Yesterday morning it became apparent that it would be impossible to bury the dead even in trenches, and arrangements were made to take them to sea. Barges and tugs were quickly made ready for the purpose, but it was diffcult to get men to do the work. The city's firemen worked hard in bringing bodies to the wharves, but outside of them there were few who helped. The work was in the hands of Alderman C. H. McMasters, M. P. Morrisey, Captain Chas. Clarke and Joseph B Hughes, and they were ably assisted by Mr. J. H. Johnson and Jack Morrisey. These men p tched in handling the bodies themselves and urging the few men they could pick up to work. Rev. Father Kirwin, who went out to summon men for the work, reported that it was impossible to get any considerable number and he urged that all able bodied men be impressed. Soldies and policemen were sent out and every able bodied man they found was march to the wharf front. The men were worked in relays and were liberally, but not too plentifully supplied with stimulents to nerve them for thir task.

At nightfall three barge loads, containing about 700 human bodies had been taken to sea. Darkness compelled suspension of the work until this morning. Toward night great difficulty was experienced in handling the bodies of negroes which were badly decomposed The work to-day will be still more difficult. No effort was made after 9 o'clock yesterday morning to place the bodies in morgues for identification. It was imperative that the dead should be gotten to sea as soon as soon as possible. Many of the bodies taken out are unidentified They are placed on the barges as quickly as possible and lists are made while the barges are being towed to sea.

A large number of dead animals were hauled to the bay and dumped in, to be carried to sea by the tides.

One hundred and twenty-five men worked all day yesterday and last night in uncovering the machinery of the water works from debris. It is hoped that it will be possible to turn on the water for a while to-day, and it is planned to set fire to the debris under the direction of the chief of the fire department and cremate the bodies under it.

THE NEWS hopes to be able to resume regular editions Wednesday and Thursday. The list of dead got out under date of Sunday, and the sheet issued Monday were printed on the Clarke & Courts hand press. While working on a small sheet Tuesday morning, alarm was given that the Clarke & Courts building was about to fall and all withdrew. Later five of the Clarke & Courts men volunteered to return to the building to bring out type and copy, which were turned over to THE NEWS. Some of the names turnnd into THE NEWS were lost. Until regular editions are resumed THE NEWS will endeavor to print hand circulars from time to time in its own job department.

THE NEWS desires to print as early as possible a correct list of the dead, and will be glad to receive information which will aid in giving the public authentic information. The NEWS would ask citizens to send in corrections of the list as presented. In many cases it has been impossible to ascertain the full names of victims.

Mayor Jones has given very full scope to Chief-of-Police Ketchum and Mr. J. H. Hawley, chairman of the committee on public safety, to swear in citizens of good character as officers, and has told them that able-bodied men must be made to work or get off the island. Picket lines have been established around the large stores. and guards placed on duty. The soldiers and police are instructed to shoot any one caught looting or attempting to loot. The jails are full and summary measures are necessary.

The shooting of eight negroes for looting was reported last evening. One soldier at guard mount reported to Captain Rafferty thot he had been forced to shoot five negroes.

They were in the act of taking jewelry from a dead woman's body, the soldier ordered them to desist and placed them under arrest. One of the number whipped out a revolver and the soldier shot him. The others made for the soldier and he laid them out with four shots.

As the work of collecting the bodies increases, and as reports come in of deaths, it becomes apparent that the death list will run much higher than was at fisrt supposed. Conservative estimates place the number of dead in the city at 2,000.

A relief train from Houston with 250 men aboard and two car loads of provisions came down over the Galveston, Houston & Northern Railroad to a point about five miles from Virginia Point. It was impossible for them to get the provisions or any number of men to Galveston and they turned their attention to burying the dead lying around the mainland country. Mr. James Hays Quarles came over in a skiff to Galveston and reported that the steamer Lawrence had left Houston with provisions and one hundred thousand gallons of fresh water.

There is no fresh water famine here, as the pipes from the supply wells are running at the receiving tanks. It is dificult, however, to get it to the parts of the city where it is needed.

Bridge foreman Patterson, of the Gulf & Interstate Railway, reached here last evening from Beaumont, having walked about half the distance from Beaumont. He reports that Beaumont did not suffer much from the storm; two lives were lost from live wires.

From Beaumont down to High Island there was little damage, but the country below that place was greatly ravaged, and hundreds of bodies are scatterred along the beach.

Last evening Col. L. Polk, general manager of the Guf, Colorado and Santa Fe R'y, states that all of the bridges across Galveston bay are gone, nothing remaining but the piles.

THE DEATH LIST

The following is a list of the dead as accurate as NEWS men have been able to make it. Those who lost have lost relatives should report same at NEWS office. This list will be corrected and added to as returns come in.

Allen, Mr. and Mrs.
Albertson, M., wife and daughter.
Betts, Walter.
Boecker, Mr. and Mrs. John F. and two children.
Burrows, Mrs.
Baxter, Mrs and child
Bell, Mrs. Dudley
Burnett, Mrs. George and child.
Bowe, Mrs. John and two children.
Benn, Mrs. Annie and two naughters.
Burnett, Mrs. Gary and two children.
Burns, Mrs.
Cramer, Miss Bessie.
Coryell, Patti Rose.
Cline, wife of Dr. I. M.
Clark, Mrs. C. T. and child.
Coryell, Mrs. J. R.
Collins, daughter of Mr. Ira.
Coates, Mrs. William A.
Caddou, Alex, and five children.
Dailey, William
Day, Alf
Delany, Capt Jack, wife and son.
Davis, Gussie.
Davenport, 3 children of Mr. and Mrs.
Dorian, Mrs. George and five children.
Davies, John R. and wife.
Ewing, Miss.
Engelke, John, wife and child
Evans, Mrs. Katy and two daughters.
Ellisor, two children of Capt. Will.
Eichler, Edward.
Fredrickson, Viola.
Fredrickson, Mrs. and baby.
Fordtram, Mrs. Claud G.
Flash, Mr. William.
Foster, Mr. and Mrs. Harry and three children.
Guest, Mamie.
Gordon, Mrs. Abe and three children.
Gordon, Miss.
Garnaud, John H, wife and two children.
Gernaud, Mrs. John and two daughters.
Hughes, Mrs.
Howth, Mrs. Clarence.
Hill, Mrs. Ben and child.
Harris, Miss Rebecca.
Harris, Mrs. (colored)
Hobeck—and boy.
Humburg, Mrs. Peter and four children.
Hawkins, Mattie Lee.
Huhn, Mr. F.
Hausinger, Mr. H. A., daughter and mother-in law.
Hughs, Joe.
Hess, Miss Irene.
Howe, Adolph, wife and five children.
Jones, Mr. and Mrs. and daughter.
Johnson, Richard (Colored)
Jones, Mrs. W. R. and child.
Kelner, Sr., Charles L.
Kelly, Barney.
Kelly, Willie.
Krauss, Miss Kate.
Lauderdale, Mrs. Robert, two daughters, one son and Mrs. Lauderdale's mother.
Lisbony, W. H.
Labbatt, Joe.
Lynch, John.
Lord, Richard
Lafayette, Mrs. and two children.
Longnecker, Mrs. A.
Lenker, Tommy.
Lasoeco, Mrs.
Love, R. A. officer.
Magua, Mr. two daughters and son
McCauley, Annie.
McKenna, five members families of P. J. and J. P.
Monroe, (colored), Mrs. and three children.
Munn, Sr., Mrs. J. W.
Munn, Mrs. J. W.
Motter, Mrs. and two daughters.
Norton, Mrs. and two children.
Nolley, Mrs. Sam and four children.
O'Keefe, Mrs. Mike and brother.
O'Harrow, Wm.
O'Dell, Miss Nellie and brother.
Palmer, Mrs. J. B. and child.
Parker, Miss Mollie.
Plitt, Harmon.
Peek, Capt. R. H., wife and 5 children.
Porette, Josephine.
Parker, Mrs. Frank and two children
Ptolmey, Paul.
Parker, Angeline.
Parker, Sullivan, wife and 3 children.
Poree, Henry.
Pix, C. H.
Quester, Bessie.
Questor, Mrs. M. son and daughter.
Roudadaux, Murray.
Roll, J. F., wife and four children.
Ripley, Henry.
Regan, Mike, wife and mother-in-law.
Rose, Mrs. Franklin.
Rhymes. Mr. Thomas, wife and 2 children.
Ruhter, Albert and wife.
Richards, officer.
Swain, Richard D.
Spencer, Stanley G.
Stickloch, Miss Mabel
Spanish sailor; Steamship Telesfora
Scofield, Miss Ida
Sommers, Miss Helen.
Sweigel, George, mother and sister.
Schwartzbach, Joe.
Smith, Mrs. Mamie.
Schuler, Mr. and Mrs. Charles and five children.
Sharp, Mr. and Mrs.
Sharp, Miss Annie.
Schuzte, Mr. and Mrs.
Summers, Sarah.
Sylvester, Miss.
Schroeder, Mrs. George M. and four children.
Schuler, Adolph, mother and five sisters.
Treadwell, Mrs. J. B. and child.
Taylor, (colored), Mrs.
Trebosius, Mrs. George.
Trebosius, two sisters of George Trebosius.
Watkins, Mr. S.
Wensmore, family of seven members
Wenman, Mrs. John C. and two children
Wilson, Mrs. B.
Webster, Edward and two sisters.
Woodward, Miss Hattie.
Woollam, C.
Wilson, Mary and child.
Wood, mother of deputy U. S. Marshal
Webster, Sr., Thomas.
Wolfe, Charles.
Walter, Mrs. Charles and three children.
Williams, Miss.
Weinberger, Mrs. Frederick.
Weinberger, Fritz J.
Wharton.
Warren, James, wife and 6 children.
Wood, Mrs. S. W.
Woodward, Mrs. R. L. and two children.
Wakelee, Mrs. David.
Masterson, Mrs. B. T.
Wallis, Lee and four children.
Minor, Lucian.
Eggert, Fred and father.
League, Mrs. and two children.
Johnson, Mrs. H. B. and cnild.
Anderson family, four people.
Bell, George, wife and four children.
Feigle, George and daughter.
Coers, Dr.
Boatwright, Mrs.
Warren, John.
Holmes, Florence.
Park, Mrs. M. L.
Youngblood, L. J., wife and child.
McManus, Mrs. W. H.
Zinke, August, Richard C. and Johanna.
Herman, Martin and two children.
Pix, C. H.
Hock, Mrs. and son.
Eggert, Wm. and son Charles.
Mutti, A., killed in rescue work.
Lucas, Mr. and Mrs. H., 2 children white nurse.
Pauls, Willie and Cecelia.
Stockfleth, Peter, wife and 6 children.
Schwoabel, George, wife and daughter Lulu.
Krauss, Mr. Joseph J., wife and 2 daughters—mother, father and sister of jailer Fred Krauss.
Ducos, 2 children of Leon.
Olsen, Mrs. Matilda and 2 children.
Kelso, Munson J. jr.
Kelso, Roy, baby boy of J. C. Kelso.
Grothcar, Mrs. John and child.
Bush, Charles, wife and three children.
Kauffman, H., wife and children.
Popular, Mr. and Mrs. A. and four children, Agnes, Mamie, Clarence and tony.
Opperman, Miss May of Palestine, and Marguerite and Gussie Opperman.
Williams, Mrs. Frank and child.
Beveridge, Mrs. J. L. and two children.
Davis, Mrs. and daughter Grace.
Levine, Mrs. P. and family.
Sherwood, W. T.
Schwarzback, child of Theo.
Andrew, Mrs. and three children.
Ellis, Mrs. and family.
Zipp, Mrs. and daughter.
Stenzel, Mr. and family.
English, John, wife and child.
Weyer, Judge and wife.
Olfson, Mrs.
Turner, Mrs. K. and little girl.
Johnson, Mrs. Wm.
Dowel, Mrs. Sam.
Dowel, Miss Nona.
Wheless, J. S.
Burnett, Mrs. mother of Gary and George Burnett.
Dinter, Mrs. and daughter.
Lysler, W. W.
McGill, Dr.
Moran, James.
Tovera, Officer.
Hatch, D. B. and family.
Bisbey, and family.
North, and family.
Segers, and family.
Castenane (milkman).
Byrd, Mrs. J. C. and child.
Ritzler, Mrs.
Geoppinger, Leopold.
Gottleib, Mrs. and seven children.
Ashley, Mr. and Mrs. F. C.
Faucett, Mrs. Bell.
Edmonson, Mrs.
Borden, Mr. and Mrs. J. F.
Balzman, Mrs.
Delaya, Paul and two daughters.
Mati, Amedio.
Junemann, Charles, wife and daughter.
Harris, Mrs. John and 3 children.
Darley, John, wife and daughter Belle.
Goldmann, Mr. and Mrs. Theodore and son Will.
Dean, child of R. F.
Mitchell, Miss Nola.
Johnson, Mrs. Ben and 2 children.
Rowan, Mrs. John and three children
Bird, Mrs. Joseph and five children
Tovrea, Sam wife and four children
Armstrong, Mrs. Dora wife of C. F. and four children
Swanson, Mrs. Martin
Rice, William J. of (Galv. News) and little daughter, Mildred
Windman, Mrs.
Sherwood, Charles L. wife and two children
Sherwood, Thomas wife and two or three children
Amundsen, Mrs. Anna Marie
Amundsen, Louis
Fisher, Walter wife and three children.
Aguilo, Joe B. and two children
Agin, George and child.
Casey, Mrs.
Shike, Mrs. son and infant.
Warrah, Martin.
Warwarvosky, Adolph, mother and sister.
Homburg, Peter.
Hannamann, Mrs. August.
Andreson, Nick, and sons Henry and John.
Oppe, Fritz (milkman).
Schneider, Henry, and family.
Long, two children of Sergeant.
Thomas, Mrs. and one child.
Schaf, Mrs. and three children.
Worral, Mr., wife and child.
Stenzel, wife and three children.
Burge, Wm., wife and child.
Kleimcke family.
Sugar, Mrs., and two children.
Johnson, Oakey, wife, child and brother.
Dixon, Mrs. Tom and three children.
Williams, father of Frances (colored).
Vamey, Mrs. B. (colored).
Johnson, Harry.
Morse, Albert P., wife and three children.
Lloyd, W.
Irvin, child of Wm. H.
Irwin, wife and two sisters of Will.
Vidovich, Mike.
Miller, S. and wife.
Poland, Ed., and sister.
White, ———
Tickle, H. J., wife and two children.
Hunter, Mrs. Alice, and brother and father and three children.
Bailey, Geo., wife and three children.
Graft, Mrs. George and three children.
Schwoebel, Geo., wife and daughter.
Fiegel, John, Sr.
Fiegel, Martin.
Muller, Henry (painter).
Levine, Mrs. P., daughter and sons Leo and Carroll.
Hauser, I., and wife.
Harris, L.
Hennessy. Mrs. M. P. and two nieces.
Weber, W. J., wife and two children.
Haslers, Charles, wife and child.
Drewa, H. A.
Kelley, Dan., Sr.
Hester, Charlie.
Emanuel, Joe.
Labatt, H. J., Sr., wife and daughtea Nellie.
Paisley, William.
Agin, George.
Migel, Meyer.

Owing to limited facilities and a lack of space The News is unable in this issue to publish the complete list of names reported. Those omitted, together with all additional names secured, will appear in the list tomorrow.

The Galveston Daily News.

59TH YEAR—NO 172. GALVESTON, TEXAS, WEDNESDAY, SEPTEMBER 12, 1900. ESTABLISHED 1842.

STORY OF THE HURRICANE WHICH SWEPT GALVESTON

Loss of Life Is Estimated at Between 4000 and 5000---Not a Single Individual Escaped Property Loss---The Total Property Loss From Fifteen to Twenty Million Dollars.

REVIEW OF THE SITUATION.

Galveston, Wednesday. — Galveston has been the scene of one of the greatest catastrophes in the world's history. The story of the great storm of Saturday, September 8, 1900, will never be told. Words are too weak to express the horror, the awfulness, of the storm itself; to even faintly picture the scene of devastation, wreck and ruin, misery, suffering and grief. Even those who were miraculously saved after terrible experiences, who were spared to learn that their families and property had been swept away, spared to witness scenes as horrible as the eye of man ever looked upon—even those can not tell the story. There are stories of horrible deaths, thousands of stories of individual heroism, stories of wonderful rescues and escapes, each of which at another time would be a marvel in itself and would command the interest of the world. But in a time like this, when a storm so intense in its fury, so prolonged in its work of destruction, so wide in its scope and so infinitely terrible in its consequences has swept an entire city and neighboring towns for many miles on either side, the human mind can not comprehend all of the horror, can not learn or know all of the dreadful particulars. One stands speechless and powerless to relate even that which he has felt and knows.

Gifted writers have told of storms at sea, of the wrecking of vessels, where hundreds of lives were at stake and lost. That task pales into insignificance when compared with the task of telling of a storm which threatened the lives of perhaps 60,000 people, sent to their death perhaps 6000 people and left other thousands wounded, homeless and destitute, and still others to cope with grave responsibilities to relieve the stricken, to grapple with and prevent anarchy's reign, to clear the water sodden land of putrefying bodies and rotting carcasses, to perform tasks that try men's souls and sicken their hearts. The storm at sea is terrible, but there are no such dreadful consequences as those which have followed the storm on this seacoast. And it is men who passed through the terrors of the storm, who faced death for hours, men ruined in property and bereft of families, who took up the herculean and well nigh impossible task of bringing order out of chaos, of caring for the living and getting the dead away before they made life impossible here.

The storm came not without warning, but the danger which threatened was not realized, not even when the storm was upon the city. Friday night the sea was angry. Saturday morning it had grown in fury and the wrecking of the beach resorts began. The waters of the gulf pushed inland. The wind came at a terrific rate from the north. Still men went to their business and about their work, while hundreds went to the beach to witness the grand spectacle which the raging sea presented. As the hours rolled on the wind gained in velocity and the waters crept higher and higher. The wind changed from the north to the northeast, and the water came in from the bay, filling the streets and running like a mill race. Still the great danger was not realized. Men attempted to reach their homes in carriages, wagons, boats, afoot, in any way possible. Others went out in the storm for a lark. As the day wore on the water increased in depth, and the wind tore more madly over the island. Men who had delayed starting for home, hoping for an abatement of the storm, concluded that the storm would grow worse, and went out in that howling, raging, furious storm, wading through water almost to their necks, dodging flying missiles swept by a wind blowing 100 miles an hour.

Still the wind increased in velocity, even after it seemed impossible that it should be more swift. It changed from east to southeast, veering constantly, calming for a second, and then coming with awful, terrific jerks, so terrible in their power that no building could withstand them, and none wholly escaped injury. The maximum velocity of the wind will never be known. The gauge at the weather bureau registered 100 miles an hour and blew away at 5.10 o'clock. But the storm at that hour was as nothing when compared with what followed and the maximum velocity must have been as great as 120 miles an hour. The most intense period and the most anxious time was between 8.30 and 9 o'clock. With a raging sea rolling around them, with a wind so terrific that none could hope to escape its fury, with roofs being torn away and buildings crashing all around them, men, women and children were huddled in buildings, caught like rats, expecting to be crushed to death or drowned in the sea, yet cut off from escape. Buildings were torn down, burying their hundreds, and were swept inland, piling up great heaps of wreckage. Hundreds of people were thrown into the water in the height of the storm, some to meet instant death, others to struggle for a time in vain, and thousands of others to escape death in most miraculous and marvelous ways. Hundreds of the dead were washed across the island and the bay, many miles inland. Hundreds of bodies were buried in the wreckage. Many who escaped were in the water for hours, clinging to drift wood, and were landed, bruised and battered and torn on the mainland. Others were picked up at sea.

And all during the terrible storm acts of the greatest heroism were performed. Hundreds and hundreds of brave men, as brave as the world ever knew, buffeted with the waves and rescued hundreds and hundreds of their fellow men. Hundreds of them went to their death—the death that they knew they must inevitably meet in their efforts; hundreds of them perished after saving others—heroes, martyrs, men who exemplified that supreme degree of love of which the Master spoke:

"Greater love hath no man than this, that he lay down his life for his friend."

Many of the men who laid down their lives in this storm did so in efforts to save their families, many to save friends, many more to save people of whom they had never heard; they simply knew that human beings were in danger, and they counted their own lives as naught.

It is the irony of fate that many of those who left their own homes to seek seeming safety in other buildings perished beneath ruins or in the water, while their own homes remained standing. Scores and scores of people took refuge in the homes that had been deserted by their owners and were lost. Some who remained in seemingly insecure buildings, in structures long since deemed unsafe, escaped unhurt.

As the great danger of the storm was not realized in advance, neither was it realized by many even during its progress. Many slept while it was intense. And even the horror and extent of the storm was not realized when it had passed. As the days grow on the awfulness of the catastrophe is being ascertained and appreciated.

The waters fell even more rapidly than they came, but the wind did not abate sufficiently to quiet fears until about 1 o'clock Sunday morning. Then men ventured out—those who were not homeless—saw an awful scene of wreckage. They learned that many buildings had been destroyed and that lives had been lost. They stood aghast, appalled; but they did not realize the extent of devastation and destruction. Sunday morning came and bright sunshine fell upon a wrecked city. Everywhere was wreck and ruin, everywhere was death and desolation. The streets were a tangle of debris, of broken timbers, brick and mortar, tangled wires and poles. Human bodies and the carcasses of animals lay all around. And yet the awfulness of the calamity was not felt. The mortality was estimated at 150 to 300; men put away the horrible thought that a greater number of their fellow men had perished. But every hour since then has brought fresh knowledge of the work of the storm, and estimates of the dead have passed into the thousands, until now it appears that the population of the city has been decimated.

Sunday the city was demoralized and little was accomplished toward the great work which had to be done. Citizens met and organized for relief work, for burying the dead and clearing away the debris, but no very effective work was done until the next day. On Sunday provisions were made for bringing the dead to improvised morgues, and committees were directed to bury the bodies. Then it was thought that hundreds would have to be buried. Monday morning it was realized that there would be more than a thousand. It was also realized that it would be impossible even to dig trenches to cover the dead, so filled was the ground with water. Corpses were decaying, carcasses were rotting. Then it was that the survivors from the storm began to appreciate that conditions of the gravest character confronted them. The city was being looted, dead bodies were shorn of fingers by human ghouls, thieving the jewelry. Not enough men could be gotten to dig the dead out from the ruins or to haul them. It was decided to take the bodies to sea, as being the most expeditious way to dispose of them. But men refused to touch the bodies. This was especially true of the negroes. Some few were secured to undertake the grewsome task by reason of the example set them by M. P. Morrissey, Alderman McMaster, Captain Charles Clarke, Captain Fred Chase, Mr. J. H. Johnston, Mr. Joseph Hughes and other citizens, who handled the putrefying corpses all day long, although their very souls revolted at the task.

Monday the city was practically placed under martial law. Soldiers and hundreds of special officers were placed on guard. The citizens' committee sequestered all food supplies, and ordered that no able-bodied man should be allowed to eat unless he worked. Men were impressed at the point of the bayonet to do the work that must be done.

Quite a number of negroes were killed for looting. No one was allowed in certain parts of the city without a pass, nor anywhere after 9 o'clock at night without a permit from the authorities.

Seven hundred bodies were buried at sea on Monday. When night fell it was known that there were thousands more to be disposed of. Many of them were lying on the beach; many others were buried beneath the ruins of buildings. They were decomposing rapidly and giving off a horrible stench. The situation looked desperate. On Tuesday morning the bodies had decomposed so greatly that it was absolutely impossible to handle them to send them to sea. Fortunately, however, the waters surrounding the island had receded somewhat, and the water in the ground had fallen so that it was possible in places to bury the bodies where found. The wind had also abated and the day was calm, so that it was comparatively safe to set fire to some of the debris, although the waterworks were not in operation. Many bodies of human beings and animals were burned.

Several times on Monday and on Tuesday there were riots caused by the impressment of men to do the public work. But by Tuesday evening there was better organization all around; the law officers had a firmer grip on the city and authority was better respected. Still the situation was grave. The stench arising from human bodies, dead animals, damaged goods and wreckage of all kinds was terrible. The need of disinfectants in enormous quantities was keenly realized and appeals went out for help of this kind.

Fortunately there has been moonlight ever since the storm, otherwise the city would be in total darkness. All wires are down and the electric light plants are badly damaged, and the gas works torn. Fortunately also the water works supply pipe from the wells at Alta Loma remained intact, and has poured a steady stream into the receiving wells, where people could go for water. This was an encouraging feature, as it took away the horrible prospect of perishing for want of water. But the machinery of the waterworks was covered in the ruins of the building, and the pipes were torn in many parts of the city. It was impossible to distribute the water through the mains. It has been a godsend that there have been no fires. Water was badly needed for fire protection, and badly needed that the work of burning the wreckage could be carried on without endangering the entire city. Early this morning the force of men at work in restoring the plant succeeded in turning water into the mains from the receiving tank. The elevation was so slight and there were so many open service pipes that the water did not reach many premises. Work is being pushed, however, and the prospect is that the pumps will be going this evening.

Cut off from all rail communication, cut off from telegraphic communication, absolutely cut off from the outside world, the people of Galveston have gone ahead with their appalling task, confident that the world would come to their relief as speedily as possible. Houston came nobly to the rescue as quickly as possible, Beaumont and New Orleans sent relief, and now the cheering news is received that relief is coming from all quarters of the country. Help is needed and needed quickly. Money, provisions and disinfectants are needed. Brave men who will help are needed. But sightseers ought by all means to remain away. The congregation of hundreds or thousands of strangers here at this time would be unspeakably horrible. Provisions are needed for the thousands of destitute people here, and all the transportation facilities possible are needed to get the women and children out of the city. The people of the state will do Galveston a great kindness in keeping sightseers away from Galveston at this terrible time.

ARMY OFFICERS HERE.

Galveston, Tuesday.—General McKibben, U. S. A., commanding the department of Texas, and Adjutant General Tom Scurry, Texas volunteer guard, arrived here to-night to co-operate with the local authorities.

SUMMARY OF SITUATION.

Sent to Associated Press—Estimate of Losses.

The following telegrams explain themselves:

New York, Sept. 11.—Major R. G. Lowe, Galveston: Please send at the earliest moment signed statement giving summary of conditions prevailing at Galveston.

CHARLES H. DIEHL,
Gen. M'gr. Associated Press.

✣ ✣ ✣

Charles S. Diehl, General Manager Associated Press, New York: A summary of conditions prevailing at Galveston is more than a human intellect can master. Briefly stated, the damage to property is anywhere between fifteen and twenty millions. The loss of life can not be computed. No lists could be kept, and all is simple guess work. Those thrown out to sea and buried on the ground wherever found will reach the horrible total of at least three thousand souls. My estimate of the loss on the island of Galveston and intermediate surrounding district as between four and five thousand deaths. I do not make this statement in fright or excitement. The whole story will never be told, because it can not be told.

The necessities of those living are total. Not a single individual escaped property loss. The property on the island is wrecked, fully one-half totally swept out of existence altogether. What our needs are can be computed by the world at large from the statement herewith submitted much better than I could possibly summarize them. The help must be immediate.

R. G. LOWE,
Manager Galveston News.

SITUATION WEDNESDAY.

Improvements in Policing the City—Effort to Get Women and Children Away.

Galveston, Wednesday Noon.—At 1 o'clock last night water was turned into the city mains from the receiving tank, connection having been completed. A portion of the pipe was built up of wood. This difficult task was accomplished by Charles Rube, a carpenter, who worked steadily for twenty-four hours. The water reached many premises throughout the city, but on account of broken mains and service pipes there were many places not reached. Alderman McMaster, who is superintending the job of restoring the works to running order, and who has been at work night and day, said this morning that he had eight squads of men out plugging the broken service pipes. He expects to have the pumps going some time this afternoon and this will supply water to a large part of the city. The plumbers, steam fitters and machinists of the Galveston City railroad worked on the job last night. This morning the machinists of the government dredgeboat Comstock and of the revenue cutter Galveston tendered their services and are at work. Engineer Mercer of the City railroad tendered his services to operate the plant.

Last night General McKibbon, commander of the department of Texas, United States army, arrived in Galveston. He came in accordance with an order of the secretary of war to render all the assistance possible. He said he was followed by 20,000 rations and 1000 tents, coming by barge from Hoston, and that he had 20,000 rations following by express. Colonel Robert, adjutant general of the department, was here during the storm and has since been rendering assistance in the work of relief. Lieutenant Perry, aide de camp, came with General McKibbon.

Adjutant General Thomas Scurry, Texas volunteer guard, arrived here last night. Mayor Jones had telegraphed for him. The mayor, General McKibbon and General Scurry had a long conference last night, and afterwards General Scurry had a conference with Chief of Police Ketchum.

Mayor Jones said to a News reporter that he had practically placed the policing of the city in the hands of General Scurry. He said he had sent for him, knowing that a man who had not passed through the experiences here would be better able to handle the situation, and also because General Scurry was so well equipped for that kind of work, and his reputation would give confidence to the people. The mayor said the police situation had greatly improved within the past two days.

The pass system was abrogated last evening and the police and soldiers were told to use their judgment about letting people pass. The wrecked wholesale houses and the great piles of debris are still surrounded by sentinels and no one is allowed to pass except upon written permission from police headquarters. This morning in impressing men for the public work the officers were told not to molest men engaged in legitimate work on private premises. Some of the ward chairmen claim this new order is interfering greatly with their work, as they can not get men. So many men have been put to work on buildings, and so many have donned deputy sheriff badges that the supply of men for the gruesome task of burying or burning the dead humans and animals and clearing away the debris is not adequate to the requirements.

The committee on transportation this morning began its service to Texas City, where the Galveston, Houston and Henderson is operating trains. When the boats left here it was not known that they would be able to get the passengers ashore, and the trip was experimental. The Lawrence took 400 pay passengers, and the Brunswick took over a hundred destitute people free of charge. Upon the return of the boats the committee will know what can be done in the way of regular service. Colonel Polk, general manager of the Gulf, Colorado and Santa Fe, says, they expect to carry passengers from the wharves to Virginia Point to-day and take them thence by train. They expect to have their track rebuilt from the city to the bridge this evening, and to-morrow will operate trains to the bridge, and will send the boats across the bay from that point. The committee on transportation expresses the hope that every effort will be made to keep sightseers from coming to Galveston; every available boat is needed to send women and children out of town.

CONDITIONS BETTERING.

Order Gradually Coming Out of Chaos--Water for Fire Protection--Burning the Dead.

Galveston, Tuesday, 8 p. m.—This evening the committees in charge of cleaning up the city, caring for the destitute and arranging for transportation feel much encouraged. Something like order has been brought out of chaos. There is organized effort and the day's work has been big. It was impossible to handle the dead bodies of human beings or the carcasses of animals to take them to sea, because of putrefaction. Hundreds were buried in trenches and many were cremated. It was necessary to handle fire with great caution as there is not water supply as yet. The city is not suffering much for drinking water, but water is needed in the mains that fire may be controlled. The water has been flowing steadily from the Alta Loma supply pipe into the receiving tank. Unfortunately there was no connection from the receiving tank to the mains except through the pumps, and it is impossible to get the water through by that route. Alderman McMaster, who has been directing the work, to-day is taking out the connection from the pumps to the mains andis making a connection from receiving tank to mains. Some of the large pipe needed was not available, but carpenters are making a wooden section which will stand the slight pressure. It is expected that water can be turned into the mains from the receiving tank before morning. This will give a supply in yard hydrants and at fire plugs from which the steamers can work. The men at work on the pumps and pipes are well along with their work, but the boiler makers are not so far along. Mr. McMaster thinks the pumps can be started by tomorrow afternoon, which will give the usual pressure in the mains.

In addition to the arrangements made for handling people from here to Texas City and thence via the Galveston, Houstdn and Henderson railroad to Houston, the prospect is that the Santa Fe and Southern Pacific will be ready for passengers within the next few days. Mr. W. S. Keenan, general passenger agent of the Santa Fe, said this evening that he expected their track would be completed to both ends of the bridge by to-morrow evening. The company has chartered three boats and will take passengers by train from Galveston to the bridge and there transfer by boats to trains on the mainland.

Quite a large number of people reached here to-day from Houston and other points. Some of them came to lend a helping hand and are doing noble work; others came to look for relatives. But there are many who come out of sheer curiosity and who do naught but eat up provisions and drink the water. They are taking up room in boats returning to the mainland which women and children ought to have. People who are not coming to help or on other urgent missions ought to remain away. Sightseers are not wanted, and those who have no higher purpose in coming will do Galveston the greatest service within their power by staying away. The police and soldiers have orders not to permit the landing of strangers, and the order is being carried out as far as possible. The committee on transportation proposes to see that women and children get a chance to leave during the first few days. If sightseers come anyway they will find it difficult to get in and still more difficult to get out of the city.

Mayor Jones received a telegram to-day from President McKinley expressing his sorrow that Texas had been visited by such a dreadful calamity and advising that he had instructed the secretary of war to render all the assistance possible. The mayor also received a telegram from the Kansas City chamber of commerce saying that body stood ready to help and asking what it could do.

The steamer George Hudson arrived from Beaumont this afternoon with a carload of ice, 5000 barrels of water and provisions. Mr. John F. Keith, who came with the tug, said he would take one hundred people back with him in the morning and would bring the tug on another trip with lime and provisions.

Fortunately Galveston has not been entirely without ice. The Red Snapper company had a large supply on hand and it has been letting the people have it at wholesale prices. This supply will last but a day or two and ice will be gladly received. Three of the schooners of the Red Snapper company reached here from Campeche banks to-day filled with fish. The fish were given away by the thousands to all who came for them.

R. A. Brown, E. A. Mayo and Charles Yolland reached here from Dickinson today. They report that little town almost completely demolished.

Captain Robert Talfor of the United States engineer department returned last night from the mouth of the Brazos on the tug Anna. The Anna went to Quintana Saturday to save people. Fifty-four buildings at that town collapsed and twenty-five are total wrecks. Velasco was flattened out; very few houses are left; the hotel collapsed, killing two people. Seven deaths are reported so far. Angleton was wiped away. Hon. J. R. Duff's back was broken and his son was killed.

Sam Swinford of Houston, who came as far as the first relief train would bring him, nearly to Virginia Point, reached the city this afternoon. He says the Houston relief parties buried three hundred bodies in the immediate vicinity of Virginia Point.

The labor situation has not been so bad to-day as it was yesterday. The police system is better organized, for one thing. George H. Neviells, chairman of the republican county executive committee, and ex-Alderman Cornelius J. Williams, both colored, reported to the relief committee this morning and did good work in inducing the members of their race to work for the good of the community.

The following are missing from Bolivar Point, near Roll Over: Mr. Bishoff and wife, Charles Atkins and six children, Will Statum, wife and two children, Mrs. Statum and two daughters, F. Venson, wife and five children.

J. S. Gregory of Pepper Grove came to The News office this evening and reported that the dead animals which are being dumped into the bay and which go out with the tide, are coming ashore by the hundreds on Bolivar peninsula. He said they started to bury them but the few people on the peninsula found it impossible. He came to the city to implore the authorities to send men there to bury these animals and to quit throwing them in the bay. The dumping in the bay had already been stopped, as there was little wind to-day, and the carcasses were cremated.

STORM THEORY.

The Galveston Hurricane Not the Same as That Off the Coast of Florida.

Galveston, Wednesday—Dr. J. T. Fry, who has been an observer of the weather for a great many years, has a theory that the storm which visited Galveston originated in the vicinity of Port Eads, and was not the hurricane which was reported on the Florida coast. On Thursday a storm was reported moving in a northeasterly direction from Key West. It moved up the Atlantic coast. The Mallory steamer Comal ran into it and reported a great number of wrecks, as were reported in The News at the time. The supposition that this was the same storm that reached Galveston by doubling back on its tracks is a mistake. The first knowledge of the Galveston storm was the report of a wind velocity of forty-eight miles an hour at Port Eads on Saturday morning. The News also reported high winds at Pass Christian. The Port Eads storm was a distinct storm from that of Florida and was confined to the gulf. The proof of this is that the steamer Comal came in from Florida in beautiful weather and apparently followed in the wake of the storm.

BODIES NUMBERED.

Galveston, Wednesday. — Bodies going ashore on the mainland have been buried. At Texas City a large number have been placed in the ground, and if anything by which they could be identified was found on them it was removed and taken in charge by the officials for better identification. The bodies were numbered as they were interred and the identification articles were given corresponding numbers. On No. 46 it is reported that a plain gold ring was found and taken from the body of a well dressed woman whose body was beyond identification. On the inside of the ring was the inscription: "E. E. S. to C. E. G., Dec. 31, 1868." These are the initials of the late E. E. Seixas and Mrs. Seixas' initials of her given name were C. E., so it is quite probable that the body buried as No. 46 is that of Mrs. Seixas.

The Messenger is the Old Stand-by Paper of Milam County; And Stands on its Record of Twenty-Eight Years of Unflinching and Uninterrupted Service.

Rockdale Messenger.

OFFICE OF PUBLICATION, 107 SOUTH CAMERON STREET. ENTERED AT THE POSTOFFICE, AT ROCKDALE, AS SECOND-CLASS MATTER.

TWENTY-EIGHTH YEAR. ROCKDALE, MILAM COUNTY, TEXAS, THURSDAY, SEPTEMBER 13. 1900. EIGHT PAGES

DIED.

Rubie, a little six year old daughter of Mr. and Mrs. H. W. McBurnett of the Lewis School House neighborhood died on Sunday Sept, 2, with congestion.

Fifty cent whips at thirty five cents at Dudleys.

A LARGE PEAR.

Brother H. Henniger brought a Keiffer pear to the Messenger office last Friday that weighed a fraction over twenty ounces or 1¼ pounds, it is the largest ever brought to Rockdale that we know of, and as large as the premium pear the Dallas fair last fall.

Put your team up at J, R. Rowland's wagon yard when in town.

W. R. BRITTON.

In this issue appears the announcement of W. R. Britton for Justice of the Peace of Precinct No. 5.

Brother Britton has bought him a home near Tracy, and many of the voters of his beat have been insisting on his making the race for some time until they have prevailed. If the people of Beat 5 elect him as their justice they will certainly have as good a man as ever filled the office.

Try those unbreakable goblets at Dudley's.

A HORSE BADLY CUT ON WIRE.

Last week Mr. Wade Harris, son of J. H. Harris, living one mile north of Rockdale, saw a good horse get badly cut on a wire fence near his house and went to the horses relief. After Mr. Harris saw how bad it was cut he took the poor animal home with him, and came to town and got Linement with which he doctored the horse with. He was told that the horse belonged to a man named Ferguson living on or near Briar Branch. Mr. Harris wishes the owner to come and get the horse and pay for this notice.

For wheat bran go to J. R. Rowland. Only 75 cents.

Some days since a Messenger man overheard one of this papers subscribers call for a hat at one of our principal business houses, and he boldly stated that the firm's hat ad in the Messenger the week previous had been the means of him making the purchase. Every body reads advertisements but few think to mention the fact when they make their purchases. The Messenger wishes to tender to the above mentioned gentleman its sincere thanks for so kindly giving the paper credit for the purchase which he made.

Our goods must, go prices down to bed rock to make room for big Xmas line, says the novelty man.

Doctors say that there is not as much sickness in the country as there was a few weeks ago, still there is a great deal existing yet.

Wonderful bargains at Dudley's to make room for new goods on the way.

WILL URGE RELIEF

GOVERNOR WILL SEND IN SPECIAL MESSAGE NEXT WEEK CONCERNING STORM DISTRICT.

TO INCREASE TRADE

COMMITTEE TO SEARCH IN SOUTH AMERICAN MARKETS FOR THE PRODUCTS OF TEXAS.

CHANGES IN CONSTITUTION

Proposed "Hogg Amendments" to Be Considered Next Week—Legislative Proceedings Yesterday.

SPECIAL TO THE NEWS.

Austin, Tex., Jan. 16.—In the absence of Lieut. Gov. Browning, President Pro Tem Miller called the Senate to order this morning. The roll showed only eighteen Senators present, three less than the number required to make a quorum. On motion of Senator Hanger a call of the Senate was ordered for the purpose of getting and maintaining a quorum. After a few minutes' wait enough Senators came in to make a quorum.

Bills were introduced as follows:

By Messrs. Miller and Hanger, to create the office of State Fire Marshal, whose duty it shall be to investigate fires that occur in Texas

By Mr. Savage—Applying the provisions of the present law governing the Sam Houston Normal to the North Texas Normal at Denton.

By Messrs. Wilson and Staples—Increasing the Confederate pension appropriation to the maximum limit, $250,000 for each year, commencing Oct. 1 next.

By Mr. Davidson of DeWitt—Delegating upon the Railroad Commission the power to make police rules and regulations to the extent that such could be prescribed by the Legislature.

By Mr. Patterson—An act to protect discharged employes against blacklisting, to define blacklisting and prescribing penalties therefor.

By Mr. Wheeler—Amending the code of criminal procedure with reference to appeals from inferior courts to county courts. Referred to Judiciary No. 2

By Mr. Harris of Hunt—Regulating the printing of election tickets.

By Mr. Davidson of DeWitt—Prescribing a penalty of not more than $5,000 for violating decrees of the Railroad Commission issued as police orders.

By Messrs. Lloyd and McGee—Making vaccination compulsory in counties where smallpox is prevalent.

By Mr. Lloyd—Providing that fifty pounds shall constitute and be the standard weight of a bushel of peaches and fifty-five pounds shall constitute and be the standard weight of a bushel of tomatoes.

By Mr. Lloyd—Increasing the powers of the State Health Officer with reference to fumigating and disinfecting vessels entering Texas ports.

By Mr. Paulus—To prohibit traffic in teachers' examination questions.

By Mr. Hanger—Regulating the sale of cocaine, opium and other poisonous drugs.

By Mr. Swan—An act to punish laborers who violate either written or verbal contracts and to provide a penalty for effecting breaches of contract between employer and employe.

Mr. Savage obtained passage of his resolution authorizing the Sergeant-at-Arms to purchase stationery from whom he pleases, where the State contractor is not prompt in deliveries or the articles furnished are inferior.

Mr. Lipscomb's resolution was adopted inviting President McKinley to visit Austin while the Legislature is in session, in the event he carries out his intention to visit Texas in the near future.

The Committee on Constitutional Amendments reported favorably on Mr. Davidson's joint resolution requiring a poll tax receipt in order to vote in Texas.

Adjourned until 10 o'clock tomorrow.

HOUSE PROCEEDINGS.

Bill to Prohibit Private Gambling Was Under Discussion.

SPECIAL TO THE NEWS.

Austin, Tex., Jan. 16.—The House convened at 9:30 o'clock this morning, Speaker Prince in the chair.

Mr. Griggs offered a resolution which was signed also by Messrs. Kennedy of Harrison, Tarpley, Bridges, Nolan, Stewart, Callan, Little, Mugg, Goodlett and Lane, providing for the appointment of a committee of five to investigate the question of establishing closer relations between the United States and the southern Republics. It was referred to a special committee of five to be named by the Speaker.

Mr. Mills of Red River was added to the Committee on Education.

Mr. Edwards of Fannin was added to the Committee on Agriculture.

Mr. Robertson of Williamson was added to the Committee on Labor.

A resolution by Mr. Seabury providing for printing 300 copies of the Legislative Manual for the use of the members was adopted.

Speaker Prince appointed the following Committee on Railroad Commission: Mr. Robinson of Williamson, chairman; Messrs. Hogsett, Fears, Ackerman, Stewart, Talbot, Meece, Lane, Nolan, Fountain, Jones, Waller, Wells of Red River, Henderson of Lamar, McMeans, Robertson of Harrison, Pierson and Still.

The resolution by Mr. Lane providing for a joint committee of three from the House and three from the Senate to investigate the claims of victims of the Galveston storm to State aid, came up as a special order and was referred to the Committee on State Affairs.

Majority and minority reports were made from the Committee on Judiciary No. 2 on the bill by Messrs. Rowland, Evans and Calvin amending the gambling law so as to prohibit private games of cards for money. The majority report was adverse.

Mr. Walker, who signed with Messrs. Wells of Red River, Allred, Aldrich and Hill, the minority report, moved that the latter be substituted for the majority report. After much debate the motion was adopted.

Mr. Moore offered a substitute for the bill, simplifying its verbiage. It was adopted. The debate was not concluded before adjournment.

The Speaker appointed the following special committee to consider the Griggs resolution: Messrs. Griggs, Little, Bridges, Russell and Goodlett.

Adjourned to 9:30 tomorrow

BILLS IN THE HOUSE.

Measure to Prohibit the Sale of Adulterated Food Products.

SPECIAL TO THE NEWS.

Austin, Tex., Jan. 16.—The following bills were introduced in the House:

By Mr. Gay—An act amending the seduction law, providing that an indictment may be retired for five years, but may be revived if the defendant deserts his wife.

By Mr. Clements—An amendment to act providing for the appointments of boards of health in towns and cities by Commissioners' Courts.

By Mr. Strother—An amendatory act providing that original marriage licenses shall be returned to the contracting parties.

By Mr. Bridgers—An act making the theft of a bicycle a felony.

By Mr. Goodlet—An amendment providing a stock law for Ellis and other counties.

By Mr. Goodlet—An act requiring mercantile agencies to obtain permits to do business in Texas from the Secretary of State.

By Mr. Thorp—An amendatory act exempting those who gamble at private residences from indictment.

By Mr. Pierson—An act to prohibit the use of money in primary elections.

By Mr. Beaty—An act appropriating $100,000 for the establishment of a branch asylum for idiots and imbeciles.

By Mr. Gresham—An act repealing the law defining the offense of affray.

By Mr. Terrell of Cherokee—To prohibit the traffic in examination questions used by the County School Boards of Examiners or by summer normal boards of examiners, in the examination of applicants for teacher's certificate.

By Mr. Satterwhite—Providing that taxes may be paid in scrip issued by the counties.

By Mr. Looney—To prohibit the manufacture and sale of adulterated food products.

TRADE WITH SOUTHERN REPUBLICS.

Resolution Looking to an Investigation by Texas Legislators.

SPECIAL TO THE NEWS.

Austin, Tex., Jan. 16.—The following resolution was introduced in the House today:

Whereas, The United States of America is essentially a commercial nation, rapidily extending its arms of trade into every portion of the habitable globe; and

Whereas, Mexico, Central and South America, lie at the very door of the United States, and the trade of said countries, as well as their everlasting friendship, is more to be desired than any other foreign countries; and

Whereas, Said Southern Republics are now and have been for a number of years, courting the friendship and extended trade relations of our country; and

Whereas, The State of Texas is the natural gateway, both by land and sea, to said Southern Republics, and by and through which all trade, travel and commerce must eventually pass by reason of location, situation and the ever increasing facilities of transportation; and

Whereas, This subject is one of vital interest to the United States of America and particularly to the State of Texas, and should have prompt and proper attention at the hands of our national Government; now therefore be it

Resolved, That a committee of five members be appointed to investigate the best method and manner of cultivating the acquaintance and extending our trade relations with the people of these Southern Republics as well as the particular advantages to be derived thereby by the State of Texas, and that said committee, at some future day of the term, report back what steps, if any, the State of Texas should take looking toward the consummation of such object, and that such report be accompanied by recommedations of said committee. Signed by Messrs. Griggs, Kennedy of Harris, Torpey, Bridgers, Nolan of Galveston, Stewart, Callan, Little, Lane, Mugg, Goodlett.

HOUSE COMMITTEE WORK.

Hogg Amendments Will Be Considered Next Wednesday.

SPECIAL TO THE NEWS.

Austin, Tex., Dec. 16.—The House Committee on Constitutional Amendments at its meeting this afternoon decided to hold a public hearing next Wednesday on the Hogg amendments. An invitation is extended to ex-Gov. Hogg and all others interested to attend.

The committee discussed informally but did not act upon the bill by Mr. Kennedy of Limestone directing the Governor to submit to the people the question whether a constitutional convention shall be held.

Mr. Griggs of Harris favored a constitutional convention, but thought the bill should be changed so as to bring it about as speedily as possible.

Mr. Moran opposed the holding of a constitutional convention at all.

At the request of the author the bill was allowed to lay on the table for further discussion.

House Judiciary Committee No. 1 at its meeting this afternoon again postponed action on the Greenwood libel bill, laying it over informally.

SENATE COMMITTEE REPORTS.

Staples' Libel Bill Will Be Recommended for Passage.

SPECIAL TO THE NEWS.

Austin, Tex., Jan. 16.—Senate Judiciary Committee No. 1 this evening decided to report favorably Staples' bill defining libel. Mr. Hanger gave notice of an adverse minority report.

Senate Judiciary Committee No. 2 decided to report favorably a bill by Mr. Harris of Hunt prohibiting the use of money in primary elections.

The same committee agreed to report adversely Mr. Swann's bill to punish laborers who violate either written or verbal contracts and to provide a penalty for effecting breaches of contract between employes and employer. Mr. Swann gave notice of filing of a favorable minority report.

TRAIN PORTER HAD SMALLPOX.

Was Walking the Streets of Paris When Arrested.

SPECIAL TO THE NEWS.

Paris, Tex., Jan. 16.—Considerable excitement was caused this morning by the appearance of a negro on the square with the smallpox broken out over his face. He was a porter on the Frisco and came in last night from Monett, Mo. He was made to back up in a stairway off the sidewalk and was held a prisoner there until some person who had had the smallpox could be found to escort him to the pesthouse. Pedestrians were warned to give the sidewalk in front of him a wide berth. He was finally marched down the middle of the street to the pesthouse, and indignant and excited persons enjoined the guard to shoot him if he attempted to escape.

FIFTY CASES AT AQUILLA.

Smallpox Has Made Rapid Headway in a Hill County Town.

SPECIAL TO THE NEWS.

Hillsboro, Tex., Jan. 16.—Judge L. C. Hill returned from Aquilla last night, where he went to investigate the smallpox situation. To The News correspondent he said that in the negro settlement near Aquilla there were nineteen families and about fifty persons affected with the disease. The district was quarantined so as to prevent any one from going out or in. It is proposed by this method to confine the disease until it exhausts itself.

QUARANTINE AGAINST CISCO.

Case Which One Physician Calls Chickenpox Has Broken Out.

SPECIAL TO THE NEWS.

Cisco, Tex., Jan. 16.—A case which one of the physicians has pronounced smallpox has been discovered here. There have been several cases like it, but heretofore the physicians have diagnosed it as chickenpox. The Council has made an investigation, but has not ordered a quarantine. Eastland has declared a quarantine and citizens going there to attend court have been turned back.

Death from Smallpox.

SPECIAL TO THE NEWS.

Bonham, Tex., Jan. 16.—Ed Kincaid died of smallpox at Edhube yesterday. Several persons were exposed to the disease. The Commissioners' Court is in session here and this afternoon contracted for the erection of a pesthouse on the county farm.

Two Cases in Comanche County.

SPECIAL TO THE NEWS.

Comanche, Tex., Jan. 16.—County Health Officer, Dr. J. J. Eargle, reports that there are two well developed cases of smallpox at Proctor.

One Case at Dawson.

SPECIAL TO THE NEWS.

Corsicana, Tex., Jan. 16.—A well developed case of smallpox is reported at Dawson.

Killed by His Partner.

Helena, Ark., Jan. 15.—Gen. McDowell, a well-to-do storekeeper at Spring Creek, near here, was shot and killed yesterday by Dr. Snipes, his friend and partner. Reports are that the two men had quarreled over business matters and, meeting in the road, renewed the argument with pistols. Snipes fired three times, killing McDowell, who was attempting to escape. Snipes' parents live in Jackson, Tenn.

Found Dead in His Room.

SPECIAL TO THE NEWS.

Eufaula, I. T., Jan. 15.—D. B. Delzell, Modern Woodmen organizer from Durant, who had been at this point for about a month, was found dead in his room at the National Hotel this morning. A post-mortem examination proved heart failure to be the cause of his death. The body was found lying on the floor with one foot resting on the bed. The Wagoner Camp Woodmen took charge of the body.

PALESTINE AFTER A COLLEGE.

Establishment of an Episcopal Institution There Is Wanted.

SPECIAL TO THE NEWS.

Palestine, Tex., Jan. 16.—A movement is on foot to procure the location of an Episcopal college in this city., Mayor Powers and the Business Men's League are in correspondence with Rev. Wallace Carnahan of San Antonio, who has the movement in charge, and who will place the institution here, should Palestine want it. It will be made one of the leading educational institutions of the South, and the citizens here have gone to work with an earnest effort to secure the enterprise for Palestine.

POLITICS IN HILLSBORO.

Democratic Committee's Call for a White Primary Was Approved.

SPECIAL TO THE NEWS.

Hillsboro, Tex., Jan. 16.—The report of the mass meeting here last night contained an error in that it stated that the resolution requesting the Democratic committee to revoke its order for a white man's primary was adopted, whereas it was defeated and a substitute, approving the committee's action, was adopted by a large majority.

WON'T REMOVE QUARANTINE.

Gov. Sayers Denies an Appeal from El Paso Citizens.

SPECIAL TO THE NEWS.

Austin, Tex., Jan. 16.—Representatives Bridgers and Vansickle called on Gov. Sayers today in reference to removing the Frisco quarantine and were informed by the executive that he did not purpose to assume responsibility over such a technical matter. He referred them to State Health Officer Blunt, who asserted that the quarantine would remain for the time and that rules were only being enforced against passenger and freight traffic from Chinatown not able to show certificates of Dr. Charles F. Horton, his San Francisco representative.

Gov. Sayers was positive in his position, asserting that one case of plague at El Paso would mean a granite wall quarantine around the town if it required the service of a regiment of soldiers.

DIED ON THE TRAIN.

Agent for Lemp's Brewery at Galveston a Victim of Bright's Disease.

SPECIAL TO THE NEWS.

Galveston, Tex., Jan. 15.—William G. H. Janesen, agent for Lemp's Brewery at Galveston, died this morning on the train en route to Galveston from St. Louis, where he went a few weeks ago for treatment. He was suffering from acute Bright's disease. Deceased was 35 years of age, and leaves a widow and father living in this city. He came to Galveston eight years ago from St. Louis.

Bank Officers at Hillsboro.

SPECIAL TO THE NEWS.

Hillsboro, Tex., Jan. 16.—The Farmers' National Bank gave out the election of directors this afternoon as follows: E. M. Turner, J. S. Casey, H. G. Gibson, W. W. Boyd, Nelson Phillips, E. S. Davis and W. M. Williams. The directors held a meeting and elected the following officers: E. M. Turner, president; W. M. Williams, cashier; W. L. Embree, assistant cashier; J. M. Abernathy, collector.

SPOUTS FUEL OIL

PRODUCT OF THE BIG BEAUMONT GEYSER IS TOO LIGHT FOR ILLUMINATING PURPOSES.

BEAUMONT IS WEARY

THE INTENSE EXCITEMENT OF THE WEEK IS ABATING AND SPECULATING FEVER LOWER.

FLOW STILL UNDIMINISHED

Effort to Control It Will Be Made Today—Few Outside Investments Made Yet.

SPECIAL TO THE NEWS.

Beaumont, Tex., Jan. 16.—Beaumont is becoming both accustomed to and relieved of the oil excitement kept up here now for six days. The intensity of the strain has exhausted everybody, and all are willing to lay aside the wild speculation and take hold of this oil matter with calmness and deliberation. It has been developed here in this thing that outside capital is not going to invest in this field with conditions at such a strained point as they have been. It is a certain fact that none of them have invested very heavily save in oil leases. Notwithstanding all the talk of hundred thousand-dollar deals and millions of dollars capital, the fact remains that no big deals have been made, and a yet more significant fact is that all these deals have been made by home people. This bearish tendency is not forced. It is the result of the conditions themselves. Excitement could not keep up the same as it has been during the last week, and by virtue of the very fact that speculations were so flighty and uncertain, the situation must turn bearish. Those who have kept the situation closely in hand predict that tomorrow the people, the real estate agents and land owners, will get down to actual conditions, lay aside the deals and awaken to facts.

Beaumont has been fearfully wrought up, there is no denying that. The frenzy has penetrated every mind and the blood has coursed like fire through the hearts of every one who owned a bit of land somewhere in this section. The mind has been stunned with the possibilities of great wealth and men have been carried further from sound business principles than they care to admit. The fight is practically over now, however, and no one is seriously hurt. Tomorrow matters will be straightened out much more than they were today, and then the oil men and capitalists will begin to talk business.

Heretofore they have stood from under and watched the wildness of uncontrollable throngs. Substantial development is dawning. Men will begin to get into the field, and it will soon be known what the field is worth. If it produces like the Lucas well there is a revolution in store for the people of the West who use fuel. The oil is only good for fuel, there is no longer any doubt of that. Its specific gravity is not more than 24, and no one would undertake to refine that oil, no matter what it contained.

J. H. Galey, part owner of the Lucas well, on this question said to The News correspondent: "It is the most fortunate thing that could have happened in connection with this well, that it is not illuminating oil. If it had been a light oil the oil markets would have been demoralized and the oil could not have been sold at the cost of production. As it is, there will be a good market for fuel oil when the country has had time to adjust itself to using liquid oil. The railroads will use it, every factory will make steam with it, and the steamships can carry much more power in oil than they can in coal."

Mr. Galey is not disappointed over the grade of the oil. To the contrary, he is pleased with it.

Preparations to stop the well today were not completed. Some necessary machinery has not arrived and the checking of the flow will not be attempted before tomorrow, if then.

Visitors continue to arrive here in large numbers. Several large parties of oil men from Marietta, Ohio, and Parkersburg, W. Va., reached here this morning, and more men from Pittsburg arrived today.

Mayor Jones of Galveston and several other Galvestonians are sight-seers here today. Mr. Hugh Hamilton was here from Houston yesterday endeavoring to negotiate for the purchase of 600,000 barrels of the oil for fuel.

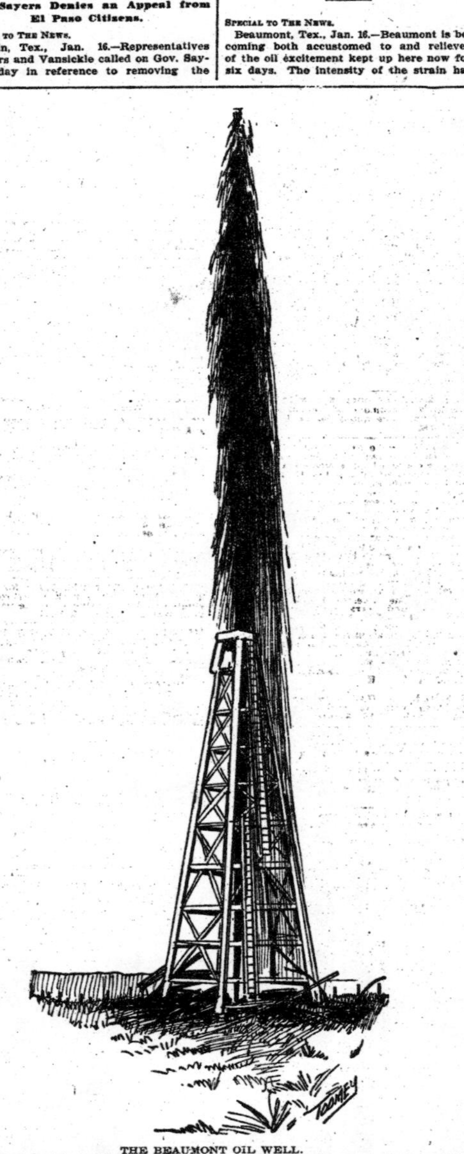

THE BEAUMONT OIL WELL.

This is a picture of the remarkable oil well which was discovered about one mile south of the city limits of Beaumont on Jan. 10. The well is estimated by conservative oil men of experience to be flowing 20,000 barrels of oil per day of twenty-four hours. The oil is considered to be a very good grade, though an analysis of it has not yet been made. The well was discovered by Capt. A. F. Lucas, a geologist of Washington, D. C., who has been operating in the Beaumont territory for over two years. This well was begun about Oct. 15. It is supposed to be 1,340 feet deep. The stream is six inches in diameter. The derrick is sixty feet high and as the picture shows, the main body of the stream is going fully the length of the derrick above its top.

MIKE WELKER.

INTEREST IN NEW YORK.

Capitalists Inquiring of the Big Oil Well at Beaumont.

SPECIAL TO THE NEWS.

New York, Jan. 16.—The wonderful oil discovery in southeastern Texas is attracting considerable attention here. A number of capitalists and speculators have already started for Texas, expecting to get in the swim. There is a great deal of land in Jefferson County and counties adjoining owned by New Yorkers, and they have received many inquiries from prospectors and speculators. One of the owners of Jefferson County land, which is said to be near the well which is such a wonderful producer, said: "From what I hear the whole country down there has gone crazy over oil. I have never known anything to compare with it anywhere, and they must certainly have discovered an oil field equal to anything in the United States. I guess I will go down and take a look at things myself."

WILL PROSPECT FOR OIL.

Outlook in the Neighborhood of Palestine Regarded as Good.

SPECIAL TO THE NEWS.

Palestine, Tex., Jan. 16.—Col. C. J. Grainger, president of the Palestine Coal and Mining Company, in conversation with The News correspondent, said that he was going to begin at once experimenting for oil. Mr. Grainger said:

"A stock company is being formed among the leading business men of this city, and it will be the intention of the company to sink a number of oil wells near here. We have had experts go over the ground, and reports as to the existence of oil around Palestine are very flattering. In some places where the men have conducted their examinations the oil has been found seething from the rocks. We expect to get this oil, and our company will begin work at once. We have ordered the necessary machinery, and when it arrives a force of workmen will be engaged to place it in position."

TWO CAPERS OF FORTUNE.

Man Who Formerly Owned Beaumont's Oil Land Is in Ennis.

SPECIAL TO THE NEWS.

Ennis, Tex., Jan. 16.—The fortunes in Beaumont property are varied and strike people in other sections in varying ways. Mr. Robert H. Smith of Ennis, a Wells-Fargo express messenger running on the Fort Worth branch of the Central, bought some lots at Beaumont a few weeks ago and he was offered a profit of 300 per cent on his investment. Mr. W. F. Gilbert, a merchant of this city, owned the identical land on which the wonderful oil well is situated and sold it about a year ago at a moderate price.

ORANGE GETS THE FUMES.

Odor of Oil Wafted from Beaumont Twenty-five Miles Away.

SPECIAL TO THE NEWS.

Orange, Tex., Jan. 16.—From 11 o'clock this morning until 2 in the afternoon a west wind blew here, and fumes from the great oil well at Beaumont were distinctly noticeable in the atmosphere. The distance is fully twenty-five miles. Later the wind veered to the north and no further evidence of the gas was traceable. About half of the town has been to Beaumont.

Another Cut in Oil.

SPECIAL TO THE NEWS.

Corsicana, Tex., Jan. 16.—Cullinan Pipe Line Company has posted another bulletin reducing the price of heavy crude petroleum from 58c to 50c per barrel.

Bank Officers at Tyler.

SPECIAL TO THE NEWS.

Tyler, Tex., Jan. 15.—The stockholders of the Citizens' National Bank in this city elected the following officers: John W. Wright, president; R. Bergfeld, vice president; H. J. McIntosh, cashier. Directors: S. H. Cox, J. W. Wright, R. Bergfeld, G. C. Wimberly, J. Lipstate, H. B. Marsh, Dr. C. A. Smith, G. W. Burkett and T. M. Campbell of Palestine.

The Morning News

A. H. BELO & CO., PUBLISHERS.

Also of The Galveston News. Distance between the two publication offices—315 miles.

Entered at Postoffice at Dallas as Second-class Matter. Office of Publication, Nos. 199 and 201 Commerce Street. Eastern Office 90 Tribune Building, New York.

TERMS OF SUBSCRIPTION.

DAILY.

PER COPY	.05
ONE MONTH	$1.00
THREE MONTHS (by mail)	2.50
SIX MONTHS (by mail)	5.00
TWELVE MONTHS (by mail)	10.00

SUNDAY.

TWELVE MONTHS (by mail)	$1.50
SIX MONTHS (by mail)	.75
FOUR MONTHS (by mail)	.50

SEMI-WEEKLY.
(Issued Tuesdays and Fridays.)
Enlarged, Improved and Specially Edited. Comprising eight pages of fifty-six columns made up from the cream of the daily edition. It is the largest and cheapest Newspaper in the south.

ONE COPY ONE YEAR	$1.00
ONE COPY SIX MONTHS	.50
ONE COPY THREE MONTHS	.25

Invariably in advance.
FREE OF POSTAGE TO ALL PARTS OF THE UNITED STATES, CANADA AND MEXICO.

ALL PAPERS DISCONTINUED AT THE EXPIRATION OF THE TIME PAID FOR.

Look at printed label on your paper. The date thereon shows when the subscription expires. Forward your money in ample time for renewal if you desire unbroken files, as we can not always furnish back numbers.

Subscribers desiring the address of their paper changed will please state in their communication both the old and the new address.

Remit by draft on Dallas, Galveston or New York (if on any other point add 25c to cover cost of collection), postoffice money order or express money order. If sent otherwise we will not be responsible for miscarriage. Address A. H. BELO & CO., Dallas or Galveston, Tex.

Specimen copies sent free on application.

THE NEWS' TRAVELING AGENTS.—The following are the traveling representatives of The Galveston News and The Dallas News, who are authorized to solicit and receipt for subscriptions and advertisements for either publication: J. A. Sloan, H. C. Scott, Joe M. London, T. B. Baldwin, J. R. Johnson, Tom C. Swope, Roy Smith, G. J. Hudson, A. R. Carnes and W. R. Marchman.
Jan. 10, 1901. A. H. BELO & CO.

TEN PAGES.

FRIDAY, JANUARY 18, 1901.

NOTICE TO THE PUBLIC.

Any erroneous reflection upon the character, standing or reputation of any person, firm or corporation which may appear in the columns of The News will be gladly corrected upon its being brought to the attention of the publishers.

WHY BRITISH INDUSTRIES ARE LOSING GROUND.

That England is losing ground in the industrial world is very generally conceded. The London Standard, on the authority of an expert who has visited various countries, claims that the cause is found in the ability and willingness of laboring men of other nations to do more than the trades unions permit the British workman to do. The Spectator takes the matter up and declares the unproductiveness of British labor reveals the trades union at its worst during a time when foreign competition is most severe. It quotes the following opinion of a critic who had investigated conditions in the engineering trade: "From a careful calculation, made after comparing notes with other observers and taking the figure 1 to 1¼ as representing the producing capacity of the ordinary British workman, I consider the Swiss-German as fairly represented by 1¾ and the Yankee by 2¼." The Spectator charges that "the trade union has actually reinforced by its jealous and short-sighted rules that tendency to do the least for the most pay which is an infirmity of human nature. No wonder the British workman is called upon to cease digging a pit for himself. He has put himself into the hands of leaders who are adepts at organization, but who, with all their thoroughness in providing for immediate objects of the trade union, are fatally short-sighted with regard to ultimate results. The hope of improving the situation lies in opening the eyes of these leaders and enlisting their sympathies with those of employers in a resolute attempt to increase output to the utmost extent during working hours. It seems that after the unions have secured shorter hours they have adopted the policy of doing the least possible amount of work in them. They have not wakened yet to the fact that if they keep up this sort of self-deception it will not be long before their pet scheme of a restricted output will be forced back upon them permanently with disastrous result by their economic enemies abroad." Another cause assigned by an English journal is the "aptness of the American workman aided by improved machinery." He is easily able, as this authority has it, to look after twice as many irons in the fire as the European is able or willing to look after. A circular issued by a temperance union of Boston and bearing the signature of Mary H. Hunt notes that "American trade supremacy is just now a topic of newspaper discussion in Europe. A recent number of a London paper, the Express, published an article with the startling headline, 'Wake Up, England,' the purpose of which was to rouse interest in the question, 'Is England losing commercial position?'" The circular continues:

Another London paper in searching for the cause of England's lack of ability to compete, after citing as an illustration the fact that in one shipyard alone there was last year an injury to its output of 25 per cent from drinking men, said: "If we are not able to produce better, faster and cheaper than other countries our sober rivals will come and capture our trade." The same paper quotes the British Medical Journal as authority for the fact that Great Britain's per capita consumption of alcohol is nearly twice that of the United States. Again it is the schoolmaster. Sixteen years ago, in obedience to laws enacted by Congress and State Legislatures, the public schools in this country began to teach all pupils that one of the effects of alcoholic drinks is so to injure the brain and muscles that the drinker can not do as good work as the abstainer. Soon after banks, railroads, manufactories and responsible business of almost all kinds in the United States began to demand that their employes should be total abstainers. The effect of this upon the industrial ability of our nation is manifest.

In other words, it is held by these good women that intemperance is dragging down British industries and trade. Other theories are being discussed and the discussion leads one to conclude, whatever the cause may be, that, beyond any doubt, industrial England is losing prestige and is in a fair way to lose much of the trade upon which the prosperity and peace of the old country depend.

The Democrats in the Massachusetts Legislature placed Mr. Richard Olney in nomination as their candidate for Senator. Mr. Olney will be remembered as the great Attorney General and Secretary of State of Mr. Cleveland's second administration.

Close readers of The News will have noticed in a dispatch a few days ago that 550 bales of cotton were shipped in lump from this State to Japan. These same readers will perhaps begin to calculate how much profit would have fallen to the State if these bales had been turned into cloth by Texas mills and shipped to their destination in a finished rather than in the raw state. The question is, Shall the Texan content himself with furnishing the raw product to other countries, foregoing the profit from the finished product?

The leading business men of Atlanta, Ga., are already at work on the project to hold a great textile exposition in that city in 1902. The executive committee of the proposed exposition has decided to raise the preliminary fund from $100,000 to $200,000, of which the City Council is asked to appropriate one-half. The committee in appealing to the Council for an appropriation says the purpose of the exposition is to demonstrate to the world the marvelous progress already made in the manufacture of textiles in the South, and, through the agency of operating exhibits, to demonstrate to Southern manufacturers the various methods and processes by which they may improve the quality and quantity of their product.

LOOTING AMERICAN CITIES.

It is complained by citizens of Kansas City that thieves are carrying away their fences, fine trees of the parks and lawns, and even houses. This is quite bad enough, but it is not asserted that the asportation is performed by members of the upper tendom. In Chicago it is otherwise. In a dispatch to the New York World it is charged that the society women of that place have fallen into the habit of carrying away with them parts of the table furnishings at banquets which they attend in the fashionable clubs of that city. One woman went so far, it is alleged, as to carry away a candlestick three feet in length, and it is said to be a common thing to take home glasses, spoons, knives, whisky decanters, napkins and salt cellars. Some Chicago women are reported to have made unique collections in this way of banquet souvenirs from all parts of the world, and the habit is not looked upon adversely even by the men who run the clubs, restaurants and hotels. It is considered, according to the World's bright young man, a dainty and delicate expression of the Chicago society woman's appreciation of the beautiful and useful, and is supposed to indicate her desire to perpetuate in memory the name of the cafe or club and the delightful occasion on which the article was obtained. Of course the World's story must be taken with many grains of allowance. It would be sad indeed if it should become necessary for the Chicago housewife to chain every piece of silver to the table, take a check for every chair, nail down every table napkin, and employ a full force of detectives and guards every time she is moved to indulge in a little social function. If all that the World says is true it is about to come to this. Do not believe the World. Because one guest carried away a sewing machine, shall we conclude that the whole fashionable party was made up of kleptomaniacs? Not at all. Reports of this kind are apt to be grievously exaggerated. Kansas City is still there and Chicago is not a Tien Tsin.

ABOUT CHARLIE ROSS.

A great many people are under the impression that the fate of Charlie Ross has never been revealed, but according to a statement recently made by Senator Plunkitt in the New York Legislature, this is a mistake. The facts as set forth by the New York Senator confirm the story published by the press long ago. However, as the Senator based his statement on knowledge obtained at first hand, the facts are interesting in their repetition. According to his statement, Charlie Ross was abducted by New York river thieves—a notorious ruffian named Mosher and his companion. The former hired the wagon in which the boy was placed, near his father's home in New York, and drove it to Philadelphia to destroy an important clew. The wagon was driven about thirty miles out of Philadelphia and was there abandoned. Mosher and his companion, accompanied by their victim, taking passage on the train to New York. Fear kept the boy quiet. In New York he was placed by Mosher on a river craft, and when the meshes began to tighten around the abductors the lad was weighted with iron and thrown overboard and drowned. Mosher was shot while committing a burglary in New York and tried to explain the abduction, but was able only to indicate that the detective theory of the case was correct. There is no longer any mystery about the celebrated case. Mr. Ross died fully convinced that his boy had been murdered. So says Senator Plunkitt.

The Supreme Court of the United States has determined that Mr. Neely, who gathered in the Cuban postal funds, must return to the Gem of the Antilles and stand his trial. The wonder is that he did not return voluntarily. With what he had paid out for lawyers in this country he might have made a telling argument with the Cuban courts. According to some accounts they are both poor and sympathetic.

Mrs. Lease has "made up" with her husband, Mrs. Nation is out of jail and Mrs. Diggs is preparing to enter actively into the work of raising chickens as soon as spring opens. These items of news may be properly put under the head of "Kansas Politico-Social Happenings."

The civilized world has been holding up its hands in horror over the report that De-Wet, the Boer leader, subjected to a flogging three peace commissioners who were sent to him by the English to request him to surrender, but no comment is made on the action of an officer of the American forces in the Philippines who, when visited by a Filipino officer for the purpose of inducing him to surrender, deliberately "booted" the patriot out of camp.

From the showings or statistics now brought forward in the work of purifying New York it is plain that the very bad people of that town are persistently bled by other very bad people. The good people who have no friends or sympathy with the bad are being led to the cold-blooded verdict that it is a case of "dog eat dog." As a rule there can be no reform unless the good are here and there getting the worst of it.

The fact that all the excitement over the murder cases in Kentucky has about subsided may be attributable to the fact that the Republicans succeeded in electing a member of their party to the supreme bench in that State at the last election, thus giving them a majority in that tribunal. The indicted parties were convicted before a Democratic court and their appeals will be heard by a Republican court, which, to said convicted persons, makes a difference.

Hon. John P. Hopkins of the city of Chicago has been elected chairman of the Illinois Democratic State central committee. It is not necessary in order to make the item of news interesting to go further than to state that Mr. Hopkins was an earnest worker for Palmer and Buckner at a time which it is not necessary to set forth in figures.

The Louisville Courier-Journal of the Bourbon State is apparently disgusted and disgruntled over recent happenings in this land of the free and easy. It says:

With Mrs. Nation out of jail again, ready to resume smashing the saloons, and Congress smashing the army canteens, there should be some definite modus vivendi between these workers in the cause of teetotalism. Mrs. Nation should at least agree to smash only her side of the street, leaving the cold tea purlieus of the capitol to the discretion of Congress.

Col. Gordon of the Tennessee Legislature raised a breeze by offering a resolution to remove the portraits of W. G. Brownlow and Gen. George H. Thomas from the State library. The resolution was tabled.

SNAP SHOTS.

Some martyrs are self-made.

The kidnaper is all the go. He must go.

When the canteen is smashed and the idle hero can not get any beer he can play mumblepeg.

All the preachers seem to look upon Mr. Croker as Satan rebuking sin.

A rigid rule providing that either hazing or the hazer must go will work a noticeable change at a free school like West Point.

The method by which the soulless trust reads out every man who refuses to surrender to it is merely the party method (which has been in force in this country for almost a hundred years) brought down into private business.

The butter with which oleomargarine competes is not as good as its competitor. The best butter of the dairies has no competitor and always brings a fair price. It is the man who peddles what-is-it? who demands the passage of the Grout bill.

An Arkansas editor expresses the wish that every American belle who marries a foreign title may be brought down to the washtub.

The man who stands with Honor and Truth can afford to have the majority against him.

Ambitious men have never hesitated to misuse the people when the people would permit them to do it.

First-class butter speaks for itself. Certain other classes are no better than oleomargarine, and nobody will be hurt if indifferent butter is left to compete with the artificial product. Such competition may render it necessary to improve the methods of some of the dairies, and may thus tend to protect the consumer.

STATE PRESS.

Hico Vidette: It is estimated that the past year has produced about one bale of cotton for every person, white and black, old and young, in the State, which, with the cotton seed means over $50 per capita.

That is an encouraging statement, but it will not be read with pleasure by those people who several years ago made the air ring with their talks about the "per capity." They believed the way to get the per capita necessary to the happiness of the people was for the Government to take hold of the proposition and issue enough money to make up the amount. The cotton crop is but one thing sold in Texas this year. If the wheat, hogs, cattle and all things sold or kept by the people are considered, the per capita will run up even higher. The State has been blessed within the last twelve months, and the prospects are good for a repetition of the blessing.

✣ ✣ ✣

Granbury News: Texas wheat, Texas corn, Texas cotton, Texas tobacco and Texas pecans all took first prizes at the Paris exposition.

And now new oil fields, which exceed in richness anything of the kind ever known, have been discovered. The greatness of the Commonwealth is being realized. It staggers the mind to contemplate what the State will be in a few years at the rate it is going.

✣ ✣ ✣

Hill County Mirror: Hill County farmers will, as a rule, begin the new year with the largest cash balances they have ever had, and if they diversify next year as they did this, one year hence their cash balances will be larger still.

Only a few years ago there was a broadcast prejudice against the banks. By some bankers were looked on as something like enemies of the people. But this feeling has given way to a sympathy for them. The people feel sorry for them because they are unable to lend out their money.

✣ ✣ ✣

Yoakum Times: There is money in beans, and the trucker who is onto his business will soon commence preparing the soil for a crop of this salable product of the garden.

Last year the great part of the country lying north and northeast of Texas began to look to Texas for its early vegetables and its fruit. Texas peaches were the best on the market and brought fair prices when handled properly. Texas melons were considered as good as the best. Texas cabbages came in earlier than cabbages from other States, and it looked as if South Texas was destined to be the garden for Chicago, St. Louis, Kansas City, Denver and many other cities. But for some reason the south Texas products fell off. In time the country will, with the price it will pay, impress on south Texas the importance of truck gardening and fruit raising. However, all of the people have not abandoned the profitable business of raising vegetables and the like, as witness the following from the Sulphur Springs News:

Representative Willacy of Nueces County says his constituency is cultivating 4,000 acres of cabbage, which they sell for $1.25 and $1.50 per 100 pounds. Mr. Willacy claimed to have raised a patch of cabbage last year that netted him $337 per acre.

✣ ✣ ✣

Blooming Grove Rustler: We need to reduce the army, make peace with the Filipinos and help them establish a nice little republic.

It is highly probable that when this country withdraws its troops and admits that it can not whip the Filipinos, a confession which would be made by such withdrawal, the Filipinos may not be willing to permit us to assist them in organizing "a nice little republic."

✣ ✣ ✣

Paris Advocate: Diversification has brought Texas out of the kinks and the way to keep from getting back into them is to keep on diversifying.

Diversification is admitted to be the thing which brings comfort and peace to the farmer, hence to the public. But let us not diversify too much in legislation. The legislative period is on the State now, and when that is the case there is more or less danger. The word from one end of the State to the other should be to the farmer, "Diversify," and to the lawmaker, "Be careful about diversifying or engaging in experiments in legislation."

✣ ✣ ✣

Roxton Wide-Awake: Will the Christian nations stand with folded arms and watch England completely annihilate the Boers?

It seems that some of said nations are busy now in the work of annihilating China. They are well into the business themselves.

✣ ✣ ✣

Montague Democrat: The average Texas farmer is now beginning to pay less attention to politics and more to economics. He is beginning to raise more at home and to buy less away from home. His stock of hogs, cattle, horses and other domestic animals he is improving. His apple orchard is no longer in Arkansas nor his smokehouse in Kansas. He is "living at home."

If any farmer in Texas can lay his hand on his heart and truthfully point out any benefit he ever got out of ordinary agitation of politics, then he ought to come forward at once and go in a side show as a "wonder." And if there is any one of them who has built up himself and family save by attending to his own affairs he is not known. The farmer who can tell offhand how many things he sold and got the money for has more pianos and organs in the house than that farmer who can tell what some politician said on the stump about what Thomas Jefferson did or did not believe. So it is in other lines.

✣ ✣ ✣

Tyler Courier: Why not have a greater Swan, a greater Flint or a greater Burlingame? The cry is for a greater Waco, a greater Slabtown and a greater Pulltight; and we see just as much sense in a greater any other place as we see in a greater Waco or a greater Corsicana.

Waco Times-Herald: Double-header egg nogg must be plentiful over about Tyler. "Greater Waco" is a fact. Why that particular phrase—"Greater?" Simply a rallying point—that's all. In all movement here is a catch phrase—something easily remembered and voicing the common aspiration. Waco was indulging in sleepy content. "Greater Waco" was proclaimed. It passed down the line. Men, women and children took it up. It was discussed at the breakfast table. It was talked on the street cars. The entire population became enthused, and the thing was done. The old town became a thing of life and activity, and has just closed the most prosperous year in her history. In the meantime, the Tyler papers complain because the populace break young mules on the public square!

Sitting in the supreme delights of satisfaction, as they do at Tyler, it is not to be wondered at that the Tylerite should snigger at any frantic efforts of Pulltight to become greater and more prosperous. It must be said to the credit of the Tyler papers, however, that they have been working in the line of the people of Pulltight and other places, that is to say, they have been trying to arouse the people to the necessity of doing something for the town in the way of factory building. They have done it in a conservative way, as befits newspapers of such a staid and dignified place, and have avoided what might be called the harsh cries, such as "On to Topolobampo," "A Greater City of Artesian Wells," and the like. They have solemnly told the people that this is a race for supremacy and if Tyler would win and keep in the procession of prominent towns Tylerites must stop breaking young mules on the public square, and come to consider whether a cotton mill might not be built to give the people chances of work and the town the profits of the business.

✣ ✣ ✣

Gatesville Messenger: Such institutions as our oil mill, our compress, our flour mill, gins, laundry and soda pop factory are the kind of institutions that make a city and deserve the united support of our people during 1901.

Whenever a town has factories in it of the kind enumerated by the Messenger it will in time have larger factories. For, after all, the ability of a town to build factories is measured by the energy in getting the few it has. If there is the necessary energy to build even a soda pop factory the energy to build a cotton mill is there, and it will come forth after a while.

AN APPEAL FROM WALLER.

It Is Planting Time and There Is No Seed to Plant.

The following communication was received yesterday by a Dallas man, and is self-explanatory:

Hempstead, Tex., Jan. 14.—Dear Sir: The $2 Rev. Dr. Buckner handed me in your office is all that your county has given Waller for seed. Does this mean that your people just ignore our appeal for help? I see in The News and other papers that north Texas never had such a surplus of money or so much on deposit, and yet it is about planting time here and these people, who have lost everything, can not get seed to plant. What shall we do? Your friend, E. P. PENICK.

The Commissioners' Court appointed a committee of farmers to solicit seed for the impoverished people of Waller some weeks ago.

GRIP CAUSES DESTITUTION.

Result of Investigations Made by the United Charities.

At the headquarters of the United Charities yesterday afternoon it was announced that an average of about eight persons per day had been cared for thus far this winter. In a majority of the cases investigated grip is the cause of destitution, in many instances all of the male portion of the family being afflicted and unable to work. In addition to this, attacks of pneumonia are by no means rare.

Contributions by the citizens this year have been very liberal, and assurance is given that the work of relief is being conducted along the same systematic lines as in past years.

DERAILED FREIGHT CARS.

They Were Cause of Delay of East Bound Texas and Pacific.

It was reported last night that there had been a freight wreck on the Texas and Pacific east of Arlington. The eastbound passenger train due in Dallas about 9 o'clock was delayed several hours.

The office of the general manager was called by phone and the information was given that there was no wreck, but that the delay was caused by freight cars getting off the track.

ROUND ABOUT TOWN.

Paul M. Gallaway returned yesterday after six weeks' absence in Honduras, Jamaica and Cuba on business and pleasure.

Speaking of the resources of Honduras he said: "The principal products of the section which I visited are fruits, mahogany and minerals. The timber resources are enormous, but transportation facilities are lacking for their development. One firm is now building a wagon road to some copper mines at great cost.

"I traveled on a burro and slept in a hammock during my stay there. On Christmas Day I was in the Province of Copan, near the wonderful remains of ancient temples and for dinner I had plantains and frijoles, with sardines for dessert.

"Across the bay from Puerto Cortez the principal city of Honduras, lies the old Morro Castle built by Cortez nearly 400 years ago at a cost, it is said, of $20,000,000. The old town beside the fortress contained 60,000 inhabitants 100 years ago, but now has a population of 150.

"On my return voyage I stopped at the Island of Jamaica and visited the royal botanical gardens, which are extremely beautiful. I passed around the eastern end of Cuba, caught a view of the battered walls of Matanzas and landed at Havana for a sight of that regenerated city. The streets looked remarkably clean and beautiful and health seemed to prevail. Many Americans are to be found there, but it is to be regretted that many of the laboring class are there, too, without means and many calls are made upon tourists for help.

"I am much pleased with my trip and can say that for Americans with some capital Central America offers remarkable inducements."

AMUSEMENTS.

Dallas Operahouse.

"A Hot Old Time," a roaring farce in three acts, was the attraction at the operahouse last night. The audience was not large, but it was a well-pleased gathering.

The cast is composed of vaudeville people, such as John and Miss B. Gleeson and Miss Anna Suits and Frank Hayes, all of whom were features of the large vaudeville houses in the North and East the past season. Taken as a whole, "A Hot Old Time" as presented last night was creative of much laughter and deserves praise for the introduction of neat, clever specialties. John W. Jess is a capable light comedian.

Herrmann.

The next attraction will be Herrmann, Saturday matinee and night.

Huge Electric Scheme in Australia.

According to a Sydney correspondent a colossal scheme for supplying the whole of Sydney with electro-motive power, not only for lighting, but for transportation and general motive purposes, is now being worked out by the Public Works Department. For the generation of the necessary force it is proposed to utilize the Blue Mountain Rivers and to provide for water storage on a large scale. The plant is to be of the most modern type and is to be supplemented by storage batteries in order to fully utilize the available energy during the hours of least demand. For the Sydney train and tramway service alone some 25,000 horsepower is required, and the scheme contemplates the generation of sufficient force to supply this, in addition to street lighting in the city and the mountain resorts and the rental of electric power to manufacturers. The total cost of the scheme is under £1,500,000.

Licensed to Wed.

J. E. Amos and Miss Margaret Smith.

CAP ON THE WELL

FLOW OF THE BIG GEYSER AT BEAUMONT CAN NOT BE PLACED UNDER CONTROL.

BIG DEALS ARE MADE

COMPANIES BEING ORGANIZED WITH LARGE CAPITAL TO DEVELOP THE TERRITORY.

STOCKS JUMP TO PREMIUM

Speculators Continue to Flock in from Distant Points in All Directions. Some Other Enterprises.

SPECIAL TO THE NEWS.

Beaumont, Tex., Jan. 17.—Notwithstanding last night's trains brought in large numbers of sightseers, investors, oil men and well digging machinery agents, the day has been more quiet than any since the bursting of the Lucas oil well, and yet more real business has been transacted today than during the whole of this week. This is because men with money to invest and experienced oil men have been waiting for the excitement over the well to subside in order that business might be transacted intelligently. Several large deals have been negotiated today and a few have been closed.

The charter for the Higgins Oil Company was forwarded to Austin last night for approval. The company will have a capital stock of $100,000 and will operate many rigs on land owned and controlled by the stockholders. It is said that there was such a demand for stock of this company as soon as organization was completed that the price advanced to 200 per cent premium on the face of the stock.

There is a world of money here, seeking investment, and it will gradually find its way into the development of the oil field. Several prominent oil men from New York, Pennsylvania, Ohio and other fields reached here last night. Among them is ex-State Senator M. L. Lockwood of Harmony, Pa., who is president of the Anti-Trust League of America. Mr. Lockwood came from his home in the Keystone State to see the Lucas well, and to investigate the fields. He is undecided whether he will identify himself with the development or not. There can be no doubt but that this field will be one of the most extensive in the United States.

The universal opinion of all oil men is that this is one of the richest fields of oil ever struck and many predict that there will be other wells as large as the Lucas strike.

Dr. Chauncey B. Forward, secretary and general manager of the Forward Reduction Company of Cleveland, Ohio, and Edward L. Buckwalter, vice president of the same company, from Springfield, Ohio, arrived here last night and are enthusiastic over the field.

The Forward Reduction Company is interested in this field, and has been represented here for about two years by J. A. Paul Lamus, who has several wells in the lower part of the country. Dr. Forward talks of building a large plant here for the utilization of the oil, and the manufacturing of gas.

The big Lucas well has been mastered by its owners. Last evening about 6 o'clock a joint was placed over the stream and the valve on the upright pipe was closed, thus directing the stream through the horizontal pipe and shooting oil on to the ground. When preparations have been completed this valve on the horizontal pipe will be closed and the well stopped. This destroys the wonderful sight furnished by the oil spouting in the air, but it is a cause for rejoicing with Capt. Lucas and the owners of the well.

The oil can now be managed and will be turned into immense iron tanks which are being built for the purpose. A company is being organized here tonight which will have a capital stock of $1,000,000 and will be the largest factor in the working of the field in this country.

BUYING OIL LANDS.

Developments at Beaumont Have Greatly Quickened Speculation.

SPECIAL TO THE NEWS.

Austin, Tex., Jan. 17.—The recent great oil discovery near Beaumont is the subject of much comment among the members of the Legislature, a number of whom are owners of tracts of land in that locality.

Hon. W. W. Dies, Representative from Hardin County, said today that he had just purchased 2,500 acres located within ten miles of the big gusher. He will probably put down a number of wells on the property if it is found that the oil field extends in his district.

Hon. R. A. Greer, the member of the House from Beaumont, is at home on business. A photograph of the great well was received by some of his fellow members from him today.

ERA OF OIL FOR FUEL.

Mayor Jones of Toledo Thinks It Is About to Dawn.

SPECIAL TO THE NEWS.

Corsicana, Tex., Jan. 17.—Mayor Jones of Toledo, Ohio, and his son, Paul H. Jones, left the city this evening for their home in Toledo, Ohio. Mr. Jones is very enthusiastic over the outlook for Texas and thinks that an era of liquid fuel is about to dawn, and says that when the consumers can feel sure that the output of heavy oil will be sufficient to meet all demands they will readily adopt it and dispense with coal and wood.

THINK THEY'LL GET OIL.

Prospecting Wells Will Be Sunk at Morgan at Once.

SPECIAL TO THE NEWS.

Morgan, Tex., Jan. 17.—The Morgan Oil and Gas Company now has the machinery on the ground to drill 3,000 feet in prospecting for petroleum. Work will begin on the first well next Saturday. The company is composed of such men as Capt. Garitty of Corsicana, Col. R. P. Lowe of Weatherford and Harry Schear of Dallas.

To Prospect Near Ennis.

SPECIAL TO THE NEWS.

Ennis, Tex., Jan. 17.—Preparations are being made to prospect near Ennis for oil.

EXCITEMENT AT BEAUMONT.

A. G. Newsum Says It Surpasses Anything He Ever Saw.

A. G. Newsum, division passenger agent of the Houston and Texas Central, returned yesterday from Beaumont, where he spent the preceding day. He says he might have stayed longer if he could have found a place to sleep. He describes the excitement there as wonderful, and the big spouting oil well as surpassing anything in his experience.

"I have been in the oil fields of Pennsylvania, West Virginia and other States," said Mr. Newsum, "during periods of discovery and excitement, but never witnessed anything to equal what may now be seen at Beaumont.

"The scene around the gusher is impressive. The huge volume of dark liquid spurting high in the air conveys but a faint idea of the tremendous force behind the stream and of the enormous resources of oil lying beneath the surface. All round the derrick lies the broken, twisted casing, 600 feet of which was thrown out of the well by the force of the geyser.

"The breaking forth of that stream is the greatest thing that has ever happened in Texas, even if the oil is only fit for fuel, as is now stated. It is a great thing for Beaumont and for all other cities near there. The Standard Oil Company has already been granted a concession for a pipe line to Port Arthur and the oil may in time be pumped to Houston and Galveston, furnishing cheap fuel in abundance for those cities.

"Beaumont is chock full of all classes of people, speculators, investors, grafters, oil experts and business men from all parts of Texas and the United States and every place of accommodation is crowded to suffocation.

"The hotels remind one of the wheat pits in Chicago and New York in the turmoil of buying and selling property and the attempts to get options on oil land.

"The whole population thinks and talks of nothing but oil—white, black, old and young—all are busy making fortunes, on paper, and the few lucky ones are really getting rich.

"One attempt has been made to stop the flow of oil from the Lucas well, but the cap placed on the pipe was blown off with such terrific force that other measures are being planned to stop it.

"There is danger of the oil catching fire, and such a catastrophe would be disastrous, as the lake just south of the city contains over 100,000 barrels of oil. A man dropped a cigar in the dry grass the other day and a score or more of excited men fought the flames desperately until they were extinguished, for fear the fire would reach the oil. No one is now allowed near the well or stream of oil at any place with a pipe or a cigar."

THE CANAL TREATY

According to Editorials in London Papers England May Reject the Treaty.

London, Jan. 16.—Nicaraguan Canal matters were brought forcibly before the public today by means of an editorial in the Daily Telegraph and a lengthy dispatch from the American correspondent of the London Times. Each takes exactly opposite views. The Associated Press is officially informed that neither can be taken to represent the Government views for the excellent reasons that these views are not yet concentrated into a decision. The conferences so far held between United States Ambassador Choate and Secretary of State for Foreign Affairs Lord Lansdowne have occurred at the instigation of the latter and were for the purpose of enlightening Lord Lansdowne on various technicalities so as to enable him to explain them to the Cabinet meeting on Friday. Until that is held Great Britain's attitude will not be known. The forecast thus develops into speculation. The United States embassy officials appear to be hopeful of the acceptance of amendments to the Hay-Pauncefote treaty. In spite of this impression and taking full consideration of the opportunities of the embassy officials in determining which way the cat is likely to jump, the Associated Press has excellent reason to believe that if Lord Lansdowne's voice predominates the Cabinet of Great Britain will not accept the amendments. There is no shadow of doubt that if the Foreign Office is followed Great Britain will either regretfully express her inability to comply with the amendments or fail to take any action whatever, in which case the treaty will lapse of itself. Several of Lord Lansdowne's advisers favor the latter course. Their feelings can well be judged from a statement of one of the foremost of his advisers who, replying to a remark that the canal was not worth a row, said: "Perhaps not, but it does not do to apply that principle in every case."

A BITTER INVOCATION.

England Is Called Upon Not to Yield to America's Demands.

London, Jan. 16.—The dispatch of the American correspondent of the London Times is a bitter invocation of Great Britain not to give anti-English Americans an opportunity for exultation over her surrender, and finds a hearty editorial echo in the Globe, which declares that though Americans as a whole are learning to take a more sober view of the relations with Great Britain, "there is still a group of politicians whose main object is to annoy and humiliate Great Britain."

Various American dispatches refer pointedly to Washington's growing assumption that Great Britain will accept the amendments. According to rumors here this is greatly due to private conversations with Lord Pauncefote some time ago. Whatever truth there is in the reported conversations with Lord Pauncefote, and they are not credited at the Foreign Office, it can be said that the matter has now gone beyond the phase where Lord Pauncefote's views are likely to turn the scale one way or the other. Were not the question regarded from the broad standpoint of Great Britain's general policy toward the United States it would be safe to say the Senate's amendments would meet with a prompt refusal, and if that does occur it will be done with a full appreciation on the part of Great Britain of any and all consequences.

GLENNY & CO.'S COTTON LETTER.

Poor Condition of Dry Goods Trade Is a Bearish Factor.

SPECIAL TO THE NEWS.

New Orleans, La., Jan. 17—Mr. Neill's circular was published today, as expected, reaffirming his previous estimate of 9,750,000. It had not the effect anticipated, as Liverpool lost sharply and only partially recovered. Our market was also disappointing, the conspicuous feature being selling by longs, who had bought in anticipation of the estimate advancing Liverpool. Port receipts today were moderate and so were receipts expected tomorrow at New Orleans and Houston. This was counteracted by the stress laid by bears on condition of dry goods trade and an increase in the Bombay movement. The day's business resulted in a decline of about 10 points, March 9.25-26c. Spots were quoted steady, prices unchanged. Some buyers claimed they could buy at easier prices. Some others deny this claim. To summarize, the immediate market is disappointing, irresponsive to what should be a distinctly bullish feature. It seems under the spell of comparisons with last season and those who claim much cotton remaining in the interior. The Bombay movement and the action of Eastern mill owners is deterring those bulls who are getting tired of waiting for decreased movements. Still if bulls are correct in believing the movement to date brisker than the average they should not be surprised that it still continues free. We must soon reckon with last year's very large February and later on with its immense July and August to hold the gain for which its extremely small December is largely responsible. Perhaps there is some truth in the theory that Southern mills have not yet removed from sight the cotton for which the weekly movements have had to give them credit. We continue to run well behind year before last, which brought into sight from now on less cotton than last year. Each week we fall heavily behind three years ago, though to reach about 10,250,000 we must more than equal it from now on. We are to date far behind the only crop of near the size of the present average expectations, 1895-94, of 9,900,000 bales. Our Liverpool friends assert present prices are safe for summer months unless crop exceeds 10,300,000.

I. E. GLENNY & CO.

H. & B. BEER'S COTTON LETTER.

Neill's Bullish Estimate Had No Influence in the Market.

SPECIAL TO THE NEWS.

New Orleans, La., Jan. 17.—Much interest was centered in the course of Liverpool today, as that market had taken the lead in the advance. Advices from there, however, stated that Mr. Neill had confirmed his previous estimate, which was disbelieved, causing longs to resell. Our market, in sympathy, opened 8 points lower, declined 4 additional points on the free port and interior movement and the large Bombay weekly receipts, which were 86,000 bales this year against 41,000 last year.

Near the close short covering caused a slight rally, making the net loss on the day 10 to 11 points. Spots locally are officially quoted steady and unchanged, with sales of 2,750 bales, including 650 to arrive. Buyers claim, though, that purchases can be made from 1-16c to 1/8c under quotations. The enthusiasm apparent yesterday was lacking, and it is beginning to dawn on a good many that the recent reports from all over the South, to the effect that the holdings are heavier than any one expected, are being borne out by the large interior receipts.

The restricted export demand for spots causes cotton to accumulate in the interior and prevents it coming to the ports. Should exporters enter the market freely receipts would immediately increase. The cotton goods trade in this country is not encouraging, while on the Continent outside of France trade is generally poor. Consequently, considering the high level of values, the poor condition of trade generally and the probability that the crop has been underestimated, it is no wonder that operators are commencing to do something; therefore daily receipts will continue to rule prices until definite conclusions are reached as to the size of the crop.

H. & B. BEER.

WORDS OF WARNING

EX-PRESIDENT GROVER CLEVELAND SPEAKS OF NATIONAL DANGER AT A NEW YORK BANQUET.

EXAMPLE OF NATIONS

ENGLAND AND THE UNITED STATES PORTRAYED AS ENCOMPASSED BY SIMILAR TROUBLES.

VAST PROBLEMS OF FUTURE

Patriotism and Good Sense Are Relied Upon to Rescue from Impending Dangers.

New York, Jan. 17.—The Holland Society held its sixteenth annual dinner at the Waldorf-Astoria tonight. Among the speakers was Grover Cleveland, who said:

"The cordial welcome you extended to me is exceedingly grateful and comforting, for it gives me a grain of satisfaction in the ordeal that confronts me. I am convinced that the art of making an after dinner speech without distress is for me a sealed book, and as the years pass I am only saved from complete wretchedness in my efforts in that direction by the kindness and toleration of those who are good enough to listen to me.

"I can not resent the charge that I am apt to preach sermons on subjects of this kind, for I am afraid the accusation is justified. At any rate, I am quite willing to take an humble place among the sermonizers, in this time of headlong national heedlessness and to invoke the cultivation and saving grace of Dutch conservatism. In this assemblage the question is suggested whether in present conditions this conservatism characterized the conduct or guides the sentiment of our people. There can be but one answer to this question. Conservatism has in a great degree been jauntily cast aside or condemned as opposed to our country's welfare and glory. A strange voyage has been entered upon without count of cost and without chart or compass. The tried and sure foundations of our liberty and national happiness have been discredited. Reverence for our national traditions has been relaxed, and satisfaction with our country's mission has been undermined. The restraints and limitations of our Constitution have become galling and irksome under the temptations of national greed and aggrandizement. Our old love of peace, honor and justice has been weakened and frugality and contentment are not now traits inseparable from American character. War even with the world's advanced civilization may still be sometimes necessary and justifiable, but whether necessary and justifiable or not, the demoralization that follows in its train can never be evaded. It teaches bloody instructions which, in a country whose citizens do the fighting, can not fail to leave their impress for a time at least upon public and private life in time of peace.

"Thirty years after the close of the war for the preservation of the Union, a treaty of arbitration was formulated between the United States and Great Britain, which, if completed, would have gone far towards removing every pretext of war between the two countries. Thus these two great English-speaking nations then assumed leaderships in the path of peace and in advocacy of the abolition of war—with the hope and expectation that the example would be followed by other nations, and that a more general adoption of arbitration as a means of settling international disputes would result in a great advance towards the abandonment of war throughout the world. This treaty failed of confirmation in the Senate of the United States. Less than five years passed, and these English-speaking champions of peace and arbitration are still operating in parallel lines—one in the Philippines and the other in South Africa—but no longer for peace and arbitration. Both are killing natives in an effort to possess their lands. This indicates a sad relapse, and in our case it is a most serious one. If England succeeds in her attempt in South Africa she will but add another to her list of similar acquisitions: a brave people will be subjugated, and because of our engagement in a similar venture in another quarters they will miss the expressions of American sympathy which we are accustomed to extend to those who struggle for national life and independence. On the other hand, with success in our subjugation effort, a new, untried and exceedingly perilous situation will be forced upon us.

"We can conquer the Philippines, and after conquering them, we can probably govern them. It is in the strain upon our institutions, the demoralization of our people, the evasion of our constitutional limitations and the perversion of our national mission that our danger lies. As a distinguished bishop has said: 'The question is not what we shall do with the Philippines, but what the Philippines will do to us.'

"Our country will never be the same again. For weal or woe, we have already irrevocably passed beyond the old lines.

"The Republic will in some way be saved. Shall it be only in name, in semblance, with fair external appearance, but with the germs of decay fastened upon it vitals, or shall it, though changed, still survive in such vigor and strength as to remain the hope and pride of free Americans?

"The problem is a momentous one. Its solution depends upon the extent to which the old patriotism and good sense of our countrymen can be rescued from impending danger. Thus these are sober days for thoughtful citizens—days for preaching—days for sermonizing. If we are to be saved from disaster it must be through the cultivation and enforcement of that sort of conservatism that would find a congenial home in the Holland Society. In the midst of reckless tumult and in the confused rage of national greed and bloodiness, this conservatism should defiantly stand forth and demand a hearing. Let it be known that American freedom and popular rule can not perish except through the madness of those who have them in their keeping and by the blood and sacrifices of our fathers, by the lofty achievements of the free institutions they established, by our glorious victories of peace, and by our reliance on the promises of God, let Dutch conservatism enjoin upon our people a faithful discharge of their sacred trust."

Boer Delegate Arrested.

Standerton, Jan. 17.—Boer women brought in the military report that William Stein, who was appointed a delegate of the Boers here to ask the fighting Boers to surrender under Lord Kitchener's proclamation, was made a prisoner and sent to Piertewieff, accused of treason. The Boers are still active around Standerton.

A SHOW OF DOCUMENTS.

COLLECTION OF MANY BEARING UPON NEW-YORK HISTORY EXHIBITED AT THE LENOX LIBRARY.

Controller Coler and Librarian Eames, of the Lenox Library, between them have done a laudable and public spirited thing in arranging an exhibition of documents bearing upon New-York history. The exhibition as it is at present is only an affair of three weeks' or a month's duration, beginning from last Monday, but if all goes well the bulk of the documents may be permanently on exhibition in the new and consolidated Library of the City of New-York, when that magnificent anticipation attains reality.

In calling this an exhibition of documents, the term is used in its more proper and wider sense, to include a great variety of things—manuscripts and printed books, maps, drawings, prints, old newspapers and broadsides, deeds and, above all, charters. All these things afford historical information at first hand, and are, for so much, historical documents. For the largest class of New-Yorkers who may be supposed to take any interest whatever in the history of their city, the cynosure of the whole display will be found at the end of one of the long showcases arranged down the middle of the lower hall, on the left as you enter. Here are the two earliest charters of the English province of New-York. They are two thick wads made up of many sheets of parchment. To the earlier of the two, the Dongan charter, is attached the seal (presumably that known as the Privy Seal) of the King of Great Britain, France and Ireland, who at that date (1686) happened to be James II, some time known as Duke of York, and in whose honor its new name of New-York was given to the settlement of the New-Netherlands. The wax seal is inclosed in a silver box, upon the lid of which is inscribed "N. Bayard, Mayor, 1686." "N." stands here for Nicholas, and in that name of Nicholas Bayard lies a whole volume or more of early colonial romance. The later is the Montgomerie (so spelled) charter of 1731, to which is attached the seal of the province.

Both of these documents are the property of the city of New-York, and have been so for longer than any one can remember, but their resting place has long been in the darkness of the archives where no human eye has looked upon them from year's end to year's end. Controller Coler even now keeps a fearful watch over their safety, as he should do. At least three New-York newspapers, The Tribune among the number, have asked his permission to make special photographs of the precious charters, but in vain. Only one photograph, or, rather, artograph, has been made, and that upon the Controller's own commission, and under his superintendence, by Bierstadt. The experts on old writings, known as diplomatists, have pronounced it hazardous to allow the parchments to be taken out and handled as often as they must be if all the photographers who wish to are to be allowed to photograph them.

Among the exhibits in the upper hall are a number of rare contemporary prints illustrating the earlier history of the city, many of them lent for the exhibition by John D. Crimmins, but most of them the property of the library. As one instance of the light which contemporary prints may shed upon history, there is in the upper hall a colored print, the property of the New-York Library, showing the mob in the act of pulling down the statue of King George at Bowling Green, and another of "The Victorious Entry of the Royal Troops into New-York." Both of these bear the imprint of the Imperial Institute of Arts, at Augsburg. Even though no date can be found on either, it is evident enough to any one who has seen many old prints that these are contemporary, and, this being so, it may be taken for granted that they show the events as those events were supposed by persons then living to have taken place. The display of New-York newspapers is also valuable and deeply interesting in this quality of introducing one to bygone events as they were seen by contemporaries. "The New-York Gazette and Mercury" of 1776 exhibits two of the most impudent journalistic faces on record, having broken itself into two like an amœba when the war began, and printing "The Gazette" in New-York with a British view of the war news, and "The Mercury" in Newark with an American view. Another newspaper of especial historical interest is one entitled "The War," the first number of which is dated June 27, 1812, published by S. Woodworth & Co., at No. 437 Pearl-st. Those who were interested in this journalistic collection will probably be glad to look at the two autographs, on a deed of the year 1729, of William Bradford, the first printer in New-York.

To a great many people, indeed, the autographs of the great names of history, to be found on instruments of the most various degrees of importance, from grants of land to complaints in the city court and mere business letters, will be the most interesting exhibits. There is the signature of Peter Stuyvesant, Director-General of the New-Netherlands, for instance, on a Dutch original document, so exquisitely inset in an extra illustrated copy of Booth's "History of New-York" that most visitors are sure to mistake it for a facsimile lithographed on toned paper. A long minute of certain proceedings before Mayor Francis Rombout on Christmas Eve of 1679, about a ketch which had been wrongfully appraised, contains the name of the first Lord of the Manor of Sleepy Hollow, and it is interesting to note that the name is here written neither "Flypse" nor "Philipse," but "Mr. Frederick Phillips." Other interesting autographs are those of Jacobus Kipp, Peter Minuit, several Bayards and Francis Rombout.

The great pity is that, for the present at least, all this wealth of historical interest must be only for people who can spare the time to enjoy it during the working hours of the day. The library closes at 6 p. m. and all day on Sundays. While there are two divisions of the New-York Public Library, entailing much expense, which will be eliminated after consolidation, the authorities do not feel justified in incurring the further expense of prolonging the open hours of either branch.

TRICKED OUT OF HIS CLAIM.

From The Joplin (Mo.) News-Herald.

"Many things occurred during the opening and settlement of the Cherokee Strip in Oklahoma in 1893, the like of which had never been seen or heard," said a Joplin printer, who was mixed up in the race at the opening, and secured a number of town lots at Pawnee. "I remember a young fellow who came down to Perry from Iowa and staked out a nice corner lot. And, by the way, merely staking out a claim did not give one the complete right of possession. You had to sit down on it and hold it fast, and the Iowa chap was a stayer. He ate his meals on the lot and rolled himself in a blanket and slept on it at night. Unscrupulous schemers were ever present, beating the unwary out of their claims. But the Iowa man held his base and played safe.

"One night four men silently approached the sleeper. They carried a tent, a table and four seats. They quietly erected the tent over the Iowa man, got out a deck of cards and began playing seven up. The Iowa man slept on. After a while one of the players gave him a poke in the ribs with his foot. The man in the blanket awoke, rubbed his eyes and stared about inquiringly and in a very much bewildered manner. 'What the h—— are you doing here, young fellow?' demanded the man who had kicked him. 'Why—why—I don't exactly know,' faltered the Iowan, as he extricated himself from the blanket. 'I—I must have been walking in my sleep.' 'Right sure you ain't tryin' to steal this lot from me,' demanded the other, scowling in a threatening manner at the Iowan. 'No, sir, I am not. I had no tent or anything on my lot and I do not wish to beat you out of this claim.' 'I believe you're lying to me, young feller, an' I'm a great mind to fix you right now, but I won't. If you will hold up your right hand in the presence of these three men and swear this is not your lot and that you will not try to claim it an' make me trouble, I'll let you off this time. Some of you guys are too d—— tricky to live in this neighborhood, anyway. What do you say?' 'Gentlemen, I swear this is not my lot and that I will make no claim on it whatever,' said the Iowan, with uplifted hand. 'That's enough. Now hit the grit.' The young man gathered up his blanket and departed. He spent the rest of the night trying to find his choice corner lot. The day broke and the sun arose, but he was yet unsuccessful in locating it. The men in the tent threw up a shack, opened a saloon and a thriving business on the corner lot, and in a few days the Iowan traded his Winchester for a lame mule and sorrowfully rode out of the Territory."

NEW EXCAVATIONS NEAR NAPLES.

From The London News.

While awaiting the approval of the new bill on works of ancient art, the Italian Minister of Public Instruction has decided to permit at present no private excavations. This, says our Naples correspondent, is a pity, for there are two excavations near Naples which, if continued, would probably be most interesting. One is at a place between Torre Annunziata and Castellammaret, where caves have been found not far from the sea, which seemingly served the ancient Romans as baths and boathouses. At the end of these caves paintings of some value have been found.

The other excavation is at Camaldoli di Torre in a walled territory called, from its position, the Corona, with vineyards and cornfields and a large wood, the whole about eighty acres in extent. In the wood at the foot of the wall, where a road was being made and pozzolana dug out, there was discovered an old Roman wall. Excavation was made, and other walls were discovered, those of a large building. Soon some frescos in lively colors were uncovered, and then amphoræ, bits of glass, pieces of marble, bones of men and animals came to light, as well as a metal statuette, so thickly incrusted that as yet its quality and value cannot be ascertained. The proprietor informed the Ministry of this discovery, and asked permission to continue the excavation at his own expense. After long delay the Ministry decided to send the Extraordinary Commission, now busy at the Naples Museum, to inspect the works. The Commission, which began the inspection with some prejudice, advised the proprietor not to continue the excavation, as the building must have belonged to poor peasants, and the work would not be remunerative. The proprietor, however, objected that there was too much elegance in the manner of building for a humble abode, and that the position, on an elevated stretch of country, was at the spot where the rich inhabitants of Herculaneum were likely to have villas, and therefore interesting discoveries were probable. The Commission, however, proposed the prohibition of further excavation, and now the decision of the Ministry is awaited.

THE DESTRUCTION OF THE STATUE OF GEORGE III.
(From an old colored print on exhibition at the Lenox Library.)

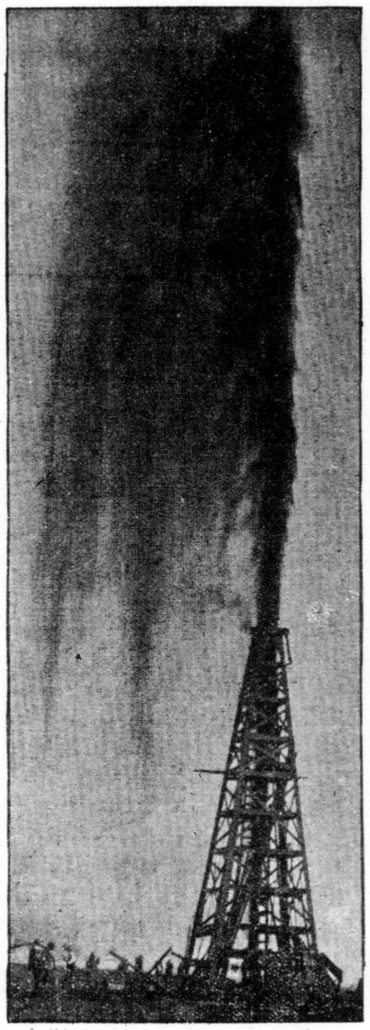

NEW OIL WELL AT BEAUMONT, TEXAS.
Which yields fifteen thousand barrels in twenty-four hours.

OIL GUSHER CAUSES A BOOM.

GREAT WELL AT BEAUMONT, TEX., SENDS LAND VALUES SOARING.

Announcement was made last week of the wonderful oil well at Beaumont, Tex., on the property of the Kansas City Southern Railroad. The well is a gusher, and it had a slightly depressing effect on the petroleum market when it was first struck. Its record production thus far is 15,000 barrels in twenty-four hours. Reports from Beaumont indicate that the gusher has caused the wildest excitement and a boom in land values. Many other borings are being made in the neighborhood. The gusher that has caused the commotion is 1,500 feet deep, and the oil at first shot 144 feet in the air, which is eighty feet above the derrick built over the well.

A BELL WITH A HISTORY.

IT IS A RELIC OF THE WORST STEAMBOAT ACCIDENT ON THE MISSOURI RIVER.

From The Charleston News and Courier.

There hangs in the belfry of the little Christian Church in the town of Savannah, in Andrew County, Mo., a bell which has a remarkable history. In 1852—forty-eight years ago—there occurred at Lexington the most disastrous accident which ever befell a steamboat on the Missouri River and one attended with the greatest loss of human life. The Saluda, a sidewheel steamer, with a battery of two boilers, was on its way up the river with a cargo of general merchandise and its cabin and lower deck crowded with passengers, the most of whom were Mormons. The river was unusually high and the current, as it came around the point just above the town, was extremely strong. Captain Francis T. Belt had made repeated efforts to stem the rapid current, but had as often failed. At last, after waiting several days for the flood to subside, he asked the engineer how many more pounds of steam it could stand. On being answered that it had already every pound that it could safely carry, he gave the command, "Fill it up, put on more steam," and remarked to the engineer, with an oath, that he would round the point or blow it up. He then retired to the hurricane roof, rang the bell and gave the final command to "cast loose the lines." The bow of the boat turned gently out into the stream as it was caught by the current. The engines made but one revolution. Then came the terrible explosion—and all was chaos, darkness and death. The number of those who lost their lives by the explosion was never known. About one hundred bodies were recovered, and it was supposed that there were as many more victims whose remains were never found. Nearly all the officers of the boat were killed. The bell which had just sounded the death knell of so many unfortunate ones was blown high up on the bank, where it was found uninjured.

PLOUGH MONDAY.

From The London Chronicle.

Yesterday being Plough Monday, the Lord Mayor went in pomp to the Guildhall, where he held a Grand Court of Wardmote, at which all ward officers who were elected in December were presented, and were confirmed in their appointments, no objections being offered. In the evening there was the customary dinner at the Mansion House. The origin of Plough Monday is to be sought not in London, but, as the name implies, in rural districts, where the ploughmen arranged a procession in order to collect money for the maintenance of the candles which, as dependents on the soil, they kept burning before the images of certain saints in the churches. Ploughs, candles and images are scarce in the City to-day, but Plough Monday still brings its Grand Wardmote.

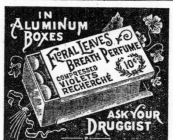

BEAUMONT AND ITS BOOM.

CHARACTERISTICS OF THE TEXAS OIL TOWN—WILD SPECULATION SUBSIDING.

Beaumont, Tex., May 20.—Oil operations here have reached a period of suspense. The reaction that must follow a gambling fever is setting in. Three weeks ago indiscriminate land buying raged like an epidemic. To-day the sellers are far more numerous than the buyers, and nothing but a marked extension of the known oil field will change things. Men's heads were turned by the petroleum geysers, and one day options and dubious titles were traded in at rapidly ascending figures. Now the holders of oil lands are beginning to realize that they have a vast problem on hand, and that a flood of oil cannot be converted into money until a market has been found and means of transportation and of refining have been provided.

A. F. LUCAS.
The discoverer of oil at Beaumont.

The Beaumont oil strike is the most wonderful and the most spectacular in the history of oil fields, but its market must be created. That will take time and capital. The extent of the field must be determined by persistent drilling, and pipe lines, refineries and tank steamers constructed. That also will take time and money. Meanwhile, it is pretty certain that great losses will be sustained by a large body of speculators who have purchased distant acres at fancy prices, or have read too credulously the prospectuses of irresponsible corporations.

The fact remains, however, that a few miles out from this little Texas village, within an area of about 118 acres so far developed, have been drilled nine of the largest oil wells in the world. What their total capacity is can only be conjectured. Wells that spout a six or eight inch stream of petroleum 150 feet in the air are beyond ordinary standards of measurement. An expert guess, backed by an incomplete test, has put the production of the Lucas well alone at from fifty thousand to seventy thousand barrels in twenty-four hours. The previous total output of the world is stated, on authority that ought to be sufficient, to have been something more than 375,000 barrels daily. Is Beaumont to outdo the rest of the earth? Probably not, but the figures are instructive, nevertheless.

The now famous Lucas "gusher" came in (as the jargon of the oil fields has it) on January 10, 1901; the latest of its eight companions spouted on May 9. Probably no one has counted the number of derricks that dot the prairie for miles in all directions and mark the spots where the drills are at work or preparations for drilling have been made. A very few of these wells are certain to reach the oil sands; it is whispered that about eight or nine of them are certainly dry holes; the fate of the remainder cannot be even approximately foretold.

Interest is centred on the outcome of two or three wells situated outside the present "gusher" district. The drilling of these wells has been in progress for weeks, and speculation hangs breathless upon the results. Should they develop oil, it would mean an extension of the known field, with a great rise in values of the surrounding lands; the other alternative will mean a heart breaking limitation of the field. Suspicion has it that these holes have already reached below the depth at which their great neighbors began to spout forth liquid wealth. But operations are conducted with a burglar's secretiveness, and the tale of the drill is sacred. Suspicion is at a discount in such a place; yet if these particular wells are not successful, others will be, for it is not to be conceived that this oil flood cannot be tapped at other spots than those already found. Prospectors are busy northeast into Louisiana, northwest to Corsicana, southeast to Sabine Lake, and southwest to High Island. The Lucas well alone produces more oil daily than the whole of the California field. What the Texas output will be when the field is fully developed can be surmised only in superlatives.

Unfortunately, many of the land titles are in a woful state of defectiveness. At prairie values of $1 to $3 an acre niceties in title were of no moment. Even the most uncertain of these same prairies, from the point of view of oil speculation, are now held at $50 to $100 an acre; tracts near the gusher district have sold readily at from $5,000 to $20,000 an acre, while the gusher area itself has climbed up to $100,000 an acre. At one particularly choice spot an offer of $75,000 was made and refused for a plot twenty-five feet square—just room enough to rig a derrick. At such figures titles have become of immense importance, and a long calendar of law suits is now confronting the Jefferson County courts. Texas lawyers will reap a little harvest of their own.

Beaumont is said to have a population of ten thousand. It is the county seat of Jefferson County, but despite its premiership it straggles along the Neches River in a careless, undignified manner. It has great sawmills, where the long leaf yellow pine of Louisiana is prepared for market, and rice mills, where the crop of the surrounding prairies is handled. Rice has been king in this country, albeit a youthful one, but oil has now usurped the throne. For the rest little can be said about the town in its external aspects except in line of unfavorable criticism. It has the filth that goes with surface drainage. Its supply of drinking water is dependent upon the rains or the muddy bottoms of the Neches. Smallpox is prevalent, physicians placing the number of cases to-day as high as two hundred. To a Northerner's conception the townspeople are astonishingly regardless of the pest, and if it attacks them they simply murmur "Allah is Allah," or its Texas equivalent, and turn in. Beaumont is, in truth, ugly and inadequate.

To this town unexpectedly a phenomenal flow of petroleum brought a stream of humanity. The hitherto lazy streets were transformed into oil exchanges, where unwonted crowds pushed and struggled and where lands and options found a clamorous market at high figures. Land offices sprang up in corridors of business buildings, in hotel piazzas, street booths and temporary wooden buildings. An oil and stock exchange was established. Several hundred corporations for dealing in and prospecting oil lands were formed and exploited. Men, women and boys bought and sold options and stocks at prices that doubled overnight. Land in all directions was traded in with small regard to titles, and blocks of corporate stock were absorbed without adequate conception of the values represented. All this means that the crowd perhaps equalled that of a block or two of lower Broadway at noontime, and a day's transactions approximated five minutes' trading on the New-York Stock Exchange on a quiet day. For Beaumont it was tremendous, and old oil men say that all previous "booms" were outclassed.

Many people made money in the trading and realized on their profits. Many others will make fortunes from the oil. For the most part, however, it is probable that the speculative public, as usual, will have to pay the piper.

Digging for oil here began as long ago as 1867, and it was found in small quantities in from three hundred to five hundred feet. For illuminating purposes that oil had little value, and as the use of oil for fuel had not been thought of the wells were abandoned. The Lucas well was begun last winter about three miles south of Beaumont, on a little wriggle in the land dignified by the name of a hill and known as Spindle Top. Its owners had the nerve and persistence to send the drill down nearly one thousand feet. One day in January, 1901, with a roar and with tremblings of the earth, the oil rushed up and blew the machinery out of the hole. A 6-inch stream of petroleum shot sixty-four feet, to the top of the derrick, and then one hundred feet above that into the air. For ten days the geyser played uncontrolled, and a lake of half a million barrels of oil was formed. Then a spark from a passing engine set the mass on fire. The conflagration that followed was an unparalleled celebration of the discovery.

The latest of the gushers, that of May 9, is scarcely more than two hundred yards from the Lucas. The Tribune representative saw it playing on the afternoon of that day, just before its owners succeeded in getting the valve gate closed. Its capacity is not known, nor, indeed, has that of any of its predecessors been much more than guessed at. When the Lucas well was struck oil men said it was producing at least twenty thousand barrels a day. When a tank was built and a pipeline laid an approximate test was had that indicated a production of seventy thousand barrels a day. The subterranean pressure will diminish as the field is developed, and eventually, no doubt, nature will have to be reinforced by the pumps.

When the fame of the Lucas well was first noised abroad, wise men from the California fields and from Ohio and Pittsburg hastened here, and acquired what is now known as the gusher district before the tide of wild speculation set in. These men and their Texas associates are now the leading factors in the legitimate development of the field and in arranging to market the oil. Already the largest domestic corporation ever formed in Texas has been organized for refining and handling the Beaumont oil. By far the larger part of the product will be fuel oil, but it is expected that illuminating and lubricating oils will also be obtained in profitable percentages.

The scarcity of fuel has long retarded industries in Southern Texas, and business men now expect an industrial revolution.

It is estimated that two and a half barrels of oil are equal to one ton of coal for fuel purposes. Coal costs from $6 to $8 a ton in Southern Texas and is scarce at that; while it will undoubtedly be possible to get an unlimited supply of fuel oil at from 60 cents to 80 cents a barrel. An Ohio oil man has figured out, however, that if all the present users of power in the Southern States, including the railroads, should immediately equip their engines and boilers for the use of oil, their total consumption would not amount to a quarter of the present production of the Beaumont field. It is not impossible that the Ohio man may be "bearing" the market, but his figures illustrate the difficulty of the situation. Engines and boilers are not equipped for oil, and it will take a long time to bring about the change and to build up in addition the export trade that will be essential to the prosperity of the oil producers.

For foreign markets, Beaumont has an enormous advantage over all other oil fields in that Port Arthur lies only eighteen miles away. There Sabine Lake and the 25-foot ship canal offer ample facilities for ocean-going vessels. A short pipe line becomes the only necessary link between the producing well and the tank steamer. For home consumption it is expected that the lumber industry, already great, will assume much larger proportions; that cotton mills will be established, and that the hitherto undeveloped iron regions of Eastern Texas will be opened up. Altogether the outlook is most promising for business interests here, not the least hopeful feature being the fact that speculators are retiring from the field and actual investors taking their places.

THE NAME "KENTUCKY."

ITS ORIGIN AND MEANING.

Extract from "Boonesborough," in The Louisville Courier-Journal,

Both the country and the river that now bear the beautiful name "Kentucky" were called so by the Indians ages before the coming of their white destroyers. The Indians also called the river "Chenoca," a word which still distinguishes a mountain spur in Bell County, Ky., but the name they used by far the most was "Kentucky." In coming into use among the whites early in the eighteenth century, the word varied as to form and pronunciation according to the user's knowledge of the Indian tongue. John Salling, who was a prisoner among the Cherokees for some years before 1736, and who must have been somewhat familiar with their language, gives the name as we now have it, when he says they took him "to the salt licks of Kentucky." Alexander Maginty, who had also been held by the Indians, deposed in 1753 that they captured him "on the south bank of the Cantucky," and Colonel George Croghan (not the Major Croghan, of Fort Stephenson), who was for so many years British agent among the Six Nations, and an authority in savage matters, speaks in his journal of 1765 of "the river Kentucky." Dr. Thomas Walker (1750) ignores the Indian name, if he knew it. Christopher Gist (1751) gives it in a corrupted form as "Cuttaway," and Lewis Evans (1755), who only caught the name from traders, put it down on his map as "Cuttawa."

Kentucky seems never to have been known by any but Indian names until a short time before 1775, when "Louisa" came into limited use, among the whites. The generally accurate Bradford helped to perpetuate the error that the Kentucky River was given the English name "Louisa" by Dr. Walker, but not only does Marshall declare that Walker did not reach the interior of the country, but later writers assert that it was a tributary of the Big Sandy—as given on Jefferson's map—that the explorer of 1750 so named. It was some time after Walker's tour before the name of this tributary was applied to the country itself, and then, fortunately, it quickly subsided before the original and ancient Indian name, which after many vicissitudes among the whites as to spelling and pronunciation came into prominent use as the Indians themselves pronounced it, "Kentucky."

Authors differ as to the meaning of the name. According to Darlington, in "Archives Americana," it is a Mohawk word, signifying "among the meadows." Johnson, in "Indian Tribes of Ohio," claims it as Shawanese, meaning "at the head of a river," and others give it still different definitions. Probably the earliest writer to give its meaning as "The Dark and Bloody Ground" was Filson (1784), who says the country was so denominated by the Indians when Finley travelled through it about 1767. This statement was adopted by succeeding historians and came into use, though Filson gave no authority for it, and there is nothing extant that this writer knows of to sustain it—certainly nothing from the Indians themselves.

There is a popular impression that this phrase, "The Dark and Bloody Ground," was used as the meaning of the word Kentucky by the Cherokees at the treaty of Watauga in 1775, but that is a mistake. On that occasion Dragging Canoe, who was strongly opposed to the treaty, said in that metaphorical style which distinguished his race that there was a "dark cloud" over Kentucky, meaning by that expression, as he himself explained, the hostility of the northern tribes to its occupancy by the whites. On the same occasion an Indian opposer of the treaty, hoping to arouse the superstitious fears of the whites, said that the land desired by Henderson & Co. was a "bloody country," but in neither case was a reference made to the meaning of the word "Kentucky." What this last expression did mean is not clear. Certain writers assume that it referred to the supposed bloody extermination of the Mound Builders, but on that theory the phrase would apply with even more force to Ohio and other States of the Ohio and Mississippi valleys. One has as much authority, apparently, for calling Kentucky "The Meadow Land" as "The Dark and Bloody Ground."

THE WALL STREET OF BEAUMONT.

THE JEFFERSON AND HARDIN COUNTY OIL FIELDS.

Map Showing the Best Known Surveys and Locating Wells That Have Come in and Those Being Drilled.

There are probably 100 derricks on oil lands in Jefferson county, but the number of wells being drilled is not over thirty, according to reports received from the field. This is due mainly to the fact that many of the companies have not yet been able to secure the machinery with which to begin the work of drilling. They have put up their derricks and made every preparation for active work, but will not be able to make much progress for some weeks to come, as the demand for oil well outfits is much greater than the present supply.

The map shows the oil wells that have been brought in and those that are now being drilled. The total is thirty-four. It will be seen that there are very few outside of the Veatch and Bullock leagues. There are reports of many other wells going down in remote surveys, but it has been impossible to obtain reliable information as to the location of any except these indicated by the map.

The wells around Sour Lake are two discovered a few years ago, and two that are now being drilled.

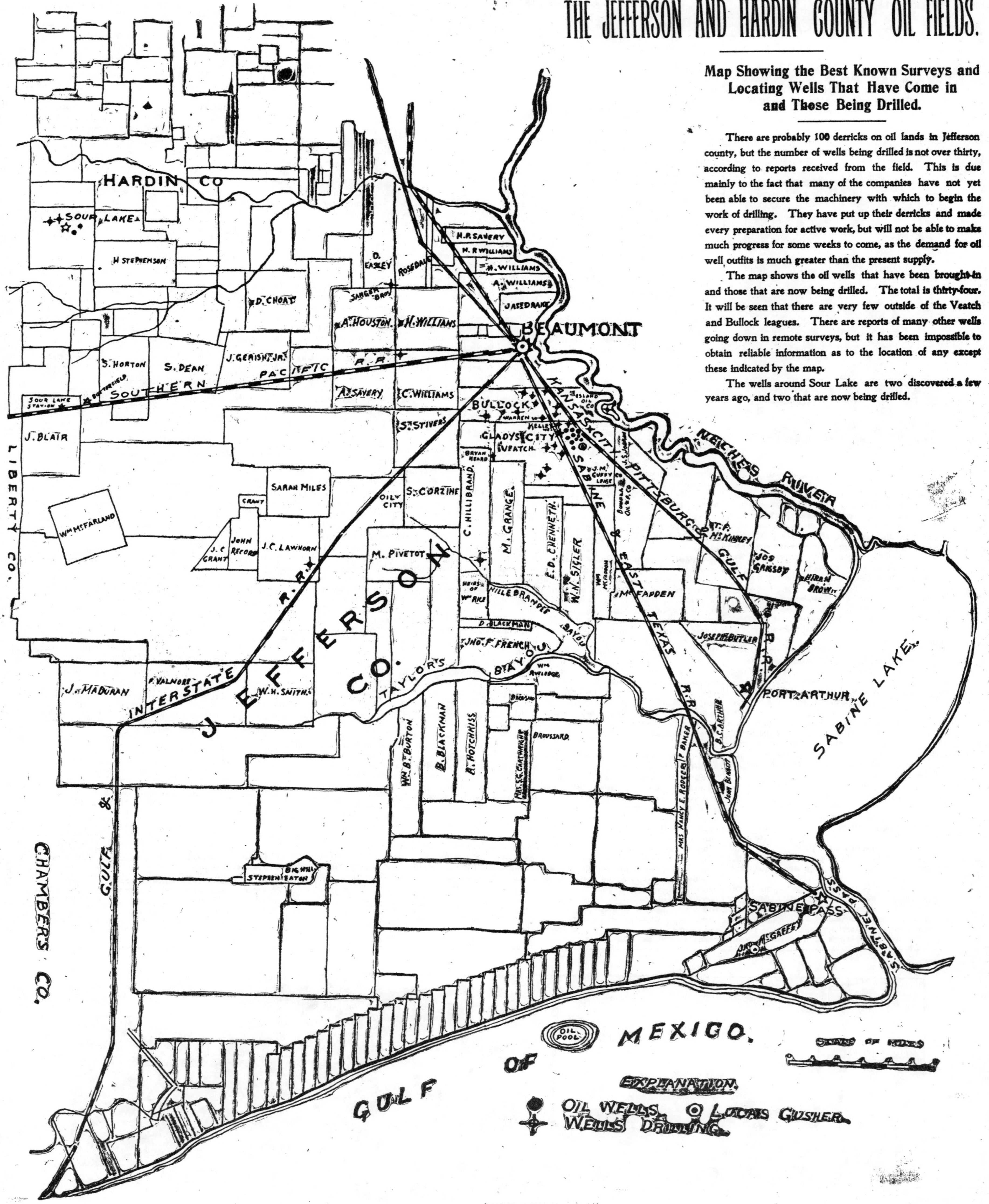

TEXAS' COTTON STOCK.

Reports from 61 Points Show Twice Last Year's Record.

COMING CROP MAY EXCEED THE LAST

An Increase in Acreage Is Generally Estimated—Some Guesses as to Total Crop.

New York Commercial.

New York, May 2.—In Texas, as in most of the other cotton States, the stock of cotton on hand, outside the mills, is larger than at this time a year ago. Reports from more than sixty Texas points show that the quantity of cotton on hand now is more than twice as much as it was at this time last May.

In Texas practically no fertilizer is used on cotton land, and therefore no line is given upon the coming crop by the quantity of fertilizer bought.

Most of the Texas cotton men who have furnished the Commercial with their best information on the subject believe the coming crop in that State will be larger than the last one.

Some of them think it will be 50 per cent larger, and an average of all the estimates shows that the general opinion places the next crop at a little more than 12 per cent in excess of the last.

The reports upon the acreage in the different sections of the State show that it has been increased, but is hardly enough greater to mean a 12 per cent increase in the total crop.

The reports to the Commercial from more than sixty different sections of the State place the acreage at a little less than 5 per cent greater than last year.

In spite of the fact that most of the Texas men think the Texas crop will be much larger than last year, they are rather conservative in their estimates of the total crop. An average of their estimates places the total at 9,955,353 bales.

Following are reports from the best posted cotton handlers in Texas:

Town—	Stock on hand. 1901. Bales.	1900. Bales.	—Estimates— State crop. Per cent.	Local acreage. Per cent.	Total crop. Bales.
Abilene	1,000	1,000	..	*25	9,250,000
Albany	15	25	same	same	....
Alvarado	3,000	2,500	*10	*20	10,250,000
Baird	.....	.....	*15	..	....
Bartlett	2,700	30	*35	..	9,835,000
Blossom	.....	150	— 10	— 5	9,000,000
Bremond	100	.....	*15	* 5	9,850,000
Bryan	500	900	..	same	....
Center	25	.....	— 10	— 10	9,500,000
Coleman	300	100	* 3	* 5	10,000,000
Connal	.....	.....	* 5	— 20	9,750,000
Corsicana	5,000	5,500	*33	* 7	9,900,000
Daingerfield	515	100	* 5	same	9,750,000
Denton	2,000	.....	*30	*25	10,250,000
Eddy	150	50	*15	*15	....
El Paso	.....	.....	*10	..	10,800,000
Fayetteville	53	500	— 50	— 15	....
Ferris	100	50	*10	* 5	10,000,000
Gilmer	150	25	*15	* 5	10,200,000
Glenrose	40	25	— 15	— 40	8,750,000
Grapeland	100	50	*10	*20	9,500,000
Groveton	.....	.....	*10	* 5	9,500,000
Hamilton	250	325	*25	— 10	9,000,000
Henderson	2,000	600	*40	same	10,250,000
Illinois Bend	.....	.....	— 5	*15	....
Kerens	.....	.....	..	* 5	9,750,000
Kerrville	50	.....	*10	* 5	10,000,000
Lancaster	100	.....	*15	*10	10,350,000
Lindale	250	50	*25	* 5	10,100,000
Llano	250	50	*10	* 5	10,500,000
Lone Oak	210	.....	*10	*15	10,300,000
Lott	65	.....	*15	*20	10,000,000
Lufkin	50	100	same	same	....
Marble Falls	150	25	*10	* 5	9,988,000
McDade	50	25	— 5	— 5	9,850,000
Midlothian	500	.....	*15	*15	10,500,000
Mineola	1,200	1,000	*20	* 5	9,950,000
Moody	210	400	*35	*10	10,100,000
Moulton	1,000	500	same	*10	10,000,000
Navasota	527	960	..	— 20	10,000,000
New Boston	600	500	* 5	* 5	9,800,000
Nocona	250	150	*10	same	10,000,000
Paris	4,000	700	*10	* 5	10,000,000
Plano	300	.....	*10	*10	10,200,000
Quanah	.....	.....	*10	* 5	10,000,000
Richmond	.....	.....	..	— 20	....
Rockwall	750	.....	*15	*15	10,500,000
San Antonio	6,000	2,000	*65	*20	10,550,000
San Marcos	2,000	1,000	*35	* 3	9,500,000
Schulenburg	250	300	* 5	same	9,900,000
Shiner	1,500	.....	same	..	10,000,000
Snyder	20	5	* 5	same	10,000,000
Sulphur Springs	1,000	.....	*50	*25	10,500,000
Uvalde	1	.....	..	— 50	....
Van Alstyne	900	.....	..	..	....
Waxahachie	1,600	.....	*10	*10	9,900,000
Weimar	20	20	*15	same	10,150,000
Whitesboro	.....	.....	*10	* 5	9,800,000
Williamsburg	30	.....	..	..	10,000,000
Willis	.....	.....	* 5	* 5	11,000,000
Wyhle	125	800	*20	— 10	9,600,000
Totals and averages	42,256	20,515	*12.23	* 4.75	9,955,353

*Plus; —minus.

HARDIN IS DEAD.

Both of the Duelists Succumbed to Their Hurts.

Palestine, Texas, May 11.—A special International and Great Northern car came up from Oakwoods last night at 8:10 bearing a number of relatives and friends of Henderson Hardin, participant in the Lake Station tragedy, previously reported in The Post. Hardin breathed his last at 10:30 last night and the body will be conveyed to his home at Oakwoods today. He was a cousin of Captain Black Hardin of Jewett, one of the early day Texans. The different members of the family have engaged in numerous bloody encounters in the past.

The trouble in which both Hardin and Holton lost their lives in the affair at Lake occurred over a trifle. Both men were under the influence of liquor.

Decoration Day at Cleburne.

Cleburne, Texas, May 10.—Today was Decoration day. The floral decorations showed unusual care in preparation and lavish profusion. Hundreds of people spent the day at the Confederate park and adjoining cemetery. Besides great wreaths and crosses of roses there had been erected a mound-shape grave, but four or five times the length, to represent the trenches where the heroes of battle were laid after the strife had closed, and this was literally covered and piled with lovely bouquets, cut floweds and all sorts of floral emblems. Around this silent square the throngs gathered and 500 voices took up the strains of "Nearer, My God, to Thee," led by Mrs. Bella McLeod Smith. After decorating the different graves in the cemetery all adjourned to the speakers' stand, where the program of recitations, old time Southern songs and addresses was concluded with a love feast. The weather was most auspicious and the large crowds were well pleased with the affair.

TWO CHILDREN BURNED TO DEATH.

They Were Kindling a Fire with Kerosene.

McKinney, Texas, May 11.—Last evening the house of Mrs. Whitsel, a widow living two miles southeast of Climax, this county, was burned. Her two children, a boy and a girl, aged 8 and 10 years respectively, were kindling a fire with coal oil, when the can of oil ignited. The house and contents quickly burned. The two children were fatally burned, from the effects of which both of them died within twelve hours time. The mother was burned and is not expected to live through tonight.

Boy Scared a Burglar Away.

Bonham, Texas, May 11.—About 9 o'clock last evening a burglar entered the residence of M. A. Bridges. All the family were away from home except Robert, a lad 10 years of age. The intruder was in a back room ransacking a trunk when the boy heard him and, securing a gun, proceeded to persuade the unwelcome visitor to depart. He fired one shot at the culprit and he immediately fled. The trunk contained four $5 bills, two of which were found near the back fence, where the fleeing burglar made his exit.

TWELVE PAGES.

The Galveston Daily News.

60TH YEAR—NO. 122. GALVESTON, TEXAS, FRIDAY, JULY 26, 1901. ESTABLISHED 1842.

TEXANS ABROAD.

In New York.

SPECIAL TO THE NEWS.

New York, July 25.—The following Texans are registered at New York hotels:

Galveston—H. H. Meyers, L. A. Meyers, Union Square.

Fort Worth—G. B. Monnig, Albert C. S. Battle, Broadway Central.

Dallas—L. Newbury, Herald Square; J. W. Dean and wife, J. B. Taylor, Grand Union; Mrs. R. Oliver, R. Oliver, Mrs. E. F. Buckley, Normandie.

McKinney—W. Purnell, Mrs. Egbert, Broadway Central.

Corsicana—A. Fox, Miss G. Fox, M. A. Fox, St. Denis; J. R. Sutton, Navarre.

Houston—R. C. Zeiss, Mrs. P. Zeiss, Vendome.

Mineola—I. G. Bromberg, Navarre.

Marlin—A. Y. Curtis, Navarre.

San Antonio—E. Goldstein, Westminster; W. B. Seeley, Grand Union; S. Carlisle, Marlborough; G. T. Gosling, Cadillac.

Navasota—R. Patouh, Herald Square.

Texarkana—W. A. Nelson, St. Denis.

Denton—R. S. Bass, Miss Halstead, St. Denis.

Paris—Miss I. McClardy, W. G. Burton, Miss J. Burton, St. Denis.

Austin—G. F. Smith, Marlborough.

Bryan—G. M. Brandon, Herald Square.

Pilot Point—A. H. Gee, Miss V. Gee, St. George.

Greenville—Miss C. Gee, St. George.

Bremond—E. W. Roberts and wife, Belvidere.

Mexia—J. E. Phillips, Continental.

Texas—O. Bailey, Grand Union.

Painfully Hurt.

SPECIAL TO THE NEWS.

Edna, Tex., July 24.—Sam Rogers, son of F. W. Rogers, the County Assessor, met with a painful accident yesterday afternoon. While working cattle on the Putnam ranch his horse ran and fell into a barbed wire fence, breaking it down. The young man's foot caught in the stirrup, and he also became entangled in the wire, and in the meantime the horse was bucking and dragging Mr. Rogers and the wire after him. The terrified animal went about 150 yards before the herders could stop him and relieve Mr. Rogers from the perilous entanglement. The scratches, bruises and kicks which Sam received were numerous and painful, but not serious.

DEFENSE OF SCHLEY

Captain Cook, Commander of Brooklyn, Describes the Famous Loop and Its Connection With the Destruction of the Spanish Fleet.

HE AFFIRMS THE STATEMENT OF EVANS

Declares That Admiral Schley and the Brooklyn Were Not in Possession of Signal Code Arranged With Cubans—Signals From the Beach Thought to Be a Trap fof American Fleet.

SPECIAL TO THE NEWS.

Washington, D. C., July 25.—The personnel of the Court of Inquiry which will investigate the charges against Admiral Schley gives general satisfaction to the Admiral's friends. It is believed the Court will give the Admiral a square deal. So far as anybody knows not one of the members is personally hostile to Schley. It will be one of the most notable Courts of Inquiry in the history of the navy and will attract the attention of the country like no similar investigation ever did. Admiral Schley will remain in New York a few weeks longer and will then return to Washington to give his personal attention to his interests.

The most interesting development in the case to-day was the interview of Captain Cook, who commanded the Brooklyn during the operations before Santiago. He described the famous loop about which so much has been said and takes full responsibility therefor. He also affirms the statement made by Admiral Evans that neither Admiral Schley nor himself had been informed of the code arranged with the insurgents on the shore. Admiral Sampson affirms that he gave orders that all captains of the fleet should be informed as to the code and he believes that Schley and Cook knew of it.

Captain Cook said: "There is nothing in the loop. It had nothing whatever to do with the battle, but was due to circumstances. It was purely a tactical and a natural movement. We had come from the west, and it was necessary to go back again. So we ported our helm to hold off the Spanish fleet and the Spanish turned to the westward while we were turning rapidly to starboard. The Spanish fleet stood out of the harbor about southwest, and it did not turn at once. We feared that it was heading in between the Brooklyn and the Texas. I said to Admiral Schley, 'We may get a cross fire here.' It looked very much to us as if we would." According to the captain's story, the situation at the time with reference to the possible cross fire was delicate in the extreme. "But then," he continued, "the Brooklyn made a beautiful turn and we were able to fire directly into the bows of the leading ship of the enemy. Our helm was put aport to head off the Spanish fleet and the Brooklyn turned rapidly and beautifully. I remember distinctly giving the order to Quartermaster. 'You see clearly the head of the leading ship,' I said to him; 'the idea is to get directly ahead of her.' That was the order. I thought we might sacrifice our ship, but I believed we would hold the fleet for our battleships. This I told Admiral Schley. When the Spanish fleet turned to the westward and the Brooklyn's helm was put hard aport she was swinging beautifully. She turned until she straightened upon her course exactly parallel to the Spanish ships, keeping up all the time a continuous fire from her port battery until the starboard battery could be brought into use. The statement has been made that the Brooklyn in turning ran two miles south. This is outrageously incorrect. The Brooklyn turned as rapidly as possible and was after the enemy as fast as any ship could have been."

To indicate exactly his meaning, Captain Cook said: "The Oregon when she joined the Brooklyn steamed between the Iowa and the Texas and must have gained distance to the north—that is, in the direction of the enemy and still on a parallel course with the Brooklyn. She was not more than 600 yards from the westward course of the Brooklyn, showing conclusively that the Brooklyn could not have gone to the southward." Captain Cook's statement that he thought he might sacrifice the ship and told Schley so, but that he believed in doing so he would leave the enemy a prey to the American battleships, adds new interest to the Brooklyn's experience at Santiago, and, indeed, to the discussion of Schley's moves during the engagement. So far as known the idea Schley and Cook had that they might have to sacrifice their ship for the sake of winning the fight, now comes to light for the first time through Captain Cook's statement. Besides, according to Captain Cook, the famous loop which the Brooklyn made at that point was a tactical movement made necessary by the position in which the Brooklyn found herself by the heading off of the Spanish fleet, and the purpose of Schley to follow the flying enemy in its unlooked-for movement in turning sharply westward.

Speaking of the signals withheld from Schley, Captain Cook said: "The Brooklyn was not put in possession of the code of signals that had been arranged for use by the insurgents and the ships of our navy. On account of our lack of knowing them we were greatly mystified by certain signs we observed on the beach at Cienfuegos. We saw one night, the date of which I can not give without my notes, three horizontal lanterns on the beach there. As we afterward learned, they were a sign from the insurgents that they wished to communicate with us, but we, having no knowledge of their import, thought the lanterns a trap of some sort, and we acted accordingly.

"At that time," continued Captain Cook, "we had no knowledge whatever of the wherabouts of Cervera. We had been informed by the captain of a vessel—the Adula—that the Spanish fleet had been seen going into Santiago, but had also been seen coming out again. The commander in chief, Admiral Schley, thought possibly they had gone past us and had gotten into Havana. When we observed the lights on the beach at Cienfuegos, the commander in chief believed they indicated the presence of the Spanish ships there.

"Not knowing that any signal code had been arranged, we looked for no signs on the beach in the day time, but the second night we again observed the horizontal lights on the shore. It was not until the next day, when Captain McCalla came up, that we learned any signals had been prearranged, and the lights we had seen for two nights on the beach expressed a desire of the insurgents to communicate with us. Captain McCalla explained that as he had some explosives for the Cubans he would go in and investigate. He did so, and as soon as he was able to inform us, he said that the lights had really been signals from the insurgents, who desired to communicate with us. Captain McCalla informed us the Spanish ships were not in Cienfuegos. That was the point we were after.

Texas Matters.

SPECIAL TO THE NEWS.

Washington, D. C., July 25.—The Comptroller of the Currency has approved the application of Thomas J. Penn, James K. Broons, George N. Gibbs, John A. Crawford and Wm. D. Doon to organize the Citizens' National Bank of Crandall, with $25,000 capital.

First Lieutenant Wm. P. Woodall, Assistant Surgeon U. S. A., recently appointed, has been assigned to duty at Fort Clark.

Pensions granted—Renewal: Abner Seymour, San Antonio, $10. Increase: Littleton Clarkson, Faught, $12; James R. Arthur, Austin, $8. War with Spain—Original: William M. Miller, Sprinkle, $12; Quinn Plant, Lexington, $10.

Postmasters appointed: Chico, Wise County, W. J. Flowers; Katy, Harris County, William E. Ule.

DAVENPORT IN FLAMES

Sparks From a Locomotive Said to Have Started a Fire, Which Threatens the Entire City.

DAVENPORT, Iowa, July 25.—At 9.45 p. m. nearly a square mile of this city is in flames. The firemen, though aided by companies from Rock Island and Moline, seem powerless to check the fire. Sparks from an engine are said to have started the fire.

LAKE CHARLES NEWS.

Sawmills Voluntarily Established the Ten-Hour Day.

SPECIAL TO THE NEWS.

Lake Charles, La., July 25.—At the meeting of the grand lodge, Knights of Pythias, held in Baton Rouge, Dr. W. A. Knapp of this city was presented with a gold jewel emblematic of the past grand chancellor. On the front side is his name in enamel and on the reverse side the words: "Presented to W. A. Knapp by Grand Lodge Knights of Pythias."

Beginning August 1, the sawmills of Lake Charles will run 10 hours, so said one of the largest mill owners of this city to The News correspondent this morning. Orange has already announced its intention of making 10 hours a day's work and Lake Charles is not disposed to be the last. At a quiet conference held by the mill owners a night or two since the subject was gone over and the determination was arrived at to adopt the 10-hour system. It has always been a matter of pride with the Lake Charles mills that the relations between the mill men and their employes have been constantly pleasant. A few weeks since the men held a meeting to consider the matter of asking a reduction of one hour, but as the press understands it, the committee appointed to bring the matter before the mill owners has not yet reported. The determination, therefore, of the mill men to make the reduction will come with greater grace and will certainly be hailed with much pleasure by the workmen. On the 1st of next month the 10-hour plan will be an established fact.

Palma Favors Cuba's Independence.

New York, July 25.—A letter has been received from Estrada Palma to Horatio Reubens, in which the former denies the utterances in favor of the annexation of Cuba to the United States attributed to him, says a dispatch from Havana to the Tribune. He also denies that General Maximo Gomez made similar declarations on the same occasion, and says that he (Palma) and Gomez both favor absolute independence and oppose annexation.

The leaders of all political parties requested the immediate publication of the letter from Senor Palma.

St. Louis World's Fair.

St. Louis, Mo., July 25.—The committee on organization of the Louisiana Purchase Exposition Company has submitted a number of highly satisfactory reports on the promotion work being done at the Pan-American Exposition among representatives from Central and South American states.

Capt. Smith Appointed Governor.

Manila, July 25.—Captain Harry A. Smith of the Fifteenth Infantry has been appointed Military Governor of Laguna Province, Luzon.

The establishment of provincial government in this province has been deferred until next February.

OIL AND LUMBER.

Organization of Two Companies by Mr. Kirby Practically Perfected.

SPECIAL TO THE NEWS.

NEW YORK, July 25.—John H. Kirby of Houston, who is prominent in the Houston Oil Company and the Kirby Lumber Company, which were incorporated in Texas with enormous capital to develop the oil and lumber resources of Texas, is stopping at the Waldorf-Astoria Hotel. While here he has been in conference with Francis Peabody, Jr., of Boston, and President J. Wilcox Brown and Secretary Scott of the Maryland Trust Company of Baltimore, which is financing the two Texas companies.

Mr. Kirby said that the organization of the two companies had practically been perfected. With reference to the oil company he said that as yet it does not own any gushers, except a few wells in the Corsicana district, which combined yield about 1000 barrels of oil per day, but the company has actually bought the land outright, instead of leasing it, and the work of development is still to be done.

With reference to the lumber industry in Texas Mr. Kirby said it has never been developed except in a very small way, because of the difficulty of getting capital into the business in Texas. He says his company has secured all the money needed, the most of the stock being taken in New York, Boston, Philadelphia and Baltimore.

Mr. Kirby will return to Texas next Sunday.

MEXICAN BUDGET.

Anti-Clerical Agitation Denounced as Savoring of Jacobinism—The Judicial Investigation.

Mexico City, July 25.—El Pais, a daily clerical organ, sold at 1 cent in order to compete with the cheap Liberal party papers, denounces the anti-clerical agitation as savoring of Jacobinism and says that a mistake has been made in leaving out of sight railways, banks, harbor improvements and new American companies to enter on a course of disorder which may cause foreign capitalists to look askance on Mexico.

The clerical scandals are now being quietly investigated by the judicial authorities and the public excitement has died out, the public being satisfied that the judicial authorities will sift out the truth in the accusations brought against clergymen.

Captain Powell Clayton, United States military attache here, has received orders to rejoin his regiment at Fort Myers, District of Columbia.

Carlos Varona, manager of the National Bank of Mexico, who was, some weeks ago, stricken with paralysis, is slowly improving.

Sebastian Mier, Mexican Minister to France, has purchased the Atlamaxac hacienda, in the State of Puebla, for half a million dollars.

MAYA REBELS SURRENDER.

Charges That Peonage Exists in Yucatan—State Officials Arrested.

Merida, Yucatan, July 25.—Seventeen Maya rebels have come in and surrendered, asking the privilege of returning to their homes as peaceable citizens.

Governor Canton ordered that they be provided with food and clothing.

Two battalions are reported lost in the jungle, not having been heard from for several days.

Two officials of the State Treasury have been arrested charged with complicity in defalcations estimated at $10,000.

There is much interest in the charges against the labor system here, the Mexico City papers averring that peonage or serfdom practically exists and that men are sold from one hacienda to another and have no liberty such as is Constitutionally guaranteed.

THE WELLS-FARGO PERMIT.

Letter of the Attorney General to the Manager.

SPECIAL TO THE NEWS.

Austin, Tex., July 25.—The following letter, written by Attorney General C. K. Bell to Mr. G. A. Taft, manager Wells-Fargo Express Company in Texas, was made public to-day:

Austin, Tex., July 17, 1901.—Mr. G. A. Taft, Manager Wells-Fargo Express Company, Houston, Tex.—Dear Sir: My attention has been called to the fact that the permit which was obtained on the 21st day of August, 1889, by the Wells-Fargo Express Company, of which you are the general manager, authorizing it to transact business in the State of Texas, has expired by limitation, and that your company has neglected to obtain a new permit, as required by law to do. I am advised by the Railroad Commission that your company has ever manifested a willingness to comply with the laws of this State, and that you have made the reports required by law and have complied with the rules of the Commission at all times. It is not the policy of the officers of this State to in any way embarrass the corporations which are willing to respect and comply with our laws, and I therefore call your attention to the dereliction, which I am sure must have resulted from an oversight, and suggest that you take the necessary steps at once to procure the requisite permit.

Before taking any further step in this matter I will wait a short time to give you an opportunity to comply with the laws which you seem to have overlooked. Very respectfully,

C. K. BELL,
Attorney General.

GOLD STAMPEDE.

A Rich Strike Reported About Ninety Miles From Nome.

Port Townsend, Wash., July 25.—The steamer Nome City arrived late last night from Nome, bringing 23 passengers, among whom was J. Wilson, manager of the North American Transportation Company. Passengers report a rich strike in the Fair Haven district, 90 miles north of Nome, and that a stampede has occurred from Nome.

Over half a million dollars has been sluiced at Winter Dumps, near Nome.

The Nome City brings news that the transport Seaward is in distress and will have to be towed to Puget Sound. Her boilers gave out, and the transport Warren will start from there with the Seaward in tow on July 16.

Killed by Lightning.

SPECIAL TO THE NEWS.

Uvalde, Tex., July 24.—Douglas Bratton, about 21 or 22 years old, was killed by lightning yesterday evening at the new asphalt mine, in this county. The young man was employed by Dan Bogard to drive a team. Three of the mules he was driving were also killed. Young Bratton formerly lived at Gonzales. His mother was notified by wire.

GREAT IS TEXAS

The Longer We Live, the More We Realize This Fact. Farmers' Congress Compared to the Three-Ring Circus of To-day.

ONE MAN CAN'T TAKE IN WHOLE SHOW

Grown So Big the College Directors Must Provide for Its Wants—Congress Has Aroused Farmers to Inquiry—Results From One Section Benefit Other Sections—Ferreting Out the State's Resources.

SPECIAL TO THE NEWS.

College Station, Brazos Co., Tex., July 25.—If the proceedings of the Farmers' Congress are not given with that continuity and clearness which should mark the record of the proceedings of such an important gathering, the fault can not be laid at the door of any individual who is engaged in the work of recording. This can be appreciated, possibly, by only those who are present. Those who want a continuous story of the proceedings are advised that the Congress is composed of different suborganizations, such as the Cotton Growers' Association, the Truck Growers' Association, the Bee Keepers' Association, and many other kinds of associations, each of which have met in a sort of general council, and yet transacts its business and discusses matters in which it is interested apart from other organizations.

In fact, to the newspaper man it is something in the character of the three-ring circus. There was never a true lover and high critic of the circus who did not deplore the advent of the three-ring affair. When you hear a man say he likes or even approves a three-ring circus, you can at once put him down as a man who knows nothing of circuses, has never experienced the thrills and ecstasies which an old time one-ring circus can produce in the heart. For while you may be intent upon a daring feat on the trapeze in one ring, your attention is snatched rudely away by the double somersault in another ring. This destroys pleasure, prevents that fixed attention which results in a knowledge of how it is done, and leaves behind a feeling of dissatisfaction, unhappiness and suspicion that you have not received your money's worth.

It is the same way with this Congress. A man may be deeply interested in bees. He may want to know the best blood to build up his native colonies in. He may want to know how to move his colonies with the least damage to them. He may want to hear something on botany, this subject being a part of bee culture and honey producing. At the same time he may want to know something about cows and hogs, which are connected with life, even if a man is a bee man. Now, at the very time the bee performance is going on in one ring, the cow performance is going on in another ring and the hog performance in still another. He may have his whole soul wrapped up in the description of the amiable and industrious character of the Italian bee, and hence the wisdom of breeding the native stock up on that kind, when in the very next ring they will be telling how to make the cow improve her milking and how the carnivorous sow can be induced to forego her appetite for young chickens. He can not hear all these things at once, any more than the ordinary man with the sweep of his eye can take in all that is going on in the three-ringed circus and appreciate and enjoy the whole.

✣ ✣ ✣

This is a defect in the proceedings which will be hard to cure. Indeed, it is not readily seen how it can be cured. For there is such an aggregation of talent under the canvass, such a varied and numerous assortment of "features," as they call them in the circus advertisements, that it would be well nigh impossible to give or produce them within the leisure time of the farmer. The programme of the congress—the subjects to be discussed are so many and so interesting that if each were taken up after another—or, to still adhere to the circus figure of speech, were confined to the single or one-ring, at least a month would be necessary for the entire performance. The question is, would it not be better that the congress should sit for at least two weeks, giving a day or two days to each subject, rather than four or five subjects should be discussed at one time? Or if this latter policy were adopted, would not the attendance be small and interest drop off because many people would not attend except on the day the matter in which he was most interested was discussed?

These are things which the congress will have to consider. For there are many people going away from here with new knowledge about bees, but without a single new idea on how to make his cow give more milk or how to stop the ravenous appetite of his sow for chickens.

The congress has been eminently satisfactory to every one who has attended. That is manifest on all sides. It is growing and its growth for the first time makes the Agricultural and Mechanical College feel that it really has something very important on its hands. Naturally the college is the place for the meeting. Hence it was invited to meet here. That was hospitable and all that, but now the college begins to feel an embarrassment. The president and directors of this institution are not officially connected with the organization, except perhaps as members here and there. Neither are the professors, and a great many of them are absent on their vacations. There is no money to entertain the guests. The officials can not be expected to go down in their pockets for the cash for entertainment. The steward of the institution undertakes to feed and lodge the guests for a dollar a day. So far, I am informed, he has laid by no great sums of money in the business. For farmers as well as newspaper men carry their appetite with them. If it were a great crowd, there would be money in feeding and lodging the visitors, but there have never been any great crowds. It is not possible to have the very best of service about the rooms. It is impossible to make good waiters at the table out of young and inexperienced negro boys from the Brazos bottoms. A dollar a day for board and lodging, and the board is good, is a cheap price and no one can expect any great amount of comfort and satisfaction for that amount of money. Yet the farmer, when he comes to his meeting at the Agricultural and Mechanical College, expects something more than he would get if he visited a town and roughed it around. In fact the college, whether it would or not, is rapidly being connected with the organization. The farmer attendant is joining the two together. It is his organization and his college. It is highly probable that he does not appreciate the fact that the institution has nothing to do with his organization. The latter meets at the former every year and the former teaches what he is learning. That connects the two with him. So, it will fall out that the college will finally have to submit to the inevitable. The directors will have to arrange the details of the entertainment of the congress and see that they are carried out. This is not meant as a criticism of the entertainment, so far. But the congress is growing in size and in importance. The entertainment of the visitors must be looked after, and in a very short time this can not be done by the steward or any one man. Of course the visitors expect to pay, but they will look about them to see just what they are paying for. The State officials may consider the entertainment and the labor involved as something that should not be imposed. They would be right in this position, but unless that entertainment is provided and provided in the very best way, in time the meetings will be held elsewhere, if the organization lives and grows. What then? The college will suffer immensely. The farmers will disconnect it from themselves. Their organization will be no longer closely associated in their minds with the institution. They will lose an interest in it if they do not lapse into an absolute indifference to the college. If it could not provide for their entertainment, when paid for, surely no one would say that a boy could be educated in details and other things necessary to make a man of him at such an institution. That's the way some of them will look at it. Then where will be the influence which will get those appropriations from the Legislature and which are so necessary to its advancement, stability and influence? With the agricultural prop pulled from under the institution the chances are that the fabric would fall like a house built of cards. The institution must go on. It wanted the farmers to gather within its grounds and eat and sleep within its walls, because they were farmers and it was a farmer's college. They wanted them for their influence. Hence it must go on and retain the organization and to do this more men are needed than two or three professors who are enthusiastic in their loyalty to the institution and their work and the single steward who must look after the physical entertainment. The directors must do it.

✣ ✣ ✣

This session of the congress proves the wisdom of its organization. That proof is in the fact that many subjects are handled more elaborately and at the same time more closely than ever before, and the discussions between members show a great advance made not only in a knowledge of subjects considered, but of the investigation of them. In fact, the papers read and the discussions engaged in show that the farmers are learning and that the congress in a great measure has aroused them to inquiry. The simplest questions were formerly asked. Deep ones, involving a journey into botany, chemistry and other scientific branches, are now asked. The A B C of the business seems to have been passed. Why, some of these farmers talk like school professors, and I don't think there is a woman present who could not make the hair of a woman's reading club curl as if a hot iron were applied to it in a talk on butter. More important than the papers read and the discussions on the floor have been the swapping of experiences.

✣ ✣ ✣

It is all well to teach, but what are the results. That matter comes up on every occasion when the members talk to each other. One man will tell of what sounds like marvelous results, and at once he is plied with questions. I have heard one man say that he netted $2500 on seven acres of land near Laredo from his onion crop. He irrigated and employed Mexican labor. He made $3200 gross from the crop and he estimated that the seven acres paid him $2500 net, anyhow, as the seven-acre crop had to bear some expenses of other crops. "How far did you plant the onions apart? How did you cultivate them, with a hoe or hand cultivator? Did you raise your own 'sets' or buy them? How large did you let them grow? When did you plant them? When did you gather them?" These were only a few of the questions asked him before he had scarcely finished his statement. Then he went on and told in detail all about how he produced his crop, and I am sure when he concluded that there will be a dozen more farmers who will raise onions for the market who never raised them before, and more than a dozen who know things about onion raising that they never knew before.

"And thus it goes all along the line. The question of the proper latitude for certain kinds of the same fruit is a matter of deep concern and thought among the fruit growers. The uninitiated think a peach is a peach and that it will grow in one part of the country as well as in another. But this is an egregious mistake which has retarded peach growing. For a mistake in planting certain kinds of fruit in one locality has the effect of creating the impression that no fruit of that character will grow there. You hear on the grounds here and in the discussion of the merits of the Chinese and Persian strains of peaches being good for this or that latitude, or grapes being worthless south of a certain point. And when one hears of it, he wonders that it was not thought of long ago.

With the Texan distances and area are not as with other people. They look on their State as a State territorially considered. It is to them as Georgia is to them—a certain amount of land embraced within the arbitrary lines which bound States. Once upon a time the Senate of the United States called on the meteorlogical department for a report on climatic conditions in Texas. Just why such a report was called for and what particular Senator was pricked by curiosity on this question, I was never able to find out. Greeley, of Arctic fame, was at the head of the bureau and he answered. In the answer was an intimation that the Senate of the United States didn't know what it was asking. Anyhow, the report was made. Briefly, it stated that the State was the least bit less than a seventh of the whole of the United States and hence a report on climatic conditions meant a report on the climatic conditions of one-seventh of the United States. Just to impress the stupid sensational mind comparisons were made. Among them was the statement that if Texas whirled around on an axis, fixed at its Northeast corner, it would lap over into West Virginia, and if it were taken up bodily and placed with its northern line running through the City of Washington, its southern line would be within 50 miles of Key West, Fla. It stated that there were sections in Texas closer to Great Salt Lake, Utah, than to the Gulf of Mexico, though the whole State was bounded on the South by this body of water.

Hence, from all this the man who thinks a fruit will grow in one part of the State as well as another is the man who thinks that a fruit planted in Labrador ought to flourish well in Virginia, and the orange which grows in Florida would do well in Washington. For Texas takes up as many degrees of latitude as does the territory between Washington to within 50 miles of Key West, according to Greeley's report. There are a lot of things to learn in Texas and about Texas, and the agricultural classes are learning.

W. G. S.

WHITECAP OUTRAGE.

A Peaceable Negro Driven From the House That He Owns.

SPECIAL TO THE NEWS.

CORSICANA, Tex., July 25.—Last night a body of armed white men made a raid on the house of Ed Elam, colored, near Raleigh, 18 miles west of this city, and fired several shots into it, wounding Elam's 16-year old daughter and frightened the negroes badly.

Elam is said to be a peaceable citizen and owns the farm on which he lives, but was ordered by the whitecappers to leave within three days. He was sick in bed when the raid was made, but was so thoroughly convinced that the mob intended violence that he and his family left this morning.

The girl is probably dangerously wounded, as it is said that a load of birdshot took effect in her neck.

This is not, however, the first event of this kind in that community. Several similar attacks have been made on negroes of that vicinity, and two other families were ordered to leave last night.

A PRISONER'S TRAGIC ACT.

Was Being Guarded in Jail and Cut His Throat.

SPECIAL TO THE NEWS.

Ballinger, Tex., July 25.—Late yesterday afternoon Sheriff Kirk received a telegram from the Sheriff of Medina County instructing him to arrest on a charge of assault to murder one Sam Moss, about 55 years old, who had arrived here from Medina County last Sunday. Sheriff Kirk immediately arrested him and not wishing to place him in a cell hired two guards to watch him during the night and they kept him in that part of the jail known as the jailer's residence. About sunrise this morning the jailer stepped into the adjoining room to light a fire in the cooking stove and in less than a minute sent his little boy into the room with the prisoner and as the boy entered the door he saw the man roll off the bed with his throat cut from ear to ear and he died in a few minutes. During the night he made the statement to the jailer that he had a family of 10 children and had just recently had trouble. Two telegrams have been received from his family to-day, one to ship the remains to Devine; the other to bury him here.

VETERANS AT MARBLE FALLS.

At Least Ten Thousand People Are Attending the Reunion.

SPECIAL TO THE NEWS.

Marble Falls, Tex., July 25.—Over one hundred more Confederate Veterans registered this, the first day, than ever before. At least ten thousand people are in attendance. The welcome address was delivered by General A. R. Johnson; response was by acting Colonel of the First regiment, T. D. Vaughn, in the absence of Tom Hill of Llano, elected to make the annual address. Speeches were made by B. Badger and Rev. M. W. Aller. In the afternoon Senator W. D. Yett made a speech. Recitations and songs by young ladies.

To-morrow is Marble Falls day. Governor Sayers is expected to make a talk and an election for place of next meeting will be held.

Aiding Prisoners to Escape.

SPECIAL TO THE NEWS.

Tyler, Tex., July 25.—Isham Strong a negro, was convicted in the County Court on a charge of aiding prisoners to escape from the county farm. His fine and costs amount to $97. The negro was a trusty and, it is alleged, aided the prisoners to escape by slipping an ax and crowbar in between the iron bars of the jail. He was taken back to the farm at noon, where he will spend 194 days working out his new fine.

Rain in Louisiana.

SPECIAL TO THE NEWS.

Jennings, La., July 25.—A heavy rain has been falling nearly all day long, and is still falling this afternoon, and the outlook is fair for a heavy all night's rain. The farmers are feeling jubilant over the rain and the crop outlook, which is now certain, owing to the heavy rains.

Dawson Telegraph Line.

Seattle, Wash., July 25.—After 18 months of continuous work, it is announced that work on the telegraph line to Dawson will be entirely completed on August 1.

ROCKY MOUNTAIN
THE NEWS

VOL. XLV: NO. 193. DENVER, COLORADO, MONDAY, JULY 11, 1904.—10 PAGES.—PRICE 5 CENTS. ESTABLISHED 1859.

MOST NOTORIOUS BANDIT AND TRAIN ROBBER OF THE WORLD IS BURIED IN THE MOUNTAINS

EAST ASKS FOR MORE

Indications That New Yorkers Will Insist on Hill's Choice of Man to Run Campaign.

CHAIRMAN JONES SAYS PARKER MUST BE SEEN

National Committee Suggests Taggart of Indiana as National Chairman but Nothing Decided Till Meeting in Gotham.

ST. LOUIS, July 10.—The Democratic national committee, new in its make-up, met at 2:30 o'clock this morning and again at 4 o'clock this afternoon, with the avowed intention on behalf of the supporters of Taggart of Indiana of electing him chairman. The early morning meeting was not fully attended and the object aimed at was not accomplished. It was pointed out by Mr. Mack of New York that it would be discourteous to take any action until Mr. Parker, as the candidate, was consulted. The Taggart men, while not having enough to elect, still suggested that Mr. Hill, Mr. Sheehan and Mr. Belmont, the candidate's friends, were still here, and adopted a resolution that they be invited to meet the committee this afternoon. When afternoon came there were three new complications in the way of electing. Chairman Jones of the old committee boldly asserted that such action as contemplated would be unprecedented and, in fact, illegal. It also turned out that at a late hour the convention adopted a resolution authorizing Chairman Jones of the old committee to call the new commitee together in New York city at such time as he might suggest.

Then the other thing was that Senator Hill and Mr. Sheehan left for New York at noon, and could not, therefore, attend the meeting.

Chairman Jones' Statement.

Senator James K. Jones, the retiring chairman of the national committee, made this statement to the Associated Press:

"The national convention, by specific instruction, last night authorized me to call the first meeting of the new committee in New York city. Until I call it the new committee cannot organize and meetings they have held are unauthorized. Now let me say, forcibly, if need be, that, acting under the convention authority, I shall call the national committee to meet in New York city at such time as Judge Parker shall designate, for before I call it I shall consult him. It would be an unprecedented thing for the new committee to organize without consultation with the candidate. Such a thing was never heard of."

Just after the afternoon session began, Mr. Taggart, who was presiding, was asked to retire so that he need not be embarrassed.

August Belmont of New York was called into the room and asked to give Judge Parker's views. He said he could not do so.

(Continued on Page 6—1st Col.)

THE OLD HOLE-IN-THE-WALL GANG OF OUTLAWS.

This choice collection of train robbers appears in the photograph in the following order: Harry Longbaugh, alias the Sundance Kid, express and train robber, whose body is worth $10,000 to his captors; Harvey Logan, alias Kid Curry; George Ceirsie, who is still in the saddle, although badly wanted; Elza Lay; George Parker, alias Butch Cassidy.

NOT TOO COARSE FOR P. C. KNOX

W. B. Childers Charged With Serious Offense of Aiding a Monopoly but Attorney General Forgave Him.

(By News Leased Wire.)

WASHINGTON, July 10.—One of the most sensational cases in the department of justice came to light here today, when it became known that William B. Childers, United States district attorney for the territory of New Mexico, was appointed in the closing days of the second Cleveland administration upon the recommendation of powerful magnates, and who was retained in office through the same influences by President McKinley and President Roosevelt, was charged with acting as an attorney for the Colorado Fuel and Iron company, of which Paul Morton, secretary of the navy department, is a director, in a suit in which that corporation was sued in the courts of New Mexico for violating the Sherman anti-trust law.

Never before in the history of the government has an officer of the United States, whose sworn duty it is to prosecute violators of the anti-Sherman trust law, not only failed to perform his duty, but actually gone into open court and boldly appeared as a champion of a trust, and as counsel for the defendant in a suit brought to punish violators of the Sherman law. In the judgment of many persons here, the case has no parallel in the history of the department of justice.

William B. Childers of Albuquerque, N. M., was appointed United States district attorney for the territory of New Mexico in the last month of the second Cleveland administration. Childers was indorsed for the position by persons influential in Southwestern industrial circles. Among his backers were the of-

(Continued on Page 3—2nd Col.)

TRAGIC CONFESSION BEFORE DEATH

Durango Man Tells of Trying to Kill His Family by Putting in Stove Dynamite Sticks With the Fuel.

Special to The News.

DURANGO, Colo., July 10.—Isaac E. Covert, who last Wednesday was frightfully injured by an explosion of dynamite in a cook stove at his home, died this morning at 1:45 o'clock. On his death bed he confessed that he had placed the dynamite in the stove intentionally in the hope that the explosion would not only kill himself, but his wife and seven children.

Covert lived with his family on a farm six miles out of Durango. He was highly respected and an industrious man. His family consists of seven children, ranging in age from an infant to a boy 18 years old. For the past few years Mr. Covert had brooded over the fact that his children were not receiving the schooling he thought they should have.

He arose early Wednesday morning to go after some horses. On returning to the house at breakfast time he placed in the stove a pan supposedly containing chips, but mixed with these chips were three sticks of giant powder a quantity of black powder and a box of giant caps. His wife was serving breakfast from the stove at the time, and his children were all in the house. The explosion which followed fatally injured Mr. Covert, inflicted severe cuts and burns about Mrs. Covert's face and eyes, and slightly injured one boy, Freddy Covert. Mr. and Mrs. Covert were taken to the hospital in Durango. Mrs. Covert will recover, but will probably lose the sight of one eye.

Until shortly before the death of Mr. Covert, when he made his confession, everyone thought he had placed the explosives in the stove by mistake.

DOMINATE PORT ARTHUR

Japanese Batteries Are Strongly Entrenched So as to Command All Parts of the Fortress.

LOSSES IN THE RECENT NAVAL ENGAGEMENTS

Chinese Say More Than 800 Dead Russians Were Carried Into Port Arthur After a Recent Engagement.

CHE FOO, July 10, 5 p. m.—A fair wind brought a fleet of junks from Port Arthur today, carrying both Chinese and Europeans. Reports which they bring of conditions at Port Arthur are contradictory, but they all say that a Japanese division from the northward is entrenching seven miles from the marine camp, while another division from the eastward is fighting continuously and with the aid of the fleet is endeavoring to gain a position commanding the town and the naval basis.

A Russian says that the Japanese occupied the summit of Takushan mountain, which is about three miles from Port Arthur, on the night of July 6, with a mounted battery of artillery.

On July 7 the Russian cruiser Novik and four gunboats went out under protection of the guns on Golden hill and shelled a Japanese battery, which was surrounded and captured finally by the Russian infantry.

The fighting to the eastward of Port Arthur has been very heavy since July 4. The Japanese ships along the shore are shelling the Russian position in the hills. The smoke from the artillery on the hills around Port Arthur is seen almost continuously. Dead and wounded are being brought in at all hours and many private houses have been turned into hospitals. Only skirmishes have occurred to the northward. The main Japanese force is ten miles away, but Japanese scouts have been seen in the vicinity of Marine camp, which commands the principal pass to the hills directly back of Port Arthur. On the nights of July 2, 3 and 4 the Japanese fleet bombarded the roads from the south of the town. The forts were not damaged. No further night attacks have been made since July 4.

(Continued on Page 3—4th Col.)

CAPTAIN OF THE HOLE-IN-THE-WALL GANG LED RIO GRANDE RAILWAY HOLDUPS

Harvey Logan, Who Broke Jail in Tennessee, Killed Himself When Cornered by Posse in Colorado.

Defied Officers of the Law Only to Die a Suicide to Escape Capture in Recent Fight Near Rifle.

To the determination of one woman the police are indebted for the death of the most desperate train robber in the world. After the Rio Grande train robbery at Parachute Mrs. Larson saw a stranger trying to steal one of her horses. She called her two boys to her aid, after remonstrating with the trespasser, and they started in pursuit, armed with carbines. On their way they met the posse that was searching for the train robbers and invoked their assistance. This act was the undoing of Harvey Logan, the bandit king, as the following story recites:

Logan was one of the most desperate bandits that ever infested the West or the country. Among his last robberies was the Denver & Rio Grande train.

On June 7, the westbound passenger train on the Denver & Rio Grande railroad was held up at Parachute, Colo. The robbers, three in number, blew the safe in the express car, rifled it, and then detached the express car from the train and escaped. Posses were organized at once and gave chase. The robbers were well mounted, but their horses had run down, and they abandoned them June 9. On the same day they stole three horses from Ranchman Bandy, near Rifle, Colo. Bandy organized a posse of young farmers and followed the three men, coming up with them between Rifle and New Castle on the afternoon of June 9.

The robbers showed fight and shot at the posse, nearly wounding one of the young men in the posse. Their fire was returned, and one of the robbers fell from his horse, seeing which one of his companions shouted out to him: "Tom, are you hurt?" The wounded robber answered: "Yes; I am all in, and I will end it right here!" saying which he drew a revolver and shot himself through the head.

Addresses found on the body of the dead robber caused inquiries to be made in Texas, where he was identified as Tap Duncan of Knickerbocker, Tex. Further investigation indicated who his companions were, and it was for a time accepted that the identification was reliable until officials of Pinkerton's National Detective agency at Chicago identified the photograph of the dead robber as being that of Harvey Logan, alias Kid Curry, alias Bob Nevilles, alias Tom Jones, alias Nelson, alias Whelan, the leader of the West and Southwest gang of train robbers, who escaped from the county jail at Knoxville, Tenn., on June 27, 1903, after having received a sentence of twenty years in the penitentiary for participating in the Great Northern Express robbery, which occurred at Wagner, Mont., July 3, 1901. In this robbery Logan was assisted by Ben Kilpatrick, who is serving fifteen years for it in the Ohio penitentiary. The third man in this robbery, O. C. Hanks, alias Deaf Charley, was shot and killed while resisting arrest at San Antonio, Tex., April 16, 1902.

Notwithstanding the identification by the Texas officers and others, William A. Pinkerton sent Assistant Superintendent Spence to Knoxville with the photograph of the dead man, and it was identified there by a dozen persons as Harvey Logan. Mr. Spence had previously identified the picture. He had attended Logan's trial and was with him more or less for a period of two weeks before his conviction, and he declared there could be no mistake and that it was Harvey Logan beyond a doubt.

Harvey Logan was a member of the famous "Wild Bunch" band of outlaws. They robbed the Butte County bank, Belle Fourche, S. D., in 1897; in June, 1899, they held up a Union Pacific train at Wilcox, Wyo.; in August, 1900, they robbed another Union Pacific train at Tipton, Wyo., and in the following month they robbed the First National bank of Winnemucca, Nev., of $32,640; in July, 1901, they held up the Great Northern Express at Wagner, Mont., and secured about $35,000. The Pinkertons were put on the trail of the gang in 1897, and since that time eleven of the fourteen members have either been killed or arrested and sent to prison.

Logan was pursued through Montana, Wyoming, Colorado, New Mexico, Kansas, Arkansas and Texas. Finally the chase grew so hot that Logan went to Tennessee, where he was arrested in November, 1901. The charge brought him into the jurisdiction of the United States court, and he was tried and sentenced to twenty years' imprisonment. Fearing that an attempt would be made to help Logan to escape, the Pinkertons recommended that he be guarded night and day by specially chosen men. Notwith-

(Continued on Page 6—2nd Col.)

HARVEY LOGAN.
From a Photograph Taken in 1900.

THE DEAD BANDIT OF RIFLE, COLO.

SEVENTEEN SLAIN IN RAILWAY WRECK

Excursion of the Plattdeutscher Club of Hoboken Ends in a Horrible Accident and Loss of Life.

NEW YORK, July 10.—Seventeen persons were killed and about fifty injured in a collision which occurred at Midvale, N. J., just before noon today, when a regular passenger train on the Greenwood Lake branch of the Erie railroad ran into an excursion train that had stopped to take water. All the dead and injured lived in Hoboken, Jersey City and New York.

The accident is believed to have resulted from a tower operator having lowered his signal too soon.

The train which was run into was a special carrying members of the First Plattdeutscher association of Hoboken on their annual outing, and had 800 passengers. It consisted of twelve cars and two engines. The first engine had taken water and the train had moved up and stopped with the second engine beside the tank, when the regular train drew near. The flagman of the special signaled the engineer of the oncoming train, but owing to a curve in the road, his flag was not seen until too late. It is claimed that the engineer of the regular train had slowed down to about ten miles an hour before he crashed into the special, but his engine tore through the rear car the greater part of its length and drove the forward end of that car into the car ahead. The killed and injured were in these two cars.

The wreckage did not catch fire and the work of taking out the dead and maimed was accomplished quickly.

The passengers from the uninjured coaches ran back and joined in the work and the residents of Midvale, many of whom had heard the crash, assisted them.

While physicians were being sent for women of Midvale brought bandages and other articles that could be used in caring for the injured.

An engine and cars were sent from Little Falls to the scene of the wreck

(Continued on Page 8—3rd Col.)

MAY SEND FLEET TO FORCE SULTAN

United States Said to Have Made Final Demand for Fair Play for American Teachers and Professional Men.

VIENNA, July 10.—A dispatch from Constantinople says that American Minister Leishman handed a note to the porte declaring that unless a prompt settlement of the school question was arranged a United States fleet would appear in Turkish waters. The sultan ordered the grand vizier to comply with the American minister's demands.

The American demands upon the sultan are for privileges to schools and colleges conducted by American teachers equal to those given to foreign teachers; for permission for American professional men to practice on even terms with foreigners, and for the direct access of the American minister to the sultan in the transaction of business.

ST. PETERSBURG, July 10.—While the Baltic fleet on its way to the Far East is not likely to be able to get coal at French ports, it is understood that the contractors will send out coal from these ports to meet the fleet beyond territorial waters.

WILLIAM B. CHILDERS,
United States District Attorney, Who Is Accused of Acting for the Colorado Fuel and Iron Company.

WILD WEST SETS IN AT BONESTEEL

Cowboys and Indians Swoop Down on Land Office Town and Many Fakirs Enticing Dollars From Homeseekers.

No Open Gambling in Sight but Liquor Flowing Freely by Backdoor Routes—Land and Lot Fever Is High.

(By News Leased Wire.)

BONESTEEL, S. D., July 10.—Indians and cowboys swooped down upon Bonesteel today and took possession. A band of Sioux has encamped in the outskirts of the town, while a party of broncho busters, with Captain Hardy, the crack shot, is entertaining the public outside the town.

No registering is going on here today or tonight and everything is quiet. There is no street gambling and the front doors of the saloons are closed. Games and drinks are as plentiful as on week days, however. Shows of all kinds are heading for Bonesteel.

The latest and most picturesque attraction is an "Uncle Tom's Cabin" company, with a prime "little Eva" and dogs galore. The first presentation is expected to create a furore and preparations are being made to entertain the actors in due Western style, a style in which six-shooters will be in evidence.

Interest at present centers in the preparation for the sale of the St. Elmo townsite lots, which will take place Thursday.

Ola Johnson of Chicago is the loser of a $500 roll. He was induced to put up $20 as security while here, and went back to Chicago to get the rest of the $500. He returned and put up the balance.

EAST WANTS IT ALL

(Continued From Page One.)

Colonel Guffey insisted that precedent showed that the committee courteously awaited Judge Parker's opinion. "In fact," he said, "the resolution of last night precluded any action until Chairman Jones issued a call for New York."

Senator Bailey of Texas said that the matter should be settled at once. It was customary for the committee to meet immediately after the adjournment and elect, and a resolution was passed last Thursday to that effect by the convention. "I guess," he said, "that we can have Judge Parker's views in a few moments from his friends here, if they care to give them."

After nearly two hours of debate, Senator Bailey offered a compromise if the committee would adopt a resolution indorsing the candidacy of Thomas Taggart for chairman of the committee. Mr. Mack agreed to this, and the resolution was adopted. The committee will therefore meet in New York on the call of former Chairman Jones.

For secretary a three-cornered contest developed. The original aspirants were the secretary of the retiring committee, Charles A. Walsh of Iowa, who had given able and tireless service, and Edward Sefton, his assistant secretary.

A third candidate, however, is Urey Woodson of Kentucky, complicating the situation. Mr. Walsh stated that he was not seeking re-election and certainly had no intention to move counter to the wishes of Judge Parker, if the nominee had other preference. For re-election as sergeant-at-arms, Colonel John I. Martin of St. Louis had no opposition discoverable in advance of the meeting of the national committee.

The following national committeemen or their proxies as designated were present, and unanimously voted in favor of the adoption of the resolution indorsing the candidacy of Thomas Taggart for chairman:

Alabama	H. D. Clayton
Arkansas	W. H. Martin (proxy)
California	M. H. Tarpey
Colorado	John I. Mullins
Connecticut	Homer S. Cummings
Florida	J. B. Browne
Georgia	Clark Howell (proxy)
Idaho	S. P. Donnelly
Illinois	R. C. Sullivan
Iowa	Charles A. Walsh
Kansas	John H. Atwood
Kentucky	Urey Woodson
Louisiana	N. C. Blanchard (proxy)
Maryland	L. V. Baughman (proxy)
Michigan	Daniel J. Campau
Mississippi	C. H. Williams
Missouri	M. A. Rothwell (proxy)
Montana	C. W. Hoffman
Nebraska	J. C. Dahlman
Nevada	John N. Dennis
New York	Norman E. Mack
Ohio	John R. McLean (proxy)
Oregon	F. V. Holman
Pennsylvania	J. M. Guffey
Rhode Island	George W. Green
South Dakota	E. S. Johnson
Tennessee	R. E. L. Mountcastle
Texas	R. M. Johnston
Utah	D. H. Peery
Washington	John Y. Terry
West Virginia	John T. McGraw
Wisconsin	T. E. Ryan
Wyoming	J. E. Osborne
Alaska	Arthur K. Dulany
Arizona	Ben M. Crawford
District of Columbia	James L. Norris
New Mexico	H. B. Ferguson
Oklahoma	Richard A. Billups
Porto Rico	David M. Field

CHRISTIAN MASSACRE WAS NARROWLY AVERTED

BEIRUT, Syria, July 10.—What threatens to become a general period of unrest, such as was experienced a year ago when an attack was made on the American Consul Magelssen, has begun in Beirut. On Friday afternoon, June 17, two Moslems, caught smuggling arms and ammunition into the Lebanon district, were fired upon by Turkish soliders and killed. One of the men killed had been for many years a lawless character. Moslems at once charged Christians with murdering the two smugglers, and before long the whole town was thrown into a wild state of excitement. Shops everywhere were closed and Christians fled to places of safety.

Change in Boulder and Fort Collins Trains Via Colorado & Southern.

Effective Sunday, July 10, train for Boulder and Fort Collins, scheduled out of Denver at 10:15 a. m., will leave at 10 o'clock. The 6 a. m. train will be discontinued. The 8 a. m. and 5 p. m. trains will serve Louisville and Lafayette.

BANDIT IDENTIFIED

(Continued From Page One.)

standing this precaution, he escaped June 27, 1903. The United States government thereupon sued the sheriff of Knox county, Tennessee, for $10,000 for his carelessness in allowing Logan to escape, and this judgment has since been affirmed by the higher courts.

Logan's escape was cleverly arranged. While his guard's back was turned Logan threw a wire over his head and lassoed him, tying him tight to the bars of the cage. Having one entire floor of the jail to himself, Logan next secured two pistols that had been placed in the corridor of the jail for use by officers if needed. When Jailer Bell appeared in answer to a knock from Logan the prisoner passed out a bottle, saying he wanted some medicine. As the jailer put out his hand Logan covered him with a pistol, forced him to unlock the door and take him to the sheriff's stable and made him saddle the sheriff's horse, on which Logan rode away.

Waiting for Union Pacific.

A short time before the Rio Grande robbery the Union Pacific company, having gotten wind of the fact that the noted outlaw, Logan, and his pals were again at large and were likely to resume business in their old haunts, put on an armored train running west from Laramie, Wyo., in order to be prepared to meet their wily foes. This train was supplied with fighting equipment, and carried a crew of well-known gunfighters, each an expert in his line and a terror to the train robbers of the West.

In some way, Logan and his gang became informed of the move of the Union Pacific to forestall operations by them along the road, and on this account it is supposed that they moved their base southward into Colorado, to a country that was also familiar to them through their operations at a previous period as cattle rustlers.

Six Murders.

There are at least six murders laid to this man. He has been associated with all the daredevil leaders in train robberies in the West and Southwest for years, having been the partner of such men as "Butch" Cassidy, Harry Longbaugh, Bob Lee, his cousin, now serving ten years in Rawlins, Wyo., for his part in the Wilcox, Wyo., train robbery; George S. Currie, alias "Flat Nose" George, who was killed by a sheriff's posse April 17, 1900, near Thompson, Utah; Elza Lay, alias McGinnis, one of the Black Jack gang, now doing a life sentence in the Santa Fe, N. M., penitentiary, and Lonnie Logan, alias Curry, his brother, who was killed by officers at Dodson, Mo., February 28, 1900, while resisting arrest for the Wilcox, Wyo., train robbery.

The pals of Logan in the Denver & Rio Grande train robbery are known, and it will be only a question of time when they are captured.

Left a Trail of Blood.

In December, 1892, Longbaugh, associated with Bill Madden and Harry Bass, held up a Great Northern train at Malta, Mont. Madden and Bass were caught, and are now serving long term sentences for the robbery, but Longbaugh escaped. June 28, 1897, Longbaugh, with several others, including Harvey Logan, robbed the Belle Fourche, S. D., bank. All were captured. Logan and Longbaugh effected a daring escape from the Deadwood, S. D., jail. Harvey Logan was also the murderer of Pike Landusky, at Landusky, Mont., December 25, 1894, and was implicated in many noted train robberies, among them the robbery of a Union Pacific train at Wilcox, Wyo., June 2, 1899, after which a posse overtook Logan and his band near Casper, Wyo., and in an attempt to arrest them Sheriff Joseph Hazen of Converse county, Wyoming, was shot and killed.

Trains were held up, and looted banks became matters of current comment. The last noted exploit of this man and his nervy lieutenants was on the night of September 19, 1900. He, with Harry Longbaugh and some others, robbed the First National bank of Winnemucca, Nev., and secured $33,000. Rewards of $1,000 for each of the robbers and 25 per cent of all the money recovered were offered.

Rock Springs was finally thrown into a fit of disgust when it realized that Butch Cassidy was himself a guest in the city in which he was so badly wanted. He played a good card in disguises, and his best friend in Rock Springs, where everybody knew him, would not have recognized him when he was trying to elude every one. His facial makeup was not amateurish. He was nearly always his own scout, and he had perfect confidence in his ability to deceive his personal friends when he so desired.

He was simply the stranger who nightly played "twenty-one" at Black Sam's place in Rock Springs during all the time he was so badly wanted in this last advent of his at Rock Springs.

Then when his plans were accomplished this big bandit chieftain quietly slipped away, and it was several days before the natives realized what had occurred.

The long list of names under which Cassidy sailed did not seem to be any drag to his memory. He was known as George Cassidy and Captain Ingefield, but his true name was George LeRoy Parker, a Texan by birth, and of Swedish-American extraction. Among the other members of this famous gang was Harry Tracy, whose famous escape and subsequent death are still fresh in public memory. Elza Lay is serving his time in Arizona, Bob Meeks was convicted for his participation in the Montpelier, Idaho, bank robbery, and Harvey Logan, one of the princes of this royal gang of robbers, is dead at his own hand.

Other Members of Gang.

Ben Kilpatrick, known as the "Tall Texan," is immured in a Southern prison; Bill Carver was killed at Sonora, Texas, while resisting an arrest for murder, and Bob Lee is serving a sentence in Montana. In addition to all the foregoing, the bandit gang missed the services of Sure Shot Sam, who was the captain of the band of American-Cuban highwaymen and cutthroats, which played its part in the Cuban province of Santa Clara.

VICTIMS OF WRECK AT CAMERON RECOVERING

Special to The News.

CRIPPLE CREEK, Colo., July 10.—The passengers injured in the wreck on the Short Line last Tuesday night are getting along nicely. Only four of them now remain in the Sisters' hospital here, and they, Dr. Hassenplug, the railroad physician, states, are getting along nicely. Miss Grace Manning, who was thought to be very seriously injured, will be taken to her home in Elkton tomorrow. The hemorrhage which developed has stopped. Mrs. M. A. McLeod will be able to sit up tomorrow. Fred Miller, who had four ribs fractured, has passed the danger point. Mrs. Frank Brainerd, while not yet able to sit up, is much better. Miss Grace Jarvis has been sent to her home in Denver and is reported to be much improved.

BOTH GAMES WENT TO THE GRIZZLIES

Denvers Are the Victors Over Omahas—A Condition Principally Due to the Bad Luck of Visitors' Pitching Talent.

Games Today.

Omaha at Denver.
Sioux City at St. Joseph.
Des Moines at Colorado Springs.

Standing of the Teams.

TEAMS.	Won.	Lost.	Pct.
Denver	41	26	.612
Colorado Springs	35	25	.583
Des Moines	35	35	.500
Omaha	33	34	.493
St. Joseph	29	34	.460
Sioux City	22	41	.349

A turn of the fickle Goddess of Luck yesterday won out for the Denvers in both games played at Broadway park with the Omahas. It was not entirely due to excellence of playing of our boys, but the visitors did not come out very well with their pitchers.

Three star twirlers were used up in the first game, Companion staying four innings, McCarthy three and Fast Man Brown stepped into the box to finish the game. The first man to face him was struck out, and had Brown pitched from the start the game would have probably gone to the Omahas.

Captain Hallman again demonstrated yesterday to the satisfaction of the spectators, and probably to the management, that he is not the right man to occupy a position at the head of the Denver club. Not only does his own misplays tend to demoralize his associates, but he is very free with advice that does not assist his team in winning, but only brings upon his own head the ridicule of the fans.

The Denvers drew first blood in the first game by making two runs in the second inning, and from that time on the sides were "neck and neck." The visitors' poor array of pitching talent was about evenly balanced by the Denvers' lack of a guiding hand.

None of the plays were in any way phenomenal, the only good thing being a three-bagger by Thomas, which let three men home. Brown showed up well as first baseman, although he appears to hug the bag too much. He accomplished two runs, as did Gonding.

The second game was not so exciting, but it was none the less interesting, as up to the ninth inning Denver had not scored a run, and only one was made by the visitors in the sixth inning, Miller being the boy who turned the trick. In the last inning, with two men out, McHale got to third on a redhot grounder and Smith followed him at the bat. By good, hard hitting Smith got McHale home and winning the second game of the afternoon for his team. Quick put out a good ball for the Omahas in this game, as did Hostetter, who pitched fast and certain. Freese caught in place of Gonding and his work compared favorably with his predecessor's.

The summaries:

First Game.

DENVER.

PLAYERS.	A.B.	R.	B.H.	P.O.	A.	E.
Ketcham, c. f.	5	0	2	0	0	0
McHale, l. f.	3	2	2	2	0	0
Hartzell, 3b	5	0	2	3	0	0
Hallman, 2b	4	2	1	3	6	1
Hayes, r. f.	3	1	2	2	0	0
Smith, s. s.	2	1	0	1	0	2
Braun, 1b	3	1	0	8	2	0
Lucia, c	2	1	0	7	1	0
Cable, p	4	1	2	1	2	0
Totals	31	9	11	27	11	3

OMAHA.

PLAYERS.	A.B.	R.	B.H.	P.O.	A.	E.
Carter, r. f.	5	0	0	1	0	0
Brown, 1b	3	2	1	8	2	1
Miller, l. f.	5	1	2	0	0	0
Welch, c. f.	3	0	0	2	0	0
Dolan, s. s.	5	0	1	3	1	0
Thomas, 2b	4	1	1	1	2	1
Shipke, 3b	3	1	2	2	4	0
Gonding, c	3	2	3	6	2	0
Companion, p	1	0	0	0	2	0
McCarthy, p	3	1	0	0	2	0
Freese, 1b	0	0	0	2	1	1
Totals	35	8	10	25	16	3

Score by innings—
Denver .... 0 2 1 0 0 3 1 1 1—9
Omaha .... 0 0 1 0 3 0 3 1 0—8

Stolen bases: McHale, Hartzell, Miller. Three-base hit: Thomas. Bases on balls: O: Cable, 4; off Companion, 6; off McCarthy, 5; off Brown, 1. Struck out: By Cable, 5; by Companion, 1; by Brown, 1. Left on bases: Denver, 15; Omaha, 6. Home run: Hayes. Two-base hits: Shipke, Brown. Wild pitch: McCarthy. Hit by pitched ball: Smith. Double play: Shipke to Gonding to Brown. Time: 2:05. Umpire:: Keefe: Attendance: 1,500.

Second Game.

DENVER.

PLAYERS.	A.B.	R.	B.H.	P.O.	A.	E.
Ketcham, c. f.	4	0	1	2	0	0
McHale, l. f.	4	0	1	0	0	0
Hartzell, 3b	3	1	0	2	1	0
Hallman, 2b	3	0	0	3	4	0
Hayes, r. f.	3	0	1	1	1	0
Smith, s. s.	4	1	2	3	2	0
Braun, 1b	4	0	1	9	0	0
Lucia, c	3	0	0	7	1	0
Hostetter, p	2	0	0	1	0	0
Totals	30	2	6	28	9	0

OMAHA.

PLAYERS.	A.B.	R.	B.H.	P.O.	A.	E.
Carter, r. f.	3	0	0	1	0	0
Brown, 1b	4	0	1	11	0	1
Miller, l. f.	4	1	1	1	0	0
Welch, c. f.	4	0	3	3	0	0
Dolan, s. s.	4	0	0	0	3	2
Thomas, 2b	4	0	1	2	4	0
Shipke, 3b	4	0	2	2	2	1
Freese, c	4	0	0	3	2	0
Quick, p	3	0	0	0	2	0
Totals	34	1	8	26	13	4

Score by innings—
Denver .... 0 0 0 0 0 0 0 0 2—2
Omaha .... 0 0 0 0 0 1 0 0 0—1

Stolen bases: McHale, 2. Bases on balls: Off Hostetter, 1; off Quick, 3. Struck out: By Hostetter, 4; by Quick, 3. Left on bases: Denver, 6; Omaha, 7. Two-base hit: Shipke. Wild pitch: Hostetter. Double play: Thomas to Brown to Dolan. Time: 1:45. Umpire: Keefe. Attendance: 1,500.

Des Moines Outplayed.

Special to The News.

COLORADO SPRINGS, July 10.—The Millionaires got into the game today for a change and took the game from the Politicians of Des Moines by the one-sided score of 11 to 3. Villeman, who did the twirling for the locals, was invincible for eight innings, allowing but four scattered hits. In the ninth inning he eased up and allowed four more. In the first eight innings Des Moines did not get a man to third, and only one to second. Skopec's brilliant fielding in right garden and some exceedingly fast work by Radcliffe were features.

Two hits in the second inning started the run getting. Baerwald singled, Blake got life on an error and Radcliffe filled the bases on a field play. Herman doubled and three runs came in. Villeman and Nill were both safe on errors, one of which allowed Villeman to score, and then a long fly to center scored Nill. In the third Blake tripled and scored on Hoffman's wild throw to the plate. In the fifth Graham singled, stole second, got third on Ryan's high fly to left, which was good for two bags, and Graham scored on Baerwald's hit. Nine men faced Leifield in the sixth. Three runs were scored. Herman got a pass, Villeman doubled and Nill singled, scoring Herman and Villeman. Nill went out at second on Skopec's hit. Graham singled and Ryan flew out. Baerwald singled, Blake drew a pass and Radcliffe flew out.

Des Moines' only runs were scored in the ninth. Fiske, who batted for Thiele, singled, as did Lobert. Then Clark's home run cleared the bases and scored three men.

The score:

COLORADO SPRINGS.

PLAYERS.	A.B.	R.	B.H.	P.O.	A.	E.
Nill, 2b.	4	1	1	5	3	1
Skopec, r. f.	5	1	0	3	0	0
Graham, 3b.	5	1	2	0	1	1
Ryan, l. f.	4	1	1	0	0	0
Baerwald, 1b.	5	1	3	11	0	0
Blake, c. f.	3	2	1	1	0	0
Radcliffe, s. s.	4	0	0	3	5	0
Herman, c.	3	2	1	4	2	0
Villeman, p.	4	2	1	0	1	0
Totals	37	11	10	27	12	2

DES MOINES.

PLAYERS.	A.B.	R.	B.H.	P.O.	A.	E.
Thiele, l. f.	3	0	0	1	0	0
Lobert, 3b.	4	0	3	0	8	1
Hoffman, s. s.	4	1	1	3	4	1
McChesney, r. f.	4	0	0	1	0	0
Clark, c. f.	4	1	2	3	0	0
Connery, 1b.	4	0	1	9	0	1
Towne, c.	4	0	0	4	0	1
Shugart, 2b.	3	0	0	3	2	1
Leifield, p.	3	0	0	0	2	0
*Fiske	1	1	1	0	0	0
Totals	34	3	8	24	11	5

*Batted for Thiele in the ninth.

Score by innings:
Colorado Springs .... 0 5 1 0 2 3 0 0 *—11
Des Moines .... 0 0 0 0 0 0 0 0 3— 3

Earned runs: Colorado Springs, 4; Des Moines, 3. Two-base hits: Villeman, Herman, Ryan. Three-base hit: Blake. Home run: Clark. Stolen bases: Graham, Hoffman. Double plays: Radcliffe to Baerwald; Radcliffe to Nill to Baerwald. Bases on balls: Off Liefield, 4. Struck out: By Villeman, 4; by Liefield, 3. First base on errors: Colorado Springs, 3; Des Moines, 2. Left on bases: Colorado Springs, 5; Des Moines, 3. Time, 1:25. Umpire, Kelley.

Chinn Was Slaughtered.

SIOUX CITY, Iowa, July 10.—St. Joseph won the first game today on Fremer's error at short. In the second game Sioux City knocked Chinn out of the box. Scores:

First game—
Sioux City .... 0 0 0 0 0 0 1 0 0—1
St. Joseph .... 1 0 0 0 0 0 0 3 0—4

Base hits: Sioux City, 10; St. Joseph, 5. Errors: Sioux City, 3. Batteries: Jarrott and Ward; Maupin and Garvin.

Second game—
Sioux City .... 4 0 2 0 0 0 1 0 *—7
St. Joseph .... 0 0 0 1 0 0 0 0 0—1

Base hits: Sioux City, 10; St. Joseph, 4. Errors: Sioux City, 2; St. Joseph, 3. Batteries: Cadawallader and Anderson; Chinn, Diehl and McConnell.

AMATEUR BASEBALL.

Cottrells Win Out.

Yesterday afternoon at Union park the Cottrells outplayed and outhit the Colorado Iron Works team at every stage of the game. Conley, the iron workers' new pitcher, of whom so much was expected, was taken out at the end of the sixth inhits, three of which were three-baggers. Schaffer, who replaced him, shared as bad a fate in the next inning. The feature of the game was the hard hitting of the Cottrells against pitchers who have been very effective against all other teams this year and clever base running and the best kind of fielding.

The score:

COTTRELLS.

PLAYERS.	A.B.	R.	B.H.	P.O.	A.	E.
Eichoff, 2b	5	2	3	6	0	0
Birkendahl	4	0	1	2	2	0
Good, s. s.	3	3	1	1	4	2
Smith, c. f.	4	2	0	2	0	0
Dudley, 1b	5	2	2	8	0	0
Mesch, l. f.	5	1	3	2	0	0
Currigan, r. f.	4	1	2	1	0	0
Reynolds, c	3	1	1	5	2	0
Ewing, p	4	2	2	0	1	0
Totals	37	14	15	27	9	2

COLORADO IRON WORKS.

PLAYERS.	A.B.	R.	B.H.	P.O.	A.	E.
Hoffer, r. f.	4	0	1	0	0	0
Warnecke, 3b	4	0	0	1	0	1
Coulehan, 1b	4	0	0	7	0	1
Stewart, c	4	0	0	7	3	0
Richter, l. f.	4	0	0	2	0	0
Seltzer, c. f.	3	0	0	0	0	0
McGeever, s. s.	4	0	2	1	4	0
Berry, 2b	4	0	0	6	1	0
Conley, p	1	0	0	1	1	0
Schaffer, p	1	0	0	0	0	0
Totals	33	0	3	24	9	2

Score by innings—
Cottrells .... 2 2 4 0 0 5 0 1 x—14
C. I. W .... 0 0 0 0 0 0 0 0 0— 0

Stolen bases: Eichoff, 3; Good, Birkendahl, Smith, Reynolds. Passed balls: Stewart, 2. Bases on balls: Off Ewing, 1; off Conley, 2; off Schaffer, 1. Struck out: By Ewing, 5; by Conley, 2; by Schaffer, 3. Left on bases: Cottrells, 9; C. I. W., 4. Two-base hits: Eichoff, Mesch, 2; Ewing. Hit by pitched ball: Schaffer. Time: 1:40. Umpire: Jones. Attendance: 485.

Las Vegas Lost by Errors.

Special to The News.

ALBUQUERQUE, N. M., July 10.—Albuquerque again defeated Las Vegas at baseball today, taking the second game of the series by the score of 6 to 4. Up to the eighth inning Las Vegas had no chance, when Gallegos, the local pitcher, let down long enough to allow the visitors four runs. Otherwise Gallegos pitched a flawless game, as did Rhodes, the Las Vegas twirler, who played wonderful ball and lost the game only because of poor support.

James Doyles Won.

The James Doyles defeated the Leyden club yesterday on the latter's home grounds by a score of 19 to 3. At every stage of the game the visiting team were in control of the situation and the hard hitting of their players won the game. The Denver boys spent a very pleasant day in the village, beside having the satisfaction of taking the game from a strong team who have lost only two games this season.

Castle Rock Defeated.

Special to The News.

CASTLE ROCK, Colo., July 10.—The most exciting game of the season was played here today between the Castle Rock team and the Denver Vulcan Iron Works. The score was 5 to 3 in favor of the visitors. Ten innings were played. This is the first game the Castle Rocks have lost this year.

BLANKED FOR EIGHT INNINGS

Corridon Let Down a Little in Ninth and Prevented a Shutout for the Bridegrooms at Chicago National Park.

Games Today.

Brooklyn att Chicago.
Philadelphia at Cincinnati.
New York at St. Louis.

Standing of the Teams.

TEAMS.	Won.	Lost.	Pct.
New York	52	17	.754
Chicago	41	27	.603
Cincinnati	40	27	.597
Pittsburg	36	30	.545
St. Louis	33	35	.485
Boston	27	43	.386
Brooklyn	28	45	.384
Philadelphia	17	40	.298

CHICAGO, July 10.—Corridon blanked the visitors for eight innings, allowing only three scattered singles, the locals having scored three runs by hard hitting. In the ninth inning the Brooklyns, by bunching a double and three singles, tallied twice. Attendance 11,200. Score:

Chicago .... 0 0 0 1 2 0 0 0 *—3
Brooklyn .... 0 0 0 0 0 0 0 0 2—2

Base hits: Chicago, 9; Brooklyn, 3. Errors: Chicago, 1; Brooklyn, 1. Batteries: CCorridon and O'Neil; Jones and Bergen. Two-base hits: McCarthy, Chance, Casey, Lumley. Struck out: By Corridon, 4; by Jones, 3. Bases on balls: Off Corridon, 3; off Jones, 2. Umpire, Moran.

Nichols Beat M'Ginnity.

ST. LOUIS, July 10.—St. Louis and New York split even on a double-header this afternoon, the home team winning the first to 2 and New York getting the second 3 to 1. Nichols was more effective than McGinnity in the opening game, the runs of both teams being made on hits. In the second Luther Taylor pitched a brilliant game for New York. Attendance 19,800. Score:

First game—
St. Louis .... 0 0 0 2 0 1 0 0 *—3
New York .... 0 1 0 1 0 0 0 0 0—2

Base hits: St. Louis, 6; New York, 8. Errors: New York, 1. Batteries: Nichols and Zearfoss; McGinnity and Warner. Earned runs: St. Louis, 3; New York, 2. Two-base hits: Mertes, McGinnity, Barclay, Dahlen. Three-base hit: McGann. Bases on balls: Off McGinnity, 1; off Nichols, 1. Struck out: By Nichols, 2; by McGinnity, 3. Umpires, O'Day and Emslie.

Second game—
St. Louis .... 0 0 0 0 0 0 0 0 1—1
New York .... 1 0 0 0 0 0 0 0 2—3

Base hits: St. Louis, 5; New York, 1. Errors: New York, 1. Batteries: O'Neill and Zearfoss; Taylor and Bowerman. Three-base hit: McGann. Bases on balls: Off O'Neill, 1; off Taylor, 1. Struck out: By O'Neill, 4; by Taylor, 4. Umpires, Emslie and O'Day.

Good Hitting the Cause.

CINCINNATI, O., July 10.—The Cincinnatis and Philadelphia split even in a double-header this afternoon. The first game went to the visitors through their opportune hitting, aided by bases on balls. In the second game McPherson was hit hard enough in the first inning to put the locals in an easy position from the start. Attendance, 10,300. Score:

First game—
Cincinnati .... 1 0 0 0 0 0 0 0 0—1
Philadelphia .... 1 0 1 0 0 2 0 0 0—4

Base hits: Cincinnati, 6; Philadelphia, 6. Errors: Philadelphia, 1. Batteries: Harper and Peitz; Frazer and Dooin. Two-base hits: Huggins, Titus 2, Dolin. Three-base hits: Dolan, Doyle. Bases on balls: Off Harper, 3; off Frazer, 1. Struck out: By Harper, 3; by Frazer, 2. Umpire, Zimmer.

Second game—
Cincinnati .... 3 0 2 0 0 0 0 2 0—7
Philadelphia .... 0 0 0 1 0 0 0 0 0—1

Base hits: Cincinnati, 10; Philadelphia, 6. Errors: Cincinnati, 1; Philadelphia, 4. Batteries: Ewing and Schlei; McPherson and Dooin. Earned runs: Cincinnati, 2. Two-base hits: Dolan, Odwell, Kelly. Three-case hit: Huggins. Bases on balls: Off Ewing, 5; off McPherson, 1. Struck out: By Ewing, 6; by McPherson, 1. Umpire, Zimmer.

AMERICAN LEAGUE.

Games Today.

Detroit at Cleveland.
Washington at Philadelphia.
Boston at New York.

Standing of the Teams.

TEAMS.	Won.	Lost.	Pct.
Boston	45	22	.672
New York	40	25	.615
Chicago	41	30	.577
Cleveland	35	27	.563
Philadelphia	34	32	.515
St. Louis	28	28	.500
Detroit	25	40	.385
Washington	12	53	.185

Dundon the Star.

ST. LOUIS, July 10.—St. Louis and Chicoga broke even here today in a double-header, the first game going to Chicago by a score of 2 to 1, while St. Louis landed the second 6 to 5. Clever fielding by Dundon was the feature of the opening game.

The feature of the second game was the batting of Burkett. Attendance 12,000. Score:

First game.
St. Louis .... 0 0 0 0 1 0 0 0 0—1
Chicago .... 1 0 0 1 0 0 0 0 0—2

Base hits: St. Louis, 7; Chicago, 4. Errors: St. Louis, 1. Batteries: Pelty and Kahoe; White and Sullivan.

Second game—
St. Louis .... 3 0 1 0 0 0 0 0 1 0 1—6
Chicago .... 0 0 1 0 0 0 0 3 1 0 0—5

Base hits: St. Louis, 11; Chicago, 12. Errors: St. Louis, 2. Batteries: Siever, Sudhoff and Sugden; Patterson and Sullivan.

AMERICAN ASSOCIATION.

Games Today.

Indianapolis at Milwaukee.
Toledo at Kansas City.
Louisville at St. Paul.
Columbus at Minneapolis.

Yesterday's Results.

At Kansas City—First game: Kansas City, 6; Toledo, 4. Second game: Kansas City, 9; Toledo, 8.

At St. Paul—St. Paul, 1; Louisville, 2.

At Milwaukee—Milwaukee, 4; Indianapolis, 2.

At Minneapolis—Minneapolis, 1; Columbus, 0.

AMATEUR BASEBALL.

Iron Workers' Waterloo.

Special to The News.

CRIPPLE CREEK, July 10.—The Cripple Creek boys again defeated the Colorado Fuel and Iron team of Pueblo today and gave the crowd, which was about 1,000 strong, the best exhibition of baseball ever witnessed in the mountains. The game was fast and furious from start to finish, lasting two hours and ten minutes. A heavy rain had made the diamond extremely muddy, making it difficult for the runners to make any time, and more than one man was put out because he could not cover the ground. Up to the fifth inning the visitors had everything their own way, but in the last half of the sixth the rooters started in with such unmerciful guying that the pitcher lost all control of himself and the Cripple Creek boys scored five runs. In the seventh inning the Cripple Creek boys made seven runs. Gail started the ball rolling in this inning by batting a home run. When McClusky came to bat there were three men on bases, and when he struck the ball it flew in the air, landing outside the grounds, permitting the men on bases to come in and himself scoring a home run, the second one in the inning. This made the crowd yell with delight. The visitors lost all heart. The score:

C. F. and I...... 0 5 0 0 1 0 0 0 0— 6
Cripple Creek .. 1 0 3 0 0 5 7 2 x—18

Batteries: Brierly, Baker and Robson; McCausland and Nash. Left on bases: C. F. and I., 12; Cripple Creek, 11. Struck out: By Nash, 6; by Baker, 4; by Robson, 1. Earned runs: Cripple Creek, 7. Home runs: Gail, McCluskey. Umpire: W. E. Dingman.

The Cripple Creek team will play the Colorado Springs league team next Friday afternoon. There is considerable speculation as to the outcome, and many are of the opinion that the local boys will do up the league team. The game today makes the twentieth they have played this season, and so far they have lost but two games.

Cozys Defeated by Reds.

Special to The News.

LITTLETON, Colo., July 10.—The Arapahoe Indians of this place today defeated the E. Z. Cozys of Denver by a score of 13 to 4. The score by innings:

Arapahoe Indians .. 1 0 4 1 0 0 4 1 2—13
E. Z. Cozys .... 1 0 0 1 0 1 0 1 0— 4

Batteries: Lemcheck and Weigel; Goddie and Wilcox.

Claytons Easy Victims.

The Claytons were easy victims for the Hardestys yesterday when they let go by a score of 12 to 8. The pitching talent of the victorious team was especially strong, S. Mossberg striking out ten men and F. Mossberg fanning four to the bench.

Red Men Scalped.

The Neefs defeated the Red Men yesterday at the new amateur ball park, Forty-third and York, by a score of 27 to 4. The Indians had no show to win at any time, but met their defeat bravely and exerted every effort to score.

JUNIOR BASEBALL.

Challenges (Answer Through News)

The Tom Moores won from the Hoovers yesterday by a score of 8 to 4.

TIPS FOR TODAY

(By News Leased Wire.)

Brighton Beach.

First race—Letola, Julia M., T. Musketeer.
Second race—Flying Buttress, Black Death, Silver Twist.
Third race—Hurst Park, Eugenia Burch, Brigand.
Fourth race—Paget entry, Schulmate, Chrysitis.
Fifth race—British, Austen Allen, Broadcloth.
Sixth race—Marmee, Belle of Portland, Lady Prudence.

Fair Grounds.

First race—Anyway, Torlo, Mengis.
Second race—Leenja, Jake Weber, Mohave.
Third race—Miss Gomes, Triple Silver, Yellow Hammer.
Fourth race—Ancke, Copperfield, First Mason.
Fifth race—Lady Savoy, Col. White, Useful Lady.
Sixth race—Thane, Jerry Hunt, Elil.

Union Park.

First race—Lady Lusk, Satin Coat, Buster.
Second race—Jetty, Half Tag, Forden entry.
Third race—Dodie S., Bluish, T. G. Scarbrough.
Fourth race—Monadnock, Planet, George W. Dasch.
Fifth race—Little Margaret, Baronesa, Eufalla.
Sixth race—Flamero, Dominis, Orme.
Seventh race—Rogers entry, Broadway, Gould.

BOWLING.

Prize Bowlers' Standing.

The leaders in the special prize contest, which runs during this month at the Brunswick alleys, stood as follows last night:

Moeller, 276, 257.
Lang, 256.
Frost, 239.
Reilly, 237.
W. Burton, 234.
Mason, 234.

The most pins made to July 25; all games count. First, $5; second, $2. Leaders:

Kerr, 2,896.
Herman, 2,516.
Langan, 2,451.
Homer, 2,378.
Barnettler, 2,353.
Birkendahl, 2,117.
Gaston, 2,002.
Patterson, 2,000.

Connors Defeated.

The Three Rules defeated the Connors in a one-sided game yesterday afternoon, the battery of the winners being responsible for the victory. Score:

Connors .... 4 0 0 0 2 0 0 0 1— 7
Three Rules .... 1 0 0 3 3 3 0 0 *—10

Change in Boulder and Fort Collins Trains Via Colorado & Southern.

Effective Sunday, July 10, train for Boulder and Fort Collins, scheduled out of Denver at 10:15 a. m., will leave at 10 o'clock. The 6 a. m. train will be discontinued. The 8 a. m. and 5 p. m. trains will serve Louisville and Lafayette.

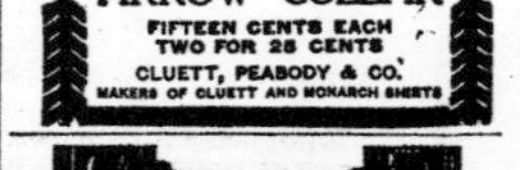

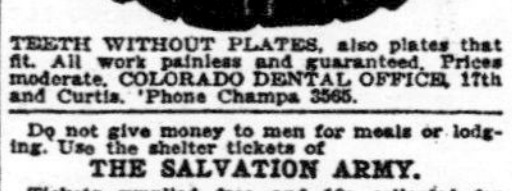

MANY ATTRACTIONS AT CHAUTAUQUA THIS WEEK

Special to The News.

BOULDER, Colo., July 10.—There were two very good events at the Colorado Chautauqua today and they were largely patronized by the citizens of Boulder. The management has this year provided a Sunday afternoon sermon and music and a grand sacred concert at night. The sermon today was by Rev. Frank G. Tyrrell of St. Louis, who is also the platform superintendent of this session. "Optimism" was the theme of the address.

This closed the first week of the session, which has been a notable one, although the attendance was not what was anticipated, owing to two rainy and cold nights. The second week begins tomorrow night with the American vitograph, which will also be the attraction on Tuesday night. Wednesday will be Maccabee day, when 5,000 members of that order are expected from all points of the state. The chief event of the day promises to be the address by Rev. Grant A. Robbins of Missouri, grand chaplain of the order. At night the Maccabees and others will be entertained by a dramatic reading by a great Chautauqua favorite, Mrs. Lulu Tyler Gates.

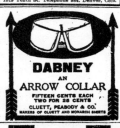

The Beeville Bee.

VOL. XXII. $1.50 Per Year. BEEVILLE, BEE COUNTY, TEXAS, FRIDAY, NOVEMBER 8, 1907. Established May 13, 1886. NO. 29

A TEXAS RANGER FIGHT.

A Tale of Old Refugio Sixty Years Ago. EntireFamily Wiped Out by Merciless Comanches.

A. J. Sowell in Galaeston News.

In the early days of the Republic of Texas, soon after the great victory at San Jacinto which freed the Lone Star State from the tyranny and misrule of a proud Mexican dictator, many people came from the old states of the American Union to find homes in this pleasant land of mild winters, sunshine and flowers. Some of these pioners lived to an advanced age, enjoying the blessings of a new and fruitful country, while others found bloody graves and desolated homes. Wild bands of indians roamed at will over the vast domain of Texas, committing many horrible depradations upon the almost defenseless settlers. They not only killed stock and drove stock away, but murdered the people, burned their houses and carried women and children into a captivity sometimes worse than death.

One of these unfortunate families was that of Johnston Gillelland. He came to Texas in 1837 from the far distant state of Pennsylvania and settled in Refugio county, south, near the gulf coast. In his settlement was the large Don Carlos ranch, where were many horses and cattle, and which fact drew to that point many Indian raids for booty. Mr. Gillelland established here a pleasant home. Peace and plenty seemed to prevail, the grass covered and flower-bedecked prairies spread away in undulating rolls in every direction, upon which grazed sleek herds of cattle and horses, while the gentle and invigorating gulf breeze wafted the sweet smell of many varieties of wild flowers across the prairies. Chilling winds seldom came. Flowers bloomed in December, but savage men, who hated the pale-faced race, marred the enjoyment at times of all this loveliness.

For the protection of the people small companies of men were banded together who scouted through the country watching for signs and trails of Indians. They were called "Texas Rangers." At the time of which we write four of these companies were in Refugio and adjoining counties under Capts Price, Albert Sidney Johnston, Mustang Grey and Peter Tumblinson. These men were brave, fine riders, good shots, hardy, and would die in defense of the helpless. The Indians soon learned to dread them, but often met and fought them in bloody battles. Soon after settling in the country Mr. Gillelland joined the company of Capt. Tumblinson and did good service in the defense of the settlement. When not on scout duty he would come home and spend some time with his family. On one occasion in 1840 he came home with the intention of remaining ten days or two weeks until a scout which were out returned. His family consisted of his wife, Mary Gillelland; son William, 6 years of age, and daughter, Rebecca, 8 years. One quiet evening the family went out for a walk only a short distance from the house, the children in high glee running here and there gathering flowers, shouting and laughing in exuberance of innocent childhood. Suddenly and without one note of warning a band of painted Comanche Indians came into view over a rising swell in the prairie. For an instant the father gazed with blanched cheeks at the savages, the mother shrieked in terror and the children tremblingly clung to them. Gillelland then seized the children, one in each arm, and made a desperate attempt to reach the house where his gun and pistols were, but fate was against him. The Indians on their quick, swift ponies, soon dashed around him and the work of death commenced. He placed the children on the ground and tried to shield them with his body, but soon fell pierced with many arrows. Mrs. Gillelland met the same fate. Their bodies were then lanced repeatedly, stripped, the scalps torn from their heads and the children placed on horses and carried away screaming. As they passed the house it was set on fire, and when the sun went down on that fearful day the mother and father lay cold in death, the house in ashes and the children carried away into captivity.

The Indians did not like the crying of the children and said they would cut off their hands and feet if they did not stop it; and no doubt would have carried this threat to execution if it had not been for an Indian squaw who was of the party. She made threats and violent motions towards the bucks, and they finally desisted and let the children alone. The Indians made no halt during the night, but pushed on through the settlement. After daylight they halted. Early in the morning Mustang Grey and a scout of his men came upon the trail and following it met a few of Capt. Price's men. They had seen the Indians, but not being strong enough to successfully fight them were hurrying to the camp of Capt. Johnston for reinforcement. During the few minutes these two parties were halted and discussing the situation another squad of men were discovered rapidly approaching them on the trail of the Commanches. These proved to be some of Capt. Sidney Johnston's men under Lieut. Hannum. Some settler had discovered the smoke of the burning house carried the news to Johnston's camp, and he had sent out this squad in persuit.

The combined force now moved rapidly upon the trail and soon came upon the Indians in open ground, but near thickets and dense timber. The rangers charged and a furious battie commenced. They saw the children at the first onset, but a few of the children ran into the thickets with them, while the others faced and fought the rangers. The battle was short. The Comanches soon broke away and scattered into the timber. After the chase was over the rangers made a search for the children, rode here and there, calling loudly for them, but no response came. Satisfied now that they were still in the hands of the Indians, or had been killed, the men dismounted, and while some deployed through the brush others skirted the edge of the timber in the prairie. The Indians who carried the captives into the brush lanced the boy and knocked the girl in the head, leaving them for dead, and continued their flight to escape the rangers. Both children soon revived and the girl took her little brother, who was unable to walk, in her arms and endeavored to get to the edge of the prairie so the white men could see them. She knew they were near for she looked back while the Indians were running into the brush with them and saw the rangers fighting the other indians in the prairie. These children had been taught to ask God for help when in trouble, and now the wounded and nearly exhausted little girl laid her brother down, and kneeling asked God to save them.

After resting and somewhat regaining her strength this devoted little sister again raised the little boy in her arms and staggered on through the brush and finally reached the edge of the prairie where she could see what was going on. The yelling, gun shots and other sounds of conflict had ceased and many men could be seen riding to and fro. Some of these came near, but the buckskin hunting shirts which some of the rangers wore frightened the child who, thinking these must be Indians also, again clasped the little boy in her arms and going back into the thicket hid under some dense underbrush. Here they lay for some time while the search for them was being made, but finally voices near by called them by name, and knowing now it was friends Rebecca once more claspsd little Willie in her arms and came out to the opening where they were soon surrounded by shouting rangers. These strong, brave men shed tears as they very tenderly lifted the bloody little captives to their saddles. Four rangers were wounded and eight dead Comanches law on the battle ground. A detail now hurriedly carried the children to the nearest ranger camp, and on the following day they were conveyed to the Don Carlos Ranch, where they were placed under the treatment of Drs. Axsom and Hammond. Soon after the girl was carried to Victoria by Captain Sidney Johnston, and was there joined by her brother, where he recovered. They found a home and kind friends in the house of a Presbyterian minister, Dr. Blair, and his good wife. They were like like father and mother to the orphans.

Many years after this Willie accidentally shot himself in the hip, badly shattering it, but he recovered from this wound also but was ever after a cripple. Rebecca married a man named Fisher and still has relatives in this state. One of them Orcenath Fisher, a Methodist preacher, died in Uvalde county in 1880, leaving a large family. Albert Sidney Johnston was a famous Confederate general in the Civil War and was killed at the battle of Shiloh in 1862.

Mabery Grey, known along the border as "Mustang Grey," fought many battles with the Indians, and finally died in Mexico. At his request some of his old comrades brought the remains across the Rio Grande and buried them in Texas soil. Among the followers of "Mustang" Grey on this occasion was Samuel H. Walker, a noted ranger under Hays in Texas and Lieutenant Colonel of his regiment in Mexico. He was killed at the battle of Humantia in 1846.

LEGAL MISCARRIAGES.

Law Becomes so Complicated That Those Versed in It Have Not Brains Enough to Try Cases.

Chicago, Ill., Nov. 1.—As a result of a recent decision of the supreme court, which held that municipal courts of Chicago could not legally try cases in which the indictments were returned by a Cook county grand jury, over a hundred murderers, highwaymen, burglars and other criminals were today turned loose from the Joliet penitentiary. This is the first batch to gain freedom by the decision, and many more will be set at liberty.

The situation is one of the worst that ever confronted Chicago. If the decision of the highest court is to stand, it means that on the eve of winter footpads, murderers and criminals of all classes are to be turned loose on the streets of the city. States Attorney John J. Healy, however, has decided to take drastic steps to prevent the wholesale liberation of criminals. He construes the decision to mean that the supreme court never intended that convicted criminals should be given liberty, but that each and every man must stand trial again this time in the criminal court.

Fourth Trial Same as Before.

Dallas, Tex., Nov. 1.—After being out forty-three hours the jury returned a verdict of murder in the first degree this morning and assessed the death penalty in the case of Burrell Oats, who was charged with murder as the result of the killing of Sol Aronoff in this city four years ago.

The case of Oats is regarded as one of the most remarkable in the criminal annals of the state, for the reason that this is the fourth trial of the defendant on the charge, the death penalty having been returned each time. The case has been reversed and remanded in each of the former three trials.

Counsel for the defendant will file a motion for a new trial to-morrow, and in the event the motion is overruled the case will again be appealed.

Was in Court 100 Years.

Staunton, Va., Nov. 5—A will case which has been occupying the various court here for more than 100 years was ended in the circuit court by Mayor W. H. Landis, receiver, entering a decree which is considered as final, showing all the disbusements in the case of Peck vs. Borden and Borden vs. Borden. More than $100,000 was involved, and the various decrees have been entered by almost every lawyer here.

Their heirs, numbering nearly 400, were from all parts of the country. The final decree approving the settlement of the receiver, William H. Landis, involved only about $5000.

One heir represented in the original suit as an infant died some years ago at the age of 96 years. Nearly every lawyer at the local bar for the last century has represented some of the heirs. The papers in the case were so voluminous that nobody was familiar with all of them.

PLOWING TIME AGAIN!

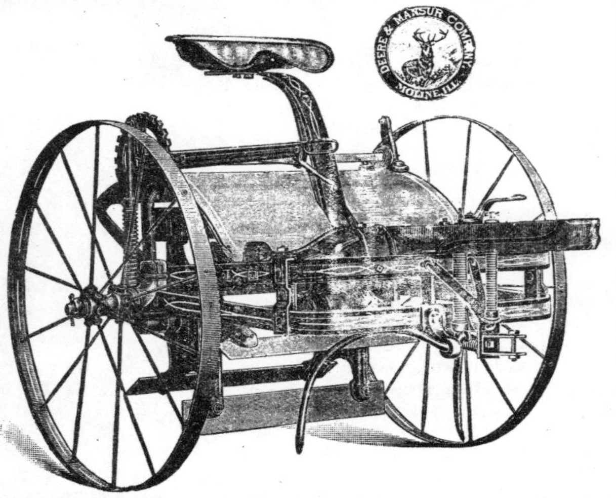

The season challenges the agriculturist again to the field of honor. According to the code the latter has choice of weapons. The farmer who chooses the "Old Reliable John Deere" implements has his battle with the soil half won before he begins. John Deere has been the standard for more than 60 years. We keep them in all sizes needed.

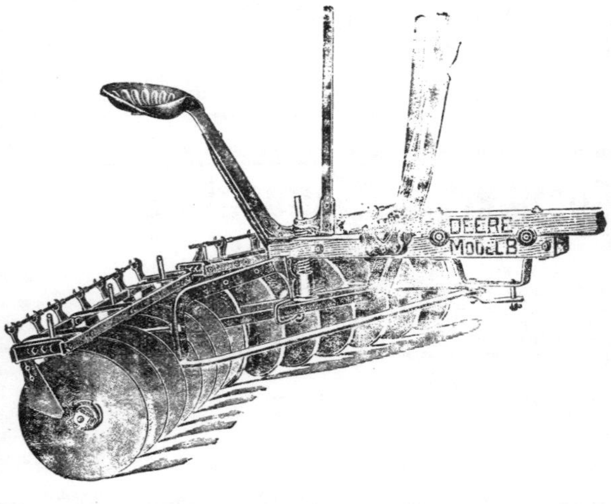

The Strongest Fence

Science proves that the strongest fence, because constructed throughout on scientific lines, is the

ELLWOOD FENCE

SIMPLE—SCIENTIFIC—STRONG

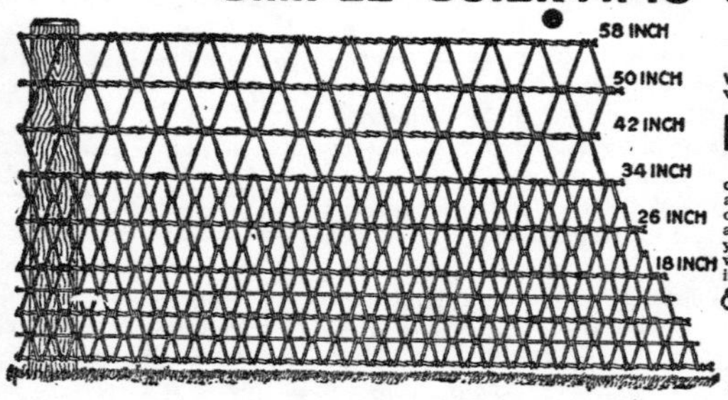

The Reasons:

1st—Each horizontal extension of the **ELLWOOD** is a ***steel cable,*** consisting of two heavy wires intertwined.

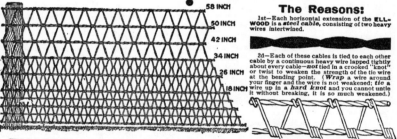

2d—Each of these cables is tied to each other cable by a continuous heavy wire lapped tightly about every cable—***not*** tied in a crooked "knot" or twist to weaken the strength of the tie wire at the bending point. (***Wrap*** a wire around your finger and the wire is not weakened; ***tie*** a wire up in a ***hard knot*** and you cannot untie it without breaking, it is so much weakened.)

THAT IS ALL THERE IS TO ELLWOOD FENCE—

Heavy steel cables lapped about and held together by steel wire, forming uniform meshes. Simple, isn't it? No chance for weakness in any part; uniformly strong. The reasons for the superiority of **ELLWOOD FENCE** are not hard to find. This company ***owns*** and operates its own iron mines and furnaces; its own wire mills and ***six*** large fence factories—***either*** one of the six being larger than any other fence factory in the world. These facts should be convincing.

MOON BUGGIES

Are the prettiest things on wheels, and what is better they wear longer and run lighter than any other buggy in the market for the money. Every stick of the timber and every piece of iron and steel that goes into them is inspected before the paint goes on. We keep a full line of them in stock, other makes and styles also, giving you a wide range of selection.

THE GEESE ARE HONKING SOUTH

Warning us of the near approach of the hunting season, and every rustle of the wind seems to sing "Johnnie Get Your Gun." If you haven't your gun, we have one for you, just the size and weight you want. We know it because we have all sizes and weights, and at prices from $4 up.

AMMUNITION FOR ALL GUNS, no matter what you shoot, either shotgun or rifle, or what gauge it may be, or whether you want smokeless or black powder. We are carrying the largest stock of ammunition in Beeville, direct from manufacturers, and are making close prices, either on a single box or a case.

THE OLD RELIABLE STUDEBAKER.

The wagon your grandfather bought, the kind your father bought, and the kind you will buy if you want a wagon to last long after the paint is gone. Been manufactured for three-quarters of a century, and stand today the "King of all Wagons."

Household Furnishings.

In our stock will be found everything needed for the kitchen or pantry. Plain and decorated china, pots, kettles and pans, in plain and enameled ware.

General Hardware.

Our stock of General Hardware embraces everything needed on the farm or in the workshop. Our tools are made to sell because they last, and they sell because the quality is there.

BUCK'S STOVES & RANGES

A. Praeger

The Beeville Bee.

VOL. XXII. $1.50 Per Year | BEEVILLE, BEE COUNTY, TEXAS, FRIDAY, JANUARY 31, 1908. | Established May 13, 1886 | NO. 41.

EARLY DAYS of SLAVERY IN TEXAS

Need of Labor Offered Extra Inducements for Traffic in Human Chattels. Last Cargo to Land in America Brought to Texas.

J. C. Moore in Houston Chronicle.

When Mexico declared her independence of Spanish rule Manuel Ferrero was appointed minister to the United States, but when his home government fell into the hands of the royalist party he took up his residence at New Orleans. Here he gathered a force composed of his countrymen who had fled from Mexico and of a number of Americans, and in the fall of 1816, with twelve or fifteen vessels, he sailed for Galvaston island. On reaching his destination he organized a government and De Aury, a Frenchman, was apionted governor, naval commander and judge of a court of admiralty. De Aury issued privateering commissions to his vessels, which swept the Gulf of Mexico for Spanish merchantmen. His fleet captured many vessels off the coasts of the West Indes laden with African slaves. As Galveston island and the rest of Texas had no need for slaves at that time, a market was found by smuggling them into Louisiana and some were sold even in the suburbs of New Orleans. Thus Galveston became a slave supply depot for Louisiana and for other plunder captured by De Aury's vessels. This trade led to collisions with United States revenue officers, and the collector at New Orleans informed the secretary of state that he was unable to prevent most shameful violations of the slave act by a motly mixture of smugglers and freebooters at Galveston under the Mexican flag.

When De Aury, having filled his private coffers with gold, finally abandoned Galveston in 1817, La Fitte, the noted pirate and bold buccaneer, pounced on that place for his future he dquarters. He had previously located on Grand Terre Island in Barrataria bay about sixty miles west of the Mississippi delta, and he held that position seven years in spite of efforts by the government of Louisiana to dislodge him, and until Commodore Patterson of the United States navy routed him with a fleet of gunboats in the summer of 1814. It is said that previous to this event some of the leading merchants in Louisiana were La Fitte's factors, and that his plunder was sold almost openly in the streets of New Orleans.

When La Fitte resumed business at Galveston in 1817 his knowledge of the bays and bayous of Louisianna enabled him to defy custom officers. Then the slave trade in Texas began in earnest. In order to fortify his plant with the semblance of legality, La Fitte declared Galveston island a republican province; a full corps of officers was elected, and allegiance to the Mexican government avowed. No qualified government officer being present, a citizen was sworn in as governor, who administered the oath of office to members of the cabinet. A subsequent avowal was made by the judge of admiralty to the effect that captured Spanish property, under what they called the Mexican flag, but without any idea of aiding the then revolution in Mexico, or any of the revolted colonies, was justifiable.

As was the case with De Aury, most of La Fitte's prizes were captured off the coasts of the West Indes, a fair proportion being slaves. Thus Galveston island would soon have resembled a section of the African Guinea coast had not the buccaneers maintained an equilibrium between supply and demand by hurrying their captures into the United States, where a market was found by advertising and canvassing. It is said that most of the purchases of captured slaves in Louisiana were made through agents who sent orders to Galveston, having contracts to deliver slaves at specified points. The favorite points were the mouths of the Sabine, Calcasieu and Bayou Larfourche, or inlets of Barrataria bay. Some purchasers went to Galveston to select their stock where slaves were sold by weight, the market price being a dollar a pound, but that beats even the present day prices for hogs and cattle.

We are told that La Fitte's most successful salesmen were the three Bouie brothers—Resin P., James and John J. Some idea of the extent of their dealings was afforded by their record book, which showed that in two years, 1818 and 1820, their profits amounted to $65,000.

In explanation of one or two points which will follow it is well to recall just here the fact that the bill adopted by congress in 1807, which prohibited the slave trade after the first of the following January, was a compromise measure by the committe in charge of the bill. The puzzling point was how to dispose of slaves smuggled into the United States and apprehended by custom officers. It was finally agreed to leave the disposition to each of the states within whose jurisdiction said slaves are apprehended—a simple, common sense decision, and democratic in principle.

One of the Bouie brothers declared he often sold negroes to Louisiana slave companies who, in order to validate their claim, surrendered them to custom officers, and when the negroes were resold in compliance with the state law the companies bought them back again, receiving, as informers, a rebate of half the last selling price.

Having grown too bold in his privateering, the United States forced La Fitte to abandon Galveston in 1825, and then the slave trade ceased in Texas for a dozen or more years.

When the next cargo of slaves reached Galveston there was a home market for that commodity, due to the influx of immigrants numbering about 20,000 up to 1830. Though peonage prevailed in Mexico, public sentiment opposed slavery, and a constituent congress in 1824 prohibited the slave trade. In 1827 the constitution of Coahuila and Texas, then combined, forbade, after six months, further introduction of slaves and provided for the gradual emancipation of those already introduced. The immigrants then adopted the shrewd policy of converting their slaves into servants indentured for life, and the legislature legalized the subterfuge. But in 1827 when President Guerrero issued a decree emancipating slaves throughout the republic, he made a special exception of those in Texas. Doubtless his object was to concilliate immigrant slave owners and to secure more uniform allegiance to the Mexican government.

About 1833, we are told, three prominent citizens of Galveston landed a full cargo of slaves at that port. As the story is told, they chartered a vessel and sailed for Cuba, but on approaching that island they found a United States frigate patrolling the coast. Then they decided on a plan to outwit Uncle Sam's watch dog. Landing at Havana, they employed an interpreter, visited the chief slave markets and harrangued crowds of Cuban slaves, describing Texas as being far superior to Cuba, a land of freedom, where the rich soil enables everybody to procure a good living with but little labor. Then they invited voluntary immigrants to go with them to Texas, promising that, in return for cost of transportation and provisions on the trip they would be required to serve only three years, and then would receive their freedom and be given a year's supply of necessaries for raising a crop for themselves. A full cargo of voluntary immigrants was procured, a contract setting forth promised terms was duly executed and, having paid the Cuban traders for the cargo of immigrants, the Galvestonians sailed for Texas, passing unmolested by the patroling frigate, the commander having learned that the cargo consists of voluntary immigrants. But before the vessel reached Galveston another contract was executed which abrogated the first one, and by which the duped slaves ignorantly bound themselves to serve their masters 99 years.

Though there is no documentary evidence to that effect, many old Texans know that slaves were imported into the state between 1850 and 1855. The best authenticated case, and probably the last, occurred in 1856. In the spring of that year the war department imported a cargo of camels for transporting army stores across the western plains, and the cargo was discharged at Indianola. In a short time afterward another vessel anchored off that port, claiming to have on board a cargo of camels for delivery to private parties, but persons interested in the enterprise know that, instead of camels, the cargo consisted of African slaves who were sold to purchasers from aboard of that vessel. Prof. Barker says he conversed with a man who declared he had seen and talked with some of the imported Africans. Probably some of those negroes are employed today on Brazos bottom plantations.

When readers of the Bee remember the environment of early settlers in Texas they will readily see that pioneers in civilization had some good ground for desiring to perpetuate the institution of slavery in Texas at that time. Texas was then a vast wilderness roamed over by numerous tribes of wild and hostile Indians. Many settlers were too poor to pay for free labor in assisting to recover the country from a state of wilderness, even if such labor could have been procured. Such men as Stephen F. Austin and others, who opposed slavery on principle, recognized and acquiesced in what seemed at least a temporary necessity for the use of slave labor.

HISTORY OF BROOM CORN.

A Native of India and Introduced Into This Country by Benj. Franklin.

The history of broom corn is somewhat interesting. Its introduction into the United States, the development of the industry, and the present magnitude of the same is not very widely known to the average consumer when he purchases a broom of his corner grocery.

Broomcorn, "Sorghum Vulgare," a plant which is a native of India, has been cultivated in a small way in some of the European countries, but its great value and its peculiar uses were not fully developed until it became extensively cultivated in the United States. The introduction of broom corn as an agricultural product into this country is attributed to Dr. Franklin, and its first production was more of a curiosity than as a plant of real value. It remained for the society of Shakers in Watervlett, New York, in the year 1791, to grow a small quantity in their gardens, and in 1798 the practical use was attempted, while crude in its way, at the same time in shape and form of the present brush or broom, and for many years all the broom corn grown was in the state of New York, and largely in Mohawk Valley. During the early development period of this industry, the supply did not keep with the demand, as the American housewife was quick to appreciate the value and importance of the good broom in her home. She at once abandoned the old hickory split broom for the new idea, the material for which she was able to produce in some cozy corner in her well kept garden. For a time broomcorn sold at fabulous prices in comparison to later years, often selling as high as $400 per ton.

The industry finally spread to Ohio, and in a small way to Tennessee, but the soil of both states was not of the character to make the industry a success, and was finally introduced in Central Illinois in 1863, and for a number of years the growing of broomcorn has been one of the most profitable and leading farm industries in central Illinois.

The Illinois farmer was quite fortunate in introducing this farm product when he did, from the fact that the question of overproduction has not yet taken place, and the supply was not equal to the demand. The country was new, and the soil exceedingly fertile and well adapted to the growing of this product, hence many Illinois farmers can look back to the time when he never sold broom corn for less than $100 per ton, and quite frequently at a much higher price. The industry was a profitable one, and many Illinois farmers today owe their financial success very largely to the broomcorn industry.

The Beeville Bee.

VOL. XXII. $1.50 Per Year. BEEVILLE, BEE COUNTY, TEXAS, FRIDAY, FEBRUARY 28, 1908. Established May 13, 1886 NO. 45.

CYNTHIA ANN PARKER AGAIN.

The Late Governor Ross, and Not Maj. Loefler Her Rescuer, as the Latter Claims.

San Antonio Express.

Austin, Tex., Feb. 22.—E. M. Phelps, assistant adjutant general, takes issue with information conveyed in a recently published interview with Major Loeffler, doorkeeper of the White House at Washington, who claims to have effected the capture of Cynthiana Parker and her baby, Quanah Parker, in the Indian fight on Pease river, December 19, 1860.

Mr. Phelps says:

"This claim on the part of Major Loaffler, as shown by the original report of Capt. L. S. Ross, commanding company Texas rangers, to Gov. Sam Houston, made on January 4, 1861, not quite two weeks after the fight, has no foundation other than he may possibly have been one of the three men of Company H, second cavalry, under Sergeant Spangler, who participated in the fight, the report showing that the capture, which Major Loeffler claims the credit of making, was made by Lieutenant Killeher of Ross' company. While it is true that General Ross (captain) only reports the capture of a white woman and her baby, as at that time her name was unknown, until afterward it was ascertained that the woman was Cynthiana Parker, who was taken into captivity in 1836, escaping the massacre at Parker Fort in Parker County. (See John Henry Brown's Indian Wars of Texas.")

"In corroboration of the above a copy of the original report, now on file in the adjutant general's department, is printed."

(Copy of Gov. L. S. Ross' report to General Sam Houston of an "Indian fight" on Pease river, December 18, 1860, as taken from the original report on file in the adjutant general's office):

Waco City, Jan. 4, 1861.—His Excellency Gen. Sam Houston—Sir: I take great pleasure in communicating to your Excellency the result of the expedition which I informed you I designed making against the Comanches in my report of December 8.

I left my station on the 11th inst. with forty men of my company, which was all my available force, and twenty men of H. Company, Second Cavalry, from Camp Cooper, under Sergeant J. W. Spangler. On the morning of the 12th I met with Capt. Jack Carrington and a gallant company of ninety-two citizens, with whom I was anxious to co-operate. With our combined forces we took up the line of march for Pease river, guided by a Mr. Stewart of Belknap, a brave and hardy frontiersman of much experience in Indian fighting, with a superior knowledge of the Indian country.

On the evening of the 18th we encamped on Pease river, having traveled up it for two days, and on the morning of the 19th I made an early start, leaving Captain Carrington's command in camp, some of his men having lost their horses during the night, and had proceeded but a few miles when I came upon a fresh trail, which I at once recognized as that of Indian spies, as it led to and from an elevated position on the prairie from which they could obtain a commanding view of the surrounding country. Hence I concluded their village could not be very far off, and after dispatching a man to inform Captain Carrington of the discovery I had made and requesting him to push forward with his company I left my company to proceed on the trail, while I rode forward with Sergeant Spangler to a prominent peak, just in advance of us, on the opposite side of the river. Upon reaching the desired position we were most agreeably surprised to find that we were in 200 yards of the village, consisting of eight or nine grass tents, which the Indians, fifteen in number, were just deserting. I gave the signal for the men to advance, and by the time they were fairly prepared for the engagement, the Indians, unconscious of our presence, had gotten out on a level plain and were never apprised of our approach until we were in 200 yards of them, in full charge, consequently many of them were killed before they could make any preparation for defense.

Several, however, were well mounted and succeeded in getting about two miles from the village before they were killed, fighting with great desperation all the while. Yet the surprise was so great to them, that they were never enabled to gain self-possession enough to shoot their arrows with much accuracy or precision, hence none of my command were hurt in the conflict. My horse and that of Private James Ireland were both wounded with arrows, twelve Indians were killed and the son of the chief and white woman and child taken prisoners.

I take great pleasure in saying that all my men acquitted themselves with great honor, proving worthy representatives of true Texas valor. Not more than twenty were able to get in the fight, owing to the starved and jaded condition of their horses, having had no grass after leaving the vicinity of Belknap, excepting "dry sedge," which the buffalo had refused, and a portion of the time we fed them on cotton wood bark.

During the engagement Lieutenant Killiher saw one Indian mounted on a fleet pony and in advance of the others, and supposing it to be a "warrior bold" he started in hot pursuit, eager for a single handed contest, but after a race of two miles, he came up with what he had supposed a formidable adversary and was just in the act of firing when a white woman threw up her baby and cried "Americano." She had been with them from childhood.

Lieutenant Sublett captured the son of the chief and took him up behind his saddle, but seeing there were others endeavoring to make their escape he threw him off, and he was afterwards taken up by F. C. Donohoe.

Lieutenant Somerville came very near being killed by the chief, who had dismounted, evidently determined to sell his life as dearly as possible. Lieutenant Somerville endeavored to charge by him and shoot, but his horse made a short halt, when the Indian, too sure of his victim, let fly his arrow just as Lieutenant Somerville fell over on the opposite side of his horse.

I had made a proposition to present the first man who should kill and scalp an Indian with a Colt's revolver, and after the battle it was awarded to Mr. C. R. Gray.

As for the three men of the Second Cavalry who were with me, it is enough to say that they were of H. Company, and under Sergeant Spangler, than whom a braver man never lived. This was one of the companies, which, while commanded by the intrepid Captain N. G. Evans, achieved for Major Van Dorn so many gallant and glorious victories. Much credit is due Captain Evans from the people of Texas for his willingness at all times to co-operate with those who desire to chastise the guilty savage.

The papers of Henry Riley, who, I believe, was killed about two months ago, were found in the possession of these Indians. Also a great many articles of clothing and the Bible of Mrs. Sherman, who was killed by them the last foray they made upon the settlements. About forty head of animals were taken, two of which were claimed by citizens belonging to Captain Carrington's company, one of them had been stolen six months and the other seven years.

The white woman informs me that the warriors had run the horses that had been stolen by them during their many visits to the frontier directly on to their main village, where there was at that time some traders from New Mexico, trading for stolen property taken from the citizens of Texas. Also, that thirty-eight warriors had left the camp or village three or four days before I reached it, for another stealing excursion in Texas, which proved correct, for I was informed as I came down that thirty-five were counted just above the Comanche Peak.

Respectfully, L. S. Ross,
Captain commanding Texas Rangers. To his Excellency, Genaral Sam Houston, Austin City, Texas.

Vandalism at Lagrange.

Lagrange, Tex., Feb. 20—The citizens of this quiet little city were shocked this morning when the sexton of the two pretty cemeteries telephoned to the Sheriff's office that some vandals had entered the old cemetery during the night and wrought havoc to some thirty of the pretty monuments and gravestones. What the motive could have been is a mystery, unless it was to create the great indignation that now exists.

The scene at the cemetery really beggars description. The vandals were not satisfied with merely toppling over a few monuments but continued in their work until some very costly statues and stones were not only turned over, but demolished as well. The damage will run high into the thousands.

Subscriptions are being taken raise funds to apprehend the culprits.

Car Loads Of Poultry.

Farm and Ranch.

While at Greenville, Texas, the writer visited a firm which has for years sent poultry cars to various parts of Texas, buying up poultry, eggs, etc., from farmers and merchants, making engagements ahead and notifying farmers by postal cards on what day the car would be at their town.

The bookkeeper gave me poultry receipts for 1907. Up to December 1st, 1907, they had paid out $298,083.19, and up to January 1st 1908, this was increased to $333,083.19. This is the amount that this firm alone has paid out for poultry and eggs during 1907. They ship principally to New York. I was surprised to learn that this firm had shipped into Texas two cars of eggs from Chicago and one car from Kansas to supply the demand in Texas for eggs—would it not pay to give poultry raising a little more attention?

27 Years Spent At One School.

New York, Feb. 25.—William Cullen Bryant Kemp has been a student at Columbia university for 27 years and he hopes to remain a student there for the rest of his life. He is finding difficulty now in discovering studies that he can take in keeping from graduating and being compelled to leave the university, but he knows most of the tricks of the curriculum and hopes to be able to keep going for another 27 years. At the beginning of his college course a relative of Kemp died and left him an annuity of $2500, to be paid while he remained in college and lived in a college dormitory. Kemp has forgotten most of the details of the bequest, but he gets his $2500, annually and that's enough. Having seen a great many classes graduate from Columbia he is perhaps the best known college man in the country. He is devoted to the university and no one takes more interest in its sports and its uudergraduate life.

Anarchists Claim Roosevelt.

New York, Feb. 22.—Alexander Berkman, the anarchist who shot Henry Freick, while addressing the socialist studies club, said that "President Roosevelt is one of us at heart, though he has not courage of his convictions as yet. Although he has many faults we must give him credit for having some sense at times. He has done much for our cause, but he did it for himself. He is selfish, his only aim is to overthrow the government for himself."

Plan War Upon Lumber Trust.

Austin, Tex., Feb. 25.—Attorneys General Hadley, Jackson and Davidson yesterday had a lengthy conference with Governor Campbell relative to the lumber trust. It is reported that Missouri, Kansas and Texas are planning a mutual campaign against this combination.

Quanah Tribune-Chief.

VOLUME XIX — QUANAH, HARDEMAN COUNTY, TEXAS, THURSDAY, OCTOBER 15, 1908 — NUMBER 2

The Cement City of Northwest Texas

Quanah has 4,500 inhabitants and growing rapidly. Good streets, fine business buildings and residences, cement sidewalks and crossings. Three railroads and more coming---Early History.

Quanah—which by the way is the best city in Texas west of Fort Worth, with Chillicothe coming along second—is located on Sections 141, 142, 149 and 150. which sections corner about where the present passenger depot of the Fort Worth & Denver Railroad stands. This city was named for Quanah Parker, chief of the Comanche Indians.

Prior to 1884 there was no Quanah—wasn't even anything to indicate where the town of Quanah would be located. It was all much alike. But Gen. G. M. Dodge had cast his eye along a possible line of railroad which should connect Denver and all the Northwest with Galveston and New Orleans and the Gulf of Mexico, that road being the Fort Worth & Denver. And he had had the survey made, and the stakes were set every 100 feet away up as far as Texline to which point the Union Pacific, Denver & Gulf was being built from Pueblo to form the connection link between the northwest and the Gulf. At that time the name of Quanah was not Quanah at all—it was proposed to call it the new town of Lubbock. However, when the townsite was finally located it was called Quanah.

In Nov. 1884, one of Sanger Bros. drummers happened to be at Wichita Falls, then the terminus of the Denver road. He was to make a drive to Vernon next day with his sample trunk and a four mule team. Judge W. J. Jones, who was in the store of a man named Goldsmith at the time the drummer mentioned his proposed trip, asked to go along.

The drummer was very anxious for company, and Judge Jones accompanied him. At Vernon Judge Jones found an old acquaintenance, J. A. Nabors, deputy county surveyor, who also had knowledge of where the new town in Hardeman county would be located, which was, as before stated, on a part of sections 141, 142, 149 and 150. Judge Jones filed on section 166, and having under the law of 1883 six months to move on, returned to Wood county to get together some supplies, etc., preliminary to returning and formally taking possession of his section. In January 1885 he came here accompanied by two negroes to help get the place in shape. When he arrived here, Judge Jones found his nearest neighbors would be Henry Kooch, who was living in the rock house on Box K ranch five miles away, Pick Gibson, then managing the Horse ranch where Acme is now located, and Joe Johnson lived near Chillicothe. Also the nearest postoffice was in a dugout at Chillicothe, the nearest physician at Vernon, and Wichita Falls was 85 miles distant by wagon road. A man named Satterwhite managed a stage line which operated between Wichita Falls and Pueblo, changing horses at the rock house, now Jno. R. Good's barn at his ranch on Groesbeck. Judge Jones wrote to Senator S. B. Maxey and asked that he try to get a postoffice established here, stating that the railroad would be built in shortly. Senator Maxey immediately took the matter up with Postmaster General Vilas who had an order issued creating this a special office.

J. A. Johnson filed on section 150, Captain Bill McDonald located in the Wanders creek district, and the Sands boys took up land southeast of Quanah. Satterwhite agreed to route his stage by Quanah and a crossing on Groesbeck was made for him near Acme.

Dr. G. H. Shaw opened a store in "town" and was appointed postmaster. His stock of groceries was small, and a few hungry men one day created a famine in Quanah by purchaisng all the eatables Shaw had on hand, causing that worthy to hitch up next morning and drive to Harrold for a supply.

The first building actually erected in Quanah was for J. A. Johnson; the second building was for Dr. Shaw in which the postoffice and a grocery were located. The first date on which town lots were sold was Dec. 1st, 1886. Lumber was hauled from Harrold, then the terminus of the road.

The first bank was operated by the Wood-Dixson Mercantile Co. on the corner of Johnson and South streets, in a frame building which has been replaced by a two story brick. In the street a little south of this building was a well and windmill, shown on page 11 of section 2, this issue.

On March 1st, 1887, first passenger train on the Fort Worth & Denver came into Quanah. The depot was a box car. and the present depot might be a heap better than it is without bankrupting the Denver road. It was hoped that Quanah would be the terminus of the railroad for some time. but that was not to be. The road built on, but Quanah was the "steel yard" for some time.

The first school in Quanah was opened in Oct., 1886. by Miss E McCann. Gen. Dodge made deed to two lots to Miss McCann, and a two room structure was built, one room being 16 by 22 feet. About a dozen pupils attended on the first day, which number increased to about 25 in a month. In this room were held for a considerable time, church and Sunday school services. The first church services held in Quanah, however, were held in Judge Jones' office, then located on the railroad right-of-way; the preacher was a missionary who passed through Quanah on horseback. The Baptists built the first church, which was all paid for before it was erected.

For a long time Quanah did some fierce standing still; she wouldn't grow at all except in age. Finally in Dec. 1889 a petition was presented to the County Commissioners Court in Margaret for an election for changing the county seat to Quanah. O! the howl that went up! A warrant was issued for the arrest of County Judge Combes, there were screeches of "fraud," etc., and Margaret blew up with a great noise. The election was ordered for Feb. 7, 1890. Judge M. M. Hankins, J. M. Doolen, D. G. Smith, J. K. Rambo, Sterling Ferguson and others who were living in Margaret, moved to Quanah. Others sold their property conditioned on Quanah being elected county seat.

At the time election was held, the law was to the effect that railroad men, and cowboys could vote in the town where they had been having their laundry work done for the preceeding six weeks. Quanah had become a prominent "laundry" town for the railroad men for some two or three months prior to the election.

It had been rumored that a solid train load of heelers were to be hauled up from Fort Worth to vote in the election, and of course the people in Margaret were very much wrought up, and had spotters in Quanah to watch what was being done, the intention being to enjoin the moving of the county seat if Quanah won it. As a matter of fact a large number of repeaters were brought up from Fort Worth, but Quanah talent loaded them on the train and shipped them back next morning before the polls were opened. However, during the day a large number of Irish railroad laborers who, under the law, could vote where they had their washing done, debarked at the coal chute and with a yell of "hooray for Quanah," proceeded to exercise their right of franchise, some voting so many times, it has been stated, that they had to ask whose name they were to vote next time. When the votes were canvassed by the county commissioners two days later, Quanah had 680 votes and Margaret 164. Margaret claimed that Quanah polled 480 fraudulent votes, but as the throwing out of the number still would have left Quanah 200 against Margaret's 164, no attempt was made to enjoin the commissioners from declaring the result, and immediately three big wagons were loaded with the county records and furniture and hauled to Quanah, the fireproof safes coming over later. The present office of the Tirbune-Chief was used for the court house and jail for some time. The population of Quanah then was estimated to be 1500.

When it came to building the business district of Quanah, choice fixed upon Mercer street and several stores were erected there. But some speculators fancying that they saw an opportunity for making 1000 per cent profit on their lots, pushed the prices up to $1500 per lot and even higher. Two lots did sell for $1750 each. Such high prices of course brought building to a standstill. The facts being made known to Gen. Dodge, he instructed his agent, Judge Jones, to act, and lots on Johnson street were sold to W. E. Johnson, Louis Simpson, Duncan G. Smith, S. W. Tenley, W. G. Lewis, J. A. Pardue and others at $600 for the lots corner of Clarke and Johnson, while inside lots on the west side of Johnson were sold at $200 each. The only stipulation made by Judge Jones was that the buyers should erect rock or brick buildings on the property. This started a rush to Johnson street and Mercer street property fell from one half to one quarter former prices.

The first newspaper printed in Quanah was the Advance, the office of which for a time was in a dugout on the north side, but which was later moved into a frame building located where the Quanah State Bank building now stands, a picture of which may be found on page 15, section 2 of this issue. The editor, proprietor, publisher, pressman, compositor and devil was W. W. West. Then the Settler made its appearance, and on Sept. 13, 1889 came the Quanah Quirt, of which J. D. Ballard was editor. The latter paper was taken over by D. E. Decker on April 4th, 1890, who changed its name to the Quanah Tribune on May 23rd following. The Quanah Chief was launched in 1890 by B. F. Colthar, and consolidated with the Tribune in 1897. The Tribune-Chief had a birthday last Thursday, having completed its 18th year of publication and starting on Vol. xix No. 1

The proprietor of the Tribune-Chief came to Quanah in August 1891, bought an interest in the Quanah Chief, bought the Tribune a few years later and has been continuously engaged in active newspaper work in this city, a little more than 17 years. If ever he has done any person a wrong through the columns of his newspaper, it has been unintentionally. With the exception of a few early years, the history of Quanah has been reflected in the columns of the Tribune-Chief.

Up to 1891 Quanah's hotels were not of much account, speaking from an architectural standpoint, and in Aug. 1890, work on The Quanah, a 3-story brick structure. with all rooms having an outside exposure. This hotel was opened to the public in the spring of 1891, by Mrs. J. D. Ballard under whose management The Quanah soon established a reputation as being the best kept hotel on the Fort Worth & Denver.

The greatest flood that visited this section for a century, according to the Indians, occurred in 1891. On the fourth of June a cloudburst took place between Gypsum and Kirkland, when it is said fourteen inches of rain fell within two hours. This sounds like exaggeration, still when we add that a man came very near drowning in front of the Quanah hotel, and that the band house on Mercer street was washed away and the band instruments scattered all over the country, the bass drum being found two days afterwards in a tree on Groesbeck, it seems some water fell within a short time.

The flood did a world of damage to crops, and the creeks and rivers rose to an unbelievable height. Every bridge in the county was washed away. Red River bridge, which had just been built by the Quanah citizens by subscription at a cost of nearly $20,000, was half destroyed, and most of the remaining lumber carried away by settlers, whose education in regard to others' property had been neglected.

Even the steel bridge across Pease river succumbed to the pressure of water, and no wonder, if one considers that a small creek like Groesbeck during this flood had become a raging torrent over half a mile wide.

In Quanah the damage was great, too; the dam below the Denver tank, had been washed out; railroad travelers had to be carried for days half a mile south to get around the draw.

Near Chillicothe three tramps, who had taken refuge upon the Wanders creek bridge were drowned.

In 1891 Quanah was a bustling little village, when the writer first saw it. A big fire in August had destroyed the buildings between Mundy's corner and the Sanders hardware store, and a number of prominent business men were temporarily doing business in the frame buildings that lined the east side of Mercer street. The Tribune had its office in a small house adjoining the old court house, while the Chief found quarters in the court house itself.

When we returned to Quanah in February 1892, the burned buildings had been replaced by better ones, but that summer fires laid waste the whole block north of the Cameron lumber yard. Only Fred Rip's store escaped. A drouth had set in, and the whole west was suffering from the low prices of farm products, and the effects of over speculation.

At Quanah, where the early town builders with splendid faith had laid off the third largest town plot in the United States, it was discovered that the corporation covered too much territory, and when suit was brought by an indignant taxpayer, the corporation was dissolved, fortunately not for long, and the town was re-organized on more modest lines.

Hard times were with us, good and strong. Hundreds of farmers unable to make a living, on account of poor crops, low prices, and long distance from market, had to leave this county. Others profiting by past mistakes, gave up exclusive wheat raising and commenced planting cotton, low priced as it was. saying there was more money for them in five cent cotton than sixty cent wheat. They began raising feedstuff, bought cattle and land, and the farmers who staid here during the hard times are nearly all independently rich now.

The cowmen, who were still here in large numbers, saw their opportunity to steal a march on the man with the hoe. They bought his land whenever he wanted to sell. They closed up roads, and assiduously spread the report that this was no farming country, and wherever a man made a failure of farming—which had happened rather often in those days, when bonus hunters made a pretense at farming, and few people. understood that the different climate called for a different method of farming from the East—the cowman found ample witnesses to prove any assertion derogatory to this country.

(continued on page 2)

A SECTIONAL VIEW OF THE BUSINESS DISTRICT OF QUANAH FROM THE COURTHOUSE

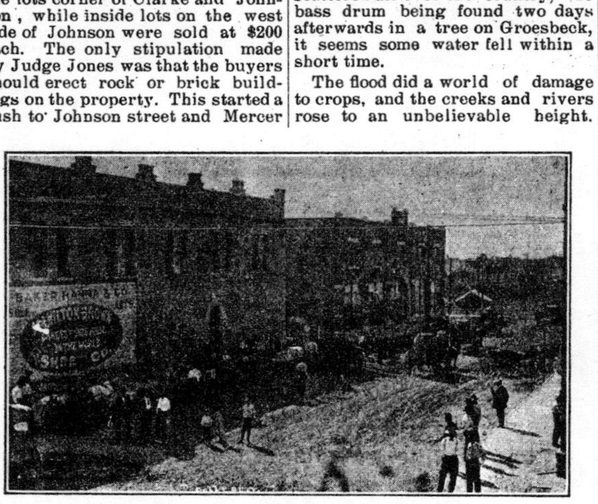

CLARK STREET LOOKING WEST FROM JOHNSON

W. E. SANDERS

REAL ESTATE DEALER

Has lived in Chillicothe for three years and is secretary and treasurer of Texas Real Estate and Industrial Association, holding the office for two years, he is also townsite agent for the Kansas City, Mexico & Orient Railway, Mr. Sanders claims to have sold more real estate than all other Chillicothe firms together during this time. ¶He was formerly a commercial traveler and consequently is a hustler. He has listed on his books the best of ranches, town lots and new town propositions and takes pleasure in giving information to those who call or write him. Reference to the Herring & Laird Banking Company and the many satisfied citizens he has transacted business for. Write him or call for anything in real estate. Chillicothe, Texas

LLOYD & SWIM

REAL ESTATE DEALERS

LLOYD & SWIM

S. E. SWIM and J. B. LLOYD

The above photograph represents J. B. Lloyd and S. E. Swim. Mr. Lloyd has resided in this town (Chillicothe) six years, and has been in the Real Estate business four years. He has sold a great amount of farm and ranch lands, and city property. In all these transactions the purchasers have made more money than could have been made in the old states by years of hard work and the strictest of economy, property having doubled in most cases and trebled in some. In fact the above man has doubled on all that he has held in his own name.

S. E. Swim is a new comer in this town, having lately bought an interest with Mr. Lloyd. Mr. Swim has lived in the State forty-one years and during his business life has held places of trust in the Insurance business, representing the best and giving his best to the work. His reputation is such that any transactions intrusted to him will receive prompt and careful attention, and his best endeavors, and he or his partner will stand any investigation. The land, lots or improved property, are just as represented and in fact they handle the best lands and will work to your interest.

Reference---Any Bank or Business House in Chillicothe, Texas

REAL ESTATE DEALERS

CHILLICOTHE TEXAS

Glover & Baker

GENERAL BLACKSMITHS

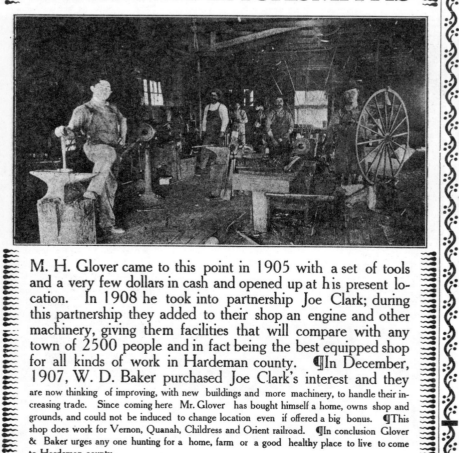

M. H. Glover came to this point in 1905 with a set of tools and a very few dollars in cash and opened up at his present location. In 1908 he took into partnership Joe Clark; during this partnership they added to their shop an engine and other machinery, giving them facilities that will compare with any town of 2500 people and in fact being the best equipped shop for all kinds of work in Hardeman county. ¶In December, 1907, W. D. Baker purchased Joe Clark's interest and they are now thinking of improving, with new buildings and more machinery, to handle their increasing trade. Since coming here Mr. Glover has bought himself a home, owns shop and grounds, and could not be induced to change location even if offered a big bonus. ¶This shop does work for Vernon, Quanah, Childress and Orient railroad. ¶In conclusion Glover & Baker urges any one hunting for a home, farm or a good healthy place to live to come to Hardeman county.

Anderson & Farrington

T. W. Anderson, of the above firm, was born in Texas fifty years ago, and has been in the wholesale and grain business for fifteen years in central Texas, and in same capacity here two years. "I believe that Hardeman county has more inducements to offer settlers than any county in Texas, and that being able to raise garden truck, fruits and all other crops, such as corn, cotton, wheat and oats, with a good market, splendid schools and churches, that no one will miss anything that is conducive to their happiness or welfare, and that we have as good a class of citizens as lives any place on earth." On Sept. 1 a partnership was formed with H. C. Farrington who is a native Texan, born in Limestone county in 1874 and moved to Hardeman county in 1891 and lived here ever since. "When I first came to this county there was nothing raised but wheat and cattle. A few years later I began raising Short Horn cattle and this is where I made my start. As soon as I had made good money on the cattle, I bought a small tract of land for $4.00 per acre, and commenced stock farming which I found to be very profitable. In a few years I began buying grain and moved to Chillicothe, and have lived here ever since. Now my land is worth $30 per acre and I have bought another tract joining the town, making 760 acres in all I own. I am handling Real Estate in partnership with Mr. Anderson, having just begun, but I believe the real estate in this county will readily sell for the prices asked for it and will not be long about it."

We have the pleasure to refer you to Herring & Laird Banking Co. Bank of Chillicothe or any newspaper in said County.

HARRY KOCH

To readers of the Quanah Tribune-Chief:

This is an uncommon communication; we realize it. But we have demanded of the editor of the Tribune-Chief space in the Booster Edition for an honest expression of our regard for one of our daily associates—Harry Koch. Mr. Koch will not even have the privilege of reading the proof of what we have to say and will know nothing of its sentiment until he reads it in his own paper.

Harry Koch came to live in Quanah in August 1891. He is a Hollander by birth, but a truer American and citizen never lived. In all the seventeen years he has lived in Quanah, he ever has been a splendid citizen, a good neighbor and an honest man. He ever has been intolerant of wrong as he saw it, ofttimes to his own financial detriment. Optimistic, he always saw the rosy side for Quanah and for Hardeman county. In the lean years when everyone was blue, Harry Koch was as cheerful through the columns of his paper as if we were all wallowing in wealth. His courage never weakened, no matter if at one time he had less than $3.00 between himself and bankruptcy. As we say, we have known him in lean years when the country was poverty stricken, and we may have smiled at his predictions that Quanah one day would be a bustling city. But those predictions, shouted over and over for seventeen years, are today come true. Many of us have known Harry Koch from the day he first set foot in Quanah, one of us has known him twenty years, none of us have known him less than ten years, and we are glad to be able to attest our high regard and love for him in this manner.

Fred Chase
Stiteler & Carroll Co.
W. J. McDonald
W. R. DuPuy
Bob Dawson
J. J. Specht
Joe Cunningham
W. J. Jones
J. L. Elbert
W. J. Williams
T. J. Rodgers
J. T. McCullough
Geo. Rowden
J. E. Woolbright
H. B. Warde
M. M. Hankins
J. H. Wilson
J. E. Ledbetter
J. B. Goodlett
Jas. A. Radford
B. F. Walker
J. C. Marshall
J. R. Sanders
J. B. Robertson
H. W. Martin
D. E. Decker
F. O. Griffith
D. F. Griffith
W. G. Crowder
E. I. Flynt
M. E. Kerrigan
J. W. Odell
T. S. Hanna
W. G. Mulkey
L. E. Robbins
Fred Rips
C. W. Hodge
J. C. Ferguson
F. D. Clisbee
L. F. Reeves
L. H. Cope
Alex M. Lewis
W. E. Givens
W. D. Jordan.
Gus Gober
Pat Dooling

RESIDENCE OF W. R. DuPUY

L. C. BRADLEY'S RESIDENCE

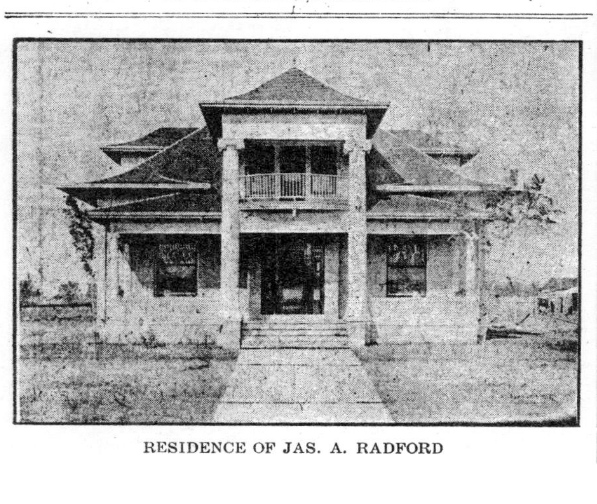

RESIDENCE OF JAS. A. RADFORD

In connection with the milling and grain business A. Moseley & Bro. own the Lake View Hereford farm, located a few miles south of Quanah in the Wanders Creek valley. The above picture was taken on the 4th inst., and shows Beau Carlos 246452, a thousand dollar male who heads their herd of 100 registered cows. This bull has no superior in the state, having taken first prize at the Fat Stock Show at Fort Worth last year, and at the National Feeders and Breeders show this year. Young stock for sale.

THE TRIBUNE-CHIEF FORCE

Standing, left to right—Philip Stovall, foreman; L. A. Dyer, pressman; Miss Y Z Hamblen, simplex operator; Tim Stovall, devil; Richard Box, job compositor; Chas. Stephenson, ad man. Sitting—Fred Chase, special writer; Harry Koch, "the Old Man;" Harry C. Moore, solicitor

JUDGE W. J. JONES

Judge W. J. Jones may well be called the father of Quanah, for he has been here longer than almost anybody, and takes more interest in the growth and prosperity of the town than anybody we know of.

Coming to this country in 1888 from Wood county, where he had served three terms as county judge, he soon became a prime factor in the upbuilding of this county. Judge Jones was one of General Dodge's most trusted

agents; a friendship existing between the two that dated back from the days of the civil war.

Through Judge Jones the General has always been kept in close touch with this town and country.

Liberal and fair in his views, hospitable and genial, Judge Jones always has been one of the most popular men in this country. He has been mayor of Quanah, judge of Hardeman, and is at present in the real estate business.

END IN SIGHT

After Six Weeks the Tribune-Chief Force Finishes the Booster Edition and Feels Thankful its no Worse

At last we are now getting ready to print the fourth and last section of the Booster Edition, and as the Tribune-Chief force is pretty well all in, after many nights of over work, everybody in the office will feel relieved when the big job is finally out of the way.

For a small printing office it was a big thing to undertake, at least within the limited scope of time at our command. When the invitation from the commercial club to get out a special edition was first received on September 2, we had a great deal of other work on hand, that had to be gotten out of the way first.

With an edition of this kind hundreds of people had to be seen, information gleaned, advertising secured, etc., which all requires much time and effort before we could get to the mechanical part of the work. After a number of photos had been secured, we experienced much delay on the part of two engraving houses, which were unable to turn out the work within as short a space of time as we had hoped for. There were other things causing delay, but by patient pegging away we managed to get out the issue on time, and of the size we had set out originally to make it, though at times it looked impossible to do so. Only for the fact that the editor was aided by an exceptionally good office force, who scorned to sleep as long as there was work to be done, did we manage to get out as large a paper in so short a time.

We now feel that something has been accomplished in which we shall take pride for years to come. Few printing offices in Texas could have printed over four tons of newspaper in such a short time, like the Tribune-Chief office has done. And to those good friends in Quanah and Chillicothe who enabled us to get out an issue like this we are going to show that their money was well spent, and is going to bring them big returns.

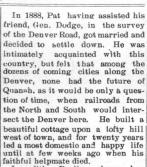

PAT DOOLING

The Tribune-Chief man had considerable difficulty in persuading Pat Dooling to sit for his picture, as the oldtimer objected to what he called advertising himself. Besides he never had sat for his picture since a tintype of his had been made when, at the head of a scouting party, he had started to fetch in the body of General Burns, who had been killed by the Indians in 1868.

From the above it is easy to surmise that our townsman, during his career of sixty-odd summers, passed through an eventful life. Born in Ohio from Irish parentage, he enlisted during the civil war, when still a boy. After the war he went to Mexico to fight for Maximillian, came back to become a union scout, and participated in a thousand skirmishes with Indians. A man of courage and rare judgment, he was a favorite among the old Union generals, who entrusted him with the most hazardous and delicate tasks.

In making horseback surveys for the T. P. and other early roads in Western Texas, New Mexico and Arizona, Dooling made his mark in the annals of the Great Southwest. And little do present day people dream of the dangers that beset the traveler before Pat Dooling and other men like him, made traveling safe in the West after undergoing hardships that called for hearts of oak and muscles of steel.

In 1888, Pat having assisted his friend, Gen. Dodge, in the survey of the Denver Road, got married and decided to settle down. He was intimately acquainted with this country, but felt that among the dozens of coming cities along the Denver, none had the future of Quanah, as it would be only a question of time, when railroads from the North and South would intersect the Denver here. He built a beautiful cottage upon a lofty hill west of town, and for twenty years led a most domestic and happy life until at few weeks ago when his faithful helpmate died.

In politics Dooling always has been republican of the uncompromising kind. Like all western men he was loyal to his friends and expected loyalty in return. His tact made him a natural politician, while his good judgment made him a leader wherever he went. In a strictly democratic community he was alderman for long years, and could have held the job for life, nad he so chosen.

In 1896 Pat stampeded the republican state convention by casting the proxies of over eighty western counties, after which he ran the convention to suit himself. An ardent McKinley man, he had himself elected delegate to the St. Louis convention that nominated his favorite candidate, and while there the St. Louis and New York papers were full of pictures and write-ups of the Quanah man.

For years he has been claim agent for the Denver road, and the many thousands he has saved his company by his handling of claims has made him one of their most valued and trusted employees.

PROF. C. G. GREEN

Superintendent of the Quanah Public Schools

DR. A. J. BALL

The above his a very good likeness of Dr. A. J. Ball, the oldest member of the firm of Drs. Ball, Frizzell & Hargraves.

Dr. Ball came to Quanah from Corinth, Ark., a little over eight years ago. Being a man of sunny, genial disposition, and a good physician

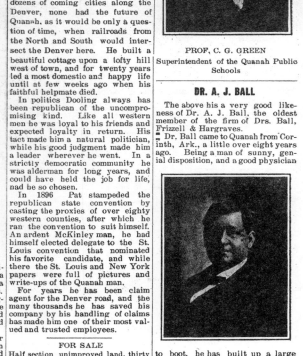

to boot, he has built up a large practice. Last spring he associated himself with Dr. T. D. Frizzell, a prominent medical man from Powell, Texas, and this fall they strengthened their already strong firm, still more by taking in Dr. Hargrave, one of the best known surgeons of East Texas, who came here from Sulphur Springs recently.

Section of Huge Crowd Before News Building Yesterday to Watch Houdini's Feat

QUICKLY FREES SELF FROM STRAITJACKET

HARRY HOUDINI DOES FEAT HANGING HEAD DOWN BEFORE NEWS BUILDING.

BIG CROWD SEES STUNT

Probably 10,000 Persons Fill Street. Liberator Takes 2¼ Minutes to Work Off Garment.

Houdini escaped in two minutes and fifteen seconds.

Ten thousand people saw Houdini liberate himself from a strait-jacket yesterday at noon while suspended head downward fifty feet above the sidewalk in front of The News Building at Commerce and Lamar streets. Ten thousand cheered him. Houdini, who is appearing at the Majestic Theater, extricated himself seemingly without difficulty from the close confinement of the heavy leather and canvas garment.

The crowd gathered to watch Houdini filled Lamar street from Commerce past the Main street intersection, making a solid lane of humanity nearly 100 feet wide and more than a block long.

Houdini had announced previously that he had "graduated" from strait-jacket feats, and the manner in which he slipped out of the jacket yesterday showed that he is an adept at the art. Thousands from all points of Dallas came to The News Building presumably expecting to watch a man struggle hard and long to extricate himself from a garment from which it is said no prisoner or insane person has ever liberated himself.

Hoisted on Time.

Exactly at 12:30 o'clock, the time announced for the feat, Harry Houdini was hoisted by a block and tackle until he was even with the third floor windows of The News Building. Immediately he began to squirm. At first the straps bound the performer so tightly that his struggles were hardly discernible to the 20,000 eyes focused upon him. Gradually the extent of his contortions increased, and suddenly he held up both of his hands—free. The crowd cheered. Only two minutes had elapsed, but the spectators had another surprise in store. With his hands free, although they were still inside of the strait-jacket arms, the man had little difficulty in unbuckling the straps buckled tightly about his body. Fifteen seconds after his arms were free Houdini threw the strait-jacket to the ground.

Ten thousand people cheered, and many seemed unwilling to believe that such a feat had been accomplished within such an extremely short time. Houdini could have struggled for half an hour to make the spectators think it was extremely difficult work, but he evidently preferred to show just how easily and how quickly he could get out of a strait-jacket, a feat he has been performing successfully for many years.

Right in the midst of the crowd Sergeant C. D. McKeehan and Traffic Officer W. H. Tonn of the Dallas police department had buckled the jacket upon Houdini. With a rope tied to his feet he had been intensely silent and still until it became evident that he was succeeding in his effort, when cheering began and continued until Houdini was free.

The crowd began gathering before noon, and at 12:30 o'clock there was not even "standing room only" within view of the feat. Many of the spectators were women.

TO SEEK EXIT FROM BIG BOX.

Harry Houdini Accepts Challenge of Expert Packers, Who Will Nail Him in Heavy Case.

Under challenge from expert packers employed by Butler Brothers, Harry Houdini, "genius of escape," will be nailed into an especially constructed box upon the stage of the Majestic Theater at tonight's show, and it will be up to him to extricate himself without leaving any trace of his means of exit. The challengers of Houdini are Thomas B. Jackson, G. B. Cone, Le Mar Ramel, R. H. Brooke, G. C. Sams and J. D. Barlow. The box in which Houdini will be nailed has been constructed by the challengers from two-inch-thick lumber. Before Houdini is secured in the packing case the box will be renailed in order to forestall any preparation that the "arch mystifier" may have made while the box has been on exhibition in the lobby of the Majestic. A committee from the audience will be invited upon the stage to witness the conduct of the test. Houdini has escaped from every device that has been brought forth to test his ability as a self liberator. He is known all over the world as "The Elusive American" and "The Arch Mystifier." He claims an undefeated record to date.

DALLAS ZIONISTS MEET TONIGHT.

Musical Program to Follow Business Session at Y. M. H. A. Hall.

The Dallas Zionist Society will meet at 8 o'clock tonight in the Young Men's Hebrew Association Hall. The business session will be followed by a program, including a piano selection, "Mendelssohn's Song Without Words," by Mrs. Robert Roth; "The Life of Mendelssohn," a paper, by Mrs. J. A. Rosenfield, and an original poem by Charles Klein.

The society is arranging to bring to Dallas for a series of lectures Dr. Stephen S. Wise and Dr. Magnew, well-known Eastern orators.

AD MEN ADVOCATE ADVERTISING LAW

WEEKLY SESSION OF DALLAS LEAGUE DEVOTED TO DISCUSSION OF EDWARDS BILL.

The bill recently introduced in the House of Representatives by Charles G. Edwards of Georgia, which in effect, if passed, will be a companion law with reference to advertising to the law now obtaining with reference to use of the United States mails, was discussed by the Dallas Ad League at its weekly luncheon yesterday.

The committee on honest advertising submitted its report through its chairman, J. C. Phelps, recommending the passage of such a law. Mr. Phelps pointed out that under the terms of a written contract, the purchaser now has recourse by law if the facts in that contract are misrepresented. He said that there ought to be a law that will protect in the same manner the man who buys an article on the representation of its seller in his advertising if that representation proves to be false. Mr. Phelps said the operation of the Edwards Bill said the operation of the purchaser this protection. In discussing the question, Mr. Phelps pointed out that in this day of specialization in every line of business, no man is in position to know the details of construction or to discover the faults of the numerous articles he must buy. The man who specializes in the manufacture of automobiles knows better than any other man the worth of the article he produces, and the purchaser of that article must rely to a large extent on the representation of its worth set forth by the manufacturer in his advertising, Mr. Phelps said. Therefore, the passage of such a law is timely and advisable, he concluded.

Copies of the Edwards Bill were circulated among the members. The bill provides a penalty of $1,000 or imprisonment for not more than one year for any person who knowingly circulates, through the United States mails, in whatever form, any advertising that is false or misleading.

Talks were made by several members on the subject. [illegible]enator McNealus said he endorses the [illegible]rts of the league for truthful advertising and would support any legislation toward that end. W. H. Benners of The Dallas News said his firm has turned down as much as $40,000 worth of improper advertising in one year, and that carrying bad advertising is a bad business policy.

J. H. Foreman of the Dallas Dispatch and Herman Philipson of the Times Herald made short talks favoring the passage of such a law as that contemplated.

"This is a day when the minds of men turn largely toward public service and betterment of social conditions," said Will T. Henry, speaking from a legal standpoint. "but I believe those men who are bound together with the purpose of raising the standards of advertising in the daily papers and magazines are doing a noble service."

R. E. L. Saner expressed himself as being heartily in favor of honest advertising, and in favor of a law to that end if such a law is made effective.

AUTOMOBILE CLUB MEETING.

Election of Officers Is Scheduled to Take Place at Luncheon Today.

Election of officers for the year is the order of business at the weekly luncheon of the Dallas Automobile Club at the Oriental Hotel today at 12:15 o'clock. The men nominated last week will be voted on, and it is expected they will all be elected unanimously. President Fred E. Johnson does not anticipate any dark horses.

The names to be voted on today are Z. E. Marvin, president; W. C. Rice, vice president; F. R. Slater, vice president; W. M. Freeman, secretary-treasurer; S. H. Boren, Frank G. Jester, E. T. Peter, directors for a term of three years.

The remainder of the meeting will be devoted to speeches by the incoming and outgoing administrations.

Donations for today will be five one-gallon cans of automobile oil and five one-gallon cans of cup grease.

WILL BANQUET NEWCOMERS.

Local Bankers to Honor Judge W. F. Ramsey and Edward Rotan of Federal Reserve Bank of Dallas.

Judge W. F. Ramsey, newly appointed chairman of the Federal Reserve Bank and Federal reserve agent at Dallas, and Edward Rotan of Waco, recently named as vice chairman of the board of directors of the Federal Reserve Bank of Dallas, will be the guests of honor at a banquet to be arranged within the next few days by the Dallas Clearing House Association. Plans for the dinner were left to the discretion of a committee composed of Edwin Hobby, L. L. Henderson and Tucker Royall.

This same committee was also named to prepare plans for the entertainment of the meeting of the Texas Bankers' Association, fifth district, at Dallas on Feb. 15.

Trinity Lodge, I. O. O. F., Election.

Trinity Lodge No. 198, I. O. O. F., installed the following officers last night: C. A. Taylor, noble grand; W. H. Kelley, vice grand; F. T. Payne, recording secretary; G. W. Godfrey, financial secretary; H. J. Emmins, treasurer; W. E. Tribble, warden; O. F. Heath, chaplain; S. W. Clark, right supporter to noble grand; T. W. Hallmark, left supporter to noble grand; Leon Taylor, right supporter to vice grand; James McLure, left supporter to vice grand.

Houdini Liberating Self From Strait-Jacket While High in Air.

AT THE PICTURE SHOWS TODAY.

Hippodrome Theater

Playing a return engagement by special request for today only at the Hippodrome, Edna Mayo will appear in "The Blindness of Virtue." Miss Mayo shows to advantage in the role of the innocent, unsuspecting girl. Opposite Miss Mayo Bryant Washburn, prominent Essanay actor, plays.

"The Blindness of Virtue" tells a tale of human nature. The Hon. Archibald Graham is expelled from college and his indignant father sends him to a little English village to study under the Rev. Harry Pemberton. Misunderstood by his father he has grown up somewhat reckless and dissipated. All this is changed under the tutelage of the minister.

Effie Pemberton is a young girl of 17. She has never been told of the fundamental principles of life and has been brought up in innocence and ignorance. She and Archie become fast friends.

Winstanley, a friend of Archie's, comes to the village to visit him. He is a shallow youth with no moral principles. He meets Mary Ann, a beautiful girl, the daughter of a washwoman in the village. She longs for pretty clothes and all the gayeties she has been denied, and being as innocent of life as Effie, is persuaded by Winstanley to elope to London with him.

Archie follows them with the intention of saving her from his friend. In this he fails. He returns to the village early in the morning. Effie, in her innocence, rushes to his room in her kimono, to tell him how glad she is to see him again. He tries to get her out of the room but she refuses to go.

The minister bursts into the room and accuses Archie of evil intentions. Archie, in honest indignation, tells the minister some wholesome truths about his leaving his daughter in such total ignorance, which opens his eyes. Mary Ann returns home, a wreck of her former self, and tells the minister her story.

Pemberton and his wife then awake. Effie is told the truths of life. Finally Archie and Effie discover that they have been in love and receive the blessing of her parents.

Old Mill Theater.

Alexander Bisson's "Madame X" has been screened by the Pathe company. With the original star in the title role, it will show at the Old Mill today.

Dorothy Donnelly created the role of Madame X in the stage play that ran seven consecutive seasons in New York City and broke all records in box receipts in that city. So when the play was to be screened, the title role went to Dorothy Donnelly. Her wonderful interpretation of the heart-hungry wife who sought companionship elsewhere when her husband refused it, and who, when turned from her home and little son, was aided by circumstance and society in falling gradually to the lowest depths, is the same on the screen as it was on the stage. Edwin Fosberg, Ralph Morgan, John Bowers, Robert Fisher, and Charles Brunnell are in the supporting cast.

Soon after marriage, Jacqueline finds that her husband does not give full measure for the worship she accords him. Absorbed in his career as a lawyer, he neglects her more and more until the overflow of her heart is caught by another. For one mistake the husband, Floriet, sends her from home and away from her little son. Abandoned and heartbroken she tries to find work, but work is scarce. One thing only is plentiful—lovers. And from one to the other of these she is finally obliged to go until she reaches the lowest depths. Then in a curious mingling of lives, she meets her son. Rather than have him learn of her shame, the mother, now known as Madame X, kills a man who would have told. Brought before the Judge for trial, the unknown woman gives no name but Madame X. The climax is unbelievably pathetic and leaves no heart untouched. "Madame X" will play the rest of this week at the Old Mill.

Crystal Theater.

"Man and Morality," a special three-reel feature at the Crystal today, offers a new solution to an old problem,—whether there should be one standard for women and an entirely different moral code for men, a question argued by moralists for years. Both sides have found champions for their own individual theories. In nearly every case wherein the man has sowed his wild oats he demands in the woman he wants for his mate one free from any suggestion of a past. Such a man was Henry Anstruther, the protagonist in this drama of emotions, "Man and Morality." He loved Rosemary Trent with a rare devotion, but had his own narrow standards of morals where woman was concerned.

He insisted that the woman of his choice be without suspicion. When Rosemary confesses an indiscretion of her early girlhood, Henry bitterly casts aside her love to satisfy his self-conscious pride. In an effort to forget Rosemary, he goes to the Philippines. There he meets a dusky native dancer, who bears a striking resemblence to Rosemary. Here he is confronted with a problem, which confronts almost every man sometime during his lifetime. The story is handled in a masterly manner by Harry Myers, assisted by Miss Rosemary Theby. Critics say it is among the best screen plays produced.

The Animated Weekly, on the same program, consists of some interesting scenes of activities aboard Henry Ford's peace ship, and the latest winter fashions, showing newest sport coats. The models are Universal stars, Mary Fuller, Edna Hunter, and Dorothy Phillips.

Queen Theater.

The very fact that many of the experiences of the young opera singer, Renee, as told in the Lasky picture, "Temptation," featuring Miss Geraldine Farrar and showing at the Queen for a return engagement today, are the true life experiences of the famous star, makes the play of double interest. This American girl, the world's most famous grand opera singer, can not but have sympathy for the character she portrays. The play is the second Farrar picture produced by the same company and directed by the same men as "Carmen." Supporting Miss Farrar are Pedro de Cordoba, the dashing toreador of "Carmen;" Theodore Roberts, Elsie Jane Wilson, Raymond Hatton and Anita King.

The young American singer, Renee Dupree, and Julian, a composer and violinist, are devoted to each other, and while they are both poor and ambitious, they expect to marry as soon as Julian is successful in selling the opera on which he spends all his time. Renee's wonderful voice attracts Otto Muller, the impresario, and he makes her an offer of a trial in opera singing. She makes a splendid success of the role of Madame Butterfly, and Muller offers her a fabulous salary and a gorgeous suite of rooms. But when the girl learns why these things are offered, she spurns Muller and returns to Julian. Muller follows and learning of the love affair, threatens to kill their careers. As good as his word, Muller prevents the sale of Julian's opera and neither artist can find work in the professions. Julian falls very ill and the doctors say it is from worry; to save his life Renee goes to Muller and agrees to pay if he will produce Julian's opera. He does so and Renee, in the title role, wins fame for herself and Julian, who is now about well. Then she goes to pay the price to Muller. The sudden turn in affairs that leads to a startling climax is the sensation of the story. "The Temptation" will show at the Queen no more after today's performance.

Washington Theater.

"The Fourth Estate," declared to be one of the best and most interesting newspaper stories ever written, will start a four days' engagement at the Washington Theater today. Miss Ruth Blair, Clifford Bruce and Samuel Ryan are seen in the leading roles. Many newspaper dramas have been produced and placed on the moving picture market, but few are as true to life as "The Fourth Estate." The atmosphere of newspaperdom has been filmed. The scenes are true to life. The entire plant of the Chicago Herald was used in the making of the production. The story tells of a man who amasses a fortune and buys a paper and exposes a political Judge who has impoverished widows and orphans. The making up of a newspaper from beginning to end is shown and the climax is one very seldom seen in motion pictures.

TROLLEY POLES BEING REMOVED.

Temporary Roadbed for Electric Cars Toward Oak Cliff Expected to Be Completed Tomorrow Night.

Within the next forty-eight hours Dallas-Oak Cliff street cars and interurban cars will pass almost within an arm's length of a row of small houses that face east on Jefferson street. The west track used for outgoing cars will be shifted more than fifty feet from its old position for temporary use, while the new electric line viaduct is being erected by the Northern Texas Traction Company over the railroad tracks that lead into the new Union Station.

Yesterday workmen made tangible headway in removing several hundred feet of trolley and feed wire poles from Jefferson street. These poles were placed on private property between Jefferson and Houston streets. The overhead wire will be placed today, and the work is expected to be completed by tomorrow night.

Track men also put in several hours during the day, removing ballast and loosening ties from the roadbed. This work will continue until a point is reached where the fill starts, a few feet of the railroad crossings.

The two-story frame building that will serve as offices for the engineers and paymaster of the viaduct construction was completed yesterday and Engineer Gardner has removed his headquarters there.

It was announced yesterday that the contract will probably be let today for the purchase of steel for the viaduct. Quick delivery will be one of the specifications of the order.

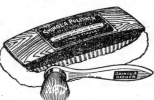

CALIFORNIA FORECAST
Los Angeles and vicinity: Fair Thursday, cloudy or fog in morning; light southerly wind.
San Francisco and vicinity: Fair Thursday except for cloudiness or fog in morning; light southerly wind.
COAST TEMPERATURES
Los Angeles..... 61 San Francisco... 54
Portland .... 51 Spokane 44
Sacramento ...... 65 Tacoma 45
San Diego....... 57

Los Angeles Examiner
AN AMERICAN PAPER FOR THE AMERICAN PEOPLE
The Great Newspaper of The Great Southwest

VOL. XIII—NO. 96 Registered in U. S. Patent Office Official Forecast—Fair LOS ANGELES, MARCH 16, 1916 THURSDAY PRICE 2½ CENTS Delivered to Subscribers 5 CENTS On News Stands and Trains

INVADING U. S. ARMY HEADS FOR CASAS GRANDES

U. S. TROOPS WHICH CROSSED BORDER, UNDER GENERAL PERSHING, TO BEGIN DRIVE FOR CAPTURE OF VILLA, "DEAD OR ALIVE."

Copyright International Film Service Photo.

CARRANZA TROOPS CO-OPERATE WITH ADVANCE IN MEXICO

Riding at Head of Thirteenth Cavalry, General Pershing Leads 4000 Men Across Line; Forced Marches for Four Days Are Planned by Leader

UNREST OF PEONS CAUSES APPREHENSION AT BORDER

BULLETIN

EL PASO, March 15.—From confidential Government sources it has been learned that General Pershing plans to reach Casas Grandes in four days. The distance is a little more than 100 miles. This will necessitate forced marches of twenty-five miles or better each day. This would indicate that the first effort of the American forces will be to rescue the 500 Mormons reported imperiled at Casas Grandes.

By H. H. Stansbury
(BY INTERNATIONAL NEWS SERVICE)

EL PASO, Texas, March 15.—(*By Telephone and Courier From Columbus*)—The United States army expeditionary forces organized to capture Francisco Villa crossed the border into Mexico just before noon today.

Brigadier General John J. Pershing, riding at the head of the Thirteenth cavalry, led the expedition from Columbus along the cattle trail which crosses the theoretical border line at a point known as "the gap." The Mexican town on the opposite side is Palomas.

The censorship still in force prohibits the announcement of the strength of the expedition except to say it is approximately 4000 mounted men. With pack train and munition train attendants this number is increased several hundred.

The advance guard was followed by the aeroplane corps. The flying machines were loaded on forty huge motor trucks. These were followed by another motor truck train which carried light artillery and ammunition. Next came the hospital corps. The supply train, consisting of both motor trucks and packmules, brought up the rear.

SPECIAL TRAIN CARRIES RESERVE WATER SUPPLY

When the head of the column was well across the border a halt was made to permit the supply trucks to catch up. Many of these were held at Columbus for the supplies which arrived at the last moment. The column was actually in motion before the last trainload of provisions reached Columbus.

A reserve supply of water for the troops, who know but little of the character of the country into which they are going, is being carried in a special train of tank cars. Every motor tank car in this part of the country, such as is used for street sprinkling purposes, has been impressed into service.

Oliver L. Dawson, a chemist, who belongs to the United States customs service, is one of the most important members of the advance guard. Orders have been issued by General Pershing that no water shall be used, either by the men or by the animals, unless it has been analyzed for poisons. This precaution was taken through fear that the Mexicans would put cyanide in the limited supply of water that the desert offered. This deadly poison is easily obtainable in this section and its use is one of the well known tricks of Mexican warfare.

OFFICERS AND TROOPS IN HIGH SPIRITS

C. K. Warren, a Michigan millionaire, who owns and spends the greater part of his time on the Alamo-Huacora ranch near Hachita, N. M., was one of the first Americans to reach El Paso from Columbus after the expedition started. He said:

> I saw the last of the Pershing column passing through the gap which is just half way between Columbus and Palomas as I started away. Earlier in the day I talked with some of the officers. They were all in high good humor and the troops seemed in excellent shape.
>
> I asked one officer what time they expected to cross the border. He seemed to voice the spirit of the command.
>
> "We are going to pick the border up and take (

CANAL WILL REOPEN BY APRIL 15TH

Restoration of Waterway Declared as Feat Only Second to Building of Mighty Project; Millions of Tons of Rock, Earth Moved

(By Associated Press)

WASHINGTON, March 15.—An official prediction that the Panama Canal will be reopened by April 15 for the passage of deep-draft vessels was announced tonight by the War Department.

Re-opening of the great waterways is regarded as an engineering feat second only to the construction of the canal. Millions of tons of rock and earth have been torn our of the collapsed excavations. New dredges of a size and capacity never before employed have labored night and day for months. Steam shovels have driven their way into the obstructions wherever there was ground sufficiently firm to hold them.

In the meantime the construction work at the terminals and about the locks has proceeded without pause. When the canal is re-opened it will have advanced in equipment far beyond the point it had reached when the slides began.

Rainfall Blamed and Drainage Urged as Remedy

Conditions in Gaillard cut, scene of the principal earth movement which blocked the waterway last fall, are regarded as justifying the forecast.

Colonel Harding, Acting Governor of the canal zone, telegraphed the War Department today as follows:

> Conditions in Gaillard cut justify predictions that canal will be available for ships of 30-foot draught on April 15, subject to probable temporary delays thereafter to meet exigencies of dredging fleet in completing canal to full width and depth and in removing shoals that may possibly develop.

Until this report came, canal officials had refused since the closure to make any estimate of the probable date of re-opening.

Colonel Harding's telegram is taken to mean that, short of another great movement of earth, the canal will be practically in full operation again after April 15.

Ex-Convict With Prison Petitions Urges Prohibition

(By Associated Press)

ALBANY, N. Y., March 15.—Petitions said to contain the names of 1000 inmates of Sing Sing, Auburn and Dannemora State prisons were filed with a legislative committee today by an ex-convict, who appeared at a hearing in support of the Wilson-Fullagar State-wide prohibition bill. The former prisoner, whose name was not disclosed, was introduced as No. 11,221." He said that if the future of the bill lay with prison inmates it would be made law in ten minutes.

The former prisoner said:

"Most of these men know the effects of intemperance. They know it was intemperance largely that put them where they are."

Samuel Gompers, president of the American Federation of Labor, in opposing the measure, said that prohibition was not the cure for intemperance and its attendant evils.

Ex-Mexican Minister to France Is Dead

(By Associated Press)

PARIS, March 15, 4:55 p. m.—The death of Sebastian Mier, who was Mexican minister to France under the Diaz administration, was announced today.

'BATTLE AT VERDUN NOW FAVORS US'

—Gen. De La Croix

Tide Has Turned Favorably to Entente Arms as Third Phase of Struggle Begins, Says Former Paris War Council Chief

By General de la Croix
Former Chief of the French War Council
(BY INTERNATIONAL NEWS SERVICE SPECIAL CABLE.)

PARIS, March 15.—The battle of Verdun has turned favorably to our arms. We can confidently await the issue of the gigantic struggle.

The third phase of the battle seems to have begun.

In the first phase we had to give ground, inflicting the maximum loss possible as we retreated, till we came to Douaumont, where we have held on, preventing any further German advance.

The second phase, fought during the first ten days of March, consisted of local attacks on positions on the Paris side of the Meuse. It

((Continued on Page 8, Column 5)

Von Tirpitz, in Reported Clash With Kaiser, Out

(BY INTERNATIONAL NEWS SERVICE SPECIAL CABLE)

LONDON, March 15.—Grand Admiral von Tirpitz, head of the German navy and author of the U-boat war, has retired according to unofficial dispatches reaching here by way of Copenhagen and Rotterdam tonight. **It was reported earlier in the day that he had been dismissed.**

The reports state that Admiral von Capelle has been selected as Von Tirpitz's successor.

Mrs. Phoebe Hearst Adds to U. C. Gifts

SAN FRANCISCO, March 15.—A large part of the mineral exhibits which were shown at the exposition have been presented to the University of California. The gifts have been accepted by the board of regents and will be placed in the Hearst Memorial Mining Building, which was erected by Mrs. Phoebe Hearst as a memorial to Senator Hearst.

Mrs. Hearst added to her list of donations thirty samples of ore from Peru. Mrs. Hearst also presented to the Museum of Anthropology twenty pieces of pottery and bead work made by Pueblo and plains Indians.

Morgenthau Sued in $25,000 Libel Case

(By International News Service)

NEW YORK, March 15.—Henry Morgenthau, ambassador to Turkey, was sued today by Eugene H. Lehman for $25,000 damages for libel. The plaintiff, a writer, prior to September 24, 1912, was the director of religious education of the Free Synagogue, of which Mr. Morgenthau is president. He was dismissed on the above date. The alleged libel consists of a statement made by the ambassador to the American Hebrew, in which Mr. Morgenthau is quoted as saying that Mr. Lehman was "grossly disloyal."

Girl, 18, Seeks to Enlist in Militia

(By International News Service)

SAN ANTONIO, Texas, March 15.—An eighteen-year-old girl presented herself at a local national guard recruiting station today and asked to be allowed to enlist.

When told that men only were accepted, she said indignantly:

"Yes, I know I'm a woman and you're a man, but I can lick you just the same."

The sergeant in charge mustered his waning courage and told her to call on the adjutant at Austin.

MEXICANS FIRE ON U. S. LINE GUARD

Bandit Gang Routed at Brownsville; Troopers From Train Join in Counter-Attack; 100 Shots Exchanged; Report None Hurt

(By Associated Press)

KINGSVILLE, Texas, March 15.—Mexican bandits, said to have numbered about 30, fired upon 16 American soldiers guarding the Barreda bridge on the St. Louis, Brownsville and Mexico railroad about 14 miles north of Brownsville at 10 o'clock tonight. At least 100 shots were exchanged. None of the Americans was injured. It is not known if the bandits suffered any casualties.

While the fight was in progress a train approaching from the south was flagged and stopped by an American soldier. A guard of five soldiers on the train rushed forward and reinforced the men fighting at the bridge. With the arrival of these reinforcements the bandits fled and are believed to have escaped into Mexico.

This was the first bandit trouble in the Brownsville region since last October.

Troops guarding the railway line have been ordered increased.

'America Can Stop War'—Morgenthau

(By Associated Press)

NEW YORK, March 15.—Europeans look upon America as typifying justice and honor, Henry Morgenthau, United States ambassador to Turkey declared in an address at a reception given in his honor today by Manhattan borough officials.

"America is the only nation powerful and resourceful enough," continued Mr. Morgenthau, "to rearrange the machinery of civilization which has been entirely upset by the war that is now devastating Europe. Only America can stop this war before it runs its full course."

President of Peru, Ill, Resigns Post

(By Associated Press)

LIMA, Peru, March 15.—President Pardo has decided to resign next month in favor of Ricardo Bentin, the First Vice President, on account of ill health. He will go to New York about the middle of April on the way to Europe to recuperate. He will be accompanied by his wife and his brother, Luis.

Police Comb City for Gypsies and Two Missing Boys

A little white boy who is fond of animals and who is likely to ask for "Unkie Newt" or "Billie Brown," and another toddler who doesn't talk very plainly are being sought by the police in the gypsy camps near the city since the receipt yesterday of an appeal from Chief of Police D. A. White of San Francisco.

A reward of $500 and no questions asked is promised for the recovery of either of the children, whose names are James Douglas Glass and Robert Allen Striker.

The Striker child is 4½ years old and was last seen in St. Petersburg, Fla., December 12, 1914. The stepfather, William C. Richter of 698 Macon street, Brooklyn, and Inspector Joseph A. Faurot of New York police offer the reward.

The other boy was last seen in Greeley, Pike County, Pa., on May 12, 1915. He is four years old.

The recent arrival in the neighborhood of Los Angeles of a party of suspected gypsies has led to the fixing of suspicion on them, and both the police and the sheriff's office are prepared to round up the entire crowd and conduct a searching investigation.

Garrison Joins Law Firm in New York

(By Associated Press)

NEW YORK, March 15.—Lindley M. Garrison, former Secretary of War, has become a resident of New York City and, as soon as admitted to the New York bar, will practice law here as a member of the firm of Hornblower, Miller, Potter & Earle, it was announced by that firm today. Mr. Garrison was formerly a Vice Chancellor of the State of New Jersey.

Illness of Queen Marie Grows Worse

(By Associated Press)

LONDON, March 15, 2:52 p. m.—German press dispatches from Bucharest, as forwarded from Zurich by the Exchange Telegraph Company, say that Queen Marie of Rumania is seriously ill and that her condition is gradually growing worse.

Jane Addams Visits San Diego for Health

(By Associated Press)

SAN DIEGO, March 15.—Miss Jane Addams, noted woman worker of Chicago and peace advocate, arrived here today for a stay of several weeks to benefit her health.

AMERICAN FORCES BEGIN HUNT FOR BANDIT VILLA

AEROPLANE CORPS IN FIRST WAR SERVICE

it with us," he said. "At least that is what we believe will be the outcome."

A trail of dust hovered over the border long after the last of the column had disappeared. I am afraid these tell-tale dust-clouds will be of much embarrassment to General Pershing, in revealing his division to the unfriendly Mexicans. The section into which the troops are moving is exceedingly dry, and the rainy season will not set in for more than a month.

An attempt was made to overthrow the garrison in Juarez last night. A party of Villa sympathizers marched through the streets shouting "Viva, viva, Villa!" The entire town was in an uproar of excitement in less time than it takes to tell it. Fortunately, the commander of the garrison effected the arrest of the disturbers before the mutiny of the garrison had been accomplished.

Until positive proof that the Pershing expedition was already on Mexican soil, General Gavira refused to believe that the start would ever be made. Later he said: "I had hoped the Americans would not go into Mexico. Since they have started, I will do all in my power to co-operate with General Pershing. General Carranza has just informed me that he does not wish the Mexican troops to make any demonstration against the American forces. General Carranza's message concluded with the statement that he favored the step, as it was for the best interests of the Mexican people."

Consul Garcia has just informed the El Paso authorities that he will co-operate in every way to maintain order and assist General Pershing in his undertaking.

Notwithstanding the passiveness of the Mexican authorities, feeling with the peon class is that of bitter resentment.

Destroyer Rushes to Guard Ensenada

SAN DIEGO, March 15.—The torpedo boat destroyer Stewart will leave here at midnight for Ensenada under orders from Admiral Winslow following instructions received today from the Navy Department. This action follows reports brought here by fishermen of a threatened revolt in the garrison there.

The guard at the international bridge, which was doubled last night, was again doubled today.

The discovery was made today by Lieutenant Shellenbarger, aide to General Pershing, that Mexican spies have been furnishing their people with copies of nearly all the telegraphic correspondence which has passed through the local telegraph offices between Fort Bliss and General Funston's headquarters at San Antonio. The spies had secured employment as operators. Steps were taken to prevent a recurrence of the trouble in the future.

DODD EXPEDITION READY TO GO

(BY INTERNATIONAL NEWS SERVICE.)

EL PASO, Texas, March 15.—Long distance telephone communication established with Hachita revealed that General Pershing returned to to that point by automobile tonight. He came to superintend the start of the second column which will get under way some time tomorrow. The second column will be commanded by Col. George A. Dodd of the Second Cavalry Brigade. It will consist of the Seventh Cavalry, Tenth Cavalry and a battery of the Sixth field artillery left behind by the first column. It is understood the second column will parallel the first column.

A base of supplies is to be established at Guzman, on the Mexico Northwestern railroad.

By Joseph Timmons

Staff Correspondent of the Inter- national News Service

HACHITA, N. M., March 15.—Col. George A. Dodd's second column of the punitive expedition is poised from the continental divide nearly a mile above sea level, within a few miles of the line of white monuments that mark the border, prepared to swing into Mexico at a trot whenever the word of command comes from General Pershing. Despite reports and rumors to the contrary, Dodd's column has not started yet. A week may elapse and New Mexicans will believe the line is to be crossed by the army only when their cowpunchers come in with the word that the unbelievable has happened.

The men who are planning the campaign have taken the utmost precautions here, as elsewhere, that plans be kept secret. Colonel Dodd has requested newspaper men not to visit the camp down on the border and if the subordinate officers have an inkling of the hour of the start they are revealing nothing. While they wait, their invariable question is "What is happening at Verdun?"

Three Mules to Troop

Three mules to the troop is the order, two for packing food and one for ammunition. It is to be another Geronimo campaign, so far as the advance of the cavalry is concerned, at the start, at least, and all the officers have been instructed "to lighten baggage." In consequence a mule team came to Hachita this afternoon with a big load of suit cases and packages of what the average civilian would consider absolutely necessary for life in the open, but what officers must get along without.

The First Cavalry, if it is to march through from Douglas, may not arrive in time to get away with the column. In that case it will be able to overtake the brigade within a few days, as scouting will somewhat retard the advance of the main body.

Ranchers Are Eager

The border ranch where part of the troops are camped is a great dry range with forty thousand head of cattle on its valleys and hills. Seven or eight cowpunchers and as many "mud hens" go about their daily tasks restlessly with thoughts only of adventure that is coming to the men in uniform. "Red," the cook, has spoiled every mess of biscuits since the sudden influx of soldiers. Every plainsman in this region has been trying to get into the service either as a guide or scout and sharpshooter.

Colonel Dodd has his headquarters in a low adobe house, and a long adobe structure has become a temporary warehouse of army goods.

Seven miles northeast at another water hole another camp is established. This second camp is "somewhere in New Mexico." Juncture will be quickly effected when camp is broken and the march begun. The actual point of crossing the boundary line may be any one of three or four passes that lead into the Mexican road.

WHERE AMERICANS AND MEXICANS ARE MOBILIZING FOR BORDER WARFARE

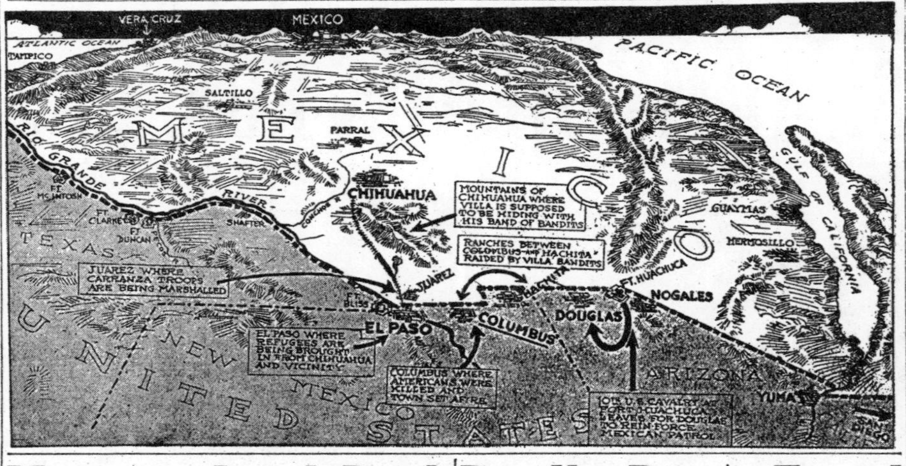

Mexicans Lead Dash Join Pershing Column

(BY INTERNATIONAL NEWS SERVICE.)

SAN ANTONIO, Texas, March 15.—"Now that our troops have gone into Mexico they will not come back until Francisco Villa is either dead, captured or entirely eliminated."

This was the statement of Major General Frederick Funston tonight to the International News Service.

According to General Funston's statement issued earlier, American troops under the command of Brigadier General J. Pershing crossed the international boundary near Columbus between 12 noon and 1 o'clock this afternoon. They were met at the custom house on the Mexican side by Colonel Juan Alfredo Bertani, commanding 500 Mexican cavalrymen at Palomas, four miles south.

Colonel Bertani greeted General Pershing and told him that he was under orders from his commanding general to accompany the American expedition with his force in the capacity of guide. General Pershing thanked him and the two commanders rode side by side into Palomas. Here half the Mexican troops took the lead and the other half the rear guard. No American flag was displayed by the troops on their entrance into Mexico.

General Pershing's command will go directly south to some point on the Northwestern line and there cross to Galeana, in which district Villa is now reported to be.

Information reaching Fort Sam Houston tonight was to the effect that Villa is steadily adding to his force and now has an army of about 3000 men, poorly armed and badly mounted.

The aeroplanes have not yet crossed but are expected to fly south tomorrow.

The American troops under General Pershing are camping tonight probably about twenty miles in the interior of Mexico.

A command of Carranza troops under Col. Manuel Herrera is reported to be marching from Casas Grandes to Sabinal to meet the American force there.

VILLA FIRES 100 MORMON HOMES

(BY INTERNATIONAL NEWS SERVICE.)

EL PASO, Texas, March 15.—Colonia Dublan, the Morman settlement in the Casas Grandes Valley, is in ruins as a result of an invasion of Villa bandits, according to a report which reached El Paso from Columbus, N. M., tonight. The news of the burning of the Mormon village of more than 100 homes was brought to Columbus by Alexander Straut, who barely escaped with his life.

Whether the Mormons were murdered or whether they escaped to the Carranza garrison at Casas Grandes, is not known. Mr. Straut, who was on top of one of the one-story houses when he saw the Villa band of 300 soldiers approaching, leaped to the ground, mounted a horse and rode away as the bandits entered the town on their mission of destruction. As Mr. Straut rode away, the flames from the burning buildings could be seen for miles.

With Mr. Straut was a man named Tracy, who also was a member of the Mormon colony. Tracy also barely escaped with his life. He remained at Columbus to act as scout for the United States army.

According to Straut's story the five male members of the Polanco family were murdered by Villa bandits while at the Corralitos ranch on Monday, but the three Polanco girls were taken prisoners. The men who were shot to death were Gregory, Mucio, Geronimo, Davis A., and Valentine Polanco.

Whether the bandits will attempt to attack the Carranza soldiers and Mormon settlers at Casas Grandes is not known. The direction said to have been taken by the bandits was to the south and east of Casas Grandes in the Galena district.

Infantry Maintains Line of Communication

(By International News Service)

EL PASO, March 15.—The Sixteenth and Sixth regiments of infantry are employed tonight in keeping open the line of communication between the Pershing expedition and Columbus, N. M.

Munitions Shipments to Carranza Permitted

Customs authorities here became alert yesterday following the receipt of a telegram from William P. Malburn, Assistant Secretary of the Treasury, containing instructions to keep all arms, munitions and explosives, believed to be in preparation for shipment out of the district, under strict surveillance until it is definitely ascertained that such munitions and war materials are not for the revolutionary factions of Mexico.

The message is as follows:

> Hold for the present all shipments of arms, munitions or explosives for Mexico except those you are certain, after careful investigation, are for the Carranza forces.

The order, if effectively carried out, it is believed, will contribute appreciably to cutting off General Villa's war supplies. According to Frank Cretcher, chief deputy in the office of the Collector of Customs, there have been no reports of shipments of war materials out of this district recently.

SAN FRANCISCO, March 15.—Similar instructions permitting shipments of arms, explosives and munitions to Mexican territory not menaced by Villa were received by the collector of the port here. Two days ago port authorities here were instructed by the Treasury Department not to clear munitions cargoes to Mexican ports.

It is left now to the discretion of the port authorities whether there is a likelihood that shipments destined to West Coast ports might reach Villa territory. One shipment of dynamite already has been held up.

Sheriff Buys 40 Rifles to Meet Emergencies

In order that the sheriff may be prepared for instant action in the event of an outbreak among the Villistas of this city, the Board of Supervisors yesterday purchased forty carbines and 5000 rounds of ammunition. With these additional arms, Sheriff Cline stated that he would be able to cope with any sort of disorder that did not necessitate calling out the militia.

For several days the local authorities have received reports of various threatened outbreaks and a constant watch is kept.

Deadly Route Faced Desert Lies in Path

EL PASO, Tex., March 15.—The territory chosen for the entrance of the punitive expedition into Mexico is at the verge of a dreary, desolate plain, inhabited principally by coyotes and prairie dogs, swept by sandstorms and denuded of vegetation except the cactus and a few other spiky and objectionable growths.

For at least thirty miles the soldiers of the United States must make their way across this desert. They then reach the lowest range of the Sierre Madre Mountains, rising to a height of 3000 to 3500 feet, broken and twisted into all manner of fantastic shapes by volcanic action, and as barren of any verdure worthy of the name as the desert over which they frown. Lonely, half-civilized ranchmen are found here and there in the valleys, nursing their cattle at the infrequent and scanty water holes and subsisting almost entirely on beef. To offset the evil results of a continuous diet of cow flesh, they drink the blood of the cattle, which contains supposedly healthy salts.

No Roads To Follow

There are no roads of any kind in all this region. An ancient track, known as the "smugglers' trail," is used by such traffic as passes through. The expeditionary force must carry all its own provisions and must, in a large measure, rely also on its base for water.

After fighting its way against nature, assisted by whatever guerrilla troops Villa may be able to muster for about 125 miles through this country, the punitive expedition will reach the Sierra Madre proper, a range of mountains rising from 8000 to 10,000 feet. Americans who have penetrated these fastnesses claim that the region is the wildest, most barren and desolate that it is possible to find anywhere in the world. The mountains are split by mighty canyons, some of which have a sheer depth of between 2000 and 3000 feet, and there is not even a recognized trail through their solitudes.

Forage Is Lacking

From Casas Grandes south, however, the country is thickly wooded, although devoid of vegetation which could provide forage for horses or food of any kind for men. In the Casas Grandes section the expedition would strike the Casas Grandes River, which sweeps westward, and here splits into three considerable branches. By following one of the branches the soldiers would be able to obtain sufficient water, but between the streams the mountains rise in great barriers, presenting a country almost inaccessible even to men on foot, and, according to the few Americans who have ventured there, impassable to wheeled transports of any sort.

It is in these wilds that Pancho Villa is said to have taken refuge, and there to be prepared to wage a guerrilla warfare on the troops who have been ordered to pursue him to death or capture.

Irish Commander of Japanese Liner Dies

(By Associated Press)

SAN FRANCISCO, March 15.—Capt. William Woodus Greene, commander of the Toyo Kisen Kaisha liner Tenyo Maru, died today in Honolulu, according to word received here at the office of the steamship company.

Captain Greene was stricken during the voyage. He was 53 years old and a native of Ireland and was in the service of the Japanese line as master for sixteen years.

Dental Board Moves Headquarters Here

(By Associated Press)

SAN FRANCISCO, March 15.—The State Board of Dental Examiners has removed its headquarters from San Francisco to Los Angeles, it was announced today, and the next meeting of the board will be held there March 19.

The change was decided upon at the last meeting of the board, at which Dr. C. E. Rice of Los Angeles, retiring president, was elected secretary to succeed Dr. C. A. Herrick of San Francisco, whose term had expired. Dr. F. H. Houck of Anaheim was elected president and Dr. L. T. Corwin of Piedmont vice president.

Chino Votes Road and Sewer Bonds

CHINO, March 15.—The election here today for $73,000 road bonds and $55,000 sewer bonds, for which the Chamber of Commerce has been actively campaigning for six weeks, resulted in an easy victory for the improvements. The vote follows: Road bonds, 468 for and 94 against; sewer bonds, 435 for and 123 against. The carrying of the road bonds means that two thoroughfares running through Chino will be put into a condition which will make them fitting parts of the county highway system.

City Brevities

Ray Benjamin of San Francisco, past grand exalted ruler of the Elks, and several other men noted for their oratorical ability, as well as for their prominence in political and public affairs, will speak at the twenty-seventh annual banquet of the Union League Club which is to be given at 6:30 o'clock next Wednesday evening. Tickets are available at the club. The guest privilege has been fixed at one for each member.

Plans for the convention to be held in Salt Lake City the last of June were discussed last night at a meeting of the local "Greeters" at the Hotel Angelus. Walter Heister presided and F. E. Zonne of St. Paul, ex-president of the Twin Cities Hotel Men's Association, and E. L. Wille of Salt Lake, manager of the Hotel Wilson, spoke.

A new organization was formed yesterday at the College of Law, U. S. C., for the purpose of cultivating the art of extemporaneous speaking and debating. The name of the new organization is the Rialto Club. Officers are: Leo Freund, president; G. F. Baker, vice president; H. M. Linneman, secretary, and W. H. Devereaux, treasurer.

For the benefit of the war sufferers of Russia, the Russian Association of Los Angeles will present Tolstoy's "The Power of Darkness," at the Gamut Theater, 1044 South Hope street, on the night of March 28.

The Dayton Improvement Association will hold an important meeting in its hall at the corner of Dayton avenue and Avenue 28, at 8 o'clock tonight.

The meeting of the Federated Improvement Association will be held tomorrow evening at 8 o'clock in Burbank Hall, 542 South Main street. Lawrence Holmes will speak on the Bunker Hill open cut.

Councilman John Topham will address the association on viaducts.

The Southern California section of the American Chemical Society will hold its regular monthly meeting tonight at the University Club. Dr. Wilhelm Hirschkind will speak.

A meeting open to men and women will be held today at 2 o'clock at Blanchard Hall, when Prof. H. W. Rolfe will speak on "True Democracy."

CALIFORNIA FORECAST

Los Angeles and vicinity — Clearing weather Tuesday; light west wind.

San Francisco and vicinity—Fair Tuesday; light northwest wind.

COAST TEMPERATURES

Los Angeles .... 61 Portland 53
San Diego ...... 62 Spokane 51
San Francisco .. 57 Tacoma 53
Sacramento ..... 60 Santa Barbara... 68

Los Angeles Examiner

AN AMERICAN PAPER FOR THE AMERICAN PEOPLE

The Great Newspaper of The Great Southwest

VOL. XIII—NO. 101 | Registered in U. S. Patent Office | Official Forecast—Clearing. | LOS ANGELES, MARCH 21, 1916 | TUESDAY | PRICE 2½ CENTS Delivered to Subscribers 5 CENTS On News Stands and Trains

U. S. TROOPS MAY FIGHT VILLA BY DAWN

PEACE TALK IS DENIED BY J. P. MORGAN

Announcement Follows Rumors on Wall Street That End of War Is in Sight; Galveston Report Adds to Stock Flurry

Paris Political and Military Authorities Declare Battle of Verdun Is Practically Over and Net Result Is Defeat for Germany

(By International News Service)

NEW YORK, March 20.—The unsettled condition of the stock market today caused rumors to be circulated in Wall Street that J. Piermont Morgan had said peace was in sight. A member of the firm of J. P. Morgan & Company said:

"Mr. Morgan has made no statement predicting that peace in Europe was in sight. Mr. Morgan does not contemplate any statement. We are perfectly satisfied with the market today."

A dispatch from Galveston stated that a prominent British ship chartering firm had canceled arrangements for a large amount of tonnage in Galveston on the plea that "immediate peace is in sight." The source of the story could not be learned.

(By Associated Press)

NEW YORK, March 20.—Reports from Galveston that tonnage arrangements had been canceled there by receipt of a dispatch from a London chartering firm saying, "immediate peace is in sight in Europe," brought from large shipping firms here the statement that no word of a confirmatory character had been received here and that no cancellation had been made here. Insurance brokers who handle marine risks also said they had received no intimation of the step reported in the Galveston dispatch. The peace rumors were reflected in the stock market, where abrupt declines occurred. The New York Maritime Exchange also was without confirmation of the report.

'Verdun Victory Is Ours,' Is Paris View

(BY INTERNATIONAL NEWS SERVICE SPECIAL CABLE)

PARIS, March 20.—Heavy fighting preceded by terrific bombardments and marked by ferocious hand-to-hand conflicts left the situation but little changed tonight, with the French victors on the west and the Germans on the east of the Meuse.

When General Cadorna arrived today his first words as he grasped General Joffre's hand were:

"I congratulate you on the magnificent and heroic victory at Verdun."

General Joffre was evidently immensely pleased.

Many of the leading authorities here, political and military, declare in most positive terms that the battle of Verdun is practically finished, save for some desultory fighting here and there on the line and that the net result is a disastrous defeat for Germany.

In the Avocourt-Malancourt district, northwest of Verdun, the Germans made an infantry attack in force, aided by "liquid fire," but made only a slight gain, according to the French headquarters report tonight, which reads:

"We energetically bombarded the sector of Avocourt-Malancourt, and disposed of groups of the enemy reported assembling to the north of Montfancon wood.

"West of the Meuse, the Germans, in the course of the day, after an intense bombardment with shells of large caliber, made an attempt to enlarge their front. An attack by a fresh enemy division, recently brought up from a point remote from the front, was directed with great

(Continued on Page 9, Column 1.)

U. S. Must Have Railroad Lines to Canal--Sibert

Military Lines Through Mexico Necessary in Time of War, Asserts Army Officer

(By Associated Press)

OAKLAND, March 20.—A system of railroads controlled by the United States, extending from the southern boundary of the country to the Panama Canal zone, would help to make certain the possession of the Panama Canal in time of war, according to Brigadier General William L. Sibert, U. S. A., who addressed members of the Oakland Chamber of Commerce today.

"It will ultimately come to this," he said, "that this country will have to operate railroads through Mexico and South American republics for military purposes, so we can transport supplies and men to the canal zone without depending upon the sea lanes entirely."

Panama, the general said, was by far the most important of our outlying possessions. Military need first prompted the construction of the canal and "steps must be taken for its proper protection against the encroachments of any power."

Large forces of regular soldiers, he declared, should be kept at all outlying posts, made up of men who were familiar with conditions and able to meet any emergency.

Liver Pill Bandit Scorns Mere Gold

Hear ye, hear ye!

We have with us the hold-up man with liver complaint—who lurks in the shadows, waylays innocent pedestrians at the point of a gun and robs them of liver pills, ignoring the jingle of dollars in the pockets of his victims.

Joseph Gordon, 942 Potter Park avenue, and clerk to Secretary McKeag of the police commission, met him unexpectedly last night and today he is minus one box of liver pills. The hold-up man seized Gorden's two wallets, handed back one containing the cash, and beat a hasty retreat with his haul of liver regulators.

Juan J. Carrillo Is Seriously Ill Here

SANTA MONICA, March 20.—Juan J. Carrillo, at one time Mayor of this city and later police judge, is seriously ill at the home of his daughter, Mrs. A. H. Calkins, in Los Angeles. Much anxiety is felt by the members of his family. An X-ray examination was made today to determine the cause of his trouble. He is 74 years of age and before his present illness had never known a sick day. He is a member of one of the old Spanish families and a pioneer resident of Santa Monica. He is one of the heirs to the De Baker estate.

BRYAN TAKES 'LIAR' WITH MEEKNESS

'Peace-at-Any-Price' Apostle Holds to Creed and Temper When Politician at Lincoln Applies 'Short and Ugly' Word

'You Are Tied Up With Man Who Is Friendly to Brewers,' Charge to 'Commoner' in Dispute on Prohibition Campaign Speech

(By International News Service)

LINCOLN, Neb., March 20.—The lie was passed to William J. Bryan this afternoon by Col. John G. Maher, a local politician. The insult was received by the former Secretary of State with **becoming meekness**, no effort whatever being made to resent it.

The "short but ugly" word came as the climax to an altercation following an inquiry made by Colonel Maher of Judge S. D. Wakely of Birmingham, Ala., as to whether the latter was being paid for his speech at a mass meeting tonight, held to celebrate Bryan's birthday and open the prohibition campaign in the State.

Mr. Bryan heard the inquiry and coming forward said to Judge Wakely:

"Maher is the only man who would ask that question. He thinks of nothing but money, and money will get him to do anything."

"Mr. Bryan, That Statement Is a Lie"

"Mr. Bryan, that statement is a lie," Maher retorted.. "Anyone who says I ever took money in a political way utters a lie, **and you know it is a lie."**

Bryan merely replied that that was "Mr. Maher's opinion" and with Judge Wakely walked away.

A few minutes later Bryan returned alone and said to Maher:

"You are the only man I know who would insult a guest of this city."

An exchange of words followed, and finally Colonel Maher flashed forth:

"Mr. Bryan, I have never taken any money in a political way, but what have you done? You were a candidate six times and every time you received the support of the brewers. You are tied up right now with Jim Dahlman (Mayor of Omaha) who is friendly to the brewers, and with others who helped collect money for your campaign from brewers."

"I have your enmity and it is a benefit to me," Bryan retorted as he turned away.

HERE Is the Latest Photograph of Francisco Villa. It Was Taken Within a Month by Fred Leroy Granville of the Universal Film Company. He Secured Letters of Introduction to Villa and Filmed Him in his Mountain Fastnesses.

Photo Copyrighted, 1916, International Film Service.

U. S. Recruits Only 507 Men in 5 Days

(By International News Service)

WASHINGTON, March 20.—Reports to the War Department today showed that in the first five days of the campaign to recruit the army up to war strength, 507 men have enlisted.

Reports received today cover only forty-six of the fifty-four recruiting districts. The rate of enlistment for the last five days was more than double the average rate. The figures show that at the present rate it would take more than six months to obtain the 20,000 recruits provided for by the Hay resolution.

630 Quarts of Nitro Explode; No Damage

(By International News Service)

SPENCERVILLE, Ohio, March 20.—An explosion of 630 quarts of nitroglycerine at the magazine of the American Glycerine Company's plant, a mile and a half north of here, early this evening, broke windows and rocked buildings in many surrounding towns, the force of the explosion being felt in towns fully fifty miles away, but practically no damage was done here.

No one was near the magazine when it exploded and no one was injured. Windows were smashed in Lima, Findlay, St. Mary's, Vanwert and Ottawa.

American Party to Tour Chinese Wilds

NEW YORK, March 20.—Roy C. Andrews, leader of an Asiatic zoological expedition organized by the American Museum of Natural History, left here today for China, via San Francisco.

Mr. Andrews was accompanied by his wife and will be joined in China by Edmund Heller and Harry C. Caldwell. They will seek rare specimens of big game. Mrs. Andrews is official photographer of the party.

Angry Bull Starts Panic at Bay City

BAY CITY, Mich., March 20. — Maddened at the sight of a red handkerchief, a bull went on a rampage here and after creating a panic among the residents and blocking traffic on a street car line, was killed by the police.

Two traders bought the animal from a farmer, five miles out in the country.

Allies Gather for Paris War Parley

(By Associated Press)

PARIS, March 20, 10:30 a. m.—Lieutenant General Count Cadorna, the Italian commander-in-chief, arrived in Paris today to take part in the military and political conference of the entente allies. Crown Prince Alexander of Serbia is due here tomorrow with Premier Pachitch.

The conference is looked upon here as of the greatest importance, as it will decide the joint policies to be pursued during the next period of the war.

Professor Stephens Is Honored by King

(By Associated Press)

BERKELEY, March 20.—Professor Henry Morse Stephens of the department of history, University of California, received today from Madrid, Spain, information that the Spanish King had appointed him comendador of the Royal Order of Isabella the Catholic.

The decoration was awarded in recognition for researches into the old Spanish traditions and history of California.

Four Middies 'Fired' for Intoxication

(By Associated Press)

WASHINGTON, March 20.—Four midshipmen were ordered dismissed from the Annapolis Academy for intoxication and misconduct in shielding intoxicated fellow students from detection. Secretary Daniels declined to divulge the names.

Assassin Shoots at Bulgarian Premier

(By Associated Press)

LONDON, March 20, 3:35 p. m.—An unsuccessful attempt to assassinate Premier Radoslavoff of Bulgaria is reported in an Exchange Telegraph dispatch from Rome.

PARIS, March 20, 5:25 p. m.—A Bucharest dispatch says that the attack on Premier Radoslavoff of Bulgaria was made by a postoffice employe named Ivanof, who fired two shots at the premier while he was riding in an open carriage. Ivanof was disarmed by a student.

Professor Goodnow to Hold China Post

(By Associated Press)

WASHINGTON, March 20.—The Chinese legation announced tonight that the agreement with Professor Frank J. Goodnow, professor of Johns Hopkins University, to serve as constitutional adviser of the Chinese Government, had been renewed for a year from May next. Professor W. W. Willoughby of Johns Hopkins has been retained as deputy constitutional adviser to succeed his brother, Professor W. F. Willoughby.

King Manuel Would Fight for Portugal

(L. A. EXAMINER AND LONDON DAILY TELEGRAPH EXCLUSIVE WAR SERVICE)

MADRID, March 20.—King Manuel, deposed King of Portugal, has telegraphed to Lisbon offering his services to Portugal. He said in his dispatch:

"My only thoughts are for the welfare of my country."

CARRANZA'S MEN FIERCELY ATTACK OUTLAW'S FORCE

Fugitive, Reinforced, Having Band of 1200, Suddenly Makes a Stand at Namiquipa, After Running Battle With His Pursuers Lasting Hours

DODD'S CAVALRYMEN HURRY FORWARD TO ENTER FRAY

BULLETIN

(BY INTERNATIONAL NEWS SERVICE.)

EL PASO, March 20.—A band of Villistas swooped down on one of General Pershing's supply caravans Sunday night, capturing several horses, according to a report received by General Gavira.

By H. H. Stansbury

(BY INTERNATIONAL NEWS SERVICE.)

EL PASO, March 20.—Francisco Villa was in a desperate battle with Carranza forces under Colonel Cano at Namiquipa tonight at 7 o'clock, El Paso time. Here the bandit leader turned on his pursuers and made a stand after a running fight which started at Las Cruces during the forenoon.

United States troops from the command of Colonel George A. Dodd are hurrying to the support of the Carranzistas from El Valle. Another detachment is following the trail which leads to the pass through the mountains to Babicora. It is believed Villa will retreat in the direction of Laguna Babicora.

The total number of United States troops now in Mexico was fixed at 8000 by an army authority today. Half of this number have crossed the border since the original expeditions started out. Others are still going south.

Reports indicate the Americans will be in the midst of the fighting before daylight, either at Namiquipa or the mountain pass. An engagement at the latter point would give Villa distinct advantage, as he is expected to give fight from the mountain slopes.

VILLA SAID TO HAVE 1200 MEN; CARRANZISTAS LESS THAN 900

Villa is said to have about 1200 men. He is able to stand and fight only because 500 sympathizers, working northward, well supplied with ammunition, joined him at Namiquipa. The Carranza force is estimated at less than 900 men. The strength of the detachments is not given.

General Pershing is believed to be hurrying to the scene of battle. The section of the Mexican Northwestern Railroad, south from Casas Grandes to Cumbre and beyond, is understood to have been taken in charge by General Pershing to send reinforcements and supplies to Dodd's men.

The news of the fighting sent a thrill through El Paso such as had not been experienced since the last time Juarez was taken. First a wireless leak told that Pershing had reported to Funston that Carranzistas had engaged Villa at Las Cruces and defeated him.

Then General Cavira, commander of the Juarez garrison, began getting messages over the Mexican Federal telegraph lines. The information was only fragmentary during the first two hours.

'WE'RE HELPING AMERICANS,' CRIES MEXICAN CONSUL

At 6:30 o'clock, Mexican Consul Andres Garcia rushed breathlessly into the International News Bureau with this dispatch:

"Colonel Cano, engaged Villa in battle at Namiquipa, district of Guerrero, Chihuahua. Hard fighting started at 4:30 o'clock."

Having acted as messenger himself to get the news out first, Garcia turned to me and said with a dramatic gesture:

"Now you can see the Carranza soldiers are helping the Americans to catch Villa. We are fighting him right now, and I hope the Americans will get there soon." General Luis Gutierrez, commander of all the forces in Chihuahua, is rushing to the scene from the capital of the State.

General Gavira is now loading 200 men at Juarez and will

'LOOKING HOPEFUL,' ASSERTS FUNSTON

CARRANZISTAS NOT HOLDING UP THEIR END

Detachment Refuses to Fight Villa; Troops Withdrawn From Casas Grandes to Juarez

start them south immediately. Those will be followed by the cavalry command of General Maldonado, who arrived today from Saltillo.

The next confirmation came over the wires of the Mexican Northwestern, but details were lacking.

General Pershing's first wireless to General Funston was sent from Galeana. He is believed to have been working south when couriers from the Carranzistas brought news of the fighting.

It is evident that he did not expect Villa to stand and fight as he has done at Namiquipa. This theory is based on the disposition of United States troops in a effort to entrap the bandit.

One detachment was sent to Carmen on the Rio Carmen, which is east and considerably to the north. These men are believed by army strategists here to have been recalled. The flying squadron which started for El Valle is moving in a direct line south for Namiquipa. The distance to be covered is nearly thirty miles, but the roads are good and they should be within range of the fighting by midnight.

The dispatching of a strong detachment along the trail to Babicora indicates that General Pershing was fully informed of the intention of Villa to go in that direction. This detachment is believed to run a better chance of getting a shot at the bandit and his army than any of the others.

General Gavira is following the movements of the Americans, Carranzistas and Villistas by a large map which hangs in his room at the Cuartel Generale in Juarez. The positions of several commands are designated by different colored thumb tacks.

The amber heads give the locations of the Americans. White heads designate position occupied by Carranzistas and to Villa the somber black headed tacks are assigned.

Americans 120 Miles Below Line

This morning the Mexican general's information placed a part of the American advance at Cumbre, the point near which the Cumbre tunnel disaster occured. This is just 120 miles southwest of Columbus, the starting point.

Another force was at Almo, ten miles south in a straight line from Galeana and 110 miles from the border. Almo is on the Santa Maria river, thirty miles east of the railroad.

The guard of the American force was at Casas Grandes, 100 miles south of the border.

At noon General Gavira said Villa was between Las Cruces and Namiquipa and intended to take the trail from the last named point to Babicora. Private information received in El Paso verified this information, as well as later developments.

There is a Carranza garrison at Santa Ana, twenty-five miles south of Namiquipa. As the column of Villistas from the south which reinforced their chieftain at Namiquipa came over this route some apprehension is felt about them. It is certain that they either ran away or joined the Villista column.

There is a force of less than 100 Carranza soldiers on the Babicora ranch.

Carranzistas Retire From Villa Pursuit

(By Associated Press)

EL PASO, March 20.—The Carranza forces have failed to hold their end of the net that was closing about Pancho Villa, and the bandit chief has escaped to his mountain haunts about Guerrero, where he is now fighting according to reliable information received here today.

A feature of the gravest importance was injected into the situation by substantial confirmation of the numerous reports received for the past week that the Mexican government troops were not only failing to co-operate with the American troops, but in certain instances at least were actually withdrawing from the field of operations.

The Associated Press learned on unquestionable authority that the troops of the de facto government which had been stationed at Casas Grandes have been withdrawn and are now in and about Juarez. From the same source it was learned that at least one detachment of Carranza troops had refused to fight Villa and had withdrawn on the bandit's approach, leaving him free to pass into his favorite mountain fastnesses in the great continental divide south of Namiquipa. This detachment withdrew on receipt of a message that he was warring not on Mexicans, but the enemies of Mexicans.

High Hopes Dashed

The extraordinary rapidity with which the American cavalry had pushed into Mexico gave rise to high hopes yesterday that the unexpected had happened and the notorious bandit was cornered. This seemed inevitable if the Carranza soldiers did their part and if the account of the strength of their field forces was correct. Villa, cut off from the north by the forward sweep of the American columns, from the west by the Sierra Madre barring the approaches to the State of Sonora, was suppossed to be equally barred from east and south by powerful Carranza forces. Those hopes have been completely dashed by the day's developments.

More than this it now seems certain that Villa is moving freely in at least a large section of the country supposed to be held by the troops of the First Chief. In the last few days he has been variously reported by General Gavira, the Carranza commander at Juarez, at points along a line reaching north and south from Galeana to Namiquipa, a distance of about seventy-five miles. By the same accounts he has not been moving steadily south but roving north and east. The mountainous, canyon-split, roadless country in which he is operating adds many miles to the country he has covered as compared with its distance on the map.

Movement Unexplained

The reason for the Carranza troops moving to the border remains unexplained. It is impossible even to make a fair estimate of the number of men under General Gavira at Juarez. The large staff at his headquarters and the fact that new troops are arriving daily indicates that his force is a large one.

The most conservative estimate places it at 3000 and calculations range from that point upward to 8000. Every precaution has been taken to prevent the facts being known and most of the men are kept outside the town among the hills. Reports from Agua Prieta and Ojinaga tell of Mexican reinforcements reaching those points also, but nothing is known as to their numbers.

There is no question that there is serious and growing uneasiness in El Paso.

1000 Picked U.S. Troopers Believed Pursuing Bandit

(BY ASSOCIATED PRESS)

COLUMBUS, N. M., March 20.—*(By wireless from General Pershing's headquarters in Mexico)*—Six biplanes of the First Aero Squadron under the command of Captain B. D. Foulois arrived today to scout in the mountains for Villa. Two machines left Columbus last night, one this morning. Four spent the night in the vicinity of La Ascencion.

Additional troops arrived here to take the place of the thousand men sent from the temporary base to try to pursue Villa.

(The above dispatch was passed by the military censor.)

No location of the temporary base is given in the dispatch passed by the censor, but yesterday's wireless intimated that General Pershing had established headquarters near Casas Grandes, from which point he was sending out columns in pursuit of Villa. Today's dispatch apparently means that only 1000 men, probably picked cavalry, are actually engaged in the chase after the bandit in the mountain retreats in which he has taken refuge, while the remainder, about 4000 in all, representing artillery, infantry and cavalry, are held at the Mexican base.

U. S.-MEXICAN PROTOCOL ON VILLA HUNT FAVORED

(BY ASSOCIATED PRESS)

WASHINGTON, March 20.—The de facto government of Mexico proposed to the United States today the drafting of a protocol, under which American and Mexican troops may co-operate in running to earth Francisco Villa and his bandits without danger or misunderstanding or conflict. **The terms of such a formal convention would be designed to meet all questions which may arise in the future, setting forth the rights of the American expeditionary forces now in pursuit of the bandit chieftain and the nature of the co-operation expected from the troops of the Carranza government.**

These facts became known at the conclusion of a conference between Eliseo Arredondo, Mexican ambassador-designate, and Acting Secretary Polk of the State Department. Negotiations on the details will be in progress for several days, but the two governments are in agreement on the general principles involved.

Meanwhile the troops of the de facto government actually are co-operating with the American forces, and according to information received by the War Department, planning to render even greater assistance. High military officials let it be known that the Carranza government had promised to move a large force of its troops from Central Mexico to the north, forming a trap into which the American cavalrymen under General Pershing may chase Villa and his followers.

Proposals for the protocol, which it is planned to have remain in force until Villa is captured, came from Mr. Arredondo and was a direct result of the request of the United States for permission to use the railway from El Paso and Casas Grandes for the shipment of supplies to the American expeditionary forces. Mr. Arrendondo is understood to have received instructions from General Carranza to discuss the request with the State Department, and to propose the agreement by which a complete understanding will be had by both governments.

While the convention will provide for all matters such as the use of Mexican railroads by American troops, the specific request for permission to ship supplies from El Paso will be disposed of separately. General Carranza has asked for additional information upon that subject and it will be forwarded to him immediately. State Department officials declined to discuss the nature of the information desired, on the ground that while the negotiations are in progress they must be held to be confidential.

After his conference with Mr. Polk, Mr. Arredondo started to prepare a tentative draft of the agreement, which will be submitted to General Carranza as soon as an agreement on details is reached with the State Department.

New Line Opened in Government-S.P. Suit

The Government yesterday introduced a new phase of the litigation with the Southern Pacific Company concerning the petroleum lands which, it is claimed, were obtained by that corporation through fraudulent representations, when Sutherland Hutton, a veteran oil operator was called to the witness stand in the hearing before Judge B. F. Bledsoe.

Mr. Hutton's testimony is held to support the Government's theory that the Southern Pacific Company would not have equipped its locomotives with oil burners had it not been convinced that there existed in the undeveloped fields of Kern County an unlimited supply of fuel petroleum and that the Southern Pacific knew it was acquiring mineral lands when it took advantage of the Congressional grant of 1866.

Building Workers in Meeting Weigh Party

(By Associated Press)

SACRAMENTO, March 20.—Although President P. H. McCarthy announced to the opening session of the annual convention of the State Building Trades Coucil that the Los Angeles Building Trades Council had suggested to the State organization and the California Federation of Labor that labor could best enforce its demands through the organization of a political party, McCarthy tonight denied that the convention would support the organization of a separate party. Probable action, he declared, would be limited to a movement to support solidly candidates pledged to carry out labor's demands.

Brakes on Train Save Autoist's Life

PASADENA, March 20.—While a large crowd of pedestrians and automobilists looked helplessly on, C. Willis Six of 1839 South Main street, Los Angeles, maneuvered an automobile in an effort to save his life from a fast-approaching train on the Colorado street crossing of the Santa Fe tracks this afternoon.

Six was caught within the gates as they were lowered.

He turned his machine on the track and backed up before the oncoming train. The engineer applied emergency brakes and the train was stopped with the locomotive almost touching Six's car.

CALLES RUSHES FORCE TO CLOSE PASS TO VILLA

Sends 4000 Men to Stop Bandit's Flight; Plans to End State Concessions

By Joseph Timmons

Staff Correspondent of the International News Service.

DOUGLAS, Ariz., March 20.—General Miguel Dieguez, in charge of Carranza troops operating against the Yaqui Indian rebels, has detached 4000 of his men. They are being sent under command of General Enrique Estrada to Tonichi by railroad from Corral, and from Tonichi they will march to Sahuaripa, within easy distance of Dolores Pass, which they will guard against Villa invasion.

This announcement was made today on the authority of Governor Calles of Sonora by Ives Lelevier, Carranza consul here. Villa is believed to be most likely to try this pass if he desires to escape into Sonora.

Will Abolish State Concessions

Lelevier also announced that Governor Calles will issue within a few days a decree abolishing all State concessions in Sonora granted under former regimes. This will not affect the big American mining interests, which are federal grants, nor big ranches with federal titles. It will affect many concessions for control of commodities and State land concessions. These concessions are to be re-issued in accordance with Calles' conception of the better chance the under dog ought to have.

The movement of troops, as described by the consul, has large importance. A rumor spread here that Dieguez was sending a big force of his men up to the border. Lelevier denies this.

Scouts Will Give Warning

Corral is in the Yaqui Valley. The consul says Estrada's men will entrain there and go to the northern terminus of this section of the railroad, Tonichi, and from there march to a base at Sahuaripa. If Villa approaches Dolores Pass, Calles' scouts on the Chihuahua side will bring the word through and Estrada will rush men to the pass to hold it against the bandit invader.

The town of Dolores, in the southernmost pass of the Chihuahua-Sonora boundary line of mountains, is but forty miles west of Madera, which is fifty miles west of Namiquipa.

Dieguez, who was a rival for the governorship with Calles, has 18,000 soldiers, according to the Mexican claim, which places the entire number of Constitutionalist troops in Sonora at 25,000. American army officers do not credit Sonora with so many soldiers.

Rancher to Escape Death Abandons $250,000 Estate

(By International News Service)

EL PASO, March 20.—At least a quarter of a million dollars worth of property and 6000 head of cattle, valued at about $50,000, were abandoned at Moctezuma, Sonora, by R. L. Slaughter, when he fled from there last week to escape possible death from the hands of Mexican bandits. Mr. Slaughter arrived in El Paso today with his son. He said:

"Moctezuma and the neighboring country is practically all Villa territory. The inhabitants there look on Villa as their liberator—their hero. I practically believe they would do anything at his bidding.

"So far the Villistas have done nothing but raid and loot.

"We were the only Americans within miles of Moctezuma and as the insults began to grow more frequent we thought it was a pretty good time to move. And we did."

Antonio Flores Arrested in Nogales Arms Search

NOGALES, Ariz., March 20.—Following his proclamation requesting citizens to register arms and ammunition in their possession by the 18th, Sheriff McKnight, assisted by twenty soldiers of the Twelfth Infantry, searched the houses of several Mexicans under suspicion. Search failed to disclose many rifles, as those not registering evidently concealed their arms. During the search Antonio Ortez Flores, who formerly held a commission as colonel under Villa, was arrested and is being held. Among his papers was found a telegram from a prominent ex-Villista at Alhambra, Cal., offering him transportation to that city.

Carranza Captain Urges War on U. S., Is Arrested

(By International News Service)

CANANEA, Sonora, March 20 (via El Paso).—A captain in the Carranza army has been arrested here for delivering an address to his troops urging them to attack all Americans. The Carranza officer urged his men to murder every American in that district, of which there are nearly one hundred.

His address incited the troopers, and for a time the situation was tense. They had started to pillage when the commanding officer ordered the captain's arrest and said he would be tried before a drumhead courtmartial. Order has been restored for the time being.

Four U. S. Soldiers Back From Mexico, in Hospital

(By International News Service)

EL PASO, March 20.—A colored trooper from the Tenth cavalry whose name is withheld by the authorities, was blinded by the glare of the desert on the first day's march. He was brought to Fort Bliss hospital today. Three infantrymen who started out with the column are also in the hospital with inconsequential injuries.

3 U. S. COLUMNS SPREAD; AIM TO ENVELOP VILLA

Funston Hears 'Unofficially' That Carranzistas Repulse Bandit Band at Las Cruces

By Otheman Stevens

Staff Correspondent of Los Angeles "Examiner"

SAN ANTONIO, Texas, March 20.—General Funston's late afternoon wireless today from General Pershing placed Villa near Las Cruces, after having been defeated in a battle by Carranzista troops. **Three cavalry columns of Pershing's force are spreading out from Casas Grandes in the hope of enveloping Villa.**

One of these columns is well on its way to Lake Babicora, below the Cumbre tunnel, seventy miles as a wise crow would fly from Casas Grandes. The second is bound for El Valle, twenty miles south of Galeana. The third is galloping for Carmen, sixty-two miles southeast of Casas Grandes.

Meanwhile the troops of what is termed the main column are working out of the main line betwen Columbus and Casas Grandes.

General Pershing's message said that Villa's defeat by Carranzistas at Las Cruces was "unofficially" learned, but it was evident that he placed considerable reliance on the report. **That Villa is northbound, as the message indicates, shows that he is hard pressed. Villa's loss in the Columbus raid is now known to have been 200 men.**

General Is Hopeful

"It begins to look hopeful," said General Funston. The General is satisfied that Pershing's men are in the neighborhood of Villa, but he is not exaltedly hopeful because, as he says, "Villa is in a wide country."

After General Funston had placed the positions of the United States troops on the big map in his office, he grimly remarked: "Our troops are well into the region; a good bit from the border."

Though Carranza's delay in acceding to the request of the United States for permission to use the Northwestern railway from El Paso to Casas Grandes for the shipment of supplies is embarrassing, news from the front shows that the troops are getting some supplies from the Mormon colonies and that a supply of alfalfa is on hand for the horses.

General Funston is taking no chances on the railway question, and today requisitioned fifty-four more motor trucks for use on the line between Columbus and Casas Grandes.

All Requirements Being Met

The aero corps are now at Casas Grandes or probably beyond with the three flying columns. Every requirement of the forces in being met and the cavalry is doing the chasing, with the infantry plugging along holding positions of restraint against Villa, while the biplanes are spying his hiding places.

It is a tremendous task to maintain supplies by motors cars in such an abominable country, but it is being done, and will be done, until General Carranza determines whether he really wants Villa caught, and opens his railway facilities.

Even then it would take some time to replace the bridges Villa destroyed, but General Funston makes rather light of that. He believes the army engineers would make a quick job of opening the line.

The Carranza garrison at Casas Grandes is described as still being "friendly but passive." So far there has been no co-operation, nor has there been a proffer of co-operation from the Carranza forces anywhere.

MOTOR TRAIN AND BIG BODY OF CAVALRY LEAVE COLUMBUS

(BY ASSOCIATED PRESS)

COLUMBUS, N. M., March 20.—A large body of American cavalry left here today. The troops which were brought here from Texas border points were preceded by a motor train carrying supplies. Whether the detachment will serve as a separate command in the effort to capture Francisco Villa or whether it is to join the punitive expedition force now in the field under General Pershing somewhere in Northern Chihuahua, was not indicated by military authorities here.

Accompanying the troops were a number of American civilian scouts, said to know the mountain trails of Chihuahua, in which Villa is reported to be fleeing, as the city man knows his front yard. Wearing the sombrero of the frontier, heavily roweled spurs, and with little wrinkles at the corners of their eyes, bespeaking lives spent in the open, these scouts form what is said to be the most picturesque group of men in the expeditionary force.

Military men frankly admit that upon their knowledge of the district in which Villa is reported fleeing rests much of the hope for the capture of the bandit. It is these volunteers, many of whom Villa drove from their homes and their property in Mexico, that are leading the American columns to the waterholes and to the hiding places in the mountains in which the bandit and a few of his followers might seek to evade the American pursuit.

That more Villistas than the seventy-nine already accounted for were killed in the running engagement following the raid on Columbus, was indicated in the discovery of three additional bodies reported here today by H. K. Lemmon, a ranchman.

SCHOOLBOYS ON BORDER ARM

By Kent A. Hunter

(BY INTERNATIONAL NEWS SERVICE)

COLUMBUS, N. M., March 20.—(Passed by United States army censor.)—School re-opened today. Several boys of thirteen or fourteen, who have to ride for miles across the mesa to reach the town, walked in to school with man-sized revolvers and cartridge belts strapped around them.

Activity of the military forces is again at top sped. The aviation squadron was up again this morning and for an hour Columbus was given a chance to see eight airmen maneuver at once.

That a movement of some kind is contemplated is apparent by the care with which the big motor trucks and the smaller troop wagons have been packed and prepared during the day. But the movement, as far as civilian Columbus is concerned, might just as well not take place.

Some morning when they awake the citizens will find blank stretches of tramped earth where a tent city existed the night before. And even the troop camped next to the vacant place will know nothing of where the missing organization has gone.

The town, in the absence of many of the residents, is overrun with dogs. They are of all kinds and descriptions and appear everywhere. Big dogs, little dogs, woolly ones and the hairless kind try to make friends with any one who looks like ready food.

The different troops have contributed to the general surplus of animal life by leaving behind on orders of the commanding officers all pets and mascots. Two burros that formerly were mascots of troops of a cavalry regiment are now doing duty as mounts for the messenger boys of the Western Union, and a parrot that belonged to an infantry company is acting as announcer for a Chinese restaurant. The parrot can say "Pork chops, steak and bacon and eggs," and has more than paid for his lodging by business attracted to the place.

'U. S. UNPREPARED'---GARFIELD

PASADENA, March 20.—James R. Garfield, son of President Garfield, and Secretary of the Interior under President Roosevelt, made a vigorous plea for preparedness in an address at this morning's assembly at Throop College of Technology. He urged universal military training. He said:

> The volunteer system is wrong in principle and worse than useless. Why should one man volunteer and another stay at home? Citizenship means the duty of giving life, if necessary, for the nation, and every man should go through enough training to know how to take care of himself in the field and be an intelligent unit in an army.

We have the splendid example of France before us.

In America an invading force could go through the country from end to end and meet no effective opposition, except in a few places.

As to our lack of preparation, the situation in Mexico is an example. For four years we have known such an attack might come; for four years lives have been sacrificed across the border, and property destroyed, and for three or four years our soldiers have been fired upon from across the border and were not permitted to reply.

The doctrine of preparedness has fallen on deaf ears. The nation has been "too proud to fight;" Mexico has been trying to work out her own salvation, and now an armed force shoots up an army camp and burns an American town, killing the inhabitants, and we are a whole week getting ready to pursue it, all because of the doctrine of unpreparedness.

Many New Recruiting Stations in California

Two new recruiting stations for the United States Army will be opened this week in Southern California, one in San Diego and the other in San Bernardino. Lieutenant Colonel W. E. Purviance, in charge of recruiting at the Los Angeles headquarters, will go to San Diego today to organize a station and immediately following that will open a second in San Bernardino.

Six recruiting stations were opened yesterday in Central and Southern California at the following points: Bakersfield, Fresno, Sacramento, Chico, Stockton and San Jose. Before the week is out additional offices will be opened at San Luis Obispo, Salinas, Santa Rosa, Grass Valley, Marysville, Modesto, Visalia and in Reno, Nev. They will be under the general direction of Lieutenant J. H. Gardner, in charge of recruiting for the San Francisco district.

GALVESTON BEACH, THE PLAYGROUND OF TEXAS, ALREADY POPULAR WITH BATHERS

Recent Warm Weather Brought Out Hundreds of Fair Fun Lovers and the Sands Are Dotted With Dancing and Lounging Groups

There May Be Wars and Rumors of Wars, but the Bathing Girl on Galveston Beach, While Ready for Enlistment in Whatever Branch of Service She May Qualify For, Has a Good Time While She Is Waiting:::The News Photographer Has Caught the First Invasion of the Beach by the Bathers, and Soon Thousands Will Have Caught the Enthusiasm.

More Lords Than Commons.

Correspondence of the Associated Press.

London.—The House of Lords this year, for the first time in history, has more members than the Commons. The membership of the lower house is fixed at 670, while the roll of the upper house has increased during the last year by nineteen, to 673.

The House of Lords would have been still larger but for the fact that minors succeeded to several peerages, while three peerages become extinct through lack of heirs—the baronies of Fitshardings, Llangattock and Somerhill.

Twenty-one new peerages were created during the year, including Lords Astor, Beresford, Rhondda, Shaughnessy and Viscounts Grey and French. There are five new peers, whose choice of titles has not yet been announced—Max Aitken, John Dewar, J. A. Pease, Stuart Wortley and Edward Partington.

Six titles have been temporarily removed from the roll of the House of Lords by the succession of minors to the Earldoms of Feversham, Longford, Kinnoull and St. Aldwyn and to the Viscounty of Ridley, and a lady to the Barony of Lucas. The Barony of Scarsdale had lapsed, because the heir already held a higher grade in the peerage, Earl Curzon of Kedleston.

Three peers who were "infants" at the opening of last year—the Earls of Carlisle and Lathom and Viscount Gage—have since come of age. In addition to the tour peers whose death led to the extinction of titles and to the six who were followed by children of women, sixteen died during the year. The Earls of Longford and Feversham and Lord Lucas were killed in action and Earl Kitchener died on war service. Other deaths included Lord Burnham, the Earl of Sandwich, Lord Redesdale and the Earl of Essex.

Five old baronies were revived during the year and another old title was restored in the granting of a viscounty to Lewis Harcourt.

KING'S OATH.

Budapest.—The oath which the new King of Hungary took at the coronation ceremonies here, as prepared by the Hungarian Parliamentary Committee, was expressly worded so that in connection with any peace arrangement it will be almost impossible for the King-Emperor to make any cession of territory without the consent of the Austrian and Hungarian Parliaments. The oath reads: "We, Charles the First, Emperor of Austria, the fourth King of Hungary by this name, etc., swear by God and all his saints that we will respect the freedom, liberties and rights of all our subjects * * * and that we shall under no circumstances alienate any parts of Hungary, Croatia, Slavonia and Dalmatia; on the contrary, we shall so far as in our power, increase their territories and extend their boundaries, and shall do all we can in the interests and glory of all these States of ours."

Quarter Million Gift.

Budapest.—The newly crowned Emperor Charles has received from the Hungarian people a popular gift of $250,000 in gold, which the Emperor has ordered to be devoted to national purposes.

Cardiff Booms Like Pittsburgh

Correspondence of the Associated Press.

Cardiff, Wales.—Cardiff has become known as the Pittsburgh of the British Isles. Like the American city, the coal mines are largely responsible for its boom, although shipping has played no small part. Men who were shipping clerks two years ago now own a string of ships, and coal miners are making $100 a week.

Just to show that it has made a lot of money, Cardiff invested £30,000,000 in the last British war loan. This works out at the rate of more than £150 a head of the population, and is the most remarkable of all the contributions that came from any city in the British Isles.

Shortage of Copper.

Amsterdam.—An alleged sign of Germany's shortage of copper is found in the fact that all 2½c pieces (one American cent in value) are being bought up by certain unknown persons in places along the frontier at four Dutch cents each. They are destined for export to Germany, where they bring as much as two groschen (five American cents) apiece, it is said.

Closer Relations Between China and Japan

Correspondence of the Associated Press.

Tokio.—Liu-tsung-yu, former Chinese Minister to Japan, is in Tokio on a mission which may have a far-reaching importance in bringing about closer working relations between Japan and China. Mr. Liu is here privately, but he is authorized by his Government to consult Japanese officials and leading business men to work out a system of practical co-operation.

The position of Japan in Shantung Province is one of the questions under discussion with the Foreign Office. Japan's place in the quintuple group which the United States is expected to join also is under consideration. Japan is seeking the right to appoint a Japanese financial adviser at Pekin, but China is opposing this.

Check Payments in France.

Paris.—Further efforts are being made to extend the popularity of the checking system in France. Some of the railway companies have decided that all provincial stations may hereafter accept payment in certain specified forms of checks. In order to induce small shippers to adopt this form of payment, the companies will allow shippers who pay in checks to settle their accounts weekly instead of daily as heretofore required.

The News MAGAZINE Supplement AND CHILDREN'S DEPARTMENT

DALLAS, TEXAS, SUNDAY, APRIL 15, 1917

MONSTER PATRIOTIC PARADE OF DALLAS PEOPLE

Unprecedented Demonstration by Thousands of Texas Patriots Resulted in Tremendous Outpouring of Enthusiasts on April 10.

SOME ENORMOUS FLAGS WERE CARRIED BY HUSKY YOUNGSTERS.

HUNDREDS OF WHITE CLAD WOMEN WERE IN THE PARADE.

BATTERY DRAWN BY TRACTION ENGINE IN PARADE.

HELLA TEMPLE PATROL.

Shipping Facilities in Algeria

Correspondence of The Associated Press.

Oran, Algeria.—The movement of shipping in the ports of Algeria gives an indication of the state to which any purely Mediterranean country has been reduced by lack of shipping facilities, even before submarines entered into serious consideration. Between Algeria and France alone, on Aug. 1, 1914, 109 ships were plying, with an annual tonnage of 11,290,600. On July 1, 1915, before the submarine campaign in the Mediterranean had assumed formidable proportions, the number of ships plying between Algeria and France alone had been reduced to fifty, totaling an annual tonnage of 3,631,000. About 50 per cent of the bottoms had disappeared, 75 per cent of their net tonnage and 65 per cent of their annual carrying capacity. Of the vessels withdrawn from the Algerian trade, twenty-four had been requisitioned and fifteen had been sunk. No figures are available on the results since that time, but a very great many ships serving one or another of the Algerian ports are known to have been sunk by submarines.

Oran has suffered least of the Northwest African ports. Since 1913 the loss in tonnage of Algieria has been 60 per cent, that of Oran only 6 per cent, the latter now virtually equaling the tonnage of the capital. This disparity is attributed to the fact that 30 per cent of the entire Algerian income from wines and 45 per cent of Algeria's total product of cereals pass through the port of Oran, and while the commerce in other products has been vastly reduced or suspended by the war, that in wines and cereals has been agumented. Business in special lines, which in 1913 amounted to $237,604,200 for all Algeria, had been reduced by the war to $169,170,600 in 1915. Oran, however, suffered only in point of its large production of early vegetables usually grown for the winter Paris market.

In 1914 the shipping in the Mediterranean was still safe, few of the fast fruit and vegetable-carrying vessels had been requisitioned for transport purposes, and Oran shipped some 10,250 tons of aritchokes, peas, green beans, tomatoes and other vegetables to France in the course of the year. The extension of the war to the eastern Mediterranean in 1915 reduced this output to 6,000 tons for that year and almost annihilated it last year. An annual exportation ot 10,169 tons of fruits and melons in 1914 suffered a similar fate. Even potatoes, more easily transportable than either early vegetables or fruits, fell from 3,704 tons in 1914 to 2,594 tons in 1915, and less than half that in 1916. As Oran is the gate of the principal vegetable garden of France, these figures, due almost entirely to the lack of means of transport, are regarded as explaining in large measure the greatly augmented cost of living in France, as well as the tightness of money and general hard times in Algeria.

Male Customer — Er — er — er. Um. Ah. Er—He—he.

Jeweler (to his assistant)—Bring that tray of engagement rings here, Henry.

Protest Against Allied Blockade

Correspondence of The Associated Press.

Piraeus.—The presidents of the 300 labor unions of Piraeus and Athens have presented American Minister Droppers with a protest for transmission to the President of the United States against the allied blockade of Greek ports.

"What is most painful," says the protest," is that the blockade is being continued even after the Government has accepted and executed the onerous conditions of the last ultimatum of the Powers, which have formulated no new demands whose acceptance could bring about a lifting of the blockade. This last measure touches the harmless population of women, old folks and children, whose lives are respected even in time of war.

"Under the protection of the blockade, a revolutionary movement, conducted by a small number of traitors, has been spread in the Aegean Islands by brandishing the specter of hunger. The foodstuffs consigned to the commission charged with supplying food to the country are seized by the very Powers maintaining the blockade and turned over, in violation of all justice, to those who have fomented and directed the Saloniki movement. This arrangement makes it evident that even when the blockade is raised the country will be menaced by famine. This situation has greatly upset the commercial relations with all neutral countries, and especially with the United States.

"All the unions and syndicates of working men, through the signatories of these presents, address the liveliest protest to all the neutral lands against this violation of every human and divine right, and particularly approach the Government of the United States, in the hope that it will be willing to use its voice to bring about a cessation of these unheard-of measures against a neutral State."

Increase in Docking Facilities in London

Correspondence of The Associated Press.

London.—In spite of the war, a great deal of progress has been made in establishing increased docking facilities here. They are expected to help restore much of the lost trade of the Thames and to make London a stronger competitor of other ports in the United Kingdom. When the war ends gigantic efforts are to be made to regain for London much of the trans-shipment traffic which in recent years was captured by Antwerp, Rotterdam and Hamburg.

The scheme now being carried out calls for dockage for bigger ships. At Tilbury, where a big landing stage is being built, berths are now ready for steamers of 25,000 gross tons, or nearly double the tonnage that could have been accommodated there before the war began.

THE Dallas Establishment of the Coca-Cola Co., located at 2019-21 North Lamar Street, is under the personal management of Mr. Daniel B. Candler, through whose energetic efforts the sales in Texas and the Southwest have increased enormously. The public is invited to call and inspect this plant, which is one of the best equipped in the United States, for the purpose for which it is intended. A rigid standard of cleanliness is maintained in every department.

COCA-COLA BUILDING, DALLAS, TEXAS.

THE Coca-Cola Company, manufacturers of that delicious and popular beverage, "Coca-Cola," is recognized as one of the leading industrial enterprises of the South. From a small beginning in Atlanta, Ga., a little over a quarter of a century ago, the business has increased to such an extent that branch houses and distributing depots are maintained throughout the United States, and in nearly every country of the civilized world.

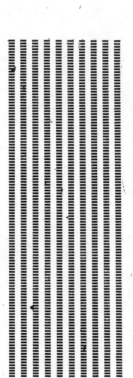

COCA-COLA is a drink for every member of the family, every day of the year —pure, wholesome and palatable—a beverage which meets the requirements of the entire system, and is today easily the peer of all fountain beverages. Bright, sparkling, teeming with effervescence, it is, indeed, the ideal thirst-quencher for persons in all walks of life. When you feel that thirst coming on, seek "first-aid"—Coca-Cola.

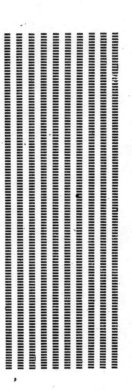

STYLES

Evening functions, especially the formal dinner, will find this simple gown an attraction this fall. The low back, the suggestion of a double train, the rich eggshell satin, gives this dress its quiet charm.

A.P. Photo

Dance of Eve's Daughters in Fox Movietone

A beautiful winter coat, in deep Burgundy with a luxurious trim of Kolinsky fur, which, with the turban chapeau gives milady a distinguished ensemble for late fall and early winter.

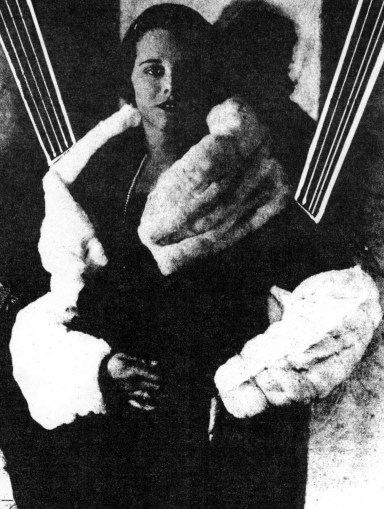

Sport ensemble for football weather—white satin blouse, trimmed in red, with gray tweed coat and dress, with large fox coat trim and chapeau in neutral tones—gives an ensemble which is wholly charming.

A.P. Photo

Henri Bendel is featuring ermine for evening wraps. The wrap here shown, which Mr. Bendel has created, is of black chiffon velvet and has a huge collar and very deep cuffs of Russian ermine. A new method of using ermine is illustrated — applying the fur wound around flat—(as though a large animal were being used) — about the sleeve — reaching above the elbow. The skins are thus used in the soft crushed collar, making the coat very lovely and soft.

A lovely evening gown, suggestive of an older day, created for milady who loves the feminine touch—tulip pattern warp print taffetas with scalloped peplum and long scalloped hemline.

A.P. Photo

CURRENT SHOWS

News of the Players

COMING Attractions

FILMS OVERSHADOW STAGE BILLS AS THEATERS OFFER VARIED AMUSEMENT FARE

By BESS WHITEHEAD SCOTT.

With the caprice which is much of the charm of amusements, the pendulum of favor has swung back to program pictures in local theater bills for the week. Stage shows are interesting on the average, but with few exceptions offer nothing out of the ordinary. There is a choice of two stage programs, a third variety house dispensing with the vaudeville program because of the length of the picture.

These screen offerings are the first musical revue of the screen; a world famous cowboy humorist in a talking feature; a continuation of the comedy and drama of the most famous blackface pair of entertainers, and a quiet love story of groping youth presented in natural manner by one of the most appealing of screen celebrities.

+++

METROPOLITAN.

"Young Nowheres" is this idyl of young love in which sentiment is the continual keynote, but does not cloy or lose interest because of the fine work of Richard Barthelmess and Marion Nixon. The picture, showing at the Metropolitan, is an all talking one.

There is nothing sensational about the story or development. On the contrary, it is merely a narrative of the friendship and love of a pair of inarticulate young waifs, beaten by the terrible loneliness of a big city, written with the characteristic sympathy and charm of I. A. R. Wylie. Those whose screen appetites are whetted to the enjoyment of mystery thrills or elaborate extravaganzas will not be satisfied with "Young Nowheres." But given a fair chance, the simple story is apt to touch springs of sympathy unsuspected in the heart of the beholder and linger in his mind.

Not since his first fine pictures, notably "Toler'ble David," has Barthelmess done the naturally fine work displayed as the hotel elevator boy, clean minded, slow thinking, but faithful to some inner sense of right, in "Young Nowheres." He never for a moment steps out of character, continuing "dumb" to the undiscerning to the last scene. Miss Nixon, graduated from Western thrillers to prominence in the talking pictures, also does a remarkably fine piece of work. Bert Roach's souse bit affords entertainment.

All actors of the stage show deserve appreciation for their specialties, but the show on a whole is much the same as many others. Caperton and Biddle, adagio dancers, do difficult routines gracefully. Harry Downing, comedian with a high soprano, gets many laughs, but frequently descends to exceedingly low comedy levels to inspire them.

The Merrymakers, a male quartet, is stingy with its excellent harmony and funny delivery. Bert and Hazel Skatell (the latter a double for Polly Moran) dancing on roller skates, gives the most unusual performances. The chorus has three attractive costume changes. "Parisian Life" is the title of the unit.

George Parish, unassuming and popular pianist of the Met orchestra, is featured in an arrangement of Goddard's Allegro and introduction, a commendable performance, directed by Lou Forbes.

+++

MAJESTIC

The Majestic puts the big pot in the little one for its Blue Ribbon annual program. Will Rogers' wisecracking from the screen is a made-to-order story to suit his homely personality, is the principal course of the amusement feast.

Owen Davis is given credit for the story, "They Had to See Paris," which takes Pike Peters from the garage business in Claremore, Okla., through a sudden rise to riches from an oil gusher, and a trip to Paris to satisfy the social ambitions of "Idy," the school teacher wife. But it is said that Rogers provided many of the original wisecracks.

Comedy, unostentious drama sprung from natural situations, and not a little of keen satire is contained in "They Had to See Paris." From the minute Pike rolls his gum under his tongue and brushes his forelock from his eyes to observe "I've fixed a many a one of these things (Fords), and I ain't never found the same thing wrong with any two of 'em," the story is off to a good start. And the interest increases until the climax of Pike's philosophy as expounded to his family, sick of Paris artificialities and ready to return to Claremore. The chamber of commerce of this town should give Rogers a vote of thanks.

While Rogers is nine-tenths of the picture, other characters deserve high praise. Irene Rich is wonderful as Idy, loving her family, but with head a bit turned by sudden wealth, and Fifi Dorsay, the French girl, all but runs away with the show. Her accent is delicious, and her whole performance of the baby siren is perfect. Margaret Churchill is acceptable as the young daughter, but Owen Davis Jr., makes little impression as the boy of the family.

If it were not for Natacha Nattova and her stalwart company of three men the Majestic stage show would just about be a total loss. But this dainty little originator and exponent of the adagio in duet, trio, and quartet, with the muscles of steel, make up for any deficiencies in the rest of the entertainment.

Exhilirating and arresting are the "dance with death" and the closing impression of "the spirit of the modern age"—age of iron, power and labor. The effect of strength and power given is startling.

Other acts are the Zellias Sisters, dainty aerialists; Princeton and Yale, a trio in a series of gags of tab show caliber; Jane Green, "siren of syncopation," an attractive blond, and Jack George, in a funny take off on the old-time negro preacher, giving an oration on modern times and customs.

+++

LOEW'S STATE.

It is difficult to make a review of "The Hollywood Revue" more than a roster of famous screen names. The Loew's State specialty, called the first screen musical revue, has 20 stars and a chorus of 200, many of whom are also well enough known to screen audiences to be classed as "stars."

With the exception of two, every member of the Metro-Goldwyn-Mayer organization of players whose names mean anything to the public, and many who do not, are seen and heard in this picture. These two are Lon Chaney and Greta Garbo, both of whom declined to do a "specialty" on the ground that such was not in their line. Maybe they are right. It is often the better part of wisdom on the part of a screen actor never to step from his screen personality before his public.

At any rate, these two are not greatly missed in the peppy aggregation of "The Hollywood Revue." Few of the players attempt to be anything other than the selves the public knows, but John Gilbert does surprise with a burlesque and Conrad Nagel blossoms out as a singing lover.

In the amazing medley of specialty acts — the picture is strictly a revue, with no story—the comedy skit of little Bessie Love, Polly Moran and big Marie Dressler, and the "Dance of the Sea" by Buster Keaton are the funniest; "Singing In the Rain" and "Orange Blossom Time" the most enjoyable chorus ensembles, and the adagio number of Natacha Nattova the most startling.

William Haines is his usual perky self in "The Cut-Up." Laurel and Hardy appear as "magicians." Joan Crawford and Marion Davies go back to their stage musical comedy specialties, and Gus Edwards, Charles King, Cliff Edwards, James Burroughs and the Brox sisters lead song specialties, aided by a chorus of beauties who are both dancers and singers. The Albertina Rasch ballet appears in many of the beautiful tableaux numbers.

John Gilbert and Norma Shearer give the balcony scene from "Romeo and Juliet," in technicolor, and then burlesque the same scene. Lionel Barrymore adds interest to this sketch.

As the numbers reel on, although offering much variety and favorite faces, the picture becomes a bit monotonous. And then comes the finale—and folks, what a finale! Gorgeous and glittering, and all the old ballyhoo adjectives are needed to describe the finish, in which are mingled the virile tenor of Charles King, the grace and beauty of the Rasch ballet, the entire M-G-M ensemble of stars and chorus, all embellished with dazzling sets and technicolor. Don't fail to see "The Hollywood Revue," if for no other reason than to discuss and dispute about it with your neighbor.

+++

KIRBY.

Held over for the second week, Charlie Mack and George Moran continue to "stand 'em out" at the Kirby, where they are appearing in "Why Bring That Up?"

Fortunately an adequate and suitable story is afforded the "Two Black Crows" for their first screen program picture, and the production is given fine direction and staging. The elements of the picture—comedy, melodrama, back stage scenes and show-within-a-show flash acts, are presented in admirable proportion.

Charlie Mack dominates every scene he is in, but Harry Green, stage star of "Kabitzer," is of equal excelence in his characterization of the penny watchful stage manager. Noran and Evelyn Brent are the other principals. The story concerns the start of the blackface team, their close friendship through five years of success, and the experience of Moran in being "taken to the cleaners" by a chorus gold digger, which almost disrupts the partnership. Interest is added to the story by the report that Moran and Mack have dissolved partnership in reality.

"Moonshine," a dramatic playlet written by Willard Mack and played by James Barton; a cartoon illustrated song, and news reel are the short offerings of the Kirby program.

+++

QUEEN.

Little Sally O'Neil, one of the Young sisters trinity, who has made good in a big way, plays at the Queen through Monday in "The Girl of the Barge." Thus she returns to the sort of characterization in which she made her first screen hit—that of "Mike."

As the daughter of a crusty barge captain, overzealous in protecting his motherless brood, she falls in love with a handsome tugboat pilot and finds the course of true love obstructed by choppy squalls. Matters are brought to a climax by a storm, and the lovers united with parental blessings. Malcolm MacGregor is handsome and convincing as the lover, and Jean Hersholt at home in the role of the dominant father.

Backgrounds of the barge canals in upper New York, and a well photographed storm at sea lend the picture interest. Dialogue sequences are well interposed, and voices record satisfactorily.

An interesting variety is offered in the Queen short reels.

+++

TEXAN.

A tantalizing Garbo with wavy, windblown bob and at times exuding an exuberance thought foreign to her, is found in "The Single Standard," the Texan attraction. Greta has, for the time at least, abandoned her sleek, sveldt type of attraction, but certainly none of the seductiveness and indefinable charm which is her natural personality.

She plays the young wife (with a past) of Johnny Mack Brown, a staid young business man. Her past affair with Nils Asther, an artist, is pictured in frank detail, and is well known by her husband and their circle of friends. In the artist's absence, and in the apparently happy home life of the couple with their young son, the girl's indiscretions are overlooked.

Of course, the artist returns to complicate matters, and the girl again asserts her right to live her own life according to the dictates of her own heart and conscience. The ending is thoroughly satisfactory, but never obvious until the last scene. Asther and Brown play admirable seconds to the Garbo, and others deserving commendation for good work are Dorothy Sebastian, Lane Chandler and Kathlyn Williams, formerly a serial star of great brilliance.

"The Single Standard" is not a talking picture. Dialogue and music are furnished in adequate form on the Texan bill by a variety of short features and a news reel.

WITH THE 101 RANCH

GLASS FIRM IS HOLDING SALE

Celebrating 20 years of successful business in Houston, A. Schwartz, Inc., 815 Main street, is holding its twentieth anniversary all during the past week and the next, with a store-wide sale covering every department. The growth of A. Schwartz, Inc., is not only a story of the growth and development of Houston, but also is the personal story of a remarkable business woman, Mrs. A. Schwartz, who from a small beginning, has built up one of the outstanding businesses, in its line, in this city.

The original business was founded by Mr. and Mrs. A. Schwartz at 516 Travis street, Chronicle building, who claim the distinction of opening the first exclusive high class china and glassware store in Houston. When, four years later, Mr. Schwartz passed on, Mrs. Schwartz took over the business and under her direction and management it has grown to its present commanding position in its line. A year after Mr. Schwartz's death the store moved to its present location on Main street. With the remodeling of the West building, the store was enlarged and today occupies nearly 4000 square feet of floor space, besides a large reserved stock room in the basement.

From the beginning A. Schwartz, Inc., has handled such famous and nationally known lines of chinaware and glassware as Minto, Wedgewood, Black Knight, Theodore Haviland and Lennox of which it is the exclusive Houston representative.

During these years Mrs. Schwartz has built up a personnel of experts who are in charge of the various departments of the store, whose knowledge and familiarity with china and glassware are at the services and aid of patrons. These include: Miss Mollie Westheimer, Miss Lillie Berle Emden, Mrs. J. V. Suggs, Miss Margaret Motheral, Miss Alma Cherry, J. D. Rothschild and Richard Schwartz.

HOUSTON BOYS ON MUSIC BILL

In what probably will prove to be a musical discovery in Houston, Herbert and Alfred Teltschik will be presented in a joint piano recital in Foley Bros. Town Hall Wednesday, October 23, at 3 p. m.

These two youngsters, 10 and 11 years old respectively, are still in the elementary grades of the Houston public schools.

One afternoon the father of the two boys brought them to the musical director of Foley Bros., to have them play for him. They had never before appeared in public. In fact, they have been studying only three years, beginning first with their father, who taught them notation, and then were put under the tutelage of Aldridge B. Kidd.

Their unusual talent and promise, particularly in view of their youth, was immediately recognized and, in conformity with one of the aims of the Foley Bros. Town Hall musicales to bring out the most promising youthful talent of Houston, the boys were engaged for a concert in Town Hall. Not only the elementary compositions of beginners do they play, but they demonstrated their ability on such compositions as Mozart's concertos, Chopin, Grieg and MacDowell.

Their program will include two Mozart concertos as well as compositions of the above composers. It is to be hoped that the forth coming recital will demonstrate the fact that Houston may produce two musical proteges.

Woman Faces Charge After Plea to Court

ALTADENA, Cal., Oct. 20.—(AP) Because she wrote a letter asking Superior Judge Charles Allison of San Bernardino to "go easy with" six young persons charged with communistic activities, Mrs. Kate Crane Garz, wealthy Altadena resident, was under summons Saturday to appear before the jurist next Wednesday on contempt charges.

Judge Allison quoted Mrs. Garz as having asked him, in her letter, to "go easy with these young enthusiasts." Six persons were convicted of conspiracy in the operation of an alleged communist camp in Yucaipa valley.

The judge charged Mrs. Garz with having "knowingly, wilfully and unlawfully" written the letter "for the purpose of unlawfully influencing, coercing and prejudicing" him.

CELEBRATES ANNIVERSARY

Mrs. A. Schwartz of A. Schwartz, Inc., who is celebrating the twentieth anniversary of the founding of the firm. Mrs. Schwartz has been the head of the firm for the past 15 years and by her ability and business acumen has built up one of the outstanding exclusive retail china and glassware concerns in Houston.

Woman Under Wagon at Night Heard Panther Cry in War Days

Nights of sleeping beneath wagon beds and listening to the nearby cry of a roving panther. Days of weary plodding behind a yoke of oxen. The creaking and sighing of ungreased wagons as they inched along into a virgin land. Youthful rapture at the unfolding of a new country.

Such are the unstilled memories of Mrs. M. A. Robinson of 7735 Baltimore street, Harrisburg, who as a girl of 7 or 8 years came to Texas from Alabama in a covered wagon before the Civil war.

A girl unafraid of wild animals then roaming about—a girl who at 15 would ride the mail weekly between Spring and Harrisburg. And one, who in the evening freshness, would scamper high into the trees and laugh in delight as the wind tossed the limbs to and fro.

Pioneer Texan.

Pioneer Texan, nourished largely on venison, bear meat and pressed clabber, and required to do many home chores while the men were at war, Mrs. Robinson, now nearly 85, loves to hark back to the early days of the state. In reminiscent mood, she will recall the trials and hardships of the families which trekked across country to settle near the Sabine.

One memory revives another, and she brings to mind wild days of horse breaking, and watching the men folks as they stood just outside the homestead door and shot wild turkeys by the score. At that time Houston was not even the nebula from which dreams are made, and, Harrisburg "was only a puddle of water."

On November 5 Mrs. Robinson will celebrate her 85th birthday.

In Covered Wagon.

Years ago, as Millay Ann Dunn, she left Macon, Ala., with her parents and other members of the family. Forty-seven families were represented in the determined group which set out in covered wagons to find a new abiding place. Millay Ann was about 7 then.

Others of the family who made the trip were her parents, Mr. and Mrs. J. W. Dunn; a brother, James Greenleaf Dunn, now dead; her grandmother, Mrs. Polly Cook; and an uncle and aunt, Mr. and Mrs. William Stillwell.

From Macon the homeseekers set out westward toward the Mississippi. Reaching that stream some days later they boarded river craft of that time, and with their teams, wagons and other belongings, passed eight days and nights on the river.

Resume Journey.

At some point which Mrs. Robinson did not recall, they disembarked and resumed their overland journey, making a few miles daily. At times they would find a suitable camping spot and halt for three or four days to rest up, overhaul the wagons and bring in fresh supplies of meat.

"At night my brother and I would sleep under the wagons," she said. "I remember one night when it rained very hard and we woke the next morning to find our mattress floating in several inches of water.

"Then we would again move on, with the men driving the cattle on ahead, the hogs and other animals following the wagons. Hitched to our outfit were two oxen and two cows. At night and in the mornings we would milk the cows.

No Matches.

"Of course we had no matches in those days with which to light a fire. Instead, we'd strike sparks from a skillet, setting fire to tufts of cotton or 'punk' taken from decayed trees. Sometimes we hastened the process with powder."

After crossing the Sabine, the families settled in Shelby county, where the men immediately set to erecting log cabins and clearing the land. They named their settlement Buckslort because of the countless deer, turkeys and wild game of the region.

"I remember one day we counted 25 turkeys right in front of the house," Mrs. Robinson said. "Panthers and wolves often stole our venison and when the men were away working, the women would throw firebrands to scare the animals off. Almost any time we could kill six or eight turkeys on the fence. And the prairie chickens soon got to laying with our hens."

Gruesome Story Told.

This pioneer existence, of course, was not unmarked by tragedy. Mrs. Robinson tells the gruesome story of how one woman in the settlement was left alone after dusk, waiting for the men to return. With her in the cabin was her baby.

"Suddenly a panther sprung in from the darkness, snatched the infant from its mother's breast, and bearing it outside, devoured the baby right in front of the cabin.

After clearing away the timber, the men built a crude but efficient sort of grist mill, where they ground up corn grown in fields adjoining the houses. Wild meat was abundant.

Many times the settlers were without bread, however, the place of which was usually taken by pressed clabber cheese.

"We became so used to this wholesome cheese that when we were able to get bread we didn't care anything about it," Mrs. Robinson tells.

130 Miles for Coffee.

Later the men would make infrequent trips of 130 miles to Shreveport for coffee, flour and other commodities. From two to three months was usually required for the trip.

Womenfolks of the little town manufactured all of the clothes. So inured to the spinning wheel and its uses did Mrs. Robinson become that not long ago in Beaumont she was with her daughter and heard a whirring sound coming from about a block away. Mrs. Robinson immediately knew what it was and was not satisfied until the instrument had been located.

Young people had more fun those days, Mrs. Robinson claims, simple though the amusements were. They had hunting and exploration parties. Around home they spent hours climbing and playing in the trees. And best of all there was the riding of wild horses.

Break Horses.

During the war, Millay Ann and her brother would break horses at $5 each, realizing enough to purchase nine yoke of oxen by the time their father returned from the army.

"Riding horses was heaps of fun," Mrs. Robinson declares. "Once I was mounted, they'd pitch and pitch until my hair was tied in knots. Of course girls nowadays couldn't get their hair tied in knots from riding.

"I wish I had a horse now."

"Well, I don't know where you'd get one," Mrs. Brewer, her daughter, replied. Even at 85, Mrs. Robinson is confident she can still ride.

War When Young.

While she was still a young girl, the Civil war broke out in all its fury. Her father, John Wesley Dunn, participated, being a member of Stevenson's company in Elmo's regiment of the Confederate army. For much of the duration of the conflict, these troops were stationed near Harrisburg on Buffalo bayou.

After their residence in Shelby county, the family moved to Old Hardin in Harris county. During the war, Millay Ann, about 15, rode the mail once a week between Spring and Harrisburg. Hair flying and galloping her horse, she made the trip alone and capably.

Harrisburg was not much in those days and Houston even less, from Mrs. Robinson's account.

On their trek to Texas, the families had brought negro slaves with them and utilized the blacks in working the farm lands.

Sold Girl for $1500.

"My father sold one of the negro slave girls for $1500 during the Civil war," she says. But the buyer didn't pay until after the war was over. Confederate money then was worthless. Though we had enough bills to paper the house, it wouldn't buy us things we needed."

Part of the time following the struggles between the states Mr. Dunn floated logs down Pile Island bayou to Orange.

Mrs. Robinson has spent most of her life in the vicinity of Houston, watching it grow and new developments supercede the old. She resides at present with her daughter, Mrs. Ida Brewer, at 7735 Baltimore. Mrs. H. Block, who lives in the Smith addition, is another daughter. Mrs. Robinson also has 10 grandchildren and 12 greatgrandchildren. Her brothers have all died.

Mrs. Robinson has never voted. She declares voting is "not a woman's business." She also upbraids the modern girl, particularly for her bobbed hair. Of her own she says:

"God gave me my hair and intended that I keep it, and I'm going to," she says.

At 85 years of age, Mrs. Robinson has retained most of her faculties, though she does not see as well as she would like. She is active and still proficient in the execution of the old-time dances.

101 RANCH WILL SHOW IN CITY ON OCTOBER 23

Houston citizens will be transported back to the time when the white man plunged into an unknown country where the savage red men roamed and ruled the plains and valleys, when the 101 Ranch Wild West show arrives in Houston, October 23, for a two-day stay.

Scouts, chieftains, hunters and pioneers will be brought to the present day in the many acts and exhibitions connected with the show. Famous adventurous epochs of the early history of the West will be unfolded in the two performances to be given here at the Sampson and Calhoun streets show grounds.

This famous show of the Miller Brothers will give an afternoon and evening performance, 2 and 8 p. m. each day. A parade downtown with all members of the large show taking part will be held at 11 a. m. the first day.

Tickets for the performance will be on sale at a downtown office (show day), location to be announced later.

REVUE SHOW PACKS LOEW'S

Thousands of Houstonians packed Loew's State theater Saturday from the time the doors opened in the morning until the last flicker on the silver screen near midnight. The unusual magnet for theatergoers was "The Hollywood Review" of 1929 with a cast of 20 famous movie and stage stars and a chorus of more than 100 show girls.

In connection with the screen attraction, Atwater Kent dealers and distributors are staging the first annual Atwater Kent-Loew's State theater radio show. A score of radio sets are on display, latest models of the Kent factory, little sets, big sets, old time sets, novelty combination sets and many other unusual receivers.

The table set on the mezzanine floor attracted considerable attention from the visitors Saturday. It was a complete Atwater Kent set built into a gate leg table. When the drawers of the table are closed one would never suspect that the beautiful article of furniture contained an up-to-date radio.

Another set which came in for a good share of attention was the combination buffet and radio. It contains glasses, decanters and silverware, everything necessary for the serving of a light lunch. The two millionth set made by the Atwater Kent factory also was on exhibition.

"The Hollywood Revue" was billed as the talking, dancing and singing sensation of the year, and the manner in which it was received by the large Saturday crowd indicates that it must be all of that.

Payroll Bandits Take $1500 in New Orleans

NEW ORLEANS, La., Oct. 20.—(AP)—Two unmasked bandits Saturday held up Louis McGarlin, paymaster of the Globe Construction company at Chartes and St. Ferdinand streets here and escaped with $1500.

SINGER

Corrine Hart, billed as "The Gem of Syncopation," will be one of the bright spots featured at the annual Firemen's Frolic and dance at the City Auditorium October 30 and 31. The frolic is for the benefit of the firemen's burial fund and tickets can be bought from city fire stations or direct from any fireman.

Health Education News

The health education department held a gym supper on Tuesday, October 15. Each member of a business woman's gym class was invited and brought a guest with her. A program was held during the supper hour. Miss Lucille Wilkins gave a tap dance. Miss Lucille Williamson, associate director of the health education department, also danced. Misses Edna Feeny, Louise Mulhausen and Victoria Moore put on an athletic stunt.

The Hiking club held the first meeting of the year on Sunday, October 13, and planned a program for the fall months.

The Hiking club is open to all women and girls who enjoy long country hikes and the outdoors.

The first hike of the year is to be taken Sunday, October 20. The girls will meet at the Y. W. C. A. at 6:30 a. m. and hike to Memorial park where breakfast will be cooked. Hikes for Saturday and Sunday evenings are planned for the coming months. All interested in joining the Hiking club are asked to call the Y. W. C. A., Fairfax 4346, and register.

A meeting will be held at the Y. W. C. A. on Friday, October 25, at 7:30 p. m. for representatives of all the different churches to discuss the possibilities of forming an inter-church basketball league for girls over 17 years of age.

The class for small girls in natural dancing opened last Saturday morning at 10:30 with Miss Lucille Williamson, associate director of the health education department as the teacher. The instruction in this class consists of rhythmic exercises, calisthenics and exercise for perfection of bodily poise and dancing technique. The dancing is interpretive of music and is one of the best recognized forms of exercise and development for young girls. The ages of this class are from six to ten.

Swimming lessons are being given for beginners and advanced pupils and will be given throughout the winter months. The water will be heated to 80 degrees.

Mrs. Johnnie Watson Murray is conducting the work in American Red Cross life saving tests and the corps which is sponsored by the health education department of the Y. W. C. A. is planning some interesting events for the winter months. All of those who are interested in becoming a senior American Red Cross life saver are asked to call the Y. W. C. A., Fairfax 4346, and register.

+++

Pine View Jolly Club

The Pine View Jolly Thimble club met at the home of Mrs. S. A. Rogers Tuesday. Lovely refreshments were served following the games and the social hour.

Mrs. C. A. Pattison, 116 Pine View drive, will be the next hostess.

DIALOGUE HIKES JOB OF WRITERS

The advent of the dialogue picture has increased the responsibilities and the importance of screen writers, just as it has lessened the authority of the director.

Motion picture scripts are more carefully prepared for dialogue pictures than they were for silent pictures. Usually when they are turned over to the director the story is complete and requires no changing on his part.

With the increased importance of writers, many are being elevated to executive positions and being placed in charge of production, with authority over the directors. Such a situation would have been considered next to impossible in the days of the silent drama.

Executive Writer.

One such writer who has just been placed in an executive position of great responsibility is C. Graham Baker, formerly in charge of the story department at First National studios, who is now associate executive, and acting jointly with Hal Wallis, is in complete charge of all production activities at this large and important producing plant.

Baker was appointed to this position by officials of First National because they realized that the writer's viewpoint is highly essential in the management of motion picture production.

Baker has had extensive experience as a screen writer and editor. He has been connected with motion picture work since 1914. At that time he was a cartoonist on a Brooklyn newspaper, and another cartoonist who had just been signed as a movie comedian, asked him to write a series of short comedies. The other cartoonist was the late Larry Semon, and Baker wrote 52 short comedies for Semon the first year he was in pictures.

Wrote Features.

Later he wrote features and then serials. He became story editor for Vitagraph and wrote for Inspiration, Fox, Universal and Warner Brothers. One of the best known pictures was Al Jolson's "The Singing Fool."

Several months ago he went to First National as story editor, and now shares with Wallis the responsibility of the entire plant, with its expenditures of millions each month. One of Baker's first official acts as associate executive was the naming of Walter Anthony, formerly a title writer, as story editor at First National.

Baker declares that the writer's responsibility has increased greatly with the advent of dialogue pictures.

"The ignorant and uncultured writer who 'got by' because he could shout louder than the director or the actors, has passed out of pictures," he declares.

"A picture now in no better than its dialogue, and this dialogue must sparkle in every line. It requires writers of background and education to write successful screen stories now."

Missouri War Veteran And Builder Expires

ST. JOSEPH, Mo., Oct. 20.—(AP) Col. Joseph A. Corby, 82, Civil and Spanish-American war veteran and retired financier, who built St. Joseph's first street car line and operated the first telephone exchange here, died Saturday at his home.

Committee Thanks Clubs

The W. C. T. U. social morality committee, Mrs. J. L. Abbe, wished to take this means of thanking each and every club, organization and newspaper for their splendid help and co-operation in securing a full time matron at the city jail.

The committee members feel that through combined effort a great good has been accomplished for the city and the unfortunate women and girls who are sent there.

Woolworth's New Lunch Counter Opens Today!

F. W. WOOLWORTH CO.
NEW LUNCH COUNTER
OPENING TO THE PUBLIC TODAY
Will Feature

TAYSTEE BREAD
THE READY SLICED LOAF
Also
DIXIE AND SWEETHEART BREAD
Quality Products of the
TEXAS BREAD CO.
Telephone Preston 0793

We Wish to Extend Our Congratulations

F. W. WOOLWORTH CO.
MAIN STREET

Upon the Opening of Their New

LUNCH COUNTER

Where You May Be Served at All Times With The Famous

DR. PEPPER
DELAWARE PUNCH

and Many Other Delicious Drinks

UNION BOTTLING WORKS
"Growing With Houston"

48 Years on the City's Pioneer Map

38 Riesner Street — Preston 0366

GRADE "A" MILK
For the New
F. W. WOOLWORTH CO. LUNCH COUNTER
Will Be Furnished by the
Cloverdale Creameries
INCORPORATED

Drink More Milk—More Cloverdale Creameries Milk—If You Please

Two Phones
Preston 2977 and 2978

F. W. WOOLWORTH CO.

5, 10 and 15 Cent Store — 513-17 Main Street, Houston, Texas

NEW SANITARY LUNCH DEPARTMENT

OPENS FOR BUSINESS TODAY (SATURDAY), OCTOBER 26, 8:30 A. M.

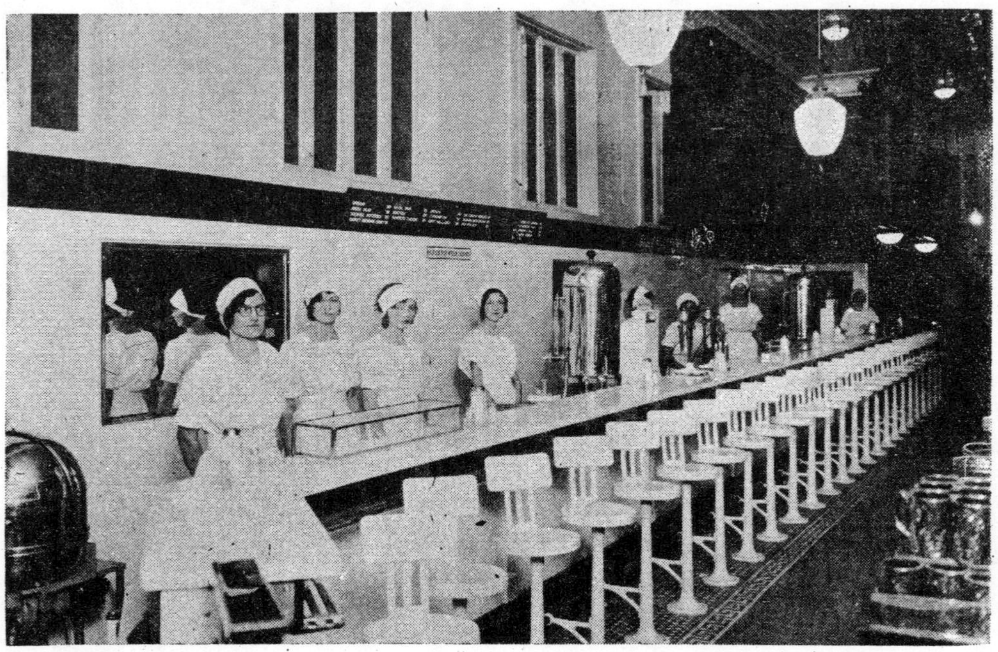

Our alterations have been completed and we are now prepared to serve you at our SANITARY LUNCH COUNTER with seating accommodations for 46 people and the latest equipment throughout. NOTHING BUT THE BEST FOODS WILL BE SERVED IN A STRICTLY SANITARY WAY AT WOOLWORTH PRICES.

Special Menu for Saturday, October 26th

SPECIAL TODAY
BIG BANANA SPLIT
10c

Home-Made Chili and Crackers
15c

TURKEY DINNER
Roast Young Turkey and Celery Dressing 15c
Cranberry Sauce 5c
Creamed Potatoes 5c
Green Peas 5c
Bread and Butter

SPECIAL TODAY
Double Rich Chocolate Malted Milk
5c

Spring Vegetable Soup and Crackers
10c

~PLATE LUNCHES~

No. 1 Plate Lunch
Breaded Veal Cutlets 15c
Mashed Potatoes 5c
Cold Slaw 5c
Bread and Butter

No. 2 Plate Lunch
Baked Ham 15c
Potato Salad 5c
Head Lettuce and Dressing 5c
Bread and Butter

No. 3 Plate Lunch
Chicken Sandwich 15c
Potato Chips 5c
Combination Salad 5c

Hot or Cold Tea, Coffee, Sweet Milk or Buttermilk 5c

SALADS
Chicken 15c
Potato 10c
Combination 15c
Egg and Potato 15c

VEGETABLES
Spinach 10c
Creamed Potatoes 10c
Green Peas 10c
Candied Yams 10c

SATURDAY EVENING FEATURE—5 to 8 p.m.
Sirloin Steak 15c
French Fried Potatoes ... 5c
Sliced Tomatoes 5c
Bread and Butter

ENTREES
Boston Baked Beans 15c
Beef Stew and Vegetables. 15c
Hot Vegetable Dinner 15c
Roast Beef and Mashed Potatoes 15c
Roast Pork and Dressing .. 15c
Hot Roast Beef Sandwich. 15c
Hot Roast Pork Sandwich. 15c
Tomato, Stuffed with Chicken 15c
Turkey Dressing and Gravy 10c
Baked Ham Sandwich 15c
Chicken Sandwich 15c
Pimento Cheese Sandwich. 15c
Home Made Chili 15c
Baked Ham and Potato Salad 15c
Breaded Veal Cutlets 15c

DESSERTS
Vanilla Cherry Parfait ... 15c
Banana Splits 10c
Pies, per cut 10c
Bananas and Cream 10c

FOUNTAIN
Chocolate Sundae 10c
Strawberry Sundae 10c
Pineapple Sundae 10c

VEGETABLE DINNER
Creamed Peas, Baked Corn, Mashed Potatoes and Corn Muffin
15c

Turkey Dinner Ready to Serve 11 a. m. Saturday

WHOLESOME, WELL-COOKED FOOD AT MINIMUM PRICES

F. W. WOOLWORTH CO.

5, 10 and 15c STORE — 513-17 Main Street — HOUSTON, TEXAS

SERVING THE BEST THE MARKET PRODUCES

South Texas Agricultural and Industrial

IN AND AROUND CONVENTION HALL

EXPOSITION

IN AND AROUND CONVENTION HALL

Opens Wednesday, October 30th

11 Big Days—Continues to November 9th—11 Big Days

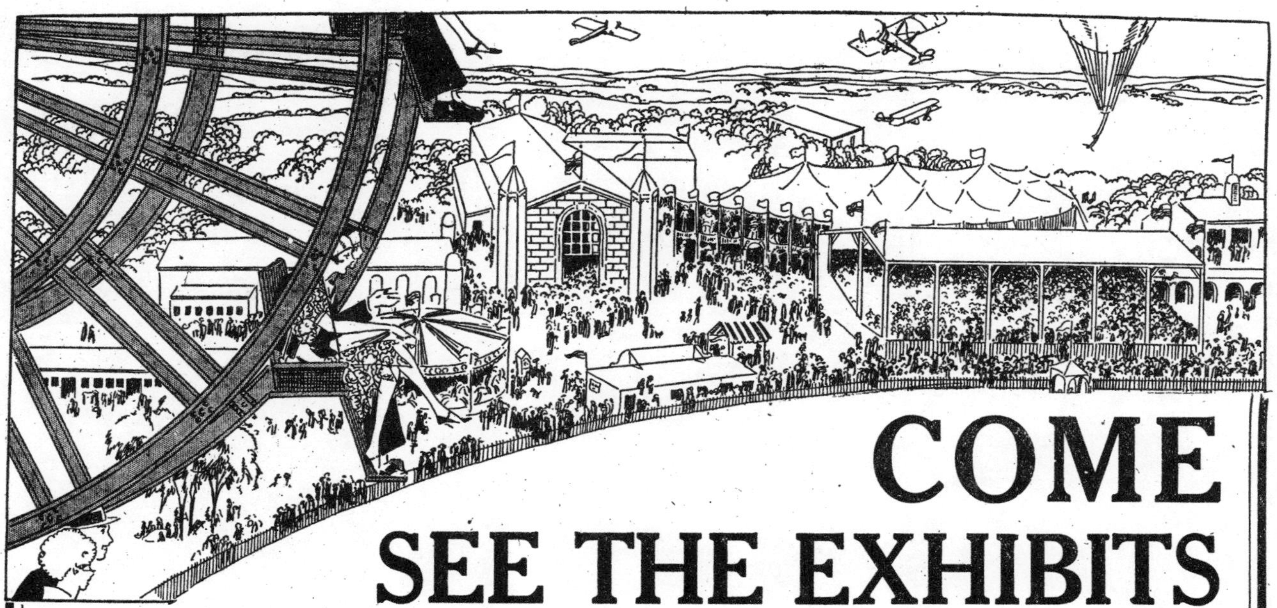

COME SEE THE EXHIBITS

Industrial - Agricultural - Poultry - Rabbits - Aviation

A. & M. College Agricultural Display

Illustrating Proper and Improper Methods of Farming

Boys' 4-H Club Exhibits

Farm products grown by members of Boys' 4-H Clubs under supervision of Extension Service of A. and M. College.

Girls' 4-H Club Exhibit

Exhibits of work done by 4-H Club Girls and by members of Women's Home Demonstration Clubs

Vocational Agricultural Exhibit

Showing work done by farm boys enrolled in vocational agriculture classes in rural high schools. This exhibit being entered by vocational teachers of Luther Burbank, Katy, Tomball and Angleton schools.

Poultry Show

Staged by South Texas Poultry Association, Julian A. Weslow, president. Get dope from him. Phone Preston 2404

Rabbit Show

Staged by South Texas Rabbit Breeders' Association, Hampton Ellis, secretary, South Texas Commercial National Bank Building. Preston 4381.

ADMISSION FREE *to* EXPOSITION *and* MIDWAY

REDUCED FARES ON ALL RAILROADS

Aviation Exhibit

A most interesting exhibit of present-day airplanes, parachutes, navigation instruments and flying accessories with *licensed well known pilots* in attendance day and night to answer all questions. A set of preliminary test questions prepared by Instructor Glenn Loomis, president of the Loomis School of Aviation—who will be present personally—will be given FREE to those interested.

County Agricultural Exhibits

The following counties will have county agricultural ehibits at the South Texas Agricultural and Industrial Exposition:

Gonzales, Wharton, Brazoria, Austin, Chambers, Liberty, Grimes, Walker, Madison, Angelina, Rusk, Harrison, Marion, Hunt, Hemphill, Houston, Washington, Lee, Henderson, Galveston, Ellis, Fort Bend (not definite), Bee.

Community Exhibits

Tomball, Hufsmith, Highlands

MIDWAY OPENS TUESDAY NIGHT

COMING DIRECT FROM STATE FAIR OF TEXAS (DALLAS)
MORRIS & CASTLE SHOWS
"The SHOW THAT SHOWS"

40 — Double Length Circus Cars — 40
483—People, Performers, Actors—483
20 Clean, Meritorious Attractions 20
12—New Thrilling Riding Devices—12

TEXAS GULF COAST BOOSTS OIL PRODUCTION

MOST FIELDS IN THAT AREA REPORT GAINS

Registering an increase of 4950 barrels in corrected daily average production of crude oil for the week ending October 19 the gulf coast Texas district registered a new high of 143,500 barrels.

Majority of the fields in the gulf coast district registered small increases for the period under consideration, marking the first time in several months that the gulf coast Texas district has increased to any great extent during a seven-day period.

Increases, however, were general in the districts in this section of the state, gulf coast Louisiana being the only one to decline during the period under consideration.

The gulf coast Louisiana district dropped off 1850 barrels to 24,750 barrels, while the East Central Texas district increased 1300 barrels, corrected daily average production figures for the district being 18,400 barrels.

Southwest Texas, and particularly the Refugio field in Refugio county, increased during the week ending October 19. The gain for the entire Southwest Texas district was 2850 barrels, bringing daily average production to 73,000 barrels. The gain for the Refugio field in Refugio county was 3350 barrels, bringing daily average production to 10,550 barrels.

Corrected daily average production in the various fields in the gulf coast Texas, Louisiana, East Central Texas and Southwest Texas districts follow:

Gulf Coast Texas.

Field—	Barrels
Barbers Hill	20,700
Batson	1,300
Big Creek	4,450
Blue Ridge	2,150
Boling	1,400
Damon Mound	600
Goose Creek	5,700
Hull	10,800
Humble	13,100
Orange	2,750
Pierce Junction	11,400
Raccoon Bend	8,650
Saratoga	1,000
Somerville	2,000
Sour Lake	2,600
South Liberty	5,850
Spindle Top	23,300
Sugar Land	11,400
West Columbia	6,700
Others	7,650
Total week end October 19	143,500
Total week end Ocotber 12	138,550
Increase week end Oct. 19.	4,950

Gulf Coast Louisiana.

Field—	Barrels
Bayou Boullion	200
East Hackberry	1,800
Old Hackberry	2,300
Edgerly	600
Evangeline	1,700
Lockport	4,100
Sorrento	150
Sulphur	7,600
Vinton	4,200
Others	2,100
Total week end October 19	24,750
Total week end October 12	26,600
Decline week end Oct. 19	1,850

East Central Texas.

Field—	Barrels
Boggy Creek	3,400
Corsicana-Powell	6,800
Currie	400
Mexia	5,150
[illegible] Creek	300
[illegible]	350
Wortham	1,050
Van Zandt county	1,000
Total week end October 19	18,400
Total week end October 12	17,100
Increase week end Oct. 19	1,300

Southwest Texas.

Field—	Barrels
Dale	400
Laredo	9,350
Luling	10,500
Lytton Springs	900
Refugio	10,550
Salt Flat	37,000
Somerset	1,200
Others	3,100
Total week end October 19	73,000
Total week end October 12	70,150
Increase week end Oct. 19	2,850

Petroleum Institute Figures Show Increase

NEW YORK, Oct. 27.—(AP)—The daily average gross crude oil production in the United States increased 65,100 barrels for the week ended October 19, totaling 2,903,200 barrels, says the weekly summary of the American Petroleum Institute. The daily average production east of California was 2,020,700 barrels, an increase of 55,100 barrels.

Refineries representing 94.9 per cent of the estimated daily potential refining capacity, operating at 85.1 per cent of their capacity, reported daily average run of crude oil to stills as 2,798,800 barrels. Daily average the previous week was 2,788,400 barrels for refineries representing 95.4 per cent of potential capacity operating at 84.3 per cent of their capacity.

Daily Average Production Difference.

	Barrels		Barrels
Oklahoma	708,250	a	57,700
Kansas	111,500	b	600
Panhandle Texas	107,650	a	1,450
North Texas	92,900	b	1,100
West Cent. Texas	57,300	a	1,100
West Texas	364,500	b	7,400
East Cent. Texas	18,450	a	1,350
Southwest Texas	73,000	a	2,850
North Louisiana	39,450	b	1,750
Arkansas	64,800	a	350
Coastal Texas	143,500	a	4,950
Coastal Louisiana	24,750	b	1,850
Eastern (not including Mich.)	120,250	a	250
Michigan	16,800	b	550
Wyoming	54,950	b	1,350
Montana	10,750	b	50
Colorado	5,450	b	150
New Mexico	6,450	b	100
California	822,500	a	10,000
Total	2,903,200	a	65,100

a—Increase.
b—Decrease.

Daily average imports of petroleum at principal ports for the week ended October 19 were 317,286 barrels compared with 261,857 for the previous week, and 308,929 for the four weeks ended October 19.

Daily average receipts of California oil at Atlantic and gulf coast ports for the week ended October 19 were 119,429 barrels compared with 63,000 for the previous week, and 74,000 for the four weeks ended October 19.

Refinery operation:

October 19—Week ended crude run to stills, 19,592,000 barrels; total daily average, 2,798,800 barrels; gasoline stocks, 32,160,000; gas and fuel stocks, 146,421,000 barrels.

October 12—Week ended crude run to stills, 19,518,700 barrels; total daily average, 2,788,400 barrels; gasoline stocks, 32,324,000 barrels; gas and fuel stocks, 145,208,000 barrels.

Development to Start Soon Near Brenham

BRENHAM, Oct. 27.—(Sp)—Oil development will start in the near future in the Niederauer block, about two miles north of Brenham. A derrick has been erected on the T. S. Estes place, machinery has arrived and drilling will start by November 1.

Several thousands of aces have been leased for oil purposes, and geologists who have made surveys are hopeful that some good producers will be brought in.

DAILY OIL REVIEW

Completion of two wells on the Dewalt structure, near Sugar Land in Fort Bend county, was reported at the close of the week. Humble Oil and Refining company brought in their Nelson No. 6 for an initial production of 632 barrels from a total depth of 3690 feet, and their Camp No. 8 for an initial production of 600 barrels from a total depth of 3622 feet.

Locations also were announced for their Nelson No. 7 and Camp No. 9, while their Hagerson No. 1 is to go on the pump at 3811 feet, and their Brazos Farms No. 8 was waiting on cement at 3096 feet.

Other drilling activities in the field are: Sugar Land No. 12, drilling cement at 3734 feet; Sugar Land No. 13 is a derrick; Sugar Land No. B-1 is in sticky shale at 2891 feet; Peterson No. 1 is in sandy shale at 3692 feet; Bankers Mortgage No. C-1 is in shale and lime at 2400 feet.

Several completions are expected in the Barbers Hill field in Chambers county the early part of this week, as two wells were standing cemented on oil-showing sands.

The Texas Company's Wilburn No. 3 will drill in at 5000 feet, while Yount-Lee Oil company's Chambers No. 8 set screen at 5136 feet.

Other drilling operations in the field follow: Mills Bennett Production company's Collier No. 1, drilling at 5320 feet; Collier No. 2 a derrick; Smith No. 3 to pump at 5160 feet; Smith No. 4 in lime at 1125 feet; Wilburn No. 1 is a derrick; Barber No. 2 is in gumbo at 1325 feet; Hammon No. 3 in gumbo at 1236 feet.

The Humphreys corporation's Kirby No. A-8 is fishing at 6440 feet; Kirby No. H-6 has set casing at 4940 feet; Kirby No. C-2 is in shale and lime at 4000 feet; Kirby No. B-6 is milling at 4085 feet; Scott No. 1 is rigging up. Sinclair Oil and Gas company's McKinney No. 1 is bailing.

The Texas Company's Lawrence No. 1 is in shale at 3188 feet; their Wilburn No. 1 is in sandy shale at 4900 feet and their Wilburn No. 2 is in hard sand at 4001 feet. Gulf Production company's Wilburn No. 1 is sidetracking at 2150 feet, the well has a total depth of 2700 feet.

In Harris county at Humble the Texas company's Landslide No. 270 is in gumbo at 2072 feet; their House No. 23 is in sticky shale at 4194 feet; their Dunman No. 1 has set 6 5-8-inch casing at 4587 feet; their Stevenson No. 41 is in gumbo at 868 feet.

The Humble Oil and Refining company's Williams No. 5 will bail at 5378 feet; their Williams No. 7 is rigging up; their Glass No. 1 is in packed sand at 6331 feet; their Oats No. 1 is in shale at 4244 feet; their Trahon No. 1 is in shale and lime at 2590 feet. The Sun Oil company is rigging up its Bender No. 1.

The South Texas Production company's Morris No. 12 has spudded in; their Morris No. 11 is sidetracking at 4950 feet, and their Lee No. 1 has set screen at 4550 feet.

At Goose Creek the Humble Oil and Refining company's Simms-Smith No. 76 is in gumbo and boulders at 3182 feet.

At Genoa their Woodburn No. 2 is waiting on cement at 1830 feet; at Mykawa their Slad[illegible]s No. 1 is testing at 3394 feet. At [illegible]ekley their Warren No. 6 is reaming at 4496 feet.

At Big Creek, in Fort Bend county, the Gulf Production company completed their T. W. Davis No. 56 for an initial production of 3500 barrels from a total depth of 4175 feet, and made location for their T. W. Davis No. 57. Their Davis No. 25 is drilling at 3080 feet.

At Blue Ridge the Gulf Production company's Lutscher No. 17 is sidetracking. The well has a total depth of 4200 feet. At Orchard their Moore No. 19 is drilling at 6300 feet, and at Long Point their Trone No. 12 is drilling at 6120 feet.

At Boling the Texas company has abandoned its Pleasant No. 2 at a total depth of 5299 feet.

In Jefferson county at Fannette the Gulf Production company is rigging up its Burrell No. 4 and Bordages No. 8. Their Junker No. 1 has set strainer at 4870 feet.

At Big Hill the Texas company's Pipkin No. 2 is in sand and shale at 5165 feet, and their Fitzhugh No. 1 is in hard lime at 3708 feet.

In Brazoria county at West Columbia the Texas company has made location for their Arnold No. 25. The Humble Oil and Refining company's Smith No. 3 is drilling at 4809 feet. The Gulf Production company's Tom Hogg No. B-3 is drilling at 3150 feet.

In Liberty county at the Hankamer dome the Gulf Production company's Weiser No. 1 is drilling at 3665 feet; their Boyt No. 3 is drilling at 1200 feet.

At Hull the Humble Oil and Refining company's Hooks-Spell No. 12 is in sand at 301 feet. At Moss Bluff their R. S. Sterling No. 6 is in hard sand and lime at 4666 feet.

Completion of two gas wells were reported in the Refugio field in Refugio county Saturday.

Mission Drilling company's Fox No. 2 came in as a gasser with 1250 pounds pressure, through quarter inch choke from a sand at 3660-70 feet.

The Houston Oil company completed their Rooke No. F-2 as a gas well with 1275 pounds pressure through a quarter inch choke from a sand at 3672-82 feet.

Queen Marie Directing Royal Palace Building

BUCHAREST, Oct. 27.—(AP)—Under direct supervision of Queen Marie, the royal palace, which burned down while the late King Ferdinand was lying on his deathbed, is being rebuilt. She is assisted by a commission of the leading Rumanian architects, engineers and decorative artists, who advise the department of public works.

The palace is to be considerably more spacious than the old building.

Contract Awarded for State Cop Motorcycles

AUSTIN, Oct. 27.—(AP)—The board of control Saturday let the contract for the purchase of 40 motorcycles to be used by state highway patrolmen.

The contract was let to the Mutual Motor company of Abilene at $358.35 each, a total of $14,334.

Fire Destroys Homes of Colony on Pacific Coast

LOS ANGELES, Oct. 27.—(AP)—Ten houses at Malibu Beach, fashionable seaside colony, where the pretentious summer homes of many wealthy people and motion picture stars are located, were destroyed by a fire Saturday.

The damage was estimated at $200,000.

NACOGDOCHES MAN DIES.

NACOGDOCHES, Oct. 27.—Dude Stallings, 72, prominent Nacogdoches county citizen, died at his home in the Oak Ridge community Saturday. Burial will be at Fairview Sunday.

West Texas Permian Basin Offers Several High Points of Interest

MIDLAND, Oct. 27.—(Sp)—High points of field activity in the West Texas Permian basin during the past week comes from an extension effected in the Fisher county area, a well of unusual performance in Upton county, and the Pecos county area.

In Fisher county the semi-wildcat test of Mid-West Exploration company, Steele No. 1, extended the proven area around a mile to the southeast while pay lime was encountered from 3192-93 feet, total depth. The well is estimated good for 200 to 300 barrels and has taken in only one foot of the pay sand. The new producer figures around 20 feet higher on top of the lime pay than of the Sinclair Oil and Gas company, Steele No. 1, which topped the pay at 3209 feet, and was completed for initial of 602 barrels per day at total depth of 3225 feet. Operators are expecting a good-sized performance from the Mid-West Exploration company's well as soon as storage can be erected, and same is carried deeper into the pay.

Proves Up Acreage.

This extension will serve to prove up acreage held by the Sinclair Oil and Gas company, Texas company, Roeser & Pendleton, Cosden Oil company and Cranfill & Reynolds. It is thought the well will require as many as two offsets, possibly three. Any other activity which may spring up will, no doubt, fall farther to the south and east, as a number of tests which were made to the north of the Sinclair well in section 72 and the Texas company's Stephens No. 1 in section 79, proved dusters.

Farther to the west in the Permian basin district, what proved to be the sensation of the week was the White Eagle Oil and Refining company Ed S. Hughes No. 2, located in the William Teer survey. This well started flowing at the rate of 100 barrels per hour from pay topped at 2273, total depth 2275 feet. The well produced around 2000 barrels the first 24 hours, and has not fallen below 1700 barrels per day for any 24-hour period since being placed on production.

While this well is located in a proven sector, it has shown up so much larger than other wells in the area that it can be considered nothing less than a sensation for Upton county. Upton county is one of the oldest producing districts in the Permian basin. Outside of Pecos county it has probably furnished more dry holes than any other county in the basin. While a good per cent of the most favorable acreage in this county has been under lease for several years, it is still being given attention. The Shell Petroleum corporation is the principal one buying in the county, but such acreage as it acquires is taken only after exploration by core drills. Only recently the Shell has leased three different blocks following core drill work.

Two New Producers.

In Pecos county nice producers were furnished, both in the Yates pool and the Taylor-Link district. In the Yates district the one big well for the week was that of the Gulf Production company, I. G. Yates, No. 25. It showed up good for 1000 barrels per hour from 1321-22 feet, and at this depth the tools were blown up in the hole, later sticking five feet off bottom.

The Taylor-Link pool offered a new well producing at the rate of 40 barrels the first hour, later settling down to around 30 barrels per hour, in the Landreth Production and World Oil company No. 2-8 University. The well is making its oil from 1602-20 feet, which conforms with the lower producing horizon of this district.

QUIET RULES IN ABILENE AREA

ABILENE, Oct. 27.—(Sp)—No new developments had been reported as a result of the discovery of commercial production in north central Taylor county in Dunigan Brothers No. 1 Hunter. No. 1 rated as a 200-barrel pumper from a stray line formation at 2389.91 feet.

The Hunter well has been shut-in while the owners have been attempting to secure a pipeline outlet for the oil. Thursday no arrangements had been made for a line and it was reported that additional storage tanks were to be put on the lease in order to allow producing the well.

Few trades on leases and royalty have been reported on acreage in the vicinity of the new discovery. Gibson and Johnson of Abilene bought 429 acres a mile south of the well for $20 an acre and agreed to start a test on the tract within 90 days. Several other deals were reported but none of them had been confirmed.

All indications point to a slow development of the Hunter area. In the first place the surrounding acreage is in the hands of Dunigan Brothers, owners of the well, and of Shell Petroleum corporation, to a large extent and neither of them are likely to start any new operations until the price of oil begins to show advancements.

The only features of the week in this area were in Jones county, where a new location was announced and a wildcat test in the central part of the county was reported dry.

Mid-Tex Oil and Gas company have spudded its W. A. Minter No. 1. This test is to go to 2300 feet and will be drilled with a Super-D spudder. Jay A. McCartney of San Angelo has the drilling contract. The test is four miles north of Hawley.

Sedgwich Oil and Gas company's J. C. Brown No. 1 five miles southwest of Anson in the central part of Jones county is being plugged as dry at a depth of 2750 feet.

CHURCH PARLEY TALKS BUDGET

M'KINNEY, Oct. 27—(AP)—Greenville Saturday was selected as the next meeting place of the North Texas conference of the Methodist Episcopal Church, South. The Wesley church of that city will act as the conference's host. Denison also sought the meeting.

The annual conference here will close Sunday night with assignment of pastors for the next year.

The task of paring board requests to meet the financial condition of the conference is facing the conference.

The financial condition of the conference is said to be acute, due to dry weather over a large part of the conference territory. The only bright spots in the picture as presented were the reports of preachers, showing claims against the church were in a much better shape than last year.

One of the things depending upon the budget allowance was the naming of a conference superintendent of religious education. More money was necessary for the place before one of the younger men, whom the general board wished to see appointed, might be named to this place.

College Proposal Before Conference

SAN ANTONIO, Oct. 27.—(AP)—With indications pointing to favorable action, the West Texas Methodist conference had before it Saturday the plans of trustees of Westmoorland college to make the institution a senior co-educational college.

If the conference approves, the college plans a campaign for a million dollar fund for expansion.

Horse Stands Against Automobile in Spain

MADRID, Oct. 27. — (AP) — The horse drawn carriage still makes in Spain a stand against the encroachment of the automobile, but it is a losing fight.

In the capital some old families, if also possessed of wealth, continue to keep their grand carriage and fine-blooded steeds, their liveried coachmen and footmen, and drive of afternoons in the parks.

But the horses for which Spain was famous, whose ancestors went to Mexico with Cortes and whose increase populated the Western plains, are seen less and less, as taxis honk through the streets of Spanish cities.

However, the humble mule and donkey still hold their own. They plod along just as patiently and numerously over every road and highway, still packing or pulling incredible loads, still being cussed constantly in the ancient, approved fashion of muleteers the world over.

ACTIVITY IN OIL CIRCLES GAINS

GONZALES, Oct. 27.—(Sp)—Oil operations in Gonzales county are beginning to take on considerable proportions, as shown by the extensive leasing in nearly all parts of the county.

Cranfield and Reynolds company spudded in their well on the F. J. Land place east of Peach creek in the eastern part of the county and are going down at a lively rate. They have about 15,000 acres of land leased in this section.

A well is being drilled on the F. C. Reid farm about eight miles southeast of Gonzales near the Middle Buster highway, and Adams and Liles Independent Oil company has nearly 4000 acres of land leased near this location.

The Shell company, Magnolia, Gulf, Empire and Sun and other large companies are leasing in many sections of the county. Another location has been made about one mile east of Dilworth, where oil has been found at 383 feet, with a small drilling outfit, and a large derrick is being placed on the ground.

There are two wells being drilled about three miles north of Waelder, and L. J. Jones has made a location on the A. S. Kindred survey about 10 miles northeast of Gonzales. Burt and Burt will start operations on a test about two miles north of Gonzales shortly. The North and South Oil company plan to start drilling near Cheapside within 90 days. Beeman and Staton are down about 650 feet at the Staton place about 7 miles west of Gonzales, and the Norwood No. 1 near Ottine is still producing oil in paying quatities.

Coleman County Field Gets 500-Barrel Well

COLEMAN, Oct. 27.—(Sp)—The outstanding completion in Coleman county's oil field is Permian Oil company and Gibson & Johnson Crowder No. 4, which has been completed for approximately 500 barrels. This well is located between the Eastland Oil company's Crowder No. 1 and Permian Oil company and Gibson & Johnson Crowder No. 1.

The Eastlands well is producing approximately 130 barrels a day, and the Gibson & Johnson and Permian Oil company 1000 barrels.

There is still one other well drilling between the Permian Oil company and Gibson & Johnson No. 1 and their recent completion offsetting the Tower & McKanna lease to the north. Levi Smith completed his Nos. 4 and 5 Morris. Neither of these wells looked large until after being shot. They are rating from 100 to 150 barrels each.

Petrolia Again Is Agog Over Two New Wells

PETROLIA, Oct. 27.—(AP)—This North Clay county town, center of one of Texas' earliest oil fields, the Petrolia shallow oil and gas development in 1900, again finds itself agog with oil excitement.

Completion of a 100-barrel flowing well by Merrick & Goldsmith just southeast of the public school, in a sand 1015 feet, was followed within 10 days by a 300-barrel offset drilled by Art & Taxman of Wichita Falls. Three rigs are being moved on to nearby locations and town lots are included in some of the lease deals which followed the discovery.

Port Arthur Oil Man Named to Committee

Appointment of G. N. Bliss, assistant general manager of the marine department, Gulf Refining company, Port Arthur, as a member of the American Petroleum institute's technical committee on prevention of pollution was announced by D. V. Stroop, chairman.

Mr. Bliss is chairman of the gulf coast sectional committee on oil pollution. Members are: S. W. Oberg, Humble Oil and Refining company, Houston; John Carlstrom, the Texas company, Port Arthur, and Claude F. Reynaud, Standard Oil company of Louisiana, Baton Rouge.

Magnolia Plans Building Pipe Line in Oklahoma

OKLAHOMA CITY, Oct. 27.—(UP)—The Magnolia Petroleum company will start construction of a $700,-eight-inch pipe line to run to the company's main trunk line at Purcell, 41 miles away from the Oklahoma City field, shortly, company officials announced.

More than 150 men have been employed for the work, it was said. Pipe has been ordered, and officials expect the crude carrier will be completed in 90 days. Two 55,000-barrel capacity storage tanks are to be constructed. Total capacity of the pipe lines will be about 125,000 barrels daily.

TWO OFFETS TO GUADALUPE GUSHER LOOM

SAN ANTONIO, Oct. 27.—(Sp)—Two offsets to the company's R. C. Appling No. 1, new Guadalupe county gusher, have been announced by the Magnolia Petroleum company. South offset to the well, production of which was estimated at the rate of 6400 barrels daily after it came in last week, will be on the L. V. Echols tract. A southwest offset will be on another tract.

It was reported that Cranfill & Reynolds also were preparing to drill and offset 300 feet west of Magnolia's No. 1, this well to be on the R. C. Appling tract.

Although admitting they were not certain, Magnolia officials expressed belief the new well is producing from the Edwards lime. Some geologists voiced the opinion that the oil was coming from the chalk.

It is known that the last core was taken from the chalk at 2532 feet. When the plug was drilled in, the driller, it is said, went between eight and 10 feet deeper before pay was struck.

Luling reports this week were to the effect that five acres in the southeast corner of the tract adjoining the Appling farm was leased to a Tulsa party for consideration of $1000 per acre, overriding royalties and a drilling contract.

The Magnolia gusher again put Guadalupe county in the spotlight of Southwest Texas oil and gas operations. It is between Luling, Caldwell county, and the Darst Creek pool in Guadalupe, where drilling has been largely closed down since the first two producers were brought in. The No. 1 Appling, however, is nearer the Penn Manford No. 1 wildcat, a 1000-barrel producer brought in a few months ago, than it is to either Luling or Darst Creek.

At last reports, the Magnolia well was pinched in pending completion of pipeline from the well to the company's tank farm at Luling. The oil was said to test 36.50 gravity, corrected.

NEW REFINERY IS MAKING GAS

PALESTINE, Oct. 27.—(Sp)—Another area of development in the Anderson county oil field was reached when gasoline from the new refinery located four miles northeast of Neches was turned into the pipe lines of the Humble Oil and Refining company and carried to loading stations in both Neches and Jacksonville.

This refinery, although not completed in all its detail, is doing business. The deliveries to the loading stations is for railroad shipments to points more than 50 miles distant from the plant. Big tanker trucks will furnish delivery to all points within a radius of 50 miles of the new plant.

The Humble Oil and Refining company, owner and developer of the local oil field, has completed a number of stations in Jacksonville and other East Texas towns and is building three stations in Palestine.

Iowa Company to Make Test Near San Marcos

SAN MARCOS, Oct. 27.—(Sp)—The Weber oil interests of Davenport, Iowa, represented by W. L. Richards and H. A. Lang, have leased 2000 acres of land some 18 miles northeast of San Marcos, on the Buda-Niederwald road, adjacent to what is known as the Martin church.

Material for the derrick and the drilling rig are being placed on the grounds, and drilling will start shortly.

The company has had this particular acreage under examination for several months, and Richards, the geologist, who has operated extensively and successfully in the Laredo oil fields, states that the outlook for production is extremely good. His contract with the Weber Oil company takes him to the depth of the Edwards lime, a geological formation in this country, where oil is usually found.

OIL FIRE FIGHTERS

F. T. Kinley (left) and M. M. Kinley are Tulsa boys who made good by squelching oil field candles. Their latest feat was the dousing of this blaze from a 50,000,000-foot gas well in Oklahoma City.

BOATS BOUGHT TO SHIP CRUDE

Increase in their equipment for transporting oil from the Barbers Hill field in Chambers county to points on the Houston ship channel and at Texas City, was announced Saturday by the Liberty Pipe Line company.

The increase in equipment consists of a towboat and an oil carrying barge. With this new equipment the company will be able to transport around 15,000 barrels of oil a day from the Barbers Hill field.

At present the company is operating two towboats and a like number of barges.

Another item of interest relative to the transportation of oil from this field is that the war department has appropriated funds for the dredging of Cedar bayou to a depth of 8 feet at mean low tide. This increased depth will enable faster navigation of the waterway, and also will permit the use of larger towboats and barges.

Work of dredging Cedar bayou is expected to start about November 15, and will be rushed to completion.

Terminal of the Liberty Pipe Line company is on Cedar bayou, near the town of Cedar Bayou, and transportation of the oil by water has been going on for the past several years.

Haley Young Test Near Teague Has Fishing Job

TEAGUE, Oct. 27.—(Sp)—The Haley Young oil test seven miles east of Teague is at a depth of 5000 feet with casing set at 4300 feet.

While boring through the concrete a slight mishap has caused a temporary delay in drilling. The fishing job is only temporary, and drilling will be resumed shortly.

Prospects are bright for bringing in a paying well. The promoters have bought up practically all the leases for an area of eight by two miles, and one-half of all the royalty available.

This well is on the same trend as the Van well in Van Zandt county. Other major oil companies have leased up over 100,000 acres near the site of this test.

OIL OUTPUT AT REFUGIO GAINS

With oil production hitting a high average of 13,000 barrels a day, the Refugio field is fast taking major rank as an oil producing area in the coastal territory. Karona Oil company's Reilly No. 3 was showing for a well during the midweek when this was written. From a total depth of 3669 feet the well was flowing around 75 barrels of pipe line oil. It will be tubed and this should increase the production. Mission Drilling company developed a pressure of 1475 pounds on its Shelly No. 2 from a sand encountered by the drill at 3641-50 feet. The gas will be killed and the test cored deeper.

A number of tests are developing oil showing sands and have either set or are in process of setting casing. The more interesting ones follow:

Houston Gulf Gas company is setting casing in its Fannie Heard No. 8, which has an oil showing sand at 3649-52 feet; its No. 4, same, is coring a sand at 3666 feet and its Shelly No. 8 is in sticky shale at 3295 feet.

Mission Drilling company's Shelly No. 3 is in gumbo and lime at 3406 feet; its Mitchell No. 2 is in hard sand at 3824 feet. Houston Oil company has three tests cemented as follows: Rooke No. 2-F at 3672 feet; Pratt-Hewit-Rooke No. 10, at 3691 feet and Rooke No. 13 at 3678 feet. Pearson Properties, Inc., is coring a sand in its Swift et al No. 1 at 3680 feet. Sun Oil company's Leisering No. 1 has set at 3670 feet. Morgan Oil corporation's City No. 2 has set at 3676 feet. Refugio Oil corporation's Murphy No. 1 is preparing to set screen to test an oil showing sand, total depth 3676 feet.

There are no less than 40 strings of tools in operation at Refugio at this time, counting locations rigged and ready to spud.

SALAMANDERS OF OIL FIELDS IN RISKY GAME

TULSA, Okla., Oct. 27.—(AP)—Into an inferno consuming enough fuel to heat a city, two nonchalant men drag a huge bomb.

It is a steel barrel containing a charge of high explosive.

They retire to shelter. An electric contact is made and—boom! A colossal candle that has lit the countryside for miles around is out.

Thus human ingenuity conquers oil field fires which defeat ordinary methods of fire-fighting.

Tulsa is the seat of a small closed corporation of these death-defying firemen whose business is to squelch unruly blazes in the midcontinent oil area of Kansas, Oklahoma and Texas.

Tex Works Alone.

Outstanding is the Kinley company, with M. M. and F. T. Kinley, brothers, as officers, directors and staff. Then there is Tex Thornton, who works alone.

Suggest to "Mack" that there is anything dramatic or heroic in his calling, and one receives a snort of disdain in reply.

Asbestos suits for protection in approaching terrific heat of oil and gas fires have become standard equipment, but the Kinley brothers scorn the 60-pound suits as cumbersome. Instead they wear two or three pairs of khaki work trousers, as many shirts, and caps with ear muffs. They keep their clothing soaked with water.

A Recent Task.

Extinguishing fire from a gas well of 50,000,000 cubic feet in the Oklahoma City field was the Kinley brothers' most recent task. Its intense heat melted a 100-foot steel derrick over the well.

For more than a day, the Kinley brothers and aides cut away that steel so they might approach the well. Then, facing maddening heat, they rolled the bomb and fired it.

The brothers left the field unconcernedly after they were satisfied the fire was out.

Their pay for those two days' work was reported as $10,000. And few envy them their job.

Texas Children

Staff Photo's—Houston Photo Service
Andrew A. Moss Manager.

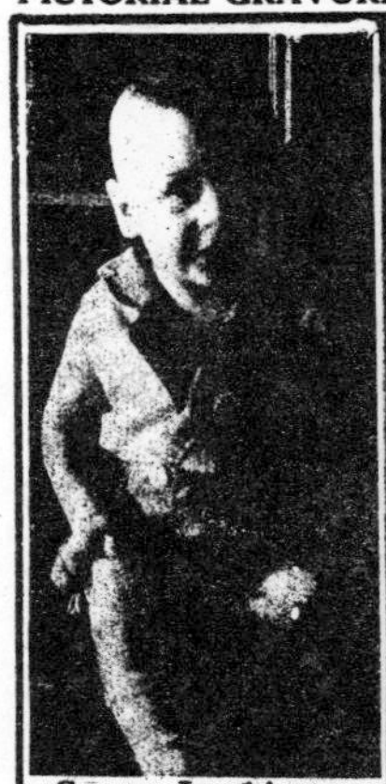

Carson Jr., 14 mos., son of Mr. and Mrs. C. C. Reneham, Texas City

Jesse Elmer Jr., 4, son of Mr. and Mrs. J. E. Hylton, Highlands

Ruba May, 9, and Wanda Ruth, 3, daughters of Mr. and Mrs. Tom Trevathan, Crosby

Ethel Murl, 18 months, daughter of Mrs. Lucille Butler, Sugarland

Gayle, 7, son of Mr. and Mrs. Jake Vicic of Sugarland

Wilfred Clyde, 2 son of Dr. and Mrs. W. C. Hooper, Rosenberg

Emily Flora, 10½; Viola, 8, daughters of Mr. and Mrs. J. C. Stucklick, Rosenberg

Wayne, 2, son of Mr. and Mrs. J. A. Henderson, 718 Hts. Blvd.

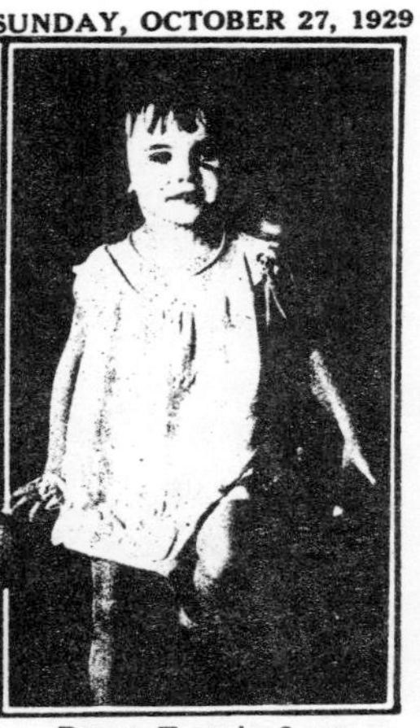

Denny Francis, 3, son of Mr. and Mrs. J. R. Wisenbaker, Crosby

James Carter, 11 months, son of Mr. and Mrs. J. E. Johnston, Highlands

Emmie, 8; Jearld Eugene, 6, and Ralph Jr., 6, children of Mr. and Mrs. Ralph Swan, Highlands

Geraldine, 9, and Shirley, 3, daughters of Mr. and Mrs. C. J. Landry, Highlands

Nina Beth, 6, and Joseph, 2, children of Mr. and Mrs. J. M. Gay, Texas City

Clarence, 10, and Kenneth, 6, sons of Mr. and Mrs. Edward Roberts, Texas City

Howard Russell, 4, and Paul Edward, 2, sons of Mr. and Mrs. G. H. Taylor, Humble

Lee, 9; George, 5; Walter, 2, sons of Mr. and Mrs. R. L. Loflin, Humble

Frances Harrell, granddaughter of Mr. and Mrs. R. A. Harrell of 1105 Yale

Dorothy Adele, 9, and Nancy, 6, daughters of Mr. and Mrs. L. G. Wade, Texas City

Velah, 7, daughter of Mr. and Mrs. A. A. Rister of Sugarland

Doris, 5, and Samuel, 13, children of Mr. and Mrs. S. F. Alexander, Rosenberg

Edwin, 11, and Bill, 7, sons of Mr. and Mrs. E. B. McLaurin, 4440 McKinney

Delma, 10; Guroa, 7; Jose, 4; Clovis, 2, and Travis, 8 mos., sons of Mr. and Mrs. E. M. Archer, Humble

James, 13; Wilson, 11, and Wayne, 9, sons of Mr. and Mrs. Fred G. Deats, Dickinson

Connie Lea, 6, daughter of Mr. and Mrs. J. L. Hopkins, Texas City

Jack Dempsey, 2, son of Mr. and Mrs. H. H. Zipprian, Texas City

Esther, 11; James Edward, 8; Faurette, 6; Blake, 4, and Eldon, 1, children of Mr. and Mrs. J. J. Farmes, Highlands

Leedon, 11; Elouise, 9, and R. L., 8, children of Mr. and Mrs. L. R. Beard, Rosenberg

Pauline, 9, and Luther, 5 months, children of Mr. and Mrs. M. L. Williams, Humble

Woodrow, 13, and Douglas, 9, sons of Mr. and Mrs. J. L. Hopkins, Texas City

At left: Yvonne, 15 months, and Mickey, 10, children of Mr. and Mrs. R. E. Kenser, 1137 Allston

At right— Leverda, 3, and David Mayson, 5 months, children of Mr. and Mrs. A. M. Mings, Texas City

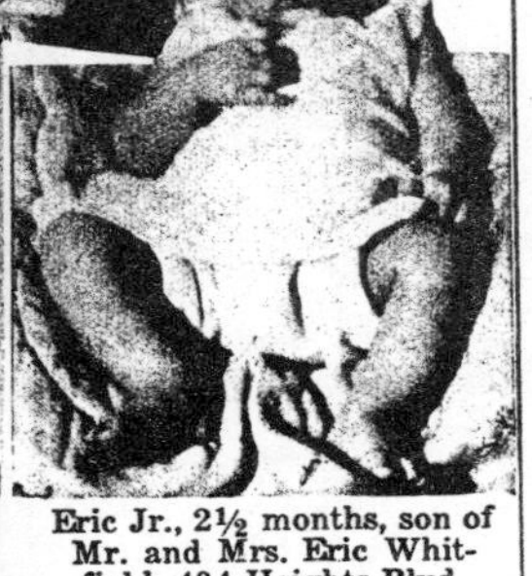

Eric Jr., 2½ months, son of Mr. and Mrs. Eric Whitfield, 404 Heights Blvd.

The baby pictures shown on this page were made by the Houston Photo Service. The original picture measures 9¼ inches deep and 7 inches wide, in a nice folder 11¾ inches deep and 8¾ inches wide.

If you are interested in any of these pictures, additional copies may be obtained by filling in the coupon below and mailing it to the Houston Photo Service, 2318 Polk Avenue, Houston, Texas.

Name ....

Street Address ....

City ....

State ....

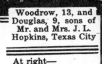

Inside Today
"Inside stuff" on the news at Washington by Rodney Dutcher. —Page 4

MUSKOGEE TIMES-DEMOCRAT

ASSOCIATED PRESS — UNITED PRESS — N. E. A. SERVICE

AP Means Associated Press

VOL. XL.— NO. 79 | CITY EDITION | MUSKOGEE, OKLA., MONDAY EVENING, APRIL 2, 1934 | CITY EDITION | PRICE FIVE CENTS

$1,800,000,000 to Carry on PWA Work Throughout Nation to Be Requested

TEXAS KILLERS ELUDE NET OF OFFICERS

CONGRESS FACES DRIVING FINISH BEFORE QUITTING

Members Are Anxious to Get Through in Washington and Start Electioneering

WIRT PROBE TO START

Speaker Rainey to Name Special Committee to Investigate 'Brain Trust' Charges

WASHINGTON, April 2—(AP)—Congress is up to its ears in work and the end is not yet. President Roosevelt is expected to give the legislators more labor when he gets back from fishing.

Democratic leaders understand he will ask for about $1,800,000,000 additional for the PWA.

There was no official business today, because of the death of Rep. Pou of North Carolina, dean of the house, but both branches will plunge into their tasks tomorrow. They are anxious to adjourn and get to their home-work in preparation for coming elections.

Stock Regulation Up

Democratic leaders plan to push for action on such important administration legislation as the revised sugar control and 330 million dollars revenue bills.

Besides acting on the sugar bill tomorrow, the house is to vote on the Johnson measure, already adopted by the senate. This would prevent defaulting war debtors from obtaining loans here. Action may be reached also on the Rankin resolution, calling for an investigation of utility rates by the power commissions.

The senate will plunge into tax bill debate tomorrow with a view to a vote late in the week. The senate banking committee again planned to take up in private the highly contested stock market regulation bill.

To Name Probers

Speaker Rainey will soon appoint a special congressional committee to inquire into the charges of Dr. William A. Wirt, Gary, Ind., educator, that the "brain trust" is plotting a revolution. He will also name a committee to look into nazi propaganda and activities in this country.

House action on the senate bill to guarantee the principal as well as interest of the two billion dollars in home loan bank bonds is scheduled for late in the week.

Chairman Rayburn (d) Texas, of the interstate commerce committee hopes to report the stock market regulation bill to the house late in the week.

RFC CHIEF DECLARES MONEY NOW EASIER; BANKS MAKING LOANS

WASHINGTON, April 2—(AP)—Jesse H. Jones, RFC chairman, told reporters today indications are that money is getting easier to borrow over the country and that the demand for government loans is less than anticipated. The corporation still has unused borrowing power of one billion dollars.

Bankers are seeking to make loans, he said, and he looks for a pickup after congress adjourns.

The fact that the Reconstruction Finance Corp. expects to run more than 500 million dollars under budget estimates for the fiscal year ended June 30 he ascribed to better business conditions.

TRANSFER NEGRO PATIENTS TO TAFT HOSPITAL BY BUS

OKLAHOMA CITY, April 2—(AP)—Three buses with 27 insane negro patients each began the transfer of negro inmates today from the central state hospital, Norman, to the new hospital for negro insane at Taft.

W. C. Hughes, chairman of the state board of affairs, said arrangements had been made for three trips by the three buses at this time. The remainder of the 600 negro patients will be moved from Norman later in the spring.

Hugh Askew, vice chairman of the board, and medical attendants accompanied the buses. Hughes said the less violent patients were included in the first transfers.

THREE KILLED, BIG DAMAGE IN HAVANA GARAGE BLAZE

HAVANA, April 2—(AP)—Three employes were killed and 35 buses were destroyed by a fire of undetermined origin which wrecked the garage of the Omnibus de la Havana Co., today.

Property damage was estimated at $300,000.

The company is in the midst of labor difficulties.

BANK TRANSACTIONS

Bank transactions for Monday, $501,-664.

KING OF SWEDEN IS OUT TO HALT RAVAGES OF LOVE

PRINCE BERTIL OF SWEDEN

CANNES, France, April 2—(AP) Word that another prince is "that way" about a commoner was responsible, friends said today, for a hurried packing of bags by King Gustaf V, racquet-swinging ruler of Sweden.

He planned a hasty return to his capital—there to put the royal foot down upon the reported marriage plans of his grandson, Prince Bertil, and Christina Brambeck, daughter of an army captain.

Apparently he is determined to deal more firmly with this case than he has with similar affairs in the not-too-distant past.

It was only a few weeks ago that 22-year-old Bertil's older brother, Prince Sigvard, poo-poohed royal rights when he and Fraulein Erika Patzek were married at a London registry. The romance had blossomed on the movie lots in Berlin. He's an up-and-coming director; she—blond and trim—is an actress.

The royal family tried everything; even to rushing an envoy to London by plane, before giving up efforts to halt Prince Sigvard's marriage.

That, however, wasn't the first time one of the king's grandsons had picked a pretty commoner for a wife. In 1932, Prince Lennart—cousin of Sigvard and Betril—married Karin Nissvandt, daughter of a Stockholm businessman.

Now, say those who ought to know, the king has decided the royal family has had enough of such romances.

JAPANESE GIRL LOSES A PRINCE

Plan to Marry Her to Heir to Ethiopian Throne Blocked By Mussolini

TOKYO, April 2—(AP)—The projected picture-bride marriage of the Ethiopian prince Lij Araya and Miss Masako Kuroda, daughter of Viscount Hiroyuki Kuroda, has been cancelled and, despite official denials of interference, vernacular newspapers surmised today that the match had run afoul of powerful forces of international politics.

The Addis-Ababa, Ethiopia, correspondent of the Tokyo newspaper Nichi Nichi reported that the foreign minister of Ethiopia had announced the marriage plans had been called off, quoting the prospective bridegroom to the effect that the machinations of "a certain power" had interfered.

The foreign minister, according to the correspondent, said he notified Ethiopia's minister in Rome concerning the cancellation of the marriage plans from which the vernacular newspaper conjectured that Italy disliked the prospect of Japanese penetration in Ethiopia in view of Premier Mussocini's recent declarations of Italy's mission in Africa.

The family of Viscount Kuroda asserted that it was ignorant of cancellation of plans.

THE WEATHER

MUSKOGEE: Cloudy, cooler.

OKLAHOMA: Mostly cloudy, colder in northwest portion tonight; Tuesday cloudy, local showers in north portion, colder.

ARKANSAS: Increasing cloudiness tonight; Tuesday cloudy, showers and cooler in northwest portion.

EAST TEXAS: Cloudy and unsettled, probably showers in southwest portion tonight and Tuesday; colder in north portion Tuesday. Moderate to fresh southerly winds on the coast.

WEST TEXAS: Mostly cloudy, probably showers in southeast portion, tonight and Tuesday. Colder in north and west portions tonight; colder Tuesday.

MISSOURI: Cloudy, showers probable tonight and in east and south portions Tuesday; much cooler Tuesday and in extreme west portion tonight.

KANSAS: Scattered showers followed by somewhat colder tonight; Tuesday generally fair, colder in east and central portions.

CITY WILL ELECT 11 COUNCILMEN, MAYOR TUESDAY

Campaigns of Both Will Close Tonight; Vote of Between 7000 and 8000 Anticipated

HEATED COUNCIL RACE

Two Charter Amendments Also On Ballots; Siren Tomorrow Will Summon Voters

With anything like favorable weather tomorrow 7000 or 8000 voters are expected to turn out to the polls to elect a mayor and 11 members of the city council and to approve or reject two proposed amendments to the city charter. Both the incumbent, E. J. Phelps, and Dr. John Reynolds, mayoralty nominees, were winding up their campaigns today and tonight, with campaign managers of each expressing complete confidence in the outcome of tomorrow's balloting.

Both camps were sponsoring mass meetings among the negro voters tonight, Mr. Phelps' backers having arranged a meeting at Second and Denison streets and Dr. Reynolds' candidacy to be urged at a second meeting a block away, at Bronzman hall, Second and Court streets. Both meetings were scheduled to start at about 7:30 o'clock.

> **TO PRECINCT INSPECTORS**
> To expedite the compilation for publication in an "election extra" of returns from tomorrow's election, the Phoenix and Times-Democrat would appreciate your calling in the final vote on mayor, councilmen and charter amendments in each precinct as soon as the count has been completed tomorrow night. Use telephones 122 or 1302.

Interesting Council Races

Despite the marked interest in the mayoralty race, some of the races among councilmen were crowding the mayoralty candidates for attention.

Although both Dr. Reynolds and Mr. Phelps repeatedly have stated they are heading no tickets, their names have appeared with printed slates being passed around by campaign workers.

The name of each of the 22 council nominees has appeared on at least one such printed slip and some of them have appeared in two and three different combinations of endorsed nominees, the duplication furnishing weight to the emphatic assertions of many of the nominees that they are personally running absolutely independent, although they have been powerless to prevent various groups from endorsing them and printing their names on tickets.

Voters will be reminded throughout the day that they have a duty to perform at the polls by the sounding of a siren. Firemen, who have endorsed the proposed civil service charter amendment for the fire department, have arranged to have the siren sounded at 8 o'clock in the morning, 12 noon, 1 o'clock in the afternoon and again at 4 o'clock.

They have been conducting a vigorous campaign the past few days in support of the amendment that would place their department under a civil

(See Number THREE on Page Two)

ACTRESS FILES CHARGE MOVIE FRIEND SOUGHT A 'CAVE MAN' WEDDING

LOS ANGELES, April 2—(AP)—Her story of being kidnaped by R. C. Dowling, movie actor, taken to Yuma, Ariz., and threatened with harm unless she married him was to be related today to the district attorney by Marjorie Crawford, 25-year-old flier and movie player.

Dowling is held in jail at Yuma, pending further investigation. He denied Miss Crawford's story, saying she agreed to accompany him there voluntarily and to marry him.

Miss Crawford, former wife of William Wellman, motion picture director, said Dowling locked her in a hotel room when she refused to marry him but that guests heard her screams and liberated her.

NINE K. C. COPS REMOVED IN POST-ELECTION SHAKEUP

KANSAS CITY, April 2—(AP)—The scrutiny which was turned on Kansas City's police department after municipal election day slayings resulted today in a "shakeup," nine members of the department being dismissed upon order by Chief of Police Robert J. Coffey.

It was the second major move in the police department, the first being the resignation of Eugene C. Reppert, director of police, which was submitted Saturday.

AN EDITORIAL

VOTE TOMORROW

There is a challenge to Muskogee citizens in tomorrow's general election. It is a challenge that each voter should willingly accept — the challenge to do his part in giving the city the best government obtainable.

From the standpoint of candidates to be voted on it is one of the most important elections in years There are 22 nominees for the city council, 11 of whom will become members of the body by virtue of majority votes tomorrow.

They hold it in their power, if they choose to employ it, to control the council for at least the next two years since only five of the 16 members of the council hold over for another term.

Their names have been before the public sufficiently for every voter to have determined which 11 men in his opinion would best serve the city as councilmen.

Likewise the names of the two mayoralty nominees, both long-time residents of Muskogee, have been before the voters sufficiently long to allow for deliberate decision as to the qualifications of each for the office both seek.

The two proposed charter amendments, one providing for civil service for the city fire department and the other allowing for employment, for audit of the city's books, of other than auditors from the office of the state examiner and inspector, should be given studied consideration.

Let each voter mark his ballot in accordance with the opinion he has formed on the various candidates and the amendment proposals. Each qualified voter has the privilege of casting a ballot tomorrow; more, he has a civic duty to perform in casting that ballot in this strictly non-partisan election.

Let Muskogee cast a record vote in a record field of candidates. Go to the polls tomorrow. VOTE!

MURDER OF SIX STILL A PUZZLE

Washington Police Hold Three For Questioning but Do Not Suspect Any of Them

BREMERTON, Wash., April 2—(AP)—By an underworld roundup police strove today to capture killers who slaughtered six persons attending a gay party in a summer home.

Three men were in custody and were questioned for hours, but police said none of them was suspected of being the maddened slayers who stabbed, beat and shot six victims to death after binding them.

The topsy-turvy condition of the house and the absence of two diamond rings, belonging to Mrs. Frank Flieder, hostess at the party, led investigators to adopt robbery as the most plausible theory for the crime.

Beaten, Shot, Slashed

When police broke into the home late Saturday they found the place a shambles. In various parts of the house they found the bodies of:

Frank Flieder, 45, owner of the home;

Mrs. Anna Taylor Flieder, 50, his wife;

Eugene Chenevert, 38, better known as Bert Vincent, the "singing bartender" and former vaudeville player;

Mrs. Peggy Chenevert, 30, his wife;

Magnus Jordan, 50, retired navy man and caretaker of summer homes;

Fred Balcom, bartender at a Bremerton beer parlor.

All of the victims had been beaten with a blackjack and a hammer. Some of them had been shot. The throats of both Mrs. Flieder and Balcom had been slashed. Flieder's jaw was broken, his head had been hammered 11 times, and a knife thrust in the back of his neck.

Card Dealer Held

Evidence indicated all had been first tied up or had their mouths and eyes taped. Luke S. May, Seattle criminologist, said Chenevert, Flieder and Balcom apparently made a desperate fight for life.

Jerry Murphy, described as a card dealer, was one of the three taken into custody. The names of the others held were not disclosed.

The tragedy was discovered when a neighbor, Tom Sanders, noticed that three dogs had been left for hours in an automobile parked outside the house. He investigated and, looking through a window, saw two of the bodies.

FIFTH SUSPECT HELD

JOPLIN, Mo., April 2—(AP)—Sheriff Oll Rogers brought William B. Moors, a taxicab driver, to Jasper county yesterday from Kansas City to face charges of connection with the slaying March 3 of B. L. Van Hoose, Carthage capitalist, at his home near there. Moors is the fifth man to be arrested in the slaying.

RICHARDS RITES BEING HELD TODAY AT INDIAN'S HOME

Wealthy and Colorful Creek Succumbs in Hospital After Lingering Illness

LONG TRIBAL SERVICES

Ceremonies Began Yesterday At Richardsvilie; Story of Life Highly Romantic

Last honors were being paid to Eastman Richards, wealthy Creek Indian, this afternoon, at Richardsville, the town which he founded and in which he lived. The noted tribesman died Saturday evening at the Muskogee General hospital after an illness of many months. Richards was first a patient at the hospital in November, 1932, suffering from a kidney ailment, and early this year again became very ill. On February 28, he consented to be moved to the hospital again, after spending several weeks in bed at his home.

The life of Eastman Richards is almost impossibly romantic. It combines almost the complete history of his tribe, and shows the transition from the life of Indians as it was lived before the coming of the white man, to modern civilization.

Dire poverty, fabulous wealth; leadership of Indian warriors in the fight against encroaching settlers; leadership of his people in the ways of today, all these he knew. No man was better loved by the Creeks, for when a youth he was one of the trusted lieutenants of Chitto Harjo in the Crazy Snake rebellion, and in more mature years, he spent his money generously in their behalf.

Hunted to Support Family

Richards was born in 1872 in a one-room log cabin in Arbeker township in McIntosh county in the Creek nation. His father was a fullblood Creek and his mother of mixed Indian blood. During his boyhood, his father deserted his mother and young Eastman supported the family, did it in the manner in which Indians had secured food for their dependents since the beginning of history, by hunting. He could bring down a deer in full flight with a bow and arrow, it was said, and was a crack shot with a rifle.

When Chitto Harjo and his followers rebelled against the decision of the federal government to divide the tribal land into allotments, Richards became one of his trusted lieutenants. Finally, when the rebellion was put down, and the Dawes commission gave allotments to the Creeks, the rebels received the poorest land, the rich farm land having been given to the Indians who accepted the white man's rule more meekly. The rebels had insisted that land west of the Mississippi had been given to them to have and to hold "as long as grass grows and water runs."

Richards received 160 acres of land of which only about 10 was tillable. "White man give me rock pile," Richards said later. "Rock pile worth more than all white man government."

(See Number ONE on Page Two)

CLEVELAND'S RICHEST MAN FACES CHARGES OF BANKING FRAUD

CLEVELAND, April 2—(AP)—Kenyon V. Painter, former director and largest single stockholder of the closed Union Trust Co., and Wilbur M. Baldwin, former president of the bank, were indicated today by a county grand jury on charges of misapplying bank funds and abstracting collateral posted as part security for three million dollars in bank loans.

Last week indictments were returned by a federal grand jury against three former officials of the Guardion Trust Co., the other large Cleveland bank which was unable to resume operations following the banking holiday a year ago.

Painter, for years regarded as Cleveland's wealthiest capitalist, also was widely known for his numerous hunting and natural history excursions to Africa and elsewhere.

CHRYSLER HIKES PRICES

DETROIT, April 2—(AP)—Increases ranging from $35 to $130 were announced today by three units of the Chrysler corporation. The Plymouth announced a $35 increase on its standard model; Dodge increased $45 on all models and the Chrysler models were increased from $40 on standard types to $130 on its imperial model.

APPOINT COUNTY COMMISSIONER

OKLAHOMA CITY, April 2—(AP)—Governor Murray today appointed R. E. Rader, of Newkirk to succeed the late Marshall Hiatt as Kay county commissioner.

HEIRESS TO 50 MILLIONS SEEKS A PARIS DIVORCE

The only daughter of the late George W. Vanderbilt, from whom she inherited 50 million dollars, Mrs. Cornelia Vanderbilt Cecil (above) has asked court permission in Paris to sue John Francis Amherst Cecil, a former member of the British diplomatic corps, for divorce. The couple, married in 1924, have two sons, aged 8 and 4.

JAIL PLAN HEADS FOR JUNK HEAP

Commissioners Indicate They May Abandon Idea in Face of Probable Injunction

Intimation that the "county jail by the courthouse" plan of present county commissioners may follow other bastile suggestions to the junk heap was given today by commissioners in conversation with Ben Martin, attorney for a group of Muskogeeans protesting building a jail at the proposed site.

Martin, with numerous other protestants who asserted a jail built by a courthouse would destroy the value of nearby property, appeared before commissioners Thursday and spoke volumes against the jail site. Commissioners told them at that time that today they would consider their protests.

'No Use Starting'

While no official action was taken today, Martin appeared and was told by county commissioners that if no jail could be built due east of the courthouse, no jail probably would be built.

"There's no use in starting a jail when we figure injunctions will be filed to delay construction," they told Martin. Injunctions, they said, would injure the county's chances to obtain government money for workers.

Commissioners said that it was out of the question at the present time to plan building a jail a block north of the courthouse where the city owns a lot. They argued that a jail there, which would be a two-story affair and require a separate boiler, would cost more than the $12,000 commissioners have on hand for a jail.

Jail Chances Dim

One of their ideas in constructing a jail near the courthouse was to save the expense of purchasing an extra boiler. Commissioners planned to use the one supplying the courthouse with heat.

If the present county jail plan falls through it is a question if the county will have a new bastile for some time to come, it was said. Once the county attempted to build a jail atop the courthouse only to have the Hotel Severs protest. Again a former board of county commissioners attempted to build a jail due north of the courthouse, only to be balked by protests from the First Christian church.

Now, with government aid assured, two groups of Muskogee county men have protested construction of a jail south of the courthouse.

REFINERY SHUTS DOWN

BRISTOW, April 2—(AP)—The Wilcox refinery here was shut down again today pending "improvement in the price structure." Fifty of the 60 employes are affected.

Will Rogers Says:

SANTA MONICA, Calif., April 2 Not much news last couple of days from Astors fishing smack. Pretty nice of England to let our president in their ocean. Speaking of oceans, our grand fleet of 110 ships have to leave this coast this week. Japan says they have been in their ocean long enough. We are about the only nation that has a fleet, but no ocean to put it on. The thing we ought to do is dig a canal right smack dab across the U. S. from east to west. Then when there is objections from the proprietors of the Atlantic and Pacific we could cruise in our own waters, something we can't do now. Yours,

WILL ROGERS.

BONNIE PARKER, CIGAR SMOKING WOMAN, HUNTED

Clyde Barrow, Accused of Slaying Two Fort Worth Officers, Steals Gasoline

STATE CRISS-CROSSED

No Late Clues to Whereabouts Of His Pal Hamilton; $1500 In Rewards Offered

By The Associated Press

Elusive Clyde Barrow and Raymond Hamilton, robbers and killers, apparently dashed back and forth across Texas at will today, while officers of the state and federal government sought clues to two slayings, a bank robbery and a kidnaping for which the desperadoes were blamed.

Spurred on by rewards of $1500, local police, state rangers and highway patrolmen and agents of the department of justice frantically tried to catch up with Barrow, whom they directly accused of directing a burst of gunfire which killed E. D. Wheeler, 26, and H. D. Murphy, 23, state highway patrolmen, near Grapevine yesterday. They learned that Barrow's fingerprints were on a whisky bottle near the scene.

Detective A. C. Howerton of the Fort Worth police department, was one of the investigating officers who was convinced the killing was done by Barrow and Bonnie Parker. He said a cigar stub was found near where the car had been parked, bearing the imprint of small teeth on the butt. Bonnie Parker's liking for cigars is well known to officers.

Hamilton's Trail Lost

In the same type and color car as the assassins used, two persons believed to be Barrow and Bonnie Parker, his woman traveling companion, drove up to a filling station at Blanket, 10 miles northeast of Brownwood, held Howard Strickland, night watchman, at bay and stole a tank full of gasoline. They dashed away to the east, with Strickland firing at them.

Officers could only speculate on the whereabouts of Hamilton. He was identified as the robber of a bank at West Saturday, as the kidnaper of Mrs. Cam Gunter of Mexia several hours later and as the thief who stole an automobile in Houston yesterday morning after she was released.

For a time it was thought he was heading north yesterday and perhaps planned to meet Barrow on the side road where Wheeler and Murphy were slain. First information on the Blanket holdup indicated he might have been one of the two persons involved.

Other Tips on Progress

Highway patrolmen at Abilene, however, said the description of the automobile used at Blanket tallied with that in which two persons fled from Grapevine.

In addition to these reports, other tips said Barrow might be found in southeastern Denton county and that two persons in a speeding automobile had passed through Alvord and were headed for Sunset and Wichita Falls.

L. G. Phares, chief of the highway patrol, at Austin guaranteed $1000 of the reward, for "the apprehension and conviction, or the dead bodies," of the Grapevine slayers.

Gov. Miriam A. Ferguson posted a $500 reward for each desperado, "dead or alive."

John Reese, deputy sheriff at Comanche, said he felt certain that Hamilton was the Blanket holdup man.

Sure It Is Them

Williamson county officers, state rangers and highway patrolmen spread a dragnet over the sector of Texas after a report was received that Barrow and Bonnie stopped at a filling station in Round Rock between last midnight and dawn. They were in a black sedan and carried a machine gun.

Frank J. Blake, in charge of department of justice agents at Dallas, said he had "no doubt but that Clyde Barrow and Bonnie Parker killed" the highway patrolmen.

"There is no one else in southwest who would kill so coldbloodedly."

BARROW AND BONNIE ON WAY TO OKLAHOMA?

MIAMI, Okla., April 2—(AP)—Clyde Barrow and Bonnie "Suicide Sal" Parker, his feminine companion, were reported headed in the direction of Miami and Picher, Okla., today, Sheriff Dee Waters was advised.

Texas authorities believed Barrow participated in the slaying of two officers near Grapevine during the week-end.

Barrow abandoned a stolen car near Picher last winter, and is known to have friends in the vicinity.

EXTRA **The Dallas Morning News** EXTRA

49TH YEAR NO. 184 (AP)—Associated Press. (UP)—United Press. (NANA)—North American Newspaper Alliance. DALLAS, TEXAS, MONDAY, APRIL 2, 1934—FOURTEEN PAGES Oldest Business Institution in Texas—Founded in Galveston April 11, 1842.—Established in Dallas October 1, 1885. 5c PER COPY.

Clyde Barrow, Fleeing, Kills Two Patrolmen

Insull Ashore, To Be Turned Over to U. S.

Former Utilities King Taken From Floating Refuge to Hear Edict of Turkish Court

Action Protested

Through Pouring Rain Fugitive Is Escorted by Maritime Police

ISTANBUL, Turkey, April 1 (AP).—Bewildered Samuel Insull, virtually a prisoner of the Turkish Government, will be told Monday that he is to be turned over to American authorities for extradition.

A decision of the Turkish Cabinet to hand him over was communicated Sunday night to the Governor General of Istanbul, who will inform the former Chicago financier. After notification he will be placed formally under arrest.

Removed from the Greek freighter Maiotis, his floating haven for the last fifteen days, Insull heard a Turkish court declare the offense of which he is accused a common crime and was escorted to a room in a modest hotel for the night.

The final scenes of Insull's long fight to escape American authorities who seek him on embezzlement charges, flashed in kaleidoscopic fashion across the most significant Easter Sunday of the 74-year-old man's life.

It was generally conceded that he had reached the end of his rope.

Cabinet Makes Up Mind.

The Turkish Cabinet, sitting at Ankara, the capital, wasted no time in making up its mind to grant a request from Washington for his extradition when word was flashed from Istanbul that the court had found Turkish law would uphold the action.

Insull's last request of the authorities was for permission to send telegrams. This was granted. Authorities ordered him left alone for the night in his hotel room in the old city of Istanbul.

Insull himself did not know his own status when he left the court and was taken to the hotel.

"What is my legal position?" he asked.

"We can not tell you anything until Monday," officials answered.

Insull had asked to be allowed to

See INSULL on Page 5.

Retired Pastor Dies At End of Services

BALTIMORE, April 1 (AP).—As the Easter festival service ended in the Church of the Ascension and the Prince of Peace, the Rev. Robert Kell, retired Protestant Episcopal rector, collapsed and was dead before aid reached him.

Only a few minutes earlier, the Rev. Mr. Kell, assisting the Rev. Robert E. Browning, had read from an epistle "for ye are dead, and your life is hid with Christ in God. When Christ who is your light shall appear then shall ye also be with Him in glory."

The Weather

NEW ORLEANS, La., April 1 (AP).—Government weather forecast:

East Texas (including Dallas and vicinity): Monday cloudy, probably thundershowers in east portion.

West Texas: Monday fair.

Arkansas: Monday partly cloudy, cooler.

Oklahoma: Monday partly cloudy.

Louisiana: Monday unsettled, probably thundershowers, cooler in northwest portion.

Dallas Temperatures.

Temperatures in Dallas Sunday April 1, 1934, and for the same date last year, as reported by the United States Weather Bureau, follow:

	1934.	1933.		1934.	1933.
Midnight	65	62	Noon	70	74
2 a. m.	62	62	2 p. m.	73	77
4 a. m.	59	59	4 p. m.	78	80
6 a. m.	60	58	6 p. m.	79	80
7 a. m.	60	58	7 p. m.	74	79
10 a. m.	67	69			

Maximum temperature April 2, last year, 71 degrees; minimum, 48 degrees. Total precipitation so far this year, 6.24 inches.

RENDEZVOUS.

FOR just a brief while every day,
I steal away from duty
And leave the indoor tasks undone,
To keep a tryst with beauty:

Bird-song and lily-bell,
Music thin and sweet;
Sun-gold and starry bloom
Flash about my feet;
Cool mist, with crystal beads
Gleaming everywhere;
Wild-plum and pink-thorne
Hanging on the air.

Swiftly, then, I can return
To tread the rounds of duty—
Since for one fleet half-breath I stood
Hand-in-hand with beauty.

—Mary S. Fitzgerald, in Progressive Farmer.

Convicted Felon, Luke Trammell, Caught on Farm

House Dean Dies

EDWARD W. POU.

Edward W. Pou, 70, Of North Carolina, Claimed by Death

Was Oldest Member in Point of Service in National House

WASHINGTON, April 1 (AP).—The Dean of the House—Rep. Edward W. Pou, 70, of Smithfield, N. C.—died Sunday of a heart attack following a siege of influenza.

Pou was chairman of the powerful House Rules Committee, which formulates the legislative program of the party in power. He also held this post during the administrations of Woodrow Wilson, who was his close friend.

Funeral services will be held at a joint session of the House and Senate at 1 p. m. Monday in the House chamber. Burial will be at Smithfield, the boyhood home of the veteran legislator, beside the grave of Ensign Edward Smith Pou, naval aviator son who was killed in action during the World War.

Entered Congress in 1900.

The quiet spoken but courageous North Carolinian came to Congress in 1900 and had served continually since from the Fourth District. He was a leader in the democratic party for many years and handled many of President Wilson's war time legislative proposals.

Twice Pou sacrificed his prerogative of seniority for the speakership because of his health. He stepped aside for the election of John N. Garner, now Vice President, as speaker in 1931, and again for Speaker Rainey in 1933.

Pou suffered an attack of influenza

See POU on Page 2.

Spring Business Saved When Auto Dispute Settled

Removes Curtailment in Major Industries, Says National City Bank

NEW YORK, April 1 (AP).—Peaceful settlement of the threatened strike in the automobile industry has saved spring business from a severe setback, the National City Bank of New York says in its monthly review of business conditions.

"The settlement accomplished by President Roosevelt," the survey asserts, "is a very important achievement. It removes the danger of enforced curtailment of automobile operations, which would cause curtailment in other industries; and if the formula upon which the settlement was reached works in one major industry it will probably work in others, wherever controversy over similar issues may arise. Thus the danger of a series of great strikes over questions of union jurisdiction appears to be averted."

Business Improves.

The survey finds that business generally continued to improve in March, but that the gains were more irregular and at a slower pace than in February.

Building lines showed a pronounced improvement during the month, the bank notes, and cotton mills continued busy. The coal industry gave more support to general business than for some time, owing to the prevalence of abnormally cold weather, and retail figures showed the broadest gains in several years.

The bank states that the request of the Government that industry pay

See BANK SURVEY on Page 2.

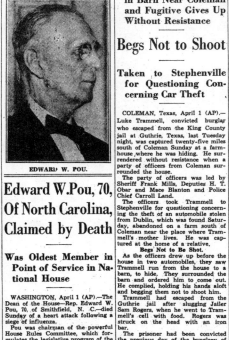

Officers Surround Him in Barn Near Coleman and Fugitive Gives Up Without Resistance

Begs Not to Shoot

Taken to Stephenville for Questioning Concerning Car Theft

COLEMAN, Texas, April 1 (AP).—Luke Trammell, convicted burglar who escaped from the King County jail at Guthrie, Texas, last Tuesday night, was captured twenty-five miles south of Coleman Sunday at a farmhouse where he was hiding. He surrendered without resistance when a party of officers from Coleman surrounded the house.

The party of officers was led by Sheriff Frank Mills, Deputies H. T. Obar and Mace Blanton and Police Chief Carroll Land.

The officers took Trammell to Stephenville for questioning concerning the theft of an automobile stolen from Dublin, which was found Saturday, abandoned on a farm south of Coleman near the place where Trammell's mother lives. He was captured at the home of a relative.

Begs Not to Be Shot.

As the officers drew up before the house in two automobiles, they saw Trammell run from the house to a barn, to hide. They surrounded the barn and ordered him to come out. He complied, holding his hands aloft and begging them not to shoot him.

Trammell had escaped from the Guthrie jail after slugging Jailer Sam Rogers, when he went to Trammell's cell with food. Rogers was struck on the head with an iron bar.

The prisoner had been convicted the previous day of the burglary of a store at Dumont, King County, in which a safe was broken open and

See TRAMMELL on Page 2.

Securities Act Again Under Fire Of U. S. Chamber

Claim Is Made Proposed Law Harmful to Industry of the Nation

WASHINGTON, April 1 (AP).—The Chamber of Commerce of the United States Sunday renewed its attack on the truth in securities act, adding its voice again to what has become a virtually unanimous assault on the law by major organized business and industrial groups.

In a special report drafted by a committee of experts, the chamber said the act, designed to protect investors by giving them full information about securities, had practically stopped the issuance of high grade corporate issues.

The act was condemned in a general way because, the committee contended, it imposed liabilities on persons who might be in no way to blame for errors.

Earlier this week similar opinion was expressed by the National Automobile Chamber of Commerce, and previously the American Bar Association had demanded revision.

The consumers goods and capital

See SECURITIES on Page 2.

Dallas Girl Slated for Stardom

—Associated Press Photo.

Jacqueline Wells (left) of Dallas was one of the three lucky thirteen young motion picture actresses who were selected out of a field of thirty-eight nominees by the Western Association of Motion Picture Advertisers at Hollywood recently as the ones most likely to reach stardom. The others are Jean Gale (center), San Francisco, and Lucille Lund, Buckley, Wash.

Easter Is Celebrated World Over in Song, Service and Festivity

Churches Jammed and Fashionable Display Finery on Streets

(By the Associated Press.)

All the creeds of Christendom joined Sunday in hallelujahs for the risen Lord as they celebrated Easter in song, service and festivities.

In Jerusalem where Christ made His triumphal entry, thousands of Christians from over the globe knelt in adoration at His tomb. Temple bells rang out paens of praise calling the faithful to worship.

A beneficent sun shone down on the city that cradled Christianity to bathe in bright light the colorful parades of the pilgrims. Mohammedans flocked to the Mosque of Omar to pray before the sacred stone as a prelude to a pilgrimage to one of their holy places, the site of the Tomb of Moses. Christian and pagan brushed shoulders without disorders.

Rome, the city that nurtured the

See EASTER on Page 2.

Guggenheim Trust 10th Year Awards Cover Wide Range

Forty Fellowships Include Theater, Arts, Sciences, Literature

NEW YORK, April 1 (AP).—Six artists, nine authors, two composers of music, two workers in the arts of the theater and twenty-one scholars studying in as many different fields of knowledge were announced Sunday as winners of the tenth annual fellowship awards of the John Simon Guggenheim Memorial Foundation.

The fellowships, normally $2,000, are adjusted to meet the needs of the individual fellows. Periods for which the fellowships are granted vary with the necessities of the work. The recipients this year will work in four Continents and in the islands of the East and West Indies.

Trustees of the foundation said these awards bring the total grants of the foundation to more than $1,200,000, and the total number of fellowships to 577. Another series of grants to Latin-American scholars will be made next June.

Former United States Senator and Mrs. Simon Guggenheim established the foundation in 1925 as a memorial to a son. Heretofore the fellowships have been granted only for work abroad, but this year provision is made to permit some fellows to work in the United States.

Theatrical Fellowships.

The theatrical fellowships were awarded to:

Miss Angna Enters of New York, a

See AWARDS on Page 2.

Frenchmen to Fight Duel With Pistols

CARCASSONNE, France, April 1. (AP).—Pistols at twenty paces were decided upon in principle Sunday for a duel between Deputy Jean Mistler, Minister of Commerce in the Daladier Cabinet, and Roger de Tour, Royalist sympathizer.

Seconds were arranging details for the encounter, which is the outcome of a political dispute in a cafe Saturday night. Witnesses said De Tour struck Mistler as the latter was putting on his overcoat.

Cards were immediately exchanged and seconds, one of whom is the Mayor of Carcassonne, were designated. The time and place of the meeting have not been decided.

Card Dealer Is Held After Six Persons Killed

Detained After Taking Blood-Stained Suit to Tailor in Bremerton

BREMERTON, Wash, April 1 (AP).—A roundup of all persons who might be able to shed some light on the brutal slayings of two women and four men in the summer colony home of Mr. and Mrs. Frank Flieder at Erlander's Point, was started by authorities Sunday. Their deaths, believed to have occurred Thursday night, were discovered late Saturday.

Among those held was a man named Murphy, described by police as a card dealer. Authorities emphasized, however, no one was now directly under suspicion.

Attention was called to Murphy when Isadore Laschbin, Bremerton tailor, reported to Sheriff D. L. Blankenship of Kitesap County that Murphy had brought a blood-stained suit to his shop Friday for cleaning, explaining he had a hemorrhage. Laschbin, who was also questioned, reported the incident to police after he had read of the slayings.

Blankenship and Luke S. May, Seattle detective chief and well known criminologist, declined to discuss details of their investigations for the present.

Shots Discharged Into Prone Body, Witnesses Relate

Dallas Couple, Driving, Hear Report, Return to Road and See Tall Man Firing Shotgun

Miss Being Chased

Get Away and Assailants Turn Car Into Highway, Speeds to Dallas

The experience of being eyewitness to the fatal shooting Sunday of State Highway Patrolmen E. B. Wheeler and H. D. Murphy near Grapevine, Tarrant County, and of being threatened with pursuit by the slayers was related by Mrs. Fred A. Giggal of Dallas upon her return from the scene of the double killing.

Mrs. Giggal and her husband, of 4226 Prescott, were taking a Sunday afternoon drive on the Northwest highway to Rhome. The couple, with Mr. Giggal at the wheel, had noticed two highway patrolmen turn up a dirt side road, and as they passed the road, saw a black sedan parked there. Mr. and Mrs. Giggal had hardly driven by the road when they heard a volley of shots.

See Men on Ground.

Mr. Giggal immediately slowed down and turned back, trying to see through a screen of trees. As he got to the entrance of the dirt road, he and his wife saw the two patrolmen stretched out on the ground with the

See EYEWITNESS on Page 2.

Minnesota Police Hold Eight Men In Dillinger Hunt

Believed Bandit, Eluding St. Paul Officers, Was Planning Robbery

ST. PAUL, Minn., April 1 (AP).—Underworld haunts were combed Sunday for clues to the outlaw killer, John Dillinger, and his gangster pal, John Hamilton, as Department of Justice agents questioned eight men in custody.

Theorizing the men who masked their flight from an apartment house Saturday behind a curtain of submachine gunfire when surprised by authorities, were still in town and ready to carry out a planned bank robbery, investigators sought the fugitives' trial in Twin City hoodlums' hideouts.

Clarence Colton, acquitted in the Third Northwestern National Bank robbery in Minneapolis and killing of two policemen several years ago, was one of those held, together with his brother Doc Colton, alias Devol.

Police believed Dillinger had gathered the remnants of other gangs, and, with his new mob, planned a bank robbery in the Twin Cities. Examination of the apartment indicated the gang was ready for a robbery, police said, and orders were issued for all officers to be on the alert for the next two days particularly.

A check of hospitals and physicians on the chance they might have treated the woman who fled with the desperadoes, also was made. She was wounded by a shot from the gun of Detective Henry Cummings as she and one of the men scuttled down the rear stairway of their third floor apartment.

Killed

E. B. WHEELER.

E. B. Wheeler of Fort Worth was one of the two State highway patrolmen killed Sunday by Clyde Barrow.

Freed by Bandit

MRS. CAM GUNTER.

Woman Hostage Of Bandit Tells Story of Capture

Stopping to Offer Aid, Loses Her Auto and Taken to Houston

HOUSTON, Texas, April 1 (AP).—Mrs. Cam Gunter of Mexia was forced to accompany a man identified as Raymond Hamilton, notorius desperado, more than 175 miles Saturday and Saturday night as a result of her desire to be of assistance to an ill-fated motorist.

The attractive 27-year-old brunette told of the kidnaping and the all-night ride after she was freed here shortly before 9:30 a. m. Sunday. She said she was treated courteously and that the desperado left her $30 to have her car fixed up. The automobile had been badly used, she explained.

Mrs. Gunter said she left her home in Mexia about 9:30 o'clock Saturday morning and drove her husband, an oil gauger, downtown. She then drove to Thelma to get her 4-year-old son,

See HOSTAGE on Page 2.

Bandit Shoots Officers Down On Side Road

Parked Near Grapevine, Robber and Woman Companion Fire as Officers Approach Car

Flee Toward Dallas

Believed to Be Waiting for Hamilton When Killings Occurred

FORT WORTH, Texas, April 1 (AP).—Gunfire pouring from an automobile believed occupied by Clyde Barrow, Texas' public enemy No. 1, and a red-haired woman companion, possibly Bonnie Parker, almost instantly killed two State Highway Patrol officers Sunday afternoon near Grapevine.

Detective A. C. Howerton of the homicide squad of the Fort Worth police department said there was no doubt the killer was Clyde Barrow.

The officers, E. B. Wheeler and H. D. Murphy, both of Fort Worth, were shot down as they approached the car parked on a side road.

Barrow and the cigar-smoking Bonnie Parker had been there since mid-morning, officers believed, awaiting the arrival of Raymond Hamilton, freed recently from a prison farm under a barrage thought laid down by Barrow and whose latest exploit was the single-handed hold-up of a bank in West yesterday.

Fled Toward Dallas.

The direction in which the death car headed after the fusillade that cost the lives of the two officers was not immediately determined, though it was thought to have gone toward Grapevine or Dallas.

State Motorcycle Patrol Officers Polk Ivy, Wheeler and Murphy were riding on Highway 114 between Grapevine and Rhome. Ivy, who was several hundred yards in advance of the other two officers, noticed a black Ford sedan with yellow wire wheels parked on a side road fifty yards from the highway five miles northwest of Grapevine.

He thought nothing of it, however, until having gone a quarter of a mile he glanced back and saw that Wheeler and Murphy were not following him. Turning back he discovered them lying near their motorcycles at the spot where the car had been parked. Wheeler was dead and Murphy dying from buckshot wounds. Their pistols still were in their holsters, indicatin gthat as they drew near the machine the deadly fire from within began.

An ambulance was summoned but

See CLYDE BARROW on Page 2.

Slaying of Pair Is Attributed to Clyde and Bonnie

Chief Deputy Checks Descriptions and Opines Hamilton Not Present

Belief that the killer of the two highway patrolmen was Clyde Barrow, noted desperado, accompanied by Bonnie Parker, was expressed Sunday night by Chief Deputy Sheriff Bill Decker. Mr. Decker was called to the scene of the shooting a few minutes after it happened and checked all angles of it.

"The car which Patrolmen Murphy and Wheeler approached just before they were shot by its occupants had been seen there since 11 o'clock Sunday morning," Mr. Decker said. "If Raymond Hamilton let out his prisoner, Mrs. Cam Gunter, at Houston at 9:15 o'clock Sunday morning, he couldn't have been at Grapevine two hours later, particularly by back roads. It doubtless was Clyde Barrow and Bonnie Parker."

The possibility also was suggested that Barrow had been waiting for Hamilton, whom he freed recently from the State prison farm near Huntsville. The deputy did not believe Barrow took part in the West bank robbery Saturday.

Mr. Decker also did not believe the killer had driven on to Dallas. Although the car was reported headed for this city, he thought Barrow had turned north soon after passing through Grapevine.

Late descriptions of the pair seen in the car tallied more nearly with Barrow and his woman than with Hamilton. The man was said to be about five feet six inches, weighing around 140 pounds, dressed in dark tan riding pants and blue shirt. His companion also was dressed in riding pants, which gave rise to reports there were two men in the car. It was a woman, however, wearing brown riding pants and a brown blouse, Dallas police were informed.

News Behind the News

By PAUL MALLON

(Copyright, 1934, by Paul Mallon)

Mr. Hull Is Not a Mr. Milquetoast; It's Unsafe to Step on His Toes

Perseverance.

WASHINGTON, April 1.—The mild demeanor of State Secretary Hull is deceiving.

Behind it he hides the heart of a Canadian Northwest policeman. He always gets his man.

This time the man is none other than President Roosevelt's own special foreign trade adviser, George Peck. When Mr. Peek's appointment was announced it was generally assumed around the State Department that Mr. Hull's influence on that subject was on the wane. Mr. Peek was supposed to be the big influence on foreign trade, overriding the executive commercial policy committee started by Mr. Hull.

Mr. Hull said nothing, but was annoyed. A week ago the White House gave out an executive order formally installing Mr. Peek and giving him $100,000 to work with.

The laugh was on Mr. Hull—but not for long.

Retribution.

Two days after Mr. Roosevelt left on his fishing trip Mr. Hull's State Department made public a supplemental executive order the President had signed before he left.

Why its announcement was delayed forty-eight hours was not explained, but the fact is that by that time Mr. Roosevelt was out on the Astor yacht, out of reach of Mr. Peek and everyone else.

This supplemental order specifically instructed Mr. Peek not to interfere with the executive policy committee. It did not say directly, but clearly implied that Mr. Peek was also not to interfere with Mr. Hull, and gave Mr. Hull the right to name a representative on the policy committee.

The inner departmental circlers nudged each other and allowed that many influential persons have found it distinctly unprofitable to step on Mr. Hull's toes. He is decidedly not a Mr. Milquetoast.

NRA.

Those on the inside at the NRA are talking among themselves about the radical changes which have been quietly going on within the organization.

For instance, W. Averill Harriman has virtually taken the entire routine off General Johnson during the last few weeks. He appears to be running the show since he was made first assistant administrator.

One job General Johnson has taken on recently is the writing of office orders. They are supposed to be more secret than a Supreme Court decision. If anyone is caught disclosing an order outside the organization it constitutes grounds for dismissal.

Lately the orders have been more picturesquely worded than when they were written by Executive Director Alvin Brown.

Opposition.

These and other signs have led to considerable discussion as to the future of the NRA. Some wise boys are saying the outfit will grow less and less important. They expect that a compliance drive will be started soon by the legal division. The show will then center around technical individual cases of enforcement. Any broad further curtailment of hours seems to be out of the question.

The tendency of the administration is to temporize with the existing setup and await developments in hopes that more reforms may be forced later.

But industry is getting its back up. It is organizing quite effectively backstage against the Wagner Labor Board bill. Three of the largest industries have sent letters to all stockholders urging them to campaign actively against the measure.

They will probably be able to block it for this session.

Regrets.

The White House crowd took the defeat on the veterans' pay restoration bill very hard. Their advance information was to the effect that the Senate would save them by sustaining the veto.

It is rather important politically, but not financially.

When the figures are all in June 30 you will find that Mr. Roosevelt's budget estimate of this year's deficit will be just about half what he thought it would be. He has been unable to spend money as fast as he estimated.

The condition of the Treasury will not be as seriously affected by the $228,000,000 additional expense of the veterans' pay restorations.

That is only a drop in a $7,000,000,000 budget bucket.

Hitler.

The inner group at the State Department believes it is going to be a long time before anyone gets any money out of Berlin.

Germany's gold reserves, according to their calculations, are only 8 per cent of her total currency outstanding Her gold position is so bad she can not pay for current foreign purchases and has slapped an embargo on cotton, wool, etc.

Hitler's diplomats have been sounding us out on a proposition whereby they would pay in kind for their domestic purchases. That means we would have to buy in Germany as much as they buy here.

We will not fall for that one.

Trick.

There is more than a desire for reform behind this democratic movement for revision of the electoral college system.

If they succeed, the Republicans may never get back in the White House.

The constitutional amendment approved by Mr. Roosevelt the other day provides that the electoral vote of each State be split in accordance with the popular vote. For instance, Hoover carried Pennsylvania last year with a total vote of 1,453,540, against Roosevelt's 1,295,948, and thus won the whole block of thirty-six electoral votes.

Under the proposed amendment, Pennsylvania's electoral vote would have been split, about twenty for Hoover and sixteen for Roosevelt.

It would mean that the Democrats would get electoral votes out of their minority representation in normally Republican States, but would lose little in their stronghold, the solid South, where Republican voting is nil.

Dents in Fender Lead to Arrest In Murder Case

Taxi Driver Fifth Taken in Slaying of Mining Man in Missouri

KANSAS CITY, Mo., April 1 (AP).—Two dents in the fender of a motor car led to the arrest here Sunday of a fifth man, William B. Moore, 34, a taxi driver, in connection with the slaying of Brooks L. Van Hoose, 64, wealthy retired mining operator, near Carthage March 3.

Other arrests in the case had been made previously in Los Angeles, Denver an din the vicinity of Carthage.

W. W. Graves Jr., Jackson County Prosecutor, quoted Moore as admitting he drov esome men to and from Carthage at the time of the slaying, but insisted he was in no way involved in the plot to kidnap or rob Van Hoose, which ended in the murder.

Paid $15 for Trip.

Moore said he was approached here March 2 by a Dr. Glenn, believed by authorities to have been Glenn Harmon, who was slain recently in Los Angeles by officers seeking him in connection with a holdup. The man offered to pay Moore $15 to drive him to Carthage. The trip was made the next day with three men as passengers.

Moore said he drove the car to a tourist camp near Carthage and there two other men, one a cripple, joined the party. The night of the slaying, Moore said, the men drove around in the car with him while he slept. Later he was arcused by a pistol which was pushed against him by Dr. Glenn, who ordered Moore to drive to Kansas City. Moore said he was threatened with death if he ever told of having made the trip.

Dents Identify Car.

Moore's motor car was identified by two dents which authorities were informed were noted in the fender of a motor car seen in the vicinity of the Van Hoose home.

Byron Wolff, a suspect in the case, was arrested in Los Angeles the day Harmon was slain. Victor E. Powell, another suspect, was arrested in Denver. L. B. Harmon, a brother of Glenn Harmon, and Charles Napper, said by officers to be an ex-convict from Illinois, were arrested in the Carthage vicinity.

Motion picture theaters in the world now total 60,347.

Easter

CONTINUED FROM FIRST PAGE.

Catholic church, was filled by thousands of the devoted who went to the Vatican to hear Pope Pius XI give his Easter message and cannonize Don Viovanni Bosco, celebrated social worker of the nineteenth century, as a saint.

From the central balcony of the basilica the Pontiff gave his benediction to the throngs of the famous and the unknown united in common worship.

In the United States citizens knelt in sunrise services, jammed churches and joined in Easter cantatas. On a rockly hillside in Nebraska, church people enacted the Easter drama on ground legend says was regarded as holy by the Indians.

The Nation's capital celebrated with two attractions—the President and the usual cherry blooms—absent. President Roosevelt, on vacation aboard a yacht in the blue waters of the Bahamas, laid aside hir rod and reel to commemora'e the holiday quietly. The cold weather preceding Sunday's sunshine retarded the Easter debut of the cherry blossoms.

Services in Hospital.

Acting for the President, Mrs. Roosevelt attended sunrise services in Arlington National Cemetery. At the same time the ill and wounded of the World War held services in the Walter Reed Military Hospital. Mrs. Roosevelt later attended St. Thomas Episcopal Church. Monday she will direct the annual Easter egg roll on the White House lawn for the children.

Not all the celebration, however, was religious. The fashionable paraded in finery. In New York the weather man relented after a contemplated April Fool joke of rain, the sun peeped out and the four hundred and lesser lights took to the avenues in colorful costume in sharp contrast. Several hundred poorly dressed men, women and children surged through the streets to the chants of "Work! Work! Jobs! Jobs!—We want jobs!" —A discord in the counterpoint of the holiday.

Chicago Displays Finery.

Chicago's "boul mich" saw its finery too, but paraders had to duck for cover at noon when rain splattered down.

South America celebrated by church services and fiestas. Cathedrals in European capitals were as crowded as small parish churches attended by peasants. The only disturbances were reported in Spain, where at Cuidad Real shots were fired into a procession and the church-goers attempted to lynch the disturbers. El Grade at a Fascist meeting was suspended with two priests and forty-four other persons arrested.

Peculiarly on Easter Island—a dot in the Pacific belonging to Chile—Easter was just another day of sadness. The pitiful inhabitants are members of a leper colony awaiting freedom from the bondage of disease. But they still had hope as they joined with other Christians in prayer.

Securities

CONTINUED FROM FIRST PAGE.

goods committees of the NRA code authorities also have criticized the act, as has also the business advisory and planning council of the Department of Commerce, composed of some sixty big business men, and the National Association of Manufacturers, and the Investment Bankers' Association.

President Roosevelt, however, has said he wanted no changes made in the securities law which would weaken it.

Criticism Based on Survey.

The chamber of commerce said its criticism was based on a careful canvass of industrial and commercial firms, financing houses, accountants, attorneys and other interested parties. This investigation, it said, disclosed:

"A general belief that the act in its present form is so severe and uncertain in its consequences as to be prohibitory of normal financial transactions.

"Few will venture to originate and market new or refunding issues of merit. This appears to be the fact, even after full allowance is made for needless and unwarranted fears concerning some provisions that have been brought into question."

To prove this assertion figures were presented to show that whereas securities coming under the act have fallen off greatly under its operation, other securities exempt from the act have been maintained at almost the same levels.

Corporate Issues Decline.

In the seven months prior to the act, the report said, corporate issues amounted to $314,000,000 but in the following five months, under the act, slumped to only $67,000,000.

At the same time noncorporate issues, exempt from the act, showed no comparable decline. For the similar seven months prior to the act, their total was $363,000,000, while for the next five months the total was $309,000,000.

Members of the chamber's committee included Thomas S. Gates, president of the University of Pennsylvania; Alexander Dana Noyes, financial editor of the New York Times, and David F. Edwards, president of the Saco-Lowell Shops, Boston. Edwards was chairman of the committee.

The act was condemned as unconstitutional in a supplementary statement by William V. Hodges of Hodges, Wilson & Rogers, Denver, Colo., who said it was in all respect a harmful and useless piece of legislation.

Pou

CONTINUED FROM FIRST PAGE.

about two months ago but insisted upon remaining on duty. He handled many of President Roosevelt's recovery proposals and led the fight for a number of them during the special session last spring and in the present session.

Ordered to Take Rest.

Only last week he was ordered by his physician to takc a rest and Saturday it was announced at his office that he was in better physical condition. He died at 7:30 a. m. Sunday.

Mrs. Pou, a son, George R. Pou of Raleigh, North Carolina State Highway Commissioner, and a daughter, Mrs. Thomas Anthony Wadden of Washington, were present. Another daughter, Mrs. Edwin Fuller Parham of Henderson, N. C., returned to her home two days ago, when her father's condition appeared tc be improving.

Immediately after the announcement of the death, Vice President Garner and Speaker Rainey, both of whom served more than thirty years with him in the House, called at the Pou apartment. A message accompanied by flowers was sent from the White House.

Arrangements were made by the Vice President and speaker for the joint funeral service. Senator Robinson of Arkansas, the democratic leader; Senator McNary of Oregon, Republican leader; Mr. Garner and Speaker Rainey will deliver addresses.

Pou was the only member of the House to regain chairmanship of a committee he formerly controlled when the Democrats recaptured the House in 1930. He had been chairman of the Rules Committee from 1912 to 1920.

Trammell

CONTINUED FROM FIRST PAGE.

a sum of money stolen. Trammell was given a two-year sentence.

Under Heavy Sentence.

Trammell, then a fugitive from the Lynn County jail, at Tahoka, surrendered in Coleman last July 7, when his younger brother, Starkweather (Doc) Trammell, was wounded fatally in a gun fight with officers. The capture and killing brought to a climax an intensive search lasting ten days in which the brothers had eluded posses of rangers, county officers and citizens and had terrorized Taylor, Coleman and Runnels Counties with a series of holdups. Trammell was tried in Abilene for the holdup of Dr. C. W. Dunn and drew a twenty-five-year sentence. In Coleman County, he received sentences totaling thirty-five years for two robberies.

Later, he was tried in Sweetwater for the fatal shooting of John Lamkin, night watchman at Blackwell, last June 1, and received an additional sentence of fifty years.

Awards

CONTINUED FROM FIRST PAGE.

dancer, who will go to Greece to study the ancient Greek art forms.

Charles Norris Houghton, graduate of Princeton University, who has done work in New York and Baltimore.

Fellowships were awarded the following persons to assist them to carry on their literary work:

Conrad Aiken, poet and novelist; Miss Kay Boyle, poet and novelist; Albert Halper, novelist and short story writer; Alexander Laing of Hanover, N. H., poet and novelist; George Milburn of Oklahoma, novelist, and Isidor Schneider, poet and novelist.

Fellowships granted Leonard Ehrlich and Younghill Kang, a Korean, for literary work last year, were renewed.

Tom Tippett, writer on economic subjects, to prepare a volume dealing with certain aspects of the coal industry in the United States.

All of the authors, except Ehrlich and Tippett, will carry on their work abroad.

Two Composers in List.

The two composers are: William Grant Still, who will work in this country, and Prof. Douglas Moore of Columbia University.

The artists receiving awards are: Peggy Bacon, a satirist in the graphic arts; Frank Mechau of Denver, Colo., a painter of Western scenes; Francis Criss, who will study fresco painting in Italy; Rosella Hartman of Woodstock, N. Y., who will study the lithographers' craft in Paris, and Maurice Glickman, a sculptor.

Howard Cook of Springfield, Mass., has been granted a second fellowship to enable him to carry on studies. He now is in Springfield doing a mural painting under PWA auspices.

The scholars are:

Dr. Michael Heidelberger, associate professor of biological chemistry at Columbia University, for research at the University of Upsala, Sweden, on the molecular weight of thyroglobulin, the hormone of the thyroid gland.

Arthur Loveridge, now in Kenya on a fellowship, was granted a continuation of the fellowship to continue his studies in East Africa. He formerly was curator of reptiles and amphibians in the museum of comparative zoology at Harvard University.

Woman Scientist Gets Award.

Dr. Grace Lee Nute, assistant professor of history at Hamline University, St. Paul, Minn., for research abroad for biographical material. Miss Nute is the only woman scholar to receive a fellowship, although four were awarded to women artists.

Dr. Fulmer Mood, renewal of a fellowship to continue his research into early American colonization.

Dr. Lowell J. Ragataz, associate professor of history at George Washington University in Washington, D. C., a renewal of a fellowship to continue his studies into the social and economic studies of the French Antilles during the seventeenth and eighteenth centuries.

William Henry Chamberlin, a renewal of his fellowship. Chamberlin, a newspaper man, is writing a history of the Russian revolution from 1917 to 1921.

Dr. Frank Tannenbaum, a renewed scholarship, to continue his studies of the agrarian problems of Peru and Argentina.

Dr. Douglas Bush, professor of English at the University of Minnesota, for work on a critical study of English poetry.

Sterling Dow of Harvard University, for studies on Athenian public documents in Greece.

Dr. Geoffroy Atkinson, professor of romance languages at Amherst College Massachusette, for study on the French Renaissance.

Dr. Rudolf M. Riofstahl of New York University, for research into certain Islamic ceramics in Italy.

Dr. Ernest Nagel of Columbia University, research in mathematics.

Dr. Robert B. Brode, professor of physics, University of California, research at the University of Cambridge, England, on collisions of electrons with atoms.

Dr. Frank H. Spedding, instructor of chemistry, University of California, to make European investigations into heterocyclic compounds containing nitrogen.

Dr. Arnold Dresden, professor of mathematics, Swarthmore College, for preparation of a book on the calculus of variations.

Dr. Harold Kriby Jr., associate professor of zoology at the University of California, for studies in South Africa.

Dr. George Oswald Burr, associate professor of biology at the University of Minnesota, for European research in the field of photosynthesis.

Dr. Allan Lyle Grafflin, instructor in anatomy at Harvard University, for research at Naples, Italy, and Plymouth, England.

Eyewitnesses

CONTINUED FROM FIRST PAGE.

taller of the two men shooting with a shotgun into the body of one of the officers. With the killer was a shorter fellow.

Seeing themselves watched the pair hastily jumped into their car and started it. Mr. Giggal debated whether to drive up and try to stop them, but Mrs. Giggal urged him to speed away as they had no pistol or gun. As he complied, the black sedan jumped into motion apparently to chase them. Mr. Giggal stepped on the accelerator and the bandits' car suddenly whirled around in the road and headed toward Dallas, gathering speed rapidly.

Mr. Giggal saw a third patrolman coming toward them, and flagged him down to tell him of the shooting. The patrolman hurried back to the aid of his comrades, being joined by the Giggal and some farmers living near by who had heard the shots. Other cars arrived soon, too, occupants reporting a black sedan traveling at a furious rate of speed had passed them going toward Dallas.

Dies in Ambulance.

One of the patrolmen was found dead and the other seriously wounded, dying later in an ambulance en route to Grapevine. The pistols of both were still in their holsters, the officers not having been given a chance to draw them.

Farmers living near by reported the car had been parked on the side road for some time, and one of them was said to have informed highway officers of his suspicions in regard to it.

The car tore through the town of Grapevine at an estimated speed of seventy-five miles an hour, traveling toward Dallas. A hitchhiker who narrowly missed being run down said the car contained two men who seemed to be laughing and having an enjoyable time in general. There was no woman in the car as far as he could see, the hitchhiker, William Pike, reported. Others who saw the car said one of the pair was a woman dressed in riding breeches.

Bank Survey

CONTINUED FROM FIRST PAGE.

more wages and shorten hours of work was an event of the month of greatest moment to the future of business.

Anxiety Over Hours.

"There can be no doubt," it says, "but that the proposal of the Government to shorten hours of work and increase the rate of pay has caused a great deal of anxiety among business men.

"There is no wish on the part of American business men to be niggardly with labor. Industry in this country believes in the doctrine of good wages and for many months after the onset of the depression employers in general withheld wage cuts, hoping that an improvement in business conditions would make them unnecessary.

"Business men know, however, that increased wages and shorter hours mean higher prices and they are fearful of the effect of price advances upon consumption in the present state of the markets and of reduced buying power."

Clyde Barrow

CONTINUED FROM FIRST PAGE.

before Grapevine was reached Murphy was dead.

Wheeler, 26, had been with the State highway patrol nearly four years. He was married. Murphy, 24, had been assigned to duty here last fall upon completing the training course at headquarters in Austin.

Sixteen Fort Worth detectives, Tarrant and Dallas County Sheriffs and deputies as well as Rangers Hanna and Weems took up the hunt for the occupants of the car. The description of the machine and the occupants was sent out of the Fort Worth police radio and given officers in all parts of the State.

Authorities at first thought that the man in the automobile was Raymond Hamilton, but the fact that a farmer living near the scene said that the car had been parked there since 10:30 a. m. destroyed this theory, as Hamilton had stolen a car in Houston at 9:30 a. m. Sunday.

First Thought Hamilton.

When the slaying of the two highway patrolmen was first reported, officers believed that Raymond Hamilton, escaped convict and bank robber and pal of Barrow's, had done the killing. Hamilton had robbed a bank at West, near Waco, Saturday, and had abducted a woman motorist, who sought to aid him after his car had gone in the ditch near Mexia. The woman was released in Houston early Sunday and later identified her abductor as Hamilton, from photographs i nthe Houston police files.

However, it later developed that Hamilton could not have been in Tarrant County so soon after his reported flight from Houston. The fact that the car whose occupants killed the highway patrolmen had been parked for some time, apparently waiting, also destroyed this theory.

Woman Is Released.

At Houston, Mrs. Cam Gunter, wife of an oil field gauger, the abducted woman, told her story, and of the escape of Hamilton in a second car, stolen after hers had been restored there. Mrs. Gunter, resident of Mexia, said Hamilton had a woman companion with him. It then was believed that Hamilton was fleeing back to his old North Texas haunts.

Shortly afterward Houston officers advised that the car in which the killers fled, a black 1934 Ford sedan, bore the same license as a machine stolen in Houston by Hamilton Sunday morning shortly after he released Mrs. Gunter.

Third Officer in Advance.

State Highway Patrolman Polk Ivy of Fort Worth, who was riding in advance of his comrades, said he noticed the car parked on a side road fifty yards from the highway but thought nothing of it until he glanced back, after he had gone a quarter of a mile, and saw that Wheeler and Murphy were not following him.

Retracing his route, he found Wheeler dead and Murphy dying from buckshot wounds. They lay near their motorcycles. Their weapons had not been drawn. Apparently, he said, they were shot down as they drew up to the parked machine, which, meanwhile, had disappeared in the direction of Grapevine.

She said his companion was an attractive young woman who spoke to Hamilton in terms of endearment, addressing him as darling and sweetheart.

Identified as Robber.

Officers of the State National Bank of West, near Waco, which was robbed of $1,865 Saturday morning, and farmers who had assisted the robber in getting his car out of a mudhole, also identified photographs of Hamilton as the blond young bandit they had seen.

Hamilton, convicted of killing John Bucher, Hillsboro filling station operator and of numerous robberies, was liberated with five other convicts from the Eastham State prison farm near Huntsville, last Jan. 16, in a dawn machine-gun raid during a dense fog, believed engineered by Clyde Barrow, eel-like desperado from West Dallas sought by officers throughout the Middle West.

He entered the West bank at 10:30 a. m. Saturday, ordered several officers, employes and customers into the vault and drove rapidly away after seizing $1,865 from a teller's cage.

Shortly afterward a farmer helped him get the car out of a mudhole east of West and Hamilton sped on toward Mexia. At a turn in the road near Thelma the machine plunged into a ditch and was wrecked against an embankment.

While two farmers had gone to get a chain Mrs. Gunter and her 4-year-old son, Jolly, drove up and Mrs. Gunter offered assistance.

Tells Woman of Robbery.

The farmers, returning with the chain, heard the robber say to Mrs. Gunter, "Lady, I've just robbed a bank and I'll have to have your car." She screamed and when the farmers attempted to come to her assistance with a shotgun, the robber fired one shot at them and ordered them to drop the gun. His red-haired woman companion helped him transfer his machine gun and the bank loot from the wrecked car to Mrs. Gunter's machine and after forcing Mrs. Gunter to get in with them the robber and his companion drove away, leaving Jolly Gunter with the farmers.

Central Texas officers searched throughout the night for the fugitives and no word was heard of them until Mrs. Gunter notified Houston police Sunday morning she had been released there. Her husband, the Sheriff and Chief of Police at Mexia left immediately for Houston.

Idetnified From Pictures.

She said the robber, whom she identified positively from pictures as Hamilton, gave her $30 and told her to have her car fixed up. After leaving her the man stole an automobile there and escaped.

Hamilton's trail next appeared unexpectedly in North Texas with the shooting of two officers near Grapevine.

Highway Patrolman Ivy said he did not hear the shots that killed his two companions, the noise of his motorcycle apparently drowning out the roar of the shotgun.

Sixteen Fort Worth detectives armed with rifles and shotguns and a force from the Sheriff's office began searching highways and country roads for the fugitives.

The death car had been halted on the side road for some time, William Sheeper, farmer living about 400 yards away, said. A man and a woman, both wearing knickers or trousers, were the occupants. He described the man as five feet six inches and weighing 140 pounds, the woman five feet four inches and weighing 115 pounds.

Near the spot that the car had been parked were three sixteen-gauge shotgun shells, five forty-five caliber automatic shells, three twelve-gauge shells and one rifle shell, all empty.

Murphy, who formerly lived in Nacogdoches, was assigned to Fort Worth for duty after completing his training period in the Austin headquarters Oct. 1. He lived in the Fort Worth Y. M. C. A.

Wheeler was a member of the original patrol, having enrolled Jan. 10, 1930. He resided at 1101 Fairmount, Fort Worth.

Hostage

CONTINUED FROM FIRST PAGE.

Jolly, who had been staying with friends.

"We started out of Thelma and a short distance away we saw a car wrecked in a ditch," she continued. "A man and a woman were in it, and I stopped to see if I could be of aid. The man had a scratch on his nose and the woman a scratch on her forehead where she had bumped the windshield.

"A boy came up on horseback. He knew me, but I did not know him. The boy got in my car and tried to pull the wrecked car out of the ditch with a rope, but the rope broke. I don't think the car could have been driven if they could have got it out.

"Then the man told the boy to go to a house up the road and try to get a chain, and he started off. He had gone a little ways when the man turned to me.

"He had a machine gun in his hands and said he had just robbed a bank about twenty or thirty minutes before.

"I screamed and the boy on horseback started coming back. The man shot into the ground in front of him. "The woman was taking things out of the wrecked car and putting them in mine. Then they made me get in the car. I begged them to leave my little boy and they finally said they would. I told him to go to the house where he had been staying.

Went Through Mexia.

"I was in the back seat and the man and the girl were in front. The man drove full speed over the rough roads and when we got to a highway he told me to guide them through Mexia by side streets and keep out of the downtown district.

"I was dreadfully scared and I did as they told me. We drove through and then got back into country lanes and drove over winding country lanes for hours. I was lost.

"Finally, some time after nightfall, we drove onto the Houston-Dallas highway. The first town I remember passing through on the highway was Buffalo.

"Just the other side of Conroe something went wrong with the car and the man drove into a filling station. The filling station man worked on it a long time and finally got it so it would run better. Then we drove off again and passed through Conroe a little after midnight, I think. I judge it was about 1 o'clock when the man drove us off into the woods, away from the road, and told us to get some sleep.

Got a Little Sleep.

"They had treated me so nicely that I was not afraid like I had been and I did doze off some in the car. The girl seemed to sleep pretty well, but I don't think the man ever went to sleep. He sat around or walked around with a machine gun most of the night.

"We came on into Houston after sun-up and got here about 8:30, I guess, and drove around the town. The man said he wanted to find a car to steal.

"Finally he found the car and he drove off in it. The girl sat beside me and made me follow in my car. She said she had a pistol and kept her hand in the folds of her clothes. I think she had a little pistol, about a .32, for I had seen her with one earlier.

"He drove all around and finally stopped and the girl got out and got in the car with him and they drove off."

Girl Cute and Sweet.

Mrs. Gunter said both Hamilton and his companion tried to be pleasant to her and calm her fears during the all-night ride. She described the girl as being "cute and sweet, at least as far as I was concerned."

She told officers that the couple spoke freely of criminal exploits but were not specific about anything except robbery of the West bank. The girl used good English and did not smoke, she said.

The man and young woman counted the loot in their possession as they drove along, Mrs. Gunter said. "There was around $2,000, mostly in currency," she said.

The automobile stolen belonged to Clyde Clayton. Clayton had driven to his mother's home to take her some flowers for Easter. He had barely reached the door of the house when he looked around and saw a man driving off in his car, which had been parked in front.

Robert T. Johnson Weds Miss Maggie Kinsey

Miss Maggie Kinsey, daughter of Mr. and Mrs. W. J. Kinsey, 1001 Sunset, was married Sunday evening to Robert H. Johnson, son of Mrs. C. M. Johnson of Calvert. The ceremony was performed by Dr. George W. Truett, pastor of the First Baptist Church, at the minister's residence, with relatives present.

The bride wore a pink ensemble and carried talisman roses and lilies of the calley. Following the ceremony, a reception was held at the home of the bride's sister, Mrs. H. W. Garrett, 5625 Ridgedale.

The couple will make their home at 725 West Eighth.

Shepherds in the Orient in ancient times kept track of the number of sheep in their care by carrying a hollow clay cylinder with a pebble in it for each sheep in the flock.

El Paso Herald-Post

Home Edition

THREE CENTS IN EL PASO
FIVE CENTS OUTSIDE EL PASO

SIXTEEN PAGES

Weather Forecast: F... and tomorrow; not much change in tem perature

VOL. LIV. NO. 82 — EL PASO, ...S, THURSDAY, APRIL 5, 1934

WOMEN VOTERS ATTACK REGAN FOR STAND ON CHILD LABOR

LONG REBUKED AFTER THREAT TO HIT LAWYER

Senator Tells Huey Nation Gives Him Little Respect

ROW AT HEARING

'Kingfish' Offers to Fight Attorney Outside Over Racetrack Charge

By Associated Press

WASHINGTON, April 5.—Antagonism between Huey Long and administration leadership burst forth in the senate today with Pat Harrison of Mississippi saying "the opinion of the senator from Louisiana is less respected by the membership of this body as a whole and by the country than that of any other senator here."

The two outspoken legislators had been in several lesser disputes a while before at a senate finance committee hearing on the confirmation of D. D. Moore as internal revenue collector in Louisiana, opposed by Long. Long charges Moore is linked with Louisiana racetrack promoters.

Edward Rightor, Moore's attorney, was invited by Long to "go outside" after Rightor had said of Jefferson race track in Louisiana "that's your track, senator." Long called that statement an "infamous falsehood."

Replies to Speech

The exchanges between the Louisiana senator and Harrison, who heads the finance committee, pertained to conduct of the hearing.

Again a crowd was on hand, many of whom went to the senate floor later and heard Long in a speech calling for heavier taxes on the wealthy.

Then Harrison undertook a reply to a speech yesterday by Long, blaming the Democratic leadership for "helping the Hoover administration to send the country to hell."

"A surplusage speech," Harrison termed Long's earlier address.

"I shall offer no defense of what this side of the aisle did during the Hoover administration. It needs no defense on the part of good Democrats and I am sure the country appreciates the fact when men charged with a high responsibility here attempt to cooperate in trying to bring the country back to economic normalcy.

Huey Interrupts

"Of course the leader on this side of the aisle (Robinson of Arkansas) needs no eulogy from me because what is in my heart, and my estimate of him and his labors and services here is shared by every member of the senate on both sides of the aisle, with possibly one exception."

Here Long interrupted:

"In speaking of the leadership I had more particularly in mind, as well as anybody else, the senator from Mississippi. I was not speaking only of the senator from Arkansas. When I speak of the leadership, I think the senator knows I certainly had him in mind for the tax policy he had pursued. He need make no defense of anyone else; let him take care of himself."

Rebuked

"I am glad," Harrison replied, "the senator looks on me as included in the leadership, but if others care no more about his estimate of me than I care about it, it makes no difference because in my opinion the opinion of the senator from Louisiana is less respected by the membership of this body as a whole and by the country than that of any other senator here."

PLANE CRASH VICTIM ALIVE IN JUNGLE

Engineer Found With Four Dead; Ship Crashed March 10

By United Press

CALI, Colombia, April 5.—Indians reported today the finding in the jungles of Newton C. Marshall, American mining engineer, sole survivor of a passenger plane that crashed on the banks of the Sipi river in Colombia three weeks ago.

The plane, the Von Khorn of the Scadta line (Colombian-German air Transport Co.) left Buenaventura on the Pacific coast of Colombia March 10, for Medellin, in the interior. Five persons were aboard.

Desperado and Cigar-Smoking Pal

Clyde Barrow and his cigar smoking woman companion, Bonnie Parker, was hunted by hundreds of police today, following the slaying of two state highway motorcycle police near Dallas, Sunday. They were shot to death when they investigated a car parked near the highway. Barrow first drew the attention of police when he was held in Dallas in connection with chicken theft.

CALLES GRAVELY ILL OF MALARIA

Former Mexico President Is Stricken After Visit to Tropical States

By United Press

MEXICO CITY, April 5.—Plutarco Elias Calles, Mexico's foremost statesman, was gravely ill of malaria today at his Cuernavaca home.

Recently he paid a visit to the tropical tsates of Fabasco and Campeche. Malaria, from which he had suffered, recurred and he was ordered to bed.

Calles is former president of Mexico.

WIRT'S SUPPORTERS CALLED 'JACKASSES'

Committee Named to Investigate Revolt Charges

WASHINGTON, April 5.—Champions of Dr. William Wirt's "red plot" charges were denounced today as "intellectual jackasses" by Rep. George Foulkes, Dem. Mich., leading defender of the "brain trust" in congress.

A committee of five was named to investigate the charge of Dr. William Wirt, Gary, Ind., that administration brain trusters are planning a revolution.

WOMAN WHIPS JACK DEMPSEY

Wife of Wrestler Attacks Ex-Champ After He Hits Husband on Chin

By Associated Press

ALEXANDRIA, La., April 5.—Jack Dempsey lost a ring battle here last night. Worse than that, he was forced into ignominous retreat from the scene of contest. It all happened as the ex-heavy champion was referreeing a heavyweight wrestling match and the 95 pound wife of one of the participants climbed into the rope square and took a hand in the proceedings.

Dempsey lost his shirt and a good deal of hair.

Mrs. Johnny Plummer, whose husband was tying up with Bruce Noland in the feature of a mat card, gave the fans the unexpected extra thrill when she challenged the former pugilistic king and won at least a temporary victory.

Mrs. Plummer Rises

It all started when Dempsey warned Plummer that he would not allow any kicking of Noland when the latter was on the floor. One thing led to another and Referee Dempsey closed the argument by delivering three quick upper-cuts to the chin, which ended the evening's entertainment for Plummer.

But not for Mrs. Plummer. She was through the ropes from her ringside seat in a second and going after Dempsey's shirt and his hair before anybody could do anything about it.

Lots of Excitement

Dempsey retreated as far as the ropes would allow and stood there for a while, proving he could still take it, without raising a hand in defense. When Mrs. Plummer really got organized, however, Dempsey slipped through the ropes and retreated into the crowd.

By that time, Promoter Mike Mule was in the ring trying to make everyone listen to reason, but when Mrs. Plummer turned her attention to him, he quickly pinned her arms behind her and held them thus while Dempsey slipped back into the ring and raised Noland's arm in token of victory by default on a foul.

There was lots of excitement, but really very little damage to anyone.

SENATE BANS HIKE IN INCOME TAXES

Refuses to Increase Levy on Small Incomes

By Associated Press

WASHINGTON, April 5. — The senate today rejected a proposal to increase from four to six per cent the existing normal income tax and to levy surtaxes ranging from six to 71 per cent as against an existing range of one to 55 per cent.

By this action the senate retained the less severe finance committtee schedule for a flat four per cent normal rate and surtaxes ranging from five to 59 per cent.

The committee surtaxes run through 29 brackets as compared with 28 in the house bill and begin the five per cent on net incomes between $4000 and $6000 and reach 59 per cent on those over $1,000,000.

U. S. OFFICER'S CONTRACT WITH CELIA UPHELD

Inspector Says Locke Acted Properly in Villa Case

SIGNED VOLUNTARILY

Mystery Woman Again Asks Movie Manager for $500 For 'Information'

T. A. Arnold, inspector in charge of the plant quarantine bureau, said today that a thorough investigation showed that Clarence M. Locke, plant quarantine inspector at the bridge, acted properly in signing a contract as manager for Celia Villa.

"I talked with the girl in Las Cruces yesterday and she said she signed the contract voluntarily," said Mr. Arnold.

Miss Villa, daughter of Gen Francisco (Pancho) Villa, spurned a Metro - Goldwyn - Mayer publicity tour contract to take her chances with Mr. Locke as her manager.

Mr. Locke is trying to get her a job in Hollywood.

The woman who asked Metro-Goldwyn-Mayer for $500 in return for revealing the whereabouts of Miss Villa is still trying to collect the $500.

She appeared at the Plaza theater Monday and told E. B. Coleman, M.-G.-M. representative, that Celia, who had signed a contract with Coleman, would be at the El Paso courthouse at 11:45 a. m. Monday.

Miss Villa, after signing the contract, had left El Paso and Mr. Coleman could not find her.

He waited at the courthouse for nearly an hour. At that time, Celia was in the Las Cruces courthouse, where her cousin, Fermin Torres, was taking out guardianship papers.

Mr. Coleman left in disgust when Celia did not return. He was informed that she had signed a previous contract with Clarence M. Locke, plant quarantine inspector at the bridge.

John Paxton, Plaza theater, today had received a letter from the "mystery" woman asking him to send the $50 0to a Las Cruces address. The letter was unsigned.

FLOOD DEATHS GROW TO 40

11 More Bodies Are Found In Oklahoma Ruins; Million Damage

By THE ASSOCIATED PRESS

Texas entered into the nation's flood picture today with four victims, as 11 bodies were recovered in a western Oklahoma flood in which nearly a score may have perished.

Recovery of the 11 bodies brought flood deaths to 40.

As was the case in the Oklahoma flood which centered around Elk City and Hammon, the southwest Texas deaths near Menard occurred when a stream, usually shallow, became a torrent because of heavy rains.

C. P. Smith district FERA engineer, reported the Oklahoma flood damage at $625,000.

It was estimated that damage of several millions dollars was done in northern and western Wisconsin by rain and melting snow.

Seven channel projects on the upper Mississippi were endangered today when the river reached a high stage and continued its rise.

Storms in Ohio caused damage estimated at $100,000. A man was killed by lightning at Canton.

In Kansas, the rains continued but were less serious. Farmers expected their crops to benefit.

Snow held up highway and air traffic in the Rocky Mountains región and lay as deep as 15 inches in places in the Dakota hills.

In the east, 10 families near Hartford, Conn., abandoned their homes when the Connecticut river rose more than two feet above flood stage.

MACHINE GUNNERS ROUTED FROM BANK

Two Employes Battle Bandits And Foil Robbery

By United Press

BISHOP, Texas, April 5—Two machine gun bandits were routed in a gun battle at the First State bank here today by Cashier William A. Harlan and his assistant, Leon Hagan.

No one was injured.

The bandits held the trigger down on their machine gun while the two bankers emptied their two automatics.

Where Six Were Brutally Slain at House Party

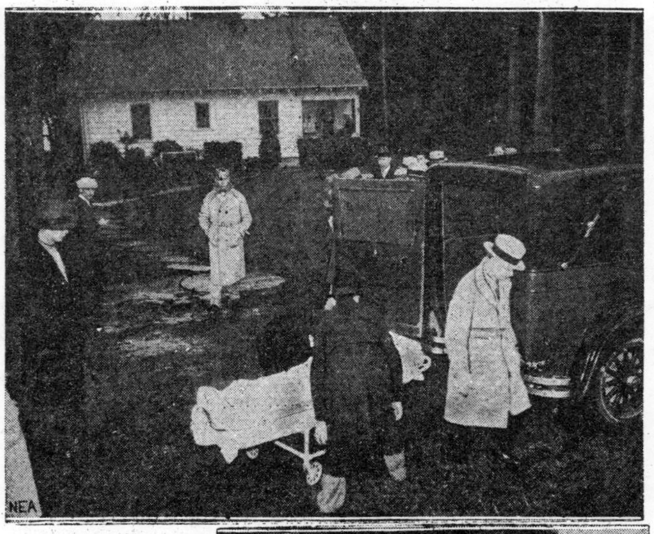

Above is the scene of the Pacific northwest's most gruesome murder—the home of Frank Fileder, near Bremerton, Wash., where Fileder, his wife and four guests were blindfolded, bound, then beaten to death. Photo shows exterior of the murder house, with authorities removing one of the victim's bodies.

Below, a corner of the blood-drenched house—a closet where the body of Fred Balsom was found in pools of blood. Police are mystified.

TURNER ATTACKS EDITOR PERRY

Board President Charges That Publisher Seeks Control Of School Affairs

Dr. George Turner, school board president, asserted today that a faction opposing him on the school board is trying to give control of the board to Wallace Perry, Herald-Post editor, and a group of school teachers.

Dr. Turner said:

"It appears from editorials published in the Herald-Post that Mr. Perry has forgotten about Dr. E. J. Cummins running for election to the school board and has taken out after me. He seems to have taken a lot for granted and shaped a background and attitude for me to suit his own purpose.

"The background of my candidacy a year ago was no faction or group as Mr. Perry pointed out. I was requested to run by a number of prominent citizens for the sole purpose if elected to use my best judgment in helping to work out for El Paso a nine months' term of school with the small amount of money which every one knew would be available and to keep if possible the school system on a cash basis for the general good of the teachers, taxpayers and all concerned.

"Product of Imagination"

"The statement that I was supported and elected by a group of teachers playing politics for the purpose of favoring them through my actions on the board is a product of Mr. Perry's imagination.

"The only reference made to 'Hughey and anti-Hughey politics' was when the candidates got together for the first time. This was in Mr. Harwell's office. Mr. Harwell, Mr. Covington, Mr. Wilcox, Mr. Roy Hoard, Mr. Robert Price and others were present and discussing Mr. Hughey when I arrived.

"After listening for a few minutes, I said these words: "If the purpose of organizing this ticket is to oust Mr. Hughey and put a new man at the head of the school system who is unfamiliar with its organization and operation at a time when drastic reductions must be made, I thank you for the compliment of asking me to run with you, but I have plenty of work to do and will be going."

Says Perry Changed

"Speaking of some one changing. How about Mr. Perry?

"Just what is back of his supporting Mrs. Burnett?

"He couldn't know anything of her value on the board as compared with Dr. Cummins because he has spoken long and well of Dr. Cummins and admits he did not know Mrs. Burnett until the time of her announcement. Just what does Mr. Perry want to do, anyway?

"Does he want to control the school board himself through teacher group politics at the expense of public school disruption? Judging from previous editorials and his attitude toward the advancement of the school system this would seem to be the case.

"The Herald-Post bitterly opposed

(Continued on Page 9)

He's 'Yes' and 'No' Man, Cummins Replies to Critics

School Trustee Denies He Is 'Yes Man' for Dr. George Turner, President of Board

Dr. E. J. Cummins, candidate for election to the school board, answered "yes" and "no" today when asked if he is "yes man" for Dr. George Turner, board president, as charged by a group of teachers.

Dr. Cummins said:

"If they mean that I vote with Dr. Turner on a question I think is right, then I am 'yes man.' If they mean when I vote against him, then I am his 'no man.'

Dr. Cummins replied to a statement attributed to Mrs. Burnett that Mrs. Susan Buck, Bowie High school teacher, was saved from dismissal by Joseph G. Bennis, C. K. Jameson, and Roland Harwell, board members assertedly composing the "anti-Hughey" faction.

"If those three members favored Mrs. Buck, then the implication is that C. C. Covington, Harvey Wilcox and I opposed her," said Dr. Cummins.

"If that is true, then the vote of Dr. Turner, board president, was necessary in case of a tie, and Dr. Turner is the one who must have 'saved' her.

"As a matter of fact, Mrs. Buck's rating is such that there never was any discussion as to whether she should be retained."

Solicitation of Fund For Mrs. Buck Charged

Friends of Mrs. Susan Buck, president of the El Paso Teachers' Assn., are collecting 10 cents each from school teachers to buy Mrs. Buck a present, Dr. E. J. Cummins, candidate for reelection to the school board, and Dr. George Tur-

(Continued on page 16)

Mrs. Burnett's Children Sick

Mrs. T. R. Burnett, candidate for election to the school board, lost interest in the campaign today when her two children became ill.

She spent the day conferring with physicians about the health of her children. It is believed they have the measles.

Mrs. Burnett said she is sure she will win a place on the board in the voting Saturday.

Dr. E. J. Cummins, her opponent, predicted victory for himself.

TEMPERATURES

Chicago	44	40	New York	48	34
Denver	38	30	Phoenix	76	46
EL PASO	68	44	Roswell	70	36
Kansas City	68	54	San Antonio	78	58
Los Angeles	74	54	Seattle	60	46

Criticize State Senator For Opposing Texas Amendment

URGE SEX EDUCATION

Speaker Says Adolescents Should Be Told About Origin of Life

League of Women Voters members today criticized State Sen. Ken M. Regan for voting against Texas ratification of the child labor amendment.

"When he comes up for re-election we'll put him on the spot by making him put his name on the dotted line for or against the child labor amendment," members said at the league's citizenship school at the College of Mines today.

Mrs. W. P. Hobby, Houston, charged that eastern manufacturers are fostering paid propaganda in Texas to defeat state ratification.

"They know the amendment will be ratified unless they can get farmers excited about some misconception," she said.

"They are telling the farmers that children won't be permitted to milk a cow until they are 18 years old, if the amendment is ratified. The amendment excepts farm labor of children.

"That line of attack against it is contemptible, ridiculous."

She advised the league to request every candidate in the next election to answer a questionnaire about his views on child labor and the amendment.

Sex Education Advocated By Dr. Joseph M. Roth

Shildren today develop into adolescence faster than in previous generations because of oversexed stimulation in modern life, Dr. Joseph M. Roth, College of Mines psychology professor, told the League of Women Voters citizenship school today.

Dr. Roth blamed "the type of news some newspapers carry, the type of moving pictures, risque literature and irregularities in actual life" for the serious problem of too early adolescence.

"The need for sex education starts with the child in his cradle," he said. "Clement of Alexandria said: 'No one should be ashamed to name what God was not ashamed to create.'"

He warned mothers that chaildren know more about sex than "many of the foolish people who do not care to discuss the subject."

Should Answer Questions

Questions of children about sex never should be disregarded, he warned. They should be answered as fully as the age, interest and capacity to the child to understand permits, he said.

He advised gradual education of children in sex matters, beginning with illustrations from animal life.

"Puppy love which often begins between eight and 10 years of age, is an essential preparation for future love and the great work of married life," Dr. Roth said.

"The child who is teased and ridiculed about puppy love may become surreptitious. He will not seek advice from the parent when he needs it, because of lost confidence in the parent."

Appeal to Courage

He advised parents to appeal to manliness, courage and heroism in boys and the motherhood instinct in girls of growing years, to keep them from mis-steps.

"Adolescence is a dream time," he said. "It is unfortunate that some parents goad their adolescent children into activity by poking fun at their dreams. Their dreams and ideals should be encouraged."

He advised hobbies for children, such as scoutcraft, or stamp collecting, athletics for boys and less strenuous exercise for girls.

The dangers of social disease should be impressed upon youth, but this must be convincing, or parents had better leave such negative sex education phases to their ministers or physicians, he advised.

Discuss Dress

Dr. Roth advocated sex instruction in high schools and colleges, especially in connection with biology courses.

During a discussion following his talk, women members of the audience asked Dr. Roth what can be done about immodest dress on bathing beaches.

"Ideas of what is modest change with age and decade," Dr. Roth replied. "In Japan, it is immodest for a woman to appear in a drawing room without long sleeves, yet the same women see nothing immodest in going nude on the beach. Customs and the norm set ideas of modesty. Uncovering the body is not a sign of immodesty, where we are accustomed to it."

Speaker Says E. P. Lacks Public Health Nurses

El Paso always will have a high infant death rate because of its great percentage of foreign population, poor sanitation, economic conditions, and excessive child bearing among some classes, Mrs. Lois Huffaker told the League of Women Voters citizenship school today.

She said El Paso has only one public health nurse to each 11,200 persons, whereas one to each 2500 population is the ideal.

Harvard Student Follows Freudian Impulse and Socks Sea Serpent

EDITOR'S NOTE: Coast-guards and fishermen saw Thomas G. Ratcliffe, Harvard junior and member of a prominent St. Louis family, seize an oar and strike at an object in Vineyard Sound yesterday. Ratcliffe thus became perhaps the first person ever to engage in actual combat with a sea serpent—if sea serpent it was—although Jonah is said to have gotten in some infighting with a whale. In the following article, Ratcliffe tells of the "Freudian impulse" which led him to wallop the monster.

By THOMAS G. RATCLIFFE
(Written for U. P.)

PENZANCE POINT, Mass., April 5.—Eric Warbasse and I took the outboard about 3 p. m. yesterday afternoon and made a complete circle of great harbor. I had bet Eric he could not start the motor but he did and I lost five cents. We headed for the hole.

On the way I saw an object and thought it was the body of William Hulten, who was drowned a week ago. I said to Eric, "That must be the boy's body." We started for it and then I saw that it was a serpent. It was by the spindle near the rock and not far from the steamer wharf.

When I saw the thing close up my first thought was of Loch Ness, but I said to Eric, "There is no Scotch mist here." Remembering the days when knighthood was in flower, I socked it on the head. The head was not defined from the body but tapered to a snub nose. When we got to within 10 feet of the monster, we noticed for the first time a tail out of the water about 20 feet away.

Eric cut the motor and we came alongside just a foot or two away. It looked like a gigantic eel head and was six inches out of the water.

After it was struck, it slowly slipped down under the water, apparently arching its body, though it had never been completely out of the water. It slipped alongside the boat for probably 15 seconds and we had ample time to see the monster. I did not strike it again because by that time I had realized what I had done.

As the tail came slowly along I noticed that it tapered to a point and appeared to carry a fin. The body did not lash or writhe and the beast simply sounded, like a submarine or a whale. We followed slowly on the surface in the direction the monster was headed into Great Head but nothing more was seen of it.

The center of the body was about three feet in diameter; it was quite large and about 30 feet in length.

I don't know why I hit it—just a Freudian impulse, I suppose—but I bashed it hard. Then when I saw it move I decided that discretion would have been the better part of valor but the snake, or monster, or whatever you want to call it, seemed perfectly bored with the situation, and remembering Harvard indifference, it simply pushed off.

ONLY NEWSPAPER IN THIS AREA WITH FULL LEASED WIRE NEWS, INTERNATIONAL ILLUSTRATED NEWS AND KING SYNDICATE FEATURES, FULL LOCAL, SPORTS, POLITICAL NEWS.

PALESTINE IS THE CENTER OF THE WORLD'S GREATEST OIL AREA.

PALESTINE DAILY HERALD

and ANDERSON COUNTY HERALD

FULL LEASED WIRE

VOL. 32, No. 97. Palestine, Texas, * * "The City Beautiful" * * Wednesday Afternoon, May 23, 1934. Member Associated Press Price Five Cents

Barrow and Bonnie Parker Riddled With Bullets

Chinese Say Japan Bombarding Manchuria

1000 Killed By Bombs In Farm Section

Reports Not Confirmed From Other Sources Say Bombardment Begun Against Chinese.

Shanghai, May 24. (Thursday) (AP)—Chinese reports from Peiping today alleged a Japanese air squadron bombed a wide area around Chinchow in Southeast Manchuria yesterday (Wednesday) killing 1,000 Manchurian farmers and destroying 20 villages.

These dispatches said the onslaught followed the farmers' refusal to comply with Japanese army demands that the Chinese give up their arms.

The allegations claim that the Japanese bombers had injured hundreds of persons in addition to those killed and that numerous villages were still burning from Japanese incendiary bombs.

The report was not confirmed from other sources.

New Cars.

Tide Water and Texas Seaboard, Palestine, Ford V-8 sedan.

O. T. Coburn, Fort Worth, Chevrolet coupe.

River Report.

Trinity river stage at Long Lake, 7.0 feet, falling; partly cloudy.

ABOUT TOWN

About Town wishes these companies that specialize in scaring the daylights out of you in order to get you to buy their products would quit the scare racket and let About Town get some rest at night.

—o—

Honestly, About Town's scared stiff for fear that he'll wake up some morning to find himself all broken out with "Athlete's Foot" or "Pink Tooth Brush," or something else equally as horrible.

—o—

Just about the time he thinks he's got all the preparations it takes to assure good health and happiness, here comes a new batch of them with scares that are just as scary as the others, and often more so. Seeing visions of these big bare feet with spots on them gives About Town many a bad dream. Just feeling those great big toes twining around his neck and doing all kinds of things to make unpleasant dreams the order of the night.

—o—

Yessir, you've got to buy this and that until there just isn't anything you haven't prepared yourself against having. There's only one thing that you can't be assured of being warded against. That's a nervous breakdown from trying to keep up with all the new preventatives.

—o—

Looks like About Town will go through life just being a tube squeezer and a drug store inquirer. Maybe that isn't an unpleasant prospect.

—o—

They don't even let you go free and unwarned when you start out for a nice fishing trip or something else to try to escape for a day the tribulations of civilization. You've got to remember that you don't have the mystic "golden ply" in your tires, because the car didn't come equipped with them, and you may have a blowout, and have to send a telegram saying "BLOW OUT ON HIGHWAY MOTHER AND CHILDREN MANGLED BEST WISHES DADDY STOP."

Scot Defeats American In British Open

Prestwick, Scotland, May 22. (AP)—Jack McLean, Scottish Walker cup star and the pride of Prestwick, today defeated Johnny Fischer, sensational Cincinnati youngster, by 2 and 1, in the third round of the British amateur golf championship.

Putting brilliantly, sinking the ball from distances as far as 20 feet from the cup, McLean was out in a scorching sub par 33 for this strenuous seaside course to be two up on Fischer at the halfway mark.

Fischer, who was the medalist in the last two American amateur championships, toured the outward holes in par 35 and try as valiantly as he did, he was never able to overcome that two hole deficit.

As the result of his defeat Fischer joined his other beaten Walker cup brethren on the sidelines—Captain Frances Ouimet, H. Chandler Egan, Max Marston, and Gus Moreland.

Jesse Guilford, former American amateur king and looming more and more as a serious threat in this cahmpionship, gained the fourth round with a one-sided triumph over Lt. Col. T. J. Mitchell of Prestwick. Guilford won by 6 and 4 and will meet McLean tomorrow.

Johnny Goodman, U. S. open champion, and W. Lawson Little of San Francisco, caught up with the field today, winning their second round matches without any difficulty. They play again this afternoon.

George Terry Dunlap, Jr., amateur champion of the United States and regarded by old links disciples here as a "man of destiny" after his first and second round comeback victories, made short shrift of George D. Hanay, former French amateur titleholder. The American king won, 6 and 4.

Rotund Cyril Tolley, champion in 1920 and 1929, was eliminated in the third round by James Wallace, who won by 4 and 3.

Cayuga Outpost Nearing Top of Woodbine Sand

Coring was due to start today in the J. R. Meeker No. 1 H. H. Duncan, eastern extension in the Cayuga area. The well is now regarded the most important in the new field. On the basis of calls on top of the Austin chalk, the No. 1 Duncan is running a few feet lower than the Hill & Hill et al No. 1 Tubbs producer.

No. 2 Edens of Tide Water and Seaboard is drilling in Austin chalk below 2241 feet. Chalk was topped at 2146 feet.

No. 2 Wills, plugged-back to 4089 feet, is still waiting on cement.

Wills No. 4, Robertson No. 1 and Louella Hartin No. 1 are rigging up.

On the opposite side of the field, Roeser & Pendleton are rigging up their No. 1 Virginia Bowyer, in the Everett Ritter survey.

Barnsdall No. 1 Tubbs, offsetting the Hill & Hill well, was due to top the Woodbine today.

WATER TANK CRASH THROUGH BUILDING KILLS THREE TODAY

Seven Others Injured and Three Missing After a Heavy Tank Crashes Through Four Floors.

Chicago, May 23. (AP)—The thundering plunge of a steel water tank through the upper floors of a seven story buildini left three dead and seven injured today. Three others were missing.

The tank, weighing 330,000 pounds, crashed through four floors of the Oakley building.

SHERIFF SAYS BANK JOB TIP LED TO AMBUSH

Louisiana Sheriff Says Barrow and Bonnie Had Been Seen In Area Yesterday and Today.

Arcadia, La., May 23. (AP)—Sheriff Jordan of Bienville parish said that he had received a tip that the First National Bank of Arcadia was to be robbed, and that he notified Texas officers of the fact.

He said Clyde Barrow and Bonnie Parker came from Benton, La., yesterday afternoon and passed through Gibsland about 4 or 5 o'clock in the afternoon, and again this morning shortly before the killing.

In the group of officers who awaited the pair on the highway were: Sheriff Jordan, his deputy, Paul M. Oakley, both of Bienville parish; former Ranger Captain Frank Hamer of Austin; Bob Alcorn, a member of the sheriff's department at Dallas, Texas; B. M. Gault, Austin, member of the Texas highway officers department; and Officer Hinton.

The officers were stationed in a ring on top of a hill.

They were concealed in high grass over a distance of about half a block when they sighted Barrow's car approaching the hill. There were two trucks on the Castor-Gibsland road, going in opposite directions.

These trucks served as an extra shield against discovery by Barrow and his companion, who were first fired upon by Deputy Sheriff Oakley. He used a shotgun loaded with buckshot and fired quickly after ordering Barrow to stop, which warning Barrow ignored.

Barrow opened a door of the car evidently to fire a sawed-off shotgun which he held in one hand, but Deputy Oakley and the five other officers who immediately joined in the shooting were too quick.

Sheriff Jordan said it was pos-

(Continued on Page 8)

Barrow On Spot.

Dallas, May 23. (AP)—The Dallas Times Herald today said it was informed by an unimpeachable authority that Clyde Barrow and Bonnie Parker had been "put on the spot" by the father of an escaped Texas convict who hoped thereby to gain clemency for his offspring.

The newspaper said that a Texas prison official learned that the father of the convict, who recently escaped while serving a 99-year sentence, lived in Louisiana and perfected an agreement whereby "consideration" would be given the escaped convict if the father would cooperate in having the desperado couple "spotted."

President Asks Congress Tight Control of Oil

Washington, May 23. (AP)—President Roosevelt today asked congress to tighten up the oil control program at this session.

This was among the developments made known today at the president's semi-weekly press conference.

Another was that the president had consented to a summer furlough for Frank C. Walker, chairman of the National Emergency Council, but has asked him to return to his government post in the fall.

Mr. Roosevelt also said he would send a message to congress very soon relating to the controversial war debts issue.

In a letter to Chairman Logan of the senate mines committee and Chairman Rayburn of the house interstate commerce committee, the president asserted that illegal production of oil is threatening the structure of the newly organized oil production control system.

HAMER SAYS BARROW JUST "DROVE INTO IT"

Dallas, May 23. (AP)—L. G. Phares, chief of the State Highway Patrol, announced today that he was informed by Frank Hamer, in a telephone conversation, that Clyde Barrow, notorious Southwest desperado, and Bonnie Parker, his companion, were killed today near Shreveport, La.

Hamer, former Texas Ranger; B. M. Gault, highway patrolman, and Ted Hinton and Bob Alcorn, Dallas county sheriffs, encountered Barrow and the Parker woman at Black Lake, 90 miles south of Shrevepot, Phares was advised.

"The job is done," Hamer told Phares over the telephone.

"We killed Clyde and Bonnie at 9:15 this morning. They were at Black Lake, a hideout we had been watching for weeks. Clyde and Bonnie did not get to fire a shot. Their car was full of guns and ammunition, but they did not get a chance to use them."

In a later conversation with Hamer, Phares asked the veteran officer to tell him "all about it."

"Well, Chief, there ain't much to it," Hamer replied. "They just drove into the wrong place. Both of them died with their guns in their hands, but they did not have a chance to use them. We got them as they drove into their hide-out?"

"Who did the shooting?" asked Phares.

"All of us," Hamer replied.

Phares said payment of rewards for Barrow and the woman "dead or alive," would be withheld pending trial of Billie Mace and Floyd Hamilton at Fort Worth. The patrol chief had guaranteed a reward of $1,000 for slayers of the patrolmen. He had collected about $4,000 in free-will contributions. He said from this amount would come some expenditures for expenses incurred incident to the hunt for the killers.

JUDGMENT AGAINST FORMER CONSTABLE IS RENDERED HERE

Judge Lex Smith Holds Will Gordon and Bonding Company Liable for $1353 In Fees.

Special Judge Lex Smith this afternoon rendered judgment for $1,353.60 against Will Gordon, former constable of Precinct No. 1, and his bonding company, the American Surety Company, for uncollected fees from justice court cases in 1931 and 1932.

Attorneys W. C. Campbell and Joe N. Davis, representing Gordon, gave notice of appeal.

Gordon carried only $1000 bond, and the American Surety Company is not held liable for more than this amount.

Gordon and the bonding company were being sued by Anderson county, represented by County Attorney Tom Pickett and Attorney J. D. Pickett. Judge Smith's judgment against Gordon asked payment of $633.60 in uncollected fees in 1931. The judgment held that the county is due $352.80 for the 1932 cases, and that County Attorney Tom Pickett is entitled to $367.20 in fees for that year. The previous year, however, the county attorney made the maximum amount allowed in fees and is entitled to no further remuneration.

Judge Smith upheld a recent decision of the Waco court, which held that suit against a bonding company can be brought by a third party.

Out of 165 separate causes involved in the suit, the judgment was against Gordon in all except twenty-nine, who were shown not to have been in his custody after the cases were filed.

Second Crash Victim Dies at Sherman

Sherman, May 23. (AP)—The second fatality of the airplane crash at the Sherman airport Monday, was counted when William Curry, 20, died here today. Mortimer Riley, 21, of Hewlett, Long Island, his companion died three hours after the accident.

Man Questioned Concerning the Robles Kidnap

Tucson, Ariz., May 23. (AP)—An alleged participant in the nation's largest mail train robbery was questioned by authorities here today concerning the $15,000 kidnaping of June Robles, six-year-old heiress.

The suspect, Joe Newton, refused to make any statements regarding the kidnaping, in which the ransom was not paid, or the robbery of a Medford, Okla., bank, the charge on which he was arrested here last night.

Officers said Newton had been under surveillance for several days, during which time he had made nocturnal visits here from a mine in Sonora, Mexico, a locality in which an intensive search was conducted for the Robles girl before she was found.

Sheriff's investigators said Newton made telephone calls to Tucson from the old Robles ranch between here and Sasabe at the border. They said they had learned he lived at the mine, 45 miles below the international line, with a brother, Tull.

THE WEATHER

U. S. Department of Agriculture Weather Bureau.
Arthur W. Pugh, Meteorologist.

Temperature Yesterday.

	Low	High	Rain
Palestine	67	89	
Temp. Year Ago	72	89	

Average temperature yesterday 79, normal 74.

Barometric Pressure.

Reduced to sea level, 29.96 in.
Station pressure at altitude of 510 feet, 29.439 inches.

Relative Humidity.

7 a. m. today, 86 per cent.
Lowest yesterday, 44 per cent.

Thursday.

Sunrise 5:20 a. m. Set 7:19 p. m.

Weather Forecast.

Palestine and Vicinity: Partly cloudy tonight and Thursday.

East Texas (east of 100th meridian): Partly cloudy, probably thundershowers northwest portion tonight and Thursda .

Car Speeding 85 Miles Per Hour When Officers Shower Them With Fire

Shreveport, La., May 23. (AP)—The eight year trail of murder and robbery of Clyde Barrow, dangerous bandit of the Southwest, was ended today beside Bonnie Parker, his woman companion in crime, in a hail of bullets from a sheriff's posse, fifty miles east of here near the town of Gibsland.

Both the man and woman were killed instantly before they could fire a shot and their bodies and automobile were riddled with bullets. They drove into a posse's ambush, arranged by the former captain of Texas Rangers, Frank Hamer, who had followed Barrow's trail relentlessly.

With the posse, heavily armed, hiding in the brush along the paved highway, Barrow's car broke over the horizon racing at an 85 mile rate. As the car approached, an officer yelled "Halt." Barrow and the woman answered by reaching for their guns and were met by a fusillade from a dozen guns. Bonnie Parker died with her head between her knees and a machine gun on her lap. Barrow slumped behind the steering wheel with a revolver in his grip.

The automobile careened from the road and smashed into an embankment. The officers continued to fire until the car virtually was shot to pieces and the bodies were riddled.

The bandits' trail was picked up this morning by Hamer and three Texas Ranger associates in Bossier Parish, where Barrow was reported to have relatives residing.

They followed the bandit car to Bienville Parish where the Rangers were joined by Sheriff Henderson Jordan and a staff of deputies.

The officers got ahead of the bandit car and laid in waiting until Barrow ran his car into the ambush.

In the wrecked bandit car, officers found three army rifles, two sawed-off shotguns, a machine gun, a dozen pistols and large quantities of ammunition.

Govenor O. K. Allen was given a graphic description of the slayings over long distance by Sheriff Jordan and Governor Allen officially congratulated the officers in the name of the state.

The governor was told that shortly after 9 a. m., the officers, who were hidden in the brush along the roadside, recognized the grey sedan in which they knew the two were traveling. Barrow was driving.

Some of the officers quickly walked out into the road, the governor was told, and called for a halt, but Barrow reached for a sawed-off shotgun and stepped hard on the accelerator. As the little car leaped forward, the officers poured a barrage of fire in- [illegible] and the two inside [illegible] and the car careen- [illegible] and against an [illegible] people from the [illegible] to the scene [illegible] of America's [illegible] of Gibs- [illegible] the scene [illegible] graphic story of the transportation of the dead bodies to Arcadia in their "death car."

"The officers brought the bodies through here about 11:30," he said, "They just left the [illegible] the car and tied it to another car and hauled it to Arcadia.

"Bonnie Parker's head was almost shot off, and it just dangled. Barrow was badly shot up. There must have been 15 or 20 bullet holes in the windshield of the car. The sides of the car were just peppered full of holes.

"Several people here noticed Barrow's car in the last three or four days. It was an almost new car (of a light make—Ford V-8) and was sandy in color It had an Arkansas license and a big trunk on the back.

"The officers had automatic rifles, sawed-off shotguns and pistols.

"The officers had been hiding along the road since 3 o'clock this morning and I heard an ex-convict had tipped them off that Barrow was coming that way.

"The ex-convict went out in the road to flag the car and when Barrow reached for his gun that's when the officers fired."

ROGERS,

PATROLMAN'S WIDOW GLAD

Austin, May 23. (AP)(AP)—"Thank God." sighed Mrs. E. B. Wheeler, widow of one of the highway patrolmen slain at Grapevine Easter Sunday, when news was received today that Clyde Barrow and Bonnie Parker had been killed.

BARROW, RUTHLESS MURDERER, KILLED AT SLIGHTEST MOVE

Most of the Victims of the Furtive Southwest Desperado Fell Without a Chance.

Dallas, May 23. (AP)—Clyde Barrow, furtive killer reported shot to death with Bonnie Parker, his woman companion, in a clash with officers in Louisiana, became one of the nation's most dangerous outlaws through his ruthless resort to firearms whenever he encountered difficulties in carrying out the robberies he undertook.

Most of the victims credited to his deadly machine gun and pistol fire fell without having a chance to protect themselves. Barrow, who started out as an automobile thief in Dallas and blamed his subsequent depredations on officers mistreating him, displayed a bitter hatred of the law and its enforcers, especially in the last two years when he has been hunted incessantly throughout the Southwest.

He was first arrested in Dallas for automobile theft in December, 1926, but got off light. In 1930 he was convicted of automobile theft at Waco and sentenced to 14 years. Ross S. Sterling, former governor of Texas, granted the young desperado a general parole in Feb. 1932. From that time Barrow blazed a bloody trail across the Southwest and, aided by his bank robbing partner, Raymond Hamilton, was involved in several raids on small - town banks.

The first murder charged against him was that of a Hillsboro filling station operator, J. N. Bucher, in a petty hold-up. Then he was mixed up in the killing of an officer at Atoka, Okla. The murder of Howard Hall, grocery clerk at Sherman, also was attributed to him. These three killings occurred in 1932.

Last year Barrow, still a relatively small-time robber, had gained a reputation as a killer and officers were hot on his trail. In January officers set a trap for him in Dallas and Deputy Sheriff Malcolmn Davis of Tarrant county was killed in it.

Barrow jumped to Joplin, Mo., and there was credited with another murder.

The next killing laid to him was that of Marshal Henry Humphrey, in Van Buran, Ark., in July. He shot his way out of a posse of officers in Iowa. His brother, Buck, was killed in that affray. In November, he shot out of another group of officers near Dallas.

Easter Sunday of this year two Texas highway patrolmen rode up to an automobile parked on a side road near Grapevine. As they dismounted from their motorcycles and started walking toward the car, utterly unaware of danger, a man and a woman leaped out of the car and cut them down with shotgun charges at close range. The officers died without having a chance to draw their pistols. A whisky bottle found at the scene of the cold-blooded killing bore Barrow's finger prints. The woman was thought to be Bonnie Parker.

Barrow has displayed an arrogant, boastful disrespect for the law and has been vainglorious in his black record. Pictures showing the outlaw posing with a machine gun in his hands have fallen into the hands of officers and captured confederates have told of his cocky attitude. Bonnie Parker, the wife of a convict, demonstrated almost equal vanity as a criminal. She, too, has posed for numerous pictures with her belt weighed down with pistols and another pointed at the photographer.

For many months the two [illegible] been living a precarious [illegible] ly eluding officers or [illegible] occasions. They hav[illegible] wood, eating cann[illegible] sandwiches, th[illegible] dreds of miles [illegible] lated spot to [illegible] their trail. The

(Continued

Mothers Sob at Deaths.

Dallas, May 23. (AP)—Mrs. Henry Barrow, mother of Clyde Barrow, Southwest killer slain in Louisiana, cried out in anguish today when informed her son had been shot down.

"And, I prayed only last night that I might see him alive again, just once more," she sobbed.

Mrs. Emma Parker, mother of Bonnie Parker, killed with Clyde, fainted when informed by telephone that her child, too, had been killed. Relatives at the home said she suffered a breakdown.

Not Surprised.

Fort Worth, May 23. (AP)—"I'm not surprised," Mrs. Billie Mace, 21, said quietly when told that her notorious sister, Bonnie Parker, had been slain in Louisiana.

"I have been expecting it to end this way."

Mrs. Mace is in the county jail on murder charges growing out of the slaying of Highway Patrolmen Wheeler and Murphy near Grapevine on April 1—a crime for which her sister and Clyde Barrow already had been indicted.

To Set Casing For Testing of Cherokee W[illegible]

Casing is due to be set at [illegible] in the New Birmingham Dev[illegible] ment Company No. 1 T. J. Wo[illegible] Cherokee county wildcat, loca[illegible] six miles southwest of Rusk, whic[illegible] stole the spotlight of East Texa[illegible] exploration when it cored into o[illegible] saturated sand.

While no official reports we[illegible] available here today over outcom[illegible] of a Schlumberger test last nig[illegible] local operators were informed t[illegible] casing would be run for a tes[illegible] the sand. The well showed oil [illegible] after passing through a very [illegible] streak of shale, the format[illegible] running very similar to those of the Byrd-Frost, Inc., Stanolind Oil & Gas Company No. 1 Scott well at Slocum.

Another section of the Scott well was scheduled to be tested today.

Royall Bank Given Judgment In Suit On 1146 Acres La[illegible]

Royall National Bank was [illegible] en judgment in district court [illegible] day against R. A. Gatewood [illegible] foreclosure of a deed of trust on 1146 acres of land in the no[illegible] western part of the county. [illegible] bank was given judgment for ne[illegible] ly $14,000. The Houston Lan[illegible] Bank holds first mortgage on the land in question, it was shown in testimony. Gatewood testified that the top lease value of the land was $15 an acre, but admitted he had not been offered as much as $5 per acre.

THE vanity of human life is like a river, constantly passing away, and yet constantly coming on.
—Pope.

The Dallas Morning News

Section One
General News

49TH YEAR | NO. 236 | (AP)—Associated Press. (UP)—United Press. (NANA)—North American Newspaper Alliance. | DALLAS, TEXAS, THURSDAY, MAY 24, 1934—TWENTY PAGES | Oldest Business Institution in Texas—Founded in Galveston April 11, 1842.—Established in Dallas October 1, 1885. | 5c PER COPY

Posse Kills Clyde Barrow and Bonnie Parker

Manchukuan Farm Villages Wrecked By Japanese Bombs

Chinese Sources Claim 1,000 Dead as Planes Drop Explosives on Twenty Towns

Fires Still Raging

Refusal of Settlers to Give Up Arms Alleged Cause of Reprisals

SHANGHAI, May 24 (Thursday) (AP).—Reports that Japanese military airplanes had destroyed twenty farm villages in Southeast Manchukuo, killing 1,000 persons and injuring hundreds of others, reached here Thursday from Peiping.

The reports, not confirmed from other sources, were that Chinese farmers in Manchuria refused to give up their arms on demand of the Japanese Army and that the bombing of their homes resulted.

The bombing was said to have occurred Wednesday and many villages were reported still burning from incendiary bombs.

The efforts of Japanese troops to clear out opposition elements in the Japanese-sponsored Empire of Manchukuo have given rise to reports of numerous clashes with Chinese.

Communication with the territory involved is extremely difficult and the interpretations placed upon activities of the troops and of citizens and irregular Chinese forces vary with the source of the reports.

Attention has been called several times by the Soviet Union to allegations that Japanese military planes are active in Manchukuo and several months ago charges were made that they were flying over the Russian border.

Japanese sources at that time denied that Russian territory had been trespassed upon and said only a few planes were in Manchukuo.

Relief Is Promised For Drouth Sections

KANSAS CITY, Mo., May 23 (AP).—Promising that Texas would receive a substantial amount for relief purposes, particularly in the drouth-stricken Panhandle counties, Federal relief administration Harry L. Hopkins said Wednesday a definite agreement with the Texas relief delegation would be drafted Thursday morning.

The Weather

NEW ORLEANS, La., May 23 (AP).—Government weather forecast:

East Texas (including Dallas and vicinity): Partly cloudy to cloudy, thundershowers in northwest portion Thursday; Friday partly cloudy.

West Texas: Partly cloudy Thursday and Friday.

Arkansas: Cloudy and unsettled Thursday and Friday.

Oklahoma: Cloudy and unsettled Thursday and Friday.

Louisiana: Partly cloudy Thursday; Friday cloudy and unsettled.

Dallas Temperatures.

Temperatures in Dallas Wednesday, May 23, 1934, and for same date last year, as reported by United States Weather Bureau, follow:

	1934.	1933.		1934.	1933.
Midnight	76	78	Noon	86	84
2 a. m.	74	75	2 p. m.	87	87
4 a. m.	72	75	4 p. m.	89	90
6 a. m.	70	74	6 p. m.	86	88
7 a. m.	72	74	7 p. m.	84	86
10 a. m.	80	81			

Maximum temperature May 24 last year 81 degrees, minimum 65 degrees. Total precipitation so far this year 10.38 inches.

Full weather report on Page 11, Section II.

BIRD SANCTUARY.

THIS is a spot where God might choose to rest
And look upon the beauty He has made;
The suulight filtering through the leafy shade;
The mourning dove contented on her nest;
The tanager in scarlet raiment dressed—
A flash of lightning in the dewy glade—
The oriole in rainbow hues arrayed;
And bluebird with a pink rose at his breast.

The yellowhammer beats his brave tattoo;
The bobolink calls from the underbrush;
The mocking bird sings songs forever new;
The jaunty waxwing and the timid thrush.

Yes, God might choose to come and rest Him here,
For He and His high heaven seem very near.
—Fitzhugh L. Minnigerode in New York Times.

Salutatorian at Rusk Not Only Gets Diplamo, But Check for $11,600

RUSK, Texas, May 23 (AP).—Graduation was a big event for Ruth Moseley. In addition to being class salutatorian and receiving her diploma, she received a share of an $11,600 oil lease check. She and her brothers, orphans, shared the check.

Dr. E. M. Moseley, her guardian, took advantage of Rusk's infant oil boom to cash in.

Dillinger's Girl And Doctor Aiding Him Get 2 Years

Another Woman in Conspiracy Also Convicted and Third Acquitted

ST. PAUL, Min., May 23 (AP).—The law won two more associates of desperado John Dillinger Wednesday, while the outlaw himself roamed free, outside its clutches.

A Federal Court jury convicted Evelyn Frechette, his sweetheart, and Dr. Clayton May, Minneapolis physician, of conspiracy to hide the fugitive, and sentenced each to a prison term of two years and to pay a fine of $1,000.

Mrs. Augusta Salt, in whose apartment Dr. May was alleged to have treated Dillinger after he was wounded in escaping March 31 from an apartment where he lived with Miss Frechette, was acquitted.

Mrs. Beth Green, indicted with the three whose case was concluded Wednesday, was sentenced to fifteen months in prison. She pleaded guilty several days before the trial started.

Granted Week's Stay.

Miss Frechette and Dr. May were granted a week's stay of execution and their attorneys announced an appeal would be taken to the circuit court of appeals.

The half Indian girl, who was ar-

See DILLINGER on Page 4.

New Australian Flight Mark Set By Plucky Girl

Jean Batten Makes Trip From England After Two Attempts Fail

PORT DARWIN, Northern Australia, May 23 (AP).—Petite Jean Batten, who refused to quit trying after two failures, Wednesday made a new aviation record for women by completing a flight from England to Australia in 14 days, 23 hours and 25 minutes.

The 24-year-old New Zealand girl brought her old Wooden Moth plane, which has been in use for nearly five years, down at 3 p. m. to cut four and a half days off the previous woman's record, set by Amy Johnson, wife of Capt. James A. Mollison.

"I had an adventurous trip" she said upon her arrival, "the weather was frightful throughout—where can I get a cup of tea?"

Battled Headwinds.

On the last stage of her trip, across the Timor Sea, headwinds blew her plane miles south of the course, she said, but she managed to battle

See FLIGHT on Page 4.

America's Silver Plan Blocks Hope For Gold Return

(Copyright, 1934, by the Associated Press.)

LONDON, May 23.—British financial leaders were pictured in well-informed quarters Wednesday as being highly alarmed by the prospect that President Roosevelt's silvar monetization program will blast their hopes for the return of Great Britain to the gold standard in the near future.

Despite the nonchalant attitude they assumed toward the American President's message, financial circles were pictured as being thrown into gloom.

"Financial leaders here have been hoping for some time that President Roosevelt would head off the silverites, so there would be no further steps in the direction of world-wide bimetallism," said a well-informed observer.

Forestalls Return to Gold.

"Roosevelt's capitulation to the silverites will only give new impetus to

See SILVER on Page 4.

Leading Principals in Slaying of Outlaws

Here are some of those who figured in the killing Wednesday morning of Clyde Barrow and Bonnie Barker, Dallas outlaws. Left to right above are Clyde Barrow, Bonnie Parker and Frank Hamer, former Texas ranger and at present special highway patrolman. Below, left to right, are Deputy Sheriffs Bob Alcorn and Ted Hinton of Dallas County. Other officers, not shown here, who took part in the shooting down of the pair were M. T. Gault, also a former Texas ranger and at present a special highway patrolman; Sheriff Henderson Jordan of Bienville Parish, Louisiana, and his deputy, Curtis Oakley.

Church Must Aid New Deal Because Taught by Christ

Praise for Program of Roosevelt Government Given Presbyterians

CLEVELAND, Ohio, May 23 (AP).—National leaders of the Presbyterian Church in the United States of America were told Wednesday night the new deal in the Government is based on the fundamental tenets of Christ himself. The speaker was Secretary of the Interior Harold L. Ickes.

Addressing a public meeting here sponsored by the church's general council, Ickes pictured the social objectives of Christianity and the new deal as being identical.

"Christ wanted men and women to live upright lives, but He also wanted them to have for each other understanding and good will and mutual helpfulness," the Secretary said. "He wished them to be good neighbors. He hated injustice with a righteous hatred. His life was a fight against oppression. This was the man who drove

See CHURCH on Page 4.

Small Industries Granted Millions Of Federal Credit

House Passes Bill, Now to Go to Conference With Senate

WASHINGTON, May 23 (UP).—Federal credits of $440,000,000 to grease the wheels of small industries were authorized by the House Wednesday.

The vote was 178 to 6.

RFC loans of $75,000,000 to cities to pay school teachers' salaries also were authorized.

The bill for these new recovery credits now goes to the conference with the Senate, which has authorized Federal Reserve Banks and the RFC to lend $700,000,000 to small business.

Dallas Deputy Tells Of Ending Long Chase

Bob Alcorn Says All He Has Done for Months Is Hunt for Bandits

BY BOB ALCORN,
Dallas County Deputy Sheriff.
(Copyright, 1934, NANA, Inc.)

ARCADIA, La., May 23.—With other officers for ten months I've been trying to get Clyde and Bonnie, ten months when I did little else except look for them, hope I'd find them and get them dead or alive. Today we got them. They won't kill anyone else now. We got them as they came along the road. It was all over in a moment. Both of them were dead as their car nosed into a sandbank and came to a stop. They didn't even fire a shot but they had grabbed at their guns when our bullets knocked them over.

I began following Clyde and Bonnie last summer. I got reports they were here, there and yonder but always when the other officers and I got there they were gone. Only once last November we ran onto them near Dallas but they got away when we let them have it and they weren't even hit.

Since then I've been after them and for the last four weeks I've done nothing else, all over East and South Tex-

See ALCORN on Page 4.

Planes Complete 1,000-Mile Flight To Aid Newlywed

Surgeons Go Prepared to Help Appendicitis-Stricken Bridegroom

LOS ANGELES, Cal., May 23 (AP).—Roaring across the equator, two nava planes from Coco Solo, Canal Zone, Wednesday completed a 1,000-mile flight to Tagus Cove of the Galapagos Islands with medical aid for William Albert Robinson, Cambridge, Mass., textile engineer and explorer, stricken with appendicitis.

Safe landing of the planes was reported by the Mackay Radio Corporation in a message relayed from the lonely equatorial archipelago by a fishing trawler that for two days has been standing by the little thirty-two-foot, round-the-world ketch on which the explorer is confined with appendicitis.

Naval surgeons who flew from the Canal Zone at dawn Wednesday were prepared for an immediate operation.

Since Sunday night, in the most remote spot in the world from medical aid that such a drama has been enacted, Florence Crane Robinson, Chicago heiress and socially prominent bride, has maintained a vigil by the bunk of her distressed bridegroom in the tragic interruption of their romantic honeymoon that started last June when the little craft sailed from New York.

The quickly executed flight, accomplished with the aid of two destroyers which set out from Coco Solo ahead of the planes, was the response of the navy to the frantic appeal of Mrs. Robinson.

Quick action followed the relaying of the appeal to Washington Tuesday and the planes set out at 6:40 a. m. Wednesday.

Body of Naval Officer Found Beside Road

GREENSBURG, Kan., May 23 (AP).—The body of Lieut. Commander S. J. Trowbridge, naval physician slain last Saturday night, was found about fifteen miles northwest of here beside a little used road in Edwards County. The skull was crushed.

The body was not removed pending the arrival of Leo Hudgins, 24-year-old hitchhiker, who admitted to authorities at Marietta, Ok., Tuesday that he killed the naval officer during a drunken orgy. He said he struck Trowbridge on the head with a hammer after a quarrel precipitated by back-seat driving.

Elusive Dallas Desperadoes Shot to Death in Louisiana

Long Hunt Over Three States Is Ended as Six Officers Ambush Pair in Speeding Auto

BY J. R. BRADFIELD JR.,
Staff Correspondent of The News.

ARCADIA, La., May 23.—Volleys of lead from the guns of six ambuscaded officers brought swift death Wednesday morning to Clyde Barrow, notorious Dallas desperado, and Bonnie Parker, his woman companion down the trail of crime. The Dallas Deputy Sheriffs, Bob Alcorn and Ted Hinton; two former Texas rangers, Frank Hamer and M. T. Gault, who are members of the Texas highway patrol working under special orders to "Get Barrow;" Sheriff Henderson Jordan and Deputy Sheriff Curtis Oakley of Bienville Paris, comprised the posse which shot down the much-hunted pair on the highway eight miles from Gibsland at 9:15 a. m. Wednesday.

Not a shot was fired by either Barrow or Parker but the bandit was reaching down for his gun when the officers turned loose their deadly fusillade. The car careened to one side of the road as the man fell backward and the woman forward. Fearing the two might be stalling, the officers stepped out from their ambuscade and poured more bullets into the wrecked auto, but they were not needed. Both Barrow and Parker were dead. Their bodies were brought in later to an undertaking establishment here, which quickly was jammed by ever-growing crowds of people, all anxious to get a look at the notorious couple.

It was a long and hard trail that ended on a lonely road near the little Louisiana town of Gibsland. Alcorn and Hinton had been following the elusive desperadoes for many days. Their hunt had been all over Northern Louisiana and East Texas and had dipped into Mississippi and South Texas. The father of Henry Methyn, freed from a Texas prison farm with Raymond Hamilton by the daring Barrow, lives in this vicinity. The officers learned definitely that Clyde and Bonnie had traversed the Gibsland road a few days ago. They figured the two would return.

Find Perfect Ambush.

"We took a chance that they would come," Alcorn said. "We found a perfect ambush behind an embankment and took our places at 2 o'clock Wednesday morning. Sheriff Jordan had been tipped off that Clyde was planning to rob a bank at Arcadia. Hamer and Gault had information that led them to believe the pair would come this way. So we laid down and waited.

"Daylight came, but no desperadoes. At 9 o'clock we were about ready to give up, but while we were discussing whether to stay or leave, I glanced down the road and, some distance away, saw a car whizzing along that looked like the one we knew Barrow was driving.

"'That's Clyde, sure as the world,' I exclaimed, and we kept perfectly still and watched as it came over a

See BARROW-PARKER on Page 4.

Failure of Clyde To Pay for Guns' Delivery Is Fatal

Henchman, Caught by Officers, Gives Valuable Information

Special to The News.

LONGVIEW, Texas, May 23.—Clyde Barrow and Bonnie Parker, will-o'-the-wisp killers, whose sanguine trail was terminated in a blast of gunfire and death in a small and rural Louisiana town Wednesday, frequently moved in and out of Gregg County, but so far as is known their sorties into this sector were made as sociable calls on relatives and were bloodless.

In recent weeks there have been a number of developments along a far-flung East Texas and Louisiana front to indicate the capture or death of the elusive Barrow and Bonnie Parker, was imminent. Officers, grim-faced and heavily armed, have moved out of Longview on several occasions during recent weeks, following tips on the desperate pair. Those enforcers of the law were serious. They went to kill, capture or face the hazards of battles with Barrow and his woman.

A posse of officers, among them Charles Gant and Marvin Utzman, slipped quietly out of Longview Tuesday night, turning their automobiles toward Winnsboro where the Barrows had arranged for a clandestine meeting with a henchman, a man who had delivered guns and ammunition to them in a stolen automobile. That trip to a Barrow rendezvous, in a stolen Dallas machine, proved to be the man's undoing, and hardened his heart toward the outlaw pair which he previously had served as contact man and aid.

Gun Runner in Jail.

The man is in jail here now. He gave his name as J. A. Nichols, Dallas, and officers say he is facing eleven charges in Dallas. The trend of his conversation indicates he had connection with one of the greatest rings in Dallas' history. He was taken in custody earlier in the week by Deputies Marvin Utzman and Charles Gant at a Gladewater road cottage.

When officers told him Wednesday that Barrow and Bonnie had failed in their efforts to reach their guns—met the fate which they have so unrelent-

See GUN DELIVERER on Page 4.

State Candidate Dies After Being Shot at Trinity

Rail Clerk Is Held as Treasurer Aspirant, E. R. Waller, Expires

HOUSTON, Texas, May 23 (AP).—Edward Rex Waller, 34, candidate for State Treasurer, who was shot in front of the postoffice at Trinity on Wednesday, died here at night. Waller was brought here aboard a train. He died as physicians prepared to operate on him.

Will Splettstoesser, a railroad clerk, surrendered to officers after the shooting. He was taken to Groveton, the county seat, to make bond.

Waller had been interested in politics for many years. At one time he was city manager at Goose Creek.

Splettstoesser was charged with assault to murder before Justice Bert Dunlap at Trinity. Sheriff Joseph S. Evans of Trinity County attributed the shooting to family trouble."

Comrades Praise Men That Trapped Barrow and Parker

Job Done, Message Sent by Ex-Rangers, Now on Highway Patrol

From the Austin Bureau of The News.

AUSTIN, Texas, May 23.—Frank Hamer and B. M. Gault, two Austin men who played the principal roles in trailing and slaying Clyde Barrow and Bonnie Parker, are veteran officers and former members of the rangers. Hamer retired as ranger Captain when the Fergusons entered the Governor's office and was succeeded by his brother, D. E. Hamer. It was Frank Hamer and Gault who did the work and their comrades here are paying them tribute.

Hamer has ferreted out a number of noted crimes and has had many brushes with so-called bad men. He is about six feet three inches tall and does not wear the boots and accoutrements of other rangers. Gault is a smaller, spare man with benevolent features and as gentle as men get to be. No one would pick him as a fearless chaser of desperadoes, as he has been for many years.

Commissioned as Patrolmen.

Under recent commissions as patrolmen from the Highway Department, Hamer and Gault have been seeking the hiding places of Barrow and Bonnie, and they laid the trap that caught them. "The job is done," was the telephone message from Hamer to Capt. L. G. Phares, chief of the highway patrol. Phares has been almost sleepless in his efforts to have the Easter Sunday killers of his two patrolmen, H. D. Murphy and E. B. Wheeler, run down. It was Phares who put Hamer and Gault on the trail with instructions to go the limit. Phares chartered a plane and flew to Arcadia, La., when apprised of the deaths.

Rewards to Be Paid.

Since his retirement from the rangers Hamer has worked under private employment in a number of crime investigations and has others on his list now.

Phares had accumulated a fund of more than $4,000 to chase the slayers of the patrolmen and only a part of it has been spent. The remainder is expected to paid in rewards. The Governor offered a $500 reward and the Legislature tried to offer $1,000 each for Barrow and Raymond Hamilton, but the bill was defeated.

Arcadia Sheriff Tells How Barrow Drove Into Trap

Report That Outlaws Planned to Rob Bank Led to Ambuscade

BY SHERIFF HENDERSON JORDAN,
Of Bienville Parish, Louisiana,
Eyewitness to the slaying of Bonnie Parker and Clyde Barrow.
(Written exclusively for Associated Press.)

ARCADIA, La., May 23.—I have been working on this case about six weeks. I received a tip Wednesday that Clyde Barrow and Bonnie Parker were coming through the lower part of Bienville Parish and going to the northern part of Natchitoches Parish. We began checking on this. I put an undercover man on this job. I had him stationed in Shreveport. Upon getting a tip that Barrow and Parker figured on robbing the First National Bank of Arcadia, I got in touch with Frank Hamer, ex-Captain of the Texas rangers, and R. F. Alcorn, Dallas County Deputy Sheriff, I had to get some one who knew Barrow and Parker personally in order not to make a mistake in shooting them if we found them.

Tuesday night I received a tip they

See SHERIFF on Page 4.

State Troopers Asked at Toledo To Quell Strike

Disorders at Autolite Plant Involve 4,500 Workers—Four Hurt

TOLEDO, Ohio, May 23 (AP).—Sheriff David Kreiger Wednesday night asked Gov. George White and Adjutant Gen. Frank D. Henderson to send State troops to Toledo to quell the Auto-Lite plant disorders.

Three thousand angry strike pickets any sympathizers held 1,500 day shift workmen at the plant virtual prisoners Wednesday evening as riots which started in the afternoon continued. Four persons were in hospitals.

Meanwhile State and Federal conciliators were working to bring about a truce in the strike of 1,900 automotive workers, which has been under way here for five weeks. The situation was complicated by a threat of a general strike in sympathy with the automotive workers. A third of the local unions in Toledo were reported to have voted in favor of the general strike.

Wednesday's rioting began shortly after 100 policemen arrived at the plant to protect day shift workers leaving the building.

News Behind the News

By PAUL MALLON
(Copyright, 1934, by Paul Mallon)

Revolting Democratic Congressmen Creeping Back in Fold as Primaries Near

Sweet Harmony.

WASHINGTON, May 23.—You can not believe all you hear from Washington. As an instance, it now appears that the wrath of the administration will not descend, as advertised, upon the heads of all rebellious Democratic Congressmen.

Speaker Rainey has, in fact, quietly been striking names off his secret blacklist so fast that there are few left.

One of the names on it was that of a semi-Southern Democrat. Early in the session he was bitter against the Rainey-Byrnes leadership and frequently opposed Roosevelt legislation.

The other day he made a public statement of praise for Speaker Rainey and almost immediately he was appointed to a juicy position on the Democratic patronage committee.

Another Prodigal.

A Democrat from a Pacific Coast State fared even better. He was the No. 1 man on the original blacklist.

Recently he paid tribute to the gr-r-eat Rainey-Byrnes generalship in a speech from the floor. Soon thereafter Floor Leader Byrnes wrote him a letter strongly approving him for re-election.

Hoopla.

The backslapping has replaced backbiting so extensively that Mr. Rainey recently appeared in the sound movie news reels with a first-term Democrat from Montana. Floor Leader Byrnes wrote another letter covering four pages of the Congressional Record (cost to the Government estimated at $55 per page), praising a Gulf States Democratic Congressman. A Texas Representative is using letters from both Rainey and Byrnes saying how good he is. In answer to an inquiry from the Middle West, Rainey also publicly approved a Congresswoman, although she had "opposed the administration on veterans' legislation."

Such tactics are extremely unusual in advance of the primaries. These Congressmen are not running for reelection yet, but only for renomination as Democrats.

The participation of Mr. Byrnes is even more extraordinary because he is chairman of the Democratic Congressional Campaign Committee, which keeps out of the primaries and acts only after Democratic nominations have been made.

Co-operation.

The reason for it is not hard to find.

When the House was in revolt on veterans' restorations, pay cuts and other matters, an impression was created by the party leaders that the revolters were going to be made to suffer. Aspiring young Democrats out through the country thought that afforded a splendid opportunity for them to get elected to Congress. They announced themselves in great numbers as opponents of sitting Congressmen on the ground that those now holding office did not stand with President Roosevelt.

As a result, the Congressmen have been running to Rainey and Byrnes on their hands and knees, asking for statements of approval.

When the bars were let down nearly all the wolves had to be given sheep's clothing.

Underlying it all is the fact that both the House and the Senate have a certain cameraderie and clublike atmosphere on the inside.

When misfortune befalls them they usually let bygones be bygones and sympathize and help each other.

Silver.

The silverites were not as enthusiastic about their new silver bill as they pretended, although it was exactly what Mr. Roosevelt promised them weeks ago.

Floor Leader Robinson picked Senator Key Pittman to introduce the bill in the Senate because Pittman has been the only silverite with whom the administration has worked closely. The final draft came from the Treasury and White House, where the administration worked it out in conference with all the silver group.

On silver enthusiast, in his despair, described it in the cloakroom as "a rimless zero." Another said: "It authorizes them to do something for silver when and if they want to."

Motives.

The reasons for such feelings are numerous. One is there are just as many different kinds of silverites as there are mosquitoes. Each likes a little different kind of meat. For instance, the main reason Senator Thomas has been so active for silver is that he wants to get that issue out of the way so we can have some real inflation.

Another reason is that the silverites doubt if the administration will carry out the flexible mandate of the act as enthusiastically as they would like. They noticed that the administration has lately placed stress on the international aspects of the program.

If they wait until they get an international silver agreement they will wait a long time. Otherwise they might be able to establish the 25 per cent silver base in thirty years.

Notes.

When S-2817 came up in the House last Monday Congressman Carter of California objected and the bill was blocked. It is the bill authorizing Congressmen to borrow from the farm credit administration and HOLC. If three Congressmen object the next time the bill comes up it will be killed.

Nothing will be done about the Darrow charges of malfeasance against the coal code authorities. The Government takes the position that, inasmuch as it will be a party to the price and marketing arrangement made by the code authorities, it can not prosecute even if it wanted to.

Among the industries on which Mr. Darrow is yet to report is oil.

The Darrow board was privately amazed at the public response to its recommendations. Members thought they did a splendid job.

Sheriff's Slayer Will Go to Chair, High Court Rules

Rehearing Denied Perch Mouth Stanton in Killing of Officer

From the Austin Bureau of The News.

AUSTIN, Texas, May 23.—A Court of Criminal Appeals' opinion affirming the death penalty given Ed Stanton, alias Perch-Mouth Stanton, for the murder in Swisher County of Sheriff John Moseley, Jan. 23, 1933, was made final Wednesday when the court overruled Stanton's motion for a rehearing.

Indicted jointly with Stanton were Glenn Hunsucker and Bernice Inman. Hunsucker was killed in a gun battle with officers in New Mexico. Inman has not been found. Moseley was killed after he had arrested the trio near Tulia.

A fifty year sentence given John Barr on a charge of the murder of John Mayhugh in Coryell County Jan. 5, 1933, was reversed and the case remanded for another trial. Mayhugh was beaten to death with a stick of wood.

Murder Sentences Affirmed.

The court affirmed the cases of George L. Lafferty and J. W. Hillman, convicted in Upton County of the murder of George E. Berry July 28, 1933. Lafferty was sentenced to twenty years and Hillman to thirty-five. Berry was beaten to death with a piece of iron.

A two-year sentence given R. S. Dilworth on a charge of receiving a deposit of $60 in an insolvent bank at Gonzales was reversed and the case remanded. The trial was in Gaudalupe County on a charge of venue. Dilworth had been interested in a private bank but had had nothing to do with its management for some time prior to the commission of the alleged offense.

Because of insufficient testimony, the case of Burton Houston, convicted under the habitual criminal act, an indictment charging burglary, with a sentence to life imprisonment, was reversed and remanded.

Roark Appeal Dismissed.

The court granted the application of Noah Roark for dismissal of his appeal on his conviction at Dallas of murder of Justin Stein, manager of an office building, and sentenced to forty years.

Cases affirmed were those of Willie Pool, Dallas County, assault to murder, fifteen pears; A. J. Midgett, Collin County, arson, ten years; Mrs. A .J. Midgett, Collin County, perjury, three years; J. P. Hickey, Reeves County, criminal assault, five years; Sam Stewart, Dallas County, misdemeanor theft, twenty days, and Husie Bailey, Freestone County, murder. ten years.

The case of C. A. Sheffield, Lubbock County, negligent homicide, fined $1,500, was reversed and remanded.

Entemio Longaria, Hidalgo County, accused of paying the poll tax for another, and fined $100, was denied a rehearing.

Council Will Gravel Street at Lee School

Bids for rocking and graveling Delmar street from Goodwin to Vanderbilt will be received by the council June 6. Councilmen agreed to make this improvement at a cost of about $550 after a delegation from the Robert E. Lee Parent-Teacher Association asked it on behalf of school children in that vicinity.

New Refinery Law Test Case Advanced

From the Austin Bureau of The News.

AUSTIN, Texas, May 23.—The Third Court of Civil Appeals Wednesday refused to certify to the Supreme Court but advanced the case of George L. Culver et al vs. Railroad Commission in a proceeding attacking the validity of House bill No. 99, the new act vesting the commission with power to enter refinery premises and to exact periodical reports from refineries. This is one of the new laws to aid the commission in stopping illegal oil.

District Judge J. D. Moore sustained the State's demurrer to Culver's petition, thereby upholding the constitutionality of the new law and Culver appealed. Argument on his appeal will be heard June 13.

Cotton Seed Rate Continued.

AUSTIN, Texas, May 23 (AP).—Temporary reduced freight rates on cotton see and its produces, due to expire May 31, Wednesday were continued to June 30 by the Railroad Commission. It also postponed the effectiveness of a new general schedule of rates on the commodities from June 1 to Aug. 1. Previous standard rates will apply during July.

Barrow-Parker

CONTINUED FROM FIRST PAGE.

hill, just a little way north of us. It was coming fast, but just before it got to us, a truckload of logs coming form the other direction made Clyde slow down. I got a good look then and told the bunch, 'That's them.'

"We raised up. Clyde saw us and reached down, we knew for his gun. We began firing. Bonnie never raised the machine gun, which she had on her lap. Clyde fell back before he could get hold of the weapon his hand sought. Our long chase was over."

Runs Right Into Trap.

(Copyright, 1934, by the Associated Press.)

ARCADIA, La., May 23.—Clyde Barrow, notorious Texas outlaw, and his cigar-smoking gunwoman, Bonnie Parker, were ambushed and shot to death near here Wednesday in a sensational encounter with a posse led by an old-time Texas ranger.

The law-breaking desperado, whizzing along the Big Road highway at eighty-five miles an hour, ran right into a trap set for him.

Before he or Bonnie Parker could get their guns into action, the officers riddled them with bullets.

Barrow's car, running wild, careened from the road and smashed into an embankment. As the wheels spun, the posse continued to fire until the car was almost shot to pieces.

The body of the gunman, who four years ago was a minor hoodlum scarcely known outside of Dallas, was found slumped behind the steering wheel, a revolver in one hand.

Girl Still Clutched Gun.

Bonnie Parker died with her head between her knees. She still was clutching the machine gun.

"We killed Clyde and Bonnie at 9:15 this morning," reported Ted Hinton, one of the Texas officers, to the Sheriff's office in Dallas. "They were at Black Lake, a hideout we had been watching for weeks."

Frank Hamer, former captain of the Texas rangers, who had been waiting in the brush for days for Barrow to come by on his regular run, added:

"Barrow and Parker did not get to fire a shot. Their car was full of guns and ammunition, but they did not get a chance to use them."

In the wrecked car were three army rifles, two sawed-off shotguns, a dozen pistols and large quantities of ammunition, besides Bonnie Parker's machine gun. The bodies were left temporarily in the automobile awaiting the Coroner's arrival.

Dillinger Friend Sentenced.

While the law was scoring this victory in Louisiana, Evelyn Frechette, friend of the fugitive John Dillinger, and Dr. Clayton May, convicted of harboring the Indiana criminal, were sentenced in St. Paul, Minn., to two years in prison and were fined $1,000.

In Chicago James Lacey and Benjamin Wolfram pleaded guilty to the attempted abduction of Emanuel Philip Adler, Davenport, Iowa, newspaper publisher.

With Hamer and Hinton in the ambush near here were B. M. Gault, highway patrolman; Bob Alcorn of Dallas County, Texas, and Louisiana officers.

Sheriff Jordan of Bienville Parish said he had received a tip that the First National Bank of Arcadia was to be robbed Wednesday or Thursday and immediately had notified Texas officers.

Barrow came from Benton Tuesday afternoon and passed through Gibsland about 4 o'clock and again Wednesday morning, Jordan said. Jordan and his deputy, Paul M. Oakley, were waiting at the top of the hill with the Texans.

In Dallas Mrs. Henry Barrow, mother of Barrow, cried in anguish.

"And, I prayed only last night," she sobbed, "that I might see him alive again, just once more."

Barrow's father, working at his filling station. west of Dallas, made only one remark. He said he guessed his wife would be going to Louisiana.

Bonnie Parker's mother, Mrs. Emma Parker, also a resident of Dallas, fainted when informed by telephone of her daughter's death.

Hamer Maps Roads.

Bit by bit, Hamer, one of the best known peace officers in Texas, and his aids had pieced together a map of the highways Barrow was in the habit of using. Several weeks ago they barely missed the outlaw and his companion in this same section.

Since then the officers had been sitting and waiting.

Barrow, whose custom was to shoot on the drop of a hat and to escape in high-powered automobiles, was wanted in several States for charges ranging from small thefts to murder. He was accused to killing a dozen men, most of them officers.

Bonnie Parker, wife of a convict, was charged by officers with having taken an active part in most of Barrow's recent crimes. She, too, was known as vain and boastful.

Several times she was photographed with her belt weighted down with pistols.

The couple's life became more and more harried of late as the law gradually closed in around them. Darting out of an isolated retreat at midnight, they would drive at furious speeds to some other rendezvous—sometimes several hundred miles away. Resting only a few hours, they would dash on again.

Bonnie Parker was believed to have been with Barrow and his brother, Buck, when a posse cornered the gang near Dexter, Iowa, July 24, 1933. Buck was killed, but Clyde and Bonnie Parker escaped.

Hamer Tells of Killing.

ST. LOUIS, Mo., May 23 (AP).—"We just shot the devil out of them."

Thus Frank Hamer, former Texas Ranger Captain, Wednesday described in a copyrighted telephone interview with the St. Louis Post-Dispatch the slaying near Arcadia, La., of Clyde Barrow and his woman companion Bonnie Parker.

"Sure," he said, "I can tell you what happened this morning. We just shot the devil out of them, that's all. That's all there was to it. We just laid a trap for them. A steel trap. You know, Bessemer steel, like gun barrels are made of.

"There were six of us, two Deputy Sheriffs from Dallas, a Texas State highway patrolman, Sheriff Henderson Jordan of Arcadia and his deputy, Mr. Oakley, and myself.

"They Reached Too Slow."

"We were hiding beside the road All six of us on one side—we didn't want any cross-fire—and when they came along we hollered at them to stop. They both reached for their guns, but were kind of slow. Seemed like they must have had cramps or something.

"They were too slow. They didn't get to fire a shot. The car smashed into an embankment after we fired. Clyde was driving when we tried to stop them. Bonnie was sitting beside him.

"Now don't, please, put in your paper that I'm with the rangers. I'm not. I was for twenty-seven years, but when they elected a woman Governor, I quit. That was on Nov. 1, 1932, just before she took office."

Hamer said he had been searching for Barrow and Parker for the last six months. He said he had been employed by a law officer to make the search but declined to say what agency employed him "because there's some other tough-shooting fellows I may be hired to go after."

Bonnie's Sister Not Surprised.

From the Fort Worth Bureau of The News.

FORT WORTH, Texas, May 23.—"I've been expecting it to end this way," said Mrs. Billie Mace, 21, Bonnie Parker's sister, Wednesday when she was informed of the killing of Clyde Barrow and her sister, Bonnie Parker, by officers in Louisiana.

Mrs. Mace is in the Tarrant County jail under murder charges growing out of the slaying of Highway Patrolmen Wheeler and Murphy near Grapevine on Easter Sunday, a crime for which her sister and Barrow already had been indicted.

Floyd Hamilton, brother of Raymond Hamilton, who was charged with Mrs. Mace, is still in jail at Crockett and probably will not be brought here until the grand jury acts on the case.

Slain Officer's Widow Pleased.

AUSTIN, Texas, May 23 (AP).—"Thank God." sighed Mrs. E. B. Wheeler, widow of one of the highway patrolmen slain at Grapevine Easter Sunday, when news was received that Clyde Barrow and Bonnie Parker had been killed. Mrs. Wheeler is employed in the State patrol offices here.

She was given the place by L. G. Phares, chief of the patrol, after Wheeler and a companion officer, H. D. Murphy, were shot from their motorcycles by a couple believed to be Clyde and Bonnie.

"Easiest Way," Says Blanche Barrow.

JEFFERSON CITY, Mo., May 23 (AP).—"I'm glad they were both killed; it was the easiest way out."

That was the first comment made here Wednesday by Blanche Barrow, auburn-haired inmate of the Missouri State prison farm for women, when informed her brother-in-law, Clyde Barrow, and his companion, Bonnie Parker, were killed in Louisiana.

Blanche is the widow of Clyde's brother, Marvin (Buck) Barrow, who was killed last July near Dexter, Iowa, where the Barrows with Bonnie and Blanche, fled after participating in a shooting affair with officers at Platte City, Mo.

Blanche, who was captured and returned to Missouri, pleaded guilty to a charge of assault with intent to kill and was sentenced to ten years' imprisonment for her part in the Platte City episode. Clyde and Bonnie escaped.

"I'm glad it's all over," she added. "It is much better that they were both killed rather than to have been taken alive."

Aunt Not Sorry.

CARLSBAD, N. M., May 23 (AP).—Breaking a two-year silence forced upon her by fear of her own life, Mrs. E. M. Stamps, aunt of Bonnie Parker, slain with Clyde Barrow in Louisiana, said Wednesday night she was not sorry her niece was dead but did regret the manner in which she was killed.

"I am glad she is dead, but I am sorry she had to go the way she did, without repenting, because she surely is in hell," Mrs. Stamps said.

Miss Parker brought Barrow and Raymond Hamilton, whose identity she then only suspected, to the Stamps home near here for a four-day cooling-off in August, 1932.

Mrs. Stamps telephoned the Sheriff and Joe Johns, a deputy. They arrived alone and unarmed and were covered by Barrow and Hamilton. Johns was kidnaped and taken as hostage to San Antonio where he was released unharmed.

"From that day to this," Mrs. Stamps said, "I have lived in mortal fear of my life. I have hardly slept a wink for fear they would return and punish me for reporting them."

Special Medals Proposed.

Special to The News.

SAN ANTONIO, Texas, May 23.—Representative Harold Kayton Wednesday said he would propose that the Legislature authorize special medals for slayers of Clyde Barrow and Bonnie Parker. Police recalled that Barrow was once arrested in San Antonio about seven years ago on a chicken-stealing charge.

Part of Parker's Childhood Was Lived in Oklahoma Town Where Pair Killed Constable

MIAMI, Ok., May 23 (AP).—The crime-stained career of Bonnie Parker began not far from the little mining town of Commerce, ten miles north of here, where she and her gangster companion, Clyde Barrow, made their last cold-blooded attack on the law last April 6.

At Commerce she and Barrow and another man, believed to have been Henry Methvin, a fugitive convict, shot and killed Cal Campbell, 63-year-old Constable, and wounded and kidnaped Percy Boyd, police chief.

The two officers had tried to question the trio, whose car had been pulled from a mudhole a few moments before.

While the officers reached for their pistols they were shot down by the rapid fire of automatic rifles. Boyd was taken as hostage for a fourteen-hour ride through Oklahoma and Kansas before being released near Fort Smith at midnight.

Bonnie was born and reared at Caney, Kan., not far over the Kansas-Oklahoma line, and from 1925 through 1928 lived at Commerce and Picher. Ok.

She had no criminal record here, however, prior to the Commerce affray.

During her residence in the county she made many contacts that provided refuge for herself and Barrow when they were hard pressed, O. F. Mason, former County Attorney, said. Ottawa County was a favorite resting place for the gang.

Last winter, after a bloody battle with Fort Worth officers, she and Barrow abandoned a stolen auto near here and were flushed a few nights later from a temporarily unoccupied house in Vinita, where they had hidden.

Boyd exulted Wednesday when told that Barrow and Bonnie were shot down in Louisiana.

"It's lucky some officers were not killed," he said.

Sheriff Dee Waters, advised of their deaths, withdrew special deputies who had been assigned a ceaseless watch at two alleged Barrow hideouts near Miami.

Deputy Sheriff Wesley Gage of Creek County also ended a day and night vigil at a home he had believed that of Bonnie's mother near Sapulpa.

Alcorn

CONTINUED FROM FIRST PAGE.

as. Southern Arkansas, Northern Louisiana and even over into Mississippi where we heard they had been but they were always gone when we got there.

Hung Around and Watched.

A few days ago we got reports that Clyde and Bonnie had been through this part of the country and had been over the road through Gibsland. We hung around watching but nothing happened. We didn't give up, though, and decided to stick around a while longer.

At 2 o'clock Wednesday morning we hid our car in the woods eight miles south of Gibsland and lay down behind a little knoll. The grass was wet with heavy dew and it was awful just lying there and waiting. We were right on top of a hill and could see the road until it went over the top of the hill north of us and the other hill south of us. Six of us were watching all the time, Deputy Ted Hinton, M. Gault of the Texas Highway Patrol, former Ranger Captain Frank Hamer, Sheriff Henderson Jordan and Deputy Prentis M. Oakley of Bienville Parish.

Daylight came and still no Clyde. By 9 o'clock we had just about decided to give up, but waited a few minutes. At 9:15 I saw a light tan Ford V-8 head south over the hill north of us. I knew that was the kind of car Clyde was driving. He came closer at good speed. I knew it was Clyde. I told the other officers it was Clyde.

He came still closer. I was positive. A truckload of logs was coming from the other way. Clyde began to slow down. All of us jumped up from behind that little mound. We had rifles and shotguns pointed at him.

"We Let Him Have It."

By this time he was in fifty feet of us. He saw us and reached over grabbing for what we later learned was his gun. We let him have it. His head flew back. Bonnie toppled forward. The car careened to the left and ran into a sandbank. We didn't know whether we had killed them or not.

I ran out into the road and to the right side of the car. I had a rifle. I fired into the rear of the car and again into the right side of the car. The other officers fired again. Nothing happened. We waited. Still nothing.

We slowly walked up to the car and Bonnie and Clyde were both dead in the front seat. Clyde's Browning automatic rifle was lying at his feet. It had been hit by a rifle bullet. He had reached for it and one of the shots had knocked it out of his hand. Bonnie had a .45 automatic pistol in her lap but she hadn't fired it either. There they were, those two bandits and killers, dead, just as they had killed so many others in their murderous career.

We got a wrecker from Gibsland, hitched it onto the front end of their car and without moving their bodies brought the car to Arcadia. The bodies were taken out, a Coroner's jury called, evidence given, the pair identified and the jury held that they had come to their death from gunshot wounds.

Worker Insurance Not for Employes Of Relief Program

From the Austin Bureau of The News.

AUSTIN, Texas, May 23.—The Texas Relief Commission has no authority to spend any of the funds derived from the sale of bonds for workmen's compensation and disability insurance for its employes, Attorney General James V. Allred ruled Wednesday in an opinion to C. B. Braun, secretary of the commission.

The opinion said the Legislature repeatedly has refused to enact laws subjecting the State or its employes to the provisions of the compensation law, nor has it provided compensation for State employes killed or injured in the course of their work.

"It could not be contended that persons engaged on relief programs are entitled to any greater degree of consideration than ordinary employes working for the State, nor do I think it fair to presume that the Legislature intended to provide protection for persons engaged in relief work programs by compensation insurance, and wholly failed to provide any such protection for the State's ordinary employes," said the ruling.

Gun Deliverer

CONTINUED FROM FIRST PAGE.

lessly meted out to others—his head dropped to his chest. He said nothing. Apparently gone, momentarily at least, was his desire to have the law deal with those whom he charged caused his arrest.

Nichols' story was a long one. Officers weighed it thoroughly and were inclined to believe him. He appeared to be too much "in the know" to be leading officers astray.

He told of taking an automobile in Dallas, loading guns and ammunition into it and driving it to Winnsboro where he met Barrow and Bonnie Parker who were to pay him $100 for the trip.

Barrow Delayed Paying.

The delivery was made and Barrow purportedly stalled, ordering Nichols to return Tuesday night for his money. Nichols was willing, but in the meantime officers had arrested him, confiscated his delivery machine. Thus angered, Nichols told officers he would accompany them to Winnsboro, but the posse thought twice, left Nichols behind in the Gregg County jail and made the trip as a strictly official party and no spectators.

The desperado and his moll were in the Winnsboro area, but the Longview posse missed them. Barrow and Bonnie didn't know it, but the trail which led through the Winnsboro sector also was leading them to their death in a burst of gunfire touched off by such fearless men as Frank Hamer, who for many years was captain of headquarters company, Texas Rangers.

The Dallas man told of pilfering autos for the theft ring and when he decided to talk, called for a Dallas Deputy Sheriff who had served in an old and sensational political ring.

State highway patrolmen who have worked under but one order since the slaying of two patrolmen at Grapevine—"get Barrow"—joined the Longview and Dallas officers in Winnsboro Wednesday night to lay in wait for the outlaws.

Shooting Exposes Trap.

Weeks of watching and waiting in the Gladewater area were to no avail as officers turned to Gregg County, as they did to many others, tracing the network of Barrow trails. An unexpected shooting near Gladewater probably prolonged the quest for Barrow and Bonnie, and that came about with such suddenness that officers gasped. They also realized that another trap for Barrow had been exposed.

The Gladewater shooting claimed no lives, but it gained momentum over the grapevine telegraph and the outlaws undoubtedly were warned that Gladewater was, on their map and in their parlance, plenty hot. Two undercover men were sent by the State to Gladewater, arriving only hours after Billie Mace or Billie White, a sister of Bonnie Parker, began working at a beer garden on the Gilmer road. Drinks were exchanged. The undercover men were getting along, making contact, gaining information from the rough and the tough side of life through which they hoped to bring the ruthless desperadoes to the end of their bloody career.

Then the information leaked out that the men were laws in disguise. The shooting broke out quickly. John Gregory, highway officer stationed at Tyler, spent many sleepless nights on a bridge in the Gladewater sector, waiting for Barrow and Bonnie. But the elusive ones went elsewhere. Gregory and other officers several weeks ago took Billie Mace and several of her relatives in custody, grilling them here about the Barrows. Nothing apparently came of that investigation. All of the information gained, however, little by little, word by word, eventually led to the slaying of the hunted pair.

Dillinger

CONTINUED FROM FIRST PAGE.

rested in Chicago after participating with Dillinger in several raids and who said she planned to marry him, heard the decision without show of emotion she refused to comment. Dr. May, however, said he was surprised.

The jury deliberated seven hours. Dr. May and Mrs. Salt admitted on the witness stand during the trial that they had treated the notorious fugitive, but asserte dthey did so in fear of their lives. Miss Frechette admitted accompanying himb in his wanderings and escapades, but testified all her movements were directed by him. Her attorney pleaded that she be sent back to an Indian reservation.

The two women will serve their terms in the women's reformatory at Alderson, W. Va., while Dr. May will be sent to an undesignated Federal prison.

Attorney General Pleased.

WASHINGTON, May 23 (AP).—Attorney General Cummings Wednesday termed extremely gratifying the convictions of Evelyn Frechette and Dr. Clayton May for aiding John Dillinger.

The Attorney General said: "Our campaign is not only against the criminal himself but also against those who intentionally co-operate with him, and their punishment is essential to success in the adequate enforcement of law."

Funerals to Inscribe Finis On Bloody Saga of Outlaws

By their ignominious deaths, shorn of the glamour that small minds saw in the sneaking and bloody exploits of their brief careers, Clyde Barrow, 24, and Bonnie Parker, 21, were being prepared Wednesday night for their return home.

With the unexpected and startling suddenness that characterized their deaths, the two were all but chopped to pieces by gunfire Wednesday morning near Gibsland, La.

Their bodies, badly mangled by the spray of bullets poured into them by officers in a highway trap, at night were in a morgue at Arcadia, La., being prepared for burial and John Bulloch of the McKamy-Campbell funeral home was waiting to bring them to Dallas.

Father Claims Son.

Henry Barrow, father of the not?orious outlaw, went with Bullock to accompany the bodies back to Dallas.

Funeral services will be conducted in Dallas probably Thursday afternoon, members of the family said.

Clyde Barrow, whose career in crime during the last two and a half years made him one of the most notorious and widely sought outlaws in Southwestern history, first ran afoul of the law while little more than a child, officers recalled Wednesday night. When 12 or 13 years old he was a member of a small West Dallas gang that specialized in stealing chickens and in other petty thefts. In 1926, when he was 16 years old, he was arrested on a charge of automobile theft. It was then his name was first entered in the records of the Dallas police department.

Branded Troublesome Punk.

Following that he was arrested with fair regularity for various offenses by Dallas officers who branded him as a troublesome punk, but never dreamed he would develop into a dangerous killer.

Though he had been arrested on charges of theft, burglary and robbery in Fort Worth and Dallas on numerous occasions it was not until 1930 that he received his first and only sentence to the penitentiary, following a conviction at Waco on a charge of burglary. The sentence was for fourteen years but in February, 1932, he was given a general parole by Gov. Ross Sterling. He almost immediately began his ruthless campaign in which he is accused of having committed twelve brutal murders, several kidnapings and numerous holdups. He also is accused of having criminally assaulted one woman in Arkansas, but many Dallas officers believe this to be a crime charged against him that he did not commit.

Joined by Parker Woman.

Bonnie Parker, of whom officers had heard but little before she associated herself with Barrow, joined the outlaw shortly after he was paroled and was either present or assisting in most of the holdups and killings in which her outlaw consort took part, officers say. She was the wife of Roy Thornton, known as the torch man for a gang of burglars and robbers and who now is in the Texas penitentiary.

The mothers of the two waited grimly and fearfully for what they felt certain was to come, and did come Wednesday, to their children.

Mrs. Emma Davis, mother of the Parker woman, fainted when first notified of the deaths of the pair. After being revived she left her home in the afternoon, some said to visit relatives in Fort Worth.

"Oh!" said Mrs. Barrow between choking sobs and in a voice of anguish, "and I asked God in prayer last night to let me see my boy just once more."

The report that Barrow and his consort had been killed brought out expressions of jubilation and sighs of relief among Dallas officers generally. Dallas police had been seeking him since J. D. Bucher was robbed and killed at Hillsboro on April 30, 1932. Sheriff Smoot Schmid and several of his deputies had been devoting much time to the trail. Deputy Sheriff Malcolm Davis was shot and killed in West Dallas on Jan. 7, 1933, a week from the day that Schmid took office.

Church

CONTINUED FROM FIRST PAGE.

out the money changers from the temple."

Church Should Aid New Deal.

Asserting the new deal is an opportunity for the church to aid in a Christian work, the Secretary then inquired, "will the leaders in the church follow the banner which has been boldly raised by President Roosevelt in his determination to establish social and economic justice so far as lies within the power of man, wholeheartedly or only reluctantly?"

The answer to this question, he said, "Is important because if the moral aspirations of the church should reenforce the political efforts now being made to establish a new social order, the advance all along the line would be irresistible and that new social and economic order, certain as it is to be realized in the end in any event, would be accomplished much more quickly and with infinitely less disturbance."

Between the close of the World War and the beginning of President Roosevelt's administration, "rugged individualism ran riot," Ickes asserted. "Social injustices were taken for granted.

Laissez Faire Presidents.

"Laissez faire presidents," the Secretary continued, "were model statesmen in the eyes of a grasping, selfish crowd. No 'brain trust' to worry about at this period, only 'best minds' who were little concerned about helping to build an ideal commonwealth in which men, woman and children could live happier and more worthwhile lives."

"The new deal," he said, "is grounded on the theory that one should do unto others what he would that others should do unto him."

He listed among the administration's objectives the adoption of the constitutional amendment abolishing child labor, fair wages, an end of sweatshops and unhealthy working conditions, a clean-up of slum areas, "an end to wasteful and disregardful exploitation of our natural resources," the adoption of old age, unemployment, maternity and disability insurance, and the assessment of taxes in proportion to the ability to pay.

"We would make it impossible for a merehandful of ruthless, acquisitive men to accumulate unearned fortunes from the oppression of less fortunate people in no position to protect themselves." he said.

Sheriff

CONTINUED FROM FIRST PAGE.

would be on the Jamestown-Sailes road Wednesday morning. With Captain Hamer, Bob Alcorn and Ted Hinton, Dallas Deputy Sheriffs; M. T. Gault, Texas highway patrolman, and P. M. Oakley, one of my Bienville Parish deputies, I drove out the road and picked out a place to wait for them.

We chose a natural barricade at the top of a little hill, and we secreted ourselves on the left-hand side of the road and waited for the car to come by.

Alcorn, who personally knew Barrow and Parker, sighted their car a quarter of a mile away and told us that was them. When the car got within 100 yards coming up the grade, Alcorn said: 'That's them boys.'

About that time the car, which was meeting a truck, slowed down. We hollered to Barrow to halt as we wished to give them a chance. They went for their guns and we let them have it.

In the car we found three submachine guns, two automatic sawed-off shotguns, four .45-caliber automatic pistols, two .38-caliber automatic pistols and one .45-caliber revolver, also a large quantity of ammunition.

School Events

Special to The News.

PLANO, Texas, May 23.—Commencement exercises of the Plano public school were held Monday evening. The following thirty-seven students received diplomas: Dale Armstrong, Ervin Arnold, Lawrence Bailey, Robert Blaine, Frank Bray, Eva Bess Brisendine, Bowman Bryan, Ruth Alto Bryan, Elizabeth Brown, Marion Cowherd, Johnnie Egnew, Marguerite Garrett, Emmajean Haggard, Ida Mae Hartline, Furmon Hefner, Kathleen Hollon, Flora James, Maxie Lee Jones, Bill Krodel, Rudd Mann, S. J. Mathews Jr., Gleen Moulden, Douglas O'Neal Jr., Inez Ritchey, Ouida Saigling, Myrtle Sarver, Inez Shuffler, Dorothy Stogner, Herman Tennell, Mary Sue Thompson, Clark Turner Jr., Anna May Vavra, Bernice Vines, William H. L. Wells, James Earl Wetsel, Earl White Jr. and Pauline Wilson.

OVERTON, Texas, May 23.—Supt. H. W. Stilwell, past president of the Texas State Teachers' Association, present vice president of National Educational Association, and head of public schools of Texarkana, Texas, delivered the closing address to the 1934 graduating class of the London High School Monday night. Diplomas were awarded to seventeen graduates by Supt. W. C. Shaw of London. The valedictory address was given by Derwood Duncan. Miss Iva Rae Peters was the salutatorian, and Miss Helen Fulton was the junior representative.

CALVERT, Texas, May 23.—Calvert High School graduates received their diplomas Tuesday. The personnel of the class is Eloise Noles, Florine Smithermon, Helen Heath, Arthur Tyson, Edith Smith, honor pupils in the order of their grades: W. W. Boggan, Ben Burns, Dallas Criswell, George Erck, Robert Foster, Robert Ford, Beth Holloman, Fredrick Knapp, Eugene Linam, Robert B. McKneely, Helen Newman and Henry G. Taliaferro.

Silver

CONTINUED FROM FIRST PAGE.

the two-base currency movement, which the British distinctly do not want. If bimetallism becomes popular it may be good-bye forever to the gold standard.

"At least it tends to forestall the hopes and plans of Great Britain for return to the gold basis at any time in the near future."

The informant declared that Britain has little interest in silver sales, since India is far less a factor in the white metal market than five years ago and China is far more important.

In Government quarters little support was found for the proposal to invoke a world conference for the rehabilitation of silver.

It was the general view that the white metal would not play as important a part in economic recovery as anticipated by the supporters of the Washington program.

Alarm Not Shared.

In Government quarters the alarm of the financial leaders was not shared, for the reason that the British Treasury officials do not have expectations of return to the gold standard soon.

The city of London, Britain's Wall street, and the Treasury have held divergent views on return to gold for some time, the latter favoring immediate action and the latter holding that the time is inopportune.

The official view toward gold was said to have been unchanged from that voiced as long as two years ago —that return would be made only when conditions are such as to assure that it will be permanent.

Answers to questioners in the House of Commons during recent weeks have indicated that the official view is that the time for a gold basis is not yet in sight.

Flight

CONTINUED FROM FIRST PAGE.

through and had no difficulty in finally locating Port Darwin.

Miss Batten, who acted as her own mechanic, said her plane functioned perfectly all the way. She plans to leave Thursday for Brisbane, but will not attempt to fly to her native New Zealand, she said, because her machine does not have sufficient range to cross the Tasman Sea, a distance of 1,200 miles.

The small, attractive girl flyer reached Rome on the first day of her trip and made principal stops later at Athens, Nicosia, Cyprus, Bagdad, Karachi, British India; Calcutta, Rangoon, Batavia, Dutch East Indies; Lombok Island, Malay Archipelago.

First Studied Music.

Miss Batten went to England several years ago to study music, but soon turned her attention to aviation and won a grudging consent from her parents to take it up. Sir Charles Kingsford-Smith, the Australian air hero, was her inspiration and she determined to join him as an England-to-Australia record holder.

Kingsford-Smith holds the men's record of 7 days, 4 hours and 47 minutes.

The first attempt of Miss Batten ended in Karachi, India, where her plane broke down in April, 1933. Last month, trying again, she cracked up in Rome and was slightly injured.

When she could get the plane, which once belonged to the Prince of Wales, repaired, she flew back to England and started again.

The net PAID circulation of The Austin American and The Austin Statesman Wednesday was
30,669
Clyde Barrow died — thousands wanted the details. They bought and paid for more copies of these newspapers ever before sold in one day.

The Austin Statesman.
Second Oldest Daily in Texas—Est. July 26, 1871—Founded by the Democratic Convention of Texas

WEATHER FORECAST
For Austin and vicinity: Partly cloudy tonight and Saturday, warmer Saturday.
For East Texas: Partly cloudy tonight and Saturday, warmer in the west and north portions Saturday.
For West Texas: Partly cloudy, warmer in Panhandle tonight; Saturday partly cloudy, warmer in northeast portion.

VOL. 66—NO. 229 AUSTIN, TEXAS, FRIDAY, MAY 25, 1934. PRICE FIVE CENTS

MOBS SURGE PAST BONNIE, CLYDE

KIDNAPERS KILL TEXAS DAIRYMAN

COLON, Panama, May 25.—(AP)—William Albert Robinson, author and explorer, stricken with appendicitis in the Galapagos Islands, sailed aboard the destroyer Hale for the Panama Canal zone and American medical attention at 7:30 a. m. today, the destroyer reported by wireless to headquarters here. (Robinson is shown here with his wife.)

ALLAN EXERCISES TO BE DIFFERENT

Graduation exercises with a different slant will be the theme at the Allan Junior high Friday, June 1 when the program is held

A pageant dramatizing the entire history of public schools in Austin will be presented by a selected group from the 250 students who are scheduled to get their diplomas at this time. The exercises will be held at the school auditorium at 9 o'clock.

After the processional of the graduating class, a welcoming speech will be made by the president of the class, Henry Bernheim.

The pageant shows the events of historical and academic importance in the development of public schools in Austin with pictures on the screen to be accompanied by explanation from different pupils, dramatic sketches in pantomime, folk dances and music by the school orchestra.

Prologue Reading

Billy Brill will give the prologue reading. The background of the history from the organization of the first public schools in Austin in 1880 to their present stage of development will be shown by pictures on the screen accompanied by explanatory remarks from Alice Ann Nitschke, Helen Robinson, and Henry Bernheim. A costumed pantomime by Lucille Browne, Sybil Catterall, Doris Heath, Marie Johnson, Eleanor Mills and Dorothy Wright will be presented showing how the schools acquired the well equipped libraries in all the buildings. Charles Donoho will explain the part which John T. Allan and A. J. Zilker have played in the history of the schools as benefactors and philanthropists.

The next division of the program will show how culture is acquired through the study of music, art, public speaking, and how physical education supplements academic work. Musical division will be represented by the John T. Allan orchestra; public speaking, Lewis Labenske; and art, 8B students. Physical education will be represented with a folk dance by Margaret Easey, Louise Brown, Roberta Mapes, Alice Ann Nitschke, Oma Ray and Frances Webb.

Regina Brelsford will make a talk on the new child centered program in elementary schools.

Dorothy Albert, Gene Howard, Rose Kassouf, Janie Peacock, Benjamin Soto, and Walter Wilde will

Continued on page 2, col. 4.

SEA ADVENTURER IS OPERATED ON

LOS ANGELES, May 25.—(AP) William Albert Robinson, wealthy explorer, was reported "doing as well as could be expected" today following an appendicitis operation performed by U.S. navy surgeons who made a 1000-mile aerial dash to dis bedside at Tagus Cove in the lonely Galapagos islands of the Pacific.

Robinson, who was stricken Sunday aboard his tiny world-girdling honeymoon craft, the Svaap, was operated upon last night after the arrival of the U.S. destroyer Hale, which had been dispatched from the Canal Zone. Two navy seaplanes carrying medical officers and supplies, had preceded it.

A message to the Associated Press from wireless operator King aboard the trawler Santa Cruz, which has been standing by the Svaap since the Cambridge, Mass., textile engineer became ill, said:

"Hale reports operation performed and Robinson doing as well as could be expected. Planes leaving at dawn to return to Balboa."

When medical officers, Lieut. Com. Rollo W. Hutchinson and Lieut. Oscar D. Yarbrough, arrived at Tagus Cove Wednesday night they found Robinson's appendix apparently was ruptured and delayed an operation until Hale arrived with better facilities.

LOCKER COMPANY SUIT AGAINST STATE FAILS

A three-judge federal court here Friday dismissed the suit brought by the American Locker Co., Inc., against State Comptroller George H. Sheppard for injunction to restrain enforcement of a law that placed a tax on parcel checking lockers.

The court, in dismissing the suit, pointed out that it raised a moot question because the court of civil appeals already had held the locker taxing law invalid.

The federal court, composed of Circuit Judge Joseph C. Hutcheson of Houston and Dist. Judges Duval West and Robert J. McMillan of San Antonio, Friday was hearing a suit brought by the trustees of the estate of Mrs. M. M. Cook against state officials attacking the validity of the oil taxing law, known as house bill 154, and passed by the 43rd legislature.

'IT IS BEST,' JAP MOTHER DIES WITH SON IN FIRE

SAN FRANCISCO, May 25.—(AP)—Leaving a note saying "it is best that I do this," a Japanese mother carried her 11-months-old son to a flaming death with her 11-months-old son to a flaming last night in the Japanese tea garden at Golden Gate park.

The woman, Mrs Iako Hagiwara, 23, police said, drenched herself and her son with gasoline, applied a match and leaped into a rubbish pit at the tea garden here. A short time before she had served guests.

LEAD CODE APPROVED

WASHINGTON, May 25.—(AP) A 40-hour work week was established in the lead mining industry by the code approved by Hugh S. Johnson last night. The work will be restricted to five days of eight hours each.

2 BANK BANDITS SHOT DOWN; 4 ESCAPE

CHICAGO, May 25.—(AP)—One bandit was killed and another wounded, perhaps mortally, today in an attempted robbery of the South Holland, Ill., trust and savings bank.

Bank employes fought it out with the invaders in the bank and killed one outright.

The proximity of South Holland, a hamlet south of Chicago near the Indiana line, to the scene of the killing of two East Chicago policemen last night gave rise to a report the bandits might have been the assailants of the Indiana officers.

Four men and two women were in the bandit gang.

While the two women stayed at the wheel of the car, the quartet of robbers marched into the bank at 10 o'clock, the moment the time locks released the vault.

Guards had been posted in the balcony for the bank, alert for just such a raid. A machine gun was turned loose on the robbers below and two of them fell.

The other two raced for the door and scrambled into their car, speeding away while vigilantes already gathering around the bank riddled the rear of the automobile with bullets. The fugitives sped northward toward Chicago.

TWO OFFICERS KILLED BY GANG

EAST CHICAGO, Ind., May 25.—(AP)—Two more police officers are dead today in the bloody game of "get Dillinger."

In this city where Policeman William P. O'Malley was slain Jan. 4 by a man definitely identified as John Dillinger, two officers, Martin O'Brien, 44, and Lloyd Mulvihill, 28, were machine-gunned to death late last night.

There was no clue to the identity of the killers. Dillinger, fugitive from the Crown Point jail where he was held for trial for murder of O'Malley, was suspected, but it was only a suspicion. The only two men who might have been able to

Continued on page 2, col. 3.

PRESBYTERIAN CHURCH SELECTS MODERATOR

MONTREAT, N. C., May 25.—(AP)—Judge Samuel H. Sibley of Marietta, Ga., was elected moderator of the Presbyterian church in the United States today succeeding Dr. Ernest Thompson of Charleston, W. Va.

The new moderator is a graduate of the University of Georgia and a widely known attorney. He was appointed judge of the United States court for the northern district of Georgia in 1919 by Pres. Wilson and 12 years later was named to the circuit court of appeals at New Orleans by Pres. Hoover.

He is the sixth ruling elder to be elected moderator in the 73 years of the church. The last was R. A. Dunn of Charlotte who served as moderator in 1931.

AUSTINITE ASKS $10,000 FOR ACCIDENT INJURIES

Suit for $10,210 damages was filed Friday in 126th district court by G. S. Baker against B. W. Randolph and company for alleged injuries received by Baker as result of an automobile accident on South Congress avenue, April 16.

Baker's petition asserts that Theo Moore was driving a truck belonging to the Randolph company and that the truck and Baker's car figured in the collision.

PITTINGER TO SPEAK

TAYLOR, May 25.—(Spl)—Dr. B. F. Pittinger, dean of the school of education of the University of Texas, will address the 96 seniors of the Taylor high school in annual commencement Friday evening. Welton House, class orator, will deliver the class address and the diplomas will be delivered by H. A. Bittick, president of the board of education.

Here is Pete Kreis, Knoxville daredevil driver, who was killed at Indianapolis this morning in a practice spin for the automobile races there next Wednesday.

2 RACERS KILLED AT INDIANAPOLIS

INDIANAPOLIS, Ind., May 25.—(UP)—A driver and his mechanic were killed today when their automobile crashed into the wall during a test run at the Indianapolis motor speedway.

The dead were Peter Kreis, Knoxville, Tenn., and his mechanic, Robert Hahn.

Hahn was from Chino, Calif.

The crash came during a warm-up run preparatory to a qualifying test for the annual memorial day 500-mile race but it was as spectacular as any in the classic itself. Kreis' car cleared the three-foot retaining wall, struck a tree and was cut in two.

Kreis was a construction engineer by profession and annually took his month's vacation at this time of the year in order to participate in the speedway classic. He had raced in earlier years throughout America and abroad.

The Kreis family is prominent in Knoxville. Kreis was 34 years old.

County Campaign Begins Tonight

Fledgling candidates for Travis county public offices will take their first flight with old timers in the ancient game called politics Friday night at Kimbro, scene of the opening speaking program in the 1934 county political campaign.

County Democratic Chmn. J. M. Patterson announced at noon that a barbecue supper, prepared by citizens of the Kimbro community in the extreme eastern section of the county will precede the speaking program. The barbecue supper will be served about 6 p. m.

The speaking program is scheduled to begin at 7:30 p. m.

Immediately before the speeches get under way, candidates will draw for places on the program.

Although almost all of the aspirants to county office have filed their applications with Chmn. Patterson, those who have not yet filed will not be denied a place on the program.

The county democratic chairman also announced that the second political rally of the present campaign will be held next Friday, June 1, at Creedmoor. Date and place of the third program has not yet been set but it will be held north of the Colorado river, Mr. Patterson said.

TREASURY RECEIPTS

WASHINGTON, May 25.—(AP)—The position of the treasury May 23 was: Receipts, $6,799,414.21; expenditures, $86,024,298.36; balance, $2,062,970,688.96; customs receipts for the month, $15,874,141.08.

Receipts for the fiscal year (since July 1) $2,684,319,411.84; expenditures, $6,291,353,212.50 (including $3,526,829,122.13 of emergency expenditures); excess of expenditures $3,607,033,800.66; gold assets, $7,765,564,500.35.

HAMER IS URGED TO HELP TRACK SLAYERS

MEXIA, May 25.—(AP) Kidnapers who ruthlessly slew their victim when they found they had abducted a dairyman instead of the rich man they intended holding for ransom were credited today with killing John L. Adams and dumping his body in a tank.

With a bullet hole in his temple, a handkerchief gag in his mouth and a belt tightly fastened about his throat, the 50-year-old dairyman's body was found in the tank today, about a mile south of Groesbeck, his home. The slayers had taken all his valuables, hastily turning out his pockets.

Suspect Held

Sheriff Will Adams revealed that he had under investigation a man who failed to give satisfactory answers to questions concerning his activities Monday night—the night Adams disappeared from his home. The sheriff kept secret the identity of the suspect.

A note received Tuesday by Dwaine Adams, son of the slain man, was the basis for officers believing the kidnapers got the "wrong man" and, in their efforts to conceal the unprofitable crime, silenced Adams forever by murdering him.

"Your old man is safe—excuse us, we got the wrong man," the note read. The note was mailed from a rural box near Groesbeck. Adams lived next door to Joe Morris, a wealthy man.

Body Found By

Sheriff Adams also disclosed that he was trying to locate Frank Hamer, the straight-shooting former Texas ranger who, with other officers, wiped out Clyde Barrow and Bonnie Parker, in a roadside shooting south of Shreveport, La., Wednesday morning. Hamer had been on the trail of Barrow and his woman companion for weeks.

The sheriff said he intended to offer Hamer the job of solving the murder and kidnaping of the dairyman.

Fred Herring, tenant on a farm south of Groesbeck, found the body in the tank, 200 yards from his house, and reported his gruesome discovery to the sheriff.

RURAL ESSAY CONTEST WINNERS ARE NAMED

Winners of the Travis county rural school "made-in-Texas" essay contest were announced Friday by the county superintendent's office as follows:

Ethel Ruth Duke, Pleasant Hill; Dorothy Nell Bustin, Turnerville; Ollie Lee Camp, Gregg; Hazel Ekdahl, Decker; Bobbie Jo Kolmberg New Sweden; Louis Nelson, Carlson; Beruth Tatum, Haynie Flat; Candelaria Torres, Pecan Springs, and Herbert Lehman, Pilot Knob.

CLUCKS TO PARLEY

Mr. and Mrs. Cictor S. Cluck are leaving Friday afternoon for Marlin to attend the closing sessions of the Texas Chamber of Commerce Managers association which opened its convention Thursday. They plan to return Sunday. Mr. Cluck, asistant manager of the Austin Chamber of Commerce, will join Walter E. Long in Marlin.

CC DELEGATES

Austin Chamber of Commerce representatives who attended the annual meeting of the Giddings Chamber of Commerce Thursday night were A. C. Bull, Austin president, who addressed the Giddings body; Victor S. Cluck, Alfred Ellison and Morris Burns.

PLAY PLANNED

Colorado school Parent-Teacher association will entertain Saturday at 8 p. m. with a play, "It's All Over Town," Mrs. J. W. Kelly, president of the organization, announced Friday.

PROGRAM SET

Esperanza school Friday announced a program for Wednesday, May 30.

Horsenapers Demand $250

LOUISA, Ky., May 25.—(AP)—The ransom racket has invaded the Kentucky mountains.

A registered stallion owned by Dr. R. C. Moore, veterinarian and former Lawrence county judge, was taken from his stall in the dead of night.

The horsenapers tacked a ransom note on the barn door. It demanded $500, but a postcript added, "This horse ain't worth what we furst thot; bring $250."

Dr. Moore, who values the four-year-old Percheron at $500 no matter what the horsenapers think he is worth, was instructed to "come to Town Hill tonight at 12. Start walking from Bill Fisher house to gate. Go in cemetery, when you hear whistle like Bob White drop money on road and keep walking."

Dr. Moore turned the note over to authorities, and announced he would not meet the ransom demand.

CYLDE HAD CHANCE, SCRIBE SAYS, AFTER TWO-HOUR TALK WITH HAMER ABOUT KILLING

By L. E. HARWOOD
The Statesman Staff

Did Clyde Barrow really reach for his gun before the fusillade from the rifles of six officers killed him Wednesday morning?

That is one of the leading questions I have heard asked since I returned to Austin Thursday afternoon from the scene of the killing. The answer of many persons is:

"What's the difference?"

The reputation of Frank Hamer is that he always gives a cornered fugitive a chance to surrender.

After talking to him for two hours in his hotel room at Shreveport the night after Barrow was killed, I firmly believe that Clyde had his chance.

Always Gives Man Chance

An inspection of the spot where the shooting occurred further leads me to believe that officers gave Barrow and Bonnie Parker a chance to give themselves up.

Barrow had been in many traps before and he always had shot his way out, but this was the first time he ever had been in a Frank Hamer trap.

"I always give a man a chance, I don't care who he is," Hamer said. "But when we raised up and shouted halt at Clyde Barrow, I was looking down my gun barrel at him and when I do that I know a man isn't going to shoot his way out."

Had Drop on Clyde

In other words, the crack shot former Texas ranger, 27 years in the service, had the drop on Clyde, and when the desperado reached for his gun instead of for the air, it was curtains for him.

The officers were well protected in case Barrow had succeeded in getting his gun into play. It is a straight road at that point, which is at the crest of a hill. In cutting through the hill, engineers left a bank several feet high on the left side. The road runs north and south and from the crest of this hill a person standing in the road can see for a quarter of a mile in both directions.

It would have been an ideal location for one of Barrow's mail boxes, for here he could have gotten out of his car, looked for his mail and at the same time watched the road in both directions far enough to allow him to get back into his machine and speed away in just a few minutes.

Barrow Drove Slowly

Officers admitted Barrow was driving slowly when they commanded him to halt. It might have been that he was about to stop and look at his "mail box."

The car came up the hill from the north and for several miles before it came into view, according to one of the officers lying in wait, they could hear it "roaring through the country."

Now a hill with the gentle slope that one had is not one to slow a V-8 down to 30 miles an hour. No, Clyde must have been slowing down for a stop.

The officers, behind bushes up on that bank, were in a straight line parallel with the road. P. M. Oakley, deputy sheriff of Bienville parish, was the man at the north end of the line, the direction from which Barrow approached.

Deputy Fired First

Hamer, 25 or 30 feet from Oakley, was at the other end of the line. Between them were the others Manny Gault, Sheriff Henderson Jordan, Ted Hinton and Bob Alcorn. Officers credited Oakley with firing the first shot. It was all over in just a few minuntes.

The car door on the left side shows how the gunfire was aimed at Clyde. Bonnie's death appears to have been incidental.

That place where the desperado and his sweetheart companion were trapped is typical of the country roads on which they drove most of the time. Slender pine trees lined

Continued on page 12, col 5.

CROWDS RENEW TOLEDO RIOTING

TOLEDO, O., May 25.—(AP)—A crowd of 1500 strikers and sympathizers, bringing more bricks and assorted missiles, gathered at the plant of the Electric Auto-Lite company here at noon today and reopened the bombardment of the building and troops which already had cost the lives of two men.

The crowd gathered at street intersections still strewn with wreckage and debris of three days of rioting. Guardsmen, laying a field telephone communication system, made no attempt to break up the crowd as paving bricks and chunks of concrete came hurtling up toward the factory building.

The attack was aimless and less spirited than the fighting yesterday, which led to hand-to-hand slugging and bullets. The militiamen had bayonets fixed but did not use them.

Hard pressed, the soldiers fired into the jeering, taunting rioters yesterday afternoon, killing Frank Hubay, 27, and Steve Cygon, 20, and wounding several.

Stopped for a time, the rioters strengthened their forces and returned to battle last night. Two men were shot and three others were injured. The crowd numbered 6000 at the height of the riots.

Many Women Hurt

Prospects for peace negotiations were complicated by new developments toward a general strike in Toledo.

Fifty-three persons were arrested by the militia for civil authorities and charged with rioting.

Quiet was restored shortly after midnight in the area of machine guns and bayonets just five blocks northeast of the city hall.

Scores of injured—including many women—were included in the casualties. In previous rioting during a three-day period approximately 100 suffered minor injuries from clubs, stones and tear gas.

Four more companies of guardsmen, an armored car and trucks loaded with gas bombs were ordered into Toledo to tighten the hold of the military authorities, bringing to nearly 1000 the forces of the militia.

10 Per Cent Hike Asked

Adjt. Gen. Frank D. Henderson announced that officials of the company had agreed to shut down the plant today and tomorrow.

Charles P. Taft, who was dispatched here by the federal department of labor, took the lead in negotiations.

Union leaders clung to the orig-

Continued on page 12, col. 2.

HAMER BANQUET PLANS PROGRESS

Plans for the proposed testimonial dinner for Former Ranger Capt. Frank Hamer and State Highway Patrolman Manny Gault, who participated in the killing of Clyde Barrow and Bonnie Parker, were being made Friday.

Sheriff Lee O. Allen, who first proposed the affair Thursday, said it probably will not be held before Monday or Tuesday and likely will be a barbecue given at Zilker park.

The dinner will be an informal affair, to be attended by fellow peace officers here including members of the state highway patrol, the state ranger force, the sheriff's department, city police and the constable's department, Sheriff Allen said. Other state, county and city dignitaries also likely will be asked to the dinner.

Allen said he had conferred with Police Chief Raymond D. Thorp, ranger officials, and Chief L. G. Phares of the state highway patrol regarding the dinner and that all those to whom he had talked are in favor of it.

Hamer and Gault were working as members of the highway patrol when they "sprung the trap" in Louisiana in which the young desperado and his red-haired "moll" were shot to death.

Sheriff Allen at first suggested that the testimonial dinner be held Saturday night, but Friday said Hamer and Gault will be permitted a few days of rest before the affair in their honor is given.

Showers Yield To Fair Weather

FOLLOWING two days of intermittent showers which totaled .73 of an inch, Austin faces a dry if partly cloudy week-end, according to U. S. weather bureau forecast for tonight and Saturday.

Warmer weather has been predicted for Saturday.

Last night's .13 of an inch of rain is likely to be the last for several days at least, bureau officials said. The month's total was increased to 1.84, still considerably under the 4.64 inches which are the normal for May, but the year's total exceeds the normal by 6.18 inches. To date Austin has had 21.17 inches of rain since Jan. 1.

Temperatures ranged from 88 degrees Thursday afternoon to 69 during the night.

BARROW BURIAL TODAY WHILE GIRL'S TO BE SATURDAY

DALLAS, May 25.—(AP) The bullet-riddled bodies of Clyde Barrow and Bonnie Parker lay in the noisy atmosphere created by thousands of morbidly excited spectators today while families of the outlaw lovers planned private funerals to end the spectacle.

The southwest's No. 1 gunman will be buried at Sunset in the West Dallas cemetery, close to the grave of his brother, Marvin (Buck) Barrow, after what the family plans as a private service.

The body of his 23-year-old, red-headed consort will be taken from a funeral home tonight and will be placed in the home of her mother, Mrs. Emma Parker. Burial probably will be held Sunday at the Fishtrap cemetery, less than a mile from the spot where her marauding companion of two years will be laid to rest.

Many Scars Removed

Officials of the two undertaking establishments where the bodies had laid for 24 hours estimated that 50,000 persons will have viewed the bullet-torn bodies before burial. Mobs took over both homes last night, trampled the lawns and shrubs and ruined the carpets of the parlors before they dispersed about midnight.

Clyde, attired in an expensive suit and a stiff collar, lay in a wood casket, battleship gray with cream satin plush interior. In the center of a gray tie was a pearl stickpin and the tip of a white handkerchief was visible in the coat pocket. Embalmers had removed many indications of the barrage of gunfire he and Bonnie met when they sped over the top of a hill east of Shreveport, La., Wednesday. Only a small hole under the left ear remained to indicate how he met his death.

$2000 Funeral For Bonnie

Bonnie was clad in a blue silk negligee and her hair was freshly marcelled. Her nails again were tinted, just as she wore them for two years since she began her fast life with Clyde. She lay in a steel casket with satin plush interior. Her family arranged for a steel vault at a cost of $1000, bringing the total expense for her funeral to more than $2000.

Mrs. Parker stayed close to her daughter's body all night. She was prostrated this morning and her sister, Mrs. Lelia Plummer, said she would be unable to attend the funeral unless she recovered rapidly.

Another sister, Mrs. Lillie Smith, and Bonnie's brother, Hubert, also stayed up all night.

Mrs. Henry Barrow, the frail mother who anxiously watched for her son at their West Dallas home whenever she felt he could come to her with a measure of safety, was at Clyde's bier last night.

Someone asked Henry Barrow about funeral arrangements.

"We'll have to see mamma about that," he would reply.

The Curtain Goes Down

Beginning at dawn, crowds of curious began to gather at the funeral establishments in opposite sectors of the city, but not until 10 o'clock were they permitted to file past Bonnie's casket. Attaches said the procession would be stopped at 3 p. m.

Only slightly fewer persons surrounded the building where Clyde lay. Guards kept them in front of the building and the hosts extended almost to the street. Their automobiles clogged the street, one of the main thoroughfares from the north pat of the city to the business sector.

The more agile spectators who could not enter the room where Clyde lay last night climbed trees on one side of the building and looked down through a large window. Today, however, the curtains were drawn.

Mrs. Parker fainted when she twice visited the home where the torn body of her daughter lay yesterday. She was unconscious more than an hour one time. Officials

Continued on page 2, col. 2.

Austin Today

Colorado River Stages 7 a. m.

Flood stage 21 feet, height above zero .3 foot, 24-hour change, none, rainfall .13 inch. Stage expected Saturday, .3 foot.

Sunrise 5:32 a. m., sunset 7:24 p. m., moonrise 5:24 p. m., moonset 3:26 a. m.

SPOT COTTON

Austin middling 11.20

BANK CLEARINGS

Friday $84,318.81

Spring Training to Climax in Round-Up Game

Chevigny To Pit 'Round-Up' Team Against 'Texas'

Football Exhibition Shows Prospective Stars Of Coming Season

One of the leading attractions that will bid for the attention of Round-Up visitors again this year will be the intra-squad Round-Up football game in Memorial Stadium on Saturday afternoon.

This colorful event was originated last year by Coach Jack Chevigny with a view to giving interested ex-students and visitors a sort of preview of what his first Longhorn football team would be like in the season of 1934. Though the brand of football displayed was a bit ragged in parts, an enthusiastic audience praised the contest highly, causing its adoption as a part of the annual Round-Up program.

Despite the fact that last year's game was not truly a classy bit of football, it was colorful and served to point out some of the promising sophomore stars of this past season. The 50-yard touchdown run of Hugh Wolfe, the passing of Bill Pitzer and Ney Sheridan, and the pass receiving of Jack Collins marked them as men of great promise last spring, and they were some of the first year men who were found regularly in the starting lineup this past season.

It is highly probable that several stars will again be found this year from among the group of youngsters who will be working under Coach Chevigny for the first time. Giant Tarlton Jones, six-foot seven-inch sophomore who has regained his eligibility, is expected to show great promise at one of the tackle positions, as is Nick Frankovic, another husky 200-pound freshman. Bill Dunne at center, Warren Wiggins and James Voss at ends, T. J. King and Vincent Vallone at guards; Judson Atchison, John Morrow, Frank O'Rourke, Ed Strout, Henry Mittemeyer, and several others in the backfield—all are expected to be pressing some of the Varsity men for positions after the four-week training session.

The Round-Up game will be handled in the same manner as last year, Coach Chevigny said when he announced that it would be held again. The entire squad reporting for spring training will be drilled in fundamentals for about three weeks before being divided into "Texas" and Round-Up" squads. The final week will be spent in shaping up the two teams for the game, and it is likely that Coaches Tim Moynihan and Marty Karow will again be designated as the coaches of the two teams.

This arrangement allows Coach Chevigny ample freedom to be of some assistance to both teams, and of great help in "putting over the show" as he did last year.

Varsity vs. Notre Dame

The highlight of the 1934 football season was the Longhorn 7 to 6 victory over Notre Dame. The picture shows Hilliard being brought down by Michuta, giant Notre Dame tackle, after gaining 12 yards on an off-tackle smash. Co-Captains Hilliard and Coates were the leaders in this fight to victory, just as they were the mainstays of the team throughout the season. Next year other men must take their place. Who will they be? The exhibition game during the Round-Up should point to next year's stars.

Peregrinus Destroyed While Laws and Engineers Battle

Peregrinus was destroyed.

Another episode took place just before Christmas in the interesting series of episodes centering around the patron saint of the School of Law and the fight between the Laws and the Engineers.

The first law banquet in three years was scheduled for Monday night, December 17. The main lounge of the Union Building was converted into the dining room. Union officials anxiously guarded the doors that night. While the banquet was going on, little groups of engineers gathered here and there around the Union Building. Some of the guardian lawyers began to wonder if they should prepare to resist a mass rush.

But the engineers decided to try strategy. Ralph Immel, junior engineer, clad in a waiter's jacket, borrowed for the occasion, made his way into the banquet hall. When he came close to Perigrinus, he made a grab for the Saint. Before he could go far with the Saint in his hands he was grabbed by a number of lawyers. In the fight that followed Perigrinus crumbled and fell in pieces to the floor. Tha was the end of Perigrinus.

But the lawyers are determined that Perigrinus shall not stay dead. Tuesday a campaign was made to raise a fund to have Perigrinus born again, this time out of wood. The destroyed Perigrinus was apparently a plaster cast. And Perigrinus will continue to be the patron Saint of the Laws.

The Engineers are gleeful in their claims of victory. The Laws deny that the victory amounted to much. They point out the fact that Immel did not escape with Perigrinus and assert that, had the Saint not crumbled, they would have regained possession.

And thus endeth another episode on the fight between the Laws and the Engineers.

Round-Up

(Continued from Page 1)

D. B. Hardeman, Editor, Daily Texan.
Jack Taylor, Student.
Bob Ford, Student.
Elizabeth Cameron, Student.
John A. McCurdy, Executive Secretary of the Ex-Students' Association.

The Texas Union will serve as Round-Up headquarters. Registration and Campus Inspection will be directed by Read C. Granberry; the Revue and Ball will be under the chairmanship of George Stephens; the Parade will be directed by Arno Nowotny; Publicity by DeWitt Reddick; Athletic Events by W. E. Metzenthin; Student Organization Activities will be directed by Jack Taylor, Bob Ford, and Elizabeth Cameron; Ex-Students' Association Meetings by Ralph C. Goeth and Fred W. Adams.

Ex-Clubs Participate

The presidents of all Texas Ex Clubs will be ex-officio vice-chairmen of the 1935 Round-Up. All club officers will attend the club officers' meeting on Saturday, April 6. Special invitations will be sent to all clubs urging them to send delegations to the Round-Up and to have a club entry in the Round-Up Parade.

Mail invitations are going out to all dads and mothers of students now in the University. Invitations also are being sent to the alumni of all active student organizations.

Reunion Classes

Reunion classes for the 1935 Round-Up start with the Class of '85 and include '90, '95, '00, '05, '10, '15, '20, '25, and '30. Members of the Class of '85 will be Round-Up guests of honor. Not many of them are still living but most of the survivors are expected back. The Class of '85 included among its number such names as: Thomas Watt Gregory, Yancey Lewis, James R. Hamilton, and William C. Wear. Surviving members are: Dr. Samuel C. Red of Houston, Mr. James C. Burns of Goliad, Mr. Owen P. Hale of California, Mr. Virgil B. Harris of Quitman, Texas, Judge A. J. Peeler of San Antonio, and Mr. Venable B. Proctor of Victoria.

With the end of this school year our University will have completed fifty-two years of active service to the State of Texas. Approximately 63,000 students have enrolled during these years and it is estimated that 45,000 are now residing in the State of Texas. It would be a happy day for students and faculty if all 45,000 would come home on the occasion of this Sixth Annual Texas Ex Round-Up.

Freakish Floats To Liven Parade

Again this year a Varsity parade with its ingenious floats devised by fraternity, sorority, boarding house, and other campus groups will entertain the Round-Up visitors. The parade may be supplemented by floats arranged by ex-student groups from Texas cities if plans now under consideration are put into effect.

The Round-Up parade of last year was the first Varsity parade in a number of years. Sixty-five entries paraded down Guadalupe Street, Lavaca Street, and thence down Congress Avenue. About 100 entries are expected in the 1935 parade.

Some of the outstanding floats of last year were: a Fiji island scene; the old woman who lived in a shoe and her family of sorority girls; a rusty old box-like wagon enclosed with iron bars like a cage (formerly used to transport slaves) serving as a prison wagon for a group of stripe-clad fraternity prisoners; Carrie Nation's visit to the campus. Campus groups are already at work collecting ideas to make the 1935 floats even more original than those of 1934.

50,000 Relics In Indian Collection

Exes who return to the campus for the Round-Up this spring will find that one important step has been taken toward the building up of a museum at the University. An Anthropology Museum has been opened on the fourth floor of Waggener Hall. Inside this museum is housed the largest collection of native archaeological material in the south and southwest.

Under the direction of Dr. J. E. Pearce, chairman of the Department of Anthropology, careful excavations have been made over a period of years in a number of sections of Texas. Archaeological material of the type which hitherto had been dug up by expeditions from northern colleges and taken out of the state was brought to the University. Year after year this invaluable collection grew; yet there was no place available for display. Now, the Anthropology Museum has supplied the need.

March 2—

(Continued from Page 1)

versity faculty, President Winston thought the idea preposterous.

Liberty Reigns

Notwithstanding his opinion, students went on with their plans. They dragged a cannon from the Capitol grounds to the campus, and from there they took it to Clark Field, where they began their celebration by discharging shot after shot from the old cannon.

Judge J. C. Townes and Judge R. L. Batts of the law faculty accepted invitations to make speeches on the occasion. Students had a difficult time getting President Winston to attend the demonstration. Finally he acceded and joined the gathering.

"Speech! Speech!" the crowd shouted when they saw him. Apparently out of humor, he made his speech.

"I was born in a land of liberty," he said, "nursed on the bottle of liberty, rocked in the cradle of liberty, and grew up a son of liberty, but the students of the University of Texas take more liberties than anybody I ever saw."

Coach Disch Plans Baseball Game for Round-Up Visitors

Longhorns Seek Twentieth Conference Pennant With Untried Squad

That shrewd coach and maker of baseball players, William "Uncle Billy" Disch, will place his 1935 Longhorn team on the diamond in a game especially arranged for Round-Up visitors; and the visitors will be given a chance to form their opinions as to whether or not he has the material available to add another pennant to the many which he has brought to The University of Texas. The game will be played Friday afternoon during the Round-Up.

Much of the success of the Longhorn's baseball season will probably depend on two redheads, Norman "Red" Branch from Montgomery and Richard "Freck" Midkiff from Gonzales. Both are juniors and both are pitchers.

Behind the plate Coach Disch will have to develop a youngster to take the place of the veterans of last year. Joe Fitzsimmons of Dallas seems the best prospect, though the place will be hotly contested by Jimmy Phipps of Waco, Norman Powell of Texarkana, and Dan Jarvis of Aransas Pass.

First place apparently belongs to John C. Munro, letterman from the 1934 season. Bohn Hilliard, who last year played in the outfield and pitched, will probably be developed into a second baseman. His lightning quickness fits him for the infield.

Red Preibisch, slugging outfielder of 1934, may be moved into the shortstop position before the 1935 season progresses very far. Captain Buster Baebel will be the regular guardian of centerfield.

Baseball has given way in popularity to football in many colleges; but in this America where the public follows with eager interest the outcome of a World series there will always be an enthusiastic following for Disch-coached baseball teams. A spectator with a knowledge of the game appreciates the strategy that marks every game played by the Longhorns under the direction of the man with the keen eyes and the iron gray hair.

Round-Up Revue Honors Beauties

Every year since the first Round-Up, the Revue and Ball, which is the social climax of the homecoming celebration, has increased in splendor. The Revue and Ball is centered around the coronation of the Sweetheart of The University of Texas. The coronation is followed by a dance.

As a court for the Sweetheart serve the Cactus Beauty candidates, nominated by various sororities and dormitories and other girls' groups. From 60 Cactus Beauty candidates as appeared in the first revue, the number has increased steadily until 130 took part in the 1934 revue. About 150 are expected for this year's revue.

The Sweetheart is chosen by popular election. Nominations may be made by any student or student group. In a preliminary election the five highest candidates are chosen, and a run-off election is held in which the girl receiving the highest number of votes gets the honor of being Sweetheart.

As part of the court of the Sweetheart each of the other six colleges of the Southwest Conference elect a Sweetheart who is one of the honor guests of the Round-Up and who is presented during the revue.

Miss Janet Collett, who directed the revue last year, has already begun planning for the new revue. Preceding the presentation, a number of exhibition dances and songs liven the revue. George Stephens and Charles Zivley are chairmen of the Revue and Ball Committee.